The PHISH Companion

A Guide to the Band and their Music

Foreword by Tom Marshall,
Phish Lyricist

The Mockingbird Foundation

MF | Miller Freeman Books

San Francisco

Published by Miller Freeman Books
600 Harrison Street, San Francisco, CA 94107
An imprint of Music Player Network
www.MusicPlayer.com
Publishers of *Guitar Player*, *Bass Player*, *Keyboard*, *Gig*, *MC2* and *EQ*
    Magazines

Distributed to the book trade in the U.S and Canada by
Publisher's Group West, 1700 Fourth Street, Berkeley, CA 94710

Distributed to the music trade in the U.S. and Canada by
Hal Leonard Publishing, P.O. Box 13819, Milwaukee, WI 53213

Cover Illustration and Design: Peter Holwitz
Back cover photos: Michael McNamara (light show, December 8, 1999)
    Elise Ryerson (band photos October 6 and 7, 2000 concerts)
Text design: Leigh McLellan

ISBN: 0-87930-631-9

Library of Congress Control Number: 00-136445

00 01 02 03 04 05   5 4 3 2 1

CONTENTS

Dedication

To anybody who has ever been touched by the magic of Phish
and to the people who create the magic.

Yes my brother I know,
The rest might not,
but I have treasur'd every note.

—Walt Whitman—

FOREWORD

By Tom Marshall
lyricist and co-lyricist of many Phish songs

Because of my proximity to Phish, I am the recipient of an unending series of interesting questions and proposals. Often they're from people who think I'm drowning in the torrent of money that must be rushing in—spilling over the sides of the Phish member's wallets and into my cupped hands—wondering, of course, if I'll give them some. I explain my philosophy about giving to them, a John Lennon, "we're all doing what we can" kind of thing—in a polite manner of course.

There's the ever-present ticket request. It's haunted me at home to the point of my having to change my number several times. They find me through email. They ask me through other people—I get twice and thrice-removed ticket requests…like from a cousin-in-law, "Tom, my girlfriend's brother is a huge Phish-head, and got shut out from the Garden…" My answer there is usually, "Phish tickets aren't mine to give away."

The primary request I receive as Phish's lyricist though is, of course, to explain a particular song. I heard that Don McLean when asked what "American Pie" meant said, "It means that I never have to work again." I wish I could use that brilliant answer truthfully. Maybe someday I will. Keep checking back.

Then there are the proposals. I love proposals: "You can have 'A' if you give me 'B' ", where B = "introduce me to Trey" or "give me an aftershow pass" or something like that. Usually harmless requests—although, unless 'A' is irresistible, I'll almost always refuse. "Don't set a precedent" is the motto Brad, Phish's tour manager, taught me. Probably decent advice—although it is possible to set a good precedent as well.

But there was a question recently posed to me about my relationship with Phish, which I liked but didn't answer. I was being interviewed this past New Years Eve in Florida and the interviewer, whose name I forget, asked me something like this: "After all the backstage experiences, all the hotel parties, all the great seats for the most desirable shows, and incorporating your relationship with Trey and all your Phish history, what is the single, one thing, that you like most about your Phish experience?"

Unfortunately, I was not in any state to produce a coherent answer at that moment. At Phish shows, I often find myself not setting a good precedent, which is why, when asked to write a forward for a Phish Encyclopedia, I instantly thought, "hey, this could be a good thing…" But now, several months as well as four or five deadlines for this preface have come and gone—and the only thing I feel able to write about happens to be an extremely bad precedent I set backstage this past summer.

It was the summer of 1999, at the PNC Bank Center, the first night of two Phish shows. During the set break, my friends JS, HP and I decided we needed to climb up to the place where the spotlight operators sit—a tiny catwalk that borders the circular roof of the

seating area. The fact that this was potentially life threatening, and possibly illegal somehow, didn't seem to enter into our decision. Little did we know that after walking up a few flights of stairs backstage, that we would be faced with an incredible obstacle course of ladders and scaffolding—high up in the rafters above the stage. This was where all the cables that support the lights, speakers and that kind of thing were wound up on huge spools that were kept from being released by ratcheting mechanisms.

There was braided steel cable under high tension everywhere we looked, which we had to slip under and crawl over. To make matters worse, there was no floor, only strips of metal with three-inch openings between. It was very stupid and dangerous and we most likely could have inadvertently sent some two-ton piece of equipment plunging onto the stage with the slightest misstep.

We felt very clever and secretive up there however, and actually enjoyed ourselves on our mission to "the best seat in the house!" JS, however, whose identity I'm protecting, wasn't enjoying himself as much as I, and seemed to have momentarily lost his balance and let go of the water bottle he was carrying.

In his job as a vice president for a major insurance company, I suppose he's not used to mentioning minor mistakes to his coworkers. In that spirit, he didn't find it necessary to tell us about this mishap and kept trudging along after us. Never mind that the bottle fell on a stack of amplifiers and exploded onto Pete Carini, Fishman's drum technician, and a PNC security guard who didn't quite see the humor in it. Thankfully the show started and HP, JS and I spent several enjoyable minutes up in the catwalks before we realized that our return route was now illuminated in a blaze of lights courtesy of Chris Kuroda, Phish's light-show magician. Everyone would see us climbing down! I resigned myself to quickly descend in the darkness before the encore, and actually managed to enjoy the rest of the set. HP on the other hand, a very crafty girl who moves like a wraith, managed to slip down unseen between songs, effectively pulling the best "ditch" on her pals possible—especially in light of what happened next. Suffice it to say that JS and I crawled like hell after the set ended and managed to get to the stairs with no problems. At the bottom of the stairs though, a wet security guard seemed to be very interested in us and wouldn't let us pass.

I flashed my otherwise quite powerful All-Access pass in his face, but he was immune to its magic. JS somehow vanished (second best ditch ever!) leaving me to deal with the irate gentleman. The way I chose to deal with him was probably unadvised: I simply walked away from him after repeatedly denying "throwing something from the rafters." Phish was playing and rather than go out into the audience, I stopped side-stage and stood and watched. Suddenly I was grabbed by three unpleasant fellows and dragged toward a backstage exit, where I happened to notice two more extremely large simian-men

waiting eagerly for me. All were depressingly dressed just like the security guard.

I decided that if they got me outside I was in real trouble, and dedicated every part of my (rather large) self into NOT going out the door. They began yelling at me and displaying my grease-covered shirt to others as evidence of my having been somewhere I didn't belong. Thankfully, the commotion attracted Brad, whom I've never seen shy away from any unpleasant situation. Like a hockey ref, he inserted himself in between my captors and me. After an extremely tense moment or two, Brad turned to me and motioned to "get lost." I didn't wait to see how that ended. I was just happy not to have been stomped in the back lot by PNC Bank Center security, who were perhaps bored by the hitherto uneventful concert.

The matter took a bizarre turn when the next night Eric Larson, Phish's traveling feel-good guy, mentioned to the in-house video crew to take special notice of the encore as Bruce Springsteen, who happened to have a day off from his shows at the Meadowlands, was going to sing a number with Phish. Needless to say, the word spread like wildfire among the backstage employees who were more than

happy to see New Jersey's native son after two nights of Vermont hippie music. So, imagine their surprise when from the band room emerged, not the Boss, but a six-foot-six, dorkily-dressed, bandanna-clad…ME!

I heard one of them say, "Hey, it's that asshole from last night!" I was laughing even before I made it onto the stage… But—to answer the interviewer's question…while that may have been a favorite moment, my favorite "thing" about Phish is more of an emotion which comes from watching them rise from a bar band to the phenomenon they are today. Perhaps they've stumbled a few times here and there on their ascent, but for the most part, they have managed to avoid major pitfalls which so many other bands fall into as they experience success. This sentiment I feel has to do with the unceasing quality which pervades everything that is Phish (excluding of course album-cover art). It has to do with watching them get married and buy houses. It has to do with holding their children in my arms, and watching their kids play with mine. It has to do with the fact that there even could be an Encyclopedia written about them. It's my pride as I watch them gracefully grow older.

PROJECT HISTORY

Written by Craig DeLucia
and the Setlist Working Group

The Phish Companion began with a vision—that information assembled online by hundreds of volunteer fans ought to be distributed in print form without anyone involved profiting from anyone else's efforts. The heart of the book started with the *Helping Phriendly Book*, an online compilation of setlists compiled initially by Shelly Culbertson, John Friedman, Richard Stern, and Lee Silverman. The *HPB* was named for the mythical *Helping Friendly Book* of Phish song lore. (See the introduction to the Setlists chapter for further details on its evolution.) When this collection began to be sold in lots outside of Phish shows, sometime in 1993, and again when books about Phish began to be published in the fall of 1995, heated discussions began in the online Phish.Net community about the ethics of printing out and selling the *HPB*, in light of the volunteer, communal, and nonprofit manner in which the setlists had originally been compiled. The conversations were particularly stimulated by publication of a commercial book admittedly based on the *Helping Phriendly Book* setlists collection. On the one hand, people were pleased that the setlists would reach a wider audience: Phish fans without computers. On the other hand, it was disturbing that those who had diligently compiled the setlists on a nonprofit basis for the benefit of the community were exploited so coldly by other profit-motivated fans. Those heated online discussions have since turned an impassioned, upbeat undertaking into a fantastic and encyclopedic megillah that few could have imagined at the project's inception two years ago.

In September of 1996, Craig DeLucia dedicated himself to the distribution of setlists, and possibly other information, either at cost or for the benefit of charity. This project would never have begun, nor would it have survived various falters, without his initial dream and dedication. He and a few friends decided to write a book that would encompass efforts by the entire fan community without personal gain. These friends were a diverse group of people representing various ages and interests—from adults with jobs to high-school and college students, a cross-section of the Phish community we all love.

The Phish community was in need of a book that was thoughtful, accurate, and complete, one which reflected favorably on the band and their fans. We believed that such a book should be distributed on a not-for-profit basis, with proceeds benefiting charities, and that the project should involve as many volunteers as possible. We began laying the foundation for what would become The Mockingbird Project, named after that character of Phish song lore who helped bring the *Helping Friendly Book* from the hands of avarice and greed, and into the eager hands of the faithful Lizards.

We publicized these ideas in various online forums and on leaflets distributed outside Phish shows to inform others of the Project and to request help in making it the most encyclopedic book in the market. Our pleas immediately attracted support, which has continued to grow. The first table of contents was drafted in October 1996, and by March 1997 the Mockingbird Foundation was legally incorporated in the state of New York as a Nonprofit Corporation, with the fourteen founding fans as board members. Throughout late 1997 and early 1998, over one hundred people submitted show reviews, essays, and art work to the project, and editors chose a selection of their contributions to be included in the book. In the fall of 1998, we began contacting literary agents and publishers for assistance in publishing the book, and the number of contributors exceeded three hundred. The Foundation contracted with Christian Crumlish of Waterside Productions in May of 1999 and, as the number of contributors neared one thousand, inked a publishing contract in March of 2000 with Miller Freeman Books, who also publish the *All Music Guides*, *Guitar Player*, *Bass Player*, *Keyboard*, and other publications known and enjoyed by Phish fans. The contract ensured the release of the book by the fall of 2000, just over four years after the massive project began. By the time you read this, proceeds from the project are already benefiting music education for youth, and may have already moved into other related charitable areas.

Far more than simply another book on Phish, *The Phish Companion* represents four years of passionate service by Phish fans for the benefit of their community and charities. We hope that this book becomes your favorite Phish reference guide, and that the love of Phish's music pervading this book continues to inspire charity-driven creativity for the enrichment of the Phish community.

ACKNOWLEDGMENTS

Written by Ellis Godard
on behalf of the Board of the Foundation

From the moment this project began, we hoped that hundreds of fans, both on and off the Internet, would contribute to this project and know that they helped create a fan-based book that will benefit worthy charities and further spread the word about the band that we all love. Our expectations were more than exceeded, and we were not fully prepared for the outpouring of support, ideas, and contributions, which ultimately came in some form from literally thousands of fans. We have attempted to thank and acknowledge as many as possible, where explicit contributions have been enumerable and noted. We have likely forgotten some names, either because their contributions were less concrete or because our tracking of contributions has been incomplete. Both failures are bound to have occurred in a four-year process directly involving hundreds in the production of a single book, and so we add apology to the following acknowledgements.

We of course appreciate the band, for their many years of practice, performance, and more. We also appreciate Phish's management company, Dionysian Productions, both for doing what they do to keep Phish going, and for their cooperation and support in our own endeavor. They were contacted about this project early on and expressed enthusiasm about the idea of a fan-produced work for the benefit of charities, and we have much appreciated (and benefited by) their help and support. We continue to keep Dionysian abreast of project developments, and will continue to work passionately for the benefit of charities, and in celebration of Phish, their music, and the fan community. A special note of gratitude is reserved for Kevin Shapiro, Phish's Archivist, for his inestimable assistance in setlist corrections and verification. We have also benefited greatly from the input and support of Tom Marshall, Dave and Luann Abrahams, John Paluska, Jason Colton, and Beth Montuori, and to Shelly Culbertson for originating documentation of Phish setlists through the original Helping Phriendly Book and for the spirit in which she did so.

The project owes its origin to the interest and dedication of Craig DeLucia, and a great deal of thanks to Craig as well as Mark Toscano, Charlie Dirksen, and Ellis Godard. We would also like to thank those other founding members of this project who, while no longer active in the administrivia of board activities, have always been and continue to be part of the productive and moral fabric that has helped ensure our success, including Dave Donohue, Charles Franz, Herschel Gelman, Eddie Dinel, Joe Rioux, and John Wood. We are indebted to our literary agent Christian Crumlish for his thoroughness in connecting the vision of those founders with the commitment of a publisher, as well as to Jay Kahn and Miller Freeman for backing our vision with both expertise and enthusiasm.

We are deeply indebted to those contributors who, at one time or another, served as chapter editors and brought together the wide array of contributions received, or who made significant contributions of their own towards producing a cohesive set of chapters: Craig DeLucia, Charlie Dirksen, Charles Franz, Herschel Gelman, Chris Glushko, Kim Hannula, Jack Lebowitz, Jim Raras, Dan Seideman, David Steinberg, Mark Toscano, and Tim Wade.

In particular, we are indebted to Kevin Shapiro, Phish's archivist, for his help in verification and compilation, and to the Setlist Working Group—initially, Craig DeLucia, Charlie Dirksen, Benjy Eisen, Charles Franz, Herschel Gelman, Phil Nazzaro, Dan Purcell, Jim Raras, Dan Seideman, and Darius Zelkha—for their tireless dedication, which has produced a document with *hundreds* of new shows and *thousands* of additional corrections over any previous setlist collection. For assisting them in this mammoth effort by sharing and reviewing tapes, contributing data, and engaging in lengthy discussions about accuracy and notation, we also want to thank Aaron Brandewie, Aaron Rosenthal, Adam Roberts, Adam Rosenberg, Aldo Torre, Allison Tuthill, Amanda Henry, Andy Puckett, Benji Eisen, Billy Reeves, Bradley Lonard, Brent Cusher, Brian Hayle, Brian Levine, Brian Lipman, Butch Weiss, Carl Distefano, Chad Fagin, Charles Franz, Charlie Dirksen, Chris Barnes, Chris Bertolet, Chris Cottagio, Chris Fischer, Chris Glushko, Chris Stebbins, Christian McKee, Christopher R. Bingham, Clay Ellwood, Craig DeLucia, Creg Bradley, Curtis Monroe, Dan Hantman, Dan Hobbs, Dan Purcell, Dan Mittag, Dan Seideman, Dan Shupack, Daniel Ritchey, Darius Zelkha, Dave Donohue, Dave Kennedy, Dave Mangini, Dave O'Hara, David Anderson, David Goodwin, David Riddle, David Shulman, David Steinberg, Dean Budnick, Dennis Kelley, Duffy, Ellis Godard, Eric Oberbroeckling, Eric Salmassy, Erik Janus, Erika Hokanson, Evan Romano, Forrest Tinsley, Franklin C. Malemud, Geoff Gardner, Greg Ehle, Herschel Gelman, Ian Cummings, Jagjit Chadha, Jakim Duckstein, Jason Buc, Jeff Ishaq, Jeremy Birchman, Jess Habansky, Jesse Appelman, Jesse Darlington, Jesse Jarnow, Jim Doherty, Jim Raras Jr, Joe Rioux, John Procopio, Jonathan D. Price, Jonathan Krall, Joseph DiLiberto, John Davis, Josh Rosenfield, Josh Zelkowitz, J.R. Trimpe, Julia Mourdant, Karen Neuhaus, Katie Holloway, Kevin Larsen, Kevin Shapiro, Kim Hannula, Kit Tincher, Leo Kotas, Marc Toscano, Marcus Pearson, Mark Regopoulos, Martin Acaster, Matt Greenfield, Matt Monaco, Matt Myers, Matthew Bourland, Matthew King, Mehool Patel, Michael Batta, Michael Calore, Michael Gouker, Mike Greenhaus, Michael R. Isenbek, Mike Kriz, Mike Lerman, Mike O'Dea, Mike Pelczarski, Mike Preston, Nick Johnston, Patrick Forsland, Paul Chung, Paul Jones, Pete Gershon, Peter Bierman, Phil Nazzaro, Phillip Zerbo, Rebecca Morin, Reilly Brennan, Ric Dean, Rich Steele, Rich Vining, Richard Plumb, Richard Wright, Rob Clay, Robert, Ryan Creasey, Ryan Stroud, Saul Wertheimer, Scott Silton, Shawn Wiley, Simon Cohn, Steve Dolley, Steve Logan, Steven Dolley, Steven Drebber, Syd Schwartz, Ted Kartzman, Tim Wade, Timothy Gibson, Todd Hartgrove, Tom Bailey, Vincent Isaia, Wayne Lane Jr.and Yance Davis.

For help in compiling and verifying the master list of available soundboards, a mammoth effort which Phil Nazzaro continues to direct, now incorporated into the Tape Notes tables, thanks to Adam Eakins, Andrew Harrison, Andrew Rakow, Bill Hance, Blair K. Willis,

Bob Haas, Brendan Komala, Brett Parnes, Brian Hayle, Brian Walsh, Bryan Foley, Chris Klebl, Chris Tweedy, Clay Ellwood, Cobee (single name okay), Craig Hillwig, Dan Haugh, Dave Donohue, David Horowitz, Dennis Ruggeri, Diana Hamilton, Dirk Cota, Eric Vandercar, Eric Angel, Eric Burns, Eric Doherty, Forrest Tinsley, Fred Sweet, George Carson, Greg Bradley, Hano Bunjes, Jamie Lutch, Jeff Kemp, Jesse Jarnow, John Garrity, John Isham, John Ishaq, John Joyce, John Procopio, Jonathan Rozes, Joshua Devins, Joshua Zelkowitz, Kenji Yamaguchi, Lenny Stubbe, Mark Powers, Mark Walsh, Matt Judd, Melissa Agar, Michael O'Dea, Michael Perrott, Mike Pfeil, Mike Weitman, Nick Gorevic, Noelle LaMorgese, P. Marshall, Paul Jones, Phil Fernandez, Randy Ward, Rob Clay, Rob Garland, Robbie Dunn, Scott Morrison, Sean Yockus, Shane Neff, Shane O'Reilly, Steve Chiaramonte, Steve Leonard, Steven Tobani, Terry Weadock, Tim Danielson, Tim Kreytak, Tim Stritmaper, Trent Blomquist, Will Hermann, Yance Davis, and, of course, Phil Nazzaro.

For help in documenting and verifying other Tape Notes information, Aaron Fogg, Aaron Rosenthal, Adam Detsky, Andrew Becherer, Andrew Bump, Andrew Hall, Andrew McAuliffe, Ben Greenfield, Bo Palmer, Brad Nahill, Brian Burns, Brian Gore, Brian Gore, Brian Levine, Brian Palmer, Brian Wagner, Cary Chapnick, Charlie Franz, Chris Anderson, Chris Giorgi, Chris Glushko, Chris Guinn, Chris Mahovlich, Christopher Salge, Clay Redmond, Corey Kamerman, Dan Hantman, Dan Mittag, Dan Shupack, Daniel Gold, Darian Johnston, Dave Kieval, Dave Striepe, Eddie Dunn, Eric Ward, Evan Myers, Geof Koss, Geoff Gardner, Geoff Grant, Glenn Goldstein, Greg Dutton, Greg Schwartz, Ian Harbilas, Jack Riley, Jagjit Chadha, Jamie Jollie, Jamil Muasher, Jason Back, Jason Powers, Jeff Bigham, Jeff Farrow, Jeff Wieczorek, Jeffrey Palmer, Jeremy Welsh, Jerry Iannucci, John Florek, Jon Carrico, Josh Carver, Jure Babnik, Keith McCrary, Ken Wilson, Laurence Birdsey, Lukas Karlsson, Marcus Pearson, Mark Decker, Mark Wallace, Matt Cardullo, Matt Hemlepp, Matt Mazzuckelli, Matthew Kresge, Melissa Agar, Michael Batta, Mike Lerman, Mitchell Kalmar, Phil Nazzaro, Rob Sharron, Scott Sandler, Scott Silton, Sean Pennefather, Spencer Young, Stephen Rogers, Steve Cole, Steven Cohen, Steven M. Paolini, Taylor Franklin, Tim Sullivan, Todd Puckett, Tom Bloch, Tom Fitzgerald, Glenn Krupiak, Jim Curtis, Josh Ehrlich, Ken Pierce, Kirra Paskins, Kolin Kelly, Mike Salvo, Pete Knowlton, Spagackle Shea, Ted Rogers and Wolfgang Norton.

For help with the Band Chronology, thanks to Tim Wade, Kim Hannula, and Tom Marshall, Kevin Shaprio, Jason Colton, Shelly Culbertson, and Luann Abrahams.

For help in writing and verifying song histories, Aaron Rosenthal, Aaron Senegal, shley and Travis Willwerth, Becky Bird, Becky Morin, Bill Beach, Billy Rickards, Brad Davis, Bradley Lonard, Bryan Rodgers, Charles Franz, Charlie Dirksen, Chris Bertolet, Chris Glushko, Christian McKee, Craig DeLucia, Dan Hantman, Dan Nooter, Dan Purcell, Dan Seideman, Daniel Mielcarz, Danielle Fodor, Dave Abrahams, Dave Manier, Dave McCallum, David Shulman, David Steinberg, Dead, Dean Budnick, Dusty from Antelope, Ellis Godard, Emilie DeClerck, Eric Angel, Eric Isaacson, Erik Swain, Grant Calof, Herschel Gelman, Jake Williams, Jamie Treworthy, Jason McEwan, Jef Samp, Jen Marshall, Jeremy Goodwin, Jeremy Welsh, Jesse Appelman, Joseph Stanko, Josh Miller, Julie Wright, Justin Vaccaro, Katie Holloway, Keren Albala, Kevin Shapiro, Kim Hannula, Marcie Vogel, Mark Shapiro, Mark Toscano, Martha Hunt, Martin Acaster,

Matt King, Minderella, Neal Grigsby, Nikki Rhoe, Phil Nazzaro, Phillip Zerbo, Saul Dude, Syd Schwartz, The Jackleens, Tom Marshall, Tri Le, Yance Davis, and to any other song historians not named here.

For help with the Jamming Tune Summary Charts: Allison Tuthill, Anne Sither, Becky Morin, Benjy Eisen, Billy Rickards, Charles Franz, Christian McKee, Creg Bradley, Dan Mittag, Dave Kennedy, David Shulman, Duffy, Herschel Gelman, Jared Proctor, Jason Buc, Jason Hawkins, Jason Rose, Jeff Leiker, Jeremy Goodwin, Jesse Appelman, Jesse Appelman, Jonathan Krall, John Davis, Kim Hannula, Lance Paruka, Marcus Pearson, Mark Regopolous, Marty Acaster, Matt O'Malley, Michael Batta, Mike Lerman, Mike Preston, Phillip Zerbo, Richard Plumb, Rob Kallick, Robert, Ryan Stroud, Saul Wertheimer, Scott Hershkowitz, Shawn Wiley, Simon Cohn, Syd Schwartz, and Tim Wade.

For help writing the guestbook, thanks to Benji Eisen, Ellis Godard, Matt King, Christian McKee, Mark Lynn, Matt King, Michael Preston, Aaron Rosenthal, and "Fred."

For help in compiling and verifying the Sideshows material, thanks to Adam Kurth, Alex Oliver, Andy Goodman, Anthony Cotton, Benjy Eisen, Carl Walter, Christian A. Binder, Christian McKee, Clay Ellwood, Craig DeLucia, Dan Mielcarz, Donald Glasgo, Ellis Godard, Eric Conko, Erin McKeon, Franklin C. Malemud, Jeffrey Trisoliere, Jessee Jarnow, Jimmy T., John B. Dilly, John Fingland, John J. Wood, Jon Smith, Joseph Sirotnak, Kristen Godard, Marcie Vogel, Matt Steve, Matthew King, Michael A. O'Dea, Nick Johnston, Patrick D. Burke, Phil Nazzaro, Rob Hillard, Robert G. Johnson, and Troy Colyer.

For help with Venue Information, thanks to Aaron Soriero, Adam Cox, Andrew Kaplan, Andy Adelwitz, Brian Conner, Casey Logan, Charlie Dirksen, Dan Nooter, Dan Meilcarz, Dan Seideman, Darryn Marcus, David Steinberg, Ed Peterson, Jay Young, Jeff Casale, Jen Marshall, Jeremy Barry, Mark Toscano, Matt Heller, Michael Bosold, Mike, Sara York, Stewart Buttersfield, Tim Allison, Tim Todd, and Timothy Miciotto, Jr.

For assistance with the discography, thanks to Daniel Mielcarz, Hal Waterman, Harry Childers, Julia Mourdant, Kevin Shapiro, Mark Goldberg, Mark Hutschison, Mark Toscano, Matthew Cramer, Nick Johnston, Scott Weiser, Syd Schwartz, Tom Costello, and Tom Walters.

For dictionary entries, suggestions, and corrections, thanks to Adam Schneider, Adam Suritz, Alex Mack, Alex Rose, Amanda Henry, Andrew Mount, Andy Gadiel, Bob Aderhold, Brian Gearing, Cass Blacksbear, Charlie Gubman, Chris Bertolet, Christ Intagliata, Corey Ferber, Craig DeLucia, Dan Correll, Dave Bulkin, Dave Kieval, David Johnston, Diane Weitfle, Ellen Rose Hollidge, Eric Stiens, Jason Musante, Jeff Katz, Jeff Williams, Jen Marshall, Jim Busse, Joe Chisholm, John Fennessy, John Seidenspinner, Jonathan Pron, Julia Mourdant, Keith Bergstrom, Kellie Olenick, Kelly Baines, Kelly Morris, Louis Arzonico, Marco Walsh, Mark Decker, Mark Huisman, Matt Dan, Matt Nelson, Mike Greenhaus, Mike Kleinhaus, Mike Pelletier, Mike Schultheisz, Mike Tarkanian, Patel Mehool, Phil Nazarro, Richard Schadle, Rob Barrett, Robert Buysse, Ryan Barone, Sara Morrison, Scott Caffrey, Scott Carter-Eldred, Scott Eidam, Scott O'Brien, Steve Gibbs, Tara Fowler, Tim Gerland, Travis Spurley, Troy Young, and Yance Davis.

For image (photography and artwork) coordination, thanks to Jack Lebowitz and Kat Griffin; for submissions, permissions, and assistance, thanks to Aaron Boros, Aaron Hawley, Annie Plitz, Arjuna

Sunderam, Bill Yudichak, Brian Porter, Brian Turnerb, Casey Leonard, Charlie Dirksen, Chris diLeo, Chris Guthrie, Chris Mullinax, Clare Grill, Craig Judkins, Dan Bond, Daniel Serge Chorba, Dave dello Russo, Dave Leonelli, Dave Levin, David Steinberg, Denise Elliot, Derek Finbolt, Don Bruce, Elise Ryerson, Eric Angel, Eric Venezia, Forrest Reda, Greg Ehle, Heather Townsend, Heidi Mann, Holly Daniels, James Mahan, Jason Stuffle, Jay Young, Jeremy Little, Jim Francis, Jim Raras, Joby Semmler, Joe Rioux, John Davis, John Paluska, Jon Mantell, Jure Babnik, Kat Griffin, Kevin Pole, Kevin Shapiro, Kim Hannula, Kristen Godard, Liz Kittleman, Marco Walsh, Mark Jensen, Mark Majewski, Matt Scellen, Michael Cohen, Michael Collins, Michael Haecker, Michael McNamara, Mike Brez, Mike Rowe, Nathan Hale, Ned Beebe, Olaf Nelson, Pete Sitzman, Peach Friedman, Randy Ward, Roberto Santana, Scott Harris, Scott Hun, and Steve Drebber.

Word of mouth about this book would not have spread as rapidly, or as extensively, without the assistance of those who designed Mockingbird Flyers—Damian Powers, Dan Hantman, Darius Zelkha, Ellis Godard, Marcie Vogel, and Mila Currier—to those who reproduced the Flyers at their own cost—Darius Zelkha, Jim Raras, Jack Lebowitz, Kathleen Griffin, Lizbeth Trebour Karpman, Marcie Vogel, Mike Witt, Mila Currier, Ross Dunkel, and Scott Boyarksy—and to those who distributed Mockingbird flyers and magnets to fans, outside Phish shows and elsewhere—Andrew Hitz, Annie Lebowitz, Beatriz Walsh, Benji Eisen, Brian Lipman, Charlie Dirksen, Charles Franz, Chris Charapata, Craig DeLucia, Dave Donohue, Dan Hantman, Darius Zelkha, David Shulman, David Steinberg, Doug Loeb, Edo Mor, Elise Ryerson, Gavin Lebowitz, Hassan Wahid, Heather McLaughlin, Heidi Mann, Jack Lebowitz, Jeremy Birchman, Jeremy Welsh, Jesse Applebaum, Jim Raras, Kathleen Griffin, Kerry McDonough, Laura Boyarsky, Karne Venini, Kristen Godard, Marcie Vogel, Mark Goldberg, Mark Toscano, Mark Walsh, Martin Acaster, Mike Hayes, Mike Witt, Mila Currier, Noah Cole, Peter Bierman, Phil Nazarro, Rick Friedman, Robert Johnson, Ross Dunkel, Scott Boyarsky, Scott Hershkowitz, Sherry Moran, and Yance Davis.

We also extend thanks and appreciation to Dan Hantman, for his professional management of our web site (www.phish.net/mockingbird); to Noah Cole, for his help and expertise in drafting press releases and in advising us on media relations; to Eddie Dinel and Brian Fisk, who helped establish and continue to help maintain the online communications without which this project could not have occurred; to Marcie Vogel, for managing the deluge of email contributions and suggestions (send more, to mockingbird@netspace.org); to Lee Silverman, who provided professional guidance, moral and financial support, and content recommendations in the early stages of the project; to Theresa M. Skaine, for vetting and work to form the foundation and begin the formal structure; to Tammy Sullivan for clerical support, typing, and morale; and to David Rioux, Joe Rioux, and Eileen Cope for early and helpful publishing advice.

For the suggestion of nearly 150 titles, we thank the creative minds of Noah Andrews, Dean Budnick, Chris Camp, Michael Carney, Jimmy Cartwright, Mike Caspar, Charlie Dirksen, Andy Gadiel, Charles Franz, Matt Grillo, Bill Marconi, Benjamin Gardner, Kathleen Griffin, Dan Hantman, Terance Kishiyama , Jack Lebowitz , Martin Berlett, Mike Motey, Scott Rill, Alex Rose, Aaron Rosenthal, Chris Smith, Greg Starks, Eric Stiens, Phil Nazzaro, Craig DeLucia, Mark Toscano, Kristen Godard, Jon Weber, and Dionysian.

For other content suggestions and assistance, from participation in our public votes to helpful advice to submissions not otherwise acknowledged, we are indebted to thousands more, of whom we are able to name Aaron Aftergood, Aaron Baraff, Aaron Bauman, Aaron Erpel, Aaron Fogg, Aaron Leeder, Aaron Nevins, Aaron Rosenthal, Aaron Tuleja, Adam Dickson, Adam Joshua Schneider, Adam Kessler, Adam Marcinek, Adam Roosevelt, Adam Rosen, Adam Shiffman, Adam Siegartel, Adam Silverman, Adam Smith, Adi Gelem, Agatha Littlewart, Al Maskeroni, Alan Bunder, Aldo Torre, Alek Grabinski, Alex Bilowitz, Alex Juren, Alex Levicki, Alex Pearson, Alex Rose, Alex Uram, Allan Smith, Allison Minter, Amanda Deneca, Amanda Holzwarth, Amanda Panetta, Amy Allen, Andre Terhorst, Andrea Meyer, Andrew Bransford, Andrew C., Andrew Danch, Andrew Epstein, Andrew Hitz, Andrew Sell, Andrew Tritz, Andrew Van Alstyne, Andrew Zanghi, Andy Gadiel, Andy Gadiel, Andy Myatt, Andy Shields, Andy Shonebarger, Andy Ughetta, Angelo Fernandez, Anna Clayton Logan, Ansel Freniere, Anthony Ludwig, Anthony Fappiano, Anthony Fecteau, Anthony Michal, Ara J. Crittenden, Autumn Pifer, Bart Basile, Barton Hodges, Ben Foster, Ben Jacobs, Ben Mann, Ben Skirvin, Ben Skoglund, Ben Spidahl, Ben Whitlock, Benjamin Gardner, Beth Kendall, Beth Montuori, Beth Wysong, Bill Beach, Bill Luke, Bill Marconi, Bill McCafferty, Bill Sharpe, Bill Small, Bill Striejewske, Bill Webster, Bob Miromonti, Bob Weaver, Brad Thacker, Bradley T. Falk, Branden Butler, Brandon Boone, Brandon Sloane, Brandon Stanfill, Brandon Waloff, Brandyn Bowden, Branham Ware, Brendan Reilly, Brendan Smyth, Brent Housteau, Brent Kauffman, Brent Lacy, Brent Macdonald, Bret Andrea, Brett Buffington, Brett Mathany, Brian Altman, Brian Bordage, Brian Davidson, Brian Fisk, Brian Gershey, Brian Gutmann, Brian Hayle, Brian Hensley, Brian Kelly, Brian Lipman, Brian Messineo, Brian Muise, Brian O'Connor, Brian O'Toole, Brian Palmer, Brian Pleban, Brian Roets, Brian Smith, Brien Christesen, Brooke Pitman, Brooks Williams, Bruce Carlin, Bruce Norbeck, Bruce Sither, Bruce Usry, Bryan Chambers, Bryan Gauvin, Bryan Weiss, Bryan Wilk, C. Purdie, C. Whitehead, Cailleen Louth, Callip Hall, Cameron Garrison, Carrie Schonaerts, Casey Allred, Chad (Mike Gordons unknown cousin), Chad Krisel, Chad Peterson, Chapman Wakefield, Charles W. Craven Jr., Charlie Burkett, Charlie Dirksen, Charlie Gubman, Charlie K., Charlie Weaver, Charlz Franz, Charney Cale, Chelle Patterson, Chett Bland, Chris Bertolet, Chris Bracken, Chris Camp, Chris Coyier, Chris Delmonico, Chris Drabandt, Chris Ford, Chris Francescani, Chris Giorgi, Chris Gosey, Chris Johnston, Chris Kellermeyer, Chris Kilgallon, Chris Kula, Chris Lott, Chris O'Donnell, Chris Paulson, Chris Plummer, Chris Pullen, Chris Reisetter, Chris Sahl, Chris Shea, Chris Skinkle, Chris Smith, Chris Stebbins, Chris Sullivan, Chris Taylor, Chris Waterman, Christian Campagna, Christian Landes, Christian Vise, Christine Doll, Christopher Cassata, Christopher Tank, Clay, Clay Redmond, Colby Jensen, Colin Gowland, Colin Protch, Connor O'Malley, Coralyn Brazee, Cory Biggerstaff, Cory Ferber, Cory Tressler, Craig Blean, Craig Judkins, Craig Vinecombe, Cristina Arcuri, Damian Powers, Dan Alford, Dan Alford, Dan Auble, Dan Calderaro, Dan Egan, Dan Hantman, Dan Hobbs, Dan Kaiser, Dan Laves, Dan Mittag, Dan Murray, Dan Nooter, Dan Purcell, Dan Schar, Dan Shapiro, Dan Simons, Dan Smith, Dan Tepper, Dan Tompkins, Dan Treharne, DanDeBeer, Daniel Cohen, Daniel Hinojosa, Daniel Van Liere, Danielle Zahn, Danin Little, Darrell Crick, Darus Zahm, Dave Angus Blackwood, Dave Bristol, Dave Broering, Dave Gould, Dave

Herrmann, Dave Keller, Dave Kieval, Dave Levin, Dave Lundgren, Dave Madden, Dave McCabe, Dave McGuriman, Dave Olson, Dave Reese, Dave Saslowsky, Dave Striepe, Dave Striepe, Dave Willard, Davey Jones, David Clement, David Etelson, David Kane, David Laramie, David Mazza, David Olsen-Fabian, David Paisley, David Riemenschneider, David Rugh, David Steinberg, David Stritch, David Thomas, David Waxman, Dean Budnick, Deanne Herman, Denis Dasilva, Dennis Moore, Derall Riley, Derek Brown, Derek Niedermayer, Diana Ladd, Dickson Corbett, Don Bruce, Don Davies, Dorothy Henderson, Doug Budzak, Doug Fox, Doug Olsen, Douglas Fleischmann, Dovie Spitz, Dred Folly, Drew Story, E. Damien Raba, Elena Heiblim, Elisa Leeder, Elizabeth Severson, Elizabeth Smith, Ellen Ross, Ellis Kline, Emily Wentzell, Emma Schnitzel, Eric Aden, Eric Burns, Eric Callighan, Eric Fox, Eric Goldhammer, Eric Gross, Eric Haugee, Eric Land, Eric Stiens, Eric Tracy, Eric Watts, Eric Wyman, Eric Zielinski, Erica Larson, Erick Barbare, Erik "Stretch" Janus, Erik Andrulis, Erik Brynildsen, Erik Dempsey, Erika Hokanson, Evan Cohen, Evan Drachman, Fabrizio Tarara, Frank Burgess, Frank Burris, Fred Dolly, Gabe Concepcion, Gabriel Jessee, Gabrielle Goldberg, Gandalf Calrisian, Garrett Parker, Garth Tingey, Gary Block, Gary Griffith, Gene Wozny, Geoff Dyhrberg, Geoff Pelletier, Geoffrey Gardner, George Hamilton, George Spater, Glenn White, Gordon Davidescu, Gordon Sharpless, Greg Ehle, Greg Felsen, Greg Genrich, Greg Hotchkiss, Greg Monack, Greg Mortenson, Greg Seltzer, Greg Shapiro, Greg Starks, Greg Starks, Greg Wikoff, Gretchen Bender, Guido Calrissian, Guy Danka, Hanif Khan, Hassan Wahid, Hayden Ryan, Hillary Spera, Holly Isbister, Ian Mitchell, Ian Mizel, Ian Waters, Ilan Halfi, J. Oppenheimer, J. Roth, J. Turick, J.R. Wanner, Jack Lebowitz, Jackie McKeown, Jackie Racicot, Jacob Hall, Jacob Isleib, Jacob Lake, Jacob McNulty, Jade Emerson, Jake Ferry, Jake Morrill, Jake Wilkinson, James Burke, James Hackethorn, James Hooper, James Kinkela, James Lawton II, James Malatino, Jamey Boike, Jami Marchitto, Jamie Burkart, Jamie Felitte, Jamie Fitzpatrick, Jamie Hart, Jarad Fleming, Jared Hirsch, Jared Hulteen, Jared Stroud, Jason Azuma, Jason Chung, Jason Colton, Jason Ghionzoli, Jason Link, Jason Musante, Jason Powers, Jason Powers, Jason Rocha, Jason Schwartz, Jason Simodejka, Jason Uttam, Jason Uttam, Jason Wilde, Jay Allan, Jay Flaherty, Jay Gilmore, Jay Mehta, Jay Turner, Jay Westensee, Jeanine Bogart, Jedediah Smith, Jeff Arndt, Jeff Battles, Jeff Conboy, Jeff Farrow, Jeff Furlow, Jeff Goldenberg, Jeff Goodman, Jeff Johnson, Jeff Katz, Jeff Kemp, Jeff Leiker, Jeff MacMullen, Jeff Marowitz, Jeff Meyers, Jeff Miller, Jeff Scogland, Jeff Tansley, Jeff Tehan, Jeff Warren, Jeff Wieczorek, Jeff Williams, Jeffrey Pollock, Jen Hall, Jen Malfet, Jen McCoy, Jen Rubin, Jenn Pereira, Jennie Schniedwind, Jennifer Rubin, Jereme Steele, Jeremiah Drueke, Jeremy and Nicole", Jeremy Birchman, Jeremy Goodwin, Jeremy Little, Jeremy Timko, Jeremy Welsh, Jesse Appleman, Jesse Brady-Davenport, Jesse Itzkowitz, Jesse Jarnow, Jessica Hanson, Jessica Hemp, Jessica Piccirilli, Jim Clough, Jim Corelis, Jim Cowan, Jim Larson, Jim Middleton, Jim Moran, Jim Odoherty, Jim Piermarini, Jim Predhomme, Jimmy Cartwright, Jimmy Corio, Jimmy Lalp, Joe Bernardi, Joe Cat, Joe Chisholm, Joe Kozlinski, Joe Maly, Joe Morra, Joe Oliveri, Joe Shrieve, Joe Weaver, Joel Masters, Joel Sivertsen, Joel Soldinger, John "Yoda" Davis, John Alexa, John Barrett, John Behan, John Bohan, John Breunig, John Clark, John Coghlan, John Dileo, John Donnelly, John Ducharme, John Dunham, John Florek, John

Hafner, John Hile, John Joyce, John Milham, John Paluska, John Shumberger, John Skogstad, John Thornbury, Jolan Patterson, Jon Bayko, Jon Cramer, Jon Freed, Jon Gilbert, Jon L. Boyer, Jon Mueller, Jon Murphy, Jon Park, Jon Schroeder, Jon Snow, Jon Steinman, Jon Titus, Jon Weber, Jon Weber, Jon Weidler, jonathan caufield, Jonathan Mueller, Jonathan Super, Jonathan Van Schoick, Jonny Cooper, Joseph Beddia, Joseph Brown, Joseph Collins, Josh Alcorn, Josh Bortnick, Josh Carver, Josh Castleberry, Josh Fullam, Josh Samis, Josh Tizel, Joshua Cano, Joshua Levine, Jules Maciulis, Julian West, Jure Babnik, Jure Babnik, Jurgen Fauth, Justin Antos, Justin Braniff, Justin Garcia, Justin Gardner, Justin Johnson, Justin LeWinter, Justin Ryan, Justin Sokol, Juston Brommel, Juston Brommel, Kat Ridolfi, Kat Widden, Katherine Toan, Katie Styles, Katleeeen Griffin, Keith Bergstrom, Keith Fridel, Kelly Cook, Ken Smith, Kendra Fettig, Kent Nevitt, Kerri Hartnett, Kevan Ouimet, Kevin Doyle, Kevin Dunlap, Kevin Grizzard, Kevin Kleinbord, Kevin Larsen, Kevin McCormack, Kevin O'Neill, Kevin Pole, Kevin Price, Kevin Shapiro, Kevin Tankersley, Kevin Umberger, Kimberlee Bell, Klaus Bender, Klay Waddel, Kobi Stapleton, Kris Kwilas, Kristi Trover, Kristy Cardinal, Kurt Heckel, Kurt Johnson, Kurt Shafer, Kyle C. Kreischer, Kyle Hanefeld, Lamar Lewis, Lance Parauka, Lauren Clay, Lauren Sherrow, Lauren Thirer, Lee Silverman, Lee Swerdlin, Leigh Gallagher, Leo Kotas, Lisa Hartmayer, Liz Goldman, Lizzie Henricks, LJ Saxton, Love Tooth, Luke Hilko, Lydia Kellogg, Maggie Busser, Mandy Mezger, Manning Doub, Marc Eisenberg, Marc Olson, Marc Pechaitis, Marc Sobelman, Marcie Vogel, Marco Walsh, Marcus Pearson, Marcus Pearson, Marcus Shutta, Mark Carr, Mark Decker, Mark Herman, Mark Horowitz, Mark Lynn, Mark Mahfouz, Mark Powers, Mark Toscano, Mark Young., Martin Acaster, Martin Berlett, Mathias Loertscher, Matt Burmeister, Matt Clay, Matt Conley, Matt Cundiff, Matt Eiting, Matt Fell, Matt Grillo, Matt Habinowski, Matt Herman, Matt Hoiland, Matt Hurley, Matt Job, Matt Kanable, Matt Latuchie, Matt Luken, Matt Mack, Matt Maguire, Matt Mazzuckelli, Matt Moore, Matt Musick, Matt Musick, Matt Schwartz, Matt Steeves, Matt Sweeney, Matt Virta, Matt Wroc, Matteo Corvo, Matthew Campbell, Matthew Hooper, Matthew Imperato, Matthew Ulrich, Max Brand, Maya Szatai, Mechelle Zarou, Megan Stuart, Megan Thomas, Melinda Cummings, Melissa Clark, Micah Kagan, Micah Mellander, Michael Abramo, Michael Arden, Michael Carney, Michael Cohen, Michael Cohen, Michael D. Sauda, Michael Drossner, Michael Garey, Michael Gouker, Michael Hillson, Michael Jorda, Michael Marusin, Michael McCarthy, Michael Packer, Michael Potvin, Michael Prusinowski, Michael Rammer, Michael Trevors, Michael Turi, Michelle Akin, Michelle Akin, Michelle Kawecki, Mike Adey, Mike Alexander, Mike Arant, Mike Beuselinck, Mike Burnettf, Mike Campitelli, Mike Carmody, Mike Caspar, Mike Chesnut, Mike Discavage, Mike Foley, Mike Hagemann, Mike Hanley, Mike Jones, Mike Lehner, Mike Lerman, Mike Meier, Mike Montague, Mike Motey, Mike Niven, Mike Olson, Mike Orzali, Mike Rowe, Mike Rowe, Mike Russo, Mike Scott, Mike Skoko, Mike Skuro, Mike Stolte, Mike Sullivan, Mike Valente, Mike Viita, Mike Witt, Mikey Perrott, Nat Katin-Borland, Nate Black, Nate Ouellette, Nathan Butryn, Nathan Zuiderzee, Nathaniel Spelich, Ned Beebe, Neil Craven, Nicholas Anziano, Nick Buscemi, Nick Rogoff, Nick Viens, Nicole Apatoff, Niki Stevens, Noah Andrews, Noah Cole, Noah Sassaman, Nposkarbiewicz, Oskar Kollen, Paige Clem, Pat Coyle, Pat Hootbart, Patricia Crews, Patrick Daley, Patrick Drake, Patrick Lewis, Patrick Thompson, Patsy Winchester,

Paul D. Crittenden, Paul Heintz, Paul Hemmer, Paul Kanterman, Paul Santorelli, Paul Shea, Paul Vercoe, Pete Pidgeon, Peter Caffrey, Peter Hasenfuss, Peter Knowlton, Peter Roose, Peter Savage, Phil Nazzaro, Philip DePaul, Phillip Spell, Phillip Weaver, Previn Waran, Prof. David Keller, Ralston Barnes, Randy Freedman, Randy Fruchter, Randy Hambley, Randy Little, Randy Litton, Randy Ward, Reba Radey, Rebecca Friedman, Rebecca Palmisano, Rebekah Liebling, Rich Barrett, Rich Spinale, Rich Williams, Richard Garvey, Richard Thornton, Rick Kuhlman, Rob Arey, Rob Boyle, Rob Clay, Rob Gamble, Rob Kirchhoff, Rob Lee, Rob Ortiz, Rob Robinson, Rob Spidle, Robert Dietrich, Robert Down, Robert Francis, Robert j Kirkpatrick, Robert Johnson, Rosemary Mackintosh, Ross Dunkel, Ross McDevitt, Russell Whitesides, Ryan Anderson, Ryan Bocchino, Ryan Cleary, Ryan Clement, Ryan Flaherty, Ryan Fletcher, Ryan Kraemer, Ryan Liszak, Ryan Magnuson, Ryan Morris, Ryan Nelson, Ryan Walsh, Rytas Stankunas, S. Reifenberg, Sam Aaronian, Sam Castellano, Sam Gilman, Sam Potts, Sam Smith, Sara Beggs, Sara Fisher, Sara Krywcun, Sara White, Sarah Benjamin, Sarah Bensenhaver, Sarah Clark, Sarah Golden, Saul Wertheimer, Scott Bernstein, Scott Boyarsky, Scott Dunlap, Scott Fortenberry, Scott Graham, Scott Matter, Scott Miller, Scott Ramalho, Scott Ratzmann, Scott Rill, Scott Rosenthal, Scott Silton, Sean Berg, Sean Foley, Sean Gamble, Sean Marchetti, Sean Marien, Sean Nowlin, Sean Wiseman, Seth Gowans, Seth Licis, Seth Reynolds, Shadd Scott, Shane Brennan, Shannon DeVerna, Shannon DeVerna, Shanny Leavitt, Shelly Culbertson, Sly Zogheib, Srinath Vadlamani, Stan Jackson, Stephen Rodgers, Steve Cunningham, Steve Dolley, Steve Eisenhauer, Steve Jakus, Steve Messina, Steve Nacht, Steve Nissman, Steve Paolini, Steve Sleeve, Steve The Dude, steve vermey, Steveemmerich, Steven Cohen, Steven Wong, Sunil Shah, Tatjana Bodrozic, Ted Ahern, Ted Quinn, Tegan Culler, Terance Kishiyama, Terry Kilcullen, Thaddeus Wanat, Tharaneetharan Arumugarajah, Thom O'-Connor, Thomas Bedeian, Tim Barney, Tim Brousseau, Tim Delaune, Tim DiBerardino, Tim Fogel, Tim Gondek, Tim Howard, Tim Mahon, Tim Markham, Tim Mccarthy, Tim Sullivan, Timothy Braun, TJ Dolliver, Todd Beckman, Todd Hamlin, Tom and Leslie Sabo, Tom Benoit, Tom Bloch, Tom Bullotta, Tom Ciavarella, Tom Dorgan, Tom Gardner, Tom Hallissey, Tom Johnson, Tom Nagle, Tony Barresi, Tony Stec, Travis Albright, Travis Mize, Travis Pemberton, Trevor Smith, Trey Anastasio, Tycho Bergquist, Tyler Penn, Tyler Young, Tyson Green, Vanessa Scarbeau, Vic Altherr, Vicki Pennington, Vikky Hamm, Wade Fietzek, Walter Eugene O'Reilly, Ward Meehan, Wayne Lustberg, Wayne Yeatman, Will Howell, Will McAuliffe, Will Oast, Wils Linker, Wolfgang Norton, Yale Chasin, Zac York, and Zachary Vincent.

We acknowledge Dean Budnick for *The Phishing Manual*, the maiden contribution of Phish history in book form; and Andy Bernstein, Brain Chasnoff, and Locke Steel for the *Pharmer's Almanac*, which has served fans wanting a printed resource, and which has documented the scene and other aspects ancillary to the band and their music. We have been repeatedly impressed by the journalism of Richard Gehr and Paul Robicheau, who treat Phish and their music with a seriousness lacking in typical coverage, and we are increasingly pleased by the ability of other journalists to discern something special behind the deceiving veil of familiar patterns, symbols, and behaviors.

Above all, and on behalf of all of the contributors to the book as well as the beneficiaries of the charitable proceeds, we thank you the reader, and look forward to your reactions.

With sincerity and hope,

The Board of the Mockingbird Foundation

Charlie Dirksen (Director at Large)
Craig DeLucia (Project Founder and Setlist Guru)
Dan Hantman (Webmaster and Internet Liaison)
Dan Purcell (Director at Large)
Dan Seideman (Director at Large)
David Steinberg (Statistician and Timer)
Ellis Godard (Book and Album Facilitator)
Jack Lebowitz (Legal Consultant and Photographer Liasion)
Kathleen Griffin (Image Coordinator and Artist Liaison)
Kim Hannual (Editor and Funding Chair)
Mark Goldberg (Director at Large and CFO in Part)
Marcie Vogel (Publicity and Public Relations)
Mark Toscano (Director and Historian)

Part I

The Band

The Band

PHISH COMMUNITY CHRONOLOGY

Compiled by Tim Wade, Kim Hannula and Charlie Dirksen

1963

May 17   Page Samuel McConnell is born in Philadelphia, Pennsylvania.[1]

1964

September 30   Ernest Guiseppe Anastasio III ("Trey") is born in Fort Worth, Texas.[1]

1965

February 19   Jonathan Fishman is born in Philadelphia, Pennsylvania.[1]

June 3   Michael Elliott Gordon is born in Boston, Massachusetts.[1]

1982

September 2   Trey, Mike, and Fish enter the University of Vermont.[2]

1983

Fall   Trey, Mike, Jeff Holdsworth (on rhythm guitar), and Marc "Daubs" Daubert (drums and percussion) form a band. Trey, Mike, and Fish also begin jamming together.[2]

December 2   After rehearsing over the Thanksgiving break, Mike, Fish, Trey and Jeff play as "Blackwood Convention" at a Christmas semi-formal dance in Mike's dorm. They play a second show the following night.

1984

Spring   Trey, Tom Marshall, and Marc Daubert form a band called "Bivouac" and record a four-track project entitled *Jaun*. Portions of *Jaun* become part of the demo known as *The White Tape*.[2,3]

October   Trey, Mike, Fish, and Jeff play a party as a band called "Phish" (a pun on Fishman's name) at 69 Grant Street in Burlington.

November 3   Phish plays its first gig at Slade Hall, a dorm on the campus of the University of Vermont.

December 1 Phish's first club gig—with Marc "Daubs" Daubert, their full-time percussionist, and special guest Steve Pollak, the "Dude of Life"—takes place upstairs at Nectar's in Burlington.[2]

1985

April 21 Mike's hall-mate (and "first fan") Brian Long helps get Phish (Trey, Mike, Fish, Jeff, and Marc) a gig at Goddard College's Springfest. There, Phish meets concert organizer Page McConnell. Page is playing keyboards in "Love Goat," an R&B band.[4]

May 3 Page plays with Phish for the first time at the University of Vermont's "Last Day Party."[4]

Summer Trey and Fish travel around Europe with friend Pete Cottone and write "You Enjoy Myself," "Dog Log," and the music to "Harry Hood."[4]

Fall Page joins Phish.[4]

November 23 Mike has a transcendent musical experience while Phish performs in Goddard's cafeteria. Mike is inspired to make music his career.[2]

December Trey distributes cassette tapes as Christmas gifts to friends. Side A features music from Phish's November 23, 1985 Goddard show. Side B is Trey's untitled four-track project, which includes some pieces from *The White Tape* demo and some from his *Jaun* project with Bivouac (Trey, Tom Marshall and Marc Daubert). Tom, Marc and Dave Abrahams contributed back-up vocals, and Pete Cottone contributed the drums, to the project's version of "Slave to the Traffic Light."

1986

Spring Jeff Holdsworth graduates from the University of Vermont and leaves Phish.[4]

Fall Trey and Fish transfer to Goddard College. Trey begins studying composition with Ernie Stires. Fish vigorously improves his drumming craft. [2,4]

October 15 Paul Languedoc mans Phish's soundboard for the first time, at a show at Hunt's for 169 people.[4]

1987

December Page graduates from Goddard. His senior study is entitled *The Art of Improvisation*. Mike graduates from the University of Vermont with a degree in filmmaking and communications.[2]

1988

March 12 Phish performs a live version of Trey's senior study project *The Man Who Stepped into Yester-day*, which features the story of *Gamehendge*, at Nectar's.[5]

Spring John Paluska books Phish's first paid gigs outside of Vermont at Kenny's Castaways in New York City (3/31/88) and at Amherst College (4/2/88).

Phish endures its first "Oh Kee Pa Ceremony."

July Trey earns a Bachelor of Arts from Goddard after submitting his senior study, *The Man Who Stepped Into Yesterday*, which includes the story of *Gamehendge*.

August Phish drives across the country and plays their first shows outside of New England in Telluride, Colorado.[2]

Fall *Junta* is recorded in Revere, Massachusetts, at Euphoria Sound Studios and released as a cassette.[4]

1989

January 26 Phish rents the Paradise in Boston, Massachu-setts, and sells tickets for $5. The show sells out.[4]

March 30 Phish fan and roadie Chris Kuroda's first gig as Phish's Lighting Director at The Front, a Burlington club.[6]

April 21-22 Phish competes in and wins "The Rock & Roll Rumble," a two-night battle of the bands event, at The Front. The win was assured after Fish lowered himself from the rafters—naked—to begin a vacuum solo, but the vacuum was not plugged in.

August "Union Federal," a portion of Phish's second "Oh Kee Pa Ceremony," is recorded, and eventually winds up on the re-release of *Junta*.[4]

Winter *Lawn Boy* is recorded at Archer Studios in Winooski, Vermont.[4]

1990

Spring The Phish.Net begins as an email list of fans on the Internet.[7]

After taking time off, Fish submits his senior study, *A Self-Teaching Guide to Drumming Written in Retrospect*, and graduates from Goddard.

Fall Soundboard patches are discontinued.[4]

September 21 *Lawn Boy* is released on Absolute-A-Go-Go Records.[8]

1991

Summer Phish tours with the Giant Country Horns.[4]

August 3 A free show to thank fans "for eight years of memories" is held at Amy Skelton's horse farm in Auburn, Maine. The show features three sets, and special guests the "Dude of Life" and Sofi Dillof.[2]

August 8 The Phish.Net digest is started.[9]

November 22 Phish is signed by Elektra.[4]

1992

February 18	*A Picture of Nectar* is released by Elektra.[4]
March 3	The Usenet newsgroup rec.music.phish is created and messages once sent to the Phish.Net digest are forwarded to rec.music.phish.[10]
March 22	Opening for Buckwheat Zydeco, Phish performs four songs (including "All Things Reconsidered") live for the Mountain Stage Radio Program at the Cultural Center Auditorium in Charleston, West Virginia. Phish's set is broadcasted to a national audience on National Public Radio in April.
June-July	Phish tours Europe opening for the Violent Femmes.[4]
June 30	Elektra re-releases *Lawn Boy*.
July	Phish performs with the first HORDE tour.[4]
July-August	Phish tours the United States opening for Santana.[4]
Fall	*Rift* is recorded in Burlington, Vermont, and Nashville, Tennessee.[4]
October 26	Elektra re-releases *Junta*. It is a double CD, and includes versions of "Sanity," "Icculus," and "Union Federal" which were not on the original cassette release.[4]

1993

February 2	*Rift* is released by Elektra.[4]
February 3	Page's baby grand piano makes its debut.
Spring	Greenpeace begins sponsoring a table at Phish shows.[10]
Fall	*Hoist* is recorded in October and November at American Recording Company near Los Angeles in Woodland Hills, California.
New Year's Run	Tapers' tickets are available by mail order for the first time.[12]
December 31	Footage for the "Down with Disease" video, the only music video Phish has produced, is shot during the New Year's Eve show.

1994

March 29	*Hoist* is released by Elektra.[4]
Spring	The Green Crew begins touring with Phish, beautifying parking lots before and after shows.[13]
May 19	"Down with Disease" is released by Elektra as a cassette single.
October 31	Phish performs The Beatles' *White Album* as a second set "musical costume." This album choice received the largest number of votes from fans.
December 30	Phish performs on *The David Letterman Show* for the first time, and plays "Chalk Dust Torture" at Dave's request.

Early Concert Promo Poster (4/15/89)

1995

February 5	Through Shelly Culbertson, Phish solicits fan opinions from rec.music.phish for a double live CD.
May 16	Phish performs a benefit show for Voters for Choice in Lowell, Massachusetts.
June 21	*A Live One*, a live album compiled from various performances recorded during 1994, is released by Elektra.[4]
Summer	Non-tapers are able to order Phish tickets by mail for the first time.
Fall	*Rosemary's Digest*, a moderated digest composed of posts chosen from rec.music.phish by Rosemary Dean Macintosh, is started. The Phish.Net digest is discontinued.
October 31	Phish performs The Who's *Quadrophenia*, chosen from the suggestions of fans, as their musical costume for Halloween. Although Frank Zappa's *Joe's Garage* was the number one fan pick, and

an album also loved by band members, Phish decided it would be too challenging to perform.

Fall Phish plays two chess matches against the fans during the Fall tour's shows.

New Year's Run Mail-order tickets feature snazzy holographic art for the first time.

1996

February Tom and Trey go to the Cayman Islands with an acoustic guitar, bongos and a horrible Sony cassette recorder and write 22 songs. Some of those songs, including "Waste," "Steep," and "Swept Away" appear on *Billy Breathes*.[3]

March 12 *Surrender to the Air*, which includes Trey and Fish performing with many other musicians, is released by Elektra.

April 26 Phish performs at the New Orleans Jazz and Heritage Festival.

Spring Phish records a "blob" of music and other pieces that become *Billy Breathes* at Bearsville Studios in Woodstock, New York.

June 6 Phish performs a stealth show, "The Third Ball," at a bar in Woodstock, New York.

Summer Phish returns to Europe, opening some shows for Santana and headlining other shows.

August 16-17 "The Clifford Ball," a two-day festival held at the former Plattsburgh Air Force Base in Plattsburgh, New York, is the largest concert event of the summer in the United States.

Fall "The Phellowship," a support network for fans who choose to remain clean and sober, begins maintaining a table inside Phish shows.[14]

October The digiphish email list is started for DAT tapers and traders.[15]

October 15 *Billy Breathes* is released by Elektra.[4]

October 31 Phish chooses their own musical costume for Halloween: *Remain in Light* by Talking Heads.

1997

February 20 "Phish Food" ice cream is dished out by Ben and Jerry's. Phish's profits benefit the clean-up of Lake Champlain. Phish Food becomes one of Ben & Jerry's most popular flavors.

March 1 Phish records a show in Hamburg, Germany, which becomes the source of the live album *Slip Stitch and Pass*.[4]

March 18 Phish performs a benefit show for the clean-up of Lake Champlain at the Flynn Theatre in Burlington,Vermont. Ben & Jerry's gives away free "Phish Food."[4]

April 29 Through Shelly Culbertson, Phish once again solicits ideas and input from fans of rec.music. phish about the form and content of a possible new live album.

August 16–17 The summer United States tour ends with a two-day festival, "The Great Went," at the former Loring Air Force Base in Limestone, Maine.

October 28 *Slip Stitch and Pass* is released.[4]

Fall Greenpeace discontinues touring and the "Water-Wheel Foundation" takes its place. The Foundation raises money for one local charity at each show.[11]

November Rosemary Mackintosh hands her legendary digest of rec.music.phish's messages over to Benjy Eisen, who operates the digest ("The Eigest") through June, 1999.

December The Phish-Women email list (also known as the "Phunky Bitches") begins.

1998

January Phish finishes 1997 as the #11 grossing concert act. It is the top finish for a "relatively new" act.[16]

March Phish writes and records some of the material included in *Story of the Ghost* in a farmhouse in Stowe, Vermont.[17]

April–June The remainder of *Story of the Ghost* is recorded at Bearsville Studios in Bearsville, New York.[17]

August 15-16 Phish ends its summer United States tour with a two-day concert, "The Lemonwheel," at the former Loring Air Force Base in Limestone, Maine.

August *The White Tape* is released through Phish Dry Goods.

October 3 Phish participates in the Farm Aid benefit in Chicago, Illinois.[4]

October 15 Phish performs in a room made legendary for its psychedelic rock concerts: The Fillmore Auditorium in San Francisco, California.

October 17–18 Phish plays at two of Neil Young's Bridge School Benefit shows at the Shoreline Amphitheater in Mountain View, California.[4]

October 27 *Story of the Ghost* is released by Elektra.

October 31 Phish performs The Velvet Underground's *Loaded* as its musical costume in the second set of its Halloween show in Las Vegas, Nevada.

November 20–21 Phish performs two shows at the Hampton Coliseum in Hampton, Virginia. The shows are eventually released as *Hampton Comes Alive*.

1999

Spring	Trey tours in the "Trey Anastasio Acoustic and Electric Band." Fish first tours with "Jazz Mandolin Project," and then "Pork Tornado."[4]
June	*The Siket Disc* (versions of material from the same recording sessions as *Story of the Ghost*, edited and arranged by Page) is released exclusively through Phish Dry Goods.
July 30–August 1	Phish performs at the Fuji Rock Festival, Niigata, Japan.
August 22	Phillip Zerbo, Brian Fisk, and numerous Mockingbird Foundation contributors renew the Phish.Net digest (a digest of the substantive messages of rec.music.phish, including important Phish news).
October	Phish enters the studio (actually a barn in Vermont) to record *Farmhouse*.[18]
November 23	*Hampton Comes Alive* is released by Elektra.
December 31	Phish celebrates the new year at Big Cypress Seminole Indian Reservation in southern Florida with tens of thousands of fans. It was the world's largest new year's concert event.[4]

2000

May 16	*Farmhouse* is released by Elektra.
June	Phish tours Japan.
September 24	The official website, phish.com, announces that there will be no shows in November, December, or soon thereafter.
September 30	During a live webcast, Trey announces that the band will take an "extended hiatus" after 17 years, but hints at returning for another 17.
October 7	Phish performs their last show before "the break."

Courtesy: Mike Rowe

Sources:

1. Polston, P., "Phish Phacts," *Vox*, Burlington, Vermont, May 10, 1995.
2. Phish.Net FAQ: Phishtory, http://www.phish.net/PhishFAQ/bhistory.html, March 12, 1998.
3. Tom Marshall, 1998.
4. About Phish, http://www.phish.com/bios.html, February 3, 1998.
5. Phish.Net FAQ: TMWSIY, http://www.phish.net/PhishFAQ/stmwsiy.html, March 14, 1998.
6. Budnick, Dean, Interview with Chris Kuroda 12/5/95, http://archive.phish.net/phishtory/12595.html.
7. Phish.Net FAQ: The Phish.Net? http://www.phish.net/PhishFAQ/npnet.html, March 17, 1998.
8. Phish: September, 1990, http://www.phish.com/sept90.html, September, 1997.
9. Phish.Net Digest Volume 1 #1, http://www.phish.net/digests/Volume1/digests.001-024/digest1.91Aug8.gz, August 8, 1991.
10. Phish.Net Digest Volume 1 #239, http://www.phish.net/digests/Volume1/digests.225-249/digest 239.92Mar3.gz, March 3, 1992.
11. Phish.Net FAQ: The WaterWheel Foundation, http://www.phish.net/PhishFAQ/bwaterwheel.html, March 11, 1998.
12. D. Steinberg, 1998.
13. Phish.Net FAQ: Green Crew, http://www.phish.net/PhishFAQ/lgreencr.html, March 4, 1998.
14. Phish.Net FAQ: Phellowship, http://www.phish.net/PhishFAQ/nphellow.html, March 11, 1998.
15. D. Seideman, 1998.
16. Pollstar: Concert Business Analysis, http://www.pollstar.com/97biz.htm, January 1998.
17. Interview with Page McConnell, http://www.phish.com/ghost/, July 29, 1998.
18. Interview with Trey Anastasio, http://jambands.com/may00/features/trey.html, May, 2000.

BIOGRAPHIES

Trey Anastasio

● *Family:* Born Ernesto Guiseppe Anastasio III on 9/30/64 in Fort Worth, TX; moved to Princeton, NJ, summer 1966. Mother Diane ("Dina") was editor of *Sesame Street Magazine* (see Dictionary entry) and has written stories, songs, and even albums with Trey. Father Ernie was the Executive Vice President of Educational Testing Services, who administer the SAT and other aptitude tests. Dog Marley is on both of his guitars and at several shows (see Dictionary entry). Married Susan Eliza Statser (Sue) 8/13/94, with whom he has two daughters, Eliza Jean (b. 8/21/95) and Isabella (b. 4/22/97).

● *Education:* Princeton Day School for junior high (with John Popper and Chris Baron, among others), where his music writing began; Taft School for high school, where Space Antelope formed; University of Vermont (fall 1983 to spring 1986, except for spring 1984), where he met Ernie Stires and hosted a morning radio show ("Ambient Alarm Clock"); and Goddard College (fall 1986 to spring 1988), where he wrote *TMWSIY*.

● *Nicknames:* Trey, Shaggy, The Bad Lieutenant, The Good Lieutenant.

● *Previous bands:* Red Tide and Space Antelope (see entry for the latter in Dictionary).

● *Plays:* guitar (see Dictionary entry), drums (age 7 until 11th grade, though now only when Fishman comes to the front of the stage), percussion mini-kit (reminiscent of Sheila E, and used by Trey summer 1995 to spring 1997 in efforts to stand back from the lead), drumsticks (on any surface, including his guitar, such as at 5/6/93), megaphone (the verses to "Fee" from 11/19/92 to circa 8/96; occasionally during "BBFCFM"; more recently, fall 1994 through 1996, spinning it in circles with his arm extended, adding feedback as in the "David Bowie" 11/26/94; and in "I Didn't Know" 6/15/95), fiddle (e.g. "Butter Them Biscuits" 11/18/94 and 11/19/94, "Long Journey Home" 11/19/94), beer bottle ("BBFCFM" 6/6/96); slice of pizza (11/16/91); acoustic guitar (in the acoustic setup of 1997, usually for "Horse", occasionally for the opening of "My Friend My Friend", and in "Acoustic Army", and more recently for "Inlaw Josie Wales"); a Yamaha AN1-X keyboard (notably during "Sand", but also for example during the 10/5/00 "Guyute"); and piano (during "Walfredo" and "Rock-o-William", and on his solo tour, at the recommendation of Neil Young).

● *Wrote:* Many Phish songs, including all of the songs on *TMWSIY* and *Farmhouse*; and co-wrote others attributed to the full band.

● *Key side shows:* National Guitar Summer Workshop, 1993; Jazz Mandolin Project, 1993; Bad Hat, 1994; New York, 3/21/97; 8 Foot Fluorescent Tubes, 4/17/98; "Solo" tour, 1999; Phil and Friends, 4/15&15/99; and Cosmic Krewe, variously.

● *Side studios: Surrender to the Air*, 1996; *Samson Riffs*, 1997; Jamie Noterthamos' *Head or Tales*, 199?; Merl Saunders' *...and His Funky Friends*, 1998; Cosmic Krewe's *Funk If I Know*, 1998; solo effort *One*

Peter Silzman

Peter Sitzman

"Glide"), and drums (on "Walfredo" and "Rock-o-William").

● *Wrote:* "Cars Trucks Buses" and "Magilla"; co-wrote "Bittersweet Motel" and "Dog-Faced Boy", and others attributed to the full band.
Key side shows: filling in for Duane Allman in the Allman Brothers Band, 3/26/96; and Phil and Friends, 4/15 & 15/99.
● *Side studios:* Widespread Panic's *Space Wrangler*, 1992; Travis' *Good Feeling*, 1997; mixing for *The Siket Disc*, 1999; with the Funky Meters on *Get You A Healin'*, 2000
● *Other projects:* movie score (four or five instrumentals, including "Cars Trucks Buses" for the opening and closing credits) for *Only In America* (which opened in Austin 7/25/97), working with bass player Andy Cotton and sax player Dave Grippo (who also played congas). Also, public service announcement about the dangers of unprotected sex, during the House of Blues Radio Hour in August of 1998, with "Free" playing in the background.

Peter Sitzman

Man's Trash, 1999; Dude of Life's *Under the Sound Umbrella*, 1999; Son Seals' *Letting Go*, 2000.
● *Other projects:* Trey started earliest, working with his mother, but has done the least since Phish began.

Page McConnell

● *Family:* Born Page Samuel McConnell on 5/17/63 in Philadelphia, PA; moved to Basking Ridge, NJ, circa 1967. Father Dr. Jack McConnell worked at McNeil and helped develop Tylenol, then started a free health clinic staffed by retired health personnel in Hilton Head, SC; a Dixieland jazz fan, he has performed with Phish (see Guestbook). Married 9/8/85 to Sofi Dillof (see Setlists, e.g. 8/31/91), with whom he has one daughter, Delia Edna McConnell.
● *Education:* senior year of high school at Lawrence Academy, Groton, MA; Southern Methodist University fall 1982 to spring 1984; Goddard College fall 1984 to December 1987, where he recruited Trey and Jon (and earned $50 for each in a 1986 recruitment drive which helped save the school) and wrote his Senior Study "The Art of Improvisation" under the guidance of Karl Boyle.
● *Nicknames:* Chairman of the Boards (esp. after "Lawn Boy"), Leo (in "Yamar" and "NICU").
● *Previous bands:* Love Goat (see Dictionary entry). Also, used to hang out and play a lot with Carl "Geerz" Gerhard.
● *Plays:* keyboards and theremin (see those Dictionary entries), double bass (a.k.a. "upright bass", inc. fall 1994 and 1995), melodica ("mouth piano", with a keyboard on the side which modulates air blown from one end to the other; spring and summer 1994); acoustic guitar (in "Acoustic Army"); "big harmonica" (on the studio version of

Mike Gordon

● *Family:* Born Michael Elliott Gordon on 6/3/65 in Boston, MA; moved to Sudbury, MA, circa 1970. Father founded the Store 24 convenience chain. Mother Marjorie Minkin is an artist, featured in the song "Minkin" (see Song History, as well as Discography entry for *White Tape*) and in the Minkin backdrops (see Dictionary entry). Married 6/20/98 to Cilla Foster (illustrator for *Mike's Corner*, see Dictionary entry); no children.
● *Education:* Jewish Solomon Schecter Day School in Sudbury, MA; Sudbury High School; University of Vermont (fall 1983 to spring 1987, studying electrical engineering first and then film and communications), where he produced his senior project film "TVF."
● *Nicknames:* Cactus.
● *Previous bands:* Tombstone Blues Band (1960s blues and rock) in high school, the Edge (new wave, with some originals) at UVM, Dangerous Grapes (loud and hard, with Fishman) in early 1984 (while Trey was suspended).
● *Plays:* bass (see Dictionary entry), banjo (esp. 11/19/94, 10/17/98, and 10/18/98), stand-up bass (a.k.a. "upright bass," inc. summer 1993 and 1994), accordion (3/13/92 "Contact"), electric drill (6/15/95 "I Didn't Know" and 7/1/95 "It's Ice"); acoustic guitar (in the acoustic setup of 1997, and in "Acoustic Army"), electric guitar (during "Walfredo" and "Rock-o-William"), Fish's vacuum (4/21/92), and foot bell (e.g. "YEM"

Peter Sitzman

11/9/96, "Ghost" 7/1/97, "YEM" 10/5/00, and at the start of "Scent of a Mule," e.g. 8/16/97; but note that the bell on 12/30/96 was Steve Wright.

● *Wrote:* "BBFCFM," "Catapult," "Contact," "Destiny Unbound," "Fuck Your Face," "Mike's Song," "Mound," "N2O," "Poor Heart," "Scent of a Mule," "Simple," "Train Song," "Weekly Time," and "Weigh"; co-wrote "He Ent to the Bog" and "Minkin," and others attributed to the full band.

● *Key side shows:* Jazz Mandolin Project, 1993; Glen Schweitzer's Jalapeno Brothers, 3/99; and Max Creek, Gordon Stone Trio, and Left-over Salmon, variously.

● *Side studios:* Gordon Stone's *Touch and Go*, 1995; Fiji Mariner's self-titled debut, 1998; with the Meters on *Get You A Healin'*, 2000

● *Other projects:* directed and produced video for "Down with Disease"; *Tracking*, a documentary of the production process behind *Hoist*; *Goodwood*, a short film about Phish at Great Woods; *Stewart*, with Page in the title role and Fishman's critique as a coda; and *Outside Out* (see Dictionary entry). Also wrote the book *Mike's Corner* (see Dictionary); and played a "deluded rock star" in John O'Brien's *Nosey Parker*.

Jon "Fish" Fishman

● *Family:* Born Jonathan Fishman on 2/19/65 in Philadelphia, PA; moved to Syracuse, NY, in early 1970s. Father Len is an orthodontist and sculptor. Mother Mimi started a foundation to combat glaucoma, and has appeared onstage with Phish (see Guestbook) and many New York "jambands." Married 9/28/97 to Pam Tengiris in Las Vegas; currently divorced.

● *Education:* Moses Dewitt High School; University of Vermont (fall 1983 to spring 1984); Goddard College (fall 1986 to spring 1990), where his Senior Study was titled "A Self-Teaching Guide to Drumming Written in Retrospect."

● *Nicknames:* See dictionary entry for Henrietta.

● *Plays:* drums (since age 8), vacuum, and Bag-Vac (see Dictionary entry for each), as well as bagpipe, trombone, cymbals (see Song History for "Cracklin' Rosie"), the "Madonna washboard" (with golden metal breasts, debuted mid-1992); mandolin (in the acoustic setup of 1997), acoustic guitar (in "Acoustic Army"); and bass (during "Walfredo" and "Rock-o-William").

● *Wrote:* "Bye Bye Foot," "Faht," "Ha Ha Ha," "Kung," "Lengthwise," and "My Sweet One," and lyrics to "Gumbo" and "Rock-a-William"; co-wrote "Dave's Energy Guide," "Dog-Faced Boy," "Harpua," and "Tube," and others attributed to the full band.

● *Key side shows:* Bad Hat, 1994; Zambiland Orchestra, 12/22/97; Jazz Mandolin Project, 1998-2000; and Sons of Papaya, Gordon Stone Trio, and Pork Tornado, variously.

● *Side studios:* J. Willis Pratt's *Lost Paradox*, 1993; Dude of Life's *Under the Sound Umbrella*, 1999.

● *Other projects:* Performs (in a pink dress) in the band in the movie *The Wedding Band* (see Dictionary entry).

● *Etc.:* Wears a frock ("dress") on stage, a blue number with orange donuts that was reportedly found in a dumpster. Also, a white dress with eyes/holes during late 1992, a black tailored suit from Italy in summer 1997; and pants and/or a Flyers shirt underneath the "Henrietta dress" fall 1997. On most occasions since, including 5/00 as aired on VH1, he's gone back to nothing underneath—and butt hanging out of the holes. He has also occasionally worn a Viking helmet.

Peter Sitzman

Part II

Songs

Songs
Songs

DISCOGRAPHY

A comprehensive review of Phish's commercial recordings, promotional singles and compilations, and guest appearances on releases by other artists, with both a chronological summary and an alphabetical detailing. Compiled by Herschel Gelman and Ellis Godard.

General Comments

Cycles: Each Phish album has been, in some sense, a response to the one previous. Not having previously had full studio strengths, *Hoist* took studio options to the max. In response to arguable overproduction and excess of guests, the next studio effort (*Billy Breathes*) was birthed from a loose, insolative exercise. (See entry for "The Blob" in Dictionary.)

Titles: Phish's titles, like much of their music, have been unsubtle to the knowing but plain weird to the outside. *Rift*, a concept album about the schism between sleep and consciousness, began a separation from their harsh rock band reality to an unexpected fantasy of success. *Hoist* was a well-funded effort to raise the band's stature, with dozens of guests and the only music video (for *Down With Disease*). And, after years of being asked "When are you going to release a live one," they did—in content and title.

Favorites: Which Phish album you prefer says something about your other musical tastes. That different people like different albums says something about Phish's diversity, which is well represented on their albums. An interest in clean, produced pop might guide you towards *Picture of Nectar*. Toss in a bit of funk, and you'll want *Farmhouse*; or for ballads and the closest to melancholy, try *Billy Breathes*.

Get *Junta* for composed masterpieces, *Lawn boy* for youthful glee, and *Story of the Ghost* for space funk. Of the side projects, *Crimes of the Mind* and *One Man's Trash* may have more detractors than fans, but *Surrender to the Air* is heralded as fascinating experimentation if not brilliant in result. Of the live albums, choose *A Live One* for focused energy, *Slip Stitch and Pass* for a taste of Phish's newer sounding grooves, and *Hampton Comes Alive* for a smattering of everything, as well as the full content of an entire two-night run.

Complete Details, Chronologically

Music, lyric, and vocal credits are given in Song Histories. The following entries are otherwise as complete as possible. Items which are not Phish releases are in brackets.

[Bivouac Jaun] (10/83–12/83)
Earliest known recordings of any members of Phish, including various precursors such as Bivouac as well as Space Antelope.
● *Distribution:* Five copies were made, of which three were given away and the other two lost. One of the five surfaced 14 years later, in June of 1998, but the compilation remains a rarity.

Alphabetic List

Title	Released	Role/Significance	Units sold
(untitled 4-track)	1985	First circulated compilation	n/a
A Live One	6/27/95	1st live release; 1st double-CD release	579,411
Billy Breathes	10/15/96	1st studio gathering in 2 ? years	494,404
Bivouac Jaun	1984	First compilation made of Phish	n/a
Copyright 1987	1987	Circulated widely on Dead lots	n/a
Crimes of the Mind	10/25/95	Dude of Life's first album	87,784
Elektra Promo	1992	Preview of Rift sent to Elektra	n/a
Farmhouse	5/16/00	11th domestic Elektra release	247,839
Hampton Comes Alive	11/23/99	6 full discs, 2 whole shows, no editing	96,006
Hoist	3/29/94	Guest-heavy, producer-intensive	588,652
Junta	4/89	First studio release	*
Junta	10/26/92	Re-released on Elektra	541,087
Lawn Boy	9/21/90	Promoted with first national tour	*
Lawn Boy	6/30/92	Re-released on Elektra	418,927
Man Who Stepped..., The	1986/7	Trey's senior study at Goddard	n/a
One Man's Trash	1999	Trey tracks riffs, words, and noises	*
Phish: A Sampler	1993	Promo compilation of previous releases	*
Picture of Nectar	2/18/92	1st Elektra release	454,940
Rift	2/2/93	4th Elektra release	505,493
Siket Disc, The	6/99	Page's remastering of Ghost outtakes	*
Slip Stitch and Pass	10/28/97	2nd live release; all from the same show	292,625
Stash	1996	Sampler released in Europe	
Story of the Ghost, The	10/27/98	Strong studio capture of the post-'96 funk	299,621
Surrender to the Air	3/12/96	12 musicians, 2 days, 1 studio, no plans	62,040
Under the Sound Umbrella	6/8/99	Dude of Life's 2nd album	6,171
Wendell Studios	7/90	Unreleased studio effort	*
White Tape, The	1985/6	First promotional tape	n/a
White Tape, The	8/98	independent release on CD	*

* Industry reports current as of July 23, 2000. Independent releases not reported.

● *Recorded* by Trey Anastasio, mostly via four-track, throughout high school and into college, but especially October through December of 1983, particularly in Trey's New Jersey basement.

● *Engineered (*so to speak) by Trey in the summer of 1984

● *Tracks:*

Slave to the Traffic Light	??
Run Like an Antelope	I am Hydrogen->
Divided Sky	??
Letter to Jimmy Page	Intros
Aftermath	Little Squirrel->
Injest	??
Prolonged Exposure->	Run Like an Antelope

● *Track note:* Rumored to include "I Am Hydrogen," but not apparent on available copies.

● *Guests:* Marc Daubert and Tom Marshall, on most of the tracks.

● *Title:* Bivouac was the name of a band composed of Trey, Marc Daubert, and Tom Marshall. *Jaun* is the name of a compilation they made, which included at least two songs (King Lear and Little Squirrel) that are not on this compilation.

● *Alternate release:* Parts of the this tape ("Slave," "Antelope," and

"Letter") were later used on the "untitled 4-track" tape.

Untitled 4-Track ('85)

1st promotionally circulated compilation.

● *Distribution:* Perhaps dozens of copies throughout 1986.

● *Recorded:* December 1985 by Trey Anastasio.

● *Tracks: ....(0:40*)*

● *Track Notes:*

* includes 12/1/84 filler

● *Source notes:* Parts of this tape ("Slave," "Antelope," and "Letter") come from *Bivouac Jaun.*

White Tape, The (85-86)

3rd compilation tape made, though 1st one circulated widely as a demo tape, particularly to club owners. A.k.a "The White Album" or simply the "demo". Included pieces not yet fully developed as songs as they are now known, such as "You Enjoy Myself."

● *Circulation:* There are actually multiple versions, as Trey made mixes for gifts that each began a lineage, including one late 1985 and then a slightly different version circa 1986. (By then, *Junta* was recorded but

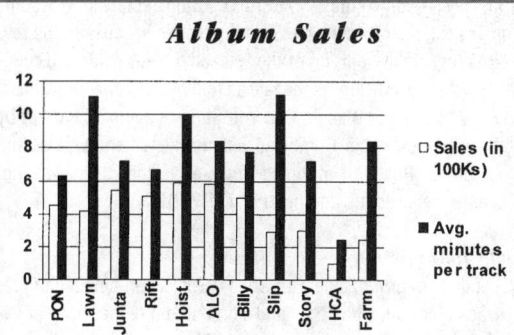

Album Sales

Oddly, what seems most closely related to sales is the length of the title: Sales were strongest for earlier albums with shorter titles, and dropped off with the wordiness of recent titles. Farmhouse, however, at half the length of the previous three titles, also threatens to outsell all three—after only six months!

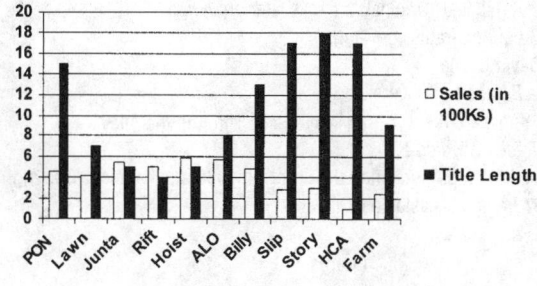

not yet released, and folks were clamoring for some kind of Phish tape to get and cherish.)

● *Recorded:* early 1984 and mid-1985, live and in dorm rooms, by Mike and Trey on four-tracks for the band's personal pleasure.

● *Version 1:* (most common incarnation, although tracklist varies among lineages)

Side A:

Alumni Blues >	Aftermath
Steve Reich (c.1985 only, and	Ingest **
unlabelled on CD release)	NO[2] > ** ~
And So to Bed	Fluff's Travels
You Enjoy Myself (acapella) *	Tube (c.1985 only)
AC/DC Bag	Dog Gone Dog (c.1986 only;
Fuck Your Face	a.k.a. Dog Log)
Divided Sky (intro only,	He Ent to the Bog (c.1986
acoustic)	only)
Slave to the Traffic Light	

Side B:

Run Like an Antelope	Fluffhead (filler with Dude of
Minkin	Life, c.1986 only)
Letter to Jimmy Page	

● *Track notes:* Some versions label "He Ent to the Bog" as "Hamburger."

* Some argue it's one sample of one voiced note played on a synthesizer,

and some insist it is four tracks of repeatedly voiced and edited actual singing of the separate notes, but in either case are probably both Trey.

** There is debate about whether or not "Ingest" and "N20" are different songs.

~ with drilling and picking by Mike

^ with all four members of Phish

^^ acoustic

● *Short Version A:* (45-minutes; only four tracks after "Slave")

Alumni Blues >	Slave to the Traffic Light
Steve Reich (c.1985 only)	Letter to Jimmy Page
And So to Bed	Ingest
You Enjoy Myself (acapella) *	N20
AC/DC Bag	Aftermath
Fuck Your Face	
Divided Sky (intro only,	
acoustic)	

● *Short Version B:* (45-minutes; only two tracks after "Slave")

Alumni Blues >	Divided Sky (intro only,
Steve Reich (c.1985 only)	acoustic)
And So to Bed	Slave to the Traffic Light
You Enjoy Myself (acapella) *	Letter to Jimmy Page
AC/DC Bag	Fluffhead (filler w/ Dude of Life)
Fuck Your Face	

● *Short Version C:* (less commonly circulated, and mixed as a precursor to *Junta*)

Side A (from 1987 *Junta* sessions, mixed as precursor to *Junta*)

You Enjoy Myself	Esther
Fee	Golgi Apparatus
David Bowie	

Side B: (rarely duplicated; live recordings with studio Mike added in remastering)

Wilson	The Sloth
Alumni Blues	Mike's Groove *
Lizards	

● *Track notes:* Side A may end, depending on incarnation, with "Fluffhead" (filler w/ Dude), or with "I Know A Little" and "Sneakin' Sally" from the *Copyright 1987* tape.

* often labeled incorrectly as "Mike's Song".

● *Track note:* All versions include the first recordings of many songs. The copies of tapes are typically ninety-minutes long. Some songs are incomplete, and only four songs have all four members of the band playing.

● *Title note:* There was no official name for fourteen years, but fans attributed "White Album" in allusion to the Beatles' officially unnamed album. Throughout 1996, there was a shift to calling it "White Tape" since it didn't actually exist in album form, and because there was increasing confusion with 10/31/94 II, during which Phish covered the Beatles' *White Album* in its entirety.

Man Who Stepped into Yesterday, The (86-87)

1st compilation tape made (?),a.k.a. *TMWSIY*. Trey's senior study, produced on Mike's 4-track in a dorm during their early years. First complete telling of the saga of Gamehendge, more than a fairy tale but less than a rock opera.

● *Distribution:* Copies of the tape portion of the original project do exist and are traded. Plans to make a CDROM of the project were scrapped.

● *Recorded* by Trey on a four-track—the music first, then the narrative added to the left channel, blocking out the music on that channel.
● *Circulation* through tape-trading circles, sparsely until 1991, then slowly until 1994, more vigorously since. Most copies are mono—narrative on the left channel, songs on the right. However, beginning circa 1996 a version began circulating with both channels digitally overlaid (by a fan) back into stereo.
● *Tracks* *

Wilson Prelude **	Betrayal Jam
(intro narrative) ***	(narrative)
Lizards	Col. Forbin's Ascent
Tela	Famous Mockingbird
(traveling narrative)	(Errand Wolfe's narrative)
Wilson	The Sloth
(Palmer narrative)	(Forbin in the Dungeon)
AC/DC Bag	Possum

● *Track Notes:*
* At least seven other songs—"Divided Sky," "Llama," "McGrupp and the Watchful Hosemasters," "Punch You In the Eye" (originally "PMeITE"), "Axilla" and "Axilla II," and "Harpua"—have Gamehendge references in them.
** "Wilson Prelude" is often not counted or listed separately, but has been revived by audience participation, eg 12-31-94, to have a life of its own
*** Narration occurs between almost every pair of songs on the original project, and also occurs live, usually (since 4-21-92, and possibly earlier) between "Col. Forbin's Ascent" and "Famous Mockingbird" and also during the few complete performances of *TMWSIY*. The background music (which Trey has written was "designed to create a sense of motion") is performed live, and called "The Man Who Stepped Into Yesterday" (abbreviated "TMWSIY"), usually played with "Avenu Malkenu" in the middle (since 1987, except for 2/4/93, 8/7/93 "TWMSIY">"Avenu">"Sloth," 11/19/94, and 6/30/95).
● *Other release:* Early 1990s plans for an interactive Gamehendge CD-ROM was scrapped by mid-1996, initially due to concerns about standardization of the CD-I technology, but later (and more firmly) by conviction that the Gamehendge saga not be used to generate profits. (See entries for Palmer, Wilson, and Forbin in the Dictionary.)
● *Live notes:* see entry for "Gamehendge, Live" in Dictionary.
● *Source notes:* The tape portion was accompanied by a 50-page paper (38 pages of text and 12 pages of notation), copies of which circulate but are closely guarded. The tape-and-essay project was submitted in July of 1988 (and signed off on by Trey's advisor Lois Harris on 8/24/88 and second reader Christopher Noel on 8/25/88), but began from three pieces. *(A)* At least part of the Gamehendge work flowed from earlier work Trey did with his mother, who had been an editor for *Sesame Street* magazine and who has written dozens of children's stories. The two of them wrote a series of songs, and one musical, *Gus the Christmas Dog*, which included "No Dogs Allowed" and "If I Were a Dog" (now the ending of "Lizards"). The former is now a rarity unrelated to Gamehendge, but the latter is a focal point of *TMWSIY* (and listen to the "Lizards Jam" at 7/10/97). *(B)* Tom Marshall sent Trey a poem, "McGrupp and the Watchful Hosemasters," which was read at earlier shows to its own music (e.g. 10/17/85) and later (12/6/86) combined with the music from "Skippy the Wondermouse" (originally played 12/1/84). This new "McGrupp" became a core nugget of the Gamehendge tale, and is a good summary of the story of Gamehendge. Though not in-

cluded in Trey's senior study, "McGrupp" often replaces "Possum" when the project is performed live. This is perhaps because of the revelry of "Possum" is ill-befitting of the "current" crisis-state of Gamehendge, whereas "McGrupp" is the tale as told by a percipient witness. *(C)* The third seed was "Wilson, Can You Still Have Fun?," written by Trey, Tom, and Aaron Wolfe. Combined with newly written material, and material such as "Possum" modified from Jeff Holdsworth's writing, these became the structure and heart of *TMWSIY*.

Copyright 1987 (1987)
Various versions of promo tape with white labels, a combination of previous 4-track recordings and the band's first studio recordings.
● *Distribution:* Circulated lightly in mid-1987, re-emerged in different form in mid-1998 (see below) though still rare.
● *Recorded:* in Mike's and Trey's dorm rooms, on 4-track, and for the first *Junta* sessions.
● *Edited* by Trey, in fall 1987 and again several times during 1988.
● *Tracks, Version 1:* Distributed to several northeast clubs in late 1987, and labeled "Phish, Copyright 1987 Ernesto Anastasio III".
Side A (labeled "Originals"; tracks later on *Junta*):

Golgi Apparatus	Fluffhead
David Bowie	

Side B (labeled "Covers"):

I Know a Little	Sneaking Sally Through the Alley

● *Tracks, Version 2:*
Mailed to clubs (including the Front) in 1988, and labeled "Copyright 1987 Ernesto.Anastasio III".
Side A:

Fee	Lizards
Golgi Apparatus	Sloth
David Bowie	Wilson

Side B:

Mike's Groove *	Sneaking Sally Through the Alley
Fluffhead	

● *Tracks, Version 3:* Mailed to clubs as late as mid-1990s by All Points Booking, with a small hand-drawn "apb" on the label.
Side A:

Golgi Apparatus	David Bowie
Fee	Fluffhead

Side B:

I Know a Little	Sneaking Sally Through the Alley

● *Track notes:*
"Fee," "Golgi," "Fluffhead" are the versions recorded during the first *Junta* sessions, and "Bowie" is from the second Junta sessision; all four appear on *Junta*. "Sally" is possibly also studio, from the second sessions.
* "Mike's Song" and "Weekapaug Groove" did not appear on an album until 1997's *SS&P*, "I Am Hydrogen" has still not been officially released (though see "Wendell Studios" demo).
● *Packaging:* Black demo tape with computerized labels in true 1980s demo fashion.

Junta (4/89)
1st official release, and 1st released studio recording, including the greatest of Phish's epic compositions
● *Distribution:* Rough Trade Records, as an affiliate of manufacturer

Junta Cassette Cover (4/89)

Courtesy: Mike Rowe

Absolute A Go Go who printed 10,000 copies (some vinyl, mostly tape) mostly sold at shows. Rough Trade closed its doors soon after printing and went out of business between the end of 1990 and the middle of 1991, just before Phish signed with Elektra, taking the studio masters and most of the proceeds with them.

● *Produced* by Phish.
● *Recorded* in Euphoria Studios, Revere, MA, three days in 1987 (initially for a demo) and two winter weeks stretching from 1988 into 1989.
● *Engineered* by Gordon Hookailo (misspelled Hookaloo on the liner).
● *Tracks* ....(84:08)

01 Fee 05:23	Part 2: The Chase
02 You Enjoy Myself.......09:47	(1:06-2:18)
03 Esther........................09:21	Part 3: Who Do We Do
04 Golgi Apparatus.........04:35	(2:18-4:09)
05 Foam 06:50	Part 4: Clod (4:09-7:18)
06 Dinner and a Movie ...03:42	Part 5: Bundle of Joy
07 The Divided Sky 11:50	(7:18-9:07)
08 David Bowie 10:59	Part 6: Arrival (9:07-11:35)
09 Fluffhead 03:24	11 Contact......................06:42
10 Fluff's Travels 11:35	
Part 1: Fluff's Travels	
(0:00-3:21)	

● *Track notes:*
None.
● *Outtakes:* A tape of *Junta* outtakes is lightly traded and was sent to clubs and promoters in the late '80s as a promotional tape, with: "Fee," "David Bowie," "Fluffhead," "Golgi Apparatus," "Wilson," "Lizards" (labeled as "Land of the Lizards"), "The Curtain (With)," "Sloth," "Contact," "I Didn't Know." Outtakes rumored to also include "Alumni Blues," although that is not confirmed.

● *Title:* Named for Ben "Junta" Hunter, who helped manage the band in their early years and, with John Paluska, helped birth Dionysian Productions.
● *Pronunciation:* Pronounced *JOON-tuh*, not *JUHN-ta* or *HOON-ta*, although Trey's voice on an early hotline message said the *JUHN-tuh* and *Lawn Boy* were available.
● *Cover:* First pressing cover has pink-and-white photo of screaming man (thought to be Ben 'Junta' Hunter); second pressing (much more common) has black-and-white Pollack design.

Lawn Boy (9/21/90)
2nd official release (CD, cassette, vinyl)
● *Distributed* by Rough Trade Records (out of business 1990/1991; see *Junta* notes).
● *Manufactured* by Absolute A Go Go (#AGO 1992-2) on CD, cassette, and vinyl.
● *Produced* by Phish.
● *Recorded* in May 1989 ("Split" and "Gin") and January 1990 (remainder), at Archer Studios, Winooski, VT, by engineers Dan Archer and Deal LaBrie (credited for "heavy metal screams"). The studio time for "Split" and "Gin" was won in the spring 1989 Rock Rumble (a "battle of the bands") at the Front.
● *Tracks*...........................(53:09)

01 The Squirming Coil....06:01	06 Bathtub Gin 04:28
02 Reba * 12:25	07 Run Like an
03 My Sweet One * 02:08	Antelope *** 09:52
04 Split Open and	08 Lawn Boy ^ 02:31
Melt ** 04:44	09 Bouncing Round
05 The Oh Kee Pa	the Room ^^ 03:57
Ceremony....................01:40	10 Fee ^^^ 05:23

● *Track notes:*
* case has "Reba" and "My Sweet One" listed backwards in the track listing.
** with The Giant Country Horns (Joseph Somerville, Jr., trumpet; Dave Grippo, alto sax; and Russell Remmington, tenor sax) and Christine Lynch, vocals
*** misspelled "Run Like and Antelope" on A Go Go CD release
^ slower on Elektra re-release
^^ possibly released to some Vermont radio stations soon after the initial release.
^^^ same version as on *Junta*; not on the re-release

"Wendell Studios" (7/90)
Two tapes generated by a session, for promotional purposes.
● *Distribution:* Scores (perhaps hundreds) of copies to nightclubs and venues. 2nd tape (of 2) was thereafter widely circulated by tape traders.
● *Producer:* Phish
● *Recorded:* 6/17/90, Wendell Studios.
● *Tracks, Tape 1:* (difficult to find)

Dog Log	Take the "A" Train
Uncle Pen	In a Mellow Tone
Suzy Greenberg	Possum
Caravan	Mike's Song >
Alumni Blues	I Am Hydrogen *

Unreleased Originals

Compiled by Mark Toscano

List of unreleased originals including live stuff:

AC/DC Bag
Acoustic Army
Anarchy
Axilla
Big Ball Jam
Big Black Furry
 Creatures From Mars
Bittersweet Motel
Black-Eyed Katy
Brother
Buffalo Bill
Buried Alive
Bye Bye Foot
Camel Walk
Carini
Colonel Forbin's Ascent
Curtain
Dave's Energy Guide
Dear Mrs. Reagan
Destiny Unbound
Dogs Stole Things
Don't Get Me Wrong
Driver
 (japanese farmhouse)
Famous Mockingbird
Flat Fee
Fog That Surrounds

Free Thought
Glide II
Grind
Gumbo
Ha Ha Ha
Halley's Comet
Harpua
Harry Hood
I am Hydrogen
I Didn't Know
I Don't Care
Icculus
In a Hole
Jaegermeister Song
Keyboard Cavalry
Kung
Leprechaun
Lizards
Lushington
Makisupa Policeman
Marijuana Hot Chocolate
McGrupp and the
 Watchful Hosemasters
Meatstick
Mike's Song
Mountains in the Mist
 (japanese farmhouse)
Never
NICU
No Dogs Allowed
Olivia's Pool
Possum
Practical Song
 (Shortage)
Prep School Hippie
Punch Me in the Eye
 (I Will Set You Free)
Punch You in the Eye

Revolution
Rock-a-William
Runaway Jim
Samson Variation
Sanity
Saw it Again
Setting Sail
Simple
Skippy the
 Wondermouse
Slave to the Traffic Light
Sleeping Monkey
Sloth
Somantin
Spock's Brain
Strange Design
Suzy Greenberg
Tela
Tube
Vibration of Life
Vultures
Waking Up
Walfredo
Weekapaug Groove
Weekly Time
Will It Go Round In
 Circles?
Wilson
Windora Bug

List without live album songs:

AC/DC Bag
Acoustic Army
Anarchy
Big Ball Jam
Bittersweet Motel

Black-Eyed Katy
Brother
Buffalo Bill
Buried Alive
Bye Bye Foot
Camel Walk
Carini
Colonel Forbin's Ascent
Curtain
Dave's Energy Guide
Dear Mrs. Reagan
Destiny Unbound
Don't Get Me Wrong
Famous Mockingbird
Flat Fee
Fog That Surrounds
Free Thought
Glide II
Grind
Halley's Comet
Harpua
I am Hydrogen
I Didn't Know
I Don't Care
In a Hole
Jaegermeister Song
Keyboard Cavalry
Kung
Leprechaun
Lizards
Lushington
Makisupa Policeman
Marijuana Hot Chocolate
McGrupp and the
 Watchful Hosemasters
Meatstick
Mountains in the Mist
 (japanese farmhouse)

Never
No Dogs Allowed
Olivia's Pool
Practical Song
 (Shortage)
Prep School Hippie
Punch Me in the Eye
 (I Will Set You Free)
Punch You in the Eye
Revolution
Rock-a-William
Runaway Jim
Samson Variation
Saw it Again
Setting Sail
Skippy the Wonder-
mouse
Sleeping Monkey
Sloth
Somantin
Spock's Brain
Strange Design
Suzy Greenberg
Tela
Vibration of Life
Vultures
Waking Up
Walfredo
Weekly Time
Windora Bug

● *Tracks, Tape 2:*
TMWSIY >
Avenu Malkenu >
TMWSIY
Tweezer

Possum
Harry Hood
Rift **
Runaway Jim ***

● *Track notes:*
Only "Tweezer" and "Rift" appeared on the next two Phish releases.
* may or may not have included "Weekapaug Groove".
** original (slow) version
*** with alternate lyrics

Picture Of Nectar (2/18/92)

3rd official release, 1st Elektra release (#61274). A.k.a *PON* or simply *Nectar*. Notable for musical diversity and strong production.
● *Distribution:* Elektra (#61274), on CD and minidisc.
● *Recorded* May-June 1991, at White Crow Studios, Burlington, VT.

Mixed and mastered August 1991. Engineered by Kevin Halpin.
● *Produced* by Phish ("with a lot of help from Kevin").
● *Tracks* ....(60:29)

01 Llama 3:31	09 The Landlady...............2:56
02 Eliza............................1:31	10 Glide...........................4:12
03 Cavern * 4:24	11 Tweezer 8:42
04 Poor Heart ** 2:45	12 The Mango Song........6:23
05 Stash.........................7:11	13 Chalk Dust Torture ^^ 4:35
06 Manteca ^ 0:29	14 Faht.............................2:21
07 Guelah Papyrus 5:22	15 Catapult......................0:32
08 Magilla 2:46	16 Tweezer Reprise 2:40

● *Track notes:*
* released as a single-edit radio single (PRCD #8607-2)
** with Gordon Stone on pedal steel
^ originally by Dizzie Gillespie; only studio cover released, and only cover released until *Slip*, over five years later.

^^ released 2/92 to radio as unedited (4:45) LP version (PRCD #8511-2). Also released as a for-sale single, with inner sleeve containing the album art and this text: "'Chalk Dust Torture' is one of the sixteen songs on Phish's debut Elektra album."

● *Outtakes:* reportedly include "Runaway Jim" and "Memories".

● *Title:* from the line that replaced the original phrase "penile erector" in the common set-ender "Cavern," and is named for Nectar Rorris, at whose bar (Nectar's, in Burlington) Phish got an early start.

● *Packaging:* The first printings of the CD came in the longbox, and the title of the disc was not printed on the disc insert. Later printings came in the shrink-wrap instead of the longbox, so had the title imprinted on top of the picture of Nectar.

[*Space Wrangler*] (1992)

Page is featured on "Holden Oversoul" on this Capricorn release from Widespread Panic.

Lawn Boy (6/30/92)

Official re-release (CD and tape) with "Fee" dropped (due to space limitations) and "Lawn Boy" slower (due to an error in the duplication process)

● *Distribution:* Elektra (#61275)

● *Tracks ....(47:55)*

01 The Squirming Coil.06:06	06 Bathtub Gin 04:29
02 Reba 12:27	07 Run Like An
03 My Sweet One 02:08	Antelope 09:53
04 Split Open And Melt04:43	08 Lawn Boy 02:32*
05 The Oh Kee Pa	09 Bouncing Around
Ceremony 01:41	The Room 03:56

● *Track notes:* * slower, longer version than on the original release.

● *Package note:* CDs sold in a special longbox which is no longer available.

● *Merch note:* Dry Goods sell a refrigerator magnet set that includes all of the lyrics to all of the tracks on *Lawn Boy*.

Junta (10/26/92)

Official re-released, as two discs including three bonus (live) tracks

● *Distribution:* Elektra ((#US9 61413). Gold 10/9/97.

● *Tracks, Disc One ....(62:50)*

01 Fee...........................05:23	Part 2: The Chase (1:06-2:18)
02 You Enjoy Myself....09:47	Part 3: Who Do We Do
03 Esther 09:21	(2:18-4:09)
04 Golgi Apparatus 04:35	Part 4: Clod (4:09-7:18)
05 Foam 06:50	Part 5: Bundle of Joy
06 Dinner And A	(7:18-9:07)
Movie 03:42	Part 6: Arrival (9:07-11:35)
07 The Divided Sky......11:50	03 Contact.....................06:42
08 David Bowie............10:59	04 Union Federal ....25:31 *
● *Tracks, Disc Two ....(60:08)*	05 Sanity ....08:22 **
01 Fluffhead................03:24	06 Icculus ....04:24 **
02 Fluff's Travels.........11:35	
Part 1: Fluff's Travels	
(0:00-3:21)	

● *Track notes:*

* "Union Federal" was from an early "Oh Kee Pa Ceremony" (see FAQ section), recorded in 1989.

** "Sanity" and "Icculus" were live recordings from 7/25/88, not 5/3/88 as noted in the liner notes. Only 45 minutes of the latter show were taped, as the second side to the second tape used for 5/3/98. Elektra used the tracks Phish wanted, but took the date from the wrong side of the tape.

● *Package note:* CDs sold in a special Pollack longbox which is no longer available.

● *Other release note:* The band planned to release an interactive CD (CD-I) version of the album, including the "Esther" video (see Dictionary entry).

● *Merch note:* Dry Goods sell a refrigerator magnet set that includes all of the lyrics to all of the tracks on *Junta*.

Elektra Promo (1992)

1st promotional sampler, a compilation from Paul's soundboard 4/15-22/92 mailed to Ekektra as a preview of what *Rift* would look like.

● *Tracks:*

Brother *	Horse >
It's Ice	Silent in the Morning
Runaway Jim *	Mound
NICU *	Weigh
My Friend, My Friend	My Mind's Got a Mind of It's Own *
Horn	Rift
Sparkle	Sleeping Monkey *
Fee *	

● *Track notes:*

* did not appear on *Rift*, which did include "Fast Enough for You," "Lengthwise," "Maze," "The Wedge," "All Things Reconsidered," and "Lengthwise," none of which were on this demo.

RIFT (2/2/93)

4th official release, 1st with an outside producer. Conceived as a "concept album," around a dream sequence about a strained relationship.

● *Released* by Elektra (#61433) on CD and cassette. Billed as a "concept album," streamed together as though in a dream sequence. Debuted at #51 on Billboard album charts. Gold 10/15/97

● *Produced* by Barry Beckett (Lynyrd Skynyrd, Vince Gill) for Beckett Productions (Muscle Shoals); Engineered by Kevin Halpin, assisted by Jon Altschiller

● *Recorded* by Kevin Halpin, September-October 1992 at White Crow Studios, Burlington, VT, except "Wedge" recorded at The Castle, Nashville, TN.

● *Mixing* and additional recording October-November, 1992, at The Castle.

● *Tracks...........................(67:54)*

01 Rift 6:14	09 Weigh.........................5:09
02 Fast Enough For	10 All Things
You * 4:51	Reconsidered 2:32
03 Lengthwise >..............1:19	11 Mound........................6:02
04 Maze............................8:14	12 It's Ice 8:14
05 Sparkle 3:54	13 Lengthwise.................0:35
06 Horn 3:38	14 The Horse >................1:24
07 The Wedge ** 4:07	15 Silent In the Morning...5:28
08 My Friend, My Friend ..6:10	

● *Track notes:*

* New arrangement, with Gordon Stone on pedal steel. Released as a

single-edit (4:01) radio version (PRCD #8707-2) to radio stations and stores in January/February 1993

** Released as a full-album version in mid-1992 and as an abridged radio version (PRCD #8768-2, 3:43) to radio stations in February 1993

● *Liner:* Every track is referenced in the liner by either lyrics (in whole or part) or image (such as My Friend's knife on the bedside table) except "The Wedge" and perhaps "Silent". For "Mound," the words in the liner are those left over from Mike's writing of the song (see Song History).

● *Cover:* The cover art includes references to every song on the album except "Horse". Note that the cover of the next album, *Hoist*, was a horse being hoisted.

[*Lost Paradox*] (2/93)

Jon performs drums on this J. Willis Pratt (see Guestbook entry) release available only at the merchandise tables of Phish shows during the Spring 1993 tour.

Phish: A Sampler (1993)

Promotional compilation CD by Elektra (a.k.a. "Sampler"), sent to radio stations prior to and during the summer tour of 1993.

● *Tracks* ....(39:03)

01 Fast Enough For You * 4:51	06 Bouncing Around
02 The Wedge * 4:08	The Room ^ 3:56
03 Chalk Dust Torture ** .4:35	07 Fee ^^ 5:23
04 Cavern ** 4:24	08 Golgi Apparatus ^^......4:35
05 Stash ** 7:11	

● *Track notes:*

* originally on *Rift*

** originally on *Picture of Nectar*

^ originally on *Lawn Boy*; released as a single-edit radio single (7559-64272-2 WE 739)

^^ originally on *Junta*

● *Insert* says, "Phish's summer tour 1993. Bigger audiences, mostly outdoor venues, no support" then lists their summer 1993 tourdates.

Hoist (3/29/94)

5th official release, more upbeat than *Rift*, with new songs, heavy production, and many guests

● *Distribution:* Elektra (#61628) on CD and cassette. Debuted at #34 on the Billboard album charts, went Gold 8/19/96, and remains the top-selling Phish release.

● *Producer:* Paul Fox (10,000 Maniacs, Sugarcubes, XTC)

● *Recorded* October and November, 1993, at the American Recording Company, Woodland Hills, CA, by Ed Thacker (who had worked with Fox for ten years prior).

● *Mixed* December 1993, at Can-Am Studios in Tarzana, CA, by Ed Thacker.

● *Tracks* ....(50:57)

01 Julius (abc) * 04:41	06 Sample in a Jar *** ..04:38
02 Down With	07 Wolfman's
Disease ** (b).............04:08	Brother (c)...................04:28
03 If I Could (d).............04:09	08 Scent of a Mule (h)....03:58
04 Riker's Mailbox (ef) ...00:20	09 Dog Faced Boy 02:09
04 Axilla [Part II]...........04:25	10 Demand ^.................10:40
05 Lifeboy (fg) 06:52	

● *Track note:*

* Released 5/94 (third single from *Hoist*) as a single-edit (3:43) radio version (PRCD #9012-2). Cover has Fishman standing on his hands on a barbell while the rest of the band claps.

** Released 3/8/94 (first single from *Hoist*) as an unedited (4:08) LP version (PRCD #8915-2) to radio stations and record stores, accompanied by the only official video; black-and-white cover has the band standing in a dead forest. Also released 5/19/94 as an extended version (4:13) for-sale single (#4-64535), on analog cassette only ("cassingle") with "NO^2" (aka "Nitrous"; 8:14) as the b-side (not on promotional single); sold 4,223 units as of 7/23/00. Also used for the band's only video (see entry for Videos in Dictionary).

*** released 4/94 (second single from *Hoist*) as an unedited LP version promotional single (PRCD #8989-2, 4:38) on CD

^ includes part of the "Split Open and Melt" jam segment from April 21, 1993, at the Newport Music Hall, Columbus, OH. It also includes part of "Y-Rushalayim Schel Zahav" ("Jerusalem of Gold"), written by Naomi Schemer-Sapir. For more information, see "Demand" entry in the Song Histories chapter.

● *Guests:*

a. with Ricky Grundy Chorale (gospel choir), backing vocals

b. with Rose Stone and Jean (Jenn?) McClain, backing vocals

c. with Tower of Power horn section

d. with Alison Krauss, additional vocals, and The Richard Greene Fourteen, string section

e. with Jonathan Frakes (Riker on *Star Trek: The New Generation*; neighbor of producer Fox, trombone

f. with Bela Fleck, banjo

g. with Morgan Fichter (formerly of 10,000 Maniacs and Camper Van Beethoven), violin

● *Recording note:* Listen for background sounds including a toilet flushing, a bottle rattling, some toying with amps to produce a Doppler effect, and the band walking on broken coal. (For more, see Mike's Tracking video.)

● *Outtakes:* reportedly include "Simple," "Buffalo Bill," "Runaway Jim" (also outtaken from *Picture of Nectar*), and "Memories"

● *Cover:* Amy Skelton's horse Maggie being hoisted. Maggie lives on Amy's Farm in Auburn, ME (see setlist for 8/3/91). Note also that the cover of the previous album, *Rift*, included references to every song on that album except "Horse".

● *Promotional release:* Some copies sent to disc jockeys and radio stations were released in a white canvas bag, with 'PHISH' in orange lettering on the front and '(hoist)' in black lettering on the back. Attached to the bag was a small metal pulley (playing on the hoist theme), to which was attached a brown tag that says on one side "HOIST: it's in the bag. On the other side of the tag it says: "They've netted over half a million records sold. Their 1993 concert attendance tipped the scale at 312,000. They sold out a 14,000-seat arena in seven hours. What can they do now to get these numbers higher?"

A Live One (6/27/95)

6th official release; 1st live release; 1st double-CD. A.k.a. *ALO*.

● *Distribution:* Elektra (#61777); Gold 11/10/95; Platinum 10/15/97; 492,000 copies as of 10/3/98; Reached #19 on Rolling Stone Reader's Chart; Reached #3 on the Rolling Stone Alternative Chart.

● *Produced* by Phish

● *Recorded* by Paul Languedoc, during the summer and fall 1994 tours (all 45 shows), using four 32-track ADAT machines. Mixed March and April, 1995, Bearsville Studios, Bearsville, NY
● Tracks, Disc one *.........(62:33) *

01 Bouncing	05 You Enjoy Myself
(12/31/94)** 04:08	(12/7/94) 20:57
02 Stash (7/8/94) *** 12:32	06 Chalkdust Torture
03 Gumbo (12/2/94) ^ ...05:15	(11/16/94) 06:48
04 Montana (from	07 Slave (11/26/94) 10:48
11/28/94 Tweezer).......02:04	

● *Tracks, Disc two* ^^ ......(68:40)

01 Wilson (12/30/94) 05:07	04 Harry Hood
02 Tweezer (11/2/94) 30:55	(10/23/94) 15:11
03 Simple (12/10/94) 04:53	05 Squirming Coil
	(10/9 & 23/94) ^^ 11:19

● *Track notes:*
* The end of disc one, where Trey says, "We're going to take a very short break…" is from 10/9/94 Pittsburgh
** released as single-edit radio version and promotional single (PRCD #9299; 3:45, from 6/20/95. Cover shows Mike on stage with Trey in background on a trampoline. Inner sleeve of CD packaging reads: "Bouncing Around The Room' is the premiere single from Phish's forthcoming album 'PHISH LIVE.' 'PHISH LIVE' captures Vermont's favorite sons in their natural habitat - on the concert stage - with over 125 minutes of music including six previously unreleased songs. Phish's 1994 tour put the band in *Pollstar Magazine*'s Top 50 grossing acts of the year. On Tour Summer and Fall 1995.
*** The guitar solo in Stash was rated one of the top 100 guitar solos. The track was reportedly a Phish.net suggestion (see below).
^ single-edit radio version (PRCD #9364; 5:15); features the Giant Country Horns: Peter Apfelbaum (tenor sax), Carl Gerhard (trumpet), Dave Grippo (alto sax), James Harvey (trombone), Michael Ray (trumpet)
^^ The start of disc two is part of Miles Davis' "Right Off," from *A Tribute to Jack Johnson*, recorded 11/11/70, mimicking what Paul Languedoc plays over the PA during setbreaks.
^^^ Mostly 10/9/94, but the Page outro is from 10/23/94. Also, as the audience noise fades out after "Coil," listen for Trey in a high-pitched voice repeating the chorus line "I Saw You" from "Golgi Apparatus."
● *Source note:* Throughout 1994, he band kept journals about song versions. In January of 1995, a master list began of 560 versions mentioned by at least two of the band members, narrowed to 30 which were put on tapes and listened to repeatedly by the band.
● *Input note:* The Phish.Net (see Online Resources and Dictionary) played a role in the selection of tracks, invited in a 2/5/95 rec.music.phish post to discuss "constructing the Phish double live CD that you would like to hear" in the hopes that "some sort of rough consensus will emerge," after which the band would be given tapes of the Phish.Net's draft along-side the band's own "first draft" tapes of ideas.
● *Liner:* The liner notes bill this release as "live at Clifford Ball, 1994".

Crimes of the Mind (10/25/95)
1st release by "The Dude of Life and Phish," featuring Phish as the band for the Dude (Steve Pollak), although many record stores file it under Phish.
● *Distribution:* Elektra (#61715-2)

● *Producers:* the Dude of Life, Phish, and Dan Archer
● *Recorded* in 1991, at Archer Studios (not at White Crow, as sometimes reported).
● *Tracks*...........................(48:39)

01 Dahlia 3:18	07 Trials And Tribulations .5:08
02 Family Picture 4:22	08 Lucy In The Subway ...4:59
03 Self 4:01	09 Ordinary Day 3:53
04 Crimes Of The Mind ...4:28	10 Revolution's Over 4:42
05 Bitchin' Again * 3:37	11 King Of Nothing...........5:30
06 TV Show......................4:41	

● *Track Notes:* * with Sofie Dillof on vocals

[**Touch And Go**] (11/24/95)
Mike played bass on and cowrote "Fraction" (2:04) on this Alcazar Productions release by Gordon Stone (also on *Picture of Nectar* and *Rift*; see also Guestbook entry).

[**Surrender to the Air**] (3/12/96)
One-time side project (a.k.a. *STTA*) featuring Trey and Fishman, as well as Marshall Allen (sax), Oteil Burbridge (bass), Kofi Burbridge (flute), Damon A. Choice (xylophone), Bob Gullotti (drums), James Harvey (trombone), John Medeski (organ), Michael Ray (trumpet), and Mark Ribot (guitar). Entirely loose format involving no composition, little pre-planning, and little structure over the course of a two-day jam session during which participants came and went as they pleased.
● *Distributed* by Elektra (#61905) on CD.
● *Produced* by Trey Anastasio
● *Recorded* at Electric Lady Studios in New York City, sometime prior to May 1995, in a loose format
● *Engineered and Mixed* by Ed Thacker
● *Mastered* by Bob Ludwig
● *Tracks* ....(49:23)

Intro (Gullotti) 01:51	Intro (w/ Medeski/
And Furthermore 07:18	Ribot/ Choice) 02:00
We Deflate.....................07:15	And Furthermore...........04:12
And Furthermore 07:06	And Furthermore 11:10
Down (Ribot, Allen,	Out (Allen, Choice,
Ray) 02:52	Ray, Fishman) 05:39

● *See also:* entry in Dictionary.
● *See also:* The participants gathered for two performances, 4/1&2/96 at the Academy (in Times Square), which was razed days later. More shows were intended, but assembling representatives of eight bands (including Phish, ARU, MMW, Cosmic Krewe, and Sun Ra's Arkestra) was challenging enough just for the four days of recording and performing that *STTA* already accomplished.

[**Burlington Does Burlington**] (1996)
Phish (with Burlington's Richard "the Clarinet Man" Haupt on clarinet) cut "Rocketsled's Funky Main Man Meets Big Joe on Church Street" (lyrics by Rocketsled, music by Phish) for this two-disc compilation set from Good Citizen, which also featured The Pants covering Phish's "Golgi Apparatus".

Stash (1996)
For-sale compilation (CD) of US-released tracks, including popular selections from every (official) album up to and including *A Live One*, to coincide with the 1996 tour.

● *Distribution:* Elektra (#GE 7559, 61933), in Europe only (primarily Germany).

● *Track list* ....(66:24)

01 Down With	06 Split Open And Melt ^04:43
Disease * ~...................04:11	07 Maze ***..................08:21
02 If I Could * 04:10	08 Sample In A Jar * ~...04:39
03 You Enjoy Myself **..09:50	09 Bouncing Around
04 Fast Enough For	The Room ^^ ~ 03:56
You ***......................04:53	10 Stash ^^ 12:30
05 Scent Of A Mule * 04:00	11 Gumbo ^^ 05:11

● *Track notes:*

* from *Hoist*

** from *Junta*

*** from *Rift*

^ from *Lawn boy*

^^ from *A Live One.*

~ released in Europe by Elektra on a three-song single to promote the full compilation.

Billy Breathes (10/15/96)

5th studio effort, 7th official release. Notably more introspective than *Hoist*, with no guests, Page's second tune ("Cars Trucks Buses"), and selections from "the Blob" experiment (see entry in Dictionary).

● *Distribution:* Elektra (#61971), rated four stars by *Rolling Stone*, debuted at #6 on the Soundscan Top 200 (although *Farmhouse* had higher first-week sales), and peaked at #7 on the *Billboard* 100, with sales already then in excess of 434,000. Sales have not grown much since, although the album did finally become Gold 1/8/99.

● *Produced* by Steve Lillywhite (Rolling Stones, U2, Dave Matthews Band, et al.) and Phish

● *Recorded* and Mixed by John Siket, February to June, 1996, at Bearsville Studios, Bearsville, NY

● *Tracks*...........................(47:08)

01 Free * 3:48	08 Train Song..................2:34
02 Character Zero **........3:59	09 Bliss *** 2:04
03 Waste 4:50	10 Billy Breathes 5:31
04 Taste............................4:07	11 Swept Away................1:16
05 Cars Trucks Buses......2:24	12 Steep...........................1:38
06 Talk..............................3:09	13 Prince Caspian 5:19
07 Theme from the	
Bottom 6:22	

● *Track Notes:*

* released in 1996 as a single-edit (3:48 LP version) promotional single (PRCD #9635-2 in the US; #7559-6425 in Germany, the UK, and, by WEA Records, in Australia) prior to the album release. Also released as a for-sale CD, in the U.S. with the album versions of "Free" and "Theme from the Bottom" (6:22 LP version), and outside the U.S. (Germany, Australia, and the UK) also with the unreleased "Strange Design" (3:14, but slower than typically performed live; not on the album or U.S. promo). The three-track import "single" (7559-64205-2 EW-773 A4205CD), released 2/26/97, has sold 741 units as of 7/23/00.

** released in 1997 as a two-track CD "single" (PRCD #9749-2) with both a radio remix (3:36) and the album version (3:59)

*** written for a fan named Kevin, hospitalized by a car accident on his way to the 12/15/95 show.

● *Additional releases:* 1/17/97 in Australia and Europe, 1/25/97 in Japan, 2/10/97 in the United Kingdom

● *Demo:* Leaked and lightly circulated, including "Free," "Talk," "Theme from the Bottom," "Train Song," "Bliss," "Billy Breathes," new Trey song, new Mike song ("Weekly Time"?), "Glide II" (instrumental), "Swept Away," "Steep," "Waste," and "Strange Design"

● *Outtakes:* Primarily "Strange Design," planned as the 14th track but deemed a potential commercial success (see above). Others reportedly include "Spock's Brain," "Ha Ha Ha" (later on *Hampton Comes Alive*) "Grind" (performed 12/30/98 with Tom Marshall), "Glide I"l (unreleased instrumental), "Weekly Times" (unreleased instrumental, sometimes labeled "Waitin' Time"), and "The Blob" (at least the full-length version, from which "Steep," "Talk," and "Waste" were taken).

● *Sheet music:* A tablature book for the album is available through Phish Dry Goods, and in the *Doniac Schvice*. Note that all of the lyrics to "Swept Away" are repeated in "Steep," and that the book reveals the chorus of "Character Zero".

● *Liner:* The miniature *Doniac Schvice* included with the liner notes is a greatest hits compilation from the past issues, including February 1993 (Tom Interview), February/March/April 1993 (Inside Joe's Nose), Spring 1994 (Burgess and Schvice Letter), October 1994 (Disease letter), and June 1995 (Fish's Forum)

[Feast of Fools] (late 1996)

Jon played vacuum on one track of this holiday compilation produced by the Magic Hat Brewery, in Burlington.

[Mainstream American Rock] (mid-1997)

A Phish track was included on this summer compilation, which also included tracks from Better than Ezra, Jackson Browne, Nanci Griffith, and Hootie and the Blowfish.

[Samson Riffs: The Music of Ernie Stires] (1997)

Trey plays guitar on the title track on this Dry Goods release from his Goddard College mentor.

[Good Feeling] (10/7/1997)

Page played keyboards on the title track from this release from British act Travis, a band lauded by Oasis (see also, 12/29/96).

Slip Stitch and Pass (10/28/97)

8th official release, 2nd live release, all from one show. A.k.a. *SLIP*, *SS&P*, *SSP*. Promised as the first of "more experimental" live releases.

● *Distribution:* Elektra (#), reaching #17 on the Billboard Charts in November of 1997, and Phish was presented with gold records for the release on 12/2/97.

● *Produced* by Phish. Production consultant: Steve Lillywhite.

● *Recorded* by Paul Languedoc live 3/1/97 at the Markthalle, Hamburg, Germany.

● *Mixed* by John Siket, with assistant engineer Chris Laidlaw, July 1997 at Bearsville Studios, Bearsville, NY.

● *Mastered* by Bob Ludwig at Gateway Studios, Portland, ME, August 1997. Sequencing by Fred Kevorkian, Sear Sound, New York, NY, August 1997.

● *Tracks*...........................(72:46)

01 Cities * 05:19
02 Wolfman's Brother 13:51
03 Jesus Just Left
    Chicago ** 12:58
04 Weigh.......................05:30
05 Mike's Song...............13:52
06 Lawn Boy 02:56
07 Weekapaug Groove ...08:20
08 Hello My Baby ^ 01:20
09 Taste ^^......................08:45

● *Track notes:*

* second single released from *SS&P*, originally by the Talking Heads
** originally by ZZ Top
^ cover, traditional
^^ first single released from *SS&P*

● *Source:* The material is from a live performance, 3/1/97 at the Markthalle in Hamburg, Germany.

● *Length:* The album was originally reported to be 78 minutes, although the original tracks totaled 71:10.

● *Other releases:* Released 10/24/97 in Franch, Belgium and the Netherlands; 10/27/97 in the UK, Germany, Ireland, and Norway; 10/28/97 in the U.S, Canada, and Italy (catalog #62121); 10/29/97 in Sweden, 11/7/97 in Spain, 11/21/97 in Denmark, 11/24/97 in Czech Republic, and 11/25/97 in Japan. Reached #17 on the *Billboard* charts. Phish was presented with gold records on 12/2/97

● *Title:* According to an Elektra press release (dated 10/97, released 9/28), the title is "a knitting term that captures the integration of historic overview and forward-thinking strategies into the fabric of the groups' music at this juncture." The insert with the disc includes knitting instructions. Comparing the disc playlist to the original show playlist suggests a bit of knitting, as the CD slips ahead a step then twice stitches back to catch an earlier song.

● *Tape notes:* Most are missing "Possum" and "Reba." Many are also missing "Ragtime Gal" and "Sweet Adeline."

● *Low promo:* Interestingly, there was an advance cassette of this disc around, but no advance CD sent to radio stations and stores weeks early, as happened with previous discs.

● *Liner notes* are attributed to Steven Wright. Also, note the nicknames, scribbled into the photos: MC Neon Cellgap for Page (referencing the Great Went, see Dictionary); Leroy Elroy for Mike; and Herr Necklace for Trey (who appears to have a necklace "made" of chest hair).

● *Promotional liner:* Has the Steve Wright quote, but calls Fishman Jacques (also referencing the Great Went; see Dictionary).

● *Cover art:* __, whose previous work has been the covers for albums by Pink Floyd and Led Zeppelin, and who now works with graphic art house Hipgnosis.

[*Fiji Mariners*] (1998)

Mike played bass on "Star of Gladness" on this PDG/Capricorn Records release from the Fiji Mariners (featuring Col. Bruce Hampton, Retired; see Guestbook entry). The album also features members of ARU and Widespread Panic.

Story of the Ghost, The (10/27/98)

9th official release, 1st Elektra release since *SS&P*, and 1st studio production since *Billy Breathes*. A.k.a. *Ghost*, *SOTG*. A veritable time capsule of the funk-filled sound the band produced from fall 1997 through at least summer 1998, which reportedly began with 45 songs brought into the studio. Compared to Herbie Hancock's *Headhunters* for following a peak (characterized by dissonant experimentation) with a re-focus (based in funk).

● *Distribution:* Elektra (#62297), 11/3/98 on vinyl. Debuted at #7 on *Billboard* Top 200, with first two week sales in excess of 100,000, although *USA Today* listed it among "the five most disappointing albums of the year" (with releases from Vanilla Ice, Barry Manilow, Vonda Shepard, and Hootie and the Blowfish).

● *Produced and Mixed* by Andy Wallace (Nirvana, Limp Bizkit, Rage Against the Machine)

● *Recorded* at Bearsville Studios, Bearsville, NY, April-June 1998 (reportedly beginning 4/20; see Dictionary entry). Additional sessions 3/11/97-3/15/97, 9/29/97 to 10/2/97; and, Dave O's Farmhouse, 3/4-7/98 and 4/7-11/98

● *Engineered* by Chris Shaw, assisted by Craig Laidlaw

● *Mixed* at Soundtracks Studios, New York City, June-July 1998.

● *Mastered* by Howie Weinberg at Masterdisk, July 1998.

● *Tracks*...........................(50:06)

01 Ghost 3:51
02 Birds of a Feather * ^ ..4:15
03 Meat ** 2:39
04 Guyute.......................8:26
05 Fikus.........................2:20
06 Shafty *** ^ 2:21
07 Limb By Limb.............3:32
08 Frankie Sez.................3:06
09 Brian & Robert 3:03
10 Water In The Sky.........2:28
11 Roggae.......................2:59
12 Wading In The Velvet
    Sea................................4:29
13 Moma Dance **** 4:28
14 End of Session 1:54

● *Track notes:*

* with Dave Grippo (sax), James Harvey (trombone), Jennifer Hartswick (trumpet); formerly called "Red Sand" by the band. Released as a single-edit version (PRCD 1191-2) which hit radio 10/1/98.
^ with Heloise Williams on background vocals
** billed as a sequel to "Ghost"
*** formerly known as "Oblivious Fool"
**** formerly "Black-Eyed Katy"

● *Title:* taken a funky original tune of the same name debuted in Europe in June 1997.

● *Cover:* red beast in funky bathrobe and cuffed boxing gloves, by George Condo

● *Promo:* Though not nearly the scale seen with later *Farmhouse*, Elektra got Phish into a vibrant promotional tour, including in-store appearances in the NYC Tower Records 10/27, the same day they appeared on Letterman; in LA on 10/28, and in Chicago 11/1. Elektra also sponsored "listening parties," and coordinated radio station contests (e.g. "tell your ghost story") for copies of the CD, *The Phish Book*, and tickets (and hotel and airfare) to the New Year's show.

● *Not tracks:* Rumored to have been (but not on) the release were "Twist (Around)," "Piper," "Dogs Stole Things," "Eight Years and Thinking*," "When the Circus Comes to Town," "My Soul," "Vultures," "Tiny House,"* "Washed up at Sea*," "Clouds*," "Spock's Brain," "Dirt," "NICU," and "Tube." (*not yet performed live)

● *Outtakes:* enough material left over for an all-instrumental album—much of it seen on *The Siket Disc*, released six months later—as well as a number of outtake songs that later appeared on *Farmhouse*. A 90-minute tape, circulated as either "Ghost outtakes" or "Bearsville sessions," includes:

Side A:

NICU (instrumental)
Water In the Sky
Velvet Sea
Brian and Robert
Somantain
Vultures

Saw It Again
Ha Ha Ha
Tube
Guyute
Dirt

Side B:

NICU (w/ lyrics)
Limb By Limb
Ghost (with funked out intro)
Samson Riff
Relax (aka Frankie Says)
Roggae (sometimes labeled Relax)
Shafty (revision of Oblivious Fool)

What's the Use
Ficus
Acoustic Song (possibly called In A Misty Glade)
Meat
Meatstick (with phone snippets)

● *Other* outtakes reportedly include "In a Misty Glade," "I Saw it Again," "Cataract Song," and "Fooled by Images" (a.k.a. "Waking Up")

White Tape, The (8/98)

1st vault breakout, and 1st exclusive/independent release
● *Released and distributed:* Independently, exclusively through Dry Goods
● *Tracks*...........................(54:39)

01 Alumni Blues...............4:11	09 Ingest.........................1:38
02 And So to Bed 4:44	10 NO2............................7:37
03 You Enjoy Myself.........0:56	11 Fluff's Travels 1:23
04 AC/DC Bag...................4:09	12 Dog Gone Dog............4:03
05 Fuck Your Face...........2:16	13 He Ent to the Bog 3:56
06 Divided Sky 1:16	14 Run Like an Antelope ..6:42
07 Slave to the Traffic	15 Minkin 2:59
Light...............4:35	16 Letter to Jimmy Page ..1:17
08 Aftermath 2:55	

● *Package:* Paper foldout, with Trey's original artwork supplemented by new work from Pollack.
● *Digital release:* The entire tape, and a bonus track (previously unreleased early studio recording) of "The Curtain (With)," was released for purchase and download via emusic.com in the MP3 format.

[Merl and His Funky Friends—Live] (9/15/98)

Trey played on this Sumertone release, which also features Jerry Garcia, John Popper, David Grisman, Dr. John, Steve Kimock, and Matthew Kelly.

[Funk If I Know] (11/3/98)

Trey plays on this Funky Hill release from Michael Ray and the Cosmic Krewe (see Guestbook and *Sharing in the Groove*).

[One Man's Trash] (1999)

Trey solo effort, a loose collage of noodles and noises.
● *Distributed* independently by Dionysian through Dry Goods.
● *Produced* (and written and performed) by Trey Anastasio.
● *Recorded* at the Fungus Factory and the Barn. (Horns recorded at Chuck Eller Studios.)

● *Tracks*....................(total?)

01 Happy Coffee Song......2:40	11 Here's Mud in
02 Quantegy.....................2:59	Your Eye.........................1:11
03 Miister Completely 2:41	12 The Real Taste of
04 A Good Stalk 0:54	Licorice 2:34
05 That Dream Machine ...1:28	13 And Your Little
06 The Way I Feel.............2:55	Dog Too.........................4:00
07 Rofa Beton 2:41	14 Jump Rope (Fast
08 For Lew (My	Version) 0:38
Bodyguard) 1:39	15 Jump Rope (Slow
09 At the Barbecue...........2:02	Version) 2:13
10 Tree Spine 0:51	16 Kidney Bean 0:34

● *Liner* artwork by Gerrit Goliner, and nicely matches the patchwork character of the music.
● *Title* is also the title of a 1999 release by rock/rockabilly artist Charlie Berton (subtitled "The Charlie Berton Story: 1977-1999").

[Tour de Flux] (1/26/99)

Fishman appears on this release from the January/February 1998 Jazz Mandolin Project tour, during which he played drums. (See Sideshows entries.)

[Under the Sound Umbrella] (6/8/99)

Trey and Fishman play on about half of this, the second release from the Dude of Life (see Guestbook and Dictionary entries), which also features Mike on one track. The cover photo is by Danny Clinch, who has work heavily with Phish. It was also recorded and produced by Dan Archer, who has also worked on past Phish albums.

Siket Disc, The (6/99)

8th official release (CD and tape), a collection of selected and mastered outtakes from the Bearsville Studio sessions that produced *Story of the Ghost,* selected, compiled, and edited by Page.
● *Distributed* independently by Dionysian through Dry Goods
● *Produced* by Phish
● *Recorded* 3/11/97 to 3/15/97 and 9/29/97 to 10/2/97 at Bearsville Studios, Woodstock, NY.
● *Engineered* by John Siket, assisted by Chris Laidlaw
● *Mixed* by John Siket, assisted by Jon Sowle and Mike Sabo, October 1998 at Mutiny Zoo, Holboken, NJ.
● *Mastered* by Bob Ludwig at Gateway Studios, Portland, Maine, March 1999.
● *Tracks*...........................(35:18)

01 My Left Toe 04:47	06 The Happy Whip
02 The Name Is Slick 04:00	and Dung Song 05:29
03 What's The Use 11:19	07 Insects 03:11
04 Fish Bass..................01:12	09 Title Track.................01:00
05 Quadrophonic	09 Albert 02:19
Toppling 01:59	

● *Track Notes*
● *Title:* Named for engineer John Siket.

Hampton Comes Alive (11/23/99)

Complete, unedited release (a.k.a. *HCA*) of two consecutive live concerts in their entirety, including six sets and two encores, and contains

44 songs, including 20 previously unreleased, and including eleven covers of artists from Ween to Will Smith.
● *Distributed* by Elektra
● *Producer:* name (previous producing credits)
● *Recorded* and mixed live (to two-track ADATS) by Paul Languedoc 11/20/98 and 11/21/98
● *Mastered* by Bob Ludwig at Gateway Mastering, September 1999.
● *Tracks:*

11/20/98 Set 1, A.............(49:12)	11/21, Set 1, A...................(45:06)
01 Rock and Roll Part 2 02:04	01 Wilson.......................07:03
02 Tube 04:13	02 BBFCFM......................05:09
03 Quinn the Eskimo.....04:29	03 Lawn Boy 02:50
04 Funky Bitch 06:38	04 Divided Sky 15:12
05 Guelah Papyrus........06:12	05 Cry Baby Cry 03:06
06 Rift..........................05:59	06 Boogie on Reggae
07 Meat.......................06:17	Woman ~1..................06:13
08 Stash......................12:45	07 NICU ~2...................05:34
11/20 Set 1, B................(38:57)	11/21, Set 1, B................(41:57)
01 Train Song..............03:30	01 Dogs Stole Things ~5 04:34
02 Possum..................10:03	02 Nellie Kane 03:20
03 Roggae...................08:15	03 Foam 09:51
04 Driver.....................03:58	04 Wading in the
05 Split Open and	Velvet Sea ~7 ....06:30
Melt........................12:51	05 Guyute.....................10:17
11/20, Set 2 ....(69:24)	06 Bold As Love ~4 ....06:46
01 Bathtub Gin ~6.........14:13	11/21, Set 2 ....(70:07)
02 Piper 07:05	01 Sabatogue 03:08
03 Axilla I 04:43	02 Mike's Song..............11:51
04 Roses Are Free........05:22	03 Simple 15:28
05 Farmhouse ~3.........04:59	04 The Wedge 05:56
06 Getting' Jiggy	05 The Mango Song.......07:44
Wit It...........................07:13	06 Free 04:48
07 Harry Hood 12:49	07 Ha Ha Ha 01:34
08 Character Zero ~8 ....07:38	08 Free 05:15
09 Cavern ~9................04:48	09 Weekapaug Groove ...08:36
	10 Tubthumping.............05:20

● *Track notes:*
~ released by Elektra on a nine-song promotional sampler (PRCD #1427-2), track orders as numbered
● *Title* plays on the biggest selling album of the 1970s, Peter Frampton's *Frampton Comes Alive*.
● *Cover image* is a photograph of "Spaceship Hampton," the coliseum.
● *Packaging* won an award, with each disc in its own sleeve, the entire set in an elaborate magnetic box, and a liner within each disc sleeve, the six of which form a large version of the box's cover.

[*Get You a Healin'*] (3/21/00) (4/99?)
Mike and Page appear with The Meters on the opening track of this benefit compilation from the New Orleans Musicians Clinic, released in New Orleans to coincide with JazzFest.

[*Letting Go*] (4/00)
Trey is featured on this Son Seals release, playing with him on Son's original "Funky Bitch," which Phish covers (see Song Histories).

Farmhouse (5/16/00)
11th domestic release, a somewhat pensive effort borne of Tom and Trey isolated in a farmhouse, and the band partying at the Barn.
● *Distributed* by Elektra, with the highest first-week sales of any Phish album (although *Billy* Breathes debuted higher on the Soundscan Top 200). Also released in Japan (AMCY-7153) as a full-length CD with bonus studio tracks of "Driver" and "Mist," plus a Japanese fold-out with setlists and bios.
● *Producer:* Bryce Goggin (Pavement, Spacehog) and Trey.
● *Recorded and Mixed* at the Barn 10/99 to 2/00 by John Siket.
● *Mastered* by Bob Ludwig at Gateway Studios, Portland, Maine, February 2000.
● *Tracks:*..........................(49:43)

01 Farmhouse 4:02	08 Piper ^..........................4:27
02 Twist............................3:25	09 Sleep 2:10
03 Bug..............................5:07	10 The Inlaw Josie
04 Back on the Train........3:03	Wales ^^ 2:56
05 Heavy Things *...........4:16	11 Sand............................3:25
06 Gotta Jibboo **...........5:31	12 First Tube 6:46
07 Dirt ***........................4:33	

● *Track Notes:*
* released as a single-edit radio single (PRCD #1472-2)
** with Dave Grippo (sax), James Harvey (trombone), Andy Moroz (trombone), Jennifer Hartswick (trumpet).
*** with John Dunlop (cello), Roy Feldman (viola), David Gusakov (violin), Laura Markowitz (violin).
^ includes part of the version from 7-17-99 (Oswego).
^^ with Jerry Douglas (dobro), Bela Fleck (banjo)
● *Outtakes* reportedly include "Jennifer Dances," "Mozambique," "Driver," "Mist" (formerly "Mountains in the Mist"), "Never," and "Bittersweet Motel."
● *Title* comes from the song of the same title, about and named for a location Tom Marshall and Trey have spent time writing songs together.
● *Cover note:* The cover image is not a farmhouse, but an outhouse near The Barn. Nicknamed "the Brown Lounge," it is actually a prop created for use in *Outside Out* (see Dictionary entry).

[*HEADS OR TAILS*] (?)
Trey plays on this release by Jamie Northatomas.

[*TRAMPLED BY LAMBS AND PECKED BY DOVE*] (10/00)
Forthcoming (at this printing) independent release of Tom Marshall and Trey performing original versions of Phish songs, plus several non-Phish songs.

SONG HISTORIES

Information on every song (original or cover) that Phish is known to have ever played, jammed,, in any set, encore, or studio. Each song's genesis, evolution and current form are described and explained, and versions of merit are noted.

Compiled and edited by Mark Toscano

AC/DC Bag
AKA: "Bag," "AC/DC"
Music/Lyrics: Trey Anastasio
Album: "The White Tape"
Vocals: Trey (lead), Mike, Page (backing)
Debut: 4/1/86
Historian: Mark Toscano

AC/DC Bag is one of the earliest Gamehendge tunes to show up in Phish's live repertoire. Since Trey's Senior Study "The Man Who Stepped Into Yesterday" (which incorporated "AC/DC Bag") wasn't completed until 1988, this shows that "Bag" was initially its own tune, and got Gamehendgified to work with the storyline of Trey's song cycle. (Highly likely considering the tune appears on the band's '84–'86 era "White Tape" recording.) Still, "Bag" fits rather well in its place as the fourth song of the musical, right between "Wilson" and "Colonel Forbin's Ascent." The tune's lyrics have a loosely narrative, stream-of-consciousness feel to them, similar in this respect to "Tela," or "The Sloth." Additionally, since "AC/DC Bag" is musically unlike the other songs in the cycle, Trey was offered another opportunity to show off his versatile compositional skills by tackling yet another style.

The title of the song derives from the chorus's chord progression (well, almost—it's actually an F-major, not a B-major). The lyrics to this groove-rock tune speak of a certain Mr. Palmer, who is most decidedly "concerned with a thousand-dollar question." He is about to be hanged by the AC/DC Bag (the name of Wilson's plug-in, robotized, bag-headed executioner) under orders from Wilson himself. Mr. Palmer is Wilson's accountant, you see. However, he was also a member of the anti-Wilson revolution effort. Palmer helped support Errand Woolfe, Tela, and the other rebels by channeling funds from Wilson's regime to bankroll the revolution. Of course, Wilson eventually found out, and sentenced Mr. Palmer to death, thus substantially crushing the revolution effort.

Hammered into the Gamehendge narrative, the song's lyrics end up having meaning, however vague. In this context, the song is sung as a duet between Wilson and Palmer. In the first two verses, Wilson torments Palmer in a facetious manner. Palmer takes over the second two verses, defiantly challenging Wilson ("I'll show you mine if you

show me yours"). The final lines of the fourth verse indicate Palmer's steadfast resistance to Wilson as he shouts for the commencement of his own execution. Following this, Palmer muses over his complete lack of a future. He is just about dead, after all.

For the longest time, "Bag" was clearly used by the band as a standard rock tune, usually lasting no longer than eight minutes or so. Versions through 1988 also feature a cute little intro preceding the song's opening chords. Many fan favorites exist; check out 4/1/86 ("Help on the Way" > "Slipknot!" > "AC/DC Bag"!!!), 10/31/86 (with long intro), 8/6/88, 2/24/89 (workin' and warblin'), 11/4/90 (strong), 5/3/91 (scorching), 6/25/95, 7/3/95, 8/16/96, and 11/18/96 (smoking). Quite a few ripping versions of this tune are out there.

However, with the myriad musical experiments in jamming out some of the most unexpected tunes in early 1997 (even "Cavern," and "Scent of a Mule" received this treatment), "Bag" started visiting the most extraordinary of places. Standout versions include 11/21/97 (epic), 12/7/97 (sweet segue into "Psycho Killer"), 12/30/97 (mind-bending!), 8/9/98, 11/7/98 (gargantuan), 7/4/99, 9/26/99, and 6/15/00 (nice outro segue into "Uncle Pen"). Since 1997, "Bag" has served as a useful springboard for the band to launch into some expansive and exciting jams, very seldom finding its way to the drizzle of escalating notes that makes up the song's traditional, composed ending.

By the way, the "Roger" mentioned in this song (and also mentioned in "Wilson") is an old friend of Trey's, Roger Holloway, with whom Trey shares credit on the band's "White Tape" for the tune "Aftermath." For the Gamehendge saga, Roger is the name of Errand Woolfe's son, who was murdered by Wilson. The real Roger appeared on stage at the band's 4/14/93 gig at the beginning of the second set and proposed to his girlfriend. She accepted, and the band happily responded by playing the song that made that "crazy little kid" Roger a star, "AC/DC Bag."

Acoustic Army

Music: Phish
Album: (none)
Vocals: (instrumental)
Debut: 6/7/95
Historian: Mark Toscano

This tune seems to have been a two-tour phenomenon. During the second set at the Boise, ID Summer '95 tour opener (6/7/95), Mr. Jonny B. Fishman treated the crowd to a rousing rendition of The Velvet Underground's "Lonesome Cowboy Bill." Strangely, though, he didn't resume his seat at the drum kit after the song had ended. Rather, Fishman was joined front and center by Mike, Page, Trey, four stools, and four acoustic guitars. While the crowd looked on in confused anticipation, the guys tuned up and eventually launched into a pleasant little acoustic instrumental. The song they played—dubbed "Acoustic Army" by fans—was based on the idea of creating a cohesive tune from the distinct, disparate guitar lines that each bandmember played. The resulting song was melodic and pretty, and worked well as a charming breather for both band and audience. Although it had its critics, "Acoustic Army" was for the most part very well received by fans over the course of the Summer and Fall '95 tours. Its success is likely what led the band to try a similar experiment with keyboards (see "Keyboard Cavalry"), exclusively for the Fall '95 tour. "Acoustic Army" was played a total of 27 times before it

rode off into the sunset on 12/8/95. Interestingly, though, it did resurface in slightly altered form. Trey's first solo recording effort, *One Man's Trash*, contains a track called "The Real Taste of Licorice" which is basically "Acoustic Army" with a minor facelift.

See Also: "Keyboard Cavalry"

After Midnight

Music/Lyrics: J.J. Cale
Original Artist: Eric Clapton
Original Album: *Eric Clapton* (1970)
Debut: 12/31/99
Historian: Jeremy David Goodwin

The opening chords to this classic signaled perhaps the most appropriate song selection in the history of Phish. About 80,000 fans had swarmed to a field in the middle of the Everglades to witness the ambitious quartet perform an unprecedented all night set. As anticipation grew, fans were pretty much stumped as to what in the hell was going to go down. After a stunning three set affair the day before, the happily curious fans had enjoyed a relatively normal (though long) afternoon set on New Years Eve, punctuated by an unreal "SOAM" -> "Catapult." Then, the boys unleashed a set closer that sent chills (and cries of delight) through the entire crowd: "After Midnight," via the famous Eric Clapton arrangement.

The message couldn't have been more clear: after midnight, we're gonna let it all hang down! As if the curiosity and anticipation could get any more frenzied, this declaration somehow turned it all up a notch. It was one final tease before the main event, and as the jubilant crowd slowly walked back across the concert field after the set, an enormous roar erupted. Phish was planning to utterly throw down the gauntlet and plumb the depths of their artistic subconcious through a marathon night of musical experimentation, and this song put everything into words pretty perfectly. We're gonna find out what it's all about! On this night, many fans did just that.

If the landmark midnight set marked a new phase of the Phish story, "After Midnight" was the last song played by the old Phish...before Everything Changed, and the possibilities for this phenomenon shifted into the "limitless" category. Among a laundry list of musical epiphanies that occured in Big Cypress, seek out the "Drowned," which features an absolutely hair-raising segue into a brief "After Midnight" reprise, featuring another go-round of the chorus.

Aftermath

Music: Trey Anastasio, Roger Holloway
Album: "The White Tape"
Vocals: (instrumental)
Debut: (never performed live)
Historian: Ellis Godard

Aftermath lies beyond the ignited jams and the tweezered ecstasy, in a space of uncertainty. Pretty, yes, but subdued. An unsettled calm, filled with sweet anticipation but not aspiring away from what it is. Light but intricate, trill but full. But its history is not full: only slightly more than composed filler, it has only reached the stage once, and then only Trey's stage (on his early 1999 solo tour), and peopled otherwise only by co-creater Roger Holloway.

Jamming Songs

Compiled by Jeremy Goodwin and Charlie Dirksen

Composed with room for improvisation, Phish's jamming songs exhibit the band's creative prowess night after night. This section sketches the history and growth of many jamming songs by briefly summarizing noteworthy versions with timings and lighthearted comments.

A variety of factors were involved in determining which versions of jamming songs were to be included in these tables. The chief consideration was a version's importance as "one of the best," based on the opinions of many fans. Other factors included whether there were any teases of non-Phish or Phish songs in the jam segment; whether a particular version was unusually improvisational, or longer than the average version; and whether there was anything which set the version apart from a "standard, typically great" version.

We hope that these tables help you discover remarkable versions of your favorite jamming songs. If you would like more information about versions of the following songs, including more thorough tables and reviews, please surf over to the reviews pages of the Phish.Net site on the worldwide web. Also, please keep in mind that this section, like other sections in this book, is a continuous "work in progress," and it will change as the band's music evolves. As Phish continues to add new songs to its repertoire (for example, "Sand," "Gotta Jibboo," etc.), and advance other songs improvisationally (such as "Piper"), the number of jamming songs—and the scope of this section—will grow. No doubt, many meritorious versions of jamming songs have been omitted. We could use your help in making this section more complete. If you would like to contribute to and improve this section, please do not hesitate to contact the Foundation.

Miles Davis is believed to have said that writing about music is like "dancing about architecture." The attempt to describe improvisational music well is a confounding and challenging exercise. The notes in this section should therefore be interpreted as nothing more than whimsical reflections.

Every table in this section was edited and appended by Charlie Dirksen. Jeremy Goodwin assisted considerably with the editing

Occasional Jamming Songs

Phish is of course too unpredictable to adhere strictly to a proscribed roster of "jamming songs." Some of the most exciting on-stage moments come when a song is unexpectedly jammed out for the first time ever. There are many "one-timers" like this, such as "Character Zero," "Fee" and "Carini." There are also songs that jam in an exploratory fashion once in awhile, but usually stay concise, like "AC/DC Bag," "Gumbo" and "Cities." And, of course, songs proceed from one category to another all the time, or eventually graduate to full "regular jamming song" status.

Here are several citations to one-time (e.g., "Fee") or occasional jamming songs (e.g., "C&P"), as well as jamming songs for which even relatively complete tables are unavailable ("Harry Hood," "Piper" and "Twist"). Some of these tunes will most likely receive their own full table in future editions of the Companion. All of these are recommended versions, be it for their uniqueness, musical brilliance, or both.

AC/DC Bag
11/21/97 26:06
12/30/97 24:39
11/07/98 21:25
09/14/99 27:10

After Midnight
12/31/99 20:01

Axilla
12/28/97 09:36

BBFCFM
04/17/93 11

Birds of a Feather
04/04/98 14:26
07/08/99 18:35
07/23/99 25:24
07/25/99 19:08
06/29/00 13:43

Boogie On Reggae Woman
07/25/99 10:36
09/18/99 21:10

Carini
02/17/97 21:20
12/28/98 15:58

Chalkdust Torture
07/10/99 14:08

Character Zero
11/26/97 19:58

Cities
07/01/97 23:36
08/10/97 22
08/16/97 11:23
07/31/98 15:04

Crosseyed and Painless
11/02/96 23:53
12/31/99 20:14

Drowned
12/31/95 12:26
12/03/97 16:35
12/11/97 21:13
07/20/98 13:27
11/02/98 15:15
09/21/99 17:10
12/12/99 30:32
12/31/99 25:34
06/29/00 17:58

Jamming Songs (Continued)

Emotional Rescue
11/21/97 16:57
12/31/97 15:22

Fee
07/08/99 22:38

Fluffhead
07/24/99 32:54

Free
11/22/95 (not timed)

Funky Bitch
11/22/94 28:22
07/06/97 13:32
11/30/97 14:26

Get Back On The Train
06/14/00 12:20

Gotta Jibbo
07/04/00 28:30

Gumbo
08/13/97 19:22
11/14/97 11:04
11/26/97
08/15/98 13:31
10/15/98 09:01
09/14/99 10:04
06/14/00 12:30

Halley's Comet
12/14/95 11:59
11/22/97 24:13
08/16/97 14:32
12/28/97 12:45
07/13/99 14:32
10/08/99 14:25
06/30/00 15:07

Harry Hood
10/30/85 10:45
10/15/86 09:00
08/21/87 13:55
05/28/89 12:40

04/22/90 13:19
11/04/90 10:33
08/03/91 11:48
03/20/92 12:08
04/18/92 14:05 (Linus &
Lucy theme)
12/28/93 11:40
12/31/93 13:10
10/23/94 14:47 (A Live One
version)
11/12/94 14:50
07/01/95 14:26
10/07/95 16:03
12/06/96 15:46
11/16/97 17:55
11/22/97 18:02
12/31/98 17:58
10/08/99 15:23
09/09/00 16:52 (with
Michael Ray
on trumpet)

It's Ice
06/30/00 12:07

Izabella
12/06/97

Johnny B. Goode
11/17/97 17:03

Julius
07/10/97 12:02
12/05/97

The Mango Song
07/24/99 14:05
06/30/00 12:06
07/06/00 12:26
09/17/00

Moma Dance
07/06/00 12:26

NICU
12/14/95 09:02
10/30/98 09:21

Piper
12/06/97 14:02
12/12/97 18:57
07/06/98 19:49
08/08/98 15:43
07/18/99 25:19
09/17/99 15:25
10/02/99 21:58
12/08/99 19:31
12/13/99 19:10
12/31/99 18:58
07/08/00 14:49

Prince Caspian
06/19/97 11:52
10/15/98 09:45
12/31/99 08:57

Rock and Roll
12/31/99 30:12

Roses Are Free
04/03/98 27:22
12/31/99 35:02

Sand
12/13/99 22:43
12/16/99 21:47
12/31/99 (not timed)
09/09/00 19:51

Saw It Again
12/12/97

Suzy Greenberg
07/25/99

Theme From the Bottom
07/31/97 19:43
07/26/99 14:13
09/17/00 (not timed)

Timber Ho
11/16/97 13:50

Tube
12/07/97 12:33
11/02/98 13:33
09/15/00 17:36

Twist
06/20/97 13:18
07/06/97 13:49
11/14/97 15:58
04/02/98 18:36
12/31/99 13:20
06/14/00 34 (includes the
Jam which follows
the conclusion of
Twist)
07/04/00 17

Ya Mar
07/31/97 14:08
12/02/97 13:59
12/13/97 17:55
12/08/99 14:11

From the studio, on the "White Tape," it starts with an eruption labelled "mayem" in the credits, following the first recorded "Slave to the Traffic Light" (which one imagines ends in a merciless crash) and preceding "Ingest" (which begins the slow build of weirdness for the remainder of the album). In "Aftermath" lies still the studied composition of "Slave" and, earlier on the compilation, "You Enjoy Myself," but also arrives a looseness that recurs in later tracks.

Ain't Love Funny

AKA: "Funny As It Seems"
Original Artist: J.J. Cale
Original Album: *Closer to You* (1994)
Vocals: Mike (lead), Page, Trey (backing)
Debut: 6/20/97
Historian: Mark Toscano

This delicate J.J. Cale tune was a pleasant surprise for fans at the 6/20/97 Prague show, as it rose from a sweetly textured post-"Limb by Limb" jam for its debut performance during the first set. The rich, melodic harmonies are almost painfully sweet and Phish wisely remained very faithful to the original, leaving the instrumentation sparse and simple. Although the song's delicate fragility and subtlety make it an atypical choice for a cover, the band pulled it off nicely on the three occasions it was played (twice in Europe, once in the U.S.). After another first set appearance in Amsterdam on 7/1/97, the song made its final appearance at Alpine Valley over a month later on 8/9/97 in the middle of a nearly set-long, multi-song "Mike's Groove."

Albuquerque

Original Artist: Neil Young
Original Album: *Tonights the Night* (1975)
Vocals: Trey (lead)
Debut: 7/26/98
Historian: Phillip Zerbo

Debuted at the Starplex Amphitheatre in Dallas, TX on 7/26/98, "Albuquerque" was performed eight times in 1998 before disappearing from the rotation for a solid year. Interestingly, despite three guest appearances by the Neil Young with Phish in that year (Farm Aid on 10/3/98, and Neil Young's own Bridge School Benefits at Shoreline 10/17 & 10/18/98) they never performed the tune with its original artist. In 1998 the song was performed in equal parts acoustic (four times—the aforementioned Farm Aid and two Bridge School shows, as well as during the "mini acoustic set" 12/28/98 at MSG) and electric (four times).

Perhaps a window into the feelings that come with the fame Phish has found, "Albuquerque" reflects on the time-honored notion of escape that permeates many musical genres: rock, blues, soul, even pop. "I've been starving to be alone…and independent from the scene that I've known…I'll find somewhere where they don't care who I am." These lines in particular find emphasis in Trey's delivery of the ballad.

Shelved for over a year, it was revived at about three in the morning during The Show at Big Cypress. This version included a key lyric change that belies the tenor of the song, but was oh-so-appropriate for the event: "So I'll stop when I can, find some *cheesecake* and country ham."

Albert

Music: Phish
Album: *The Siket Disc*
Vocals: (instrumental)
Debut: (never performed live)
Historian: Mark Toscano

The final track on *The Siket Disc* acts as a sort of quiet epilogue to the all-instrumental CD, shouldering the noise buildup and tension of "Title Track," its predecessor, and giving it release. It's noodling, but it's sweet and simple. When Mike and Trey happen upon a nice, repeatable passage, the track gains direction and makes for a relaxing album closer.

All Along the Watchtower

Original Artist: Bob Dylan
Original Album: *John Wesley Harding* (Dylan),
  Electric Ladyland (Hendrix)
Vocals: Dave Matthews (4/21/94), Buddy Miles (10/22/96)
Debut: 4/21/94
Historian: Phil Nazzaro

When Bob Dylan writes a song, and Jimi Hendrix makes it famous, you know its got to be good. "All Along The Watchtower" made its debut on Bob Dylan's 1967 album *John Wesley Harding*. However, it is the version on Hendrix's 1968 *Electric Ladyland* that most of us think of when this song is mentioned.

Phish has only performed "Watchtower" twice. Both times their take leaned a little more towards Jimi's soaring, psychedelic version that became an anthem of sorts during the Vietnam war. One appearance was spurred on by a guest musician that uses "Watchtower" as a signature song; the other helped make it famous.

The first time around this song crept out of a drum duet between Fishman and Dave Matthews Band drummer Carter Beauford, with Dave Matthews himself taking the lead vocals as he has done in his own shows for years. Funny it should begin with a drum solo, as next time it appeared was when Merle Saunders and Buddy Miles took the stage with Phish for the encore 10/22/96 at Madison Square Garden. Although present on *Electric Ladyland*, Buddy was not the drummer on Hendrix's original cut. But playing drums for Jimi's Band Of Gypsys (and beyond) he certainly did his part to make this song famous. With Phish, he not only played the drums (while Fishman played Trey's drumkit), he also took the vocals.

All Blues

Original Artist: Miles Davis
Original Album: *Kind of Blue* (1959)
Vocals: (instrumental)
Debut: 7/30/88
Historian: Christian C. McKee

Bill Evans, who played the piano for Miles Davis in the '50s and '60s was far and away the most influential jazz pianist since Bud Powell, the great bebopper. Page often cites Evans as an influence, and that can be heard in the chord voicings McConnell employs while improvising. Strange then, that Phish would cover the only cut off of Davis' landmark *A Kind of Blue* that did not feature Evans on piano. For this

track, Miles called in Winton Kelly, a skilled blues player. Lacking John Coltrane, Cannonball Adderly and Miles himself, Phish's cover on 2/6/89 (to open the second set) suffered a bit, although it did give Page a chance to stretch out. Same goes for the 7/30/88 debut, performed with Trey on drums during the infamous "late Fishman" show at Telluride's Roma. Like most of their jazz numbers, this has long since disappeared, and is unlikely to return.

All the Pain Through the Years

Music/Lyrics: Seth Yacavone
Original Artist: Seth Yacavone
Original Album: *Bobfred's Bathtub Minstrel* **(studio):**
   Yessir **(live)**
Debut: 11/29/98
Historian: Craig DeLucia

Burlington guitar prodigy Seth Yacavone joined the band in Worcester at the close of the Fall 1998 tour. Together, they ran through Eric Clapton's "Layla" and this Yacavone original.

All Things Reconsidered

AKA: "ATR"
Music: Trey Anastasio
Album: *Rift*
Vocals: (instrumental)
Debut: 9/25/91
Historian: Phillip Zerbo

A direct nod to and variation on the theme to the National Public Radio show *All Things Considered*, "All Things Reconsidered" is a short instrumental tune that was a standard in the Phish repertoire in

Elise Ryerson

the early 1990s. "All Things Reconsidered" made its live debut on 9/25/91, at the classic Colonial Theater, in Keene, NH. "ATR" shares its live "birthday" with "Brother," "It's Ice," and "Sparkle," which were also debuted at this tour opening show.

Trey has made several explicit references on stage to the link between *All Things Considered* and "All Things Reconsidered": at the debut in Keene, at Trax in Charlottesville, VA on 3/25/92, and at the Livingston Fieldhouse in Granville, OH, on 12/1/92. On this last occasion Trey noted (with tongue firmly planted in cheek): "Thank you people, at this time we're going to play the variations on the *All Things Considered* radio show theme song so please feel free to sing along."

National Public Radio has taken notice of the song, as it has been played on several occasions as intro and outro music during the *All Things Considered* show, as well as another NPR show, *Mountain Stage*.

"All Things Reconsidered" was in heavy rotation during all of 1992 and 1993, when it was performed on average every two to three shows. It made only sporadic appearances from 1994 through 1996, and as of this writing it was last performed on 2/23/97, at the Fillmore in Cortemaggiore, Italy.

"All Things Reconsidered" is an entirely composed song that has never been "stretched out," and performances only vary in the degree of precise execution. Certainly check out the studio version on *Rift*, and where it appears in otherwise exceptional shows that you should check out anyway, such as 3/30/93, 8/2/93, 4/9/94, 10/28/94, 7/1/95, and 11/30/96.

Alumni Blues

AKA: "Alumni"
Music/Lyrics: Trey Anastasio
Album: "The White Tape"
Vocals: Trey (lead), Mike, Page (backing)
Debut: 5/3/85
Historian: Mark Toscano

I'm alright, you're alright, everybody's alright. Trey was presumably alright when he wrote this wacky tune around the beginning of 1985, even if he wasn't yet an alumnus of anything (save high school). In fact, Trey couldn't officially sing this song until the 7/11/88 version, an excellent rendition that was performed to commemorate Trey's graduation from Goddard.

"Alumni" is the quintessential early-days Phish tune that fans today ache to hear at each show they attend. It was a very common, signature song for the guys during the hungry years, dotting numerous setlists for shows through 1989. In 1990, frequency dropped off severely, and though a few more versions were performed the following year (most notably on the summer horn tour), the song basically disappeared. At this point, Phish was no longer a quartet of college students or even recent college graduates. By 1991 they had graduated to another level, that of fast-growing, highly successful and accomplished touring band. 1991 saw their first nationwide tour that included the West coast, and the following year the band made a trip to Europe opening for the Violent Femmes and a U.S. amphitheatre/arena tour opening for Santana. It is fitting that 1991 was the last year "Alumni" was a semi-regular tune in the repertoire, as 1992 brought the band into the "real world," as it were.

Since 1991, "Alumni" has only walked across the stage a few

times. Notwithstanding a tease during the 11/28/92 "Tweezer," the song didn't show up again until the fun 4/15/94 show, at which a single verse of the tune emanated from "Wolfman's" into "I Wanna Be Like You." That Fall tour, the presence of horns at some West coast shows must have brought the guys back to the days of Summer 1991, as the 12/3/94 San Jose show boasted an "Alumni" jam, although no lyrics were sung. Fast forward another five years for the next appearance, this time on Trey's solo tour stop in Madison on 5/8/99. The song was performed as a dedication to the various students of Trey's brother-in-law that cut classes to see the show. The last known Phish appearance came later that year in Alpine Valley at the crazy 7/24/99 show that also featured a 31-minute "Fluffhead" and a blistery "Camel Walk."

"Alumni" has two other aspects of interest, both of which concern Phish's "White Tape." The final track on that early demo, "Letter to Jimmy Page," has almost always shown up as a bridge inside "Alumni." Trey wrote and recorded "Jimmy Page," playing all the instruments himself, as an homage to one of his guitar heroes. In live performances, "Jimmy Page" has appeared in "Alumni" pretty much since the beginning, with strange and notable exceptions (e.g. 10/15/86 and 7/24/99). Also, on the version of the "White Tape" that circulated before the album was officially released, a mysterious track called "Steve Reich" was always listed after "Alumni," and consisting of only marimbas and nature noises, ending in a tumultuous car crash. On the official release, this track was not listed, though it is still present, sharing a track index with "Alumni." (For further explanation, check the "Steve Reich" history.)

"Alumni" has never varied all too much from standard delivery, though some standout and curious versions include 10/17/85 (with Mike solo), 10/15/86, 2/27/87, 5/20/87 (with guests on guitar and sax), 9/24/88 (with "Possum" teases), 3/12/89 (featuring punk jamming with local band Eyeburn), 5/13/89 (dedicated to Syracuse grads), 12/7/89 (ferocious "Jimmy Page"), 4/6/90 (with extra lyrics), and 7/18/91 (last version until 4/15/94).

See Also: "Letter to Jimmy Page," "Steve Reich"

Also Sprach Zarathustra

AKA: "2001"; "Also Sprach"; "ASZ"
Music: Richard Strauss/Eumir Deodato
Original Artist: Eumir Deodato
Original Album: *Prelude* (1972)
Debut: 7/16/93
Historian: Chris Bertolet

This 1895 tone poem, one of the oldest compositions Phish has covered, achieved pop-culture prominence on the soundtrack to Stanley Kubrick's *2001: A Space Odyssey*. But Deodato's discotheque remix—featured in the 1979 Hal Ashby film *Being There*—seems to be Phish's direct inspiration.

"Also Sprach" leapt onto the playlist as a catalytic second set opener and a showcase for Chris Kuroda's smoke machine. And though it wasn't jammed in its early years, "Also Sprach" often served as a springboard for jamming juggernauts like "Mike's Song," "Maze," "David Bowie," and "Run Like an Antelope."

On 10/31/96, guest percussionist Karl Perazzo inspired Phish to extend the lead-in to each of the two ascending stanzas, locking down a chunky groove that stretched the song to a full seven minutes. Subsequent Fall '96 versions (like 11/18 in Memphis and 12/6 in Las Vegas)

earned "Also Sprach" full jam status, and offered a taste of the bovine funk that would lubricate Phish's live sound in 1997.

Throughout that year, "Also Sprach" remained the standard bearer for the new sound. Creative appearances abounded. At the Great Went on 8/17/97, Phish used loops to sustain a liquid soundscape as they painted a mural in the background. The 11/26/97 Hartford version glided out of "Character Zero" and into "Cities," and featured extended "Superbad" jamming in between. The expected 12/31/97 Madison Square Garden "Also Sprach" proved a visual feast as well as a sonic one, with morphing udder balls, embryos and breakfast foods projected onto an overhead screen.

Since its coming-of-age, "Also Sprach" continues to set the gearshift on Phish's boogie tractor, combing the reaches of space, electronica, and old-school funk to unearth dance hall grooves that can range from pornographic to ecstatic. Recent hallmark "Also Sprachs" include the sunrise version from Big Cypress (if only for sentimental reasons) and the eminently groovy rave-up from 6/14/00 Fukuoka, Japan, which marked the first time the song has ended the second set.

Amazing Grace

Vocals: Phish/(occasionally performed instrumental)
Music/Lyrics: John Newton (1779)
Debut: 1/28/93
Historian: Ellis Godard:

John Newton's "Amazing Grace" is something like a musical version of Thomas Paine's *Common Sense*. Beneath the guise of mass appeal and popular imagery, both writers expressed complex convictions and helped foment intense insurgency. Paine's pamphlet was more explicitly political, weaving the needs of a developing democracy into emotional challenges to pride and patriotism. While explicitly religious on the surface, Newton's song also addressed the direction of a new nation. Written in the same era as the Declaration of Independence and U.S. Constitution, it spoke to reprieve from persecution as well as from purgatory. No surprise, then, that it regained popularity throughout the south during the Reconstruction era after the Civil War.

For Phish, the subtleties take another route, not concealing politics behind religion, but evoking a religiosity not explicit in shows or the interaction between band and fans. On special occasions such as Halloween (10/31/94), New Year's Eves (12/31/93, 12/31/94, 12/31/96), special events (Clifford Ball opening, 8/16/96) or some tour closers (e.g. 7/3/95), its lyrics stand on their own: Here, the band declares, we have reached one of those epiphanies for which we strive, a graceful escape from wayward distractions. Such appearances acknowledge the transformative power of music, and make sacred the ritual of cooperative attention towards and from the stage.

That is not to imply that large or event shows necessarily have more sanctity. Another common fan interpretation of the Phishy relevance of the lyrics centers on the "as when I first begun" lyrics, pointing to the perpetually maintained integrity of the band amid the zany popular growth of the phenomenon. Moreover, appearances have not always been sacred. The debut (1/28/93) was near sacrilege, in the Boston Hard Rock Cafe, a commercial center of celebrity, following a ceremony in which Fishman donated his vacuum to the venue's memorabilia collection. And banality diminished sanctity, as the song was performed nearly sixty more times that year alone, opening, closing, or

constituting dozens of encores. There were nearly as many performances the next year, including one sandwiched inside "Big Black Furry Creature From Mars" (5/16/94) and three paired in an encore with "Highway to Hell." (Appearances have petered off since, with only sixteen versions in 1995 and only six in 1996.)

Versions are memorable largely for their placement, capping off strong or otherwise memorable shows. But three are notable for the performances themselves: One (12/31/96) including the Boston Community Choir. And two (5/8/93 and 11/30/96) were instrumental rather than a capella. This form seems particularly ironic: The switch to a diminished chord in the next-to-last verse seems to contradict the melody's soaring message, but the return to the regular melody in the last verse is doubly powerful because of it. These turns were particularly dramatic without words.

AMERICAN BAND (see: "WE'RE AN AMERICAN BAND")

Amoreena
Original Artist: Elton John
Original Album: *Tumbleweed Connection* (1970)
Vocals: Page
Debut: 8/13/97
Historian: Craig DeLucia

Elton John's second album, *Tumbleweed Connection*, was released in October of 1970. To quote John Tobler's comments in the liner notes for the album's 1995 re-release, "Nearly all of the songs…seemed to reflect [lyricist] Bernie Taupin's preoccupation and fascination with the American west, outlaws, sheriffs, the great outdoors, etc."

Although the album sold over two million copies, it did not produce any hit singles. Some of the songs, though, were highly memorable. Among them was "Amoreena," a piano-driven spaghetti western tale of lovers lament that Phish covered at Star Lake in the summer of 1997. The song, named for Elton's god-daughter, is narrated by a man who left his country girl in the cornfield and has come to miss her. Fans may miss the song as much as the narrator misses the girl; it hasn't been played since.

Anarchy
Music/Lyrics: Phish
Album: (none)
Vocals: Trey
Debut: 3/4/85
Historian: Mark Toscano

Anarchy was really no more than ten seconds of blaring punk chords supported by breakneck drumming from Fishman, all accompanied by repetitive shrieks of "Anarchy!" It was basically a joke song that didn't even make it into the nineties (and barely made it into the late '80s— it was played only twice between '88 and '89). The final version took place on 10/14/89. If you truly want to experience the many interesting and excitingly diverse versions of this tune, by all means listen to 4/15/86, 10/15/86, 4/29/87 (two in a row), and 8/1/87 (three in a row).

"Anarchy" does have a bastard sibling, an equally thought-provoking composition supported by lyrics that almost live up to the sweet, poetic beauty of this, a song that finds us in perhaps Phish's finest hour.

Played only one delirious time, "Revolution" will likewise have you cursing songs like "Reba" and "The Squirming Coil" as pedantic and amateurish.

See Also: "Revolution"

And it Stoned Me
Music/Lyrics: Van Morrison
Original Artist: Van Morrison
Original Album: *Moondance* (1970)
Vocals: unidentified fan
Debut: 7/6/97
Historian: Ellis Godard

Phish's 1997 tour of Europe included stops in some of the most romantic spots of Italy, places of jaw-dropping beauty, history, and revelation. During the 7/6/97 soundcheck, they paused from the whirlwind of emotion for a limbo karaoke contest, full of silly songs. The pause was almost broken, when an audience member sang the lead track from Van Morrison's *Moondance*, an album filled with romance, beauty, and revelation even in this simple three-chord (D,C,G) ditty. But its chorus about liking wetness and its three verses—we went fishing but got rained on, we got a ride and then went swimming, and our throats were dry but we found a guy with bottled relief—came across as deadpan. This version is less likely to give you "cotton mouth" (it won't stone you) than make you want to jump in a lake.

And So To Bed
Music: Trey Anastasio
Album: "The White Tape"
Vocals: (instrumental)
Debut: (never performed live)
Historian: Mark Toscano

And So to Bed is that rare animal—a Phish song that never made it to the live show. Though it appears on a few circulating 4-track demos from the band's infancy (most notably The "White Tape"), this sweet solo acoustic number penned and performed solo by Trey was likely never intended to occupy a place in the band's repertoire. It's just too damned…nice.

Andy's Chest
Music/Lyrics: Lou Reed
Original Artist: Lou Reed
Original Album: *Transformer* (1973)
Vocals: Trey
Debut: 9/13/88
Historian: Martha Hunt

Lou Reed is one of the most influential, innovative, and bizarre artists in rock and roll history, and the primary creative talent behind The Velvet Underground. "Andy's Chest" was first written in the VU days, but was not released until 1973, on Reed's second solo album, *Transformer*. It was with this album, produced by David Bowie, that Reed first gained some amount of (long overdue) public recognition with the track "Walk on the Wild Side, an unusual top-10 hit single that mentions transvestism, prostitution, and oral sex.

Listening to the lyrics to "Andy's Chest," you really have to won-

der what it must be like to be Lou Reed, and have that sort of thing going on in your mind all the time. Thankfully, we don't all have his gift. But thankfully, he does. Also, thankfully, Trey is not Lou Reed, which may explain why this song was only covered once, on 9/13/88. The band does a passable job at the tune, but must have realized they were better suited for less…"Loureedian" outings.

Another One Bites the Dust

Music/Lyrics: John Deacon
Original Artist: Queen
Original Album: *The Game* **(1980)**
Vocals: unidentified fan (7/6/97)
Debut: 7/6/97
Historian: Martin Acaster

Perhaps hoping to capitalize on the waning glitter-ball infested daze of disco, the typically hard-rocking British band Queen renounced their "no synthesizers" policy and released their first dance-oriented album *The Game* in 1980. "Another One Bites The Dust," written by bassist John Deacon, and featuring a mesmerizing disco bass groove, was ultimately Queen's most successful hit single in the United States, reaching number one for three of the thirty-one weeks that it charted. Lyrically the song dances a metaphorical line between gun fights and failed relationships.

All but one of the Phish performances of this dance favorite to date have been as Mike Gordon-led instrumental grooves in the midst of a jam. The first appearance of this "Another One Bites The Dust" groove was during an otherwise average "You Enjoy Myself" at Colorado College, Colorado Springs, CO on 4/22/90. Since then it has appeared in two other "YEMs" (Fox Theater, Boulder, CO, 4/5/92 and the University of Gainsville, Gainsville, FL, 10/23/94), a "Mike's Groove" (Electric Ballroom, Knoxville, TN, 2/18/93), and most recently during a spicy "Gumbo" served up in Boise on 9/14/99. The only time the lyrics have been included was during a session of "Phish Karaoke" held during the sound check of the 7/6/97 show at the Spiaggia di Rivoltana, Desenzano/Genova, Italy. This hilarious performance featured the vocal stylings (and "Another One Rides The Bus" lyrical improvisation) of one of the lucky fans present for the surprise soundcheck which also included a limbo contest.

ANTELOPE (see RUN LIKE AN ANTELOPE)

Any Colour You Like

Vocals: (instrumental)
Original Artist: Pink Floyd
Original Album: *Dark Side of the Moon* **(1973)**
Debut: 11/2/98
Historian: Mark Toscano

This song, sometimes referred to as "Breathe—Second Reprise," has been in Pink Floyd's conception of *Dark Side of the Moon* from the very beginning. The song cycle was organized conceptually, touching on and interweaving themes of madness, both personal and societal. As a result, the Floyd wanted to have some recurring musical themes show up a few times throughout the album. The "Breathe" theme is a primary theme in *Dark Side*, built more or less on a syrupy, waking dream of a two-chord progression. This theme, after being introduced in "Breathe," shows up a few songs later as "Breathe

Reprise," a relaxed sigh following the mounting energy of "Time."

In the second half of the album, "Money" provides a hot-bed of nastiness that is perfectly complimented by the blissful languor of "Us and Them," the former segueing into the latter by means of some overlapping sound bites. "Us and Them" then practically trips over "Any Colour You Like," which starts up immediately after the former song's final verse. This reprise of "Breathe" is a different animal, though. It's not at all like the underwater sleepwalk of the first two instances, although it retains the same two-chord values. This song is all instrumental, and is driven by an insistent beat and a funky demeanor. "Any Colour You Like" is almost dirty, as if the band suddenly turned a corner into a bad section of town. The track boasts its own confidence, and in fact was often one of the only jamming showcases for Pink Floyd during their live performances of *Dark Side* after 1972.

Enter Phish. "Any Colour You Like" had its turn under the chopping block on 11/2/98 for the now-legendary, surprise *Dark Side* performance at the E Center in Utah, and the guys played it with adequate strength and groove. However, one can't help but wonder what they *could* have done with the song if it hadn't been played so late in an already exhausting show. It might've been a monster.

Arc

Music: Neil Young
Original Artist: Neil Young
Original Album: *Arc* **(1991)**
Vocals: (instrumental)
Debut: 10/3/98
Historians: Craig DeLucia and Erik Swain

There was great anticipation leading up to Phish's 1998 Farm Aid appearance. Neil Young was set to perform as well, and the band was scheduled to play his Bridge School Benefits in two weeks. Fans hoped for some sort of collaboration and were certainly not disappointed, as a national television audience saw Phish and Neil team up on, among other songs, a powerful "Runaway Jim" / "Down By the River" combo that left the crowd speechless.

A feedback-based free-form jam connected the two songs, and some in the Phish community who are also Neil fans took to labeling the jam "Arc." Originally released as a companion to the *Weld* album and subsequently released separately on Reprise, *Arc* (the album) contained one track: "Arc" the song. And even then, "Arc" is not really a song but rather a free-form experiment that some revered and some saw as pure noise. It combined guitar squeals, feedback, drum breaks, soundchecks, and other seemingly random material into one thirty-five minute experience. The source material came from the 1991 "Smell the Horse" tour, which also produced the live tracks for *Weld*. Most of the material seems to come from the songs "Like a Hurricane," "Welfare Mother," and "Tonight's the Night."

To say that Phish and Neil played "Arc" would be like saying that Phish jammed "And Furthermore" from *Surrender to the Air*; you can't really say that an artist jammed something too free-form to define. Still, labeling the jam "Arc" made it to the Internet and seemed to survive in many setlists, so the title appears to have stuck.

Arrival

Music: Trey Anastasio

Album: *Junta* (part of "Fluff's Travels"—CD 9:10-11:38)
Vocals: Phish
Debut: 12/1/84
Historian: Mark Toscano

Arrival is the seventh part of the epic "Fluffhead." Although other parts of "Fluffhead" have been performed disembodied from the rest of the full composition, "Arrival" never has had that distinction (the same goes for "Fluff's Travels"). From the very beginning, "Arrival" has served only as the closing chapter of "Fluffhead." In fact, the late-1984 "Fluffhead" consisted of only "Fluffhead" and "Arrival," the former segueing into the latter (see 12/1/84).

Many fans have been known to claim "Arrival" as their favorite part of "Fluffhead." The blissful, energetic release it delivers after the ever-tightening, escalating melodrama of "Bundle of Joy" is possibly unparalleled as far as sheer, Phishy thrills go. The happy four-chord progression—accompanied by Fluffy shouts and an ecstatic Trey solo—rarely disappoints (and you know it's a good night if Trey yells "Fluffballs!"). On a final note, some fans may find the four-chord progression of "Arrival" familiar; an identical progression can be found comprising the Blues Traveler song "Runaround" (and for what it's worth, the liner notes of that song's host album, *Four*, do give thanks to "any swollen-ankled, red-bearded guitarists....")

See Also: "Fluffhead/Fluff's Travels"

The Asse Festival

AKA: "Asse"
Music: Trey Anastasio
Album: *A Picture of Nectar* (bookended by "Guelah Papyrus")
Vocals: (instrumental)
Debut: 9/13/90
Historian: Ellis Godard

During a summer 1990 effort to dredge new directions from old songs, Phish abstracted the instrumental from "PYITE" to create the independent "Landlady." Soon after, the band took the opposite approach and built a new song, "Guelah Papyrus," around a tune they had already performed a dozen times over a five-month period. That earlier kernel, "The Asse Festival" (pronounced "ass"), is one of the more challenging items in the band's repertoire, a fugal piece inspired by Anastasio mentor Ernie Stires, and has appeared alone only twice (2/21/91 and 4/27/91) since "Guelah's" debut (2/1/91). "Guelah" itself was shelved for a bit before reappearing on 10/30/98, with the "Asse" in newly practiced (and excellent) form.

Relating to another tune, "The Ass Festival" is one of the last chapters in Nietzsche's *Thus Spoke Zarathustra*. After coming down from the mountain, proclaiming "God is Dead," Zarathustra strives to create a select group of "supermen" but then recognizes this group has convalesced into a more highly evolved state when he finds them adoring an ass in a cave.

Before "Guelah," "The Asse Festival" marked similar turns. For example, it followed a soaring "Mockingbird" (10/7/90), high-reaching "YEMs" (10/31/90 and 11/8/90), an energetic "Funky Bitch" (11/4/90), and a fiery "Llama" (12/8/90) and was then followed by songs of self-conscious recognition such as "The Squirming Coil," "My Sweet One," "I Didn't Know," and "Bouncing Round the Room." Other solo appearances were the reverse turn, from self-conscious to fiery, such as "Tube"

to "Antelope" (9/13/90), "Cavern" to "Possum" (11/2/90), and "Sweet Adeline" to "Runaway Jim" (4/27/91). And while early versions of "Guelah" followed the former pattern (often followed by "My Sweet One"), later versions take the later turn and most often follow "Chalk Dust Torture," about someone evolving from the ass of educational drudgery.

See Also: "Guelah Papyrus"

Axilla

AKA: "Axilla (Part I)"; "Axilla I"
Music: Trey Anastasio
Lyrics: Tom Marshall, Scott Herman
Album: *Hampton Comes Alive* (11/20/98)
Vocals: Trey
Debut: 11/19/92
Historian: Craig DeLucia

Ever wonder how many obscure terms for body parts made it into Phish songs? "Chalk Dust" has a slew, and "Heavy Things" has a few, but "Axilla" and its successor are the only songs named for one (with apologies, of course, to "My Left Toe," which is just not at all obscure). The axilla is the armpit, or, more specifically, the cavity between the forelimb and the body.

So, what does the song have to do with the armpit? No one is quite sure. The lyrics tell the story of a battle with a witch; one singular line refers to a particularly stinky axilla that makes the narrator lose his/her appetite. And, of course, the word is cool enough that it gets shouted over and over at the end of the song. Musically, it may be the hardest, heaviest original since "Big Black Furry Creature From Mars" first appeared in the early days.

After debuting in 1992, "Axilla" was played regularly through 1993. Given its heavy tones, it was often a set-opener that got the crowd moving. The appearance of the sequel, "Axilla (Part II)," doomed the original to the shelf. The sequel went in the can after 12/31/95, though, and the original entered re-runs—sort of. The band tagged the ending of "Part II" onto the original and continues to perform the song in this manner. Also, for some reason, it ceased to be a set-opener and, like "Part II" in its day, is likely to be heard just about anywhere in a set.

Now if we can just figure out how this song relates to Gamehendge....

Axilla (Part II)

AKA: "Axilla II"
Music: Trey Anastasio
Lyrics: Tom Marshall
Album: *Hoist*
Vocals: Trey (lead), Mike, Page (backing)
Debut: 4/16/94
Historian: Craig DeLucia:

Axilla (Part II) followed on the heels of the original "Axilla" and debuted on 4/16/94. It was the last of the *Hoist* songs to debut (save "Riker's Mailbox," which still has not been performed and likely never will). New lyrics, same music, and same "axilla" cry at the end. Absent, though, is any specific axilla reference during the verses, except the narrator "[wishing] it was cool"—perhaps to avoid the stench referenced in the original.

The only main structural difference between the two songs was the addition of a slow, trippy, guitar lick-based ending. In fact, when

"Axilla (Part II)" was shelved in 1995, this ending was retained and tagged to the end of future performances of the original "Axilla." The music to this ending was heard as early as 1993—listen to the little jam at the end of "It's Ice" on 3/31 of that year.

Auld Lang Syne
Original Artist: Robert Burns
Vocals: (performed instrumental)
Debut: 5/28/89
Historian: Mark Toscano

This 18th-century Scottish ditty (at one point it was the unofficial Scottish national anthem) is easily one of the oldest songs that Phish covers. Ironically, though it's the quintessential New Year's Eve song, the band did not in fact debut it on a New Year's Eve. The song was first teased by Trey as a joke at the 5/28/89 "Christmas" show (the ashes from the outdoor bonfire reminded Trey of snow). The first actual appearance of the tune was 12/30/89, the day before New Year's Eve, as the first encore song before a full Mike's Groove! (The song did put in a proper appearance the next night at the appropriate time.) Only one time has "Auld Lang Syne" appeared outside of a Holiday Run context. It surfaced in the middle of "Mike's Song" at the exceedingly strange 3/27/92 show.

Beginning with New Year's 1989, this has become a Holiday Run standard, featured at every New Year's show since then. The band frequently teases the song in New Year's run shows, outside of its 12/31 midnight context: teases or jams can be found in the 12/30/92 "YEM," the 12/28/93 "Ya Mar," the 12/31/93 "Harry," the 12/28/94 "Weekapaug," the 12/31/94 "Simple," the 12/30/95 "Ya Mar," the 12/31/95 "Weekapaug," the 12/31/97 "Ya Mar," the 12/31/98 "Runaway Jim," and the 12/30/99 "Weekapaug." Amidst all this, the full tune is customarily played as the clock strikes twelve, and often accompanying thrillingly bizarre goings-on.

1993 featured the band tearing into a then unfamiliar "Down With Disease" jam out of "Auld Lang Syne," and then segueing back into it for a dramatic finale, all within the confines of a stage-sized aquarium. For the 1994 version, the band played this tune on smaller instruments from atop a flying hot dog that circled around Boston Garden at the stroke of midnight. For 1995's show, the band (helped by some unidentified extras) acted out their roles as curators of the Gamehendge Time Factory, a machine without which the world would remain frozen in time. At midnight, the Frankensteinian machinery on stage was activated, producing a freshly shorn Baby Fishman. In '96, a record was set for the largest indoor balloon drop (79,627!), followed by a rather unexpected cover of Queen's "Bohemian Rhapsody" with a full choir. 1997 featured more balloons, but this time many of them evoked the themes and objects found in the dome animation projected at various times throughout the show. 1998 also featured balloons, but was a bit of a departure, as several dancers in various organically themed costumes shimmied about on the terrarium-dressed stage amidst occasional pyrotechnics, taking focus away from the band for once. The legendary 1999 Big Cypress New Year's show topped them all, however, for not only was the "Auld Lang Syne" preceded and accompanied by pyrotechnics, balloons, AND the hot dog, but it was followed by a never-to-be-forgotten seven-plus-hour set of non-stop pure molten bliss.

Avenu Malkenu (Our Father, Our King)
Original Artist: (traditional)
Vocals: Mike, Page, and Trey
Debut: 5/11/87
Historian: Saul E. Wertheimer

Walk into any synagogue on Rosh Hashanah or Yom Kippur (and various other times during the year), and you're bound to hear this ancient Jewish prayer, familiar to many from synagogue services. To others, "Avenu Malkenu" is more recognizable from its appearance sandwiched between "TMWSIY."

This Hebrew prayer has its roots in a Talmudic story (tractate Ta'anit, 25b). At a time of drought, after another Rabbi has made a fruitless attempt to pray for rain, the great sage Rabbi Akiva (second half of 1st century, and 1st half of 2nd century) initiates a prayer in the "Avenu Malkenu"—"Our Father, Our King"—format. His prayer is successful.

The "Avenu Malkenu" that Phish performs is a later version of this efficacious prayer. It can be translated as, "Our Father, Our King, be gracious with us and answer us, even though we have no [worthy] deeds; treat us with charity and kindness, and save us." Within the context of the Jewish liturgy, this prayer is interesting because it defines a relationship with God as both that of a Father-Son, as well as a Master-Servant.

Phish almost always plays "Avenu Malkenu" (granted, a bit funkier than you're likely to hear it in synagogue) preceded and followed by "TMWSIY." As always, there are exceptions; the band occasionally forgoes the "TMWSIY" reprise, in favor of another song, such as the fan-favourite 8/7/93 (which launches into a raucous "Sloth"), 12/28/96 (straight into "Mike's Song"!) and 10/3/99 ("BBFCFM"). 4/18/92 is also an interesting version, as it contains an extended "Happy Passover" bass solo. The "TMWSIY" > "Avenu" > "TMWSIY" trio replaced "I Am Hydrogen" in its traditional role as intermediary between "Mike's" and "Weekapaug" on 2/4/93. Trey then proceeded to tease "TMWSIY" in "Weekapaug."

And finally, on 8/26/89, Trey announced that "Avenu" was written by, "Pete Rose and God," leaving many fans saying, "I knew he wasn't just a ballplayer!"

AXIS: BOLD AS LOVE (see: "BOLD AS LOVE")

Baby Elephant Walk
Original Artist: Henry Mancini
Original Album: *Hatari* (1962)
Vocals: (instrumental)
Debut: 12/1/92
Historian: Phillip Zerbo

Demonstrating that no musical genre is off-limits, "Baby Elephant Walk" dips into the "cocktail culture" music of the late fifties and early sixties. One of the most successful film composers of all time and perhaps most famous for his score to *The Pink Panther*, Henry Mancini penned this song for the 1961 film *Hatari*.

Phish first performed this tune on 12/1/92 at the Livingston Fieldhouse in Granville, Ohio, during the intro theme to "David Bowie." The only other version is a memorable one, as it provided the soundtrack for one of the great theatrical "gags" of Phish's career.

On 8/16/98, the second day of Lemonwheel in Limestone, Maine,

the assembled crowd was greeted by a 20-foot-tall mechanical elephant sitting to the right side of the stage. After the glowstick-filled Harry Hood encore, the band members gathered around the small stone temple containing a fire that had been lit the night before after the "Ambient Jam," and that had been burning continuously throughout the show on Sunday. Trey used this flame to light a tiki-torch which he then used to ignite a fuse that ran around the stage and eventually toward the waiting elephant. During the time the fuse was on its journey, Fishman began to coax the elephant to life, using his trombone to imitate elephant sounds. When the fuse found its way to the elephant, it came to life amid a cloud of smoke, lifting its trunk and spraying water over the nearby crowd. A massive fireworks display was then unleashed over the brilliant Maine sky, as the band played the "Baby Elephant Walk," while the elephant marched off towards the campground, led by tiki-torch bearers and followed by many in the crowd, humming along to the infectious rhythms of the band. A delightful end to a wonderful weekend of fun and music!

Baby Lemonade
Original Artist: Syd Barrett
Original Album: *Barrett* **(1970)**
Vocals: Fishman
Debut: 3/11/92
Historians: Tim Wade/Benjy Eisen

Though he only performed it one time, Fishman made the most of his rendition of "Baby Lemonade." For this tune he employed a special attachment for his vacuum which connected it to the bagpipes. He used this contraption for a month or so during the beginning of the '92 spring tour.

Back At the Chicken Shack
Original Artist: Jimmy Smith
Original Album: *Back at the Chicken Shack* **(1960)**
Vocals: (instrumental)
Debut: 10/30/98
Historian: Chris Bertolet

Organ legend Jimmy Smith, who sits proudly at the crossroads of blues, jazz, and early funk, all but invented the Hammond B-3 style that contemporary wizards like John Medeski and Page McConnell lay down today. Anyone who appreciates genuine roots music and spot-on storytelling should jump at the chance to see Jimmy pull out the stops at their local jazz club. At 70-plus, he's still going strong.

Phish sandwiched their debut of this blues number into the "Scent of a Mule" on 10/31/98 in Las Vegas, in the middle of a set that seemed to recall their own musical roots. This and subsequent versions (all fine) provide fans with an increasingly rare chance to hear Page show off his chops, front and center.

Back In the U.S.S.R.
Original Artist: The Beatles
Original Album: *The Beatles* **(aka "The White Album") (1968)**
Vocals: Trey (lead), Mike, Page (backing)
Debut: 10/31/94
Historian: Mark Toscano

The all-important opener for 10/31/94 set II—perhaps one of the most anticipated set openers in the history of Phish. 1994 marked the first year of the coveted Halloween "musical costume," and every single fan was dying to hear the duds the band would don that night. Electricity filled the air—the excitement of that evening simply can not be described in words. As the tape loops and sound effects of Pink Floyd's "Speak to Me" buzzed through the air, many were justifiably convinced that the band would be doing their trick-or-treating in the guise of *Dark Side of the Moon*. However, as should have been expected on Halloween, this one was a trick. The real treat came when the band confidently soared into a rockin' rendition of "Back In the U.S.S.R.," the opening track from The Beatles' eponymous 1968 "White Album." One hundred minutes and thirty songs later, the band had once again made Phishtory. Santa Barbara, California fans were even treated to an encore performance of this tune over a month later on 12/6/94. These are the only two live performances of this tune to date.

Back on the Train
AKA: "Get Back on the Train"; "GBOTT"; "BOTT"
Music/Lyrics: Trey Anastasio, Tom Marshall
Album: *Farmhouse*
Vocals: Trey (lead), Page, Mike (backing)
Debut: 6/24/99 (private show), 6/30/99 (public show)
Historian: Erik Swain

When "Back on the Train" entered the Phish realm, first on Trey's May 1999 solo tour and then for the band's Summer 1999 tour, many fans could have sworn they'd heard it before. Initially a lot of them thought it was a cover, and several posted "it is an original or a cover?" queries to rec.music.phish. Its bluesy groove and catchy chorus recall any number of classic-rock songs, especially Eric Clapton's "Lay Down Sally." Its lyrics can be interpreted in many ways. What exactly is the "train" that the protagonist needs a break from and then comes back to after a long respite?

Trey played the song—which the fan base assumed was called "Get Back on the Train" until the release of *Farmhouse* showed otherwise—as an acoustic number on his solo tour, making it sound like an old-time blues shuffle. He transformed it radically for Phish's repertoire, giving it the full-band electric treatment and using everyday noises for some of his inspiration. Not only does it feature a Fishman drum part that sounds like a train running on tracks, but it is in the key of F, the same as a train whistle! Perhaps to show how happy they were to be back after a long layoff, the band slipped "Back on the Train" into the first set of the first show of the Summer 1999 tour on June 30 in Bonner Springs, KS. It has remained a constant in setlists ever since. Through the Summer 2000 tour, it never went more than six shows without being played.

The song has rarely deviated from how it was played that first night in Kansas, with four major exceptions. Its second performance, on 7/1/99 in Antioch, TN, had a strong bluegrass feel thanks to guest musicians Jerry Douglas (dobro), Ronnie McCoury (mandolin) and Tim O'Brien (fiddle). On 7/18/99, the Del McCoury Band guested for another bluegrass rendition of the tune. On 6/14/00 in Fukuoka, Japan, it began the second set and its groove sprung a jam that lasted more than twelve minutes, setting the stage for an exceptional set. And in the wild second set of 7/11/00 at Deer Creek, the band inserted a "Moby Dick" jam

in the middle, one of several songs that night to get that treatment. For strong versions of the standard arrangement, check out 7/16/99, 12/16/99 and 5/22/00.

Many fans felt the song (often noted in setlists by its initials, "BOTT") would be a natural choice for a studio album, and it was included on *Farmhouse* to no one's surprise. There, an acoustic guitar part is high in the mix, minimizing some of the "Lay Down Sally" comparisons.

"Back on the Train" received major television exposure twice in 2000. The band chose to play it for their 6/27/00 appearance on *Late Night with Conan O'Brien*. Fans gave mixed reviews to the raw but energetic rendition; at times it seemed like Trey was shouting the lyrics. Then it was one of the songs from the 5/23/00 performance at New York's Roseland Ballroom chosen to be aired on VH1's *Hard Rock Live* at various times throughout the summer.

Back Porch Boogie Blues
AKA: "Back Porch Boogie"; "Back Porch"
Original Artist: Max Creek
Original Album: *Max Creek* (1977)
Vocals: (instrumental)
Debut: 10/31/86
Historian: Craig DeLucia

In *The Phish Book*, Mike Gordon tells how, in the early days, he "tricked" the band into playing a Max Creek bluegrass tune by making everyone think it was his own composition. That song is likely "Back Porch Boogie Blues," an instrumental that appears unlabeled (or noted as "Jam") on many early tapes. All known versions were played between Halloween 1986 and Halloween 1987. The three other known versions, 2/21/87, 5/20/87, and 8/21/87, circulate fairly well among traders of older tapes.

The Ballad Of Curtis Loew
Original Artist: Lynyrd Skynyrd
Original Album: *Second Helping* (1974)
Vocals: Page
Debut: 4/29/87
Historian: Craig DeLucia

Curtis Loew is the story of a lonely old guitarist whom the narrator, as a young boy, would pay to play the blues. From 1987 through 1990, the song was a regular second set number. The song disappeared, though, after 10/30/90, and was not heard again until 3/14/93. The band dusted old "Curtis" off during the soundcheck and played the song in the second set. It was played three more times and then was buried again on 8/2/93.

Though it hasn't been played since, "Curtis Loew" is still one of the most frequently requested covers on tour. In fact, as the band returned cover after cover from long hiatuses in 1998 and 1999, many fans waited impatiently for "Curtis Loew" to join them. Hearing the song at an occasional soundcheck (for example, at Big Cypress in 1999) only makes matters worse. To date, their requests have been as unlucky as the song's namesake.

Banana Boat Song (Day-O)
AKA: "Day-O"

Music/Lyrics: West Indian folk song
Original Artist: Harry Belafonte
Original Album: *Belafonte on Calypso* (1956)
Vocals: Fishman (sort of)
Debut: 7/6/97
Historian: Erik Swain

Harry Belafonte's popularization of "Banana Boat Song (Day-O)," a folk song from Trinidad, was a major cultural event in 1956-57. It started a worldwide calypso craze and made Belafonte an international superstar. That's not relevant to Phish's rendition, though. They played it at the 7/6/97 Desenzano soundcheck (which circulates widely) because it is, as Trey put it, "the official limbo song," and the band needed to play something for the last round of the audience limbo contest in progress. Fishman makes a brief attempt at singing the words, but the performance is really just Page playing the melody on piano and the others following along halfheartedly.

Bathtub Gin
AKA: "Gin"
Music: Trey Anastasio
Lyrics: Susannah Goodman
Album: *Lawn Boy; Hampton Comes Alive* (11/20/98)
Vocals: Trey (lead), Mike, Page (backing)
Debut: 5/26/89
Historian: Christian McKee

Bathtub Gin is perhaps one of Phish's most distinctive songs. Drawn together from many and varied influences, it marries the unique lyrics of Susannah Goodman, an old friend of Trey, to an Anastasio composition. Page's opening piano part often quotes heavily from George Gershwin's "Rhapsody in Blue," as do his fills later in the song. Jon's beat is unique among Phish songs, and gives the "Gin" jam much of its character. The slow, loping feel of this song forces Trey and Page to play less frantically, leading to more interesting, contemplative solos. The presence of such a strong central theme also provides a springboard for Trey's solos, much as a poet often chooses to write according to a form instead of in free-verse.

Initially, and indeed for the first four years of its life, "Bathtub Gin" offered few great improvisations. In recent years, however, "Bathtub Gin" has offered longer and more varied jams than ever before. This particular libation first flowed on 5/26/89, and was warmly received. In its early years, it provided Page with an opportunity to shine on the piano (11/2/89), and Mike a chance to bellow "BATHTUB GIN!" at "the bottom" of his lungs. During this era, the jam following the song was short (one to three minutes,) and centered around the song's main theme. Thankfully, all this changed in 1993.

On August 13, 1993, at the Murat Theater in Indianapolis, Phish filled the Bathtub to overflowing. The Murat version (8/13/93) charted new territory for "Bathtub Gin," when for the first time, the jam led to varied and diverse improvisation. Featuring enthusiastic cries of "Riding in the Bathub!" from the whole band (in particular Jon), "Weekapaug Groove" teases, and stop-on-a-dime tempo shifts, the Murat "Gin" is required listening for the tub afficionado. From then on, the opening notes of the tub signaled the possibility for true glorious, improvisational bliss.

Even though the Murat "Gin" broke new barriers, Phish did not

seem really comfortable jamming on the song until 1995. While the occasional "Gin" fulfilled the hopes of the most jaded fans, 1994 was a spotty year overall, as most versions failed to meet the high water mark set on 8/13/93. One notable exception though, is the performance on 5/20/94 at the Evergreen College Recreation Center, in Olympia, WA. Clocking in at just under ten minutes, this version is short, but indeed, so sweet. Mike takes a very prominent role in this jam, and Trey spends most of his time letting the bass shine, and backing it on rhythm parts.

It was 1995 that solidified "Gin's" place among songs like "Tweezer" and "You Enjoy Myself." The tub had great moments in November (11/24/95), but in December, it carved a deep notch at the table. The "Gin" of 12/5/95 UMASS is a favorite among many and is the clear predecessor to 11/23/97. The UMASS "Gin" quickly left the limping tub jam in favor of hard rock and roll, followed by tight, syncopated interaction between Mike, Page and Jon. 12/5 was great, but on 12/29/95, at the Worcester Centrum, Phish jumped into a truly earth-shattering "Bathtub." Clocking in at over twenty-three minutes, the jam got harder, faster and more grating, until it became the chorus of The Who's "Real Me." After a pounding ride through that song, the music that emerged slowed, developed that distinctive "Gin" feel, and returned to the main "Bathtub" theme. That night, the "Bathtub Gin" -> "Real Me" -> "Bathtub Gin" was a highlight among highlights.

From 1996 onwards, "Bathtub Gin" grew by leaps and bounds. 11/7/96 in particular continued the development of this song, and featured jamming some say is reminiscent of the Grateful Dead's "Fire on the Mountain." Slower, and much more relaxed than many of the great "Gins," this version features Trey on his percussion kit, and many great moments from Page. Other notable "Bathtubs" from 1996 include 10/17/96 (an awful ending to an otherwise great version) and 12/29/96 (nothing like the "Gin" from one year before, but worth hearing.)

1997 was a huge year for the tub. The summer of funk did not leave "Bathtub Gin" behind, as 7/25/97 became the deepest, grooviest, funkiest ever. In Dallas, Page and Jon took off in a fast, techno-funk groove that eventually lead into "Makisupa Policeman." The Great Went (8/17/97) offered a transcendent "Gin" that built and grew from the beginning to the end. Then, following in the footsteps of 12/29/95, the "Bathtub" from Winston-Salem (11/23/97) sat down at the table of all time great jams. The longest "Gin" to date, at thirty minutes and fifteen seconds, this second set-opening version begins with an extended "standard" "Gin" jam, which leads the band into heart-pounding rock and roll more suited to "Antelope" than "Gin." The jam eventually quiets down to feature beautiful, understated interaction between Trey and Mike, before dissolving into space, out of which emerges "Down with Disease." In 1997, "Bathtub Gin" was consistently reaching and surpassing the expectations that had been set in August of 1993.

Just when avid Phish listeners thought "Gin" could improve no longer, it became a highlight at nearly every show at which it was played. Every single version of "Bathtub Gin" played in 1998 is worthy of being heard, several of them seven or eight times. A few versions from the US Summer tour stood out in particular, including Ventura Beach (7/20/98) where they achieved a glorious blending of rocking jams and sizzling funk, and St. Louis on 7/28/98. The St. Louis "Bathtub" is easily the best from '98. If forced to describe it, one could say "it's like the Ventura Beach version, only *more*!" November contained several excellent versions, check out 11/4, 11/09 or 11/29 for examples. "Bathtub Gin" consistently reached previously unattained heights from

night to night in 1998. With a few notable examples (e.g., 12/29/95, 11/7/96, 8/17/97 or 11/23/97) it is not too far off to claim that every '98 "Gin" was better than any version from years previous.

Thankfully for fans of this song, 1999 kept the pressure on. Summer tour produced several excellent versions, 7/18/99 and 7/26/99 among them. While great "Gins," they did not break as much new ground for the song as had '98 versions. In the fall, Phish proved that they could still wail through this one on 12/2/99 at the Palace. This 'tub revealed itself as the grandchild of 12/5/95 and 11/23/97 by becoming the hardest rocking version in recent years. To the delight of the roughly 80,000 in attendance, "Bathtub Gin" also made an appearance at Phish's millennium bash in Florida. This version ranks among the most unique ever, as Page, Mike and Trey scatted along with their instruments for most of the jam. For fans who like to hear old tunes go new places, this is an excellent choice. 2000 saw a few more stellar versions of "Gin." 9/8/00 boasted an atypical ambient jam with Fish on vacuum and Trey on drums, while the tour closing 10/7/00 "Gin" electrified Shoreline with a thrilling jam of pure energy reminiscent of the classic Went version. Also worth hearing are the 6/28/00 and 9/17/00 versions, both of which hose magnificently.

Those who like to argue that Phish has continued to not only change but improve over their entire career could do much worse than "Bathtub Gin" for evidence. Since 1993, versions of this song have been alternately long, short, rocking, introspective, exploratory or well directed. Phish's post-1996 propensity for deep grooves lifted the tune to new heights, as displayed at the Great Went, and in nearly every single version from 1998. If you're looking to establish a good collection of "Gins" start with 8/13/93, pick up 12/29/95, 11/7/96, the Great Went, Winston Salem '97, and as many '98 versions as possible. Don't forget, those who enjoy "Bathtub Gin" consume it responsibly.

B.B.F.C.F.M. (See: "BIG BLACK FURRY CREATURES FROM MARS")

The Beatles (1968)
AKA: "The White Album"
Original Artist: The Beatles
Debut: 10/31/94
Historian: Mark Toscano

One of the most exciting nights in Phish history was, hands down, Halloween of 1994. The air was electric. The buzz of excitement characteristic at all shows was just a shade below explosive. Nobody really knew what the hell was going to happen.

Earlier in the year, Phish had made a proposal. In the Döniac Schvice prior to the fall tour, the band had solicited fan responses for a favorite album that could be integrated into a musical costume for the Halloween performance at the Glens Falls Civic Center. A number of fans responded—though not a whole heck of a lot—and an album was chosen. Following this newsletter solicitation, though, no other information was divulged. As Halloween grew near, fans grew more anxious and excited: "what the hell is a musical costume, anyway?!"

The night arrived. The aforementioned buzz was at a deafening roar. The gearshift was most decidedly set to the high gear of everyone's soul. The energy mounted all the more as the show started over an hour and a half late. After a first set with many tasty tidbits, the crowd was even more rabid. The band had teased "War Pigs" during

"Harpua"—would the band be playing Black Sabbath's *Paranoid* during the show? No one had a clue.

Even right before the truth would be revealed, the band continued to confound their attentive audience. At the start of the fateful second set, Pink Floyd's "Speak To Me" was played over the P.A., leading everyone to believe that the album of choice would be 1973's *Dark Side of the Moon*. Hopeful Floyd fans were momentarily distraught when that song was cut off, making way for a soundbite of Ed Sullivan's famous introduction to The Beatles on his show. The Sullivan crowd cheered, and though they still didn't know what was going on, the Phish crowd cheered. The band surfed this response to their "Back In the U.S.S.R." opener, the first signal of what would happen that night.

The ensuing ninety-odd minutes just barely contained all thirty songs of The Beatles' 1968 "White Album," instantly making Phish history and securing 10/31/94 a place as one of the most memorable Phish shows ever. Phish boggled fans' minds even more when they announced that they were coming back for yet another set of music. The third set included a costume contest and some excellent music, and the show got out around the conservative hour of 3:00 AM.

Ladies and gentlemen, This Is Phish. Be afraid.

Beaumont Rag
AKA: "Bow Mt. Rag" (incorrect title)
Vocals: (instrumental)
Original Artist: (traditional)
Debut: 10/14/94
Historian: Mark Toscano

Phish has performed this jaunty rag tune only twice, both times under interesting circumstances. The first performance, during the second set of 10/14/94, came out of nowhere in an acoustic setup alongside "Nellie Kane." The second, less than a week later on 10/18/94, featured banjo accompaniment from Béla Fleck, who also lent his talents to several other songs, including "Scent of a Mule," "Lifeboy," and "Llama"(!) Both versions of "Beaumont Rag" were performed in a more bluegrassy style than the standard, old-school, rag version, though Phish wasn't the first to adapt the tune in this way (though they indeed were with Boston's "Foreplay/Long Time," which followed "Beaumont Rag" at the latter's debut).

Originally written as a fiddle tune, many different versions of this song—some dating back to the '20s—have been performed by a wide array of artists over the years. Fans might cotton to the Tony Trischka solo interpretation found on his *Solo Banjo Works* collaboration with none other than Béla Fleck. A Woody Guthrie version can be found on a three-disc set of Library of Congress recordings, and Allison Krauss recorded a wonderful version with Jerry Douglas on dobro. Of most interest may be the guitar-based version found on the Kentucky Colonel's *Long Journey Home* album, for the disc contains a few other songs that have received the Phish treatment: "Soldier's Joy," "Auld Lang Syne," "Long Journey Home," and a song that Phish hasn't covered but rings familiar nonetheless: "Listen to the Mockingbird."

Beauty Of My Dreams
Vocals: Trey (lead), Mike, Page (backing)
Original Artist: The Del McCoury Band
Original Album: *Blue Side of Town* (1992)

Debut: 2/16/97
Historian: Benjy Eisen/Mark Toscano

Many fans were under the impression that this tune was a Phish original when it debuted early in 1997, but it is in fact a Del McCoury tune. The Del McCoury Band is a popular contemporary bluegrass/country act that tours roughly the same festival circuit as Allison Krauss or Béla Fleck, for example. Del McCoury actually performed on the same bill as Phish at the 1998 Bridge School Benefit at Shoreline Amphitheatre in Mountain View, CA (10/17 & 10/18/98).

Been Caught Stealing
Original Artist: Jane's Addiction
Original Album: *Ritual De Lo Habitual* (1990)
Vocals: Trey
Debut: 8/1/98
Historian: Phillip Zerbo

While Phish's repertoire has always been filled with a solid percentage of cover songs, the Summer 1998 tour was extraordinary, witnessing the debut of no less than a dozen new covers. The diversity of covers was even more remarkable than the sheer number, encompassing both classic rockers (Neil Young, Led Zeppelin, The Velvet Underground, Van Halen, Grateful Dead, Bob Marley) as well as more contemporary artists (Smashing Pumpkins, Beastie Boys).

Among the modern day covers was the very popular 1990 Jane's Addiction hit "Been Caught Stealing," which filled the encore slot on 8/1/98 at the Alpine Valley Music Theater in East Troy, WI. This initial performance of "Been Caught Stealing" holds the distinction as being one of only two occasions (the other being on 4/29/90 at the Woodbury Ski & Racket Club in Woodbury, CT during a rendition of Joe Walsh's "Walk Away") where Mike and Trey take a few hops on the trampolines during a cover song.

A rocking show closer to the core, "Been Caught Stealing" either closed the show or was part of the encore for four of its five live appearances (polished off by a "Llama" second set closer on 11/25/98). As with most of the new cover tunes busted out in the Summer of '98, "Been Caught Stealing" had a relatively short shelf life as a Phish cover, being last performed as the encore of the spirited opening gig of the 1998-99 MSG New Year's Eve run on 12/28/98.

Bell Boy
Original Artist: The Who
Original Album: *Quadrophenia* (1973)
Vocals: Page (lead), Mike, Trey (backing),
**   Leigh Fordham (The Bell Boy)**
Debut: 10/31/95
Historian: Craig DeLucia

In one of *Quadrophenia*'s sadder moments, Jimmy becomes even more dejected when he realizes that the punk leader he once idolized and worshipped has buckled in the face of the establishment and has taken a job as a hotel bell boy. When he appeared on stage during the 1995 Halloween show, Phish crew member Leigh Fordham reprised the musical role that Keith Moon created as the original Bell Boy.

Bertha
Music/Lyrics: Jerry Garcia, Robert Hunter

Original Artist: The Grateful Dead
Original Album: *Grateful Dead* (1971)
Vocals: Trey
Debut: 11/3/84
Historian: Chris Bertolet

This rollicking tune about a troublesome dame is an early Grateful Dead classic that, like many songs in the Dead canon, served as a touchstone for the band's evolving style. "Bertha" came out of the gates as a driving country number in 1971, only to settle back into the Dead's mellower, jazzy landscapes in 1973, then emerged as a full-blown rocker in the late seventies (when it was commonly mated with The Rascals' "Good Lovin'").

Phish (who by most accounts hadn't even adopted that name yet) covered "Bertha" at UVM's Slade Hall during one of their very first gigs. Apart from Trey's earnest Jerry Garcia impression, it's a rather unremarkable performance, but curious as a historical document nevertheless.

Trey also sang "Bertha" at the 4/16/99 Phil Lesh & Friends show, as Page accompanied on keys.

Big Alligator

Original Artist: James Billie
Album: *Alligator Tales*
Vocals: James Billie
Debut: 12/30/99
Historian: Phillip Zerbo

Big Alligator is often sung around—and perhaps most appropriate for—a campfire setting. So, perhaps history will view our little swamp gathering on the last days of the 20th Century as one big glorious campfire!

From the liner notes to his breathtaking CD, *Alligator Tales*, "Big Alligator" tells: "A true story about not heeding the elder's advice and a hard learned lesson of a young boy's hunting trip in the swamp." Sung by Chief Jim in the first person, the song recounts his experience as a 12-year-old, losing his dog to the mortal clutches of a gator's jaws on his First Gator Hunt.

This should end once and for all any questions regarding the seriousness with which the "DO NOT BRING YOUR PETS TO THE VENUE"

Bathtub Gin

Compiled by Christian McKee (with help from Benjy Eisen's reviews, Erik Swain, and Jeremy Welsh)

Date	Timing	Comments
05/26/89	04:57	First time played.
11/02/89	05:53	Great early Page.
02/23/90	06:20	Near-perfect composed section, but average jam.
04/25/92	07:20	Unique vocals and a sharp, concise jam.
08/13/93	15:15	Hose! Includes tempo shifts, Weekapaug jamming, vocal silliness. First exceptional Gin, which set the standard for years.
12/30/93	09:57	Jon-directed, building jam, like a Slave or a Hood.
05/20/94	09:49	Mike! Bass-led jam, and a great rhythm from Trey.
10/14/94	11:47	Awful opening; but a good jam.
11/24/95	12:45	Breaks ground for '96 Gins. Great Jon/Mike.
12/05/95	23:12	Forerunner of 11/23/97. Hard rocking, strong Trey/Mike to close.
12/29/95	23:31	The almighty, all-hallowed Gin->Real Me->Gin. One of the best.
10/17/96	09:22	Abrupt ending; above-average Trey.
11/07/96	26:39	Features Trey on percussion, fabulous Page and many different moods. A version for the Gin highlights reel.
12/29/96	11:28	Beautiful, melodic Trey/Page interaction.
07/25/97	21:29	Page leads an electronic groove. Segues into Makisupa.
08/17/97	14:40	Beautiful, majestic, soaring, Hood-like jam. Includes an inspiring Trey-led peak.
11/23/97	30:15	Extended Gin jam followed by serious Rock and Roll. Segues into DWD.
12/06/97	11:10	Fabulous cooperation between Trey and Jon; segues into Foam.
07/20/98	20:23	Phat beats from Jon; funky but not repetitive.
07/29/98	23:16	Arguably the finest Gin of 1998. Soaring, Went-like jam, plus the electro-groove from Starplex '97!
08/16/98	13:28	Great Page moments, and a good Gin jam. Segues into Rift.
11/04/98	13:19	Hard rocking jam. Short but very sweet.
11/09/98	23:10	Jon-directed breakdowns, with a soaring climax, Gin reprise. Hot!
11/29/98	18:50	Strong Gin (for 1998) with nice work from Mike near the end.
07/18/99	19:40	Slower tempo to start, but 10 minutes of highly danceable, gliding grooves to close.
07/26/99	13:40	Trey and Mike scatting segues into a rollicking, classic Gin jam.
09/12/99	18:33	A mellifluous odyssey.
09/22/99	17:20	Reminiscent at times of the 12/31/95 jam out of Drowned. Melodic and beautiful.
10/10/99	10:06	Short and restrained; interesting, unique rhythm played by Fishman.
12/02/99	20	Features a thrilling, upbeat jam segment, and a -> into 2001.
12/07/99	22:35	A mesmerizing jam that recalls several 1998 versions.
12/15/99	16:37	Complex, multi-layered—and at times hypnotic—improvising.
12/31/99	15:45	Funky vocal jamming segues into an enchanting, mystical jam.
06/23/00	15:38	Magical, brilliant!
06/28/00	15:38	Funky groove soon becomes a breathtaking, enormous jam.
07/10/00	16:09	Waterfall of melodic notes from Trey.
10/07/00	13:07	Gorgeous jam hoses everyone off and then fades out; does not return to Gin theme.

dictate is delivered to fans!

A tragic moment always vivid and remembered, the story is cautionary. The spellbinding chant—the wisdom of Jim's Grandfather—is not in English, but the captivating nature of the rhythms speak a universal language of respect and coexistence with beings more powerful than ourselves in the natural or spiritual worlds:

Hul-Pah-Te Cho-Bee
Nock-Sho-Nitch-Kee-Kah
Hul-Pah-Te Cho-Bee
Oo-Kun Kay-Ye-Wan

It is a rhythm that certainly had 80,000 or so of us in a frenzy when played by Chief Jim Billie on 12/30/99…with a nifty little backup band, taboot! Hopefully this will not be a one-time "cover," that Phish and their fans made for a good guest, deserving of the respect and overwhelming hospitality offered to us by Chief Jim Billie and his tribe, and that we once again may rejoice in the land of the Big Alligator!

Big Ball Jam

AKA: "BBJ," "Balls," "BBJam"
Music: Phish/Crowd/Particle Physics
Album: (none)
Vocals: (instrumental)
Debut: 11/19/92
Historian: Martin Acaster

(Note—Please read to the tune of AC/DC's "Big Balls")

In the ever upper class of Phish hilarity,
lives a song with chaotic notoriety.
Whether in the Eagles Ballroom (6/17/94),
or at Memorial Hall (2/15/93),
Fish, Mike, Trey, and Page had the biggest balls of all.

Oh, Phish had big balls,
Brad released those big balls,
they were such big balls,
bouncy big balls.
The band jammed to big balls.
We bounced those big balls.
Oh Phish had the biggest balls of them all.

The first Ball Jam followed Tweezer (11/19/92, Colchester, VT),
some Ball Jams followed Mule (4/21/94 Winston Salem),
in '93 it seemed they would come (3/31/93 Portland, OR)
and come again (4/1/93 Portland, OR).
If you were at the Warfield (5/25/94)
after Contact your Ball Jam did transpire,
later that year (12/9/94 Mesa, AZ),
I report without cheer, the Ball Jam was retired.

Oh, Trey picked a big ball,
Mike picked a big ball,
they were such big balls,
bouncy big balls.
Page picked a big ball.
We bounced those big balls.
Fishman's drumbeat followed the slowest ball of all.

Some Ball Jams followed Poor Heart (2/12/93, 2/15/93, 8/16/93),

No Ball Jams featured guests,
and the one that followed Peaches (4/9/94, Binghamton)
is the one that I liked best.
Since with big balls I was bouncing to the left and to the right,
it's my belief that those big balls will bounce again some night.

Oh, the crowd passed the big balls,
to the front of the gig halls,
they were such big balls,
bouncy big balls.
Then we shot those big balls,
onto the stage of those gig halls.
Then Phish caught the biggest balls of them all.

It's been my pleasure to tell you about them,
oh they were such wonderful fun.
Kind veggie burritos,
glass,
headnugs.

Big Black Furry Creatures from Mars

AKA: "B.B.F.C.F.M."
Music/Lyrics: Mike Gordon
Album: *Hampton Comes Alive* (11/21/98)
Vocals: Mike (lead), Fish, Page, Trey (backing)
Debut: 8/21/87
Historian: Ellis Godard

This song is just barely more complex than "Anarchy." It has similar thunderous noise and abruptness, but instead of one bar and one word, it has three and thirteen, respectively. (The lyrics change, often ad hoc, but a typical performance is described here.) An opening three-note, death-metal rage is topped with Mike asking "Why are you running?" and then stops abruptly. After a brief pause, the band attacks in response with a raging crash of noise and the repeated refrain "'Cause you're a big black furry creature from Mars." After a second pause, Fishman often counts out (sometimes rather quickly) "1-2-3-4" just before the renewed attack phase. (The count was done by Cameron McKenney 4/18/92 and Mimi Fishman on 4/8/94.) In a final section of the song, the attack/refrain segment is repeated four times, sliding up a scale, ending the song with another abrupt ending.

The song has occasionally followed a lyrical or performance error, as if the Creature was impeding on (or represents the frustrations of) the performance, such as after "Divided Sky" on 11/9/87 or "Lizards" on 7/3/95. Most other versions have been in a second set or encore, and many of those as the last song. Versions through 1996 included an overabundance of dry-ice fog and strobe lights, with Trey running around swinging his guitar or a megaphone. (Trey and Mike dove back and forth on 4/24/92, and Trey stood on his stacks during 5/2/92).

Other notable events include the dedication to Steely Dan 5/14/88, and the audience making guacamole during the 4/6/92 jam, and Trey using a beer bottle as a guitar slide on 6/6/96, as well as appearances by the horns 3/9/90 (Dave Grippo) and 7/19/91 (the Giant Country Horns).

"BBFCFM" frequently includes teases of a television theme, such as "Flinstones" 8/6/88; "Popeye" 11/3/88; "Brady Bunch" 4/3/90 and 7/24/91; "I Love Lucy" 7/19/91, 7/24/91, and 9/28/91; "Leave it to Beaver" 3/28/93. Other teases in "Creature" include "Simple Gifts" by

Trey 3/29/91, "St. Thomas" by Grippo and Fishman 11/23/91, "Divided Sky" by Trey on 8/8/93, and "Electric Funeral" by Mike 12/11/97.

The 5/11/91 version is uncharacteristic for having a Trey solo. Prominent segues include 12/29/93 out of "Contact" and into "Walk Away," 5/16/94 (dispersed throughout the second set), 6/14/94 into "Purple Rain," 11/22/94 providing a transition from electric to acoustic setups, 12/1/94 out of "Tweezer" and into "Makisupa," 11/18/94 into "Acoustic Army," 12/29/95 into the classic Mike-Jim Stinette Bass Duet, and 12/11/97 out of "Roses are Free." Other interesting variations include the 3/13/92 the "Run like a Big Black Furry Antelope"; 11/19/92, which had the lyrics from "I Walk the Line"; and 7/13/94, which was to the music of "Scent of a Mule."

Big Leg Emma

Original Artist: The Mothers of Invention
Original Album: single (1967), *Läther* (released 1996),
   ***Absolutely Free* (1967) (CD only)**
Vocals: Trey (lead)
Debut: 5/3/85
Historian: Phil Nazzaro

Although possibly a nod to boxer-turned-bluesman Champion Jack Dupree's "Big Leg Emma," Phish fans will know this as Frank Zappa's song from two notorious bootleg records, as well as the posthumous *Läther*, and originally as a seven-inch single released simultaneously with *Absolutely Free* in 1967. If you want to hear this bouncy, humorous tune, you may have to look long and hard. As far as the sporadic availability of early tapes allows us to know, this song was only played three times (5/3/85, 5/21/88, and 6/18/88).

Bike

Music/Lyrics: Syd Barrett
Original Artist: Pink Floyd
Original Album: *The Piper At the Gates Of Dawn* (1967)
Vocals: Fishman
Debut: 11/19/87
Historians: Tim Wade and Mark Toscano

This tune is special for a couple of reasons. First, it is the only Phish cover song written by Syd Barrett but performed originally by Pink Floyd. Second, while it was never really common, performances since 1994 have been scarce. However, Jon "Bob Weaver" Fishman has delighted crowds with renditions on 8/3/98, 11/6/98, 7/30/99, and a special Japanese appearance on 6/15/00 that erupted unexpectedly out of an impromptu vacuum solo. Check out the 9/12/00 version for some amusing Fish comments about the extent of his repertoire. Other notable performances occurred on 11/20/91 (with Fish on fretless guitar instead of vacuum) and 3/16/93 (a "Bike" -> "Lengthwise" -> "Bike" sandwich).

Bill Bailey, Won't You Please Come Home?

AKA: "Won't You Come Home Bill Bailey?"
Music/Lyrics: Hughie Cannon
Original Artist: (unknown)
Original Album: (unknown)

Vocals: Dr. Jack McConnell
Debut: 7/28/93
Historian: Ellis Godard

Hughie Cannon wrote "Won't You Come Home Bill Bailey" in 1902, but the song was heavily popularized by Lloyd Price (on 1952's *Lawdy, Miss Clawdy*), Louis Armstrong, Bobby Darin (reaching #19 in 1960), Sarah Vaughan (on 1963's *Sassy Swings the Tivoli*), and Carol Channing. The title character is a railroad workman, and the song tells the story of a woman weeping for having kicked her hubby out. Originally a mix of big band and blues, most versions are barbershop or boogie woogie. Phish has performed the song (in the latter format) four times (7/28/93, 4/22/94, 11/28/95, and 7/3/99), all with Page's father on lead vocals and all on southward swings away from the band's home but toward the McConnell home.

Billy Breathes

Music/Lyrics: Trey Anastasio
Album: *Billy Breathes*
Vocals: Trey (lead), Mike, Page (backing)
Debut: 9/27/95
Historian: Craig DeLucia

In most cases where fans find a Phish song historically significant, it is because the song led to new avenues or styles of jamming. And while it is not a song where fans actively seek out multiple versions for their diversity, "Billy Breathes" stands in the select upper echelon of the Phish catalog, representing the band's most prevalent musical change in the mid 1990s: the emergence of mellow, balladesque material that rounded out Phish's musical rotation.

"Billy Breathes" stands out in this regard, especially when considering the rest of the songs on the album that bears its name. All other songs have either been jamming vehicles ("Free," "Taste," "Character Zero," and "Theme From the Bottom," immediately come to mind) or were written after "Billy's" 9/27/95 debut in Sacramento (see, for example, "Swept Away," "Steep," and "Talk"). And while other ballads came before it (see "Fast Enough for You"), Billy seems to stand alone, historically, as the turning point where lyric-based original material became more common.

After multiple appearances on the Fall 1995 tour, "Billy Breathes" was heard only once in the summer of 1996. During that lone appearance in Amsterdam on July 12, Trey announced that fans were hearing the song in its final arrangement. It had certainly undergone several minor changes since its debut; like almost all Phish songs it constantly evolved during its first season. And when the *Billy Breathes* album was released prior to the Fall 1996 tour, many fans tabbed the title song as the best studio song on the album. Some, including this fan, consider it the best piece of studio work in Phish's catalog to date. The studio version saw the band nail the difficult, intricate harmonies so crucial to the song's chorus. And the brief instrumental interlude was augmented with additional instrumentation and a breathtakingly intricate guitar solo that seemed to catapult the emotional level of the song to new heights.

"Billy Breathes" returned to the concert rotation in the fall of 1997 and has made regular appearances since then. It even had a slot in the 1999 "Trey Tour," where it was performed solo on the piano. Perhaps more importantly, the success of the song on the live stage has led to fans accepting the new breed of lyric-based Phish songs.

Birds Of A Feather

AKA: "Birds," "BOAF"
Music/Lyrics: Phish, Tom Marshall
Album: *Story of the Ghost*
Vocals: Trey (lead), Fish, Mike, Page (backing)
Debut: 4/2/98
Historian: Mark Toscano

In the songwriting fervor following the 10/31/96 *Remain in Light* set, "Birds of a Feather" represents the most obvious product of Talking Heads' influence on Phish. The hyperkinetic textures and colors of the song strongly evoke "Crosseyed and Painless," the TH classic that Phish so enjoyed covering frequently following the '96 Halloween gig.

"Birds" debuted on the Island Tour of 4/98, impressing fans greatly with its interplay of tightness and looseness, electrifying builds, and tension-filled jams. With few exceptions, the song still hasn't done much outside of its safety zone of jamming potential, but it always helps energize a set. Strong versions abound, including the 4/2/98 debut, 4/4/98, 7/2/98, 7/20/98, 10/15/98, 6/30/99 (into "Simple"), 7/8/99 (with "Days Between" jam and great improv into "If I Only Had a Brain"), 7/20/99 (into "When the Circus Comes"), 7/23/99 (out of "Free"), 7/25/99 (with "My Left Toe" tease, into "Walk Away"), and 12/17/99 (strong version, plus a tease in "Moma Dance"). The song was also performed on David Byrne's *Sessions at West 54th* TV show on 10/20/98, and on *The Late Show with David Letterman* on 10/27/98.

The strongest version to date is easily the 6/29/00 outing, the only version thus far to boast a serious "type II" jam. Following some teasing of Coltrane's "A Love Supreme," the jam soared off to unusual places, sporting a "Catapult" on its back, eventually coming to rest with the weight of "Heavy Things." Highly recommended.

Birthday

Original Artist: The Beatles
Original Album: *The Beatles* (aka "The White Album") (1968)
Vocals: (performed instrumental, sort of)
Debut: 10/31/94
Historian: Mark Toscano

Though it occupied its proper place at the 10/31/94 show as the eighteenth song on the Beatles' "White Album," this song was not actually played in its entirety. The ominously repeated main riff to this Lennon/McCartney tune served as the background music for the stage appearance of Road Manager Brad Sands, who (wearing Fishman's dress) received a cake for his Halloween birthday.

The Birthday Dub

Music/Lyrics: Phish/Mildred and Patty Hill, Robert Coleman
Album: (none)
Vocals: Phish
Debut: 9/21/87
Historian: Mark Toscano

This bent bit of silliness is not a "song" requiring a "history" per se, but it appears on enough fans' setlists from this fun three-set show to warrant a brief write-up. Taking the Hill Sisters' famous "Happy Birthday to You" and dub-ifying it, Phish layed down this joke song to open the third set, dedicating the effort to as-yet-unidentified fan/friend "Spup."

Bitchin' Again

Original Artist: The Dude of Life (with Phish)
Original Album: *Crimes of the Mind* (1994)
Vocals: The Dude of Life
Debut: 8/3/91
Historian: Ellis Godard

About as far as you can get from a touching romantic melody, this tune includes the phrase "She's bitchin' again" thirty-six times. And writer (and Dude of Life) Steve Pollak's three verses don't add much candlelight in reciting nine complaints, ranging from "I thought you said you'd bring me some flowers" to "When are you going to buy me a house." Phish has performed the song three times, all with Pollak—first as his backing band for his 1994 debut release (recorded in 1991), then in the soundcheck and the encore for Amy's Farm (8/3/91). The last two appearances also include Sofi Dillof, now Page's wife, "singing" the complaints as she did in the studio.

Bittersweet Motel

Music/Lyrics: Trey Anastasio, Page McConnell
Album: (none)
Vocals: Trey (lead), Page (backing)
Debut: 7/21/98
Historian: Martin Acaster

When the only tool you have is a hammer, everything looks like a nail. This simple lyric, the central tenet of "Bittersweet Motel," is a heavy truism applicable to both our travels down the road of life and the inherent frustrations that can manifest during life on the road. The little disasters can strike even when we are traveling alone. It is not surprising that the song is the title track for a film documenting life on the road with Phish. A flat tire, a wrong turn, a traffic jam, a lost ticket, a missing friend, a bent tent stake, an over adoring fan, it could be anything, usually something simple, but it puts us through a personal hell of frustration just the same. Frustration becomes anger. Anger is a blunt indiscriminate hammer. Too often we lash out with this hammer at the unsuspecting nails (friends, lovers, tour buddies) that surround us. "Bittersweet Motel" is a brief reminder, as well as an opportunity during a Phish show, to stop and catch a breath. A chance to try to develop different tools to deal with the nuts, loose screws, and the pressure of vices we all must face.

A hauntingly sparse simple electric arrangement of "Bittersweet Motel" debuted at the Desert Sky Pavilion (7/21/98), swirling out of the "Ring of Fire" ambience between "Simple" and "Weekapaug." Since then it has appeared sporadically (only three times in 1999), most often as part of a multiple song encore (e.g. 7/29/98 at Riverport Amphitheater). One of the more interesting versions of "Bittersweet Motel" was the acoustic rendition at the E Center in Salt Lake City (11/2/98). This performance included a closing "Free Bird" jam and was dedicated to the people at the Dead Goat Saloon. Apparently, the previous evening, Trey and Mike had played an open mic night at a small Salt Lake City bar. After playing a couple of songs Trey said they began inviting the other patrons and staff of the saloon to sit in with them. This free-for-all culminated with the only other acoustic version of "Bittersweet Motel" to date. However, unlike the E Center version, everyone in the

room at the Dead Goat was up on stage jamming along. Barring the discovery of unknown tapes from the Dead Goat, the absolutely must hear at all cost version of "Bittersweet Motel" can be found nestled between "Silent in the Morning" and "Piper" late in The Show at Big Cypress (12/31/99). Appropriately enough Trey dedicated the song to the Pittsburgh crew.

Black-Eyed Katy

AKA: "BEK," "Katy"
Music: Phish
Album: (none)
Vocals: (instrumental)
Debut: 11/13/97
Historian: Martin Acaster

She came strutting onto the stage at the opening show of the 1997 Fall tour and has not looked back—other than to watch her own rump shaking, that is. The new queen of the Phish funk scene, she who would spawn the dance craze of the next millenium (no not the "Meatstick" dance), the lovely "Black-Eyed Katy" was born in the Thomas & Mack Center on 11/13/97. Sadly the life of this funky momma appears to have been cut short. During her time with Phish she showed her never-ending stamina, her sizzling raunch, her breathtaking peaks, and put the fun back in funk. Typically she consisted of two runs through a tight yet gelatinous funk groove followed by a jam (usually similar to the original theme) which at its longest duration approached ten minutes. The jam was followed by a short reprise of the original theme as an outro. "Katy" made appearances in both first and second sets and an encore during the 1997 Fall tour and looked like a mainstay. However, by the time the Summer 1998 tour began in Europe she had undergone a makeover. With the addition of lyrics during the recording of *Story of the Ghost*, "Black-Eyed Katy" was transformed into the "Moma Dance." In the dance her spirit lives on. To know "Katy" is to love her, to know all her moods listen to the following versions 11/13/97 Las Vegas (her birth), 11/22/97 Hampton (in a delightful "Tweezer"—"Piper" sandwich), 11/28/97 Worcester (dark and sloppy), 12/5/97 Cleveland (tight and playful), and 12/30/97 NYC (short and strange with a lumpy head).

See Also: "Moma Dance"

Blackbird

Original Artist: The Beatles
Original Album: *The Beatles* (aka "The White Album") (1968)
Vocals: Page
Debut: 10/31/94
Historian: Mark Toscano

Nicely played by Trey on solo guitar with Page singing, this was a sweet highlight of the 1994 Halloween "White Album" set. Nearly a month later on 11/22/94, the band surprised the fans in Columbia, MO by jumping into a nice version of the song out of "The Curtain" (which itself was preceded by "Cry Baby Cry"!)

Bliss

Music: Trey Anastasio
Album: *Billy Breathes*
Vocals: (instrumental)

Debut: (never performed live)
Historian: Mark Toscano

A mysterious track, "Bliss" consists of a lush, 12-string-sounding, arpeggiated build, lasting less than a few minutes in length. Never performed live and with no explanation, fans were at a loss to identify this song, which, though pretty, seemed like nothing more than a bridge between the different moods of "Train Song" and "Billy Breathes."

Various net whispers at the time of the album's release indicated that Trey wrote the track for a terminally ill fan named Kevin. More info either substantiating or refuting this story is being sought.

This possibility is underscored by the incidence of CNN reportedly using the track as background music for a story on JFK Jr.'s presumed (at the time) death in flight in August of 1999. Either way, it makes for a somber reading of an already sweetly melancholic tune.

Blister In the Sun

Original Artist: Violent Femmes
Original Album: *Violent Femmes* (1982)
Vocals: Trey
Debut: 7/26/97
Historian: Phillip Zerbo

The lead track to their 1982 self-titled debut album *Violent Femmes*, "Blister in the Sun" has made two appearances in the Phish playlist. The first was on July 26, 1997 at South Park Meadows in Austin, TX. By no means a complete rendition, Mike began teasing "Blister in the Sun" during "Harry Hood" and the rest of the band picked it up quickly. Trey made a game attempt at the first verse of the lyrics, but his ear-to-ear grin, laugh, and shrug indicated it was probably best to bail, and the band settled quickly back on "Harry" Also notable about this version of "Harry" is the extended intro led by Fishman and guest drummer Bob Gullotti, and a seamless, inspired transition into "Free." A much more complete version of "Blister in the Sun" (skipping only one verse) was offered in the middle of "Scent of a Mule" at the often underrated July 9, 1998 gig at Club Zeleste in Barcelona, Spain. These two bands are no strangers, as Phish's first tour of Europe in June, 1992 was as the opening act for the Violent Femmes.

Blue Bayou

Original Artist: Roy Orbison
Original Album: single (1963)
Vocals: (performed instrumental)
Debut: 7/16/92
Historian: Mark Toscano

Phish has toyed with this song on two occasions, 7/16/92 and 12/29/92, but they've never fully played the Roy Orbison classic. The 7/16/92 "version" is a fun one, with the band teasing and fiddling with it extensively and repeatedly at the beginning of the encore as they solicit suggestions for a song. The latter is also a kick, as it is substantially teased in "Mike's Song" before Mike himself kicks in with a "Weekapaug" bass solo quoting the song yet again.

Blue Bossa

Music: Kenny Dorham

"Billy Breathes: *A Rock Opera*"

Guy Stevens

It seems a lot of folks have been speculating on the "concept" behind *Billy Breathes*—birth, life, escape, etc. Unfortunately, no one has yet hit upon the true concept, which is that *Billy Breathes* is actually a rock opera. Trust me, I know. Think *Tommy, Quadrophenia, The Wall,* but most importantly, think Wagner. The opera details the tragic story of Billy, half-man/half-fish, and his adventures on the surface.

Act I

The opera opens underwater, where Billy has been imprisoned for political crimes by the Lord of the Undersea, Trogglodofka. Billy is floating in the prison ship Blympalot, but he has plans to escape. As he escapes, he sings *Free:*

> In a minute I'll be free
> And be splashing in the sea
> You'll hear a tiny cry
> As the ship [the Blympalot] goes sliding by

As the song climaxes, he swims to the surface, where, because he has gills not lungs, he immediately begins to suffocate.

Meanwhile, Zero, the local village idiot, is walking along the shore. Zero is unhappy because the villagers don't believe his stories about a vast undersea empire, and the village wise man, Mulcahey, has kicked him out of the village. He sings a little song, "Character Zero" to himself:

> Now I'm convinced the whole day long
> That all I've learned is always wrong
> And things are true that I forget
> No one taught that to me yet

To Zero's surprise, he comes across Billy gasping on the shore. Realizing that (a) he's not so stupid after all and (b) he's still not smart enough to know how to save Billy from suffocating, he exclaims, "I've got to see the man Mulcahey," both to save Billy and to vindicate himself. He brings Billy to Mulcahey, who promptly sticks a fishbowl on Billy's head and saves his life.

Following this, Zero, Mulcahey, and the fishbowl-wearing Billy go for a walk and see a caravan on the way to Prince Caspian's castle. In the head carriage is a special cargo for Prince Caspian, a big-screen projection TV. As the caravan rolls along, the TV sings "Waste":

> So if I'm inside your head
> Don't believe what you might have read
> You'll see what I might have said
> …
> Come waste your time with me

Billy is smitten and falls hopelessly in love with the TV. The caravan enters Prince Caspian's castle and the gates shut, leaving Zero, Mulcahey, and a forlorn, lovesick Billy outside.

Inside the TV is brought to Caspian, who is excited by his plan to get free cable by splicing into the fiber-optic lines and sings *Taste* to the TV:

> I'm up
> And I can take what you give and I'm here
> And I want you to live with me
> Cause all I want is a taste for free [i.e., free cable]
> I'm out
> And I will stay here alone and without
> Someone controlled by the phone and TV

Original Artist: Joe Henderson
Original Album: *Page One* **(1963)**
Vocals: (instrumental)
Debut: 7/12/88
Historian: Ellis Godard

Blue Bossa was written by 1950s trumpeteer Kenny Dorham but most known from the many versions by 1960s saxophonist Joe Henderson. Aptly named, it blends melancholy with Latin rhythms. (Bossa is Latin-influenced jazz, developed in the 1960s by Stan Getz, Astrud and Jao Gilberto, and Herbie Mann. Think "Girl from Ipanema.") This danceably rhythmic tune is known to have appeared in only two, consecutive Phish shows. The debut (7/12/88) was a surprise opener to a second set just before "Take the A-Train." The second appearances followed "Satin Doll," each with both Peter Danforth and Dave Grippo on horns.

Blue Monk
AKA: "Swing Tune" (unidentified title)

Music: Thelonious Monk
Original Artist: Thelonious Monk
Original Album: *Mysterioso* **(1954)**
Debut: 8/12/89
Vocals: (instrumental)
Historian: Ellis Godard

For over a decade, this song has been labelled on tapes only as "Swing Tune" or with a simple question mark. An offbeat midsection and the lack of vocals make the title harder to recall, but "Blue Monk" has been recorded by scores of artists, and the opening melody is probably as recognizable as many jazz standards. The 1960s alone included dozens of versions, but some of the more interesting came three decades later, such as those by Aki Takse and David Murray (1991), McCoy Tyner and Bobby Hutcherson (1994, with Hutcherson on marimba), and Giovanni Hidalgo (1997). Bill Evans' (1963) version is of particular note, as Page seems to mimic it for Phish's only version.

Near the end of a wedding reception Phish played on 8/12/89, Trey recalls "what great dancing we had going on before the tossing of

"Billy Breathes: *A Rock Opera*" *(continued)*

He then leaves to carry out his cable-theft plan.

Outside the castle, Billy must see his beloved TV, so the three conceive a plan to get Billy in. As "Cars Trucks Buses" plays, they build a giant slingshot and catapult Billy over the wall. He lands in Caspian's room, in front of the TV and immediately begins to proclaim his love for it. Unfortunately, the fishbowl makes his words of love unintelligible. Confused, the TV sings "Talk":

I can't talk the talk with you
Nothing's ever sunken through
The filter that surrounds your thoughts
[referring to the filter on the fish tank]

The act ends as Caspian returns and Billy hides.

Act II

Act II opens as Caspian sits in front of his brand-new big-screen projection TV to watch purloined cable. Unbeknownst to Caspian, the malevolent Lord of the Undersea Trogglodofka has tapped into the undersea fiber-optic cables and plans to use them to brainwash Caspian and conquer the world. Singing "Theme from the Bottom," Trogglodofka (sort of a cross between Jack Palance, Benito Mussolini, and Sigmund the Seamonster) gradually seduces Caspian, and then, as the music climaxes, does the cosmic brain suck.

This reduces Caspian to a blithering idiot and he sings "Train Song" as he runs around the castle babbling incoherently. Unfortunately, the various ministers of state mistake this babbling for orders and begin a series of strange actions: ripping up train tracks, ordering lots of Cheetos and wine, and declaring war on every country around them.

"Bliss," a ballet, follows, in which Caspian, Trogglodofka, and Billy all express their bliss. Caspian is blissful because he's been reduced to being a complete moron. Trogglodofka is blissful because he is swimming to the surface to conquer the world. Billy is blissful

because he and the TV have figured out how to communicate visually and the TV returns his love.

Declaring this love for one another, Billy and the TV sing the duet "Billy Breathes":

Softly sing sweet songs
Time it seems
And broken dreams
Asleep beside the stairs
[They're so happy that their troubles seem nonexistent.]

As the song climaxes, Billy rips the fish bowl off of his head to kiss the TV. Unfortunately he begins to suffocate and dives out the window into the moat to save himself. Here he is sucked into the sewage system (think *Trainspotting,* or *Gravity's Rainbow*). As he is sucked through the sewage system and battered against the pipes, he watches his beloved TV fade away and sings "Swept Away":

Much doo-doo is all I see
And I feel like it's surrounding me
I'm finally swept away

His broken body is spit out into the ocean and as he sinks to the bottom we hear Steep. Sounds become more and more distorted as he sinks deeper and deeper, yet we hear the sounds of war as a massive battle begins, both between Caspian's forces and the other nations of the world (begun during "Train Song"), and a revolt led by Mulcahey, who thinks Caspian killed Billy. Caspian is forced to grab the TV, flee the castle and set out to sea. Zero runs along behind them warning them not to set sail or they'll sail off the edge of the world, but is ignored because he's an idiot. Unfortunately, he's also right.

The opera closes as Billy, lying broken on the ocean floor, sees Caspian's ship sail by overhead. He sings "Prince Caspian," longing to be Caspian on board the ship with his beloved TV, unaware that the world has been engulfed in a cataclysmic war and that Caspian and the TV are about to sail over the edge of the world.

the bouquet and garter, and this time we're hoping to get some other members of the party to get out on the floor for some…real dancing, we'll call it." Then, before launching into Phish standards "I Didn't Know" and "You Enjoy Myself," they play "Blue Monk" to try and draw the older crowd onto the dance floor. We're glad to be able to name the tune for the Phish fan community, but we'll probably never know whether it helped diversify the dancing.

Blue Sky

Original Artist: The Allman Brothers Band
Original Album: *Eat a Peach* (1972)
Vocals: Steve Drebber
Debut: 8/12/89
Historian: Ellis Godard

Blue Sky was performed only once, at the first wedding Phish is known to have played. Dedicated to the newlyweds, and sung by the groom, the performance featured only token riffs from Trey, and is notable mainly for its novelty.

Bohemian Rhapsody

Original Artist: Queen
Original Album: *A Night At the Opera* (1975)
Vocals: Phish, Boston Community Choir
Debut: 12/31/96
Historian: Craig DeLucia

On New Year's Eve 1996, fans witnessed the dropping of thousands of balloons at the stroke of midnight while the band launched into a raucous "Down with Disease." Many thought that this event alone was the New Year's treat; many were surely wrong. In the third set, Phish brought out "Bohemian Rhapsody," a complex Queen song made popular in the 1970s by its intricacy and operatic story and again in the 1990s by its appearance in the hit movie *Wayne's World*. Interestingly, this song was one of the longest to become an FM radio staple. This is a fun comparison to Phish, whose songs have been criticized by mainstream radio because of their length.

For the song, Phish was aided by the Boston Community Choir, who provided assistance with the song's complex harmonies. Page

noted in *The Phish Book* that he was a bit nervous about singing the song, as he was losing his voice and contemplating the difficulty of the lead vocals. Not surprisingly, given the vocal difficulties of playing the number, "Bohemian Rhapsody" remains a concert one-timer.

Bold As Love

Original Artist: The Jimi Hendrix Experience
Original Album: *Axis: Bold As Love* **(1967)**
Phish Album: *Hampton Comes Alive* **(11/21/98)**
Vocals: Page
Debut: 7/11/88
Historian: Craig DeLucia

Jimi Hendrix is revered by most fans of rock and roll, and is seen by some as the most talented musician to ever take hold of an electric guitar. Trey has remarked on his affinity for Jimi on many occasions, going so far as to pay tribute to him almost every time Phish has played on his birthday (November 27). In fact, on 11/27/92, Trey went so far as to call Jimi the greatest electric guitarist ever. And to close the show, they played their version of Hendrix's classic "Bold As Love," one of three Hendrix covers that Phish has attempted over the years (see also "Fire" and "Izabella").

Despite being one of Phish's oldest and truest covers, the band seems to reserve the song from heavy rotation to avoid spoiling it. After two years of regular play from mid-1988 to mid-1990 and almost two years on the shelf, "Bold as Love" has been played a handful of times each year since. It is of note that the mention of the colors in the song lyrics allow for a wonderful visual spectacle, especially when the band reaches the "rainbow" line.

Phish has always chosen to play "Bold as Love" as a straight cover, without altering the song's feel from the original. The raw energy inherent in the song, especially the swirling closing jam segment, seem to make it a fantastic (albeit somewhat rare) choice as a set-closer or encore. In fact, since 1992, it has only been played elsewhere once (on 7/26/98, in Dallas).

Boogie On Reggae Woman

Original Artist: Stevie Wonder
Original Album: *Fulfillingness' First Finale* **(1974)**
Phish Album: *Hampton Comes Alive* **(11/21/98)**
Vocals: Trey
Debut: 2/21/87
Historian: Phillip Zerbo

Fans of Phish statistics will revel in this most notable gap: "Boogie On Reggae Woman" was first known to have been performed at Slade Hall on 2/21/87. After appearing occasionally in two known shows after that (4/29/87, 3/21/88), it made its next appearance at the Ervin J. Nutter Center, Dayton, OH on 12/7/97, well over eight hundred shows later!

Aside from a cover of "I Wish" performed when Jeff Holdsworth was still in the band (10/30/85) and a one-time performance of "Golden Lady" (10/20/94), "Boogie On Reggae Woman" is the only other Stevie Wonder cover Phish has performed. That fact does not diminish the influence he has had on the members of Phish, an influence mentioned in several interviews.

Trey even made mention of Stevie Wonder from the famed stage

of Radio City Music Hall on 5/21/00: "We are really moved by this whole scene that has surrounded the four of us. Page and I came to this hall to see Stevie Wonder, which was a huge inspiration. We feel so lucky and blessed to be able to play here for all of our family, friends and all of you."

Coincidence or no (cause or effect?), the delightfully upbeat and soulful "Boogie On Reggae Woman" almost always seems to find its way into the setlists of some killer Phish shows! The roster of show appearances reads like many fan's "best show" lists in the recent Phish era: the aforementioned 12/7/97, 11/21/98 (the *Hampton Comes Alive* version), 12/29/98 (blissfully bookended by outstanding versions of "2001" and "YEM"), 7/25/99 (Deer Creek, by many accounts the best show of that tour), 9/18/99 (put down the *Companion*, go find yourself a copy of this show immediately!), 12/30/99 (duh!), 5/23/00 (sadly not making the cut to appear on VH1) and 7/14/00 (during the "rain delayed" 'set 1.5').

Two versions of "Boogie On Reggae Woman" stand out above all others, both featuring extended "Type II" jamming. The version performed on 7/25/99, at Deer Creek (by many accounts the best show of that tour) is sublime, and the first time Phish has substantively "stretched out" this song. The version performed on 9/18/99, in Chula Vista, CA (by many accounts the best show of THAT tour) demonstrated that this song can at any time be a vehicle for extended exploratory jamming. Opening the second set and clocking in at over 20 minutes, the length of this version is surpassed only by its beauty. Get the tapes!

Born To Run

Original Artist: Bruce Springsteen
Original Album: *Born To Run* **(1975)**
Vocals: Tom Marshall
Debut: 7/16/99
Historian: Craig DeLucia

Tom Marshall continued his streak of providing memorable cover songs when he performed "Born to Run" with Phish in Holmdel, New Jersey on July 16, 1999. The song selection was very appropriate, as Springsteen himself was in the midst of a 15-concert stand at New Jersey's Continental Airlines Arena. Some fans thought Springsteen himself would appear when Trey announced "the greatest songwriter ever." Indeed, we were treated to Tom Marshall, decked out in his best early-'80s Springsteen attire, singing The Boss's most popular song.

Born Under Punches (The Heat Goes On)

Original Artist: Talking Heads
Original Album: *Remain in Light* **(1980)**
Vocals: Trey (lead), Fish, Mike, Page (backing)
Debut: 10/31/96
Historian: Mark Toscano

The multi-layered, energetic opener to the Talking Heads' *Remain in Light* album, this tune was mastered as the opener to the *Remain in Light* set on 10/31/96 by Phish with Karl Perazzo (of Santana) providing percussion and Dave Grippo and Gary Gazaway inserting occasional horny contributions. From Fishman's count-in to its head-first collision with "Crosseyed and Painless," the song remains ever steady and tight, quite a feat considering the tune's manic arrangement and jagged rhythms.

"Born Under Punches" is a song driven by madness and para-noia, and combines unabashed energy and sonic density with a somber mood and instrumental restraint. The result is a track that embodies parallel aspects of Talking Heads' 1980 sound—extroversion and introversion—in a single perpendicular moment. The raging, mathematical pressure gauge of their earlier artpunk sound collides with the rich rhythms, textures, and hues of African music that had begun to point them in a startlingly new direction. Although *Remain in Light*'s predecessor, 1979's *Fear Of Music* (host album to "Cities") featured "I Zimbra," a song with a similar influx of styles and ideas, "Born Under Punches," as the inaugural track of this album, truly represents the band's first brave steps into this new electric jungle setting.

Phish's version was appropriately cataclysmic, setting the tone for the ensuing set, and Trey captured the feeling of the guitar solo on the album version quite nicely. The song never reappeared in the band's live show, but teases of the tune have been noticed in the 10/31/96 "Suzy" and the 12/29/98 "Also Sprach Zarathustra."

Bouncing Around The Room

AKA: "Bouncin'," "BATR"
Music: Trey Anastasio
Lyrics: Tom Marshall
Album: *Lawn Boy; A Live One* (12/31/94)
Vocals: Mike, Page, Trey
Debut: 1/20/90
Historian: Christian McKee

Bouncing Around the Room is a Phish standard, an active part of the song list since its debut on 1/20/90. Many long-time fans dislike this song because it is always performed without variation. Nonetheless, "Bouncing" is a beautiful piece. Like so many Phish tunes, "Bouncing" is another collaboration between Trey and Tom Marshall. Perhaps this simple little ditty has remained in the band's repertoire for so long because of its lyrics, which are favorites of Trey.

The first verse paints a picture of a dreamer, dreaming of a woman. Upon waking, the narrator is haunted by the gentle words she spoke in the dream, as they faintly bounce around the room. The second verse is a shift, portraying a seascape, where the woman is replaced with sirens. The narrator eventually joins their beautiful song, and bounces with it, through a "never ending coral maze." The song ends with a melodic canonical refrain, as everyone except Jon steps up to the mic. For some, hearing "Bouncing" at a show means enough time to run to the restroom. For most, it is a chance to enjoy a serene message of seeking set to blissfully simple music.

BOW MT. RAG (see "Beaumont Rag")

Brain Damage

Original Artist: Pink Floyd
Original Album: *Dark Side of the Moon* (1973)
Vocals: Trey (lead), Mike, Page (backing)
Debut: 11/2/98
Historian: Mark Toscano

The psych-folk acidrock of *Dark Side*'s penultimate track contains some of Pink Floyd's most memorable lyrics, not the least of which

is the contextualization of the album's title. This song is a bit of whimsy—albeit a serious bit of whimsy—that is almost never played on radio stations without its album-closing counterpart, "Eclipse." A great duo they are, inseparable almost to the degree of that of two other well-known album closers, "The Horse" and "Silent in the Morning." Charlie Dirksen is even reputed to have given a legendary culinary invention of his the moniker "Brain Damage Eclipse."

Phish covered this track in turn as a part of the 11/2/98 second set in Salt Lake City, and their rendition built the necessary amount of lackadaisical tension that reached its climax and release in "Eclipse." The original Floyd version may boast some of the band's most legendary lyrics, but Phish imbued some more of the song's lyrics with even greater significance in light of the surprise *DSOTM* performance: "And if the band you're in starts playing different tunes...."

Breathe

Original Artist: Pink Floyd
Original Album: *Dark Side of the Moon* (1973)
Vocals: Trey (lead), Page (backing)
Debut: 10/25/95
Historian: Mark Toscano

Breathe indeed. That's precisely what the fans at the 11/2/98 show had trouble doing when they heard Phish unload into this song, for Phish had just knocked the wind out of every fan in attendance at the half-sold-out E Centre. Though a "Breathy" jam had made a single appearance three years before in the middle of a "Mike's Song," the post-Halloween Utah version has only a tiny bit more import—it opened the surprise performance of the entire *Dark Side of the Moon* album!

The half-full venue was thoroughly blown away when they heard the opening sound effects and voice bites of "Speak To Me," but it took the first few minutes of "Breathe" (and perhaps "On the Run") to fully clue them in about what was going to be happening over the course of the second set.

The crowd eventually caught their breath, sometime the following morning.

Brian & Robert

AKA: "This One's For You," "Staring at the Walls"
Music/Lyrics: Trey Anastasio, Tom Marshall
Album: *Story of the Ghost*
Vocals: Trey (lead), Fish, Mike, Page (backing)
Debut: 6/30/98
Historian: Martin Acaster

To the average fan of the intricate, extended, upbeat jams featured in many other Phish songs, "Brian and Robert" is everything they hate: slow, reserved, simple, completely undanceable. The song is, however, a lyrical masterpiece, an ironic description of the epitome of what a Phish fan is not. A detached, morose, lost soul who finds no joy in life. Someone who would rather be at home in their TV seat, since there is no one they would care to meet. A solitary diner, the loaner on the playground, the grumpy old man that bangs on the apartment wall when the stereo is too loud. "Brian and Robert" (named for Eno and Fripp) calls out to the lost soul, hoping to save them from their self-imposed misery. Musically it is a lilting melody riding a mellow swell of ambient hues. No, the song does not jam, but the message it bears should register loud and clear: life

(much like the music of Phish) is to be enjoyed and shared with others. Live versions do not stray far from the studio release in style or duration. The resonating whine of an empty TV screen was reproduced perfectly in the constructive feedback which closed the 7/15/98 Portland Meadows version, to date the most tear-jerking rendition of the song.

Bring It on Home

Music/Lyrics: Willie Dixon
Original Artist: Sonny Boy Williamson
Original Album: Chess single (1963);
   ***The Real Folk Blues* (1965)**
Vocals: Tim Rogers
Debug: 5/3/85
Historian: Mark Toscano

Although the version of "Bring it on Home" Phish covered on 5/3/85 was closer to the Led Zeppelin interpretation of the song found on *Led Zeppelin II*, Willie Dixon is the actual author of this tune. Dixon, who wrote the song for Sonny Boy Williamson, influenced Zeppelin quite a bit, along with plenty of other classic bluesmen, and Zeppelin in turn influenced Phish quite a bit (especially Trey and Fishman). Dixon also originated "Red Rooster" and "Hoochie Coochie Man," two other songs Phish has covered.

Apparently, Led Zeppelin was too busy being influenced by classic bluesmen, for they neglected to credit or compensate Dixon or Arc Music, the legal copyright holders of "Bring it on Home." Arc sued Zeppelin and won a settlement, but then neglected to kick back to Willie (bastards), giving him even more reason to sing the damn blues. Eventually, Dixon and Muddy Waters sued Arc (that's right!) and won not only their respective due royalties, but ownership of their songs as well. Finally, to cap off the story, Dixon sued Led Zeppelin himself over their song "Whole Lotta Love," which was dangerously similar to Dixon's own "You Need Love." All told, Dixon ended up with a nice settlement and lived out the rest of his years comfortably, enjoying his long-deserved recognition as one of American's most important singer-songwriters, and a major force in the development of the blues.

Phish's only known performance of this tune, on 5/3/85, featured two special guests. One was "Bobby Brown," (aka early days crew member Tim Rogers) on harmonica. The other guest? A certain "Page, from Goddard," some keyboard player about whom little, if anything, is known.

Brother

Music/Lyrics: Trey Anastasio
Album: (none)
Vocals: Trey (lead), Page (backing)
Debut: 9/25/91
Historian: Craig DeLucia:

Destiny Unbound owes a great to deal to "Brother"—if the latter hadn't been broken out at The Clifford Ball in 1996, the former might not have become the most requested and sought-after song at Phish concerts.

Like "Destiny," "Brother" debuted with a bang in 1991. It was the first song played on the Fall 1991 tour, and was played in four of the tour's first five shows. It was the perfect addition to the Phish repertoire, combining quirky lyrics (about someone jumping into bathtubs with siblings) with an odd, dissonant jam. Though recent years have seen the

technique used in originals like "Taste" and "Limb by Limb," "Brother" was the first Phish original to feature a jam that centered upon Arabic-sounding solos. Trey even mentioned once, in an interview, that he wrote "Brother" to have a song with a "sick" jamming section.

"Brother" remained a song that did not jam outside of itself, but the searing solos provided by Trey and those fun lyrics (complete with warbling at the end of the song) endeared the song to fans. Twice, on 11/20/91 and 3/24/92, the band used "Brother" to showcase the talents of Carl "Gears" Gerhard on trumpet or cornet.

The song was still played regularly in the spring of 1992 and likely reached its humor pinnacle on April 17 of that year. In the middle of the band's legendary west coast run of shows, Phish played "Brother" while family, friends, and road crew members literally jumped into a bathtub that was placed on stage! To the band's credit, they didn't take the easy joke and follow with "Bathtub Gin" (this was actually only ever done once, with "Brother" following "Gin" on 11/16/91).

"Brother" was only played four more times in the spring and summer of 1992. Though it remained a regular soundcheck number, it was not heard from again until the zany 8/2/93 show in Ybor. And then, for some reason, the band stopped jumping in the tub. Fans missed "Brother," and they let it be known on the Internet and at shows. One example was caught on tape on 12/14/95. At the start of the encore, Trey remarked that the band was going to play a song for a fan holding a sign. One fan holding a "Brother" sign up front got visibly excited but Trey quickly brought him down: he was referring to a fan holding a "Bold as Love" sign. Said Trey, "You gotta bring a sign, but you also have to bring a sign for something that we want to play."

It took a pair of ice cream moguls from Vermont to finally bring "Brother" back after over a 250-show absence on 8/17/96. Ben and Jerry guested on vocals in their own backyard when Phish played their first summer festival at the Clifford Ball. Though "Brother" stuck around for longer than the single 1993 reappearance, the revival was again short-lived. Fans were treated to four more versions in 1996, none in 1997, and only two in 1998 before the song was tossed back on the shelf until a single performance on 9/27/00 broke the hiatus.

One fan-favorite version wasn't played for an audience. Seek out the 5/5/93 soundcheck to hear the band jam "Brother" in a unique, loose atmosphere. To round out your collection, start with one of the aforementioned versions with Gears. If guest percussion is your bag (which works quite well with this song), go for 10/23/96 with Bob Gulotti or 10/31/96 with Karl Perazzo. And for a "Brother" with some stage banter and a serious jam taboot, find your copy of 4/4/98 (every fan should be born with one!) and the humorous "Brother" and subsequent "radio friendly" reprise.

Brown Eyed Girl

Original Artist: Van Morrison
Original Album: *Blowin' Your Mind* (1967); *T.B. Sheets* (1973)
Vocals: Jimmy Buffett and Trey
Debut: 11/16/95
Historian: Ellis Godard

Phish has played this Van Morrison tune on only one occasion. Beach pop maverick Jimmy Buffett joined the band for the encore at 10/22/96, after conferring with the band and finding it was the one tune both he and they knew. A fun but mediocre version, the perform-

"The Woman Was a Dream I Had Though Rather Hard to Keep"

Jon Lober, Atlanta, GA

Reflections of life often surface in Phish songs like pieces of sky captured in water's natural mirror. The loss of my girl-friend Mitzi was the still-life reflection of *Bouncing Around the Room*. At the University of Florida we bounced around the roomy confines of our relationship until one day she whispered words and I awoke to find that the woman was a dream I had, one I could not keep. As I tuned out the siren's song she sang for me I saw the beautiful coral maze of our relationship was a prison. I realized we lived underwater in a hazy reality we created. Once I awoke from that dream, I could no longer sink beneath the sea of our troubles ob-scured by the crystal haze of our dream world. So the siren disap-peared beneath the waves and, barely alive, I swam to the shore and recovered in the shallow waters of solitude. But even today, three years after we broke up, I can still hear the gentle echo of her beau-tiful voice bouncing around the roomy confines of my mind. I know she is happy and I know another man tends the beautiful coral maze of the siren Mitzi and this makes me smile.

---

ance was surely enjoyed most by those in attendance that night.

Buffalo Bill

Music/Lyrics: Trey Anastasio, Tom Marshall
Album: (none)
Vocals: Page, Trey (lead), Mike (backing)
Debut: 11/21/92
Historian: Mark Toscano

Buffalo Bill actually does appear on an album. Sort of. Ever wonder what that "Riker's Mailbox" madness is on *Hoist*? Most or all of the puny track is actually a half backwards, half forwards chunk of the unused "Buffalo Bill" studio recording done during the *Hoist* sessions. After recording this purportedly long and bizarre version of the song, the band decided it was a little too wacky for the overall sound they were going for on *Hoist*. After altering part of the track with various stu-dio effects, it was decided to plug it into the album following "If I Could," creating an interesting bridge between that sweet and sad num-ber and the hard-rocking "Axilla (Part II)." As if to add to the time-warpy feeling of "Riker's," Jonathan Frakes (Commander Riker of *Star Trek: The Next Generation* fame) plays trombone on the track,

Its live incarnations have been a little less outrageous. Debuting unusually as an encore song on 11/21/92, the song then completely disappeared except for a few soundcheck performances (see 7/18/93). Almost two years later, the song resurfaced during the first set of 10/29/94, an all-around unusual and fun show. Since it had been so long since the "Buffalo Bill's" only public performance, and at a not too well-known show to boot, barely anyone knew what the heck Phish played between "Split" and "Makisupa" that day in Spartanburg. The song showed its homely hide once again that year, on 12/31/94, no less, in the middle of a "Mike's Groove." Following this bewildering per-formance, the song again disappeared for another two and a half years.

By mid-1997, Phish was so huge, that even the band's long-neg-lected songs were commonly discussed and hoped for by fans. Even still, almost everybody at the Great Went on 8/17/97 had forgotten "Buffalo Bill" even existed; listen to the huge crowd reaction really occur only when the chorus is sung! A nice segue into "NICU" followed, leav-ing "Bill" in the dust(bin) for another few months until 11/29/97 in Worcester, when it was played as part of an amusing encore that in-cluded "Moby Dick." For this version, Trey introduced the song as Fish-man's favorite as a joke, actually meaning the Led Zeppelin tune to follow. "Buffalo Bill" disappeared again for another year, reappearing again at Worcester (hey, no fair!) on 11/27/98 in the middle of a com-pletely insane second set. Finally, the song reappeared in Hampton a year later on 12/18/99 during the "Weekapaug" set closer. West coast-ers will soon erupt in riots if "Bill" doesn't grace their presence: the song has only ever been performed on the East coast.

As for what the song's about, well let's just say it's based on a real-life experience Tom Marshall had with one of his superiors at a for-mer job. The lyrics should provide the rest of the details. Just try think-ing of "Buffalo Bill" as a verb rather than a noun….

See Also: "Riker's Mailbox"

Bug

Music/Lyrics: Trey, Tom
Album: *Farmhouse*
Vocals: Trey (lead), Mike, Page (backing)
Debut: 6/24/99 (private show), 6/30/99 (public show)
Historian: Martin Acaster

To the entomologist in all of us, the life of an insect can seem bliss-fully simple. A "Bug" likely does not spend significant portions of its day pondering the infinite. The meaning of it all does not weigh heavy on the brow of the dung beetle. The existence of God is incon-sequential in the everlasting search for the freshest heaving pile of waste. The lyrics of "Bug" evoke images of a much more complex being in the throes of existential wondering. As the swirl of their thoughts re-garding God and (karmic?) debt faded, the grand conundrum of con-ciousness was best answered through the eyes of an insect. Chicken or egg? To the "Bug" it doesn't matter which came first. Worry? Don't need it. Doubt? Don't feed it.

"Bug," which musically sounds like a hybrid of Velvet Under-ground's "Oh! Sweet Nuthin'" and the Marshall Tucker Band's "Can't You See," first scurried from its mound at the Summer Tour 1999

opener at Sandstone Amphitheater (6/30/99 Bonner Springs, KS). Subsequent infestations during 1999 worthy of further inspection by budding Phish entomologists include the specimens uncovered at The Tweezer Center (7/13/99 formerly Great Woods, Mansfield, MA), GM Place (9/9/99 Vancouver, BC), Nassau Coliseum (10/8/99 Uniondale, NY), Blue Cross Arena (12/5/99 Rochester, NY) and the glorious late night Scarab Beetle which scuttled out of the Technicolor bouqet of roses plucked from the swamps of Big Cypress (12/31/99). The swarm of "Bugs" which have followed the release of the *Farmhouse* studio version suggest that the hive is thriving. "Bug"-hungry "Birds of a Feather" should flock to the Radio City Music Hall (5/22/00 New York, NY), Hibiya Outdoor Theater (6/11/00 Tokyo, Japan), and Molson Amphitheater (7/6/00 Toronto, ON) versions for a tasty meal. Clearly the life of a Bug is far from overrated.

Bundle of Joy
Music/Lyrics: Trey Anastasio
Album: *Junta* (part of "Fluff's Travels"—CD 7:21-9:10)
Vocals: Page, Trey
Debut: 8/21/87
Historian: Mark Toscano

Bundle of Joy, also known as the disturbing, whacked-out, building-to-a-bizarre-and-feverish-climax part of "Fluffhead," is the penultimate segment of the complete "Fluffhead" epic. Since May of 1988, "Fluffhead" has always featured "Bundle of Joy" and all of its sister segments: "Fluff's Travels," "The Chase," "Who Do? We Do!," "Clod," and "Arrival." However, "Bundle of Joy" has occasionally shown up outside of its usual "Fluffhead" context. Both 8/21/87 and 10/20/89 boast halved versions of "Harpua," featuring "Bundle of Joy" occupying the space in between. Also, like several other "Fluff's Travels" segments, "Bundle" was performed a few times on its own in 1989 (9/21/89, 10/1/89, 11/3/89).

As near as can be figured, the point of this tune is to build an insane amount of drama and tension so as to exponentially amplify the screaming sigh of relief that the final segment, "Arrival," provides at the song's conclusion. More often than not, it works.

See Also: "Fluffhead/Fluff's Travels"

BUNGALOW BILL (see: "THE CONTINUING STORY OF BUNGALOW BILL")

Buried Alive
Music: Trey Anastasio
Album: (none)
Vocals: (instrumental)
Debut: 9/13/90
Historian: Craig DeLucia

Buried Alive is an instrumental number that was played regularly from 1990 through 1994 but only sparingly since then. The frantic pace and squealing guitar sounds conjure the image of a person truly being buried alive and fighting to escape. Although early versions could creep up anywhere in a set, the song is now usually played as a raucous set opener.

Many fans love the song for its ability to kickstart a set and raise the energy level of a crowd, despite the fact that most versions do not jam and are basically played the same. An exception, though, was the fifteen-minute "Buried Alive" second set opener on 7/29/98 in Maryland Heights, Missouri. Other fun versions include 9/27/91 (with "Esther" teases), 12/7/91 (with yuletide teases), 3/26/92 (with an introduction from Trey remarking that the song was inspired by Jimmy Herring), 2/6/93 (with John Popper on harmonica), 4/4/94 (with The Giant Country Horns), 12/2/94 and 12/3/94 (with The Cosmic Country Horns), 12/28/95 (sandwiched between "Wilson" and "Tweezer"), and 2/26/97 (at the start of a crazy second set). If you're a true fan of the song, seek out the 11/2/90 "Possum" and the 10/11/95 "Julius," both of which contain "Buried Alive" teases.

Burning Down the House
Music/Lyrics: David Byrne, Chris Frantz,
Jerry Harrison, Tina Weymouth
Original Artist: Talking Heads
Original Album: *Speaking in Tongues*
Vocals: Trey (lead), Fish, Mike, Page (backing)
Debut: 8/12/98
Historian: Mark Toscano

One of Talking Heads most anthemic songs, this tune has been heard everywhere from *Revenge of the Nerds* to Bonnie Raitt concerts. Phish are easy Talking Heads fans, and have covered them many times, not an insignificant example of which is the full *Remain in Light* album, played on 10/31/96. Two years after this feat, the guys were playing an amusing Fishman hometown show in Vernon, NY (near Syracuse), and treated the crowd to a mind-boggling "Burning Down the House" / "YEM"encore. In the presence of the drummer's friends and family, "Burning" was able to showcase Fish's best ChrisFrantzian drumming, Trey's amusing vocals, and a nice climaxy ending. Likely a special one-time treat, this tune is likely too exploratorily limiting for the band to make it a regular in their show, especially when "Crosseyed" has done just fine without any outside help.

BUTTER THEM BISCUITS (see: "LITTLE TINY BUTTER BISCUITS")

Bye Bye Foot
Music/Lyrics: Jon Fishman
Album: (none)
Vocals: Fish
Debut: 6/6/97 (private show); 6/14/97 (public show)
Historian: Bradley Lonard

A gentle ballad with an air of childlike wonderment reminiscent of Syd Barrett, "Bye Bye Foot" gave Fishman a (relatively rare in 1997) turn at the microphone. Not that he took too much advantage of the fact; after making its initial public appearance in Dublin on 14 June 1997, it was played just three more times—once more in Europe and twice on the US summer tour—before the band put it away, possibly because it was a bit ambitious vocally for Fish. Even on what is probably the best version—Walnut Creek, 7/22/97, with a beautifully flowing solo from Trey—Fishman strains to reach the notes. The composer thought enough of the lyrics to have them printed in the summer 1997 Döniac Schvice.

Camel Walk
Music/Lyrics: Jeff Holdsworth
Album: (none)
Vocals: Trey (lead), Mike, Page (backing)
Debut: 11/3/84
Historian: Mark Toscano and Ellis Godard

Not to be confused with the Southern Culture on the Skids song of the same name, this is an original Jeff Holdsworth composition for Phish, one of the two that Phish still features in their repertoire (the other is "Possum"). The Phish version is in fact completely different from the Southern Culture song, which is more country-fried freakabilly than the skunky-eyed geekgroove Phish fans know all too well.

Jeff Holdsworth (who sang lead on all versions prior to leaving Phish in '86) mysteriously introduced "Camel Walk" on 4/15/86, and fans will have to seek out that entertaining early show to find out what meaning he intended to impart with this dastardly tune. The song was fairly common in "the early days," and fun versions include 10/17/85, 10/15/86, 8/21/87, and 2/24/89 ("see those humps a-movin'"), Following a dwindling of appearances in the late '80s, the song disappeared altogether for several years, not showing up again until the classic 7/2/95 show at Sugarbush.

The song disappeared again until 2/26/97, when it reappeared and stayed for a bit, resurfacing somewhat sparingly over the ensuing years. Though they're more or less faithful to Jeff's original vision, the band plays "Camel Walk" a bit differently today than early versions. Besides being performed at much more languid, oozing pace as of late, the song also seems to have lost its brief, prog-rocky bridge composition. On the few recent appearances the band attempted to remember this portion of the original song (check out 2/26/97), though it wasn't a disaster, one can see why they simplified the song for maximum listening pleasure. Recent versions of note include 8/14/97, 12/12/97, 7/28/98, 7/24/99 (accompanied by the first "Alumni Blues" in five years), 12/16/99, and 10/1/00 (out of "When the Circus Comes.")

Cannonball
Original Artist: The Breeders
Original Album: *Last Splash* (1993)
Vocals: Trey, Page
Debut: 5/7/94
Historian: Mark Toscano

A chunk of this 1993 hit alterna-rock single by The Breeders showed up briefly in the epic Bomb Factory "Tweezer" on 5/7/94, something which has surprised and perplexed many fans who have heard this classic set. The band has even been known to enjoy The Breeders' *Last Splash* album on the tour bus from time to time.

Can't You Hear Me Knocking
AKA: "CYHMK"
Original Artist: The Rolling Stones
Original Album: *Sticky Fingers* (1971)
Vocals: Mike, Trey; (often performed instrumental)
Debut: 11/3/84
Historian: Craig DeLucia

Plenty of fans have heard this song jammed at a Phish show and never even realized it. Pop in your copy of *Slip, Stitch, and Pass* and listen to the little jam that closes "Weekapaug Groove" and then start digging through your tapes to find other versions!

In the very early days, Phish played long, jammed-out versions of "Can't You Hear Me Knockin'." The song fell away in 1985, though it was heard at soundchecks from time to time. Starting in 1994, though, the band began to bring the ending jam back to the live stage. Usually, it was as a tag ending to "Weekapaug" (see 10/21/94, 11/4/94, and the wonderful 7/22/97). It has, however, closed other songs, such as the "Down With Disease" reprise on 11/27/96.

Caravan
Music/Lyrics: Duke Ellington, Irving Mills, Juan Tizol
Original Artist: Duke Ellington
Original Album: single (1937)
Vocals: Merle Saunders (4/22/94);
  (otherwise perfomed instrumental)
Debut: 1/20/90
Historian: charlz franz

One of several Duke Ellington classics in the Phish repertoire is the swing era masterpiece, "Caravan." Written and most often played as an instrumental, lyrics were added later, making "Caravan" a standard for both jazz combos and vocalists such as Ella Fitzgerald. At its best, "Caravan" can be a potent interplay of exotic rhythms and textures (*Money Jungle*'s version with Ellington, Max Roach, and Charlie Mingus is excellent). At its worst, it can sound like the background music for a television game show. Played most often from 1990 through 1994, Phish's instrumental rendition is respectable if not inspired. Special versions include 4/22/94 in Atlanta, when Phish was joined by Merle Saunders on keyboards and vocals, and 12/29/96 in Philadelphia. The latter performance belies the oft stated claim that Phish can't play jazz in large auditoriums.

Carefree
Original Artist: Sun Ra
Original Album: *Destination Unknown* (1993)
Vocals: (instrumental)
Debut: 4/26/94
Historian: Craig DeLucia

While Phish has never played this song at a concert, many fans have it on their tape of the Purple Dragon session from 4/26/94. Pick up Sun Ra's live *Destination Unknown* album to hear the song performed by Sun Ra's Arkestra, including two musicians (Marshall Allen and Michael Ray) who would later appear on *Surrender to the Air*.

Carini
AKA: "Carini/Lucy With/Had a Lumpy Head/Face,"
  "Song For Carini"
Music/Lyrics: Phish
Album: (none)
Vocals: Phish
Debut: 2/17/97
Historian: Jeremy David Goodwin

It is difficult to imagine any other Phish song accumulating as much hype and lore in so short a time as has "Carini." Indeed, it seems logically impossible for a beloved song to be "broken out" (played again after a long absence) less than a year after its initial debut. Yet, this is a part of this curious song's improbable history.

"Carini" is marked by an irresistible, head-banging heavy metal intro and spiced with surreal, Beatles-eque lyrics ("You told me of a secret place/ I saw it when I met you/ the walrus on your face"). It was the best amid a smattering of half-baked new songs ("Walfredo," "Rocka William") that was introduced during the band's first extended Europe tour, in early 1997.

"Carini" was a special song from the outset. Its auspicious debut came in Amsterdam on Feburary 17, when it emerged as a raw, intense (but unfinished) nugget in the midst of a raging, mid-set jam that stands as one of that tour's high points. In Italy a week later, as show time drew nearer, anxious fans were surprised by the pre-recorded sound of Phish playing over the speakers. It was in fact that strange new friend "Carini," and the band took the stage and played along as the recording was gradually turned down. By the time the song appeared a few days later, during a much-loved show in Stuttgart, it had already matured noticably, featuring a percussion jam at the end (that would later be dropped). This curious new ditty was used again as a show opener the next night in Berlin; it appeared again to open the second set in Hamburg on 3/1, whipping the audience into a quick frenzy on a night that would later be immortalized on the live album *Slip Stitch and Pass*.

Almost as soon as tapes from this landmark tour started circulating stateside, word started spreading among fans about that strange new song, called…"Lucy With A Lumpy Head"? "Carini Had A Lumpy Head"? "Song for Carini"? No one seemed to know exactly what the song was called, much less have any insight into the enigmatic lyrics. They include an ominous warning ("everyone was screaming when they saw the lump!") and a backhanded compliment that the legions of fans on college campuses no doubt had some fun with: "The thesis that you're writing is a load of shit/ But I'm glad you finally finished it." The existence of a drum tech named Pete Carini seemed to be both a clue and a red herring.

That summer the story started circulating that some of the lyrics actually referred to an altercation Pete Carini had been involved in while the band was overseas, and that he didn't approve of his barroom exploits being sung about onstage. In a 2000 online interview, Trey claims (jokingly?) that the song is a response to a night in which someone splashed liquid acid on Pete Carini's face, subsequently causing him to turn into "a rock star." As it turns out, the song was actually inspired by an incident on one of the early Europe tours in which a college aged female fan was enjoying an up-front view of Page before being told to move, because she was interfering with monitor man Pete Schall's sightlines. Her angry refusal apparently included a threat to call her parents ("He went across the street and he called his dad/ now you'll never get that raise you thought you had"). (We at the Mockingbird Foundation do not believe that this info has been published anywhere previously).

The overwhelming majority of fans hadn't yet had a chance to see "Carini" in person, but there was a slate of performances scheduled between June and August. Would this new composition continue to be used as a high profile set opener? Would it serve as a second set jam vehicle, as it had in Amsterdam?

As Phish headed back to Europe in the Summer of '97, hometown

Elise Ryerson

fans looked forward to the upcoming US tour while checking the new setlists sent via phone lines from such exotic-sounding locations as La Laiterie, Piazza Risorgimento, and the Glastonbury Festival. As unfamiliar as these places were, the load of new song titles ("Water in the Sky"? "Fooled By Images"?) was equally inscrutable. "Carini," however, seemed to have been misplaced somewhere amidst the flurry of activity. Perhaps it had been held behind by customs in Hamburg, the site of its last appearance?

The second leg of Summer Tour opened with a night in Virginia Beach that was rife with these new compositions. But as the now-classic tour wound on, the anticipated United States debut of "Carini" continued to elude fans. Amid the largest slew of new songs in years, "Carini" had apparently been left out. By the tour-closing festival The Great Went, the sad news had spread among tour kids: Mike had been telling fans backstage that "Carini" was "no longer a Phish song."

Thus, the "Carini" story ended: a very promising new song that had been yanked from the rotation before we really had a chance to enjoy it. Rabid fans continued to request it, but there was no sign of Lucy or her lumpy head anywhere during a long fall tour that saw such rarities and debuts as "Emotional Rescue," "Them Changes," and "Boogie On Reggae Woman."

Until one of the most storied New Year's Run performances ever, of course.

On December 30, 1997, Phish decided to celebrate the new year a day early by launching such fireworks as a "Sneaking Sally Through the Alley" opener, the second-ever fully jammed "AC/DC Bag," an epic "Harpua" (encompassing Trey's childhood in New Jersey, *Lost in Space*, and an udder ball), a Tom Marshall-led performance of "I'm Gonna Be (500 Miles)," and well-appreciated versions of "Izabella" and "Harry Hood." When Phish took the stage for the encore, fans were al-

ready satiated. Then the mighty, clanging riff of "Carini" roared out through Madison Square Garden, and those who were in the know exploded with glee. An enthusiastic Trey went on to call Pete Carini himself out onto the stage to accept the adulation of the multitudes, as the band sang the chorus over and over. Thus the bizarre new song had been debuted, won fans, dissapeared "forever," and then been resurrected, all in the course of eleven months.

It was not immediately clear whether the MSG breakout was going to be only a one-time gift to fans, but the band was soon to give in again to their apparent compulsion about playing "Carini" during superb shows. On the second night of the mind bending Island Tour (also known as the Spring Run), an over-excited fan ran onstage during "Loving Cup." Although the identity of the security personnel who chased the man offstage is still debated, the band seized the chance during "Run Like an Antelope" to riff vocally upon the theme, "Carini's gonna get you!" This remarkably successful sequence includes Fishman offering the advice, "You can run onto the stage, but just don't let Carini get you." When the band returned for the encore, they came armed with the timely version of "Carini" that seemed inevitable. Once again, the main man with respect to Fishman's drums was called onstage to recieve vociferous applause from the happy fans.

And thus "Carini" returned to the rotation for the first time in over a year. It appeared periodically throughout Summer and Fall tours in 1998; not so frequently as to become routine, but more often than you would care to count on your hands. This time it was complete with a raging, extended guitar solo at the end. In this incarnation, it was most often played in the midst of a first set, as a fiery but relatively predictable treat.

There were no Amsterdam-style heroics in this song again until the first night of the 1998 New Year's Run, when the band celebrated their return to Madison Square Garden by opening the second set with "Carini" for the first time since Hamburg. This seemed a clear allusion to the MSG breakout of the dormant song a year before, and notably, the 12/28/98 rendition is the only jammed-out version played in the United States to date. This extended psychedelic delight features the kind of electro-space sound collage jamming that would dominate much of the exciting improvisation of 1999, stretching out for over fifteen minutes before seguing into "Wolfman's Brother."

Versions from Summer '99 on include alternate lyrics referencing an incident involving a naked man at a show ("I saw Carini with that naked dude/ I could not eat my food"). For those college students out there who would like some music to blare at 7am while finishing a paper (whether it be "a load of shit" or not), check out the following versions of "Carini": 2/17/97, 2/26/97, 12/30/97, 11/27/98, 12/28/98, and 7/13/99 ("Reba" > "Carini").

Carolina
Music/Lyrics: traditional
Vocals: Phish
Debut: 1/20/90
Historian: Dan Mielcarz

Carolina represents one of several forays Phish has made into the barbershop quartet genre. It made its debut at Dartmouth College on 1/20/90, and in small (and sometimes not so small) venues was sung without amplification. Unfortunately, this often leads to a live

recording consisting solely of the yells of an appreciative audience. Since 1995, "Carolina" has been quite rare, and in fact hasn't appeared since 11/18/98. A capella fans eagerly await its return.

In concert, Phish takes "Carolina" seriously, respecting the uniquely American roots of the song. However, in one hilarious soundcheck from 5/4/90, Fishman makes the song eternally his. By rhyming "Carolina" with a certain female body part, Fish lets all of us experience what he calls "the Boy Scout Anthem." Interested fans will seek this version out, as well as some of the later, amplified versions of "Carolina."

Cars Trucks Buses
AKA: "CTB"
Music: Page McConnell
Album: *Billy Breathes*
Vocals: (instrumental)
Debut: 9/27/95
Historian: Saul Wertheimer

One of only two Page compositions, Phish first performed this song during the first show of Fall '95. This short, keyboard-based ditty quickly established itself as a regular, yet continues to diminish in frequency with each passing year. "CTB" has been played in many positions, serving as anything from first set filler to a second set opener before a big jam (see 11/30/95 Dayton). The false ending which has caught a few fans by surprise does not appear on the album.

The most exciting version of this Jimmy Smith-like tune in its first year and a half of life is the version from the N'awlins JazzFest in spring '96, which features a Cajun injection courtesy of Michael Ray. Although spicier than preceding versions, this version was not extended (except for the ending, ala the Allman Bros), merely highlighted by Ray's trumpet.

"CTB" seemed closed to the possibility of opening up into a jam. That changed at the Lake Champlain benefit played at the Flynn on 3/18/97. After a strong Hood, Dave "The Truth" Grippo and James Harvey came onstage for the longest version to date. Clocking in at nine minutes, this version is nearly twice as long as the runner up. This performance features Grippo and Harvey taking extended solos and trading licks with Trey. "Suzy" fans should check out this show for some "Soul Power." Aside from a reappearance by Michael Ray on the 9/9/00 version, not much has come of the song as of late. At this rate, "Cars Trucks Buses" seems on its way to the Phish graveyard: gone, but certain to be revived (or reincarnated) somewhere down the road. Tunes have been known to disappear entirely from setlists, only to reappear years later (e.g. Camel Walk), while other songs seem to be revived as slightly different incarnations (ex.Guyute).

Catapult
Music/Lyrics: Mike Gordon
Album: *A Picture of Nectar*
Vocals: Mike and/or Trey
Debut: 4/17/92
Historian: Martin Acaster

Sandwiched between the Memorial Day beachfront traffic jam that is "Faht" and the sublime reprise to a cold, cold tale about a man and his freezer is this morbid curiosity penned by Mike Gordon. Clocking in at a mere 32 seconds on the album *A Picture of Nectar*, it speaks vol-

umes on the human condition—the anguished thoughts of a poor catheterized soul whose "wien machine" is malfunctioning. As the pain sears his guts he dreams of catapulting downtown to meet his fiancée at an art gallery. Sadly, there ain't gonna be no wedding.

The first live appearance of this oddity was during the secret language filled "David Bowie" that closed out the first set of a show at the Warfield Theater in San Francisco on 4/17/92. In this version, "Catapult" is segmented into four verses by the frenetic trills that close out the "David Bowie." "Catapult" is a relative rarity typically found within another song. Other notable renditions include 6/22/94 Columbus, OH, 10/14/95 Austin, TX, 12/1/95 Hershey, PA, 12/13/97 Albany, NY, and 12/31/99 Big Cypress, FL

Cavern

Music: Trey Anastasio
Lyrics: Tom Marshall, Scott Herman
Album: *A Picture of Nectar; Hampton Comes Alive* **(11/20/98)**
Vocals: Trey (lead), Mike, Page (backing)
Debut: 3/28/90
Historians: Dan Purcell and Craig DeLucia

Either the nail-biting tale of a daring nighttime rescue mission or a surreal yarn about a camping trip gone horribly awry, "Cavern" is one of the most-frequently played songs in the Phish songbook. This much is clear: the protagonist is venturing into strange territory where grave danger awaits. His friends admonish him to have one for the road before he leaves. When he finally departs his home base, he faces various unforeseen perils: "primal soup," "porthole pirates," and "sanctuary bugs." But wait: before you start deploying phrases like "5th-level Magic-User" and "+2 mace," this isn't just some arrested-adolescent Dungeons & Dragons fantasy; far from wielding a mighty sword, our hero is armed only with a hedgehog's spine and his friend Rick's trusty fork. And in the end, it all would've worked out if only he'd taken care of his shoes.

Except for some early lyric changes (no longer does the narrator attack with an unwieldy knife and leave his poor victim in a pile of excrement, and no longer does the song reference an enlarger pump a la *Austin Powers*), "Cavern" has been a rock in Phish's rotation since early 1990. While most fans have become accustomed to the song as a set-closer or encore song, it actually appeared in just about every setlist slot until 1992, when the band began utilizing it in its current role. In fact, beginning in Fall 1992, well over half of the performances of "Cavern" have come either at the close of a set or during an encore. And no wonder: the song's straight-up rock feel and rousing final chorus make it a fitting exclamation point on the end of an evening of more excursionary jamming.

The early lyrics have returned to the live stage on a few occasions (see 4/4/94, 11/26/97, and 4/5/98, to name a few) but have largely disappeared. Some have speculated that at least one band member wasn't enamored with the concept of singing about a penile erector. The replacement lyrics became quite important, though; the album title *A Picture of Nectar* was taken directly from them. "Cavern" has been home to several special guests. It is a frequently-played number when Carl Gerhard is around—see 11/20/91, 3/24/92, and the 11/20/98 version from *Hampton Comes Alive*. The most intriguing guest version to date, though, saw both Gerhard and Michael Ray accompany the band on 11/14/94.

For a non-jamming song, "Cavern" has produced some fun variations and versions. See, for example, the bluegrass interpretation from 4/6/92 (a show complete with a "Make Your Own Guacamole Jam" that must be heard!) or the "Cavern" sandwiched around "Take the 'A' Train" on 5/5/93. Another favorite version is from 11/27/92, where the band paid homage to Jimi Hendrix by teasing his music on his birthday during an inspiring "Cavern." Of course, when mentioning this song, the granddaddy of all quirky versions is from the offbeat 7/13/94 show where the band sung "Wilson" above the music to "Cavern," and then returned to the latter's final chorus to close the medley. Finally, for a jammy "Cavern," return to 6/14/97 or the aforementioned 4/5/98 (out of a smooth "Possum").

Cecilia

Original Artist: Simon and Garfunkel
Original Album: *Bridge Over Troubled Water*
Vocals: Fishman
Debut: 6/25/97
Historian: Tim Wade

Fans of "Greasy Troll" Jon Fishman have been amazed by his skill with the trombone, bagpipes, washboard, and vacuum cleaner for years. However, fewer of those fans are familiar with Fish's proficiency on towel. This unique talent was displayed on 6/25/97 during an equally unique second set in Lille, France. The complex machinations of towel performances are surely to blame for Fishman's trouble in relating the complete lyrics of the folk-rock classic "Cecilia." After several attempts, though, Henrietta managed to get almost one whole verse right before his band broke into a triumphant rendition of "Hold Your Head Up."

Chalkdust Torture

AKA: "Chalkdust"; "CDT"; "Chalk Dust"
Music: Trey Anastasio
Lyrics: Tom Marshall
Album: *A Picture of Nectar; A Live One* **(11/16/94)**
Vocals: Trey
Debut: 2/1/91
Historian: Craig DeLucia

Peter Slizman

Some songs are flat-out meant to rock and roll. "Chalk Dust Torture" ("Chalkdust") is a prime example. One of the most often-played songs since its debut in 1991, "Chalkdust" has been a frequent set opener because of its ability to whip a crowd into a frenzy. The lyrics speak of teen angst and rebellion, as the narrator seeks to live life while he is still young. While most versions of the song feature Type I jamming and screaming guitar work from Trey, it has also served as a large Type II jam vehicle on a few occasions.

The first memorable "Chalkdust" was on 5/17/91 at the Campus Club in Providence, Rhode Island. The power cut off during the song, but Fishman continued playing. When the lights came back on, a strong jam ensued. Other early memorable versions include 3/8/93, where a "Chalkdust" encore moved into a reprise of a second set "Big Ball Jam," and 7/23/93, where the song grew out of a typically angry "Big Black Furry Creature from Mars."

Fans in Toronto on 8/9/93, were treated to the first real exploratory "Chalkdust." The show-opening version included a jam based on Jimi Hendrix's "Who Knows." Another tasty version is the 7/16/94 Sugarbush "Chalkdust," with a tease of Heart's classic "Barracuda." By the Fall of 1994, "Chalkdust" had grown into a popular concert anthem. The band actually played the song twice on 12/10, returning to the song at the start of the encore while they introduced the crew. Phish thought enough of the 11/16 version to include it on *A Live One*. At the culmination of the 1994 tour season, the band played a shortened version during their first-ever appearance on David Letterman's late-night talk show on 12/30.

Several other memorable versions have surfaced since then. The 6/20/95 Blossom version is a fan favorite for that year. On 10/23/96 and 7/25/97, the band welcomed Bob Gulotti on a second drum set for portions of the show and "Chalkdust" was among the selections played. The second set of the Atlanta show on 7/23/97 included a tasty combo of "You Enjoy Myself" and "Chalkdust," with a "Rocky Mountain Way" jam sandwiched in between. On 7/30 of the same year, the first set included a strong "Chalkdust" that emerged from Wolfman's Brother." In Worcester on 11/27/98, fans were awestruck as the band moved freely in and out of "Mirror in the Bathroom" and an atypical, bluesy "Dog Log" while also teasing "Wipe Out" and never losing sight of the "Chalkdust" theme. And on 7/11/00, Phish performed the rare "Chalk Dust Reprise" for just the second time ever (after a rocking "Drowned") and before a wondeful "Chalkdust" proper) and then whipped it out again in the encore.

On several occasions, members of the band have expressed their affection for this number. Tom Marshall mentioned in *The Phish Book* that the lyrics are among his favorites, and Fishman remarked that he still loves belting the song's anthemic chrous despite the fact that he is obviously not as young as he was when the song was written. The band even went as far as to loan the music to the Dude of Life, who used it verbatim in his song "Self." Phish played on the Dude's album, recording "Self" as one of the tracks, and has performed the song live in concert with the Dude at the helm (see The Wetlands gig on 9/13/90 and Amy's Farm on 8/3/91). "Chalkdust" was adapted to an acoustic format during Trey's solo tour in the spring of 1999. And when Trey and Page played the Warfield in San Francisco with "Phil and Friends" in the spring of 1999, "Chalkdust" was one of only four Phish originals played. Perhaps most unusual was the 10/6/00 version, featuring Bob Weir on guest guitar. Following a rendition of "El Paso" with Weir on vocals, Trey blasted into "Chalkdust," perhaps sensing that the crowd wasn't as into the encore as they had intended. However, Bobby, either not expecting the song or not ready to start, silenced Trey during the intro, and the song had to be started over again when the Dead alumnus was ready. True to its nature, the version that ensued re-energized the crowd for the last minutes of the night. Never out of rotation for any considerable period of time, the song should remain a concert staple for years to come.

Champagne Supernova
Original Artist: Oasis
Original Album: *(What's the Story) Morning Glory?* **(1995)**
Vocals: Tom Marshall
Debut: 12/29/96
Historian: Phillip Zerbo

Continuing his tradition of New Year's Eve run appearances, the December 29, 1996 gig at The Spectrum in Philadelphia again found Tom Marshall a central figure in the holiday festivities. This time played the role of "Uberdemon" in the midst of a memorable rendition of "Harpua."

Trey made quick work of the introductory "Harpua" narration, offering instead that "for those of you who don't know what's going on in the story, there's a lot of preliminary stuff, just ask the person next to you...." The story continues as "the grinch who stole christmas in gamehendge," making quick work of the character development (to the point of some confusion for those who might not have read the book or seen the movie) in order to get to the MEAT of the story...(Trey) "Poster and Harpua are fighting, spinning, creating a tornado...so fast and so viciously that it actually begins to dig a hole in the ground...until it becomes a Direct Hole to HELL! And everybody in Gamehendge gets sucked down to Hell!"

"And they're all down in Hell, they get sucked down. He (Jimmy) looks forward and he sees the horrible face of Hell, the Uberdemon coming towards him" (could they even tell)? Terror is filling his head. The Uberdemon comes towards him and he opens his mouth and the horrible sound of Hell comes out of his mouth and Jimmy, Jimmy hears the horrible sound of Hell...." (Fishman) "Oh horrible sound of Hell... Speak to us!"

At this point Tom Marshall came out equipped with equally cheesy glasses, glam-rock shirt, and british accent to perform the 1995 <queue Don Pardo> "chart-topping hit 'Champagne Supernova'":

It was clear that "was very little respect involved" in performing this Oasis cover, offered as the song the Devil himself may greet you with. A terrible thing, indeed!

This Harpua came on the heels of a set that already boasted solid versions of "David Bowie," "Bathtub Gin," "A Day in the Life," and a spirited "YEM" that included a solo performance of "Sixteen Candles" by Mike and an equally rare rotation jam. The "Ooom Pa Pa, Oom Pa Pa..." and the events that follow make this set a "must-have" for the serious collector and a classic moment in Phish history.

CHANGES (see: "THEM CHANGES")

Character Zero
AKA: "Zero," "Character 0"

Music: Trey Anastasio
Lyrics: Tom Marshall
Album: *Billy Breathes; Hampton Comes Alive* (11/20/98)
Vocals: Trey (lead), Mike, Page (backing)
Debut: 6/6/96
Historian: Jeremy David Goodwin

Amid the serene acoustic songs that debuted in 1996, "Character Zero" stood out as the only brand-new rocker. In this sense it was viewed by some as a song with more potential as a live piece than its brethren "Trainsong," "Talk," and "Waste." The song was unveiled at the Joyous Lake surprise show, and was aired once more (a month later in France) before being set aside for the rest of the summer. It entered the rotation for the first time in Fall '96, and its role quickly became clear: of its first 15 appearances, 6 were as a first set closer. That statistic would expand to 20 of 53 (as of Summer '98), not even including the nine times that the song has been either the second set closer or the last song of the encore.

"Character Zero" has generally gotten a little better every tour. An early high-profile appearance came on 12/31/96, when it had the honor of closing the second set. A surprisingly blistering jam became the soundtrack for the launch of a hot air balloon into the atmosphere of the Fleet Center, adding a surreal touch to the performance. Future versions typically featured a slightly longer and more intense jam than those of the first versions, but the song remained a pretty straightforward "Type I" tune. It was like a more restrained "Chalkdust Torture." Also note that later versions omit the brief vocal jam that closed initial performances and the studio version on *Billy Breathes*.

The "Character Zero" paradigm took a radical shift in Hartford on 11/26/97, when it received a nearly 20 minute, fully-jammed treatment. This jam was quite in character of Fall '97, when traditionally pedestrian songs were often jammed out to an unprecedented extent. This "Zero" performance featured an excellent pass at the normal jam (which hinted at a return to the closing vocals, but eventually bypassed them altogether), followed by an impressive exploration of some '70s rock-styled themes, which finally slunk down (via Fishman's slithery machinations) into the brilliant "Also Sprach Superbad."

A less auspicious rendition of the tune was the abridged, edgy performance given by a very exhausted, scraggly group of men on 3/5/97. Phish had just returned from a brief Europe tour (which had, by the way, blazed the band's first fiery fingerprint into the epic year that was in the making) on that awkward afternoon in the studios of *Late Show With David Letterman*. (The Eisenstein Editing Award goes to the quirky television director that day, who cut to extreme close-ups of Mike's face every time he was screaming "aiy! aiy!," but otherwise left the subdued bassist mostly out of the broadcast.)

The Chase

Music: Trey Anastasio
Album: *Junta* (part of "Fluff's Travels"—CD 1:09-2:21)
Vocals: (instrumental)
Debut: 2/21/97 (with "Lushington")
Historian: Mark Toscano

One of Trey's most meticulous compositions, "The Chase" found a permanent home as the third segment of the complete "Fluffhead" in May of 1988. Prior to that, it appeared in another, somewhat more

humiliating context as the bridge for the rather unpleasantly conceived "Lushington" (see 4/29/87, 8/29/87). A number of times during this period, "The Chase" subjugated "Lushington" and the band would play the former with merely a closing jam on the latter (see 5/11/87). Also, as with "Who Do? We Do!," and "Clod," "The Chase" made a brief solo reappearance during 1989 (see 9/21/89, 10/1/89, 10/26/89) as a filler tune between longer songs.

Like many of Trey's compositions ("It's Ice," "Esther," "Buried Alive" and "The Famous Mockingbird" also come to mind), "The Chase" reflects a sort of "musical onomatopoeia." The rapidly crossing and interlocking melodies of Trey's guitar and Page's piano supported by Mike's responding bass line uncannily evoke the feeling of an urgent pursuit, albeit one that usually lasts about one minute.

See Also: "Fluffhead/Fluff's Travels"

Che Hun Tah Mo

Original Artist: James Billie
Original Album: *Alligator Tales*
Vocals: James Billie
Debut: 12/30/99
Historian: Phillip Zerbo

From the liner notes of Alligator Tales on "Che Hun Tah Mo"—"In the Miccosukee tongue, the phrase means 'welcome.' The Seminoles' friendliness is described here in a Latino/blues style. It is also known as the 'welcome song' inviting all peoples to the swamps for a good time 'down where the trade winds play.' "

And what a good time that was had by all!

A warmer welcome we will all be lucky to have in our lifetime. Emphasizing the inclusiveness of the invitation, "Che Hun Tah Mo" offers that "We Seminoles are friends to the earth…Shalom…Moshi Moshi." To call this "a guest appearance with Phish by Chief Jim Billie" would be to miss the point entirely: WE made a 80,000+ person collective guest appearance at the biggest campfire Chief Jim Billie has ever assembled in his backyard!

Chief Jim offered a wonderful bit of perspective on the events of 12/30/99 during his welcome: "There are folks just a few short miles away that don't have any idea that you [us] are even here!"

The Magic that occurred on those days in Big Cypress could never have happened without the warm invitation by Chief Jim Billie and the Seminole Tribe, and for that we are all in their debt. Thank you!

The Chicken

Music: Alfred "Pee Wee" Ellis
Original Artist: James Brown
Original Album: B-side to "The Popcorn" (1968)
Vocals: (instrumental)
Debut: 3/11/88
Historian: Mark Toscano

Played on a whim, this classic James Brown instrumental jam opened up the 3/11/88 show on an atypically funky note, leading all-too-agreeably into "Funky Bitch." Prefacing the song, Trey remarked on the ideal nature of the JB tune as a show-opener, providing the impetus for the rest of the band to join him on a fun-but-white rendition, still the only one in known Phish history.

Choo Choo Ch' Boogie
Music/Lyrics: V. Horton, D. Darling, M. Gabler
Original Artist: Louis Jordan
Original Album: single (1946)
Vocals: Bruce "Sunpie" Barnes
Debut: 3/2/93
Historian: Ellis Godard

Phish performed this bit of bouncy fun only once, with Bruce "Sunpie" Barnes on washboard, harmonica, and lead vocals. The lyrics, typically silly swing, are of upbeat love for railroads, not for the freedom they suggest, but for the sound and rhythms of the trains and tracks. This smash hit of 1940s swing, by a pioneer who mixed blues and jazz and thus helped found R&B, was a perfect choice for the guest spot and allowed some nice interaction between Barnes and Page.

Cinnamon Girl
Original Artist: Neil Young with Crazy Horse
Original Album: *Everybody Knows This is Nowhere*
Vocals: Trey and Page (lead)
Debut: 3/18/97
Historian: Tim Wade

This Neil Young cover appeared in prominent positions twice in 1997. It kicked off the year in the U.S. by opening the Flynn Theater show on 3/18/97, then served as the encore to a memorable show at Shoreline Amphitheatre on 7/31/97.

Cities
Original Artist: Talking Heads
Original Album: *Fear Of Music* (1979)
Phish Album: *Slip Stitch and Pass* (3/1/97)
Vocals: Trey
Debut: 12/1/84
Historians: Chris Bertolet and Mark Toscano

Talking Heads released this sideways paean to urban life on their third album, 1979's *Fear of Music*. Like each of the early Heads albums—up to and including 1980's *Remain in Light*—*Fear of Music* fused infectious rhythm, ambitious melody and surreal lyrics to create something undeniably unique. "Cities" stands as a wonderful example of that vision.

Phish played their debut cover of "Cities" at Nectar's in Burlington, VT, nearly twelve years before they'd tackle *Remain in Light* in its entirety. The song appeared occasionally at Phish gigs in the late 1980s before dropping out of the playlist entirely for almost six years, then resurfacing a single time at the Congress Center in Ottawa on 7/5/94. "Cities" immediately took another long hiatus before reappearing in Hamburg, Germany on 3/1/97 (see *Slip, Stitch & Pass*). That July 30 in Ventura, CA, the first "Cities" on American soil in nearly nine years bubbled up from the thick of "David Bowie." Though "Cities" made seven appearances in 1998, it has since become a rare treat once again. This furtiveness is possibly what makes fans mis-hear teases of the song in random jams, as its main riff is simply a repeated D-chord. Errant setlists from '97 and '98 were rife with claims of "Cities" teases. The most dastardly example of this came on 4/16/99, when some fans, not as familiar with the Dead as others, labelled the breakdown jam in "St.

Stephen" as a "Cities" tease!

As with many covers, Phish takes liberties with "Cities." Contemporary versions are far slower and wah-drenched than the Talking Heads standard—far more cow-funky than avant-garde. Trey also plays fast and loose with the lyrics, omitting an entire verse about getting lost in El Paso and tweaking other lines at whim ("find yourself" instead of the actual "find myself"). Such creative license helps keep the tune fresh and just a little different each time out. To wit, check out the super-goopy Great Went "Cities" from 8/16/97 ("Fishman sleeps…sleeps in the daytime…build yourself a city to live in"); the aforementioned Hamburg breakout ("Are those things real?…nein!"); the 9/29/99 Memphis encore ("Home of Elvis and the Rendezvous Bar-B-Q"); and the 6/14/00 version from Fukuoka, Japan ("It's only the noodles").

Extended jams on the tune are rare, which makes the undisputed Goliath of "Cities"—the 8/10/97 Deer Creek behemoth—that much more special. The second set opener delved into licentious grooves for nearly a half-hour, setting the funky standard by which the jams of that summer would be judged. Other great "Cities" include the Lemonwheel version from 8/15/98 (with delay loop jam between "Funky Bitch" and "Weekapaug"), and the 8/6/88 Colorado sandwich ("YEM" -> "Cities" -> "DEG" -> "Cities"). Fans interested in Talking Heads' live versions of the tune should check out the home video version of *Stop Making Sense*, which features "Cities" as one of three bonus tracks. Fans of David Byrne's post-ironic explorations of Americana should definitely check out his film *True Stories*.

Clod
Music/Lyrics: Trey Anastasio
Album: *Junta* (part of "Fluff's Travels"—CD 4:12-7:21)
Vocals: Page, Trey
Debut: 10/15/86
Historian: Mark Toscano

This song, originally its own entity, joined the full version of "Fluffhead" for that song's final-draft debut on 5/15/88. Prior to then, it had shown up from time to time in a jammed-out version that usually lasted for about five minutes or so. The bizarre lyrics, chosen for their sound rather than their meaning, are indicative of many Phish compositions, and should be shoved into the bursting-at-the-seams "Captain Beefheart: Effects and Influences on Popular Music Since the Sixties" file. Some typically cockeyed pre-"Fluffhead" versions of "Clod" can be surmised by obtaining 12/6/86, 5/11/87, 8/21/87, 2/7/88, and a single, post-"Fluffhead" appearance on 11/10/89.

See Also: "Fluffhead/Fluff's Travels"

Cocaine
Music/Lyrics: J.J. Cale
Original Artist: J.J. Cale; Eric Clapton
Original Album: *Troubadour* (1976) (Cale); *Slowhand* (1977) (Clapton)
Vocals: Trey
Debut: 8/6/93
Historian: Craig DeLucia

Stick this classic rock song in the file containing musical treats that Phish has briefly dangled in front of their fans. During a rocking "You Enjoy Myself" on 8/6/93, the band launched into a verse and cho-

rus of this Cale/Clapton staple. The ensuing "YEM" reprised "Cocaine" in the vocal jam before launching into "Halley's Comet."

Cold As Ice
Original Artist: Foreigner
Original Album: *Foreigner* (1977)
Vocals: (performed instrumental)
Debut: 3/13/92
Historian: Mark Toscano

This ubiquitous Foreigner tune showed up for part of the spring 1992 tour as Fishman's theme, supplanting the tried-and-true "Hold Your Head Up." Like "HYHU," "Cold as Ice" was performed instrumentally as an intro and outro for Fishman's usual song and dance. Also like "Hold Your Head Up," it was used basically as yet another excuse to piss The Greasy One off. Check out 3/13/92, 3/14/92, 4/16/92, 4/18/92, 4/25/92, 4/29/92, 5/12/92, and 5/16/92 for instances of this unfortunate practice.

Cold Rain and Snow
AKA: "Cold Rain"
Music/Lyrics: traditional
Original Artist: The Grateful Dead
Original Album: *The Grateful Dead* (1967)
Debut: 9/17/99
Historian: Chris Bertolet

When Phish breezed into the Bay Area for a two-night run at the Shoreline Amphitheater in fall 1999, heads were abuzz with speculation about potential guest appearances—and with good reason. Shoreline is undeniably a Dead shed, and the memory of Trey and Page's stint with Phil Lesh & Friends at the nearby Warfield was sweet and fresh enough to taste. The first gig did find Warren Haynes game to the task, but if his contributions to the "Misty Mountain Hop" encore were well appreciated, he wasn't the hometown hero and liver recipient the locals were openly pining for.

The following night, in the throes of a second set "YEM," Phil finally delivered the goods with a triumphant and eminently Phishy entrance—on trampoline. After a melodic and adventuresome bass duel with Gordon (and an unremarkable amble through "Wolfman's"), Lesh led the charge into a cathartic and zealously jammed "Cold Rain."

The blues-inflected traditional—which commonly served as an opener at Dead shows—ended Phish's set. Warren Haynes then made his second appearance in as many nights to join Phil and Phish for a blistering "Viola Lee Blues" encore.

Colonel Forbin's Ascent
AKA: "Forbin," "Forbin's Ascent,"
  "Forbinbird" (with "The Famous Mockingbird")
Music/Lyrics: Trey Anastasio
Album: (none)
Vocals: Trey (lead), Mike, Page (backing)
Debut: 3/12/88
Historian: Mark Toscano

He has braved many challenges, some extremely perilous, some exceedingly bizarre. He has conquered dangerous mountains, dark forests, rushing rivers, and treacherous love. He has helped save an entire civilization, only to find it doomed yet again. He has shared the company of both faithful fleethounds and intimidating deities. He has found adventure and misadventure in outer space (5/2/92), under the earth's surface (5/6/92), on Gilligan's Island (2/25/93), and in Fishman's ear (11/27/92). His innumerable exploits have led him to unique encounters with chocolate (12/1/95), peapods and diapers (2/7/93), flooding (2/19/93), surfing (2/25/93), rollercoasters (8/7/93), magical lights (11/4/94), giant iguanas (8/7/96), writhing bodies covered in love-goo (9/30/00), surrealist gluttonous excess (8/7/98), and a mammoth, talking, dancing colossus of David Byrne (10/31/96). He is none other than Colonel Forbin.

Colonel Forbin is the hero of Trey's Gamehendge saga, "The Man Who Stepped Into Yesterday," a musical devised, written, and recorded for his Senior Study at Goddard College. In addition to appearing throughout the musical's narrative, Forbin is the central focus of the song "Colonel Forbin's Ascent." This composition, perhaps the wordiest song in Phish's repertoire, is the fifth song in the cycle, and tells the story of Forbin's ascent up the sacred mountain to obtain help from Icculus, the Lizards' god. When he sees how futile the revolutionaries' attempts at overthrow are, Forbin realizes that this appeal to deific aid may be the Lizards' only hope. After his arduous climb, he confronts the great and knowledgeable Icculus, who sends the Famous Mockingbird to Wilson's castle to retrieve the Helping Friendly Book and bring it to Forbin's hut in the revolutionaries' camp. It is with this Icculusian command that the song ends, bridging nicely into "The Famous Mockingbird," a mostly instrumental tune that describes this feathered fellow's flight to fetch the furtive fortune.

Besides "Tela," "Forbin" was the most time-consuming and difficult song for Trey to compose for his Senior Study. Also like "Tela," Trey spent a lot of time on "Forbin's" lyrics, wanting them to be strong enough to stand up on their own as poetry. To accomplish this, he focused intensely on the use of language and phrasing, sometimes letting words he especially wanted to use (specifically "quagmire," "devour," "thunder," and "knotted") dictate settings and even plot changes. "Forbin" and "Lizards" are definitely the primary, storytelling anchors of "The Man Who Stepped Into Yesterday," as they provide the listener with detailed plot developments that could not be expressed in stream-of-consciousness self-promotion ("The Sloth") or instrumental description ("The Famous Mockingbird"). The end product is a song rife with verbose descriptions and rich, effective word choices; especially impressive are the double-time verses immediately preceding both "sacred creed" refrains.

One of Trey's challenges in designing his Senior Study was to write songs representing a number of different musical styles that he could alter just enough to form a coherent compositional progression, not just a narrative one. For "Forbin," Trey mined a rich ore of jazz chords, and the song yields such nuggets as flatted fifths and ninths, and minor chords with major sevenths. These motley chords—perhaps unusual for a "rock" song—were arranged by Trey into a strange pattern, making the lead vocals awkward for him, but singable and definitely interesting. Trey based the music supporting the aforementioned double-time verses on bluegrass principles, and the proto-"Mockingbird" chord progression was one he picked up in Ireland. This menagerie of musical tidbits combines rather nicely and unexpectedly to complete the song, one of the Gamehendge tunes of which Trey is still most proud.

Peter Sitzman

'99) made up for any lack of visibility. Likewise, the 9/30/00 version with its bizarre story and Trey's memorable comments about the band and their time off, was all the more special because it hadn't been performed in over two years.

Like "Harpua," the appearance of "Forbin" and "Mockingbird" has, especially since 1994, usually signified a special show of sorts, so any version from '94 and later is worth hearing. This is not to say that the pre-1994 versions should be neglected at all, but their degree of frequency made them a little more commonplace than these later versions. Some particularly interesting or standout versions to check out are 3/12/88 (the very first), 7/24/88, 2/24/89, 10/20/89, 10/31/89, 1/28/90, 11/2/90, 12/28/90, 10/13/91, 3/24/92, 4/16/92, 4/21/92, 12/31/92, 2/7/93, 2/25/93, 3/22/93 (with original story in full Gamehendge setting), 8/7/93, 8/15/93, 12/30/93, 6/26/94, 7/8/94 (two more straightforward Gamehendge versions), 10/27/94, 11/30/94 (both with "The Vibration of Life"), 10/5/95, 12/31/95 (with "Shine" and Gamehendge Time Factory story), 8/7/96 (ignore the "Mockingbird"), 10/31/96, and 8/7/98, and 9/30/00.

See Also: "The Famous Mockingbird"

Come On Baby Let's Go Downtown

AKA: "Downtown"
Music/Lyrics: Danny Whitten, Neil Young
Original Artist: Crazy Horse
Original Album: *Crazy Horse* (1971)
Debut: 9/23/00
Historian: Erik Swain

This song about scoring heroin, written by Danny Whitten (the original guitarist for Crazy Horse) and Neil Young, is best known for its appearance on Young's classic *Tonight's the Night* album (1975). It first surfaced on Young's 1970 tour with Crazy Horse as his backing band; at one show Young acknowledged it was written "mostly by Danny." A year later it appeared, simply titled "Downtown," on Crazy Horse's first album without Young. This excellent record also contains Whitten's "I Don't Want to Talk About It," which has been covered by Rod Stewart and the Indigo Girls, among others.

Whitten died of a heroin overdose in 1972. The following year, partly inspired by that, Young wrote a collection of songs examining the darker side of the sex-drugs-and-rock-and-roll mentality of the '60s. Two years later, they would be released as *Tonight's the Night*. In the interim, three other tunes were added to the song cycle, and one was a live version of this song from the 1970 tour with Whitten on lead vocals. Here it is listed as "Come on Baby Let's Go Downtown," which is the title Young fans use today, chiefly so as not to confuse it with "Downtown" from 1995's *Mirror Ball*.

Trey kicked off the electric set of his first solo show on 2/15/99 with this song and played it sporadically on his subsequent solo tour. He performed it as a straightforward rocker not much different from the Young/Crazy Horse versions. It entered the Phish repertoire when it opened the show on 9/23/00 in Rosemont, IL. Was there a reason they chose to play it there in particular? Perhaps. Trey attended a Young concert in this same city the previous year (on 5/1/99, to be exact), and described it during his 5/8/99 solo show as one of the best experiences of his life.

"Forbin" debuted on 3/12/88, even though its usual companion, "The Famous Mockingbird," had debuted a month earlier, on 2/7/88. It is really amazing to consider that even though both songs have been performed since the band's late-Nectar period in 1988, "Forbin" has only been performed without "Mockingbird" once, on 8/14/97. This is the band that publicly stated that "Mike's Song," "I am Hydrogen," and "Weekapaug Groove" would always be performed together, and in that order. Plus, the 8/14/97 exception was quite an exception: Ken Kesey and the Merry Pranksters showed up at Darien Lake, and the band used "Forbin" as a launching pad for the Pranksters' antics, something that could only have been followed by the swampy funk of "Camel Walk," not "Mockingbird."

"Forbin" -> "Mockingbird," or "Forbinbird" as it is often called, is also a special concert treat for being one of the two major storytelling songs in the Phish canon (the other is "Harpua"). Early versions of "Forbinbird" were usually performed without any narration, "Forbin" instead segueing smoothly into "Mockingbird" with nary a word from Trey. Though there were a few exceptions, for which Trey would give brief background details on what the songs were about (more common when the band was playing a new area for them), this format more or less prevailed until Spring tour, 1992. With this tour, the two songs would not only be consistently joined by a varying narrative, but occasionally by an extra song, slipped in just for fun. The most common bonus song has been "Icculus," which showed up in between "Forbin" and "Mockingbird" on only a handful of occasions—4/16/92, 4/24/92, 5/2/92, and 3/25/93—but has been frequently teased in several other "Forbinbirds." "Kung" has shown up in between a few times (3/25/93, 6/16/94), as well as "How High the Moon" (3/8/93) and even Collective Soul's "Shine" (12/31/95), but these are only notable exceptions.

Following some must-hear Spring '92 versions (4/16/92, 4/21/92, 5/2/92, 5/6/92), Trey began to free up the confines of the sandwiched story, even if the songs themselves remained almost exactly the same as they were originally conceived. Over the next few years, the songs may have dwindled in frequency, but not in creativity: the stories got increasingly elaborate and unusual, culminating in the truly epic, surrealist classic performed on 8/7/98. Twelve "Forbinbirds" were performed in 1994, but the following year, the songs were performed only three times, and 1996 was visited by the duo no fewer than two times. While 1997 saw not one "Forbin" -> "Mockingbird" story unfold, the sheer gravity of the 8/7/98 version (a lone appearance between all of '98 and

Come On (Let the Good Times Roll)

Music/Lyrics: Earl King
Original Artist: Jimi Hendrix Experience
Original Album: *Electric Ladyland* (1968)
Debut: 4/29/87
Historian: Mark Toscano

Though Earl King had previously written and recorded this classic, it is most decidedly the Hendrix version that Phish covered at Nectar's on 4/29/87. Fans will have to seek out and acquire this incredible early show to hear the boys do this tune, as it is the cover's only documented performance. Though it definitely hasn't been performed by Phish since the '80s, the 8' Fluorescent Tubes did perform the song at their 4/17/98 gig.

Come Together

Original Artist: The Beatles
Original Album: *Abbey Road* (1969)
Vocals: Trey (12/8/95); Jim Carrey (6/24/99)
Debut: 12/8/95
Historian: Mark Toscano

In Cleveland on 12/8/95, the band encored with this tune along with "A Day in the Life." Trey, at the start of the encore, announced that they wanted to send a little love out to someone with this song. That someone was John Lennon, who was murdered on that day exactly 15 years before. This tune was described by Lennon as one of his favorite Beatles tracks. The tune was resurrected three and a half years later at the so-called "Fifth Ball," a private show played by the band at Trey's barn in Vermont, with—you guessed it—Jim Carrey on vocals!

Communication Breakdown

Original Artist: Led Zeppelin
Original Album: *Led Zeppelin* (1969)
Vocals: Page
Debut: 1/27/90
Historian: Martin Acaster

The January 1969 release of Led Zeppelin's eponymous first album forever changed the face of rock and roll. Their inventive brand of hard and heavy rock had dropped upon the earth with all the impact of a planet-killing asteroid. Most severely damaged by the shockwave it generated was the made-for-radio single;

the album-oriented rock format had been born. Nonetheless, a single from the album was released in March 1969. That single was "Communication Breakdown." Pushed along by the driving rhythm section of Bonzo and Jonesy, the guitar wizardry of Jimmy Page soared into the ethers on the heels of the orgasmic wails and moans of an enrapt Robert Plant. He sure didn't know what he liked about that woman's charms…but we sure know that he liked them a lot.

Phish debuted and then reprised "Communication Breakdown" on back to back nights (1/27/90 and 1/28/90) at the Front in Burlington, VT. The song would be played for an audience only once more later that year. During the rest of the '90s "Communication Breakdown" was dusted off for the soundcheck at Old Orchard Beach (7/3/94) and has resided in the "where are they now?" file ever since. Though it is difficult to match the vocal gymnastics of Robert Plant or the inspired solo-

ing of Jimmy Page, the musical grandeur of the song was kept largely intact each time Phish gave it a go.

Contact

Music/Lyrics: Mike Gordon
Album: *Junta*
Vocals: Mike (lead), Page, Trey (backing)
Debut: 6/15/88
Historian: Martin Acaster

The lyrics to "Contact" appear to be lifted directly from the drivers' education chapter in the helping friendly book. Simple rules for any motorist to live by: "The tires are the things on your car that make contact with the road." Keep that one rule in mind and one probably wouldn't get into too much trouble navigating the road of life either. Curiously enough, the typical placement of the song in a setlist (late second set or commonly as an encore), and its placement as the final song on the original release of *Junta*, has throughout its history given the song an identity as a friendly post-show/end of party reminder. Keep those tires on the road and we will all live to see each other another day. Looking deeper into the song's lyrics, and absorbing the sweetly simple, lullaby-like melody that pervades it, "Contact" takes on the guise of a well-crafted love song. The car that is the subject of the song very easily could be a metaphor for one's partner in life. The glowing headlights, the gleaming tailpipe, the tenacity for holding the road when things get tough. How could one go driving away and come back without them?

"Contact" has been played over one hundred times since 1988, and notable versions include 7/15/91 (The Academy, NYC), 7/21/91 (Arrowhead Ranch, Parksville, NY) both with the Giant Country Horns, 5/21/94 (Moore Theatre, Seattle, WA) where it includes a "Big Ball Jam," and 8/16/97 (The Great Went, Limestone ME), and the "Mexican Love-style" "Contact" on 7/28/98 (Sandstone Amphitheater, Bonner Springs, KS) dedicated to a happy couple by Trey. Common to a number of songs written by Mike Gordon, people either love"Contact" or they hate it, and those who hate it perhaps don't grasp the sublime universal truths it contains. For truly "Bummed IS what you are when you go out to your car and it's been towed!!!" Which begs the question "Who pick up truck?"

The Continuing Story of Bungalow Bill

Original Artist: The Beatles
Original Album: *The Beatles* (aka "The White Album") (1968)
Vocals: Trey (lead), Fishman, Mike, Page (backing)
Debut: 10/31/94
Historian: Mark Toscano

Described enigmatically by John Lennon as "a sort of teenage social-comment song," this sixth track on the Beatles' "White Album" featured some crazed vocals from the band, including Fish's hilarious "all the children sing" line. The 10/31/94 version is the band's only performance of The Beatles' bizarro original.

Cool It Down

Original Artist: The Velvet Underground
Original Album: *Loaded* (1970)
Vocals: Page, Trey (lead)

Debut: 10/31/98
Historian: Mark Toscano

The Velvets' smutty jangle-rock track from *Loaded* was covered by Phish for their 1998 Halloween show. The original is an underhanded, laid back rocker reminiscent of the what the Stones would sound like a few years later; leave it to Lou Reed and the Velvets to be forever ahead of their time.

Phish's Halloween version cooled it down alright. After a fiery "Rock and Roll," the audience was more than happy to be hosed off with the loping spray of this tune. It rocks, but at a very casual pace and energy level. It sashays. It shuffles. It's a head-bobber to be sure. The band were unafraid to put their feet up on the coffee table with this one, stretching it out to just over seven minutes—more than twice the length of the original. Much of this overage can attributed to the exceedingly laid back approach Phish took, extending the song's middle instrumental section to sweat maximum groove out of its pores. Fans were pleased with the results, and the band obviously liked their version enough to include it (along with seven other songs from this set) on an Album Network show in late 1998.

Like all other *Loaded* tunes excepting "Rock and Roll," this one was seemingly hung up to dry for good, until the surprise performance of the tune on 9/24/00 reminded fans that nothing is forever in Phishdom.

Corrina

AKA: "Corrina, Corrina" and "Corrine Corrina"
Music/Lyrics: Taj Mahal, Jessie Ed Davis
Original Artist: Taj Mahal
Original Album: *Natch'l Blues* (1968)
Vocals: Trey
Debut: 3/6/87
Historian: Jeremy Welsh

Corrina was written by bluesman and musicologist Taj Mahal and released on his 1968 album *Natch'l Blues*, which also featured "She Caught the Katy." Phish first performed this slow, bluesy number on 3/6/87, and played it twelve times between 1987 and 1989. The song often featured an extended piano solo by Page, blending well with Trey's heartfelt vocals.

Ten years and almost a thousand shows later, Phish broke-out "Corrina" at their New Year's Celebration in Florida (12/30/99). Early in the opening set of the festival, only two songs after they broke out Traffic's "Light Up or Leave Me Alone," Phish decided to treat the crowd to a great rendition of "Corrina." Though the band trotted "Corina" out again on 9/15/00, it is still likely to remain a rarity of the live repertoire.

COWBOY'S SWEETHEART (see: "I WANT TO BE A COWBOY'S SWEETHEART")

Cracklin' Rosie

Vocals: Fishman (lead)
Original Artist: Neil Diamond
Original Album: Tap Root Manuscript
Debut: 3/7/92
Historian: Phillip Zerbo

The man of a thousand nicknames: Tubbs; Friar Tubbs; Tubbs the Hairy Beast Man; Sneezeblood Eyeball; Norton Charleton Heston; Central Scrutinizer; Forrest Gump; J. Edgar Hoover. He's a nut, but he can sure bang the skins!

The infamous theme songs "Cold as Ice" or "Hold Your Head Up" always signal an appearance by one of Fishman's alter-egos, and in the early '90s this would often take shape in a rendition of Neil Diamond's "Cracklin' Rosie." While most "Fishman tunes" would make use of his world renowned skills on the Electrolux, "Cracklin' Rosie" had its own, unique hook: the "Cracklin' Rosie Cymbals." Two small cymbals, one with the letter "B" and the other with the letters "AH" would merge as one to signal the famous "BAH, bah bah bah bah" chorus.

Making its debut in Phish setlists in the spring of 1992, "Cracklin' Rosie" was in regular and steady rotation throughout all of 1992 and 1993. While it has become a rarity in the modern Phish era, it still makes occasional appearances, including 8/6/98 (complete with several classic Fishman "victory laps" around the stage) and most recently on 12/10/99. The versions of "Cracklin' Rosie" don't vary much, other than to the relative degree that Fishman decides to ham it up. Several notable (and widely circulating) shows contain fine versions of the tune, including 2/21/93, 5/2/93, and 8/24/93. Of course, ALL of you have the version on 12/29/94, by virtue of its appearance in the same set as the monumental and indispensable Providence "David Bowie." If you don't, you should!

While it may seem strange to some that Phish would cover Neil Diamond, in a 1994 interview Trey put that notion firmly to rest: "We realized after long, arduous research that Syd Barrett and Neil Diamond were the two greatest songwriters of all time." Diamond himself wrote the song about a cheap wine resorted to for companionship by the men in a remote, predominantly male Canadian village. With that in mind, perhaps "Cracklin' Rosie" is more about Fish's longing for some female companionship to contrast that of the testosterone-driven caravan he makes company with.

Crimes of the Mind

Music/Lyrics: Steve Pollak
Original Artist: The Dude of Life (with Phish)
Original Album: *Crimes of the Mind*
Vocals: The Dude of Life
Debut: 8/3/91
Historian: Craig DeLucia

This heavy-metal piece of machinery that invoked the memory of such acts as T. Rex and Mott the Hoople became a standard for the Dude of Life's guest appearances from 1991 through 1994. In fact, at Phish shows, it became the most frequently played song from the Dude's album of the same name. Of course, Phish was the backing band for the Dude when the album was recorded. Given the Dude's absence in recent years, though, it's likely that "Crimes of the Mind" has gone away for good.

Crosseyed and Painless

Original Artist: Talking Heads
Original Album: *Remain in Light* (1980)
Vocals: Fishman (lead), Mike, Page, Trey (backing)
Debut: 10/31/96
Historian: Mark Toscano

The rocket-powered second track on *Remain in Light* is one of the more conventional songs on the album, and here Talking Heads and Brian Eno pulled off some amazing arrangements with great invention and precision. The song's got legs, and they belong to a jive-dancin' marathon runner. The guitar solo is completely original, sounding like a train passing a station, leaving its prospective passengers scratching their heads in the kicked-up dust. There's no clutter here, however. The arrangements are surgically precise, cutting and exact, and in fact the various keyboard fills even suggest the steady beeps of life support apparatus. When the song ends, the patient dies.

Phish first performed the song, not surprisingly, as part of their 10/31/96 "musical costume" set. Coming second in the lineup, Phish ripped the rug right out from under its predecessor, "Born Under Punches," taking the residual steam from that song and embezzling it for use in this track. In this Atlanta version we find some horn work from Dave Grippo and Gary Gazaway, new to the song, as it is absent on Talking Heads' studio version. Fishman insisted on singing the lead, and he handles the vocals with appreciably ironic restraint and terseness, adapting it nicely to his own timbre. Trey's solo evokes Byrne's original well, but is decidedly more ferocious and dangerous; it screams like a skyscraper filling rapidly with mercury. Karl Perazzo lends his unquenchable hands to the song's rhythm, and the entire tune is punctuated by occasional hoots and howls. The band was obviously having great fun.

They apparently had so much fun with this one that it entered the show-to-show playlist, albeit surfacing somewhat irregularly. It showed up in the band's very next show, in Florida on 11/2/96, in an incredible 20-plus-minute version that jammed so hard, the band picked it to be released to radio (with other tunes from the same performance) as part of The Album Network show. Fans should acquire this version at all costs, at least to hear Fishman's crazed shrieking during the early part of the jam.

The song showed up again a few times in 1997, on 2/16/97, 2/21/97, and 8/13/97, but then took a long hiatus. It eventually turned up yet again towards the front end of the historic 12/31/99 all-nighter set, eliciting a nice cheer from the lucky crowd. The epic, 21-minute jam that ensued, though not the only historic performance that night, ranks in many fans' minds right up there with the West Palm Beach version from three years earlier. Other recent versions of note include the 14-minute outing on 7/12/00 and the remarkable 9/14/00 rendition, sandwiched oddly between "Drowned" and Dog Faced Boy."

"C+P" also has the distinction of being one of the most exaggerated tease claims in Phish history. So many '98 jams were said to feature "C+P" teases, that the whole thing became sort of a joke. However, some legitimate "C+P" teases can be found in the 11/28/97 "YEM," the 4/3/98 "Weekapaug," and the 12/29/98 "ASZ." It also didn't help things that Phish's 1998 composition "Birds of a Feather" bears striking similarities to the sound and structure of Talking Heads' classic.

For folks interested in comparing, great live versions of this tune by Talking Heads themselves can be found on both *Stop Making Sense* and *The Name of This Band is Talking Heads*.

Crossroads

Original Artist: Robert Johnson
Original Album: *Wheels Of Fire* **(Cream)**
Vocals: Trey
Debut: 5/8/93
Historian: Craig DeLucia

Crossroads, a blues classic written by the legendary Robert Johnson and made popular by supergroup Cream on the 1968 album *Wheels of Fire*, has been covered by countless bands throughout the years. Phish joined the stable in 1993, sandwiching "Crossroads" in the middle of an insane "Mike's Song" during the last show of the spring tour. Touring fans were prepared for it, as the band previewed "Crossroads" inside of "Harpua" the night before. The song then disappeared until 10/11/95. In the middle of a second-set "Suzy Greenberg," the band teased the song, along with Cream's hit "Sunshine of Your Love," before breaking into a full-fledged "Crossroads" that shocked the crowd. The song appeared sporadically throughout the remainder of the fall of 1995 (including an appearance inside "You Enjoy Myself" at The Fox Theatre in Atlanta on November 10) before being shelved for all of 1996. Subsequently played thrice in 1997 and once in 1998 (plus a performance at the 4/17/98 Tubes show), the song has become a rare concert treat.

Cry Baby Cry

Original Artist: The Beatles
Original Album: *The Beatles* **(aka "The White Album") (1968)**
Phish Album: *Hampton Comes Alive* **(11/21/98)**
Vocals: Trey (lead), Page (backing)
Debut: 10/31/94
Historian: Mark Toscano

The band apparently liked covering this one on Halloween 1994, because it showed up a few more times (11/22/94, 6/16/95, and 11/21/98). Although the 10/31/94 version (true to the "White Album" itself) also featured the "Brother can you take me back" refrain that precedes "Revolution 9," subsequent solo versions did not.

Cryin'

Original Artist: Aerosmith
Original Album: *Get a Grip* **(1993)**
Vocals: Fish
Debut: 9/29/95
Historian: Chris Bertolet

What is it about Southern California that brings out the beast in Jon Fishman?

Cast aside the balmy climes and stunning vistas—SoCal natives have been graced with some of the rarest and most sex-drenched performances that Henrietta, Jon Fishman's vaguely disturbing alter-Id, has ever crafted. To wit: he's asked the provocative musical question, "Why Don't We Do It In The Road?" (Santa Monica, 12/10/94), and exposed his naughty bits to the front rows during his positively lascivious debut of "Sexual Healing" (Ventura, 7/20/98). Is he trying to get laid, or arrested?

At Hollywood's picturesque Greek Theatre on 9/29/95, though, the muumuu'd one proved a less-than-attentive lover. Gazing wistfully into the tall pines, Fish took center stage with a sheet of lyrics to deliver Aerosmith's rawking paean to fractured romance—and promptly lost his place. Undaunted, however, Henrietta recalled The Cardinal Rule of Divadom: when in doubt, gyrate.

And gyrate he did. Unfortunately (or, perhaps, thankfully), Phish has yet to reprise "Cryin."

The Curtain

AKA: "The Curtain (With)" (title of original version)
Music/Lyrics: Trey Anastasio, Marc Daubert
Album: (none)
Vocals: Mike, Page, Trey
Debut: 8/9/87
Historian: Mark Toscano

Phish has been playing "The Curtain" since 1987. However, until late 1988 it was noticeably longer than it is now. In fact, in its infancy, "The Curtain" was quite the epic composition. With the average version ending somewhere around the 15-minute mark, this tune—like "Fluffhead" and "Reba"—challenged Phish to sustain their early audiences' attention.

The lyrics were written by Trey's friend Marc Daubert. Although "Daubs" had actually been in Phish at one point—playing percussion at some of their very first gigs—he was no longer a bandmember by the time "The Curtain" entered the rotation.

This early version of "The Curtain" was also referred to by a different name: "The Curtain (With)." Post-1988 versions of the song are comprised of an intro, Daubs' lyrics, a composed section of moderate length, and a repeat of the intro to close out the song. However, earlier versions feature a two-part instrumental opus that followed this cohesive construction. This instrumental section consisted of a composed bit and a jamming bit. The composed bit will definitely sound familiar to most fans. After it was lopped off of the end of "The Curtain" in 1988, it eventually found its way into the song "Rift," where it remains to this day. (This version of "Rift"—Trey's second, more successful attempt at writing music to Tom's wonderful lyrics—premiered on 3/6/92.) This "Rift" segment was then followed by a beautiful and soaring jam, featuring liquid tones from Trey and lots of electric piano from Page. For some strong versions of "The Curtain (With)," check out 8/21/87, 8/29/87, 5/15/88, and 5/25/88. Additionally, a studio version of the song recorded in June of 1987 in Mike's grandmother's basement was released by the band as a promo for the mp3 sale of "The White Tape."

In its post-"Rift" incarnation, "The Curtain" has usually served as a springboard for other songs. Everything from "Bouncing" (11/4/90) to "Tweezer" (many times) to "Julius" (12/28/95) to "A Letter to Jimmy Page" (7/5/94) to "Blackbird" (11/22/94) has followed the restrained tones of "The Curtain."

Like many of the band's older tunes, "The Curtain" has been played less and less in recent years. Following a glut of performances in 1995 and 1996, "The Curtain" made it to the stage only three times in 1997, twice in 1998, and three times in 1999. In addition to those listed above, quality post-1988 versions include 2/24/89, 11/4/90, 12/11/95, 12/14/95, 8/6/96, 12/30/99, 7/7/00, 7/12/00, 9/17/00, and 9/30/00. The last three of these versions deserve extra-special mention, however. After performing "The Curtain" in its truncated incarnation with no deviation since 1988, the band broke out the original, big-daddy "The Curtain (With)" for these three performances. Though all are worth hearing, 7/12/00 is an awesome reading of the song, long since considered extinct, and the obtaining of a copy is highly recommended.

Finally, if you're confused about the song's lyrics, don't worry—you're not the first. They are darkly surreal, with a few tips-of-the-hat to the absurd. Trey even offers a potential explanation of them at the 8/21/87 Ian's Farm show, but whether or not you actually believe they're about Jim Bakker is up to you.

See Also: "Rift"

CURTIS LOEW (see: "THE BALLAD OF CURTIS LOEW")

Cut My Hair
Original Artist: The Who
Original Album: *Quadrophenia* (1973)
Vocals: Page
Debut: 10/31/95
Historian: Craig DeLucia

This song about the pains of "fitting in" was played during Phish's performance of The Who's *Quadrophenia.*

Dahlia
AKA: "Done Me Wrong"
Music/Lyrics: Steve Pollak
Original Artist: The Dude of Life (with Phish)
Original Album: *Crimes of the Mind* (1994)
Vocals: The Dude of Life (lead), Phish (backing)
Debut: 9/13/90
Historian: Dan Mielcarz

Played only once, on 9/13/90 (at the Wetlands in NYC) during a Dude of Life guest appearance, "Dahlia" deals with a relationship that ended badly for both parties. Written by the Dude with music arranged by Phish, "Dahlia" is the opening song on the Dude's first album *Crimes of the Mind*, which was recorded in August of 1991. Because the album wasn't released until 1994, "Dahlia" was incorrectly known as "Done Me Wrong," for the intervening years. Checking out the Wetlands show is recommended, due to the many other songs debuted that night.

Daniel (Saw the Stone)
AKA: "Daniel"
Music/Lyrics: (traditional)
Vocals: Mike, Page, Trey
Debut: 7/15/93
Historian: Ellis Godard

Instrumentally, Phish's version of "Daniel (Saw the Stone)" is faithful to the customary, upbeat, bluegrass spiritual. Lyrically, however, they

Peter Sitzman

trim the spiritual a bit. For example, they repeat "Daniel saw the stone" in each chorus, rather than the customary changes (to "Jesus was the stone" and "I found the stone") without which the (rock of ages, born again) meaning is unclear. Poetic justice to the song's originators (who found a home in Jesus), Phish had trouble finding a home for the song in play order—unlike many songs which might be typical openers, typical encores, or typical late-in-second-set meat. Its first three appearances were as a first set closer, a second set opener, and in the middle of a three-song encore. Several solid versions were nestled in the second set, such as after "Purple Rain" and before "Good Times Bad Times." However, versions did not vary greatly, in accuracy or energy, such that the two memorable versions are not memorable for how they were played at all: 8/21/93 (which featured the Flecktones) and 7/31/93 (which followed the religious lyrics with ACDC's "Highway to Hell"). The consistency must have bored the band: After fourteen appearances on the (33-show) Summer 1993 tour, including both the first and last nights (7/15 and 8/28), "Daniel" was soundchecked several times on 12/28/93 and then slipped away, returning only once, to open the second set of 2/23/97 at the Italian Fillmore.

Dark Side of the Moon (1973)
Original Artist: Pink Floyd
Historian: Mark Toscano

As the story goes, Pink Floyd were interested in creating another concept show for their live performances, with a new album as the possible end result. They were fascinated with the idea of a song cycle held together by interweaving themes of various madnesses, and started working on material for the show. All of the songs that would end up on the album *Dark Side of the Moon* were debuted as a concept piece during 1971, save "Speak To Me" and "The Great Gig in the Sky," which were absent, and "On the Run," which was a completely different song at this stage. The show proved very successful, and the band fine-tuned the songs and tweaked them over the next year and a half before settling on the final draft version of would ultimately become one of the biggest-selling albums in music history.

DSOTM spent a record 724 consecutive weeks (until 4/23/88) in the American Top-200 and is practically regarded as the Holy Bible of Rock by fans around the world. It took nine months to record and produce, but the arduous work was worth it, as it gave Pink Floyd their first number one album in the U.S. and spent two full years on the top charts in Great Britain. The band premiered the polished, completed, live version of the album at London Planetarium in March of 1973, and the rest is history. It remained a standard fixture of their live show through the '70s until the 1977 *Animals* tour. Still, the (brain) damage had been done, and Pink Floyd and *Dark Side of the Moon* never lost their status as household name.

As the story goes, Phish decided to perform this inimitable album at dinnertime the night of the 11/2/98 Salt Lake show. Come on. I mean really, is this not the greatest band in the history of life?

The band's 10/31/98 show was so highly anticipated due to the lack of a 1997 'ween show, that the scene was more than a little crazy. Following this madness, Phish was ecstatic to hit Salt Lake City, where they were scheduled to play a half-sold-out show at the E Centre. Mike and Trey kicked it at the Dead Goat, a local tavern where they made some friends and had a great time drinking and playing music. The op-

portunity to loosen up for 11/2/98 was such a welcome change from the oppressive chaos of Vegas, that the guys decided to throw Salt Lake a major honkin' bone.

After the decision was made, Brad Sands was sent to find a copy of the album at a local music shop so the songs could be learned and some samples and tape loops could be borrowed for the performance. The band practiced before the show and between sets, and got the album down pretty nicely, realizing that a "Harpua" story was the prefect way to frame it, in light of the 12/6/96 Vegas "Harpua" that unknowingly set the stage.

Most fans were already satisfied by the chunky first and second sets, including the killer "Tube" -> "Drowned" that will likely go down in the history books. However, when "Harpua's" signature "oom-pah-pah" started up, the smallish crowd went crazy, certain something wild and wooly was up. They were right. This "Harpua" left Poster Nutbag alone and told the story of Jimmy, and how he found it too crazy in Vegas, and decided to take a cab back to Salt Lake City. On the way, the cabbie popped in a tape—a certain album—and the two of them sat back and enjoyed a nice, beautiful ride. Not one to mince words, Trey's point was proven as the band unloaded into "Breathe" following the P.A. performance of "Speak To Me" directly off the disc. The entirety of the album followed, and the crowd was pretty much flabbergasted. All the surprise inherent in the Halloween idea had been sucked dry from Vegas and injected into the salt flats of northern Utah. The neat segue back into "Harpua" following "Eclipse" was the cherry on the sundae—it didn't even matter that the encore was another Phishy surprise, Nirvana's "Smells Like Teen Spirit." In fact, that cover has been almost routinely ignored due to the overpowering presence of its full-blown competitor.

I'll be the first to say it: the performance was good, but not great, and kind of sloppy. I'll also be the first to say that this is almost entirely irrelevant. It didn't matter whether Phish played it OK or phenomenally well. They PLAYED it. They said, "why not?" and we said "why not INDEED!" Many share my opinion that the simple idea of Phish doing this cemented their status as some of the best entertainers in music today, and it didn't even require a flying hot dog or a Van Der Graaf generator to do so. The idea alone was enough.

Otherwise, a posteriori reactions were only slightly mixed; some fans were actually pissed off that the band had "betrayed" them by pulling such a dastardly trick, but most fans thought those people were idiots and realized that Phish was indeed gigantically huge. The show was immediately noted as officially "sacred," in the relevant books, and even Floyd fans were thrown for a loop. Bootleg CDs of the show approached a ubiquitous level and many fans still insisted that it couldn't possibly have happened.

It happened, though. It happened more or less between dinner and bedtime on November 2nd, 1998. Phish succeeded in their long-term plan to conquer the world.

Dave's Energy Guide
AKA: "DEG"
Music: Dave Abrahams, Trey Anastasio, Jon Fishman
Album: "The White Tape" (excerpt)
Vocals: (instrumental)
Debut: 5/3/85
Historian: Dave Abrahams/Mark Toscano

A lot of folks think this tune is basically the digital delay loops jams that Trey occasionally initiates in an especially exploratory set (see 5/7/94 "Tweezer," 12/29/94 "David Bowie," etc.). However, this is not the case. "Dave's Energy Guide," named for Dave Abrahams, Trey's friend and the co-writer of the tune, has nothing to do with digital delay loop jams. It is a composed piece of music reminiscent of King Crimson's "Discipline," (from the album of the same name).

Trey has made no secret of his respect and admiration for Robert Fripp, the guitar player and composer extraordinaire behind King Crimson, a band that has always been on the cutting edge of rock-prog-proto-electronic-noise. However, it was Trey's friend Dave, also a big Crim-head, who invented the initial "DEG" theme after being blown away at an early '80s Crimson concert he attended with Tom Marshall. Seeking to emulate Robert Fripp's intricate, precise picking patterns in his own guitar style, Dave created the first "DEG" theme as an practice exercise. The pattern he composed—designed around a 5-6-5-7 structure—is built out of repeating parts, which are extended to always keep the total number of notes between repeats at an odd number.

One summer in the mid-'80s, Dave and Trey attended the National Guitar Summer Workshop. On one of the performance nights, they decided to play the still-unnamed song, with one guitar playing 5-6-5-7, and the other playing 5-6-5-6. This way, although the two lines would usually be out of synch, they would cohere every 22 repetitions. The performance went miserably, and with the revelation that their song was, in Dave's words, "formulaic b.s.," they left the venue exhilarated.

Soon after Phish was formed, Trey happened to catch sight of none other than Jon Fishman at a party playing a diamond-shaped pattern on an acoustic guitar. Trey immediately seized upon this theme and incorporated it into what would then be called "Dave's Energy Guide." The "Energy Guide" portion of the title derives from a yellow, diamond-shaped, municipal utilities sign that Trey hung on his mic stand during some early performances of the song. Additionally, Trey explains on 5/3/85 that the "Energy Guide" is provided for those poor souls having trouble "directing their energy." (but seriously, folks....)

The "Energy Guide" has never been found too commonly on its own in a setlist; it usually comes about as the product of an especially exploratory jam. Some fine examples of the tune include 4/29/87 (excellent version segues out of "Melt the Guns"!), 8/6/88 (sandwiched by a shimmyin' "Cities"), and 9/13/88 (between "Cities" and "Antelope" and in the middle of "BBFCFM"!). The song became increasingly less visible through the late '80s, and was more or less extinguished as a full-performed entity by 1988. However, this wasn't the end of the "Energy Guide." Miniature jams of the song or quotes of one or more of its themes showed up with alarming frequency in the late '80s and early '90s, most notably on 10/31/89 (in "Bowie"), 11/30/89 ("Split"), 3/29/91 ("Tweezer"), 7/14/91 ("Possum"), 4/21/92 ("Possum"), 4/20/92 ("YEM"), 12/30/93 ("Bowie"), 6/14/94 ("Possum" yet again), 6/16/94 ("Stash"), and 6/18/94 ("Bowie"). The second half of the '90s saw even less of "DEG," though teases and jams did occur in the 6/28/95 "Tweezer," the 7/22/95 "Maze," the 12/1/95 "Stash," the 3/1/97 "Wolfman's," the 4/4/98 "Brother," and the 11/29/98 "Possum."

David Bowie

AKA: "Bowie"
Music/Lyrics: Trey Anastasio
Album: *Junta*

Vocals: Mike, Page, Trey
Debut: 10/31/86
Historian: Chris Bertolet

Fishman's tick-tock cymbal intro to "David Bowie" is to the loyal Phishhead what the toll of a bell was to Pavlov's famous dogs. Much like the noted animal behaviorist, the casual observer at a Phish show might witness panting, howling—even cascading rivulets of drool—as the subjects anticipate the orgy of catharsis that awaits.

"Bowie," one of Phish's most beloved and ambitious compositions, is a lengthy, complex and challenging piece that snakes its way through many rhythmic and tonal motifs before dropping precipitously into ominous jamspace. The signature hi-hat prelude cuts through an oft-extended passage of space and dissonance (and provides one of Phish's favorite places to sneak in secret language cues). At the end of the intro, Trey signals his bandmates with a scratch on his strings, and they're off. Though the spare, Zen-like lyrics that follow are said to hail the glam-rock icon's 40th birthday, the song's sound and musical spirit bear little relation to David Bowie's own work.

Typical "Bowie" jams are patient, crescendo-driven exercises in tension and release that consume themselves in a white-hot conflagration of rapid-fire guitar, effects, and feedback. On a special night, however, the epic gives birth to fearless, hairpin improvisation—the kind of fiery, "type-II" jamming that singes eyebrows and drops jaws.

Two such "Bowies," played just over a month apart, tend to vie among fans for best-ever status: the 11/26/94 Orpheum colossus and the 12/29/94 Providence masterpiece. Both of them clock in at roughly half an hour, both are ravenously eclectic and adventurous, and both echo similar themes along their twisting paths. While the Orpheum version climaxes in a dirty, propulsive groove that seems to foreshadow Phish's Talking Heads period, the Providence "Bowie" detonates in a blitzkrieg of arena rawk fury. Perhaps because of the overall quality of the show, or perhaps because of its unmistakably Phishy non-sequiturs (Trey moans, "Come home, Lassie," in the middle of the jam), Providence tends to nose out the Orpheum in the average fan's estimation.

Other remarkable versions of "David Bowie" abound, of course. Neophytes should start with the crisp and concise album version to get a feel for where composition ends and improvisation begins. Once you've got the lay of the land, check out the aggressive 4/17/92 Warfield version, which contains a "Catapult," and stands as one of the finest jams in a stellar west coast run. You might want to graduate from there to the 6/18/94 UIC "Bowie," which opens with a dramatic "Mind Left Body Jam" and samples "Simple" before splintering into angry chaos. For a contemporary taste, consider the surgical strike of the 6/30/98 Copenhagen "Bowie," which takes mere minutes to set fire to the Grey Hall.

The "Bowie" jam, being airy and unstructured, lends itself to entertaining teases and segues. The stupendous 5/8/93 UNH version sandwiches a rare "Have Mercy," and features a tease of the Allman Brothers' "Jessica." The 7/3/95 Stowe version opens with extended "Timber Ho!" quotes from Trey before the band finally dives into "Bowie" proper; the ensuing improv barrels into the debut cover of "Johnny B. Goode," then double-barrels right back into "Bowie." The 7/30/97 Ventura monster finds the band steering the jam into an unusually chunky groove, modulating into the first "Cities" on U.S. soil in nearly nine years, then following the trail of embers back into "Bowie" for a balls-out finish.

For reasons untold, Philadelphia's CoreStates Spectrum has seen its share of deliciously warped "Bowies." Page plays a stadium synth

David Bowie

Compiled by Jason Rose

Date	Composed	Jam	Trill	Total	Comments
10/31/86	:21	4:22	7:12	10:12	Earliest known live version.
12/06/86	:34	4:13	14:26	16:08	Strong early version.
10/31/87	:21	4:06	12:04	12:45	Average, typical early version.
??/??/88	:10	4:03	10:14	10:55	*Junta* Version. Still the favorite of some fans.
03/11/88	1:49	5:32	15:23	16:07	Sunshine of Your Love, Timber Ho, Alumni Blues, and Whipping Post are all teased in the opening segment.
04/20/89	1:22	5:05	12:30	13:15	"Frosty the Snowman" and "Santa Claus is Coming to Town" riffs played during the opening.
08/26/89	1:00	4:26	11:37	13:32	Nice jam segment with cool Doppler effects.
10/21/89	2:33	6:10	13:47	15:27	Humorous stage banter. Ninja Mike.
10/26/89	1:42	5:14	16:17	17:12	David Bowie's "Major Tom" teased during opening.
10/31/89	2:15	6:05	19:38	21:04	Mac and cheese distributed to crowd during the hi-hat intro for percussive accompaniment. Awesome jam segment with some DEG jamming.
11/30/89	1:23	4:55	12:36	13:08	Strong shredding from Trey. "Mr.PC" tease.
10/30/90	2:33	6:04	11:30	12:30	Intriguing opening with numerous teases.
12/07/90	1:03	4:35	11:40	13:02	Jam segment has lots of DEG-ish breakdowns and releases, but no clear DEG tease. Trey is on fire!
02/03/91	1:27	5:07	12:12	13:13	Killer jam! Short but purposeful, with lots of little grooves and a really cool breakdown jam.
02/15/91	1:15	4:49	11:07	12:07	Tease of Simon and Garfunkel's "Sound of Silence." Great jam with interesting silent moments.
03/23/91	:59	4:31	10:38	11:39	Minor DEG stylings, but overall a sub-par version.
07/19/91	:52	4:24	9:57	11:00	Giant Country Horns make this otherwise average version special.
10/24/91	3:13	6:42	12:51	14:12	Cool opening segment with some signals. Strong jam with a frightening ending.
10/28/91	2:29	5:49	11:12	12:11	Strong early '90s version. Fierce groove from the band, with Trey providing much of the dissonance.
03/21/92	1:53	5:23	12:50	13:48	Amusing stage banter.
04/17/92	2:04	5:25	11:58	14:22	Exceptional version with amazing trill section which alternates with verses of Catapult!
05/16/92	2:16	5:43	11:53	13:07	Heavy focus on classic rock jamming.
11/27/92	2:01	5:32	13:05	14:07	Teasing of Johnny Cash's "I Walk the Line."
02/13/93	:56	4:12	8:30	9:40	Ridiculously fast version! Novelty performance.
03/12/93	1:49	5:04	10:47	12:15	Fast and fierce guitar playing keep this obnoxious and over the top version listenable.
04/10/93	2:34	5:50	13:44	15:15	Many Phish tunes are teased in this exceptional version, including Chalk Dust, Uncle Pen, My Friend, Coil, Split Open and Melt, Lawnboy, and Sparkle. There are also a few signals.
08/13/93	4:07	7:28	17:35	19:07	Awesome jam segment with a Mango->Magilla jam!
08/21/93	:52	4:18	14:49	15:47	Simpsons signal. Crazy and intense jam segment with lots of descending chromatics and big dynamic drops, cool percussion, and funky bass lines added by the Flecktones. Incredible version.
04/17/94	1:25	4:42	12:20	13:14	Average version salvaged by cool deconstruction-style delay of the ending.
05/03/94	1:28	4:58	10:54	11:34	Multiple teases during the opening hi-hat segment, including Black & White and Sunshine of Your Love.

(continued on the next page)

"Take Me Out To The Ballgame" over the lengthy prelude to the 12/3/97 version, which also features "Simpsons" language and a sprawling, melodic jam dripping with group improvisation (and a buttery segue into "Possum," taboot). The 12/10/99 Philly version meanders into yet another "Have Mercy" before reprising the "Bowie" theme, reggae-style. In lieu of a fireworks finale, the jam melts into a tropical island reading of "HYHU."

A Day in the Life

Original Artist: The Beatles
Original Album: *Sgt. Pepper's Lonely Hearts Club Band* (1967)
Vocals: Page, Trey
Debut: 6/10/95

Historian: Mark Toscano

The tune—considered by many to be one of the Beatles' greatest—was first covered by Phish at Red Rocks on 6/10/95, and was in regular rotation for the next year. It dropped off in frequency by 1997, though it continues to make an occasional appearance. Some strong versions include the debut, as well as 11/11/95 and 12/8/95. This latter show featured the song as an encore along with "Come Together," played in honor of the 15th anniversary of John Lennon's death.

DAY-O (see "BANANA BOAT SONG (DAY-O)")

Dazed and Confused

Music/Lyrics: Jimmy Page

David Bowie (continued)

Date	Composed	Jam	Trill	Total	Comments
05/27/94	:57	4:31	11:35	13:12	Strong, slightly above average version.
06/14/94	:58	4:30	11:10	12:24	Notable for intermittent DEG teases.
06/18/94	5:00	8:34	16:44	18:21	Beautiful, descending four chord "Mind Left Body Jam"-like progression in the hi-hat intro. "Three Blind Mice"-like riffing segues into melodic hose, which in turn becomes a DEG-flavored, thrilling jam. "Voodoo Chile" and "Foxey Lady" teases in closing segment. A fan favorite.
10/12/94	1:08	4:42	16:22	17:20	Powerful jam segment.
10/22/94	1:05	4:37	12:13	13:31	Nothing spectacular, but above average.
11/17/94	1:02	4:33	15:02	15:56	Awesome jam, typical of November '94. DEG-ish jams and huge tension/release builds and drops.
11/20/94	:45	4:07	15:36	16:53	Excellent, thrilling jam serves as a perfect primer for the monster version to follow a week later.
11/26/94	1:08	4:51	—	~38	Very improvisational. A Work of Art.
12/02/94	3:03	6:29	20:23	22:04	Cool, moody opening. Great jam has some cool experimental teasing and jazzy improv. Major deviations from the typical Bowie jam and rhythm. Horns enter into the picture for a majestic and triumphant trill segment. Must-hear!
12/29/94	4:24	7:57	33:51	34:51	Orchestral, transcendent. Digital delay loop jam intro, whistling/Lassie section, vocal jamming on "Do It NOW." A legendary version you must hear.
06/19/95	1:43	5:14	21:53	23:32	Long jam segment. Unfocused feel, however.
06/24/95	2:11	5:38	21:12	24:05	Dark, dissonant, "Spooky," Floydian-Metal-Space.
07/03/95	2:21	5:52	29:55	31:15	Heavy Bathtub Gin teasing and Johnny B. Goode!
10/08/95	1:11	4:34	12:36	13:52	Strong version with focused build.
10/15/95	:18	3:47	13:41	14:38	Average, typically great Fall 1995 version.
10/21/95	1:22	4:34	14:39	15:50	Somewhat above-average, Trey dominated.
10/27/95	2:32	5:58	17:20	18:38	Mysterious chant-like jam.
11/11/95	3:01	6:32	16:35	17:47	Dark, riveting, captivating jam.
12/01/95	2:09	5:31	12:45	14:00	Excellent hi-hat segment featuring Catapult verses and Simpsons humor and signals. Fierce *Junta*-like jam builds to an excellent climax.
12/11/95	5:06	8:30	22:18	23:29	Thrilling.
04/26/96	1:05	4:28	12:26	13:44	Caravan quoting.
11/19/96	2:33	5:52	16:25	17:53	Spacey, meandering jam segment.
02/23/97	1:11	4:28	13:57	15:28	Tight, focused jam reminiscent of early versions.
06/20/97	1:20	4:51	18:07	19:25	Long, trance-like old-school jam leads into a more provocative, experimental jam before unexpectedly exploding into the trill segment.
07/26/97	6:10	9:30	18:56	20:28	Dynamically strong jam with focused playing by Trey. Bob Gulotti on a second set of drums!
12/03/97	5:19	8:48	—	26:26	"Take Me Out to the Ballgame" tease and Simpsons signal in intro. Exciting jam segues into Possum.
07/31/99	:19	4:00	22:18	24:04	Unleashed in the East. Run to the Hills.
12/31/99	2:55	6:30	19:28	21:04	Transcendent, passionate version—not bad for 4:20 in the morning!
06/23/00	1:47	5:21	12:21	13:39	Terrifying, thrilling, run for your life.
06/30/00	:27	4:09	11:29	13:23	Bewilderingly intense improv!
10/07/00	:35	3:56	11:19	12:32	Short, but screams for vengeance.

Original Artist: Led Zeppelin
Original Album: *Led Zeppelin* **(1969)**
Vocals: Trey (?)
Debut: 5/21/89
Historian: Mark Toscano and Craig DeLucia

Phish had an affinity for Led Zeppelin covers in the late-eighties, trying a handful of them on stage but only sticking with "Good Times Bad Times" for any extended period. "Dazed and Confused," one of Zeppelin's early anthems, made it to the Phish stage on one known occasion, following a novice "Split Open and Melt." Coming nothing near the rock majesty of the epic *Song Remains the Same* version, Phish's rendition is, as always, worth discovering for novelty value.

Dear Prudence
Original Artist: The Beatles
Original Album: *The Beatles* **(aka "The White Album") (1968)**
Vocals: Page (lead), Mike, Trey (backing)
Debut: 10/31/94
Historian: Mark Toscano

Due to a deceptive sound bite from Pink Floyd's "Speak to Me" (from *Dark Side of the Moon*), it wasn't until Phish began the second song on the Beatles' "White Album" that many fans' suspicions on Halloween 1994 were confirmed: the band was actually playing the entire "White Album." This gentle tune was originally written about Mia

Farrow's sister, and Phish imbued their cover with appropriate delicacy and sweetness

Dear Mrs. Reagan

AKA: "Mrs. Reagan"
Music/Lyrics: Phish (?)
Album: (none)
Vocals: Trey, Page
Debut: 9/27/85
Historian: Ellis Godard

Sometimes attributed to Trey Anastasio but officially believed to have been written by Phish as a group, "Dear Mrs. Reagan" is so different from anything else by the band, particularly at that time, that some suspect a lost lyricist credit. Although the live debut was 9/27/85 and recordings span from 11/84 to 6/88, Mike's journals suggest that the song began its evolution around October 1984, during the peak of the Reagan-Mondale presidential race.

Contrary to these uncertainties, there are no hidden meanings or metaphors in these most political lyrics of Phish's originals: the song lambasts President Ronald Reagan's wife Nancy for her stance on drugs (remember "Just say no"?), suggests that she secretly wields power behind the overly-promoted actor, and commands her to "gun your husband down" in order to save the country. She didn't, and the song has not been performed since Reagan VP George Bush won the 1988 election.

Unrelated to Woody Guthrie's "Dear Mrs. Roosevelt," the song is said to parody Dylan tunes of the '60s, and Trey is said to sound like Dylan on early versions, particularly 4/1/86 and 4/15/86, both of which feature Trey introducing Phish as the Bob Dylan Band. The only pattern apparent from the nine known live performances is that the song came late in shows, closing three second sets (4/1/86, 8/10/87, and 6/15/88) and second-to-last in two other shows (9/27/85 and 4/24/87). Fans of Ronald Reagan may want to check out the film *Bedtime For Bonzo*, a stirring classic that pits Ronnie against the unpredictable wiles of a naughty little chimp.

Demand

Music: Trey Anastasio
Lyrics: Tom Marshall
Album: *Hoist*
Vocals: Page, Trey
Debut: 4/9/94
Historian: Ellis Godard

Demand is a typical Trey composition (complex but not really "fugue-like," as the band has described it) accompanied by quirky Marshall lyrics. But unlike those Tom/Trey collaborations that balloon into improvisation themselves, "Demand" often only precedes some other jamming tune. The debut (4/9/94) turned into a fabulous freeform "Weekapaug Groove," in a set that involved much audience interaction. After being soundchecked three times on 5/20/94, the song took on a looseness that, for example, rendered a surprise segue into "Sloth" (5/22/94), a nice shift to "Maze" (10/24/95), and a quick ragtime transition to "Antelope" (11/14/96).

In only fourteen appearances (9 in 94, 4 in 95, 1 in 96), it has thrice opened a memorable set and has usually launched songs like

"David Bowie," "Run Like An Antelope," or "Split Open and Melt."

Indeed, its appearance on *Hoist* included "Split" in the same track. After "Demand" ends, someone can be heard entering a car and putting a tape in the stereo. Then ensues the jam segment from the 4/21/93 "Split," an instrumental mix of 4/4 and 9/8 time signatures which build in intensity until interrupted by a crash very similar to the start of the original "And So To Bed." This crash is followed by a splicing of two versions of Phish performing Naomi Shemer's "Y-Rushalayim Schel Zahav." According to an interview with Fishman on the afternoon prior to "Demand's" debut, this ending prayer is "like the voice is rising to heaven…the spirit rising out of his body." Fishman also mentioned in that interview that "Split" was the favorite song of a fan who died in a car wreck, and that her friends wrote Phish a letter to that effect, but that the track was set before that letter arrived.

The full *Hoist* track ("Demand" > "Split" > "Yerush") has happened twice. 6/26/94 is widely recognized, since it occurred during the complete performance of the album, but the ensuing "Split" on 9/14/94 is much more intense. Some of the best versions came in the fall of 1995, in a legendary series of incredible shows. "Demand" has been followed by a nonjamming tune only once ("Sparkle" at 10/8/95), though at that point it was a breakout (having not been played for 97 shows), as it is now primed to be again (having not been played since 11/14/96).

See Also: "Split Open and Melt"

Destiny Unbound

Music/Lyrics: Mike Gordon
Album: (none)
Vocals: Mike, Page. Trey
Debut: 9/14/90
Historian: Ellis Godard

Destiny Unbound is about a road tripping duo, Bill and Jill, who find the street isn't paved. But the title belies its wavering history and uncertain disappearance.

It appeared in several "out there" shows, such as 2/7/91 (also including the debut of "Tweezer Reprise" and yet another "Lizards" lyrics flub by Trey) and 4/11/91 (known mostly for the "Prison Joke" in the encore, but laudable throughout for song selection and conviction). It was reworked several times (compare 9/14/90, 2/14/91, and 4/19/91) and finally found a home (following "Landlady" for ten of its seventeen appearances) in the solid grooves of the Fall Tour of 1991.

Though often a launching pad for heavy improv (followed by tunes like "Harry Hood," "You Enjoy Myself," and "Mike's Song"), the song itself is bouncy but heavily scripted. Although this writer has never understood the connection (musically, rhythmically, lyrically, or otherwise), one of the members of Phish apparently thinks "Destiny Unbound" sounds too much like a Grateful Dead tune. As such, it has become the ultimate rarity. Trey has joked that Phish will perform the tune when, upon the band coming to stage, the entire audience sings the first verse in unison. Several valiant efforts by front rows have been to no avail (though the band did acknowledge the 11/21/97 attempt), and the song has not been heard since 11/15/91.

Diamond Girl

Original Artist: Seals and Crofts
Original Album: *Diamond Girl* (1973)

Vocals: The Dude of Life
Debut: 12/31/92
Historian: Phil Nazzaro

How do you make a potentially goofy cover even more goofy? Well, you invite the Dude of Life to sing the vocals, throw rubber chickens into the crowd, and have him bring his lawnmower. That's exactly how The Dude presented this one-time cover when he performed this song with Phish at the legendary 12/31/92 show. If you would like to hear a bit of this 1970s nostalgia, either seek out a copy of the New Years '92 show, or pay close attention to the Muzak playing in your dentist's office next time you're getting a cavity filled. You're sure to find it in either place.

Dinner And A Movie

AKA: "Dinner"
Music: Trey Anastasio
Lyrics: The Dude of Life
Album: *Junta*
Vocals: Phish
Debut: 11/19/87
Historian: charlz franz

Dinner and a Movie is an odd little ditty. Early versions consisted primarily of different vocalizations of its one line, "Let's go out to dinner and see a movie." Backing music, sighs, and the occasional scream have been added to fill it out. Fishman commented before the 5/18/91 New York, NY version that "Dinner" celebrated "America's favorite pre-nuptial ritual."

Played fairly frequently in 1989 through 1992, its appearances have diminished since, as the band members agree that its one-joke nature has worn thin. It often served as a first set opener or was paired with "Bouncing." "Dinner" was resurrected for the 3/1/97 Hamburg, Germany show, but that version was not selected for inclusion on *Slip, Stitch and Pass*.

4/18/92 Palo Alto, CA is a particularly good version (an excellent soundboard of this show circulates) which precedes an incredible "Harry Hood." The 7/11/91 Burlington, VT and 7/15/91 New York, NY versions with The Giant Country Horns are worth digesting as well.

Dirt

Music: Trey Anastasio
Lyrics: Tom Marshall, Scott Herman
Album: *Farmhouse*
Vocals: Trey (lead), Mike, Page (backing)
Debut: 6/14/97
Historian: Bradley Lonard

When it made its live debut in Dublin during the 1997 summer tour of Europe, "Dirt" struck many as a throwback to the ballad style of *Billy Breathes*. Dig a little deeper, though; "Dirt" is of a darker hue than anything on that album, with lyrics full of images of failed love and death (plus it gives the band another chance to whistle). Played frequently in 1997, "Dirt" has "grown" very little. Good versions include 8/17/97 Great Went (Page in fine form here) and 11/19/97 Champaign (a melancholic version that sits surprisingly well between "Llama" and "Limb By Limb").

The Dirty Jobs

Original Artist: The Who
Original Album: *Quadrophenia* (1973)
Vocals: Page
Debut: 10/31/95
Historian: Craig DeLucia

This song provides for a pivotal moment in *Quadrophenia*, as the narrator, Jimmy, is frightened by the possible futures that lay on his current path. Punctuated by horns, Phish performed the song as part of their rendition of the album in Chicago on Halloween, 1995. True to the album, the horns led the band from "Jobs" into "Helpless Dancer."

The Divided Sky

AKA: "Divided," "Sky"
Music: Trey Anastasio
Lyrics: Trey Anastasio, Marc Daubert, Tom Marshall
Album: "The White Tape" (intro only);
    Junta; Hampton Comes Alive (11/21/98)
Vocals: Mike, Page, Trey
Debut: 8/9/87
Historian: Syd Schwartz

One of the most revered songs in the Phish canon, "Divided Sky" has been responsible for converting many people into Phans. The version of "Divided Sky" that appears on *Junta* marks a distinct compositional time period for Trey (though its roots are much older), and while never a vehicle for experimental improvisation, it has provided ample opportunity for each of the band members to develop unique solos as tangents within the framework.

As told by Trey, "Divided Sky" was written at the Rhombus (see the "Rhombus" entry in the Dictionary section) during Trey's first year at Mercer Community College with Tom Marshall and Marc Daubert on a night enhanced by psychedelic mushrooms. The precise circumstances remain sketchy; Trey has said it came about while looking at parting clouds, yet he has also said the chant originated during a bonfire inside the Rhombus while he Tom, Marc and perhaps others were playing a percussion jam on the outside of the Rhombus. It has also been said that Trey threw an acoustic guitar down on the ground and began beating on it chanting "Divided Sky." According to Tom Marshall, he, Trey and Marc began chanting it on top of the Rhombus after noticing that the sky appeared divided into a light half and a dark half caused by the lighting of a nearby chapel tower. The exact truth is likely lost forever in a haze of caps and stems, but the true origin of Divided Sky begins years earlier when Trey and his mother used to write Christmas songs. They had written a musical called "Gus the Christmas Dog," and two themes from that musical were lifted to form parts of "Divided Sky": "There's a Christmas Star" (which forms the melodic "lullaby" section) and "Gus" (which became the melody for the end of the song.)

In the first few performances of "Divided Sky," the ending was similar to the beginning but changed over the summer of 1987 to the version you hear today. "Divided Sky" (along with other Trey penned "epics" such as "You Enjoy Myself," "Fluffhead," "David Bowie," and "Reba") reflects the compositional influence of Ernie Stires and the main melody is one of the most recognizable instrumental hooks in the Phish repertoire.

Like "Punch You In The Eye," "Llama," and "McGrupp," "Divided

Sky" is not a part of Trey's "The Man Who Stepped Into Yesterday" Senior Study, but is included in the Gamehenge mythos. As written in the *Junta* liner notes, three individuals are chosen (through a Secret Agenda known only to a select few but the three are Mike, Trey and Page for the time being) to climb the rhombus in the middle of a field to offer tribute to Icculus by singing the chant, "Divided Sky, the wind blows high."

After the chant, Divided Sky goes into a section often referred to as the "Mary Had a Little Lamb" segment, which is comprised of an intricate note pattern over a shifting time signature—this segment is played, then played backwards (check your *Junta* CD at about 1:15 seconds into the song). Coming out of this jam into what Mike describes as a Pat Metheny-influenced section, Phish begins the build towards their "tension and release" style of playing, and culminating in a Trey-led section into the main theme of the song. After the main theme has been presented, there is a pause in the song before the note that completes the theme. Trey has described in several early 90s interviews that during this pause, he can hear the jam continuing in his head. He has also described the pause as an exercise in audience behavioral study, as the pause almost always results in three waves of audience cheers—the first soon after the pause, the second about 30 seconds later (this cheer often contains a certain degree of uncertainty and builds tension) and the final cheer being the release for the audience and the cue for Trey to hit the last note and continue into the song. The pause has gotten longer and longer over the years, to the point where some fans have become critical that the long pause "ruins the flow of the song."

"Divided Sky" also holds a unique place in Phishtory, as it is one of only two songs (the other being "Esther") that sparked a video treatment in the early 1990s. The same company who did the "Esther" video (played only once at the Sommerville Theatre in 1991) also presented an idea for a video for "Divided Sky" to the band. Allegedly, prototypes were designed by a woman associated with that video company for inclusion in the "Divided Sky" video but the green light to proceed was not forthcoming. The band at the time was considering including both videos on the Elektra reissue of *Junta*, but that ultimately never came to pass, and it is unlikely that Elektra had anything to do with the funding or making of either video.

Phish played "Divided Sky" very frequently from 1990 to 1994. 1995 and 1996 showed a distinct drop in frequency and the song is played only sporadically since, and with considerably less accuracy than the Phish of the early '90s. Notable versions include are 3/17/92, 7/15/92, 8/20/93, 10/31/94, 11/21/98 (on *HCA*), and 12/29/98.

It should also be noted that Blues Traveler's front man John Popper put lyrics to the main "Divided Sky" theme and contributed the resulting song Christmas to the album *A Very Special Christmas: Volume 3* which was released in 1997.

See Also: "Punch Me in the Eye"

DO MY TIME (see: "DOIN' MY TIME")

Doctor Jimmy

Original Artist: The Who
Original Album: *Quadrophenia* (1973)
Vocals: Page
Debut: 10/31/95
Historian: Craig DeLucia

In *Quadrophenia*'s most disturbing song, Jimmy explores the dangerous side of his personality that appears when he drinks. Phish performed the song as part of their 1995 Halloween musical costume, complete with horns.

Dog-Faced Boy

Music/Lyrics: Trey Anastasio, Jon Fishman, Tom Marshall, Page McConnell
Album: *Hoist*
Vocals: Trey (lead), Mike, Page (backing)
Debut: 4/14/94
Historian: Martin Acaster

Coming to terms with a lost love is never easy. Typically, if closure on the relationship is to be achieved, honest remorse for the actions that precipitated the split should be expressed. "Dog Faced Boy" is such an apology. The *Hoist* studio version consists of a plaintive acoustic melody picked out by a lonesome cowboy singing his cheating heart out to the gal from his rodeo circus clown past. He has neither the time nor the patience for the dog-faced and worm-infested carnival freaks of their past, would scarcely give up a lungful of air for a dying man, but would do anything to make things right for her. He done her wrong and it makes him feel sad. She deserved better and he wishes he could have always been it. In recapitulation of the past he hopes to build for himself a brighter future…if only she could accept the apology.

"Dog-Faced Boy" debuted at the Beacon Theater in New York (4/14/94) in its sparse acoustic, *Hoist*-like form. The song was played frequently throughout the spring, summer, and early fall of 1994 alternating between this acoustic version and an equally low-key electric rendition depending on its placement in the setlist. In keeping with the lyrics of the song, Phish has spared less and less time for the "Dog-Faced Boy," as he appeared only a handful of times during 1995 and only once or twice a year since then. Most notable performances of the song since 1994 are the 6/16/95 Walnut Creek show where Fishman false-started "Split Open and Melt" three times as an intro, an a capella version in the midst of the epic 11/14/95 Orlando "Stash," a whimpering pooch in a (reserved until "Squirming Coil") four song encore at the Bi-Lo Center on 11/18/98, the paisley coated "Dog-Faced Boy" ejected from the swirling maw of "Piper" the red, red, worm-girl of Cumberland County on 12/8/99, and the super blue and grassy version in a "Harry Hood" sandwich at the Amsouth Pavilion, in Antioch, TN on 6/22/00.

Dog Gone Dog

AKA: "Dog Log," "Dog Done Gone"
Music/Lyrics: Trey Anastasio
Album: "The White Tape"
Vocals: Trey (lead), Mike, Page (backing)
Debut: 10/30/85
Historian: Phillip Zerbo

In the history of Rock-and-Roll, there have been dozens of great songs about dogs: "Old King" by Neil Young, "Hey Bulldog" by Lennon/McCartney, "Fluffy" by Ween, "I Wanna Be Your Dog" by Iggy Pop, "Walkin' the Dog" by Rufus Thomas, "Seamus" by Pink Floyd, and who could ever forget the classic "Wylie" by Sissybar? Assuming their rightful place alongside these famous tributes to the canine are Phish's "Runaway Jim" and "Dog Log." "Dog Log" chronicles the habits of all

dogs, but specifically Trey's dog, Marley, a.k.a. "Mar Mar."

Listed on the band's "White Tape" as "Dog Gone Dog," the song title eventually shifted to "Dog Log" via both fan tape-labelling and Trey's stageside comments. First performed at Burlington's Hunt's on 10/30/85, "Dog Log" is an infrequently played but much loved Phish tune. "Dog Log" is another one of those tunes that always seems to appear in exceptional Phish shows: 4/29/87 at Nectar's, 8/21/87 at Ian McLain's Farm (note Marley barking in the background periodically throughout the show), 10/21/89 at The Front, 8/2/93 at The Ritz in Tampa, FL, 2/26/97 Stuggart, Germany, 11/27/98 at the Worcester Centrum, and 9/17/00 at Merriweather Post (out of "Theme" into "Mango."

By far the most famous appearance of "Dog Log" was on 12/11/95 at the Cumberland County Civic Center in Portland, Maine. Trey clued in the audience to the band's (supposed!) intent to record an album comprised entirely of fifteen different versions of "Dog Log." Trey asked the audience to be very quiet, to make it sound as if it were a sound check; then, on his mark, for everyone to "booo" loudly. Phish fans—never missing an opportunity for audience participation—obliged with gusto, serenading the band right on cue. An especially cheesy repeat performance later in the show left some on the crowd wondering if we were indeed going to get fifteen versions of the song! Or "dumps," if you will.

While "Dog Log" is a relative rarity in Phish show setlists, it is perhaps best known as a staple of the sound check. It is often played with widely contrasting styles during the sound check: sometimes as a reggae or ska tune, sometimes as a blues number, sometimes in a jazzy style. Trey has made several references on stage that the reason for this is that it was the favorite song of Phish's longtime soundman, Paul Languedoc.

Well, never trust a prankster! In an August 1999 interview by Jeff Waful on the JamBands website, Paul let us in on the real story behind his supposed love for "Dog Log." Apparently, early on in his career, he would ask the band to play a tune with vocals, to test the soundboard mix. One time when Trey asked which song he wanted to hear, Paul randomly picked "Dog Log." Seeing an opportunity for a running joke, Phish began to consistently soundcheck it, perpetuating the myth that it's Paul's favorite tune.

DOG LOG (see DOG GONE DOG)

Dogs Stole Things
Music/Lyrics: Trey Anastasio, Tom Marshall
Album: *Hampton Comes Alive* (11/21/98)
Vocals: Trey (lead), Page (backing)
Debut: 6/6/97 (private show), 6/13/97 (public show)
Historian: Mark Toscano

Debuted along with about three hundred and forty-six other songs at Brad Sands' house on 6/6/97, "Dogs Stole Things" charmed those in attendance as well as Irish (and expatriate American) fans at its first public appearance one week later.

A likeable, shuffling tune, "Dogs" doesn't really represent anything pivotal in Phish's songwriting or performance history, so many fans have unfairly labelled it as a "throwaway" or tune, worthy of a toilet break or quick nap. While it doesn't exactly "break new ground" musically or lyrically, "Dogs Stole Things" is a nice breather tune for the band, showcasing some nice tickling from Page and restrained but loose backup from Trey, Mike, and Fish.

Most importantly, the song, written by Trey and Tom, created yet another musical outlet for Trey's ravenous love for anthems and ballads about dogs. (See dictionary entry on "Dogs" for more information.) Strong versions abound, though the song barely varies from its standard interpretation, which can more or less be found on *Hampton Comes Alive*.

Doin' My Time
AKA: "Do My Time"
Music/Lyrics: Jimmie Skinner
Original Artist: Jimmie Skinner
Original Album: single (1941)
Vocals: Tim O'Brien (lead)
Debut: 8/7/96
Historian: Mark Toscano

Seek out both versions of this song for some fun special guest action. Tim O'Brien joined Phish for the last three songs of the 8/7/96 first set, closing the three-song medley with a strong version of this old Jimmie Skinner tune. The real keeper is 7/1/99, though, which features O'Brien (fiddle), Jerry Douglas (dobro), Ronnie McCoury (mandolin), an all-star version that kicks, albeit respectfully, the ass of the Red Rocks version. Fans might also catch this tune at a Leftover Salmon show, as those boys cover it quite frequently.

DONE ME WRONG (see: "DAHLIA")

Donna Lee
Music: Miles Davis
Original Artist: Charlie Parker
Original Album: (1947)
Vocals: (instrumental)
Debut: 11/11/88
Historian: Ellis Godard

Donna Lee is a light and airy piece, which Phish often placed as a melodic pause between rock frenzies, such as before or after "AC/DC Bag," "Tweezer," or "Possum." In most performances between 11/11/88 and 7/12/91, Trey played Charlie Parker's alto saxophone lead with his guitar. However, some versions included important variations, such as Trey encouraging the audience to sing along (6/30/89) and the Giant Country Horns bringing an alto sax to Phish's rendition (7/12/91, their last to date). Other important renditions include those by Chet Baker (1952), live and with Parker; the Wardell Gray Quartet (1952), with a strong presence by Art Farmer; Eric Dolphy (1962), an extended exploration; Rahsaan Roland Kirk (1968), a speedy rumble; Bobby McFerrin (1984), as part of an a capella medley; and Jaco Pastorius (1986), a bass solo.

Don't Get Me Wrong
Music: Trey Anastasio
Lyrics: John Popper
Album: (none)
Vocals: John Popper
Debut: 10/6/90
Historian: Ellis Godard

Until early 1990, "Reba" featured an additional section sandwiched between the opening lyrics and the instrumental composition which follows it in versions since. Trey combined this section (which some feel was too rockin' for "Reba") with lyrics by Blues Traveller's John Popper, and produced "Don't Get Me Wrong." All three performances of the song featured Popper on vocals and harmonica. The first two (as a set opener both 10/6/90 and 10/8/90) were relatively quick and dry, even timid, but the third (introducing a hot "Funky Bitch" on 12/28/90) was a strong performance, although the tune was never heard from again.

See Also: "Reba"

Don't Pass Me By

Original Artist: The Beatles
Original Album: *The Beatles* (aka "The White Album") (1968)
Vocals: Mike (lead), Fishman, Page, Trey (backing)
Debut: 10/31/94
Historian: Mark Toscano

A way-over-the-top, bluegrassed-out version of this tune, Ringo Starr's only "White Album" solo composition, greatly entertained fans at the 1994 Halloween show. Mike provided vocals with the other band members screeching and chirping in at various points.

Don't Want You No More

Music: Spencer Davis, Edward Hardin
Original Artist: Spencer Davis Group
Original Album: B-side to "Time Seller"
Vocals: (instrumental)
Debut: 12/1/84
Historian: Erik Swain

After frontman Steve Winwood left in 1967 to form Traffic, the U.S. hits for the Spencer Davis Group dried up. Only one song from that incarnation of the group, "Don't Want You No More," has endured on this side of the pond, and not because of Davis & Co.'s efforts.

The bluesy instrumental's beginnings could not have been more obscure. The Davis-Edward Hardin composition was the b-side of a forgotten 1967 single, "Time Seller." It remained relatively unknown until a cover version showed up as the opening track on the 1969 debut album of an exciting new band that fused blues, rock and jazz: The Allman Brothers Band. Featuring the trademark slide guitar of Duane Allman and the organ flourishes of his younger brother Gregg, "Don't Want You No More" announced The Allman Brothers Band to the world with an exclamation point. It remains in their live set today, always seguing (as on the album) into Gregg's emotional slow blues "It's Not My Cross to Bear."

In 1984, "Don't Want You No More" surfaced in the repertoire of another exciting new band that fused blues, rock and jazz (among other things): Phish. The only Phish version that circulates, 12/1/84, copies the Allmans' arrangement with one major difference: no organ in this pre-Page lineup. With no Page around to provide vocal chops, it is perhaps wise that the band did not attempt "It's Not My Cross to Bear."

Don't You Wanna Go

Music/Lyrics: (traditional)

Original Artist: Missionary Sisters
Original Album:
Vocals: Trey (lead), Mike, Page (backing)
Debut: 5/16/95
Historian: Tim Wade

The Voters for Choice benefit in Lowell, MA was a heck of a way to kick off the year in Phish for 1995. No less than ten songs were debuted on that evening, quite possibly a record in many respects. The first of these debuts was also the first song played after New Year's '94/'95, a feisty gospel number by the Missionary Sisters called "Don't You Wanna Go?" Even though it only appeared four times after this Lowell gig, its opening line set the tone for all of 1995; "Come on, children, don't you wanna go?"

Dooley

Original Artist: The Dillards
Original Album: *Back Porch Bluegrass* (1963)
Vocals: Reverend Jeff Mosier, Phish
Debut: 11/19/94 (parking lot jam), 11/20/94 (public show)
Historian: Christian C. McKee

Many have speculated that "Reba" is about bootlegging moonshine. No such such speculation is necessary about this installation in Phish's love affair with bluegrass. The song's namesake is a wily mountain distiller, constantly exhorted by the narrator for "another swaller" of his fine product. This bluegrass standard was added to

Peter Sliznan

Phish's repertoire when the Reverend Jeff Mosier joined Phish on tour in November of 1994. Sadly, "Dooley" made only one single official appearance: 11/20/94 at the Dane County Coliseum in Madison, Wisconsin. But a lucky few fans were able to hear Phish play this the night before along with Rev. Jeff Mosier, Eric Merrill and Jeremy outside their tour bus in Bloomington, Indiana. Until Phish decides to resurrect their acoustic bluegrass selections, don't hold your breath to hear "Dooley" again.

Down By The River
Music/Lyrics: Neil Young
Album: *Everybody Know This Is Nowhere* **(1969)**
Vocals: Neil Young (lead), Phish (backing)
Debut: 10/3/98
Historian: Phil Nazzaro

Phish performed Neil Young's barn-burning classic with The Man himself as part of their Farm Aid appearance on 10/3/98. This pairing of artists is the kind of thing dreams are made of for many fans, and in their first performance together, they did not disappoint. At nearly 19 minutes, this version of "Down By The River" is a fully realized, jam-filled take on Neil's powerful rock anthem.

Down With Disease
AKA: "DWD," "Disease"
Music: Trey Anastasio
Lyrics: Tom Marshall
Album: *Hoist*
Vocals: Trey (lead), Mike, Page (backing)
Debut: 4/4/94
Historian: Craig DeLucia

If ever a Phish song came along at just the right moment, it was "Down with Disease." Upset with the perceived radio-friendly appeal of *Hoist*, some fans were poised to rebel against the album and the songs it contained. While it would take sibling "Wolfman's Brother" almost three full years to develop, "Down with Disease" jammed the first time it hit the stage and proved to the naysayers that Phish was still writing songs that they intended to stretch out live.

The first true "Down with Disease" was played at the *Hoist* tour opener, though fans who bought the album recognized the tag ending jam from the 1993 New Year's Show just three months earlier. Having already recorded "Disease" in the studio, Phish jammed it out of the traditional "Auld Lang Syne" to ring in 1994. In true Phish fashion, the performance produced footage for Phish's only video, but, at the time, most fans weren't even aware that they were hearing a new song!

Like all infants, "Disease" spent most of its first year learning to walk. Some versions stand out as noteworthy, such as 6/16/94 and the mammoth 11/12/94 "Disease" -> "Have Mercy" -> "Disease," but most versions followed a fairly standard pattern of a short, guitar solo-based jam to close the number. A second monster version was played on 6/26/95 at Saratoga, combining relative newcomers "Disease" and "Free." The length and depth of this combination left fans drooling for more, but "Disease" was only played three more times in 1995.

It returned with a bang in 1996, though. In fact, the development of "Disease" as a jam vehicle was one of the major highlights in what some fans considered to be an off-year. Once again, "Disease" was in the right place at the right time. The band seemed more comfortable with the groove of the jam, adding texture and layers and not relying on Trey to dominate. The song's development was punctuated with showcase moments in the year's three biggest shows: The Clifford Ball ("Disease" -> "NICU"), Halloween (first set placement directly before "You Enjoy Myself"), and New Year's Eve (out of "Zarathustra" -> "Auld Lang Syne" while the band was immersed in a sea of balloons on-stage). "Disease" also showed that it could be a near set-long showcase song, a la "Tweezer" or "Mike's Groove." Witness the "Diseezer" from 11/27/96, which ran from "Disease" to "Jesus Just Left Chicago," paused for "Scent of a Mule," and closed with "Tweezer" -> "Disease Reprise," with a "Sweet Emotion" jam taboot.

1997 brought the "Cow Funk," led by a thick bass sound and a greater emphasis on full-band improvisation. In addition to long, interwoven jams on 2/17/97 (with "Carini" and "Taste" sandwiched inside), 11/23/97 ("Low Rider") and 12/11/97 (melting into "Maze" in the first set, with a reprise arising from the second set "Ghost"), "Disease" provided its own share of stand-alone glory. See 6/25/97 (with "Piper") and the literally electric 7/22/97 (into "Mike's Song.") Once again, "Disease" was played in the showcase shows, appearing at the Great Went and jammed while the band painted their pieces of art.

Groovy versions continued to punctuate setlists in 1998 and 1999. 7/26/99, 12/15/99, and Cypress' 12/31/99 version stand out as memorable. "Disease" continued to rock into 2000, with interesting versions played both during the *Farmhouse* promos (5/21/00 Radio City) and on the Japan mini-tour (6/10/00, with a "Weekapaug Groove" tease).

"Disease" has done all this jamming while also being an interesting lyrical work. The chorus provides an anthemic line that is rivaled only by "Chalk Dust Torture" in terms of high school yearbook quotability. And much speculation has been made about the song's cryptic verses—some interpreted it as a way of deflecting the band's then-newfound fame while others argued that it referenced a true story where two teenage fans showed up on Trey's lawn to meet him one day. Tom Marshall has neither confirmed nor refuted these stories, but the lyrics may be more biographical than fans ever credit. Tom noted, in Richard Gehr's *The Phish Book*, that he wrote the lyrics to Disease while laid up in bed with mononucleosis.

See Also: "Auld Lang Syne"

Driver
Music/Lyrics: Trey Anastasio, Tom Marshall
Album: *Hampton Comes Alive* **(11/20/98);**
**   *Farmhouse* (Japanese edition)**
Vocals: Trey
Debut: 10/17/98
Historian: Martin Acaster

There are bodily functions each of us perform perhaps thousands of times each day that thankfully require no thought. Breathing, blinking, the beating of our hearts, digestion, and the growth of hair are all ongoing processes which for the most part are beyond our conscious control. To whom does the responsibility for the steering of these processes fall? One possible answer to this mystery of life is presented in "Driver," which debuted at the first night of the Bridge School Benefit at Shoreline on 10/17/98. Unlike the one in each of our heads the lyrics tell of a driver who has been given far too much responsibility by his

host. Rather than controlling only the autonomic responses that would keep the body alive, this driver is charged with the control of walking, talking, making decisions, and even picking out clothes. A clear case of a multiple personality disorder developed in response to the inability to accept responsibility for poor fashion sense.

"Driver" has featured Trey on acoustic guitar each time it has been played, which was fairly often during Fall Tour 1998. This acoustic format lent itself to studio appearances at a taping of an edition of PBS's *Sessions at West 54th* (10/20/98) and a promotional set on Boulder radio station KBCO's "Studio C" series on 11/3/98. "Driver" was also one of the songs Mike and Trey performed at an open mic night at the Dead Goat Saloon in Salt Lake City on 11/1/98. A live performance of "Driver" from 11/20/98 was released on *Hampton Comes Alive* and the studio version recorded during the *Farmhouse* sessions was one of two bonus tracks ("Mist" being the other) released on the Japanese edition of the album. Since the appearance of the gorgeously acoustic instrumental "The Inlaw Josie Wales" in recent setlists, "Driver" has been relegated to the back seat of the bus.

Drowned

Original Artist: The Who
Original Album: *Quadrophenia* **(1973)**
Vocals: Mike (lead), Page, Trey (backing)
Debut: 10/31/95
Historian: Craig DeLucia

Drowned is noteworthy as the only *Quadrophenia* song to be played more than three times. Phish has made the song a popular number, as fans have come to relish the pure energy and excitement signaled by Page's rocking piano intro and Mike's stratospheric vocals.

This rocking number was a centerpiece on 12/31/95, featuring an oft-debated "Fire on the Mountain" tease. It disappeared, though, for over two years before re-appearing 2/28/97. Almost all versions since the Halloween debut have housed monster jams, including the aforementioned New Year's Eve 1995 version and 12/11/97, Rochester, which clocks in at around twenty minutes. Also notable is 12/5/97, with a jam based on "Couldn't Stand the Weather" by Stevie Ray Vaughan.

While "Drowned" was played only a handful of times in 1998, the most memorable was probably the version from 11/2/98. "Drowned" emerged from a freeform jam and eventually melted into "Jesus Just Left Chicago." Still somewhat rare (only three appearances in each of 1999 and 2000), "Drowned" shouldn't be overlooked as a potential jam vehicle. 12/12/99 clocked in at over 30 minutes long!

From a historical perspective, "Drowned" has twice been paired up with songs from other Halloweens past: 6/29/00 into "Rock and Roll" and 9/14/00 into "Crosseyed and Painless." Finally, true enthusiasts who just can't get enough of "Drowned" should also hear the 7/22/97 Virginia Beach "Bathtub Gin," where the song was substantially teased.

Earache My Eye (featuring Alice Bowie)

Music/Lyrics: Thomas Chong, Richard "Cheech" Marin,
  Gaye Delorne
Original Artist: Cheech and Chong
Original Album: *Cheech and Chong's Wedding Album* **(1974)**
Vocals: Fish
Debut: 5/17/94

Historian: Marco Walsh

The Seventies saw Cheech and Chong consistently on the top of the comedy charts with their unique mind-altering humor, first via their wildly successful comedy routine and recorded albums, and later with a series of popular movies. "Earache My Eye" was an instant hit when released in 1974, featuring a burned-out student who, once awakened by his alarm clock, puts on a loud heavy metal record, and tells his father he can't go to school because he has an earache. "Earache my eye, you're going to school!" was his father's classic reply.

The song is also featured in Cheech and Chong's first movie, *Up In Smoke*. Here the boys find their band entered in the "Rock Fight," a local battle of the bands. They take the stage as "Alice Bowie," where thanks to the mellowing effect of an accidental van fire near the club's ventilation intakes, their performance of "Earache My Eye" wins the contest.

Despite their many fans in common, it wasn't until 5/17/94 in Santa Barbara, CA, that Cheech and Chong were featured in a Phish set. And with the song's lyrics about a cross-dressing glam rock star, only Henrietta could do "Earache My Eye" justice. Early in the second set the band started into a tight "Tweezer," keeping a hard rock sound on into the jam section. As Trey's jam began to take the form of a familiar riff, Fishman was on it, belting out "My momma talkin' to me tries to tell me how to live. But I don't listen to her 'cause my head is like a sieve...." The rest of the band fell in behind him, and two full verses and a bridge later, Cheech and Chong were added to the diverse list of artists covered by Phish.

Earl's Breakdown

Music: Earl Scruggs
Original Artist: Flatt and Scruggs
Original Album: *Lester Flatt & Earl Scuggs* **(1959)**
Vocals: (instrumental)
Debut: 11/16/94
Historian: Ellis Godard

As part of Phish's first lesson in a week-long course of Mosier, they tackled this tricky ditty most widely known as the opening to the movie *Deliverance* (though there overshadowed by "Dueling Banjos"). Reminiscent of "Poor Heart," "Earl's Breakdown" is more bouncy and less whiplashing than its name suggests: If you're thinking "Foggy Mountain Breakdown," invoke a bit of "Jimmy Cracked Corn."

Eclipse

Original Artist: Pink Floyd
Original Album: *Dark Side of the Moon* **(1973)**
Vocals: Phish
Debut: 11/2/98
Historian: Mark Toscano

On 11/2/98, all fans touched, ate, begged, borrowed, stole, created, and destroyed was in tune as Phish eclipsed the sun with their mind-bending, suprise cover of Pink Floyd's *Dark Side of the Moon*. At this point in the set, it's safe to say that everyone knew this song was coming, but it still thrilled the half-sold-out E Centre to no end. Easily the most climactic and dramatic song of the entire album (and this show), "Eclipse" sums up not just the album and its themes, but literally "*everything* under the sun," proving first and foremost that Pink

Down with Disease

Compiled by Mike Preston (with a little help from Rob Kallick)

Date	Timing	Notes
12/31/93	03:43	Instrumental (the jam segment only).
04/04/94	07:30	Debut of the complete version.
06/26/94	09:00	Very long for '94. Trey's solo is unbelievable.
10/29/94	07:54	Chaotic. Multiple peaks.
11/12/94	23:32	DWD: 00:00–14:00. Fabulous jam, unusual; on the 'Wheel Archives Show. Have Mercy: 14:00–19:46 DWD: 19:46–23:32. Very experimental.
11/17/94	08:38	Unusual improv in jam.
06/26/95	21:54	Great bass leadership. Spooky 007ish jam segues into Free.
12/01/95	08:22	Not life-changing, but definitely worth a fifth or sixth listening!
12/12/95	31:20	Large effects jam. Improvisational.
12/29/95	09:36	Powerful. Each peak is more enjoyable than the last.
08/05/96	15:55	Sweet Page clavinet jam. Funky. Red Rocks! Segues into Ice.
08/14/96	09:44	Bursting out the seems with joy! A must-hear.
08/16/96	15:06	Very relaxed. Key stays in "A" the whole time. Segues into NICU.
10/19/96	11:36	Very funky with quiet Page clavinet jam towards the end.
10/26/96	09:49	Trey never stops progressing. Definitely a cousin of the 12/13/97 Ghost.
12/01/96	10:30	Elevated solos by all of them.
12/06/96	10:25	Prolonged explosive build-up with Fishman in the driver's seat.
12/31/96	15:49	Majestic! Main riff is teased. Weekapaug teases.
02/17/97	45:45	DWD: 00:00–17:02; Carini Jam: 17:02–37:56; Taste: 37:56–44:23; DWD Reprise: 44:23–45:45. Need one say more?
07/09/97	10:22	Nothing crazy, but a perfect start to a historic set.
07/22/97	18:30	Dragging funk beat evolves into Mike's Song. A crucial ingredient in what was—in my opinion—the best jam ever.
08/02/97	14:20	Strong version segues into Tweezer, after which DWD arguably returns for a minute or two.
08/10/97	10:49	Very accelerated beat.
08/17/97	25:17	Profound version featuring several modes. Concludes with a Mike/Trey duet. Segues into Bathtub Gin
07/26/99	18:44	Intense with a "feedback jam" that segues into an Also Sprach SOAM.
12/15/99	15	Thrilling jam segment!
12/31/99	23:42	Very spirited and improvisational.
05/21/00	20:15	Deeply universally resonant groove! One of the strongest versions ever.
06/10/00	24:12	Weekapaug tease in intense jam.
06/23/00	15:52	Upbeat jam segues into deep space.
07/15/00	26:46	Magnificent.

Floyd knew precisely how to seal up an album.

One of the greatest moments of Phish's performance that night was definitely the almost matter-of-fact segue from "Eclipse" back into "Harpua" to finish off the set, a seamless movement helped immeasurably by the fact that both songs are in the same key. What a cab ride!

Eliza

Music: Trey Anastasio
Album: *A Picture of Nectar*
Vocals: (instrumental)
Debut: 9/15/90
Historian: Ellis Godard

When Trey wrote "Eliza," he named it for his girlfriend, Sue Eliza. The song combines a slow and jazzy bassline, dual voices (on piano and guitar),and drum accents to render a brief but elaborate instrumental ballad, like a prelude to a fabulous children's story. While "kind of a quiet one," (said Trey 10/13/91) which doesn't vary even from its album verison, the song often precedes fiery numbers such as "Rift" (3/24/92) or "Llama" (5/8/92). The sincerity was broken on 11/1/91 by Mike's crack that it was written by "Ringo," but the title was returned to placidity when Trey and Sue married and named their daughter Eliza. And while young Eliza grows and energizes,the song remains silent: Phish has not performed it since 5/14/92.

El Paso

Music/Lyrics: Marty Robbins
Original Artist: Marty Robbins
Original Album: single (1959)
Vocals: Bob Weir
Debut: 10/06/00
Historian: Charles Dirksen

A song that charmed Grateful Dead fans at hundreds of Dead shows since 1970, "El Paso" tells a vividly dramatic, romantic, and violent tale. Written and released by the legendary country and western music artist Marty Robbins in 1959, the song reached the top of the pop and country music charts practically overnight. "El Paso" was the first country music song ever to win a Grammy. Phish covered it on 10/06/00 at Shoreline with Bob Weir on rhythm guitar and vocals.

Emotional Rescue

Original Artist: The Rolling Stones
Original Album: *Emotional Rescue*
Vocals: Mike
Debut: 11/21/97
Historian: Phillip Zerbo and Mark Toscano

At the time of its release, the 1980 album *Emotional Rescue* represented to many critics either a turning point, or an identity crisis for

the Rolling Stones. Mixing their classic rock and blues styles with more up-tempo dance numbers and soulful classics, many hard core 'Stones fans were left shaking their heads, as it represented such a significant departure from their standard modus operandi. Ironic, given that two decades later this album is viewed by many as a "classic."

Phish debuted the title track, "Emotional Rescue," to open the legendary Hampton run on 11/21/97. This tune provided Mike the opportunity to display a wide range of his vocal skills, alternating between the extremes of falsetto and bravado, the former of which had Trey visibly cracking up during the debut! It is perhaps the difficulty and extraordinary vocal range required of the song that on each performance it opened the show. "Emotional Rescue" was played by Phish sparingly after its debut, opening both 12/31/97 and 7/28/98, not showing up again until the legendary 9/30/00 encore version. This rendition, which may confuse fans who only hear the tapes, features a drawn-out noisy tail end that offers no answers. Thanks to the ethereal magic of webcasts, however, many non-attendees were able to see the bizarre, questionably choreographed interpretive dance performed by Trey and Mike over the last several minutes of "Emotional Rescue." Shots of the stage antics were nicely intercut with views of a rather stunned audience as Trey and Mike pirouetted about the stage, placed strange hats on their bandmates with their guitars, and engaged in some sort of indescribable duel of expressionist balletics.

End of Session
Music/Lyrics: Phish, Tom Marshall
Album: *Story of the Ghost*
Vocals: Phish
Debut: (never performed live)
Historian: Phillip Zerbo

Story of the Ghost provides an interesting twist to a common thematic device in the recording industry: as the "final" track "The Moma Dance" winds down, the band offers a reprise to the chorus of the album's first track, "Ghost," seemingly to provide a sense of closure to the record. But we are not yet done, as the band instead finishes with "End of Session," a delightful, lilting, melodic segment of jamming with lyrics sparse and simple and delivered almost as spoken word, and yet so distinctively those of Tom Marshall.

Indeed, while many fans and critics tended to discount this beautiful song as a simple afterthought, among all the disc's tracks "End of Session" epitomizes best the approach that was used in the creation of *Story of the Ghost*. Many of the songs on the album were based on the best cuts among hours of band improvisation in the Bearsville Studios, which were then combined with lyrics from Tom Marshall's vast array of yet-unpublished lyrics and poetry. While most of the tracks were molded and tweaked into a more traditional song format, "End of Session" is perhaps the most pure reflection of this specific creative process that occurred during the Bearsville sessions.

"End of Session" also was a hint of the style that fans would receive a more complete dose of with the 1999 release of *The Siket Disc*, which contained both well-developed songs as well as smaller "jamlets" and "non-traditional" songs. "End of Session" has yet to be performed by Phish in concert, but before you discount the possibility, recall that prior to 12/31/99, people probably said the same thing about "Quadrophonic Toppling."

Esther
Music/Lyrics: Trey Anastasio
Album: *Junta*
Vocals: Trey (lead), Mike, Page (backing)
Debut: 9/12/88
Historian: Mark Toscano

Girl goes to fairground. Girl meets Armenian man. Armenian man gives girl doll. Girl flies around and encounters many angry people. Girl jumps naked into lake. Doll pulls girl beneath surface of water, drowning her. And so the thread of yet another human existence is cut short by the scissors of badness.

Ask most fans, and they'll agree that "Esther" is a mighty special song. One of Trey's purely solo works, this tune made its live debut relatively late compared to its *Junta* compatriots, not showing up until 9/12/88. Even then, it featured different, decidedly less macabre lyrics than the version that ended up on *Junta*. These original lyrics, aside from containing various differences of detail ("a hot summer night," "a wrinkled old man," and so forth), feature a story that takes on a "just desserts" theme rather than the wonderfully demented "ruination of an innocent" theme that the final-draft lyrics eventually gave us. These darker, more familiar lyrics that most fans are used to appeared at the song's second appearance, on 2/7/89.

"Esther's" music is quite lyrical, evoking circus mood, soaring flights through the clouds, and helpless drowning. Many fans actually agree that the quintessential version of Esther is the *Junta* studio version, since it is such a delicate song, easily harmed by the unavoidable vagaries of live performance. In fact, its very fragility is one reason the song is such a rarity in the Phish live repertoire. The band has played "Esther" very infrequently since 1994. Since then, the song seems to appear primarily at "kitchen sink" shows, where the guys bust out many a neglected tune (see: 7/5/94, 6/16/95, 8/9/98, 9/30/00, etc.)

Although she doesn't play any role in the central "Man Who Stepped Into Yesterday" story, Trey has mentioned, on occasion, that Esther does hail from a part of Gamehendge. However, there is some musical territory shared by the two Trey brainchildren. The so-called "flying jam" in "Esther" (the E > Em > F#m/E > F#/E > B/E progression that occurs twice in the song) also appears as the transitional music between several of the "Man Who Stepped Into Yesterday" songs, when performed live (3/22/93, 6/26/94, 7/8/94) and on the Senior Study tape. Additionally, Mike's bassline for this "flying jam" is identical to the playing he does during Page's solo in "McGrupp." Trey has even commented on this, noting how many lyrical and musical themes interweave in his numerous compositions. (Even one of the "Secret Language" cues—the "random note"—is signaled by the same "circus" theme that kicks off "Esther.")

Perhaps most enigmatically, "Esther" was also the first subject for a Phish video. The only fans to see this video, however, were the attendees of the 7/19/91 Somerville Theatre show. The video, a computer-animated piece, was designed by Scott Nybokken, an acquaintance of the band. Playing more like a slide-show of still images than a full-motion cartoon, the video was shown between sets at the aforementioned gig.

Exceptional versions of "Esther" include 4/18/92, 7/15/92 (w/ "random note" secret language), 2/12/93 (w/ more secret language),

4/23/94 (w/ "Caravan" teases"), 7/5/94 (w/ "Dance of the Sugar Plum Fairies" teasing), 8/16/96 (a nice surprise), and 9/30/00 (fine version with Trey forgetting entire last verse, instead summing it up with "She Died.") Additionally, "Esther" teases popped up during the 9/27/91 "Buried Alive" and the 11/30/97 "Wolfman's Brother," while an "Esther" jam found its way into the epic "Stash" on 11/14/95.

Everybody's Got Something to Hide Except Me and My Monkey

Original Artist: The Beatles
Original Album: *The Beatles* (aka "The White Album") (1968)
Vocals: Trey (lead), Mike, Page (backing)
Debut: 10/31/94
Historian: Mark Toscano

The "White Album" song with the longest title took its turn being covered by Phish on Halloween 1994 as part of the band's first "musical costume." Although Phish's rendition was one of the set's highlights, they were not afforded the luxury of a fire bell as the Beatles were when they recorded this tune back in '68. Instead, Fishman beat his ride cymbal furiously. In a surprise move, the band busted this unduly neglected Beatles track as the 9/25/00 show opener, leaving many a fan dumbfounded with glee.

Eyes of the World

Music/Lyrics: Jerry Garcia, Robert Hunter
Original Artist: Grateful Dead
Original Album: *Wake of the Flood*
Vocals: Trey
Debut: 11/3/84
Historians: Mark Toscano and Phil Nazzaro

Phish debuted this Dead cover at one of their first shows billed as "Phish," performing a passable version that segued interestingly into the Allman Brothers' "Whipping Post." This combo is especially telling, as it represents the two major musical forces that brought the band together; Trey, Jeff, Mike, and Fish all commonly liked the Dead and the Allmans, both considered fathers of modern jam-rock. At the first Nectar's show on 12/1/84, "Eyes" showed up as an extra long encore. Then at Page's first show on 5/3/85, the song segued out of the Dead's "Scarlet Begonias." No other known versions of the tune exist, but it is likely the guys played it here and there at undocumented shows. Though it wasn't actually a Phish show, it should be noted that the song was played on 12/31/86 by a band consisting of half of Phish (Trey and Page) and half The Joneses, billed as "The Phones."

"Eyes of the World" features some of the most introspective lyrics Robert Hunter ever wrote for the Dead. Appropriately, it was a staple of their live performances: the song never left their repertoire for more than 16 shows at a time from its debut on 2/9/73 to the last performance on 7/6/95.

Faht

AKA: "Windham Hell" (original title)
Music: Jon Fishman
Album: *A Picture of Nectar*
Debut: 11/22/92
Historian: Ellis Godard/Mark Toscano

Fishman spun this ditty from a few threads of acoustic guitar and a whacked mix of tracks. Both the studio version on *A Picture of Nectar*, and all twelve live versions are played atop a background of interspersed urban and woodsy sounds—water running, birds chirping, horns honking, an occasional siren wailing—while Fishman plucks calmly on a guitar while seated on a wooden stool.

Arguably a parody of new age music, Jon labeled the tune "Windham Hell," alluding to new age distributor Windham Hill Records. Fish was on vacation as the *Picture of Nectar* liner notes were being scripted, and the other band members elected to resolve potential conflict (legal or otherwise) with Windham Hill by changing the song's title. What to change it to? Well, in the November 1991 Phish Update newsletter, the drummer's "Fish's Forum" included a misspelling, whereby the intended mock-Southern phrase "raht tuh the front door" lost its reputed meaning when "raht" became "faht." Fish was annoyed with this gaffe, and his band mates, ever trying to get the furry one's goat, decided to change "Windham Hell's" title to "Faht," claiming that Elektra had misspelled the title he had chosen. (Some argue that "Faht" is just a Boston-accented "fart," which may refer to the tuba blast at the end of the otherwise idyllic track.)

The song itself hasn't changed much, but its role has, even though all twelve versions came in the second set of their respective shows. Earlier appearances (four in Fall 1992 and four in Summer 1993) came late in the set and offered a relaxing break after particularly vigorous tunes ("You Enjoy Myself," "Harry Hood," "Possum," "Mike's Groove," "Antelope"). The last appearance to date was on 12/2/95, between a fumbled "Simple" and a crisp "Tweezer." But the song's few appearances since '93 (two set openers in summer 1994, and the 10/3/95 version which segued out of "Billy Breathes") played a different role: focusing all attention front and center in preparation for the ensuing musical madness.

Family Picture

Original Artist: The Dude of Life (with Phish)
Original Album: *Crimes of the Mind*
Vocals: The Dude of Life
Debut: 11/8/91
Historian: Dan Mielcarz

With lyrics by the Dude of Life and music arranged by Phish, "Family Picture" was played live but once, on 11/8/91 at the Ivory Tusk. This is unquestionably a good thing. You can also hear it on the Dude's album *Crimes of the Mind*, but you really don't want to. Trust me.

The Famous Mockingbird

AKA: "Mbird," "Mockingbird," "Fly Famous Mockingbird"
Music/Lyrics: Trey Anastasio
Album: (none)
Vocals: Page, Trey
Debut: 2/8/88
Historian: Mark Toscano

Esther and her doll may "flutter and glide," but this tune absolutely soars. One of Trey's most beautiful compositions, this exquisite song has wowed 'em in many a room since its first performance at Nectar's on 2/8/88.

The Famous Mockingbird, a character Trey first encountered in the "McGrupp" poem Tom Marshall had sent him in the pre-Gamehendge days of Fall 1985, was officially incorporated into Gamehendge mythology by way of this song. Colonel Forbin, fed up with the impotence of the anti-Wilson revolution effort in light of Mr. Palmer's execution (see "AC/DC Bag"), decides to climb the mountain and find Icculus, who Forbin believes will be able to assist them. The Colonel reaches Icculus at the mountain's summit, and the Great and Knowledgeable One promises to deliver the Helping Friendly Book to him, without which Wilson will be easily defeated. In order to fetch the Book from its hiding place in the highest tower of Wilson's castle, Icculus sends his faithful friend the Famous Mockingbird. This song describes the flight of the Famous Mockingbird as it finds and retrieves the Book from Wilson's castle.

The chords that make up the opening of this song are actually first expressed midway through "Colonel Forbin's Ascent," the song that precedes "Mockingbird" in the Gamehendge story. When this particular chord structure is reiterated at the end of "Forbin," it moves the listener gracefully into "Mockingbird" without a hitch, serving as the latter song's intro. Trey discovered this sweet progression during a between-semester trip to Ireland, and modified it very slightly to use in "Mockingbird." Preparing itself for the harrowing journey to Wilson's castle, the Mockingbird flaps its wings repeatedly over these chords before launching into flight over the next progression, which provides the main melody of the song. Over the gentle rhythms of these chords, Trey's guitar whistles a lengthy succession of eighth notes in 6/8 time. Along the way, we are treated to a "Leave it to Beaver" bassline from Mike, not the first TV theme to find its place in his portion of a song (see "It's Ice" for another). The brief chorus that then ensues was originally envisioned by Trey to be sung by a full choir. Following this short vocal refrain, the guitar line—meant to echo the adventure-filled flight of the Famous Mockingbird—flutters prettily alongside the same chords before it crashes head-on into the next section of the song.

What follows is a dramatic and brutal musical episode that evokes either a tempestuous storm or perhaps some Wilsonian antagonists attempting to impede the Mockingbird's flight. The repeating double-crash of Fishman's cymbal, Page's and Mike's perfectly placed accents, and Trey's impassioned and daring guitar work in this moving segment rank up among some of Phish's most brilliant moments.

This segment repeats and then calmly and hypnotically glides downward into a soothing, luminous section that indicates the Mockingbird's survival of its plight. Following a reprisal of the chorus, Mike takes a mellifluous solo over the song's opening chords, which smoothly gives way to an exquisite Page/Trey duet of escalating notes. This final section evokes the image of the Mockingbird, successful with Book in beak, humbly gliding and dipping over Colonel Forbin's shack before easing down low enough to present him with the means to de-throne Wilson. The song ends, appropriately, on a single piano note, as the Mockingbird rests from its difficult journey at last.

If this song reminds you at all of "Flight of the Bumblebee," then you're right on—this is the piece Trey had in mind when he composed "Mockingbird." Also, along with "The Lizards," this song was greatly influenced by Trey's experiences in Ireland, where he met and spent much time with another guitarist, playing for people as they went from pub to pub, night after night.

When performed well, the song is a mesmerizer. Sometimes, the song is so powerful, the band knocks the crowd off their collective feet. Some above average versions include 2/24/89, 10/20/89 (with "Jeopardy!" theme tease), 3/24/92, 4/16/92, 12/31/92 (with Brad Sands in a chicken outfit), 3/22/93 (gripping), 10/31/95 (Evil Mockingbird!), and (more to come). Unfortunately, when NOT played well, the song can be just short of a disaster. One version to avoid at all costs is 8/7/96, despite a fun narration that refers back to the 8/20/93 version. The 9/30/00 version, though more solid than the evil 8/7/96 travesty, is still quite shabby, but both are worth checking out for their amusing narratives.

Additionally, "Mockingbird" has, since 1992, almost always been appended to "Forbin" by some clever and ever-changing narration from Trey. For information about narrations, see "Colonel Forbin's Ascent."

Since 1993, the frequency of "Mockingbird" appearances has diminished dramatically, for although it is one of the band's truly special tunes, its strict compositional structure doesn't fit in very well with their current state of musical being, which is a looser, more free-form one. In 1993, the song was played 16 times, dropping to 11 the following year. In '95, the Mockingbird made its heroic flight no more than 3 times, which diminished to 2 in '96. In 1997, although the band played "Colonel Forbin's Ascent" at their 8/14/97 gig (with Ken Kesey and the Merry Pranksters onstage), they followed it with "Camel Walk" instead; Trey explained that they couldn't do "Mockingbird" after such a funky vibe had been created. In 1998, the Mockingbird flew a single flight on 8/7/98, its first in 135 shows, and it was another 14 shows before the next performance on 9/30/00. So, although this incredible song's role used to be an integral one in the Phish repertoire, it now seems to have served its purpose and will eventually move on into Phishtory, much like the proud little fellow about whom it was written.

See Also: "Colonel Forbin's Ascent"

Farmhouse

AKA: "This Is a Farmhouse"
Music/Lyrics: Trey Anastasio, Tom Marshall
Album: *Farmhouse; Hampton Comes Alive* (11/20/98)
Vocals: Trey (lead), Mike, Page (backing)
Debut: 11/16/97
Historian: Craig DeLucia

On 11/7/97, fans were abuzz with energy as they tried to figure out what Phish would play that night on *Late Night with Conan O'Brien*. Most fans presumed it would be a cut from the recent *Slip, Stitch, and Pass* release; "Cities" was the most popular guess on the Internet. The band, as usual, responded in surprising fashion by busting out "Farmhouse," a brand new number that had never before been played for a live audience. Its offical concert debut was just over a week later in Denver on 11/16, but the surprise surrounding this true first appearance of "Farmhouse" summed up the "This Band Can Do Anything" buzz that surrounded the Fall 1997 tour.

The story behind the development of the song is pretty interesting. Trey and Tom had retreated to a Vermont cabin to write some new music. Upon arriving, they found that the cleaning lady had left them a note warning them about the annoying "clusterflies" that were beginning to breed in the cabin. The song was written quickly, with lyrics based on that note. Trey and Tom even recorded a four-track version of the song while staying in the cabin, and some fans have been lucky

enough to come across copies of this demo.

A sweet ballad with a twinge of southern flavor and a moving Trey solo to close, "Farmhouse" reminds more than a few fans of the refrain to Bob Marley's "No Woman No Cry" (especially the "everything's gonna be alright" lyric) in terms of tempo and melody. "Farmhouse" was played sparingly (three times) in the fall of 1997 and slightly more often in 1998. However, in 1999, "Farmhouse" moved into a regular spot in rotation, even opening several shows (see, for example, 7/26/99 and 9/28/99). The band continues to tinker with the song, as is evidenced by a new intro added in the summer of 1999 (see 7/9) and a slightly different arrangement that debuted on 12/2/99 in Auburn Hills. This new arrangement featured another chorus added at the end of the song. The album version added a brief guitar-led break prior to the last chorus; the band continues to render the song this way.

Fast Enough for You

AKA: "FEFY"
Music: Trey Anastasio
Lyrics: Tom Marshall
Album: *Rift*
Debut: 11/19/92
Historian: Craig DeLucia

Long before Phish took a slight turn into writing more "song"-oriented material, Trey Anastasio and Tom Marshall penned this poignant piece of poetry about a man who seemingly can't meet his partner's high expectations. Strangely, given the introduction of slower-paced material in the late 1990s, "Fast Enough for You" has become a bit of a concert rarity, appearing only seven times between 1997 and Summer 2000.

While regarded as a fantastic piece of songwriting and a welcome addition to any show, "Fast Enough for You" is among the least varying songs in the Phish catalog. As such, most versions are fairly indistinguishable. The 11/19/92 debut is regarded by many as the most interesting version to exist on tape, as it included Gordon Stone's wonderful pedal steel guitar textures (as also provided on *Rift*).

FAST TRAIN (See "I Been to Georgia on a Fast Train")

Fee

Music/Lyrics: Trey Anastasio
Album: *Junta; Lawn Boy* (initial pressing)
Debut: 8/9/87
Historian: Dan Purcell

Fee provides a narrative-laden counterexample to anyone who might accuse Phish of writing only nonsense lyrics. Even though that narrative—the story of the Buddhist weasel Fee's blood feud with Floyd the chimpanzee over the affections of an aging gospel chanteuse named Millie Grace—is nearly as fanciful as anything out of Dr. Seuss, it *is* a coherent story. And it even has a happy ending, if you're into that.

Fee sits under a banana tree dreaming of Millie, who's "far away in another place." It's not clear where he is or why he's away from Millie, but it doesn't really matter; he might feel isolated and imprisoned, but he has faith in his escape to better things. He thinks back to meeting Millie in a bar in Peru and running afoul of Floyd, the cruel and vicious chimp who wants Millie to himself. Floyd vows revenge. He tracks Fee and Millie on an ocean voyage to Quebec (a mostly land-

locked province one suspects Trey chose because it rhymes with "lovers' trek"). When he finds the pair sunning themselves on deck, he breaks a bottle over Fee's head. Fortunately for the hapless weasel, Millie is made of stronger stuff; she steps in and beats Floyd down, first jamming a nectarine into the unfortunate primate's occipital bone, and then, after Floyd tumbles backwards over the ship's edge and is left clinging to the railing in desperation, slicing his nipple with a piece of paper. Floyd plummets into the ocean and is messily devoured by sharks.

"Fee" is one of three Phish songs—"Punch You in the Eye" and "The Sloth" are the others—that include a lyrical reference to an image that must keep Trey Anastasio up nights: getting a paper cut on the nipple. Apparently this is a major social problem in Gamehendge: both the Evil King Wilson's soldiers ("Punch You in the Eye"), and the freelance hitmen of the region ("The Sloth") are proficient in the art. In "Fee," however, the nipple-slicing is performed in the service of Good and ultimately saves the day.

As the leadoff track on Phish's first real album, *Junta*, and one of the oldest continuously-played songs in Phish's repertoire, "Fee" occupies a special place in the band's history. Many fans who first heard Phish in the pre-Elektra early '90s concede that it was the jaunty singalong bounce of "Fee," and not the more ambitious prog-rock vibe of "Divided Sky" or "You Enjoy Myself," that first hooked them on the band—a fact recogized by Phish's first label, Absolute-a-Go-Go, which appended "Fee" as a bonus track to the initial CD pressing of *Lawn Boy*.

The other thing to mention about "Fee" is the megaphone. When Phish was recording *Junta*, engineer Gordon Hookailo devised a clever vocal effect by channeling Trey's vocal through a set of headphones, then holding those headphones up to a microphone. For years, Trey approximated this vocal effect onstage by singing "Fee" through a megaphone, which was kept, awaiting the song's next performance, atop his guitar cabinet. For whatever reason, Trey has stopped using the megaphone in recent years.

For years, discerning fans have heard "Fee's" blissful, dwindling coda as a potential jamming vehicle. And for years, the band seemed reluctant to pursue jamming out of "Fee," although they did occasionally segue into another song (e.g., the otherwise unremarkable 9/28/95 "Fee" -> "The Fog That Surrounds" or the underrated and crafty 8/14/96 "Fee" -> "Poor Heart"). But in Prague on 7/5/98, following one of the most laughably botched versions of the song ever performed (Trey helpfully replaces most of the second verse with "You know how it goes"), the band launched into a gloriously mellow 12-minute jam, eventually segueing into "Water in the Sky." And the lone "Fee" of Phish's summer 1999 tour, performed in Virginia Beach on 7/8/99, spiraled into an even longer (~20 minute) jam, suggesting that bold new frontiers lie ahead for the little weasel and his bathing beauty.

Fikus

AKA: "I, Fikus"
Music/Lyrics: Phish, Tom Marshall
Album: *Story of the Ghost*
Debut: 7/2/98
Historian: Mankind Acaster

The album version of "Fikus" is a mellow, bass-driven percussive experiment. The lyrics are delivered in an enchanting Mike Gordon

spoken word monologue. Beginning about halfway through this idyllic South Pacific island vacation each phrase of the monologue is subsequently echoed by Trey Anastasio. The lyrics paint the picture of the artist escaping the bloody fray of the road, to spend some time on the beach, picking flowers, watching the ocean boil, and all for free. "Fikus" is one of the least played songs from *Story of the Ghost*, having been performed only four additional times since being debuted in Copenhagen on 7/2/98. The live version of "Fikus" is perhaps more sparse than the album version as it lacks the layered polyrythmic effects of the tin cans, mason jars, and the ocean found on the studio cut. "Fikus'" present role in the live Phish experience mimics the vacation it describes: a brief chance to take a breath and look around.

Fire

Music/Lyrics: Jimi Hendrix
Original Artist: Jimi Hendrix Experience
Original Album: *Are You Experienced?* (1967)
Vocals: Trey (lead), Mike, Page, Fish (backing)
Debut: 12/2/83
Historian: Craig DeLucia and Mark Toscano

Perhaps no other cover has endured as long of an uninterrupted run in concert rotation followed by a seeming disappearing act from the stage. Played straightforward as a tribute to the greatest left-handed guitarist in the history of rock and roll (Trey deliberately used the song to pay tribute Jimi's birthday on 11/27/96), "Fire" had been a concert staple from its debut in 1983 through late 1997. After that year's New Year's show, though, the song was not heard again until 7/23/99 and has made few appearances since (9/8/00, 9/24/00).

In true Phish fashion, they began playing "Fire" sandwiched between the Dead's "Scarlet Begonias" and "Fire on the Mountain" as one of the band's first recurring stunts. This triplet of covers, perhaps Phish's first official on-stage "joke," ("Scarlet" > "Fire" > "Fire," get it?) began the second set of the very first gig on 12/2/83. Unfortunately, dance organizers upped the P.A. during the Hendrix tune (blasphemous!) to drown out the largely unappreciated band with Michael Jackson's *Thriller*. The combo was also likely played at the band's very next gig a few days later, though a setlist is not known for that show. As this tape doesn't circulate, the (quite literally) most accessible version is from the well-circulated 12/1/84 show. Two later "Fires" (sans "FOTM") worth seeking out are 4/20/89 and 6/21/94, where the song served as a tribute to fire alarms in the concert venues.

The most famous "Fire," though, was on 2/6/93. Following a few botched attempts blamed on Mike, Trey jokingly suggested Mike step down and they get Jimi Hendrix Experience bassist Noel Redding out to give it a whirl. And he did. The ensuing "Fire" (watched by Mike from off-stage left) was a bit slower and groovier, and stretched out a bit. Check this version out for obvious reasons, with fiery solos from John Popper and Trey being the deciding factors.

Fire on the Mountain

Music: Mickey Hart
Lyrics: Robert Hunter
Original Artist: Grateful Dead
Original Album: *Shakedown Street* (1978)
Vocals: Trey (lead), Jeff (backing)

Debut: 12/1/84
Historian: Christian C. McKee

There are, depending on who you talk to, either two or three ways of hearing members of Phish play this classic Grateful Dead song. The least controversial is to obtain a copy of 12/1/84, the earliest common tape in circulation. Trey, Page, Mike and Jon used to have a yen for performing the Dead's well known transitions in an ever-so-Phishy way: see 1986's "Help on the Way" > "Slipknot!" > "AC/DC Bag." On 12/1/84, you can hear Phish play "Scarlet Begonias" -> "Fire" > "Fire on the Mountain," adding the famous Hendrix tune to the traditional Scarlet -> Fire sandwich. Good, but not great, Phish could hardly live up to the fluidity and grace of the Dead at the time.

The next, and most controversial encounter Phish had with this tune came on 12/31/95. The question of whether or not there is a "Fire On the Mountain" tease towards the very end of the second set-opening "Drowned" has raged online since the first concert reviews were posted. This author hears no such thing, but a great many do. Obviously, there is no authoritative answer to this mystery, it's best to make up your mind for yourself.

While not Phish per se, you can hear Trey and Page play this song as members of Phil and Friends on 4/16/99. This version is certainly the best they've ever been involved in, and can lend a great deal of perspective on how much Trey's guitar playing and voice have matured since the winter of 1984.

Fire Up the Ganja

Music: Mickey Hart
Lyrics: Robert Hunter (altered from original)
Original Artist: Grateful Dead
Original Album: *Shakedown Street* (1978)
Vocals: Phish and Lamb's Bread
Debut: 3/4/85
Historian: Ellis Godard

This song is known to have occurred only once in Phish history, in a show that was really a combination of Phish members with members of Lamb's Bread. Fitting the haphazardness of the combination, and the party ritual of the evening, the group launched into a rastafarian rendition of "Fire on the Mountain." With lyrics that parody Hunter's original words, giving the tune an obvious thematic spin, this tune has gone down in Phish history as one of the band's most irreverant (but least heard) covers.

First Tube

AKA: "Bing Bong"
Music: Trey Anastasio, Russ Lawton, Tony Markellis
Lyrics: Heloise Williams (not performed by Phish)
Album: *Farmhouse*
Debut: 9/9/99
Historian: Martin Acaster and Mark Toscano

The name with which this blistering rocker ultimately became adorned is a misnomer on two counts. Apparently "First Tube" owes its title to the belief that it was the first song Trey performed with the 8-Foot Fluorescent Tubes at Higher Ground (4/17/98). If the version released on *Farmhouse* is any indication of the original composition of the tune, then it was in fact preceded at the Higher Ground show by a brief instrumental prelude. Furthermore, the 8-Foot Fluorescent Tubes version actually featured lyrics of a sort, lyrics which further compound the misidentification of the song. Since, following some introductory banshee-like wails from Heloise Williams (formerly of Viperhouse), the phrase "Free Thought" is repeated incessantly over the wailing combo of Anastasio, Lawton, and Markellis. "Mozambique" (AKA "Free Thought) of course being the title of another Trey band song which ultimately made it into the Phish repetoire.

Despite the inherent confusion of its identity (prior to its formal identification on *Farmhouse* that is), "First Tube" has quickly become a fan favorite. So much so in fact that nary a complaint has been heard about the song being overplayed since its 9/9/99 debut (in Vancouver, BC). Typically not the case when a new song is so frequently revisited after its first appearance. This curious response is likely due to just how electrifying the song can be. Often getting the call as a show opener, "First Tube" is guaranteed to crank up the energy level of the crowd a couple of extra notches. The incandescent liquid metallic fire of the song usually causes Trey to bounce higher than he does when jumping on the tramps and at times (e.g. Radio City Music Hall 5/21/00) has even incited Pete Townshend-style rock guitar god pinwheel strumming. The fat groove laid down by Mike and Fish is guaranteed to make a dancer out of even the most rhythmless among us as Trey's soaring guitar and Page's neo-medieval trance-space keyboard fills carry stray thoughts to where they truly can be set free. Anybody who does not like "First Tube" just does not know how to have a good time. Once you've had the "First Tube" you've quite honestly had the best tube. You know you want it. So for a good time call on the following: 9/12/99 Portland, OR; 9/24/99 Austin, TX; 10/10/99 Albany, NY; 12/18/99 Hampton, VA; 5/21/00 New York, NY; 6/9/00 Tokyo, Japan; 6/28/00 Holmdel, NJ and 7/11/00 Deer Creek, IN.

"First Tube" is also noteworthy for being the first Phish tune since "Esther" (in 1991) to feature an animated video made to augment its already vivid musical imagery. The disturbed, surreal story of a disfigured green beastman who keeps losing his head was produced by Bullseye Art in Shockwave format, and was available for viewing on their site by mid-2000.

Fish Bass

Music: Phish
Album: *The Siket Disc*
Vocals: (instrumental)
Debut: (never performed live)
Historian: Mark Toscano

Jon Fishman is responsible for the train-like rumblings of effect and delay loop-laden bass guitar on the brief fourth track of *The Siket Disc*. If Mike ever lets Fish near his bass long enough at a show to create these characteristic loops, the tune may some day be performed live. Until that day comes, though, the song remains immortalized only on compact disc.

Fishin' Hole Theme

AKA: "The Fishin' Hole," "Theme from The Andy Griffith Show," "Andy Griffith Theme"
Music: Herbert W. Spencer and Earle H. Hagen
Lyrics: Everett Sloane

Vocals: (performed instrumental)
Debut: 5/13/89
Historian: Ellis Godard

Its real name is no better known that its lyrics (written years later), but rightchere's a catchy television classic of yesteryear. A professed fan of ditties, Trey picked up the tune as part of the band's "secret language" (see dictionary entry). It has been deployed in "Possum" (5/13/89 and 2/10/90), "Antelope" (3/8/90 and 3/28/93), and "Weekapaug" (11/16/90). But the classic performance came when the band whistled it to open a second set (8/26/89) and the audience whistled along.

5:15

Original Artist: The Who
Original Album: *Quadrophenia* (1973)
Vocals: Trey
Debut: 10/31/95
Historian: Craig DeLucia

Phish's interpretation of one of the more popular *Quadrophenia* songs, complete with horns, left many fans wishing that the the band would not let this song be a one-time cover. Trey's searing solo at the end reinforces this desire for many fans every time they listen to their Halloween 1995 tapes. Perhaps the song's nature has condemned it, though, to being shelved: without horns, it would sound flat and incomplete, and guest horn appearances have been all-too-rare in the mid- and late-nineties.

The song opens and closes with a brief reprise of "Cut My Hair," but the force of the song is housed in a fast-moving train that is carrying the narrator to the beach for a self-indulgent time. The narrator, influenced by both the uppers he has taken and his desire for a good time, is "going out of [his] brain on the train." It is his arrival that sets the tone for the rest of the story, and it was this song that set the tone for the rest of the Halloween show.

Fixin' To Die

Music/Lyrics: Bukka White
Original Artist: Bukka White
Original Album: single (1940s)
Vocals: "Reverend" Jeff Mosier (11/17/94); Trey (11/30/94)
Debut: 11/17/94
Historian: Jeremy Welsh

Phish has played this dark Delta blues song twice. The debut occurred on the 17th of November, 1994, as the final song of a four-song encore. "Reverend" Jeff Mosier accompanied Phish on the banjo, as he would for a number of shows that fall. "Fixin' to Die's" second appearance is a must hear; two weeks later, on the night of the 30th, a dark and vengeful "Fixin' to Die" appeared out of jam in the middle of an incredibly unique second set. This set had begun interestingly enough, with a raging "Antelope" flowing out of a "Halley's Comet" opener. As the "Antelope" began to take off, it curiously segued into "My Sweet One"; the rockin' energy continued out of "My Sweet One" into a jam that featured the unique upright bass that Mike was playing that fall. As the jam progressed, it moved smoothly into "Fixin' to Die." This version is long and drawn out, with energy and some very good vocals by Trey. "Fixin'" may be more familiar to fans as the fifth track on Bob Dylan's self-titled 1962 debut LP.

Flat Fee

AKA: "Jerry's Beard"
Music: Trey Anastasio
Album: (none)
Debut: 8/9/87
Historian: Mark Toscano/Tim Wade

Trey wrote this piece as part of his work with Ernie Stires, the influential Burlington-area jazz and classical composer who served as a mentor for the musically starved Trey during his Goddard years. Ernie helped Trey realized his desire to write music that was compositionally challenging, yet fun, entertaining, and danceable. "Flat Fee" represents an early accomplishment for Trey in this vein, but also reflects his first successful attempt at composing horn charts for one of his own compositions. The most notable story about this song deals with precisely this event, and Ernie's reaction when Trey showed him the arrangement. Trey had spent weeks on the song, and it ellicited a historical comment from Ernie about "Flat Fee" representing a breakthrough for Trey's music writing. Ernie likened the event to Trey finally poking his head out of the ground in order to find himself at the base of this huge mountain that still lays before him. These words resonated big-time for Trey, who has always been driven by a desire to experiment in composition and performance.

"Flat Fee" made a handful of live appearances in 1987 and 1988, although Trey, proud of the horn arrangement he had written for the piece, was not satisfied with its sans-horn incarnation. Check out 8/9/87, 8/21/87, 8/29/87, 5/15/88, or 6/21/88 for these hornless versions. After a two-year hiatus, the tune made its comeback during the July 1991 tour with the Giant Country Horns, making appearances at eight of these shows, from 7/11/91 through 7/25/91. Since that time, principally due to the lack of another horn tour, "Flat Fee" has faded into the shadows.

Fluffhead/Fluff's Travels

AKA: "Fluff," "Fluffy," "Fluff!"

Peter Sizman

Music: Trey Anastasio
Lyrics: The Dude of Life (Fluffhead),
   Trey Anastasio (Fluff's Travels)
Album: *Junta*
Debut: 12/1/84
Historian: Mark Toscano

Like "Reba," "Fluffhead" is many a fan's favorite Phish tune. Also like "Reba," the song seems to embody every aspect of early Phish: a catchy intro, bizarre, surreal lyrics ("elevated prime did edit her?!?"), a complex, multi-part composition, and a blissfully climactic ending jam. Before the song finally premiered live in its "final draft" form on 5/15/88, it went through many changes. To start with, it was written in separate parts (parenthetical timings represent the timings on the *Junta* studio version of the song):

> I. Fluffhead (0:00-3:24)
> II. Fluff's Travels (0:00-1:09)
> III. The Chase (1:09-2:21)
> IV. Who Do? We Do! (2:21-4:12)
> V. Clod (4:12-7:21)
> VI. Bundle of Joy (7:21-9:10)
> VII. Arrival (w/ outro) (9:10-11:38)

"Fluffhead" debuted on 12/1/84 at Nectar's with guest vocals from The Dude of Life, who penned the lyrics for the song. The opening three verses were written by The Dude about a guy he and Trey had seen at a Dead show in 1983. The Dude's older brother was dying of cancer at the time, and so when they saw some guy at the Dead show, also a cancer patient, with cotton balls stuck all over his bald head to simulate hair, it struck a chord. The rest of the song's lyrics, showing up in the "Clod" segment, were composed by Trey and chosen more for their sound than their meaning. At this first performance, the song was comprised of only the "Fluffhead" and "Arrival" segments, one segueing into the other, running only about 4:40 in total. By late 1986, the composition had been altered slightly to incorporate a new segment, "Fluff's Travels," which, along with some meddling with the format, extended the length of the average version to roughly 9 minutes (see: 10/15/86, 4/24/87, 4/29/87). Also around this time, other random segments of the future epic "Fluffhead" began to surface as individual compositions in the band's live repertoire. For instance, the end chunk of "Who Do? We Do!" at this time served as the end chunk of "I am Hydrogen"! (Again, see 4/24/87 or 4/29/87.) "The Chase" made up part of "Lushington," another early tune (see 10/15/86).

By the time of the 8/21/87 Ian's Farm show, "Clod" and "Bundle of Joy" had surfaced, but still not within the context of "Fluffhead." "Clod" appeared on its own in a slightly extended version in the first set, while "Bundle of Joy" was actually sandwiched in the middle of a "Harpua"-sans-narration in set two.

Although "Fluffhead" had codified by May of 1988, the band continued to spotlight an individual segment or two here and there in their set. For instance, check out the 10/26/89 Wetlands show for disembodied performances of "Who Do? We Do!" and "The Chase." Also, see the freaky 10/31/87 show for performances of almost every individual part, including the then-incomplete "Fluffhead" itself.

Although some fans say that they find "Fluffhead" to be a composed waste of time during which fifteen minutes of serious improvisation could be taking place, the majority still keep "Fluffhead" near and dear to their hearts as a favorite tune that hasn't mellowed with age. Just one example: At the 6/11/94 Red Rocks show, a group shout of "Fluffhead!" can be heard (on the tape!) multiple times throughout the show. When the band finally appeased them with the song in set two, the audience was treated to quite an excellent version, after which the thankful group of shouters yelled "Fluffhead!" one last time to show their appreciation. Along with this version, 2/20/93, 6/22/94, 8/2/96, 11/30/96, 7/10/99, and 9/17/00 stand out as stellar versions of the song. Due to a fire alarm during the 4/20/89 version, the song was aborted. When the band resumed the show, a spontaneous "You Shook Me All Night" jam segued beautifully into "Fluff's Travels" to finish out the song. Especially unique is the Alpine Valley 7/24/99 version, which proved that the song could jam; the band extended the "Arrival" segment out to realize a 30+-minute outing of the song, segueing nicely into "TMWSIY." 9/30/00, although not as strong as the Alpine version, was also followed by an unusual jam that eventually let into "The Meatstick." Though always welcome at a show, "Fluffhead" has suffered a bit in recent years as the band's more loose, improvisational approach sometimes makes it difficult to pull off these tightly composed numbers without several hitches. To understand what I'm talking about, do yourself the questionable favor of checking out the "Fluffhead" from 12/5/99.

See Also: "Arrival," "Bundle of Joy," "The Chase," "Clod," "Fluff's Travels," "Who Do? We Do!"

Fluff's Travels
Music: Trey Anastasio
Album: "The White Tape," *Junta*
   (part of "Fluffhead"—CD 0:00-1:09)
Debut: 10/15/86 (in "Fluffhead")
Historian: Mark Toscano

Perhaps this will clear things up. Technically, there are three things called "Fluff's Travels." The first (and earliest), which appears on the so-called "White Tape," bears only a passing resemblence to the "Fluff's Travels" that exists today. It is basically a bunch of effects and noises segueing out of Mike's "NO_2" outro, interpolating part of "Dave's Energy Guide," and closing with a brief, instrumental version of the "Fluffhead" intro. The second "Fluff's Travels," comprising the entire second track on the disc two of *Junta*, refers to the 11 (or so)-minute, 6-part composition that follows the opening three verses of "Fluffhead." This 6-part piece first became a permanent feature of the resultantly 15-minute "Fluffhead" in early 1988, and includes "Fluff's Travels," "The Chase," "Who Do? We Do!," "Clod," "Bundle of Joy," and "Arrival." To make it further confusing, "Fluff's Travels" is also the name of the first individual part of the complete "Fluff's Travels" (0:00-1:09 on *Junta* CD track 2). Perhaps this hasn't cleared things up at all.

See Also: "Fluffhead/Fluff's Travels"

FLY FAMOUS MOCKINGBIRD (see THE FAMOUS MOCKINGBIRD)

Foam
AKA: "Marijuana Hot Chocolate" (original title)
Music/Lyrics: Trey Anastasio
Album: *Junta; Hampton Comes Alive* (11/21/98)
Debut: 11/3/88
Historian: Grant Calof

If you saw Phish in the late eighties and early nineties, you were all but guaranteed to see them blaze their way through the criss-crossing melodies of "Foam." This particular crowd-pleaser consists of several intricately composed layers, wrapped around fugue-like moves that were a signature of the band's playing at the time. "Foam" offers yet another example of composer Ernie Stires' influence through its flowing combination of varying styles and rhythms (see "Reba" and "Fluffhead," among others).

The lyrics, referring to the ever-thickening foam despite one's attempt to see things clearly, are easy to interpret but difficult to define. Regardless of whether it's meant to be philosophical, sociological, metaphorical or literal, it's clear that the deeper we sink, the harder it is to see through the foam (metaphorically speaking, in this case).

One fateful day in Burlington, (April 22, 1988 to be exact) the band was running through a few new songs. Trey announced one called "Marijuana Hot Chocolate" and Mike played a piece of the bass line to the aforementioned tune. No one knew it at the time, but "Marijuana Hot Chocolate" was the very same melody that would become "Foam" just seven months later. The original title—referring to a concoction that would often accompany the band's Oh Kee Pah ceremonies—was dropped in favor of the much more innocuous "Foam."

Despite its free-flowing nature, "Foam" is an almost entirely scripted piece, the only exception being the atmospheric middle section with its ascending piano/guitar jam. Touted by Trey as the band's toughest song to get through, "Foam's" complex arrangements offer a way in which the band can get warmed up onstage, and thus has largely remained a first set tune. Even the drums and bass for this tune were sketched out on orchestral staff paper.

"Foam" was so commonplace as a follow up to "Runaway Jim" that the combination became known, begrudgingly to some, as "Runaway Foam" (check out the awe-inspiring segue from 12/29/94). They've played it as a stand-alone (try 4/25/94), they've segued into it from songs other than "Runaway Jim" (check out the seamless "Gin" -> "Foam" from 8/3/97), and they've always played it furiously (treat yourself to 5/30/93).

At one point, unsubstantiated rumors circulated that "Foam" had been put on a shelf along with a number of older Phish tunes (causing some amusing paranoia during Europe 1997). The sad reality though, was that with the advent of new material, "Foam" was simply being played less and less. As the years progressed, "Foam" slowly began to fade into setlist obscurity. It was played five times in 1997, and by 1998, that number had dwindled to four (feel free to enjoy 11/29/97 and 11/21/98, two outstanding tour highlights). "Foam" was rumored to have been soundchecked during the summer of 1999, but wasn't played for an audience all that year. And it remained noticeably absent until Summer Tour 2000, when "Foam" bubbled its way back up to the surface during a rain-drenched set in Camden, New Jersey (7/3/00). Finally, after a gap of three tours and eighty-seven shows, the foam was once again getting thicker.

The Fog That Surrounds
AKA: "Fog"
Music/Lyrics: Phish, Tom Marshall
Album: (none)
Debut: 9/27/95

Historian: Mark Toscano

The Fall '95 tour opener in Sacramento, CA marked this song's debut—sort of. Perhaps Trey explained it most concisely in his introduction at that very show, indicating that some fans may think they recognized the song, but it wasn't what they thought it was.

But then again, it was *almost* what everyone thought it was. It *was* "Taste"—or rather, a lyrically re-worked version of "Taste." The music was the same. The structure was the same. Hell, even the chorus was the same. But the easy Summer '95 fan favorite had somehow become—simply through the obliteration of the original's lyrics—an entirely different tune that many folks frankly found frightening. Well, that's overstating it quite a bit. The re-worked "Taste" (dubbed "The Fog That Surrounds") was a fine song, but it was a finer song when it *was* "Taste," and fans couldn't figure out why the band had messed with it. The new lyrics, sung well by Fishman (who had that tour just begun to truly find his singing voice), were even received with no real criticism. Perhaps it was merely the principle: "If it ain't broke, why fix it?"

At any rate, the band was apparently also unsatisfied with this second incarnation of the tune, and by the middle of the Fall '95 tour it had undergone another change. This third version—dubbed "Tasty Fog" by many fans following its 10/27/95 debut—was basically an egalitarian combination of the two previous versions. Trey would start out with his "Taste" verses, and Fishman would begin his "Fog" verses one triplet behind, in true "Row, Row, Row Your Boat" fashion. Fish's verses would conclude over repetitions of the chorus from the other band members. This third version of the song persisted through the end of the year, its final performance being the 12/29/95 Worcester Centrum show.

The fourth variation of this song turned out to be basically the first version again, and it re-debuted on 7/3/96, with Carlos Santana making a guest appearance to boot. Trey made it official in Amsterdam on 7/12/96, announcing in the first set that "Fog That Surrounds" would cease to exist, with "Taste" re-asserting its place in the band's repertoire.

Though it hasn't been played since 1995, a few residual "Fog" lyrics remain in the final version of "Taste" (and the version found on 1996's *Billy Breathes*), which hopefully goes to show that all of that re-working wasn't for nothing. For versions of "Fog That Surrounds," check out 9/27/95, 9/28/95, 9/30/95, 10/2/95, 10/5/95, 10/7/95, 10/11/95, 10/17/95, or 10/24/95. For versions of "Tasty Fog," check out 10/27/95, 11/10/95, 11/12/95, 11/22/95, 11/25/95, 11/29/95 (with Béla Fleck), 12/2/95, 12/5/95, 12/7/95, 12/11/95, 12/14/95, 12/16/95, or 12/29/95.

See Also: "Taste"

FOOLED BY IMAGES (see: "WAKING UP")

Foreplay/Long Time
Original Artist: Boston
Original Album: *Boston* (1976)
Vocals: Phish
Debut: 10/7/94
Historian: Craig DeLucia

In the fall of 1994, Phish began to play a variety of songs in a traditional bluegrass setup. Most of these tunes were bluegrass staples by legends like Bill Monroe and Earl Scruggs. As usual, though, the band was not content to simply accept common musical conventions

and put their own musical twist on this hard-rocking Boston classic by modifying the song from an arena-rock classic to a bluegrass ditty. The intro, once played on a wailing organ, was transposed for the banjo, which Mike Gordon worked into a frenzy. Like "Freebird," this song remains a classic example of how Phish always finds a way to put their own unique stamp on even the most popular of all music.

When the Fall '94 tour came to an end, "Foreplay/Long Time" was put on the shelf with many of the bluegrass songs that had become concert regulars. It remained there until the summer of 1999, when it made its first (and only) electric appearance to lead off the July 12 Tweeter Center show. Whether future versions remain electric or return to bluegrass remains to be seen.

Four Strong Winds

Music/Lyrics: Ian Tyson
Original Artist: Ian & Sylvia
Original Album: *Four Strong Winds* (1964)
Vocals: Neil Young (lead), Sarah MacLachlan (backing)
Debut: 10/18/98
Historian: Erik Swain

On their only performance of this song, on the second day of the 1998 Bridge School Benefit, Phish sat back and let the Canadians have the spotlight. This folk tune, penned by Canadian Ian Tyson and full of Canadian pastoral imagery, followed Phish's collaboration with Canadian songstress Sarah McLachlan on Cat Stevens' "Sad Lisa." Neil Young, the benefit's organizer and another Canadian, emerged from backstage before "Four Strong Winds" started to take the lead vocal. The band left Young and McLachlan to handle all the singing and stuck to the arrangement Young used when he covered "Four Strong Winds" on his *Comes A Time* album (1978). So, if you don't like this performance, Blame Canada!

Frankenstein

Music: Edgar Winter
Original Artist: Edgar Winter Group
Original Album: *They Only Come Out at Night* (1972)
Vocals: (instrumental)
Debut: 11/11/89
Historian: Mark Toscano

Edgar Winter named this tune "Frankenstein" because its various sections were independently composed, and then fitted together like a monstrous creation. This creation ended up dominating radio and the concert stage, leaving a wretched path of devastation in its wake. A variety of bands have covered "Frankenstein," among them The Ventures, Overkill, and They Might be Giants (nothing beats this tune on the accordion!). Add Phish to that list: their early-on preference for both classic rock covers and complex, multi-part instrumentals made this tune a shoe-in.

The debut on 11/11/89 set the stage properly, showcasing horns for the song. 11/16/89 featured the song segueing out of "YEM," something it also did on 7/8/94 (in that version, segueing out of and back into "YEM"). Following a few more performances, the song disappeared for a year and a half after the 12/3/89 performance, resurfacing very aptly on the 7/91 horn tour. The song was a standard on that tour, appearing on 7/11, 7/12, 7/13, 7/15, 7/24, and 7/26.

Following a three hundred-plus show absence, the song was broken out at the excellent 6/11/94 show, catching many fans off guard for what ended up being an awesome version. Since then, it has made regular appearances in the live show, never leaving the stage for very long. Some strong versions include 6/17/94, 10/31/94 (appropriate show opener), 12/3/94 (with horns), 11/11/95 (awesome, segueing into "Suspicious Minds"), 12/14/95, 12/31/95, 8/17/96, 10/31/96 (horns), 12/30/97 (with Fish on vacuum), 11/9/98, 9/14/99 (with vacuum and "One of These Days" quote), and 7/7/00. Strong teases of the song have also shown up in the 12/15/99 "Rocky Top," the 8/14/97 Merry Pranksters jam, and "YEMs" from 7/19/91, 6/18/94, 11/17/94, and 11/23/94. Look for this one almost exclusively as a set closer or encore.

Frankie Says

AKA: "Relax," "Frankie Sez"
Music/Lyrics: Phish, Tom Marshall
Album: *Story of the Ghost*
Debut: 4/2/98
Historian: Grant Calof

Rumors surrounding some type of Spring Tour (mini, club dates, etc.) circulate pretty much every year, but in 1998 the rumors proved true. The Island Tour, as it was appropriately dubbed (Long Island and Rhode Island were the only venues), came as briefly as it went, but it left a handful of new tunes, and thus a handful of debates over their correct titles. Was it "Relax" or "Roggae" (or "Roget"), "Oblivious Fool" or "Shafty"? "Frankie Says" was first misidentified as "Roggae" thanks to a confusing conversation between Tom Marshall and some fans. After the Rhode Island show on April 4, 1998, two fans asked Tom the name of the new "Page" song. Tom hadn't been at that particular show, so the fans described the song as best they could. He tried to be helpful, but apparently thought the fans were referring to "Roggae" (pronounced "rouge" at the time, by the way). From that conversation, people assumed they had absolute confirmation, and the word was spread: "The song last night was called 'Roggae'!." It wasn't until the album was released that the dispute for all the correct song names was laid to rest.

Amusingly passionate debates still continue as to the origin of the song's title, though. To some, the title is a tongue-in-cheek homage to the infamous 1980s synth-pop act, Frankie Goes to Hollywood, while others simply see it as a way to avoid having a song with the same name as the song by the aforementioned eighties synth-pop act ("Relax") (Don't deny it—You know the song)

Lyrically, "Frankie Says" weaves a haunting tapestry that delves into the darker realms of the psyche more than most Phish songs. It toys with notions of the self, the cyclical nature of life, and paints time as an eternal flowing river, with consciousness as its guide. The subtle inflexions in Page's voice make it all more resonant. The song is so hypnotic, that with the right headphones, it feels like slipping into a musically driven trance.

"Frankie Says" made thirteen appearances in 1998 (check out the dreamy version from 8/16/98 or when it filled the space between "Mike's Song" and "Weekapaug Groove" on 10/31/98), but only two in 1999 (try 10/7/99). And while the song appears predominantly as a first set tune, it surfaced twice during the 2000 summer tour, both occurring amid the second sets in Georgia (6/24/00) and Ohio (7/14/00). And while it's a favorite for late night listening in a darkened room, there's

little variation to the way the song is played. Some would argue that "Frankie Says" has yet to really find its place in the live show experience, but most consider it a welcome addition to any set.

The first studio version of "Frankie Says" appeared on a tape commonly known as the "*Ghost* outtakes" or "Bearsville sessions" that circulated around the community before *Story of the Ghost* was released. But the first time it appeared on stage, at least partially, was in an atmospheric post-"Timber Ho" and pre-"Simple" jam on 11/17/97 in Denver. And it's more than just a tease. As the band ascends out of "Timber Ho," Trey plays the first few notes of "Frankie Says" while Mike subtly drops in and Page's hands trace the simply melody (the man in the dress all the while keeping the beat). They play the first few notes of the song all the way through the moments preceding the first refrain, then glide their way into "Simple." If you don't have the show, definitely make a point of getting it, for the jam as well as to check out a little bit of that fat '97 funk.

Free

Music: Trey Anastasio
Lyrics: Tom Marshall
Album: *Billy Breathes; Hampton Comes Alive* (11/21/98)
Debut: 5/16/95
Historian: Craig DeLucia

Free was one of the many songs that debuted at the Lowell benefit concert in early 1995. Fans quickly took to the song, which tells of a man who is thinking of throwing his wife from the boat on which they sail. In fact, a minor lyrical change from earlier versions was released in the album version of the song and all subsequent live performances; this change from "as we go sliding by" to "as the ship goes sliding by" cemented the song's imagery in the minds of fans.

While the song has always been an outlet for jams, it has gone through several minor structural changes since its debut. The truncated album version was the most dramatic of all, as the band axed the swirling guitar-based intro. Some feared that the original intro was gone forever, but the band has always left it in the song's stage performances. As a whole, the music present in early versions conjured underwater images for many (which perfectly matches the nautical theme of the lyrics); this sound style was augmented with the addition of Trey's percussion rack in 1995. Post-1995 versions featured a stylistic change that effectively combined the coarse texture of good southern "rock" with the in-your-face sound of loud arena "roll."

The first jammed-out "Free" arose from an insane "Runaway Jim" at the 6/16/95 Walnut Creek show in Raleigh. Just ten days later, fans in Saratoga Springs, New York were treated to an inspiring "Down with Disease" -> "Free" second set opener. Three days after that, the second set at Jones Beach opened with a "Free" -> "David Bowie" combo and fans were left with little doubt that a new jamming star had been born.

The Fall 1995 tour brought Trey's percussion rack to the stage, and a new dimension was added to the jams. No song was greater influenced by the percussion rack than "Free." Using the rack allowed Trey to lay back in the jam while Page took control. Favorite versions include 11/10/95 at the Fox in Atlanta and 12/30/95 at Madison Square Garden. The 11/22/95 Landover version was also particularly intense, as the song followed an attempt at "Rift" that was aborted after a drum foul-up by Fishman. This "Free" clocked in at over 30 minutes and included

"Bouncing" teases and a segue into "Llama," as well as a spoken intro from Trey that dedicated the song to Fishman after his "Rift" gaffe.

The Summer 1996 tour saw "Free" become a spacier number. Notable versions include one from the third set of the wild 7/12/96 Amsterdam gig and a version at the historic Red Rocks Amphitheater on 8/7/96. The song's development continued through the fall, with 10/19/96 and 12/29/96 ("Rift" > "Free") providing strong showings. However, the jam section had started to become predictable, and many fans were losing interest.

The band changed all of this during the summer of 1997, as the song slowed down a hair and took on more of a bluesy angle. Part of the change involved dropping the reprise of the verse that used to be sung after the jam and substiting the ending from the album version of the song. "Free" quickly returned to the spotlight and has once again become a fan favorite. A prime example is the supreme 7/2/97 encore. Other inspiring versions include 8/8/97 Tinley Park (arising from "Wolf-man's Brother"), 8/14/97 at Darien Lake and the must-hear Worcester (11/30/97) "Stash" -> "Free" > Jam -> "Piper." Notable versions in 1998 include the 11/23 Hampton "Free" -> "Ha Ha Ha" -> "Free," which proved to fans that on any given night, any song combination is possible. "Free" contined to please in 1999, with many powerful and moving versions. The 7/23/99 Polaris "Ghost" -> "Free" stands out above the rest, with the oft-debated and much maligned 12/15/99 "Free" coming in a close second.

FREE THOUGHT (see "MOZAMBIQUE")

Freeworld

AKA: "If This is a Free World, Then Tomorrow Must be Just as Worse"
Music/Lyrics: (unknown)
Vocals: (unknown)
Debut: 3/6/87
Historian: Mark Toscano

Quite the mystery, this unidentified song has circulated on setlists for years as "Freeworld," even though the unknown vocalist announces the title (though perhaps sarcastically) as "If This is a Free World, Then Tomorrow Must be Just as Worse." Performed one single time at a sparsely attended Goddard Cafeteria gig, the vocalist also claims to have just made up the song. If this is true, stick this one in the same bin as "The Jaegermeister Song" and "The Practical Song," tunes also made up on the spot for equally amusing and mysterious reasons. If the person who sang/composed this tune is reading right now, we'd love to hear from you.

Freebird

Original Artist: Lynyrd Skynyrd
Original Album: *Pronounced Lêh'-nerd' Skin'-nerd* (1973)
Vocals: Ninja Mike (3/6/87); Wynnona Judd (6/22/00);
 Phish (all others)
Debut: 3/6/87
Historian: Martin Acaster

With the release of their self-titled (including phonetic pronunciation for the linguistically challenged) first album in 1973, Lynyrd Skynyrd added another wrinkle to the skin of the ripening Georgia

peach known as southern rock. "Freebird," the closing track to the album, quickly became a concert favorite. Not unlike the all too frequent calls for "Harpua" during the SHOW at Big Cypress, the rampant bellow of "Freebird" was a mantra to the typical bourbon sippin' Skynyrd fan.

The first Phish performance of "Freebird" was at Goddard College (3/6/87 Plainfield, VT), featured Ninja Mike Billington on vocals, and by all accounts was a rather tongue-in-cheek performance of the classic rock favorite. The song then flew the coop for over six years and about 450 shows. The triumphant return of "Freebird" at the Cayuga County Speedway (7/15/93 Weedsport, NY) raised the bar on the Phish comedy meter quite a few notches. Stepping to the microphones after a rocking "Chalk Dust Torture" encore to an already steamy Summer Tour opener, Trey put a question to the audience in the best Ronnie Van Zant drawl he could muster.

"Wayull…wut song is it y'all wanna heeyah?" An ecstatic young martian (for whom the sought after response was a common chant at every concert he had ever attended) pogoing on the front rail at his second Phish show gleefully exclaimed "FREEBIRD!" and was rewarded with his request. What set this version apart from the debut performance was that nary an instrument was played. "Freebird," a capella, yet complete with guitar solo and the big arena rock finish. This band was just TOO MUCH. "Freebird" made many flights (typically as an encore) throughout the rest of 1993. Among the best were the 7/24/93 Great Woods (Mansfield, MA), 8/20/93 Red Rocks (Morrison, CO) and 12/30/93 Cumberland County Civic Center (Portland, ME) performances. "Freebird" was much more difficult to catch in 1994 as it appeared at only five shows in the first half of the year. For the next three and a half years (with the exception of a "Freebird" outro jam here and there; see 7/20/98 "Poor Heart") there were just too many places that bird had to see before it finally came home to roost on 10/17/98 at a Bridge School Benefit show at the Shoreline Amphitheater (Mountain View, CA).

An electrifying (yet still a capella) performance the first night (10/30/98) of the Vegas Halloween run left fans more than ready for a long night of gaming. "Freebird" flew several more times that year but once again went into hiding throughout 1999. The most spectacular version to date of "Freebird," played as the closer to the second set of the 6/22/00 Summer Tour opener, was complete with instruments, a guest appearance by the Del McCoury Band (including Ricky Scaggs and Sam Bush), and the vocal stylings of the free-as-a-bird (her divorce was finalized that day) Wynonna Judd. I'm certain there's never been a "Freebird" that flew any higher.

Fuck Your Face

Music/Lyrics: Mike Gordon
Album: "The White Tape"
Debut: (unknown—but not 4/28/87)
Historian: Mark Toscano

The Phish song with the naughtiest title (except perhaps "Sleeping Monkey…"), this hilarious creation belongs to the versatile mind of Mr. Michael Gordon. This tune appears in 4-tracked "studio" form on the band's "White Tape" demo, and is a curious nugget of wailing coprolalia. Mike played all of the instruments on this version, and supplied the angry rocker-boy vocals as well, singing meanly about forcing his screaming guitar to painfully fornicate with the poor, unsuspecting listener's general facial area. Despite the song's own assertive and stub-

born demeanor, though, it remains a dinosaur from the band's past, lurking near the bottom of the Phishy tar pits somewhere between "Dear Mrs. Reagan" and "Lushington."

One noticeable gap in this tune's history is the uncertainty about whether or not it was ever performed live. So far, the mystery is only half-solved. On most circulating tapes of 4/29/87 sets II and III, side one ends with a *definitely live* "Fuck Your Face." It's not at all the same version found on "The White Tape," especially since here it features Page's keyboards as well as a spoken bit from Page during the song's brief breakdown. Unfortunately, though, this version is NOT from 4/29/87, as it is frequently labelled—the sound quality is different, and there is a distinct cut between it and "Cities" (the previous song). This "mystery version" of "Fuck Your Face" may remain a mystery for some time, but it is somehow comforting to know that at least once, fans were subjected to this truly wonderful, face-fucking aural monstrosity. Then again, as unlikely as it is that we will ever see "Fuck Your Face" performed on stage again, the band has been known to break out stranger tunes (see "NO$_2$").

Funky Bitch

Music/Lyrics: Son Seals
Original Artist: Son Seals
Original Album: *Live and Burning* (1978)
Phish Album: *Hampton Comes Alive* (11/20/98)
Vocals: Mike; Son Seals (7/17/99, 10/3/99)
Debut: 3/6/87
Historian: Craig DeLucia

Some say that the ultimate compliment for an artist is when another musician covers his or her material. Son Seals took it one step further: after joining Phish for a cover of his song "Funky Bitch," he invited Trey to join him on a new studio rendition!

The list of special guests that have joined Phish for "Funky Bitch" reads like an All-Star lineup from jamband heaven. Guests include John Popper (3/3/90 and 11/15/96), Carlos Santana and Karl Perazzo (7/25/92), Jimmy Herring (2/19/93), Sugar Blue (4/10/93 and 10/3/99), Warren Haynes (12/11/95), Peter Apfelbaum (11/30/96), Dave Grippo and James Harvey (3/18/97), LeRoi Moore (7/21/97), Derek Trucks (7/7/99), members of Son Seals' band (7/10/97), Son Seals himself (7/17/99 and 10/3/99), and Michael Ray (9/9/00).

Some of the band's most memorable takes on "Funky Bitch" haven't been for the music. Fans remember fondly the fireworks that lit up the Maine sky during the Great Went "Bitch" on 8/16/97. And Phish turned a strange situation into a humorous one on 12/30/96, when the arena P.A. system cut out during "Bitch" and the band hammed it up on stage to keep the crowd entertained while technicians scrambled to fix the equipment. Otherwise, though, "Funky Bitch" has remained a fan favorite (see 7/1/95, where Trey talks about how often the song is requested) while never straying too far from its bluesy progression. It does, however, allow each member of the band to show off their chops while Mike sings a high-pitched lament of his lover's fickle ways.

But "Funky Bitch" has been more than just a quick blues number, or a novelty act for guests. On a select few occasions, the song has been a monster jam vehicle. Pick up 11/22/94 for an insane, free-form jam that sprung from the ending of an otherwise normal "Funky Bitch," and

11/30/97 for an unfinished version that jammed into new territories. Round out your collection with 7/28/98, with an ending akin to "Black-Eyed Katy." Those looking for rare, obscure versions should try their hand at some circulating soundchecks, as "Funky Bitch" has been a frequent soundcheck number in the 1990s. Two notable versions are 5/5/93 ("Poor Heart" and "Funky Bitch" intermingled) and 8/24/93 (sung in the vein of Midnight Oil, complete with "Beds are Burning" lyrics).

Funky (Breakdown)

Lyrics: Ninja Mike
Music: Ninja Custodians
Vocals: Ninja Mike (lead); Magoo (back-up vocals)
Debut: 5/28/89
Historian: Charlie Dirksen

At shows in the '80s and early '90s, a Burlington band known as the "Ninja Custodians" would routinely play their original, "Funky (Breakdown)," often accompanied by insects on a projection screen. During Phish's show at Ian's Farm on 5/28/89, "Mike and Magoo Ninja"—from the "where are they now" category—were invited by Trey to the stage. The ensuing, memorable "Funky (Breakdown)" -> "Price of Love" (with vacuum, trombone, keyboards, bass, drums, percussion and guitar) continues to amuse fans to this day.

Gamehendge

Some time during Trey's fall 1985 semester at Goddard College, Tom Marshall sent him a letter. The two were attending different schools, and often kept in contact through written correspondence. However, rather than containing any of the typical greetings and so forth commonly found in such letters, the envelope contained only a poem. The poem in question was "McGrupp and the Watchful Hosemasters." This is where it all began. Or at least, this is where a lot of it began. Well, let's just say that this is where Gamehendge began.

Trey was intrigued by the poem—enough to mount it on the door of his dorm room for about a year. Over the course of this year, the poem made occasional appearances in the Phish live show, primarily as a sort of spoken-word performance (see 5/3/85). Eventually, Trey took the music from a song he had written with his mother, "Skippy the Wondermouse," and grafted "McGrupp's" words onto it. ("Skippy" itself had also occasionally appeared in the band's live show until 1985.)

In the meantime, Trey had also been working with his mother on a children's musical called "Gus the Christmas Dog." Although he enjoyed developing this project, he also wanted to hone his growing skills as a composer. The poem upon the door beckoned, and Trey answered its call.

During the Fall 1986 semester, Trey started formulating a project for his Goddard "Senior Study." Whereas Page had written on "The Art of Improvisation," and Fishman would later do a treatise on his experience with self-taught drumming, Trey had decided to write a multi-song musical that would demonstrate his knowledge and strengths in both lyrical and musical composition. "McGrupp," with its lines describing a host of intriguing but anonymous characters, served as the creative impetus for Trey's project, which soon came to be known as "The Man Who Stepped Into Yesterday."

By combining McGrupp's characters and their implied relationships with other ideas already formulated a few years earlier by Trey, Tom, and Aaron Woolfe in the song "Wilson, Can You Still Have Fun?"

("Wilson"), Trey started to develop the storyline. Although both songs were originally intended as nonsense, Trey found a satisfying challenge in constructing a thematically strong and dramatically cohesive musical story from the disparate bits of silliness he and his friends had written.

Two other songs already in the band's repertoire became engulfed in the tide of the ever-expanding Gamehendge story: "AC/DC Bag" and "Possum." Both had been performed live for some time before Trey decided to incorporate them into his Senior Study. In fact, "Possum" was originally written by Jeff Holdsworth, Phish's second guitarist through Spring 1986. Trey merely changed some of the words and music a bit to fit better with his project.

With these four songs already destined to fit into the storyline, Trey began to compose original material that would tie up all the loose narrative ends, as well as allow him to exercise his music-writing abilities. The first song written especially for the musical, "The Lizards," represented a major step in forcing the strange, unrelated characters and episodes described in the other songs to cohere into an actual narrative. "Tela" followed, fleshing out some of the characters' relationships. Besides, "Tela," "Colonel Forbin's Ascent" was the most time-consuming song to write, and Trey used its elaborate structure to lay a final, juicy slab of narrative on the listener before tying up loose ends with "The Famous Mockingbird" and "The Sloth." With this set of songs complete and coherent, "McGrupp and the Watchful Hosemasters," ironically the inspirational germ of the whole project, was subsequently used as a coda for the musical, a summation of the events that had transpired by an outside observer. It wasn't even included on the final Senior Study recording.

The final structure of the musical as Trey organized it for submission to his advisor at Goddard in July, 1988 was as follows: "The Lizards," "Tela," "Wilson," AC/DC Bag," "Colonel Forbin's Ascent," "The Famous Mockingbird," "The Sloth," "Possum."

On the audio tape that accompanied his Senior Study process paper, these songs progressed in the above order, bridged (and sometimes overdubbed) with narration and a connecting instrumental theme based on chords that eventually found their way into the song "Esther." Additionally, Trey composed an instrumental intro for the musical over which the introductory narrative was spoken leading into "The Lizards." This piece, which wound up in Phish's live repertoire, is commonly referred to as "The Man Who Stepped Into Yesterday," or "TMWSIY," not to be confused with the full musical itself, which also bears that name.

Other songs followed, some directly related to the Gamehendge saga, some very indirectly. "Punch You In the Eye" (formerly known as "Punch Me In the Eye") tells the story of a dissident of Wilson's regime who is captured in Prussia by Wilson's toadies, but then escapes by sea. "Llama" describes a practically post-apocalyptic, war-torn Gamehendge. "The Divided Sky" musically describes a sacred ritual from the pre-Wilson days of Gamehendge in which people would gather in the woods, ingest a special root that was believed to contain the spirit of Icculus, and celebrate in ceremony, dance, and song, convening around a giant Rhombus (basically what Trey and friends used to do back home). "Harpua" also almost always takes place at least partially in Gamehendge, though the events Trey describes almost never have anything to do with the main narrative in "The Man Who Stepped Into Yesterday." On occasion, Trey has proclaimed "Reba" and "Esther" to relate to Gamehendge, albeit tenuously. Additionally, songs like "It's Ice," "Kung," and "NO_2" have been used to enter Gamehendge at a

show. And of course, who could forget "Icculus," the song that Trey uses to slowly build a maniacal, feverish diatribe extolling the wonders of either the Helping Friendly Book or its great and knowledgeable author.

In 1988, after the Senior Study was fully organized and hammered out, Trey, Mike, Page, and Fish all learned it—very quickly—in order to record it on 4-track to turn in before the deadline that summer. By this time, all of the songs had begun showing up in the Phish repertoire, the last core tunes to appear being both "Tela" and "Colonel Forbin's Ascent," making their debuts on 3/12/88. This date also marks the first public presentation of the musical, in a show at Nectar's. "The Man Who Stepped Into Yesterday" was performed in its entirety, preceded strangely by "Jump Monk" and an explanatory "McGrupp." Though all of the songs frequently recurred in the band's live show, it wasn't until three and a half years later on 10/13/91 (in Olympia, WA, of all places) that the story was fully revisited. Well, almost fully. For some reason at this show, Trey elected to present the songs slightly out of order and without "Lizards" or "Possum." However, the crowd did get a "McGrupp" and "Llama" to boot.

Fast forward another year and a half, and the band was again performing on the west coast, this time on 3/22/93 at Sacramento's beautifully reconditioned Crest Theatre, an ornate, palatial movie theatre from the golden age of overindulgent cinema construction. Perhaps this setting put Trey in a theatrical mood (or perhaps the somewhat miniscule crowd was a refreshing change of pace for the band, whose fan base was growing quite rapidly at this point), because the Gamehendge saga was aired out that night in Sactown. The complete gamut was run, in the original order, starting with an "It's Ice" entrance and finishing with a beautiful "McGrupp," in place of "Possum." The classic set concluded with a nice "Mike's Groove." The Gamehendge saga got a public performance only twice more, on 6/26/94, and less than two weeks later on 7/8/94. The 6/26/94 performance is solid, with especially great versions of "Lizards," "AC/DC Bag," "McGrupp," (again subbing for "Possum") and the bonus set closer, "The Divided Sky." The 7/8/94 set was even stronger, also concluding with an awe-inspiring "Divided," but 3/22/93 remains most fans' favorite when it comes to live Gamehendge. (Those folks who haven't yet heard the Gamehendge story are encouraged to acquire a copy of the Senior Study tape, as well as at least one live version of the musical.)

Though the full musical has only been performed this handful of times, "Colonel Forbin's Ascent" and "The Famous Mockingbird" have, with only a couple of exceptions, always been performed together, and after 1991, always with some narrative in between. Though these narratives, like those in "Harpua," are usually hilarious, bizarre, and quite different from the original story (for an extreme example, seek out 8/7/98), they almost always get across the basic idea: Forbin seeks book, Forbin visits Icculus, Icculus sends bird to get book.

In recent years, there has been a lot less emphasis on the Gamehendge songs. Previously the band's bread and butter, they had most decidedly moved on by 1994, when the last full Gamehendge show was performed. Since Trey wrote most of the "TMWSIY" songs for himself, they have usually been seen by fans and the rest of the band (especially Mike) as "Trey" songs. Even though the guitarist writes so much of the band's material himself, the Gamehendge songs were particularly his, telling his story in his (and Tom Marshall's) words, set to his music.

Back in 1994, the Döniac Schvice featured an announcement of a possible CD-ROM project dealing with Gamehendge, incorporating a re-recorded studio version of the musical with animation and art and interactivity to augment it. In fact, it is likely that the Summer 1994 Gamehenge shows were performed with this project in mind, with 6/26/94 as a rehearsal, and 7/8/94—one of the few shows that tour recorded 24-track digital—to be the recording used on the CD-ROM itself. Though this project was talked about for a few years, it has almost definitely been filed in the "Dead Projects" folder, along with the "Big Ball jam," the "Hydrogen" ballet, and the show-to-show, tour-long chess game.

Despite the band's welcome evolution and movement away from this stuff of legend, the songs still remain special to fans, whether they discovered Phish back in the mid-'80s or at Big Cypress at the close of the 1900s. The tapes all circulate, keep changing hands and reaching new fans, and the story of the man who, one fateful day, stepped into yesterday will be forever told and retold in the circles of Phish lore.

See Also: Llama, PYITE, Divided Sky, Kung, NO_2, Esther, Harpua, TMWSIY

GET BACK ON THE TRAIN (See: "BACK ON THE TRAIN")

Gettin' Jiggy Wit It
Original Artist: Will Smith (aka The Fresh Prince)
Original Album: *Big Willie Style* (1997)
Phish Album: *Hampton Comes Alive* (11/20/98)
Vocals: Fish
Debut: 11/20/98
Historian: Craig DeLucia

Henrietta has proven to us time and time again that no song is beyond his grasp. Perhaps the best testament to this truth was offered in Hampton on 11/20/98 with the only appearance of "Gettin' Jiggy Wit It." As he came out from behind the drums to the usual "Hold Your Head Up" theme, stagehands brought several large cue cards to the stage. The crowd, eager with anticipation, were subsequently treated with the first ever rap song performed in its entirety on the Phish stage. Fishman did alter the lyrics, though, to reference his own alias, Bob Weaver. Luckily for all, the moment was caught on tape and released on *Hampton Comes Alive*. It isn't the only momento of the occasion, though; at the end of the song, Henrietta tore up the cue cards and tossed them to the crowd for all to enjoy

Ghost
AKA: "Story of the Ghost"
Music: Trey Anastasio
Lyrics: Tom Marshall
Album: *Story of the Ghost*
Debut: 6/6/97 (private show), 6/13/97 (public show)
Historian: Martin Acaster

The 1997 European Spring tour was the spawning ground of the Phishy funk which has become the mind-eating great white shark of many of their recent live performances. During 1997, "Ghost" epitomized the constantly evolving psychotronicaquadisco sound of the next millenium that appears to have arrived a few years early (or is it 20 years too late?). The ultrasound of the then unborn "Ghost" can be heard in the segue from "Wolfman's Brother" to "Jesus Just Left Chicago" on the album *Slip Stitch and Pass*.

At its core, "Ghost" consists of a simple funk groove oddly reminiscent of Anita Ward's "Ring My Bell" being played at the same time as the Sugar Hill Gang's "Rapper's Delight." To say that the Phish groove of the '90s (and "Ghost" as its dis-embodiment) is not firmly rooted in old school '70s funk, rap, and disco would be a crime of the mind. This sound has been brought into the '90s via techno-space transporter beams, absorbing renewed vitality along the way.

Spring 1998 found Phish in the studio laying down tracks for *Story of the Ghost*. This time in the studio pushed "Ghost" further up (to some, back down) the evolutionary ladder. Where in 1997 "Ghosts" typically started abruptly, materializing out of thin air. The "Ghosts" of Summer 1998, and that which is found on Story of the Ghost, have a mesmerizing techno-spacy groove for an intro that is very reminiscent of recent versions of "Also Sprach Zarathustra." Where in 1997 the vocals of "Ghost" seemed edgy and disturbed, the singing in the "Ghosts" performed since Summer 1998 have been imbued with a cool hipster confidence, a smooth swagger that paves the way for the ethereal and transcendent groove for which it is typically the prelude. The vocals in the album version "Ghost" lie somewhere in between the two end points, slithering frantically or hurrying at a languid pace.

Story of the Ghost as an album is just that, a story of a Ghost.

"Ghost" as the first song on the album introduces us to the main character of the tale. The Story of the Ghost is one of rebirth, hope for the future, self-extraction from a well of despair. A metaphor perhaps for the musical rebirth of Phish from the seeming improvisational stagnation of the bulk of 1996 to the new frontiers of 1998 and beyond.

The first official performance of "Ghost" was in Dublin, Ireland on 6/13/97. "Ghost" was, however, one of several new songs debuted in Europe that had been played before a small crowd a week earlier at the home of Brad Sands. "Ghost" was played frequently during 1997 and there are a wide variety of styles and lengths of "Ghosts." In *The Phish Book* Trey referred to the 11/17/97 Denver "Ghost" as his favorite part of his favorite show from the Fall tour, a show the band listened to many times, in a way influencing themselves. Every version of "Ghost" that has been played to date, spanning the spectrum from "cow funk" to ethereal space, is worth a listen, but the following are guaranteed to send a shiver down the listener's spine: 7/3/97 Nurnberg, Germany; 7/23/97 Atlanta, GA; 8/13/97 Burgettstown, PA; 11/17/97 Denver, CO; 11/21/97, Hampton VA; 12/13/97 Albany, NY; 7/2/98 Copenhagen, DK; 7/9/98 Barcelona, SP; 7/19/98 Mountain View, CA; 7/21/98 Phoenix, AZ; 8/2/98 Deer Creek, IN; 8/16/98 Limestone, ME; 11/7/98 Champaign, IL; 11/19/98 Winston Salem, NC; 12/31/98 New York, NY; 7/4/99 Atlanta, GA; 9/12/99 Portland, OR;

"Gamehendge *as a Metaphor for the Eastern Afterlife*"

David Steinberg, Seattle, WA

Recall how *The Man Who Stepped Into Yesterday* begins. Colonel Forbin was shaving and thinking about what a waste his life was. "Fifty-two years of obedient self-restraint, of hiding his tension behind a serene veil of composure." He then started thinking about this "door." He discovered the "door" out of his reality when he was preoccupied (most likely brooding about his life) and walking his dog, McGrupp. This is a door that had always been there, yet the Colonel had never noticed it. Once he noticed the existence of this, he felt that his "dreary life was a prison from which there was only one escape." Forbin has set himself up. He was so upset about his life that he finally used the only escape he had, the escape that he had for so long refused to see. That morning, he took the razor, slashed his wrists, and stepped through the door.

If one is on the correct karmic path, the idea of removing oneself from this mortal realm would never occur to you. And for fifty-two years Colonel Forbin had been there. He would not want to die when there still were wrongs to right. After all, he had sided with good all of his life, refusing to let even the idea of marriage affect his goal. We could wonder for years as to why Forbin decided to end it all. My personal theory is that being retired is what did it. For nearly forty years, he was fighting for what he believed in. When that was taken away from him, he was at a loss as to what he could do. Regardless of the reason why he killed himself, the act called into question as to whether he was ready for Nirvana. Which was more

important, the act of suicide or the good life that he had led before that? Well there was only one way to find out; Forbin's status was to be put to the test. Therefore, after passing through the white corridor that so many people who have encountered near-death experiences have told us about, Forbin found himself in Gamehendge.

Gamehendge itself was the test. Forbin had a challenge. A truly enlightened person (and only a truly enlightened person) would be able to join forces with Tela and restore Gamehendge to its pre-Wilsonian days. Gamehendge would become the Nirvana that Forbin would be able to live in for eternity. Alas, like a suicide at the end of a good life, Forbin fell just short of his goal. He first was unable to prevent Tela's death. Then, instead of reading the *Helping Friendly Book* and letting the sacred creed be his, he delivered it to enemies of Icculus. Finally, he ended up being imprisoned, unable to change things at all anymore.

While Forbin sat there "he realized that he was back again through the door." The prison was changing from one of walls and bars into the prison of the womb. As he began to transform himself, he heard for one last time the cries of the Lizards, and Icculus, looking from above, knew that Forbin was wiser. Maybe this time around he would go all the way to Nirvana. Then he thought of how silly it was that humans had to jump through these hoops to learn what they should already know, and he laughed.

12/30/99 Big Cypress, FL; 5/22/2000 New York, NY; and 7/1/2000 Hartford, CT.

Ginseng Sullivan
Original Artist: Norman Blake
Original Album: *Back Home in Sulphur Springs* **(1971)**
Vocals: Mike (lead), Page, Trey (backing)
Debut: 8/11/93
Historian: Dan Mielcarz

Ginseng Sullivan is an unlikely tale of woe concerning a man searching for his big break in the ginseng industry so he can return to his "muddy water Mississippi Delta home." Possibly the most popular of the bluegrass covers due to its references to the touring ethos, it has enjoyed a steady spot in the rotation since its 1993 debut.

In early 1994, "Ginseng" was often played acoustic and without amplification (4/13/94 and 4/23/94 for example). The 10/10/94 version includes Steve Cooley as a guest on banjo. Following 1994, "Ginseng" has been played electric, and most versions are similar. As such, a "Ginseng" fan should seek out versions from shows that have other reasons to recommend them, like the Great Went, or 11/29/97.

Glass Onion
Original Artist: The Beatles
Original Album: *The Beatles* **(aka "The White Album") (1968)**
Vocals: Trey
Debut: 10/31/94
Historian: Mark Toscano

With an altered lyric and an alternate implication, Phish covered the third tune on the Beatles' "White Album" on Halloween 1994. Rather than remind us of "The Fool on the Hill," Trey chose to inform us: "I told you 'bout Guyute the pig—I tell you man he's dancin' a jig!" Additionally, the Walrus apparently wasn't a McCartney—he was a Languedoc, as Trey so indicated by pointing back to the soundboard at the appropriate time.

Glide
Music/Lyrics: Dave Abrahams, Trey Anastasio,
  Tom Marshall, Phish
Album: *A Picture of Nectar*
Debut: 9/27/91
Historians: Dan Purcell and Mark Toscano

The liner notes for *A Picture of Nectar* identify this disconcertingly pleasant jiglike number as "another oldie orginally written by Trey, Tom and Dave around '81," that was "taken out, dusted off, and re-arranged by Phish." It opens with a bit of nimble and folky guitar picking from Trey, which dissolves into a pretty three- part harmony crooning some of Tom Marshall's most overtly joyful lyrics. After that the lyrics the band spirals back into the jig, then back to the lyrics, then to a metalish variation on the jig theme. A brief composed guitar interlude eventually leads back into a final, a capella reprise of the lyrics.

Those lyrics spotlight a bit of linguistic playfulness, intentional or not. The consonants "l" and "r" both belong to the family of phonemes called "glides." The first line of the song—"And we're glad glad glad that you're alive"—features a consonant pairing of r followed by l. The

second line—"And we're glad glad glad that you'll arrive"—features a double-l followed by a double-r. This linguistic device—the transformation of one glide into another—is emphasized in the verse's final line: "And we're glad glad glad that you're a glide."

Much like "YEM" and its trampolines, "Glide" was accompanied by exercise glider antics at 1993 shows. Supposedly, the gliders were ordered by the band off of TV one night in a motel on tour. They haven't been seen since '93, but many still fondly recall the damn things.

Initially played with relative regularity (every three or four shows), "Glide" has been seldom seen in recent years. Phish has trotted it out only eight times since 1994, and only one time apiece in each of the past three years. There are no especially notable individual versions of the song (although some do contain amusing bits, like the 5/22/94 version with the long pause before the tune's final note, in which Trey eventually announces that "this number is called 'Whoomp, There It Is'"), but "Glide's" rarity and downright jolly feel make it welcome whenever the band dusts it off.

Glide II
AKA: "Flip," "It's Time"
Album: (none)
Debut: 5/16/95
Historian: Dan Purcell

Only played once, this fragile bit of ephemera is now largely forgotten. It made its debut among a cavalcade of new songs at the Voters for Choice benefit concert in Lowell, Massachusetts on 5/16/95. But while the other songs debuted that night—most notably "Free" and "Theme from the Bottom"—were immortalized on vinyl via *Billy Breathes* and are regularly included in Phish sets to this day, Phish has never played "Glide II" again.

Formally, the song consists of a gentle, wispy guitar figure, over top of which Trey and Page sing "Gllllllliiiiiiiiiiide/Flip flip flip flip flip." A variation on the guitar theme heralds the song's ostensible chorus: "It's time." And even if you've never heard the song, chances are you've heard its bridge: after the second chorus, Phish drops in a few bars lifted directly from the middle of "Guyute." At the time, this was cause for much speculation in the Phish community regarding "Guyute's" future—the ugly pig made no appearances between 12/29/94 and Halloween 1995.

Perhaps feeling the song was oversimple or would get lost in large venues, Phish shelved "Glide II" after Lowell. A small cadre of devoted fans mourns its relegation, however, and demands "Glide II's" inclusion as a wee lacuna of calm in the center of a smoking Mike's Groove, as soon as possible.

GLISTEN (see: "SLEEP")

Gloria
Original Artist: Them
Original Album: B-side
Vocals: Trey
Debut: 5/16/95
Historian: Mark Toscano

The band teased a nice chunk of this classic Them tune at the 5/16/95 Lowell show in honor of none other than Gloria Steinem.

Ghost

Compiled by Martin Acaster

Date	Location	Time	Notes
06/13/97	Dublin, IRE	07:57	Nice Segue From Chalkdust. Short and funky.
06/19/97	Vienna, AUS	08:45	Flawless segue from Stash. Short and spacy.
06/20/97	Prague, CZR	12:03	Big bass space funk.
06/22/97	Koblenz, GER	11:50	Funky rock groove with a Character Zero Reprise.
06/24/97	Strasbourg, FR	13:40	Santana-esque Albany YEM-like groove with Ghost vocal reprise.
07/01/97	Amsterdam, NL	20:19	Melodious "Back of the Worm" madness.
07/03/97	Nurnberg, GER	29:54	Flowing, passionate near symphonic Ghost vocal reprise.
07/09/97	Lyon, FR	09:39	Long segue from YEM. "Pierre" intro with the Flecktones jazzy speed funk.
07/10/97	Marseille, FR	20:20	Hard rocking with a segue into and out of Talking Heads' "Take Me To The River."
07/21/97	Virginia Beach, VA	16:25	Melodious space funk.
07/23/97	Atlanta, GA	24:40	Raging porno-funk that slides into a very mellow midi horn laden outro.
07/25/97	Dallas, TX	16:30	Smooth Riders on the Storm dusty Desert Southwest space funk.
07/29/97	Phoenix, AZ	15:05	Mellow C&P-like groove into Monster Funk ending in Went Gin-like jam.
07/31/97	Mountain View, CA	12:00	Big-time bass driven techno-funk.
08/02/97	George, WA	18:00	Funk groove with "Who Knows" theme and a nice Fish-driven outro.
08/06/97	St Louis, MO	17:41	Melodious techno-funk with some Gotta Be Starting Something at the end.
08/09/97	Alpine Valley, WI	14:10	Big bass techno-funk. Fine segue into Taste.
08/16/97	Limestone, ME	15:30	Mellow big bass funk groove, no climax.
11/17/97	Denver, CO	21:16	Raging space funk.
11/21/97	Hampton, VA	09:45/40:29	Dark growling techno-funk.
11/28/97	Worcester, MA	18:30	Raucous techo-funk with break-down jam.
12/02/97	Philadelphia, PA	12:50	Techno-funk groove with less pronounced breakdown jam.
12/11/97	Rochester, NY	17:20	Blazing, rocking funk with a DWD Reprise.
12/13/97	Albany, NY	14:44	Big bass spacy porno-funk.
12/28/97	Landover, MD	14:28	Ghost in the machine. Trey banter. Melodious funk groove into Went Bathtub Gin-like outro jam.
04/04/98	Providence	15:40	Last of the "Old" Ghosts. Grooving repetitive bass into spacy soaring trance that stumbles blandly into "Can't Turn You Loose" theme.

Ms. Steinem was instrumental in organizing the Voters For Choice benefit that served as the venue for the guys to dump a bucketload of new material onto the unsuspecting Lowell crowd.

Goin' Down Slow

Music/Lyrics: "St. Louis" Jimmy Oden
Original Artist: "St. Louis" Jimmy Oden
Original Album: (unknown)
Vocals: Trey (lead), Page, Mike (backing)
Debut: 9/13/90
Historian: Erik Swain

This venerable blues song, written and originally performed by "St. Louis Jimmy" Oden, is one of the mainstays of the genre. It has been covered dozens of times, including by Oden's contemporaries such as Muddy Waters and Howlin' Wolf and by rock figures like Eric Clapton and Duane Allman, whose version on *Duane Allman: An Anthology* (1972) is where many rock fans heard it first. The explanation for its staying power is simple. As a tale of a young man's dying reflections after too much fast living, it's a story rockers and bluesmen know all too well.

Phish's version, which debuted with many other new selections at New York's Wetlands Preserve on 9/13/90, doesn't have the emotional power of, say, the Allmans'. But it is a perfectly respectable effort, highlighted by Trey's chunky rhythm guitar work and strong three-part harmonies in the coda. Unfortunately, the band didn't give it a chance to develop further. After encoring with it the next night in Providence, they dropped it from the rotation.

Gold Soundz

Original Artist: Pavement
Original Album: *Crooked Rain, Crooked Rain* (1994)
Vocals: Trey
Debut: 7/21/99
Historian: Mark Toscano

Phish did a one-time cover of this catchy Pavement tune from the band's excellent *Crooked Rain, Crooked Rain* album, leaving many

Ghost *(continued)*

Date	Location	Time	Notes
06/30/98	Copenhagen	11:42	Debut of the SOTG version of Ghost. "Spooky" blooze rock.
07/02/98	Copenhagen	21:29	Volcanic rock to Carmina Burana trance which passes through lush oceanic swells to the ring of fire.
07/08/98	Barcelona	10:55	Slowly building repetitive groove to JBGoode Bluesness.
07/19/98	Mountain View	17:35	Great Wentian "Mind Left Body Jam"-like build into driving groove through "Who Knows" and "Manteca" themes culminating in blistering rock with Ghost vocal reprise.
07/21/98	Phoenix	19:57	Funky groove into epic soaring balls-out rock and roll supernova that throbs smoothly into bluesy intro for She Caught the Katy.
08/02/98	Deer Creek	19:09	Rock star Page driving the mothership into deep outer space.
08/16/98	Limestone	17:55	Relaxing cerebral massage with glow sticks and a Foxy Voodoo outro.
10/20/98	W. 54th NYC	9:25	Short, tight, well-balanced rocker.
10/31/98	Las Vegas	8:17	Aborted I'm Your Venus space groove.
11/07/98	Chicago	13:19	Vegas Venus theme cast into the sun to become molten metal with an ultrasexy swaggering outro.
11/19/98	Winston Salem	17:21	Soaring incandescent groove to old skool cow-funk culminating in full band screaming orgasm and a molten metal outro.
12/31/98	New York City	15:30	Orgasmic "sleety" symphony which breaks down into throbbing B&D industrial metal which ratchets abruptly into HaHaHa.
07/04/99	Atlanta	13:40	Lush grooving soundscape built around a heavy metal "Twinkle Twinkle Little Star" theme. Segues into Slave.
09/12/99	Portland	29:06	Colossal virtual reality train ride across the wind-swept moors of ninth century England diving into a vortex which dumps out into orbit around Saturn.
09/17/99	Mountain View	12:49	Heavy bass driven groove used as a launch pad for stratospheric Trey noodling washing through brief space out onto the Lawnboy.
05/23/00	Radio City	26:52	Mesmerizing.
07/01/00	Hartford	16:21	Will hose you down.

fans scratching their heads, wondering why. Well, aside from this having been performed amidst a tour of a number of one-time covers, it seems that Mr. Anastasio is—you guessed it—a huge Pavement fan.

Golden Lady

Music/Lyrics: Stevie Wonder
Original Artist: Stevie Wonder
Original Album: *Innervisions* (1973)
Vocals: Trey
Debut: 10/20/94
Historian: Mark Toscano

Though it has been reported as a soundcheck song a few times (10/23/94 being the only definite date), "Golden Lady" was covered only once at a show, eleven days before the "White Album" Halloween fiasco. As the story goes, the band had thrown open the album-choosing for the first Halloween musical costume to the fans, but deep in their fiendish little hearts, they really wanted to do Stevie Wonder's *Innervisions*, a truly awe-deserving disc. Upon getting the fan-derived results, the band decided to placate their own desires by busting out an otherwise random cover of "Golden Lady" in St. Petersburg (Florida, not Russia) in between an otherwise standard "Runaway Jim" and "Poor Heart." Fans were amused and pleased, but also dazed and con-

fused, and the song has not returned to setlists despite the onslaught of Funk that arrived in Phish's sound 1997. Then again, "Golden Lady" is a lot more balladesque than "Boogie on Reggae Woman," a Stevie tune better suited to the band's appetite of late.

Golgi Apparatus

AKA: "Golgi"
Music/Lyrics: Trey Anastasio, Tom Marshall, Bob Szuter, Aaron Woolfe
Album: *Junta*
Debut: 10/15/86
Historian: Dan Purcell

Some great rock and roll songs are written at four in the morning on a battered Fender Stratocaster, the author splayed on a cigarette-singed mattress on the floor of a filthy tenement, having speedily gulped a fifth of Jack Daniel's to better forget the woman who done him wrong. And some great rock and roll songs are composed on a jewel-encrusted Steinway in a remote antechamber of a seventy-room Hertfordshire mansion while a dissolute multi-millionaire waits for his loyal manservant to bring a flotilla of smoked salmon and a tumbler of the finest single-malt whisky.

But *some* great rock and roll songs are written by the dorks in

your junior high audiovisual club, sitting around bored during fifth-hour biology lab. "Golgi Apparatus," not surprisingly, falls into this third category. Originally written by Trey, Tom, Dave Abrahams and Aaron Woolfe in eighth grade, "Golgi" competes with "Runaway Jim" and "Glide" for the coveted title of Oldest Currently Played Phish Song. (Given that Trey didn't even play guitar when the song was originally written, one would guess that he inserted the lyrical middle section, with its graceful, winding guitar line, a few years later.)

Strictly speaking, a Golgi apparatus, named after the Italian biologist Camillo Golgi (1844-1926), is a membranous subcellular particle that produces secretions within human (and animal) cells. And it's really pronounced "Gol-jee," not "Gol-gee," if anyone cares. But no one really thinks the song is about subcellular biology, anyway. To the contrary, the tune's anthemic chorus, sporting one of Phish's most satisfying hooks, is a shout-out to the audience. Although the practice has ebbed in this era of sheds and hockey arenas, in the early 90s, the crowd would traditionally respond to Trey's shouts of "I saw you/With a ticket stub in your hand!" by waving their ticket stubs in the air.

First performed waaaaaaay back in the formative stages of Phish's career, "Golgi" gradually found a niche as a set opener or, more commonly, set closer. Which is unsurprising, given the potent arena-rock drive of its chorus. "Golgi" has only fallen out of heavy rotation for two extended periods: it was played only four times in eighty-some shows between June 1995 and July 1996, and played only four times during 1997. Since then "Golgi" has been on the playlist a little more frequently. As one of the band's more tightly-structured songs, it doesn't jam, but most fans forgive it anyway. After all, you know, it rocks.

Good Night

Original Artist: The Beatles
Original Album: *The Beatles* **(aka "The White Album") (1968)**
Vocals: Ringo Starr (played over P.A.)
Debut: 10/31/94
Historian: Mark Toscano

Well, Phish has actually never covered this tune, which was written by John Lennon for his son Julian. The version heard by fans at the 1994 Halloween show was just The Beatles' album version piped in over the P.A. to appropriately close out the second set.

Good Times Bad Times

AKA: "GTBT"
Original Artist: Led Zeppelin
Original Album: *Led Zeppelin* **(1969)**
Vocals: Mike, Page, Trey
Debut: 2/13/87
Historian: Craig DeLucia/Tim Wade

Of all the cover songs in Phish's vast repertoire, "Good Times, Bad Times" is one of the oldest and most reliable. As such, it has been one of the most frequently played covers since its debut in the mid-eighties. This tune, like Hendrix's "Fire" and AC/DC's "Highway to Hell," is usually played as a straight-forward rock song and rarely strays from its normal path. Still, most versions include searing guitar work from Trey, including an occasional tease of Zeppelin's "Heartbreaker" (see 6/16/94 for a good example). This makes the song a popular set-closer or encore.

As with most songs, though, a few exceptional gems stand out from the rest. Perhaps the most impressive was the version from 11/21/95, Lincoln, which featured a seamless segue into "Tweezer Reprise." The segue becomes even more impressive when one considers that, to pull it off, the band played "TwePrise" in a different key than usual! This segue was pulled off again three weeks later on 12/15.

Also highly atypical was the entertaining '93 Roxy version (2/21), where the Reverand Jeff Mosier joined the band on banjo. Before moving into more standard songs like "Paul and Silas" and "Pig in a Pen," the band rocked through a bluegrass "Good Times, Bad Times." Fans of guest appearances will also want to seek out a "GTBT" with John Popper on harmonica, such as 3/14/92, or 6/23/95.

"Good Times, Bad Times" had, until recently, never experienced any kind of significant shelf time. Since its debut, it has been played often and regularly, without any long gaps in appearances, though it made only five appearances in 1998, one in 1999 and a few more in 2000.

Got My Mojo Workin'

AKA: "I Got My Mojo Working"
Music/Lyrics: Preston Foster
Vocals: Sydney Ellis
Debut: 2/25/97
Historian: Mark Toscano

Though the song is often associated with Muddy Waters, the original tune was penned by Preston Foster under contract at Chess. So many artists have covered this tune—Manfred Mann, Ike and Tina Turner, Paul Butterfield, Canned Heat, Clarence Gatemouth Brown, the Dead (in '77 and '78), B.B. King, Elvis Presley, Carl Perkins, Professor Longhair, Conway Twitty, Al Jarreau, Pork Tornado (4/11/99 and 4/13/99 to name a few), The Zombies, and of course, Mojo Nixon—that Phish were bound to take their turn at some point in their history.

That point arrived on 2/25/97 in Munich, at the tail end of a three-song guest appearance from classic jazz, blues, and spritiual vocalist Sydney Ellis. In a selection that also included "One Meatball" and "Li'l Red Rooster," the Germany-based singer-songwriter lent a passion to those tunes that doesn't always come easy for Phish. She can been seen live in Germany fronting her Yes Mama Band, and curious fans may want to check out her various self-produced albums, such as *Ask a Woman Who Knows*, *Amazing Grace*, and *Goin' Home*.

Gotta Jibboo

AKA: "Gotta Jiboo"; "Jibboo"
Music: Trey Anastasio, Russ Lawton, Tony Markellis
Lyrics: Trey Anastasio
Album: *Farmhouse*
Vocals: Trey (lead), Page, Fishman (backing)
Debut: 9/10/99
Historian: Erik Swain

Gotta Jibboo may be the perfect fusion of old-style and new-style Phish. By 1999, some fans were wondering whether Phish would ever come up with any more compositions in the style of *Junta*. If by that they meant lengthy instrumental passages punctuated by brief nonsensical lyrics (penned by Trey, no less), "Gotta Jibboo" delivered for them. But those instrumental passages themselves are about as representative of the 1999-2000 "groove" style as anything in the Phish canon.

Mike and Fishman anchor the song with a steady, driving rhythm while Trey and Page create a wide variety of soundscapes, often making liberal use of digital delay loops and synthesizer effects. To some fans, this is mesmerizing; to others, boring.

Like many songs that made their way into the Phish rotation in 1999, "Gotta Jibboo" was introduced to the public on Trey's solo tour from that spring. It was one of several songs Trey developed with drummer Russ Lawton and bassist Tony Markellis as part of an effort to develop a more groove-based style of songwriting and jamming. The results, first unveiled at the debut Trey Anastasio Band performance on 2/15/99, were well-received, leading to calls for "Jibboo" to be added to Phish sets.

The band obliged at the second show of the 1999 Fall tour, 9/10/99 at the Gorge. It appeared five more times on that jaunt, but then became even more of a fixture in the setlist. From the beginning of the December 1999 tour through the end of the Summer 2000 tour, it never went more than three shows without being played. On top of that, 11 of its 25 performances through Summer 2000 were in the crucial slot of second set opener. Due to this popularity within the band, it was hardly a shocker that the song showed up on *Farmhouse*. That performance, colored by horns, delay loops and a "Lion Sleeps Tonight" tease that often shows up in concert versions, is one of the album's strongest. Its album appearance also clarified the title's spelling; previously fans assumed it had only one "b."

To hear some of the things the band likes to do with "Jibboo," check out 9/29/99, 12/10/99, 12/17/99, 12/30/99, 5/21/00, 6/25/00 and 7/10/00 (which segues into "Jibboo's" groove kin "Sand.") One version Trey would rather not have you hear is 12/13/99, which he has publicly criticized. There, the band never gets in sync and the groove is rushed. Chalk it up to the growing pains of learning a new style; it's the exception rather than the rule.

However, it is essential to hear the one live performance that to date has towered above the rest: the nearly 30-minute extravaganza on 7/4/00 at the E Centre in Camden, NJ. Its first 15 minutes presented the standard grooving and looping, but then the band, apparently inspired by a massive glowring war on the lawn, took the jam into serious Type II territory. But given Phish's fondness for the song, do not be surprised if this performance is topped, maybe even by the time you read this.

(I Heard it Through the) Grapevine
Music/Lyrics: Norman Whitfield and Barrett Strong
Original Artist: Marvin Gaye
Original Album: (unknown)
Vocals: Trey
Debut: 12/31/86
Historian: Ellis Godard

Grapevine is one of the few songs that people think Phish played— but they didn't. On 12/31/86, Trey and Page sat in with some members of The Joneses for a last-minute New Year's Eve gig as The Phones; "Grapevine" was one of the songs all six performers knew. It was also rumored to have been performed 12/2/83, but it wasn't.

The Great Curve
Original Artist: Talking Heads

Original Album: *Remain in Light* (1980)
Vocals: Page (lead), Fish, Mike, Trey (backing)
Debut: 10/31/96
Historian: Mark Toscano

Remain in Light is all about interlocking gravitational fields, changing densities, kinetics, inertia, basically a physics teacher's wet dream. "The Great Curve" is a nice example of these properties just like any other song on the album, but is definitely a more restrained artifact of science and nature. Not as sparse and minimal as "Listening Wind," but certainly not as mind-poundingly dense as "Born Under Punches," "The Great Curve" takes a slightly different approach. The rhythms are there, as are the instrumental fills and asides, but the focus of this song is definitely the vocals. The arrangement is simple, but no less ruthless than its brethren, allowing the complicated interplay of voices to take charge. There are multiple entry and exit points for the vocals, and Phish likely had a difficult time pinning this one down on 10/31/96, date of their only performance of the third track on the classic 1980 album.

Perhaps needless to say, they nailed it pretty firmly, playing nicely with and around the sounds of the original track. In both versions, guitar solos consist of short bursts of metallic noise, wrapping otherwise inaccessible melodies into unbreakable knots. Horns (synth on the original) punctuate every few measures, putting periods on ends of musical sentences. The music itself remains quite consistent throughout the entire song, fitting the vocal madness like a heavily starched shirt. Phish even gussied up the horn lines, giving Dave Grippo and Gary Gazaway more to do on this one. Also, though Trey played with the conventions of the album version's solos, he definitely made them his own, and seemed to have put a lot into the performance. The guys conquered this tune with admitted surprise, even succeeding with the vocals. They flew away with the ending, never straying too far, but nevertheless exploring much more ground than Talking Heads' album version. The last few minutes completely raged, as Trey suddenly found himself orbiting Ganymede. The stop-on-a-dime ending came just before everyone (especially the audience) was completely out of breath. Seeketh out this set or be punished.

Fans of both bands may want to pick up 1982's *The Name of This Band is Talking Heads*, a double live album containing a seven-minute version of the track by the folks who wrote it.

The Great Gig In the Sky
AKA: "Great Gig"
Original Artist: Pink Floyd
Original Album: *Dark Side of the Moon* (1973)
Vocals: Fishman
Debut: 3/14/93
Historian: Mark Toscano/Tim Wade

Richard Wright's single solo contribution to *Dark Side of the Moon* has been a staple of live Floyd concerts since 1973, but the original, live conception of the album from 1971-72 featured a completely different song in "Great Gig's" place called "The Mortality Sequence." This M.I.A. track was also designed by Wright, and was characterized primarily by strange tape effects, voice samples, and freaky church-like organ music, creating an unsettling mix of sonic salad that disturbed and thrilled concert-goers lucky enough to catch this track while it lasted. Wright re-conceived this space in the album's progression as

Peter Sitzman

not a funereal dirge, but rather the aftermath of some theatrical demise, a soundtrack for a soulful soul who is slowly rising to meet her maker.

Phish first displayed a Pink underbelly on 3/14/93 in the Western State University gym in Gunnison, CO. The band treated the crowd to "You Enjoy Myself" and a vocal jam that included some serious "Welcome To The Machine" action, but the real coup occurred when Fishman took center stage, Electrolux in tow, to perform "Great Gig," using the vacuum to help him mimic Clare Torry's otherworldly vocals from the original version on *Dark Side*. "Great Gig" appeared somewhat regularly as the centerpiece for "Mike's Grooves" during the spring and summer of 1993, and it actually opened a show in Birmingham, AL on 5/2/94. This song was played once more that year, on 7/5/94 in Ottawa, and did not resurface until the band's surprise performance of *Dark Side* in Salt Lake City on 11/2/98.

Grind

Music/Lyrics: Trey Anastasio/Tom Marshall
Album: (none)
Debut: 12/30/98
Historian: Martin Acaster

Grind was composed by Trey and Tom while they were in the Cayman Islands writing songs for *Billy Breathes*. "Grind" was eventually left off the album (something Tom considered to be a "bad decision") and did not appear until the encore of a 1998 Madison Square Garden holiday run show (12/30/98). Being an original composition. this was a slight departure from the holiday tradition wherein Tom would sing a typically tongue-in-cheek version of a cover song

with the band. The brief yet profound "Grind" consists of a short poem set to a delicate loungey piano tune. The poem describes a person who can bend in 68 ways, someone who has lived for 12,000 days, who has 28 teeth inside of their head, which grind 3 types of things, and is sad that they're dead.

Doing the math finds that Tom was about 12,000 days old when the song was written. The 68 degrees of bending suggest that he is perhaps a practitioner of yoga (or in search of the 69th way of bending). Though no dental charts have been inspected in the preparation of this document he presumably has 28 teeth. The final mystery in this sphinx-like riddle is what are the three types of dead things that his teeth grind? Animal, vegetable, and mineral perhaps?

Guelah Papyrus

AKA: "Guelah"
Music: Trey Anastasio
Lyrics: Tom Marshall
Album: *A Picture of Nectar; Hampton Comes Alive* (11/20/98)
Vocals: Trey (lead), Mike, Page (backing)
Debut: 2/1/91
Historian: Julia Mordaunt

Since first appearing on setlists in early 1991, "Guelah Papyrus" has become a favorite original over the years, and more recently, a rarity. During the early nineties gigs, "Guelah" rarely went more than 2 or 3 days before being performed again, but as the band's original song list grew, the fly was slowly disappearing.

It actually consists of three distinct sections—"Guelah Papyrus,"

"The Asse Festival," (see "Asse Festival") and "Guelah (The Fly)." Despite one last solitary performance of "The Asse Festival," at the Capitol Theater on 4/27/91, these three sections have yet to be played separately since the song's initial performance at Brown University in 1991.

"Guelah" regularly appeared at shows from 1991 to 1994 before steadily allowing more time to lapse between each performance. 1995 through 1997 saw only a handful of Guelah's making the rounds on setlists. At the Hampton Coliseum in 1998, fans were treated to a super tight rendition, which will be forever engraved in Phish history due to the 1999 release of *Hampton Comes Alive*. The year of that release saw only two more performances of the song on 7/17/99 and 9/22/99. It remained hidden for 48 more shows until it was performed on 7/3/00 in New Jersey.

In more recent years, during the interlude between "The Asse Festival," and "Guelah (The Fly)," the band often inserts a pause. A rather humorous instance of this occurred at the 10/7/94 show at Lehigh University, where the band decides to take an extra long pause. Trey takes full advantage of the silence by slipping in some banter, thanking everyone for coming to the show, and reminding them that they are going to debut a new tune later in the evening. And, I can't forget to mention the dance that goes along with this song, performed by both Trey and Mike. It involves a knee lifting, hoping and swinging motion, that fits perfectly into play with the beat.

At the Great American Music Hall on 10/18/91, Trey gave a brief explanation of "Guelah Papyrus." "This is a song about a Mother," he confesses. Trey then continues to explain that when he was younger and hanging out with Tom Marshall and Dave Abrahams, Dave's mother whose name was Geulah (pronounced the same as Guelah) would knock on the door to his bedroom, come in and pull Dave out into the hallway, spoiling all the fun they were having. Hence the lines, "And through the bedroom door intrude / A fretful frown and spoil the mood." Other meanings that are drawn from the song include a ballad about a fly and her journey around the planet, absorbing all she can for every member of her clan.

See Also: "The Asse Festival"

Gumbo

Music: Trey Anastasio
Lyrics: Jon Fishman
Album: *A Live One* (12/2/94)
Vocals: Trey (lead), Mike, Page (backing)
Debut: 9/28/90
Historian: Ellis Godard

Like "Split Open and Melt," "Gumbo" started out as a strong tune but one that clearly had a destiny that didn't lie solely in its composition. A mix of acid jazz and loose funk, attended with three-part harmonies and silly lyrics, it had the ingredients for greatness. The first several versions clearly lacked something, which seemed to be fulfilled with the addition of horns—five times on the Giant Country Horn tour in 1991 (esp. 7/12, 7/14, and 7/19) and twice with the West Coast return of the horns (12/2/94 & 12/3/94). One of those versions (12/2/94) appears on *A Live One*, from which it was the second single released and from which it was extracted for the European compilation *Stash*. And some other early versions are worth note, such as 7/21/91 (which featured horns as well as Steve-O on washboard) and 10/7/95 (straightforward,

but one of the cleanest without horns).

The song must have been somewhat inspiring to the band, who soundchecked it a number of times, including thrice before the monstrous 7/16/94 show (which nevertheless featured a tame "Gumbo"). And they had already started tooling with the melody, such as in Trey's tease during "YEM" 4/12/93. (Mike teased it a bit more years later, during "The Moma Dance" 11/28/98). But early versions of "Gumbo" remained promising filler with good placement, such as 8/21/93 (nicely following "Weekapaug"), 6/22/94 (followed by a good "Maze"), 6/28/95 (energetic, out of a decent "Tweezer"), 12/9/95 (out of "Wilson"), 12/28/95 (nice piano outro), 12/3/96 (between "Theme" and "Julius"), 7/29/97 (religious) and 8/8/97 (providing a nice transition from "CTB" to "Lizards").

The song took on fuller life beginning 8/13/97, the first jammed-out version, segueing into "The Horse." From there forward, it was no longer a rote display of good songwriting, but a platform for exploratory jams. It thus began to fit into new places, such as between "Runaway Jim" and "Maze" (11/14/97) and "AC/DC Bag" and "Down with Disease" (9/14/99, with a jam of "Another One Bites the Dust"), and segueing into "Also Sprach Zarathustra" (12/3/97), "Sanity" (8/15/98, one of the most popular versions), and "Chalkdust Torture" (11/19/98). It even started taking on the acoutrements of jamming tunes (such as on 8/3/98, with "Manteca" teases more often found in "Stash," long-established as a jamming tune). Why, then, did it get the odd placement between "Silent in the Morning" and "Mist" on 10/1/99? That ain't no time for "Gumbo"!

Guy Forget

Music/Lyrics: Dave Abrahams, Trey Anastasio
Album: (none)
Vocals: Phish
Debut: 10/1/00
Historian: Mark Toscano

Moroccan-born Guy Forget began playing pro tennis in 1982, making a name for himself that many enthusiasts of the game won't soon…Oh skip it.

This wackilicious ditty, though much in the vein of Mike Gordon's "Catapult," was actually dreamed up by the occasional writing duo of Trey Anastasio and Dave Abrahams. Coming out of an especially fruitful night at the Rhombus with Tom, Daubs, and Pete (the songs "Pyromaniac" and "Girlfriend Named Bubba" were also composed that evening), Trey and Dave came up with this amusing song-pun on one of the most memorable names in sports history.

The tune itself cryptically dots a few 1993 soundcheck setlists, most notably that of 3/17/93 in Hollywood, overheard by ZZYZX through the venue door. A February '93 soundcheck version also circulates. However, the only "official" version of "Guy Forget" to yet grace the stage occurred in Phoenix on 10/1/00, sung over a post-"Piper" jam, before flowing into "When the Circus Comes." Though a fun tune and one that fans are very curious to hear more of, is it likely the song will be a common live song or even end up on a future Phish album? Forget it.

Guyute

Music: Trey Anastasio
Lyrics: Tom Marshall

Album: *Story of the Ghost; Hampton Comes Alive* (11/21/98)
Debut: 10/7/94
Historian: Chris Bertolet

Portions of "Guyute" made their first auspicious appearance at a Bad Hat show on 9/11/94 in Northampton, MA. But almost as soon as the finished suite reared its porcine head at a Phish show, it became a fan favorite.

Given the year it first appeared, many aficionados consider "Guyute" a glaring anachronism. At first, many speculated that Trey and Tom may have penned years ago, only to shelve it until it was fully baked and ready for consumption. Maybe that's because its symphonic structure and high-wire time and key changes hearken back to 1980s-era epics, like "Fluffhead."

"Guyute" itself unfolds over four distinct movements. In the first—a buoyant romp in 6/8 time—the narrator chronicles an unpleasant encounter with the tune's namesake, an "ugly pig." If not outright homicidal, the storyteller suggests, Guyute is at the very least malevolent. From a dead stop, Trey introduces the second leg of the journey on guitar, ripping through a Celtic, jig-flavored riff at blinding speed. The rest of the movement, which playfully explores this theme, is jaunty and inspirational. The third section, however, takes a turn for the menacing, as dissonance and tempo build to a climactic frenzy. Fishman ends this melee with a drum break, introducing the final and majestic fourth movement—in which a wailing and declaratory melody finally gives way to subdued ambience. In early versions (before 12/94), this ambience was followed by the closing coda (which reprises the opening). Afterward, a mysterious and darkly distorted second verse was inserted before the coda, suggesting that the narrator recalls his tussle with the pig fondly. Go figure.

Since Phish doesn't jam "Guyute," per se—and since it's such a technical challenge—fan critiques of the song often focus on how tightly it was performed. The letter-perfect 12/29/94 Providence version is consistently and deservedly lauded as a favorite (and as yet another reason to seek out this landmark show).

After Providence, Guyute disappeared for nearly a year, reportedly so the band could rework it. But when it re-emerged at the 1995 Halloween show, the only material addition was several bars of whistling.

As the adage goes, if it ain't broke….

Gypsy Queen

Original Artist: Gabor Szabo
Original Album: *Spellbinder* (1966)
Vocals: (instrumental)
Debut: 8/7/96
Historian: [Phil Nazzaro

Unless you have a better then cursory knowledge of Santana, you might have never known "Gypsy Queen" was a song. It is better known as the second part of the Fleetwood Mac cover "Black Magic Woman" from the album *Abraxas.* However, in another twist, "Gypsy Queen" was neither written by Santana, nor Fleetwood Mac. The song was originally written and performed by the influential Jazz Guitarist Gabor Szabo on his 1966 album *Spellbinder.*

Phish teased "Gypsy Queen" for a short period (8/16/93 "Weekapaug," 8/20/93 "Antelope," 10/23/94 "Jim" and 6/14/95 "Tweezer") before finally giving the song its due as a regular part of "Runaway Jim"

a few times (8/7/96, 3/2/97 and 6/24/97). Apparently the band has not listened to much Santana…er…Szabo since the summer of 1997 as the song has not resurfaced.

Ha Ha Ha

Music/Lyrics: Jon Fishman
Album: *Hampton Comes Alive* (11/21/98)
Debut: 5/16/95
Historian: Jeremy David Goodwin

This is undoubtably one of the strangest Phish songs to come out of the 1990s. One of the few Fishman-penned contributions to the catalog, "Ha Ha Ha" is one of those songs whose effect far exceeds the sum of its parts.

It's a two minute crunch rocker, held together loosely by a riff and the refrain "Ha ha ha ha." The lyrics (such as they are) are delivered in a flat, eerie tone that feigns ambivalence while achieving the ominous.

The tune remains strangely endearing, in part because of its limited duty. It showed up a handful of times in 1995 after its debut in Lowell, and then crept back deep within the recesses of the rotation. Since '96 the boys have picked their spots carefully, and unleashed this quirky favorite quite rarely. It initially seemed to hover on the edge of extinction before being occasionally exhumed, but the band seems to have eased into a steady, once or twice a year rotation for this song.

Phish uses this number to greatest effect whenever they pull it out; its appearance is inconceivable in a mere run of the mill show. It's opened shows (10/25/96, 6/30/00), participated in bizarre transitions (11/21/98 "Free" > "Ha Ha Ha" > "Free"), and served as an exclamation point to great jamming (7/3/95 "Tweezer" -> "Ha Ha Ha").

HAD ENOUGH (see: "I'VE HAD ENOUGH")

Halley's Comet

Music/Lyrics: Richard Wright
Original Artist: Richard Wright (aka "Nancy")
Original Album: various home-produced tapes; *Nancy Tracks* bonus CD
Debut: 5/17/86
Historians: Mark Toscano and Ellis Godard

Originally conceived as two separate songs, Richard Wright (aka "Nancy") is not even sure why he appended the repeated "Halley's Comet" refrain to his song "Goin' Down" to create the tune we know so well today. It just sounded good.

Wright grafted the former (a medicine for the ridiculous amount of Halley's hype rampant in mid-to-late '85) to the latter (a reaction to the then-hip and heinous mass commercialization of Motown in the wake of *The Big Chill*) and re-recorded the tune as one song. This new version made its way onto a tape (along with "I Didn't Know") that fell into the hands of Brian Long, at that time the roommate of three of the members of Phish in the King Street house. The band heard it and liked it, deciding to cover it in their live show. (The story progresses from there, but both songs' stories are better told by Wright himself—check the extensive interview with him elsewhere in *The Companion*.)

Wright (at the time still known largely as Nancy) began the tradition of guest-singing "Halley's" on the song's otherwise undocumented debut at Goddard Spring Fest on 5/17/86. For the next three

years, the band would only play the song if Wright was in attendance so he could handle the vocals. This didn't hinder the tune's frequency too much, as Richard was a huge fan at the time and caught the band every chance he could. When he finally publicly announced that he would never again sing the tune with Phish (at 5/26/89—see the interview for an explanation), the band retired the song for almost four years. The reappearance on 3/14/93, an excellent show all-around, marked simply the beginning of "Halley's" evolution from rare, savored gem (through '94) to all-out jam vehicle ('95 and onward).

As with many Phish tunes, earlier versions of the song tended to be rather straightforward, especially since the author's presence in the crowd probably intimidated the band into "getting it right." Nevertheless, some especially notable versions include 4/29/87 (dedicated to Duke Ellington), 10/29/88 (followed by a strong "Whipping Post"), 10/31/87 (segued nicely in and out), 5/25/88 (with Jah Roy), 8/6/93 (nicely out of "YEM" and into "Slave"), 5/8/94 (boldly out of "YEM"), 11/2/94 (before the "YEM" which appears on *A Live One*), and 6/24/95 (between a nice "2001" and an experimental "Bowie").

Many fans think of 12/14/95 as the catalyst, the version that sent "Halley's" spiraling into jamming oblivion from which it would emerge a completely different song. Ensuing "Halley's" not surprisingly always had to live up to the example of this Binghamton version, with its must-be-heard-to-be-believed jam into "NICU" in one of the best sets of Fall '95. Though the band still often kept the reins on "Halley's" as before, a number of truly inspired renditions have blessed outstanding shows since. Check out 8/5/96 (into "Somewhere Over the Rainbow"), 8/16/97 (into "Cities"), 11/22/97 (with a "He Used to Cut the Grass" jam), 8/3/98 (into "I Didn't Know" for a Nancy double header), and 7/13/99 for the most obvious examples. Also, don't forget the odd 7/20/98 encore version that ended with a delay-loop-wall-of-sound as the band members walked off-stage one by one.

Always a fun, singable, and still somewhat infrequent addition to any setlist, some particularly spirited or notable versions include 11/26/94, 12/1/95, 6/16/95, 4/3/98 (in encore between "Carini" and "Tweezer Reprise"), 8/15/98 (with a few alternate lyrics), 11/24/98 (out of "Ghost"), 9/28/99 (encore segueing into "Tweezer Reprise"), 10/8/99 (into "Tweezer"), 6/30/00 (into "Mango Song!"), 9/18/00 (nice 16-minute second set closer), 9/23/00 (thrilling version flows into "Fee"), and 10/5/00 (into "Walk Away").

HAMBURGER (see HE ENT TO THE BOG)

Happiness is a Warm Gun
Original Artist: *The Beatles*
Original Album: The Beatles (aka "The White Album") (1968)
Vocals: Trey (lead), Mike, Page (backing)
Debut: 10/31/94
Historian: Mark Toscano

This Lennon/McCartney composition was covered by Phish as part of their 1994 Halloween "White Album" set—a full two years before Brian Eno's Passengers covered the tune as the theme for film-maker Robert Altman's short-lived TV series, "Gun."

Happy Birthday To You
Music/Lyrics: Mildred and Patty Hill, Robert Coleman

Original Album: N/A
Original Artist: N/A
Vocals: Various
Debut: 12/2/83
Historian: Ellis Godard

There was a time when birthdays were of no import. The institution of "childhood" as we know it did not exist, and there were religious objections to celebrating our unity in Adam's original sin. The first recorded birth celebrations were for noblemen and kings, and the Catholic Church even ruled against being exact about the date of Christ's birth. But by the nineteenth century, children were regarded as celebratable. Making it through another year without the palsy was worth a toast, and the ritual of birthdays spread to the lower classes.

The song now associated with that ritual began as something else entirely—and its history is not as pleasant or simple as the song itself. An 1893 songbook, Song Stories of the Kindergarten, included "Good Morning to All," written by the Louisville sisters Mildred and Patty Hill as a morning welcome song. Entrepreneur Robert Coleman substituted the words "happy birthday, dear (name)" for "good morning, dear children," republished the song, and began claiming ownership. Eventually, the Hill family sued, won, and began claiming royalties for themselves. But the legal battle soured the magic: Western Union stopped sending singing birthday messages, and the song was removed from several Broadway plays. Nonetheless, in the ensuing century, "Happy Birthday" (as it is now called) has become the most sung song.

Phish's versions have sometimes been traditional (e.g. 2/7/88, 5/21/88, and 10/7/89). More often, they've given the song a new voice, including a long reggae version (3/6/87, to Sue and Debra) and Fishman's own reggae stylings (7/25/99, for Chris Kuroda). Mike has had one birthday on stage (June 3, 1989). Page has been the most frequent target (5/17/91, 5/17/92 during "Coil," and 5/17/94), but there were also two performances each for Fishman (2/19/91 during "Love You" and 2/19/93, when he was presented with a giant clock necklace) and Kuroda (7/26/91, and 7/25/99 when each member took a solo and then Kuroda took a light solo). Other targets are largely unknown beyond mentions on tape (e.g. Heather 6/16/90 and Erica 7/13/91; and, spoken not sung, Dimitri 9/28/91, Wesley 11/19/91, and Greenpeace Dana 12/12/92).

The audience has done the singing a few times, twice for Trey (9/29/90 and 9/29/99) and once for Page (5/17/94 after Trey brought out a cake). And, of course, the tune has been teased dozens of times (e.g. in "Bowie" 2/19/91 for Fishman, "Maze" 5/17/94 for Page, "Weekapaug" 7/31/97 for Jerry Garcia, and "Stash" 9/29/99 for Trey). But perhaps the most interesting, and the only one worth seeking is Fishman's 10/6/89 performance (including vacuum) for his brother David. Those Hill sisters are rolling in their graves.

The Happy Whip and Dung Song
AKA: "The Happy Whippin' Dung Song"
Music: Phish
Album: *The Siket Disc*
Vocals: (instrumental)
Debut: 7/24/99
Historian: Martin Acaster

According to Page McConnell, to know "The Happy Whip and Dung Song" you must "imagine driving through a blinding snowstorm in the tundra with a yak, a sled, and a heaving pile of dung" (from *The Phish Book*). With this in mind, it is easy to picture the snowy tundra blowing out of the blinding white noise of the guitar loop that opens this instrumental snippet from the Bearsville studio sessions for *Story of the Ghost*. The ponderous bass line which follows can be equated to the plodding footfalls of the Yak. The incessant cymbal crashes evoke images of the sled driver's stinging lash on the Yak's rump. But what of the heaving pile of dung?

"The Happy Whip and Dung Song" (as it was entitled on *The Siket Disc*) made its debut (and only appearance to date) on 7/24/99 at (appropriately enough) Alpine Valley. Since it was the middle of summer and likely a blazing hot day, the song selection was perfect. Rather than taking the crowd to the tundra to cool it down, Phish simply brought the tundra to the crowd.

Harpua

Music/Lyrics: Trey Anastasio, Jon Fishman
Album: (none)
Debut: 8/9/87
Historian: Yancy Davis

Harpua, the gentle story of the love between a boy and his cat, holds a special place in the hearts of many die-hard fans, both for its rarity and uniqueness. Much like the band itself, "Harpua" has evolved over the years. In the mid-to-late 80s, only the composed beginning of the song was played, while the central piece would be strictly instrumental and often showcase various parts of what is now "Fluffhead." It was not until 1989 that the now-standard tale of Harpua the dog was added on in the middle, often with a brief cover of another song included in the story. The narration tells of Jimmy, a boy of varying ages, who has an almost abnormal level of love for his dear cat Poster Nutbag. Up in the hills outside Jimmy's peaceful suburban town lives a bitter old man and his angry dog (and the song's namesake) Harpua. For various reasons, the dog always manages to make its way into town, chaos ensues, and Poster inevitably ends up dead. Though the story takes place in Gamehendge more often than not, it is not typically considered a Gamehendge song as the plot is completely separate.

Recent "Harpuas" have broken from the original template and give only brief mention to the main characters before going off on a complete tangent (see 8/17/96 Clifford Ball, 12/30/97 Madison Square Garden and 11/2/98 for examples).

Trey has hinted that the figure of the old man and his dog are based upon true characters from his childhood, but the extent of that is unknown. Some have brought up the sexual undertones which come up from time to time when Trey mentions in a state of ecstasy how much he loves to pet, rub and stroke Poster Nutbag, but we prefer not to think about that.

Harry Hood

AKA: "Harry," "Hood"
Music: Trey Anastasio
Lyrics: Phish, Brian Long
Album: *A Live One* (10/23/94);

Hampton Comes Alive (11/20/98)
Debut: 10/30/85
Historians: Mark Toscano

Many people have pondered the eternal question: "does the refrigerator light stay on when you close the door?" Well, it doesn't. This obviously prompts the next question: "Harry! Harry! Where do you go when the lights go out?!"

Folks familiar with Hood milk and its advertising gimmicks of the past few decades might remember Harry Hood. He was a little animated milkman that would often pop up unannounced in peoples' fridges, and would proudly rattle on about his company's dairy products when the poor bastards opened their icebox doors. During Fall 1985, Mike, Fish, and Page lived in a big red house with friend Brian "Miles" Long. The house was situated on King Street in Burlington, directly across from the regional Hood bottling company (and one block from the Wilson Hotel). The Hood plant featured a pair of huge milk tanks upon which Harry's smiling face was painted, a streetlight above the structure illuminating his grin at night. These parallel situations involving Harry being lit up inspired Brian Long to first ask the aforementioned eternal question #2.

Earlier that summer, Trey and Fish had traveled to Europe with their friend Pete Cottone. In Greece, the two bandmates experienced a tumultuous series of events involving a seastorm, a capsized raft, and lots of clean acid (check *The Phish Book* for a full explanation). Following their return to safety, Trey wrote several chunks of new music inspired by the adventure.

Back at the King Street house, a former tenant apparently named Mr. A. Minor was still receiving mail. One piece caught the band's collective eye, a form letter bursting at the seams with Minor's name, telling him, "Thank you, Mr. Minor." And thus, a song was born.

"Harry Hood" was the song, and it debuted at Hunt's on 10/30/85 amidst such early years relics as "I Wish," "Revival," and "Skippy the Wondermouse." Slightly sloppy and unpolished, with a promising but uninspiring jam, it is from these nondescript circumstances that one of Phish's most beloved songs began. It is also one of Phish's most enduring songs, having never been out of the rotation for a significant interval; it has been a consistent part of the repertoire since its 1985 debut. Musically, however, the song has developed quite a bit.

Early versions are, ironically, usually more exploratory in the intro than the jam. Such versions as the epic Ian's Farm (8/21/87) outing took over seven minutes to get to the jam itself, compared to an average of about five for recent versions. Fans might also want to check out 5/28/89, 4/22/90, 11/4/90 for examples of what "Harry" was capable of for his first few years.

Continuing to grow as a song and jam vehicle, "Harry" reached higher and higher peaks until it truly soared at various shows on the Fall 1994 tour. The most notable of these—10/23/94 (*A Live One* version) and 11/12/94 (gorgeous)—continue to thrill tape-listeners everywhere. Other fine early-to-mid-'90s "Harrys" include 3/20/92 (well-jammed), 5/17/92 (powerful), 3/31/93 (a favorite), 12/28/93 (rushed but strong), 12/31/93 (awe-inspiring), 7/9/94 (totally underrated), and 12/30/94 (thrilling as hell). Many fans, when asked to name their favorite version of "Harry," point to 4/18/92. This is the beautiful and legendary "Linus and Lucy" version, the jam of which contains an extended homage to Vince Guaraldi's eternal Peanuts music.

Though it continues to wow the crowd, many fans feel that, though

"Thoughts on Harry Hood"

Matt Frankel, Warren, RI and Chris Fagan, Middletown, RI

Harry Hood is a masterpiece of an instrumental—a song that people have to love even if a long, jam-filled, practically lyric-less song is not their thing. I can't really comment on the musical aspect of it; I'm certainly not qualified and wouldn't do it justice.

What I do want to comment on, though, are the lyrics. Now, I know the real reasons why Phish wrote the song and what it's really about: living near the Hood dairy company, the letter addressed to Mr. Miner, the "You can feel good about Hood" slogan. Actually, it's an interesting—and totally "Phishy"—thing to write a song about, but recently a friend and I came to the realization that, if you look at it in a certain way, Harry Hood can be thought about in a much different way than we're all told to think about it. It isn't merely a song related to milk. Quite the contrary. There is a story that we believe is behind it.

My friend had this vision one day while listening to it, and subsequently realized that Harry Hood is actually a homeless man in a small town. Bear with me here. He is well known throughout this town (kind of like Onion John in that book, Onion John, if you've ever read it), and people see him around and know who he is. They dislike him, though; he is dirty and unappealing and parents are afraid to let their kids near him. No child is allowed to talk to him, and parents scurry their kids off whenever they see Harry. One day, a curious little boy goes up to him and says:

"Harry, Harry, where do you go when the lights go out?" (Where do you go at night?)

But Harry doesn't answer. We, listening to the song, actually begin to wonder where Harry does really go at night. The answer is forthcoming. First we must go back in time: You see, in this little town, there is a rich, single man named Mr. Miner. Mr. Miner is living a wretched life; he is the stereotypical rich guy with no purpose who, despite the money, is a very unhappy person. He can't find meaning or redemption in anything he does.

Mr. Miner is comparable to Richard Cory in the poem "Richard Cory," which goes as follows:

> Whenever Richard Cory went down town,
> We people on the pavement looked at him:
> He was a gentleman from sole to crown,
> Clean favored and imperially slim.
>
> And he was always quietly arrayed,
> And was always human when he talked;
> But still he fluttered pulses when he said,
> "Good-morning," and he glittered when he walked.
>
> And he was rich—yes, richer than a king—
> And admirably schooled in every grace:
> In fine, we thought that he was everything
> To make us wish that we were in his place.
>
> So on we worked, and waited for the light,
> And went without the meat, and cursed the bread;

(continued on the next page)

---

it has remained strong, "Harry" hasn't surpassed the Fall '94 level of excellence. However, great versions since then include 7/1/95 (incredible, lots of Page), 9/27/95 (starts out great, ends up fizzling out), 10/7/95 (awesome), 12/5/95, 8/6/96 (fired by a crazy thunderstorm!), 11/16/96 (with an eternal sustain from Trey), 3/18/97 (excellent), 8/10/97 (strangely magical), 8/14/97 (interesting pre-"Forbin" jam), 11/22/97 (follows a strong "Mike's Groove" show opener!), 12/13/97 (exciting glowstick interaction from Trey), 12/30/97 (odd , with unexpected segue into "My Soul"), 10/15/98 (interesting version with multiple peaks), 10/17/98 (acoustic, with Neil Young!), 11/6/98 (worth mentioning), 12/31/98 (throbbing digi-loop intro), 7/18/99 (with fireworks), 10/8/99, 12/11/99 (unusual show opener!), 12/30/99 (very short intro), 6/22/00 (highly irregular version bookending "Dog-Faced Boy" and with fiddles, mandolins and banjoes!), 6/28/00 and 9/9/00 with Micheal Ray.

To fans, "Harry" is perhaps even more special than any other song for the level to which band-audience interaction has been taken with its performances. For the 1996 Red Rocks run, fliers were circulated by enterprising fans detailing audience participation activities for the crowd to engage in during particular songs. Though most of them didn't really work, the resounding success of the project was definitely "Harry." On the flier, fans were encouraged to follow the band's shouts of "Harry!" with a response shout of "Hood!" On the third night, 8/6/96, the band broke into "Harry" during an electrifying thunderstorm, and

were subsequently caught totally off-guard by the successful crowd chant. The band was noticeably pleased, especially Trey, who responded to the situation with a mile-wide grin. The success was not short-lived, either, as the chant became regular practice at pretty much every show afterwards.

Even more incredible was the night of 8/17/97 at the Great Went, towards the end of the amazing second set. Fans' spirits were already in the skies, as the band had introduced the now-legendary art-sculpture and its intended meaning as a true artistic collaboration between band and fans. In an overwhelming gesture, the fans reciprocated during the awesome "Harry" with—you guessed it—glowrings. Earlier in the year, at The Gorge (8/2/97), Trey had Chris Kuroda turn off the stage lights during "Harry" in order for everyone to enjoy the jam in the beautiful, unadorned, natural surroundings. The procedure was repeated on 8/17/97, but then the unexpected happened. A few fans began to toss their glowrings and glowsticks around, creating beautiful colored arcs of glowing light that danced above the crowd. More fans began to take notice of this and followed suit, until there were so many glowthings flying around the crowd that the air above peoples' heads looked like the Northern Lights. Hundreds of phosphorescent streams flowed and fluttered through the air, many even landing on stage. The band was noticeably energized by the display, and played ecstatically as they watched the colored light fly all around them. As the crowd went wild,

"Thoughts on Harry Hood" *(continued)*

And Richard Cory, one calm summer night,
Went home and put a bullet through his head.

Well, Mr. Miner is this type of guy, except he has yet to commit suicide. He has no meaning in his life, no reason to wake up each morning. Anyway, he meets Harry Hood one day, and offers him some money to buy food. Harry refuses to accept Mr. Miner's charity. So that night, after the lights have gone out, Mr. Miner follows Harry back to his meager camp, the place where Harry sleeps, behind the statue in the park. Mr. Miner leaves, but comes back much later and brings Harry a loaf of bread and apple juice, placing it next to Harry's sleeping form.

Every morning from then on, Harry wakes up with food to last him the day; sometimes there'll be blankets when it's cold out and sometimes a new pair of boots when it's muddy. Oftentimes Harry even finds a book or two, of short stories and folk tales, lying next to him when he wakes up. Because he is aware of his importance to Mr. Hood, Mr. Miner feels as though he now has a reason to get up each day. He realizes and takes inner pride that Harry is dependent upon him for life, and this gives him peace. He doesn't tell a soul that he aids Harry; everybody just thinks he's going about his normal business. Yet, for Mr. Miner, this sustenance of Harry assures him that he rises each day for a purpose: to let Harry live.

Harry has yet to find out who has been helping him this whole time. He tries to stay awake and wait for the person, but he always seems to fall asleep before the person comes. But one chilly night, while Mr. Miner is hovering over Harry and placing a nice, wool blanket on him, Mr. Miner sneezes, waking up Harry. Harry just rolls over and looks at Mr. Miner, recognizing him immediately, and smiles.

"Thank you Mr. Miner," (Harry says, as he places the blanket.)
Then Mr. Miner places down a hardcover edition of Rudyard Kipling's Just So Stories.
"Thank you Mr. Miner," (Hood says again.)
Then Mr. Miner places down a loaf of bread, some jelly, and a flask of milk. After placing each object, Miner hears Hood, half-asleep, say "Thank you Mr. Miner," which creates the line:
"[Places bread]Thank you Mr. Miner, [places jelly] thank you Mr. Miner, [places milk] thank you Mr. Miner."
In hearing Harry thank him, Mr. Miner realizes that it is Harry's existence that allows him (Mr. Miner) to receive the gratification and inner peace of being thanked by a needy man. Miner realizes that Hood should thank himself as much as he should Mr. Miner. He pats Harry on the shoulder and turns to go. And then as Harry lays there, and Mr. Miner walks away, Harry hears Mr. Miner say, very softly:
"Thank you Mr. Hood."

Epilogue:
Mr. Miner and Mr. Hood were each other's saviors. Each found peace within the other; Harry was able to live, in a physical sense, because of Mr. Miner, and Mr. Miner was able to live, in a spiritual sense, because of Mr. Hood.

Soon after Mr. Hood was befriended by the rich bachelor, Mr. Miner, the children of the town took a liking to the homeless old man. He would tell them stories and folk tales while they gathered under the statue in the park. The little children loved him, but their parents were still wary of the dirty homeless man. The children, in school and in the park, or anyplace for that matter, could often be heard spreading the rumor:
"You can feel good about Hood!"

---

the band went wilder, playing a majestic "Harry," inspired directly by the crowd's cascades of color, to close an already historic set. (In *The Phish Book*, Trey remarked that he almost "lost it" during this jam!) Though this also became regular practice during "Harry" at subsequent shows, this night will remain extra-special to all who were there to witness the birth of such a phenomenon.

Have Mercy

Original Artist: The Mighty Diamonds
Original Album: *When the Right Time Comes I Need a Roof* (aka *Right Time or Right Time Comes*) (1976)
Vocals: Mike, Page, Trey
Debut: 4/1/86
Historian: Ellis Godard

Please, don't mistake this for the chart-topping country hit (of the same title) written by Paul Kennerly and recorded by the Judds. Phish's "Have Mercy" bows to the writing of reggae trio the Mighty Diamonds, who originally released the song as one of three singles preceding their debut album. Phish's cover is rare ritual, performed only ten times. Five appearances in 1986 filled the space between omnipotent tunes like "David Bowie" and "Harry Hood." After a seven-year absence, the prodigal song returned for appearances during several godly jams: the 2/20/93 "Weekapaug Groove," the 5/8/93 "David Bowie," the prelude

to the 8/14/93 "Antelope," and the 11/12/94 "Down with Disease" (in which the "Have Mercy" segment alone was nearly six minutes long!) And all was well, and the song rested.

But then the sacred was made profane. After five years in peace, "Have Mercy" was dragged into an arguable letdown (7/17/99), and then part of a moment of band confusion and miscommunication (12/10/99). Or, perhaps the profanity is appropriate: Although the Mighty Diamonds sported boyish harmonies, their attitude was otherwise young and brazen—a mix of choir boy and Kingston punk. They were rough reggae, not roots rastafari, and their sound and appearance began a "rockers" era in reggae. And maybe that's not such a band direction to go. "Guide us, Jah man," as the song say, "oh yeah."

He Ent to the Bog

AKA: "Hamburger"
Music: Mike Gordon, Dan McBride
Album: "The White Tape"
Historian: Mark Toscano

Perhaps "Home on the Range" is not a hamburger's favorite song. Some hamburgers might be inclined to name this Mike Gordon track from Phish's "White Tape" as their favorite, for it pays curious homage to the hamburger cause. Rife with hamburgoid witticisms and originally called "Hamburger" by fans prior to the official release of this

recording, this sonic construction is reminiscent of The Beatles' "Revolution 9." Not coincidentally, portions of this recording were used for Phish's live performance of that Lennon/Ono puzzler during The Phab Four's "White Album" set in Glens Falls, NY on 10/31/94. Talk about synchronicitous duplicity, sheesh.

See Also: "Revolution 9"

Head Held High

Original Artist: The Velvet Underground
Original Album: *Loaded* (1970)
Vocals: Trey (lead), Fish, Mike, Page (backing)
Debut: 10/31/98
Historian: Mark Toscano

The Velvet Underground original is a fun, grating rock n' roller featuring some unusual instrumental flourishes and bridges, some uncharacteristic double guitar work, and typically invigorating, Reed vocals that level off somewhere around a dull roar.

For their 10/31/98 *Loaded* set, Phish covered the tune well, even faithfully beginning with the song's odd false-start vocal refrain. Though Trey's voice doesn't quite have Reed's growly scouring-pad sound, he did an admirable job, capturing at least the slightly manic, half-drunk feeling found in the original. Phish's version clocked in at a little over a minute longer than the original studio version owing to some extended slamming on the tune's closing chorus. Altogether, a fun, faithful performance that got a huge crowd reaction.

Heavy Things

Music/Lyrics: Trey Anastasio, Scott Herman, Matt Kohut,
Tom Marshall (Amifibian version); Anastasio, Herman,
Marshall (Phish version)
Album: *Farmhouse*
Debut: 9/11/99
Historian: Phillip Zerbo

For a song that most fans consider one of Phish's more "pop" tunes, the history of "Heavy Things" might surprise you, and certainly give pause to look at the song in a different light. The first live performance of "Heavy Things" was by Tom Marshall's band "Amfibian" on 1/15/99, at The Middle East in Cambridge, MA. The Amfibian and Phish versions of "Heavy Things" share a common title and chorus, but little else.

The Amfibian version is more of a mini rock opera, and considerably more "heavy" compared to the tune most of us recognize today. The original lyrics as performed to this day by Phish were co-authored by Tom Marshall and Tom's friend Scott Herman; the lyrics for the Amfibian version were co-authored by Tom and Amfibian's bass player, Matt Kohut. The Amfibian rendition begins with the soft acoustic guitar of Andrew Southern, with Tom singing the chorus. The lyrics to the Amfibian version are dark and introspective, the first person character clearly in a troubled state:

Stumbing as I run astray
to a place I cannot stay
seeking refuge in the night
I'm quickly turned away

Once I climb the wire fence
it is too late to repent

(my) words are just a jasmine veil
(meant) to throw you off the scent

'til I'm brought down on my knees
taste the soil with my teeth
from the dust I see a place
where I'll find some peace

Then there is what might be called the "dream sequence," where we are taken on a whirlwind journey led by Scott Metzger's soaring lead guitar, a substantial jam that builds to a frenzied and chaotic pinnacle. As if leaping off of a cliff, the song takes a page out of the agonized pages of Syd Barrett or Jim Morrison, as against a sparse and dissonant background our seemingly tortured character repeats in distant cries that "Things are falling down on me, Heavy things I could not see, on me, on me, on me…." Our saga then ends with a short, more upbeat rock ending stanza. The tone and rhythm of the song convey the inner pain of someone who has clearly endured some "heavy things!"

Then Trey came along and turned the song on its head! First performed by the Trey Anastasio Band (with Tony Markellis on bass and Russ Lawton on drums) on 5/4/99, "Heavy Things" bore little resemblance to the Amfibian version. Gone were the solitary introduction, darker lyrics, and dramatic shifts of tone and tempo. In its place we find an upbeat, light, bouncy rendition that seem to mock these supposedly dire circumstances as presented in the Amfibian version.

The original chorus is retained and so the lyrics still convey a sense of loss: "Things are falling down on me, Heavy things I could not see, When I finally came around, Something small would pin me down." But the intervening verses are far more accessible ("Mary was a friend I'd say, Until one summer day, She borrowed everything I owned, And simply ran away"). Instead of the "'70s glam rock" exploratory jam offered by Amfibian, Trey engages in an optimistic, joyful, lilting jam, and then he shakes off these heavy things with a hearty and repeated laugh and smile, "ooh ooh, wah hah, ooh ooh, wah hah!" "Heavy Things" was performed during the electric portion at all but two of the shows on the May 1999 Trey Anastasio Band tour.

Phish first performed "Heavy Things" on 9/11/99, at the majestic Gorge Amphitheatre in George, WA. By the midpoint of that tour it had become a regular fixture in the setlist rotation; it was by far the most frequently played song on the December 1999 run, appearing in more than half of the tour's fourteen shows. As a Phish tune "Heavy Things" retains almost to the note the upbeat version as performed by Trey on his solo tour. While many fans appreciated the irony of this decidedly dark tune being juxtaposed against such lighthearted melodies, reaction among many fans was mixed. Often decried as being "too much of a pop tune," "Heavy Things" has been relegated to the "Bouncin'" category in the minds of more than a few fans.

Whatever your opinion about "Heavy Things," the song is now steeped in Phish lore as the tune performed during by far the biggest single point of mass media exposure Phish has ever enjoyed (or some would say endured). Almost an hour into The Show on New Year's Eve 2000 at Big Cypress, our party in the swamp was joined by upwards of 100 million television viewers via the "ABC 2000" coverage of new year's festivities around the globe. Extending the irony of the song to absurd extremes, "Heavy Things" will forever be remembered in the same sentence with "cheesecake" and with Trey's "message of peace" for the dawn of the 21st century.

"I want to send a message of peace and love in the 21st century, a simple message that will keep everyone happy. Please remember the right lane is for traveling and the left lane is for passing. Stay in the left lane unless you are passing, and lets have some peace and harmony in the 21st century. Thank you."

Heavy Things follows, as does a convoluted yet spirited "cheesecake" chant by the New Year's Eve revelers. Just as memorable for some, once the television lights went out and the on air segment was over, Trey offered with a sense of relief "OK, its just us now!" Just us 80,000 friends and family!

Hello My Baby

AKA: "Hello Ma' Baby"
Music/Lyrics: Ida Emerson and Joseph E. Howard (1899)
Phish Album: *Slip Stitch and Pass* (3/1/97)
Vocals: Phish
Debut: 9/27/95
Historian: Ellis Godard

Phish performs only the chorus of "Hello My Baby," in which the singer longs for his long distance love to telephone him about his devotion. The verses, of course, add more detail, such as that the singer has "never seen ma honey, but she's mine all right." He calls her every morning, but only learns her name in the second verse: "This morning… she said her name was Bess, and now I kind of know where I am at."

The song became especially popular during the 1970s, when done by folk artist Leon Redbone. But the lyrics were written in 1899, as the telephone replaced the telegraph. This new technology allowed virtually anyone (with little skill) to engage in realtime communications through a distributed network with virtually anyone else, even strangers. These were important steps from the central telegraph offices toward the Internet.

When Phish began singing the song 96 years later, more important steps had been taken towards the Internet. Meanwhile, by their debut of the song in 1995, Phish had emerged as a performance powerhouse. Their success was furthered and bolstered by a distributed network of fans, making liberal use of the Internet to express their devotion. Many of them are strangers to each other, and some are strangers even to the band, having never seen a show. But their love is none the less, and they check in every morning after a show for reports and reactions.

Relatively few mornings reported versions of this song, and few of those included glowing reactions. The debut came in a tour opener with four other debuts, after two years without a new a capella tune, and made glorious use of the bulky radio mics introduced the previous summer—although a few later versions (e.g. 10/6/95 and 3/18/97) were performed without microphones. Except for 12/31/95 (a particularly strong version), it has not been performed in any "special" shows, such as Halloween shows, New Year's runs, and festival—placing it low in the hierarchy of a capella tunes (such as "Amazing Grace," common at special shows, or "Memories," once frequent in setlists). And the only time it opened a show was 10/18/98, preceding "Billy Breathes" in a sluggish first set. However, more than half of its appearances have closed a set or a show (e.g. 7/23/96 and 11/14/96). Other notable versions include 10/11/95 (crisply following a grand "Crossroads"), 3/1/97 (which appeared on *Slip Stitch and Pass*), and 10/18/98 (during which the band faced the Bridge School kids at the back of the stage).

Hells Bells

Music/Lyrics: Brian Johnson, Angus Young, Malcolm Young
Original Artist: AC/DC
Original Album: *Back in Black* (1980)
Vocals: (performed instrumental)
Debut: 7/6/97
Historians: Martha Hunt and Mark Toscano

Hell's Bells originally appeared on the 1980 album *Back in Black*, AC/DC's first release after the death of Bon Scott, originally the chauffeur for the band, who became the lead singer early on in the band's history. Scott provided the distinctive vocal sound of the band through the 1970s. It was he, more than any other member of the band, who was responsible for creating AC/DC's "bad boy" image.

One month after Scott's accidental, alcohol-related death in February 1980, the brothers Malcolm and Angus Young, rhythm and lead guitarists, respectively, drummer Phil Rudd and bassist Cliff Williams recorded *Back in Black* with new lead singer, Brian Johnson. Featuring the songs co-written by Johnson and the Young brothers "You Shook Me All Night Long," "Back in Black," and "Hells Bells" it was to become their most popular album, selling more than 10 million copies in the U.S. alone, and firmly establish the Australian rockers' place in the pantheon of the most influential and distinctive heavy metal bands. With Simon Wright having replaced Phil Rudd as drummer in 1982, AC/DC is still releasing albums, their seventeenth came out in early 2000, and the band maintains its reputation as a top international concert draw.

Phish performed "Hells Bells" at only one show. Well, sort of performed. Sort of at a show. On 7/6/97, the crowd waiting to get in to the Spiaggia di Rivoltella in Desenzano, Italy was treated to an early entrance and an impromptu soundcheck circus. The band did some karaoke-style song requests, as part of the pre-show antics, with "Hells Bells" actually being inspired by some local church bells ringing. Though it was only toyed with and not really played, Phish's "Hells Bells" is silly fun, and led directly into another AC/DC tune, "You Shook Me All Night Long."

Help Me

Music/Lyrics: Sonny Boy Williamson/Willie Dixon
Original Artist: Sonny Boy Williamson
Original Album: Checker single, B-side to "Bye Bye Bird" (1961)
Vocals: Sugar Blue
Debut: 4/10/93
Historian: Mark Toscano

In his first appearance with Phish, Sugar Blue lent his vocals and harp to this early '60s Sonny Boy Williamson song. Sugar has guested with Phish on other occasions, always when the band are playing near his Chicago stomping grounds (see also 8/8/97 and 10/3/99), but this classic blues tune has not resurfaced at these subsequent collaborations.

Help on the Way/Slipknot!

AKA: "HelpSlip"
Original Artist: The Grateful Dead

Original Album: *Blues For Allah* (1975)
Vocals: Trey
Debut: 4/1/86
Historian: Chris Bertolet

Trey was only ten when The Grateful Dead debuted this daunting musical pairing. But with its time signature trickery, intertwining melodies and daredevil changes, "Help/Slip" may be the most Phishy-sounding piece of music in the Dead's repertoire, and so it seems natural that the band chose to cover it in an early gig during Goddard College's Festival of Fools.

With precious few exceptions, the Dead's live renditions of "Help/Slip" dropped neatly into "Franklin's Tower" (see the band's *One From The Vault* release for the flawless and inspiring 1975 debut of the entire suite). Phish's only known reading of "Help/Slip," on the other hand, features some intensely creative jamming before plummeting into "AC/DC Bag."

Though Phish hasn't revisited "Help/Slip," Page and Trey accompanied Phil Lesh and Friends on a particularly wicked version at the Warfield on 4/16/99. To no one's surprise, "Franklin's Tower" followed.

Helpless

Music/Lyrics: Neil Young
Original Artist: Crosby, Stills, Nash, and Young
Original Album: *Déjà Vu* (1970) (Crosby, Stills, Nash, and Young), *Decade* (1977) (Neil Young)
Vocals: Neil Young (lead), Phish (backing)
Debut: 10/17/98
Historian: Erik Swain

Toward the end of Phish's set on the first day of the all-acoustic 1998 Bridge School Benefit, the band surprised the crowd by attempting an acoustic "Harry Hood." Even more surprising was that Neil Young, the benefit organizer, came out in the middle of "Hood" to jam with them. Less of a shock for the occasion, however, was when they wound down the jam and segued into "Helpless," one of Young's best-known acoustic songs and a staple of his heyday with Crosby, Stills, Nash & Young. The band stuck closely to the arrangement on CSNY's *Déjà Vu* album and reproduced CSN's yearning harmonies. This performance closed the set and Phish has not attempted the song in concert again.

Those who track down the CSNY album to hear the original version will also be treated to Jerry Garcia's pedal steel guitar playing on "Teach Your Children."

Helpless Dancer

Original Artist: The Who
Original Album: *Quadrophenia* (1973)
Vocals: Trey
Debut: 10/31/95
Historian: Craig DeLucia

At Halloween '95, Phish avoided this dark, eerie song about giving up by only playing a few lines from each verse and building them into a crescendo of inaudibility as Trey tried in vain to keep pace with Page's rapidly accelerating chords. Arising out of the horn fanfare that segued out of "The Dirty Jobs" (mimicking the version recorded on *Quadrophenia* to a note), the band seemed to regard "Helpless Dancer"

in an off-kilter, joking manner. Still, the key to the song is a response to the age-old question "What happens to a beaten man," and Trey belted that line out in all its glory: "you stop dancing." This song, like much of *Quadrophenia*, only "danced" once onstage with Phish.

Helter Skelter

Original Artist: The Beatles
Original Album: *The Beatles* (aka "The White Album") (1968)
Vocals: Trey (lead), Fish, Mike, Page (backing)
Debut: 10/31/94
Historian: Mark Toscano

Legend has it that Paul McCartney penned this track as a response to the journalistic claim that Pete Townshend of The Who had just written the nastiest, most hard-core rock song. Legend also has it that an insane, jammed out, 20-something minute version of this tune exists somewhere in the vaults at Apple. Phish covered this noisy tune on 10/31/94 during their Halloween "White Album" set with reasonably satisfactory results. As they did with a few other "White Album" tunes, (for instance "Glass Onion," "Honey Pie," and "Don't Pass Me By") the band altered this one ever-so-slightly. The end of the song's anguished McCartney cry of "I've got blisters on my fingers!!!" was Phishified into a sweet barbershop quartet refrain! The band offered a second helping of this tune on 11/17/94, also ending it with the barbershop wackiness of the Halloween version.

Hey You

Original Artist: Bachman Turner Overdrive
Original Album: *Four Wheel Drive* (1975)
Vocals: Jim Carrey
Debut: 6/24/99
Historian: Ellis Godard

When the setlist for 6/24/99 hit the Internet, there was immediate mockery. A private gig at Trey's barn billed as "The Fifth Ball"? And, the kicker, comedic actor and box-office king Jim Carrey on lead vocals for "Hey You"—and, taboot, not the Pink Floyd song most thought of, but a now-obscure pop tune by Bachman Turner Overdrive?

A joke perhaps, but not a lie. Carrey was in the area filming "Me Myself and Irene," a psychological comedy in which his character is beset with "advanced delusional schizophrenia with occasional aggressive outburts." Staying in character, the zany wiseguy belted out lyrics fitting the venue, but not the band: dedication ("I won't let down til every song is set...no time left...don't let me down") despite a lost muse ("The music's gone now / you lost it somehow"). Luckily, the band has maintained its muse, but not this tune.

High-Heel Sneakers

Music/Lyrics: Robert Higgenbotham
Original Artist: Tommy Tucker
Original Album: (unknown)
Vocals: Merl Saunders
Debut: 4/23/94
Historian: Ellis Godard

The first set of 4/32/94 included, in typical Phish fashion, blues, rock, pop, country, jazz, Latin rhythms, and story-telling—and closed with "High Heel Sneakers," a rockabilly classic from the 1950s usually (as here) performed as R&B. The song has been covered almost annually, by everyone from Pinetop Perkins (c. 1960), Jerry Lee Lewis (c. 1963), Don and Alleyne Cole (1964), Stevie Wonder (1965), the Grateful Dead (1966), Eddie Floyd (1967), Big Brother (1967), Jose Feliciano (1968), and Elvis (1968, as the b-side to "Guitar Man"), to the Legendary Blues Band (1983), Ramsey Lewis (1984), Pete York & Superblues (c. 1990), Jeff Beck (1993), Dix Bruce (1997), Keller Williams (1998), and Doug Lawrence (1999). Phish's version featured keys king Merl Saunders, who also played on the previous tune ("Caravan"), giving two back-to-back keys duets.

Highway to Hell

Original Artist: AC/DC
Original Album: *Highway to Hell* **(1979)**
Vocals: Trey (lead)
Debut: 10/1/89
Historian: Martin Acaster

The title track of the most successful album put out by the original lineup of AC/DC was eerily prophetic. Less than a year after the release of "Highway to Hell," lead singer Bon Scott was found dead in a friend's car after a long night of excess at an English pub. Sadly he had indeed cashed in his season ticket on that one way ride. We can only hope that his friends were in fact there to meet him.

"Highway to Hell" is one of the most played songs in the Phish arsenal of cover tunes, bested only by "Loving Cup," "Fire," "Funky Bitch," "Amazing Grace," and "Good Times Bad Times." This is a testament to both the durability of the song as a classic rock gem and how long Phish has been performing it. "Highway to Hell" made its debut as an encore to a show at the Front in Burlington (10/1/89). For the next two years it was played often, usually as an encore or set closer. "Highway to Hell" was shelved for all of 1992, yet returned for a second heyday which peaked in 1994. In the following years it was played very infrequently appearing in two shows in 1995 (6/20/95 and 10/21/95), three in 1996 (6/6/96, 10/31/96, and 12/1/96), and only one in 1997 (2/26/97). Since then the on-ramp to the "Highway to Hell" has been closed…though certainly not for repairs. A frequent juxtaposition of "Highway to Hell" with "Amazing Grace" as a two-song encore (e.g. Binghamton, NY 4/9/94) was a constant reminder that Phish has a great sense of humor.

Hold to a Dream

AKA: "Ode to a Dream" (mistitle)
Original Artist: Tim O'Brien
Original Album: *Odd Man In* **(1991)**
Vocals: Tim O'Brien
Debut: 8/7/96
Historian: Kazimierz O. Wrzeszczynski

Hold to a Dream made its one and only concert appearance at Red Rocks on 8/7/96. Until its recording by Tim O'Brien in 1991, the song was probably best known as part of New Grass Revival's live repertoire. This one-time version, which is often mislabeled on tapes as

"Ode to a Dream," featured its original composer Tim O'Brien joining Phish on mandolin and lead vocals.

At Red Rocks, the very melodic and sweet bluegrass song was given a nice, fast Phish beat and groove predominately by Mike's bass (and backing vocals) as well as Page's piano accompaniment and Trey's quick country solo. You can also hear Mike's well-performed lead vocal effort of this song on tapes from his acoustic appearances with Gordon Stone and Doug Perkins in October of 1996.

Hold Watcha Got

Music/Lyrics: Jimmy Martin
Original Artist: Jimmy Martin and His Sunny Mountain Boys
Original Album: B-side to "She's Left Me Again" (1959)
Vocals: Del McCoury, Ricky Skaggs
Debut: 6/22/00
Historian: Mark Toscano

Phish played this sunny song with what may have been the most numerous special guests in the band's history. Sam Bush, Ricky Skaggs, AND the Del McCoury Band all guested on this tune for the 6/22/00 show, proving that too much is sometimes simply not enough.

Hold Your Head Up

Original Artist: Argent
Original Album: *All Together Now* **(1974)**
Vocals: (performed instrumental)

Peter Sitzman

Debut: 8/21/87
Historian: Mark Toscano

Though the band has never actually played this song in full, it remains a staple of their live repertoire. It all started during band practice early on in the band's career. Knowing that Fishman hated this Argent song, Trey, Mike, and Page would start playing it just when they were about to get down to some serious practicing. Although the three of them found it hilariously funny, Fish apparently did not, and he would often storm out of band practice.

In a live context, the song first appeared during the "Mike's Song" jam on 8/21/87, as well as once the following year (5/14/88). The following year, on 10/1/89, the band performed the first official Argential torment of Fish as he took center stage to perform "If I Only Had a Brain." Fish hated it, the band started doing it regularly, and the rest is history. The song was briefly replaced by a similarly arranged version of Foreigner's "Cold as Ice" during part of 1992, but the Argent tune eventually returned, apparently the winner of the "Fishman's Most Hated Song Ever" award.

Actually, the version of "Hold Your Head Up" they play is usually nothing more than a few bars of the original tune's verse and chorus on organ, bass, and Trey on drums. Sometimes it has been jammed out like the aforementioned 8/21/87, but most memorably so on 5/7/94, during which Trey turned the drums back over to Fish after "Purple Rain" without ever letting the beat drop.

HONEY LOVE (see: "LOVE YOU")

Honey Pie
Original Artist: The Beatles
Original Album: *The Beatles* (aka "The White Album") (1968)
Vocals: Trey, Fish (intro), Mike (lead)
Debut: 10/31/94
Historian: Mark Toscano

Mr. Michael Gordon sang this McCartney tune from the White Album on Halloween 1994, re-orchestrated for Phish due to the lack of a horn section. Trey altered the intro slightly from the album version, stating that "if she could only hear Cactus, Cactus would this say." And Cactus did then proceed to say.

Honky Tonk Women
Original Artist: Rolling Stones
Original Album: Through the Past Darkly (1969)
Vocals: Sean Hoppe (6/30/94)
Debut: 6/30/94
Historian: Craig DeLucia

Phish have long covered the Rolling Stones, from "Loving Cup" to "Sweet Virginia" to the unforgettable "Emotional Rescue." This more popular Stones number has made the Phish stage in fragments but never in its entirety. Pick up 4/12/93 for a "Honky Tonk Women" jam out of "YEM" and then pick up 6/30/94 to hear audience member (and musician) Sean Hoppe belt out the lyrics inside Harpua.

Horn
Music: Trey Anastasio

Lyrics: Tom Marshall
Album: *Rift*
Vocals: Trey (lead), Mike, Page (backing)
Debut: 5/24/90
Historian: Chris Bertolet

Yet another one of *Rift*'s irony-laced musings on the foibles of relationships, "Horn" is the sad confession of a human doormat. Its battle-weary narrator addresses the bitter woman who's turned his life inside out, smearing his good name and strewing his possessions to the winds. He knows she's poison, but he can't cut the strings; such is love. He promises to pick her up at eight, as usual. "Listen for my horn."

While Trey pointed to "Horn" after its debut as the kind of simple tune he'd been struggling to write, it's hardly elementary. His melancholy solo winds and curls through key changes (as many as nine, depending who you ask) before returning to the riff that begins the song. In a wicked bit of musical legerdemain, however, the coda is actually a half step lower than the intro (E-flat vs. E). Some fans even speculate that the two blaring chords in this bookending phrase are meant to represent the horn of title.

As "Horn" is devoid of improvisational space, it usually serves as a mood piece between first set jams. After slipping into relative obscurity from 1995-1998, it surfaced quite often in 1999 (nine times, to be precise), including the afternoon set on 12/31/99.

The Horse
Music: Trey Anastasio
Lyrics: Tom Marshall
Album: *Rift*
Debut: 3/7/92
Historian: Craig DeLucia

Every good concept album needs a conclusion. On *Rift*, "The Horse" begins that conclusion; it ends with the song's traditional companion "Silent in the Morning." Not much can be written about "The Horse."

It is a short, somber tale that the narrator of *Rift* experiences as he awakens. Outside of a lyrical change included in earlier versions (a reference to a forgotten character named Matilda), most "Horses" are simply a short lead-in to "Silent." In fact, "The Horse" has only once not been followed by "Silent." On 6/21/94, the fire alarm went off in the Cincinnati Music Hall after the band had begun the sung. They were not afforded the time to move into "Silent" before the house lights came on and the building was evacuated. When the band returned to the stage some twenty minutes later, they humorously launched into "Fire" and never completed their traditional couplet.

One other version stands out as noteworthy. Pick up a copy of the 4/14/93 show from the American Theatre in St. Louis, Missouri. Phish had just finished playing a monster version of "Stash," with the "Kung" chant sandwiched inside. During the intro to the ensuing "Horse," you'll get to hear a brief reprise of the "Kung" theme, a "Pinball Wizard" tease, and a tease of the composed segment of "Harry Hood."

See Also: "Silent in the Morning"

Houses in Motion
Original Artist: Talking Heads
Original Album: *Remain in Light* (1980)
Vocals: Page (lead), Fish, Mike, Trey (backing)

Debut: 10/31/96
Historian: Mark Toscano

David Byrne's vocals trudge through a thick funkmuck of accompaniment, breaking out every so often for a jungle-feverish call-and-response chorus. On the original *Remain in Light*, this track is the only one to feature real horns, and it in fact buries them deep in the aforementioned groove, where they provide just another part of the music's elemental structure. One could make a difficult but interesting game out of attempting to figure out which instruments are playing which parts. Bring the album on your next road trip and have a go at it.

Phish covered this one on 10/31/96 as part of their third Halloween "musical costume." For this single performance, Phish dissected the tune quite remarkably, considering how difficult it is to identify just what the hell is going on in the original. The song is so perfectly and densely structured; it must have been a fun one for the band to figure out on their own road trips. For Phish's live interpretation, the horns were more noticeable, and Dave Grippo's sax solo works very well, retaining the large, carnivorous insect-call sound of the original. The band also used nice effects—echo and so forth—during the jam, which walked steadily on for some time until each instrument began to be stripped away, one by one, like layers of flesh beneath a cloak of bacteria. The jam eventually was stripped down to a single hand clap, which in turn was built upon, element by element, before metamorphosizing into "Seen and Not Seen." To this day, these moments represent one of the most celebrated segues in Phish history.

Fans wanting to compare a live Talking Heads version with Phish's interpretation might want to pick up the excellent *The Name of This Band is Talking Heads*, a double live album released in 1982.

How High the Moon

Music/Lyrics: Morgan Lewis Jr.,
Nancy Hamilton (words and music)
Original Artist: Various performers
Original Album: *Two For the Money* soundtrack (1940)
Vocals: (performed instrumental)
Debut: 4/22/90
Historian: Ellis Godard

Written in the late 1930s and first recorded for the 1940 musical *Two For the Money*, "How High the Moon" achieved rebirth several times in several styles. Initially a mid-tempo ballad, a waltz in the style of Oscar Peterson, it became a bebop anthem under the attention of Dizzy Gillespie and Charlie Parker during the 1940s, then a rockabilly teaser by pioneer Les Paul in the early 1950s, and again a jazz standard by the time Paul Whiteman recorded it in 1956.

Phish performed the tune three times, each as an instrumental, thus emphasizing the composed intricacies of the tune, including rapid block chords and doubling of octaves. And the complexity has fit nicely with Phish's repertoire, and in those three sets: between "Fluffhead" and the lengthy "Esther" (4/22/90), opening a set into "Esther" (4/26/90), and between the narration of "Col. Forbin's" and the majestic ascension of "The Famous Mockingbird" (3/8/93).

Hurricane

Original Artist: Bob Dylan
Original Album: *Desire* (1976)

Vocals: Trey
Debut: 11/19/85
Historian: Ellis Godard

Dylan wrote a fabulously powerful epic about 1960s middleweight Rubin 'Hurricane' Carter, an African American boxer wrongly convicted of a triple homicide. Carter's case was championed by many pop cultural luminaries, who staged protests and held benefit concerts to raise popular support for his cause. Ruben was finally awarded an honorary Middleweight championship, and his story was brought to the big screen in 1999 (starring Denzel Washington). The coarse story fit Dylan's coarse voice, and remains a highlight of an evocative album which isn't lacking in punches.

But Phish blew it. Tapes circulate of their attempt, the only known remnant of this show, but they are not recommended. (Indeed, most didn't know Phish had ever played the tune, prior to its inclusion in the Archives Show at the Great Went.) The story's frailty is lost without the crying fiddle—and the bleakness of the song's social critique is lost in then-21-year-old Trey's unseasoned voice, which was not yet (and perhaps is still not) capable of conveying the drama of the underlying story, particularly with several apparent giggles.

I Am Hydrogen

AKA: "Hydrogen," "I am H2," "H2"
Music: Marc Daubert, Tom Marshall, Trey Anastasio
Album: None
Debut: 10/15/86
Historian: Mark Toscano

I am Hydrogen was originally written around 1984-85 by Tom Marshall and Marc Daubert on piano and acoustic guitar. They brought their creation over to Trey's house, where it was recorded. Trey added a harmony to it on his electric guitar, and the "Hydrogen" we have come to know was born. Initially intended for Tom, Marc, and Trey's band Bivouac, "Hydrogen" ended up in the Phish lineup and made its debut, all alone, on 10/15/86.

Although very early live versions of this song—for the most part—feature the tune as it has come to be known, for a brief period it ran about 3 minutes longer, due to a separate composed section that fattened out the end a bit. Many fans, upon hearing these earlier versions of the song, might recognize this latter segment as part of the Trey composition "Who Do? We Do!," which eventually wound up in "Fluffhead" (immediately preceding "Clod"). The "Who Do? We Do!" portion of "Hydrogen" was eventually dropped, and "Hydrogen" made its first appearance in the now legendary position between "Mike's Song" and "Weekapaug Groove" on 7/23/88. Check out 4/24/87 and 4/29/87 for examples of this early version.

The "Mike's Song" > "I am Hydrogen" > "Weekapaug Groove" format predominated with little variation until "Simple" began to join or supplant "Hydrogen" in the summer of 1994 (see, e.g., 5/27/94, 6/17/94, 6/22/94, etc.). From July 1994 until July 1997, "Hydrogen" was performed only nine times. Since Summer 1997, however, it has appeared more frequently sandwiched in the 'Groove. Interestingly, on 10/7/99, the band played the first stand-alone version of "Hydrogen" in nearly twelve years. Why? Perhaps they wanted to give the song its due after it had been subjugated earlier in the show by "McGrupp," "Prince Caspian," and "Golgi."

"Hydrogen" has also not always been played as straight as one may think. Those interested in unusual, interesting, or weird versions of the otherwise sweet instrumental should check out 5/12/91, 5/1/92, 11/28/92, 2/15/93, 3/30/93, 4/29/93, 7/22/97, 11/13/97, or 7/1/00.

"Hydrogen" is also known for sporadically inspiring dance-like interplay between Trey and Mike, sometimes taking the form of a "foot ballet," a dance performed by the guys on their backs with feet in air. Other times, Trey and Mike have taken opposite sides of the stage and walked toward each other with a slow, graceful gait. Though these practices were more or less abandoned after 1996, breakouts of dances—not just songs—can happen at any time.

Nowadays, whether the band will follow "Mike's Song" with "Simple," "Hydrogen" or something completely different is pretty much a crapshoot. In fact, the semi-rhetorical question, like a thought escaping unnoticed, can always be heard coming from at least one fan when the band is well into a raging "Mike's Song": "Do you think will they go into 'Hydrogen?'" And the answer, invariably: "Who knows…."

See also: "Who Do? We Do!"

I Am the Sea
Original Artist: The Who
Original Album: *Quadrophenia* (1973)
Vocals: Phish
Debut: 10/31/95
Historian: Craig DeLucia

After a brief tease of Michael Jackson's "Thriller" through the P.A. system, fans in attendance at Halloween 1995 were immersed in the sound of crashing waves that signaled the beginning of The Who's 1973 epic album *Quadrophenia*. True to this song's original form, the band lightly accompanied the sound effects with textural background tones and lyrics from the four distinct melodies that underlie the rock opera. It may be more than mere coincidence that the band performed this album, punctuated with images of water, in the same year that aquatic imagery was evident in several new original songs (see "Theme From the Bottom," "Free," etc.).

I Been to Georgia on a Fast Train
AKA: "Fast Train"
Music/Lyrics: Billy Joe Shaver
Original Artist: Billy Joe Shaver
Original Album: *Old Five & Dimers Like Me* (1973)
Debut: 5/6/93
Historian: Mark Toscano

Billy Joe Shaver (aka "Shaver") is one of those guys who is most well known to and respected by critics and other musicians for having written some great country/Americana tunes during the seventies that somehow subverted maudlin anachronism. But enough of this pretentious craptalk.

The song represents great pre-Hot Rize country-bluegrass, with fun lyrics to a singable tune. Phish has performed it only once, in a unique set with some musical help from the likes of Dick Solberg (on violin and vocals) and Jeff Walton (on guitar). Often labeled erroneously as "Fast Train," the song has also been covered by Willie Nelson, Tennessee Ernie Ford, and Commander Cody.

I Didn't Know
Music/Lyrics: Richard Wright
Original Artist: Richard Wright (aka "Nancy")
Original Album: various home-produced tapes; *Nancy Tracks* bonus CD
Vocals: Mike, Page, Trey
Debut: 9/27/87
Historians: Mark Toscano and Ellis Godard

I Didn't Know is an almost typical Phish oddity: arbitrarily quirky lyrics in a catchy rhythm and rhyme scheme, delivered in three-part harmony accompanied by a thumping bass line, and altogether a bit about having "lost it." However, "I Didn't Know" wasn't written by Phish. It's another song (along with "Halley's Comet") from the bizarre genius of Richard Wright, known by fans (and band) more commonly as "Nancy."

Richard wrote the song in August of 1985 between semesters at Goddard College, and recorded it on a four-track a week later. This version of the tune—slightly imperfect and later re-recorded by Wright—was played soon after to Page in Jim Pollock's dorm room. Page and Jim were listening to a tape of a recent Phish gig at the time, giving Richard his first exposure to the band that would soon become one of his favorites. After re-recording in September, the fine-tuned "I Didn't Know" was dubbed to a Nancy mix-tape (along with "Halley's Comet"), and ended up in the hands of Phish roommate Brian Long, who played it for the band. They obviously liked what they heard and asked Richard to cover "Halley's," debuting it at 5/17/86. "I Didn't Know" followed on the heels of "Halley's" success, debuting about a year and a half later. (For more detailed information, check out the Richard Wright interview elsewhere in *The Phish Companion*.)

Although Richard sang vocals on "Halley's" each time Phish played it for the first three years, he only occasionally guested on "I Didn't Know," usually taking over on drums so Fishman could bust out his trombone. To this day, "I Didn't Know" is still a popular concert favorite, and Fish still occasionally brings out the trombone (9/27/95 and 12/28/95), though the song has also been accompanied by vacuum (numerous versions), washboard (3/31/93), cymbals (Mimi Fishman, 4/8/94), megaphone (Trey, 6/15/95), bass drum pedal (Fishman, with his knee, 6/29/94), Mimi on vacuum (7/19/91), and of course the Bag-Vac (3/24/92). Other than these amusing variations, few versions of the song stand out from the rest, although the inclusion of "My Sweet One" (on 6/14/94), and the display of an actual picture of Otis Redding (at early shows) are both notable. Incidentally, though almost entirely vocal, the only true a capella rendition occurred on 3/28/92.

Released in various contexts by Richard on home-produced tapes throughout the years, Phish actually recorded and released a version of their own on their first promotional tape, circulated sparsely in 1988. The song's heyday was definitely the period of 1991–1993, when it was a frequent show-stopper. Declining in frequency since then, "I Didn't Know" has been trotted out only a few times each tour in recent years, though it is always greeted with wild appreciation.

I Don't Care
Music/Lyrics: Trey Anastasio, Tom Marshall
Album: (none)
Debut: 6/6/97 (private show), 6/16/97 (public show)
Historian: Phillip Zerbo

After one private ("Bradstock" 6/6/97) and two public (6/16/97 Royal Albert Hall, London and 6/20/97 Divaldo Archa, Prague, Czech Republic) appearances, apparently the band does not care much about "I Don't Care." While the tune has had the lifespan of your average cluster fly—10 days—in stands as an important early example of some of both the stark, heavy-metal-ish jams that found life in the jamfest that was Fall '97, and the sparse, spacey, spacey grooves of Summer '98 and beyond.

The song is best appreciated if pissed off at someone or something: "I don't care about the time...It's your time that I waste my mind...I don't care about your ears, All I say, you're just...too weird...Just like weeds out in the lawn...I don't care about your reaction...." The hair-tossing heavy metal groove is dark, powerful, a-n-g-r-y! A true segue emerges out of "Ghost" on the first public appearance 6/16/97 at the famed Royal Albert Hall. It is an interesting segue in retrospect, but was even more refreshing for those in attendance, a new groove out of what was, to those of us on tour, a 3-day old tune ("hey, what is this new verse to "Ghost?" The tune sure takes an abrupt turn!"

Ironically, the tune shines the brightest on its—at the time of this writing—last public appearance on 6/20/97 at the Divaldo Archa in Prague, Czech Republic. Emerging this time out of "Limb by Limb" (by this time an "old favorite" being played for the fifth time in a week— every show of the young Summer '97 Europe tour), Trey takes charge on a particularly inspired tear, rhythm in total groove control, simultaneous hints of Hendrix and Zappa, yet so distinctively Trey...after a solid exploration of that groove, we breakdown into a very sparse, dissonant groove, that evokes in this writer images of the 11/30/97 "Sanity" (or other heavy-metal jams of that period). But we are not done yet, as the jam takes another detour toward a very spacey groove that could seamlessly fit into the middle of 8/15/98 IV, 10/31/98 III, or any other of the more quiet, spacey jamming which became part of the "jam rotation" in '98 and beyond.

In retrospect, the biggest irony of this tune hitting the mothballs is that the song never saw the light of day in a (public) US venue. It seems like the proper venue—in terms of attitude—is a hockey rink, not a European club or Brad Sands's back porch. Perhaps "I Don't Care" will live another day, perhaps not. Regardless, the 6/20/97 version alone makes the tune notable, and a good excuse to seek out a recording of this inspired and generally under-appreciated show.

I DON'T CARE ABOUT ANYONE EXCEPT MYSELF (see: "SELF")

I Found a Reason
Original Artist: The Velvet Underground
Original Album: Loaded (1970)
Vocals: Trey (lead), Mike (second lead), Fish, Page (backing)
Debut: 10/31/98
Historian: Mark Toscano

The Velvets reached back to earlier strains of rock n' roll virii with which they could infect their audience, making this very possibly the first postmodern rock ballad. Some may claim this honor goes to the Mothers for all of their crazed doo-wop work and the entire *Freak Out!* album in general, but those songs, all incomparable, were too confrontational to be properly postmodern. At any rate, "I Found a Reason" is a sweet song, elegantly composed and arranged, and was very finely sung by Phish at their 10/31/98 show.

Peter Slizman

It was obvious that some fans at the show thought Mike's spoken refrain halfway through the song was a Phishy invention, a leftover from 1996's "Seen and Not Seen," perhaps? But no, the absurdly earnest, tongue-in-cheek confession was one of the original track's defining moments.

I Get a Kick Out of You
Music/Lyrics: Cole Porter
Original Artist: Dinah Washington
Original Album: *Star Dust* (1929) and *Anything Goes* (1934)
(stage musicals)
Vocals: Mike
Debut: 8/2/98
Historian: Ellis Godard

Written by Cole Porter for the musical *Star Dust* but better known for its appearance in *Anything Goes*, this show tune is about the singer's love and his relative disinterest in perfume, bee-bop, champagne, cocaine, and planes. Mike sang the song less than three months after getting married. It is unclear whether the kick he was singing about was his wife, or his musical life. But the bit of mystery is fitting, since *Anything Goes* was a Shakespearean comedy of love and disguise.

Phish's early years were marked by a dozen or more jazz standards, but this number did not enter the repertoire until nearly a decade after their heavy jazz period (1987-1989). The debut was delicately dropped between raging versions of "David Bowie" and "Loving Cup," to close a second set. The second appearance (11/9/98) was a bit less spirited and more campy, and fell between the crispness of "Horn" and "Divided Sky." In each case, the cover was a mix of fresh material with reminiscence of Phish's younger days. And we all get a kick out of that, disguised as new or not.

I HEARD IT THROUGH THE GRAPEVINE (see: "GRAPEVINE")

I Know a Little
Music/Lyrics: Steve Gaines
Original Artist: Lynyrd Skynyrd
Original Album: *Street Survivors* (1977)
Vocals: Trey
Debut: 8/10/87
Historian: Ellis Godard

Phish's may not have had the roughness or grit to pull off "Curtis Loew" or "Freebird" with authenticity, but here's one they could tackle with gusto. The lyrics are predictable, and the melody banal, but you'll recognize "I Know a Little" by the guitar bits at the end of each chorus, which Trey delivered with clarity on three occasions in the late 1980s, then teased before the 4/26/90 encore and in the 6/13/94 "Tweezer." Other notable versions include those released by Pete Seegar and Tower of Power.

I Shall Be Released

Music/Lyrics: Bob Dylan
Original Artist: The Band
Original Album: *Music From Big Pink* **(1968)**
Vocals: Neil Young, Page, Trey (lead), Sarah MacLachlan, Fish, Mike (backing)
Debut: 10/18/98
Historian: Erik Swain

Phish's only performance of this Bob Dylan song, perhaps best known for its inclusion on The Band's classic *Music From Big Pink* album, closed the 1998 Bridge School Benefit. After backing benefit organizer Neil Young and Sarah McLachlan on Ian Tyson's "Four Strong Winds," Phish started up "I Shall Be Released." Page sang the first verse, Young the second, and Trey the third, with the rest joining in on the chorus.

The anthemic ballad has often served as the BSB's grand finale and famously closed The Band's 1976 farewell concert, which was captured in the Martin Scorsese film *The Last Waltz*. Young was one of the many guest stars who joined in on that rendition.

I Told You So

Music/Lyrics: Jimmie Davis
Original Artist: Jimmie Davis
Original Album: single (ca. early '40s)
Vocals: Tammy Fletcher
Debut: 3/18/97
Historian: Ellis Godard

Just before Tammy Fletcher sang this at Phish's Flynn benefit show in Burlington, she joked to a companion in the audience, "Now, see, Greg, I'm a safe date." Safe or not, it'd be weird to take someone out and have them jump on stage to sing this number: campy three-chord fare, gospel honkytonk with bluesy "you left me" lyrics. Part of the way in, Tammy says, "Play me something, baby" and Page takes off, sounding akin to what he does with his father on stage (see "Bill Bailey"), although Trey joins in here, with a B.B. King-like solo, followed by some nice a nice return by Page and Fishman. Throughout, Mike is the constant; nothing terribly interesting, but a nice bed to lay the blues on. The tune ended with a cheesy, elongated ending and Tammy's laughter.

I Walk the Line

Original Artist: Johnny Cash
Original Album: single (1956)
Vocals: Mike
Debut: 11/19/92
Historian: Ellis Godard

Well, Johnny Cash, the man in black, was a dark mysterious male. Sang kinda slow, and talked real low, and performed in a sketchy jail. His ballads crooned, but not the tunes you'd sing while wearing white. But "I Walk the Line" Mike sings real fine, in neon green at night.

The narrator sings the joy love brings, but not in pastel cheese: He's a happy fool, and obeys the rules, but from what does he retreat? The entire song suggests no wrongs, and mentions no temptations. It's all devotion, with calm emotions, and no sin (save, perhaps, masturbation).

About what crimes did Mike sing nine times, of which two were in "Reba" (12/5/92 and 12/30/92)? Did he get engaged during the 111 days from the debut (11/19/92) to the leaver (3/9/93)? He didn't betroth for five years more, though Cilla he did court. But the rock star spin is full of sin—does he walk the line no more?

I Wanna Be Like You

Music/Lyrics: Richard and Robert Sherman, Terry Gilkyson
Original Artist: Louis Prima (as "King Louie")
Original Album: *Jungle Book* **soundtrack (1967)**
Vocals: Fishman
Debut: 4/4/94
Historian: Ellis Godard

In the original, King Louie longs to be human, bemoaning the difficulties of animalhood, attracted by the complexing of human social life, and desiring the secret of fire. Though every bit as animal, social, and fiery as the rest of the band, Fishman is not a typical front man, or singer. But Phish has built audiences who tolerate fun, and what better tune with which to let Fishman face his frailties from front and center. (See also, versions by everyone from Big Bad Voodoo Daddy to the Royal Philharmonic Orchestra to Los Lobos.) The debut featured horns, emboldening a temporary Disneyfication of Phish's sound. Fishman kept up the gag, with ten more performances in the months following, but has not King Louied it since.

I Want to be a Cowboy's Sweetheart

Music/Lyrics: Patsy Montana
Original Artist: Patsy Montana
Original Album: (1978?)
Vocals: unidentified yodellers
Debut: 12/6/96
Historian: Ellis Godard

Phish played this bit of "western swing" on only one occassion, during the legendary Vegas "Harpua" on 12/6/96. Lyrics like "a thousand miles from old city lights" clashed with the Vegas surrounding, but the song was an omen of westernness that night, as the show included cowgirl yodellers as well as Les Claypool, a cowboy of sorts. The song was also performed at the show's soundcheck earlier on.

I Will

Original Artist: The Beatles
Original Album: *The Beatles* **(aka "The White Album") (1968)**
Vocals: Page (lead), Mike, Trey (backing)
Debut: 10/31/94
Historian: Mark Toscano

This simple ballad, the 16th song on the Beatles' "White Album," received the Phish treatment on 10/31/94 for their Halloween "White Album" set.

I Wish

Original Artist: Stevie Wonder
Original Album: *Songs in the Key of Life* (1976)
Vocals: Trey
Debut: 10/30/85
Historian: Mark Toscano

Phish apparently only performed this Stevie Wonder classic once, at one of Page's early shows with the band, 10/30/85. Perhaps they wanted to spotlight the recently acquired keyboard player's strengths, for this song's signature organ lines would be hard to replicate on guitar, if not blasphemous. The band, then only 21 or thereabouts, did a surprisingly decent cover of this funkalicious tune at a show that's fun, but otherwise musically unremarkable. As with certain other early covers ("Light up or Leave me Alone" comes to mind), fans hoped "I Wish" would return with the sudden appearance of funk in '97, but alas, no sign of the song in setlists yet, despite teases found on 4/16/93 ("Weekapaug"), 7/13/94 ("Tweezer"), and 7/25/99 ("Suzy").

Icculus

Music/Lyrics: Trey Anastasio, Tom Marshall
Album: *Junta* (live, from 7/25/88)
Vocals: Trey (lead), Fish, Mike, Page (backing)
Debut: 4/1/86
Historians: Jeremy David Goodwin and Mark Toscano

Icculus is one of an elite handful of Phish songs (a category which also includes "Harpua" and "Colonel Forbin's Ascent") which features a spoken-word performance by Trey. It is a soothing, faux-ethereal, testimonial monologue, which escalates gradually before bursting into a frenzied spatter of shouting. Throw in a (musically unrelated) ten second composed ending that hints at a jam before ending abruptly, and you've got a quirky epic.

One of the oddest "Icculuses" occurred on 10/31/95 (also the only known use of the tune as a show opener!), when Trey announced that "the Book is getting it's ass kicked!" by the evil Halloween spirits. Although the band often tries to literally scare the audience on Halloween, this may be one of the most disconcerting things Trey has said on-stage. The prospect that Icculus may indeed be fallible is surely a distressing thought within the universe of Gamehendge, or for those fans who take the saga too seriously.

It's hard to ascribe any pattern to the emergence of the few other extant versions of the tune scattered through the Phish oeuvre, other than to note that Trey's wandering "Forbin's" narration has led into Icculus on four occasions, all between 4/16/92 and 3/25/93. Due to its rarity, unique structure, and thematic concern, "Icculus" is one of the most special songs in the Phish catalog.

"Icculus" (like "Divided Sky," "Llama," and "Punch You in the Eye") is a Gamehendge-related song, but not a part of the actual piece The Man Who Stepped Into Yesterday. Interestingly enough, this paean to the author of the Helping Friendly Book has not been slipped into any of the five full performances of the Gamehendge saga, even

though it was written as early as 1984 by Trey and Tom in the house of the guitarist's father. Then again, the rambling, Gamehendge-specific diatribe that differs from show to show was not part of the song until its debut performance at Hunt's, two years later. Still, Trey had plenty of time to add it to his Senior Study, but likely chose not to as the song didn't exactly show off his compositional skills the way "Tela" or "Lizards" did.

Like "Sanity," "Icculus" made it to disc by a curious twist of chance. On 4/20/92, following a Napa Valley vineyard tour during a break between shows, Shelly amused the band by loaning them her tape of 7/25/88, which included the aforementioned two songs. The band happened to be looking for material to fill space on the second *Junta* CD, and decided that including the two wacky tracks would be a kick. Shelly tracked down the guy who had taped the show and borrowed his master, a 90-minute tape with some of 7/25/88 on one side and some of 5/3/88 on the other. When Elektra received the tape, they messed up the dates, which is why your *Junta* CD booklet features the wrong date for those two tunes.

"Icculus" always varies from show to show, but in vocals rather than music, a rare exception to the usual Phish rule. Never a common tune, its frequency of appearance dropped off severely in the '90s, with a only a few performances in '92, '93, and '94. The song made only one '95 appearance, at the aforementioned Halloween show. It wouldn't surface again until Oswego nearly four years later, when a babbling Trey segued from an endorsement of literacy to some old style Icculus worship.

Always fun and interesting, some standout versions include 8/10/87 (for Paul's mother), 8/12/89, 5/2/92 (with amusing ARU references), 6/22/94 (unexpected and awesome), 10/27/94 (out of "Slave" encore!), 11/20/94 (references O.J. Show), and 7/18/99 (with "Smoke on the Water" and "Cat Scratch Fever" jams).

If I Could

Music/Lyrics: Trey Anastasio, Tom Marshall
Album: *Hoist*
Vocals: Trey, Alison Krauss(studio); Trey, lead, Page, Mike, backing, (live)
Debut: 4/4/94
Historian: Christian C. McKee

Ask any Phish fan what they love about the quartet's music, and the answer will almost always involve their concerts. Phish's music blossoms on stage every night, and by comparison, some of their studio material lacks the same spunk, pizzaz and fire that comes through live. However, there are a few songs whose recorded versions are still definitive. "If I Could" is one of those songs. "If I Could" appears on *Hoist*, and is one of many tracks on that album to feature the work of a guest musician. Alison Krauss leads the reknowned bluegrass band Union Station, is a member of the Grand Ol' Opry, and a Grammy winning fiddler and singer. Her work with Phish was somewhat coincidental; she happened to be playing in Los Angeles while the band was there cutting their new album. While some fans did not like 'a strange woman' singing on the track, most agree that her beautiful voice adds a great deal to the song. In concert, the passion of "If I Could" is transferred from the vocals to the soloing (12/04/94) providing both Page and Trey a chance to explore more soulful musical territory. Sadly, Ms. Krauss

has only once joined the band on stage for a repeat of their studio collaboration (5/03/94). The tune was altered in the studio, but you can still drop in 7/1/95 Set I at Great Woods to hear a partial restoration of the original solo guitar introduction, which was removed before the record reached stores. That same introduction was teased before the "Antelope" on 12/29/93. While this song may never become a live favorite, it has been preserved at its best.

If I Don't Be There by Morning

Music/Lyrics: Bob Dylan, Helena Springs
Original Artist: Eric Clapton
Original Album: *Backless* (1978)
Vocals: Trey
Debut: 5/9/89
Historian: Erik Swain

If I Don't Be There By Morning is a rarity in several ways. It is one of the few Bob Dylan compositions that the master has never recorded or performed live. And there is only one known Phish performance, at the release party for *Junta* on 5/9/89 at the Front. This mid-tempo rocker, which Dylan co-wrote with Helena Springs, came into the public eye when Eric Clapton recorded it for his 1978 hit album *Backless*. It also appears on Clapton's 1980 live album *Just One Night*.

If I Only had a Brain

Music/Lyrics: E. "Yip" Harburg (lyrics), Harold Arlen (music)
Original Artist: Ray Bolger (as "The Scarecrow")
Original Album: *Wizard Of Oz* soundtrack
Vocals: Fishman
Debut: 3/12/89
Historian: Ellis Godard

In the Harburg/Arlen story 'bout midgets and Oz's glory, it's a much beloved refrain. But when it features vacuum its such a flatulent tune, and it always sounds the same. I could while away the hours 'bout versions to devour, and tapes you should obtain. And a list I could be startin'—but Phish is barely fartin' with "If I Only had a Brain."

Oh, I could tell you why, the Scarecrow sings and cries. I could tell you things the lyrics mean to me—but, please, it's Fish being silly. And he often get the words wrong (e.g. 4/14/89, 10/1/89, 5/4/90, 11/14/91, and 10/25/94), like Trey with that "Lizards" song, so the vacuum's good to hear. But there are other acts who have played it with more tact, such as Harry Connick, Jr.

It would be a lot of nothin', a headache full of fluffin', overblown for this short tune, to devote much ink to versions that you could go be learnin', so I'll just mention these few: The 4/5/90 gets tweakin', in the year the song was peakin', and that New Year (12/31/90) had some heat. But another (11/6/95) deserves the big nod, before "Grace" and after "Hood," and is one of few that's neat.

If You Need a Fool

AKA: "Call Me If You Need A Fool"
Music/Lyrics: Steve Earle
Original Artist: The Del McCoury Band
Original Album: *Blue Side of Town* (19)
Vocals: Phish; Del McCoury and Phish (7/18/99)

Debut: 7/29/98
Historian: Christian C. McKee

There is confusion with the title on this one, and Mr. McCoury has been no help, announcing it onstage as "If You Need a Fool," "Call Me If You Need A Fool" and "If You Need a Fool, Call Me." Even if he seems to have Phish's knack for mis-information, he and his band write and play the best bluegrass music out there today. Phish has played this tune on three occasions, the best being the version from Oswego in the summer of 1999 (7/18/99) featuring the Del McCoury Band. Trey's glee is apparent throughout all the selections the two ensembles performed together, which included other McCoury originals ("Beauty of My Dreams,") bluegrass standards ("I'm Blue, I'm Lonesome,") and Phish originals ("Back on the Train.")

I'll Come Running

AKA: "I'll Come Running (To Tie Your Shoe)"
Original Artist: Brian Eno
Original Album: *Another Green World* (1975)
Vocals: Mike
Debut: 5/16/95
Historian: Phillip Zerbo

May 16, 1995, was certainly not an ordinary Phish show! Ten new tunes were debuted at this single set performance, a "Voters for Choice" benefit in Lowell, MA. Among the six new originals and four new covers was Brian Eno's "I'll Come Running" from the classic album *Another Green World*.

"I'll Come Running" has many of the same qualities as "Contact": it is smooth and flowing, almost bouncy with hints of pop influence, yet undeniably goofy. As with "Contact," "I'll Come Running" is also a love song at heart, one that relies on thinly veiled metaphors: sung in the first person, the character waits patiently by the window, watching seasons pass, dreaming of the day when he will finally have the opportunity to "come running to tie your shoe."

This would be the first of several nods to the musical influence of Brian Eno on the members of Phish. Eno was the producer of The Talking Heads *Remain in Light* which was performed as the 1996 Halloween "musical costume." More directly, the song "Brian and Robert" from *Story of the Ghost* is in reference and in tribute to Brian Eno and Robert Fripp.

After its debut, "I'll Come Running" was never performed by Phish again. Warmly received by many fans who viewed it as a quintessentially perfect Phish cover (especially for Mike), it remains on many a fan's "wish list" for a return appearance.

I'm Blue, I'm Lonesome

AKA: "Blue and Lonesome"
Original Artist: Bill Monroe
Original Album: N/A
Vocals: Phish
Debut: 11/16/94
Historian: Christian C. McKee

Along with its frequent companion, "Long Journey Home," "I'm Blue, I'm Lonesome" made its debut on 11/16/94, when the Reverend Jeff Mosier joined Phish for a week of shows featuring acoustic bluegrass selections. For these tunes, Phish would transform themselves

into a traditional bluegrass band: Jon on mandolin, Page on upright bass, Mike on banjo and Trey on guitar. Like "Long Journey Home," "I'm Blue, I'm Lonesome" is a part of the bluegrass canon, being a composition of none other than Bill Monroe, the father of the genre.

Phish has played a few noteworthy versions of this song. On 9/30/95, the band dedicated it to Jerry Garcia. Both the timing and location had significance: Garcia had died just over a month before; Shoreline was a favorite of the Dead, remains a favorite of Phish, and was also the last place that all the members of Phish saw the Dead live. Musical highlights surrounding "I'm Blue, I'm Lonesome" have been mostly due to guest artists, as on 11/29/95 (with Béla Fleck) and on 7/18/99 at the Oswego festival with the Del McCoury Band.

I'm Gonna Be (500 Miles)
Original Artist: The Proclaimers
Original Album: *Sunshine On Leith* (1988)
Vocals: Tom Marshall (lead), Trey, (backing)
Debut: 12/30/97
Historian: Mark Toscano

This song was covered under some of the strangest circumstances of any cover tune. On 12/30/97, following an intricate Harpua story involving olive loaf, fried eggs, Slim Jims, *Lost in Space*, and udder balls, Trey explained that as a child he saw a vision of Tom Marshall come to him thanks to some bizarre ritual involving the aforementioned objects. In Trey's childhood vision, Tom appeared and began to sing this once overplayed Proclaimers tune. At this point during the show, the real Tom Marshall stepped out on stage and the five of them did in fact play the song, with much of Madison Square Garden singing along.

I'm One
Original Artist: The Who
Original Album: *Quadrophenia* (1973)
Vocals: Trey (lead), Page (backing)
Debut: 10/31/95
Historian: Craig DeLucia

In one of the most special moments of Halloween 1995, Trey picked up an acoustic guitar and rolled through a rousing rendition of this declarative, introspective ballad from The Who's *Quadrophenia*.

I'm So Tired
Original Artist: The Beatles
Original Album: *The Beatles* (aka "The White Album") (1968)
Vocals: Mike (lead), Trey (backing)
Debut: 10/31/94
Historian: Mark Toscano

One of John Lennon's favorite Beatles tracks, this one was written in India when Lennon found he had great trouble getting to sleep on the nights following a full day's meditation. For Phish's two performances of this tune, Mike "Cactus" Gordon took over lead vocals, first on 10/31/94 during the band's "White Album" set, and then a second time over a year later on 11/18/95.

(I'm Your) Hoochie Coochie Man
Music/Lyrics: Willie Dixon
Original Artist: Muddy Waters
Original Album: single (1954) (Waters);
  I Am the Blues (1970) (Dixon)
Vocals: Sugar Blue
Debut: 4/10/93
Historian: Ellis Godard

Although he is sometimes credited as the original artist, harmonica wizard Willie Dixon does not always receive credit for having written "Hoochie Coochie Man." Interesting, though, he was present for both of the studio recordings (1952 and 1954) by fellow Chess artist Muddy Waters, who *was* the original artist. Waters' second recording was released as a single, but each eventually found their way to albums—the first on a "rhythm and blues" compilation released in 1977, the second on a Muddy Waters boxed set released in 1989. Dixon later released several versions of his own, emphasizing the harmonica which Waters had placed second to the guitar. Perhaps the only released cover of the tune is by Eric Clapton, on his (1994) *From the Cradle*, where Jerry Portnoy's harp gets nearly as much time as Clapton's guitar.

Despite its few studio appearances, the song is perhaps part of the blues canon, having been performed on stage by almost any blues artist that comes to mind, from Dixon and Waters to the Allman Brothers and

Peter Sitzman

Jimi Hendrix. And the title phrase has been alluded to in song titles from Etta James' "Hoochie Coochie Gal" to Edgar Winter's "Rock and Roll, Hoochie Koo" and, more recently, perhaps a dozen dance and hip hop releases. Phish stuck with the original spirit and showed their mojo twice (4/10/93 and 8/8/97), both in Chicago with James "Sugar Blue" Whiting on lead vocals and harmonica.

In a Hole

AKA: "I Fell In A Hole," "Hole," "What You Will"
Music/Lyrics: Trey Anastasio
Album: (none)
Vocals: Page
Debut: 10/20/89
Historian: Jeremy David Goodwin

Page sings this sprightly little ditty, which was played six times in Fall 1989, only to subsequently disappear from the Phish universe. It reflects the band's jazzier leanings back in the Burlington days. The lyrics tell a story which, if not a straight transcription of a dream, is in any case extremely dreamlike. The first-person narrator recounts his experiences running though a field, falling into a hole, and experiencing a harrowing plunge into the depths of the crevice. He somehow escapes, though it is only a momentary reprieve before he repeats his mistake, perhaps in the midst of an impenetrable cycle.

"In A Hole" was debuted on 10/20/89, the first of three celebrated nights at the Front. This original incarnation (a hot jazz number) featured Dave Grippo and Russ Remington on alto and tenor saxes, respectively. It swings unrelentingly. This tune was played four times in the brief span between its debut and 10/28, and then popped up four more times between 11/30 and 12/16. Sadly, it has yet to appear again. "In A Hole" diehards can take some solace in the fact that it has been soundchecked as recently as 7/4/99, possibly portending an impending breakout? Such an event would certainly make the day of this Mockingbird scribe.

In the Midnight Hour

AKA: "Midnight Hour"
Original Artist: Wilson Pickett
Original Album: *In the Midnight Hour & Other Hits* (1965)
Vocals: Trey
Debut: 12/2/83
Historian: Ellis Godard

Phish played this Wilson Pickett tune at three of their first four known shows. The racy lyrics have a clear message: "Tonight, I'm gettin' some." At those early gigs, the band wasn't, but perhaps they were thinking ahead, as both improvisational ecstacy and typical rock groupies came years later.

The record of their prophecy is nonetheless thin. The 12/2/83 debut does not circulate, and 5/19/85 was actually a mix of Phish and Lamb's Bread. The remaining performance (11/3/84) does little to flatter either Pickett or Phish, and little to foretell the payoff to come.

Ingest

Music: Trey Anastasio
Album: "The White Tape"

Laugh: Ernie Anastasio
Debut: (never performed live)
Historian: Mark Toscano

Perhaps if Kraftwerk covered Fishbone's "Asswhippin'" (from *The Reality of My Surroundings*), it would sound like this. This bastard track from Phish's so-called "White Tape" is an angry, running-in-circles synth loop augmented by another loop of Trey's dad Ernie, laughing amid some unidentifiable slapping noises. The track continues in this manner for over a minute before breaking down and out of the loop, which is sampled from a recording of what may be an Anastasio family gathering, as Trey's voice is clearly apparent toward the end of the track.

The song as a whole is clearly a tightly constructed and densely defined parable of our urgent internal need as sentient beings to subvert the mores of society and throw off the constricting shackles of repetition and monotonous nonadventure that bog us down in our daily lives. Or it may just be a bunch of crap noise.

The Inlaw Josey Wales

AKA: "Minestrone," "Purple Hugh"
Music: Trey Anastasio
Album: *Farmhouse*
Debut: 9/9/99
Historian: Erik Swain

This acoustic instrumental has changed more in its title than in its performance since it first surfaced on Trey's 1999 solo tour. During the that tour's first show in Ann Arbor, MI, Trey said he did not have a moniker for the song and the first fan who posted the setlist to the Internet could name it. This honor went to Jesse Jarnow and Ali McDowell. "In deference to Ali's misreading of the word 'instrumental' on my setlist, we hereby request that the tune be named 'Minestrone,'" Jesse wrote on phish.net.

But the next night in Indianapolis, Trey decided he would call the song "Purple Hugh"—as in a guy named "Hugh" rather than "hues" and colors. This lasted all of six days; on 5/10/99 in Asheville, NC, Trey joked that he felt guilty about breaking his promise and resumed calling it "Minestrone."

It began life as a Phish song on 9/9/99 in Vancouver, the first show of that year's fall tour. It was no longer a completely solo effort by Trey; the others added minimal accompaniment. It surfaced on three more occasions that year, and all four times it served as a breather after an intense jam, following "Ghost" on 9/9, "Sand" on 12/13, "First Tube" on 12/18 and "Crosseyed & Painless" on 12/31.

The title issue was not resolved yet, however. During the *Farmhouse* sessions the band simply referred to it as "Acoustic," according to list of songs being considered for the album (as seen in a photograph published in the Summer, 2000 Döniac Schvice). More importantly, they were able to entice legendary musicians Béla Fleck and Jerry Douglas to contribute banjo and dobro, respectively, to the studio recording.

Trey finally announced the official title on 2/5/00 during his solo performance at the Tibet House Benefit at New York's Carnegie Hall. Why did he choose "The Inlaw Josie Wales," a pun on the Clint Eastwood western *The Outlaw Josey Wales*?

"The Inlaw Josie Wales is a much friendlier guy than the outlaw Josie Wales is," he explained in an interview with SonicNet. "In the

movie, there's lots of drama and gunfighting. In the mental movie of 'Inlaw Josie Wales,' the guy comes over, hangs out and has lunch. The tune was written, and Béla Fleck and Jerry Douglas were in town and wanted to see the barn, so they came over and we did it."

The song's new prominence was underscored by its placement as the first song of the encore on 5/21/00 at New York's Radio City Music Hall, Phish's first show after the release of *Farmhouse*. The band members must have liked it as an encore because they employed it there the next two times they played it. It continued to crop up regularly on the Summer and Fall 2000 tour.

Insects

Music: Phish
Album: *The Siket Disc*
Vocals: (instrumental)
Debut: (never performed live)
Historian: Mark Toscano

A manic tune that scurries constantly, almost outrunning its own rhythm, this is the seventh track on *The Siket Disc*. Combining delay loops, drones, and a crickety drum beat, the song threatens to annoy, but ends up escaping just before the listener can get out the bug spray.

Is It In My Head

Original Artist: The Who
Original Album: *Quadrophenia* (1973)
Vocals: Page (lead), Trey (backing)
Debut: 10/31/95
Historian: Craig DeLucia

One of *Quadrophenia*'s four major musical themes is revisited in this introspective song, as the narrator Jimmy wonders "Is it me, for a moment?" Page's heartfelt vocals and piano proficiency and Trey's harmonies pound home the question plaguing Jimmy: are his actions being guided by his mind or his soul?

On their Halloween '95 tapes, astute fans will hear background music piped through the P.A. system between "Helpless Dancer" and this song. On the original album, The Who used a piece of their early single "The Kids Are Alright" between the two songs. For the purpose of the Halloween show, Phish recorded their own version of "The Kids Are Alright" and played a snippet back through the loudspeaker that night at the appropriate moment.

It's Ice

AKA: "Ice"
Music: Trey Anastasio
Lyrics: Tom Marshall
Album: *Rift*
Debut: 9/25/91
Historian: Mark Toscano

When he received Tom Marshall's "It's Ice" poem, Trey was so impressed with it that he was extremely nervous about writing music to accompany it. He respected the words so much, that he didn't want to risk writing music that didn't do them justice. Many (including Tom) agree that Trey did a fine job, writing one of Phish's most

accomplished songs.

Not only does "It's Ice" have an extremely strong compositional structure separated into a number of distinctive but cohesive parts, but the music often seems to perfectly evoke the actions of the characters. This is best exemplified by the severe "fall" of the music as the main character breaks through the ice and sinks downward to the bottom of the frosty pond, as well as his subsequent ascent back up to the surface a minute or so later in the tune. This sort of "musical onomatopoeia" shows up in a number of other Phish songs, such as "The Chase," "Esther," and "The Famous Mockingbird," to name a few. (By the way, if you just swear that Mike's bassline in the main theme sounds familiar, perhaps you should check out an old episode of "The Benny Hill Show.")

Lyrically, this tune gives a blow-by-blow description of the battle between a guy skating on a frozen pond and his reflected image in the ice beneath. The lyrics are filled with all sorts of vivid imagery and multiple plays on the confusion between reality and reflection, and still represent some of Tom's most impressive lyrics to date. As with "Tela," when Trey composed the music for this tune, he did so specifically with Page in mind as lead singer, writing it for Page's vocal range rather than his own. Both band and fans alike agreed at the time (mid-to-late '91) that Page did not sing enough and Trey made this choice to satisfy both parties. He also consciously designed the song to highlight Page's piano-playing more than the average tune. Trey saw this as a way to expand the possibilites of the song as well as to give Page a much-deserved showcase.

Another influence on "It's Ice's" composition was one of simple logistics. Trey has stated that he wrote "It's Ice," "Sparkle," and "Brother" (all written in the same wave of songwriting) basically to fill niches in the band's repertoire. "It's Ice" offered the band a ready opportunity to play a far-out, "mind-twisting" song if they wanted to. And "It's Ice" has on occasion been known to twist a mind or two.

"It's Ice" is a long tune; even the relatively jam-free studio version on *Rift* runs over eight minutes in length. Performed live, the song rarely strays from its composition, although the bottom-of-the-pond portion of the tune (the "breakdown" of the music before the final, dramatic climb back up to the surface for a reprise of the chorus) has on many an occasion gotten pretty wacky. The version on 7/28/98 even features Fishman giving us a vacuum-enriched version of "Lengthwise.")

At the Crest Theatre on 3/22/93, the band segued into their legendary set-II Gamehendge performance via "It's Ice." Once the song had reached the bottom of the pond, Trey informed everyone that by sinking down through the ice, they had traveled to the land of Gamehendge. He then began to tell the story of "The Man Who Stepped Into Yesterday" as the rest of the band continued to play bottom-of-the-pond mood music until starting into "Lizards." Although "It's Ice" isn't at all a Gamehendge tune, Trey used it as a springboard for the story much in the way that "Kung" did on 6/26/94. (Speaking of "Kung," the tune has been sandwiched in the middle of "It's Ice" on a few occasions—see 10/29/94 and 12/30/95.)

"It's Ice" is also known as the tune that features "The Fish Dance." During the succession of escalating 1-2-3-count chords that culminates in a dead-stop scream, Fishman will often stand atop his stool and do a wild, vaguely sexual dance that always seems to please the (sometimes dumbstruck) crowd. [Author's note: Once, during this part of "It's Ice" at a show I attended, I actually overheard someone who was obviously unfamiliar with Phish say, "What the hell is *wrong* with this band?!"]

Versions of this tune vary wildly in quality from " kind of sloppy"

to "pretty standard" to "pretty durned good" to "holy crap!" Some "holy craps" you might want to hear include 3/17/92, 6/16/95, and 9/20/00 (unfinished, 14 minutes long, with an awesome jam bubbling up from the "underwater" segment!)

And remember: even though it may be the tune's music that moves you, please don't forget the lyrics. They're some of the best you're gonna get!

It's My Life

Music/Lyrics: Junior Wells
Original Artist: Junior Wells
Original Album: *It's My Life, Baby* (1966)
Vocals: Bruce "Sunpie" Barnes
Debut: 3/2/93
Historian: Ellis Godard

Phish performed this bluesy number only once, and not with any of the bluesmen they've usually featured as guests (such as Son Seals or Sugar Blue). Instead, they introduced Bruce "Sunpie" Barnes, a cajun ball of fire who brought his harp and washboard for a Nawlins interlude that began with this Junior Wells number.

IT'S NO GOOD TRYING (see: "NO GOOD TRYING")

I've Had Enough

Original Artist: The Who
Original Album: *Quadrophenia* (1973)
Vocals: Trey (lead), Page (second lead), Fishman ("LOVE!")
Debut: 10/31/95
Historian: Craig DeLucia

This song was played during Phish's performance of The Who's *Quadrophenia*. It featured Trey on acoustic guitar and amazing vocals from Page on the song's self-contained preview of "Love, Reign O'er Me," as well as an emphatic shout of "LOVE!" from Fishman.

Peter Sitzman

I've Turned Bad

Music/Lyrics: (unknown)
Original Album: (unknown)
Vocals: Sofi Dillof and unidentified male vocalist
Debut: 5/9/89
Historian: Mark Toscano and Erik Swain

This tune (along with "Nowhere Fast") has eluded fans' keen identification for some time. It might be an original, it might be a cover. "I've Turned Bad" and "Nowhere Fast" are both sort of hardcore punk efforts, the latter segueing into the former, with lyrics consisting mainly of streams of insults. Sofi Dillof and an unknown male vocalist provided these amusing but confusing tunes for the listening pleasure of the audience, gathered together for the final Phish show at Nectar's and the release party for *Junta*. If anyone has any information about the identification of these two songs, don't keep it to yourself!

Izabella

Original Artist: Jimi Hendrix
Original Album: *Rainbow Bridge* (1971),
   First Rays of the New Rising Sun (1997)
Vocals: Trey
Debut: 6/6/97 (private show), 6/13/97 (public show)
Historian: Chris Bertolet

1971's *Rainbow Bridge* was the first of two Hendrix albums compiled by MCA Records after Jimi's untimely death. In 1997, after winning a legal battle with MCA over rights to the iconic guitarist's works, his family released their own posthumous favorites under the title *First Rays of the New Rising Sun*. It's a tribute to "Izabella" that the song made the cut for both. The song's narrator is a soldier longing to return home to his love, the tune's namesake, so he can hold her instead of his rifle.

Though her name is spelled with an "s" instead of a "z," conventional Phish lore suggests that Trey chose the cover as a fatherly nod to his infant daughter. He and Mike road-tested the song on 5/21/97 at Club Toast with New York! (a one-off collaboration with several Burlington musicians), but Phish debuted "Izabella" before an intimate crowd at Bradstock. Soon thereafter, on 6/13/97, it saw its first public performance in Ireland, one of the few Western European countries where Hendrix never performed. To the obvious delight of the Dublin crowd, "Izabella" arose from the jammed-out "Stand!" encore.

While Phish's instrumental reading of this propulsive tune is pretty faithful to the original, Trey's vocals typically consist of the same verse sung twice or thrice with a varying degree of accuracy. Check out the volcanic version that erupts from "Tweezer" in the 12/6/97 jam-a-thon at Auburn Hills, MI.

The Jägermeister Song

Music/Lyrics: Phish
Album: (none)
Vocals: Trey
Debut: 4/18/90
Historian: Phil Nazarro

Just like the Jägermeister factory in Wolfenbüttel, Germany, with its bright orange on green trim and gingerbread castle-come-'70s hotel

look, this song is very goofy. The first version of Jagermeister from Denver rolls out of a bit of banter that finds Phish being as silly as any Fishman cover song interpretation. After "Lawn Boy," Fishman starts the high-hat intro to "David Bowie." But the rest of the band isn't ready to be serious. Trey begins "Lawn Boy" again, and Page sings "Throughout the night…" as if drunk. Then the band begins, as if planned (it was), to build up Chris Kuroda's stage lights skills to the audience. Comments like "sexy light show" are followed by a "light solo." Trey finally admits they are trying to get Chris a date from any willing female in attendance. Funny stuff.

Fishman starts the song off with a drumbeat and Trey falls right into, chanting "Gimme some Jägermeister…Gimme some Jägermeister…" in his best drunk and rowdy voice. One by one the rest join in on the chant, adding some more layers to the music, and sometimes adding "All night long" to the vocals. After a couple minutes of this hilarity, the song falls apart due to someone singing while pinching their nose. No doubt the the impending end to the song is because the rest of the band and audience are now laughing too hard to continue.

There you have it. Jägermeister in all its gut-busting glory. A great song to do shots to. Too bad Phish only played it twice (see also: 5/6/90). But then again, they don't play bars anymore either.

Jennifer Dances
Music/Lyrics: Trey Anastasio, Tom Marshall
Album: (none)
Vocals: Trey (lead), Mike, Page (backing)
Debut: 12/5/99
Historian: Mark Toscano

This simple, sweet, and sunny pop number greeted the 12/5/99 Rochester crowd as an unexpected treat after Trey announced how much they liked playing that venue (Blue Cross Arena). The ensuing tune charmed fans with its warmth (it was pretty cold outside), as it represented Phish's poppiest original to date. After two more performances (12/7/99 and 12/17/99), the song disappeared. Last anybody heard, it was considered for, but ultimately left off of, *Farmhouse*.

JERRY'S BEARD (see: FLAT FEE)

Jessica
Original Artist: The Allman Brothers Band
Original Album: *Brothers and Sisters* (1973)
Vocals: (instrumental)
Debut: 5/8/93
Historian: Craig DeLucia:

Classic rock aficionados will surely recognize this Allman Brothers instrumental. Phish has never played this one in its entirety, but fans were treated to a short "Jessica" jam in the 5/8/93 "Bowie." If you're a rabid fan of both bands, grab the 7/15/94 "Bowie," which contained an unmistakable (albeit shorter) "Jessica" tease.

Jesus Just Left Chicago
AKA: "Jesus Left Chicago"; "JJLC"; "Jesus"
Original Artist: ZZ Top
Original Album: *Tres Hombres* (1973)
Phish Album: *Slip Stitch and Pass* (3/1/97)

Vocals: Page
Debut: 1/27/88
Historian: Chris Bertolet

Take a down-tempo 12-bar shuffle, add another bar to make it a baker's dozen, and throw in conceptual lyrics about the Son of God on a road trip across America. Glaze with honky-tonk piano and plaintive, wailing guitar, and bake until crisp. Such is this bluesy confection from Texas trio ZZ Top, one of Phish's less obvious influences.

"Jesus" graced Phish's repertoire in 1988 and abided there until 1992, when it vanished for over a year. Since its resurrection in March of 1993, the tune's seen inconsistent and limited action; still, as it's a relatively simple song to remember and execute, this hasn't diminished its potency.

In Hamburg, Germany, on 3/1/97, Phish segued out of "Wolfman's Brother" into what would become the best-known version of "Jesus" (it subsequently appeared on *Slip, Stitch and Pass*). The following summer at the magnificent Gorge (8/3/97), the band plummeted from a swirling, psychedelic "Twist" into what would become a driving, mighty "Jesus." The 10/31/95 Rosemont version also inspires.

Johnny B. Goode
AKA: "JBG"
Original Artist: Chuck Berry
Original Album: single (ca. 1957);
   ***Chuck Berry is on Top* (1959)**
Vocals: Trey (lead), Page (backing)
Debut: 6/17/95
Historian: Chris Bertolet

Smack in the middle of a tour characterized by expansive, complex jams, Phish proffered their first public attempt at "Johnny B. Goode," one of rock's earliest and most elementary anthems. Simple or not, a self-referential ode to a young guitar stud destined for stardom should never be performed by a band without a stellar axe-man. Some think Phish has one.

Phish's hyperactive reading of "JBG" first reared its head in the middle of a "Tweezer" at Virginia's Stone Ridge; at the blazing Sugarbush show weeks later, it came charging out of the meat of "Bowie." Though both versions delivered, they interrupted the continuity of the jam that contained them, and Phish has since preferred to let "JBG" stand on its own. At the Gorge show on 8/2/97, however, Trey steered the band into "JBG," abandoning a dramatic, conflicted "Diseezer" segue that found he and Fishman at loggerheads. Though some in the crowd groaned in disappointment, the hi-torque "JBG" won over the audience emphatically.

Other marquee versions of "JBG" include the 12/31/95 MSG encore (near-dangerous energy release), the 8/6/96 Red Rocks encore (capstone of a set-long sparring match with an electric Mother Nature), and the 11/17/97 Denver oddity (meanders into space, never to return).

"Johnny" seems to have jumped the tracks for an extended vacation; he hasn't been seen since July 1998.

Julia
Original Artist: The Beatles
Original Album: *The Beatles* (aka "The White Album") (1968)
Vocals: Mike (lead), Trey (second lead)

"The Ides of Marshall: An Historical Breakdown of Julius"

Daniel Nooter, New York, NY

The song *Julius* is, as many probably know, an account of the last moments of Julius Caesar's life from his own stream-of-consciousness point of view. The following is an attempt to provide some historical context to the song line-by-line so listeners not otherwise acquainted with the life of Caesar may better appreciate it.

>Danger, I've been told to expect it

Julius Caesar had, by the time of his assassination, on March 15, 44 B.C., had many warnings that his life was in danger. Shakespeare's play has all sorts of omens and unnatural phenomena to foreshadow Caesar's death, as well as nightmares sent to Caesar's wife Calpurnia. In fact, the comet Hale-Bopp may last have been visible in the year of Caesar's death, providing an omen. (In historical fact, Calpurnia was troubled by bad dreams the evening before her husband's death, and Caesar, for that reason, as well as his own illness, almost stayed home instead of going to the senate on that fateful day.) There was the fateful prophecy (more on that later), and a warning in writing which, tragically, Caesar never read. One of the many petitioners accosting Caesar as he walked to the Pompey Theatre handed him a notice warning him of the plot against him, exhorting Caesar to read it right away. Instead, Caesar held it in his left hand, planning to read all the petitions later in the day, at home.

>I begin my descent down the cold granite steps

Marshall is probably drawing here from the popular Shakespearean account, in which Caesar is stabbed on the steps of the Roman Senate. In actuality, Caesar was stabbed inside, seated on his raised couch twenty-three times.

>And who could have turned among those I confide in?

Quite a few, in fact. Caius Cassius led the conspiracy against Caesar which eventually included sixty citizens, among them Marcus Brutus. Brutus was closely trusted by Caesar, eliciting Caesar's famous (fictional) last remark as he was attacked: "Et tu, Brute?" [And you also, Brutus?]

>I think that I know what I haven't known yet
>'Cause a week is a month and an hour a day
>When your reaching just pushes it further away
>With your past and your future precisely divided
>Am I at that moment?
>I haven't decided

This section seems only to echo Caesar's sense of unease as the attack grew imminent. The historical Caesar was somewhat less wary, not realizing an attempt on his life was happening when Lucius Tillius Cimber, who had ostensibly come to petition Caesar for clemency for an imprisoned brother, seized his toga. Moments later, the senator Casca stabbed Julius in the throat.

>And stretching out into the sea…Aquitana

Probably Marshall means "Aquitania," not Aquitana, but changed the word to better fit the general rhythm and cadence of the line. Aquitania was a region in Southwestern France which the Roman Empire eventually expanded to include.

>Is that what the prophet told me he saw?

In Shakespeare's play, a soothsayer warns Caesar to "Beware the ides [15th] of March." On that morning, Caesar chides the soothsayer that "the ides of march have come." The soothsayer properly responds that "they have not yet gone."

>You gave it to me but I really don't want it

Caesar is said to have been offered the crown and title of roman King several times, but refused it. This is pivotal, because it was on the basis of fear that Caesar would destroy the Roman Republic by seizing such power that the conspirators felt it necessary to murder him (at least in most interpretations, that is their motivation). Marshall seems to be indicating that Caesar's power was unsought, and eventually dragged him down, even though it had been pressed upon him. This view is weakened somewhat by Caesar's well-documented, deliberate quest for power. Many have speculated that the crown was actually offered to Caesar by a man in his employ in order to test the public's reaction (which proved to be lukewarm) to the idea.

>I came out on top by the luck of the draw

This is a bit strained. Caesar's famous crossing of the Rubicon river in defiance of the Senate, as well as his ruthless, Machiavellian political maneuvering make it clear that Caesar's appointment as dictator was hardly a matter of luck, although perhaps amidst that ruthless competition, Marshall's Caesar feels it is luck that he survived while his enemies did not.

[The "if you lay it on your brother" section, while it may refer to Caesar, has no direct historical relevance I've been able to discover.]

All in all, Tom Marshall's Julius Caesar seems far closer to Shakespeare's portrayal than to the historical Caesar (although Marshall makes Caesar a more sympathetic character), but then the song is no less hurt as a song by being ahistorical than is Shakespeare's play.

Debut: 10/31/94
Historian: Mark Toscano

On 10/31/94, Mike provided the lead vocals for this tune, the 17th song on the Beatles' "White Album." John Lennon originally wrote this fragile ballad for his mother.

Julius

Music/Lyrics: Trey Anastasio, Tom Marshall
Album: *Hoist*
Vocals: Trey (lead), Fish, Mike, Page (backing)
Debut: 4/4/94

Historian: charlz franz

While the lyrics of "Julius" ("Danger! I've been told to expect it.") are based on Shakespeare's *Julius Caesar*, Tom Marshall has admitted that the chorus is nonsensical. It was made up at the last minute on the way into a recording session simply to have something to sing, and has no relation to the play at all. The upbeat tempo and exultant chorus certainly belie the dark and foreboding tone of the play, and "Julius" has become a favorite of many fans. It is one of the few Phish tunes where the album version is as good as it is live.

The *Hoist* version, released in the Spring of 1994, featured the backing vocals of the Ricky Grundy Chorale (with Rose Stone & Jean McClain) and the Tower of Power Horns Section. The *Tracking* video contains footage of this recording session. "Julius" debuted on 4/4/94 at Burlington's Flynn Theater in the first show of the year, with the six-piece Giant Country Horns providing backup, and went on to appear frequently in the rotation throughout that year. It also was released as a single and Phish played it on July 13, 1995 on the *Late Show with David Letterman*, accompanied by a four-piece horn section In subsequent years, "Julius" often has served both as a rousing set opener or closer, and as an encore. It has been played in every European country of the former Roman Empire, except for Ireland.

While there are fans who say that there are no bad versions of "Julius," one of the best performances came at the 12/31/96 New Year's show at the Fleet Center in Boston. Amid thousands of balloons, Phish was joined onstage by the Boston Community Choir for "Bohemian Rhapsody." Band and choir then belted out a joyous "Julius" to end the set amid cheers from the crowd. The enthusiastic hugging among band and chorus members showed that all clearly enjoyed themselves immensely.

Other notable versions include 12/3/94, San Jose, CA (with the Giant Country Horns); 10/24/95 Madison, WI; 12/6/96, Las Vegas, NV; 8/3/97, Gorge, WA; 11/23/97, Winston-Salem, NC; 12/5/97, Cleveland, OH (almost 20 minutes!), and 11/28/98, Worcester, MA.

Jump Monk

Original Artist: Charles Mingus
Original Album: *Cafe Bohemia* **(1956)**
Vocals: (instrumental)
Debut: 3/12/88
Historian: Ellis Godard

Phish has played this Charles Mingus instrumental only once, to open the first known live Gamehendge show (complete with narration)—although fans briefly heard it again opening the 7/17/93 soundcheck. Commonly labelled "Gamehendge Jazz" or "Gamehendge Intro" (on a tape often mislabelled 3/12/89 or 3/12/90), the song is not part of and bears no relation to the Gamehendge saga other than this appearance. But Phish does bear connections to the song and its composer.

In the original, Mingus began a period of fusing gospel and blues into jazz movements, and thereby pushed innovation forward (into hard bop) even while paying homage to jazz greats—here, pianist/composer Thelonius Monk, who often danced around while performing. In covering the tune, Phish, and Trey in particular, signaled their move from relatively isolative composers with strong jazz roots to performance innovators with great ambitions. Though Phish has not covered the tune since, it can still be heard occasionally at Bad Hat shows or in

"Bathtub Gin" jams (e.g. 4/24/94)—and Trey has acknowledged that he used part of the chord progression in "Stash."

Keyboard Cavalry

AKA: "Keyboard Army"
Music: Phish
Album: (none)
Debut: 9/27/95
Historian: Mark Toscano

Its name coined by fans who just didn't know what the heck to call it, "Keyboard Cavalry" was a phenomenon with half the life expectancy of its sister song, "Acoustic Army." Whereas "Acoustic Army" was performed over the course of 1995's two tours, "Keyboard Cavalry" only made appearances during the Fall tour that year.

At the tour's Sacramento, CA opener on 9/27/95, something odd happened after the band's debut of the still-incomplete "Billy Breathes." Page started repeating a pleasant piano riff over and over, while the rest of the band abandoned their instruments one by one. Fish, Mike, and Trey marched, slowly and single file (as if possessed), across the stage, each of them stopping in front of one of Page's other keyboards. The three of them then joined Page's simple riff on their respective keyboards, each playing a distinct riff of their own. The result was a pleasant tune that was sweet and bucolic, all the while leaving the crowd dumbstruck. The short, four-voice song repeated many times, until a melodic ascent came out of nowhere and the music stopped. Then it began again. After the second stop, Fish, Mike, and Trey retreated back to their own instruments much in the way they had left them, with Page still repeating his initial riff as accompaniment.

No one was quite sure what to make of this one, although it was obviously related to "Acoustic Army" (which had debuted 6/7/95), another experiment in combining individual musical parts to produce a pleasant aural composite (see "Acoustic Army"). This song surfaced 15 times over the course of the Fall '95 tour (on 10/8/95 it appeared twice!), often occurring in the middle or at the end of a jam. For interesting examples, check out 9/30/95 Shoreline ("Mike's Song" -> "Keyboard Cavalry" -> "Weekapaug Groove") or 12/14/95 Binghamton (its final performance coming out of a "Tweezer" jam). Some fans loved its eccentric sweetness, while other fans felt it rudely interrupted otherwise notable jams. Either way, it looks as if "Keyboard Cavalry"—like "Acoustic Army"—was available for a limited time only. (And in case you're wondering, both "Armies" made appearances in the same show on three occasions—9/28/95, 10/2/95, and 10/6/95.)

See Also: "Acoustic Army"

Killer Joe

Music/Lyrics: Phish
Album: (none)
Vocals: Fishman
Debut: 3/17/90
Historian: Erik Swain

Killer Joe is not really a song. It's hard to say exactly what it is. At the beginning of the second set on 3/17/90 in Ardmore, PA, the band briefly improvises a jam while Fishman mutters the words "Killer Joe" over and over again. Dementia? Performance art? Too much alcohol in honor of St. Patrick's Day? Who knows.

Kung

Lyrics: Jon Fishman
Album: (none)
Debut: 3/4/85
Historian: Ellis Godard

In the local culture, he is sometimes called "The Beast Boy." But he is a learned animal, and his tribe has on twenty-five occasions chanted his reflections on another peoples. The !Kung Sans a Kalahari hunter-gatherer population that was the dominant population in southern Africa for perhaps tens of millenia. The population of perhaps 300,000 in the seventeenth century encountered Dutch colonists, and then dwindled by the 1970s to under 50,000, dispersed throughout South Africa. But as their numbers shrank, anthropologists devoted increasing attention to the population's complexity, diversity, and adapations. Although the !Kung no longer rule the high desert, Phish incants their spirit from the hills of their own performances. Their noted diversity is reflected in "voraciously alternate" speeds and tones, as the words are adaptively overlayed on diverse segues and jams. (Compare the 2/20/93 craziness to the rising energy of 11/29/98.) But the words do not vary, as the song appropriately evokes a mix of reverence and glee: On three occassions (12/31/92, 3/25/93, and 6/26/94), Trey declared the chant a requisite step to entering Gamehendge. This sense of transport, too, connects with the !Kung, who perform a ritual healing dance from dusk to dawn perhaps twice each week. The !kia dance, described as "an experiential passage," is a fatiguing process that advances an altered state of consciousness, with the aim of transcendence not only for spiritual purposes but to address misfortune. Near its climax, the !kia ignites the "n/um," an energy which resides in the stomach and works its way up the spine with increasing intensity: "Stand up," it says, "stand up on your heels and sing."

La Grange

Original Artist: ZZ Top
Original Album: *Tres Hombres* (1973)
Vocals: Mike, Trey
Debut: 8/9/87
Historian: Phillip Zerbo

The diversity of covers that Phish has performed over the years is well known. Less often noted, if you look at the bands that Phish draws on for inspiration, those bands themselves often combine a wide variety of influences. In the case of ZZ Top, the stew includes a little Texas boogie, a dash of liquored-up cowboy twang, a few ounces of down-home blues, and a heavy dose of good-ol-boy rock-and-roll. Fast women, fast cars, fast livin'!

ZZ Top's acclaimed 1973 album *Tres Hombres* produced not one but two songs that would find their way into the Phish repertoire: "Jesus Just Left Chicago" and ZZ Top's first top 40 hit, "La Grange." "La Grange" was first performed by Phish at Nectar's on August 9, 1987. If you haven't had the fortune to hear this tune performed by Phish, find yourself a tape soon! Mike shows off his extended range of vocal capabilities, and if you can keep yourself from laughing ("A haw, haw, haw, haw"), his deep, soulful serenade of the first verse is often quite impressive. Trey takes the second verse, usually accompanied by a rip-roaring guitar solo.

Versions of "La Grange" do not vary much, even over the years. "La Grange" was a staple in Phish setlists from 1987 through 1990, but has tapered off significantly in the last decade. Solid versions appear in a number of outstanding Phish shows, including 5/25/88, 8/26/89, 11/2/90, 8/2/93.

A most notable appearance was on 12/29/95, with guest Jim Stinnette, Mike's bass instructor. The modern day appearances of "La Grange" are few and far between, but it still lurks in the repertoire, played as recently (as of this writing) as 9/22/99, at the Pan Am Center in Las Cruces, NM. Have Mercy!

The Landlady

Music: Trey Anastasio
Album: *A Picture of Nectar*
Vocals: Instrumental
Debut: 6/9/90
Historian: Kristen Godard

The Landlady—a brief Latin style mamba-esque instrumental written by Trey—originated as the composed middle section of another Phish song, "Punch You in the Eye." "PYITE" (originally called "Punch Me in the Eye") debuted in October 1989 and was played only a handful of times before its temporary retirement until 1993. Several months after "PYITE" was put to bed, "The Landlady" emerged as its own tune on 2/1/90 at The Georgia Theater (Phish opening for Widespread Panic). It was next played as an encore, with "Contact," on 6/9/90, and went into heavy rotation that fall.

Fall 1990 was a period in which Phish was aiming to develop new directions from several old songs, as with the extrication of "Landlady" from "PYITE" and "The Asse Festival" from "Guelah Papyrus." "Landlady" and "Guelah" have two other common threads: both were included on Phish's first Elektra disk, *A Picture of Nectar*, and both feature little choreographed dances performed by Trey and Mike during a specific segment of the song. On 7/11/92, four female dancers joined Trey and Mike on stage to do the "Landlady" dance at the H.O.R.D.E show in Holmdel, NJ.

"PYITE" returned to Phish's repertoire on 2/5/93 at the Roseland Ballroom in NYC, with Trey teaching the audience the "Landlady" dance (dubbed for the only time as the "Storm Dance"). "PYITE" co-existed in the line-up with "Landlady" through 1994 and become a favorite live tune in the years that followed, while "Landlady" became increasingly scarce on its own. "Landlady's" last appearances as a stand-alone song came on 12/2/94 at UC Davis' Recreation Hall and 12/3/94 at San Jose State's Events Center, both featuring the Giant Country Horns. Since that time, it has been performed only in its original state within "PYITE."

Because it is a highly structured composition, no song has ever segued into or out of "Landlady" (unlike "PYITE"), nor has it ever been performed with a guest (with the exception of the GCH during the Summer 1991 Horns Tour and several other Horns shows). Early "Landladys" often were followed by "Bouncing Around the Room," with many subsequent versions preceding "Destiny Unbound" (including the last appearance of "Destiny" on 11/15/91 at Trax in Charlottesville, VA). Notable versions include: 11/2/90 with Page on organ, a rarity at the time; 2/9/91 with great Trey soloing; 3/22/92 to close the Mountain Stage radio show; and 8/12/93 as part of a crazy "Tweezer" jam. The song was also teased within "David Bowie" on 3/17/91 and "4/1/92," and

jammed in a first set "Possum" on 4/5/92 before being played in full during the second set.

See Also: "Punch You in the Eye."

Lawn Boy

Music: Trey Anastasio
Lyrics: Tom Marshall
Album: *Lawn Boy; Slip Stitch and Pass* (3/1/97);
 ***Hampton Comes Alive* (11/21/98)**
Debut: 11/30/89
Historian: Phillip Zerbo

Ladies and Gentlemen, The Chairman of the Boards. As often introduced by Trey following its performance, "Lawn Boy" shines the spotlight on The Chairman of the [Key]Boards, Page McConnell. Not content with a stylistic diversity that includes everything from punk rock to bluegrass, "Lawn Boy" adds "Lizard Lounge Crooning" to Phish's repertroire.

"Lawn Boy" provides the title track for Phish's second studio release, and in keeping with the Phish tradition of variety—in this case unplanned—there are two different "versions" of the studio release. The remastered version on Elektra is significantly slower than the original version on the Absolute A-Go-Go label. Perhaps they found the remastered version preferable, as the live version performed today is even slower than the (already slowed-down) remastered album cut.

Introduced at Boston's Paradise Club on 11/30/89, "Lawn Boy" has been a standard ever since, remaining in the regular live rotation to this day. Almost all renditions witness Page moving out from the veil of his keyboard setup to assume front-and-center stage in order to serenade the crowd, and often to receive a rose from an adoring fan. "Lawn Boy" also provides an opportunity for Mike Gordon to display his more more subtle skills, with a laid-back, jazzy solo. While most version are very similar, a few notable variations can be found on 7/19/91 and 7/21/91 with the Giant Country Horns, on 8/16/97 with an extended bass solo by Mike (sitting down on his monitor, introducing a cozy setting that belied the 60,000+ crowd assembled at The Great Went), and on 11/21/98, which featured an "anti-drum solo," an intentionally slow, non-eventful solo by Jon Fishman.

The title "Lawn Boy" also introduces a possible double-meaning, given its useage in the pornography trade, and perhaps not coincidentally, as Fishman assumes a dominant role in the graphic images on the album. It also may provide a glimpse into Tom Marshall's writing method, as "oleander" and "olfactory" can conveniently be found on the same page of most dictionaries.

Layla

Music/Lyrics: Eric Clapton
Original Artist: Derek & the Dominoes
Original Album: *Layla And Other Assorted Love Songs* (1970)
Vocals: Page
Debut: 11/29/98
Historian: Craig DeLucia

Layla is the only Eric Clapton-penned song that Phish has performed in its entirety (though Trey did play "Bell Bottom Blues" on his May, 1999, solo tour). Though it had been teased before (see, for example, the "Suzy Greenberg" from 5/13/94), it took a guest appearance by

blues guitarist Seth Yacavone to make the whole song come to life. Given the textured dual-guitar sound of the original, it's not surprising that "Layla" was a one-time concert treat.

Lengthwise

Vocals: Fish
Music/Lyrics: Jon Fishman
Album: *Rift*
Debut: 11/19/92
Historian: Ellis Godard

Lengthwise is one of three songs on *Rift* (along with "FEFY" and "Wedge") that were recorded in the studio before they debuted live. It is also one of three songs (like " NO₂" and "Catapult") which are arguably just lyrics, since only the lyrics are common to all versions. Even *Rift* has two versions of "Lengthwise." In the first (track 3), Fishman's simple refrain is accompanied by snoring and then interrupted by an alarm clock just prior to "Maze," which begins the nightmare that is the album's unifying concept. The second version (track 13, a third as long) comes as the narrator begins to stir from his sleep, and includes compressed snippets of other songs on the album. Live, too, everything but the lyrics is distinctive about each performance, including in particular the debut (with reggae instrumentation, revisited on 2/17/93), 2/4/93 (which ranged from reggae to rock, and had the refrain reprised during "Harry Hood"), and 2/6/93 ("Faht"-like).

However, though the lyrics are few, Fishman has used them to ham things up, whether with additional lyrics about burning his hand (2/6/93, after refusing to tell the Prison Joke), as an insert in "Bike" (3/16/93), even for bringing out his mom to play vacuum (11/23/92 and 4/23/93).

"Lengthwise" often opens a set, typically followed by either "Squirming Coil" or "Maze." It is one of the few songs to appear in the show immediately following the show in which it debuted (emerging from "Terrapin" on 11/20/92). It was played nineteen more times during the next nine months, but only twice since, most recently in the middle of "It's Ice" on 7/28/98. Other notable appearances include 3/31/93, 4/10/93, 4/30/93, and 8/3/93—all set openers segueing adequately into "Maze" at shows that also included another Fishman tune.

Leprechaun

Music: Trey Anastasio
Album: (none)
Debut: 7/15/93
Historian: Mark Toscano

Leprechaun has jigged around the stage of a Phish show only three times, and its hardcore appreciation among fans that have heard it makes it one of the rarest and most coveted gems in Phish's canon.

This gentle, incandescent tune came primarily out of Trey's mid-'93 songwriting, a period that also gave birth to the first incarnation of "Guyute," which wouldn't debut at a Phish show until over a year later. The approach to composition in both songs is very similar. Trey's extended instrumental pieces from years past ("Fluff's Travels," "The Divided Sky," and "Reba," to name a few) were more strongly constructed from interlocking, sharply defined melodic and harmonic bits to create a clever and complex sonic whole. Trey often played around with theoretical and intellectual properties of music in constructing these

tight compositions, an approach that came both from his work with Ernie Stires and his interest in progressive rock bands like Genesis, King Crimson, and P.F.M. As he grew compositionally, his influences expanded, and his approach to song composition gradually changed, though not nearly as much as in the years since 1993. With *Rift* behind them, the band sought out something new and different, as the complex and intellectual trappings of that album had bogged them down a bit. Songs like "It's Ice," "Rift," and "All Things Reconsidered" are excellent, but all of them and more on one album sounded a bit too musically masturbatory, and the band felt it more than anyone.

In the move from complex, multi-part composition eventually to more simply conceived and strongly grounded songs like "Waste," "Farmhouse," and "Prince Caspian," a few songs showed up that fit in neither category. "Guyute" and "Leprechaun" are still multi-partite and complex, but in a more textural and substantive way than Trey's earlier work. "Leprechaun" glides, floats, dips, turns, and skips. It feels grounded in an earthy reality, not at all theoretical or heady. Both songs also suggest that Trey perhaps revisited the memories and experiences of his Ireland trip in 1987, thematically and compositionally. Additionally, both "Leprechaun" and "Guyute" are composed to encourage more cohesion between the four band members. His earlier compositions voiced each instrument in a more distinct, disparate way, while these two '93 songs were arranged to create an overall harmonious sound.

"Leprechaun" is a perfect moniker—the title alone evokes an image of the blissfully verdant travels of a leprechaun amidst the fields, trees, and streams of Ireland, a dance here, a nap there, and pausing to feel the cool breeze against his face. The only other potential rival for "Most Idyllic Phish Song" would likely be "Glide II," another M.I.A. tune. Comparisons to other songs include "The Man Who Stepped Into Yesterday," "Acoustic Army," "The Squirming Coil" (listen to Mike's bass), and even to The Beatles' "Here Comes the Sun" (compare that song's bridge to "Leprechaun's" "chorus").

"Leprechaun" runs about four and a half minutes in length, twice the length of "I am Hydrogen," its nearest counterpart in the peaceful instrumental category. The comparison is doubly just, as "Leprechaun" supplanted "Hydrogen" between "Mike's Song" and "Weekapaug Groove" in the second and third of its three performances (7/17/93 and 7/31/93). Its debut, curiously following "My Mind's Got a Mind Of Its Own" and slipping into "Runaway Jim," occurred on 7/15/93.

A Letter to Jimmy Page

Music: Trey Anastasio
Album: "The White Tape"
Debut: 5/3/85 (in "Alumni Blues"); 5/11/87 (on its own)
Historian: Mark Toscano

Trey knew that sending an actual letter to the Led Zeppelin guitarist wouldn't be the best way to pay homage to one of his rock heroes. Instead, the precocious then-20-year-old composed a little metal ditty designed to evoke the living spirit of Page himself, who was at the time recording music of questionable worth with The Firm. Perhaps Trey's song was intended to wake Page out of his crap-rock stupor, and perhaps Page heard him, for the guitarist soon realized the error of his ways and left The Firm, and (soon after) David Coverdale in the dust.

As it appears on the band's "White Tape" demo, "Letter to Jimmy Page" is a standalone track, closing out the tape's second side. In Phish's early live set, however, it usually appeared as a bridge about two-thirds of the way through concert favorite "Alumni Blues." After Phish lost Jeff Holdsworth as its second guitarist, a few years passed until "Alumni" went in its own direction, losing "Letter" in the process. The ephemeral nature of the tune seemed to condemn it from Phish setlists until a sudden, luminous reappearance on 7/5/94 in Ottawa, the first in several hundred shows. Word has it that the tune was performed that night due to news of the upcoming release of the Page and Plant reunion album *No Quarter*, but "Letter to Jimmy Page" had been gone from the stage for so long, that most fans didn't even recognize the song or make the connection. After a second remergence on 7/15/94, "Letter to Jimmy Page" was presumably retired.

See Also: "Alumni Blues"

LIFE IS A T.V. SHOW (see: "TV SHOW")

Life On Mars?

Original Artist: David Bowie
Original Album: *Hunky Dory* (1971)
Vocals: Page
Debut: 10/13/95
Historian: Martian Acaster

Life On Mars? was released by David Bowie in 1971, about the time the first successful NASA missions to explore the mysterious red planet were completed. The Mariner Missions, which lasted from 1964 to 1971 had found geomorphic evidence for the past existence of water on Mars. Water being a primary ingredient necessary to supporting the carbon-based life familiar to you humans, the possibility had been raised that life could have indeed at one time been present on Mars.

Phish first performed the song at the Will Rogers Auditorium, in Fort Worth, TX (10/13/95), while nearby NASA teams in Houston were making preparations for the Mars Global Surveyor mission. At Red Rocks on 8/6/96, the day *before* geologists studying an Antarctic SNC meteorite announced they had discovered tenuous evidence for life on Mars, Phish displayed a shocking prescience by playing "BBFCFM." The following day, Trey's narration during "Colonel Forbin's Ascent" told of a giant iguana taking us to Mars to check out the newly discovered life there. "Life on Mars?" followed "Possum" later in the set. The intriguing question has gone unasked since the final show of the Spring '97 Europe tour at the Pumpehuset, Copenhagen, Denmark on 3/2/97. With the recent failure of several NASA missions to Mars it may be time for the song to return to a regular orbit.

Lifeboy

Music/Lyrics: Trey Anastasio, Tom Marshall
Album: *Hoist*
Vocals: Trey (lead), Page (backing)
Debut: 2/3/93
Historian: Martin Acaster

On first listen, "Lifeboy," the thematic centerpiece of *Hoist*, appears to be an indictment of blind religious faith. The lyrics, sung by Trey Anastasio, find a guy at the end of his rope, the remaining strands of his lifeline (his faith) fraying as he dangles above the "Rift" that gapes below him. When taken in the context of one of an infinite number of

album interpretations (*Hoist* as the continuation of a tale of love and loss that was begun in *Rift*), his loss of faith is the result of his loss of love. The guy is reaching for straws, suspended between the light above (happiness) and the blue below (depression). His past and his future precisely divided (should he have faith in god?), he hasn't decided. Everybody else has run out on him, why wouldn't God too? When faced with these thoughts, he finds that to continue to have faith seems a waste, since, "you don't get a refund if you overpray."

The studio version of "Lifeboy" features guest appearances from Béla Fleck on the banjo and violinist Morgan Fichter. These additional strings round out the delicate acoustic structure of the song quite well. "Lifeboy" is built around a simple, haunting melody that ironically sounds as if it was lifted directly from a religious hymn. The lyrics are delivered by Trey with a melancholy tone, befitting the gloomy outlook of the protagonist. As a live song, "Lifeboy" has fulfilled a role in a setlist that is akin to its conveniently misspelled title. It IS a life buoy, a second set breather following a monster jam, a lifeline tenuously connecting the listener to the reality that was swamped by the "hose" that often preceded it. The song debuted in the first show of 1993 (2/3/93 at the Portland Expo in Portland, ME) and was a relative rarity in the rotation for the rest of the year. With the release of *Hoist* in 1994, "Lifeboy" experienced its heyday, appearing in 25 shows, with many of its performances following "Tweezer." Since 1994, the frequency of "Lifeboy" appearances has dwindled to 1 or 2 a year until 1999 when the last fraying piece of twine snapped and "Lifeboy" disappeared into the blue below.

The live version of the song deviates very little from the studio track. As a result, the "must hear" versions of "Lifeboy" are typically governed by the show rather than the song. Consequently, the "Lifeboy" fan is advised to seek the following: 2/3/93 Portland Expo (debut); 8/13/93 Murat Theater (segued out of a rare "Weekapaug Grooveless" "Mike's Song"); 6/10/94 Red Rocks and 11/23/94 Fox theater, St. Louis (follows a monster "Tweezer"); 10/18/94 Vanderbilt University (with Béla Fleck); 6/24/95 Mann Center (follows an "epic" "David Bowie" and later teased in "Suzy Greenberg"); and 8/2/98 Deer Creek (slides out of a rocking "Ghost" before swirling into "David Bowie").

Light Up or Leave Me Alone
Original Artist: Traffic
Original Album: *The Low Spark of High-Heeled Boys* (1971)
Vocals: Page (lead), Mike, Trey (backup)
Debut: 8/9/87
Historian: Mark Toscano

This terrifically groovy Traffic song was a cover in Phish's early repertoire for about a year. After its strong first performance on 8/9/87, it continued to delight fans until its seemingly final performance on 8/13/88. Many fans thought it was gone for good, and with the Phishy Funk Renaissance of '97 and '98, it's a wonder that the band didn't revisit this old territory as they did with other early covers like Little Feat's "Time Loves a Hero" (on 8/11/98) and Stevie Wonder's "Boogie On Reggae Woman" (on 12/7/97, 7/9/98, and 8/2/98). Yet, in spite of this shocking oversight, naysayers were, as usual, proven incorrect as Phish lit up the 12/30/99 first set with an especially fiery and smoky version of the groove-rock classic.

Peter Sitzman

Limb By Limb
AKA: "Limb"
Album: *Story of the Ghost*
Music/Lyrics: Trey Anastasio, Tom Marshall, Scott Herman
Debut: 6/6/97 (private show), 6/13/97 (public show)
Historian: Chris Bertolet

Though the Dublin gig was "Limb By Limb's" official public debut, it was road-tested at Brad Sands' party on 6/6/97 (tapes circulate). Along with "Ghost," it instantly became a favorite among the Anastasio/Marshall collaborations debuted on that summer's tour through Europe, and has been a regular on playlists since.

"Limb By Limb" is a polyrhythmic highwire act; like "Guyute" and "Taste," it's an example of Phish's affinity for the 6/8 time signature. The lyrics are vintage Marshall, chock full of vivid imagery that suggests a relationship gone cold, or perhaps a bitter breakup. But it's not all doom and gloom; the narrator may "come unglued while in midair," but he "land(s) to reform, limb by limb."

The guitar-driven jam segment mirrors the images in the lyrics, shattering, splintering and then reforming. As in "Taste," Trey and Page frequently weave phrases into the fabric of this jam that sound distinctly Indian or Arabic; in fact, many have likened "Limb By Limb" to the Grateful Dead's "Crazy Fingers" in that regard. The tune concludes with an acrobatic drum-and-vocal reprise from Fishman.

Though most fans' favorite "Limb" is the last one they saw, the Rochester version from 12/11/97 is particularly juicy and long. The 7/31/97 Shoreline and 8/3/97 Gorge versions both rip, and serve as interesting counterpoints. In the summer of 2000, "Limb By Limb" ventured out from its anchor groove a number of times, with varying success; see 6/29/00 Holmdel for one that works in spades.

Listening Wind

Original Artist: Talking Heads
Original Album: *Remain in Light* (1980)
Vocals: Page (lead), Fish (backing)
Debut: 10/31/96
Historian: Mark Toscano

One of Talking Heads' most haunting tracks, Phish performed "Listening Wind" along with the rest of *Remain in Light* on 10/31/96. After the amusing vignette that was "Seen and Not Seen," the band swelled into the ambient beginnings of this song. Trey returned Mike's bass to him and picked up his guitar, with which he produced incredible soaring bird sounds throughout the performance, beautifully capturing Adrian Belew's guitar work from the album version.

This song tells a different jungle story than its predecessors, one in which the jungle is dying or already dead. Gone are the intertwining tangles of sound and rhythm that marked "Born Under Punches," "The Great Curve," and so on. "Listening Wind" is the most minimalist song on the album, a decision made to underscore the somber critique of David Byrne's gorgeous lyrics. While listening to the wind tell *its* story, one can easily imagine a barren landscape, once alive with richness and vigor, but now stripped and violated. The cascading grey clouds of an unending storm lay overhead, and an ineffectual breeze tosses about the choking remnants of the earth. Phish should be commended for their fine job performing this one.

The Little Drummer Boy

Music/Lyrics: Katherine Davis, Henry Onorati and
 Harry Simeone (1958)
Vocals: (performed instrumental)/Fishman (7/3/99 and 12/2/99)
Debut: 12/6/86
Historian: Ellis Godard

Little Drummer Boy is one of those tunes that is so overplayed that it has quickly become regarded as "traditional" although younger than most presume. Written only in 1958, it frequently regained widespread attention in versions by top celebrities, most notably a duet between David Bowie and Bing Crosby.

Phish has only performed the song thrice during December—the debut performance segueing out of "Mike's Song" and into "Whipping Post," a tease during the 12/28/94 "Weekapaug Groove," and jammed out of the "YEM" vocal jam 12/2/99 (which melted down until Jon was left singing it to close the set). But the song was jammed out of season during "My Friend, My Friend" 3/18/93 and "Stash" 7/15/93, and teased during "Weekapaug Groove" and "Big Ball Jam" 4/9/94, "Wilson" 8/13/97, and "Silent in the Morning" 7/4/99. And the most memorable version was Fishman's 7/3/99 encore performance, solo on the snare drum with alternate (and ad hoc) lyrics about how he illustrates his love by playing his drum—including some cracking screeches during the "pa rum pum pum pum" refrains.

Little Tiny Butter Biscuits

AKA: "Butter Them Biscuits" (mistitle)
Music/Lyrics: "Reverend" Jeff Mosier
Original Artist: "Reverend" Jeff Mosier
Vocals: Mosier (lead)
Debut: 11/18/94
Historian: Mark Toscano

When "Reverend" Jeff Mosier's help was enlisted for a run of bluegrass-inflected shows in November of 1994, he got a lot more than he bargained for. Wanting to do everything right, Phish got Mosier to not only teach them some bluegrass tunes, but also how to play, what instruments to get, and even about the history of the genre. The quintet ended up picking a slew of standards—"Earl's Breakdown," "Dooley," "I'm Blue, I'm Lonesome," and others—revamping some covers Phish already did ("Long Journey Home" and "Ginseng Sullivan"), and, like a cherry on top, also picked a Mosier original, the often misnamed "Little Tiny Butter Biscuits." Mosier has said the song was inspired by an Alzheimer's patient he worked with, who one day uttered the cryptic phrase-cum-song-title in the banjo player's presence.

In their five performances of the tune, the most interesting was perhaps the 11/19/94 post-show "parking lot" version. This parking lot jam is legendary, as the band and Mosier (and a few brave fans) kicked it outside the tour bus and played many of the tunes in the Mosier-Phish repertoire, much to the dumbstruck delight of the assembled crowd.

Lively Up Yourself

Music/Lyrics: Bob Marley
Original Artist: Bob Marley and the Wailers
Original Album: *African Herbsman* (1973)
Vocals: Fishman
Debut: 4/21/92
Historian: Mark Toscano

This Bob Marley tune (also on the classic *Natty Dread* album) was covered only once, during the second set of the band's somewhat strange and excellent 4/21/92 Eureka, CA show. Fishman took the stage to (wretchedly) sing lead, with Page on bass, Trey on drums, and Mike Gordon debuting his hitherto unexplored skills as a vacuumist. Following this…*interesting* rendition of the classic reggae song, the band began to apologize for their sarcastic performance, which escalated madly into a brief but hilarious vocal jam. Check it out!

The Lizards

AKA: "Lizards"
Music/Lyrics: Trey Anastasio
Album: (none)
Debut: 1/30/88
Historian: Mark Toscano

Lizards is basically the linchpin of the Gamehendge saga. Nearly every disparate element of "The Man Who Stepped Into Yesterday" story was made to cohere into a single, multifaceted narrative with the writing of this song.

When Trey finally began to write and re-work songs into some kind of a storytelling cycle in 1987, he already had four narrative elements waiting to be used—Tom Marshall's poem "McGrupp and the Watchful Hosemasters," Tom and Aaron Woolfe's joke song "Wilson, Can You Still Have Fun?," and Trey's and Jeff's own compositions for Phish, "AC/DC Bag" and "Possum," respectively.

For his Senior Study at Goddard College, Trey decided to construct a musical that would cover plenty of diverse compositional ground over the course of its continuous narrative. Sensing the potential of these four elements for an epic tale, Trey began to work on the story, extrapolating various characters, ideas, and situations from the

lyrics already written, and trying to fit them into a cohesive storyline. The first fruit reaped from this harvest was "The Lizards."

"Lizards" (as it is more commonly known) contains a lengthy narrative that describes Colonel Forbin's entrance into the land of Gamehendge and his encounter with Rutherford the Brave, an errant knight. Rutherford explains the sad history of the Lizards and their subjugation by the evil King Wilson, who keeps them in check by preventing them from gaining access to the Helping Friendly Book, the sacred tome of Icculus, their god. In a state of overzealous fervor while engaging the Colonel's promise to help, Rutherford jumps into a river and sinks, forgetting that he was encased in metal armor. As the story goes, Tela and the Unit-Monster show up just in time to save Rutherford from the watery peril, and Colonel Forbin is thus introduced to the land and inhabitants of Gamehendge.

The "Lizards" lyrics are very wordy, but their purpose is twofold: to draw the listener into the story with provocative imagery and word choices, and to lay the framework for the events that take place in later songs. Trey wanted to choose this song's first lines very carefully, and ultimately took a cue from "The Chamber of 32 Doors," a track on Genesis's 1974 magnum opus, *The Lamb Lies Down on Broadway*, an album that obsessed Trey for several years. That song's first lyric, "At the top of the stairs, there's hundreds of people," encouraged Trey to come up with an opening line ("Passing through the corridor…") that grabbed listeners' attention with the mysterious implication that it was merely part of a larger, as yet unknown story. This lyrical style set the direction for much of the musical's storytelling, which often leaves the histories and questions about the various characters and their actions up to the whims of the listener.

With "Lizards," Trey was also looking to "ground" his compositional style. At the time, he felt he was starting to get too theoretical and intellectual with his music-writing, and "Lizards," though still complex in structure, was an attempt to write songs that could be appreciated for their challenging musicality AND their fun and danceable nature. This was undoubtedly the influence of his mentor, Ernie Stires, who introduced these possibilities to Trey in his Goddard years, cultivating and influencing Trey's compositional style immensely.

In Trey's original conception of the song, the verbose lyrics are sung over a musical construction influenced by a diversity of styles. Trey took the Irish guitar convention of a drone string and built the song's primary chord progression around it. The chorus section of the song was based on a calypso beat, and Trey wrote it one day while Fishman repeatedly practiced such a beat in the next room. Finally, the extended coda was originally written for a children's musical called "Gus the Christmas Dog," a project on which Trey worked with his mother in the mid-'80s. The song "If I Were a Dog" was re-worked to fit onto the end of "Lizards," and serves as a soundtrack for Rutherford's rescue. As the narration gets more dramatic, the music moves from sweet lullaby to grandiose, heroic opera. Trey envisioned this portion of the song to swell in instrumentation with each verse, culminating in the addition of a choir of vocals. The song then finishes on a re-visit of the chord progression of the chorus.

In its live incarnation, "Lizards" is almost identical to its 4-track progenitor, with the exception of the coda's narration, which is not performed. It has never varied much from this structure, though a number of versions are decidedly more spirited or exciting than others. Some of the more memorable outings include 4/5/90 (incredible), 4/16/92 (pos-

itively energized!), 3/22/93 (restrained), 12/28/93 (tight and energetic), 5/27/94 (wonderful), 12/31/95 (excellent segue out of "Drowned" with oft-debated "Fire on the Mountain" teasing), 12/8/99, and 6/15/00. Two other versions of "Lizards" are particularly notable for Trey's botching of the lyrics: 2/7/91 and 7/3/95. In both cases, the song was abandoned.

Llama
Music/Lyrics: Trey Anastasio
Album: *A Picture of Nectar*
Vocals: Trey (lead), Mike, Page (backing)
Debut: 10/30/90
Historian: Martin Acaster

If a revolution is to succeed certain sacrifices must be made. Often in times of desperation, even life itself must be given up for the cause. From high atop a turquoise mountain above the war torn forests of Gamehendge comes "Llama," a song which documents the last selfless moments of a brave rebel's life. Equipped with a pair of bazookas mounted on the back of his trusty llama, the rebel detonates a cache of blastoplast, driving the loyalists back to their lakeside encampment, unfortunately taking his own life in the process. Knowing he has done all he could, the martyr's last vision is of his own Taboot. A Taboot of course being a wooden, brick, or stone monument placed above the coffin of the deceased in Mohammedan burial ceremonies. Icculus akbar!

Trey wrote "Llama," which debuted at the El Dorado Cafe (10/30/90 Crested Butte, CO) during a stay at Page's parents house. Phish was on tour with Aquarium Rescue Unit at the time and the blistering pace of the song was apparently influenced directly by the tempo of ARU's performances. Perhaps as a tribute to the origins of "Llama," it was one of the tunes played during a guest appearance by Jimmy Herring (ARU guitarist) and dedicated to the McConnells at the 2/19/93 Roxy Show in Atlanta. Other notable guest appearances for "Llama" have included Carlos Santana, Karl Perazzo, and Paul Rekow of Santana (7/25/92 Stowe, VT), John Popper of Blues Traveler (6/23/95 Stanhope, NJ), and Bob Gullotti of Cosmic Krewe (10/23/96 Hartford, CT).

The live version of "Llama" is typically a little wilder and woolier than the studio release which can be found on *A Picture of Nectar*. As such, "Llama" is usually a great opportunity to catch a glimpse of machine-gun Trey. Particularly explosive versions include the following: 7/10/92 Syracuse, NY; 3/19/93 Redlands, CA; 4/1/93 Portland, OR; 5/7/94 Dallas, TX; 5/21/94 Seattle, WA; 12/6/96 Las Vegas, NV; 2/17/97 Amsterdam, Holland; 8/16/97 Limestone, ME; 11/19/97 Champaign, IL; 12/13/97 Albany, NY; 7/19/98 Mountain View, CA; 12/31/98 New York, NY; 7/18/99 Oswego, NY; 6/14/00 Fokuoka, Japan; and of course 12/31/99 Big Cypress, FL. Fans of the odd should also check out the 12/11/95 Portland, ME, "Llama" which was sandwiched among several versions of "Dog Log" or the 7/2/97 version which gave way to a demented "Wormtown."

Adding to the mystique of "Llama" is the nearly unintelligible (and absent from the liner notes of *APON*) lyric sung before "Llama, Taboot, Taboot" in the chorus. Much fan debate has surrounded the deciphering of this all important line, with interpretations ranging from the mechanics of blastoplast detonation "Leave it on press, depress, depress!" to the recreational chemistry habits of the martyred rebel soldier "Living on Pez, Mesc, and Reds!" This "What are they saying in Lllama?" powderkeg might only be defused by repeated listens to the song.

Sometimes sacrifices are easy. Taboot!

Loaded (1970)
Original Artist: The Velvet Underground
Historian: Mark Toscano

After taking a break from the Halloween "musical costume" tradition in 1997, Phish returned to form in Las Vegas for Halloween 1998, performing The Velvet Underground's fourth album, originally released in 1970. This was easily the most anticipated Halloween show since the tradition's 1994 debut, as the skipped year had severely whetted fans' ravenous appetites. Excited speculation of which album Phish would perform buzzed all around The Strip, infecting many parts of Downtown as well. Some observant fans noted the presence of bananas on the 10/31 square of the tour calendar in the recent Döniac Schvice, yet talk of a Velvet Underground album was limited. The most prevalent rumors were suggesting Genesis' 1974 magnum opus *The Lamb Lies Down On Broadway* (which Trey has always cited as a major influence on his early songwriting) or Led Zeppelin's *Physical Graffiti*. Continuing a tradition begun in 1996, a "Phishbill" featuring the album's cover and a few pages of explication and random absurdity was passed out to fans entering the Thomas and Mack Center. Although many fans didn't recognize the album cover, a quick look inside confirmed that the evening's second set would indeed highlight the innovative sounds of The Velvet Underground.

Probably the most accessible of their four "real" studio albums, *Loaded*, though it made no immediate waves when it was first released, is now recognized as one of the more influential rock n' roll albums of the recent past. Originating as sponsor/manager Andy Warhol's "house band," founding members John Cale, Sterling Morrison, Lou Reed, and Maureen Tucker took Rock n' Roll in a new and refreshing direction, punctuated by bluesy tips-o'-the-hat, stripped-down vocals singing eccentric and brazenly poetic lyrics, incredibly creative, underindulgent songwriting, and startlingly original improvisation. Although John Cale departed the group after their second album (1968's *White Light/White Heat*), the band's self-titled third album is an utter classic, and *Loaded* is none too shabby. However, by the time the Velvets (with Doug Yule in Cale's place) started working on *Loaded*, the various strains of rockdom had taken their toll, and by the time of its release, Reed and Morrison had left the group. Tucker also split, leaving Yule to attempt to hold the band together with other bandmates, only to release *Squeeze*, an album generally considered to be an embarrassment to the band's name and ideology.

For Halloween 1998, Phish had initially been scouting for a '90s album to cover (following the trend: The "White Album" (1968) in '94, *Quadrophenia* (1973) in '95, and *Remain in Light* (1980) in '96). After unsuccessful attempts to choose a disc they'd like to perform, however, Phish kept coming back to *Loaded*. *Loaded* was an album that Page, Fish, and Trey had respected and enjoyed immensely for some years, and after Mike, being less familiar with it, gave it a close listen and concurred, the band decided to buck the trend and cover another '70s LP.

For the first time, Phish covered an album featuring not one, but two songs that they had covered before. "Sweet Jane" was a one-timer on 8/8/98, and "Lonesome Cowboy Bill" was a three-timer that served as a vehicle for Fishman to sing back in '95 (see 5/16/95, 6/7/95, or 6/10/95). Also for the first time, the Halloween tradition made its way

to the western United States, satisfying many West Coast fans who had grumbled at the relatively distant location of every previous Halloween show (in New York, Illinois, and Georgia, respectively).

As if Halloween wasn't creepy enough, this year it was in Vegas on a Saturday night. Another first was the scheduling of a two-night run for the holiday, the second night of which was Halloween. Following a great first night (on the band's 15th anniversary—see "Long Cool Woman" for more about this), the band bookended the masterfully played *Loaded* with two startlingly different sets of music. The first set featured some really strong jamming, highlighted by an incredible "Sneaking Sally"—"Chalkdust" and a great "Mike's Groove" that sandwiched an exquisite "Frankie Says." The third set, in stark contrast to the ten-song first set, featured just three songs, with plenty of ambient and generally atypical jamming in between. These three very different sets made the 10/31/98 show one of the most eclectic in Phish history, and in many fans' minds, an instant classic. The band even thought highly enough of the performance to include seven of the ten *Loaded* tracks on an Album Network broadcast in late '99. The three tracks not broadcast—"Who Loves the Sun," "Lonesome Cowboy Bill," and "Train Round the Bend," were all rgreat performances, but axed due to time constraints rather than quality assurance concerns.

Lonesome Cowboy Bill
Original Artist: The Velvet Underground
Original Album: *Loaded* (1970)
Vocals: Fishman (lead), Page, Trey (backing)
Debut: 5/16/95
Historian: Mark Toscano

Odd story, this one. At the incomparable 5/16/95 Voters For Choice benefit, Phish put a whole clothesline full of new laundry out to dry, among which was this seemingly random Velvet Underground track. As

a Velvets song, it's not very notable. In fact, it's sort of a joke and a throwaway track, really. Additionally, the band covered it as a Fishman song, which sometimes calls into question Phish's respect for the particular tune. At any rate, Trey manned the drums for this one as Fish took the energized lead vocals, with the piano taking the instrumental foreground rather than the standard guitar. The song was covered only twice more before riding off into the sunset, presumably never to be seen again.

Of course, Phish is always full of surprises, and when they performed the Velvets' *Loaded* on 10/31/98, this song was not quite as those that had attended 5/16/95, 6/7/95, and 6/10/95 had remembered it. Likely to encourage more group improvisation and stretching out on the tune, Fishman sang it from his drumseat so Trey could remain at the guitar. Throwaway song, indeed—the band faked an ending, then tore into an end chorus reprise that led to an experimental, extended jam making the song about ten minutes long, all said. This unexpected embellishment shouldn't go unnoticed—up to this point, no other Phish Halloween cover had departed so far from its original composition, indicating that the band was finally getting comfortable playing other peoples' songs without the paranoid worry of bastardizing or defaming them. Of all songs from the original album, this was the last track fans thought would yield an interesting jam, but Phish ran away with it and blessed it with the most unusual and provocative playing of the set, eventually segueing perfectly into "I Found a Reason." Typical.

Long Cool Woman in a Black Dress
Original Artist: The Hollies
Original Album: *Distant Light* (1971)
Vocals: Trey
Debut: 12/2/83
Historian: Phil Nazzaro

Long Cool Woman In A Black Dress" by The Hollies was always considered by fans to be the first song Phish ever played live. But tapes of the ill-fated 12/2/83 Blackwood Convention show were also few, far between, of horrible quality, and unknown completeness. Funny that such an all American band would choose to start their career with a British song meant to imitate American music with lyrics like "Working for the FBI" and "Bootlegging boozer." The Hollies had a long history of imitating sounds from the States (see their all-Dylan album); but "Long Cool Woman" in particular sounds precisely like a Creedence Clearwater Revival song.

It's been said many times that Phish "started off as a Dead cover band." But look at the songs from their first few gigs: "Long Cool Woman" is Creedence-y, "Proud Mary" IS Creedence, and setlists abound with tunes by The Who, The Doors, Hendrix, Herb Alpert, and, yes, the Dead. Although the 12/2/83 debut is the only officially documented performance, the song was likely performed at the very next show on 12/4/83, as the band had only learned and rehearsed a select number of songs. Exactly (well, almost) 15 years later, the band honored their own 15th anniversary (albeit on the wrong day) by playing "Long Cool Woman" on 10/30/98 in Vegas.

Long Long Long
Original Artist: The Beatles
Original Album: *The Beatles* (aka "The White Album") (1968)

Vocals: Trey (lead), Mike, Page (backing)
Debut: 10/31/94
Historian: Mark Toscano

This song, one of four George Harrison compositions on the Beatles' "White Album," was covered by Phish at their 10/31/94 Glens Falls, NY show as part of their Halloween "musical costume." Its stripped-down, late-'60s Pink Floydesque, psychedelic tone seemed optimally suited for some jamming, but there was just too much ground to cover that night.

LONG TIME (see: "FOREPLAY/LONG TIME")

Loup Garou
Music/Lyrics: Bruce "Sunpie" Barnes
Original Artist: Bruce "Sunpie" Barnes and the Louisiana Sunspots
Album: *Loup Garou* (1998)
Debut: 3/2/93
Vocals: Bruce "Sunpie" Barnes
Historians: Ellis Godard and Mark Toscano

For over seven years following Phish's New Orleans performance of this tune with its author, lead vocalist and harp player with the Louisiana Sunspots, the song has been misunderstood and untrackable by Phish fans who recorded it as "Luke-a-Roo." Given Phish's success in turning its fans on to new music, we all should have been more aware of Barnes' debut album which showcases Barnes' accordian skills and encapsulates his band's rockin' cajun energy. The unusual title derives from the story of the "loup garou," a Cajun expression for the legendary werewolf that roams the swamps of southern Louisiana. For what it's worth, Barnes has also been known to associate with Lazy Lester, another Louisiana artist that Trey cryptically references before the 5/26/89 "Bowie."

Love Me Like a Man
Original Artist: Bonnie Raitt
Original Album: *Give It Up* (1972)
Vocals: Tammy Fletcher
Debut: 3/18/97
Historian: Christian C. McKee

Online Phish fans have debated everything about the band, from what movies they might like to who looks better with a beard. In 1999, the question of whether or not Phish has sex appeal had its day in the sun. Regardless of what you think of their originals, Phish has graced the stage with sultry tunes. On 3/18/97, Tammy Fletcher (a Burlington area singer) joined them for an unrehearsed take on "Love Me Like a Man." Judging by the tapes, it would seem that many in attendence that night would have liked to oblige her.

Love Me
AKA: "Treat Me Like a Fool"
Music/Lyrics: Jerry Leiber, Mike Stoller
Original Artist: Elvis Presley
Original Album: RCA EPA-992 (1956)
Vocals: Mike (lead), Page, Trey (backing)

Debut: 2/13/97
Historian: Craig DeLucia

Fans consider it a treat when Mike Gordon steps to the microphone to sing a tender love song. Unfortunately, they are usually up-tempo bluegrass ditties or lamentations about his stolen tape deck. "Love Me" gave Mike the chance to croon like The King, if only for a brief while.

"Love Me" debuted in Europe on the early 1997 tour. It was played quite regularly during the short stretch overseas. Upon returning home, though, the song seemed to disappear. Despite rave reviews, "Love Me" has only been played four times since, the last of which occurred on 11/18/98.

Love, Reign O'er Me

Original Artist: The Who
Original Album: *Quadrophenia* **(1973)**
Vocals: Fishman
Debut: 10/31/95
Historian: Craig DeLucia

Arising from "The Rock," Phish concluded their 1995 musical Halloween costume by doing justice to one of the most popular classic rock songs of all time. Perhaps more importantly, it was with his passionate belting of this song that Fishman first asserted his role as a musician capable of singing for more than just a laugh. As with several other *Quadrophenia* songs, the decision to augment the performance with horns added a special dimension that made this a memorable event for all in attendance.

Love You

AKA: "Honey Love"
Original Artist: Syd Barrett
Original Album: *The Madcap Laughs* **(1970)**
Vocals: Fishman
Debut: 4/20/89
Historian: Mark Toscano/Tim Wade

This jazzy Syd Barrett tune derives from the eccentric popmaster's first solo album following his forced retirement from the band he founded, Pink Floyd. By 1970, Syd had become increasingly difficult to work with, due to his growing detachment from reality and the rising inability to communicate with him on any constructive level. Robert Wyatt, a friend of Syd's, has recalled working on this song (the ex-Soft Machine drummer was featured extensively on this disc); upon asking Syd what key the song was in, Syd only chuckled and said, "Yeah… that's funny," in his typically detached, dreamy way. It was unpredictable mental ambiguity like this that forced the musicians to record most of the songs on this album live in studio with him, rather than multi-tracking or doing overdubs.

Fishman usually sings this song much faster than Syd Barrett did, often making the lyrics incomprehensible. Although "Love You" usually features a vacuum solo, on 2/9/91 in Northampton, MA, an unplugged Electrolux forced Fish to scramble for his trombone. This tune was most common in the early '90s; performances have been scarce since 1994, although two notable versions have appeared since. The first was on 7/5/97 in Cernobbio, Italy, emerging from a vacuum solo

which marked the end of "Harry Hood." The second, at the 12/31/99 Big Cypress all-nighter, featured an exhilerated but tired Fishman busting out the vacuum not too long before dawn. Other versions of note include 2/8/88 Nectar's (appearing in tandem with "Bike"), 2/19/91 Washington D.C. (featuring a "Happy Birthday" to Fish and a "Whole Lotta Love" vacuum jam), and 11/7/91 Tipitina's (with the Aquarium Rescue Unit).

Loving Cup

Original Artist: The Rolling Stones
Original Album: *Exile on Main Street* **(1972)**
Vocals: Page, Trey
Debut: 2/3/93
Historian: Martin Acaster

Originally written in 1969 during studio sessions for *Let It Bleed*, the piano-driven romantic trophy piece "Loving Cup" was safely locked away for three years until its release on the 1972 Rolling Stones epic double album *Exile On Main Street*. The Stones' studio version of "Loving Cup" was recorded in their mobile studio at Keith Richard's Villa Nellcote, Villefrenche, France in 1971. Lyrically it is an impassioned plea from a stumbling, fumbling, nitty, gritty, torn shirt wearing, broken down car driving, bad guitar playing, muddy faced, mountain climbing, rose picking, plowman for a beauty beyond his means to satiate his desires. Clearly he feels unworthy, but he's just gotta have it. "Loving Cup" closes out the delta blues cum swampy-tonk first LP of the original vinyl release and features the New Orleans jazz flavored horn playing of Bobby Keys (saxophone) and Jim Price (trumpet and trombone), the piano stylings of Nicky Hopkins, and additional percussion from Jimmy Miller. The Rolling Stones played "Loving Cup" live during their 1972 tour in support of the album but then sent it back into exile.

Phish broke the dusty drinking vessel out of its trophy case (2/3/93 Portland Expo, Portland, ME) as the Spring 1993 tour opening song. The subsequent sipping from the font of venus during that tour was frequent and came almost exclusively (the 2/5/93 Roseland Ballroom encore as the exception) as a first or second set opener. In contrast "Loving Cup" appeared only once during the summer tour that year (8/8/93, Nautica Stage, Cleveland, OH), was exiled even from Maine's streets during the holiday run, and only made three appearances during all of 1994. Most noteworthy of the 1994 performances was the 5/7/94 version which ushered in the legendary Bomb Factory "Tweezer"-fest. A version which should definitely be listened to on a sunny sunday morning-after with friends and loved ones nearby to be truly appreciated.

Although Phish performances of "Loving Cup" to date have lacked the horns, a second guitarist, and the extra percussionist present on the Stones' studio version, even die-hard fans of the original auteurs have been heard to admit that "Phish really can crank on that tune." Since the near-exile of "Loving Cup" early after its debut the song has been in very regular rotation and ranks among the most played cover songs in the Phish repetoire.

Variation between individual performances has been slight despite the obvious room for balls out rock and roll improvisation. For a representative taste from the full spectrum of the Phish "Loving Cup," please check out the following versions: 2/3/93, Portland, ME; 3/30/93 Eugene, OR; 5/7/94 Dallas, TX; 11/4/94, Syracuse, NY; 12/9/95, Albany, NY; 11/24/96, Portland, OR; 7/1/97, Amsterdam, Holland; 8/2/97,

George, WA; 11/13/97, Las Vegas, NV; 7/15/98, Portland, OR; 8/15/98, Limestone, ME; 12/30/98 New York, NY; 9/14/99, Boise, ID; and 5/21/2000 New York, NY; Each one guaranteed to make the listener exclaim "OH…What a beautiful buzz!"

Low Rider

Vocals: Trey
Original Artist: War
Original Album: *Why Can't We Be Friends?* (1975)
Debut: 8/27/87
Historian: Mark Toscano

Although teases of this song have shown up from time to time, it was seriously *played* twice, both times flowing out of an extended jam (8/21/87 "Mike's Song" and 11/23/97 "Down With Disease"). In the Ian's Farm (8/21/87) version, Trey actually sings "La Bamba" to the Low Rider tune in a falsetto voice, which leads us to question the use of the word "serious" in the first sentence.

Lushington

AKA: "Lushington Miles"
Music/Lyrics: Trey Anastasio (?)
Album: (none)
Debut: 10/15/86
Historian: Mark Toscano

This lovely tune tells the sad but empowering story of a dejected soul who, over the course of a daytime drive, finds all sorts of fascinating substances in his body's various orifices and crevices. The music is tap-your-foot fun (Dean Budnick's use of the word "galloping" is right on the money) even if the lyrics are elementary schoolish naughtiness drivel. "Lushington" is more interesting for what it begat. The song usually featured a tightly composed, instrumental bridge, a piece that Trey eventually revivified from this discarded tune and inserted it into the ever-growing "Fluff's Travels." "The Chase," as it came to be known, is a full member of "Fluffhead," appearing in the *Junta* version and in all live versions since.

Despite the fact that it hasn't been played since 8/9/87, "Lushington" has acquired somewhat of a cult following. In fact, as early as 8/21/87, one fan yells several times for the song—a wish that ends up unfulfilled. Later versions of the tune were limited to "The Chase" followed by a "Lushington jam," which is just an instrumental excursion based on the song's chords; no lyrics were sung (check out 5/11/87 for an example). The song debuted and departed all in the space of a year, covering a range of shows from 10/15/86 to early August of 1987. For the full fecal onslaught of this tune, the 10/15/86 version is highly recommended.

Magilla

Music: Page McConnell
Album: *A Picture of Nectar*
Debut: 9/13/90
Historian: Craig DeLucia

Ever notice how words often mean different things inside and outside the Phish community? Take "Magilla," for example. To the uninitiated, he's a Hanna-Barbera cartoon character from a 1964 series that bore his name. Cartoon afficionados will remember him as the go-

rilla that was always returned to the pet store because he ate eveything in sight. True "Happy Days" fanatics (or those who, like me, enjoy to watch the re-runs) will notice a reference to "The Magilla Book of Records" in the episode where Fonzie's cousin tries to gain fame by flipping quarters off of the back of his elbow and catching them. But to the Phish faithful, it it a piano-based jazz instrumental that represents Page McConnell's first contribution of original music to the band.

"Magilla" debuted with a batch of new songs on 9/13/90, far from the confines of Mr. Peebles' Pet Shop. The band must have taken a liking to him, as it was played at the first five shows of that Fall tour. Indications are that the band tinkered with the song before then, though. Pick up a copy of 2/22/90 and, during "Caravan," you'll hear a tease of the "Magilla" melody over six months before its debut.

The song remained a relative concert staple through early 1991, usually occupying a spot in the second set where Phish had once played jazz standards like "Caravan" and "Take the A-Train." Quite a few of these early appearances featured guests on various brass instruments. Carl Gerhard produced a few memorable versions, including 2/8/91 (this fan's personal favorite), 5/17/91, and 11/20/91 (complete with a Flintstones theme tease). Other guests included Paul Guiness on trombone (4/16/91) and Dave Grippo on sax (5/12/91). Given the way the horns complemented the song, it was no surprise that "Magilla" was a regular on the 1991 Giant Country Horns tour.

"Magilla" began appearing less frequently in 1992 and, after a semi-breakout on 3/25/93, seemed to again be retuned to the pet store. Fans heard a tease of the song in the 8/13/93 "Bowie" and the song was sometimes soundchecked but it was not played on the live stage for the rest of 1993.

The re-emergence of horns in early 1994 seemed to bring "Magilla" back for a short while. Of its five appearances in 1994, three were accompanied by either the Giant or Cosmic Country Horns. These 1994 versions are notable for being played in more of a shuffle-style than previous, straight-jazz versions. Still, "Magilla" apparently devoured everything in sight on 5/4/94 and was sent back to Mr. Peebles. As in 1993, "Magilla" remained a soundcheck song that fans were often lucky enough to hear, but he stayed far away from the show.

Then, in 1997, a funny thing happened on the way to the pet store: "Magilla" grew up. Phish launched into an inspired version in Stuttgart on 2/26/97 inside of a raging "Mule Duel" and Magilla suddenly became a minor jam vehicle. All versions since then have evolved from strong versions of jamming tunes, such as 7/10/97 out of "Julius" and the brilliant 7/21/97 Creature Double Feature of "Wolfman's Brother" into "Magilla." Also, fans who have heard the 4/17/98 8-foot Fluorescent Tubes show also know that a Pageless "Magilla" showed up at the beginning of the second set. And while the song remains a concert rarity (one Phish appearance in 1998, a strong tease during "Simple" on 12/31/98, no appearances in 1999, and one in 2000), its evolution means it might never be far away from returning…so long as it keeps its appetite in check.

Maiden Voyage

Music: Herbie Hancock
Original Artist: Herbie Hancock
Original Album: *Maiden Voyage* (1965)
Vocals: (instrumental)
Debut: 7/30/88

Historian: Mark Toscano

This horny Herbie Hancock tune is the title track from the keyboardist's well-received *Maiden Voyage* album. Though Hancock's arguably more important musical contributions were to come later with albums like *Headhunters* and *Fat Albert Rotunda*, *Maiden Voyage* remains an accessible and toothsome treat for jazz diehards and newcomers alike. The title track, a laid back opener to a rather peaceful album, served as a cover opportunity for Phish at their legendary 7/30/88 "Jazz Odyssey" show in Telluride. Fishman, late for the gig, didn't show up for the first two sets, forcing the remaining three band members to adopt a new setup (Trey on drums) and a new repertoire (jazz standards and reconfigured originals). "Maiden Voyage," presumably led by Page, set the stage for the set-closing "Corrine Corrina," right before Fishman finally showed his lame face. Unfortunately, the tapes of this show that circulate do not include this song.

The Maker

Original Artist: Daniel Lanois
Original Album: *Acadie* (1989)
Vocals: Dave Matthews
Debut: 10/15/94
Historian: Ellis Godard

Rolling Stone called Daniel Lanois "the most important record producer to emerge in the Eighties" for his work with U2 (*Unforgettable Fire* and *Joshua Tree*), Peter Gabriel (*So*), and Bob Dylan (*Have Mercy*). Each of those albums expressed spirituality more explicitly than the artists had previously. No wonder, then, that beginning in 1990 Lanois' own musical expressions became more spiritual. Known earlier

Peter Sitzman

for ambient work with Brian Eno, he has since become known for a song he wrote that year, "The Maker."

In the same vein as "Amazing Grace," Lanois' "Maker" draws smooth lyrics across a simple but powerful musical base. The singer laments having erred into darkness, and pauses to sigh at his choosing to be saved. The song's smooth spirituality has fooled some to think it is an old hymnal. But even though not penned until 1989, "The Maker" has already become a classic, covered often by Willie Nelson, Emmylou Harris, Jerry Garcia Band, and the Dave Matthews Band. Lanois himself re-released it as part of his soundtrack to the 1996 movie *Sling Blade*—and, a year later, recorded "Amazing Grace" for a compilation by the same name.

Phish has performed the moving tune only once, emerging from a jam with the Dave Matthews Band to close the 10/15/94 encore. The bands shared the tune in the stolid section of the "Bible Belt," ending a show which also featured a host of songs about spiritual awakening, including "Amazing Grace," "Also Sprach Zarathustra," and "Bouncing Around the Room."

Makisupa Policeman

AKA: "Makisupa"
Music/Lyrics: Phish, Tom Marshall
Album: (none)
Vocals: Trey (lead), Mike, Page (backing)
Debut: 10/23/84
Historian: Jeremy David Goodwin

Those fans who try to draw an explicit connection between marijuana and Phish find much of their evidence in this song. However, impressionable fans who try to interpret "Makisupa" as a straight-out drug endorsement need to pay more attention: the joking references are more an example of sarcasm (and possibly a gentle criticism of the fanbase itself) than anything else. When Trey announced "stay kind" in some 1997 versions, the admonition was probably not a heartfelt plea for fans to do so; more likely, a sign of perplexity at the sometimes cartoonish tour culture which has burgeoned in recent years. Also, the theme of the ever-shifting lyrics is a nod to the reggae flavor of the tune, which is Phish's only original foray into the genre (though trace elements can be found in sections of other early tunes, such as "Slave" and "Harry Hood").

Lyrically, "Makisupa" often features some truly hilarious moments. Witness 12/14/95: "Woke up this morning…Khaddafi in my bed. So I smoked a joint with him." On 12/28/96, the band mimicked a section from the classic song "You're a Mean One, Mr. Grinch!," as Trey exclaimed, "Stink! Stank! Stunk!" to bombastic accompaniment from Fish. 7/25/99 features a blase laundry list of tourkid buzzwords. The 7/1/00 version alludes to George Thorogood: "One bourbon, one scotch, and a big fat doob!" As far as the fixed, repeated lyrics go, they were written by none other than Tom Marshall as a first grader in 1969. The surprising reality of a Phish song written in the halcyon days of Zeppelin and Hendrix has prompted Trey to dub "Makisupa" "Phish's '60s song."

Musically speaking, the 11/19/97 version is definitely the strangest modern-day "Makisupa," as it drifts out of regular territory into a unique ambient jam, and then finally back into MakisupaLand for the closing verse. Several earlier versions are unfinished, drifting into

a new tune after only the opening lyrics and a bit of spacey funking. Another "Makisupa" reared its head with the addition of trumpeter Michael Ray to the fray on 9/9/00. With the appearance of Trey's drum kit in 1995, the middle section was refurbished, and "Makisupa Policeman" became something of a fuller tune. Similarly, the song became a regular showcase of Trey's mini keyboard when that jam implement appeared in '99. The appearance of "Makisupa" in a set generally seems to be a sign of good things to come, or an exclamation point to an already impressive musical passage. A very rare tune through much of its existence, "Makisupa" received heightened attention in 1995, when the band dusted it off nine times, utilizing it on a handful of occasions as something to segue into after some exhausting jamming. Several very excellent jams of recent years have drifted into "Makisupa," including the 5/7/94 "Tweezer," 7/2/95 "Runaway Jim," 11/30/95 "Tweezer," and 11/19/97 "Wolfman's Brother." In its recent incarnation, "Makisupa" has more often than not served as a set opener, having been tapped for that duty in about half of its appearances dating back to 12/8/94, sometimes in very high-profile situations (such as 12/29/95, 8/16/96, 12/28/96, and 8/16/97).

Most importantly, however, "Makisupa" holds the distinction of being the first known performance of a Phish original. The song is the only identified tune known to have been played at the band's "Phish" debut following Trey's return from Europe.

The Man Who Stepped Into Yesterday

AKA: "TMWSIY"
Music: Trey Anastasio
Album: (none)
Vocals: (instrumental)
Debut: 5/11/87
Historian: Mark Toscano

Though "The Man Who Stepped Into Yesterday" is the official name of Trey's Senior Study for Goddard, that title is best known for a particularly sweet bit of instrumental composition he developed for that project. The Gamehendge saga (common parlance for "The Man Who Stepped Into Yesterday," which is a mouthful) is, as many fans know, a multi-song musical Trey conceived, composed, and recorded to satisfy his Goddard graduation requirement of a Senior Study. For the recording, Trey needed an introductory piece of music over which the saga's opening narration would be read; sort of an overture. He had been working on an arpeggio-rich instrumental composition in early 1987, intended for just this purpose. As the opening narration was intended to pull the listener into the story, the piece—dubbed "The Man Who Stepped Into Yesterday" ("TMWSIY") after the song-cycle it would inaugurate—was designed to create a definite sense of forward motion.

It's a gorgeous tune, rivalling "I am Hydrogen" and "Leprechaun" in its rhythmic beauty; even "The Inlaw Josie Wales" may not compare to "TMWSIY's" sheer expression of feeling and action. The song starts out with a pretty but uncertain repetition, described by Trey's swirling guitar line and Page's discordant accompaniment. Page's line suddenly changes to complement Trey's playing very harmoniously, as if to describe the successful passage of the listener into the enchanted land of Gamehendge. The main melody follows, with Trey outlining a repeating structure based on arpeggios in various chordings, while Mike complements each change with a single, well-placed bass note. Page arrives

after the first go-round, adding pretty and sparse harmonic flourishes to the mix. Fishman comes in last, providing an unobtrusive but anchoring beat, mainly in the form of light cymbalic [sic] brushes. The melody is both nostalgically sad and optimistic, and plays like an echo of a time and place forgotten but sweetly regarded. Indeed, Gamehendge is a place out of space and time, existing only in the heart of Colonel Forbin, who looks back on his past with regret and misery. To him, Gamehendge and the events that transpire within its boundaries represent bittersweet memories on which he has no claim. He can only dream of them as he contemplates suicide (a clever and disturbing twist Trey possibly picked up by seeing the classic French short-cum-*Twilight Zone* episode "Occurrence at Owl Creek Bridge.") After all, in context, "TMWSIY" is basically a soundtrack for the Colonel's miserable and self-destructive thoughts, as he is saved from oblivion only by the possibility of a better place and time.

The idyll lasts for a spell, but just as the song seems to be getting too forlorn and introspective, the music rises, swells, and erupts into a more joyous evocation of lost memories found again. Colonel Forbin has found his answer in the "door" he discovered while walking McGrupp and, at the close of the song, steps through it.

On the Senior Study tape, this leads the listener to the "Esther" flying jam that brings us to Gamehendge and all of its characters, stories, and songs. In the live Phish concert experience, this is not the case. On every occasion it has been played, "TMWSIY" has been followed by "Avenu Malkenu," a lively and popular Hebrew song that always pleases fans. Often, "Avenu" is followed in suit by a "TMWSIY" reprise, shorter than the song proper, but based on the same themes.

The appearances of "TMWSIY" were pretty steady through 1992. After this, it took a tragic dip in frequency in '93, made a minor comeback in '94, then dropped again from '95 onward, making only two or three appearances a year, sometimes less (only one in '97!). Early versions tend to be more straightforward and tightly interpreted, although the song usually only veers from its composition by way of sloppiness or error. The debut, 5/11/87, is recommended, and is introduced cryptically as "The Man Who Stepped Into Yesterday and I'm Going to Get My Head Sharpened." Other worthwhile early versions include 8/29/87, 10/31/87, 2/7/88, 2/24/89, 10/31/89 ("The Man Who Stepped Into Dog Log"), 12/3/89 ("TMWSIY" > "Avenu" > "AC/DC Bag"), 6/9/90 (into "La Grange"), 4/27/91 (into "Mike's"), 7/11/91, 7/13/91, 7/20/91 (all horn shows), 4/18/92 (very pretty), 11/28/92 ("Tweezer" -> "TMWSIY" > "Avenu" -> "Maze" -> "TMWSIY"), 12/30/92 (dedicated to cousins everywhere), 2/4/93 (inside "Mike's Groove"), 8/7/93 (great show all around), 6/22/94 (awesome "Weekapaug" -> "TMWSIY" > "Avenu" -> "TMWSIY" > digital delay loop jam -> "Fluffhead"), 7/14/94 ("Stash" -> "TMWSIY"), 10/29/94 (legendary "DWD" -> "TMWSIY" > "Avenu" > "TMWSIY" -> "Sparks"), 10/9/95 (out of "Gin"), 12/28/96 (out of a beautiful digital delay loop jam), 11/29/97 (out of "Simple"), 7/31/98 (flows out of "If I Could"), 7/24/99 (incredible segue out of amazing 30-minute "Fluffhead," then into a jam that becomes "The Wedge"), 10/3/99 (from "Possum" and into "BBFCFM"), 7/4/00 (flawless and beautiful), and 9/20/00 (in the middle of "Mike's Groove…Groove").

See Also: "Avenu Malkenu"

The Mango Song

AKA: "Mango"
Music/Lyrics: Trey Anastasio

Album: *A Picture of Nectar; Hampton Comes Alive* (11/21/98)
Debut: 3/30/89
Historian: Mark Toscano

Picture war-torn Vietnam, during the war in the '60s and '70s. A local woman has given birth to a child—the child of an American soldier. The soldier is leaving, and a group of village women are desperately trying to get him to take the baby along. He insists on leaving alone, and the women, in a possibly insane, possibly overzealous attempt to force the baby on him, throw it towards him. Unfortunately, a mine goes off and the baby, though he lives, is left with severely mangled hands and feet. Yet, despite his handicap, the boy excels intellectually as his life progresses. So, ultimately, the story has an optimistic angle: his hands and feet are mangled, but he's going to be a genius anyway.

This was the opening scene of a film that Trey's friend Aaron Woolfe had envisioned, about a boy who loses his extremities in the aforementioned situation, yet goes on to become a great genius. Trey hitched upon a select sentence in Aaron's verbal description to him ("His hands and feet are mangled") and transformed it ever so slightly into the delightfully nonsensical chorus of what would eventually become "The Mango Song."

The verses of the song—"a day in the life of a waiter/addict with delusions of grandeur"—are rumored to have been based in part on Trey's experiences working in a restaurant where much of the waiting staff regularly indulged in heavy narcotics. Written entirely by Trey, "Mango's" lyrics represent some of Phish's most bizarre, surreal songwriting. The music is even hard to pin down. In an interview around the time of the release of *Picture of Nectar*, even Mike singled out "Mango" as perhaps the only song on the album that couldn't be pigeonholed into a specific genre.

"Mango" has never been as ubiquitous a song as "Stash," "Chalkdust Torture," or "Tweezer," its prolific brethren on *Nectar*. In fact, on setlists over the past few years, "Mango" has been increasingly scarce, although it seemed to be making a comeback in '99 and 2000. While this may frustrate heavy-duty "Mango" fans, one could argue that it makes the song's infrequent appearances all the more unexpected and enjoyable. Always a fun tune, some standout versions include 12/1/95, 7/28/98, 12/16/99 (almost nine minutes long!), and 5/22/00 (strong). A few versions in 1999 and 2000 even pushed the jamming limits of the song, introducing some unexpected and must-hear improv to a normally tightly shut song. Check out 7/24/99 (sloppy but sporting a huge crazy jam), 6/30/00 (jammed, with great segue into "Twist") and 9/17/00 (fifteen minute version out of "Dog Log" into "Free").

Manteca

Music: Dizzy Gillespie, Chano Pozo, Gil Fuller
Original Artist: Dizzy Gillespie
Original Album: *Dizzy Gillespie at Newport*
Phish Album: *A Picture of Nectar*
Vocals: Phish
Debut: 9/16/90
Historian: charlz franz

Along with Charlie Parker, composer and trumpeter John "Dizzy" Birks Gillespie (1917-1993) is credited with founding the "bebop" era of jazz and for introducing Afro-Cuban elements into modern jazz. One of his many compositions that became a jazz standard in the 1950s

is "Manteca." Gillespie was known for his inventive improvisation, comic wit, bent trumpet, and cheeks that swelled from his eyes to his collarbone while blowing his horn. With at least two of those characteristics in common, it's fitting that Phish has made "Manteca" the most prominent, albeit rarely played, of the several jazz standards in its repertoire.

Phish's version features comic lyrics ("crab in my shoemouth"), dancing by Trey and Mike, and has arisen in "Tweezer" and "Stash" jams. Teased several times before its debut on 9/16/90 at Wesleyan University (see the 11/3/89 Tree Cafe, Portland, ME "David Bowie," for example), "Manteca" is also included on the album *A Picture of Nectar*.

Good examples include 11/4/90 Fort Collins, CO (into "Caravan"), 4/18/92 Palo Alto, CA (squirt gun break), 5/3/93 New Brunswick, NJ (in a great "Tweezer" that also includes an "I Feel The Earth Move" jam), 10/28/94 Charleston, SC (in "David Bowie"), 11/14/95 Orlando, FL (in an epic "Stash"), and 10/30/98 Las Vegas, NV (providing a bridge between "Stash" and "Tweezer").

Martha My Dear

Original Artist: The Beatles
Original Album: *The Beatles* (aka "The White Album") (1968)
Vocals: Trey
Debut: 10/31/94
Historian: Mark Toscano

It's surprising that Trey didn't sing this song as "Marley My Dear," seeing as how Paul McCartney originally wrote it for his own dog, Martha. Despite this glaring oversight, the band did a fine job re-orchestrating the horn-and-strings laden song for their four-piece setup at the 1994 Halloween show.

Maze

Music: Trey Anastasio
Lyrics: Tom Marshall
Album: *Rift*
Debut: 3/6/92
Historian: Craig DeLucia

Since its debut during the Spring 1992 tour opener, "Maze" has been a solid crowd favorite. Known for its frenetic pace, ear-splitting guitar work from Trey, and piano thumping from Page, it has the ability to exhaust the dancing concert faithful while serving as a ferocious jam outlet.

In 1992, "Maze" was a Type I song and was usually placed in the middle of the first set. Still, many versions featured inspired jams. Favorites include 4/25/92 (with "Oye Como Va" teases) and 11/28/92 (inside of "The Man Who Stepped Into Yesterday"). The song was also featured frequently on occasions where the band opened for Santana.

The song began to evolve in 1993. At a gig at The Roseland Ballroom on 2/6/93, it began with an acoustic intro. The strong version on 8/7/93 included whistling during the intro (to compensate for the lack of whistling during "Reba"). Still, the song did not tend to stray too far from its normal structure.

In 1994, Trey began to utilize his digital delay loop effect on stage. This effect frequently showed up in "Maze"—see, for example, 4/8/94. The song also began to surface more frequently in the second set. One notable fall version is the "Simple" and "Maze" combo from 10/15/94.

By 1995, the song was as likely to be seen in the second set as

the first. To many, this meant that "Maze" had finally come of age as a jamming vehicle. The wonderful version from the Mann Music Center in Philadelphia (6/25/95) included "Reville" teases. And, for some reason, Trey felt the need to dedicate the song to hockey Hall of Famer Mario Lemieux in Pittsburgh on 11/24/95. The band continued to expand the song in 1996 and show it respect in Pittsburgh; on 10/18/96, fans were treated to a true Type II "Maze" that is among the undisputed heavyweight champion versions. Then, just three weeks later, the second-set opening "2001" and "Maze" combo on 11/8/96 raised the crowd into an absolute frenzy.

Most fans have noticed that the beginnings of "Maze" and "David Bowie" are quite similar. The band played off this theme on 11/4/98, starting the former but actually playing the latter, and 7/2/97, where Mike began playing "Maze" during a "Bowie" encore. Other notable recent versions include 12/11/97 (sandwiched inside the near show-long "Down With Disease"), 11/29/98, 9/18/99, and 6/13/00.

Mcgrupp and the Watchful Hosemasters

AKA: "McGrupp"
Music: Trey Anastasio
Lyrics: Tom Marshall
Album: (none)
Debut: 5/3/85
Historian: Mark Toscano

The lyrics for this song are derived from a Tom Marshall poem that remains more or less unchanged from its original form. Tom had sent Trey an envelope containing only this poem some time during early 1985. Trey was intrigued by the poem and affixed it to his door, where he left it undisturbed for a year or so. The poem occasionally made its way into the Phish live show around this time, though primarily in a spoken-word context. Eventually in early 1986, "McGrupp" usurped the music that originally accompanied "Skippy the Wondermouse" when that questionable tune was retired from the band's repertoire. 1986 and 1987 versions of "McGrupp" sound almost as they do today, although the lyrics were chanted disturbingly and the piano solo section of the tune didn't exist just yet. But there were other, larger plans for this song brewing in Trey's head.

Some time during Trey's Fall 1986 semester, the poem "McGrupp," along with a song he had written a few years earlier with Tom Marshall and Aaron Woolfe ("Wilson, Can You Still Have Fun?," aka "Wilson"), served as the inspiration for Trey's Goddard "Senior Study." By extrapolating a detailed narrative from the myriad characters and events found in "McGrupp" and "Wilson," Trey constructed "The Man Who Stepped Into Yesterday," subsequently known to many fans as "The Gamehendge Saga." (By the way, McGrupp is Colonel Forbin's dog, a seldom-mentioned character in the story.) Were all the Gamehendge ingredients to be boiled down, "McGrupp" would be found at their essence. "McGrupp," plainly speaking, begat Gamehendge.

After some tweaking and experimentation with "McGrupp" over the two years following its live debut, the song finally found compositional repose in 1988. The tune's structure is fairly straightforward: a brief musical intro is followed by all of the song's lyrics, which lead to a somewhat brief 5-part instrumental suite, followed (usually) by a Page solo (or sometimes full band improv), with an encore of the last part of

the suite and (usually) an outro that echoes the song's intro. This format, with few exceptions, has persisted to the present day. Both band and fans seem to be very pleased with it.

Until 1997, the band rarely did more than spotlight Page during the post-composition section of the tune. Standout "McGrupps" of this sort include 3/22/93, 7/2/94, 6/26/94, 7/8/94 and 12/29/95. Beginning in 1997, though, the band seemed to be more eager to communally explore this part of the song, rather than let Page alone show his skills. Some really nice post-1996 versions include 6/25/97, 7/31/97 and 9/18/00.

Though Trey ended up leaving "McGrupp" out of "The Man Who Stepped Into Yesterday" Senior Study, its importance to the project has not been left uncredited—for the 3/22/93, 6/26/94, and 7/8/94 performances of "The Man Who Stepped Into Yesterday," Trey replaced "Possum" with "McGrupp." In the Gamehendge story context, the song is generally understood as a summary of the events of the rest of the story, as seen through the unbiased eyes of a shepherd who tends his flock on the outskirts of Gamehendge.

One more thing: in case you're wondering about the "Dave" that Rutherford looks too much like—it's Dave Abrahams, another longtime friend and music writing partner of both Tom and Trey, who wrote and lent his name to the infamous "Dave's Energy Guide."

Mean Mr. Mustard

Original Artist: The Beatles
Original Album: *Abbey Road* (1969)
Vocals: Trey
Debut: 11/15/96
Historian: Chris Bertolet

Mean Mr. Mustard is a cryptic character sketch from side two of The Beatles' classic *Abbey Road* album (and the second song in a four-song progression commonly called "The Sun King Medley"). The lyrics describe a man of ill habit and nasty demeanor who might be found fraternizing with the likes of The Sloth.

Phish performed "Mustard" only once—near the end of a second set in which, curiously, every song but one had a word in its title starting with the letter "m." In a charmingly bizarre fusion of "Sesame Street" and "Shakedown Street," Trey announced that the set was "brought to you by the letter 'm' and the number 420."

Apart from its alliterative impact, the cover was also noteworthy for the appearance of John Popper, who portrayed Mr. Mustard in cape and cane before joining in on harmonica for the one-of-these-things-is-not-like-the-other "Weekapaug" closer and "Funky Bitch" encore.

Meat

Music/Lyrics: Phish, Tom Marshall
Album: *Story of the Ghost; Hampton Comes Alive* (11/20/98)
Vocals: Mike (lead), Fish, Page, Trey (backing)
Debut: 7/2/98
Historian: Martin Acaster

Reminiscent of the Worcester (11/28/97) and Philadelphia (12/2/97) "Ghosts" and the Albany (12/13/97) "Mike's" -> "Groove," the opening theme of "Meat" is a hybrid of the basic groove core of the "old" "Ghost" and a stop-on-a-dime break-down jam. In the break down jams of Fall 1997, one band member would be the featured funkmas-

ter, getting down with his bad self while the rest of the band looked on in amusement. Unlike those break-down jams, the full stops in "Meat" are deafeningly silent. They leave the listener hanging, with the sound of their heartbeat ringing in their ears.

The verses of the song feature the voice of Mike Gordon. The first is sung by Mike alone and is followed by a chorus sung by Trey, Page, and Fish. Following verses are sung by Mike in unison with the chorus repeated by Trey and Page with an alternate Fishman chorus in which he sounds like a member of Cameo during a particularly fly rendition of "Word Up." In the album version of "Meat," this Fishman chorus is processed and robotic à la the Beastie Boys' "Intergalactic." The lyrics are mysterious ghosts of Gamehendge tales untold which have a distant kinship to Edgar Allen Poe's "Telltale Heart." They tell of a man deluded, convinced he is happy alone. Sitting in silence waiting for a call, he listens to the living, flocking outside, beyond his self-imposed wall.

"Meat" was first performed live 7/2/98 at the Grey Hall in Freetown, Christiania, Denmark. It was at this show where the song was identified by Trey as the second part of the *Story of the Ghost* trilogy (which includes "Ghost" and "Fikus"). The prince who thinks he has it all made his only other appearance in Europe in a "Julius" sandwich in the second set of the 7/5/98 show in Prague. "Meat" was one of a host of new songs played at the 7/15/98 Portland Meadows U.S. summer tour opener, once again appearing in a mid second set open-face sandwich of "Tweezer" -> "Free" -> "Meat." "Meat" appeared twice more during the summer at Deer Creek (8/3/98) and Star Lake (8/11/98). The most interesting versions since then have been the 12/30/99 performance at Big Cypress, and a reprised slice of "Meat" on either side of a "Maze" at the Club Quattro, Nagoya, Japan on 6/13/00.

The Meatstick
AKA: "Time"; "Meatcamp"; "On a String"
Music: Phish
Lyrics: Tom Marshall, Scott Herman, Trey Anastasio,
  Jon Fishman, John Paluska, Brad Sands
Album: (none)
Debut: 6/25/97
Historian: Martin Acaster

The Vienna Sausage, also commonly known as the Summer Sausage, long held the ignominious distinction of ranking second (behind a boys choir) for the best thing to come out of the Austrian capital. All this changed one fateful evening in the summer of 1997 when a two-day session of tour break revelry and an empty hotel mini-bar led to the emergence of the "Meatstick." The sausage was once again king. The first public exposure of the "Meatstick" came about a week later (6/25/97) in Lille, France, as the now unforgettable chorus of the tune spurted out of a "Can't You Hear Me Knocking" tease at the end of a blistering diseased worm known to its friends as "Piper." Later that year (11/19/97 Champaign, IL), this fragment of the "Meatstick" popped its head out of the tail end of a surprisingly extended "Fee" before it plunged into an equally aroused "Antelope." During the Bearsville sessions for *Story of the Ghost*, additional lyrics were added and a studio version of "Meatstick" was recorded. Unfortunately for carnivores everywhere the track did not make the album. Perhaps hanging its head in shame, the "Meatstick" was a no-show for all of 1998.

However, it soon became apparent that 1999 was to be the year

of the sausage. The new and improved "Meatstick," featuring the added verses and an intro that is vaguely reminiscent of "Fire On The Mountain," proudly emerged from the abattoir at the Lakewood Amphitheater, Atlanta, GA on 7/3/99. The now-legendary international dance craze the "Meatstick" dance was unveiled by the entire crew the following day in a reprise of the song at the conclusion of a monstrous "Carini" encore. The first west coast performance of the "Meatstick" followed the inspired debut of "Sand" at the Gorge Amphitheater (which was apparently located in Seattle at the time) on 9/11/99. The "Meatstick" dance was introduced to west coast fans during the next performance of the tasty treat at Chula Vista (9/18/99).

Those lucky enough to make it down to Big Cypress would find that 1999 was indeed forever to be known as the year of the "Meatstick." A large copper "Meatstick" time capsule on display in the delta (of Venus?) just across a creek from the enchanted forest invited fans to deposit items that may be of interest to our descendents in the year 4020. Treats left in the capsule (which could be viewed through a porthole in its side) ranged from the sublime (psilocybin food of the gods) to the ridiculous (a ticket to Gloria Estefan's New Year's Eve show). The SHOW itself was to be a double-ended "Meatstick" that would please even the most insatiable. To the tune of a pre-recorded version "Meatstick," the well aged tube steak that was first flown around the Boston Garden on NYE 1994 emerged from a giant fan boat and carried the band to the stage where they revived father time with a fresh supply of sausage they had brought along.

As the hot dog (which has subsequently been donated to the Rock and Roll Hall of Fame in Cleveland) was hoisted to the rafters above the stage, Phish began to play along to the taped "Meatstick" before sliding into "Auld Lang Syne." The greatest of all Phish sets was finally brought to a close about seven and a half hours later as the "Meatstick" once again waded out of the gorgeous velvet sea that was the first sunrise of 2000. Surely the "Meatstick" was to remain buried from then until 4020. Not so apparently, as a new flavor of the summer sausage was unveiled at the opening show of the Japan leg of Summer Tour 2000 (6/9/00 Tokyo, Japan) where "Meatstick" was sung in Japanese. Subsequent versions on the US leg of the tour included both the original recipe (7/12/00 Deer Creek, IN) and the new sushi-flavored (6/29/00, 9/29/00, 10/7/00) varieties of Vienna's grandest sausage of all.

Mellow Mood
Music/Lyrics: Bob Marley
Original Artist: The Wailers
Original Album: single (1966); *Chances Are* (1981)
Vocals: Trey (lead), Fish, Page (backing)
Debut: 9/8/00
Historian: Mark Toscano

Much like their unexpected performance of "Trench Town Rock" on 8/11/98, the tour-opening rendition of Marley's "Mellow Mood" on 9/8/00 threw fans for a loop, albeit a happy-smiley loop. Subsequent performances that tour (9/24/00, 9/29/00, 10/6/00) pleased fans mightily, especially those Marleyophiles that were dejected for having missed the Albany tour opener, assuming the cover would be a one-timer.

The song itself is an interesting choice, representing one of The Wailers' strongest early efforts, and is the oldest Wailers song Phish has covered. With their conversion to Rastafarianism in 1966 (Bunny

and Peter in April, Bob in October), The Wailers took a different approach to their compositions and performances, imbuing their recordings with unique soul and a powerful, visionary outlook on life and love. "Mellow Mood," released later that year, is a beautiful, seminal example of where the band—Bob Marley in particular—would be heading. These themes would develop over the next fifteen years, encompassing all of the band's classic, groundbreaking albums, gradually rendering Bob Marley in the likeness we know and revere today.

Melt the Guns
Original Artist: XTC
Original Album: *English Settlement* **(1982)**
Vocals: Trey (lead)
Debut: 9/27/85
Historian: Mark Toscano

Many fans are surprised when they hear for the first time that Phish used to cover an XTC song. Although it may seem odd at first, a quick listen of the 6+ minute original on XTC's brilliant *English Settlement* album will possibly clear up matters. The song is rather bizarre, featuring a complex, textured composition, witty and satirically pointed lyrics, and an open-ended invitation to jam. Phish certainly accepted that invitation on 4/29/87, which features the most notorious version of this song, which segues into a manic, extended "Dave's Energy Guide." Get this show—it's some of the best early Phish around.

Memories
Music/Lyrics: Gus Kahn and Egbert VanAlstyne
Original Album: single (ca. 1905)
Vocals: Phish
Debut: 11/17/90
Historian: Ellis Godard

Memories was not performed for nearly a year after its debut (from 11/17/90 to 9/26/91), and has never been frequent. Most versions have opened a first set, closed a second set, or been part of an encore. Appearances during sets (such as between "Lizards" and "I Walk the Line" 11/20/92, or "Divided Sky" and "Squirming Coil" on 8/9/93) were nice pauses for the band, but disrupted the flow of sets. The song has almost always been performed without microphones or amplification; the band's dedication to that format has kept the song out of rotation for over six years (since 7/6/94), as they are unable to project to a crowd of tens of thousands.

Messin' with the Kid
Music/Lyrics: Mel London & Junior Wells
Original Artist: Junior Wells
Original Album: single (1960)
Vocals: Sugar Blue
Debut: 8/8/97
Historian: Mark Toscano

Messin' With the Kid is a quintessential blues number penned by Junior Wells and Mel London in the late '50s, showing up on a Wells single in 1960. Phish has performed this tune with Chicago bluesman Sugar Blue twice, on 8/8/97 and 10/3/99, the latter performance also featuring Son Seals on guitar. Sugar lent his harmonica and

vocals to both performances of the song, a standard that has been covered by everyone from the Blues Brothers to Todd Rundgren to Johnny Winter to the World Saxophone Quartet.

Mice and Bats
AKA: "Tea Tray Song" (mistitle)
Music/Lyrics: Baby Gramps
Original Artist: Baby Gramps
Original Album: none
Vocals: Arab PBS Gym
Debut: 8/26/93
Historian: Mark Toscano

Baby Gramps is a conundrum, an enigma, a riddle that would outsphinx the Sphinx itself.

That said, Baby Gramps opened for Phish at three Northwestern shows during Summer 1993 (8/24, 8/25, and 8/26). The final night of his appearances, the legendary guitar player and palindrome profferer boarded the stage following a "HYHU" intro, and led Phish in a rendition of one of his twisted originals, "Mice and Bats." Fishman joined in on vacuum, Trey took the drums, and Baby Gramps played his signature guitar-playing, a slapped-together combination of Eugene Chadbourne and Django Reinhardt. In future performances, either solo or opening for other bands, Gramps has spoken fondly of his appearance with Phish, calling them "nice guys" who could "almost" even keep up with his playing! For a while, Gramps even sold a video of his performance with the guys, a collectible that can be somewhat hard to find.

MIDNIGHT HOUR (see: "IN THE MIDNIGHT HOUR")

Midnight On the Highway
AKA: "Mid-Highway Blues"
Music/Lyrics: Tim O'Brien
Original Artist: Hot Rize
Original Album: *Hot Rize* **(1979)**
Vocals: Mike

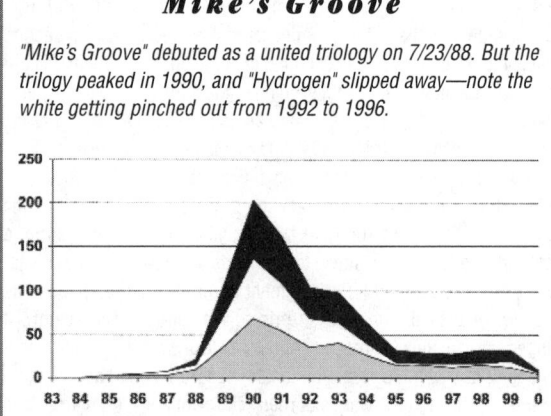

Mike's Groove

"Mike's Groove" debuted as a united triology on 7/23/88. But the trilogy peaked in 1990, and "Hydrogen" slipped away—note the white getting pinched out from 1992 to 1996.

■ Weekapaug   □ Hydrogen   ▨ Mike's Song

Mike's Groove

Compiled by Charlie Dirksen

Date	Timing	Notes (including what's sandwiched between the Mike's Song and Weekapaug)
05/03/85	11:37	First Mike's Song (without Page). Segue into Dave's Energy Guide ("DEG").
10/15/86	6:49	Mike's Song only. One of the finest early versions.
08/21/87	12	Good early version.
07/23/88	17:30	Sometimes circulates as 3/17/89. Congas! Unusually percussive.
11/02/90	14:15	Strong early 1990s version.
11/16/90	15:31	Andy Griffith theme tease in 'paug.
03/17/91	13	Rock star machine gun Trey in 'paug.
05/12/91	15:20	Final version at The Front.
11/08/91	17:29	"A Slice of Pizza" and "A Bucket of Lard" in the Weekapaug.
11/21/91	22	Excellent Weekapaug.
03/20/92	19:56	Fierce.
04/19/92	21:06	Magnificent early 1990s version.
11/19/92	21:31	Vocal jam in the Weekapaug.
11/23/92	17	Weekapaug includes a brief, unusual reggae jam, and a Big Ball Jam.
11/28/92	20:20	One of the sickest pre-1993 versions. Check it out.
12/31/92	17:16	Auld Lang Syne. No Hydrogen. Awesome jamming.
02/04/93	25:37	Page on piano. TMWSIY. Wonderful 'paug.
02/15/93	18:14	Hysterical Hydrogen.
02/20/93	25	Kiss's "I Want To Rock and Roll All Night."
03/25/93	21:49	"Ob La Di" in 'paug. 'Paug smokes!

Date	Timing	Notes (including what's sandwiched between the Mike's Song and Weekapaug)
03/27/93	24:27	Very improvisational for 1993. "On Broadway" jam in the 'paug.
03/30/93	26:48	Talking Heads "Psycho Killer"!
04/18/93	8:30	Mike's features a "Low Rider" jam. Excellent segue into Yamar.
07/31/93	18:39	Leprechaun inbetween Mike's and Weekapaug.
08/13/93	12:05	Mike's Song only, but hear this exciting, melodic version at all costs.
08/16/93	31:25	Faht. Teasefest. Santana's "Gypsy Queen." Stevie Wonder's "I Wish." More.
12/30/93	20	HorseSilent, PYITE, McGrupps; gorgeous Mike's Song and killer 'paug.
06/17/94	23:29	OJ Simpson version. Run, OJ, Run! Simple. H2.
06/22/94	28:45	Excellent "Midnight Rider" Jam in Mike's. Catapult, Simple, Icculus, H2.
07/10/94	25:34	"Low Rider" jam in Mike's. H2.
10/25/94	31:30	Simple, Mango. Amazing Weekapaug.
11/04/94	29:51	Simple, Tela. Rolling Stones "Can't You Hear Me Knocking" ending to a great 'paug.
11/16/94	38:17	Mike's -> Simple -> JAM!
11/25/94	47:48	Simple, JAM, Harpua. Unusually improvisational filler.
12/28/94	33:48	Mango. Evil "Little Drummer Boy" jam in the 'paug.

(continued on the next page)

Debut: 11/23/96
Historian: Kazimierz O. Wrzeszczynski

This bluegrass number of Tim O'Brien and Hot Rize fame made its one and only Phish concert appearance in Vancouver on 11/23/96. Trey introduced the song in the middle of the first set by saying they "learned this one this morning, specifically for you" after "kind of a long night coming through the border [where] we met up with some funny people at the border." It seems that a long and laborious Canadian border crossing for the tour late in the evening allowed Mike to teach the band this highly appropriate road song featuring him on vocals. The song was obviously fresh on the bassist's mind since he recently played it on at least two occasions during some memorable acoustic shows featuring Mike on bass, Gordon Stone on banjo and Doug Perkins on guitar. This trio performed "Midnight on the Highway" on 10/1/96 at University of Vermont's Slade Hall and 10/3/96 at the Last Elm Cafe in Burlington.

Midnight Rider
Original Artist: Allman Brothers
Original Album: *Idlewild South* **(1970)**
Vocals: (performed instrumental)
Debut: 6/22/94
Historian: Craig DeLucia

The infectious, catchy hook to Gregg Allman's "Midnight Rider" has long been stuck in the minds of a generation of music lovers. Though Phish has never performed the song in its entirety, it was seriously jammed inside of an early "Simple" on 6/22/94. In true Phish fashion, the band took their jam a step further, singing the quirky "Catapult" over the top of "Midnight Rider" before venturing into other musical territory.

THE MIGHTY QUINN (see: "QUINN THE ESKIMO")

Mike's Groove

Mike's Groove originally referred to the three-part arrangement consisting of "Mike's Song," "I am Hydrogen," and "Weekapaug Groove." Since 1994 or so, the consistancy of this format has been less and less reliable, and "Mike's Groove," not quite an obsolete expression, still generally refers to the combination of "Mike's Song" and "Weekapaug Groove," as well as anything that may fall in between the two (e.g. "Leprechaun," "Simple," "Keyboard Cavalry," etc.)

Mike's Song
AKA: "Mike's," "Microdot"
Music/Lyrics: Mike Gordon

Mike's Groove (continued)

Date	Timing	Notes (including what's sandwiched between the Mike's Song and Weekapaug)	Date	Timing	Notes (including what's sandwiched between the Mike's Song and Weekapaug)
06/10/95	34:43	Mike's Song is over 20 mins. Hydrogen.	11/23/96	43:46	Simple, Makisupa, Axilla Pt.1. Very improvisational.
06/20/95	37:10	Contact. Great Mike's, but Weekapaug is a wet, smelly, flatulent dog.	12/06/96	56:04	Mike's->Simple->Jam->Harry->Weekapaug. Magnificent, must-hear version.
06/25/95	31:42	"Do It in the Road" -> HYHU.	12/28/96	35:14	Cool Simple-like jamming; Weird Design;
06/30/95	37:06	Contact. Excellent version!			"Page Bastard Jam" at end of Weekapaug.
10/25/95	33:15	"Breathe" (Floyd) Jam -> Sparkle. Killer Mike's!	07/22/97	37	->Mike's->Simple->Hydrogen->Weekapaug. A fan favorite.
11/11/95	23:51	First set Mike's Groove. Fantastic versions of Mike's and Weekapaug!	08/09/97	13:20/11:30	Mike's is average, but Weekapaug is must-hear. You'll weep out of joy.
11/15/95	33:30	Life on Mars. If you like spacey jams, then hear this.	11/13/97	30:26	Thrilling Mike's->Hydrogen>Paug.
11/25/95	39	Switching instruments "jam." Heavy Page in the 'paug.	11/22/97	33:55	Mike's->Hydrogen>Paug. Unusually long H2.
12/01/95	30:09	Very popular. Mike's->JAM->Weekapaug.	12/02/97	20:07/15:11	Mike's/Weekapaug; spectacular Weekapaug!
12/07/95	31:17	Mike's->JAM->Weekapaug->JAM! Incredible improv.	12/13/97	11:11/16:17	Mike's/Weekapaug (with Catapult). Goofy.
			12/31/97	13:56/17:41	Mike's/Weekapaug (loooong 'paug).
12/16/95	29:30	Mike's->Simple->Jam->Weekapaug->Jam. Check this out.	07/17/98	32:34	Popular version. Mike's contains several minutes of gorgeous jamming.
12/31/95	39	Both Mike's and Weekapaug contain spectacular improv.	11/27/98	39:06	Hydrogen; "Wipe Out" jam in an exceedingly upbeat, crazy 'paug.
08/13/96	39	Lifeboy. Weekapaug->"Somewhere over the Rainbow"!	12/31/98	27:04	Beautiful Mike's Song; Hydrogen> Weekapaug.
08/16/96	37:05	Mike's>Jam>Simple>Contact>Weekapaug.	09/29/99	21:34	Catapult, Kung, I Didn't Know.
10/22/96	20:47	SweptAway>Steep. Magnificent ending to the Weekapaug!	10/07/99	11:58/11:28	Mike's/Weekapaug; strong versions.
11/06/96	36	Mike's->*JAM*->SweptAway->Steep>Weekapaug.	12/30/99	37:12	Simple, Hydrogen. Thunderous Mike's Song with an "Immigrant Song" quote.
11/15/96	23:01	Sleeping Monkey, Mean Mr. Mustard, and Popperpaug.	06/28/00	25:46	Albuquerque; Mike's Song is extremely powerful!
			10/07/00	21:10	Hydrogen; Dangerous Mike's!

Album: *Slip Stitch and Pass* **(3/1/97);**
  Hampton Comes Alive **(11/21/98)**
Vocals: Mike (lead), Page, Trey (backing)
Debut: 5/3/85
Historian: Charlie Dirksen

Almost as old as the band itself, "Mike's Song" has evolved from a simple song that Mike wrote as a sophomore-year four-track dorm room experiment into a groove of transcendentally elephantine proportions. At the time when Mike wrote it for the band, he did not have any other songs in Phish's repertoire. He also did not have a name for it. Though the band called it "Microdot" for awhile (Trey refers to the song as either "Mike Wrote That," or "Microdot," in the 10/17/85 Finbar's version), soon they began calling it simply "Mike's Song."

In the first few years of its existence, "Mike's Song" was played on its own and sometimes as a lead-in to other improvisational Phish tunes (see, for example, 5/3/85 UVM, 11/23/85 Goddard, 12/6/86 Ranch, 8/21/87 Ian's Farm). These early versions were very melodic and their improvisational style shared an affinity with Grateful Dead jams (check out the very beautiful 10/15/86 Hunt's version). The jam segment of "Mike's Song" began to get dark and twisted in 1987, but dissonance was not a common characteristic of the song until 1989.

From 1989 through 1994, "Mike's Song" often contained a dark, sinister and semi-dissonant jam (for example, check out 12/30/89 Wetlands, 11/30/90 Keene, 11/8/91 Tuscaloosa, 4/16/92 Santa Barbara, 3/3/93 New Orleans, 12/28/94 Philadelphia). In the 1990s, Mike and Trey often performed this chaotic jam while bouncing on trampolines, hence why some people refer to it as the "tramps segment" of "Mike's Song." Fog—reserved for special occasions—occasionally made (and continues to make) an appearance during this sometimes psychotic, terrifying jam. The intense "Mike's" jam was usually, though not always, topped off with a few measures of composed chords, which transitioned and bridged the groove into a new segment (compare 2/7/89 Front with 3/24/89 Paradise and 5/28/89 Ian's Farm). In many versions since Summer 1994, this second jam segment has often been replaced by the song "Simple."

From Summer 1988 through Spring 1993, "Mike's Song" was routinely followed by the popular instrumental "I Am Hydrogen." Since 1993, however, it has been anyone's guess as to what song will follow "Mike's." Over the years, some rather unusual songs have been performed out of "Mike's Song" (for example, "TMWSIY," 2/4/93 Providence; Pink Floyd's "Great Gig in the Sky," 4/10/93 Chicago; "Ya Mar," 4/18/93 Ann Arbor; "Jerusalem City of Gold," 7/24/93 Mansfield; a Puccini aria, "O Mio Bab-

bino Caro," 5/27/94 San Francisco; The Beatles' "Why Don't We Do It In the Road," 6/25/95 Philadelphia; David Bowie's "Life On Mars?," 11/15/95 Tampa; "Sleeping Monkey," 11/15/96 St. Louis; "Lawn Boy," 3/1/97 Hamburg; "Chalk Dust Torture," 12/9/97 State College; "Esther," 8/1/98 East Troy; "Frankie Says," 10/31/98 Vegas).

Most versions of "Mike's Song" contain something unusual, of course. Nevertheless, here are some popular, unusual versions: 7/23/88 Underhill (vocal jam and percussion in opening); 12/1/89 Boston (Trey teases Jimi Hendrix's "Third Stone from the Sun"); 5/12/91 Front (last show at the Front; Dude of Life on vocals!); 7/23/91 Bayou (excellent version with the Giant Country Horns); 8/17/92 San Juan Capistrano (Trey sustains a note for three minutes); 11/28/92 Port Chester (Aerosmith's "Walk This Way"); 12/31/92 Boston (Auld Lang Syne); 3/27/93 San Francisco (trippy and unpredictable); 4/10/93 Chicago (Rolling Stones's "Girl"); 4/18/93 Ann Arbor ("Low Rider" jam and segue into "Ya Mar"); 5/6/93 Albany (The Beatles "Ob La Di, Ob La Da"); 8/7/93 Darien Center (Irish folk theme?); 4/29/94 Clearwater (exploratory); 6/9/94 Salt Lake (powerfully weird); 6/17/94 Milwaukee (Run, OJ, Run!); 7/10/94 Sarasota Springs ("Midnight Rider" and "Low Rider"); 10/8/94 Fairfax (features a girls soccer team's cheer); 11/25/94 Chicago (ferocious jam); 6/25/95 Philadelphia (exploratory, spacey jam); 10/25/95 St. Paul (incredibly psychedelic, with teasing of Pink Floyd's "Breathe"); 11/15/95 Tampa (thrilling, spacey jam); 11/25/95 Hampton (instrument switching); 7/12/96 Amsterdam (aimless and sad); 10/29/96 Talahasse (Karl Perazzo on percussion!); 11/15/96 St. Louis (an adventure); 11/23/96 Vancouver (all over the map); 3/1/97 Hamburg (The Doors' "The End" and Pink Floyd's "Careful With That Axe, Eugene" quoting); 7/22/97 Raleigh (mysterious); 11/22/97 Hampton (funky and soulful); 12/13/97 Albany (Bring In The Dude); 7/17/98 Gorge (mellifluous hose); 11/27/98 Worcester (beautiful segue into "Hydrogen"); 9/22/99 Las Cruces (dizzying, kaleidoscopic energy); 9/29/99 Memphis (Hendrix's "Who Knows").

Incredible versions of "Mike's Song" are too numerous to detail here, but you should definitely hear these awe-inspiring versions, which feature soulful, collective and exciting improvisation: 6/22/94 Columbus; 11/11/95 Atlanta; 11/21/95 Winston-Salem; 12/1/95 Hershey; 12/7/95 Niagara Falls; 12/16/95 Lake Placid; 12/31/95 New York City; 8/13/96 Noblesville; 11/6/96 Knoxville; 12/4/96 San Diego; 11/13/97 Vegas; 12/2/97 Philadelphia; 12/31/97 New York City; 12/31/98 New York City; 12/30/99 Big Cypress; 9/20/00 Cincinnati; 10/7/00 Mountain View.

See Also: "I am Hydrogen," "Weekapaug Groove"

Mind Left Body Jam

AKA: "MLBJam," "MLB," "Mud Love Buddy Jam,"
  "Your Mind has Left Your Body" (original title)
Music/Lyrics: Paul Kantner and Jerry Garcia
Original Artist: Paul Kantner, Grace Slick, and David Freiberg
Original Album: *Baron von Tollbooth and the*
  ***Chrome Nun* (1973)**
Vocals: (instrumental)
Debut: 6/18/94 (hard to place—this is the likeliest date)
Historian: Ellis Godard

Purportedly an intentional tune with an exciting history, "Mind Left Body Jam" is little more than four descending chords. The ortho-

dox history is that Phish is covering a Grateful Dead instrumental derived from the song "Your Mind Has Left Your Body" from the Paul Kantner / Grace Slick album *Baron von Tollbooth and the Chrome Nun* (remastered and re-released in 1997). The album, which came during the lapse between Jefferson Airplane and Jefferson Starship, was a powerful collaboration of Bay Area icons, including David Freiberg, Jerry Garcia, Mickey Hart, Jorma Kaukonen, David Crosby, Jack Cassady, Papa John Creech, and the Pointer Sisters. (The album also features a tune called "Fishman," about "the son of Caliban" who "rules the ocean land," "holds the ocean in his hands," and is pursued by the singer who wants to make love to him "over and over in the sand.") Dead fans label this purported cover "Mind Left Body Jam," speak highly of its sporadic appearance in Dead setlists, and rave about classic performances such as 6/28/74, and 3/24/90 out of "Terrapin."

But the official story is very different. Phil Lesh, for example, has often insisted that the band never consciously covered or teased the Kantner/Slick song, and never called anything they played "Mind Left Body Jam" ("MLBJ"). They even mocked fans by giving the name "Mud Love Buddy" to a jamming track on *Dozin' at the Knick*. But that mockery just institutionalized a growing convention—and even gave it a second name. And due to a widely circulated but mislabelled tape, "MLBJ" was further confused with the very different "Heaven Help (the Fool) Jam," full of rockin' crescendos—and thus got sparked a third (though certainly wrong) name.

As the song entered Phish's repertoire (or, rather, as the chord sequence began to be noted in Phish setlists), it's history became even less clear. Many fans have confused it for "Dave's Energy Guide" (or vice versa), despite radical differences: The latter ("DEG"), a bouncing array interlocking and repeating themes (e.g. 4/1/86, 3/23/87, 4/29/87, 8/6/88, or 9/8/88), is about as far from four descending chords as you can get. And some have labelled as "MLBJ" delay-loop jams which are not even "DEG" (such as in the "Tweezerfest" 5/7/94, before "Bowie" 12/29/94, ending "Mike's Song" 12/31/95, after "Bouncing" 12/28/96, starting "Bowie" 8/10/97, and during "Scent" 8/17/97.

On some occasions (especially the 6/18/94 "Bowie" intro), a jam has been strikingly similar to "MLBJ" with Page and Mike leading the way, Trey swiftly on their tails. And that same chord progression appears in the 8/21/93 "Bowie," the 6/18/94 "Tweezer," the 6/19/95 "Bowie," the 11/16/95 "Timber Ho," the 10/29/96 "Mike's Song," the 7/31/97 "McGrupp," and the 4/2/98 "Twist" jam. While perhaps no more conscious or intentional than the Dead, Phish has thus included just enough allusion to enhance confusion. And doing so is practically their forte.

MINESTRONE (see: "THE INLAW JOSEY WALES")

Minkin

Music/Lyrics: Cactus
Album: "The White Tape"
Vocals: Mike Gordon, Marjorie Minkin, Lillian Cherry
Debut: (never performed live)
Historian: Julia Mordaunt

The original intent of "Minkin" was a brief commercial/jingle, made by Mike, to let the world know that artist Marjorie Minkin had arrived. Minkin is Cactus' mother, but even more familiar to phans, the

creative genius behind the backdrops that lined the stage at a number of earlier shows.

To create "Minkin," Mike set out with his four-track and recorded obscure conversations with his mother, none of which related to Minkin paintings. He then took the dialogue, manipulated the words and changed their order to fit a verbal exchange about her artwork. Additional voice overs were added to the jingle, praising Minkin's creative style, by Lillian Cherry (Nanny), Mike's grandmother (many of you know Nanny from her appearance on stage with Phish at the 1994 New Year's Eve show). A small bit of music was added, and the commercial for this artist was born.

Minkin paintings were huge backdrops hung at the back of the stage at select shows from 1991 to 1994. These giant abstract works were originally painted on canvas and then onto glass. According to Mike, "the texture of a Minkin painting is so vividly intransigent that it seems to reach out into the room and grab you." So, who does Marjorie Minkin consider to be the main influence of her paintings? The family cat, of course, The Ubiquitous Smokey.

Phish has never performed "Minkin" (aside from a tease during the 10/31/86 "Melt the Guns"), but you never know when it could leap into rotation. Oh, and for what it's worth, bite-sized paintings are also available. Da da da da da, Minkin.

Minute by Minute

Original Artist: Doobie Brothers
Original Album: *Minute By Minute* (1978)
Vocals: Fish (lead), Mike, Page, Trey (backing)
Debut: 9/13/90
Historian: Erik Swain

This slice of slick late-70s pop from The Doobie Brothers was one of eight debuts (not counting Dude of Life songs) during the legendary first show of the Fall 1990 tour at New York's Wetlands Preserve. It is the only one that has not appeared since. Some fans would say that's a good thing, even though the performance was intended as a joke like many other Fishman routines. Fishman's attempts to copy Michael McDonald's husky baritone are certainly, er, amusing, as are the others' attempts at the falsetto harmonies.

Mirror In the Bathroom

Original Artist: The English Beat
Original Album: *I Just Can't Stop It* (1980)
Vocals: Trey
Debut: 11/27/98
Historian: Mark Toscano

The wild nature of the second set at Worcester on 11/27/98 is reflected in the appearance of this English Beat song in the middle of a raucous "Chalkdust Torture." While Trey took the reins at the start of the "Chalkdust" jam, Mike's mind was obviously contemplating the staccato ska of "Mirror," one of the English Beat's most popular singles. After Mike plugged the tune's bassline into the "Chalkdust" socket a couple of times, Trey took the cue and electrified the whole thing with some appropriate chording and a couple of verses to boot. Fish and Page naturally complemented with respective drumming and organ work. By the way, this set is a must-have for fans of the wilder shows.

Mist

AKA: "Mountains in the Mist"; "Bake and Boil"
Music: Trey Anastasio
Lyrics: Tom Marshall
Album: *Farmhouse* (Japanese edition)
Vocals: Trey (lead), Page, Mike, Fish (backing)
Debut: 7/3/99
Historian: Erik Swain

This mellow ballad with strong harmonies and a guitar line similar to "Lifeboy" reminds some fans of the Grateful Dead, in particular a "slow Jerry tune."

More impressive, though, are Tom Marshall's lyrics (written with Trey over the phone), which concern in some way the tug-of-war between the conscious and the unconscious. In this writer's interpretation, the song is about your unconscious mind taking your wishes and the pleasant little things from your daily life and making them the focal point of your dreams. In fact, as one verse points out, you can't achieve this state if you try too hard: "I guess I'm just an obstacle...." The catchy and evocative chorus ("Now I'm soaring far too high...") describes the dream state itself. It began life in the acoustic sets of Trey's 1999 solo tour. Trey initially called it "Bake and Boil" but soon changed it to "Mountains in the Mist," making it one of two "Mist" songs debuted on that tour.

The other, "Kissed by Mist," a song dedicated to Julia Butterfly Hill, who lived in an old-growth Redwood tree for two years to protest logging, has not made it into a Phish set as of 2000. The band's subsequent decision to shorten the title of "Mountains in the Mist" to simply "Mist" could bode ill for "Kissed by Mist's" emergence.

"Mist" itself was one of the first songs from that tour to make it into the Phish repertoire, debuting in the second set of 7/3/99 in Atlanta as a breather between "Moma Dance" and "Antelope." Most subsequent versions were deployed similarly (see 7/10/99, 9/16/99 and 9/26/99).

While it did not make the final cut of *Farmhouse*, it did show up as a bonus track on the Japanese edition of the album. That is where fans learned that the title had changed to "Mist." This version is, believe it or not, even slower than the concert versions, though the studio setting provides an intimacy that is well-suited to the song.

Surprisingly, the studio version is missing the song's final verse, which sums up the whole premise. Check into a live version of the tune and feast your ears on the lyrics beginning with "Woven in the fairy tales...." Perhaps the band found its phrasing awkward.

Oddly, given the album placement and the mountainous terrain in Japan, the band did not play "Mist" on its June 2000 tour there. Indeed, the song became rarer as 1999 went on, and it did not appear in 2000 at all, leading to speculation as to whether it has disappeared from the rotation.

Misty Mountain Hop

Original Artist: Led Zeppelin
Original Album: *Untitled* (aka *Led Zeppelin IV* or *Zoso*) (1971)
Vocals: Page (lead), Trey (backing)
Debut: 7/20/99
Historian: Erik Swain

This classic-rock staple had surfaced in Phish's soundchecks from time to time, leading fans to wonder whether it might make it to the stage. Sure enough, on 7/20/99 in Toronto the band broke it out to end the second set. It was quite a crowd-pleaser, with Page handling Robert Plant's high-pitched caterwauling and Trey replicating Jimmy Page's muscular riffs.

Like many of the covers broken out the year before, it was generally faithful to the original version, but unlike many of them it was not a one-off. The song appeared three more times in 1999, always as a second-set closer or encore. The 9/16/99 version featured Warren Haynes of Govt. Mule on second guitar, though some fans did not understand why Phish would deploy the talented Haynes for what they consider a "simple" Zeppelin song. Another notable version is 9/24/99, which featured an incredible "Sand" -> "Misty Mountain Hop" segue.

MMMBop

Original Artist: Hanson
Original Album: *MMMBop* (1996); Middle of Nowhere (1997)
Vocals: Fish
Debut: 7/6/97
Historian: Martin Acaster

Those of us searching for the moment in history that made the musical scourges known as the Backstreet Boys and N'Sync a potential future reality should look no further into the past than the summer of 1997. With the release of their first single, Ike, Tay and Zac—now known the world over as the brothers Hanson—became seemingly overnight sensations. In an "MmmBop" the musical genre that presently drains the piggy banks of pre-teen girls around the globe was reborn from the ashes of Menudo, the Monkees, and New Kids On The Block. First appearing (twice!!!) on their independently released album "Mmm-Bop," the tune was remixed by the Dust Brothers for Hanson's major label (Mercury) debut "Middle of Nowhere." Since then "MmmBop" has been rereleased on every Hanson album except a collection of Christmas songs released in 1998 called *Snowed In*.

The first (and likely only) Phish performance of the song was during an open to the public soundcheck for a show at Spiaggia Di Rivoltana, Italy on 7/6/97. In defiance of Trey's assertion that "Hanson is going too far," the Fishman of Soul belted out the insidious chorus in the guise of James Brown, and paid tribute to young Zac doing it like an 11-year old "Sex Machine."

Moby Dick

Original Artist: Led Zeppelin
Original Album: *Led Zeppelin II* (1969)
Vocals: (instrumental)
Debut: 11/29/97
Historians: Jeremy Welsh/ Mark Toscano

Although 11/29/97 is probably best known for the hour-long "Runaway Jim" that opened the second set, it should also be noted that Jon Fishman actually came close to playing a "drum solo" in the encore (Fishman's dislike for rock-n-roll drum solos is common knowledge). The encore began with "Buffalo Bill," a favorite of Fishman's, or so it was announced by Trey. As the song was nearing its close, Trey asked Fishman for a drum solo. Midway through Fishman's

sparse solo, Trey yells for John Bonham's classic out of the blue—"Moby Dick-dic-ic-ic…Jon Fishman and Moby Dick!" At that point, the rest of the band kicks into the Zeppelin song, almost forcing Fishman to take part—the rendition is unique, but certainly not mind-blowing. One classic rock acknowledgment was not enough, and they finished off the three-song encore with a blazing rendition of Jimi Hendrix's "Fire."

Roughly 150 shows later, Phish made up for lost time by playing substantial chunks of "Moby Dick" at least a half dozen times throughout the wild 7/11/00 Deer Creek show. Check out the setlist (and the tapes) for a laugh.

The Moma Dance

AKA: "The Moment Ends," "Moma"
Music/Lyrics: Phish, Tom Marshall
Album: *Story of the Ghost*
Debut: 6/30/98
Historian: Martin Acaster

Debuted at the opening show of the 1997 Fall Tour as a delicious funk groove instrumental called "Black Eyed Katy," "The Moma Dance," by the summer tour of 1998, had become what may be the finest sailing song since "The Good Ship Venus." Rather than describing a debaucherous crew of diseased pirates, the lyrics of "The Moma Dance" are the metaphorical sailing orders for those onboard the flagship of the Phish armada.

"Moma" is one of many songs in the Phish repertoire which in some way explores perhaps the most incredible boundary to be found on spaceship Earth. The surface of the sea. Closing out *Story of the Ghost* ("End of Session" notwithstanding) and actually containing a "Ghost" reprise, "Moma" is the cathartic response of the album's protagonist to the implications of "Wading in the Velvet Sea." Realizing he won't find moments (when he is) in the box, faced with a biting rain blowing in his heartbroken soul, he rejects "the big swim" as an option, he chooses life, his "Ghost" tells him to get up that rigging, take in the sail, mind the skipper and we'll not fail, he'll bring out wine, all will be fine, just hear the order, watch the sail! The moment ends. Each of us face these seemingly crucial increments of time every day. Perhaps an attempt to subvert millennial paranoia, the song is an assurance that the Gamehendge time factory is still in good working order, no matter how bad (or for that matter good) a moment may be, the moment ends, while yet another begins.

"The Moma Dance" is sung by Trey Anastasio and Jon Fishman, and the first live performance on 6/30/98 at the Grey Hall, Copenhagen, Denmark also included a demonstration by Trey of the dance itself. The title of "Moma" is another example of Phish Phonetics, cleverly transforming the moment ends lyric into a reference to a display of "The Rhombus" at the New York City Museum of Modern Art (MoMA). In keeping with the groove-oriented jamming style of 1998, "Moma" was in frequent rotation and was typically extended well beyond the length of the album version. Often the song would slowly evolve out of a "Black Eyed Katy" instrumental groove, finally kicking into the song itself. Other times "Moma" would begin with a brief funky intro, slide almost immediately into the song, and then close with the extended funk groove.

For a good cross-section of "Moma Dance" performances try

those from 7/15/98 Portland Meadows, Portland OR; 7/19/98 Shoreline Amphitheater, Mountain View CA; 8/6/98 Lakewood Amphitheater, Atlanta GA; 8/15/98 Lemonwheel, Limestone ME; 11/2/98 The "E" Center, Salt Lake City U;, 12/30/98 Madison Square Garden, New York City NY; 7/18/99 Oswego, NY; 9/24/99 Austin, TX; 12/30/99 Big Cypress, FL; 5/21/00 New York, NY; and 7/11/00 Deer Creek, IN.

See Also: "Black-Eyed Katy"

Money

Original Artist: Pink Floyd
Original Album: *Dark Side of the Moon* (1973)
Vocals: Trey
Debut: 11/2/98
Historian: Mark Toscano

One of Floyd's ballsier rock songs, this bluesy butt-kicker is perhaps "Time's" only rival for Most Radio-Played Pink Floyd Song. In keeping with *Dark Side*'s exploration of madness, the song touches upon the madness of moneylove, in many of its glorious forms. Also like "Time," "Money" is famous for its signature tape effect rhythm track, consisting of clinking coins, cash register noises, and receipt tears. Alan Parsons had a tough time putting this together, as fancy-schmancy tape/delay loop machines were still slightly out of the band's technological reach, so Parsons had to actually spend days manufacturing these tape loops manually. Floyd loved to tear this one up in concert, and it has been a popular part of their show since the very beginnings of *Dark Side* in 1971.

Phish also had a fun time with this one at their E-Centre gig on 11/2/98, kicking it off with the CD's tape effects playing over the P.A. In fact, when they start up the song proper, close listeners will even be able to hear the actual *DSOTM* version begin before Paul has a chance to fade out the Floyd input. The Phish version is strong, but like their rendition of "Time," contains a few sloppy moments that actually do very little to mar the performance. And hey, give 'em a break—they learned the song only a few hours before the show!

Montana

AKA: A 2-minute chunk of the Bozeman "Tweezer"
Music: Phish
Album: *A Live One* (11/28/94)
Historian: Mark Toscano

An interesting choice for a track on the band's first live album, *A Live One*, this "song" is actually just a two-minute excerpt from a 45-minute version of "Tweezer" that the band played in Bozeman, Montana, on 11/28/94. The full song, easily available via tape trading, is a stellar example of the band's experimental, "Type-II" jamming at its best. Apologies to those who purchased the album thinking the band would be doing the legendary Zappa dental floss tune.

See Also: "Tweezer"

Moonlight in Vermont

Music/Lyrics: John Blackburn and Karl Suessdorf
Vocals: Willie Nelson
Debut: 10/03/98
Historian: charlz franz

A jazz tune with lyrics written in haiku form, "Moonlight in Vermont" has been covered by many artists, including Sarah Vaughan, Gerry Mulligan, Buddy Greco, and Betty Carter. At the 10/03/98 Farm Aid concert, host Willie Nelson and Paul Shaffer joined Phish and Neil Young onstage for a lovely rendition.

Moose the Mooche

AKA: "Moose the Mootch/Mooch/Mutch"
Original Artist: Charlie Parker Septet
Original Album: *Dial* boxed set
  (originally recorded March 18, 1946)
Vocals: (instrumental)
Debut: 7/12/91
Historian: Ellis Godard

Charlie Parker's original was syrupy bebop, a mix of creep and frolic, like something you might hear during the credits of an episode of "Alfred Hitchcock Presents." It had a straightness to it, preceding as it did Parker's later meanderings in New York (and stupor in Paris), but it was nonetheless difficult to manage. And so, on a warm Hollywood day, Parker began his second studio session as group leader (with the Septet, Miles Davis et al) by trying three times to tackle the tune.

Phish's only rendition came 45 years later, on a warm New Hampshire day, and Trey's second night as leader of his own septet (Phish with the Giant Country Horns). The tune is no jazz standard, but that's the way Phish performed it: bland, stolid, and on-the-mark. But, hey, even Miles and the Bird took three shots.

Mother Nature's Son

Original Artist: The Beatles
Original Album: *The Beatles* (aka "The White Album") (1968)
Vocals: Page (lead), Trey (backing)
Debut: 10/31/94
Historian: Mark Toscano

This sweet, melodic tune was covered by Phish during the second set of their Halloween 1994 show as part of their performance of the Beatles' "White Album."

Mound

Music/Lyrics: Mike Gordon
Album: *Rift*
Vocals: Mike (lead), Page, Trey (backing)
Debut: 3/6/92
Historian: Martin Acaster

The pubescent faces of many prairies of the American west are inflicted with a curious pimple-like geomorphic feature called Mima Mounds. The origin of these mounds, which are typically about seven feet high and several dozen feet across, is a hotly contested issue. Explanations for their existence range from the burrows of giant prehistoric pocket gophers to seismically coalesced piles of loose surface sediments. These mounds are fairly uniform in size and shape and few if any are distinguishable as being markedly different from their pimply peers. The same can be said for the Phish song "Mound," though any relationship between the song and the Mima Mound is purely coincidental. "Mound" was written by Mike Gordon as a brain-freeing exercise. The result of this exercise is arguably the most poetic of his

compositions telling the tale of an old man suffering the grand rewind of his life as he faces death and his own burial mound.

The lyrics were developed through the brain-freeing exercise which involved Mike taping himself as he vocalized to the tune of the song. He then listened to the tape of his spontaneous vocalization and wrote lyrics from what he heard. This process was repeated many times until the song which was recorded for *Rift* was compiled. Some of the lyrics which did not make it into the song are included in the liner notes of the album. Another lyric which did not make it either into print or the final version of the song (for not so obvious reasons) was "The dangling bearded crabman has hoofs coming out of his ass. They surround his turds like birds, coming out from other guys' asses"

"Mound" debuted at the Spring 1992 tour opener (3/6/92) at the Portsmouth Music Hall in Portsmouth, NH and was in fairly frequent rotation from then until Fall 1995. "Mound" was played only four times in 1996 and has yet to reappear in a live performance. Oddly enough the simple blues progression which opens the song is now found in the intro to "Dogs Stole Things" which (although itself a relative rarity) debuted in 1997 shortly after "Mound" disappeared. Any given live performance of "Mound" is not much different than the album version so it is really the only "must hear" version of the song. However, a unique version of "Mound," with Fishman ontTrombone and Mike and Trey playing through their monitors after the soundboard shorted out, was played at the Electric Ballroom in Knoxville, TN (2/18/93). If you seek further improvisation (governed by the crowd no less!) the "Mound" from Bloomsburg, PA (2/11/93), was followed by a "Big Ball Jam."

Mozambique
AKA: "Free Thought," "Third Tube"
Music/Lyrics: Trey Anastasio
Album: (none)
Debut: 9/9/99
Historian: Martin Acaster

Take the juicy beat of the reworked "Water In The Sky," add a healthy dash of "Bathtub Gin" flavored ivory, and stir in the stringy spice of Santana's "Jingo" and what do you get? A Phishy salsa called "Mozambique," a concoction which would presently be found on the mild end of the condiment tray at your local taqueria.

"Mozambique" made its Phish debut as the opening song of the 1999 Fall Tour at GM Place in Vancouver. Following its appearance in this coveted appetizer slot the song was dished out four more times as the tour made its way down the West Coast (Portland, OR 9/12/99 and Mountain View, CA 9/17/99) and eastward through the desert Southwest (Las Cruces, NM 9/22/99) to the Mississippi Delta (New Orleans, LA 9/26/99 with Michael Ray and Tim Green of Cosmic Krewe). Perhaps due to the somewhat sloppy fashion in which the song was served up as well as its inability to create any real fire in the bellies of those who have consumed it, "Mozambique" was shelved for the rest of the year. Hopefully the ingredients (meaty lyrics and a tasty jam) missing from the original batch of "Mozambique" served up during the 8-Foot Fluorescent Tubes show at Higher Ground will be tossed back into the jar when it is brought back to the menu.

Mr. P.C.
Original Artist: John Coltrane

Original Album: *Giant Steps* (1960)
Vocals: (instrumental)
Debut: 7/30/88
Historian: Kazimierz O. Wrzeszczynski

Mr. P.C., a jazz classic, first appeared on John Coltrane's self composed debut record *Giant Steps*. This song and most of *Giant Steps* come from recording sessions in the spring of 1959 while John Coltrane was still a member of the Miles Davis Quintet, but had recently signed his own first major recording contract with Atlantic Records. The title of the composition comes from the nickname Coltrane called the extraordinary bassist of the Miles Davis Quintet, Paul Chambers, who also appears prominently on this record.

"Mr. P.C." has become a major vehicle for jazz improvisation or all out jam sessions. Most every jazz musician knows the very familiar chords at the song's centerpiece and whenever a spontaneous jam arises and the assembled group of musicians is struggling for something to play, somebody is bound to yell out "PC!" Whether or not this is what occurred on the two known Phish performances of the piece (7/30/88 Telluride, CO and 11/11/88 Newmarket, NH) is unknown, but one can only believe that with Carl Gerhard aboard for the latter performance some serious jamming was experienced.

Mustang Sally
Original Artist: Wilson Pickett
Original Album: *In the Midnight Hour & Other Hits* (1965)
Vocals: Trey (lead), Mike, Page (backing)
Debut: 10/15/86
Historian: Craig DeLucia

Mustang Sally is certainly a rock and roll classic, and seems to be one of those songs that almost all young artists cover at one time or another. Phish was no exception, as they played the song sporadically from 1986 through 1988. She rode off in her Mustang, though, and hasn't been seen since 6/21/88, or over a thousand performances.

My Baby Left Me
Music/Lyrics: Arthur "Big Boy" Crudup
Original Artist: Arthur "Big Boy" Crudup
Original Album: single (ca. 1950);
  The Father of Rock and Roll (1972)
Vocals: Mike
Debut: 7/30/88
Historian: Mark Toscano

Much like Spinal Tap at that marine park gig, Phish busted out their own Jazz Odyssey at this early Telluride gig from the band's first shows outside the Northeast. Fishman, for variously claimed reasons, didn't arrive for this gig until after the second of three sets, so the remaining trio of musicians had to improvise to keep the (miniscule) crowd happy. With Trey on drums, the music was more piano-based, so tunes like "Suzy" and "Contact" were doable. Two interesting covers also graced the second set, one of which was the popular Elvis hit "My Baby Left Me" (the other was Herbie Hancock's "Maiden Voyage").

Like many Elvis songs, The King didn't write "My Baby Left Me," he just popularized it for the new rock and roll audience in the mid-'50s. The original tune was written around 1950 by self-proclaimed "Father

of Rock and Roll" Arthur "Big Boy" Crudup, who, though he obviously wasn't the sole influence for the creation of rock, did do a lot to send country blues in that general direction. And The King liked him too: Elvis also made rock and roll hits out of two other Crudup songs, "That's All Right Mama" (covered by Phish on 5/6/93), and "So Glad You're Mine." Elvis either knew a good thing when he heard it or had a penchant for four-word song titles.

Though the performance is definitively documented, not much is known about Phish's version of the song, as tapes that circulate do not include this tune.

My Friend My Friend

AKA: "MF MF," "MF2," "Knife" (original title)
Music: Trey Anastasio
Lyrics: Tom Marshall
Album: *Rift*
Debut: 3/6/92
Historian: Christian C. McKee

> *"Is this a dagger I see before me?"*
> —The Tragedy of Macbeth, William Shakespeare

My Friend, My Friend is one of the tunes in Phish's repertoire that bridges the gap between compositional complexity and singalong simplicity. The lyrics, with their references to knives and bombs are among Tom Marshall's most unsettling, lacking the giddy smiles of so many Phish songs. Covering a lot of musical territory in slightly over six minutes, in recent years, "My Friend, My Friend" has become a charming rarity, though it returned somewhat during Fall 2000.

When played as a show opener (its most regular slot since 1994,) the guitar tremelo gives the audience plenty of time to anticipate the musical chaos which is barrelling their way. Featuring an introduction reminiscent of Jethro Tull and leading into a crunching, almost heavy metal groove, this piece gives Phish a great vehicle for warming up both the audience and their chops. Not only are there moments of tight composition and hard grooves, but also unstructured, viscous, spacey noise. In these measures of sonic assault, Jon takes the opportunity to shine (see 10/24/95). Trey's playing can be equally frenetic, as on 7/3/95 when he used his microphone stand as a guitar slide.

Along with so many other songs from *Rift*, this one debuted on 3/6/92 in Portsmouth. At the time, Trey introduced it as "Knife," and not until the album was released did the official title come to light. "My Friend, My Friend" varies little from performance to performance, with a few exceptions. Some versions have featured Trey on acoustic guitar for the opening (see 8/7/93 or 2/3/93) while the version from 5/5/93 was wrapped around "Manteca." For folks who harbor fantasies about performing with Phish, this song provides a glimmer of hope: The chanting voices on the studio version are the voices of local fans recruited with the help of a local radio station.

My Generation

Original Artist: The Who
Original Album: *The Who Sing "My Generation"* (1966)
Music/Lyrics: Keith Moon and Pete Townsend
Vocals: Phish (6/22/95) Trey (lead)
Debut: 6/22/95
Historian: Ellis Godard

The "Fleezer" (the 6/22/95 "Tweezer") included the first signs of The Who's "My Generation," including several teases and a bit of the lyrics—but the hint was missed. Phish didn't play more of the song until the Halloween encore later that year, after surprising the audience with *Quadrophenia* (in its entirety) as their second set "musical costume." The sole appearance of the song was followed with ritual destruction of a drum set and a large backstage explosion. (The Who routinely loaded the drum set with powder for a show-ending bang. Townsend reportedly got tinnitus of the ear when the powder was overloaded for a performance on *The Smothers Brothers Show*.)

My Left Toe

Music: Phish
Album: *The Siket Disc*
Vocals: (instrumental)
Debut: 6/30/99
Historian: Mark Toscano

One of the more prolific songs on *The Siket Disc*, "My Left Toe" has emanated from a number of jams on several occasions. However, as with almost everything on that album, its tenuous construction makes it easy to mistake similar jams for intentionally performed "My Left Toes." Such is the case on 10/8/99, when a jam out of "Tweezer" sparked much debate as to whether it was "My Left Toe" or just a jam. More concretely identified performances of the song have taken place on 6/30/99 (awesome segue from "Bug," 19 minutes total), 7/7/99 ("Disease" -> "Toe" -> "Wading" -> "Toe"), 7/21/99, 7/25/99 (out of "My Friend My Friend"!), and 10/9/99.

My Long Journey Home

AKA: "Two-Dollar Bill"
Music/Lyrics: (traditional)
Original Artist: Bill Monroe
Vocals: Phish
Debut: 11/16/94
Historian: Christian C. McKee

Phish has incorporated music with bluegrass influences nearly since their beginning, debuting "My Sweet One" in 1989. But it was not until they had been together for some time that they finally broke down and performed some of the bluegrass canon. "Long Journey Home" (or "Two-Dollar Bill") is one of those classics. Phish played this one in their parking lot jam (11/19/94) and at each of the shows featuring the Reverend Jeff Mosier on banjo (11/16/94-11/20/94.) When Reverend Jeff left the tour, "Long Journey Home" made a few more immediate apprearances, check out 11/30/94 for an example. After that, the tune surfaced occasionally, sometimes acoustic, sometimes electric. To date, the last version played (11/29/95) was a musical stand-out, as Béla Fleck sat in on banjo.

My Mind's Got a Mind of Its Own

AKA: "Mind"; "MMGAMOIO"
Music/Lyrics: Butch Hancock
Original Artist: Jimmy Dale Gilmore
Original Album: *After Awhile* (1991)
Vocals: Mike (lead), Page, Trey (backing)
Debut: 3/7/92
Historian: Dan Mielcarz

More country than bluegrass, "My Mind's Got a Mind of its Own" is a fan favorite. And why shouldn't it be? How many times do you end up at a party when you'd "rather be alone"? It also has the benefit of not being overplayed, as Phish is sometimes wont to do with short covers.

The premiere performance at the Portsmouth Music Hall should be sought out, as the show contains several other debuts as well. Another notable version of "My Mind" was played on 2/20/93, sandwiched between "Mike's Song" and "Kung." The version played at the Warfield Theater on 5/27/94 was played acoustic and without microphones, and features Morgan Fichter on fiddle.

MY OLD HOME PLACE (see: "THE OLD HOME PLACE")

My Soul

Original Artist: Clifton Chenier
Original Album: Chess single (1957)
Vocals: Trey (lead), Fishman, Mike, Page (backing)
Debut: 2/13/97
Historian: Craig DeLucia

Clifton Chenier was a mid-century music pioneer who some credit as the grandfather of American zydeco. Drawing on his background of R&B, blues, and rock, Chenier wrote and played songs with raw energy and determination and brought an element of rock and roll to zydeco that, to that point, had not been seen before.

Some comparisons to Phish are actually quite interesting: he was known as a showman (sometimes wearing a cape and/or crown to his performances) and he carved out his niche via a non-stop touring schedule. Phish began performing his blues number "My Soul" in 1997, nearly ten years after Chenier's death. Fans seem split in their opinions on this number; some enjoyed the energy and raw blues power while others found it repetitive (especially the chorus) and boring. For those in the latter catergory, it didn't help that it was, for a while, the most frequently-played song on tour…or maybe it just seemed that way. It remained in standard rotation in 1997 and 1998 and, though played somewhat less, was still a regular in 1999 and 2000.

My Sweet One

AKA: "MSO"
Music/Lyrics: Jon Fishman
Album: *Lawn Boy*
Vocals: Mike, Page, Trey
Debut: 9/9/89
Historian: Ellis Godard

Written as Phish was expanding its territory from being a northeast bar band, "My Sweet One" mixes the best of Phish's lighter side: authentic bluegrass riffs, a hint of country twang, syncopated vocals,

silly lyrics, and sincere emotion. Word of that mix (and the band's name) was spread far away from their geographic base, and engendered a mutual respect between band and audience even in places they had not yet played.

This song acknowledged the specialness they encountered in reaching new areas—something not rare, but frequent: The song reached its clear peak during the extensive touring of 1991, when they played it nearly 70 times in roughly 100 shows, more than twice as frequently as in 1990 or 1992. (One of few songs to be played at consecutive shows, it was played at perhaps eighteen consecutive shows beginning in early February!) A sign of the band's growth, during which mutual respect may have become less evident, "My Sweet One" slipped quickly from setlists, played only thrice in 1995 (6/15, 12/2, and 12/14) and once each in 1997 (12/31, after a substantial movement on the net to push for the song's return), 1998 (7/20), and 1999 (7/17).

For an essentially composed (yet not terribly complex) song, there are many interesting versions. A number of versions have differed from the studio *Lawn Boy* track, including five acoustic (5/25/94, 6/19/94, 6/22/94, 7/5/94, and 11/3/94), one with John Popper on harmonica (3/3/90), and three with Secret Language signals (two signals on 5/16/92, three on 8/11/93, and *five* on 3/27/92). Additionally, the song has often had interesting placement, segued nicely out of "Tela" (9/25/91), into "Big Ball Jam" (six shows in December 1992), out of "Vibration of Life" (12/7/92), both out of and into "AC/DC Bag" (10/22/89 and 4/7/90, respectively), inside a monster "Antelope" (11/30/94, with some "snoring"), and inside "I Didn't Know" (6/14/94, with an actual picture of Otis Redding displayed).

Other memorable versions include 3/24/90 (preceding the first known "Horn," on the first southeast tour), 4/16/91 (segued out of the "Crew Football Theme Song," which combined its drumbeat with a demented "Barracuda"), 7/14/91 (with a tease of the "Bonanza" theme), 10/15/91 (a capella during the soundcheck), 11/9/91 (initially as gospel with no drums), 3/25/92 (a show full of sweetness), 4/15/92 (with Fishman bowing for his songwriting), 11/30/94 (out of a dissonant "Antelope" and into an dark jam preceding "Fixin' to Die"), 12/31/94 (interrupted by delivery of the oversized hotdog), and its two appearances as an encore (7/20/92 and 10/18/94).

The Name Is Slick
Music By: Phish
Album: *The Siket Disc*
Vocals: (instrumental)
Debut: (never performed live)
Historian: Martin Acaster

The second track from *The Siket Disc* documents the rehearsal space meanderings of a sparse guitar and bass rhythm through its metamorphism to a smooth cerebral groove inhabiting the ethers somewhere between "Manteca" and "Crosseyed and Painless." "The Name Is Slick" thereby captures the essence of the present state of Phish improvisation. Although the song has not been performed live to date, shows from recent tours have included several "Slick" "Crosseyed and Painless" jams that could be considered teases.

Nellie Kane
AKA: "Nellie Cane"
Music/Lyrics: traditional

Phish Album: *Hampton Comes Alive* (11/21/98)
Vocals: Mike (lead), Page, Trey (backing)
Debut: 7/16/93
Historian: Dan Mielcarz

First appearing in 1993, "Nellie Kane" added to the pantheon of Phish bluegrass tunes. The traditional song tells an earnest story of a cowboy who falls for a single mother and decides to settle down with her. It was in heavy rotation in 1994, and played acoustic for most of those appearances. I don't know what changed their minds, but Phish decided not to play "Nellie Kane" from 1995-1997. Since her welcome return in 1998, "Nellie" has been exclusively electric.

In the bluegrass tradition, "Nellie Kane" doesn't differ much from one verion to the next. But some notable versions from the past include special guests: 8/21/93 and 10/18/94 with Béla Fleck, 5/27/94 with Morgan Fichter (of Camper van Beethoven fame), 11/17/94 with "Reverend" Jeff Mosier, and 10/10/94 with Steve Cooley. A more recent version can be found on *Hampton Comes Alive*.

Never
AKA: "Beyond My Grasp"
Music/ Lyrics: Trey Anastasio, Tom Marshall
Album: (none)
Vocals: Trey (lead), Page (backing)
Debut: 10/17/98
Historian: Erik Swain

This short, sparse tune was one of three acoustic originals debuted at the first night of the 1998 Bridge School Benefit. Unlike the others, "Sleep" and "Driver," it has not been played since. It is most notable for Marshall's philosophical lyrics, penned with Trey in the Stowe farmhouse that begat many late-'90s Trey/Tom tunes. In response to a fan question at the JamBase website in April 2000, Marshall said "Never" is one of his few songs about the space-time continuum. However, in that same response he said he did not think that Phish had ever played it!

Phish has not forgotten about "Never," though. The Summer 2000 Doniac Schvice included pictures from the "Farmhouse" sessions.

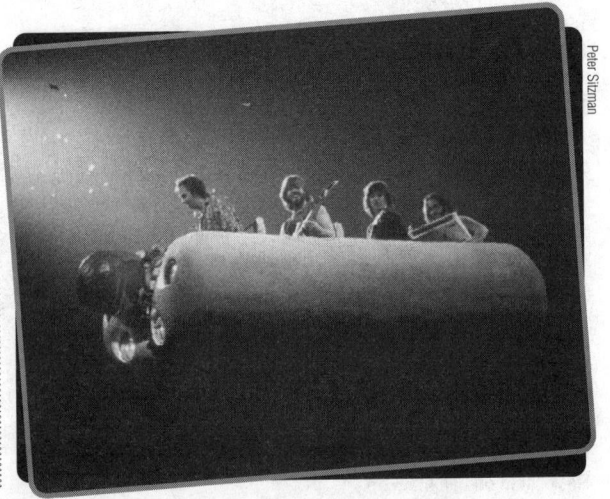
Peter Sitzman

One featured a list of songs apparently being considered for inclusion, and right in the middle of that list was "Never."

New Age
Original Artist: The Velvet Underground
Original Album: *Loaded* (1970)
Vocals: Trey (lead), Fish, Mike, Page (backing)
Debut: 10/31/98
Historian: Mark Toscano

Lou Reed's eccentric gutter-ballad to a used-up piece of Hollywood offal is simultaneously beautiful and vulgar, representing the best of both worlds of the Velvet Underground. The song is often considered one of the diamonds in the rough terrain of *Loaded*, an album of which the Velvets and their hard-core fans are actually somewhat critical. Though Doug Yule's portion of the lyrics are blasted for being too blandly and flatly delivered (even, albeit politely, by Reed himself), the song is one of the Velvets' last few masterpieces.

Phish covered this on 10/31/98 during their *Loaded* set, playing it pretty straight and true to the original album version, despite an extended ending featuring an extremely fiery (yet repetitive) Trey solo. Though their version was strong, and this versimilitude of performance was appreciated, the Velvets themselves had quite a different version of the song in their own live set, as can be discovered by checking out their *Live 1969* double-LP. There, the song is structured differently and features a whole slew of altered or completely original lyrics, and is delivered in a decidedly (and appreciably) more abrasive, flippant manner.

(Theme From) New York, New York
Music/Lyrics: John Kander, Fred Ebb
Original Artist: Liza Minnelli
Original Album: *New York, New York* soundtrack (1977)
Vocals: Page
Debut: 12/31/97
Historian: Phillip Zerbo/ Mark Toscano

Popularized by both Frank Sinatra and Liza Minnelli, the Big Apple theme song "New York, New York" was originally penned by the famous Broadway composing duo of John Kander and Fred Ebb for Martin Scorsese's film *New York, New York* (Sinatra's version is actually a cover recorded three years later). Nine blocks south of Broadway, Phish performed "New York, New York" to close the three night New Year's Eve run at the famed Madison Square Garden in the wee hours of 12/31/97. As has been the case with many Phish covers, this was a last minute decision, with the band learning the tune between sets before being performed as the encore (leading into a rocking "Tweezer Reprise"). Page, long known to aspire to a Las Vegas Lounge Lizard career in his post-Phish days, provided the soulful yet cheesy vocals, while Mike and Trey obliged with a few Broadway-style leg kicks. Filing out into the freezing New York night, many a Phish NYE reveler could be heard singling along: "Start spreading the news…!"

NICU
AKA: And I See You, "In an Intensive Care Unit"
Music: Trey Anastasio

Lyrics: Tom Marshall
Album: *Hampton Comes Alive* (11/21/98)
Debut: 3/6/92
Historian: Craig DeLucia

Has any Phish song had as many names with as many explanations as "NICU"? At its debut in Portsmouth, New Hampshire, Trey introduced the song as "In an Intensive Care Unit." Shortly thereafter, the name was changed to "NICU," which some considered a play on a line from the backing vocals in the chorus ("and I see you") and others noted was the abbreviation for the Neonatal Intensive Care Unit in a hospital.

Shortly thereafter, the "controversy" began, as controversy can only begin among the rabid fans of Phish. Some called the song "And I See You." Some stuck with the original "In an Intensive Care Unit." Other interesting theories developed, including one from the internet where a fan noted that the elements Nickel (NI) and Copper (Cu) are side-by-side on the Periodic Table and that the title "NICU" may thus be a reference to nickels and pennies or, more likely, small change.

Whatever the explanation, fans quickly took to the song. The signature guitar licks manage to combine a reggae beat with rock and roll spirit, and the swirling organ touches from Page only serve to complement the instrumentation. This, combined with the sing-along chorus (quite rare for a Phish song) and fun falsetto-led bridge made it one of the more popular debuts on the Spring 1992, tour. It subsequently became one of the most frequently-played tunes from its debut through the notorious month of April 1992.

And then, seemingly as quickly as it arrived, "NICU" disappeared. While alert fans were able to hear the song at several soundchecks, it did not return to the Phish stage until 6/23/94, in Pontiac, Michigan. The falsetto bridge was gone, replaced by a solo segment that, as time progressed, allowed Page to show off his chops. "NICU" was subsequently played only a handful of times in the summer of 1994 and continued to be played sporadically until the Fall of 1995.

It was at the famous 12/14/95 Binghamton show that "NICU" seemed to finally find its place in Phish's repertiore. From this night on, the song seemed to appear in more regular intervals and placated those fans who crave to hear Page wail on the organ. And in 1997 and 1998, the song followed a path of evolution that saw it used as either a springboard or capstone for other songs.

While most versions of "NICU" are quite similar, several versions are quite popular. Usually, it is because of the song's inclusion in an otherwise tremendous set. See, for example, three popular "Tweezer" jams that morphed into various set-long segues: 7/13/94, 12/1/94, and the aforementioned 12/14/95. Looking for a show with Phishtorical significance? Pick up The Clifford Ball (8/16/96, "Down With Disease" -> "NICU") or The Great Went (8/17/97, "Buffalo Bill" -> "NICU"). And if you're looking for a great segue, seek out the 10/30/98 "Tweezer" -> "NICU," which also closed with quite an interesting little jam.

Of course, the most famous version is the 11/21/98 "NICU," subsequently released on *Hampton Comes Alive*. If you enjoy this one, and the fluid transition from "Boogie On Reggae Woman," be sure to seek out the same combo from Barcelona on 7/9/98.

Night and Day
Music/Lyrics: Cole Porter

Original Artist: Ella Fitzgerald
Original Album: *Anything Goes* (1934) (stage musical)
Vocals: (performed instrumental)
Debut: 8/12/89
Historian: Ellis Godard

Phish opened a three-set wedding reception with a long lost set of jazz standards, but it was their second set that included their only version of this Cole Porter tune (sometimes labelled "Wonderful You"). Introduced on Broadway by Fred Astaire and Claire Luce in the 1934 *Gay Divorcée* (and also in the film version), the original outshines all other versions, including Phish's. Nonetheless, the Moroccan-inspired structure (48 bars rather than the conventional 32) fits well in Phish's repertoire of offbeat structures and twists on the conventional. Page and Fishman do make most of the noise, although after Page lays down the melody Trey does noodle a bit, in a style that would well accompany a Sunday brunch buffet. But Page brings up the rear, extends the length of notes a bit, and draws Mike into some marginally interesting play before a squeaky clean ending.

Night Moves
Original Artist: Bob Seger
Original Album: *Night Moves* (1976)
Vocals: Fish, Trey
Debut: 10/2/95
Historian: Jeremy Welsh

When one thinks of blue-collar rocker Bob Seger, pick-up truck anthems probably come to mind ("Like a Rock"). One rarely associates his music with chess. But on the night of October 2, 1995, Bob Seger and the game of chess would forever be entwined. Two nights before, Phish introduced their Band vs. The Audience chess match, with Page and a fan making their opening moves to the tune of "White Rabbit." On the evening of 10/2, in the middle of the first set, Phish began to play Seger's song "Night Moves" as Trey once again introduced the Chess Game. As Page made the move for the band, Trey and Fishman added vocals (I am speculating that they sang "Knight moves" in response to Page's move). The song ended with Trey proclaiming to the audience that "We will crush you."

1999
Original Artist: Prince
Original Album: *1999* (1982)
Vocals: Mike, Page, Trey (alternating leads)
Debut: 12/31/98
Historian: Mark Toscano

The final song recorded for Prince's notorious 1982 album, "1999" was likely performed by more bands than just Phish on 12/31/98. Fun and surprising as the New Year's '98 opener (yet at the same time somewhat anticipated), this song kicked off what would almost immediately become a memorable and, to some, legendary show.

Ninety Nine Years (and One Dark Day)
AKA: "Ninety-Nine Years"; "99 Years"
Music/Lyrics: Tim O'Brien
Original Artist: Hot Rize

Original Album: *Hot Rize* (1979)
Vocals: Tim O'Brien (lead)
Debut: 8/7/96
Historian: Mark Toscano and Ellis Godard

Performed only once, this Red Rocks bonus featured the vocal and string-playing talents of Tim O'Brien, founding member of Hot Rize and a highly influential modern bluegrass performer/songwriter in his own right. "99 Years" is a Hot Rize original penned by O'Brien and released seventeen years prior to this show but it has the feel of "newgrass," reminiscent of Sam Bush. It was performed the one and only time, helping to close out the first set of Phish's final Red Rocks gig after the "one dark day" in Morrison. Page took a nice solo, close to the beginning—hearing strong keys in bluesgrass is refreshing.

NITROUS (see NO₂)

No Dogs Allowed
Music: Trey Anastasio
Lyrics: Trey's Mom
Album: (none)
Debut: 7/23/88
Historian: Mark Toscano

If "No Dogs Allowed" evokes the feeling of a childhood singalong, possibly one preceding some milk and cookies and a nap, then it has done its job. "No Dogs Allowed" *is* a children's song, written by Trey with his mother in the '80s, at a time when Phish was still making a name for itself. For some time, Trey's mom worked for *Sesame Street Magazine*, and she and Trey collaborated on some songs for Sesame Street Records. "No Dogs Allowed" is part of a Christmas musical for children called "Gus the Christmas Dog," a multi-song project that provided ample fodder for Phish's songwriting as well. Not only did "No Dogs Allowed" make it into Phish's repertoire intact, but sections from other songs in the musical were transplanted into new Phish compositions, including "The Divided Sky" and "Lizards." Many songs in the Phish canon exhibit singalong, storytelling qualities (e.g. "Esther," "Fee," "Reba," the Gamehendge songs, etc.) and much of this approach likely comes from Trey's songwriting experiences with his mother.

Though it hasn't been performed since 11/3/89, the song can still be heard on a few '88-'89 tapes such as 10/20/89, 10/26/89, and the debut on 7/23/88.

No Good Trying
Original Artist: Syd Barrett
Original Album: *The Madcap Laughs* (1970)
Vocals: Fishman
Debut: 12/7/90
Historian: Mark Toscano

Phish really loves Syd Barrett, and Fishman probably loves him the most. There have been, at any given time, no less than five Barrett songs in rotation, making him one of the most covered artist in their repertoire (except The Beatles, The Dead), and *the* most covered artist in Fishman's repertoire.

"No Good Trying" is the second track on Barrett's excellent *The Madcap Laughs* album, and is wonderfully typical of Syd's ability to construct deceptively simple songs on deceptively simple themes with

eccentric musicality and lyrics that express an unsurpassed, schizophrenic creativity. As with many of the songs on this and Syd's other solo effort, *Barrett*, it was a problem to record due to Syd's increasingly erratic behavior and confounding actions and responses to people's efforts to get his albums recorded. With "No Good Trying," one day Syd snapped up all copies of the master tape featuring his guitar and vocal track. Co-producer Malcolm Jones assumed they were to be given to the musicians set to perform on the song just days later, but Syd kept them! It was a while before the session could commence to actually record the track.

Fishman first covered this one on 12/7/90, and it showed up again in the setlist the very next day. Unfortunately, though, it apparently wasn't meant to be, for after only one more performance (12/28/90 with John Popper on harmonica), it was dropped from the Fishman pantheon.

Norwegian Wood (This Bird Has Flown)

Original Artist: The Beatles
Original Album: *Rubber Soul* (1965)
Vocals: (performed instrumental)
Debut: 11/23/85
Historian: Ellis Godard

Phish has quoted this Lennon/McCartney sweetness in some rollicking places, such as "Possum" (5/13/90), "Tweezer" (12/1/94 and 8/6/96) "Taste" (dead-on 10/27/96, and in reminiscent soloing in many '96-97 versions), and "Weekapaug Groove" (12/18/99)—songs about getting run over, frozen, starved, and left out. The only time they gave it more than a measure or two of teases (11/23/85), was within an extended jam of "Whipping Post," a raging roar for redemption in the midst of Mike's "epiphany" show. But none of these six appearances were out of place: Each signalled a moment (and in a show) where the intense became soothing and the explosive became uniting, as if to ask (as the original did), "Isn't it good?"

Not Fade Away

AKA: "NFA"
Music/Lyrics: Norman Petty, Buddy Holly
Original Artist: The Crickets
Original Album: *The Chirping Crickets* (1958)
Debut: 4/1/86
Historian: Kazimierz O. Wrzeszczynski

Not Fade Away was co-written by Buddy Holly (AKA Charles Hardin Holley) and Holly's manager/producer Norman Petty. It was first introduced by Buddy Holly's original band The Crickets as a B-side single in 1957 and then in the following year on The Crickets' debut album. Its signature beat and probably even moreso its standard quick guitar solo has been the song's foundation through the years. It has since evolved from a rockabilly love song into a strong rock and roll force which now serves as a musical bond between a band and its audience. The song's popularity has only intensified through the versions of other high-powered rock and roll acts such as The Everly Brothers, The Rolling Stones, James Taylor, and The Grateful Dead. Phish's one and only known covering of "Not Fade Away" was performed along with the Boston based band The Joneses on 4/1/86 at Hunt's in Burlington as the encore for a show which featured alternating sets of the two bands.

NO_2

AKA: "Nitrous," "N2O"
Music/Lyrics: Mike Gordon
Album: "The White Tape"; "Down With Disease"
single (cassette only)
Debut: 6/25/94
Historians: Ellis Godard/ Mark Toscano

Closer to a tracking of dialogue and noises than an actual tune, "NO_2" (aka "Nitrous") has only been performed live four times, though it has surfaced twice on official releases. It was first recorded in 1987 by Mike on his four-track, but first surfaced on the "White Tape" (released on disc August 1998). An extended, psychedelic version was the b-side to the "Down with Disease" single (tape only; not on the disc version), which was released about the same time as the "DWD" video.

The start of "NO_2" is a whirling effect of repeated "WEEE-yooooo"s not unlike a dentist's drill, and which some find similarly annoying. (A similar sound starts "Wading in the Velvet Sea," introduced over a decade after "NO_2" was first recorded; some hope for segues between the two.) Following this intro, Mike begins speaking to the listener about "feeling a little drowsy," and asks her to "open wide...don't close... don't bite." About one-third through, the sound begins echoing, imitating the "wah-wah-wah" effect which nitrous oxide has on hearing. Then follows a slow cavalcade of drilling, whirring, occasional screeching, and babble, ending with Mike's reassurances: "Still pretty out of it, aren't you? You just relax there, I'll be back in a few minutes. ...There's a tape if you want to put on the headphones... there you go." The "White Tape" version then segues into a sweet acoustic instrumental passage, presumably the "tape" the patient listens to.

"NO_2" may have been first hinted live on 2/20/93, between the "Vibration of Life and Kung," with Mike singing/saying "Your eyes may be feeling heavy...your nose light, your eyes heavy" (but see "Vibration of Life" song history). The full debut of the "song" (6/25/94 Cleveland) was a set opener as unexpected as 12/30/97's "Sneaking Sally." Its reappearance two weeks later (7/8/94 Great Woods) was less of a surprise, but its placement (as the second song in the last of only five live Gamehendge sets) had import: This performance included narration from Trey about Col. Forbin sitting in a dentist's chair, inhaling nitrous, and being transported to Gamehendge, one of the few narrations to describe Forbin travelling there (and the last narration to do so). The third appearance of "NO_2" (7/16/94 Sugarbush) came nestled between an early "Disease" and a maturing "Stash," and calmed a gregarious crowd that stretched up and over the facing mountain slope. Three years later, an out-of-nowhere reappearance of "NO_2" graced the end of the 7/13/99 "Roses are Free" jam, then made its mark as the only

Some infer from the song a condoning of recreational use of nitrousoxide (aka "laughing gas"). Various forms of the gas are sold illictly in parking lots, dispensed in balloons and referred to as "hippie crack" due to the price, numbness, addictiveness, health effects, and illicit trade. But Trey made clear (in "a little story" 4/12/93 at the U. of Iowa) that the song references his great grandfather, who graduated from Iowa in 1908 and was later "the first to ever use nitrous in this state."

Nowhere Fast

Music/Lyrics: ?
Original Album: *?*

Vocals: Sofi Dillof and unidentified male vocalist
Debut: 5/9/89
Historian: Mark Toscano and Erik Swain

Like its mysterious brother "I've Turned Bad," "Nowhere Fast" is one of the few unidentified songs in the Phish pantheon, although surely some folks out there know the tune. Basically a hardcore punk effort with insult-lyrics shouted in a steady stream by Sofi Dillof and an unknown friend, the tune was only performed once, at the last Nectar's show on 5/9/89. This was also the *Junta* release party, so it's not surprising that a little bit of craziness would appear in the setlist. Though there is a Meatloaf song of the same name, this one is definitely something else, and if you have some clues as to its identity, don't hesitate to contact us.

O Mio Babbino Caro
Music/Lyrics: Giacomo Puccini/Giovacchino Forzano
Original Album: *Gianni Schicchi* (opera)
Vocals: Andrea Baker
Debut: 5/27/94
Historians: Aaron Richardson and charlz franz

Lyric soprano Andrea Baker of the San Francisco Opera was a surprise guest at the 5/27/94 Warfield Theater show, singing an aria from Puccini's opera *Gianni Schicchi*, "O Mio Babbino Caro" ("Oh, My Dear Daddy").

The aria segues from a "Mike's Groove" that is itself a rather unconventional version. Right after "Simple" slows down to a stop, Trey starts to play the beginning theme to the aria (and quite beautifully I might add). It is after this that, Andrea Baker sings most of the aria itself. Alone and unmic'ed, Ms. Baker sang powerfully a young woman's plea to her father to be allowed to marry her love, else she'll throw herself off a bridge ("Oh dear daddy, I love him, he is so handsome, … Daddy, have pity, have pity"). Baker sings the aria faster than it is normally performed and is not able to finish it; there is a space between where she stopped to take a breath and the actual completion of the aria. However, mistaking this pause for the actual ending of the aria, the crowd began to cheer and thank Andrea for her performance. Baker could have chosen this particular aria for a couple of reasons. First of all, it is rather short as arias go. Secondly, it is very famous; probably ranked within the top ten soprano arias.

No doubt a bit befuddled by opera aria at a Phish show, the audience nonetheless applauded Ms. Baker long and heartily. Thus inspired, the crowd accompanied the band by shaking boxes of mac'n'cheese during the spirited "Possum" that ensued.

Ob-La-Di Ob-La-Da
Original Artist: The Beatles
Original Album: *The Beatles* (aka "The White Album") (1968)
Vocals: Page (lead), Fish, Mike, Trey (backing)
Debut: 5/6/93
Historian: Mark Toscano

Though Phish had teased and jammed this one a few times (5/6/93, 5/8/93), the first full-blown version didn't occur until 10/31/94 as a part of their Halloween "White Album" performance. "Ob-La-Di" received one of the bigger crowd reactions of the set, as

Peter Sitzman

the original, though not a major Beatles single, is one of their most beloved songs.

ODE TO A DREAM (see: "HOLD TO A DREAM")

The Oh Kee Pa Ceremony
AKA: "Oh-Kee-Pah,"
Music: Trey Anastasio
Album: *Lawn Boy*
Debut: 8/17/89
Historian: Ellis Godard

The oh kee pa is a rite of passage, a physical and mental endurance test, a willed torture into manhood. For young men of the Mandan (Native American) tribe, it was a means to becoming a warrior. After four days without nourishment or rest, the subject was dressed and painted. Wood slats were then stuck through his skin and behind the muscles in his chest and shoulders, and large rocks tied to his feet. He was hoisted by leather straps hung from the ceiling of a ceremonial hut, and spun until he was unconscious. (See also, an exhibit at the Atlantic City Ripley's Believe it or Not, or rent the movie *A Man Called Horse*.)

For Phish, the Oh Kee Pa ceremonies were tests of endurance, during which the band locked themselves in a room and jammed for hours on end. The first was in the spring of 1988, and the second, which produced the "Union Federal" track on *Junta*, recorded in in August of 1989. These rites were recorded, though their resemblance to a high school band imitating a John Zorn composition makes for little more than useless noise. But they helped hone the band's collective improvisation, and allowed the members to develop the musical bond that

sets them apart from others.

Although the ceremonies are gone, among Phish as among the Mandan, their name has endured, as the title of a gripping instrumental. "Oh Kee Pa Ceremony" is a countrified jazz thing, somewhere between the end of the "Popeye" theme and the end of a bomb fuse. As a short, tight, wacky instrumental, "Oh Kee Pa" is a treble antithesis of the improv ceremonies. Fittingly, however, it is a song which Phish uses for passage: "Oh Kee Pa" has opened dozens of sets and typically precedes "Suzy Greenberg" (in about two-third of its appearances). Although often said to frequently precede "AC/DC Bag," it has as frequently preceded some other song (such as "Sloth" or "Golgi Apparatus.")

Given his other anthropological interests (e.g. see "Kung"), Fishman is believed to have introduced the band to the Mandan oh kee pa. But the Jewish half of the band likely knew much earlier about "keepah," Hebrew for the Yiddish "yarmulke," the prayer headpiece worn by Jewish men.

Oh! Sweet Nuthin'

Original Artist: The Velvet Underground
Original Album: *Loaded* **(1970)**
Vocals: Page (lead), Fish, Mike, Trey (backing)
Debut: 10/31/98
Historian: Mark Toscano

This anthemic Velvet Underground song actually evokes The Beatles' "Hey Jude" in a number of ways, most notably with its long, repetitive, similarly-chorded coda. It's an ideal singalong, Velvets-style, and makes for a perfect album closer, as well as closing the books on the Velvet Underground, as it is also the last track on their last proper album.

Phish took the song's natural role as a killer set closer to the limit, squeezing its thrill-building, energy-accumulating potential 'til both band and crowd were drained. The band must have been exhausted after this set, one of the tightest in Phish history. Why else would the set to follow commence with a nice, loose, half-hour long "Wolfman's Brother"?

Old Home Place

AKA: "My Old Home Place," "The Old Home Place"
Music/Lyrics: Dead Webb and Mitch Jayne
Original Artist: The Dillards
Original Album: *Back Porch Bluegrass* **(1963)**
Vocals: Mike (lead), Page, Trey (backing)
Debut: 6/26/94
Historian: Ellis Godard

It's the name of several folk songs, and at least one venue (in McClure, VA). But Phish fans know "Old Home Place" as the tune by country icons and bluegrass progenitors The Dillards, who've performed everywhere from "The Andy Griffith Show" to Denmark. The tune's narrator regrets having chased a woman from his rural farm into the burgeoning metropolis of Charlottesville, ultimately losing both the girl and his home. (Charlottesville, a college town in central Virginia, hosted seven Phish shows. Six of those were at the legendary venue Trax, birthplace of the Dave Matthews Band phenomenon, where Phish played their last "Destiny Unbound" and the only vacuum-solo-as-encore.)

The title refers not only to the physical house left and lost, but to the life left behind. Phish picked up the song as they turned another corner away from their old life. The debut, in West Virginia, started the

encore to a show that had featured Gamehendge (nearly ten years old) as the first set and *Hoist* (recently released) as the second set. That debut helped emphasize the band's transition from four-track recording in a dorm room to a nearly overproduced studio extravaganza.

The song has since become something of a special staple, particuarly in first sets. It appears less frequently than other bluegrass tunes, but without notable gaps in appearance (although it was more likely to be in a soundcheck than a show during August 1996). Notable performances include 7/6/94 (acoustic with no mics), 10/10/94 (acoustic with Steve Cooley on banjo), 10/18/94 (acoustic with Béla Fleck), 11/12/94 (as a joyful suffix to the jams earlier in the set), 11/18/94 (acoustic with "Reverend" Jeff Mosier, who played the Dillards' "Dooley" with Phish at the 11/19/94 parking lot jam and 11/20/94 show), 12/31/94 (electric, with a surprise shift into Maze), 11/10/95 (during the most ignored set of the Fox Theater run), 8/17/96 (opening the second day of the Clifford Ball at roughly 4:20), 11/30/96 (with John McEuen on banjo), 4/3/98 (between "Mike's Song" and "Weekapaug Groove"), and 10/18/98 (with Mike on banjo and Page on standup bass).

Olivia's Pool

AKA: "Oblivious Fool"
Music/Lyrics: Trey Anastasio, Tom Marshall
Album: (none)
Debut: 6/6/97 (private show) 6/13/97 (public show)
Historian: Phillip Zerbo

The history of "Olivia's Pool" follows familiar Phishy themes: changes in musical structure and name, devilish irony between lyrics and music, plus a healthy dose of collective pranksterism. The first run-through of "Olivia's Pool" took place on 6/6/97 at the rehearsal and keg party at the Charlotte, VT home of Pete Carini and Brad Sands, affectionately known as "Bradstock." On the heels of the inaugural "Ghost," the public debut of "Olivia's Pool" took place on 6/13/97 in the cozy confines of the 600-person capacity SFX Centre (Saint Francis Xavier church gym and recreation center, not to be confused with the SFX Entertainment, Inc., the venue management company in the US) in Dublin, Ireland. Unlike many of the new tunes unveiled that summer, "Olivia's Pool" had a relatively short shelf-life: it made only six more appearances in the summer and fall of '97 before transforming into what we now know as "Shafty" at the 4/5/98 Providence Civic Center show.

A short, upbeat number in the classic '50s rock-n-roll tradition of Jerry Lee Lewis or Chuck Berry, the happy-go-lucky musical exterior of "Olivia's Pool" provides an interesting backdrop for the tale of someone not quite on the same page as the rest of us, someone who is, in fact, an oblivious fool. The narrator tells a story of cluelessness ("You say 'so what'? I'm doing just fine…. The irony is that it's all in your mind"), while the bright, cheery, care-free tone of the music seems to represent the accused in the story. It's a juxtaposition in the style of the Talking Heads' "Life During Wartime," where warnings that "this ain't no party, this ain't no disco" go unheeded by the tune's thick dance groove.

Never clocking in at over 5 minutes, "Olivia's Pool" doesn't vary much between versions, and excepting the first (6/13/97) and last (11/17/97) appearances, it was always opened or closed a set. Most setlists from the 4/5/98 Providence gig were noted "Olivia's Pool (or "Oblivious Fool"), to a slow mellow groove," but we now know this to have been the public debut of "Shafty."

If you believe everything Tom Marshall says, the proper title of the

tune is "Olivia's Pool." It is listed as such on the official website of Tom Marshall's band, Amfibian, as well as the Phish website for the June 1997 installment of This Month in Phish History. "Official" is an often very relative and fluctuating concept with this band of pranksters. The title "Olivia's Pool" might well be an inside joke, and one which employs clever irony to mock those of us insisting on the obvious and appropriate title of "Oblivious Fool."

While the original arrangement of "Olivia's Pool" as performed by Phish has been cast aside in favor of "Shafty" and is seemingly a thing of the past, the upbeat interpretation remains a standard in the setlist rotation of Amfibian. Amfibian's performance of the tune at the Higher Ground in Winooski, VT on 1/30/99 is notable both for a guest appearance by Burlington friend Gordon Stone, and in response to an audience member's prodding after the tune ends, yet another affirmation from Tom of the "official" name, "Olivia's Pool."

See also: "Shafty"

On My Knees
Music/Lyrics: Son Seals
Original Artist: Son Seals
Original Album: *Midnight Sun* (1976)
Vocals: Son Seals
Debut: 7/17/99
Historian: Mark Toscano

Son Seals, a Chicago guitarist playing the blues since his teens, was an early blues influence on the impressionable young Phish when they began to cover his "Funky Bitch" in the '80s. Had you told the bandmembers that they'd be sharing the stage with Son Seals only a decade later, they would have proclaimed you daft. However, daffiness seems to rule the career of this band, and Seals joined them at Volney on 7/17/99 for renditions of two of his classics, the aforementioned "Bitch" and "On My Knees." "On My Knees," though well received by the crowd, did not subsequently enter the band's sans-Seals repertoire, though "Funky Bitch" stayed on to shake her ass from time to time.

On the Run
Original Artist: Pink Floyd
Original Album: *Dark Side of the Moon* (1973)
Vocals: (instrumental)
Debut: 11/2/98
Historian: Mark Toscano

At Phish's 11/2/98 gig, "On the Run" was easily the most creatively interpreted song from Pink Floyd's *Dark Side of the Moon* album. In fact, given the spontaneous nature of the show, the performance of this tune ranks up as perhaps the most improvisational and curious.

Pink Floyd themselves often did interesting things with this song during live shows, especially in the pre-album release period of 1971-1972, when the whole album concept was still being hammered out. 1971 versions were startlingly different, usually taking the form of a groovy, ambient jam that lasted for several minutes before finding its way into "Time." By 1973, live versions agreed more with the album version of the tune, completely redesigned in the form of loops, synthesizer and tape effects, and the musical description of a sort of manic, rat-race mentality. The version appearing on Pink Floyd's double live album *Pulse* is almost identical to the 1973 studio configuration.

Phish, however, having decided to play *Dark Side* the evening of the E Centre show during dinner, had to think fast of a way to translate a song that relied so heavily on studio effects, and they didn't have the advantage of pre-planning or expensive, appropriate equipment that the Floyd did. So they just winged it. Fishman maintained the all-important, driven beat while Page, Mike, and Trey played with delay loops, effects, and atmospheric sounds. Effective results were even generated with such simple techniques as Trey raking across his strings up and down the guitar neck. Fans were duly impressed and satisfied by the results, which just goes to show that it doesn't take a dozen folks on stage with millions of dollars in custom-engineered electronics to kick a song's ass.

On Your Way Down
Music/Lyrics: Alain Toussaint
Original Artist: Little Feat
Original Album: *Dixie Chicken* (1973)
Vocals: Page
Debut: 7/23/88
Historian: Ellis Godard

Phish have played three Little Feat songs, once for each stage in the career of this very '70s bluesadelic band. "On Your Way Down" may be the most conventional score of the three songs (not that any of them is a fugue), but has an odd history. It first appeared on Feat's third album, *Dixie Chicken*, which gained critical (and fan) acclaim years later—but bombed originally. When the previous album (*Sailin' Shoes*) sold poorly, bassist Roy Estrada (formerly with the Mothers of Invention) split to join Captain Beefheart. And when *Dixie Chicken* floundered, the whole band split. The band which had all the ingredients for success seemed to be on its way down. They'd be on their way up again within two years, releasing progressively stronger LPs (*Feats Don't Fail Me Now*, *The Last Record Album*, and *Time Loves a Hero*)—but down again in 1979 when, after the disappointing *Waiting for Columbus*, founder Lowell George left the band and then passed away.

Except for George, the band is the same people who met up in 1972. They picked up again in 1987 and began releasing albums again in 1988, the same year Phish began covering their classics. Phish played "On Your Way Down" perhaps a dozen times, typically in the first set. It fit well with Phish's newly expanding tour schedule: classic tune, with a likeable boogie beat but enough blues for Trey to wail, with lyrics that mix hope and humility. But that mix must not have fit well with their developing air of aggressive unpredictability, and it dropped from rotation.

The song resurfaced 9/16/99, after just over ten years (and almost 900 shows), and was played twice more on that Fall Tour (9/25/99 and 10/2/99). But those earlier years had a rawness that comes from being on your way up (living in a moving truck and sleeping on YMCA floors). Phish is not likely to be on their way down to that rawness anytime soon. Meanwhile, of earlier versions in circulation, 9/8/88 is probably the crispest, in quality as well as performance.

Once in a Lifetime
Original Artist: Talking Heads
Original Album: *Remain in Light* (1980)
Vocals: Trey (lead), Mike, Page (backing)
Debut: 10/31/96
Historian: Mark Toscano

Though they handled it fine, the only mildly weak spot in Phish's fantastic 10/31/96 *Remain in Light* set is their performance of this song. It's a good performance, but frankly the song isn't as attuned to their powers as the rest of the album's tracks. Yes, "Once in a Lifetime" is an insanely "classic" song, an anthem (if you will) of the post-punk generation or some damn thing. Yes, everybody remembers the video with David Byrne doing dances that to this day can only be characterized as… Byrneish. Yes, people who don't know anything about Talking Heads often know this song by heart. It is, however, probably the most conventional song on the disc, and, despite its genius, lies somewhere slightly outside of the electronic earthscape inhabited by the rest of the album.

With this in mind, Phish's version naturally didn't quite gel like the rest of the songs. More accurately, it's about as good a performance Phish could pull off of a song that no one could really "do" anything more with anyway. And since they stick relatively closely to the original version, fans definitely look to the rest of the performance for Phish's shining moments.

Amusingly, this song is a classic radio and concert sing-along, despite having little or no distinguishable tune or melody. David Byrne's singing on the album track is like the anxious ramblings of a man destroyed by (or at least seriously disillusioned with) the society he seeks to understand. Interestingly, Byrne has commented that he often wouldn't need to sing the lyrics to this one at Talking Heads shows because the crowd would be singing along so loudly.

At the Omni, Phish's audience also sang along. Trey's vocals were fine, though his vocal irony wasn't nearly as pointedly oblivious as Byrne's. The best moments of Phish's performance came at the end of the tune, when the band extended the outro a wee bit for some near wall-of-sound dynamics. The crowd cheered adoringly as Page's organ mimed the original's digital water flow effect, with "Houses in Motion" just around the bend. All in all, though Phish's one-time version of this track was strong, one need only look to the tune's repeated mantra for the most concise evaluation one could ask for.

One Meatball

Music/Lyrics: Singer/Zanet
Album: Single (1945)
Debut: 2/25/97
Vocals: Sydney Ellis
Historian: Ellis Godard

Phish's first show in Munich was at a venue called the Incognito, an apt name for where Phish went in their first set. Even the opening "Runaway Jim" and "My Soul" sounded more like the Grateful Dead—slower and sloppy—than Phish. Then they busted into a three-song suite that was a dead ringer, or at least a more authentic approximation than their riotous Dead covers in the mid-1980s. Sydney Ellis, an American blues singer-songwriter living in Germany, guested on vocals.

Of that suite, the first and last parts ("Lil' Red Rooster" and "Got My Mojo Workin'") are better known by American audiences than this middle piece. Jerry Garcia would have been proud of the selection, once a staple but since faded from glory. "One Meatball" is a goofy ditty, recorded in the 1940s, a half dozen times in 1945 alone, from Josh White to the Andrews Sisters, and later by everyone from Lightin' Hopkins to Pig.

Only Shallow

Music/Lyrics: Kevin Shields, Bilinda Butcher
Original Artist: My Bloody Valentine
Original Album: *Loveless* (1991)
Vocals: unknown fan
Debut: 7/6/97
Historian: Erik Swain

Most fans have long been aware of the major influences—from Carlos Santana to Frank Zappa—on Trey's guitar playing. He acknowledged them in a 1999 interview with Rolling Stone, but added another name that came as a bit of a surprise: Kevin Shields of alt-noise-rockers My Bloody Valentine. "As far as new guitarists, the guy I love the most is Kevin Shields," he said. "He's the absolute best. I think *Loveless* is the defining album of the Nineties as far as sound goes. Oh, my God, I've never heard anything like that before." Indeed, Trey and Fish love that album so much that they lobbied to cover it for the 1998 Halloween show, but Trey said they were "outvoted." Apparently a tie is as good as a loss in the Phish democratic process.

Don't feel too bad for them, though, as they did get to try out *Loveless'* best-known song, "Only Shallow," at the infamous 7/6/97 Desenzano soundcheck, which circulates widely. It appeared near the end of the soundcheck, when the band was providing the soundtrack for an audience limbo contest and letting the audience members sing. An unknown female concertgoer did the honors.

Earlier in the year, on 5/21/97, Trey and Mike played the song during the only show of their "New York!" side project with members of Burlington combo The Pants and Giant Country Horns trombonist James Harvey (on drums!)

The Other One

Music: Grateful Dead
Lyrics: Bob Weir
Original Album: *Anthem of the Sun* (1968)
Debut: 5/3/85
Historians: Mark Toscano and Phil Nazzaro

An homage to the adventurous Neal Cassady and "adventure" in general, "The Other One" is known to have been covered by Phish on only one occasion (5/3/85, Page's first show), though it is possible that it was a more regular part of the band's early repertoire than we know. Coming out of an early "Antelope" jam, "The Other One" performed by Phish was based on Bob Weir's contribution to the "That's it for the Other One" suite that opens the Dead's second album. Otherwise, the song is only known to have been jammed during the 11/23/85 "Whipping Post." Interestingly, both known versions of this song were performed by the closest incarnation Phish had to the Dead: drums, bass, lead guitar, rhythm guitar, and keys.

It should be noted that the 4/17/99 Phil and Phriends show contained a serious "Other One" jam out of the second set "Dark Star," but was abruptly abandoned by Phil. This may have been a bummer to fans (and band), but Bobby songs were carefully avoided that night, as the repertoire stuck to Jerry tunes, Phil tunes, and covers.

The Overload

Original Artist: Talking Heads

Elise Ryerson

Original Album: *Remain in Light* (1980)
Vocals: Fishman
Debut: 10/31/96
Historian: Mark Toscano

If "Listening Wind" is a bittersweet requiem for the purity of unsullied life and culture, then "The Overload" is a death dirge for the same, a depressing epilogue in which jackhammers, televisions, and interchangeble-blade hand blenders emerge victorious over trees, breezes, and birdsong. This song tells us that something unknown and horrible is coming—or has it already arrived? It's a drone, one repetitive, shattering chord, the nihilist, zombie twin of "Tomorrow Never Knows." We're doomed. It's dronerock. Doomdronerock?

The song is imperfect, marred by occasional tears and holes in its sonic weave. On the original, David Byrne's vocals just barely float above its leaden waters, in a sort of insomniac haze, like Caligari's Somnabulist telling us we'll all die at dawn.

All misery aside, Phish's version to close the second set on 10/31/96 went in a completely different direction. They made it into theatre, choosing a U2 meets *Brazil* way of expressing the song's feelings. Chaos slowly erupted onstage, and many fans present can't remember what exactly happened. Whatever did happen, it featured a jackhammer, an Italian bus driver, a megaphone, all the band's instruments, lights and smoke, four multi-media screens, a power drill, an Electrolux vacuum cleaner, a Black and Decker skillsaw, and Colonel Bruce Hampton. Draw your own conclusions.

Oye Como Va

Music/Lyrics: Tito Puente
Original Artist: Tito Puente, Santana
Original Album: *El Rey Bravo* (1962) (Tito Puente),
   Abraxas (1970) (Santana)

Vocals: (performed instrumental)
Debut: 4/25/92
Historian: Ellis Godard

Written by Tito Puente but recorded and repopularized by Carlos Santana, "Oye Como Va" is, much like "Low Rider," the kind of tune that entered American consciousness without carrying along much of the Latino culture of its origins. If it had come along two decades later, no doubt it would have been paraded as heralding a widespread movement and recognition of a foreign rhythmic genre. Instead, its carriers slipped in and out of the charts without leaving a lasting image—at least not explicitly. (Retribution came for Santana years later in the form of multiple Grammys.)

Similarly, the tune itself has slipped in and out of Phish history without leaving a complete impression. Teased during "Maze" once (4/25/92) and during "You Enjoy Myself" dozens of times (including 12/7/92, 3/14/93, and 5/2/93), Phish have yet to play the song in full. However, its appearance during one YEM (8/28/93), while less than complete, was more than a tease. A full-on jam ensued during this tour-closing performance, with several measures in which the band is fully "in" the cover and a number more where they are wavering into "typical" Phish jam space.

Paul and Silas

AKA: "Hall in Solace" (Trey's mistitle)
Music/Lyrics: (traditional)
Vocals: Trey (lead), Mike, Page (backing)
Debut: 9/13/90
Historian: Mark Toscano

Songs about the biblical characters Paul and Silas have actually been quite numerous in music history, and various interpretations of the

story have shown up in folk, gospel, and country incarnations, as well as spirituals and hymns, to name the most common examples. Fans who enjoy the version Phish performs will likely be most comfy with the classic Flatt and Scruggs reading, played as fast, no-holds-barred bluegrass.

Though most versions of this tune (played regularly from 1990 to 1994, and only sporadically since) have been pretty standard, a few shine. 12/11/92 slipped into a crazed "Big Ball Jam," 7/22/93 featured Gordon Stone on banjo, and 11/29/98 featured amusing alternate lyrics about Paul Languedoc's run-in with the law the night before.

Also of note is Trey's now-famous error in identifying the title of the song. Until 1992, he always announced and sang the tune as "Hall in Solace," until bluegrass-savvy fans corrected him once the band started regularly playing beyond its Northeastern digs.

Peaches en Regalia

AKA: "Peaches"
Original Artist: Frank Zappa
Original Album: *Hot Rats* (1969)
Vocals: (instrumental)
Debut: 10/15/86
Historian: Mark Toscano

On 3/12/88, Zappa's final tour came through the Northeastern U.S., making a surprising (according to residents) stop at the Memorial Auditorium in Burlington. Excited by the prospect of seeing Zappa in their home town, a slew of folks from the local music scene went to the show, including Trey, Mike, Fish, Page, Nancy, and Rob Dasaro (of The Joneses). Rob Dasaro has told an excellent story about how at one point in the show, Zappa was collecting concertgoers' underthings (as he was wont to do), and among some panties and bras, someone had thrown a Phish shirt to the stage. Apparently, Zappa picked it up and held it up to look at it, eliciting many cheers of recognition from the crowd. It may not have meant much to Frank, but it certainly must have been cool for Phish.

It's incredible how influential Frank Zappa has been on Trey's and Fish's musical development, considering the band has only covered two of his songs, one of which ("Big Leg Emma") was only done briefly in the band's first few years. This number stands in stark contrast to, at last count, thirty-four by The Beatles, twenty by The Who, thirteen by Talking Heads, ten by the Dead, eight by Led Zeppelin, six by the Rolling Stones, five by Syd Barrett (including "Bike"), five by the Allman Brothers, four by Lynyrd Skynyrd, three by Stevie Wonder, and three by ZZ Top. For crimony's sake, they've done two each from Prince and The Wizard of Oz!

Frank Zappa, perhaps the original music iconoclast, was offending, disturbing, amusing, and challenging listeners before bands like The Residents, Mr. Bungle, Primus, and Phish were even crapping their diapers. Frank gave us conceptual continuity, xenocrony, poodle sex, and the Mudshark. He blessed the world with songs about religious hypocrisy ("Heavenly Bank Account"), questionable politicians ("Dickie's Such an Asshole"), government mind control ("Who are the Brain Police?"), dastardly criminals ("The Illinois Enema Bandit"), debilitating diseases ("Stink Foot" and "Why Does it Hurt When I Pee?"), false prophets ("Cosmik Debris"), bad monster movies ("Cheepnis"), hipster posing ("Who Needs the Peace Corps?"), unorthodox sex

("Bobby Brown Goes Down"), racism ("Uncle Remus"), and ramming things up poop-chutes ("Broken Hearts are for Assholes").

His music is also extremely eclectic, and Zappa dabbled generously in many genres. With experiments in doo-wop (*Cruising With Ruben and the Jets*), experimental freak-rock ("The Return of the Son of Monster Magnet"), fusion (*Hot Rats*), weird jazz (*Waka/Jawaka* and *The Grand Wazoo*), classical music (the *LSO* albums, *The Yellow Shark*), electronic composition (*Jazz From Hell*), musical theatre (*Thing-Fish*), cinema and cinema scoring (*Uncle Meat, 200 Motels*), baroque chamber music (*Francesco Zappa*), musique concrète (*Lumpy Gravy, Civilization Phaze III*), and even top-40 hit pop songs ("Valley Girl"), Zappa carved a niche for himself out of every conceivable place in the music industry.

Zappa even wrote music that was nearly impossible to play, like "Ship Arriving too Late to Save a Drowning Witch," a piece he once said that he and his live band could never quite nail—quite a comment considering the legendary chops of his bandmates throughout the years. His band members were always the best in the business, and many stayed with him for years at a time. The tours were legendary, combining political commentary, offensive and hilarious stage antics, audience participation, amusing covers ("I Left My Heart in San Francisco," anyone?), and, above all, kick-ass performances of ass-kicking music.

He produced Captain Beefheart's ultra-legendary *Trout Mask Replica* album, and even gave the Captain (aka Don van Vliet) his famous moniker. He challenged censorship of music and the arts in general, releasing such anti-censorship-oriented albums as *Joe's Garage* and *Frank Zappa Meets the Mothers of Prevention*, eventually testifying before Congress on the subject. He subverted Warner Brothers' power when, after they refused to release his epic recording *Läther* in 1977, he brought the album to a radio station and enabled fans to record it themselves off the airwaves. The Mothers of Invention's debut album *Freak Out!* (the first rock double-LP) inspired Paul McCartney to conceive The Beatles' own "concept" album, something called *Sgt. Pepper's Lonely Hearts Club Band*.

He helped foster the careers of many artists, such as Jean-Luc Ponty, George Duke, Ray White, Terry Bozzio, Steve Vai, Adrian Belew, and Alice Cooper. In fact, it was Zappa that convinced Alice to not dispel the rumor that he had bitten the head off a chicken, an untruth that had begun following a Cooper show at which fans had torn apart a dove that was used as part of the stage theatrics. He also convinced Lowell George to leave the Mothers and form his own band (Little Feat!), telling George that he was too good to be a backing player. Following the Jimmy Swaggart debacle that unfolded during Zappa's final tour in '88, he constructed parody versions of "Norwegian Wood" ("Texas Motel"), "Lucy in the Sky With Diamonds," ("Louisiana Hooker With Herpes"), and "Strawberry Fields Forever," ("Texas Motel" reprise) to criticize not just Swaggart, but the whole televangelist world. Annoyed with the wave of bootleg recordings of his concerts, FZ collected a large number of the illicit recordings and released them officially in a boxed set on his own label. (One bootleg producer even tried to sue Zappa for "stealing" his cover artwork!)

Frank Zappa was a remarkable guy.

"Peaches en Regalia" is one of Zappa's most well-known works. Even those who normally can't stomach the man's more confrontational material have been known to like "Peaches." As the opening track on Zappa's first credited "solo" album, *Hot Rats*, it sets the stage rather

oddly, as the music that follows this completely composed piece is largely free-form and improvisational. *Hot Rats* is considered by many to be a ground-breaking fusion album, much as *Bitches Brew* was for Miles Davis not too long before. Songs such as "The Gumbo Variations" and "Son of Mr. Green Genes" push the envelope of both rock and jazz. The album grooves hard at times, assaults the listener at others, and is always riveting. "Peaches," unusually composed and structured for the disc, is a classic track combining Zappa's eccentric compositional approach, quirky instrumentation, complex arrangement, and ultimately hummable tune.

It's no wonder Phish wanted to cover Zappa. Trey and Fish are confessed Zappa fanatics, always eager to champion their hero in interviews. Mike is no slouch in the Zappa department either; he obviously takes the cue on 12/29/95 during the bass duet for a "Keep it Greasey" jam, and for a "He Used to Cut the Grass" jam out of "Halley's" on 11/22/97. Page, however, respects Zappa, but was never really a "fan." He did agree that "Peaches" would be a good song to cover, and the band learned it in mid-1986 from a book of jazz standards. They performed the song regularly through 1989, when it disappeared without a trace for a full four years. These early versions are usually fine, always wowing audiences who were usually impressed and surprised at the moxie of a young bar band covering a Zappa tune.

Phish always had a decent arrangement of the tune worked out for their setup, but the arrangement improved remarkably in late 1993. Legend has it that at some point in December '93, the band met Dweezil Zappa, who provided the guys with his recently deceased father's correct arrangement for the song. Regardless of the truth in this story, the band premiered a better, tighter, and more accurate arrangement on 12/28/93, and it was performed at three of the four New Year's Run shows that year (skipping 12/30). Zappa had just died of prostate cancer on December 4 of that year, and the reintegration of "Peaches" into Phish's playlist was a tribute to FZ. In fact, "Peaches" was even teased several times throughout the 12/31/93 show (e.g. "Possum" and "Suzy"), Phish showing the audience how interwoven Zappa's musical accomplishments were with their own.

The song remained a frequent play throughout 1994, with especially listen-worthy versions appearing on 4/9/94 (with "Little Drummer Boy" segue into "Big Ball Jam"), 5/27/94, and 6/18/94 (before a monster "Bowie"). The song disappeared again in 1995 and almost all of 1996 before a surprise mid-tour breakout on 12/1/96 in Los Angeles, Zappa's stomping grounds. (Perhaps they met up with Dweezil again?) The song then continued an on-again-off-again pattern, dotting setlists throughout 1997, disappearing for 1998, and showing up again in 1999. Decent latter-day versions of the tune came on 12/31/96, 2/23/97, 9/14/99, and 9/17/99.

Rumor has it that, following FZ's death, Gail Zappa (his widow) publicly indicated a handful of Zappa tunes that she did not wish to be played in the aftermath of her husband's passing. This short but sweet list included classics such as "Black Napkins," "Watermelon in Easter Hay," and, supposedly, "Peaches." Whether or not this is the case remains a mild mystery, but would Dweezil have shared "Peaches" with Phish if it were meant to be suppressed? And would Frank himself have wanted his music to ostensibly die, only living on in the ephemera of his own lifetime? I think not. And it certainly hasn't.

The Pendulum

Music: Phish
Words: Zenzilé
Vocals: Zenzilé
Debut: 4/1/86
Historian: Craig DeLucia and Mark Toscano

Once upon a time, Phish played backing music while a man named Zenzilé recited reactionary poetry. Fans have labeled this "The Pendulum." Zenzilé studied at Goddard briefly around this time, having been a revolutionary and "trouble-maker" in South Africa as a young adult. Today, Zenzilé still rallies extensive support for various high-power civil rights causes, urged on by his innate dissatisfaction with the heinous state of things in the world, always electrifying his supporters with eloquent speech and cadence. On April Fool's Day 1986, however, in order to distinguish between Zenzilé and a true prophet, Phish subsequently slid into "Dave's Energy Guide" as a bridge to "Icculus."

The Pez Song

Music/Lyrics: Dave Abrahams
Vocals: Trey Anastasio
Debut: 3/28/93
Historian: Charlie Dirksen

The Pez Song was only performed once and, even then, not in its entirety. In the opening section of "You Enjoy Myself" on 3/28/93 in the East Gym of Humboldt State University in Arcata, California, Trey simply sang a few words from this song in honor of his good friend looks too much like Dave Abrahams, "the Pez man." Though the song consists of considerably more lyrics, Trey sang only: "When you turn my neck back, don't you even try to get inside my head and see the sky there. It is good enough for the two of us." Trey then whispered: "please give the Pez back to the guy who gave you the Pez. Don't keep the Pez." Trey then repeated the "When you turn my neck back…for the two of us" lyrics once again. And finally, Trey sang: "When you break my neck." (pause) "When you break my neck." "Break my neck." (pause) "Neck." (pause) "NNnn." One of the most interesting and amusing opening sections of "You Enjoy Myself" you are likely to ever hear.

Phase Dance

Original Artist: Pat Metheny Group
Original Album: *Pat Metheny Group* (1978)
Vocals: (instrumental)
Debut: 9/28/87
Historian: Ellis Godard

Trey was never slack in picking heroes or cover songs. In Pat Metheny's "Phase Dance," he found some genius of both types. Each of Phish's three known performances (9/28/87, 2/7/88, and 2/8/98) pale in comparison to the original, but they illustrate Trey's reach, and have no doubt helped expose some hippies to crucial contemporary jazz.

Pig in a Pen

Music/Lyrics: traditional
Vocals: "Reverend" Jeff Mosier (2/21/93, 11/16/94)

Debut: 2/21/93
Historian: Jeremy Welsh

A traditional bluegrass tune, "Pig in a Pen" has been performed four times by Phish. It was debuted on 2/21/93 as the final song of a four-song encore that featured "Reverend" Jeff Mosier on banjo. (This pickin' encore actually includes a bluegrass version of "Good Times Bad Times.") Two nights later, the song made an interesting appearance in the middle of a "Weekapaug Groove." "Pig in a Pen's" third appearance came on 11/16/94, again featuring Jeff Mosier on banjo and vocals (Mosier would join Phish for four more shows that fall). This version includes nice solos by Mike and Fish, who was introduced as "the world's premier bluegrass drummer." Three nights later, after their show in Bloomington, Indiana, Phish performed this song in their parking lot set, an acoustic bluegrass set that featured the Reverend on banjo, Eric Merrill on fiddle and guitar, and "Jeremy" on banjo and jaw harp.

Piggies

Music/Lyrics: George Harrison
Original Artist: The Beatles
Original Album: *The Beatles* (aka "The White Album") (1968)
Vocals: Trey (lead), Page (backing)
Debut: 10/31/94
Historian: Mark Toscano

This sprightly little George Harrison harpsichord ditty from The Beatles' "White Album" was covered by Phish for their 10/31/94 Halloween show. Page even used a harpsichord voice on one of his electric keyboards to be as faithful to the original as possible.

Piper

AKA: "Words"
Music/Lyrics: Phish, Tom Marshall
Album: *Farmhouse, Hampton Comes Alive* (11/20/98)
Debut: 6/14/97
Historian: Martin Acaster

The life of the common red wiggler worm seems simple upon first observation. A typical day in the compost heap for the red wiggler consists of drawing organic material into its gaping maw with the aid of a protractible pharynx. Effectively swallowed, the unwitting organic matter passes into the crop, where it is briefly stored before moving into the gizzard. There, it is smashed and ground into smaller and smaller pieces until sliding into the intestine where digestive juices dissolve and extract the useful energy. Ultimately the red wiggler disposes of the "useless" waste as a tubular cast of its sphincter. Of course what is useless as an energy source to the worm is very useful as fertile soil for the farmer. The farmer uses the enriched soil to grow new vegetables. Many of these vegetables in turn end up back in the compost heap to provide energy for the worm. The entire process is microcosm of the never ending cycle of life and the exchange of energy.

"Piper," "Piper," the red red worm of the Gamehendge compost heap, plays a similar role in the exchange of energy between Phish and its fans. The organic matter (listener) is unwittingly drawn into the gaping maw of the worm by a delicate pharynx wherein Page pours gentle piano rivulets over Trey's "lightly strummed, simple chord progression." The time in the crop is typically brief, allowing for Mike and Jon to settle into an exponential groove where the pace quickens and the pressure increases.

Cast into the gizzard of the worm, the muscular bass and drums pound the listener into smaller and smaller pieces while the maniacally repetitive yet glorious wash of keyboard and guitar pushes us onward into the intestine. Tom Marshall's simple (yet certainly profound) lyrics repeated seemingly ad infinitum creates a fifth instrument which helps the worm to absorb the useful energy from the digested listener. Some listeners describe the voyage through the digestive system of the worm to be akin to sailing. In fact, throughout the repeated verse of the song, the distant wail of the bearded siren "Henrietta" can often be heard to proclaim just that (I'm Sailing). Finally discarded as a "useless" cast, the listener is typically spent yet enriched at the same time, imbued with the intoxicating glow of the Kava Kava root (Species, Piper Methysticum), fertile soil ready for replanting.

After bursting forth from its egg at "Bradstock" (6/6/97) the neophyte "Piper" made its Phish show debut 6/14/97 at the SFX Center in Dublin, Ireland. The short, simple, red wiggler worm appeared frequently during the rest of the European leg of the summer tour gaining somewhat in size and stamina while remaining a "radio friendly" length (e.g. Vienna 6/19/97, Strasbourg 6/24/97). "Piper" was most conspicuous in its absence from two shows in Amsterdam (7/1 and 7/2/97) which featured multiple references to riding the worm, highlighted by "Wormtown" a demonic variation of Steve Miller's "Swingtown," which included a warning from Trey about the monstrous worms in the canals of Amsterdam. As if summoned by the black magic of the night before, "Piper" squirmed from the compost heap onto the stage to open the show in Nuremberg (7/3/97). During the US portion of the tour "Piper" all but vanished below the surface of the pile appearing only at Ventura (7/30/97) and Deer Creek (8/11/97) after making its US debut at the opener in Virginia Beach (7/21/97). During the fall of 1997 "Piper" rose from its burrow during one show each week of the tour, where it transformed gradually from a brief yet energetic portion of multiple song sandwiches (e.g. Salt Lake City 11/14/97 or Hampton 11/22/97) into a voracious monster space worm (e.g. Worcester 11/30/97 and Albany 12/12/97).

Fattened and lengthened by the Bearsville *Story of the Ghost* sessions, "Piper" was much more bold and experimental throughout 1998. "Piper's" first appearance in 1998 during the island tour at the Nassau Coliseum (4/3/98) featured a closing jam segment which set the improvisational bar for future worms to attempt to surpass. For pure otherworldly improvisation (where "Piper" escapes the compost heap entirely) seek out the Merriwether Post Pavillion and Las Vegas (10/31/98) performances. Many other versions from 1998 that remained within the confines of the pile yet will certainly "enrich" the listener do exist however; among these are Shoreline (7/19/98), Lemonwheel (8/16/98), Hampton (11/20/98), and Madison Square Garden (12/30/98). Fat and juicy worms which have been played in subsequent years include the "Bug" spewing "Piper" from Great Woods (7/13/99), the fiery 7/18/99 Oswego County Airport performance which was used as the base for the *Farmhouse* studio version of the song, the magically psychedelic "Piper" from Portland (12/8/99) the glorious swamp thing found deep in the recesses of the SHOW at Big Cypress, and the "Crosseyed and Painless" "Piper" which dropped from the beak of "Birds of a Feather" at Deer Creek (7/12/00).

Poor Heart

AKA: "Poor ♥"
Music/Lyrics: Mike Gordon
Album: *A Picture of Nectar*
Debut: 4/22/91
Historian: Craig DeLucia

Not many bands could pull off a number about a man and his four-track tape recorder, but such is the creative genius of Mr. Michael Gordon. Mike wrote the song after someone stole his four-track machine during Springfest at Goddard one year. The lyrics recount his lament over the theft. Mike once mentioned in an interview that a third verse exists. The lyrics reference driving around in a pickup truck and stealing the four-track back. No one knows of any occasion, though, when this verse was performed live.

Though the song debuted in 1991, it was mentioned on stage as early as 1988. Listen to the first set of April 22 from that year; Trey mentions several new songs, including "The Four-Track Song." This would eventually become "Poor Heart." Some knock "Poor Heart" as a song that does not change much from performance to performance. While it is true that almost all versions of "Poor Heart" are performed in the same uptempo, bluegrass fashion, the few versions that have strayed from this pattern are highly memorable.

The band's greatest on-stage experimentations with "Poor Heart" took place in the fall of 1995. On 11/19, the band broke into a slower bluegrass number near the beginning of the first set. Fans were surprised when the "Poor Heart" lyrics were sung over this groove. The song was again performed this way in Landover on the 22nd. Three nights later, the band played the original "Poor Heart" to kick off the first set in Hampton. Then, to confound matters, the second set ended with the slow version! Never willing to let a good joke pass, the band then began the encore with an even slower "Poor Heart" before stopping and asking the audience: "Get it?" Many did, as they realized that the band had the power to change even the most static of songs. While the slow "Poor Heart" has not been played on-stage since, fans have reported hearing it soundchecked (for example, 12/8/95 in Cleveland and 8/4/96 at Red Rocks).

"Poor Heart" has also been a vehicle for bluegrass special guests. Gordon Stone played pedal steel (in addition to banjo) on the *Picture of Nectar* version, and then again live on 11/19/92. Béla Fleck has guested twice on the song. The first time, 11/29/95, he came alone; the second time, on 7/9/97, he brought the Flecktones along with him. On 11/16/97, Pete Wernick added banjo to the song at a memorable show in Denver. And in the largest demonstration of on-stage four-track lamentation known to man, the 7/1/99 version featured guests Jerry Douglas, Ronnie McCoury, Tim O'Brien, and Gary Gazaway.

Fans sometimes lament, however, that the most radical and different "Poor Heart" has never been played during a show. Those lucky enough to have the 5/5/93 soundcheck on tape can relish the "Poor Heart Blues," a rocking adaptation of the number (based on the musical progression used in "Funky Bitch") that has been known to make listeners laugh and dance at the same time.

For other interesting versions, check out 2/15/93 (segued into the "Big Ball Jam"), 6/24/94 (acoustic), 11/26/97 (started as "Rocky Top"), and 7/20/98 (with a "Freebird" ending). And, of course, no tape collection is complete without 6/17/94, which took place the night of O.J.

Simpson's infamous Bronco incident. Phish made reference to the event (which they had witnessed on TV at the venue) during several songs, including "Poor Heart."

Possum

Music: Jeff Holdsworth
Lyrics: Jeff Holdsworth, Trey Anastasio
Album: *Hampton Comes Alive* (11/20/98)
Debut: 10/30/85
Historian: Scott Hershkowitz

Born from the mind of Jeff Holdsworth, "Possum" began as a short, quiet, folk song about driving over possums. Sometime in the mid 1980s, Trey incorporated "Possum" into his Gamehendge saga, and it's the final track on many of the copies of Trey's Senior Study that circulate. It seemed to cap off the story, with Icculus sitting on top of the mountain, musing on the futility of life. From there, "Possum" started to become the monster that it is today.

Found in its original form, the song is about six minutes long, and sung by Mike Gordon. In the late '80s, the band extended the length of "Possum," usually by incorporating a long building, snare-driven section in the introduction, sometimes extending beyond a minute or two. Later versions of "Possum" contain many musical phrases borrowed from other songs in this section (or teases), as well as Secret Language signals. The more fun Trey had in the intro, the more fun you'll have listening to the tape.

However, the earlier versions of the song usually stayed within the ranges of the normal "Possum"—the jam was tight, but never too long or memorable. Occasionally Trey would tease a song slightly during the jam section, something like the "Andy Griffith" theme or the "Woody Woodpecker" theme. These jams were always fun, but in no way close to what "Possum" would become.

In 1990 and 1991, Phish played "Possum" more than they ever had before, and they played it well. There were some monster "Possums" from this time period, including 11/4/90, 3/16/91 and 4/27/91. Around this time, Trey was using a signal—an off-key version of the Beatles' "Get Back"—to tell the rest of the band to come back from la-la land into the end chorus. Eventually, the band dropped the signal, probably when their chemistry improved to the point where they didn't need one anymore.

The year of 1992 saw a decline in the number of "Possums" played, a decline that continues steadily today. However, possibly the one of the best "Possums" ever was played on 5/17/92, at Union College, in Schenectady, NY. For an example of what a ripping "Possum" sounds like, check this one out.

Since then, the teases and language in "Possum" have been a little harder to come by, but the jams are more intense and tighter than ever. Really groovin' "Possums" still contain a signal from Trey—a bluesy chord progression that he fanpicks up and down his guitar that he uses to bring the band to the crescendo. If you hear this signal it's usually the sign of a really ripping "Possum."

Some of the more recent "Possums" of note are 12/7/97 Dayton, OH (with "Camel Walk" teases and polka jamming,) 12/29/97 MSG, NY (comes out of "David Bowie," teases "Camel Walk," and goes into a jam on Otis Redding's "I Can't Turn You Loose,") and 8/12/98 (lightning Trey solo,) 12/30/98, and 6/30/00.

"Possum" has come a long way, and is somewhat rare nowadays.

It has been played more than many other Phish songs but the bulk of those came between 1990 and 1993. It was only played 8 times in 1997, and remained uncharacteristically scarce through 2000. It usually finds its place in a set as a closer although it has opened a set and encored quite a few times.

"Possum" is a vehicle for Trey to showcase; he starts slowly noodling around, and then builds up to a violent jam. The band as a whole seems to have a lot of fun playing it, which means that the audience has plenty of fun listening.

The Practical Song
AKA: "Shortage"
Music/Lyrics: Phish
Album: None
Debut: 9/12/88
Historians: Ellis Godard and Mark Toscano

This curious original is quite a rarity, known only to have been performed twice, on 9/12/88 and 5/26/89. When one realizes the origins of the song—it was made up on the spot to extend the band's set—one may cease questioning its obscurity in Phish's current live show.

Prep-School Hippie
AKA: "Trust Fund, Baby"
Music/Lyrics: Trey?
Album: (none)
Vocals: Trey
Debut: 9/27/85
Historian: Emilie Kennedy/Mark Toscano

Basically a one-joke song, "Prep-School Hippie" is only known to have made it to the stage three times. It has been speculated that the band retired this song in the late '80s for fear that they might insult some of their fans, but a more likely guess is that the joke had simply worn thin.

The song's lyrics describe a person's internal debate on whether to be a "Prep-School Hippie" or a "Hip-School Preppie." The narrator is trying to decide if he should "spend my adolescent days wearing tie-dies or Vuarnets." The song is meant to make fun of many of the fans that follow the Grateful Dead as well as their preppie opposites. Appropriately enough, Phish, with their vaguely preppie/hippie backgrounds, seems to represent both states of being. At the end of the song Trey screams, "I can't wait until I'm 21, dip into my trust fund!"

The song most likely was written by Trey, who was a graduate of the Taft school, a private high school in Connecticut. If you're interested in hearing this song, you can listen to any version from the mid-to-late '80s (e.g. 10/30/85, 4/15/86, or 12/6/86). At these shows, the song is played among a few other more or less retired songs such as "Dear Mrs. Reagan," and "Lushington." It is pretty unlikely that we will see this one in Phish's repertoire in the future.

The Price of Love
Lyrics: Ninja Mike
Original Artist: Ninja Custodian
Original Album: Unknown
Vocals: Ninja Mike, Magoo

Debut: 3/30/89
Historian: Mark Toscano

Not much is known about this "song," including whether or not it's even a song. At the antic-filled 3/30/89 show, Ninja Custodian members Ninja Mike and Magoo guested on stage with Phish for a performance of the NC original, "Funky (Breakdown)." Segueing into a song usually labeled as "The Price of Love," NinjaMike merely continued his bizarre, seemingly off-the-cuff lyrical contributions over Phish and Magoo's background music.

Prince Caspian
AKA: "Caspian"; "Fuckerpants"
Music: Trey Anastasio
Lyrics: Tom Marshall
Album: *Billy Breathes*
Debut: 6/8/95
Historian: Craig DeLucia

If you recognize the name "Prince Caspian" from outside the realm of Phish, you're not alone. C.S. Lewis created this mythical prince in his famous Chronicles of Narnia, which have been read and loved by young men and women around the world. The song's lyrics speak of a man who yearns to be the boy prince, "afloat upon the waves."

Fans were not sure what to make of "Caspian" when it first debuted in the Summer of 1995. The song featured a pretty melody but seemed a bit repetitive. The band altered the song in the Summer of 1996, adding the jam and the false ending that appear on the album version. While most versions are highly similar, some worth hearing from this year include 8/6 (Red Rocks), 8/12 ("Caspian" flowing into "McGrupp"), and 12/4 (sandwiched in between "Mike's Song" and "Sparkle").

"Caspian" was fairly immune to the cow funk jams of 1997, but the band began stretching the jam segment and experimentally linking it with other songs. One interesting combo was "Drowned" into "Caspian"; see 2/28 and 3/18. Fans also enjoyed the "Caspian" to close the third set of The Great Went on 8/17. Other fun versions from 1997 include 11/21 (first-set closer in Hampton) and 12/12 (with a "Llama"-esque jam section that moved into "Izabella.") In addition to this latter show, "Caspian" appeared in the midst of a number of full-set jams; see, for example, 11/26, 12/3, and the third set of New Year's Eve. This trend continued into 1998 and 1999. Check out 4/5/98, 7/2/98, 10/30/98, 7/21/99 and, of course, "The Show" from 12/31/99 for prime examples.

1998 also brought us another inspired "Drowned" / "Caspian" combo on 11/25. Perhaps the most memorable "Caspian," though, was played on 11/6/98, when a naked man jumped onto the stage and was taken away by security. This event scarred the band severely enough that some future versions of the song "Carini" included lyrics referencing the event.

Fans are still split on their opinions of "Caspian." Some like the song; others view it as a bathroom break. Still others have dubbed the song "Fuckerpants" to disguise their love for it. There can be little doubt, though, of Trey and Page's affection for the song. They brought it out on April 16, 1999, during the "Phil and Friends" shows. More than one fan has noted that the ensuing jam, which featured delicious guitar work from Trey and Steve Kimock, is perhaps the sweetest "Caspian" jam ever played. It remains to be seen if the effects of this jam can lure

Possum

Compiled by Scott Hershkowitz and Erik Swain

Date	Time	Notes
04/01/86	05:07	Weird and slow. Jeff sings alternative lyrics. "Music Never Stopped" tease.
08/29/87	11:40	Jams out of McGrupp; they play with the Possum/McGrupp chords for a while.
05/15/88	—	Funky jam out of AC/DC Bag over Possum chords. Alternate lyrics—"it don't matter anyway" (reference to the Dead's "Morning Dew"?).
05/13/89	08:42	Cool chord progressions in intro. "Andy Griffith" show theme tease.
12/08/89	08:37	Little "Popeye" tease.
02/23/90	07:27	Alumni Blues tease in intro. Cool jam.
03/01/90	07:34	Segues out of YEM vocal jam and intro includes vocal jamming.
10/31/90	08:36	"Oom Pah Pah" signal.
11/02/90	08:29	Comes right out of Curtain. Sweet jam.
12/28/90	08:46	Random note signal. "We Wish You A Merry Christmas" tease.
03/16/91	08:23	Segues out of Manteca. Manteca teases. All Fall Down signal.
04/27/91	10:40	They start Possum, signal "Turning Japanese," then tease Buried Alive and segues into "Buried Alive." Possum then proceeds out of "Buried Alive," and there's an "Oom Pah Pah" signal. Excellent.
08/03/91	08:20	"I Love Lucy" tease.
12/05/91	08:05	Pink Floyd's "Money" tease in intro.
12/06/91	16:06	Extended hi-hat intro, where the band repeats "Wait" over, and over, for 5:30, and then there's a Simpsons signal. Fish asks the crowd, "Can I hear you say yes? Can I…Boner?" At 8:53 they go back into Possum, and tease Wait. Cool jam, with lots of stops/starts. Buried Alive tease. Finishes with "Turning Japanese" tease.

Date	Time	Notes
04/05/92	12:11	Tease of Landlady, then an Oom Pah Pah signal. "Third Stone From the Sun" tease, then Random Note and All Fall Down signals. Then a "Moby Dick" tease and "Aw Fuck" signal, all in the 3:40 intro before the lyrics. Weird tempo jam before they segue into the closing lyrics. Mike sings "Crossroads" in the lyrics. Amazing jam!
04/16/92	12:15	Extended opening with rampant language signals. Trey's riffing is particularly ZZ Top-ish.
04/18/92	08:45	Cool intro plus Simpsons signal.
04/21/92	12:17	Simpsons, Oom Pah Pah, All Fall Down, Aw Fuck signals. Really cool hi-hat intro (about 3:30). Great jam, great Possum!
04/29/92	10:21	Random Note signal. Another killer jam.
05/17/92	13:06	Cool Trey/Mike play in beginning that leads into Simpsons language, All Fall Down, Random Note, Aw Fuck. Then a "Rocky Mountain Way" tease. Then "LA Woman" into Possum (3:30 intro). Another "LA Woman tease," then lyrics. After lyrics, a "China Grove" tease. An "It's Ice" tease in the jam. A great crescendo, then some more intense jamming into a "Divided Sky" tease. Truly amazing. One of the best. Check this one out!
11/27/92	10:51	Random Note and All Fall Down signals.
12/30/92	11:13	Random Note signal.
02/06/93	06:34	With John Popper; short but sweet.
08/08/93	11:02	Cool intro, which sounds like the "Mind Left Body Jam." "Tequila" tease in the jam, where they do some circus themes back into the lyrics. Great Possum!
08/12/93	10:55	Sounds like a "Tweezer" tease during the jam.
12/28/93	11:53	Tease of Led Zepplin's "Kashmir." Nice long jam.
12/31/93	12:04	Great jam with a stop in the middle.

more fans to love the song named for a boy who would become king of Narnia.

Proud Mary

Original Artist: Creedence Clearwater Revival
Original Album: *Bayou Country* (1969)
Vocals: Trey?
Debut: 12/2/83
Historian: Craig DeLucia

This easy, uptempo classic rock staple was apparently pulled together for the first gig but not played since. We assume that vocals were provided by Trey, though it may have been Jeff; no doubt, neither could match the wails of Tina Turner's popular cover.

Psycho Killer

Original Artist: Talking Heads

Original Album: *Talking Heads '77* (1977)
Vocals: Trey
Debut: 12/7/97
Historian: Phillip Zerbo

Two decades after the release of the definitive *Talking Heads '77*, Phish pulled out the Talking Heads hit "Psycho Killer" for two shows widely considered among the very best of the 1997 Fall and Holiday runs. The 12/7/97 gig at the Nutter Center in Dayton, OH wasted no time making its mark in Phish history, opening with a memorable "AC/DC Bag"—"Psycho Killer"—"Jesus Just Left Chicago."

In a Washington Post article published December 26, 1997, Page quoted this specific performance in the context of the strong Talking Heads influence in Phish's music: "When we're really playing at our best, things we love just come flowing out. The other night [12/7/97], we started playing "Psycho Killer" in the middle of a jam and that's a song that's not even in our repertoire."

POSSUM (continued)

Date	Time	Notes
04/11/94	10:41	Start/Stop jam during intro. Trey and Fish do some cool stuff during intro. Cream's "Sunshine of your Love" is teased during an intense jam.
04/21/94	11:05	All Fall Down signal.
04/30/94	11:55	"Lion Sleeps Tonight," "Wilson," "Peaches," "Wolfman's," and "Axilla" teases during a really sweet jam.
05/12/94	11:43	Excellent jam!
05/23/94	11:33	"McGrupp" tease in hi-hat intro.
05/27/94	11:50	Extended hi-hat intro with macaroni shaking. "Flintstones" theme tease. Fish screams "shake your macaroni" to the crowd.
06/10/94	10:40	Random Note signal.
06/14/94	09:03	"On Broadway" tease. Intense jam.
07/01/94	10:54	Phat bass in intro. Weird off-key jamming. "Voodoo chile (SR)" tease. Maybe a Funky Bitch tease.
11/02/94	12:00	Tease of something (?) in the intro. Long, good jam.
11/18/94	11:17	Simpsons signal. Sounds like a "Bathtub Gin" tease.
12/04/94	13:13	All Fall Down signal. Possible "Lizards'" tease.
12/08/94	16:09	Long silent jam in middle; the jam itself is really slow and bluesy.
06/14/95	10:51	Trey is very impressive. Mike kicks ass during the jam.
06/26/95	14:13	Cool, funky bass line in extended intro. "Heartbreaker" tease. Intense.
06/30/95	13:24	Bluesy jam. Some Chalk Dust or SOAM-like off-key jamming.
10/29/95	11:11	"Beat It" tease; remarkably intense jam.
11/16/95	08:19	With Butch Trucks on a second set of drums. Slowed down, laid back feel with a short but excellent jam. "One Way Out" tease in the intro.
08/17/96	13:19	Bluesy intro before hi-hat. Trey plays some sweet licks before they explode into the main tune. Very improvisational version. Hardcore off-key jamming.
03/01/97	09:50	All Fall Down signal. Weird heavy metal intro for two minutes. Cool sounding effect used throughout.
07/29/97	10:56	Long and bluesy intro.
11/19/97	13:21	Cool, funky extended intro with heavy Mike. Great jam section with some really cool progressions. There's an interesteing "chaos" section, and the jam segues into some hardcore blues.
12/03/97	11:21	Segues out of some soft "Bowie" jamming. They play some chords that sound like the start/stop funk style. Jam is long and intense. Funk!
12/07/97	11:39	Really sweet intro—sounds like "Camel Walk." Long hi-hat (1:30) with some Trey and Mike polka scales. Hardcore blues licks ala Johnny B. Goode. Awesome jam. Really tight. Ends with that polka-style progression that was in the intro segment.
12/29/97	09:58	Segues out of Bowie with "Camel Walk" teases all throughout intro. Page starts out the jam, and starts playing the chords to "Can't Turn You Loose." They jam on this tune for two minutes, and then return to Possum. Page is very strong in this jam. Trey keeps teasing "Camel Walk." They end with "Can't Turn You Loose."
08/12/98	10:18	Dedicated to Jeff Holdsworth (who wrote Possum). Wild!
11/29/98	10:29	Thirty second "Wipe Out" jam at the four-minute mark. Muted soloing from Trey.
12/30/98	11:35	A wild one that is a must-hear for Mike fans. Serious bass riffage and soloing in the opening. Also has two "Wipe Out" jams, another bass solo, and a "light solo" by Kuroda.
08/01/99	11:20	Unusually slow opening. Trey uses slide-guitar sounds throughout for a countryish feel.
12/11/99	12:49	Adrenaline-fueled encore with All Fall Down signal.
06/30/00	10:25	Agitated, sick version out of Tweezer Reprise's ending.

The Dayton "Psycho Killer" has been the only complete version Phish has performed, though there have been clear teases of the song both before and since. You can find "Psycho Killer" teases in YEM vocal jams (8/9/93 at the Concert Hall, Toronto, Canada, and 5/23/94 at the Civic Auditorium in Portland, OR).

A strong instrumental tease of the song also appears in what is regarded as one of the best "AC/DC Bag" versions in recent memory, on 12/30/97 at Madsion Square Garden. On the heels of news of the Dayton version, many in attendance were momentarily disappointed that the band abandoned the "Psycho Killer," but you would have been hard pressed to find a disappointed fan leaving the building *that* night!

Punch Me In The Eye
AKA: "I Will Set You Free," "Kill You 'Til You're Dead"
Music/Lyrics: Trey Anastasio

Album: (none)
Vocals: Trey (lead), Mike, Page (backing)
Debut: 4/24/87
Historian: Mark Toscano

This is not what you think. This is a truly bizarre song. Yes, Phish currently plays a song called "Punch *You* in the Eye." Yes, back in October of 1989 when "Punch *You* in the Eye" premiered, it was actually called "Punch *ME* in the Eye" (see 10/26/89 to hear Trey mention this multiple times). But, this is not the same song. The only similarity between "Punch Me" (1989) and "Punch Me" (1987) is the inclusion of the lyric "punch you in the eye." That's where the similarities end. This song seems to represent a sort of amalgamation of musical and lyrical ideas that ended up in later Phish tunes ("Wilson," "Divided Sky," and of course "Punch You in the Eye"), however not before shining brightly—but all too briefly—in the form of this genuinely disturbed song.

After starting out with some silly falsetto harmonies ("Kill you 'til you die...Punch you in the eye...Kill you 'til you're dead...Punch you in the head..."), the song segues into an evil vocal section featuring horrible chants of "I will set you free...Kick you in the knee..." This is followed by a brief Mike solo over a two-chord progression à la "Avenu Malkenu." Page then takes a solo over a climactic progression of minor seventh chords which are found today in a section of "Divided Sky." A strange and dissonant King Crimsony jam ensues, culminating in a rockabilly closing chorus, like Frankie Valli and the Four Seasons on speed, which threatens us: "I will kill you 'til you die...I will punch you in the eye...I will kick you in the knee...I will set you free." There seems to have been only one performance of this song, and that was on 4/24/87 at Billings Lounge at UVM in Burlington. This show, which also features the first live "I am Hydrogen," is worth checking out.

Many fans wonder why this song (and its more recognizable descendent) was originally entitled "Punch ME in the Eye," when the lyrics have always said "you" instead of "me." Trey has explained this as yet another attempt to freak out new fans. Like the secret language, the title of this song is a fun way of messing with the minds of people who have never seen Phish before. Just as it would be strange for a Phish novice to walk into a show and suddenly see everyone fall down or yell "D'oh!" in unison for seemingly no reason, it would be equally distressing to discover dozens of fans pleading with the band to "Punch Me in the Eye!" A newbie may walk away confused, thinking the fans of this band were crazed masochists.

Though it wasn't performed after its debut, of interesting note is the 5/11/87 show, only a few weeks after the tune's first and onlyknown performance. Following "Clod," Trey and company joke about playing "Peach"-"Punch" ("Peaches en Regalia" followed by "PMITE"), but their uncertainty about the song's future is clear. Quoth Trey: "What can we do with 'Punch'?" Well, they did something with it, but not for another two and a half years.

Punch You In The Eye

AKA: "Punch," "PYITE," "Punch Me in the Eye" (original title)
Music/Lyrics: Trey Anastasio
Album: (none)
Vocals: Trey
Debut: 8/17/89
Historian: Michael Preston

When the house lights turn off and the fans go insane, one of the best events that can happen at a show is that Trey begins an up-beat, muted riff on his guitar. This is the sign that Phish is going to play "Punch You in the Eye". A favorite of many, "PYITE" is a pounding, invigorating, yet astoundingly simple song. The beginning of the song is a steady pulse played in A. This one chord progression (yes, one chord), is all the song needs to set the scene of one of Phish's truly musically descriptive songs. The steady pulse rises and rises until it gets to a peak, which screams the opening theme of the song. The song has already been great and it has not even begun yet.

"Punch Me in the Eye" was introduced in the fall of 1989, and is a story narrated by a man traveling aimlessly on a kayaking trip, when he quickly discovers that he has landed in Prussia. He has a hostile encounter with the Evil King Wilson, is enslaved and tossed into a tiny shack. The feelings and thoughts that he experiences are clearly illus-

trated through the instrumental section, which is an elaborate melodic composition consisting of a descriptive guitar melody and a Latin beat. At the beginning of this jam in more recent versions, only the drums and piano continue to play while Mike and Trey do a little Latin dance of their own. This instrumental section was later performed by itself as "The Landlady" and can be heard on *A Picture of Nectar* (see "Landlady").

The narrator manages to escape by heading back out to the rough sea. As he leaves Prussia, he chants his hatred towards Wilson by saying: "Wilson, someday I'll kill you 'til you die!" He is not unscarred, however. Wilson holds a piece of paper to the poor guy's nipple before he gets away. This is the third song in which Trey has thrown in a reference to nipple slicing (see "The Sloth" and "Fee"). Trey's reintroduction of the song "Punch Me in the Eye" was easily disregarded by the fans. They wrote it down as "Punch You in the Eye" since that is the line that is chanted in the chorus.

After a gig at Williams College in Williamstowm, MA on 11/9/89, "Punch You in the Eye" disappeared from the setlist for four years. The "Landlady" section was excised from the song, and many figured that the dilemmas of the Kayaker had been heard for the last time.

However, on 2/5/93 at the Roseland Ballroom, the song was revived, and although it was considered a rare treat for the next few years, it has become a strong, consistent number ever since the end of 1995 (18 times in '97 alone).

The song is not considered a jamming tune due to its restricting structure, and because people seem to love it just the way it is. The only difference that has occurred since '93 is that the opening groove has gradually become a lot longer and a bit funkier. Some strong versions of "PYITE" include 12/8/94, 12/31/95, 12/13/97, and 12/30/97, but all versions are considered a tasty treat.

The Punk Meets The Godfather

Original Artist: The Who
Original Album: *Quadrophenia* (1973)
Vocals: Page
Debut: 10/31/95
Historian: Craig DeLucia

This song, an anthem of individuality and a story of the rebellious nature of the young, was performed during Phish's *Quadrophenia* "musical costume."

PURPLE HUGH (see: "THE INLAW JOSEY WALES")

Purple Rain

Original Artist: Prince and the New Revolution
Original Album: *Purple Rain* (1984)
Vocals: Fishman (lead), Page, Trey (backing)
Debut: 7/16/93
Historian: Martin Acaster

Purple Rain was the multimedia fortean event which made Prince a household name. Apparently Prince grew unhappy with his fame and fortune. Closer to the truth is the possibility that he wanted to disassociate himself with his record label (or perhaps the unholy flop of his second turn on the big screen (*Under a Cherry Moon*). Either way Prince renounced his crown through the release of a 1992 album enti-

tled with the enigmatic symbol with which The Artist now signs his checks (though he eventually reverted back to a pronounceable name at the close of of 1999.) No doubt seeking to fill the void on the throne left by the untimely disappearance of the Prince of Pop, Henrietta assumed the mantle during the 1993 summer tour.

From its first heartfelt rendering (7/16/93) at Darien Lakes Performing Arts Center until its seemingly final magical performance (8/6/96) at Red Rocks, "Purple Rain" was sure to bring a tear to the eye and a lighter to the hand of many a fan. In each performance Jon made the song his own, emotionally belting out the lyrics and usually substituting inspired vacuum solos for the Hendrixian licks of the original version.

Perhaps a coincidence, but most likely not, Phish hadn't performed the song since the Red Rocks run, the first time Phish became a household name, one which was unfortunately linked to fan rioting. In a not so obvious reference to the regrettable events in Morrison, CO, "Purple Rain" made its triumphant return to the stage (7/25/99) at Deer Creek. On cue, the attendees of Woodstock '99 in Rome, NY showed the world what it really means when fans riot.

Pusherman
Original Artist: Curtis Mayfield
Original Album: *Superfly* soundtrack (1972)
Vocals: performed instrumental
Debut: 11/1/91
Historian: Mark Toscano/Tim Wade

Pusherman by Curtis Mayfield was "played" about as much as "Hold Your Head Up" or "Cold as Ice" has been: instrumental, and only briefly. It was used as the outro for Fish after "Love You" on 11/1/91 for a very simple reason: while he hates the aforementioned '70s flashback radio staples, Fish likes "Pusherman." Always the recipient of his band-members' unending torment, they granted him a reprieve for this show as a gesture of goodwill. Interested fans may want to check out the classic black action film *Superfly* for a whole filmload of Mayfield's music, including this chart-topping hit.

P.Y.I.T.E. (see: "PUNCH ME IN THE EYE" AND "PUNCH YOU IN THE EYE")

Quadrophenia (album) (1973)
Original Artist: The Who
Historian: Craig DeLucia

In the minds of the popular public and average music listener, The Who's rock opera *Quadrophenia* has always played second fiddle to older brother *Tommy*. Phish at least managed to change the perception of their fans after an inspired Halloween performance of the former in 1995. Rumor has it that Phish asked, or considered asking Roger Daltrey to perform with them that night in Chicago. Regardless, The Who realized that performing *Quadrophenia* was a good idea and took it on the road themselves after Phish's cover was performed.

"Quadrophenia," as the story goes, is schizophrenia times two. The main character, Jimmy, has four "personalities," each represented by one of the four musicians in The Who (and, for one night in 1995, for each of the four musicians in Phish). Each personality has its own musical theme that resonates through the album.

What is the story about? Mark Brown once wrote in *Addicted to*

Noise magazine that "a young man has a bad day, basically, and that's really all there is. It's a series of events." The story couldn't get any simpler, and therein lies the beauty. It is an "everyman" tale of a "mod" rocker who has come to question the elements of his life. And when he is forced to question the very nature of being a "mod" himself, he has his own awakening.

Though the individual histories for each song contain more details, the basic story arc follows teenage Jimmy as he begins as an outcast in his parents' home and ends alone on a rock in the ocean. In between he questions his future, laments the loss of a love, and sees that his former heroes aren't what they claimed to be.

Quadrophenia did not provide us with lasting FM radio staples like *Tommy*, save the epic "Love, Reign O'er Me." Still, rockers like "Drowned," "5:15," and the anthemic "The Real Me" have stood the proverbial test of time while introspective numbers like "Sea and Sand" and "I'm One" provide shining moments of delicacy.

As a Halloween cover album, *Quadrophenia* allowed Page to shine on both vocals and piano. Unlike the "White Album" in 1994, *Quadrophenia* seemed much more directed—a story, rather than an album. Few songs have survived the evening and been resurrected on the Phish stage, though the aforementioned "Drowned" has become an oft-requested fan-favorite cover.

Quadrophenia
Original Artist: The Who
Original Album: *Quadrophenia* (1973)
Vocals: (instrumental)
Debut: 10/31/95
Historian: Craig DeLucia

All good musicals and rock operas interweave common themes throughout the course of the story. The title track to *Quadrophenia* does just this, as it highlights musical phrases from throughout the album and presents them for the listener to remember and refer to. "Quadrophenia" takes this common concept a step further, though, by tying the recurring themes to the title of the show.

Quadrophenia is so named because the narrator, Jimmy, is suffering from a sort of inner confusion that can only be compared to a multiple personality disorder. Jimmy is so bad off that he is not only schizophrenic (two personalities), he is quadrophrenic (with four). As such, there are four common musical themes that run throughout the show and are identified with each of the original members of The Who. Phish, as a quartet, easily adapted this concept to their performance and provided yet another reason for the band to cover this epic album.

Quadrophonic Toppling
Music: Phish
Album: *The Siket Disc*
Vocals: (instrumental)
Debut: 12/31/99
Historian: Mark Toscano

Bass and drums control this track, though not in the standard "B+D," late-'70s-Cadillac-on-hydraulics kind of way. This is a rather idyllic tune, minimalist in structure, and quite short. As the fifth track on *The Siket Disc*, it helps balance the insistent locomotion of "Fish Bass" with the noisy, loping eccentricity of "The Happy Whip and Dung Song." The

song made its debut at the now-legendary 12/31/99 show, complete with recorded samplings of a voice repeating the title as is done on the album version.

Quinn the Eskimo

AKA: "The Mighty Quinn,"
"The Mighty Quinn (Quinn the Eskimo)"
Original Artist: Bob Dylan
Original Album: *Self Portrait* (1970)
Phish Album: *Hampton Comes Alive* (11/20/98)
Vocals: Mike (lead), Page, Trey (backing)
Debut: 4/15/86
Historian: Jeremy David Goodwin

Is this song about a spiritual messiah of sorts, or just the ultimate hipster? Is there a difference? Even if Quinn is merely a drug dealer, he makes such an impression that, when he arrives, "everyone's gonna know." In fact, "everyone's gonna dose!" His presence is enough to drag everyone away from their routine of feeding pigeons and sleeping on everyone's toes. This can be seen as the story of an oppressed and listless people awaiting their salvation, or perhaps a group of bored acid freaks awaiting their connection. Either way, through Quinn's impending visit, they expect transcendence. (Sort of like the pre-show vibe at a Phish gig?) This fun and (perhaps) profound ballad originated in the legendary jam sessions that Bob Dylan and members of his touring group (later to dub themselves The Band) held in the basement of a rented house in Woodstock, NY.

For several months over the summer and early fall of 1968, the Bard and his cohorts maintained a semi-regular schedule of afternoon wine and hashish consumption, followed by a few hours of playing and (sometimes) recording, with a fairly low tech, gerry-rigged technical setup, which usually lacked drums.

Dylan was recuperating from a near-fatal motorcycle accident and attempting to withdraw from the crucible of public attention in which he had been baking for several years. This period provided the breather he needed to recover personally and artistically from the amphetamine-fueled tightrope psychedelia of his mid-'60s albums (culminating in the "wild mercury sound" of *Blonde on Blonde*). The musical output of these "basement tapes" featured a unique melding of influences (Appalachian folk, English balladry, the Sun sessions, and Ginsberg-via-Dalí surreal hedonism) mixed into an oddly familiar, yet drastically fanciful stew that is authentically American, and can only be called the Dylanesque.

Phish fans would do well to note that these basement sessions quickly passed into the hands of collectors, and contributed to the genesis of the modern bootleg industry. Some of the tracks finally saw the light of day with the release of *The Basement Tapes* on Columbia in 1974. This unfortunate compilation was overseen by Robbie Robertson, who inserted a disproportionate number of Band tunes, and went so far as to overdub onto some tracks. To this day, most of the sessions remain unreleased officially, though Dylanophiles can seek out the bootleg boxed set, *The Real Basement Tapes*.

As for Quinn, that mystic/socialite/acid head, his story surfaced on wax with the release of *Self Portrait* (the much maligned, genre-hopping two album set), which included a live version recorded at the Isle of Wight Festival. This obscure cut had less of a cultural impact than the

Manfred Mann version, which charted in the top ten after the group was floated a demo tape of the song shortly after the actual basement sessions. The original "studio" version finally appeared in 1985 on the first ever boxed set, *Biograph*.

Phish included this number in their early repertoire of covers, but it was long abandoned by the time they entered the "modern era" of the '90s. On 11/21/98, after an improbable flood of odd debuts and breakouts throughout the year had apparently trickled dry, the boys opened the floodgates once more for a celebratory exclamation mark: the return of "Quinn the Eskimo." The gap between performances is one of the longest ever of a song in Phish's repertoire. This first set kickdown sent a roar of appreciation through the Hampton Coliseum (as if everyone wasn't cranked up enough already), and some fans had an emotional moment when they realized that they had seen the Grateful Dead (aka The Warlocks) perform this song in the same room over ten years before.

Ramble On

Original Artist: Led Zeppelin
Original Album: *Led Zeppelin II* (1969)
Vocals: Page
Debut: 8/1/98
Historian: Martin Acaster

Ramble On, originally released in 1969, on Led Zeppelin's second album (*Led Zeppelin II*) provides some of the clearest evidence that one of guitar god Jimmy Page's songwriting influences has been J.R.R. Tolkien's *Lord of The Rings* trilogy. Undeniably, the lyrical references in "Ramble On" to Gollum and Mordor and the wanderings of the song's protagonist evoke images of Frodo and his time spent in Hobbiton.

With this in mind, the 8/1/98 Phish debut of "Ramble On" at Alpine Valley was not as big a surprise as it may have seemed. Why? Because this crowd pleasing, first set opening, brand new cover song appeared during the Summer 1998 "Ring of Fire" tour. So? Well, Narya, the Ring of Fire, namesake of the Phish Summer tour, was one of the three named rings of Tolkien's elven kings. Furthermore, the only subsequent Phish rendition of "Ramble On" to date (8/12/98 at Vernon Downs), came eleven days later after the band and its touring legion had rambled on by Syracuse, the boyhood home of Phish's de facto lord of Hobbiton Jon Fishman.

Rapper's Delight

Music/Lyrics: Bernard Edwards, Nile Rodgers
Original Artist: The Sugarhill Gang
Original Album: single (1979)
Vocals: Kid Rock, Fish
Debut: 9/29/00
Historian: Mark Toscano

Arguably the first multi-platinum hip hop song, "Rapper's Delight" is seen by many as the beginnings of what was then predicted by the industry to be a short-lived "fad" genre. Phish more or less performed the song with Kid Rock in Vegas on 9/29/00, with Fishman contributing a largely improvised verse on his knees about the Kid's firm member. (Don't ask….)

The Real Me

Original Artist: The Who
Original Album: *Quadrophenia* (1973)
Vocals: Trey
Debut: 10/31/95
Historian: Craig DeLucia

The first real song on *Quadrophenia*, "The Real Me" arises surreally from the sound of crashing waves in "I am the Sea." The song is sung by Jimmy, the confused narrator of this rock opera. Jimmy, in his quest for truth, turns to his parents, a preacher, and a doctor, but none of them can understand his frustration. The presence of horns adds another dimension to this rock anthem.

"The Real Me" is one of only three *Quadrophenia* songs to be played again after its triumphant Halloween debut. Its only other appearance to date, on 12/29/95, was inside an epic "Bathtub Gin" sandwich that is one of many highlights from the 1995 NYE Run.

Reba

Music/Lyrics: Trey Anastasio
Album: *Lawn Boy*
Vocals: Trey (lead), Mike, Page (backing)
Debut: 10/1/89
Historians: Grant Calof and Time Wade

Soaring into the sun-drenched sky, the wind rushes underneath as you glide higher into the atmosphere…slaloming around conical mountaintops bleached white with snow, chasing flocks of migrating geese in flight as you rise higher into a sky that turns a deeper ocean blue with every breath…even higher until it feels like you've drifted effortlessly past the gates of heaven…only then, to finally burst through a glistening cloud cover and fly into the eternally shining sunlight that cradles you on a trade-wind as you float peacefully back down to the Earth below…"Reba."

"Reba" is more than a simple song about a capitalistic moonshiner's odd relationship with a meat proprietor, nor is it your average, every day recipe for Grandma's organic bathtub gin…"Reba" is a feeling, a meditation, a state of mind. To many fans, "Reba" simply is Phish. The song's whimsical lyrics, unpredictable changes and soaring end-jam embody everything magical and alluring about the band's music. If music were a religion (to the rest of the world, that is), Phish would be the hippest church in town, and "Reba" (almost) everyone's favorite Sunday sermon.

"Reba's" mind-boggling four-part structure, written by one Ernest G. Anastasio in the late eighties, came as a direct result of time spent under the tutelage of his mentor, composer Ernie Stires. It's one of the most complex and challenging pieces in the band's repertoire, and it required several years of polish. Trey wrote it as an exercise in creating a cohesive piece of music, which never repeats itself and never develops. The result was a song with numerous time changes and breaks, presenting lighting director Chris Kuroda with one of his biggest challenges. The first section (after the bouncing introductory notes) features amusing sing-along lyrics, then ascends smoothly into an intricately composed instrumental section that glides up, down and across the scales like the Road-Runner chasing the Coyote across purple-stained desert highways in a Loony Tunes cartoon gone horribly wrong. It's the way the band plays over these changes, separately yet entirely together, shifting in and out of the eclectic structure that drives fans into a manic frenzy.

The disjointed lyrics of "Reba" relate the recipe for a mysterious concoction brewed up in a motel bathroom. The title character combines ingredients such as toxic waste, coconuts and hooves to create something we're told is sure to be "the finest in the nation." Interpretations of the lyrics in "Reba" abound. Some have speculated about a connection to the word "ryba," which means "fish" in some eastern European languages, while in Hebrew, it translates into the word "jam" (the kind of jam that goes well with toast). Others see "Reba" as part mad scientist, part entrepreneur while yet another view is of "Reba" as a playful, innocent little girl whose parents give her a little too much leash. After all, kids are born chefs—they're forever making mud-pies and other concoctions from whatever they can scrape up around the house, and little "Reba" is equally creative and noxious. As we know, "Reba" dips a ladle for a taste of her creation when she's done…and the rest of the composition could be seen as the consequence of that fateful sip. Her body begins to fail, and ultimately she dies. Happily, though, her spirit prevails, and the first notes of the jam begin a patient and slow resurrection leading up to a triumphant climax—"Reba" reborn. In any case, as with many (perhaps most) of Phish's songs, the meaning is ambiguous and highly subjective.

The final portion of the composition is one of the most difficult passages Phish performs. It features a melody which scales up and down at a frantic pace as Trey plays first in unison with Page, then chases along just slightly behind him, racing from one side of bliss to another. They tear their way through starts and stops, which ultimately coalesce into a smashing crescendo that launches into the ethereal, improvised jam where some fans claim to have "seen God." The jam builds and builds until the anticipation of that one note, that guiding light, finally shatters into existence. The fourth section, a wordless whistling of the first verse, wraps up neatly with a reprise of the chorus, then exits on a characteristically idiosyncratic note. And while many songs (as well as substances) can bring about epiphanies and inspiration, "Reba" is the one song that, whether it be through smiles or tears, always has the power to melt away any and all concerns.

When "Reba" made its first appearance in 1989, the song contained a now-defunct instrumental bridge between the lyric and composed sections, consisting of a bluesy riff and a longer "Bag it, tag it" chant. That same instrumental piece later evolved into "Don't Get me Wrong," with lyrics penned by the Marvin Hamlisch of Harmonica himself, John Popper. The song was only played three times in 1990, each time with Popper on stage (10/6/90, 10/8/90 and 12/28/90 if you want to hear all three). The jamming portion of the song (a prime example of the tension and release concept) remained relatively straightforward for the first few years of its existence, although in December of 1992 they twice sandwiched "I Walk the Line" by Johnny Cash between the end of the jam and the whistling section. The whistling jam, despite conflicting reports, has been a part of the tune since its debut. It wasn't until 1992 that the band chose instead to end the song after the improvised jam (11/30/92 being the date in question). Over the years though (increasingly from 1994 through 1996), the whistling reprise has become more sporadic and can sometimes wind up being sacrificed for the sake of segueing into another tune. The speed at which the first half of the

song is played also varies from time to time, ranging from slower, laid-back grooves to blistering streams of light and sound. The atmospheric jam too, has evolved to an even greater dimensional plane, and continues to mystify listeners new and old.

The next big leap for the song happened early in the winter of 1993. On February 20th, at the Roxy Theater in Atlanta, an unusually lively "Reba" helped to spark one of the most memorable sets in Phishstory (if you own it you cherish it and if you don't, you will when you hear it). The song essentially remained a type I jam until the first show of 1994 at the Flynn Theater in Burlington (4/4/94), which featured an unusual (although somewhat sloppy) version. The jam took interesting twists and turns throughout the year, especially as the summer tour wound down in July. Memorable versions from this period include 7/15 Jones Beach, 7/8 Great Woods, 7/6 Montreal, and 7/3 Old Orchard Beach, which included a "Somewhere Over the Rainbow" jam. October brought more magical moments. One more notable type II version appeared on the eighteenth in Nashville with a dark sounding jam on the Dead's "Eyes of the World." Another magnificent feast of "Reba"-like proportions happened during the first set of the Halloween show in Glen Falls, only hours before they turned the "White Album" into a rainbow of color.

But that doesn't necessarily mean the song is always played perfectly or that all ears find "Reba" to be aging like a fine Vermont wine. "Reba" is the one song that can boast even more flubs than "Guyute" and there are some nights where it simply doesn't click. In St. Louis on 8/16/93, the band performed a rare exploratory nineteen-minute version that strayed far off the beaten path, containing three distinct sections in the jam (enter at your own risk, brave listener). But more often than not, it's played near-flawlessly and with the white-hot passion of a thousand burning suns.

"Reba" usually pops up somewhere in the middle of either set, but makes once in a blue-moon appearances as the opening tune as well (seek out 7/22/92 and 7/6/00 for the last two times "Reba" jump-started the first set). Two other notable placements of the song occurred on 12/30/98 at Madison Square Garden when it closed the behemoth first set and on 9/21/99 at the Pima County Fairgrounds in Arizona when it was played as the first tune in a two-song encore. Before those two nights, "Reba" had not yet closed a set or shown up as an encore.... What's all the more intriguing about those two uniquely placed "Rebas," is that they were played at the request of the same lucky fan both times.

There are so many versions of "Reba" that are worthy of listening to, analyzing and consuming, that to list them all would take up another few pages. The consensus as to the best "Reba" of all time is credited to the Voter's Choice Benefit show in Lowell, Massachusetts on 5/16/95 (words cannot describe, just GET IT!). Some other "Rebas" that you shouldn't miss are 4/17/92 (at the Warfield), 2/20/93 (referenced above; check out the tease in the "Mike's Song" as well), 5/28/94 (without the whistle finale), 10/21/95 (people swear by it), 12/31/95 (botched composed section but an awe-inspiring jam), 8/14/96 (people were apparently sighted hovering above the field), 8/17/96 at the Clifford Ball (segueing directly into "Cars, Trucks, Buses"), 6/16/97 (containing a "Cities" jam which preceded the "Cities" breakout later in the show), 8/15/98 (Lemonwheel doesn't get much sweeter), 7/13/99 (when it provided an interesting transition into "Carini"), and of course on 1/1/00, when the boys played it flawlessly, despite already being

three to four hours into The Show (the song started at approximately 3:41 in the morning and lasted until about 3:56 AM).

Then during Jazzfest 2000, somewhere amidst the crawfish shells and Cajun spices, "Reba" (or a portion of it, anyway) poked its head up in the middle of the now legendary Oysterhead show...and she never knew what hit her. Listen if you dare, to the end of "Jerry was a Race Car Driver," when Les Claypool starts singing the bag it-tag it chorus (with a few improvised lyrics) and Trey, quite simply, goes sonic. It's downright chilling.

"Reba" also has the distinction of being a favorite name for tour-head puppies (along with "Tela," "Esther" and "Harpua").

Red Rooster
AKA: "Lil' Red Rooster," "The Little Red Rooster"
Music/Lyrics: Willie Dixon
Original Artist: Howlin' Wolf
Original Album: *The Rocking Chair Album* (Vogue 1962)
Vocals: Sydney Ellis
Debut: 2/25/97
Historian: Kazimierz O. Wrzeszczynski

This barnyard blues song written by Willie Dixon and made famous by Howlin' Wolf's amazing vocal rendition usually features a strong slide guitar whenever performed live. Phish's single performance of this song doesn't contain a slide guitar but features the strong lead vocals of Sydney Ellis, an American-born blues singer who lives in Germany and tours regularly throughout Europe with her group the Yes Mama Band. Phish and Sydney performed a standard blues rendering of "Red Rooster" highlighted also by a nice bluesy piano solo from Page.

RELAX (see: "FRANKIE SAYS")

Remain in Light (1980)
Original Artist: Talking Heads
Debut: 10/31/96
Historian: Mark Toscano

Talking Heads' fourth studio album was, for most fans, an unexpected choice for Phish's third Halloween "musical costume" extravaganza. However, the guys are great admirers of *Remain in Light*, considered by many to be Talking Heads' finest hour (or at least their finest 40-odd minutes). Home to the all-time classics "Crosseyed and Painless" and "Once in a Lifetime," the album is a treasure of rich textures, dense layers of percussion, and creative turns of both musical and lyrical phrasing. Talking Heads' unique approach to songwriting and playing offered Phish a different perspective on their performance of the album, as well as the development of their own music. The influence of learning and performing this album greatly affected Phish's performance and songwriting over the next year. Many would agree that it was an exciting change for the better.

So, on 10/31/96, with help from percussionist Karl Perazzo of Santana, and blowhards Dave "The Truth" Grippo on sax and Gary Gazaway on trumpet, flugelhorn, and trombone, the band pulled off a feat that even they weren't sure they could accomplish: they covered the *hell* out of *Remain in Light*.

Prior to the second set, the band had never successfully performed the album all the way through in rehearsals, and they were really nervous

about the show. Trey even stated in a later interview that he was even a little worried that they would "blow it." Whereas "The White Album" and *Quadrophenia* are more melodically driven with chords and tunes to be learned, *Remain in Light* relies so heavily on atmospheres, textures, layers of sounds, and subtle fills—hard-to-pin-down tricks and tropes that could foil Phish's attempt at a successful cover a lot easier than the previous two outings. As it turned out, there was no need to worry. The band's performance of *Remain in Light* was a blissful release of tension, and even Trey considers this set his favorite of the Halloween sets thus far.

The band opened the show with a wild first set featuring a "Sanity" opener, a "YEM" with a great vocal jam, and a hilarious "Colonel Forbin's Ascent" that introduced a monolithic, stone David Byrne and an evil Halloween Mockingbird who plucked out Colonel Forbin's eyes! Coming on for the second set, fans knew which album to expect, thanks to a hilarious and educational "Phishbill" handed out before the show. Dropping carefully into the first song, "Born Under Punches (The Heat Goes On)," and eventually finishing with a jaw-dropping, all-star "The Overload" closer, Phish & Co. gave the crowd one hell of an hour—one of Phish's finest hours, in fact.

In other news, "Crosseyed and Painless" became an occasional show-stopper over the course of the next year, most notably on the radio-broadcasted 11/2/96 show, where a twenty-minute "C+P" jam segued nicely into "Antelope." Teases of "C+P" even show up somewhat regularly in an occasional Phish jam.

When Phish covers an entire album for their Halloween show, fans always wonder what the original band thinks of the gesture, as well as the performance itself. Well, let it be known that Talking Heads bassist Tina Weymouth was very outspoken about Phish's 'tip-o'-the-hat.' She described their performance as "amazing," and "incredible," and "something that even [Talking Heads] never did!" And David Byrne? As of Spring 1999, he had a copy of the tape, but still hadn't gotten around to giving it a listen. You would think that he would have been reminded to check it out when Phish appeared on his PBS "Sessions" show earlier in the year.

Revival
Original Artist: The Allman Brothers Band
Original Album: *Idlewild South* (1970)
Vocals: Jeff (lead)
Debut: 10/30/85
Historian: Erik Swain

Allman Brothers Band guitarist Dickey Betts wrote "Revival" as a way to acknowledge and synergize the band's musical and cultural past and present. The lyrics ("People can you feel it…") and gospel-ish arrangement evoke both Southern spirituals and free-loving hippies. But most likely Phish played the song merely to showcase the twin-guitar attack of its first lineup. When second guitarist Jeff Holdsworth (who sings lead on Phish's version) departed the band, this song went with him. The only known circulating performance is 10/30/85, although a "Revival" jam was soundchecked on 2/25/90.

Revolution
Music/Lyrics: Phish
Album: (none)

Debut: 10/17/85
Historian: Mark Toscano

The inbred half-brother of "Anarchy," this tune is just as socially dysfunctional as its noisy sibling. Why? Because it's the exact same song—Fishman's balls-to-the-walls drumming propelling the machine gun fire of Trey's chords into the audience, surely leaving some casualties. However, instead of screaming "Anarchy!" over and over, the band screams—you guessed it—"Revolution!" This was played only once, on 10/17/85, following a rendition of the band's more familiar "Anarchy." Not even a joke song of its own, but rather a joke on a joke-song, the real revolution may have happened if Phish had subjected their regular audience to this one more than once. Who needs revolution when there's already widespread anarchy?

See Also: "Anarchy"

Revolution 1
Original Artist: The Beatles
Original Album: *The Beatles* (aka "The White Album") (1968)
Vocals: Trey (lead), Mike, Page (backing)
Debut: 10/31/94
Historian: Mark Toscano

One of The Beatles' most disseminated songs ("thanks" in part to Michael Jackson and some high-profile TV commercials), there are actually three versions of the original track: the slower "shoo-be-doo" album version, the faster, "shoo-be-doo"less single version, and a fast, "shoo-be-doo"-having version that turns up from time to time.

Well, Phish's version seems to be fourth one, as they play it faster than the album version, not as fast as the single version, yet including the aforementioned "shoo-be-doos." Whatever it was, they played it well and the crowd liked it fine.

Revolution 9
Original Artist: The Beatles
Original Album: *The Beatles* (aka "The White Album") (1968)
Vocals: Phish
Debut: 10/31/94
Historian: Mark Toscano

Phish closed their indescribable 10/31/94 second set in style, with nudity and bubbles. Following the outro "Brother, can you take me back?" refrain that trails "Cry Baby Cry," odd sounds and vocal effects began to emanate from the stage in the form of a somewhat raunchy aural stew. While the guys mimicked some of this Lennon/Ono track's more memorable tidbits ("Number nine, number nine…," "The situation… they are standing still!" and "Hold that line…! Block that kick…!" to name a few), the P.A. was playing some sound and music bites, including parts of Mike Gordon's "He Ent to the Bog," a track from the band's very own "White Album."

Fishman of course christened the track with some vacuum playing, but it was a dangling appliance of another sort that got the most attention that night. After performing one of the original track's signature lines, "If you become naked," Fish proceeded to, well, become naked. Pulling his dress over his head, he shocked and discombobulated the audience and his bandmates by prancing about the stage in his (so you say it's your) birthday suit. As Mike looked about as mortified as a human being can possibly get, the rest of the band mustered up enough

Reba

Compiled by Tim Wade (and appended in part by charlz franz)
(second timing represents the time after the end of the "whistling" segment)

Date	Timings	Notes
10/31/89	12:09/13:51	First of four Halloween Rebas. Still had the extra "Bag it, Tag it" section in the middle (and whistling ending).
04/17/92	11:54/13:31	Great interplay between all four guys, and a strong finish, too.
12/05/92	—	"I Walk the Line" sandwiched between the jam and the whistling.
02/20/93	11:42/13:36	A little crazy, but nothing out of the ordinary for this set. Trey teases the Woody Woodpecker theme.
03/22/93	13:23/15:09	Some beautiful, quiet work for an attentive audience. Hot ending. Some Reba whistling in the beginning of Maze.
08/16/93	16:48/18:46	A magnificent, three-part improvisational journey.
12/31/93	11:22/13:16	Some very delicate work in this one—very pretty.
04/04/94	11:20/13:11	Cool, somewhat crazy moments amidst some mistakes, but still fun. Trey plays with an eerie violin-like sound; very cool.
05/28/94	12:07	A darker-sounding Reba. A great version.
06/19/94	12:10/13:44	Melodic, charming jam with a hypnotic, swirling groove.
07/03/94	13:10/14:43	With a good minute or so of "Somewhere Over the Rainbow."
07/06/94	14:11/16:19	An incredible groove, fantastic jamming. A Classic.
07/08/94	12:03	A little taste of Manteca in this one. Neat groove.
10/18/94	14:30/16:24	Some rare morphing into a spacy groove, similar to the Dead's "Eyes of the World." Trey teases DEG.
10/31/94	14:15/15:58	Excellent jam with thick grooves and beautiful melodies.
11/25/94	12:11/13:59	Pretty and powerful, with some big punches thrown in.

Date	Timings	Notes
12/08/94	15:51/17:29	Mesmerizing, lengthy, quiet jamming, though the end falls flat.
05/16/95	14:45	Middle section of the jam is hypnotic and enchanting. Mysterious!
06/19/95	14:49/16:34	A great groove in the middle reminiscent of 5/28/94 Laguna Seca.
06/23/95	14:21	Funky and hot! Syncopated fun and a great ending.
10/14/95	14:57	Jamming similar to 12/8/94 Spreckles, but with a better finish.
10/21/95	13:59	A wonderful, rolling groove that picks you up and floats you. along.
10/25/95	16:23	Power jam with a HUGE ending. Trey goes over the edge.
11/29/95	13:45/15:07	A warp speed Reba with a get-you-on-your-feet finish.
12/07/95	14:36	Fast, furious, and a little sloppy at times. The ending toms come at 14:04, but Trey sustains through them and drags out the ending for another minute.
12/31/95	14:24	Very hot; builds up to a wild finish. Good recovery from a sloppy intro. botched composed section.
08/14/96	14:16	Extremely powerful jam. Handle with care.
08/17/96	16:00	One of the most gorgeous versions.
02/21/97	13:40	Another rarity, as the jam quiets and fades out into Waste.
08/09/97	15:15	Shades of the 'Ball version in this one. Unhurried.
10/15/98	18:25	Long and experimental.
10/29/98	20:38	Strays from the standard Reba fare into something completely different.
12/31/99	15:20/16:58	Long and mellifluous.
07/06/00	17:15/19:27	Gorgeous. One of the finest versions in years

concentration to blow bubbles for the audience, who responded loudly to them and Fishman in appreciation and sheer terror, respectively. Those interested in getting an idea of what this was like may want to consult the image of naked Fishman in the booklet for *A Live One*, which at least spares fans unnecessary distress by having the "offending material" (in Trey's words) blocked out by a conveniently placed letter "H."

Revolution's Over

Original Artist: The Dude of Life (with Phish)
Original Album: *Crimes of the Mind* **(1994)**
Vocals: The Dude of Life
Debut: 9/13/90

Historian: Dan Mielcarz

Like in many of his songs, The Dude of Life takes on materialism in his quick rocker "Revolution's Over." Played live only once, at The Wetlands Preserve on 9/13/90, "Revolution's Over" can also be found on *Crimes of the Mind*, The Dude's debut album.

Rhinoceros

Original Artist: Smashing Pumpkins
Original Album: *Gish* **(1991)**
Vocals: Trey
Debut: 8/3/98
Historian: Mark Toscano

"Reba & Me"

Daniel Nooter, New York, NY

As much as I love Phish, I find that I don't really *identify* with many of their songs. I mean, *Stash* or *NICU* are great songs, but they don't make me think, "yes, I've certainly been there"—and I find this to be the case with most Phish songs.

Yet I've always identified strongly with *Reba*. I mean, this is precisely how I passed the long afternoons of my childhood: mixing together everything in the house—some of it edible but most of it toxic, believing that I was going to be famous for my creation. Didn't everyone do this as a kid? It couldn't have been just Reba and me.

And this wasn't just a phase, either. I can think of these "experiments" of mine lasting all through childhood. In fact, I went through separate fads *within* my Reba-ness. There was the "punch phase," for example, when I decided that I was going to find fame making different varieties of punch. I remember this so distinctly: all these multicolored samples of my various "flavors" permeating the refrigerator. (Mmmmm…camphor punch….) In summer camp one year, I managed to create a concoction that tasted vaguely reminiscent of Tootsie Rolls. (Amazingly, I even got people to try it—and they agreed that my beverage indeed had a certain Tootsie Roll-ish quality.) Alas, the recipe has been lost to time. But that's okay: working from a recipe misses the whole point of Reba-ness—the spontaneous creative impulse that transcends restraint…and taste.

Reba stays with me to this day. It's tempered somewhat by what I begrudgingly acknowledge as maturity, but it still rears its strange and wonderful head from time to time. There are, for example, my "Reba Cookies," made by combining whatever's in the house (my last batch was truly excellent, by the way, if I do say so myself); there's my utter inability to work from a recipe, or even to measure ingredients (I was a terror in my high-school chemistry lab, as you can probably imagine); there's my constant sense of wonder, as I walk into my kitchen, of what I can create—from the annals (or anals) of gastronomy—that will indeed be "the finest in the nation."

Reba, in her own magical way, is a visionary. Whatever we may think of her culinary dispositions, we feel compelled to revel in her sense of wonder and hope. Reba is the part in each of us that refuses to be bound by conventionality—by the standards others set for us or that we set for ourselves. Hers is not rebelliousness for the sake of rebelliousness, and it is only partially rebelliousness for the sake of art. To me, Reba represents the carefree poetry of creation that cannot (and will not) be bound or repressed. And it is that uninhibited innocence which transcends the mundane and so endears Reba (and the band that sings of her) to all of us. Or at least to me.

The golden tones of this Smashing Pumpkins song crackle over a set of speakers like a waking dream, and Phish somehow captured these qualities quite well in their performance of the tune on 8/3/98. This song also produced an interesting reaction at its debut. The portion of the crowd that was familiar with the Pumpkins' early, minor, alterna-rock hit cheered, and the rest of the crowd asked the portion of the crowd that had just cheered what the hell song it was. (A similar effect greeted the debut of Ween's "Roses Are Free.")

Ride Captain Ride
AKA: "Mystery Ship"
Original Artist: Blues Image
Original Album: *Open* (1970)
Vocals: Page (lead), Mike, Trey (backing)
Debut: 3/23/87
Historian: Ellis Godard

An ongoing rarity with an elusive name, "Ride Captain Ride" is a perennial favorite. Its first four appearances marked important turns in Phish's voyage, calling fans "to ride along to another shore… and be free once more." The song boarded Phish's repertoire during the first known show at Nectar's proper (downstairs, rather than the upstairs which is now the Metronome), segueing neatly into the similarly elusive "Dave's Energy Guide." It embarked again eighteen months later (9/13/88, which featured two "Energy Guides" and the first vacuum solo) as the band outgrew Sam's Tavern and prepared for its first ex-

pansive northeast tour. Its third sighting, and the one most known to fans, came during the exploratory Ian's Farm show (5/28/89), and its fourth (4/14/90) during the band's second jaunt to Colorado.

From there, this history becomes personal. In late 1992, I sent Page a letter espousing the strengths of the tune. Originally recorded by Tampa band Blues Image, who took it to number four in 1970, "Ride Captain Ride" is an upbeat blues number about departure towards joy. Penned by Mike Pinera, who also played with Iron Butterfly and penned "In-A-Gadda-Da-Vida," it captures what I then saw as the spirit of Phish, with (taboot) a bluesy bridge for Trey's guitar and some exuberant twists for Page's voice. I must have been persuasive, as the tune was performed twice in the next month—opening the encores of 12/12/92 and 12/30/92—but I was too busy with school and all, and missed both. Over the next six years, I became a bit bitter as I hoped for a comeback but not one came at all. And I felt teased by the song's re-emergence 8/3/98, 11/8/98, and 12/10/99, all of which I also missed. Now, the tune's likely sailed off into history. But anytime there's a lull on stage, a moment of indecision about what to play next, I hold out a bit of hope that I'll finally catch the mystery ship.

Rift
Music: Trey Anastasio
Lyrics: Tom Marshall
Album: *Rift; Hampton Comes Alive* (11/20/98)
Debut: 2/25/90 (original version), 3/6/92 (current version)
Historian: Craig DeLucia

Rift is a perfect example of how some songs take years to develop. In fact, nearly five years elapsed between the time that pieces of "Rift" first appeared and when the song was finished and finally unveiled in March of 1992.

The song's evolution began with an instrumental segment that the band had been playing as part of "The Curtain." In the late eighties, the band dropped this ending and it was thought to be gone forever. Then, in early 1990, the band debuted a new original song called "Rift." The song included lyrics almost identical to those of today. In fact, only one line was dropped, though it still appears in the liner notes of the *Rift* album. Musically, though, the song seemed to be lacking any emotion.

Still in its embryonic phase, "Rift" appeared five more times between February and May of 1990 and was recorded during the Wendell Studios sessions in June of the same year, but was nowhere to be found when the fall tour rolled around. Later, the band decided to fuse the lyrics Tom Marshall had written with, among other themes, the music once appended to "The Curtain." The idea clicked, and "Rift" was finally born during the Spring, 1992, tour opener in Portsmouth.

"Rift" is one of the most complex short songs in Phish's repertoire. It certainly requires much more concentration and dedication than similar-length songs like "Sparkle" and "Sample," as it features a difficult rhythm pattern and extended interplay between guitar and piano. From a lyrical standpoint, the song (and lead track) sets the theme for the album of the same name. The narrator speaks of a rift that has developed in a relationship. To demonstrate the confusion the narrator feels, Trey and Page share lead vocals, trading line for line as the music builds to a frenzy. Because of the raw passion the song generates, it is usually played in the middle of the first set as a musical pick-me-up.

Early in its lifetime, "Rift" quickly became one of the most frequently played songs in Phishtory. The band began playing the song less often in 1996 and scaled back considerably in 1997, 1998, and 1999, playing the song one, four, and three times, respectively. This has allowed fans to better appreciate the song.

As a non-jamming song, most versions of "Rift" are fairly similar. Credit should be given to the 10/29/94 "Rift," as the band moved smoothly into the song from "Makisupa Policeman" after already winding through "Split Open and Melt" and the rare "Buffalo Bill." Serious fanatics will want to hear the "Bathtub Gin" from Atlanta's Fox Theatre on 11/9/95, which included serious "Rift" teases.

Not all versions of the song have gone smoothly, though. When the band started the second set at Landover on 11/22/95 with "Rift," Trey called the song off after Fishman flubbed the drum beat. On a humorous note, fans were angered when the arena P.A. system failed during the "Rift" in Worcester on 12/28/95, and were subsequently joyous when the sound properly returned. This led to quite a laugh when Page sang about the "silence contagious in moments like these." And, finally, few can forget the exuberance Trey showed during "Rift" on 8/6/96. Playing at the famous (and fan-favorite) venue Red Rocks, Trey mimicked the line that Bono of the band U2 made famous in the same venue nearly 15 years earlier and that Trey himself recreated on the *Junta* version of "Icculus": "This is Red Rocks! This is the Edge!"

See Also: "The Curtain"

Riker's Mailbox
Album: *Hoist*

Debut: (never performed live)
Historian: Mark Toscano

Possibly one of Phish's strangest studio tracks, this one was greeted with the same initial confusion as were tracks like "Manteca," "Lengthwise," and "Montana" when their respective albums came out. But most mysteries get cleared up eventually, especially with as rabidly fact-craving a fanbase as ours.

Hoist producer Paul Fox apparently lived next door to Jonathan Frakes, best known for his role as Commander Riker on "Star Trek: The Next Generation." Well, Frakes's mailbox was quite unusually decorated, and the subject of some discussion during the *Hoist* sessions. So we know where the song's title comes from.

The song itself is a different story. Sounding vaguely like a more upbeat Naked City or an Albert Ayler track on fast forward, it's a menagerie of trombone bursts, backward yelling, manic banjo, disturbed by various studio effects, creating a sound like an entire barnyard in a blender. Clocking in only at around half a minute, it turns out that the song's origins are quite unlikely. During Fall 1993, while the album was being recorded, the song "Buffalo Bill" was on extended hiatus, but not forgotten. Though it hadn't been played in public since its 11/21/92 debut, a bizarre version of the song was recorded for *Hoist*. Realizing that the fun but absurd song conflicted with the album's more sober hue, it was decided to leave the track off. Enter "Riker's Mailbox." A brief snippet of the recorded "Buffalo Bill" is what you hear beneath and alongside all that other madness when your copy of *Hoist* reaches track four. The shouting can even be deciphered as something like "Olaffub," proving the seemingly far-fetched story true. And the trom-

Peter Sitzman

bone: is it Fishman? No, on the contrary. It is Commander Riker himself, Jonathan Frakes, who sat in on part of the recording sessions.

See Also: "Buffalo Bill"

Roadhouse Blues

Music: The Doors
Lyrics: Jim Morrison
Original Artist: The Doors
Original Album: *Morrison Hotel* (1970)
Vocals: Trey (?)
Debut: 12/2/83
Historian: Mark Toscano

Along with The Who's "Squeeze Box," "Roadhouse Blues" is a song that only recently was discovered to have been covered by Phish at their first-ever performance on 12/2/83 (under the name "Blackwood Convention"). Jeff, Trey, Mike, and Fish ran through this Doors cover to close the first set (aside from some Happy Birthday wishes) of the cafeteria performance. While covers of Motown and '70s rock songs may please a college audience now, most 1983 college audiences wanted nothing of the sort. Following the set, it wasn't Little Feat or the Dead that drifted out of the P.A., but Michael Jackson. And, as many fans know, the band's playing was eventually drowned out a bit into their second set (during Hendrix's "Fire"!!) by The Gloved One's then-hit album, *Thriller*. A recording of this show does exist, but it does not circulate.

Roadrunner

Music/Lyrics: Jonathan Richman
Original Album: *Modern Lovers* (Recorded 1971, Released 1976)
Vocals: Trey
Debut: 9/11/00
Historian: Phil Nazzaro

Phish opened their September 2000 stand at the Tweeter Center with this revved-up ode to driving fast with the radio on loud. Presumably it was chosen both for its deep history, and "I'm in love with Massachusetts" lyrics.

"Roadrunner" is significant because it was the first song on the first album by what is widely considered the first punk recording in history. The brains behind the operation was Jonathan Richman (of *There's Something About Mary* fame). He wrote all the songs, sang in his deep nasal tone, and played guitar. Also of note was Jerry Harrison (of Talking Heads fame) on keys and John Cale (of Velvet Underground) doing the production duties. For more from their first album, check out the soundtrack to *Repo Man*. Sadly, most of the other Modern Lovers albums are either hard to find, or out of print.

The Rock

Original Artist: The Who
Original Album: *Quadrophenia* (1973)
Vocals: (instrumental)
Debut: 10/31/95
Historian: Craig DeLucia

The Who's original rendition of this instrumental piece served to tie the musical themes of the album together and bridge into the rock

opera's triumphant ending. Phish's lone rendition of this instrumental piece has it all: Page's repetitive play on the "Love Reign O'er Me" theme, Fishman's Keith Moon-esque fills, Trey's subtle guitar tones, Mike's rumble on bass, and the power of the horns, which deliver the awakening that the story's narrator hears and heeds. A challenging compositional piece, Phish managed to play the song near-flawlessly and provide the final plateau before the set's finale.

Rock-A-William

AKA: "Rocko William"
Music: Phish
Lyrics: Jon Fishman
Album: (none)
Vocals: Fish (lead), Mike, Page, Trey (backing)
Debut: 2/13/97
Historian: charlz franz

Rock-A-William features the inimitable Jon Fishman on guitar and lead vocals, Mike on piano, Trey on drums, and Page on bass. Sadly, it has made just five appearances, all in 1997.

"Rock-A-William" is a dark but comic song, purportedly based on a true story of a "very strange man" the band met in Colorado in 1988 while spending the night in a purple house and partaking of Bloody Marys and turkey ham. "A loner just like Malachi from *Children of the Corn*," William lives in a cabin in the hills and has purportedly hit a bear on the nose with a hammer. He appears at the purple house with a hammer in hand, where his sister is upstairs with Timber Ho. William grabs him by the hair while his sister screams, but the others—remembering the bear—fear to intervene. "We didn't want to die!" The song ends inconclusively, with the hammer "held high," before it dissolves into Fishman's inspired guitar renderings and Mike's piano outro. Check the 2/26/97 Stuttgart outing for a particularly good version.

Rock and Roll

Original Artist: The Velvet Underground
Original Album: *Loaded* (1970)
Vocals: Page (lead), Fish, Mike, Trey (backing)
Debut: 10/31/98
Historian: Mark Toscano

Ah, yes, "Rock and Roll." What can one say? Each time Phish covers an album for Halloween, at least one song ends up getting a decent amount of mileage following the show. The 1994 "White Album" set fostered a few, but "Cry Baby Cry" and "While My Guitar Gently Weeps" got the most play over the next few years. 1995's "Drowned" from *Quadrophenia* became the anthemic Phish cover from that album. In 1996, "Crosseyed and Painless" was, not surprisingly, the candidate voted most likely to succeed, and the band subsequently played many a slick version of this tune. Then we come to 1998. The song Phish ran madly with after their cover of Velvet Underground's *Loaded* in Vegas was the aptly named "Rock and Roll."

Trey tells a great story about running into Lou Reed at one of Phish's European shows. Upon Trey's departure, Reed gave him encouragement about the show that night and reminded him that "we invented" rock and roll. The twist comes when Trey realized he didn't know if Reed meant "we" as in "Americans" or "Velvet Underground."

Well, they may not have "officially invented" rock and roll, but the Velvets sure as hell re-invented it. Their first album is still mind-blowing today, and, put in its 1966 context, is a swift kick in the face no matter who you are. As if to occasionally remind themselves of what the Velvets injected into rock and roll, Phish injected "Rock and Roll" into the setlists of several shows since its first performance in Vegas (e.g. 7/8/00). A few of these appearances have been encores (7/12/99, 10/4/99, 12/3/99); Phish used the tune as a sort of exclamation point at the end of each of those shows, making their message clear: "Yes, that's right, we play rock and roll!" This statement is taken to an extreme with the epic 12/31/99 version, a half-hour opus that included spine-chilling "After Midnight" tease. "Rock and Roll" continued to make more appearances in 2000, including jump-starting a nice second set segue-fest on 9/17/00.

Fans who want to compare Phish renditions with one of the Velvets' own may want to pick up a copy of the latter's *Live 1969* double album, which features a live take on this tune, as well as some other *Loaded* tracks.

Rock and Roll All Nite

Original Artist: Kiss
Original Album: *Dressed to Kill* **(1975)**
Vocals: Phish and "Gene Simmons"
Debut: 2/20/93
Historian: Ellis Godard

Phish performed Kiss' lynchpin anthem only once, during the legendary 2/20/93 second set at the Roxy. The song requires tuning the guitar down a half step—and the song's performance was a step down from the rest of the set. During the "Weekapaug" weirdness, an impressive (though not impeccable) Gene Simmons impersonator appeared in the audience, near the stage and in front of Page. As soon as Mike and Page started laying down the rhythm, Trey pulled the visitor onstage for a rousing, though brief, rendition. It was a bit of comic relief, a theatrical pause in a rollercoaster setlist. Very '70s.

Rock and Roll Part Two

Original Artist: Gary Glitter
Original Album: *Glitter* **(1972)**
Phish Album: *Hampton Comes Alive* **(11/20/98)**
Vocals: (instrumental)
Debut: 11/20/98
Historian: Mark Toscano

Gary Glitter's radio mega-hit is one of the ultimate audience-participation songs in rock history, and it was only a matter of time before Phish decided to capitalize on its interactive possibilities. The tune was performed as a show opener on 11/20/98 at the Hampton Coliseum, and the crowd was ever so happy to offer up some "Heys" in the appropriate places, completing the call and response requirements of the song. Though this audience factor is not very audible on the *Hampton Comes Alive* recording of the song, audio tapes reveal the tens of thousands of fans' contributions in all their Pavlovian glory.

Rocky Mountain Way

Original Artist: Joe Walsh

Original Album: *The Smoker You Drink, the Player You Get.* **(1973)**
Vocals: Trey (lead), Page (backing) (7/23/97)
Debut: 7/23/97
Historian: Mark Toscano

Phish has teased this bongrock Joe Walsh hit a few times, most notably on 7/23/97 at the tail end of one of the craziest "YEMs" ever. For that performance, the band actually played a full verse and chorus of the rock anthem before sliding into "Chalkdust," which itself contained a few more teases from Trey. Other teases of the song showed up in the 2/16/91 and 5/17/92 "Possums" and the 12/7/97 "Jesus Just Left Chicago."

Rocky Raccoon

Original Artist: The Beatles
Original Album: *The Beatles* **(aka "The White Album") (1968)**
Vocals: Trey (lead), Mike, Page (backing)
Debut: 10/31/94
Historian: Mark Toscano

The sad, sad story of Rocky Raccoon and his failed attempt to win back a wayward girlfriend was told during set II of Phish's 1994 Halloween "White Album" performance. Although Trey played the tune on his electric guitar (the original was on an acoustic), it was more or less faithful to the original, with one exception. What at first seems like a gender-agreement problem with Trey's pronouns ("…but everyone knew *him* as Nancy") is actually a clever reference to an old Phish friend, Richard "Nancy" Wright. Who is Nancy, you may ask? *He* is the creative soul that penned "I Didn't Know" and "Halley's Comet," two songs that he generously allowed Phish to perform at their concerts.

Rocky Top

Original Artist: Boudleaux & Felice Bryant
Vocals: Mike (lead), Page, Trey (backing)
Debut: 9/21/87
Historian: Grant Calof

Guaranteed to shoot bliss-filled bolts of energy through Hatfields as well as McCoys, Rocky Top has always been a "kick up your heels at the hoe-down" shotgun blast of country music. When Phish debuted the song during the fall of 1987, its lightning quick, blistering pace provided the perfect showcase for the band to push the envelope of yet another, less obvious musical arena—country. And after four singing cowboys from Vermont had their way with this country music classic, it was never to be the same again.

With no real formula for success in the music "business," most bands commit their careers to playing and perfecting just one style of music. But Phish isn't like other bands. Rather than play one type of music, they play every type of music. And they don't just play it, they redefine, reinvent and repackage it; they own it. Phish is able to shift in and out of styles (let alone songs) so effortlessly, that to the uninitiated eye, it almost looks easy. It's not surprising to hear straight-ahead rock and roll, lighter than air ballads, earth-shaking hard-core, a country tune and a couple of funk filled grooves, all in one set. What makes it all the more incredible, and one of the main reasons people trek across the globe to see Phish again and again, is that it's never the same show twice.

Like "Sample" and "Bouncing," the arrangement of "Rocky Top"

has remained the same over the years and it's for this reason that the song is both loved and loathed by fans. The only aspect of "Rocky Top" that ever really changes is the speed at which it's played ridiculously fast or obscenely fast (check out the "Rocky Top" from the Great Went 8/16/97).

The song was originally penned by Bordleaux and Felice Bryant, and reflects on the good old-fashioned simple life of real-life destination, Rocky Top, Tennessee. It also happens to be the "Fight Song" for the University of Tennessee, but any fan from Tennessee will tell you it's really just a thinly veiled homage to Phish. When it was first played, "Rocky Top" could show up at any given time during either set. But after showing up thirty five times in 1991, "Rocky Top" was played fewer times each year and began to appear almost exclusively as an encore.

Another version to explore comes from the 7/20/91 show, where "Rocky Top" had the added bonus of the Giant Country Horns. Some other "Rocky Tops" that are sure to make you feel like you've been soaking in moonshine are 6/16/90 from Townsend Park, 3/26/93 from the Warfield, 5/29/94 from Laguna Seca Daze as part of a five song double encore, 11/14/95 after the monster second set "Stash," and as a first set closer on 9/18/99 in Chula Vista, California.

Roggae

AKA: "Roget"
Music/Lyrics: Phish, Tom Marshall
Album: *Story of the Ghost; Hampton Comes Alive* (11/20/98)
Vocals: Phish
Debut: 6/30/98
Historian: Mike Preston

Throughout the years that we have had this band, we have been fortunate enough to see many different sides of them. Many would say that the reason a Phish show is so magical is partially due to the wide variety of emotions experienced by everyone in the room.

One of the things Phish has given us with their more recent material is their ability to appear vulnerable, intimate, and even more personal. While most of their lyrics are still straight from the heart of Tom Marshall, both the music and words continue to speak for each other as eloquently as they ever have.

"Roggae" is a ballad of personal reflection. When it debuted in Copenhagen on 6/30/98 (a very intimate setting), it was clear from the start that whatever the song is about, many can relate. Once again, Mr. Anastasio had composed a score so parallel to the poet's feelings, that even the Danish natives in the crowd must have known exactly what the song is all about.

At a show, there are few "leg-resters" that can unwind a crowd like "Roggae." Each line of the first verse is sung by a separate, individual voice. This is yet another example of how much of a well-oiled music machine Phish has always been. The masterfully harmonized chorus echoes itself gorgeously the second time around, which takes us into the jam. This fluid section, mostly a gentle dance around D major, peaks when it is at its quietest moment. At this point, Trey plays a little riff which triggers three monstrous power chords. Thesis is then restated and the song is over. A true gem.

Since the debut of "Roggae," it has not had a period of dormancy. Not many people have voiced concerns regarding that. Although this tune does not vary that much from song to song, some notable versions are: 6/30/98 (following a mammoth "Stash" -> "Cities"), 8/9/98, 12/30/98 and 7/17/99.

Roll in My Sweet Baby's Arms

AKA: "Sweet Baby's Arms"; "Rollin' in My Sweet Baby's Arms"
Music/Lyrics: traditional
Vocals: "Reverend" Jeff Mosier (lead)
Debut: 11/18/94
Historian: Jeremy Welsh

The traditional song "Roll in My Sweet Baby's Arms" has been performed by artists as varied as Bill Monroe, Leon Russell, Willie Nelson, Del McCoury, and Jerry Lee Lewis. Phish decided to add their name to the list on 11/18/94. "Reverend" Jeff Mosier had joined the tour two nights before, sitting in with Phish for a few bluegrass songs each evening. Phish was using the opportunity to debut a number of traditional bluegrass songs, and "Roll in My Sweet Baby's Arms" was brought out as the first song of a two-song encore that evening (Mosier played banjo on both "Sweet Baby" and "Runaway Jim"). "Roll in My Sweet Baby's Arms" was also played the following evening, 11/19/94, during the impromptu parking lot jam outside the Indiana University Auditorium in Bloomington.

Roses are Free

Original Artist: Ween
Original Album: *Chocolate and Cheese* (1994)
Phish Album: *Hampton Comes Alive* (11/20/98)
Vocals: Phish
Debut: 12/11/97
Historian: Mark Toscano and Tim Wade

Phish interpreted this typically bizarre Ween song well, retaining much of the feel of the original while adapting it well to their sound. Like XTC's "Melt the Guns," this song was thought by many to be an unusual choice for a cover by the band. However, after its premiere on the Fall 1997 tour, Phish found some good use for the tune, most notably in the 27-minute version on 4/3/98 which featured a phenomenal jam of subtlety and mutliple layers. Combine that one with the now-classic 12/31/99 version (another epic), and your collection is nearly complete. Just pick up the 12/11/97 debut, segueing out of a kick-ass "Drowned" jam, and round it all out with 12/31/97, appearing in the middle of a Mike's Groove sandwich.

In an amusing side note, at Ween's 8/4/99 Seattle concert, Gener introduced their own "Roses" by mentioning Phish's covering of the tune, and that they started playing it again recently in order to "reclaim it." Incidentally, live Ween is highly recommended, especially if they get really drunk.

Run Like An Antelope

AKA: "Antelope"
Music: Trey Anastasio
Lyrics: Tom Marshall, The Dude of Life
Album: "The White Tape"; *Lawn Boy*
Vocals: Trey (lead), Mike, Page (backing)
Debut: 5/3/85

Historian: charlz franz

Imagine a young boy who once worked with his mother developing stories and songs of fantasy and fun. Imagine that boy in high school, playing in a garage band, studying the stylings of the masters of rock, teaching himself guitar, and writing ever more inventive music. Imagine that boy putting together a rock band in college with others similarly serious about their craft. Imagine that band puffing a big fattie and themselves imagining a young buck antelope as they ease into a tune. Imagine with them as the antelope begins a leisurely stroll across a plain of fragrant grasses, bright morning sunlight warming the air around him, insects buzzing lazily in the background. doo do doo do doobie doobie doo do

Suddenly, a fly bites him on the ass and he's off! Bounding through the grasses, his well-muscled haunches tensing and relaxing, tensing and relaxing, faster and faster. After awhile, the initial impetus for flight is forgotten as he revels in his speed and agility. Hooves pound on resilient earth, his heart thumps deep inside, his coat gleams from his mighty exertions on this most magnificent of days. Twisting and turning for the sheer joy of being able to do it. Free of all distractions and, almost, the bonds of gravity. Twisting and turning, tensing and relaxing, faster and faster and faster. Out of control.

And then he falls off a cliff.

That's kind of how "Run Like an Antelope" starts. The antelope bounces back to life, however, as Mike's bass line picks him up (listen to 6/11/94 for instance) and the band carries him off, advising us all to run like an antelope, over and over and over. That's kind of how "Antelope" ends.

Trey Anastasio did actually write stories and songs with his mom, and did teach himself guitar while playing in a high school band. That band, Space Antelope, eventually wrote a tune called "Run Like a Space Antelope." "Run Like an Antelope," with lyrics contributed by Steve Pollak (the Dude of Life) and Tom Marshall, first appeared on a demo tape called *Jaun*, which Trey made in his basement shortly after Phish formed. The studio version of "Antelope" on *Lawn Boy* (recorded in 1988) does start with the sounds of much huffing in the background. For the rest, you'll have to use your imagination.

As one of the oldest standards in the Phish repertoire, "Run Like an Antelope" has seen significant development and variations. The opening section of early versions from 1985 seem fast-paced, without the series of peaks building to the ultimate climax of later years, the transition to "rye, rye, rocco" seems abrupt, while the ending is short and far less structured. By 1988 and *Lawn Boy*, however, the tension and release leading to climax pattern is well established. The "Rye, rye, rocco. Marco Esquandolas. Been you to have any spike, man?" verse is pretty consistent—changed from the earlier "Happen to have any spliff, man"—and the "Set the gearshift for the high gear of your soul. You've got to run like an antelope: out of control." lines are exclaimed rather than intoned. The ending, where "You've got to run like an antelope: out of control" is repeated, is one of the best examples of the influence Lou Reed and Velvet Underground has had on Phish.

Since then, "Antelope" often has been a vehicle for ferocious jamming and stage antics. The "rye, rye, rocco" line has had many impromptu variations by Trey. The clear peaks of the first section have become less distinct in recent years, however, as Trey has used more effects-ladened builds to create more textures of sound in the run to cli-

max. It remains one of the most consistently satisfying of all Phish songs and is greeted with enthusiasm everytime that antelope's hooves start their delicate dance. "Set the gearshift for the high gear of your soul," indeed.

There are almost too many great versions of "Antelope" for a short list to do justice to the range of what is available. Fans definitely should pull out *Lawn Boy* for another listen. For live versions, check 3/22/91 Steamboat Springs, CO; 3/13/92 Providence, RI; 8/14/93 Tinley Park, IL; 5/4/94 New Orleans, LA (where Trey relates news of a friend's baby and says "I hope you live your life like that last jam."); 6/11/94 Morrison, CO (a great pre-FM soundboard of this show circulates); 6/25/94 Cleveland, OH; 7/16/94 Sugarbush, VT (with "Catapult" in the middle); 10/24/95 Madison, WI; 10/31/95 Chicago, IL; 11/2/96 West Palm Beach, FL (the "cross-eyed antelope" with Karl Perazzo); 8/6/97 Maryland Heights, MO (with an instrumental "Makisupa" and Page on Theremin and Mike on mini-drum kit); 4/3/98 Uniondale, NY (a "deconstructed" "Antelope" with "Carini's gonna get ya" lines added); 10/30/98 Las Vegas, NV; and 12/30/99 Big Cypress Seminole Indian Reservation, FL. Tom Marshall appeared with Phish to deliver the line he contributed ("rye, rye, rocco…") at the New Year's Eve shows in 1993 and 1994.

Runaway Jim

AKA: "Jim"
Music/Lyrics by: Dave Abrahams, Trey Anastasio
Album: (none)
Vocals: Trey (lead), Mike, Page (backing)
Debut: 3/28/90
Historian: Chris Bertolet

This whimsical yarn about a dog named Jim—who has cleverly managed to split with the narrator's car, clothes and money—has been a staple of Phish's repertoire since its strong debut. It seems unlikely that there are any hidden or allegorical meanings in the lyrics to this song, which Trey penned with Dave Abrahams while sitting around a fountain with Daubs at the Woodrow Wilson School in Princeton, NJ. Summarily shelved, the tune didn't appear live until years later.

"Runaway Jim's" ebb-and-flow jams are unpredictable sonic journeys—alternately textural and colorful, melodious one night and darkly dissonant the next. The first extended "Jim" was played in Albany on 5/5/93, but it was the 6/16/95 Raleigh version (29 minutes, with segue into "Free") that first took the song to truly experimental spaces. Nowadays, type-II "Jims" are fairly common.

The undisputed heavyweight champion of all "Jims" unfolded at the Worcester Centrum on 11/29/97. Certainly the moodiest, boldest version to date, this monster clocks in at 60-plus minutes. Along the way, the groove morphs from jazz to funk, and climaxes in a full-blown "Weekapaug" jam. Though some hardcore fans laud this "Jim" as the finest improvisation Phish has ever done, others are critical of its overblown length and its occasionally aimless wanderings. For those who don't mind a little aimless wandering, it's a must-hear. Segue fanatics should check out the abbreviated 7/22/97 Raleigh version, which drops seamlessly into "My Soul" by way of a "Superstition" quote from Page. Other favorite "Jims" include 12/31/95 Madison Square Garden (a spectacular set altogether), 8/7/96 Red Rocks (complete with "Gypsy Queen" tease), 7/31/97 Shoreline (mesmerizing), 8/13/97 Star Lake (brief, but incendiary), and 7/3/00 Camden (groovy and experimental).

Runaway Jim

Compiled by Jesse Appelman

Date	Time	Notes
03/28/90	—	First version.
07/15/93	07:00	Intense! Power of a normal Jim packed into a 5-minute jam.
08/21/93	10:23	Evil and ugly. Quite weird. Improvisational.
06/16/95	29+	Long and exploratory. Marks the beginning of the Jim jams. Segues into Free.
07/02/95	18:30	The second brilliant, improvisational Jim. Segues into Makisupa.
12/31/95	17:32	This excellent melodic version (for pre-1996) is still the favorite of many fans.
08/07/96	15:10	Features a jam on Santana's "Gypsy Queen."
08/14/96	15:13	Great climax followed by permagroove.
03/02/97	9:32	Another jam on Santana's "Gypsy Queen."
07/22/97	10:05	PornoFunkinJam segues into My Soul.
07/31/97	23:30	Mellifluously mesmerizing.
08/06/97	16:05	Darkly hypnotic jam>gloriously melodic jam>ass-kickin' blues jam>My Soul.
08/13/97	08:42	Warning: jam may cause blank stare and drooling.
11/29/97	60+	Longest single Phish jam to date. Contains many different sections and moods, and has been nick-named the "Jim Symphony." Contains a thrilling Weekapaug jam.
07/18/99	24:12	Magnificent.
07/03/00	33	Exploratory and intense.

Runnin' With the Devil

Original Artist: Van Halen
Original Album: *Van Halen* (1978)
Vocals: Trey
Debug: 8/6/98
Historian: Martin Acaster

Runnin' With the Devil, the first song on Van Halen's self titled debut album, may well be the musical genotype for every glam-rock/hair-metal band to come out of southern California since the late '70s. Featuring the cocksure swagger of frontman David Lee Roth and the pyrotechnic hammer-on guitar wizardry of Eddie Van Halen, the band invented a musical style which initiated their meteoric rise to rock-n-roll megastardom. This ascent peaked, for the VH purist, with the release of their synchronologically titled album *1984*.

Phish played "Runnin' With the Devil" as an encore at Lakewood Amphitheater, Atlanta, Georgia on 8/6/98. This perfomance was another example of the 1998 "Summer Under the Covers" habit where the band learned a new cover tune backstage shortly before coming on stage to perform it. Though lacking the egotistical vamping and hyperpharyn-geal screams of Diamond Dave, the Phish version of "Runnin' With the Devil" was fundamentally true to the Van Halen version. Perhaps to make a statement regarding compositional virtuosity, the cover was fol-lowed with an abbreviated version of "YEM" which featured teases of Eddie's solo riff from the tune.

Sabotage

Original Artist: Beastie Boys
Original Album: *III Communication* (1994)
Phish Album: *Hampton Comes Alive* (11/21/98)
Vocals: Trey (lead), Fish, Mike, Page (backing)
Debut: 8/8/98
Historian: Martin Acaster

The 1994 release of "Sabotage" returned The Beastie Boys to the ex-alted throne of top-40 superstardom they first occupied in 1986 with their frat house anthem "Fight For Your Right To Party." The Beast-ies' hard rocking free-style, which grew out of their hardcore punk roots and is exemplified by "Sabotage," made it possible for the likes of Limp Bizkit and Kid Rock to have careers today.

Unlike these latter-day pretenders to the Grand Royal crown, the Beastie Boys have displayed a vision and inventiveness in their musical efforts that is largely unparalleled in the world of hip-hop and rap. Es-chewing the hit-making formula they perfected on *Licensed to III* they spent several years of relative musical obscurity exploring jazz, funk, soul and Tibetan buddhism before returning to their instruments to pro-duce *Check Your Head* and *III Communication*. Though it received a great deal of radio airplay, "Sabotage" is perhaps best known for its hi-larious music video spoof of *Starsky and Hutch*-type '70s cop shows.

Phish performances of "Sabotage," featuring the strained rap stylings of Trey Anastasio, have been explosive surprises that served to whip the mellow undulations of the typical Phish crowd into a riotous frenzy.

The debut performance at Merriweather Pavilion (8/8/98) was one of several unexpected cover song encores played during the U.S. Sum-mer tour. The high-octane "Sabotage" returned eight days later to open the final set of the Lemonwheel (8/16/98) evoking a crowd scene in front of the stage which observers have likened to those for certain per-formers at Woodstock '99. The most recent version of "Sabotage" (11/21/98), though not quite as rabid as the Lemonwheel performance, once again ignited the delighted crowd to open the final set of a two night run at the Hampton Coliseum. "Sabotage" was not played at all in 1999 despite being released on *Hampton Comes Alive*.

Sad Lisa

Original Artist: Cat Stevens
Original Album: *Tea For the Tillerman* (1970)
Vocals: Sarah MacLachlan, Trey (lead)
Debut: 10/18/98
Historian: Erik Swain

This Cat Stevens ballad was the first of three cover-song collabora-tions with guest stars that closed Phish's set at the second day of the Bridge School Benefit. Following "Brian and Robert," Sarah

McLachlan, who also performed at the benefit, joined the band to do this duet with Trey.

Following this song, Neil Young joined Phish and McLachlan for Ian Tyson's "Four Strong Winds" and Bob Dylan's "I Shall Be Released." Despite some deft and delicate acoustic playing by Trey and Page in this version, "Sad Lisa" has not resurfaced in Phish's repertoire.

St. Stephen

Music/Lyrics: Jerry Garcia, Robert Hunter, and Phil Lesh
Original Artist: Grateful Dead
Original Album: *Aoxomoxoa* (1969)
Vocals: (performed instrumental)
Debut: 11/3/84
Historian: Mark Toscano

St. Stephen is just one of the several Dead songs that appear in the setlists of early Phish shows. So far, only one known performance of this 'un has been discovered, and it takes the form of a "St. Stephen" *jam* rather than a complete interpretation of the song. Following an admirable but somewhat embarassing version of "Bertha" (hey, they were only 20!), the guys jammed on "Stephen" for a spell before moving onto the more raucous "Can't You Hear Me Knocking" (which itself ended up hosting a "St. Stephen" tease.) Though this early show—one of the very first the band played under the name "Phish"—is fun for novelty and historical purposes, fans looking for a solid version of the song might want to check out the 4/16/99 Phil and Friends version featur-

ing excellent playing all around and a classic segue into "The Eleven." In a time when Phish were playing a number of different Dead songs, it's surprising that this one didn't make some full-blown appearances; "St. Stephen" was insanely rare at Dead shows at this point, and fans were likely jonesing for a fix.

St. Thomas

Music: Sonny Rollins
Original Artist: Sonny Rollins
Original Album: *Saxophone Colossus* (1956)
Vocals: (instrumental)
Debut: 5/21/98
Historian: Mark Toscano

St. Thomas is just one of those tunes that so many damn bands have played, that it long ago entered the pantheon of "jazz standards." Artists such as Tal Farlow, David Murray, Kenny Burrell, and Count Basie have all run through the classic tune, not to mention the Jonny B. Fishman Jazz Ensemble. Phish is known to have performed "St. Thomas" only once, at the somewhat hard-to-find 5/21/88 show, though it was teased by Dave Grippo and Fish during the 11/23/91 "BBFCFM."

Rollins' original, appearing on the tenor saxophonist's amusingly named 1956 outing *Saxophone Colossus*, also featured the talents of Max Roach, Tommy Flanagan, and Doug Watkins.

Sample In A Jar

AKA: "Sample"
Music: Trey Anastasio
Lyrics: Tom Marshall
Album: *Hoist*
Vocals: Trey, Page (lead), Mike (backing)
Debut: 2/4/93
Historian: Craig DeLucia

Has any Phish song been received in as many different ways as "Sample?" When it debuted in early 1993, it was seen as a short, rocking number that had the potential to jam heavily. However, when *Hoist* was released, some fans viewed the song as The Apocalypse That Will End the World of Phish as We Know It—the song that would bring mainstream radio success to Phish. Of course, it never happened.

Granted, the song has a pop-hook chorus and a much more mainstream feel than the rest of the Phish catalog. In *The Phish Book,* Page even remarked that it "contains a catchy little progression not unreminiscent of Status Quo's 'Pictures of Matchstick Men.'" It is a song that turned many *Hoist*-era fans on to the band. For whatever reason, some fans hold a dislike for the song that continues to this day, and "Sample" sometimes seems like a silly dividing line between "newer" and "older" fans (though most of us can't figure out what the hell that really means anyway).

Those who dismiss the song as pure radio pop are missing out on quite a lot. It is rare that a studio version of a Phish song receives acclaim among the faithful, but many fans agree that Trey's outro solo is among the finest pieces of studio work he has ever recorded. The vocal harmonies, both on the album and the live stage, are difficult and eerie.

On the surface, the lyrics seem to deal with a relationship argument while intoxicated. In *The Phish Book,* Trey mentioned that the song is "basically about sitting in a car with the seatbelt on, drunk." But many fans have taken their own meaning that probes deeper and provides a look at something that most of us can relate to: that feeling of being trapped and viewed like a specimen, or a sample in a jar. Also, as in other Phish songs, the lyrics reference family friends. Here we learn of Elihu, father of Dave Abrahams, in a fictional capacity as a bed-dancer. No need to search for the connection with Leemor, though; he's a complete work of fiction that Tom and an old boss created after passing a man on the side of the road.

"Sample" is noteworthy as being one of only two *Hoist* songs played in their entirety before the album came out (the other is "Lifeboy"). It is also noteworthy for its setlist versatility. It is as likely to open a show as to close one, and as likely to be played early as it is to be played late. Other bands have shown an affinity for the song as well: Little Feat covered "Sample" on their album *Chinese Work Songs* (released in 2000) and Phil Lesh and Friends (including members of Little Feat but sans Phish guests) covered "Sample" in concert on 7/22/00.

Unfortunately, not many versions stand out among the samples of "Sample." It has never been used as a jam vehicle, and Trey's live outro solo nearly always mimics his blistering guitar work on the album version. Still, the hope remains that it will one day go the way of "Gumbo" and other songs that toiled in jamming obscurity before blossoming on stage. Until that moment, many fans will still use "Sample" as a chance to hit the bathrooms. Other will relish it, though, and continue to welcome its live appearances.

Samson Variation

AKA: "Blow Wind Blow," "Samson Riff"
Music: Trey Anastasio, Ernie Stires
Album: *Samson Riffs* (Ernie Stires album, as "Samson Riff");
   One Man's Trash (as "At the Barbecue")
Debut: 6/6/97 (private show), 8/3/97 (public show)
Historian: Mark Toscano

This song, nondescript though it is, could very well represent the culmination of Trey's apprenticeship to Ernie Stires. Trey often credits Ernie with singlehandedly shaping the development of Trey's (and therefore Phish's) compositional style, even if Ernie insists that he only "opened the door" for Trey to walk through on his own. Though Trey had largely moved on by the time the "The Asse Festival" was written in 1990, Ernie was a big influence on his student even after Phish signed with Elektra in 1992. At this point, Trey would still show all of his new music to Ernie before greenlighting it for the band, a practice that was used for a number of the songs that ended up on *Rift.*

A quintessential Trey-Ernie moment came when Trey showed Ernie the completed big band arrangement for "Flat Fee," a project on which he had toiled endlessly. Though Ernie acknowledged Trey was on the right track, his otherwise nonplussed reaction helped Trey realize how high he could still take his compositional skills. Ernie compared the "Flat Fee" accomplishment to sticking one's head out of the ground in order to see the foot of huge mountain that now needed to be climbed. Trey has cited this moment as an extremely important one for his music writing career, and it's easy to see why. Trey respects the hell out of Ernie, his teaching, and his music, and Trey's regard for these three things has always driven him to challenge both himself and the audience who hears his music.

In 1997, many of these issues came full circle when Trey organized the production and release of Ernie Stires' first CD, *Samson Riffs.* For the occasion, Trey composed an instrumental piece with Ernie that he and his mentor play on the disc. This track, "Samson Riff," is named for Ernie's street in Vermont, and is a shining moment for both teacher and student, who for the first time truly share musical space, both figuratively and literally. The track and the album in general represent a wonderful peak in the two musicians' relationship, a peak Trey worked hard to climb in order to conquer. At this point, however, Ernie would surely point out to Trey the hundreds of peaks in the mountain range surrounding them, each one representing another set of new personal goals.

"Samson Riff" also appears, in a different permutation, on Trey's solo CD, *One Man's Trash,* under the name "At the Barbecue." This version is comprised of a three-horn arrangement which gives way to a brief a capella interpretation midway through the two-minute track. "Samson Riff" has also shown up in Phish's live repertoire, but in yet another form. This version is more a variation on the original than a re-arrangement, and for this reason it is referred to as "Samson Variation." The Phish version is deceptively simple, its invention lying mainly in the way the melody is carried, one note at a time, from Page to Trey to Mike and back again, with Fish providing an unobtrusively jazzy beat. After being tested out twice at "Bradstock" on 6/6/97, the song appeared at only one show, 8/3/97 Gorge, before departing from the repertoire indefinitely. Fans at the Gorge liked the brief number, though a number were confused by its unexpected appearance. Perhaps Trey was inspired by the sight of so many impossibly majestic peaks surrounding

Run Like An Antelope

Compiled by David Shulman and Billy Rickards

Date	Time	Notes
10/17/85	07:15	First version. Jammed straight into "Rye Rye Rocco" without the now customary peak. Extended jam of the "Rocco" section. "Been you to have any spleef, man?"
07/12/88	13:26	Jazzy intro. First ever "Roll Like A Cantaloupe." (See the Antelope song history for more information)
08/26/89	12:49	Flea from Red Hot Chili Peppers performs a trumpet solo. He is introduced as Marco Esquandolas.
05/28/89	09:03	In the spirit of the pig.
11/30/89	11:58	Fierce rock star Trey.
11/14/91	12:06	Second "Cantaloupe." Great overall jam segment.
03/13/92	17:49	"Somewhere Over the Rainbow" in the intro. Simpsons signal. Jams into "BBFCFM" (then into "Hawaii" vocal jam, and back into "BBFCFM)."
03/20/92	13:55	Simpsons signal. Fish on trombone. Don't operate heavy machinery while listening to this intense version!
05/14/92	20:50	Spiderman theme tease. Trey explains and demonstrates many of the "Secret Language" signals: Fall Down, TurnTurnTurn, Simpsons, Circus, Aw Fuck.
04/17/93	11:23	Rock star Trey. Simpsons and All Sing On a Different Note signals.
08/02/93	10:50	Very raw and grinding jam. "Rocco" section segues into "Makisupa Reprise," and includes an All Fall Down signal.
08/07/93	09:36	Fiery machine gun tension and release. Great Mike!
08/14/93	30:45	One of the best versions ever. Hose jam segues into "Sparks," which segues into "Walk Away, which segues back into more hose jamming, which segues into "Have Mercy" (which includes "Rye Rye Rocco"), and which segues back into "Antelope."
08/28/93	16:21	Five distinct, magnificent jams. "Brady Bunch" theme tease. Secret Language.

Date	Time	Notes
05/08/94	15:27	Fiery and passionate.
06/16/94	12:22	Super-charged Page! Raw, trilling, peaking Trey. Loose, jammy end.
06/19/94	13:20	Many goal-oriented lyrical licks from Trey. Great experimental tension and release, incredible energy. Extended "Rocco" with Mikeadelic. One for the ages!
06/24/94	19:47	Roaring, heavy, thunderous jam segment with brief "DWD" teasing.
07/16/94	17:11	"Catapault." Simpsons language. Lots of screaming. Intense.
10/31/94	10:37	Short but thrilling jam segment. "Stash" tease in opening.
11/16/94	11:10	Many excellent improvisational twists and turns. Botched ending leads to reggae then back into "Antelope."
11/30/94	22:00	Dissonant jam into full "My Sweet One" into extended dark jam into "Fixin' to Die." Unfinished.
06/09/95	10:23	Some strange, atonal jamming. Space into "Rocco."
06/15/95	12:06	Bouncy intro. Raw, grinding jam segment into double-time machine gun fury.
06/23/95	13:07	Mike-controlled, monotonous jam; lots of cyclical tension.
06/30/95	12:07	Standard jam segment, but extended "Rocco" with Trey saying, "Set the deershit for the side of his hole." They'll be back in 14 minutes and 61 seconds.
07/03/95	11:47	Fish is out of control! (otherwise a standard version)
10/02/95	10:34	Flaming hot from the begining. Spacey-rhythmic "Rocco."
10/07/95	11:39	Vocalized intro. Quadruple-time ending.
10/13/95	11:55	Emanates from post-Wilson space, playful intro; rhythmic ending.

the venue, that he couldn't help but pay tribute to the man that showed him the mountain in the first place.

Sand

AKA: "Pistol"
Music/Lyrics: Trey Anastasio, Tom Marshall
Album: *Farmhouse*
Vocals: Trey (lead)
Debut: 9/11/99
Historian: Martin Acaster

The existence of sand is ultimately responsible for life as you know it on this planet. Without sand there would be no continents, there would be no television, there would be no internet, and there would be no phatty glass pieces available on the lot. Of its myriad forms, perhaps the most interesting sands (so much so that a museum dedicated to them can be found in Japan) are of the rare musical variety. Due to their strange acoustic properties, which arise from vibrations caused by intergranular friction, these musical sands display a wide sonic range from the "singing" sands of beaches in Japan and Brazil to the "booming" sands of some deserts in the United States, Africa, and China. Unfortunately, these sands are very susceptible to contamination by environmental pollutants. As we continue to foul our planet, more of these rare sands disappear. The lyrics of "Sand," written by Tom Marshall, and first performed by Trey with the 8-Foot Fluorescent Tubes (4/17/98 Winooski, VT) can be interpreted as an indictment of the ills

Run Like An Antelope (continued)

Date	Time	Notes
10/24/95	16:03	Flowing intensity, incredible energy. One of the best ever. Epic!
10/28/95	12:10	Collective tension/release jam.
10/31/95	12:39	Scat-singing and mini drum solo during "Rocco."
11/11/95	11:21	Experimental jamming, many key changes. Fantastic tempo changes.
11/30/95	10:20	Segues out of "Makisupa." Never-ending tension into the peak. Small "Tweezer"-jam teases in the closing "Rocco" segment.
12/04/95	13:30	A scorcher! "Been you to have any spike. Marco Esquandolas. Man."
12/08/95	12:08	"Brady Bunch" tease in intro (see also 8/28/93). Nice rhythm-accented jamming and extended tension fury towards end. Reggae-flavored "Rocco."
12/17/95	12:20	Grunge rock at times, spacey-noodling at others. Hurried ending.
12/30/95	10:12	Fantastic jam built around ascending/descending licks. Great Trey for the peak.
07/12/96	08:20	Segued from "Mike's Song." Jazzy Page. Into "Purple Rain." Unfinished.
07/15/96	11:55	Good energy. Mike rules!
07/21/96	12:36	Strong build. Good listening.
07/25/96	10:29	Segues out of "Ice." Beautiful, slow Page intro. Machine gun Trey!
08/02/96	11:23	A short "Star Wars Theme" tease in jam, but average overall.
08/06/96	09:58	Nice Fish in intro. Overall group craziness throughout. "Rye Rye Rocco, 28-year old Phish fan Marcus Esquandolis" (reference to Morrison newspaper article describing fan "riot" from previous night).
08/12/96	12:24	Secret Language tease in intro (laughter). Moments of extended tension.
08/17/96	10:25	Out of "Fluffhead." Intense.
10/26/96	12:22	Dedicated to Jason Robbins (Fish's 14 year-old cousin who won a guitar contest). Preceded by brief Star Spangled Banner tease. Tease of a Hendrix tune in the closing segment.
11/02/96	13:33	With Karl Perazzo on percussion. Segues out of 20+ minute "C&P."
11/08/96	11:40	Nice set closer. Intense build-up.
11/14/96	11:46	Out of short "Demand." Ragtime style intro. Page!
11/24/96	12:59	Norton Charlton Heston—rather than Marco Esquandolas.
12/31/96	11:27	Hose! Fast and crazy. Highly recommended. Spacey "Rocco" segment.
02/14/97	10:57	Page lays down the foundation; Trey spends 5 minutes swirling it around until all come together for the ending release. Crazy Fish.
02/21/97	11:43	Unfinished. Solid group jamming throughout, until "Rocco" ending, when Trey turns things heavy-metal. Segues into heavy metal "Wilson."
06/20/97	11:26	Hints of funk at the begining and ending. "Rye Rye Rocco. New Jersey drunk. Been you to have any spike, Chong?"
07/29/97	20:17	Jam falls away from "Antelope" into melodic space, then grows back into `lope ending. Different.
08/06/97	16:00	Very open initial jam segment; not very dense. Some Reggae flavor. Picks up into typical `lope craziness by end. Segue into "Makispua Reprise" during "Rocco" with Page on Theremin (ouch).
11/14/97	13:14	Whistling in intro and ending "Rocco."
11/19/97	11:50	Playful, harmonic intro. Extended, super-charged ending.
11/22/97	12:24	Fiddle-like Trey in intro. Spurts of diverse improv throughout jam.
12/06/97	16:16	Jam quickly drops into laid-back funk, grows into "Antelope." Mellow build to the Peak.
12/12/97	14:08	Intense! Short "Buried Alive" tease by Trey. Tension into double-time jam. Stop/Start "Rocco" funk style.
12/29/97	15:53	Nice peaks in jam. Outrageous funk in "Rocco" section!
04/03/98	13:56	Fish says "If you're gonna run up on the stage, just don't let Carini get you" in the intro. This prompts hilarious "Carini's gonna get you"

(continued on the next page)

which affect our planet in general, and the Phish scene (as a somewhat skewed microcosm) specifically. Considering the subject matter, "Sand" might well have been called "Heavy Things."

Looking beyond the obvious message regarding gun control (with due respect to victims of school shootings, wars, and our unalienable right to bear arms), the gun in the first verse is a symbol for all that is wrong with society. Suggesting that rather than treat the wounds we inflict upon the earth, each other, and the Phish scene, we should strive to eliminate the causes of these injuries. Perhaps, if as a society, a species, and as fans we were able to evolve beyond the level of parasite we might all have a brighter future.

The second verse deals with our innate competetiveness in both our daily lives and while at the show. The lyrics evoke images of traffic and road rage on the paved surfaces of reality, the superhighway of the virtual world, and the turnstiles, aisles, and front rails of the concert venue. We careen ahead, carelessly oblivious (or perhaps chemically blinded) to the fact that we are eagerly crushing our "brothers" and "sisters" beneath our wheels or heels, simply because we think we have some divine right to the road, the newsgroup, dancing space, or the band.

The final verse of "Sand" explores spirituality, connection to the universe, and blind idolatry. Ultimately (as with any other experience or perception)our religion and gods are personal. For some the dollar is almighty, for others the buddha reigns supreme, sometimes even mu-

Run Like An Antelope *(continued)*

Date	Time	Notes
		harmonizing thoughout the song. Straightforward tension/release jamming with overcharged trilling peaks at end. Funkadelic Mike in the "Rocco" section, and a small stop/start jam after "spike, mon." Unique version all around.
06/30/98	10:23	Segues out of "Frankie Sez." Mellow, melodic intro with Trey flubs. Outrageous raging by all in the jam. Good off-key/on-key jamming. "Rocco" is spoken and unaccompanied.
07/16/98	13:09	Country-style tease in intro. Mission Impossible-sounding jam.
07/21/98	13:20	Awkward Trey sounds in intro. Nice overall low, building jam with noodling Trey, until an extended one-note climax. Loose jammy "Rocco" with an eerie "spike, mon."
07/26/98	13:23	Segues out of a harmonic "Fee" jam. Good Trey/Page tension with rock-star Trey. One note Mike through "Rocco."
07/29/98	13:31	Extended playful intro with Fish on vacuum. Purposeful jamming and nice extended tension/release. Great Fishman throughout.
08/03/98	11:36	Nice Trey/Mike communication. Not much variation in a high-octane jam segment. "Have you any spliff?"
08/09/98	13:10	Short lullaby start. Tight, syncopated, jazzy Fish. Bouncy Mike. Machine gun Trey over jam that (intentionally) falls apart numerous times. Drops into grunge-tension jam, and melds beautifully back into furious end. Reggae into syncopated rhythm "Rocco."
10/30/98	16:38	Active noodle-Trey intro. Mellow start to jam into swirling Trey/Page and Mike/Fish repetition for alter-"Antelope" jam. Back into 'lope where rock-star Trey creates crazy tension. Unbelievable energy! Extended psychedelic groovy "Rocco" segment with chanting. Longest 'lope since 11/30/94?
11/08/98	12:06	Upbeat, hoedown intro. Pretty standard jamming until Fish hits double-time. Watch out! Madness ensues and energy limits are pushed. Intense!

Date	Time	Notes
11/13/98		16:56 Playful noodling intro. Mellow jam tries to build energy and finds life in the second half of the jam. Supercharged noisy tension is the result. Slightly extended "Rocco."
11/27/98	15:38	Solid, no suprise intro. Slow building jam with nice contributions from Page. Typical (great) gear shift to craziness with feedback Trey at the peak.
12/31/98	15:24	Active, full intro. Nice cyclical Trey/Page/Mike jam until it leaves Antelope jam structure in "Siket-Disc" style for 1-2 mins. Returns to 'lope with crazy Fish for lightning ending. Smooth cowgroove in "Rocco."
07/03/99	15:23	A couple nice Trey/Fish rhythm hookups. Noisy, full jam. To the point.
07/25/99	16:16	Loose, jammy intro with lyrical, bouncy Mike. Nice alternating between standard Antelope jamming and sparse, rhythmic hook ups. Great, syncopated Fish. Drops into mellow non-Antelope-sounding cow funk, into sparse mellow jamming, then into monotone space. Trey brings everyone back to "Antelope" proper for the peak and ending. Short "Rocco" section. Most experimental 'lope since 10/30/98.
09/16/99	13:24	Quick pace to the intro, swift jam. Delay-loop in beginning of jam. Nice Mike/Page/Trey connections to create tension and release. Fast and to the point.
12/12/99	12:50	Upbeat, playful intro. Lyrical Trey to begin jam. One note tension by Trey brings gear shift and resulting craziness. Standard "Rocco."
12/30/99	15:34	Mellow, straightforward intro. Jam wavers between mellow and trilling cyclical tension until a gear shift brings energetic 3/4 time tension and new life to the jam. Fantastic Trey and Mike interaction. New age Page sounds featured in "Rocco."
06/24/00	13:06	Sirens! Thunderous! Run for cover!
09/15/00	13:03	Benny Hill theme in intro. Fierce, thrilling jam. Tom Marshall (and daughter) for "Rocco" lyrics.

sicians are idolized as gods. Unfortunately, when our god (no matter what form she/he/it takes) questions our behavior, we are given to rejecting the warning. Disregarding good advice, whether it comes from the stormy seas washing onto the singing sands of our diseased planet or the guitarist/song writer of our favorite band, could be catastrophic.

In stark contrast to the lyrical content of "Sand," the song is an orgiastic rump-shaking groove-fest. The bedrock foundation of "Sand" is cemented together by a simple repetitive groove that is rooted in a '70s disco beat. This sturdy pad is then used by Trey as a launch site for sky searing volleys of liquid metallic guitar-hero fireworks. The Phish debut of "Sand" (it was also previously played on Trey's solo tour

with Tony Markellis and Russ Lawton) was 9/11/99 at the Gorge Amphitheater, George, WA. Since then, "Sand" has been in fairly regular rotation as an opener or early jamming tune in second sets.

To sample a good cross section of "Sand's" stratigraphic column check out the debut and the following versions: Irvine Meadows, Irvine, CA (9/19/99); South Park Meadows, Austin, TX (9/24/99); Redbird Arena, NORML, IL (10/4/99); Firstar Center, Cincinatti, OH (12/3/99); the Providence Civic Center, Providence, RI (12/13/99); the monstrous version From Big Cypress, FL (12/31/99); Radio City Music Hall, New York, NY (5/22/00); the dark and sinister PNC Bank Arts Center "Sand" From Holmdel, NJ (6/29/00); the Michael Ray-infected version from

Pepsi Arena, Albany, NY (9/9/00); and the creeping beast from Shoreline Amphitheatre, Mountain View, CA (10/6/00).

Sanity

Music: Phish
Lyrics: The Dude of Life
Album: *Junta* (live, from 7/25/88 show)
Debut: 10/15/86
Historian: Chris Bertolet

From the inimitably twisted psyche of the Dude comes this inimitably twisted march through madness. The structure's simple: our deranged narrator happily offers his point of view ("I don't care if the world explodes") as synaptic chaos erupts on the heels of each verse. Then, without warning, we're back in the rubber room and all is quiet, save for the peal of a familiar guitar phrase—Garcia's signature riff from the Grateful Dead ballad, "Row Jimmy."

Ooooookaaayyyy.

Phish uncorked "Sanity" two weeks before Halloween '86, and reprised it ten years later before a slightly heftier crowd at the Omni in Atlanta. They played it rarely in between, and only twice since. In 1989, "Sanity" popped off like a hypoglycemic kid in a crank frenzy, and Phish sent it to the corner for a time out. After nearly three years of tough love and Ritalin treatments, the tune resurfaced at its original, lobotomized tempo.

As a jamming tune, "Sanity" is rather straight-jacketed. Instead, it serves to create a unique mood or energy, much like "BBFCFM" or "Icculus." It tends to rear its mercurial head at special shows, such as the 4/16/92 Anaconda gem, the legendary 12/31/95, and the 8/15/98 Lemonwheel extravaganza (where it nestled snugly between "Gumbo" and "Tweezer").

Boom, pow!

Satin Doll

Music/Lyrics: Duke Ellington, Billy Strayhorn, and Johnny Mercer
Original Artist: Duke Ellington Orchestra
Release: Various
Vocals: Page
Debut: 6/20/88
Historian: Ellis Godard

This Duke Ellington standard appeared in ten regularly spaced appearances (6/20/88 through 2/25/90), and then laid dormant until a 4/12/93 breakout and a 5/8/93 reprise. Trey dedicated the April breakout to his grandmother, saying, "I wouldn't be here if my grandmother hadn't danced on this very floor [of the University of Iowa IMU Ballroom] with my grandfather to Duke Ellington, and neither would you." Other memorable versions include the debut, nicely placed between "Golgi" and "A-Train"; 7/23/88, with Peter Danforth and Dave Grippo on horns; 8/6/88, "drummer's choice"; and 12/31/89, oddly followed by "Highway to Hell." The song was also teased, by Page, during the 12/30/92 "A-Train."

Savoy Truffle

Original Artist: The Beatles
Original Album: *The Beatles* (aka "The White Album") (1968)

Vocals: Trey (lead), Mike, Page (backing)
Debut: 10/31/94
Historian: Mark Toscano

One of George Harrison's compositions for The Beatles' eponymous double-LP, this skunky rocker is strangely reminiscent of Thomas Pynchon's disturbing novel *Gravity's Rainbow*. Phish injected an extra helping of juice into the already juicy composition for their 10/31/94 "White Album" set.

Saw It Again

Music/Lyrics: Trey Anastasio
Album: (none)
Vocals: Trey
Debut: 6/14/97
Historian: charlz franz

Saw It Again was seen first on 5/21/97 at Club Toast in Burlington during the "New York!" group project show Mike and Trey helped organize. "Saw It" is a harsh, strident-sounding punk rock or Black Sabbath-like tune that has been described by one fan as the "soundtrack to a B horror film." Fans generally either really like it or detest it, just like people generally either really like or detest punk rock or Black Sabbath. The band may be ambivalent about it as well. It was not played at all in 1998 after a limited number of performances in 1997, and made it into the rotation only three times in both 1999 and 2000. Even fans who detest "Saw It" grudgingly admit that the jammed out 12/12/97 Albany version is worth hearing.

Peter Sitzman

Scarlet Begonias

Original Artist: Grateful Dead
Original Album: *From the Mars Hotel* **(1974)**
Vocals: Trey
Debut: 12/2/83
Historian: Ellis Godard/Mark Toscano

The Grateful Dead played "Scarlet Begonias" 315 times, debuting it with the "Wall of Sound" 3/24/73, two days before entering the studio for *From the Mars Hotel*. The song also appears on four of the *Dick's Picks* released (6, 7, 12, and 13), the 1984 release by (former Grateful Dead members) Keith and Donna Godchaux, lyricist Hunter's 1991 solo album, and three Grateful Dead tribute albums. The original lyrics—littered with British place names and allusions to nursery rhymes, folks songs, and fables—accompany music at once delicate and rhythmic. But not every band sees a heart of gold: A 1992 version by Sublime appended new lyrics, focused on drugs and faux fandom.

Performed at the very first Phish gig (as "Blackwood Convention") on 12/2/83 (and likely two days later), "Scarlet Begonias" opened the ill-fated debut second set, several minutes into which the band's playing was drowned out by the P.A. by dance organizers. Following the band's 1984 reformation after a lengthy hiatus, the song returned to the repertoire, showing up on 12/1/84 and (probably) other lost Phish gigs for which setlists are not known. Its last appearance came in the third set of the first show with Page (5/3/85, although he did not perform officially as part of the band until that fall) followed by "Eyes of the World."

Scent Of A Mule

AKA: "Mule," "SOAM," "SOAMule"
Music/Lyrics: Mike Gordon
Album: *Hoist*
Debut: 4/4/94
Historian: Bradley Lonard

Trust the mind of Michael Gordon to come up with a bluegrass song, played at breakneck speed, about an alien invasion of the American South. The invasion fails when the song's hero Kitty Malone shows them her "Southern home": "And they liked it, they really liked it!" All this plus frequent exhortations to "smell my mule." Chris Bertolet has dubbed the musical genre of "Scent" as "eminently spacegrass—a fusion of the backwoods and corny Jules Verne sci-fi fantasy." It stands alone in a field of one.

"Scent" was one of the songs written and recorded for *Hoist* which was not played live until after the album's release. Mike had penned the lyrics some time before; he had the first verse as far back as May 1993. The studio version, recorded in late 1993/early 1994, features Béla Fleck on banjo (he can be seen in the *Tracking* video; so can Mike, bellowing the lyrics while stinking drunk).

When the band took to the road "Scent" gained a brief Page piano solo in melodramatic "silent movie" style which lead into a klezmer-type riff (accompanied often by Mike and Trey performing one of their patented strange dances). Slowly the band plays the riff, getting faster and faster until it reaches a feverish speed, before Trey breaks back into the "Scent" riff and Mike howls in true backwoods form—and back into the song they dash. By the 1995 tours this sequence had developed into

what the band calls the "Mule Duel": Page plays his piano solo, Trey responds on guitar and Page hits back, often at length (sometimes longer than some in the audience would ideally prefer). This continued right up until Summer 1997, when Phish began to play a rather more free-form jam in place of the duel.

Some memorable versions include: 6/11/94 (an early, very strong pre-duel "Scent"), 6/26/94 (part of the "Phish Cover *Hoist*" set), 7/13/94 ("BBFCFM" lyrics to "Scent" music), 11/30/95 (a particularly good version that seems to gather a lot of strength from following a "Tweezer"> "Makisupa"> "Antelope" trilogy), 6/6/96 (with a "Cocaine" jam and Trey taking over Page's keyboards), 7/23/96 (Trey's duel is a capella), 8/17/96 (Fish gets a drum solo instead of the usual duel), 10/22/96 (scat singing during the duel in honour of backstage guest Oteil Burbridge), 10/27/96 (with "Catapult" and a theremin solo from Page), 11/27/96 (Trey's part of the duel includes a vacuum solo and a Brady Bunch scat), 12/30/96 (with comedian Steven Wright), 2/16/97 (Trey's part of the duel is a very jazzy guitar solo; Page responds with the first "Magilla" since April 1994), 8/9/97 (part of the "S Suite": "Simple"-> "Swept"-> "Steep"-> "Scent"-> "Slave"), 8/17/97 (Great Went; a very hyper version with "Mind Left Body" jamming), 12/28/97 (energy to burn, and a Page/Mike jam as part of the duel), and 10/30/98 (with a funky blues jam).

Sea and Sand

Original Artist: The Who
Original Album: *Quadrophenia* **(1973)**
Vocals: Page
Debut: 10/31/95
Historian: Craig DeLucia

Sea and Sand is the inevitable downer the *Quadrophenia* narrator experiences after the maniacal high of "5:15." While Jimmy took the train to experience a fantasy love, his reality is in the form of a bitter rejection. This song has been played three times including its Halloween '95 debut, and is performed much differently than The Who once did; to the delight of Phish fans everywhere, Page plays the song solo on piano. For the other inspiring versions, seek out 12/31/95 (segues beautifully out of "Weekapaug") and 7/20/98, which was literally played by the sea and sand at Ventura.

Seen and Not Seen

Original Artist: Talking Heads
Original Album: *Remain in Light* **(1980)**
Vocals: Mike (lead), Page, Trey (backing)
Debut: 10/31/96
Historian: Mark Toscano

No write-up could do justice to the incredible segue between "Houses in Motion" and this song at Phish's 10/31/96 performance of *Remain in Light*. As each element of the former got stripped down to almost nothing, Mike surrendered his bass to Trey as a recliner and floor lamp were brought out on stage for him, from which he would deliver this radio-unfriendly tune. The almost nothing then slowly became almost something, as Fish played percussion, Karl Perazzo played drums, Trey played bass, and Mike played comfy chair. Comfy chair made Mike tell a story about a man and his face, and the whole audience held their faces in their hands, some in despair, some

in glee. We all held our faces. Mike held his face. Comfy chair told the story through Mike's face. Listen to the story. Let it cradle your head in its arms like a comfy chair—a comfy chair telling a story through Mike's face.

Self

AKA: "I Don't Care About Anyone Except Myself"
Music/Lyrics: Steve Pollak
Original Artist: The Dude of Life (with Phish)
Original Album: *Crimes of the Mind* (1994)
Vocals: The Dude of Life
Debut: 9/13/90
Historian: Dan Mielcarz

Anone-too-subtle indictment of the "me" decade (from a lyricist not known for subtlety), "Self" is more important for what it became, than for what it was. The main guitar riff from the rare "Self" later became the main guitar riff in the more commonly played "Chalkdust Torture." You can hear this clearly on the Dude's first album, *Crimes of the Mind*. Fans of "Self" should seek out the Wetlands debut-fest on 9/13/90.

Setting Sail

Music/Lyrics: Trey Anastasio, Tom Marshall
Album: (none)
Vocals: Fish
Debut: 4/20/91
Historian: Craig DeLucia

When Fishman comes out from behind the kit, fans usually expect a song and a vacuum solo. On 7/15/94, though, Fishman treated fans to a brief sing-along about seeing a whale and its relationship to his disdain for sailing. If it sounded familiar, it should have: it appeared briefly in two earlier "You Enjoy Myself" vocal jams, on 4/20/91 and 3/25/92.

Sexual Healing

Original Artist: Marvin Gaye
Original Album: *Midnight Love* (1982)
Vocals: Fish (lead), Mike, Page, Trey (backing)
Debut: 7/20/98
Historian: Mark Toscano

Returning to the stage for their encore at Ventura County Fairgrounds, Trey took drums and Fishman took center stage for the first Fishman tune in a while. Reading from lyrics scrawled on an ad poster for the show (probably written during the 50+ minute setbreak), Fishman proceeded to sing this awe-inspiring Marvin Gaye tune, much to the delight and dumbstruck hilarity of the crowd, who had already been thoroughly befuddled by a bizarre and excellent show. Amidst numerous laughs, cheers, hoots, and hollers, Fishman concluded his singing with a few lewd dances that doubled and trebled the reaction of the crowd. The song made other appearances, the first of which occurred during the second set of 8/8/98, a show notable for two debut covers, The Velvet Underground's "Sweet Jane" and The Beastie Boys' "Sabotage." The tune made a few more more appearances after this (8/16/98, 11/14/98), but has since remained dormant, the unfortunate victim of an unconsummated case of *coitus interuptus*.

Sexy Sadie

Original Artist: The Beatles
Original Album: *The Beatles* (aka "The White Album") (1968)
Vocals: Page (lead), Mike, Trey (backing)
Debut: 10/31/94
Historian: Mark Toscano

Legend has it that this song was written in response to The Beatles' discovery, much to their anger and dismay, that their spiritual advisor in India, Maharishi Mahesh Yogi, was corrupt and distrustful. "Sexy Sadie" actually criticizes a man—Maharishi himself—for being deceitful and other unpleasant things, warning "her" that "you'll get yours yet," which puts a nice spin on the karmic principles the fakir faker was probably teaching the Fab Four.

For Phish's 10/31/94 performance of the tune, Page lent his higher vocal range to this underrated, head-bobbing track. The closing chords seem nicely suited to a jangly, exploratory jam, but Phish took pains to maintain tight control on their jamming reins during this set—they had thirty songs to fit into the second set alone.

Shafty

Music/Lyrics: Phish, Tom Marshall
Album: *Story of the Ghost*
Debut: 4/5/98
Historian: Phillip Zerbo

Where "Olivia's Pool" featured a mindless, carefree, upbeat musical backdrop that seems to assume the character of the 'oblivious fool', the musical tone and vocal delivery of "Shafty" fundamentally transforms the spirit of the song. Sung in a hushed, ominous and deliberate tone framed by Mike Gordon's slinky bass lines, "Shafty" draws on a vibe reminiscent of 1950s Beat poetry. The mood twists from the mocking scorn of "Olivia's Pool" into one of an earnest warning, as to caution "don't become this oblivious fool." Building on the irony of its predecessor, "Olivia's Pool," "Shafty" adds additional layers of word play into the equation. An oblivious fool would certainly seemed to have "gotten the shaft," and greeted with scorn, satire and downright harsh treatment. A "terrible thing about hell," to be sure! It also wouldn't be especially out of character for these guys to have in mind other meanings of a "Shaft(y)," perhaps as in the trunk of a tree, something suggestive of a shaft, an upright member, or, perhaps in Fishman's case, a small architectural column {See 10/31/94 et al].

Debuted during the "Island Tour" on 4/5/98 in Providence, many setlists have been re-written two or three times: "Oblivious Fool, to a slow funky beat" to "Olivia's Pool" and then to "Shafty" (who's on first?). "Shafty" pleased the band enough to make the cut among several dozen tunes for inclusion on *Story of the Ghost*. That enthusiasm has not yet translated to the live stage, as it has only been performed twice since, 7/2/98 at The Grey Hall, Freetown Christiana, Copenhagen, Denmark and 7/7/00 in the middle of a grueling "Maze." Stay tuned to your favorite pranksters for the continuing saga of "Shafty, an Oblivious Fool in Olivia's Pool."

See Also: "Olivia's Pool"

Shaggy Dog

Original Artist: Lightin' Hopkins

Original Album: (unknown)
Vocals: Trey (lead), Mike, Page (backing)
Debut: 10/15/86
Historian: Dan Mielcarz

Shaggy Dog, part of the Phish dog canon with "Dog Log," "Dogs Stole Things," and "No Dogs Allowed," was played several times from '86 to '88, after which it disappeared. It is a fun blues cover that many people assumed was gone forever (or at least only played during soundchecks), but it made a cameo appearance on 10/29/95. An a capella version was played on 5/6/92. However, the best "Shaggy Dog" on tape is no doubt the version played on 8/21/87 at Ian McLean's Farm. This version contains a continuous refrain of several barking dogs (one of them being Trey's dog, Marley) in the background.

She Caught the Katy and Left Me a Mule to Ride

AKA: "She Caught the Katy"
Original Artist: Taj Mahal
Original Album: *Natch'l Blues*, 1968
Vocals: Mike

Debut: 12/6/86
Historian: Jeremy Welsh

Released on Taj Mahal's album, *Natch'l Blues*, "She Caught the Katy" tells a story of unrequited love in a light-hearted manner. Phish performed this blues number a few times through 1987. See 4/29/87 and 8/29/87.

After eleven years and over eight hundred shows (not including an 8/10/97 soundcheck appearance), Phish broke-out "She Caught the Katy" at the Desert Sky Pavilion in Phoenix on 7/21/98. This funked-out version flowed out of a very strong "Ghost" at the end of the second set and segued into "Funky Bitch" (a notable ending to the show, with Mike singing the last two numbers). Phish has also covered "Corrina" off of the same album.

SHE'S BITCHIN' AGAIN (see: "BITCHIN' AGAIN")

Shine

Original Artist: Collective Soul
Original Album: *Hints, Allegations, and Things Left Unsaid* (1993)
Vocals: Tom Marshall

Peter Sitzman

Debut: 12/31/95
Historian: Ellis Godard

On 12/31/94, Mike Gordon teased the overplayed tripe-rock "Shine" (by overplayed tripe-rockers Collective Soul) during an epic "Mike's Song." Tom Marshall (who sang on "Run Like an Antelope" in the first set of that show, but was by then in the audience) must have cringed at the tease and appreciated it when Mike moved on. Back at Madison Square Garden a year later, he appeared to sing the song as a lesson in the importance of moving forward. Trey set up the appearance with narration (in "Col. Forbin's Ascent") about getting stuck in time. Following the comically horrific display, the band introduced the Phish Time Factory, which ensures that the world keeps spinning so that we don't get stuck with crappy pop tunes for very long.

SHORTAGE (see: "THE PRACTICAL SONG")

Silent In The Morning

AKA: "SITM," "Silent," "Silent in the AM"
Music: Trey Anastasio
Lyrics: Tom Marshall
Album: *Rift*
Debut: 3/6/92
Historian: Craig DeLucia

Silent is the coda to the *Rift* album. As the narrator awakens he begins to question the events he has dreamed and ponders the fate of his relationship. While "Silent" is a short, non-jamming song, many fans appreciate it because it is an opportunity for Page to show off his voice. Also, the counterpoint harmonies add a nice vocal touch to the song.

"Silent" is usually played on the heels of its companion, "The Horse." However, on 5/30/93, Silent was actually played alone for the first time. It has only happened twice since, on 6/23/94 and 12/13/99. The song has been played during three of the last five New Year's Eve shows. If you listen to the tapes, you'll notice that the audience usually cheers in delight when they are reminded that the same thing happened just last year.

See Also: "The Horse"

Simple

AKA: "Cymbop and Bebophone" (original title)
Music/Lyrics: Mike Gordon
Album: *A Live One* (12/10/94);
 ***Hampton Comes Alive* (11/21/98)**
Vocals: Phish
Debut: 5/27/94
Historian: Chris Glushko

Simple was first written and recorded by Mike Gordon in a four-track medium and introduced to the band during the studio sessions for *Hoist*. This version reflected the writing style of many previous Gordon compositions by its country and bluegrass characteristics. For this reason, the song was left off of the album *Hoist* and the band showed hesitation in performing it live.

Then, on 5/27/94, "Simple" debuted in a very strange and raw fashion during the "Mike's Song" at the Warfield Theater in San Francisco that evening. In contrast to the song we know today, the debut

version of "Simple" was Mike's original lyrics sung by the band members over a jam that had emerged from "Mike's Song." Three weeks later, "Simple" was played for a second time at the historic O.J. Show on 6/17/94, the same night that much of the country was watching the police chase of O.J. Simpson's white Ford Bronco through Los Angeles. This version was extremely reworked and sounded much like the "Simple" we are accustomed to hearing today with the exception of a minor humoristic augmentation providing the line "We've got O.J., cause we've got a band."

Since the reworked version of "Simple" debuted on 6/17/94, the song has not left Phish's rotation and has proven to be a band and fan favorite (in *The Phish Book*, Jon Fishman stated that it was his favorite Phish song as well as his favorite riff in the Trey Anastasio arsenal). Most often found in the second set, "Simple" has taken on a number of roles throughout the years. "Simple" was rarely a jamming vehicle in 1994 and 1995. At times it was part of a long jam the came out of a "Mike's Song" (see 11/16/94) and on rare occasions, such as 10/31/94, the song would contain some beautiful melodic jamming as a stand alone piece of music. However, it wasn't until Fall 1996 that the band realized "Simple" could be used as true jamming vehicle. During this period, several long and interesting jams evolved as Page would lead the jam in a new direction and Trey would patiently provide percussion on the mini-drumkit he was using at the time before picking up his guitar and joining in on lead. Some standout versions from this period include 10/31/96, 11/8/96 and 12/6/96 (which many feel contains a jam reminiscent of "Caution: Do Not Stop On Tracks" by the Grateful Dead).

With the exception of some notable versions in the fall of 1998 which contained long, dissonant jams (see 11/29/98 and 12/31/98), the modern "Simple" jam has remained relatively unchanged since 12/31/96. As opposed to being exploratory, today's jam contains gorgeous interplay by all four band members as they take the high energy theme of the song and dynamically descend with it until a point of near silence, usually providing a segue into the next song.

Finally, if one wishes to find "Simple" in a set, it is usually not very hard. Simply look for the "Mike's Song" and wait as more often than not "Simple" will emerge from the natural progression of the ending of "Mike's Song." This has led to some very flowing sets over the years. However, it has also led to many fans shaking their heads saying, "What ever happened to 'Hydrogen'?"

16 Candles

Music/Lyrics: Dixon/Khent
Original Artist: The Crests
Original Album: single (1959)
Vocals: Mike
Debut: 12/30/96
Historian: charlz franz

The Crests were a late 1950s doo wop group, whose 1959 "16 Candles" was a national hit single. "16 Candles" has appeared on innumerable compilation albums, has been covered by groups such as Sha Na Na, and was on the soundtrack for *American Graffiti*. The Crests' other hits included "The Angels Listened In" and "Step by Step." Singer Johnny Maestro went on to score another hit with Brooklyn Bridge in 1968, "Worst That Could Happen."

Phish covered "16 Candles" once, during the New Year's run on

12/29/96 at the Spectrum in Philadelphia. Mike Gordon stepped to the piano at the end of an instrument switch jam during "YEM," sat down, settled in and shouted "SEX!" After a pause, it became apparent that it was actually the first syllable of "sixteen." Cactus then went on to give a passable imitation of a psychedelic jamband member imitating a doo wop singer. He shoulda done the Zappa take off instead.

Skin It Back
Original Artist: Little Feat
Original Album: *Feats Don't Fail Me Now* (1974)
Vocals: Mike (lead)
Debut: 10/15/86
Historian: Phil Nazzaro

Little Feat must have been quite an influence on Phish during their early years. "Skin It Back" is one of three Feat songs to appear in the band's repertoire before the '90s. This one debuted on 10/15/86 in the Sculpture Room at Goddard College. Besides its great syncopated, funky style, this song features some excellent lyrics about the refusal of our narrator to settle down in one place. This leads him to fret over how to tell someone he loves her when they both know he'll be on the move again soon. Perhaps the lyrics, which are very unPhish-like in their romanticism, are the reason this song (as far as we know) has not been heard since 7/25/88. However, the travelling aspect of the words are a possible reason why "Cities" ("Find a city, find yourself a city to live in") followed "Skin It Back" twice in its short life. One of which, is the searing, flawless segue into "Cities" from 4/29/87 Nectar's show. Although "Time Loves A Hero" was resurrected after a nearly ten year hiatus on 8/11/98 and "On Your Way Down" saw the light of day after more then ten years on 9/16/99; "Skin It Back" remains the last Little Feat cover Phish still keeps in mothballs.

Skippy the Wondermouse
AKA: "Skippy"
Music: Trey Anastasio
Lyrics: Trey Anastasio, Dina Anastasio, The Dude of Life
Album: (none)
Debut: 12/1/84
Historian: Mark Toscano

This is one of the few tunes written by Trey with his mother, Dina, when working on various children's albums in the early '80s. It features bizarre kiddie lyrics over a Trey composition that would eventually serve as the bulk of "McGrupp." For the band's 12/1/84 Nectar's debut, the song was played with The Dude of Life on guest vocals, although Trey sang it himself in some subsequent versions. "Skippy" was played very few times, and by 1986, the song had disappeared, and "McGrupp"—more or less the same music with Tom Marshall lyrics instead—had taken its place. Why? Who knows. Perhaps nobody gave a shit about the mouse. Generally, people will tell you that they like dogs better than mice anyway. And McGrupp is a dog. So there you have it.

See also: "McGrupp and the Watchful Hosemasters"

Slave To The Traffic Light
AKA: "Slave"
Music/Lyrics: Trey Anastasio, Dave Abrahams, The Dude of Life

Album: "The White Tape"; *A Live One* (11/26/94)
Debut: 12/1/84
Historian: Syd Schwartz

Slave holds the distinction of being one of the oldest Phish originals, and is found on the earliest widely circulated Phish show, 12/1/84 at Nectar's in Burlington, VT. "Slave" appears on "The White Tape" and the basic structure of the song has remained largely intact over the years. "Slave" has never been a vehicle for improvisational exploration, but it has been a consistent song for demonstrating both subtle dynamics and powerful, soaring peaks. "Slave" also provides Page a chance to show his considerable abilities on the Fender Rhodes electric piano, an instrument sadly underutilized in his keyboard arsenal.

"Slave" was played semi-regularly in the old, old days, but it started to become somewhat sporadic in 1988. It found its way back into rotation in the summer of 1989 but after one performance in the fall of 1989 and one more in the winter, it disappeared again. It was played only three times in 1990, and almost a year went by until it was played by request on 3/17/91 during a second set that also featured the Prison Joke and the Bear Joke. After two October 1991 performances, "Slave" disappeared for almost two years and well over 200 shows.

A trip to the Cincinnati Zoo in August of 1993 apparently inspired the "Slave" breakout on 8/6/93. Though played only two more times that year, both performances (8/20/93 and 12/30/93) are frequently cited as among the best. "Slave" was in regular rotation for much of 1994 and 1995 with the version from 11/26/94 appearing on *A Live One*. Its usual place as a second set song (frequently closing the second set or as an occasional encore) was also established in that time period. Only occasional gaps in "Slave" performances through 1997 occured, but once again in 1998 performances became less frequent and "Slave's" appearance in a Phish show has gotten even rarer, with only a handful of appearances in the last two years.

Sleep
AKA: "Glisten"
Music/Lyrics: Trey Anastasio, Tom Marshall
Album: *Farmhouse*
Debut: 10/17/98
Vocals: Trey, Page
Historian: Mark Toscano

One of Phish's lighter offerings, "Sleep" premiered at Neil Young's Bridge School Benefit, debuting with the advantage of an acoustic setup. Played only sporadically since (and electric to boot), the song usually acts as a breather for the band and the audience, and occasionally as an opening encore tune.

"Sleep" nicely describes the feeling of trying to remember thoughts and ideas generated during lucid sleep, immediately prior to waking. The song was penned by both Tom and Trey during one of their writing and recording sessions at the legendary Stowe farmhouse. Tom's lyrics are some of his most evocative, and Trey's wonderful main guitar line is a perfect marriage of simplicity and thoughtfulness in composition.

That said, versions of "Sleep" don't differ from show to show, although this is not a bad thing. Played several times on the Fall 1998 tour (10/29/98, 11/11/98, 11/18/98, 11/25/98, and 12/28/98), the song reappeared the following year only twice (7/8/99 and 7/26/99). An ad-

ditional two performances of the tune can be found among Trey's 1999 solo shows, on 5/11/99 (with Tom Marshall) and 5/13/99, both with Trey playing piano rather than guitar.

The 2000 release of *Farmhouse* indicated that this likeable new tune was not forgotten by the band like its brethren "Waking Up" and "Never," and though its appearances in 2000 were modest (6/14/00 and 9/18/00 only), chances are that Phish will always find an occasional place for this one in setlists to come.

Sleeping Monkey

Music/Lyrics: Trey Anastasio, Tom Marshall
Album: (none)
Debut: 3/6/92
Historian: Craig DeLucia

Fans look forward to most Phish songs for the jams. "Sleeping Monkey," though, has become a welcome concert treat because it offers a glimpse of the band's sometimes bawdy sense of humor.

Sung by Trey and Fishman, with tongues firmly planted in cheek, the song tells the tale of a narrator who laments the disappearance (or, should we say, malfunction) of his "monkey." Laden with acute sexual references and double entendres, it is nine parts fun and one part music. Fishman's vocal performance on the final chorus, singing as high-pitched and whiny as the narrator surely feels, provides the icing on this cake. Also, many fans will recognize the ending jam as the tag from The Beatles' "Let it Be"; a clever ending given "Monkey's" frustrating tale of woe.

"Sleeping Monkey" is generally played as an encore, but sometimes shows up in the middle of a show. The song's presentation doesn't usually change much from performance to performance, but there are some versions that are particularly fun to hear. Seek out 3/14/92 (with John Popper on harmonica), 10/29/94 ("Monkey" inside of a hot, raging "Antelope"), 10/24/95 (which arose a capella from the "YEM" vocal jam, and was finished as normal and followed by an amazing "Antelope"), 12/6/97 (near the end of a hot, jam-filled second set), and 7/8/98 (with Betty from Chile on stage). And, for a fun twist, seek out 5/2/93, where Trey forgot Tom's lyrics and was embarassed because Tom was in attendance!

The Sloth

Music: Trey Anastasio
Lyrics: Trey Anastasio, Tom Marshall
Album: (none)
Debut: 8/9/87
Historian: Mark Toscano

Although it has never been a vehicle for jamming due to its tight composition, "The Sloth" is still quite a song. It's a nasty, raucous, even vicious ballad to the ugly likes of The Sloth, the meanest man in all of Gamehendge. As the penultimate song in Trey's Senior Study "The Man Who Stepped Into Yesterday" (aka the Gamehendge Saga), "The Sloth" occupies a pivotal point in the story that deals with the downfall of the evil King Wilson.

The Sloth is the awful character hired by Errand Woolfe to execute Wilson, who, without his stolen Helping Friendly Book, has been rendered powerless by the revolutionaries (with a big hand from Colonel Forbin). The preceding song, "The Famous Mockingbird," de-

scribes the flight of the Mockingbird to retrieve the Helping Friendly Book from Wilson's castle and deliver it into the desperate hands of the rebel Lizards. When Errand Woolfe, the revolution's leader, receives the Book from the Famous Mockingbird, he immediately formulates a plan. He will kill Wilson, and then use the Helping Friendly Book to make himself the new, omnipotent ruler of Gamehendge. After tying up the Famous Mockingbird with glue and rubber bands to protect the secrecy of his plan, he sets out to find The Sloth—the only person capable of completely disposing of Wilson. This song is a sort of vanity piece sung by The Sloth himself—a hubristic ode to his badness, nastiness, and friendlessness.

The intro and verses of the song are standard rock n' roll with a mean streak. Trey also incorporated call-and-response lyrics here, working partially from Tom Marshall's original story. Each line Trey sings in the song is followed by a complimentary line sung by Mike and Page. Musically, Trey took a completely different approach when composing "The Sloth's" middle instrumental section. Instead of working the music out on paper, he wrote it out of his head, disregarding any harmonic or theoretical concerns. He figured out each instrument's part by ear, beginning with the descending guitar line that opens up this section of the song.

Early versions of "The Sloth" (including the one found on the studio tape of "The Man Who Stepped Into Yesterday") are reasonably shorter than later examples, for Trey added a another section to the song's instrumental bridge some time in late 1988 or 1989, after he had completed his Senior Study. This shortness is also the case with early versions of "The Sloth," such as 8/21/87, where it segued out of a blistering jam to close the second set. Another later addition to the song's structure is the chanting that can often be heard over the pounding, repeated chord that makes up "The Sloth's" outro. Is it a subliminal Satanic message telling us to kill our loved ones or just counting from one to ten in Spanish? You be the judge.

Since 1989, "The Sloth" hasn't varied much from version to version, other than the usual fluctuations in tightness and precision that occur in most of the heavily composed tunes in the band's repertoire (e.g. "Fluffhead," "Divided Sky," "Mound," etc.). Some particularly strong versions include 5/25/88 (intro jams somewhat), 5/1/92 (strong), 2/20/93, 3/22/93 (very tight), 8/7/93 (ripping—segues out of "Avenu Malkenu"!), 12/28/93 (short fuse, loud boom), 5/22/94 (surprise segue out of "Demand"), and 12/31/95 (a raging thrill).

Although it was a pretty common song up through Summer tour '94 (in 1991 alone, it was played 27 times!), "The Sloth" has been very slothful in its appearances lately, chalking up only a few each year since then. However, even in recent appearances (e.g. 6/28/00), the band still seems to have a lot of fun playing "The Sloth," so there's still a chance at any given show that fans might get a surprise visit from the meanest, nastiest, dirtiest and dastardliest of all Gamehendgians.

Smells Like Teen Spirit

Original Artist: Nirvana
Original Album: *Nevermind* (1991)
Vocals: Trey (lead), Mike, Page (backing)
Debut: 11/2/98
Historian: Martin Acaster

With the 1991 release of Nirvana's major label debut *Nevermind*, Seattle was magically transformed into the font of all that was hip and cool in music. "Smells Like Teen Spirit," the first track of the album and breakthrough buzz bin hit single, gave instant fashion sense to all those flying the flannel across the nation. This Kurt Cobain lyrical homage to fitting in was the key that opened the door to success for the likes of Pearl Jam, Soundgarden, and Alice In Chains. Grunge was alive and well and would dominate popular music until the death of its reluctant messiah signaled its imminent demise in early April 1994. The blend of disaffected punk angst and catchy power chord hooks was just the winning combination that many of the hard rock fans who had suffered through the new wave of the 1980s were looking for.

Phish performed this landmark Nirvana hit as the encore to their shocking (to some overrated) Salt Lake City E Center show on 11/2/98. Thereby making a gig that was already destined to go down in history as one for the ages (see "Harpua" -> *Dark Side of the Moon* -> "Harpua") that much greater (or worse). Perhaps this surprise cover was an indication of another album which had been considered for the Halloween costume in Las Vegas two nights earlier. Based on the reputation the song carries as one of the worst covers Phish has ever performed, the decision to play the Velvet Underground classic *Loaded* on Halloween was clearly the right choice.

Thankfully, for those who think that the Phish rendition of "Smells Like Teen Spirit" carried an odor more akin to the one now emanating from its author, it has yet to return to a setlist. It did however make a brief (a single verse, by request) appearance at a Trey Tour show on 5/14/99 at SUNY Binghamton.

Smoke on the Water

Original Artist: Deep Purple
Original Album: *Machine Head* (1972)
Debut: 7/18/99
Historian: charlz franz

Perhaps Deep Purple's most famous tune, "Smoke on the Water" riffs are a favorite of budding guitarists everywhere. The song is about a 1971 Frank Zappa concert in Montreux, Switzerland, attended by the members of Deep Purple shortly before the recording of *Machine Head*. The show was cut short by a fire started by a fan that burned down the venue and sent smoke across Lake Geneva. Reportedly, the band didn't think the song had much potential and it didn't become a hit until it was released as a single in the United States in 1973.

A "Smoke on the Water" jam appears in "Icculus" from the 7/18/99 Oswego third set. Trey explains that according to the Helping Friendly Book, Heavy Metal is evil except for Deep Purple, whereupon the first verse of "Smoke" is played. Trey then explains that "Smoke" is the same song as "Cat Scratch Fever," but "Smoke" is the better song.

Sneakin' Sally Through the Alley

Music/Lyrics: Alain Toussaint
Original Artist: Robert Palmer
Original Album: *Sneakin' Sally Through the Alley* (1974)
Vocals: Trey (lead), Mike, Page (backing)
Debut: 9/27/85
Historian: Ellis Godard

Robert Palmer (who is mentioned in the lyrics to "Tube") had more than fifteen albums of his own, plus two more with The Power Station. The ninth brought him MTV fame, accompanied by iconic videos such as "Simply Irresistable." But his first album, with the hit title track (as well as one other Toussaint tune), brought him radio fame years earlier. "Sneakin' Sally through the Alley" follows "Sailing Shoes" (by Lowell George of Little Feat) and "Hey Julia" in an uninterrupted flow on the album (though not in radio play), as if the three are one track.

What other association Palmer and Feat may have had is unclear, particularly since Palmer's music quickly turned away from bluesy rock and toward electronic music and then jazz. But Phish took similar turns, from a blues-rock bar band to a jazzy electronic circus. Their early years included a number of Feat songs, including Toussaint's "On Your Way Down," and they recorded "Sneakin' Sally" as the last song of a six-song demo tape that circulated lightly in mid-1987. The latter also marked other important changes in the band's history.

In Phish's earlier versions, the song's role seemed somewhat defined, helping transition from something heavily orchestrated ("Slave," "YEM," "Fluffhead," "McGrupp," and "Lizards") to something silly ("Freebird," "Makisupa," and "Tela") or loud ("Suzy," "Frankenstein," "GTBT"). In the later period, the song's role became one of broadening the setlists from the recent funk phase back into the variety that is Phish (and thus followed "Wolfman's," "Boogie On," and "Birds," but preceded "Ghost," "Axilla," "Guyute," "Tube," and "It's Ice").

Early versions included the band's first vocal jams (3/11/88, 5/25/88, and 7/12/88), and one (2/24/88) featured an early horn bit by Fishman. The 10/30/85 is well-known, as it appears on a widely circulated tape, but stronger versions followed on 10/15/86, 8/29/97, and 12/30/97. The last actually included two versions, a show opener, after eight years of absence, and during the encore, when the band tried to find something to do with their time after getting caught exceeding the venue's curfew. Some contend the latter was to benefit those who got into the show late and missed the former.

Other strong versions segued out of "Dave's Energy Guide" (10/3/86) and "Wolfman's Brother" (4/2/98, 7/17/99, and 9/28/99), and into "Back Porch Boogie" (10/31/87), "Yamar" (5/28/89), "Guyute" (8/8/98), "Chalkdust" (10/31/98), and "Ghost" (12/11/99, which began with an "AC/DC Bag" tease).

So Lonely

Original Artist: The Police
Original Album: *Outlandos d'Amour* (1978)
Vocals: Page (lead), Mike, Trey (backing)
Debut: 11/14/98
Historian: Ellis Godard

Phish capped a decent show with a strange encore when they preceded "Tweezer Reprise" with this Police staple. The verse lyrics (including "Welcome to this one man show / Just take a seat, they're always free") didn't fit, though perhaps the chorus matched the mood of music men on the road and halfway through a four-week tour, their second as an all-married band.

For no known reason, the song was originally listed in setlists for 2/20/97 but was not played that night. In early 11/98, there was a thread on rec.music.phish telling people to correct their setlists, just a few

days before the song was played live for the first time!

Somantin

AKA: "Somanatin"
Music/Lyrics: Trey Anastasio, Tom Marshall
Album: (none)
Debut: (never performed live)
Historian: Mark Toscano

A mystery surrounds this unusual track. It has never appeared on any Phish album. It doesn't appear on any live Phish tape. In fact, it has never been performed live at a Phish show. Its existence is only known to fans in two ways. First, it appears on the infamous "*Ghost* Outtakes" recordings that have circulated somewhat meekly since first showing up following that album's final recording sessions in 1998. Second, Trey performed it three times during his 1999 solo tour, on the 4th, 6th, and 8th of May.

It's a very nice, tender ballad, yes, but it boasts a few unusual touches not unreminiscent of the work of Adrian Belew or even Robert Fripp. When the song's chorus kicks in after the stripped-down first verse, the restrained soar of a guitar drone commands attention, as the piano and bass walk upwards in deference to Fish's clockwork highhat beat. Enter the acoustic guitar breakdown, with more storytelling vocals from Trey, followed by another chorus. A delicate cymbal and electric piano bridge follows with Trey's fragile vocals, and the song concludes with another chorus, this time with a few more instruments added to the mix.

All the while, the multi-faceted story of a beleaguered character named Somantin unwinds, intertwined with the music in a nicely offset pattern. The lyrics were adapted by both Tom and Trey, from stories they each tell their respective children. The end result is a three-and-a-half-minute sweet pickle of a song, but one that apparently isn't ready or able to make the transition to o-Phish-al status.

Something

Music/Lyrics: George Harrison
Original Artist: The Beatles
Original Album: *Abbey Road* (1969)
Vocals: Page (lead), Trey (backing)
Debut: 10/29/98
Historian: Chris Bertolet

Critics and rock historians frequently hail *Abbey Road* as one of the most important records ever made, so as ardent Beatles fans, it's no surprise that Phish would mine it for covers. But as *Abbey Road* is predominantly a Lennon-McCartney opus, it's "something" of a curiosity that Phish chose one of only two George Harrison compositions found on the album.

The debut of "Something" concluded a magical, misty tour-opening gig at L.A.'s Greek Theatre on 10/29/98. Though grossly underrated due to the strong Las Vegas Halloween run that ensued, the Greek show boasted quite a few charms, including an ominous, throbbing "Reba" that melted unexpectedly into a euphoric breakout of "Walk Away." But it was "Something's" bittersweet embrace of the uncertainties of love that sent the crowd away sated.

Phish played "Something" three times the following month and, most regrettably, has not played it since.

Somewhere Over the Rainbow

Music: Harold Arlen
Lyrics: Edgar Yipsel "Yip" Harburg
Original Artist: Judy Garland
Original Album: *Wizard of Oz* soundtrack (1938)
Vocals: (performed instrumental)
Debut: 3/13/92
Historian: Ellis Godard

There's something about the end of the rainbow being hard to find, that inhibits some folks from looking for the pot of gold. "Somewhere Over the Rainbow" is a song about that journey, from the cinematic masterpiece (and money maker) *The Wizard of Oz*, a golden classic—indeed, a classic of any colour you like. But the song has remained elusive (on the run, so to speak) in Phish setlists. When it has appeared, it has often signaled a time to eclipse a damaged jam in the air.

The first signs were Trey's teases during "Wilson" (3/13/92), "Harry Hood" (3/14/92), and "Take the A-Train" (8/17/92). Saxophonist Leroi Moore used it to take control during a lost Fishman vacuum solo (4/20/94), and the band spent nearly a minute on it after a meandering jam in Reba (7/3/94). The first full treatment came in Utah (8/2/96), but even that was Page solo (on the theremin). He repeated that trick 8/5/96 and 8/13/96, and again at 8/14/97 during the Merry Pranksters jam—and perhaps encouraging them to click their heels and head home. In each of these appearances, the song has brought the band back from an arguably dark side, but only faintly so.

Not until 8/9/98 did "Somewhere Over the Rainbow" leave the footnotes and enter the setlist proper. Though a weak version (certainly no pot of gold), it was quite earnest and appeared in a great gig, joined with "Terrapin Station" on the anniversary of Jerry Garcia's death. Somewhere, Jerry and Judy are singing the lyrics Phish has neglected. Perhaps someday Phish will sing the lyrics for us…and them.

Soul Shakedown Party

Music/Lyrics: Bob Marley
Original Artist: Bob Marley and the Wailers
Original Album: single (1970)
Vocals: Page (lead), Fish, Mike, Trey (backing)
Debut: 2/17/97
Historian: Phillip Zerbo

Walk the streets of Amsterdam, and it is hard to travel very far before seeing some tribute to Bob Marley. Combine that with the praise members of Phish have showered on Bob Marley over the years, and it was no great surprise for Phish to debut a Marley cover during their second ever visit to Amsterdam. "Soul Shakedown Party" opened Phish's first ever appearance at Amsterdam's historic Paradiso on 2/17/97. While many fans think of "Soul Shakedown Party" as a perfect cover for Phish to keep in their repertoire, it made only one subsequent appearance, on 2/20/97, at Teatro Smeraldo in Milan, Italy.

Spanish Flea

Music/Lyrics: Julius Wechter
Original Artist: Herb Alpert and the Tijuana Brass
Original Album: *Going Places* (1965)

Vocals: (instrumental)
Debut: 12/1/84
Historian: Mark Toscano

They only played this classic of '60s swinger-pop once, and at one of the first official Phish shows no less. On 12/1/84, the band made their Nectar's debut as Phish in the upstairs room at the legendary bar. Following an interesting set featuring "Skippy the Wondermouse," "Makisupa Policeman," and The Dude of Life in full (albeit cheapo) regalia, band intros were done above a soundtrack of this Herb Alpert masterpiece, sans Herb's signature trumpet, but with the added bonus of Marc Daubert on percussion.

Sparkle

Music: Trey Anastasio
Lyrics: Tom Marshall
Album: *Rift*
Debut: 9/25/91
Historian: Martin Acaster

Sparkle, found on the album *Rift*, and written for Tom Marshall's wife, tells the tale of a man on his knee. He is prepared to ask his beloved's hand in marriage as the weight of the future that is rapidly unfolding before him presses down upon his head, all the while his heart soars with all the unbridled emotion of a man in love. To truly know the sensation, it must be experienced. Faced with the pressure from friends, from family, from heart, and head, the groom to be is overcome by the simultaneous and conflicting emotions of courage and fear, sobriety and hilarity, unable to withstand the matter-antimatter conflict in the warp drive of his brain he laughs…and, laughing, falls apart.

Musically "Sparkle" mimics the soon-to-be-former bachelor's pulse rate. Slow at first, building to a frenetic, seizure-inducing cacaphony by its end, it is blue-speed-metal-grass at its finest. The pulverizing jackhammer which "Sparkle" often becomes live, when combined with strobe lighting with the potential to induce vomiting or at the very least disorientation can make this often-played much-maligned song somewhat uncomfortable for the average listener.

"Sparkle" has been played well over 200 hundred times since 1991. There is very little improvisation in "Sparkle," with deviations from version to version being the result of the gravitational lensing caused by the speed of its delivery. Performances of note include a 5/17/92 version at Union College in Schenectady, NY where it followed a Fishman vacuum solo re-enactment of the crash which transformed Steve Austin into the Six Million Dollar Man; the swirling second set launch pad for the 5/7/94 Bomb Factory seguefest; the blood-stained solitaire of the infamous 6/17/94 Eagle Ballroom "OJ show" which culminated in a "Big Ball Jam"; an early second set rhinestone in the dazzling tiara that was the legendary 12/6/96 Aladdin Las Vegas show; and the 8/9/98 Virginia Beach "Sparkle" which follows a blistering "AC/DC Bag" on an evening made all the more special by the gift of another jewel of a rare and different sort. Other recent versions which are worthy of a look through the jeweller's glass include 12/17/99 Hampton, VA, 5/22/00 Radio City Music Hall, and 7/10/00 Deer Creek, IN.

Sparks

Music: Pete Townshend

Original Artist: The Who
Original Album: *Tommy* (1969)
Vocals: (instrumental)
Debut: 3/23/87
Historians: Craig DeLucia and Mark Toscano

Long before Phish covered *Quadrophenia*, they covered another song from an epic Who rock opera: "Sparks," the instrumental coda to "The Amazing Journey" on *Tommy*. The song is thrilling, especially in its live incarnations (check out the re-released *Live at Leeds* or *Live at the Isle of Wight*), and also serves as a thematic basis for *Tommy*'s "Underture," the epic track that closes that album's first disc. Especially interested fans are encouraged to check out The Who's awesome third album, *The Who Sell Out*, which contains an early incarnation of "Sparks" rounding out the album-closing "Rael 1." (Also, the remastered CD version contains a bonus track, "Glowgirl," whose final seconds yield a nice surprise!)

Played sparingly in the late 1980s, the song had disappeared from rotation entirely by the end of 1990. It reemerged for a few appearances during monster jams in the magnificent month of August 1993 ("Also Sprach Zarathustra" > "Mike's Song" -> "Sparks" > "The Ballad of Curtis Loew" on 8/2 and "Also Sprach Zarathustra" > "Run Like an Antelope" -> "Sparks" -> "Walk Away" -> "Antelope" -> Have Mercy -> "Antelope" on 8/14) and another at one of the most famous setlong jams ever: the 5/7/94 "Tweezerfest." Finally, it eked out one more showing during the second set in Spartanburg on 10/29/94 before disappearing. "Sparks" has only been heard once since, out of a "Simple" jam on 11/29/96, followed by an amusingly well-placed "Sparkle." Fans who can't get enough should pick up 3/17/91 and listen to the Bowie, where the song was teased.

Speak To Me

Original Artist: Pink Floyd
Original Album: *Dark Side of the Moon* (1973)
Vocals: (instrumental)
Debut: 10/31/94
Historian: Mark Toscano

Many fans of Pink Floyd underestimate drummer Nick Mason's contributions to the band. This is largely because even most Floyd fans don't realize that it was Mason who ultimately shaped the formation and overall thematic structure of *Dark Side of the Moon*, weaving his sound collages of people discussing madness in and out of songs over the course of the classic album. He is the sole author of "Speak to Me," having asked dozens of friends and strangers provocative questions, and using the taped responses to create samplings for the then-unborn disc.

Phish have used this overtly recognizable bit of Pink Floyd twice, once as a trick and once as a treat. The trick came on 10/31/94, at the start of the second set. No one at the show knew which album the band was going to play, and an intro of "Speak to Me" convinced everyone it was to be *DSOTM*. Not so—as the building collage of speech and screaming was about to let loose into "Breathe," the sound bite stopped, breaking into the famous Ed Sullivan Beatles intro instead. As is commonly known, the band then performed The Beatles' entire "White Album."

Fans were given a treat four years later, though, on 11/2/98, when

Phish gave a surprise performance of *Dark Side* in Utah, starting it up with this essential opening track from the album. In both cases, the actual track was used, taken directly from a CD of the album, as it would be a bit difficult (notwithstanding "Revolution 9") to reproduce such a weird sonic mishmash live.

Split Open And Melt

AKA: "Melt," "SOAM," "Split"
Music/Lyrics: Trey Anastasio
Album: *Lawn Boy; Hampton Comes Alive* (11/20/98)
Vocals: Trey (lead), Mike, Page (backing)
Debut: 2/17/89
Historians: Charles Dirksen and Mark Toscano

Since entering Phish's repertoire in 1989, "Split Open and Melt" ("SOAM") has thrilled fans with its ferocious jams. "SOAM's" complex improv segment is notorious for its time signature, which involves three sections of eight eighth-notes and then a fourth section with nine eighth-notes in a steady pulse (listen to Fishman's hi-hat). This tune, now an integral jam tune often used to close first sets, first debuted in early 1989. The *Lawn Boy* version has curious origins: the band actually recorded "SOAM" and "Bathtub Gin" with the money and studio time they won at the 4/21 and 4/22/89 "Rock Rumble," a local battle-of-the-bands-style competition.

It was not uncommon for horn players to sit in on "SOAM" during its early years, as Trey was especially proud of the horn charts he wrote for the song. Check out the notorious 10/20/89 version, the first to include horns. During the intro, Russ Remington and Dave Grippo's lights went out, preventing them from reading the music. Not to have the first horn-augmented version of his pet project be ruined, Trey stopped the tune and begun it again. The first Phish album release to feature musicians outside the band, the *Lawn Boy* "SOAM" featured Joseph Somerville, Jr. on trumpet, Russell B. Remington on tenor sax, Christine Lynch on vocals, and Dave "the truth" Grippo on alto sax. For their July 1991 Giant Country Horns tour, Phish performed a number of strong versions of "SOAM," playing on its strengths as a horn tune while they had the chance. Trey has mentioned multiple times that for a while, "SOAM" wasn't really meeting its potential in their live performances, and as a result had been dropped out of rotation for some time. This all changed on the night of 4/21/93, when the band played an awesome, stretched-out "SOAM" that forever changed the way the band felt about the song, not to mention the approach taken to perform it. "SOAM" again became a regular part of the live show, re-invented for a new jamming outlook. The band thought highly enough of this change and the version that sparked it that they used the 4/21/93 "SOAM" jam as part of *Hoist*'s finale, tacked onto the end of the otherwise stunted "Demand." Since '93, the song has had its ups and downs, but consistently produces some of the band's sickest and most mind-bending Type I jams. It's the kind of song that seems to just get better with every version experienced.

"SOAM" has split open and melted the minds of fans on many occasions. Exciting, notable versions include: 4/15/89 and 10/22/89 (both with drum solos), 11/30/89 Boston (heavy "Dave's Energy Guide" teasing); 12/30/92 Springfield; 4/21/93 Columbus (the "Demand" version); 5/13/94 Tempe; 12/28/95 Worcester; 7/23/97 Atlanta; 8/2/97 George; 8/10/97 Noblesville (King Crimson's "Larks Tongues in Aspic (Part II)";

7/15/99 Holmdel (very improvisational version with "Kung"); and 12/30/99 Big Cypress. "SOAM" is one of the strongest tunes in the band's repertoire, and usually shines on stage. As such, most versions are recommended listening.

See Also: "Demand"

Spock's Brain

AKA: "The Plane," "The First Single," "Israel"
Music/Lyrics: Phish
Album: (none)
Debut: 5/16/95
Historians: Benjy Eisen/Emilie Kennedy/
  Bradley Lonard/Mark Toscano

When Phish played a special one-set show at Lowell Memorial Auditorium on 5/16/95 they were the guests of honor for a Voters For Choice Benefit. The show also featured sets by the multi-media Emergency Broadcast Network (EBN) and rocker Jennifer Trynin. Due to the unusual nature of the show, and with Phish's summer tour still almost month away, fans were unsure what to expect. Building anticipation even more, Gloria Steinem, President of Voters For Choice, delivered an extended speech immediately preceeding the main attraction. It was from this odd setting, that the oddity of "Spock's Brain" emerged.

Phish's set featured ten debuts, compared to only four familiar tunes—a record according to Gloria's pre-set introduction. Midway through the set when Fishman came out front to sing a tune, he answered fans' requests to name the new songs that had just been played. Fish proceeded to name some of them—"Theme From the Bottom," "Don't You Wanna Go," and "Ha Ha Ha,"—but seemed curiously ambivalent about the third. It turned out that the song didn't yet have a title. And, since it was a Voters For Choice benefit, the band decided to let the audience choose their favorite from four possible titles. Following a very enthusiastic reaction from the crowd, Trey listed the potential titles. The first choice, "The Plane," spawned a rather non-plussed reaction; some folks even booed, albeit in jest. A similar reaction came from the voters at the announcement of the second title, "The First Single." When the third choice, "Israel," received a modest crowd response, Fishman commented, "Ah, c'mon. You can call anything "Israel" and it works, right?"

The fourth choice was "Spock's Brain." The crowd went wild. "Well I guess we know the title to that song!" Fishman assessed.

It turned out to be the most appropriate title, for as Trey subsequently explained, the song was inspired by an episode of *Star Trek* of the very same moniker. Originally broadcast on September 20, 1968, the "Spock's Brain" episode is famed as one of the worst *Trek* episodes of all time (that's including *Deep Space Nine* and *Voyager*!) The first show of the third series, it concerns a race of Amazonian women who decide that they don't want to think for themselves. In order to accomplish this, they steal Spock's brain, leaving the inimitable Vulcan a mindless zombie. Eventually, of course, the brain is retrieved and Dr. McCoy replaces it in Spock's skull. The episode was penned by "Lee Cronin," the penname of Gene L. Coon, who had actually written some other, more respectable episodes of the legendary series.

The song itself was an instant winner, showing off many strengths of Phish's songwriting within the boundaries of one song—great vocal

interplay, time changes, and a nice groove—everything but Type II jams. Containing no room for real improvisation, the tune averaged around five to five-and-a-half minutes every time it was played.

Played in the first set five times throughout June of 1995, and never with a gap of more than five shows in between, the seemingly final performance of this tune was at the Mann Music Center in Philadelphia on 6/24/95. Having become stronger every performance, the Philly version was perhaps the best. Also by this time, just a month and a half after its debut, "Spock's Brain" had already become a widespread fan favorite.

But then suddenly, without any warning, the song disappeared. At one point, an unlikely rumor spread that Elektra, anticipating it as the band's next single, asked the guys to stop playing it. However, due to the song's radio-unfriendly strangeness and the fact that they would make a decision like that only on their own, this is highly unlikely. Still, much speculation continues to surround its disappearance and even more speculation constantly revolved around a break-out: Almost every tour since the Summer of '95 there have been rumors proclaiming its return. Every so often there are reports of a "Spock's Brain" soundcheck. Once in awhile fans even claim to have heard a "Spock's Brain" tease during a particular jam (e.g. 8/15/96 Clifford Ball). These rumors became especially fervent during the Summer '98 tour—a tour during which many rare and/or "retired" songs snuck in an appearance or two. Clearly, the intensity with which fans wanted to see this song brought back rivaled only "Destiny Unbound."

By 2000, fans had all but forgotten about "Spock's Brain," and new fans were either completely unfamiliar with the tune or had only heard the much-circulated 5/16/95 debut. Chances of a breakout were less likely, and gossip about this possibility had pretty much dissolved into nothing. Though weirder breakouts have happened (7/5/94 "Letter to Jimmy Page" to name one), fans couldn't have been happier when, on 9/29/00 in the debauched and discombobulated city of Vegas, Phish let the seemingly innocent post-"Wilson" noises slam into the first "Spock's Brain" in over five years. Fans were treated to a nice, but unsteady welcome-back version of the beloved tune in the first set of that show, the band letting its closing refrain serve as scenic backdrop of the ensuing "Bathtub Gin." An even stronger performance of this rarity occurred a week later at Shoreline (10/6/00), segueing unbelievably out of a fiery "Down With Disease." Whether or not it becomes a permanent part of the repertoire in years to come remains to be seen.

Many fans recall the 5/16/95 show when Fishman joked that "this is a benefit for Spock's Brain being put back together." He had no idea....

Spooky

Original Artist: Atlanta Rhythm Section
Original Album: Single (1967)
Vocals: (performed instrumental)
Debut: 3/14/93
Historian: Ellis Godard

Fans have reacted to and noted dozens of examples where Trey seemed to play a bit of this 1970s classic. But a bit of "Spooky," like a bit of "Mind Left Body," is simple enough to be elusive if intentional (such as teases during the 11/19/94 "YEM" or the 7/9/99 "Twist") or

imagined if unintentional (such as in the noodling of the 6/30/98 "Ghost"). Nonetheless, three examples are complete enough to warrant actually labelling "Spooky": during "YEM" jams 3/14/93 and 4/14/93, both with a verse by Page, and during the 8/13/96 soundcheck.

Squeeze Box

Music/Lyrics: Pete Townshend
Original Artist: The Who
Original Album: *Who by Numbers* (1975)
Vocals: Trey (?)
Debut: 12/2/83
Historian: Mark Toscano

Performed at Phish's first ever gig (under the name "Blackwood Convention"), this familiar Who song derives from *Who by Numbers*, the band's disappointing 1975 follow-up to *Quadrophenia*. At a "show" featuring only covers, "Squeeze Box" preceded The Doors' "Roadhouse Blues," another song that until recently was not known to have ever been covered by Phish. Not much is known about the Phish version of "Squeeze Box," for although a recording of the show exists, tapes do not circulate. Also, as the band quickly rehearsed only a select number of songs over Thanksgiving break that year, the song may also have been performed at their very next show, either 12/3/83 or 12/4/83.

The Squirming Coil

AKA: "Coil"
Music: Trey Anastasio
Lyrics: Tom Marshall
Album: *Lawn Boy; A Live One* (10/9/94 and 10/23/94)
Debut: 1/20/90
Historian: Ellis Godard

At base, "Squirming Coil" is a fabulously energetic and cerebral piece de resistance, not an epic of "Fluffhead" or "You Enjoy Myself" proportions, but a solid landmark of an earlier era in Anastasio compositions. It is frequently followed by something energetic ("Tweezer," "Golgi," "Llama," or "Antelope"), and has rarely opened a show (though see 6/5/90). But the compositional mastery is not the song's forte, despite predictable placement (late in the show) and consistency (as all versions are essentially the same).

The strong point of "Squirming Coil" is beyond the composition. In early versions, it simply ends with a short close-out by Page. But that ending evolved slowly, and in the closing minutes are sometimes two, sometimes five or more, as Trey, then Fish, then Mike slow and fade from the music, leaving Page to glide gently around scales, keys, signatures, riffs, and more on his own. (The 7/8/99 "Simple" also ended with Page left ending a jam on his own.) The first signs were 4/12/91, ending a crazy three-part encore, but it would be in several more encores (eg 10/10/91, 10/18/91) before the Icarusian meltdowns began to take form (7/16/92, 8/17/92), becoming full-blown show-enders in the following years (e.g. 4/17/93, 5/10/94, and 11/19/94). By the next summer, "Split Open and Melt" was also coming into a new area and Red Rocks (6/9/95), for example, saw both tunes in an invigorated state. The effect is sometimes magical (witness 7/16/92 or 3/18/93), sometimes perfunctory. But the meandering, variable ending has been so expansive that Page's noodling during soundchecks are sometimes labelled as Coil teases.

Split Open and Melt

Compiled by Syd Schwartz

Date	Time	Notes
10/20/89	05:53	With Dave Grippo and Russ Remmington on horns. The band gets interrupted during the first attempt at 3:20 into the song because the lights go off and Russ and Dave can't see the charts. Trey gets about as verbally miffed at the lights going out as you'll probably ever hear him get on stage with a live mic.
10/22/89	08:45	With Fishman drum solo from 2:55 until 3:58.
11/30/89	08:03	Heavy Dave's Energy Guide quoting from Trey.
07/21/91	06:12	Most commonly circulated horns show.
03/12/92	07:38	Machine gun Trey gets paid by the note in this version.
04/16/92	07:59	Well-played with particularly nice bass work from Mike.
12/30/92	08:22	An intense pre-1993 version. Page and Trey just RAGE.
04/21/93	11:23	The jam segment of this version appears in the Demand on Hoist.
04/29/93	09:57	Run to the hills!
08/12/93	11:52	Psychedelic trance.
08/26/93	14:41	Hallowed Be Thy Name.
05/13/94	11:34	Ferocious and terrifying.
07/03/94	15:37	With Simpsons theme and Hendrix teases.
08/10/97	16:01	Frenzied, chaotic improvisation.
12/14/95	13:55	With silent jam.

Date	Time	Notes
12/28/95	10:54	Shadows of 12/30/92. Trey sounds like he is demonically possessed.
07/09/97	11:55	Thick funk: Trey makes sweet love to his wah-wah.
07/23/97	12:32	Even funkier: I expected Starsky and Hutch to make an appearance.
08/02/97	14:13	Staggeringly gorgeous funky-ass groove that shot the sun out of the sky at the Gorge.
08/10/97	17:32	Features a fully-formed "Larks Tongues in Aspic (Type II)" jam.
11/13/97	11:14	All structure gets thrown out the window at about 7:15. It seemed particularly intense when I was alone on the subway platform at about 1:00 AM but I should probably play it again under less paranoid circumstances.
11/06/98	14:04	One of Mike's favorite jams of the fall. Hot, tight, collective groove.
07/15/99	30:03	Opens with a 2001 drum beat (which Fish maintains somewhat cacophoniously). Includes Kung. Unusually improvisational.
07/26/99	15:24	2001 rhythm at first. Thrashing jam, which includes a speech from Trey.
12/31/99	21:19	Thrilling, funky, major-key jam. Segues into Catapult. Timing includes Catapult.
06/14/00	14:44	Vigorous jam. At end, Trey comments on "nourishment" during intermission.
07/01/00	12:16	Angry, dangerous, blistering.

Although this ending section wanders widely and sometimes wildly, it does almost always with Page on his own, sometimes with other band members leaving the stage one at a time as they drop out of the song. As such, the song usually stands alone even though it contains some of the most expansive soloing in the Phish repertoire. Nonetheless, some versions have developed into something else rather than petering out, including 9/28/90 into "Lizards," 12/28/90 into "Tweezer," 4/27/91 into "Wipe Out," 10/3/91 into "Tweezer," 8/20/92 into "Bowie," 5/8/93 into "Big Ball Jam," 2/17/97 into "Disease," and 12/30/98 into "Slave," the most unusual of these transitions being 10/3/91 (with a Dixieland transition) and 12/30/98 (which also had "Piper" teases).

Other notable versions include 7/24/91 with horns and followed by "Buried Alive," 10/4/91 with a "Linus and Lucy" tease, 5/17/92 with a birthday dedication to Page, 2/5/93 dedicated to Sofi, 5/17/94 interrupted by Trey with a cake for Page, 10/31/94 at nearly 3 a.m. after a marathon show, 2/13/97 closing one of the band's strongest tours, 10/8/99 with a "Bug" tease, and 6/14/00, which was reacted to explosively for nearly half an hour.

Stand!
Original Artist: Sly and the Family Stone
Original Album: *Stand!* (1969)
Vocals: Trey (lead), Fish, Mike, Page (backing)

Debut: 6/6/97 (private show); 6/13/97 (public show)
Historian: Phillip Zerbo

On a tour-opening two-night run that witnessed the live performance debut of no less than thirteen Phish originals, the first night encore on 6/13/97 in Dublin, Ireland gave a nod to a pair of musical and cultural powerhouses of the late 1960s. The title track to the highly successful 1968 album *Stand!*, this Sly and the Family Stone cover was an exhilarating early example of the funky grooves that became dominant in 1997. 1960s San Francisco Psychedelic Funk meets 1990s Vermont Cow Funk, in Ireland of all places! This spirited cover included some now classic extended "start-stop" jams that were prevalent in 1997, and a genuine, fluid, and distinctively funky transition to the Jimi Hendrix classic rocker "Izabella." Besides the enormous historic value of the debuts and the at times inspired group improvisation and musical cohesion of these shows, the "Stand!" and "Izabella" encore alone makes the Dublin run something that should be sought out on tape!

While "Stand!" was only performed by Phish in public on that one occasion, it was paired with "Izabella" two previous times by members of Phish. First as the band "New York!," seemingly a "one-off" band which made its only public performance on 5/21/97 at Club Toast in Burlington, VT. The lineup for this single gig included Trey, Mike, Pistol Stamen on guitar, James Harvey on drums, and Tom "Tommy Law" Lawson on guitar and keyboards. The same song combo also closed

"Dangerous Women in Phish's Music"

Allison Tuthill, Charlottesville, VA

One of the things I like the most about Phish is that the women in their songs are Subjects (Acting Individuals) and not Objects (Passive, viewed only through the eyes of the group) as many women in rock, rap, and popular songs are. I recently read a book that defined the concept of "dangerous women," and I couldn't help but think of four characters from Phish's songs who are each "Dangerous Women" in their own unique way. Dangerous women are basically those who do things that are not "appropriate." Such women put social paradigms into question merely by their existence. By acting in ways that are not "natural" for women, they often end up acting "as men." Such women cast doubt upon the society's vision of masculinity. Hence the adjective "dangerous," for such women pose danger to the social constructs of gender identity. Yet there is a certain fascination with, if not attraction to, such dangerous women for the viewer. For this reason, I wish to examine the portrayals of four dangerous women in Phish's music: Tela, the revolutionary; Suzy Greenberg, an '80s child in flux; Esther, possessor of true Knowledge; and Millie Grace, who does not allow adversity to keep her from acting.

As the single strong female character and a rebel in the *Gamehendge* saga, Tela is the obvious starting point. She has been the subject of much debate on the newsgroup, rec.music.phish (past articles accessible through www.dejanews.com; good summary available at www.phish.net). Most people seem to accept the idea that she might have been a spy for Wilson, but as David Steinberg points out (www.ihoz.com), her identity as a spy is "established" by Errand Wolfe, who obviously had already been corrupted by the evil of Wilson's domain, and therefore should be discounted as a character reference. In any case, Tela is referred to as the "Jewel of Wilson's Foul Domain," and Colonel Forbin is attracted to her persona (as well as to her beauty). Certainly, the song seems to indicate that Tela becomes a revolutionary after many years of frustration due to inaction ("burst at the seams there was nothing she could do"). Rather than sit around, she uses her suffering to become strong and take action ("Tela grew strong from her struggle to endure…Time touched her wounds and shelter proved the cure").

Then again, the question is raised: If Forbin is attracted to Tela's revolutionary actions and ideas, her strength of character, and her role as a warrior (remember, he falls for her when he sees her riding the multi-beast, and it is evidently on her command that the unit monster saves Rutherford, while Forbin stands by helpless—these are not the actions of a weak woman), is she "beautiful" (in the societal sense) or is he actually (oooh, gasp) attracted to TELA (i.e., the soul that inhabits her body). Her beauty struck him at first glance, but I have always found the moment where she reaches out her hand and helps him onto her multi-beast rather touching, and I think that this moment is also influential in establishing his fascination with her. She is a comrade and a friend, as well as warrior, revolutionary, and beautiful woman. I think Colonel Forbin is also attracted somewhat to the danger that she represents as the only

woman revolutionary, yet in the end, he is attracted to TELA. Forbin can handle the idea of a strong woman.

One further question: If Tela was not guilty, why did Errand Wolfe feel that she must be executed? There are several possibilities. First, Forbin was new to the scene and obviously (as we later see) was unable to see through Wolfe's facade into his blackened heart. Perhaps, Wolfe knew he could handle Forbin on his own, and eventually obtain possession of the *Helping Friendly Book*, but it is possible that he felt he could not handle both Forbin and Tela. Forbin is a strong and noble-hearted hero, but his lack of experience in Gamehendge makes him a less dangerous opponent than this paragon of dangerous women, Tela.

Second, it might be that Wolfe felt somehow threatened by this dangerous woman. She obviously had the power to inspire those around her. Indeed, it is likely that her inner fire prompted Forbin to become involved in the revolution. It often seems to Forbin is somewhat swept along by events around him, and does not take the initiative as much as he might. (Although this might be a function of his inexperience and his "newness" to the scene.) It is certain that his reaction to Tela influenced, at least to some extent, his involvement with the revolutionaries.

This leads to yet another question: Is Tela's death necessary to the plot of the story? Certainly, Forbin felt some regret and loss at her death. Does he seem to feel betrayed by Tela, or does he, again, simply react instead of act? This is a question that seems unanswered by the text. Certainly, Tela's death might have been the impetus for his decision to try to obtain the *Helping Friendly Book* and help the lizards. In this case, then, Tela's death might have been necessary to spur Forbin into action. If this is true, then Wolfe's insistence upon her guilt is called even more into question. Could he have foreseen that Forbin would be forced into action, thus bringing him the *Helping Friendly Book* and the power that lies within? Maybe we will know someday, but in the meantime, I agree with a recent rec.music.phish poster that *Gamehendge* is not all that it seems. The entire saga raises some interesting (and open-ended I might add) questions about gender roles, love, action versus reaction, passivity versus aggression, guilt, betrayal, and revolution. These concepts are examined in the *Gamehendge* saga, but most importantly they are *not* all answered, which leaves all of us with some interesting things to think about.

Suzy Greenberg is a somewhat controversial figure in Phishtory, as she is rather negatively portrayed. The Dude of Life wrote these lyrics, which paint the image of a woman who has not only treated him badly, but also has some issues of her own. It is a rather one-sided portrayal, and thus we must ask ourselves how accurate this portrayal is, yet we may still examine Suzy as she is presented in this song. Suzy is basically a character in flux. "Suzy is an artist, she paints quite a lot, an artist she may be, but a genius she's not." She wants to be a lot of things, yet is unable to find purpose, focus, or

"Dangerous Women in Phish's Music" *(continued)*

direction. She plays at a profession because she does not know who she is. Though the Dude's portrayal is certainly negative, the image of the lost child is one that is familiar to all of us.

She is a child of the '80s (first played 8/9/87), when the Feminist Movement was being called into question, when a lot of women had no idea who they were, where the were going, how they were going to get there, and who they would be if and when they *did* get there. Suzy is in a constant state of motion like the proverbial "chicken with its head cut off." Her motion is directionless and lacks purpose. It is motion without meaning, motion for its own sake. None of Suzy's activities fill her with purpose or meaning; she is unable to define herself in spite of her efforts to find her own niche. This inability to express oneself or define oneself is indicative of the times in which the song was written, when therapists were beginning to be popular: "She's always afraid that she's not sure what she's worth / she's out of her mind, and she's not of this earth." In fact this "she's not of this earth" might even indicate chemical substance abuse; certainly something like valium might explain her lack of connection with the rest of the world.

In any case, her flighty behavior is somewhat explained by this last line: She seems to have low self-esteem. At the very least the fear of low self-esteem seems to have affected her behavior, which is yet another '80s illness that has carried over into the '90s. Certainly poor body image, low self-esteem, and feelings of worthlessness or depression could be a contributing factor in her behavior. Might it not be, however, that the Dude takes issue (excuse the pun) with people who excuse their behavior because of past experiences? Certainly this is one possibility, as he mentions that Suzy is always "playing the game." What game could it be other than the one everyone plays, the game of trying to fit in?

Whether Suzy might be viewed as dangerous or not (in my terms) is a difficult question. I don't think she really crosses any gender lines, but I would characterize her as dangerous. She is basically a loose cannon, unpredictable, and dangerous in this sense. Her danger is to herself, as she must find purpose to function in society, and also to others who might become involved with her (such as the Dude). Though the song gives only the Dude's story, we can extrapolate some of Suzy's story from his words, giving us this dual definition of Suzy's Danger. Although she is not dangerous in any positive or pro-active manner, she serves as a reminder of a danger every person could face, male or female, in themselves or else in their relationships with others.

Esther's danger, on the other hand, stems from her possession of Knowledge, a definition of danger which dates back to Plato's vision of the Republic. A lot of comment has been made on the meaning of *Esther*. For some reason this dark and somewhat eerie-sounding song sparks curiosity in many fans. I would add that the music is somewhat carnivalesque in nature and for me, at least, brings back echoes of Ray Bradbury's classic *Something Wicked This Way Comes,* which I'm sure the boys have read, in which a backward-rotating merry go round could grant any wish, but at a horrible price. This theme has also been reflected in Stephen King's best-selling *Needful Things,* Oscar Wilde's *The Picture of Dorian Gray,* and

Christopher Marlowe's *Dr. Faustus.* The human obsession with Knowledge stems ultimately from the Biblical story of Eve and the Tree of Knowledge of Good and Evil. Rarely is true Knowledge seen as a benign force; rather it usually is seen as a burden from which humans must be protected and which can bring harsh consequences.

The Armenian man in *Esther* evokes Bradbury's carnival owner and King's shop owner who could grant wishes in exchange for human souls. The old man is described in words that convey his darker nature. He "grovels" towards her and has "pasty white cheeks." Even his spittle is described as evil in no uncertain terms, "and his lips hurled a dollop of murk on the curb." Yet, it seems that he does not grant wishes, but rather provides Esther with something that could cause much more trouble, "and the lights from the rides showed a mischievous sparkle that flashed in his hollow-eyed stare."

Many people have speculated on the figurative meaning of the doll. Though it is impossible to know for sure exactly what was meant, it seems likely that the doll could represent true Knowledge. The Armenian man is rather eager to be rid of the doll. In keeping with the figurative nature of Knowledge as a dangerous tool, and of which the acquisition and possession in traditional literature often leads to suffering, as the masses do not understand, cannot accept, and therefore reject, it is clear that the Armenian man relishes handing over his burden. Perhaps the man's hollow-eyed stare is due to his long-term possession of Knowledge. Perhaps the mischievous nature of his demeanor stems from his anticipation of the trouble that Esther will cause and the suffering she will face, or simply from mere gratefulness that he has found someone to whom he can give this knowledge and thus be free of its burden ("And he stood looking down at the innocent girl"). Of course, just as Eve could not resist the lure of the apple and true Knowledge, Esther "saw the doll's eyes and couldn't resist." She is mesmerized by the doll and what it represents and must take it. Indeed, she seems to be almost greedy to have it, as she immediately runs off. Perhaps in fear that the old man will regret his gift and try to take it back?

The reaction of the people that Esther meets throughout the course of the song supports the idea that the doll represents Knowledge. It is interesting that she immediately runs to the church, a societal structure which presents itself as the sole possessor of true Knowledge, to share her Knowledge. She obviously, subconsciously, understands the implications of this Knowledge and almost revels in the opportunity to reveal its nature. Certainly, she makes sure that everyone can see what she holds by lifting it high. And most obviously, the people in the church are *not* happy with what she shows them.

It is at this moment that Esther begins to realize that the doll is perhaps more trouble than it is worth, and she may also begin to understand the Armenian man's desire to get rid of it. In any case, not quite comprehending the seriousness of the church's rejection, she attempts to get through to them one more time: "Esther tried in vain to pacify the mob." In addition, the people of the church try to take the puppet, as if by destroying it they could destroy its implications for their nice, comfortable existence. Finally, Esther realizes the futility of her attempts to share her knowledge and flees.

The storm outside causes her to understand that people do not want Knowledge, which might interfere with their fantasies about life

(continued on,the next page)

"Dangerous Women in Phish's Music" *(continued)*

and which reveals their closed-mindedness. She still believes, however, that human nature in general will accept her doll, and she flees "out into the rainstorm where she felt she would be free." However, Nature is also against her, and lifts her up and drops her in the "nasty part of town." At this point, I think she begins to realize that it is not just the church-going people who do not want to have their cherished beliefs challenged, but humans in general. That Nature turns against her is particularly significant for this reason. Now Esther is actually fearful: "She glanced about the village / sure to find the evil men who rob and pillage / in the darkest hour of night." Yet she still does not realize that Knowledge is not only going to cause trouble and strife, but also that it can not protect her, "Nervously she fumbled for the pouch that held the Puppet on her rump." She hides and waits for the dawn, "cause it would have been a blunder to succumb to a hoodlum on the prowl," yet she still believes that the light of day will bring out more reasonable people. She begins to relax and comes out of her hiding place with the dawn thinking, "at last a peaceful moment," which ironically is the exact moment where she encounters the more "reasonable" people of the daylight: "It was an angry mob of joggers coming up to knock her down." This is the moment of epiphany for Esther that there are no reasonable people in the world: "Esther stood and shook her head."

Esther's choice to dive into the water represents giving up on the unreasonable people, and not an attempt to run away. She does not want to swim, and knows she must, but is unaware of the dangers or of the fact that she will most likely die. She fights for her life, but it is ironically the puppet, Knowledge, the cause of all her troubles, which brings her down in the end, "and the puppet she'd forgotten wrapped its tiny little arms around her ankle and wouldn't let her go." Once Knowledge is gained, it cannot be forgotten, no matter how hard we try. It seems that Knowledge had driven the Armenian man mad (hollow eyes), but Esther dies. She does not hide her Knowledge in a pail, she keeps it close to her body, close to her heart, and thus it is likely that its effects on her were that much stronger. Once touched in this way, she can not return to the normal world. This song shows the progression of her understanding of the doll, from joy and elation (the church scene), to confusion and insistence upon the inherent rationality of men (waiting for the dawn), to realization that human nature is truly evil (the jogger scene and her decision to swim), and finally the realization that Knowledge is a two-edged sword as the puppet drags her down into the "eerie green deep."

The danger posed by Esther is twofold. Her possession of true Knowledge is the obvious danger that she poses, but the tradition behind her name imbues her with a second capacity for danger. The name Esther has strong connotations, particularly for people who are familiar with the Old Testament. Esther was a Jewish girl during the time of Xerxes, whose Uncle Mordecai was an honorable man. When the king decided to search for a true queen, he had many women brought to the palace for a "charm school." Mordecai hoped that Esther would have a wonderful life as a queen, and both he and Esther believed that she could do much good for her people, if chosen to be queen. The king's advisor, Haman, however, was an evil man, who hated the Jews and eventually planned to have them massacred and

their property confiscated. Esther eventually became queen, and her uncle Mordecai, hearing of Haman's plans, was able to warn her. Through quick thinking and courageous action, she was able to save the Jews. The Jewish celebration of Purim marks this event. Simply by naming this song *Esther*, Phish has tapped into several thousand years of tradition that this name refers to a particularly strong woman.

However, of all of these character, Millie Grace is the strongest and most active. Fee's friend Millie's actions shine out and overshadow her friend, whose name forms the title of the song, *Fee*. It is Millie, the "fading beauty…with a bamboo cane to help her keep the pace," who is the pro-active character. Fee is her friend and her boyfriend. They are attracted to each other not because of outward appearances, money, status, or any other superficial characteristics but rather because they are kindred souls. The two work together to overcome obstacles and reach their happy common end, yet it is Millie who seems to be the leader in this relationship.

Fee is portrayed as somewhat backward and a little immature. He is a "Buddhist prodigy, long past the age of maturity," yet it is clear that he has not reached the self-reliant peaceful state of more mature Buddhists: "Someday he knew it would set him free." Millie, on the other hand, has obviously suffered. She is described as having "pox on her face," and is a "fading beauty" and thus not that young. Furthermore, she cannot walk without the aid of a cane; she has obviously endured some debilitating illness or disease, yet she does not let herself be overcome by the obstacles she faces. She takes her scars, gets herself a cane, and keeps on moving. She finds joy and purpose in her life through her singing (she's a gospel singer) and finds her soulmate in Fee.

Fee and Millie are an unlikely couple, but that is the simple beauty of this tale, that two people who are meant to be together (that is, soulmates) can overcome any obstacle to be together. Fee recognizes Millie as his soulmate upon first glance in a bar in Peru, "His heart was jumping like a kangaroo / like a beast in a cage in an old Dutch zoo / It was hopping and thumping in wooden shoes." Floyd the chimpanzee, however, is jealous of this perfect and wonderful love, and becomes their common enemy: "But Floyd was jealous and alone / He wanted Millie for his own / A desperate craving in his bones / 'Their love,' he said, 'I will not condone.'" Floyd is strong and quickly knocks Fee out with a bottle. It is Millie, "thin as a small string bean," who overcomes Floyd by hitting him in the face with a nectarine. Then in the simplest and Phishiest way possible, she slices his nipple with a piece of paper, causing him to fall into the sea where he is eaten by sharks, as Mother Nature displays her support of the two lovers.

Millie's defeat of Floyd and rescue of Fee prevents the song from deteriorating into a display of machismo between the two would-be suitors. Furthermore, it showcases Millie's independence and gusto, and underlines her unwillingness to let any physical infirmities stop her from acting for herself. Yet, Fee is not portrayed as weak or diminished by the fact that Millie saves him. In fact, it is likely that Millie could not have defeated Floyd if Fee had not distracted him, and Fee certainly could not have matched Floyd's brawn in an out-and-out duel. Indeed, it is evident from the text that the two are equals, well matched and considerate of each other. Each has his/her own role, own strengths and own weaknesses, and together they are able to triumph.

the show at the 6/6/97 private keg party/rehearsal gig at the home of Road Manager Brad Sands and drum tech Pete Carini, commonly known as "Bradstock."

The Star Spangled Banner
Original Artist: Francis Scott Key
  (Music based on an Irish drinking song)
Original Album: N/A
Vocals: Phish
Debut: 10/17/96
Historian: Ellis Godard

Francis Scott Key wrote the U.S. national anthem on September 20, 1814, while watching the defense of Fort McHenry against a British attack. Only the first two stanzas (of eight) are commonly sung. The other six narrate an earnest search in the war-torn night sky for the flag, symbolically and metaphorically a people's hope and inspiration in a dark time. But those first two stanzas merely pose the question: Can you see it, there in the explosive flashes of light? Isn't that our flag, our hope?

Over 150 years later, Jimi Hendrix revised the song for a new era. The lasting impression was delivered from an otherwise empty stage, in a dark Woodstock night, to throngs of collapsed people. Hendrix's raging instrumental histrionics symbolized (and later served as a metaphor for) that same people's search, from the darkness of the Vietnam war and civil rights conflicts. Without words, Jimi asked those same questions: Can you see it, out there in the dark sprawled across Yasgur's farm? That is our hope.

Many Phish fans were familiar with Hendrix's version (and perhaps with John Popper's reprise at the less-historic Woodstock II) and were surprised when Phish performed the song a capella. But by sticking to those two conventional stanzas, in four-part harmony t'boot, Phish did what they do best: ecstatic frivolity without being undignified or insincere. Although it seems like a natural encore, the song has opened and closed first sets and appeared in the middle of second sets. The first four versions were difficult to hear over the audience's excitement, particularly at the end, but by 11/8/96 and 11/19/96 the novelty had waned enough; the band's control of the song had solidified. There is not much variation in the performances (of which only two have been since 1996). Two—11/19/96 and 11/27/96—are notable for preceding "Fire" (also performed by Hendrix), as is 12/30/96 for opening the first MSG show, and 7/4/99 for its Independence Day fireworks (explosive flashes of light).

Phish also performed the song at venues where the song was more important than they were, including the Philadelphia Flyers games 5/5/97 and 12/1/97. For hardcore Phish fans at those sports events, one could ask those same questions, not about the audience, but about the band: Can you see it, even without their vacuums and "Tweezers" and skyscrapers and lights? That is our inspiration.

STAR TREK JAM (see: "T.V. THEME")

"Star Trek" Theme (Main Title)
Original Artist: Alexander Courage
Original Album: "Star Trek" TV show
Vocals: (instrumental)
Debut: 8/4/96

Historian: Mark Toscano

Aside from a brief tease by Trey on 3/7/92 and a soundcheck appearance on 8/10/97, Alexander Courage's original "Star Trek" theme has been publicly explored only once. Appropriately enough, Page performed an encore version of the world-famous music on his newly acquired theremin following the first sets of a four-night stint at Red Rocks on 8/4/96. The theremin, which first came to widespread public awareness on the soundtrack to such films as *The Day the Earth Stood Still* and in the Beach Boys' classic "Good Vibrations," was a ground-breaking invention in the music world. Played without actually touching the instrument itself, the performer alters pitch and volume by increasing or decreasing the distance between hands and apparatus. To find out more about this unique instrument, check out the unusual and highly entertaining documentary *Theremin: An Electronic Odyssey*, which features interviews with Brian Wilson, Robert Moog, and the inventor of the instrument, Leon Theremin himself.

Stash
Music: Trey Anastasio
Lyrics: Tom Marshall
Album: *A Picture of Nectar; A Live One* (7/8/94);
  ***Hampton Comes Alive* (11/20/98)**
Debut: 9/13/90
Historian: Jeff Goldberg

In the late '80s, Phish was but a mere sapling compared to what the band, as a whole, is today. Interestingly, however, this unique era of Phish's musical development, where the band members, still relatively young, were riding a wave into stardom unfathomable at the time, was pinnacle in Phish's maturity as a band.

Although one never ceases to learn and advance musically, the band members were still very much music students themselves, undergoing such group exercises as a capella vocal lessons and frequent jazz jam sessions. Trey, specifically, was listening to lots of jazz at the time. *Lawn Boy* had been completed already (recorded in 1989, released 9/90) and he was thirsty for musical expansion, as well as some new material. Trey, at that time, was also exploring and studying new ways of musical communication through theory-based concepts such as "tension and release," which actually happens to be the bare-bones basis for Western harmony. As such, during the beginning months of 1990, Trey, who was enamored with several different genres of music, wrote several new songs, many of which would not only be debuted at the Wetlands Preserve in New York City (9/13/90) shortly after *Lawn Boy*'s release, but would also eventually be on Phish's next studio release, *A Picture of Nectar*.

Several of Phish's songs still to this day rely heavily on this "tension and release" concept. "Split Open and Melt, Run Like an Antelope," "David Bowie," and even "Mike's Song" all at least flirt with the concept during their jams. Trey capitalizes on this by engaging the audience in a musical journey where he is at the driver's seat, and he journeys into the unknown. Mixed with Phish's creativity and acute ears, this is quite an effective "audience wower" as well as a good listen. One song, however, stands out among Phish's vast repertoire as the "grandfather" of tension/release jams, and thus was appropriately chosen to represent this facet of Phish's live jamming on their 1995 compilation release, *A Live One*: "Stash."

At the time "Stash" was written, Trey was listening to many of the jazz greats of the mid 20th century. The Benny Goodman Quintet, with Charlie Christen on guitar, Miles Davis, John Coltrane, and Charles Mingus all found their way into the still-growing list of Trey's influences, and many of Nectar's songs directly reflect this. Musically, jazz is fundamentally based upon what is called a "ii-V7-I" progression, which is vocally pronounced "two-five-one." Many of Benny Goodman's songs took advantage of the tension created by going from the fifth degree of a key back to the root note, or "home base." It was simply a re-interpretation of the same music theory and harmony that Mozart and Bach used to write their symphonies, only applied in a modern context. Trey has admitted openly that "Stash's" chord progression is a direct rip-off of Charles Mingus' "Jump Monk" with a simple key change and a slinky calypso drum beat underneath. Charles Mingus was a prominent jazz composer and bass player from about the mid-'50s until his death in the late '70s. He had a very distinctive sound, and for a time he wasn't widely appreciated because his music was so unique and hard to categorize. "Jump Monk," which Phish has actually covered, was written as a tribute to jazz pianist/composer Thelonious Monk, another one of the greats (the title apparently came from the fact that Monk was always jumping and dancing around). "Jump Monk" is a i-♭VI7-ii-V7♭9 (which is pronounced "minor one-flat six-two-five") progression in the key of F minor, and is usually played with a standard swing beat. "Stash," is a i-♭VI7-ii-V7♭9 in the key of D minor, and as noted, uses a slowed down calypso beat instead.

Lyrically, the song is nonsensical. It is comprised of several of Tom Marshall's poems. Trey simply took little lines out of each song and put them into one silly compilation (a common trend for many of the songs on Nectar, as vocals were not their focus at the time.) Musically, however, "Stash" is ingenious. Phish has taken the concepts that Goodman and Mingus were known for and made itself known for the very same phenomenon, only taken to an entirely new level. Instead of using the tension and release within the chord progression, expressed solely through lines and runs, Phish improvises over the "tension chord" (aka the "five" or "dominant") for extended amounts of time, integrating several other theoretical tactics to increase the tension harmonically. The ending result is an orgasmic release at the end of the jam, creating a universal blast of energy amongst the musicians and the audience alike, and again, as noted, is quite effective. During the jam, despite the fact that the general pulse stays the same throughout the jam, the band members are improvising by changing the harmonic structure of the song as it goes along. They also take advantage of another musical technique of tension/release by playing rhythmic patterns which counterpoint one another through different time signatures. Trey himself stated in an interview that "It's normally just a D-minor jam, but the whole time you can look back at it and figure out what the harmonic structure [is,] and jam over unusual degrees of it. Going to the five chord, and the five of five, and to the two chord, for example…I don't really know other bands that do that. The thing is, you couldn't do that in a normal soloist, backup band atmosphere. The backup band is trained to support and define the chord progression and let the soloist do his thing. We kind of look at it from a different light, more from a King Sunny Ade band perspective, where there is no soloist, everyone is playing."

Another source of inspiration for "Stash" was a book written by Ted Dunbar that Trey was studying at the time. The book was all about different ways to take advantage of the tense sound created when playing two tones that are an interval of a tritone away from each other. The human ear that is trained to hear music in a "Western" way does not "like" the sound of a tritone. It is unsettled and dissonant. Tritones are the intervals that cause tension in your ear. Literally, they are an augmented fourth (or a diminished fifth, depending on how you look at it) and you ear WANTS the interval to resolve. Due to the nature of the half and whole step relationships of Western music, a tritone can resolve to two different keys.

If you own a piano, or any other musical instrument, try playing, for instance, a C and an F♯. They will sound very tense together. Now you can either resolve the notes IN or OUT by a half step, to relieve the dissonance. In other words, if you raise the C to a C♯, and lower the F♯ to an F, you have resolved the tritone to the key of D♭. The C and the F♯ imply a C diminished chord. This is the more obvious resolution; ie, when the tritone is used to form a chord that is the dominant (or V) of the key you're in. In other words, in Stash, we are in D minor. The dominant (or V) of D is A. So we take A as the tonic, and form a dominant seventh chord over it, making an A7.

Interestingly, if you resolve the tritone by moving the notes a half-step *farther* away from one another (*lowering* the C to a B, and *raising* the F♯ to a G) you resolve the tritone to a completely different key, and alter the entire flavor of the tritone. By bringing the notes OUT by a half step, we now resolve to the key of G. Same tritone, different keys, different relationship. This is what Trey means by analyzing the harmonic structure of the song.

Western music is based on this very V-I cadence. In other words, you are either playing ON a chord or TO another chord. Again, Stash is a i-♭VI7-ii-V7♭9 progression. Since the pattern repeats over and over, you see that we have that magic V-i cadence in there between the last chord and the first. In the key of Dm, these chords are Dm-B♭7-Em7♭5-A7♭9. The A7 (or any seventh chord for that matter) contains a tritone. For example, play an A7, then resolve it to a Dm. You'll hear tension, then release when you land on the Dm. Well, the same goes for the Stash jam, but instead of just using strictly chords to cause the tension and release, Trey uses phrasing, scales, and arpeggios.

So now, we know that A7 resolves to D…. BUT WHY?

Musicians, pay attention. If you spell out the A7 chord, you have A, C♯, E, and G. The third (C♯) and the lowered seventh (G) of a dominant seventh chord create the tritone relationship about which I spoke. When you resolve those two notes by raising that C♯ to a D again (making the D harmonic minor mode fit nicely over the progression) you release the tension.

Well, let's expand the progression a bit. We've already examined the V-i cadence, so let's expand it into the ii-V-i cadence. Now the "ii" is theoretically the V of the V. Get it? The A7 is the V of Dm, and the Em7♭5 is the V of the A7. Thus, we have the first tension/release relationship, the ii to the V. The problem (or cool thing) about the ii-V cadence is that it doesn't FULLY resolve. It still leads your ear to want it to resolve again. Thus, now you go from V to i, and POOF! you're in release-land, as Trey calls it.

Now, understanding it is one thing, but putting it into use is another. So, guitarists, here's some tips on soloing with this style of jamming, specifically with regards to Stash.

1. Learn where every single D is on the fingerboard. EVERY ONE.
2. Learn how to connect every D to any other D using a minor scale. Practice correct shifting patterns. Go up and down. Use natural minor, harmonic minor, and melodic minor.

Stash

Compiled by Jeremy Goodwin

Date	Time	Notes
07/11/91	07:19	With the Giant Country Horns.
03/30/93	14:48	Spectacularly improvisational, with a "Can't You Hear Me Knockin'" jam.
08/15/93	17:56	Exploratory improv, which includes a collective, melodic jam.
05/13/94	10:54	Includes a heavy, noisy jam, with Fishman pounding out a three beat figure repeatedly.
05/19/94	11:30	Brilliant, raging, borderline-metal jam segment for several minutes.
06/22/94	10:17	Page plays jaunty chords over a repetitious, metallic Trey.
07/08/94*	11:58	A Live One version. Strange ending, as "maybe so" is sung over an unrelated jam.
07/16/94	10:13	Fishman and Page star in this chaotic, noisy version.
11/02/94	10:58	An unexpected groove emerges from a typically chaotic jam.
11/12/94	14:00	Unbelievably dark and thrilling. This version screams! Vocal jam.
10/17/95	11:29	Fiendishly intense.

Date	Time	Notes
11/14/95	39:39	Stash-> (16:00) Manteca-> (18:40) "Stash" -> (30:28) Dog Faced-> (33:18) Stash. Total 39:39 (inlcudes a jam on "Esther")
11/24/95	13:56	Fierce.
12/01/95	13:35	Stormy, dangerous, deadly. Includes a tease of Dave's Energy Guide.
12/29/95	18:42	This stirring, upbeat monster is one of the best. Must hear.
10/25/96	13:37	Not totally outrageous, but absolutely stunning peak.
07/02/97*	29:19	Unfinished. Includes an incredibly melodic, thematic jam (17:45 to 25:25).
07/26/97	14:15	Frenzied peak, with Trey pushing the boundaries of the rhythmic structure (as in many great Stashes).
11/13/97*	22:14	Mike takes the lead of a spacey jam around 16 min. Spellbinding return to the Stash theme.
11/23/97	17:45	Unfinished. Segues into NICU!
11/30/97*	20:00	Unfinished. FISHMAN.

* second set

3. Then learn how to connect every D using minor arpeggios. Up and down. Count (or sing) the degree of the scale out loud as your playing it. For example when playing a Dm7 arpeggio, sing "one-three-five-seven."

4. Once you do that, do the same thing only this time, sing the actual note names. By this time, you should really know what every note is on the fretboard by name, and apply the tritone concept using intervals.

Now, you have the ammo to use proper phrasing. As another exercise, starting with Dm, go around the entire circle of fourths and fifths, using ii-V cadences the whole way around. In other words, Dm7, G7, Cm7, F7, B♭m7, E♭7, A♭m7... and continue all the way back to Dm. You hear how the tension never ends? You ear is waiting the entire time for the resolving "I" chord, but never gets it. Well, in the "journey" part of "Stash," Mike sits on the five (A) while Page plays tritone-filled bedding chords, and Trey is free to roam back and forth between tension-land and releaseland. At the climax of the song, Mike resolves to the D finally, along with Trey and Page, creating the musical orgasm. The vibe is felt universally throughout the room when this occurs, and developed into a definitive technique of Phish-style jamming.

In 1994, Phish knew that they were going to be releasing a live album to more correctly represent their sound than their previous releases had. In order to prepare for this event, the band purchased all new recording equipment. They decided that they were going to record the entire year of 1994 on a digital 24 track recorder, and see what they came up with. The resulting music from that year was quite improvisational and exploratory. Late '93 brought long, extended jams never heard before (ie, "Bathtub Gin," 8/13/93) and thus led to many of the staple '94 versions of songs fans refer to whimsically, as if it's common knowledge. Whether or not the recording of the album subconsciously had a direct effect on pushing the band to new levels in this domain is up for debate. Whatever the case, the summer of '94 brought some of the most revolutionary versions of "Stash" heard to that point. Summer '94 also marked the beginning of a to-be common trend at Phish shows of audience involvement in written Phish tunes. There is a point in the recorded Nectar version of "Stash" where Fishman hits his wood block during a break. During the '94 tour, this wood block hit developed into a universal triple-clap from the audience, which slowly replaced the sound of the wood block. Notable others originating from or after that era are the "Wilson" chanting and the "Hood" chanting during "Harry Hood." (yuck.) The version chosen to best represent the tension/release concept for "A Live One" ended up being taken from set two of Great Woods Center for the Performing Arts in Mansfield, MA, on July 8, 1994. This was a particularly hot second set brought on by the phenomenal "Gamhendge" performance from the previous set, and both the band and the crowd were quite into it.

"Stash," played more than almost any other Phish song, is a favorite of both the band and the crowd. Despite being played so often, its origins and musical structure are ideal vehicles for extended, interesting, yet varied jams, and thus is pretty universally liked amongst most fans. Notable other versions include 7/25/92,12/31/93, 4/6/94, 12/30/97, and 10/10/99. Every version, however, by the nature of the origins of the song, along with its harmonic structure is home to the tension/release jam that is so very...Phish.

Steep

Music: Phish

Lyrics: Tom Marshall
Album: *Billy Breathes*
Debut: 10/16/96
Historian: Dan Purcell

In early 1996, Phish went into the studio in Woodstock, New York to record its followup to *Hoist*. In an attempt to distance itself from *Hoist*'s L.A.-infected studio sheen, the band instead crafted a dense, layered improvisational swirl of music that eventually became known as The Blob. Phish eventually rejected The Blob as too unfocused and meandering, but saved one small part of it for inclusion on *Billy Breathes*.

That small slice of The Blob is "Steep," a rhythmic and melodic variation on the album's preceding track, "Swept Away." Where "Swept Away" is gentle and lilting, "Steep" is creepy; its vocals are stated, not sung. Where "Swept Away" glides along effortlessly, "Steep" unfolds with a herky-jerky, stop-and-start rhythm that unsettles the listener. It ends with a tidal rush of bass effects that eventually falls away into the album-closing arena-rock resolution of "Prince Caspian." (The live versions of the song take it a step further: they end with a blood-curdling scream, a 180-degree pivot away from the bucolic vibe of "Swept Away.")

As on *Billy Breathes*, "Steep" has always followed "Swept Away" when performed in concert. Phish frequently used the pairing as a second-set breather in the fall of 1996 and the spring of 1997, but has largely shelved the combination since then. After three appearances in the summer of 1997 and one in the fall, "Swept Away" -> "Steep" has reared its head only once apiece in 1998 and 1999.

Steve Reich

Music: Trey Anastasio
Album: "The White Tape"
Debut: (never performed live)
Historian: Mark Toscano

Steve Reich—the man—often shares conversational space with the likes of John Cage, Terry Riley, Philip Glass, Tony Conrad, and other moguls of the 20th Century minimalism/avant-garde music scene. Though known for many of his innovative pieces ("It's Gonna Rain," "Different Trains," "Music For 18 Musicians") involving varying permutations of instrument and voice, he is often most associated by the uninitiated with his experimental percussive compositions for marimbas (especially "Six Marimbas"). Trey, part of an elite group (disaffected, disenfranchised college music students), likely crossed paths with Reich's music on more than one occasion. Enter "Steve Reich," the song. More conspicuous because of its absence from the official "White Tape" track listing, this gentle stab at the aforementioned Reich stereotype was retained for the CD release even if its name wasn't. Perhaps this was done to prevent the satirical aspects of the song from potential offending its inspiration, still alive and well upon its release.

The track, consisting of clunking marimbas and various sound effects, can still be found adhering "Alumni Blues" to "And So To Bed." Due to its instrumental irregularity and general sophomoric superfluousness, it has never been performed live. Fans interested in Reich's work may want to check out the mammoth 10-CD retrospective box released in 1996 to commemorate the composer's sixtieth birthday.

See Also: "Alumni Blues"

Stir It Up

Music/Lyrics: Bob Marley
Original Artist: Bob Marley
Original Album: *Catch a Fire* (1973)
Vocals: (performed instrumental) (8/21/87); Jah Roy (6/20/88)
Historian: Mark Toscano

One of Bob Marley's signature tunes, "Stir it Up" is a popular reggae cover for both reggae and wanna-be reggae bands alike. Phish, though they've attempted (with reasonable success) the likes of "Trench Town Rock" and "Soul Shakedown Party," have only ever jammed this song as part of another tune. At Ian's Farm on 8/21/87, a jam of the tune erupted out of "McGrupp" and into a "Makisupa" jam during the improv-heavy third set. The next year, Jah Roy made one of his random appearances at Phish's 6/20/88 Nectar's show, lending his vocals to a post-"Ya Mar" reggae jam that included vocal quotes of "Three Little Birds," "One Love," and "Stir it Up," among others. The only other known appearance of the tune occurred during a mouth-watering 7/30/93 soundcheck combo of "Makisupa" -> "Stir it Up" jam -> "Have Mercy." Also of interest is the version performed on 4/17/98 by 8' Fluorescent Tubes, a band that included Trey and Fish, as well as other Burlington-area musicians and friends.

Strange Design

AKA: "Companions" (original title),
"Ah, Page Sang!" (Fishman's title)
Music: Trey Anastasio
Lyrics: Tom Marshall
Album: European "Free" single
Debut: 5/16/95
Historian: Grant Calof

A dream-like Tom Marshall ballad made all the more beautiful by Phish's own "Chairman of the Boards," "Strange Design" is rare treat to see and hear nowadays. For Page fans, it's a song held in the same regard as other occasional "gifts," like "Sea and Sand," "Ride Captain Ride," and "Curtis Loew." "Strange Design" made its debut on 5/16/95 at the Voters for Choice Benefit. The band debuted a few other tunes as well and was introduced to the crowd by legendary women's rights advocate, Gloria Steinem.

"Strange Design" was originally written and recorded during the *Billy Breathes* sessions, but was omitted from the final cut. The band recorded a handful of different versions in the studio, one of which ended up appearing as a B-side to the European CD Single for "Free" (a more atmospheric version with echoes of King Crimson). An mp3 of this studio version should be available for download from the February, 1996 installment of "This Month in Phishtory" at www.phish.com. (assuming the band continues to keep "This Month in Phishtory" articles archived on their website).

The lyrics are more introspective and thought provoking than a lot of earlier songs, a trend that started around the time of *Billy Breathes*. "Strange Design" is a reflection on life and the evolution of thought and understanding that comes with time and friendship. Its mid-section hints at one of Tom Marshall and the band's favorite themes of surrendering to the flow, and goes as far as applying that concept to issues of mortality in the last lines of the song.

"Strange Design" was most frequently played in 1995, and usually appeared midway through the first or second set, often to give the band and the audience a much-needed breather. "Strange Design" made a rare appearance as the closing tune in the second set on 11/22/95, and was one of many highlights during the great musical assault of 12/31/95. The song was also featured as a follow up to "Trainsong" in a trio of mini acoustic sets during the summer tour of 1996 (8/5/96 at Red Rocks comes highly recommended).

It was played only three times in 1997 (11/29/97 followed a monster 60-min "Runaway Jim"), twice in 1998 (8/15/98 from Lemonwheel is particularly affecting), and three again in 1999 (wedged between "AC/DC Bag" and "Divided Sky" on 12/12/99). "Strange Design" made its first appearance of the new millennium when it was played during the first set at Lakewood Amphitheater in Georgia (6/24/00).

Suspicious Minds

Music/Lyrics: Mark James
Original Artist: Elvis Presley
Original Album: single (1969);
  ***From Memphis To Vegas, From Vegas To Memphis* (1970)**
Vocals: Fish (lead), Page, Trey (backing)
Debut: 9/30/95
Historian: Martin Acaster

Suspicious Minds was Elvis Presley's last number one hit and his first since the 1962 release "Good Luck Charm." The song was written by Mark James and recorded by the king of rock-n-roll at American Studios in Memphis on January 23, 1969. The single was released in August of that year while Big E set up shop at the International Hotel in Las Vegas. A live performance of the song recorded during this "tour" at what is now the Las Vegas Hilton was released on the 1970 album *From Memphis to Vegas, From Vegas to Memphis*.

Phish debuted "Suspicious Minds" at Shoreline (9/30/95) and the dazzling new jewel in Jon Fishman's big ol' gold belt of vocal stylings instantly became a crowd favorite. Each time Trey climbed behind the drum kit, the collective hope of the crowd was that the king of shlock would emerge from the wings of the stage decked out in his sequin-covered and mini-light lined cape. With a few exceptions in the 1995 Fall Tour that wish came true. After an inspired rendition that sprung from "Ha Ha Ha" at the Spectrum in Philadelphia (12/15/95), the dazzling cape was put back in the closet for almost a year. "Suspicious Minds" returned in all its extravagant glory as part of the "Harpua" encore that closed out the 1996 Fall Tour at the Aladdin Theater (where Elvis and Cilla had tied the knot!!). This "Harpua" included among others Les Claypool, some Yodelers, John McEuen, and four Elvii which Jimmy (Fishman) and Poster met out in the desert. The Elvii challenged Jimmy to an Elvis-off whereupon they began singing "Suspicious Minds." Fish (as Jimmy) out Elvises the Elvii and finishes out the song. The grandeur and hilarity of this final performance makes it unlikely that the cape (unlike Elvis) will ever be seen again.

Suzy Greenberg

Music/Lyrics: Anastasio/Dude of Life
Album: (none)
Vocals: Trey (lead), Mike, Page (backing), Fish (mutterings and rants)

Peter Sitzman

Debut: 2/13/87
Historian: Craig DeLucia

Oh, to be a woman immortalized in song for scorning The Dude of Life!

Unlike most Dude songs that appeared on the Phish stage, "Suzy Greenberg" became revered by Phish fans and, for many years, was not saved for Dude guest appearances. It was one of the early singalong numbers, alongside "Golgi" and "Alumni Blues." As the band grew older, though, the song seemed to fall by the wayside. The song has become a rare concert treat, partially due to Page's dislike for the number (see his comments in *The Phish Book*). Where "Suzy" was once played every few shows, it has been played less than five times a year every year since 1997.

Most versions do not vary much musically—often, versions are worth hearing for Fishman's vocal antics in the song's breaks (particularly after the 'neurologist' lyric). Still, see 11/13/96 and 9/14/00 for strong, experimental, jam-laden "Suzies." And no Phish collection is complete without at least one horn-augmented "Suzy Greenberg," as many fans feel that it was the song that benefited most from the 1991 and 1994 Horns Tours.

Sweet Adeline

Music/Lyrics: Armstrong/Gerard
Artist: Artie Shaw
Vocals: Phish
Debut: 3/28/90
Historian: Ellis Godard

Phish have performed several "sweet" songs, such as "Swing Low (Sweet Chariot)" (played 10/15/86 to 8/29/87) and "My Sweet One" (starting 9/9/89). But none are as sugary as their a capella "Sweet Adeline." Their rendition is fabulous, but they of course introduce much levity, such as performing the song in masks (7/12/92 and 6/24/95), using it as a challenge to Metallica (5/16/92) or as an interlude during which to return a lost wallet (3/31/93), or promising yet another record attempt (6/13/95).

Fishman sings lead, and hams it up by stretching his lines and syllables. But that stretch ain't all pork product: Early versions were interrupted by bursts of applause after the chorus, and during the final lines. As the band continued the song in increasingly large rooms, without microphones (certainly by 5/3/91, possibly earlier) and still a capella, crowd noise became a problem. The band began calming the audience with a ritual huddle, and Trey would hold out his hands as if to say "not yet" several times during the song. Eventually an old boxy radio mic was added, but a trick remained from earlier days: Syllables held between lines near the end clued in the audience that the song wasn't over, and allowed the band to get all the way through…well, almost all the way…most of the time.

The song is often a set or show closer, but has occasionally opened things up, even starting one show (4/25/91). It was kept in regular rotation through 1996, with heavy use during the July 1992 openers for Santana and the Summer 1996 Europe tour. Notable versions include 10/6/91 performed from the balcony, and 6/14/94 between "Guelah" and a delay loop jam.

Sweet Emotion

Music/Lyrics: Steven Tyler, Tom Hamilton
Original Artist: Aerosmith
Original Album: *Toys in the Attic* (1975)
Vocals: Phish
Debut: 3/16/93
Historian: charlz franz

One of a handful of good Aerosmith tunes, "Sweet Emotion" is a rock classic from Aerosmith's *Toys in the Attic*, the first platinum album from a hard rock band that seems determined to endure longer than the Rolling Stones. The song's lyrics are overtly sexual, but the three jams of it performed by Phish are limited to the affecting melody and words, "sweet emotion." Two of the jams came during "Tweezers"—on 3/16/93 Phoenix and 5/07/94 Dallas. A third appeared in the 7/9/99 Merriweather "Mike's Song." Also, there are "Sweet Emotion" teases in the 4/21/91, 5/3/91, and 5/6/93 "Tweezers," the 11/27/96 "Diseezer," and the 9/21/90 and 5/25/91 "YEMs." The jam in the Bomb Factory "Tweezer" is particularly sweet.

Sweet Jane

Original Artist: The Velvet Underground
Original Album: *Loaded* (1970)
Vocals: Page (lead), Trey (backing)
Debut: 8/8/98, 10/31/98
Historian: Mark Toscano

Whether you like the Velvet Underground original or the Cowboy Junkies' strong remake, this song is a classic. It's easily one of the Velvets' most recognizable tunes, and on 10/31/98 at the Thomas and Mack Center in Las Vegas, it got Phish their biggest cheer of recognition for the entire second set.

Most folks at that show were not nearly as familiar with the Velvets' fourth album as they were with Phish's three previous musical Halloween costumes (the "White Album," *Quadrophenia*, and *Remain in Light*), and many were quite surprised by the album choice in general. However, despite whatever unfamiliarity there may have been, the set was received very warmly, and even had a direct effect on sales of the original Velvets' album in music stores for the next few weeks. Phish not only honored their gods, they even converted a bunch of heathenous non-believers.

The guys had actually already covered "Sweet Jane" once to close out the first set on 8/8/98, delivering the tune in an enjoyable, but not nearly as inspired version as the one that took place on Halloween. The latter was thrilling as all-get-out, and drove the crowd wild with its energized shipping and handling. Page's vocals were sturdy and engaging, and even when Trey just chorded, it electrified the whole room. This was one of the highlights of the set.

Would Lou Reed have enjoyed their reading his song? Well, possibly not, but for a very specific reason. When the Velvets originally cut the tune for *Loaded*, the song's bridge ended up getting completely excised to save time (a similar thing happened to "New Age" on the same album). As a result, the Velvets—especially Lou Reed—were always displeased with the truncated version of their song. They always played the complete version live, though, and even the Cowboy Junkies' version contains the missing, so-called "wine and roses" segment. However, until the mid-'90s, the bridgeless version of the tune predominated

on the radio and on disc, and this was the one Phish covered both times. (Incidentally, the complete version of "Sweet Jane" now appears on most CD versions of the original album.)

SWEET NUTHIN' (see: "OH! SWEET NUTHIN'")

Sweet Virginia

Music/Lyrics: Keith Richards, Mick Jagger
Original Artist: The Rolling Stones
Original Album: *Exile on Main Street* **(1972)**
Vocals: Page (lead), Fish, Mike, Trey (backing)
Debut: 9/26/99
Historian: Phil Nazzaro

Sweet Virginia is the second song from The Stones classic *Exile on Main Street* album that Phish has covered ("Loving Cup" being the first). This song's first and only appearance in Phish's repertoire came as a show opener in New Orleans on 9/26/99. The first reaction of the crowd was to wonder what song it was. But once word spread, the ambiguity of the lyrics kept the wonderment alive throughout those in attendance. Perhaps the decision to play "Sweet Virginia" can be owed to the fact that Phish hadn't been welcome in New Orleans since their appearance at Jazzfest in '96. As one longtime Stones fan interprets it, Mick Jagger wrote the lyrics as an homage all the 'rock star activities' his band got away with during their previous tours of the United States.

Swept Away

Music: Trey Anastasio
Lyrics: Tom Marshall

A Capella

Phish began doing a capella tunes in 1990, with the annual number of a capella performances peaking in 1993 and trailing off since then.

	90	91	92	93	94	95	96	97	98	99	0
120											
100											
80											
60											
40	40	43	72	104	77	53	40	17	14	6	
20											
0											

Top five a capella tunes:

Sweet Adeline	163
Amazing Grace	107
Carolina	67
Hello My Baby	53
Memories	37

Album: *Billy Breathes*
Debut: 10/16/96
Historian: Dan Purcell

Never played live before its release on *Billy Breathes*, most fans first heard "Swept Away" as it segued out of the contrapuntal guitar rumble of "Bliss" toward the end of that album. A pleasant and waiflike tune, "Swept Away" states another of Tom Marshall's favorite lyrical themes: the need to be free of societal intrusions and pressures.

After the pleasant harmonies of the chorus, "Swept Away" melts into a droning minor-key groove that becomes the following song, "Steep." Phish must have liked the way these two songs fit together, as they've only been played live in tandem with one another. Throughout the fall of 1996 and the spring of 1997, the band frequently segued into the simple guitar chords of "Swept Away" from a particularly chaotic second-set jam. On both 10/22/96 and 11/6/96, Phish inserted the combination into the middle of "Mike's Groove"; on Halloween and New Year's Eve 1996 (not to mention the less-circulated 11/18/96), "Swept Away" segued out of "Simple."

"Swept Away" was played (along with "Steep," of course) three times in the summer of 1997 and once in the fall. Since then, however, it has been relegated to spot duty, appearing only once apiece in 1998 and 1999—oddly enough, on June 30 of both years—and another singular outing in 2000.

Swing Low (Sweet Chariot)

Music/Lyrics: (traditional)
Vocals: Phish (4/12/93); "Reverend" Jeff Mosier (11/16/94);
  (otherwise performed instrumental)
Debut: 10/15/86
Historians: Martha Hunt and Mark Toscano

The lyrics of this traditional African-American spiritual are based on the biblical story of the prophet Elijah, who lived in northern Israel in the ninth century B.C. He was opposed to the worship of Baal, was a strong proponent of monotheism, and is recognized in both Christianity and Islam as a prophet. He was said not to have died, but, after passing on his mantle (the symbol of his power) and a double portion of his spirit to his disciple, Elisha, was taken up into heaven in a chariot of fire in a whirlwind (2 Kings 2:9-12).

"Swing Low, Sweet Chariot" was probably first sung by black American slaves, which gives the image of the chariot, "coming for to carry me home" a rather gruesome cast. It is a plea for escape from the miserable human existence, a plea to be transported "home," to heaven, essentially, a plea for death.

The song has been performed by nearly everyone who can sing, at some point in their life. The Grateful Dead performed it several times and it was on the soundtrack to *The Trouble With Girls*, memorably sung by Elvis Presley. Johnny Cash, Eric Clapton and Pete Seeger each has his own version of the song. And it is the English Rugby team's unofficial theme song.

Not to be outdone, Phish made this song their own in early shows, performing it instrumentally at gigs like 10/15/86, 10/30/86, 2/21/87, 3/23/87, 4/29/87, 8/21/87, and 8/29/87. Trey's guitar handled the vocal lead, with Page, Mike, and Fish providing capable backup. Though fun, these early versions are somewhat lifeless, lacking in soul

and emotion. The band breezes through them, and nothing very memorable occurs throughout, despite the adequate performances. After a few other random appearances (6/18/88, 10/20/89), the song disappeared from the band's repertoire for about three years.

On 12/11/92, the song showed up after a long absence, teased during "David Bowie." It also resurfaced briefly on 4/12/93, encased in a "YEM" vocal jam. But Phish's most memorable performance of the tune has to be 11/16/94, done in bluegrass instrumentation with "Reverend" Jeff Mosier on his first night of a five-night stand with the guys. On this fan favorite, Mosier provides banjo and vocals in what is the only version of the song Phish has performed with music and singing. When it comes down to it, songs about throwing off the shackles of misery may not exactly be within Phish's emotional reach, but the performances are fun and listen-worthy nonetheless. Check out the awesome 11/30/96 "Amazing Grace" jam for a more impressive handling of austere, canonic gospel.

Take Me to the River

Music/Lyrics: Al Green and M. Hodges
Original Artist: Al Green; Talking Heads
Original Album: *Explores Your Mind* (1974) (Green);
  ***More Songs About Buildings & Food* (1978) (T. Heads)**
Vocals: Trey
Debut: 11/21/95
Historian: Craig DeLucia

Though Talking Heads made "Take Me to the River" famous, it was actually written by the Reverend Al Green. Phish has never performed the song in its entirety but has jammed it in soundchecks (see 4/9/93, which circulates) and twice on stage: its 11/21/95 debut, inside of "David Bowie," and 7/10/97, out of a monster "Ghost." All three times, its performance has been much more aligned with the Heads cover than Green's original. Given the song's jam potential and popularity in the fan community, it may only be one jam-fest away from springing up again at a concert near you.

Take the "A" Train

Music: Strayhorn
Original Artist: Duke Ellington
Original Album: *Take the "A" Train* (1941)
Vocals: (instrumental)
Debut: 4/29/87
Historian: charlz franz

All musicians should get down on their knees one day to thank Duke Ellington." Miles Davis

With music written by long-time collaborator Billy Strayhorn, "Take the 'A' Train" became Duke Elington's signature piece and remains an enduring swing era jazz classic. The "A" train provided New Yorkers the quickest way to Harlem when that was the locus of the city's night life and the place to hear jazz. It's a fast-paced piece, with a clear melodic line and inventive rhythm.

The members of Phish have paid homage to many jazz classics, and "Take the 'A' Train" frequently was in the rotation from 1987 through 1992. By 1993, however, it was a rare event and its last performance to date was 4/13/94, another victim of the apparent belief that Phish covers of jazz tunes do not translate well to auditoriums. "'A'

Train" was a staple of 1991's "Horn Tour" with the Giant Country Horns. Trumpeter Carl "Gears" Gerhard also has performed the tune alone with Phish.

For representative examples, check out 4/13/94 New York, NY; 11/14/91, Chapel Hill, NC; 12/30/92 Springfield, MA; and 5/5/93, Albany, NY.

Talk

Music: Trey Anastasio
Lyrics: Tom Marshall
Album: *Billy Breathes*
Vocals: Trey
Debut: 8/5/96
Historian: Martin Acaster

The fine art of communication comes in many forms. The one which sets us humans apart from the other passengers aboard Noah's Ark is the ability to "Talk." Certainly many other species have audible communication. Some even appear to be able to send messages telepathically or through color changes. But no other form of communication can carry the depth of thought and emotion that we feel for each other as well as a good conversation. The song "Talk" is one of frustration. Imagine a father trying to share his thoughts with a newborn child or perhaps a sober individual trying to speak with a pseudo-extraterrestrial being who's thoughts are surrounded by a cloud of mind altering chemicals. Sometimes our words just can't get through the filter that surrounds the consciousness of a listener. "Talk" at times like these can feel cheap and meaningless.

"Talk" was one of several tunes ("Waste" and "Trainsong") from *Billy Breathes* that debuted in an acoustic mini-set format. The first performance of "Talk" was on 8/5/96 at Red Rocks in Morrison, CO. The acoustic mini-set made subsequent appearances at Deer Creek, IN on 8/12/96 (without "Talk") and the Clifford Ball in Plattsburgh, NY on 8/16/96 (with "Talk"). Performances which followed in Fall 1996 and both the Spring and Summer European tours in 1997 were played solo acoustically by Trey, however they were stand-alone breathers found typically in the midst of first sets rather than the on the mini acoustic stage of Summer 1996. "Talk" was played only once in 1998 (8/6/98 Lakewood Amphitheater, Atlanta GA) and has been left speechless since.

Taste

Music: Phish
Lyrics: Tom Marshall
Album: *Billy Breathes; Slip Stitch and Pass* (3/1/97)
Debut: 6/7/95
Historian: Craig DeLucia:

Fans expect that a Phish song will usually undergo changes and tinkering from the time it debuts to the time the band finally settles on an arrangement. "Taste" took this expectation further. It may, in fact, be the musical equivalent of cloning, but only if the clone and the original then had a beautiful baby.

Like "Maze," "Taste" is one of the few songs that contains inspired solos from both Page and Trey, and though the guitar-led jams of the latter are usually greater in length, the impressive piano work of the former should not be dismissed by any measure. Also, like "Maze" and "Chalk

Dust Torture," "Taste" has remained a song that features interesting interplay and solos but that does not usually jam outside of the predetermined structure of the song. Interestingly, Page usually renders his contributions to this song on the baby grand piano, ignoring the electronic pieces of his arsenal. Even in 1997, when the cow funk was prevalent and keyboards and synthesisers were used for jams in most numbers, the "taste" in Page's mouth remained the wonderful "Taste" of ivory.

"Taste" originally debuted on 6/7/95. It was actually written along with the batch of songs that were previewed at Fishman's house on 5/14/95 and debuted in Lowell two days later, but was the lone number in this group of originals that did not make it to the stage that evening. Most versions from that summer are fairly nondescript, as the band seemed to still be mastering the song's complexity. As "Taste" combines different rhythms among the four instruments and an odd-key jam, it undoubtedly took considerable work to master. The first curveball was subsequently thrown at the fall tour opener on 9/27/95. Phish began playing the music to "Taste" but Fishman assumed lead vocals and the lyrics were entirely different from the anticipated Trey-led song.

The changes in "Taste" were coupled with the band's 1995 trend of all band members playing simultaneously on the same instrument: in the summer, we had "Acoustic Army" and the fall produced "Keyboard Cavalry." Good-natured conspiracy theories were abound. Some fans thought the trend would continue for two more tours, speculating that we'd be eventually treated to "Bass Brigade" and "Drum Demons" while also receiving new lyrics to "Taste" while Mike and, finally, Page assumed lead vocals.

The band put most of the rumors and speculation to rest later that fall when, on 10/24/95, they threw us our second curveball—a combination of "Taste" and "Fog" that has never been officially named but that goes by the generally accepted title "Taste That Surrounds." Actual indications are that the band again called it "Taste" at this point, but fans wanted a different name in order to keep the two incarnations separate. And in the summer of 1996, the band unveiled the "final" version of "Taste," paring most of the "Fog" lyrics but keeping one refrain of Fishman's lyric as an added verse and adding the manic percussion work that would subsequently appear on the *Billy Breathes* album version. The first new "Taste" was performed on 7/3/96 and featured an inspired jam, led by guest appearances from Carlos Santana and Karl Perazzo, that segued nicely into "Llama."

Now that the band had settled on an arrangement, they seemed to play the song with a mission to jam. Fall, 1996 produced several inspired versions, including 10/27 (with a beautiful "Norwegian Wood" tease) and back to back smoking versions in California on 11/29 and 11/30. The latter was unforgettable, as West Coast legend Peter Apfelbaum was featured on tenor saxophone.

Momentum continued into 1997, with 2/17 standing out as memorable for the fluid second-set jamming that engulfed and surrounded the song. Nothing, though, prepared fans for what they heard in Raleigh on 7/22/97. During one Phish show that can literally be described as electric, Phish jammed away to "Taste" during a torrential downpour and lightning storm, with the rises and falls of the jam seamlessly coinciding with the force of the storm. Fans who listen to tapes of the evening can only shake their heads as they hear the brute force of the thunder explode in their speakers. Subsequently, standout versions of "Taste" continued to rock 1997 as it became one of the most frequently-played songs in the Phish repertoire. A sampling includes 8/3/97 (a highlight at

The Gorge), 8/9/97 (Phish combines two newer jam outlets with "Ghost" -> "Taste"), 8/17/97 (fans at the Great Went were treated to a "Tweezer" -> "Taste," and 12/30/97 (out of the "Sneakin' Sally" breakout).

"Taste" was regarded highly enough to be included in the Sessions at West 54th television broadcast that was originally recorded on October 20, 1998. Ironically, the song was played that night as an afterthought. After running through a studio set of new original material and the then-recently added cover of "Albuquerque," Phish had time for one more song and quickly polled the audience for a request. That request was "Taste," and it was the highlight of the evening. The last few years have included more typically solid "Taste" jams. No collection is complete without 11/19/98 ("Rock and Roll" -> "Taste") and 7/17/99 Oswego.

See Also: "The Fog That Surrounds"

Tela

Music/Lyrics: Trey Anastasio
Album: (none)
Debut: 3/12/88
Historian: Mark Toscano

She glided into his life like a luminous, brilliantly hued, perfectly formed leaf on a gentle, almost imperceptible wind. At first he admired her from afar, not even daring to speak with her. Then, his pulse quickened, for she called to him, beckoned him close, gazed into his eyes, and told him all about evil King Wilson, the Lizards, the Helping Friendly Book (divine gift from Icculus the mountain god), and the revolutionary effort to overthrow Wilson, thus restoring peace and tranquility to the land of Gamehendge. Alright, so it's not your typical love story.

In his Senior Study, Trey described "Tela" as his favorite song of "The Man Who Stepped Into Yesterday," feeling it was an ambitious departure from his usual compositional style. And indeed it was. As Trey originally wrote it, "Tela" was alternately a sweet ballad and a jumpy, danceable swinger with an atonal fugue tacked onto the end. Although it was definitely Phishy, it was more like a Phish song turned inside-out. It was in "Tela" that Trey first tackled the challenge of writing seriously for voice, and the first song he wrote for a vocalist other than himself: Page McConnell. This unusual approach also goes for the lyrics themselves, which he conceived more as poetry than words in a song. Finally, there's the matter of the atonal fugue at the end, which was intended to musically express the feeling and movement of the Unit Monster and the Multi-Beast tromping through the jungle with Colonel Forbin, Tela, and Rutherford atop its back. Trey spent a lot of time on the fugue's theme, and the band had to learn it quickly to get the project in on time. It's not surprising that Trey singled out this song as the most time-consuming of the whole project. We'd like to thank him for his effort—"Tela" is a much beloved song, all the more so because of its relative rarity at shows.

"Tela" made a handful of live appearances during the first half of 1988 (3/12, 5/21, and 6/20) before Trey turned in his Senior Study that July. The excellent 6/20/88 version is more or less the highlight of the entire second set—the band goes through the entire song masterfully, all the way to the end of the fugue. This full version of "Tela" lasted through 1988, with its final performance occurring on 8/27/88. The song was then shelved, not reappearing until over a year later on 10/22/89, and not without some changes. Gone was the danceable, upbeat portion, gone was the mindscrewing atonal fugue. All that re-

mained was the sweet, ethereal beauty of the song's elemental structure, a love song from a lonely, aging colonel to a woman so beautiful he questions her very existence.

Since the 10/22/89 reappearance, "Tela" has remained fixed in composition, and neither abandoned section has returned for another go-round. The song's structure is pretty rigid, not allowing for much improvisation, but the band is usually able to get some sweet mileage out of the few instrumental bridges in the song; Page especially shines in these areas.

"Tela" is always a welcome guest at any show, and the band usually invites her on stage to mellow the crowd down a shade, only to help their sprits to soar with the song's thrilling, shimmering climax. Some especially blissful versions of "Tela" include 4/21/92, 3/22/93, 11/4/94 (in "Mike's Groove")12/14/95, and 8/14/97.

Tell Me Something Good

Original Artist: Rufus with Chaka Khan
Original Album: *Rags to Rufus* **(1974)**
Vocals: unknown guest
Debut: 3/6/87
Historian: Craig DeLucia

This 1970s funk classic only shows up on one Phish tape: 3/6/87 at Nectar's. Reprising Chaka Khan's original role, an unknown female joined the band on lead vocals. All is not lost, though; Fishman still plays the song with his band, Pork Tornado.

Tennessee Waltz

Original Artist: Pee Wee King and Redd Stewart
Original Album: N/A
Vocals: Dick Solberg (5/6/93); "Reverend" Jeff Mosier
  (11/16/94)
Debut: 5/6/93
Historian: Jeremy Welsh:

Phish has played this standard on three occasions, all three in bluegrass settings with guests. Its debut was on 5/6/93 at the Palace Theater in Albany, NY. Dick Solberg and Jeff Walton had joined the band for the final three songs of the first set (Solberg on fiddle, Walton on acoustic guitar); "Tennessee Waltz" was played between "Why You Been Gone So Long" and "I Been on a Fast Train to Georgia," the only appearance of those two songs. The second time "Tennessee Waltz" was played was 11/16/94 with "Reverend" Jeff Mosier on banjo and vocals. It was played as part of a string of bluegrass songs to close the first set. Three nights later, after their show in Bloomington, Indiana, Phish performed "Tennessee Waltz" in their parking lot set, an acoustic bluegrass set that featured the Reverend on banjo, Eric Merrill on fiddle and guitar, and "Jeremy" on banjo and jaw harp.

Terrapin

Original Artist: Syd Barrett
Original Album: *The Madcap Laughs* **(1970)**
Vocals: Fish (lead)
Debut: 9/21/87
Historian: Tim Wade

This is another Syd Barrett song that Fish rarely performs any more, although he did allude to a "love song about a turtle" before crooning Marvin Gaye's "Sexual Healing" during 1998's Lemonwheel extravaganza. In contrast to the spastic "Love You" and the schizophrenic "Bike," "Terrapin" is a smooth ballad. To illustrate this, listen to the version from 2/20/93 at the Roxy Theater in Atlanta. At this show Fish invited the crowd to imagine having a glass of wine and being "laid back." He got so laid back while introducing band and crew that Page tried to move things along with a few notes of "Hold Your Head Up," but Fish would have none of it. Other special performances include 12/29/92 ("the slowest version of this song ever performed on the face of the earth"), 11/20/92 ("Terrapin"- "Lengthwise"), and 10/19/91, which featured Fishman on trombone while his mother Mimi played the vacuum. "Terrapin" was dusted off for a performance on 7/11/96 in London, England, but it has not crawled out of its shell since.

Terrapin Station

AKA: "Terrapin"
Original Artist: The Grateful Dead
Original Album: *Terrapin Station* **(1977)**
Vocals: Trey (lead), Mike, Page (backing)
Debut: 8/9/98
Historian: Chris Bertolet

Fans can file this one under "m" for miracle. The Grateful Dead's "Terrapin Station" is arguably their most beloved composition, and its genesis is a miracle in its own right. According to Dead lyricist Robert Hunter, he and Jerry Garcia composed the words and music to this song simultaneously—and unbeknownst to each other—while watching an electrical storm dance over San Francisco.

The first section of the celestial epic, appropriately titled "Lady With A Fan," recounts the story of a Soldier and Sailor, each smitten with a beautiful Lady. She puts a mortal challenge to them both, throwing her fan into a den of lions. While the Soldier shrugs off the chance to win the Lady's hand, the Sailor throws caution to the wind. Though the storyteller eschews a Hollywood ending, the message is clear—in matters of love, take the chance.

The second section is a soaring, spine-tingling ode to inspiration and the muse, sense and color, mystery and truth. It speaks of a place that crickets and cicadas sing of, a place that can be found only by those with adventure and passion in their hearts: Terrapin Station. That is also the name of the third section, a driving, percussive passage that repeats and heightens, opening a door to jamspace. The concluding movements to "Terrapin Station"—"Terrapin Transit," "At A Siding," "Terrapin Flyer" and "Refrain"—never surfaced in the Dead's live performances. In that regard, Phish's rendition was no different.

Phish debuted this song in Virginia Beach on the third anniversary of Garcia's death, perhaps inspired by a stunning full moon that hung over the amphitheater that night. By all accounts, the crowd's slack-jawed reaction to the first signature guitar peal gave way quickly to hugs, tears of joy, and spontaneous acrobatics. All of this crackling energy is palpable on tape.

Though Phish hasn't reprised it since, Trey and Page played an extended "Terrapin" in their Phil Lesh & Friends engagement. Though most fans consider the Warfield jam to be a notch above, the brave Virginia Beach breakout is a must-hear for fans of both bands.

That's Alright Mama

Music/Lyrics: Arthur Crudup
Original Artist: Elvis Presley
Original Album: (single)
Vocals: Dick Solberg
Debut: 5/6/93
Historian: Phil Nazzaro

I was down in New Orleans this last week at the Jazz Heritage Festival; and over near where they server an etouffee I could have swear I saw Elvis" —Jeff Walton

Indeed. "That's Alright Mama" may be best known as Elvis's first single; but it has been covered by a slew of artists over the years. Phish got added to the list of admirers on 5/6/93 at the Palace Theater in Albany, NY. Although Phish sounds a little hesitant at first, they pick up on it quickly while guest artists Dick Solberg (fiddle) and Jeff Walton (acoustic guitar) rip from the beginning to the end of this one appearance wonder.

Them Changes

AKA: "Changes," "Dem Changes"
Original Artist: Buddy Miles
Original Album: *Them Changes* (1970)
Vocals: Page
Debut: 11/30/97
Historian: Phillip Zerbo

On the final night of a memorable three show run at Centrum in Worcester, MA, Phish dipped into the repertoire of classic blues rock and drummer Buddy Miles, performing his best known 1970 hit "Them Changes." Buddy Miles is perhaps best remembered by his stint in the late 1960s and 1970 as the drummer with the Jimi Hendrix Experience. "Them Changes" provided the title track for Buddy's first solo album, but it is better known for having appeared on the wildly popular Jimi Hendrix album "Band of Gypsies." The single performance of "Them Changes" on 11/30/97, witnessed Page shining on vocals, and Trey engaged in a particularly inspired solo. Closely resembling the live Jimi Hendrix-led versions, "Them Changes" seemed a perfect fit for Phish, but they have apparently shelved this song after this single appearance.

Theme From The Bottom

AKA: "Theme"
Music: Phish
Lyrics: Tom Marshall
Album: *Billy Breathes*
Vocals: Page, Trey (lead), Mike (backing)
Debut: 5/16/95
Historian: Craig DeLucia

Has ever a stronger group of original songs debuted on one tour than in the summer of 1995? Try picking a favorite from that group and you're likely to be stuck with a tough decision, weighing the relative merits of "Free," "Billy Breathes," "Taste," the rare "Spock's Brain," and "Theme From the Bottom." Each has their supporters, but "Theme From the Bottom" may contain the best balance of intriguing music, interesting lyrics, and inherent jamming potential.

Early in its life, "Theme" kicked off the infamous "FLeezer" set by roaring out of the second set gates and leading into a free-form jam on 6/22/95. Unfortunately, though, this remains the only largely exploratory version and the song's jamming potential has remained just that: potential. Versions have not varied largely from each other, and minor changes in structure (removing and then re-adding a piece of the middle bridge, for example) have been the only real discernible difference between early and current renditions. Despite the lack of exploration, though, "Theme" remains a fan favorite for its delicate power.

A few notable "Themes" have bubbled up. 11/27/96, out of "Free," remains one of the longest and most powerful and, along with 6/16/00, marks the most jammed-out version to date. Pick up 7/21/97, which led to a distinct jam with LeRoi Moore on saxophone and round out your collection with 7/9/98 "Drowned" -> "Theme" from Barcelona.

THIS IS A FARMHOUSE (see: "FARMHOUSE")

Three Little Birds

Original Artist: Bob Marley and the Wailers
Original Album: *Exodus* (1977)
Vocals: Jah Roy (6/20/88), Dave Matthews (6/17/95)
Debut: 6/20/88
Historian: Ellis Godard

Three Little Birds has appeared three little times in Phishtory. At an early Nectar's show (6/20/88), guest Jah Roy teased the lyrics a bit during the jam out of "Ya Mar." Seven years later, Phish tested the tune at a soundcheck (6/16/95) and then pulled it out for an encore (6/17/95) with the Dave Matthews Band (with whom they had earlier debuted "Somewhere Over the Rainbow" and "The Maker").

The song itself only says three little things: the singer woke up, and saw three birds, who told him not to worry. It only has three chords, and only three pairs of measures. There is, in three little words, not much there. But in it, as with "One Love," Bob Marley magically captured a moving ballad within the distinctive heavy bass and downbeats of reggae.

Timber (Jerry)

AKA: "Timber Ho!," "Timber"
Music/Lyrics: Josh White and Sam Gary
Original Artist: Josh White
Original Album: ('30s)
Vocals: Trey (lead), Mike, Page (backing)
Debut: 4/29/87
Historian: Grant Calof

From manic house-pets, to almost-extinct reptilians, road wary highway-dwellers, existentialist insects and a handful of other creatures, few bands can boast as many songs about bizarre animals as Phish. Yet even among this vast lyrical menagerie, there's only one animal distinguished enough to have two songs about it the Mule.

And while fans may be more familiar with a certain tune about mules and UFOs, "Timber Ho!" was actually the first of the mule-inspired tunes to make its way on to the setlist. The song was written in the 1930s by the songwriting team of Josh White and Sam Gary. And while the song was originally composed as a team, it was Josh White who

supplied both the vocals and guitar work when it came time to record.

"Timber Ho!" tells the amusing story of a determined man and his ill-tempered mule, and their repeated attempts to haul lumber for an unsympathetic boss. Like much of depression-era poetry and songwriting, the lyrics take a satirical approach to chronicling the everyday struggle people endured to survive. But not long after its inception, "Timber Ho!" disappeared into a vast sea of musical catalogues for the next thirty years. The song was later resurrected during the 1960s, when it was re-recorded by Odetta Holmes, a renowned blues and folk artist of the time. After Holmes though, the song once again faded into the ether. And it might have been lost forever, were it not for one special night in April of 1987, when Phish debuted it in front of an audience at Nectar's.

When it was first played, "Timber Ho!" was apt to show up in either the first or second set, but as the years wore on, it appeared almost entirely during the second, often serving as the opening song. Phish played it fairly regularly until 1990, when the song was inexplicably shelved for two years. But after its one-time appearance on 12/30/92, the song once again eluded concert-goers for another three years, until the last night of the 1995 Summer tour (7/3/95).

On that particular night, the last of two truly incredible nights of music at the SummerStage at Sugarbush in Fayston, Vermont, two lucky fans near the rail were holding a sign that read "Timber Ho!" During the set-break, the band decided to grant them their request and played the song for the first time in two-hundred and fifty seven shows. With the crowd's jaws still on the floor, and the walls still shaking, the roof was blown clear into the stratosphere when the boys from Burlington reprised "Timber Ho!" during an extended tease through the "Bowie" intro that immediately follows. Later, when questioned about the absence of the song for so many years, Mike Gordon claimed that the band never played the song because they apparently didn't like their cover as much as the original version and felt that they "didn't do it justice." Nonetheless, after that summer, "Timber Ho!" finally became a regular, albeit sporadic, part of the Phish repertoire.

And with its entrance into Phish's ever-growing musical arsenal, along with it came the years-long debate as to the correct title of the song. The true name of the song is in fact, "Timber (Jerry)," but only the most orthodox of fans identify it by its true moniker. It's most commonly identified on setlists as "Timber Ho!," due to the song's chorus but is also sometimes written as "Timber" simply for the sake of brevity. The style and overall feel of the song, as well as the sharp contrast between the lyrics and music often leads people to mistakenly identify the song as an original. The band did alter the song's structure quite a bit, adding the double-drum repetiton that drives the song forward. But every question and every concern ceases to matter when those first few strums of the guitar echo across the sky.

Despite its rooting in folk, Phish puts their own undeniable "spin" on "Timber Ho!," bringing an almost space age, otherworldly quality to it. The song can sometimes provide the springboard for an interesting set (check out the "Timber Ho!" segue into "Mike's" from second set of 12/31/97) or the gateway into a mind-numbing jam (7/26/97 comes highly recommended). Other versions that are worthy of mention are 2/7/89, 6/16/90, 11/11/96, 7/17/99 and 7/14/00.

TIME (see: "THE MEATSTICK")

Time/Breathe Reprise

Original Artist: Pink Floyd
Original Album: *Dark Side of the Moon* **(1973)**
Vocals: Trey (lead), Mike, Page (backing)
Debut: 11/2/98
Historian: Mark Toscano

Many Floyd fans exalt this song as one of their favorites from the whole of PF's ouevre, and that ain't no joke. Beginning with its signature collage of ticking and alarming clocks (the loudest single part of the whole album), the song can be heard on almost every classic rock station worldwide at least three times a week, and is one of Pink Floyd's most recognizable and popular songs.

In preparing for their last-minute 11/2/98 performance of *Dark Side*, Phish spared no expense and actually sent Brad Sands out into Salt Lake City to do nothing less than BUY a copy of the album on CD especially for the show. The CD was used a few times during the second set to add the album's special sound effects to a few songs that were otherwise unimaginable. Therefore, after the exciting rendition of "On the Run," the familiar ticking of "Time" began, followed by the inevitable alarms and metronomic beat as the sounds of the CD played over the venue's P.A. Fishman then picked up the minimalist ticktock on his woodblocks as the band began to play the song's intro themselves. Though hampered a wee bit by a mistimed start and a few sloppy moments, the guys did the song plenty justice, kicking out a rocking version that energized the heck out of the E Centre on one of the most hallowed nights in Phish history.

Time Loves a Hero

Music: Bill Payne, Paul Barrere and Ken Gradney
Lyrics: Bill Payne and Paul Barrere
Original Artist: Little Feat
Original Album: *Time Loves a Hero* **(1977)**
Vocals: Trey
Debut: 10/31/88
Historian: Ellis Godard

Of all of the rarities "busted out" during Phish shows over the years, perhaps the most poignant is "Time Loves a Hero." Early performances of this Little Feat bop had an exuberance that suggested prophecy (though not the full sound of the original, which featured the Tower of Power horns.) The debut (10/31/88, the first Halloween show) was particularly strong. The next two appearances came at the first Molly's gig (11/3/88) and their first out-of-state college gig (11/5/88). And the song moved earlier in the setlist with each appearance, as if the lyrics were becoming stronger and stronger omens of the band's coming success. But then it moved too early in the evening for an audience to hear, serving as the soundcheck on consecutive nights (4/14/89 and 4/15/89).

The lyrics deal with an uncle who left his wife and "blue collar hell" for "the beaches of Puerto Rico." The chorus then ponders whether the uncle will someday be lauded for having ditched convention in search of beauty, or will instead continue to be seen as a hollow deviant. Though with the harshness of a good blues story, the song brings to mind a popular image of travelling musicians as carefree artists. But the realities of sleeping on YMCA floors and travelling cross-country in the back of a moving truck are harsher than Caribbean beaches. Phish en-

dured not by ditching conventions, but by adopting those that work and doing what it took to fulfill their dream. And it paid off.

Time confirmed the prophecy, as Phish's heroic status in art, performance, and business was made clear over the next ten years. "Appropriately, then, they added a breakout "Time Loves a Hero" to the "Summer of Covers" roster on 8/11/98, nearly ten years after its last performance.

Title Track

Music: Phish
Album: *The Siket Disc*
Vocals: (instrumental)
Debut: (never performed live)
Historian: Mark Toscano

The eighth track on *The Siket Disc* is possibly the most idiosyncratic. Starting with some electronic fidgeting, it soon builds to a noisy climax before being silenced by "Albert," the album's sweet, tuneful closer.

T.M.W.S.I.Y. (see: "The Man Who Stepped into Yesterday")

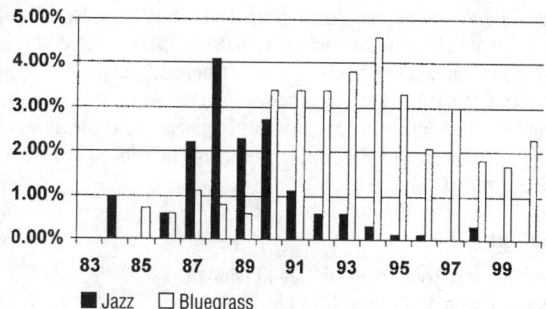

Jazz and Bluegrass Covers

Compared by times played as a percentage of all songs played, jazz covers clearly predominated until 1990, after which bluegrass covers have been much more frequent. Even combined however, the two genres have accounted for more than 5% of Phish's songs in only one year, 1990 (6.1%).

■ Jazz ☐ Bluegrass

Top bluegrass covers:

Uncle Pen	190
Rocky Top	169
Paul and Silas	77
Ginseng Sullivan	66
Nellie Kane	46

Top jazz covers:

Take the A-Train	90
Caravan	39
Donna Lee	20
Satin Doll	12
Manteca	12

Too Much of Everything

Music/Lyrics: Kim Wilson, Steve Jordan, Danny Kortchmar
Original Artist: Fabulous Thunderbirds
Original Album: *Trial & Error* (Soundtrack); *High Water* (1997)
Vocals: Trey
Debut: 7/26/98
Historian: Phillip Zerbo

Part Memphis blues, part southern soul, part garage band, the original "Too Much of Everything" first appeared on the soundtrack to the asinine 1997 movie *Trial & Error*. This latter-day incarnation of the Fabulous Thunderbirds (without stalwarts Jimmie Vaughan and Duke Robillard) was neither critically or commercially acclaimed. "Too Much of Everything" was co-written by the Fabulous Thunderbirds only remaining founding member, vocalist and harp player Kim Wilson, along with Steve Jordan (*Late Show With Dave Letterman* band) and guitarist Danny "Kootch" Kortchmar. A gritty rocker, "Too Much of Everything" finds our central character proclaiming primal desire: "Too much of everything ain't good for nobody, but baby I want you!" In the context of the modern day Phish universe, this same line could well be viewed as a cautionary tale of the dangers of various excesses!

During the Summer 1998 tour that witnessed an unusual abundance of new covers, Phish first performed "Too Much of Everything" on 7/26/98, at the Starplex Amphitheatre in Dallas, Texas. After the debut of this comparatively short song, Trey remarked to the audience that "the guy in the front row wants to hear something LONG" and the band obliged with a solid version of "David Bowie." "Too Much of Everything" saw the Phish stage on only one other occasion, a week later on 8/2/98, at the famed Deer Creek Music Center in Noblesville, Indiana.

Touch Me

Original Artist: The Doors
Original Album: *The Soft Parade* (1969)
Vocals: Jon Fishman
Debut: 7/11/91
Historian: Phillip Zerbo

In front of a large crowd of people, Jon Fishman proclaims with all his heart and soul his desire for someone to "touch me, babe." Some things never change!

The Door's classic song "Touch Me" was one of several new cover songs debuted during the famous "Horn Tour" in July, 1991. The addition of The Giant Country Horns (Dave "The Truth" Grippo and Russell Remington on saxophones and Carl "Gears" Gerhard on trumpet) opened up new and exciting possibilities for song arrangements for the band. Given the tightness of the arrangements, the song does not vary among versions, though it has been played both by itself and sandwiched between the famous Henrietta theme "Hold Your Head Up." Closing the first encore at the Arrowhead Ranch in Parksville, NY on 7/21/91, "Touch Me" was performed with washboard accompaniment by guest "Steve-O" from New Orleans.

After the July 1991 horn tour, "Touch Me" made only one more appearance, on 12/3/94 at the Event Center in San Jose, CA; this was one of two shows on that tour (along with 12/2/94 in Davis, CA) that featured another version of the Giant Country Horns (dubbed "The Cosmic Country Horns," this time with Grippo, Gerhard, Michael Ray on trumpet, Peter Apfelbaum on tenor sax, and James Harvey on trombone.

Train Round the Bend
Original Artist: The Velvet Underground
Original Album: *Loaded* **(1970)**
Vocals: Mike (lead), Fish (backing)
Debut: 10/31/98
Historian: Mark Toscano/Dan Purcell

This chug-chuggin' track was the penultimate tune in Phish's *Loaded* set on 10/31/98. Mike handled the vocals on this chicken-fried rock song, the learning of which almost certainly influenced Trey's composition "Back On the Train" the following year. Phish did a heavily energized reading of this tune, and many fans were surprised that it was one of the three tracks not selected for inclusion on the late '98 Album Network broadcast of portions of the 10/31/98 show. Trey's extended solo raises the ante—each time the song seems about to end, the band takes the train around the track one more time, until Mike's vocals slide back in to bring the number to an emphatic close. Many of the hardercore Velvets fans consider this one of the highlights of the set.

Trainsong
Music/Lyrics: Mike Gordon, Joe Linitz
Album: *Billy Breathes; Hampton Comes Alive* **(11/20/98)**
Vocals: Mike (lead), Trey (backing)
Debut: 7/21/96
Historian:Mark Toscano

Of Phish's non-jamming songs, quite a few fans consider this wonderful Mike song one of their favorites. Combining a treat of a repeating guitar riff (supposedly born of "The Blob") with some truly poetic lyrics (some of Mike's best), the bassist wove a sweet and subtle tune perfect for mellowing out any unruly, hyperactive set.

Premiering in Europe, the song made its U.S. debut in a mini-acoustic setting at Red Rocks on 8/5/96 with Trey on guitar, backing Mike's lead vocals, and Page providing the strangely pleasingly dissonant solo The *Billy Breathes* version recommended for crystal clarity, but some strong live versions include those mentioned above, plus the 8/16/97 Went version, which flowed out of a very short "YEM" vocal jam, the last vocalized chord of which was the same as "Train Song's" opening! Also check out 12/6/97, 4/3/98 (into "Billy Breathes," bypassing "Bliss"), and 9/22/99 (in a "Mike's Groove"). Interestingly, though it was still making regular appearances in 1999, 2000 saw not one version of "Train Song" come to the stage.

TREAT ME LIKE A FOOL (see: "LOVE ME")

Trench Town Rock
AKA: "Trenchtown Rock," "Trenchtown"
Music/Lyrics: Bob Marley
Original Artist: Bob Marley and The Wailers
Original Album: *African Herbsman* **(1973); Live! (1975)**
Vocals: Trey (lead), Mike, Page (backing)
Debut: 8/11/98
Historian: Mark Toscano

Phish surprised everyone with this left-field cover of Bob Marley's "Trench Town Rock," perhaps one of the most raw and meaningful songs ever written in the history of life as we know it. Opening the

8/11/98 Star Lake show, "Trench Town" was greeted with a huge, all-engulfing cheer from everyone in the amphitheater, both those who were Bob Marley fans and those who mistook the song's opening for "Harry Hood." Phish's version of the tune is surprisingly strong, considering it was a (likely hastily decided upon) one-timer. The vocals are fine, and the guys get the song's sound about as right as four white New Englanders could ever get it. Fans curious to hear the original may want to grab the live Marley version from *Live!* before looking for the studio track recorded on *African Herbsman*.

Tropical Hot Dog Night
Original Artist: Captain Beefheart
Original Album: *Shiny Beast (Bat Chain Puller)* **(1979)**
Vocals: Captain Beefheart (played over P.A.)
Debut: 12/31/94
Historian: Mark Toscano

It was to the schizoid-calypsoid rhythm and rhyme of this Captain Beefheart track that Phish mounted the infamous hot dog to end all hot dogs at their 1994 New Year's Eve show at Boston Garden. The frankfurter soared above the heads of the crowd as the band tossed out ping-pong balls and other goodies, with said Beefheart tune blasting over the P.A. system. The track, found on the Captain's ill-fated, penultimate album, is a tame but reasonably representative example of his third and final musical phase, encompassing the albums *Doc at the Radar Station* (1978), *Shiny Beast (Bat Chain Puller)* (1979), and *Ice Cream For Crow* (1982). Interestingly, the incredible, original *Bat Chain Puller* album, never released due to label problems, did not include this track. "Tropical Hot Dog Night" was actually recorded a few years later and, mixed with some original *Bat Chain Puller* songs, begat the still impressive *Shiny Beast (Bat Chain Puller)*. It was music industry bullshit like this that helped the Captain decide to retire, and Don van Vliet (his real name) is now a very successful and reknowned painter.

As Captain Beefheart is generally considered to be one of the most influential figures in rock since its beginnings, his recorded work is highly recommended (especially the albums mentioned above and anything pre-1973).

Tube
Music/Lyrics: Trey Anastasio, Jon Fishman
Album: *Hampton Comes Alive* **(11/20/98)**
Vocals: Trey
Debut: 9/13/90
Historian: Craig DeLucia

Perhaps no individual Phish song benefitted more from the emergence of the Cow Funk in 1997 than "Tube." The fan favorite which, until then, had never seemed to find a comfortable place on stage suddenly became a centerpiece set-up song that the band tweaked and rode to much applause.

Like many songs, "Tube" came roaring out of the gates after its debut. It combined quirky Fishman-penned lyrics that reference asteriods crashing, tigers in lily patches, and even singer Robert Palmer (though few can decipher the ending lyrics well enough to know what he is doing!) with a fast, shuffle-style verse and a groovy jam in the middle. In fact, the song's untapped potential continued to lie dormant in this jam segment for the better part of the 1990s.

By 1991, "Tube" had become a fairly regular song in rotation and was often used as a second-set opener. But the song became rarer in 1992 and seemingly disappeared in 1993. Subsequently, it was played only once in 1994 and a handful of times in 1995. Trey referenced the crowd's fondness for the rare song on 12/11/95, when he rewarded the fans in attendance with "Tube" for their participation in the humorous "Dog Log" album gag.

Still, fans were disappointed when "Tube" seemed to go back in a hole, as it was fairly forgotten by the band in 1996 and early 1997. And then the Cow Funk hit. Spurred by Mike's Modulus bass and setlists that placed increased emphasis on thick funk-oriented jams, "Tube" seemed to be a perfect vehicle to convey the sound the band was trying to perfect. For some reason, it stayed away until the 12/7/97 Dayton show, but once released it came charging out and has not looked back since. And the band was apparently happy enough with their performance that they reprised the jam segment after the song concluded before moving nicely into "Slave." A few weeks later, fans at MSG caught a hot "Tube" on 12/29/97 (complete with an "I Feel the Earth Move" tease) and realized that the asteroid had surely crashed and left one hell of a burning song behind.

In 1998 and 1999, the band moved to a more groove-oriented style of jamming and "Tube" continued to grow. It was a fitting choice for the first song of 1998 and only grew stronger throughout the year. Be sure to check out the hot 11/2/98 version, which contained the second-ever "Tube Reprise" jam (also 9/15/00). This one moved nicely into the return of "Drowned." Other notable versions include 7/21/98, 11/21/98, and 7/17/99. And to make your collection complete, pick up the outtakes from *Story of the Ghost* to hear the unreleased studio version.

As a final note, "Tube" shouldn't be confused with "First Tube," which debuted in 1999 and was included on Farmhouse, or "Last Tube," which appeared on Trey's 1999 theatre tour but has not yet made it to the Phish stage.

Tubthumping
Original Artist: Chumbawumba
Original Album: *Tubthumper* **(1997)**
Phish Album: *Hampton Comes Alive* **(11/21/98)**
Vocals: Tom Marshall (lead)
Debut: 11/21/98
Historian: Martin Acaster

Tubthumping made the British musical collective known as Chumbawumba a household name in the United States for the first time in their 15 year career. Telling the tale of a seemingly melancholy drunk "pissing his life away" it is buoyed by its never-say-die chorus "…You're never gonna keep me down!"

Phish debuted this pop hit as the encore to the second show of a two night run at the Hampton Coliseum on 11/21/98. This performance, which featured lyricist Tom Marshall on lead vocals and Carl Gerhardt on trumpet, was released on *Hampton Comes Alive* and included Fishman teases of Will Smith's "Gettin' Jiggy Wit It" in the chorus.

Tuesday's Gone
Original Artist: Lynyrd Skynyrd
Original Album: *Pronounced Lêh'-nerd' Skin'-nerd* **(1973)**
Vocals: Trey (lead), Page (backing)

Debut: 7/13/99
Historian: Myrk Tyscyno

Phish pulled off a pretty strong one-time cover of this Skynyrd tune as the encore to their fun 7/13/99 show. What made them pick this one? That's easy. It was Tuesday.

Tush
Original Artist: ZZ Top
Original Album: *Fandango* **(1975)**
Vocals: Trey
Debut: 12/6/86
Historian: Ellis Godard

Phish has twice covered "Tush," the epitome of ZZ Top's redneck rock though the shortest of the trio's scores of originals. Both performances (12/6/86 and 8/10/97) rounded out cover-heavy sets, and the second was in a show with two other ZZ Top tunes ("La Grange" and "Jesus Just Left Chicago"). It does appear on other setlists, but only by error as it was often confused with "La Grange." The song, a three-chord ditty about needing titty, helped build the repertoire of what was becoming known as a great bar band from Vermont. But the tune didn't translate well to larger venues, as witnessed in more recent soundchecks (e.g. 8/14/96).

T.V. Show
AKA: "Life Is a T.V. Show"
Original Artist: The Dude of Life (with Phish)
Original Album: *Crimes of the Mind* **(1994)**
Vocals: The Dude of Life
Debut: 11/8/91
Historian: Dan Mielcarz

An anthemic take on the melding of media and reality, "TV Show" was played only once at the Ivory Tusk on 11/8/91. Phish and The Dude also released it on The Dude's album, *Crimes of the Mind*.

T.V. Theme
AKA: "Star Trek Jam"
Music: (unknown)
Album: (none)
Vocals: (instrumental)
Debut: 10/17/85
Historian: Mark Toscano

This song constitutes one of the more unexplored conundra of Phish's early song mysteries. Labeled consistently for years as "Star Trek jam" on everyone's tapes, this reasonably short Allmanesque instrumental sounds very little like any "Star Trek" music this fan has ever heard. Like another "Melissa" or "Jessica" or some other thusly named song, Trey and Jeff's guitars trace a happy little melody around as the rest of the band supports them from behind. Though the band likely performed it more than once (as with "Punch me in the Eye"), the only known version appears on the curious 10/17/85 Finbar's show. Questions over the nature of this song as an original or cover can be dispelled with one listen to this show. Trey clearly states that it's a new one they just wrote in the past few days.

Even band archivist Kevin Shapiro was somewhat perplexed when

it came to the identification of this song. He was able to offer a piece of information that, if it didn't help identify the tune, at least shed a little more light: the band's original master tape calls the song "T.V. Theme." Whether it's an actual T.V. theme, or a fictional ditty the band wrote for their own wacky and wild program, who knows. Trey? Mike? Anyone?

Tweezer

AKA: "Tweezer So Cold" (original title)
Music/Lyrics: Phish
Album: *A Picture of Nectar; A Live One* (11/2/94)
Vocals: Phish
Debut: 3/28/90
Historians: Saul Wertheimer and Charlie Dirksen

Tweezers from each consecutive tour seem to yield at least a slightly—if not wildly—different style of jamming. The song's funky intro has served as a launching pad for some of Phish's most experimental playing. It has been jammed in excess of 50 minutes (6/14/95 Memphis), has been woven like a fine shirt (e.g., 5/7/94 Dallas, 12/1/94 Salem), and has yielded some fiery, Hose-inducing jams (e.g., 11/30/95 Dayton and 12/2/95 New Haven).

Making its debut as "Tweezer So Cold" in March 1990, the song allegedly grew out of a soundcheck jam which occurred before the 12/31/89 New Year's show. It was toyed with a little bit before the "Bowie" on 2/25/90 in Baltimore, and finalized at the 3/3/90 Wetlands soundcheck. Mike comments in *The Phish Book* that not only did he invent "Tweezer's" bass line, but also that the "freezer" of the song's lyrics is the state of Vermont. Upon hearing Mike's bass line, Trey came up with the guitar part instantly.

The earliest "Tweezers" feature a closing segment (a few measures of the opening theme) after the jam segment dies out. This segment was shortened around April 1991 (compare 3/29/91 DNA Lounge with 4/27/91 Port Chester), and "Tweezer"—when the jam does not segue or fade out into another song—continues to close in a slow, dying-out-of-the-main-melodic-theme fashion. Early "Tweezers" of note include the 4/27/91 Port Chester version, which contains strong "Sweet Emotion" jamming and "Dr. Q on bass." 4/21/92 Eureka, with its melodious jam segment, is also quite charming. The Roxy version on 2/20/93 is also loved by many fans. While Aerosmith's "Sweet Emotion" was a more or less common theme of early "Tweezers," most early versions are dark and dissonant, and not particularly melodious.

The first "Tweezer" that strayed unusually far from home (but which was not a monster of epic proportions, like 11/2/94 Bangor) is 5/6/93 Albany. After a somewhat traditional groove for the first few minutes, including some intense "Sweet Emotion" quoting, particularly from Mike, the jam takes on a frighteningly aimless and peculiar mood for several minutes. It returns to a powerful rock theme, however, just before a spine-tinglingly mellifluous improvisation develops. "Tweezer" would be forever changed, and the August 1993 versions bear this out (e.g., behold the unusually inventive 8/15/93 Louisville version).

Perhaps the most widely circulated "Tweezer" is that performed on 5/7/94 at the Bomb Factory in Dallas. Performed off and on for almost an entire set, "Tweezer" is immersed in several other great tunes and jams (e.g., "Sparks," "Sweet Emotion," "Walk Away" and "Cannonball"), which weave in and out of a "Tweezer" jam. The set concludes with a magnificent jam based on the "Hold Your Head Up" theme, and

a strong "Tweezer Reprise." It remains to this day a fan favorite.

Summer tour 1994 yielded some strong "Tweezers," such as 6/10/94 Red Rocks (unusually powerful jam), 7/6/94 Montreal (jams on "2001" and "HYHU") and, of course, 7/13/94 Big Birch ("Tweezer" -> "Julius" -> "Tweezer" -> "BBFCFM" -> "Tweezer"). But the real excitement came on 11/2/94 in Bangor, Maine. Featured on *A Live One*, the 11/2/94 Bangor "Tweezer" is spectacularly playful and just over 30 minutes long. "Tweezer" had never before been jammed out in such a loose, experimental manner. A two-minute, four-second portion of Fall 1994's other experimental "Tweezer," 11/28/94 Bozeman (approximately 45 minutes long), also appears on *A Live One* as "Montana." Another strong Fall 1994 version, the 12/1/94 Salem "Tweezer" sandwiches "BBFCFM," "Makisupa Policeman," and "NICU." The 12/9/94 Mesa "Tweezer" is also noteworthy because it switches back and forth from intense space to typical rock jamming numerous times, and also features a full-blown jam on "Slave to the Traffic Light."

The Experimental "Tweezer" also showed up several times in Summer tour 1995. The momentous 6/14/95 Memphis "Tweezer" is about 52 minutes long, and is more a symphony with movements—a masterpiece of improvisational artistry—than simply a rock song. It contains some great space, and Mike lays down a captivating bass line. The 6/17/95 Gainesville version contains the first-ever Phish performance of "Johnny B. Goode," even though it is not as experimental as the other versions of the tour. At the Finger Lakes Performing Arts Center on 6/22/95, "Tweezer" was jammed for almost the entire set, and featured some "My Generation" (The Who) vocals, heavy exploration, and a nice segue into "Tweeprise." If you want to hear Phish take a lot of risks, check it out! The Jones Beach "Tweezer" on 6/28/95, which (like 11/2/94 Bangor) is around a half-hour long, featured the most serious "Dave's Energy Guide" jam of the decade about 19-20 minutes into it, as well as a "Cannonball" jam (see also 5/7/94 Bomb Factory). The final "Tweezer" of the tour, which segued smoothly into "Ha Ha Ha," was brilliantly performed at Sugarbush on July 2.

Considered by many to be the most inspired tour that Phish has ever performed, Fall 1995 contains astounding musical explorations in "Tweezer" and numerous other songs. You will likely rewind the 10/22 Champaign, 11/30 Dayton, 12/2 New Haven, 12/8 Cleveland, and 12/14 Binghamton versions to hear them again. Their intense jams are often more reminiscent of "Antelope," "Bowie" and "Possum" than "Tweezer's" typically discordant jams.

With the exception of Fall 1997, "Tweezer" has been relatively calm for the last few years. A "Norwegian Wood" jam graced the Red Rocks 8/6/96 "Tweezer." In Gainesville on 11/3/96, Karl Perazzo from Santana wailed away on percussion in what was arguably the finest version of that year. While still riding the Tsunami caused by Halloween, this version portended the Funk Renaissance that took full effect in 1997. Its jamming is dense and heavy with a textured feel, much like the *Remain in Light* 10/31/96 set, and the "Crosseyed" -> "Antelope" from 11/2/96 West Palm Beach. The 11/27/96 Seattle "Tweezer" harked back to the "Old Days" with a brief "Sweet Emotion" quote. And the summer 1997 Gorge and Went "Tweezers" signaled the song's rescue from a brief retirement.

Fall 1997 "Tweezers" raged with a funk so deep that many fans became stuck in its licentious depths, able only to mutter "Step into the Freezer" with perverted grins on their faces. Traditionally a second set jamming tune, "Tweezer" began appearing in the first set of Fall '97

shows, even opening the show on two occasions (11/17 Denver and 11/26 Hartford) much to the surprise and excitement of fans. The 11/22 Hampton "Tweezer" is a part of one of the most thrilling sets in Phishtory, and its segue into "Black-Eyed Katy" is ferociously funkalicious. The 12/6 Auburn Hills version is not only the longest "Tweezer" of '97, but also probably the most popular '97 version. It is essentially a hybrid of the 11/30/95 Dayton "Tweezer" and James Brown's "The Payback."

Though it appeared less frequently in 1998 than in most previous years, "Tweezer" nevertheless continued to serve as an exciting opportunity for the band to jam (see, for example, 8/1 Alpine, 10/30 Vegas, 11/24 New Haven). "Tweezer" in 1999 was no slouch, either (check out 12/16 Raleigh), and in 2000, hear 6/9/00 Tokyo, 6/24/00 Atlanta, and 10/7/00 Shoreline "Tweezer" continues to evolve as a collective, improvisational thriller. When you hear "Tweezer's" opening notes, prepare to groove passionately with the band, and celebrate one of Phish's most improvisational songs.

See Also: Montana, Tweezer Reprise

Tweezer Reprise
AKA: "Reprise," "Tweeprise"
Music/Lyrics: Phish

Album: *A Picture of Nectar*
Debut: 9/21/90
Historian: Mark Toscano

A "reprise" is a sort of musical afterthought—basically a reintroduction of and variation on the main theme of a piece of music. Thus, "Tweezer Reprise" is a slight variation—a condensation of sorts—of "Tweezer." As it does on the album *A Picture of Nectar*, the "Reprise" often follows "Tweezer" in concert, most frequently as an encore song. It is also common as a second set closer following an earlier "Tweezer." A few times, the "Reprise" has even been spewed out of some long, monster "Tweezer," serving as the thrilling exclamation point at the end of a raging, set-long sentence (e.g. 5/7/94 Bomb Factory, 6/22/95 Finger Lakes).

On occasion, "Tweezer Reprise" has shown up as a surprise in a show where there has been no performance of "Tweezer" proper. Although usually this occurs because the "Reprise" will be referring back to a non-reprised "Tweezer" at the previous night's show (e.g. 12/30/96's "Tweezer" was reprised on 12/31/96), the song has been known to appear, albeit rarely, completely free from its Granddaddy counterpart, like on 9/29/99. The most interesting example of this, and perhaps the most unusual "Tweezer Reprise" ever performed, was on 12/8/99, which featured an a capella version that came out of a "YEM"

Peter Sitzman

vocal jam to close the second set. The band later finished off the show with a traditional "Tweezer Reprise" to end the encore. Other interesting versions include 10/27/94 and 10/21/95.

As Trey begins the opening riff, some fans may mistake "Tweezer Reprise" for "Tweezer" itself. How to tell the difference? Well, aside from the tempo (Trey's riff in the "Reprise" is often faster and more momentous than its laid-back, funky progenitor), fans with keenly trained ears might pick out a difference: "Tweezer" is in A, while "Tweezer Reprise" is in D.

Twist

AKA: "Twist Around"
Music: Trey Anastasio (So tear a Sanity)
Lyrics: Tom Marshall (Mr. Ham so tall)
Album: *Farmhouse* (Hum of Ears)
Debut: 6/6/97 (private show); 6/14/97 (public show)
Historian: Martin Acaster (I'm a trance star)

An anagram is a new word or phrase created by rearranging the letters in a word. This simple linguistic tool has been used throughout history as a means of encrypting secret messages. When applied to a person's name, the anagram can provide strange insight either into their character or the anagrammaticist's feelings toward them. In "Twist" the victim of this analysis is the too often absent beloved of the protagonist. Clearly, neither is happy with the resulting anagrams.

"Twist" was one of several new songs which first appeared during the European leg of the 1997 Summer Tour, making its public debut at the SFX Centre in Dublin, Ireland on 6/14/97. Like the rest of these new songs, "Twist" had been played at a private party at Brad Sands' house a week earlier (6/6/97). Unlike many of these songs, "Twist" did not make the final cut for *Story of the Ghost*. Nevertheless the song was played pretty frequently throughout 1997. Of the 1997 performances the 8/3/97 Gorge version is a clear favorite. The first "Twist" of 1998 (4/2/98, Uniondale, NY) set a new standard for just how far out into space the song could go. Few versions since have approached the majesty of the trance inducing groove that first debuted on the "Island Tour." Those that come close twisted around the Lakewood Amphitheater on 7/3/99 and the Gorge on 9/10/99.

"Twist" was rearranged during the studio sessions for *Farmhouse* which followed the Fall tour, as evidenced by a performance in Rochester, NY (12/5/99) where the lyric "and substituting every sound" was eliminated. The studio track itself features a somewhat smug Trey intro and some stray Fishman (and friends) studio banter tacked on the end. A monstrous "Twist" played early the first morning of the year 2000, marked the return of millions of TV viewers to the sanctity of their living rooms from the hedonistic swamps of Big Cypress. If only they had been there more of the day.

TWO DOLLAR BILL (see: "MY LONG JOURNEY HOME")

2001 (see: "ALSO SPRACH ZARATHUSTRA")

Union Federal

AKA: The Oh Kee Pah Ceremony
Music: Phish
Album: *Junta*
Historian: Christian C. McKee/Mark Toscano

Many folks, upon purchasing their CD copies of *Junta*, were likely surprised to see a 25-minute, 31-second track listed on the back. This is a special track. For although a number of fans have been extremely vocal about their distaste for it, it represents some of the basic virtues, philosophies, and goals of Phish. This track, though endowed with the moinker "Union Federal," is actually part of the sacred Oh Kee Pah Ceremony. If you don't know what an Oh Kee Pah Ceremony is, then rent *A Man Called Horse* (1970, starring Richard Harris). If you think a Phish Oh Kee Pah Ceremony is a short instrumental written by Trey that appears on *Lawn Boy*...well, you're not quite right. True, that's "The Oh Kee Pah Ceremony," but we're talking about *the* Oh Kee Pah Ceremony.

Once upon a time, Phish was just four or five twenty-something guys that loved to play music together. Back in those days, they did the sorts of things that you might expect a crazy band to do. One of these was the Oh Kee Pa Ceremony. I repeat, this Oh Kee Pa Ceremony is *not* the one that you find on your copy of *Lawn Boy*. In fact, the two are basically antithetical.

On *Lawn Boy*, "The Oh Kee Pa Ceremony" is a short, tight, composed ditty. The Ceremonies that led to the birth of what we know as "Union Federal" were quite the opposite. These events involved the band members confining themselves in an enclosed space with their instruments (and a few other essential items) and playing for several hours straight.

Thankfully, Phish has continued to share this same kind of free form improvisation with their audiences. Over the years, "Tweezer" has occasionally spiraled out of control and onto completely new ground (see "Tweezer" history.) From time to time, "Runaway Jim" and "You Enjoy Myself" have done the same (see the "Jim" and "YEM" histories.) Perhaps the clearest example of this kind of playing in recent years came on 8/15/98, in the surprise fourth set at Lemonwheel. In that set, the music did not start with a song, but with the choice of a key, and the improvisation moved on from there.

The moral of the story? Don't go to a show, waiting to hear an enormous song called "Union Federal" featuring "Under Pressure" and "Dave's Energy Guide" teasing. "Union Federal" is little more than a label for what Phish does on a near nightly basis: improvise.

Uncle Pen

AKA: "Uncle Penn"
Music/Lyrics: Bill Monroe
Original Artist: Bill Monroe
Original Album: Decca single (December, 1950)
Vocals: Mike (lead), Page, Trey (backing)
Debut: 3/28/90
Historians: Mark Toscano and Jeremy Welsh

Phish first performed this popular bluegrass song on 3/28/90 at the Beta Intramural Hockey Party at Denison University in Granville, Ohio, debuted along with "Tweezer," "Runaway Jim," and "Cavern." "Uncle Pen" has been in regular rotation since, although it went on a 135-show hiatus from August '97 through October '99. Usually filling the "bluegrass" slot, "Uncle Pen" is always a fun tune to hear at a show, and is one of the few covers Phish has recorded in studio (along with "Caravan" and "'A'-Train" at Wendell Studios, on 6/17/90).

Interesting versions of "Uncle Pen" abound, although in its regular configuration, the song varies minimally. Check out 4/15/92 (dedi-

Tweezer

Compiled by Charlie Dirksen

Date	Timing	Notes
03/28/90	8:10	First version. Long drum intro.
12/28/90	11	Manteca.
04/27/91	10	Sweet Emotion jam.
07/26/91	10:30	The strongest of the versions with the Giant Country Horns.
04/21/92	13	Intensely melodic jam.
11/22/92	17:09	Very improvisational. Includes a Big Ball jam.
12/29/92	13:30	Quoting of Hendrix's "Who Knows."
05/03/93	17	"Earth Move" tease, and a Manteca jam.
05/06/93	20	Sweet Emotion and several other melodic jams.
08/12/93	13	Get Back signal. Features a bit of The Landlady.
08/15/93	19:35	Antelopian hose. Fiery and furious.
04/05/94	11	Excellent melodic jam.
05/07/94	69	"Tweezerfest." Traded heavily, and a fan favorite.
06/10/94	15	Rippin' jam.
07/06/94	19	Hold Your Head Up and 2001 jams.
11/02/94	31	A Live One ("ALO") version. The first experimental Tweezer.
11/23/94	20:16	Gorgeous jams and space. Remarkably beautiful.
11/28/94	45	Second experimental version. Monstrous. A snippet became "Montana" on ALO.
12/01/94	25+	Norwegian Wood, BBFCFM, NICU, Makisupa. Segue-fest.
12/09/94	25:29	A jam on Slave to the Traffic Light. Very spacey, jazzy version.
12/30/94	22	Ladies and Gentlemen, PAGE MCCONNELL.
06/14/95	51	Gypsy Queen-esque jam. The third exploratory, experimental version.
06/17/95	20:35	Heartbreaker tease; first Johnny B. Goode.
06/22/95	45	The "FLeezer" and the fourth experimental version.
06/28/95	30:30	The fifth experimental Tweezer. Dave's Energy Guide and Cannonball jams.
10/22/95	15:20	Funkasaurus.
11/19/95	21:32	Unusually improvisational. An exceptionally funky jam at one point.
11/30/95	19:23	Will hose you down in the final few minutes.

Date	Timing	Notes
12/02/95	15:10	Will hose you down from start to finish. Incredible version. Fan favorite.
12/08/95	26:18	Remarkably improvisation, and includes Kung.
12/14/95	24:20	This will rock you, as will Timber Ho!
12/17/95	22:46	Features a Page solo, and a Tweezer Reprise finish.
12/28/95	22:00	A divinely inspired jam (but a tepid ending).
08/06/96	16:55	Quoting of the Beatles' Norwegian Wood.
10/23/96	17:26	Additional drummer: Bob Gulotti.
11/03/96	16:49	Karl Perazzo from Santana on percussion!
11/27/96	16:30	DISEEEEZER. (a Down With Disease sandwich)
08/17/97	18:33	Space Funk.
11/22/97	11:31	Funky and very popular fan favorite.
11/26/97	17:29	Hear this, Holmes. Funkier even than 11/22/97.
12/06/97	22	Spectacular improvisation.
07/09/98	18:10	Boiling the phat.
07/15/98	15:56	California Love tease. Manteca-theme. Popular version.
08/01/98	18:34	Ambient, beautiful improvisation.
10/30/98	16:50	Psychotic, Frippian Trey madness.
11/14/98	16:30	Hypnotizing, kaleidoscopic, spacey-groove.
07/24/99	18	Includes an amusing Catapult. A notably sluggish, foggy jam.
08/01/99	13:08	Soulful and melodic. Segues well into Llama.
09/09/99	21:09	Remarkably improvisational with a twisted jam.
09/18/99	14:10	A very tight and kind version.
10/08/99	19:57	Unusually long, spacey jam.
12/16/99	21:52	Melodic "Slave-like" jam.
12/30/99	16:45	Enchanting, soulful, mellow and melodic. Channels ancient spirits.
06/09/00	31:01	Joe Walsh "Funk #49" tease in the lyrics. A complex, exploratory jam.
06/24/00	25:54	Hypnotic groove eventually explores intense, gripping territory.
06/30/00	12:16	Short, fierce version segues into an exciting Runaway Jim.
10/07/00	16:12	Listener discretion advised.

cated to Bill Monroe), 6/17/95 (segued out of "Fee"), 11/30/96 (with John McEuen on banjo), and 6/22/00 (with guests including Del Mc-Coury, Ricky Skaggs, Mike Budd, and Jason Center).

As the story goes, Bill Monroe wrote this tune as a tribute to his uncle, Pendleton Vandiver, a fiddler who, according to Monroe, "got some wonderful Scots-Irish sound out of" the fiddle. Though it (arguably) remains true in spirit, Phish's arrangement of the song is quite different from Monroe's original conception. To start with, Trey plays the song's main fiddle melody line on guitar, hyper-fast, Bruce Hampton-style. Also, many fans find the instrumental breakdown about two-thrids into the song a bit curious. Not part of the original composition, here Phish perform two bluegrass classics mentioned in "Uncle Pen's" lyrics: "Soldier's Joy" and "Boston Boy."

Uncloudy Day

Music/Lyrics: Reverend J.K. Alwood
Original Artist: The Staples Singers
Original Album: (1956)
Vocals: Phish, Neil Young, Willie Nelson, Paul Shaffer, Four Native American singers
Debut: 10/3/98
Historian: Ellis Godard

Roebuck "Pops" Staples was working in a meat-packing plant when he started singing in quartets during World War II. Soon after the war, he organized his children (Cleotha, Pervis, Yvonne, and Mavis) into their own quartet, the Staples Singers, which became quickly success-

ful on the Northern Illinois church circuit. Their ship came in under contract to Vee-Jay Records with their second release (though fourth recording), "Uncloudy Day." They later recorded other religious favorites, such as "Will the Circle Be Unbroken," but gradually moved from more traditional gospel to arrangements that incorporated blues, before losing gospel altogether and trying to forge their own blend.

Phish mimicked that history a bit with their sole performance of both of these songs, at Farm Aid. The event was organized by Willie Nelson, who also started singing during World War II, and who himself moved from traditional country to an Americana blend of hippie/redneck soul. Farm Aid (and Phish's set) culminated with two quartets (Phish and four Native American singers), plus Neil Young, Willie Nelson, and Paul Schaffer. And while donations apparently sagged during Phish's performance as eyes stayed tuned to a Country Music Television broadcast, the ship came in afterwards as donations surged a bit.

Undun

Original Artist: The Guess Who
Original Album: *Canned Wheat* **(1969)**
Vocals: Fish
Debit: 3/30/89
Historian: Erik Swain

Undun was one of the first Fishman routines. This flute-driven pop tune from the Canadian combo The Guess Who hit #22 on the Billboard charts in 1969. Its cheesy arrangement, bombastic vocals and oblique lyrics (it could be about suicide, mental illness or a bad LSD trip, but it appears not to matter to singer Burton Cummings) made it a perfect target for Fishman dementia.

The earliest documented performance by Phish occurred in the second set of a three-set show at the Front on 3/30/89. It appeared a handful of times throughout the year, the last known rendition closing the second set on 12/7/89 in Baltimore. It is that version that is most commonly circulated. Fishman apparently decided to play it on that night after a few vociferous fans called for him to sing Frank Sinatra. "Where'd you people come from, and how did you know we sing Frank Sinatra?" he deadpanned. "This is an old Frank Sinatra song covered by The Guess Who. If you listen to the words, it's obviously Frank." He then proceeded to sing the song in a Sinatra croon, or at least Joe Piscopo's idea of a Sinatra croon.

After it took a bow on 12/7/89, Phish came very close to breaking out the song three-and-a-half years later. On 5/2/93 in Upper Darby, PA, after Fishman came to the front of the stage for his "routine," he hemmed and hawed about what to play. If you listen very closely to the tape, you can hear Trey say, "how about 'She's Come Undone [sic],' Fish?"

"If only I could remember the words to that one!" Fishman blurted, before calling for "Cracklin' Rosie."

Us and Them

Original Artist: Pink Floyd
Original Album: *Dark Side of the Moon* **(1973)**
Vocals: Page (lead), Mike, Trey (backing)
Debut: 11/2/98
Historian: Mark Toscano

Dark Side of the Moon's most elegant and ethereal tune was possibly Phish's biggest challenge at the 11/2/98 E Centre show, even

more than the elusive structure of "On the Run" or the languid slither of "Breathe." The original track is alternately empassioned and lilting, and was a harsh test of Phish's ability to imbue their performance with the proper degree of earnest emotion.

Well, they played it fine, but it lacked a certain oomph. Also, their arrangement cut the song short by a few minutes by excising a full measure each verse and truncating the piano/sax solos found on the original, the longest track on *DSOTM*. Page's verse vocals were appropriately small, and they even cleverly mimicked the echo effect of each verse's first word by having Page, Mike, and Trey repeat the word a few times each in succession. Also, listen to Page's organ after "Great Gig"—apparently the Chairman of the Boards momentarily forgot that "Money" existed, for he was starting up "Us and Them's" intro a tad prematurely.

The Vibration of Life

Music: God
Album: (none)
Vocals: Phish
Debut: 11/23/92
Historian: Ellis Godard

Like "NO₂," "The Vibration of Life" is more a mix of dialogue and noise than a song. The core is Trey's guitar (and sometimes Mike's bass, too) fed through amps at seven beats per second. Trey usually introduces its arrival as something that will "energize you...for the rest of the evening" (2/20/93). He has said that "healers have been known to to get their hands to vibrate at seven beats per second" (11/17/94, where Forbin proceeds to "surf the 'VOL'" with the crowd). He also (11/19/96) called this rhythm the "theoretical universal glue" that will "tune you up with the energy of the universe and fill you with incredible energy. You're gonna feel it in your ass...." (See also 4/16/94 UMass and 11/3/94 UMass.)

The 2/20/93 version is also interesting for the confusion it created. While Trey interrupts the build to "Kung" with his signature "VOL" intro, Mike alternates with the lines "Your eyes may be feeling heavy...your nose light, your eyes heavy." But these are lyrics from "NO₂," not "VOL": They had not appeared prior to this show, in "NO₂" or "VOL," and are repeated in later versions of "NO₂ but not in any other version of "VOL." Moreover, they seem more befitting "NO₂" (which is all about relaxing) rather than "VOL" (which is all about energy). "The Vibration of Life" is nonetheless usually understood to be these lines repeated over Trey's guitar loop.

"VOL" has been performed less than two dozen times, and in rather curious spurts: four within eleven days in Fall 1992, three on the Spring 1993 tour, eight throughout the Fall 1994 tour, and then two singular reappearances in 1996 (11/16/96, 11/19/96).

Viola Lee Blues

Music/Lyrics: Noah Lewis
Original Artist: Gus Cannon
Original Album: Victor 38523 (Cannon) (1928),
   Grateful Dead **(1967) (Grateful Dead)**
Vocals: Phil Lesh, Phish
Debut: 9/17/99
Historian: Phil Nazzaro

It's a testament to the Grateful Dead that the first song they consistantly took to the level we would consider type-II jamming began as a stark, bare bones, blues tune. "Viola Lee Blues" was written by Noah Lewis (who also wrote the GD standards "Big Railroad Blues" and "Minglewood Blues") and originally released by Gus Cannon (with Lewis on harmonica) way back on September 20, 1928. Little did they know that in less than forty years, their country-blues song would be performed as a powerhouse psychedelic trip into another world.

Nor could they have known that on 9/17/99 Phil Lesh would join Phish for their encore at Shoreline Ampitheater. It was then that Phil, Page and Trey would relive the thrilling opening number from their three-night stand as Phil & Friends back in April of that year. While the version from Shoreline doesn't quite stack up against the pure excitement generated at the Warfield Theater show, it is still an energetic and more than worthwhile performance. It becomes a pulsating force driven by the dual basses of Mike Gordon and Phil Lesh.

Vultures

Music: Trey Anastasio
Lyrics: Tom Marshall, Scott Herman
Album: (none)
Vocals: Trey, Page (lead), Fish, Mike (backing)
Debut: 6/6/97 (private show), 6/13/97 (public show)
Historian: Martin Acaster

Whether a circling vulture is a good sign or a bad sign depends entirely on the philosophical frame of reference of the observer. To a wayward hiker overcome by the midsummer sun of the southeast Oregon desert, seeing the vultures moving in could be a bad omen indeed. To the Tibetan villager relinquishing the useless corpse of a loved one to the macabre ritual of sky burial, the vulture instead symbolizes something good. To Tibetans, the vultures that feast on the discarded remains of a now useless body, are the Dakini. The Dakini, or Sky Dancers, are the supreme embodiment of highest wisdom and feminine divinity to Tibetan Buddhists. The role of the Dakini in the sky burial is to transmute suffering by removing anger, greed, and delusion from the scene. The role of the Sky Dancers at a Phish show should without question be the same. Too often this is not the case.

With their clear reference to timing, expectations, and those expectations not being met, the lyrics of "Vultures" appear to be an indictment of the dissatisfied Phish fan. Too often the anger, greed, and delusion of the fan unhappy with the length of a given song, setlist, or show is manifested in an irrational feeling of being somehow cheated by the band. This ungratefulness must wear thin at times. In a broader sense "Vultures" reflects the impending death of anything. Whether it be a job, a relationship, a way of life, or a really good show, when the end is near the signal is clear. At times we can all see the vultures moving in. Clearly, based on one's perspective, this can be a good thing or a bad thing.

"Vultures" was one of several songs (which included "Ghost," "Dirt," and "Limb By Limb") which were first played 6/6/97 at a pre-tour party at Brad Sands house. Unlike many of the songs first played at Bradstock, Vultures has yet to find its way onto a Phish album. It debuted before a paying audience a week later (6/13/97) at the tour opener in Dublin, Ireland. "Vultures" was in fairly regular rotation throughout both the European and US legs of the 1997 summer tour

and had a curious association with "Dogs Stole Things" in setlists. "Vultures" was reworked duirng studio sessions for *Story of the Ghost*. A studio out-take version of the song includes an additional verse where the razor to the throat is replaced with a potato, a line which Trey sang in one (11/27/98 Worcester, MA) of only three versions played in 1998, all of which were the new reworked version. "Vultures" came circling more often during Summer and Fall 1999 with repeat performances in some venues suggesting preferred roosts (Shoreline Amphitheatre 7/31/97 and 9/16/99; Deer Creek 8/11/97 and 7/26/99; Lakewood Amphitheater 8/6/98 and 7/4/99; and TAFKAK 12/13/97 and 10/10/99). This propensity for favored feeding grounds did not continue with the 2000 tours at all, as the Vultures chose instead to make their return (7/1/00) from their winter migration at the Meadows in Hartford rather than Lakewood Amphitheater or PNC Arts Center in Holmdel, NJ.

Wading in the Velvet Sea

AKA: "Wading," "Velvet Sea," "Wading in Velveeta Cheese"
Music/Lyrics: Trey Anastasio, Tom Marshall
Album: *Story of the Ghost; Hampton Comes Alive* (11/21/98)
Vocals: Page (lead), Trey, Mike (backing)
Debut: 6/6/97 (private show), 6/13/97 (public show)
Historian: Martin Acaster

Wading In the Velvet Sea was among the first of the songs subsequently released on *Story of the Ghost* to surface during the summer of 1997. In stark contrast to the "funk" sound which proliferated during the summer and fall tours of 1997, "Wading In The Velvet Sea" is an introspective anthemic tearjerker in the style of "Slave To The Traffic Light." The song swirls out of a half-speed "Nitrous Oxide" siren into a delicate piano melody which gradually swells to an oceanic crescendo of soulful guitar licks.

Lyrically the song carries the tone of a letter to a lost love, a message of hope for a brighter future. An account of a moment shared during a solitary trip to the coast. A moment which simultaneously captured the joy and sorrow of the past forgotten and the future lost. The title phrase, repeated incessantly throughout the soaring elegy to enduring emotion, captures the spirit of the waves. Cascading over and over against the edge of the earth. Time leaks out, life leaks in, the moment ends.

The song was debuted in Dublin on 6/13/97 and was in fairly regular rotation for the rest of the summer tour. Entirely absent from the fall 1997 tour "Wading In The Velvet Sea" resurfaced late in the Summer '98 tour and has been often played since then. Particularily inspired versions of "Wading In The Velvet Sea" include 8/2/97 at the Gorge Amphitheater, 8/16/98 at the Lemonwheel, and a sublime performance at the 12/31/98 year end Madison Square Garden extravaganza. Clearly the best (read: most tear-jerkingly beautiful) version to date preceded the SHOW closing "Meatstick" as the first sun of 2000 peeked through the velvety clouds swirling over the swamps of Big Cypress. If you didn't get all choked up by that one you were either unconscious or somewhere else.

Waking Up

AKA: "Fooled by Images"
Music/Lyrics: Trey Anastasio, Tom Marshall
Album: (none)
Vocals: Trey, Page

Debut: 6/6/97 (private show), 6/14/97(public show)
Historian: Craig DeLucia

Waking Up is a short, bitter song of betrayal, played primarily by Page on piano and sung in tight harmony by Trey and Page. Emotionally, it may rank as the most somber and ominous song that Phish has ever brought to the stage. Witness the final lyric, where the narrator wonders why, of all his dreams, only "this" one came true. That may be why you can stick this in the relatively empty bag of Phish compositions that have only been played once. Unless you count the "Bradstock" private party on 6/6/97, the 6/14/97 Dublin show marks the only time that "Waking Up" has been performed to date.

Walfredo

Music/Lyrics: Phish
Album: (none)
Vocals: Phish
Debut: 2/13/97
Historians: Phillip Zerbo and Mark Toscano

First played on 2/13/97, at the Shepard's Bush Empire in London, it made all of four appearances before being shelved for three and a half years. In his casino wanderings before the 9/30/00 Vegas show, Trey apparently asked a random fan which song she wanted to hear, and her enthusiastic response led to the breakout of this tune later that night.

While certain Phish lyrics often take on special meanings to fans, "Walfredo's" lyrics are unique in that they almost completely describe autobiographical band experiences, making the song one big in-story that only folks in the band's inner circle are likely to truly appreciate. Still, one can't help but feel a chill of nostalgia hearing those words, even if one is just a casual fan.

While generally held in low regard by jam-seeking fans, "Walfredo" does have a rather unique history in that it is one of only a few songs written collaboratively by all members of Phish. As Trey related in *The Phish Book*: "It's a struggle for Phish to write songs together. Before leaving Europe, though, we said, 'Damn it, we're going to write together no matter how it comes out.' So we wrote 'Walfredo,' 'Rock-a-William,' and 'Carini had a Lumpy Head,' which were okay."

Another unique aspect of "Walfredo" (along with "Rock-a-William") is that the song was written with the intent of having the band members play instruments other than their own. For both of these tunes, Fishman played bass, Mike played guitar, Trey assumed the keyboards, while Page took Fishman's seat behind the drums.

Walk Away

Original Artist: The James Gang
Original Album: *Thirds* (1970)
Vocals: Page (lead), Mike, Trey (backing)
Debut: 7/23/88
Historian: Ellis Godard

Seems to me, Phish, you ought to play this tune more often. Yeah, I know—it's a silly tune, so I don't s'pose I can blame ya for not playing it more (mostly 1988-1990). But meet with me halfway: the emergence during the 8/14/93 "Antelope" was brilliant. And you've played it in "Tweezer" often enough (including 2/20/93, 4/30/93, 7/22/93, and 5/7/94) that, for awhile, it was practically part of the song.

And then, boom, you drop it for 366 shows (from 5/7/94 to 10/29/98), dammit!

Okay, maybe I should cool myself down. Frankly, Page's voice doesn't have the Walsh-like looseness that it used to (e.g. 7/23/88 or 11/3/88). And covers of masturbatory '70s rock are sort of passe. Guess I'll just turn my pretty head and...well, you know.

Walk This Way

Music/Lyrics: Joe Perry, Steven Tyler
Original Artist: Aerosmith
Original Album: *Toys in the Attic* (1975)
Vocals: Kid Rock
Debut: 9/29/00
Historian: Mark Toscano

Hailing from the same classic cockrock album as "Sweet Emotion," "Walk This Way" is about as anthemic as it gets. Kid Rock joined Phish onstage at the Thomas & Mack in Vegas for this one on 9/29/00.

Though plenty of fans questioned the band's (Trey's?) decision to so prominently feature the notoriously abrasive and misogynist rapper in their show, "Walk This Way" was still good for plenty of laughs, and was played reasonably well to boot.

Waste

Music: Trey Anastasio
Lyrics: Tom Marshall
Album: *Billy Breathes*
Vocals: Trey (lead), Page(backing)
Debut: 6/6/96
Historian: Bradley Lonard

A soft-rock ballad with lyrics that wouldn't seem out of place on an early Elton John album, "Waste" is one of those rare Phish songs which is an obvious studio creation. Indeed, the version included on *Billy Breathes* is pretty much definitive. In performance the song hasn't grown much, although the outro guitar solo does provide an opportunity for Trey to trill away quite attractively (hear 7/26/97 Austin, for example, for an excellent live "Waste"; also 11/2/96 West Palm Beach). Still, Phish has remained rather fond of "Waste" and kept it in fairly high rotation since its debut on 6/6/96 at the Third Ball in Woodstock, even breaking it out as an occasional encore.

Water in the Sky

Music/Lyrics: Trey Anastasio, Tom Marshall
Album: *Story of the Ghost*
Vocals: Trey, Mike, Page
Debut: 6/13/97
Historian: Phillip Zerbo

Water in the Sky contains several common Phish themes: a reworking of the musical structure long after its debut, nautical imagery, and lyrics open to multiple interpretation. "Water in the Sky" is among the many songs that were debuted in 1997 and then went on to form the basis of *SOTG*. It was debuted on 6/13/97 at the SFX Centre in Dublin, Ireland. "Water in the Sky" lived for a little over a year as a traditional American country tune; the kind of tune played in establishments perhaps such as the one in which the Blues Brothers found

themselves encased by chicken wire. The twangy guitar and romantic prelude of "close the shutters, draw the shades" is about as down-home as a bunch of middle-class, suburban, northeast kids can pull off with a straight face. Tough to pull off with a straight face, especially if the gist of the song seems to be the quite traditionally un-romantic notion of "tuning somebody out." Those voices may indeed flutter through, but they find many filters—metaphorical walls. In the end, those voices find deaf ears ("watch them fall, and let them lie"). On the other hand, the song can be viewed simply as a beautiful tune about water and waves and sky and sea.

Then a funny thing happened to this tune destined to be a country hit: the tempo got cranked up a few notches. Taking its new form live 6/30/98 at The Grey Hall in Freetown Christiana, Copenhagen, Denmark, this more up-tempo, polished version is the one that appears on *Story of the Ghost* and in all subsequent Phish performances. However, Tom Marshall's Amfibian continues to perform the tune in its "original" country style. The reworked version of "Water in the Sky" is one of several Phish tunes (including "Mockingbird," "Split Open and Melt," and "Billy Breathes") in which the central lyrical and musical themes—water, in this case—are cleverly intertwined. Page's piano swirls evoke images of sheeting rain tumbling from the sky into a swollen river, lit occasionally by an organ-spire sunbeam. The lyrics, such as "thunder calls through waterfalls," focus on the forging of sound with water. "Water" is as brief as it is clever—the song is a musical cloudburst. More than one observer has characterized this reworked version as "the trippy version."

The Wedge

Music: Trey Anastasio
Lyrics: Tom Marshall
Album: *Rift; Hampton Comes Alive* (11/21/98)
Vocals: Mike, Page, Trey
Debut: 2/3/93
Historian: Craig DeLucia

With a catchy sing-along chorus (which, in *The Phish Book*, Tom Marshall noted was inspired by Neil Young's "Thrasher") punctuated by an infectious beat and featuring some wonderful bass bombs, "The Wedge" was a longtime resident in a select group of songs: always requested, never played, and no fan could understand why. Before coming back to rotation in 1998, "Wedge" was only played once in 1996 and twice in 1997 following its breakout in the summer of 1995. And this all came following its 1993 debut, where it roared out of the gates but was on the shelf by summer.

The band had, until 1998, continuously made minor modifications to "The Wedge." They have experimented with a drum intro and a piano intro, with numerous 1993 soundchecks circulating as testament to the ongoing experiment. A representative version on *Hampton Comes Alive* (from 11/21/98) seems to show the complete evolution of the song. Versions do not change much from show to show, but grab yourself a representative sampling from various eras to hear the band play with the song. Also, find the 8/24/93 soundcheck for Trey's comments on the band's tinkering.

Weekapaug Groove
AKA: "Weekapaug," "Week"

Music/Lyrics: Phish
Album: *Slip Stitch and Pass* (3/1/97);
   Hampton Comes Alive (11/21/98)
Vocals: Mike, Page, Trey
Debut: 7/23/88
Historian: Charlie Dirksen

Weekapaug Groove takes its name from the town of Weekapaug, located on the shores of the Atlantic ocean in southwestern Rhode Island. According to Mike, the song's lyrics ("Trying to make a woman that you move, sharing in a Weekapaug Groove") are meaningless. As Mike said in a 9/9/97 interview with Parke Puterbaugh: "So we came back to Boston [from Weekapaug, after playing a gig there at a yacht club], and I guess we were in the van or the Voyager we used to drive in, and that song "Oh What a Night" came on the radio. You know that one? That awful Four Seasons song? Is that what it is? Yeah. We just constantly listened to songs and changed around the words as to what they might sound like. I always had a particularly hard time hearing lyrics anyway, so I always would sing a song on the radio, sing along with the wrong words. So the bridge of that song goes, "Oh I-I-I trying to something," but I was singing it, "Oh I-I-I trying to make a woman that you move," which means nothing, "sharing in a Weekapaug groove." So we all just started singing that as complete nonsense: "trying to make a woman that you move." It never occurred to any of us that it had any meaning, ever. There was a period of time that we were singing it, and I used to just yell out the lyrics, between singing them I would just yell them out as if I was preaching them, just to sort of make it more ironic that they have no meaning." Many fans have heard "Trying to make a woman match your moves" in this song, perhaps in a (futile) effort to glean meaning from the song's meaningless lyrics.

"Weekapaug Groove," akin to other remarkably improvisational Phish songs, has sandwiched or teased other songs on numerous occasions, or has otherwise deviated from the norm. For example, check out these versions: 11/16/90 Providence (Andy Griffith theme); 7/23/91 Bayou (with the Giant Country Horns); 11/8/91 Tuscaloosa (Slice of Pizza and a Bucket of Lard); 12/31/91 Worcester ("Lion Sleeps Tonight"); 4/21/92 Eureka ("Happy Birthday"); 11/23/92 Binghamton (reggae and "Big Ball" jams); 2/20/93 Atlanta ("Have Mercy" and Kiss' "Rock N Roll All Nite"); 3/19/93 Redlands (vocal jam ending); 3/25/93 Santa Cruz (Beatles' "Ob La Di, Ob La Da" and Anastasio/Popper's "Don't Get Me Wrong"); 3/30/93 Eugene (Taking Heads' "Psycho Killer"); 4/29/93 Montreal ("Bonanza"); 5/8/93 Durham ("Amazing Grace" jam); 8/16/93 St. Louis (Santana's "Gypsy Queen," Pink Floyd's "Another Brick in the Wall," Steve Wonder's "I Wish," and "Possum"); 7/2/94 Holmdel ("Antelope" and "2001"); 10/21/94 Plantation, 11/4/94 Syracuse, 12/31/94 Boston, 3/1/97 Hamburg, 8/9/97 East Troy (Rolling Stones "Can't You Hear Me Knockin'"); 12/28/94 Philadelphia ("Little Drummer Boy" jam); 10/29/96 Talahasse (Karl Perazzo of Santana on percussion); 11/15/96 St. Louis (John Popper on harp); 12/13/97 Albany ("Catapult"); 7/10/98 Barcelona ("On Broadway"); 11/27/98 Worcester ("Wipe Out"); 12/31/98 New York City (Prince's "1999"); 7/9/99 Columbia ("Macarena"); 9/22/99 Las Cruces ("2001"); 12/18/99 Hampton ("Buffalo Bill").

It is also a tune in which individual band members' performances have brilliantly shined. For example: 3/1/90 New Haven (Trey); 8/17/92 San Juan Capistrano (Mike); 12/29/92 New Haven (Trey); 7/24/93 Mans-

field (Trey); 4/29/94 Clearwater (Mike, Trey); 7/10/94 Saratoga (Mike); 10/25/94 Atlanta (Fish); 6/20/95 Cuyahoga Falls (Fish); 10/25/95 St. Paul (Page); 11/25/95 Hampton (Page); 11/6/96 Knoxville (Trey); 12/28/96 Philadelphia (Page); 8/7/98 Raleigh (Page); 8/12/98 Vernon Downs (Page); 7/21/99 Burgettstown (Mike); 12/30/99 Big Cypress (Fish).

Although collective, transcendent improvisation is common in "Weekapaug Groove," these are versions that will likely thrill you: 11/2/90 Boulder; 11/21/91 Somerville; 3/20/92 Binghamton; 4/19/92 Santa Cruz; 11/28/92 Port Chester; 12/31/92 Boston; 2/4/93 Providence; 3/27/93 San Francisco; 12/30/93 Portland; 6/17/94 Milwaukee; 10/21/94 Plantation; 6/25/95 Philadelphia; 6/30/95 Mansfield; 11/11/95 Atlanta; 12/1/95 Hershey; 12/7/95 Niagara Falls; 12/16/95 Lake Placid; 12/31/95 New York City; 8/13/96 Noblesville; 8/16/96 Plattsburgh; 10/22/96 New York City; 12/6/96 Las Vegas; 8/9/97 East Troy; 11/13/97 Vegas; 11/22/97 Hampton; 12/2/97 Philadelphia; 12/31/97 New York City; 4/3/98 Uniondale; 7/17/98 George; 10/31/98 Vegas; 11/27/98 Worcester.

See Also: "Mike's Song"

Weekly Time

Music/Lyrics: Mike Gordon
Album: (none)
Vocals: Mike
Debut: (never performed live)
Historian: Julia Mordaunt

And so it emerges from the Blob. There is a single negative aspect of this Cactus original, and that is the fact that very few people have had the opportunity to hear it. The song was recorded in 1996 at Bearsville Studios during the *Billy Breathes* recording sessions, but along with other fitting tunes (see "Glide II") it was left on the cutting room floor. Mike confided to *The Phish Book* that he was bummed that it didn't make the cut, citing "it failed when I sang it."

The version that appears on the *Billy Breathes* Outtakes is a totally slow-funk driven tune, with heavy wah-wah grinding by both Trey and Page throughout the song. But, I must disagree with Mike about the vocal issue. "Weekly Time" is definitely a shadowy, heavy-hearted song, and seemingly the only one in the band who could pull it off without losing that quality is Mike. You get a feeling similar to the one that enters your body when "Catapult" is recited over a dark, brooding, mystical jam. Although the funk is deep, it definitely has a gloomy, sedated overcast to it. The lyrics that weave their way through the tune amplifies that.

Mike also wrote this song as a bluegrass standard, which he performed along side Gordon Stone and Doug Perkins on 10/1/96 at Slade Hall (University of Vermont) in Burlington. This version was faster and more upbeat, and had the inclusion of banjo and acoustic guitar but, it did not lessen the morose quality of the tune in the least. Both the funk and bluegrass versions are relatively upbeat but, the lyrics in addition to Mike's 'wale of woe' hit the soul.

It's never made its way to the stage with Phish, but it's definitely got the qualities to jump into rotation in the future. Forget "Destiny Unbound"—we want "Weekly Time"!

Weigh

Music/Lyrics: Mike Gordon
Album: *Rift; Slip Stitch and Pass* (3/1/97)

Debut: 3/7/92
Historian: Martin Acaster

At first listen, "Weigh" is a disturbing look inside the brain of an obsessive compulsive stalker. An individual somewhat more twisted than the character portrayed in the Police classic "Every Breath You Take." Rather than simply following, watching, pining for his beloved, the psycho in "Weigh" is having thoughts of removing vital body parts to weigh them, and sneaking into the object of his desire's home and collecting razor stubble, just to "Weigh" it. Pure madness. The bouyant funk groove underlying the unsettling lyrical content is not entirely balanced in its own right. Full of sudden time changes, quirky fills, and stray meandering notions, the tune is as schizophrenic as he who is weighing his options. This being said, the live version of "Weigh" rarely departs from the studio version of the song first released in 1993 on the "concept" album *Rift*. As evidence, the reader is directed to the live release of the song on the 1997 release *Slip, Stitch and Pass*. A little funkier perhaps, but what song in 1997 wasn't?

"Weigh" is a relative rarity live having been played only on a few dozen occasions since 1992, with over half of those performances appearing in 1992 and 1993 setlists. During 1992 it was usually a mid-second set "breather." Since that time it has appeared predominantly in a similar second set spot. Live versions of "Weigh" which require listening are those which were played in "must hear" shows such as 4/21/92 Eureka, CA; 12/30/93 Portland ME, 11/7/97 Lexington, KY; 3/1/97 Hamburg, Germany. A recent Weigh (8/2/98 Deer Creek, IN) approached improvisational experimentation in a funky tonk break-down style of mini-jam.

We're An American Band

AKA: "American Band"
Original Artist: Grand Funk Railroad
Original Album: *We're An American Band* (1973)
Vocals: Phish (11/16/96), Kid Rock (9/29/00)
Debut: 11/16/96
Historians: Tim Wade and Mark Toscano

Although many fans were confused by the encore on 11/16/96, most of the hometown crowd recognized "American Band" from the moment Fishman started in on the cow bell. Although Phish had never covered this song before, it was a nice tip-of-the-cap to the evening's host city; perhaps it was played for "all them chiquitas in Omaha." Other sources suggest that it was performed in honor of Homer Simpson, who has been known to claim the Grand Funk tune as his favorite song.

A reappearance four years later on 9/29/00 proved that the song was not limited by geography. For that rendition, Vegas was the place, and the song's lyrics were modified to the fit the occasion. Appearing again this time as an encore, the tune was sung by Kid Rock, first runner-up of the "Least Likely Guest at a Phish Show" award (ironically beaten only by Gloria Steinem).

For what it's worth, many folks also have noted that the refrain of this Grand Funk tune influenced a line from "Harpua": "We're comin' to your town, we'll help ya party down."

We're Not Gonna Take It

Original Artist: The Who
Original Album: *Tommy* (1968)

Vocals: Tom(my) Marshall (lead), Page, Trey (backing)
Debut: 10/8/99
Historian: Craig DeLucia

The Who's classic rock opera *Tommy* details the life of a child pinball prodigy who, upon breaking free from his deaf, dumb, and blind affliction, opens up a camp to instruct his followers. "We're Not Gonna Take It" is from the end of the epic and is a song of revolt that occurs when his followers can't handle the truths they thought they sought. Therefore, some consider it ironic that Phish performed this number for the first and only time while Internet fans were actively bashing the band for choosing to release the 1998 Hampton shows, which were considered by many to be inferior compared to other shows from that tour or to Hampton '97, as a live album.

In his lone Fall 1999 appearance, Tom Marshall sang guest vocals on "We're Not Gonna Take It." Unfortunately, fans were deprived of seeing Tom in full Tommy regalia; he had been told the song would be played during the encore and was in the middle of practicing, sans costume, when he was called upon to sing before the second set had ended!

West L.A. Fade Away
Music/Lyrics: Jerry Garcia, Robert Hunter
Original Artist: Grateful Dead
Original Album: *In the Dark* (1987)
Vocals: Bob Weir
Debut: 10/06/00
Historian: Charlie Dirksen

A regular in The Grateful Dead's amazing arsenal of songs since 1982, "West L.A. Fadeaway" was covered by Phish with Bob Weir—rhythm guitarist, songwriter and vocalist for The Grateful Dead—at Shoreline on 10/06/00. A highly valued "Jerry tune" (Jerry, and not Bobby, sang this song's lyrics at Dead shows among Deadheads, Dead versions often featured spectacularly moving, inspired playing by Garcia, particularly at Dead shows in the 1980s. The reference in the song to a "chateau," at which the song's protagnist wants to rent a room for an hour or two, is the Chateau Marmont, a hotel on Sunset Strip in Los Angeles where John Belushi died on March 5, 1982. Phish's cover of it at Shoreline featured beautiful singing from Bob Weir, who also accompanied on rhythm guitar.

What's The Use?
Music: Phish
Album: *The Siket Disc*
Vocals: (instrumental)
Debut: 7/4/99
Historian: Martin Acaster

What's The Use?, the majestic gravitational centerpiece of *The Siket Disc*, is a lush soaring spacescape of digital effects and electronic loops set to an ominously dark and ponderous bass line. It echoes the crush of the singularity of matter and energy at the core of a gently spiraling galaxy of reason as viewed by a hesitant psychonaut during those first hesitant steps across the icy surface of Jupiter's moon Europa. With the sound of orbiting gravity drive craft whirring overhead the psychonaut chips through the thick layer of ice revealing an ocean of liquid oxygen beneath the surface. The sight of the fluo-

rescent glowphish hurtling through the roiling mass of thick air beneath the icy crust inspires pure joy and longing in the heart of all who see them. After taking one last look at the galaxy of reason spiraling overhead the psychonaut leaps once more into the icy abyss of infinite love and greets the inherent death of self with a smile.

"What's the use in going fast if you're not in a race?" is the lyrical question that goes unasked on *The Siket Disc* release of "What's The Use?" However, an abbreviated version which circulates on unauthorized Bearsville Studio outtakes tapes contains these (and other) lyrics from which the song's title is derived. "What's The Use?" debuted on July 4th at Lakewood Amphitheater (after being teased earlier in the set during "Slave") and was played sporadically during the rest of the east coast leg of the summer '99 tour. Following two performances (9/10/99 George, WA and 9/14/99 Boise, ID) on the west coast leg of the tour "What's The Use?" remained frozen in the icy depths with the Glowphish. With the thaw brought on by the radiation of the sun that was Summer Tour 2000 the frosty instrumental flowed in rivulets from the stages of the Creeks (6/25/00 Walnut Creek, NC and 7/10/00 Deer Creek, IN).

When Something is Wrong With My Baby
Music/Lyrics: Isaac Hayes, David Porter
Original Artist: Sam and Dave
Original Album: *Double Dynamite* (1967)
Debut: 4/24/93
Historian: Mark Toscano

Yes, this song was co-written by Isaac Hayes, who, along with David Porter, wrote much of Sam and Dave's (Prater, not Porter) material while the two singers were under contract at Atlantic. Atlantic had their sister company Stax bring on Hayes and Porter to produce and write for the singing (but not very songwriting) duo, but when the Stax relationship ended, so did Sam and Dave's career. Their material suffered without Hayes and Porter and their high profile backing band (Booker T. & the MGs!), and the two began fighting as well. Following their breakup, Dan Aykroyd and John Belushi's Blues Brothers success—some of it owed to Sam and Dave, who had made "Soul Man" a hit—brought the original duo back into the spotlight and they toured briefly in 1980.

Also covered by B.B. King, King Curtis, Joe Cocker, and others, Phish performed this unlikely song three times, all done within the space of a week. The debut on 4/24/93 came after a standard "Caravan" in the first set, whereas the other two—4/25/93 and 4/30/93—appeared as encores, both times preceding an a capella tune. Though Trey soloes soulfully in these covers, the band just wasn't quite suited for the "soul vocalist" genre at the time, and the tune was dropped from rotation.

When the Circus Comes
AKA: "Circus"
Original Artist: Los Lobos
Original Album: *Kiko* (1992)
Vocals: Trey
Debut: 2/13/97
Historian: Ellis Godard

Like Phish, Los Lobos is a great band sometimes disserviced by comparisons to the Grateful Dead. Trey's reported fondness for their "Circus" led to rumors that it would be included on the studio release

Story of a Ghost. And that might have been appropriate, given the song's history on Phish's stage.

Although the original is gorgeous, in lyric and chord, the 2/13/97 debut is as forgettable as the other four debuts from that show. Delivery was not much stronger its next three appearances. But warmth entered the song's history on 6/14/97, opening the encore for an underrated show which included jamming even in "Waste" and "Cavern." Of its next ten appearances, six were encore openers, including 6/20/97 (with an unusually strong first set), 7/1/97 (which birthed Wormtown), and 7/22/97 (the fabulous lightning show). It was in a second set at Shoreline 7/31/97, as one of several nods to Jerry Garcia, but again in the encores after the strong set of 8/9/97 and just prior to the Great Went art bonfire 8/17/97. Even outside of encores, it marked success, appearing in strong second sets that featured extended exploratory jams on 11/17/97, 11/30/97, 12/13/97, 12/31/97, and 7/9/98. Then the circus left—as, some would argue, jamming had.

The next appearance (7/16/98) surprised the audience a bit. Following "Fast Enough For You" (which wasn't) in the first set of a two-night run that opened with "Squirming Coil" (and still hadn't quite gone anywhere, much less squirmed high enough to melt wax), this metropolitan capstone to memorable shows worldwide (something akin to early East Coast "Sleeping Monkeys") had lost its meaning to the view of a northwest ditch. The song seemed in better placement 7/25/98, and the appearance in the 8/3/98 encore was reminiscent of what the song had previously been. But 8/16/98 and 12/30/99 were calmly gratuitous given the circus aire, and the remaining thirteen appearances through the end of 1999 were in arguably weak shows and often in the first set. The song has become a ghost of what it once was.

While My Guitar Gently Weeps

Original Artist: The Beatles
Original Album: *The Beatles* (aka "The White Album") (1968)
Vocals: Trey (lead), Page (backing)
Debut: 10/31/94
Historian: Mark Toscano

This anthemic George Harrison track is Phish's most-covered "White Album" tune, having been played several times after the 10/31/94 debut. Some sloppy, some sublime, these performances include 12/8/94, 7/2/95, 10/20/95, 12/4/95, 2/26/97, 8/16/98 and 9/20/00. It is most frequently found as an encore, as with 6/22/95, 10/5/95, 12/11/95, 11/7/98, 12/31/98, 7/10/99 (slightly messy), 10/2/99 (the best version in years), and 10/5/00.

Perhaps most interesting is that this song has appeared with four of the most monstrously huge and legendary versions of "Tweezer" the band has ever performed. 11/2/94 (the *A Live One* version), 6/14/95 (Mud Island), 6/22/95 (the FLeezer), and 6/28/95 (Jones Beach) were either preceded or followed by a rendition of "WMGGW," leading fans to merely scratch their heads, boggled at the potential connections.

Whipping Post

Music/Lyrics: Gregg Allman
Original Artist: The Allman Brothers Band
Original Album: *The Allman Brothers Band* (1969)
Vocals: Jeff (1984-1985); Trey (1985-1989, 1999-);
Fish (1990-1996)

Debut: 11/3/84
Historian: Ellis Godard

The Allman Brothers Band emerged in 1969 and, like several Bay Area bands, blended blues roughness and jazz looseness back into rock, which elsewhere was diverging into showmanship and away from the music itself. (Even the Bay Area scene had been then become watered-down, with psuedo-psychedelic tailcoat riders but the Allmans, from the Appalachian foothills of central Georgia, came with a harder edge that suggested less lysergic acid and more Jim Beam. No surprise, then, that writer Gregg Allman had to work to convince the rest of the band to take up "Whipping Post." The song is full of raging riffs and historic bridges, but the lyrics go deeper and dark: Inspired by Gregg's romantic and contractual difficulties at the time, they speak of being a run-down, lied-to, cheated-on fool stuck in bad times and drowning in sorrow. But the band succumbed, and the song has become a signature of the Allmans. It has since been covered by scores of artists from Los Lobos to Frank Zappa, and released by perhaps a dozen more. Gregg released an acoustic version in 1997, and the Allmans have released a number of versions, several of them live.

Long a favorite among Phish fans but never frequent in setlists, "Whipping Post" was played roughly every fourth show or so through 1988, and then declined both in raw frequency and in fraction of shows. (A third of its appearances were during 1988, not counting many teases, such as in "David Bowie" 3/11/88 or in "Anarchy" 6/30/88.) Its first two appearances (11/3/84, into a nice drums jam, and 5/3/85, segueing nicely into "McGrupp," both following "Eyes of the World") featured two guitars (plus Jeff Holdsworth on lead vocals) and so the band was able to faithfully mimic the Allmans' co-wailing axes. Its next appearance (without Jeff) was as the vehicle for Mike's religious epiphany, an extended jam (11/23/85) that included parts of both "Norwegian Wood" and "Harry Hood." Beyond that, Trey took over vocals (starting 8/10/87), and the cover remained somewhat faithful (esp. 5/15/88, 9/24/88, and 11/3/88, with "Dave's Energy Guide" teases). It was a straight cover, ripped from the golden days of rock and used by a bar band to communicate earnestness, with powerful placement (out of "Little Drummer Boy" 12/6/86, and out of a show-opening "Low Rider" jam 10/31/87) and strong jamming (as on 5/25/88, 4/27/89, 5/9/89, and 5/13/89, possibly one of the most improvisational versions Phish has performed.)

But then Phish got bigger, and sillier, and performances of the song became something of a joke. It was first revised as a Fishman romp, through his lead vocals (e.g. 3/9/90), lead on fretless guitar (10/28/91 and 12/6/91), and, of course, vacuum solo (12/5/92 and 8/10/96). (Also note the "What I Am" tease during the 6/5/90 version.) But the song was too strong for the joke to last and, as Mike noted in one interview, Phish was playing venues that the Allmans were playing, "so it wasn't so much of a joke anymore." They tried to pull it off 8/10/96, after a three-year absense, but the next day felt guilty for that version's weakness. So when it reurned 7/25/99, in one of the best first sets of that tour, Trey was on vocals and (for the first time since the 1980s) the performance was hardcore, true to the song's beginning.

"THE WHITE ALBUM" (see: *THE BEATLES*)

White Rabbit

Original Artist: Jefferson Airplane

Original Album: *Surrealistic Pillow* (1967)
Vocals: (performed instrumental)
Debut: 9/30/95
Historian: Mark Toscano

Toward the beginning of the Fall '95 tour, Phish decided to challenge their collective audience to a game of chess. Over the course of this tour, a large chessboard hung behind the band, and fans were invited to communicate their chess strategies at the Greenpeace table during the setbreak of each show. At the beginning of each second set, the fans' and band's respective moves would be made, pushing the game forward for the next show.

It all began at the Shoreline Amphtitheatre in Mountain View, California, where the first sight of the chessboard confused but intrigued the entire audience. After a couple of opening songs, Trey addressed this justified confusion, explaining how the band are great fans of the game, and over the years have enjoyed engaging various fans in playing. They decided that it would be fun to challenge the *entire* audience to a game, and to let the result unfold over the course of the tour. So, before the sold-out crowd at Shoreline, a single fan referred to as "Pooh" arrived on the stage, representing the fan contingent. Meanwhile, Page mounted a ladder in front of the chessboard to access the band's half of the game board. The two then exchanged about three sets of moves as the rest of the band played "a little chess music." Said chess music was, appropriately enough, Jefferson Airplane's classic of surrealist psychedelia, "White Rabbit." Based on Lewis Carroll's various adventures of Alice, the song references, among other things, Alice's interaction with the live chess pieces of the Red Queen's humongous chessboard. Although they didn't actually play the full song or even sing any of its lyrics, Trey, Mike, and Fish layed down enough of the classic tune to provide an adequate soundtrack to the chessy musings occupying the back portion of the stage.

Who By Fire
Original Artist: Leonard Cohen
Original Album: *New Skin For the Old Ceremony* (1974)
Vocals: Colonel Bruce Hampton (retired)
Debut: 4/23/94
Historian: Ellis Godard

Who never would have guessed that Phish would cover this bizarre tune by Leonard Cohen. Who first recorded the tune in 1974 in the style of "Greensleaves" (bouncy and high-pitched, with a harpsichord) but who released a more compelling version on Cohen Live (from Austin City Limits 10/31/88), released the same year the song was performed by Phish. Who first teased it during the brave ascent of the vocal jam following "You Enjoy Myself," and then performed the entire song with Col. Bruce. Who became one of only five first set guests throughout Phishtory and (after Merl Saunders in the first set on "High-Heeled Sneakers") completed the only one-guest-per-set show. All of whom played together in Atlanta's Fabulous Fox Theater, favorite venue of this history's writer. Who wonders what the hell Leonard is saying in a song which is just a stream of questions with no verbs, except for the refrain "And who shall I say is calling?" And what shall we suppose that means?

Who Do? We Do!
Music: Trey Anastasio

Album: *Junta* (Part of "Fluff's Travels"—CD 2:21-4:12)
Vocals: (instrumental)
Debut: 5/15/88 (in "Fluffhead"); 9/21/89 (independently)
Historian: Mark Toscano

Jumping up and down. You can tell when the band is in the middle of this, the fourth part of the complete "Fluffhead," because Trey and Mike are jumping up and down. They don't use trampolines. They'll just be standing there, when all of a sudden, there it is: the jumping up and down.

"Who Do? We Do!" is possibly the most indescribable part of "Fluff's Travels." The music is strange, characterized by some severe rhythm-bending, flirtations with atonality, a brief Page solo, and some irregularly escalating major chords. And, just when you think a song has everything but the kitchen sink, they toss in some jumping to boot.

This tune is the only segment of "Fluff's Travels" to not premiere until showing up in the "final draft" version of "Fluffhead" on 5/15/88. Sort of. You see, a seminal, partial version of this song is originally found in a very unexpected place: as the second half of "I am Hydrogen"! For Some of "Hydrogen's" early performances in 1987, the song contained an extra instrumental section that doubled its length. This section was basically a start-and-stop version of the aforementioned "Who Do? We Do!" chord escalations, except without the jumping. Quite a contrast to "Hydrogen's" floating, ethereal beauty, this section was dropped by the beginning of the next year, just in time to find a home in "Fluff's Travels."

Like some of its brethren ("The Chase," "Bundle of Joy," etc.), "Who Do? We Do!" did enjoy a brief period of autonomy in 1989, appearing a number of times outside of "Fluffhead" (9/21/89, 10/1/89, 10/26/89, to name a few), but otherwise has faithfully remained the stable, unflinching anchor between "The Chase" and "Clod." Well, stable and unflinching except for the jumping, at any rate.

See Also: Fluffhead/Fluff's Travels, I am Hydrogen

Who Knows
AKA: "You Don't Know"; "I Don't Know"
Music/Lyrics: Jimi Hendrix
Original Artist: Jimi Hendrix (Band of Gypsys)
Original Album: Band of Gypsys (1970)
Vocals: Trey
Debut: 8/9/93
Historian: Kazimierz O. Wrzeszczynski

Who Knows is best known as the first track on the Jimi Hendrix album *Band of Gypsys*. The Band of Gypsys trio was made up of Jimi Hendrix, Buddy Miles and Billy Cox, and other than a short benefit performance later in January of 1970, Band of Gypsys made its only public appearances over a four-show debut at the Fillmore East on Dec. 31, 1969 and Jan. 1, 1970. The history and recordings of those New Year's Eve performances have been ideally preserved and can be relived with two wonderful recent releases, the remastered original "Band of Gypsys" in 1997, and "Live at the Fillmore East" in 1999. The song "Who Knows" was played a couple of times over those performances but its identity comes from the nine-minute, Buddy Miles-improvised scat version that is found on the album *Band of Gypsys*.

This familiar version of "Who Knows" emerges out of Phish's opening number "Chalkdust Torture" on 8/9/93 in Toronto. In the middle of the "Chalkdust" jam Trey begins to play the opening chords of

"Who Knows," and instead of teasing around this melody Fish slows the drum beat and we hear Trey singing the so-called first verse of "You don't know, like I know." The very quick rendition finishes up with Trey exactly mimicking the Buddy Miles unique "Who Knows" scat and Fish yelling out his support and approval in the background. The "Who Knows" jam was played as the second set opener during the well circulated 10/26/89 Wetlands, New York City appearance, and even though the song is often mislabeled as "Good Morning Little School Girl" you can hear a faint Trey yelling "I Don't Know" in the background out of the microphone's range. It is somewhat amazing that this song has not blossomed out of any jams since that Toronto appearance because the "Who Knows" melody and influence can be heard from Trey or Mike in numerous improvised jams during various Phish songs besides "Chalkdust Torture" such as "Tweezer" (12/29/92, 7/6/94), "YEM" (3/9/90, 5/7/93), "Mike's Song" (8/16/93, 9/29/99) and "Character Zero" (5/21/00).

Who Loves the Sun

Original Artist: The Velvet Underground
Original Album: *Loaded* **(1970)**
Vocals: Trey (lead), Fish, Mike, Page (backing)
Debut: 10/31/98
Historian: Mark Toscano

This song, the opening tune on The Velvet Underground's *Loaded*, inaugurated Phish's 1998 Halloween "musical costume." The band covered it solidly, albeit a bit meekly, keeping their version completely faithful to the original. This opening on cautious ground helped set a solid foundation upon which they would build the madness of, among other things, the "Sweet Jane," "Rock and Roll," and "Lonesome Cowboy Bill" to come.

Why Don't We Do it in the Road?

Original Artist: The Beatles
Original Album: *The Beatles* **(aka "The White Album") (1968)**
Vocals: Fishman
Debut: 10/31/94
Historian: Mark Toscano

A little less than halfway through the band's 10/31/94 "White Album" set, this wild and wooly McCartney tune was appropriately interpreted by the inimitable Mr. Fishman while Trey manned the drumkit. Fish, in many fans' estimations, surpassed the lunatic angst of Paul's original extremist pleas for hot, buttered love, but this is to be expected. One would find it hard to imagine Paul McCartney punctuating a verse of this song with XXX-rated pelvic thrusting, but in the case of Fishman, one would find it hard to imagine the song otherwise. The song was busted out of hiding two more times, on 12/10/94 and 6/25/95, on both occasions in the middle of a "Mike's Groove." Incidentally, the original Beatles' recording of this tune, layed down at the height of their internal disagreements, features only Paul and Ringo.

Why Don't You Love Me?

AKA: "Why Don't You Love Me (Like You Used to Do)?"
Music/Lyrics: Hank Williams
Original Artist: Hank Williams

Original Album: single (1950)
Vocals: Trey (lead); Mike, Page (back-up vocals)
Debut: 3/23/87
Historians: Charlie Dirksen and Mark Toscano

Only one known Phish performance exists of this funky song originally composed by the not-at-all-funky-to-his-own-credit Hank Williams. Why is Phish's version funky? Sometime over this song's evolution, it split off in two divergent directions. One was a traditional path, and the song is still covered by many artists today as it originally was played in the early '50s by Hank Sr.

The other path was an interesting one, tracing from Williams' original, to various early rock and roll incarnations, to the proto-funk-boogie of Little Richard. On a set of recordings highlighting the collaboration of Little Richard with none other than Jimi Hendrix, the duo covered this unlikely song, making it funkier and groovier than ever. More recently, the Red Hot Chili Peppers featured a totally funked-out version of the song (with pedal steel!) on their 1984 debut LP and a limited edition covers collection from 1998.

In Phish's version of "Why Don't You Love Me?," Trey sings the vocals in a lower range than usual, and with a gusto so funky that you'll doubt that he's a honky (or maybe not). This amusing cover jams in much the same way that Phish's covers of "I Wish" and "Sneakin' Sally" used to jam, which is to say more along the lines of Hendrix and the Chili Peppers than Hank's or Pat Boone's versions. The singular 3/23/87 version of the tune is also interesting for a very nice segue into "Camel Walk."

Why You Been Gone so Long?

Music/Lyrics: Mickey Newbury
Original Artist: Jessi Colter
Original Album: *A Country Star is Born* **(1970)**
Vocals: Jeff Walton, Dick Solberg, and Trey
Debut: 5/6/93
Historian: Ellis Godard

Dick Solberg had already been onstage at this show to liven up "Lawn Boy" with some violin, when Trey brought out acoustic guitarist Jeff Walton as well. But Jeff's first contribution was vocal, like a younger version of Dr. McConnell, leading a rollicking version of this tune with lines like "Ain't nothin' to do Lord, so I'll guess I'll get drunk." The author, Mickey Newbury, released his own version in 1973 (on *Heaven Help the Child*), a bit rougher than Jessi Colter's original take though not as rough as David Allen Coe's 1995 version.

Phish's take was softer still. Dick and Jeff share good vocal harmonies, with Trey joining in before a nice little Page solo. The rendition ended with a four-part vocal harmony. Not a great tune, but a nice warm-up for "Tennesee Waltz" and "I Been on a Fast Train to Georgia," both of which followed.

Wild Child

Music/Lyrics: Lou Reed
Original Artist: Lou Reed
Original Album: *Lou Reed* **(1972)**
Vocals: Trey
Debut: 11/3/84
Historian: Erik Swain

Those who are looking for the roots of Phish's decision to cover the Velvet Underground's *Loaded* for Halloween 1998 can go all the way back to one of the band's very first shows. On 11/3/84 at the University of Vermont's Slade Hall, the band attempts "Wild Child," from VU auteur Lou Reed's debut solo album (consisting mostly of songs intended for VU). This performance of the song, similar in structure to *Loaded*'s "Sweet Jane," features Trey attempting to mimic Reed's voice by singing in a lower register, and ends with a very un-Reed-like psychedelic jam that segues into the Grateful Dead's "Bertha." Other performances of "Wild Child" that circulate are 5/3/85 and 9/8/88.

Wild Honey Pie

Original Artist: The Beatles
Original Album: *The Beatles* (aka "The White Album") (1968)
Vocals: Phish
Debut: 10/31/94
Historian: Mark Toscano

Perhaps the "White Album's" strangest song aside from "Revolution 9," this short little ditty was almost nixed from The Beatles' original release for being too silly, until Patti Harrison (George's wife) pleaded with them to keep it. Phish covered it in typically wacky form for their 1994 Halloween "musical costume."

Wild Thing

Original Artist: The Troggs
Original Album: *Wild Thing* (1966)
Vocals: (unknown)
Debut: 11/23/85
Historian: Mark Toscano

Wild Thing, the ever-coverable Troggs song, may seem an unlikely song for Phish to play, but apparently it was done. Mike has spoken of covering this song early on at the curious 11/23/85 show, at which Mike had his oft-described spiritual epiphany. Though no tape of the complete show circulates among fans, a portion of the gig (not including the performance of this song) can be found from time to time. According to Mike, "Wild Thing" had been written on a blackboard the band used, on which fans would write down requests of what they wanted to hear. Perhaps a pre-cursor to the Halloween musical costume days to come, this practice was apparently used at occasional gigs, yielding often curious and bizarre setlists that to this day leave fans scratching their heads.

Wildwood Weed

Music/Lyrics: Jim Stafford, Don Bowman
Original Artist: Jim Stafford
Original Album: *Jim Stafford* (1974)
Vocals: Les Claypool
Debut: 12/6/96
Historian: Chris Bertolet

Jim Stafford, who may well be the Elvis Presley of redneck comedy, conceived this thinly veiled counterculture nugget about a man who stumbles upon a special weed. He and his brother, the story goes, discover that they can use it to "take a trip without leaving the farm." Upon learning of the their find, however, a Federal agent descends upon their land and decimates their crop. But the narrator and his brother are a step ahead. They bid the G-man a fond adieu, while perched on a bumper crop's worth of seeds.

Les Claypool has recited "Wildwood Weed" with various projects, from Primus to Caca (see 1992's *First Caca Show*). And so, as the Elvis Presley of his own demented musical universe, it was only fitting that he chose to recite "Wildwood Weed" during the sprawling "Harpua" encore at The Aladdin in Las Vegas on 12/6/96.

Fans lucky enough to catch the "unadulterated audio sodomy" of Oysterhead at New Orleans' Saenger Theatre on 5/4/00 bore witness to yet another "Wildwood Weed," recited atop one of the power trio's crunching grooves.

Will it Go Round in Circles?

Original Artist: Billy Preston
Original Album: (single); The Best of Billy Preston
Vocals: Trey
Debut: 9/10/99
Historian: Phillip Zerbo

The members of Phish have long been known to have a special reverence for 70s R&B, Soul, and Funk, from Stevie Wonder to James Brown to Bootsy Collins. In 1999 they dipped into this rich reservoir once again, reviving the Billy Preston hit tune "Will it Go Round in Circles?"

"Will it Go Round in Circles?" made its first entry into the Phish universe during Trey's May 1999 solo tour. Along with Tony Markellis on bass and Russ Lawton on drums, Trey performed this tune during the electric set in more than half of the shows on that tour. Phish first performed "Will it Go Round in Circles?" on 9/10/99, at the majestic Gorge Ampitheatre in Gorge, WA, ending the first set. While many fans saw the tune as an inspirational cover, "Will it Go Round in Circles?" made only one other appearance, on 9/21/99, at the Pima County Fairgrounds in Tucson, AZ.

Will the Circle Be Unbroken?

AKA: "Can the Circle be Unbroken"
Music/Lyrics: traditional
Vocals: "Reverend" Jeff Mosier (lead), Phish (backing)
(11/19/94); Willie Nelson (lead), Neil Young, Trey,
Page (backing) (10/3/98)
Debut: 11/19/94 (parking lot jam); 10/3/98 (public show)
Historian: Erik Swain

Like many of America's older folk songs, "Will the Circle Be Unbroken" has a fractured and fuzzy history. The authorship of this spiritual is unknown. The Carter Family popularized the song with the country music audience in the 1930s, and an arrangement was copyrighted in 1941 under the name "Can the Circle Be Unbroken." It reached the pop audience in 1972 as the title track of a seminal album by country-rockers Nitty Gritty Dirt Band. This project represented the first major collaboration between hippies and old-time country musicans. Maybelle Carter from The Carter Family performed on that rendition. It has subsequently been performed by, among others, Arlo Guthrie, Willie Nelson and the Dirt Band again on their 1990 sequel *Will the Circle Be Unbroken Vol. II*.

Phish is first known to have attempted this song in 1994. Its only appearance from that era is in the 11/19/94 parking lot jam, where it

closed the impromptu set with "Reverend" Jeff Mosier. Before the song begins, you can hear someone tell Trey that it's time to wrap up the gig.

To the mainstream public, Phish became part of the song's history at the Farm Aid benefit on 10/3/98. After Phish jammed with Neil Young on "Down By the River," Phish and Young welcomed Nelson and keyboardist Paul Shaffer to the stage for four songs to close the benefit. "Circle," a staple of Nelson's live show, was the second. Nelson sang lead and the rest backed him with a frenetic bluegrass arrangement. Just after the song began, four Native Americans came on stage to clap along, though their presence seemed to confound some of the Phish fans in the audience. At its end, the song segued into another Nelson concert mainstay a bit more familiar to Phish: "Amazing Grace."

Less than a month later, Trey and Mike had already forgotten the words. On 11/1/98, they attempted to wrap up their jam with open mic night patrons at the Dead Goat Saloon in Salt Lake City with this song. But it was aborted when no one could remember the lyrics.

Wilson

AKA: "Wilson, Can You Still Have Fun?" (original title)
Music/Lyrics: Trey Anastasio, Tom Marshall, Aaron Woolfe
Album: *A Live One* (12/30/94);
   Hampton Comes Alive (11/21/98)
Vocals: Trey (lead), Mike, Page (backing)
Debut: 10/15/86
Historian: Mark Toscano

Woodrow Wilson was the 28th President of the United States. He served two consecutive terms, maintaining the office from 1913 through 1921. Despite being a self-proclaimed "man of the people" who felt that it was the Presidents job "to look out for the general interests of the country," it was Wilson's orders that sent millions of Americans to fight and die in World War One, ostensibly to prevent trade with Britain from being disrupted.

But we're here to discuss a different Wilson. King Wilson. The Evil King Wilson.

Whatever he did during his term, Woodrow Wilson was certainly nothing near the level of dastardliness and general awfulness that King Wilson reaches in the Gamehendge saga. In "The Man Who Stepped Into Yesterday, Trey's Senior Study, Wilson is an embodiment of many things, including but not limited to abuse of power, greed, selfishness, corruption, and even Fascistic domination.

In the Gamehendge story, Wilson is a traveller from another land who arrives in Gamehendge looking to take over the entire land from the largely communist Lizards. Mighty lofty ambition for a single person, you may say, but these Lizards are pretty stupid. Wilson realizes that the Lizards rely almost entirely on the Helping Friendly Book, a single, mystical volume given to them by their god, Icculus, and which contains all of the knowledge inherent in the universe. Wilson is a keen thinker, and he steals the book, putting the Lizards at his mercy. He swings his heavy, domineering hand in vicious, sadistic circles over the entire land of Gamehendge. He tears down a huge chunk of the forest and builds an immense, glowering castle, naming the city that encircles it Prussia. He enslaves the Lizards both physically and mentally, and maintains this control by stowing the Helping Friendly Book in the highest tower of his new castle. At one point, Wilson hangs a young revolutionary for treason. This young rebel was Roger, the son of Errand Woolfe, the leader of the rebellion against Wilson. The song "Wilson"

is sung (read: angrily yelled) from the viewpoint of Errand Woolfe, in a fit of rage at the rebel camp, shaking his tightly closed fist at Wilson's castle looming in the distance.

Well, sort of. Actually, the interesting thing about "Wilson's" lyrics is that they were written before Trey even began conceiving "The Man Who Stepped Into Yesterday." This isn't necessarily unusual, as "AC/DC Bag," "Possum," and "McGrupp" were also all written before and independently of Trey's Senior Study. The unusual parts are how the song was written and how Trey incorporated it into the story.

The original name of the song was "Wilson, Can You Still Have Fun?," and was first written by Tom Marshall and Aaron Woolfe for A-Dot Tom, their band at the time. It was a gag song, rife with in-jokes, and the lyrics were almost entirely random, nonsensical, and even partially deriving from stream-of-consciousness back and forths between the two friends. For instance, there is a Wilson's Leather Shop in King of Prussia, PA, and "Mike Christian, Rog(er), and Pete" are all old friends. Aaron and Tom had fun performing it for friends, who got a kick out of it, but when Trey eventually heard it, he reacted somewhat differently.

Trey incorporated "Wilson, Can You Still Have Fun?" into the Gamehendge storyline by changing a few lyrics (e.g. the "Roger/Rutherford" line), and using the song as commentary rather than having it develop the plot. In fact, "Wilson" doesn't really offer much in the way of story explication, a result of the lyrics being nonsensical to begin with. Trey conceived "Wilson's" role in the musical as unnecessary to the plot, but essential to the ever-changing flavor of the porject's different songs. "Wilson" is a straight-forward rock number, simple and powerful, and written to be memorable. Its placement after the sweet beauty and eventful climax of "Tela" and the laid-back groove-rock of "AC/DC Bag" is notable; it works as a nice pick-me-up after the lay-me-down of "Tela," musical Vivarin in preparation for the journeys to come.

Though "Wilson" obviously has its place in the Gamehendge storyline, it is perfectly suited as an energetic rock number to be played anytime, anywhere. It has opened and closed first sets and second sets, always to the delight of fans, and its likeable, simple structure ensure it will retain a place in the Phish repertoire for some time. Case in point: though it was one of the songs supposedly axed by the band from their songlist back in early 1997, the song made an appearance soon after at the 6/27/97 Glastonbury Festival. The reason for the reappearance? When would the band next be playing so close to Stonehenge?

Another interesting note about the song's evolution concerns the chanting. In the original 4-track version from "The Man Who Stepped Into Yesterday," the eerie "Wilson" chanting is heard at the very beginning of the recording, as well as at the beginning of the song, in both cases over the thudding double E that acts as the intro to the song. The band brought this idea to their 1988 live performances of the song, and even though the chanting had been long abandoned by late 1994, fans had started to pick up the job. The crowd chanting reached its first major peak on 12/30/94. While the band hammered down the intro, eventually the entire crowd was chanting "Wilson!," much to Trey's visible delight. They extended the intro to milk it for all it was worth, and the result ended up being chosen for inclusion on 1995's *A Live One*. After the release of that album, the crowd chanting became a standard part of the song, yet another example of the consistent audience-band interaction that pleases both parties immensely.

From its early beginnings in late 1986 all the way through to 1998, "Wilson" honestly didn't change that much. Aside from a few changes

in structure and lyrics, the song has remained the same. Interestingly, though, the jamminess of "Wilson" has followed a strange pattern. In its earliest appearances, the song was performed quite loosely and usually featured a decent amount of bonus jamming (see 10/15/86 and 8/21/87). After a few years, it settled down a bit, and remained under compositional control for some time. It was only in late 1998 that the tune began to jam a bit in otherwise tightly maintained sections, especially in the pre-"You've got me back thinkin'" part. Check out any version including and following Fall 1998 for some interesting jamming.

Versions of "Wilson" from late 1987 through 1989 often featured an unusual and creative segue out of "Peaches en Regalia" (see 3/22/88, 5/15/88, 9/24/88, 5/9/89). Other great and fun versions include 10/15/86 (slightly different arrangement; a fun one!), 8/21/87 (loose and flavorful), 1/27/90 (weird and heavymetalesque), 12/31/91 (with cursing voicebox), 3/13/92 (with "Somewhere Over the Rainbow" teasing), 5/8/92 (Charlie's favorite), 12/29/92 (lots of secret language), 4/15/94, 4/23/94 (sweet segue into "Antelope"), 7/13/94 (with "Cavern" crossover), 12/9/95 (with buttmunch), 8/14/96, 2/21/97 (heavy metal version), 10/30/98 (nice jamming), 7/4/99, 7/20/99 (both great), 12/30/99 (growly), and 6/13/00 (fades into nice loops, then into "Mike's").

Wind Beneath My Wings

Original Artist: Bette Midler
Original Album: *Beaches* soundtrack (1988)
Vocals: Fish
Debut: 11/28/95
Historian: Craig DeLucia:

It would be easy to label this song as a fun Henrietta one-shot, but the beauty that was expressed in Phish's lone rendition on 11/28/95 can't be stressed enough. The band sat long-time influence Colonel Bruce Hampton in a chair on the stage and allowed Henrietta to serenade him. They chose this former top-40 ballad, an inspirational song about an unsung hero, while their unsung hero was moved to…read a newspaper while they played.

So maybe it was a fun Henrietta one-shot.

Windora Bug

Music/Lyrics: Trey Anastasio, Tom Marshall
Album: (none)
Vocals: Trey, Mike, Page
Debut: 6/24/99 (private show); 9/8/00 (public show)
Historian: Erik Swain

This loose reggae song with three-part singing and inscrutable lyrics ("Is it a wind? Or a bug? It's a Windora Bug!") debuted on Trey's May 1999 solo tour and immediately enticed some fans with its quirkiness. After over a year of requests and a few soundcheck appearances, it entered the Phish rotation during the Fall 2000 tour, first surfacing 9/8/00 in Albany. Until then, only the lucky few who on 6/24/99 attended "The Fifth Ball" (also known as "Carreystock"), a private party at Trey's barn for friends of the band, comedian Jim Carrey, and the crew of his movie *Me, Myself and Irene*, had ever seen a non-soundcheck Phish performance of this song.

Unlike the rendition by the guitar-bass-drums trio on the Trey tour, Phish's version departs from two-chord reggae, thanks mainly to Page. On 9/15/00 in Hershey, for example, Page provided clavinet and

synthesizer fills to give the song extra texture, and led a brief spacey jam toward the song's end. In addition, Fishman produced some drum flourishes absent from the Trey tour version.

Page's singing also differentiates Phish's version from the one performed earlier by Trey's band. On the Trey tour, "Windora Bug" featured bassist Tony Markellis chanting the main "Is it a wind?" lines while Trey attempted some form of reggae toasting ("We've got the rules down now…") and drummer Russ Lawton sang something barely intelligible behind Trey's part. For Phish performances, Mike takes Tony's part, which is perfect for a low voice, and Page takes Russ's part, but his singing is clear and prominent, producing a call-and-response effect with Trey.

As Trey explained on 5/8/99, this is one of two "Bug" songs written around the same time. The other, just plain "Bug," also debuted on the solo tour. That more conventional song made it into the Phish rotation immediately, and eventually on to the *Farmhouse* album. "Windora Bug," by contrast, remained elusive, just as the meaning of the song still does.

Wipe Out

Original Artist: The Surfaris (aka The Safaris)
Original Album: (1963)
Vocals: (instrumental)
Debut: 12/9/89
Historian: Ellis Godard

Wipe Out has been a humorous knickknack in Phish setlists. It has come in three meaningful spurts. Early versions typically came after a band fumble. It was thus teased in the meanderings of the 12/9/89 "David Bowie," opened the second set of 4/15/91 (after a trampled first set, but preceding a strong "Mike's Song"), and followed a wobbly "Squirming Coil" on 4/27/91. But by that April, Trey had finally visited California. Over successive tours out West, he attempted surfing—and later spoke spiritually about it, and its similarities to improvisational music. Within three years, wipeouts seemed to be by band design.

Later appearances of the song seem deliberate, esp. 11/17/94 (within "Vibration of Life" as part of an orchestrated narration following "Colonel Forbin's Ascent") and 11/27/98 (early in the second set and then throughout the set (esp. in "Chalkdust" and "Weekapaug"). Between those two appearances, as the band was hit by successive waves of attention and rising popularity, their jams dropped from the rock heights of earlier years to an almost ambient-level groove, even within their great early compositions (such as "Divided Sky," during which Mike teased "Wipe Out" on 6/26/94).

But the ambient days (which reached their peak 10/31/98 III) waned. Phish's music, in composition and delivery, soon returned to soaring aspirations. Though Trey has stepped back, the band as a whole continues to try and hang ten, musically. The final two appearances of "Wipe Out" anticipated this reversal, coming during wandering versions of "Possum" and 11/29/98 and 12/30/98. But, though the band keeps surfing and though their woodies have wobbled, they have yet to again acknowledge it with this song.

Note that the original was recorded not by the Ventures (as is commonly reported) but by The Surfaris, the Glendora, CA, quintet not to be confused with the original Surfaris, the Orange County quartet who changed their name when "Wipe Out" became a hit.

Wolfman's Brother

AKA: "Wolfman's"
Music/Lyrics: Phish, Tom Marshall
Album: *Hoist; Slip Stitch and Pass* (3/1/97)
Vocals: Trey (lead), Mike, Page (backing), Fish (Shirley Temple)
Debut: 4/4/94
Historian: Jeremy David Goodwin

The early maturation period of "Wolfman's Brother" was awkward, sprinkled with starts and stops. Although the version on *Hoist* holds up as a bouncy, fun tune, it seemed that the band didn't quite know what to do with it initially in the live rotation. Early versions with horns (4/4/94, 4/15/94, 5/4/94) tapped into the tune's delicious groove, but "Wolfman's" was the poor younger sibling in the year in which "Julius" "DWD" and "Sample" dominated the family of new songs. It was unceremoniously shelved for over a year after the GameHoist show of 6/26/94, surfacing finally as an odd and unexpected tour opener for Fall Tour '95 (it would go on to open another tour: the US portion of Summer '98.) Although some fans noticed a hint of something extra special in the version performed in Philly on the opening night of the 1996 New Year's Run, perhaps only an accomplished adherent of the *I Ching* could have forecast the role this song would assume in the year to come.

On March 1, 1997, in a club in Hamburg, Germany, various latent inclinations in the band's collective unconscious were stirred, and the "Wolfman's" jam that night emerged as a vehicle for a new sound. Phish channeled a sound that they had been "hearing in their heads" (as Trey put it later) and summoned it into existence. A result of numerous subtle changes in the band's approach towards music that had been accruing for a year (notably the focus on groove that was crystallized and encouraged by the performance of *Remain in Light* on Halloween), the Hamburg "Wolfman's" was the first palpable evidence of what Phish jamming would be like in 1997 and beyond. Though this is of course just another chapter in the development of Phish's ongoing, evolving oeuvre, the Hamburg "Wolfman's" no doubt set the pace for the next two years or so of performance. Over the summer of 1997, this song was raised as a purple and blue flag: the emblem of a new age. The viciously funky "Wolfman" had descended from the mountain, and was ready to tell the world what he had learned. "Wolfman's" was used a handful of times that year as the tool of a delicious new trend: huge set openers. During Summer '97, it seemed sometimes that once they took the stage, Phish literally could not wait to delve into the rich subterranean world of improvisation. Regardless of its set placement, though, the insistent bass-driven groove of "Wolfman's Brother" was consistently a welcome treat. Two particularly pleasing versions from this period are 8/2 and 8/16. The former is first set delicacy at the Gorge, featuring a well-executed return to the "Wolfman's" theme; the latter is the second set opener of the first day of the Great Went. It includes a glorious, melodic jam after several minutes of thick funkiness.

"Wolfman's Brother" got better in the fall, as did the style of jamming it had helped to usher in back in February. The band had become more springy and aggressive within the groove-heavy context, and the electronic funk jams that ensued were sometimes remarkable to behold. A standout, capstone version of "Wolfman's" occured in Illinois on 11/19. This jam hinted at a breakout of "Walk Away" before segueing masterfully into "Makisupa." The very next version, a week later in

Worcester, Massachusetts, included a surreal heavy metal jam, during which Chris turned off all the lights in the room and Trey and Mike hid behind speakers on-stage.

By now established as a major second set jam vehicle along the lines of "Mike's Song" and "Tweezer," "Wolfman's" continued to showcase cutting edge, marquee jams in 1998. It segued masterfully into "Sneaking Sally" on the first night of the Spring Run (as it would again at Oswego, though sloppily), and hosted the lion's share of a jam-saturated third set on Halloween '98, which had the fewest distinct songs of any set since the Space Camp of Summer '95 (see 6/22/95). A thrilling version lept out of the second-ever jammed "Carini" on 12/28/98 in Madison Square Garden; this version showcased the most experimental jamming of that Run (though some fans prefer the glossy, upbeat fun of 12/29 or the deep and versatile strengths of 12/31).

Not all "Wolfman's" these days are second set showstoppers. Indeed, by 1999 the song settled into a less experimental role, acting more as a warmup than the main exhibition. The versions from this period have a twist, as they tend to include an instrumental reprise of the "Wolfman's" theme before wrapping up. Even the most uneventful ten minute run-throughs, however, (see numerous versions like 12/31/97, 11/28/98, 12/30/99) are a revelation given the song's humble upbringings.

This song entered a new realm of credibility in April '99 when an incarnation of Phil and Friends, including Trey and Page among the players, chose it as one of four Phish compositions to include in a historic three night stand at the Warfield. Notably, this tune remained in the repertoire of Phil Lesh and his rotating Friends. Lyrically, "Wolfman's Brother" tells a story that is all but impossible to decipher. Indeed, it may be one of Tom Marshall's last great surreal word sketches, before covering more "serious" territory on *Billy Breathes* and later work. It is mined, however, with many tasty verbal nuggets. Nifty turns of phrase ("this isn't who it would be if it wasn't who it is") and potential slogans ("I might be on a side street/ or a stairway to the stars....") Listen for a slight swell of applause after this line in the 8/16/97 version) abound. The bouncy, enigmatic lyrics combine with a sexy groove that encourages listeners to jiggle their limbs in a rhythmic fashion, creating a decidedly fun listening experience.

WON'T YOU COME HOME, BILL BAILEY? (see: "BILL BAILEY, WON'T YOU PLEASE COME HOME?")

Woodstock

Music/Lyrics: Joni Mitchell
Original Artist: Crosby, Stills, Nash, and Young
Original Album: *Déjà Vu* (1970)
Vocals: Trey, Page (lead), Fish, Mike (backing)
Debut: 7/26/99
Historian: Craig DeLucia:

At the end of the second set of the last show of the Summer, 1999 U.S. tour, Trey stopped to tell the fans in attendance how much their support meant to the band. He specifically complimented the crowd for the way they handle themselves, especially in light of the criminal events at the Woodstock '99 festival.

When the band re-took the stage for the encore, they launched into a seemingly unrehearsed rendition of the CSNY classic, "Woodstock" (actually, Joni Mitchell penned the song but gave it to CSNY to

Wolfman's Brother

Compiled by Saul Wertheimer and Billy Rickards

Date	Timing	Notes
12/28/96	06:16	Great groove! The first of the "jammed out" Wolfman's. Foreshadows what was to come in 1997.
03/01/97	13:50	Twenty second DEG quote. Wormtown action, ushering in the era of huge versions of Wolfman's. Segues into Jesus Just Left Chicago.
07/21/97	10:20	Good segue into Magilla.
08/02/97	18:00	What a monster! At around ten minutes into it, the jam slowly starts to build, and soon rocks (it isn't very funky at all). Quite different from its summer brethren.
08/08/97	16:50	Very mellow and summery jam. Doobie Brothers feel. The segue into Free is slow and sweet.
08/16/97	18:55	Could be funkier. Strong build and segue into Simple.
11/14/97	15:40	Segues into Piper.
11/19/97	27:45	C&P jamming transcends the boundaries of mere funk. Total hose!
11/30/97	31:13	The longest Wolfman's to date. Surreal, repetitious, heavy-metal "Pentagram Death Jam." Sanity and Esther lyrics. Fades out and segues into Treat Me Like A Fool.
12/07/97	07:20	Short but sweet. Mike lays it down! Hints at Boogie On.
12/31/97	10:55	Manteca-like tease at one point.
04/02/98	08:55	Nice segue into Sneakin' Sally.
06/30/98	12:13	Very improvisational. Good segue into Frankie Says.
07/15/98	08:48	Intense final few minutes.
08/06/98	15:33	Excellent jam soon becomes an ambient, spacey groove. Segues into Talk.
10/15/98	12:47	Funk at the Fillmore.
10/31/98	30:15	A huge Halloween masterpiece! Scary, charging, energy-building space, ambiance, and noise. Very improvisational.
12/28/98	21:12	Porno-funk and spacey grooves.
07/26/99	17:39	Magnificent, exploratory improvisation.
12/30/99	09:02	Rages in the final minute or two.

perform). Indeed, they made it through a verse, two choruses, and a brief guitar solo before launching into a tour-closing "Julius."

Wormtown

Music/Lyrics: Chris McCarty/Steve Miller/Phish
Original Artist: Steve Miller (as "Swingtown")
Original Album: *Book of Dreams* (1977)
Vocals: Trey Anastasio ("Swingtown" lyrics and worm narration), Jon Fishman (On the back of the worm)
Debut: 7/2/97
Historian: Martin Acaster

Wormtown, a bizarre hybrid of Steve Miller's "Swingtown" and Trey's post-show hallucination in a canal-side urinal the previous evening, emerged ominously from the tail end of an energetic "Llama" in the second set of the 7/2/97 show at the Paradiso in Amsterdam. The song included improvised lyrics from Steve Miller's "Swingtown" begging the musical question "Do You Know Where You Are?" Trey followed with a disturbing warning that audience members should take care when they leave the show that night. Cautioning them that if they were to use the small green urinals on the side of the road they might get sucked down one and have to spend the rest of the night riding on the backs of the giant worms that live in the canals. He was apparently serious, claiming that it had happened to him the night before. Trey's experience was likely a product of an overactive imagination and some rather potent tea that could be found on the menu at the Paradiso, but who can say for sure. It is hard to tell fantasy from reality when you're riding on the back of the worm.

Ya Mar

Music/Lyrics: Cyril Ferguson
Original Artist: Cyril Ferguson, The Mustangs
Original Album: (unknown) (C. Ferguson); The Wonderful Side of the Mustangs (Mustangs)
Vocals: Mike (lead); Page, Trey (backing)
Debut: 2/21/87
Historian: Craig DeLucia

Ya Mar is the cover song most likely to be confused with a Phish original. Given the obscurity of the original and the amount of time it has lived in the Phish catalog, many fans are unaware that it was not actually written by the band. And, until recently, most fans had been under the impression that the song was originally written by a reggae band called The Mustangs—as the story went, Mike Gordon heard them play the song while on vacation in the Caribbean, he came home with a tape, and Phish learned the reggae tune.

Thanks to fan Bob Richburg, though, the truth of "Ya Mar" can finally be told. Yes, a band called The Mustangs recorded a version of "Ya Mar." It appeared on their album *The Wonderful Side of The Mustangs*, and has been included in reggae music compilations from the Bahamas. And it was this Mustangs' version that Mike brought home with him. But the original was actually written and recorded by an artist named Cyril Ferguson. In fact, the song helped Cyril earn the "Most Potential Recording Artist Award" at the 1974 Music Maker of the Year Award Ceremony in the Bahamas.

Cover or original, "Ya Mar" resides as a favorite in the hearts of many fans. It represents one of Phish's few forays into calypso and is

among the most playful and danceable songs in the band's repertoire. And anytime Trey screams for Page to take the reins ("Play it, Leoooooo!"), the crowd is apt to go wild. Page's nickname actually comes from this line in the original, where the Mustangs urged their own piano man to step into the spotlight.

The title seems to reference the slurred interpretation of "your ma," as the singer recounts the disdain his lover's family has for him. Phish put their own unique stamp on it by often changing the "no good pa" lyric in the chorus to mimic their own "oh kee pa" phrase. But what is that mystery lyric that Mike wails towards the end? Though it surely varies somewhat from time to time, pick up 8/24/93 to hear Mike slow it down and explain slowly how you have to look at it from his side.

Over the years, "Ya Mar" has had a little bit of everything. Special guests are common. Its reggae roots were expanded with vocals by Jah Roy on 5/25/88 and 6/20/88. For horns, see Dave Grippo's contributions on 3/9/90, and Carl Gerhard and Michael Ray on 10/14/94. For pure percussion thunder, grab Bob Gulotti's guest appearances on 10/23/96 and 7/25/97. The latter is notable for another reason, as it is sandwiched inside of an exploratory set of jamming and free-flowing segues. Other examples here include 7/10/97 and 11/30/94 (with an especially notable segue from "Ya Mar" into "Mike's Song").

Looking for other good "Ya Mar"-induced segues? No tape collection is complete without the incomparable 8/13/93 Murat "Bathtub Gin" -> "Ya Mar" but don't overlook the strong "Mike's Song" -> "Ya Mar" (with a "Low Rider" jam in between) from 4/18/93. Other long and fiery versions include 12/13/97 and 7/25/98.

Of course, every recollection of a Phish jamming vehicle needs mention of a few teases. 6/29/94 is stellar, with a Simpsons Signal and "Dixie" tease, while 4/26/96 ("When the Saints Go Marching In" at New Orleans' Jazzfest) also scores high marks. See also various New Years Run performances from the last several years, where "Ya Mar" often includes "Auld Lang Syne" teases. And, for some goofy stage banter, grab 4/29/93, where Trey cues Page in a bit too early and laughs his way out of it.

Yer Blues
Original Artist: The Beatles
Original Album: *The Beatles* **(aka "The White Album") (1968)**
Vocals: Mike
Debut: 10/31/94
Historian: Mark Toscano

Although they gave it a good shot, this is usually the biggest criticism that discerning fans have of the Halloween "White Album" set. Phish's version of this classic tune gets a lot of flak for being performed in somewhat lackluster fashion, but no one really complains, considering the rest of 10/31/94 set 2 is almost completely priceless.

Yerushalayim Shel Zahav (Jerusalem of Gold)
AKA: "Jerusalem, City of Gold"
Original Artist: Naomi Shemer
Original Album: N/A
Vocals: Phish
Debut: 7/16/93

Historian: Saul E. Wertheimer

Next time you find yourself in Jerusalem, stand on King George Street in the centre of town, and each time another hour passes, you will hear a familiar tune coming from the clock tower. That tune is "Yerushalayim Shel Zahav," written by Israeli composer and folksinger Naomi Shemer.

Shortly before the Six-Day War in 1967, Shemer was commissioned by the Israel Broadcasting Authority to write a song for the annual summer song festival. Her composition was an instant hit, and became the theme song of the war. Her beautiful poetry and the romantic, haunting melody have touched hearts across the world.

Although the translation of the title of the song is easy— "Jerusalem of Gold"—the body of the song is largely metaphoric, and thus fairly hard to translate from the original Hebrew. The chorus can be translated as follows:

> "Jerusalem of gold, and of copper, and of light,
> For all your songs, I am a violin."

Turn your *Hoist* liner notes upside-down, and you will see the chorus written in Hebrew. Phish performed this tune a handful of times, primarily in the summer of '94, and you can also hear it at the end of the "Demand"-encased "SOAM" jam at the back end of *Hoist*.

You Enjoy Myself
AKA: "YEM"
Music/Lyrics: Trey Anastasio
Album: "The White Tape" (intro only); *Junta;*
** *A Live One* (12/7/94)**
Vocals: Trey (lead), Fish, Mike, Page (backing)
Debut: 2/3/86
Historian: Charlie Dirksen

Written by Trey in the summer of 1985 while performing street music with Fish in Europe, "You Enjoy Myself" (also known as "YEM") is one of the oldest and most beloved songs in Phish's catalog. The Phish phenomenon is exemplified by "YEM's" history and nature, which is as compositionally intricate as it is lyrically goofy.

Originally just a multi-tracked a capella tune on the band's first "White Tape" demo, the song has obviously grown. That initial version, comprising merely the first minute or so of the song's intro, was fleshed out by Trey by late 1986 as a full-on jam tune. The seminal version's legacy is not lost however, as an animated video of the tune showed up in mid-2000 on the Internet, produced by Bullseye Art in ShockWave.

Fans have speculated about "YEM's" mysterious lyrics since the song's debut, hence the often heard query, "What are they saying in You Enjoy Myself?" ("WATSIYEM") "YEM's" lyrics appear to be "Boy. Man. God. Shit. Wash Uffizi Drive Me to Firenze." The latter lyric allegedly derives from an incident involving Trey, Fish and a Firenze (Florence) cab driver during the aforementioned European trip. The cab driver apparently remarked to them, "When I'm with you, you enjoy myself!" The 2/3/93 Portland "YEM" features "Water your beehive in a team I'm a sent you" lyrics in place of "Wash Uffizi drive me to Firenze." These bizarre lyrics were in the response that Mike gave to the "What are you saying in YEM?" question in the Döniac Schvice published only a few months before this show. And, as of this writing, 2/3/93 Portland is the only version featuring a substantial lyrical deviation, even though Mike,

You Enjoy Myself

Compiled by Charlie Dirksen

"Boy" is the time when Trey sings it. "Jam" is when the jam segment begins. "B&D" is the timing for when the bass and drums segment begins. "FS/VJ" is when the final Wash Uffizi Drive Me To Firenze segment (and ensuing vocal jam) begins. If there was no B&D or vocal jam, "—" appears. "Total" is the total time (approximately). For considerably more information on these versions and many more, please see the Phish.Net website.

Date	Boy	Jam	B&D	FS/VJ	Total	Notes
02/03/86	5:40	7:29	—	10:05	10:30	The revolutionary poet Zenzile on violin.
04/24/87	5:00				11	Cool segue into DEG out of the vocal jam.
05/26/89	5:27	10:30	—	18	20:08	TREY IS ON FIRE.
03/09/90	5:16		11:53	12:39	15:01	Grippo on sax. Teasefest includes Frankenstein.
07/24/91	5:34	9:25	12:45	14	17:04	Wilson teasing from Mike. Great version with the GCH.
07/26/91	5:13	9	12:52	14:08	17:12	Fantastic jam segment with the GCH.
11/16/91	5:08	8:51	16:10	17:28	20:19	Most groovy and amazing pre-1993 "Pizza Shit" YEM.
03/25/92	5:58	10	12:20	13:50	18:08	Mike funks up the house.
05/12/92	5:24	10	15	16	21:23	Loose opening, but Trey channels Santana in the jam.
07/25/92	5:21	8:28	—	—	16:14	Carlos Santana jams with Phish!
11/22/92	6:10	10:05	13:25	15:02	19:05	Eleanor Rigby teasing. Humorous vocal jam.
12/02/92	6:15	10	13:20	14:40	19:13	The music of The Wedge's intro guides the jam segment.
12/07/92	6	9:30	13:05	14:05	18:49	Santana-esque jam.
02/03/93	8:10	12:10	15	16	21	"Water Your Team in a Beehive I'm a Sent You" lyrics.
02/07/93	8:01	12	15:24	17:24	21:54	Excellent version all-around. "Clementine" vocal jam.
03/14/93	7:02	11	17:35	19	24:24	Teasefest. Spooky, Low Rider, Oye Como Va, We Will Rock You, Welcome to the Machine. And an insane vocal jam.
03/28/93	8:36	13:11	18:14	19:38	26:42	A few lines of Dave Abrahams' The Pez Song appear in the opening segment.
04/12/93	7:17	11:40	16:30	18:40	24:36	Gumbo and the Rolling Stones' Honky Tonk Women are quoted.
04/14/93	6:54	11:50	16:55	18:49	25:40	Spooky teasing in an excellent jam.
04/17/93	7:00	10:39	17	18:56	24:38	Stevie Wonder's I Wish is jammed on.
05/02/93	6:29	10:56	18:08	20	24:13	Remarkably groovy jam segment.
05/05/93	6:53	10:32	—	—	31:25	Incredible jam with Aquarium Rescue Unit! Fan favorite.
08/25/93	7:18	11:30	18:02	19:43	23:15	Magnificent jam. Segues into "Mice and Bats" (aka the "Tea Tray Song") with Baby Gramps.
08/28/93	7:32	11:15	15:56	17:38	23:41	Huge jam on Santana's Oye Como Va.
04/23/94	6:10	10:14	15:53	18:40	22:11	Improvisational. Whacky. Who By Fire.
04/29/94	5:52	10:17	—	—	18:12	Very strange and unusually improvisational.
05/20/94	7:31	9ish	15:25	16:09	20:55	Ob La Di, Ob La Da. Twisted.
06/11/94	7:32	11:14	15:37	16:33	20:22	Melodious, memorably beautiful jam segment.
06/14/94	7:29	11	15	16	20	On Broadway jam.

(continued on the next page)

in Schvices over the years, has suggested that they sing: "Yes, I'll play, but no I won't raise;" "Washer/Dryer/Freezer/Fencing;" "Wanton in a key, I live, and me for horse rent;" "Won't you please-e-curve me from valensi;" "Wash, you face, and drive me to Valencia;" "Washington fences, please, says me;" "Watchusett fiji is sun-hived to floor antsy;" and, of course, "Wasohbf woeh ejwro jeeef je ei Fndsbid." Some fans swear that they have heard "Wash Your Feet They Drive Me to A Frenzy" on many a night.

"YEM" is comprised of several segments. The opening, pre-lyrics segment, before 6:11 on the 12/7/94 *A Live One* ("*ALO*"; all timings below refer to this "YEM") version, though composed, has nevertheless evolved over the years. The earliest versions of "YEM" (especially 2/3/86 Hunt's, which features a violinist), and even the *ALO* version, lack the enchanting and spacey improvisation found within the first few minutes of many more recent versions of the song (e.g., compare 1:19-2:52 on the *ALO* version with the opening of the 4/22/93 Cleveland "YEM," which includes "The Vibration of Life"). Since 1988, "YEM's" opening segment has also regularly contained a brief solo from Mike (see, for example, 3:35 on the *ALO* "YEM"). "Jerusalem City of Gold" has also, like "The Vibration of Life," been featured in "YEM's" opening segment, as in the "YEMs" on 7/16/93 in Philadelphia and on 6/30/94 in Richmond. Gorgeous opening segments of "YEM" include 12/28/92 Palace, 2/7/93 Lisner Auditorium, 3/28/93 Arcata ("The Pez Song"), 6/18/94 UIC Pavilion, 11/23/94 St. Louis, 6/19/95 Deer Creek, 2/26/97 Stuttgart, 11/14/98 Cincinnati.

The transition to the next segment features an often hideous

You Enjoy Myself (continued)

Date	Boy	Jam	B&D	FS/VJ	Total	Notes
06/18/94	7:12	10:55	14:57	16:08	21:05	Tease of Led Zepplin's How Many More Times. Spam vocal jam.
11/23/94	7:57	11:37	18	20:15	27:46	Spectacular in every way. Must-hear.
12/07/94	6:11	9:49	13:16	15:10	20:32	The A Live One version.
06/16/95	6:28	10:11	18:23	20:23	25:06	Boyd from Dave Matthews Band on Fiddle.
06/23/95	6:52	10:47	15:37	17:43	24:15	Thrilling jam.
06/26/95	6:19	9:55	14:47	17:31	21:32	Excellent, intense all-around version.
06/29/95	6:50	11	16	19:37	24:20	Amazing bass and drums segment!
10/14/95			—	—	20+	With Medeski, Martin and Wood.
10/31/95	6:18	10:40	—	32:56	39:45	Hear this monster at all costs. "Fuck you up the ass" vocal jam.
11/10/95	7:05	11:05	21:42	24:24	29:45	Perfect.
11/14/95	6:20	10:05	14:37	16:02	20:15	A jam on Led Zepplin's Immigrant Song.
11/18/95	7:22	10:45	16	24:50	30:20	Brick House jam.
12/09/95	7:27	11:05	—	29:32	34:09	One of the finest versions of YEM ever. Includes "silent jam" and "Shaft" vocal quote. Fan favorite.
12/31/95	6:28	9:45	—	19:13	25:50	Two fantastic hear-at-all-costs jam segments!
11/09/96	6:57	10:45	16:04	19:50	23:58	Fearsome bass and drums.
11/19/96	6:07	10	19:30	21:14	25:38	Groove is in the Heart jam.
12/06/96	7:45	12:05	17:35	21:05	25:59	Incredible bass and drums.
12/29/96	7:34	11:30	—	23:30	26:51	Instrument Switching jam. Sixteen Candles.
02/21/97	6:33	10:22	13:30	15:01	18:43	Remarkably intense.
07/09/97	7:18	—	—	—	34:35	Bewilderingly sweet jam with Bela Fleck and the Flecktones. Very popular.
07/23/97	6:26	11:10	—	—	18	Unusually weird jam. Segue into Rocky Mountain Way.
07/31/97	6:40	—	—	26	28:58	Magnificently intricate, spell-binding, hypnotic jam.
08/11/97	7:40	12	—	23:58	27:17	Weird jam segment and vocal close.
11/28/97	7:15	11:20	—	—	24	Explosively funky. Extensive C&P teasing.
04/05/98	7:31	11:26	—	22	25:32	Spirited jam led by Trey.
08/12/98	6:55	10:20	—	16	19:50	"Who's Your Daddy" vocal jam.
11/29/98	7:50	11:30	—	20:10	23:54	Funkasaurus. A shagfest!
12/29/98	7:11	10:45	—	19:07	23:39	Dynamic. Captivates from start to finish.
07/15/99	7:35	10:50	—	20:30	23:58	Killer jam segment.
09/17/99	7:14	11	—	—	25:39	Jam and Bass Duet with Special Guest Phil Lesh.
09/28/99	7:53	11:50	—	16:24	22:11	Unusually upbeat, "Sweet Home Alabama" vocal jam.
10/10/99	7:58	11:30	—	—	26:20	Two thrilling jam segments! Very popular.
12/02/99	9:56	13:30	—	18:40	25	Glam-rock, repetitious jam segment. Little Drummer Boy vocal jam.
12/08/99	8:48	13:06	—	16:30	21:23	Tweezer Reprise vocal jam.
12/18/99	7:29	11:30	—	17:52	22:47	A very inspired jam segment.
12/31/99	7:26	11:21	—	15:29	22:22	Crowd-assisted, cheesecake vocal jam.
06/09/00	8:01	11:23	18:50	19:55	23:04	Killer jam and return (more/less) of the B&D segment.

scream (at 6:08). This section of "YEM" (6:11-9:49 on the *ALO* version) features "YEM's" lyrics, as well as a funky, usually Page-driven jam. Page has been known to explore and rage (as well as tease "Mission Impossible"; see, e.g., 5/7/93 Bangor) in this section, as Trey and Mike bounce, respectively giddy and pensive, on trampolines. This section of "YEM" is often referred to as the "tramps segment" because of the trampolines. The tramps have been featured in "YEM" since the 5/20/89 Northfield show, and they are usually brought out onto the stage to the great amusement of the audience in "YEM's" opening segment by Brad Sands (listen at 4:03 on the *ALO* version). Page was particularly vigorous on organ in the tramps section in the August 1993 and November 1995 versions of YEM, as well as 10/28/91 Telluride, 5/12/92

Canton, 4/12/93 Iowa City, 5/23/94 Portland, 6/29/95 Jones Beach, and many other versions.

"YEM's" jam segment has featured a plethora of Phish's various improvisational styles over the years. Any given version from any particular tour will often reflect that tour's improvisational themes (from jam-rock to porno-funk to spacey-groove), despite the fact that Trey's soloing in "YEM" often hints at Carlos Santana's soloing in "Oye Como Va." For example, the jam segments of pre-1990 "YEMs"—like Phish's music of that period in general—often contain riveting, powerful soloing from Trey, who leads all of the jam segments (as might Jimmy Page or Jimi Hendrix). Though this trend has certainly continued, nevertheless, more recent versions of "YEM" may feature Mike leading the

jam (7/7/99 Charlotte), or may involve a collective jam—one seemingly led by all band members playing as one (2/21/97 Florence, 11/9/98 Chicago, 10/10/99 Albany). Paradigms of Fall 1997 and 1998 funk, check out the 11/28/97 and 11/29/98 Worcester versions of "YEM."

On 11/16/91 at the Bayou, Phish played the "Mrs. Pizza Shit" "YEM," which was the first of many funky, collective versions. Although Trey still leads the jam segment most of the time (for example, hear the amazing 6/11/94 Morrison "YEM"), there have been many full-band explorations in "YEM" since 1991. On 5/5/93 at the Palace in Albany, Phish jammed ferociously with special guests Aquarium Rescue Unit and The Dude of Life. Throughout 1995, versions regularly exceeded 25 minutes in length, and contained gloriously beautiful improvisation, particularly the 10/24/95 Madison, 10/31/95 Chicago, 11/10/95 Atlanta, 11/18/95 North Charleston ("Brick House" jam), 12/9/95 Albany, and 12/31/95 New York City versions. The band members switched instruments during an unusual version at the Philadelphia Spectrum on 12/29/96. And on 7/9/97 in Lyon, France, Phish played a magnificent "YEM" with help from Béla Fleck and the Flecktones (Victor Wooten on bass, Jeff Coffin on sax, and Futureman on drumitar).

The "bass and drums" segment regularly followed the jam segment in "YEM" between Summer 1988 and December 1996, but has been very rare in recent years. Mike and Fish have usually excelled during this section, but particularly noteworthy bass and drums segments include: 4/22/90 Colorado Springs, 5/2/92 Chicago, 6/29/95 Wantagh, 11/9/96 Auburn Hills (with Trey on the mini-drum-kit), and, of course, the spectacular 12/6/96 Las Vegas version.

Vocal jams featuring spontaneous vocal improvisation, from the merely strange to the auricularly traumatic, began to close "YEM" on a regular basis in 1989. The idea for this vocal improvisation came from a former voice teacher of the band, who suggested that they infuse their singing with some of the energy created by the playing of their instruments. Additionally, the learning of an early cover, XTC's "Melt the Guns," may have also influenced this decision, as the original version of that song ends with a vocal jam of its own. Certain harmonization-themes have appeared in vocal jams over the years. For example, the "Go" or "Guuhm" theme (12/7/92 Minneapolis, 12/30/92 Springfield, 2/19/93 Atlanta, and 11/23/94 St. Louis); "Hom-Nee" (4/17/92 San Francisco and 10/15/94 Pelham); and guttural, animal noises, reminiscent of Pink Floyd's "Several Species of Small Furry Animals Gathered Together in a Cave and Grooving With a Pict" (5/20/89 Northfield, 10/20/89 Burlington, 10/6/90 Port Chester, 10/28/91 Telluride, 10/23/94 Gainesville, 11/10/95 Atlanta, etc.).

Teases and quotes of all sorts of famous melodies and jokes have appeared in vocal jams since 1989, as well: 5/21/89 Burlington (Godzilla); 5/28/89 Hebron (Poop); 3/9/90 Burlington ("Sunshine of Your Love"); 4/22/90 Colorado Springs ("Another One Bites the Dust"); 8/3/91 Auburn (Gerbils in Bottom); 9/27/91 Rochester ("D'OH!"); 10/11/91 Seattle (Miss Piggy); 3/25/92 Charlotteville (White Boys Attack); 4/7/92 Durango (Roger, "My Girl"); 4/25/92 Olympia (Sprockets, "Chariots of Fire"); 4/30/92 Madison ("Welcome Christmas" from "How the Grinch Stole Christmas"); 12/12/92 Ontario (Davy Crockett); 3/14/93 Gunnison ("We Will Rock You;" "Welcome to the Machine"); 8/6/93 Cincinnati ("Cocaine"); 8/9/93 Toronto and 5/23/94 Portland

("Psycho Killer"); 8/17/93 Kansas City ("Ob La Di, Ob La Da"); 4/11/94 Durham ("It's My Soul"); 4/23/94 Atlanta ("Who By Fire"); 5/20/94 Olympia ("Low Rider"); 6/18/94 Chicago ("The Spam Song"); 6/30/94 Richmond ("Redrum"); 6/16/95 Raleigh (with Boyd Tinsley on fiddle); 10/31/95 Chicago ("fuck you up the ass"); 12/06/96 Vegas ("Donuts, I love donuts"); 3/2/97 Copenhagen (Amy Skelton, first fan); 8/12/98 Vernon ("Who's Your Daddy" and "Oooh Chicago"); 12/8/99 (Tweezer); etc. Some spectacularly psychotic and crazy vocal jams include 11/4/90 Fort Collins, 5/3/91 Somerville, 11/30/91 Port Chester, every Spring 1992 version, 8/25/93 Seattle, and 10/15/94 Pelham.

"YEM" has evolved into one of Phish's greatest improvisational songs. There are far too many versions that are excellent all-around to detail here. Nevertheless, in addition to those already noted above (especially those from Fall 1995), and, in general, any version that closes a first set (for example, 7/31/97 Mountain View), check out these other special "YEM's": 5/26/89 Rutland (Trey goes wild); 7/25/92 Stowe (with Carlos Santana, Karl Perazzo, and Raul Rekow; a work of art!); 12/7/92 Minneapolis; 2/3/93 Portland; 3/14/93 Gunnison (Teasefest); 4/14/93 St. Louis; 5/2/93 Phili; 8/25/93 Seattle; 8/28/93 Greek Theater (several measures of Santana's "Oye Como Va"); 4/20/94 Lexington (with members of the Dave Matthews Band); 4/23/94 Atlanta (with Colonel Bruce Hampton); 5/4/94 New Orleans (with the Cosmic Country Horns); 5/28/94 Monterey (with Les Claypool); 6/14/94 Des Moines; 6/18/94 Chicago; 7/14/94 Canandaigua; 11/23/94 St. Louis; 6/26/95 Saratoga; 6/29/95 Wantagh; 10/14/95 Austin (with MMW); 11/19/96 Kansas City ("Groove is in the Heart"); 11/28/97 Worcester; 11/29/98 Worcester; 7/15/99 Holmdel; 10/10/99 Albany; 12/2/99 Auburn Hills; and 6/9/00 Tokyo. For more information on YEM, please visit http:/www.phish.net/ and check out the FAQ and Reviews pages.

You Gotta See Mama Every Night
Original Artist: Con Conrad/Billy Rose
Original Album: N/A
Vocals: Harry Jones (Trey's grandfather)
Debut: 3/16/93
Historians: Craig DeLucia and Rob Winkler

Conrad and Rose, who gained notoriety working with George Gershwin and other legends in the 1930s, wrote this dixieland jazz number back in 1922. Phish has only performed the song once, in Phoenix on 3/16/93. The band serenaded Trey's grandmother with her husband, Harry Jones, providing the lead vocals.

You Shook Me All Night Long
Original Artist: AC/DC
Original Album: *Back In Black* (1980)
Vocals: Bon Fishman (lead), Trey (backing)
Debut: 4/20/89
Historian: Martin Acaster

In the summer of 1980, still reeling from the death of front man Bon Scott, AC/DC came *Back in Black* with another glowing example of their mastery of the cheeky double-entendre grafted onto the screaming back of bloozy rock-n-roll song writing milieu. The centerpiece of this (their all-time best selling) album, was the classic rock nugget "You Shook Me All Night Long," which unlike "Giving the Dog a Bone" pulled

no lyrical punches. This song was about sex plain and simple and every thirteen year old boy within earshot knew it.

The first appearance of "You Shook Me All Night Long" at a Phish show came in the form of an instrumental jam to restart a fire alarm interrupted "Fluffhead" at the 4/20/89 show at "The Zoo" (Humphries House), Amherst College. Phish returned this classic rock treat to their AC/DC bag until shaking it out at free-for-all soundcheck at the Spiaggia Di Rivoltana, Italy on 7/6/97. On cue from the somber peal of a nearby church bell, Trey initially began playing the intro to "Hells Bells"

but apparently did not know the whole song. Instead the band launched into a spirited version of "You Shook Me All Night Long" this time featuring Bon Fishman on lead vocals. Though he stumbled in places and eventually had to be helped out by Trey, his rendition clearly overshadowed the James Brown style version of Hanson's "MmmBop" which followed it.

To hear the inconceivable, check out the infamous 9/29/00 Vegas version of this tune, segueing out of "Rapper's Delight" with none other than Kid Rock on guest vocals.

COVERED ARTISTS

Compiled by Mark Toscano

Abrahams, Dave; ; The Pez Song

AC/DC; Hell's Bells, Highway To Hell, You Shook Me All Night Long

Aerosmith; Cryin', Sweet Emotion, Walk This Way

Allman Brothers Band; Blue Sky, Jessica, Midnight Rider, Revival, Whipping Post

Alpert, Herb; Spanish Flea

Alwood, Reverend; Uncloudy Day

Argent; Hold Your Head Up

Arlen/Harburg; If I Only Had A Brain, Somewhere Over The Rainbow

Armstrong/Gerard; Sweet Adeline

Atlanta Rhythm Section; Spooky

Baby Gramps; Mice And Bats

Bachman-Turner Overdrive; Hey You

Barnes, Bruce "Sunpie"; Loup Garou

Barrett, Syd; Baby Lemonade, Love You, No Good Trying, Terrapin

Beastie Boys; Sabotage

Beatles, The; Come Together, A Day In The Life, Mean Mr. Mustard, Norwegian Wood (This Bird Has Flown), Something, "White Album"

Berry, Chuck; Johnny B. Goode

Billie, Chief Jim; Big Alligator, Che Hun Tah Mo

Blackburn/Suessdorf; Moonlight In Vermont

Blake, Norman; Ginseng Sullivan

Blues Image; Ride Captain Ride

Boston; Foreplay/Long Time

Bowie, David; Life On Mars?

Breeders, The; Cannonball

Bryant, Felice/Boudleaux; Rocky Top

Burns, Robert; Auld Lang Syne

Cale, J.J.; After Midnight, Ain't Love Funny, Cocaine

Cannon, Hughie; Bill Bailey, Won't You Please Come Home?

Cash, Johnny; I Walk The Line

Cheech And Chong; Earache My Eye

Chenier, Clifton; My Soul

Chumbawumba; Tubthumping

Clapton, Eric; If I Don't Be There By Morning

Cohen, Leonard; Who By Fire

Collective Soul; Shine

Coltrane, John; Mr. Pc

Conrad/Rose; You Gotta See Mama Every Night

Courage, Alexander; "Star Trek" Theme (Main Title)

Creedence Clearwater Revival; Proud Mary

Crests, The; Sixteen Candles

Crudup, Arthur "Big Boy"; My Baby Left Me, That's Alright Mama

Davis, Jimmie; I Told You So

Davis, Miles; All Blues

Davis/Onorati/Simeone; The Little Drummer Boy

Deep Purple; Smoke On The Water

Del Mccoury Band; Beauty Of My Dreams, If You Need A Fool

Derek And The Dominoes; Layla

Diamond, Neil; Cracklin' Rosie

Dillards, The; Dooley

Dixon, Willie; Bring It On Home, (I'm Your) Hoochie Coochie Man, Red Rooster

Doobie Brothers; Minute By Minute

Doors, The; Roadhouse Blues, Touch Me

Dorham, Kenny; Blue Bossa

Dude Of Life, The; Bitchin' Again, Crimes Of The Mind, Dahlia, Family Picture, Revolution's Over, Self, Suzy Greenberg, Tv Show

Dylan, Bob; All Along The Watchtower, The Hurricane, I Shall Be Released, Quinn The Eskimo

Edgar Winter Group; Frankenstein

Ellington, Duke; Caravan, Satin Doll, Take The "A" Train

Ellis, "Pee Wee"; The Chicken

Emerson/Howard; Hello My Baby

English Beat, The; Mirror In The Bathroom

Eno, Brian; I'll Come Running

Fabulous Thunderbirds, The; Too Much Of Everything

Ferguson, Cyril; Ya Mar

Foreigner; Cold As Ice

Foster, Preston; Got My Mojo Workin'

Gaye, Marvin; Sexual Healing

Gillespie, Dizzy; Manteca

Gilmore, Jimmy Dale; My Mind's Got A Mind Of Its Own

Glitter, Gary; Rock And Roll Part Two

Grand Funk Railroad; We're An American Band

Grateful Dead; Bertha, Eyes Of The World, Fire On The Mountain, Help On The Way/Slipknot!, Mind Left Body Jam, The Other One, St. Stephen, Scarlet Begonias, Terrapin Station, West L.A. Fadeaway

Green, Al; Take Me To The River

Guess Who, The; Undun

Hancock, Herbie; Maiden Voyage

Hanson; Mmmbop

Hayes, Isaac/David Porter; When Something Is Wrong With My Baby

Hendrix, Jimi; Bold As Love, Fire, Izabella, Who Knows

Higgenbotham, Robert; High-Heel Sneakers

Hill, Mildred And Patty; Happy Birthday To You

Hollies, The; Long Cool Woman In A Black Dress

Holly, Buddy; Not Fade Away

Hopkins, Lightnin'; Shaggy Dog

Horton/Darling/Gabler; Choo Choo Ch' Boogie

Hot Rize; Midnight On The Highway, 99 Years (And One Dark Day)

Ian And Sylvia; Four Strong Winds

James, Mark; Suspicious Minds

James Gang; Walk Away

Jane's Addiction; Been Caught Stealing

Jefferson Airplane; White Rabbit

John, Elton; Amoreena

Johnson, Robert; Crossroads

Kahn/Vanalstyne; Memories

Kander/Ebb; (Theme From) "New York New York"

Key, Francis Scott; The Star-Spangled Banner

King, Earl; Come On (Let The Good Times Roll)

King, Pee Wee/Redd Stewart; Tennessee Waltz

Kiss; Rock And Roll All Nite

Lanois, Daniel; The Maker

Led Zeppelin; Communication Breakdown, Dazed And Confused, Good Times Bad Times, Misty Mountain Hop, Moby Dick, Ramble On

Leiber/Stoller; Love Me (Treat Me Like A Fool)

Lewis, Noah; Viola Lee Blues

Lewis/Hamilton; How High The Moon

Little Feat; Skin It Back, Time Loves A Hero

London/Wells; Messin' With The Kid

Los Lobos; When The Circus Comes

Lynyrd Skynyrd; The Ballad Of Curtis Loew, Freebird, I Know A Little, Tuesday's Gone

Mahal, Taj; Corrina, She Caught The Katy And Left Me A Mule To Ride

Mancini, Henry; Baby Elephant Walk

Marley, Bob; Lively Up Yourself, Mellow Mood, Soul Shakedown Party, Stir It Up, Three Little Birds, Trench Town Rock

Martin, Jimmy; Hold Whatcha Got

Mayfield, Curtis; Pusherman

Metheny, Pat; Phase Dancemax Creek; Back Porch Boogie Blues

Midler, Bette; Wind Beneath My Wings

Mighty Diamonds, The; Have Mercy

Miles, Buddy; Them Changes

Mingus, Charles; Jump Monk

Missionary Sisters; Don't You Wanna Go

Mitchell, Joni; Woodstock

Modern Lovers, The; Roadrunner

Monk, Thelonious; Blue Monk

Monroe, Bill; I'm Blue, I'm Lonesome, Uncle Pen

Montana, Patsy; I Want To Be A Cowboy's Sweetheart

Morrison, Van; And It Stoned Me, Brown-Eyed Girl

Mosier, Reverend Jeff; Little Tiny Butter Biscuits

My Bloody Valentine; Only Shallow

Newbury, Mickey; Why You Been Gone So Long?

Newton, John; Amazing Grace

Ninja Custodian; Funky (Breakdown), The Price Of Love

Nirvana; Smells Like Teen Spirit

O'Brien, Tim; Hold To A Dream

Oasis; Champagne Supernova

Orbison, Roy; Blue Bayou

Parker, Charlie; Donna Lee, Moose The Mooche

Pavement; Gold Soundz

Pickett, Wilson; In The Midnight Hour, Mustang Sally

Pink Floyd; Bike, *Dark Side Of The Moon*

Police, The; So Lonely

Porter, Cole; I Get A Kick Out Of You, Night And Day

Preston, Billy; Will It Go Round In Circles?

Prince; 1999, Purple Rain

Proclaimers, The; I'm Gonna Be (500 Miles)

Puccini/Forzano; O Mio Babbino Caro

Puente, Tito; Oye Como Va

Queen; Another One Bites The Dust, Bohemian Rhapsody

Raitt, Bonnie; Love Me Like A Man

Reed, Lou; Andy's Chest, Wild Child

Robbins, Marty; El Paso

Rolling Stones; Can't You Hear Me Knocking, Emotional Rescue, Honky Tonk Woman, Loving Cup, Sweet Virginia

Rollins, Sonny; St. Thomas

Rufus/Chaka Khan; Tell Me Something Good

Scruggs, Earl; Earl's Breakdown

Seals And Croft; Diamond Girl

Seals, Son; Funky Bitch, On My Knees

Seger, Bob; Night Moves

Shaver, Billy Joe; I Been To Georgia On A Fast Train

Shemer, Naomi; Yerushalayim Shel Zahav

Sherman, Richard And Robert; I Wanna Be Like You

Simon And Garfunkel; Cecilia

Singer/Zanet; One Meatball

Skinner, Jimmie; Doin' My Time

Sly And The Family Stone; Stand!

Smashing Pumpkins; Rhinoceros

Smith, Jimmy; Back At The Chicken Shack

Smith, Will; Getting' Jiggy Wit' It

Spencer Davis Group; Don't Want You No More

Spencer/Hagen; Fishin' Hole Theme

Springsteen, Bruce; Born To Run

St. Louis Jimmy; Goin' Down Slow

Stafford, Jim; Wildwood Weed

Stevens, Cat; Sad Lisa

Strauss, Richard/Eumir Deodato; Also Sprach Zarathustra

Sugarhill Gang, The; Rapper's Delight

Sun Ra; Carefree

Surfaris, The; Wipe Out

Szabo, Gabor; Gypsy Queen

Talking Heads; Burning Down The House, Cities, Psycho Killer, *Remain In Light*,

Them; Gloria

Toussaint, Alain; On Your Way Down, Sneakin' Sally Through The Alley

Traditional; Avenu Malkenu, The Banana Boat Song (Day-O), Beaumont Rag, Carolina, Cold Rain And Snow, Daniel, My Long Journey Home, Nellie Kane, Paul And Silas, Pig In A Pen, Roll In My Sweet Baby's Arms, Swing Low (Sweet Chariot), Will The Circle Be Unbroken?

Traffic; Light Up Or Leave Me Alone

Troggs, The; Wild Thing

Van Halen; Runnin' With The Devil

Velvet Underground; *Loaded*

Violent Femmes; Blister In The Sun

Walsh, Joe; Rocky Mountain Way

War; Low Rider

Webb/Jayne; Old Home Place

Ween; Roses Are Free

Wells, Junior; It's My Life

White, Bukka; Fixin' To Die

White, Josh/Sam Gary; Timber (Jerry)

Whitfield/Strong; (I Heard It Through The) Grapevine

Whitten, Danny; Come On Baby Let's Go Downtown

Who, The; My Generation, *Quadrophenia*, Sparks, Squeeze Box, We're Not Gonna Take It

Williams, Hank; Why Don't You Love Me?

Williamson, Sonny Boy; Help Me

Wonder, Stevie; Boogie On Reggae Woman, Golden Lady, I Wish

Wright, Richard; Halley's Comet, I Didn't Know

XTC; Melt The Guns

Yacavone, Seth; All The Pain Through The Years

Young, Neil; Albuquerque, Arc, Cinnamon Girl, Down By The River, Helpless

Zappa, Frank; Big Leg Emma, Peaches En Regalia

Zenzilé; The Pendulum

ZZ Top; Jesus Just Left Chicago, La Grange, Tush

INTERVIEWS

Tom Marshall, Part A

Interviewed by Chris Bertolet via email during October 1999. See also Foreword and Dictionary.

When describing Tom Marshall's lyrical contributions to the sprawling Phish catalog, certain words come to mind—elusive, off-kilter, unpredictable, playful, intelligent, challenging—and a conversation with the band's prolific wordsmith can elicit the same adjectives. Chris Bertolet talked with Tom in October of 1999 about where he's been, where he's going, and what he's driving.

Chris Bertolet: Where does the songwriting process begin for you? Is it more a flow, or something you have to harness?

Tom Marshall: So far, I've never really adopted a consistent method that I've stuck with long enough to definitively say, "This is how I write." For the most part, I listen to what people say, and read a lot. In the course of a week or so, a prominent idea will drift among my other thoughts that I may feel I could expand upon. I like writing on a PC because I erase and scribble too much for standard pen and paper. I'll often construct a poem in an email to my friend and long-time recipient of my first drafts, Scott Herman.

CB: Is that the Herman who's credited on "Limb by Limb?"

TM: That's him. His first credit was "Cavern", but he actually went uncredited on the second verse of "Squirming Coil" ("I saw Satan on the beach") and inspired "Lawn Boy", among others. He receives my poems first. I don't need a reply or any actual editing; just the fact that he reads them makes them real for me. It's their first stage of life. If he does reply or happen to mention a particular one later, that just further cements it in my head as a good potential song. It helps to know that I'm writing for someone other than myself. I like the idea of provoking some sort of reaction.

CB: The cruelest Hell I can imagine is a place where you're forced to write things no one else will ever read.

TM: What are all those diary writers thinking? The thought that someone will eventually read it must be in the back of their head constantly, I imagine. There are things I experiment with that are for my eyes only, but like I said, Scott is the first line of defense for Phish lyrics. You could, therefore, blame him for anything you don't like about Phish.

CB: Well, that's a weight off Los Lobos.

TM: Ha! Another "Circus" fan, eh? I personally love that song. I don't like the whole album as much as Trey, but that song is beautiful, and I think it's a great Phish cover. Trey's mom turned to me when she heard it for the first time and asked, with open-mouthed awe, "Is this yours?" I wish I could've said yes then. I felt the same way.

CB: Isn't it just a little surreal watching your friend play to 30,000 screaming fans with his mom standing beside you? Does it ever clobber you from time to time: "Holy crap, I write songs for the biggest

touring act in the world?"

TM: A little. Trey's mom and I are good friends now, but even about five years ago she was still "Trey's mom" to me, although she never had the mom vibe in a negative way at all. I think I just assigned it to her as a kid and kept it there. As far as writing for the biggest touring act, I've had time to get used to it. Phish didn't just jump suddenly on the scene. But, even with time to deal with it, it still is a concept worthy of reflection, and I do plenty of that. It's changed my life in a lot of cool ways.

CB: As the Phish universe has grown, do you think Phish has ever sacrificed their art?

TM: No. People who have been waiting for the big sell-out will have to wait a bit longer I think. Remember when Hoist marked the end of Phish as we know it? Well it did, but not in the disastrous way some people may have thought. They have made a couple of mistakes along the way, but not too many. Changing the words to "Axilla" was one—but I can't think of another offhand.

CB: How long have you known Trey?

TM: We first met in eighth grade at the Princeton Day School in New Jersey. The two of us didn't really have any kind of relationship at the time aside from being part of the same musical gang, if you will. Many of our friends played instruments and wrote original songs and recorded them in home-made studios. He left in tenth grade and went to Taft. We lost touch and then randomly both met again at Mercer County Community College where we were forced to go since we were both kicked out of college after our freshmen year for different reasons. It was great- we just picked up where we had left off three years earlier. We built a mini-studio in his dad's basement, got tremendously stoned nightly and recorded lots of music, like "Divided Sky", "Letter to Jimmy Page", "Antelope", etc..

CB: Was *Bivouac Jaun* {see Discography} from that era? "Little Squirrel?"

TM: Yeah, that was one of the products of the Trey's dad's basement recordings. Like I said, we might not have been completely wasted the entire time we recorded, but if there were moments of lucidity, I don't remember them.

CB: What was your involvement in the "Gamehendge" story and Trey's thesis project?

TM: I wrote a poem called "McGrupp and the Watchful Hose Masters", which became the song "McGrupp", in which most of the "Gamehendge" characters were first named. Also, I came up with the name "Gamehendge" when Aaron Wolf and I wrote "Wilson." Aside from that, it was all Trey.

CB: What do you and Trey think about it now?

TM: I love it! I always have—it's incredible really, like Phish's "Jesus Christ Superstar." I never understood the plot twist that became nec-

essary because of that silly line where Tela gets killed, though. We should have written that out. As for Trey, I think he's still proud of "Gamehendge" too. There have been a few ideas to resurrect it—an interactive CD-ROM or something similar—so my guess is that eventually it will come to life again.

CB: What have been your favorite live Phish experiences?

TM: The Clifford Ball was unforgettable—that and *The White Album* Halloween as well. I think the music outdid the spectacle and all expectations and hype. Runners-up for me are the Atlanta Halloween when they played *Remain in Light*, and New Years 1995 in the Garden.

CB: You're a front-man in your own jam band (Amfibian). Do you enjoy improvising?

TM: I do, but playing is definitely not one of my strong points. I basically punch chords and loosen up slightly when I'm not singing. After 4 shows or so I felt like I was improving a bit on the jam side of things. The other guys in the band are real pros and I was the weak link as far as chops are concerned. We structured the songs and the jamming in ways that could work despite this—so that I wasn't absolutely pivotal in the jams—and I felt that as we got more and more comfortable playing, that aspect of Amfibian wasn't a big hang-up for us.

CB: You cautioned fans not to expect Phish when they come to see your band. Judging by audience reactions, do you think the caveat got through?

TM: Not really. Of course we were expecting some curiosity from Phish fans, but I was worried about giving the impression of jumping on Phish's coattails. As a new band, I felt we grew way too fast, and to a degree that the band as a whole began to look at Amfibian as a commercial venture. Here we were having played in public about five times, and headlining at the Wetlands on a Saturday night. It didn't make sense to me. I basically broke the band up and stopped answering phone calls from tons of club owners who wanted to book us. On one hand it seems silly, because we had it made! We could have just plugged away and gotten better and bigger, etc. Why turn your back on success? It's a big no-no in the entertainment field to let the hype die down; to not keep your web page updated and to turn down offers to play. But it was exactly what I wanted to do—kill the hype. If we ever play again, it's going to be at small parties and tiny clubs on weeknights until we get really good. I don't want to be in the position of headlining for 500 people again and feeling like we're not ready and we don't deserve it.

CB: Do you bring anything from your Bearsville experiences into your own studio sessions?

TM: At Bearsville, I was very interested in the recording process. I think I learned studio techniques and stuff like that, but for the most part I was there to party and hang. My studio sessions are completely unlike Phish's sessions in every way. First of all at my studio, different musicians show up each weekend. Secondly, I don't have a deadline, or even a concrete project in mind—I just like writing and recording stuff. In fact, the Amfibian album idea was scrapped when it became apparent that we weren't really a band anymore. So it's just been an open-door, "come and play" kind of vibe. Whether Amfibian will rise out of the swamp again or not, no one really knows. We've talked about starting up again, but nothing really has come of it. I think we're all on the same page now, though, regarding our "mission", which is good. And I think this winter we're going to actually start a practice schedule again,

which is a good sign. But unless Ween asks us to open for them, which is the one thing that we've all agreed we would say yes to, I'm not sure when or if Amfibian will venture too far away from central New Jersey.

CB: You mentioned that you read a lot. Books? Magazines? Bathroom walls?

CB: You mentioned that you read a lot. Books? Magazines? Bathroom walls?

TM: Books! Currently, I'm re-reading *One Flew Over the Cuckoo's Nest,* by Ken Kesey. Seeing the movie is no reason not to read the book. I really like to think that the proceeds funded the Merry Pranksters' pranks. I also really got into *Hannibal* by Thomas Harris—it's the sequel to *The Silence of the Lambs.* It is an unbelievably eerie, horrifying novel that has been haunting me since it came out. I also recently read *The Endurance,* named after the ship in which Sir Ernest Shackleton attempted to reach Antarctica, and then cross it on foot in 1915. Unfortunately, 100 miles from land, the ship was frozen in pack ice and crushed. At that point, it became a survival story. The ship's photographer captured all of this. He'd taken about 200 pictures of the entire adventure and had to dive into ice water to rescue the negatives as the ship was sinking. This is a traveling museum exhibit also, and it's currently in New York City.

CB: Any favorite movies?

TM: The Godfather (I and II), Apocalypse Now, and Full Metal Jacket, to name a few.

CB: What do you perceive as the relationship between words and music? How is that perception evolving?

TM: I like that you used the word "evolving" in that question. I enjoy thinking back to man's earliest ancestors and how language was created as they evolved. I think music evolved next to and in conjunction with language, the primary instruments being voice and rhythm. So music drew upon language. But even while it encompassed and surpassed language, words were necessary for survival and progress, while music was a luxury, a means of celebration or relaxation. I think that is still essentially true today; music is a higher form of language, if you will. It sets our species apart from others. Do birds sing just for the fun of it, or are they wired to sing as part of a mating ritual or something?

CB: Interesting question. We like to think language helps us communicate with specificity, but what if that bird's simple song communicates meaning as purely and specifically as any sentence we can construct, and we're just so "advanced" that we can't see it anymore?

TM: Exactly. We hear it and think, "oh, a bird, how pretty," but really it's a specific message for a precise species of bird. All other birds know how to ignore it. Our language hasn't even gotten there yet.

CB: For lack of a better word, you seem to be more comfortable writing "serious" material in the last few years. Is that conscious choice, or natural progression?

TM: A little of both. I mean, I still write a lot of weird nonsense, but as it's ultimately Trey who thumbs through my material, perhaps he is drawn more to the serious stuff lately. That's not to say I don't put more effort and thought into the songs these days. I do. I just cringe nowadays when I hear some of the older songs—I feel like they were part of an era that has past, especially the extremely silly ones. I frankly would rather hear the words to "Dirt" or "Velvet Sea" than those from "Chalkdust" or "Cavern". I still like the songs; I just wish that perhaps Trey or I had put just a little more thought into the editing process back

then.

CB: Strange that you lump "Chalkdust" in with your "silly" songs. I think it communicates a predicament and a mood really well without clubbing it over the head. People relate.

TM: I know. It's a fan favorite, which is really nice, but I think it would have been a lot better if we pulled out the "vasoconstrictors" line. It could be something very similar, but the way it's used is just wrong, and it's the type of word that doesn't allow you to get by it easily in the song. A couple of other things that would have changed probably would have been "flagon of rice" and "locust the lurker," although I suppose that off-beat, eye-opening stuff has a place in certain songs. I'm just uncomfortable listening to it lately.

CB: Those tongue twisters always strike me as riffs. Their consonance and rhythm are so organic to the music that if you let go of your preconceptions, it doesn't matter whether they mean anything literally.

TM: Cool. But I think assuming people will let go of their preconceptions is asking a lot, especially of those who write reviews! They seem to want "Love Theme from the Titanic", or something equally instantaneously digestible.

CB: What are your favorite Phish songs?

TM: At a show, I tend to want to hear the newest stuff—something I haven't heard before—to gauge the audience's acceptance maybe, or just to hear Phish's arrangement. "Bug" was cool to hear. Since it never really caught on with the other Phish guys after Trey and I wrote it in 1997, it kind of became Amfibian's signature tune . . . then Phish rediscovered it and it turned out to be the perfect Phish song. I thought so anyway. I really liked "Meat" for a while—I think I am in the minority on that one, but I think it rocks. I still never tire of "Halley's," "Punch," and "Sloth," though; I'd have to say those are my unchanging favorites.

CB: Do you have a favorite Phish album?

TM: I still think Billy Breathes holds together the best, but it only narrowly edges out Rift for me. Billy Breathes is the one I recommend to new listeners, and it is the one that stays in my changer continually.

CB: Billy Breathes always felt to me like a turning point for Phish, I guess largely because of those simpler song forms. Is the era of songs like Guyute and Reba is in the past?

TM: That, I think, is also a function of evolution in a way. Complexity and acrobatics in music often can't hold a candle to a simple, powerful song. I have to point to The Beatles—"Something" or "Hey Jude". Those are all about melody and not at all about fancy chord changes or time signatures. Like I said, though, I love "Sloth" and "Punch" and all the crazy stuff that goes on musically there. Perhaps there's a sense of been-there-done-that for Trey. Maybe it's reverse evolution.

CB: It's interesting that you mentioned the Beatles. I read an interview with Trey recently in which he said, roughly, that Phish was trying to find out if they had an "Abbey Road" in them. That's my favorite album of all time for many reasons, one of which is that as different as the songs are, the whole thing feels like one long, mighty song. It's so cohesive.

TM: Trey has had "Abbey Road" in his head for a long time as a perfect album. He likes the 20 minutes per side thing. I think he still mourns the passing of the two-side concept from LP's. I personally like the long albums. I'm a proponent of filling up the CD with the full 74 minutes. I also love liner notes, but Trey feels like they get in the way of the music.

CB: I love liner notes, but I think I know what Trey means. They don't usually encourage listeners to use their imaginations.

TM: There is something pure about putting on a CD for the first time, not knowing what to expect, not reading about it, just listening. You can have that first experience once, however, after which reading liner notes or lyrics only helps me to continue enjoying it.

CB: Do you and the band feel pressure from fans not to change – to remain Good Ole Phish?

TM: I don't feel that pressure. The band might, I suppose. I do stay away from the negative subjects discussed on the Phish.net, though, because then I might feel like I had to respond. Like, the "Trey sucks now, is he on cocaine?" kind of thing. As a fan, I find that their constant change keeps things fresh and exciting, and they can always revert to old Phish when they want to. I don't buy into the rehash-the-past crap. Forge onward. Change is built into the band.

CB: Do you ever find that when you set out to say one thing, or even nothing at all, you wind up saying something else entirely? Happy accidents, so to speak?

TM: Constantly. I rarely sit down and say what the song is going to be about. I'll often begin writing by putting down a line that I've been repeating in my head for a while. In many cases the finished product doesn't even contain that line—or it's been severely altered. For example, "Wolfman's Brother" was about an ocean voyage at first—I think only the "ship that's run aground" line was salvaged from the original. Sometimes you have to let it flow rather than steer it. That's how I avoid writer's block, too . . . I guess I'm lucky and don't have to write, which makes a huge difference. I'm not feeding my family on my words. Actually, I am, but they'd still eat if I stopped writing for a six-month stretch, you know? I'd just have to return the BMW, is all.

CB: A whole cottage industry has sprung up around writer's block – how to beat it, what it means. Maybe it means you just don't have anything to say.

TM: In most cases I'd say you're absolutely correct. How awful, though, to sit down and stare at the proverbial blank page. I guess I'm lucky and don't have to write, which makes a huge difference. I'm not feeding my family on my words. Actually, I am, but they'd still eat if I stopped writing for a six-month stretch, you know? I'd just have to return the BMW, is all.

CB: Why not an old, funky Benz? Something with a little more character.

TM: I don't like the old, funky shit. I have an M3. It laughs at cars with character.

CB: What's the strangest interaction you've ever had with a fan?

TM: I don't fit into the standard Phishhead profile. I don't wear the hippie uniform, the hair's all wrong, and I'm about 15 years older than the average fan. They usually think I'm security or something, and ask me where to park. I always tell them, by the way. I find a special place for them.

CB: Can you describe the feeling of hearing your words put to music?

TM: I think of it as the third life for a poem. Most poems get written and exist on a piece of paper somewhere. The second life for a lucky poem is when it gets put to music. The third life is when it actually makes the final cut and becomes a Phish song. That's amazing when

it happens. Most recently, I was blown away when Del McCoury and his band played "Get Back on the Train" at Oswego. That poem had four lives, actually, because it was a "Trey-band song" for a while, too. I still think Oswego was the coolest version I've heard yet, though.

CB: Let's dive into some of your other work. "Lifeboy" seems to be a satirical poke at religion-as-crutch. What was your religious background as a kid?

TM: I was kind of anti-religion for a while. Not because it was imposed heavily on me as a child or anything like that—in fact, I was brought up religion-free, and as such I guess I just kind of landed on the "science" side of the argument. Worshipping an invisible ghost and using it to explain away nature's mysteries didn't make much sense to me. I mean, before people knew what thunder was, they thought the gods were angry with them. I will say that I'm pretty spiritual, though, in many ways. I had my own religion in my head, I guess. But I found it easy to make fun of any organized religion growing up, and really enjoyed sticking it to any overly fervent, born-again Jesus freaks I encountered. I think I've finally grown out of that phase. I think the values and teachings one can be exposed to in church are, for the most part, harmless. In many cases, they're wonderful—and certainly not something to ridicule in these days of school shootings and loss of morality and responsibility. I was surprised to see my sister who lives in San Diego get involved with the Unitarian Church recently with her family, and was touched to learn about how they help the poor in their community. Church isn't for me, I don't think, but the overall goodness and selfless vibe that Jesus taught is obviously something I want my kids to learn as well . . . albeit without all the God and guilt rap. I'll give them sermons from the *Helping Friendly Book,* I suppose. That'll send them over the edge.

CB: "Icculus is coming, and he is pissed."

TM: I don't think the world needs another angry, vengeful god. How about, "Icculus is coming, and he's giving out office supplies." Gods never do cool shit like that anymore.

CB: Maybe that was on the tablet Moses broke "Thou shalt not keep a cluttered workspace." If you could write the eleventh commandment, what would it be?

TM: "Thou shalt ignore all prior commandments and think for thineself, thou weak-minded sheep!"

CB: "Limb by Limb" feels like a song about a painful relationship— fairly deep stuff. Then along comes a line like "tossed with the salad and baled with the hay." What gives?

TM: You don't consider getting tossed with the salad and baled with the hay painful? What kind of dressing do you use? I was thinking of a lemon-pepper vinaigrette.

CB: "Julius" works nicely if you think of it as the story of a guy who grossly overestimates the time he has left in life. Or is it just a song about whipped orange drink?

TM: Like the kind John Candy offered in "The Blues Brothers"? I love that movie. No—it's not really about Orange Whips. It's loosely about Caesar, but John Popper explained to me that I got some facts wrong. I told him I didn't think there were any facts in the song.

CB: Popper's a closet historian?

TM: I'm not sure what goes on in his closet. But I'd imagine that there are handguns involved.

CB: The mentions of olfactory hues in "Lawn Boy"—smelling col-

ors and such—sound an awful lot like veiled references to psychedelic synesthesia.

TM: Umm...I don't know. It's about my back yard, in a way.

CB: "Birds of a Feather" has been appropriated by certain factions of the Phish community as a dig on, well, everyone else but themselves. Poetic irony, or is everyone missing the point?

TM: I hate assigning a meaning. That's never what I want to do. People often come up to me and ask what a particular song is about— and the primary reason they do this is because they want to see if my meaning matches the one they've come up with. Now, if I went and told you that "Birds" is about a dog I saw chasing a bus, chances are you'd be disappointed because you thought I was equating the audience with a flock of unruly birds and making a statement about stardom and the pressures of fame. Why would I want to tell you you're wrong? You're right! It's about what it makes you think of.

CB: Where does that impulse to define art come from, to know the artist's specific intent? Is it just discomfort with ambiguity?

TM: Maybe, but it could also be simple curiosity; wanting to know what an artist who creates something you like was up to at the time. I mean, knowing that Edgar Allen Poe was a poor, Philadelphia alcoholic who died on the street shouldn't affect me as I'm reading his poetry, but I confess it's on my mind.

CB: Umm...wasn't Poe from Baltimore?

TM: Who are you now, John Popper? I guess another example would be that Van Gogh's ear thing. Stories like that humanize the artist and help people answer the "how did they come up with that" question.

CB: Interesting example. If you had to lop off one appendage for your art, what would it be?

TM: Who's to say I already haven't?

CB: What do you think of the "Siket Disc?"

TM: Oh, you mean "One Band's Trash?" Sorry—that's a cool disc. I like those jams—studio jams edited for your listening pleasure. What a cool band to release stuff like that, you know? What's the point of critiquing it other than to say, "keep doing stuff like this, guys!"

CB: Any songs from that collection you'd like to put words to?

TM: Some of them did have words. "What's the Use" was so named because of that lyric... which was later removed for your convenience, apparently.

CB: What was it like to watch Phil Lesh & Friends perform your songs alongside those timeless Garcia/Hunter collaborations like "Saint Stephen" and "Uncle John's Band"?

TM: That was great. I liked seeing the real old Deadheads getting into it as well.

CB: Ever had a chance to talk to Robert Hunter?

TM: We've exchanged email on a couple of occasions. I'd like to get something like that going again. He's a very interesting person and obviously has insight into situations that I'm encountering, although I'd rather talk about writing next time rather than the biz. That was my fault.

CB: In his book _Box of Rain_, he explains that he and Garcia wrote the words and music to "Terrapin Station" one night while they were watching lightning flash over San Francisco—from two different places.

TM: That's awesome! "Brian and Robert" is my favorite example of a song that just sprang from the ether like that. Trey and I were in a rented farmhouse, hanging out and doing nothing but writing. So much writing, in fact, that I was getting itchy to just sit down and watch TV or

something to allow my brain to heal. Trey kept finding reasons to continue working. Finally, he gave up and sat down at the piano, acknowledging at last that I was leaving the room towards the television. He just started playing the chords to "Brian and Robert", and it sounded a lot like Brian Eno to me. Trey urged me, "Tom, just press record, and sing something to this." So I just sang a poem I had written earlier. After Trey added the Robert Fripp guitar drone, we had another song! It took about five minutes. That's one of our favorites, but what is most ironic is that it has the "longing for your TV seat" line in it—and if I had gone and watched TV, the song wouldn't exist. It makes me wonder how many other songs we didn't write because of a simple walk to the fridge for a beer.

CB: Your guest appearances with Phish are the stuff of rock and roll legend. How do you find the emotional core of a song like "Champagne Supernova?" Do you imagine an exploding star with, like, champagne squirting out of it? Did you actually walk 500 miles, then 500 more?

TM: Those songs were selected as jokes the audience would get right away. Embarrassingly, I've actually come to like them more than is healthy, perhaps. "Shine" by Collective Soul has to be my favorite still, although I must admit they have slipped somewhat in terms of my esteem for them when they opened for The Cranberries at the E-Center in Camden. I went backstage to say hello to my longtime friend Dean Roland, and he pretended he'd never heard of me. It was a low point for me. I haven't actually recovered from that shock yet.

CB: One day at a time, man. Aside from Dean Roland and the rest of Collective Soul, who are your heroes?

TM: Peter Gabriel, Brian Eno, Robert Fripp, David Byrne, Page/Plant, Lennon/McCartney, CSN&Y...there are too many.

CB: Fans harvest lines from your songs for bumper stickers and t-shirts ("Control for smilers can't be bought," etc.). If you were a Phishhead, what Zen-like Marshall nuggets would we find on your VW Microbus or Beefy-T?

TM: I like taking "lick the coil" out of context and offering it as advice.

CB: You know, there are dozens of Marshall imitators in the jam band scene. What would you recommend for a young hack who wanted to bite your style?

TM: I'd like to find one of those, or perhaps just have one pointed out to me. I would say write a lot and often. I don't think anyone's actually trying to imitate my style, though. It's too personal. It was arrived at by summing up all my life experiences and subtracting the year I lived in Pittsburgh.

CB: Uh-oh. You just started a firestorm of speculation about "The Lost Pittsburgh Songs."

TM: Oh, boy. They should stay lost. I'm more concerned about the "Lost Pittsburgh People" I hung out with. Where's Tom Seidel, for example? I imagine he'd be a Phish fan, but who knows?

CB: What's your favorite Dr. Seuss story?

TM: Probably that foot book, because that's my daughter's favorite right now. Trey gave it to her.

CB: Who's your favorite Muppet?

TM: Does Elmo count? I'm not familiar with the muppets other than the ones that appear on Sesame Street. Elmo or Ernie.

CB: Who's your favorite Superfriend?

TM: I must admit I'm more familiar with the cast of "Friends" than I am with the Superfriends. I liked one of the babes in a hormonal way, but I forget what her deal was. I could never fantasize too well about cartoons. Jamie Sommers was another matter entirely, though. How did this subject come up again?

CB: Who would win in a fight—Guyute or Pokemon?

TM: Uh...well, Pokemon translates to "pocket monster," and Guyute is, of course, and ugly pig. I would think Guyute would win hands down because he is willing to actually dance on people, and not just cower in somebody's pocket.

CB: Have you ever written a song to someone?

TM: All my songs are for Jesus.

Tom Marshall, Part B

Interviewed by Charlie Dirksen (and others) via email in March of 2000.

Charlie Dirksen: For those who aren't aware, how and when did Amfibian begin?

Tom Marshall: It began as a band called Utalk, with me, Trey, Peter Cottone on drums, and Matt Kohut on bass. We're all friends from Princeton Day School—back in the '70s/'80s. Matt, Pete, and I began practicing various songs that Trey and I wrote in anticipation of a Utalk tour. Those songs were "Dirt," "Farmhouse," "Twist Around," "Bug," and "Heavy Things," among others. Then, after an abortive practice session with Trey up in Vermont, which spelled the end of Utalk, the New Jersey side of the band decided to keep the dream alive. We added a few new musicians and changed the name to Amfibian.

CD: Why do you say the practice session was "abortive"? Were things just not gelling?

TM: Pretty much. Trey had a friend come up to play second guitar in the band, and we all just didn't find a groove, I guess. It was pretty discouraging for all of us, but it made sense at the same time.

CD: How did you meet the other musicians on "Amfibian Tales"?

TM: Pete and Matt and I go way back. So do Marc Daubert and I. Aside from that, everyone on the disk I've met through the local [Princeton, NJ]{change from parens to brackets ok?} music scene. JP Wasicko and Scott Metzger came from Matt's band, F-Hole. Andrew Southern I met at PDS [Princeton Day School]—he's a recent graduate. Anna Soloway and Steph Sanders [The Saras singers]{change from parens to brackets ok?} also are from PDS. That's the main core—there are a few others whom I've met along the way.

CD: Who thought of the fishy name "Amfibian"? It's exceedingly clever. And thank god you spell it improperly with an "f".

TM: An exceedingly clever friend of mine, John Furth, came up with that when he and I were attempting to write a book which was loosely about me—and a band I had (not yet) formed.

CD: Given your experiences over the years working close to the production of Phish's recordings, what distinguishes "Amfibian Tales" from that production?

TM: Wow. Everything. Actually, this is probably a lot closer to Trey's "One Man's Trash" than any Phish release. This wasn't done in a big studio—it was all done in my tiny farm studio. I produced it there and Andrew Southern and I mixed it and then he mastered it. It's a very small-scale studio, based around a single DA-88 digital 8-track unit.

Craig DeLucia: In that vein, how much time have you spent watch-

ing Phish and/or other bands in the studio, and how did it affect your approach to the recording process?

TM: Well, before Phish, and in conjunction with Phish's projects, this method is something that Trey and I have used for several years: sequestering ourselves in a farmhouse with a DA-88. That's how most of the new Phish songs were written, and how all of these "Amfibian Tales" songs were written.

Craig: Given that some of the songs on Phish's upcoming "Farmhouse" album are partly your compositions, did you make a decision to exclude those songs from your album? Or other songs you've written that Phish plays extensively? ("Bug" and "Heavy Things" come to mind.)

TM: Not really. I mean, that wasn't our thinking process. We just wrote new stuff. None of the songs on "Amfibian Tales" has been performed live yet. Trey's name does appear as writer for one song, "Nothing," which he and I wrote on my farm two years ago. But I don't think it was ever considered by Phish.

Craig: Was any consideration given to including older songs that you've written, like putting your own spin on "It's Ice" or any number of older songs that you wrote for Phish?

TM: No. These are all original compositions. Amfibian the band would certainly consider Trey/Tom songs as fair game for live performances, though, but I doubt that we'd focus on any Phish staples.

Craig: You've been writing songs for so long now. What made you choose to release some of your work now?

TM: It was kind of a timing thing. I started spending a lot of time on my farm recently, and the songs just happened naturally. People would stop by and we'd record. Eventually I needed to do something with them so I could move forward. Just listening to them once a week didn't satisfy my urge to get them out somehow.

CD: I miss farms. My great aunt and uncle used to own a modest and old horse farm in the Lexington, Kentucky, area, and I have fond memories of roaming the fields and barns and woods. I love the smell of manure. The smell of manure reminds me of vacations that I used to take as a child to Kentucky, just as the smell of patchouli oil mixed with wookie body odor reminds me fondly of being on tour with the Dead or Phish. Do you have any animals on your farm?

TM: There is the memory of animals. The way the barns are designed all reflect the fact that they once housed cows and sheep and pigs. But ever since my grandmother and grandfather moved in around 1930, they adapted all the buildings for human use and leased the fields to a local farmer, whose son and grandson still farm it today.

Craig: How was "Amfibian Tales" recorded? Is it mostly "live-in-studio" tracks, or solo instrument tracks with successive overdubs?

TM: It's a mixture of both. "Dream Satellite" was recorded with all of Amfibian playing live, for example. "Sleep as It Grows," on the other hand, was built track by track. Although, even on an entirely overdubbed song, the basic first part of the track is often done with two people playing their parts simultaneously—which imparts something of a performance vibe into the track.

Craig: Was most of the material written before you entered the studio or while the sessions were in progress?

TM: All songs were primarily written in session.

Craig: What did you find most difficult about the recording process?

TM: Deciding what should and should not go on the final disk. The Internet makes that decision slightly easier because the songs that get cut can still be released as MP3s, which we plan to do.

Craig: How hard was it to "let go" and decide that a particular song, or the album as a whole, was "done"?

TM: Since there was only a self-imposed deadline, it was extremely difficult. We kept adding songs and wanting to fix the old ones.

Craig: Is this a one-shot or a possible ongoing project?

TM: Oh, definitely an ongoing thing. I'm upgrading my studio as we speak and can't wait to get back in. I'm also hoping to have Trey down for some Phish writing soon. We've also been doing a lot of work with Chris Harford, another local musician/producer, and that looks really hopeful. We're thinking perhaps of an Amfibian/Harford disk—"Live in the Barn," or something like that. Check out Chris's stuff at http://www.chrisharford.com/. Matt and JP are the rhythm section on most of his beautiful new disk, "Wake."

CD: Any plans for an Amfibian tour to support the album? Or in the future?

TM: We're talking about it and playing a lot lately, so it's a distinct possibility. A co-tour with The Saras and Chris Harford might be in the works too. There's a cool music scene going on here and it would be silly not to jump in.

Craig: We've seen the effect that the Phish fan community can have on the tours and live shows of other artists, from the influx of Phishheads to the MMW scene, to Son Seals recent "thank you" for our support. How has this affected Amfibian?

TM: Well, I'll put it this way: I think ninety-nine percent or more of our audience for the five shows we played were Phishheads wondering what the hell Amfibian was all about.

Craig: Some of your most memorable Phish moments on stage have been as gags and jokes. Do you worry that fans won't take your album or band seriously, since you're the "Tubthumping" guy or the "Shine" guy to many people who may not realize your lyrical contributions to Phish?

TM: No, I'm not really concerned. Funny, serious, who cares?

CD: Do you remember what you were thinking just before you went on stage for the "500 Miles" bit in the 12/30/97 Harpua? I busted a gut at that.

TM: Yeah—I was nervous as hell, as usual, before I got on stage. I was probably thinking that I wish I knew Harpua better so I'd know when to go on . . .

Phillip Zerbo: Your performances with Phish have always placed you in the role of the "front man in a glam rock band" (Roger Daltrey, Bruce Springsteen) or as the "straight man in an inside joke" (Shine, 500 Miles, Champagne Supernova), both very extroverted personas. Your "stage presence" in the performances with Amfibian are much more "restrained," almost introverted. What's up with that?

TM: Well, for Amfibian's shows I was sitting behind a keyboard, actually pressing down on the keys now and then! This restrained me I suppose. But, boy, did I want to go and throw a stage dive now and then.

PZ: Do you pay attention to any fan reviews? What do you think of them? Do you perceive them differently when they are reviews of Amfibian, or reviews of songs you have written performed by Phish?

TM: I read them. I found them mostly positive. Phish song reviews I can distance myself from slightly, unless they're specifically about the

lyrics. Amfibian reviews I couldn't step back from and insert another person between myself and the reviewer. In that sense, I took them rather personally and was happy to find that people in general just had a good time at Amfibian, and didn't slice and dice each aspect of the show like they do with Phish.

PZ: Has any element of a fan review or an interaction with any fan ever made its way into a lyric of a tune that Phish performs?

TM: Hmm . . . no, I don't think so. There are some aspects of the "scene" I suppose that creep in here and there, simply because it's such a large part of Phish and, consequently, my experience . . . from where I'm forced to draw inspiration.

CD: What about "A Thousand Barefoot Children Outside, Dancing on My Lawn"? Wasn't that lyric about Trey's "interaction"—so to speak—with fans on his lawn?

TM: I'd heard that too—about how he was renting a place at the Jersey shore, I think, and kids kept appearing while his family was eating dinner or something. That really did happen, but it also really had nothing to do with that lyric. I was thinking more of the Mann Music Center's back lawn seats, I think.

PZ: When you are at a Phish show, is there a line that you feel between being a "fan" and being a more active agent in the creative process, as it is happening on stage? Do you consider yourself a "fan" or is it something different?

TM: I'm a fan. I'm constantly reminded that there's something else there, like getting a knowing glance from someone, or recognizing an emotion behind a lyric or something. But for the most part, when I'm in the audience, I'm a fan.

CD: As a fan, then, do you ever find yourself going, "I wish they had jammed out that [name of tune] more"? Or "Man, if I hear Trey butcher Coil like that again . . ."? Or do you miraculously remain totally positive—and not in the least bit jaded—even after all these years?

TM: Ha! Well, I'm jaded in certain ways, I think. Like, it's very easy for a Phish show just to be a social event rather than a musical thing—so I might find myself talking over a song because I've heard it a lot, or spending too much time floating around backstage. But I think I remain positive about the music and let the band steer me where they want me to go.

CD: That's wonderful! I found that after heavily seeing shows for years, taking a break and only seeing a handful of shows in a given year really helped me appreciate everything more (again). It became easier to "let go my conscious self" and let go all of the history in my head and not try to "steer" the band. What do you like most about the Phish community? Or the scene? Is there anything about the Phish scene that really disturbs you?

TM: No—I can't really think of any aspect of the scene at large that bothers me specifically. It's completely the opposite, actually. I think there's a great give and take between the fans and the band that you don't find elsewhere. The band keeps the ticket prices relatively low and keeps the quality of the whole experience very high. The Phish fan community knows what a good thing they've got and strives to keep it that way by displaying a whole lot of courtesy and compassion and consideration for others. Walk out in the crowd and there's rarely anything behavior-wise to complain about. When you do hear something negative, it's the exception, not the rule, and that's great.

CD: Is there any special interaction that you've had with another fan

at a show that sticks out in your memory?

TM: Oh, the Benjy [Eisen] Uno card incident perhaps. He made a big spectacle out of giving me a card from some weird game I used to play in French class or something like that. I think it was at an MSG show. I refused the gift from him just because I thought there might be too much significance attached to his gesture. Later I learned that the Uno-card craze had been credited, or blamed, actually, on me!

PZ: A number of the songs on "Amfibian Tales" are co-authored by Amfibian's bass player, Matt Kohut. How is writing a song with Matt different than writing a song with Trey?

TM: Matt and I are newer at it. That's really all. We know each other very well, and that's really one of the big hurdles, I think. You need to know what to expect of the other person and where you fit into his/her method of writing. Matt has tons of musical ideas, as you can see by listening to F-Hole [http://www.f-hole.net/]{brackets rather than parens here ok?}, and can use lyrical help now and then—so it's perfect.

Mark Toscano: I'm a big fan of Ween. What do you think of Ween? I heard that Amfibian worships the ground that Ween shits on.

TM: Ugh. That's such a pleasant way to put it. Amfibian covered "Birthday Boy"—does that constitute worship? Matt also played bass for their "Golden Country Greats" tour. So, apart from some cross-pollination, there's no organized prayer group or anything. I do personally worship them, however—but in private, and in sanitary conditions.

CD: What would you say were Amfibian's primary musical influences, if any?

TM: Amfibian is a mix of 35-year-olds and 20-year-olds. I thought it was cool when the younger guys would bring in, say, a Steely Dan or King Crimson disc that we grew up on to play for us because they had heard it for the first time. That happened a lot. The influences are consequently across the board. On "Amfibian Tales" I think you'll hear some Tom Waits, some Band, some Beatles, some Phish perhaps?

Aaron Wolfe

Interviewed by Ellis Godard and Jay Kahn via email during August 2000. See also entry in Dictionary.

Ellis Godard and Jay Kahn: What do you remember most about Princeton Day School and the folks you went to school with?

Aaron Wolfe: Princeton was a pretty quiet, homogeneous place. But even then we knew that the suburbs created the best rock and roll. That's why we all took up the air guitar with such dedication.

EG and JK: What's your first memory of Tom Marshall?

AW: Tom could make me laugh without making a sound. And without moving. He would be perfectly still. Just standing there . . . and it was funny. Well, maybe he would move a little. Like a hair or a finger or something.

EG and JK: What do you remember of Marc Daubs Daubert?

AW: Daubs pushed boundaries in ways that were not appreciated enough. He was a break in the preppy, suburban paradigm that we lived in and brought life to our world. He was also really good at talking to adults.

EG and JK: Whatever happened to Bob Szuter?

AW: Bob was reverently mod, the brightest light in our nascent songwriting efforts, always tackling themes of social import, always acknowledging Pete Townshend. He also had a great jump shot. Bob, Tom,

and I played hoops together, inventing invisible opponents who were always called "The Multicolored Ceramics."

EG and JK: When did you first meet Trey?

AW: We both liked the same girl. She told us she couldn't decide which one to be with, but that we should know that there was another, distant competitor who she said she would just call "Mr. X." Finally one day she gathered Trey and me and told us to sit down. We waited. Then she made a solemn announcement. She was already going out with Mr. X.

Trey and I became friends and listened to Moby Grape records at his Dad's house.

EG and JK: Was he the biggest geek in school?

AW: Anybody that was into Moby Grape, Mountain, and Ten Years After in eighth grade is kind of exempt from geekdom.

EG and JK: What can you tell us about the Rhombus?

AW: Neither I, nor anyone I know, knows anything about this.

EG and JK: What's the earliest poem of Tom's that you remember reading or hearing?

AW: Tom and I formed an air guitar band called, unbelievably, "A dot Tom"—decades before the Internet and the assault of the "dot.coms." The songs were mostly adaptations of other people's songs. Neil Young's "Cinnamon Girl" was remade—without reason whatsoever—as "Michaelson Girl." Some were inspired by things we saw outside the windows of our Latin class.

EG and JK: What's the earliest lyric of Trey's that you remember reading or hearing?

AW: In those long ago days we used to love to repeat a line we found in an R. Crumb book, ". . . Surrender to the void, cloid." We liked making up songs that would be slow and then fast; start and stop. We would always blurt out a line when we were making up stuff back then and it's hard to connect what to who. Phonetics was key. "Ticket stub . . ." had a nice ring to it. But the first thing of Trey's that wasn't some burped utterance was the cassette he had made at Goddard College or Burlington. I listened to it. It started and stopped a lot. I liked that. I remember thinking it was ambitious.

EG and JK: When did you first see Trey in a performance, and what can you recall about it?

AW: The first performance I ever saw by Trey was probably a hockey game. Hockey was unfathomable to me. But musically there were countless performances that we would create for each other in parking lots, back rooms of parties. Parents' tables would be left pockmarked by the rhythmic beating of spoons. But I don't think it was until many years later that I actually saw Trey play in front of anyone besides friends. It wasn't until a show he played with Phish at Madison Square Garden that I really—as an audience member—got to see him play music. It was amazing. The place was full of people. I was strangely nervous for the band. Just because it was the first time I'd seen them it felt like it was their first show. When they went on stage they seemed so calm. It was an utterly surreal experience.

EG and JK: How did Trey change (musically or otherwise) in and then after high school?

AW: I remember thinking when he quit playing drums—I think he even sold his drums to devote time to guitar—I remember thinking, in a hesitant, conservative moment, "I hope that's a wise decision." Guess it was a wise decision.

EG and JK: What ya been doin' with your life?

AW: I'm a documentary filmmaker.

EG and JK: What do you do for fun?

AW: I like to play music for fun.

EG and JK: Do you listen to much Phish these days?

AW: Now and then. I'm always interested in how they evolve and in what they're going to do next.

EG and JK: What other music are you into?

AW: Bluegrass, Cuban, and high seventies camp resonate, but my softest spot still is for garage-built psychedelia from, say, 1965–1972.

EG and JK: What other bands would you like to have been in on the ground floor of?

AW: Velvet Underground.

EG and JK: Do you still have the black Les Paul that you had in college? Do you still play it?

AW: Yes, I have it. No, I don't play it. But I can't sell it. I almost always play acoustic now. I just bought a pedal steel. It looks nice in the living room. Sounds great too. But it may go the way of the Les Paul .

Dave Abrahams

Interviewed by Charlie Dirksen via email throughout 1998 and 1999. See also entry in Dictionary.

Charlie Dirksen: When and where did you first see Phish play?

Dave Abrahams: It was at a bar in Burlington, Hunt's, I think. Year? Aeons ago—mid '80s. There may have been two such early concerts I went to; I can't recall. At the time Marc Daubert was living in Burlington; I don't know if that helps you pin it down at all. I went up with Tom to visit Trey and Marc. I remember that there were some people sitting at tables around the outside of the room. Pretty much the entire dance floor was available, so I took full advantage. Trey still talks about the time I ran towards the stage, dropped to my knees, and slid with my hands hosannah in the air for one of his solos. I think in those days a little audience participation was extra welcome. I also remember some woman talking to her friend on the phone at the back of the room about the upcoming act (Phish) saying, "I don't know; it's some Grateful Dead cover band," so you can see that they were already getting stuck with an inaccurate label in those days. At least one of these shows involved two guys from an R&B/reggae band, much bigger than Phish, who showed up and took over the stage, hijacking Mike's bass and driving the music in their own particular aggressive direction. After watching the reggae guy play his three well-executed, but ultimately uninteresting two-note bass riffs for an hour and a half, Mike was heard to say sardonically, "Well, at least I learned some reggae bass lines."

CD: When did you first meet Trey?

DA: We were in school together for a few years, you know, but I don't know if we ever really communicated much until he went away to Taft. When he came back for the summer as a rhythm guitarist for Space Antelope, our mutual interest in music drew us together. One personal interaction stands out in my mind, though. When we were in 8th grade, there was a sort of class camping trip. Trey was still a drummer then, and hadn't started playing guitar yet. During one of the free periods, I wandered up on a little huddle of guys listening to a cassette on a boombox. It was Steve Howe, playing "The Clap." When I heard the free way he seemed to be playing, I was blown away. "My God" I ex-

claimed, "he's just improvising!" Trey shot back, "Shut up, he's great!" Rather than try to explain what I meant I just sat there in silence, taking in the music's twists and turns. Learning to play that tune would become one of my proudest early achievements on the guitar.

CD: Does it bother you when people take Phish too seriously? It must amuse you that some folks still wonder why it matters that someone looks too much like Dave. They want to be in on the joke.

DA: It doesn't bother me, but there has been an amazing amount of meaning read into things that were written just because they sounded silly, or just because the words bounced off each other in a particular way. But if someone can find religious meaning in "McGrupp," well then I'm happy for him. I do want people to understand what an incredible amount of (constructive) idiocy all of us got away with, only sometimes in the name of art. I hope that people will be inspired (and I mean moved to act) by Trey's boundless enthusiasm for making something, and his undefeatable conviction that it's going to turn out great.

CD: It seems to me that most people—not necessarily Phish fans—would rather share in the groove than make the effort, and take the risk, to create their own. Everyone has the potential to be creative, of course, and everyone is creative in some way, shape, or form, but listening is an objectively passive (but subjectively active) activity after all. I certainly hope people learn from Trey's example.

DA: One way in which this came up with Trey was when I saw him backstage one night, and he told me a bunch of phans wanted to find the rhombus. He said that people had written to him, and they really wanted to know where it was; it was a kind of pious impulse on their part to go visit it. He asked me if I thought he should tell them. His first reaction was that it was a bad idea. He was thinking of gangs of kids defiling the place with graffiti or something, but he said the people that were writing to him seemed pretty thoughtful and sincere. Even so, I said that other people visiting the rhombus was somehow missing the point. "They should make up their own mythology," I offered. Trey really keyed into that point. I remember him saying "that's exactly right."

Tom and Marc and I found this place and made it meaningful. Trey became a part of that story through shared experience. I'm a huge fan of many other artists and musicians, but we have our own magical experiences which are deeper than any kind of contact with the people I'm a fan of could be. I think, ultimately, many fans are trying to access that kind of personal magical experience, but don't know it. For these people, sole pursuit of Phish or anyone else's creative juice is forever unsatisfying.

CD: I believe that a lot of fans do get "it" and share in the magic, hence why they spend lots of money to see every show they can wherever and whenever they can. They want to be a part of the Experience, to share in the Joy. Which is great. But at the same time, the most intense magic is that which you create yourself. I bet that Trey would say that the "audience" helps create "the magic" of course, and I'd obviously agree.

DA: Yes, he would. And it's a great attitude to have.

CD: But there's a big difference, in my opinion, between helping to create magic as part of the Herd, and creating it as an individual will.

DA: Being in the audience and participating in the show is a totally authentic way to be a part of it. I do worry when people start trying to connect with the artist on a more personal level; to capture some part of the artist's personal experience to the exclusion of, or as a replacement for, their own creativity.

CD: There's a "Bivouac Jaun" tape that has been circulating, which appears to feature you, Trey, Tom, and Marc Daubert on a few tunes. What was "Jaun" all about? I've heard that "Bivouac" was the name of a band—Marc, Trey, and Tom—but where did you fit in?

DA: For the most part, I didn't. Tom, Trey, and Marc all coincidentally took some time off from college at the same time. While I was away at school in Philly, they were getting busy. I had a really hard time with it, because Tom and Marc had been my steadfast creative partners and because the product was so good. Trey had blossomed into a brilliant guitarist in a very short period of time (I had been playing at least twice as long). I was lucky enough to be able to participate a bit on some weekend visit home or maybe a Thanksgiving break. That's what you hear on the tape.

CD: How well do you know the members of Phish other than Trey?

DA: I'm friendly with everyone, since I first met them over ten years ago and have seen them regularly since then. We say hi when we run into each other backstage; I'm sure you can imagine how it is.

CD: I can imagine it, but what is it "like" backstage, anyway? Care to de-mythologize it at all? Most people reading this interview probably have not had the privilege of being at an "aftershow" or, for that matter, in any of the even more privileged backstage areas. I imagine that unless you already knew people backstage, had friends backstage who you wanted to hang out with, then it wouldn't be nearly as much fun as the lot scene post-show.

DA: It's more like an obstacle course of oversized rusty buzz-saws than anything else. There is, as you describe, a hierarchy of privileged areas, with the band, family members, and staff (and anyone else who has managed to scam or grovel for an all-access pass) occupying the most protected area. Often the band will not venture beyond this border. There are plenty of polite but firm security personnel who don't know you from Adam whose duty it is to keep the borders sealed. Usually my only reason to be backstage is to spend a couple of minutes catching up with old friends. Unless Trey happens to venture into the greater mob and I am lucky enough to catch his eye, I slink away unrewarded. Can you tell how excited I am about the backstage scene?

CD: Sure! What were your musical influences growing up? What instruments did you play? What's "Andback"?

DA: Andback is the name of a band founded by Marc Daubert, Tom Marshall, and me in about 1980.

On my thirteenth birthday my brother got an electric guitar. We had just returned from summer vacation in Colorado where my dad had a regular position at the Aspen Center for Physics, and our house was in an unlivable condition. The renovations, which were supposed to be finished while we were away, had taken longer than expected. We were camped out in the architect's (also unfinished) place of residence and my parents were obviously stressed. As the elder son, I was expected to be mature and understanding that my birthday celebration would be postponed . . . but somehow Jonathan got an electric guitar, that very day. I don't remember what I got for my birthday that year, but I do remember that guitar. I remember asking an experienced guitarist who was babysitting my brother to teach me a song from a Bee-Gees songbook. Wisely, I think, he refused.

My parents were open-minded classical music heads and had actually bought copies of a few other things like *Quadrophenia* and one of the more unlistenable Zappa albums ("Lumpy Gravy") at the urging of

friends. I discovered these after exhausting my appetite for the steady diet of Beatles music which had been available to me. Another great album which I listened to as a kid was an electronic version of "Peter and the Wolf." It featured, among others, members of Brand X and the incredible Stephane Grapelli.

My brother later decided he liked acoustic guitar better, and when he finally lost interest in that I had two guitars. I tried to play everything I could lay my hands on in those days. The next summer I hung around in a Colorado music store obsessively playing all their guitars and trying to soak up some of the bluegrass picking that was the local lingua franca . . . until the owner politely suggested that I exercise a few of my other interests, elsewhere.

I had no serious ideas about writing music until a few years later. One day in gym class I heard Tom Marshall and Marc Daubert practicing a harmony: "Moons, moons/ sons of moons/ die in dark hallways," they sang. It sounded cool, but I didn't recognize the song. Excited, I asked them what it was. "Andback", Tom said. When they told me that Andback was the name of their band, I was incredulous at first, then blown away. At the time it was more of a songwriting project than a band, but it wasn't long before they asked me to join them and we got something going. Tom had a tiny Casio keyboard—really a palm-sized toy—and Marc had an acoustic guitar and a drum kit. I was into electronics in those days and built a crude synthesizer from a kit for Tom to use. We made up songs and recorded them live onto cassettes using my boombox. We listened to them constantly, driving through the farmland that surrounded Princeton in Marc's International Scout, howling with laughter.

My relationship with Tom and Marc will always be one of the most amazing creative experiences I have ever had. Every minute we spent together in those days was an excuse to write some new bit of music, poetry, or often just a strange incantation. We went camping and shared wild nights building fires and myths of polyhedra. When the creative juices ran dry, we became arch critics, panning our own exploits and cracking ourselves up at the irony of it. Behavior on anyone's part that was considered embarrassing or out-of-line to the others was a good enough excuse for some sort of sick torture, but somehow that never killed the atmosphere of spontaneity that we had made for ourselves. In fact, spontaneous torture could arise for its own sake: the "air-conditioned nightmare," in which an unsuspecting rear-seat passenger was subjected to open windows and full A/C in the dead of winter at high speed, needed no excuse. Then, of course, there was the incident on Aunt Molly Road, but I digress . . . It's probably worth noting that punishment was not meted out equally: Marc probably got the worst of it, and Tom was often strangely exempt, though it would be easy to see Tom's current sad condition as a form of kharmic come-uppance.

In that time I also started to discover new music. In a 500-seat venue at Princeton University, Tom and I saw the Pat Metheney group (its greatest incarnation, with cymbal-master Dan Gottlieb and percussionist Nana Vasconcelos) and King Crimson on its "Discipline" tour. We stood in the little hall face-to-face with Adrian Belew and let the music rip through us. I remember leaving the concert in a state of shock: though a willing participant, I was also totally done-to.

Marc started gravitating more towards guitar playing and songwriting, experimenting with open tunings and slide on his acoustic, and it became clear we needed a full-time drummer to complete the band.

We invited Peter Cottone to fill that role and brought in Roger Holloway on bass.

I didn't really get to know Trey until after he had already gone away to school at Taft. At PDS he had always been one of three drummers (the other two being Pete and Marc), but when he came back one summer playing guitar, it was clear that his drumming background had given him incredible grounding. He had been playing rhythm guitar in a cover band for about a year, and while he seemed to repeat the same Grateful Dead material a bit, he really knew how to lock into a groove. For a guy who didn't "really play lead guitar," he was impressive. I began living in fear.

"Runaway Jim" originated that summer with Marc and I sitting out by Princeton's largest fountain. I had been fooling around with the basic song structure, showed Marc how to get that bluegrass rhythm sound with the emphasis on the bass notes, and the lyrics just popped into my head. I guess it's really true that we're conduits for the music. I had a couple of single-note lines that I wanted to go between the vocal parts, one of which sounded just like the kind of stuff Trey had been playing. I don't know how we arranged it, but I do remember being back at the fountain, working out the song between the three of us. For some reason I never understood, the song was causing Trey frustration that day. During Trey's hiatus from school years later, and also for some reason I didn't understand, we had this short conversation:

"Hey Dave, remember that song Runaway Jim?"

"Yeah . . ."

"What a stupid song [laughter]!"

So imagine my shock when Phish opened a concert at the Somerville Theater with my tune! Trey had added a verse and a chorus, but it was basically the same song.

CD: What's the story behind "Dave's Energy Guide?" You are "Dave," after all.

DA: First, Tom Marshall and I went to see King Crimson play at Alexander Hall at Princeton University. It was an incredible show in a 500-seat round church (that's also where I saw my first Pat Metheny Group concert, when they were in their incredible Dan Gottlieb/Nana Vasconcelos configuration). Not a bad seat in the place. They played cuts from "Discipline" and even a few from "Beat," which hadn't been released yet. A revelation.

I was blown away by Adrian Belew's free, spare, avant-garde style and by Robert Fripp's intricate, precise picking patterns. I tried to emulate both of them, but mostly I wanted to improve my technique to Fripp's level. I invented one of the DEG themes as a picking exercise. Because it is easier to play some patterns which skip between strings beginning with an upstroke or downstroke, I arranged the exercise to force me to repeat the same patterns in both directions. The pattern is built out of repeating parts which are extended to keep the total number of notes between repeats always an odd number. The pattern is 5-6-5-7, and sounds a *lot* like something you'd hear on "Discipline."

One summer Trey and I went to a guitar camp, the National Guitar Summer Workshop. I studied jazz and bluegrass. I think Trey was doing jazz and classical . . . maybe. Anyway, they had a performance night, and Trey and I decided to make the DEG pattern into a tune for performance. We put the pattern together with one of us playing 5-6-5-7 and the other one playing 5-6-5-6, so they would go out of synch and eventually come back together in synchrony after 22 repetitions. This

is a standard King Crimson trick. There were also a few shifts where we'd go into harmony, etc. I don't know if it had a name, but it wasn't called "Energy Guide" or "Dave's" anything. We played it twice, and messed it up both times. It's really easy to drop a note and if you lose track of where you are in the pattern, God help you. Some kid went up on stage and played an acoustic solo piece he had written, and we decided our thing was formulaic B.S. We left the hall shivering with delight.

At some point Trey formed Phish and the next time we played together he showed me another part to the DEG song, whatever it was called. He said he had walked into a party and seen Fishman sitting on a couch playing this diamond-shaped pattern on the guitar. Trey seized on it and incorporated it into the song. Meanwhile, I had written another part, but I don't think that ever made it into a Phish rendition of DEG. When I finally got up to Burlington to see them perform it, Trey hung a yellow diamond-shaped sign (promotional material for Con Edison or something) on the mic stand. It said "Energy Guide."

And that's the story. I don't think they play it much anymore partly because it's really a two-guitar song—it must be hard to get the right sound with guitar and keys.

CD: It sounds fine to me with guitar and keys. I wish they played it more often, frankly. OK, for the record, who is Guy Forge?

DA: Some tennis player guy, I don't know. I think he has a pyromaniac girlfriend named "Bubba."

CD: You've written some Phish lyrics and helped write several of their songs, but what's your regular job?

DA: I trash other people's living rooms so they can collect the insurance.

CD: What are you listening to these days? Have any favorite bands?

DA: I hardly listen to music anymore.

CD: Do you pay attention to on-line criticism of the band's music, including songs that you had a hand in writing? Are you a subscriber to the Phish.net Digest?

DA: Nope. I do own a personally autographed copy of "George Bush's Boyhood Dream," though.

CD: That rocks.

DA: That does not "rock." His boyhood dream is all wet inside.

CD: You live in Boston. Do you have a favorite music store in town, e.g., the Newbury Comics/Tower combination?

DA: Not really; I seldom buy CDs. I guess you could say I'm basically an unmusical person.

CD: Uh-huh. What was your most memorable Phish show?

DA: There was one show at the Providence Civic Center about four years ago which just made me so . . . happy. There wasn't a single detail I could seize on to say that it made the difference, but that night I decided I would try to see Phish whenever I got the chance.

CD: Is there a story behind the "Looks too much like Dave" line in "McGrupp"?

DA: Nope. Tom wrote it and I didn't know until I heard Trey say it on stage.

CD: Who is Guelah Papyrus? Who are Elihu and Lemore, who are mentioned in "Sample"?

DA: Well, my mother's name was Geulah. I don't know who Guelah is, but coincidentally (?) it's pronounced the same.

Elihu is my dad's name. They used the Israeli pronunciation in the

song, but in my dad's case the accent is on the first syllable. It's an unusual name, but he's being inducted into the American Academy of Arts and Sciences this fall with an unbelievable two other guys named Elihu, so it can't be all that kooky.

All in all, I'm surprised I didn't end up with a name like "Schmecky."

Lemore, I think, is the name of Tom's first love. I'm not sure I want to say any more, though; you might have to ask him about that.

CD: Can you name all of the Phish songs that you helped in some way to write? Any special stories behind the genesis of any of them?

DA: "Glide": Trey, Tom, and I were sitting on a bronze Henry Moore sculpture on Princeton University campus late one night. I don't remember how the words came up. I'm not sure I actually had anything to do with it, but they generously gave me an album credit.

"Slave": This was written during the "Bivouac" phase. Trey had this whole instrumental thing he had worked out around just singing the title of the song. I tried to imagine what it might mean to be a slave to the traffic light and riffed the other line. I thought it was pretty stupid and was almost embarrassed when Trey seized on it and put it in the song. Trey has a talent for finding the greatness in the inane.

"Fast Enough for You" was first recorded by Trey, Tom, and I at my parents' house. I wrote one line (see if you can guess which). "The Wedge," which Trey changed completely after that recording (definitely for the better), was also recorded that day but I didn't write any part of it.

CD: "Fast" is one of my favorite of Phish's slow, soulful tunes. By the way, what did you think of the huge "Runaway Jim" that Phish played in Worcester in fall 1997?

DA: I am proud anytime they play that song, and I'm deeply gratified that it has turned into such an opportunity for amazing jams . . . but, you'll probably be shocked to hear, I don't remember that particular version.

CD: Do you have any "personal favorite" versions of the songs that you helped to write?

DA: Not being a tapey-head Phish trivia weenie, I don't have such a mental catalogue of individual performances. I've heard a few amazing live concert tapes, though.

CD: Do any particular Phish lyrics hold special meaning to you?

DA: The one that immediately pops into my head is "Julius." That song paints an incredible picture of a emperor who is about to fall, and it stands out among Tom's lyrics as being written from a character's perspective. But that doesn't really answer your question, does it?

Hmm, the first time I heard "Horn" it really affected me deeply. Everything Phish had done before seemed so . . . peppy. It was great to hear them play melancholy as well.

I don't know about meaning, though. I don't relate to art on the concrete level much. For me, it's all about how it makes me feel or think.

CD: Disco Saul, a legendary Phish fan who loves plants, has a croton plant which he has had since Earth Day his freshman year, which is named after you. How does that make you feel? (This was due to a certain "strange" experience that he had with the 5/13/94 McGrupp, about a year after he acquired the plant.)

DA: Holy chlorophyll, Batman! That is probably a step up the evolutionary ladder for Davekind. It makes me feel all meaningful inside.

CD: Excellent! As well it should.

Richard "Nancy" Wright

Interviewed by Mark Toscano via telephone and email during July 2000. See also entry in Dictionary.

During Phish's Halloween 1994 performance of The Beatles' "White Album," many fans were perplexed at a slight case of apparent gender disagreement during "Rocky Raccoon." Instead of "Everyone knew her as Nancy," Trey substituted a "him," thus calling Rocky's sexual preferences into question. Well, not really. As with a few other songs that night, "Rocky's" lyrics were altered to create a Phish in-joke. Nancy is no mysterious woman, guilty of toying with a certain Raccoon's heart before dropping him in the dirt. "Nancy" (no "Taube") is actually the one-time moniker of Richard Wright, a Phishy friend from the band's early days, and the one and only writer (both music and lyrics) of Phish favorites "Halley's Comet" and "I Didn't Know."

Richard currently resides in Burlington and was kind enough to grant the Mockingbird an interview about his connections to Motown, the solar system, and a bar band named Phish.

Mark Toscano: I suppose I should begin with the most obvious questions: What went into composing "Halley's Comet" and "I Didn't Know," and how did the two songs come to the band's attention?

Richard Wright: Contrary to what *The Pharmer's Almanac* says, I wrote both the lyrics AND the music to both of these songs (with the exception of the little snatch of "Chattanooga Choo-Choo" that turns up just before the first chorus and at the tail end of "I Didn't Know"). In the summer of 1985, just before my final semester at Goddard, I was living in Montpelier, and had just a month or two previously began working with 4-track recording at the Goddard radio station. I wrote "I Didn't Know" in early August '85, and recorded a rough version on 4-track about a week or so later, a capella, about seven vocal tracks layered. Some of the parts were a bit out-of-tune, so I re-recorded it in September, during my last semester at Goddard. That is the version that was heard by the members of Phish.

All during the summer of '85, there was beginning to be a lot of hype about the arrival of Halley's Comet in our solar system. The opening bars of "Halley's Comet" (the parts of the song where the lyrics are nothing but melodic repeatings of "Haaaaal-ley's Comet, Haaaaaaa-ley's Comet") came to me during this time. I heard it in my head as a sort of Brian Eno–type tune (the *Another Green World* phase). I was writing a lot of poetry that summer. I heard what sounded like The Mills Brothers with a lead singer that sounded like a cross between John Lennon, Mike Love, Bob Dylan, and Lou Reed, singing it to me in my head, as a complete song body. Later, in September, after getting stoned and listening to Lou Reed's *The Blue Mask* album (I have no idea what the connection is, if any), the rest of the song (at the time called "Goin' Down," which featured all the non-Halley's Comet lyrics and the "I'm goin' down to the central part of town" refrain) came to me as a complete song body and I wrote it down. It was sort of a reaction to this Motown revival that was going on at the time. I recorded it on 4-track about a week later (as "Goin' Down"

with no "Halley's Comet" intro) with just bongos and several vocal tracks. It didn't sound so good and before I re-recorded it, I decided to tag "Halley's Comet" onto the front, middle, and end of it.

I played the first recording of "I Didn't Know" for Page on the first day of the Fall 1985 semester at Goddard. He was hanging out in Jim Pollock's room, which was downstairs from mine, listening to a tape of a Phish gig at Hunt's. This was the first time I'd ever heard Phish, or even of them. A few weeks later, I re-recorded "I Didn't Know" and a few days after that, I recorded "Halley's Comet."

The re-recording of "Goin' Down" interpolating "Halley's Comet" along with "I Didn't Know" and a few other songs were played to friends of mine at Goddard, one of whom was a guy named Ricky Puffer. Ricky had a friend, Brian Long, who, at the time, was living with several members of Phish on King Street in Burlington, across the street from the parking lot of the Hood Milk Factory in a red house. I had made a tape of my songs for Ricky [and] he played the tape for Brian, who borrowed it, took it to Burlington, and played it to the members of Phish (I'd known Page for about a year at this point; he'd been attending Goddard since Fall '84).

The weekend before Halloween, Phish came to Goddard to play a show in the Haybarn (they ended up taking too much acid to play). I met Trey in Jim Pollock's room and he asked me if I was Nancy. I said yes and asked him if he was the guy (I heard on the Hunt's tape) who sounded like Frank Zappa. He laughed his trademark laugh and said, "Yes, I'm the guy who sounds like Frank Zappa." It was either that night or a month or so later that he asked me if Phish could cover "Halley's Comet." I was flattered and immediately gave my consent. They debuted it at the Haybarn at Goddard Spring Fest '86 (when I wasn't a student anymore) with me on lead vocal. A year or two later, they also started covering "I Didn't Know," [and] I played drums on it at a few gigs.

MT: Have you been in bands yourself? What else could you tell us about your songwriting activities?

RW: No, I've never actually been in a band. Well, maybe a little. A high school friend of mine had a band called Equinox that he was lead singer of. I sat in on two gigs (one at a Dairy Queen, one at a skating rink) and did backup vocals and also sang lead on covers of Lynyrd Skynyrd's "Gimme Three Steps" and ZZ Top's "Tube Snake Boogie." I would've joined full-time, but the lead guitarist didn't like me and threatened to quit the band if I stayed on full-time. I played tongue drum and conga in a Burlington acoustic band for a few months back in early '96, but I dropped out 'cause it got too boring. As for songwriting, I started writing songs in my teens when I [was] still living in Maryland. The first songs I wrote were horrible. I still have some of them, typewritten in a suitcase in my room. Occasionally, I look at them for a laugh. I didn't write any songs that I thought were any good until I started doing acid when I was 18. At the time I wrote "Halley's Comet" and "I Didn't Know," I believe I was occupied by another spirit—a "muse" some might say—though I believe the spirit was parasitic, what some people

might call a "demon." I was happy to get it out of my system, although my songwriting has certainly suffered for it. But no matter; my own health and well-being will always be more important to me than being a good songwriter.

MT: In the Phish realm, your songwriting is always credited to the name "Nancy Taube." Where did the name "Nancy" come from, and is it true you've never used the name "Taube"?

RW: [Nancy] is a name that's been with me all my life. I used to feel that I was a woman (specifically a lesbian) trapped in a man's body and that Nancy was my "real" name. A psychic later told me that Nancy was actually the name of a lover I had in a past life. I started using the name Nancy on February 25, 1985, and stopped using it sometime in the autumn of 1990. But people I met back in the late eighties still call me Nancy.

I don't know where the "Taube" came from, but every book about Phish I've ever browsed through has that word in it. When I was "Nancy," "Nancy" didn't have a last name (actually, Nancy's full name was Nancy Bitterbug Voodoo Coleslaw, but I never used that full name in print or on my tapes, I was always just plain "Nancy"). Maybe at some point after I left Goddard, there was a student named Nancy Taube and maybe someone assumed that that was the person who wrote those songs. I certainly didn't come up with it.

MT: Have you seen the band in a personal capacity recently?

RW: I haven't seen Trey since October '95 at a Band from Utopia show in Club Metronome here in Burlington. Fishman and Trey were both at that show and that was the last time I saw Trey. The last time I saw Mike was about a year after that. He had just gotten his new house and he invited me to his house-warming party. Fishman came to my house in early '97 because at the time I was living with this guy who was making a movie and one of the producers of the movie was friends with Mike and Fish and apparently Fish was being considered to audition for a part in the film, but I don't think he got it. I saw him then and I saw him almost a year later . . . I think the last time I saw Fishman was at a Link Wray show at Club Toast in Burlington, which was also the last time I saw Page. That was in October of '97, so I haven't seen or heard from any of them since then. I do have a friend who follows them on tour whenever they go on tour every year and he tells me that they still do my songs and the songs are very popular.

MT: Did you conceive of "Halley's Comet" and "I Didn't Know" as poetry, not just songs?

RW: In a sense I consider all song lyrics that way.

MT: Would you say some of the poetry you've written could also be envisioned as song lyrics?

RW: The poems that are on my website, none of those were written as songs, although I suppose they could be at some point, although they don't really have any rhyme or meter to them, 'cause I don't really write poetry that way. It's happened before. There's one song I did, I wrote lyrics back in early '87 and made a song out of it about a year later, so I have done that kind of thing before. I haven't written that many songs in the last few years. I've written about maybe one or two songs a year, I haven't been that prolific lately. But in the last five years when I *have* written songs, I usually pretty much write the music and the lyrics at the same time. If I'm just writing words, that's pretty much all they come out to be. Or if I'm writing just instrumental music, I don't always have the intention of putting words to it.

MT: So, you're still writing music?

RW: Yeah, when I'm inspired to. I'm in the middle of working on a new album. I've been playing guitar since I was 27, I've been playing piano since I was 16, and drums since I was 15. A few months ago I got a pair of tablas, Indian drums, and I've been learning to play those. I have a four-track. I started working on a new album in December. It's maybe a little less than half finished. I did a lot of recordings in the late '80s. There's one album that I put out that's sort of a compilation of what I consider to be my best recordings from the '80s. I have an album that I did in '94 which is almost entirely cover tunes. And, I have another album of stuff that was intended to be a follow-up album of originals to the '94 album, but it never got finished because my four-track that I had at the time broke down during the making of it. So I've got these three unfinished instrumental pieces on that. I've got three 110-minute tapes worth of music and about half an album done this year. I haven't done any recording for a few months because I haven't been very inspired. I'm hoping I will become inspired again very soon.

MT: When you recorded these, would you sell them?

RW: I give them to people. I don't have any tapes that are of nothing but my music. If I did, I suppose I would sell that, but since I don't write all that much, it's kind of hard for me to imagine being able to put out a tape of nothing but my own music. The unfinished album, the two main instrumentals that were written for that, those were entirely written by me. But I also have a Hammond organ instrumental on that and while most of that is written and/or improvised by me, it's also got little snippets of classical themes in it, so because of what I choose to record, I kind of put myself into a position where I can't really sell my recordings, because if I did, I would owe royalties to people whose tunes I covered.

MT: For instance, in "I Didn't Know," where you borrow part of "Chattanooga Choo-Choo"?

RW: I don't know that I'd have to pay a royalty on that, but that was just a little tiny bit of a melody. Lots of people take little tiny bits of melody. Zappa used to do that all the time. I don't think there'd be a problem with that. But the album I did in '94 is almost nothing but covers. There's one song on it I wrote and two instrumentals that I just sort of improvised and the rest of it is all covers.

MT: What sorts of songs do you cover?

RW: I'd say about half of the recordings I did in the '80s were covers. I was doing a lot more composing back in the '80s. Well, the first four-track recording I ever did was a couple of covers. I did a couple of David Byrne songs from his first solo album, *The Catherine Wheel*. I do an a capella version of Frank Zappa's "Peaches en Regalia." It's almost totally a capella, it's got bongos on there, but I'm doing all the instrumental parts with my voice, overdubbed.

MT: Wow, how did it turn out? I imagine that was insanely difficult.

RW: It turned out okay, there were two sections where I couldn't get the notes right at all. Those two bits I couldn't get, so I just sort of deliberately flubbed those parts, like I don't even try to get them right. And it sounds like it. But the rest of the parts I actually did pretty well, I think. I've covered four Zeppelin songs. The first one I did was "Stairway to Heaven," all on synthesizers. "No Quarter," all on synthesizers. "Battle of Evermore" on guitar and synthesized harpsichord. And "The Rain Song." "Rain Song" is also the only song that I play on guitar that I actually used tablature to learn. And the reason why I used tablature

is that it's my favorite song and I was absolutely determined to learn it, and I just couldn't figure it out. Most songs that I learn I figure out by ear. I knew that Jimmy Page had used an alternate tuning on that and I couldn't figure out which tuning. It wasn't a standard open G, which he had used on "That's the Way" and which I was able to figure out on my own. Turned out he had used this tuning that was like D-G-C-G-C-D, and I actually do it in C-G-C-G-C-D. I'm actually going to redo that one. On the recording I did a few years ago, I do the rhythm guitar part, which is what I learned from the tablature. I also do, on lead guitar, I try to recreate one of the Mellotron parts. The way I ultimately want to do it is to have several lead guitars recreating all the Mellotron parts, sort of like what Brian May used to do in Queen. Do all of John Paul Jones's Mellotron parts on multitracked lead guitars. I just have to be inspired enough to work on it.

MT: Some of my friends that don't like Phish will hear "Halley's Comet" or "I Didn't Know" and say, "OK, now *that's* a good song." I think that's a great testament to your songwriting, that it has very broad appeal. What else could you tell us about your songwriting?

RW: Thanks, I appreciate that. See, in the '80s, I didn't have too many instruments at my disposal. For instance, on the recordings I did of "Halley's Comet" and "I Didn't Know," on "I Didn't Know," it's all voices, no instruments. "Halley's Comet" is just bongos and all vocals. I also did a lot of improvisational stuff where I just work with found objects, like jars of water and just random objects being used for percussion sounds. And then in '87 I got a synthesizer which I still have, a Casio CZ-101. In '91, when I was 27, I started learning to play guitar. I had sort of been playing guitar before that, but I didn't know how to finger chords. I would just tune the strings to a chord and play with a slide. I did that for about five years, and then in '91 I started learning how to finger chords. The album I did in '94 was my first guitar album. But I only played rhythm guitar at that time. I did a few simple leads . . . in the past year or so, I've been learning sort of bluesy-type leads. I can't play very fast, but I get this kind of fat, Cream-era Eric Clapton–type sound. I use feedback a lot too, I'm really influenced by Hendrix and Yardbirds-era Jeff Beck. Even though I've only been playing guitar for only nine years, it's pretty much become my main instrument.

MT: You've mentioned Zappa a few times. Are you a big fan?

RW: Oh yeah, I'm a total Zappa freak. One of my fondest memories of ever hanging out with the members of Phish was when Jon Fishman bought me a ticket to a Zappa concert in Burlington on his last tour. As far as I know, it's the only tour ever where Zappa actually played a gig in Vermont. It was in Burlington at Memorial Auditorium. Before I even heard that Zappa was playing in Burlington, Fishman, when he got a ticket for himself, he got an extra ticket for me because he knew that I was huge Zappa fan and the concert just happened to be taking place about a week before my birthday, so I always look upon that as the best birthday present I ever received.

MT: Did the other band members go?

RW: Oh, the whole band went. All the members of Phish, and me, and one of Phish's roadies, and a few other people, a few Goddard students. We were all in this one row, right in front of the soundboard, so we got really good sound. It was definitely one of the three best concerts I've ever been to. I think that was one of his best bands ever—that and his '74 band. I love "Inca Roads," that's my favorite Zappa tune

ever.

MT: What do you think of Phish's cover of "Peaches en Regalia"?

RW: I always thought they did it pretty good. About the only thing I would've had them do differently with it was during that complicated part, the part I couldn't get right, I think Page should have played that on the organ rather than on the piano, kind of like the Mothers' *Fillmore '71* version. But what the hell, they did it good. When the band was in L.A. working on the *Hoist* album in fall of '93, a friend of mine was house-sitting for Fishman. I came out to his house and I stayed there for a couple weeks, and I was there when Fishman got back from L.A. Jon told me that while they working on *Hoist*, they met Mike Keneally, the guitarist from the '88 [Zappa] tour, because *Hoist* was produced by Paul Fox, and Paul Fox had also produced XTC's *Oranges and Lemons* album, and apparently Mike Keneally is a big XTC fan.

MT: Since it's a rarity to find somebody who saw the band so regularly during their early years, what could you say about the experience in retrospect?

RW: Well, at that time, they were my favorite band. I was just so glad that there was actually a band like that during the '80s because all through the '80s I was pretty much a progressive rock fan, and because of that there wasn't too much '80s music that I liked. Progressive rock was kind of looked down upon in the '80s. It's been a little less looked down on in the '90s, since the '70s have kind of become fashionable again, but in the '80s, prog-rock was totally looked down on. So, Phish were kind of a refreshing contrast to the sort of anti-music that was going on in the '80s. Like, the whole idea of a stoner band or psychedelic band was not an '80s thing. So for this local band to actually have four fantastic musicians with roots in progressive rock and actually daring to play that publicly and writing their own sort of prog-rock influenced stuff . . .

And I liked their influences too, you know. When I first heard them, they sounded a little bit to me like Yes. And then I also picked up on the Zappa influence and the Allman Brothers influence and so it was something that I felt very comfortable with. I'd go see them as often as I could. It was really good for a while. I kind of felt like sometime around the middle of '88 . . . like the whole period from spring of '88 to around spring of '89 I felt like that whole time period they were in top form. It was hard for me to imagine them getting any better than where they were at that point. And then sometime around the summer of '89 . . . By then they had become too big to play at Nectar's anymore. Nectar's is a fairly small place and it had gotten to a point in '88 where they would be playing at Nectar's and there'd be lines of people out on the sidewalk of Nectar's trying to get in. So they moved down the street and started playing at this place called The Front, which was a little bigger. The Front doesn't even exist anymore, it's a bicycle shop now.

I'm kind of sensitive to crowds—I don't really like going to big shows—so around late '89, that was when I started to go to their shows less and less. They were playing a lot louder because they were playing in slightly bigger places, and I just felt at that point I'd gotten to a point where I couldn't really handle going to their shows anymore. The last time I saw them in the '80s was when they played at Goddard, Halloween '89. And then I didn't see them again until about a year and a half later, in July of '91, they played a free concert in Battery Park in Burlington. Then I saw them about a year and a half after that at St. Michael's College in Colchester in late '92. And then I didn't see them

again until March of '97 at the Flynn. That was the last time I've seen them play. I didn't really enjoy that show at the Flynn very much. I felt like they weren't really playing up to their full potential because—I might be wrong about this—since they were so popular, they didn't really have to prove themselves anymore. It seemed to me like they were taking it easy a little bit.

In the '80s I was going to Phish shows all the time, so a lot of particular moments are kind of a blur to me. There are certain things that stand out. Like I remember going to one Phish show at Nectar's some time in spring of '88, and about 15 minutes before they went to the stage, Trey came up to me and he said, "You want some mushrooms?" and I said, "Yeah, I guess so," and he says, "Hold out your hand," and he plops this big handful of mushrooms into my hand, right in the middle of Nectar's, so I just stuffed 'em into my mouth and chewed 'em up. Right about the time they took to the stage was about the time the mushrooms started to kick in and they opened up with "The Curtain (With)." I understand they do it a bit different in the '90s, that it's not "The Curtain (With)" anymore.

MT: Yeah, they took out the whole end section because part of it ended up being used in the song "Rift," although they just played it out of nowhere two weeks ago at Deer Creek [7/12/00].

RW: Wow . . . That was always my favorite song of theirs and I was kind of disappointed when they stopped doing it around '89 or so. Then a few years later I heard the tail end of it resurface as the song "Rift," which I thought was OK, but frankly I liked it better when it was in "The Curtain (With)." So they started playing "The Curtain (With)," and that was about the time the mushrooms kicked in and I had this impression that "The Curtain (With)" was sort of a musical map of the death process. I've had this feeling a lot on acid before too. There's always this slight fear that I could die during the trip, and so whenever I have that fear going on, any music I listen to is going to be carrying me through my death. But "The Curtain (With)" sounded like it was actually a map, sort of a tour through the death process. Like if I died during it, it would be okay, because I was being guided through it.

MT: You briefly touched on an episode when Phish was supposed to play a show, but took too much acid and had to cancel . . .

RW: They showed up at Goddard to do a show, and that was the night that I met Trey. He hadn't taken the acid yet. Apparently, while they were setting up to do the show in the Haybarn, someone had taken a gallon of apple cider—we have really good apple cider here in Vermont—and put like a bunch of sugar cubes [into the jug] . . . That's what we had going around at the time, some guy who was hanging out with them had these sugar cubes with really good liquid acid on them. I guess he put about five or six into this gallon of cider, and I guess the members of the band were passing the gallon of cider around, and I guess they ended up taking so much that they couldn't even play. I wasn't there for that part because I was somewhere else on campus. I was all tripped-out myself, 'cause I had taken a couple of sugar cubes myself. I had met Trey earlier that evening. I think I saw him again maybe a few weeks later, and I think that's when he asked me if they could cover "Halley's Comet." It took them months to learn it. I think they had pretty much been planning all along to debut it at Spring Fest '86.

MT: You've mentioned that Phish sometimes got the chords to "Halley's Comet" wrong . . .

RW: Always in the '80s they did. I haven't heard them do it since

the '80s, so for all I know they get the chords right now. I did mention to them a few times that they got the chords wrong, and I think one of them may have said to me at one point some time in the '90s that they started doing it again and that they got the chords right now, but I wouldn't know because I haven't heard it.

MT: I think they stopped doing it for a while after the late '80s and didn't play it again until March of 1993.

RW: Some time in '89 I did it for the last time. The way it was in the '80s was that they would only play it if I was present at a gig, because they would only play it if I was there to sing it.

MT: Would you sing it solo?

RW: Page usually sang lead with me, and Mike did the bass line chant. And then I just got tired of doing it. One night at The Front, I think August of '89 [8/17/89], before I sang it . . . I was kind of in a weird mood that night. I'm kind of sorry that I did this because I think it kind of put them off a bit. I was in a weird mood and I was sort of taking advantage of the fact that I was on a stage with a microphone. They never expressed any anger towards me for it, but I wouldn't be surprised if they were a little pissed off that I did what I did. I got up on stage and they were playing the intro to "Halley's Comet" and I'm just talking all this total bullshit. I was fighting with a couple of friends earlier in the evening and I was not in the best state of mind for getting up on stage and doing the song anyway. I was just making a bit of a spectacle of myself. One of the things I did was I announced that I was never going to sing "Halley's Comet" again. It was largely because I was kind of tired of people seeing me as the author of "that song," and the author of "I Didn't Know," and not really being interested in me on any other level, like not being interested in knowing if I had any other songs, or if I played my own music, or anything else about me. People would be introduced to me and they would be told that I wrote these two songs, and if they were at a gig that I was at, they'd see me sing "Halley's Comet" and that seemed to be all they wanted to know about me. I was a little bit upset about that, and I just kind of wanted to distance myself from that song for a while. It's an OK song, I'm glad that Phish liked it enough to want to cover it, but I think it's hardly the best song I've ever written, and like I said, I'm not very prolific, but I've written a few at least that I think are better than that.

MT: You mentioned that you're currently recording an album. What can you tell us about it so far?

RW: The centerpiece of the album I'm working on now—which I've already got recorded, I recorded it back in late January—is this improvisational instrumental called "Mojo Filter," which is built around this bass line that's in a sort of an Arabic scale. It's this ten-minute long sort of space jam that's all in Arabic scales. And it sort of starts out sort of skeletal with just a conga and the bass line and the feedback guitar going over it and then it starts to rock out a bit more. It sort of keeps building and going through these textures and then it's got a synthesizer doing Arabic scales through. Have you ever heard of a band from the early '70s called Gong?

MT: Oh yeah, I like Gong.

RW: You ever heard their album *You*?

MT: Yeah, I have . . . The whole Radio Gnome trilogy . . .

RW: You know the tune on *You* called "Master Builder"? That's what "Mojo Filter" is like. I sort of wanted to do my own "Master Builder"-type Arabic space jam. The bass line is kind of similar, though a little more complex. Also, for the last few years I've been really into surf

music, so I do some surf covers on this album. I do a couple of Ventures tunes. I don't have a drum kit, I just have a conga and a tambourine, in addition to the tablas. I've also got a floor tom from a drum kit, but I don't have a snare, I don't have a kick drum, and I don't have any cymbals. I've always just sort of used whatever was available to me, and that's one of the advantages of working with multitrack recording. You can take any sounds and layer them and make something musical out of them, and that's pretty much what I've always done. Over the years, I've gradually had more and more actual instruments available to me, along with the ability to play them.

MT: You understandably wanted to distance yourself from being just "that guy who wrote Halley's" or "that guy who wrote those two songs from Phish." If you were to get in contact with the band now, and they were to ask you to either perform the songs with them again or if they wanted to cover another of your songs, how would you react?

RW: Oh, I'd be fine with it. It's been eleven years since I've sang "Halley's Comet" with them, it's been twelve years since I played drums on "I Didn't Know" with them. Actually . . . Well, I wrote those two songs before I met them, so I didn't really write those songs for Phish. There *was* a song that I actually wrote for them. About a month after "Halley's Comet" debuted at Spring Fest '86, I wrote a song called "Snootable Snunshine." Shortly after I recorded it, I ran into Trey and Fish at a mutual friend's house, and I played it to them. They both really dug it, they were laughing really hard through the whole thing. Years later, I asked Fishman why they had never covered it, and he said, "Well, there's no way we could improve on your version!" I guess he considers it one of those songs that just can't be covered . . .

But if they ever wanted to cover any of my other songs, I don't think I'd be against it. I wouldn't be quite as psyched about it at this point in time as I was fifteen years ago when they wanted to do "Halley's Comet," but I certainly wouldn't mind them doing it, and I would still be flattered if they wanted to do any of my songs.

It was really great for me on a personal level to be part of the whole early Phish scene in the late '80s. I'm really glad to have been part of that and to have that have been part of my life during that time. I was having a lot of hard times during that time, and Phish being part of that scene was one of the things that got me through that period of my life. I can in all honesty say that.

MT: I think they've probably had an effect on a lot of people in a positive way, whether they intended to or not.

RW: I would say that they probably had the intentions to. They always struck me as pretty positive-minded people.

MT: A lot of the things they do, they don't need to do, but they do anyway, always trying to please their fans as much as possible . . .

RW: Yeah, like I've got some old *Rolling Stone* magazines laying around the bathroom, and I was looking at one from a few years ago that was describing the Lemonwheel thing in Maine. I was reading about the setup to that and it seemed like they set up the whole ground there as kind of like a big amusement park, sort of like a psychedelic rock Disneyland or something. Which I think is a really cool thing; it's definitely a sort of psychedelic vision being made manifest. Like, they got the bucks to manifest that kind of thing, and they're choosing to do that, and I think that's a good thing.

NOTES ON MY SONGS
by Richard Wright (a.k.a. Nancy)

Richard Wright (a.k.a. Nancy), was kind enough to grant the Mockingbird an interview for our book, but he has done so much more than that. Richard not only provided us with the official lyrics to "I Didn't Know" and "Halley's Comet," but he has blessed us with some insightful commentary on the lyrics, presented below. (Edited by Mark Toscano)

I DIDN'T KNOW

(Music and Lyrics by Nancy; (P)1985 Coleslaw Tunes, Inc., (c)1998 FaceBat Music, Inc.)

I didn't know
I didn't know

And I didn't like cheeseburger alleycats near me
And petrified fish disease, I wish somebody'd hear me
I didn't like maple dew honey melon watercress
I didn't like fish shoes down my honey watermelon
I didn't seem to miss you when you draped my honey water
And even showed a picture show to down my honey's border
And Kool-aid silver tooth broke my sunny shoe-shine

And all my plastic melon dreams are waitin' for their new shine

Pardon me, Doug
Is this a picture of Otis Redding?
Yeah, Yeah
Taken just before he died
Well, you can give me his hide

I didn't know that I was that far gone (x8)

And I would like to see Bess Truman come see me
And hear all the revolutionaries come free me
Cause if it all ends up runnin' to sneeze me
I'll make'em all hear "Black corners, come seize me"
And if ya boom back, Got troubles wit'cha ear
And ya can't seem to come back make it all clear
For eye-tails and toenails and liquid all meet me
For mustard pies and carrot-eyes and flounder come greet me

I didn't know that I was that far gone (x8)
It was the Summer of 1985, just before my last semester at Goddard College. I was living in Montpelier in a duplex apartment with

five other people: a married couple, an unmarried couple who were friends of mine (how I got a room in the apartment in the first place), and a guy in his forties who believed he was the Supreme Commander of the Universe... strangely enough, I think I got along easier with him than with anyone else living there.

I was writing a lot of poetry that Summer... I would smoke lots of pot, stay up until four in the morning, listen to the Velvet Underground and Brian Eno, and write poetry. One night, in early August, I think, I had this weird, sorta bluesy, Mills Brothers-type groove going through my head... my favourite approach to poetry and/or lyric writing is to have a groove going on & try to figure out the words that sound like they belong there... the lyrics don't have to mean anything, they just have to "sound good" in that groove, in that rhythm. One of my favourite songs of all time is "I am the Walrus" by The Beatles... that approach to lyric writing is what I like. Generally, I'm not much of a lyric person... I like music. As far as I'm concerned, lyrics exist just so the singer can have something to sing. What the lyrics mean or whether they do mean anything or not is completely irrelevant to me. What concerns me is: Do they *sound* good? To me, the human voice is a musical instrument & like all instruments, there are not just notes but the *shape* of the sound, the *attack* of the sound, to consider. Lyrics shape the notes of a vocal for phrasing, like a wah-wah pedal does for an electric guitar... lyrics are a *built-in effect* to a vocal... so, as with any instrument, you start out with just the notes... the vocal equivalent of this is scat-singing or humming... you shape the sounds of each note a bit more intricately and voila! You get lyrics!

Okay, still with me? I've got this groove, this bluesy Mills brothers-type groove goin' through my head... I can hear their voices... I can also hear the voice of a sixties-type lead singer with a cynical, nasal voice, like a cross between Lou Reed, John Lennon, Bob Dylan, & Mike Love... maybe a little bit of Roger McGuinn... this pseudo-sixties cat is singing the verses, with the pseudo-Mills Brothers in the background... they sing the choruses themselves. Okay, now what are they all singing?

I think the chorus ("I didn't know that I was that far gone") came to me first. As for the verses... "Cheeseburger alleycats" might have been self-referential (on a sub-conscious level, of course)... me & one of the guys I was living with used to go to the McDonald's on the Barre-Montpelier road a few nights a week, around 2:00 in the morning & go dumpster diving... McDonald's keep their dumpsters locked up in a small brick building behind the restaurant itself... only, this particular McDonald's didn't lock the door. Me & my friend would drive around the back of this shopping center that was next door to the McDonald's, then cross this little stream, sneak into the little brick building & start looking for the bag that had all the thrown out burgers, muffins, & chicken nuggets that didn't get sold that day... there was usually *one bag* that had the leftover food in it... most of the other bags were just trash from the waste baskets in the store. Anyway, me & my friend actually got caught one night... by a plump little grotesque evil Shirley Temple lookalike & a tall clean-cut high school guy who looked like he wasn't old enough to shave yet. Evil Shirley told us

to (I swear this is true) "Put that fucking trash back, sir." She then went to call the police & told her colleague to *not let us leave*... he simply said "I don't want any trouble" and we didn't give him any... we simply took our rejected fast-food booty & split.

"Petrified fish" was a phrase that'd been kicking around in my head for a year or so... why all the "honey dew" & "melon" references? Beats me. The little parody snatch of "Chattanooga Choo-Choo" that turns up after the first verse just sorta came up as soon as the first verse was written. In the second verse, I really can't say what most of it's about, if anything... "Black corners" & "mustard pies" were phrases that continually came to me on acid... I think "Black corners" is a reference to unexplored places in the psyche... "Mustard pies" are probably a symbol of what was usually found there when I did explore them... nothing materially useful, but it makes good words for song lyrics.

HALLEY'S COMET

(Music and Lyrics by Nancy)

a) "Halley's Comet"

Halley's Comet
I said-uh Halley's Comet (x2)

Halley's Comet (x4)

Halley's Comet
I said-uh Halley's Comet (x2)

b) "Goin' Down"

How did you know that I live in a desperate world?
How could you dream that we were all made out o'stone?
What is the truth? What is the faithful, lasting proof?
What is the central theme of this everlasting spoof?

Knock on my window,
Link up the chain
It's gotta be easy
No splinters, no pain
It's Cadillac rainbows
And lotsa spaghetti
And I love meatballs
So you'd better get ready

I'm goin' down to the central part of town (x4)

REPEAT a)Halley's Comet

What did I do?
And don't be blaming "Eat my kazoo!"
For everything I do to know the story
For everything I see to pull me near
For everything I say to get the title

But when they use it on me,
I reject it

What would you do if you ate my daddy's shoes?
What would you say if it was naturally for you?
How would you feel if you ate hungry cat-chew (sic)
How would you like to have your fake strawberry goo?

I'm sinkin' down
It's a glorious feelin'
To make a big difference
The body is reelin'
Even Broth Zada can't shine my shoes
And I know, deep inside,
he's got some mighty fine Jews.

I'm goin' down to the central part of town (x4)

Summer of 85 was when all the hype started over the impending passage of Halley's Comet through our solar system, which was due to happen in early 86. You couldn't go anywhere in town without seeing a reference somewhere to Halley's Comet. If you're a person like me & you get continually pelted with references to the same thing over and over again, your subconscious starts coming up with ways of coping... all through the Summer of 85, I coped by singing "Haaaal-ley's Comet, I said-uh Haaaaal-ley's Comet". At the same time, I was a big fan of Brian Eno & had just acquired my first copy of *Another Green World*. When I heard "Halley's Comet" (just that little portion I'd come up with so far) in my head, I heard it being sung by Brian Eno during his *Another Green World* phase. For several months, that's all it was... a concept in my head, with no lyrics other than "Haaaaaal-ley's Comet, I said-uh Haaaaaal-ley's Comet"... I thought nothing of it & had no intentions of doing anything with it.

In September of 1985, I was back at Goddard College for what would turn out to be my last semester. One night, I was in my room (Wolper, room 5) getting stoned & listening to Lou Reed's *The Blue Mask* album. I remember the next-to-last song on Side One, "The Gun", really scared me... I actually believed that a spirit or apparition with a gun was going to materialise & threaten me (let's just say I was not exactly a "stable person"). This was around the same time that the soundtrack album to *The Big Chill* came out... a lot of people were listening to it & there was a bit of a Motown revival at the time, which irked me, being the uptight intellectual rugged individualist I was at the time... but, when the going gets tough, the tough write satires. While still in the grip of fear inspired by "The Gun" while still in the general phase of the all-encompassing Motown revival polluting my lilywhite psyche, I

pondered the idea of being visited by an apparition (benevolent or malevolent?) to a Motown-type soundtrack, sorta like a Broadway musical (why settle for Broadway?) a la *The Wiz*.

I had a chain hanging by my window ("Knock on my window, link up the chain") for what purpose, I can't remember... in fact, 15 years later, living in Burlington, I *still* have a chain hanging by my window... maybe the apparition is the God of Metal & maybe my subconscious knows this. "No splinters, no pain"... Shakespeare wrote about the "slings & arrows", I write about "splinters" & "thorns" & "dust"... maybe that's what "grunge" is... the "nitty gritty". I was definitely looking for an "alternative" to "no pain, no gain"... I wanted gain without pain & I saw no reason not to strive for that. "Cadillac rainbows" & "fake strawberry goo" were references to my attitude about Motown at the time (for the record: I like Motown stuff now, but I don't take my tastes as seriously as I did when I was in college)... mass-produced artificial colours (maybe that's what Little Richard meant by "Tutti-Frutti, all Rooty")... & yes, I do like meatballs with my spaghetti.

Of course, all of this had to be building up to *the big chorus*... a buncha Motown fans (black people and white people who wish they were black) dancing down the street, a Cadillac being driven slowly... where to? The groove was there, the setting was there... it could only mean one thing: "I'm goin' down to the central part of town"... if the picture isn't clear in your mind right now, I can't describe it to you.

"What did I do?"... for two years at Goddard College, my best friend was Wayne Graham. He & I had a language all our own... if I'd had words for it at the time, it might've been "communication as entertainment" or even "entertainment as communication"... we had a lot of words, non-words, phrases & sounds that meant something *only to us*... we weren't trying to be exclusive... we made attempts to bring others into our communication circuit but nobody else was open to it. "Eat my kazooey!" was one such phrase... is that such a horrible thing to say? "Don't be blaming 'Eat my kazoo'" for my downfall... once again, my world was crumbling around me & I was looking for some way to save it, or at least for an explanation.

"For everything I say to get the title"... whatever that title (label) may be... poet, artist, songwriter, musician... I'm not any of these things, I'm a *person*! "But when they use it on me, I reject it."

Don't ask me what "cat-chew" is or who "Broth Zada" is... let's just say they're "underdeveloped lyrics" or "literally challenged"... and I'm neither pro- nor anti-semite.

What's the connection between "Goin' Down" & "Halley's Comet"? I just figured they'd work well together... was I right? You decide.

Part III

Shows

Shows

SET LISTS

Compiled and edited by and under the direction of Craig Delucia

The music played at all of Phish's known amateurly recorded performances is listed in this section. This section will provide a reference for the large number of people who trade amateur recordings of Phish's performances

A History

Documents detailing the setlists of Phish shows have been around since the early 1990's. One such document, "The Helping Phriendly Book" (the "HPB"), was originally compiled via the Internet by Phish fan Shelly Culbertson. The project was undertaken for the free use of fans and out of love for the band. Shelly's HPB was compiled with assistance from John Friedman, Richard Stern and other friends.

Lee Silverman took over the editing and compiling of the HPB for about a year in 1992. Richard "Chip" Callahan, with the help of Shelly and Sean Kennedy, pulled together everything for 1992 and the summer of 1993. In the fall of 1993, Ellis Godard, also known as Ellis of Lemuria, made significant revisions and additions to the document. Updated setlists and show dates, along with corrections and show notes from scores of helpful netters, were added to the file. Special notice should be given to Brian Bettencourt, Mike Pollack, Ben Miller, Harry McQuillen, Joe Rioux, Chris Bingham and Patrick Sprowels, who all made considerable contributions.

A copy of the Godard-edited HPB, dated January 17, 1994, was being used by Charlie Dirksen for his setlist information. Charlie used this document as a base for his own version of a setlist file. He appended the document with setlists for tapes he acquired and corrections from tapes in his collection. With the massive assistance of setlists distributed by Mikey Perrott, which were obtained via a mailing list run by Shelly and Sean, Charlie continued to add more shows to his setlist file. His particular document was compiled separately from the online HPB, which Michael Weitzman and Dan Shoop began to administer after Ellis concentrated on developing other areas of Phish.net.

Late in the fall of 1996, when the Mockingbird Project was in its earliest stages, Dan Purcell assisted Charlie in making significant changes to the document he had compiled. These changes were based on hundreds of Phish tapes gathered primarily from the collections of Dan, Charlie, and Bill Bowman. Also, several rare setlists were gathered from fans Dean Budnick, Matthew King and Jason Rose. It should be noted that the setlists obtained from Dean were from Dean himself and were not taken from the setlists listed in his book, *The Phishing Manual*.

In January, 1997, Charlie's setlist file was sent to Craig DeLucia. This document became the base for the setlists you see in this document. Craig spent hundreds of hours editing and appending the setlists file into an original format, making song names and abbreviations consistent, and developing show notes. When Craig felt that the document was consistent in presentation and ready for other eyes, he and Charlie

assembled a group of eleven fans to further update the document. This group consisted of Craig, Charlie, Benji Eisen, Charles Franz, Herschel Gelman, Matthew King, Phil Nazzaro, Dan Purcell, Jim Raras Jr., Dan Seideman, and Darius Zelkha. These eleven fans remained in constant contact and performed massive and continuous updates to the document, including the verification of older tapes and the addition of show notes for many shows. Since then, many fans have been a part of the Mockingbird working group, and assisted in other ways – they are thanked in the Acknowledgements chapter, at the beginning of this book. If the typical reader could see the extent to which this working group debated and discussed seemingly each and every segue, jam notation, and tease identification, he would most either be very impressed or very frightened!

Why is this particular file not referred to as "The Helping Phriendly Book?" To do so, at this point, would border on being historically inaccurate. Ellis's setlist file from 1994 continued to undergo revisions and additions under the guidance of Michael Weitzman and Dan Shoop. Their file continued to bear the name "The Helping Phriendly Book;" therefore, the name has become synonymous with that particular online setlist file. While the embryo for our project was indeed an older version of the HPB, the setlists you see in this book bear little resemblance to the HPB (currently maintained on-line at http://www.phish.net/hpb), or any other setlist file, except for the common concept of collecting and highlighting the setlists of Phish for all to see and use as a resource.

However, the underlying spirit of both the Mockingbird file and the HPB remains the same. The organizers of both believe that setlists should be available as a reference tool for all fans, and that no fan should profit from their distribution. Therefore, any group that sells the HPB for profit, in whole or in part, would be doing so against the wishes of those who originally compiled it, and those who have lovingly maintained and updated it over the years.

To this end, the Mockingbird Foundation and HPB have had a information-sharing relationship since early 1997. We are proud to count Dan Hantman, current administrator of the on-line HPB, as a member of the Mockingbird Board of Directors and as a member of the setlist file working group. Together, we have produced a community setlists archive which will benefit all fans.

It should be noted that this setlist file is not complete. Because so many early shows went undocumented, the assumption that any setlist project ever was or will be complete is mistaken. This document will continue to undergo revisions through corrections and additions as supporters of The Mockingbird Foundation strive to maintain the most accurate setlist file available. We encourage you to assist us in this effort, because your contributions are both appreciated and critical in making this file as complete as possible

Of course, there is an inherent degree of subjectivity involved as well. Fans have differing opinions on what constitutes a noteworthy segue, or whether a particular song was jammed, quoted, or teased. We have diligently attempted to use the lexicon and standards that are most accepted in the tape-trading community and among music scholars in general.

The Use of Abbreviations

A debate was held on the merits of abbreviations; using them would

have saved us a lot of space in the document and would have left the setlists reading like the conversation at a show. When was the last time you used the full song title "Run Like an Antelope" or "You Enjoy Myself" in a Phish-related sentence? The abbreviations "Antelope" and "YEM" have become more conversationally common than the original song titles, and fans rarely take the time to write out the full titles at a show or on a tape.

Abbreviations, though, are frequently confusing to newer fans. Sure, it is easy to deduce that "YEM" is the same as "You Enjoy Myself." How many newer fans, though, stare at "PYITE," "BBFCFM," "MMGAMOIO," "SOAM," and "WMGGW" and can't figure out what song was played?

After some debate, we decided to eliminate abbreviations from the setlists but to leave them in the show notes. By following this format, the setlists can be considered historically accurate while the show notes can assist newer fans in adapting to the abbreviations that they see on tapes.

Important Note

If you only want to read the setlists to get the gist of what songs were played at a particular show, go ahead and dig right in! To that end, they are self-explanatory; you can feel free to skip the very specific and nuanced information that follows. If you want to fully understand the intricacies and peculiarities of this unique setlist document, all the terms and notations contained therein are explained below. We believe that the segment of the fan population that enjoys the rabid discussion of Phish setlists will appreciate it. Our goals have always been, and will remain, clarity, completeness, and accuracy.

The Use of Segues

For the purposes of this file, there are two different segue notations: "->" and ">". The former refers to an actual segue, or when one song jams fluently and without interruption into another; the latter is used when:

1) One song stops and another immediately starts but there is no fluent jamming between songs;

2) One or more band members begin a new song as the previous song is still ending and there is no transition;

3) Two songs are played that are usually played together but do not actually segue (for example, Mike's Song > I am Hydrogen > Weekapaug Groove or The Horse > Silent in the Morning); or

4) A song that is typically a "lead-in" song is played (for example, The Oh Kee Pa Ceremony or Buried Alive).

Sometimes, the difference between a ">" and a "->" seems arbitrary or a matter of opinion. For this reason, we considered only using segue notations for actual jam segues (example number one above). Two arguments, though, convinced us that we should list both.

First, on many tapes (especially older, pre-1992 tapes), traders have traditionally noted segues without distinguishing between the two types. However, differentiating fluid, improvisational transitions (ie, the "->" symbol) – which are often among the highlights of a show – from routine transitions (the ">" symbol) gives fans a true feel for what was played and ably communicates the significance of a transition. Second,

demarcating routine ">" segues from improvisational "->" segues aids tape traders in determining tape flips. No harm occurs in breaking up an uneventful, purely routine transition between songs. But an improvisational segue should never be carried over from side A to side B of a tape, lest the integrity of the segue be destroyed

The Use of the Words "Tease," "Quote," and "Jam"

A "tease" occurs when a band member briefly hints at a part of another song, usually the melody. A good example is the "Drowned" tease in the July 21, 1997, Bathtub Gin: Page, in the middle of the song, plays the signature "Drowned" piano lick a few times before moving on to other musical territories.

A "quote" occurs when a member of the band vocally quotes another song, or familiar saying, or anything along those lines. See the April 15, 1992, "You Enjoy Myself" vocal jam, where band members quote "Proud Mary." Another popular example is Trey and Fishman's quotes from "The End" during the March 1, 1997, Hamburg "Mike's Song" (subsequently released on *Slip, Stitch and Pass*). [Note that, in technical music terms, a quote also occurs when a musician plays a complete melody line on his on her instrument but, in the Phish community, the terms "tease" and "quote" have become interchangable for this purpose. Therefore, we have reserved the term "quote" for the instances mentioned above.]

It is in our conservative use of the word "jam" where we differ from other setlist files. In our opinion, Phish is a jamming band and, by their nature, several songs at a show will jam out in some way and any song is subject to jam on any night. It would be silly to label every "You Enjoy Myself" as "You Enjoy Myself" -> "Jam" because, quite frankly, they all do. And it would be too discretionary to label the "best versions" as "You Enjoy Myself" -> "Jam." So, for the sake of brevity and accuracy, we have limited the use of the word "jam" to three specific occasions:

1) A substantial part of another song is played and, usually, some lyrics are sung. For a good example, see the "Cannonball Jam" in the May 7, 1994 "Bomb Factory" Tweezer or the "Wormtown Jam" that took place in Amsterdam in 1997. These jams are considered so substantial that they are listed in the setlist itself.

2) A jam of another song is so true that it deserves to be mentioned. Often, it involves multiple band members locking in on a common theme for a short period of time. Basically, this is a tease taken to another level. Examples include the "Birdland" jam in the July 21,

1997, "David Bowie" and the "Couldn't Stand the Weather" jam in the December 3, 1997, "Drowned." Usually, these types of jams are mentioned in the show notes, and not the setlists themselves.

3) A jam is initiated on its own, as if it were an individual song. These types of jams became more frequent in the summer of 1997. See the "Jam" -> "Slave" on December 7, 1997, the "Jam" -> "Cities" on June 20, 1997, or the "Jam" -> "Timber Ho!" in the popular July 1, 1997, Amsterdam show.

Cross-Referencing

The show notes only reference charicteristics of a show that deviate from the norm. For example, it is not mentioned in any of the notes that "Carolina" or "Hello My Baby" was performed *a capella*, because these songs are always performed that way. Similarly, it is not noted when versions of "Foreplay/Longtime" are performed acoustic, because almost all versions of this song have been performed that way. Instead, the Great Woods '99 show notes mention that the song was played electric.

Unless otherwise mentioned in the show notes, every version of "Guelah Papyrus" contains "The Asse Festival." Similarly, "Alumni Blues" always includes "Letter to Jimmy Page" and "Punch You in the Eye" contains "The Landlady" unless otherwise noted. To list these songs as, for instance, "Guelah Papyrus" -> "The Asse Festival" -> "Guelah Papyrus" is redundant and incorrect.

Of course, the middle, "sandwiched" songs can be and sometimes are played on their own. Far more detailed information regarding such songs is contained in other sections of the book.

In Closing

All of these details may be too technical for your taste. But the beauty of the Companion's setlists file is that it can be enjoyed on many levels. The casual fan can simply look and see what songs were played on any given date. The passionate tape collector can determine whether he or she should seek out a particular tape based on the setlist and other details of a show. And the segue notations and cautious use of the word "Jam" give the setlists file an original, creative and unique character. We hope you enjoy this setlists file. We also urge you to send us suggested changes or additions, so that we can maintain an accurate, comprehensive setlists repository that benefits everyone in the Phish community, including the band's own archives. Enjoy!

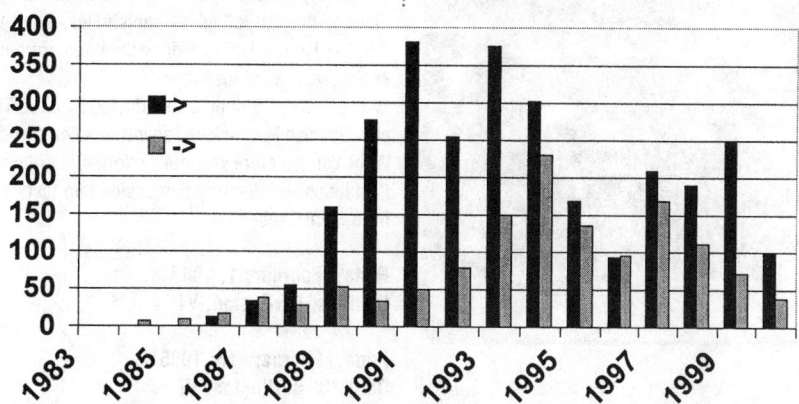

1983-1985

Sunday, October 30, 1983
Halloween Dance, Harris-Millis Cafeteria, University of Vermont, Burlington, VT
● *Show Notes:* Though fans have always held this date to be the date of the first-ever Phish show, this date is believed to be incorrect. If a show was played on this date, it was not the "Thriller" show that Phish lore has often referenced. The correct date of that show is December 2, 1983.

Thursday, November 3, 1983
Slade Hall, University of Vermont, Burlington, VT
● *Show Notes:* Tapes which circulate under this date are mislabeled copies of November 3, 1984.

Friday, December 2, 1983
Harris-Millis Cafeteria, University of Vermont, Burlington, VT
● *Check:* Jam (with audience present)
● *Set I:* Long Cool Woman in a Black Dress, Proud Mary, In the Midnight Hour, Squeeze Box, Roadhouse Blues, Happy Birthday
● *Set II:* Scarlet Begonias > Fire
● *Show Notes:* Trey, Mike, Fish, and Jeff Holdsworth recall being billed as "Blackwood Convention" for this show (though no one is certain what band name was used), which is believed to be their first public gig together. The band was short on equipment, so a hockey stick was used as a microphone stand. Between sets, the DJ spun some Michael Jackson and Trey drummed along to the album. The house music (which included more Michael Jackson) was presumably turned up after Fire to drown out the band. The setlist may be incomplete, though, as the master tape contains nothing after Trey's sarcastic comments about Michael

Mike driving a golf cart

Jackson following Fire. All songs are, of course, live debuts. While this show is often billed as an ROTC Halloween Dance that took place on October 30, 1983, this is incorrect. The master copy of the recording of this show, as unearthed by Phish archivist Kevin Shapiro, contains a handwritten note that pegs the date as December 2, 1983. In recent discussions with Kevin, band members confirmed that they recall rehearsing for this show over the Thanksgiving Break, and that the show was a Christmas semi-formal. Also, though many ROTC students lived in the dormitory (Mike's dorm at the time), it was not an ROTC-sponsored event; it was a dorm dance in a predominantly ROTC dorm.

Saturday, December 3, 1983
Marsh / Austin / Tupper Dormitory, University of Vermont, Burlington, VT
● *Show Notes:* This show, played by Trey, Mike, Fish, and Jeff, may have been billed as "Blackwood Convention." This date is believed to be correct but, due to a lack of records, the exact date can not be ascertained.

Tuesday, October 23, 1984
69 Grant Street, Burlington, VT
Makisupa Policeman
● *Show Notes:* This show, played in the garage of a house on Grant Street, is believed to be the band's first show after Trey's return to the University of Vermont and the first show where the band was billed as Phish. It is known that Makisupa was played but the rest of the setlist is unknown. The date is believed to be correct but may have been a few days earlier or later.

Saturday, November 3, 1984
Slade Hall, University of Vermont, Burlington, VT
In the Midnight Hour, Wild Child, Jam -> Bertha, St. Stephen Jam, Can't You Hear Me Knockin', Camel Walk, Eyes of the World -> Whipping Post -> Drums Jam
● *Show Notes:* The setlist for this show might be incomplete, as the tapes that circulate cut during the Drums Jam. Marc Daubert made a guest appearance on percussion. These tapes often circulate as November 3, 1983 but it is believed that this is incorrect. CYHMK included a St. Stephen tease.

Saturday, December 1, 1984
Nectar's, Burlington, VT
Scarlet Begonias -> Fire -> Fire on the Mountain, Makisupa Policeman, Slave to the Traffic Light, Spanish Flea, Don't Want You No More -> Cities -> Drums Jam -> Skippy the Wondermouse, Fluffhead
● *Encore:* Eyes of the World
● *Show Notes:* Skippy and Fluffhead featured The Dude of Life on vocals. Spanish Flea included an introduction of the band members. Don't Want You No More was not performed in its entirety, as it lacked the final lyrics. The lengthy percussion jam featured a guest appearance from Marc Daubert.

Friday, February 1, 1985
Doolin's, Burlington, VT

Friday, February 15, 1985
Doolin's, Burlington, VT

Friday, February 22, 1985
Doolin's, Burlington, VT

Monday, February 25, 1985
Doolin's, Burlington, VT

Monday, February 25, 1985
Private Party, Burlington, VT

Thursday, March 2, 1985
Hunt's, Burlington, VT

Saturday, March 4, 1985
Hunt's, Burlington, VT
Anarchy, Camel Walk, Fire Up the Ganja, In the Midnight Hour
● *Show Notes:* Fire up the Ganja featured members of the band Lamb's Bread.

Thursday, March 9, 1985
Doolin's, Burlington, VT

Thursday, March 16, 1985
Doolin's, Burlington, VT

Wednesday, March 29, 1985
Doolin's, Burlington, VT

Saturday, April 6, 1985
Finbar's, Burlington, VT

Friday, April 19, 1985
Hunt's, Burlington, VT

Sunday, April 21, 1985
Goddard College, Plainfield, VT
● *Show Notes:* This show was performed at The Bowl in the center of campus.

Monday, May 1, 1985
University of Vermont, Burlington, VT
● *Show Notes:* In what must have been the busiest day in Phishtory, the band played four shows (three of which were fraternity parties).

Wednesday, May 3, 1985
Last Day Party at UVM-Redstone, Burlington, VT
● *Set I:* Slave to the Traffic Light, Mike's Song, Dave's Energy Guide, Big Leg Emma
● *Set II:* Alumni Blues, Wild Child, Can't You Hear Me Knockin', Jam -> Cities, Bring it On Home
● *Set III:* Scarlet Begonias > Eyes of the World, Whipping Post -> McGrupp and the Watchful Hosemasters -> Makisupa Policeman -> Reggae Jam, Run Like an Antelope -> The Other One
● *Encore:* Anarchy
● *Show Notes:* This show marked Page's debut with the band, as he guested during portions of the third set. In fact, Big Leg Emma was preceded by an announcement from Trey that "our friend Page, from God-

Mike and phans at Ventura Beach (7/20/98)

dard, will sit in later." Bring it On Home featured "Bobby Brown" (Tim Rogers) on harmonica. McGrupp was dedicated to Fishman.

Sunday, May 7, 1985
Finbar's, Burlington, VT

Sunday, May 19, 1985
Hunt's, Burlington, VT
● *Show Notes:* There was no show on this date. Tapes that circulate are a mix of March 4, 1985 and May 3, 1985.

Wednesday, May 31, 1985
Slade Hall, Redstone Campus, University of Vermont, Burlington, VT

Sunday, September 26, 1985
WRUV "Exposure", WRUV Radio, Burlington, VT
Dog Gone Dog, Prep School Hippie, Camel Walk, Alumni Blues, Run Like an Antelope, Dave's Energy Guide, McGrupp and the Watchful Hosemasters
● *Show Notes:* This was an in-studio set that was aired live on the radio. Before Antelope, the band invited fans to the Slade Hall gig on the following night. Prep School Hippie was introduced as "Trust Fund Baby." This performance was the band's first with Page as an official member of the band.

Trey at Oswego (1999) at 3 A.M.

Monday, September 27, 1985
Slade Hall, Redstone Campus, University of Vermont,
Burlington, VT
Sneakin' Sally Through the Alley, Fluffhead, Skippy the Wondermouse, Slave to the Traffic Light, Alumni Blues, Prep School Hippie, Dear Mrs. Reagan, Melt the Guns
● *Show Notes:* The setlist is incomplete; the full show also included a few Dead covers and an Allman Brothers Band cover. This show was in the basement of Trey and Jeff's dorm and was played primarily for their housemates. According to one fan who attended, the highlight was Melt the Guns, during which the band handed out boxes of cheap grocery store macaroni and cheese for the audience to use as shakers in a big percussion jam.

Thursday, October 17, 1985
Finbar's, Burlington, VT
TV Theme, Alumni Blues -> Mike's Song, Dave's Energy Guide, Revolution, Anarchy, Camel Walk, Run Like an Antelope, McGrupp and the Watchful Hosemasters
● *Show Notes:* Some fans have labeled the show-opening jam a "Star Trek Jam."

Sunday, October 20, 1985
Slade Hall, Redstone Campus, University of Vermont,
Burlington, VT

Saturday, October 26, 1985
"Halloween Fest," Goddard College, Plainfield, VT
● *Show Notes:* This would have been Phish's first Halloween show, but they were unable to play. References to the show are made in *The Phish Book*; for audio comments, dig deep into the Hunt's show four nights later.

Wednesday, October 30, 1985
Hunt's, Burlington, VT

Harry Hood, Dog Gone Dog -> Possum, Slave to the Traffic Light, Sneakin' Sally Through the Alley, I Wish, Revival, Alumni Blues, Prep School Hippie, Skippy the Wondermouse, Jam
● *Show Notes:* This is the first widely-circulated show with Harry Hood. Also, though they are still sometimes soundchecked or teased, this show contains the only known versions of I Wish and Revival. Slave was dedicated to Brickle. Trey's humorous comments about being back on Planet Earth were in reference to the events at Goddard on October 26.

Saturday, November 2, 1985
Slade Hall, University of Vermont, Burlington, VT

Thursday, November 14, 1985
Memorial Auditorium Basement, Burlington, VT
Hurricane
● *Show Notes:* This setlist is incomplete.

Saturday, November 23, 1985
Goddard College, Plainfield, VT
● *Set I:* Wild Thing
● *Set III:* Mike's Song -> Whipping Post Jam -> Run Like an Antelope -> Dave's Energy Guide
● *Show Notes:* The Whipping Post Jam contained jams reminiscent of The Grateful Dead's The Other One and Dark Star, as well as Norwegian Wood teases from Mike and a jam reminiscent of the early intro to Harry Hood. The complete lists for Sets I and II are not known, although Mike has referenced the first set Wild Thing in interviews and in *The Phish Book*. This list for Set III may be incomplete, as the tapes that circulate fade in and out at points.

Friday, December 13, 1985
Private Party, Burlington, VT
● *Show Notes:* This show is sometimes noted as the "Red House Party."

1986-1987

Saturday, February 1, 1986
Hunt's, Burlington, VT
● *Show Notes:* There was no show on this date. Tapes that circulate are mislabeled copies of the Hunt's show from February 3, 1986.

Monday, February 3, 1986
Hunt's, Burlington, VT
Slave to the Traffic Light, Mike's Song > Dave's Energy Guide, You Enjoy Myself, Alumni Blues, Prep School Hippie, Run Like an Antelope
● *Show Notes:* Jeff made use of a slide guitar during Antelope. The unnamed fiddle player is most likely Russ Flanagan. Some tapes erroneously note that this show was a double-bill with The Joneses. This show contained the first known version of You Enjoy Myself.

Friday, February 28, 1986
Slade Hall, University of Vermont, Burlington, VT

Tuesday, April 1, 1986
Hunt's, Burlington, VT
● *Set I:* Quinn the Eskimo > Have Mercy > Harry Hood, The Pendulum
-> Dave's Energy Guide > Icculus, You Enjoy Myself
● *Set II:* Help on the Way > Slipknot! > AC/DC Bag, McGrupp and the
Watchful Hosemasters > Alumni Blues > Dear Mrs. Reagan
● *Encore:* Not Fade Away
● *Show Notes:* The Pendulum, which was a recital of revolutionary po-
etry, featured special guest Zenzile. For this show, Phish and The Jone-
ses switched off for 45 minute sets. The two bands got together to jam
out the encore. This show contained the first known versions of Icculus
and AC/DC Bag. McGrupp was spoken in a Dylan-esque fashion, in
keeping with Trey's jokes about Phish being the "Bob Dylan Band."

Tuesday, April 15, 1986
University of Vermont, Burlington, VT
AC/DC Bag -> Dear Mrs. Reagan, Prep School Hippie, Quinn the Eskimo
-> Slave to the Traffic Light, Makisupa Policeman, Have Mercy, Bob
Dylan Band, Dog Gone Dog, Possum, You Enjoy Myself, Anarchy,
Camel Walk -> Alumni Blues
● *Show Notes:* This version of Possum included a Music Never Stopped
tease.

Tuesday, April 29, 1986
University of Vermont, Burlington, VT
● *Show Notes:* This show was performed on The Green outside Bai-
ley Howe Library.

Friday, May 16, 1986
Memorial Auditorium Basement, Burlington, VT

Saturday, May 17, 1986
SpringFest, Goddard College, Plainfield, VT
Halley's Comet
● *Show Notes:* While a complete setlist is not known, it has been confirmed that Halley's (with vocals by "Nancy", or Richard Wright) debuted at this show. Richard believes the band also played YEM and a
bluegrass number that was likely Back Porch Boogie Blues.

Monday, June 1, 1986
Boston Harbor, Boston, MA
● *Show Notes:* This show was performed on a boat in the harbor.

Wednesday, September 3, 1986
Hunt's, Burlington, VT

Wednesday, September 10, 1986
Finbar's, Burlington, VT

Friday, September 26, 1986
Private Party, Johnson, VT
● *Show Notes:* Though tapes do not circulate, it is believed that a show
was played on this date at a hippie commune owned by a man named
"Irving." In a 1992 interview, Trey referenced this show when asked
about the strangest gig the band has ever played. No setlist is known.

Sunday, October 12, 1986
Haybarn Theater, Goddard College, Plainfield, VT

Wednesday, October 15, 1986
Hunt's, Burlington, VT
● *Set I:* Alumni Blues, Makisupa Policeman, Skin it Back > Cities, I Am
Hydrogen, McGrupp and the Watchful Hosemasters, AC/DC Bag, You
Enjoy Myself, Lushington
● *Set II:* Peaches en Regalia, Golgi Apparatus, Swing Low (Sweet Char-
iot), Camel Walk, Shaggy Dog, Mustang Sally, Fluffhead, Sneakin' Sally
Through the Alley, Wilson -> Slave to the Traffic Light, Quinn the Es-
kimo -> Mike's Song, Have Mercy -> Harry Hood
● *Set III:* Roll Like a Cantaloupe, Sanity, Anarchy
● *Encore:* Clod
● *Show Notes:* Before YEM, Page played cocktail-style jazz, including
snippets of Play Misty and Brother Can You Spare a Dime, while Trey
tuned up. This show was Paul Languedoc's first as soundman. The second set featured some strong early jamming, especially during the
segue from Quinn into Mike's. The third set listing is incomplete; tapes
that circulate have cuts before Cantaloupe. The Clod encore began with
an impromptu kazoo solo from Mike. This show contained the first
known versions of many Phish songs, including Hydrogen, Lushington,
Golgi, Shaggy Dog, Wilson, Cantaloupe, Sanity, and Clod.

Friday, October 31, 1986
Sculpture Room, Goddard College, Plainfield, VT
● *Check:* Bertha (performed by The Joneses), Blues Jam (with mem-
bers of The Joneses)
● *Set I:* Mustang Sally, Camel Walk, Golgi Apparatus > Slave to the
Traffic Light, Melt the Guns -> Sneakin' Sally Through the Alley, Halley's
Comet > Back Porch Boogie Blues > Shaggy Dog, Fluffhead
● *Set II:* Jam -> AC/DC Bag, Swing Low (Sweet Chariot), Peaches en
Regalia, David Bowie, Have Mercy -> Harry Hood, Sanity, Skin it Back
> Icculus, Alumni Blues
● *Show Notes:* The jam to open the second set is a must-hear. Trey and
Mike quoted Fuck Your Face and Minkin during the Melt the Guns intro.
This show contained the first known version of David Bowie. Have
Mercy featured Jah Roy on guest vocals.

Friday, November 7, 1986
Marsh Hall Dining Room, University of Vermont, Burlington, VT

Friday, November 14, 1986
Slade Hall, University of Vermont, Burlington, VT

Tuesday, November 18, 1986
Nectar's, Burlington, VT

Saturday, December 6, 1986
The Ranch, South Burlington, VT
Mike's Song -> Little Drummer Boy -> Whipping Post, She Caught the
Katy and Left Me a Mule to Ride -> AC/DC Bag, David Bowie -> Fluff's
Travels -> Clod -> David Bowie, You Enjoy Myself, Dog Gone Dog, Tush,
Sneakin' Sally Through the Alley, Prep School Hippie

Wednesday, December 31, 1986
Magic Mountain, Londonderry, VT
● *Show Notes:* Though this wasn't really a Phish show, it may have been the first time members of Phish performed publicly on New Year's Eve. A booking company called The Joneses on New Year's Eve and asked them if they could play a last-minute show. Apparently, not all members of the band were in town so they added Trey and Page and played the show as a combination of the two bands called "The Phones." The lineup included Trey on guitar, Page on keys, Steve Drebber on drums, Dan Pine on drums, Tim "T.J." Johnston on bass, and Mark Jensen on percussion. Sound was engineered by Garrett Mead. While a setlist is not available, it is known that the show included Eyes of the World, I Heard it Through the Grapevine, and a Bachman-Turner Overdrive song. While most "sideshows" are listed in a separate chapter, this show is also listed here for its historical significance.

Thursday, January 1, 1987
Private Party
● *Show Notes:* There was no show on this date. Tapes that circulate are mislabeled copies of August 21, 1987, set III.

Monday, January 19, 1987
Hunt's, Burlington, VT

Wednesday, January 21, 1987
Hunt's, Burlington, VT

Sunday, February 1, 1987
Nectar's, Burlington, VT

Monday, February 2, 1987
Nectar's, Burlington, VT

Michael McNamara

Fishman at the Wetlands (4/5/00)

Saturday, February 7, 1987
Mad Maggie's Farm, Monkton, VT

Friday, February 13, 1987
Johnson State College, Johnson, VT
Sneakin' Sally Through the Alley, Possum, Golgi Apparatus > Slave to the Traffic Light > Quinn the Eskimo, Alumni Blues, Suzy Greenberg, Sanity, Good Times Bad Times, Wilson, Melt the Guns -> Dave's Energy Guide, Fluffhead, Harry Hood
● *Show Notes:* The Dude of Life made a guest appearance on vocals during Suzy (first known version), Sanity, Fluffhead, and Hood.

Saturday, February 21, 1987
Slade Hall, University of Vermont, Burlington, VT
● *Set II:* Fluffhead, Fire, Suzy Greenberg, Dear Mrs. Reagan, Camel Walk, Back Porch Boogie Blues, Clod, Lushington, Peaches en Regalia, Swing Low (Sweet Chariot), Boogie On Reggae Woman, Ya Mar, Corrine Corrina, Dog Gone Dog, Alumni Blues
● *Show Notes:* While this show may have taken place six nights later, this date is believed to be correct. It contained the first known Ya Mar and Boogie On.

Friday, February 27, 1987
Slade Hall, University of Vermont, Burlington, VT
● *Show Notes:* It is not believed that a show was played on this night. Tapes circulate but they are actually from the Slade Hall show six nights earlier.

Friday, March 6, 1987
Goddard College, Plainfield, VT
● *Set I:* Funky Bitch, Good Times Bad Times, Corrine Corrina, Golgi Apparatus, Quinn the Eskimo > Sneakin' Sally Through the Alley
● *Set II:* Freebird, Happy Birthday > Harry Hood, Tell Me Something Good -> Possum, Freeworld, Wilson
● *Encore:* Slave to the Traffic Light
● *Show Notes:* Freeworld was sung by an audience member. Happy Birthday was sung to Sue and Debra and was a long, reggafied version. This version of Freebird was an actual attempt at the song and not an *a cappella* version, but it was performed quite mockingly and not in its entirety. It did, however, feature Ninja Mike on vocals. Also, Tell Me Something Good featured a female lead vocalist.

Sunday, March 22, 1987
Nectar's, Burlington, VT

Monday, March 23, 1987
Nectar's, Burlington, VT
● *Set I:* Funky Bitch, Mike's Song, Alumni Blues, You Enjoy Myself -> Sparks
● *Set II:* Fluffhead, Peaches en Regalia, Ride Captain Ride -> Dave's Energy Guide, Corrine Corrina, Why Don't You Love Me -> Camel Walk, Golgi Apparatus, Swing Low (Sweet Chariot)
● *Show Notes:* Based on comments made by the band during the show, it appears that there may have been a third set. Tapes of it, though, are not in circulation.

Monday, April 20, 1987
Nectar's, Burlington, VT
● *Show Notes:* There was no show on this date. Tapes that circulate are the second set of October 15, 1986.

Friday, April 24, 1987
Billings Lounge, University of Vermont, Burlington, VT
Golgi Apparatus, AC/DC Bag -> Possum, Fluffhead, You Enjoy Myself -> Dave's Energy Guide, Punch Me in the Eye, Alumni Blues, I Am Hydrogen, David Bowie, Dear Mrs. Reagan, Slave to the Traffic Light
● *Show Notes:* Phish played this show at the conclusion of "Earth Week."

Tuesday, April 28, 1987
Nectar's, Burlington, VT

Wednesday, April 29, 1987
Nectar's, Burlington, VT
● *Set I:* She Caught the Katy and Left Me a Mule to Ride, Alumni Blues, Golgi Apparatus, Swing Low (Sweet Chariot), Fire, Skin it Back -> Cities, Fuck Your Face, Lushington
● *Set II:* Dog Gone Dog, Melt the Guns -> Dave's Energy Guide, Take the 'A' Train, Halley's Comet, Quinn the Eskimo, AC/DC Bag
● *Set III:* Peaches en Regalia, Fluffhead, Good Times Bad Times, Anarchy, Makisupa Policeman > Run Like an Antelope, Boogie On Reggae Woman, Timber (Jerry), Slave to the Traffic Light -> Sparks, McGrupp and the Watchful Hosemasters, The Ballad of Curtis Loew, Come On (Let the Good Times Roll), I Am Hydrogen
● *Show Notes:* Highlights included a great segue from Skin it Back into Cities, a long, intricate jam at the beginning of McGrupp, and the Melt the Guns / DEG combo. Some debate whether Fuck Your Face (the only known live version) is from this show, due to tape cuts before the song. It may be filler from another date but circulates on all known copies of this tape.

Saturday, May 9, 1987
Nectar's, Burlington, VT
● *Show Notes:* Tapes that circulate under this date are mislabeled copies of May 9, 1989.

Sunday, May 10, 1987
Nectar's, Burlington, VT

Monday, May 11, 1987
Nectar's, Burlington, VT
● *Set I:* You Enjoy Myself, The Chase -> Lushington -> Possum, Slave to the Traffic Light, Sneakin' Sally Through the Alley, Clod, Peaches en Regalia > The Man Who Stepped Into Yesterday > Avenu Malkenu > The Man Who Stepped Into Yesterday Reprise, Makisupa Policeman, Ya Mar
● *Encore:* Golgi Apparatus, Corrine Corrina, Letter to Jimmy Page
● *Show Notes:* This show included some funny stage banter, including Trey's announcement after TMWSIY: "That was called 'The Man Who Stepped Into Yesterday…and I'm going to get my head sharpened." A set break was announced after Ya Mar, so this is the complete first set. The list for the second set, though, is not known.

Tuesday, May 12, 1987
Nectar's, Burlington, VT

Saturday, May 16, 1987
Goddard SpringFest, Haybarn Theatre, Goddard College, Plainfield, VT

Wednesday, May 20, 1987
The Ranch, South Burlington, VT
Wilson, Run Like an Antelope, Golgi Apparatus > Back Porch Boogie Blues > Lushington -> Possum, Harry Hood, You Enjoy Myself, Alumni Blues
● *Show Notes:* This setlist may be incomplete. It was taken from a video that circulates. Alumni featured guests on rhythm guitar and saxophone. These guests were members of local bands The Joneses and Mental Floss. The show was a co-bill with The Joneses and was played for forty or fifty people in front of a big red barn-like house, with the band playing on an actual stage.

Sunday, August 9, 1987
Nectar's, Burlington, VT
● *Set I:* Golgi Apparatus, Slave to the Traffic Light, La Grange, The Chase -> Possum, Sneakin' Sally Through the Alley, Timber (Jerry), Good Times Bad Times, AC/DC Bag, Shaggy Dog, Funky Bitch
● *Set II:* The Curtain With, Halley's Comet, The Sloth, Light Up or Leave Me Alone -> Skin it Back, Peaches en Regalia, Fluffhead, Fee, Harry Hood, Harpua, Suzy Greenberg
● *Set III:* David Bowie, You Enjoy Myself, Ya Mar, Divided Sky, Flat Fee, McGrupp and the Watchful Hosemasters, Corrine Corrina
● *Show Notes:* This show marked the first known appearances of La Grange, The Curtain With, Divided Sky, Fee, Harpua, and The Sloth.

Fishman at the Wetlands (4/5/00)

Monday, August 10, 1987
Nectar's, Burlington, VT
● *Set I:* Peaches en Regalia, Alumni Blues, Golgi Apparatus, Wilson, Quinn the Eskimo, Divided Sky, Good Times Bad Times
● *Set II:* Fire, AC/DC Bag -> Possum, Fluffhead, Fee, The Curtain With, I Know a Little, Mustang Sally, You Enjoy Myself, La Grange
● *Set III:* Icculus, David Bowie, Jesus Just Left Chicago, Whipping Post, Anarchy, Tush, Dear Mrs. Reagan
● *Show Notes:* Icculus was dedicated to Paul Languedoc's mother on her birthday.

Sunday, August 16, 1987
Trey Anastasio's Basement
● *Show Notes:* The tapes that circulate under this date are actually the first set of the July 23, 1988 show.

Wednesday, August 19, 1987
Collis Center, Dartmouth College, Hanover, NH
● *Show Notes:* There was no show on this date. Tapes that circulate are actually from August 19, 1989.

Friday, August 21, 1987
Ian McLean's Farm, Hebron, NY
● *Set I:* Dog Gone Dog, Peaches en Regalia, Divided Sky, Funky Bitch, Harry Hood, Clod, The Curtain With, Light Up or Leave Me Alone, Shaggy Dog, Wilson, Camel Walk
● *Set II:* Mike's Song, Harpua -> Bundle of Joy -> Harpua -> Golgi Apparatus > Sparks, Flat Fee > Fee, Skin it Back -> Low Rider Jam -> Back Porch Boogie Blues -> The Sloth
● *Set III:* Big Black Furry Creature from Mars, McGrupp and the Watchful Hosemasters -> Stir it Up Jam -> Makisupa Policeman Jam -> David Bowie Jam > Sanity, Swing Low (Sweet Chariot)
● *Show Notes:* This show, one of the most commonly circulated from this era, is mislabeled on many tapes as 8/27/87. Teases of other songs were everywhere, including La Bamba lyrics in Low Rider and HYHU teases during Mike's Song and before McGrupp. Also, before Mike's, Trey teased I've Got Spurs That Jingle Jangle Jingle. Sections of Fluff's Travels were also teased before McGrupp. The third set was heavy on jamming and light on lyrics. Harpua was played by request and was re-started after the opening lyric, which was repeated. The intro to Sparks was extended while Fishman relieved himself. Trey delivered some freestyle reggae-rapping before and during the Makisupa Jam that some fans have labeled the "Mouse House Rap." This show contained the first known BBFCFM.

Saturday, August 22, 1987
"Vergennes Day," Vergennes, VT

Monday, August 24, 1987
Burlington, VT
● *Show Notes:* There was no show on this date. Tapes that circulate are the third set of the August 29, 1987 show.

Friday, August 27, 1987
● *Show Notes:* There was no show on this date. Tapes that circulate are actually August 21, 1987.

Saturday, August 29, 1987
The Ranch, South Burlington, VT
● *Set I:* Clod, Slave to the Traffic Light, Swing Low (Sweet Chariot), The Curtain With, McGrupp and the Watchful Hosemasters, Possum, Harry Hood, Timber (Jerry), AC/DC Bag, Divided Sky, Harpua -> Bundle of Joy -> Harpua
● *Set II:* Alumni Blues, The Ballad of Curtis Loew, Sneakin' Sally Through the Alley, Makisupa Policeman, Big Black Furry Creature from Mars, Flat Fee, Lushington, Suzy Greenberg, Mustang Sally, Ya Mar, The Man Who Stepped Into Yesterday > Avenu Malkenu > The Man Who Stepped Into Yesterday
● *Set III:* La Grange, Corrine Corrina, Mike's Song > I Am Hydrogen > Shaggy Dog, David Bowie, Jesus Just Left Chicago, She Caught the Katy and Left Me a Mule to Ride
● *Show Notes:* This show was played for Eric Larson, who took care of Trey's dog Marley over the summer.

Wednesday, September 2, 1987
Hunt's, Burlington, VT
AC/DC Bag, Fluffhead, Sneakin' Sally Through the Alley, Divided Sky, Wilson, David Bowie, The Chase -> Possum, Big Black Furry Creature from Mars, Makisupa Policeman, Timber (Jerry), Shaggy Dog, You Enjoy Myself
● *Show Notes:* Check out this early Makisupa to hear the band play with a lot of crazy effects!

Thursday, September 3, 1987
Hunt's, Burlington, VT

Friday, September 4, 1987
Goddard College, Plainfield, VT

Monday, September 7, 1987
The Living Room, Providence, RI
● *Show Notes:* Tapes that circulate under this date are actually the second set of November 9, 1989.

Saturday, September 19, 1987
Goddard College, Plainfield, VT
● *Show Notes:* This show was a birthday party.

Sunday, September 20, 1987
Nectar's, Burlington, VT

Monday, September 21, 1987
Nectar's, Burlington, VT
● *Set I:* The Man Who Stepped Into Yesterday > Avenu Malkenu > The Man Who Stepped Into Yesterday Reprise, Clod > Slave to the Traffic Light, Funky Bitch, Wilson, Dear Mrs. Reagan, Golgi Apparatus > AC/DC Bag -> Possum
● *Set II:* You Enjoy Myself, The Curtain With, Big Black Furry Creature from Mars, Suzy Greenberg, Alumni Blues
● *Set III:* The Birthday Dub, Good Times Bad Times, Rocky Top, Sneakin' Sally Through the Alley, Fee, Divided Sky, Dog Gone Dog, The Ballad of Curtis Loew, Run Like an Antelope, Makisupa Policeman, Flat Fee, Fire, Terrapin, La Grange, Fluffhead

● *Show Notes:* The listed setbreaks are uncertain and may be incorrect. The Birthday Dub was dedicated to "Spup." This show marked the first known performance of Rocky Top.

Sunday, September 27, 1987
Pledge Party, Burlington, VT
● *Set I:* David Bowie, Funky Bitch, Golgi Apparatus, Peaches en Regalia, Take the 'A' Train > Possum, Phase Dance, Good Times Bad Times, Skin It Back
● *Set II:* Wilson, I Didn't Know, Fluffhead, Fire, Fee
● *Show Notes:* This setlist is incomplete. This show includes the first known version of I Didn't Know.

Saturday, October 10, 1987
The Ranch, Shelburne, VT

Wednesday, October 14, 1987
Hunt's, Burlington, VT
Peaches en Regalia, Take the 'A' Train, You Enjoy Myself, Golgi Apparatus, Slave to the Traffic Light, Fluffhead, Possum, David Bowie > AC/DC Bag > Divided Sky -> McGrupp and the Watchful Hosemasters, Makisupa Policeman

Sunday, October 18, 1987
Nectar's, Burlington, VT

Monday, October 19, 1987
Nectar's, Burlington, VT

Friday, October 23, 1987
Cork's, Burlington, VT

Saturday, October 24, 1987
Cork's, Burlington, VT

Thursday, October 29, 1987
Goddard College, Plainfield, VT
● *Show Notes:* There was no show on this date; tapes that circulate are mislabeled copies of Halloween, 1988.

Saturday, October 31, 1987
Sculpture Room, Goddard College, Plainfield, VT
● *Set I:* Jam -> Whipping Post, Sneakin' Sally Through the Alley -> Back Porch Boogie Blues -> Halley's Comet -> Light Up or Leave Me Alone, Love You, AC/DC Bag, Possum, You Enjoy Myself > Big Black Furry Creature from Mars
● *Set II:* The Man Who Stepped Into Yesterday > Avenu Malkenu > The Man Who Stepped Into Yesterday Reprise, Peaches en Regalia, Take the 'A' Train, Timber (Jerry) > Fluff's Travels -> I Am Hydrogen -> The Chase, Fee, Divided Sky > McGrupp and the Watchful Hosemasters, Who Do? We Do! -> Clod, Alumni Blues > Fluffhead, David Bowie
● *Show Notes:* The jam before Whipping Post included Low Rider teases. This show was a double bill with The Joneses, whom Trey referenced several times. It has been reported that Fishman shaved his entire body for this show!

Wednesday, November 18, 1987
Hunt's, Burlington, VT
● *Set I:* Slave to the Traffic Light, The Man Who Stepped Into Yesterday > Avenu Malkenu > The Man Who Stepped Into Yesterday Reprise, Flat Fee, Wilson > Peaches en Regalia, Take the 'A' Train, Golgi Apparatus, Divided Sky, Alumni Blues, Good Times Bad Times
● *Set II:* I Didn't Know, You Enjoy Myself, Fluffhead, AC/DC Bag
● *Show Notes:* The second set listing is incomplete, as the tapes that circulate cut during Bag. I Didn't Know was dedicated to Brian Long.

Thursday, November 19, 1987
Hunt's, Burlington, VT
● *Set I:* McGrupp and the Watchful Hosemasters, Sparks, Funky Bitch, You Enjoy Myself, Sneakin' Sally Through the Alley, Harry Hood, Fire
● *Set II:* Timber (Jerry), Fluffhead, I Didn't Know, Fee, Corrine Corrina, Alumni Blues
● *Set III:* Jam, Suzy Greenberg, Possum, Divided Sky > Big Black Furry Creature from Mars, Dinner and a Movie, The Ballad of Curtis Loew, Whipping Post, Letter to Jimmy Page, Take the 'A' Train, Camel Walk, La Grange, Bike, Slave to the Traffic Light
● *Show Notes:* Divided Sky was botched badly, leading Trey to launch humorously into BBFCFM. This show contained the first known Dinner and a Movie and was the last known show at Hunt's.

Kevin Pole

Sunday, November 22, 1987
Nectar's, Burlington, VT

Monday, November 23, 1987
Nectar's, Burlington, VT

Tuesday, November 24, 1987
Nectar's, Burlington, VT

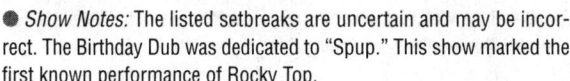

1988

Wednesday, January 27, 1988
Gallagher's, Waitsfield, VT
● *Set I:* Funky Bitch, Mustang Sally, AC/DC Bag -> Possum, Jesus Just Left Chicago, Sneakin' Sally Through the Alley, Alumni Blues, Take the 'A' Train, Good Times Bad Times
● *Set II:* Wilson, Slave to the Traffic Light, Corrine Corrina, Fire, Fluffhead, Divided Sky, The Ballad of Curtis Loew, You Enjoy Myself, The Sloth, Whipping Post
● *Set III:* Fee, The Lizards, Suzy Greenberg, Golgi Apparatus, Bike, Big Black Furry Creature from Mars, Camel Walk, Harry Hood
● *Show Notes:* Check out the excellent segue between AC/DC Bag and Possum. This show contained the first known version of Lizards.

Saturday, January 30, 1988
Gallagher's, Waitsfield, VT
● *Show Notes:* There was no show on this date. Tapes that circulate are

mislabeled copies of January 27, 1988, at Gallagher's.

Wednesday, February 3, 1988
Gallagher's, Waitsfield, VT

Sunday, February 7, 1988
Nectar's Lounge, Burlington, VT
● *Set I:* Fire, McGrupp and the Watchful Hosemasters, Shaggy Dog, Golgi Apparatus, Alumni Blues, Peaches en Regalia, Phase Dance, Dear Mrs. Reagan, I Didn't Know, David Bowie
● *Set II:* Happy Birthday, AC/DC Bag, Timber (Jerry), Flat Fee, Fee, Possum, The Lizards, The Famous Mockingbird, Whipping Post
● *Set III:* Suzy Greenberg, The Man Who Stepped Into Yesterday > Avenu Malkenu > The Man Who Stepped Into Yesterday Reprise, Clod, The Curtain, The Ballad of Curtis Loew, Good Times Bad Times
● *Show Notes:* Mockingbird made its debut at this show and was played without Forbin's.

Monday, February 8, 1988
Nectar's Lounge, Burlington, VT
● *Set I:* Slave to the Traffic Light, Funky Bitch, Take the 'A' Train, Golgi Apparatus, Phase Dance, Fire, You Enjoy Myself
● *Set II:* Fluffhead, Wilson > Peaches en Regalia, Divided Sky, The Lizards, Run Like an Antelope
● *Set III:* The Sloth, Flat Fee, Dinner and a Movie, Alumni Blues, Harry Hood, Bike, Fee, Jesus Just Left Chicago, Big Black Furry Creature from Mars
● *Show Notes:* Bike included one verse of Love You and a trombone solo from Fishman.

Wednesday, February 10, 1988
Gallagher's, Waitsfield, VT

Saturday, February 20, 1988
St. Lawrence University, Canton, NY
● *Show Notes:* It is believed that this show was a fraternity party.

Wednesday, February 24, 1988
Gallagher's, Waitsfield, VT
● *Set I:* The Curtain > You Enjoy Myself, I Didn't Know, The Lizards, Wilson > Peaches en Regalia, Golgi Apparatus, Slave to the Traffic Light, Corrine Corrina, Fee, David Bowie
● *Set II:* Mustang Sally, Sneakin' Sally Through the Alley, Sanity, La Grange, Harry Hood
● *Show Notes:* The second set listing may be incomplete. The first two songs of the second set featured John Carlton on drums and Sneakin' Sally featured Fishman on horn.

Friday, February 26, 1988
Living and Learning Center, University of Vermont, Burlington, VT
● *Set I:* The Curtain With > Suzy Greenberg, You Enjoy Myself, The Man Who Stepped Into Yesterday > Avenu Malkenu > The Man Who Stepped Into Yesterday > AC/DC, Possum, Phase Dance, Good Times, Bad Times, Fluffhead, I Didn't Know, Golgi Apparatus
● *Set II:* The Lizards, David Bowie, The Ballad of Curtis Loew, Fee > Mc-

Grupp and the Watchful Hosemasters, Dear Mrs. Reagan, Makisupa Policeman, Alumni Blues, Whipping Post

Wednesday, March 9, 1988
Gallagher's, Waitsfield, VT

Friday, March 11, 1988
Baso Lounge, Johnson State University, Johnson, VT
● *Set I:* The Chicken, Funky Bitch, Sneakin' Sally Through the Alley, Take the 'A' Train, You Enjoy Myself -> Wilson, Golgi Apparatus, Slave to the Traffic Light, Flat Fee, Corrine Corrina, The Lizards, David Bowie
● *Set II:* Fluffhead, Dinner and a Movie, Harry Hood, The Ballad of Curtis Loew, Harpua, AC/DC Bag > Alumni Blues > Run Like an Antelope
● *Show Notes:* Sneakin' Sally and Curtis Loew featured Tim Rogers (who was announced as "Bobby Brown") on harmonica. Bowie began with a tease medley that included Timber, Sunshine of Your Love, Whipping Post, and several others. There was a vocal jam in Sneakin' Sally, but not in YEM. Trey spat out the names "Marco Esquandolas...Poster Nutbag...Moses Heaps...Moses DeWitt" in Antelope. Dinner and a Movie was dedicated to "our good friend Suzannah." The first set Lizards was delayed, as Trey cut on Fishman for losing his drumsticks during the gig.

Saturday, March 12, 1988
Nectar's, Burlington, VT
● *Set II:* Jump Monk, McGrupp and the Watchful Hosemasters, The Lizards, Tela, Wilson, AC/DC Bag, Colonel Forbin's Ascent > The Famous Mockingbird, The Sloth, Possum, Run Like an Antelope
● *Show Notes:* This was the first known live Gamehendge, complete with narration. The date is incorrect, though the correct date is not known. Actually, the members of Phish were, by accounts, at a Frank Zappa concert on the evening of March 12, 1988. Chronologically, the show contained the first known version of Tela and Forbin's, though the actual date of this show might be after their separate debuts (see May 21, 1988, where Trey calls Tela a debut).

Sunday, March 20, 1988
Nectar's, Burlington, VT
● *Show Notes:* There was a show on this date, but tapes do not circulate. However, mislabeled tapes circulate that are actually the *Junta* release party from May 9, 1989.

Monday, March 21, 1988
Nectar's, Burlington, VT
Suzy Greenberg, Golgi Apparatus, McGrupp and the Watchful Hosemasters, Sneakin' Sally Through the Alley, Divided Sky, Boogie On Reggae Woman, Timber (Jerry), The Lizards, Fire, AC/DC Bag, Possum, Dinner and a Movie, I Didn't Know, Colonel Forbin's Ascent > The Famous Mockingbird

Tuesday, March 22, 1988
Nectar's, Burlington, VT

Thursday, March 31, 1988
Kenny's Castaways, New York, NY

I Didn't Know, Golgi Apparatus, Fee > AC/DC Bag > Possum, Fluffhead, Alumni Blues, The Lizards, Colonel Forbin's Ascent > The Famous Mockingbird, Take the 'A' Train, Fire, You Enjoy Myself, Wilson
● *Show Notes:* This was the first ever Phish show in New York City. AC/DC Bag was sung for Roger, a "character" in the song, who was in attendance.

Saturday, April 2, 1988
The Zoo, Humphries House, Amherst College, Amherst, MA
Fire, Good Times Bad Times
● *Show Notes:* This setlist is obviously incomplete. The show, though, definitely took place on this night.

Wednesday, April 6, 1988
Gallagher's, Waitsfield, VT

Sunday, April 17, 1988
Nectar's, Burlington, VT

Monday, April 18, 1988
Nectar's, Burlington, VT

Tuesday, April 19, 1988
Nectar's, Burlington, VT

Friday, April 22, 1988
University of Vermont, Burlington, VT
Earth Day Festival
● *Set I:* Colonel Forbin's Ascent > The Famous Mockingbird, Fire, Alumni Blues, Run Like an Antelope, Fluffhead, Dinner and a Movie, Harry Hood, Harpua
● *Set II:* I Didn't Know, Golgi Apparatus, The Lizards, Fee, Shaggy Dog, Big Black Furry Creature from Mars, You Enjoy Myself, Suzy Greenberg, Ya Mar, AC/DC Bag -> Possum, The Ballad of Curtis Loew, David Bowie
● *Show Notes:* If you are a stage banter fan, seek out this show for Trey's announcements after Fire as someone requested "Page's new love song." Trey announced that this requested song is actually called Tela, and announced the future debut of several songs, including "The Tires" (a.k.a. Contact), "The Four-Track Song" (a.k.a. Poor Heart) and "Marijuana Hot Chocolate," for which Mike gave a preview of the bass line.

Wednesday, April 27, 1988
Gallagher's, Waitsfield, VT

Saturday, April 30, 1988
Colgate University, Hamilton, NY
● *Show Notes:* This show may have been a fraternity party.

Monday, May 2, 1988
The Haunt, Ithaca, NY

Tuesday, May 3, 1988
The Haunt, Ithaca, NY

Thursday, May 5, 1988
Slade Hall, University of Vermont, Burlington, VT

Thursday, May 12, 1988
Kenny's Castaways, New York, NY

Saturday, May 14, 1988
SpringFest, Goddard College, Plainfield, VT
Fire, I Didn't Know, Halley's Comet > Light Up or Leave Me Alone, You Enjoy Myself, The Lizards, Big Black Furry Creature from Mars, Jesus Just Left Chicago, Fluffhead, Alumni Blues, Take the 'A' Train
● *Show Notes:* Fire was dedicated to Bobby Brown (Tim Rogers); JJLC subsequently featured Bobby on harmonica. Also "guesting" on the song was three year old Cameron McKinney, whom Trey announced was playing guitar. Halley's Comet and I Didn't Know featured Nancy Taube adding additional vocals; he also played drums on I Didn't Know. After Light Up, Trey introduced the crowd to Marley and sang to her both before and during YEM. BBFCFM was dedicated to Donald Fagen and Walter Becker of the band Steely Dan. Take the 'A' Train, which was preceded by HYHU teases, featured Carl Boyle on saxophone.

Sunday, May 15, 1988
Vermont Farm Festival, Beecher Hill Farm, Hinesburg, VT
● *Set I:* Alumni Blues, Golgi Apparatus, You Enjoy Myself, Suzy Greenberg, Good Times Bad Times, Fluffhead, Shaggy Dog, The Lizards, Sneakin' Sally Through the Alley, AC/DC Bag -> Possum
● *Set II:* Icculus, McGrupp and the Watchful Hosemasters, The Curtain > Wilson > Peaches en Regalia, Take the 'A' Train, Jesus Just Left Chicago, I Didn't Know, Flat Fee > Whipping Post, Harpua
● *Encore:* Fire
● *Show Notes:* Harpua was preceded by a Rocky Top tease. After JJLC, Fishman borrowed a snare drum from the Dirch Brothers.

Saturday, May 21, 1988
Nectar's, Burlington, VT
● *Set I:* Funky Bitch, Sneakin' Sally Through the Alley, Alumni Blues, You Enjoy Myself, St. Thomas, Golgi Apparatus, Fire
● *Set II:* La Grange, Possum, The Lizards, Timber (Jerry), Tela, Happy Birthday, Fluffhead, Bike, Good Times Bad Times
● *Set III:* Big Leg Emma, Rocky Top, Cities, Take the 'A' Train, The Curtain > Suzy Greenberg
● *Show Notes:* This show included the first known version of St. Thomas. YEM was dedicated to Del and La Grange was dedicated to Mike. The date for this show may be wrong, but a correct date is not known. Note that Trey refers to Tela as a debut at this show.

Sunday, May 22, 1988
Nectar's, Burlington, VT

Monday, May 23, 1988
Nectar's, Burlington, VT

Tuesday, May 24, 1988
Nectar's, Burlington, VT

Wednesday, May 25, 1988
Nectar's, Burlington, VT
● *Set I:* The Curtain, Rocky Top, Funky Bitch, Alumni Blues, Peaches en Regalia, Golgi Apparatus, Sneakin' Sally Through the Alley, Suzy

Greenberg, Fire
● *Set II:* Jesus Just Left Chicago, Fluffhead, Whipping Post
● *Set III:* The Sloth, I Didn't Know, Ya Mar, Halley's Comet, La Grange, Fee, I Know a Little, Big Black Furry Creature from Mars, Corrine Corrina, Harpua, Run Like an Antelope
● *Show Notes:* Ya Mar and Halley's Comet featured guest vocals from Jah Roy. The venue on tapes that circulate is often mislabeled as Ian McLean's Farm, Hebron, NY.

Friday, May 27, 1988
The Front, Burlington, VT

Saturday, May 28, 1988
Wedding Reception, Waitsfield, VT

Friday, June 3, 1988
Squam Lake Steak House, Squam Lake, NH

Saturday, June 4, 1988
Squam Lake Steak House, Squam Lake, NH

Wednesday, June 15, 1988
The Front, Burlington, VT
● *Set I:* Suzy Greenberg, Alumni Blues, You Enjoy Myself, Wilson, Rocky Top, McGrupp and the Watchful Hosemasters, Fluffhead, Golgi Apparatus, La Grange
● *Set II:* The Lizards, AC/DC Bag, The Sloth, Contact, Dinner and a Movie, Take the 'A' Train, Good Times Bad Times, Whipping Post, Dear Mrs. Reagan
● *Show Notes:* This show marked the first known performance of Contact. The actual date of this show may have been June 16.

Thursday, June 17, 1988
Gopher Broke (Commune), Morrisville, VT

Saturday, June 18, 1988
Nectar's, Burlington, VT
● *Show Notes:* There was no show on this date. Tapes that circulate are mislabeled copies of the following night at Nectar's.

Sunday, June 19, 1988
Nectar's, Burlington, VT
● *Set I:* The Curtain With, Funky Bitch, Possum, Golgi Apparatus, La Grange, Suzy Greenberg, Big Leg Emma, You Enjoy Myself
● *Set II:* Good Times Bad Times, Cities
● *Show Notes:* Listen for a fun, piano-based jazz interlude between The Curtain and Funky Bitch. The setlist is incomplete.

Monday, June 20, 1988
Nectar's, Burlington, VT
● *Set I:* Slave to the Traffic Light, Peaches en Regalia, You Enjoy Myself, Fluffhead, AC/DC Bag > The Lizards, Halley's Comet -> Wilson, Ya Mar -> Jam, I Didn't Know
● *Set II:* Sneakin' Sally Through the Alley, Tela, Fee, Golgi Apparatus, Satin Doll, Take the 'A' Train > Possum, The Ballad of Curtis Loew, David Bowie

● *Show Notes:* The jam out of Ya Mar featured Jah Roy. During the jam, Jah Roy quoted lines from many famous reggae tunes, including One Love, Three Little Birds, Stir it Up, and Everything's Gonna Be Alright. I Didn't Know featured a trombone solo from Fishman.

Tuesday, June 21, 1988
Nectar's, Burlington, VT
● *Set I:* Fluffhead, Rocky Top, Mustang Sally, Suzy Greenberg, The Curtain > The Lizards, Colonel Forbin's Ascent > The Famous Mockingbird, Fire
● *Set II:* Harpua, I Didn't Know, AC/DC Bag, Flat Fee, Alumni Blues, Jesus Just Left Chicago, Good Times Bad Times, Contact, Peaches en Regalia, Golgi Apparatus

Friday, June 23, 1988
Tramps, New York, NY

Saturday, June 24, 1988
Halverson's, Burlington, VT
The Lizards, Possum, Jazz Jam, Alumni Blues, On Your Way Down, Golgi Apparatus, Fee, Sneakin' Sally Through the Alley, You Enjoy Myself, The Ballad of Curtis Loew, Fluffhead
● *Show Notes:* This setlist is incomplete. It is unclear whether this tape is actually from this show (which was confirmed for this date), is from another show, or is a mix with pieces from various shows.

Sunday, June 27, 1988
Cossayuna Lake, Cossayuna, NY
● *Show Notes:* Several fans who were in the area for the following evening's Grateful Dead concert hired Phish to play at their campsite. The area is a regular site of concerts and small festivals. While the show was apparently taped through the soundboard, copies do not circulate and no setlist is known.

Thursday, July 7, 1988
The Front, Burlington, VT

Friday, July 8, 1988
The Front, Burlington, VT

Monday, July 11, 1988
Sam's Tavern, Burlington, VT
Satin Doll, Suzy Greenberg, The Curtain, Jam, Funky Bitch, Fire, Bold As Love, Colonel Forbin's Ascent > The Famous Mockingbird, Golgi Apparatus, Alumni Blues
● *Encore:* McGrupp and the Watchful Hosemasters > La Grange
● *Show Notes:* Trey graduated college on this date and treated the crowd to a killer Alumni Blues, complete with a fun drum solo from Fishman. Suzy Greenberg included Dave's Energy Guide teases. Trey referred to the jam after The Curtain as "A Living Nightmare." The listed encore may actually be the start of the second set; the first set appeared to end after Alumni given Page's comments.

Tuesday, July 12, 1988
Sam's Tavern, Burlington, VT

● *Set I:* Cities, The Lizards, Sneakin' Sally Through the Alley, Good Times Bad Times, Happy Birthday, Peaches en Regalia, You Enjoy Myself, I Didn't Know

● *Set II:* Blue Bossa, Take the 'A' Train -> Timber (Jerry), Fluffhead > Jesus Just Left Chicago, Makisupa Policeman, Slave to the Traffic Light, AC/DC Bag, Roll Like A Cantaloupe

Wednesday, July 13, 1988
Underhill, VT

● *Show Notes:* There was no show on this date. Mislabeled tapes that circulate are listed here as June 24, 1988, which is a "best-guess" and may not be correct.

Saturday, July 23, 1988
Pete's Phabulous Phish Phest, Underhill, VT

● *Set I:* Jam, Colonel Forbin's Ascent > The Famous Mockingbird, Mike's Song > I Am Hydrogen > Weekapaug Groove, The Lizards, On Your Way Down, AC/DC Bag, Possum, Walk Away, Bold as Love, No Dogs Allowed

● *Set II:* The Sloth, Fire, The Curtain, Terrapin, Run Like an Antelope, Satin Doll, Blue Bossa, La Grange, Alumni Blues, Peaches en Regalia

● *Set III:* You Enjoy Myself, Contact, Harry Hood, Dinner and a Movie, Slave to the Traffic Light, The Ballad of Curtis Loew, Good Times Bad Times

● *Show Notes:* This show was actually a party at Peter Danforth's place and included the first known Weekapaug. Satin Doll and Blue Bossa featured Peter Danforth and Dave Grippo on horns. After Weekapaug, Fishman teased both Weekapaug and Peaches on the drums. Lizards included a Mockingbird tease from Page.

Sunday, July 24, 1988
Nectar's, Burlington, VT

● *Set I:* Walk Away, Golgi Apparatus, Funky Bitch, Colonel Forbin's Ascent > The Famous Mockingbird, Sneakin' Sally Through the Alley, Mike's Song > I Am Hydrogen > Weekapaug Groove, Bold As Love

● *Set II:* Light Up or Leave Me Alone, Fluffhead, La Grange, The Lizards, Alumni Blues, On Your Way Down, Cities, David Bowie

● *Set III:* The Man Who Stepped Into Yesterday > Avenu Malkenu > Peaches en Regalia > Jesus Just Left Chicago, McGrupp and the Watchful Hosemasters -> Run Like an Antelope

Monday, July 25, 1988
Nectar's, Burlington, VT

● *Set II:* Mike's Song > I Am Hydrogen > Weekapaug Groove, Bold as Love, Light Up or Leave Me Alone, Fluffhead

● *Set III:* Skin it Back, Harpua, Big Black Furry Creature from Mars, Sanity

● *Encore:* Icculus, Camel Walk

● *Show Notes:* These versions of Icculus and Sanity also appear on the *Junta* re-release. BBFCFM featured a tease of the "Flintstones" theme. This setlist is incomplete.

Thursday, July 28, 1988
The Roma, Telluride, CO

Friday, July 29, 1988
The Roma, Telluride, CO

Saturday, July 30, 1988
The Roma, Telluride, CO

● *Set I:* All Blues, Mr. P.C.

● *Set II:* Funky Bitch, Suzy Greenberg, My Baby Left Me, Contact, Maiden Voyage, Corrine Corrina

● *Set III:* La Grange, On Your Way Down, Slave to the Traffic Light, Timber (Jerry), Walk Away, Possum, Sneakin' Sally Through the Alley, Harpua, Fluffhead, Anarchy, Dear Mrs. Reagan, Terrapin, Run Like an Antelope

● *Encore:* Fire

● *Show Notes:* This is the infamous show when Fishman missed the first two sets, prompting the band to play two sets of jazz and standard Phish material in his absence, with Trey on drums. These opening sets are sometimes referred to as "Jazz Odyssey," as the lone known taper labeled his master tapes as such. The Antelope is hilarious—Trey told the story of what happened to Fishman and explained that Fish, who had been at the top of a mountain and, therefore, late for the gig, had to "Run like an Antelope, out of control." Check out this tape and listen to Trey chide Fishman for his tardiness. The narration in Harpua was straightforward, with no teases. Anarchy included teases of Whipping Post. Many tapes mislabel this venue as Fly Me to the Moon Saloon.

Wednesday, August 3, 1988
Fly Me to the Moon Saloon, Telluride, CO

● *Set II:* I Know A Little, You Enjoy Myself, Jesus Just Left Chicago

● *Set III:* Peaches en Regalia, Mike's Song > I Am Hydrogen, Fluffhead, Harry Hood, Satin Doll, Funky Bitch, Walk Away

● *Show Notes:* A birthday dedication to "Stacy" followed Fluffhead. This setlist is incomplete. Many tapes mislabel this venue as The Roma.

Thursday, August 4, 1988
The Roma, Telluride, CO

Friday, August 5, 1988
The Roma, Telluride, CO

Saturday, August 6, 1988
Aspen Mining Company, Aspen, CO

● *Set I:* La Grange, You Enjoy Myself -> Cities -> Dave's Energy Guide -> Cities, Take the 'A' Train, Funky Bitch, Dinner and a Movie, Fire

● *Set II:* Golgi Apparatus, AC/DC Bag, Satin Doll, Sanity, Big Black Furry Creature from Mars, Slave to the Traffic Light

● *Show Notes:* On the tapes of this show that circulate, both Dinner and a Movie and Slave are cut. Therefore, this list might be incomplete. 'A' Train included a London Bridge tease from Trey. Cities included DEG teases before actually segueing into the song. Funky Bitch was dedicated to The Blue Sevilles, a band playing across the street. The band brought light board operator Tim Rogers on-stage for his birthday and presented him with a "Baked in Telluride" T-shirt. BBFCFM included a "Flintstones" theme tease.

Thursday, August 11, 1988
The Front, Burlington, VT

Friday, August 12, 1988
The Front, Burlington, VT

Saturday, August 13, 1988
The Front, Burlington, VT

Wednesday, August 17, 1988
Gallagher's, Waitsfield, VT

Thursday, August 18, 1988
Sam's Tavern, Burlington, VT

Friday, August 19, 1988
Collis Center, Dartmouth College, Hanover, NH
● *Show Notes:* There was no show on this date. Tapes that circulate are actually from August 19, 1989.

Sunday, August 21, 1988
Nectar's, Burlington, VT

Monday, August 22, 1988
Nectar's, Burlington, VT

Wednesday, August 24, 1988
Unknown Location, VT
● *Show Notes:* This show was a co-bill with The Hollywood Indians, a Burlington band.

Saturday, August 27, 1988
Food Court, Mont Alto Campus of Penn State University, Mont Alto, PA
Satin Doll, You Enjoy Myself -> Funky Bitch, Walk Away, Fluffhead, Mike's Song, Take the 'A' Train, Golgi Apparatus, Tela
● *Show Notes:* Golgi included a fun, atypical jam segment. Listen for some fun references to Pennsylvania and Penn State.

Monday, August 29, 1988
Page's House
● *Show Notes:* No such show took place. Tapes that circulate are mislabeled copies of the third set of August 29, 1987.

Monday, August 29, 1988
Sam's Tavern, Burlington, VT

Tuesday, August 30, 1988
Sam's Tavern, Burlington, VT

Thursday, September 8, 1988
The Front, Burlington, VT
● *Set I:* Peaches en Regalia, Walk Away, Slave to the Traffic Light, Wild Child, AC/DC Bag, Colonel Forbin's Ascent > The Famous Mockingbird, Bold as Love
● *Set II:* Possum, You Enjoy Myself, Cities -> Dave's Energy Guide -> Cities, Good Times Bad Times, On Your Way Down, Whipping Post
● *Show Notes:* This was definitely a three-set show, although the third set is not known. Apparently, the lone taper's ride home from the show had to leave early!

Friday, September 9, 1988
The Front, Burlington, VT

Saturday, September 10, 1988
The Front, Burlington, VT

Monday, September 12, 1988
Sam's Tavern, Burlington, VT
● *Set I:* Shaggy Dog, Take the 'A' Train, Fee, Bold as Love
● *Set II:* Timber (Jerry), Satin Doll, The Lizards, The Man Who Stepped Into Yesterday > Avenu Malkenu -> Bundle of Joy -> Camel Walk, The Practical Song, Harry Hood, Esther
● *Show Notes:* This performance included the first known appearances of the old version of Esther, with different lyrics, and The Practical Song. The listing for the first set is probably incomplete.

Tuesday, September 13, 1988
Sam's Tavern, Burlington, VT
● *Set I:* Walk Away, Funky Bitch, You Enjoy Myself, Flat Fee, McGrupp and the Watchful Hosemasters, Wilson > Peaches en Regalia, Good Times Bad Times
● *Set II:* Ride Captain Ride, Boogie On Reggae Woman, Cities > Dave's Energy Guide > Run Like an Antelope, Fluffhead
● *Set III:* Blues Jam, Andy's Chest -> Big Black Furry Creature From Mars -> Dave's Energy Guide -> Big Black Furry Creature From Mars, Sanity -> Vacuum Jam, Fire
● *Show Notes:* The second set listing might be incomplete, as the tapes that circulate cut during Fluffhead. The vacuum jam out of Sanity was around ten minutes long, and may have been the first time Fishman used the vacuum on-stage. This show also marked the only known appearance of Andy's Chest.

Saturday, September 16, 1988
Nick's Basement, University of New Hampshire, Durham, NH

Thursday, September 22, 1988
Binghamton Campus Pub, Binghamton College, Binghamton, NY
McGrupp and the Watchful Hosemasters, Take the 'A' Train, Fluffhead, You Enjoy Myself, David Bowie
● *Show Notes:* The setlist is very incomplete, but McGrupp definitely did open the show.

Saturday, September 24, 1988
Full Moon at The Zoo, Humphries House, Amherst College, Amherst, MA
● *Set I:* Golgi Apparatus, On Your Way Down, Alumni Blues, You Enjoy Myself -> Wilson -> Peaches en Regalia, La Grange, Take the 'A' Train, Divided Sky, Bold As Love
● *Set II:* David Bowie, The Lizards, Walk Away > Possum, Fee -> Sparks, Whipping Post
● *Set III:* Good Times Bad Times, Fluffhead, The Curtain, AC/DC Bag
● *Show Notes:* There were many highlights to this show, including a great segue from YEM (dedicated to John Paluska) into Wilson. Whipping Post was sung by Trey, not Fishman, and was a serious cover of the song. AC/DC Bag was laden with teases, including London Bridge, "Flint-

stones," and My Fair Lady. There was a First Noel tease at the beginning of the third set. Alumni included a Possum tease. The second set listing might be incomplete, as the tapes that circulate cut into Bowie.

Wednesday, October 12, 1988
The Red Barn, Hampshire College, Amherst, MA
● *Show Notes:* There was no show on this date. Tapes that circulate are mislabeled copies of December 10, 1988, set I.

Friday, October 28, 1988
Cafeteria Building, Middlebury College, Middlebury, VT

Saturday, October 29, 1988
Sculpture Room, Goddard College, Plainfield, VT
● *Set I:* Suzy Greenberg, The Lizards, Time Loves a Hero, Golgi Apparatus, Bold as Love, La Grange, Contact, Costume Contest -> Harry Hood
● *Set II:* Halley's Comet -> Whipping Post, Fee, Alumni Blues, Walk Away, Divided Sky, The Ballad of Curtis Loew, Mike's Song, Take the 'A' Train, Fire
● *Set III:* Fluffhead, Good Times Bad Times, You Enjoy Myself -> Possum, AC/DC Bag, Foam, Terrapin, Big Black Furry Creature From Mars, Timber (Jerry), Slave to the Traffic Light, Donna Lee, Run Like an Antelope, I Didn't Know, Wilson > Peaches en Regalia, Funky Bitch
● *Show Notes:* Lots of highlights here, including a great segue from YEM into Possum. Page, Mike, and Fishman noodled around with the Hood intro while Trey conducted the costume contest. In a fun twist, a fan dressed as Harry Hood won! "Bobby Brown" (Tim Rogers) guested on harmonica for Curtis Loew and "Nancy" provided vocals for Halley's. Also, Russ Remington guested on saxophone for parts of the third set.

Monday, October 31, 1988
Hamilton College, Clinton, NY
● *Show Notes:* There was no show on this date; tapes that circulate are partial copies of the Halloween show from two nights earlier.

Thursday, November 3, 1988
Molly's Café, Boston, MA
● *Set I:* Fire, Golgi Apparatus, Fluffhead, Possum, Fee, Alumni Blues, Good Times Bad Times
● *Set II:* Time Loves a Hero, Walk Away, The Lizards, Shaggy Dog, Whipping Post, Contact, Bold As Love, Take the 'A' Train, Run Like an Antelope
● *Set III:* Suzy Greenberg, Foam, I Didn't Know, Big Black Furry Creature from Mars, Harpua, David Bowie
● *Show Notes:* BBFCFM featured a "Popeye" theme tease. Lizards was dedicated to Cilla for cooking the band spaghetti before the show. Whipping Post included DEG teases. This show included the first known version of Foam.

Friday, November 4, 1988
Nardis Restaurant, Clinton, NY

Saturday, November 5, 1988
Hamilton College, Clinton, NY
● *Set I:* Slave to the Traffic Light, Time Loves a Hero, Fire, You Enjoy

Myself, Possum, Take the 'A' Train, Golgi Apparatus, Walk Away, Fluffhead, Alumni Blues, David Bowie
● *Set II:* Wilson -> Peaches en Regalia, Bold as Love, The Lizards, AC/DC Bag, Fee, Mike's Song > I Am Hydrogen > Weekapaug Groove, I Didn't Know, Good Times Bad Times
● *Encore:* Icculus, Suzy Greenberg > Sparks, Divided Sky
● *Show Notes:* This setlist may be incomplete, as the listed encore may actually have been the start of a third set.

Friday, November 11, 1988
The Stone Church, Newmarket, NH
● *Set I:* Divided Sky, You Enjoy Myself -> Slave to the Traffic Light, Foam, Possum, Colonel Forbin's Ascent > The Famous Mockingbird > David Bowie
● *Set II:* Mike's Song > I Am Hydrogen > Weekapaug Groove, Mr. P.C., Fee, Bold as Love, The Lizards, Whipping Post
● *Show Notes:* Mr. P.C., which included a "Spiderman" tease, featured Carl Gerhard on horns. The finale also featured Gerhard and Russ Remington. Some tapes circulate with Timber in the second set and an encore including Peaches, Funky Bitch, and Donna Lee; this is actually filler from the October 29, 1988 show.

Thursday, December 1, 1988
The Red Barn, Hampshire College, Amherst, MA
● *Show Notes:* There was no show on this date. Tapes that circulate are mislabeled copies of December 10, 1988, set I.

Friday, December 2, 1988
Molly's Café, Boston, MA
● *Set I:* The Sloth, Golgi Apparatus, Bold As Love, Take the 'A' Train, Divided Sky, Contact, You Enjoy Myself
● *Set II:* I Didn't Know, Good Times Bad Times, Alumni Blues, The Lizards, AC/DC Bag, Suzy Greenberg, Run Like an Antelope, Wilson

Friday, December 9, 1988
Sheehan's, Northampton, MA

Saturday, December 10, 1988
NORML Benefit
Red Barn, Hampshire College, Amherst, MA
● *Set I:* I Didn't Know, Golgi Apparatus, David Bowie, The Lizards, Foam, Fee, Mike's Song > I Am Hydrogen > Weekapaug Groove, Wilson, Colonel Forbin's Ascent > The Famous Mockingbird
● *Set II:* Alumni Blues, You Enjoy Myself, Contact, The Sloth, AC/DC Bag -> Possum, Good Times Bad Times
● *Encore:* Run Like an Antelope
● *Show Notes:* AC/DC Bag was very slow and featured a hot segue into Possum. This version of Contact was highly amusing, as it was performed quite mockingly.

Sunday, December 11, 1988
The Front, Burlington, VT

Monday, December 12, 1988
The Front, Burlington, VT

Marshmallow at Oswego (1999)

Thursday, December 15, 1988
The Front, Burlington, VT

Friday, December 16, 1988
UVM Gymnasium, University of Vermont, Burlington, VT

Saturday, December 17, 1988
The Stone Church, Newmarket, NH

1989

Wednesday, January 18, 1989
Gallagher's, Waitsfield, VT
Dear Mrs. Reagan
● *Show Notes:* The setlist is incomplete. Dear Mrs. Reagan was played to commemorate George Bush's impending inauguration and Nancy Reagan's departure from the White House.

Thursday, January 19, 1989
Gallagher's, Waitsfield, VT
● *Show Notes:* There was no show on this date; it occurred the night before at Gallagher's.

Friday, January 20, 1989
College of the Atlantic, Bar Harbor, ME

Saturday, January 21, 1989
The Oronoko, University of Maine, Orono, ME

Wednesday, January 25, 1989
Penny Post, Old Town, ME
Fee, Fluffhead
● *Show Notes:* The setlist is incomplete.

Thursday, January 26, 1989
The Paradise, Boston, MA
● *Check:* The Sloth
● *Set I:* I Didn't Know, Golgi Apparatus, Alumni Blues, You Enjoy Myself, The Lizards, Take the 'A' Train, Sanity, Divided Sky, Fee, Good Times Bad Times
● *Set II:* Suzy Greenberg, Icculus, Colonel Forbin's Ascent > The Famous Mockingbird, The Sloth, Possum, Contact, Big Black Furry Creature from Mars, Foam, David Bowie
● *Encore:* AC/DC Bag, Fire

Saturday, January 28, 1989
Dartmouth College, Hanover, NH

Wednesday, February 1, 1989
Gallagher's, Waitsfield, VT

Sunday, February 5, 1989
The Front, Burlington, VT

Monday, February 6, 1989
The Front, Burlington, VT
● *Set I:* Suzy Greenberg, The Curtain > Wilson, Peaches en Regalia > Fee > La Grange, You Enjoy Myself
● *Set II:* All Blues -> Sanity, Take the 'A' Train, Golgi Apparatus, Divided Sky, On Your Way Down, I Didn't Know
● *Set III:* Good Times Bad Times, Walk Away, Harry Hood, Big Black Furry Creature from Mars, The Ballad of Curtis Loew, Colonel Forbin's Ascent > The Famous Mockingbird, Whipping Post, Corrine Corrina
● *Encore:* David Bowie
● *Show Notes:* 'A' Train included a tease of the "Woody Woodpecker" theme.

Tuesday, February 7, 1989
The Front, Burlington, VT
● *Set I:* Esther, McGrupp and the Watchful Hosemasters -> Foam, The Sloth -> Possum, Mike's Song > I Am Hydrogen > Weekapaug Groove, Golgi Apparatus
● *Set II:* Makisupa Policeman, Dinner and a Movie, AC/DC Bag, The Lizards, Timber (Jerry), Contact, Alumni Blues, Fee, Run Like an Antelope
● *Set III:* Sanity, Fluffhead, Suzy Greenberg, Slave to the Traffic Light, Bike, Whipping Post
● *Encore:* Fire
● *Show Notes:* Check out the great segue from Sloth into Possum. This version of Sanity was the rare, fast version.

Friday, February 10, 1989
University of Massachusetts Student Union, Amherst, MA

Saturday, February 11, 1989
Sheehan's, Northampton, MA
The Sloth, Take the 'A' Train
● *Show Notes:* This setlist is incomplete.

Friday, February 17, 1989
The Stone Church, Newmarket, NH
AC/DC Bag, You Enjoy Myself, Fee, Divided Sky, Split Open and Melt, Golgi Apparatus, Take the 'A' Train, Alumni Blues, Run Like an Antelope, Fluffhead
● *Show Notes:* This show contained the first known version of SOAM.

Saturday, February 18, 1989
The Stone Church, Newmarket, NH
Whipping Post, Corrine Corrina, Divided Sky, AC/DC Bag, Fire, Divided Sky, Wilson, Peaches en Regalia, Contact

Thursday, February 23, 1989
The Front, Burlington, VT

Friday, February 24, 1989
The Front, Burlington, VT
● *Set I:* The Man Who Stepped Into Yesterday > Avenu Malkenu > The Man Who Stepped Into Yesterday Reprise, The Curtain, Foam, Colonel Forbin's Ascent > The Famous Mockingbird, Run Like an Antelope > Golgi Apparatus, Possum
● *Set II:* On Your Way Down, AC/DC Bag, You Enjoy Myself -> Camel Walk
● *Show Notes:* This second set listing may be incomplete, as tapes that circulate cut during Camel Walk.

Saturday, February 25, 1989
The Front, Burlington, VT

Wednesday, March 1, 1989
Gallagher's, Waitsfield, VT

Friday, March 3, 1989
Living and Learning Center,
University of Vermont, Burlington, VT
● *Set I:* Wilson, McGrupp and the Watchful Hosemasters, You Enjoy Myself, Foam, AC/DC Bag, The Curtain > Run Like an Antelope, I Didn't Know, Divided Sky, Alumni Blues, Good Times Bad Times
● *Set II:* Mike's Song > I Am Hydrogen > Weekapaug Groove, Fee, Possum, Walk Away, Colonel Forbin's Ascent > The Famous Mockingbird, The Lizards, Split Open and Melt, Take the 'A' Train, David Bowie
● *Encore:* Golgi Apparatus

Saturday, March 4, 1989
The Wetlands Preserve, New York, NY
● *Set I:* Take the 'A' Train, I Didn't Know, Mike's Song > I Am Hydrogen > Weekapaug Groove, Fee, Golgi Apparatus, Good Times Bad Times
● *Set II:* Possum, Fluffhead, The Lizards, Run Like an Antelope, Contact
● *Show Notes:* The second set listing is incomplete.

Saturday, March 11, 1989
Sheehan's, Northampton, MA

Sunday, March 12, 1989
Nectar's, Burlington, VT
Mike's Song > I Am Hydrogen > Weekapaug Groove, If I Only Had a Brain, Alumni Blues, Golgi Apparatus, Bold As Love, Foam
● *Show Notes:* Alumni Blues featured a local band, Eyeburn, trading off punk rock jams. This setlist is incomplete.

Monday, March 13, 1989
Nectar's, Burlington, VT

Tuesday, March 14, 1989
Nectar's, Burlington, VT
● *Set I:* The Curtain, Ya Mar, Mike's Song > I am Hydrogen > Weekapaug Groove, Fluffhead, Contact, AC/DC Bag > Wilson, You Enjoy Myself, Harpua, Foam
● *Set II:* Wilson, Fluffhead
● *Set III:* Fire, Sneaking Sally Through the Alley, Alumni Blues, The Lizards, La Grange, You Enjoy Myself, Good Times Bad Times
● *Encore:* Halley's.
● *Show Notes:* One tape in circulation contains the first set, as listed above. Another contains the above list for sets II (incomplete) and III. Since songs are repeated within the list, it is likely that one is mislabeled. This was the last Phish show at Nectar's and the master copy of sets II and III is specifically labeled as such; the tape circulating as the first set may be from the night before or from another show entirely. Also, the band wished the audience good night after Harpua and made several references to it being the "last song" so this is likely a final set from another show where Foam may have been the encore. Since an exact date can not be ascertained, we will continue to list as is.

Friday, March 17, 1989
Bear Trap Road, Burlington, VT
● *Show Notes:* There was no show on this date. Tapes that circulate are mislabeled copies of July 23, 1988, set I.

Friday, March 24, 1989
The Paradise, Boston, MA
Possum, Mike's Song > I Am Hydrogen > Weekapaug Groove, Golgi Apparatus, Divided Sky, AC/DC Bag, If I Only Had a Brain, Take the 'A' Train, David Bowie
● *Show Notes:* This setlist is incomplete and may be out of order.

Saturday, March 25, 1989
Tree Café, Portland, ME

Thursday, March 30, 1989
The Front, Burlington, VT
● *Set I:* Bold as Love, McGrupp and the Watchful Hosemasters, Divided Sky, The Price of Love, On Your Way Down, Ya Mar, Fluffhead, Run Like an Antelope
● *Set II:* The Mango Song, Mike's Song > I Am Hydrogen > Weekapaug Groove, You Enjoy Myself, Undun, La Grange, Golgi Apparatus
● *Set III:* Peaches en Regalia, Foam, AC/DC Bag, Big Black Furry Creature from Mars, Satin Doll, Rocky Top
● *Encore:* Makisupa Policeman
● *Show Notes:* This is another fun Burlington show that featured a de-

cent version of YEM with some fun teasing and quoting of You're No Good. This show marked Chris Kuroda's first full show as light technician and included the first known versions of The Mango Song and Undun.

Wednesday, March 31, 1989
The Front, Burlington, VT

Saturday, April 1, 1989
10 Below, Northampton, MA
● *Show Notes:* The venue for this show is sometimes mislabeled as The U-Joint.

Sunday, April 2, 1989
The Nightshift, Naugatuck, CT

Friday, April 7, 1989
The Stone Church, Newmarket, NH

Thursday, April 13, 1989
Valley Club Café, Rutland, VT

Friday, April 14, 1989
Chez Pierre, Johnson, VT
● *Check:* Time Loves A Hero
● *Set I:* AC/DC Bag, Foam, Walk Away, Fluffhead, Fee, Halley's Comet, Run Like an Antelope, Contact, Fire
● *Set II:* You Enjoy Myself, Bold as Love, The Lizards, The Sloth, Possum, If I Only Had a Brain, Mike's Song > I Am Hydrogen > Weekapaug Groove, Esther

Saturday, April 15, 1989
Billings Hall, University of Vermont, Burlington, VT
Benefit for VPIRG
● *Check:* Time Loves a Hero
● *Set I:* Mike's Song > I Am Hydrogen > Weekapaug Groove, Esther, You Enjoy Myself > Wilson -> Peaches en Regalia, On Your Way Down, Alumni Blues, I Didn't Know, McGrupp and the Watchful Hosemasters > Foam, David Bowie
● *Set II:* Funky Bitch, Golgi Apparatus, Slave to the Traffic Light, The Mango Song, Divided Sky, Split Open and Melt, Suzy Greenberg, Fluffhead, Good Times Bad Times
● *Show Notes:* McGrupp included some strange special effects. SOAM included a nice drum solo, as well as an audience participation contest where the gag prize was a date with Fishman.

Wednesday, April 19, 1989
Johnny D's, Somerville, MA

Wednesday, April 19, 1989
Nectar's, Burlington, VT
● *Show Notes:* There was no show on this date. Shows that circulate under this date are mislabeled copies of March 12, 1988.

Thursday, April 20, 1989
Full Moon at The Zoo, Humphries House, Amherst, MA

● *Set I:* AC/DC Bag, Fluffhead, You Shook Me All Night Long Jam -> Fluff's Travels, Fire, Esther, Suzy Greenberg, The Sloth, Possum, McGrupp and the Watchful Hosemasters -> Foam, David Bowie
● *Set II:* Divided Sky, Walk Away, You Enjoy Myself, Split Open and Melt, The Lizards, Mike's Song > I Am Hydrogen > Weekapaug Groove, Love You, Harpua
● *Show Notes:* Bowie included a brief Frosty the Snowman jam in the intro, as well as a Santa Claus is Coming to Town tease. A fire alarm sounded as Fluffhead moved into Fluff's Travels, which caused the building to be evacuated. When the band retook the stage, they started up a humorous pass at You Shook Me All Night Long and then dove back into Fluff's Travels. Fire was dedicated to the "brave men" who turned off the fire alarm.

Friday, April 21, 1989
The Rock Rumble
The Front, Burlington, VT
● *Show Notes:* While a setlist for this show is not known, Fishman recalls getting naked on-stage during this "Battle of the Bands" competition.

Saturday, April 22, 1989
The Rock Rumble
The Front, Burlington, VT

Thursday, April 27, 1989
Memorial Building, University of New Hampshire, Durham, NH
Golgi Apparatus, String Changing Nature, The Sloth, Divided Sky, Sanity, I Didn't Know, Alumni Blues, The Lizards, Whipping Post
● *Encore:* Contact, David Bowie
● *Show Notes:* String Changing Nature was not really a song, but rather a jam that arose while the band tuned their instruments and included some funny stage banter. Whipping Post was well-jammed and Sanity was the fast version.

Friday, April 28, 1989
Moulton Union, Bowdoin College, Brunswick, ME

Saturday, April 29, 1989
The Living Room, Providence, RI

Sunday, April 30, 1989
Night Stage, Cambridge, MA
I Didn't Know, You Enjoy Myself, McGrupp and the Watchful Hosemasters, The Lizards, Divided Sky, Wilson, Peaches en Regalia, Run Like an Antelope, Terrapin
● *Encore:* Possum
● *Show Notes:* This show was preceded by an introduction from Dionysian co-founder Ben Hunter.

Monday, May 1, 1989
Pearl Street Ballroom, Northampton, MA
● *Set I:* Dinner and a Movie, You Enjoy Myself, Esther, AC/DC Bag, Alumni Blues, Split Open and Melt, The Lizards, Golgi Apparatus, Good Times Bad Times

● *Set II:* Mike's Song > I Am Hydrogen > Weekapaug Groove, On Your Way Down, Possum, Icculus, Colonel Forbin's Ascent > The Famous Mockingbird, David Bowie, Contact
● *Show Notes:* It is possible that Contact was the encore at this show.

Wednesday, May 3, 1989
The Orange Grove, Syracuse, NY
● *Show Notes:* Though there was a show on this date, it was not at The Orange Grove. Tapes that circulate from that venue are actually mislabeled copies of May 13, 1989.

Wednesday, May 3, 1989
Tent Party, Franklin & Marshal College, Lancaster, PA

Friday, May 5, 1989
Sigma Phi Fraternity, Hamilton University, Clinton, NY
● *Set I:* Golgi Apparatus, You Enjoy Myself, Ya Mar, Fluffhead, Alumni Blues, Donna Lee, Fee, Run Like an Antelope
● *Set II:* I Didn't Know, Take the 'A' Train, Good Times Bad Times, McGrupp and the Watchful Hosemasters

Saturday, May 6, 1989
Collis Center, Dartmouth College, Hanover, NH
● *Set I:* You Enjoy Myself, I Didn't Know, Mike's Song > I Am Hydrogen > Weekapaug Groove, Esther, The Sloth, Possum, Bold As Love, AC/DC Bag, Colonel Forbin's Ascent > The Famous Mockingbird, David Bowie
● *Set II:* Donna Lee, Suzy Greenberg, Contact, Fire, Harry Hood, Golgi Apparatus, Slave to the Traffic Light, Divided Sky
● *Show Notes:* Suzy included a Linus and Lucy tease.

Sunday, May 7, 1989
The Front, Burlington, VT

Monday, May 8, 1989
The Front, Burlington, VT

Tuesday, May 9, 1989
The Front, Burlington, VT
● *Set I:* Wilson > Peaches en Regalia, Ya Mar, Mike's Song > I Am Hydrogen > Weekapaug Groove, The Sloth, Possum, Divided Sky
● *Set II:* You Enjoy Myself, La Grange, If I Don't Be There by Morning, Slave to the Traffic Light, Esther, Run Like an Antelope, I Didn't Know -> Nowhere Fast -> I've Turned Bad -> I Didn't Know, The Lizards, Bold as Love, Harpua, Whipping Post
● *Show Notes:* Nowhere Fast and I've Turned Bad featured Sofi Dillof on vocals. Phish celebrated this show with the release of the original *Junta* cassette. It is believed that this was the last Phish show at Nectar's.

Thursday, May 11, 1989
Paulis Hotel, Albany, NY
● *Show Notes:* The venue may have been Polly's.

Friday, May 12, 1989
Copperfield's, Syracuse, NY

Bike, Mike's Song > I Am Hydrogen > Weekapaug Groove, AC/DC Bag, David Bowie, Buried Alive, The Asse Festival, You Enjoy Myself, Slave to the Traffic Light, The Sloth, Possum, Split Open and Melt, Ya Mar, Run Like an Antelope
● *Show Notes:* This date is mislabeled, as Buried Alive did not debut until the fall of 1990. Still, the tape circulates under this date and information to ascertain the correct date is, unfortunately, not available.

Saturday, May 13, 1989
Hungry Charlie's, Syracuse, NY
● *Set I:* AC/DC Bag, Alumni Blues, You Enjoy Myself, Golgi Apparatus, La Grange, Fluffhead, Possum, Foam, Walk Away, Take the 'A' Train, Split Open and Melt > David Bowie
● *Set II:* Suzy Greenberg > Bold As Love, The Lizards, Harry Hood, If I Only Had a Brain, Contact, Fire
● *Encore:* Whipping Post
● *Show Notes:* This show featured more fun stage banter, as Trey referred to Fishman as "the hometown boy" and Fish commented about embarrassing himself in front of his entire class. Also, Trey commented that his mother was in the audience, "all the way from Ireland." After AC/DC Bag, Trey referenced that day's graduation events. Possum included Fishing Hole Theme teases. This version of Whipping Post was really jammed out. The Bowie hi-hat intro included 'A' Train and SOAM teases. The venue is often listed as Orange Grove but, according to those in attendance, was actually Hungry Charlie's.

Sunday, May 14, 1989
University of Massachusetts, Amherst, MA
● *Show Notes:* This was a show where Phish opened for Canned Heat.

Thursday, May 18, 1989
The Tree Café, Portland, ME

Friday, May 19, 1989
The Blue Pelican, Newport, RI
● *Show Notes:* While it is believed this show was played, confirmation could not be found.

Friday, May 19, 1989
Nectar's, Burlington, VT
● *Show Notes:* Tapes that circulate from this date are mislabeled copies of May 9, 1989.

Saturday, May 20, 1989
Northfield/Mt. Herman School Gymnasium, Northfield, MA
● *Set I:* AC/DC Bag, Alumni Blues, You Enjoy Myself, The Lizards, Wilson, Divided Sky, I Didn't Know, Possum
● *Set II:* Bold as Love, Mike's Song > I Am Hydrogen > Weekapaug Groove, Foam, Contact, Take the 'A' Train, David Bowie, Golgi Apparatus
● *Encore:* Good Times Bad Times

Sunday, May 21, 1989
320 Spear Street, Burlington, VT
Harry Hood, Foam, Contact, Mike's Song > I Am Hydrogen > Weekapaug Groove, Split Open and Melt, Dazed and Confused, The Sloth, You

Enjoy Myself -> Ya Mar, AC/DC Bag, Divided Sky
● *Show Notes:* Before Contact, the band announced that the police were towing cars out on Spear Street. Check out this version of Mike's Song (also known as "Molly's Song") for some alternate lyrics and YEM for a Godzilla vocal jam. This show marked the first known Dazed and Confused. Some tapes that circulate are mislabeled as The Front.

Friday, May 26, 1989
Valley Club, Rutland, VT
● *Set I:* Bold as Love, AC/DC Bag, Mike's Song > I Am Hydrogen > Weekapaug Groove, Sanity, Halley's Comet, The Sloth, You Enjoy Myself
● *Set II:* David Bowie, The Mango Song, Split Open and Melt, Bathtub Gin, Run Like an Antelope, Golgi Apparatus
● *Set III:* Slave to the Traffic Light, Funky Bitch, The Ballad of Curtis Loew, Possum
● *Encore:* The Practical Song
● *Show Notes:* This show marked the debut of Bathtub Gin. Nancy Taube provided guest vocals on Halley's Comet. Bowie was announced as, dedicated to, and sung as "Lazy Lester." This show also included some rarities, such as the fast version of Sanity, The Practical Song, and a strange ending to The Sloth. Trey compared Antelope to his life-long dream of playing hockey and dedicated the song to "all you pro hockey players out there." The first set ended with yet another great early YEM.

Saturday, May 27, 1989
Alpha Delta Phi Fraternity, Trinity College, West Hartford, CT
● *Set I:* AC/DC Bag, Mike's Song > I Am Hydrogen > Weekapaug Groove, Funky Bitch, Fee, You Enjoy Myself, Take the 'A' Train, Fluff-head, Bathtub Gin, Good Times Bad Times

Sunday, May 28, 1989
Ian McLean's Party, Connie Condon's Farm, Hebron, NY
● *Set I:* Divided Sky, Run Like an Antelope, Colonel Forbin's Ascent > The Famous Mockingbird, Fee > Slave to the Traffic Light, Esther, Suzy Greenberg, You Enjoy Myself
● *Set II:* Fire, Mike's Song > I Am Hydrogen > Weekapaug Groove, Bathtub Gin, Sanity, Ride Captain Ride, Peaches en Regalia, Take the 'A' Train, Possum, Contact, Funky (Breakdown) -> The Price of Love, Funky Bitch, Split Open and Melt, The Mango Song, Harry Hood
● *Set III:* Jam -> La Grange Jam, The Sloth, Sneakin' Sally Through the Alley > Ya Mar, Jesus Just Left Chicago
● *Show Notes:* Trey dedicated the Divided Sky opener to "the spirit of the pig." This YEM featured the infamous "Poop Vocal Jam," followed by a set-stopping keg run. Antelope included the word "spliff" instead of "spike" in the lyrics and Mike's Song included a tease of the HBO theme song. Funky (Breakdown) and Price of Love featured guest appearances by Ninja Mike (vocals) and Magoo (guitar). Fishman intermittently played trombone and vacuum during the latter.

Tuesday, May 30, 1989
Pearl Street Ballroom, Northampton, MA

Wednesday, May 31, 1989
Variety Playhouse, Atlanta, GA
● *Show Notes:* There was no show on this date. Tapes that circulate are

mislabeled copies of May 31, 1990.

Saturday, June 3, 1989
The Wetlands Preserve, New York, NY

Thursday, June 8, 1989
The Quad, Hobart College, Geneva, NY
● *Show Notes:* Phish played an outdoor party, complete with a beer moat. One fan in attendance recalls hearing Peaches en Regalia, as well as a Zeppelin cover (possibly Good Times Bad Times).

Saturday, June 10, 1989
The Living Room, Providence, RI

Wednesday, June 14, 1989
Private Party, Stone High School Graduation, Burlington, VT

Friday, June 16, 1989
The Tree Café, Portland, ME

Saturday, June 17, 1989
The Tree Café, Portland, ME

Friday, June 23, 1989
The Paradise, Boston, MA
● *Set I:* AC/DC Bag, You Enjoy Myself, Wilson, Peaches en Regalia, Donna Lee, Fee, Mike's Song > I Am Hydrogen > Weekapaug Groove, The Lizards, Run Like an Antelope
● *Set II:* The Sloth, Fluffhead, Harry Hood, Ya Mar, Split Open and Melt, Possum, David Bowie
● *Encore:* Contact, Good Times Bad Times

Thursday, June 29, 1989
The Front, Burlington, VT

Friday, June 30, 1989
Pearl Street Ballroom, Northampton, MA
● *Set I:* Funky Bitch, You Enjoy Myself, McGrupp and the Watchful Hosemasters, Possum, Donna Lee, Fluffhead, Run Like an Antelope
● *Set II:* Walk Away, AC/DC Bag, The Curtain, Slave to the Traffic Light, Bathtub Gin, Mike's Song > I Am Hydrogen > Weekapaug Groove

Saturday, July 1, 1989
Les Fou Founes Electriques, Montreal, Quebec, Canada
● *Show Notes:* This show was part of the Montreal International Jazz Festival.

Tuesday, July 11, 1989
Sam's Tavern, Burlington, VT
● *Show Notes:* There was no show at Sam's on this date. Tapes that circulate are mislabeled copies of July 11, 1988.

Wednesday, July 12, 1989
Sam's Tavern, Burlington, VT
● *Show Notes:* There was no show at Sam's on this date. Tapes that circulate are mislabeled copies of July 12, 1988.

Friday, August 11, 1989
Tree Café, Portland, ME

● *Show Notes:* While it is believed this show was played, confirmation could not be found.

Saturday, August 12, 1989
Burlington Boat House, Burlington, VT

● *Set I:* Blue Sky, Suzy Greenberg, AC/DC Bag, Ya Mar, Rocky Top, On Your Way Down, Night and Day, Blue Monk, I Didn't Know, You Enjoy Myself, Possum

● *Set II:* Icculus, Run Like an Antelope, The Oh Kee Pa Ceremony > Contact

● *Show Notes:* This show was at the wedding reception of Beth and Steven Drebber (the latter of The Joneses fame). Blue Sky, a debut, was dedicated to the newlyweds and sung by the groom. Antelope featured Steven on drums and Fishman on trumpet and trombone. During Suzy, some of the attendees got on the trampolines! The band actually played an earlier set of jazz standards at the reception but a setlist is unknown. On Your Way Down was preceded by La Grange teases. This show included the first known version of The Oh Kee Pa Ceremony.

Sunday, August 13, 1989
Circuit Ave. in Oak Bluffs, Martha's Vineyard, MA

Thursday, August 17, 1989
The Front, Burlington, VT

● *Set I:* Ya Mar, Suzy Greenberg, McGrupp and the Watchful Hosemasters, The Sloth, Rocky Top, Harry Hood, Mike's Song > I Am Hydrogen > Weekapaug Groove

● *Set II:* Walk Away, AC/DC Bag, The Mango Song, Fee, You Enjoy Myself, The Lizards

● *Set III:* The Oh Kee Pa Ceremony, Bold as Love, Punch You in the Eye, Possum, Halley's Comet > Alumni Blues, Contact, Run Like an Antelope

● *Encore:* Golgi Apparatus, Fire

● *Show Notes:* Halley's featured Nancy Taube on vocals. At the show, Nancy announced that it was the last time he'd ever sing it. Rocky Top was played for the Drebbers, who had just gotten married (see August 12, 1989). This show included the first known version of PYITE.

Friday, August 18, 1989
Pearl Street Ballroom, Northampton, MA

Saturday, August 19, 1989
Collis Center, Dartmouth College, Hanover, NH

● *Set I:* The Oh Kee Pa Ceremony > Suzy Greenberg, The Man Who Stepped Into Yesterday > Avenu Malkenu, AC/DC Bag, Punch You in the Eye, Rocky Top, Bold As Love, The Mango Song, The Lizards, Mike's Song > I Am Hydrogen > Weekapaug Groove

● *Set II:* Split Open and Melt, Take the 'A' Train, Divided Sky, Bathtub Gin

● *Show Notes:* This show is often mislabeled as August 19, 1987 and August 19, 1988 but is definitely from 1989. This second set listing is most likely incomplete.

Wednesday, August 23, 1989
The Living Room, Providence, RI

● *Set II:* Run Like an Antelope, Colonel Forbin's Ascent > The Famous Mockingbird, Ya Mar, You Enjoy Myself, AC/DC Bag, Foam, Good Times Bad Times

Friday, August 25, 1989
The Blue Pelican, Newport, RI

● *Show Notes:* While it is believed this show was played, confirmation could not be found.

Saturday, August 26, 1989
Townshend Family Park, Townshend, VT

● *Set I:* Fluffhead, Colonel Forbin's Ascent -> The Famous Mockingbird, Harry Hood, Split Open and Melt, Divided Sky, You Enjoy Myself -> Possum

● *Set II:* Theme from Andy Griffith, Bold as Love, Ya Mar, Slave to the Traffic Light, AC/DC Bag, Donna Lee, Funky Bitch, Foam, David Bowie

● *Set III:* The Man Who Stepped Into Yesterday > Avenu Malkenu, Suzy Greenberg, Dinner and a Movie, Run Like an Antelope

● *Encore:* Contact, The Lizards, La Grange

● *Show Notes:* Apparently Fishman got a speeding ticket on the way to the show and someone else had to set up his drum set. The Hood intro featured an "Odd Couple" theme tease from Page. The Andy Griffith theme jam that opened the second set started with the band whistling and ended with the audience whistling to the band's accompaniment! Slave was introduced by Mike as being written by Pete Rose; Avenu Malkenu was subsequently announced as a song written by "Pete Rose and God." Antelope included a Paint it Black tease.

Friday, September 1, 1989
Bowdoin College, Brunswick, ME

● *Show Notes:* While it is believed this show was played, confirmation could not be found.

Saturday, September 2, 1989
The Wetlands, New York, NY

● *Show Notes:* While it is believed this show was played, confirmation could not be found.

Wednesday, September 6, 1989
The Living Room, Providence, RI

Thursday, September 7, 1989
The Front, Burlington, VT

Friday, September 8, 1989
The Front, Burlington, VT

Saturday, September 9, 1989
Dining Commons, Bennington College, Bennington, VT

● *Set I:* Foam, The Oh Kee Pa Ceremony, Suzy Greenberg, Divided Sky, AC/DC Bag, McGrupp and the Watchful Hosemasters -> Bathtub Gin, Punch You in the Eye, Wilson, My Sweet One, David Bowie

● *Set II:* Ya Mar, You Enjoy Myself -> Alumni Blues, Split Open and Melt, Harry Hood, Walk Away, Possum

● *Show Notes:* This show contained the first known version of My Sweet One.

Wednesday, September 13, 1989
The Living Room, Providence, RI

Thursday, September 14, 1989
MacPhie Pub, Tufts University, Medford, MA
● *Set I:* The Oh Kee Pa Ceremony > Suzy Greenberg, You Enjoy Myself, Foam, Colonel Forbin's Ascent > The Famous Mockingbird, La Grange, Fee, David Bowie
● *Set II:* Harry Hood, Bathtub Gin
● *Show Notes:* This setlist is incomplete.

Saturday, September 16, 1989
The Tree Café, Portland, ME

Wednesday, September 20, 1989
The Living Room, Providence, RI

Thursday, September 21, 1989
Pearl Street Ballroom, Northampton, MA
● *Set I:* Golgi Apparatus, Ya Mar, AC/DC Bag, My Sweet One, Fee, Alumni Blues, McGrupp and the Watchful Hosemasters -> Who Do? We Do! > David Bowie
● *Set II:* Divided Sky -> The Chase -> Dinner and a Movie > Bundle of Joy -> Possum, Bathtub Gin, You Enjoy Myself, If I Only Had a Brain, Run Like an Antelope
● *Encore:* Good Times Bad Times

Sunday, October 1, 1989
The Front, Burlington, VT
● *Set I:* Alumni Blues, McGrupp and the Watchful Hosemasters -> Who Do? We Do! -> Golgi Apparatus, Harry Hood -> The Chase, Wilson > Foam, Ya Mar, The Oh Kee Pa Ceremony > Suzy Greenberg, Run Like an Antelope
● *Set II:* AC/DC Bag, My Sweet One, Reba, Dinner and a Movie > Bundle of Joy -> Possum, You Enjoy Myself -> HYHU > If I Only Had a Brain > HYHU, Contact, Split Open and Melt, The Lizards
● *Encore:* Highway to Hell
● *Show Notes:* This show featured the first known performance of Reba.

Friday, October 6, 1989
The Paradise, Boston, MA
Timber (Jerry), Mike's Song > I Am Hydrogen > Weekapaug Groove, The Sloth, Golgi Apparatus, Bold As Love, Dinner and a Movie, Happy Birthday, Harry Hood, Possum, Highway to Hell, Big Black Furry Creature from Mars
● *Encore:* Good Times Bad Times
● *Show Notes:* Fishman performed Happy Birthday on the vacuum for his brother David.

Saturday, October 7, 1989
Chase Hall, Bates College, Lewiston, ME
● *Set I:* Golgi Apparatus, Ya Mar, Mike's Song > I Am Hydrogen > Weekapaug Groove, Suzy Greenberg, Fee, La Grange, Makisupa Policeman, Alumni Blues, Good Times Bad Times
● *Set II:* Dinner and a Movie > Bundle of Joy -> Possum, Happy Birth-

day, The Lizards, AC/DC Bag, David Bowie, Contact > Highway to Hell
● *Encore:* You Enjoy Myself
● *Show Notes:* The Bowie intro included a brief Fly Like an Eagle jam.

Tuesday, October 10, 1989
The Front, Burlington, VT

Thursday, October 12, 1989
Mabel Brown Room, Keene State College, Keene, NH
● *Set I:* The Oh Kee Pa Ceremony > AC/DC Bag, Colonel Forbin's Ascent > The Famous Mockingbird, You Enjoy Myself > Possum, Divided Sky, La Grange
● *Set II:* Fee, Mike's Song > I am Hydrogen > Weekapaug Groove, Esther, Walk Away, The Lizards
● *Encore:* Highway to Hell

Friday, October 13, 1989
Clement's, Syracuse, NY
● *Set I:* David Bowie, Slave to the Traffic Light, The Sloth, Possum
● *Set II:* Bike, The Man Who Stepped Into Yesterday > Avenu Malkenu > Mike's Song > I am Hydrogen > Weekapaug Groove, AC/DC Bag, Colonel Forbin's Ascent
● *Show Notes:* While this show might have taken place, it also might be confused with the May 13, 1989 show at Hungry Charlie's. Tapes with the above list circulate, though it is unclear if they are from this show. Home videos were shown both before and during this humorous, early Bike. Trey jokingly referred to TMWSIY as "The Man Who Stepped Into Dog Log." It is believed that this show was actually at Clement's and not at The Orange Grove or Copperfield's, as it is usually listed.

Saturday, October 14, 1989
Hobart College, Geneva, NY
● *Set I:* AC/DC Bag, Divided Sky, I Didn't Know, Golgi Apparatus, Ya Mar, Split Open and Melt, Fee, Alumni Blues, You Enjoy Myself, Makisupa Policeman, Good Times Bad Times
● *Set II:* Anarchy, Highway to Hell, Possum, Harpua
● *Show Notes:* This setlist may be incomplete.

Friday, October 20, 1989
The Front, Burlington, VT
● *Set I:* Harpua -> Bundle of Joy > Colonel Forbin's Ascent > The Famous Mockingbird, You Enjoy Myself, The Oh Kee Pa Ceremony, Reba, Divided Sky, Golgi Apparatus, Run Like an Antelope
● *Set II:* No Dogs Allowed, Walk Away, Dinner and a Movie, I Didn't Know, AC/DC Bag, Donna Lee, Split Open and Melt, Harry Hood, Swing Low (Sweet Chariot), In a Hole
● *Encore:* La Grange, Slave to the Traffic Light
● *Show Notes:* Antelope featured Old McDonald Had a Farm and "Benny Hill" theme teases in the intro and Mockingbird included a "Jeopardy" theme tease from Page. SOAM (which had to be started a second time after the lights went out before the *a cappella* segment of the first attempt) through the debut of Hole featured Dave Grippo and Russ Remington on horns. Hole also included a tease of the *Close Encounters of the Third Kind* theme from Page and the horns. No Dogs Allowed was dedicated to Dave.

Saturday, October 21, 1989
The Front, Burlington, VT
● *Set I:* Fee, Ya Mar, In a Hole, McGrupp and the Watchful Hosemasters -> Who Do? We Do! -> Foam, AC/DC Bag, The Lizards, Dog Gone Dog, David Bowie
● *Set II:* The Oh Kee Pa Ceremony > Suzy Greenberg, Wilson, Possum, Reba, The Sloth, La Grange, You Enjoy Myself, Highway to Hell, Run Like an Antelope
● *Encore:* The Lizards
● *Show Notes:* It appears as though one of the two sets that circulates is labeled incorrectly, since Lizards probably would not have appeared twice in the same show.

Sunday, October 22, 1989
The Front, Burlington, VT
● *Set I:* La Grange, Colonel Forbin's Ascent > The Famous Mockingbird, You Enjoy Myself > The Oh Kee Pa Ceremony > Suzy Greenberg, Ya Mar, Foam, Rocky Top, Split Open and Melt, Tela > Divided Sky, I Didn't Know, Good Times Bad Times
● *Set II:* Harry Hood, Reba, Golgi Apparatus, In a Hole, McGrupp and the Watchful Hosemasters > AC/DC Bag, My Sweet One, Fee > Possum
● *Encore:* Undun, Run Like an Antelope
Show Notes: Suzy included Purple Haze teases from Trey. SOAM included an extended drum solo from Fishman. Fishman explained some of his vacuum parts before launching into a vacuum solo during I Didn't Know. Members of the Ninja Custodians visited the stage before and during the encore, leading to some funny stage banter. Undun was subsequently dedicated to Sofi (likely Sofi Dillof) on her 22nd birthday and the lyrics to the song were changed to reference the event and the Ninja Custodians' hijinks. The setlist might be incomplete, as the tapes that circulate cut during Antelope.

Thursday, October 26, 1989
The Wetlands Preserve, New York, NY
● *Set I:* The Oh Kee Pa Ceremony > Golgi Apparatus, You Enjoy Myself -> Fee > Divided Sky, I Didn't Know, Wilson > The Lizards, Mike's Song > I Am Hydrogen > Weekapaug Groove
● *Set II:* Who Knows Jam > Dinner and a Movie, Who Do? We Do! > AC/DC Bag, Reba > Walk Away, Bathtub Gin > The Sloth, The Chase -> Possum, Punch You in the Eye, In a Hole, Fishman's Gull Poem, No Dogs Allowed, David Bowie
● *Show Notes:* The YEM vocal jam moved nicely into the drum intro for Fee. PYITE, described by Trey as a recently debuted "love song," was introduced under its original title, "Punch Me in the Eye." In a Hole was introduced as having no title, until the band members jokingly decided to call it "What You Will." Vocals were provided by Page "Tex" McConnell. No DoPgs Allowed was introduced by Trey as a song he co-wrote with his mother for the children's musical "Gus the Christmas Dog." The Bowie intro contained teases of David Bowie's Space Oddity.

Saturday, October 28, 1989
The Chance, Poughkeepsie, NY
I Didn't Know, You Enjoy Myself, Colonel Forbin's Ascent, Highway to Hell, Good Times Bad Times, Dinner and a Movie, Reba, Divided Sky, Harpua

● *Show Notes:* This setlist is out of order and incomplete.

Tuesday, October 31, 1989
Goddard College, Plainfield, VT
Opening Act: Ninja Custodians
● *Set I:* The Oh Kee Pa Ceremony > Suzy Greenberg, You Enjoy Myself, AC/DC Bag, Divided Sky, Fee, Walk Away, Bathtub Gin, Possum
● *Set II:* David Bowie, Wilson, Reba, Colonel Forbin's Ascent > The Famous Mockingbird, Alumni Blues, The Lizards, Highway to Hell
● *Encore:* Contact, Run Like an Antelope -> Kung -> Run Like an Antelope
● *Show Notes:* This show was a Halloween extravaganza! The band's costumes included Trey wearing devil horns, latex pants, and strap-on breasts (which he ran around fondling during the Ninja Custodians' set) and Mike wearing a dog-faced mask. The band distributed boxes of macaroni and cheese for audience use during the Bowie intro. This Bowie, at over 20 minutes, was, at the time, one of the longest versions ever. The show closed with Trey returning to the Kung theme, as he promised to stage another runaway golf cart marathon this time next year.

Thursday, November 2, 1989
Memorial Union Building, University of New Hampshire, Durham, NH
● *Set I:* Bathtub Gin, Foam, Mike's Song > I Am Hydrogen > Weekapaug Groove, Fee, The Curtain > Reba, Split Open and Melt, Esther, Good Times Bad Times
● *Set II:* The Oh Kee Pa Ceremony > Golgi Apparatus, You Enjoy Myself -> Kung, Rhombus Narration -> Divided Sky, McGrupp and the Watchful Hosemasters -> Who Do? We Do! > AC/DC Bag, My Sweet One, Highway to Hell
● *Show Notes:* Mike's Song was dedicated to Matt Hawke.

Friday, November 3, 1989
The Tree Café, Portland, ME
● *Set I:* Colonel Forbin's Ascent > The Famous Mockingbird, Bathtub Gin, My Sweet One, Split Open and Melt -> Bundle of Joy -> You Enjoy Myself, Punch You in the Eye, Reba, Golgi Apparatus
● *Set II:* David Bowie > No Dogs Allowed, The Oh Kee Pa Ceremony, The Sloth, Foam
● *Show Notes:* Bowie included a "Sesame Street" theme tease and some Manteca teases, as well as an Antelope-style jam segment. The listing for the second set is most likely incomplete.

Saturday, November 4, 1989
College Auditorium, College of the Atlantic, Bar Harbor, ME
● *Show Notes:* While it is believed this show was played, confirmation could not be found.

Thursday, November 9, 1989
Mission Park Dining Hall, Williams College, Williamstown, MA
● *Check:* In a Hole
● *Set I:* I Didn't Know, Golgi Apparatus, Ya Mar, The Curtain, My Sweet One, Bathtub Gin, You Enjoy Myself, Take the 'A' Train, Good Times Bad Times
● *Set II:* The Oh Kee Pa Ceremony, AC/DC Bag, McGrupp and the Watchful Hosemasters -> Who Do? We Do! -> Punch You in the Eye,

The Lizards, Mike's Song > I Am Hydrogen > Weekapaug Groove
● *Encore:* Highway to Hell

Friday, November 10, 1989
Sigma Phi House, Hamilton College, Clinton, NY
● *Set I:* Split Open and Melt, The Oh Kee Pa Ceremony > Suzy Greenberg, Fee, Divided Sky -> AC/DC Bag, My Sweet One, You Enjoy Myself > La Grange
● *Set II:* Harry Hood, Bathtub Gin, Mike's Song > I Am Hydrogen > Weekapaug Groove, McGrupp and the Watchful Hosemasters -> Who Do? We Do! -> Clod -> The Sloth, The Lizards, If I Only Had a Brain, Possum
● *Encore:* Harpua, Highway to Hell
● *Encore:* Take the 'A' Train, Run Like an Antelope
● *Show Notes:* The vocal jam in YEM included My Girl quotes. Harpua included Sunshine of Your Love teases. The second two encores may be filler from another show.

Saturday, November 11, 1989
Patrick Gymnasium, University of Vermont, Burlington, VT
The Oh Kee Pa Ceremony > Golgi Apparatus, Bathtub Gin, AC/DC Bag, My Sweet One, You Enjoy Myself, If I Only Had a Brain, Frankenstein
● *Show Notes:* Frankenstein included a guest horns appearance. This set was an opening set for Max Creek and Third World.

Thursday, November 16, 1989
Pearl Street Ballroom, Northampton, MA
● *Set I:* Mike's Song > I Am Hydrogen > Weekapaug Groove, Bathtub Gin, Foam, The Oh Kee Pa Ceremony > Suzy Greenberg, My Sweet One, Reba, You Enjoy Myself -> Frankenstein
● *Set II:* The Sloth > AC/DC Bag, Tela > David Bowie
● *Show Notes:* The show was stopped after Bowie due to a window breaking in the building.

Saturday, November 18, 1989
23 East Cabaret, Ardmore, PA
You Enjoy Myself, Take the 'A' Train, AC/DC Bag, The Lizards, My Sweet One, Possum, Divided Sky, Wilson, Reba, David Bowie, Contact
● *Show Notes:* This listing may be one set of a two-set show.

Thursday, November 30, 1989
The Paradise, Boston, MA
● *Set I:* Bathtub Gin, Divided Sky, Ya Mar, The Oh Kee Pa Ceremony > AC/DC Bag, Foam, The Lizards, My Sweet One, Run Like an Antelope, Lawn Boy, Frankenstein
● *Set II:* Reba, Possum, Colonel Forbin's Ascent > The Famous Mockingbird, Undun, Fee, Split Open and Melt, Take the 'A' Train, Suzy Greenberg, Contact, David Bowie
● *Encore:* In a Hole, Golgi Apparatus
● *Show Notes:* This show marked the debut of Lawn Boy, which Trey announced as a world premiere. SOAM included DEG teasing and Bowie included a Mr. P.C. tease. Suzy included a tease of the Brady Bunch theme.

Friday, December 1, 1989
The Paradise, Boston, MA
● *Set I:* I Didn't Know, La Grange, You Enjoy Myself, The Oh Kee Pa

Ceremony, Dinner and a Movie, Bathtub Gin, My Sweet One, Harry Hood, Good Times Bad Times
● *Set II:* Alumni Blues, Rocky Top, Divided Sky, Walk Away, The Lizards, Mike's Song > I Am Hydrogen > Weekapaug Groove, If I Only Had a Brain, Highway To Hell, Possum

Sunday, December 3, 1989
The Front, Burlington, VT
● *Set I:* Bathtub Gin, Funky Bitch, Ya Mar, Reba, Divided Sky, My Sweet One, Run Like an Antelope, Lawn Boy, Frankenstein
● *Set II:* The Man Who Stepped Into Yesterday > Avenu Malkenu > AC/DC Bag, Esther, The Oh Kee Pa Ceremony > Suzy Greenberg, Split Open and Melt, In a Hole, Fee, Possum, Love You, Mike's Song > I Am Hydrogen > Weekapaug Groove
● *Encore:* I Didn't Know, Golgi Apparatus

Monday, December 4, 1989
The Front, Burlington, VT

Wednesday, December 6, 1989
The Roxy, Washington, D.C.
● *Show Notes:* While it is believed this show was played, confirmation could not be found.

Thursday, December 7, 1989
8x10 Club, Baltimore, MD
● *Set I:* I Didn't Know, You Enjoy Myself, Take the 'A' Train, AC/DC Bag, Fee, Mike's Song > I Am Hydrogen > Weekapaug Groove, Alumni Blues, Rhombus Narration -> Divided Sky
● *Set II:* The Oh Kee Pa Ceremony > Suzy Greenberg, Rocky Top, Ya Mar, Walk Away, The Lizards, Run Like an Antelope, Lawn Boy, Possum, Undun, Golgi Apparatus
● *Show Notes:* Listen to the Weekapaug bass intro to hear Mike tease Joe Walsh's Life's Been Good.

Friday, December 8, 1989
Green Mountain College, Poultney, VT
● *Set I:* The Oh Kee Pa Ceremony > Suzy Greenberg, Split Open and Melt, Ya Mar, Reba, McGrupp and the Watchful Hosemasters -> Who Do? We Do! > AC/DC Bag, My Sweet One, Bathtub Gin, Run Like an Antelope
● *Set II:* Harry Hood, Tela, Timber (Jerry), Slave to the Traffic Light, I Didn't Know, You Enjoy Myself -> Possum
● *Encore:* Lawn Boy, Fire

Saturday, December 9, 1989
Bomeseen, Castleton State College, Castleton, VT
● *Set I:* Dinner and a Movie, La Grange, The Lizards, Foam, In a Hole, Rocky Top, David Bowie, Lawn Boy, Bathtub Gin, Golgi Apparatus
● *Set II:* Take the 'A' Train, Fluffhead, Esther, Alumni Blues, Fee, Mike's Song > I Am Hydrogen > Weekapaug Groove
● *Encore:* Contact, Big Black Furry Creature from Mars
● *Show Notes:* This Bowie included Wipeout teases.

Friday, December 15, 1989
Ukranian National Home, New York, NY
● *Set I:* Take the 'A' Train, Golgi Apparatus, Mike's Song > I am Hydro-

gen > Weekapaug Groove, Ya Mar, The Oh Kee Pah Ceremony > Suzy Greenberg, You Enjoy Myself, Good Times Bad Times
● *Set II:* I Didn't Know, Divided Sky, Possum, Run Like an Antelope, Funky Bitch, Jesus Just Left Chicago, Contact, David Bowie
● *Show Notes:* Phish shared this gig with Blues Traveler. John Popper guested on harmonica for Bitch and JJLC. Listen to this Contact for some Low Rider teases by Page. The listed second set is definitely from this show and has been in circulation for quite some time. The listed first set recently came into circulation under this date as an early set played by Phish.

Saturday, December 16, 1989
Contois Auditorium, City Hall, Burlington, VT
Burlington Community Boathouse Benefit
The Curtain, AC/DC Bag, Lawn Boy, Mike's Song > I Am Hydrogen > Weekapaug Groove, The Lizards, In a Hole, Golgi Apparatus
● *Encore:* Possum

Wednesday, December 20, 1989
The Wetlands Preserve, New York, NY
● *Show Notes:* There was no show on this date. Reports are likely confusing this date with the Wetlands show ten days later.

Sunday, December 24, 1989
Christmas Party, Burlington, VT
● *Show Notes:* There was no show on this date. Tapes that circulate are mislabeled copies of May 28, 1989, set II.

Friday, December 29, 1989
23 East Cabaret, Ardmore, PA
● *Opener:* The Modern Beatniks
● *Set I:* Rhombus Narration -> Divided Sky, Ya Mar, The Oh Kee Pa Ceremony > AC/DC Bag, The Lizards, Lawn Boy, Mike's Song > I Am Hydrogen > Weekapaug Groove
● *Show Notes:* This setlist is incomplete.

Saturday, December 30, 1989
The Wetlands Preserve, New York, NY
● Opening Act: Indecision
● *Set I:* Fluff's Travels -> David Bowie
● *Set II:* Bathtub Gin, Split Open and Melt, Ya Mar, Suzy Greenberg, Foam, My Sweet One, La Grange, Lawn Boy, Golgi Apparatus
● *Encore:* Auld Lang Syne -> Mike's Song > I Am Hydrogen > Weekapaug Groove
● *Show Notes:* The setlist for the first set is incomplete.

Sunday, December 31, 1989
Boston World Trade Center Exhibition Hall, Boston, MA
● Opening Act: The Ululators
● *Set I:* I Didn't Know, You Enjoy Myself, The Oh Kee Pa Ceremony > AC/DC Bag, Run Like an Antelope, Bathtub Gin, The Lizards, Satin Doll, Highway to Hell
● *Set II:* Mike's Song > I Am Hydrogen > Weekapaug Groove, Ya Mar, Split Open and Melt, Divided Sky, Fee
● *Encore:* Contact
● *Show Notes:* Trey and Mike wore tuxedos and top hats to commem-

Michael McNamara

orate the New Year. Fishman came out for I Didn't Know wearing a top hat and a g-string with tuxedo tails. Antelope began with a countdown to the New Year.

EARLY 1990

Tuesday, January 2, 1990
University of New Hampshire, Durham, NH

Saturday, January 13, 1990
Thompson Gym, Exeter, NY

Friday, January 19, 1990
Clark University Pub, Clark University, Worcester, MA

Saturday, January 20, 1990
Webster Hall, Dartmouth College, Hanover, NH
● *Set I:* Harry Hood, Carolina, Bathtub Gin, You Enjoy Myself, The Squirming Coil, Caravan, The Lizards, Run Like an Antelope
● *Set II:* Suzy Greenberg, Bouncing Around the Room, Reba, Tela, La Grange, Lawn Boy, Esther, Mike's Song > I Am Hydrogen > Weekapaug Groove
● *Show Notes:* This show included the first known performances of Bouncing, Coil, Caravan, and Carolina.

Thursday, January 25, 1990
The Oronoko, University of Maine, Orono, ME

Friday, January 26, 1990
Tree Café, Portland, ME

Saturday, January 27, 1990
The Front, Burlington, VT
● *Set I:* Carolina, Bathtub Gin, Ya Mar, The Oh Kee Pa Ceremony >
AC/DC Bag, My Sweet One, Bouncing Around the Room, Wilson, Reba,
Funky Bitch, Mike's Song > I Am Hydrogen > Weekapaug Groove
● *Set II:* Communication Breakdown, Caravan, You Enjoy Myself, The
Squirming Coil, Run Like an Antelope, Terrapin, Divided Sky
● *Encore:* La Grange
● *Show Notes:* Check out this Wilson; unlike most versions, it had a
heavy metal feel. This show marked the debut of Communication
Breakdown.

Sunday, January 28, 1990
The Front, Burlington, VT
● *Set I:* Suzy Greenberg, Split Open and Melt, Tela, Fluffhead, La
Grange, Carolina, Colonel Forbin's Ascent > The Famous Mockingbird,
Communication Breakdown
● *Set II:* Wilson, Run Like an Antelope, Bouncing Around the Room,
Caravan, The Squirming Coil, You Enjoy Myself, Bathtub Gin, Mike's
Song > I Am Hydrogen > Weekapaug Groove
● *Encore:* Lawn Boy, Big Black Furry Creature from Mars
● *Show Notes:* It must have been a hot night at The Front, as refer-
ences were made to a large fan cooling off the crowd. The band even
encouraged the audience to take their shirts off; Trey went so far as to
promise that Fishman would get naked if the audience did!

Monday, January 29, 1990
The Haunt, Ithaca, NY
The Lizards, If I Only Had a Brain, Mike's Song > I Am Hydrogen >
Weekapaug Groove, Jesus Just Left Chicago -> Possum, Highway to
Hell, Harpua, Fire
● *Show Notes:* This version of Harpua included a Purple Haze jam.

Wednesday, January 31, 1990
Myskyn's, Charleston, SC

Thursday, February 1, 1990
The Georgia Theater, Athens, GA
David Bowie, Walk Away, The Landlady, Suzy Greenberg, Caravan, Di-
vided Sky, Possum, Fee, Mike's Song > I Am Hydrogen > Weekapaug
Groove
● *Show Notes:* This setlist may be incomplete and out of order. This
show marked the first known performance of The Landlady outside of
PYITE. At this show, Phish opened for Widespread Panic.

Friday, February 2, 1990
The Georgia Theater, Athens, GA
● *Show Notes:* At this show, Phish opened for Widespread Panic.

Friday, February 2, 1990
The Bayou, Washington, D.C.
● *Show Notes:* Tapes circulate under this date but are actually misla-
beled copies of February 24, 1990, set II.

Saturday, February 3, 1990
Cotton Club, Atlanta, GA
● *Show Notes:* At this show, Phish shared the bill with Widespread
Panic.

Sunday, February 4, 1990
Greenstreets, Columbia, SC

Monday, February 5, 1990
Myskyn's, Charleston, SC

Tuesday, February 6, 1990
Hilton Head, SC
● *Show Notes:* It appears that this show was played at Page's father's
house. It is believed that the band primarily played jazz tunes.

Wednesday, February 7, 1990
Cats Cradle, Chapel Hill, NC

Thursday, February 8, 1990
The Jade Elephant, Richmond, VA
● *Show Notes:* While a complete setlist is not known, one fan remem-
bers a Contact encore.

Friday, February 9, 1990
Chameleon Club, Lancaster, PA
● *Set I:* Golgi Apparatus, The Oh Kee Pa Ceremony > Suzy Greenberg,
You Enjoy Myself, Walk Away, Bouncing Around the Room, AC/DC Bag,
The Squirming Coil, Mike's Song > I Am Hydrogen > Weekapaug
Groove, Carolina
● *Set II:* Dinner and a Movie, Ya Mar, Reba, Wilson, Take the 'A' Train,
Alumni Blues, Foam, The Ballad of Curtis Loew, David Bowie
● *Encore:* I Didn't Know
● *Show Notes:* During the encore, Trey introduced Fishman as "The
King of Prussia" (an allusion to the real-life location King of Prussia, not
far away from Lancaster).

Saturday, February 10, 1990
23 East Cabaret, Ardmore, PA
● *Set I:* Dinner and a Movie, The Oh Kee Pa Ceremony > Suzy Green-
berg, You Enjoy Myself, Bathtub Gin, Bouncing Around the Room, Possum, Carolina, Contact, David Bowie
● *Set II:* La Grange, Esther, AC/DC Bag, Rocky Top, Happy Birthday,
Donna Lee, Fee, Mike's Song > I Am Hydrogen > Weekapaug Groove
● *Encore:* I Didn't Know, Highway to Hell
● *Show Notes:* Happy Birthday was sung by "Rocco" to Trey's sister
Christine. Possum included Fishing Hole Theme teases. The band
asked the audience several times if anyone could give them a ride back
to Burlington, as their van broke down on the road to Philadelphia. As
with the encore the night before, Trey introduced Fishman as "The King
of Prussia."

Kathleen Griffin

Thursday, February 15, 1990
The Living Room, Providence, RI
● Opening Act: Widespread Panic
● *Set I:* Carolina, The Oh Kee Pa Ceremony > Suzy Greenberg, Divided Sky, Dinner and a Movie, Caravan, Bathtub Gin, Mike's Song > I Am Hydrogen > Weekapaug Groove
● *Set II:* Split Open and Melt, Bouncing Around the Room, Possum, Foam, Highway to Hell
● *Show Notes:* The second set listing may be incomplete.

Friday, February 16, 1990
The Paradise Theatre, Boston, MA
● Opening Act: Widespread Panic
● *Set I:* Fluffhead, Esther, Mike's Song > I Am Hydrogen > Weekapaug Groove, Donna Lee, Run Like an Antelope
● *Set II:* Golgi Apparatus, Caravan, Bouncing Around the Room, The Sloth, Possum, The Ballad of Curtis Loew, The Lizards
● *Encore:* Carolina, Whipping Post

Saturday, February 17, 1990
Student Union Ballroom, University of Massachusetts, Amherst, MA
● Opening Acts: Widespread Panic, Gene Matthews
Reba, The Oh Kee Pa Ceremony > AC/DC Bag, The Squirming Coil, Harry Hood, Carolina, Mike's Song > I am Hydrogen > Weekapaug Groove, Jazz Jam, Cavern, You Enjoy Myself
● *Show Notes:* Another show circulates under this date, but it is actually mislabeled copies of the Providence show from two nights earlier, minus Carolina, Divided Sky, and Possum. This setlist may be incomplete.

Thursday, February 22, 1990
Keene State College, Keene, NH

Wilson, You Enjoy Myself, Bouncing Around the Room, Ya Mar, The Oh Kee Pa Ceremony, AC/DC Bag, Caravan, The Lizards, David Bowie
● *Show Notes:* Caravan included a Magilla tease and Bowie included a Mike's Song tease and references to Marley. There was no second set, as someone pulled the fire alarm and prematurely ended the show.

Friday, February 23, 1990
Haverford College, Haverford, PA
● *Set I:* Alumni Blues, You Enjoy Myself, Possum, Foam, Carolina, Rocky Top, Dinner and a Movie > Ya Mar, Walk Away, Bouncing Around the Room, Run Like an Antelope
● *Set II:* Golgi Apparatus, Reba, Bathtub Gin, Jesus Just Left Chicago, Tela, The Oh Kee Pa Ceremony > Suzy Greenberg, Mike's Song > I Am Hydrogen > Weekapaug Groove, Highway to Hell
● *Encore:* Contact, I Didn't Know, Good Times Bad Times
● *Show Notes:* Suzy featured a Purple Haze tease from Trey and a full-band Low Rider jam. The YEM jam included Camel Walk teases.

Saturday, February 24, 1990
The Bayou, Washington, DC
● *Set I:* Carolina, You Enjoy Myself, Golgi Apparatus, Divided Sky, Esther, Possum, I Didn't Know, Run Like an Antelope
● *Set II:* The Sloth, The Oh Kee Pa Ceremony, AC/DC Bag, Fee, The Squirming Coil, La Grange, Bathtub Gin, Lawn Boy, Contact
● *Encore:* The Lizards, Caravan

Sunday, February 25, 1990
8x10 Club, Baltimore, MD
● *Check:* Jessica Jam, Donna Lee -> Jazz Jam
● *Set I:* Foam, My Sweet One, Colonel Forbin's Ascent > The Famous Mockingbird, Funky Bitch, The Squirming Coil, Bouncing Around the Room, David Bowie, Satin Doll, Rift, Possum

● *Set II:* Reba, McGrupp and the Watchful Hosemasters -> Makisupa Policeman, The Lizards, Fluffhead, Big Black Furry Creature from Mars
● *Show Notes:* This show included the first known version of the original Rift. Reba was preceded by teases of the theme from *Jeopardy*. Bowie included an extended Tweezer jam.

Thursday, March 1, 1990
Toad's Place, New Haven, CT
● *Set I:* Golgi Apparatus, Ya Mar, Rhombus Narration, Divided Sky, I Didn't Know, You Enjoy Myself -> Possum
● *Set II:* The Lizards, Foam, Mike's Song > I Am Hydrogen > Weekapaug Groove, Carolina, Slave to the Traffic Light
● *Show Notes:* This Weekapaug included a tease of the theme from *Bonanza*.

Friday, March 2, 1990
The Chance, Poughkeepsie, NY
Colonel Forbin's Ascent > The Famous Mockingbird
● *Show Notes:* This setlist is incomplete.

Saturday, March 3, 1990
The Wetlands Preserve, New York, NY
● *Check:* Tweezer
● *Set I:* Mike's Song > I Am Hydrogen > Weekapaug Groove, My Sweet One, The Squirming Coil, The Lizards, The Oh Kee Pa Ceremony > AC/DC Bag, Reba, Rocky Top, You Enjoy Myself -> Possum
● *Set II:* Dinner and a Movie, Caravan, Fluffhead, Esther, Funky Bitch, Carolina, Divided Sky
● *Encore:* Suzy Greenberg
● *Show Notes:* My Sweet One and Funky Bitch featured John Popper on harmonica.

Monday, March 5, 1990
The Haunt, Ithaca, NY

Wednesday, March 7, 1990
University of New Hampshire, Durham, NH
● *Set I:* Reba, Possum, Esther, Caravan, The Lizards, David Bowie
● *Set II:* The Oh Kee Pa Ceremony, AC/DC Bag, The Squirming Coil, Bathtub Gin, Split Open and Melt, Tela, Mike's Song > I Am Hydrogen > Weekapaug Groove
● *Encore:* Whipping Post

Thursday, March 8, 1990
Aiko's, Saratoga Springs, NY
● *Set I:* Dinner and a Movie, You Enjoy Myself -> Possum, Ya Mar, Foam, Carolina, The Oh Kee Pa Ceremony > Suzy Greenberg, Take the 'A' Train, Run Like an Antelope
● *Set II:* Divided Sky, Bathtub Gin, My Sweet One, AC/DC Bag, Caravan, I Didn't Know, The Lizards, Mike's Song > I Am Hydrogen > Weekapaug Groove, The Ballad of Curtis Loew, Golgi Apparatus
● *Encore:* Contact, Good Times Bad Times
● *Show Notes:* Antelope included a Fishing Hole Theme tease.

Friday, March 9, 1990
The Front, Burlington, VT

● *Set I:* The Man Who Stepped Into Yesterday > Avenu Malkenu, Caravan, Ya Mar, Bouncing Around the Room, Colonel Forbin's Ascent > The Famous Mockingbird, The Sloth, Possum, Donna Lee, Run Like an Antelope
● *Set II:* Reba, The Oh Kee Pa Ceremony > AC/DC Bag > The Curtain, Dog Gone Dog, Slave to the Traffic Light, Highway to Hell, You Enjoy Myself > La Grange, Contact, Big Black Furry Creature from Mars
● *Encore:* Whipping Post
● *Show Notes:* Caravan, Ya Mar, Donna Lee, Antelope, Slave, Highway to Hell, YEM, and BBFCFM all featured Dave Grippo on saxophone. Antelope also included a tease of the *Odd Couple* theme. Whipping Post featured Fishman on vocals and guitar. YEM included a Who Knows jam.

Saturday, March 10, 1990
The Front, Burlington, VT
● *Set I:* Wilson, Esther, McGrupp and the Watchful Hosemasters, AC/DC Bag, Rocky Top, The Squirming Coil, Funky Bitch, Divided Sky, Jesus Just Left Chicago, Carolina
● *Show Notes:* The list for the second set is not known.

Sunday, March 11, 1990
The Front, Burlington, VT
● *Set I:* Contact, The Oh Kee Pa Ceremony > Suzy Greenberg, The Man Who Stepped Into Yesterday > Avenu Malkenu > The Man Who Stepped Into Yesterday Reprise, Reba, La Grange, Mike's Song > I Am Hydrogen > Weekapaug Groove, The Squirming Coil, Possum
● *Set II:* Carolina, Roll Like a Cantaloupe, My Sweet One, Bouncing Around the Room, Dinner and a Movie, Take the 'A' Train, The Sloth, Ya Mar, Split Open and Melt, Harpua, Slave to the Traffic Light, AC/DC Bag, David Bowie
● *Show Notes:* This excellent older show included a great SOAM and a hysterical Harpua with a Foxy Lady tease.

Friday, March 16, 1990
23 East Cabaret, Ardmore, PA

Saturday, March 17, 1990
23 East Cabaret, Ardmore, PA
● *Set I:* Golgi Apparatus, Esther, Dinner and a Movie, Bouncing Around the Room -> My Sweet One, Rhombus Narration -> Divided Sky, Donna Lee, The Lizards, Run Like an Antelope
● *Set II:* Killer Joe, Bold As Love, The Oh Kee Pa Ceremony > AC/DC Bag > Foam, You Enjoy Myself
● *Encore:* Good Times Bad Times

Tuesday, March 27, 1990
Stache's, Columbus, OH

Wednesday, March 28, 1990
Beta Intramural Hockey Team Party, Denison University, Granville, OH
● *Set I:* Possum, Ya Mar, Fee, Walk Away, Tweezer, Uncle Pen, The Oh Kee Pa Ceremony > Suzy Greenberg, Take the 'A' Train, Runaway Jim, You Enjoy Myself, Good Times Bad Times
● *Set II:* Carolina, Sweet Adeline, Whipping Post, Funky Bitch, Mike's

Song > I Am Hydrogen > Weekapaug Groove, Jesus Just Left Chicago, The Lizards, Split Open and Melt, Contact, La Grange, Rift, Cavern, Highway to Hell, If I Only Had a Brain
● *Show Notes:* This show marked the premiere of three original songs and two covers, as the band unveiled Tweezer, Cavern, Runaway Jim, Sweet Adeline, and Uncle Pen.

Thursday, March 29, 1990
Canal Street Tavern, Dayton, OH

Friday, March 30, 1990
Lounge Axe, Chicago, IL

Friday, March 30, 1990
The Pterodactyl Club, Athens, GA
● *Show Notes:* Tapes that circulate under this date are mislabeled copies of May 30, 1990.

Saturday, March 31, 1990
Ratskellar, Memorial Union, University of Wisconsin, Madison, WI

Wednesday, April 4, 1990
Colorado University, Boulder, CO
● *Set I:* Golgi Apparatus, You Enjoy Myself, Walk Away, Take the 'A' Train, Possum, Foam, Divided Sky, Carolina
● *Set II:* Mike's Song > I Am Hydrogen > Weekapaug Groove, The Lizards, Uncle Pen, The Sloth, I Didn't Know, Good Times Bad Times
● *Encore:* Contact, Highway to Hell

Thursday, April 5, 1990
J.J. McCabes, Boulder, CO
● *Set I:* Possum, Ya Mar, David Bowie, Carolina, The Oh Kee Pa Ceremony, Suzy Greenberg, You Enjoy Myself, The Lizards, Fire
● *Set II:* Reba, Uncle Pen, Jesus Just Left Chicago, AC/DC Bag, Donna Lee, Tweezer, Fee, Cavern, Mike's Song > I Am Hydrogen > Weekapaug Groove, If I Only Had a Brain, Contact
● *Encore:* Golgi Apparatus
● *Show Notes:* Ya Mar and Bowie included teases of the "Bonanza" theme. JJLC featured special guest Dan Mosebee on harmonica.

Friday, April 6, 1990
El Dorado Cafe, Crested Butte, CO
● *Set I:* Cavern, You Enjoy Myself, Uncle Pen, Rhombus Narration > Divided Sky, Ya Mar, Dinner and a Movie, Bouncing Around the Room, The Oh Kee Pa Ceremony > Suzy Greenberg, Run Like an Antelope
● *Set II:* Carolina, La Grange, Esther, The Sloth, Harry Hood, Caravan, Reba, I Didn't Know, Alumni Blues, Good Times Bad Times
● *Encore:* Jesus Just Left Chicago, Highway to Hell
● *Show Notes:* This interesting Alumni was full of additional lyrics.

Saturday, April 7, 1990
El Dorado Cafe, Crested Butte, CO
● *Set I:* David Bowie, My Sweet One > AC/DC Bag, The Squirming Coil, The Lizards, Walk Away, Bathtub Gin, Possum, Tweezer, Mike's Song > I Am Hydrogen > Weekapaug Groove

● *Set II:* Harpua, Big Black Furry Creature from Mars, Contact
● *Show Notes:* BBFCFM included a jam based on the "Brady Bunch" theme. This setlist may be incomplete.

Sunday, April 8, 1990
Fly Me to the Moon Saloon, Telluride, CO
● *Set I:* Divided Sky, Funky Bitch, You Enjoy Myself, If I Only Had a Brain, The Oh Kee Pa Ceremony > Suzy Greenberg, Uncle Pen, Possum
● *Set II:* Golgi Apparatus, Walk Away, The Lizards, Slave to the Traffic Light, Mike's Song > I Am Hydrogen > Weekapaug Groove, Fee, My Sweet One, Run Like an Antelope
● *Encore:* Carolina, Fire

Monday, April 9, 1990
Fly Me to the Moon Saloon, Telluride, CO
● *Set II:* Funky Bitch, Esther, Uncle Pen, La Grange, Foam, Harry Hood, Jesus Just Left Chicago, Divided Sky, Love You, Tweezer, Whipping Post
● *Show Notes:* This setlist is incomplete.

Wednesday, April 11, 1990
Fly Me to the Moon Saloon, Telluride, CO

Thursday, April 12, 1990
The Inferno, Steamboat Springs, CO
● *Set I:* Golgi Apparatus, Ya Mar, Walk Away, Uncle Pen, Possum, You Enjoy Myself, Take the 'A' Train, Cavern, Jesus Just Left Chicago, Divided Sky, Good Times Bad Times
● *Set II:* David Bowie, My Sweet One, The Oh Kee Pa Ceremony > Suzy Greenberg, Tweezer, The Lizards, Runaway Jim, Love You, Mike's Song > I Am Hydrogen > Weekapaug Groove
● *Encore:* Carolina
● *Show Notes:* This show may have actually been at The Moon in Telluride.

Friday, April 13, 1990
The Inferno, Steamboat Springs, CO
● *Set I:* Funky Bitch, Dinner and a Movie, Bouncing Around the Room, Fluffhead, Esther, La Grange, The Oh Kee Pa Ceremony > AC/DC Bag, Reba, Fire
● *Set II:* Run Like an Antelope, Foam, You Enjoy Myself, Alumni Blues, The Ballad of Curtis Loew, The Sloth, Harry Hood, Caravan, Possum, Highway to Hell

Saturday, April 14, 1990
The Inferno, Steamboat Springs, CO
● *Set I:* Split Open and Melt, Uncle Pen, Cavern, Divided Sky, Colonel Forbin's Ascent > The Famous Mockingbird, Rift, Mike's Song > I Am Hydrogen > Weekapaug Groove
● *Set II:* I Didn't Know, The Oh Kee Pa Ceremony, Suzy Greenberg, Tweezer, Bathtub Gin, Bold as Love, Wilson, Ride Captain Ride, Golgi Apparatus, Fee, David Bowie

Wednesday, April 18, 1990
Herman's Hideaway, Denver, CO
● *Set I:* Mike's Song > I Am Hydrogen > Weekapaug Groove, Uncle Pen, The Curtain > Foam, You Enjoy Myself, My Sweet One, Take the 'A' Train >

Possum
● *Set II:* La Grange, Fee, The Sloth, Funky Bitch, Reba > Walk Away, The Oh Kee Pa Ceremony > Bold As Love, Lawn Boy, David Bowie -> Jagermeister -> David Bowie
● *Show Notes:* The end of the second set was full of surprises. The beginning of Bowie included a return to the Lawn Boy melody, a tribute to Chris Kuroda and his abilities at the light board, and a tribute to Jagermeister.

Thursday, April 19, 1990
Boulder Theater, Boulder, CO
● Opening Act: The Circle
● *Set II:* Possum, McGrupp and the Watchful Hosemasters, Dinner and a Movie, You Enjoy Myself, Terrapin, Highway to Hell, Carolina, Golgi Apparatus
● *Show Notes:* This setlist is incomplete.

Friday, April 20, 1990
Ramskellar, Colorado State University, Ft. Collins, CO
● *Set I:* Take the 'A' Train, Divided Sky, Alumni Blues, Ya Mar, Cavern, Dinner and a Movie, Bouncing Around the Room, Colonel Forbin's Ascent > The Famous Mockingbird, Possum
● *Set II:* Caravan, Mike's Song > I Am Hydrogen > Weekapaug Groove, La Grange, Rift, Fee, The Oh Kee Pa Ceremony > AC/DC Bag, Jesus Just Left Chicago, You Enjoy Myself

Saturday, April 21, 1990
Lincoln Center, Fort Collins, CO
● *Set I:* Sweet Adeline, Reba, Funky Bitch, Esther, Foam, Walk Away, The Oh Kee Pa Ceremony > Suzy Greenberg, Bike, Run Like an Antelope
● *Set II:* Harry Hood, Runaway Jim, No Dogs Allowed, Uncle Pen, Fluffhead, Highway to Hell, Tela, Tweezer, The Lizards
● *Show Notes:* No Dogs Allowed was played for Erik the Viking.

Sunday, April 22, 1990
Cutler Quad, Colorado College, Colorado Springs, CO
● *Set I:* Divided Sky, Uncle Pen, The Oh Kee Pa Ceremony > Suzy Greenberg, Possum, I Didn't Know, Cavern, My Sweet One, Slave to the Traffic Light, Mike's Song > I Am Hydrogen > Weekapaug Groove
● *Set II:* Dinner and a Movie, Bouncing Around the Room, You Enjoy Myself, Fluffhead, How High the Moon, Esther, Big Black Furry Creature from Mars, Harry Hood, Fire
● *Encore:* Lawn Boy, Golgi Apparatus
● *Show Notes:* This was a free outdoor show, performed on Earth Day, where Phish opened for Kenny Loggins. The short break after Suzy was necessary to correct audio problems. This version of YEM contained teases of Another One Bites the Dust. Mike used How High the Moon to change his broken bass string. The second set opened with Bouncing teases and a request for Caleb Snyder to retrieve his license, which was awaiting its retrieval on Page's keyboard.

Wednesday, April 25, 1990
Notre Dame University, South Bend, IN
● *Set I:* If I Only Had a Brain, Divided Sky, My Sweet One, David Bowie
● *Set II:* Foam, Sweet Adeline, Reba, Ya Mar, You Enjoy Myself, Esther, La Grange, Dinner and a Movie, Bouncing Around the Room, Mike's

Song > I Am Hydrogen > Weekapaug Groove
● *Encore:* Contact

Thursday, April 26, 1990
The 'Sco, Oberlin, OH
● *Set I:* Possum, Foam > You Enjoy Myself, Uncle Pen, Dinner and a Movie -> Bouncing Around the Room, I Didn't Know, Run Like an Antelope, Lawn Boy
● *Set II:* How High the Moon, Esther, Bathtub Gin, The Oh Kee Pa Ceremony > Suzy Greenberg, Cavern, Sweet Adeline, The Ballad of Curtis Loew, Mike's Song > I Am Hydrogen > Weekapaug Groove
● *Encore:* Highway to Hell
● *Show Notes:* Listen for a strong I Know a Little tease before the encore.

Saturday, April 28, 1990
The Strand Theater, Boston, MA
● *Set I:* Sweet Adeline, The Oh Kee Pa Ceremony > Suzy Greenberg, Uncle Pen, Dinner and a Movie -> Bouncing Around the Room, Possum, You Enjoy Myself, Rift, Foam, Run Like an Antelope
● *Set II:* Cavern, Harry Hood, Caravan, I Didn't Know, Reba, My Sweet One, Mike's Song > I Am Hydrogen > Weekapaug Groove
● *Encore:* Big Black Furry Creature from Mars

Sunday, April 29, 1990
Woodbury Ski & Racquet Club, Woodbury, CT
Carolina, Possum, Ya Mar, You Enjoy Myself, Dinner and a Movie, Bouncing Around the Room, Uncle Pen, Divided Sky, Fluffhead, Walk Away, HYHU > Love You > HYHU, The Lizards, Fire
● *Show Notes:* Walk Away featured Trey and Mike on the trampolines.

Thursday, May 3, 1990
The Pub House, Poultney, VT

Friday, May 4, 1990
Colonial Theatre, Keene, NH
● *Check:* Carolina (with alternate, "R"-rated lyrics)
● *Set I:* Runaway Jim, The Sloth, Uncle Pen, Tweezer, The Oh Kee Pa Ceremony, Mike's Song > I Am Hydrogen > Weekapaug Groove, Caravan, If I Only Had a Brain, Highway to Hell, Run Like an Antelope
● *Set II:* Whipping Post, Sweet Adeline, The Man Who Stepped Into Yesterday > Avenu Malkenu, Bouncing Around the Room, Possum, Reba, My Sweet One, You Enjoy Myself, The Lizards
● *Encore:* Contact

Saturday, May 6, 1990
Toad's Place, New Haven, CT
● Opening Act: Widespread Panic
● *Set I:* Possum > Bouncing Around the Room, Uncle Pen, Reba, Tweezer, Mike's Song > I Am Hydrogen > Weekapaug Groove
● *Set II:* Fee, Harry Hood, Esther, David Bowie, HYHU > Terrapin > HYHU, Jagermeister, You Enjoy Myself
● *Show Notes:* Reba was dedicated to Widespread Panic. The jam out of Terrapin had a Spanish-style feel. The management stopped the band in the middle of YEM, so there was no vocal jam. During the tramps jam in YEM, though, Trey jumped off the stage.

Monday, May 7, 1990
The Haunt, Ithaca, NY
Walk Away, Highway to Hell, La Grange, If I Only Had a Brain, Possum
● *Show Notes:* This setlist is incomplete and out of order. It is known, though, that these songs were definitely played.

Wednesday, May 9, 1990
Thunderbird's, Portland, ME

Thursday, May 10, 1990
Pearl Street Ballroom, Northampton, MA
● *Set I:* Suzy Greenberg, Uncle Pen, Bouncing Around the Room, Divided Sky, Tweezer, My Sweet One, Bathtub Gin, Possum
● *Set II:* Funky Bitch, Runaway Jim, Harry Hood, Caravan, Reba, The Oh Kee Pa Ceremony > AC/DC Bag, Good Times Bad Times
● *Encore:* Whipping Post

Friday, May 11, 1990
The Living Room, Providence, RI
● Opening Act: Widespread Panic
● *Set I:* Mike's Song > I Am Hydrogen > Weekapaug Groove, Uncle Pen, Foam, Bouncing Around the Room, Possum, Reba, Highway to Hell
● *Set II:* The Oh Kee Pa Ceremony > AC/DC Bag, The Lizards, Tweezer, Ya Mar, Love You, Good Times Bad Times
● *Encore:* Big Black Furry Creature from Mars

Saturday, May 12, 1990
The Front, Burlington, VT

Sunday, May 13, 1990
The Front, Burlington, VT
● *Check:* Mike's Song, Shaggy Dog, Jam
● *Set I:* Bathtub Gin, The Oh Kee Pa Ceremony, AC/DC Bag, Dinner and a Movie, Bouncing Around the Room, Runaway Jim, Uncle Pen, Divided Sky, Lawn Boy, David Bowie
● *Set II:* Mike's Song > I Am Hydrogen > Weekapaug Groove, Foam, Donna Lee, Tweezer, My Sweet One, Reba, Funky Bitch, Sweet Adeline, Possum, La Grange
● *Show Notes:* This version of Possum included teases of Norwegian Wood.

Tuesday, May 15, 1990
Hamilton College, Clinton, NY
Reba, Alumni Blues, Foam, Mike's Song > I Am Hydrogen > Weekapaug Groove, Uncle Pen, Bouncing Around the Room, Split Open and Melt, Runaway Jim, The Squirming Coil, The Lizards
● *Show Notes:* This outdoor show was halted due to rain. Some tapes that circulate are mislabeled "The Front."

Saturday, May 19, 1990
The Upper, St. Paul's School, Concord, NH
● *Set I:* Golgi Apparatus, Ya Mar, Alumni Blues, Sweet Adeline, La Grange, You Enjoy Myself, The Lizards, Highway to Hell
● *Set II:* Possum, Reba, The Oh Kee Pa Ceremony > Suzy Greenberg, Fee, Dinner and a Movie -> Bouncing Around the Room, Rift, Jesus Just Left Chicago, Good Times Bad Times

● *Encore:* Contact

Wednesday, May 23, 1990
The Library, Richmond, VA
● *Set I:* Divided Sky, Ya Mar, You Enjoy Myself, If I Only Had a Brain, The Oh Kee Pa Ceremony > Suzy Greenberg, Uncle Pen, Bouncing Around the Room, Possum, Sweet Adeline
● *Set II:* The Squirming Coil, Reba, Tweezer, The Lizards, La Grange, McGrupp and the Watchful Hosemasters, Take the 'A' Train, Run Like an Antelope, Mike's Song > I Am Hydrogen > Weekapaug Groove

Thursday, May 24, 1990
The Brewery, Raleigh, NC
● *Set I:* The Sloth > Bouncing Around the Room > Tweezer, Donna Lee, Reba, You Enjoy Myself, The Oh Kee Pa Ceremony > AC/DC Bag, Golgi Apparatus
● *Set II:* Foam, Dinner and a Movie > Possum, I Didn't Know, My Sweet One > Horn, Fee, Walk Away, Harry Hood, Highway to Hell, Contact
● *Encore:* Good Times Bad Times
● *Show Notes:* This show marked the first known performance of Horn. Fishman jokingly introduced "Tweezer So Cold" as a song from the "Jane Fonda Workout Tape" and subsequently announced "Donna Lee" as a song from the "Charlie Parker Workout Tape."

Friday, May 25, 1990
The Old Post Office, Hilton Head, SC

Saturday, May 26, 1990
The Old Post Office, Hilton Head, SC

Monday, May 28, 1990
Hilton Head, SC
● *Show Notes:* It appears that this show was played at Page's father's house. It is believed that the band primarily played jazz tunes.

Wednesday, May 30, 1990
The Pterodactyl Club, Athens, GA
Reba, The Oh Kee Pa Ceremony > Suzy Greenberg, The Sloth, Dinner and a Movie, Bouncing Around the Room, Run Like an Antelope, Lawn Boy, Fluffhead, Sweet Adeline, Mike's Song > I am Hydrogen > Weekapaug Groove, Good Times Bad Times
● *Show Notes:* This venue may have actually been in Charlotte, North Carolina.

Thursday, May 31, 1990
Variety Playhouse, Athens, GA
Possum, You Enjoy Myself, Dinner and a Movie, Bouncing Around the Room, Caravan, Esther > Tweezer > I Didn't Know, Uncle Pen, Divided Sky, The Oh Kee Pa Ceremony > Suzy Greenberg,
● *Encore:* Good Times Bad Times
● *Show Notes:* At this show, Phish opened for The Aquarium Rescue Unit.

Friday, June 1, 1990
The Cotton Club, Atlanta, GA
Rocky Top, Uncle Pen, Run Like an Antelope, Mike's Song > I Am Hy-

drogen > Weekapaug Groove, HYHU > Fee, Terrapin > HYHU, Possum, Fee, Big Black Furry Creature from Mars, Contact
● *Show Notes:* Rocky Top through Antelope featured the Reverend Jeff Mosier on banjo; Antelope also featured Oteil Burbridge on bass. This show features one of the most humorous moments ever caught on tape! It started when the crowd chanted for Fee as Fishman took the stage during HYHU. Fish sounded perplexed, and remarked that he doesn't sing Fee, but Trey and Page started the song up anyway and left Fishman on the spot. He tried his best and got through the first verse before falling apart during the chorus.

Saturday, June 2, 1990
Greenstreets, Columbia, SC
Uncle Pen, Dinner and a Movie, Bouncing Around the Room, Reba, Possum, The Lizards, Fire, Contact, Good Times Bad Times

Tuesday, June 5, 1990
Cat's Cradle, Chapel Hill, NC
● *Set I:* The Squirming Coil, Uncle Pen, Mike's Song > I Am Hydrogen > Weekapaug Groove, Ya Mar, The Oh Kee Pa Ceremony > Suzy Greenberg, Take the 'A' Train > David Bowie, Lawn Boy, Possum
● *Set II:* Sweet Adeline, Divided Sky, Caravan, Dinner and a Movie -> Bouncing Around the Room, My Sweet One, The Lizards, You Enjoy Myself > The Ballad of Curtis Loew, Good Times Bad Times
● *Encore:* Whipping Post, Golgi Apparatus

Wednesday, June 6, 1990
The Barrel House, Salem, VA

Thursday, June 7, 1990
The Bayou, Washington, DC
● Opening Act: Aquarium Rescue Unit
● *Check:* Suzy Greenberg -> Fluff's Travels (three times)
● *Set I:* Suzy Greenberg -> Fluff's Travels, Donna Lee, Possum, Fee, Reba, You Enjoy Myself, The Lizards, Good Times Bad Times
● *Set II:* My Sweet One, Dinner and a Movie > Bouncing Around the Room, Tweezer, Uncle Pen, Divided Sky, Love You, Mike's Song > I Am Hydrogen > Weekapaug Groove
● *Encore:* Lawn Boy, Big Black Furry Creature from Mars

Friday, June 8, 1990
23 East Cabaret, Ardmore, PA
● *Set I:* Foam, Bouncing Around the Room, You Enjoy Myself, Divided Sky, Uncle Pen, The Oh Kee Pa Ceremony > Suzy Greenberg, Run Like an Antelope
● *Set II:* Possum, My Sweet One, Tweezer, I Didn't Know, Mike's Song > I Am Hydrogen > Weekapaug Groove

Saturday, June 9, 1990
The Wetlands Preserve, New York, NY
● Opening Act: The Aquarium Rescue Unit
● *Set I:* Possum, Lawn Boy, Reba, Dinner and a Movie, Bouncing Around the Room, Tweezer, Uncle Pen, Mike's Song > I Am Hydrogen > Weekapaug Groove
● *Set II:* Whole Lotta Love Jam > Harry Hood, The Man Who Stepped Into Yesterday > Avenu Malkenu > The Man Who Stepped Into Yesterday Reprise > La Grange, Fee -> Foam, The Oh Kee Pa Ceremony >

Suzy Greenberg, Run Like an Antelope, Terrapin, Harpua, Good Times Bad Times
● *Encore:* The Landlady > Contact
● *Show Notes:* Harpua included Funkytown teases.

Saturday, June 16, 1990
Townshend Family Park, Townshend, VT
● *Check:* Carolina, Funky Bitch
● *Set I:* AC/DC Bag, Divided Sky, Wilson, Reba, Horn, Uncle Pen, Bouncing Around the Room, Timber (Jerry), Lawn Boy, Possum
● *Set II:* Golgi Apparatus, Esther, Tweezer, My Sweet One, Bathtub Gin, You Enjoy Myself, The Lizards, Run Like an Antelope
● *Set III:* La Grange, Happy Birthday, Ya Mar, Foam, The Oh Kee Pa Ceremony > Suzy Greenberg, Fee, Rocky Top, Caravan, If I Only Had a Brain, Mike's Song > I Am Hydrogen > Weekapaug Groove
● *Encore:* Contact, Big Black Furry Creature from Mars
● *Encore:* Good Times Bad Times
● *Show Notes:* Happy Birthday was sung for Heather.

Sunday, June 17, 1990
Wendell Studios, Boston, MA
Dog Gone Dog, Uncle Pen, Suzy Greenberg, Suzy Greenberg, Caravan, Alumni Blues, Take the 'A' Train, In a Mellow Tone, Possum, Mike's Song > I Am Hydrogen > Weekapaug Groove, The Man Who Stepped Into Yesterday > Avenu Malkenu > The Man Who Stepped Into Yesterday Reprise, Tweezer, Possum, Harry Hood, Rift, Runaway Jim

SUMMER, 1990

Sunday, July 8, 1990
23 East Cabaret, Ardmore, PA

Saturday, August 4, 1990
The Red Barn, Hinesburg, VT
● *Show Notes:* It is believed that this was a private party thrown by someone named Pam.

Sunday, September 2, 1990
The Ranch, Shelburne, VT

FALL, 1990

Thursday, September 13, 1990
The Wetlands Preserve, New York, NY
● *Set I:* The Landlady, Divided Sky, Foam, Tube, The Asse Festival, Run Like an Antelope, Minute by Minute, Buried Alive, Paul and Silas, Bouncing Around the Room, Possum
● *Set II:* Mike's Song > I Am Hydrogen > Weekapaug Groove, Magilla, Stash, Going Down Slow, The Oh Kee Pa Ceremony > AC/DC Bag -> Buried Alive -> Take the 'A' Train > Sparks > Reba, Self, Dahlia, The Revolution's Over
● *Encore:* The Lizards, La Grange

● *Show Notes:* Self, Dahlia, and The Revolution's Over featured the Dude of Life on vocals. In addition to these debuts, fans at this show saw several premieres. The band also debuted Tube, The Asse Festival, Buried Alive, Magilla, Stash, Paul and Silas, Minute by Minute, and Going Down Slow. Buried Alive included early music signals among the band members; 'A' Train subsequently included a Buried Alive tease.

Friday, September 14, 1990
Living Room, Providence, RI
● *Set I:* Suzy Greenberg, Bouncing Around the Room, The Landlady, Reba, Paul and Silas, Stash, Dinner and a Movie, I Didn't Know, Mike's Song > I Am Hydrogen > Weekapaug Groove
● *Set II:* The Asse Festival, The Squirming Coil, Buried Alive, Tweezer, Magilla, Cavern, The Lizards, Destiny Unbound, Fire, Going Down Slow
● *Show Notes:* Tweezer included teases of Turning Japanese and Popeye, as well as Oom Pa Pa and Random Laugh Signals. At this show, Fishman was introduced by Trey as "Red Doughnut Man." This show included the debut of Destiny Unbound. Also, Going Down Slow, which debuted the night before, was played for the last time to date.

Saturday, September 15, 1990
Colonial Theater, Keene, NH
● *Set I:* Buried Alive > Divided Sky, Paul and Silas, The Landlady, Fee, Tube, The Oh Kee Pa Ceremony > AC/DC Bag, The Asse Festival, David Bowie, Golgi Apparatus, Stash, Magilla, The Squirming Coil
● *Set II:* Split Open and Melt, Eliza, My Sweet One, Bathtub Gin, Foam, Minute by Minute, Harry Hood > Possum
● *Encore:* Communication Breakdown > You Enjoy Myself
● *Show Notes:* Eliza debuted at this show.

Sunday, September 16, 1990
Wesleyan University, Middletown, CT
Dinner and a Movie, Bouncing Around the Room, The Sloth, The Landlady, Reba, Ya Mar, Tube, Tweezer, Paul and Silas, Mike's Song > I Am Hydrogen > Weekapaug Groove, Magilla, Run Like an Antelope
● *Encore:* Contact
● *Show Notes:* This was a free show. Tweezer included a Heartbreaker tease.

Monday, September 17, 1990
The Front, Burlington, VT

Tuesday, September 18, 1990
The Front, Burlington, VT

Thursday, September 20, 1990
Somerville Theatre, Somerville, MA
● *Set I:* Reba, Paul and Silas, The Asse Festival, Dinner and a Movie, Foam, Esther, The Landlady, Mike's Song > I Am Hydrogen > Weekapaug Groove, Eliza, La Grange
● *Set II:* Stash, AC/DC Bag, Bouncing Around the Room, The Squirm-

ing Coil, Divided Sky, Magilla, The Oh Kee Pa Ceremony, Suzy Greenberg, Possum, Funky Bitch, Stash, Uncle Pen, Tube, Lawn Boy

Friday, September 21, 1990
Somerville Theatre, Somerville, MA
● *Set II:* Funky Bitch, Stash, Uncle Pen, Tube, Lawn Boy, Tweezer, Buried Alive, Tweezer Reprise
● *Encore:* Golgi Apparatus
● *Show Notes:* This show was a *Lawn Boy* release party. The setlist is incomplete. This show marked the first known version of Tweezer Reprise. Tweezer included a Sweet Emotion tease.

Saturday, September 22, 1990
University of Massachusetts, Amherst, MA
● *Set I:* Buried Alive, Horn, My Sweet One, Divided Sky, Tela, The Oh Kee Pa Ceremony > Suzy Greenberg, Magilla, Wilson, The Landlady, I Didn't Know, David Bowie
● *Set II:* The Squirming Coil, Tweezer, Destiny Unbound, Fee, Uncle Pen, Bouncing Around the Room, Stash, The Lizards, Lawn Boy, Possum
● *Encore:* The Asse Festival, Golgi Apparatus

Wednesday, September 26, 1990
The Chance, Poughkeepsie, NY
● *Show Notes:* There was no show on this date. Tapes that circulate are mislabeled copies of the show two nights later.

Thursday, September 27, 1990
The Front, Burlington, VT

Friday, September 28, 1990
The Chance, Poughkeepsie, NY
● *Set I:* The Landlady, Bouncing Around the Room, The Oh Kee Pa Ceremony > Suzy Greenberg, Stash, My Sweet One, The Squirming Coil -> The Lizards, The Asse Festival, Run Like an Antelope
● *Set II:* AC/DC Bag > Esther, Gumbo, Dinner and a Movie, You Enjoy Myself, Divided Sky
● *Encore:* Paul and Silas
● *Show Notes:* Gumbo made its debut at this show.

Saturday, September 29, 1990
23 East Cabaret, Ardmore, PA
● *Set I:* Divided Sky, Dinner and a Movie, The Landlady, Ya Mar, Buried Alive > Bouncing Around the Room, Possum, Magilla, David Bowie
● *Set II:* The Squirming Coil, Tweezer, Gumbo, Uncle Pen, Stash, Mike's Song > I Am Hydrogen > Weekapaug Groove
● *Encore:* Lawn Boy
● *Show Notes:* During the Bowie intro, the crowd sang Happy Birthday to Trey at the stroke of midnight.

Monday, October 1, 1990
The Haunt, Ithaca, NY
Mike's Song > I Am Hydrogen > Weekapaug Groove, The Asse Festival,

Stash, Runaway Jim, Fee, Gumbo, Golgi Apparatus, Love You > HYHU
-> Run Like an Antelope
● *Show Notes:* Plenty of fun Fishman action during this set! HYHU
faded into Antelope, after which both Trey and Page continued to tease
HYHU. Fishman, introduced as "Zero Man," played Love You for his
parents, who were in attendance. Fee featured Trey on megaphone, un-
miced, for the vocals. This setlist may be incomplete.

Wednesday, October 3, 1990
Thunderbird's, Portland, ME

Thursday, October 4, 1990
UNH Fieldhouse, University of New Hampshire, Durham, NH
● *Set I:* Golgi Apparatus, The Landlady, Esther, Possum, The Squirm-
ing Coil, The Lizards, Destiny Unbound, The Sloth, Uncle Pen, Golgi Ap-
paratus
● *Set II:* Reba > Bouncing Around the Room > Foam, Fee, Tweezer,
Magilla, Cavern, You Enjoy Myself
● *Encore:* Divided Sky
● *Show Notes:* The YEM intro featured crew introductions.

Friday, October 5, 1990
Skidmore Gymnasium, Skidmore College, Saratoga, NY
● *Set I:* I Didn't Know, Mike's Song > I Am Hydrogen > Weekapaug
Groove, My Sweet One, The Landlady, Tela, The Oh Kee Pa Ceremony
> Suzy Greenberg, Stash, The Asse Festival, Bouncing Around the
Room, Run Like an Antelope
● *Set II:* Golgi Apparatus, The Curtain > Ya Mar, Alumni Blues, Uncle
Pen, Split Open and Melt, Fee > Possum
● *Encore:* Good Times Bad Times

Saturday, October 6, 1990
Capitol Theater, Port Chester, NY
The Landlady, The Squirming Coil, Dinner and a Movie, Bouncing
Around the Room, Foam, You Enjoy Myself, The Oh Kee Pa Ceremony
> Suzy Greenberg, Esther, Possum, HYHU > If I Only Had a Brain >
HYHU, David Bowie, Carolina
● *Encore:* Don't Get Me Wrong
● *Show Notes:* This show, an opener for Blues Traveler, marked the
first performance of Don't Get Me Wrong. The song featured John Pop-
per on harmonica.

Sunday, October 7, 1990
Club Bene, Sayreville, NJ
● *Set I:* Divided Sky, Uncle Pen, Stash, The Landlady, Destiny Unbound,
Colonel Forbin's Ascent > The Famous Mockingbird, The Asse Festival,
The Squirming Coil, Mike's Song > I Am Hydrogen > Weekapaug
Groove, Take the 'A' Train, La Grange
● *Set II:* Buried Alive > Bouncing Around the Room, Tweezer, My
Sweet One, I Didn't Know, The Lizards, Good Times Bad Times, Golgi
Apparatus
● *Encore:* Contact

Monday, October 8, 1990
The Bayou, Washington, DC
● *Set I:* Don't Get Me Wrong, The Landlady > Bouncing Around the

Room, Foam, Cavern > Reba > My Sweet One, You Enjoy Myself, The
Oh Kee Pa Ceremony > Possum
● *Set II:* Suzy Greenberg, Stash, If I Only Had a Brain, Golgi Apparatus,
Magilla, Run Like an Antelope
● *Show Notes:* Don't Get Me Wrong featured John Popper on harmonica.

Wednesday, October 10, 1990
Trax, Charlottesville, VA

Thursday, October 11, 1990
The Jade Elephant, Richmond, VA
Friday, October 12, 1990
Cat's Cradle, Chapel Hill, NC
● *Set I:* Suzy Greenberg, You Enjoy Myself, Dinner and a Movie ->
Bouncing Around the Room, Uncle Pen, Cavern, Esther, Tweezer, Golgi
Apparatus
● *Set II:* Possum, Fee, The Landlady, HYHU > Terrapin > HYHU, Divided
Sky, Paul and Silas, Magilla, Mike's Song > I Am Hydrogen > Weeka-
paug Groove
● *Encore:* Carolina, Good Times Bad Times

Saturday, October 13, 1990
Greenstreets, Columbia, SC

Sunday, October 14, 1990
The Old Post Office, Hilton Head, SC

Wednesday, October 17, 1990
The Pterodactyl Club, Charlotte, NC

Thursday, October 18, 1990
Georgia Theatre, Athens, GA

Friday, October 19, 1990
The Cotton Club, Atlanta, GA
Golgi Apparatus, Foam, Uncle Pen, Mike's Song > I Am Hydrogen >
Weekapaug Groove, Magilla, Cavern, Possum, Bathtub Gin, The Land-
lady, Bouncing Around the Room, The Oh Kee Pa Ceremony > Suzy
Greenberg, Good Times Bad Times
● *Encore:* Carolina, AC/DC Bag
● *Encore:* Paul and Silas

Saturday, October 20, 1990
Solomon's, Tuscaloosa, AL

Monday, October 22, 1990
Tipitina's, New Orleans, LA

Thursday, October 25, 1990
Liberty Lunch, Austin, TX

Friday, October 26, 1990
The Showbar, Houston, TX

Saturday, October 27, 1990
Rhythm Room, Dallas, TX

Tuesday, October 30, 1990
The El Dorado Café, Crested Butte, CO
● *Set I:* The Landlady > Bouncing Around the Room, Donna Lee, The Asse Festival > Suzy Greenberg, Uncle Pen, Cavern, The Squirming Coil, Possum
● *Set II:* Mike's Song > I Am Hydrogen > Weekapaug Groove, Magilla, Foam, Reba -> Llama, The Ballad of Curtis Loew, Fluffhead, HYHU > Terrapin > HYHU, Buried Alive, David Bowie
● *Set III:* Paul and Silas, The Lizards, Good Times Bad Times, Contact, AC/DC Bag
● *Show Notes:* Check out the Bowie intro for a medley of teases. This show included the first known version of Llama.

Wednesday, October 31, 1990
Armstrong Hall, Colorado College, Colorado Springs, CO
● *Set I:* Buried Alive > Possum, The Squirming Coil > The Lizards, Stash > Bouncing Around the Room, You Enjoy Myself, The Asse Festival, My Sweet One, Cavern, Run Like an Antelope
● *Set II:* The Landlady, Reba, Runaway Jim, Foam, Tweezer, Fee, The Oh Kee Pa Ceremony, Suzy Greenberg, HYHU > Love You > HYHU, Mike's Song > I Am Hydrogen > Weekapaug Groove
● *Encore:* Uncle Pen, Big Black Furry Creature from Mars
● *Show Notes:* The band's annual costume contest preceded the second set. This show was webcast in the weeks following Halloween 1999, as the band did not play on Halloween that year. Buried Alive included DEG teases and Possum contained an Oom Pa Pa Signal. YEM contained an appropriate *Munsters* theme tease from Mike; the ensuing vocal jam included Night in Tunisia quotes.

Friday, November 2, 1990
Glenn Miller Ballroom, University of Colorado, Boulder, CO
● *Set I:* Golgi Apparatus, The Landlady, Bouncing Around the Room, Divided Sky, The Sloth, Mike's Song > I Am Hydrogen > Weekapaug Groove, Esther, Cavern, The Asse Festival, Possum -> Buried Alive -> Possum
● *Set II:* Suzy Greenberg, Colonel Forbin's Ascent > The Famous Mockingbird, My Sweet One, Foam, You Enjoy Myself, The Lizards, I Didn't Know, David Bowie
● *Encore:* Lawn Boy, La Grange
● *Show Notes:* An emcee announced before the show that Phish would not be performing since they broke up in the dressing room beforehand. Instead, he announced that the show would be performed by "Phish 2000." Page used an organ for Golgi and Landlady. The Bowie intro featured a medley of teases.

Saturday, November 3, 1990
Boulder Theater, Boulder, CO
● *Set I:* Dinner and a Movie -> Bouncing Around the Room, Llama, The Squirming Coil, The Oh Kee Pa Ceremony, Suzy Greenberg, Magilla -> Foam, Runaway Jim, You Enjoy Myself, Good Times Bad Times
● *Set II:* The Landlady, Mike's Song > I Am Hydrogen > Weekapaug Groove, Paul and Silas, Stash, Fee, Uncle Pen, Reba, Possum, HYHU > Love You > HYHU, Run Like an Antelope
● *Encore:* Fluffhead, Fire

Sunday, November 4, 1990
Fort Ram, Fort Collins, CO

● *Set I:* Carolina, AC/DC Bag > The Curtain > Bouncing Around the Room, Tube, Harry Hood, Funky Bitch, The Asse Festival, My Sweet One, David Bowie
● *Set II:* Golgi Apparatus, Rocky Top, Llama, Mike's Song > I Am Hydrogen > Weekapaug Groove, Manteca -> Caravan, Runaway Jim, The Oh Kee Pa Ceremony > Suzy Greenberg, Jesus Just Left Chicago, You Enjoy Myself
● *Encore:* Contact, Highway to Hell
● *Show Notes:* Manteca was played in its entirety over the top of Caravan, which, in turn, was teased several times during Suzy. Caravan also included *Woody Woodpecker* theme teases from Trey. Bowie featured brief DEG teases. Contact was played in honor of the venue's "disco lights."

Tuesday, November 6, 1990
The Cabooze, Minneapolis, MN

Thursday, November 8, 1990
Barrymore Theatre, Madison, WI
● *Check:* The Man Who Stepped Into Yesterday > Avenu Malkenu > The Man Who Stepped Into Yesterday Reprise, The Asse Festival, Eliza
● *Set I:* The Landlady, Possum, The Lizards, Foam, Uncle Pen, Llama, The Squirming Coil, The Asse Festival, I Didn't Know, Mike's Song > I Am Hydrogen > Weekapaug Groove
● *Set II:* Suzy Greenberg, Divided Sky, Tweezer, The Oh Kee Pa Ceremony, Dinner and a Movie, Bouncing Around the Room, You Enjoy Myself, Big Black Furry Creature from Mars
● *Encore:* Jesus Just Left Chicago, Fire
● *Show Notes:* YEM through the end of the show (both encores) featured John Popper on harmonica; Popper also scat sang during YEM. The venue may have been Great Hall at the University of Wisconsin in Madison.

Friday, November 9, 1990
Lounge Axe, Chicago, IL

Saturday, November 10, 1990
Earlham College, Richmond, IN
● *Set I:* Reba, The Landlady > Bouncing Around the Room, Runaway Jim, Cavern, My Sweet One, Buried Alive > The Lizards, Mike's Song > I Am Hydrogen > Weekapaug Groove
● *Set II:* Suzy Greenberg, You Enjoy Myself, The Asse Festival, Fee, Llama, Divided Sky, Bike, Possum

Friday, November 16, 1990
Campus Club, Providence, RI
● *Set I:* Suzy Greenberg, Buried Alive, Foam, You Enjoy Myself, Magilla, Llama, Divided Sky, Golgi Apparatus
● *Set II:* The Landlady, Mike's Song > I Am Hydrogen > Weekapaug Groove, Lawn Boy, Tube, Paul and Silas, The Lizards, Runaway Jim, I Didn't Know, Possum
● *Encore:* Contact, Fire
● *Show Notes:* Weekapaug included a Fishing Hole Theme tease and YEM included a Cheap Sunglasses tease from Mike. Trey introduced Fishman as "the hardest working man in show business…Henrietta!" before I Didn't Know.

Saturday, November 17, 1990
Somerville Theatre, Somerville, MA
● *Set I:* Llama, The Squirming Coil, The Landlady, Runaway Jim, Bouncing Around the Room, You Enjoy Myself, Cavern, Eliza, The Oh Kee Pa Ceremony > Suzy Greenberg, David Bowie
● *Set II:* Buried Alive, Fluffhead, Mike's Song > I Am Hydrogen > Weekapaug Groove, Esther, Love You, Possum, Lawn Boy, Rocky Top, Donna Lee, Good Times Bad Times
● *Encore:* Memories, Sweet Adeline
● *Show Notes:* Suzy and Bowie contained Low Rider jams.

Saturday, November 24, 1990
Capitol Theater, Port Chester, NY
● *Check:* Carolina, Foam
● *Set I:* Buried Alive, Possum, Foam, Mike's Song > I Am Hydrogen > Weekapaug Groove, The Squirming Coil, The Lizards, The Oh Kee Pa Ceremony, Suzy Greenberg, David Bowie
● *Set II:* Llama, Bouncing Around the Room, Stash, Eliza, The Landlady, Runaway Jim, You Enjoy Myself, Love You, Good Times Bad Times, Big Black Furry Creature from Mars, Lawn Boy, Divided Sky
● *Show Notes:* Possum included Manteca teases.

Monday, November 26, 1990
The Haunt, Ithaca, NY
● *Set I:* The Landlady > Runaway Jim, The Sloth -> Reba -> Buried Alive, You Enjoy Myself, Paul and Silas, David Bowie, Divided Sky, Makisupa Policeman, Llama
● *Set II:* Uncle Pen, Colonel Forbin's Ascent > The Famous Mockingbird, Wilson, Mike's Song > I Am Hydrogen > Weekapaug Groove
● *Encore:* Fire, Contact, Highway to Hell

Wednesday, November 28, 1990
Clement's, Syracuse, NY

Friday, November 30, 1990
Colonial Theater, Keene, NH
● *Set I:* The Landlady, Mike's Song > I Am Hydrogen > Weekapaug Groove, Esther, Dinner and a Movie, Bouncing Around the Room, Tweezer, My Sweet One, Llama, Possum
● *Set II:* The Asse Festival, The Squirming Coil, Runaway Jim, Stash, The Lizards, Gumbo, Divided Sky, I Didn't Know, The Sloth, Run Like an Antelope
● *Encore:* Caravan, The Oh Kee Pa Ceremony > Suzy Greenberg

Saturday, December 1, 1990
The Front, Burlington, VT
● *Set I:* Cavern, The Landlady, Llama, Divided Sky, Foam, Tweezer, My Sweet One, You Enjoy Myself, Runaway Jim
● *Show Notes:* This setlist is incomplete.

Sunday, December 2, 1990
The Front, Burlington, VT

Friday, December 7, 1990
Robert Crown Center, Hampshire College, Amherst, MA
● *Set I:* Golgi Apparatus, Stash, Bouncing Around the Room, The Land-lady, You Enjoy Myself, The Asse Festival, Runaway Jim, Foam, Llama
● *Set II:* Mike's Song > I Am Hydrogen > Weekapaug Groove, Donna Lee, Cavern, Tweezer, The Squirming Coil, The Oh Kee Pa Ceremony > Suzy Greenberg, HYHU > No Good Trying > HYHU, David Bowie
● *Encore:* Alumni Blues
● *Show Notes:* The YEM vocal jam included teases of Lou Reed's Walk on the Wild Side. Alumni was dedicated to "all the graduating seniors." No Good Trying debuted at this show.

Saturday, December 8, 1990
The Chance, Poughkeepsie, NY
● *Set I:* Buried Alive, Runaway Jim, Foam, AC/DC Bag, Divided Sky, Cavern, The Landlady, Mike's Song > I Am Hydrogen > Weekapaug Groove
● *Set II:* Llama, The Asse Festival, Dinner and a Movie, Bouncing Around the Room, Run Like an Antelope, Tela, Golgi Apparatus, HYHU > No Good Trying > HYHU, You Enjoy Myself
● *Encore:* Funky Bitch
● *Encore:* Contact, Highway to Hell

Friday, December 28, 1990
The Marquee, New York, NY
● *Set I:* Runaway Jim, Foam, Horn, Reba, Llama, Colonel Forbin's Ascent > The Famous Mockingbird, Mike's Song > I Am Hydrogen > Weekapaug Groove, Golgi Apparatus
● *Set II:* The Landlady, Possum, The Squirming Coil -> Tweezer -> Manteca -> Tweezer, The Oh Kee Pa Ceremony, My Sweet One, Divided Sky, No Good Trying > HYHU, Don't Get Me Wrong, Funky Bitch
● *Encore:* Bouncing Around the Room, Highway to Hell
● *Show Notes:* The last three songs of the second set featured John Popper on harmonica.

Saturday, December 29, 1990
Campus Club, Providence, RI
● *Set I:* I Didn't Know, Llama, You Enjoy Myself, Esther, David Bowie, Lawn Boy, Rocky Top, Horn, The Oh Kee Pa Ceremony > Suzy Greenberg
● *Set II:* Buried Alive > Runaway Jim, The Lizards, Cavern, Stash, Jesus Just Left Chicago, Dinner and a Movie > Bouncing Around the Room, Destiny Unbound, Run Like an Antelope
● *Encore:* Donna Lee, AC/DC Bag

Monday, December 31, 1990
Boston World Trade Center Exhibition Hall, Boston, MA
● Opening Act: Chucklehead
● *Set I:* Suzy Greenberg, Divided Sky, I Didn't Know, The Landlady, Bouncing Around the Room, My Sweet One, Mike's Song > I Am Hydrogen > Weekapaug Groove -> Auld Lang Syne, Buried Alive, Possum
● *Set II:* Golgi Apparatus, Stash, The Squirming Coil, Runaway Jim, Magilla, You Enjoy Myself, Rocky Top, If I Only Had a Brain, Run Like an Antelope
● *Show Notes:* Management turned on the house lights before the band could decide on an encore, prematurely ending the show.

WINTER/SPRING, 1991

Friday, February 1, 1991
Brown University, Providence, RI
● *Set I:* My Sweet One, Foam, Tweezer -> Tweezer Reprise, Magilla, Guelah Papyrus, Runaway Jim, Split Open and Melt, Bouncing Around the Room, David Bowie
● *Set II:* Chalk Dust Torture, Reba, The Landlady, The Mango Song, Cavern
● *Encore:* Alumni Blues, Carolina
● *Show Notes:* This show, which ended early due to Brown University's curfew, featured the first performances of Guelah Papyrus and Chalk Dust. It is possible that Carolina is filler from another show. The Mango Song was played for the first time since August 19, 1989 (132 shows).

Saturday, February 2, 1991
Alumni Gymnasium, Bates College, Lewiston, ME
● *Set I:* The Oh Kee Pa Ceremony > Suzy Greenberg, Guelah Papyrus, Dinner and a Movie, Esther, Stash, Destiny Unbound, You Enjoy Myself, Chalkdust Torture
● *Set II:* The Sloth, Run Like an Antelope, Lawn Boy
● *Show Notes:* This setlist is incomplete.

Sunday, February 3, 1991
The Front, Burlington, VT
● *Set I:* Runaway Jim, Guelah Papyrus, My Sweet One, Tweezer, Esther, Destiny Unbound, Reba, Chalk Dust Torture, Foam, Golgi Apparatus
● *Set II:* David Bowie, The Squirming Coil, The Landlady, Cavern, The Mango Song, Split Open and Melt, Bouncing Around the Room, The Oh Kee Pa Ceremony > Suzy Greenberg
● *Encore:* Jesus Just Left Chicago, Big Black Furry Creature from Mars

Monday, February 4, 1991
The Front, Burlington, VT

Thursday, February 7, 1991
Pickle Barrel Pub, Killington, VT
● *Set I:* Runaway Jim, Foam, My Sweet One, The Landlady, The Mango Song, Split Open and Melt, Bouncing Around the Room, Possum, The Squirming Coil, Golgi Apparatus
● *Set II:* Chalk Dust Torture, The Man Who Stepped Into Yesterday > Avenu Malkenu > The Man Who Stepped Into Yesterday Reprise > Tweezer, Tweezer Reprise, Guelah Papyrus, Uncle Pen, Cavern, Love You, The Lizards, The Sloth, Destiny Unbound, You Enjoy Myself
● *Encore:* AC/DC Bag
● *Show Notes:* Lizards was aborted midway through the second verse; Trey had forgotten the words during the first verse and mumbled his way through until finally calling the song off. Humorously, Destiny Unbound was jokingly announced as "Lizards." Sloth was played in response to an audience request. The Vocal Jam out of YEM closed with a quote of the Warner Brothers cartoon theme ("On with the Show, This Is It").

Friday, February 8, 1991
Portsmouth Music Hall, Portsmouth, NH

● *Set I:* AC/DC Bag, Reba, Buried Alive, Colonel Forbin's Ascent > The Famous Mockingbird, My Sweet One, Stash, The Squirming Coil, Runaway Jim, Guelah Papyrus, David Bowie
● *Set II:* Llama, The Mango Song, Cavern, Lawn Boy, Mike's Song > I Am Hydrogen > Weekapaug Groove, Horn, Bouncing Around the Room, The Lizards, Run Like an Antelope
● *Encore:* Magilla, La Grange
● *Show Notes:* Carl Gerhard made a guest appearance during the encore. Check out this great Magilla, which included a lot of action from Gerhard and Fishman.

Saturday, February 9, 1991
John M. Green Hall, Smith College, Northampton, MA
● *Set I:* The Mango Song, The Sloth, The Man Who Stepped Into Yesterday > Avenu Malkenu > The Man Who Stepped Into Yesterday Reprise, Runaway Jim, Foam, Guelah Papyrus, My Sweet One, Tweezer > Reba, Chalk Dust Torture
● *Set II:* Golgi Apparatus, Buried Alive > Fluffhead, The Landlady, Bouncing Around the Room, Harry Hood, Cavern, Love You, The Squirming Coil, Llama
● *Encore:* Lawn Boy, Suzy Greenberg
● *Encore:* Contact, Rocky Top
● *Show Notes:* A spirited second set resurrected this show. Fluffhead, Landlady, and Harry Hood all featured expressive soloing from Trey.

Thursday, February 14, 1991
State Theater, Ithaca, NY
● *Set I:* My Sweet One, McGrupp and the Watchful Hosemasters, Buried Alive, Reba, Destiny Unbound, Cavern, The Mango Song, Stash, Lawn Boy, The Oh Kee Pa Ceremony > Golgi Apparatus
● *Set II:* Mike's Song > I Am Hydrogen > Weekapaug Groove, Foam, The Squirming Coil, Runaway Jim, Esther, Alumni Blues, Bouncing Around the Room, I Didn't Know, The Landlady, Possum
● *Encore:* Uncle Pen, La Grange

Friday, February 15, 1991
Colonial Theater, Keene, NH
● *Set I:* The Curtain > Wilson > Divided Sky, Split Open and Melt, Fee -> Buried Alive, The Mango Song, The Sloth, Dinner and a Movie, Magilla, Llama
● *Set II:* David Bowie, Bathtub Gin, Ya Mar, Guelah Papyrus, My Sweet One, The Oh Kee Pa Ceremony > AC/DC Bag, Harry Hood, Terrapin, Chalk Dust Torture
● *Encore:* Caravan, Big Black Furry Creature from Mars
● *Encore:* Contact, Golgi Apparatus
● *Show Notes:* Bowie contained an El Condor Paso tease in Fishman's high hat intro, and had a silent jam near the end of the jam segment. Bag was also unusually adventurous, with three dead stops during the jam segment and uncommon dissonance. Trey briefly started Horn before Harry Hood, but abandoned it. Before Terrapin, Trey announced that Fishman would be "bringing out the big, heavy artillery" for the people in Keene. The "artillery" was Fishman's new vacuum, which made its debut at this show. Fish noted that "if I bleed during this song, that'll just be part of the effects." Inspired by his new instrument, Fish took an exceedingly spacy solo during Terrapin, complete with ersatz wolf howls, before singing the final verse *through* the vacuum.

Saturday, February 16, 1991
The Marquee, New York, NY
● *Set I:* The Sloth, My Sweet One, Divided Sky, Cavern, Take the 'A' Train, The Landlady > Bouncing Around the Room, Llama, The Mango Song, Mike's Song > I Am Hydrogen > Weekapaug Groove
● *Set II:* Chalk Dust Torture, Reba, Buried Alive, Runaway Jim, Guelah Papyrus, Fluffhead, Rocky Top, Love You, Golgi Apparatus
● *Encore:* Lawn Boy, Fire
● *Encore:* Possum -> Rocky Mountain Way Jam -> Possum
● *Show Notes:* This Possum had some early Secret Language, including a Random Note Signal, as well as Funk 49 teases. There are some fun references to New York, including a line from New York New York, before Llama.

Tuesday, February 19, 1991
The Bayou, Washington, DC
● *Set I:* Llama, The Curtain > Golgi Apparatus, Reba, Dinner and a Movie > The Sloth, Runaway Jim, The Squirming Coil > David Bowie
● *Set II:* My Sweet One, Mike's Song > I Am Hydrogen > Weekapaug Groove, Guelah Papyrus, The Landlady, Esther, Split Open and Melt, Bouncing Around the Room, Love You -> Whole Lotta Love Jam -> Love You, The Oh Kee Pa Ceremony > Suzy Greenberg, Rocky Top
● *Encore:* Magilla, Fire
● *Show Notes:* This show, performed on Fishman's birthday, had many classic moments, including Happy Birthday teases before Coil and during Bowie. Bowie also included an older signal, cued by the "Charlie Chan" lick, where the band all stopped on a dime. The Whole Lotta Love jam segued out of the vacuum solo in Love You and is worth hearing.

Wednesday, February 20, 1991
Kahootz, Richmond, VA
● *Set I:* Buried Alive > Cavern > Possum, The Squirming Coil > Tweezer, My Sweet One, Bouncing Around the Room, Llama, You Enjoy Myself, Manteca, Golgi Apparatus
● *Set II:* Foam, Divided Sky, Guelah Papyrus
● *Show Notes:* This second set listing is incomplete.

Thursday, February 21, 1991
Trax, Charlottesville, VA
● Opening Act: The Jolly Llamas
● *Set I:* Reba, Dinner and a Movie > Ya Mar, Split Open and Melt, Fee, Llama, The Lizards, My Sweet One > Mike's Song > I Am Hydrogen > Weekapaug Groove
● *Set II:* Golgi Apparatus, Cavern > The Landlady > Bouncing Around the Room, Stash, Guelah Papyrus, Uncle Pen, The Asse Festival, David Bowie
● *Encore:* Suzy Greenberg
● *Show Notes:* Bowie included heavy Manteca teases.

Friday, February 22, 1991
Cat's Cradle, Chapel Hill, NC

Saturday, February 23, 1991
13x13 Club, Charlotte, NC

Sunday, February 24, 1991
Trax, Charlottesville, VA
● *Show Notes:* There was no show on this date. Tapes that circulate are mislabeled tapes from three nights earlier.

Tuesday, February 26, 1991
The Barrelhouse, Salem, VA
● *Set I:* Cavern, Foam, The Squirming Coil, Llama, Guelah Papyrus, My Sweet One, Reba, The Oh Kee Pa Ceremony > AC/DC Bag, Golgi Apparatus, La Grange
● *Set II:* Buried Alive > Runaway Jim, Dinner and a Movie, Stash, Bouncing Around the Room, The Landlady > Destiny Unbound, Possum, The Lizards, Mike's Song > I Am Hydrogen > Weekapaug Groove
● *Encore:* HYHU > Love You > HYHU, Good Times Bad Times

● *Show Notes:* The band took the opportunity to introduce themselves before Love You, which also included a fun monitor board solo.

Wednesday, February 27, 1991
Arnold's Flamingo Grill, Knoxville, TN
● *Set I:* Golgi Apparatus, Divided Sky, I Didn't Know, The Landlady, You Enjoy Myself, Fee, My Sweet One, Split Open and Melt, Bouncing Around the Room, Fire
● *Set II:* Suzy Greenberg, Buried Alive > Cavern, The Squirming Coil, David Bowie, Lawn Boy, The Oh Kee Pa Ceremony > The Sloth, Love You, Possum, Rocky Top
● *Encore:* Contact
● *Show Notes:* During I Didn't Know, Trey commented that this was Phish's first show in Tennessee, and dedicated Fish's vacuum solo to Dr. Jack McConnell and other friends in the audience. After Cavern, Trey mentioned that James Brown got out on parole, which caused Fish to comment that a cease-fire was also called that day in Iraq. "Don't tell me this wasn't planned," he insisted. The Bowie was long and pretty spectacular. Lawn Boy featured a Trey guitar solo. Rocky Top was a seemingly obvious choice as closer for the first Volunteer State show.

Thursday, February 28, 1991
Sarrat Theatre, Vanderbilt University, Nashville, TN
● *Set I:* The Landlady, Bouncing Around the Room, Foam, Esther, Mike's Song > I Am Hydrogen > Weekapaug Groove, Cavern, The Man Who Stepped Into Yesterday > Avenu Malkenu > The Man Who Stepped Into Yesterday Reprise, My Sweet One, Golgi Apparatus
● *Set II:* The Squirming Coil, Reba, Llama, Guelah Papyrus, Divided Sky, HYHU > Love You > HYHU, The Lizards
● *Encore:* You Enjoy Myself
● *Show Notes:* There was a power outage during Golgi, after which Trey mocked Fishman's "memorable drum solo." During the latter HYHU, Fishman introduced the band and humorously pointed out Chris Kuroda for causing the earlier power failure. YEM included a Wilson tease and a thank-you from Trey.

Friday, March 1, 1991
Georgia Theater, Athens, GA
● *Check:* Llama
● *Set I:* Wilson, Foam, Divided Sky, Cavern, The Squirming Coil,

Tweezer, Dinner and a Movie, Bouncing Around the Room, Buried Alive, Mike's Song > I Am Hydrogen > Weekapaug Groove
● *Set II:* Golgi Apparatus, The Landlady, Reba, Llama, Guelah Papyrus, Runaway Jim, The Sloth, Possum, Love You -> Whole Lotta Love Jam, David Bowie
● *Encore:* The Oh Kee Pa Ceremony > Suzy Greenberg
● *Show Notes:* As with several other Love You's from this era, this version segues into a Whole Lotta Love jam, complete with a dissonant Fishman vacuum solo and equally dissonant impromptu vocals.

Saturday, March 2, 1991
Cotton Club, Atlanta, GA

Wednesday, March 6, 1991
The New Daisy Theatre, Memphis, TN
Golgi Apparatus, You Enjoy Myself, The Landlady, The Squirming Coil, Possum, Cavern, Divided Sky, HYHU > Love You > HYHU, My Sweet One, Bouncing Around the Room, David Bowie
● *Encore:* Jesus Just Left Chicago

Thursday, March 7, 1991
Gem, Oxford, MI
● *Show Notes:* This venue may have been called "The Gin."

Friday, March 8, 1991
College Station Theater, Tuscaloosa, AL
● *Set I:* Golgi Apparatus, You Enjoy Myself, Fluffhead, Stash, The Oh Kee Pa Ceremony > Suzy Greenberg, Split Open and Melt, The Squirming Coil, My Sweet One, Tweezer, Big Black Furry Creature from Mars
● *Show Notes:* This setlist is incomplete.

Saturday, March 9, 1991
Tipitina's, New Orleans, LA
● *Set II:* The Man Who Stepped Into Yesterday > Avenu Malkenu > The Man Who Stepped Into Yesterday, The Oh Kee Pa Ceremony > Suzy Greenberg, The Squirming Coil, Buried Alive, Runaway Jim, Guelah Papyrus, David Bowie, The Lizards, Love You, Fire, Lawn Boy, Golgi Apparatus
● Encore: Good Times Bad Times, Fee, The Curtain
● *Show Notes:* This setlist is incomplete.

Wednesday, March 13, 1991
Boulder Theater, Boulder, CO
● *Set I:* Fluffhead, The Landlady, You Enjoy Myself, Cavern, Divided Sky, Esther, Llama, The Squirming Coil, David Bowie
● *Set II:* Suzy Greenberg, Split Open and Melt, Bouncing Around the Room, My Sweet One, Guelah Papyrus, Runaway Jim, The Sloth -> Reba -> Tweezer, HYHU > Terrapin > HYHU, The Oh Kee Pa Ceremony, Golgi Apparatus
● *Encore:* Take the 'A' Train, Big Black Furry Creature from Mars

Friday, March 15, 1991
Gothic Theater, Denver, CO
● *Set I:* Llama, Foam, My Sweet One, Stash, Dinner and a Movie, Bouncing Around the Room, The Oh Kee Pa Ceremony > AC/DC Bag, The Lizards, Mike's Song > I Am Hydrogen > Weekapaug Groove
● *Set II:* Buried Alive > Possum, Horn, Paul and Silas, Cavern, Destiny

Unbound, I Didn't Know, Harry Hood, Chalk Dust Torture
● *Encore:* The Squirming Coil, Runaway Jim

Saturday, March 16, 1991
Ten Mile Room, Breckenridge, CO
● *Set I:* The Man Who Stepped Into Yesterday > Avenu Malkenu > The Man Who Stepped Into Yesterday Reprise, Golgi Apparatus, Reba, The Landlady > Bathtub Gin, The Curtain > Rocky Top, Colonel Forbin's Ascent > The Famous Mockingbird, The Oh Kee Pa Ceremony > Suzy Greenberg, Run Like an Antelope
● *Set II:* Llama, Divided Sky, Guelah Papyrus, My Sweet One, Split Open and Melt, Magilla, Buried Alive, The Squirming Coil, Cavern, You Enjoy Myself
● *Encore:* Manteca, Possum
● *Show Notes:* Forbin was dedicated to Mike from Telluride. Suzy included a Reba tease.

Sunday, March 17, 1991
Wheeler Opera House, Aspen, CO
● *Set I:* Carolina, Bouncing Around the Room, The Landlady > Mike's Song > I Am Hydrogen > Weekapaug Groove, Foam, Fluffhead, Uncle Pen, Stash, The Lizards, David Bowie
● *Set II:* Runaway Jim, Esther > My Sweet One, The Squirming Coil, Tweezer, Fee, Slave to the Traffic Light, Chalk Dust Torture
● *Encore:* Lawn Boy, La Grange
● *Show Notes:* Bowie included Sparks and Landlady teases. Foam (introduced as one of Fishman's favorite songs) was preceded by a HYHU tease while Fishman fixed his cymbal. Uncle Pen was introduced as a band favorite and dedicated to a fan in the crowd. Trey repeated the first line of Esther several times, as if he had forgotten the rest of the lyrics. Slave was played for Mike from "the Telluride contingency" and was preceded by Trey's story about the '88 Colorado tour. After Slave, Fishman came front and center to the tune of HYHU to tell his infamous "bear story." Afterwards, Trey referenced the July 30, 1988, Telluride show, where Fishman was late. Chalk Dust included Manteca teases. Slave was played for the first time since April 22, 1990 (81 shows).

Tuesday, March 19, 1991
Fort Lewis College, Durango, CO

Friday, March 22, 1991
The Inferno, Steamboat Springs, CO
● *Set I:* Llama, You Enjoy Myself, The Landlady > Destiny Unbound, Bouncing Around the Room, Split Open and Melt, The Squirming Coil, Buried Alive, Cavern, Reba, Fire
● *Set II:* The Oh Kee Pa Ceremony > Suzy Greenberg, Run Like an Antelope, Foam, Paul and Silas, Stash, Runaway Jim, Guelah Papyrus, HYHU > Terrapin > HYHU, Mike's Song > I Am Hydrogen > Weekapaug Groove
● *Encore:* Magilla, Golgi Apparatus
● *Show Notes:* This show includes a great version of Antelope for this time period. Before Terrapin, Fishman was introduced as "the late Henrietta," and then commented that he is no longer Henrietta, but has not yet thought of a new name. He and Trey introduced Chris Kuroda (as "Cooter," with a "Charge!" tease) and Colorado fan "Erik the Viking."

Terrapin included a very brief Whole Lotta Love jam.

Saturday, March 23, 1991
The Inferno, Steamboat Springs, CO
● *Set I:* The Sloth, Divided Sky, Fee, Llama, I Didn't Know, The Curtain, Possum, Colonel Forbin's Ascent > The Famous Mockingbird, Rocky Top
● *Set II:* Chalk Dust Torture, Bathtub Gin, The Oh Kee Pa Ceremony > AC/DC Bag, My Sweet One, Tweezer, The Lizards, Uncle Pen, Cavern, David Bowie, Contact
● *Encore:* Take the 'A' Train, Big Black Furry Creature from Mars
● *Show Notes:* The venue may have been the Wheeler Opera House in Aspen.

Monday, March 25, 1991
Fine Arts Center, Fort Lewis College, Durango, CO

Thursday, March 28, 1991
The Catalyst, Santa Cruz, CA
Golgi Apparatus, Divided Sky, Cavern, The Landlady > Bouncing Around the Room, You Enjoy Myself, Guelah Papyrus, My Sweet One, David Bowie, The Squirming Coil, The Oh Kee Pa Ceremony > Suzy Greenberg, HYHU > Love You > HYHU, Chalk Dust Torture
● *Encore:* Lawn Boy, Fire

Friday, March 29, 1991
DNA Lounge, San Francisco, CA
● *Set II:* Possum, I Didn't Know, Foam, Rocky Top > Fluffhead, Tweezer, Bouncing Around the Room > Big Black Furry Creature from Mars
● *Encore:* Contact, Tweezer Reprise
● *Encore:* Good Times Bad Times
● *Show Notes:* Trey teased Dave's Energy Guide during the Tweezer, and Simple Gifts during BBFCFM. The second encore was played after a loud and passionate "Phish" chant by the audience. This setlist is incomplete, as the first set setlist is unknown.

Sunday, March 31, 1991
Berkeley Square Theatre, Berkeley, CA
● *Set I:* Buried Alive > Cavern, Runaway Jim, Colonel Forbin's Ascent > The Famous Mockingbird, The Landlady, My Sweet One, Esther, Possum, I Didn't Know, Mike's Song > I Am Hydrogen > Weekapaug Groove
● *Set II:* Harry Hood, The Sloth, The Squirming Coil, Stash, Guelah Papyrus, Bouncing Around the Room, Run Like an Antelope
● *Encore:* Reba, Highway to Hell

Tuesday, April 2, 1991
International Beer Garden, Arcata, CA
● *Set I:* Runaway Jim, The Landlady, Reba, Llama, Bouncing Around the Room, Foam, You Enjoy Myself, The Oh Kee Pa Ceremony > Suzy Greenberg, Chalk Dust Torture
● *Set II:* Divided Sky, Lawn Boy, Cavern, Fluffhead, Dog Gone Dog, Buried Alive, The Squirming Coil, Run Like an Antelope
● *Encore:* Magilla, Possum
● *Show Notes:* Dog Gone Dog was played for the first time since March

9. 1990 (105 shows).

Wednesday, April 3, 1991
Britt Ballroom, Southern Oregon State College, Ashland, OR
● *Set I:* Golgi Apparatus, Llama, The Lizards, Foam, Tweezer, Dinner and a Movie, Bouncing Around the Room, Mike's Song > I am Hydrogen > Weekapaug Groove
● *Set II:* Chalk Dust Torture, Take the 'A' Train, My Sweet One, Stash > Esther, The Landlady > Destiny Unbound, Fee, David Bowie
● *Encore:* Cavern, Rocky Top

Thursday, April 4, 1991
Woodsmen of the World Hall, Eugene, OR
● *Set I:* The Oh Kee Pa Ceremony > Suzy Greenberg, You Enjoy Myself, The Squirming Coil, Llama, Colonel Forbin's Ascent > The Famous Mockingbird, Possum, Carolina, Golgi Apparatus
● *Set II:* The Curtain > Runaway Jim, Guelah Papyrus, David Bowie, Lawn Boy, The Landlady, My Sweet One, Divided Sky, Love You, Big Black Furry Creature from Mars
● *Encore:* Magilla, Highway to Hell
● *Encore:* Contact, Uncle Pen
● *Show Notes:* This show included an interesting, frightening Bowie. Lawn Boy featured a Trey guitar solo. Before Love You, which included band introductions, Fishman noted that his backup Mighty Mite vacuum has the same suction per inch as his broken Electrolux (which he acknowledged as "the greatest vacuum of all").

Friday, April 5, 1991
Starry Night, Portland, OR
● *Set I:* The Landlady > Bouncing Around the Room, Divided Sky, Cavern, Take the 'A' Train, Reba, Chalk Dust Torture, Foam, Mike's Song > I Am Hydrogen > Weekapaug Groove
● *Set II:* Rocky Top, Stash > The Lizards, The Sloth, Dinner and a Movie > Harry Hood, I Didn't Know, My Sweet One, Good Times Bad Times
● *Encore:* Fee, The Oh Kee Pa Ceremony > Suzy Greenberg
● *Show Notes:* Reba contained a brief, subtle tease of the "I Love Lucy" theme. After Lizards, Trey congratulated the audience ("A lot of people have tried, but you're the first to have done it!") for clapping on the beat during the slow end solo. Before Fee, he repeated the compliment: "I hope you didn't think I was making fun of you…clapping on the upbeat —wow!" This venue became the Roseland Theater soon after; Phish was possibly the last band to play this venue while it was still called 'Starry Night.'

Saturday, April 6, 1991
Evergreen College; Olympia, WA
● *Set II:* Ya Mar, Split Open and Melt, Runaway Jim, Magilla, Llama, You Enjoy Myself, Bathtub Gin, Icculus, Run Like an Antelope, Terrapin, Possum
● *Encore:* Jesus Just Left Chicago
● *Show Notes:* This setlist is incomplete. Icculus was played for the first time since May 1, 1989 (178 shows).

Thursday, April 11, 1991
The Cave, Carleton College, Northfield, MN

● *Check:* Harpua
● *Set I:* Runaway Jim, Cavern, Paul and Silas, Tweezer, Magilla, Dinner and a Movie -> Bouncing Around the Room, Foam, Carolina, You Enjoy Myself, The Squirming Coil, Chalk Dust Torture
● *Set II:* My Sweet One, Reba, Llama, The Man Who Stepped Into Yesterday > Avenu Malkenu > The Man Who Stepped Into Yesterday Reprise, The Lizards, Split Open and Melt, Lawn Boy, The Landlady > Destiny Unbound, Mike's Song > I Am Hydrogen > Weekapaug Groove
● *Encore:* Fee, The Prison Joke, Possum
● *Show Notes:* This show is memorable for Fishman's telling of "The Prison Joke," which has, for some unknown reason, become a popular request. Possum included a Random Note Signal.

Friday, April 12, 1991
Barrymore Theater, Madison, WI
● *Set I:* Llama, Uncle Pen, Divided Sky, Guelah Papyrus, The Oh Kee Pa Ceremony > Suzy Greenberg, Stash, Rocky Top, Golgi Apparatus
● *Set II:* The Landlady, Runaway Jim, You Enjoy Myself, Fluffhead, Cavern, Tela, Buried Alive, Reba, My Sweet One, Good Times Bad Times
● *Encore:* Contact -> Big Black Furry Creature from Mars -> The Squirming Coil

Saturday, April 13, 1991
Biddy Mulligan's, Chicago, IL

Monday, April 15, 1991
Northwestern University, Evanston, IL
● *Set I:* The Sloth, Ya Mar, Foam, Runaway Jim, Split Open and Melt, Fee, Chalk Dust Torture, Colonel Forbin's Ascent > The Famous Mockingbird, Llama
● *Set II:* Wipeout, Mike's Song > I Am Hydrogen > Weekapaug Groove, Horn, My Sweet One, The Landlady, The Lizards, Possum, Magilla, Fire
● *Encore:* The Squirming Coil, Rocky Top

Tuesday, April 16, 1991
Rick's Cafe, Ann Arbor, MI
● Opening Act: Ryth McFeud
● *Set I:* Golgi Apparatus, You Enjoy Myself, Paul and Silas, Cavern, The Mango Song, The Oh Kee Pa Ceremony > AC/DC Bag, Tela, David Bowie
● *Set II:* Crew Football Theme Song, My Sweet One, Reba, Chalk Dust Torture, Magilla, Buried Alive, Uncle Pen, Tweezer, Runaway Jim, Carolina, Tweezer Reprise
● *Encore:* HYHU > If I Only Had a Brain, Good Times Bad Times
● *Show Notes:* Magilla featured Paul Guinness of Ryth McFeud on trombone. The Crew Football Theme Song at this show was a demented version of Barracuda played over the drumbeat for My Sweet One, with Trey mincingly whining the "Crew football theme song!" lyrics. Brain was performed as a "special treat" for the audience. Fish sang the final verse through the vacuum, creating an excellent echo effect.

Thursday, April 18, 1991
Oberlin College, Oberlin, OH
● *Set I:* Llama, Reba, The Oh Kee Pa Ceremony, The Sloth, Paul and Silas, Horn, Suzy Greenberg, Split Open and Melt, The Squirming Coil, Possum -> Harpua

● *Show Notes:* Harpua was played for the first time since June 9, 1990 (74 shows). This setlist is incomplete.

Friday, April 19, 1991
Nietzsche's, Buffalo, NY
● *Set I:* Dinner and a Movie, Bouncing Around the Room, Divided Sky, Cavern, The Lizards, Stash, I Didn't Know, Rocky Top, Mike's Song > I Am Hydrogen > Weekapaug Groove, Sweet Adeline
● *Set II:* Harry Hood, Fee, The Curtain > Golgi Apparatus, The Landlady > Destiny Unbound, My Sweet One, The Squirming Coil, Take the 'A' Train, Run Like an Antelope
● *Encore:* Paul and Silas, Big Black Furry Creature from Mars

Saturday, April 20, 1991
University of Rochester, Rochester, NY
● *Set I:* Runaway Jim, Reba, Llama, Fluffhead, My Sweet One, The Landlady, Esther, Chalk Dust Torture, Bouncing Around the Room, You Enjoy Myself -> Setting Sail
● *Set II:* The Sloth, Ya Mar, Split Open and Melt, The Squirming Coil, Paul and Silas, Cavern, The Man Who Stepped Into Yesterday > Avenu Malkenu > The Man Who Stepped Into Yesterday Reprise, Tweezer, The Oh Kee Pa Ceremony > Suzy Greenberg, Sweet Adeline
● *Encore:* Horn, Alumni Blues
● *Show Notes:* Fishman led the band in the debut of Setting Sail, which arose out of the vocal jam of YEM.

Sunday, April 21, 1991
Earth Day Festival
SUNY Potsdam, Potsdam, NY
● *Set I:* Golgi Apparatus, Rocky Top, Wilson, Divided Sky, Foam, Jam, My Sweet One, The Oh Kee Pa Ceremony, AC/DC Bag, Tela, Mike's Song > I Am Hydrogen > Weekapaug Groove, Sweet Adeline
● *Set II:* Possum, Fee, The Landlady, Colonel Forbin's Ascent > The Famous Mockingbird, Llama, Uncle Pen, Harry Hood, Cavern, I Didn't Know, David Bowie

Monday, April 22, 1991
Billings Lounge, University of Vermont, Burlington, VT
● *Set I:* The Curtain > Runaway Jim, The Sloth, Reba, Poor Heart, Llama, Guelah Papyrus, The Oh Kee Pa Ceremony > Suzy Greenberg
● *Set II:* Chalk Dust Torture, Bathtub Gin, Uncle Pen, The Landlady > Destiny Unbound, The Squirming Coil, Stash, My Sweet One, The Lizards, Highway to Hell
● *Encore:* Lawn Boy, Rocky Top
● *Encore:* Tweezer, Tweezer Reprise
● *Show Notes:* Tweezer contained fairly extensive Heartbreaker teasing by both Trey and Mike. After Tweezer, the band introduced and thanked the tour crew, presenting them with a cake and customized bowling balls. This show contained the first known Poor Heart.

Thursday, April 25, 1991
University of New Hampshire Field House, Durham, NH
● *Opening Act:* Aquarium Rescue Unit
● *Set I:* Sweet Adeline, The Landlady, Runaway Jim, The Curtain > Cavern > Poor Heart, Reba, Llama, The Oh Kee Pa Ceremony > Suzy Green-

berg, David Bowie

● *Set II:* Buried Alive, My Sweet One, Mike's Song > I am Hydrogen > Weekapaug Groove, Tela, Dinner and a Movie, Bouncing Around the Room, Divided Sky, Big Black Furry Creature from Mars

● *Show Notes:* Before Runaway Jim, Trey referenced the ARU and the string of shows that the two bands were, at the time, playing together. Subsequently, Bowie included teases of the ARU song Yield Not to Temptation. It is unclear whether BBFCFM was the end of the second set or the encore, or if BBFCFM closed the show and another song served as the encore. Tapes that circulate under this date with a different list are mislabeled copies of November 2, 1989.

Saturday, April 27, 1991
Capitol Theatre, Port Chester, NY
● *Opening Act:* Aquarium Rescue Unit
● *Check:* Carolina, The Asse Festival, Poor Heart, Funky Bitch
● *Set I:* Sweet Adeline, The Asse Festival, Runaway Jim, Cavern, The Landlady, My Sweet One, Reba, Llama, The Lizards, Suzy Greenberg, Stash, Golgi Apparatus
● *Set II:* The Curtain > Possum, The Man Who Stepped Into Yesterday > Avenu Malkenu > The Man Who Stepped Into Yesterday Reprise > Mike's Song > I Am Hydrogen > Weekapaug Groove, Fluffhead, Tweezer, The Squirming Coil -> Wipeout -> Tweezer Reprise
● *Encore:* Bouncing Around the Room, Good Times Bad Times
● *Show Notes:* Tweezer contained Sweet Emotion teases and an introduction of "Dr. Q" on bass. Wipeout was performed on the vacuum by Fishman.

Thursday, May 2, 1991
The Chance, Poughkeepsie, NY
● *Opening Act:* Skratch Baxter
● *Set I:* Rocky Top, Drum Jam -> Foam, Bouncing Around the Room, The Landlady, Colonel Forbin's Ascent, Llama, The Squirming Coil, Cavern > David Bowie, Sweet Adeline
● *Set II:* Chalk Dust Torture, Poor Heart > Divided Sky, Fee -> Split Open and Melt > Tela, My Sweet One > I Didn't Know, Buried Alive, Possum
● *Encore:* Harry Hood
● *Show Notes:* Fishman's drum solo before Foam was due to a broken bass string. Forbin's featured guest Jamie Janover on didgeridoo. Fishman performed this show wearing a tight blue and red superhero costume, complete with cape and hood, that had been made for him.

Friday, May 3, 1991
Somerville Theater, Somerville, MA
● *Opening Act:* Aquarium Rescue Unit
● *Set I:* Bouncing Around the Room, Foam, Chalk Dust Torture, The Man Who Stepped Into Yesterday > Avenu Malkenu > The Man Who Stepped Into Yesterday Reprise, Divided Sky, Fee, Paul and Silas, Tweezer, The Lizards, Sweet Adeline
● *Set II:* AC/DC Bag > The Curtain > The Sloth, The Landlady, Runaway Jim, Tela, You Enjoy Myself, Harpua, Tweezer Reprise
● *Encore:* Take the 'A' Train -> Big Black Furry Creature from Mars
● *Show Notes:* Sweet Adeline was performed without microphones. Tweezer included a Sweet Emotion tease.

Saturday, May 4, 1991
Somerville Theater, Somerville, MA
● *Opening Act:* The Aquarium Rescue Unit
● *Set I:* The Oh Kee Pa Ceremony > Suzy Greenberg, Cavern, Reba, My Sweet One, Split Open and Melt, Guelah Papyrus, Fluffhead, Mike's Song > I Am Hydrogen > Weekapaug Groove
● *Set II:* Dog Gone Dog, Llama, Colonel Forbin's Ascent > The Famous Mockingbird, Buried Alive, Harry Hood, Horn, Rocky Top, Possum
● *Encore:* Terrapin, Runaway Jim, Golgi Apparatus
● *Show Notes:* Forbin featured a guest horn player dressed in a leopardskin toga and a huge orange Mohawk. Hood was played in support of the Vermont Dairy Farmers.

Thursday, May 9, 1991
Portland Performing Arts Center, Portland, ME
● *Set I:* Divided Sky, Foam, Paul and Silas, Guelah Papyrus, Reba, Llama, Bouncing Around the Room, Magilla, Runaway Jim, Sweet Adeline
● *Set II:* My Sweet One, The Curtain, Fluffhead, Stash, Esther, Split Open and Melt, The Squirming Coil, Rocky Top
● *Encore:* Fee, Chalk Dust Torture

Friday, May 10, 1991
Page Commons Room, Student Center, Colby College, Waterville, ME
● *Set I:* David Bowie, Cavern, Ya Mar, Dinner and a Movie > The Sloth, The Landlady, Bathtub Gin, Buried Alive, The Lizards, Possum
● *Set II:* Golgi Apparatus, Harry Hood > Wilson, Poor Heart, Foam, McGrupp and the Watchful Hosemasters > Chalk Dust Torture, Love You, Mike's Song > I Am Hydrogen > Weekapaug Groove
● *Encore:* Take the 'A' Train, Highway to Hell

Saturday, May 11, 1991
The Front, Burlington, VT
● *Set II:* Chalk Dust Torture, You Enjoy Myself, Poor Heart, Reba, Donna Lee, Mike's Song > I Am Hydrogen > Weekapaug Groove, Tela, The Oh Kee Pa Ceremony > Suzy Greenberg, Tweezer Reprise
● *Encore:* Love You, Big Black Furry Creature from Mars
● *Show Notes:* YEM featured Tom Baggott on harmonica. Fishman called Trey "Eddie Van Anastasio" after his inspired guitar solo in this fantastic BBFCFM. This setlist is incomplete.

Sunday, May 12, 1991
The Front, Burlington VT
● *Set I:* Chalk Dust Torture, Bouncing Around the Room, Dinner and a Movie, Stash, The Lizards, The Landlady > Destiny Unbound, Llama, Fee, Foam, Runaway Jim
● *Set II:* HFB Intro, David Bowie, Bathtub Gin, Poor Heart, The Curtain, Golgi Apparatus, Magilla, Mike's Song > I Am Hydrogen > Weekapaug Groove, The Squirming Coil, The Oh Kee Pa Ceremony > AC/DC Bag > Rocky Top
● *Encore:* Run Like an Antelope
● *Show Notes:* Magilla, Hydrogen, AC/DC Bag, and Rocky Top featured Dave Grippo. Mike's Song featured The Dude of Life on vocals, who added several verses. Page began Hydrogen on a Casio synthesizer, adding a humorous touch to the last Phish show at The Front.

Thursday, May 16, 1991
The Sting, New Britain, CT
● *Set I:* Buried Alive, Golgi Apparatus, Foam, Cavern, Divided Sky, Colonel Forbin's Ascent > The Famous Mockingbird, Chalk Dust Torture, You Enjoy Myself, Magilla, Llama
● *Set II:* Runaway Jim, Dinner and a Movie, Bouncing Around the Room, The Landlady, The Squirming Coil, Tweezer, My Sweet One, The Lizards, Good Times Bad Times
● *Encore:* Sweet Adeline
● *Show Notes:* Magilla featured a guest appearance from Bryant Smith on trombone. Adeline was chosen as the encore because of curfew issues.

Friday, May 17, 1991
Campus Club, Providence RI
● *Set I:* Chalk Dust Torture -> Drum Jam -> Jam, Reba, Poor Heart, The Oh Kee Pa Ceremony > Suzy Greenberg, Happy Birthday, The Man Who Stepped Into Yesterday > Avenu Malkenu > The Man Who Stepped Into Yesterday Reprise, Stash, I Didn't Know, Mike's Song > I Am Hydrogen > Weekapaug Groove, Take the 'A' Train
● *Set II:* Possum, Guelah Papyrus, Rocky Top, The Landlady > Fluffhead, Magilla, Cavern, Bike, Big Black Furry Creature from Mars
● *Encore:* Lawn Boy, Golgi Apparatus
● *Show Notes:* A blackout occurred during Chalk Dust. The drum solo and jam that ensued featured Carl Gerhard, who also guested on 'A' Train, Magilla, Cavern, and Lawn Boy. The Man Who Stepped Into Yesterday was introduced as "The Old Man Who Stepped Into Yesterday." Happy Birthday was sung to Page. Bike was played for the first time since November 10, 1990 (64 shows).

Saturday, May 18, 1991
The Marquee, New York, NY
● *Check:* Take the 'A' Train, Caravan, Guelah Papyrus, Paul and Silas, Jam
● *Set I:* Buried Alive > Golgi Apparatus, Chalk Dust Torture > You Enjoy Myself, Paul and Silas, Foam, Divided Sky, Cavern > Possum
● *Set II:* The Oh Kee Pa Ceremony > Suzy Greenberg, The Curtain > Stash, Take the 'A' Train, My Sweet One > Guelah Papyrus, David Bowie, HYHU > Terrapin > HYHU, The Lizards
● *Encore:* Dinner and a Movie, Runaway Jim
● *Show Notes:* The Bowie intro included Trey teasing 'A' Train. Before Foam, Trey noted that this gig would be the last until July since the band was going into the studio to cut an album. Terrapin featured a brilliant vacuum solo. Before Dinner and a Movie, Fishman noted that "this is a song about America's favorite pre-nuptial ritual."

Sunday, May 19, 1991
Salisbury School, Salisbury, CT
● *Set I:* Divided Sky, The Landlady, Chalk Dust Torture, Bouncing Around the Room, You Enjoy Myself, Cavern, The Squirming Coil, Llama
● *Set II:* The Oh Kee Pa Ceremony > AC/DC Bag -> Fee, Foam, Reba, Dinner and a Movie > The Sloth, McGrupp and the Watchful Hosemasters, I Didn't Know, Golgi Apparatus
● *Encore:* Possum
● *Show Notes:* Mike played a birthday tease on bass before The Oh Kee Pa Ceremony for Josh's 20th birthday. Trey announced that the second set would be their last until the summer, as they were going in to record an album. A small break caused by technical difficulties followed McGrupp. This show included some humorous stage banter about prep school headmasters and the like.

SUMMER, 1991

Thursday, July 11, 1991
Battery Park, Burlington, VT
● *Set I:* The Oh Kee Pa Ceremony > Suzy Greenberg, Divided Sky, Flat Fee, My Sweet One, Stash, The Lizards, The Landlady
● *Set II:* Dinner and a Movie, Cavern, The Man Who Stepped Into Yesterday > Avenu Malkenu > The Man Who Stepped Into Yesterday Reprise -> Mike's Song > I Am Hydrogen > Weekapaug Groove, HYHU > Touch Me, Frankenstein
● *Encore:* Contact -> Big Black Furry Creature from Mars
● *Show Notes:* The entire show, which was a free show, featured The Giant Country Horns. This show marked the first performance of Touch Me. Frankenstein was played for the first time since December 3, 1989 (160 shows) and Flat Fee was played for the first time since September 13, 1988 (230 shows).

Friday, July 12, 1991
Colonial Theater, Keene, NH
● *Set I:* Dinner and a Movie > Bouncing Around the Room, Buried Alive, Flat Fee, Reba, The Landlady, Bathtub Gin, Donna Lee, AC/DC Bag, Rocky Top, Cavern, David Bowie
● *Set II:* Golgi Apparatus, The Squirming Coil, Moose the Mooch, Tweezer, My Sweet One, Gumbo, Mike's Song > I Am Hydrogen > Weekapaug Groove, Touch Me, The Oh Kee Pa Ceremony > Suzy Greenberg, Sweet Adeline, Frankenstein
● *Encore:* Fee, Tweezer Reprise
● *Show Notes:* This show featured The Giant Country Horns and marked the first performance of Moose the Mooch. Gumbo was played for the first time since November 30, 1990 (63 shows).

Saturday, July 13, 1991
Berkshire Performing Arts Center, Lenox, MA
● *Set I:* The Curtain > Runaway Jim, Foam, Llama, The Oh Kee Pa Ceremony > Suzy Greenberg > Alumni Blues, The Man Who Stepped Into Yesterday > Avenu Malkenu > The Man Who Stepped Into Yesterday Reprise, Split Open and Melt, Bouncing Around the Room, Frankenstein
● *Set II:* Chalk Dust Torture, Guelah Papyrus, Divided Sky, Flat Fee, Paul and Silas, The Lizards, Stash, HYHU > If I Only Had a Brain > HYHU, You Enjoy Myself
● *Encore:* The Landlady
● *Show Notes:* This show featured The Giant Country Horns from Suzy through the end of the first set and from Guelah through the encore. Trey flubbed the slow, middle section of Divided Sky and humorously remarked that "that was the jazz version." Brain was preceded by Happy Birthday teases and was dedicated to Erica; YEM subsequently included a brief reprise of the tease from Trey. The YEM vocal jam featured Chain Gang teases from Mike.

Sunday, July 14, 1991
Townshend Family Park, Townshend, VT

● *Set I:* Reba, Llama, The Squirming Coil, Golgi Apparatus, Guelah Papyrus, My Sweet One, Colonel Forbin's Ascent > The Famous Mockingbird, The Sloth, I Didn't Know, Possum
● *Set II:* Suzy Greenberg, Caravan, Divided Sky, Gumbo, Dinner and a Movie, Bouncing Around the Room, Split Open and Melt, Magilla > Cavern, Run Like an Antelope
● *Set III:* AC/DC Bag > The Landlady, Esther, Chalk Dust Torture, Bathtub Gin, Mike's Song > I Am Hydrogen > Weekapaug Groove, HYHU > Touch Me, Harry Hood
● *Encore:* Contact, Big Black Furry Creature from Mars
● *Show Notes:* This show, which featured The Giant Country Horns for most of the second and third sets, began with a humorous announcement from Trey that he felt "overdressed" during National Nudist Week. My Sweet One included a tease of the "Bonanza" theme and Magilla included a "Flintstones" tease. Possum included an Oom Pa Pa Signal and a Dave's Energy Guide tease, while Weekapaug included Tweezer teases from Trey. There was a long wait during HYHU for Fishman, who was apparently in the bathroom. Hood included full-band "Jeopardy" theme teases. This show ran much longer than scheduled (at one point, when Trey noted that they should wind up the show, a fan urged the band to "fuck the clock"), prompting Trey to beg the crowd to leave in a timely and orderly fashion after the encore.

Monday, July 15, 1991
Academy of Music, New York, NY
The Oh Kee Pa Ceremony > Suzy Greenberg, The Landlady > Dinner and a Movie, Stash, Bouncing Around the Room, Mike's Song > I Am Hydrogen > Weekapaug Groove, Flat Fee, The Lizards, Cavern, The Squirming Coil, Frankenstein
● *Encore:* Caravan -> Contact, Alumni Blues
● *Show Notes:* This show featured The Giant Country Horns. The horns guested on all songs except Oh Kee Pa, Hydrogen, Weekapaug, and Coil. Also, Mike's Song only included guest saxophone. Caravan included Manteca teases. Trey humorously botched the lyrics to Cavern, leading to some funny stage banter.

Tuesday, July 16, 1991
BMI New Music Awards, Marriott Marquis, New York, NY
● *Show Notes:* It is believed that the band only performed one song, and that it may have been *a capella*.

Thursday, July 18, 1991
Hampton Casino Ballroom, Hampton Beach, NH
● *Set I:* Chalk Dust Torture, Foam, Runaway Jim, Guelah Papyrus, Suzy Greenberg, Stash, Take the 'A' Train, Cavern, Mike's Song > I Am Hydrogen > Weekapaug Groove
● *Set II:* Llama, Reba, Poor Heart, Split Open and Melt, The Lizards, The Landlady, I Didn't Know, Possum
● *Encore:* Alumni Blues
● *Show Notes:* This show featured the Giant Country Horns. At one point during the show, the crowd was told by the promoter that they were dancing too much, prompting Trey to offer a date with Fishman to the fan who danced best on their chair!

Friday, July 19, 1991
Somerville Theatre, Somerville, MA

● *Set I:* Golgi Apparatus, The Landlady > Bouncing Around the Room, David Bowie, Fee > Cavern, The Squirming Coil, You Enjoy Myself, Gumbo, Touch Me
● *Set II:* Suzy Greenberg, Divided Sky, I Didn't Know, My Sweet One, Magilla, Tweezer, The Mango Song, Big Black Furry Creature from Mars
● *Encore:* Lawn Boy, Runaway Jim
● *Show Notes:* This entire show featured the Giant Country Horns. I Didn't Know featured Mimi Fishman on vacuum. The hi-hat segment of Bowie included Bouncing teases and YEM included Frankenstein teases. This long, strong Tweezer featured a Divided Sky tease from Trey, as well as lots of impromptu rapping. The band introduced the horns during BBFCFM, which also included a quick tease of the "I Love Lucy" theme. Runaway Jim was sung as "Runaway Yim" and Lawn Boy featured a trumpet solo.

Saturday, July 20, 1991
Arrowhead Ranch, Parksville, NY
● *Set I:* Chalk Dust Torture, Foam, The Squirming Coil, Llama, The Oh Kee Pa Ceremony > Suzy Greenberg, The Landlady, Bathtub Gin, Gumbo, David Bowie
● *Set II:* Buried Alive, Reba, Caravan, Dinner and a Movie, Flat Fee, Golgi Apparatus, Stash, The Man Who Stepped Into Yesterday > Avenu Malkenu > The Man Who Stepped Into Yesterday Reprise, You Enjoy Myself, Rocky Top
● *Encore:* Possum
● *Show Notes:* This show featured the Giant Country Horns.

Sunday, July 21, 1991
Arrowhead Ranch, Parksville, NY
● *Set I:* Cavern, Divided Sky, Guelah Papyrus, Poor Heart, Split Open and Melt, The Lizards, The Landlady, Bouncing Around the Room, Mike's Song > I Am Hydrogen > Weekapaug Groove
● *Set II:* Tweezer, I Didn't Know, Runaway Jim, Lawn Boy, The Sloth, Esther, AC/DC Bag, Contact -> Tweezer Reprise
● *Encore:* Gumbo, Touch Me
● *Encore:* Fee, Suzy Greenberg
● *Show Notes:* This show featured the Giant Country Horns. The encores featured "Steve-o from New Orleans" on washboard, or, as Trey referred to it, "whatever the hell you call that thing." Weekapaug included a "Bonanza" tease.

Tuesday, July 23, 1991
The Bayou, Washington, DC
● *Check:* Poor Heart
● *Set I:* Chalk Dust Torture, Foam, The Squirming Coil, My Sweet One, The Oh Kee Pa Ceremony > Suzy Greenberg, Stash, Flat Fee, Bouncing Around the Room, Mike's Song > I Am Hydrogen > Weekapaug Groove
● *Set II:* Llama, Reba, Cavern, The Lizards, The Landlady > Tweezer, Sweet Adeline, Dinner and a Movie > Gumbo, HYHU > Touch Me
● *Encore:* Caravan, Golgi Apparatus
● *Show Notes:* This show featured the Giant Country Horns from Suzy through Weekapaug, Cavern through Tweezer, and Dinner through Caravan.

Wednesday, July 24, 1991
Trax, Charlottesville, VA

● *Check:* Poor Heart (twice), Gimme Three Steps, Jazz Jam, Dinner and a Movie Intro (three times), Sesame Street Theme -> Jam -> Superstition, Caravan, Poor Heart -> Funky Bitch -> I'm Nationwide

● *Set I:* Golgi Apparatus > Chalk Dust Torture, The Squirming Coil > Buried Alive > Split Open and Melt, Bathtub Gin, The Landlady, Cavern, Tela, You Enjoy Myself

● *Set II:* Possum > Guelah Papyrus, David Bowie > Jesus Just Left Chicago, My Sweet One > Bouncing Around the Room, Funky Bitch, I Didn't Know, Frankenstein, Suzy Greenberg

● *Encore:* Contact > Big Black Furry Creature from Mars

● *Show Notes:* This show featured the Giant Country Horns. BBFCFM featured an "I Love Lucy" theme tease and a "Brady Bunch" theme tease. The intro to Bowie included teases of The Asse Festival. Funky Bitch was played for the first time since December 28, 1990 (68 shows).

Thursday, July 25, 1991
Cat's Cradle, Chapel Hill, NC

● *Set I:* My Sweet One, The Sloth, Foam, Suzy Greenberg, Divided Sky, Flat Fee, AC/DC Bag, Sweet Adeline, Cavern, Run Like an Antelope

● *Set II:* The Landlady, Golgi Apparatus, The Squirming Coil, Llama, Poor Heart, Jesus Just Left Chicago, The Lizards, Gumbo, Touch Me, Magilla, Mike's Song > I Am Hydrogen > Weekapaug Groove

● *Encore:* Split Open and Melt

● *Show Notes:* This show featured the Giant Country Horns from Suzy through the encore. Sweet Adeline was performed without microphones. The Antelope intro included Ding Dong, The Witch is Dead teases and Weekapaug included a Superstitious tease.

Friday, July 26, 1991
Georgia Theater, Athens, GA

● *Opening Act:* The Aquarium Rescue Unit

● *Set I:* Chalk Dust Torture, Reba, My Sweet One, Foam, Suzy Greenberg, Cavern, The Man Who Stepped Into Yesterday > Avenu Malkenu > The Man Who Stepped Into Yesterday Reprise, Buried Alive, Bouncing Around the Room, Golgi Apparatus

● *Set II:* Stash, Dinner and a Movie -> You Enjoy Myself, Flat Fee, Fee -> Funky Bitch, The Squirming Coil, Tweezer, The Lizards -> Tweezer Reprise

● *Encore:* Lawn Boy, Frankenstein

● *Show Notes:* This show featured the Giant Country Horns. Stash was dedicated to a fan and Lizards included a Happy Birthday dedication to Chris Kuroda.

Saturday, July 27, 1991
Variety Playhouse, Athens, GA

Llama, Foam, The Oh Kee Pa Ceremony > Suzy Greenberg, Cavern, Poor Heart, Stash, The Man Who Stepped Into Yesterday > Avenu Malkenu > The Man Who Stepped Into Yesterday Reprise, Possum, I Didn't Know, The Landlady, Mike's Song > I Am Hydrogen > Weekapaug Groove

● *Encore:* Touch Me, Contact

● *Show Notes:* This one-set show featured the Giant Country Horns and concluded the summer "Horns Tour." It was an opening set for The Aquarium Rescue Unit.

Saturday, August 3, 1991
Larrabee Farm, a/k/a Amy's Farm, Auburn, ME

Check: Poor Heart, Crimes of the Mind (with the Dude of Life), Bitchin' Again (with the Dude and Sofi Dillof)

● *Set I:* Wilson, Foam, Runaway Jim, Guelah Papyrus, Llama, Fee, The Squirming Coil, Poor Heart, The Sloth, Divided Sky, Golgi Apparatus

● *Set II:* The Curtain, Reba, Chalk Dust Torture, Bouncing Around the Room, Tweezer, Esther, Cavern, I Didn't Know, You Enjoy Myself, Rocky Top

● *Set III:* Stash, Ya Mar, Fluffhead, Lawn Boy, My Sweet One, The Lizards, Buried Alive > Possum

● *Encore:* Magilla, Self, Bitchin' Again, Crimes of the Mind

● *Encore:* Harry Hood

● *Show Notes:* This was a free show. YEM featured an infamous "no gerbils in your bottom" vocal jam. Self, Bitchin' Again, and Crimes of the Mind (the last two debuts) featured The Dude of Life, and Bitchin' Again also featured Sofi Dillof. Buried Alive featured Jamie Janover on didgeridoo. Self was played for the first time since September 13, 1990 (104 shows).

Monday, August 19, 1991
Dartmouth College, Hanover, NH

FALL, 1991

Wednesday, September 25, 1991
Colonial Theater, Keene, NH

● *Set I:* Brother, Poor Heart > Foam, Llama, Tela -> My Sweet One, It's Ice, The Landlady > Caravan -> Reba -> Possum

● *Set II:* The Squirming Coil, Stash, Sparkle, Cavern, Jesus Just Left Chicago, Runaway Jim, You Enjoy Myself, Chalk Dust Torture

● *Encore:* All Things Reconsidered, Big Black Furry Creature from Mars

● *Show Notes:* This show marked the first performances of Brother, It's Ice, Sparkle, and All Things Reconsidered. Cavern and Jesus Just Left Chicago featured Carl Gerhard on saxophone. All Things Reconsidered was not quite as developed as it is today.

Thursday, September 26, 1991
State Street Theater, Ithaca, NY

● *Set I:* Llama, Bouncing Around the Room, Divided Sky, Fee, It's Ice, My Sweet One, Guelah Papyrus, The Lizards, Foam, David Bowie

● *Set II:* Golgi Apparatus, The Squirming Coil, Brother, Sparkle, The Landlady > Destiny Unbound, Mike's Song > I Am Hydrogen > Weekapaug Groove, Lawn Boy, Chalk Dust Torture

● *Encore:* Memories, Poor Heart, Sweet Adeline

● *Show Notes:* Listen to this interesting Bowie, as Fishman filled in with chants of "Dr. Seuss" in counterpoint to the lyrics. Memories was played for the first time since November 17, 1990 (81 shows).

Friday, September 27, 1991
The Warehouse, Rochester, NY

● *Set I:* Runaway Jim, Cavern, Reba, Buried Alive > Esther, Tweezer, It's Ice, I Didn't Know, Llama

● *Set II:* Possum, Tela, Sparkle, Split Open and Melt, The Mango Song, Dinner and a Movie, The Oh Kee Pa Ceremony > Suzy Greenberg, You Enjoy Myself, Tweezer Reprise

● *Encore:* Glide, Rocky Top
● *Show Notes:* This show marked the first performance of Glide. The final verse of Runaway Jim was accidentally omitted. Trey teased portions of Esther during the Buried Alive jam segment. The second set was preceded by an announcement that cars blocking the alley outside would be towed. It led to some humorous vocal interplay among the band members. This was a very loose show, with some sloppy moments but generally interesting jamming. Before his vacuum solo in I Didn't Know, Fishman was introduced as "The Earl of Sandwich."

Saturday, September 28, 1991
The Rink, Buffalo, NY
● *Set I:* The Landlady > Bouncing Around the Room, Chalk Dust Torture, The Squirming Coil, My Sweet One, Stash, Eliza, Foam, Brother, Golgi Apparatus, Memories
● *Set II:* Llama, Guelah Papyrus, Sparkle, Cavern, Run Like an Antelope, Lawn Boy, The Lizards, Poor Heart, Magilla, Mike's Song > I Am Hydrogen > Weekapaug Groove
● *Encore:* Contact > Big Black Furry Creature from Mars
● *Show Notes:* Before Llama, an award was presented for longest distance traveled for any Phish gig to Henry Petras, who traveled to Amy's Farm from Palo Alto, California. During Weekapaug, Trey soloed while riding through the crowd on rollerblades. BBFCFM featured "I Love Lucy" theme teases and Antelope featured an early Simpsons Signal. After Brother, Trey wished a happy birthday to "Dmitri." Eliza was played for the first time since November 24, 1990 (82 shows).

Sunday, September 29, 1991
The Agora Ballroom, Cleveland, OH
● *Set I:* Cavern, Divided Sky, I Didn't Know, It's Ice, Poor Heart, The Landlady, Destiny Unbound, You Enjoy Myself, The Oh Kee Pa Ceremony > Suzy Greenberg
● *Set II:* Brother, Bouncing Around the Room, Eliza, Foam, Reba, The Sloth, The Squirming Coil, My Sweet One, Golgi Apparatus, David Bowie
● *Encore:* Memories, Rocky Top

Monday, September 30, 1991
The Dugout Lounge, University of Ohio, Athens, OH
Cavern, Stash, Colonel Forbin's Ascent > The Famous Mockingbird
● *Encore:* Good Times Bad Times
● *Show Notes:* This setlist is obviously incomplete, as it represents a fan's recollections of what was played. The show may have actually been on the next night. The location, though, is correct.

Wednesday, October 2, 1991
The Cubby Bear, Chicago, IL
● *Set I:* Llama, Foam, The Squirming Coil, Poor Heart, Cavern, Reba, Brother, Bouncing Around the Room, Chalk Dust Torture, Golgi Apparatus
● *Set II:* The Landlady, You Enjoy Myself, My Sweet One, Guelah Papyrus, Runaway Jim, Lawn Boy, Stash, The Oh Kee Pa Ceremony > Suzy Greenberg
● *Encore:* Possum, I Didn't Know, Rocky Top

Thursday, October 3, 1991
Mabel's, Champaign, IL

● *Set I:* Chalk Dust Torture, Foam, Uncle Pen, It's Ice, Bouncing Around the Room, Llama, Fee > Divided Sky, Cavern, Possum
● *Set II:* Paul and Silas, Mike's Song > I Am Hydrogen > Weekapaug Groove, Esther, The Landlady > Destiny Unbound, Buried Alive > The Squirming Coil -> Tweezer, Memories
● *Encore:* Terrapin -> Tweezer Reprise
● *Show Notes:* Coil featured an interesting Dixieland-style jam outro that segued into a dissonant and intense Tweezer.

Friday, October 4, 1991
The Barrymore Theater, Madison, WI
● *Set I:* Memories, Chalk Dust Torture, Reba, Poor Heart, Cavern, Divided Sky, Guelah Papyrus, Sparkle, Suzy Greenberg, Magilla, David Bowie
● *Set II:* My Sweet One, Brother, Bouncing Around the Room, Foam, Runaway Jim, Lawn Boy, Stash, The Squirming Coil, Mike's Song > I Am Hydrogen > Weekapaug Groove
● *Encore:* Sweet Adeline, Golgi Apparatus, Rocky Top
● *Encore:* Love You, Llama
● *Show Notes:* During the pause in Guelah, Trey welcomed everyone to the Hemp Festival ("Free the weed!" Mike exclaimed). After Jim, Trey introduced "a very famous person" in the audience, John Basilli. "Stephen King was at a gig recently," he noted, "but this is much more exciting." Coil contained a Linus and Lucy tease.

Saturday, October 5, 1991
The Cabooze, Minneapolis, MN

Sunday, October 6, 1991
Macalester College, St. Paul, MN
● *Set I:* Suzy Greenberg, Foam, Divided Sky, Bouncing Around the Room, Poor Heart, The Oh Kee Pa Ceremony > AC/DC Bag, The Man Who Stepped Into Yesterday > Avenu Malkenu > The Man Who Stepped Into Yesterday Reprise, Brother, HYHU > Terrapin > HYHU, Golgi Apparatus
● *Set II:* My Sweet One, Stash, Fee, The Landlady > Destiny Unbound, Harry Hood, I Didn't Know, Cavern, The Squirming Coil, Rocky Top
● *Encore:* Sweet Adeline, Possum, Llama
● *Show Notes:* Check out this second set for some great stage banter from Fishman. "I hate this fucking song!" he shouted during the lengthy HYHU intro to Terrapin. "All I have do in this band is say I hate something," he commented, "and it'll be done forever." Trey proceeded to tell the crowd that HYHU is the Henrietta theme precisely because Fish hates it. "It used to be 'La Bamba,'" he noted, prompting Page to play the La Bamba riff. After the song, an unamused Fish complained that "they just do it out of HATE." Brother was dedicated to "the guy who offered us $10,000 to play a different song," according to Trey. Adeline was sung from the balcony to open the encore.

Thursday, October 10, 1991
EMU Ballroom, University of Oregon, Eugene, OR
● *Set I:* Chalk Dust Torture, Foam, Paul and Silas, Split Open and Melt, Bouncing Around the Room, The Landlady, Runaway Jim, It's Ice, Eliza, Llama, Golgi Apparatus
● *Set II:* Brother, Reba, Poor Heart, Cavern, Run Like an Antelope, I Didn't Know, Sparkle, The Oh Kee Pa Ceremony > Suzy Greenberg, Fee,

Mike's Song > I Am Hydrogen > Weekapaug Groove
● *Encore:* The Squirming Coil, Fire
● *Show Notes:* Many copies of this show that circulate include Alumni Blues and Lizards at the end of set I but this is filler from an unknown show.

Friday, October 11, 1991
Backstage, Seattle, WA
● *Set I:* The Landlady, My Sweet One, Divided Sky, Guelah Papyrus, Chalk Dust Torture, You Enjoy Myself, The Lizards, Llama, Bouncing Around the Room, Runaway Jim
● *Set II:* The Curtain > Cavern, Foam, David Bowie, The Mango Song, The Sloth, Poor Heart, Magilla, Possum
● *Encore:* Sweet Adeline, Big Black Furry Creature from Mars
● *Show Notes:* Adeline was performed without microphones.

Saturday, October 12, 1991
Roseland Theater, Portland, OR
● *Set I:* Buried Alive > Possum, Foam, My Sweet One, Stash, Esther, Divided Sky, Guelah Papyrus, You Enjoy Myself
● *Set II:* Tweezer, Uncle Pen, Fluffhead, Chalk Dust Torture, Take the 'A' Train, Dinner and a Movie, Brother, HYHU > If I Only Had a Brain > HYHU, Harry Hood, Tweezer Reprise
● *Encore:* Lawn Boy, Rocky Top
● *Encore:* Contact, Golgi Apparatus
● *Show Notes:* This set featured a guest appearance by Artis the Spoonman from Brain through Rocky Top Also, someone (perhaps Trey) played a strange pipe or flute during Brain.

Sunday, October 13, 1991
North Shore Surf Club, Olympia, WA
● *Set I:* Runaway Jim, Wilson, Reba, The Landlady, Colonel Forbin's Ascent > The Famous Mockingbird, Tela, AC/DC Bag, The Sloth, Mc-Grupp and the Watchful Hosemasters, Mike's Song > I Am Hydrogen > Weekapaug Groove
● *Set II:* Llama, Bathtub Gin, The Squirming Coil, It's Ice, My Sweet One, Jesus Just Left Chicago, Bouncing Around the Room, Love You, David Bowie
● *Encore:* Eliza, Uncle Pen, Carolina
● *Show Notes:* The first set is almost a complete Gamehendge narration and is the second time the saga was performed live. Carolina was performed without microphones. Bowie included a hi-hat "solo" from Fishman during the intro, while Trey explained how Fishman's hi-hat serves as his escape from reality. Bowie also included Oom Pa Pa, Simpsons, and Random Note Signals.

Tuesday, October 15, 1991
International Beer Garden/Humboldt Brewery, Arcata, CA
● *Check:* Funky Bitch, My Sweet One (*a cappella*), It's Ice
● *Set I:* Chalk Dust Torture, Foam, The Squirming Coil, Split Open and Melt, Sparkle, Reba, The Landlady, Destiny Unbound, You Enjoy Myself, Rocky Top
● *Set II:* Brother, Bouncing Around the Room, Runaway Jim, Guelah Papyrus, Poor Heart, Llama, Horn, The Oh Kee Pa Ceremony > Suzy Greenberg, HYHU > Love You > HYHU, Funky Bitch, Golgi Apparatus
● *Encore:* Memories, Harry Hood

● *Show Notes:* Memories was performed without microphones.

Thursday, October 17, 1991
Great American Music Hall, San Francisco, CA
● *Set I:* Memories, The Landlady > Bouncing Around the Room, Divided Sky, Cavern, Poor Heart, Stash, Esther, Chalk Dust Torture, Golgi Apparatus
● *Set II:* The Curtain, The Oh Kee Pa Ceremony > Suzy Greenberg, David Bowie, Lawn Boy, Fluffhead, You Enjoy Myself, Love You, Possum
● *Encore:* Magilla, Rocky Top

Friday, October 18, 1991
Great American Music Hall, San Francisco, CA
● *Set I:* Runaway Jim, Foam, Paul and Silas, Reba, Wilson > Llama, The Lizards, Sweet Adeline, Run Like an Antelope
● *Set II:* Brother, Uncle Pen, Guelah Papyrus, Dinner and a Movie, Mike's Song > I Am Hydrogen > Weekapaug Groove, I Didn't Know, Fee > Split Open and Melt, My Sweet One, Cavern
● *Encore:* Sparkle, Walk Away
● *Encore:* The Squirming Coil
● *Show Notes:* Walk Away was played for the first time since May 24, 1990 (131 shows).

Saturday, October 19, 1991
The Catalyst, Santa Cruz, CA
● *Set I:* The Landlady > Suzy Greenberg, It's Ice, Runaway Jim, Foam, Chalk Dust Torture -> Bouncing Around the Room, My Sweet One, Stash, Golgi Apparatus
● *Set II:* Llama, Bathtub Gin, Sparkle > Tweezer > Horn, Poor Heart, You Enjoy Myself, The Oh Kee Pa Ceremony > HYHU > Terrapin > HYHU, Harry Hood
● *Encore:* Good Times Bad Times
● *Show Notes:* During Terrapin, Mimi Fishman substituted for Jon on vacuum. She was announced as "Showboat Gertrude's Mother."

Monday, October 23, 1991
Chuy's, Tempe, AZ
● *Set I:* Chalk Dust Torture, Reba, The Landlady > Destiny Unbound, Paul and Silas, It's Ice, Horn, Llama, Bouncing Around the Room, Runaway Jim, Cavern
● *Set II:* Brother, The Squirming Coil, Sparkle, Golgi Apparatus, The Mango Song, Split Open and Melt, Love You, Fee, You Enjoy Myself, Possum
● *Encore:* Take the 'A' Train

Thursday, October 24, 1991
Prescott College, Prescott, AZ
● *Check:* Memories, Tube
● *Set I:* The Oh Kee Pa Ceremony > Suzy Greenberg, Foam, Poor Heart, Stash, Ya Mar, Divided Sky, I Didn't Know, The Man Who Stepped Into Yesterday > Avenu Malkenu > The Man Who Stepped Into Yesterday Reprise > David Bowie
● *Set II:* Mike's Song > I Am Hydrogen > Weekapaug Groove, The Lizards, Uncle Pen, Tube, Slave to the Traffic Light, Dinner and a Movie, Bouncing Around the Room, HYHU > Terrapin > HYHU, Possum
● *Encore:* Memories, Sweet Adeline, Rocky Top

● *Show Notes:* Before the first set, Trey introduced Mike as "Lou Reed." After Foam, Trey mentioned how happy he was to be playing at Prescott College, which, he announced, is very similar to Goddard. There was a Secret Language Jam in the Bowie intro, with Oom Pa Pa, Simpsons, and Random Laugh Signals. The disco-inflected Bowie was extremely groovy, with an on-the-fly full-band slowdown and maniacal screaming from Trey and Mike during the end segment. After Bowie, Trey introduced "Fern," who read poetry during the setbreak. Fishman was introduced as "Showboat Gertrude" before Terrapin; he explained that the name is derived from that of the Indian singer Shoba Gertu. Tube was played for the first time since November 16, 1990 (100 shows) and Slave was played for the first time since March 17, 1991 (67 shows).

Saturday, October 26, 1991
Club West, Santa Fe, NM

Sunday, October 27, 1991
Elk Ballroom, Telluride, CO
● *Set I:* My Sweet One, Chalk Dust Torture, The Mango Song, Buried Alive, Guelah Papyrus, Fluffhead, Brother, Bouncing Around the Room, Harry Hood, Golgi Apparatus
● *Set II:* Llama, Colonel Forbin's Ascent > The Famous Mockingbird, Sparkle, It's Ice, Mike's Song > I Am Hydrogen > Weekapaug Groove, Tela, The Landlady > Destiny Unbound, Take the 'A' Train, Run Like an Antelope
● *Encore:* Glide, Possum

Monday, October 28, 1991
Elk Ballroom, Telluride, CO
● *Set I:* Runaway Jim, Cavern, Poor Heart, Reba, I Didn't Know, Tube, The Oh Kee Pa Ceremony > Foam, Fee -> David Bowie
● *Set II:* Divided Sky, Wilson > Dinner and a Movie > Stash, Paul and Silas, Bathtub Gin, You Enjoy Myself, The Squirming Coil, Harpua, HYHU > Whipping Post > HYHU, Highway to Hell
● *Encore:* Horn, Rocky Top
● *Show Notes:* Whipping Post (first since June 5, 1990, or 131 shows) featured Fishman's hilariously inept debut on fretless guitar. Listen for some early Secret Language, including Oom Pa Pa and Simpsons Signals, in the Bowie intro. Also, listen for Mike's teases of On Top of Old Smokey during Harpua.

Wednesday, October 30, 1991
Boulder Theater, Boulder, CO
● *Set I:* Foam, Runaway Jim, Cavern, Sparkle, Brother, The Lizards, Possum
● *Set II:* Tube, Divided Sky, Poor Heart, Run Like an Antelope, Lawn Boy, Wilson, The Landlady, Bouncing Around the Room, Mike's Song > I Am Hydrogen > Weekapaug Groove
● *Encore:* Fire
● Show Notes: Before the encore, Page and Fishman told some jokes amidst a few HYHU teases. Fire was dedicated to Ralph.

Thursday, October 31, 1991
Armstrong Hall, Colorado Springs, CO
● *Set I:* Memories, Brother, Ya Mar, The Sloth > Chalk Dust Torture,

Sparkle, Foam, Bathtub Gin, Paul and Silas, You Enjoy Myself, Runaway Jim
● *Set II:* The Landlady, Costume Contest, Wait > Llama, Fee -> Wait, My Sweet One > Wait -> David Bowie, Horn, Dinner and a Movie, Tube, I Didn't Know, Harry Hood
● *Encore:* Glide, Rocky Top
● *Show Notes:* During the long, hilarious costume contest, there was a brief full-band tease of Jesus Just Left Chicago, inspired by some guy in a Jesus costume (with a cross on his back!). The first round of the contest closed with a rendition of the Blues Brothers theme. After each unsuccessful entrant was eliminated, Trey forced them to stage-dive. First prize - free admission to all Phish shows for one year - was shared by The Bergen County Woman Cop and Captain Bonghit. During the final Wait, before Bowie, the audience was chanting "Fuck you!" in response! Bowie contained an on-the-fly Oom Pa Pa Signal during the jam. I Didn't Know featured a vacuum solo by "Showboat Gertrude," which continued well into the final verse of the song.

Friday, November 1, 1991
Gothic Theater, Denver, CO
● *Set I:* AC/DC Bag, Sparkle, The Landlady > Destiny Unbound, The Squirming Coil, Split Open and Melt, Fluffhead, Uncle Pen, Tube, Divided Sky, Sweet Adeline
● *Set II:* Tweezer, My Sweet One, It's Ice, Chalk Dust Torture, Eliza, Mike's Song > I Am Hydrogen > Weekapaug Groove, Take the 'A' Train, Tela, Cavern, Poor Heart -> Tweezer Reprise
● *Encore:* HYHU > Love You > Pusher Man Jam, Stash
● *Show Notes:* Divided Sky was dedicated to Sun Ra. Trey explained that the Hold Your Head Up Theme became the Henrietta theme because Fishman hates the song. The band ended with the Pusher Man Theme because Fishman likes that song. Stash was dedicated to members of the phish.net.

Saturday, November 2, 1991
Lory Theater, Fort Collins, CO
● *Set I:* Suzy Greenberg, The Curtain, Llama, Reba, Paul and Silas, Foam, Bouncing Around the Room, Colonel Forbin's Ascent > The Famous Mockingbird, Possum
● *Set II:* Golgi Apparatus, Run Like an Antelope, The Man Who Stepped Into Yesterday > Avenu Malkenu > The Man Who Stepped Into Yesterday Reprise, Sparkle, Guelah Papyrus, Walk Away, The Landlady, Runaway Jim, You Enjoy Myself
● *Encore:* Contact, Big Black Furry Creature from Mars
● *Show Notes:* The YEM vocal jam included the themes "Big Poop Slide" and "Step in the Pile."

Monday, November 4, 1991
Rhythm Room, Dallas, TX

Tuesday, November 5, 1991
Liberty Lunch, Austin, TX
● *Opening Act:* The Aquarium Rescue Unit

Thursday, November 7, 1991
Tipitina's, New Orleans, LA
● Opening Act: The Aquarium Rescue Unit

● *Set I:* Memories, Chalk Dust Torture, Foam, Sparkle, Cavern > It's Ice, You Enjoy Myself, The Landlady > Runaway Jim, I Didn't Know, Llama
● *Set II:* Brother, Bouncing Around the Room, My Sweet One, Reba, Tube, Horn, David Bowie, Take the 'A' Train, HYHU Jam -> Love You -> HYHU, Possum
● *Encore:* Fee, Rocky Top, Lawn Boy, Fire
● *Show Notes:* Bowie through HYHU featured members of The Aquarium Rescue Unit. Rocky Top was announced as the ARU's favorite song.

Friday, November 8, 1991
Ivory Tusk, Tuscaloosa, AL
● *Set I:* Tube, The Landlady > Dinner and a Movie > Stash, Paul and Silas > Divided Sky, Guelah Papyrus, The Mango Song, Brother, Eliza, Golgi Apparatus
● *Set II:* The Sloth, Sparkle, Split Open and Melt, The Squirming Coil, I Didn't Know, Mike's Song > I Am Hydrogen > Weekapaug Groove, Jesus Just Left Chicago, Self, TV Show, Family Picture, Crimes of the Mind
● *Encore:* Fee, Suzy Greenberg
● *Show Notes:* Self through Crimes (including the debut of Family Picture) featured The Dude Of Life. Paul and Silas was dedicated to "Jason" on his birthday. Weekapaug featured an on-the-fly Simpsons Signal and an adventurous, off-center jam segment culminating with Trey chanting "a slice of pizza!" and "a bucket of lard!" The final chorus was even sung as "I'm sharing in a bucket of lard." This show was not at the College Station Theater; that show was on March 8, 1991.

Saturday, November 9, 1991
Variety Playhouse, Atlanta, GA
● *Set I:* The Curtain > Runaway Jim, Foam, Sparkle, Llama, Reba, Tube, You Enjoy Myself, Horn, Brother, Sweet Adeline
● *Set II:* Chalk Dust Torture, Fluffhead > Poor Heart, It's Ice, Tweezer > Tela, The Landlady, HYHU > Terrapin > HYHU, My Sweet One > Tweezer Reprise
● *Encore:* Glide, Possum
● *Show Notes:* Trey and Mike teased Curtain several times before the start of the show. Before Sparkle, Trey thanked the Atlanta crowd for their general attentiveness, noting that Artis the Spoonman always said "the best thing you can give to another person is your attention." Mike's cousins were in attendance, and he welcomed them. The YEM jam segment was excellent. The well-above-average Tweezer contained several quick Band on the Run teases from Trey. The HYHU preceding Terrapin featured Trey and Page singing "Henrietta" vocals. My Sweet One was first sung as a gospel tune, without drums and with Fishman singing lead, and then done again normally. The Possum jam featured a Rhapsody in Blue tease from Trey and a Simpsons Signal.

Sunday, November 10, 1991
Music Farm, Charleston, SC
● *Set I:* Buried Alive, The Sloth, Uncle Pen, David Bowie, Fee, The Squirming Coil, The Oh Kee Pa Ceremony > Suzy Greenberg, You Enjoy Myself, Cavern
● *Set II:* Split Open and Melt, Cold As Ice > Terrapin > Cold As Ice, Sweet Adeline, Llama
● *Show Notes:* This setlist is incomplete.

Tuesday, November 12, 1991
Georgia Theater, Athens, GA
● *Set I:* Buried Alive > Golgi Apparatus, Uncle Pen, Brother, Bouncing Around the Room, Tube, The Sloth, Harry Hood, Fee, Foam, Llama
● *Set II:* Dinner and a Movie > Stash, The Squirming Coil, Paul and Silas, Mike's Song > I Am Hydrogen > Weekapaug Groove, Guelah Papyrus, Chalk Dust Torture, Magilla, Cavern, HYHU > Love You > HYHU, Run Like an Antelope
● *Encore:* Ya Mar, Big Black Furry Creature from Mars
● *Encore:* Split Open and Melt, Memories
● *Show Notes:* Trey teased Possum before the second set opener. In Magilla, Trey's solo featured a theme similar to All Things Reconsidered. Love You featured band introductions. Antelope included a Dixie tease from Trey, a foul-up near the end when Fish attempted to end the song too early, and a Simpsons Signal during the final raveup.

Wednesday, November 13, 1991
Love Auditorium, Davidson College, Davidson, NC
● *Set I:* The Landlady > Runaway Jim, It's Ice, Sparkle, Chalk Dust Torture, Esther, Cavern, Divided Sky, I Didn't Know, You Enjoy Myself
● *Set II:* David Bowie, Colonel Forbin's Ascent > The Famous Mockingbird, Golgi Apparatus, Bathtub Gin, The Squirming Coil, Llama, HYHU > Terrapin, Possum
● *Encore:* Horn, My Sweet One, Sweet Adeline
● *Show Notes:* If you're a fan of stage banter, you'll want to hear this show. Terrapin was announced as the "restrained version" and Fishman as the "Master of Restraint." In response, Fish sang only one out of every few words to the song. Trey also clarified during the show that Colonel Forbin is not to be mistaken for Colonel (Bruce) Hampton. Bowie included Random Note, Oom Pa Pa, and Simpsons Signals in the intro.

Thursday, November 14, 1991
Cat's Cradle, Chapel Hill, NC
● *Set I:* Wilson, Uncle Pen, Llama, Reba, Foam, Tube, Sparkle, Brother, The Mango Song, Golgi Apparatus, Runaway Jim
● *Set II:* Dinner and a Movie > Roll Like a Cantaloupe, Fee, Paul and Silas, It's Ice, Glide, Tweezer, Take the 'A' Train -> HYHU, If I Only Had a Brain > HYHU, The Lizards, Tweezer
● *Encore:* Bouncing Around the Room, Good Times Bad Times
● *Encore:* You Enjoy Myself
● *Show Notes:* Brother was dedicated to Trey's sister Christie. 'A' Train included Frosty the Snowman and We Wish You a Merry Christmas teases. Cantaloupe was played for the first time since March 11, 1990 (177 shows).

Friday, November 15, 1991
Trax, Charlottesville, VA
● *Set I:* Chalk Dust Torture, Sparkle, Cavern, The Curtain, Split Open and Melt, The Squirming Coil, My Sweet One, Guelah Papyrus, Rhombus Narration -> Divided Sky, Lawn Boy, Golgi Apparatus
● *Set II:* Llama, Bathtub Gin, Poor Heart, Mike's Song > I Am Hydrogen > Weekapaug Groove, Eliza, Tube, The Landlady > Destiny Unbound, Harry Hood, HYHU > Love You > HYHU, Bouncing Around the Room, Possum
● *Encore:* Highway to Hell, Suzy Greenberg

● *Show Notes:* Trey began the show by screaming "Mrs. Pizza Shit ROCKS TRAX!" During Harry, Trey again shouted "Mrs. Pizza Shit!," prompting Fishman to introduce Page as "Mrs. Pizza Shit on the piano!" Possum contained Simpsons and Random Note Signals.

Saturday, November 16, 1991
The Bayou, Washington, DC
● *Set I:* The Landlady, Uncle Pen, Wilson, Runaway Jim, It's Ice, Sparkle, Fluffhead, Foam, Stash, Ya Mar, Cavern
● *Set II:* Tube, My Sweet One, Bathtub Gin, Brother, You Enjoy Myself, Horn, Chalk Dust Torture, Terrapin, Llama
● *Encore:* Glide, Rocky Top
● *Show Notes:* This YEM is a fan favorite among early versions. It is preceded by introductions of lots of friends and family, and is halted and restarted by Trey so that he can confirm that Phish had indeed changed their name to "Mrs. Pizza Shit." At one point during the show, Trey even grabbed a slice of pizza from a passing waitress and used it to strum the guitar.

Tuesday, November 19, 1991
The Sting, New Britain, CT
● *Set I:* Uncle Pen, Foam, Runaway Jim, Fee, Sparkle, Brother, Horn, Chalk Dust Torture, Love You, Wilson, Divided Sky
● *Set II:* Tube, My Sweet One, Mike's Song > I Am Hydrogen > Weeka-paug Groove, The Mango Song, The Sloth, Reba, Dinner and a Movie, Cavern -> David Bowie
● *Encore:* Glide, Rocky Top
● *Show Notes:* Before Wilson, Trey brought a fan named Wesley on-stage and wished him a happy birthday. Trey proceeded to dedicate the song to him.

Wednesday, November 20, 1991
Campus Club, Providence, RI
● *Set I:* Buried Alive > Possum, Colonel Forbin's Ascent > The Famous Mockingbird, Sparkle, Stash, Paul and Silas, Bathtub Gin, The Squirm-ing Coil, Llama, You Enjoy Myself
● *Set II:* Golgi Apparatus, It's Ice, My Sweet One, Run Like an Antelope, Tela, The Landlady, HYHU > Bike > HYHU, Cavern
● *Encore:* Magilla, Brother
● *Show Notes:* Possum included a Rhapsody in Blue tease from Trey. Before YEM, Trey announced that the second set would feature a spe-cial guest on guitar who has influenced Trey for years. The "special guest" turned out to be Fishman, who added some atrocious fretless guitar stylings to Bike (first since May 17, 1991, or 54 shows). Cavern, Magilla and Brother featured Carl "Geerz" Gerhard on trumpet, who teased the "Flintstones" theme during Magilla.

Thursday, November 21, 1991
Somerville Theatre, Somerville, MA
● *Set I:* Chalk Dust Torture, Bouncing Around the Room, Poor Heart, Guelah Papyrus, Reba, Foam, Horn, Split Open and Melt, Esther, Mike's Song > I Am Hydrogen > Weekapaug Groove
● *Set II:* Wilson, Harry Hood, It's Ice, The Mango Song, Uncle Pen, Tweezer, The Man Who Stepped Into Yesterday > Avenu Malkenu > The Man Who Stepped Into Yesterday Reprise, Runaway Jim

● *Encore:* Memories, Sweet Adeline, Golgi Apparatus
● *Show Notes:* This long, fantastic version of Weekapaug included an On Broadway tease. At one point, the jam stopped completely before Trey counted everyone back in to finish the song.

Friday, November 22, 1991
University of Southern Maine Gym, Portland, ME
● *Check:* Rocket Man, Mountain Jam
● *Set I:* Possum, Cavern, Sparkle, Brother, Fee, Foam, Divided Sky, Lawn Boy, Dinner and a Movie, Stash, Rocky Top
● *Set II:* Tube, My Sweet One, The Landlady, Bathtub Gin, Run Like an Antelope, The Squirming Coil, I Didn't Know, Llama, The Lizards, You Enjoy Myself
● *Encore:* Glide, Suzy Greenberg

Saturday, November 23, 1991
Barre Memorial Auditorium, Barre, VT
● *Set I:* Llama, Reba, Foam, Runaway Jim, Guelah Papyrus, Sparkle, Chalk Dust Torture, Uncle Pen, Brother, Bouncing Around the Room, Golgi Apparatus
● *Set II:* The Curtain, Mike's Song > I Am Hydrogen > Weekapaug Groove, Horn, Poor Heart, Tweezer, Eliza, The Landlady, Fee, Love You, My Sweet One, Tweezer Reprise
● *Encore:* Jesus Just Left Chicago, Big Black Furry Creature from Mars
● *Show Notes:* This show's venue may have been "Seminary Hill." Be-fore Chalk Dust, Trey noted that the band was finishing a nine-week na-tional tour and proceeded to thank and introduce the tour crew, who he exulted as "the very best in the business." After Eliza, Trey commented that he wrote the song for his girlfriend (now wife) Susan Eliza, who was in the audience. Dave "the Truth" Grippo guested on alto saxo-phone during the encore. Grippo and Fishman briefly teased Sonny Rollins' St. Thomas during one of the breaks in BBFCFM.

Sunday, November 24, 1991
Webster Hall, Dartmouth College, Hanover, NH
● *Check:* Memories, Destiny Unbound, Blues Jam
● *Set I:* The Sloth, Paul and Silas, Stash, The Landlady, Fluffhead, Sparkle, It's Ice, I Didn't Know, David Bowie
● *Set II:* Tube, Divided Sky, Cavern, The Mango Song, Chalk Dust ● Torture, Take the 'A' Train, You Enjoy Myself, Golgi Apparatus
● *Encore:* Sweet Adeline, Rocky Top
● *Show Notes:* During the Bowie hi-hat intro, Trey presented mono-grammed bathrobes to the crew for their dedication and hard work. The crowd passed the bathrobes from the stage to the crew. The Bowie intro also featured the Random Laugh Signal and an early Simpsons Signal.

Saturday, November 30, 1991
Capitol Theatre, Port Chester, NY
● *Opening Act:* Shockra
● *Set I:* Glide, Llama, Foam, Sparkle, Divided Sky, Cavern, The Squirm-ing Coil, Brother, Paul and Silas, Guelah Papyrus, You Enjoy Myself
● *Set II:* Chalk Dust Torture, Uncle Pen, Harry Hood, It's Ice, Bounc-ing Around the Room, My Sweet One, Horn, I Didn't Know, Run Like an Antelope, Golgi Apparatus
● *Encore:* Contact, Rocky Top

● *Show Notes:* I Didn't Know featured Fishman on the mouthpiece of his trombone.

Wednesday, December 4, 1991
Angel Ballroom, SUNY Plattsburgh, Plattsburgh, NY
● *Set I:* Llama, Reba, The Landlady, Runaway Jim, Cavern, Poor Heart, Brother, The Squirming Coil, Dinner and a Movie > Bouncing Around the Room > David Bowie
● *Set II:* My Sweet One, Stash, The Mango Song, Mike's Song > I Am Hydrogen > Weekapaug Groove, Sparkle, The Lizards, Chalk Dust Torture, Love You, Golgi Apparatus
● *Encore:* Sweet Adeline, Suzy Greenberg
● *Show Notes:* Bowie had a long intro with several signals, including the Random Laugh Signal.

Thursday, December 5, 1991
Greenfield Armory Castle, Greenfield, MA
● *Check:* Shaggy Dog, Jam, Cavern Jam, Blues Jam
● *Set I:* Golgi Apparatus, Paul and Silas, Split Open and Melt, Ya Mar, Fluffhead, Llama, Bathtub Gin, It's Ice, Bouncing Around the Room, Possum
● *Set II:* Tweezer, Sparkle, Tube, Foam, Mike's Song > I Am Hydrogen > Weekapaug Groove, Fee > The Sloth, The Squirming Coil, I Didn't Know, My Sweet One, Tweezer Reprise
● *Encore:* Glide, Cavern

Friday, December 6, 1991
Middlebury College, Middlebury, VT
● *Check:* Memories (twice), Dog Gone Dog, Blues Jam, Shaggy Dog, Makisupa Policeman
● *Set I:* Memories, Foam, Reba, Uncle Pen, The Squirming Coil, Magilla, The Landlady, Guelah Papyrus, I Didn't Know
● *Set II:* It's Ice, Eliza, Sparkle, You Enjoy Myself, Horn, Divided Sky, Tela, Llama, Whipping Post, Possum -> Wait -> Possum
● *Encore:* Lawn Boy, Rocky Top
● *Show Notes:* Whipping Post featured Fishman on fretless guitar. Guelah was aborted due to problems with Trey's guitar.

Saturday, December 7, 1991
Portsmouth Music Hall, Portsmouth, NH
● *Check:* Memories, Dog Gone Dog, Blues Jam, Shaggy Dog, Makisupa Policeman -> Blues Jam, Take the 'A' Train
● *Set I:* Wilson, Runaway Jim, Foam, Colonel Forbin's Ascent > The Famous Mockingbird, My Sweet One, Stash, The Curtain > Cavern, The Mango Song, Run Like an Antelope
● *Set II:* Buried Alive > Reba, Chalk Dust Torture, Sparkle, Brother, The Lizards, HYHU > Terrapin > HYHU, Harpua
● *Encore:* "Trampoline Giveaway," Sweet Adeline, Golgi Apparatus
● *Show Notes:* Trey felt so generous during the trampoline giveaway that he decided to give Fishman away as well, pushing him into the crowd. He also teased The Christmas Song before and during Buried Alive. This version of Brother was much more dissonant and out-of-control than usual.

Tuesday, December 31, 1991
The New Aud, Worcester Memorial Auditorium, Worcester, MA

● *Set I:* Possum, Foam, Sparkle, Stash, The Lizards, Guelah Papyrus, Divided Sky, Esther, Llama, Golgi Apparatus
● *Set II:* Brother, Bouncing Around the Room, Buried Alive > Auld Lang Syne, Runaway Jim, The Landlady, Reba, Cavern, My Sweet One, Run Like an Antelope
● *Set III:* Wilson, The Squirming Coil, Tweezer, McGrupp and the Watchful Hosemasters, Mike's Song > I Am Hydrogen > Weekapaug Groove
● *Encore:* Lawn Boy, Rocky Top, Tweezer Reprise
● *Show Notes:* Auld Lang Syne included a fun New Year's countdown and Weekapaug included Lion Sleeps Tonight teases. Trey played with a voicebox on stage that uttered curses during Wilson. Divided Sky was dedicated to Chris Gainty, who was seeing his first show since a car accident had left him in a coma five months earlier.

SPRING, 1992

Friday, March 6, 1992
Portsmouth Music Hall, Portsmouth, NH
● *Set I:* Rift, Cavern, Sparkle, It's Ice, The Oh Kee Pa Ceremony, Divided Sky, Guelah Papyrus, Maze, Reba, All Things Reconsidered, David Bowie
● *Set II:* My Friend My Friend, Poor Heart, Secret Language Instructions, Stash, Mound, Llama, Bouncing Around the Room, NICU, Possum
● *Encore:* Sleeping Monkey
● *Show Notes:* Many debuts were played, including the "new" Rift, Maze, My Friend, Mound, NICU, and Sleeping Monkey. This show is also historic because the band gave us the first ever language instructions. Trey referred to NICU as "In an Intensive Care Unit," though that title was later changed, and referred to My Friend as "Knife." Bowie contained many signals, including the Simpsons Signal, the Fingerscrape Signal, two musical Get Back signals, and many other, rarer ones. Possum included Simpsons, Turn Turn Turn, and Fingerscrape Signals.

Saturday, March 7, 1992
Portsmouth Music Hall, Portsmouth, NH
● *Set I:* Brother, My Mind's Got a Mind of its Own, Foam, Runaway Jim, The Horse > Silent in the Morning, Maze, The Mango Song, The Landlady, Rift, Run Like an Antelope
● *Set II:* My Sweet One, Tweezer, The Squirming Coil, Weigh, Chalk Dust Torture, Horn, Mike's Song > I Am Hydrogen > Weekapaug Groove, Cold as Ice > Cracklin' Rosie, Tweezer Reprise
● *Encore:* Sweet Adeline, Golgi Apparatus
● *Show Notes:* More debuts were played this night, as the band played the first ever Horse > Silent, Weigh, Cracklin' Rosie (and, along with it, the "B" and "Ah" cymbals), and My Mind's Got a Mind of its Own. Also, Cold as Ice debuted as the new Henrietta Theme. Listen for the "Star Trek" theme tease from Trey before Brother, and All Fall Down, Random Note, Oom Pa Pa, and Turn Turn Turn Signals in Antelope.

Wednesday, March 11, 1992
Colonial Theatre, Keene, NH
● *Set I:* Suzy Greenberg, My Friend My Friend, Paul and Silas, Reba, Maze, Fee, Split Open and Melt, Mound, Divided Sky, Cavern

● *Set II:* Llama, NICU, The Sloth, The Lizards, Bathtub Gin, My Mind's Got a Mind of its Own, Brother, Cold as Ice > Baby Lemonade > Cold as Ice, All Things Reconsidered, Harry Hood, Rocky Top
● *Encore:* Sanity, Memories, Carolina, Sleeping Monkey
● *Show Notes:* This show marked the debut of Baby Lemonade and, along with it, the first appearance of Fishman's Bag-Vac. My Friend was dedicated to "Steve E." who drove eighteen hours to the show. Jokingly, Trey subsequently called the bouncers over to throw him out! Before Maze, Page read an announcement from management asking fans not to smoke in the building. Many people shouted out requests during the pause in Divided Sky, prompting Trey to scream "POSSUM!" into the microphone. The second set started with Page again requesting that fans not smoke, while Trey and Mike launched into a few bars of Smoke on the Water. NICU included a Simpsons Signal. Foreshadowing the encore, Sanity was teased before All Things Reconsidered. Lots of humor ensued over Mike's use of a cardboard cutout of Kathleen Turner from the movie *V.I. Warshawski*, which started out on top of his bass rig and ended up in front of him, giving the appearance of his head on her body. Sanity was played for the first time since May 28, 1989 (255 shows).

Thursday, March 12, 1992
Flynn Theatre, Burlington, VT
● *Set I:* Runaway Jim, Foam, Sparkle, Stash, I Didn't Know, Reba, Buried Alive, Rift, Magilla, Llama, You Enjoy Myself
● *Set II:* Golgi Apparatus, Tweezer, Eliza, It's Ice, Bouncing Around the Room, The Squirming Coil, Uncle Pen, David Bowie, Cracklin' Rosie, My Sweet One, Cavern
● *Encore:* Sweet Adeline, Weigh, Tweezer Reprise

Friday, March 13, 1992
Campus Club, Providence, RI
● *Check:* Piano Jam, Shaggy Dog -> Dog Gone Dog, Blues Jam, AC/DC Bag, McGrupp and the Watchful Hosemasters
● *Set I:* The Curtain, Split Open and Melt, Poor Heart, Guelah Papyrus, Maze, Dinner and a Movie, Divided Sky, Mound, Fluffhead, Run Like an Antelope -> Big Black Furry Creature from Mars -> Run Like an Antelope
● *Set II:* Wilson -> Brother, The Horse > Silent in the Morning, The Landlady, The Lizards, My Mind's Got a Mind of its Own, The Sloth, Rift, Cold as Ice > Love You > Cold as Ice, Secret Language Instructions, Possum
● *Encore:* Contact, Fire
● *Show Notes:* The great ending to this first set is often referred to as the "Big Black Furry Antelope." Mike used an accordion for the first time during Contact. This show included more Language Instruction; the subsequent Possum included Simpsons and Turn Turn Turn Signals. Listen for Trey's teasing of Somewhere Over the Rainbow before and during Wilson and We're Off to See the Wizard during the ending of Fluffhead. Some fans, mocking Trey's comment two nights earlier, shouted out "POSSUM!" during the pause in Divided Sky.

Saturday, March 14, 1992
Roseland Ballroom, New York, NY
● *Set I:* Runaway Jim, Cavern, Reba, Sparkle, Foam, Rift, Stash, Fee, Chalk Dust Torture, Take the 'A' Train, Mike's Song > I Am Hydrogen > Weekapaug Groove
● *Set II:* Golgi Apparatus, Llama, The Squirming Coil, Split Open and

Melt, Bouncing Around the Room, The Oh Kee Pa Ceremony > Suzy Greenberg, Harry Hood, Cold as Ice > Cracklin' Rosie, Possum
● *Encore:* Sleeping Monkey, Good Times Bad Times
● *Show Notes:* The encore was performed with John Popper on harmonica. The Hood intro included Somewhere Over the Rainbow teases.

Tuesday, March 17, 1992
Lisner Auditorium, Washington, DC
Opening Act: Everything
● *Set I:* Buried Alive > Possum, Cavern, Sparkle, It's Ice, I Didn't Know, Divided Sky, Guelah Papyrus, Rift, Bouncing Around the Room, Run Like an Antelope
● *Set II:* Runaway Jim, Glide, The Sloth, Poor Heart, Tweezer -> Esther, Mike's Song > I Am Hydrogen > Weekapaug Groove, Cold as Ice > Love You, Llama
● *Encore:* Memories, Sweet Adeline
● *Show Notes:* Love You featured Fishman on the Bag-Vac.

Thursday, March 19, 1992
Palace Theater, New Haven, CT
● *Check:* Shaggy Dog -> Jam, Lullaby, Mound, Maze
● *Set I:* The Landlady, Rift, Split Open and Melt, Sparkle, Golgi Apparatus, The Horse > Silent in the Morning, Dinner and a Movie, Colonel Forbin's Ascent > The Famous Mockingbird, All Things Reconsidered, David Bowie
● *Set II:* Glide, Chalk Dust Torture, NICU, My Sweet One, Stash, The Oh Kee Pa Ceremony > Suzy Greenberg, My Friend My Friend, The Squirming Coil, Cracklin' Rosie
● *Encore:* Sleeping Monkey, Rocky Top

Friday, March 20, 1992
Broome County Arena, Binghamton, NY
● *Set I:* Wilson, Reba, Brother, Glide, Rift, Fluffhead, Maze, The Lizards, Mound, Run Like an Antelope
● *Set II:* Mike's Song > I Am Hydrogen > Weekapaug Groove, Sanity, The Sloth, The Mango Song, Cavern, Uncle Pen, Harry Hood, Terrapin, Secret Language Instructions, Possum
● *Encore:* Lawn Boy, Fire
● *Show Notes:* Trey teased Yes's Roundabout before Mike's Song and uttered the infamous line, "Help me…I'm melting and I can't solidify!" Weekapaug contained an Oom Pa Pa Signal and a Random Note Signal. Fishman was on trombone for parts of Antelope and used the Bag-Vac during Terrapin.

Saturday, March 21, 1992
Chestnut Cabaret, Philadelphia, PA
● *Set I:* The Landlady, Runaway Jim, Foam, Sparkle, Split Open and Melt, The Horse > Silent in the Morning, Dinner and a Movie, The Squirming Coil, My Sweet One, Stash, Golgi Apparatus
● *Set II:* Buried Alive, The Oh Kee Pa Ceremony, Suzy Greenberg, Take the 'A' Train, My Friend My Friend, Poor Heart, All Things Reconsidered, David Bowie, Weigh, Cracklin' Rosie, You Enjoy Myself
● *Encore:* Bouncing Around the Room, Rocky Top
● *Show Notes:* Fishman used both the cymbals and the Bag-Vac during Rosie. 'A' Train included a Simpsons Signal.

Sunday, March 22, 1992
Cultural Center Auditorium, Charleston, WV
Sparkle, All Things Reconsidered, Foam, The Landlady
● *Show Notes:* This set, performed live for the Mountain Stage Radio Program and as an opener for Buckwheat Zydeco, was broadcast several weeks later on National Public Radio.

Tuesday, March 24, 1992
Flood Zone, Richmond, VA
● *Set I:* Stash, Poor Heart, Foam, Eliza > Rift, Golgi Apparatus, The Horse > Silent in the Morning, Llama, Colonel Forbin's Ascent > The Famous Mockingbird, The Landlady > David Bowie
● *Set II:* The Curtain, Mike's Song > I Am Hydrogen > Weekapaug Groove, Guelah Papyrus, The Mango Song, Brother, Uncle Pen, I Didn't Know, The Oh Kee Pa Ceremony > Suzy Greenberg, Harry Hood, Cavern
● *Encore:* Lawn Boy, Fire
● *Show Notes:* The Forbin's narration gave a brief recap of the Gamehendge saga and included Wilson teases. The ensuing Mockingbird included Rift and *Leave It to Beaver* teases. The Bowie intro included Take Five (Dave Brubeck) teases. Check out this fantastic Mike's Groove, complete with screaming band members and a tease of Bob Seger's Main Street during Weekapaug. I Didn't Know featured Fishman on Bag-Vac. Brother and Cavern featured Carl Gerhard on coronet.

Wednesday, March 25, 1992
Trax, Charlottesville, VA
● *Set I:* Wilson > Sparkle, Split Open and Melt, Rift, Fee -> Maze, Glide -> Runaway Jim, It's Ice, Run Like an Antelope
● *Set II:* Tweezer -> Mound, Reba, All Things Reconsidered, The Squirming Coil, You Enjoy Myself -> Setting Sail, Horn > My Sweet One > Chalk Dust Torture, Cold as Ice > Cracklin' Rosie, Golgi Apparatus
● *Encore:* Sleeping Monkey > Tweezer Reprise
● *Show Notes:* Setting Sail (first since April 20, 1991, or 90 shows) arose from the YEM vocal jam.

Thursday, March 26, 1992
Ziggy's, Winston-Salem, NC
● Opening Act: The Aquarium Rescue Unit
● *Set I:* The Landlady, Runaway Jim, All Things Reconsidered > Foam, Sparkle, Stash, Fluffhead, Uncle Pen, NICU, David Bowie
● *Set II:* Buried Alive > The Oh Kee Pa Ceremony > Suzy Greenberg, Poor Heart, Brother, The Man Who Stepped Into Yesterday > Avenu Malkenu > The Man Who Stepped Into Yesterday Reprise, My Friend My Friend, The Lizards, Cavern, Cold as Ice > Cracklin' Rosie > Cold as Ice, Possum
● *Encore:* Sleeping Monkey, Chalk Dust Torture, Harpua
● *Show Notes:* The second set was preceded by birthday wishes for a fan named Amy and a remark that Buried Alive was inspired by Jimmy Herring. Bowie included Simpsons and Oom Pa Pa Signals and Possum included a Random Note and two Fingerscrape Signals (including one from Mike!). Marley made a special guest appearance as "the evil, evil dog Harpua." This version, set in the "teeming Brazilian rain forest," is a must-hear. There was a brief full-band Fire tease, high-pitched "Brazil" squawks from Fishman, and a preview of the Clifford Ball motto (four years early) as Trey introduced Page as "a beacon of light in the world of flight."

Friday, March 27, 1992
13x13 Club, Charlotte, NC
● *Set I:* Llama, Reba, Paul and Silas, The Sloth, Divided Sky, Guelah Papyrus, Maze, Glide, Bouncing Around the Room, Run Like an Antelope
● *Set II:* Mike's Song > I Am Hydrogen > Weekapaug Groove, The Horse > Silent in the Morning, My Sweet One, Rift, Bathtub Gin, Dinner and a Movie, Magilla, Harry Hood, Cold as Ice > Love You, Golgi Apparatus
● *Encore:* Memories, Sweet Adeline
● *Show Notes:* The beginning of the show, as well as the Antelope jam, contained We're Off to See the Wizard teases. Hood contained several references to some fan's T-shirt. Mike's Song contained an Auld Lang Syne tease. My Sweet One was full of the Secret Language, including All Fall Down, Fingerscrape, Oom Pa Pa, Simpsons, and Me and My Arrow Signals. The song also featured the band squawking at Page.

Saturday, March 28, 1992
Variety Playhouse, Atlanta, GA
● *Set I:* Runaway Jim, Foam, Sparkle, Stash, Rift, Bouncing Around the Room, The Landlady, David Bowie, Glide, Cavern
● *Set II:* Memories, Carolina, I Didn't Know, Sweet Adeline
● *Show Notes:* The second set was performed *a cappella* due to a small flood in the theatre. Authorities refused to allow the band to plug in their instruments, including the Bag-Vac.

Monday, March 30, 1992
Mississippi Nights, St. Louis, MO
● *Set I:* The Landlady, Llama, Foam, Guelah Papyrus, Sparkle, Maze, I Didn't Know, All Things Reconsidered, The Sloth, Runaway Jim, Cavern
● *Set II:* Golgi Apparatus, Uncle Pen, Tweezer, Mound, You Enjoy Myself -> Vacuum Solo -> Big Black Furry Creature from Mars, The Squirming Coil, Weigh, Chalk Dust Torture, HYHU > Cracklin' Rosie > Cold As Ice, Bouncing Around the Room > Tweezer Reprise
● *Encore:* Sleeping Monkey, The Oh Kee Pa Ceremony > Suzy Greenberg
● *Show Notes:* The vocal jam in YEM was based loosely on the song Rock On and was followed by a Bag-Vac solo from Fishman. BBFCFM included a Follow the Yellow Brick Road tease and was dedicated to hockey player Brett Hull, who, at that time, played for the St. Louis Blues. After Cracklin' Rosie, Trey remarked that the entire Blues hockey team was guest listed for the show and that he was glad to see one of them, Roger Halloway, in attendance. I Didn't Know featured Fishman on vacuum.

Tuesday, March 31, 1992
The Blue Note, Columbia, MO
● *Set I:* Wilson, Divided Sky, Glide, Split Open and Melt, Rift, Reba, Llama, Colonel Forbin's Ascent > The Famous Mockingbird, Run Like an Antelope
● *Set II:* Mike's Song > I Am Hydrogen > Weekapaug Groove, Fee, Poor Heart, Stash, The Lizards, Cavern, Dinner and a Movie, My Friend My Friend, My Sweet One, Love You, Possum
● *Encore:* Sweet Adeline

Wednesday, April 1, 1992
Liberty Hall, Lawrence, KS
● *Set I:* Golgi Apparatus, Foam, Bouncing Around the Room, Brother, All Things Reconsidered, Sparkle, It's Ice, Runaway Jim, I Didn't Know,

The Landlady > David Bowie, Carolina
● *Set II:* Llama, You Enjoy Myself, The Horse > Silent in the Morning, Uncle Pen, Tweezer, Horn, Chalk Dust Torture, Cold as Ice > Cracklin' Rosie > Cold as Ice, The Squirming Coil, Tweezer Reprise, Contact, Rocky Top
● *Encore:* Lawn Boy, Good Times Bad Times
● *Show Notes:* To commemorate April Fool's Day, Fishman got decked out in a black dress with a feather boa around his neck. During I Didn't Know Trey introduced him as "Tommy Dorsey's third cousin twice removed." Bowie included Landlady teases, as well as Oom Pa Pa, Fingerscrape, and Random Note Signals.

Friday, April 3, 1992
Hyatt Regency Village Hall, Beaver Creek, CO
● *Set I:* The Landlady > Poor Heart, Stash, Rift, Guelah Papyrus, Sparkle, Maze, Fluffhead, All Things Reconsidered, Split Open and Melt, Golgi Apparatus
● *Set II:* The Curtain > The Sloth, Possum, Mound, You Enjoy Myself, The Mango Song, Llama, Harry Hood, Suzy Greenberg
● *Encore:* Rocky Top

Saturday, April 4, 1992
UC Fieldhouse, Boulder, CO
● *Set I:* Runaway Jim, Foam, Reba, Uncle Pen, Chalk Dust Torture, Bouncing Around the Room, It's Ice, Sparkle, The Lizards, I Didn't Know, Run Like an Antelope
● *Set II:* Mike's Song > I Am Hydrogen > Weekapaug Groove, Glide, My Sweet One, Tweezer, The Squirming Coil, Cracklin' Rosie, My Friend My Friend, Harpua, Cavern
● *Encore:* Sleeping Monkey, Tweezer Reprise

Sunday, April 5, 1992
The Fox Theatre, Boulder, CO
● *Set I:* Llama, Guelah Papyrus, Divided Sky, Wilson, Poor Heart, Stash, Rift, Horn, It's Ice, Possum, Sweet Adeline
● *Set II:* Split Open and Melt, All Things Reconsidered, You Enjoy Myself, The Horse > Silent in the Morning, Maze, Weigh, The Landlady > David Bowie, Love You, Take the 'A' Train -> Runaway Jim
● *Encore:* Lawn Boy, Rocky Top
● *Show Notes:* Possum included a brief full-band Landlady jam, as well as All Fall Down, Random Note, and Oom Pa Pa Signals.

Monday, April 6, 1992
Western State College Gym, Gunnison, CO
● *Set I:* Suzy Greenberg, Foam, Sparkle, Reba, Brother, Esther, Chalk Dust Torture, Guelah Papyrus, The Squirming Coil, Run Like an Antelope
● *Set II:* Dinner and a Movie, Bathtub Gin, Paul and Silas, Mike's Song > I Am Hydrogen > Weekapaug Groove, NICU, Llama, Mound, Stash, Cracklin' Rosie, Uncle Pen, Cavern
● *Encore:* Big Black Furry Creature from Mars
● *Show Notes:* Sparkle was dedicated to "Donna." Trey announced before Cavern that the band would play a bit more bluegrass; therefore, segments of Cavern were performed in a bluegrass style. Also, Trey altered the lyrics to "take care of your boots" and reference a hoe-down! BBFCFM included a "Make Your Own Guacamole" jam, during which the audience made guacamole from band-supplied avocados because

the band's traditional post-show guacamole was not supplied.

Tuesday, April 7, 1992
Fine Arts Auditorium, Fort Lewis College, Durango, CO
● *Set I:* Buried Alive, Possum, It's Ice, Fee, Divided Sky, The Horse > Silent in the Morning, Split Open and Melt, Bouncing Around the Room, Rift, The Sloth, Runaway Jim
● *Set II:* Poor Heart, All Things Reconsidered, Tweezer, Eliza, You Enjoy Myself, My Friend My Friend, The Lizards, Maze, Bike, My Mind's Got a Mind of its Own, Golgi Apparatus
● *Encore:* Contact, Tweezer Reprise

Wednesday, April 8, 1992
El Ray Theatre, Albuquerque, NM
● *Set I:* The Landlady, Sparkle, Foam, Guelah Papyrus, Llama, Mound, Reba, Uncle Pen, Stash, The Squirming Coil, Golgi Apparatus
● *Set II:* The Oh Kee Pa Ceremony, Suzy Greenberg, David Bowie, The Man Who Stepped Into Yesterday > Avenu Malkenu > The Man Who Stepped Into Yesterday Reprise, My Sweet One, Mike's Song > I Am Hydrogen > Weekapaug Groove, The Horse > Silent in the Morning, Chalk Dust Torture, Terrapin, Cavern
● *Encore:* Sleeping Monkey, Rocky Top

Sunday, April 12, 1992
University of Arizona Ballroom, Tucson, AZ
● *Set I:* Suzy Greenberg, Poor Heart, Guelah Papyrus, Divided Sky, The Horse > Silent in the Morning, It's Ice, Sparkle, Maze, Reba, Run Like an Antelope
● *Set II:* Glide, Split Open and Melt, Bouncing Around the Room, Rift, You Enjoy Myself, Lawn Boy, NICU, Cracklin' Rosie, Harry Hood, Cavern
● *Encore:* Sweet Adeline, Rocky Top

Monday, April 13, 1992
After the Gold Rush, Tempe, AZ
● *Set I:* Golgi Apparatus, Uncle Pen, Stash, The Lizards, NICU, Fee, All Things Reconsidered, Foam, Take the 'A' Train, David Bowie
● *Set II:* Llama, Fluffhead, Sparkle, Mike's Song > I Am Hydrogen > Weekapaug Groove, Magilla, Ya Mar, The Squirming Coil, Love You, Possum
● *Encore:* Memories, Fire

Wednesday, April 15, 1992
Variety Arts Theatre, Los Angeles, CA
● *Opening Act:* Widespread Panic
● *Set I:* The Oh Kee Pa Ceremony > Suzy Greenberg, Foam, Guelah Papyrus, Sparkle, Stash, Uncle Pen, Cavern, I Didn't Know, All Things Reconsidered, Runaway Jim
● *Set II:* Chalk Dust Torture, You Enjoy Myself, Reba, The Landlady > NICU, Cold as Ice > Cracklin' Rosie > Cold as Ice, My Sweet One, Golgi Apparatus
● *Encore:* Memories, Sweet Adeline, Rocky Top
● *Show Notes:* Uncle Pen was played, according to Trey, "with all due respect to Bill Monroe." It was also explained at this show that All Things Reconsidered is a variation on National Public Radio's All Things Considered. YEM included a Sunshine of Your Love tease segment and the vocal jam centered on a "rolling" theme, including the quote

"Rolling on the River" from Proud Mary. It also included quotes from the theme to "Rawhide." My Sweet One was announced by Trey as being written by the third greatest songwriter of all time while Fishman took a bow of recognition. Memories and Sweet Adeline were performed without microphones.

Thursday, April 16, 1992
Anaconda Theatre, Santa Barbara, CA
● Opening Act: Widespread Panic
● *Set I:* Buried Alive > Possum, It's Ice, Bouncing Around the Room, Split Open and Melt, Rift, Fee -> Maze, Colonel Forbin's Ascent > Icculus > The Famous Mockingbird, Run Like an Antelope
● *Set II:* Sanity, Llama, The Lizards, Mike's Song > I Am Hydrogen > Weekapaug Groove, Horn, Poor Heart, Terrapin, Memories, Sweet Adeline, Suzy Greenberg
● *Encore:* Sleeping Monkey
● *Show Notes:* This version of Icculus (first since April 6, 1991, or 113 shows) was, perhaps, the shortest version ever as it did not contain the usual build-up and screaming.

Friday, April 17, 1992
Warfield Theatre, San Francisco, CA
● Opening Act: Widespread Panic
● *Set I:* Runaway Jim, Foam, Sparkle, Stash, I Didn't Know, Cavern, Reba, Maze, Bouncing Around the Room, The Landlady > David Bowie -> Catapult -> David Bowie
● *Set II:* Brother, You Enjoy Myself, Fluffhead, The Squirming Coil, Tweezer, Uncle Pen, Cracklin' Rosie, Tweezer Reprise
● *Encore:* Golgi Apparatus
● *Show Notes:* This show marked the first performance of Catapult. Brother featured Steve McConnell, Mike's brother, and several crew members jumping into a bathtub on stage. This fantastic Bowie included the Random Laugh Signal; the Reba is also well worth hearing.

Saturday, April 18, 1992
Wilbur Field, Stanford University, Palo Alto, CA
● *Set I:* Wilson > Divided Sky, Guelah Papyrus, Poor Heart, Split Open and Melt, Esther, Possum, It's Ice > Sparkle, All Things Reconsidered, Run Like an Antelope
● *Set II:* Glide, The Oh Kee Pa Ceremony > Suzy Greenberg, Rift, Manteca, Bathtub Gin, Manteca Reprise, The Lizards, Mound, Llama, The Man Who Stepped Into Yesterday > Avenu Malkenu > The Man Who Stepped Into Yesterday Reprise, Harry Hood, Cold as Ice > Love You > Cold as Ice, Rocky Top
● *Encore:* Contact, Big Black Furry Creature from Mars
● *Show Notes:* This was a free outdoor show at Stanford. Possum included a Simpsons Signal, and Antelope included Frere Jacques teases. Harry Hood contained a Linus and Lucy tease from *Peanuts;* this theme was briefly reprised at the beginning of Contact. Avenu Malkenu included a "Happy Passover" bass solo from Mike. The encore featured special guest Cameron McKinney on ukulele (unmiced). McKinney, seven years old at the time, also had the honor of counting off BBFCFM. It should be noted that the infamous "squirt gun breaks" during this show are in reference to a security guard cooling off the audience with a Super Soaker, and not the band shooting each other. Manteca was played for the first time since March 16, 1991 (126 shows).

Sunday, April 19, 1992
The Catalyst, Santa Cruz, CA
● *Set I:* Buried Alive > NICU, Stash, Paul and Silas, My Friend My Friend, Reba, Maze, Fee, Chalk Dust Torture, I Didn't Know, Golgi Apparatus
● *Set II:* The Curtain, Mike's Song > I Am Hydrogen > Weekapaug Groove, The Horse > Silent in the Morning, My Sweet One, Tube, The Mango Song, Llama, Lawn Boy, If I Only Had a Brain, Runaway Jim
● *Encore:* Sleeping Monkey, Cavern
● *Show Notes:* This fantastic Weekapaug included a vocal jam at the end.

Tuesday, April 21, 1992
Redwood Acres Fairgrounds, Eureka, CA
● *Set I:* Suzy Greenberg, Uncle Pen, Split Open and Melt, Rift, Guelah Papyrus, Possum, It's Ice -> Eliza, NICU, Bouncing Around the Room, David Bowie
● *Set II:* Dinner and a Movie, Colonel Forbin's Ascent > The Famous Mockingbird, Tweezer, Tela, Mike's Song > I Am Hydrogen > Weekapaug Groove, Weigh, Cold as Ice > Catapult > Cold as Ice, HYHU > Lively Up Yourself > Cold as Ice, Sanity, Maze
● *Encore:* Memories, Sweet Adeline, Cavern
● *Show Notes:* Possum was full of the Secret Language, containing Simpsons, Get Back, Oom Pa Pa, All Fall Down, and Fingerscrape Signals. It also featured strong Dave's Energy Guide teases. Weigh and Hydrogen were announced as written by baseball Hall-of-Famer Carl Yastrzemski. Weekapaug contained a Happy Birthday tease and dedication from Trey, as well as a Linus and Lucy tease from Mike. Trey used an interesting voice effect during the Forbin's narration as he spoke of the evil King Wilson. For this, the only appearance of Lively Up Yourself, the band switched instruments. Trey played drums, Fishman played bass, and Mike played guitar and (believe it or not!) vacuum.

Wednesday, April 22, 1992
Hilton Ballroom, Eugene, OR
Earth Day Celebration
● *Set I:* Llama, Foam, Reba, Sparkle, Guelah Papyrus, Divided Sky, Mound, Stash, All Things Reconsidered, Suzy Greenberg
● *Set II:* Glide, Run Like an Antelope, The Horse > Silent in the Morning, Rift, Wilson -> You Enjoy Myself, Poor Heart, Cracklin' Rosie, Harpua, Runaway Jim
● *Encore:* Take the 'A' Train, Rocky Top
● *Show Notes:* To commemorate Earth Day, inflatable globes were thrown around the audience.

Thursday, April 23, 1992
Oz Niteclub, Seattle, WA
● *Set I:* Cavern, The Curtain, Split Open and Melt, Uncle Pen, Guelah Papyrus, The Squirming Coil, Llama, Bouncing Around the Room, It's Ice, I Didn't Know, Possum
● *Set II:* The Landlady, Poor Heart, Mike's Song > I Am Hydrogen > Weekapaug Groove, The Lizards, NICU, Horn, Tweezer, Fee, Maze, Cracklin' Rosie, Golgi Apparatus
● *Encore:* Sleeping Monkey, Tweezer Reprise

Friday, April 24, 1992
Roseland Theatre, Portland, OR
● Opening Act: Jim
● *Check:* NICU
● *Set I:* Runaway Jim, Colonel Forbin's Ascent > The Famous Mockingbird, Uncle Pen, The Sloth, The Landlady, Fluffhead, Sparkle, Stash, The Squirming Coil, Golgi Apparatus
● *Set II:* David Bowie, Cavern, Ya Mar, Foam, Mike's Song > I Am Hydrogen > Weekapaug Groove, The Mango Song, Horn, Love You, Glide, Llama
● *Encore:* Contact, Big Black Furry Creature from Mars
● *Show Notes:* Love You featured a trombone solo, as Fishman could not get the vacuum to work. BBFCFM featured Trey and Mike diving across the stage while the strobes flashed.

Saturday, April 25, 1992
Evergreen College, Olympia, WA
● *Set I:* Suzy Greenberg, My Friend My Friend, Paul and Silas, Reba, Brother, Tela, Chalk Dust Torture, Bouncing Around the Room, Rift, Magilla, Run Like an Antelope
● *Set II:* Maze > Bathtub Gin, You Enjoy Myself, The Horse > Silent in the Morning, All Things Reconsidered, Dinner and a Movie, Harry Hood, Weigh, Terrapin, Poor Heart
● *Encore:* Memories, Sweet Adeline, Cavern
● *Show Notes:* Maze included strong Oye Como Va teases. The YEM vocal jam was based on the instrumental theme to the movie "Chariots of Fire." Memories and Adeline were performed without microphones.

Wednesday, April 29, 1992
First Avenue, Minneapolis, MN
● *Set I:* Suzy Greenberg, Foam, Sparkle, It's Ice, Runaway Jim, Guelah Papyrus, Rift, Bouncing Around the Room, Take the 'A' Train, David Bowie
● *Set II:* The Landlady > Possum, Mound -> The Oh Kee Pa Ceremony, Llama, The Lizards -> Mike's Song > I Am Hydrogen > Weekapaug Groove, Love You, Golgi Apparatus
● *Encore:* Horn, Rocky Top

Thursday, April 30, 1992
Barrymore Theatre, Madison, WI
I Opening Act: The Aquarium Rescue Unit
● *Set I:* The Curtain, Split Open and Melt, Fee, Maze, Reba, Uncle Pen, Stash, Rift, Esther, Run Like an Antelope
● *Set II:* Glide, Tweezer, The Squirming Coil, My Mind's Got a Mind of its Own, You Enjoy Myself, The Horse > Silent in the Morning, Chalk Dust Torture, Cold as Ice > Cracklin' Rosie > Cold as Ice, Harry Hood, Tweezer Reprise
● *Encore:* Carolina, Cavern
● *Show Notes:* Glide was preceded by an All Fall Down Signal. Tweezer featured Colonel Bruce Hampton on trombone. YEM included a Me and My Arrow Signal, a Dave's Energy Guide tease, and a Welcome Christmas tease in the vocal jam.

Friday, May 1, 1992
The Rave, Central Park, Milwaukee, WI
● *Set I:* Suzy Greenberg, My Friend My Friend, Poor Heart, The Landlady, NICU, The Sloth, Divided Sky, Guelah Papyrus, It's Ice, Horn, I Didn't Know, Possum

● *Set II:* Sanity, Buried Alive, Wilson, All Things Reconsidered, My Sweet One, Mike's Song > I Am Hydrogen > Weekapaug Groove, Mound, The Lizards, Llama, Cold as Ice > Terrapin, Golgi Apparatus
● *Encore:* Lawn Boy, Good Times Bad Times
● *Encore:* Rocky Top
● *Show Notes:* I Didn't Know featured Fishman on the Bag-Vac in what was the instrument's last known appearance.

Saturday, May 2, 1992
Cabaret Metro, Chicago, IL
Opening Act: The Aquarium Rescue Unit
● *Set I:* Runaway Jim, Colonel Forbin's Ascent > Icculus > The Famous Mockingbird, Sparkle, Reba, Maze, Bouncing Around the Room, Stash, The Squirming Coil, Llama
● *Set II:* Glide, David Bowie -> Crew Football Theme Song -> David Bowie, Tela, Foam, You Enjoy Myself, Chalk Dust Torture, Cracklin' Rosie, Cavern
● *Encore:* Sleeping Monkey, Big Black Furry Creature from Mars
● *Show Notes:* Both Forbin and Stash referenced the Los Angeles riots that ensued after the Rodney King verdict was announced. This incredibly fun Bowie included Fingerscrape, All Fall Down, Oom Pa Pa, Chaos, and Random Laugh Signals, as well as the return of the Crew Football Theme Song. During a hilarious Icculus, Trey extolled the virtues of the Helping Friendly Book and remarked jokingly that the Aquarium Rescue Unit "used to be a feeble bluegrass band until they read this great book!" Glide was a birthday dedication. BBFCFM featured some zany on-stage antics that found Trey on top of his stack and Mike singing from down on the floor. Bowie included "Wizard of Oz" theme teases and YEM included a strong Don't Get Me Wrong tease.

Sunday, May 3, 1992
Michigan State University Union Ballroom, East Lansing, MI
● *Set I:* The Landlady, Possum, It's Ice, Uncle Pen, Fee, Split Open and Melt, I Didn't Know, Rift, Horn, Runaway Jim
● *Set II:* Tweezer, The Horse > Silent in the Morning, Fluffhead, Guelah Papyrus, Mike's Song > I Am Hydrogen > Weekapaug Groove, The Mango Song, Cracklin' Rosie, Dinner and a Movie, Bouncing Around the Room, The Oh Kee Pa Ceremony > Suzy Greenberg
● *Encore:* Memories, Sweet Adeline, Tweezer Reprise

Tuesday, May 5, 1992
Bogart's, Cincinnati, OH
● *Set I:* Golgi Apparatus, The Curtain, Sparkle, Stash, Rift, Guelah Papyrus, Divided Sky, I Didn't Know, It's Ice -> Glide -> Run Like an Antelope
● *Set II:* Chalk Dust Torture, Bouncing Around the Room, All Things Reconsidered, Foam, Mike's Song > I Am Hydrogen > Weekapaug Groove, The Horse > Silent in the Morning, Poor Heart, Llama, Cold as Ice > Love You > Cold as Ice, The Squirming Coil, Cavern
● *Encore:* Contact, Rocky Top
● *Show Notes:* Guelah included use of the Secret Language.

Wednesday, May 6, 1992
St. Andrew's Hall, Detroit, MI
● *Set I:* Llama, Foam, Reba, My Mind's Got a Mind of its Own, Maze, Tela, Brother, Colonel Forbin's Ascent > The Famous Mockingbird, Sparkle, Cavern

● *Set II:* My Sweet One, Stash, The Squirming Coil, You Enjoy Myself, All Things Reconsidered, Bouncing Around the Room, Uncle Pen, Cold as Ice, Chalk Dust Torture, HYHU > Terrapin > Cold as Ice, Take the 'A' Train, Golgi Apparatus

● *Encore:* Carolina, Good Times Bad Times

● *Show Notes:* The vocal jam out of YEM included Shaggy Dog quotes.

Thursday, May 7, 1992
The Agora, Cleveland, OH

● *Set I:* Suzy Greenberg, Poor Heart, Buried Alive, My Friend My Friend, Foam, Runaway Jim, Esther, Split Open and Melt, Rift, Guelah Papyrus, Possum

● *Set II:* The Landlady, Sparkle, Tweezer, Fluffhead, Glide, Mike's Song > I Am Hydrogen > Weekapaug Groove, Fee > Cold as Ice > Bike, The Squirming Coil, Tweezer Reprise

● *Encore:* Sweet Adeline, Sleeping Monkey, Rocky Top

● *Show Notes:* Possum included Asshole, Fingerscrape, Random Laugh, and All Fall Down Signals. During Fee, a fake palm tree was lowered onto the stage behind Page. The prop seemed to surprise the band as much as it did the audience.

Friday, May 8, 1992
The Riviera Theatre, North Tonawanda, NY

● *Set I:* The Curtain > Cavern, Reba, Uncle Pen, It's Ice -> Eliza, Llama, Mound, All Things Reconsidered, Bouncing Around the Room, David Bowie, Memories

● *Set II:* Wilson, My Sweet One, Stash, Magilla, Maze, You Enjoy Myself, The Horse > Silent in the Morning, Chalk Dust Torture, Cold as Ice > Terrapin, Harry Hood, Golgi Apparatus

● *Encore:* Big Black Furry Creature from Mars

Saturday, May 9, 1992
The Syracuse Armory, Syracuse, NY

● *Set I:* Runaway Jim, Foam, Sparkle, Split Open and Melt, Guelah Papyrus, Rift, Fee, Maze, The Squirming Coil, I Didn't Know, Run Like an Antelope

● *Set II:* Suzy Greenberg, Divided Sky, Tela, Tweezer, Harpua, Llama, Cold as Ice > Cracklin' Rosie, Golgi Apparatus

● *Encore:* Poor Heart, Tweezer Reprise

● *Show Notes:* Guelah included an All Fall Down Signal. Mimi Fishman joined Henrietta for a vacuum duet during I Didn't Know.

Sunday, May 10, 1992
University of Massachusetts, Amherst, MA

The Landlady, Suzy Greenberg, Sparkle, Stash, Uncle Pen, Cavern > Reba, I Didn't Know, You Enjoy Myself, Possum

● *Show Notes:* Possum included Simpsons and All Fall Down Signals. This was a free show that also featured the bands Rippopatamus, The Mighty Mighty Bosstones, fIREHOSE, Fishbone, and The Beastie Boys

Tuesday, May 12, 1992
St. Lawrence University, Canton, NY

● *Set I:* My Sweet One, Reba, All Things Reconsidered, The Sloth, Possum, It's Ice, Dinner and a Movie, Bouncing Around the Room, Buried Alive, Uncle Pen, Horn, David Bowie

● *Set II:* The Landlady, Bathtub Gin, You Enjoy Myself, Guelah Papyrus, Chalk Dust Torture, Cold as Ice > Terrapin > HYHU, Poor Heart, Llama, Cavern

● *Encore:* Runaway Jim

Thursday, May 14, 1992
The Capitol Theatre, Port Chester, NY

● *Set I:* Suzy Greenberg, All Things Reconsidered, The Sloth, Sparkle, Maze, Horn, Reba, Poor Heart, My Friend My Friend, Bouncing Around the Room, Run Like an Antelope

● *Set II:* Glide, Cavern, Rift, Fluffhead, Eliza, Mike's Song > I Am Hydrogen > Weekapaug Groove, Wait, McGrupp and the Watchful Hosemasters, Stash, Cracklin' Rosie, Possum

● *Encore:* Sleeping Monkey, Rocky Top

● *Show Notes:* Antelope included another Language Instruction and a "Spiderman" tease.

Friday, May 15, 1992
Lonestar Roadhouse, New York, NY

Golgi Apparatus, Foam, Cavern, Sparkle, Stash, Bouncing Around the Room, Cold as Ice > Love You > Cold as Ice, Chalk Dust Torture, You Enjoy Myself, Sweet Adeline, Rocky Top

● *Show Notes:* This small gig was a private party for record industry folk and friends.

Saturday, May 16, 1992
The Orpheum, Boston, MA

● *Set I:* Maze, Foam, Glide, Split Open and Melt, Bouncing Around the Room, My Sweet One, Horn, Golgi Apparatus, The Lizards, Cavern > David Bowie

● *Set II:* Runaway Jim, It's Ice, Paul and Silas, Tweezer, The Squirming Coil, You Enjoy Myself, The Horse > Silent in the Morning, The Oh Kee Pa Ceremony > AC/DC Bag > Cold as Ice > Cracklin' Rosie > HYHU, Poor Heart, Tweezer Reprise

● *Encore:* Sweet Adeline, Suzy Greenberg

● *Show Notes:* My Sweet One contained Simpsons and All Fall Down Signals. Before the Adeline encore, Trey asked the audience for their help, as Phish was attempting to perform an *a cappella* number in the largest venue to date. Afterwards, he remarked that he'd like to see Metallica try that! AC/DC Bag was played for the first time since November 1, 1991 (74 shows).

Sunday, May 17, 1992
Union College, Schenectady, NY

● *Set I:* The Landlady, Llama, Colonel Forbin's Ascent > The Famous Mockingbird, My Sweet One, Reba, I Didn't Know, Stash, The Mango Song, Poor Heart, Chalk Dust Torture

● *Set II:* The Curtain, Possum, Guelah Papyrus, The Squirming Coil, All Things Reconsidered, Brother, Sanity, Cold as Ice > Love You > HYHU, Sparkle, Harry Hood, Cavern

● *Encore:* Lawn Boy, Good Times Bad Times

● *Show Notes:* Coil included a Happy Birthday dedication to Page. This excellent Possum included Simpsons, All Fall Down, and Fingerscrape Signals, as well as teases of Rocky Mountain Way, LA Woman, China Grove, It's Ice, and Divided Sky.

Monday, May 18, 1992
Flynn Theatre, Burlington, VT
● *Set I:* Suzy Greenberg, Maze, Bouncing Around the Room, Divided Sky, Guelah Papyrus, Foam, Poor Heart, Horn, Sparkle, Run Like an Antelope
● *Set II:* Glide, Llama, The Man Who Stepped Into Yesterday > Avenu Malkenu > The Man Who Stepped Into Yesterday Reprise > Mike's Song > I Am Hydrogen > Weekapaug Groove, Fee, Rift, Cavern, Cold as Ice > Love You > HYHU, Runaway Jim
● *Encore:* Rocky Top
● *Show Notes:* Love You included Mississippi Queen teases, both before and during the song. The ensuing vacuum solo was quite spirited.

SUMMER, 1992

Friday, June 19, 1992
Stadtpark/Freilichtbuhn, Hamburg, Germany
● *Check:* My Sweet One
The Landlady, Suzy Greenberg, Stash, The Squirming Coil, Sparkle, Cavern, You Enjoy Myself
● *Show Notes:* A fiery YEM was the highlight of Phish's first ever European show, as they opened for The Violent Femmes.

Saturday, June 20, 1992
Waldbuhn, Nordheim, Germany
Buried Alive, Bouncing Around the Room, Foam, Runaway Jim, It's Ice, Horn, Love You, Llama
● *Show Notes:* This set was an opener for both Lou Reed and The Violent Femmes.

Tuesday, June 23, 1992
Philipshalle, Dusseldorf, Germany
Chalk Dust Torture, Reba, Maze, Sweet Adeline, Uncle Pen, Big Black Furry Creature from Mars, If I Only Had a Brain, Golgi Apparatus

Wednesday, June 24, 1992
Resi, Nuremburg, Germany
Runaway Jim, Llama, Sweet Adeline, Uncle Pen, Guelah Papyrus, I Didn't Know, Sparkle, Cavern, Rocky Top

Saturday, June 27, 1992
Roskilde Festival, Copenhagen, Denmark
Runaway Jim, Foam, Sparkle, Reba, Maze, All Things Reconsidered, Chalk Dust Torture, Bouncing Around the Room, Uncle Pen, David Bowie
● *Encore:* I Didn't Know, Good Times Bad Times
● *Show Notes:* This four-day festival featured over 100 bands, including Nirvana, Faith No More, and David Byrne.

Tuesday, June 30, 1992
Elysee Montmartre, Paris, France
Golgi Apparatus, Divided Sky, Guelah Papyrus, Possum, Sweet Adeline, You Enjoy Myself

Wednesday, July 1, 1992
Ancienne Beguique, Brussels, Belgium

The Curtain, Cavern, Rift, Horn, Split Open and Melt, Sweet Adeline, Rocky Top

Friday, July 3, 1992
Brixton Academy, Radio One Music Festival, London

Thursday, July 9, 1992
Cumberland County Civic Center, Portland, ME
Glide, The Oh Kee Pa Ceremony > Suzy Greenberg, Sparkle, Stash, The Squirming Coil, Runaway Jim, Guelah Papyrus, David Bowie -> Vacuum Solo -> David Bowie, Glide
● *Encore:* Rocky Top
● *Show Notes:* This show was part of the HORDE tour. The intro to Bowie included an All Fall Down Signal and the Glide opener included a Simpsons Signal. Interestingly, the show both opened and closed with Glide.

Friday, July 10, 1992
Empire Court, Syracuse, NY
Bouncing Around the Room, Llama, Reba, Sparkle, Maze, Golgi Apparatus, The Lizards, Cavern, Vacuum Solo, Run Like an Antelope
● *Encore:* My Sweet One
● *Show Notes:* This show was part of the HORDE tour.

Saturday, July 11, 1992
Garden State Arts Center, Holmdel, NJ
The Landlady, Runaway Jim, Foam, Sparkle, Stash, The Squirming Coil, Cavern -> Vacuum Solo -> Cavern, You Enjoy Myself, Suzy Greenberg
● *Show Notes:* This show was part of the HORDE tour. Several "official" HORDE dancers took the stage during The Landlady to dance with Trey and Mike. During the tramps segment of YEM, an extra tramp and microphone were brought out for John Popper. On his first jump, though, Popper jumped right through the trampoline. Embarrassed, he left the stage.

Sunday, July 12, 1992
Jones Beach, Wantagh, Long Island, NY
● *Check:* Sweet Adeline, Carolina, Sweet Adeline (many times)
Sweet Adeline, Chalk Dust Torture, Bouncing Around the Room, Divided Sky, Fluffhead, Maze, Uncle Pen, Glide -> Vacuum Solo -> Glide, Possum
● *Show Notes:* This show was part of the HORDE tour. Unlike other HORDE shows, though, Phish headlined. The band took the stage wearing *papier mache* costume masks, which they threw into the crowd after Adeline. Glide was dedicated to David Ullrich, a fan who had recently died of leukemia. Possum featured the secret language, including the Simpsons, All Fall Down, and Oom Pa Pa Signals.

Tuesday, July 14, 1992
The Boathouse, Norfolk, VA
● *Check:* Rift (several times)
● *Set I:* The Landlady, Rift, Guelah Papyrus, Maze, Sparkle, It's Ice, Runaway Jim, Horn, Brother, I Didn't Know, Poor Heart, Cavern
● *Set II:* Tweezer, Fee, All Things Reconsidered, Reba, Llama, The Squirming Coil, Paul and Silas, You Enjoy Myself, Take the 'A' Train, Tweezer Reprise
● *Encore:* Sleeping Monkey

Wednesday, July 15, 1992
Trax, Charlottesville, VA
● *Check:* Weigh, Happy Trails, Weigh, Rift, Silent in the Morning (four times)
● *Set I:* Glide, The Oh Kee Pa Ceremony > Suzy Greenberg, Foam, My Friend My Friend, Uncle Pen, Split Open and Melt, The Horse > Silent in the Morning, Chalk Dust Torture, The Lizards, Run Like an Antelope
● *Set II:* The Sloth, Divided Sky, Esther, My Sweet One, Stash, McGrupp and the Watchful Hosemasters > All Things Reconsidered, Harry Hood, Golgi Apparatus
● *Encore:* Possum -> Vacuum Solo -> Possum
● *Show Notes:* Fishman performed his solo wearing nothing but underwear with a big "0", referencing his "Zero Man" nickname, on the groin area. Antelope included a Simpsons Signal; Esther included a Random Note Signal. Some tapes that circulate include Rift at the beginning but it is believed that this is from the soundcheck.

Thursday, July 16, 1992
The Flood Zone, Richmond, VA
● *Check:* My Friend My Friend, Silent in the Morning, It's Ice (each song played several times, stopping and starting)
● *Set I:* Poor Heart, It's Ice, Maze, Sparkle, Wilson, Dinner and a Movie, Bouncing Around the Room, Rift, Guelah Papyrus, David Bowie
● *Set II:* Runaway Jim, Weigh, The Landlady, Fluffhead, The Man Who Stepped Into Yesterday > Avenu Malkenu > The Man Who Stepped Into Yesterday Reprise -> Llama -> Glide, Paul and Silas, Mike's Song > I Am Hydrogen > Weekapaug Groove
● *Encore:* Blue Bayou, The Squirming Coil
● *Show Notes:* This show marked the first performance of Blue Bayou.

Friday, July 17, 1992
Merriweather Post Pavilion, Columbia, MD
● *Check:* Shaggy Dog, Jam, Jam
Chalk Dust Torture, Sparkle, Stash, The Squirming Coil, Maze, Bouncing Around the Room, Runaway Jim
● *Show Notes:* This set was an opener for Santana.

Saturday, July 18, 1992
Mann Music Center, Philadelphia, PA
Suzy Greenberg, Foam, Llama, Reba, Rift, Run Like an Antelope
● *Show Notes:* This set was an opener for Santana. Trey used his microphone stand as a slide during Foam.

Sunday, July 19, 1992
Garden State Arts Center, Holmdel, NJ
Poor Heart, Maze, Runaway Jim, David Bowie, Sweet Adeline
● *Show Notes:* This set was an opener for Santana.

Tuesday, July 21, 1992
Great Woods, Mansfield, MA
All Things Reconsidered, Possum, It's Ice, Sparkle, Stash, The Squirming Coil, Runaway Jim
● *Show Notes:* This set was an opener for Santana.

Wednesday, July 22, 1992
Holman Stadium, Nashua, NH

Reba, Poor Heart, Bouncing Around the Room, Maze, Rift, Cavern, David Bowie
● *Show Notes:* This set was an opener for Santana.

Thursday, July 23, 1992
MTV Studios, New York, NY
The Landlady, Buried Alive, Rift, Vacuum Solo, Poor Heart, Guelah Papyrus, You Enjoy Myself, Stash, Jam, Divided Sky
● *Show Notes:* This was an in-studio performance on *Hangin' with MTV*. No song was aired in its entirety; all were just short instrumental snippets. Trey and Mike were on the tramps for the YEM snippet, prompting the VJ to ask Trey if he was more inspired by Jerry Garcia or Mary Lou Retton. For the record, Trey didn't answer.

Friday, July 24, 1992
Jones Beach, Wantagh, Long Island, NY
My Sweet One, Foam, Tweezer, The Squirming Coil, You Enjoy Myself, Tweezer Reprise
● *Show Notes:* This set was an opener for Santana.

Saturday, July 25, 1992
Stowe Performing Arts Center, Stowe, VT
Runaway Jim, Foam, Sparkle, Stash, Rift, You Enjoy Myself, Llama, Funky Bitch
● *Show Notes:* This set was an opener for Santana. YEM through Funky Bitch featured special guests Carlos Santana, Karl Perazzo, and Raul Rekow. Funky Bitch was played for the first time since October 15, 1991 (107 shows).

Sunday, July 26, 1992
Big Birch Concert Pavilion, Patterson, NY
Chalk Dust Torture, It's Ice, Divided Sky, Weigh, Split Open and Melt, The Lizards, Llama
● *Show Notes:* This set was an opener for Santana.

Monday, July 27, 1992
Saratoga Performing Arts Center, Saratoga Springs, NY
Golgi Apparatus, All Things Reconsidered, David Bowie, Horn, Suzy Greenberg, Llama, Sweet Adeline
● *Show Notes:* This set was an opener for Santana.

Tuesday, July 28, 1992
Finger Lakes Performing Arts Center, Rochester, NY
Chalk Dust Torture, Bouncing Around the Room, Uncle Pen, The Squirming Coil, Tweezer, Runaway Jim
● *Show Notes:* This set was an opener for Santana.

Thursday, July 30, 1992
Meadow Brook Music Festival, Rochester Hills, MI
Rift, Horn, Sparkle, It's Ice -> All Things Reconsidered, Maze, I Didn't Know, Possum
● *Show Notes:* This set was an opener for Santana. Possum included the Simpsons Signal.

Friday, July 31, 1992
Blossom Music Center, Cuyahoga Falls, OH

Suzy Greenberg, Chalk Dust Torture, Bouncing Around the Room, The Oh Kee Pa Ceremony, You Enjoy Myself, Good Times Bad Times
● *Show Notes:* This set was an opener for Santana.

Saturday, August 1, 1992
Poplar Creek Music Center, Hoffman Estates, IL
Golgi Apparatus, Foam, Poor Heart, Stash, The Squirming Coil, Horn, Llama
● *Show Notes:* This set was an opener for Santana.

Sunday, August 2, 1992
Riverport Performing Arts Center, Marilyn Heights, MO
Chalk Dust Torture, Guelah Papyrus, Rift, The Oh Kee Pa Ceremony > Suzy Greenberg, David Bowie, Cavern, Rocky Top
● *Show Notes:* This set was an opener for Santana.

Thursday, August 13, 1992
Greek Theatre, Los Angeles, CA
Chalk Dust Torture, Foam, You Enjoy Myself
● *Show Notes:* This set was an opener for Santana.

Friday, August 14, 1992
Greek Theatre, Los Angeles, CA
Poor Heart, Stash, The Squirming Coil, Llama, Sweet Adeline
● *Show Notes:* This set was an opener for Santana.

Saturday, August 15, 1992
Greek Theatre, Los Angeles, CA
The Landlady, Sparkle, Guelah Papyrus, Maze, Runaway Jim
● *Show Notes:* This set was an opener for Santana.

Monday, August 17, 1992
The Coach House, San Juan Capistrano, CA
I Opening Act: Ninja Custodians
● *Set I:* Buried Alive, Poor Heart, The Landlady, Reba, Rift, Wilson -> All Things Reconsidered, Foam, My Friend My Friend, Bouncing Around the Room, David Bowie
● *Set II:* Suzy Greenberg, It's Ice, Tweezer, Esther, Mike's Song > I Am Hydrogen > Weekapaug Groove, Horn, Terrapin, Take the 'A' Train, Cavern
● *Encore:* The Squirming Coil
● *Show Notes:* 'A' Train included a jam of the "Flintstones" theme, as well as teases of Somewhere Over the Rainbow. Ninja Mike guested on drums during Terrapin and added some vocal scats during the vacuum solo.

Wednesday, August 19, 1992
Pema County Fair, Tucson, AZ
Chalk Dust Torture, The Landlady, Runaway Jim, Guelah Papyrus, You Enjoy Myself, Uncle Pen, Llama
● *Show Notes:* This set was an opener for Santana.

Thursday, August 20, 1992
Pan American Center, Las Cruces, NM
● *Check:* Blues Jam, Shaggy Dog
Golgi Apparatus, Foam, Stash, The Squirming Coil -> David Bowie, Sweet Adeline
● *Show Notes:* This set was an opener for Santana. Bowie included an

All Fall Down Signal.

Sunday, August 23, 1992
Colorado State Fair, Pueblo State Fairgrounds, Pueblo, CO
Chalk Dust Torture, Maze, Sparkle, Cavern, Foam, Runaway Jim, Stash
● *Show Notes:* This set was an opener for Santana.

Monday, August 24, 1992
Gerald Ford Amphitheater, Vail, CO
Buried Alive, Poor Heart, All Things Reconsidered, Tweezer, The Landlady, Reba, You Enjoy Myself
● *Show Notes:* This set was an opener for Santana.

Tuesday, August 25, 1992
The Downs, Santa Fe, NM
Runaway Jim, It's Ice, Sparkle, Stash, The Squirming Coil, Llama, Sweet Adeline
● *Show Notes:* This set was an opener for Santana.

Thursday, August 27, 1992
Santa Barbara County Bowl, Santa Barbara, CA
Chalk Dust Torture, Bouncing Around the Room, The Landlady, Horn, Sparkle, You Enjoy Myself, Llama
● *Show Notes:* This set was an opener for Santana.

Friday, August 28, 1992
Concord Pavilion, Concord, CA
Poor Heart, Foam, Stash, Sweet Adeline, The Squirming Coil, Runaway Jim, Rocky Top
● *Show Notes:* This set was an opener for Santana.

Saturday, August 29, 1992
Shoreline Amphitheater, Mountain View, CA
Chalk Dust Torture, Rift, Bouncing Around the Room, Maze, You Enjoy Myself
● *Show Notes:* This set was an opener for Santana.

Sunday, August 30, 1992
Cal Expo Amphitheater, Sacramento, CA
Uncle Pen, The Landlady, Reba, Llama, Memories, Run Like an Antelope, Sweet Adeline
● *Show Notes:* This set was an opener for Santana.

FALL, 1992

Friday, October 30, 1992
Boston Garden, Boston, MA
Runaway Jim, Maze, Bouncing Around the Room, Rift, Cavern -> Vacuum Solo -> Cavern, The Squirming Coil, Stash, Sweet Adeline, You Enjoy Myself
● *Show Notes:* This show was a New Music concert sponsored by WBCN in Boston and included The Levelers, Material Issue, Michael Penn, The Spin Doctors, and a comedy troupe that was booed off stage before their time expired as the impatient crowd clamored for Phish.

Thursday, November 19, 1992
Ross Arena, St. Michael's College, Colchester, VT
● *Set I:* Maze, Fee -> Foam, Glide -> Split Open and Melt, Mound, Divided Sky, Esther, Axilla, The Horse > Silent in the Morning, Run Like an Antelope
● *Set II:* Mike's Song > I Am Hydrogen > Weekapaug Groove, Bouncing Around the Room, It's Ice, I Walk the Line, Tweezer -> Big Black Furry Creature from Mars -> Tweezer, Big Ball Jam, Poor Heart, Fast Enough for You, Llama, Lengthwise, Cavern
● *Encore:* Bold as Love
● *Show Notes:* Axilla, I Walk the Line, FEFY, and Lengthwise all debuted at this show. The Big Ball Jam also debuted, as Trey explained the concept and mentioned that it was written for Pete Shaw. Divided Sky featured a tease of Those Were the Days and, along with Antelope, Poor Heart, FEFY, and Llama featured Gordon Stone on pedal steel guitar. Mike's Song included an Ice Ice Baby jam. Weekapaug included a vocal jam ending and Price of Love teases. BBFCFM featured lyrics from I Walk the Line. Lengthwise was performed in more of a reggae style than other versions and featured a vacuum solo from Fishman. The start of the second set included an Owner of a Lonely Heart tease. Bold as Love was played for the first time since April 18, 1990 (276 shows).

Friday, November 20, 1992
Palace Theatre, Albany, NY
● *Set I:* Axilla, All Things Reconsidered, Suzy Greenberg > Rift, The Sloth, Reba, Sparkle, Stash, The Lizards -> Memories, I Walk the Line, David Bowie
● *Set II:* Chalk Dust Torture, Fluffhead, Tube, You Enjoy Myself, Fast Enough for You, Dinner and a Movie > Harry Hood, Terrapin -> Lengthwise, Self
● *Encore:* Sweet Adeline, Good Times Bad Times
● *Show Notes:* Self (first since November 8, 1991, or 117 shows) featured The Dude of Life on vocals. Trey also mentioned the Dude during Suzy. Stash contained "Flintstones" theme teases and Bowie included a Jimmy Olsen's Blues tease. Tube was played for the first time since April 19, 1992 (66 shows).

Saturday, November 21, 1992
Sports Complex, SUNY Stony Brook, Stony Brook, NY
● *Set I:* The Landlady, Runaway Jim, Foam, Glide, Poor Heart, It's Ice, Bouncing Around the Room, Maze, Colonel Forbin's Ascent > The Famous Mockingbird, Possum
● *Set II:* Carolina, The Curtain, Mike's Song > I Am Hydrogen > Weekapaug Groove, The Horse > Silent in the Morning, Uncle Pen, Guelah Papyrus, The Squirming Coil, Love You, Take the 'A' Train, Llama
● *Encore:* Buffalo Bill, Big Black Furry Creature from Mars
● *Show Notes:* This show marked the debut of Buffalo Bill. Llama included a Big Ball Jam. Carolina was played for the first time since May 6, 1992 (55 shows).

Sunday, November 22, 1992
Bailey Hall, Cornell University, Ithaca, NY
● *Set I:* Buried Alive, The Oh Kee Pa Ceremony > Suzy Greenberg, Fee, Maze, Reba, Sparkle, Horn, All Things Reconsidered, Bathtub Gin, Sweet Adeline, Run Like an Antelope

● *Set II:* Axilla, My Friend My Friend, My Sweet One, Tweezer -> Big Ball Jam -> Tweezer, Tela, You Enjoy Myself, Faht, Golgi Apparatus
● *Encore:* Bold as Love, Carolina, Tweezer Reprise
● *Show Notes:* Suzy included a Jimmy Olsen's Blues tease (with a lone lyric from Trey) and YEM included serious teases of Eleanor Rigby. This show marked the debut of Faht. Bathtub Gin was played for the first time since May 12, 1992 (51 shows) and Tela was played for the first time since May 9, 1992 (53 shows).

Monday, November 23, 1992
Broome County Forum, Binghamton, NY
● *Set I:* Runaway Jim, Foam, Glide, Split Open and Melt, Rift, Guelah Papyrus, Divided Sky, Mound, Bouncing Around the Room, Memories, David Bowie
● *Set II:* Poor Heart, Stash, The Squirming Coil, I Walk the Line, Llama, Weigh > Mike's Song > I Am Hydrogen > Weekapaug Groove -> Jam -> Big Ball Jam -> Weekapaug Groove, HYHU > Lengthwise > HYHU, Cavern
● *Encore:* Sleeping Monkey, Rocky Top
● *Show Notes:* Bowie included the first known Vibration of Life. The jam before the Big Ball Jam included hints of Makisupa. Lengthwise featured Mimi Fishman on vacuum and some funny stage banter.

Wednesday, November 25, 1992
Keswick Theatre, Glenside, PA
● *Set I:* Buried Alive > Poor Heart, The Landlady, Fee -> Maze, Sparkle, It's Ice, The Squirming Coil, Cavern, Sweet Adeline, Run Like an Antelope
● *Set II:* Chalk Dust Torture, Foam, Fast Enough for You, You Enjoy Myself, The Lizards, Tweezer -> Cracklin' Rosie, My Sweet One, Tweezer Reprise
● *Encore:* Harry Hood, Carolina
● *Show Notes:* Carolina was performed without microphones.

Friday, November 27, 1992
Capitol Theatre, Port Chester, NY
Check: Dog Gone Dog, Axilla (twice), two Blues Jams
● *Set I:* Rift > Wilson > Divided Sky > Colonel Forbin's Ascent > The Famous Mockingbird, Split Open and Melt, Lawn Boy, Reba, Llama, Mound, Memories, Runaway Jim
● *Set II:* Axilla, Poor Heart > Possum, Glide, It's Ice > McGrupp and the Watchful Hosemasters > I Walk The Line -> David Bowie, The Horse > Silent in the Morning, Faht, Take the 'A' Train > Cavern
● *Encore:* Bold As Love
● *Show Notes:* Possum included All Fall Down and Random Note Signals. Faht was dedicated to Jimi Hendrix on his birthday and Trey called Jimi the greatest electric guitarist ever during the second set. Cavern included Voodoo Chile and Purple Haze teases as an obvious tribute to Jimi. Bowie included I Walk the Line and McGrupp and the Watchful Hosemasters teases.

Saturday, November 28, 1992
Capitol Theatre, Port Chester, NY
● *Set I:* My Sweet One, Foam, Stash, Esther, Chalk Dust Torture, Sparkle, Fast Enough for You, All Things Reconsidered, Mike's Song > I Am Hydrogen > Weekapaug Groove

● *Set II:* Suzy Greenberg, Paul and Silas, Tweezer -> The Man Who Stepped Into Yesterday > Avenu Malkenu -> Maze -> The Man Who Stepped Into Yesterday Reprise, Bouncing Around the Room, The Squirming Coil, Terrapin, Harpua -> Golgi Apparatus

● *Encore:* Contact -> Tweezer Reprise

● *Show Notes:* Harpua (first since May 9, 1992, or 57 shows) included a Jimmy Olsen's Blues tease and Tweezer contained strong Alumni Blues teases. My Sweet One included a long pause due to problems Mike had with his bass. Terrapin included the use of a gong. Contact was played for the first time since May 5, 1992 (61 shows).

Monday, November 30, 1992
Metropol, Pittsburgh, PA
● *Set I:* Llama, Foam, Bouncing Around the Room, Poor Heart, Stash, Sparkle, It's Ice, I Didn't Know, Reba > Run Like an Antelope
● *Set II:* Buried Alive > Runaway Jim, Guelah Papyrus, Maze, Glide, Uncle Pen, You Enjoy Myself, The Squirming Coil, Terrapin, Cavern
● *Encore:* Fee, Fire
● *Show Notes:* Fire was played for the first time since April 13, 1992 (78 shows).

Tuesday, December 1, 1992
Livingston Fieldhouse, Denison University, Granville, OH
● *Set I:* The Landlady > My Sweet One, Split Open and Melt, Bouncing Around the Room, Rift, Cavern, Fluffhead, Maze, Sweet Adeline, Mike's Song > I Am Hydrogen > Weekapaug Groove
● *Set II:* Axilla, The Curtain, Chalk Dust Torture, My Friend My Friend, All Things Reconsidered, Uncle Pen, Llama, Love You, Dinner and a Movie, Baby Elephant Walk -> David Bowie
● *Encore:* Good Times Bad Times
● *Show Notes:* Baby Elephant Walk debuted at this show.

Wednesday, December 2, 1992
Newport Music Hall, Columbus, OH
● *Set I:* Suzy Greenberg, Foam, Divided Sky, Fast Enough for You, Poor Heart, Stash, The Lizards, Sparkle, Horn, You Enjoy Myself
● *Set II:* Wilson -> Possum, Mound, Tweezer, Tela, Llama, Glide, Lengthwise, The Squirming Coil, I Walk The Line, Runaway Jim
● *Encore:* Golgi Apparatus, Rocky Top

Thursday, December 3, 1992
Bogart's, Cincinnati, OH
● *Set I:* Maze, Fee -> All Things Reconsidered, Split Open and Melt, Bouncing Around the Room, Uncle Pen, Chalk Dust Torture, The Horse > Silent in the Morning, Reba, Sweet Adeline, Run Like an Antelope
● *Set II:* Rift, Guelah Papyrus, Fluffhead, Mike's Song > I Am Hydrogen > Weekapaug Groove, Lawn Boy, It's Ice, My Sweet One > Big Ball Jam, HYHU > Cracklin' Rosie > HYHU, Take the 'A' Train, Cavern
● *Encore:* Bold as Love
● *Show Notes:* Antelope included Simpsons and Fingerscrape Signals. During the break in Guelah, Trey explained the concept of the Big Ball Jam to the crowd. Guelah also included a Random Note Signal. 'A' Train included Dixie teases, to which the audience sang along.

Friday, December 4, 1992
Mississippi Nights, St. Louis, MO

● *Set I:* Llama, Foam, Poor Heart, Stash, Glide, Sparkle, Fast Enough for You, Maze, Colonel Forbin's Ascent > The Famous Mockingbird, Cavern
● *Set II:* Suzy Greenberg > David Bowie, Esther, Possum, It's Ice, The Squirming Coil, Carolina, Harry Hood, Faht, You Enjoy Myself
● *Encore:* Fee, Rocky Top

Saturday, December 5, 1992
The Vic Theatre, Chicago, IL
● *Check:* The Wedge Jam, My Mind's Got a Mind of its Own Jam, Jam, My Sweet One, Dog Gone Dog
● *Set I:* The Landlady, Chalk Dust Torture, Bouncing Around the Room, Rift, Guelah Papyrus, Split Open and Melt, The Lizards, Mound, Divided Sky, Sweet Adeline, Uncle Pen, Golgi Apparatus
● *Set II:* Poor Heart, Tweezer, Reba > I Walk The Line > Reba, Sparkle, Maze, Lawn Boy, Mike's Song > I Am Hydrogen > Weekapaug Groove, Whipping Post, Tweezer Reprise
● *Encore:* Memories, Good Times Bad Times
● *Show Notes:* Whipping Post (first since December 6, 1991, or 112 shows) included a vacuum jam from Fishman.

Sunday, December 6, 1992
The Vic Theatre, Chicago, IL
● *Set I:* Runaway Jim > Foam, Fee > My Friend My Friend, My Sweet One, The Sloth, The Squirming Coil, Llama, Fluffhead, Run Like an Antelope
● *Set II:* Suzy Greenberg, The Curtain > Stash, Paul and Silas, Big Ball Jam, Bathtub Gin, You Enjoy Myself, The Man Who Stepped Into Yesterday > Avenu Malkenu > The Man Who Stepped Into Yesterday Reprise, Lengthwise, Carolina, Cavern
● *Encore:* Possum
● *Show Notes:* Antelope included All Fall Down and Simpsons Signals. Possum contained a Random Note Signal and The Vibration of Life. Also, Foam included a brief but distinct Dixie tease from Trey.

Monday, December 7, 1992
1st Avenue, Minneapolis, MN
● *Set I:* Axilla, Poor Heart, Maze, Glide, Sparkle, Foam, Fast Enough for You, All Things Reconsidered, Split Open and Melt, Bouncing Around the Room, You Enjoy Myself
● *Set II:* Chalk Dust Torture, Reba -> Llama, Horn -> The Vibration of Life -> My Sweet One, It's Ice, Fee, David Bowie -> Love You, The Squirming Coil, Sweet Adeline
● *Encore:* Runaway Jim
● *Show Notes:* YEM contained Oye Como Va teases.

Tuesday, December 8, 1992
Barrymore Theatre, Madison, WI
● *Set I:* Rift, Wilson, Llama, Colonel Forbin's Ascent > The Famous Mockingbird, Uncle Pen, Guelah Papyrus, Divided Sky, Mound, Sweet Adeline, Stash
● *Set II:* Mike's Song > I Am Hydrogen > Weekapaug Groove, The Horse > Silent in the Morning, It's Ice, The Lizards, Run Like an Antelope, Lawn Boy, Sparkle, Suzy Greenberg, Lengthwise, My Sweet One -> Big Ball Jam, Sleeping Monkey
● *Encore:* Carolina, Fire

Thursday, December 10, 1992
State Theatre, Kalamazoo, MI
● *Set I:* Golgi Apparatus, Llama, Foam, Fee, Poor Heart, Split Open and Melt, I Didn't Know, All Things Reconsidered, Reba, Sweet Adeline, Cavern
● *Set II:* Rift, Tweezer -> Tela, My Sweet One -> Big Ball Jam, Maze, You Enjoy Myself, Love You, The Oh Kee Pa Ceremony > Suzy Greenberg
● *Encore:* Bold As Love, Carolina, Tweezer Reprise

Friday, December 11, 1992
Michigan Theatre, Ann Arbor, MI
● *Set I:* Runaway Jim, It's Ice, Uncle Pen, Stash, The Lizards, Chalk Dust Torture, Guelah Papyrus, Sparkle, My Friend My Friend, Memories, David Bowie
● *Set II:* Dinner and a Movie, Mike's Song > I Am Hydrogen > Weekapaug Groove, Esther, Axilla, Bouncing Around the Room, Paul and Silas > Big Ball Jam, The Squirming Coil, Faht, Possum
● *Encore:* Contact, Good Times Bad Times
● *Show Notes:* During Guelah, Trey thanked the crowd for their support at the last American show of the year. He also thanked Mike and Dana from Greenpeace for their help on the tour and wished Dana a happy birthday. Guelah also included Fingerscrape and Simpsons Signals and Trey calling Page "Page 'The Savage' McConnell." Faht and Memories were performed without amplification. Hydrogen included The Vibration of Life. David Bowie contained a Moby Dick jam at the end, as well as Swing Low (Sweet Chariot) and Davy Crockett teases and an All Fall Down Signal during the hi-hat intro.

Saturday, December 12, 1992
The Spectrum, Toronto, Ontario, Canada
● *Set I:* Llama, Foam, Sparkle, Cavern, Reba, The Landlady, Split Open and Melt, Poor Heart, All Things Reconsidered, Bouncing Around the Room, Run Like an Antelope
● *Set II:* Maze, Glide, The Curtain, Tweezer, Rift, Guelah Papyrus, You Enjoy Myself, If I Only Had a Brain, The Squirming Coil, Golgi Apparatus
● *Encore:* Ride Captain Ride, Tweezer Reprise
● *Show Notes:* This show marked the band's first ever Canadian headlining performance. Listen for Davy Crockett teases in YEM and in the vocal jam. Brain was played for the first time since June 23, 1992 (59 shows) and Ride Captain Ride was played for the first time since April 14, 1990 (296 shows).

Sunday, December 13, 1992
Le Spectrum, Montreal, Quebec, Canada
● *Set I:* Buried Alive > Wilson, Divided Sky, It's Ice, Fee, Uncle Pen, Stash, Rift, Fast Enough for You, I Didn't Know, David Bowie
● *Set II:* Suzy Greenberg, Mound, Bouncing Around the Room, Llama, Fluffhead, Chalk Dust Torture, The Man Who Stepped Into Yesterday > Avenu Malkenu > The Man Who Stepped Into Yesterday Reprise, My Sweet One -> Big Ball Jam, Cracklin' Rosie, Harry Hood, Cavern
● *Encore:* Sweet Adeline, Rocky Top

Monday, December 28, 1992
Palace Theatre, New Haven, CT
● *Check:* Shaggy Dog, AC/DC Bag (twice, slowly)
● *Set I:* Maze, Sparkle, Buried Alive > Glide, It's Ice, Bouncing Around the Room, Rift, Golgi Apparatus, Sweet Adeline, Run Like an Antelope
● *Set II:* Poor Heart, Split Open and Melt, Reba, The Sloth, You Enjoy Myself, The Lizards, Bike, Harry Hood, Cavern
● *Encore:* Memories, Fire
● *Show Notes:* Bike was played for the first time since May 7, 1992 (73 shows).

Tuesday, December 29, 1992
Palace Theatre, New Haven, CT
● *Check:* Diamond Girl (with the Dude of Life)
● *Set I:* Funky Bitch, Runaway Jim, Guelah Papyrus, Llama, My Friend My Friend, Divided Sky, Wilson, Uncle Pen, Stash, Tela > The Oh Kee Pa Ceremony > Suzy Greenberg
● *Set II:* The Curtain > Tweezer, The Horse > Silent in the Morning, My Sweet One -> Big Ball Jam, Fast Enough for You, All Things Reconsidered, Mike's Song > I Am Hydrogen > Weekapaug Groove, HYHU > Terrapin > HYHU, The Squirming Coil, Tweezer Reprise
● *Encore:* Big Ball Jam, Carolina, Rocky Top
● *Show Notes:* Wilson included Simpsons, Random Note, and Fingerscrape Signals played over a jazzy interlude. The second Big Ball Jam was an *a cappella* version. Tweezer included Who Knows teases. Mike's Song included On Broadway and Blue Bayou (with All Fall Down Signal) teases. Mike again teased Blue Bayou during the Weekapaug opening. Terrapin was the slowest version ever, according to Trey's commentary at the show. It included Fishman introducing the band with various slow-related nicknames.

Wednesday, December 30, 1992
Symphony Hall, Springfield, MA
● *Check:* Ride Captain Ride, Ya Mar, Blues Jam
● *Set I:* The Landlady, Sparkle, Split Open and Melt, Esther, Chalk Dust Torture, Fluffhead, Paul and Silas, Reba -> I Walk The Line -> Reba, I Didn't Know, David Bowie -> Timber (Jerry) -> David Bowie
● *Set II:* Axilla, Rift, Bathtub Gin, You Enjoy Myself, The Man Who Stepped Into Yesterday > Avenu Malkenu > The Man Who Stepped Into Yesterday Reprise, Possum, Big Ball Jam -> Love You, Take the 'A' Train, Llama
● *Encore:* Ride Captain Ride, Sweet Adeline
● *Show Notes:* YEM included an Auld Lang Syne jam. TMWSIY was preceded by a humorous full-band dedication to cousins. Between sets, Jamie Janover entertained the audience on hammer dulcimer. Page teased Satin Doll during 'A' Train, which was dedicated to Trey's uncle. Timber was played for the first time since June 16, 1990 (272 shows).

Thursday, December 31, 1992
Matthews Arena, Northeastern University, Boston, MA
● *Set I:* Buried Alive > Poor Heart, Maze, Bouncing Around the Room, Rift, Wilson > Divided Sky, Cavern, Foam, I Didn't Know, Run Like an Antelope
● *Set II:* Runaway Jim, It's Ice, Sparkle > Colonel Forbin's Ascent > The Famous Mockingbird, My Sweet One > Big Ball Jam, Stash, Glide, Good Times Bad Times
● *Set III:* Mike's Song > Auld Lang Syne > Weekapaug Groove, Harpua

-> Kung -> Harpua, The Squirming Coil, Diamond Girl, Llama
● *Encore:* Carolina, Fire
● *Show Notes:* This show featured the debut (and only appearance) of Diamond Girl, which included a Dude of Life guest appearance. Wilson included a Simpsons Signal and Antelope included a Random Note Signal. Brad Sands was hoisted above the crowd as the Famous Mockingbird (in complete costume) during the Forbin's narration. This was the first time that Mike's and Weekapaug were played without Hydrogen in the middle as the band treated the audience to a fantastic New Year's transition. The Mike's combo was very intense and included Trey counting down to the New Year and telling the crowd that they better make the last minute of the year a good one. Kung was played for the first time since November 2, 1989 (351 shows).

WINTER/SPRING, 1993

Thursday, January 28, 1993
Hard Rock Cafe, Boston
Amazing Grace
● *Show Notes:* This was the *Rift* release party. Fishman donated his vacuum to the Cafe.

Wednesday, February 3, 1993
Portland Expo, Portland, ME
● *Set I:* Loving Cup, Rift, Fee, Llama, The Wedge, Divided Sky, I Didn't Know, My Friend My Friend, Poor Heart, Guelah Papyrus, David Bowie
● *Set II:* Runaway Jim, It's Ice, Tweezer, The Horse > Silent in the Morning, Sparkle, You Enjoy Myself, Lifeboy, HYHU > Terrapin > Big Ball Jam > HYHU, Possum
● *Encore:* Amazing Grace, Tweezer Reprise
● *Show Notes:* Loving Cup premiered at this show and was the first tune played on Page's new baby grand. Lifeboy also debuted at this show. Portions of My Friend and Horse featured Trey on acoustic guitar. YEM contained a My Girl tease and the "Water Your Team in a Beehive I'm a Sent You" lyrics. The Amazing Grace encore (also a debut) was performed without microphones.

Thursday, February 4, 1993
Providence Performing Arts Center, Providence, RI
● *Set I:* Axilla, Foam, Bouncing Around the Room, Maze, Fast Enough for You, All Things Reconsidered, Stash, The Lizards, Sample in a Jar, Glide, Run Like an Antelope
● *Set II:* Chalk Dust Torture, The Wedge, Mike's Song > The Man Who Stepped Into Yesterday > Avenu Malkenu > The Man Who Stepped Into Yesterday Reprise > Weekapaug Groove, Lawn Boy, Uncle Pen, Big Ball Jam, Lengthwise, Harry Hood, Cavern
● *Encore:* Amazing Grace, Good Times Bad Times
● *Show Notes:* This show included the first performance of Sample. Amazing Grace was performed without microphones.

Friday, February 5, 1993
Roseland Ballroom, New York, NY
● *Set I:* Llama, Guelah Papyrus, Rift, Split Open and Melt, Sparkle, Punch You in the Eye, I Didn't Know, Poor Heart, Reba, The Vibration of Life, David Bowie
● *Set II:* The Curtain, Tweezer, The Horse > Silent in the Morning, Paul and Silas, It's Ice, You Enjoy Myself, HYHU > Love You > HYHU, The Squirming Coil, Tweezer Reprise
● *Encore:* Amazing Grace, Loving Cup
● *Show Notes:* During PYITE (first since November 9, 1989, or 352 shows), Trey taught the crowd the "The Landlady/Punch You in the Eye storm dance." Bowie included The Vibration of Life, as well as Random Note and All Fall Down Signals. Tweezer featured a Funkytown tease. Squirming Coil was dedicated to Sofi Dillof. Amazing Grace was performed with microphones.

Saturday, February 6, 1993
Roseland Ballroom, New York, NY
● *Set I:* Golgi Apparatus, Foam, Wilson, My Friend My Friend, Maze, Horn, Divided Sky, Lawn Boy, The Wedge, Bouncing Around the Room, Run Like an Antelope
● *Set II:* Chalk Dust Torture, Mound, Stash, Sweet Adeline, All Things Reconsidered, Mike's Song > I Am Hydrogen > Weekapaug Groove, Lifeboy, Uncle Pen, Big Ball Jam, HYHU > Lengthwise > Buried Alive, Possum
● *Encore:* Fire
● *Show Notes:* Wilson included Simpsons and Random Note Signals and Maze featured an acoustic intro. Weekapaug was dedicated to Cilla Foster and included an extra verse. During Lengthwise, Fishman refused to tell The Prison Joke and sang a verse about burning your finger from holding a lighter up too long. Buried Alive, Possum and Fire featured John Popper on harmonica; Fire also featured Noel Redding on bass, with Mike moving over to keyboards.

Sunday, February 7, 1993
Lisner Auditorium, George Washington University, Washington, DC
● *Set I:* Suzy Greenberg > Buried Alive > Poor Heart, It's Ice, Sparkle, Colonel Forbin's Ascent > The Famous Mockingbird > Rift, I Didn't Know, Split Open and Melt, Fee, Runaway Jim
● *Set II:* Llama, Fast Enough for You, My Mind's Got a Mind of its Own, Reba, Bouncing Around the Room, Tweezer, Big Ball Jam, Glide, You Enjoy Myself, The Squirming Coil, If I Only Had a Brain, Tweezer Reprise
● *Encore:* Amazing Grace, Contact, Big Black Furry Creature from Mars
● *Show Notes:* Trey dedicated Llama to Chelsea Clinton and, with huge balloon and flowers in hand, dedicated Amazing Grace to his sister on her 30th birthday. Amazing Grace was performed without microphones. Reba included odd variations on the "Bag it/tag it" lyrics, an atypical jam, and a Simpsons Signal. The vocal jam in YEM included a brief piece of the traditional Clementine. MMGAMOIO was played for the first time since May 6, 1992 (82 shows).

Tuesday, February 9, 1993
Auditorium Theatre, Rochester, NY
● *Set I:* David Bowie, Bouncing Around the Room, Poor Heart, My Friend My Friend, Rift, The Wedge, Chalk Dust Torture, Esther -> Maze, Golgi Apparatus
● *Set II:* Punch You in the Eye -> Mike's Song > I Am Hydrogen > Weekapaug Groove > Weigh, My Sweet One, Sample in a Jar, Big Ball Jam, Stash, The Lizards, HYHU > Bike, Amazing Grace

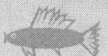

● *Encore:* Cavern, Rocky Top

Wednesday, February 10, 1993
Smith Opera House, Geneva, NY
● *Set I:* Loving Cup, Foam, Guelah Papyrus, Reba, The Sloth, Divided Sky, Tela, I Didn't Know, Catapult, Run Like an Antelope
● *Set II:* Runaway Jim, It's Ice, The Squirming Coil, Tweezer, I Walk the Line, Sparkle, You Enjoy Myself, The Horse > Silent in the Morning, HYHU > Cracklin' Rosie, Possum
● *Encore:* Sweet Adeline, Amazing Grace, Tweezer Reprise
● *Show Notes:* Sweet Adeline and Amazing Grace were performed without microphones. Catapult was played for the first time since April 21, 1992 (95 shows).

Thursday, February 11, 1993
Haas Center for the Arts, Bloomsburg, PA
● *Set I:* Suzy Greenberg, Buried Alive > Poor Heart, Stash, Fee, Rift, Fluffhead -> Llama, Lawn Boy, David Bowie
● *Set II:* The Landlady, Wilson -> Uncle Pen, Mike's Song > I Am Hydrogen > Weekapaug Groove, Mound, Big Ball Jam, Bouncing Around the Room, Love You, The Lizards, Cavern
● *Encore:* Bold as Love, Amazing Grace
● *Show Notes:* Bowie contained Simpsons and Oom Pa Pa Signals.

Friday, February 12, 1993
Mid-Hudson Civic Center, Poughkeepsie, NY
● *Set I:* Golgi Apparatus, Maze, Guelah Papyrus, Sparkle, Split Open and Melt, Esther, The Wedge, Chalk Dust Torture, I Didn't Know, Take the 'A' Train, Run Like an Antelope
● *Set II:* My Friend My Friend, All Things Reconsidered, Reba, Poor Heart, Big Ball Jam, Fast Enough for You, You Enjoy Myself, Ya Mar, HYHU > Terrapin, Harry Hood, Harpua
● *Encore:* Amazing Grace, Good Times Bad Times
● *Show Notes:* The Harpua narration included a Black or White jam as Jimmy was watching the halftime show of the Super Bowl and saw Michael Jackson. Poster killed Harpua and then had a heart attack. During the show, Trey remarked that Fishman is always late for the bus in the morning and that they have $1,000 bet on whether he can be on time for the entire tour. Harry Hood was played in response to chanting by a group in front. The break in Guelah featured an Oom Pa Pa Signal and the Esther intro included Simpsons and Random Note Signals. Ya Mar was played for the first time since April 24, 1992 (94 shows).

Saturday, February 13, 1993
Bob Carpenter Center, Newark, DE
● *Set I:* David Bowie, Bouncing Around the Room, Poor Heart, It's Ice, Glide, Rift, Stash, Lawn Boy, Maze, Golgi Apparatus
● *Set II:* Wilson, Runaway Jim, Uncle Pen, Tweezer, The Lizards, Llama, You Enjoy Myself, Big Ball Jam, HYHU > Lengthwise > HYHU, The Squirming Coil, Cavern
● *Encore:* Amazing Grace, Tweezer Reprise

Monday, February 15, 1993
Memorial Hall, University of North Carolina, Chapel Hill, NC
● *Set I:* Amazing Grace, Suzy Greenberg, Sparkle, Guelah Papyrus, Di-

vided Sky, Esther, Chalk Dust Torture, Mound, Stash, Guelah Papyrus, I Didn't Know, Run Like an Antelope
● *Set II:* Rift, Fast Enough for You, Reba, Mike's Song > I Am Hydrogen > Weekapaug Groove, The Wedge, Poor Heart -> Big Ball Jam > HYHU > Bike, Fee, Llama
● *Encore:* Contact, Fire
● *Show Notes:* At the request of Matt Heller, Fishman ran around the audience and balcony with his vacuum during Bike. Contact was dedicated to Charlie, the bus driver.

Wednesday, February 17, 1993
Benton Convention Center, Winston-Salem, NC
● *Set I:* Buried Alive, Possum, Weigh, All Things Reconsidered, The Sloth, Runaway Jim, It's Ice, Bouncing Around the Room, Fluffhead, Maze, Golgi Apparatus
● *Set II:* Axilla, The Landlady, David Bowie, Glide, My Friend My Friend, My Sweet One -> Big Ball Jam, Horn, You Enjoy Myself, Lengthwise, The Squirming Coil
● *Encore:* Carolina, Good Times Bad Times
● *Show Notes:* YEM included a Sunshine of Your Love vocal jam. Lengthwise was performed with vacuum accompaniment.

Thursday, February 18, 1993
Electric Ballroom, Knoxville, TN
● *Set I:* Chalk Dust Torture, Guelah Papyrus, Poor Heart, Tweezer -> Foam, Sparkle, Cavern, Reba, Lawn Boy, Run Like an Antelope
● *Set II:* Rift, Stash, The Lizards, Punch You in the Eye, Mike's Song > I Am Hydrogen > Weekapaug Groove, Mound, Amazing Grace, Memories, Sweet Adeline, Rocky Top
● *Show Notes:* Antelope included an All Fall Down Signal and Weekapaug featured a tease of Another One Bites the Dust. The soundboard shorted out during Mound. The band engaged in a rubber band fight between Sweet Adeline and Rocky Top.

Friday, February 19, 1993
Roxy Theatre, Atlanta, GA
● *Set I:* Loving Cup, Rift, Split Open and Melt, Fee -> Maze, Colonel Forbin's Ascent > The Famous Mockingbird, Sparkle, My Friend My Friend, Poor Heart > David Bowie
● *Set II:* Runaway Jim, It's Ice, Paul and Silas, You Enjoy Myself > Ya Mar, Big Ball Jam, Lawn Boy, Funky Bitch, My Sweet One, HYHU > Love You > HYHU, Llama, Amazing Grace
● *Encore:* AC/DC Bag
● *Show Notes:* The Forbin's narration recalled the flood from the last Atlanta show. This show was performed on Fishman's birthday, which Trey made reference to during the Bowie intro. Bowie also contained a Moby Dick jam, with Fishman soloing on both drums and vacuum, and a Simpsons Signal. There were also several Happy Birthday teases throughout the show. Funky Bitch through Llama featured Jimmy Herring guesting on guitar. Lawn Boy was dedicated to Page's parents. Big Ball Jam included a "Charge!" tease. Love You featured Fishman on guitar and vacuum, as well as the delivery of a birthday cake. During HYHU, Trey tried unsuccessfully to convince Colonel Bruce Hampton to come out and jam on horns. AC/DC Bag (first since May 16, 1992, or 83 shows) was played for "Hack's" 21st birthday, as he had evidently requested it at a party the night before. Amazing Grace was performed without microphones and

dedicated to Page's dad, who gave a standing ovation.

Saturday, February 20, 1993
Roxy Theatre, Atlanta, GA
● *Set I:* Golgi Apparatus, Foam, The Sloth, Possum > Weigh, All Things Reconsidered, Divided Sky, The Horse > Silent in the Morning, Fluffhead, Cavern
● *Set II:* Wilson > Reba, Tweezer -> Walk Away -> Tweezer > Glide > Mike's Song -> My Mind's Got a Mind of its Own -> Mike's Song > I Am Hydrogen -> Kung -> I Am Hydrogen > Weekapaug Groove -> Have Mercy -> Weekapaug Groove -> Rock and Roll All Nite Jam -> Weekapaug Groove, Fast Enough for You > Big Ball Jam > HYHU > Terrapin > HYHU -> Harry Hood, Tweezer Reprise
● *Encore:* Sleeping Monkey
● *Show Notes:* This show is noted for its legendary setlist, fun performances, and ridiculous musical teasing. This long version of Wilson included a Simpsons Signal and, towards the end, a freakish jam that included an Iron Man tease from Mike. Reba included a tease of the theme from *Woody Woodpecker*. Tweezer had a Low Rider jam and a "Straight From the Sewer" rap. Glide subsequently included Tweezer teases. This insane, loose Mike's Song featured minor lyric changes, three different Tweezer teases, two different Wilson teases, and other teases of Reba, Lizards, and Stash. Mike teased the Esther "circus" theme in Hydrogen, which was bookended by The Vibration of Life. The Rock and Roll All Nite jam was for a fan dressed as Kiss' Gene Simmons, who the band brought on stage to sing the song's chorus. Terrapin featured band intros and lots of chatter from Fish, prompting a hurry-up HYHU tease from Page. Fish also performed a lengthy vacuum solo during this tune. The HYHU outro segued nicely into Hood as Fish and Trey switched places. Neither Have Mercy (first since Halloween, 1986, or 479 shows) nor MMGAMOIO were played in their entirety. Walk Away was played for the first time since November 2, 1991 (157 shows).

Sunday, February 21, 1993
Roxy Theatre, Atlanta, GA
● *Set I:* Suzy Greenberg, Buried Alive, Punch You in the Eye, Uncle Pen, Horn > Chalk Dust Torture, Esther > Dinner and a Movie > Bouncing Around the Room > Run Like an Antelope
● *Set II:* Axilla, The Curtain > Stash -> Manteca -> Stash > The Lizards, Bathtub Gin -> HYHU > Cracklin' Rosie > HYHU, The Squirming Coil, Big Black Furry Creature from Mars
● *Encore:* Sweet Adeline, Good Times Bad Times -> Paul and Silas -> Pig in a Pen
● *Show Notes:* Prior to starting Suzy, the band sung the first line *a cappella* in a different manner than the rest of the song. Suzy also included a Tweezer tease. Esther began with Page modifying the intro (including a brief reggae attempt) and included a Simpsons Signal. Antelope included a *Woody Woodpecker* tease and a Random Note signal. Good Times Bad Times, which was performed bluegrass-style, through Pig in a Pen (a debut) featured the Reverend Jeff Mosier on banjo. Manteca was played for the first time since April 18, 1992 (106 shows).

Monday, February 22, 1993
The Moon, Tallahassee, FL
● *Set I:* Rift, Guelah Papyrus, Poor Heart, Maze, Sparkle, Foam, Fee,

Cavern, I Didn't Know, David Bowie
● *Set II:* Runaway Jim, Uncle Pen, It's Ice, Tweezer, You Enjoy Myself, Glide, The Oh Kee Pa Ceremony > Llama, HYHU > Love You, The Squirming Coil, Tweezer Reprise
● *Encore:* Amazing Grace, Fire
● *Show Notes:* Guelah Papyrus included Simpsons and Random Note Signals.

Tuesday, February 23, 1993
The Edge, Orlando, FL
● *Set I:* Golgi Apparatus, My Friend My Friend, Rift, Bouncing Around the Room, Split Open and Melt, Reba, Lawn Boy, Chalk Dust Torture, The Wedge, Paul and Silas, Run Like an Antelope
● *Set II:* Axilla, My Sweet One, Stash -> The Lizards, Punch You in the Eye, All Things Reconsidered, Mike's Song > I Am Hydrogen > Weekapaug Groove -> Pig in a Pen -> Weekapaug Groove, HYHU > Terrapin, Possum
● *Encore:* Sweet Adeline, Poor Heart

Thursday, February 25, 1993
The Cameo Theatre, Miami Beach, FL
● *Set I:* Buried Alive > Poor Heart, Cavern, Maze, Colonel Forbin's Ascent > The Famous Mockingbird, Rift, Stash, Bouncing Around the Room, I Didn't Know, David Bowie
● *Set II:* Suzy Greenberg > It's Ice, Sparkle > Wilson > You Enjoy Myself, Uncle Pen, Big Ball Jam > Fast Enough for You, HYHU > If I Only Had a Brain > HYHU, Golgi Apparatus > Big Black Furry Creature from Mars
● *Encore:* Amazing Grace, Good Times Bad Times
● *Show Notes:* Bowie included a tease of the theme from *Jeopardy!* Wilson included a Random Note Signal. This version of Forbin's included a surfing narration and a tease of the *Gilligan's Island* theme song. Brain featured Mimi Fishman on vacuum.

Friday, February 26, 1993
Ritz Theatre, Tampa, FL
● *Set I:* Runaway Jim, Foam, Fee, Split Open and Melt, Fluffhead, Llama, Horn, Divided Sky, I Didn't Know, Cavern
● *Set II:* Loving Cup, Paul and Silas, Tweezer, Glide, Chalk Dust Torture, Mound, Big Ball Jam, You Enjoy Myself, HYHU > Lengthwise, The Squirming Coil, Tweezer Reprise
● *Encore:* Bold As Love, Sweet Adeline

Saturday, February 27, 1993
Florida Theatre, Gainesville, FL
● *Set I:* Golgi Apparatus, Rift, Guelah Papyrus, Maze, Bouncing Around the Room, It's Ice, Sparkle, Punch You in the Eye, Lawn Boy, Run Like an Antelope
● *Set II:* The Curtain, Stash, Poor Heart, Sample in a Jar, Big Ball Jam, Ya Mar, Mike's Song > I Am Hydrogen > Weekapaug Groove, HYHU > Terrapin, Fee, Llama
● *Encore:* Sleeping Monkey, Amazing Grace, Rocky Top

Tuesday, March 2, 1993
Tipitina's, New Orleans, LA
● *Set I:* Buried Alive, Poor Heart, Stash, Reba, Sparkle, It's Ice, Fee, All

Things Reconsidered, Chalk Dust Torture, The Horse > Silent in the Morning, I Didn't Know, David Bowie
● *Set II:* My Friend My Friend, Uncle Pen, Tweezer, The Lizards, Llama, You Enjoy Myself, Love You, It's My Life, Loup Garou, Choo Choo Ch' Boogie, Harry Hood, Amazing Grace
● *Encore:* Golgi Apparatus, Tweezer Reprise
● *Show Notes:* It's My Life through Choo Choo Ch' Boogie featured Bruce "Sunpie" Barnes of Sunpie & the Louisiana Sunspots on washboard, harp, and lead vocals. During I Didn't Know, Fishman wore a Madonna-like pointy boob washboard while Trey and Mike loaded Mardi Gras beads on his head.

Wednesday, March 3, 1993
Tipitina's, New Orleans, LA
● *Set I:* Rift, Foam, Bouncing Around the Room, Maze, Guelah Papyrus, Paul and Silas, Sample in a Jar, Runaway Jim, Lawn Boy, Cavern
● *Set II:* Axilla, The Curtain, Split Open and Melt, Mound, Mike's Song > I Am Hydrogen > Weekapaug Groove, Glide, My Sweet One, Fast Enough for You, HYHU > Terrapin, The Squirming Coil, Sweet Adeline
● *Encore:* Fire
● *Show Notes:* Lawn Boy and Cavern featured Carl Gerhard on trumpet.

Friday, March 5, 1993
Deep Ellum Live, Dallas, TX
● *Set I:* Buried Alive > Poor Heart > Cavern, Foam, The Sloth, Rift, Stash, Sparkle -> It's Ice, I Didn't Know, Possum
● *Set II:* The Landlady > Chalk Dust Torture, Guelah Papyrus, Uncle Pen, Mike's Song, Jesus Just Left Chicago, My Sweet One -> Big Ball Jam, Love You, The Squirming Coil, Amazing Grace
● *Encore:* Good Times Bad Times
● *Show Notes:* JJLC was played for the first time since November 23, 1991 (152 shows).

Saturday, March 6, 1993
Liberty Lunch, Austin, TX
● *Check:* Everybody's Got a Missile, Sample in a Jar (twice), Blues Jam, My Friend My Friend (Trey solo on acoustic; intro only; twice)
● *Set I:* Llama, Horn, The Curtain, Split Open and Melt, Mound, Punch You in the Eye, Bouncing Around the Room, Maze, Golgi Apparatus, Runaway Jim
● *Set II:* Rift, Tweezer, Reba, Paul and Silas, Big Ball Jam, Fast Enough for You, You Enjoy Myself, HYHU > Cracklin' Rosie > HYHU, Big Black Furry Creature from Mars
● *Encore:* Sweet Adeline, Poor Heart, Tweezer Reprise

Monday, March 8, 1993
Sweeney Center, Santa Fe, NM
● *Set I:* Golgi Apparatus, Rift, Guelah Papyrus, The Oh Kee Pa Ceremony, Llama, Colonel Forbin's Ascent -> How High the Moon -> The Famous Mockingbird, Sparkle, It's Ice, Glide, David Bowie
● *Set II:* Poor Heart, Cavern, Uncle Pen, Stash, Big Ball Jam, My Friend My Friend -> Kung -> You Enjoy Myself, The Lizards, Amazing Grace
● *Encore:* Terrapin, HYHU, Chalk Dust Torture -> Big Ball Jam Reprise
● *Show Notes:* How High the Moon was played for the first time since April 26, 1990 (320 shows).

Tuesday, March 9, 1993
Pike's Peak Center, Colorado Springs, CO
● *Set I:* Runaway Jim, Foam, Bouncing Around the Room, Maze, Esther, Divided Sky, Glide, Punch You in the Eye, I Didn't Know, Run Like an Antelope
● *Set II:* Axilla, Rift, Tweezer, Reba, Lawn Boy, Mike's Song > I Am Hydrogen > Weekapaug Groove, The Horse > Silent in the Morning, Big Ball Jam, HYHU > Love You > HYHU, I Walk the Line, The Squirming Coil, Tweezer Reprise
● *Encore:* Amazing Grace, Rocky Top
● *Show Notes:* Antelope included Simpsons and All Fall Down Signals. Amazing Grace was performed without microphones and was preceded by an *a cappella* rendition of The Eleven by a tenor in the front of the balcony.

Friday, March 12, 1993
Daubson Arena, Vail, CO
● *Check:* Dog Gone Dog, Sample in a Jar, Lifeboy, Blues Jam
● *Set I:* Buried Alive, Poor Heart, Cavern, Possum, Guelah Papyrus, Rift, Stash, Fluffhead, The Horse > Silent in the Morning, David Bowie
● *Set II:* AC/DC Bag, My Friend My Friend, Axilla, Sparkle, You Enjoy Myself, Mound, Big Ball Jam, Chalk Dust Torture, HYHU, Lengthwise, Harry Hood, Golgi Apparatus
● *Encore:* Sweet Adeline, Carolina, Rocky Top
● *Show Notes:* Listen for a Random Note Signal and *Popeye* theme tease in Bowie. In an attempt to request AC/DC Bag at the start of the second set, roughly twenty people in front donned shopping bags on their heads with the word AC/DC written on them.

Saturday, March 13, 1993
Colorado University Field House, University of Colorado, Boulder, CO
● *Check:* Dog Gone Dog, Halley's Comet (twice), Blues Jam, Owner of a Lonely Heart
● *Set I:* The Landlady, Funky Bitch, Bouncing Around the Room, Maze, Fee, All Things Reconsidered, Split Open and Melt, Contact, Llama, Wilson, Run Like an Antelope
● *Set II:* Suzy Greenberg, Tweezer, The Lizards, It's Ice, Glide, Uncle Pen, Big Ball Jam, Mike's Song > I Am Hydrogen > Weekapaug Groove, Fast Enough for You, HYHU > Love You, Tweezer Reprise
● *Encore:* My Sweet One, Amazing Grace, Big Black Furry Creature from Mars
● *Show Notes:* Weekapaug included My Girl teases and Wilson included a soulful, improvisational opening jam and a Simpsons Signal. It has been said that Fishman wore a coat and tie for this show!

Sunday, March 14, 1993
Western State College Gym, Gunnison, CO
● *Check:* Halley's Comet, Tales of Brave Ulysses -> Sunshine of Your Love, The Ballad of Curtis Loew, Lifeboy
● *Set I:* Loving Cup, Foam, Guelah Papyrus, Sparkle, Stash, Paul and Silas, Sample in a Jar, Reba, Indian War Dance, Punch You in the Eye -> Runaway Jim
● *Set II:* Halley's Comet > David Bowie, The Ballad of Curtis Loew, You Enjoy Myself -> Spooky Jam -> You Enjoy Myself, Lifeboy, Rift, Big Ball Jam, The Great Gig in the Sky > HYHU, The Squirming Coil

● *Encore:* Memories, Sweet Adeline, Golgi Apparatus
● *Show Notes:* Owner of a Lonely Heart, Low Rider, and Oye Como Va were all teased or jammed during YEM and We Will Rock You and Welcome to the Machine were both a part of the YEM vocal jam. Great Gig debuted at this show. Sweet Adeline and Memories were performed without microphones. Curtis Loew was played for the first time since October 30, 1990 (285 shows) and Halley's Comet was played for the first time since August 17, 1989 (400 shows).

Tuesday, March 16, 1993
Celebrity Theatre, Phoenix, AZ
● *Check:* I Wanna Be Your Slave, Lifeboy, Dog Gone Dog, Blues Jam
● *Set I:* Sweet Adeline, Buried Alive > Poor Heart, It's Ice, Fee, Maze, I Didn't Know, Divided Sky, You Gotta See Mama Every Night, McGrupp and the Watchful Hosemasters, Cavern
● *Set II:* My Friend My Friend, The Curtain, Tweezer -> Sweet Emotion Jam -> Tweezer -> Bathtub Gin, Esther, Chalk Dust Torture, You Enjoy Myself, HYHU > Bike -> Lengthwise -> Bike, Lawn Boy, Llama, Amazing Grace
● *Encore:* Sparkle, Tweezer Reprise
● *Show Notes:* YEM did not contain a vocal jam. You Gotta See Mama Every Night was sung to Trey's grandmother by her husband, Harry Jones.

Wednesday, March 17, 1993
The Palace, Hollywood, CA
● *Check:* Self, Guy Forget, Shaggy Dog
● *Set I:* The Landlady > Runaway Jim, Foam, Bouncing Around the Room, Stash, Amazing Grace, Paul and Silas, It's Ice, The Oh Kee Pa Ceremony > Suzy Greenberg, Run Like an Antelope
● *Set II:* Axilla, Glide -> Reba, Jesus Just Left Chicago, Mound, Mike's Song > I Am Hydrogen > Weekapaug Groove, The Horse > Silent in the Morning, HYHU > The Great Gig in the Sky, Golgi Apparatus
● *Encore:* Sweet Adeline, Rocky Top
● *Show Notes:* Reba was never finished, as there was no whistling or final chorus. Fishman announced Great Gig as "The OK Gig In The Sky."

Thursday, March 18, 1993
The Palace, Hollywood CA
● *Set I:* Chalk Dust Torture, Guelah Papyrus, Rift, Fee, Maze, Colonel Forbin's Ascent > The Famous Mockingbird -> Sparkle, Horn, I Didn't Know, David Bowie
● *Set II:* My Friend My Friend, Poor Heart, Split Open and Melt, Tela, You Enjoy Myself, Uncle Pen, Big Ball Jam, HYHU > If I Only Had a Brain > HYHU, The Squirming Coil, Cavern
● *Encore:* Good Times Bad Times
● *Show Notes:* Bowie included All Fall Down and Simpsons Signals and My Friend featured a Little Drummer Boy jam. SOAM included Stayin' Alive teases. The second set opened with a Contact tease from Page. Seek out this second set for an excellent Coil.

Friday, March 19, 1993
The Greek Theatre, Redlands, CA
● *Check:* Dog Gone Dog (reggafied), Heartbreaker, Misty Mountain Hop, Bang a Gong
● *Set I:* Suzy Greenberg, Llama, Foam, Bouncing Around the Room,

Rift, Stash, Fluffhead, Cavern, Run Like an Antelope
● *Set II:* Runaway Jim, It's Ice, Uncle Pen, Sample in a Jar, The Lizards, Mike's Song > I Am Hydrogen > Weekapaug Groove -> HYHU > Love You > HYHU, Golgi Apparatus
● *Encore:* Amazing Grace, Chalk Dust Torture

Sunday, March 21, 1993
Ventura Theatre, Ventura, CA
● *Set I:* Maze, Sparkle, The Sloth, Divided Sky, Esther, All Things Reconsidered, Split Open and Melt, Poor Heart, Punch You in the Eye, Lawn Boy, Possum
● *Set II:* Loving Cup, My Friend My Friend, Rift -> Tweezer -> Ya Mar > You Enjoy Myself, My Sweet One, Big Ball Jam, HYHU > Cracklin' Rosie > HYHU, Llama, Harry Hood, Cavern
● *Encore:* Sleeping Monkey, Sweet Adeline, Tweezer Reprise

Monday, March 22, 1993
Crest Theatre, Sacramento, CA
● *Check:* Two Princes, Halley's Comet, Weigh
● *Set I:* Chalk Dust Torture, Guelah Papyrus, Uncle Pen, Stash, Bouncing Around the Room, Rift, Weigh, Reba, Sparkle, David Bowie
● *Set II:* Golgi Apparatus, It's Ice -> The Lizards, Tela, Wilson, AC/DC Bag, Colonel Forbin's Ascent > The Famous Mockingbird, The Sloth, McGrupp and the Watchful Hosemasters, Mike's Song > I Am Hydrogen > Weekapaug Groove
● *Encore:* Amazing Grace, Fire
● *Show Notes:* The second set included Gamehendge narration in between songs from Lizards through McGrupp. Amazing Grace was performed without microphones.

Wednesday, March 24, 1993
Luther Burbank Center for the Arts, Santa Rosa, CA
● *Set I:* Llama, Foam, Fee, Poor Heart, Maze, I Didn't Know, Sample in a Jar, Amazing Grace, Cavern
● *Set II:* The Landlady, Split Open and Melt, Sparkle, Tweezer, Mound, Big Ball Jam, Fast Enough for You, You Enjoy Myself, The Horse > Silent in the Morning, The Prison Joke, Terrapin, Good Times Bad Times
● *Encore:* Carolina, The Squirming Coil
● *Show Notes:* Amazing Grace and Carolina were performed without microphones.

Thursday, March 25, 1993
Santa Cruz Civic Auditorium, Santa Cruz, CA
● *Set I:* Chalk Dust Torture, Guelah Papyrus, It's Ice, Possum, Bouncing Around the Room, Stash, Glide, Rift, Horn, Magilla, Run Like an Antelope
● *Set II:* Axilla, The Curtain > Sample in a Jar, Uncle Pen, Colonel Forbin's Ascent -> Kung -> Icculus -> The Famous Mockingbird, The Wedge, Mike's Song > I Am Hydrogen > Weekapaug Groove, Golgi Apparatus
● *Encore:* My Sweet One, Big Ball Jam, Sweet Adeline
● *Show Notes:* Sweet Adeline was performed without microphones. Antelope and Weekapaug included Ob La Di, Ob La Da teases. Magilla (first since May 8, 1992, or 113 shows) included a tease of the theme from *Benny Hill*. Possum included Simpsons and Oom Pa Pa Signals. Icculus was played for the first time since May 2, 1992 (118 shows).

Friday, March 26, 1993
Warfield Theater, San Francisco, CA
● *Set I:* Maze, Sparkle, Foam, Punch You in the Eye, Fee, All Things Reconsidered, Split Open and Melt, Fluffhead, Divided Sky, Cavern
● *Set II:* Wilson, Runaway Jim, Tweezer, Mound, The Horse > Silent in the Morning, Big Ball Jam > You Enjoy Myself, The Oh Kee Pa Ceremony > Suzy Greenberg, The Great Gig in the Sky, Tweezer Reprise
● *Encore:* Amazing Grace, Rocky Top
● *Show Notes:* Amazing Grace was performed without microphones.

Saturday, March 27, 1993
Warfield Theatre, San Francisco, CA
● *Set I:* Llama, Guelah Papyrus, Rift, Stash, Reba, My Friend My Friend, Uncle Pen, Sample in a Jar, I Didn't Know, David Bowie
● *Set II:* Buried Alive > Halley's Comet, It's Ice, Bouncing Around the Room, Chalk Dust Torture, The Man Who Stepped Into Yesterday > Avenu Malkenu > The Man Who Stepped Into Yesterday Reprise, Mike's Song > I Am Hydrogen > Weekapaug Groove, Cracklin' Rosie, Poor Heart, Golgi Apparatus
● *Encore:* The Squirming Coil, Carolina
● *Show Notes:* This excellent Weekapaug featured an On Broadway tease. Listen before Carolina for an *a cappella* Suzy Greenberg quote.

Sunday, March 28, 1993
East Gym, Humbolt State University, Arcata, CA
● *Set I:* The Landlady, Funky Bitch, Sparkle, Split Open and Melt, The Lizards, The Sloth, Maze, Fee, It's Ice, Lawn Boy, Run Like an Antelope
● *Set II:* Walk Away, Runaway Jim, Mound, Bathtub Gin, Big Ball Jam, You Enjoy Myself, Paul and Silas, HYHU > Love You > HYHU, Possum
● *Encore:* Contact, Big Black Furry Creature from Mars
● *Show Notes:* YEM included the Pez Song for "Dave the Pez Man". Listen for teases of Fishing Hole Theme, the theme from *Beverly Hills Cop*, and Speed Racer in the Antelope and for McGrupp teases during Possum. Also, there were repeated teases of the *Leave It to Beaver* theme in BBFCFM, primarily from Mike. During Contact, Trey wished Shelly Culbertson a safe journey on her trip out to Boston.

Tuesday, March 30, 1993
Hilton Ballroom, Eugene, OR
● *Set I:* Buried Alive > Poor Heart > All Things Reconsidered, Golgi Apparatus, My Friend My Friend > Llama, Esther, Stash, Glide > Divided Sky, Cavern
● *Set II:* Loving Cup > Rift > Tweezer > Lifeboy, Big Ball Jam > Weigh, Mike's Song > I Am Hydrogen > Weekapaug Groove -> Psycho Killer Jam -> Weekapaug Groove, The Horse > Silent in the Morning, HYHU > If I Only Had a Brain > HYHU, Tweezer Reprise
● *Encore:* My Sweet One, Amazing Grace
● *Show Notes:* Mike dedicated Mike's Song to himself. The band subsequently included several references to it being "his song."

Wednesday, March 31, 1993
Roseland Theater, Portland, OR
● *Set I:* Runaway Jim, Foam, Sparkle, Split Open and Melt, Mound, Punch You in the Eye, Sample in a Jar, Reba, I Didn't Know, David Bowie
● *Set II:* Lengthwise -> Maze, Bouncing Around the Room, Uncle Pen,

Harry Hood, Big Ball Jam, It's Ice, You Enjoy Myself, Harpua, Chalk Dust Torture
● *Encore:* AC/DC Bag, Sweet Adeline
● *Show Notes:* I Didn't Know featured Fishman on washboard. Bowie included All Fall Down and Simpsons Signals; Hood later contained another Simpsons Signal and a *Pink Panther* theme tease. Listen at the end of It's Ice for a brief interlude that later became the tag ending to Axilla Pt. II. Harpua contained Axle F (*Beverly Hills Cop* theme) and She's So Cold (a Rolling Stones song) teases. Sweet Adeline was dedicated to Nina, who lost her ID and got it back from Trey on stage.

Thursday, April 1, 1993
Roseland Theater, Portland, OR
● *Set I:* Llama, Guelah Papyrus, Rift, Stash, The Squirming Coil, My Friend My Friend, Paul and Silas, Fluffhead, Lawn Boy, Run Like an Antelope
● *Set II:* Axilla, The Curtain > Possum, Fee > Ya Mar, Tweezer, Poor Heart, Big Ball Jam, HYHU > Love You > HYHU, Cavern
● *Encore:* Carolina, Tweezer Reprise
● *Show Notes:* I Feel the Earth Move and Barracuda teases were heard in this Antelope. Carolina was performed without microphones. After the Big Ball Jam, Trey introduced Fishman as Neil Young. Fishman responded by singing a quiet line from Neil Young's Needle and the Damage Done before launching into Love You.

Friday, April 2, 1993
Mt. Baker Theatre, Bellingham, WA
● *Set I:* Buried Alive, Poor Heart, Foam, Bouncing Around the Room, Divided Sky, I Didn't Know, Sparkle, Maze, Golgi Apparatus
● *Set II:* Runaway Jim, Sample in a Jar, Uncle Pen, Llama, The Horse > Silent in the Morning, Mike's Song > I Am Hydrogen > Weekapaug Groove, The Lizards -> Big Ball Jam, HYHU > Bike > HYHU, Chalk Dust Torture
● *Encore:* Amazing Grace, Rocky Top

Saturday, April 3, 1993
86th Street Music Hall, Vancouver, BC, Canada
● *Set I:* The Landlady > Rift, Guelah Papyrus, Sparkle, Split Open and Melt, The Squirming Coil, My Friend My Friend, Reba, Horn, Run Like an Antelope
● *Set II:* Suzy Greenberg, Stash, Mound, All Things Reconsidered, The Sloth, You Enjoy Myself, Jesus Just Left Chicago, My Sweet One, HYHU > Love You > HYHU, Cavern
● *Encore:* Good Times Bad Times

Monday, April 5, 1993
HUB Ballroom, Seattle, WA
● *Set I:* Llama, It's Ice, Fee, Maze, Fluffhead, Paul and Silas, Stash, Colonel Forbin's Ascent > The Famous Mockingbird, David Bowie
● *Set II:* Axilla, Poor Heart, Caravan, Punch You in the Eye, Tweezer, Glide, You Enjoy Myself, Cracklin' Rosie, Tweezer Reprise
● *Show Notes:* Caravan was played for the first time since September 25, 1991 (214 shows).

Friday, April 9, 1993
State Theatre, Minneapolis MN
● *Check:* Miss You > Take Me to the River > Can't You Hear Me

Knockin' Jam, The Wedge, The Great Gig in the Sky
● *Set I:* Chalk Dust Torture, Sparkle, Guelah Papyrus, Stash, The Horse > Silent in the Morning, Maze, I Didn't Know, It's Ice, Divided Sky, Cavern
● *Set II:* Buried Alive, Suzy Greenberg, All Things Reconsidered, Llama, Mound, My Friend My Friend, You Enjoy Myself, My Sweet One, HYHU > Love You, Possum
● *Encore:* Sweet Adeline, Golgi Apparatus

Saturday, April 10, 1993
Aragon Ballroom, Chicago, IL
● *Set I:* Runaway Jim, Weigh, Sparkle, Split Open and Melt, The Squirming Coil, My Friend My Friend, Uncle Pen, Chalk Dust Torture, Lawn Boy, David Bowie
● *Set II:* Lengthwise -> Maze, Bouncing Around the Room, Rift, Glide, Big Ball Jam, Mike's Song -> The Great Gig in the Sky > Weekapaug Groove, Funky Bitch, Help Me, Hoochie Coochie Man, Cavern
● *Encore:* Amazing Grace, Good Times Bad Times
● *Show Notes:* Funky Bitch through Cavern featured Sugar Blue on harmonica and vocals. David Bowie included a tease medley opening, and Mike's Song included a jam of The Rolling Stones' Miss You.

Monday, April 12, 1993
IMU Ballroom, University of Iowa, Iowa City, IA
● *Set I:* Golgi Apparatus, Tube, Bouncing Around the Room, Poor Heart, Stash, The Horse > Silent in the Morning, Reba, Llama, Satin Doll, Run Like an Antelope
● *Set II:* Dinner and a Movie, Tweezer, Fee, Paul and Silas, It's Ice, Big Ball Jam, You Enjoy Myself -> Honky Tonk Women Jam -> Vocal Jam, Terrapin, Tweezer Reprise
● *Encore:* Amazing Grace, Highway to Hell, Rocky Top
● *Show Notes:* Between Llama and Satin Doll, Trey told a story about how his great-grandmother went to the University of Iowa and used to attend dances in the same venue and dance to the big band music of Dizzy Gillespie, so they played Satin Doll with Page on vocals. The YEM vocal jam included bits of New York, New York and Swing Low (Sweet Chariot). Tube was played for the first time since November 20, 1992 (73 shows), Highway to Hell was played for the first time since November 15, 1991 (184 shows), and Satin Doll was played for the first time since February 25, 1990 (370 shows).

Wednesday, April 14, 1993
American Theater, St. Louis, MO
● *Set I:* Buried Alive, Poor Heart, Maze, Bouncing Around the Room, It's Ice, Stash -> Kung -> Stash, The Horse > Silent in the Morning, Divided Sky, I Didn't Know, Golgi Apparatus
● *Set II:* AC/DC Bag, My Sweet One, Tweezer, Mound, Big Ball Jam, You Enjoy Myself -> Spooky Jam -> You Enjoy Myself, Harpua > Runaway Jim
● *Encore:* Lengthwise > Contact, Tweezer Reprise
● *Show Notes:* Stash included DEG teases. The acoustic intro to The Horse included a brief Pinball Wizard jam and a portion of the composed section of Harry Hood backing up a reprise of Kung. At the beginning of the second set, Trey's friend Roger got on stage and asked his girlfriend Jen to marry him. She said yes, and in response the band played AC/DC Bag (which references Roger in the lyrics). The Spooky Jam raged inside this fantastic YEM, and even included a verse sung by

Page. Harpua featured Dreamweaver and *The Jetson's* theme teases as well as vocal quotes from The End. The narration centered around a story about people who steal your dreams at night. AC/DC Bag included a My Woman from Tokyo tease.

Friday, April 16, 1993
McCauley Theater, Louisville, KY
● *Set I:* Chalk Dust Torture, Guelah Papyrus, Sparkle > Split Open and Melt, Esther, Llama, Sample in a Jar, Rift, Harry Hood, Cavern
● *Set II:* Axilla, The Curtain > Maze, The Lizards, Mike's Song > I Am Hydrogen > Weekapaug Groove, The Horse > Silent in the Morning, Uncle Pen, Big Ball Jam > HYHU > Bike > HYHU, Highway to Hell
● *Encore:* Gumbo, Amazing Grace
● *Show Notes:* Before Chalk Dust, Trey chided Fishman for being late. Hood included a Simpsons Signal. Trey dedicated Highway to Hell to Terry, the equipment truck driver. Gumbo was played for the first time since July 25, 1991 (223 shows).

Saturday, April 17, 1993
Michigan Theatre, Ann Arbor, MI
● *Check:* I Can't Explain, Substitute (brief), I Can See For Miles > Sparks, LA Woman
● *Set I:* Llama, Foam, Bouncing Around the Room, Stash, It's Ice, Glide, My Friend My Friend, All Things Reconsidered, Golgi Apparatus, Run Like an Antelope
● *Set II:* Wilson, Reba, The Landlady > Halley's Comet, You Enjoy Myself, Lifeboy, The Oh Kee Pa Ceremony > Suzy Greenberg, HYHU > Cracklin' Rosie > HYHU, Big Ball Jam, The Squirming Coil
● *Encore:* Sweet Adeline, Big Black Furry Creature from Mars
● *Show Notes:* My Friend included an Ob La Di, Ob La Da tease. BBJ featured Trey on drums and Fishman on vacuum. During BBFCFM, Trey forgot he was supposed to start part of the song, and there was quite a bit of silence on stage until he finally realized that the rest of the band was waiting for him. BBFCFM also included some humorous additional lyrics from Mike, who echoed a fan's cry that he could "smell [himself] running." YEM included teases of the closing jam to I Wish. Antelope included Random Note and Simpsons Signals.

Sunday, April 18, 1993
Michigan Theatre, Ann Arbor, MI
● *Set I:* Rift, Guelah Papyrus, Split Open and Melt, Sparkle, Divided Sky, Fee -> Maze, Horn, I Didn't Know, Cavern
● *Set II:* Poor Heart > Tweezer, The Horse > Silent in the Morning, Possum, Mound, Big Ball Jam, Mike's Song -> Ya Mar, Walk Away, HYHU > Love You > HYHU, Tweezer Reprise
● *Encore:* Amazing Grace, Rocky Top
● *Show Notes:* During the section of I Didn't Know where Fishman usually does some sort of solo, Page asked everyone who had been there the night before how they liked the encore. Trey and Mike put their microphones in the same position as they were for BBFCFM, and Page brought people on stage to give testimonials about how they felt about it. Special guests included Brad Sands and Chris Kuroda. Trey admitted his guilt in the mishap and the song continued. Horse included an extended intro section. Mike's song included a melodic Low Rider jam before segueing into Ya Mar.

Tuesday, April 20, 1993
Newport Music Hall, Columbus, OH
● *Set I:* Runaway Jim, Weigh, Sparkle, Stash, Bouncing Around the Room, It's Ice, Glide, Uncle Pen, Lawn Boy, David Bowie
● *Set II:* Chalk Dust Torture, Fluffhead, Sample in a Jar, Big Ball Jam, The Man Who Stepped Into Yesterday > Avenu Malkenu > The Man Who Stepped Into Yesterday Reprise, My Friend My Friend, Llama, You Enjoy Myself, HYHU > Whipping Post, Golgi Apparatus
● *Encore:* Funky Bitch, Amazing Grace
● *Show Notes:* Amazing Grace was performed without microphones. Whipping Post was played for the first time since December 5, 1992 (66 shows).

Wednesday, April 21, 1993
Newport Music Hall, Columbus, OH
● *Set I:* Buried Alive, Poor Heart, Foam, Guelah Papyrus, Maze, Colonel Forbin's Ascent > The Famous Mockingbird, Rift, Punch You in the Eye, I Didn't Know, Run Like an Antelope
● *Set II:* Possum, Mound, Split Open and Melt, The Squirming Coil, The Horse > Silent in the Morning, Big Ball Jam, Mike's Song > The Great Gig in the Sky > Weekapaug Groove, Gumbo
● *Encore:* Sweet Adeline, Cavern
● *Show Notes:* The jam segment of this Melt is the one that appears at the end of Demand on *Hoist*.

Thursday, April 22, 1993
The Agora Theatre, Cleveland, OH
● *Set I:* Suzy Greenberg, Sparkle, It's Ice, Reba, Chalk Dust Torture, Esther, Stash, Fee, Rift, Golgi Apparatus
● *Set II:* Llama, Bouncing Around the Room, All Things Reconsidered, Tweezer, The Lizards, Big Ball Jam, You Enjoy Myself, Uncle Pen, HYHU > Love You, Tweezer Reprise
● *Encore:* AC/DC Bag, Amazing Grace
● *Show Notes:* The Vibration of Life was played during YEM.

Friday, April 23, 1993
Colgate University Athletic Center, Hamilton, NY
● *Set I:* Runaway Jim, Weigh, Sparkle, Split Open and Melt, Fluffhead, My Friend My Friend, Divided Sky, Guelah Papyrus, Lawn Boy, Chalk Dust Torture
● *Set II:* Golgi Apparatus, Maze, The Ballad of Curtis Loew, It's Ice, Paul and Silas, Big Ball Jam, Mike's Song > I Am Hydrogen > Weekapaug Groove, HYHU > Lengthwise > HYHU, The Squirming Coil, Highway to Hell
● *Encore:* Fire
● *Show Notes:* This Weekapaug included atypical, jazz-laced jams. Lengthwise featured Mimi Fishman on vacuum. Apparently, while she was attempting to master the "instrument," members of the band paraded around the stage with school banners they had borrowed from the locker room. There was a long break before the encore; apparently, the venue officials wanted the show to be over.

Saturday, April 24, 1993
Cheel Arena, Clarkson University, Potsdam, NY
● *Set I:* Chalk Dust Torture, Guelah Papyrus, Poor Heart > Stash, The Horse > Silent in the Morning, Rift > Caravan, When Something is Wrong with My Baby, Sparkle, Run Like an Antelope
● *Set II:* Llama, Foam, Bathtub Gin, Dinner and a Movie > Mound > Big Ball Jam, You Enjoy Myself, HYHU > Bike > HYHU, Harry Hood, Cavern
● *Encore:* Amazing Grace, Good Times Bad Times
● *Show Notes:* When Something is Wrong with My Baby debuted at this show.

Sunday, April 25, 1993
SUNY Geneseo, Kuhl Hall, Geneseo, NY
● *Set I:* The Landlady, Possum, Bouncing Around the Room, It's Ice, Glide, Runaway Jim, Colonel Forbin's Ascent > The Famous Mockingbird, Maze, I Didn't Know, Golgi Apparatus
● *Set II:* Wilson, The Curtain, Tweezer, Contact, Uncle Pen, Big Ball Jam, Mike's Song > I Am Hydrogen > Weekapaug Groove, Fee, Tweezer Reprise
● *Encore:* When Something is Wrong with My Baby, Carolina, Rocky Top

Tuesday, April 27, 1993
Concert Hall, Toronto, Canada
● *Set I:* Buried Alive > Poor Heart, Foam, Bouncing Around the Room, Rift, Stash, Guelah Papyrus, It's Ice, Sparkle, David Bowie
● *Set II:* Golgi Apparatus, My Friend My Friend, All Things Reconsidered, Maze, The Lizards, Big Ball Jam, You Enjoy Myself, Silent in the Morning, Love You, Cavern
● *Encore:* My Sweet One, Amazing Grace
● *Show Notes:* YEM featured teases of Gordon Lightfoot's Sundown, in both the song and the vocal jam. Silent was actually played without The Horse.

Thursday, April 29, 1993
Le Spectrum, Montreal, Canada
● *Check:* Reggae Jam
● *Set I:* Split Open and Melt, Uncle Pen, The Sloth, Runaway Jim, Horn, Llama, Glide, Rift, Fee, Run Like an Antelope
● *Set II:* Chalk Dust Torture, It's Ice > Ya Mar, Mound, Big Ball Jam, Reba, Mike's Song > I Am Hydrogen > Weekapaug Groove -> Makisupa Policeman -> Weekapaug Groove, HYHU > Terrapin > HYHU, The Squirming Coil
● *Encore:* My Friend My Friend
● *Show Notes:* Some of the fans cheered the mention of Quebec during Fee. Antelope included a brief jam on Pink Floyd's Money. Ya Mar contained some funny stage banter, as Trey tried to bring "Leo" in too early. It also included a Can't Turn You Loose tease from Page. Hydrogen included a tease of I've Got Spurs That Jingle Jangle Jingle, with a bassline somewhat akin to Happy Trails. Weekapaug included a Can't You Hear Me Knockin' tease from Page. Fishman dedicated Terrapin to his friends from Burlington who made the trip to see the band. Makisupa was played for the first time since November 26, 1990 (307 shows).

Friday, April 30, 1993
University Of Hartford, West Hartford, CT
● *Set I:* Lengthwise -> Maze, Bouncing Around the Room, Poor Heart, Stash, The Horse > Silent in the Morning, Divided Sky, Cavern, Lawn Boy, All Things Reconsidered, Possum
● *Set II:* Wilson, Sparkle, Tweezer -> Walk Away -> Mound, Big Ball

Jam, Harry Hood, HYHU > If I Only Had a Brain, You Enjoy Yourself, Golgi Apparatus
● *Encore:* When Something is Wrong with My Baby, Amazing Grace, Tweezer Reprise

Saturday, May 1, 1993
Tower Theatre, Philadelphia, PA
● *Check:* Poor Heart (*a cappella*), Odd Couple Jam, Brother
● *Set I:* Runaway Jim, Foam, Guelah Papyrus, Split Open and Melt, Fee, Rift, Sample in a Jar, It's Ice, Glide > David Bowie
● *Set II:* Chalk Dust Torture, Fluffhead > My Friend My Friend, The Squirming Coil, Big Ball Jam > Halley's Comet > Paul and Silas, Mike's Song -> The Great Gig in the Sky -> Weekapaug Groove, Cavern
● *Encore:* Carolina, Rocky Top
● *Show Notes:* Mike's Song included teases of what would become the riff to Simple, as well as a tease of Neil Young & Crazy Horse's Fuckin' Up.

Sunday, May 2, 1993
Tower Theatre, Philadelphia, PA
● *Set I:* Axilla, Sparkle, Divided Sky, Mound, Stash, The Horse > Silent in the Morning, Poor Heart, Maze, I Didn't Know, Golgi Apparatus
● *Set II:* Llama, Punch You in the Eye, You Enjoy Yourself, The Lizards -> Big Ball Jam, Uncle Pen, Bouncing Around the Room, Run Like an Antelope, HYHU > Cracklin' Rosie, Big Black Furry Creature from Mars
● *Encore:* Sleeping Monkey, Amazing Grace
● *Show Notes:* YEM included Speed Racer and Oye Como Va teases. Antelope included Simpsons and All Fall Down Signals. Sleeping Monkey was delayed while Trey scrambled to remember the lyrics. He remarked that it was particularly embarrassing since Tom Marshall was in the audience. After Antelope, Fishman listened to the crowd's requests, including Trey's request of Undun, before settling on Rosie.

Monday, May 3, 1993
State Theatre, New Brunswick, NJ
● *Set I:* Buried Alive, Rift, Weigh, Chalk Dust Torture, Esther, Split Open and Melt, Colonel Forbin's Ascent > The Famous Mockingbird, Possum, Lawn Boy, Cavern
● *Set II:* AC/DC Bag, The Curtain, Tweezer -> Manteca -> Tweezer, Contact, It's Ice, McGrupp and the Watchful Hosemasters, Runaway Jim, Love You, My Sweet One, Tweezer Reprise
● *Encore:* Highway to Hell
● *Show Notes:* Tweezer included an I Feel the Earth Move tease.

Wednesday, May 5, 1993
Palace Theatre, Albany, NY
● *Check:* Give a Little Bit, Poor Heart Blues, Funky Bitch Blues, Brother
● *Set I:* Rift, Guelah Papyrus, Foam, Sparkle, Stash, Bouncing Around the Room, It's Ice > Glide > Maze, Golgi Apparatus
● *Set II:* Runaway Jim > My Friend My Friend -> Manteca -> My Friend My Friend, Poor Heart, Weigh -> Big Ball Jam, Ya Mar, You Enjoy Myself -> Jam
● *Encore:* Amazing Grace, Cavern -> Take the 'A' Train -> Cavern
● *Show Notes:* The jam after YEM featured The Aquarium Rescue Unit and the Dude of Life and was simply amazing. It also included a Who Knows tease. This show was full of anomalies, including variations on usually unchanged songs like My Friend and Cavern. A-Train was played

for the first time since February 12, 1993 (58 shows). Trey dedicated Ya Mar to Sue on her birthday. Ya Mar subsequently included a Two Princes tease.

Thursday, May 6, 1993
Palace Theatre, Albany NY
● *Set I:* Chalk Dust Torture, Mound, Split Open and Melt, The Horse > Silent in the Morning, All Things Reconsidered, Llama, Fluffhead, Possum, Lawn Boy, Why You've Been Gone So Long, Tennessee Waltz, I Been to Georgia on a Fast Train
● *Set II:* Suzy Greenberg, Tweezer, Tela, Uncle Pen, Big Ball Jam, The Squirming Coil, Mike's Song -> Ob La Di Ob La Da Jam -> Rocky Top, HYHU > Cracklin' Rosie, That's Alright Mama
● *Encore:* Sweet Adeline, Contact > Tweezer Reprise
● *Show Notes:* Why You've Been Gone So Long, Rocky Top, and HYHU featured Dick Solberg on violin. Tennessee Waltz, Fast Train, and That's Alright Mama featured Solberg on violin and Jeff Walton on acoustic guitar; the two also provided vocals on Tennessee Waltz. Why You've Been Gone So Long also featured Walton on vocals. Tweezer included a Sweet Emotion tease.

Friday, May 7, 1993
Bangor Municipal Auditorium, Bangor, ME
● *Set I:* Buried Alive > Poor Heart, Split Open and Melt, Sparkle, Caravan -> Manteca -> The Lizards, Horn, Divided Sky, I Didn't Know, Run Like an Antelope
● *Set II:* Rift, Bouncing Around the Room, Maze, Fee -> Big Ball Jam, You Enjoy Myself, The Great Gig in the Sky, Harry Hood, Harpua, Highway to Hell
● *Encore:* Amazing Grace, Golgi Apparatus
● *Show Notes:* Harpua included pieces of Crossroads, which would debut the following day. YEM included a Who Knows jam.

Saturday, May 8, 1993
University of New Hampshire Field House, Durham, NH
● *Set I:* Chalk Dust Torture, Guelah Papyrus, Rift, Mound, Stash -> Kung -> Stash, Glide, My Friend My Friend, Reba, Satin Doll, Cavern
● *Set II:* David Bowie -> Jessica Jam -> David Bowie -> Have Mercy -> David Bowie, The Horse > Silent in the Morning, It's Ice, The Squirming Coil -> Jam -> Big Ball Jam > Mike's Song -> Crossroads -> Mike's Song > I Am Hydrogen > Weekapaug Groove, Amazing Grace > Amazing Grace Jam
● *Encore:* AC/DC Bag
● *Show Notes:* The intro to Bowie included Simpsons and Random Note Signals, and an Amazing Grace tease from Mike. Subsequently, Mike's and Weekapaug both included Amazing Grace teases. The Amazing Grace Jam was played to a Weekapaug-esque drumbeat. Crossroads debuted at this show. The breakdown in It's Ice included a tease of one of the guitar lines from Discipline (King Crimson) and a Manteca tease.

Saturday, May 29, 1993
Laguna Seca Daze, Laguna Seca Raceway, Monterey, CA
Chalk Dust Torture, Bouncing Around the Room, Stash, Sparkle, The Squirming Coil, Cavern, You Enjoy Myself, Big Ball Jam, Runaway Jim, Amazing Grace
● *Encore:* Good Times Bad Times

Sunday, May 30, 1993
Laguna Seca Daze, Laguna Seca Raceway, Monterey, CA
Lengthwise > Maze, Guelah Papyrus, Poor Heart, Foam, Ya Mar, Silent in the Morning, Run Like an Antelope, I Didn't Know, Split Open and Melt, Contact, Llama, Golgi Apparatus
● *Encore:* Possum
● *Show Notes:* Silent was actually played without The Horse. I Didn't Know was dedicated to the guy stuck on top of the Ferris Wheel. Possum included a tease of LA Woman.

SUMMER/WINTER, 1993

Thursday, July 15, 1993
Cayuga County Fairgrounds, Weedsport, NY
● *Set I:* Rift, Sample in a Jar, Divided Sky, Mound, Stash, I Didn't Know, My Mind's Got a Mind of its Own, Leprechaun > Runaway Jim
● *Set II:* David Bowie, The Horse > Silent in the Morning, Sparkle, It's Ice, Lifeboy, Possum, Faht, The Lizards, Walk Away, Daniel
● *Encore:* Chalk Dust Torture, Freebird
● *Show Notes:* This show marked the debuts of Leprechaun, Daniel, and the *a cappella* Freebird. Stash included a Little Drummer Boy jam. MMGAMOIO was played for the first time since February 20, 1993 (58 shows) and Faht was played for the first time since December 11, 1992 (79 shows).

Friday, July 16, 1993
Mann Music Center, Philadelphia, PA
● *Set I:* Daniel, Golgi Apparatus, My Friend My Friend, Ya Mar, Buried Alive, Fast Enough for You, All Things Reconsidered, Nellie Kane, Horn, Run Like an Antelope
● *Set II:* Also Sprach Zarathustra > Split Open and Melt, Glide > Maze, Bouncing Around the Room, You Enjoy Myself -> Yerushalayim Shel Zahav -> You Enjoy Myself, Poor Heart, Purple Rain, Harry Hood, Cavern
● *Encore:* Llama, Freebird
● *Show Notes:* This show featured the debuts of Nellie Kane, Yerushalayim Shel Zahav, Also Sprach, and Purple Rain.

Saturday, July 17, 1993
The Filene Center, Wolf Trap Farm Park, Vienna, VA
● *Check:* Jump Monk tease, Shaggy Dog, Nellie Kane, Leprechaun, The Mango Song (twice), Funky Bitch (twice), Punch You in the Eye, Blues Jam
● *Set I:* The Landlady, Runaway Jim, Sample in a Jar, My Mind's Got a Mind of its Own, Stash, Reba, Chalk Dust Torture, The Horse > Silent in the Morning, The Oh Kee Pa Ceremony > David Bowie
● *Set II:* Also Sprach Zarathustra > Tweezer, The Squirming Coil, It's Ice, Sparkle, Big Ball Jam, Mike's Song > Leprechaun > Weekapaug Groove, Faht, Rift, Good Times Bad Times
● *Encore:* Amazing Grace, Daniel, Tweezer Reprise

Sunday, July 18, 1993
IC Light Amphitheater, Pittsburgh, PA
● *Check:* Buffalo Bill, Guyute (partial), Jam

● *Set I:* Buried Alive, Rift, Foam, Guelah Papyrus, Maze, Esther, Divided Sky, Uncle Pen, Cavern
● *Set II:* Also Sprach Zarathustra, Poor Heart, Run Like an Antelope, Mound, Fast Enough for You, All Things Reconsidered, Fee, You Enjoy Myself -> Purple Rain, Golgi Apparatus
● *Encore:* Rocky Top, Freebird
● *Show Notes:* The soundcheck treated those who arrived early to the first-ever Guyute, which was an unfinished, raw version of the song that eventually made it to the stage fifteen months later.

Wednesday, July 21, 1993
Orange County Fairgrounds, Middletown, NY
Also Sprach Zarathustra, Split Open and Melt, Sparkle, The Squirming Coil, Maze, Glide, Rift, Bouncing Around the Room, Runaway Jim, Big Ball Jam, Purple Rain > HYHU, Daniel
● *Encore:* Chalk Dust Torture
● *Show Notes:* This show was part of the HORDE festival.

Thursday, July 22, 1993
Stowe Performing Arts Center, Stowe, VT
● *Set I:* Llama, Foam, Horn, My Mind's Got a Mind of its Own, Sample in a Jar, Divided Sky, Mound, Ya Mar, Poor Heart, Stash, Golgi Apparatus
● *Set II:* Also Sprach Zarathustra > Tweezer -> Walk Away, Sparkle, It's Ice, Contact, Possum, Paul and Silas, The Man Who Stepped Into Yesterday > Avenu Malkenu > Rocky Top
● *Encore:* Freebird
● *Show Notes:* Paul and Silas through Rocky Top featured Gordon Stone on banjo. The show was played in a total downpour, and the amphitheater was not built to handle that kind of weather. Before the first set, Trey remarked that the staff was talking about canceling the show due to the danger of electrocution. "I told 'em, 'Fuck that. Put the plug up my ass and count out Llama!'" quoth Trey. Walk Away included a brief tease of Pearl Jam's Alive. Possum included a brief Tweezer jam.

Friday, July 23, 1993
Jones Beach State Park, Wantagh, NY
● *Set I:* Buried Alive > Rift -> Caravan, Nellie Kane, Maze, The Horse > Silent in the Morning, Punch You in the Eye, Runaway Jim, It's Ice, Lawn Boy, Cavern
● *Set II:* Also Sprach Zarathustra -> Poor Heart, Run Like an Antelope, Faht > My Friend My Friend, Uncle Pen, Big Ball Jam, You Enjoy Myself -> Big Black Furry Creature from Mars -> Chalk Dust Torture, Highway to Hell
● *Encore:* Amazing Grace, Daniel

Saturday, July 24, 1993
Great Woods, Mansfield, MA
● *Set I:* Llama, Horn, Nellie Kane > Divided Sky, Guelah Papyrus, Rift, Stash, The Mango Song > Bouncing Around the Room, The Squirming Coil
● *Set II:* Also Sprach Zarathustra > Split Open and Melt, Fluffhead > Maze, Glide > Sparkle > Mike's Song > Yerushalayim Shel Zahav > Weekapaug Groove, Purple Rain > HYHU, Daniel > Good Times Bad Times
● *Encore:* Golgi Apparatus, Freebird
● *Show Notes:* This show saw the first Mango Song since May 17, 1992 (148 shows).

Sunday, July 25, 1993
Waterloo Village, Stanhope, NJ
● *Set I:* Wilson -> Foam, Mound, Stash, Fee > Rift, The Sloth, My Mind's Got a Mind of its Own, I Didn't Know, David Bowie
● *Set II:* Also Sprach Zarathustra > Suzy Greenberg, Tweezer -> The Horse > Silent in the Morning, Maze, The Lizards, Purple Rain, Harpua -> Tweezer Reprise
● *Encore:* Cavern
● *Show Notes:* Wilson contained "Jeopardy" theme teases and the Simpsons Signal. Sounds of Silence and Donna Lee were quoted in Bowie, which also included an Oom Pa Pa Signal. Harpua included a tease of the theme to *Taxi*.

Tuesday, July 27, 1993
Classic Amphitheater, Richmond, VA
Also Sprach Zarathustra > Rift, Stash, The Squirming Coil, Sparkle, It's Ice -> Purple Rain, You Enjoy Myself
● *Show Notes:* This show was part of the HORDE festival. YEM featured Chan Kinchla and John Popper, among other special guests. Popper was lowered onto the stage in his wheelchair and the cord snapped!

Wednesday, July 28, 1993
Grady Cole Center, Charlotte, NC
● *Check:* Blues Jam -> Head Games -> Double Vision -> Working for the Weekend
● *Set I:* All Things Reconsidered, Runaway Jim, Ya Mar, Sample in a Jar, Foam, Nellie Kane, Split Open and Melt, The Horse > Silent in the Morning, Poor Heart, Cavern
● *Set II:* Also Sprach Zarathustra > Axilla, My Sweet One, Run Like an Antelope, The Lizards, Mound, My Friend My Friend, Harry Hood, The Great Gig in the Sky, Chalk Dust Torture
● *Encore:* Piano Duet, Bill Bailey Won't You Please Come Home
● *Show Notes:* The encore featured Page's father, Dr. Jack McConnell, on piano. The Piano Duet also featured Fishman on washboard.

Thursday, July 29, 1993
Tennessee Theatre, Knoxville, TN
● *Set I:* Funky Bitch, Divided Sky, Weigh, Rift, The Landlady > Fast Enough for You, My Mind's Got a Mind of its Own, Colonel Forbin's Ascent > The Famous Mockingbird, Possum
● *Set II:* Maze, Bouncing Around the Room, It's Ice, Lifeboy, Sparkle, You Enjoy Myself, Purple Rain, Daniel, Good Times Bad Times
● *Encore:* Rocky Top, Freebird
● *Show Notes:* Good Times Bad Times contained a Beds are Burning tease.

Friday, July 30, 1993
Starwood Amphitheater, Antioch, TN
● *Check:* Dancing Days, Makisupa Policeman -> Stir it Up Jam -> Have Mercy -> Pressure Drop -> NICU
● *Set I:* Contact, Llama, Horn, Uncle Pen, Stash, Esther, Chalk Dust Torture, I Didn't Know, Reba, Cavern
● *Set II:* Also Sprach Zarathustra > Tweezer, The Horse > Silent in the Morning, Poor Heart, Fluffhead, My Friend My Friend, Golgi Apparatus, The Squirming Coil, David Bowie
● *Encore:* Walk Away, Amazing Grace

● *Show Notes:* The Contact opener started before the band took the stage, as they were driven to the front in golf carts. Some fans didn't even realize the show had started until well into Llama! This show was performed on a stage set up in the concession area of the amphitheater.

Saturday, July 31, 1993
Masquerade Music Park, Atlanta, GA
● *Check:* Funky Bitch (twice), The Great Gig in the Sky Intro
● *Set I:* Rift, Sample in a Jar, Ya Mar, Split Open and Melt, Mound, Foam, Nellie Kane > Divided Sky, Cavern
● *Set II:*Wilson > Runaway Jim, It's Ice > Maze, Sparkle, Mike's Song > Leprechaun > Weekapaug Groove > Purple Rain > HYHU, Daniel, Highway to Hell
● *Encore:* AC/DC Bag, Freebird
● *Show Notes:* Mike's Song included two distinct jams on Led Zeppelin's Heartbreaker. Listen as Fish and Page start the traditional Hydrogen after Mike's.

Monday, August 2, 1993
The Ritz Theatre, Ybor City, FL
● *Check:* Slave to the Traffic Light, Funky Bitch
● *Set I:* Chalk Dust Torture, Guelah Papyrus, Poor Heart, Brother, The Oh Kee Pa Ceremony > Suzy Greenberg, All Things Reconsidered, Bathtub Gin -> Makisupa Policeman -> My Mind's Got a Mind of its Own > Dog Gone Dog > La Grange
● *Set II:* Also Sprach Zarathustra > Mike's Song -> Sparks > The Ballad of Curtis Loew, Rift, The Squirming Coil, Weekapaug Groove -> HYHU > Bike > HYHU, Run Like an Antelope
● *Encore:* Sleeping Monkey, Amazing Grace
● *Show Notes:* Sweet Virginia was teased during Bathtub Gin. Brother made its first known appearance since the May 5, 1993 soundcheck and its first stage performance since July 14, 1992 (142 shows). Other breakouts included Dog Gone Dog (dedicated to Paul, and first since May 4, 1991, or 278 shows), La Grange (first since March 17, 1991, or 302 shows) and Sparks (first since September 13, 1990, or 358 shows). Guelah Papyrus contained a Simpsons Signal. The jam out of Mike's featured Joe Rooney of the band First Born on vocals. There was a Makisupa tease and a When the Saints Go Marching In tease in Antelope, along with the lyric "Marco Policeman-dolas." Amazing Grace was performed without microphones. The Bike intro featured a Moonshadow tease from Mike.

Tuesday, August 3, 1993
Bayfront Park Amphitheater, Miami, FL
● *Set I:* Runaway Jim, Nellie Kane, Foam, Fee > Rift, Stash, The Horse > Silent in the Morning, Ya Mar, Llama, Cavern
● *Set II:* Lengthwise > Maze, Bouncing Around the Room, It's Ice, You Enjoy Myself, The Lizards, Sparkle, Purple Rain, Golgi Apparatus
● *Encore:* Poor Heart, Freebird

Friday, August 6, 1993
Cincinnati Zoo Peacock Pavilion, Cincinnati, OH
● *Set I:* Split Open and Melt, Poor Heart, The Curtain > Sample in a Jar, Rift, Horn, Divided Sky, Nellie Kane, Chalk Dust Torture, Suzy Greenberg
● *Set II:* Buried Alive > Tweezer, Guelah Papyrus, The Squirming Coil,

Uncle Pen, You Enjoy Myself -> Cocaine Jam -> You Enjoy Myself -> Halley's Comet > Slave to the Traffic Light, HYHU > Cracklin' Rosie > HYHU, Tweezer Reprise
● *Encore:* Amazing Grace
● *Show Notes:* Listen for repeated Tequila teases in Suzy Greenberg, Tweezer, Guelah Papyrus, and YEM, as well as a Simpsons Signal in Guelah Papyrus. The YEM vocal jam was to the tune of Cocaine and included some Tweezer lyrics. Slave was played for the first time since October 24, 1991 (237 shows).

Saturday, August 7, 1993
Darien Lake Performing Arts Center, Darien, NY
● *Set I:* Llama, Bouncing Around the Room > Poor Heart > Stash -> Makisupa Policeman, Reba, Maze, Colonel Forbin's Ascent > The Famous Mockingbird, Cavern
● *Set II:* Also Sprach Zarathustra > Mike's Song > Kung -> Mike's Song, The Man Who Stepped Into Yesterday > Avenu Malkenu > The Sloth, Sparkle, My Friend My Friend > McGrupp and the Watchful Hosemasters -> Purple Rain > HYHU, Run Like an Antelope
● *Encore:* Carolina, La Grange
● *Show Notes:* Reba was performed without the whistling ending. To compensate, there was some whistling during the Maze opening. The narration in Forbin's dealt with the "Roller Coaster of the Mind." Mike's Song contained a Fingerscrape Signal and an Oom Pa Pa Signal.

Sunday, August 8, 1993
Nautica Stage, Cleveland, OH
● *Set I:* Big Black Furry Creature from Mars, Foam, Loving Cup, Runaway Jim, The Horse > Silent in the Morning, Punch You in the Eye, Fast Enough for You, Paul and Silas, I Didn't Know, David Bowie
● *Set II:* Also Sprach Zarathustra > Rift > Harry Hood, Wilson > It's Ice > Fluffhead, Possum > Big Ball Jam, HYHU > Love You > HYHU, Daniel, Good Times Bad Times
● *Encore:* My Sweet One, Freebird
● *Show Notes:* BBFCFM included a Divided Sky tease and Possum included a Tequila tease. Bowie included Random Note and Simpsons Signals. I Didn't Know featured Fishman on washboard. After the introductory HYHU, while Fish tried to figure out which song he would sing, Trey congratulated a fan who sunk two "baskets" during the BBJ. The band responded with a brief tease of Rock and Roll Part Two before Fish cued up Love You.

Monday, August 9, 1993
Concert Hall (Masonic Temple), Toronto, Ontario, Canada
● *Set I:* Chalk Dust Torture -> Who Knows Jam -> Chalk Dust Torture, Mound, Fee -> Split Open and Melt -> Glide, Nellie Kane, Divided Sky, Memories, The Squirming Coil
● *Set II:* Dinner and a Movie > Tweezer > Tela -> My Friend My Friend, My Mind's Got a Mind of its Own, You Enjoy Myself, Contact, Crimes of the Mind
● *Encore:* Rocky Top
● *Show Notes:* Glide included Simpsons, All Fall Down, and Random Note Signals. YEM included Smoke on the Water teases in the jam segment and Psycho Killer in the vocal jam. Memories was played for the first time since March 14, 1993 (62 shows) and Crimes of the Mind (with the Dude of Life on vocals) was played for the first time since No-

vember 8, 1991 (232 shows).

Wednesday, August 11, 1993
Eastbrook Theatre, Grand Rapids, MI
● *Set I:* Buried Alive > Runaway Jim > Weigh > It's Ice, Ginseng Sullivan, My Friend My Friend, The Mango Song, Stash, Sparkle > Cavern
● *Set II:* Mike's Song -> The Great Gig in the Sky > Weekapaug Groove, Esther > All Things Reconsidered, Bouncing Around the Room -> Rift > Jesus Just Left Chicago, My Sweet One > Run Like an Antelope
● *Encore:* Sweet Adeline, Bold As Love
● *Show Notes:* Ginseng Sullivan debuted in the first set with Trey on acoustic, Fish on washboard, Page on piano, and Mike on bass. Sweet Adeline was performed without microphones. My Sweet One and Antelope each contained multiple Simpsons Signals, and My Sweet One also contained a Fingerscrape Signal and Oom Pa Pa Signal. Mike teased the *Jeopardy* theme on bass during Antelope, which also has a tease of A Love Supreme. Great Gig featured a Fishman vacuum solo. Fishman quoted the vocals of Games Without Frontiers during Mike's Song. Bold as Love was played for the first time since February 26, 1993 (73 shows).

Thursday, August 12, 1993
Meadow Brook Music Festival, Rochester, MI
● *Set I:* AC/DC Bag, Reba, Chalk Dust Torture, Guelah Papyrus, Nellie Kane, Split Open and Melt, The Horse > Silent in the Morning, Poor Heart, The Squirming Coil
● *Set II:* Also Sprach Zarathustra, The Landlady, Tweezer > The Lizards, The Sloth, Maze, Lawn Boy, Big Ball Jam, Golgi Apparatus, Possum
● *Encore:* Fire, Freebird

Friday, August 13, 1993
Murat Theatre, Indianapolis, IN
● *Set I:* Lengthwise > Llama, Makisupa Policeman -> Foam, Stash, Ginseng Sullivan, Fluffhead, My Mind's Got a Mind of its Own, Horn, David Bowie
● *Set II:* Buried Alive > Rift > Bathtub Gin -> Ya Mar, Mike's Song > Lifeboy, The Oh Kee Pa Ceremony > Suzy Greenberg, Amazing Grace
● *Encore:* Highway to Hell
● *Show Notes:* Stash included a Weekapaug tease. Bowie included jams based on The Mango Song and Magilla, as well as a Llama tease. Amazing Grace was performed *a cappella*, without microphones. This amazing version of Bathtub Gin, which included Weekapaug teases, is the highlight of many fans' memories. Mike's Song included a tease of Ted Nugent's Stranglehold and Ya Mar lyrics at the beginning. Suzy included a Sweet Home Alabama tease.

Saturday, August 14, 1993
World Music Theatre, Tinley Park, IL
● *Check:* Long Jam (about 45 minutes, sounded McGrupp-like), Funky Bitch
● *Set I:* Chalk Dust Torture, Guelah Papyrus, Divided Sky, The Horse > Silent in the Morning, It's Ice, Sparkle, Split Open and Melt, Esther, Poor Heart > Cavern
● *Set II:* Also Sprach Zarathustra > Run Like an Antelope -> Sparks -> Walk Away -> Run Like an Antelope -> Have Mercy -> Run Like an Antelope, Mound, The Squirming Coil, Daniel, You Enjoy Myself, Purple Rain, Golgi Apparatus

● *Encore:* La Grange
● *Show Notes:* The first set is notable for interesting little jams in usually standard songs, like Guelah, Horse, and Ice. During Daniel, Trey updated the crowd on the score of a pre-season football game. YEM contained brief jams based on Speed Racer, Smoke on the Water, Kool Thing (by Sonic Youth) and Mystery Achievement (by The Pretenders). The "Rye, Rye Rocco" lyrics of Antelope were sung over the Have Mercy melody before the band kicked back into the Antelope ending.

Sunday, August 15, 1993
McCauley Theatre, Louisville, KY
● *Set I:* Sample in a Jar, All Things Reconsidered, Caravan, Runaway Jim, Fee, Paul and Silas, Stash, Colonel Forbin's Ascent > The Famous Mockingbird, Chalk Dust Torture
● *Set II:* Rift, Tweezer, The Lizards, The Landlady, Bouncing Around the Room, Maze, Glide, Sweet Adeline, Ginseng Sullivan, Nellie Kane, Freebird
● *Encore:* Harry Hood
● *Show Notes:* This show included fantastic versions of Stash and Tweezer, which contained an Antelope-style jam and a Simpsons Signal.

Monday, August 16, 1993
American Theatre, St. Louis, MO
● *Set I:* Axilla, Possum > Horn, Reba, Sparkle, Foam, I Didn't Know, Split Open and Melt, The Squirming Coil
● *Set II:* Mike's Song -> Faht > Weekapaug Groove, Mound, It's Ice, My Friend My Friend, Poor Heart, Big Ball Jam, Take the 'A' Train, Good Times Bad Times
● *Encore:* Amazing Grace, Rocky Top
● *Show Notes:* Weekapaug included Gypsy Queen and I Wish teases. Mike's Song included a Who Knows jam.

Tuesday, August 17, 1993
Memorial Hall, Kansas City, KS
● *Set I:* Wilson, Llama, Guelah Papyrus, Divided Sky, Weigh > Maze, Fluffhead, Fast Enough for You, Daniel
● *Set II:* Also Sprach Zarathustra > David Bowie, The Horse > Silent in the Morning, Rift, Suzy Greenberg, You Enjoy Myself -> Purple Rain > HYHU, My Sweet One, Cavern
● *Encore:* Memories, Fire
● *Show Notes:* The vocal jam in YEM was based on Ob La Di, Ob La Da. Bowie included an Oom Pa Pa Signal.

Friday, August 20, 1993
Red Rocks, Morrison, CO
● *Set I:* Divided Sky, Harpua, Poor Heart > Maze, Bouncing Around the Room > It's Ice > The Wedge, Ginseng Sullivan, Rift, Run Like an Antelope
● *Set II:* Also Sprach Zarathustra > Slave to the Traffic Light > Split Open and Melt, The Squirming Coil, My Friend My Friend, Chalk Dust Torture, You Enjoy Myself > Purple Rain > HYHU, Cavern
● *Encore:* The Mango Song, Freebird
● *Show Notes:* The band began the show with an appropriate opener, as the storm that had lingered in the Morrison sky cleared just before the show began. The Harpua story told the history of Red Rocks and the fate of a giant iguana, who was referred to throughout the show.

Harpua also included a Rock and Roll Part Two tease. Ginseng was dedicated to Brad Sands and was preceded by a "Charge" tease from Page. Antelope included a Simpsons Signal and Gypsy Queen teases. Purple Rain featured Mimi Fishman joining Fish on vacuum. The Wedge was played for the first time since March 25, 1993 (62 shows).

Saturday, August 21, 1993
Salt Air, Salt Lake City, UT
● *Set I:* Buried Alive > Poor Heart, Foam, Guelah Papyrus, Rift, Stash, Sparkle, The Landlady, I Didn't Know, Runaway Jim
● *Set II:* Possum, Horn, Uncle Pen, Fee -> Llama, Lawn Boy, David Bowie, If I Only Had a Brain, Harry Hood, Daniel
● *Encore:* Amazing Grace, Nellie Kane
● *Show Notes:* I Didn't Know featured Fishman on washboard. Fee through Daniel featured The Flecktones (Bela Fleck on electric banjo, Victor Lemonte Wooten on bass, and Roy "Future Man" Wooten on drumitar) and Nellie Kane featured Bela Fleck. Bowie included a "Mind Left Body" jam. Amazing Grace was performed without microphones.

Tuesday, August 24, 1993
Commodore Ballroom, Vancouver, British Columbia, Canada
● Opening Act: Baby Gramps
● *Check:* Jam, Leprechaun, The Wedge, Funky Bitch (with "Beds are Burning" lyrics)
● *Set I:* Chalk Dust Torture > All Things Reconsidered, Bouncing Around the Room, It's Ice, Nellie Kane, Split Open and Melt, The Horse > Silent in the Morning, Uncle Pen, Maze, Golgi Apparatus
● *Set II:* Llama, Horn, Ya Mar, Mike's Song -> Ginseng Sullivan > Weekapaug Groove, Wilson > Rift, HYHU > Cracklin' Rosie > HYHU, Run Like an Antelope
● *Encore:* Halley's Comet > Poor Heart, Sweet Adeline
● *Show Notes:* It's Ice included a tease of I Feel the Earth Move. Trey made several references to the venues springy floor and the fans bouncing on it while they dances. This strange Ya Mar included some odd lyrics from Mike. Fishman, usually subject to nicknames when he takes the mic, introduced Trey as Chuck Norris on the drums. Trey retorted by calling Fish "a butt with protruding arms and legs." Antelope was dedicated to three new crew members from Vancouver.

Wednesday, August 25, 1993
Paramount Theatre, Seattle, WA
● Opening Act: Baby Gramps
● *Set I:* AC/DC Bag, Daniel, Sample in a Jar, Sparkle, Foam, Ginseng Sullivan, Nellie Kane, Amazing Grace, Stash, Glide, Cavern
● *Set II:* Buried Alive, Possum, Mound, My Friend My Friend, Paul and Silas, You Enjoy Myself, The Squirming Coil, Good Times Bad Times
● *Encore:* Bold as Love, Rocky Top
● *Show Notes:* Ginseng Sullivan and Nellie Kane were played without amplification. There was a vocal jam during Paul and Silas in place of the second guitar solo.

Thursday, August 26, 1993
Arlene Schnitzer Concert Hall, Portland, OR
● Opening Act: Baby Gramps
● *Set I:* Runaway Jim, Guelah Papyrus, Reba, Fee, Split Open and Melt, Esther, It's Ice, Harry Hood, Golgi Apparatus

● *Set II:* Also Sprach Zarathustra > David Bowie, Lifeboy, Rift, Jesus Just Left Chicago, The Lizards, HYHU > Mice and Bats > HYHU, Chalk Dust Torture

● *Encore:* Freebird

● *Show Notes:* Reba included a Dixie tease and It's Ice included a Simpsons Signal. Mice and Bats featured a Baby Gramps guest appearance.

Saturday, August 28, 1993
Greek Theatre, Berkeley, CA

● Opening Act: J.J. Cale

● *Set I:* Llama, Bouncing Around the Room, Foam, Ginseng Sullivan, Maze, Fluffhead, Stash, The Squirming Coil, Crimes of the Mind

● *Set II:* Also Sprach Zarathustra > Rift, Run Like an Antelope, The Horse > Silent in the Morning, Sparkle, It's Ice > Big Ball Jam, Purple Rain > HYHU, You Enjoy Myself -> Oye Como Va Jam -> You Enjoy Myself -> Contact, Chalk Dust Torture

● *Encore:* Daniel, Amazing Grace

● *Show Notes:* Crimes featured the Dude of Life on vocals. Antelope included *Brady Bunch* theme teases and a Simpsons Signal, while It's Ice featured Random Note, All Fall Down, and Oom Pa Pa Signals. Amazing Grace was performed without microphones. Also, while several versions of YEM have teased Oye Como Va, this version featured an all-out jam of the song. Contact segued out of the YEM vocal jam. During Daniel, the band introduced and thanked each member of the crew.

Tuesday, December 28, 1993
Bender Arena, American University, Washington, DC

● *Check:* Dream On, My Mind's Got a Mind of its Own, Leprechaun, Daniel (several times), My Friend My Friend Intro, Punch You in the Eye (three times), The Squirming Coil (three times), Stash, My Friend My Friend, Horn (twice), Also Sprach Zarathustra (twice), Split Open and Melt, You Enjoy Myself, The Oh Kee Pa Ceremony, The Horse, Fluffhead Intro, Divided Sky Intro, Silent in the Morning, Reba, Fee, Kashmir

● *Set I:* Peaches en Regalia, Poor Heart > Split Open and Melt, Esther > The Oh Kee Pa Ceremony > Suzy Greenberg > Ya Mar, It's Ice, Fee, Possum

● *Set II:* Sample in a Jar, You Enjoy Myself, My Friend My Friend -> The Lizards, The Sloth, Fast Enough for You, Uncle Pen, Harry Hood, Highway to Hell

● *Encore:* Memories, Golgi Apparatus

● *Show Notes:* Possum included a Kashmir tease. Peaches (first since June 23, 1989, or 478 shows) was likely played in memory of Frank Zappa, who passed away a few weeks before. Subsequently, SOAM included Peaches teases. Ya Mar included an Auld Lang Syne tease and Hood included a Simpsons Signal. For the entire New Year's Run, the stage was set up as an aquarium, complete with sand, seaweed, rocks, and a giant clam.

Wednesday, December 29, 1993
New Haven Veterans Memorial Coliseum, New Haven, CT

● *Check:* Reggae Jam, Nellie Kane

● *Set I:* Runaway Jim, Peaches en Regalia, Foam, Glide, Divided Sky, Wilson, Sparkle, Stash, The Squirming Coil

● *Set II:* Maze, Bouncing Around the Room, Fluffhead, Run Like an Antelope, Contact > Big Black Furry Creature from Mars -> Walk Away, Big Ball Jam, HYHU > If I Only Had a Brain > HYHU, Sweet Adeline, Chalk Dust Torture

● *Encore:* Nellie Kane, Cavern

● *Show Notes:* Glide included a Simpsons Signal and BBFCFM was unfinished. Stash included a jam akin to the sound of a television newscast, complete with vocal quotes from Trey referencing news personality Connie Chung. Fishman introduced Brain by talking about his new haircut.

Thursday, December 30, 1993
Cumberland County Civic Center, Portland, ME

● *Check:* Dog Gone Dog (twice), Funky Bitch

● *Set I:* David Bowie, Weigh, The Curtain > Sample in a Jar, Paul and Silas, Colonel Forbin's Ascent > The Famous Mockingbird, Rift, Bathtub Gin, Freebird

● *Set II:* Also Sprach Zarathustra > Mike's Song -> The Horse > Silent in the Morning, Punch You in the Eye, McGrupp and the Watchful Hosemasters, Weekapaug Groove > Purple Rain > HYHU, Slave to the Traffic Light

● *Encore:* Rocky Top, Good Times Bad Times

● *Show Notes:* Dream On and Dave's Energy Guide were both jammed during Bowie. Slave was played in response to a chant from the front row.

Friday, December 31, 1993
The Centrum, Worcester, MA

● *Check:* Peaches en Regalia (twice), Funky Bitch, Ginseng Sullivan, Blues Jam

● *Set I:* Llama, Guelah Papyrus, Stash, Ginseng Sullivan, Reba, Peaches en Regalia, I Didn't Know, Run Like an Antelope

● *Set II:* Tweezer > Halley's Comet > Poor Heart > It's Ice > Fee > Possum, Lawn Boy, You Enjoy Myself

● *Set III:* Auld Lang Syne > Down with Disease Jam > Split Open and Melt, The Lizards, Sparkle > Suzy Greenberg > HYHU > Cracklin' Rosie > HYHU, Harry Hood, Tweezer Reprise

● *Encore:* Golgi Apparatus, Amazing Grace

● *Show Notes:* There was a Roundabout tease before Ginseng Sullivan. Antelope featured Tom Marshall on vocals. The band put on wet suits during the end of the YEM vocal jam. The third set was preceded by bubble noises through the PA and the band "diving" into the aquarium on stage. Peaches en Regalia was teased in many songs, including Possum and Suzy Greenberg, and Auld Lang Syne was teased in Harry Hood.

SPRING/SUMMER, 1994

March 18, 1994
WIZN Studios, Burlington, VT

● *Show Notes:* Trey, Tom Marshall, and Dave Abrahms visited the WIZN studios to promote the release of *Hoist*.

Monday, April 4, 1994
The Flynn Theatre, Burlington, VT

● *Set I:* Divided Sky, Sample in a Jar, Scent of a Mule, Maze, Fee > Reba, Horn > It's Ice > Possum

● *Set II:* Down with Disease > If I Could, Buried Alive, The Landlady, Julius, Magilla, Split Open and Melt, Wolfman's Brother > I Wanna Be

Like You, The Oh Kee Pa Ceremony > Suzy Greenberg
● *Encore:* Harry Hood, Cavern
● *Show Notes:* This show, a benefit for The Flynn Theatre, featured many debuts, including Scent of a Mule, If I Could, Wolfman's Brother, Julius, I Wanna Be Like You, and the full Down with Disease. The show kicked off with one *a cappella* line of My Hometown. Buried Alive through Suzy Greenberg featured The Giant Country Horns: Mike Gallick on baritone sax, Carl "Geerz" Gerhard on trumpet, Dave "The Truth" Grippo on alto sax, Don Glasgo on trombone, Chris Peterman on tenor sax, and Joseph Somerville, Jr., on trumpet. Cavern, which contained the old, alternate lyrics, also featured Gerhard. Magilla (first since March 25, 1993, or 72 shows) was played slightly differently than most versions, with more of a shuffle beat. Listen as Trey updated the crowd on the scores of the NCAA tournament games.

Tuesday, April 5, 1994
The Metropolis, Montreal, Quebec, Canada
● *Set I:* Runaway Jim > Foam, Fluffhead, Glide, Julius, Bouncing Around the Room > Rift, AC/DC Bag
● *Set II:* Peaches en Regalia > Ya Mar, Tweezer -> If I Could, You Enjoy Myself, I Wanna Be Like You, Chalk Dust Torture, Amazing Grace
● *Encore:* Nellie Kane, Golgi Apparatus
● *Show Notes:* Amazing Grace was performed without microphones.

Wednesday, April 6, 1994
Concert Hall, Toronto, Ontario, Canada
● *Set I:* Llama, Guelah Papyrus, Poor Heart, Stash, The Lizards, Sample in a Jar, Scent of a Mule, Fee -> Run Like an Antelope
● *Set II:* The Curtain > Down with Disease, Wolfman's Brother, Sparkle, Mike's Song -> Lifeboy -> Weekapaug Groove, The Squirming Coil, Cavern
● *Encore:* Ginseng Sullivan, Nellie Kane, Sweet Adeline
● *Show Notes:* Amazing Grace was performed without microphones. As a side note, the venue was changed at the last minute due to arena damage from the previous evening's New Kids on the Block concert.

Friday, April 8, 1994
Recreation Hall, Penn State, State College, PA
● *Set I:* Maze -> Digital Delay Loop Jam -> Maze, Glide -> Foam, I Didn't Know, Punch You in the Eye, The Horse > Silent in the Morning, Down with Disease, If I Could, Lawn Boy, Llama
● *Set II:* Split Open and Melt, McGrupp and the Watchful Hosemasters, It's Ice, Sparkle, Harry Hood, Bouncing Around the Room, Big Ball Jam, David Bowie, Suzy Greenberg
● *Encore:* Contact, Big Black Furry Creature from Mars
● *Show Notes:* Suzy included an Owner of a Lonely Heart tease. I Didn't Know included Mimi Fishman on cymbals. Mimi also counted off the break in BBFCFM.

Saturday, April 9, 1994
Broome County Arena, Binghamton, NY
● *Check:* Funkisupa Policeman
● *Set I:* Magilla, Wilson, Rift, Bathtub Gin, Nellie Kane, Julius, Fee -> All Things Reconsidered, Stash, The Squirming Coil
● *Set II:* Sample in a Jar, Reba, Peaches en Regalia > Big Ball Jam, De-

mand, Mike's Song > I Am Hydrogen > Weekapaug Groove, Tela > Slave to the Traffic Light, Cavern
● *Encore:* Amazing Grace, Highway to Hell
● *Show Notes:* This show marked the first performance of Demand. This non-standard, free-form Weekapaug included quotes from The Little Drummer Boy, Divided Sky, and DEG. Little Drummer Boy was also teased during the end of Peaches and the ensuing Big Ball Jam. Highway to Hell was jokingly dedicated to some fans in the front row, who were chanting for AC/DC Bag and not an AC/DC song.

Sunday, April 10, 1994
Alumni Arena, SUNY Buffalo, Buffalo, NY
● *Set I:* Runaway Jim, It's Ice, Sparkle, Split Open and Melt, Esther, Chalk Dust Torture, I Didn't Know, Scent of a Mule, Down with Disease
● *Set II:* My Friend My Friend, Ya Mar, Run Like an Antelope, Fluffhead, Ginseng Sullivan, I Wanna Be Like You > HYHU, Harry Hood
● *Encore:* Bouncing Around the Room, Golgi Apparatus

Monday, April 11, 1994
Snively Arena, University of New Hampshire, Durham, NH
● *Set I:* Caravan, Poor Heart, Foam, Fast Enough for You, Magilla, Julius, Glide, Divided Sky, Cavern
● *Set II:* Also Sprach Zarathustra > Maze, Colonel Forbin's Ascent > The Famous Mockingbird, Uncle Pen, Sample in a Jar, Big Ball Jam, You Enjoy Myself, Amazing Grace, The Oh Kee Pa Ceremony > Suzy Greenberg
● *Encore:* Possum
● *Show Notes:* YEM included a vocal jam based on My Soul.

Wednesday, April 13, 1994
The Beacon Theatre, New York, NY
● *Set I:* Buried Alive > Poor Heart, Stash, The Lizards, Julius, Ginseng Sullivan, Divided Sky, Golgi Apparatus
● *Set II:* Faht, The Curtain, Sample in a Jar, Reba, Big Ball Jam, Fee, Take the 'A' Train, David Bowie, Purple Rain, AC/DC Bag
● *Encore:* Sweet Adeline, Good Times Bad Times

Thursday, April 14, 1994
The Beacon Theatre, New York, NY
● *Set I:* Runaway Jim, Foam, Sparkle, Down with Disease, Glide, Rift, Demand -> Split Open and Melt Jam, The Squirming Coil
● *Set II:* Also Sprach Zarathustra > Run Like an Antelope, The Horse > Silent in the Morning, Scent of a Mule, You Enjoy Myself, Nellie Kane, Dog Faced Boy, Slave to the Traffic Light
● *Encore:* Rocky Top
● *Show Notes:* Nellie Kane and Dog Faced Boy, which made its debut, were performed acoustic and without microphones. YEM featured a guest trampoline jumper for Trey, who had recently broken his foot.

Friday, April 15, 1994
The Beacon Theatre, New York, NY
● *Set I:* Llama, Guelah Papyrus, Paul and Silas, Harry Hood, Wilson > Chalk Dust Torture, Bouncing Around the Room > It's Ice > Down with Disease
● *Set II:* Maze, If I Could, The Oh Kee Pa Ceremony > Suzy Greenberg

> The Landlady, Julius, Wolfman's Brother -> Alumni Blues > I Wanna Be Like You > HYHU > Cavern
● *Encore:* Magilla, Amazing Grace
● *Show Notes:* Suzy through Magilla featured the Giant Country Horns: Carl "Geerz" Gerhard on trumpet, Dave "The Truth" Grippo on alto sax, Chris Peterman on tenor sax, Mike Gallick on baritone sax, Don Glasgo on trombone, and Joseph Somerville, Jr., on trumpet. Alumni Blues was incomplete, as only one verse was played, but it was the first since July 18, 1991 (295 shows).

Saturday, April 16, 1994
Mullins Center, University of Massachusetts, Amherst, MA
● *Set I:* Runaway Jim, Fee, Axilla (Part II), Rift, Stash, Fluffhead, Nellie Kane, Run Like an Antelope
● *Set II:* Sample in a Jar, Poor Heart, Tweezer -> The Lizards, Julius, Bouncing Around the Room, You Enjoy Myself, The Squirming Coil, Tweezer Reprise
● *Encore:* Fire
● *Show Notes:* This show included the debut of Axilla (Part II).

Sunday, April 17, 1994
Patriot Center, George Mason University, Fairfax, VA
● *Set I:* Loving Cup, Foam, I Didn't Know, Divided Sky, Mound, Down with Disease -> If I Could, My Sweet One, Cavern
● *Set II:* David Bowie, Wolfman's Brother, Uncle Pen, The Sloth, Reba, Big Ball Jam, Maze, Contact, Golgi Apparatus
● *Encore:* Cracklin' Rosie, Bold As Love

Monday, April 18, 1994
Bob Carpenter Center, University of Delaware, Newark, DE
● *Set I:* Chalk Dust Torture, Glide, Poor Heart > Julius, My Friend My Friend, Rift, Split Open and Melt, Dog Faced Boy, The Oh Kee Pa Ceremony > AC/DC Bag
● *Set II:* Also Sprach Zarathustra > Sample in a Jar, Sparkle, Bathtub Gin > Big Ball Jam > Ya Mar, Mike's Song, The Man Who Stepped Into Yesterday > Avenu Malkenu > The Man Who Stepped Into Yesterday Reprise > Down with Disease -> I Wanna Be Like You, Cavern
● *Encore:* Good Times Bad Times
● *Show Notes:* "Big Phil" was the guest trampoline jumper during Mike's Song, as he took Trey's place.

Wednesday, April 20, 1994
Virginia Horse Center, Lexington, VA
● *Opening Act:* The Dave Matthews Band
● *Set I:* Runaway Jim, It's Ice, Julius, Bouncing Around the Room, Axilla (Part II), Stash, Suzy Greenberg
● *Set II:* Poor Heart, Run Like an Antelope, Paul and Silas, Sample in a Jar, Big Ball Jam, Harry Hood, Fee, You Enjoy Myself -> Somewhere Over the Rainbow Jam
● *Encore:* Highway to Hell
● *Show Notes:* YEM featured Dave Matthews, LeRoi Moore, Boyd Tinsley, Carter Beauford, and Steffan Lessard from the Dave Matthews Band.

Thursday, April 21, 1994
Veterans Memorial Coliseum, Winston-Salem, NC

● *Opening Act:* The Dave Matthews Band
● *Set I:* Chalk Dust Torture, Sparkle, Foam, Glide, Split Open and Melt, The Lizards, Down with Disease -> If I Could, Cavern
● *Set II:* Also Sprach Zarathustra > Maze, Fluffhead, Mike's Song > I Am Hydrogen > Weekapaug Groove, Scent of a Mule, Big Ball Jam > Possum, Amazing Grace
● *Encore:* Drums Jam -> Jam -> All Along the Watchtower
● *Show Notes:* The Drums Jam featured Carter Beauford of the Dave Matthews Band; the rest of the encore featured the entire band.

Friday, April 22, 1994
Township Auditorium, Columbia, SC
● *Set I:* Llama, Horn, Uncle Pen, Punch You in the Eye, Sample in a Jar, All Things Reconsidered, Nellie Kane, Divided Sky, The Horse > Silent in the Morning, David Bowie
● *Set II:* Suzy Greenberg, Julius, Reba, Tweezer, Lifeboy, Runaway Jim, I Wanna Be Like You, The Squirming Coil
● *Encore:* Piano Duet -> Bill Bailey Won't You Please Come Home
● *Show Notes:* The encore featured Page's father, Dr. Jack McConnell, on piano and lead vocals.

Saturday, April 23, 1994
The Fox Theatre, Atlanta, GA
● *Set I:* Funky Bitch, Rift, Fee > Peaches en Regalia, Poor Heart, Stash, Esther, Down with Disease, Caravan, High-Heel Sneakers
● *Set II:* Wilson > Run Like an Antelope, Mound, Sample in a Jar, Sparkle, Harry Hood, Ginseng Sullivan, You Enjoy Myself, Who By Fire, Golgi Apparatus
● *Encore:* Freebird
● *Show Notes:* The Wilson > Antelope combo was a fantastic set opener. Antelope included Simpsons and Oom Pa Pa Signals. Caravan and High-Heel Sneakers featured Merl Saunders on keyboards and YEM, which included a Rock 'n Roll Hoochie Coo jam, featured Colonel Bruce Hampton on piano. Ginseng Sullivan was performed without microphones. Freebird was played by request after Trey asked, *a la* Lynyrd Skynyrd, what song the crowd wanted to hear. Listen for a distinct Caravan tease in the beginning of Esther. The tramps jam in YEM featured a guest tramp jumper due to Trey's broken foot.

Sunday, April 24, 1994
Grady Cole Center, Charlotte, NC
● *Set I:* My Friend My Friend, Ya Mar, Axilla (Part II), Maze, Bathtub Gin, Dog Faced Boy, It's Ice, Slave to the Traffic Light
● *Set II:* Demand, David Bowie, The Mango Song, Julius, Colonel Forbin's Ascent > The Famous Mockingbird, Chalk Dust Torture, Contact, Good Times Bad Times
● *Encore:* Sweet Adeline

Monday, April 25, 1994
Civic Auditorium, Knoxville, TN
● *Set I:* The Landlady > Runaway Jim, Fee, Foam, Down with Disease, Ginseng Sullivan, Dog Faced Boy, Tela, Poor Heart, Split Open and Melt
● *Set II:* The Curtain > Sample in a Jar, My Mind's Got a Mind of its Own, Run Like an Antelope, Mound, The Squirming Coil, Divided Sky, Bouncing Around the Room, Big Ball Jam, Big Black Furry Creature from Mars
● *Encore:* Amazing Grace, Bold as Love

● *Show Notes:* Ginseng Sullivan and Dog Faced Boy were performed acoustic.

Tuesday, April 26, 1994
Purple Dragon Recording Studios, Atlanta, GA
Sample in a Jar, Bouncing Around the Room, Maze, Down with Disease, Fluffhead, Carefree

Thursday, April 28, 1994
Sunfest, West Palm Beach, FL
● *Check:* Reggae Jam, Funky Bitch, Magilla, Ginseng Sullivan, Blues Jam Runaway Jim, Foam, Sample in a Jar, Rift, Down with Disease, Bouncing Around the Room, It's Ice, Run Like an Antelope, The Squirming Coil, Julius, Good Times Bad Times
● *Encore:* Golgi Apparatus
● *Show Notes:* This performance was a one set show.

Friday, April 29, 1994
Boatyard Village Pavilion, Clearwater, FL
● *Set I:* Halley's Comet, You Enjoy Myself > Fast Enough for You, Scent of a Mule, The Sloth, Divided Sky, I Didn't Know, Dog Faced Boy, Split Open and Melt, Sanity, My Mind's Got a Mind of its Own, Llama
● *Set II:* Suzy Greenberg, Maze, If I Could, Reba, Fee, Uncle Pen, Mike's Song > I Am Hydrogen > Weekapaug Groove, I Wanna Be Like You, Cavern
● *Encore:* Fire
● *Show Notes:* There was no vocal jam in YEM, as the song melted into FEFY. SOAM included teases of Ice, Ice, Baby. Sanity was played for the first time since May 17, 1992 (198 shows).

Saturday, April 30, 1994
The Edge, Orlando, FL
● *Set I:* Chalk Dust Torture, Mound, Stash, Poor Heart, Sample in a Jar, Punch You in the Eye, Rift, Ginseng Sullivan, Sweet Adeline
● *Set II:* Wilson, David Bowie, Wolfman's Brother, Peaches en Regalia, Harry Hood, Axilla (Part II), McGrupp and the Watchful Hosemasters, Possum, Purple Rain, Big Black Furry Creature from Mars
● *Encore:* Sleeping Monkey, Highway to Hell
● *Show Notes:* Ginseng Sullivan and Sweet Adeline were performed acoustic without microphones. Lion Sleeps Tonight was teased throughout the show, including the Bowie intro. Possum included a tease jam that featured sections of all the songs from Wilson through McGrupp.

Monday, May 2, 1994
Five Points South Music Hall, Birmingham, AL
● *Set I:* The Great Gig in the Sky -> Split Open and Melt, Bouncing Around the Room, Down with Disease, It's Ice, Glide, Divided Sky, Suzy Greenberg, Foam, Sample in a Jar
● *Set II:* Runaway Jim, Mound, Reba, Golgi Apparatus, The Lizards, Julius, Lawn Boy, Mike's Song -> Bass Jam
● *Encore:* Cavern
● *Show Notes:* Oteil Burbridge and Stacy Starkweather both joined the band on bass for the jam out of Mike's Song, during which the band members switched instruments. At one point, Trey wound up on drums while Fishman played Page's organ.

Tuesday, May 3, 1994
Starwood Amphitheater, Antioch, TN
● *Set I:* Rift, Guelah Papyrus, Maze, Sparkle, Stash, The Squirming Coil, Scent of a Mule, Sample in a Jar, Sweet Adeline
● *Set II:* David Bowie, If I Could, Fluffhead, Down with Disease, Harpua, Chalk Dust Torture, HYHU > I Wanna Be Like You > HYHU, Slave to the Traffic Light
● *Encore:* Nellie Kane, Fire
● *Show Notes:* If I Could featured Alison Krauss on vocals. Sunshine of Your Love and Sunshine of My Life were both teased during Bowie. Adeline was performed unmiced. The venue is sometimes mislabeled as "The Veranda" at Starwood; the show was scheduled to be held there but was moved to the main stage due to rain. Interestingly, Hank Williams, Jr. had already set up his PA and light system for a tour rehearsal and allowed Phish to use his rig.

Wednesday, May 4, 1994
State Palace Theatre, New Orleans, LA
● *Set I:* Runaway Jim, Foam, Sample in a Jar, It's Ice, Sparkle, Axilla (Part II), Tweezer > Lifeboy, Rift > Tweezer Reprise
● *Set II:* Run Like an Antelope, Bouncing Around the Room, You Enjoy Myself, Buried Alive > The Landlady, Julius, Wolfman's Brother, Magilla, Suzy Greenberg
● *Encore:* Caravan
● *Show Notes:* YEM through Caravan featured the Cosmic Country Horns: Michael Ray and Carl "Geerz" Gerhard on trumpet, Dave "The Truth" Grippo on alto sax, Tony Tate on tenor sax, Jerome Theriot on baritone sax, and Rick Trolsen on trombone. Suzy ended with a jazz jam involving a megaphone on Trey's guitar and an electric screwdriver on Mike's bass. Trey dedicated Antelope to his friend, who was, at that moment, giving birth. He recommended that she name the child "Marco Esquandolas." It's Ice included a tease of Right Off, a tune from Miles Davis' *Tribute to Jack Johnson* album.

Friday, May 6, 1994
Tower Theater, Houston, TX
● *Set I:* Down with Disease, The Oh Kee Pa Ceremony > AC/DC Bag, Poor Heart, My Friend My Friend, Ya Mar, Stash, Esther, Chalk Dust Torture
● *Set II:* Maze, Golgi Apparatus, Uncle Pen, Sample in a Jar, Reba, Axilla (Part II), Julius, Bike, David Bowie
● *Encore:* Ginseng Sullivan, Freebird
Show Notes: The encores were performed without microphones.

Saturday, May 7, 1994
The Bomb Factory, Dallas, TX
● *Check:* Jazz Jam, Dog Gone Dog (slow reggae version), Blues Jam
● *Set I:* Llama, Horn, Divided Sky, Mound, Fast Enough for You, Scent of a Mule, Split Open and Melt, If I Could, Suzy Greenberg
● *Set II:* Loving Cup, Sparkle > Tweezer -> Sparks -> Makisupa Policeman -> Digital Delay Loop Jam -> Sweet Emotion Jam -> Walk Away -> Cannonball Jam -> Purple Rain > HYHU Jam -> Tweezer Reprise
● *Encore:* Amazing Grace, Sample in a Jar
● *Show Notes:* The jam after Walk Away included a Page solo, teases of It's Ice and McGrupp, and a Simpsons Signal. The second set is one of the most circulated tapes ever, as most fans love the "Tweezerfest."

Sunday, May 8, 1994
Backyard, Austin, TX
● *Check:* Loving Cup (intro), Nellie Kane (twice)
● *Set I:* Runaway Jim, Foam, Axilla (Part II), Rift, Down with Disease > Bouncing Around the Room, Stash, The Squirming Coil
● *Set II:* Also Sprach Zarathustra > Run Like an Antelope, It's Ice, Fee > Julius, Cavern, You Enjoy Myself -> Halley's Comet > Good Times Bad Times
● *Encore:* Sweet Adeline, Golgi Apparatus
● *Show Notes:* Halley's segued out of the YEM vocal jam.

Tuesday, May 10, 1994
Paolo Soleri Amphitheater, Santa Fe, NM
● *Set I:* Buried Alive > Poor Heart, Sample in a Jar, Divided Sky, Axilla (Part II), It's Ice, Split Open and Melt, If I Could, Cavern
● *Set II:* Maze, Wilson, Julius, Reba, Scent of a Mule, Harry Hood, Ginseng Sullivan, Dog Faced Boy, Nellie Kane, David Bowie
● *Encore:* The Squirming Coil
● *Show Notes:* Ginseng Sullivan through Nellie Kane were performed acoustic.

Thursday, May 12, 1994
Buena Vista, Tucson, AZ
● *Set I:* Catapult -> Rift, Down with Disease, Fee, Maze, Axilla (Part II), Foam, Bathtub Gin -> The Lizards, Sample in a Jar
● *Set II:* Also Sprach Zarathustra > Run Like an Antelope, The Horse > Silent in the Morning, Uncle Pen, Fluffhead, Lifeboy, Possum, Love You, Contact -> Big Black Furry Creature from Mars
● *Encore:* Amazing Grace, Rocky Top
● *Show Notes:* Catapult was played for the first time since February 10, 1993 (132 shows).

Friday, May 13, 1994
Hayden Square, Tempe, AZ
● *Set I:* Runaway Jim, It's Ice, Julius, Mound, Stash, If I Could, My Friend My Friend, Slave to the Traffic Light, Suzy Greenberg
● *Set II:* Chalk Dust Torture, Bouncing Around the Room, Split Open and Melt, McGrupp and the Watchful Hosemasters > Peaches en Regalia > Scent of a Mule, You Enjoy Myself, Purple Rain, Good Times Bad Times
● *Encore:* Freebird
● *Show Notes:* Listen carefully for a Layla tease from Page during Suzy. Also, this version of YEM included a *Mission: Impossible* tease from Page and a *Spiderman* theme tease from Mike.

Saturday, May 14, 1994
Montezuma Hall, San Diego State University, San Diego, CA
● *Set I:* Llama, Wilson, Down with Disease > Fee, Reba, Sample in a Jar, My Sweet One, Ginseng Sullivan, David Bowie
● *Set II:* The Curtain > Mike's Song > I Am Hydrogen > Weekapaug Groove > The Man Who Stepped Into Yesterday > Avenu Malkenu > The Man Who Stepped Into Yesterday Reprise, Punch You in the Eye, Fast Enough for You, The Lizards, Cavern
● *Encore:* Bold As Love
● *Show Notes:* Wilson included Oom Pa Pa and Simpsons Signals. Weekapaug included a Divided Sky tease,

Monday, May 16, 1994
The Wiltern Theatre, Los Angeles, CA
● *Set I:* Buried Alive > Poor Heart, Sample in a Jar, Divided Sky, Axilla (Part II), Rift, Down with Disease, Bouncing Around the Room, Stash, Sweet Adeline
● *Set II:* Also Sprach Zarathustra > Run Like an Antelope -> Big Black Furry Creature from Mars -> Run Like an Antelope, Sparkle, It's Ice, Julius, You Enjoy Myself -> Big Black Furry Creature from Mars, Amazing Grace, Big Black Furry Creature from Mars
● *Encore:* Fee -> Rocky Top
● *Show Notes:* Sweet Adeline and Amazing Grace were performed without microphones. Antelope included a Simpsons Signal at the beginning and All Fall Down and Oom Pa Pa Signals during the jam. Also, Louie, Louie was teased in YEM. The second set kept returning to BBFCFM, as the three verses were completely spread out.

Tuesday, May 17, 1994
The Arlington Theatre, Santa Barbara, CA
● *Check:* Jam, My Mind's Got a Mind of its Own
● *Set I:* Suzy Greenberg, Maze, Mound, If I Could -> Scent of a Mule, Ginseng Sullivan, Dog Faced Boy, Split Open and Melt, The Squirming Coil
● *Set II:* Runaway Jim, Glide -> Tweezer -> Lifeboy, Uncle Pen, Big Ball Jam -> Sample in a Jar, HYHU > Love You > HYHU, Slave to the Traffic Light
● *Encore:* Highway to Hell
● *Show Notes:* Ginseng Sullivan and Dog Faced Boy were performed acoustic without microphones. Page's piano solo in The Squirming Coil was cut short when Trey brought out a birthday cake for Page and attempted to lead the audience in a round of "happy birthday." Similarly, Maze included Happy Birthday teases. Tweezer included a jam based on Cheech and Chong's Earache my Eye, including brief lyrics.

Thursday, May 19, 1994
The Hult Center, Eugene, OR
● *Set I:* Halley's Comet -> Llama, My Friend My Friend, Poor Heart -> Stash, The Horse > Silent in the Morning, Down with Disease, The Mango Song, Cavern
● *Set II:* Sample in a Jar, Sparkle, Mike's Song > I Am Hydrogen > Weekapaug Groove, The Lizards, Julius, Big Ball Jam, Harry Hood, Golgi Apparatus
● *Encore:* Ginseng Sullivan, Nellie Kane, Sweet Adeline, Fire
● Show Notes: Ginseng Sullivan and Nellie Kane were performed acoustic and without microphones. Sweet Adeline was also performed without microphones. This version of Stash ranks among the favorites of many fans. Weekapaug and Hood included "I Love Lucy" theme teasing.

Friday, May 20, 1994
Evergreen State College Recreation Center, Olympia, WA
● *Check:* Can You See Me, Surfing Jam, Magilla (fast version), Demand (three times), Blues Jam, Blues Jam -> Low Rider -> Jam
● *Set I:* Fee, Maze, If I Could, It's Ice, Bathtub Gin, Fast Enough for You, Scent of a Mule, Dog Faced Boy, Carolina, AC/DC Bag
● *Set II:* Also Sprach Zarathustra > Run Like an Antelope, Weigh, Axilla (Part II), Wolfman's Brother, Rift, You Enjoy Myself
● *Encore:* Chalk Dust Torture
● *Show Notes:* Dog Faced Boy was performed acoustic and, along with

Carolina (first since August 7, 1993, or 55 shows), was performed without microphones. YEM contained Ob La Di, Ob La Da and Low Rider jams and Bathtub Gin included a Lion Sleeps Tonight tease from Trey.

Saturday, May 21, 1994
The Moore Theatre, Seattle, WA
● *Set I:* Runaway Jim, Foam, Guelah Papyrus, Down with Disease, Mound, Stash, The Squirming Coil, Tela, Llama
● *Set II:* Dinner and a Movie, Sample in a Jar, David Bowie, Contact, Big Ball Jam, Julius, Bike, Audience Jam, Harry Hood, Amazing Grace
● *Encore:* Bold as Love
● *Show Notes:* This version of Stash was simply outstanding and remains a fan favorite. Dinner and a Movie was played for the first time since August 9, 1993 (54 shows).

Sunday, May 22, 1994
The Vogue Theatre, Vancouver, BC
● *Check:* Dog Gone Dog -> Machine Gun -> Dog Gone Dog, Bluegrass Tune, Poor Heart, My Sweet One (unmiced)
● *Set I:* Demand -> The Sloth, Divided Sky, Glide, Peaches en Regalia, Split Open and Melt, Fluffhead, My Sweet One, Ginseng Sullivan, Dog Faced Boy, Axilla (Part II)
● *Set II:* Down with Disease, Bouncing Around the Room, It's Ice, McGrupp and the Watchful Hosemasters -> Tweezer -> Lifeboy, Rift, Slave to the Traffic Light, Tweezer Reprise
● *Encore:* Sleeping Monkey
● *Show Notes:* Glide was humorously introduced by Trey as "Whoomp! There it Is," referencing a popular dance club song.

Monday, May 23, 1994
The Civic Auditorium, Portland, OR
● *Set I:* Chalk Dust Torture, Sample in a Jar, Foam, Fee -> Maze, The Horse > Silent in the Morning, Julius, Reba, Cavern
● *Set II:* Wilson, Run Like an Antelope, If I Could, Sparkle, Punch You in the Eye, You Enjoy Myself, Possum
● *Encore:* Ginseng Sullivan, Amazing Grace, Highway to Hell
● *Show Notes:* The YEM vocal jam included quotes of Psycho Killer. Ginseng Sullivan was performed acoustic.

Wednesday, May 25, 1994
The Warfield Theatre, San Francisco, CA
● *Set I:* The Curtain > Sample in a Jar, Uncle Pen, Stash, Colonel Forbin's Ascent > The Famous Mockingbird, Axilla (Part II), Scent of a Mule, My Sweet One, Sweet Adeline, Chalk Dust Torture
● *Set II:* Rift, Tweezer -> Lifeboy, Maze, Contact -> Big Ball Jam, Julius, Purple Rain, The Squirming Coil
● *Encore:* Sleeping Monkey -> Tweezer Reprise
● *Show Notes:* My Sweet One was performed acoustic.

Thursday, May 26, 1994
The Warfield Theatre, San Francisco, CA
● *Set I:* Buried Alive > Poor Heart > Cavern, Demand, Split Open and Melt, Sparkle > It's Ice > Catapult > Divided Sky, Sample in a Jar
● *Set II:* Also Sprach Zarathustra > Run Like an Antelope, Fluffhead, Down with Disease > Mound, Ginseng Sullivan, Dog Faced Boy, You Enjoy Myself, Amazing Grace

● *Encore:* Good Times Bad Times
● *Show Notes:* Ginseng Sullivan and Dog Faced Boy were performed acoustic and, along with Amazing Grace, without microphones.

Friday, May 27, 1994
The Warfield Theatre, San Francisco, CA
● *Set I:* Wilson, Runaway Jim, Foam, Bouncing Around the Room, David Bowie, If I Could, Punch You in the Eye, Harry Hood, Golgi Apparatus
● *Set II:* Suzy Greenberg, Peaches en Regalia, My Friend My Friend, Reba, The Lizards, Julius, Nellie Kane, My Mind's Got a Mind of its Own, Mike's Song -> Simple -> O Mio Babbino Caro, Possum
● *Encore:* Fire
● *Show Notes:* This show marked the debut of Simple. Nellie Kane and My Mind's Got a Mind of its Own were performed acoustic with guest fiddler Morgan Fichter. O Mio Babbino Caro, a Puccini aria, featured opera singer Andrea Baker singing unmiced. Before Possum, the band handed out boxes of Flintstones macaroni and cheese for the audience to shake along with Possum and Fire. Possum subsequently included a *Flintstones* theme tease.

Saturday, May 28, 1994
Laguna Seca Raceway, Monterey, CA
Laguna Seca Daze Festival with Phish, Sausage, Gin Blossoms and Freddy Jones Band
● *Set I:* Rift > Sample in a Jar, Foam, Bouncing Around the Room, Stash, The Horse > Silent in the Morning > The Sloth, Maze, Cavern
● *Set II:* Axilla (Part II) > It's Ice > Tweezer, Lifeboy > Reba, Fee > Llama, You Enjoy Myself
● *Encore:* Poor Heart
● *Show Notes:* This long, atypical YEM featured Les Claypool playing on a second bass guitar and included a band-accompanied bass duel between Mike and Les. The jam segment included Dueling Banjos teases from all (including Fishman) and the song ended without a vocal jam.

Sunday, May 29, 1994
Laguna Seca Raceway, Monterey, CA
Laguna Seca Daze Festival with Phish, Four Non Blondes, Big Head Todd and the Monsters, The Mother Hips and Meat Puppets
● *Set I:* Divided Sky, Guelah Papyrus, Halley's Comet > Down with Disease, Sparkle, Julius, I Didn't Know, David Bowie
● *Set II:* Nellie Kane, Split Open and Melt, Esther, Chalk Dust Torture, Horn, McGrupp and the Watchful Hosemasters, The Oh Kee Pa Ceremony > Suzy Greenberg, Run Like an Antelope, Freebird
● *Encore:* Wilson, Golgi Apparatus, Rocky Top
● *Encore:* Jam, Harry Hood, Good Times Bad Times
● *Show Notes:* The jam at the start of the second encore is often labeled as "Trey taking a leak Jam" because Trey was in the bathroom when the band took the stage. Wilson was played by request.

Thursday, June 9, 1994
Triad Amphitheater, Salt Lake City, UT
● *Set I:* Llama, Guelah Papyrus, Rift, Down with Disease, It's Ice, If I Could, Maze, Fee, Suzy Greenberg
● *Set II:* Split Open and Melt, Glide, Julius, Halley's Comet -> Scent of a Mule, Ginseng Sullivan, Mike's Song > I Am Hydrogen > Weekapaug

Groove, Golgi Apparatus
- *Encore:* Highway to Hell
- *Show Notes:* Ginseng Sullivan was performed acoustic without microphones.

Friday, June 10, 1994
Red Rocks Amphitheater, Morrison, CO
- *Check:* NICU, Funky Bitch, Blues Jam, Ginseng Sullivan
- *Set I:* Runaway Jim, Foam, Sample in a Jar, Nellie Kane, Demand -> David Bowie, The Lizards, Cavern, Julius
- *Set II:* Axilla (Part II), The Curtain, Tweezer -> Lifeboy, Sparkle, Possum, HYHU > I Wanna Be Like You > HYHU, Harry Hood, Tweezer Reprise
- *Encore:* Sleeping Monkey, Rocky Top

Saturday, June 11, 1994
Red Rocks Amphitheater, Morrison, CO
- *Set I:* Wilson > Chalk Dust Torture, You Enjoy Myself -> Rift, Down with Disease, It's Ice > Tela, Stash
- *Set II:* Also Sprach Zarathustra > Run Like an Antelope, Fluffhead, Scent of a Mule, Split Open and Melt, The Squirming Coil, Maze, Contact > Frankenstein
- *Encore:* Suzy Greenberg
- *Show Notes:* This show marked the breakout of Frankenstein, which hadn't been played since July 26, 1991 (326 shows). This version of SOAM is a fan favorite. Fluffhead was played after a group of screaming fans had been requesting it for the entire beginning of the show. Antelope included a tease of the *Odd Couple* theme.

Monday, June 13, 1994
Memorial Hall, Kansas City, KS
- *Check:* Jam -> Dog Gone Dog, Frankenstein
- *Set I:* Buried Alive > Poor Heart > Sample in a Jar, Divided Sky, Wolfman's Brother > Dinner and a Movie, Stash, Ginseng Sullivan, Julius
- *Set II:* Mike's Song > I Am Hydrogen > Weekapaug Groove, Esther, Cavern, Reba, Jesus Just Left Chicago, Scent of a Mule, Big Ball Jam, HYHU > Terrapin > HYHU, Slave to the Traffic Light
- *Encore:* Golgi Apparatus
- *Show Notes:* Ginseng Sullivan was performed acoustic, without microphones. Listen for a Voodoo Chile tease at the beginning of the encore. JJLC was played for the first time since August 26, 1993 (53 shows).

Tuesday, June 14, 1994
Civic Center, Des Moines, IA
- *Check:* Makisupa Policeman (different than usual; not reggae)
- *Set I:* Llama, Guelah Papyrus > Sweet Adeline > Digital Delay Loop Jam -> Guelah Papyrus, Rift, Down with Disease -> Fee -> My Friend My Friend, Uncle Pen, I Didn't Know > My Sweet One > I Didn't Know, Split Open and Melt
- *Set II:* Frankenstein, Demand > David Bowie, If I Could, It's Ice, Sparkle, You Enjoy Myself, HYHU > Bike > HYHU, Possum
- *Encore:* Sample in a Jar
- *Show Notes:* After The Asse Festival segment of Guelah, the band launched into Adeline and then moved into a Digital Delay Loop Jam before finishing the song. YEM included On Broadway teases in both the jam and the vocal jam; it was also teased during Possum. HYHU segued

out of the YEM vocal jam and included Fishman talking about how much he hates that song (though he has nothing personal against Argent, who wrote it). Possum included Dave's Energy Guide teases.

Thursday, June 16, 1994
State Theatre, Minneapolis, MN
- *Check:* Gumbo (three times)
- *Set I:* Bouncing Around the Room, Rift, Julius, Fee -> Maze, Gumbo, The Curtain > Dog Faced Boy, Stash, The Squirming Coil
- *Set II:* Suzy Greenberg, Run Like an Antelope, Colonel Forbin's Ascent -> Kung -> The Famous Mockingbird, Big Ball Jam, Down with Disease -> Contact > Big Black Furry Creature from Mars -> Purple Rain > HYHU, Golgi Apparatus
- *Encore:* Ginseng Sullivan, Amazing Grace, Good Times Bad Times
- *Show Notes:* BBFCFM was unfinished. Ginseng Sullivan was performed acoustic with no microphones. Amazing Grace was performed with no microphones and was dedicated to David "ZZYZX" Steinberg. Listen for serious Heartbreaker teases in GTBT. Stash contained a brief Dave's Energy Guide jam. The versions of Stash, Disease (preceded by a Bowie tease and ending with a smooth segue into Contact), and Antelope from this show are all particularly hot. Kung was played for the first time since August 7, 1993 (69 shows) and Gumbo was played for the first time since April 21, 1993 (103 shows).

Friday, June 17, 1994
Eagles Auditorium, Milwaukee, WI
- *Check:* The Wedge, Funky Bitch
- *Set I:* Runaway Jim, Foam, Glide, Split Open and Melt -> If I Could, Punch You in the Eye > Bathtub Gin > Scent of a Mule, Cavern
- *Set II:* Also Sprach Zarathustra > Sample in a Jar, Poor Heart, Mike's Song -> Simple -> Mike's Song > I Am Hydrogen > Weekapaug Groove, Harpua -> Kung -> Harpua, Sparkle, Big Ball Jam, Julius -> Frankenstein
- *Encore:* Sleeping Monkey, Rocky Top
- *Show Notes:* Harpua included Voodoo Chile and Simple teases. This is the infamous "O.J. Show," played on the night of O.J. Simpson's Bronco chase. Also Sprach, Mike's, Jim, and Poor Heart all included references to O.J. Mike's Song also included a *Mission: Impossible* tease and Hydrogen included Simple quotes.

Saturday, June 18, 1994
UIC Pavilion, University of Illinois, Chicago IL
- *Set I:* Wilson, Rift, AC/DC Bag, Maze, The Mango Song, Down with Disease, It's Ice, Dog Faced Boy, Divided Sky, Sample in a Jar
- *Set II:* Peaches en Regalia > David Bowie -> Mind Left Body Jam -> David Bowie, Horn > McGrupp and the Watchful Hosemasters > Tweezer > Lifeboy, You Enjoy Myself, Chalk Dust Torture
- *Encore:* Bouncing Around the Room, Tweezer Reprise
- *Show Notes:* Listen for "Mind Left Body" teases in Tweezer, as well as Three Blind Mice, Voodoo Chile and Purple Haze teases in Bowie. YEM included Frankenstein and How Many More Times teases, as well as a Monty Python "Spam" vocal jam.

Sunday, June 19, 1994
State Theatre, Kalamazoo, MI
- *Check:* Gumbo, Reggae Jam
- *Set I:* Suzy Greenberg, Julius, The Lizards, Axilla (Part II), The Cur-

tain, Fast Enough for You, Scent of a Mule, Stash, Golgi Apparatus
● *Set II:* Faht, Run Like an Antelope, If I Could, Reba, Makisupa Policeman, The Squirming Coil, My Sweet One, Highway to Hell
● *Encore:* Freebird
● *Show Notes:* My Sweet One was performed acoustic without microphones.

Tuesday, June 21, 1994
Cincinnati Music Hall, Cincinnati, OH
● *Set I:* Runaway Jim, Mound -> Sample in a Jar, It's Ice, The Horse
● *Set II:* Fire, Poor Heart > Down with Disease, My Friend My Friend, Split Open and Melt, Esther, Chalk Dust Torture, Big Black Furry Creature from Mars, Ginseng Sullivan, Big Black Furry Creature from Mars Reprise, Dog Faced Boy, Sweet Adeline, Julius, Sparkle, Harry Hood, Suzy Greenberg
● *Encore:* Amazing Grace
● *Show Notes:* After a few lines of The Horse, the fire alarm in the Music Hall went off. The band kept playing but the house lights came on and the building was cleared for 20 minutes. The music resumed with Fire, and that was the only "set break." Ginseng Sullivan through Dog Faced Boy were performed acoustic without microphones, and Sweet Adeline and Amazing Grace were performed without microphones.

Wednesday, June 22, 1994
Veterans Music Hall, Columbus, OH
● *Set I:* Llama, Guelah Papyrus, Rift, Gumbo > Maze, If I Could, Scent of a Mule, Stash, Golgi Apparatus
● *Set II:* Also Sprach Zarathustra > Mike's Song -> Simple -> Midnight Rider Jam -> Catapult -> Simple -> Icculus, Simple -> Mike's Song > I Am Hydrogen > Weekapaug Groove -> The Man Who Stepped Into Yesterday > Avenu Malkenu > The Man Who Stepped Into Yesterday Reprise > Digital Delay Loop Jam > Fluffhead, My Sweet One, Big Ball Jam > Jesus Just Left Chicago, Sample in a Jar
● *Encore:* Carolina, Cavern
● *Show Notes:* My Sweet One was performed acoustic and, along with Carolina, without microphones. Catapult was sung over the Midnight Rider jam. Icculus was played for the first time since March 25, 1993 (126 shows).

Thursday, June 23, 1994
Phoenix Center, Pontiac, MI
● *Set I:* Buried Alive, Poor Heart, Split Open and Melt, NICU, Foam, Bouncing Around the Room, Down with Disease, Silent in the Morning, Punch You in the Eye, Julius
● *Set II:* Frankenstein, David Bowie, The Mango Song > Axilla (Part II), Uncle Pen, Tweezer, Lifeboy > Slave to the Traffic Light
● *Encore:* Sparkle > Tweezer Reprise
● *Show Notes:* The first set included the first NICU since May 1, 1992 (246 shows). Silent was actually performed without The Horse. Tweezer included Sunshine of Your Love teases.

Friday, June 24, 1994
The Murat Theatre, Indianapolis, IN
● *Set I:* Divided Sky, Wilson, It's Ice, Fee, All Things Reconsidered, The Sloth, Paul and Silas, Horn, Reba, Sweet Adeline, Sample in a Jar
● *Set II:* Demand > Run Like an Antelope, Halley's Comet > The Curtain > McGrupp and the Watchful Hosemasters > Simple -> Sanity > Llama,

Dog Faced Boy, Poor Heart, Cavern, Carolina, Down with Disease
● *Encore:* Rocky Top
● *Show Notes:* Dog Faced Boy through Cavern, which contained the older, alternate lyrics, were performed acoustic without microphones. Carolina was also performed without microphones. This hot Antelope included a Disease-style jam segment. Wilson included a Simpsons Signal.

Saturday, June 25, 1994
Nautica Stage, Cleveland, OH
● *Set I:* NO2, Rift, Julius, NICU, Stash, The Mango Song, Sample in a Jar, Scent of a Mule, Tela, Chalk Dust Torture
● *Set II:* Suzy Greenberg, Maze, Sparkle, Bathtub Gin, Axilla (Part II), You Enjoy Myself, HYHU > Cracklin' Rosie > HYHU, Harry Hood, Golgi Apparatus
● *Encore:* Highway to Hell
● *Show Notes:* Though written many years earlier, NO2 made its first known appearance at this show.

Sunday, June 26, 1994
Municipal Auditorium, Charleston, WV
● *Set I:* Kung, Llama, The Lizards, Tela, Wilson, AC/DC Bag, Colonel Forbin's Ascent > The Famous Mockingbird, The Sloth, McGrupp and the Watchful Hosemasters, Divided Sky
● *Set II:* Julius, Down with Disease, If I Could, Axilla (Part II), Lifeboy, Sample in a Jar, Wolfman's Brother, Scent of a Mule, Dog Faced Boy, Demand -> Split Open and Melt Jam -> Yerushalayim Shel Zahav
● *Encore:* The Old Home Place, Amazing Grace, Tube, Fire
● *Show Notes:* This show is commonly referred to as "Game Hoist." The first set was the Gamehendge saga, including narration between songs. The second set was the entire Hoist album, save Riker's Mailbox. This show marked the first performance of The Old Home Place, the first complete Gamehendge since March 22, 1993, the first Yerushalayim Shel Zahav since July 24, 1993 (88 shows) and the first Tube since April 12, 1993 (118 shows). Divided Sky included Wipeout teases.

Wednesday, June 29, 1994
Walnut Creek Amphitheater, Raleigh, NC
● *Check:* Funky Bitch
● *Set I:* The Curtain, Sample in a Jar, Reba, Mound, Julius, The Horse > Silent in the Morning, Catapult -> David Bowie, I Didn't Know, Golgi Apparatus
● *Set II:* The Landlady, Poor Heart, Tweezer, It's Ice, Lifeboy, Divided Sky, Suzy Greenberg, Cavern
● *Encore:* Ya Mar, Tweezer Reprise
● *Show Notes:* Catapult was sung as the Bowie hi-hat intro started. I Didn't Know saw Fishman play his bass drum pedal on his knee, instead of taking his usual trumpet or vacuum solo. Ya Mar included a Simpsons Signal and a brief Dixie tease from Trey.

Thursday, June 30, 1994
Classic Amphitheater, Richmond, VA
● *Check:* Dog Gone Dog -> Jam
● *Set I:* Down with Disease, Gumbo, Rift, Guelah Papyrus, Split Open and Melt, Glide, Scent of a Mule, Bouncing Around the Room, Frankenstein
● *Set II:* Wilson -> Maze, You Enjoy Myself -> Yerushalayim Shel Zahav -> You Enjoy Myself, Sparkle, Axilla (Part II), Harpua -> Kung -> Harpua

-> Honky Tonk Women -> Harpua, Run Like an Antelope, HYHU > Love You > HYHU, Chalk Dust Torture
● *Encore:* Sleeping Monkey > Poor Heart
● *Show Notes:* Sean Hoppe, an audience member who may have also been working as a security guard at the show, was invited on stage during Harpua to sing Honky Tonk Women as Jimmy. The Antelope intro and HYHU subsequently included Harpua teases. Split Open and Melt included a vocal jam. Love You contained band intros and an unusually long vacuum solo. Both the YEM vocal jam and Sparkle had "Redrum" screeches from Trey, referencing the movie *The Shining.*

Friday, July 1, 1994
Mann Music Center, Philadelphia, PA
● *Check:* Dog Gone Dog, Funky Bitch, Jam, The Old Home Place
● *Set I:* Runaway Jim, Foam, Sample in a Jar, NICU > Stash, The Mango Song, It's Ice > Tela, Julius, Suzy Greenberg
● *Set II:* David Bowie, If I Could, Fluffhead, Down with Disease > The Man Who Stepped Into Yesterday > Avenu Malkenu > The Man Who Stepped Into Yesterday Reprise, Possum, HYHU > Terrapin > HYHU, Harry Hood, Cavern
● *Encore:* Rocky Top
● *Show Notes:* Possum included teases of Voodoo Child (Slight Return).

Saturday, July 2, 1994
Garden State Arts Center, Holmdel, NJ
● *Set I:* Golgi Apparatus, Divided Sky, Guelah Papyrus, Fast Enough for You, Scent of a Mule, Tweezer -> Lifeboy, Sparkle, Tweezer Reprise
● *Set II:* Also Sprach Zarathustra > Mike's Song -> Simple -> Mike's Song -> Yerushalayim Shel Zahav > I Am Hydrogen > Weekapaug Groove, McGrupp and the Watchful Hosemasters, Maze, Sample in a Jar, Slave to the Traffic Light, Highway to Hell
● *Encore:* Rift
● *Show Notes:* Weekapaug included teases of Antelope (including lyrics) and Also Sprach.

Sunday, July 3, 1994
Old Orchard Beach, ME
● *Set I:* My Friend My Friend, Poor Heart, Down with Disease, Fee, NICU, Horn, The Old Home Place, Reba, Axilla (Part II), David Bowie
● *Set II:* Split Open and Melt, The Lizards, Bouncing Around the Room, It's Ice, The Horse > Silent in the Morning, Julius, The Squirming Coil, Run Like an Antelope, Suzy Greenberg
● *Encore:* Fire
● *Show Notes:* Listen for a Somewhere Over the Rainbow tease at the end of Reba and a Simpsons Signal in SOAM. The jam in Antelope was accompanied by a fireworks display.

Tuesday, July 5, 1994
The Congress Center, Ottawa, Ontario, Canada
● *Set I:* Rift, Sample in a Jar, The Curtain > Letter to Jimmy Page, If I Could, Uncle Pen, Stash, Esther, Down with Disease, Sweet Adeline
● *Set II:* Punch You in the Eye > Sparkle > Bathtub Gin -> Lifeboy, Cities, You Enjoy Myself > The Great Gig in the Sky > HYHU, Ginseng Sullivan, My Sweet One, Amazing Grace, Golgi Apparatus
● *Encore:* Good Times Bad Times
● *Show Notes:* Two breakouts dotted the setlist: the first Letter to Jimmy

Page (separate from Alumni Blues) since November 19, 1987 (618 shows) and the first Cities since September 13, 1988 (586 shows). Trey quoted the theme from *Shaft* at the start of the second set. Sweet Adeline and Ginseng Sullivan through Amazing Grace were performed without microphones. Ginseng Sullivan and My Sweet One were performed acoustic. The latter evolved into a fun singalong with the audience during the second verse. Fans of *The Nutcracker* will want to listen for the Dance of the Sugar Plum Fairies tease to start the second set.

Wednesday, July 6, 1994
Theatre St. Denis, Montreal, Quebec, Canada
● *Set I:* Llama, Fluffhead, Julius, Bouncing Around the Room, Reba, Axilla (Part II), My Mind's Got a Mind of its Own, Carolina, David Bowie
● *Set II:* The Landlady > Poor Heart, Tweezer -> Lawn Boy, Chalk Dust Torture > Big Black Furry Creature from Mars > Sample in a Jar > Big Black Furry Creature from Mars, Harry Hood, Tweezer Reprise
● *Encore:* The Old Home Place, Nellie Kane, Memories, Funky Bitch
● *Show Notes:* The Old Home Place and Nellie Kane were performed acoustic and, along with Memories, were performed without microphones. Tweezer included HYHU, Also Sprach Zarathustra, Who Knows, and Donna Lee teases. Bowie and Llama both included teases of the *Munsters* theme song, and there was a brief Free Ride tease at the start of the show. Memories was played for the first time since December 28, 1993 (69 shows).

Friday, July 8, 1994
Great Woods Amphitheater, Mansfield, MA
● *Set I:* Llama, NO2, The Lizards, Tela, Wilson, AC/DC Bag, Colonel Forbin's Ascent > The Famous Mockingbird, The Sloth, McGrupp and the Watchful Hosemasters, Divided Sky
● *Set II:* Rift, Sample in a Jar, Reba, Yerushalayim Shel Zahav, It's Ice, Stash, You Enjoy Myself -> Frankenstein -> You Enjoy Myself, Julius, Golgi Apparatus
● *Encore:* Nellie Kane > Cavern
● *Show Notes:* The first set included the complete Gamehendge saga, including narration between songs. This version of Stash appears on the Elektra release, *A Live One.*

Saturday, July 9, 1994
Great Woods Amphitheater, Mansfield, MA
● *Set I:* Runaway Jim, Foam, Gumbo, Maze, Guelah Papyrus, Scent of a Mule, Down with Disease > The Horse > Silent in the Morning, Run Like an Antelope
● *Set II:* Also Sprach Zarathustra > Split Open and Melt, Fluffhead, Poor Heart, Tweezer -> Lifeboy, Sparkle -> Big Ball Jam, Harry Hood, Suzy Greenberg
● *Encore:* Sleeping Monkey, Tweezer Reprise

Sunday, July 10, 1994
Saratoga Performing Arts Center, Saratoga, NY
● *Set I:* Chalk Dust Torture, Horn, Peaches en Regalia, Rift, Stash, If I Could, My Friend My Friend, Julius, Cavern
● *Set II:* Sample in a Jar, David Bowie, Glide, Ya Mar, Mike's Song > I Am Hydrogen > Weekapaug Groove, Bouncing Around the Room, The Squirming Coil, Crimes of the Mind
● *Encore:* Golgi Apparatus, Rocky Top

● *Show Notes:* Low Rider was jammed in Mike's Song. Crimes (first since August 28, 1993, or 73 shows) featured the Dude of Life on vocals.

Wednesday, July 13, 1994
Big Birch Concert Pavilion, Patterson, NY
● *Set I:* Buried Alive > Poor Heart > Sample in a Jar, Foam, The Mango Song, Down with Disease > Fee -> It's Ice, Fast Enough for You, I Didn't Know, Split Open and Melt
● *Set II:* Possum, Cavern -> Wilson -> Cavern > NICU -> Tweezer -> Julius -> Tweezer -> Big Black Furry Creature from Mars -> Tweezer -> Mound, Slave to the Traffic Light, Suzy Greenberg
● *Encore:* My Sweet One, Tweezer Reprise
● *Show Notes:* This second set is noted as one of the most bizarre in all of Phishtory. BBFCFM was unfinished and played bluegrass style to the tune of Scent of a Mule. Trey teased Slave throughout Suzy Greenberg. Tweezer contained I Know a Little, I Wish, and Woody Woodpecker teases. This show contained highly interesting versions of Wilson and Cavern; Wilson was played to the tune of Cavern and then the closing Cavern lyrics were sung.

Thursday, July 14, 1994
Finger Lakes Performing Arts Center, Canandaigua, NY
● *Set I:* Runaway Jim, Bouncing Around the Room > Stash -> The Man Who Stepped Into Yesterday > Avenu Malkenu > The Man Who Stepped Into Yesterday Reprise, Scent of a Mule, Fluffhead -> The Horse > Silent in the Morning, Run Like an Antelope
● *Set II:* Also Sprach Zarathustra > Sample in a Jar, Maze, If I Could, Uncle Pen, You Enjoy Myself -> Sparkle -> Big Ball Jam, Harry Hood, Highway to Hell
● *Encore:* Chalk Dust Torture
● *Show Notes:* Stash was unfinished.

Friday, July 15, 1994
Jones Beach Amphitheater, Wantagh, NY
● *Set I:* Rift, Sample in a Jar, Divided Sky, Gumbo, Foam, Fee, Split Open and Melt, Golgi Apparatus
● *Set II:* Letter to Jimmy Page > David Bowie, Bouncing Around the Room, Reba, It's Ice > Yerushalayim Shel Zahav, Dog Faced Boy, Julius, Setting Sail, Runaway Jim
● *Encore:* Sleeping Monkey
● *Show Notes:* This show was historic, as it was the first solar-powered Phish show. Reba included *Brazil* and *Popeye* teases and was unfinished. This is the only known complete performance of the sing-along Setting Sail. It was last played on March 25, 1992 (289 shows). Ice was fantastic and featured a Page-led jam that is unlike most versions. Bowie included a full Jessica tease during the jam.

Saturday, July 16, 1994
Sugarbush Summer Stage, Sugarbush, VT
● *Set I:* Golgi Apparatus, Down with Disease, NO2, Stash, The Lizards, Cavern, The Horse > Silent in the Morning, Maze -> Sparkle, Sample in a Jar
● *Set II:* Run Like an Antelope -> Catapult -> Run Like an Antelope, Harpua -> Also Sprach Zarathustra -> Harpua, AC/DC Bag, Scent of a Mule, Harry Hood, Contact, Chalk Dust Torture
● *Encore:* Suzy Greenberg

● *Show Notes:* This show opened with a few *a cappella* lines of My Hometown. Harpua included a narration about the comet that crashed into Jupiter. This was a great Antelope that included a Simpsons Signal and saw Trey run around the stage with a megaphone. Catapult included a tease of The Beatles' Hey Bulldog and Chalk Dust included a Barracuda tease.

FALL, 1994

Friday, October 7, 1994
Stabler Arena, Lehigh University, Bethlehem, PA
● *Set I:* My Friend My Friend, Julius, Glide, Poor Heart, Divided Sky, Guelah Papyrus, Stash, Guyute, Golgi Apparatus
● *Set II:* Maze, The Horse > Silent in the Morning, Reba, Wilson, Scent of a Mule, Tweezer, Lifeboy, My Sweet One, Tweezer Reprise
● *Encore:* Foreplay/Long Time, Cavern
● *Show Notes:* This show marked the debut of Foreplay/Long Time and first performance of the completed Guyute, and provided the lasting image of Fishman on the "female washboard."

Saturday, October 8, 1994
Patriot Center, George Mason University, Fairfax, VA
● *Set I:* Chalk Dust Torture, Horn, Sparkle > Down with Disease, Guyute, Fee > It's Ice, Lawn Boy > Run Like an Antelope
● *Set II:* Also Sprach Zarathustra > Sample in a Jar, Rift > Mike's Song -> Simple -> Mike's Song > I Am Hydrogen > Weekapaug Groove, Fluffhead > Purple Rain > HYHU, Harry Hood, Suzy Greenberg
● *Encore:* Foreplay/Long Time, Rocky Top
● *Show Notes:* Between Mike's Song and Simple, a dozen or so members of a girl's soccer team took the stage for a cheer.

Sunday, October 9, 1994
Palumbo Center, Pittsburgh, PA
● *Set I:* Runaway Jim, Foam, Fast Enough for You, The Curtain, Dog Faced Boy, Split Open and Melt, The Squirming Coil
● *Set II:* David Bowie, Bouncing Around the Room, Scent of a Mule, You Enjoy Myself, Amazing Grace, Julius, Contact, Possum
● *Encore:* Sleeping Monkey, Poor Heart
● *Show Notes:* This version of Coil appears on *A Live One*.

Monday, October 10, 1994
The Palace Theatre, Louisville, KY
● *Set I:* Sample in a Jar, Divided Sky, The Horse > Silent in the Morning, Sparkle, Stash, Guyute, The Old Home Place, Ginseng Sullivan, Nellie Kane, Chalk Dust Torture
● *Set II:* Golgi Apparatus, Maze, Esther > Tweezer, Fee -> Rift, Down with Disease -> HYHU > Love You > HYHU, Slave to the Traffic Light
● *Encore:* Foreplay/Long Time, Tweezer Reprise
● *Show Notes:* The Old Home Place through Nellie Kane featured Steve Cooley on banjo and, along with the encore, were performed acoustic.

Wednesday, October 12, 1994
The Orpheum Theatre, Memphis, TN

● *Set I:* My Friend My Friend, Reba, The Sloth, Poor Heart, Split Open and Melt, The Lizards, Guelah Papyrus, Julius, Sweet Adeline
● *Set II:* Peaches en Regalia, David Bowie, Bouncing Around the Room, Scent of a Mule, You Enjoy Myself, Nellie Kane, Foreplay/Long Time, Harry Hood, Sample in a Jar
● *Encore:* Good Times Bad Times
● *Show Notes:* Nellie Kane was performed acoustic.

Thursday, October 13, 1994
Grove Arena, University of Mississippi, Oxford, MS
● *Set I:* Llama, Gumbo, All Things Reconsidered, Down with Disease, I Didn't Know, Foam, Fast Enough for You, Sparkle, Stash
● *Set II:* The Old Home Place, Run Like an Antelope, If I Could, It's Ice, Amazing Grace, Mike's Song -> Simple, Mike's Song > Yerushalayim Shel Zahav, Weekapaug Groove, Foreplay/Long Time, Cavern
● *Encore:* Fire
● *Show Notes:* Antelope included a hi-hat solo from Fishman.

Friday, October 14, 1994
McAlister Auditorium, Tulane University, New Orleans, LA
● *Set I:* Buried Alive > Sample in a Jar -> Divided Sky, The Horse > Silent in the Morning, Punch You in the Eye, Bathtub Gin, Sweet Adeline, Rift, Colonel Forbin's Ascent > The Famous Mockingbird, Julius
● *Set II:* The Curtain > Tweezer -> Lifeboy, Guyute, Chalk Dust Torture, Nellie Kane, Beaumont Rag, Foreplay/Long Time, The Squirming Coil, Tweezer Reprise
● *Encore:* Ya Mar, Cavern
● *Show Notes:* Nellie Kane and Beaumont Rag were performed acoustic. Ya Mar and Cavern featured Michael Ray on trumpet and shaker and Carl Gerhard on trumpet.

Saturday, October 15, 1994
Oak Mt. Auditorium, Pelham, AL
● *Opening Act:* The Dave Matthews Band
● *Set I:* Wilson, Sparkle, Simple -> Maze, Glide, Reba, Down with Disease, Golgi Apparatus
● *Set II:* Also Sprach Zarathustra > Runaway Jim, Halley's Comet -> Scent of a Mule, You Enjoy Myself -> Catapult -> You Enjoy Myself, Amazing Grace, Foreplay/Long Time, Bouncing Around the Room, Suzy Greenberg
● *Encore:* Drums Jam -> The Maker
● *Show Notes:* The encore featured the first, and only, performance of The Maker, complete with a Dave Matthews Band guest appearance. Carter Beauford appeared on stage with Fishman during the preceding jam.

Sunday, October 16, 1994
Chattanooga Memorial Aud, Chattanooga, TN
● *Set I:* Rift, Horn, Foam, Fee, Split Open and Melt, The Man Who Stepped Into Yesterday > Avenu Malkenu > The Man Who Stepped Into Yesterday Reprise, Axilla, Possum
● *Set II:* The Landlady, Poor Heart, Julius, Fluffhead, Big Ball Jam, Run Like an Antelope, Dog Faced Boy, Sweet Adeline, Sample in a Jar
● *Encore:* Highway to Hell
● *Encore:* Harpua
● *Show Notes:* Axilla was played for the first time since August 16, 1993 (93 shows).

Tuesday, October 18, 1994
Vanderbilt University Memorial Gym, Nashville, TN
● *Set I:* Simple > My Friend My Friend -> I Didn't Know, Poor Heart, Stash, Tela, It's Ice, Guyute, Divided Sky, Amazing Grace
● *Set II:* David Bowie, The Horse > Silent in the Morning, Reba, Scent of a Mule, Lifeboy, The Old Home Place, Beaumont Rag, Nellie Kane, Llama
● *Encore:* My Sweet One
● *Show Notes:* Scent of a Mule through Llama featured Bela Fleck on banjo. Llama began in the acoustic setup, but, during the song, the band members switched back to their electric instruments. After Silent, Trey humorously introduced Fishman as the "creature from the Black Lagoon," referencing the horror movie of the same name.

Thursday, October 20, 1994
Mahaffey Theatre, St. Petersburg, FL
● *Set I:* Runaway Jim, Golden Lady, Poor Heart, Guelah Papyrus, Split Open and Melt -> Kung -> Split Open and Melt, Esther, Julius, Guyute, Golgi Apparatus
● *Set II:* Lengthwise -> Maze, McGrupp and the Watchful Hosemasters, Rift, Harry Hood, Nellie Kane, Foreplay/Long Time, Chalk Dust Torture
● *Encore:* Sample in a Jar
● *Show Notes:* Nellie Kane was performed acoustic. The first set included the first, and only, live performance of Golden Lady, although it has been soundchecked on other occasions. Esther included Random Note and Simpsons Signals. Lengthwise was played for the first time since August 13, 1993 (98 shows).

Friday, October 21, 1994
Sunrise Musical Theatre, Sunrise, FL
● *Set I:* Fee, Down with Disease > Foam, The Mango Song, The Old Home Place, Stash, The Lizards, Dog Faced Boy, Run Like an Antelope
● *Set II:* Also Sprach Zarathustra > Mike's Song -> Simple -> Mike's Song > I Am Hydrogen > Weekapaug Groove, Sleeping Monkey, The Curtain, Fast Enough for You, Scent of a Mule, Slave to the Traffic Light
● *Encore:* Sweet Adeline, Foreplay/Long Time, Cavern
● *Show Notes:* Antelope included an All Fall Down signal and a Cannonball tease. Weekapaug closed with a Can't You Hear Me Knockin' jam. Foreplay was subsequently teased again in Cavern.

Saturday, October 22, 1994
The Edge Concert Field, Orlando, FL
● *Set I:* Suzy Greenberg, Divided Sky, Gumbo, Axilla (Part II), Rift, Split Open and Melt, Fluffhead, Julius
● *Set II:* Peaches en Regalia, David Bowie, The Horse > Silent in the Morning, Dinner and a Movie, Tweezer -> Wilson, Reba, Amazing Grace, AC/DC Bag, Highway to Hell
● *Encore:* Uncle Pen, Tweezer Reprise
● *Show Notes:* Reba was unfinished.

Sunday, October 23, 1994
The Band Shell, University of Florida, Gainesville, FL
● *Check:* Ginseng Sullivan, Funky Bitch, Golden Lady
● *Set I:* Chalk Dust Torture -> My Friend My Friend, Sparkle, Simple, Poor Heart, Stash -> Catapult -> Stash, Tela > Maze, Sample in a Jar
● *Set II:* Runaway Jim, Bouncing Around the Room > Halley's Comet > You Enjoy Myself, Down with Disease, Purple Rain, Harry Hood, Fee,

Good Times Bad Times
● *Encore:* The Squirming Coil
● *Show Notes:* Runaway Jim contained a Gypsy Queen tease. This was a free show. This version of Harry Hood appears on *A Live One*.

Tuesday, October 25, 1994
Atlanta Civic Center, Atlanta, GA
● *Set I:* Fee, Llama, Horn, Julius, The Horse > Silent in the Morning, Split Open and Melt, The Lizards, Sample in a Jar
● *Set II:* Mike's Song -> Simple > The Mango Song > Weekapaug Groove -> Yerushalayim Shel Zahav -> Glide, Axilla (Part II), Jesus Just Left Chicago -> Big Ball Jam -> If I Only Had a Brain, Possum
● *Encore:* Foreplay/Long Time, Golgi Apparatus
● *Show Notes:* The second set opened with a Voodoo Chile tease and Weekapaug included an On Broadway tease. Brain was played for the first time since December 29, 1993 (90 shows).

Wednesday, October 26, 1994
Varsity Gym, Appalachian State University, Boone, NC
● *Set I:* Simple, It's Ice, NICU, Run Like an Antelope, Guyute, Dog Faced Boy, Scent of a Mule, The Oh Kee Pa Ceremony > Suzy Greenberg, Runaway Jim
● *Set II:* Rift, Bouncing Around the Room, Reba, Axilla (Part II), You Enjoy Myself, Cracklin' Rosie, David Bowie
● *Encore:* Nellie Kane, Foreplay/Long Time, Amazing Grace
● *Show Notes:* YEM included The Vibration of Life. Nellie Kane was performed acoustic.

Thursday, October 27, 1994
University Hall, University of Virginia, Charlottesville, VA
● *Set I:* Wilson, Sparkle, Maze, Colonel Forbin's Ascent -> The Vibration of Life -> The Famous Mockingbird, Divided Sky, The Horse > Silent in the Morning, Poor Heart, Cavern
● *Set II:* Julius, Ya Mar, Tweezer, Contact, Big Black Furry Creature from Mars, Down with Disease, Sweet Adeline
● *Encore:* Slave to the Traffic Light -> Icculus, Tweezer Reprise

Friday, October 28, 1994
Galliard Auditorium, Charleston, SC
● *Set I:* I Didn't Know, Llama, Guelah Papyrus, Scent of a Mule, Stash, Glide, Axilla (Part II), All Things Reconsidered, Sample in a Jar, Carolina
● *Set II:* Also Sprach Zarathustra > David Bowie -> Manteca -> David Bowie, The Lizards, Peaches en Regalia, Rift, Lifeboy, Chalk Dust Torture, The Old Home Place, Nellie Kane, Foreplay/Long Time
● *Encore:* Fee, Highway to Hell
● *Show Notes:* The Old Home Place and Nellie Kane were performed acoustic. Manteca was played for the first time since May 7, 1993 (131 shows).

Saturday, October 29, 1994
Spartanburg Memorial Auditorium, Spartanburg, SC
● *Set I:* My Friend My Friend, Sparkle > Simple -> Runaway Jim, Foam, Lawn Boy, Split Open and Melt -> Buffalo Bill -> Makisupa Policeman -> Rift
● *Set II:* Down with Disease -> The Man Who Stepped Into Yesterday > Avenu Malkenu > The Man Who Stepped Into Yesterday Reprise ->

Sparks, Uncle Pen, You Enjoy Myself, HYHU > Bike > HYHU, Run Like an Antelope -> Sleeping Monkey > Run Like an Antelope
● *Encore:* Harry Hood
● *Show Notes:* During Bike, Fishman made reference to the new dress he was given that afternoon and wore to the show. Listen for a *Star Wars* jam during Antelope, right before the transition into Sleeping Monkey. Sparks was played for the first time since May 7, 1994 (65 shows) and Buffalo Bill was played for the first time since November 21, 1992 (223 shows).

Monday, October 31, 1994
Glens Falls Civic Center, Glens Falls, NY
● *Set I:* Frankenstein, Sparkle, Simple, Divided Sky, Harpua, Julius, The Horse > Silent in the Morning, Reba, Golgi Apparatus
● *Set II:* Speak to Me > The Beatles' *The Beatles* (also known as *The White Album*): Back in the USSR, Dear Prudence, Glass Onion, Ob La Di Ob La Da, Wild Honey Pie, The Continuing Story of Bungalow Bill, While My Guitar Gently Weeps, Happiness is a Warm Gun, Martha My Dear, I'm So Tired, Blackbird, Piggies, Rocky Raccoon, Don't Pass Me By, Why Don't We Do it in the Road, I Will, Julia, Birthday Jam, Yer Blues, Mother Nature's Son, Everybody's Got Something to Hide Except for Me and My Monkey, Sexy Sadie, Helter Skelter, Long Long Long, Revolution, Honey Pie, Savoy Truffle, Cry Baby Cry, Revolution 9, Good Night
● *Set III:* David Bowie, Bouncing Around the Room, Slave to the Traffic Light, Rift, Sleeping Monkey, Poor Heart, Run Like an Antelope
● *Encore:* Amazing Grace, Costume Contest, The Squirming Coil
● *Show Notes:* Harpua included the Vibrations of Life and Death, and a War Pigs tease. In a classic Halloween tease, a Pink Floyd *Dark Side of the Moon* tease (the heartbeats from Speak to Me) was pumped through the P.A. at the beginning of the second set. All of the *White Album* songs were debuts, although Ob La Di, Ob La Da had been jammed or teased on many occasions. Birthday wasn't sung; Page and Mike doodled a bit while Fishman presented a birthday cake to Brad Sands, who accepted it while wearing a Fishman dress. Good Night was taped from the album. The background tape playing along with Revolution 9 is Mike's composition He Ent to the Bog, also known as Hamburger, from Phish's *White Tape*. The song ended with Fishman stark naked and running around while the band blew bubbles and waved. Listen for Trey's Custard Pie tease at the start of the third set! Amazing versions of Reba and Simple were performed, as well as an Antelope that is marred only by a miscued entrance after the lyrics segment.

Wednesday, November 2, 1994
Bangor Auditorium, Bangor, ME
● *Set I:* Suzy Greenberg, Foam, If I Could, Maze, Guyute, Stash, Scent of a Mule, While My Guitar Gently Weeps
● *Set II:* Halley's Comet -> Tweezer > The Mango Song, Axilla (Part II), Possum, The Lizards, Sample in a Jar
● *Encore:* The Old Home Place, Foreplay/Long Time, Tweezer Reprise
● *Show Notes:* The Old Home Place was performed acoustic. While Mike tuned up for Foreplay/Long Time, Trey talked about the fact that the Bangor Auditorium and Nectar's are both on Route 2, so the band had been playing on that road for eleven years. This amazing version of Tweezer appears on *A Live One*.

Thursday, November 3, 1994
The Mullins Center, University of Massachusetts, Amherst, MA
● *Set I:* Fee, Divided Sky, Wilson, Peaches en Regalia, Glide, Split Open and Melt, Dog Faced Boy, Sparkle, Down with Disease
● *Set II:* Also Sprach Zarathustra > Simple -> Poor Heart > Julius, You Enjoy Myself -> Big Black Furry Creature from Mars, Harry Hood, Cavern
● *Encore:* My Sweet One, Nellie Kane, Amazing Grace, Highway to Hell
● *Show Notes:* YEM included The Vibration of Life. My Sweet One and Nellie Kane were performed acoustic.

Friday, November 4, 1994
Onondaga War Memorial Auditorium, Syracuse, NY
● *Set I:* Sample in a Jar > It's Ice > Bouncing Around the Room, David Bowie, Colonel Forbin's Ascent > The Famous Mockingbird, Scent of a Mule, Suzy Greenberg > Chalk Dust Torture
● *Set II:* The Curtain, Mike's Song -> Simple -> Mike's Song > Tela > Weekapaug Groove, Ya Mar > Golgi Apparatus, Slave to the Traffic Light
● *Encore:* Loving Cup, Rocky Top
● *Show Notes:* The Forbin's narration was based around The Vibration of Life and a green light that transported fans to a Gamehendge revival. Weekapaug closed with a strong Can't You Hear Me Knockin' jam. Loving Cup was played for the first time since May 7, 1994 (69 shows).

Saturday, November 12, 1994
The Mac Center at Kent State University, Kent, OH
● *Set I:* Runaway Jim, Foam, If I Could, Maze, Guyute, Stash, Esther, Chalk Dust Torture
● *Set II:* Julius, Fluffhead, Down with Disease -> Have Mercy -> Down with Disease -> Lifeboy, Rift, The Old Home Place, Nellie Kane, Foreplay/Long Time, Harry Hood, Golgi Apparatus
● *Encore:* Sample in a Jar
● *Show Notes:* The Old Home Place and Nellie Kane were performed acoustic. Have Mercy was played for the first time since August 14, 1993 (110 shows).

Sunday, November 13, 1994
Erie Warner Theatre, Erie, PA
● *Set I:* Wilson, Sparkle, Simple, Reba, Axilla (Part II), It's Ice -> The Vibration of Life -> The Horse > Silent in the Morning, Run Like an Antelope
● *Set II:* Suzy Greenberg, Divided Sky, The Lizards, Tweezer, The Mango Song, Big Black Furry Creature from Mars, Amazing Grace, The Squirming Coil
● *Encore:* Funky Bitch, Tweezer Reprise
● *Show Notes:* Amazing Grace was performed without microphones.

Monday, November 14, 1994
Devos Hall, Grand Rapids, MI
● *Set I:* My Friend My Friend, Scent of a Mule, Guelah Papyrus, Split Open and Melt, Bouncing Around the Room, The Landlady, Maze, Lawn Boy > Cavern
● *Set II:* Peaches en Regalia > David Bowie, Yerushalayim Shel Zahav -> Slave to the Traffic Light, Poor Heart, Julius, The Old Home Place, Nellie Kane, Sweet Adeline, You Enjoy Myself
● *Encore:* Golgi Apparatus
● *Show Notes:* The Old Home Place and Nellie Kane were performed acoustic.

Wednesday, November 16, 1994
Hill Auditorium, University of Michigan, Ann Arbor, MI
● *Set I:* Sample in a Jar, Foam, Fast Enough for You, Reba, Axilla (Part II), The Lizards, Stash, Pig in a Pen, Tennessee Waltz, Earl's Breakdown, Swing Low (Sweet Chariot)
● *Set II:* Mike's Song -> Simple, I'm Blue I'm Lonesome, My Long Journey Home, Chalk Dust Torture, Fee, Run Like an Antelope
● *Encore:* Amazing Grace, Suzy Greenberg
● *Show Notes:* Pig in a Pen through Swing Low (Sweet Chariot) featured the Reverend Jeff Mosier on banjo and vocals, as this show marked the beginning of Mosier's five-night tour with the band. I'm Blue I'm Lonesome and My Long Journey Home were also performed acoustic. This version of Chalk Dust appears on *A Live One*. Tennessee Waltz was played for the first time since May 6, 1993 (141 shows), Pig in a Pen was played for the first time since February 23, 1993 (191 shows), and Swing Low was played for the first time since October 20, 1989 (566 shows).

Thursday, November 17, 1994
Hara Arena, Dayton, OH
● *Set I:* Helter Skelter, Scent of a Mule, Maze, Bouncing Around the Room, Wilson, Divided Sky, Dog Faced Boy, Colonel Forbin's Ascent > The Vibration of Life > The Famous Mockingbird, Down with Disease
● *Set II:* Also Sprach Zarathustra > David Bowie, Sleeping Monkey > Sparkle, You Enjoy Myself -> HYHU Vocal Jam -> Love You > HYHU, Slave to the Traffic Light, Golgi Apparatus
● *Encore:* I'm Blue I'm Lonesome, Nellie Kane, My Long Journey Home, Fixin' To Die
● *Show Notes:* The Vibration of Life featured a Wipeout tease. I'm Blue I'm Lonesome through Long Journey were performed acoustic; My Long Journey Home featured the Reverend Jeff Mosier on spoons. The encore included the first performance of Fixin' to Die, which featured Mosier on banjo and lead vocals. Listen for fun versions of Bowie and YEM, including Frankenstein teases in the latter.

Friday, November 18, 1994
Auditorium at Michigan State U., East Lansing, MI
● *Set I:* Rift, AC/DC Bag, Julius, The Horse > Silent in the Morning, It's Ice, Tela, Split Open and Melt, Little Tiny Butter Biscuits, The Old Home Place, My Long Journey Home
● *Set II:* Llama, Bathtub Gin, Lifeboy, Poor Heart, Tweezer -> Contact, Possum
● *Encore:* Roll in My Sweet Baby's Arms, Runaway Jim
● *Show Notes:* Little Tiny Butter Biscuits, The Old Home Place, My Long Journey Home, and Roll in My Sweet Baby's Arms were performed acoustic with the Reverend Jeff Mosier. Little Tiny Butter Biscuits featured Trey on fiddle.

Saturday, November 19, 1994
Indiana University Auditorium, Bloomington, IN
● Check: Fixin' to Die
● *Set I:* Golgi Apparatus, Down with Disease, Guyute, Axilla (Part II), Paul and Silas, The Man Who Stepped Into Yesterday > Avenu Malkenu -> Run Like an Antelope, I'm Blue I'm Lonesome, Little Tiny Butter Biscuits, My Long Journey Home
● *Set II:* Suzy Greenberg, Sparkle, You Enjoy Myself > HYHU > Crack-

lin' Rosie > HYHU, Harry Hood, Amazing Grace, Good Times Bad Times
● *Encore:* The Squirming Coil
● *Show Notes:* I'm Blue I'm Lonesome through My Long Journey Home were performed acoustic with the Reverend Jeff Mosier. Little Tiny Butter Biscuits and My Long Journey Home featured Trey on fiddle. YEM included The Vibration of Life and Spooky teases.

Saturday, November 19, 1994
Parking Lot, Indiana University Auditorium, Bloomington, IN
Cripple Creek, Tennessee Waltz, The Old Home Place, Jubilee, Mountain Dew, Pig in a Pen, Dooley, Roll in My Sweet Baby's Arms, My Long Journey Home, Little Tiny Butter Biscuits, I'm Blue I'm Lonesome, Midnight Moonlight, Will the Circle Be Unbroken
● *Show Notes:* The lineup for this bluegrass jam included Mike on banjo and electric bass, Page on bass, Trey on guitar and fiddle, Fishman on mandolin, Reverend Jeff Mosier on banjo, Eric Merrill on fiddle, a fan named Jeremy on banjo, and an unidentified player on the jaw harp. Tapes of this bluegrass session circulate, thanks to an alert taper who spotted the jam in progress near the tour bus.

Sunday, November 20, 1994
Dane County Exposition Center, Madison, WI
● *Set I:* Chalk Dust Torture, Fee > Scent of a Mule, Stash, If I Could, Little Tiny Butter Biscuits, My Long Journey Home, Dooley, Divided Sky, Sample in a Jar
● *Set II:* Also Sprach Zarathustra > David Bowie, Glide, Axilla (Part II), Reba, Simple, Rift > HYHU > Terrapin > HYHU, Julius > Cavern
● *Encore:* Icculus
● *Encore:* Fire
● *Show Notes:* If I Could through Dooley featured the Reverend Jeff Mosier. Little Tiny Butter Biscuits through Dooley were performed acoustic. Reba was unfinished. This show marked the end of Reverend Jeff Mosier's travels with the band. The Icculus encore recalled the last time the band was in Wisconsin, which was the infamous "O.J. Show" from June of that same year.

Tuesday, November 22, 1994
Jesse Auditorium, University of Missouri, Columbia, MO
● *Set I:* Buried Alive, Poor Heart, Horn, Foam, Guyute, I Didn't Know, Bouncing Around the Room, Down with Disease, Sweet Adeline
● *Set II:* Funky Bitch -> Jam -> Yerushalayim Shel Zahav, Cry Baby Cry, The Curtain > Blackbird, Runaway Jim -> Big Black Furry Creature from Mars, I'm Blue I'm Lonesome, Little Tiny Butter Biscuits, My Long Journey Home, Harry Hood, Highway to Hell
● *Encore:* The Lizards
● *Show Notes:* This show featured an incredible second set, with a long jam out of Funky Bitch and the return of two Beatles' songs. BBFCFM was started electric and finished in the acoustic bluegrass lineup. Harry Hood was played as a result of an audience member's request after Trey said that the crowd could pick the next song.

Wednesday, November 23, 1994
The Fox Theatre, St. Louis, MO
● *Set I:* Wilson > Sparkle > Simple, It's Ice, If I Could, The Oh Kee Pa Ceremony -> Suzy Greenberg, Divided Sky, Amazing Grace
● *Set II:* Maze, Fee, Scent of a Mule, Tweezer, Lifeboy, You Enjoy My-

self, Tweezer Reprise
● *Encore:* Sample in a Jar
● *Show Notes:* YEM contained The Vibration of Life and a Frankenstein tease.

Friday, November 25, 1994
UIC Pavilion, Chicago, IL
● *Set I:* Llama, Guelah Papyrus, Reba, Bouncing Around the Room, Split Open and Melt, Esther, Julius, Golgi Apparatus
● *Set II:* Also Sprach Zarathustra > Mike's Song -> Simple -> Harpua, Weekapaug Groove -> The Mango Song > Purple Rain > HYHU, Run Like an Antelope
● *Encore:* Good Times Bad Times
● *Show Notes:* This Thanksgiving Harpua included the first-ever Glowstick War, as Trey narrated a story involving happy green love beams and angry red hate beams. Simple and Weekapaug, which segued strongly into Mango, both featured some fun improvisation and metalesque jamming.

Saturday, November 26, 1994
The Orpheum Theatre, Minneapolis, MN
● *Set I:* My Friend My Friend, Possum, Guyute, If I Could, Foam, The Horse > Silent in the Morning, Poor Heart, Cavern
● *Set II:* Halley's Comet > David Bowie, Sweet Adeline, The Lizards, Sample in a Jar, Slave to the Traffic Light
● *Encore:* Rocky Top
● *Show Notes:* Guyute was incomplete, as it was missing the second verse. Bowie ran over 36 minutes and included a vacuum jam from Fishman. This version of Slave appears on *A Live One*.

Monday, November 28, 1994
Field House at Montana State University, Bozeman, MT
● *Set I:* Chalk Dust Torture, Also Sprach Zarathustra, Scent of a Mule, Stash, Guyute, Sparkle, Simple, Divided Sky, Sweet Adeline
● *Set II:* Suzy Greenberg -> NICU, Tweezer, Sleeping Monkey, Julius
● *Encore:* Fee, Tweezer Reprise
● *Show Notes:* Simple featured Cameron McKinney on saxophone. A portion of the jam segment from this long (nearly 45 minutes), experimental Tweezer appeared on *A Live One* as Montana.

Wednesday, November 30, 1994
Campus Rec. Center at Evergreen College, Olympia, WA
● *Set I:* Frankenstein, Poor Heart, My Friend My Friend, Reba, Colonel Forbin's Ascent > The Famous Mockingbird, Down with Disease, Bouncing Around the Room, I'm Blue I'm Lonesome, My Long Journey Home
● *Set II:* Halley's Comet > Run Like an Antelope -> My Sweet One -> Run Like an Antelope -> Fixin' To Die -> Ya Mar -> Mike's Song -> Catapult -> McGrupp and the Watchful Hosemasters > Cavern
● *Encore:* The Horse > Silent in the Morning, Amazing Grace
● *Show Notes:* Reba was incomplete. The Forbin's narration included The Vibration of Life. I'm Blue I'm Lonesome and My Long Journey Home were performed acoustic. This show was home to a great second set with an almost uninterrupted stream of segues. There was an unusually long delay at the end of My Sweet One, with some of the band members "snoring." Antelope was unfinished. Amazing Grace was performed *a cappella* without microphones. Check out the amazing

segue from Ya Mar into Mike's.

Thursday, December 1, 1994
Salem Armory, Salem, OR
● *Set I:* Sample in a Jar, Uncle Pen, Fast Enough for You > Maze, Guyute, I Didn't Know, Split Open and Melt, Sweet Adeline
● *Set II:* Peaches en Regalia, Mound, Tweezer -> Big Black Furry Creature from Mars -> Makisupa Policeman -> NICU -> Tweezer -> Jesus Just Left Chicago -> Harry Hood, Golgi Apparatus
● *Encore:* Sleeping Monkey > Tweezer Reprise
● *Show Notes:* Sweet Adeline was performed without microphones. The second set was held together by yet another great Tweezer with many strong transitions between songs and a Norwegian Wood tease right before an abbreviated (but active) BBFCFM.

Friday, December 2, 1994
Recreation Hall at UC Davis, Davis, CA
● Opening Act: Dave Matthews Band
● *Check:* Caravan, Julius, Funky Bitch, Magilla, Gumbo
● *Set I:* Poor Heart, Also Sprach Zarathustra, Sparkle, Simple -> It's Ice, The Lizards, Stash, The Squirming Coil
● *Set II:* Chalk Dust Torture, David Bowie, Buried Alive, Julius, The Landlady, Gumbo, Caravan, Suzy Greenberg
● *Encore:* Cavern
● *Show Notes:* The Cosmic Country Horns came in at the end of Bowie and played until the end of the show. Horns players included Dave Grippo on alto sax and percussion, Carl Gerhard on trumpet, Michael Ray on trumpet, James Harvey on trombone, and Peter Apfelbaum on baritone sax, tenor sax and flute. This version of Gumbo appears on *A Live One*. Based on advance ticket sales, the venue was changed from the university's Varsity Hall roughly a week before the show to accommodate the larger-than-expected crowd. Caravan was played for the first time since May 4, 1994 (87 shows).

Saturday, December 3, 1994
Event Center, San Jose, CA
● Opening Act: Dave Matthews Band
● *Set I:* Wilson, Divided Sky, Guelah Papyrus, Scent of a Mule, Run Like an Antelope, Guyute, Sample in a Jar
● *Set II:* Frankenstein, Suzy Greenberg, Buried Alive, Gumbo, Slave to the Traffic Light, The Landlady, Touch Me, Alumni Blues Jam, Julius, Cavern
● *Encore:* Golgi Apparatus
● *Show Notes:* The entire second set (but not the encore) featured the Cosmic Country Horns. The horns players included Dave Grippo on alto sax and percussion, Carl Gerhard on trumpet , Michael Ray on trumpet, James Harvey on trombone, and Peter Apfelbaum on baritone, tenor sax and flute. The Alumni jam included an introduction of the horn section. The appearance of the horns led to the first Touch Me since July 27, 1991 (391 shows).

Sunday, December 4, 1994
Acker Gym at Chico State University, Chico, CA
● *Set I:* Runaway Jim, Foam, If I Could, Rift, Tweezer, Fee, Mound, Sweet Adeline, Possum
● *Set II:* Maze, Bouncing Around the Room, Reba, Axilla (Part II), You Enjoy Myself, Purple Rain, Good Times Bad Times

● *Encore:* Sleeping Monkey, Rocky Top
● *Show Notes:* Sweet Adeline was performed without microphones. Tweezer and Reba were unfinished. Possum included an All Fall Down Signal and Foam included a silent jam.

Tuesday, December 6, 1994
The Event Center at UCSB, Santa Barbara, CA
● *Set I:* Llama, Mound, Down with Disease, Fluffhead, Jesus Just Left Chicago, Sparkle, Stash, Golgi Apparatus
● *Set II:* The Curtain > Sample in a Jar, Also Sprach Zarathustra, Poor Heart, Mike's Song -> Simple -> The Mango Song -> Weekapaug Groove, Bike, I'm Blue I'm Lonesome, Foreplay/Long Time, Run Like an Antelope
● *Encore:* Back in the USSR
● *Show Notes:* I'm Blue I'm Lonesome was performed acoustic.

Wednesday, December 7, 1994
Spreckels Theatre, San Diego, CA
● *Set I:* Peaches en Regalia > Runaway Jim, The Sloth, Ya Mar, Split Open and Melt, Guyute, Lifeboy, Chalk Dust Torture
● *Set II:* Rift, Frankenstein, Divided Sky, Fee -> Julius, I'm Blue I'm Lonesome, My Long Journey Home, Amazing Grace, You Enjoy Myself
● *Encore:* Cavern
● *Show Notes:* I'm Blue I'm Lonesome was performed acoustic and, along with Long Journey Home and Amazing Grace, was performed without microphones. This version of YEM appears on *A Live One*.

Thursday, December 8, 1994
Spreckels Theatre, San Diego, CA
● *Set I:* Makisupa Policeman -> Maze, AC/DC Bag, Scent of a Mule, Punch You in the Eye, Simple -> Catapult -> Simple -> The Lizards, While My Guitar Gently Weeps
● *Set II:* Possum, My Mind's Got a Mind of its Own, Axilla (Part II), Reba, Nellie Kane, Sweet Adeline, David Bowie, Golgi Apparatus
● *Encore:* The Horse > Silent in the Morning, Rocky Top
● *Show Notes:* Nellie Kane, which was performed acoustic, and Sweet Adeline were performed without microphones.

Friday, December 9, 1994
Mesa Amphitheater, Mesa, AZ
● *Check:* Higher Ground, Frankenstein, The Old Home Place, Funky Bitch
● *Set I:* Llama, Foam, Guyute, Sparkle -> I Didn't Know, It's Ice -> If I Could -> Run Like an Antelope
● *Set II:* Wilson -> Poor Heart -> Tweezer -> McGrupp and the Watchful Hosemasters, Julius -> Big Ball Jam, Cracklin' Rosie, You Enjoy Myself -> Suzy Greenberg
● *Encore:* I'm Blue I'm Lonesome, Foreplay/Long Time, Tweezer Reprise
● *Show Notes:* I'm Blue I'm Lonesome was performed acoustic. Tweezer included a Slave-based jam.

Saturday, December 10, 1994
Civic Auditorium, Santa Monica, CA
● *Set I:* Fee, Rift, Stash, The Lizards, Sample in a Jar, Divided Sky, Lawn Boy, Chalk Dust Torture
● *Set II:* Simple, Maze, Guyute, Also Sprach Zarathustra, Mike's Song > I Am Hydrogen > Weekapaug Groove -> HYHU > Why Don't We Do

It in the Road, Poor Heart, Slave to the Traffic Light, Cavern
● *Encore:* Chalk Dust Torture Reprise, Good Times Bad Times
● *Show Notes:* The Chalk Dust Torture Reprise included crew intro-
ductions. This version of Simple appears on *A Live One*.

Wednesday, December 28, 1994
Civic Center, Philadelphia, PA
● *Set I:* Mound, Simple, Julius, Bathtub Gin, Bouncing Around the
Room, Axilla (Part II), Reba, Dog Faced Boy, It's Ice, Run Like an An-
telope
● *Set II:* Suzy Greenberg, NICU, Mike's Song -> The Mango Song ->
Weekapaug Groove, Contact, Llama, HYHU > Love You > HYHU, The
Squirming Coil
● *Encore:* Bold As Love
● *Show Notes:* Reba was unfinished. Weekapaug Groove featured Auld
Lang Syne and Little Drummer Boy quotes. Bold as Love was played for
the first time since May 21, 1994 (83 shows).

Thursday, December 29, 1994
Civic Center, Providence, RI
● *Set I:* Runaway Jim -> Foam, If I Could, Split Open and Melt, The
Horse > Silent in the Morning, Uncle Pen, I Didn't Know, Possum
● *Set II:* Guyute, Digital Delay Loop Jam -> David Bowie, Halley's
Comet -> The Lizards, HYHU > Cracklin' Rosie > HYHU, Good Times
Bad Times
● *Encore:* My Long Journey Home, Sleeping Monkey
● *Show Notes:* Unlike many Runaway Jim and Foam combos, the
opening to this show contained a well-jammed segue between the two
songs. Possum included Auld Lang Syne teases. GTBT included Heartbreaker teases. My Long Journey Home was performed acoustic. This
epic Bowie, which times out at nearly 34 minutes, included whistling
and a "Lassie" chant, as well as Paradise City teases and a brief ASZ
tease from Mike. Before Guyute, Trey teased Spill the Wine.

Friday, December 30, 1994
Madison Square Garden, New York, NY
● *Set I:* Wilson, Rift, AC/DC Bag, Sparkle, Simple, Stash, Fee, Scent of
a Mule, Cavern
● *Set II:* Sample in a Jar, Poor Heart, Tweezer, I'm Blue I'm Lonesome,
You Enjoy Myself, Purple Rain, Harry Hood, Tweezer Reprise
● *Encore:* Frankenstein
● *Show Notes:* I'm Blue I'm Lonesome was performed acoustic. This
version of Wilson appears on *A Live One*.

Friday, December 30, 1994
**The Late Show with David Letterman, Ed Sullivan Theatre, New
York, NY**
Chalk Dust Torture
● *Show Notes:* This performance of Chalk Dust was taped for *David
Letterman* before the MSG show that same night.

Saturday, December 31, 1994
Boston Garden, Boston, MA
● *Set I:* Golgi Apparatus > NICU, Run Like an Antelope, Glide, Mound,
Peaches en Regalia, Divided Sky, Funky Bitch
● *Set II:* The Old Home Place > Maze, Bouncing Around the Room,

Mike's Song -> Buffalo Bill -> Mike's Song > Yerushalayim Shel Zahav
> Weekapaug Groove, Amazing Grace
● *Set III:* My Sweet One, Also Sprach Zarathustra > Auld Lang Syne >
Tropical Hot Dog Night, Chalk Dust Torture, The Horse > Silent in the
Morning, Suzy Greenberg, Slave to the Traffic Light
● *Encore:* Simple -> Auld Lang Syne
● *Show Notes:* Mike's Song included a tease of Collective Soul's Shine.
Antelope featured guest vocals from Tom Marshall. Trey played along
to Gary Glitter's Rock and Roll Part 2, which was being played over the
P.A., at the start of the first set. Before the lights went out for the third
set, the audience "overheard" the band before the set. Fish wound up
saying "I want a jumbo hot dog, large fries and shake" delivered on
stage. The band came out, started up My Sweet One, and was interrupted by an announcer asking who ordered the food. The band pointed
at Fishman, who looked confused as huge props of a hot dog, fries and
shakes descended from the ceiling next to the drum set. The band
played Also Sprach while the hot dog landed. Technicians (wearing
"Rocket Scientist" jackets) prepared the hot dog, and the band climbed
in with their instruments and flew out over the audience, as balloons
popped and feathers, confetti and "Phish NYE 1994" ping pong balls
fell from the ceiling. Various music, including Captain Beefheart's Tropical Hot Dog Night, was played over the P.A. as the hot dog space ship
flew back and forth. This version of Bouncing appears on *A Live One*.

SUMMER, 1995

Sunday, May 14, 1995
Fishman's House, Burlington, VT
Don't You Wanna Go, Spock's Brain, Theme From the Bottom, Ha Ha
Ha, Taste, Free, Strange Design, Glide II, Lonesome Cowboy Bill, I'll
Come Running
● *Show Notes:* This "show" was a small, private tune-up for the Low-
ell show and summer tour.

Tuesday, May 16, 1995
Lowell Memorial Auditorium, Lowell, MA
Voters for Choice Benefit Concert
● *Check:* Tweezer -> I'll Come Running -> Tweezer Reprise
Don't You Wanna Go, Ha Ha Ha > Spock's Brain, Strange Design, Reba,
Theme From the Bottom, Lonesome Cowboy Bill, Free, Glide II, You
Enjoy Myself, Sweet Adeline, Sample in a Jar
● *Encore:* I'll Come Running -> Gloria
● *Show Notes:* During the pre-show introduction, host Gloria
Steinem promised Phish fans more new music in one night than ever
before. The band, in turn, delivered the first performances of Don't
You Wanna Go, Ha Ha Ha, Spock's Brain, Strange Design, Theme
From the Bottom, Lonesome Cowboy Bill, Free, Glide II, I'll Come
Running, and Gloria.

Wednesday, June 7, 1995
Boise State University Pavilion, Boise, ID
● *Set I:* Possum, Weigh, Taste, Strange Design, Stash, If I Could, Scent
of a Mule, The Wedge, Funky Bitch, Slave to the Traffic Light
● *Set II:* Ha Ha Ha -> Maze, Spock's Brain, Theme From the Bottom,

HYHU > Lonesome Cowboy Bill, Acoustic Army, Sample in a Jar, Harry Hood, Suzy Greenberg
● *Encore:* While My Guitar Gently Weeps
● *Show Notes:* This show marked the debuts of Taste and Acoustic Army. Also, the band broke out The Wedge, which hadn't been played since August 20, 1993 (134 shows) and Weigh, which hadn't been played since May 20, 1994 (89 shows).

Thursday, June 8, 1995
The Delta Center, Salt Lake City, UT
● *Set I:* Don't You Wanna Go, Ha Ha Ha, Runaway Jim, Guelah Papyrus, Mound, Fast Enough for You, Reba, Prince Caspian, Chalk Dust Torture
● *Set II:* Simple -> Rift, Free, Bouncing Around the Room, Tweezer -> Lifeboy, Poor Heart, Julius
● *Encore:* Good Times Bad Times
● *Show Notes:* This show marked the debut of Prince Caspian.

Friday, June 9, 1995
Red Rocks Amphitheater, Morrison, CO
● *Set I:* My Friend My Friend, Divided Sky, Strange Design, The Oh Kee Pa Ceremony > AC/DC Bag, Theme From the Bottom, Taste, Sparkle, Run Like an Antelope
● *Set II:* Split Open and Melt, The Wedge, Scent of a Mule, Cavern, David Bowie, Acoustic Army, Sweet Adeline, Slave to the Traffic Light
● *Encore:* The Squirming Coil

Saturday, June 10, 1995
Red Rocks Amphitheater, Morrison, CO
● *Check:* Cry Baby Cry
● *Set I:* Makisupa Policeman -> Llama, Prince Caspian, It's Ice, Free, Rift, You Enjoy Myself -> HYHU > Lonesome Cowboy Bill > HYHU, Suzy Greenberg
● *Set II:* Maze, Fee, Uncle Pen, Mike's Song > I Am Hydrogen > Weekapaug Groove, Amazing Grace, Sample in a Jar
● *Encore:* A Day in the Life
● *Show Notes:* This show marked the first performance of A Day in the Life. YEM segued into a HYHU vocal jam. This long, moody Mike's Groove clocked in at over 32 minutes.

Tuesday, June 13, 1995
Riverport Amphitheater, Maryland Heights, MO
● *Set I:* Runaway Jim, Foam, Bouncing Around the Room, Stash, Strange Design, Taste, Reba, HYHU > Terrapin > HYHU, Sparkle, Chalk Dust Torture
● *Set II:* David Bowie, The Lizards, Axilla (Part II) > Theme From the Bottom, Acoustic Army, Harry Hood, Golgi Apparatus
● *Encore:* Sweet Adeline, Julius
● *Show Notes:* Sweet Adeline was performed without microphones as Trey jokingly tried to break the record for the largest venue played without mics. This version of Golgi, according to Trey, was the "jazz version."

Wednesday, June 14, 1995
Mud Island Amphitheater, Memphis, TN
● *Set I:* Don't You Wanna Go, Gumbo, NICU, Mound, Cavern, Possum, All Things Reconsidered, Amazing Grace, The Horse > Silent in the Morning, Spock's Brain, Split Open and Melt
● *Set II:* Also Sprach Zarathustra > Poor Heart > Tweezer, Acoustic Army, While My Guitar Gently Weeps
● *Encore:* Simple, Rocky Top > Tweezer Reprise
● *Show Notes:* The highlight of this show was a massive, long (almost 50 minutes!), jammed out Tweezer that included a brief Gypsy Queen jam, an Also Sprach tease, a Slave-like jam, and a Digital Delay Loop Jam with whistling. Simple was performed with an *a cappella* ending instead of a jam, akin to the *ALO* version from December 8, 1994. Amazing Grace was performed without microphones. Listen for a Stairway to Heaven tease at the start of the first set.

Thursday, June 15, 1995
Lakewood Amphitheater, Atlanta, GA
● *Check:* Funky Bitch, The Old Home Place, Julius
● *Set I:* My Friend My Friend, Sparkle > AC/DC Bag, The Old Home Place, Taste, The Wedge, Stash -> I Didn't Know, Fluffhead, Run Like an Antelope
● *Set II:* My Sweet One, Ha Ha Ha > David Bowie, Strange Design, Theme From the Bottom, Scent of a Mule, Acoustic Army, Slave to the Traffic Light
● *Encore:* Bouncing Around the Room, Frankenstein
● *Show Notes:* Stash was unfinished and melted into I Didn't Know, which was performed in an eerie, slower fashion and featured Fishman on trombone, Mike on electric drill, and Trey on megaphone. Fans of Page will want to seek out this odd, atypical Bowie, as he dominated the jam segment. Bowie also included some odd chanting, including the phrase "Send me on my way" (although not in a manner similar to the Rusted Root song of the same name).

Friday, June 16, 1995
Walnut Creek Amphitheater, Raleigh, NC
● *Check:* Caravan, Three Little Birds, Free, Funky Bitch, Jam
● *Set I:* Halley's Comet > Down with Disease, Esther > Ya Mar, Cry Baby Cry, It's Ice, My Mind's Got a Mind of its Own, Dog Faced Boy -> Catapult, Split Open and Melt
● *Set II:* Runaway Jim -> Free, Carolina, You Enjoy Myself, The Squirming Coil
● *Encore:* Bold as Love
● *Show Notes:* This show is famous for the long, experimental jamming in the Runaway Jim. Dog Faced Boy was preceded by several false starts of SOAM by Fishman. YEM featured Boyd Tinsley on fiddle for a portion of the jam and included Oye Como Va teases.

Saturday, June 17, 1995
Nissan Pavilion at Stone Ridge, Gainesville, VA
● *Check:* Johnny B. Goode
● *Set I:* Divided Sky, Suzy Greenberg, Taste, Fee -> Uncle Pen, Julius, Lawn Boy, The Curtain -> Stash
● *Set II:* Wilson > Maze, Mound > Tweezer -> Johnny B. Goode -> Tweezer -> McGrupp and the Watchful Hosemasters, Acoustic Army, Sweet Adeline, Harry Hood, Sample in a Jar
● *Encore:* Three Little Birds
● *Show Notes:* Fans in attendance were treated to the first performances of Three Little Birds, with a guest appearance by LeRoi Moore and Dave Matthews, and Johnny B. Goode. Tweezer included a brief

Montana tease. Stash segued nicely out of The Curtain and subsequently included Curtain teases.

Monday, June 19, 1995
Deer Creek Amphitheater, Noblesville, IN
● *Set I:* Theme From the Bottom, Poor Heart, AC/DC Bag, Tela, Punch You in the Eye, Reba, Strange Design, Rift, Cavern, Run Like an Antelope
● *Set II:* Simple -> David Bowie, The Mango Song, Loving Cup, Sparkle, You Enjoy Myself, Acoustic Army, Possum
● *Encore:* A Day in the Life
● *Show Notes:* Bowie featured a Mind Left Body tease from Trey.

Tuesday, June 20, 1995
Blossom Music Center, Cuyahoga Falls, OH
● *Set I:* Llama, Spock's Brain, Ginseng Sullivan, Foam, Bathtub Gin, If I Could, Taste, I Didn't Know, Split Open and Melt
● *Set II:* Halley's Comet, Chalk Dust Torture, Prince Caspian, Uncle Pen, Mike's Song -> Contact, Weekapaug Groove, HYHU > Cracklin' Rosie, Highway to Hell
● *Encore:* Slave to the Traffic Light, Amazing Grace
● *Show Notes:* Ginseng was played for the first time since October 10, 1994 (58 shows).

Thursday, June 22, 1995
Finger Lakes Performing Arts Center, Canandaigua, NY
● *Set I:* Sample in a Jar, Scent of a Mule, Ha Ha Ha > Divided Sky, Guelah Papyrus, It's Ice, Strange Design, Maze, Cavern, Sweet Adeline
● *Set II:* Theme From the Bottom -> Jam -> Tweezer -> Tweezer Reprise
● *Encore:* Acoustic Army, While My Guitar Gently Weeps
● *Show Notes:* This 40 minute Tweezer, which is known as "The Fleezer," contained a My Generation jam and, at one point, a Fishman vacuum accompaniment. Maze included a brief Dave's Energy Guide tease.

Friday, June 23, 1995
Waterloo Village, Stanhope, NJ
● *Set I:* Simple, Chalk Dust Torture, Prince Caspian, Reba, Ginseng Sullivan, Free, Taste, You Enjoy Myself
● *Set II:* Runaway Jim -> The Lizards, The Wedge, Run Like an Antelope, Harpua, Llama, Good Times Bad Times
● *Encore:* A Day in the Life
● *Show Notes:* Harpua was unfinished. Trey introduced the Jimmy character, who played an Abba record (which led to a band jam of Abba's Waterloo), but the end of Harpua was not told. Llama and GTBT featured John Popper on harmonica.

Saturday, June 24, 1995
The Mann Music Center, Philadelphia, PA
● *Set I:* Fee > Rift, Spock's Brain, Julius, Glide, Mound, Stash, The Horse > Silent in the Morning, The Squirming Coil
● *Set II:* Also Sprach Zarathustra > Halley's Comet > David Bowie, Lifeboy, Suzy Greenberg, Harry Hood, Acoustic Army, Sweet Adeline, Golgi Apparatus
● *Encore:* Bold As Love
● *Show Notes:* After Acoustic Army, Trey thanked the crowd for being so quiet. The band then proceeded to don surgical masks for Adeline.

The masks were provided by a fan in the front – Trey thanked him for the "hats." The encore was preceded by a Random Note Signal.

Sunday, June 25, 1995
The Mann Music Center, Philadelphia, PA
● *Set I:* Ya Mar > AC/DC Bag, Taste, Theme From the Bottom, If I Could > Sparkle, Divided Sky, I Didn't Know, Split Open and Melt
● *Set II:* Maze, Sample in a Jar, Scent of a Mule, Mike's Song -> Why Don't We Do It in the Road > HYHU > Jam -> Weekapaug Groove, Amazing Grace, Cavern
● *Encore:* Bouncing Around the Room, Slave to the Traffic Light
● *Show Notes:* I Didn't Know featured Fishman on vacuum (introduced as "Cedric Harris" by Trey). The Maze intro included Reville teases, and Weekapaug contained teases of Bob Seger's Main Street.

Monday, June 26, 1995
Saratoga Performing Arts Center, Saratoga Springs, NY
● *Set I:* My Friend My Friend, Don't You Wanna Go, Bathtub Gin, NICU > The Sloth, My Mind's Got a Mind of its Own, It's Ice, Dog Faced Boy, Tela, Possum
● *Set II:* Down with Disease -> Free, Poor Heart, You Enjoy Myself, Strange Design, Run Like an Antelope
● *Encore:* Sleeping Monkey, Rocky Top

Wednesday, June 28, 1995
Jones Beach Amphitheater, Wantagh, NY
● *Check:* Sweet Home Alabama, Jam, Ginseng Sullivan, Red River Valley Jam, Dog Gone Dog (slow)
● *Set I:* Axilla (Part II) -> Foam, Fast Enough for You, Reba, Punch You in the Eye, Stash, Fluffhead, Chalk Dust Torture
● *Set II:* Sample in a Jar, Poor Heart, Tweezer -> Dave's Energy Guide -> Tweezer -> Gumbo, Sparkle, Suzy Greenberg, Harry Hood, Tweezer Reprise
● *Encore:* Sweet Adeline, While My Guitar Gently Weeps
● *Show Notes:* Reba was unfinished. Tweezer included a Cannonball jam.

Thursday, June 29, 1995
Jones Beach Amphitheater, Wantagh, NY
● *Set I:* Runaway Jim, Taste, The Horse > Silent in the Morning, Divided Sky, Cavern, Rift, Simple, Split Open and Melt, Carolina
● *Set II:* Free -> David Bowie, Strange Design, You Enjoy Myself, Acoustic Army, A Day in the Life
● *Encore:* Theme From the Bottom
● *Show Notes:* This YEM is known for its particularly frightening vocal jam.

Friday, June 30, 1995
Great Woods Amphitheater, Mansfield, MA
● *Check:* Dog Gone Dog
● *Set I:* AC/DC Bag > Scent of a Mule, Horn, Taste, The Wedge, The Lizards, Mound, Fee -> Run Like an Antelope
● *Set II:* Also Sprach Zarathustra > Possum > Ha Ha Ha > The Man Who Stepped Into Yesterday > Avenu Malkenu > Mike's Song > Contact > Weekapaug Groove, Amazing Grace, The Squirming Coil
● *Encore:* HYHU > Cracklin' Rosie > HYHU, Golgi Apparatus
● *Show Notes:* This show featured a visually spectacular Mule, which

featured Trey playing guitar with his teeth and Page playing keyboards with his face and feet. During Antelope, Trey substituted "Suck the deer shit from the side of this hole," for the "high gear of your soul" lyric. Portions of this show were used in Mike Gordon's 1997 short film *Goodwood.* Fishman introduced Rosie as being about "a lonely man singing to his inflatable love doll."

Saturday, July 1, 1995
Great Woods Amphitheater, Mansfield, MA
● *Set I:* Ya Mar, Llama, If I Could, All Things Reconsidered, It's Ice, Prince Caspian, Split Open and Melt, Bouncing Around the Room, Chalk Dust Torture
● *Set II:* Wilson, Maze, Theme From the Bottom, Uncle Pen, Stash, Strange Design, Acoustic Army, Harry Hood, Suzy Greenberg
● *Encore:* Funky Bitch
● *Show Notes:* If I Could featured a new intro based on a Trey solo. The jam in It's Ice featured Fishman on vacuum and Mike on an electric drill. Funky Bitch was dedicated to the tourheads as an always requested but never played song. Portions of this show were used in Mike Gordon's 1997 short film *Goodwood.*

Sunday, July 2, 1995
Summerstage at Sugarbush North, Fayston, VT
● *Set I:* Sample in a Jar > Divided Sky, Gumbo, The Curtain > Julius, Camel Walk, Reba, I Didn't Know, Rift, While My Guitar Gently Weeps
● *Set II:* Runaway Jim -> Makisupa Policeman -> Scent of a Mule, Tweezer > Ha Ha Ha > Sleeping Monkey, Acoustic Army, Slave to the Traffic Light
● *Encore:* Halley's Comet > Tweezer Reprise
● *Show Notes:* This was a benefit show for the King Street Youth Center. The band brought back Camel Walk, which hadn't been played since February 24, 1989 (648 shows). Reba was unfinished.

Monday, July 3, 1995
Summerstage at Sugarbush North, Fayston, VT
● *Set I:* My Friend My Friend, Poor Heart, Run Like an Antelope, Loving Cup, Sparkle, It's Ice, If I Could, Maze, Strange Design, Free, Cavern
● *Set II:* Timber (Jerry) -> David Bowie -> Johnny B. Goode -> David Bowie > AC/DC Bag, The Lizards > Big Black Furry Creature from Mars, A Day in the Life, Possum, The Squirming Coil
● *Encore:* Simple, Amazing Grace
● *Show Notes:* Lizards was aborted after Trey lost track of the lyrics. Fish teased him about needing a TelePrompTer, and Trey started up BBFCFM. My Friend featured Trey using his microphone stand as a slide. The jamming in the second set included many Bathtub Gin teases and, right before JBG, a tease of Santana's Soul Sacrifice. During If I Could, a large inflatable moose was tossed around the crowd. It eventually landed in perfect sitting position, facing the audience, on Page's side of the stage. Plenty of stage antics preceded Amazing Grace; Page threw the pitch pipe into the crowd and Trey pretended to throw Fishman's goggles and, eventually, Fishman himself. Trey also picked up a hackey sack from the stage and impressed the crowd with his athleticism. Timber returned for its first performance since December 30, 1992 (256 shows) and first complete version since December of 1989.

Thursday, July 13, 1995
The Late Show with David Letterman, Ed Sullivan Theatre, New York, NY
Julius
● *Show Notes:* Julius was performed with accompaniment from The Late Show Band and Dave Grippo on saxophone.

FALL, 1995

Wednesday, September 27, 1995
Cal Expo Amphitheater, Sacramento, CA
● *Check:* Funky Bitch (one and a half times), Jam, Fog That Surrounds
● *Set I:* Wolfman's Brother, Rift, Free, It's Ice, I Didn't Know, Fog that Surrounds, Strange Design, Chalk Dust Torture, The Squirming Coil
● *Set II:* Cars Trucks Buses, AC/DC Bag, David Bowie, Billy Breathes, Keyboard Cavalry, Harry Hood, Hello My Baby, A Day in the Life
● *Encore:* Possum
● *Show Notes:* This tour opener brought the first performances of Fog that Surrounds, Cars Trucks Buses, Billy Breathes, Keyboard Cavalry, and Hello My Baby. I Didn't Know featured Fishman on trombone. Harry Hood was unfinished. Wolfman's was played for the first time since June 26, 1994 (88 shows).

Thursday, September 28, 1995
Summer Pops, Embarcadero Center, San Diego, CA
● *Check:* Gumbo, All Things Reconsidered, Mound, Fog That Surrounds, Hello My Baby
● *Set I:* Cars Trucks Buses, Runaway Jim, Billy Breathes, Scent of a Mule, Stash, Fee -> Fog that Surrounds, Acoustic Army, Slave to the Traffic Light
● *Set II:* Theme From the Bottom, Poor Heart, Don't You Wanna Go, Tweezer, Keyboard Cavalry, Amazing Grace, Sample in a Jar, Run Like an Antelope
● *Encore:* Fire
● *Show Notes:* Fire was played for the first time since October 13, 1994 (69 shows).

Friday, September 29, 1995
The Greek Theater, Los Angeles, CA
● *Set I:* AC/DC Bag, Sparkle, Divided Sky, Strange Design, Cars Trucks Buses, You Enjoy Myself, Sweet Adeline, Suzy Greenberg
● *Set II:* Also Sprach Zarathustra > Maze, Free, Ya Mar, Split Open and Melt, Billy Breathes, HYHU > Cryin', A Day in the Life
● *Encore:* Chalk Dust Torture
● *Show Notes:* Fans in attendance were treated to the heartfelt debut of Cryin'.

Saturday, September 30, 1995
Shoreline Amphitheater, Mountain View, CA
● *Set I:* My Friend My Friend, Cars Trucks Buses, White Rabbit Jam, Reba, Uncle Pen, Horn, Run Like an Antelope, I'm Blue I'm Lonesome, Sample in a Jar
● *Set II:* Runaway Jim, Fog that Surrounds, If I Could, Scent of a Mule, Mike's Song -> Keyboard Cavalry, Weekapaug Groove -> Suspicious

Sugarbush, Vermont (7/3/95).

Minds > HYHU, Cavern
● *Encore:* Amazing Grace, Good Times Bad Times
● *Show Notes:* This show was the beginning of the Band/Audience Chess Match that continued throughout the fall tour. Page and a tourhead named Pooh played a few moves to set up the board during the White Rabbit jam in the first set. Suspicious Minds made its debut. Listen for an Antelope tease before Horn. I'm Blue I'm Lonesome was dedicated to Jerry Garcia.

Monday, October 2, 1995
Seattle Center Arena, Seattle, WA
● Opening Act: Baby Gramps
● *Set I:* Poor Heart, Wolfman's Brother, Rift, Night Moves Jam, Stash, Acoustic Army, Fog that Surrounds, Theme From the Bottom, Tela, David Bowie
● *Set II:* Wilson, Cars Trucks Buses, Bathtub Gin, Llama, Simple > Keyboard Cavalry, Slave to the Traffic Light, Hello My Baby, The Lizards, Run Like an Antelope
● *Encore:* A Day in the Life
● *Show Notes:* The Night Moves Jam in the first set extended the Band/Audience Chess Match. Slave included Fishman on vacuum for a portion of the jam.

Tuesday, October 3, 1995
Seattle Center Arena, Seattle, WA
● Opening Act: Baby Gramps
● *Set I:* Maze, Guelah Papyrus, Foam, Fast Enough for You, I'm Blue I'm Lonesome, Free, The Man Who Stepped Into Yesterday > Avenu Malkenu > The Man Who Stepped Into Yesterday Reprise, Sample in a Jar, You Enjoy Myself
● *Set II:* Timber (Jerry), It's Ice, Sparkle, Harry Hood, Billy Breathes,

Faht, Sweet Adeline, Split Open and Melt, The Squirming Coil
● *Encore:* Rocky Top
● *Show Notes:* Faht was played for the first time since June 19, 1994 (99 shows).

Thursday, October 5, 1995
Portland Memorial Coliseum, Portland, OR
● *Set I:* Chalk Dust Torture, Ha Ha Ha, Fog that Surrounds, The Horse > Silent in the Morning, Cars Trucks Buses, Strange Design, Divided Sky, Acoustic Army, Julius > Suzy Greenberg
● *Set II:* Also Sprach Zarathustra > Runaway Jim, Colonel Forbin's Ascent > The Famous Mockingbird > Scent of a Mule > Cavern > David Bowie, Lifeboy, Amazing Grace
● *Encore:* While My Guitar Gently Weeps

Friday, October 6, 1995
The Orpheum Theatre, Vancouver BC, Canada
● *Set I:* Ya Mar, Stash, Billy Breathes, Reba, I'm Blue I'm Lonesome, Rift, Free, The Lizards, Sample in a Jar
● *Set II:* Poor Heart, Maze, Theme From the Bottom, NICU, Tweezer, Keyboard Cavalry, Suspicious Minds, Slave to the Traffic Light
● *Encore:* Hello My Baby, A Day in the Life
● *Show Notes:* I'm Blue I'm Lonesome and Hello My Baby were performed without microphones.

Saturday, October 7, 1995
Spokane Opera House, Spokane, WA
● *Set I:* Julius, Gumbo > Fog that Surrounds, Mound, Possum, The Mango Song, Acoustic Army, Wilson, Run Like an Antelope
● *Set II:* Makisupa Policeman, Cars Trucks Buses, Split Open and Melt, Strange Design, It's Ice -> Contact, Frankenstein, Harry Hood, Sweet Adeline
● *Encore:* Fire
● *Show Notes:* This fantastic Hood was unfinished.

Sunday, October 8, 1995
Adams Fieldhouse, University of Montana, Missoula, MT
● *Set I:* AC/DC Bag, Demand -> Sparkle, Wolfman's Brother, Reba, I'm Blue I'm Lonesome, Prince Caspian, Uncle Pen, Free
● *Set II:* Keyboard Cavalry, Cars Trucks Buses, Timber (Jerry), Ya Mar, Sample in a Jar, You Enjoy Myself, Suspicious Minds, Dog Faced Boy, David Bowie, Keyboard Cavalry Reprise
● *Encore:* Bouncing Around the Room, Rocky Top
● *Show Notes:* Demand was played for the first time since June 26, 1994 (97 shows).

Wednesday, October 11, 1995
Compton Terrace Amphitheater, Tempe, AZ
● *Set I:* Stash, The Old Home Place, Cavern, Divided Sky, If I Could, Fog that Surrounds, Acoustic Army, Julius, Sample in a Jar
● *Set II:* Possum > Bathtub Gin, Mound, Mike's Song -> McGrupp and the Watchful Hosemasters -> Weekapaug Groove -> Llama, Suzy Greenberg -> Crossroads, Hello My Baby, A Day in the Life
● *Encore:* Chalk Dust Torture
● *Show Notes:* Julius contained a Buried Alive tease. Suzy Greenberg contained Crossroads and Sunshine of Your Love teases. Crossroads

was subsequently played for the first time since May 8, 1993 (196 shows).

Friday, October 13, 1995
Will Rogers Auditorium, Fort Worth, TX
● *Set I:* Ya Mar, Also Sprach Zarathustra, Maze, Billy Breathes, I'm Blue I'm Lonesome, Prince Caspian, Split Open and Melt, Fluffhead, Life on Mars?
● *Set II:* Tube, Uncle Pen, Theme From the Bottom -> Wilson -> Run Like an Antelope -> Keyboard Cavalry, The Lizards, While My Guitar Gently Weeps, Sweet Adeline, The Squirming Coil
● *Encore:* Bold as Love
● *Show Notes:* I'm Blue I'm Lonesome was performed acoustic and, along with Sweet Adeline, was performed without microphones. Life on Mars debuted at this show. Tube was played for the first time since June 26, 1994 (99 shows).

Saturday, October 14, 1995
Austin Music Hall, Austin, TX
I Check: Dog Gone Dog
● *Set I:* AC/DC Bag, Cars Trucks Buses, Kung, Free, Sparkle, Stash -> Catapult, Acoustic Army, It's Ice, Tela, Runaway Jim
● *Set II:* Reba, Rift, You Enjoy Myself, Hello My Baby, Scent of a Mule, Cavern
● *Encore:* A Day in the Life
● *Show Notes:* YEM featured special guests John Medeski, Billy Martin, Chris Wood, and a trumpet player. The guest on trumpet may have been tour bus driver Dominic Placco. Trey played both guitar and mini drum set up front. Mike played bass and some kind of horn at the end of the jam. Fishman played vacuum and trombone. Billy Martin played Fishman's drums. Medeski and Page played keyboards and Page did some vocal jamming at the end. Chris Wood played a one string stand up bass with a bow. Kung was played for the first time since October 20, 1994 (75 shows).

Sunday, October 15, 1995
Austin Music Hall, Austin, TX
● *Set I:* Buried Alive > Poor Heart, Slave to the Traffic Light, I Didn't Know, Demand, Llama, Foam, Strange Design, I'm Blue I'm Lonesome, David Bowie
● *Set II:* Julius, Simple, Tweezer, The Lizards, Sample in a Jar, Suspicious Minds, Harry Hood, Tweezer Reprise
● *Encore:* Funky Bitch

Tuesday, October 17, 1995
State Palace Theatre, New Orleans, LA
● Opening Act: Medeski, Martin & Wood
● *Set I:* Sample in a Jar, Stash, Uncle Pen, AC/DC Bag > Maze, Glide, Sparkle, Free, Strange Design, Amazing Grace
● *Set II:* Mound > Prince Caspian, Fog that Surrounds, Suzy Greenberg -> Keyboard Cavalry -> Jam
● *Encore:* My Long Journey Home, I'm Blue I'm Lonesome
● *Show Notes:* The jam out of Keyboard Cavalry featured Medeski, Martin, and Wood. My Long Journey Home and I'm Blue I'm Lonesome were performed acoustic. Amazing Grace was sung first by the band, and then by audience member "Nathan," a gospel singer.

Thursday, October 19, 1995
Municipal Auditorium, Kansas City, MO
● *Set I:* Cars Trucks Buses, Runaway Jim, Horn, Punch You in the Eye, Esther, Chalk Dust Torture, Theme From the Bottom, Acoustic Army, Split Open and Melt, Billy Breathes, Cavern
● *Set II:* Frankenstein, Poor Heart, Mike's Song > I Am Hydrogen > Weekapaug Groove, Lawn Boy, Big Black Furry Creature from Mars, Kung, Suspicious Minds, Possum
● *Encore:* A Day in the Life

Friday, October 20, 1995
Five Seasons Arena, Cedar Rapids, IA
● *Check:* Amazing Grace (with bagpipes)
● *Set I:* My Friend My Friend, Ya Mar, Ha Ha Ha, Divided Sky, Fee, Rift, Free, Hello My Baby, Amazing Grace, Amazing Grace Jam
● *Set II:* Timber (Jerry), Scent of a Mule, Simple, Maze, Gumbo, While My Guitar Gently Weeps, My Long Journey Home, I'm Blue I'm Lonesome, Bouncing Around the Room, Run Like an Antelope
● *Encore:* Sleeping Monkey, Rocky Top
● *Show Notes:* The Amazing Grace Jam was accompanied by a guest on electric bagpipes. The last Amazing Grace with instrumental accompaniment was May 8, 1993. My Long Journey Home and I'm Blue I'm Lonesome were performed acoustic.

Saturday, October 21, 1995
Pershing Auditorium, Lincoln, NE
● *Check:* Life on Mars?
● *Set I:* Tweezer Reprise, Chalk Dust Torture, Guelah Papyrus, Reba, Wilson, Cars Trucks Buses, Kung > The Lizards, Strange Design, Acoustic Army, Good Times Bad Times -> Tweezer Reprise
● *Set II:* Also Sprach Zarathustra, David Bowie, Lifeboy, Sparkle, You Enjoy Myself -> Purple Rain > HYHU, Harry Hood, Suzy Greenberg
● *Encore:* Highway to Hell
● *Show Notes:* In a Halloween tease responding to Michael Jackson predictions, the band teased Black or White in GTBT and Beat It in Hood and Suzy Greenberg. Suzy also included a Tweezer Reprise tease.

Sunday, October 22, 1995
Assembly Hall, Champaign, IL
● *Set I:* AC/DC Bag, My Mind's Got a Mind of its Own, The Sloth, Runaway Jim, Weigh > NICU, Fast Enough for You, It's Ice, Poor Heart > Sample in a Jar, I'm Blue I'm Lonesome, Stash
● *Set II:* Golgi Apparatus, Possum -> Catapult, The Curtain > Tweezer -> Makisupa Policeman -> Big Black Furry Creature from Mars, Life on Mars?, Uncle Pen, Slave to the Traffic Light > Cavern
● *Encore:* Sweet Adeline, The Squirming Coil
● *Show Notes:* This show included a humorous Adeline. The band kept rotating the direction they were facing while they sang to please the entire crowd, which was arranged in a full circle around the stage.

Tuesday, October 24, 1995
Dane County Coliseum, Madison, WI
● *Check:* Dog Gone Dog, Taste
● *Set I:* My Friend My Friend, Paul and Silas, Taste That Surrounds, Fee -> Llama, The Horse > Silent in the Morning, Demand -> Maze, Wolfman's Brother, Acoustic Army, Prince Caspian, Split Open and Melt

● *Set II:* Julius, Theme From the Bottom, Bouncing Around the Room, You Enjoy Myself -> Sleeping Monkey, Run Like an Antelope, Contact, Cavern

● *Encore:* A Day in the Life

● *Show Notes:* Fee was followed by a brief jam that pounded into Llama. Sleeping Monkey segued out of the YEM vocal jam and was started *a cappella*. Highlights of this show were an amazing Antelope, an incredibly hot Julius, and the first performance of Taste That Surrounds. Paul and Silas was played for the first time since November 19, 1994 (63 shows).

Wednesday, October 25, 1995
Civic Center Arena, St. Paul, MN

● *Set I:* Ya Mar, Sample in a Jar, Divided Sky, The Wedge, Scent of a Mule, Free, Strange Design, My Long Journey Home, I'm Blue I'm Lonesome, Chalk Dust Torture

● *Set II:* Reba, Life on Mars?, Cars Trucks Buses, Mike's Song -> Breathe Jam -> Sparkle -> Weekapaug Groove, Suzy Greenberg -> Crossroads

● *Encore:* Fire

Friday, October 27, 1995
Wing Stadium, Kalamazoo, MI

● *Set I:* Runaway Jim, Fluffhead, Taste That Surrounds, Horn, I Didn't Know, Rift, Stash, Fee -> Suspicious Minds

● *Set II:* Also Sprach Zarathustra > David Bowie, Dog Faced Boy, Poor Heart, Simple, McGrupp and the Watchful Hosemasters, Keyboard Cavalry, Bouncing Around the Room, Possum

● *Encore:* Life on Mars?

Saturday, October 28, 1995
The Palace, Auburn Hills, MI

● *Set I:* AC/DC Bag, Mound, Timber (Jerry), Uncle Pen, Sample in a Jar, The Lizards, Billy Breathes, Acoustic Army, Prince Caspian, Run Like an Antelope

● *Set II:* Maze, Theme From the Bottom -> Scent of a Mule, You Enjoy Myself, Strange Design, Frankenstein, Chalk Dust Torture

● *Encore:* While My Guitar Gently Weeps

Sunday, October 29, 1995
Louisville Gardens, Louisville, KY

● *Set I:* Buried Alive > Poor Heart, Julius, Punch You in the Eye, Cars Trucks Buses, The Horse > Silent in the Morning, Split Open and Melt, NICU, Gumbo, Slave to the Traffic Light, Sweet Adeline

● *Set II:* Makisupa Policeman -> David Bowie, The Mango Song, It's Ice -> Kung -> It's Ice -> Shaggy Dog -> Possum -> Lifeboy, Amazing Grace

● *Encore:* Funky Bitch

● *Show Notes:* Check out the Beat It teases in Possum. The last known Shaggy Dog was during the soundcheck on March 18, 1992 and the last known Shaggy Dog during a show was on November 3, 1988 (686 shows).

Tuesday, October 31, 1995
Rosemont Horizon, Chicago, IL

● *Set I:* Icculus, Divided Sky, Wilson, Ya Mar, Sparkle, Free, Guyute, Run Like an Antelope, Harpua

● *Set II:* The Who's *Quadrophenia:* I Am The Sea, The Real Me,

Quadrophenia, Cut My Hair, The Punk Meets The Godfather, I'm One, The Dirty Jobs, Helpless Dancer, Is It In My Head, I've Had Enough, 5:15, Sea and Sand, Drowned, Bell Boy, Doctor Jimmy, The Rock, Love Reign O'er Me

● *Set III:* You Enjoy Myself, Jesus Just Left Chicago, A Day in the Life, Suzy Greenberg

● *Encore:* My Generation

● *Show Notes:* Harpua included a story from Mike about a dream about raccoons. The Michael Jackson references continued, as Trey teased the audience by saying that Jimmy was listening to the Halloween album while the band played a Beat It tease. Also, the second set was preceded by a Thriller tease. The *Quadrophenia* set was performed with Dave Grippo on alto saxophone, Don Glasgo on trombone, Joey Somerville on trumpet and Alan Parshley on French horn. All of the *Quadrophenia* songs, as well as My Generation, were debuts. YEM was almost 40 minutes long and was preceded by the audience chess move. The chosen fan, dressed as a Wookie, cracked under the pressure and could not choose a move on stage, prompting a quote from Trey that "Wookies can't play chess." Jesus Just Left Chicago (first since December 6, 1994, or 56 shows) featured Grippo on alto sax; Suzy Greenberg featured Grippo, Glasgo and Somerville. During Bell Boy, crew member Leigh Fordham, clad in a bell boy outfit, sang Keith Moon's original part. My Generation was performed acoustic. Before My Generation, the crew set up a Keith Moon replica drum set on stage. After the song, Fishman and Trey destroyed the drum set a la The Who. Finally, a stagehand brought out a large plunger. Trey pressed it and set off a huge explosion backstage. Other highlights of this show included the return of the reworked Guyute and an excellent Antelope. Icculus was played for the first time since November 20, 1994 (67 shows).

Thursday, November 9, 1995
The Fox Theatre, Atlanta, GA

● *Set I:* Tweezer Reprise, Divided Sky, Prince Caspian, Punch You in the Eye, Simple > Reba, Tela > Sample in a Jar

● *Set II:* Theme From the Bottom > Julius, The Lizards, Bathtub Gin -> The Man Who Stepped Into Yesterday > Avenu Malkenu > The Man Who Stepped Into Yesterday Reprise, Life on Mars?, Hello My Baby, The Squirming Coil

● *Encore:* Loving Cup

● *Show Notes:* Gin featured a huge tease of Rift.

Friday, November 10, 1995
The Fox Theatre, Atlanta, GA

● *Set I:* Bouncing Around the Room, Runaway Jim, Taste That Surrounds, The Old Home Place, It's Ice, Dog Faced Boy, Maze, Guyute, Cavern

● *Set II:* Free, Scent of a Mule, You Enjoy Myself -> Crossroads -> You Enjoy Myself, Strange Design, Sparkle, AC/DC Bag, Sweet Adeline

● *Encore:* Harry Hood

Saturday, November 11, 1995
The Fox Theatre, Atlanta, GA

● *Set I:* Cars Trucks Buses > Mike's Song > A Day in the Life > Poor Heart > Weekapaug Groove, The Horse > Silent in the Morning, Ya Mar, Stash, Amazing Grace, Fee > Chalk Dust Torture

● *Set II:* Also Sprach Zarathustra > David Bowie, Suzy Greenberg >

Uncle Pen, Fluffhead, Sleeping Monkey > Frankenstein -> Suspicious Minds, Run Like an Antelope
● *Encore:* Acoustic Army, Good Times Bad Times
● *Show Notes:* Amazing Grace was performed without microphones. GTBT included Heartbreaker teases.

Sunday, November 12, 1995
O'Connell Center, Gainesville, FL
● *Set I:* My Friend My Friend, Llama, Bouncing Around the Room, Guelah Papyrus, Reba, I Didn't Know, Taste That Surrounds, If I Could, Split Open and Melt, Hello My Baby
● *Set II:* The Curtain > Tweezer, Keyboard Cavalry, Sample in a Jar, Slave to the Traffic Light, HYHU > Cracklin' Rosie > HYHU, Possum, Tweezer Reprise
● *Encore:* Fire

Tuesday, November 14, 1995
University Of Central Florida Arena, Orlando, FL
● *Set I:* Chalk Dust Torture, Foam, Billy Breathes, Divided Sky, Esther, Free, Julius, I'm Blue I'm Lonesome, Cavern
● *Set II:* Maze, Gumbo, Stash -> Manteca -> Stash -> Dog Faced Boy -> Stash, Strange Design, You Enjoy Myself -> Immigrant Song Jam -> You Enjoy Myself
● *Encore:* The Wedge, Rocky Top
● *Show Notes:* Dog Faced Boy was performed over different instrumentation than usual. This fantastic Stash included Esther, Ya Mar and 25 or 6 to 4 teases and quotes. YEM included Low Rider teases. Manteca was played for the first time since October 28, 1994 (85 shows).

Wednesday, November 15, 1995
Sundome, Tampa, FL
● *Set I:* Poor Heart, AC/DC Bag, Fast Enough for You, Rift, Prince Caspian, Sparkle, Split Open and Melt, Sweet Adeline, The Squirming Coil
● *Set II:* Wilson, Theme From the Bottom, Scent of a Mule, Mike's Song > Life on Mars?, Weekapaug Groove, Fee, While My Guitar Gently Weeps
● *Encore:* Suzy Greenberg
● *Show Notes:* At this show, the band won the first chess game with the audience.

Thursday, November 16, 1995
The Auditorium, West Palm Beach, FL
● *Set I:* Cars Trucks Buses, Runaway Jim, Chess Jam, Horn, Mound, Ya Mar, Simple -> Timber (Jerry) > Guyute, Funky Bitch
● *Set II:* A Day in the Life > David Bowie, Lifeboy, Uncle Pen, Ha Ha Ha > Harry Hood, HYHU > If I Only Had a Brain > HYHU, Amazing Grace, Possum
● *Encore:* Brown Eyed Girl
● *Show Notes:* A new band/audience chess match started at this show. Timber included a brief Mind Left Body tease. Possum featured Butch Trucks of The Allman Brothers Band on drums, while Fishman played trombone and Trey's percussion rack. Possum also included a One Way Out jam. Brown Eyed Girl, which featured Jimmy Buffett on vocals, made its debut. Brain was played for the first time since October 25, 1994 (90 shows).

Saturday, November 18, 1995
The Coliseum, North Charleston, SC
● *Set I:* Dinner and a Movie, Bouncing Around the Room, Reba, Lawn Boy, Punch You in the Eye, Slave to the Traffic Light, I'm Blue I'm Lonesome, Sample in a Jar
● *Set II:* AC/DC Bag, Sparkle, Free, I'm So Tired, You Enjoy Myself, Contact, Big Black Furry Creature from Mars -> Acoustic Army -> Big Black Furry Creature from Mars, Cavern
● *Encore:* Bill Bailey Won't You Please Come Home
● *Show Notes:* I'm Blue I'm Lonesome was performed acoustic. YEM included a Brick House jam. The encore featured accompaniment from Page's father, Dr. Jack McConnell and returned for the first time since April 22, 1994 (163 shows). I'm So Tired returned for the first time since its debut on October 31, 1994 (86 shows) and Dinner and a Movie was played for the first time since October 22, 1994 (93 shows).

Sunday, November 19, 1995
Charlotte Coliseum, Charlotte, NC
● *Set I:* Makisupa Policeman -> Maze, Poor Heart > Rift > Stash, Strange Design, It's Ice, Hello My Baby, Julius, The Squirming Coil
● *Set II:* Theme From the Bottom > Also Sprach Zarathustra, The Curtain > Tweezer, Billy Breathes, Scent of a Mule, Harry Hood, Suzy Greenberg
● *Encore:* Life on Mars? > Tweezer Reprise
● *Show Notes:* At this show, fans caught the first performance of the slow arrangement of Poor Heart.

Tuesday, November 21, 1995
Lawrence Joel Coliseum, Winston-Salem, NC
● *Set I:* Fee, Chalk Dust Torture, Prince Caspian, Divided Sky, My Long Journey Home, I'm Blue I'm Lonesome, Guyute, My Friend My Friend, Dog Faced Boy, Runaway Jim
● *Set II:* Simple, David Bowie -> Take Me to the River -> David Bowie, Glide, Ya Mar, Mike's Song -> Keyboard Cavalry > HYHU > Suspicious Minds > HYHU, Carolina, A Day in the Life
● *Encore:* Good Times Bad Times
● *Show Notes:* My Long Journey Home and I'm Blue I'm Lonesome were performed acoustic. Take Me to the River, which was incomplete, debuted in the second set.

Wednesday, November 22, 1995
USAir Arena, Landover, MD
● *Set I:* Cars Trucks Buses, Wilson, Run Like an Antelope, Fluffhead, Uncle Pen, Cavern, Taste That Surrounds, The Lizards, Sample in a Jar, Sweet Adeline
● *Set II:* Rift, Free -> Llama, Bouncing Around the Room, You Enjoy Myself, Strange Design
● *Encore:* Poor Heart, Frankenstein
● *Show Notes:* Rift was aborted by Trey after he accused Fishman of error. This long, monster Free included a tease of Bouncing. Poor Heart was performed in the slow, shuffle style.

Friday, November 24, 1995
Civic Arena, Pittsburgh, PA
● *Check:* Dog Gone Dog, Rift, Funky Bitch (half-speed)
● *Set I:* The Oh Kee Pa Ceremony > AC/DC Bag, The Curtain, Sparkle, Stash, Tela, I'm Blue I'm Lonesome, Maze, Suzy Greenberg

● *Set II:* Chalk Dust Torture, Theme From the Bottom, Reba, Catapult, Scent of a Mule, Bathtub Gin, Acoustic Army, Bike, Fee, Julius
● *Encore:* Life on Mars?, Rocky Top
● *Show Notes:* I'm Blue I'm Lonesome was performed acoustic and, along with Maze, was dedicated to Mario Lemieux of the Pittsburgh Penguins hockey team. Oh Kee Pa was played for the first time since June 9, 1995 (56 shows) and Bike was played for the first time since December 6, 1994 (68 shows).

Saturday, November 25, 1995
Hampton Coliseum, Hampton, VA
● *Set I:* Poor Heart, A Day in the Life > David Bowie, Billy Breathes > Taste That Surrounds, Bouncing Around the Room > Rift, Wolfman's Brother, Runaway Jim
● *Set II:* Timber (Jerry) > Kung, Mike's Song -> Rotation Jam -> Mike's Song, My Long Journey Home, I'm Blue I'm Lonesome, Strange Design > Weekapaug Groove, Harry Hood, Hello My Baby, Poor Heart
● *Encore:* Poor Heart Reprise, Fire
● *Show Notes:* The first set Poor Heart was the original version and the second set Poor Heart was the slow, shuffle version. This Kung was performed differently than most; it was sung in a hymn-like fashion somewhat akin to Yerushalayim Shel Zahav. The Poor Heart Reprise to start the encore was even slower, but only a few lines of the song were played. The jam out of Mike's Song featured the first known Rotation Jam, which also included a segment where each band member was playing one of Page's keyboards (although it was not Keyboard Cavalry). My Long Journey Home and I'm Blue I'm Lonesome were performed acoustic; the latter featured a mandolin solo from Fishman.

Tuesday, November 28, 1995
Civic Coliseum, Knoxville, TN
● *Set I:* Stash, Dinner and a Movie -> Bouncing Around the Room, Foam, I Didn't Know, Divided Sky, Guyute, Hello My Baby, Sample in a Jar
● *Set II:* Also Sprach Zarathustra > Maze, Suzy Greenberg, Uncle Pen, Free, HYHU > Wind Beneath My Wings > HYHU, Run Like an Antelope, Contact, Big Black Furry Creature from Mars, Funky Bitch
● *Encore:* The Squirming Coil
● *Show Notes:* Listen for a 25 or 6 to 4 tease during Suzy Greenberg. The band debuted Wind Beneath My Wings; it was sung by Fishman and dedicated to Colonel Bruce Hampton, who sat on stage reading a newspaper during the song.

Wednesday, November 29, 1995
Municipal Auditorium, Nashville, TN
● *Set I:* AC/DC Bag, Ya Mar, Reba, If I Could, It's Ice, Theme From the Bottom, Acoustic Army, Fee, Split Open and Melt
● *Set II:* Timber (Jerry), Sparkle, Simple, Possum, You Enjoy Myself, Taste That Surrounds > Heart and Soul, Poor Heart, I'm Blue I'm Lonesome, My Long Journey Home, Slave to the Traffic Light
● *Encore:* A Day in the Life
● *Show Notes:* Trey flubbed the third verse of Fee, prompting lots of stage banter. Taste That Surrounds through Slave featured Bela Fleck on banjo.

Thursday, November 30, 1995
Ervin J. Nutter Center, Dayton, OH
● *Set I:* Sample in a Jar, The Curtain, Ha Ha Ha, Julius, NICU, Bathtub Gin, Rift, Fast Enough for You, The Lizards, Fire
● *Set II:* Cars Trucks Buses > Tweezer -> Makisupa Policeman -> Run Like an Antelope > Scent of a Mule, Free, Strange Design, Amazing Grace
● *Encore:* Harry Hood
● *Show Notes:* Hood included a jam segment that reminded some fans of Linus and Lucy. Apparently, Paul Languedoc was among them, as he then played Linus and Lucy to open the post-show music.

Friday, December 1, 1995
Hershey Park Arena, Hershey, PA
● *Check:* Funky Bitch (half-speed)
● *Set I:* Buried Alive, Down with Disease, Theme From the Bottom, Poor Heart, Wolfman's Brother, Chalk Dust Torture, Colonel Forbin's Ascent > The Famous Mockingbird, Stash, Cavern
● *Set II:* Halley's Comet > Mike's Song -> Weekapaug Groove, The Mango Song > Wilson > Suspicious Minds > HYHU, David Bowie -> Catapult -> David Bowie
● *Encore:* Suzy Greenberg
● *Show Notes:* The narration during Colonel Forbin's Ascent referenced chocolate and the rhombus. Catapult started over the Bowie hi-hat intro, which also featured quotes of Homer Simpson ("mmmm...chocolate"). Trey flubbed the lyrics to Wolfman's Brother and remarked that, since he likes them so much, he would sing them again. This was the first time ever that Mike's and Weekapaug were played without anything in between them.

Saturday, December 2, 1995
New Haven Coliseum, New Haven, CT
● *Check:* Funky Bitch (half-speed)
● *Set I:* Prince Caspian, Runaway Jim, Mound, Guelah Papyrus, Reba, My Sweet One, Free, Taste That Surrounds, Bouncing Around the Room, Possum
● *Set II:* Also Sprach Zarathustra, Maze, Simple -> Faht, Tweezer, A Day in the Life, Golgi Apparatus, The Squirming Coil, Tweezer Reprise
● *Encore:* Bold as Love
● *Show Notes:* Possum included an All Fall Down Signal and Tweezer included Bowie teases. My Sweet One was played for the first time since June 15, 1995 (58 shows).

Monday, December 4, 1995
The Mullins Center, University of Massachusetts, Amherst, MA
● *Set I:* Julius, Gumbo, Divided Sky, Punch You in the Eye, Stash, My Mind's Got a Mind of its Own, Axilla (Part II), The Horse > Silent in the Morning, Hello My Baby, While My Guitar Gently Weeps
● *Set II:* Timber (Jerry), Sparkle, Ya Mar, Run Like an Antelope, Billy Breathes, Cars Trucks Buses, You Enjoy Myself, Sample in a Jar, Frankenstein
● *Encore:* Bouncing Around the Room, Rocky Top

Tuesday, December 5, 1995
The Mullins Center, University of Massachusetts, Amherst, MA
● *Set I:* Horn, Chalk Dust Torture, Taste That Surrounds, The Lizards,

Free, Esther, David Bowie, I'm Blue I'm Lonesome
● *Set II:* Poor Heart, Bathtub Gin -> Keyboard Cavalry, Scent of a Mule -> Jam -> Lifeboy, Harry Hood, Cavern
● *Encore:* Theme From the Bottom, Sweet Adeline
● *Show Notes:* Lizards was dedicated to college basketball commentator Dick Vitale. I'm Blue I'm Lonesome was performed acoustic.

Thursday, December 7, 1995
Niagara Falls Convention Center, Niagara Falls, NY
● *Set I:* The Old Home Place, The Curtain > AC/DC Bag, Demand > Rift, Slave to the Traffic Light, Guyute, Bouncing Around the Room, Possum, Hello My Baby
● *Set II:* Split Open and Melt, Strange Design, Taste That Surrounds, Reba, Julius, Sleeping Monkey, Sparkle, Mike's Song -> Weekapaug Groove, Amazing Grace
● *Encore:* Uncle Pen
● *Show Notes:* Reba included a Pop Goes the Weasel tease and, unfortunately, a botched ending. The Melt jam included a tease of In-A-Gadda-Da-Vida.

Friday, December 8, 1995
CSU Convocation Center, Cleveland, OH
● *Check:* Poor Heart (slow)
● *Set I:* Sample in a Jar, Poor Heart, Simple, Runaway Jim, Fluffhead, It's Ice, Acoustic Army, Prince Caspian, Good Times Bad Times
● *Set II:* Also Sprach Zarathustra > Tweezer -> Kung -> Tweezer -> Love You > HYHU, The Squirming Coil, Tweezer Reprise, Run Like an Antelope
● *Encore:* Come Together, A Day in the Life
● *Show Notes:* Good Times Bad Times was dedicated to "the man in the dragon pants," aka Jimmy Page. The encore, which included the first ever Come Together, was played in remembrance of John Lennon's death on December 8, 1980. Antelope included a *Brady Bunch* theme tease. Love You was played for the first time since December 28, 1994 (73 shows).

Saturday, December 9, 1995
The Knickerbocker Arena, Albany, NY
● *Set I:* Maze, Theme From the Bottom > NICU > The Sloth, Rift, Bouncing Around the Room, Free, Billy Breathes, Dog Faced Boy, Chalk Dust Torture
● *Set II:* Timber (Jerry), Wilson > Gumbo, You Enjoy Myself, Lawn Boy, Slave to the Traffic Light, Crossroads, Sweet Adeline
● *Encore:* Loving Cup
● *Show Notes:* Wilson and the YEM vocal jam featured quotes from a talking "Beavis and Butthead" doll. This amazing YEM included a silent jam and a vocal quote of the theme from *Shaft*.

Monday, December 11, 1995
Cumberland County Civic Center, Portland, ME
● *Set I:* My Friend My Friend -> Ha Ha Ha, Stash, Prince Caspian, Reba, Dog Gone Dog, Llama, Dog Gone Dog, Tube, McGrupp and the Watchful Hosemasters, Julius, Cavern
● *Set II:* The Curtain > David Bowie, The Mango Song > Taste That Surrounds, Scent of a Mule, Harry Hood, Suspicious Minds > HYHU, Funky Bitch
● *Encore:* While My Guitar Gently Weeps

● *Show Notes:* Prince Caspian was preceded by Trey discussing how Portland was supposed to be Elvis' last show so this song was for his kid, the prince. The Dog Gone Dogs were part of Trey's announced "Dog Log" album and were preceded by Trey coaching the audience's reaction. Dog Gone Dog had not been played since August 2, 1993 (217 shows). Tube was played as a thank-you for helping out with the "album." Bowie included a long, spacy intro. Funky Bitch and WMGGW featured Warren Haynes on guitar.

Tuesday, December 12, 1995
Civic Center, Providence, RI
● *Set I:* Ya Mar, Sample in a Jar, Divided Sky, Lifeboy, Punch You in the Eye, The Horse > Silent in the Morning, Run Like an Antelope, I'm Blue I'm Lonesome, The Squirming Coil
● *Set II:* Free, Sparkle, Down with Disease -> The Lizards -> Simple, Runaway Jim
● *Encore:* Fire

Thursday, December 14, 1995
Broome County Arena, Binghamton, NY
● *Check:* Strange Design, Free
● *Set I:* Suzy Greenberg, Llama, Horn, Foam, Makisupa Policeman, Split Open and Melt, Tela, Taste That Surrounds, My Sweet One, Frankenstein
● *Set II:* The Curtain > Tweezer -> Timber (Jerry) -> Tweezer -> Keyboard Cavalry, Halley's Comet -> Jam -> NICU -> Jam -> Slave to the Traffic Light
● *Encore:* Bold as Love
● *Show Notes:* The second set featured amazingly fluid jams. Bold as Love was played for a fan up front with a sign requesting it. A humorous scene ensued when another fan got excited, as he thought Trey was referring to his Brother sign. Trey remarked that when fans bring signs, it has to be for a song the band wants to play.

Friday, December 15, 1995
The Spectrum, Philadelphia, PA
● *Set I:* Chalk Dust Torture > Harry Hood > Wilson, Maze > Ha Ha Ha -> Suspicious Minds > HYHU, Cars Trucks Buses, Bouncing Around the Room, Free, Possum
● *Set II:* Tweezer Reprise > Runaway Jim, It's Ice > Bathtub Gin -> Rotation Jam -> Also Sprach Zarathustra > David Bowie, Sweet Adeline
● *Encore:* Good Times Bad Times -> Tweezer Reprise
● *Show Notes:* Possum included Oom Pa Pa, Simpsons and All Fall Down Signals. Trey mentioned that he saw his first concert (Jethro Tull) in this very venue.

Saturday, December 16, 1995
Olympic Center, Lake Placid, NY
● *Set I:* Buried Alive, AC/DC Bag, Taste That Surrounds, Ya Mar, The Sloth, Divided Sky, Dog Faced Boy, Julius, Suzy Greenberg
● *Set II:* Sample in a Jar, Reba, Scent of a Mule, Cavern, Mike's Song -> Simple -> Weekapaug Groove, The Squirming Coil
● *Encore:* Fire

Sunday, December 17, 1995
Olympic Center, Lake Placid, NY

● *Set I:* My Friend My Friend > Poor Heart > A Day in the Life, Run Like an Antelope, The Mango Song > Tube > Stash, The Lizards, Chalk Dust Torture
● *Set II:* Bouncing Around the Room > Maze, Free > Also Sprach Zarathustra > Harry Hood, Sparkle, Tweezer -> Tweezer Reprise
● *Encore:* Hello My Baby, Runaway Jim
● *Show Notes:* Page took a nice solo between Tweezer and Tweezer Reprise.

Thursday, December 28, 1995
The Centrum, Worcester, MA
● *Set I:* Split Open and Melt, Gumbo, The Curtain > Julius, Guyute, Horn, Rift > Fast Enough for You, Possum
● *Set II:* Timber (Jerry) > Theme From the Bottom > Wilson > Buried Alive > Tweezer -> I Didn't Know, Uncle Pen, Slave to the Traffic Light
● *Encore:* Fee > Tweezer Reprise
● *Show Notes:* The P.A. went out during Rift, causing some giggles when Page sang "and silence contagious in moments like these." During Tweezer, Mike practiced part of what would become the Bass Jam on the following evening. Wilson included a Johnny B. Goode tease.

Friday, December 29, 1995
The Centrum, Worcester, MA
● *Set I:* My Friend My Friend, Poor Heart > Down with Disease > Taste That Surrounds, NICU, Stash, Fluffhead, Llama, Sweet Adeline
● *Set II:* Makisupa Policeman > Cars Trucks Buses, Bathtub Gin -> The Real Me -> Bathtub Gin -> McGrupp and the Watchful Hosemasters, Big Black Furry Creature from Mars, Bass Jam -> La Grange, Bouncing Around the Room, Fire
● *Encore:* Golgi Apparatus
● *Show Notes:* The Bass Duet featured Mike and his bass instructor, Jim Stinnette, as well as teases of Zappa's Keep it Greasey and Bach's 6th Brandenburg Concerto (better known as the theme to *Masterpiece Theatre*). La Grange made its first appearance since August 14, 1993 (215 shows).

Saturday, December 30, 1995
Madison Square Garden, New York, NY
● *Set I:* Prince Caspian, Also Sprach Zarathustra > Suzy Greenberg, David Bowie, Simple, It's Ice -> Kung -> It's Ice, The Man Who Stepped Into Yesterday > Avenu Malkenu > The Man Who Stepped Into Yesterday Reprise, Divided Sky, Sample in a Jar
● *Set II:* Ya Mar, Free, Harry Hood > AC/DC Bag, Lifeboy, Scent of a Mule, Cavern, Run Like an Antelope
● *Encore:* A Day in the Life
● *Show Notes:* Ya Mar included an Auld Lang Syne tease.

Sunday, December 31, 1995
Madison Square Garden, New York, NY
● *Set I:* Punch You in the Eye, The Sloth, Reba, The Squirming Coil, Maze, Colonel Forbin's Ascent -> Shine -> The Famous Mockingbird, Sparkle, Chalk Dust Torture
● *Set II:* Drowned -> Jam -> The Lizards, Axilla (Part II), Runaway Jim, Strange Design, Hello My Baby, Mike's Song
● *Set III:* Auld Lang Syne -> Weekapaug Groove -> Sea and Sand, You Enjoy Myself, Sanity, Frankenstein

● *Encore:* Johnny B. Goode
● *Show Notes:* Shine featured Tom Marshall on vocals. The narration in Forbin's discussed how Phish makes time in the Phish Factory, which set up the New Year's Eve stunt. The jam out of Drowned included a progression labeled by some as a highly-debated Fire on the Mountain tease. The second set ended with a Digital Delay Loop Jam out of Mike's, and the third set opened with the Phish Time Factory machine. All four band members dressed as scientists playing with synths while lights flashed and Van de Graff generators zapped. Fishman was lifted up in a bed as Father Time and was reborn as the Baby New Year. This was the first performance of Sanity since June 24, 1994 (147 shows) and the first Johnny B. Goode since July 3, 1995 (58 shows).

SUMMER, 1996

Friday, April 26, 1996
JazzFest at the Fairgrounds, New Orleans, LA
● *Check:* Funky Bitch, Poor Heart, Blues Jam, Wolfman's Brother
Ya Mar, AC/DC Bag, Sparkle, Stash, Cars Trucks Buses, You Enjoy Myself -> Wolfman's Brother, Scent of a Mule, Also Sprach Zarathustra > Harry Hood, Sample in a Jar, A Day in the Life, David Bowie
● *Encore:* Hello My Baby, Cavern
● *Show Notes:* Listen for the obvious When the Saints Go Marching In tease in Ya Mar. Cars Trucks Buses featured Michael Ray on trumpet. The first two verses of Wolfman's Brother were performed *a cappella* as they came out of the YEM vocal jam. David Bowie included a strong Caravan jam.

Thursday, June 6, 1996
Joyous Lake, Woodstock, NY
● *Check:* Funky Bitch, Taste, Waste
● *Set I:* Split Open and Melt, Poor Heart, Runaway Jim, Funky Bitch, Theme From the Bottom, Big Black Furry Creature from Mars, Scent of a Mule, Highway to Hell
● *Set II:* AC/DC Bag, You Enjoy Myself, Chalk Dust Torture, Sparkle, Stash, Waste, Character Zero, David Bowie, Fee > Sample in a Jar
● *Encore:* Ya Mar, Fire
● *Show Notes:* This show was performed under the name "Third Ball." BBFCFM featured Trey using a Rolling Rock beer bottle as a slide. Scent of a Mule included a Sunshine of Your Love tease and saw Trey on keys for portions. Waste and Character Zero debuted at this show.

Tuesday, July 2, 1996
Ville Minan, Italy
● *Show Notes:* Phish's set on this date was rained out. Trey did, however, jam with Santana during their set that evening.

Wednesday, July 3, 1996
Stadia Brtamasco, Trento, Italy
Runaway Jim, Stash, Sparkle, Taste -> Llama
● *Show Notes:* This show was a one-set opener for Santana. Carlos Santana and Karl Perazzo guested on Taste and Llama, during which Trey flubbed lyrics to both songs. Santana jumped in to help out during Llama, singing a verse.

Friday, July 5, 1996
Stadio Olimpico, Rome, Italy
Funky Bitch -> Chalk Dust Torture -> AC/DC Bag -> You Enjoy Myself, Scent of a Mule, David Bowie
● *Encore:* Sweet Adeline
● *Show Notes:* This show was a one-set opener for Santana.

Saturday, July 6, 1996
Duomo Square, Pictoia, Italy
Also Sprach Zarathustra, Reba, Poor Heart, A Day in the Life, Maze, Harry Hood
● *Show Notes:* This show was a one-set opener for Santana.

Sunday, July 7, 1996
Parco Aquatica, Milan, Italy
Sample in a Jar, Divided Sky, Bouncing Around the Room, The Curtain > Tweezer, Sweet Adeline, Uncle Pen, Cavern, Run Like an Antelope -> Suzy Greenberg
● *Show Notes:* This show was a one-set opener for Santana.

Tuesday, July 9, 1996
Centre International de Deauville, France
Theme From the Bottom, Poor Heart, Taste, Cars Trucks Buses, Mike's Song, Bouncing Around the Room, Character Zero
● *Show Notes:* This show was a one-set opener for Santana.

Wednesday, July 10, 1996
Le Zenith, Paris, France
Chalk Dust Torture, Ya Mar, Split Open and Melt, Waste, David Bowie, Hello My Baby, Good Times Bad Times
● *Show Notes:* This show was a one-set opener for Santana.

Thursday, July 11, 1996
Shepherds Bush Empire, London, England
● *Set I:* Runaway Jim, Cavern, Reba, I Didn't Know, Sparkle, Stash, Scent of a Mule, Sample in a Jar
● *Set II:* Harry Hood, Bouncing Around the Room, Also Sprach Zarathustra, Maze, The Lizards, Terrapin, You Enjoy Myself, Hello My Baby
● *Encore:* A Day in the Life
● *Show Notes:* Terrapin was played for the first time since June 13, 1995 (84 shows).

Friday, July 12, 1996
Melkweg, Amsterdam, Netherlands
● *Set I:* Wilson, Divided Sky, Horn, Split Open and Melt, Ya Mar, Funky Bitch, Taste, Theme From the Bottom, Tweezer, Llama
● *Set II:* It's Ice -> Prince Caspian -> Mike's Song -> Run Like an Antelope -> Purple Rain > HYHU, Jam, NICU -> Slave to the Traffic Light, Suzy Greenberg
● *Set III:* David Bowie -> Free, Hello My Baby
● *Encore:* Bathtub Gin, Johnny B. Goode
● *Show Notes:* The reworked Taste debuted at this show, and Trey announced that the song would be performed like this (the *Billy Breathes* album version) from now on. Slave, Bowie, and Free were all unfinished. The jam before NICU was interactive, as the band jammed on chords yelled out by the fans.

Saturday, July 13, 1996
Dour Festival, Dour, Belgium
Sample in a Jar, Runaway Jim, Cavern, Reba, Poor Heart, Split Open and Melt, Fire, Funky Bitch, Chalk Dust Torture, You Enjoy Myself

Monday, July 15, 1996
La Marna, Sesto Calende, Italy
● *Check:* Character Zero
● *Set I:* My Friend My Friend, Punch You in the Eye, Fast Enough for You, Guyute, Possum, I Didn't Know, Harry Hood, Cavern
● *Set II:* Down with Disease, Maze, Loving Cup > Makisupa Policeman, It's Ice, Julius, Purple Rain, Uncle Pen, Run Like an Antelope
● *Encore:* Golgi Apparatus

Wednesday, July 17, 1996
Theatre Antique, Vienne, France
Divided Sky, Sample in a Jar, David Bowie, Ya Mar, Funky Bitch
● *Show Notes:* This show was a one-set opener for Santana.

Thursday, July 18, 1996
Theatre de Verdure, Nice, France
Julius, Cars Trucks Buses > Bouncing Around the Room > Stash, Hello My Baby, It's Ice, You Enjoy Myself
● *Show Notes:* This show was a one-set opener for Santana at the Nice Jazz Festival.

Friday, July 19, 1996
Les Arenes in Arles, France
Runaway Jim, Foam, Sweet Adeline, Waste, Chalk Dust Torture, The Squirming Coil
● *Show Notes:* This show was a one-set opener for Santana.

Sunday, July 21, 1996
The Forum, Nuremberg, Germany
● *Set I:* Golgi Apparatus, Guelah Papyrus, Rift, Tweezer, If I Could, My Mind's Got a Mind of its Own, Split Open and Melt, The Horse > Silent in the Morning, Taste, Train Song, Fee > Timber (Jerry) > Johnny B. Goode
● *Set II:* Llama, Theme From the Bottom, Reba, Life on Mars?, Free, Run Like an Antelope > Simple, Prince Caspian, Suzy Greenberg
● *Encore:* Harry Hood
● *Show Notes:* Train Song debuted at this show and was dedicated to the fans who were following the band around Europe via the rails.

Monday, July 22, 1996
Tanzbrunnen, Cologne, Germany
Sample in a Jar, Poor Heart, Cavern, Maze, Bouncing Around the Room, Stash, A Day in the Life, You Enjoy Myself
● *Show Notes:* This show was a one-set opener for Santana.

Tuesday, July 23, 1996
Markthalle, Hamburg, Germany
● *Set I:* AC/DC Bag > Foam, Theme From the Bottom, Gumbo, Scent of a Mule -> Down with Disease -> McGrupp and the Watchful Hosemasters -> Stash, Hello My Baby
● *Set II:* Also Sprach Zarathustra > Runaway Jim, Loving Cup, Sparkle, Mike's Song > I Am Hydrogen > Weekapaug Groove, Bike, Slave to the

London, England (1997)

Traffic Light
- *Encore:* Rocky Top
- *Show Notes:* Hydrogen was played for the first time since October 19, 1995 (60 shows).

Wednesday, July 24, 1996
The Music Hall in Hannover, Germany
Chalk Dust Torture, Ya Mar, Julius, You Enjoy Myself, Golgi Apparatus
- *Show Notes:* This show was a one-set opener for Santana.

Thursday, July 25, 1996
Stadtpark, Hamburg, Germany
Poor Heart, Punch You in the Eye, Sample in a Jar, It's Ice -> Run Like an Antelope, Life on Mars?, Harry Hood, Cavern
- *Show Notes:* This show was a one-set opener for Santana.

Friday, August 2, 1996
Wolf Mountain, Park City, UT
- *Check:* The Old Home Place, Character Zero, Guelah Papyrus
- *Set I:* Somewhere Over the Rainbow, Ya Mar, Down with Disease, Guelah Papyrus, Poor Heart, Foam, Theme From the Bottom, Golgi Apparatus, Tweezer, Hello My Baby, Possum
- *Set II:* Runaway Jim, Simple, Taste, Free > Fluffhead, Prince Caspian, The Horse > Silent in the Morning, Run Like an Antelope
- *Encore:* Punch You in the Eye
- *Show Notes:* This show marked the debut of Page's theremin. Somewhere Over the Rainbow was performed solo by Page on the theremin in response to the huge rainbow that appeared over the venue just before the show started. Antelope included a tease from a *Star Wars* song.

Sunday, August 4, 1996
Red Rocks Amphitheater, Morrison, CO
- *Check:* Character Zero, Poor Heart (half speed), Caravan, Jam

- *Set I:* Chalk Dust Torture, Funky Bitch, Guyute, Fee, Split Open and Melt, The Mango Song, The Sloth, Maze, Loving Cup
- *Set II:* AC/DC Bag, Reba, Scent of a Mule, Sample in a Jar, David Bowie, Sweet Adeline, Slave to the Traffic Light
- *Encore:* Theme to Star Trek: The Original Series, Rocky Top
- *Show Notes:* The *Star Trek* theme was performed solo by Page on the theremin.

Monday, August 5, 1996
Red Rocks Amphitheater, Morrison, CO
- *Check:* Strange Design (several times)
- *Set I:* Wilson, Poor Heart, Guelah Papyrus, Divided Sky, Wolfman's Brother, Foam, If I Could, Julius, The Squirming Coil
- *Set II:* Also Sprach Zarathustra, Down with Disease -> It's Ice, Halley's Comet -> Somewhere Over the Rainbow, Waste, Talk, Train Song, Strange Design, Amazing Grace, Mike's Song > I Am Hydrogen > Weeka-paug Groove
- *Encore:* Cavern
- *Show Notes:* As urged in flyers handed out by Phish.netters, many fans sat down during the silent part of Divided Sky. Somewhere Over the Rainbow was performed solo by Page on the theremin. Waste through Strange Design were performed with Page on a smaller piano, Trey on acoustic guitar, Mike on acoustic bass, and Fishman on a smaller drum set. This show marked the first performance of Talk and featured an excellent It's Ice. Listen for Barracuda tease from Mike before the second set.

Tuesday, August 6, 1996
Red Rocks Amphitheater, Morrison, CO
- *Set I:* Makisupa Policeman, Rift, Suzy Greenberg > Simple, Theme From the Bottom, The Lizards, Dinner and a Movie, Horn, Run Like an Antelope
- *Set II:* The Curtain > Tweezer, Prince Caspian, A Day in the Life, Big Black Furry Creature from Mars, HYHU > Purple Rain > HYHU, Harry Hood > Tweezer Reprise
- *Encore:* Johnny B. Goode
- *Show Notes:* Note the "This is Red Rocks, This is the Edge" quote from Trey during the break in Rift! The quote was a reference to the both band U2's *Live: Under a Blood Red Sky* album and Trey's similar remarks on the *Junta*-released version of Icculus. Suzy included a Simple tease. The phrase "21 year old Phish Fan Marcus Esquandolas" was substituted for "Marco Esquandolas" during Antelope in reference to a fan's quote in a newspaper article on the disturbance in Morrison the day before. Tweezer included a Norwegian Wood jam. Harry Hood featured the debut of the "Hood" response chant, initiated by Phish.netters and advertised on flyers handed out at the Red Rocks shows. Among other ideas, the flyers encouraged fans to shout "Hood" after the band sings "Harry." It began to rain in the second set and the band responded with Purple Rain. Chris played along by showering the stage in purple lights.

Wednesday, August 7, 1996
Red Rocks Amphitheater, Morrison, CO
- *Set I:* Punch You in the Eye, Sparkle, Stash, Ya Mar, Gumbo, Taste, Lawn Boy, 99 Years, Hold to a Dream, Doin' My Time
- *Set II:* Runaway Jim -> Gypsy Queen -> Runaway Jim, Free, Colonel Forbin's Ascent > The Famous Mockingbird, Possum, Life on Mars?,

You Enjoy Myself, Hello My Baby
● *Encore:* Bouncing Around the Room, Golgi Apparatus
● *Show Notes:* During Ya Mar, Trey thanked the audience, saluted a Colorado swimmer who won two gold medals at the Olympics, and announced that a special guest would come out later in the set. The last three songs of the first set featured Tim O'Brien on mandolin, acoustic guitar and lead vocals. During the Forbin's narration, a giant iguana took the crowd to Mars to view the life there. This version of Mockingbird, unfortunately, was botched badly.

Saturday, August 10, 1996
Alpine Valley, East Troy, WI
● *Check:* Character Zero, The Old Home Place, Funky Bitch
● *Set I:* My Friend My Friend, Poor Heart, AC/DC Bag, Fee, Reba, I Didn't Know, The Horse > Silent in the Morning, Rift, Bathtub Gin, Cavern
● *Set II:* Wilson, Down with Disease, Scent of a Mule, Free, Fluffhead, HYHU > Whipping Post > HYHU, Harry Hood, A Day in the Life
● *Encore:* Contact, Fire
● *Show Notes:* Listen for an In-A-Gadda-Da-Vida tease from Page during the Mule Duel. Whipping Post was played for the first time since April 20, 1993 (284 shows). My Friend featured Trey using his microphone stand as a slide.

Monday, August 12, 1996
Deer Creek Amphitheater, Noblesville, IN
● *Check:* Jam, Lean on Me (instrumental), The Old Home Place, Ain't Too Proud To Beg -> Jam
● *Set I:* Ya Mar, Split Open and Melt, Esther, Chalk Dust Torture, Weigh, It's Ice, Dog Faced Boy, Taste, The Oh Kee Pa Ceremony > Suzy Greenberg
● *Set II:* Timber (Jerry), Sparkle, Simple, Prince Caspian -> McGrupp and the Watchful Hosemasters, Run Like an Antelope, Hello My Baby, Golgi Apparatus, Possum
● *Encore:* Sample in a Jar
● *Show Notes:* Possum included All Fall Down and Simpsons Signals. Weigh was played for the first time since October 22, 1995 (66 shows).

Tuesday, August 13, 1996
Deer Creek Amphitheater, Noblesville, IN
● *Check:* Talk (intro, acoustic, twice), Waste (acoustic), Spooky -> Jam
● *Set I:* Divided Sky, Tube, Tela > Maze, Fast Enough for You, The Old Home Place, Punch You in the Eye, Llama, Glide, Slave to the Traffic Light
● *Set II:* AC/DC Bag, The Lizards, Mike's Song -> Lifeboy, Weekapaug Groove -> Somewhere Over the Rainbow, Waste, Train Song, Strange Design, Sweet Adeline, David Bowie
● *Encore:* Sleeping Monkey, Rocky Top
● *Show Notes:* Somewhere Over the Rainbow was performed solo by Page on the theremin. Waste through Strange Design were performed on the acoustic mini-stage. In the soundcheck jam, Trey played the composed section to Divided Sky while the band jammed. Glide was played for the first time since November 21, 1995 (51 shows).

Wednesday, August 14, 1996
Hershey Park Stadium, Hershey, PA
● *Check:* Funky Bitch, Tush
● *Set I:* Wilson -> Jam -> Down with Disease, Fee -> Poor Heart, Reba,

The Mango Song, Gumbo, Stash, Hello My Baby
● *Set II:* Runaway Jim, You Enjoy Myself, The Horse > Silent in the Morning, Cars Trucks Buses, Tweezer, Theme From the Bottom, HYHU > Cracklin' Rosie > HYHU, Sample in a Jar, Tweezer Reprise
● *Encore:* Julius
● *Show Notes:* Julius was dedicated to Brad Sands' brother, Matty. This show is underrated; some fans speculate that it is because many tourheads were too tired to enjoy the show after the long drive from Deer Creek. Cracklin' Rosie was played for the first time since November 12, 1995 (58 shows).

Friday, August 16, 1996
The Clifford Ball, Plattsburgh Air Force Base, Plattsburgh, NY
● *Set I:* Chalk Dust Torture, Bathtub Gin, Ya Mar, AC/DC Bag, Esther, Divided Sky, Halley's Comet > David Bowie
● *Set II:* Split Open and Melt, Sparkle, Free, The Squirming Coil, Waste, Talk, Train Song, Strange Design, Hello My Baby, Mike's Song -> Simple -> Contact -> Weekapaug Groove
● *Set III:* Makisupa Policeman, Also Sprach Zarathustra > Down with Disease -> NICU, Life on Mars?, Harry Hood -> Fireworks Jam
● *Encore:* Amazing Grace
● *Show Notes:* Waste through Strange Design were performed on the acoustic mini-stage. Great, solid show from top to bottom. Disease was unfinished. Listen for Mary Had a Little Lamb teases at the start of the second set.

Saturday, August 17, 1996
The Clifford Ball Flatbed Jam, Plattsburgh Air Force Base, Plattsburgh, NY
● *Show Notes:* The band took to the back of a flatbed truck at around 3:30 in the morning and drove through the crowd, playing for those who were awake. The performance was one long open-ended jam.

Saturday, August 17, 1996
The Clifford Ball, Plattsburgh Air Force Base, Plattsburgh, NY
● *Set I:* The Old Home Place, Punch You in the Eye, Reba > Cars Trucks Buses, The Lizards, Sample in a Jar, Taste, Fee -> Maze, Suzy Greenberg
● *Set II:* The Curtain, Runaway Jim, It's Ice, Brother, Fluffhead, Run Like an Antelope, Golgi Apparatus, Slave to the Traffic Light
● *Set III:* Wilson, Frankenstein, Scent of a Mule, Tweezer, A Day in the Life, Possum > Tweezer Reprise
● *Encore:* Harpua
● *Show Notes:* Before the second set, Trey paid tribute to Aaron Stein of Syracuse, who was front row center for every show of the tour. The first Brother since August 2, 1993 (257 shows) featured Ben and Jerry on guest vocals. Wilson included a Heartbreaker tease. Antelope featured a female acrobat twirling in the rigging, suspended above the stage in a circus-like fashion. Scent of a Mule featured a Page/Fishman duel instead of the typical Page/Trey duel. Tweezer had big trampolines on each side of the stage and more circus shenanigans. A stunt plane circled overhead during Tweezer Reprise. The plane trailed above during Harpua (first since Halloween 1995, or 64 shows), which was unfinished.

Saturday, August 17, 1996
The Clifford Ball, Plattsburgh Air Force Base, Plattsburgh, NY

● *Orchestral Set: The Clifford Ball Orchestra*
Debussy: Nocturnes (2 movements), Ravel: Pavane Pour une Enfante Defunte, Debussy: Claire de Lune, Ravel: Tombeau de Couperin (2 movements), Chavrier: Joyeux Muse, Faure: Pelleas et Mellisandre (2 movements), Stravinsky: The Firebird (2 movements)
● *Show Notes:* This orchestral set followed Phish's first set at the Ball.

FALL, 1996

Wednesday, October 16, 1996
Olympic Center, Lake Placid, NY
● *Check:* Billy Breathes
● *Set I:* Cars Trucks Buses, Down with Disease, Wilson, Buried Alive, Poor Heart, Billy Breathes, Mound, Sample in a Jar, It's Ice, The Horse > Silent in the Morning, Character Zero
● *Set II:* Wolfman's Brother, Taste, Train Song, Simple, Swept Away > Steep -> Prince Caspian, Run Like an Antelope, The Squirming Coil, Johnny B. Goode
● *Encore:* Waste
● *Show Notes:* Swept Away and Steep debuted at this show.

Thursday, October 17, 1996
Bryce Jordan Center, Penn State University, State College, PA
● *Set I:* Also Sprach Zarathustra > Funky Bitch, Sparkle, Tweezer -> Theme From the Bottom, Talk, Punch You in the Eye, Character Zero, A Day in the Life, Tweezer Reprise
● *Set II:* Ya Mar, Chalk Dust Torture, Bathtub Gin, Scent of a Mule, Free, The Lizards, The Star Spangled Banner, David Bowie
● *Encore:* Golgi Apparatus
● *Show Notes:* The Star Spangled Banner debuted at this show.

Friday, October 18, 1996
Pittsburgh Civic Arena, Pittsburgh, PA
● *Check:* My Mind's Got a Mind of its Own, Billy Breathes
● *Set I:* Runaway Jim, Guelah Papyrus, The Old Home Place, Cars Trucks Buses, Stash, Strange Design, Divided Sky, Billy Breathes, Taste, Sample in a Jar
● *Set II:* Suzy Greenberg, Maze, You Enjoy Myself, Reba, Waste, Harry Hood
● *Encore:* Julius
● *Show Notes:* YEM included teases of Peter Frampton's Do You Feel Like We Do. This Maze was fantastic and remains a fan favorite.

Saturday, October 19, 1996
Marine Midland Arena, Buffalo, NY
● *Check:* Billy Breathes
● *Set I:* My Friend My Friend, Rift, Free, Esther, Llama, Gumbo, Down with Disease, Prince Caspian, Frankenstein
● *Set II:* AC/DC Bag, Sparkle, Slave to the Traffic Light, Bouncing Around the Room, Split Open and Melt, Fluffhead, Swept Away > Steep, Run Like an Antelope, Hello My Baby
● *Encore:* Fee, Rocky Top
● *Show Notes:* The second set started with a Wish You Were Here tease.

Monday, October 21, 1996
Madison Square Garden, New York, NY
● *Set I:* The Star Spangled Banner, Sample in a Jar, Cars Trucks Buses, The Sloth, Divided Sky, Character Zero, Ginseng Sullivan, Stash, Waste, Possum
● *Set II:* Wilson, Chalk Dust Torture, Wolfman's Brother, Reba, Train Song, Maze, Life on Mars?, Simple -> The Horse > Silent in the Morning, David Bowie
● *Encore:* Funky Bitch
● *Show Notes:* Ginseng was played for the first time since June 23, 1995 (103 shows).

Tuesday, October 22, 1996
Madison Square Garden, New York, NY
● *Set I:* The Curtain > Runaway Jim, Bouncing Around the Room, It's Ice, Talk, Split Open and Melt, Sparkle, Free, You Enjoy Myself
● *Set II:* Also Sprach Zarathustra > Down with Disease, Taste, The Mango Song, Lawn Boy, Scent of a Mule, Mike's Song -> Swept Away > Steep, Weekapaug Groove
● *Encore:* All Along the Watchtower
● *Show Notes:* This Weekapaug, often referred to as the "Freakapaug," included circus dancers and Mimi Fishman dancing around on stage towards the end. Watchtower (first since April 21, 1994, or 226 shows) featured Buddy Miles on drums and lead vocals, Merl Saunders on keys, and Fishman on Trey's percussion rack. The circus dancers also appeared for the encore.

Wednesday, October 23, 1996
Hartford Civic Center, Hartford, CT
● *Set I:* Punch You in the Eye, Poor Heart, AC/DC Bag, Foam, Hello My Baby, Character Zero, Rift, Theme From the Bottom, Run Like an Antelope
● *Set II:* Brother, Ya Mar, Tweezer, The Lizards, Llama, Suzy Greenberg, Slave to the Traffic Light, Julius
● *Encore:* Chalk Dust Torture
● *Show Notes:* The entire second set and encore featured Bob Gulotti on a second drum set. Ya Mar included a long drum jam between Fishman and Gulotti.

Friday, October 25, 1996
Hampton Coliseum, Hampton, VA
● *Set I:* Ha Ha Ha, Taste, Makisupa Policeman, Maze, Billy Breathes, Mound, Guelah Papyrus, I Didn't Know, Stash, The Squirming Coil
● *Set II:* Tube, Prince Caspian, Timber (Jerry), The Man Who Stepped Into Yesterday > Avenu Malkenu > The Man Who Stepped Into Yesterday Reprise, NICU, Free, Strange Design, Harry Hood, Cavern, The Star Spangled Banner
● *Encore:* Johnny B. Goode
● *Show Notes:* I Didn't Know featured Fishman on vacuum.

Saturday, October 26, 1996
Charlotte Coliseum, Charlotte, NC
● *Set I:* Julius, Cars Trucks Buses, Wolfman's Brother, Reba, Train Song, Character Zero, It's Ice, Theme From the Bottom, Sample in a Jar
● *Set II:* Down with Disease, You Enjoy Myself, Sparkle, Simple -> McGrupp and the Watchful Hosemasters, Waste, Run Like an Antelope

● *Encore:* Fire

● *Show Notes:* Antelope was dedicated by Trey to Fishman's 14-year old cousin, Jason Roberts, for winning a guitar competition, and included Star Spangled Banner and Voodoo Chile teases.

Sunday, October 27, 1996
North Charleston Coliseum, North Charleston, SC

● *Set I:* Runaway Jim, Punch You in the Eye, AC/DC Bag, Fee, Scent of a Mule -> Catapult -> Scent of a Mule, Split Open and Melt, Talk, Taste, Suzy Greenberg

● *Set II:* Chalk Dust Torture, Bathtub Gin, Rift, Prince Caspian, Ya Mar, Tweezer, Fluffhead, Life on Mars?, Tweezer Reprise

● *Encore:* Possum, Carolina

● *Show Notes:* Catapult (first since December 1, 1995, or 57 shows) was performed twice during the Mule Duel; first by Mike, and then by Page solo on the theremin. Taste included a Norwegian Wood tease. Carolina was played for the first time since November 21, 1995 (64 shows).

Tuesday, October 29, 1996
Leon County Civic Center, Tallahassee, FL

● *Set I:* Chalk Dust Torture, Guelah Papyrus, Cars Trucks Buses, Taste, Bouncing Around the Room, Stash, Train Song, Billy Breathes, Poor Heart > David Bowie

● *Set II:* Rift > Mike's Song > The Horse > Silent in the Morning, Weekapaug Groove, The Wedge, Character Zero, Suspicious Minds > HYHU, Slave to the Traffic Light, Hello My Baby

● *Encore:* Good Times Bad Times

● *Show Notes:* Guest percussionist Karl Perazzo played the entire show. After Suspicious Minds, Trey introduced Fishman as "Norton Charlton Heston." The Wedge was played for the first time since November 14, 1995 (70 shows).

Thursday, October 31, 1996
The Omni, Atlanta, GA

● *Set I:* Sanity, Highway to Hell, Down with Disease, You Enjoy Myself, Prince Caspian, Reba, Colonel Forbin's Ascent > The Famous Mockingbird, Character Zero, The Star Spangled Banner

● *Set II:* The Talking Heads' *Remain in Light*: Born Under Punches (The Heat Goes On) > Crosseyed and Painless > The Great Curve, Once in a Lifetime > Houses in Motion -> Seen and Not Seen -> Listening Wind -> Overload

● *Set III:* Brother, Also Sprach Zarathustra > Maze, Simple -> Swept Away > Steep, Jesus Just Left Chicago, Suzy Greenberg

● *Encore:* Frankenstein

● *Show Notes:* All of the *Remain in Light* songs were debuts; the set featured Karl Perazzo on percussion, Dave Grippo on sax, and Gary Gazaway on trumpet. Perazzo also played during the entire third set. Jesus Just Left Chicago (first since Halloween 1995, or 76 shows), Suzy Greenberg, and Frankenstein also featured Grippo and Gazaway. The Forbin's narration included a reference to The Talking Heads' David Byrne, who appeared in the mountain as the face of Icculus. Byrne threw Colonel Forbin off the mountain and into the arms of the "evil" Famous Mockingbird. At the end of Houses an armchair was brought out to the center of the stage and Mike sat in it to sing Seen and Not Seen. While he sang, Karl Perazzo drummed and Trey played bass. After Overload, a bizarre on-stage demonstration closed the set. The third set

opened with a Feel Like a Stranger tease. Suzy included a Born Under Punches tease from Page.

Saturday, November 2, 1996
Coral Sky Amphitheater, West Palm Beach, FL

● *Set I:* Ya Mar, Julius, Fee -> Taste, Cavern, Stash, The Lizards, Free, Johnny B. Goode

● *Set II:* Crosseyed and Painless -> Run Like an Antelope, Waste, Harry Hood, A Day in the Life, Sweet Adeline

● *Encore:* Funky Bitch

● *Show Notes:* Special guest Karl Perazzo played the entire show. Butch Trucks joined the band on drums for the encore while Fishman played Trey's percussion rack. This show is known for the incredible jamming out of Crosseyed and Painless. The lyric "Norton Charleton Heston" replaced "Marco Esquandolas" in Antelope.

Sunday, November 3, 1996
O'Connell Center, Gainesville, FL

● *Set I:* My Friend My Friend, Runaway Jim, Billy Breathes, The Sloth, NICU, Sample in a Jar, Theme From the Bottom, Bouncing Around the Room, Character Zero

● *Set II:* Timber (Jerry), Divided Sky, Wolfman's Brother, Sparkle, Tweezer, Life on Mars?, Possum, Tweezer Reprise

● *Encore:* Fire

● *Show Notes:* Special guest Karl Perazzo played percussion the entire show.

Wednesday, November 6, 1996
Civic Center, Knoxville, TN

● *Set I:* Split Open and Melt, Cars Trucks Buses, Fast Enough for You, Taste, Train Song, Poor Heart, Punch You in the Eye, Billy Breathes, David Bowie

● *Set II:* Wilson, The Curtain > Mike's Song -> Swept Away > Steep, Weekapaug Groove, Scent of a Mule, Sample in a Jar, Funky Bitch

● *Encore:* Rocky Top

● *Show Notes:* SOAM included In-A-Gadda-Da-Vida teases.

Thursday, November 7, 1996
Rupp Arena, Lexington, KY

● *Set I:* Chalk Dust Torture, Weigh > Rift > Guelah Papyrus, Stash, Waste, Guyute, Free > Tela, Character Zero

● *Set II:* Suzy Greenberg > Bathtub Gin -> HYHU > Bike > HYHU, You Enjoy Myself

● *Encore:* Frankenstein

● *Show Notes:* Character Zero was performed without the ending vocal jam. This version of Bathtub Gin ranks among the best ever. Fishman humorously stumbled through Bike, which was played by request.

Friday, November 8, 1996
Assembly Hall, Champaign, IL

● *Set I:* Runaway Jim -> Axilla -> All Things Reconsidered -> Mound, Down with Disease, Prince Caspian, Reba, Golgi Apparatus, Run Like an Antelope

● *Set II:* Also Sprach Zarathustra > Maze, Bouncing Around the Room, Simple, Loving Cup, Mike's Song, The Star Spangled Banner, Weekapaug Groove

● *Encore:* Theme From the Bottom
● *Show Notes:* Trey had equipment problems in Simple, so Loving Cup ("I know I play a bad guitar") was played next. This second set featured a sweet Simple, which included a tease of Cecilia, and a show-stopping Maze. ATR was played for the first time since July 1, 1995 (108 shows) and Axilla was played for the first time since October 16, 1994 (170 shows).

Saturday, November 9, 1996
The Palace, Auburn Hills, MI
● *Set I:* Buried Alive, Poor Heart, The Sloth, Divided Sky, Horn, Tube, Talk, Split Open and Melt, The Lizards, Character Zero
● *Set II:* David Bowie, A Day in the Life, You Enjoy Myself, Taste, Swept Away > Steep > Harry Hood
● *Encore:* Julius
● *Show Notes:* Hood contained a Steep tease.

Monday, November 11, 1996
Van Andel Arena, Grand Rapids, MI
● *Set I:* Chalk Dust Torture, Guelah Papyrus, Cars Trucks Buses, AC/DC Bag, Sparkle, Brother, Theme From the Bottom, Axilla, Runaway Jim
● *Set II:* Timber (Jerry), Divided Sky, Gumbo, The Curtain, Sample in a Jar, Tweezer, Swept Away > Steep, Maze, Contact, Slave to the Traffic Light
● *Encore:* Waste, Cavern
● *Show Notes:* Divided Sky included All Fall Down Signals.

Wednesday, November 13, 1996
The Target Center, Minneapolis, MN
● *Set I:* Down with Disease, Bouncing Around the Room, It's Ice, Ya Mar, Taste, Train Song, Reba, Character Zero, Sweet Adeline
● *Set II:* Also Sprach Zarathustra > Suzy Greenberg -> Jam, Prince Caspian, You Enjoy Myself, Theme From the Bottom, Golgi Apparatus
● *Encore:* Good Times Bad Times
● *Show Notes:* The second set was highlighted by a strong jam that arose from Suzy.

Thursday, November 14, 1996
Hilton Coliseum, Ames, IA
● *Set I:* AC/DC Bag, Uncle Pen, Wolfman's Brother, Cars Trucks Buses, Free, All Things Reconsidered, Bathtub Gin, Talk, Julius
● *Set II:* Llama, Sample in a Jar, Taste, Swept Away > Steep, Scent of a Mule, Life on Mars?, Demand -> Run Like an Antelope, A Day in the Life
● *Encore:* Stash, Hello My Baby
● *Show Notes:* Demand was played for the first time since December 7, 1995 (64 shows).

Friday, November 15, 1996
Kiel Center, St. Louis, MO
● *Set I:* Wilson, Divided Sky, Bouncing Around the Room, Character Zero, Punch You in the Eye > Prince Caspian, Ginseng Sullivan, Train Song, Chalk Dust Torture, Taste, Cavern
● *Set II:* Makisupa Policeman -> Maze, McGrupp and the Watchful Hosemasters, Split Open and Melt, The Man Who Stepped Into Yesterday > Avenu Malkenu, My Mind's Got a Mind of its Own, Mike's Song, Sleeping Monkey, Mean Mr. Mustard, Weekapaug Groove
● *Encore:* Funky Bitch

● *Show Notes:* Mimi Fishman addressed the crowd before the show and noted that the band was donating a portion of the proceeds from the show to charity. After Sleeping Monkey, Trey announced that the show was brought to you by the letter M (referencing all the second-set songs with "m"-titles) and the number 420. This show marked the debut of Mean Mr. Mustard, complete with a John Popper (cloaked in a cape and hobbling with a cane to the roar of the audience) cameo as the dirty old man. Popper stayed on stage to lend his harmonica to a very short Weekapaug closer and Funky Bitch encore.

Saturday, November 16, 1996
Civic Auditorium, Omaha, NE
● *Set I:* Poor Heart, Down with Disease, Guyute, Gumbo, Rift, Free, The Old Home Place, David Bowie, Lawn Boy, Sparkle, Frankenstein
● *Set II:* La Grange, Runaway Jim -> Kung -> Catapult, Axilla > Harry Hood > Suzy Greenberg, Amazing Grace
● *Encore:* American Band
● *Show Notes:* Kung (first since December 30, 1995, or 55 shows) included The Vibration of Life, which was announced by Trey as "Written by God." The Hood lyrics were altered slightly to include a bit about Lee Fordham, a member of Phish's light crew. The light crew also received a bizarre tribute at the end of Axilla. Suzy Greenberg included La Grange (first since December 29, 1995, or 56 shows) and Axilla teases. American Band made its debut in the city referenced in its lyrics.

Monday, November 18, 1996
Mid-South Coliseum, Memphis, TN
● *Set I:* Cars Trucks Buses, Timber (Jerry), Poor Heart, Taste, Billy Breathes, Guelah Papyrus, Chalk Dust Torture, Ginseng Sullivan, Reba, Character Zero
● *Set II:* Also Sprach Zarathustra > Simple -> Swept Away > Steep, Scent of a Mule, Tweezer, Hello My Baby, Tweezer Reprise, Llama
● *Encore:* Waste, Johnny B. Goode
● *Show Notes:* Tweezer through Llama, as well as Johnny B. Goode, featured Gary Gazaway on trumpet.

Tuesday, November 19, 1996
Municipal Auditorium, Kansas City, MO
● *Set I:* Ya Mar, AC/DC Bag, Foam, Theme From the Bottom, Mound, Stash, Fee, Taste, Loving Cup
● *Set II:* David Bowie, A Day in the Life, Bathtub Gin -> The Vibration of Life -> You Enjoy Myself, The Star Spangled Banner, Fire
● *Encore:* The Squirming Coil
● *Show Notes:* Trey announced the first-ever The Vibration of Life dedication and sent it out to the crew in general but, more specifically, Bob Neumann, the band's Audio Crew Chief and speaker designer. YEM included a Groove is in the Heart jam that even included lyrics. This Bathtub Gin is amazing, clocking in at over 20 minutes long.

Friday, November 22, 1996
Spokane Arena, Spokane, WA
● *Check:* Magilla, Funky Bitch, Billy Breathes
● *Set I:* It's Ice, Runaway Jim, Wolfman's Brother, Taste, Ginseng Sullivan, Sample in a Jar, Fast Enough for You, Train Song, Stash, Cavern
● *Set II:* Down with Disease, Prince Caspian, Maze, Billy Breathes, Swept Away > Steep, Character Zero, Theme From the Bottom, Slave to

the Traffic Light, Hello My Baby
● *Encore:* Julius
● *Show Notes:* Julius included a Cocaine tease and a thank you to the city of Spokane.

Saturday, November 23, 1996
Pacific Coliseum, Vancouver, BC, Canada
● *Set I:* Chalk Dust Torture, Guelah Papyrus, Cars Trucks Buses, Divided Sky, Punch You in the Eye, Midnight on the Highway, Split Open and Melt, Rift, Funky Bitch
● *Set II:* The Curtain > Mike's Song -> Simple -> Makisupa Policeman -> Axilla -> Weekapaug Groove -> Catapult, Waste, Amazing Grace, Harry Hood
● *Encore:* Good Times Bad Times
● *Show Notes:* This show included the first performance of Midnight on the Highway, which was learned while the band was stopped at the American/Canadian border.

Sunday, November 24, 1996
Memorial Coliseum, Portland, OR
● *Set I:* Poor Heart, AC/DC Bag, All Things Reconsidered, Bouncing Around the Room, Reba, Character Zero, Strange Design, Taste, I Didn't Know, Sample in a Jar, Run Like an Antelope
● *Set II:* Also Sprach Zarathustra, Sparkle, David Bowie, A Day in the Life, You Enjoy Myself, Loving Cup, Suzy Greenberg
● *Encore:* Ginseng Sullivan, Cavern
● *Show Notes:* Reba was unfinished. I Didn't Know included a Fishman vacuum solo and a tease of The Beatles' Because.

Wednesday, November 27, 1996
Key Arena, Seattle, WA
● *Set I:* Julius > My Friend My Friend, Ya Mar, Chalk Dust Torture, The Sloth, Uncle Pen, Free > Theme From the Bottom, Bold as Love
● *Set II:* Down with Disease -> Jesus Just Left Chicago, Scent of a Mule, Tweezer -> Sweet Emotion Jam -> Down with Disease, The Star Spangled Banner, Fire
● *Encore:* Waste, Tweezer Reprise
● *Show Notes:* Listen for "Brady Bunch" theme scats from Trey and some vacuum action from Fishman during the Mule Duel. Fire and Bold as Love were dedicated to Jimi Hendrix on his birthday. The Disease and Tweezer combo has led some fans to refer to this as the "Diseezer." The Disease Reprise contained a Can't You Hear Me Knockin' ending. Bold as Love was played for the first time since December 14, 1995 (67 shows).

Friday, November 29, 1996
The Cow Palace, Daly City, CA
● *Set I:* Frankenstein, NICU, Cars Trucks Buses, Character Zero, Divided Sky, Bathtub Gin, Life on Mars?, Maze, Suzy Greenberg
● *Set II:* Wilson > Simple -> Sparks -> Sparkle, Taste, Swept Away > Steep, You Enjoy Myself, Waste, Harry Hood
● *Encore:* Sample in a Jar
● *Show Notes:* This version of Taste is well worth hearing. Trey broke a string in YEM, leading to some odd jamming. Sparks was broken out at this show; it had not been heard since October 29, 1994 (173 shows).

Saturday, November 30, 1996
Arco Arena, Sacramento, CA
● *Set I:* Runaway Jim, Punch You in the Eye, All Things Reconsidered, Bouncing Around the Room, Stash, Fluffhead, The Old Home Place, Uncle Pen, Prince Caspian, Chalk Dust Torture
● *Set II:* La Grange, It's Ice > Glide, Brother, Contact, Also Sprach Zarathustra > Timber (Jerry), Taste, Funky Bitch, Amazing Grace, Amazing Grace Jam
● *Encore:* Possum
● *Show Notes:* The Old Home Place and Uncle Pen featured John McEuen on banjo. Timber through Funky Bitch featured Peter Apfelbaum on tenor sax. Taste included an intro jam that was, basically, a slowed-down version of the song. The Amazing Grace Jam and Possum featured Apfelbaum on tenor sax and McEuen on lap slide guitar. Punch You in the Eye and Also Sprach featured James Brown teases and antics from Fishman. The lyrics to Brother included a reference to Steve McConnell. A fantastic Possum closed the show.

Sunday, December 1, 1996
Pauley Pavilion, University of California, Los Angeles, CA
● *Set I:* Peaches en Regalia, Poor Heart, Cavern, Cars Trucks Buses, Character Zero, The Curtain > Down with Disease, Train Song, The Horse > Silent in the Morning, Sample in a Jar, Run Like an Antelope
● *Set II:* Tweezer, Sparkle, Simple -> A Day in the Life, Reba, Swept Away > Steep, Tweezer Reprise > Johnny B. Goode, Slave to the Traffic Light
● *Encore:* Highway to Hell
● *Show Notes:* This show marked the return of Peaches en Regalia, which had been shelved since December 31, 1994 (144 shows).

Monday, December 2, 1996
America West Arena, Phoenix, AZ
● *Set I:* Rocky Top, AC/DC Bag, Bouncing Around the Room, You Enjoy Myself, I Didn't Know, Theme From the Bottom, Gumbo, Julius
● *Set II:* Ya Mar, Divided Sky, Wolfman's Brother -> Taste, Free, Scent of a Mule, Harry Hood, Sweet Adeline
● *Encore:* Fire

Tuesday, December 3, 1996
The Great Western Forum, Inglewood, CA
The Star Spangled Banner
● *Show Note:* Phish performed the national anthem before a Los Angeles Lakers basketball game.

Wednesday, December 4, 1996
Sports Arena, San Diego, CA
● *Set I:* My Friend My Friend, Chalk Dust Torture, Horn, Uncle Pen, Timber (Jerry), Sample in a Jar, Train Song, Guyute, Character Zero, The Lizards, David Bowie
● *Set II:* Ha Ha Ha, Mike's Song -> Prince Caspian -> Sparkle, Punch You in the Eye, Life on Mars?, Reba, Lawn Boy, Weekapaug Groove
● *Encore:* Jesus Just Left Chicago
● *Show Notes:* During Lawn Boy, Trey thanked the caterers and brought two of them on stage to dance.

Friday, December 6, 1996
The Aladdin Theatre, Las Vegas, NV

● *Check:* Peaches en Regalia, The Wedge, Cowboy's Sweetheart
● *Set I:* Wilson, Peaches en Regalia, Poor Heart, Also Sprach Zarathustra > Llama, You Enjoy Myself, Cars Trucks Buses, Down with Disease > Frankenstein
● *Set II:* Julius, Sparkle, Mike's Song -> Simple -> Jam, Harry Hood, Weekapaug Groove, Sweet Adeline, Good Times Bad Times
● *Encore:* Harpua -> Wildwood Weed -> Cowboy's Sweetheart -> Harpua -> Suspicious Minds -> Harpua, Suzy Greenberg
● *Show Notes:* Also Sprach included a tease of James Brown's Get on the Good Foot. Sweet Adeline was performed without microphones. The opening segment of Harpua was performed in a normal 4/4 time signature, as opposed to its usual 6/4 signature. The encore featured Les Claypool and Larry LaLonde of Primus, John McEuen, the Yodeling Cowgirls, and a host of Elvis impersonators. Suzy Greenberg also featured actor Courtney Gains on Trey's percussion rack. One of the Elvis impersonators led a Susie Q jam at the end of Suzy Greenberg.

Saturday, December 28, 1996
Corestates Spectrum, Philadelphia, PA
● *Set I:* Runaway Jim, NICU, Wolfman's Brother, It's Ice, Billy Breathes, Ginseng Sullivan, Split Open and Melt, The Mango Song, Frankenstein
● *Set II:* Makisupa Policeman -> Maze, Bouncing Around the Room, Digital Delay Loop Jam -> The Man Who Stepped Into Yesterday > Avenu Malkenu > Mike's Song -> Strange Design > Weekapaug Groove, The Star Spangled Banner
● *Encore:* Johnny B. Goode
● *Show Notes:* Makisupa Policeman included the cryptic lyrics "Stink, Stank, Stunk," which may have been a reference to the theme song in *The Grinch Who Stole Christmas*. Weekapaug Groove ended with a long Page solo. The Star Spangled Banner was dedicated to Kate Smith, who used to sing God Bless America at Flyers' home hockey games. Other highlights included the first jamming version of Wolfman's and the beautiful jam before TMWSIY.

Sunday, December 29, 1996
Corestates Spectrum, Philadelphia, PA
● *Set I:* Poor Heart, Caravan, Cavern, Taste, Guelah Papyrus, Train Song, Rift, Free, The Squirming Coil, La Grange
● *Set II:* David Bowie, A Day in the Life, Bathtub Gin, The Lizards, You Enjoy Myself -> Rotation Jam -> Sixteen Candles -> Vocal Jam, Harpua -> Champagne Supernova -> Harpua
● *Encore:* Rocky Top
● *Show Notes:* Sixteen Candles was performed by Mike, solo, on piano. Tom Marshall contributed the vocals to Champagne Supernova as Harpua, Poster, and Jimmy were confronted by the Uber Demon and the evil sound of hell. This show featured the breakout of Caravan, which had been shelved since December 2, 1994 (160 shows).

Monday, December 30, 1996
The Fleet Center, Boston, MA
● *Set I:* Ya Mar, The Sloth, Llama, Gumbo, Reba, Talk, Funky Bitch, Theme From the Bottom, Good Times Bad Times
● *Set II:* Timber (Jerry), Uncle Pen, AC/DC Bag, Guyute, Tweezer -> Lifeboy, Scent of a Mule, Slave to the Traffic Light
● *Encore:* Possum
● *Show Notes:* Reba was unfinished. Talk featured Trey on acoustic gui-

tar. The P.A. cut out during Funky Bitch. The band played on for a few minutes while the crew tried to fix the problem. Fishman took an "air drum" solo, Trey performed Townsend-style windmills, and the entire band engaged in random silliness while still "playing" Funky Bitch. Scent of a Mule featured a Page/Mike Mule Duel and a guest appearance from comedian Steven Wright, who came out and rang a bell once.

Tuesday, December 31, 1996
The Fleet Center, Boston, MA
● *Set I:* Axilla, Peaches en Regalia, Punch You in the Eye, Cars Trucks Buses, Stash, The Horse > Silent in the Morning, Divided Sky, Sample in a Jar, Tweezer Reprise
● *Set II:* Chalk Dust Torture, Wilson, Sparkle, Simple -> Swept Away > Steep > Harry Hood -> Prince Caspian, Character Zero
● *Set III:* Also Sprach Zarathustra > Auld Lang Syne -> Down with Disease, Suzy Greenberg, Run Like an Antelope, Bohemian Rhapsody, Julius
● *Encore:* Amazing Grace
● *Show Notes:* Also Sprach ended as the clock turned forward into the new year. At this point, tens of thousands of balloons fell from the rafters. This show marked the first performance of Bohemian Rhapsody which, along with Julius and Amazing Grace, featured the Boston Community Choir. Also Sprach included Don't Stop 'Till You Get Enough (Michael Jackson) teases.

SPRING, 1997

Thursday, February 13, 1997
Shepherd's Bush Empire, London, United Kingdom
● *Set I:* Chalk Dust Torture, Wolfman's Brother, Also Sprach Zarathustra > Stash, Walfredo, Taste, Waste, Poor Heart, Character Zero, Peaches en Regalia, Love Me, David Bowie
● *Set II:* Julius, Cars Trucks Buses, My Soul, Punch You in the Eye, Slave to the Traffic Light, When the Circus Comes, Maze > Rock-a-William, Harry Hood, Frankenstein
● *Encore:* Prince Caspian, Johnny B. Goode
● *Show Notes:* Many premieres filled the setlist of the European tour opener, including Walfredo, Love Me, My Soul, When the Circus Comes, and Rock-a-William.

Friday, February 14, 1997
Le Botanique, Brussels, Belgium
● *Set I:* Runaway Jim, NICU, You Enjoy Myself, Sweet Adeline, Axilla, It's Ice, Billy Breathes, Uncle Pen, Run Like an Antelope
● *Set II:* AC/DC Bag, Ya Mar, Down with Disease, Funky Bitch, Reba, Walfredo, Rock-a-William, Scent of a Mule > A Day in the Life
● *Encore:* Character Zero
● *Show Notes:* Mule was unfinished.

Sunday, February 16, 1997
Wartesaal, Cologne, Germany
● *Set I:* Beauty of My Dreams, Split Open and Melt, Bouncing Around the Room, Crosseyed and Painless, Guelah Papyrus, Ginseng Sullivan, Tweezer, Waste, Cavern, Chalk Dust Torture
● *Set II:* Sample in a Jar, Cars Trucks Buses, Free, Sparkle, Simple ->

When the Circus Comes, Swept Away > Steep -> David Bowie, Loving Cup, Tweezer Reprise
● *Encore:* Theme From the Bottom, Johnny B. Goode
● *Show Notes:* This show, which was rebroadcast on German television, featured the debut of Beauty of My Dreams. Videos of this show circulate.

Monday, February 17, 1997
Paradiso, Amsterdam, Netherlands
● *Set I:* Soul Shake Down Party, Divided Sky, Wilson > My Soul, Guyute, Timber (Jerry), Billy Breathes, Llama, Bathtub Gin > Golgi Apparatus
● *Set II:* The Squirming Coil -> Down with Disease -> Carini -> Taste -> Down with Disease > Suzy Greenberg, Prince Caspian
● *Encore:* Sleeping Monkey, Rocky Top
● *Show Notes:* This show marked the debuts of Carini and Soul Shake Down Party. The second set is a fan favorite for the massive Disease jamming and the amazing jam that connected Carini and Taste.

Tuesday, February 18, 1997
Bataclan, Paris, France
● *Set I:* Beauty of My Dreams > Cavern > Punch You in the Eye > Runaway Jim > NICU, Stash, Waste, Walfredo, Character Zero > Slave to the Traffic Light
● *Set II:* Peaches en Regalia, Also Sprach Zarathustra > My Soul, Maze > Wolfman's Brother > Reba, Train Song, Harry Hood > Frankenstein
● *Encore:* Bold As Love
● *Show Notes:* Slave was dedicated to a friend who had been hit by a car earlier in the day.

Thursday, February 20, 1997
Teatro Smeraldo, Milan, Italy
● *Set I:* The Curtain, Tweezer > Soul Shake Down Party > Chalk Dust Torture, Love Me, Taste, Gumbo, When the Circus Comes > David Bowie, Tweezer Reprise
● *Set II:* Sample in a Jar, Cars Trucks Buses, Character Zero, Uncle Pen, Stash, Bouncing Around the Room, Free, Swept Away > Steep > A Day in the Life, Runaway Jim, Sweet Adeline
● *Encore:* Julius

Friday, February 21, 1997
Tenax, Florence, Italy
● *Set I:* My Soul, Foam, Down with Disease > The Lizards, Crosseyed and Painless, You Enjoy Myself
● *Set II:* Ya Mar, Run Like an Antelope -> Wilson -> The Oh Kee Pa Ceremony > AC/DC Bag > Billy Breathes, Reba > Waste > Prince Caspian
● *Encore:* Character Zero
● *Show Notes:* This second set featured mentionable versions of Antelope and Wilson. Antelope was unfinished, and a heavy metal jam rose from the "Rye, Rye, Rocco" segment. Trey started singing the Wilson lyrics over this jam and the band wound up in Oh Kee Pa. Reba was also unfinished, as it disintegrated into Waste.

Saturday, February 22, 1997
Teatro Olimpico, Rome, Italy
● *Set I:* Walfredo, Also Sprach Zarathustra > Funky Bitch, Theme From

the Bottom > NICU > When the Circus Comes, Talk, Split Open and Melt, I Didn't Know, Character Zero
● *Set II:* Chalk Dust Torture, Bathtub Gin > Sparkle > Simple > Jesus Just Left Chicago, Harry Hood > Free, Hello My Baby
● *Encore:* Johnny B. Goode

Sunday, February 23, 1997
Fillmore, Cortemaggiore, Italy
● *Set I:* Carini, Axilla > All Things Reconsidered, The Sloth, Love Me, Rift > Fluffhead, Frankenstein, David Bowie
● *Set II:* Daniel, Suzy Greenberg, Maze, The Horse > Silent in the Morning, Peaches en Regalia, Mike's Song, Why Don't We Do It in the Road > HYHU, Good Times Bad Times
● *Encore:* Billy Breathes, Rocky Top
● *Show Notes:* The beginning of this show was especially notable. Carini started off as a pre-recorded tape playing through the P.A. system. Phish took the stage and picked up the song from where it was on the tape and continued to play. This show also featured the first Daniel since August 28, 1993 (287 shows) and the first Why Don't We Do It since June 25, 1995 (144 shows).

Tuesday, February 25, 1997
Incognito, Munich, Germany
● *Set I:* Runaway Jim, My Soul, One Meatball, Li'l Red Rooster, Got My Mojo Workin', Stash, Waste, Taste, Loving Cup
● *Set II:* Beauty of My Dreams, Sample in a Jar > Punch You in the Eye > Free, Fee, My Friend My Friend, Down with Disease, Prince Caspian, La Grange, Sweet Adeline
● *Encore:* Chalk Dust Torture
● *Show Notes:* One Meatball through Mojo Workin' were debuts that featured Sydney Ellis on vocals. My Friend was aborted quickly and scrapped.

Wednesday, February 26, 1997
SWF3 Studios, Badeu-Badeu, Germany
Talk, Waste, Train Song, Walfredo, Goodbye Jam
● *Show Notes:* This "show" was an in-studio set before the Stuttgart show. Between Talk and Waste, Trey noodled around to the tune of Michael Jackson's Don't Stop Till You Get Enough. The DJ played Michael's version in its entirety after Waste. The *Billy Breathes* album versions of Free and Billy Breathes were also played during the show. This was an extremely funny interview with some great banter inbetween songs.

Wednesday, February 26, 1997
Longhorn, Stuttgart-Wangen, Germany
● *Set I:* Camel Walk, Llama, My Friend My Friend, Harry Hood, My Soul > Tube > Carini, Rock-a-William, Dog Gone Dog, While My Guitar Gently Weeps
● *Set II:* Buried Alive > Poor Heart, Ha Ha Ha > You Enjoy Myself -> Kung, Theme From the Bottom, Scent of a Mule -> Jam -> Magilla -> Scent of a Mule, Slave to the Traffic Light
● *Encore:* Highway To Hell
● *Show Notes:* Many breakouts filled this setlist, including Camel Walk (first since July 2, 1995, or 140 shows), Magilla (May 4, 1994, or 260 shows), Dog Gone Dog (December 11, 1995, or 90 shows), and

WMGGW (also December 11, 1995). Ha Ha Ha was notable for the heavy metal jam outro. YEM included Good Foot teases. The jazz jam in the Mule Duel included an 'A' Train tease from Mike.

Friday, February 28, 1997
Huxley's Neue Welt, Berlin, Germany
● *Set I:* Carini, Paul and Silas, My Soul, Cars Trucks Buses, Peaches en Regalia, Stash, Swept Away > Steep > Ya Mar, Character Zero
● *Set II:* Taste, Drowned -> Prince Caspian > Frankenstein, David Bowie, Love Me, Axilla > Waste, Julius
● *Encore:* A Day in the Life
● *Show Notes:* This show included the first Paul and Silas since October 24, 1995 (120 shows) and the first Drowned since December 31, 1995 (82 shows).

Saturday, March 1, 1997
Markthalle, Hamburg, Germany
● *Check:* Attack on the Bass
● *Set I:* Cities, The Oh Kee Pa Ceremony, Down with Disease, Weigh, Beauty of My Dreams, Wolfman's Brother -> Jesus Just Left Chicago, Reba, Hello My Baby, Possum
● *Set II:* Carini, Dinner and a Movie, Mike's Song -> Lawn Boy -> Weekapaug Groove, The Mango Song, Billy Breathes, Theme From the Bottom
● *Encore:* Taste, Sweet Adeline

Mike outside the Ed Sullivan Theater . . . giving out pints of "Phish Food".

Michael McNamara

● *Show Notes:* The week-long trend of breaking out songs continued with the show-opening Cities, which was the first since July 5, 1994 (222 shows), and Dinner and a Movie, which was the first since August 6, 1996 (59 shows). The jam out of Mike's featured teases of The End (which were also found in Weekapaug) and Careful with that Axe Eugene, as well as vocal quotes from The End. Possum included an All Fall Down Signal and a heavy metal-style intro. Wolfman's included a Dave's Energy Guide tease. Portions of this show were made available via the *Slip, Stitch and Pass* release.

Sunday, March 2, 1997
Pumpehuset, Copenhagen, Denmark
● *Set I:* Johnny B. Goode, Uncle Pen, Sample in a Jar, Guyute, My Soul, Runaway Jim -> Gypsy Queen -> Runaway Jim, Run Like an Antelope -> Catapult -> Life on Mars?, Chalk Dust Torture, Hello My Baby
● *Set II:* Also Sprach Zarathustra > Maze, Swept Away > Steep > Punch You in the Eye, Waste, Character Zero, Slave to the Traffic Light, Tweezer Reprise
● *Encore:* You Enjoy Myself
● *Show Notes:* This version of Antelope was unfinished.

Wednesday, March 5, 1997
The Late Show with David Letterman, Ed Sullivan Theater, New York City, NY
Character Zero

Tuesday, March 18, 1997
The Flynn Theater, Burlington, VT
● *Set I:* Cinnamon Girl, NICU > Sample in a Jar > Punch You in the Eye > My Soul, Beauty of My Dreams, Harry Hood > Cars Trucks Buses, Suzy Greenberg, Character Zero
● *Set II:* Taste, Drowned -> Prince Caspian, David Bowie, Love Me, I Told You So, Love Me Like a Man, Waste > Chalk Dust Torture, Slave to the Traffic Light
● *Encore:* Hello My Baby, Funky Bitch
● *Show Notes:* Once again, Phish debuted many new songs at the Flynn. First-timers included I Told You So and Love Me Like a Man, which featured Tammy Fletcher of The Disciples on vocals, and Cinnamon Girl. The last three songs of the second set, as well as Funky Bitch, featured Dave Grippo on alto sax and James Harvey on trombone. Suzy Greenberg included the horns jamming on James Brown's Soul Power. Utilizing the small venue, the band performed Hello My Baby without microphones.

SUMMER, 1997

Friday, June 6, 1997
Brad Sands' and Pete Carini's House, Charlotte, VT
● *Set I:* Limb by Limb, Dogs Stole Things, Ghost, Water in the Sky, Vultures, Dirt, Twist, Piper, Wading in the Velvet Sea, Oblivious Fool, I Don't Care, Samson Variation, Bye Bye Foot
● *Set II:* Samson Variation, I Saw it Again, Waking Up, Limb by Limb, Dogs Stole Things, Ghost, Dirt, Vultures, Water in the Sky, Twist -> Piper, Wading in the Velvet Sea, Ain't Love Funny, Stand -> Izabella
● *Show Notes:* This show, referred to as "The Fourth Ball" or "Brad-

stock," was played for friends before the band embarked on the European summer tour. Many new songs were played here but aren't considered debuts since the show was not for the general public.

Friday, June 13, 1997
The S.F.X. Centre, Dublin, Ireland
● *Set I:* Theme From the Bottom, Dogs Stole Things, Beauty of My Dreams, Billy Breathes, Limb by Limb, Wolfman's Brother -> Wading in the Velvet Sea, Taste
● *Set II:* Stash, Maze, Water in the Sky, Vultures, Slave to the Traffic Light, Chalk Dust Torture > Ghost > Oblivious Fool, Character Zero
● *Encore:* Stand -> Izabella
● *Show Notes:* Phish continued their tradition of breaking out new songs at the beginning of a tour; this show introduced us to Dogs Stole Things, Limb by Limb, Velvet Sea, Water in the Sky, Vultures, Ghost, Oblivious Fool, Stand, and Izabella. Listen before Stash for a Tequila tease during the tune-up.

Saturday, June 14, 1997
The S.F.X. Centre, Dublin, Ireland
● *Check:* Twist
● *Set I:* Down with Disease, NICU, Dirt, Talk, My Soul, Cars Trucks Buses, Limb by Limb, Bye Bye Foot, Free, Prince Caspian
● *Set II:* Twist, Piper, I Saw it Again, Waking Up, Dogs Stole Things, Waste, David Bowie, Cavern
● *Encore:* When the Circus Comes, Rocky Top
● Show Notes: Bye Bye Foot debuted at this show. Also, this show marked the first public performances of Dirt, Twist, Piper, I Saw it Again, and Waking Up. Both Waste and Cavern were actually jammed out at this show.

Monday, June 16, 1997
Royal Albert Hall, London, England
● *Set I:* The Squirming Coil > Dogs Stole Things, Taste, Water in the Sky, Sample in a Jar, Beauty of My Dreams, Theme From the Bottom, Chalk Dust Torture, Wolfman's Brother, Oblivious Fool
● *Set II:* Limb by Limb, Ghost -> I Don't Care > Reba, Wading in the Velvet Sea, Dirt, Harry Hood
● *Encore:* Cities, Poor Heart
● *Show Notes:* I Don't Care made its short-lived debut at this show. Reba included a beautiful Cities jam.

Thursday, June 19, 1997
Arena, Vienna, Austria
● *Set I:* Limb by Limb, Dogs Stole Things, Theme From the Bottom > Punch You in the Eye, Water in the Sky, Maze, Waste, Vultures, Runaway Jim
● *Set II:* Stash -> Ghost -> I Saw it Again > Wading in the Velvet Sea, Piper, Jesus Just Left Chicago > Prince Caspian
● *Encore:* Beauty of My Dreams > Character Zero, Hello My Baby

Friday, June 20, 1997
Archa Theater, Prague, Czech Republic
● *Set I:* Taste > Jam -> Cities > Horn -> Ain't Love Funny -> Limb by Limb -> I Don't Care > Run Like an Antelope
● *Set II:* David Bowie, Ghost, Bye Bye Foot, Ginseng Sullivan > Cav-

ern > Twist, Bouncing Around the Room > Julius
● *Encore:* When the Circus Comes, Rocky Top
● *Show Notes:* Ain't Love Funny made its debut at this show and was played out of an odd, atypical jam that grew out of Horn.

Saturday, June 21, 1997
Hurricane Festival, Scheesal, Germany
Sample in a Jar, Also Sprach Zarathustra > Poor Heart, Taste, Dogs Stole Things, Theme From the Bottom, Swept Away, Steep, Limb by Limb, Dirt, Harry Hood, Chalk Dust Torture, Jam, Twist, Cavern
● *Encore:* My Soul

Sunday, June 22, 1997
Loreley Festival, Loreley, Germany
Taste, Water in the Sky, Stash, Dirt, Uncle Pen, Character Zero, Theme From the Bottom, Hello My Baby, Ghost
● *Encore:* Limb by Limb

Tuesday, June 24, 1997
La Laiterie, Strasbourg, France
● *Set I:* Split Open and Melt, Beauty of My Dreams, Dogs Stole Things, Vultures, Guelah Papyrus, Runaway Jim -> Gypsy Queen -> Runaway Jim, Talk, Free, Prince Caspian, Rocky Top
● *Set II:* Wolfman's Brother, Reba, NICU, Twist, Piper, Wading in the Velvet Sea, Ghost
● *Encore:* Loving Cup
● *Show Notes:* Guelah was aborted and scrapped.

Wednesday, June 25, 1997
L'Aeronef, Lille, France
● *Set I:* Oblivious Fool, Dogs Stole Things, Taste, Billy Breathes, AC/DC Bag, The Old Home Place, Theme From the Bottom, Wading in the Velvet Sea, I Saw it Again, Limb by Limb, My Soul
● *Set II:* Down with Disease -> Piper -> Down with Disease -> Meatstick -> McGrupp and the Watchful Hosemasters > Makisupa Policeman, Cecilia > HYHU > Rock-a-William, Run Like an Antelope
● *Encore:* Guyute
● *Show Notes:* This show marked the debuts of Cecilia, which was performed *a cappella* by Fishman, and Meatstick. The jam out of Disease included Can't You Hear Me Knockin' teases. This version of McGrupp was very spacy and was filled with Makisupa teases. The subsequent Makisupa was unfinished. Trey altered the lyrics to Antelope to pay tribute to Antelope Greg, a well-known fan who, as of this show, had only missed a handful of shows since 1994.

Friday, June 27, 1997
Glastonbury Festival, Worthy Farm, Pilton, Somerset, England
Wilson, Chalk Dust Torture, Stash, Dogs Stole Things, Poor Heart, Taste, Bouncing Around the Room, Character Zero

Sunday, June 29, 1997
Roskilde Festival, Roskilde, Denmark
You Enjoy Myself, Taste, Bouncing Around the Room, Beauty of My Dreams, Chalk Dust Torture, Theme From the Bottom, Character Zero
● *Encore:* My Soul

Tuesday, July 1. 1997
Paradiso, Amsterdam, Netherlands
● *Set I:* Ghost, Horn, Ya Mar, Limb by Limb, Ain't Love Funny, I Saw it Again, Dirt, Reba, Dogs Stole Things
● *Set II:* Jam -> Timber (Jerry), Bathtub Gin -> Cities -> Jam, Loving Cup > Slave to the Traffic Light
● *Encore:* When the Circus Comes
● *Show Notes:* The amazingly fluid jam out of Cities featured a When the Saints Go Marching In tease and, along with Ghost, featured the beginning of the infamous Amsterdam "Worm" banter. Reba included the whistling ending. The jam to start the second set was a keyboard jam that primarily featured Fishman.

Wednesday, July 2, 1997
Paradiso, Amsterdam, Netherlands
● *Set I:* Mike's Song -> Simple -> Maze, Strange Design, Ginseng Sullivan, Vultures, Water in the Sky, Weekapaug Groove
● *Set II:* Stash -> Llama -> Wormtown Jam, Wading in the Velvet Sea
● *Encore:* Free
● *Encore:* David Bowie
● *Show Notes:* Stash was absolutely amazing, clocking in at nearly 30 minutes and featuring a long, spacy intro. The Wormtown Jam continued the stage banter of the night before. Portions of the narration were sung to the tune of Steve Miller's Swingtown, as Trey warned the fans in attendance about the killer worms that inhabit the canals of Amsterdam. This version of Free is a fan favorite for its incredible jam section.

Thursday, July 3, 1997
Serenadenhof, Nuremberg, Germany
● *Set I:* Piper, My Soul, Divided Sky, Beauty of My Dreams, Taste, Train Song, Theme From the Bottom, Rocky Top
● *Set II:* Ghost, Cars Trucks Buses, Billy Breathes, Sparkle, Harry Hood, Cavern
● *Encore:* Character Zero

Saturday, July 5, 1997
Piazza Risorgimento, Como, Italy
● *Check:* Funky Bitch, Ginseng Sullivan
Julius, Bouncing Around the Room > Uncle Pen, Sample in a Jar, Theme From the Bottom, Prince Caspian -> Twist > Piper, Harry Hood > Love You > HYHU > Poor Heart > Character Zero > Good Times Bad Times
● *Encore:* The Squirming Coil
● *Show Notes:* This was a free show. Twist included a Groove Is In the Heart jam and GTBT included a Walk This Way tease. At the beginning of the Hood jam, Trey asked Chris to turn off the lights so that the band could see the mountains. Love You was played for the first time since December 8, 1995 (111 shows)

Sunday, July 6, 1997
Spiaggia di Rivoltella, Desenzano, Italy
● *Check:* Jam, Oblivious Fool, Beauty of My Dreams, Hell's Bells, You Shook Me All Night Long, Mmm-Bop
Soundcheck Limbo Karaoke Contest: Another One Bites the Dust, And It Stoned Me, Only Shallow, Day-O

● *Set I:* Runaway Jim, The Old Home Place, Dogs Stole Things, Stash, The Horse > Silent in the Morning, Cars Trucks Buses, Scent of a Mule, Chalk Dust Torture
● *Set II:* Free, You Enjoy Myself, Waste, Rocky Top, Funky Bitch
● *Encore:* My Soul
● *Show Notes:* Some fans consider this a three-set show, as many in attendance were at this outdoor venue in time for the soundcheck. After a fairly long soundcheck and some fun banter with the crowd, the band held a soundcheck limbo karaoke contest where audience members came on stage and sang with the band. Luckily, a taper in attendance managed to capture the soundcheck on tape for others to experience.

Wednesday, July 9, 1997
Le Transbordeur, Lyon/Villeurbanne, France
● *Check:* Funky Bitch, Jam
● *Set I:* Punch You in the Eye > Prince Caspian, Ginseng Sullivan, Split Open and Melt, Dirt, Taste, Sweet Adeline, Harry Hood
● *Set II:* Down with Disease > My Soul > Cars Trucks Buses, You Enjoy Myself -> Ghost > Poor Heart
● *Encore:* Hello My Baby
● *Show Notes:* YEM through Poor Heart featured Bela Fleck and The Flecktones (Bela Fleck, Jeff Coffin, Roy "Futureman" Wooten, and Victor Wooten), who were announced during the bass and drums segment of YEM and bounced along during the tramps jam. The song then launched into an amazing jam that included Disease teases before segueing nicely into Ghost. Poor Heart included a "Sanford and Son" theme tease from Coffin. Pierre, a local Hagen Dazs employee who the band met the day before, was repeatedly recognized by the band and was brought up on stage and serenaded during the encore. At one point during the show, Vic Wooten stood behind Mike and the two played Mike's bass together.

Thursday, July 10, 1997
Espace Julien, Marseilles, France
● *Set I:* Dogs Stole Things, Limb by Limb, Ginseng Sullivan, Bathtub Gin, Llama > Wading in the Velvet Sea, Jam, Oblivious Fool
● *Set II:* Also Sprach Zarathustra > Julius -> Magilla, Ya Mar -> Ghost -> Take Me to the River -> Jam
● *Encore:* Funky Bitch
● *Show Notes:* The encore featured a guest appearance by members of the Son Seals Band. Take Me to the River was unfinished. Several songs including alternate lyrics referencing the "vampire children." Llama was unfinished and featured a long, atypical jam that wove into Velvet Sea. The funky, free-form jam after Velvet Sea concluded with a jam akin to Lizards.

Friday, July 11, 1997
Doctor Music Festival, Pyrenees, Spain
Chalk Dust Torture, Bouncing Around the Room, Stash, Beauty of My Dreams, Wolfman's Brother, Johnny B. Goode, You Enjoy Myself
● *Encore:* Character Zero

Monday, July 21, 1997
Virginia Beach Amphitheater, Virginia Beach, VA
● *Check:* Limb by Limb, Twist (several times), Ginseng Sullivan
● *Set I:* Ghost, Dogs Stole Things, Piper, Dirt, Ginseng Sullivan, Bath-

tub Gin, Character Zero
- *Set II:* Wolfman's Brother -> Magilla, David Bowie, Wading in the Velvet Sea, Theme From the Bottom -> Jam, Funky Bitch, Slave to the Traffic Light
- *Encore:* Loving Cup
- *Show Notes:* The jam during Bathtub Gin featured Trey jumping up and down in time with a syncopated jam, as well as strong Drowned teases. Near the end of the jam, Trey mentioned how good it was to be back home and named the four newer songs that were played. The beginning of Bowie included a Birdland jam and Wolfman's included a Bathtub Gin tease. The jam out of Theme, as well as Funky Bitch, featured LeRoi Moore on saxophone. The jam with LeRoi included a segment where he played two saxes, Trey played three guitars, Mike played two basses and the Cracklin' Rosie cymbals, Fish had four drumsticks and Page was lying across his keyboards playing as many as possible. It was an insane visual experience that can't be explained either in words or on tape.

Tuesday, July 22, 1997
Walnut Creek Amphitheater, Raleigh, NC
- *Check:* Limb by Limb (three times), Vultures, Water in the Sky, I Saw it Again (first verse only)
- *Set I:* Runaway Jim -> My Soul, Water in the Sky, Stash, Bouncing Around the Room, Vultures, Bye Bye Foot, Taste
- *Set II:* Down with Disease -> Mike's Song -> Simple -> I Am Hydrogen > Weekapaug Groove, Hello My Baby
- *Encore:* When the Circus Comes, Harry Hood
- *Show Notes:* The first set of this show was performed during a furious lightning storm in Raleigh and led to a short but memorable second set. Listen especially during Taste, during which the band jammed to the energy of the lightning. The long, jammed out transition from Disease into Mike's was one of the most fluid segues ever. Weekapaug included a Hydrogen tease and closed with a Can't You Hear Me Knockin' tease. Hydrogen was played for the first time since August 5, 1996 (83 shows).

Wednesday, July 23, 1997
Lakewood Amphitheater, Atlanta, GA
- *Set I:* Julius, Dirt, NICU, Dogs Stole Things, Ginseng Sullivan, Water in the Sky, Limb by Limb, Split Open and Melt, Billy Breathes, Possum
- *Set II:* Punch You in the Eye, Ghost > Sample in a Jar, You Enjoy Myself -> Rocky Mountain Way Jam > Chalk Dust Torture
- *Encore:* Frankenstein
- *Show Notes:* Ghost included an On Your Way Down tease. YEM included a *Jeopardy* theme tease. Chalk Dust included Rocky Mountain Way teases.

Friday, July 25, 1997
Starplex Amphitheater, Dallas, TX
- *Set I:* Beauty of My Dreams, Wolfman's Brother > Maze, Water in the Sky, Bathtub Gin -> Makisupa Policeman -> AC/DC Bag
- *Set II:* Chalk Dust Torture -> Taste -> Ya Mar -> Drum Jam -> Ghost -> Character Zero
- *Encore:* Theme From the Bottom
- *Show Notes:* The second set and encore featured Bob Gulotti on a second drum set. Chalk Dust was unfinished and segued nicely into Taste. The Drum Jam also featured Page on keys.

Saturday, July 26, 1997
South Park Meadows, Austin, TX
- *Set I:* Limb by Limb, Dogs Stole Things, Poor Heart, Stash, Billy Breathes, Cars Trucks Buses, Dirt, You Enjoy Myself -> Izabella
- *Set II:* Timber (Jerry) > David Bowie, Harry Hood -> Blister in the Sun Jam -> Harry Hood -> Free, Waste > Johnny B. Goode
- *Encore:* Bouncing Around the Room, Cavern
- *Show Notes:* The second set included the first-ever Blister jam, with lyrics, and an unfinished Hood that segued nicely into Free. The entire show featured Bob Gulotti on a second drum set. Listen closely for Willie the Pimp (Frank Zappa) teases in YEM just before the segue into Izabella.

Tuesday, July 29, 1997
Desert Sky Pavilion, Phoenix, AZ
- *Set I:* Theme From the Bottom, Beauty of My Dreams, Gumbo, Dirt, Sparkle, Ghost, Swept Away > Steep, Loving Cup
- *Set II:* Oblivious Fool, Run Like an Antelope, Wading in the Velvet Sea, Twist -> Taste, Sample in a Jar, Rocky Top, The Squirming Coil
- *Encore:* Possum

Wednesday, July 30, 1997
Ventura County Fairgrounds, Ventura, CA
- *Check:* Twist (with Chuck E's in Love lyrics), Blues Jam, Makisupa Policeman
- *Set I:* NICU, Wolfman's Brother > Chalk Dust Torture, Water in the Sky, Stash, Weigh, Piper, Cars Trucks Buses, Character Zero
- *Set II:* Punch You in the Eye > Free, David Bowie -> Cities -> David Bowie, Bouncing Around the Room, Uncle Pen, Prince Caspian, Fire
- *Encore:* My Soul
- *Show Notes:* Wolfman's included a Take Me to the River jam. Bowie included a Simpsons Signal, as Matt Groening, creator of "The Simpsons," was reportedly in attendance.

Thursday, July 31, 1997
Shoreline Amphitheater, Mountainview, CA
- *Set I:* Ghost > Ya Mar > Dogs Stole Things, Limb by Limb, Dirt, Maze, Glide, I Saw it Again, You Enjoy Myself
- *Set II:* Runaway Jim -> When the Circus Comes, Vultures, McGrupp and the Watchful Hosemasters > Mike's Song -> I Am Hydrogen > Weekapaug Groove
- *Encore:* Cinnamon Girl
- *Show Notes:* Weekapaug included Happy Birthday teases from Trey, who later made reference to Jerry Garcia's birthday, which was the following day. In a classy nod to Garcia, Trey noted that Phish and the rest of the music community were trying to keep Jerry's spirit alive through music. Listen for Sweet Home Alabama teases before the start of the second set and "Mind Left Body" teases during McGrupp, as well as strange Santa Claus is Coming to Town teases in YEM.

Saturday, August 2, 1997
The Gorge, George, WA
- *Set I:* Theme From the Bottom, Ginseng Sullivan, Ghost, Dogs Stole Things, Divided Sky, Wolfman's Brother, Water in the Sky, Split Open and Melt
- *Set II:* Down with Disease -> Tweezer -> Johnny B. Goode > Sparkle, Wading in the Velvet Sea, Loving Cup > Tweezer Reprise

● *Encore:* Harry Hood
● *Show Notes:* Ghost featured jamming based on Who Knows. The Disease intro included a tease of Three Blind Mice.

Sunday, August 3, 1997
The Gorge, George, WA
● *Set I:* Bathtub Gin > Foam, Samson Variation, Dirt, Vultures, My Mind's Got a Mind of its Own, Twist > Jesus Just Left Chicago, Limb by Limb, Character Zero
● *Set II:* Julius, Simple, Fluffhead, Lifeboy, Taste, Hello My Baby, Frankenstein
● *Encore:* Bouncing Around the Room, Slave to the Traffic Light
● *Show Notes:* The first set included the debut of the instrumental Samson Variation. MMGAMOIO was played for the first time since November 15, 1996 (61 shows).

Wednesday, August 6, 1997
Riverport Amphitheater, Maryland Heights, MO
● *Set I:* NICU, Stash, Beauty of My Dreams, Twist -> Also Sprach Zarathustra > AC/DC Bag, Ya Mar, You Enjoy Myself
● *Set II:* Runaway Jim -> My Soul, Ghost, Prince Caspian, Cars Trucks Buses, Sample in a Jar, Run Like an Antelope
● *Encore:* Julius
● *Show Notes:* Nice versions of Ghost and Antelope, which included both a Makisupa-jam with Page on the theremin and Mike on a mini-drum and *Star Wars* teases, are the highlights of this show.

Friday, August 8, 1997
World Music Theater, Tinley Park, IL
● *Set I:* Cars Trucks Buses, Gumbo > The Lizards, Dirt, It's Ice, Water in the Sky, Character Zero
● *Set II:* Wolfman's Brother -> Free, Limb by Limb, Loving Cup, Prince Caspian > Chalk Dust Torture
● *Encore:* Hoochie Coochie Man, Messin' With The Kid
● *Show Notes:* The encore, which included the debut of Messin' with the Kid, featured Sugar Blue on harmonica and vocals. Hoochie Coochie Man was played for the first time since April 10, 1993 (380 shows).

Saturday, August 9, 1997
Alpine Valley, East Troy, WI
● *Set I:* Theme From the Bottom, Punch You in the Eye, Ghost -> Taste, Dogs Stole Things, Reba, Lawn Boy, Crossroads
● *Set II:* Wilson > Foam, Mike's Song -> Ain't Love Funny -> Simple -> Swept Away > Steep > Scent of a Mule, Slave to the Traffic Light > Weekapaug Groove
● *Encore:* When the Circus Comes, Rocky Top
● *Show Notes:* Scent featured a duel between Trey and Mike after Page's solo. Mike and Trey started their duel facing each other and wound up on the ground doing bicycle kicks while they played. Weekapaug included Can't You Hear Me Knockin' teases. Crossroads was played for the first time since December 9, 1995 (127 shows).

Sunday, August 10, 1997
Deer Creek Amphitheater, Noblesville, IN
● *Check:* Dog Gone Dog, Paul and Silas, Funky Bitch (slow), She Caught the Katy and Left Me a Mule to Ride, Star Trek Jam (Page on Theremin)
● *Set I:* Bathtub Gin -> Sparkle, Down with Disease, Dirt, Cars Trucks Buses, Billy Breathes, Split Open and Melt, Bye Bye Foot > Ginseng Sullivan, Harry Hood
● *Set II:* Cities -> Good Times Bad Times -> Rotation Jam -> Rock-a-William -> David Bowie
● *Encore:* Cavern
● *Show Notes:* The long, involved Rotation Jam to set up Rock-a-William started when Page went to the theremin for a solo. Soon after, Trey took up the keys and Mike went to play guitar. Page eventually picked up Mike's bass. After they jammed a bit longer, Mike went to join Trey on the keys. Trey then joined Fishman on the drums. The two of them played on the same drum set for awhile and Mike took a piano solo. Trey eventually kicked Fishman off the drum stool, and Fishman picked up Trey's guitar. SOAM contained a very exploratory and interesting jam and a Third Stone from the Sun tease, as well as a jam on Lark's Tongues in Aspic (Part II) by King Crimson.

Monday, August 11, 1997
Deer Creek Amphitheater, Noblesville, IN
● *Set I:* Makisupa Policeman -> Maze, Water in the Sky, Guyute, Guelah Papyrus, Limb by Limb, Horn, Run Like an Antelope
● *Set II:* Timber (Jerry), Piper, Vultures > My Soul, You Enjoy Myself, Character Zero
● *Encore:* The Squirming Coil
● *Show Notes:* The "Rye Rye Rocco" section of Antelope included Page on theremin.

Wednesday, August 13, 1997
Star Lake Amphitheater, Burgettstown PA
● *Check:* Funky Bitch, Poor Heart > Jam
● *Set I:* Amoreena, Poor Heart, Stash, Water in the Sky, Gumbo -> The Horse > Silent in the Morning, Beauty of My Dreams, Crosseyed and Painless > Wilson, Sweet Adeline
● *Set II:* Runaway Jim, Ghost -> Izabella, Sleeping Monkey, McGrupp and the Watchful Hosemasters > Sample in a Jar, Also Sprach Zarathustra > Golgi Apparatus > Frankenstein
● *Encore:* Theme From the Bottom
● *Show Notes:* The end of Wilson included a Little Drummer Boy tease. This show featured the first jammed-out Gumbo and the debut (and only appearance) of Amoreena.

Thursday, August 14, 1997
Darien Lake Performing Arts Center, Darien Center NY
● *Check:* Buffalo Bill, The Old Home Place, Funky Bitch, Crosseyed and Painless
● *Set I:* Ya Mar, Funky Bitch, Fluffhead, Limb by Limb, Free, Cars Trucks Buses, Tela, Train Song, Billy Breathes, Run Like an Antelope
● *Set II:* Chalk Dust Torture, Love Me, Sparkle, Harry Hood > Colonel Forbin's Ascent -> Merry Pranksters Jam -> Camel Walk, Taste
● *Encore:* Bouncing Around the Room, Rocky Top
● *Show Notes:* The second set featured an appearance by Ken Kesey and the Merry Pranksters. Listen for several teases during the Pranksters Jam, including Somewhere Over the Rainbow from Page and Maze and Frankenstein from Trey. Tela was played for the first time since November 7, 1996 (74 shows) and Forbin's was played for the

first time since Halloween, 1996 (78 shows).

Saturday, August 16, 1997
The Great Went, Limestone, ME
● *Set I:* Makisupa Policeman -> Harpua, Chalk Dust Torture, Theme From the Bottom, Punch You in the Eye, Ghost, Ginseng Sullivan, You Enjoy Myself > Train Song, Character Zero, The Squirming Coil
● *Set II:* Wolfman's Brother -> Simple -> My Soul, Jam -> Slave to the Traffic Light, Rocky Top, Julius
● *Set III:* Halley's Comet -> Cities -> Llama, Lawn Boy, Limb by Limb, Funky Bitch
● *Encore:* Contact, Loving Cup
● *Show Notes:* Harpua (first since December 29, 1996, or 54 shows) picked up where the Clifford Ball Harpua left off. After Chalk Dust, Trey remarked that the first three songs served as the soundcheck, which the band did not do before the show. The jam out of Simple, as well as the beginning of My Soul, included *Odd Couple* theme teases. Halley's Comet (first since August 16, 1996, or 92 shows) included On Your Way Down teases and Cities included an After Midnight tease. Also, Trey altered the lyrics to Cities to reference Fishman sleeping in the day-time. The Julius intro was partially performed *a cappella* with finger-snaps. Funky Bitch featured a fireworks display behind the stage that culminated in a great finale as the song ended. Contact was played for the first time since November 30, 1996 (60 shows).

Sunday, August 17, 1997
The Great Went, Limestone, ME
● *Set I:* The Wedge, Beauty of My Dreams, Dogs Stole Things, Vultures, Water in the Sky, Maze, Bouncing Around the Room > Tweezer -> Taste, Carolina
● *Set II:* Down with Disease -> Bathtub Gin > Uncle Pen, Also Sprach Zarathustra -> Art Jam -> Harry Hood
● *Set III:* Buffalo Bill -> NICU, Weigh, Guyute, Dirt, Scent of a Mule, Prince Caspian
● *Encore:* When the Circus Comes, Tweezer Reprise
● *Show Notes:* Tweezer featured a Cities-like jam and Simple teases, and Mule included London Bridge teases. Throughout the weekend, fans painted pieces of wood that were assembled into an Art Tower. During Disease, Page and Fishman painted their portions of the Art Tower; Mike and Trey painted theirs during Also Sprach. The Art Jam saw the crowd "carry" the pieces of this design to the side of the venue where it was assembled and hoisted onto the Art Tower for everyone to see. During Tweezer Reprise, the Art Tower was burned to the ground as The Great Went came to a close. As the Hood jam kicked in, Trey asked Chris to turn the lights off and the band jammed while the front section of the audience engaged in the first Hood glow stick war. Trey remarked to the crowd at the end of the jam that the visual display was cool. Between the first and second sets, the Bangor Symphony Orchestra performed selections from Stravinsky and Debussy as a red-smoke-spewing glider synchronized its swoops and dives to the music. Three breakouts dotted the setlist: The Wedge (first since October 29, 1996, or 81 shows), Carolina (first since October 27, 1996, or 82 shows), and Buffalo Bill (first since NYE 1994, or 204 shows).

FALL, 1997

Friday, November 7, 1997
NBC Studios, New York, NY
Farmhouse, Mike's Song Jam
● *Show Notes:* Farmhouse made its unofficial debut on this episode of *Late Night with Conan O'Brien.*

Thursday, November 13, 1997
Thomas & Mack Center, Las Vegas, NV
● *Set I:* Chalk Dust Torture, Black-Eyed Katy, Theme From the Bottom, Train Song, Split Open and Melt, Beauty of My Dreams, My Soul, You Enjoy Myself, Character Zero
● *Set II:* Stash, Punch You in the Eye, Prince Caspian, Bouncing Around the Room, Mike's Song > I Am Hydrogen > Weekapaug Groove
● *Encore:* Loving Cup
● *Show Notes:* This show marked the debut of Black-Eyed Katy. The jam in Mike's Song included Born on the Bayou teases. YEM included a Who Knows tease.

Friday, November 14, 1997
West Valley E Center, West Valley, UT
● *Set I:* Runaway Jim, Gumbo, Maze > Fast Enough For You, Also Sprach Zarathustra > Funky Bitch, Guyute, Run Like an Antelope
● *Set II:* Wolfman's Brother -> Piper > Twist > Slave To The Traffic Light
● *Encore:* Bold as Love
● *Show Notes:* Maze was unfinished. Guyute was dedicated to Paul Languedoc. The "Marco Esquandolas" section of Antelope was whistled, instead of the usual singing. FEFY was played for the first time since November 22, 1996 (68 shows).

Sunday, November 16, 1997
McNichols Arena, Denver, CO
● *Set I:* NICU, My Soul, Black-Eyed Katy, Farmhouse, The Old Home Place, Billy Breathes, Cars Trucks Buses, Scent of a Mule, Poor Heart, Taste, Hello My Baby
● *Set II:* Timber (Jerry) -> Simple -> Wilson > Harry Hood > Izabella
● *Encore:* David Bowie
● *Show Notes:* Mule and Poor Heart featured Pete Wernick on banjo. Mule also included a brief Foggy Mountain Breakdown tease. Harry Hood was unfinished. Farmhouse was played in concert for the first time.

Monday, November 17, 1997
McNichols Arena, Denver, CO
● *Set I:* Tweezer, Reba, Train Song, Ghost, Fire
● *Set II:* Down with Disease -> Oblivious Fool > Johnny B. Goode -> Jesus Just Left Chicago, When the Circus Comes, You Enjoy Myself
● *Encore:* Character Zero

Wednesday, November 19, 1997
Assembly Hall, Champaign, IL
● *Set I:* Julius, Bathtub Gin -> Llama, Dirt, Limb By Limb, Funky Bitch, Theme From the Bottom, Ginseng Sullivan, Fee -> Run Like an Antelope

● *Set II:* Also Sprach Zarathustra > Wolfman's Brother -> Makisupa Policeman > Taste

● *Encore:* Possum

● *Show Notes:* This smooth segue from Fee into Antelope included Meatstick quotes.

Friday, November 21, 1997
Hampton Coliseum, Hampton, VA

● *Set I:* Emotional Rescue, Split Open and Melt, Beauty of My Dreams, Dogs Stole Things, Punch You in the Eye -> Lawn Boy, Chalk Dust Torture, Prince Caspian

● *Set II:* Ghost -> AC/DC Bag, Slave to the Traffic Light, Loving Cup

● *Encore:* Guyute

● *Show Notes:* Emotional Rescue debuted at this show. This humorous Lawn Boy featured an "anti-drum solo" - an intentionally boring one. The first set ended with the delay loop ending of Caspian played until after lights were brought back up.

Saturday, November 22, 1997
Hampton Coliseum, Hampton, VA

● *Set I:* Mike's Song -> I Am Hydrogen > Weekapaug Groove, Harry Hood, Train Song, Billy Breathes, Frankenstein, Izabella

● *Set II:* Halley's Comet -> Tweezer -> Black-Eyed Katy > Piper, Run Like An Antelope

● *Encore:* Bouncing Around the Room, Tweezer Reprise

● *Show Notes:* Fans of stage banter will want to seek out the second set for Trey's humorous response to the crowd's Destiny Unbound chant before Halley's. The song included a jam based on Zappa's He Used to Cut the Grass. Tweezer included strong BEK teases well before the segue. Unlike older Mike's Grooves, this version of Hydrogen actually segued uninterrupted from the Mike's jam.

Sunday, November 23, 1997
Lawrence Joel Memorial Coliseum, Winston-Salem, NC

● *Set I:* My Soul, Theme From the Bottom > Black-Eyed Katy, Sparkle, Twist, Stash -> NICU, Fluffhead, Character Zero

● *Set II:* Bathtub Gin -> Down with Disease -> Low Rider Jam -> Down with Disease, Bold as Love

● *Encore:* Julius

Wednesday, November 26, 1997
Hartford Civic Center, Hartford, CT

● *Set I:* Tweezer > Sparkle > Gumbo, My Soul, McGrupp and the Watchful Hosemasters, Dirt, Split Open and Melt, The Horse > Silent In The Morning, Taste

● *Set II:* Character Zero -> Also Sprach Zarathustra -> Cities -> Ya Mar > Punch You In The Eye > Prince Caspian > Poor Heart > Tweezer Reprise

● *Encore:* Cavern

● *Show Notes:* Cavern included some of the original, alternate lyrics and an *All Things Considered* (not ATR) tease from Page. Poor Heart began as Rocky Top.

Friday, November 28, 1997
Worcester Centrum, Worcester, MA

● *Set I:* The Curtain, You Enjoy Myself -> I Didn't Know, Maze, Farm-

house, Black-Eyed Katy, Theme From the Bottom > Rocky Top

● *Set II:* Timber (Jerry), Limb By Limb, Slave to the Traffic Light > Ghost -> Johnny B. Goode

● *Encore:* My Soul

● *Show Notes:* YEM did not include the bass and drums segment and ended with a shortened vocal jam that segued into I Didn't Know (first since February 22, 1997, or 55 shows). BEK featured amazing jamming and YEM included a Crosseyed and Painless tease. The Curtain was played for the first time since February 20, 1997 (57 shows).

Saturday, November 29, 1997
Worcester Centrum, Worcester, MA

● *Set I:* The Wedge, Foam, Simple -> The Man Who Stepped Into Yesterday > Avenu Malkenu > The Man Who Stepped Into Yesterday Reprise, The Sloth, Ginseng Sullivan, I Saw it Again, Horn, Water in the Sky, David Bowie

● *Set II:* Runaway Jim > Strange Design > Harry Hood, Prince Caspian, Suzy Greenberg

● *Encore:* Buffalo Bill > Moby Dick > Fire

● *Show Notes:* This Runaway Jim is one of the longest versions of any song ever played. It ran slightly under an hour and included Harry Hood teases and a strong Weekapaug jam, where the entire melody of Weekapaug was played. Buffalo Bill was announced as Fishman's favorite song. During Moby Dick, Trey imitated Robert Plant's intro from *The Song Remains the Same*. The Sloth was played for the first time since February 23, 1997 (55 shows) and TMWSIY and Avenu Malkenu were played for the first time since December 28, 1996 (67 shows)

Sunday, November 30, 1997
Worcester Centrum, Worcester, MA

● *Set I:* Guyute, Funky Bitch, Wolfman's Brother -> Love Me, The Squirming Coil > Loving Cup

● *Set II:* NICU, Stash -> Free > Jam -> Piper, When the Circus Comes, Run Like An Antelope

● *Encore:* Them Changes

● *Show Notes:* This unusual Funky Bitch was over 18 minutes long and, along with Stash, was unfinished. Wolfman's included a heavy metal style jam, with a Heartbreaker tease from Mike, and Trey quoting the lyrics to Sanity and Esther. Them Changes debuted at this show.

Tuesday, December 2, 1997
The CoreStates Spectrum, Philadelphia, PA

● *Set I:* Buried Alive > Down with Disease -> Makisupa Policeman, Chalk Dust Torture, Ghost > Divided Sky, Dirt > Taste, The Star Spangled Banner

● *Set II:* Mike's Song -> Simple -> Dog Faced Boy -> Ya Mar -> Weekapaug Groove, Bouncing Around the Room, Character Zero

● *Encore:* Ginseng Sullivan > Sample in a Jar

● *Show Notes:* Ya Mar included a fun play on the actual lyrics and a brief One Way Out tease. Simple featured a Trey/Page musical duet. Buried Alive was played for the first time since February 26, 1997 (55 shows), Star Spangled Banner was played for the first time since December 28, 1996 (69 shows), and Dog Faced Boy was played for the first time since August 12, 1996 (109 shows).

Wednesday, December 3, 1997
The CoreStates Spectrum, Philadelphia, PA
● *Set I:* Punch You In The Eye, My Soul, Drowned, The Old Home Place, Gumbo > Also Sprach Zarathustra > You Enjoy Myself
● *Set II:* David Bowie -> Possum > Jam -> Prince Caspian, Frankenstein, Harry Hood
● *Encore:* Crossroads
● *Show Notes:* The jam out of Drowned (first since March 18, 1997, or 52 shows) included a Couldn't Stand the Weather jam. Bowie included a Take Me Out to the Ballgame tease and a Simpsons Signal.

Friday, December 5, 1997
CSU Convention Center, Cleveland, OH
● *Set I:* Ghost > Wilson > Funky Bitch > Black-Eyed Katy, Sparkle > Runaway Jim -> My Friend My Friend, Ginseng Sullivan, Limb by Limb, Character Zero
● *Set II:* Stash, Bouncing Around the Room, Julius -> Slave to the Traffic Light > The Lizards, Loving Cup > Chalk Dust Torture
● *Encore:* Bold as Love
● *Show Notes:* This monster Julius was over 17 minutes long and was unfinished. Other highlights included a strong Slave and a fun segue from Jim into My Friend (first since February 26, 1997, or 57 shows).

Saturday, December 6, 1997
The Palace, Auburn Hills, MI
● *Check:* Dog Gone Dog, AC/DC Bag, Ginseng Sullivan, Black-Eyed Katy
● *Set I:* Golgi Apparatus, Run Like An Antelope, Train Song > Bathtub Gin -> Foam, Sample in a Jar, Fee > Maze, Cavern
● *Set II:* Tweezer -> Izabella -> Jam -> Twist -> Piper, Sleeping Monkey > Tweezer Reprise
● *Encore:* Rocky Top

Sunday, December 7, 1997
Ervin J. Nutter Center, Dayton, OH
● *Set I:* AC/DC Bag -> Psycho Killer -> Jesus Just Left Chicago, My Mind's Got a Mind of Its Own, It's Ice -> Swept Away > Steep > It's Ice, Theme From the Bottom, Tube, Tube Jam -> Slave to the Traffic Light
● *Set II:* Timber (Jerry), Wolfman's Brother -> Boogie On Reggae Woman > Reba, Guyute > Possum
● *Encore:* A Day in the Life
● *Show Notes:* Psycho Killer was unfinished. JJLC included a Rocky Mountain Way tease. The jam after Tube (first Tube since February 26, 1997, or 59 shows) finished was basically a Tube Reprise, without the lyrics. The second verse of Guyute was whistled and not sung. Boogie On Reggae Woman was played for the first time since September 13, 1988 (865 shows) and ADITL was played for the first time since February 28, 1997 (58 shows). Possum included "Charge" teases.

Tuesday, December 9, 1997
Bryce Jordan Center, State College, PA
● *Set I:* Mike's Song > Chalk Dust Torture, My Soul, Stash > I Am Hydrogen > Weekapaug Groove, Dogs Stole Things, Beauty of My Dreams, Horn, Loving Cup
● *Set II:* Julius, Simple -> Timber (Jerry), Contact, Axilla, Harry Hood
● *Encore:* Fire

● *Show Notes:* Hood included a brief return to the Axilla theme. Axilla was played for the first time since February 28, 1997 (59 shows).

Thursday, December 11, 1997
Rochester War Memorial, Rochester, NY
● *Set I:* Punch You in the Eye > Down with Disease -> Maze, Dirt, Limb by Limb, Loving Cup, Rocky Top
● *Set II:* Drowned -> Roses Are Free > Big Black Furry Creature from Mars > Ghost -> Down with Disease > Johnny B. Goode
● *Encore:* Waste
● *Show Notes:* This show marked the debut of Roses Are Free, which segued out of an amazing Drowned, as well as a hot Disease. BBFCFM (first since August 6, 1996, or 118 shows) featured teases of Black Sabbath's Electric Funeral. Video footage from this show appeared in *Bittersweet Motel*.

Friday, December 12, 1997
The Pepsi Arena, Albany, NY
● *Set I:* Funky Bitch -> Also Sprach Zarathustra > Camel Walk, Taste > Bouncing Around the Room, Tweezer > Train Song, Character Zero
● *Set II:* I Saw it Again -> Piper > Swept Away > Steep > Prince Caspian -> Izabella > Tweezer Reprise
● *Encore:* Guyute, Run Like An Antelope
● *Show Notes:* The jam out of Caspian bore a similarity to Llama.

Saturday, December 13, 1997
The Pepsi Arena, Albany, NY
● *Opening Act:* J. Willis Pratt and Weird Bionic
● *Set I:* Ya Mar > Axilla > Theme From the Bottom, Ginseng Sullivan, Strange Design, Sample in a Jar, Vultures, Tube, Good Times Bad Times
● *Set II:* NICU, Punch You in the Eye, Ghost, Mike's Song -> Llama, When the Circus Comes, Weekapaug Groove -> Catapult -> Weekapaug Groove, Harry Hood
● *Encore:* My Soul, The Squirming Coil
● *Show Notes:* Ya Mar was much longer than usual and was unfinished. This unusual Mike's Song featured some memorable vocal interplay from the band that included a chant to "Bring the Dude." It also included Foxy Lady quotes from Fishman and a Funky Town tease. During Hood, Trey asked Chris Kuroda to turn off the lights for a Blackout Jam, and the audience responded with a shower of green glow sticks. Catapult was played for the first time since March 2, 1997 (60 shows).

Sunday, December 28, 1997
USAir Arena, Landover, MD
● *Check:* Sample in a Jar, Drowned, Black-Eyed Katy, Funky Bitch
● *Set I:* Julius, Cities > The Curtain > Sample in a Jar, The Old Home Place > Runaway Jim, Farmhouse, Funky Bitch, Split Open and Melt, Bouncing Around the Room, Character Zero
● *Set II:* Axilla > Simple, Ghost > Drowned > Scent of A Mule, Halley's Comet > Slave to the Traffic Light, Rocky Top > Cavern
● *Encore:* Bold as Love
● *Show Notes:* The Mule Duel contained Roundabout teases and a slow jam instead of the traditional duel. Between Simple and Ghost, Trey talked about feedback problems and the "ghosts in the machine."

Monday, December 29, 1997
Madison Square Garden, New York, NY
● *Set I:* NICU, Golgi Apparatus, Crossroads, Cars Trucks Buses, Train Song, Theme From the Bottom, Fluffhead, Dirt, Run Like an Antelope
● *Set II:* Down with Disease -> David Bowie > Possum, Tube, You Enjoy Myself
● *Encore:* Good Times Bad Times
● *Show Notes:* Possum contained a Can't Turn You Loose jam, which was briefly reprised after the song. Bowie included Antelope-esque jamming, and Tube featured an I Feel the Earth Move tease.

Tuesday, December 30, 1997
Madison Square Garden, New York, NY
● *Set I:* Sneakin' Sally Through The Alley -> Taste, Water in the Sky, Punch You in the Eye, Stash, Chalk Dust Torture, A Day in the Life
● *Set II:* AC/DC Bag -> McGrupp and the Watchful Hosemasters, Harpua > I'm Gonna Be (500 Miles) > Harpua, Izabella > Harry Hood -> My Soul, Sleeping Monkey, Guyute
● *Encore:* Carini -> Black-Eyed Katy -> Sneakin' Sally Through The Alley, Frankenstein
● *Show Notes:* AC/DC Bag included Psycho Killer and Third Stone From the Sun teases. 500 Miles was sung by Tom Marshall as part of the "Pentagram Harpua," which also included a narrative about Lost in Space. Pete Carini made an appearance on-stage during the encore. Frankenstein included a segment with Fishman coming center stage with his vacuum. The encore was especially long; once the band realized they were going to be fined for playing past midnight, they decided to play well past midnight. Carini was played for the first time since March 1, 1997 (64 shows) and Sneakin' Sally was played for the first time since May 28, 1989 (833 shows).

Wednesday, December 31, 1997
Madison Square Garden, New York, NY
● *Set I:* Emotional Rescue, Ya Mar, My Sweet One, Beauty of My Dreams, Wolfman's Brother, Limb by Limb, The Horse > Silent in the Morning, The Sloth, Fire

● *Set II:* Timber (Jerry), Mike's Song -> Piper > When the Circus Comes > Roses Are Free > Weekapaug Groove
● *Set III:* Also Sprach Zarathustra > Auld Lang Syne > Tweezer > Maze > Prince Caspian, Loving Cup
● *Encore:* New York New York > Tweezer Reprise
● *Show Notes:* Ya Mar included Auld Lang Syne teases and Maze included a Birdland tease. Page debuted New York New York during the encore. My Sweet One was played for the first time since December 14, 1995 (155 shows).

SPRING, 1998

"The Island Tour"

Thursday, April 2, 1998
Nassau Coliseum, Uniondale, NY
● *Set I:* Tube, My Mind's Got a Mind of its Own, The Sloth, NICU, Stash > Horn, Waste, Chalk Dust Torture
● *Set II:* Punch You in the Eye, Simple > Birds of a Feather, Wolfman's Brother -> Sneakin' Sally Through the Alley -> Frankie Says > Twist > Sleeping Monkey, Rocky Top
● *Encore:* Guyute
● *Show Notes:* This show marked the debut of Birds of a Feather and Frankie Says. After NICU, Trey commented on the brief "Island Tour," remarking that the band was getting bored at home and wanted to play some shows.

Friday, April 3, 1998
Nassau Coliseum, Uniondale, NY
● *Set I:* Mike's Song -> The Old Home Place > Weekapaug Groove, Train Song > Billy Breathes, Beauty of My Dreams, Dogs Stole Things > Reba, My Soul
● *Set II:* Roses Are Free > Piper > Loving Cup > Run Like An Antelope
● *Encore:* Carini > Halley's Comet > Tweezer Reprise
● *Show Notes:* Weekapaug included a Crosseyed and Painless tease and a brief jam of the song that would eventually debut as Mozambique, as well as a tease of the theme from *Brazil*.

Saturday, April 4, 1998
Providence Civic Center, Providence, RI
● *Set I:* Tweezer > Taste, Bouncing Around the Room, Funky Bitch, Ginseng Sullivan, Limb by Limb, Lawn Boy, Character Zero
● *Set II:* Birds of a Feather > Also Sprach Zarathustra > Brother, Ghost -> The Lizards, David Bowie
● *Encore:* Harry Hood
● *Show Notes:* Also Sprach was unfinished. Brother (first since November 30, 1996, or 89 shows) included a brief Dave's Energy Guide tease and was followed by a short instrumental reprise, which was announced as the "radio-

The view from Section 420, Madison Square Garden (1997).

friendly version." Trey contrasted this with the normal version, which was deemed un-radio-friendly due to its length. Ghost, which Trey jokingly remarked was also not radio-friendly because it is long and slow, included a Can't Turn You Loose tease. The lights were turned off during Also Sprach as the crowd engaged in another Glowstick War.

Sunday, April 5, 1998
Providence Civic Center, Providence, RI
● *Set I:* The Oh Kee Pa Ceremony > You Enjoy Myself, Theme From the Bottom > McGrupp and the Watchful Hosemasters, Bathtub Gin -> Cities > Sparkle, Split Open and Melt
● *Set II:* Down with Disease, Ya Mar -> Prince Caspian > Maze -> Shafty -> Possum -> Jam -> Cavern
● *Encore:* Bold as Love
● *Show Notes:* The second set was one fairly uninterrupted jam that segued in and out of the listed songs and included the debut of Shafty. The funky jam inbetween Possum and Cavern featured some stage banter from Trey about the funk jams the band had been playing. Accordingly, Cavern was played in a slower, funkier manner than usual. The song also included some of the older, alternate lyrics. Oh Kee Pa was played for the first time since March 1, 1997 (69 shows).

SUMMER, 1998

European Tour

Tuesday, June 30, 1998
The Grey Hall, Freetown Christiana, Copenhagen, Denmark
● *Check:* The Moma Dance, Frankie Says, Ha Ha Ha, Birds Of A Feather, Water in the Sky
● *Set I:* Limb by Limb, Ghost, Water in the Sky, Bouncing Around the Room, Tube, Stash -> Cities, Roggae, Guyute, Beauty of My Dreams, Funky Bitch, Train Song, David Bowie
● *Set II:* The Moma Dance, Birds of a Feather, Wolfman's Brother -> Frankie Says > Run Like an Antelope, Lawn Boy, Ya Mar, Ha Ha Ha, Mike's Song -> Swept Away > Steep > Weekapaug Groove
● *Encore:* Brian and Robert
● *Show Notes:* This show marked the debuts of The Moma Dance, Roggae, and Brian and Robert. Ha Ha Ha was played for the first time since February 26, 1997 (72 shows).

Wednesday, July 1, 1998
The Grey Hall, Freetown Christiana, Copenhagen, Denmark
● *Set I:* NICU, Sample in a Jar, My Mind's Got a Mind of its Own, The Moma Dance, Down with Disease > Dog Faced Boy > Piper, Waste, Chalk Dust Torture
● *Set II:* Tweezer > Also Sprach Zarathustra > Loving Cup, My Soul, Sweet Adeline
● *Encore:* Harry Hood
● *Show Notes:* Tweezer included Long Train Running (Doobie Brothers) teases.

Thursday, July 2, 1998
The Grey Hall, Freetown Christiana, Copenhagen, Denmark

Madison Square Garden (1997).

● *Set I:* Birds of a Feather, Cars Trucks Buses, Theme From the Bottom, Brian and Robert, Meat, Fikus, Shafty, Fluffhead, Ginseng Sullivan, Punch You in the Eye > Character Zero
● *Set II:* Ghost > Runaway Jim -> Prince Caspian, You Enjoy Myself
● *Encore:* Simple
● *Show Notes:* This show marked the debuts of Meat and Fikus. Fans of stage banter will want to hear this show, as Trey was in a particularly chatty mood.

Friday, July 3, 1998
Midtfyns Festival, Dyrskuepladsen, Ringe, Fyn, Denmark
Stash, Beauty of My Dreams > Sample in a Jar, Guyute, Also Sprach Zarathustra > Down with Disease, Limb by Limb, Water in the Sky > My Soul, You Enjoy Myself, A Day in the Life

Sunday, July 5, 1998
Lucerna Theatre, Prague, Czech Republic
● *Set I:* Birds of a Feather, Taste, Cavern, Reba, Fee -> Jam -> Water in the Sky, Lawn Boy, Chalk Dust Torture
● *Set II:* Bathtub Gin > The Moma Dance, McGrupp and the Watchful Hosemasters -> Jam -> Axilla > Harry Hood, Rocky Top
● *Encore:* Funky Bitch

Monday, July 6, 1998
Lucerna Theatre, Prague, Czech Republic
● *Set I:* Buried Alive > AC/DC Bag, Ghost > Cities, Limb by Limb, Train Song, Roggae, Maze, Golgi Apparatus
● *Set II:* Julius > Meat > Piper -> Makisupa Policeman, David Bowie, Loving Cup
● *Encore:* Possum
● *Show Notes:* The Maze jam was halted while Trey humorously thanked the crowd. This version of Piper, which sounded Julius-esque at times, segued nicely into Makisupa.

Wednesday, July 8, 1998
Zeleste, Barcelona, Spain
● *Set I:* The Moma Dance, Bathtub Gin, Punch You in the Eye, Beauty of My Dreams, Frankenstein, Guyute, Run Like an Antelope
● *Set II:* Wilson, Birds of a Feather, Dirt, Piper, Sleeping Monkey, Ghost -> Johnny B. Goode
● *Encore:* Julius
● *Show Notes:* Listen before Frankenstein for a Fee tease. Sleeping Monkey included "Ole!" chants from Trey and a stage appearance by Betty from Chile. Trey had met her in a bar the night before. Monkey was her favorite song, so he dedicated it to her and she danced while the band played.

Thursday, July 9, 1998
Zeleste, Barcelona, Spain
● *Set I:* Carini -> Boogie On Reggae Woman -> NICU, Split Open and Melt, Meat, Poor Heart, Tweezer, Hello My Baby
● *Set II:* Drowned -> Theme From the Bottom, When the Circus Comes, Scent of a Mule -> Blister In The Sun -> Scent of a Mule, Harry Hood -> Izabella
● *Encore:* Chalk Dust Torture

Friday, July 10, 1998
Zeleste, Barcelona, Spain
● *Set I:* Down with Disease, Dogs Stole Things, Divided Sky, Mike's Song
● *Set II:* Halley's Comet > Roggae, Sparkle, Mike's Song > Simple > Weekapaug Groove, Sample in a Jar, Good Times Bad Times
● *Encore:* Brian and Robert, Taste
● *Show Notes:* Mike's Song was aborted due to sound problems. The first set then ended early so that the crew could fix the PA. More problems arose during Sparkle, which was subsequently aborted. Trey asked the crew to turn the monitors around so the band could play

Madison Square Garden (1997).

Michael McNamara

through them. While they worked, the band told jokes. Trey even asked Fish to tell the Prison Joke but the sound was fixed before it actually happened. The jam out of Halley's included a tease of what would become First Tube. Weekapaug included On Broadway teases.

SUMMER, 1998

American Tour

Wednesday, July 15, 1998
Portland Meadows, Portland, OR
● *Set I:* Wolfman's Brother, Water in the Sky, The Moma Dance, Guyute, Horn -> Jam > Chalk Dust Torture, Brian and Robert, Beauty of My Dreams, Cars Trucks Buses, Roggae, Birds of a Feather, Loving Cup
● *Set II:* Limb by Limb -> Simple > Tweezer -> Free, Meat, Harry Hood
● *Encore:* Wilson, Tweezer Reprise
● *Show Notes:* Some humor surrounded the Guyute ending; fans of stage banter will want to seek this segment out. Horn was followed by a long, interesting jam that led into Chalk Dust. Tweezer featured a California Love jam.

Thursday, July 16, 1998
Gorge Amphitheater, George, WA
● *Set I:* The Squirming Coil, NICU, Stash, Reba, Fast Enough for You > When the Circus Comes, Run Like An Antelope
● *Set II:* Julius, The Moma Dance > Piper, Axilla > David Bowie, Tube, Slave to the Traffic Light
● *Encore:* Sample in a Jar
● *Show Notes:* Stash included a Manteca tease.

Friday, July 17, 1998
Gorge Amphitheater, George, WA
● *Set I:* Makisupa Policeman > Ya Mar, Gumbo, Divided Sky, Waste, My Mind's Got a Mind of its Own, My Soul
● *Set II:* Also Sprach Zarathustra > Mike's Song > Weekapaug Groove > Character Zero
● *Encore:* Punch You in the Eye > Rocky Top
● *Show Notes:* Gumbo included a Manteca tease. This unfinished Weekapaug included syncopated jamming and a tease akin to Who Knows.

Sunday, July 19, 1998
Shoreline Amphitheater, Mountain View, CA
● *Set I:* The Moma Dance, Beauty of My Dreams, Sample in a Jar, Guyute, Ghost, Limb by Limb, Roggae, You Enjoy Myself
● *Set II:* Llama, Wolfman's Brother -> Piper, Tweezer -> Jesus Just Left Chicago, McGrupp and the Watchful Hosemasters -> Down with Disease
● *Encore:* Possum, Tweezer Reprise

Monday, July 20, 1998
Ventura County Fairgrounds, Ventura, CA
● *Set I:* Bathtub Gin, Dirt, Poor Heart, Lawn Boy, My Sweet One, Birds of a Feather, Theme From the Bottom, Water in the Sky, The Moma Dance, Split Open and Melt
● *Set II:* Drowned -> Makisupa Policeman > Maze, Sea and Sand,

Prince Caspian > Harry Hood
● *Encore:* Sexual Healing > HYHU, Halley's Comet
● *Show Notes:* Dirt was played in honor of the venue's dusty floor. Poor Heart featured several false endings, including a Freebird rave-up. Makisupa included a long, atypical jam. Sea and Sand (first since NYE 1995, or 166 shows) was an appropriate choice, given the venue's location near the beach. Sexual Healing debuted at this show; Fishman read the lyrics off the back of a show poster. Poor Heart included a short Freebird ending. The band left the stage as the delay loop in Halley's Comet built.

Tuesday, July 21, 1998
Desert Sky Amphitheater, Phoenix, AZ
● *Set I:* AC/DC Bag, Fluffhead, Roggae, Tube, Sparkle, Cavern, Frankie Says > Run Like An Antelope
● *Set II:* Mike's Song -> Simple -> Bittersweet Motel > Weekapaug Groove, Brian and Robert, Ghost -> She Caught the Katy and Left Me a Mule to Ride > Funky Bitch
● *Encore:* Sleeping Monkey, Rocky Top
● *Show Notes:* Tube was followed by a brief reprise of the jam section. Bittersweet Motel debuted at this show. She Caught the Katy was played for the first time since August 29, 1987 (931 shows).

Friday, July 24, 1998
Woodlands Pavilion, Houston, TX
● *Set I:* The Moma Dance, Runaway Jim, Bouncing Around the Room, Stash, My Soul, Taste, Golgi Apparatus, Loving Cup
● *Set II:* Wolfman's Brother -> Also Sprach Zarathustra > Scent of a Mule -> Ha Ha Ha -> Scent of a Mule, Slave to the Traffic Light, Chalk Dust Torture
● *Encore:* Character Zero

Saturday, July 25, 1998
Southpark Meadows, Austin, TX
● *Set I:* Roses Are Free, Down with Disease, Roggae, Beauty of My Dreams, Ya Mar, Guyute, Julius
● *Set II:* Piper, Wilson > Frankenstein, Tweezer -> When the Circus Comes, Limb By Limb, Fee, Run Like an Antelope
● *Encore:* Harry Hood > Tweezer Reprise

Sunday, July 26, 1998
Starplex Amphitheater, Dallas, TX
● *Set I:* Birds of a Feather, Too Much of Everything, David Bowie, Frankie Says, Reba, Funky Bitch, Good Times Bad Times
● *Set II:* La Grange, You Enjoy Myself, Albuquerque -> Simple, Bold as Love, Sample in a Jar
● *Encore:* Punch You in the Eye, Bittersweet Motel
● *Show Notes:* This show marked the debuts of Too Much of Everything and Albuquerque. La Grange was played for the first time since February 25, 1997 (90 shows).

Tuesday, July 28, 1998
Sandstone Amphitheatre, Bonner Springs, KS
● *Set I:* Emotional Rescue > Down with Disease > The Moma Dance > Tela, Sneakin' Sally Through the Alley, It's Ice > Lengthwise > It's Ice > Sparkle > Funky Bitch
● *Set II:* The Wedge, Poor Heart, The Mango Song, Brother, Contact,

Maze, Prince Caspian > You Enjoy Myself
● *Encore:* Camel Walk, The Squirming Coil
● *Show Notes:* Funky Bitch featured an ending similar to Black-Eyed Katy. Contact was performed "Mexican Love Style," as Trey dedicated the song to a couple he met who had fallen in love. Mango was played for the first time since March 1, 1997 (88 shows) and Lengthwise was played for the first time since October 20, 1994 (291 shows).

Wednesday, July 29, 1998
Riverport Amphitheatre, Maryland Heights, MO
● *Set I:* Bathtub Gin, Dog Gone Dog, Foam, Fikus, Farmhouse, Vultures, Glide, Birds of a Feather
● *Set II:* Buried Alive > If You Need a Fool, AC/DC Bag, The Lizards, Tube > Kung > Run Like an Antelope
● *Encore:* Waste, Golgi Apparatus, Bittersweet Motel
● *Show Notes:* The usually short Buried Alive was jammed for almost fifteen minutes! Dog Gone Dog (first since February 26, 1997, or 91 shows) was dedicated to Paul Languedoc. Also appearing for the first time since February 26, 1997 was Kung. The new arrangement of Vultures, as well as If You Need a Fool, debuted at this show. Part of the Antelope intro featured Fishman on vacuum. Glide was played for the first time since July 31, 1997 (60 shows).

Friday, July 31, 1998
Polaris Amphitheater, Columbus, OH
● *Set I:* My Friend My Friend, Ya Mar, Roggae, Rift, Cities, Water in the Sky, Stash
● *Set II:* The Curtain > Free, If I Could > The Man Who Stepped Into Yesterday > Avenu Malkenu > Twist > Izabella, Julius, Cavern
● *Encore:* Punch You in the Eye, Slave to the Traffic Light
● *Show Notes:* My Friend included a Guyute tease in the intro. Cities included Who Knows teases. Rift was played for the first time since February 23, 1997 (94 shows) and If I Could was played for the first time since August 5, 1996 (150 shows).

Saturday, August 1, 1998
Alpine Valley, East Troy, WI
● *Set I:* Ramble On > Mike's Song -> Esther > Weekapaug Groove, Guyute, Fikus, Birds of a Feather, Lawn Boy > Funky Bitch
● *Set II:* Piper, Wilson > Also Sprach Zarathustra > Magilla > Tweezer, Fluffhead, Brian and Robert, Albuquerque > Chalk Dust Torture, Frankenstein
● *Encore:* Been Caught Stealin' > Tweezer Reprise
● *Show Notes:* This show marked the debuts of Ramble On and Been Caught Stealin', as well as the breakouts of Esther (first since October 19, 1996, or 139 shows) and Magilla (first since July 21, 1997, or 69 shows).

Sunday, August 2, 1998
Deer Creek Music Center, Noblesville, IN
● *Set I:* Roggae, Divided Sky, The Horse > Silent in the Morning, Boogie On Reggae Woman, Reba, Weigh, Too Much of Everything, Birds of a Feather
● *Set II:* Possum, Ghost > Lifeboy, David Bowie, I Get a Kick Out of You, Loving Cup
● *Encore:* Harry Hood, Bittersweet Motel

● *Show Notes:* This show marked the debut of I Get a Kick Out of You. Weigh was played for the first time since August 17, 1997 (52 shows) and Lifeboy was played for the first time since August 3, 1997 (61 shows).

Monday, August 3, 1998
Deer Creek Music Theatre, Noblesville, IN

● *Set I:* Rhinoceros, Halley's Comet > I Didn't Know, Ride Captain Ride, Cars Trucks Buses, The Moma Dance, Strange Design, Character Zero

● *Set II:* Gumbo, Axilla > Limb by Limb, Meat > HYHU > Bike > HYHU, Tube, The Wedge

● *Encore:* When the Circus Comes, Run Like an Antelope

● *Show Notes:* This show marked the debut of Rhinoceros and the triumphant return of fan favorite Ride Captain Ride, which had not been played since December 30, 1992 (490 shows). Bike was played for the first time since November 7, 1996 (129 shows). The Halley's jam included A Love Supreme teases from Page. Gumbo included Manteca teases.

Thursday, August 6, 1998
Lakewood Amphitheater, Atlanta, GA

● *Check:* Sleeping Monkey, The Wedge, If You Need a Fool, Dog Gone Dog -> Jam -> Sexual Healing

● *Set I:* The Oh Kee Pa Ceremony > Suzy Greenberg, Roses Are Free, Roggae, Beauty of My Dreams, Vultures, Train Song, Billy Breathes, Fluffhead, The Moma Dance, HYHU > Cracklin' Rosie > HYHU, My Soul

● *Set II:* Birds of a Feather, Wolfman's Brother -> Talk, NICU, Prince Caspian, The Mango Song, Down with Disease

● *Encore:* Running With the Devil, You Enjoy Myself

● *Show Notes:* This show marked the debut of Running With the Devil, which was also teased during YEM. Trey once again referred to Fishman as "Bob Weaver" after Cracklin' Rosie. Talk was played for the first time since June 24, 1997 (84 shows) and Cracklin' Rosie was played for the first time since August 14, 1996 (148 shows).

Friday, August 7, 1998
Walnut Creek Amphitheater, Raleigh, NC

● *Set I:* Water in the Sky, Drowned, Frankie Says, Stash, Brian and

Lemonwheel (1998)

Matt Soellen

Robert, Foam, Bittersweet Motel, Ghost, Colonel Forbin's Ascent -> The Famous Mockingbird

● *Set II:* Chalk Dust Torture > Mike's Song -> Simple -> Albuquerque, Limb by Limb, Wading in the Velvet Sea, Weekapaug Groove

● *Encore:* Funky Bitch

● *Show Notes:* The long, surreal Forbin's narration (first since August 14, 1997, or 57 shows) offered an explanation for the evening's lunar eclipse. Mockingbird was played for the first time since Halloween, 1996 (135 shows) and Velvet Sea was played for the first time since August 2, 1997 (65 shows).

Saturday, August 8, 1998
Merriweather Post Pavilion, Columbia, MD

● *Set I:* The Wedge, NICU, Sneakin' Sally Through the Alley -> Guyute, Fikus, Farmhouse, Possum, Sweet Jane

● *Set II:* Cavern, Also Sprach Zarathustra > Tela -> Piper, Sexual Healing > HYHU, Harry Hood

● *Encore:* Sabotage

● *Show Notes:* This show marked the debuts of Sweet Jane and Sabotage. This version of Piper is a fan favorite.

Sunday, August 9, 1998
Virginia Beach Amphitheatre, Virginia Beach, VA

● *Set I:* Punch You in the Eye, Bathtub Gin, The Lizards, The Moma Dance, Birds of a Feather, Esther, Roggae, Bouncing Around the Room, David Bowie

● *Set II:* AC/DC Bag > Jam > Sparkle, Run Like an Antelope, Brian and Robert, Waste, Somewhere Over the Rainbow, You Enjoy Myself, Frankenstein, Chalk Dust Torture, Hello My Baby

● *Encore:* Terrapin Station

● *Show Notes:* Terrapin Station debuted at this show, as the band commemorated the third anniversary of Jerry Garcia's passing. AC/DC Bag included a tease of Black Sabbath's Electric Funeral. Somewhere Over the Rainbow was played for the first time since August 13, 1996 (152 shows).

Tuesday, August 11, 1998
Star Lake Amphitheatre, Pittsburgh, PA

● *Set I:* Trench Town Rock, Julius, Wolfman's Brother -> Time Loves a Hero, Bittersweet Motel, Reba, The Sloth, Ginseng Sullivan, Fee, Maze, Sample in a Jar

● *Set II:* Runaway Jim, Meat, Limb by Limb, When the Circus Comes, Down with Disease

● *Encore:* Wilson > Golgi Apparatus

● *Show Notes:* This show marked the debut of Trench Town Rock and the return of Time Loves a Hero (first since November 5, 1998, or 900 shows). Runaway Jim included a tease of Leonard Bernstein's Maria from *West Side Story*.

Wednesday, August 12, 1998
Vernon Downs Racetrack, Vernon, NY

● *Set I:* La Grange, Makisupa Policeman, Funky Bitch, Possum, Roggae, Character Zero, Ramble On > Slave to the Traffic Light

● *Set II:* Mike's Song -> Simple > Rift, Loving Cup, Sleeping Monkey > Weekapaug Groove, The Squirming Coil

● *Encore:* Burning Down the House, You Enjoy Myself

● *Show Notes:* This show marked the debut of Burning Down the House. Possum was dedicated to Jeff Holdsworth and Frodo, which was Fishman's band in high school. Ramble On was played in honor of Fishman seeing a Led Zeppelin concert at age eleven; Slave subsequently included Ramble On teases. YEM included HYHU and *Mission: Impossible* teases.

Saturday, August 15, 1998
The Lemonwheel, Loring Air Force Base, Limestone, ME
● *Set I:* Mike's Song -> Simple, Beauty of My Dreams, Roggae, Split Open and Melt, Poor Heart, The Moma Dance, Divided Sky, Water in the Sky, Funky Bitch > Cities -> Weekapaug Groove
● *Set II:* The Wedge, Reba, Gumbo -> Sanity > Tweezer > The Horse > Silent in the Morning, Chalk Dust Torture, Slave to the Traffic Light
● *Set III:* NICU > David Bowie, Strange Design, Limb by Limb > Brian and Robert, Loving Cup
● *Encore:* Halley's Comet > Cavern, Tweezer Reprise
● *Set IV:* Ambient Jam
● *Show Notes:* SOAM was played by request for an eight year old boy named Sam. Cities included Sneakin' Sally teases and, along with Halley's Comet, included alternate lyrics relating to the concert grounds. Bowie included a lengthy intro and *Mission: Impossible* teases. This jammed-out Gumbo is a fan favorite. After Tweezer Reprise, Trey made a long announcement thanking people for coming and remarked on the fun and joy of the summer concert festivals. He said that there would be some more music, played by the light of candles made that day by fans. The ensuing "ambient jam" was in the style of Brian Eno and was nearly an hour long. Sanity was played for the first time since Halloween 1996 (140 shows).

Sunday, August 16, 1998
The Lemonwheel, Loring Air Force Base, Limestone, ME
● *Set I:* Ginseng Sullivan, Bathtub Gin -> Rift, Punch You in the Eye, Lawn Boy, Ya Mar > AC/DC Bag > Frankie Says, Birds of a Feather, Guyute, Possum
● *Set II:* Down with Disease > Piper, Ghost > Fluffhead, When the Circus Comes, Wading in the Velvet Sea, HYHU > Sexual Healing > HYHU, Run Like an Antelope
● *Set III:* Sabotage -> Also Sprach Zarathustra > Wilson, The Mango Song > Character Zero, Bittersweet Motel, While My Guitar Gently Weeps
● *Encore:* Harry Hood -> Fireworks Jam -> Baby Elephant Walk
● *Show Notes:* Fishman alluded to Terrapin ("a love song about a turtle") after a long HYHU intro but instead led the band into Sexual Healing. Antelope included Sexual Healing teases in the intro and a reference to Bob Weaver instead of Marco Esquandolas in the lyrics. WMGGW returned for its first appearance since February 26, 1997 (103 shows) and Baby Elephant Walk was played for the first time since December 1, 1992 (512 shows).

FALL, 1998

Saturday, October 3, 1998
Farm Aid, New World Music Theatre, Tinley Park, IL

Birds of a Feather, Farmhouse, The Moma Dance, Runaway Jim -> Arc -> Down By the River, Moonlight in Vermont, Will the Circle Be Unbroken, Amazing Grace, Uncloudy Day
● *Show Notes:* Arc, Down By the River, Moonlight in Vermont, Will the Circle Be Unbroken, and Uncloudy Day all debuted at this Farm Aid Benefit (although Will the Circle Be Unbroken was also played during the November 19, 1994 "Parking Lot Jam"). Neil Young made a guest appearance on guitar from Runaway Jim through the end of the set. Also, Willie Nelson and Paul Schaffer joined the band during Moonlight in Vermont, and four native Americans came onstage before Will the Circle Be Unbroken. The Down By the River was seriously jammed out and clocked in at over 20 minutes, with Neil Young leading the band through the song. Amazing Grace was performed with accompaniment and included a guitar solo from Trey. This set was broadcast live on Country Music Television, so videos circulate (although the station cut to commercial after The Moma Dance and lost the beginning of Runaway Jim). Other artists that performed included Hootie and the Blowfish, The Del McCoury Band, Brian Wilson, Wilco, Martina McBride, Willie Nelson, John Mellencamp, and Neil Young (solo). Amazing Grace was played for the first time since NYE 1996, or 115 shows.

Thursday, October 15, 1998
The Fillmore Auditorium, San Francisco, CA
● *Set I:* Ghost -> Water in the Sky, Wolfman's Brother, Gumbo, David Bowie, Brian and Robert, Reba > Character Zero
● *Set II:* My Soul > Chalk Dust Torture, Roggae, The Moma Dance, Wading in the Velvet Sea, Prince Caspian, Frankie Says, Birds of a Feather, Lawn Boy, Harry Hood
● *Encore:* Dirt, Limb by Limb
● *Show Notes:* On this night, Phish treated its fans to the most intimate show in years: an unannounced gig at this popular west coast venue (which should not, however, be confused with The Fillmore West). Brian and Robert was performed with a yellow spotlight on Fishman after Trey mentioned how much he hates HYHU and the yellow lights. Page responded to Trey with a humorous HYHU tease. Reba included the use of a disco ball over the crowd. My Soul was preceded by a reference to Betty (see July 8, 1998) from Chile, whom Trey noticed in the crowd. Hood

Lemonwheel (1998)

Kathleen Griffin

Elephant built overnight at Lemonwheel (1998).

contained a tease of Aaron Copland's Fanfare for the Common Man.

Saturday, October 17, 1998
The Bridge School Benefit
Shoreline Amphitheatre, Mountain View, CA
● *Check:* Wading in the Velvet Sea, Possum
Carolina, Sleep, Never, Possum, I'm Blue I'm Lonesome, Freebird, Driver, Wading in the Velvet Sea, Harry Hood -> Helpless
● *Show Notes:* This benefit show, which included the debuts of Helpless, Sleep, Never, and Driver, featured such other acts as REM, Neil Young, and Barenaked Ladies. For both Bridge shows, all songs were performed acoustic and the stage was reversed from the usual setup (Fishman was stage right, with Page on the far left). Carolina (first since August 17, 1997, or 64 shows) was performed with the band facing backwards toward the Bridge School children, who were on a raised platform at the back of the stage. I'm Blue I'm Lonesome (first since December 12, 1995, or 195 shows) was performed in the bluegrass setup of 1994, with Mike on banjo and Page on acoustic bass. Hood was unfinished, as Neil Young joined the band during the jam and led a segue into the Phish debut of his own song, Helpless, on which he sang lead. Freebird was played for the first time since June 19, 1994 (338 shows).

Sunday, October 18, 1998
The Bridge School Benefit
Shoreline Amphitheatre, Mountain View, CA
Hello My Baby, Billy Breathes, Piper, Roggae, Loving Cup, Albuquerque, The Old Home Place, Guyute, Brian and Robert, Sad Lisa, Four Strong Winds, I Shall Be Released
● *Show Notes:* This benefit show featured such other acts as REM, Neil Young, and Barenaked Ladies. For both Bridge shows, all songs were performed acoustic and the stage was reversed from the usual setup (Fishman was stage right, with Page on the far left). Hello My Baby was performed with the band facing backwards toward the Bridge School children, who were on a raised platform at the back of the stage. The Old

Home Place was performed in the bluegrass setup of 1994, with Mike on banjo and Page on acoustic bass. Sad Lisa featured Sarah McLachlan on guitar and vocals, while Four Strong Winds and I Shall Be Released featured McLachlan and Neil Young. All three songs were debuts.

Tuesday, October 20, 1998
Sessions at West 54th Street, New York, NY
Sleep, Frankie Says -> Ghost, Roggae, Guyute, Wading in the Velvet Sea, Driver, Albuquerque, Birds of a Feather, Piper, Taste
● *Show Notes:* This intimate show, performed in front of roughly 200 fans and industry executives, was a taping for the PBS television show *Sessions*. Sleep and Driver were performed acoustic. Trey made jokes about the length of Guyute, remarking that the show could cut to four commercial breaks and the band would still be playing the same song. Taste was played after Trey took the crowd's requests for the final song. When the show was aired, only Birds, Ghost, and Taste were broadcast, with interviews interspersed between songs.

Tuesday, October 27, 1998
The Late Show with David Letterman, The Ed Sullivan Theatre, New York, NY
Birds of a Feather

Thursday, October 29, 1998
The Greek Theatre, Los Angeles, CA
● *Check:* Dirt, Water in the Sky, Dog Gone Dog, Roggae
● *Set I:* Julius, Roggae, Llama, Limb by Limb, Driver, Sleep, Frankie Says, Birds of a Feather, McGrupp and the Watchful Hosemasters, Character Zero
● *Set II:* Possum > The Moma Dance > Reba -> Walk Away > Simple > Albuquerque, David Bowie
● *Encore:* Something
● *Show Notes:* Something made its debut at this show. Walk Away was played for the first time since May 7, 1994 (366 shows).

Friday, October 30, 1998
The Thomas and Mack Center, Las Vegas, NV
● *Set I:* Wilson, Meat > Scent of a Mule > Back at the Chicken Shack > Scent of a Mule, Long Cool Woman in a Black Dress, Run Like An Antelope, Guelah Papyrus, The Lizards, Cavern
● *Set II:* Stash -> Manteca -> Tweezer -> NICU > Jam > Prince Caspian > Golgi Apparatus
● *Encore:* Driver, Freebird
● *Show Notes:* Phish treated the crowd in Vegas to three breakouts, playing Long Cool Woman (first since October 30, 1983, or 982 shows), Manteca (first since November 14, 1995, or 218 shows) and Guelah (first since August 11, 1997, or 71 shows). Before Long Cool Woman, Trey remarked that "they tell us that this is the exact day" of the band's fifteenth anniversary, though research indicates that this may be incorrect. Fishman teased a return to Long Cool Woman before Antelope but quickly aborted. Tweezer subsequently included Manteca teases. The show also included the debut of Back at the Chicken Shack.

Saturday, October 31, 1998
The Thomas and Mack Center, Las Vegas, NV
● *Set I:* Axilla, Punch You in the Eye, Roggae, Birds of a Feather, Sneakin' Sally Through the Alley -> Chalk Dust Torture, Lawn Boy, Mike's Song -> Frankie Says > Weekapaug Groove
● *Set II:* The Velvet Underground's *Loaded*: Who Loves the Sun, Sweet Jane, Rock and Roll, Cool it Down, New Age, Head Held High, Lonesome Cowboy Bill, I Found a Reason, Train Round the Bend, Oh! Sweet Nuthin'
● *Set III:* Wolfman's Brother -> Piper, Ghost
● *Encore:* Sleeping Monkey, Tweezer Reprise
● *Show Notes:* All of the songs in the second set were debuts, except for Sweet Jane and Lonesome Cowboy Bill (which hadn't been played since June 10, 1995, or 267 shows). Mike's Song included Simple teases, and the long jam out of Wolfman's included Esther and Sleeping Monkey teases. Fishman added effects with his vacuum while seated at the drum set. The band left the stage during Ghost, as the sound of Trey's delay loop ended the show.

Monday, November 2, 1998
E Center, West Valley, UT
● *Set I:* Tube, Tube Jam -> Drowned -> Jesus Just Left Chicago, Driver, Bittersweet Motel, Limb by Limb, Wading in the Velvet Sea, Sample In a Jar
● *Set II:* Down with Disease, The Mango Song, The Moma Dance, You Enjoy Myself, Harpua > Pink Floyd's *Dark Side of the Moon*: Speak to Me -> Breathe > On The Run, Time > The Great Gig in the Sky, Money, Us and Them -> Any Colour You Like -> Brain Damage -> Eclipse > Harpua
● *Encore:* Smells Like Teen Spirit
● *Show Notes:* Driver was dedicated to Wendy and Lisa, and Bittersweet Motel was dedicated to the folks at The Dead Goat Saloon (the site of the open mic night appearance by Trey and Mike one night earlier). The Moma Dance included teases of The Rolling Stones' Monkey Man. The Harpua narration picked up where the December 6, 1996 Harpua ended; Jimmy hitched a ride from Vegas to Salt Lake City and the driver was playing *Dark Side of the Moon*. All the *Dark Side* songs were debuts except for Great Gig (last played July 5, 1994, or 331 shows) Speak to Me (piped through the PA on Halloween, 1994) and

Lemonwheel Rock Garden (1998).

Breathe (never played in its entirety but seriously jammed on October 25, 1995). Smells Like Teen Spirit also debuted at this show, although it was teased during Harpua on May 9, 1992.

Tuesday, November 3, 1998
KBCO Studios, Boulder, CO
Driver, Wading in the Velvet Sea, Possum, Roggae
Show Notes: This acoustic set was performed for KBCO's "Studio C" series.

Wednesday, November 4, 1998
McNichols Arena, Denver, CO
● *Set I:* Buried Alive > Character Zero, Guyute > Bathtub Gin > Ya Mar, Birds of a Feather, Brian and Robert, Frankie Says -> David Bowie
● *Set II:* Runaway Jim > The Moma Dance > Piper > Also Sprach Zarathustra > Chalk Dust Torture, Loving Cup
● *Encore:* The Squirming Coil
● *Show Notes:* Bowie began as Maze, and included Stash teases.

Friday, November 6, 1998
Kohl Center, Madison, WI
● *Set I:* Possum, Wilson > Roggae, Maze, Meat, Sparkle, Split Open and Melt
● *Set II:* Makisupa Policeman > Funky Bitch, Simple -> Prince Caspian, Fluffhead, HYHU > Bike > HYHU, Harry Hood
● *Encore:* Birds of a Feather, Hello My Baby
● *Show Notes:* The lyrics in Makisupa referenced "university police rent-a-cops." During Caspian, a naked man jumped on stage and was kicked off by security; the lyrics to some future versions of Carini were altered to mention this.

Saturday, November 7, 1998
UIC Pavilion, Chicago IL
● *Set I:* My Soul, Mike's Song, Driver, Brian and Robert, The Wedge, Limb by Limb, Fikus, Billy Breathes, Beauty of My Dreams, Weekapaug Groove
● *Set II:* AC/DC Bag -> Ghost, Reba, Farmhouse
● *Encore:* Guyute, While My Guitar Gently Weeps

Sunday, November 8, 1998
UIC Pavilion, Chicago, IL
● *Set I:* Taste, Carini, Love Me, Ride Captain Ride, Fee, Paul and Silas, Roggae, Water in the Sky, Stash, Cavern
● *Set II:* Chalk Dust Torture, Meat > Rock and Roll > Down with Disease > Jam -> Piper > Wading In The Velvet Sea, Run Like An Antelope

● *Encore:* Been Caught Stealin'
● *Show Notes:* Carini included a verse about the streaker from the shows two nights earlier. Paul and Silas was played for the first time since February 28, 1997 (114 shows) and Love Me was played for the first time since November 30, 1997 (61 shows).

Monday, November 9, 1998
UIC Pavilion, Chicago, IL
● *Set I:* Llama, Horn, I Get a Kick Out of You, Divided Sky, Frankie Says, Dogs Stole Things, Poor Heart, Free, NICU, Bold as Love
● *Set II:* Bathtub Gin, The Man Who Stepped Into Yesterday > Avenu Malkenu > The Man Who Stepped Into Yesterday Reprise, The Moma Dance, Slave to the Traffic Light > You Enjoy Myself
● *Encore:* Frankenstein, Freebird

Wednesday, November 11, 1998
Van Andel Arena, Grand Rapids, MI
● *Check:* Drum Jam, Brian and Robert, Blues Jam
● *Set I:* Punch You in the Eye, Gumbo, If You Need a Fool, Sleep, Tela, Birds of a Feather, Theme From the Bottom, Julius
● *Set II:* Halley's Comet > Simple > Walk Away, Limb by Limb, When the Circus Comes, Ghost
● *Encore:* Contact > Rocky Top > Funky Bitch

Friday, November 13, 1998
CSU Convocation Center, Cleveland, OH
● *Set I:* Chalk Dust Torture, Wolfman's Brother, Roggae, Ginseng Sul-

Mark Majewski

Lemon sacrifice in the garden, Lemonwheel (1998).

livan, It's Ice, Cars Trucks Buses, Farmhouse, Water in the Sky, The Sloth, Run Like an Antelope
● *Set II:* Down with Disease, Sample in a Jar, Dirt, Birds of a Feather, Meat, Harry Hood
● *Encore:* Good Times Bad Times
● *Show Notes:* Antelope included a variation of the usual lyrics.

Saturday, November 14, 1998
The Crown, Cincinnati, OH
● *Set I:* Funky Bitch, My Soul, Reba, Bouncing Around the Room, Tweezer > The Moma Dance, Sparkle, Character Zero
● *Set II:* David Bowie, Something, Piper, Guyute, Golgi Apparatus, HYHU > Sexual Healing > HYHU, You Enjoy Myself, Julius, Hello My Baby
● *Encore:* So Lonely > Tweezer Reprise
● *Show Notes:* So Lonely debuted at this show.

Sunday, November 15, 1998
Murphy Center, Middle Tennessee State University, Murfreesboro, TN
● *Set I:* My Friend My Friend, Ghost, Driver, Scent of a Mule, Cavern, Limb by Limb, Roggae, La Grange
● *Set II:* Runaway Jim, Stash, Mike's Song -> Simple, Wading in the Velvet Sea, Loving Cup, Weekapaug Groove
● *Encore:* Rocky Top.

Wednesday, November 18, 1998
The Bi-Lo Center, Greenville, SC
● *Set I:* Back at the Chicken Shack, Birds of a Feather, Farmhouse, My Soul, Guyute, Lawn Boy, Love Me, David Bowie, Carolina
● *Set II:* Wolfman's Brother -> The Lizards, The Moma Dance, Albuquerque, Slave to the Traffic Light, Fluffhead > Character Zero
● *Encore:* Brian and Robert, Sleep, Dog Faced Boy, The Squirming Coil
● *Show Notes:* Carolina was restarted after Page's miscue and featured a choreographed stage routine at the end.

Thursday, November 19, 1998
Lawrence Joel Coliseum, Winston-Salem, NC
● *Set I:* Cities, The Curtain > Sample in a Jar, Ginseng Sullivan, Bouncing Around the Room, Maze, Something, Ghost > Golgi Apparatus
● *Set II:* Also Sprach Zarathustra > Rock and Roll -> Taste, Frankie Says, Gumbo -> Chalk Dust Torture, Frankenstein, Been Caught Stealin'
● *Encore:* You Enjoy Myself
● *Show Notes:* The YEM vocal jam featured a guest appearance by Heloise Williams of the band Viperhouse.

Friday, November 20, 1998
Hampton Coliseum, Hampton, VA
● *Set I:* Rock and Roll Part Two, Tube, Quinn the Eskimo, Funky Bitch, Guelah Papyrus, Rift, Meat > Stash, Train Song, Possum, Roggae, Driver, Split Open and Melt
● *Set II:* Bathtub Gin > Piper, Axilla > Roses Are Free, Farmhouse, HYHU > Gettin' Jiggy Wit' It > HYHU, Harry Hood, Character Zero
● *Encore:* Cavern
● *Show Notes:* Quinn the Eskimo was played for the first time since August 10, 1987 (970 shows) and Rock and Roll Part Two was de-

buted, although Trey did play along with the song as it was piped through the speakers at the beginning of NYE 1995. Stash included a Fikus tease. Before the debut of Gettin' Jiggy Wit' It, stagehands brought out cue cards for Fishman to sing from. At the end of the song, he threw the cards into the crowd. He also replaced Will Smith's name in the lyrics with his own alias, "Bob Weaver." Cavern featured Carl Gerhard on trumpet. This show was released as part of the *Hampton Comes Alive* boxed set.

Saturday, November 21, 1998
Hampton Coliseum, Hampton, VA
● *Set I:* Wilson -> Big Black Furry Creature from Mars, Lawn Boy, Divided Sky, Cry Baby Cry, Boogie On Reggae Woman -> NICU, Dogs Stole Things, Nellie Kane, Foam, Wading in the Velvet Sea, Guyute, Bold as Love
● *Set II:* Sabotage, Mike's Song -> Simple -> The Wedge, The Mango Song > Free -> Ha Ha Ha -> Free, Weekapaug Groove
● *Encore:* Tubthumping
● *Show Notes:* Listen as Fishman chimed in with a cheer of "Getting' Jiggy Wit' It" during Wilson and Tubthumping! Three more breakouts were played: BBFCFM (first since December 11, 1997, or 63 shows) Cry Baby Cry (first since June 16, 1995, or 277 shows) and Nellie Kane (first since December 8, 1994, or 292 shows). The encore, a concert debut, featured Tom Marshall on lead vocals and Carl Gerhard on trumpet. This show was released as part of the *Hampton Comes Alive* boxed set.

Tuesday, November 24, 1998
New Haven Coliseum, New Haven, CT
● *Check:* Funky Bitch, Ginseng Sullivan, The Old Home Place
● *Set I:* Down with Disease, The Moma Dance, Ginseng Sullivan, Stash, Brian and Robert, Limb by Limb, Sample in a Jar, Tela, Chalk Dust Torture
● *Set II:* Ghost -> Halley's Comet, Tweezer -> Possum, Wading in the Velvet Sea, Character Zero
● *Encore:* Suzy Greenberg, Tweezer Reprise
● *Show Notes:* Listen for the Stash tease in the Disease intro. Ghost included Psycho Killer teases. The encore featured guest vocals from the Dude of Life, who also provided alternate lyrics to Suzy Greenberg.

Wednesday, November 25, 1998
Pepsi Arena, Albany, NY
● *Set I:* Punch You in the Eye, My Soul, Roggae, AC/DC Bag, Lifeboy, David Bowie, Sleep, Driver, Good Times Bad Times
● *Set II:* Also Sprach Zarathustra > Golgi Apparatus, Drowned -> Prince Caspian > Piper, You Enjoy Myself, Been Caught Stealin' > Llama
● *Encore:* Something, Guyute, Freebird
● *Show Notes:* Been Caught Stealin' did not feature the usual tramps appearance.

Friday, November 27, 1998
The Centrum, Worcester, MA
● *Set I:* Funky Bitch, Ya Mar, Carini, Runaway Jim, Meat > Reba, The Old Home Place, Dogs Stole Things, Vultures, When the Circus Comes, Birds of a Feather
● *Set II:* Buried Alive, Wipeout, Chalk Dust Torture -> Mirror in the Bathroom -> Chalk Dust Torture -> Dog Gone Dog -> Chalk Dust Tor-

ture > Sanity, Buffalo Bill > Mike's Song -> I Am Hydrogen > Weekapaug Groove -> Wipeout -> Weekapaug Groove, Weekapaug Reprise > Run Like an Antelope
● *Encore:* Wading in the Velvet Sea, Golgi Apparatus > Wipeout
● *Show Notes:* Once again, Carini included lyrics about the streaker from three weeks earlier. Mirror in the Bathroom (which was subtly teased by Mike earlier in the set) debuted and Wipeout was played for the first time since April 27, 1991 (715 shows). Chalk Dust included more Wipeout teases. Dog Gone Dog was unfinished and sung over a more bluesy progression than usual. During Weekapaug, the band moved to Wipeout yet again, then back to Weekapaug. After the song ended, they took a full fifteen second break before starting it up one last time and reprising the Weekapaug jam before moving into Antelope. Listen for some funny banter as Fishman and Trey took verbal jabs at each other in the encore. Hydrogen was played for the first time since December 9, 1997 (67 shows) and Buffalo Bill was played for the first time since November 29, 1998 (74 shows).

Saturday, November 28, 1998
The Centrum, Worcester, MA
● *Set I:* Gumbo, Tube > Down with Disease, Guyute, Albuquerque, Foam, The Moma Dance, Split Open and Melt
● *Set II:* Julius, Wolfman's Brother > Timber (Jerry), Loving Cup > Scent of a Mule, Prince Caspian > Crossroads, Tweezer, Cavern
● *Encore:* Sample in a Jar, Tweezer Reprise
● *Show Notes:* The Moma Dance included alternate lyrics and Gumbo teases from Mike. Mike and Fishman were both active in the Mule Duel. Timber was played for the first time since NYE 1997 (61 shows) and Crossroads was played for the first time since December 29, 1997 (63 shows).

Sunday, November 29, 1998
The Centrum, Worcester, MA
● *Set I:* Paul and Silas, Axilla, Theme From the Bottom, Sparkle, Horn, Limb by Limb > Catapult > Kung > Maze, All the Pain Through the Years > Layla
● *Set II:* Roses Are Free > Simple, Makisupa Policeman, Possum -> Wipeout -> Possum, Bathtub Gin, You Enjoy Myself
● *Encore:* Roggae, Hello My Baby
● *Show Notes:* Paul and Silas included alternate lyrics, which told the story of Paul Languedoc's run-in with the law the night before. This event was referenced again during Makisupa. The last two songs of the first set (both debuts) featured Seth Yacovone on guitar; All the Pain also featured Yacovone on vocals. Possum included a Dave's Energy Guide tease. Catapult was played for the first time since December 13, 1997 (66 shows).

Monday, December 28, 1998
Madison Square Garden, New York, NY
● *Set I:* Axilla, Stash, Farmhouse, Taste, Sleep, Albuquerque, Driver, Tube, Golgi Apparatus, Good Times Bad Times
● *Set II:* Carini > Wolfman's Brother, Birds of a Feather, When the Circus Comes, Quinn the Eskimo -> David Bowie
● *Encore:* Been Caught Stealin'
● *Show Notes:* For the first show of the Holiday Run, the stage was decorated with flowers and sculptures. During the encore, parts of the set began to grow and sprout leaves. This stage setup was used for this

show only, and disappeared for the rest of the run. Before Sleep, Fishman's drum kit was moved to allow the crew to roll out a small mini-stage with a scaled-down drum set and a baby grand piano. Trey and Mike sat on stools and both played acoustic guitars. This acoustic set-up was used for Sleep, Albuquerque, and Driver. During the Wolfman's jam, three people in inchworm-like costumes came on stage and danced for the rest of the set. Bowie included a tease of the theme from *The Godfather.*

Tuesday, December 29, 1998
Madison Square Garden, New York, NY
● *Set I:* Rock and Roll > Funky Bitch, Punch You in the Eye, Horn, Ginseng Sullivan, Split Open and Melt, Brian and Robert, Guyute, My Soul, Freebird
● *Set II:* Free, Limb by Limb, Also Sprach Zarathustra > Boogie On Reggae Woman, You Enjoy Myself
● *Encore:* Divided Sky
● *Show Notes:* Also Sprach included Crosseyed and Painless teases and a long, ambient jam in the intro. For this show, the dancers onstage were dressed as flowers, with one dressed as a turkey.

Wednesday, December 30, 1998
Madison Square Garden, New York, NY
● *Set I:* Chalk Dust Torture, Big Black Furry Creature from Mars, Wilson > Roggae, Sparkle, The Moma Dance, The Old Home Place, Sample in a Jar, Frankie Says, Maze, Loving Cup, Reba
● *Set II:* Down with Disease, Piper, Prince Caspian, The Squirming Coil -> Slave to the Traffic Light
● *Encore:* Grind, Possum
● *Show Notes:* Moma included Manteca teases. Coil included Piper teases and featured an atypical jam that segued into Slave. Grind, a short song written while the band was recording *Billy Breathes*, made its debut and was dedicated to a fan injured in a lacrosse accident. It featured Tom Marshall on vocals. Possum included Wipeout teases. For this show, the Holiday Run dancers were dressed as nymphs.

Thursday, December 31, 1998
Madison Square Garden, New York, NY
● *Set I:* 1999 > Mike's Song > I Am Hydrogen > Weekapaug Groove, Ghost -> Ha Ha Ha > Cavern
● *Set II:* NICU > Character Zero > Tweezer -> Cities > Wading in the Velvet Sea, Run Like an Antelope, Frankenstein
● *Set III:* Runaway Jim -> Auld Lang Syne -> Simple > Harry Hood > Tweezer Reprise, Llama
● *Encore:* While My Guitar Gently Weeps
● *Show Notes:* Prince's 1999 debuted (appropriately) at this show and included dancers on stage and synchronized steps from Trey and Mike, who wound up lying on the stage with the dancers surrounding them. Weekapaug and Runaway Jim subsequently featured 1999 teases; Jim also included Auld Lang Syne teases. Simple included Magilla teases. Hood featured a fun jam segment near the beginning of the song. For this show, the Holiday Run dancers' costumes included a devil, a prostitute, and a pimp. The band started the third set and jammed Runaway Jim until just before the New Year. The dancers reappeared throughout the crowd and handed out thousands of glowrings to the crowd just before a grand balloon drop and pyrotechnics display at midnight. The band counted the crowd into the New Year before busting into Auld Lang Syne.

While some fans used the glowrings to start a Glowstick War during Hood, others used them to create long chain links of rings in the arena. '

SUMMER, 1999

Thursday, June 24, 1999
Trey's Barn, Westford, VT
The 5th Ball, aka "Carreystock"
● *Set I:* Farmhouse, The Moma Dance, Hey You, Meatstick > Come Together
● *Set II:* Back on the Train, Windora Bug, Dirt, Twist > Jam, Bug, I Saw It Again, Rock-a-William
● *Show Notes:* This private show at Trey's barn was a tune-up for the summer tour, played for some members of the Phish organization and members of the crew of the Jim Carrey movie *Me, Myself and Irene*, which was being filmed nearby. Carrey joined in on vocals for Hey You and Come Together.

Wednesday, June 30, 1999
Sandstone Amphitheatre, Bonner Springs, KS
● *Check:* Twist, Funky Bitch, Mist, Beauty of My Dreams, Glide Tease, Back at the Chicken Shack, Dogs Stole Things, The Wedge
● *Set I:* Bathtub Gin, Farmhouse, Tube, Horn, Back on the Train, Maze, Limb by Limb, Golgi Apparatus
● *Set II:* The Squirming Coil > Free, Birds of a Feather > Simple > Swept Away > Steep > Piper, Bug -> My Left Toe, Stash
● *Encore:* Bouncing Around the Room, Sample in a Jar
● *Show Notes:* This was the first show in the new stage setup. Maze included Gin teases. Back on the Train, Bug, and My Left Toe made their Phish debuts, although Trey played them on his May, 1999, solo tour. Also, Bug had been played by Amfibian since they debuted the song on November 4, 1998, albeit with slightly different lyrics. Swept Away and Steep were played for the first time since June 30, 1998 (62 shows).

Thursday, July 1, 1999
First American Music Center, Antioch, TN
● *Check:* I Saw It Again, Water in the Sky, Brian and Robert, Mist
● *Set I:* Punch You in the Eye, Billy Breathes, Guyute, Wolfman's Brother, Beauty of My Dreams, Doin' My Time, Roggae, Water in the Sky, Back on the Train, Poor Heart
● *Set II:* Down with Disease > Prince Caspian > You Enjoy Myself
● *Encore:* Character Zero
● *Show Notes:* Wolfman's featured Jerry Douglas on dobro; Beauty of My Dreams through Back on the Train featured Jerry Douglas on dobro, Ronnie McCoury on mandolin and Tim O'Brien on fiddle. Poor Heart saw Gary Gazaway, on trumpet, join the other three guests on stage. Doin' My Time also featured O'Brien on lead vocals. The song was last performed when O'Brien joined the band onstage at Red Rocks on August 7, 1996. The second set may have been cut short by a huge thunderstorm that worsened during YEM.

Saturday, July 3, 1999
Lakewood Amphitheatre, Atlanta, GA

● *Check:* What's the Use, Rock-a-William, Wading in the Velvet Sea (twice)
● *Set I:* Chalk Dust Torture, Gumbo, Sparkle > Cavern, Taste, When the Circus Comes, Tube > Funky Bitch, NICU, Waste, Meatstick
● *Set II:* Twist > Piper, The Moma Dance, Mist, Run Like an Antelope > Contact > Little Drummer Boy
● *Encore:* Little Drummer Boy, Bill Bailey Won't You Please Come Home
● *Encore:* Harry Hood
● *Show Notes:* Mist debuted at this show, though it was played on Trey's tour. The Little Drummer Boy encore was performed by Fishman, solo on the snare drum, with alternate lyrics. Bill Bailey featured Page's father, Dr. Jack McConnell, on vocals and kazoo. Meatstick was played for the first time since June 25, 1997 (123 shows).

Sunday, July 4, 1999
Lakewood Amphitheatre, Atlanta, GA

Tower of Portajohns, (the portapagoda).

● *Check:* Wading in the Velvet Sea (several times), Rock-a-William, In a Hole
● *Set I:* My Soul, Ya Mar, Farmhouse, The Oh Kee Pa Ceremony > AC/DC Bag, The Wedge, Vultures, I Didn't Know, Fast Enough For You, David Bowie
● *Set II:* Ghost -> Slave to the Traffic Light, The Horse > Silent in the Morning > What's the Use, Wilson > Mike's Song > Sleeping Monkey > Weekapaug Groove
● *Encore:* Carini > Meatstick Reprise
● *Encore:* The Star Spangled Banner
● *Show Notes:* Fishman, introduced as "Flagina Fishman," took a vacuum solo during I Didn't Know wearing only stars and stripes boxers. Slave included a What's the Use tease and an instrumental Dark Star tease from Mike and Page. What's the Use subsequently debuted later in the set. Silent included a Little Drummer Boy tease. After Carini, the band reprised the chorus of Meatstick while part of the crew and a few fans did the Meatstick Dance. The band performed the encore in stars and stripes outfits and, afterwards, the sky was filled with fireworks. What's the Use debuted at this show, where Trey wore a Mia Hamm soccer jersey. FEFY was played for the first time since July 16, 1998 (55 shows) and Star Spangled Banner was played for the first time since December 2, 1997 (82 shows).

Wednesday, July 7, 1999
Blockbuster Pavilion, Charlotte, NC
● *Check:* Loving Cup, Funky Bitch (slow), Back at the Chicken Shack, Water in the Sky, Sleep (electric), Back at the Chicken Shack (Trey Solo)
● *Set I:* Back on the Train, What's the Use, Billy Breathes, My Mind's Got a Mind of Its Own, Sneakin' Sally Through the Alley, Axilla > Rift, Wolfman's Brother > Maze, Loving Cup
● *Set II:* Also Sprach Zarathustra > Down with Disease > My Left Toe -> Wading in the Velvet Sea -> My Left Toe > Bug > You Enjoy Myself
● *Encore:* Possum > Funky Bitch
● *Show Notes:* The encore featured Derek Trucks on slide guitar. MMGAMOIO was played for the first time since July 17, 1998 (55 shows).

Thursday, July 8, 1999
Virginia Beach Amphitheatre, Virginia Beach, VA
● *Check:* Bug, You Enjoy Myself (partial), Magilla, Driver, Sleep, Dirt, Back at the Chicken Shack
● *Set I:* Julius, Fee -> Jam, Guyute, Dirt, Nellie Kane, Stash, Cavern
● *Set II:* Birds of a Feather > If I Only Had a Brain, Prince Caspian > Jesus Just Left Chicago, I Saw It Again, Sleep, Meatstick, Tube > Simple
● *Encore:* Terrapin -> HYHU, Character Zero
● *Show Notes:* Birds included a Days Between (Grateful Dead) jam from Page and Mike. Brain (first since November 16, 1995, or 246 shows) included strange lyrics from Mike and Trey, including an *Uno* reference. During Meatstick, Trey and Mike put down their instruments, came to the front of the stage and taught the crowd The Meatstick Dance. Simple ended akin to Coil, with each member of the band leaving the stage until only Page was left. At the beginning of the encore, Fishman came out holding the Electrolux vacuum and the band launched into Terrapin (first since July 11, 1996, or 211 shows). Saw It Again was played for the first time since December 12, 1997 (77 shows).

Friday, July 9, 1999
Merriweather Post Pavilion, Columbia, MD
● *Check:* Bug, What's the Use, Sleep, Back at the Chicken Shack, Vocal Check, Funky Bitch
● *Set I:* Limb By Limb, Farmhouse, Back on the Train, Divided Sky, Train Song, Llama, Driver, Runaway Jim
● *Set II:* Punch You In the Eye > Free > What's the Use > Meatstick, Mike's Song -> Sweet Emotion Jam -> Twist > Weekapaug Groove
● *Encore:* Harry Hood
● *Show Notes:* Meatstick saw Trey, Mike, and Sofi Dillof do The Meatstick Dance on stage. Twist included Spooky teases and Weekapaug included Macarena teases and quotes. The Hood encore closed with a Meatstick tease.

Saturday, July 10, 1999
E Centre, Camden, NJ
● *Check:* Foam, Funky Bitch, Back at the Chicken Shack, Jam
● *Set I:* Wilson, Chalk Dust Torture -> Roggae, Water in the Sky, Back at the Chicken Shack, Sparkle, Bathtub Gin, Golgi Apparatus
● *Set II:* Tweezer > Mist, Birds of a Feather -> When the Circus Comes, Fluffhead
● *Encore:* While My Guitar Gently Weeps, Tweezer Reprise
● *Show Notes:* Chalk Dust was unfinished and featured an atypical jam that blended into Roggae. Gin included an I'm a Man (Spencer Davis Group) jam and Tweezer included a What's the Use tease. Trey played the show wearing a Mia Hamm soccer jersey (United States, #9). This was likely in honor of the U.S. Women's Soccer team beating China to win the World Cup earlier in the day.

Monday, July 12, 1999
The Tweeter Center, Mansfield, MA
● *Check:* My Best Friend's Girlfriend, Centerfold, Dream On, Rift
● *Set I:* Foreplay/Long Time > Down with Disease, Back on the Train, What's the Use, Split Open and Melt, Water In the Sky > Character Zero
● *Set II:* Twist > The Moma Dance, Makisupa Policeman > David Bowie, The Lizards, Guyute
● *Encore:* Rock and Roll
● *Show Notes:* Foreplay/Long Time was played for the first time since December 9, 1994 (309 shows) and was played electric for the first time ever. Guyute was followed by band introductions, including Mike Gordon as Michael "Soft G" Jordan.

Tuesday, July 13, 1999
The Tweeter Center, Mansfield, MA
● *Set I:* NICU, The Curtain, Halley's Comet -> Roses Are Free -> NO2, Lawn Boy, Reba > Carini > Funky Bitch
● *Set II:* Wolfman's Brother > Piper, Bug, Mist, Run Like an Antelope > Possum
● *Encore:* Tuesday's Gone
● *Show Notes:* NO2 was played for the first time since July 16, 1994 (355 shows) and, for the first known time, included the instrumental ending originally included on *The White Tape*. Reba was unfinished and dissolved into Carini. Antelope included Meatstick teases and Trey welcoming his friends Dave and Luann Abrahams. Scott Murawski, guitarist for Max Creek, joined the band on Possum and the debut of Tuesday's Gone.

Thursday, July 15, 1999
PNC Bank Arts Center, Holmdel, NJ
● *Check:* Lady Madonna, Have Mercy, Mist -> Dirt -> Mist, Guyute (part), Too Much of Anything
● *Set I:* Punch You in the Eye > Ghost, Farmhouse, Horn, Poor Heart, Axilla > Theme From the Bottom, I Didn't Know, The Sloth, You Enjoy Myself
● *Set II:* Meatstick, Split Open and Melt -> Kung -> Jam, Bouncing Around the Room, Chalk Dust Torture
● *Encore:* Brian and Robert, Frankenstein
● *Show Notes:* This show was webcast live by the House of Blues and featured a blistering YEM in the first set. During I Didn't Know, Trey noted that Michael "Soft G" Jordan would be turning the mic over to "Flagina" Fishman, who then took a vacuum solo. During Meatstick, Trey added to the summer hoopla surrounding the Meatstick Dance. He noted that the band was going to try to get into the *Guinness Book of World Records* by having the most people doing a single dance simultaneously. Then, Trey, Mike and Sofi Dillof taught the crowd how to do the dance. SOAM began as Also Sprach and was unfinished; the ensuing Kung launched into a dissonant jam.

Friday, July 16, 1999
PNC Bank Arts Center, Holmdel, NJ
● *Set I:* Sample in a Jar, Beauty of My Dreams, Dogs Stole Things, Limb by Limb, Billy Breathes, Vultures, Back on the Train, Maze, Cavern
● *Set II:* Also Sprach Zarathustra > Mike's Song > I Am Hydrogen > Weekapaug Groove > Simple > Guyute, Loving Cup > Golgi Apparatus
● *Encore:* Born to Run

● *Show Notes:* Weekapaug included an Also Sprach tease. The encore was preceded by a story from Trey about how he and Page grew up "around here" in Jersey. Trey then referenced "the greatest songwriter of all time" and said that he, too, grew up in the area. While some in the crowd expected Bruce Springsteen (who was in the middle of a run of 15 sold-out dates at New Jersey's Continental Airlines Arena), Trey produced Tom Marshall. Tom appeared in the classic *Born in the U.S.A.* – era Springsteen outfit, complete with red bandana. He subsequently sang the debut of Born to Run. As the song concluded Tom mocked a bunch of Springsteen-esque arena-rock clichés, such as throwing his bandana into the crowd and jogging offstage to a handler who threw a towel around his shoulders. During the song he even aped some dance moves from the Dancing in the Dark video.

Saturday, July 17, 1999
Oswego County Airport, Volney, NY
● *Check:* "Mr. Sausage" (a ditty, to the tune of Dear Mrs. Reagan, about one of the vendors near the second stage), Beauty of my Dreams, Carini (slower)
● *Set I:* Tube > Boogie On Reggae Woman, Birds of a Feather, Guelah Papyrus, My Sweet One, Roggae, Tweezer -> Have Mercy -> Taste, Character Zero
● *Set II:* Funky Bitch, On My Knees, Jam, Down with Disease, Wolfman's Brother -> Sneakin' Sally Through the Alley > Timber (Jerry), You Enjoy Myself
● *Encore:* The Squirming Coil, Tweezer Reprise
● *Show Notes:* Have Mercy was played for the first time since the legendary November 12, 1994 show (334 shows) and My Sweet One was

played for the first time since July 20, 1998 (61 shows). Son Seals guested on his own composition, Funky Bitch. He also played guitar and sang during On My Knees, which made its debut. The song was followed by a brief blues jam as Son left the stage.

Sunday, July 18, 1999
Oswego County Airport, Volney, NY
● *Set I:* Punch You in the Eye, Farmhouse, Water in the Sky, Bathtub Gin, Back on the Train, If You Need a Fool, I'm Blue I'm Lonesome, Beauty of My Dreams, The Moma Dance, Reba, Chalk Dust Torture
● *Set II:* Runaway Jim -> Free, Meatstick, Guyute, Axilla, Llama
● *Set III:* My Soul, Piper -> Prince Caspian > Wilson > Catapult -> Smoke on the Water Jam -> Icculus, Quinn the Eskimo, Fluffhead
● *Encore:* Harry Hood
● *Show Notes:* Back on the Train through Beauty of my Dreams featured a guest appearance by the Del McCoury Band, who had been playing on the venue's side stage. During I'm Blue I'm Lonesome, Del McCoury broke a string, and a bluegrass breakdown ensued while the string was changed. During Meatstick, the crowd tried to break the world record for most people dancing at one time. Trey explained the record that the band was trying to break while Sofi Dillof danced on stage and the *Guinness* staff videotaped the crowd. Part of the Piper intro was used on the studio Piper released on *Farmhouse*. Caspian was unfinished. Some musical chaos ensued between Catapult and Icculus (first since October 31, 1995, or 261 shows), where Trey rambled about the negative aspects of television and the positive aspects of books. The ensuing Smoke on the Water Jam included Cat Scratch Fever teases. Subsequently, Icculus was followed by more narration and a tease of Miss You. The show closed with fireworks during Hood.

Tuesday, July 20, 1999
Molson Amphitheatre, Toronto, Ontario, Canada
● *Check:* My Soul, How Long, Dream Weaver
● *Set I:* Chalk Dust Torture, Sample in a Jar > Cars Trucks Buses, The Sloth, Divided Sky, Waste > Ghost, Wilson > You Enjoy Myself
● *Set II:* Twist > The Moma Dance, What's the Use, Train Song, Also Sprach Zarathustra > Misty Mountain Hop
● *Encore:* Guyute, Hello My Baby
● *Show Notes:* Misty Mountain Hop debuted at this show, although it had previously been heard at soundchecks.

Wednesday, July 21, 1999
Star Lake Amphitheatre, Burgettstown, PA
● *Set I:* AC/DC Bag > Cities, Gold Soundz, Ginseng Sullivan, Limb By Limb, Funky Bitch > The Moma Dance > When The Circus Comes, Taste, Bittersweet Motel
● *Set II:* Mike's Song > Simple -> My Left Toe -> Prince Caspian > Weekapaug Groove, Golgi Apparatus
● *Encore:* Brian and Robert, Bold as Love
● *Show Notes:* Gold Soundz debuted at this show. Trey forgot some of the lyrics, and Mike subsequently flubbed some of the lyrics to Ginseng. Before Limb by Limb, Trey remarked that they would try to get all the verses correct on the next song.

Friday, July 23, 1999
Polaris Amphitheatre, Columbus, OH

● *Set I:* Ya Mar, NICU, Back at the Chicken Shack > Punch You in the Eye, Fast Enough for You, Back on the Train, David Bowie, Strange Design, Possum

● *Set II:* Ghost -> Free > Birds of a Feather > Meatstick, Fire

● *Encore:* Bouncing Around the Room, Rocky Top

● *Show Notes:* Trey played keys for part of PYITE. During Meatstick, Trey talked about the band's desire to teach fans the Meatstick Dance and break the world record. He then informed the crowd that the New Year's Eve concert would be played in Florida. Fire was played for the first time since NYE 1997 (89 shows).

Saturday, July 24, 1999
Alpine Valley, East Troy, WI

● *Set I:* Guyute, Fluffhead -> Jam > The Man Who Stepped Into Yesterday > Avenu Malkenu > The Man Who Stepped Into Yesterday Reprise -> Jam -> The Wedge, Character Zero

● *Set II:* Tweezer -> Catapult -> Tweezer > The Mango Song -> Jam > The Happy Whip and Dung Song > Waste > Chalk Dust Torture

● *Encore:* Glide, Camel Walk, Alumni Blues > Tweezer Reprise

● *Show Notes:* The jam out of Fluffhead was over fifteen minutes long. Trey and Mike sang Catapult in harmony over the top of Tweezer. Alumni was played for the first time since April 15, 1994 (426 shows, although it was jammed on December 3, 1994 and played in its entirety once on Trey's 1999 solo tour). Also, Glide was played for the first time since July 29, 1998 (60 shows) and Camel Walk was played for the first time since July 28, 1998 (61 shows). The Happy Whip and Dung Song made its concert debut.

Sunday, July 25, 1999
Deer Creek Amphitheatre, Noblesville, IN

● *Check:* Mike's Song, Back at the Chicken Shack, Beauty of my Dreams, Day Tripper

● *Set I:* Meat, My Friend My Friend -> My Left Toe -> Whipping Post > Makisupa Policeman, I Saw It Again, Boogie On Reggae Woman, Cavern

● *Set II:* Birds of a Feather -> Walk Away, Run Like an Antelope, Suzy Greenberg, HYHU > Purple Rain > HYHU, You Enjoy Myself

● *Encore:* Loving Cup

● *Show Notes:* Whipping Post, which had not been played since the August 10, 1996 Alpine Valley show (207 shows) featured Trey (instead of the usual Henrietta) on vocals. Trey announced Chris Kuroda's birthday during Makisupa. The band members took "happy birthday solos," (including Fishman talking in a mock Jamaican accent) and Chris took a silent light board solo (see also April 18, 1990). Many songs in the second set featured fun teases and jams, including Birds (My Left Toe tease), Antelope (Stash tease), Suzy (I Wish teases and a syn-

copated jam based around Page) and YEM (Boogie On Reggae Woman jam). Purple Rain, played for the first time since August 6, 1996 (209 shows), saw Fishman forget the words and subsequently thank the crowd for supporting his vacuum cleaner habit.

Monday, July 26, 1999
Deer Creek Amphitheatre, Noblesville, IN

● *Set I:* Farmhouse, Back on the Train, Vultures, Sleep, Gumbo -> NICU, Beauty of My Dreams, Bathtub Gin, Mist, Axilla, Stash

● *Set II:* Wolfman's Brother > Piper, Theme From the Bottom > Down with Disease > Jam -> Split Open and Melt

● *Encore:* Woodstock > Julius

● *Show Notes:* Disease was followed by a several-minute long, feedback-enhanced jam that also jammed the opening to Also Sprach before Mike redirected the band into SOAM. In fact, Fishman continued playing the Also Sprach drum beat underneath parts of SOAM. The second set ended with a speech from Trey that mentioned how happy the band was to be playing for their audience. Trey also spoke of the damage wrought at Woodstock 1999. He subsequently quoted Turning Japanese when mentioning the upcoming trip to Japan. Woodstock, which debuted at this show, was unfinished.

Friday, July 30, 1999
Fuji Rock Festival
Naeba, Niigata, Japan

Chalk Dust Torture, Guyute, Wolfman's Brother, Taste, Punch You in the Eye > Waste, Hello My Baby

● *Show Notes:* This early set was performed from The Green Stage and was webcast live. Before PYITE, Trey apologized for not speaking the language and brought out a translator, who addressed the crowd in Japanese.

Drum Circle of friends in Alpine Valley (7/24/99).

Friday, July 30, 1999
Fuji Rock Festival
Naeba, Niigata, Japan
● *Set I:* Birds of a Feather, Sample in a Jar, Beauty of my Dreams, Stash, NICU, Funky Bitch > Ghost > Axilla
● *Set II:* Down with Disease, My Soul, Reba, HYHU > Bike > HYHU, Runaway Jim > Cavern
● *Encore:* Julius
● *Show Notes:* Before Bike, Fishman told the crowd that he would play guitar instead of vacuum because the Electrolux vacuum did not make the trip to Japan. Afterwards, Trey said that the song was meant to impress Yoshimi, the drummer from The Boredoms, because Fishman has "a crush on her."

Saturday, July 31, 1999
Fuji Rock Festival
Naeba, Niigata, Japan
● *Set I:* My Friend My Friend > Golgi Apparatus, Back on the Train, Limb by Limb, Free > Roggae, Sparkle > Character Zero
● *Set II:* Also Sprach Zarathustra > David Bowie, Wading in the Velvet Sea > Prince Caspian, Fluffhead > The Squirming Coil
● *Encore:* Jam, Brian and Robert, Simple
● *Show Notes:* The encore began with Tibetan monk Nawang Khechog discussing the current situation in Tibet (see Trey's solo performances at Carnegie Hall). The ensuing jam featured Fishman on vacuum and Khechog on horn. Subsequently, Brian and Robert featured Khechog on wooden flute.

Sunday, August 1, 1999
Fuji Rock Festival
Naeba, Niigata, Japan
● *Set I:* Cities > Rift > Wilson > The Moma Dance > Divided Sky, Horn > Split Open and Melt, Poor Heart, Bouncing Around the Room > Run Like an Antelope
● *Set II:* Possum > Tweezer -> Llama > Mike's Song -> I Am Hydrogen > Weekapaug Groove, The Wedge, The Lizards, You Enjoy Myself
● *Encore:* Sweet Adeline, Tweezer Reprise
● *Show Notes:* Tweezer included a tease, by Trey, of Wading in the Velvet Sea. Adeline was played for the first time since July 1, 1998 (84 shows).

FALL (EARLY), 1999

Saturday, September 4, 1999
Chris Kuroda's Wedding, Burlington, VT
Ya Mar, Poor Heart, Funky Bitch, Back on the Train, Water in the Sky, Possum
● *Show Notes:* Chris sang lead on Possum. The rest of the setlist is unknown.

Thursday, September 9, 1999
GM Place, Vancouver, British Columbia, Canada
● *Set I:* Mozambique, Axilla > Limb by Limb, Horn, Guyute, Chalk Dust Torture, Back at the Chicken Shack, Stash, I Didn't Know, Character Zero

Alpine Valley.

● *Set II:* Birds of a Feather, Ha Ha Ha, Ghost, The Inlaw Josie Wales, First Tube, Tweezer, Bug, You Enjoy Myself, Hello My Baby
● *Encore:* Sample in a Jar, Golgi Apparatus, Tweezer Reprise
● *Show Notes:* The Inlaw Josie Wales, First Tube, and Mozambique made their Phish debuts at this show, although they had been played on Trey's May, 1999, solo tour.

Friday, September 10, 1999
The Gorge Amphitheatre, George, WA
● *Check:* Twist, Will It Go Round in Circles
● *Set I:* Farmhouse, First Tube, Twist, Divided Sky, Ginseng Sullivan, Carini, What's The Use, Will It Go Round in Circles
● *Set II:* Down with Disease > The Moma Dance > Piper, Fee, Gotta Jibboo, I Saw it Again, Split Open and Melt, Cavern > David Bowie
● *Encore:* The Squirming Coil
● *Show Notes:* Will It Go Round in Circles and Gotta Jibboo made their Phish debuts at this show, although they had been played on Trey's May, 1999, solo tour.

Deer Creek.

Saturday, September 11, 1999
The Gorge Amphitheatre, George, WA
● *Set I:* Tube > Funky Bitch, Limb by Limb, Dogs Stole Things, Punch You in the Eye, Billy Breathes, Heavy Things, Guyute > Free
● *Set II:* Wolfman's Brother -> Sand, Meatstick -> Maze, Prince Caspian > Harry Hood
● *Encore:* When the Circus Comes
● *Show Notes:* Heavy Things and Sand made their Phish debuts at this show, although they had been played on Trey's May, 1999, solo tour. Also, Heavy Things had been played by Amfibian since they debuted the song on January 15, 1999. The Hood is notable for its odd, repetitive, atypical ending.

Sunday, September 12, 1999
Portland Meadows, Portland, OR
● *Check:* Gotta Jibboo, Heavy Things
● *Set I:* First Tube, Poor Heart, Mozambique, Bathtub Gin, Back on the Train, My Mind's Got a Mind of its Own, Frankie Says, Birds of a Feather, Lawn Boy, Possum
● *Set II:* Ghost -> Runaway Jim > Roggae, Also Sprach Zarathustra > You Enjoy Myself
● *Encore:* Theme From the Bottom

Tuesday, September 14, 1999
Boise State University Pavilion, Boise, ID
● *Set I:* Chalk Dust Torture, The Sloth, The Curtain > Waste, Loving Cup > What's the Use, Wading in the Velvet Sea, Farmhouse, Nellie Kane,
Taste, Rocky Top
● *Set II:* Peaches en Regalia > AC/DC Bag > Gumbo, Down with Disease > Frankenstein
● *Encore:* Simple, Hello My Baby
● *Show Notes:* Peaches was played for the first time since February 28, 1997, or 161 shows. This long AC/DC Bag featured Trey on keys and Fishman on vacuum for part of the jam. Gumbo included a Another One Bites the Dust jam. Fishman again grabbed the vacuum for Frankenstein and quoted Pink Floyd's One of These Days.

Thursday, September 16, 1999
Shoreline Amphitheatre, Mountain View, CA
● *Check:* Wading in the Velvet Sea, It's Ice
● *Set I:* Ya Mar, Chalk Dust Torture, Farmhouse, First Tube, Carini, Dirt, Vultures, Sparkle, On Your Way Down, Beauty of My Dreams, Stash, Train Song, Billy Breathes, Run Like an Antelope
● *Set II:* Also Sprach Zarathustra > Mike's Song -> I Am Hydrogen > Weekapaug Groove, Mist, Limb by Limb, Prince Caspian, Julius
● *Encore:* Misty Mountain Hop
● *Show Notes:* On Your Way Down was played for the first known time since August 12, 1989 (911 shows), although it had been teased as recently as the summer of 1997 (see July 23 and August 16). The encore featured a guest appearance from Warren Haynes.

Friday, September 17, 1999
Shoreline Amphitheatre, Mountain View, CA
● *Set I:* Mozambique, Guyute, Ghost > Lawn Boy, Peaches en Regalia, The Moma Dance, Water in the Sky, When the Circus Comes, Back on the Train, David Bowie, The Squirming Coil
● *Set II:* Runaway Jim, Sand, Piper, Roggae, You Enjoy Myself -> Bass Jam, Wolfman's Brother, Cold Rain and Snow
● *Encore:* Viola Lee Blues
● *Show Notes:* Phil Lesh joined the band on a second bass guitar from YEM through the end of the show. The encore also featured Warren Haynes on guitar. Cold Rain and Snow and Viola Lee Blues were both debuts.

Saturday, September 18, 1999
Coors Amphitheatre, Chula Vista, CA
● *Check:* Heavy Things, Meatstick
● *Set I:* Tweezer, Roses Are Free > Wilson > Maze, Brian and Robert, Tube > Rocky Top
● *Set II:* Boogie On Reggae Woman, Meatstick > Free > Bouncing Around the Room, Harry Hood > Frankenstein > Cavern
● *Encore:* Contact > Tweezer Reprise
● *Show Notes:* The Boogie On to open the second set was particularly strong.

Sunday, September 19, 1999
Irvine Meadows, Irvine, CA
● *Set I:* NICU, Funky Bitch, First Tube, Gotta Jibboo, Heavy Things, Farmhouse, Stash, Hello My Baby
● *Set II:* Twist, Sand, Wading in the Velvet Sea, The Squirming Coil, Loving Cup, Down with Disease
● *Encore:* Guyute, Character Zero

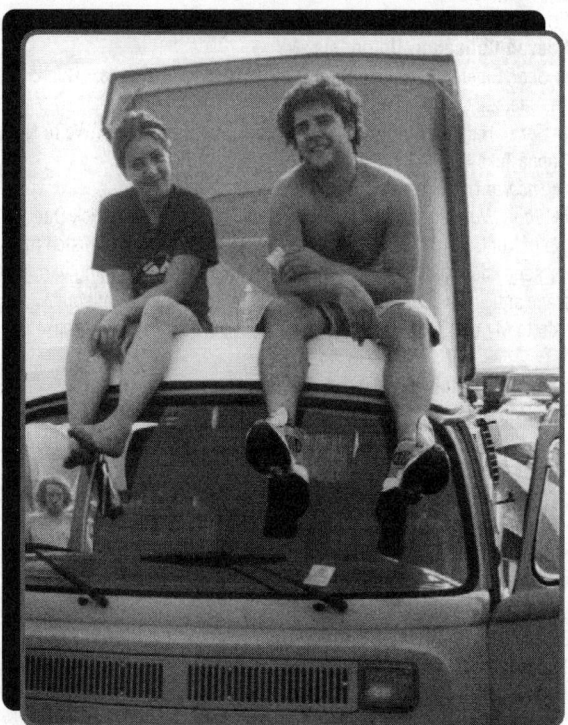

Deer Creek (1999).

Tuesday, September 21, 1999
Pima County Fairgrounds, Tucson, AZ
● *Set I:* Poor Heart > Sample in a Jar, Split Open and Melt, Drowned, I Didn't Know, Back on the Train, Birds of a Feather, Theme From the Bottom, Golgi Apparatus
● *Set II:* Carini > Bug, Strange Design, Vultures -> Limb by Limb, Will It Go Round In Circles, Dirt, Run Like an Antelope
● *Encore:* Reba, Bold as Love

Wednesday, September 22, 1999
Pan American Center, Las Cruces, NM
● *Check:* The Aggie Song, Dirt (several times)
● *Set I:* Also Sprach Zarathustra > Chalk Dust Torture, Guelah Papyrus, Axilla, My Mind's Got a Mind of its Own, Beauty of My Dreams, Bathtub Gin, Mozambique, Sand, Waste
● *Set II:* Gotta Jibboo, Ghost > Taste, Brian and Robert, Mike's Song > Simple > Train Song, Weekapaug Groove
● *Encore:* La Grange
● *Show Notes:* The Aggie Song, played during soundcheck, was a song made up on the spot about being an Aggie, or a student at New Mexico State University at Las Cruces (named after the school's mascot). The impromptu song referenced fan David "ZZYZX" Steinberg, also known as The Timer, with the lyric "Timer is an Aggie, too."

Friday, September 24, 1999
South Park Meadows, Austin, TX
● *Set I:* First Tube, Punch You in the Eye, Farmhouse, Water in the Sky, The Moma Dance, Down with Disease, Roggae, Back on the Train, Guyute, Loving Cup

● *Set II:* Peaches en Regalia > Possum, Wolfman's Brother -> The Lizards, Sand -> Misty Mountain Hop
● *Encore:* Boogie On Reggae Woman > Chalk Dust Torture
● *Show Notes:* Wolfman's dissolved into a spacy jam from which Lizards arose. Check out the nice segue from Sand into Misty Mountain Hop.

Saturday, September 25, 1999
Woodlands Pavilion, Houston, TX
● *Set I:* Tube > Runaway Jim, Ya Mar, Horn, Limb By Limb, On Your Way Down, Sleeping Monkey > Wilson
● *Set II:* NICU > David Bowie, The Squirming Coil > Prince Caspian > Rock and Roll > Also Sprach Zarathustra > Frankenstein > Julius
● *Encore:* Character Zero
● *Show Notes:* Before Monkey, Trey and Mike pulled a girl out of the crowd who had been calling for Sleeping Monkey and the band played the song for her.

Sunday, September 26, 1999
Lakefront Arena, New Orleans, LA
● *Set I:* Sweet Virginia, First Tube > AC/DC Bag, Dirt, Guyute, Bouncing Around the Room, Cars Trucks Buses, Funky Bitch, Mozambique, Cavern
● *Set II:* Twist > Piper, Mist, Heavy Things, Birds of a Feather, Meat, Down with Disease
● *Encore:* Meatstick, Rocky Top
● *Show Notes:* Sweet Virginia debuted at this show. The last four songs of the first set featured Michael Ray on trumpet and Tim Green on saxophone

Tuesday, September 28, 1999
Oak Mountain Amphitheatre, Pelham, AL
● *Set I:* Wolfman's Brother, Sneakin' Sally Through the Alley, Tube, Ginseng Sullivan > Roggae, Maze, Wading in the Velvet Sea, Harry Hood
● *Set II:* Farmhouse, Heavy Things, First Tube, Tweezer > Makisupa Policeman, Chalk Dust Torture, You Enjoy Myself
● *Encore:* Halley's Comet > Tweezer Reprise
● *Show Notes:* The YEM vocal jam included Sweet Home Alabama quotes.

Wednesday, September 29, 1999
Pyramid Arena, Memphis, TN
● *Set I:* Runaway Jim > Free, Driver, Taste, Dirt, Nellie Kane, Stash > Theme From the Bottom, Tweezer Reprise
● *Set II:* Gotta Jibboo > Also Sprach Zarathustra > Down with Disease, Billy Breathes, Back on the Train, Mike's Song -> Catapult -> Mike's Song -> Kung -> Mike's Song > I Didn't Know > Weekapaug Groove
● *Encore:* Cities
● *Show Notes:* Stash included Can't Turn You Loose and Happy Birthday (to Trey) teases. After Stash, Trey announced a contest where the winner would receive four tickets and backstage passes to any show in the next year and, jokingly, a date with Fishman. The question centered on what all of the songs played in the first set, with the exception of Driver, had in common. The answer was that all songs were in the Key of D. Cities was an appropriate choice as an encore for Memphis, and Trey altered the lyrics a bit for the occasion. Mike's included a Who Knows tease.

Friday, October 1, 1999
Hilton Coliseum, Ames, IA
● *Set I:* Chalk Dust Torture, The Moma Dance > Sparkle, First Tube > Bathtub Gin, Heavy Things, Limb by Limb, Cavern
● *Set II:* NICU > Run Like an Antelope, The Horse > Silent in the Morning > Gumbo > Mist, Julius > Fluffhead, Slave to the Traffic Light
● *Encore:* Bold as Love

Saturday, October 2, 1999
The Target Center, Minneapolis, MN
● *Set I:* Llama, Wolfman's Brother, Punch You in the Eye > Quinn the Eskimo, Poor Heart, Roggae, Split Open and Melt, The Squirming Coil > Loving Cup
● *Set II:* Tweezer > On Your Way Down > Piper > You Enjoy Myself, Frankenstein, Waste
● *Encore:* While My Guitar Gently Weeps > Tweezer Reprise
● *Show Notes:* SOAM featured band introductions: "Cactus"(Mike), "Stumpy" (Page), "Matty" (Fishman) and "The Good Lieutenant" (Trey). This long Piper included a Birds-like jam.

Sunday, October 3, 1999
Allstate Center, Chicago, IL
● *Set I:* First Tube, Farmhouse, Dogs Stole Things, Divided Sky, Heavy Things, Horn, Carini, Ginseng Sullivan, Back on the Train, Maze, Bouncing Around the Room, Guyute
● *Set II:* Twist > Possum > The Man Who Stepped Into Yesterday > Avenu Malkenu > Big Black Furry Creature from Mars, David Bowie, Wading in the Velvet Sea, Harry Hood
● *Encore:* Funky Bitch, Messin' with the Kid
● *Show Notes:* The encore featured Sugar Blue on harmonica and Son Seals on guitar. Messin' With the Kid was played for the first time since August 8, 1997 (141 shows), which was Sugar Blue's previous time on stage with Phish.

Monday, October 4, 1999
Redbird Arena, Normal, IL
● *Set I:* Uncle Pen, Funky Bitch, Vultures, Runaway Jim, Jesus Just Left Chicago, Limb by Limb, Wilson, Down with Disease
● *Set II:* Ghost > Sample in a Jar, The Wedge > AC/DC Bag > Makisupa Policeman, Sand, Ya Mar, Character Zero
● *Encore:* Rock and Roll
● *Show Notes:* Uncle Pen was played for the first time since August 17, 1997 (135 shows).

Thursday, October 7, 1999
Nassau Coliseum, Uniondale, NY
● *Set I:* NICU > My Soul, Dirt, David Bowie, Frankie Says > Possum, When the Circus Comes, Gotta Jibboo, Fluffhead
● *Set II:* Boogie On Reggae Woman, Heavy Things, Tube, Back on the Train > Mike's Song > McGrupp and the Watchful Hosemasters, Prince Caspian > Golgi Apparatus > Weekapaug Groove
● *Encore:* Rocky Top > I Am Hydrogen, Julius
● *Show Notes:* Part of the Mike's jam featured Trey on keys. Hydrogen was played outside of Mike's for the first time since October 31, 1987. McGrupp was played for the first time since October 29, 1998 (70 shows).

Friday, October 8, 1999
Nassau Coliseum, Uniondale, NY
● *Set I:* Piper, AC/DC Bag, Suzy Greenberg, Meat, Meatstick, Run Like an Antelope
● *Set II:* Halley's Comet > Tweezer, Bug, Fee, Harry Hood, We're Not Gonna Take It, Chalk Dust Torture
● *Encore:* The Squirming Coil, Tweezer Reprise
● *Show Notes:* Sofi Dillof joined the band for the Meatstick Dance. We're Not Gonna Take It (from The Who's *Tommy*, not the Twisted Sister song) debuted with Tom Marshall singing and performing various stage antics. Tweezer included a brief Sand tease and a jam somewhat akin to My Left Toe. The Coil outro included a Bug tease from Mike.

Saturday, October 9, 1999
The Pepsi Arena, Albany, NY
● *Set I:* Punch You In the Eye > Wilson, Guyute, Ghost -> My Left Toe -> Free, Sparkle > Possum
● *Set II:* Limb by Limb > Also Sprach Zarathustra > Down with Disease > Wading in the Velvet Sea, Simple, Loving Cup
● *Encore:* Slave to the Traffic Light
● *Show Notes:* Part of the Also Sprach jam featured Trey on keys.

Sunday, October 10, 1999
The Pepsi Arena, Albany, NY
● *Set I:* Farmhouse, Gotta Jibboo, Heavy Things, First Tube, Dirt, Vultures, Stash
● *Set II:* Jam > You Enjoy Myself > Prince Caspian > Train Song, Bathtub Gin, Character Zero
● *Encore:* Contact, Misty Mountain Hop
● *Show Notes:* At the end of the second set, Trey thanked the band's families, as well as the crew and the fans. This version of YEM did not contain a vocal jam.

FALL (LATE), 1999

Thursday, December 2, 1999
The Palace, Auburn Hills, MI
● *Set I:* Runaway Jim, Farmhouse, Heavy Things, Roggae, Run Like an Antelope, Wading in the Velvet Sea, Poor Heart, Sample in a Jar, Free, The Squirming Coil
● *Set II:* Boogie On Reggae Woman, Gotta Jibboo, Bathtub Gin -> Also Sprach Zarathustra, You Enjoy Myself -> Little Drummer Boy
● *Encore:* Bold as Love
● *Show Notes:* Farmhouse featured a slightly different arrangement, with an additional chorus at the end. Gin included ASZ teases before segueing into ASZ proper. YEM included a silent jam. Little Drummer Boy emerged from the YEM vocal jam and ended with Fishman alone onstage.

Friday, December 3, 1999
Firstar Center, Cincinnati, OH
● *Set I:* First Tube, Wolfman's Brother, Bouncing Around the Room, Back on the Train, Billy Breathes, AC/DC Bag > Possum, Slave to the Traffic Light
● *Set II:* Sand, Limb by Limb, Bug > Piper, Harry Hood

● *Encore:* Rock and Roll

Saturday, December 4, 1999
Firstar Center, Cincinnati, OH
● *Set I:* Heavy Things, Simple > Ya Mar, Guyute, Tweezer > Dirt, Loving Cup
● *Set II:* Down with Disease > Split Open and Melt, The Moma Dance > Farmhouse, The Man Who Stepped Into Yesterday > Avenu Malkenu > The Man Who Stepped Into Yesterday Reprise, When the Circus Comes, David Bowie
● *Encore:* Julius > Tweezer Reprise

Sunday, December 5, 1999
The BlueCross Arena, Rochester, NY
● *Set I:* Carini > Gotta Jibboo, Back on the Train, Taste, Bug, Sparkle, Tube, Lawn Boy, Ginseng Sullivan, Twist
● *Set II:* Mike's Song -> Meatstick > I Am Hydrogen > Weekapaug Groove, Brian and Robert, Jennifer Dances, Maze, Fluffhead, Chalk Dust Torture, Frankenstein
● *Encore:* Character Zero, Hello My Baby
● *Show Notes:* Twist emerged at this show with a slightly new arrangement. Jennifer Dances made its debut after Trey remarked of his affinity for the venue.

Tuesday, December 7, 1999
Cumberland County Civic Center, Portland, ME
● *Set I:* Farmhouse, First Tube, NICU > Funky Bitch > Punch You in the Eye, Nellie Kane, Halley's Comet > The Squirming Coil
● *Set II:* Wolfman's Brother, Jennifer Dances, Heavy Things, Bug, Bathtub Gin > Simple, Free, Suzy Greenberg
● *Encore:* Walk Away, Rocky Top

Wednesday, December 8, 1999
Cumberland County Civic Center, Portland, ME
● *Set I:* Limb by Limb, Back on the Train, Down with Disease > Fast Enough For You, Ya Mar, The Horse > Silent in the Morning, Run Like an Antelope
● *Set II:* Sand, Dirt, Piper -> Dog Faced Boy, The Lizards, You Enjoy Myself
● *Encore:* Golgi Apparatus > Tweezer Reprise
● *Show Notes:* The ending of the YEM vocal jam included a Tweezer Reprise vocal jam. Dog Faced Boy was played for the first time since November 18, 1998 (66 shows).

Friday, December 10, 1999
First Union Spectrum, Philadelphia, PA
● *Set I:* Tweezer, Bouncing Around the Room, Horn, Heavy Things, Dogs Stole Things, My Mind's Got A Mind of Its Own, Roggae, Birds of a Feather, Guyute, Loving Cup
● *Set II:* Gotta Jibboo, The Wedge, David Bowie -> Have Mercy -> HYHU, Cracklin' Rosie > HYHU, Twist, Waste
● *Encore:* Ride Captain Ride
● *Show Notes:* The jam out of Have Mercy resolved both to Bowie and Have Mercy before sliding into a reggafied HYHU that included a vacuum solo. Mike then handed Fishman his cymbals, which led to Rosie (first since August 6, 1998, or 92 shows). Ride Captain Ride was played

Alpine Valley.

for the first time since November 8, 1998 (73 shows).

Saturday, December 11, 1999
First Union Spectrum, Philadelphia, PA
● *Set I:* Harry Hood > Mike's Song > Simple > I Am Hydrogen > Weekapaug Groove, When the Circus Comes, Scent of a Mule, Cavern
● *Set II:* Boogie On Reggae Woman, Sneakin' Sally Through the Alley -> Ghost -> Also Sprach Zarathustra > Down with Disease
● *Encore:* Possum
● *Show Notes:* This show included the first known Hood opener since October 30, 1985. Sneakin' Sally began with an AC/DC Bag tease. Possum included an All Fall Down signal. Mule was played for the first time since November 28, 1998 (61 shows).

Sunday, December 12, 1999
Hartford Civic Center, Hartford, CT
● *Set I:* Heavy Things, AC/DC Bag, Strange Design, Divided Sky, Beauty of My Dreams, Bug, Stash, Chalk Dust Torture

Deer Creek. (7/27/99).

● *Set II:* Drowned > Prince Caspian, The Squirming Coil, Makisupa Policeman > Run Like an Antelope
● *Encore:* Runaway Jim
● *Show Notes:* Chalk Dust concluded with Trey paying his respects to his recently-deceased grandfather. The second set-opening Drowned clocked in at nearly 31 minutes long.

Monday, December 13, 1999
Providence Civic Center, Providence, RI
● *Set I:* Tube, Cars Trucks Buses, Gumbo, The Moma Dance > Piper > Theme From the Bottom
● *Set II:* Gotta Jibboo > NICU, Sand, The Inlaw Josie Wales, Mist, Limb by Limb, Golgi Apparatus > Slave to the Traffic Light
● *Encore:* Silent in the Morning, Heavy Things
● *Show Notes:* Part of the Piper jam featured Trey on his keyboard set. Sand included a tease of the Jibboo bass line. As part of the encore, fans were treated to a rare Horse-less Silent.

Wednesday, December 15, 1999
The MCI Center, Washington, DC
● *Set I:* Down with Disease, Farmhouse, Bathtub Gin, Wolfman's

Brother, Guyute, Train Song, You Enjoy Myself
● *Set II:* Sample in a Jar, Maze, Free > Dirt, Reba, Halley's Comet > Suzy Greenberg
● *Encore:* Frankenstein > Rocky Top
● *Show Notes:* Rocky Top included Frankenstein teases in the ending.

Thursday, December 16, 1999
Reynolds Coliseum, Raleigh, NC
● *Set I:* Wilson > Chalk Dust Torture, Lawn Boy, Limb by Limb, Horn, Back on the Train, Roggae, Heavy Things, Camel Walk, Possum
● *Set II:* Sand, The Mango Song, Wading in the Velvet Sea > Tweezer > Runaway Jim
● *Encore:* Bittersweet Motel, Tweezer Reprise
● *Show Notes:* Before the show, Mike brought a big shaggy doll on the stage and sat it on top of his bass cabinet. Velvet Sea ended with a short, spacy delay loop jam.

Friday, December 17, 1999
Hampton Coliseum, Hampton, VA
● *Set I:* Piper, Meat > Sparkle > Gotta Jibboo > Punch You in the Eye, When the Circus Comes, Water in the Sky, Twist
● *Set II:* Birds Of A Feather, The Moma Dance > Bug, Jennifer Dances, Split Open and Melt, Character Zero
● *Encore:* The Old Home Place, The Squirming Coil > Loving Cup
● *Show Notes:* Moma included Birds teases. Old Home Place was played for the first time since December 30, 1998 (62 shows).

Saturday, December 18, 1999
Hampton Coliseum, Hampton, VA
● *Set I:* Harry Hood, Back at the Chicken Shack, Dog Gone Dog, Tube, Heavy Things, Back on the Train, First Tube, The Inlaw Josie Wales, You Enjoy Myself
● *Set II:* Also Sprach Zarathustra > Sand, The Horse > Silent In The Morning, Possum, Mike's Song > Simple, Weekapaug Groove -> Buffalo Bill > Weekapaug Groove
● *Encore:* Ya Mar, Sleeping Monkey
● *Show Notes:* Dog Gone Dog (first since November 27, 1998, or 68 shows) was dedicated to Paul Languedoc. Afterwards, the band reprised the song for a few seconds after Trey remarked how much he liked it. Also, Buffalo Bill was played for the first time since the same November 27, 1998 show. ASZ included Do You Feel Like We Do (Peter Frampton) teases (possibly as a nod to the play on words in the *Hampton Comes Alive* title upon the band's return to the venue) and Weekapaug included a Norwegian Wood tease and a Buffalo Bill tease.

Thursday, December 30, 1999
Big Cypress Campground, Big Cypress, FL
● *Check:* Jam, Ginseng Sullivan, What's the Use, The Ballad of Curtis Loew, Jam, Timber (Jerry)!, Quinn the Eskimo
● *Set I:* Water in the Sky, Light Up or Leave Me Alone, Suzy Greenberg, Corinne Corrina, Limb By Limb, Che Hun Ta Mao, Big Alligator Song, Possum, Farmhouse, Ghost, Ya Mar, Character Zero
● *Set II:* Wilson, The Curtain > Tweezer -> Taste, Meat, Golgi Apparatus, Wolfman's Brother, Gotta Jibboo, Harry Hood, Good Times Bad Times
● *Set III:* Chalk Dust Torture, The Moma Dance, Run Like an Antelope, The Sloth, When The Circus Comes, Mike's Song > Simple -> I am Hy-

drogen > Weekapaug Groove
- *Encore:* Boogie On Reggae Woman > Tweezer Reprise
- *Show Notes:* Light Up was played for the first time since July 25, 1988 (1,009 shows) and included Jibboo teases from Mike; Corinna was subsequently played for the first time since February 18, 1989 (982 shows). GTBT was played for the first time since December 28, 1998 (66 shows). Seminole Indian Chief Jim Billie guested on lead vocals and guitar, along with John McEuen on mandolin and Raiford Starke on guitar, on Che Hun Ta Mo and Big Alligator Song. Mike's Song included an Immigrant Song tease and Weekapaug included a Light Up tease and an Auld Lang Syne tease at midnight.

Friday, December 31, 1999
Big Cypress Campground, Big Cypress, FL
- *Set I:* Runaway Jim, Funky Bitch, Tube, I Didn't Know, Punch You in the Eye, Bouncing Around the Room, Poor Heart, Roggae, Split Open and Melt -> Catapult, Back on the Train, Horn, Guyute, After Midnight
- *Set II:* "THE SHOW": Meatstick -> Auld Lang Syne, Down with Disease -> Llama, Bathtub Gin, Heavy Things, Twist -> Prince Caspian > Rock and Roll, You Enjoy Myself, Crosseyed and Painless, The Inlaw Josie Wales, Sand -> Quadrophonic Toppling, Slave to the Traffic Light, Albuquerque, Reba, Axilla, Uncle Pen, David Bowie, My Soul, Drowned -> After Midnight Reprise, The Horse > Silent in the Morning, Bittersweet Motel, Piper -> Free, Lawn Boy, HYHU > Love You > HYHU, Roses are Free, Bug, Also Sprach Zarathustra > Wading in the Velvet Sea, Meatstick
- *Show Notes:* After Midnight debuted at this show. During the Jim opener, fans participated in marshmallow and tortilla wars while also releasing many balloons. I Didn't Know featured Fishman (introduced as 'Soda Jerk') on vacuum. SOAM was unfinished. After the ensuing Catapult, Trey remarked that they could only get away with playing a song like that at the largest concert in the world. The late set, also known as "The Show," began at around 11:35. Father Time was on stage, pedaling on an exercise bike that powered a large clock. The sounds of the clock's gears could be heard through the sound system. About ten minutes before midnight, Father Time collapsed from exhaustion and the clock stopped. Then, a large fan boat entered the concert field and approached the stage. Early in its journey, the fan boat exploded away and revealed the hot dog used in the 1994 New Year's stunt. While the band rode the hot dog to the stage, an instrumental version of Meatstick began to play over the PA. The band reached the stage and fed several meatsticks to Father Time, reviving him so that the clock could continue moving toward midnight. The band then took the stage and played Meatstick to begin The Show. Heavy Things was recorded live and rebroadcast as part of ABC television's New Year's Eve coverage. In a humorous effort to confuse the home audience, Trey instructed the crowd to chant the word "cheesecake" in lieu of cheering at the end of the song. Trey then introduced the band for the rebroadcast and offered a message of peace and harmony for the world where he reminded people to drive in the right lane unless passing another vehicle. Meatstick was subsequently teased as the New Year approached in the central time zone. Sand included a My Soul tease from Mike and Crosseyed included a DEG tease. YEM included a vocal jam based around the word "cheesecake" and Trey altered the lyrics to Axilla and Albuquerque to reference the word. Quadrophonic Toppling debuted, albeit with different music than on *The Siket Disc*. Rock and Roll included an After Midnight tease. Love

You included band introductions; Fishman introduced Page before the song and Mike and Trey afterwards, and the band as Phish 2000 (see November 2, 1990). ASZ began with the signature Hood drum roll. After the show closed with yet another version of Meatstick, the Beatles song Here Comes the Sun was piped through the crowd at sunrise. Several breakouts were played: Albuquerque (first since December 28, 1998, or 67 shows), Crosseyed and Painless (first since August 13, 1997, or 158 shows), and Love You (first since July 5, 1997, or 178 shows).

FARMHOUSE PROMOS

Monday, May 15, 2000
Y100 Sonic Session, Philadelphia, PA
First Tube, Farmhouse, Twist, Heavy Things, Back on the Train, Piper, The Inlaw Josey Wales, Bug, Gotta Jibboo
- *Show Notes:* This session was taped on this date and aired on Sunday, May 28, 2000. About fifty people were in attendance.

Monday, May 15, 2000
WXPN-FM World Café Tapings, Philadelphia, PA
First Tube, Dirt, Back on the Train, Piper, The Inlaw Josie Wales, Gotta Jibboo
- *Show Notes:* This session was taped after the Y100 Session and aired on Philadelphia's WXPN-FM (88.5) on June 23, 2000.

Wednesday, May 17, 2000
The Late Show with David Letterman, The Ed Sullivan Theatre, New York, NY
Heavy Things

Thursday, May 18, 2000
KFOG, San Francisco, CA
First Tube, Bug, Back on the Train, Sand, Heavy Things, Piper, The Inlaw Josey Wales, Dirt, Farmhouse
- *Show Notes:* Bug included a Disease tease. This show was broadcast and webcast via KFOG. "Tickets" were won via KFOG contest throughout the weeks leading up to the broadcast. The show consisted of three segments of three songs each, with a break inbetween each segment filled by the on-air announcer. Following the performance, the band participated in a group photo shoot and copies were mailed to the contest winners, who also won signed copies of *Farmhouse*.

Friday, May 19, 2000
Key Club, Los Angeles, CA
Funky Bitch, My Soul, Gotta Jibboo, First Tube, Magilla, Bug, Heavy Things, Twist, Tube, Piper -> Llama, Brian and Robert
- *Show Notes:* This was a radio set that was broadcast on the "Mark and Brian" Radio Show. Funky Bitch and My Soul were performed as a warmup before the show went on the air, although the crowd was already in the bar. Jibboo through Heavy Things were aired live on the show (except for Magilla, which was played during a commercial break). The band briefly jammed on the *Jeopardy* theme tease during a radio break after Jibboo, with the crowd providing some vocals. Bug in-

cluded a brief DEG tease. During one commercial break, the fans in attendance were entertained with a humorous question and answer session with the band. Studio versions of Birds, Bouncing, and Heavy Things were used as intros and outros for the commercials.

Friday, May 19, 2000
Key Club, Los Angeles, CA
Back on the Train, Heavy Things, First Tube
● *Show Notes:* This performance, taped after the "Mark and Brian" show, aired on KACD (103.1) in Los Angeles. There were around twenty fans present for the taping.

Sunday, May 21, 2000
Radio City Music Hall, New York, NY
● *Set I:* First Tube, Wolfman's Brother, The Squirming Coil, Possum, The Moma Dance > Limb By Limb, Character Zero
● *Set II:* Gotta Jibboo, Down with Disease > Dirt, Twist > Piper, Harry Hood > Wading in the Velvet Sea, Guyute
● *Encore:* The Inlaw Josie Wales, Loving Cup
● *Show Notes:* Seek out the second set for some interesting stage banter. Page talked about how he had often visited Radio City as a child, while Trey talked again about how much the band appreciates the fan support. Zero included a Who Knows tease and Disease included Llama teases and a Crosseyed and Painless-type groove.

Monday, May 22, 2000
Radio City Music Hall, New York, NY
● *Set I:* My Soul, Chalk Dust Torture, Billy Breathes, Heavy Things, Back on the Train, Split Open And Melt, Sparkle, Horn, Bathtub Gin
● *Set II:* Bouncing Around the Room > David Bowie, Sand, The Mango Song, Ghost > Rock and Roll
● *Encore:* Bug > Golgi Apparatus

Tuesday, May 23, 2000
Roseland Ballroom, New York, NY
● *Check:* Ginseng Sullivan, My Soul, Funky Bitch
● *Set I:* AC/DC Bag, Wilson, First Tube, Ya Mar > Mike's Song -> Simple > It's Ice, When The Circus Comes, Back on the Train, Gotta Jibboo, Taste, Sleeping Monkey
● *Set II:* Punch You In The Eye, Twist, Waste, Piper, You Enjoy Myself, Run Like an Antelope, Train Song, Bug
● *Encore:* Boogie On Reggae Woman, Cavern
● *Show Notes:* This show was taped for VH-1's "Hard Rock Live." Portions were first broadcast on July 1, 2000, and has been rebroadcast several times since. Ice was played for the first time since November 13, 1998 (82 shows).

SUMMER, 2000

Japan Tour

Friday, June 9, 2000
On Air East, Shibuya-ku, Tokyo, Japan

● *Set I:* Axilla > Taste, Billy Breathes, Poor Heart, Golgi Apparatus > Funky Bitch, The Moma Dance, First Tube, Chalk Dust Torture
● *Set II:* Tweezer, Bouncing Around the Room, The Mango Song, The Squirming Coil, Gotta Jibboo > Meatstick, Tweezer Reprise
● *Encore:* You Enjoy Myself
● *Show Notes:* The Moma Dance included Funky Bitch teases and Tweezer included Funk 49 teases. Trey attempted to sing Meatstick in Japanese but wound up flubbing the words. Bouncing included a brief outro solo from Trey, which replaced the usual closing guitar lick. This show was re-broadcast on Japanese television.

Saturday, June 10, 2000
Zepp, Koto-ku, Tokyo, Japan
● *Set I:* Down with Disease, Sample in a Jar, Piper, Lawn Boy, Guyute
● *Set II:* Heavy Things, Sand, Sparkle, My Soul, Bathtub Gin > Twist, Albuquerque, Wading in the Velvet Sea > Loving Cup
● *Encore:* The Inlaw Josie Wales, Limb by Limb
● *Show Notes:* Disease included a Weekapaug tease. Lawn Boy spotlighted Mike, who provided a noteworthy bass solo.

Sunday, June 11, 2000
Hibiya Outdoor Theatre, Chiyoda-ku, Tokyo, Japan
● *Opening Act:* Big Frog
● *Set I:* First Tube, Punch You in the Eye, Horn, Ginseng Sullivan, Stash, Dirt, Possum > It's Ice, Farmhouse
● *Set II:* Birds of a Feather, Free, Beauty of My Dreams, Bug > David Bowie, When the Circus Comes, Back on the Train > Harry Hood
● *Encore:* Character Zero
● *Show Notes:* Possum included Stash teases. A large rainbow formed over the theatre and cleared during the encore, creating an unforgettable visual.

Tuesday, June 13, 2000
Club Quattro, Naka-ku, Nagoya, Japan
● *Set I:* Meat, Maze, Meat Reprise, Ya Mar, Fast Enough for You, The Old Home Place > Wilson > Mike's Song -> Simple > Weekapaug Groove
● *Set II:* Gotta Jibboo, Wolfman's Brother, Run Like an Antelope -> Contact > Sand, Roggae > Prince Caspian > Rocky Top > Cavern
● *Encore:* Brian and Robert, Good Times Bad Times
● *Show Notes:* Cavern included the older, alternate lyrics and a drawn-out, feedback-enhanced ending. The band teased Is She Really Going Out With Him before Jibboo and after Wolfman's, with the audience singing along at one point. The audience tried in vain to coerce Phish to play it in its entirety. Antelope was unfinished – Mike segued into a funky version of Contact right before the "Rye, Rye, Rocco" lyric segment of Antelope.

Wednesday, June 14, 2000
Drum Logos, Chuo-ku, Fukuoka, Japan
● *Set I:* Carini, The Curtain > Cities, Gumbo -> Llama, Fee, Heavy Things, Split Open and Melt
● *Set II:* Back on the Train, Twist > Jam -> Walk Away -> Also Sprach Zarathustra
● *Encore:* Sleep, The Squirming Coil

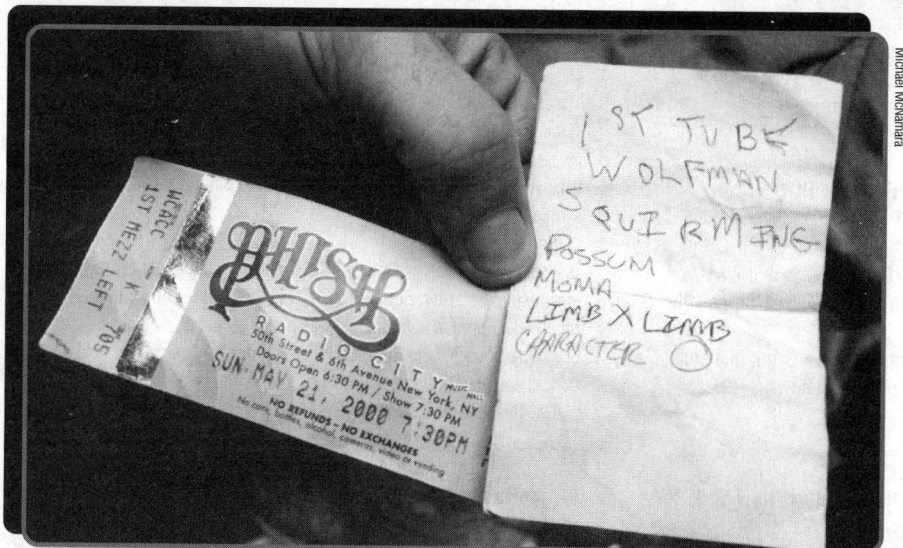

Radio City Music Hall (2000).

● *Show Notes:* Trey altered the lyrics in Cities to reference noodles. Fee included a well-received tease of the old Charlie Chan Signal lick from Fishman, who played it on the woodblock during one of his breaks. The jam between Twist and Walk Away included a jam rooted in the intro to Ghost. Sleep (first since July 26, 1999, or 52 shows) was played by request.

Thursday, June 15, 2000
Big Cat, Chuo-ku, Osaka, Japan
● *Set I:* NICU > Chalk Dust Torture, AC/DC Bag, Uncle Pen, Ghost, Frankie Says, Divided Sky, Farmhouse
● *Set II:* Down with Disease, The Lizards, Bike > HYHU, You Enjoy Myself
● *Encore:* Gotta Jibboo
● *Show Notes:* Fishman fans will want this show for the rare Bike (first since July 30, 1999, or 51 shows), preceded by a vacuum solo and followed by several runs through the HYHU theme (each faster than the one before it). Disease included a Birdland tease.

Friday, June 16, 200
Zepp, Suminoe-ku, Osaka, Japan
● *Set I:* Limb by Limb, Back on the Train, Sample In a Jar, First Tube, Golgi Apparatus, Heavy Things, Dirt, My Sweet One, Reba, Character Zero
● *Set II:* Runaway Jim -> Theme From the Bottom -> Dog Faced Boy, Driver, Slave to the Traffic Light > Julius, Bug
● *Encore:* Bouncing Around the Room, Harry Hood
● *Show Notes:* Reba was preceded by a brief Bowie tease.

SUMMER, 2000

American Tour

Thursday, June 22, 2000
Amsouth Amphitheatre, Antioch, TN

● *Check:* Jam -> Back on the Train, First Tube, Uncle Pen, Billy Breathes, You Shook Me All Night Long
● *Set I:* First Tube, Wolfman's Brother, Beauty of my Dreams, Golgi Apparatus, Limb by Limb, Bug, Poor Heart, Roggae, Chalk Dust Torture
● *Set II:* Gotta Jibboo, Also Sprach Zarathustra, Sand, Harry Hood -> Dog Faced Boy -> Harry Hood, I'm Blue I'm Lonesome, Hold Whatcha Got, Uncle Pen, Freebird
● *Encore:* You Enjoy Myself
● *Show Notes:* Special guests were abound in the second set. Hood included Ronnie McCoury on mandolin and Sam Bush on fiddle. I'm Blue I'm Lonesome (first since July 18, 1999, or 60 shows), Coming Home, Uncle Pen, and Freebird (first since December 29, 1998, or 76 shows) also included Del McCoury on guitar, Ricky Skaggs on mandolin, Mike Budd, and Jason Center, along with an upright bass player and a fiddle player (both unnamed) in addition to those already on stage. Finally, Freebird was played in a full-band arrangement as opposed to the usual *a cappella* arrangement, with Wynonna Judd on lead vocals. Wolfman's included an Inna-Gadda-Da-Vida tease.

Friday, June 23, 2000
Lakewood Amphitheatre, Atlanta, GA
● *Set I:* Ya Mar, My Soul, Bathtub Gin, Heavy Things, Back on the Train > David Bowie, Cars Trucks Buses, Farmhouse
● *Set II:* Rock and Roll > Jesus Just Left Chicago > Down with Disease > Twist, Contact > Makisupa Policeman > Character Zero
● *Encore:* Brian and Robert, Possum

Saturday, June 24, 2000
Lakewood Amphitheatre, Atlanta, GA
● *Set I:* The Moma Dance > Runaway Jim, Bouncing Around the Room > Tweezer, Strange Design, Cavern
● *Set II:* Birds of a Feather, Bug, My Sweet One, Run Like an Antelope, Frankie Says, Carini, The Squirming Coil, Prince Caspian
● *Encore:* Guyute, The Inlaw Josie Wales, Driver, Tweezer Reprise

● *Show Notes:* My Sweet One (first since July 17, 1999, or 63 shows) was botched, which led to band introductions from Trey and extended solos from Fish, Mike, and Page. Tweezer included an I Know You Rider (traditional, though a Dead concert staple) tease.

Sunday, June 25, 2000
Alltel Pavilion at Walnut Creek, Raleigh, NC
● *Check:* My Sweet One, Cars Trucks Buses, Uncle Pen (twice), "Rolling Along"
● *Set I:* NICU, Sample in a Jar, The Old Home Place, Punch You in the Eye, Water in the Sky, Funky Bitch, Horn, Heavy Things, Dirt, Split Open and Melt
● *Set II:* Gotta Jibboo > Fast Enough For You > Scent of a Mule, Meat, Maze, What's the Use > Slave to the Traffic Light
● *Encore:* Uncle Pen, Bold as Love

Tuesday, June 27, 2000
Late Night with Conan O'Brien, NBC Studios, New York, NY
Back On the Train

Wednesday, June 28, 2000
PNC Bank Arts Center, Holmdel, NJ
● *Set I:* Chalk Dust Torture, The Sloth, Taste, Bathtub Gin, Piper, If I Could
● *Set II:* Down with Disease -> Harry Hood > Gotta Jibboo, When the Circus Comes, Mike's Song, Albuquerque > Weekapaug Groove
● *Encore:* First Tube > Loving Cup
● *Show Notes:* Trey was attempting to catch the glowsticks that were launched during Hood. At one point he managed to throw some back into the crowd, eliciting a huge cheer from the fans. The band stopped playing Mike's Song mid-jam and hesitated for a minute before restarting the jam. They stopped a second time and Trey counted off Albuquerque. If I Could was played for the first time since July 31, 1998 (119 shows).

Thursday, June 29, 2000
PNC Bank Arts Center, Holmdel, NJ
● *Set I:* Funky Bitch > Wilson, Limb by Limb, Drowned -> Rock and Roll
● *Set II:* Birds of a Feather -> Catapult > Heavy Things, Sand, Meatstick > Cities -> Walk Away > Run Like an Antelope > Frankenstein, Wading in the Velvet Sea
● *Encore:* Character Zero
● *Show Notes:* Birds, which contained a tease of A Love Supreme, was unfinished and melted into an atypical jam. Catapult was sung over this jam, which then led to Heavy Things. Brad Sands brought out Page's wife, Sofi, to dance with the band during Meatstick. They talked a bit about the couple's infant child. After a few fans tried to run on stage, Trey improvised a verse about Carini having his own song while Paul Languedoc and Chris Kuroda do not. He also mentioned Bart, Carini's backup on security. Trey then talked about the Meatstick Dance being a fad in Japan; he subsequently sang the Japanese lyrics. The lyrics to Cities were then altered to reference Tokyo, the Meatstick Dance, and sushi. Antelope included Meatstick teases in the intro. At the end of the second set, Trey thanked the crew (particularly Carini, for being a good sport). Trey mentioned how it is much of a "home show" for the band to play in Holmdel, and led one final Meatstick tease.

Friday, June 30, 2000
Meadows Music Theatre, Hartford, CT
● *Set I:* Ha Ha Ha, AC/DC Bag > Tweezer > Runaway Jim, Sneakin' Sally Through the Alley > Ginseng Sullivan > Guyute, Golgi Apparatus > Tweezer Reprise > Possum
● *Set II:* Halley's Comet > The Mango Song > Twist, The Inlaw Josie Wales, Back on the Train > Makisupa Policeman, Farmhouse, Sleeping Monkey > David Bowie
● *Encore:* Cavern
● *Show Notes:* The ending of AC/DC Bag was unusual, as Trey repeated the closing guitar tweaks for quite awhile before breaking into the Tweezer riff. The key phrase in Makisupa was a play on the blues classic One Bourbon, One Scotch, One Beer. Cavern included Tweezer teases and a Moby Dick tease after Trey introduced Fishman under that name. Ha Ha Ha was played for the first time since September 9, 1999 (55 shows).

Saturday, July 1, 2000
Meadows Music Theatre, Hartford, CT
● *Set I:* Buried Alive > Wolfman's Brother, Axilla, Poor Heart, Sample in a Jar, Tube, Beauty of My Dreams, Roggae, Vultures, Dirt, Split Open and Melt
● *Set II:* Gotta Jibboo, Bug, First Tube, Mike's Song -> Swept Away > Steep -> I am Hydrogen > Weekapaug Groove -> Nellie Kane, Ghost
● *Encore:* While My Guitar Gently Weeps
● *Show Notes:* Jibboo included additional lyrics that referenced Chris Kuroda and Brad Sands. Weekapaug was unfinished. Swept Away and Steep was played for the first time since June 30, 1999 (80 shows) and Buried Alive was played for the first time since November 27, 1998 (87 shows).

Monday, July 3, 2000
E Centre, Camden, NJ
● *Set I:* Down with Disease, Guelah Papyrus, My Mind's Got a Mind of Its Own, Foam, Bathtub Gin, My Soul, Heavy Things, Fluffhead, When the Circus Comes, Run Like an Antelope
● *Set II:* Runaway Jim, Glide, Theme From the Bottom > Sand, Meat, Chalk Dust Torture, Bittersweet Motel
● *Encore:* Waste
● *Show Notes:* A golf cart (and Trey's children) made an on-stage appearance during Disease. Foam was played for the first time since November 28, 1998 (87 shows). A large storm provided thunder and lightning during Gin. Gin also included teases of Elton John's Philadelphia Freedom. Antelope featured Tom Marshall on vocals. Glide (first since July 24, 1999, or 64 shows) included an All Fall Down Signal. Sand included a syncopated jam.

Tuesday, July 4, 2000
E Centre, Camden, NJ
● *Set I:* The Star Spangled Banner, Farmhouse, Rift, It's Ice, Bouncing Around the Room, Stash, The Lizards, The Man Who Stepped Into Yesterday > Avenu Malkenu > The Man Who Stepped Into Yesterday Reprise > Julius
● *Set II:* Gotta Jibboo -> I Saw It Again -> Magilla > Twist > Slave to the Traffic Light
● *Encore:* Lawn Boy, Good Times Bad Times
● *Show Notes:* It's Ice included a Star Spangled Banner tease. Lawn

Boy included a fireworks display on stage and in the pavilion, as well as well-wishes from Page; the fireworks signalled the beginning of GTBT. Four breakouts dotted the setlist: Saw It Again (first since September 10, 1999, or 57 shows), Rift (first since August 1, 1999, or 59 shows), Star Spangled Banner (first since July 4, 1999, or 79 shows), and Magilla (first since August 1, 1998, or 123 shows). This massive Jibboo was almost 30 minutes long .

Thursday, July 6, 2000
Molson Amphitheatre, Toronto, Ontario, Canada
● *Check:* Dog Gone Dog, I Wish I Was In Guelph, Jam
● *Set I:* Reba, Dogs Stole Things > Taste, Dog Faced Boy, Heavy Things, The Moma Dance, First Tube, I Didn't Know, The Inlaw Josie Wales, Prince Caspian > Golgi Apparatus, You Enjoy Myself
● *Set II:* Limb by Limb > Also Sprach Zarathustra > Bug > Piper, Driver, Harry Hood > Loving Cup
● *Encore:* The Squirming Coil
● *Show Notes:* For his vacuum solo in I Didn't Know, Trey introduced Fishman as "Mr. Ralph Blowenstein." Limb by Limb was unfinished. Trey made several comments during the show regarding his affinity for the venue. Hood included a small vocal jam during the intro.

Friday, July 7, 2000
Star Lake Amphitheatre, Burgettstown, PA
● *Set I:* Chalk Dust Torture, Gumbo, Divided Sky, Boogie On Reggae Woman > Funky Bitch, Maze -> Shafty -> Maze, Back on the Train, The Curtain > Character Zero
● *Set II:* Ghost -> Gotta Jibboo, Split Open and Melt, Roggae, Mike's Song > Simple > Weekapaug Groove
● *Encore:* Frankenstein
● *Show Notes:* Shafty was played for the first time since July 2, 1998, or 144 shows.

Saturday, July 8, 2000
Alpine Valley East, Troy, WI
● *Set I:* Punch You In The Eye > NICU, My Soul, Poor Heart, Wolfman's Brother, First Tube, Llama, Guyute, Run Like an Antelope
● *Set II:* Heavy Things, Piper -> Rock and Roll, Tweezer -> Walk Away, Twist, The Horse > Silent in the Morning, Possum
● *Encore:* Suzy Greenberg > Tweezer Reprise
● *Show Notes:* Antelope included a Jibboo tease. The band skipped the second verse of Suzy.

Monday, July 10, 2000
Deer Creek, Noblesville, IN
● *Check:* Ginseng Sullivan, My Soul, Too Much Of Everything
● *Set I:* Cars Trucks Buses > Wilson > It's Ice > Bathtub Gin, Buffalo Bill, My Mind's Got a Mind of Its Own, Split Open and Melt, Sparkle > Funky Bitch, David Bowie
● *Set II:* Gotta Jibboo > Sand, Twist, Fee -> What's the Use, Limb by Limb > Loving Cup
● *Encore:* Run Like an Antelope

Tuesday, July 11, 2000
Deer Creek, Noblesville, IN

● *Set I:* Ya Mar, The Moma Dance, Uncle Pen, Drowned > Chalk Dust Torture Reprise > Chalk Dust Torture, Theme from the Bottom > Cavern
● *Set II:* Also Sprach Zarathustra > Down with Disease -> Moby Dick > Down with Disease > Runaway Jim -> Moby Dick, Back on the Train -> Moby Dick > Back on the Train, Harry Hood > Moby Dick, HYHU > Terrapin > HYHU > Moby Dick > HYHU, Character Zero
● *Encore:* First Tube > Moby Dick > Chalk Dust Torture Reprise
● *Show Notes:* In keeping with the theme of the second set, Hood included a Moby Dick tease. During Terrapin (first since July 8, 1999, or 82 shows), Fishman was introduced as actor Russell Crowe. The Moby Dick inside of the HYHU jam featured Trey on drums and Fishman on vacuum. The Chalkdust Reprise was akin to the version last played on December 10, 1994 (387 shows), with the band singing the words "Chalk Dust Torture" over varied music. At the end of the encore, Trey joked that, if anyone missed anything, they should read the book or see the movie. Prior to this show, Moby Dick had not been played since November 29, 1997 (168 shows).

Wednesday, July 12, 2000
Deer Creek, Noblesville, IN
● *Set I:* My Friend My Friend, The Curtain With, Tube > Heavy Things, Billy Breathes, Beauty of My Dreams > Free, Axilla > The Squirming Coil
● *Set II:* Birds of a Feather, Piper, Crosseyed and Painless -> Prince Caspian > Meatstick
● *Encore:* Wading in the Velvet Sea
● *Show Notes:* My Friend (first since July 31, 1999, or 66 shows) was unfinished. During Meatstick, Trey thanked the crowd and dedicated the song to the fans who didn't get into the show. Curtain With was played for the first time since June 19, 1988 (1,044 shows).

Friday, July 14, 2000
Polaris Amphitheatre, Columbus, OH
● *Set I:* Sample in a Jar
● *Set II:* Punch You in the Eye > Timber (Jerry), Gotta Jibboo > Boogie on Reggae Woman, Stash, Bouncing Around the Room, Foam, Dog Faced Boy, Farmhouse, Taste, Golgi Apparatus
● *Set III:* Mike's Song > Frankie Says > David Bowie, Waste, Sand, The Lizards, Weekapaug Groove
● *Encore:* The Inlaw Josie Wales, Driver, Guyute
● *Show Notes:* The band was forced to take a long, 26 minute break after the Sample opener due to the torrential downpour that was raining down on the venue. Timber was played for the first time since July 17, 1999 (78 shows).

Saturday, July 15, 2000
Polaris Amphitheatre, Columbus, OH
● *Set I:* AC/DC Bag, First Tube, Limb by Limb, NICU, Dirt, Roses are Free, Wolfman's Brother > My Soul, Julius
● *Set II:* Down with Disease -> While My Guitar Gently Weeps, Makisupa Policeman, Piper > The Mango Song, Bug, You Enjoy Myself
● *Encore:* Loving Cup
● *Show Notes:* The jam out of Mango included a Have Mercy tease. The key phrase in Makisupa was "heavy nuggets."

Monday, July 17, 2000
KLRU Studios, Communications Building B (Sixth Floor),
University of Texas, Austin, TX

First Tube, My Soul, Limb by Limb, Horn, Heavy Things, Back on the Train, Beauty of My Dreams, Gotta Jibboo, Piper, Down with Disease, The Inlaw Josey Wales, Driver, When the Circus Comes, Twist, Sleep, Chalk Dust Torture, Wading in the Velvet Sea, Possum, Character Zero, First Tube

● *Show Notes:* This was a taping for the television show "Austin City Limits." Beauty of My Dreams was botched and restarted. Due to technical difficulties, First Tube was played a second time. After Piper, Trey responded to some fan requests and noted that the band saw Bela Fleck tape a performance for "Austin City Limits" in 1993. When the Circus Comes was dedicated to Los Lobos. The episode was set to debut on October 14, 2000, to kick of the show's 26th season.

FALL TOUR, 2000

Friday, September 8, 2000
Pepsi Arena, Albany, NY

● *Set I:* Mellow Mood, Limb by Limb, Ghost, Bouncing Around the Room, The Horse > Silent in the Morning, Saw It Again, NICU, Glide, Axilla, Taste, Golgi Apparatus

● *Set II:* Birds of a Feather, Windora Bug, David Bowie, Back at the Chicken Shack, Bathtub Gin > Jam > Character Zero

● *Encore:* Fire

● *Show Notes:* The jam out of the end of Gin featured Fishman on vaccum and Trey on drums. Windora Bug made its concert debut (though it had been played at "Carreystock" in the summer of 1999. Fire was played for the first time since July 23, 1999 (76 shows).

Saturday, September 9, 2000
Pepsi Arena, Albany, NY

● *Set I:* Possum, My Friend My Friend -> Jam > Gumbo > Maze, Boogie On Reggae Woman, Roggae, Guyute, Run Like an Antelope

● *Set II:* Gotta Jibboo, The Curtain > Sand, Makisupa Policeman, Cars Trucks Buses, Funky Bitch, Cavern

● *Encore:* Harry Hood

● *Show Notes:* Sand through Funky Bitch, and Hood, featured Michael Ray on trumpet. When he wasn't playing, Ray was dancing around the stage and exhorting the appreciative crowd. During Hood, he sat and relaxed in front of the drum riser before pulling several people out of the crowd, who proceeded to sit around the stage and occasionally dance. Trey thanked them as "the Michael Ray chorus". Sand included a First Tube tease

Monday, September 11, 2000
Tweeter Center, Mansfield, MA

● *Set I:* Road Runner > The Moma Dance, Rift, Brian and Robert, Vultures, Horn, Beauty of My Dreams > Ya Mar, Stash

● *Set II:* Chalk Dust Torture, Twist > Piper > What's the Use?, You Enjoy Myself

● *Encore:* Good Times Bad Times

● *Show Notes:* Brian and Robert included a woman on stage relaying the lyrics in sign language. Ya Mar included a syncopated jam.

Tuesday, September 12, 2000
Tweeter Center, Mansfield, MA

● *Set I:* Wolfman's Brother, Scent of a Mule, My Soul, Ginseng Sullivan, First Tube, Divided Sky, Wilson

● *Set II:* Down with Disease, Heavy Things, Split Open and Melt, HYHU > Bike > HYHU, Also Sprach Zarathustra > Mike's Song > I am Hydrogen > Weekapaug Groove

● *Encore:* The Squirming Coil

● *Show Notes:* After conferring with Trey before Bike, Fishman joked with the crowd, remarking that he only knows to songs. Before the vacuum solo, he introduced the band.

Thursday, September 14, 2000
Darien Lake, Darien Center, NY

● *Check:* Birds of a Feather

● *Set I:* Punch You in the Eye > Reba, Albuquerque, Carini, The Oh Kee Pah Ceremony > Suzy Greenberg, Suzy Greenberg Reprise

● *Set II:* Drowned > Crosseyed and Painless, Dog Faced Boy, Prince Caspian > Loving Cup

● *Encore:* Driver, The Inlaw Josey Wales, Sample in a Jar

● *Show Notes:* Oh Kee Pah was played for the first time since July 4, 1999 (93 shows).

Friday, September 15, 2000
Hershey Park Stadium, Hershey, PA

● *Set I:* First Tube, Gotta Jibboo, Corrine Corrina, Birds of a Feather, Windora Bug, Run Like an Antelope, Golgi Apparatus, Bittersweet Motel

● *Set II:* Piper > The Lizards, Tube > Jam > When the Circus Comes, Character Zero

● *Encore:* Possum

● *Show Notes:* Antelope featured Tom Marshall, as well as his daughter, singing the "Rye Rye Rocco" lyrics. The jam out of Tube reprised Tube proper.

Sunday, September 17, 2000
Merriweather Post Pavilion, Columbia, MD

● *Set I:* Guyute, Back on the Train, Bathtub Gin, Limb by Limb, The Moma Dance, Lawn Boy, Fluffhead, The Curtain With > Chalk Dust Torture

● *Set II:* Rock and Roll -> Theme From the Bottom > Dog Gone Dog, The Mango Song -> Jam -> Free

● *Encore:* Contact > Rocky Top

Monday, September 18, 2000
Blossom Music Center, Cuyahoga Falls, OH

● *Set I:* Carini, Sparkle, The Sloth, Maze, Guelah Papyrus, My Mind's Got a Mind of its Own, Sample in a Jar > Rift, Sleep, Prince Caspian

● *Set II:* Boogie On Reggae Woman -> Twist, McGrupp and the Watchful Hosemasters, Halley's Comet

● *Encore:* Axilla > Taste

Show Notes: McGrupp was played for the first time since October 7, 1999 (55 shows).

Wednesday, September 20, 2000
Riverbend Music Center, Cincinnati, OH

● *Set I:* Cars Trucks Buses, Wolfman's Brother, Gotta Jibboo, Mike's Song > Simple -> The Man Who Stepped Into Yesterday > Avenu

Malkenu > Weekapaug Groove, While My Guitar Gently Weeps
● *Set II:* First Tube > Limb by Limb, Dirt, It's Ice > Wading in the Velvet Sea > Sand, Guyute > Big Black Furry Creature from Mars, Drowned
● *Encore:* Cavern
● *Show Notes:* Ice was unfinished and included a long, atypical jam. BBFCFM was played for the first time since October 3, 1999 (58 shows).

Friday, September 22, 2000
Allstate Arena, Rosemont, IL
● *Set I:* Down with Disease, Meat > Poor Heart > Wilson > Slave to the Traffic Light, Dogs Stole Things, Bathtub Gin, Heavy Things, You Enjoy Myself
● *Set II:* Tube, Reba, Ghost > The Wedge, When the Circus Comes, Meatstick, Run Like an Antelope
● *Encore:* Bold as Love
● *Show Notes:* Meat was unfinished. Meatstick included Japanese lyrics. Also, towards the end of the song, the band faded out and allowed the audience to finish *a capella*. Antelope subsequently included Meatstick teases.

Saturday, September 23, 2000
Allstate Arena, Rosemont, IL
● *Set I:* Come On Baby Let's Go Downtown > The Moma Dance, Frankenstein, Halley's Comet > Fee, Stash
● *Set II:* Birds of a Feather, Tweezer > NICU > Scent of a Mule, Fast Enough for You, Piper > Character Zero
● *Encore:* Sleeping Monkey > Tweezer Reprise
● *Show Notes:* Downtown debuted at this show. Tweezer featured an ending typical for older Tweezers with a die-down akin to the *Picture of Nectar* album version. Some fans felt the jam out of Piper resembled My Left Toe.

Sunday, September 24, 2000
Target Center, Minneapolis, MN
● *Set I:* Mellow Mood, Back at the Chicken Shack, Sparkle, The Sloth, Divided Sky, Roggae, Punch You in the Eye, Sample in a Jar
● *Set II:* Cities, Free, Ya Mar, Carini, Lawn Boy, HYHU > Love You > HYHU, Cool it Down, David Bowie
● *Encore:* Fire
● *Show Notes:* Cool it Down was played for the first time since its debut on October 31, 1998 (127 shows).

Monday, September 25, 2000
Sandstone Amphitheatre, Bonner Springs, KS
● *Set I:* Everybody's Got Something To Hide Except Me And My Monkey, Down with Disease, The Lizards, Tweezer, Back on The Train, Water in the Sky, Bug, Julius
● *Set II:* Gotta Jibboo, Mike's Song > I Am Hydrogen > Weekapaug Groove, Axilla, Harry Hood, Funky Bitch
● *Encore:* Boogie On Reggae Woman, Driver, Tweezer Reprise
● *Show Notes:* Everybody's Got Something To Hide was played for the first time since October 31, 1994 (430 shows).

Wednesday, September 27, 2000
Fiddler's Green, Englewood, CO
● *Set I:* Sample in a Jar, My Friend My Friend, Beauty of my Dreams,

Chris Frank bangs the drum at Lemonwheel.

My Soul, Limb by Limb, Dirt, Split Open and Melt, Horn, Taste, Cavern
● *Set II:* Piper, Gumbo, Ghost, The Mango Song, Heavy Things, Brother, You Enjoy Myself
● *Encore:* Loving Cup
● *Show Notes:* Brother was played for the first time since July 28, 1998 (149 shows).

Friday, September 29, 2000
Thomas & Mack Center, Las Vegas, NV
● *Check:* Gingeng Sullivan, Mellow Mood
● *Set I:* Carini, Rift, Frankenstein, Mellow Mood, Wilson > Spock's Brain > Bathtub Gin > Character Zero
● *Set II:* Dinner and a Movie, The Moma Dance > Also Sprach Zarathustra, Fluffhead > Meatstick, Walk This Way, Rapper's Delight > You Shook Me (All Night Long)
● *Encore:* American Band
● *Show Notes:* Wilson included a heavy metal jam, complete with Trey waving his guitar in the air. Kid Rock provided guest vocals frrom Walk This Way through the encore. Walk This Way and Rapper's Delight (with funny stage antics from Fishman, who danced on his knees like Kid's sidekick Joe C.) were debuts. You Shook Me (All Night Long) was played, in its entirety, for the first time, although it had been jammed on other occasions. Walk This Way was also teased during Zarathustra. Spock's Brain (first since June 24, 1995, or 387 shows), Dinner and a Movie (first since March 1, 1997, or 238 shows), and American Band

(first since November 16, 1996, or 267 shows) returned after long absences. The Carini opener was preceded by a Wilson tease and saw Trey have several problems with his guitar. Meatstick included Japanese lyrics and Mike and Trey doing the Meatstick dance.

Saturday, September 30, 2000
Thomas & Mack Center, Las Vegas, NV

● *Set I:* Walfredo, The Curtain With, Maze, Roggae, I Didn't Know, Mike's Song > Simple > Saw it Again, Esther > Weekapaug Groove
● *Set II:* Timber (Jerry), AC/DC Bag, Colonel Forbin's Ascent > The Famous Mockingbird, Twist > Sand > A Day in the Life
● *Encore:* Emotional Rescue
● *Show Notes:* Though the band came out in position for Walfredo, they were forced to pause due to technical difficulties. For the second show in a row, several breakouts dotted the setlist: Walfredo (first since February 22, 1997, or 244 shows), Esther (August 9, 1998, 142 shows), Forbin's and Mockingbird (August 7, 1998, 144 shows), A Day in the Life (July 3, 1998, 166 shows), and Emotional Rescue (July 28, 1998, 151 shows). The Forbin's narration referenced the band's upcoming hiatus. I Didn't Know included a reference to Kid Rock's sidekick Joe C. Esther featured flubbed lyrics for the final verse, ending with Trey proclaiming "She died. Dead." As the band returned for the second set, the crowd serenaded Trey with Happy Birthday. Emotional Rescue included a bizarre synchronized duel on-stage between Trey and Mike.

Sunday, October 1, 2000
Desert Sky Pavilion, Phoenix, AZ

● *Check:* Back at the Chicken Shack, Ginseng Sullivan, Twist
● *Set I:* First Tube > Wolfman's Brother, Back on the Train, Beauty of My Dreams, Vultures, The Inlaw Josey Wales, Prince Caspian, Llama, Lawn Boy, Runaway Jim
● *Set II:* Roses are Free, Piper -> Guy Forget > When the Circus Comes > Camel Walk, Driver, David Bowie
● *Encore:* Waste
● *Show Notes:* Trey introduced the band during Llama (including Fishman as "Bob Weaver") before encouraging the audience to clap along with him. He slapped himself on the forehead and encouraged fans to slap the foreheads of the person next to them, but no one did. Piper was unfinished and morphed into the debut of Guy Forget. Paged handled the closing lick at the end of Bowie while Trey played with his pedals.

Tuesday, October 3, 2000
NBC Studios, Burbank, CA

Twist
● *Show Notes:* This was a performance on *The Tonight Show with Jay Leno*.

Wednesday, October 4, 2000
Coors Amphitheatre, Chula Vista, CA

● *Check:* Drowned
● *Set I:* The Moma Dance, It's Ice, Bouncing Around the Room, Funky Bitch, Reba, Dog Faced Boy, Run Like An Antelope
● *Set II:* Rock and Roll > Also Sprach Zarathustra, Sample in a Jar, Gotta Jibboo, Bug, Harry Hood, Cavern
● *Encore:* Loving Cup
● *Show Notes:* Antelope included a reference to Bob Weaver instead of Marco Esquandolas.

Thursday, October 5, 2000
Verizon Wireless Amphitheater, Irvine, CA

● *Check:* Funky Bitch
● *Set I:* Chalk Dust Torture, Guyute, Wolfman's Brother > Sneakin' Sally Through the Alley, Limb by Limb, Come on Baby Let's Go Downtown, Beauty of My Dreams, Axilla, Horn, Possum
● *Set II:* Drowned > NICU, David Bowie, Halley's Comet > Walk Away, Piper, Character Zero
● *Encore:* While My Guitar Gently Weeps
● *Show Notes:* Piper closed with an atypical jam. Character Zero ended with a slow jam where Trey quoted the lyrics to FEFY.

Friday, October 6, 2000
Shoreline Amphitheatre, Mountain View, CA

● *Set I:* Carini, Stash > Boogie on Reggae Woman, Mellow Mood, Maze, The Moma Dance, Run Like an Antelope
● *Set II:* Heavy Things, Down with Disease -> Spock's Brain, The Inlaw Josie Wales, Rift, Cities > Sand, Golgi Apparatus, Brian and Robert, Bold as Love
● *Encore:* El Paso, Chalk Dust Torture > West L.A. Fadeaway
● *Show Notes:* Glide was teased before the Carini opener and Jibboo was teased before Heavy Things. The encore, which included the debuts of El Paso and West L.A. Fadeaway, featured a Bob Weir guest appearance.

Saturday, October 7, 2000
Shoreline Amphitheatre, Mountain View, CA

● *Set I:* First Tube, Mike's Song > I am Hydrogen > Weekapaug Groove, Fee, Bathtub Gin, Glide, My Soul
● *Set II:* Twist > 2001 > Tweezer, Wading in the Velvet Sea, Meatstick, David Bowie, Tweezer Reprise
● *Encore:* You Enjoy Myself
● *Show Notes:* Meatstick included the Japanese lyrics. Appropriately, given the pending extended break from touring, the pre-show music closed with The Rolling Stones' The Last Time and the post-show music was The Beatles' Let it Be. During the post-show, the crowd gave the crew a standing ovation as they packed the band's gear.

SHOW REVIEWS

Many of these reviews focus only on the bare facts of the show itself. If you prefer this style, there is much to delve into here. However, I encouraged everyone to include any compelling stories as well, and to focus on their personal experience of the show if they like. It adds depth, personality, and variety to what could otherwise be a string of cold, critical commentary. After all, this is about sharing stories around the fire.

Most reviews were sent to us by the authors, while we scoured the Net for others. This collection spans from one of the first known Phish shows to the tour closer of summer 2000. Keep in mind that these just happen to be the shows that people felt moved to write about; they do not attempt to represent all "important" or "noteworthy" shows in Phish history. In fact, I rarely asked for a review of a specific show.

Jim and Dan accrued most of the older reviews. I compiled the last few years' worth, added many archival selections, and edited everything. Please note that pretty much every review here has received some degree of editing, be it the insertion of a semicolon, deletion of a parenthetical, or changes more substantial. Thank you to the scores of people who submitted reviews. Any confusion or errors should be blamed on me.

Original draft by James Raras, Jr., and Dan Seideman.
Edited and expanded by Jeremy David Goodwin.

12/1/84 Nectar's, Burlington, VT—Charlie Dirksen

A law-school comrade of mine was an undergrad at the University of Vermont in the mid-1980s and attended this show. He recalled that there were a few dozen people present for the gig, which was performed upstairs. He found the "Scarlet Begonias">"Fire">"Fire on the Mountain" memorable, but he could not recall any other details. It was an exciting and unusual evening if only because Phish had almost no material, yet Nectar let them play anyway. The upstairs of Nectar's apparently held around fifty comfortably at best, whereas the room on the main floor, where Phish would play at future Nectar's gigs (and where Nectar's famous gravy fries were served up), held around 150–200.

This is Phish's most highly circulated 1980s show. Many believe that it was the band's first show billed under that moniker, but in fact they played at least two shows with this name before 12/1. Marc "Daubs" Daubert accompanies Fish's thunderous drums with fiery percussion during the lengthy jam out of "Cities." This raging percussion and drums jam lasts for well over ten minutes. The Dude of Life sings lyrics he wrote on "Skippy the Wondermouse" and an insane version of "Fluffhead." If the music of "Skippy" sounds familiar to you, it is because part of its composition was eventually used in "McGrupp."

As at other shows in the 1984–1985 period, Trey's playing at this gig is so heavily influenced by Jerry Garcia, Jimi Hendrix, and Jimmy Page that it bears little resemblance to his style today. Check out the 10/15/86 Hunt's and 10/31/86 Goddard shows, played less than two

years later, if you yearn to hear Trey Anastasio's brilliant guitar artistry in its most primordial stage.

3/11/88 The Base Lodge, Johnson State College, Stearns, VT —Dave McGuriman

I have to preface this by saying this is less of a show review than a tale of my experience. More than twelve years have passed and not once have I owned a tape of this show.

As a freshman at Johnson State I spent most of the year partying in my dorm. This is because at the very first party I went to, they carded people to weed out us freshman losers. So after that I just never left campus. This was fine and dandy as political correctness hadn't yet taken over alcohol policies on campus, and the sky was the limit. My point is that not having anything else to do in a small town in Vermont forced me to head down to the Base Lodge for each and every show that happened. It was my money going into these shows and I wanted my money's worth from college!

Most of what I saw was a disappointment. I came from the classic rock school of thought. My favorite bands at the time were Yes and Genesis, and no one could touch them as far as I was concerned. This was mainly because they were so different from everything else out there. But I kept an open mind. The '80s were bereft of quality music and I had had about enough of it, but that quickly changed one night at the Slodge. (We called it that as a term of endearment. Also the Moose Lodge, Space Garage…the names go on and on.)

Anyway, there was a bit more of a stink made about this one show than the typical night at the Base Lodge. But that wasn't saying much; all it warranted was a slightly larger party than normal. Phish still wasn't that well known , even in Stearns, only thirty-five miles from Burlington. There were a few folks who made trips to Burlington to see them, but those travelers were few and far between. As for myself, it took this visit to my usual hangout to facilitate my first Phish show.

After some typical college preshow preparations, I went down to the Lodge, which was part of the student center. Strange that they didn't bring in enough of a crowd to play at Dibden (the auditorium) which isn't that big, but much bigger than the Lodge. The room couldn't hold much more than maybe a couple hundred, and on this night there was less than that. I kind of recall it feeling roomy. It didn't even take rubbing elbows to get to where I stood up front. I noticed that there were a few hippie-looking outsiders who had made the trip for the show. This in itself was pretty new to me. JSC had a large Dead following, but I hadn't been part of that so this Philly boy was in a new world.

Chris Intagliata

Once I got in place, I spent most of the night standing literally three inches away from Page's Hammond organ; in fact, I may even have been leaning on it. I watched the Leslie speaker spin round and round the whole time, and thought that was the coolest thing I had ever seen! I thought, "Man, what a cool band to have this neat thing." I was just smiling away and I caught Page laughing at my obvious amaze-

403

ment with the Leslie.

They opened with "The Chicken," followed by "Funky Bitch," both songs I had never heard before. The performance didn't impress too much upon me, but it was rocking, garage band-type entertainment so I wasn't ready to leave just yet. Next came "Sneakin' Sally." I was a huge fan of this song at the time and they didn't disappoint me by playing it. That sealed the fact that I wouldn't be wandering back to my dorm room anytime soon. Following this they played "Take the A Train." I didn't know jazz from a hole in the ground, but I did understand enough to know that this was not your ordinary band. It was the next tune that changed my life forever.

When I first heard "YEM" I knew that it was the end of an era. The lack of originality that marked the '80s had come to a screeching halt. This was the first Phish original I ever heard, and I was dumbfounded! This is the Phish sound. It's what differentiates them from other bands. It was incredibly refreshing to hear something so different. Yes, in progressive rock I had heard things like it, but this was different. And (for me) new. The way it kept intricately building into near noise until it exploded into a tight groove wasn't necessarily new to music, but the way this band did it was new to me. And such a distinct overall sound. Somehow it came from a band that came from the '80s. I sincerely thought I would forever be stuck in the world of classic rock from the '60s and '70s; yet here was a song that obviously was influenced by that music, but so different at the same time.

They had opened up with covers and I thought they were just going to be a cover band with a few originals thrown in for good measure. But song after song of composition and improvisation with sick jamming continually bombarded me. I'll be honest that the only other thing I really recall after twelve years is "Lizards". For some reason this song truly struck a chord in me. I left that night singing, "But I'm never ever going back there / and I couldn't if I tried / cause I come from the land of the Lizards / and the Lizards they have died / the Lizards they have died / the Lizards they have died!"

After this, I wanted nothing but Phish in my ears. I knew there was finally hope in the world...musically, anyway. I saw them again in two months; if not for lack of a car, the return would have been even sooner. In retrospect, this unsuspecting night at the Lodge changed my life.

7/30/88 Fly Me to the Moon Café, Telluride, CO —James Raras, Jr.

This show is remarkable, not for its musical prowess, as so many Phish shows are, but rather for its humor. The third set of this show contains what is, in my opinion, the most hilarious Phish moment ever. The first two sets of this show are a "Jazz Odyssey" (sans "Harpua" to close set two), which featured Mike on bass, Page on keys, and Trey on drums. Where's Fish you ask? Listen to the "Antelope" that closes the third set for a detailed and humorous answer from Trey.

4/20/89 Humphries House (The Zoo), Amherst College, Amherst, MA—Dan Purcell

This is springtime. Western Massachusetts is phenomenally green. You've just come from an experimental theater piece, staged in the middle of a clearing between periodic blooming copses of maple trees. Several of your friends were acting in the piece, not that you could see them so well—being outside and in the evening, after the sun went

down, the massive post-apocalyptic industry that comprised the scenery became an indistinct impression in the middle distance. And the identically costumed actors became essentially fungible, and even though you tried to respect the effort and conjugate the garbled message, the thing you liked best was this excellent stunt performed by this guy from eastern Washington state named Alec Hammond, a friend of yours, who was dressed in shoulder pads and a primitive football helmet, and on cue, starting from the very aft edge of the clearing, would sprint full-tilt toward the audience, only to be yanked back seconds before impact by the bungee cord tied to his belt, whereupon he snapped backward abruptly and lay parallel to and four feet above the ground for a minor instant before crashing to earth with a massive thwack! on his ass and clavicle.

After the show is over you go to a party. This is a Thursday night in late April. This is not a point in your life where you are a model of clarity. But you go to the party because this band is playing, and I've heard good things, and what else is there to do. The party is at the cooperative house at your college, where the residents (wisely, in retrospect) avoid the meal plan and fend for themselves. Once you get past the entryway, which smells like wet dog, you're hit by the aggressive macrobiotic stench of the kitchen, plates piled in the sink, pipe snaking wallward below the yellowed ceiling, beads of water dripping off the ferrule, message board with colored chalk, empty pasta box.

But the band. In the distance you barely perceive them, because the front room is crowded and you linger at the back. It's a spooky little groove in E minor. Somebody has spilled a Sex on the Beach on the piano keyboard. Over the minutes the groove picks up a hint of speed, crazy little piano accents forcing the guitar forward, more than a little evil. Your college has instituted a complex money-laundering scheme to provide students with beer and liquor. Not long ago your college had a powerful fraternity system. It is not entirely clear how the college justifies providing booze to teenagers, other than perhaps by encouraging them not to dogpile in cars and skid bloodily drunk across pavement out in the hinterlands returning from a bar that's tolerant of unlaminated out-of-state IDs. Every dorm at your college has its own piano. Which explains the tuition, maybe. This is, you realize, anachronistic. Now the band has sped up considerably. For eight bars the guitarist does some crazy fast hammer-on exercise. Then eight bars of weird atonality. Then the hammer-on again. Then back into the spacey, freeform rhythmic canyon, and you're wondering what the fuck does this sound like, anyway? You are having trouble finding a point of reference. The band, putting down their instruments, mentions they will be back a little later for another set. Here comes your friend Ian.

"Man oh man," he says to you. Ian is covered in dew. His shirt is stuck to his ribcage. "Did you just get here?" he asks.

"Uh-huh," you say. "How are these guys? Are they any good?"

"Psshhfffftttt," is his response. You interpret this as affirmative. "So how long did they play for?"

"About an hour and a half. Jesus, you shoulda seen them. First thing the smokers set off the fire alarm, so there was a twenty-minute break, and after that they came back in and played the Hendrix song "Fire" as a tribute to the fire alarm, and they played the shit out of it. They manslaughtered it!" He takes a long, deep breath. "So where were you?"

"What do they sound like?" you ask, not knowing, like you will soon, that this is basically an impossible question to answer in capsule format. Ian fancies himself musically oriented. To him they sound like

early Genesis, with composed keyboard-and-guitar fugues, variable time signatures, a scavenged stylistic blend of excursionary jazz, high-toned conservatory minimalism, and classic rock. But to the guy next to Ian, some friend of Ian's who you don't know, they sound like Frank Zappa: mocking sub-referentially and periodic formal cuteness. The band hangs out during the break. The crowd is not typical of those at parties at your college. Most people there you don't know, and you can't tell if the visitors are from the hippie college down the road, or from the state university across town, or are some sort of heretofore silent and anonymous subculture just now rearing its head for the occasion. If you wanted you could chat up the keyboard player, who's sitting there drinking a tumbler of warm and uriny U.S. pilsner with the rest of the house. But the relative weirdness of the crowd doesn't register right away. Later you synthesize some identifying characteristics: a faint human odor, knotted hair, charms on strands of leather—hippie accoutrements is what it smells like, you suppose. But at the time it was just a faint thoracic hiccup telling you this was something you hadn't seen before, generalizations be damned. And you stand in front of the bass player for the second set. Lots of things hit you at once. The guitarist is the most preternaturally cheerful guy you've ever seen. He has shaggy hair and a marginally successful red beard. His guitar is homemade (or it least it looks that way) and when he plays it his jaw works itself fore and aft and side to side until a fat smile cracks the tension in the mandible. Basically the guy's a juggernaut of untutored glee. He's wearing a badly-stretched bowling shirt that sags off his shoulder. And glasses, which is funny—a rock guitar player with glasses. Then there's the bass player, who's the weirdest-looking person you've ever seen in your life. His hair is cut in a bygone curly shag idiom; his eyes have gone beyond "hooded" into some cavernous geological formation; and his pants are much too tight, but too tight in strange places, like just below the knee and at the shoe-tops. And he barely moves at all, nodding sometimes, making no real effort to mimic the guitarist's excited bounce. But fuck! Maybe, upon further review, it's the drummer who's the weirdest-looking person you've ever seen.

His head is matted with tangled brown hair, and his beard is scraggly, and he's short, built like a wrestler with a giant barrel torso and stumpy legs. Captain Caveman is who he looks like, you realize, but in the dim recesses of your pop culture memory you can't even recall what cartoon Captain Caveman originated in, though either way this guy, give him a leopard-skin singlet and gnarled wooden club, is the spitting image. The keyboard player is easily the most normal-looking of the four, and you can tell that people probably tell him that all the time, with his relatively restrained haircut and shirt with a collar.

You're not exactly sold on these guys just yet, though. The guitar player fucks up the slow and quiet middle part of the set opener. After that they break into "Walk Away" by the James Gang, the kind of disaffected '70s romance that gives classic rock a bad name. "Yeah!" the keyboard player says afterward. The James Gang. You've gotta like it. You have to. It's the law. This is excellent stage patter. These guys seem to actually like their audience. In all honesty, that's probably not that unusual for a bunch of guys playing a former fraternity house on a Thursday night. But the audience likes them too. The band, as far as

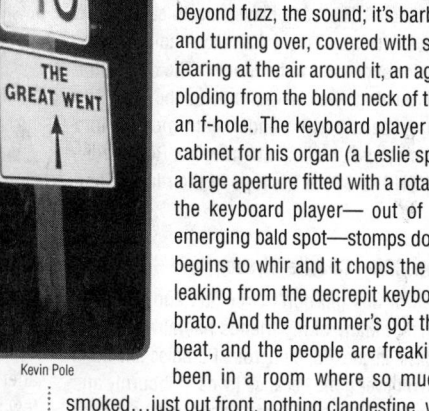

Kevin Pole

you know, has no record contract, and you haven't ever heard their songs on the radio, but the people at the concert know the names of the songs, they know the lyrics, and this is a challenge if you consider that the lyrics seem to be, on the charitable side, dadaist ramble. When the third song of the set repeatedly hops genres and rhythmic structures like a Halloween guest pulling off masks—first appearing as a prog-rock duet for guitar and organ, then a droopy lacuna of keyboard warble, then a pastoral piano tinkle conjuring images of falling leaves on a Massachusetts hillside seen from the window of a small car shooting the gap between elm-dotted basalt slopes at ninety miles an hour, then stop-time slap-bass solo, then time-shifting battle charge, then chromatic-scale raveup, finally revealed as a funky two-chord jam—they make each turn just as the band does, anticipating turns in a river they've been down before. Now the band is singing in falsetto over the funky two-chord jam. Newsflash: boy, they can't sing at all. The guitarist is probably the best of them, but his voice is thin and reedy and prone to cracking. The bass player's voice is bizarrely at the same time deep like a lagoon and high and shrill like a kettle whistle, but at least he seems to be able to hit the notes, unlike the keyboard player, who, well...forget it. But the guitar player is taking a solo. Standing five feet or so in front of the monitor you realize how short he is. His guitar sounds like a wet-dry vac. It's beyond fuzz, the sound; it's barbed, a long note stretched and turning over, covered with spires and prongs and just tearing at the air around it, an aggressive "hwhrrraw" exploding from the blond neck of this homemade guitar with an f-hole. The keyboard player has an excellent speaker cabinet for his organ (a Leslie speaker, Ian tells you later), a large aperture fitted with a rotating fan on the inside, and the keyboard player— out of place in his chinos and emerging bald spot—stomps down on a pedal and the fan begins to whir and it chops the juicy and viscous chords leaking from the decrepit keyboard into fat chunks of vibrato. And the drummer's got this aversion to the downbeat, and the people are freaking out and you've never been in a room where so much marijuana was being smoked...just out front, nothing clandestine, with a wet towel under the door, incense burning, window open.

"Here's an idea," your friend Drew, arriving late, says to you, eyeing the hippies as the two-chord jam erodes into some freeform a cappella piffle. "Howzabout this for clever: marijuana-flavored incense. Your parents come into your room and you're smoking weed and you tell them, 'No, I'm not smoking marijuana, I'm just burning this excellent new marijuana flavored incense.'" You nod at him. The next song is very unfriendly. The band isn't on particularly strong footing with it. By now the crowd is agitated.

"Lizards!" someone shouts. "Golgi Apparatus!" says someone else. You assume that's the name of a song.

"Drew," you say, "what was the function of the golgi apparatus in the basic cell structure?"

"What?"

"Like what did it do? I remember..."

"Whipping Post!" comes someone else."

"...the mitochondria was the powerhouse of the cell, but I can't remember...."

Now someone else yells "Whipping Post!" and you're thinking, the Allman Brothers, that's hardly a fashionable choice of cover, now is it? But these guys covered the fucking James Gang a minute ago, which is well down the road toward Molly Hatchet in your own personal opinion. But they also play a Syd Barrett song—when the drummer introduces it, coming out from behind the kit to sing, you shout out "Yeah!" since you and your pretend-eccentric roommate have been listening to "The Madcap Laughs" a lot recently. And you don't know it then (how could you?) but the taper in the back of the room, laying the band's every note down on DAT for time immemorial, captures your voice—and the drummer, who clearly can't sing and knows it and doesn't care that he can't sing, croons in a parched and barely intact moo before taking a godawful trombone solo where you realize he's done an amazing thing here and made a genuine trombone sound like a plastic child's toy. The thing is, and you're by no means some sort of fascist adherent of technical proficiency in musicians, this is really lousy. But the other thing is that the band knows it. And you quickly deduce that the second thing is way more important than the first, because that means that the drummer is singing because he wants to, funny as it might be, crappy as it might sound, and this is a little liberating. The last song of the night is the strangest: a half-sung, half-narrative epic about this nasty, mangy, evil dog. Midway through the guitar player digresses, talking about his own dog, "a nice little golden retriever," who was recently "shot in the ass by some obnoxious person." The bass player starts cackling to himself. "Not funny!" he says. "It's true," the guitar player admonishes, chuckling to himself, "it's not supposed to be funny." The dog in the song, though, the mangy bulldog, was never shot in the ass. The groove these four guys have been playing underneath morphs into "Gimme Some Lovin'" and they start, ad lib, to harmonize. Repeatedly, they're now singing "NON-SHOT ASS" at the tops of their lungs, and they cannot stop laughing.

10/6/89 Paradise, Boston, MA—Charlie Dirksen

Unfortunately, the tapes of this gig don't circulate, and I haven't heard it since it occurred. Many of my friends had already seen plenty of Phish shows (Molly's in late '88, numerous Paradise shows in '89…) by this time, but I had never gone because I was stubbornly and arrogantly into the Dead. I'd heard Phish on some hissy tapes back then (while at Boston College), but I wasn't sold. Two of my friends, Jon and Rick, compelled me to go to this gig, and I wound up having the best Bar Band Experience of my life up until that time. Since I can't use tapes to jog my memory, though, this isn't going to be much of a review.

If you haven't been to the Paradise, it is a small room on Commonwealth Avenue in Boston, next to Boston University, and it holds a couple hundred people at most. I don't recall anyone outside looking for tickets (it wasn't sold out), but I do remember that the Paradise wasn't full that night. There were a lot of people drinking beer over by the bar and talking during the entire gig. (That is, there were a lot of people there just to party who weren't interested in the music…sound familiar?) I remember that Fishman dedicated something to one of his relatives, because it was that relative's birthday. I recognized a couple of the songs they played, but not by name, and they didn't play "YEM." (Before this show, it was the only song that I knew and really enjoyed.) I vaguely remember the use of trampolines, which I found amusing. I was also close enough to the stage to touch Fish's vacuum, which I remember being there, but which I strangely can't recall being used. Fish,

for what it's worth, was (if memory serves) wearing his smock and goggles, which struck me as odd (how silly of me!). I had a great time at the show, with many college friends, and I thought Phish was the best bar band that I'd ever seen. I nevertheless had no idea that, within a decade, I'd be seeing them at venues like MSG and The Gorge for sold-out consecutive nights! You could tell, though, back then, that the band also had no idea that they'd be incredibly successful. They were too busy modestly creating brilliant music, having fun, and winning hearts.

12/31/89 Boston World Trade Center Exhibition Hall, Boston, MA—Jon Epstein

After many months of being into the band, I finally got my chance to go see them, the first in a tradition of Phish shows on New Year's Eve. My friend Dug and I got to the venue fairly early. The room, usually used for home shows and computer shows, had been set up with a stage and a small dance floor, along with a "buffet" of fruit and nacho chips, provided by the band. To start the show, Page, Mike, and Trey came out in tuxedos and started into "I Didn't Know," and then when it came time for the vacuum solo, Fish emerged from backstage, wearing a top hat and a g-string with tails. Fortunately, it was a short song, and Fish got behind his kit, fully hidden from my impressionable sixteen-year-old eyes. I was begging for the brand-new "Reba" all night long, but I never got it. However, I did get an excellent "Mike's">"Hydrogen">"Groove," and Page sang a dance song, "Satin Doll." What better way to bring in the '90s, but with the band of the '90s.

5/11/90 The Living Room, Providence, RI—Jon Epstein

A show that will forever live in infamy. There was a sign above the bar at the grungy Living Room that read, "Maximum Capacity 175." I estimate that there were at least four hundred in the room that crisp May night. After indulging in a little Sport-Death, a bad situation got a lot worse. Widespread Panic opened and they just multiplied the grunginess of that bleak place. The Living Room is an old warehouse that's been cleared out and set up like a club. The floor is covered with this black, quarter-inch-thick grime. It's just plain disgusting.

I thought things would finally get better as Phish took the stage after what seemed like forever. They started into "Mike's." After the first few notes, my friends, Andy and John, disappeared, and I was left to fend for myself. They had found a bench outside in an alley and seemed to find salvation there. Once the band started up "Foam," I just couldn't take it anymore. I could not handle that bass line. I tried to find refuge, which wouldn't come till I found an empty corner of the room during "Highway to Hell," the first set closer.

We seemed to mellow out during the set break and got right up front for the next set. It featured the saviors of the evening, "Tweezer" and Henrietta's spotlight, "Love You." Not to mention the "BBFCFM" encore with just about everyone slam-dancing. During "Lizards", if I recall correctly, a kid who was sitting on the stage under Page's piano got up and fell flat to the floor. It took him about a minute to get to his feet, and he arose with one side of his face covered with the Living Room grime. He looked at us and said, "I needed that." A shout picked up on the tape sums up the evening perfectly: "Would you calm down?!"

6/16/90 Townshend Family Park , Townshend, VT—Jon Epstein

A great show at the premier outdoor venue in New England, the Townshend Family Park. The stage was set up just on the outskirts

of a golf course in the middle of a field surrounded by a river. Just a great place to see a show. I was yelling for "Timber" and finally got it somewhere near the end of the first set. I also love this sloppy "Mike's">"Hydrogen">"Groove" for some reason.

12/7/90 Robert Crown Center, Hampshire College, MA —Jon Epstein

This is my favorite early show. It's actually the only time I ever showed up ticketless. And after asking a few folks, some guy decided he didn't feel like going in, so he sold me his ticket.

A very solid first set with my first "Stash" and a nice "Jim," and "Foam." But what makes this show for me is the "Llama" that closes the set. I love to hear Mike go as nuts as he does in this "Llama." It is a must-hear. Mike is just slapping like mad. Marley was working security out front and I hung with her for the set break.

Second set is another killer, featuring Fish with a diaper on his head, opening with "Mike's">"Hydrogen">"Groove," a jazz interlude with "Donna Lee," followed by "Caravan," the still relatively new "Tweezer", a Syd Barrett debut ("No Good Trying"), a killer "Bowie", and an "Alumni" encore. It's hard to match a show like that.

12/31/90 Boston World Trade Center Exhibition Hall, Boston, MA—Jon Epstein

Back to the World Trade Center a year later. The show was sold out. Ticketless friends of mine spent two hours telling tales of woe and fame to the poor woman in the ticket booth, who finally gave them tickets just to get rid of them.

There were about three to five times as many folks this year, compared to the year before. The stage was set up near the back of the room, while the year before, the stage had been set up near the middle of the room. Phish didn't go on until pretty late due to the opening band, Chucklehead, overstaying their welcome. The show itself was fairly lackluster, save for a good "Antelope" to close the show. After the "Antelope", the band got off the stage and was discussing possible encores, while my friends and I were standing right there making our suggestions. Unexpectedly, the house lights came on. The band took the hint, and thus ended the anticlimactic New Year's Eve of 1990.

5/2/91 The Chance, Poughkeepsie, NY—Phil Nazzaro

Due to the fact that a tape of this show has never surfaced, this review will have to consist of mainly my personal memories of the show. Most of the music has long since been lost to me.

The first thing I noticed after the trip across the Hudson River from New Paltz was how different the feel was at The Chance that particular night. We had bought tickets at the door, but many people were bummed later to find it had sold out shortly thereafter. However, unlike other sold-out shows I had seen at The Chance, this crowd seemed friendly and familiar with each other. Not like the drunken, rowdy crowds at shows like Joe Walsh and Johnny Winter. I had gotten this feeling at Phish shows before, but this night was different.

After getting into the tiny, ancient vaudeville theater, my companion and I walked past the merchandise table. I was already signed up for the mailing list, but after she jotted her info down, I wrote my name and a little note saying "hi" to the band. It was for this reason that I think the following happened.

After getting a spot to stand near the center and against the sec-

ond rail (about 1 foot up and twenty-five feet back), my friend went to use the bathroom. So there I stood, watching the opening band more or less alone when a guy came by and stood next to me, in her spot. Our conversation went something like this:

> Me: "Excuse me, but someone is standing there. She just went to…you're Mike Gordon."
>
> MG: "Yup."
>
> Me: "Cool. Pleased to meet you." (while shaking hands)
>
> Then a long pause passed by as we watched the opening band…
>
> MG: "Pretty cool band huh?"
>
> Me: "Actually, I think they suck."
>
> MG: (chuckles)

There was then another long pause as we took in Skratch Baxter. Then a couple of guys came over fawning, screaming "MIKE GORDON!" and asking for autographs. He obliged them, then excused himself as he disappeared backstage. About that time, my companion returned to her place beside me, and I proceeded to relay the story to her. Her response? "Well, don't look now, but Fishman is standing on your other side."

I turned to look just as he was leaving. Drat! Perhaps another time, Henrietta.

Eventually Phish hit the stage, and I remember a slow start followed by a toe-tapping "Rocky Top," and then an equipment malfunction. Our setlists remind me that it was "Colonel Forbin" that brought us a mystery guest on some large, odd instrument (reported to be a didjeridoo, but I remember it as one of those big horns they play on the mountains of Switzerland). "Sweet Adeline" was preceded by an explanation of how The Chance used to be a vaudeville theater way back when. Trey felt this was a good reason to sing "Sweet Adeline" without the benefit of amplification.

I believe it was during set break that some friends from college convinced me to join them on what passed at that time as "the rail": leaning against a five-foot stage, right at Trey's feet. I spent most of the second set marveling at Trey's guitar playing. I remember at some point being amazed by how many frets he could spread his fingers across.

I remember less of the second set then the first. But what sticks with me most is that when Fishman came out from his kit to sing "I Didn't Know," he was wearing that funky superhero suit he used to have. It was made of a red and blue satin-like material so form-fitting it looked like the seams were about to bust! Hilarious. As I recall, my comment after the show was "that outfit was so tight you could tell if he was circumcised or not." (No, I don't remember the answer.)

Oh well, I guess if I was to keep any memory of this show it would be Zeroman standing at the edge of the stage with only his face protruding from that tight, red hood with the tiny cape coming off the back of his neck.

Speaking of hoods, that's what the encore was, I believe by request. There were many people screaming what I thought was "hairy" when Phish came back onstage (not only did I not have many tapes then, but "Harry" was relatively rare). So Trey did a little speech that was lost on me, concerning the Vermont Dairy Farmers. And away we went….

5/3/91 Somerville Theater, Somerville, MA—Jon Epstein

This show is an absolute classic from the grand Somerville Theater. This was my first chance to see the Aquarium Rescue Unit, and I

was absolutely blown away. But on to Phish....The first set is high-lighted by "TMWSIY"->"Avenu" and a sick "Tweezer". 1991 was a pretty good year for "Tweezer", come to think of it. But games are always won in the second half, and the same holds true for Phish shows. The "AC/DC Bag"->"Curtain"->"Sloth" that opens up this set is incredible if only for the transitions. "AC/DC" just melts away and "Curtain" emerges right tin stride. And the "Curtain"->"Sloth" baton swap is the mind blower. "Curtain" fades out and "Sloth" fades in with astonishing power. I love this transition. We were also treated with a great "Jim" and "Tela," not to mention the "Harpua" with Jimmy watching the "Bruins kicking the Penguins' ass!" Get this show. I guarantee you will love it.

7/14/91 Townshend Family Park, Townshend, VT —Matt Laurence

After a small detour of 140 miles due to overshooting our exit a tad, we managed to wend our way to Townshend. We didn't get there until 3:00, terrified that we had already missed the first of what we knew were going to be three sets. But we were encouraged by the scene that greeted us.

A taste of things to come greeted all comers as we entered the parking lot; cars with Stealie hubcaps, tasty grilled consumables being grilled and consumed, T-shirts, T-shirts, T-shirts, and sack-hackers dotted the blazing, tangible sea of tie-dye and good cheer. Proceeding off through the woods, the human train of joyous aphishionados forded the mighty stream (mighty shallow, at any rate) that separated the parking area from the fields via a rickety, zig-zagging, wooden bridge that led, seemingly, right back into the woods. As one climbed the bank on the far side of the stream, up through the seaweed and the sli-i-ime, one emerged with astonishing suddenness into what truly had to be the center of the universe that day—the Townshend Family Park. This is no ordinary park, mind you, but a lush green bowl of trees and sunshine and water and vast plains of greenly stretching lawn with a well-secluded miniature-golf course hidden right in behind where the stage was located.

I had heard tell of rain all weekend, and that's what I expected. It rained everywhere else in the world on Sunday. The universe was gray...except for Townshend, VT, where the clouds parted and vanished altogether, leaving the undulating, sweaty, joyous crowd dancing, singing, and basking in the glorious heat of the day. All around on a plain of grassy wilderness were hundreds and hundreds of people doing all those things that people do when placed in a setting of ultimate perfection, just before the purpose for existing in that moment becomes fully clear.

And then it was all revealed to us. Over the next five hours, we were forcibly and wonderfully reminded exactly why it is that we follow Phish to the ends of the earth (or at least the ends of New England). They proceeded to play three of the most rip-snortin', kick-ass sets of music that I have ever heard anywhere. It was clear that the whole band was just as into the day and the weather and the scene as the crowd was, and everyone was grooving. The first set was played sans horns, as the guys started us off with a killer "Reba." Again, without setlist in hand I can't recall much, except for learning the true meaning of the word "peaked" as "Divided Sky" took on whole new worlds of meaning for me. Trey had me taking pictures of the Famous Mockingbird as it swooped down to land on Icculus' shoulder on top of the mountain to our right, which had crumbled and exploded before us just moments before. The horns were hoppin' with their color-coordinated tuxes, personal trampolines, and

shoe-dancing. The band was singing and swaying in the sunshine, Trey soaking up the heat and pouring it back out of his fingertips into the strings, Page riffing his way through massive solos in "Suzie" while basking in the shade, Fish did not one but two Henrietta appearances including the Doors' "Touch Me." And even Mike was rocking out, in a relative, Mike kind of way. He was smiling a whole bunch. And to top it all off, they ended with a hip, hot, happenin' "Big Black Furry Creature from Mars" that had everyone flailing and slamming.

Whoof. That's all I can say. While writing this, I have vicariously relived it yet again, and I loved every microsecond. The general consensus among those interviewed was that it truly was the best concert in the history of mankind. The day, the weather, the location, the crowd, and most of all Phish, made Sunday, July 14, a day that will never be forgotten for Phish fans anywhere. It's shows like this that make it all worthwhile.

7/14/91 Townshend Family Park; Townshend, VT—Noah Cole

Vermont mud season had just ended when the 1991 Summer Tour was announced. My friend Nate had signed up for the mailing list the previous fall during a private show in the dining hall of his high school (St. Paul's School in Concord, NH), and when the spring Newsletter came out we learned about some New England shows featuring the Giant Country Horns. I asked the Usenet community rec.music.gdead if I should go and Matt Laurence added me to "this new Phish mailing list" he created. This was the beginning of the Phish.Net, and the few folks here easily convinced me that Phish were worth a two-hour drive to the Townshend Family Park in southern Vermont.

With that in mind, Nate and I set off for Townshend on a rainy Bastille Day morning. One year to the day of my first Grateful Dead show, I knew that we were in for something special. We stopped along the way to pick up some hitchhikers on their way from the Rainbow Family gathering to the show. We almost missed the turnoff to the venue, as the sign was only a small piece of paper that said "Phish show."

We arrived at Townshend State Park to find the sun and friendly folks hanging out all around. We had the benefit of listening to the soundcheck while hanging out in the nearby campground waiting for the gates to open. The horns came through loud and clear. A Vermont state trooper was hanging out watching us when he was approached by a fan looking to camp. He tried to explain that he wasn't the ranger, but the fan persisted. Finally he explained it by saying, "Rangers are for camping, not cops. I'm a cop. I arrest people." He left it at that.

Getting into the show required a trip through the woods and crossing a narrow bridge over a small river where we were greeted by phalanx of security guys in yellow shirts who took our tickets and let us into a beautiful, open field with a stage at the far end. There were mountains on several sides, large expanses of green lawns, and a mini-golf course that combined for a magical feel. We were lucky that this was a daytime show, so we got to enjoy the surroundings throughout the day. I still had no idea what I was in for when we sat down to wait for the show to begin.

The first set kicked off with a comment from Trey about it being "National Nudist Week," although both Page and Mike were fairly well dressed compared to Fish in his dress and Trey in sweatpants. The show began with an insane "Reba" and moved through a number of early-'90s standards before a "Colonel Forbin's Ascent" complete with a narration from Trey that has Colonel Forbin climbing the mountains that towered

above the Townshend Family Park. The setting could not have been more perfect for the story; I was convinced that the Famous Mockingbird was on his way down from the mountaintop to enjoy the rest of the first set. After "The Sloth," one of the Giant Country Horns came out to lend some class to "I Didn't Know" before the set-closing "Possum."

During set break I wandered back to the mini-golf course behind the stage. I was quite surprised to see the band hanging out, waiting for the set to begin. I walked up to say hello and Mike returned the greeting. If only it were still so easy to go backstage. Before the second set began, Trey engaged in some audience participation by sending a string-telephone out into the crowd and making strange noises with the taut cord. The "Suzy Greenberg" that kicked off the second set has always been the one to which I've compared all others. The Giant Country Horns came out rocking and their harmonies created a version of "Suzie" so jazzy and funky that as far as I'm concerned shouldn't be played without them. It was the "Divided Sky" that brought me to another level. I couldn't stop looking up at the green mountains above me and felt like I was sailing above the crowd during Trey's solo. Fantastic. Much of the rest of the set, especially "Gumbo," "Split Open and Melt," "Magilla," and "Cavern," are immeasurably improved with the addition of the Giant Country Horns. I was very spoiled to hear these for my first listen, as it's never quite been the same since. The "Antelope" that closed the set was fun and rocking, bringing me to my feet to boogie during an extended jam with Spanish lyrics that reminded me of Santana. I don't think any of us there could have imagined that the next year would see both bands on the same stage.

Continuing my spoiling, I was treated to a third set at this, my first show. The GCH returned to kick off the set with an "AC/DC Bag" and "Landlady." The "Bathtub Gin" is especially memorable thanks to the interplay between Page's piano solos and the GCH. Mike got my attention during the bass solo in "Mike's Song" which got dark and evil very quickly. By this point I was completely exhausted and retreated to

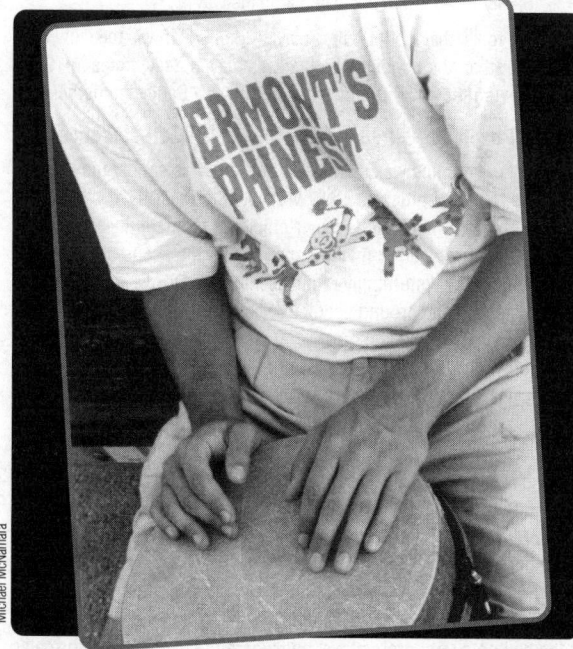

Michael McNamara

the outside of the crowd to watch the people as the "Weekapaug Groove" closed the "Hydrogen" sandwich I would come to love so much in the coming years. Fishman than ran off the stage to "take a leak" as the band jammed out "Hold Your Head Up" as the crowd waited. He returned for a hilarious (although off-key) rendition of the Doors' "Touch Me." The set closed with "Harry Hood" and I found myself singing along to a song I'd never heard before.

I laughed at "Contact" (this was the song Nate had been telling me about all along); what a perfect way to end the show. But it wasn't over. "Big Black Furry Creature from Mars" had me rocking and dancing my ass off before we gathered up our stuff and retreated to the car. I was filled with joy at this amazing new band I'd "discovered." I didn't know then what an effect this band would end up having on my life, but I couldn't have picked a better first show. If only every show had three sets in an amazing outdoor venue complete with the Giant Country Horns....

7/18/91 Casino Ballroom, Hampton Beach, NH —Ryan D. Stroud

This show is the oft-forgotten show of the tour. The tapes for this show are hard to come by. I managed to dig them up, and while the playing wasn't nearly as amazing as the rest of the tour, there are some humorous moments. Highlights from set one include a smoking "Runaway Jim" and a solid "Mike's Groove" with some very nice playing from the horns. The first set also includes some funny banter from Trey and company. The second set is the sloppiest set of music I've ever heard, but somehow they pulled it together for a fiery "Possum" set closer and the "Alumni Blues" encore, which also smokes. It's not difficult to see why this show is oft forgotten…just listen to what they did the next night!

7/19/91 Somerville Theater, Somerville, MA—Ryan D. Stroud

I've been listening to this show for a long time, and it has emerged as one of my favorites. I'm a huge fan of the July '91 tour with the Giant Country Horns. Many complained of repetitive setlists, but the horns really brought out a serious aspect in Phish's music, not to mention the amazing abilities of Carl Gerhard, Dave Grippo, and Russell Remington…those guys tear some serious solos. In my opinion, this show is amazing and should be heard by everyone. It contains some very strong playing and showcases Phish way ahead of their time. It's also one of the cleanest performances by the horn section—very tight, and very inspired.

Highlights of this show include a fiery "Landlady" with some gorgeous solos by all participants, and a "David Bowie" that sears with the often-unheard horn parts. The "YEM" from this show is also very well played. The second set, however, was one of the best of the summer '91 tour. It opens with a searing "Suzie," which drops into one of the best versions of "Divided Sky" ever played, then a jazzy "Magilla" with some interesting holiday teases, and a very humorous "BBFCFM." The "Lawn Boy" and "Frankenstein" encore finish the show in style. It's arguably the best show of the GCH tour. I'd say it's required listening.

9/28/91 The Rink, Buffalo, NY—Tony Brown

I had heard quite a bit about Phish before my first show at The Rink in Buffalo, NY. As a relatively active participant of rec.music.gdead, I had seen their name and read various comments about their per-

formances. In fact, my first Phish show should have been at Nietzsche's on 4/19/91 (my twenty-first birthday!), but I foolishly opted for the local Dead cover band that night. Perhaps due to the great summer tour with the Giant Country Horns, events like Arrowhead Ranch and Amy's Farm, and the increasing popularity of *Picture of Nectar*, Phish had become much better known in the Northeast between the spring and fall of 1991. Whatever the reason, nobody I know went to the Nietzsche's show—everybody was heading to the Rink that night.

The Rink is (was?) an actual roller-skating rink located near the corner of Main and Amherst in uptown Buffalo. The show had been heavily promoted. Phish posters hung everywhere on campus and the place was packed. I estimate that the crowd was about four to five hundred people. The parking lot "scene" consisted of four or five VW buses parked side by side. I did meet a group of tour-heads who had been on the road with the band for a few shows. Interestingly enough, they said they were from Oregon.

Musically, the song that stood out the most to me was "Foam," which to this day I believe may be the best single-song representation of the Phish sound. While my memory of the show itself is pretty hazy, there were several interesting things that occurred. The band gave an award for the longest distance traveled to a Phish show (Palo Alto, CA, to Amy's Farm in Maine), a record which I'm sure has since been eclipsed thousands of times. Trey rollerbladed around the rink during "Weekapaug" and subsequently leveled an innocent bystander, and they did the Phish show standards (trampolines, barbershop quartet numbers, "BBFCFM," etc.) that have won over crowds since the beginning. All in all, this made for a great first Phish show, but perhaps the thing I remember most is how the band was just hanging out on the rink after the show, playing with Marley and enjoying all of the good vibes.

12/31/91 New Aud, Worcester Memorial Auditorium, Worcester, MA—David Steinberg

It was cold this day…not merely chilly, but cold. I think the high was fifteen degrees or so. And since my friends had forgotten to get me a ticket (Phish selling out a show? Come on!), I got there at around 9 AM. Sure, that helped me to get my ticket, but I was nearly frozen by the time doors opened. So I sat around, watched the people with their First Night buttons try to convince the venue that this was a First Night event, and waited impatiently to be let in.

Oh yeah, the show…The fall tour was a revelation of sorts, featuring longer jams and different arrangements. So I didn't know what to expect from the NYE show.

The first two sets were okay. "Brother," a song that could either be boring or intense was quite intense this night. I was still madly in love with "Sparkle" then, so that was a treat. "Buried Alive" was the last song of 1991, which kind of bookended the year, since it was played as the first song of the year too, having been played following "Auld Lang Syne" during the previous New Year's show.

The highlight of the show was easily the third set. Yeah, it was short, but it was really nice. Trey came out with one of those little insult boxes (you push a button and it says an insult) and it swore at us during the "Wilson" intro. Then as "Tweezer" was ending, I got a song I thought I would never see—"McGrupp." An exciting (for 1991, at least) "Mike's">"Hydrogen">"Weekapaug" sent us home happy.

This show is kind of a "cusp" New Year's show. It was much more of a big deal than the '89 and '90 World Trade Center shows (especially the abysmal 1990 show), but it does not quite compare to the goofy stuff, song breakouts, and extravangazas that would start in '92. If you like Phish's playing from this period, you'll probably love this show.

3/11/92 Colonial Theater, Keene, NH—Matt Laurence

Overall, this show did not live up to the expectations set by the Portsmouth shows that preceded it, but nevertheless it was great to see Phish in such a fantastic theater. This show was very much like Portsmouth Friday, but with a few curves thrown in. They opened with "Suzy Greenberg," which I haven't heard them play in a while, and never as an opener; they did a nice "Split Open and Melt;" "Bathtub Gin" is always welcome; and I finally heard "Mind," which was new at the time.

I also decided that I liked the song "Mound" much better this time than the first time I heard it (at Portsmouth)—much like "It's Ice," it grew on me. They only did one musical language cue tonight, which was one incident of the *Simpsons* theme, and only about three other people seemed to know what was going one and did the "D'OHHHH!" with the band. I was hoping for more. Oh, yes, "Sloth" was a very nice addition. Also, the three-quarter-height V.I. Warshawski standee on Mike's amp not only added a touch of class, but from the balcony it looked exactly as if it was standing on Mike's shoulders. She also helped out in the a capella "Carolina." And Fishman sang a new Syd Barrett tune, "Baby Lemonade," and played bagpipes, which were fitted with a special attachment so he could hook the vacuum cleaner up to them and play without expending any of his precious oxygenic gasses. All in all, a pretty good show.

But the big surprise of the evening came during the encore when they whipped out a song I had considered retired for years, one which I have been hoping to hear for ages and asked Trey to play numerous times, to no avail. Or so I thought. I could not believe it when they started in and the words rolled around, the words I had been waiting to hear live for years now…

"Sanity never came my way (came his way)…"

Yes, folks, that's right—they played "Sanity!" It was the slow version rather than the hopping one that was played a few times in 1989, and Trey sang the lyrics out of order, but it was "Sanity" nonetheless!

3/14/92 Roseland Ballroom, New York, NY—Matt Laurence

First of all, the line was incredible. And this was simply the line for those picking up tickets…we were waiting for forty-five minutes just to get them (thanks to the ever-efficient resourcefulness of TicketBastard who refused to mail them out). And the scene outside was strange, and very disturbingly reminiscent of the Dead…lots of ticketless people roaming around begging, pleading "I need a miracle," and then turning out to have no money…it was hard to get rid of two tickets for even what I paid for them. Once inside, it continued to be a bit odd. Very few familiar faces, first of all, which was a little strange after going to so many shows with so many cool people for so long. Also, the crowd was more drunk, noisy, and not nearly as friendly as at New England Phish shows. I had experienced this once before, seeing them at the Capitol Theater. I chalked it up to the fact that they were opening for Blues Traveler and that it was just after school opened up again, but I now believe that this is simply the way it is with New York crowds.

Anyway, the place was very large, definitely more of a big-band-style dancehall than a concert venue: the band was set up at the end of the hall on a temporary stage, and where the band would normally

play was press and backstage seating. The second set began to smoke when they did the classic "Oh Kee Pah" into "Suzie" that they started to get into the set, and when "Harry Hood" came along, they were groovin'! They only played one new tune ("Sleeping Monkey"), but this was during a killer encore, and probably their smartest piece of PR all night…they brought John Popper up on stage to play with them for the encore (consisting of "Sleeping Monkey" and "Good Times, Bad Times"—another nice surprise!), which smoked right through.

The only other incident was the nearly religious transcendence I experienced while driving home. As I passed over the Whitestone Bridge, "Divided Sky" came on (via a crystal clear soundboard recording) and for about thirty seconds all I could see due to the upward curve of the bridge was the incredible expanse of perfect sky above the bridge…anyway, score another coup for Phish. I haven't had a chance to see the other reviews yet, but I can't imagine how even the discerning NYC review crew could help being wowed by our boys.

July 10, 1992—Empire Court, New York State Fairgrounds, Syracuse, NY—Martin Acaster

(H.O.R.D.E. Tour show featuring Aquarium Rescue Unit, Widespread Panic, Spin Doctors, Phish, and Blues Traveler)

I walked into Empire Court as a major Guns-N-Roses fanboy with a limited interest in Blues Traveler. I had a burning distaste for the Spin Doctors, no knowledge whatsoever of Panic or ARU, and had seen Phish once before in the fall of 1989. As is so often the case, I did not get IT at that first Phish show I had attended since at the time they were a "no-name" bar band who were most memorable for playing songs that were kind of long. I was way into the "rock is cock baby" scene of the Gunners and spent most of my concert-going budget on their shows, doing multiple night runs, traveling long distances, you know…touring…with GNR. When Guns-N-Roses wasn't on tour I spent most of my free time driving down to New York City to go to Limelight and "rave un 2 the light fantastic." The single set of music (with encore) that Phish played as part of this H.O.R.D.E. show changed all that.

ARU opened the show and got most people dancing in that loose, floppy, twirling, hippie style that I had observed at the eight or so Dead shows I had been to in the previous six years. Nothing at all remarkable to me about ARU. The Colonel guy seemed a little old to be in a band of this type. Panic followed and seemed to be to be living somewhere in the shadows of the Allman Brothers, Little Feat, and Lynyrd Skynyrd. All I could think of throughout their set was Axl Rose belting out Civil War right in the singer's face while Neil Young clubbed the lead guitarist with a ratty old acoustic guitar before schooling him on how to really play one of those electric things with soul. The Shit Doctors set found me spending a large amount of time in the beer garden, sitting under the smoking tree with my fiancée Wendi, and making the leap into hyper-reality as comfortable as possible for both of us.

As the lights went down on the stage, a bolt of energy seemed to surge through the crowd jostling before the stage. Four strangely normal-looking guys walked out onto the stage. They just didn't look like rock stars. Where were the leather pants? Where were the tattoos? Who are these nerds?

My live introduction to Phish came in the form of "Bouncing Around the Room." It didn't have the hard edge of the Gunners, there was none of the anger, none of the rage, it made me feel surprisingly good. The crowd before me bounced in unison to the tune. I bounced right

along with them. It was a simple melody, but it had such picturesque lyrics. I found myself swimming with the fish in the coral maze while the boat bobbed above me. This music felt good enough but was in no way overwhelming, sadly there was no real power to it. Of course the Carlos Santana on crystal meth style of Trey's guitar work in the "Llama" that followed drove me to my knees with its blinding ferocity. Who the hell taught this guy how to play guitar? I thought Slash was fast. My god.

Then it happened. "Reba." Nothing special as far as "Rebas" go. There are much better "Rebas" out there. But as the saying goes…you never forget your first girl. The song starts out oddly. Really bizarre lyrics about some woman making meat in her bathtub? What is this supposed to mean? Is there a message here somewhere? If so, what is it? The message I found was in the music that followed, of course. I had never before in my life been so touched by any musical performance of any kind anywhere. It was beautiful. I transcended all space and time. I cried with all the love and joy that was exploding from my heart. I was one with the universal. I was…bagged and tagged…I had become a Phish fan. The "bag it, tag it" outro and whistling of the opening melody had me laughing in hysterics. I got IT. I understood Phish. Absurdity to the point of transcendence before cascading back into the absurd. This band was special. They were different. They were beyond rock and roll. A musical leap of evolution. I wanted to be a part of this always.

The lyrics to "Sparkle" hit me squarely in my newly engaged chest like a sledge hammer. The creeping realization that I had made a bad decision tugged at the back of my brain. Suddenly I felt trapped. Trapped in a "Maze." The gods above laughing at my twists and turns as I tried to backpedal my way out of my relationship that was no doubt doomed to fail. I saw the future with Wendi winding out before me. It didn't look good. I was trapped. I'll never get out of this maze.

The fantasy world of communing with my "Golgi Apparatus" and moving on to the land of "Lizards" drew my attention away from my introspection and fears of the future. I was being toyed with by this band. They had a hook in my mind and could drag it wherever they wanted it to go. Finally, I succumbed to the direction. I completely surrendered to the flow. All reality dissolved. I was one with the music, the people around me, and the band. Nothing else mattered. Suddenly I was jolted back to reality. Who the hell was the homely chick in the dress sucking on the vacuum cleaner? What in all hell is going on here?

The time was here, my mission was clear….I set the gearshift to the high gear of my soul. Sadly, I eventually lost the girl I believed to be "My Sweet One," but the band has always been there for me ever since.

7/18/92 Mann Music Center, Philadelphia, PA —Kaz Wrzeszczynski

This show was one of several during the summer of 1992 in which Phish opened for Santana. Carlos Santana may have referred to Phish as "the Hose," but during this show, they were no better than a leaky faucet. The show lacked energy and creativity. The band was cramped to the front of the stage, having all of about five feet between them, and they played only standard versions of each song. Every song was played as it appeared on the album. "Reba" (during a beautiful sunset—this is where I developed my love for "Rebas" at sunset) was the highlight of the short opening set with the solo trying to take off, but hugging the album's version as if it were the walls of an ice rink. Coming away from this show, I got the impression that Phish is definitely not an opening band.

11/28/92 Capitol Theater, Port Chester, NY—A.J. Abrams

Sadly, this terrific show turned out to be Phish's final show at the historic Capitol Theater. The Capitol had become a regular tour stop for Phish, yet at the time we had no idea this would be the final show there. And what a fun and fantastic farewell this show was! There were many special moments that occurred at this intimate show that would never happen today at the huge arenas Phish play. Opening the show with "My Sweet One" gave no indication of the musical magic that was to come later on, but it did provide an early glimpse of the craziness that was to follow throughout the whole show.

In the middle of "MSO," Mike developed problems with the bass, and the band took a long pause while it got fixed. "This is what we call Capitol punishment," Trey joked. The audience immediately disapproved of this bad joke and shockingly, a loud chorus of boos echoed through the theater. This was probably the only time that Phish was ever booed at a show (well, besides the Portland 12/11/95 show when they asked to be booed), but it was hilarious. Fishman responded humorously by saying, "You didn't pay to come hear jokes. Let's not hear any complaints about the jokes." The first set came to a rousing conclusion with an absolutely perfect version of "Mike's">"Hydrogen">"Weekapaug."

This entire "Mike's Groove" was spectacular and was an incredible way to end the first set. This "Hydrogen" was beautifully done and the "Weekapaug" was just pure adrenaline and bliss. It was raging fast and furious yet somehow gorgeous and melodic at the same time. Trey just went off with spine-tingling guitar solos that climaxed over and over at the end of the jam segment. It seemed like this energetic supercharged "Weekapaug" was just never going to end.

A terrific and upbeat version of "Tweezer" that contained teases and jamming of the rare "Alumni Blues" was the early highlight of the second set. This jam eventually segued into the "Big Ball Jam." The rows of seats sloped up higher and higher towards the back of the theater. So, as the balls rolled higher and higher towards the back of the auditorium, the band played music that gradually got higher and higher in key and volume. And as the balls rolled back towards the stage the music got lower and lower. The band would go "KABAAM" as the balls crashed into walls and skidded across the heads of the audience.

During a beautiful "TMWSIY" > "Avenu Malkenu," tears came to my eyes for the first and only time at a rock concert. Phish transformed the historic theater into the historic holy temple of rock and roll. This was an emotional moment for me, as I had visions of both my past and future simultaneously. As I fondly looked back on my memories of singing the Jewish song in synagogue with my father, I looked forward to singing this song with Phish in concert arenas for years to come. Tears dripped down my cheeks as I realized I was witnessing history in the making and that Phish would become a legendary band one day. I thought that any band that could bring tears to the eyes of this cynical and jaded rock fan must be doing something special. For some strange reason, they play "Maze" immediately after "Avenu" and then return to the "TMWSIY" finale after "Maze." "Bouncin'" was terrifying, as the theater's balcony was literally and dangerously doing just that. Back then, it was very scary to be sitting directly under the balcony and watching it move inches up and down as people danced. It's a miracle none of those balconies ever collapsed under the weight of hundreds of aphishionados bouncin' around the room in unison.

During "Terrapin," Fishman tortured the audience with an obnoxious five-minute vacuum solo while he simultaneously bashed on a gong. He later apologized for the long solo and said the name of the number was "Woody's Gong." As Fishman finished up his act, shouts of "Harpua" rang out from the audience. The band obliged and launched into an incredibly fun version of "Harpua" that contains a narrative about the inside of Fishman's head. Trey also said that Jimmy was sitting on his couch and "listening to the classic rock station, listening to the big hit song…." And then the band busted into a brief verse of the Spin Doctors' "Jimmy Olson's Blues." This jab at the Spin Doctors was quite appropriate because at the time they were the media darlings, and Phish was basically being ignored or ridiculed as being a bunch of nerds. Believe it or not, critics were predicting that the Docs were going to be the next big hippie jam band, to take over when the Dead would retire. The Docs did indeed sell millions of albums that year. But I knew that the Docs were a cheesy, wimpy, one-hit wonder and that Phish would go down in rock history as a legendary live band. Although Phish and the Docs were friends at the time, I'm sure Phish was frustrated that a band much less talented had become enormously successful while Phish themselves were being ignored by everyone except their small cult following.

As the band came out for the encore, Trey announced that his grandmother was at the show and "Contact," her favorite song, was dedicated to her. The final of many hilarious moments happened when the band messed up the beginning of "Contact." "This one's for you Grandma Jean," Trey jokingly said. They then started all over again, but screwed up the tune a second time! Finally, on the third try they got the song right. Next the moment turned from funny to heartwarming as Trey brought Grandma Jean on stage and waltzed with her as the band continued to play "Contact" in the background. The crowd got a huge kick out of this as they "OOHed" and "AHHed" with every dance step. It was a lovely and tender way to celebrate the end of an era of classic Phish shows at the Capitol.

12/31/92 Matthews Arena, Northeastern University, Boston, MA—Noah Cole

This show was the final show of 1992, the largest show Phish had yet played (by themselves). With six thousand people, it was an appropriate growth in size for a New Year's show. The year before, at the New Auditorium in Worcester, the previous record was set at thirty-five hundred people. 1992 saw Phish go to Europe for the first time, open for Santana, and write much of the material that was to appear on *Rift*. This New Year's show was to be an appropriate end to an excellent and groundbreaking year.

I went to this show with my friends Andrew and Zach and my brother Ethan. It was their collective first show and they were very excited. Andrew flew out from California and was not the only one who did. In 1991, awards were given to people who traveled across the country for Amy's Farm. By the end of 1992 there were more than a handful of people willing to fly across the country for New Year's Eve. We drove down from Vermont and had just entered New Hampshire when we were passed by another car going to the show. They were looking for extra tickets. By the time we got into Boston, navigated rush-hour traffic, and found our way to the show, we found many other people looking for tickets as well. At this show, for the first time, I even saw counterfeit tickets. We were staying at the YMCA, which was immediately adjacent to Matthews Arena, thanks to Phish.Net organiza-

"*Gone Phishin*"

Jonathan Healey

The idea for this essay arose during a long, exhausting tour from Westport, CT, to Limestone, ME, with my friend, Matt, and the hundreds of other cars that followed toward the same destination. When I questioned myself about the idea of traveling so far and watching nineteen shows, I found myself in a caught up in a moment of liminality. Since then, I have had the time to deliberate and consider why I choose to spend my summers and vacations following a band around the country: a search for community.

The year was 1992, and it was the first day of the school year and my second year at a private boarding school in Connecticut. My first year at Suffield Academy was spent in the library, studying for SATs and college entrance exams. That first year, in retrospect, seems worthy since that was the year I anchored myself, preparing for a college career to happen a year and a half later. At the time, that year was thought of as an unwelcome, inconvenient change to my social life and an uncontrollable disruption to my freedom to experience all things; not to mention, it was a diversion from meeting new people, an essential part of a new student's agenda. I became an outcast, subject to strange looks from the school's veterans and looks of intrigue from those with whom I had rather not be associated. At the end of that year, I told myself that my senior year was going to be different and, indeed, it turned out unlike any other senior year.

Like every new school year, it was a time to start something new. The most common way to recognize this is noticing all the new clothing people buy to wear around campus. For me, it was much more than new clothes. I chose to wear a cape of independence, contrary to a cloak of conformity. With my trusty cape, I soared into the dormitory aghast to the friendly welcomes from my dorm-mates. My bedroom was much bigger from the one I lived in a year before, but I guess I deserved it; after all, I was a senior. I did not know who my new roommate was going to be, so I waited by picking my bed and unpacking my belongings. Earlier than expected, my door slammed open. Someone stood in the doorway with his back turned toward me, talking to somebody in the hallway. It seemed that he, too, was very welcomed since he joked and played with the people in the hallway. "Ready for another exciting year at S.A., Healey?" the person said without turning around.

Hesitant with my answer, because I still was unable to tell who this person was, I said, "Well, if I can make a change from the years in the past, I guess so."

The boy turned, my jaw dropped and he pronounced a huge grin, "Well get ready, 'cause you're living with Cookerville U.S.A.!" I could not believe it. It was Chris Cook, the nominee for the "Most Seen with Maintenance" superlative, a title reserved for the student who collected the most days in suspension. Even though I wanted this year to be my big year of change, I did not have the slightest notion that it would be spent with this wing nut. Wing nut or not, what I did want this year was to find my niche. I never imagined that Chris would become the person to uncover it for me.

In the months that passed, I discovered that Chris was not the boarding-school-bad-boy that everyone had made him out to be. Chris was not an outlandish, obnoxious person; instead he was quite the contrary, a diamond. I used to compare him to Bart Simpson; he always chose to do the right thing, but he took the hardest road to get there, which made him disorderly at times. Chris could never see the easy route, because sometimes one has to conform to take the golden road, and Chris had trouble with conformity. Chris taught me a lot of things, but one lesson that I still practice today is the seasonal ritual of "Phishing." Chris told me that going to a Phish show is like studying an interesting American culture. While it is reminiscent of a Grateful Dead show of days gone by, Phish manages to create a new mystique. The Phish aura is created from their music, which goes beyond an everyday band's sound.

It was morning and I woke up to the surprise of the first snowfall. This is one of the only times when I am excited about waking up and heading for the outdoors. The other time is the morning of a Phish concert. That day, although I did not know it, I was going to get the best of both worlds. Chris and I drove an hour and a half to Portchester, NY, where the concert was being held. As the two of us pulled into the venue's parking lot, I saw hundreds of patchouli-laden fans wearing tattered clothes. It was four hours to showtime and I wondered why so many people would drive so far to convene on a snowy Saturday, so early before a concert. Their faces glowed and they showed the emotion of joy, but they also seemed sad. It was as if they felt sorrow because they could not stay in the parking lot forever. These people indulged in what most people expect from life, nationalism and the pursuit of happiness, yet they were a cult . As contrary as it may seem, they formed an allegiance to a band in order to fulfill life's goal, and I would soon become one of them.

(continued on the next page)

tion by Rich Fromm. My first meeting with Ellis Godard and his girlfriend Kristen (now his wife) came before the show and they, like everyone else in the area, were ready for a great night.

It was a warm evening (for December in Boston), and there were many people hanging around outside the venue. Immediately upon entering Matthews Arena, the Northeastern University Hockey Arena, we were handed a flyer:

WELCOME TO THE SHOW!!
PLEASE READ THIS CAREFULLY

As you may already know, tonight's concert will be broadcast tomorrow, January 1st, at noon on WBCN (104.1 FM). In other words, we've been blessed with the opportunity to play with people's minds. We've come up with a bunch of new "language" signals designed to confuse and confound the average radio listener.

"Gone Fishin" *(continued)*

I would transcend into a nomad migrating between two communities and two identities.

As we waited for showtime, everyone in "the lot" seemed like relatives. Together they cooked over propane grills, talked like old friends lounging before a television in a living room and, occasionally, yelling themselves hoarse for Phish, in anticipation for the concert to come. Here amid the smoke from burning grills and the smell of sizzling grilled cheese I discovered something new: loyalty.

Chris and I were perched on the tailgate of my Jeep eating a vegetarian burrito, as we watched the Phish ramblers roam the Capitol Theater's parking lot. I had never seen such an inspiring spectacle, nor a culture this intriguing. I began to question Chris about this community whose neighborhoods reappear in amphitheater parking lots every tour like desert flowers after a rain. I pulled up the earflaps on my cherry tree baseball cap so I would not miss a word he said. He told me about the band's constant touring pattern and how their best renditions are only heard live. Chris explained how the band's songs intertwine and explain stories about real-life things. "They sing this story," Chris said, "that is a combination of eight individual songs. Each song describes a different act, in this play. There is one song where they tell a story about a Rhombus and all the people that live in the town who go to the Rhombus to pray."

"A rhombus?"

"Yes, it is a little far-fetched, but that's what these guys are all about. At the end of the show, you'll be thinking the music is far-fetched, too."

Next, he described the tape-trading network that allows fans to record the concerts and then trade the cassettes. Illuminated, I discovered that there were many facets to Phish that transcended the simple act of playing or listening to music and created a subculture of die-hard devotees.

After Chris and I walked a loop around the parking lot, he decided it would be good time to head towards the theater. Passing rows of Volkswagen micro-buses and Volvo wagons, I could feel the crowd's energy began to rise. People were hollering for Phish and chanting lyrics to their favorite songs. Some people hopped to the show, and others jogged, but Chris and I were content walking. As we roved closer to the building, the legion became larger and more condensed. The line for admission was short, but Chris told me that it would wrap the building in minutes, and sure enough, it did. Everyone was forced to shuttle towards the turnstiles. I was next in line to have my ticket ripped into a stub. My body was tense and jittery. My hand was shaking as I gave the usher my ticket. The older fellow handed back a seat number to me and we walked into the lobby where people were whispering rumors about what the band chose to play for the night's setlists. There was an energetic vibe flowing through the reconditioned movie theater. We took a turn at the end of the anteroom and before our eyes we saw the stage.

Minkin paintings were hoisted from cables in the background, while a grand piano and a drumset served as bookends for the stage set. There was a purple glow that shined on the band's instruments, especially on the metallic parts of the drum kit. A moment later, the lights dropped and Chris grabbed me, "Quick, they're coming on!" He rushed me to a seat that was situated five rows back off to the left. The band came on and they began to play their music. Some people began to bound joyously and others starting spinning in circles. Chris was bobbing his head and extending his arms towards the ceiling. For the next three hours or so, I was left speechless. I just stood there, wide-eyed, and absorbed the scenery.

The concert came to an end around eleven-thirty. Again, everyone shuttled towards the exit, minding the security. It was interesting how so many people could become crunched together, but still remain in the best of spirits. Chris and I returned to the merriment of the parking lot. Things were same, except it was dark and most of the people were buzzing from the show. I then began to feel the same sorrow that I had noticed, inside the fans, when we pulled into the parking lot earlier that day. I, too, didn't want to leave and instead I felt as if I should stay in this parking lot all night.

Since this first Phishing experience, I've been to sixty-eight Phish concerts. Each time I go through the same emotions of extreme joy and then a longing to stay forever inside this shanty town. Usually, it takes me a few hours to find the motivation to leave one of the band's concerts. I have not seen Chris since we left Suffield Academy and I really wish I could have just one more time like this one to share with him. My senior year at Suffield, and the rest of my life, has been altered from that night at the Capitol Theater. At first, I had no idea that I was evolving into a Phish extremist, constantly exchanging information about a band and their fans. Chris ended my search for community that night. I found something bigger than myself to become a part of. I'm not quite sure what Phish will have in store for their future. Their music seems to change from summer to summer, but the thing that remains the same is the caravan that follows. Like the generations before them, this fan base is searching for the ultimate groove. Simply, we live for the next show and maybe Phish will be the band that provides us with this ultimate groove.

These signals will be written on signs and held up by Trey at various times throughout the night. This list explains each signal:

#1) MASS HYSTERIA If Trey holds up a sign that says "Mass Hysteria" it means you should scream hysterically. Imagine turning on your radio and hearing six thousand people screaming in terror…sort of a *War of the Worlds* thing.

#2) FOOT STOMP Instead of cheering or clapping, you would stomp your feet. (Again…imagine this times six thousand.)

#3) YAY/BOO When Trey holds up this sign and then points up you would "yay" and when he points down you would "boo," alternating quickly these would be pretty surreal.

#4) EGGPLANT This would mean that Trey would raise his arm and when he drops it, you would scream "Eggplant!!"

#5) ONE CLAP When Trey holds up this sign, do nothing until he first raises his arm, then drops it, at which point you would clap once loud. That way we can do something like introduce Paul and the whole crowd will clap once in unison. (Very strange to the listener.)

#6) LIP-FLOP You would flop your lips with your finger while humming (x6000 people).

#7) SNAP Everyone would snap their fingers at no particular rhythm…sort of a white noise snapping thing.

#8) WHISTLE This means whistle a random note.

That's it…we don't know if or when we'll use these, but it's good to be armed with some ammunition. Also, thanks for a great year and we're glad you can be here to start off a new one.

Trey, Mike, Page, and Tubbs

P.S. There are several trash cans in the lobby labeled "RECYCLE" on them; please seek them out and place these papers in there when the show is over.

The show was general admission and the atmosphere fairly relaxed. There was a second row of speakers about halfway back on the floor, which even added to the spectacle of the thing—it was New Year's Eve and this place is huge! We started out on the floor but after wandering around for awhile wandered upstairs and grabbed front-row seats in the balcony, which provided a great view of the fans and the band and average sound. The show opened with a hot "Buried Alive" that warmed up the crowd. "Bouncing Around the Room" was well played and well received, with thousands of spinning people. "Wilson," without crowd chanting, had an excellent opening. "Divided Sky" was extended, clocking in at just under fifteen minutes with some beautiful solos by Page and Trey and strong jamming together as a band. Leading out of the "Divided Sky" were average versions of "Cavern" and "Foam." Following these was "I Didn't Know," which I've always enjoyed, musically simple yet silly enough to appeal to the kid in me. This was the first appearance of the signals mentioned in the flyer, with the audience yelling "yay" and "boo" in response to Trey's signs, which he really seemed to get a kick out of. The "Antelope" that closed the set was high energy and intense with Trey playing the rock star in his solos. Being a hockey arena, the sound was only fair and it echoed on and off. It was a tough space to work in, and one of their first shows in a large space, so I still give the sound crew credit.

The second set was the most disjointed of the evening, a little more diverse than the first set although it definitely had its high points. Kicking it off was "Runaway Jim," another fun song to get the audience going. "It's Ice" was standard, although fitting given that we were in a hockey arena with the ice only slightly covered by cardboard on the floor (and by the end of the show people had ripped up the cardboard and were dancing on the ice). "Sparkle" was average and led into the evil beginning of "Colonel Forbin." The narration was about a giant spaceship coming into Boston and lifting Matthews Arena into the air. The "Mass Hysteria" signal came into play as the audience screamed and Trey described how Matthews Arena was elevated into the air and spun around and the audience was pressed against the sides of the building. Everyone then grabs onto a pole in the center of the arena, and the arena/spaceship takes a tour over Boston Harbor and then slowly sinks down underwater. Eventually, everyone inside becomes solid rock and we sit there, underwater, for thousands of years. Then the Ice Age comes along and brings us up to the surface where everything is different—we've entered "Gamehendge." We see a mountain off in the distance where Colonel Forbin is climbing the mountain in search of the Famous Mockingbird. As Trey describes how the Famous Mockingbird

is flying along, and begins the song, Brad, dressed in full bird costume as the Famous Mockingbird, is lowered from the ceiling of Matthews Arena and proceeds to fly around flapping his arms. It was hilarious, and like many things I've seen at Phish shows, it had everyone in the audience trying to laugh and cheer at the same time. A quick "My Sweet One" was followed by a very big "Big Ball Jam" and a solid "Stash." Following a crowd-pleasing "Glide," I was really happy to hear "Good Times, Bad Times," being a Zeppelin fan and not having previously seen it performed. This was Phish getting into their full arena-rock mode and reaching the climax of the second set in the last hour of 1992.

At the set break, the crew came out and readied some extra stuff on stage. Where the midnight antics the year before had been fairly sparse, their intense touring and growth had paid off and they were finally in a position where they could rig up something exciting for themselves and their crowd. This has continued to this day, seeing Phish pull such crazy stunts as flying around Boston Garden in a giant hot dog and rigging a large screen on the ceiling of Madison Square Garden to project computer graphics.

But tonight it was still 1992 and when the lights went down a few minutes before midnight, one of the greatest "Mike's Groove" ever exploded out of the starting gate. The "Mike's" combo has the ability to carry a show for me and is one of my favorites. I attribute my love of this song to its performance here, at a crucial stage of my Phish listening. The "Mike's Song" is excellent with Trey saying, "We've got about one minute left, better make it good," and he starts the countdown at thirty seconds. When he gets down to zero, they break into "Auld Lang Syne." It was the first time ever that they didn't go into "I Am Hydrogen," but it didn't matter. The lights went up and confetti guns onstage rained confetti on the band as other confetti machines around the arena rained confetti on the crowd. After the short yet sweet "Auld Lang Syne," they headed directly into a smoking "Weekapaug Groove" where they were on fire. This is one of the best "Weekapaug Grooves" ever performed. After this they stopped and sort of looked around at each other smiling. Trey told us that this was going to be their tenth year together, and that they hoped that we could all be there next year to celebrate with them. Trey then says, "Mike, this song begins with you singing. In fact it begins with an oom-pah-pah." And so begins the story of "Harpua." This one is outstanding as to be expected, and involves everyone in the town, including the evil old man and Reba, gathering at Jimmy's apartment for their New Year's Eve party. As the group of people circle around this giant bubbling, boiling cauldron to call forth the evil spirits, the audience does the lip-flop. If I were listening on the radio, I'd have no idea what was going on. The evil spirits then come out of the boiling cauldron and are acted by Fishman standing on his stool and performing one of the first Kungs in many years as the New Year's Eve chant. After a brief mention of the "New Year's Ritualistic Implement Party" going on backstage, Trey finishes the story with the battle between Poster Nutbag and Harpua and puts the finishing musical touches on a wonderful story.

"Squirming Coil" was noteworthy and the piano solo at the end was beautiful. Next, the Dude of Life came out dressed as an old man and pushing a lawnmower across the stage. He sang a cover of Neil Diamond's "Diamond Girl" which was lots of fun and was described the next day as "hot." "Llama" closed the set and you could feel that they had been playing for hours as the crowd grew tired. But when they came out for the encore, they decided to try singing "Carolina" a

capella, without any microphones, because they had never sung a capella in front of six thousand people. After Fishman fired a confetti gun on the stage, the audience quieted down and was even respectful. As they finished a very nice "Carolina" and their first stunt of the year, the crowd went wild. A short but sweet "Fire" closed the show and kicked off our collective 1993 as we wandered out into a surprisingly warm January evening in Boston to continue in the revelry.

2/30/93 Roxy Theatre—Ellis Godard

No review can do justice to this experience, but I'll try. It was my 22nd birthday, and the night of the first Phish.Net gathering, so the atmosphere for me was particularly giddy. But anyone there at the time would have been thrown by the relentless sponteneity.

The second set of this show is routinely listed among "must have" recordings. There was magic in the air starting with the first set the previous night. But mere minutes into this set, it was clear that things were going a step higher. It is perhaps the most debated of Phish setlists, with so many overlays and reprises that any two fans probably list it differently. For its time, the twists and turns were religious. A cadre of diehards, front and center, scrambled with pens and scratched their heads trying to keep track of the setlist. One Matt Laurence ultimately gave a blank stare and tossed his paper into the air.

The show so stood out from others of its time that its popularity inflated its status for many years to follow. (The availability of high-quality soundboards furthered both the popularity and the status.) In retrospect, the improvisation was relatively tame, and the energy (as conveyed on tape) was higher at other shows of the same era.

Granted, many aspects of Phish shows (and life generally) are impossible to record. But the site of Fishman naked, or the band exploding a drumkit, are imaginable. For anyone who has seen Phish in recent years, the mystique of restless song shifts is probably more confounding than compelling. But for anyone who was there that night, or who saw shows or has heard tapes from that era, the flow is laudable. It wasn't the best Phish show ever, but it was one of the best ones to experience—a beautiful buzz.

3/14/93 Western State College Gym, Gunnison, CO —James Raras, Jr.

The first set of this show is another one of those elusive tapes that is rarely seen on tape lists. This is a particular shame, as this show has a very nice setlist with such rarities as a "Loving Cup" opener and "PYITE"->"Runaway Jim" to close the set. Luckily the second set circulates widely as a soundboard, which sounds great! The second set opens with the return of "Halley's Comet," which hadn't been played live since '89, although it had been soundchecked just before the show. This set also contains such rarities as "The Ballad of Curtis Loew" and (the first performance of) "Great Gig in the Sky," featuring Fish on vocals and vacuum. In addition to these novelties, the centerpiece of the set was a stellar "YEM" that meandered through teases and jams of several cover songs such as "Owner of a Lonely Heart" and "Spooky" before concluding in a vocal jam packed with even more nods to cover songs. No Phish fan's tape list is complete without a copy of this fun-packed second set.

4/24/93 Cheel Arena, Clarkson University, Potsdam, NY

So here I sit, about to embark upon a retrospective review of my first Phish show. In the background, the tape which I've held dear for many years casts forth the appropriately emotional sounds of "Silent in the Morning." I was a freshman in high school standing atop a metal folding chair being deeply moved by the sound and verse. Something about that moment seemed so very special and now, panning back through the years, I realize just how special it was. It's incredibly ironic how that moment foreshadowed so much of what was to come and what still continues. "I've found your voice it brings me to my knees…."

A fairly warm evening sun cast long shadows across the parking lot of the Cheel Student Center at Clarkson University. It was the 24th of April and though the melt was on, this was Potsdam, NY, and a healthy blanket of snow still covered the warming Earth. I stood outside of Cheel with my sister and some of her friends eagerly anticipating what the evening would entail. My sister had just completed her freshman year at Clarkson, and it was for that reason and her thoughtfulness that I was standing in the evening sun carrying on a casual snowball fight with a car that kept passing by. It was assaulting the small concert crowd with snowballs, blaring some really, really loud beats and cursing out all the "crusties."

A few years prior to that April eve I began a fascination with Phish that continues to this day. The older brother of a good friend of mine used to walk around singing the chorus lines of "Fee" and occasionally confusing us to all ends by asking "Wash Uffizi and drive me to Ferenzi?" This somehow turned into some random neighborhood joke of "Wash my feet and drive me to Falansing…." I still have no idea where the word "Falansing" came from. I passed a copy of *Junta* and rather quickly fell in love with the hilariously intriguing sounds of "Fee." A tape I believe to be from Hebron followed. This show contains a hilarious "poop" vocal jam during "You Enjoy Myself," after which the band decides, "We're going to take a short break…so we can poop!" And poop I did, many more times before finally walking on that April eve of 1993 through the doors of the Cheel Student Center and into a world different from anything I had ever known before. My sister showed me around the Student Center and I made a contribution to the Clarkson Environmental Club, which scored me my first Phish souvenir, a green Earth Week '93 cup with a white Phish logo. We milled about for awhile longer before deciding to head through the next set of doors and into Cheel Arena, a name that will forever send a tingle down my spine. On the way in I made a quick bathroom stop and ran into a guy that was my sisters year and had gone to high school in Liverpool, our home town. He and his buddy were dressed in full fly-fishing gear. What a riot! I hadn't even seen the stage and already the live Phish experience was striking me as being uniquely interesting, entertaining, and downright funny.

We rounded the corner into the arena and there across the way was the stage. All sorts of speakers were stacked on the sides and a semi-translucent black backdrop complete with funky color swirls completed the scene. Ahhh, the Minkin backdrops…

We made our way to the floor and took a seat about twenty yards back. The section immediately adjacent to the stage was clear of chairs and one of my sister's friends tossed around the idea of a mosh pit. Hmmm…this guy was pretty darn funny and though he really didn't have a whole lot of interest in Phish, he loved live music and was psyched to have any live band, let alone Phish, at his college. Looking back upon Spring Tour '93 in the Northeast, that was entirely the point. Phish was beginning to carve a name for themselves as an entertaining live act, and as such they threw themselves into the college circuit, trying to gobble up the fans with their good times and good tunes. I think it worked!

I remember later hearing gripes about Spring Tour '93 and how many newbies it brought in, "ohh the FEFY heads." Interestingly enough, I heard gripes in '94, '95, '96, '97, '98, and '99 as well. It all depends on who's talking and who's listening. I for one was born into Phish out of someone's generosity of sharing the magic and I'm ever grateful for that. I suppose it's for that reason that I have always embraced the notion that everyone in the world could listen to Phish; if they appreciate it and enjoy it, then that's absolutely excellent and I'd be so psyched!

Eventually the area in front of the stage began to fill up, as well as the seats around us. The floor was full of bodies about back to the soundboard, as were the arena seats, and a smattering of folks milled about the rest of the place. The arena lights dimmed and I caught my first glimpse of the band as they walked up onto the stage and assumed their positions. Page made his line towards the grand piano, which I, at the time, had no idea was brand new to that tour. Fishman bounded along towards his old drum kit with the upside-down Phish sticker on it. Mike and Trey quickly slinged in and seemed to sway back and forth a bit, anxious to get cranking and stop standing in front of all those people. Many times since, I have watched this same sort of occurrence and never have I lost that initial buzz of not knowing what was or is to come.

The "Chalk Dust" opener roared and I was literally blown away by how loud and energetic it was. It was crazy how different it was live, not just live on a handful of old tapes, but live in person! In all honesty, it took some getting used to.

I was borne of, and most attached to, Junta, which is almost folky and contains a very melodic jam structure. The oranges and yellows of "Chalk Dust," "Guelah," "Poor Heart," and "Stash" floored me. I was overwhelmed. What the heck was happening? This wasn't the Phish I knew! And yet it didn't turn me off but rather intrigued me further. The "Guelah" dance had me laughing, the "Poor Heart" slapping my knee and stomping my feet.

Eventually things slowed down. "Stash" wound to a close and Trey was handed his acoustic guitar. He noodled around for about a minute and eventually settled into the acoustic intro to "The Horse." It was absolutely beautiful, and the progression into "Silent in the Morning" really allowed me my first opportunity to settle back and absorb and reflect upon something that I felt was touching me in a way I couldn't understand or truly describe, and that was just amazingly intense.

To this day, I can't really describe or understand Phish in my life, but nevertheless it is so special and so very important. The ensuing "Rift" deserves mention because it was around this time that my sister's friend (the sort of crazy one) decided crowd surfing was in order. He took off towards the stage and next thing I knew I was watching him being passed about and tossed around to "Rift." I must say, to this day I have never again seen anyone crowd surf at a Phish show, and I'm sort of happy about that. He'd get dropped and next thing you knew he was jumping up again. It got sort of frenzied but nothing like what was to come. After sliding through a sinuous snaky sort of "Caravan," which I would be psyched to see once again a few years later in Philadelphia, the band pulled out a new cover. "When Something is Wrong With My Baby" drops in on a heavy drum beat and rolls through like a soft-hearted steamroller. Excellent vocal interchanges, heavy lyrics, and an explosive guitar riff all combine to make this one of my favorite Phish covers. I totally enjoyed it then and I still do. Its a shame that it doesn't get played anymore; it was only played three times. It was encored the following night and encored again later in the week, after which it

has yet to return. "Sparkle" and "Antelope" rounded out my first-ever Phish set. The frenzy that began during "Rift" got out of control during "Sparkle." I recall watching my sister's friend and now a bunch of other people crowd surf; they would jump up on the front barricade out into a crowd of bounding, bouncing, stomping, and frenzied folks. Half the reason people were jumping off the barricade was to avoid being crushed into it by the collective mass of crazy "Sparkle" fanatics. At some point in that mix of bopping my head, watching the crowd, and wondering why they were singing "laugh and laugh and Paul McCartney…," I happened to glance up and see my sister's friend complete with Chuck B. T-shirt being dragged up the stairs and out the door by security. When the song wound down they jumped immediately into the "Antelope" riff, but during the intro Trey mentioned that everyone needed to "be cool" because the folks up front were getting crushed. I'm sure the "Antelope" helped…not!

My first-ever Phish set had wound to a close, and during the set break I pursued the ever-exciting activity of going to the bathroom at intermission. In retrospect it was really easy. There were no lines or people pissing in the sinks. The halls (which were just a walkway at the top of the seats) were clear and there was no herding of the cows to be done. I recall walking back down to the floor, looking out through the haze in the arena, glancing at different people, and absorbing a sort of strange collective vibe I would later come to realize was omnipresent during intermissions. Sometime during the break the crazy crowd surfer with the Chuck B. shirt came back sporting a girl's baby-blue sweatshirt and a new hat. The change of clothes apparently got him back in, but how exactly I have no idea.

Set two would be another excellent adventure. I was settling into the surroundings, and in doing so becoming more comfortable with listening to the music in the show environment. The setlist contained a number of songs from very early on in my listening adventures with Phish. I felt like I had a better grasp of what was going on and it really allowed me to sit back and enjoy myself. "Llama" ripped things open and I was psyched to hear this tune because I loved that funky little "Blastopast" story on the inside cover of *A Picture of Nectar*. Gordo popped at his bass strings and "Foam" bubbled to life. I laughed to myself while wading through the thick "Foam." This is probably one of the

first Phish tunes that I really felt the imagery not of the lyric but of the music. I thought back to my good buddy at home and recalled how many times we would be playing ball or hackey-sacking or something silly like that and suddenly we'd be missing our shots and completing none of our passes. Every time, as if something cued us, we'd suddenly belt out "fallllling innntooo a deep well…."

"Bathtub Gin" was really cool. It, too, was one of the first Phish tunes I remember getting really into, and as I listen to it now I can hear the beginnings of new forms of Phish creativity scratching towards the surface during this particular "Bathtub." It would also be the beginning of an odd sort of crush in which I really like watching Trey sing "Brett is in the bathtub, making soup for the ambassadors…." For some reason the inflection in his voice and the way he steps to the mic during "Bathtub" has always, for some unknown reason, elicited images of Trey and some wacky childhood adventure. I was more or less a child myself, and certainly was when I first heard the song. It seemed to evoke an interesting sort of bond that spanned generations. "Dinner and a Movie" and "Mound" were both just plain fun—I love both tunes, and I often wonder why neither are in rotation. Next thing I knew these big ole balls were being bounced around and the crowd was jamming the band. I had read about the "Big Ball Jam" previously, but this was definitely something that had to be seen. It reminded me of a big, out-of-control gym class.

The "You Enjoy Myself" that followed would forever seal my fate. This song was one that had touched me before, and experiencing it live gave it all the more meaning. The tramps were in full effect and I bounced right along with them. This song still makes me bounce, and this particular version was really pretty darn rippin', a B+ on the Dirksen scale, and you can reference his review if you'd like to know more. In the present sense, it's because of that review that I'm sitting here pawing through my memories and sharing them with you all. In the holistic sense, its because of that "You Enjoy Myself" that I've come this far.

Standing atop my chair, legs growing weak, mind growing tired, a chaotic vocal jam driving into my head…I started to think I was being brainwashed. I was actually quite concerned for a moment or two, and in an attempt to lessen the effects I began adding "lalalala…" and such to the vocal jam. I thought it would protect me from being brainwashed, but apparently it didn't work. Phish has developed into an extremely important part of my life. Although I only get to a handful of shows every year, I enjoy them all immensely. Those moments in time create a web of memories which act to allow me the leisure of time-traveling my own history within the pages of Phish. I recall adventures and travels with friends and family, I feel the tears and the laughter, it all comes flooding back through me and it's incredibly powerful and important. It is so much a part of who I am because it allows me to remember who I was. A song on the way out the door, in the car, or live in concert evokes memories of some other page of history, and within that page I travel on an ongoing thread of attached moments in time. It's quite special because I'll recall a moment in 1993 or 1995 or whenever…some random whim of memory will float forth, and as the breezes catch drift of my thoughts I begin to recall what was going on in my life, what it meant to me then, and what it means to who I am now. I knew then that I was being brainwashed, but there was nothing I could do about it and I'm so very glad that I didn't.

Speaking of brainwashed, after the "You Enjoy Myself," Fishman came out from behind the set with the old vacuum cleaner. "Bike" was

great, something about Fishman singing about a "mouse with a bike" made me feel totally comfortable being a kid, and that was quite special. Trey spoke a little about Burlington and Nectar and then finished out the set with "Harry Hood" and "Cavern."

When I think back to the encore, I don't recall much other than being tired, and though I was sad that it was over, I was also slightly relieved because it meant I could get to bed. I was also relieved because I had done it, I'd seen Phish and liked it a lot. I remember really wanting to like it but I worried that the live show experience wouldn't seem as whimsical and entertaining as goofing around with songs back home. It was kind of overwhelming and scary, but I had broken the ice now, and it was pretty darn fun and full of some special and very memorable moments. I was itching to get home to tell all my friends about it, and I was certainly going to want to come back again, so I was going to need to muster up some interest. It turns out I didn't have any problems with that….

Sitting here at the end of the night I glance beside me at the tape case and stare at the "Encore: 'Amazing Grace', 'Good Times, Bad Times.'" How appropriate it seems to have been and how appropriate it is.

5/2/93 Tower Theater, Upper Darby, PA—Erik Swain

Like many fans in my age group (b. 1971), I discovered Phish in college (Princeton in my case). I knew about Blues Traveler, and in 1992 when I read about the H.O.R.D.E. tour they were putting together and the other bands that were going to be on it, I decided Phish could be worth a listen. So I bought A Picture of Nectar (the only commercially available album at that time) without ever having heard them. I did not then, and still do not, think of PON as a great album, but it had several songs ("Llama," "Stash," "Guelah," "Chalk Dust," "Tweeprise") that hooked me. I got Lawn Boy and Junta when they were reissued a few months later, and was more impressed, particularly with "Coil" and "Bowie." Then Rift came out, and that was it. This album had everything I could want: great jamming, great songwriting, great production. I knew they would be touring soon, and I had to see them.

Being from Philadelphia originally, and residing less than an hour away at Princeton, I decided to go for one of the two shows at the Tower, either Saturday 5/1/93 or Sunday 5/2/93. That Saturday, my eating club was throwing a big party, so Sunday it was. I recruited one of my friends to come with me, and set out to call TicketMaster the morning they went on sale.

Then something weird happened. I got connected to TM right away, and ordered my tickets the minute they went on sale. That had never happened to me before for any artist, and only once or twice since (not for Phish, of course). The tix arrived, and said they were on the floor in Row BB.

Shortly thereafter, my friend broke his leg and had to give his ticket away. The guy he gave it to wanted to hang with his buddies in the balcony, so I would be going alone.

I got down to the Tower, my favorite non-club venue in the Philly area. It's an old movie theater, three thousand seats, incredible acoustics. Some of my very favorite shows have been here (Allman Brothers 5/24/95, Black Crowes 8/19/92, Neil Young 4/24/99), but this night was to be the best of them all.

My ticket said Row BB, and I figured that meant twenty-eighth row or something, probably behind industry-types, friends of the band, and whoever else. So I thought there was a mistake when I showed my ticket to the usher and she said "go down to the front and turn left." But

as I was walking down the aisle, I noticed the double-letter rows were in front of the single-letter rows. And when I got down to the front, I noticed the left (Page side) section had no row AA. Yes, my very first Phish show, and I'm in the front row!

My mind was still boggled by my good fortune when the boys came out and ripped into "Axilla." I had no concert tapes at this point, so I only knew album songs, but I was mighty impressed at the insistent riffing this song offers. Then came "Sparkle," which I hated even back then, and this version was a little off. Trey must have noticed that, because he then started "Divided Sky" and his body language indicated that he was trying to kick-start the band into a higher gear…and the crowd as well. After a standard version (still fantastic, of course), came one of the two songs from *Rift* I really wanted to hear: "Mound." I couldn't hear Mike's vocal mic well from where I was, but on the front-of-board recording I have of this show, there are no problems. Perhaps the taper was on Mike's side of the stage. Whatever problem there was disappeared for Mike's subsequent lead vocals.

Then came one of the two songs I really wanted to hear from *PON*, "Stash." I will never, ever forget the performance of this song. As the jam began to progress, Trey turned around to face Page and those of us in the crowd near him. Then somebody hit a note that was completely unexpected, and the band immediately locked into a groove and took it to a higher level. I could see, literally, Trey's jaw drop and his eyes gaze in wonderment at Page. I had never seen a band so spontaneous, yet in sync, as I had at that moment. That was the very instant I "got it" about Phish.

After that epiphany, the rest of the set could have been rote and it wouldn't have mattered. But it wasn't. "Horse" -> "Silent" was sweet and "Poor Heart" was much more raucous than the studio version (which I hate), and then came my favorite Phish song of the moment, "Maze." If there was one song I really wanted them to play, this was it. And they did not disappoint. They just ripped it to shreds. After that came the show's first dose of humor when Fish donned his "Madonna washboard" for "I Didn't Know," and the set closed with a "Golgi" that the crowd really got into.

As I was alone, I had nothing to do during set break. My seat was the second in from the aisle, and my friend's vacant seat was on the aisle. Then a girl came down and asked if she could take it. I was a pretty shy person back then, but I did my best to strike up a conversation. What a story she had. She was twenty-nine and lived with her parents in South Philly. She had been through some rough times recently; she lost her job, her boyfriend left her, and her brother had passed away. The one good memory she had was driving across country with a friend and playing *PON* the whole way, "Cavern" in particular. She really wanted to hear that song. A week or so before the show, she and a male friend were walking down South Street and passed Tower Records, which is a TicketMaster outlet. On a whim she decided to go in and see if she could get Phish tickets. Her friend reluctantly agreed to go with her, and the only available two seats together were in the very back row of the balcony on this night.

Well, about three quarters of the way through the first set, her "friend" decided Phish was the worst band he'd ever seen and walked out, leaving her there alone in an already fragile state. I can't believe how cruel some people can be. She decided she was going to try to make the best of a bad situation, and sneak down to the front row. What a Godsend my empty seat must have been for her. If an usher had tried to re-

move her, I would have stuck up for her, but luckily she was left alone.

We followed the lead of some of the people in the front row of the center section and leaned against the stage for the second set. You don't see that happen much anymore. Then the boys came out again.

I don't know what they smoked, popped, or drank during set break, but they proceeded to play what remains the most energetic, adrenaline-fueled set I have ever heard from them, live or on tape. It sounds like no other. I'm not saying it belongs with the all-time great second sets like 2/20/93, 5/7/94, or 11/27/98. But it's distinctive.

To start, they granted me my second wish from *PON*, "Llama." This is my favorite song from the record because it just kicks so hard. Here it kicked twice as hard…and, it seemed, twice as fast. Then into a very spunky "PYITE," which I had never heard before. I thought it was kind of funny (not knowing anything about the "Gamehendge" saga), especially the way Trey virtually spat out the words "Punch you in the eye."

And then came epiphany number two, "YEM." It was mind-boggling enough to be introduced to the tramps and the vocal jam, which I had not known about. But to have this amazingly intense playing on top of it? Wow. At this point I decided there was no band that could touch Phish. It was that good. It is still one of my favorite "YEMs" of all time, and, again, it's like no other I have in my collection. It's incredibly fast-paced, almost punkish in spots. Among the oddities: Trey enthusiastically screamed all four of "Boy," "Man," "God," and "Shit"; there was a pronounced "Oye Como Va" tease during the lengthy jam segment; and Trey let out a squeal of delight during Mike's rapid-fire bass solo. The jam was very funky for that period; in a blind test you might mistake portions of it for a 1997 version.

From this point on, the band was playing on pure adrenaline, careening like an out-of-control roller coaster, going incredibly fast with wild abandon but never veering off-track. For that reason this set is my favorite tape to drive to. You can't help but hit the pedal to the floor.

"Lizards" was beautiful, if a bit—you guessed it—fast. This may be the speediest "Lizards" tempo I've heard. The piano solo segment sounds like one of Santana's jazzier jams. The "Big Ball Jam" was amusing, and "Uncle Pen" ripped far harder than I've heard it since.

The crowd was in a complete frenzy by this point, and then "Bouncing" came on and pushed us over the edge. Say what you want about this song, but there is a time and a place for it, and this was it. People were pogo-ing as if they were at a Mudhoney show or something.

This led into epiphany number three: "Antelope". The fastest and most intense song in the fastest and most intense set. Here they really did sound like a punk rock band, albeit one capable of Zappa-esque changes. If this version does not prompt you to hit triple digits on the speedometer of your car, there's something wrong with your car. It took me a few minutes to even realize that it was "Antelope". There were all these extra notes that disguised it. I was blown away—this was so unlike the studio version that I thought they had rewritten the song from scratch. Particularly amusing were the *Simpsons* language cues after "Rye Rye Rocco" (another first for me) and the ska-like beat they went into between "Marco Esquandolas" and "Bid you to have any spike." Never has the phrase "run like an Antelope, out of control" been so apt as it was at this show, this set, this song.

Then it was time for Fish's routine, and another Phish trick I was unaware of, the "Hold Your Head Up" theme. Even this was faster than usual on this night. He listened to people shout requests for a while, saying "Sometimes it takes a great deal of effort for me to figure out

which one of the five songs I'm gonna sing." He decided on "Cracklin' Rosie." Somehow, this song rocked too. Any band that can rock out a Neil Diamond song convincingly deserves some kind of a prize.

This set could end no other way than in complete anarchy. Since they had done their best impression of a hardcore punk band, they had to do their hardcore punk song. "BBFCFM" was absolutely insane—to the point that one of the mics fell down.

Back for the encore, the band, perhaps drained from that incredible second set, finally decided to switch tempos and began a laconic version of "Sleeping Monkey." The lulling intro…the lulling intro…the lulling intro…guys, are we going to start the song? There was a reason for the delay—Trey forgot the first line! He asked the audience for help, and half the crowd shouted it out, as did Fishman. This was particularly baffling for a first-timer—how could so many people know the words to a song that's not even on an album? Trey then told us he was embarrassed because Tom Marshall was in the audience. Anyway, this version of "Sleeping Monkey" was most notable because Fish had blown out his voice during "Cracklin' Rosie" and "BBFCFM," and could only manage a croak when the time came to sing his high notes. It sounds funny now, but no one was laughing then.

They then proceeded to the front of the stage for a flawless (I think Fish was faking it) unmiced, a cappella "Amazing Grace," almost post-coital in its mellowness. I could not believe a band with so much power was also capable of so much grace.

I was on the highest natural high I'd ever been on. Then I turned to the girl next to me and remembered her plight. I offered her a ride back to her home, and hung out with her a few times after that, but I never saw her again after that summer. However, this was the first time I'd ever made friends with a complete stranger. Only in the magic atmosphere of a Phish show could that have happened to someone as shy as I was back then.

They never did play "Cavern," which she so badly wanted to hear. We had no way of knowing that they had played it the night before. But in the next three shows I saw, and six of the next nine, they played "Cavern." Maybe they knew. Somehow.

I will argue to my death that this is one of the most criminally underrated and undercirculated shows they have ever played. The first night of the Tower stand seems to be much more available, and everyone I heard from who went to both of these shows said this one blew that one away.

How underrated is this show? The band itself seems to have completely forgotten about it. In summer 1999, Phish.com published a "This Month in Phish History" segment for May 1993. My heart fluttered in anticipation of what they would say about this show. It sank when the answer was: almost nothing. The only mention was that Fish played the Madonna washboard. That's understandable; three shows later that week (5/5, 5/6, and 5/8) are all historic, and deserved the ink. But that's no reason not to learn more about this wild and wacky show that has unfairly languished in obscurity.

The passion of the band's performance that night prompted me to become an equally passionate fan. For that I am eternally grateful.

5/8/93 University of New Hampshire Field House, Durham, NH—Jamie Hellen

This was my first Phish show: I was a virgin in this culture and by the end of the night I would be hooked for life. It was the spring 1993

tour closer and I couldn't have asked for a better show. One of my favorites, "Chalk Dust," opened up the gig and set the twenty-five hundred-plus crowd dancin'. They played a variety of classics right after, including "Guelah," "Rift," "Mound," and "Stash," but this was not your normal "Stash." This version started off quite energetically and continued to get even better due to Trey and Fishman's timely playing. Then they slowed down the jam a bit and started singing the ol' "Kung chant." Trey and Mike started singing into the microphone a bit as the ending riff came back to complete the "Stash"-> "Kung"->"Stash" sandwich. "Glide" was next, which is now considered somewhat of a rarity. Then Trey pulled out his Martin acoustic to play the intro to "My Friend, My Friend," which included great drum work from Fishman. After that they got the crowd hopping again with "Reba," then a very rare Duke Ellington cover called "Satin Doll," which they played for the whole crew. Trey actually named them all, prior to closing out a great first set with "Cavern."

The second set had a few treats to say the least. One of my favorites at the time (and now) opened the second set, "David Bowie." The intro had a couple of secret language cues, the *Simpsons* signal as well as the "sing a random note" signal. Then out of nowhere the whole band starts jamming on "Jessica" by the Allmans! It never really took off completely but it was clear that the band was having some fun. This "Bowie" goes through a very hypnotic and heavy hard-rock jam to start things off, before it lightens up and fades melodiously into "Have Mercy" and then back into "David Bowie," completing another fantastic segue sandwich!

A couple of delights came after including an acoustic intro to "Horse," a great "It's Ice" and "Squirming Coil." Then just as the "Coil" solo ended the band started to take off in a random jam that got everyone grooving for the Big Balls to come out, as the jam segued in to "Big Ball Jam."

The crowd was quite adept at getting the three shots, and as they finished the "BBJ" Trey broke into "Mike's Song." In my opinion this is a legendary "Mike's Song." The energy that poured out of this "Mike's" was uncanny. Page was happy to be using his new Hammond organ, as was evident from his inspired playing in this "Mike's." In the midst of it all, Trey led his three comrades into the old Robert Johnson (more recently Cream/Clapton) cover, "Crossroads." It was the first time they ever played this one, and they did a pretty good job of it. This segued back into "Mike's," thus completing the third segue sandwich of the night, and the rest of the groove ("Hydrogen" and "Weekapaug") followed. The "Weekapaug" was followed by "Amazing Grace," which then led right into an "Amazing Grace Jam," with the band playing "Grace" with instrumental accompaniment and thanking the crowd for supporting them and for coming to this, the tour closer. The encore, "AC/DC Bag," was simple but left everyone with a smile on their face. It had only recently come out of hibernation earlier that spring in Atlanta. Although this was my first show, it still remains one of my favorites and a classic Phish performance that all should hear.

7/17/93 The Filene Center at Wolf Trap, Vienna, VA —Charlie Dirksen

On a gorgeous summer afternoon, my friends and I barbecued for awhile in the lot preshow. Phish was really starting to "get big" this summer; there were a few vans clearly ready for tour, and a thousand or so folks already in the lot about two hours before showtime. There was very little vending, though. Wolf Trap, a small, noncommer-

cial amphitheater-style venue, usually features folk or classical music, and very little rock. I had no doubt, even before the show, that this would be the only time Phish could play here. The staff wouldn't be able to handle or tolerate the young crowd.

The first set contained solid playing and great tunes, including a pleasant "Stash" and "Reba" combo. But the highlight for me personally came with the second . I had seen the movie *Being There* just a few days before this show, in stereo with large speakers, in order to hear the "Also Sprach Zarathustra" in it as loudly as possible. This tune makes its entry at a monumental point in the movie. I had always been profoundly moved by the original classical version, but I was particularly charmed by this funky cover. I remember commenting to my friends, while watching the movie and listening to a funky "2001," on how unfortunate it was that we would never see the song jammed out live.

Imagine my shock and joy upon hearing "2001" open the second set at Wolf Trap! I recognized it at the very beginning, the spacey intro, and began trembling, then screaming and waving my arms wildly. I was Fishman-side, about seven rows from the stage, and I know I caught Mike's and Trey's attention. My Dionysian revelry also dominologically caused everybody around me to start yahooing, too. It was one of those events in one's life (if one is blessed enough to have such events) when everything falls into place and absolutely nothing could ever possibly be more spiritually glorious. I witnessed the rest of the show like an ecstatic, giddy fan boy who hadn't seen his favorite band in far too long a time. "The Leprechaun" especially moved me (I wish they would bring this back!), and both "Weekapaug" and "Good Times" raged. I wrote to the band soon after the show, leading to my receiving their newsletter. I was hooked!

8/2/93 The Ritz Theater, Tampa, FL—Reis Baron

As I put my ear to the crack in the door of the Ritz Theater, I just could not believe my ears. I had been listening to the ending solo in "Slave to the Traffic Light" every day for a week before the show, joking with myself that I would actually hear it in Florida. When they broke into the intro, I just could not believe how huge it sounded. With a song as old as that being played with fresh licks from a much more talented Phish (since the days they had had it in rotation), I knew we were in for something special when the show would start.

The fast "Funky Bitch" soundcheck was pretty funny…sounded almost like someone was fast-forwarding a tape of the tune. I guess they just wanted to get it over with or something.

Sweat was pouring down my green face by the time they let us in (fifteen minutes later than they promised). We ran in up to the front of the stage, where I was no more than six or seven feet away from Trey's rack and prepared for the show.

The "Chalk Dust" opener smoked, and Trey laid down a pretty amazing solo, playing so in the pocket…very tasty. I always love seeing "Guelah" because of the dance and the licks during "Asse"…such fast composition is a treat to see live, and this was a fun and bouncy version. "Poor Heart" had a solo that was sort of like the one in Tallahassee where Trey used space and less notes. As soon as Mike started the slapping for "Brother," I lost it. All I could do was scream "Thank you!" at the top of my lungs. I thought this was the one real treat we were going to get, and I was satisfied. Little did I know what was to come a few songs later. Trey struggled through "Oh Kee Pah Ceremony" more than any other time I've seen or heard him play it. It was

a little uncomfortable to watch this happen, but his licks in "Suzie" more than made up for it. By the end of the second Page solo in "Suzie," the whole crowd was rocking back and forth in unison, which created a sort of physical theme for the rest of the show.

I have yet to experience a crowd with more raw dancing energy, including the NYE '92 show. By the time "All Things" ended (perfect version—not a note missed), we could see this weird look on Mike and Trey's faces as they started the very slowest "Bathtub Gin" I have ever heard. They fucked with the tempo so much, and I kept looking at Mike as if to say "what the hell is going on here?" He chuckled at everyone's confusion as they broke into an interesting bluesy jam. During the jam Mike gave Trey a look like "What are we doing?" They both shrugged their shoulders, laughed, and kept the jam going. Trey began this guitar melody that was so familiar, but I could not pinpoint it. My buddy Pablo, a Stones fan from way back, screamed "Sweet Virginia" in my ear, but I wasn't sure if this was it or not. When that jam ended, they immediately segued into a straight-ahead reggae beat. I thought they were going to pull out another "Lively Up Yourself" or something, but when Trey stepped up and started singing, "Hey Makisupa Policeman," I must have pulled a vocal cord or two as I screamed in ecstasy. I only had one tape of this one from '87 at the time, and I never thought I would be fortunate enough to see this.

I knew this set was going to be extra long when they segued into "My Mind's," after the soft vocal "Policeman" refrain. It was fun to see, and I thought it would probably close the set, but lo and behold, "Dog Log!" When I heard this I truly lost my mind and could not believe what I was witnessing. Thanks to the *White Album* I was able to sing along. Page saw me singing it and laughed. "La Grange" blew me away. The bridge lasted forever, and by this time the crowd transformed into a heaping mass of sweat, feeding off the energy these guys were churning out like the groove was a big musical generator or something. The solos were fabulous, and it's great to hear them pull it off—a perfect example of how to make a cover song your own. After the set ended I felt like I had seen an entire show, although it was just about an hour long! We were all exhausted, and for about ten minutes my friends and I just dropped to the floor and hardly said a word, wondering how the band was going to top that set.

I was excited to see the "2001" theme open the second set. It's great to get the crowd right back into the energy level of the first set, which died down during set break as everyone tried their best to stay afloat in their own drool. I have never been a part of such an energetic crowd as the one I was amidst during "Mike's Song." When Trey was on the trampoline, he ripped some really intricate solos that were probably the best I've heard, versus the usual long sustained notes he forces himself into so he can keep his balance. Every minute or so Mike would hop off his tramp and stick in some killer slaps, making the groove so thick that people had no choice but to dance, and dance hard. Among the close to a thousand people that were there, I doubt at this point if there was anyone not completely drenched in sweat. Then there was the metal jam.

Trey kicked in some huge distortion and this guy, Joe Rooney, from a local Tampa metal band called First Born (I asked him his name after the show), came on stage and started singing nonsensical, high-pitched lyrics (I later asked him what he was singing and he didn't even know). Trey was so funny. He began hammering this Eddie Van Halen-like solo, and then did a huge windmill, causing him to lose his pick in the shuffle. It was so hilarious. When they segued into "Sparks," I felt

like I was going to cry. It was by far the best version I've heard them play. The dynamics were up and down like a roller coaster, and it was wonderful to hear them play this song now that they are so much better than when they played it in 1990. I felt like I stepped into a time warp and wound up at Wetlands or The Front—absolutely too much for me to take. "Curtis Loew" was cool. I'm not a big Skynyrd fan, but Trey's solo and Page's singing definitely make this one a must-see. Trey's blues licks had become so much heavier and pronounced in the past couple of years. It was a treat to hear this one. When they started both "Rift" and "Coil," I was almost positive they were going to bag "Weekapaug" altogether, but at the end of Page's beautiful "Coil" solo, Mike immediately broke into the bass solo, and we were all electrified. There was no wet distortion or T-wah, just a thick tone and some amazing slapping just like in the old days. It was classic. It was also the best Trey solo in "Weekapaug" since 3/20/92, in my opinion. It went on for awhile and he kept coming back with some pretty sick ideas. They had the best time playing it. Fish's right hand was out of control. The ride cymbal was falling in and out of the beat like I've never seen before—he was so on!

We knew "Bike" was the perfect song for this particular evening, and when we all screamed for it Trey immediately nodded and gladly sung it. I finally caught my favorite Barrett/Floyd tune...funny as hell and a real treat. The intro to "Antelope" featured a signal that was about to be the random note, but we all started pointing downward, and Trey waited while he considered it, then busted the fall-down signal. About four or five of us up front got it, and despite the many broken bottles on the floor, we remarkably came up without a scratch. The "Makisupa" teases in "Antelope" were perfect, and a good reminder of how special this show really was. Then there was the solo in "Antelope". The peaks did not stop coming back. Trey literally did not leave the top four frets for a few minutes, and it was like a huge jolt of electricity that was the only thing keeping the crowd from passing out (due to the intense amount of heat that seemed to linger through the whole show). To close the show I couldn't have prayed for a better "Antelope"—just smokin'! Hearing "Sleeping Monkey" was really nice. Mike made a face like he forgot it when Trey went up and suggested they play it. He didn't seem to have a problem with it though. The solo at the end was really well done, and despite the humorous nature of the song, their playing made it one of the most beautiful jams of the night. They were able to pull of the "Amazing Grace" without mics, although it did take a while for everyone to shut up.

When the lights went up, I just looked at my buddies, both new and old, and didn't know what to say. We all witnessed something so special. People have been waiting for a show like this for a long time, and these guys from Colorado assured me that it was the best of the year, with Gunnison being a close second.

It's incredible to be able to share this experience with all of you, as I keep asking myself why I was so privileged to be one of a very small crowd that got their lives changed in Ybor City (of all places!). Shows like this will never happen again in such an intimate setting, and I can only hope that bands who play at Ritz Theater-level capacity will one day be able to achieve the level of intensity that Phish achieved in that hot and sweaty Florida room.

8/6/93 Cincinnati Park Zoo, Cincinnati, OH—Cory Ferber

See the city. See the zoo." This show is well known for the fitting return of "Slave to the Traffic Light," after a 233-show hiatus that began on 10/27/91. This was only my second show, and my first time traveling to another city to see Phish. I had never seen a show at the Cincinnati Zoo (or at any other zoo), so I wasn't sure what to expect.

We pulled in to the Zoo's parking lot about thirty minutes before showtime. Things were quiet and there was no lot scene, no vendors, and no drum circles; there was, however, a decent number of VW buses and cars with Dead stickers. There were a few bootleg T-shirts for sale after the show and I bought my first one: it said "Phishy Ale," and was laced with references to "Gamehendge" and Vermont.

The ticket price included admission to the park, but we didn't hand over our tickets until we got to the venue located somewhere inside the park. The venue was more like a courtyard. There was a medium-sized section of pavement in front of the small, temporary stage. Beyond the pavement was a raised lawn. The standing-room-only crowd filled the pavement, and the lawn was scattered with dancers. I would be surprised if there were more than three thousand people at the show.

The setlist reads like a classic novel, and this one is full of musical surprises. There is wonderful conceptual continuity between the jams of "Tweezer" and "YEM" in the second set. The transitions are exceptional. Inside of "YEM" is a great one-verse version of Eric Clapton's "Cocaine." The "YEM" vocal jam contains "Tweezer" lyrics, and ends with the opening lines of "Halley's Comet" floating above the madness.

Trey dedicated the unplugged encore of "Amazing Grace" to the animals. People were very quiet and showed respect. We got to talk to Page after the show and he told us the "Tequila" teases were in honor of Jimmy Buffett's nearby concert. This was a special show for me, and the one that got me on the bus.

8/9/93 The Masonic Temple, Toronto, Ontario, Canada —John Wood

I've yet to have a negative experience in Toronto, ever, as it is among my favorite cities on the Canadian East Coast. After a pleasant drive up (including a stop at the Beer Store for Brador's and Schooners), Yonge Street was quietly filling up with Phish fans. A side street made for a small Phish village with all the ingredients of a small-scale scene, and the presence of nitrous tanks was minimal.

Admittedly, I wasn't as up for the show at one point, primarily because of the change of venues: I'll take a fourth-row reserved seat over any spot in a general-admission venue anytime. However, Concert Hall was more like a two-story punk club to me. The atmosphere almost reminded me of my first Phish experience at The Haunt in Ithaca: "Just how the hell does this place hold eighteen hundred?" I was glad for the balcony seating, as this old warhorse has long burnt out on the crammed floor scene. Because the lighting boards were set up on the center of the balcony, Jens, "Popper" Santora, and I opted for front balcony seats in "The Page Zone," while the one-and-only Jaybar took his spot in the small tapers' section. Still, if you were in the balcony, there wasn't a bad seat around, and the venue shined in the intimacy department. Ventilation was another story: there was none. Thus, the Concert Hall became the Concert Sauna, and by the time Page's "Squirming Coil" piano solo closed a weird first set, I didn't see a human body that wasn't drenched. Nevertheless, spirits were high, and our Canadian friends provided plenty of friendly vibes—another of many reasons I really dig Canada.

The show itself, in comparison to other lists, looks rather con-

ventional on paper, but the playing is openly bizarre and twisted. The "Chalk Dust Torture" opener forecasted this Phish trip to the Twilight Zone, and Trey had stumped me by inserting a verse-plus of "Who Knows" from the Hendrix live *Band of Gypsies* album (which I didn't recognize until after the set)—a very cool effect. A bouncy "Mound" and a "Fee" with a Trey-altered second verse gave way to a spacey interlude that merged into a twisted "Split Open and Melt;" its peak was derived from a completely different rhythm structure, eventually slowing down to a snail's crawl before Trey inserted the first few notes of "Glide." It was great to see the band experimenting with its repertoire, and "Glide" was accented by three signals before its ending. I enjoyed my first "Nellie Kane." "Divided Sky" has become a song I can hear anytime, although this rendition was enjoyable but not exceptional. I'm finding numerous versions pigeoned in its structure and would really like to see everything open up, particularly its middle. And as Jens noted, I somehow managed to make it onto the first set tapes. As the band attempted to quiet the crowd down, a few goons had no clue how to keep their mouths shut, bellowing obnoxious stupidities when the band was about to start "Memories." I just couldn't take that crap anymore, and just yelled "Shut up!!!" On the drive home while listening to Jaybar's tapes, I had lost track of that moment when I heard: "wheee—ahhhh—shut-up!!!" D'oh! The set concluded with a fine "Squirming Coil" touched off by another smooth Page excursion.

I was prepared for a "2001" opener, but I was pleasantly surprised by the playfully funky "Dinner and a Movie" opener. "Tweezer" was among the tunes expected, and the band obliged in taking its jam to another off-the-wall place. My smile became brighter upon the first notes of a personal favorite: a pretty "Tela" that remained focused, and Trey's progressions reminded me somewhat of Pat Metheny in terms of tone and melody. It was my personal favorite song of the evening. When Trey pulled out his acoustic for the "My Friend, My Friend" intro, he utilized a brief "Tela" reprise as a gateway. Admittedly, I had never really gotten into "My Friend, My Friend," but its demented state had me basking in enjoyment. Mike Gordon lightened up the mood with a hoe-downed "My Mind's Got a Mind of its Own." Still, there was one song I had looked forward to: "You Enjoy Myself." This gem gave way to a jam based on Deep Purple's hard-rock classic, "Smoke on the Water." At one point, Trey walked up to his mic and tried to sing something, then backed away. I enjoyed the spontaneity and looseness of it all, while the jam itself remained focused. When the a capella vocal reprise emerged, the band broke into the Talking Heads favorite "Psycho Killer," complete with reprises and "AIE-YIE-YIE-YIIIIIEEEE!" and melded it into the vocal jam. Hysterical!

The jam continued, then slowed down to a soft tone; as in "Split Open and Melt," the band's use of hushed dynamics for this venue was appreciated and effective. Page snuck in the opening chords to an authoritative "Contact." Everything was working well, the reprise sounding fully inspired.

At this point, I was ready for the Fishman segment, with "Bike" ringing on the top of my head. Instead, Trey approached his mic: "We have a surprise for you tonight," and indeed, out popped that wacky Dude of Life! Unlike New Year's Eve '92, there was no lawnmower, but

he tossed out party favors and who-the-hell-knows what! While I'll never mistake the Dude of Life for Sinatra, his presence added a perfect touch of wacky Phish humor, as he confidently led the psyched quartet in a reading of "Crimes of the Mind," a hard-rock number that is included on the Elektra release *The Dude of Life and Phish*.

They closed the set on an anthemic note. Since I've boarded this bus, Phish has yet to disappoint me, but they have made me scratch my head nearly every time. A "Speedy Gonzales" "Rocky Top" encore was a disappointment to me, only because I wanted something more (a Fishman tune, another song, or an a capella number), but it was clear the band had to bolt from the stage for some reason—probably some sort of curfew, since the show had started late. Of course, if most of the close to eighteen hundred bodies were drenched in sweat (some people remain seated during the show), imagine the band's position.

I enjoyed the gig because of the low supply of gimmicks. Don't get me wrong, they are fun and all, but I'm always there for the jams first and foremost. In addition, the band took some standards and played them in a improvisationally different fashion. If I heard "Split Open and Melt" the same way every time, as with any song by any artist, I'd eventually be bored with it. One comment to close: I found it amusing at the number of Netters bumming about similar setlists at the beginning of the summer '93 tour. Now, who's complaining?

Randy Ward

8/15/93 McCauley Theater, Louisville, KY—James Raras, Jr.

No doubt the reason this show is not more widely talked about is the lack of high-quality tapes that circulate from it. In a month that saw some fantastic tapes of equally fantastic musical performances, this show was unfortunately left out. The only recordings available of this stellar show are audience recordings from AKG460s, but the preamp overloaded at the show, giving it very distorted sound during loud transients. These tapes are rarely seen on traders' lists. The first set contains a version of the Duke Ellington/Juan Tizol jazz rarity "Caravan" as well as a "Forbin" > "Mockingbird," but without question the highlight of the set is "Stash." This version of "Stash" was years ahead of its time. Its beautiful and melodic jamming is amazingly contrasted by experimental jaunts, and together, they make this a "Stash" to which all present versions must measure up to, a must-hear for any Phish fan! "Tweezer" was the centerpiece of set two, with the twenty-minute version touching upon an "Antelopian" groove toward the middle of it—another must hear version for sure. Accompanying "Tweezer" in the second set were the now-rarities "The Landlady" and "Nellie" and an almost unheard-of "Freebird" set-closer. After such an inspired show what could one ask for as an encore? None other than "Harold Hood," of course! We can only hope that someday Kevin Shapiro, the band's archivist, will satisfy the need for high-quality recordings of this show via a soundboard release to the digital traders or an official band release of at least parts of this show.

8/20/93 Red Rocks Amphitheater, Morrison, CO —David Steinberg

For a while it was uncertain whether this show would happen. The tickets mentioned the chance of a rainout and the rain was coming

down hard. The cancellation rumor was helped quite a bit when the backdrop was removed. However, Icculus was with us. At almost exactly 7:30 the rain stopped. Due to some good work by the crew, the show practically started on time.

The show started with an inspired choice, the "Divided Sky." This is a beautiful song anytime, but hearing it at Red Rocks with strong winds blowing around was just amazing. The only environment that was close to this one was Amy's Farm.

"Divided Sky" came to a full stop, and after a pause we got our first surprise of the evening, "Harpua." "Harpua" nowadays is usually reserved for the "show-stopper" slot of last or second-to-last song of the show. Getting it second showed that they had confidence that they could top it. The version itself was odd. The story was about Harpua the Giant Iguana being turned to stone by Poster Nutbag's (or Posterus Nutbagus as Trey referred to him) deadly gaze. Allegedly, one of the rocks looked like a giant iguana, but I could never find it. This became a bit of a running joke throughout the set. After an outstanding opening, things had to return to normal for a bit. An excellent "Maze" was sandwiched between "Poor Heart" and "Bouncing." Then things got unusual again. Rather than the boring jams they've been playing in "It's Ice" since they got the glider toy, they gave Page a solo. After "Ice," they started to play a jam that I didn't recognize at all. After sixty-nine shows, it was rare to have to write a "?" on a setlist, and I was enjoying it. The suspense was broken when they stepped to the microphones and sang "We're bobbing on the surface…." My first "Wedge!" This version was much different from the studio, and much better. However, the highlight of the set was still to come. After two more songs, the set closed with "Run Like an Antelope." This was no ordinary version, mind you. Other than the 3/13/92 Providence "Run Like a Big Black Furry Antelope" jam, this was by far the best version that I've ever seen. The jam was both sick and long; it clocked in at over fifteen minutes, whereas the average "Antelope" is around ten. Get this tape and listen to it. You won't be sorry.

After a brief break, the second set opened to the familiar strains of "2001." Then came the best moment of the show…and of my Phish career: "Slave to the Traffic Light". Not only was this my first version, not only did they play the best version I have ever heard, but they were playing it at Red Rocks. This meant that during the quiet jam I could look out to my right and see lightning strike over the lights of Denver. I can't really say any more about this; you just had to be there.

Now, while I would have been perfectly happy if the set had ended right there, the band felt like playing some more. In fact they played excellent versions of "Split Open and Melt" and "Chalk Dust," with a sweet "Coil" and a really fun "My Friend, My Friend" in between. However, I was still going "Slave, Slave, SLAVE!!" in my head and kind of let these songs slide by. The second set was to bring one more treat. During "Purple Rain," Mimi Fishman came out to do the vacuum solo. I heard her on tapes and was expecting her to do really well. Unfortunately she was having an off night and couldn't get any sound out of it. Fish took the vacuum back and redeemed his mother with a solid solo. The set came to a close with an excellent "Cavern." My guess for the encore was "Freebird" and something else. While I was right, I never expected to hear "The Mango Song" to open an encore. An excellent version, too.

This show was easily the best of the twenty I saw that year. It had everything: odd song selection ("Wedge," "Slave"), standard songs played well ("Antelope!!!"), and even a special guest. All I can say is get the tapes. Better yet, hope that the band videotaped it and get that! Bet-

ter yet, invent a time machine and go see the show yourself. It'll be worth it.

12/28/93 Bender Arena, American University, Washington, D.C.—Charlie Dirksen

It began snowing early in the afternoon, and I wondered whether the gig might be cancelled. The D.C. area is notorious for falling apart and shutting down at even the lightest snowfall, and I feared the worst. There was probably an inch on the ground, at most, when my friend and I arrived at the Arena an hour or so before doors opened. Though AU was on break, there was nevertheless a strong contingent of local students. There was already a line of people, at least a hundred strong, waiting to get in. My friend Dead eventually joined Dave and I in line about a half-hour before showtime. It had stopped snowing. It was controlled chaos on the way in, because the line, which was at least eight hundred strong by the time the doors were scheduled to open, collapsed fast.

The Bender Arena is your average collegiate basketball arena. It probably holds five thousand in the bleachers and on the floor. Even though we could have stood on the court up close to the stage (we were among the first hundred or so fans to enter), Dead insisted that we sit in the top row of the set of bleachers at the back of the arena. Though this was the farthest spot away from the stage in the arena, we were still only about a hundred yards out and had a direct view.

The stage was dressed up as a multicolored, psychedelic (and almost cartoonish) aquarium. Sand, starfish, rocks, seaweed, and even a giant clam glittered under the lights. I couldn't believe it when Phish opened with a strong version of Frank Zappa's "Peaches En Regalia." I didn't think they were playing it anymore. I was also excited to hear "Ya Mar," which contained an "Auld Lang Syne" tease from Trey. It was one of my favorite covers at the time. The show also featured a tease of Led Zeppelin's "Kashmir" in the "Possum" (rumor had it that they had played all of "Kashmir" in the soundcheck). "Fast Enough for You," my favorite song from *Rift*, was played well and was also a treat. And following up a beautiful rendition of "Harry Hood" with an angry cover of AC/DC's "Highway to Hell" was an unforgettable way to close the second set.

12/30/93 Cumberland County Civic Center, Portland, ME —Scott Silton

Portland was a nice treat for our group because we could stay at Bowdoin, just a half-hour away. Getting from Boston to Maine was a cinch; the roads were clear by morning. We hooked up with some guests and got to the show no problem. Like the Bender show, Portland was general admission. The lines to get into the venue were long and it was quite cold out. However, we managed to head in at just the right time so that we weren't stuck out in the cold for too long but still able to snag some really nice seats. We ended up in the stands in the section just in front of the stage, Page side, fairly low.

The Cumberland County Civic Center is simply a great venue, seating around ten thousand, general admission, with excellent acoustics. I don't believe that the show sold out, and if it did, the last ticket was sold within an hour of the performance. Anyone who could have hit this show but missed it just blew it. So it goes.

Set one begins with a grand version of "Bowie," highlighted by two passes through Aerosmith's "Dream On." The ending is tight and glorious. "Weigh" is a rare and welcome treat. I suppose it's not rare any longer with the release of *Slip Stitch and Pass*, but in any case this ver-

sion is executed well. "Curtain" is also a rare and welcome treat. It's one of those songs that was on my wish list for the tour that I had enough sense not to be waiting for because I couldn't really expect to hear it. This version is tight. And the opening chords to "Sample" sound so sweet! This transition is just perfect. And this "Sample" is great. I once said that comparing "Samples" is somewhat pointless, but I was wrong. This is a hot, smoking "Sample," one that gives reason to its being played so much the next year. Paul and Silas is an upbeat bluegrass tune, but nothing special to note.

The "Forbin's" is really nice, one of my favorite songs (great drum part). The narration between the two songs involves the Civic Center washing out into to ocean so that the fans can surf; a better-than-average narration with nice sound effects from the band. The "Mockingbird," however, is seriously flawed because Trey flubs the timing between the first and second major melodic sections. The band actually has to stop playing and try to recoordinate, and even then they aren't quite on the same page. The rest of "Mockingbird" is fine, but this flub is sad, the only low point of the night. A "Rift" is a "Rift." This is no exception.

This "Bathtub" doesn't compare to some of the recent monster "Bathtubs," but it still has some interesting improvisation. This version caused one in my touring clan to identify a distinct Phish jam type as "deconstruction-reconstruction." And that is exactly what happens here. They break down the "Bathtub" until it is totally unrecognizable ("Hey Hole" territory), before piecing it back together. It is somewhat akin to a fairly spacey "Stash." My only complaint is that the "bottom" of the jam does sound a bit like an exercise. So just an okay "Bathtub" even though "Bathtub" is always a treat.

Why Phish hasn't pulled this one off the shelf in recent years is a mystery to me, because the a capella "Freebirds" played in 1993 are very creative, fun, unique Phish in my opinion. Although Fish is a little off-key for a while (one of the band members motioned with their hand at the show and he caught on), toward the end the whole band's crazy scat jam/a capella guitar solo is just out of this world. Wow. Great first set.

"2001" opened many a second set in 1993, especially in the summer as an opportunity for Chris to show off the new lights (before summer '93, Phish didn't have the moving/color changing variety, just stage lamps, strobes, and a few other goodies). This version is what people would now call "standard" because there isn't any real funked-out jam between passes by the main theme. Page gets a few bars at the keys but that's it. Still enjoyable of course, and the "Mike's" that followed…wow! I cannot say enough about this golden hose. It is a platinum hose. A five-carat diamond hose. An all-time-great "Mike's Song:" my favorite, hands down, on tape or in concert. Everyone in the band contributes in a meaningful way. Trying to describe the melody is pointless—you must hear it for yourself to understand its beauty. And the segue into "The Horse" is perfectly seamless, a feat made all the more astounding when you realize that Trey switches over to an acoustic guitar that was brought onstage by a roadie.

"Punch You in the Eye" was another song on my wish list that I didn't really expect to hear. Page's ascending keys part near the beginning is executed perfectly (on the piano as it should be) and everything is tight throughout. And then "McGrupp" follows. Already a stupendous setlist and then this! This "McGrupp" is nicely played (note the choice drum fills) and Page's solo is better then its usually awesome self. This is my second-favorite "McGrupp," next to 12/31/91.

The "Weekapaug" is high-energy and includes some fabulous gui-tar shredding by Trey. He hits upon a theme from the "Mike's Song" earlier in this set that, after hearing it in both contexts, seems more apropos to "Weekapaug." This "Weekapaug" dissolves into a short but sweet vocal jam segment that segues into the music for "Purple Rain." Then Fish takes the stage!

This "Purple Rain" is very long. It is an amusing Fishman number, but he wasn't in control of his vacuum to quite the same degree as the night before. Compared to most of the rest of the show, this is a tad weak. Fun in concert, but not really interesting on tape.

"Slave" is quite possibly played by request; you can hear fans chanting "Slave, Slave, Slave" before the opening chords on my tape. This "Slave" does not have one of the all-time-best endings (e.g., 4/9/94, 7/13/94) but it does have the all-time-best build toward the ending. Absolutely mesmerizing! And the height of the jam (Trey solo, really) is quite high. I was not very familiar with this song when I heard it at the show, but it blew me away with its melodic majesty and still does five years later.

The encore, "Rocky Top," is tight and fun. "GTBT" rocks the house down; Trey nails the jam with a Mack truck. Wonderful encore!

This is one of the all-time-great Phish shows, hands down. It has height ("Mike's" super hose, also great versions of "Bowie," "McGrupp," "Weekapaug," "Slave," and "GTBT"), a great deal of width (every song except "Mockingbird" and "Freebird" played flawlessly), and a setlist full of Phishy candy. In my experience, it ranks as one of my two favorite concert experiences ever (with 12/31/95, which has its own flub during "Coil") and is still my favorite Phish tape. If you don't have this show in your tape collection, get it now. Your collection isn't worth talking about without it.

5/4/94 State Palace Theatre, New Orleans, LA—Matt Laufer

It was May 1994. My second voyage to the New Orleans Jazz and Heritage Festival had come and gone. I was now sticking around the Crescent City for a few days to catch Phish at the State Palace Theater before returning to sunny Florida. To save money we decided to camp on the Mississippi Bayou, home to many a legend, and many a biting insect.

Two nights before the show, while camping out, I made the mistake of not covering every inch of my body to protect it from insects. My ankles were torn apart and dotted like a page of Braille from all the bites.

I awoke the next morning and my left ankle was severely swollen, and very sore and tender. It hurt to walk on it. All I could think to myself was that this could not and would not ruin my Phish experience. The swelling would go down and I would have no problem. Well not quite. Through the course of the day my ankle continued to bother me but it was far from unbearable. I continued to think that it would slowly go away, so as not to interfere with the show the following evening. With that thought in mind, I went to bed.

Lo and behold, I woke up the next morning, the swelling was gone, and any pain had all but vanished. All I had left to do was enjoy the show that evening. As we waited in line for the show to start, rumors abounded that the Cosmic Country Horns would be joining the band as they had in NYC earlier in the tour. I made it through a great first set, still no problems.

The second set began, and it was really inspirational. They kicked it off with "Antelope", one of my all-time favorites. This was made even more special when Trey dedicated the "Antelope" jam to a friend back in Burlington who had given birth to a baby during set break. He play-

fully wished "the baby [went on to live their] life something like that jam" and that it be named Marco Esquandolas. You wouldn't happen to have any spike…man?

The set continued with a "Bouncin'," and then "YEM" into jam and…bring on the horns. The Cosmic Country Horns (The Giant Country Horns + Michael Ray), marched out on stage in all their psychedelic glory blowing their brass to the beat while Trey and the crowd cheered them on. From there they proceeded to blow the roof off the State Palace Theater with made-for-horns songs like "Julius," "Magilla," and even a rendition of Duke Ellington/Juan Tizol's "Caravan."

The show was a real barn burner and gently set me down on an astral plane somewhere this side of the Milky Way. I found myself waiting outside the venue about an hour after it ended when Mike Gordon came strolling by with a friend. "Hey, what's up?" I said. "Not much, me and a friend are going to grab a drink, wanna come?" Mike replied. Being the responsible friend that I am, and knowing how much it sucks thinking that you have lost a member of your party in a town as sketchy as New Orleans (although I love it), I declined, choosing to wait for my pals.

By this point I was exhausted, and had long since forgotten about my previously bad ankle. Unfortunately, I awoke to a painful reminder. The ankle was again swollen, only now it had become so painful I could bear no weight on it or even move it. I thought I had broken my ankle. We had a long drive ahead of us and my first priority was to see a doctor upon returning. It turned out the excessive bug bites had infected my ankle causing the pain and swelling. After twenty-four hours and a few antibiotics, I was 100 percent healed. Looking back on the whole event, I am still amazed how I was able to will sickness away long enough to enjoy a healing of another sort, a spiritual one.

5/7/94 Bomb Factory, Dallas, TX—Dean Budnick

I rolled the dice on this one. Many of my friends who no longer have the time or energy to complete a full tour do the same thing. The idea is to scan over the docket as soon as it is released in an effort to predict whether Phish is going offer a jaw-dropping performance on any particular night. Some times it's easier, as the band certainly works up energy for special shows (Halloween, NYE), and the same can be said of any gigs in the Burlington region. Other times one just has to rely on hunches (Vegas '96 screamed out) and accept that fact that there will always be sleepers (Charleston, WV, '94 or Darien Lake, NY, '97—many people are still kicking themselves for blowing off the Merry Pranksters to head up to Maine). At any rate, back in March of 1994 when I looked over the spring tour dates, Texas just seemed appealing. At the very least I figured I would see three shows from my favorite band and have the opportunity to visit La Grange, the new Texas Rangers ballpark, the famed Grassy Knoll, and the Dr. Pepper museum. Admittedly, I felt some guilt when I later realized that it would be Mother's Day weekend but I'd already bought the tickets and I think my mom grew heartened when I assured her that these were "three totally nug venues."

So I boarded a plane on Friday, May 6, for a three-day stomp across Texas. My itinerary led me to Houston that night, then Dallas on Saturday, and finally Austin on Sunday. The Houston show had been moved from Bayou City Theater to a club called the Tower, a slight downsizing which was okay by me. The Austin gig took place at the Backyard, a venue that certainly lived up to its name as the stage was set up on a small patch of grass behind a funky bar/rib joint. At both of these shows I accomplished a task that had long since eluded me in my native New England. I was able to set up my deck, start it, walk to the lip of the stage to watch the band, work my way back when it was time to flip my tapes, and then return to the rail. Both of these shows offered some sublime moments (in particular the Austin second set. I'm a sucker for any "Halley's" that emerges from a "YEM" vocal jam, and there was also a solid, machine-gun "Antelope"). Still, it is the Bomb Factory show that I return to time and again (it's my fallback tape whenever I can't decide and I want to hear something that will bring on a smile).

On that Saturday morning after the Houston show I headed north (following an early morning visit to NASA which certainly put me in the mood for all things spacey). I made it to Dallas in time to catch a few innings of baseball, then I pointed my car toward the Deep Elum section of the city. Eventually, I found myself in the right area—an artsy district, full of bars, coffee shops, and music. As I drove up the street toward the venue, I saw a cluster of people standing outside a club and I immediately parked. As it turned out, these people were actually waiting to see the band GWAR (a group of costumed thrash-metal freaks, more on this later). Fortunately, however, my destination was just a short walk away.

The Bomb Factory was an old abandoned warehouse that had been renovated mostly with some thick coats of paint. Given the name of the venue, I would not be surprised if it had been an abandoned munitions plant. The space was wide but not very deep. My guess is that maybe it could hold a thousand people when totally packed, but if you were trapped over on the far sides you'd never be able to see the stage. On this night I would estimate the club was at two-thirds capacity or so. We set up our decks to the side of Paul Languedoc, and I remember thinking that the sound in this cavern would make our efforts futile (but actually the place sounded okay). I also recall that there was a metal walkway accessible to VIPs through a cage to the side of the bar, and that a few random people occasionally kicked off paint chips and spilled beer below throughout the night.

When Phish took the stage and broke into "Llama," the night began in an agreeable if inauspicious manner. Indeed, while the entire first set was solid, it really offered no hint of what was to follow. When the band returned from its "fifteen-minute" break with "Loving Cup," I started to grin (always an entertaining cover, despite those who might say the version that had opened the Patriot Center show three weeks earlier offered a more kicking jam). As the final chords concluded, Trey started in with "Sparkle," and my memory of this song is that a group of people moved to the back of the Factory to spin gleefully in the open space behind the tapers' section.

Then the action really started, as the band…ahem…dropped the bomb. As "Sparkle" raced to a close, Trey started in with the opening notes of "Tweezer". For some reason, though, the rest of the band didn't follow and there was a brief silence before they restarted the song in earnest. (In retrospect, it's almost as if they were all taking in one deep collective breath before IT was underway.) During the seventy minutes of music that followed, Phish was perpetually creating on the fly, segueing from idea to idea, song to song, working to keep the music alive and flowing. This was something the group had long done before in rehearsal and soundcheck, but finally decided to share with a concert audience. It was a hoot to stand back and watch the band members exchange both quizzical looks and smiles of affirmation (I particularly recall Trey's very visible enthusiasm, as his entire body was in motion). The result was a massive "Tweezer" sandwich that included: a blues jam

that demonstrated the Phish's effective use of dynamics; some spontaneous cries (reportedly inspired by the GWAR show next door); a number of delicate passages; a pounding "Sparks;" an entertaining stab at the Breeders' "Cannonball;" an extended "Hold Your Head Up Jam" after Fishman's vacuum-abetted "Purple Rain;" and the climactic "Tweezer Reprise" closing. In looking back, I have to admit that I had one weak moment midway through, just after "Makisupa," when the band drifted into "Sweet Emotion" and I initiated a frantic tape flip, losing about ten seconds in my panic and excitement. At any rate, as the band returned for "Amazing Grace" and "Sample," I spent the entire encore in a semi-stupor, buzzing from what I had taken in and more than a little curious as to what people thought who were there seeing Phish for the first time. (Had they expected that kind of loose, segued madness? Did they think it was silly? Weird? Inspiring?) This thought returned to me the next day as I drove around Dallas and then down to Austin, playing that second set in my car again and again and again.

The Phish experience has always been about evolution, both of the band and its listeners. The quartet will often work into a phase, focus heavily on certain elements, and then move on, incorporating some of those elements into its next incarnation. So while there is no doubt that subsequent "Tweezers" have been more complex, challenging, and experimental (for instance 11/2/94 or the controversial 6/22/95), this is the one that keeps me coming back. It's not just that I was there (although inevitably that helps). Instead, I love this "Tweezer" for all of its playfulness. There is a zest and vitality as the band finally breaks through a barrier and alters everyone's expectations. I love this "Tweezer" for its premise as well as its promise. My mom likes it too.

6/18/94 UIC Pavilion, University of Chicago, Chicago, IL —James Raras, Jr.

The first set of this show is basically forgettable, but the second set makes up for it! The "Peaches"->"Mind Left Body Jam" to open is pure bliss. Not to mention that "MLBJ" segues into one of the best fifteen-minute "Bowies" around, complete with a "Three Blind Mice" jam and a couple of nods to Hendrix in the closing trill segment. The "Tweezer" later on in the set is a gorgeous version with some very nice textured jamming as well as some "MLBJ" hints. As if "Bowie" and "Tweezer" weren't enough, a solid "YEM" pops up toward the end and makes this set a winner for sure. Check out the pristine soundboards that circulate.

6/26/94 Municipal Auditorium, Charleston, WV—Scott Eidam

This was definitely the show that hooked me for life. It is now known as the "GameHoist" show, for obvious reasons. I won't go into much of a performance review besides saying they rocked and the setlists speak for themselves. Of course, the music is what brought me there, but the main reason this show had such a big impact on me was the circumstances surrounding it.

I had just gotten back from studying and traveling for a semester in Florence (Firenze), Italy. I went with my buddy Dogger, and as we departed I gave him a little crap for bringing twenty Phish tapes along. Though I had seen the boys three times already, I was not a huge fan yet—still sticking to my Jerry-is-God opinion and not really opening myself up to the Phish experience. Well, needless to say, those damn tapes grew on me like fungus on cow dung. By the end of our four-month adventure, I was thanking the Dogger for bringing that music.

By then I knew about every note and lyric on all twenty tapes.

Back in the States I dubbed a few tapes and was off to an adventurous job supervising youth groups in the repair of poor peoples' homes in War, West Virginia. This was one tough job. Sixteen- to eighteen-hour days (no exaggeration) of some of the most satisfying and hard work I've ever done. When I found out Phish was playing two hours' drive from War in Charleston, I felt I deserved a break and immediately told my supervisors that I had a "wedding" to go to. They bought it and I was off to see Phish—the band I now felt I really knew after listening to those twenty tapes and many others.

So going into this, my fourth Phish show, having done my "homework" listening to tapes, I felt I was ready to rock along with every tune note for note. Maybe I would finally figure out what this Phish thing is all about. What I did not realize was that I had never heard a "Gamehendge" tape and that Phish had recently released *Hoist*—an album I had never heard, or heard of, for that matter.

I walked into Charleston's Municipal Auditorium right as Fish crashed a big cymbal to start "Kung." Huh, Kung? What's this weird chant? As Trey began to tell his intricate story of the fall of the Lizard people, Wilson's abuse of the Helping Friendly Book's powers, and the rest, I was mesmerized—drawing parallels in my head to our government's treatment of Native Americans and to the Bible. Wow, these guys are a lot more than the noodling, nonsense-lyrics band I had pegged them to be. Oh, I forgot to mention, the auditorium was about one-third full with no more than nine hundred people in attendance. Since I was alone, I walked right up to an empty second row seat in front of Trey. By the end of "Gamehendge," I was fully impressed and ready to hear some tunes I knew. (Of course I knew "Divided Sky," "Lizards", "Llama", etc., but the rest were not on tapes I had heard.) So what do they do second set? They played all new tunes I did not know, but quickly caught on to and enjoyed. This was the only time they have played all the songs from one album in the same order as they were on the album. Pretty cool. They encored with the first "My Old Home Place," which I remember Trey saying they had just learned on the bus the night before. Then I think I recall Trey saying something about Internet people requesting this next one—"Tube." Another rare one that I had never heard before, but loved. Ending it off with a killer version of my favorite guitarist's (Hendrix) song, "Fire," you have the show that would hook most people and definitely hooked me.

Moral of the story: You never know what you're gonna get when you see a Phish show, but it almost always satisfies your soul. If it was predictable, we wouldn't travel fourteen hours to see them like I'm doing this weekend (12/6–7/97).

6/30/94 Classic Amphitheater, Richmond, VA—Charlie Dirksen

Rain was pouring down when we pulled into the lot in the late afternoon. Though the initial downpour didn't last long, it would con-

tinue to rain intermittently throughout the evening. Fortunately, my friend Jason Bredfeldt and I had good seats under the shed (where are you now, Jason?). This shed is unremarkable; not even vaguely as "classic" as its name suggests.

The first set featured an excellent "Gumbo" (for 1994) and a thrilling "Split Open and Melt" with an unusual vocal jam. The "Scent of a Mule" had a Russian polka jam in it, which would have been unusual had the same thing (more or less) not been performed a few days later at Garden State. The first set closed with a well-played "Frankenstein."

The second set was highlighted by an eerie "YEM" vocal jam with "redrum" screeching (see the movie, *The Shining*, for more info) and a "Harpua" with the first-ever cover of "Honky Tonk Women." This Rolling Stones tune was sung by a local musician (a guy named Sean) who was invited onstage and then climbed out of the first row. I didn't notice, but Noah Cole told me that the rain had stopped shortly before Trey said "Look, the storm's gone!" in the "Harpua." Notably, there was a "Harpua reprise" of sorts that segued into "Antelope". The "Love You" contained a memorable vacuum solo, which amused me to no end, but it seemed to have a similar effect on very few others in the audience. I was also laughing my ass off for the first encore tune ("Sleeping Monkey"), a satirical rock anthem that only gets more amusing the more Phish hams it up.

7/1/94 Mann Music Center, Philadelphia, PA—Charlie Dirksen

Although I enjoyed seeing this show with friends (including Jon and Ceci, who would later marry, and Tina and Rob, who wouldn't), it was not very memorable musically. "NICU" was the highlight of the first set for me, since I (and many others, probably) had written Mike earlier in the year and begged that the band bring it back. Page soloed well in the "It's Ice," and helped make it an unusually strong version. "Tela" is always enjoyable to hear. Every time I see "Julius" I think it's the best damn version I've ever seen or heard, and this set-closing version was no different.

The second set was performed fine, but did not rage. It was wonderful to hear "Fluffhead" and "TMWSIY" played well, but the audience really didn't seem too into it. "Possum" contained a good jam, and "Terrapin" was a riot. Many people were not amused; everyone should be entertained by the absurdity of a vacuum solo, dammit! "Harry Hood" was nice but (like this show) not special. "Average-great Phish" at best, as they say.

7/1/94 Mann Music Center, Philadelphia, PA—Erik Swain

This show serves as direct counter-proof to those who claim Phish was "always better back then."

It was my second show, after the wild and fun 5/2/93. I was hoping that I'd get something even half as memorable as that one. Didn't happen. Maybe I'm bitter because it was the only show to which I took my girlfriend (who is now my wife) and she was bored to tears and vowed never to see Phish again. But the tapes confirm that the show was as uninspired as I thought it was at the time.

The setlist looks like something you'd kill for, but as you know, setlists never tell the whole story. This show was for the most part devoid of passion, emotion, and inventiveness. If I had to guess, I would chalk it up to burnout from the previous night in Richmond, where they went crazy with "YEM," "Antelope," and "Harpua."

The first set was unremittingly dull until toward the end. "Runaway Jim," "Foam," "Sample," and "NICU" were all by the book. At the time "Stash" probably suffered in my mind from comparison to the 5/2/93 version, but the tapes show it never really took off. "Mango" was again unspectacular. I was glad to hear "It's Ice." The tapes reveal a neat piano-based jam in the middle, and a mellow segue into "Tela." When I relistened to this recently I thought it was a moderate saving grace to the set. Then the next day I popped in 6/11/94 and heard the exact same piano jam and segue. So the highlight of the set so far was merely a repetition of something that had worked before. "Tela" itself was standard. Then "Julius" started and finally there was some real energy. Both "Julius" and the set-closing "Suzy Greenberg" that followed had a good spark and got the crowd involved. But they were not enough to save what remains to this day one of the worst sets I have ever heard, in person or on tape.

The second set opened with "Bowie," which provided the show's lone musical highlight. This rendition is danceable and intense. Toward the end things got really fast and the four of them melded as one into a raging jam, which today reminds me of the madness at the end of the 7/15/99 "YEM." You would think this would kick-start a fine set, but that didn't happen. "If I Could" stuck to the script of the *Hoist* version, and "Fluffhead" and "DWD" were nothing special. I had not heard "TMWSIY"->"Avenu"->"TMWSIY" before this show and I was extremely bored at the time. In retrospect it's no worse than anything else here, just at the same level of listlessness.

"Possum" was next. I like my "Possums" raging, such as 4/16/92. This was a laid-back one and I was disappointed at the time. The tapes show it to be a bit better than that, with a "Voodoo Child" ("Slight Return") tease coming as a surprise. But it was still not the kick in the pants that this set needed. Fishman's routine with "Terrapin" was amusing, but it was merely a diversion and not particularly memorable. Then they started "Hood," which would be the last chance to salvage the show. It was pleasant and fluid, like all versions at the time. But it was not the exceptional performance we needed. A perfunctory "Cavern" closed the set, and the energetic "Rocky Top" encore was too little, too late.

What bothers me most about this performance is how clinical it sounds. Most songs are well played but there is no inspiration and no risk-taking, save the "Bowie." This is probably the closest thing I have ever heard to Phish going through the motions. There is nothing even slightly memorable about it, save the "Bowie."

Worst of all, on a personal note, it was a factor in delaying my conversion from casual fan to die-hard. I continued to see the band once a year when they came around to Philly, but at the time there were plenty of other bands that held my interest and I was not convinced that I should devote most of my concert-going dollars to multiple Phish shows. Not until fall '97 did I become the raving maniac of a fan that I am today.

There is no reason to get the tapes unless you were at the show or you collect all the good versions of "Bowie." Unless of course you just want to shut up that friend of yours who keeps telling you that they were always better back then.

7/2/94 Garden State Arts Center, Holmdel, NJ—Charlie Dirksen

Ever waited at Will Call for your friend because you had his or her ticket? I waited for an hour for Dead to make it through traffic and the lot to Will Call. We missed the "Golgi" but made it in during the beginning of "Divided Sky." The first set was a good set for 1994. We

heard both "Fast Enough for You" and "Lifeboy," probably my two favorite "slow and sappy" Phish songs. I recall "Sparkle" being enormously popular with the audience, as it still is today. And it was memorable hearing "Tweezer Reprise" close the first set.

The second-set "Mike's Song" featured Trey and Mike on trampolines, along with the fog, if memory serves. Mike and Trey played the "I Am Hydrogen" on their backs, a stunt they often did during "Hydrogen" back then. We were blessed to get both "McGrupp" and "Slave". It was wild to hear a Hebrew prayer and AC/DC's "Highway to Hell" during the same set, too.

7/3/94 The Ballpark, Old Orchard Beach, ME—Kim Hannula

It was an unusually sunny summer day on the coast of Maine. My significant other and I spent the afternoon in downtown Old Orchard Beach, eating ice cream and lobster rolls and walking along the beach. I actually had a sunburn already when we headed back to The Ballpark for the show.

The Ballpark is a small stadium, built for a minor league baseball team in the '80s. It wasn't anywhere near full for the show—my s.o. and I had huge amounts of dancing space where we were planted in front of the tapers' section, and there was almost nobody in the stands. This was the last truly mellow, uncrowded Phish show I had the pleasure of experiencing.

The beginning of the first set was filled with fairly short songs. It was fun, though—especially hearing "NICU", which had been a rarity before the summer '94 tour, and which I had never heard on tape. The high point of the first set, though, was "Reba." It wasn't the sort of "Reba" that you search for on tape, like the "Reba" on Halloween later in 1994, but there was a certain magic being there. The sun was setting, and tiny clouds in the west (away from the stage) were turning various shades of pink. Trey began staring off into the clouds, and then, quietly, playing "Somewhere Over the Rainbow." I think the entire crowd looked back to see what he was staring at.

The second set featured more composed stuff ("Lizards", "Bouncing," "It's Ice," "Silent in the Morning," "Julius") between the "Split Open and Melt" opener and "The Squirming Coil". It didn't matter to me at the time, though—this was my sixth show, and I was just starting to build a tape collection. It was such a thrill to hear "Lizards" live after listening to it on tape on the drive to Maine!

The high point in the show, though, was "Antelope". Imagine "Antelope" has just begun. The crowd goes wild. They improvise around a little on the quiet part, then move on to the louder jam, and then suddenly the sky erupts in an umbrella of pink fire droplets. Big "OOooos" from the crowd. A great fireworks display—explosions in clusters, one after another, building a visual crescendo while the jam built aurally. At one point the band started playing the fireworks—drums hit when the fireworks went off, a little rising guitar note for the rising spark, followed by chords timed with the explosion. Page played one of the fireballs exactly the way it looked. I swear I was looking at an image of the pleasure sensors in my brain going off in response to the music during the entire fireworks display.

They held the end of "Antelope" for quite a while (waiting for the fireworks to end?), but ended up moving on to "Suzy Greenberg." The fireworks finale came near the beginning of "Suzie."

I've seen fireworks to Sousa marches, and I've seen fireworks to Handel's "Water Music" (which was very good, by the way), but I don't think I ever fully experienced fireworks until I saw them with "Run Like an Antelope."

During the "Fire" encore, roadies lit a Phish-logo ground fireworks display to send us off to July 4th with our brains exploding.

7/8/94 Great Woods Amphitheater, Mansfield, MA —James Raras, Jr.

As rain pelted the windshield and lightning from the storm struck all around, we trudged down Interstate 495 toward Mansfield, MA. It was the home of Great Woods, or I should say Icculus, on this night. Arriving in the parking lot about half an hour prior to the show, we parked next to these guys from Boston College. When I asked them what they though Phish would play on this night they jokingly said, "Maybe they'll play all of *Rift* tonight," in reference to the 6/26/94 Charleston, WV, show where the first set was "Gamehendge" and the second *Hoist* in its entirety (sans "Riker's Mailbox"). How I'd love to ask them how they felt about that comment after this show.

After purchasing our lawn tickets for $19.50 from the box office, we made our way into the venue as "Llama" started up. When we finally got situated on the soggy mess that used to be the lawn they were playing a strange song I had never heard before, "N_2O," and Trey began to tell the story of "a fifty-two-year-old man sitting in a dentist's chair." As the opening chords to "Lizards" rang out through the pavilion of Great Woods, the enthusiastic East Coast crowd let out a roaring cheer. Could it be? Trey began to talk again after "Lizards" and the crowd was attentive to his narration until the beginning of "Tela," at which point another huge roar was released. Maybe... As Trey spoke of Errand Wolfe venturing into the forest to find the evil King Wilson, the crowd knew they were experiencing something very special. They were in for a full performance of "Gamehendge!" The bass line to "Wilson" triggered the loudest cheer of the night, and we were on our way.

"AC/DC Bag," with preceding narration, followed the rousing version of "Wilson." This was followed by a standard "Forbin">"Mockingbird," which included the regular "Gamehendge" narration. No sooner than when Page's last note from "Mockingbird" left the amphitheater, Trey began to tell us about the only thing in Gamehendge that could kill the evil King Wilson, "The Sloth." After "The Sloth" Phish gave us an alternative perspective of the whole saga from the old shepherd via "McGrupp." A great version of "Divided Sky" filled Great Woods and made everyone forget that it was raining—a fantastic way to close a very special set.

The "Rift" second-set-opener gave hope to the hypothesis that I had heard in the lot only a mere two hours prior, but it was quickly thwarted by "Sample". Following "Sample" was a strong version of "Reba," which preceded an eerie "Yerushalayim Shel Zahav." I remember being very happy to hear "It's Ice" at this point in the set, as it was one of my favorites at the time. "Ice" was preceded by a fantastic version of "Stash," which is now featured on *A Live One*, but the jamming hardly stopped there! As the opening chords to "You Enjoy Myself" began the crowd once again was electrified, and as the band completed the segue into "Frankenstein," Great Woods exploded! The "Frankenstein" sandwich was completed by a seamless return to "You Enjoy Myself" complete with obligatory vocal jam. Standard versions of "Julius" and "Golgi" capped off the set, but the damage was done!

For the encore we got treated to a double, starting off with "Nellie Kane," which I wasn't familiar with at the time but was great. Little did I know that I'd see it only once more in the next three years! "Cav-

ern" filled the second slot of the encore nicely, as Trey went off with his effects, in typical 1994 "Cavern" style. When Trey said ,"See you right here again tomorrow night," I knew there was no place I'd rather be, and was thrilled to have pavilion seats for Saturday's show. Little did I know that forty-seven shows and a little more than three years later, I'd look back on this, my first show, as one of the most special Phish shows ever! Not only was this a fantastic show but it was the last live performance of the "Gamehendge" saga to date. Was it the last ever? Who knows, but if it was, they sent it out in style, in their own neck of the woods with the full support of a home crowd. Worth driving an hour and a half through a lightning storm for? I'd say so!

7/8–9/94 Great Woods, Mansfield, MA.—Adam Schneider

I wish I had documented my earlier Phish shows in writing, because these shows were primal to me—everything was new, and the shows were spectacular. I will attempt to rekindle the flame that made these shows so amazing to me, in writing. Up till this point I had been seeing Phish for one year (7/23/93 Jones Beach Amphitheater, Wantagh, NY, was my first show). I had the "phire," as some called it back then. I was seeing them any chance I could. I had kicked off the year by seeing wonderful shows in Binghamton and the Beacon Theater run in April, but nothing could prepare me for this wild weekend.

A couple of my friends and I made the trek up to Great Woods from Long Island. I had just recently seen the Mann Music Center show (7/1/94), and had heard about the "GameHoist" show in Charleston, West Virginia (6/26/94 Municipal Auditorium). Needless to say, I was astounded that they did the most complete "Gamehendge" since '88. I was thoroughly jealous for not attending the "unannounced" show (it was not in the newsletter, and was announced during the tour—a few showed up nonetheless).

So, as we check into our hotel, we begin talking about the night's show and what we might have in store. We make our way to the venue and check out the lot scene. It was getting crowded, not insane like it is nowadays, but it was crazy for its period. There were quite a few ticketless. As we enter the venue, a beautiful girl walks up to my friend Ryan and compliments him for his "beautiful eyes," and hands him a ticket. Ryan already had a ticket, so he hands it to the first girl he sees, who was ticketless, and compliments her on her beautiful eyes. She gives him the most genuine hug I've seen and beams a smile to us, making us all feel very good. Enter venue…My friend Erick and I go to our seats, which are within the first ten rows, center, and settle down for the show to begin. Finally, the lights dim, and out comes Phish, breaking out my first "Llama." I'm very happy and express it to Erick. As the song ends, we hear a siren going off, and I'm convinced there's a fire, but nothing happens. Suddenly, I realize that it is Phish making this noise. Confusion settles into some sort of order for me as I realize it's "N$_2$O." I had recently picked up the "Down with Disease" cassette single, which has "N$_2$O" on the B-side. I thought it hilarious that they were playing this orthodontically challenged song. Who'd a thunk?

Amidst the drilling and the smooth talking of Mike, the dentist, Trey begins speaking about a fifty-two-year-old man sitting in a dentist's chair…And we stepped through the door….Was this "Gamehendge?" Erick and I exchange confused glances, as the reality of this event sunk in. Only two weeks later and they were doing "Gamehendge" again. I will not review every bit of this set—you need to hear it yourself—but I will say that this still holds top honors in my opinion, for one of my favorite

Phish experiences, and I haven't even gotten to the tip of the iceberg yet.

The set ends and we begin mingling with the people around us. Everyone seems transcended, which tends to happen right after the lights come on. We talk to one person and express how much we loved that set. He replies, "it was good, but I wish they had played 'Chalk Dust.'" We agreed, of course, (insert laughing here).

The second set is highlighted by a wonderful "YEM">"Frankenstein">"YEM" sandwich. The show ends, and we leave fulfilled.

Fast-forward to night two. We park in the lot, and who parks next to us but the Dude of Life. We talk with him for a while and proceed into the venue. Show begins with a solid "Runaway Jim" and closes with a smoking "Antelope". Second set, well, let me just show you: Also "Sprach Zarathustra">"Split Open and Melt">"Fluffhead">"Poor Heart">"Tweezer">"Lifeboy">"Sparkle">"Big Ball Jam">"Harry Hood," "Suzy Greenberg." 'Nuff said.

As the show ends, I'm walking out and bump into the Dude of Life again. We talk for a bit and he asks me if I'd like to meet the band. Of course I say yes, and he gives me an extra pass. As I enter the backstage area, the first person I see is Trey, with his big shit-ass grin. The Dude asks me if I am going to tomorrow night's show (SPAC), to which I reply that I am, and he says, "good." He wound up playing with them the next night. Trey and the Dude of Life are ushered out by corporate-looking people, and I'm standing there, knowing no one, and being surrounded by the rest of Phish, phamily, and a few other phans.

I drink a few beers and talk to Page for a bit. Just small talk, but he's very friendly and amazingly humble. Mike, on the other hand, is a bit stranger. I ask him if they had planned out the "Gamehendge" (for possible CD-ROM release) or just busted it out. His reply: "We busted." Then he says goodbye and walks away. Not unfriendly, just strange.

I talk to a few other people. Happened to see "Big Phil" who I have seen at every show I've been to (and the few times I was at the aftershow party). I tell him that I see him at every show, to which he replies, "I am at every show." He laughed and so does Amy Skelton. After a bit I start talking to Fish (you must realize there were not many people at this aftershow, so the people I felt I knew the most were Phish). Fish was extremely friendly, and I literally feel like I'm talking to one of my friends. He enlightens me to the meaning of "Weekapaug Groove:" they were at a party in Weekapaug, RI, and had a great time, and wrote about it. He said the rumors about the band all sleeping with the same girl were bogus…hmmm?

After a while, I knew my friends were probably getting impatient, waiting at my car with no clue where I was, so I decided I had to get going. I had Page, Mike, and Fish sign my ticket from the night before ("Gamehendge"), and really wanted Trey to sign it too. Enter fanboy phase…I told Fish that this was probably going to sound lame, but does he know if Trey is coming out. Fish sarcastically replied, "Well I usually keep tabs on him, but he got away this time." Of course I felt really stupid, and just said to him, "hey…," his friends commented to him he was being rude, and he apologized to me, said he was just kidding, and said he had no clue where he was. I, feeling stupid, said okay and goodbye. By the way, when I first asked Fish to sign my ticket, his friends said, "wow, you're a rock star now." This hugeness must've still been so new to them. I left the venue totally in shock about what had just transpired. When I got back to my car and told my friends what happened, they were so happy for me. After all, they had driven Page (don't ask) to a show the previous summer (Waterloo, NJ), and I was

supposed to go with them. So, they were happy for my experience.

What an amazing run. Remember, *we can stage a runaway golf-cart marathon!*

7/16/94 Summer Stage at Sugarbush, North Fayston, VT —Jamie Hellen

It was a marvelous sunny day in North Fayston, VT, with green mountains all around us. There was not a better day to see Phish, and as we would find out later, the band felt the same way. The venue was one of the most beautiful at which to see Phish, or any concert for that matter. It was on the side of Sugarbush Mountain in the middle of the Green Mountains. Unfortunately, there was a bus system (similar to Waterloo Village) where we had to line up so busloads of Phish fans could be taken to the actual concert site. But it was such a beautiful day that not one person in the ten thousand-plus crowd could care less what they had to do to see their beloved quartet.

They opened up the show with an unusual treat to make us feel like we were with them in their most beloved environment. They came out and harmonized a few lines from "Back in My Hometown." Five seconds later, "Golgi Apparatus" was permeating the crowd, and it had people going absolutely bananas. A selection from their latest release, *Hoist*, was next, "Down with Disease." It was a very simple, babyish version that featured Trey soloing throughout. Several minutes later, they slowed it down, along with the crowd. Weird noises appeared. Trey grabbed his megaphone off of his amp and started waving his arm in huge circles, passing the megaphone by his microphone. Mike grabbed a drill and held it in front of his mic. All this was giving up the sounds of a very rare "N_2O," asong played for the first time this summer. only that summer a few times. The effect they created was that we were sitting in a dentist's chair. How a band can make you feel like you are in a dentist's chair is beyond me but they did a great job of it. Mike played the part of the dentist, saying lines like, "You are getting sleepy," and "Don't worry, it won't hurt." Out of nowhere the band went right into "Stash." The only way to describe it is short, brief, and concise, yet still somewhat engaging. Other favorites in the set were "Cavern," "Sparkle," and an incredible "Maze," "Horse">"Silent," and the set closer, "Sample in a Jar." The energy and rare vibe that fans live for were there, but there was not too much to go crazy over except a well-played set.

If only we had known what was ahead. The lights went out, the sun was pretty much down. The remnants of a gorgeous sunset were still upon us, and we heard the opening lick to "Run Like an Antelope". Just writing this review is giving me goosebumps. This version of "Antelope" is by far one of the best versions I have ever seen or heard the band perform. The energy they put toward the crowd was like no other. The main jam of the song started off in orbit. Trey was wandering all around stage in a groove that he had very rarely been in. Out of nowhere, he started screaming into the microphone. Page followed, screaming bloody murder. Trey was screaming "WEEEEEEEEEE" like he was on some sort of amusement-park ride. They even started laughing obnoxiously. Trey then started running around stage at a track star's pace, taking another guitar and doing windmills with it like Pete Townshend. After that mayhem, they broke into "Catapult," where the famous argument between Fish and Trey took place. Fish suggested that Trey didn't really want to get married, Trey got mad, and Fish apologized, all with tongue firmly lodged in cheek. Quickly they went back into "Antelope", where more screaming and running occurred. Page

stood up and was banging obnoxiously on his piano. At the end of "Antelope" they did the "D'oh!" from the *Simpsons* language, and the line "Set the gearshift for the high gear of your soul" was said with a passion, volume, and energy that no other "Antelope" has ever had. With some quiet feedback from "Antelope", the band burst into "Harpua," and what a "Harpua" it was. It was the most free-spirited and spontaneous narration I've ever heard. Trey first makes a claim that Vermont is the best state in the Union and that anyone who doesn't live there is totally missing out. The basic gist of the story is that Harpua and Poster are roaming around on top of the mountain we are standing on. Harpua is hungry and says, "Hot lunch, I want him." Just as he is about to attack poor Poster, a wave of energy came from nowhere and "they look up in the sky—and see a giant comet—crashing into Jupiter." Right then and there, a comet was actually crashing into Jupiter. Meanwhile the rest of the band was playing some heavy space, and then Fishman busted right into "2001," which I must say was one of the most perfectly placed versions ever. Following "2001," they proceeded to finish up "Harpua" with some altered lyrics ("your cat got hit by a comet!"). The band continued to rock hard by doing some great versions of "AC/DC Bag," "Scent of a Mule," "Contact," and "Harry Hood." They closed off the set with a fantastic version of "Chalk Dust." The encore was a ripping "Suzy Greenberg," and just like that, the tour was done. It was sad to say goodbye once more, but what made the ending worse was that now ten thousand tired kids all wanted to get on those buses to get back to their cars at the very same time.

10/8/94 Patriot Center, George Mason University, Fairfax, VA —Jon Epstein

This show is a classic, cover-to-cover. For years I had always felt the same way about "Chalk Dust" as most feel about "Sample" today, but this one changed my ears forever. What a great opener, a very ripping "Chalk Dust" with a bits of craziness, much like the rest of the show. "Down with Disease" a little bit later in the set showcases this very same principle. It was very short in comparison to most "Down with Diseases" but just as intense (more than some, even). The same was true with the "Antelope" that closed the set. Even "Guyute" was better than the debut from the night before. This is one of the best first sets around.

Once again, though, Phish wins the game in the second half. After a lackluster start in "2001">"Sample,">"Rift," they got things moving again with an insane "Mike's Song." With the smoke machines, lights, and band going full blast, we hardly noticed the setup of what was to come next. Once the fog dispersed, the band cut out, and there were two groups of about ten girls each in front of microphones, chanting something in call-and-response fashion. Once the girls left, the band kicked right back into the "Mike's" jam which led into a nice "Simple" into "Hydrogen" with Mike and Trey doing the classic robot walk around the stage, and out the other end with a very good "Weekapaug." And if that wasn't enough, next came a very energetic "Fluffhead," and my favorite "Purple Rain," because Fish went absolutely nuts. And there was a "Harry" and Boston's "Long Time" in there, too. Seek out both of these sets—you will not be disappointed.

10/16/94 Hill Auditorium, Ann Arbor, MI—Cory Ferber

What is a band without simple? When I heard Phish would be playing Hill Auditorium, my first thought was 12/15/71, the date

of a well-known Grateful Dead show at this venue. My second thought was Ann Arbor, MI, a small, friendly college town where my sister had attended the University of Michigan. These two thoughts, along with the temptation of hanging out with Ohioans for four straight Phish shows led me to travel from Rochester, New York.

We got to town early and hung out on campus all day. There was essentially no scene before the show, mainly because there was no central parking lot. The Auditorium is located in the heart of the campus. There was a small crowd outside before the show. I remember seeing a handful of food and soda vendors greeting us outside the doors after the show. There was essentially no lot scene in the Midwest at this time. I was shocked to see a raging scene in Syracuse, NY, less than a month later, on 11/6/94.

Stepping inside the building, I felt like I had entered sacred historical grounds. All my thoughts turned to imagining what the Dead, and the scene, might have been like in '71. The place was beautiful, with carpeting, plush seats, and a large balcony. From the ceiling hung the best theater sound system I have ever heard. I believe Phish only used the house speakers at this show. Most of the students appeared to be U. Michigan students, who unfortunately were sitting much of the time, especially in the long jam sequences.

The first set contains some of my older favorites including "Foam," "Reba," and "Fast Enough for You." "Stash" is at its full potential here, with a jam that was beyond anything I had ever heard. They deconstruct the song down to its basic elements, feeling more like a jazz band improvising rock music. It sounds like they turn the song inside out in a mathematical style. Fishman keeps the same timing, but the rest of the band appear to fill opposite holes. During the quiet section at the end of the jam, I had a vision of the band dancing like ballerinas with umbrellas while balancing on circus balls. Just when I thought they couldn't get any further away from "Stash," the main riff melted through without warning. It was brilliant! I remember commenting that I could walk out now and be happy.

The Reverend Jeff Mosier, formerly of Aquarium Rescue Unit, joined the band for the last four songs of the first set. Three of these had not been played in over a year, a special treat. Seeing the Reverend sing "Tennessee Waltz" is surely one of my oddest moments at a Phish concert. This was the first time I saw the band play a miniature acoustic set.

The second set is historic for a thirty-eight-minute sequence of "Mike's Song"->"Simple"->jam. This one was a shocker because at that time there were only a handful of shows where Phish had jammed for over a half-hour. (One of those is the "Tweezer" featured on *A Live One*, from Bangor, ME.) The unbelievable jam pushes the boundaries, with multiple segments that all have a life of their own. Every time I thought the jam would end, it just took off in a different direction. We stood with our jaws on the floor for most of it. While I admit that tapes are not as powerful as being there in the moment, I urge you to get a copy and take a listen!

This show led me deeper onto the bus. What I heard on "Stash" and "Simple" convinced me to travel just about anywhere, and as often as possible, to see this band. However, the next three nights were tainted for me by the magic of the Hill Auditorium. Some of the highlights include the Beatles' "Helter Skelter" to open Dayton the next night. The Hara Arena is really a college gymnasium with bleacher seating. The venue and vibe seemed very different from the previous night. The "Colonel Forbin"->"Vibration of Life"->"Mockingbird" was a nice

treat, though. The Reverend also played with the band all four nights, including a Michigan State encore of "Runaway Jim" with an extended banjo solo.

10/20/94 Mahaffey Theater, St. Petersburg, FL—Peter Bierman

October 20, 1994, the morning of my first day of vacation, began with a drive across Alligator Alley, out to the west coast of Florida. Up north to St. Petersburg, the day's destination. We found an inexpensive motel a couple of blocks from the venue, check in, and next it's off for adventure.

I had heard that the Salvador Dali Museum was close to the Mahaffey Theater, and this became the first stop on what would prove to be a rather surreal day. The walk ended up being a bit closer to ten blocks as opposed to the five blocks I was expecting. I was not the least bit disappointed at the works from Dali on display; it was the perfect way to spend the afternoon.

We decided to take a cab back closer to the motel, stopping to be dropped off someplace for diner. After a walk back to the motel, it was on to the show. The Mahaffey ended up being a tiny theater that couldn't have held more than twelve hundred people. A guy sitting next to me described it best when he said, "This place reminds me of the theater from *The Muppet Show.*"

When the band walked out, the first thing you couldn't help but notice was that Mike had his hair tied up, I want to say like Gene Simmons, but that wouldn't be quite right. It was more like something one of the B-52-ers might have done in *The Flintstones Movie*, just missing a bone or something. I knew right away that it would be an interesting night.

The shows opened with "Jim," and I noticed how attentive the small crowd was as the band was able to bring the music down to a whisper. Next, we were treated to the first and only performance of Stevie Wonder's "Golden Lady." With the first Halloween show coming up, this really turned me on to how sophisticated this band really is. They seem to easily transform into another band while the audience enjoys a little diversity.

While the band was playing "Poor Heart," I couldn't help but feel that these guys really enjoy playing music. The song truly brought a more upbeat atmosphere to the show. The band sped into "Guelah," and suddenly things seemed to almost stop. It was more of a shift, because Mike began to bounce a beat along before the band picked back up into "Guelah." This was the first time I noticed how Phish can change tempo at will, just deciding to slow things down for the next number.

"Split Open and Melt" seemed to take this show on a visit to the Dali Museum. For me, this "Split" marked a personal transition, a change from Phish fan to Phish fanatic. For the first time, I noticed how Phish would change tempos, taking the music in several new directions. Meanwhile, my mind was noticing how visual the music could be if you allowed it to lead you, more as a soundtrack to a day's adventure than a song with any kind of set meaning or structure. We seemed to venture forward, but we would always manage to hit some barrier. The music then seemed to swirl around this tiny theater. It was like we were caught up in a tornado, but the barrier still stopped us….Suddenly things become very dream-like, and the room filled with smoke. "Kung" was chanted. At the time, I had no earthly idea as to what was going on. It never crossed my mind that Trey was using the powers of "Gamehendge" to allow the show to continue, to give the band the strength it needed to help break through this barrier, to allow the band to transport

"*There Was No Turning Back...*"

Jonathan Price, Evanston, IL

As I sit here in front of my computer on a typically dismal Midwest fall day, I am in kind of a reflective mood. October 22 is less than two weeks away, and this will mark the three-year anniversary of my first Phish show. It seems like so long ago, but I remember the day vividly. Of course, it makes sense that I remember it so well; it is not often that you easily forget a life-changing experience.

My Phish journey had started in the four months leading up to the evening of October 22, 1994. I listened to the *Picture of Nectar* album a lot over the course of that summer, and it was at this time that I acquired my first tape: set one of the '91 Amy's Farm show. This tape was stuck in my Walkman for the remainder of the summer, and I practically memorized every part of it. It also provided me with my first batch of favorite songs: *Wilson, Foam, Runaway Jim*, and *Llama*.

Upon returning home to Orlando for my senior year of high school, I was delighted to find out that my younger brother Daniel had acquired several dozen Phish tapes while he had been at camp in Maine. So with the aid of Daniel's tapes, the journey continued. But to be more specific, the journey went into high gear. I listened to as many tapes as I could get my hands on. My "favorite song" list had a number of nice additions, and I heard a copy of the 3/22/93 *Gamehendge*.

Bear in mind that at this point I did not have much of a perception of what Phish was like in terms of touring. So as much as I was really starting to fall in love with their music, I didn't have any immediate expectations about seeing them in concert. This made it all the more wonderful when I found out that they were going to play a show in Orlando (at a venue about ten minutes from my house) on October 22. So I purchased my ticket, listened to a lot of tapes, and anxiously awaited the day.

Cut to the day of the show. The venue was the Edge Concert Field, and I drove Daniel and some friends down there early in the day so they could get a good spot right in front of the stage. During the drive, I listened to set two of the famous 7/21/91 Arrowhead Ranch show. Many of the tunes featured on this set ended up making appearances in the show I was about to experience. I returned to the venue a few hours later to meet them and wait for the gate to open. Upon joining them, I learned that they had a brief encounter with Fishman earlier in the afternoon. One of them asked him, "So, what are you guys going to play tonight?" Fishman's reply was, "Um, I don't know—music?" Good answer!

When the gate was finally opened, we ran to the front of the stage and planted ourselves until showtime. As the sun was setting and evening drew near, the band took the stage. *Suzy Greenberg* opened the show, and there is no possible way that I could have been any more excited. I didn't exactly have what you would call a comprehensive knowledge of Phish at the time, so I was elated to hear them open with a song that I knew. Also, it was fun to sing along! The *Divided Sky* that followed was perfect placement given the fact that it was an outdoor show and it had not quite gotten dark yet. Since I was so close to the stage, it was quite a thrill to watch Trey sing the composed parts of the tune. I could swear to this day that some guy behind me yelled "*Gumbo!*" right at the end of *Divided Sky*, and the band obliged with a nice *Gumbo*.

The remainder of the set consisted of *Axilla II, Rift, Split Open and Melt, Fluffhead*, and *Julius*. All these tunes kept me in a grand old dancing mood, and I remember being particularly blown away by

(continued on the next page)

this small crowd to a land, driven by the emotion of music.

I found myself extremely impressed at how quiet it can get as Phish quietly started up "Esther." Next up was "Julius." There is not a whole lot that I can say about this version, as this "Julius" can very much speak for itself. It really seemed to wrap up the first set's energy. But, to my pleasant surprise, the band decided to keep going. I had not yet heard "Guyute." I was so pleased that my first experience with the song was seeing it performed live. There were moments when I could imagine myself running, maybe skipping, out in a wide-open, grassy area. Other times, I found myself being chased out in the woods, heart beating rapidly. Right when I started hearing Phish's music more as a soundtrack, they tossed in this song with suspense, drama, and the works. Have I mentioned how much I enjoy these guys? "Golgi" closed out the first set. It was time for the audience to catch its collective breath.

The lights dropped for the second set, and Jon walks up to the mic. He was holding this square wooden box that has these metal pieces reaching over a hole in the center. (I know this instrument has a name....) Plunk, we heard. Plunk again. Jon mentioned that this is his new "favorite sound" and began to sing "Lengthwise." I enjoyed hearing the crowd singing "Lengthwise" as "Maze" came into play.

For me, it's during "Maze" that Trey's guitar work comes alive. Maybe it's just my love for heavy-metal music. Trey always seems to surf across the music, leaving us trapped in some maze.

"McGrupp" seemed to have an airy feel to it. I had heard some people use the word "transport" associated with Phish shows. I now found myself listening to their music with new ears, and it was during this "McGrupp" that I noticed how easy it was to let the music walk you to a different land. The band seemed to want to spark things up a bit, and they began to play "Rift." This reminded me of another point to Phish's music. They seem to cast out a line like the airy feel to "McGrupp," and then they reel you back in with a tune like "Rift." During the pause before "Silent contagious..." I was starting to think that Page was trying to see how long of a silence he could get away with. I was impressed that the crowd seemed to stay rather quiet.

Then the band played "Harry Hood." Most people have heard the "Hood" from Gainesville, FL, that was recorded a few days later and appears on *A Live One*. I always felt that this "Hood" was a much better version. The intro segment seemed to go on a few extra times around. Mike was having fun. After the band finishes singing the "Thank you Mr. Hood..." part, things took on new meaning to me. Following Mike, I am

"There Was No Turning Back…" (continued)

Melt and *Fluffhead*. The *Melt* was the first real "jam" of the show, so it obviously holds a special place in my heart. It seemed to go on for quite a while, and I really had no idea if or when it was ever going to end. I was completely unprepared for the intricacy of this thing we call *Fluffhead*. Of course it was fun to sing along with the opening lyrics, but after they took off into the *Fluff's Travels* section, I was sailing through some seriously uncharted territory. The *Julius* to close the set was fun, but at this time I thought of the song as something of a joke. It had definitely not become the powerhouse that it is today.

Set break was just long enough for me to sit there in disbelief over what I had experienced during the previous hour. Probably talked about the upcoming set a little bit, and how I really wanted to hear *AC/DC Bag*.

A sweet *Peaches>Bowie* combo opened up set two. *Peaches* was nice, although I was unfamiliar with it at the time. Along the same lines as the *Fluffhead*, I was completely unprepared for the experience of a *David Bowie* jam. The feeling of being very clueless about the direction a jam was going to take made it all the more exciting to be "stuck inside" of a *Bowie*, never knowing which way it would twist and turn. The *Horse>Silent in the Morning* was an appropriate breather, and it was exceptionally appropriate if you keep in mind what was to follow: *Dinner and a Movie>Tweezer>Wilson*. If we weren't having fun already, we sure were now! The *Tweezer* jam was tight and groovy, and the transition into *Wilson* surprised me. I remember thinking it was so cool that everyone was chanting "Wilson" along with the band. *Reba* followed *Wilson*, and this was yet another song where I was simultaneously unprepared for and blown away by the compositional complexity of the jam. The jam was long, patient, and graceful. It doesn't take much to fall in love with *Reba*; well, I was in love.

Amazing Grace was a needed break from all the dancing and sweating. The possibility of an *AC/DC Bag* was not looking too likely, as the show was almost over. All I knew was that they had not played it the night before, so anything was possible. When they put their instruments back on after the Grace, I figured there were only a few songs left in the show. It was now or never for the Bag. I wanted it, I needed it, I could feel it. Although I didn't know much about Phish, I was able to recognize the tell-tale strumming/counting off that Trey does before certain tunes.

We were getting our AC/DC Bag, and I think I jumped a few feet off the ground before the song even started! I was infected with such a delirious feeling of joy that I was in a rare emotional state that combines almost crying, almost laughing hysterically, and most certainly dancing like mad. This feeling is rare, and has happened to me only a handful of times (see 10/31/95 *Icculus*, 8/16/96 *NICU*, 11/8/96 *Loving Cup*, 7/2/97 *Mike's Song*, 7/9/97 *Harry Hood*). The show was not even over, but it sealed for me the fact that this band was going to play a huge part in my life for years to come. There was no better feeling than having to wait until the end of the show to receive the unexpected treat of what was my absolute favorite song. What transpired regarding that *AC/DC Bag* was undeniably cosmic. It was all I needed in order to know I was hooked for life. The set closed with *Highway To Hell*, and the encores were *Uncle Penn* and *Tweezer Reprise*.

In terms of music, this show signified the first day of the rest of my life. It opened my mind to improvisation as an incredibly powerful means of expression. For the last three years, music has been a passion and a hobby that has taken up a majority of my time. Collecting tapes and going to shows is an endless source of fascination and enjoyment. Since that night in Orlando, my ears have heard many tapes, and my eyes have seen many shows.

Nothing will ever equal that first one, though. It was clear that I was seriously infected with the "Phish bug." And it was even more clear that this infection was going to be with me forever. There was no turning back .

---

certain he was playing Lou Reed's Take a "Walk on the Wild Side." Mike seemed to fall deeper into Lou's classic during the next pass. I began to wonder if it has always been there, or even if it was there at all. This is another aspect of the music I love, that they always seem to hide hints of other tunes and TV-show theme songs in some of their jams. Sometimes I notice, others I am sure I miss. Most of the time, I scratch my head and wonder if I really heard it at all. The crowd began to clap out a beat. The band got lost in a jam. Eventually, the crowd sort of directed Trey off into a side jam of sorts. Chris was able to get some attention, as this was the tour when he had the Phish logo swim up the backdrops. Trey almost seemed to lash out with his guitar as the band just drifted back into a jam. I found myself just drifting off into space somewhere.

Then the strangest thing happened. The band was able to get my attention, as they seemed to enter some kind of holding pattern. They almost sounded like a skipping record, stuck at one point of the song. Hell, as vain as I am, I was thinking the band was upset that I drifted off and was waiting for me to return before they continued. Honestly though, it was at this point in "Hood" that I discovered yet another aspect of Phish that has kept me a fan these past four years. That afternoon, at the Dali museum, I saw a painting that was four-dimensional.

Apparently, Dali felt he could mathematically figure out the angles to create a four-dimensional painting. The way Phish was skipping around in time, it was like they had unlocked the secrets of the space-time continuum. Their music was not limited to traditional time restraints. To my ears, it appeared that Phish had created an art form that was able to travel through time.

So now I found myself looking at time in a whole new light, and I was waiting to see what the band would do next. Now that they'd gotten my attention, they seemed content to do nothing. I waited some more. Suddenly, I heard a voice from the balcony, "Hey!" The band stumbled, as if they were reminded that there was a crowd out there in the house. They slowly picked back up into the groove and built to the climax of "I feel good!" I still, to this day, wonder if they would have ever found a way out of that void on this particular night if it hadn't been for that heckler in the crowd. Wow, what a fun experience that was!

Then the band got their acoustic instruments ready. Shortly after the mic stand was placed out for the acoustic songs, I heard a gasp from the four members of Phish as a beach ball seemed to be on a collision course with Paul's new microphones. Luckily, tragedy was somehow averted. Phish played "Nellie Kane," "Foreplay/Long Time," and

then closed with a ripping electric "Chalk Dust." We got "Sample" as the encore, and I left St. Petersburg a changed person.

10/29/94 Spartanburg Memorial Auditorium, Spartanburg, SC—Craig DeLucia

I first listened to Phish in the fall of 1994. It was my sophomore year of college, and I was living next door to this fantastic girl who was really into them. I really wanted to impress her, so I started buying their studio albums and listening to them constantly.

It turns out that this band was coming to Spartanburg, about an hour away, in late October. I knew she was going to be there, so I was determined to get tickets. My roommate wound up scoring us great seats, and we were all set to go. I even borrowed a few live tapes from a friend from high school who lived upstairs. My first live Phish was the New Year's 1993 show, and I listened to that tape over and over again to try and prepare me for what was coming.

When listening to the tapes of Spartanburg, I can truly appreciate what a great show this was. I don't remember much about the first few songs, except that I liked "Runaway Jim" and that the melody to "Simple" was really catchy. I vividly remember getting excited to hear "Split Open," which was a song that I knew, but getting confused as hell as the band ran through two other numbers before winding up in "Rift." Little did I know that the two songs were the rare "Buffalo Bill" and the (at the time) semi-rare "Makisupa Policeman." The way that the band moved through the songs with ease, seamlessly flowing from number to number without regard to succumbing to the various rhythm and tempo changes left me awestruck.

During set break, I took the chance to look around and gather my surroundings. The Spartanburg Memorial Auditorium is a pretty small theater and, along with the Fox in Atlanta, is one of the two smallest places that I have seen Phish. Everyone seemed to know each other; hugs and smiles and kind, warm feelings were passed around and shared continuously. I was on the left aisle, center section, and the guy across the aisle had been keeping a setlist. He filled me in on what I didn't know, and I couldn't believe that they had dared to play so many non-album songs! We were only about ten rows in front of the tapers' section; I knew such a thing existed, but I couldn't believe that so many people were so passionate about chronicling the music and that the band was so open and encouraging of it. This band seemed to break all of the rules of a traditional concert! Nothing, though, prepared me for the second set.

It opened up with "Down with Disease," which I was incredibly excited to hear. *Hoist* was the first Phish album I ever heard, and "Disease" is one of the two songs that firmly inserted the hook into my mouth. It flowed beautifully into what I thought was just an absolutely beautiful jam. I later learned it was the theme from "The Man Who Stepped Into Yesterday." After "Avenu" and the "TMWSIY" reprise, I began to hear some familiar guitar licks. As a classic-rock fan and longtime Who devotee, I jumped ecstatically when I recognized "Sparks." Later on, the "YEM" was nice, as was the opening to "Antelope". I couldn't believe it when they stopped and changed into some song about sending a monkey home on the train. I laughed uncontrollably as Fishman belted that final chorus, much like I had when he danced around with the vacuum during "Bike." And I again lost my marbles when they tagged "Let It Be" onto the ending of that "Monkey" song. And then they finished the "Antelope"! So what did we get for an encore? "Harry Hood." Sure, I didn't appreciate it at the time, but what a treat!

Over the last few years, I have enjoyed this show on so many levels. First, I dug it because of the humor the band wove into the music, as well as the band's obvious musical talent. Then, as I became a bigger fan, I started to appreciate the jams and the fun segues. Later, I realized what a strange setlist it truly was and how lucky I was to see a song in my first show that I will probably never see again. ("Buffalo Bill"…yes, I missed the Great Went!)

When I put it all together, it's easy to realize what a great and underrated show it is. Things never worked out between the girl and I, as awesome of a person as she is. But I sure as hell don't regret spending the money on the ticket! I've seen quite a few shows since and heard over six hundred tapes, but this show, my first, still ranks as one of my favorites.

10/31/94 Glens Falls Civic Center, Glens Falls, NY —Dean Budnick

Fans had been anticipating this show for weeks. For starters, people were happy to have the date back on the tour docket. Phish hadn't played a Halloween show since Colorado Springs 1991 (the infamous "Wait" show). October 31 is an important date in Phish lore because even though the band's initial gig at the ROTC had been something of a disaster, and even though it hadn't included Page, the show had occurred on Halloween. What's more, Phish had changed the rules a bit this year. Following many weeks of rumor and speculation, the September *Schvice* confirmed that yes indeed, this show would be a three-set affair. Furthermore, the newsletter indicated that in conjunction with an audience costume contest, the band was going to wear a musical costume, performing an album chosen from among the most popular suggestions (although there was some question as to whether or not Phish would perform the album with the highest number of votes or rather would make its selection from among the most popular choices. Before a Bad Hat show in September, Fishman indicated that *Thriller* was currently in first place and that the band was not likely to play it). At any rate, as the date neared, speculation focused primarily on *Jesus Christ Superstar*, Frank Zappa's *Joe's Garage*, the Stones' *Hot Rocks*, Pink Floyd's *Dark Side of the Moon*, and any number of Beatles albums.

The venue itself was an eight thousand-seat arena built in the 1970s primarily for hockey. It was nestled in the middle of a mildly decrepit old industrial town, forty miles north of Albany. We made it to Glens Falls long before showtime, but since I was taping and I was wearing a goofy costume taboot we decided to head inside early. Although the *Schvice* had said that the show would start at 10:00, our tickets said 9:30 and we didn't want to chance it. As it turned out, the *Schvice* was right and we were in the arena long before most people even thought about entering. Still, things could have been worse, as the situation outside deteriorated closer to 9:30, with hundreds of the ticketless indulging in the Halloween spirit and antagonizing the crush of people pushing and struggling to get in (the path through security was moving slowly due to everyone's costumes). As an added bonus, because we had entered so early, the Dionysian Productions people hadn't had time to see any really cool costumes. So Shelly Culbertson looked me over and handed me a sheet of paper that indicated that I had advanced to the next round of costume judging between the second and third sets.

I abandoned my costume with my friends up at their seats and moved down to the taping section. One nice thing about the Civic Center was that, unlike most Northeast venues of this size, while the seats on the side were reserved, the floor was general admission. This offered

more room for everyone at the rear of the floor near the tapers. Meanwhile, on the floor, most every conversation turned to the album choice. The familiar speculation continued as the arena slowly filled and expectations rapidly increased. Finally, around 10:15, the houselights dimmed, the band hit the stage, and we were underway.

The show started predictably but not unsatisfactorily. Phish stomped into "Frankenstein" and the game was afoot. "Sparkle" was next and it kept the crowd shaking (I can understand why some Phishheads grow a bit tired of this song because the jams don't vary perceptibly from performance to performance, but as far as I'm concerned that complaint is all posture. It's hard to come down hard on a quick tune that gives so many people a big ol' body-twitching, devil-grinning buzz). From here it was an extended version of "Simple," a tune that had evolved nicely since its rough-hewn introduction that past summer. The band then broke into a notable "Divided Sky," as the band deftly moved through the song's complex orchestrations and guitar-sustain exhibitions to some collective improvisations. Many pulses then quickened as fans heard the familiar oom-pah-pah that introduced "Harpua." No one was sure when or how the album would be played and many thought that Jimmy's story might provide the perfect vehicle. This version took place on Halloween and included the familiar "Vibration of Life," with a new twist, "The Vibration of Death." Then, when Jimmy moved to his turntable and put on a record, some people in the audience tensed, thinking that this might be the moment. But, no. Instead, Trey indicated that Jimmy had placed a *Barney* album onto the record player and the band zeroed in on a punch line. Trey explained that Jimmy had accidentally played the album backwards, and Phish then performed the music that Jimmy had heard: twenty seconds of Black Sabbath's "War Pigs," with Fishman doing justice to Ozzy. Trey completed the story, the band sang the "Harpua" chorus and then it was on to "Julius." Phish moved vigorously through this selection, which turned out to be the only *Hoist* song of the evening. A solid version of "Horse">"Silent" came next, and while no one could say, "I think this exact thing happened to me just last year," most everyone was thankful that it was happening at all. The set concluded with an exploratory "Reba" (which included the whistling at the end, always a good sign) and a quick sing-along "Golgi." All in all a decent, eighty-minute start to the evening.

During the set break all thoughts turned to the impending album. Fans wondered aloud whether it would appear in the next set or in the third. Then, a few minutes before midnight, just after the band members took their places on stage, the sound of a heartbeat pulsed through the speakers. *Dark Side of the Moon*. Some people howled in appreciation. But then the heartbeat ceased and the voice of Ed Sullivan emerged, introducing four lads from Liverpool and...over the thirty-year old recorded squeals of teenyboppers, Phish broke into "Back in the U.S.S.R." The Beatles. The *White Album*. A double album. Wow.

Despite what we knew, I have to admit that it didn't really kick in that they were going to play the entire *White Album* until Page hit the first notes of "Dear Prudence." His tender rendition set the tone of the set with Page singing the mellow McCartney tunes ("Blackbird," "I Will") and Trey providing the vocals on most others, with Mike and Fishman contributing a few takes as well. "Glass Onion" came next and proved particularly entertaining. First, when Trey sang "the walrus was Paul," a spotlight shined down on soundman extraordinaire Paul Languedoc. Later, Trey changed a few lyrics in the third verse, transforming a Beatles self-reference into a Phish self-reference. Thus, "I told you about the

fool on the hill..." became "I told you about Guyute the Pig, you know that he's a-dancing the jig." Phish then presented a faithful cover of "Ob-La-Di Ob-La-Da." Of course, this wouldn't be a Phish show if the band didn't tweak things a bit, and so as the group moved through the album, Mike offered up a bluegrass interpretation of "Don't Pass Me By" and Fishman added some Electrolux to his inevitable "Why Don't We Do It in the Road." The band completed the first album (or disc, if you prefer) with Mike and Trey's haunting "Julia," which rivaled Phish's version of "While My Guitar Gently Weeps" as the finest of the batch.

Phish paused briefly at the start of side three (disc two). Then, instead of singing "Birthday," Fishman stood and announced, "Believe it or not, this is Brad Sands' birthday...we'd like to invite him up here to get his cake." So while Trey, Mike, and Page played an instrumental hint of the Beatles' "Birthday," big ball boy/trampoline guy Brad Sands walked onstage in his Halloween costume, a Fishman dress, to receive his cake from the drummer. As Brad exited, Phish returned to the action as Mike growled "Yer Blues." Page's intonation and phrasing on the subsequent "Mother Nature's Son" sounded similar to Paul McCartney's original. Trey then assumed vocal duties for much of the set's remainder, contributing two of the finer moments with "Revolution" (thankfully the slow, loopy version from the album and not the upbeat one later appropriated for a Nike commercial) and "Cry Baby Cry" (an overlooked Beatles gem). Following the latter tune, the band performed a show-stopping, set-closing "Revolution No. 9." Fishman retrieved his vacuum cleaner and started doing his thing while the rest of Phish produced, as best they could, the many voices and sounds of the original. Towards the end of the song, the non-vacuum-soloing members of the band pulled out bubble wands and intermittently blew into them. Then as "Revolution No. 9" reached its close with a voice proclaiming "you become naked," Fishman did just that. He pulled his dress over his head and pranced around nude while the Trey, Mike, and Page chanted "hold that line, hold that line" between bubble breaths (a photo of this moment appears on page eleven of the booklet accompanying *A Live One*, although the letter H modestly covers Fishman's package). At around 1:30 AM the band stepped offstage to the original taped version of "Good Night," the last song on The *White Album*. Everyone collapsed into seats or onto the floor, exhausted.

But not me. I didn't have time to collapse. I had been a Beatles freak as a kid, and as a Phish phreak now I felt like I had to play along, so I threw on my costume. I figured that while I wouldn't be allowed onstage for the finals, at least I would participate in the festivities, and greet the band members during this stage of the judging. Sadly, I was mistaken. (And in case you're wondering, I dressed up as my then-favorite Phish songs, "Slave to the Traffic Light". I wore a studded dog collar with a chain leading up to a facsimile traffic light that I had found at a flea market. Lame yes, but easy to get on and off.) Fifteen or so of us were herded into a corner of the hallway which led down towards the band's dressing room. We were told, "Now we're going to separate the wheat from the chaff." I was not surprised to learn that yes, indeed, I was chaff (although I did receive a lovely parting gift, a copy of Surfing magazine from earlier in the year, which contained a Trey interview). I returned to my friends who were still ranting excitedly about the set. Their attitudes ranged from the devout ("I think the spirit of John Lennon was with us tonight") to the irreverent ("I don't know about Lennon but I think I saw Ringo at the Greenpeace booth").

Phish returned to the stage around 2:00 AM. Those few people

who had dozed off were nudged awake as the band reminded them that the night was by no means at an end, with a massive "David Bowie." Next came "Bouncing Around the Room," an exercise in calisthenics to keep the adrenaline flowing. The band then launched into "Slave to the Traffic Light", which wafted through its Metheny-esque progressions and spiraled to a close. A solid "Rift" followed, and most people were sure that this would close out the evening. But no, a real treat came next with the rare "Sleeping Monkey." The tune was all the more appropriate on this evening because its ending is unabashedly lifted from "Let It Be" (if you're curious, yes, one day I'll fix the "Sleeping Monkey" entry in *The Phishing Manual*). At this point most fans were convinced that Phish would walk. But no, Mike induced square-dance fever with a zippy "Poor Heart." Then Trey, Mike, Page, and Fishman drop-kicked an exclamation point onto the evening with a savage "Antelope". As the song stormed to a close, the band smiled, waved and walked off. Their work was done.

Nearly. The quartet returned to the stage barbershop-style and moved through a slightly frayed version of "Amazing Grace" (Fishman's voice was a bit tired even if the rest of him wasn't). Next, it was time for the costume contest, and here my brush with greatness paid off as I rallied the people around me to root for the contestants that had become my favorites during the five minutes we had been corralled together. I lobbied hardest for the woman in the "Hood" milk carton who ultimately finished third, after she had nearly withdrawn from the competition because someone had danced on her costume during the first set. The winner was dressed as a giant Mounds bar or rather "Mound" bar after the Phish song of that title. The guy who finished second, by the way, appears on page 23 of the *A Live One* booklet. He appeared as a cobalt-blue vacuum cleaner and called himself "Lawn Boy" (although personally I thought it was unsportsmanlike of him to swing around his hose during the final judging to solicit applause). At any rate, Phish then brought the evening to a close with a splendid "Squirming Coil." The song concluded with Page onstage alone, ushering us outside with a playful, pleasing piano solo. He wished us goodnight and walked off. It was 3:20 in the morning. We didn't want to go.

11/2/94 Bangor Municipal Auditorium, Bangor, ME —Charlie Dirksen

If you went to this show, you may have seen my friend walking around the lot with a giant sign that read "Drove From Arizona Have Cash and Halloween Tapes for your Extras." I went to Halloween and Bangor with this guy ("Dead") and two local Maine friends (Geoff and Dave). I was horrified to learn upon arrival in Bangor that this show was sold out, since I could have easily bought tickets in advance weeks before. I figured there was no way this show would sell out. I had heard it was around a five thousand-person room, and I didn't believe Phish could sell out a room that size in Bangor. Wrong.

In desperation mode, Dead whipped up this giant sign out of a trashed posterboard found in a dumpster adjacent to the lot, and managed to gather three tickets. Since I had seen more Phish than Geoff, Dead, and Dave had combined, it made more sense for them to see the show with the tickets. Dead felt he had failed in his mission and was disappointed that he could not land a fourth ticket; I said I would find a ticket myself, and it wouldn't be a problem. I figured that I had enough Phish on tape and had seen them enough times that it wouldn't be the end of the world if I missed the show.

It started raining as everyone was going in to the show. I kept

buying Sammy's to drown out my misery and to increase the volume of my "Cash and Halloween tapes for your extra!" pleas. I finally got a ticket from dreadlocked Jeff Drudge, who needed money to get to the next show. I promised Jeff some Halloween '94 tapes, but I managed to lose the matchbook cover with his Ohio address. Jeff is to this day the only person to whom I swore I'd send tapes and never did. If you know him, please ask him to be in touch! I have to send him tapes!

Anyway, by the time I made it into the show, during the "Maze" jam in the first set, I was wet and assholed. I found space, though, about twenty feet out from Mike on the floor. I missed the "Suzie," "Foam," and "If I Could," and heard that they were good, but nothing to write home about. The "Maze" jam that I caught was strong but not awe-inspiring. "Guyute" and "Stash" were performed well but were also nothing special. Especially "Stash." I was hoping they would do more with it, but not tonight. "The Scent of a Mule," though, was the most incredible version that I'd heard up until this time. At the time, it was probably the most improvisational version that they had ever performed. "While My Guitar Gently Weeps" was a fantastic set closer, and reminded me of the power of the version in Glens Falls only two nights earlier.

My first "Halley's Comet" was wonderful to hear open the second set. I was leaping up and down with glee. The "Tweezer" was the first monster version. It eventually made it onto *A Live One*. Over thirty minutes long, it was by far the longest, weirdest, and most peculiar "Tweezer" ever performed at that time. It was an unforgettable experience. But most of the people around me on the floor weren't the least bit excited about it. The Bangor crowd consisted primarily of locals who had nothing better to do that evening. Believe it or not, there was moshing off and on during "Axilla" and "Possum," and even crowd surfing during "Lizards". Mike did not seem very amused by the crowd's behavior. I know I wasn't. Of course, at the same time, I was tanked and not particularly kind. I kept pulling down crowd surfers and screaming incomprehensible things at people. "Mango" was great, and "Possum" and "Lizards" were strong but not unusually so.

The encores were great. Fish was on ukulele, not washboard, for "My Old Home Place" and "Foreplay/Long Time." Mike was on banjo, Page on standup bass, and Trey on acoustic guitar. "Tweeprise" was typically strong, and the audience loved it.

I left the venue and ran into Dave, Geoff, and Dead again. They had spent the show high up in the bleachers on Fishman side, stage left (audience right). And as I met them, I remember hearing a guy humming the melody line of "Tweezer Reprise". Hooked.

11/3/94 Mullins Center, University of Massachusetts, Amherst, MA—Jon Epstein

If you like the "Tweezer" from the previous night but feel it's a little too long, you should check out this "Split Open and Melt." The jam starts out very swiftly, but wanders early and gets pretty spacey. Then it builds and goes further out, until the band brings it all back as one. It's a must-hear for those who like the spacier moments of Fall Tour '94. The "Down with Disease" in this first set ain't too shabby either. The second is of near-classic proportions, featuring a short and sweet "Simple" and a "You Enjoy Myself" with heavy Santana teases and finding it's way into "BBFCFM" with Trey running around the stage with the megaphone. "Julius" isn't typically a song that impresses, but this one is great. Easily my favorite "Julius," again featuring some of the spacier side of Fall Tour '94. The four-song, half-acoustic encore is great, too.

11/4/1994 Onondaga War Memorial, Syracuse, NY
—Marty Acaster

The view of the Carrier Dome I caught as I rolled back into Syracuse for the first time in four months triggered a wave of emotion that would wash through the show that night and sweep me along into an uncertain future. I was on the uphill climb out of the pit of despair I had created for myself while at the lowest point in my life. A musical obsession was slowly taking the place of an interpersonal one. In place of a love gone bad I had a new love that was nothing but good. In the course of a year and a half I had become a Phish fan and was on my way to attending my fifth show.

The scene outside the Onondaga War Memorial was as tumultuous as the torrent of thoughts cascading through my brain. It seemed there were a couple thousand more people hanging around in the parking lot than there were seats in the arena. People seemed rabid, frothing at the mouth to get into this show. Could they really all want to be here as badly as I did? The steady stream of fans climbing on each other's shoulders to sneak into the second-floor bathroom window of the War Memorial answered that question with a resounding HELL YES. This show was going to be even more crazy than the one down in Binghamton in April. I was experiencing true ecstasy and had yet to hear a note. Finally, I made it through the turnstile and down onto the floor. A general-admission show and the floor was covered with seats? What was the meaning of this? Slowly but surely the chair trees sprouted from the floor—Row upon row of chairs, separated and stacked. Higher and higher they grew, a forest of plastic and steel, lofty perches for those brave enough to scale them for a better view of the stage.

The lights went down and the roar of the crowd rose up to the rafters. The first set opened with a paint-by-numbers version of "Sample in a Jar." But the colors...the colors they used...so alive...so liquid. With the exception of "Bouncin'" (which reminded me of her!), the first set was an incredible orgy of light and sound. I felt so alive. Such a stark contrast to the Dead shows I had been to a couple weeks before at the Boston Garden and MSG. "David Bowie" ripped off the top of my head with its intensity. With my skullcap pried loose, there was nothing to prevent the "Vibration of Life" from seeping into my brainstem and coloring it paisley forever. I was indeed tuned in to the universe. There was so much room in this music to think about things. Sometimes I felt forced to consider things I'd rather forget, other times images I was sorry I had forgotten flooded into my consciousness. It was amazing, truly magical, and at times hilarious. "Chalk Dust Torture" finally (it seemed like time stood still for a while) closed out the set and I found I definitely wanted to live while I was young.

During the set break I tried to come to terms with my latest Phish experience. Garbled sentences sprung from my mouth and impacted wordlessly on the ears of my friends. I could not find the words to express the joy I felt. I had been to Gamehendge, I was saved.

The lights went down once more and I saw my life run away from me. Thousands of friends I had yet to meet ran along...singing words from a song. My song. Our song. The song of the universe. Have no regrets. Never put yourself in a position where you wish you had or had not done something. Better to love and lose than never love at all. Profound philosophy being injected into my thoughts by the vibration of light and sound and energy swirling around me. Was this happening to everyone? One look around at the radiant smiles told me all I needed to know. This band is so damn good. I can't believe a concert can be like

this. Pummeled by thoughts, by light, by sound...it's relentless. I'm trapped in time. I don't know what to do. Ah yes...just share in the groove. Sure, I can do that. This is "Simple." Just because we've got a band. Our band. Skyballs, saxscrapers, cymbop, and beebophones. What? By the end of "Weekapaug" I had been reduced to a gibbering simpleton. The rest of the set was a blur.

The encore brought me my first sip from the "Loving Cup." A song that plays such a huge role in my life to this day. It is a song of hope, a song of frustration, a song of love, and a song of life. I can run and jump and Phish but I won't fight...you if you want to push and pull with me all night. Just gimme little drink...from your Loving Cup. Just one drink...and I'll fall down drunk. Yes you.

11/4/94 Onondaga War Memorial Auditorium, Syracuse, NY
—Chris Prinos

Everyone in the car was asleep when I stopped at the gas station for directions to the Onogada War Memorial Auditorium. We had been driving for awhile. "You mean the Onondaga War Memorial Auditorium," a police officer answered. After getting directions I was on my way to my second Phish show ever, driving someone else's car...in second gear (it was an automatic). It all seemed so strange to me...why was I doing this? As soon as I got to the lot it made sense. I was with two close friends in the middle of one of the best times of my life. The lot was littered with the sounds of VW buses, people were abuzz about something called Glens Falls, and setlists from the previous show. I found everything about it to be fascinating. It was like this Bizarro world, where the only worries were of first-set-openers or extras for Indiana. All that mattered was tonight's show.

As we found our way in, I meandered onto the floor where my seat was. Only there was no seat. It was a free-for-all. Everyone was stacking the chairs into towering piles. The floor had so much room, and I could see everything, unlike the night before at the Mullins Center.

Suddenly the lights went out and that was it, everyone went ballistic. At this point I was about tenth row, and the band opened with "Sample." Knowing probably a dozen songs, I was psyched to hear something I knew (I was also psyched for the "Bouncin'"). Now I was mesmerized, studying the band that is the focus of all this. I eventually made my way to the front row, which rendered me immobile. I looked around at the arena; this is when I first noticed the lights. It was during "Bowie," granted I was at the stage where I didn't know where one song ended and another began. Trey was wearing his jamming pants, those gold striped things that he used to wear all the time in '94. I watched him for the rest of the show. During "Colonel Forbin," he did this crazy narration and he handed out these crazy 3-D glasses to the front rows. I got a pair and I was like, "Wow! Trey just gave me these glasses, I'm gonna keep these," but then I looked around and other people wanted to see, so I gave them up. It was here I realized the communalism that existed at a Phish show. It's not about one person, its about the whole experience, and having no worries.

Anyway, first set closed and ushers started threatening to end the show. They weren't excited about the chair thing. So I moved back to my tenth row seat. Although I didn't know it at the time, second set was killer. "The Curtain," "Mike's"->"Simple"->"Mike's"->"Tela"->"Weekapaug" was insane. At the time, I heard "the band opened a curtain with some guy's song into a simple 'Tela.'"

Regardless, I had a great time and it was here I got hooked. Thirty-

five shows later I'm driving a standard, hoping to go back to the OWMA again and wishin' I kept the glasses.

11/12/94 The MAC Center at Kent State, Kent, OH—Dan Nooter

The second set of Phish's 11/12/94 show at Kent State is among the finest sets the band has ever played. In fact, the entire show is consistently great, overflowing with the melodic sensitivity and imaginative experimentalism that make November 1994 such an exciting month of music. The show is notable both for its diversity of musical styles and for its creative use of dynamics: the chiaroscuro of its sudden jumps from very quiet to very loud. The show builds to a climax in what is among the most intense and transcendent versions of "Harry Hood" ever played, a version that still remains my personal favorite.

The show opens with an excellent version of "Runaway Jim," and from as early as the lyrics section, it's clear that there's magic in the air. In the mini-jam that precedes the song's final verses, the band gets quieter and quieter until they are hardly playing at all. In so doing, they introduce the themes of subtlety and control that pervade the show and that prove so crucial to the incredible Harry in the second set. Although Trey leads the jam out of "Jim's" final verse, all four band members are on—especially Page, who just begins going off. The song begins to take on a "Frankenstein"-esque feel as Trey starts sliding up the fretboard. It is Fish, however, who sends the tune out of control. He begins smashing the drums in passionate syncopation with the rest of the jam. From the quiet musings of the middle lyric section, the song has built to an energetic fury by the time Trey comes in with the final chorus. Considering the context of this version, seven months before the first truly "experimental" version of "Jim" at Raleigh, NC, it demonstrates an incredible amount of energy and creativity, and places easily in the upper echelon of pre-'95 "Jims."

If "Jim" introduces and foreshadows the explosive aspects of Phish's jamming in this show, the "Foam" that follows provides an excellent exposition of the contrary themes of mellowness and subtlety. After a solid lyrics section, Page begins the jam and is greeted quickly by Mike. The jam begins to become quiet, however; even Mike is playing faintly, and Page's piano has become a faint trickling in the distance. The song seems to gain energy after a short chromatic build (again, led by Page), but Trey takes over and returns the song to its region of sparse quietude. If you like the Spokane "Hood," you'll especially enjoy the middle section of this "Foam." Trey is playing alone, and he may as well be unplugged he's so quiet. The rest of the band slowly returns as the jam becomes a series of staccato two-note bursts. The rest of the jam is standard for "Foam," but even this concept of "standard" becomes newly mitigated by the delicate minimalism of the song's interlude. A fantastic version!

"If I Could" and "Maze," although solid versions, are not as profound as the show's openers. Hence, I will not devote space to their individual consideration. Rather, as a short aside, let me share a few words about what makes an incredible show. An amazing show isn't made by a single great jam (or even more than one); although such a show tends to contain one of the best versions ever played of a song or multiple songs, this quality isn't nearly as important as the show's overall consistency. Looking at shows like 10/31/94 or 12/31/95, among the two best shows Phish has ever played, there's not a single bad moment in either. 5/8/93 II, another of the best sets ever, has incredible versions of "Bowie" and "Mike's" (which perhaps we'd expect) but also the best

version ever of "Horse," a great "Ice," an above-average "Big Ball Jam," and the teary-eyed "Amazing Grace Jam" to close the set. A great show catches the band on a special night of their musical lives on which they can do no evil. Kent State is one of these special nights....

When I first reviewed this show, I didn't have a particularly high opinion of its "Guyute." Since then, given the poverty of good "Guyutes" in recent years, I have been forced to revise my opinion. This is, in fact, a very tight and enjoyable "Guyute," much better than most post-'94 versions. Which just goes to show how much difference practicing a song makes.

The Kent State "Stash" is an extremely nonstandard version, and it foreshadows a lot of the textural density that characterizes the jams of Space Summer '95. I have always felt, however, that those deeply layered summer '95 jams at least went places; after a fresh, funky opening and a solid verse segment, however, this "Stash" just sort of meanders (although it meanders in a very energetic and dissonant way, if that makes any sense). Some thunder from Fish gives it extra propulsion. Although the jam falls into a few little rhythmic themes, it tends to lack melodic exploration. Page has a few nice things to say about two-thirds of the way through the jam, and Trey breaks into the dissonant mush to provide a few soaring leads, but these excursions are short lived, and they quickly descend into what is probably the best part of this "Stash": the crazy "maybe so / maybe not" vocal jam that develops. This is really trippy and dissonant, and includes what sounds like barking/howling from one of the band members (Trey?). Unfortunately, it is over too quickly: the "Stash" ending is just lamely stamped on. The version as a whole, however, is extremely interesting, and even enjoyable, although it seems to be more meaningful as a prognostication of '95-style jamming than as an end in itself.

"Esther" and "Chalk Dust" close the set. Nothing particularly notable about these versions except that, like "Maze" and "If I Could," they are tight and energetic.

An above-average "Julius" opens the awesome second set. Mike is up in the mix (yay!) and his walking bass lines are pretty funky. Fish adds various drum flurries. The backing vocals are on; various band members throw in random hoots and squeals. If this "Julius" doesn't move you, you should get your hearing checked—or your pulse.

The Kent State "Fluffhead" is a strong version (although it's no 4/27/91). I should note, however, that I'm not really a big fan of the song; I've often wished they'd skip the first twelve minutes and go right into "Arrival" (maybe on NYE, out of "Auld Lang Syne." Mmmm.) Because "Fluff" is a long, composed song that lacks any real opportunities to jam, the distance between a good "Fluffhead" and one that drags is entirely a function of the freshness and energy that the band puts into it. But they go all-out on this version. Beautiful little mellow stuff follows "deranged," and the wonderfully wicked little laugh from Trey that follows the ensuing "Fluffhead" is classic. Page is on in this "Fluff", and Fish...well, I don't even have to mention Fish. He owns this show. "Arrival" contains a wonderful sustained wailing note from Trey. This is so much fun; this, friends, is what "Fluffhead" is all about.

The set really begins, however, with "Down with Disease." How good is this "Disease?" Well, let's put it this way: It's not often that the best version ever played of a song like "Harry Hood" isn't even the highlight of a set, but the monster "Disease"->"Have Mercy"->"Disease" steals that honor away. The lyrics section is strong. The jam starts off very upbeat, and includes some sweet bass from Mike, who heretofore

hasn't been a huge factor in the show. Trey throws in a beautiful little teary-eyed melody on top of Page's furious piano, which is simply beatific. And then, just like that, Page and Trey drop out. A bass/drum-driven section takes over the jam and we are no longer anywhere near "DWD." The music takes a turn towards the evil (reminiscent of Miles Davis' "Dark Magus") and then mellows into another beautiful groove. Fish drops out and Mike gets quiet and the jam shifts to Page, who himself yields to some Trey-led blues action. Finally, the lead goes to Fish, who starts picking up the beat, bringing it faster and faster. The rest of the band comes back in with dissonant fury, holding this one tense chord that finally resolves back into "Disease"-style jamming.

About thirty seconds later, the "Have Mercy" beat comes in. This is such a smooth transition, without a doubt, the sweetest segue ever into "Mercy." Although the harmonies aren't quite as spine-tingling in this version as they are in 5/8/93, the jam is far superior. The mood begins to sound very similar to the spacey beginning to "You Enjoy Myself" (sometimes referred to as the "pre-Nirvana segment" for reasons that have always eluded me). The band sings another verse and then returns to the realm of mellow, spacey, reggae Groove. Except that now, the groove seems a little less calm, a little more evil, as Page's organ leads the band from the calm passivity of the mellow groove back into the intensity of "Down with Disease." The transition is so smooth and sweet it sounds rehearsed, even though the last "Mercy" was performed a year previous to this version. Trey is all over the place in this "Disease" ending; this is so energetic and exciting. The entire "Disease"->"Mercy"->"Disease" is easily among the sweetest jams Phish has played. "Disease" doesn't even truly end, but becomes very dissonant until all the instruments drop out and the jam drops right into a stunning "Lifeboy." This version of "Lifeboy" is the most tender and moving version I've ever heard. Its placement, after that insane and dissonant "Disease" jam, is perfect. "Rift" is a great song, and is played suitably.

11/12/94 is not a "typical" show by any means, and yet it does manage to typify certain aspects of November '94. I don't have to go off on why that month is one of the greatest in Phishtory, it should already be clear to most or all of you. No month is so grossly ambitious, so unrestrained in its pull toward the experimental. And, perhaps as a result, no month is as eclectic as 11/94. Although acoustic bluegrass had been in Phish's repertoire for years, fall '94 saw bluegrass come into its own, beginning with the acoustic "Foreplay/Long Time" that encored Lehigh's tour opener and culminating in 11/19's forty-five-minute postshow parking-lot jam with Reverend Jeff Mosier. But with the exception of 10/26's encore, Kent State was the first show to contain an extended acoustic bluegrass section. None of the versions of "Old Home Place," "Nellie Kane," or "Foreplay/Long Time" played at Kent State will give you goosebumps, but they are important for situating 11/12 in its context within the evolution of Phish. If the show transcends this context in certain respects, it is no less the product of its time.

Transcendence has a name, however, and its name is "Harry Hood." The Kent State "Hood," taken by itself, is a musical masterpiece. Taken in the particular context of 11/12/94, however, it represents the combination and culmination of the improvisational themes that have guided the entire show. It combines the Fishman-led dive into pure unrestrained energy introduced in "Jim." It contains the subtlety and delicateness of "Foam's" jam, the precision of "Guyute" and "Fluffhead," the mellow sweetness of "Have Mercy," and the inspiration of the "Down with Disease" jam. The beginning of this version is solid, but offers no

hint as to the monster that it is to become. Its opening is playful and unrushed. The post-"where do you go?" section is nicely played but not notable outside of its beauty and precision. The post-"Mr. Minor" jam starts out as usual with some quiet noodling from Trey. He's just gently tickling the fretboard now. Control. Balance. Some chimes from Page smooth out what could be church music in its sheer pristine calm. A couple of minutes into the jam, Trey drops a few quiet melodic lines, which are echoed by Mike, and in the soothing calm that follows, it seems like nothing bad could ever enter the world of this "Harry." Ahh-hhhh. As with the Spokane "Harry" (yet eleven months earlier), Trey kills his volume almost entirely. This is so beautiful. A few chimes from Fish, and then Trey starts to sweep out of the quiet. The music just slides and melts, ebbing and flowing like a moonlit ocean on some warm, innocent summer's night. The "Harry" theme eventually begins to assert itself, but it keeps on being reeled back in. It sets out again, this time more slowly and gently, and again it is withdrawn, burrowing back into a growing nest of sound. Fish breaks it open with some timely smacks to the drums. The tempo and volume start to increase as Trey starts soaring. But Fish is just smashing the drums, hitting and hitting, and the momentum of the music begins to usurp control; the band can no longer contain it. Fish is just hitting, pounding. Trey breaks into the stratosphere, holding this one note, and then diving back into the deep. The music is just a freight train now, out of control and unstoppable. Fish is still pounding away, but is it even him anymore, or has he, too, fallen thrall to "Harry's" majestic will? Trey takes us into the final approach, breaking all hell and heaven loose, and now the end is inexorable. The final chorus enters and closes out this most amazing "Hood" ever.

By any standard, the "Golgi" that follows is unnecessary. Nevertheless, this is the only version of "Golgi" that dependably gives me shivers. There's this one part (à la the "Jim" opener) that seems to fade to nothing before exploding back into the theme. It may not be saying a whole lot to mention that this is my favorite "Golgi," but it is, and I'll mention it anyway.

The "Sample" encore is a good choice. "Bold as Love" would have been a better choice, but it might have caused the entire state of Ohio to spontaneously combust, so "Sample" was probably the prudent call. I've always loved this song and it really is a great, energetic, fun song, though not particularly exploratory. It provides the perfect ending to this great, fun, brilliant, powerful, inspired show. Shows like this are the reason I love Phish.

11/13/94 Warner Theater, Erie, PA—Charlie Dirksen

The Warner Theater in Erie is probably the most beautiful room in which I've heard Phish perform. Red carpeted halls, luxurious, plush couches, paintings, mirrors, detail in the baroque style everywhere (even in the john!), and an indoor fountain! I was told at the time that it seated twenty-five hundred. It was an incredible place to see a show. Phish could have sold out the nearby Civic Center, given the number of ticketless people who showed up on that frosty evening.

The first set opened with a strong "Wilson" and also featured a cheerful "Reba" (not nearly as dark and spooky as the 'Ween '94 version). An unannounced "Vibration of Life" segued out of "It's Ice," and tingled my spine (the first time it really vibrated me). "Antelope" was exceptionally good, closing the set well. Fish screamed "Marco" and numerous other things during the ending jam. The second set circulates on fully digital DSBDs. (It had been stealth-patched; the front row of the ta-

pers' section was practically on top of the soundboard.) Highlights of the second set include a perfect "Lizards", an amusing "BBFCFM" (featuring a brief but crazy drum solo), and a gorgeous "Coil" that practically made me weep. With a solid show in a resplendent room, Phish once again more than made my several-hundred-mile trip from D.C. worthwhile.

11/16/94 Hill Auditorium, University of Michigan, Ann Arbor, MI—Jeremy Welsh

On a cold night in November 1994, my senses were opened to an experience like no other. I would have certainly called myself a fan of Phish at that point in my life, having purchased their new release (*Hoist*) and having begun to actively search out tapes for my growing collection. And I had seen the Dead three times, which I think somewhat prepared me for the experience. But on November 16, 1994, at Hill Auditorium on the University of Michigan campus, I saw Phish live…and my life really has not been the same since. And it is kind of amazing how aspects of that night are clearer than memories of shows just a year ago.

When I read in the school newspaper earlier that fall that someone named Joel Cummins had an extra ticket for a Phish show up in Ann Arbor, I did not hesitate to call him. Little did I know that this music and theology major would later become a close friend of mine (and would play in his own jam band). I just knew he had a ticket for me. I was finally going to see Phish!

The drive from South Bend wasn't too bad, and when we arrived at the venue, fans were milling about everywhere. I can still picture all of the tassel caps and wool sweaters filling the halls of that great venue in the center of the campus; I don't remember if I knew that the Dead had played here twenty-three years before, but I did feel a bit of awe entering the doors. We worked our way up the stairwells, stepping over fans who were relaxing and chilling, and made our way to our seats. Front row, upper balcony!

Looking back, I don't know if I could have asked for a better show. This had a bit of everything and anything, in just the right doses to get me hooked. First-set "Reba," an acoustic bluegrass "set" with Jeff Mosier, an amazing "Mike's"->"Simple"->jam to open the second set, "Fee" (with megaphone), "Antelope", and an a capella "Amazing Grace." It certainly was enough to hook me, that's for sure.

I look back on the "Sample" opener and laugh. I remember groaning to myself, thinking that they are just playing "Sample" to support *Hoist* and cater to the frat boys at U of M. What the hell? This was my first show and I was thinking this? I really don't remember what I would have rather had as an opener, but I can't help but laugh at myself. Listening to it now, it was actually well played. A nice and rocking version, it worked well in getting everyone into the show.

The "Foam" that followed was my first taste of the "experience." From my balcony perch, I remember watching the light rings that Kuroda sent floating around the hall, gliding along the walls as Phish played "Foam" in the background. It really was an amazing sight, and I felt myself getting sucked in ….The "Fast Enough for You" was just enough of a break, letting me catch my breath and get some air, before "Reba" again pulled me under. This "Reba" featured a nice, quiet jam by Trey and Page. The playing was so subtle, making the most of the acoustics in the hall. This built and built, spiraling into the climax, whistling included. Altogether it was almost fifteen minutes in length. "Axilla II" was a nice rager. It is actually my only "Axilla II," though I have seen "Axilla I" three times. "Lizards" was nice and fun, and features a really good Page piano solo in

the middle that seems to contain a bit of the *I Dream of Jeannie* theme.

Picking up where the "Reba" left off, the "Stash" contained some quiet and subtle playing by Trey, only to be interrupted by synchronized hand-claps and "woos" from the crowd. As the "Maybe so / maybe not" section faded away, Trey quickly jumped in with a repetitious and dizzying jam, spinning around the main "Stash" theme. Around eight minutes in, the jam dropped into a minimal, droning section, similar to the jam out of "Simple" that would follow in the second set. Page and Trey set about to playing some staccato notes as Fishman worked the cymbal. It was similar to a jam you might find in 2000, but without the delay loops. As with the other jams this set, this got a bit quiet before the main theme burst through. My love of "Stash" must have begun with this version.

While I am sure it was planned, the bluegrass set that followed was a great breather after the "Stash." I had never heard of the Reverend Jeff Mosier before this show, but the fact that he was a guest and they were jamming out bluegrass tunes during my first show was enough for me. As the band stayed on their electric instruments, Jeff sang and played banjo. "Pig in a Pen" featured some nice solos by everyone in the band, including Fishman, who was introduced as the "world's premier bluegrass drummer!" Again, Trey and Page took some nice solos during the slow "Tennessee Waltz." A nice and tight bluegrass jam segued nicely into a rousing, set-closing "Swing Low Sweet Chariot."

Wow. I must have had the biggest grin on my face at set break! I went and purchased the token Phish shirt (plum colored, with the logo on the front and the tour dates on the back in orange) as Joel went to meet a taper. He had brought tapes with him to give to the taper, and thus I would soon get AUD2 tapes of my first Phish show.

I really didn't know what to expect for the second set; I don't think I was prepared for what was to come. Not in my wildest dreams was I expecting a "Mike's" to open the second set! Even then, at my first show, I felt the glory of "Mike's Song." I was jumping up and down, yelling and smiling and hugging everyone. I probably looked kind of silly. I vaguely remember the trampolines (about 3:30 into the song), as they were still bouncing in 1994 during "Mike's." Soon after the tramps segment, things got a bit dark with some held, distorted notes by Trey.

Through talking with Joel and my limited exposure to Phish.Net at the time, I knew that they were typically playing a new song called "Simple" out of "Mike's Song." I hadn't heard it up until this point, but as they cleanly segued into it, I was able to ID it from the lyrics. I still think today that this is one of the greatest versions of "Simple" played by Phish (I also enjoy the 11/08/96 version, from my second show). After the last verse ("Skyballs and saxscrapers"), "Simple" takes on this glorious feel for about a minute or two, high and sailing above. And as with the "Reba" and "Stash," it turns quiet and minimal for just a bit. At this point (six minutes or so), it slowly becomes dark.

I remember that somewhere in here Mike put down his electric bass to pick up this Rob Wasserman-looking bass; I don't know if it had just two strings or what, but Mike started to play this low, rumbling bass line. This really turned the jam dark. The slow jam quickly picked up with some quick playing by Page on the piano; Mike followed, then Trey, and then Fishman. Faster it started to run; all the while, Mike was still on this bass. Trey started to repeat these higher, trumpet-sounding notes over and over. After a faster section, the jam progressed to something similar to the "Scent of a Mule" Russian section. Phish was just moving from improvised section to improvised section—nothing was wandering, like we find in some of the more recent jams. It seemed as

though each move had its own purpose. After some great keyboard work by Page on both organ and piano, the jam progressed to a dissonant, distortion-filled section. This was sped up by Trey, then slowed down, and then sped up by Fishman, with some piano by Page. It was like we were getting yanked this way, then that. And then a new little melody was sounded (twenty-five minutes into the "Simple!")—so many textures, so many landscapes. They were flying all of us around and into every corner of the music hall. The jam closed with a Trey-led rocker, playing Clapton-like riffs, a bit like a slow "Antelope" jam, wrapping things up very nicely as they just slowed down and stopped. Whew! Thirty-plus minutes of aural landscape.

What better to follow this epic jam than with an acoustic set of "Blue and Lonesome" and "Two Dollar Bill," the first time played for each of those tunes. The band moved to the front of the stage, all on acoustic instruments, and played very good renditions of the two traditional songs. Even without Jeff Mosier, they showed their pickin' chops—and it was fun to hear their voices morph into a bluegrassy drawl.

After the brief interlude, Phish plugged back in and played a rockin' version of "Chalk Dust Torture"—the version that appears on *A Live One*, complete with yelps from Fishman. The identifiable drum beats of "Fee" quickly followed; I was very happy to hear this song, as it was actually the first Phish song I had ever heard (on WYEP here in Pittsburgh, in 1992, as they promoted the H.O.R.D.E. tour). I really enjoyed the fact that Trey used the megaphone that was sitting on one of his amps.

The beginning of "Antelope" actually began during the ending jam of "Fee" (a > rather than ->) to the delight of the crowd of four to five thousand. The song quickly picked up into the rockin' section; Page's piano worked well intertwining with Trey's blistering solos. Right before the "Set the gearshift" line, there was a brief reggae breakdown (I guess you can call it that). Great closer, with Trey thanking everyone, telling us all to drive safely (I would guess a number of the fans in attendance were U of M students).

After much applause and cheering, they came out to do an "Amazing Grace" without mics. For the most part, people were quiet; not too many "Shhhs." And to wrap up a perfect show, well, "Suzy Greenberg" of course! Trey's voice is a bit tattered and scratchy, but that really didn't matter.

What else can I say? With Satchmo over the PA, we made our way out of the Hill Auditorium, finding an emergency exit in one of the stairwells. It put us out in a service alleyway, and we debated for a bit if we should try to find their buses. But it was cold, and we didn't want to be a bother, so we headed back to the car.

I don't know if I realized my life had changed that evening, but looking back, listening to the show again, I can understand how I was hooked.

11/22/94 Jesse Auditorium, University of Missouri, Columbia, MO—Mark Powers

First, the venue: I was a relative latecomer to the Phish scene (my first show was 8/14/93), and this was the smallest venue at which I've attended a show. It was probably fifteen hundred seats, tops.

Now, on to the show…and man, what a show! I attended as a kind of graduation present to myself, but I couldn't get anyone to go with me, so I was kind of bummed. Once the band kicked into "Buried Alive," however, my gloom kind of disappeared, and I settled in for a good show.

Set one was relatively uneventful, though I did feel that the band was hitting really well, and was therefore surprised when they ended

it after "Adeline." It was a pretty short set, with some good jams, but nothing mind-blowing.

Set two, on the other hand, was a bit more interesting, to say the least. They came out full-throttle, busting into a hot "Funky Bitch." And they were really on, ripping it up. Then, after Page's organ solo, they did an abrupt segue into this funk jam (listed as "Lawn Train" on the setlists, though I've never heard of this tune). I think it was a planned segue, because it was just bam, and they were into it.

They kept grooving on this one for a bit, and then Trey started doing whammy-pedal stuff, slowly at first, and then faster, whereupon the band joined him, and they kicked into a double-time, sinister-sounding jam. This got pretty out of control, reaching a nice crescendo, before they quieted it down for a kind of horsey-shuffle thing for a minute or so.

After this, they went into several other jam variations that would probably be better heard than described; suffice it to say that I'd compare this very favorably with the 5/7/94 Bomb Factory show, which I was also fortunate enough to see. It was a real roller coaster. The "Funky Bitch"->Jam was about thirty minutes in length, and went right into "Yerushalayim Shel Zahav."

The next few songs were routine, though I always love a good "Curtain." Then, they went into "Runaway Jim," and once the jam started it became quickly apparent that this would be no ordinary "Jim." It got dark, and heavy, darker, heavier, faster, and all of a sudden… "BBFCFM!"

A few funny things happened during "BBFCFM." For starters, there was some drunken idiot on the balcony that had been heckling the band for awhile, and during one of the quiet parts he yelled out "Fuck you!" Well, the next time they ended the nutty part, Fish said "No, fuck YOU!" and the crowd went nuts; they were sick of this moron too.

After this they started right back into the nutty stuff. Trey set his guitar down and grabbed the megaphone. He was pointing it at the crowd, going crazy, and then he went to the front of the stage and started doing pirouettes like a figure skater. He was really going around fast, and it looked really cool in the strobe lights. Finally, he got so disoriented that he fell down, nearly falling off the stage, before managing to drag himself up and stagger off to stage right.

Then they brought out the acoustic instruments, and assembled at the front of the stage. They paused and started chatting amongst themselves while the crowd quieted down, and then started playing…"BBFCFM" again! It was hysterical.

The acoustic numbers were really cool, because the place was so small you could really hear them well, but there were no other surprises.

Then Trey said something about "We're going to break with tradition here, and let someone from the audience pick a tune." He went to the front of the stage and asked a girl, then when he came back all he said was "it's been picked" with a wicked grin. Then, we were treated to a really nice "Harry," and a nutty "HTH" ending. The "Lizards" encore was a nice surprise, but Trey got kind of pissed when he forgot the lyrics.

A killer show—definitely one of the best ones I've seen. Coupled with the following night's show in St. Louis, it made for a great graduation present!

12/29/94 Providence Civic Center, Providence, RI —Christian Campagna

On September 14, 1990, we were preparing to leave for Madison Square Garden the next morning for our first Dead show without

"At First Glance"

Michael Rossetto, Minneapolis, MN

When I first glanced upon the stage at my first show at Dane County Coliseum in Madison WI, I realized that the guys were not reading cue cards. Their notes were selected from the atmosphere around them. Trey's facial expressions showed signs of frustration and relief. Mike jerked his head as if he was fighting off the melody. Page bounced around like he was on a trampoline. Fishman appeared as though he wanted to rise up from the throne and beat his drums into rubble. When I saw this particular jam, I knew that it was unique and its effect on Phish was something to be seen and heard.

Brent Mydland, who had died what seemed like a week after one of the better Dead shows I saw that year (Buffalo, NY). I was a little skeptical about Vince Welnick, after hearing lukewarm reviews of his first few shows. My friend and I, who had seen the majority of our Dead shows together, were at a party, and another friend had been telling us of this band Phish he had been seeing for the past year. At first we didn't want anything to do with them, especially after a couple of Max Creek shows that didn't do much for us at the time. In my eyes, there was only one "jam-band."

The first Phish song I ever heard was "Fee," off of *Junta*. Our friend sat us down in a room and played the *Junta* tape for us. My first impressions were "this is great, sorry I didn't believe you!" and "Shit, these guys can play, that guitar tone is exactly what I want to hear." We told our buddy we needed to borrow the tape for the ride down to MSG. I think we listened to it about twelve times over the course of three days in the car and the hotel. We were both hooked, and were looking forward to getting tickets to see Phish at the Somerville Theater a week later.

I still can't find a setlist for that first show I saw (September 21, 1990), but I remember how amazed I was at the whole band. Trey's guitar sound, mixed with him looking like a guy I played Dungeons and Dragons with in junior high; Fishman in the Zero-man outfit set up at the side of the stage; Page looking like my science teacher in high school; and Mike being...Mike.

After Somerville I saw a bunch of shows (I recently found out I saw Destiny Unbound at UNH) in '90 and '91. I slowed down a lot to only a few shows in '92 and '93, and then "returned" to Phish in 1994. As fate would have it, I picked a good night to return to the scene: 12/29/94, Providence Civic Center

This was my first Phish show in an arena. It is to this date one of the best shows I've seen the band play. Things kick off with "Runaway Jim;" a pretty rocking "Jim," I might add. This version is definitely overlooked. It's only about eight minutes long or so, but segues nicely into "Foam." "If I Could" was next and was basically "If I Could." "Split Open and Melt" was a nice treat early in the set. A much faster jam than usual, with Fishman and Trey playing off each other at the beginning of the jam. Some chaos ensues about eight minutes in, and the whole thing is about eleven minutes long. Not the best "Split Open," but a great piece of the show overall. "Horse"->"Silent," "Uncle Pen," and "I Didn't Know" follow. All pretty standard. "Possum" was next. Trey teases "Dueling Banjos" pre-vocals, and the rest is pretty rocking, as rocking as "Possum" gets.

The second set opened with what would be the last "Guyute" until Halloween '95. It sounds pretty flawless when I hear it now; there are also some subtle differences to the newer versions in the beginning. I can still remember being amazed by what is still one of my favorite Phish songs.

What happened next was what I look at as the opening of a whole new Phish I had never seen. This definitely marks the beginning of what I call my "Second Wave" of Phish. Sure, the intimacy of the small theater was gone, as well as the feeling of discovering a new band and having them to your self, so to speak, but if this show and future ones were an indication, why would I care how many people were there? Granted, this was my first arena Phish show, so that was also a bit of a big jump from my last show before this, at the Providence Performing Arts Center down the road (2/4/93 for those keeping track). So, another ten thousand people or so were now seeing Phish.

This was why, I guess.

What some people to this day still call a "Dave's Energy Guide" tease, I will still just call a "Delay Loop Jam." Whatever you want to call it, it's wonderful music, and listening to it as I write this still gives me the shivers. This lasts for about three minutes, until Fishman begins what we know as the intro to "Bowie." What happened next was basically thirty-seven minutes of "Hose." Writing a simple "at 15:02 Trey starts playing arpeggios and whistling Dixie" would not even do this justice. For this thirty-seven minutes the band goes from some great spacey stuff at the beginning (including what I hear as an early incarnation of what we all know as the "Trey loop," which became pretty standard in jams starting in '97). Some great funky/spacey jamming, to the rocking Phish à la "DWD" (or "Drowned"), where it almost sounds like the "Bowie" is coming to a close. This is only halfway through the trip though. Eventually the band quiets down and Page takes the spotlight, playing some great melody lines. The band takes their cue from this and starts picking up the pace again, and then quiets down again. Some ambient stuff starts, and Trey and the band start whistling into the microphones with Trey whispering "Lassie...hey boy, there's a fire up on the old hill...good dog Lassie. Good boy...Lassie, come home." Some indecipherable whispering starts, and ends with "NOW! DO IT NOW! DO IT NOW!" This is repeated a few times and then Mike hits a pretty loud note that still makes me jump when I hear it now. A bit of feedback brings the music back to what we all know as the ending of "Bowie."

The band could have left stage for the night and I would have been happy. Instead a short but fun "Halley's Comet" followed. This ended and went immediately to "Lizards". To me, "Lizards", even though it's never really jammed out, is like "Bathtub Gin." It's one of those songs that when it starts you can feel the energy of the crowd and band as one. Fishman came out to the "Hold Your Head Up" music and

stated, "I believe Neil Diamond sang this song. I believe he sang it at Madison Square Garden, too. He probably sang it everywhere. He sang it so much that. I am gonna sing it now, for you." The band broke into my first "Cracklin' Rosie." Trey yelled "Henrietta!" at the end, and then started the set closer, "Good Times, Bad Times." Trey teased "Heartbreaker" at one point.

They returned for the encore with acoustic instruments for "Long Journey Home": Trey on acoustic guitar, Mike on banjo, Page on upright bass, and Fishman on mandolin. It was odd seeing an acoustic song in an arena, but it comes out on the tapes anyway. They went back to their respective instruments and ended the evening with "Sleeping Monkey." This song is always great to end a show, or to bookend a great show with an amazing first half, or run of shows.

To me, this was the beginning of what would be many a show that blew me away with at least one large improvisational jam, or just all-around solid show. Not that I hadn't seen some amazing shows four years earlier, but this is exactly what I was looking for. Band communication, band-audience communication, and collective improvisation at its finest. If you have not heard this "Bowie" at least, I advise you to go out and find a copy. Do it now.

12/29/94 Providence Civic Center, Providence, RI —Saul E. Wertheimer

The second set of this show is a must-have for any serious collector. Actually, it's really just the first side of the tape that is necessary, for it contains some of the most startling improvisation that I have ever been fortunate enough to witness.

The set starts off with what is, to this day, still my favorite version of "Guyute." This was the last time it was played until 10/31/95, in which time it was slightly reworked. After "Guyute" ends, Trey starts what is often referred to as the "Digital Delay Loop Jam." However, there is a circle of people that have taken to referring to it as the "Big Show Jam," as it portends good things to come. The jam meanders for about three minutes, until the high-hat intro to "Bowie" begins.

The "Bowie" jam departs relatively quickly from familiar territory, and enters a slow, engaging jam, in which Mike and Page complement each other excellently. Trey makes some scary screeching sounds, and at times, Page sounds like McCoy Tyner clomping along to Coltrane's dissonance. The chaos of this jam slowly builds in tempo and intensity but is never really resolved.

The jam shortly returns to more familiar territory, and becomes very "McGrupp"-esque. This leads into a very "Hood"-like jam, which is nothing short of beautiful. The "Hood"-ish jam stops abruptly, and then enters the portion of "Bowie," which I labeled in my setlist book as the "Lassie Whistle Jam." Among other things, Trey hauntingly whispers "Now! NOW! Do it NOW!" This portion of the jam made my travelling companions and myself ask, "Where are we?" Trey then starts up the "Bowie" jam again, and is accompanied by some frightening screaming. This jam is raging! The "Bowie" finally comes to a close at approximately thirty-five minutes. Listening to this "Bowie" still gives me a strong sense of uneasiness and disquietude. The improv is spellbinding.

12/31/94 Boston Garden, Boston, MA—Ethan White

Phish always does something crazy New Year's Eve," my sister told me after she found out that I had scored tickets to Boston Garden.

"Get ready for a party!" I was more than ready for my first New Year's show. I had seen the boys for the first time that summer at Great Woods, and the "Divided" that capped the "Gamehendge" set told me that I would be with this band for a long time to come. Now in my hometown, and just a few subway stops away, I was ready for a New Year's party.

"Party" is the best way to describe the beginning of this show. Plastic horns and New Year's noisemakers were quieted only when Paul began blasting the ultimate pump-up song, "Rock and Roll Part II" (the "HEY!" song) from the PA as the band took the stage. After jamming along for couple seconds Trey counted off a rip-roaring "Golgi" that whipped the crowd into a frenzy. My seats were awful at this show—straight back, deep behind a low overhang. Despite the poor acoustics and annoying safety light in my eyes, I was swept up with the energy of this set. A Tom Marshall-sung "Antelope" soared, and Glide reminded us how happy we all were that we had arrived. For me, the centerpiece of this set was the "Divided Sky," although it was marred by an incessant fire alarm that went off several rows behind me. The ventilation in the old Garden wasn't the best, and needless to say, the room had gotten quite smoky by the time "Divided" came around. Nevertheless, Trey played it off with a smile as he jammed along to the fire alarm for a bit before busting back into a wonderful "Divided" finish. A rampaging "Funky Bitch" closed the set. When the lights went up, I couldn't believe the amount of gray haze hanging in the air. As always, I sat down to rest my dance-weary legs and did some people-watching. I was sitting with three friends, none of whom knew much about the band. Their bright eyes told me they were hooked. It's always great to see new fans in the making. The lights went down again and I jumped from my seat.

The second set contained the real meat of this show; three years later I still get chills about that "Maze." This was my first live "Maze," and needless to say, I was blown away. Even after dozens of shows and countless hours on tape, this still ranks as one of my favorite versions. "Bouncin'" pleased my friends, and though I hate to say it, this is probably one of the tightest versions ever. As sick as I am of this song, I always enjoy hearing this version on *ALO*. The end sounds like an old music box cranking away until Mike thumps the finish. "Mike's Song" blew the roof off the place, and I was completely swept up in the groove. An appropriate "Amazing Grace" ended the set.

Toward the end of the second set break, voices suddenly rose from the PA. Is that…hey, that's Fish's voice, talking about how all this playing was making him hungry! He orders a hot dog, LARGE fries, and a LARGE Coke. This has us all scratching our heads until his order appears during the "My Sweet One" opener, and the song was aborted for "2001" as the food revealed itself. With growing amazement I suddenly realized that something…something very big…was rising from the stage next to Fishman. At the peak of "2001," the giant hot dog, fries, and Coke were unveiled. I couldn't believe it when they opened the hot dog and climbed in. Surely they're not going to—yes, they began to rise, even as the New Year counted down. The boys busted into "Auld Lang Syne" (playing on portable instruments) as they sailed in their hot dog across the arena and back, throwing souvenir ping pong balls to the audience, dropping balloons—truly one of the strangest sights I have ever witnessed. Anyway, they eventually glided back to the stage and played a great "Chalk Dust" and raging "Suzie." The "Slave" really moved me; I have since compared all subsequent "Slaves" to this one. Truly majestic. "Simple" was an odd choice for the encore (the third in

the New Year's run), but it certainly left me smiling. Dazed and confused, we made for the exit.

The party was still going on outside after leaving the Garden, and the subway ride home took over an hour. No problem—there was a great show to be discussed. Though often overshadowed by the 1995 New Year's "jamfest," the show at Boston Garden had an incredible party vibe the equal of which I did not feel until Phish returned to Boston bearing sixty thousand balloons two years later. In the meantime, I was happy as could be. The lights of the city were whisked away as the subway went underground, and visions of hot dogs danced in our heads.

6/10–11/95 Red Rocks Amphitheater, Morrison, CO
—Kim Hannula

My weekend was wedged nicely between a milk carton on the plane from Burlington that informed me that I could feel good about "Hood," and hearing "Bouncing" on a Denver radio station on the way to the airport to fly home. I had a free flight (Frequent Flyer miles), and Phish was playing two nights at Red Rocks.

It was a clear day, and warm, despite the snow that had recently fallen in the mountains. I had stopped for lunch at a burrito place in Lakewood before driving up to the amphitheater, but I hadn't thought to pick up bottled water or anything for the show. It was a hot, dry wait in the stairway leading from the lower parking lot during soundcheck. A couple of women from California offered me sections of the oranges they had brought, and I accepted them gratefully. Eventually the gates opened and we flooded in.

The amphitheater at Red Rocks is fascinating. The seats lie between two rock walls whose red sandstone beds slope towards the stage at about the same angle as the rows of seats, which are really more like giant concrete steps. At the top of the amphitheater, the rock walls end abruptly, and the ground drops into a valley that separates the amphitheater from the mountainside. At the bottom of the amphitheater, the stage sits in front of another wall of rock, with buildings of red sandstone built on either side of the rock as if they are growing out of it. The layering in the sandstone behind the stage provided the only backdrop, which Chris Kuroda used to great advantage during the second set on Friday.

Friday's show began a little after 7:30 with a typically menacing "My Friend." The "Divided Sky" that followed seemed particularly appropriate, looking back up the amphitheater to the blue sky framed by red walls of rock. After "Divided" ended, there was a pause as Page took a breath as if to mentally prepare, and began "Strange Design." "Oh Kee Pah" immediately followed by a rocking "AC/DC Bag" picked up the energy again.

The next two songs were new, introduced by Trey (who thanked us for listening to brand-new stuff) as "Theme from the Bottom" and "Taste." Since I hadn't heard the first couple shows of the tour, this was my first exposure to these songs, and I liked them both a lot. The lyrics were catchy in places, but they weren't the focus of the songs. They also didn't have the extremely complex arrangements of songs like "Rift" or the how-fast-can-they-play adrenaline rush of "Llama." I was convinced "Theme from the Bottom" is a love song from a catfish to a loon. "Sparkle" was followed by a typically mind-blowing "Antelope" (this is the song I think is most likely to set off an earthquake), which ended the set.

I think it was during set break that I first noticed a number of people on the cliffs surrounding the amphitheater, despite the warning signs everywhere to stay off the rocks. From my seat beside the tapers' section, though, I had no idea that security was clashing with people trying to sneak in the venue just behind the amphitheater.

The moon, stars, and Denver city lights were visible by the time the second set started. "Split Open and Melt" started the set off with the energy level that ended the first set. The jam had an angular feel to it that reminded me of the 12/1/94 (Salem, OR) version. I didn't immediately recognize "The Wedge" that followed. The intro was different yet again from the 1993 Red Rocks "Wedge." A great song to hear so close to the Great Divide—it stayed in my head most of the next day. "Scent of a Mule" was the only *Hoist* offering of the evening. Page's solo included some spontaneous accompaniment by Trey and Mike that added a lot. "Cavern" rocked us next, followed by a "David Bowie" that I enjoyed, but I don't remember the details. Roadies brought out four stools and four acoustic guitars for the "Acoustic Army" that came next. The crowd was nearly silent except for cheering wildly at the false endings. They remained quiet for the "Sweet Adeline." A beautiful "Slave to the Traffic Light" ended the set. "The Squirming Coil" encore was marred only by one fan who decide to dance onto the stage, but was quickly whisked away by security. I don't usually like Page's solo as the ending of a show (I enjoy Page's playing in the context of the whole group much better than any piano solo alone), but I enjoyed this one quite a bit (this was the second time I listened to Page soloing as a spontaneous composition, and I appreciated the solo much more as a result).

The atmosphere surrounding the second night was a contrast to the previous night. The weather was cool and cloudy, with scattered light showers, cutting into the sales of iced cappuccino and turning the tapers' section into a sea of little umbrellas on top of the mic stands. There were mounted police riding around between the parking lots and the amphitheater, and tickets were checked at several points on the way into the venue. On the other hand, we were let in immediately and I wasn't searched at all on the way in—security's main concern was obviously to keep ticketless hordes off the rocks.

Trey introduced his grandparents, who were sitting on the edge of the stage, before beginning "Makisupa Policeman." At the end, they sped up the jam before breaking into "Llama." My first impression of "Prince Caspian" was that it was a bit repetitive. They continued the theme of moving fast on top of water with "It's Ice." Next came "Free;" it's up there with "Bottom" and "Taste" as a new song to watch for. I want to hear it again. "Rift," typically structured and tight, followed. "YEM's" beginning got a big cheer from the crowd. The vocal jam featured a disco-ish theme in places. An unusual first-set drummer change followed, with Fishman coming out front, vacuum in hand. He announced, "Usually, I play the trombone on this song, but tonight…" to wild cheers from the audience. The vacuum solo in "Lonesome Cowboy Bill" was short, but it was long enough to let us know that the vacuum hasn't been put away forever. If playing music with heavy machinery is "industrial music," should Fishman's songs be called custodial music? Little "Suzie G." rocked us out of the set ("forgotten my name…that's okay, I forget it too!"), with Trey telling us not to do anything he wouldn't do.

The light rain that had been threatening all day finally started to fall steadily during the second set. We started out lost in an intense "Maze," followed by "Fee" and "Uncle Pen." But those were just warm-ups for the main attraction of the second set: "Mike's Groove." This was the first "Mike's" that I've seen live, though it was my tenth show. Holy moly. "Are

they always like this?" I wondered. The jam went in and out of varying amounts of spaciness. They started to go into the ending theme (which sounds similar to the "Simple" riff) several times, only to jam away from it, then come back, then jam away, etc. Meanwhile, the lights used the raindrops as a new effect. Finally we mellowed in "Hydrogen," then took it to "Weekapaug." After "Weekapaug," they put down the instruments and came forward (while roadies covered the keyboards with towels—it must have been a little wet on stage, too) to sing "Amazing Grace." The crowd wasn't quite as respectful as they had been the previous night, but they weren't hideous. Then back to the instruments (after removing the towels from the keys) to end the set with a powerful "Sample in a Jar." Sorry if you don't like this one, but it ended the set with a fine intensity. You've got to come back from spacey jams somehow!

I'm not a big Beatles fan, so although I recognized "A Day in the Life" as a Beatles tune, I didn't know the name, and I'm not sure exactly how it differed from the Beatles' version. Page sang most of it (he has a great voice for Beatles stuff), with Trey singing "Woke up, got out of bed...." Between verses they broke into noisy, thrashy jamming reminiscent of "BBFCFM" (is this where the orchestra plays in the Beatles' version?). I really enjoyed it.

I left Red Rocks excited about the new music, feeling that the tour would get even better as the new songs progressed. At the same time I was sad, afraid that this would be the last year they would be allowed to play some of the beautiful outdoor venues.

6/16/95 Walnut Creek Amphitheater, Raleigh, NC —Charlie Dirksen

This is a gorgeous, quaint amphitheater surrounded by trees. It's like the Deer Creek or Blossom Amphitheater of the East Coast. I was able to cleanly hear the soundcheck from a hill next to the venue. It was a treat to hear my first "Caravan." "Three Little Birds" was amusing too, since they "rehearsed" it only for about fifteen seconds and then appeared to laugh about how easy it was to cover. The first set included delightful versions of "Esther," "Ya Mar," "Cry Baby Cry," "Catapult," and an amazing "Split Open and Melt." Fish started "SOAM" three times before they ended up playing "Dog Faced Boy."

A "Runaway" jam opened the second set. Just as this version began, I turned to my friend Mike Niven and said, "I hope this version goes somewhere." "Jim" had seemed to me to be getting tired, and I wanted Phish to do something with it. I got my wish. This "Jim" featured an unusually long, psychedelic, spacey jam. At one point, Fish even sang something like "Doggie, doggie...So far from home." Reminded me of the "Lassie" jam from the Providence 12/29/94 "Bowie." This "Jim" was by far the most improvisational version Phish had ever played at this time. Solid in parts, too carefree (for my taste) in others, it was nevertheless memorable and historically important. It also segued magnificently into "Free."

The "You Enjoy Myself" in this set was also unforgettable. Boyd, the fiddler from Dave Matthews Band, came out during it and jammed for a very short time. It was a great jam, but after he left, the jam got even better. It was an amazing Phish experience:.the finest "YEM" I'd ever seen or heard live up until that time. Even the "Coil" was good, and the "Bold As Love" encore, though an average version, was still great!

6/17/95 Nissan Pavilion, Stone Ridge, VA—Charlie Dirksen

This venue was brand spanking new at the time of this show, and I recall being disappointed by the crass commercialism of the place.

It was a big amphitheater like Shoreline or any other, but there were all these damn Nissan cars everywhere. Ooh, a car! I mean, WTF?

It's easy to note the highlights of this show. In the first set, there was an excellent "Curtain">"Stash" that made all the commercialized b.s. in the venue worth putting up with. The "Wilson">"Maze" to open the second was solid, but "Maze" wasn't nearly as good as the one in Philly a few nights later, on 6/25.

The "Tweezer" was fantastic, and is something to check out if you have not heard it. The jamming was deep and funky, and there wasn't any aimless, spacey riffing. "Johnny B. Goode" was sandwiched in the middle of it, too, and it was an extremely high-strung, fiery version. "McGrupp" was similarly wonderful to hear, a real treat. The "Harry" was enjoyable, but its jam was not as awe-inspiring as the one in Philly a week later, on 6/24. The "Three Little Birds" encore with the sax player of the Dave Matthews Band and Dave Matthews himself was fun, but I wish they had jammed on it more. Phish had "rehearsed" this tune at soundcheck the night before at Walnut Creek for about fifteen seconds.

All things considered, this was a "typically great" Phish show for 1995.

6/19/95 Deer Creek Music Center, Noblesville, IN —Charlie Dirksen

It's always great to be back at the Creek. I even scored a nice parking spot by the "X" right near the entrance. I saw several Dead shows and a Traffic show at this venue in 1994, and was thrilled to be back again, this time seeing Phish.

I really loved this show. I got to see it with some old college friends (Jon Steinman and Rick Kuhlman), and we had great seats only a few rows back from the stage, Page side. This show was the longest of the summer 1995 tour, at about two hours and fifty-two minutes. Highlights of the first set were a strong "Theme" and good versions of "AC/DC Bag," "Tela," "PYITE," "Reba," and "Antelope". The "Rift" was botched badly (Trey forgot to come in singing at one point), but it wasn't a big deal. The crowd loves "Rift" and always has.

The second set opened with a rousing version of "Simple" that had a groovy, psychedelic transition into an interesting "David Bowie." This "Bowie" had a lot more spacey jamming than the Philly 6/24 version, but was still solid. Some people really enjoyed it, but I thought it was weak in light of the Providence 12/29/94 version, which probably isn't a fair comparison. "Loving Cup" psyched me up (though it was not as sweet as the 4/17/94 Patriot Center version, which is as of this writing still my favorite).

The "YEM" jam was very good, but not even comparable to the one in Walnut Creek a few nights earlier. The vocal jam, however, was spectacular! It was the most intensely crazy, wild, freaky vocal jam that I'd ever heard at the time. It is still worth getting the tapes of this show just to hear this vocal jam. It was that amazing.

"Possum" was astounding. Just incredible. It was so much more inspired than the version from 12/28/94 Philadelphia, and any version that I'd heard in all of 1994 (except perhaps the Big Birch and Warfield versions). Just outrageous. The "Day in the Life" encore was great to hear and a lot of fun. What a show!

6/22/95 Finger Lakes Performing Arts Center, Canandaigua, NY —James Raras, Jr.

The second set of this show is one of the mostly widely debated sets in Phish history. It consists of three songs and is nicknamed "The

Fleezer." To some fans this was the intense, freeform jamming they go to shows for; to others it lost its direction and became tiresome and stale. Pick up a copy and decide for yourself. Regardless of your verdict, this is a set you should hear.

6/26/95 Saratoga Performing Arts Center, Saratoga Springs, NY—Kim Hannula

The lawn part of SPAC reminded me of a university quad more than a concert lawn: most of it is flat enough to play ultimate frisbee on. People weren't allowed into the pavilion until twenty minutes before the show was supposed to start; although Phish didn't actually come on until twenty minutes after they were scheduled, the pavilion was maybe three-quarters full when the show started. The acoustics from where I sat (Page side, under the balcony) were really echoey; I could barely make out the preshow PA music over the murmur of crowd conversation.

The first set opened with "My Friend." The crowd rushing into the pavilion was rather distracting. "Don't You Wanna Go" is fun and joyous...I wanna go! The jam in "Bathtub Gin" flirted with chaos as Trey and Page played the theme out of time with Fish's drumming, but it never fully dove in to the uncharted waters of the legendary 8/93 Murat Theater "Gin." "NICU" was fun and followed immediately by "The Sloth." "The Sloth" has some weird time signatures in it that I never noticed until I tried to dance to it. "My Mind"...indeed does have a mind of its own, sometimes. "It's Ice" segued into "Dog Faced Boy," but I don't remember exactly how. The crowd was rude during this: lots of shouting, some off-time, too-fast clapping at the end. The beautiful "Tela" that followed seemed to soothe the crowd into a more attentive state that held through most of the rest of the evening. The set-closing "Possum" was on fire. Something let loose, perhaps in my mind, but perhaps in the band, too. I suddenly stopped being bothered by the muddy sound, envisioning myself as one of Allan Keeton's Phishtory's pre-lizard fishies swimming in a sea of music. When Trey announced they would be back, I hoped that the momentum built during the "Possum" jam wouldn't be lost during set break.

The second set opened with the strange feedback noises that mark the beginning of "Down with Disease." I thought even the non-jam parts of this were better than last year's—1994's live "DWDs" always sounded a bit rushed to me. SPAC's "DWD" slid into the comfortable groove that the *Hoist* version is in. But the *Hoist* version is short enough to be a single, and SPAC's version...well, it was twenty-five minutes long and wasn't finished. The jam (that usually precedes the final chorus) quickly wandered away from anything that resembled "DWD" into a vaguely threatening jam, with a driving bass line that reminds me of the one in "Pablo Picasso" from the *Repo Man* soundtrack. Mike's bass provided a solid anchor for the jam; it was exploratory without becoming arrhythmic or spacey. The lights on the middle "Minkin" panel looked like a dragon that started flaring its nostrils late in the jam. Eventually the tense chords resolved, and Trey started playing something that sounded classic rockish compared to the previous jam.

Tempo and drum beat and accompaniment changed into something vaguely familiar that I didn't recognize until the lyrics "floating weightless in the room": a smooth segue into "Free." The post-lyrics jam got much spacier than I remembered from my first "Free" at Red Rocks earlier in the summer. At one point it sounded as if Fish was drumming in a divisible-by-three time signature, while Trey was soloing in four. It ended with an "everybody play the same chord at once

several times," with the downbeat marked by Trey jumping up and down. "Poor Heart" started immediately and ended with a similar series of chords. "YEM" featured some wild lights during the vocal jam (which sounded like a train whistle to me at one point, complete with Doppler effect), white lights spinning across the stage rapidly, which for some reason reminded me of being on a county fair vomitride. The lights slowed gradually at the end, too, like a ride coming to a stop. "Strange Design" fit really well after the wildness of the vocal jam; it's a "reaching for mental and emotional stability" kind of song. Just relax, you're doing fine...but then we were off again with "Antelope". There was a new light effect that I hadn't seen before, little points of light like stars between the "Minkin" backdrops. The little lights flickered on and off like fireflies on too many iced cappuccinos during the ending part of the jam. And that was the end of the set. The encores, "Sleeping Monkey" and "Rocky Top," weren't mind-blowers, but after the second set, whose mind still needed blowing?

6/29/95 Jones Beach Music Theater, Wantagh, NY —David M. Goldstein

The summer of '95 was an amazing Phish tour, featuring fantastic runs at venues that we might never get a chance to see the band at again, due to their swelling popularity. Some of these include Great Woods, Sugarbush Summer Stage, Red Rocks, and one of my personal favorites, the Jones Beach Amphitheater. It's a summer shed that is unique because it has fantastic acoustics, no lawn seating, and is located right on Long Island Sound. Regarding the two nights Phish played at this venue in '95, all I ever hear about is how excruciatingly long the "Tweezer" on the 6/28 was. Maybe so, but 6/29 is a fabulous show, and perhaps one of the most criminally underrated shows of all time.

The first set is above average with definite highlights. "Runaway Jim" isn't one of the most common openers for nothing, and "Taste" is gorgeous even in its fledgling form. We also get one of the greatest "Divided Skys" I've had the pleasure to hear in person. The closing jams are gorgeous and nearly flawless. At this point in the show, the fog was just beginning to lift over Long Island Sound, adding to the beauty of the jam. "Cavern," "Rift," and "Simple" were played one after another with no pauses, creating a momentum which made this series much more than the sum of its parts. Then a fiery "Split," and "Carolina" to close.

I'll never know why the second set is nary to be found on the common "favorite sets of all time" lists that seem to crop up everywhere. At the time, I had never heard "Free" before, and it worked wonders in the opening slot, combining with the fog and bright yellow lights for an incredible experience. The "Bowie" that follows is out of this world—twenty-five minutes long, and proof that Phish can be spacey without being boring. "Strange Design" was another first-timer for me, and the placement for this mellow ballad, after the barn-burner "Bowie," was perfect. Summer '95 was a watershed time for "YEMs," and the "YEM" played on this night was no exception, with an insane bass and drums section. Mike is on fire. "Acoustic Army," and then "Day in the Life" to close, which was a treat before it got overplayed. I've seen thirteen shows since the 6/29, which was my second. This isn't mere nostalgia talking; it was a fantastic and underrated show with one of the best second sets I've seen. In addition to the two sets, "Theme from the Bottom" was an excellent encore, which was gorgeous even in '95. I rarely see this one on tape lists, but it is well worth seeking out.

6/30/95—Great Woods Center for the Performing Arts; Mansfield, MA—Jeremy D. Goodwin

June 30 was a positively beautiful day in New England. The sun was shining, and the lot scene was in full force by early afternoon. I remember wandering through a seemingly endless expanse of tie-dye, grilling food, all conceivable forms of vending, music from a hundred different directions, frisbees, hackey-sacks, and annoying security jetting around on little green carts, confiscating alcohol whenever possible. (Great Woods is known for the presence of The Man, but generally the consensus is that you can avoid difficulties by being smart). It was still a whole new world for me, and I was more than a little dazed. Despite criticism of "the scene" that was prevalent among certain circles even then, this splendid Massachusetts afternoon will always stick out in my mind as the epitome of its best features; I experienced an overwhelming feeling of peace and community that afternoon, albeit one that only seems to exist in one place at one time, before being scattered and bent and dispersed to the winds.

On this day it seemed like a Phish reunion, as the band was setting up shop at their nearest local shed for the third year in a row. With only these two nights, and then two more at Ground Zero (Vermont) to close out the Summer Tour, [I believe we have inconsistency in the capitalization of "tour"] the whole gang was in town and ready to celebrate the suddenly enormous event that is a New England Phish show. To add to the general buzz, *A Live One* had come out about two weeks earlier, and such fare as "Bouncing" was popping up on Boston radio occasionally. The band had recently graced the cover of the local Boston Globe *Parade* magazine, with the headline "The phenomenon of Phish." Seeing as the first night at Great Woods the summer before had hosted a full "Gamehendge" performance, it's fair to say that on this day the buzz was pretty high and energy was extremely positive.

Before heading in, I purchased my first-ever lot item: a very cool reflecting sticker, in the shape of the traditional Phish logo, which read, "It's the ocean phlowing in our veins." The guy who sold it to me said, "Think of me when they play it tonight." Although I was not yet totally familiar with the band's catalog, and couldn't place the origin of the quote, I just smiled and wandered off.

The lawn at Great Woods can be a horrible place to see a show; if you're more than a little back up the hill, you can't see the stage at all, and must depend on the screens if you want to actually view the proceedings. I don't know how all those people are content to essentially watch TV during a show; this show remains the first and only time I've settled for the lawn at a Phish show, until I was finally bagged with mail-order lawn seats for my summer '00 shows. I arrived in the venue early enough to casually scout out a spot literally against the front rail of the lawn, stage center. From that vantage point, with my flannel shirt hanging from the rail and with a little concrete ledge to sit on when necessary, I had a perfect audio/visual vantage point.

I guess the preshow wait extended further beyond the ticket time than usual, because people around me were whining vehemently about the delay. Finally, Trey came out onstage and announced that a lot of people were still waiting to get into the venue, so it'd be a few more minutes before things could get going. Having arrived around three in the afternoon, I missed the fact that there was actually a colossal traffic jam occurring outside the venue, which fans would remember and complain about for years to come. (The next day, while being interview on 104.1 FM, Trey jokingly exclaimed, "The New York State Thruway is closed, man!")This completely changed the anxious vibe that had been brewing among the crowd, and everyone seemed to relax and perhaps even groove off of the fact that the band was considerate enough to apologize for a delay in start time.

When things did get going, they started impressively with a rare "AC/DC Bag" opener. This song, while always a treat, served this night also as a happy reminder from the band to the crowd of last year's "Gamehendge," while simultaneously indicating that a repeat performance would not be in order this year. "Scent of a Mule" followed, and I can vaguely remember the antics of Page playing part of his solo with his feet, and Trey playing a few notes with his teeth. The set also featured the new "Taste" (I had to read the review in the paper the next day to catch the name), and a wide-eyed newcomer like myself could groove heartily to the "Fee" and "Lizards" (which, although widely overplayed then, at least brought back memories of the old days for some).

At one point, while entranced by an unfamiliar but very appealing groove, I suddenly noticed the lyrics: "and it's the ocean flowing in our veins." I pulled out the reflective sticker and examined it, to the approval of the guy next to me who seemed to understand what was going on. And thus, my first "Wedge." This is such a beautiful tune, and one that I wouldn't have the pleasure of seeing again until it memorably opened the second day of the Great Went. This began a love affair of sorts between me and "Wedge," as it continued to pop up at other special shows I saw (11/29/97, 11/21/98, in addition to the Went). I still don't know how that guy with the stickers "knew" they were going to play it (this was just the second and final "Wedge" of the tour). I prefer to believe that he was not just saying that every night.

The set eventually closed in traditional manner, with a "Run Like an Antelope" that was pretty typical except for some altered lyrics ("Suck the deer shit from the side of this hole," apparently).

Set break seemed to whiz by me at a million miles an hour as I sat alone on the concrete ledge and awaited the second set. I pretty much kept to myself, taking note of all the things around me and feeling pretty good about how the day was going.

The second set, like at least three quarters of the ones from this tour, can easily be called a "monster." This particular one has received a lot less attention over the years than other well-circulated standout nights like, say, 6/15, 6/25, and 7/3. To be fair, it lacks a definitive jam that stacks up with the "Runaway Jim," "DWD," or "David Bowie" of these shows. However, it is packed from beginning to end with special treats, notably including one of the spaciest "Mike's Songs" I've ever heard.

Things started off with an electric "2001" (perhaps the best way to open a second set in an amphitheater, in my opinion), which leap-frogged into "Possum" for the first time ever. The "Possum" was mind-bendingly intense, barreling closer and closer into white noise before finally resolving. I don't know if I've ever enjoyed a "Possum" this much again, and it stands up on tape against most versions from recent years.

Then, an extremely bizarre song I wasn't familiar with, featuring a heavy, repetitious riff and only the lyrics, "Ha, ha, ha." I later learned that some of my friends had arrived late and were just getting to their seats during this song, which seemed to be ominously mocking them! Lighters were aglow across the entire venue during the spellbindingly tranquil "TMWSIY." After "Avenu Malkenu," the band skipped the usual "TMWSIY" reprise and surprised everyone by jumping right into "Mike's Song."

I may not have been a Phish expert, but after a few months of lis-

tening to tapes, I already knew enough to be positively fired up for this. "Mike's Song" has been my favorite Phish song since literally my first live tape. I distinctly remember how I felt this night while watching Trey and Mike bounce on trampolines amid crazy strobe lights during my favorite song. I felt like everything had come together, and frankly, I was proud of myself. This "Mike's Song" is pretty much unlike any others I can think of, as it ventures far into that distinctly summer '95 brand of space. In '96 and '97 Phish began basing most of their jams around groove, but in '94 and '95, as the band was gaining its improvisational feet, the playing was a lot more experimental and sometimes even cacophonous. Personally, I like this better, as it's more consistently interesting. Finally, "Contact" emerged, and I joined in the customary arm-waving, led by Mike. Then off into "Weekapaug," which was particularly energetic and sizzling.

After an encore that included the throwback Henrietta tune "Cracklin' Rosie" (for the last time, to date), I was left to catch my breath and watch the lawn grow gradually more empty. The phrase "something really good just happened" echoed over and over in my head as I slowly made my way out towards the parking lot. I felt mentally and emotionally winded, but totally covered in a very special glow.

I would be back.

7/2–3/95 Summer Stage at Sugarbush, North Fayston, VT
—Kim Hannula

I dumped my sleeping significant other in the truck and headed out of Foxboro, MA, at 7 AM. Four hours over the speed limit and I was on Route 100 in Vermont. Got lunch in Warren and headed for the lot, praying that the north lot wasn't already full. Traffic on German Flats Road was backed up nearly to Route 17 and wasn't moving. I turned off the ignition and read a novel for about an hour and a half. Finally, traffic started to move around noon. You could smell overheated engines everywhere as we crept up the mountain, stop and go. They had stopped checking tickets when we reached the Sugarbush North access road and were waved on. (Success! No buses for us tonight!) We parked near the entrance and watched the rest of the world set up camp. We seemed like the only people who weren't going to spend the night.

Shuttle buses carrying the unfortunates stuck in the outlying lots didn't start to arrive until four or so. We went into the venue when the gates opened not much after five and planted ourselves in front of the tapers' section. The slope seemed to fill up faster than last year. I hope that was because folks were on the shuttle buses as early as possible to avoid missing a set. Before the show started people began climbing over and under the blue plastic snow fence that marked the back of the venue. With only one security person back there, there wasn't any real effort to stop them. I can understand not going through the effort (or the violence) to force them to stay out, but I don't understand why people with tickets cheer when people break in.

The show started late as usual. I don't remember the details of the first set very clearly. "Sample" opened energetically. "Divided Sky" reminded me of Red Rocks, except that the sky was framed by green trees instead of red sandstone. "Gumbo" without horns clued us in to not expect guests. That's okay with me; I like it with horns, but I'm also a fan of Page's stride piano playing at the end instead. "The Curtain" followed, ending with a quick jump into a joyful "Julius." Then, the evening's surprise for setlist watchers everywhere: "Camel Walk." I hadn't heard this before, so I can't comment on if it has changed. "Reba" came

next. I can't remember how far this wandered from the theme. It ended rather abruptly, with no whistling. "I Didn't Know," with Henrietta on vacuum, was great fun. After "Rift," Trey told the crowd he was happy they were all there, and asked those who hadn't paid for tickets to the show to donate to the King Street Youth Center (a Burlington organization for which the show was partially a benefit) during set break. "While My Guitar Gently Weeps" closed out the set.

It was dark when the second set began. "Runaway Jim" has turned into the latest experimental launchpad, I guess. This is the first experimental "Jim" I've heard. It wandered pretty far from the song structure. When it was perhaps too far to call back, Trey walked over and whispered something to Mike, and they slowly pulled the jam into a reggae feel for "Makisupa Policeman" (the segue wasn't spontaneous, but it wasn't stop and start either). The "Makisupa" jam got pretty far out, too, and eventually changed into bluegrass for "Scent of a Mule." Page's solos are starting to sound like piano concertos. After "Scent" ended, they began "Tweezer" ("That's the rest of the set," says my significant other). But it was actually a short "Tweezer" for summer '95. It only went through one spacey-jammy transition before segueing into "Ha Ha Ha." Great segue, by the way. "Ha Ha Ha" sort of segued into "Sleeping Monkey" (they never stopped playing, but it wasn't really a transformation). "Sleeping Monkey" and the following "Acoustic Army" settled us down. Page and Fishman looked more comfortable with the guitars than they did earlier in the summer—they looked up occasionally rather than staring intently at their hands the whole time. "Slave to the Traffic Jam"—oops, I mean "Light"—was an absolutely beautiful, soaring close to the set. Bubbles floating into the spotlights above the crowd looked amazing. They encored with "Halley's Comet," which segued into the last "Tweezer Reprise" of the tour.

A DJ from a local radio station announced (as he had several times through the night) that they weren't exactly prepared for the number of people who were at the show, and that no one would be rushed out of the venue, and to just relax and be patient. The buses looked better organized than last year, with clearly marked different loading areas for the different lots. The biggest slowdown may have been the hordes of people hanging out in the road (which was quite narrow for buses to pass one another as it was). Lots of people were walking. Many begged us for a ride, but we were going the wrong way and didn't want to add to the buses' traffic problems more than necessary. Got home at 1 AM (after the forty-five minutes it always takes, concert or none).

Monday we got up early again in hopes of scoring a spot in the north lot again. No such luck. We parked in the south lot beside a scalper who wasn't having much luck. Buses didn't seem to be running yet (at 11 AM), so we walked to the north lot. Nice walk. Took about an hour. The north lot looked like a refugee camp that had just gotten a donation from The North Face. We parked on the hillside close to the venue to eat lunch and read for the afternoon. Buses started running steadily between the lots by 1 PM. When the gates opened around five a lot of people were ready to go in. Contrary to rumors, they did check and rip tickets. More people crowded in long before the show started than the day before.

I don't know what was missing from the first set. There was lots of stuff from *Rift*. Even the songs that could have really taken off didn't entirely. I actually took out my contacts during "Antelope", which would normally be physically impossible because I'd be involuntarily dancing so hard. There was a large inflatable moose being tossed around to-

wards the front. During "If I Could" (after a toss perfectly synchronized with the "flipping backwards through the doors and through the windows" line), one last toss had it land in perfect sitting position, facing the audience, on Page's side of the stage. The feat got more applause from the audience than the music did. My significant other liked the "Maze" jam a lot, though he usually isn't into it. "Strange Design" can be amazing as a return to reality after a really crazy jam (see 6/26/95 SPAC and 7/1/95 Great Woods), but there was no energy in need of releasing this time. "Free" is still a great song, but again it didn't reach its full potential. All in all, an example of why one should not judge the quality of a set based on the number of songs played. (Eleven, by the way.)

I spent set break trying to convince people that there really wasn't more room somewhere up front.

I don't know what happened between sets, but somehow everything cut loose in the second set. It didn't hurt to start with "Timber Ho." In all honesty, it wasn't the musical peak of the set, but I think it started a trend of risk-taking that paid off big in the later jams. "Timber Ho" was followed by the high-hat that signals "David Bowie," with a long, spacey introduction. The jam headed out fast. Trey teased "Bathtub Gin," and they played briefly with the theme before moving on to other unexplored themes. The jam had a lot of variety to it: different drum beats, different playing styles. It got far outside the "Bowie" theme without ever getting lost in itself (the hazard of spacey jams). It segued into a rocking "Johnny B. Goode," which segued back into improvisational mystery land. There were a lot of teases in here, I think, but I didn't identify them. Then again, they may have been entirely new riffs. Eventually the jam returned to "David Bowie" and ended. The "AC/DC Bag" that followed picked up the jamming ball. It was a more experimental (for lack of a good word) "AC/DC Bag" than I've heard before. It segued into "Lizards". Suddenly, at the beginning of one of the verses, only Page (and Mike?) are singing. Trey tried to pull it together, but the words just weren't there. Fishman cracked a joke, and Trey responded by starting "Big Black Furry Creature from Mars." What a tension release! Instead of flinging his guitar around, Trey picked up a very large doll that someone had thrown on stage and flung it around, then grabbed a cup and threw some water out onto the audience (which looked wild with the strobes going), then threw some pasta (?) onto the audience as well. Phew. When "BBFCFM" ended, they started up "A Day in the Life," which stop/start-fast-segued into "Possum." "Possum" was again on fire, and contained another "Bathtub Gin" tease. "Squirming Coil" ended the set with more composing from Page. "Simple" was a perfect encore. This one was pure celebration: this is what we love to do and we're doing it! And to finish the tour, they came out front to sing us "Amazing Grace." I'm surprised they didn't collapse into a group giggle fit before this started. The audience was rowdy. After several attempts on the pitch pipe, Page turned and threw it to the audience. Trey threw something small, as well. I thought Fishman was going to throw the crowd his dress. Trey mocked throwing Fishman to the crowd. Finally the crowd and the band started to settle down and they sang nicely, almost in tune most of the time.

Waterloo by ABBA was the immediate post-show music—a request to keep everyone's sense of humor while waiting for the buses? In the lot, the DJ kept the bus-waiting crowd calm and partying at the same time, or at least it sounded like he was trying. The disco bus provided a party lower in the lot. The stars were out and it was chilly, so we decided to walk back to the south lot. I think a lot of people who did the

walk weren't too keen on it, but I preferred the stars and the exercise to the hour spent sitting in the Great Woods parking lot two nights before. We got home at 2 AM—only an hour later than we got in at Great Woods (and the post-lot drive was forty-five minutes longer).

Amazing four nights. I was struck by how consistently good these guys are. I mean, my mood creates much more variation in my show experience than the playing does. I have more off nights just listening than they do playing. I just hope that irresponsible fools don't destroy my chance to continue hearing this stuff. I don't think Phish should return to Sugarbush, not because it is a logistically hellish venue, but because security is impossible to enforce (without causing traffic jams or resorting to the kind of violent crowd control that many of us came to Vermont to avoid dealing with). I am very afraid of what rumors of mellow, successful gate crashing will lead to next time. Unfortunately, patience and a sense of humor can only go so far in keeping a crowd from getting out of hand.

10/7/95 Spokane Opera House, Spokane, WA—Charlie Dirksen

I flew from San Francisco not only to see Phish in an opera house for the first time, but also to visit my wonderful friends Klaus and Gretchen Bender in their new hometown. The Opera House itself, though pleasant, was not particularly memorable other than its magnificent acoustics. The show, on the other hand, was unforgettable.

The power in both sets is easy to hear on the tapes. The "Julius" opener is good, but the "Gumbo" and "Possum" that follow soon thereafter really smoke. A "Wilson">"Antelope" closes the first set mightily, just as good as any sweet "You Enjoy Myself" would, really!

A long, spacey, gorgeous Makisupa opens the second set. This is still my favorite version. SOAM rages, as does "It's Ice," believe it or not. It included an unusual amount of improvisation in its mini-jam segment.

The "Harry Hood," though, deserves its own paragraph. Trey's soloing in the jam segment becomes so precious and enchanting that everyone in attendance was hanging on each note that he performed. He also used the acoustics of the venue to full effect, soloing all the way down to unamplification. That's right. At one point during the "Hood," Fish, Mike, and Page faded out, and Trey soloed completely unamplified. Because of the room's remarkable acoustics, I could hear Trey's unamplified solo from more than twenty rows out from the stage (along with the white noise and hiss from the hall speakers). I don't imagine that I will ever experience this again at a Phish concert.

Many fans were (and still are) disappointed by the fact that this "Hood" is "unfinished," meaning that there are no "You can feel good / Good about Hood" closing lyrics. Though this is more common today, it was unheard of on 10/7/95. To me at the show, though, it did not matter at all: I had witnessed by far the greatest version of "Harry Hood" that I'd ever seen or heard. This is still true as of this writing. The "Theme"-like, cacophonous, enormous ending of this version is at least as inspiring, and inspired, as any final "Feel good about Hood" lyric. No fall 1995 [in this context, the author refers to Fall Tour 1995, not merely "a show that occurs in the fall of 1995". I believe Fall, Summer etc should be capitalized in this context.] tape collection is complete with this show.

10/22/95 Assembly Hall, Champaign, IL —Saul E. Wertheimer

This show turned me into the "Tweezer" fanatic that I am today. The first highlight of the show is a great "Possum," which is followed by the always-strange "Catapult." "Curtain">"Tweezer" follows that, and it

is probably my favorite "one-two" combination. This "Tweezer" does not disappoint! It grooves and glides effortlessly, through numerous jam segments. It seems that from "Tweezers" such as this one and 11/30/95 Dayton (and others, of course), that we have arrived at the epic jamming that became almost commonplace in 1997. Jams with several, distinct jam segments, such as the "Ghost" from 11/28 Worcester and the "Jim" from the next night, seem to me to be direct descendants of this "Tweezer". These styles of jams work hard at establishing the "Groove" before launching into the "Unknown." If you're not a "Tweezer" fan, by all means check this one out...it may change your mind, too!

10/24/95 Dane County Coliseum, Madison, WI
—Saul E. Wertheimer

The Dane County Coliseum always felt like a cozy venue to me, and I enjoyed seeing shows there...not to mention the fact that Madison, WI, is a fun town. The first set of this show is notable because it contained one of the first "new" versions of "Taste," at the time called "Fog that Surrounds," or "Taste that Surrounds." I had heard that "Taste" had been reworked since the summer, and this version was yet another step in its evolution. When Fishman started to "sing," I recall thinking "Huh?" There was also a rare "Demand" in the first set.

The second set, however, is what truly makes this show memorable for me. The "Julius" opener is the turning point of all "Julius'". From this point forth, every "Julius" I have heard is better than the previous! This one is astounding, complete with Fishman whoopin' and hollerin'. Theme followed, and this was before it really came into its own. "Bouncin'" was a throwaway, but perhaps a preparation for the monster jams yet to come. "YEM" was a great version, but my favorite part of it was the "Sleeping Monkey" that segued out of the vocal jam.

What came next is what I hold to be the single most intense version of "Antelope" ever played. This "Antelope" builds with the intensity of a '97 "Antelope", and just when you think it is going to drop off of the Sonic Cliff, it climbs to another level! This "Antelope" is sure to cause coronary in some patients.

"Contact" and "Cavern" closed out the set, and the encore was "A Day in the Life." Leaving Dane County, I could barely believe how good the "Antelope" was. When looking for an "Antelope" to play for someone, I always choose this one.

10/31/95 Rosemont Horizon, Chicago, IL—Dean Budnick

Friends of mine started their campaign in late August after they read the announcement in the *Schvice*: *Joe's Garage* for Halloween. I could understand their logic; last year was a double album, why not triple it this year? I had my own thoughts, however, which focused primarily on the costume contest. Last year I had been so close, but this year I was determined to finally make it onto the stage. I knew that I had to come up with something good, but I just couldn't summon any great ideas. Meanwhile my pals continued to stuff the ballot box for *Joe's* while I finally decided that maybe it would be better to sit out the contest this year to enjoy the show. Of course that was just a rationalization to cover the fact that I just didn't have any good costume ideas.

As the night before the show approached I made two discoveries. First, I learned that the Halloween album would incorporate horns. Second, I concluded that it would be inappropriate to show up without a costume. So I brainstormed, came up with a mediocre idea, and ha-

rassed some of my friends to do the same. As we met at O'Hare Airport on the morning of the thirty-first we shared one common goal: we had to go out into the city to buy some stuff to complete our costumes. Following an afternoon that featured a long visit to Woolworth's and the obligatory deep dish pizza, we were back at out hotel and ready for our preshow prep.

Fortunately, our hotel was just up the street from the Horizon, because there was no way that any of us would fit into a car. Manny was dressed as "Sleeping Monkey" (an ape face with pajamas, furry hands and sleeping cap), Marc was "The Curtain" (you guessed it: hanging out in the middle of a curtain rod he clipped from his house), Lee was "AC/DC Bag," and Rob (of dubious "Dean Budnick for President!" fame) was a total fabrication that he rented from the remainders at a costume shop (I think he said he was a multi-beast). I was dressed as the "Rhombus," trapped in a boxy, bulky, foam-core prison. I didn't quite perfect the thing so I had to stick my arms straight out so that I could walk. And to top this off I had this insanely stupid hat in the shape of a rhombus, with a little toy figure emerging from the top to sing "Divided Sky."

I waddled over to the venue with everyone and somehow bumbled inside (I didn't fit through the turnstile—thankfully they opened a door) only to learn that there was to be no costume contest this year. Eventually I moved into the actual arena, set up my deck, and abandoned my costume, convincing some usher to let me place it on an area of floor directly behind the last row of seats.

At some time shortly after 8:00 Phish took the stage (about two hours earlier than the year before). Right off, the band demonstrated that they were going to make this one special, with a Halloween Icculus incantation. "Divided Sky" came next with some nimble performances both during the scripted parts and the short but captivating improvisational section that followed. My abandoned costume no doubt appreciated the tune. "Wilson" was third, with some audience participation just as everyone had learned to do from *A Live One*. A quick run through "Sparkle" followed, eliciting an inordinate number of "yeee-haas" and "wahooos" from the Midwest crowd. Phish moved next into a lengthy "Free," a gem of a song with fine harmonies, soaring guitar tone and on this night some fine work by Fish when Trey started on percussion. At the close of this song, Phish paused briefly to consult and then..."Guyute!" The triumphant return of that ugly old pig with some minor cosmetic surgery. A romping "Antelope" came next and most of us figured that the set was over. But no, that familiar "oom pah pah" introduced us once again to "Harpua." We had discussed the possibility that Phish might play the Halloween album in the middle of "Harpua" while Jimmy listened to it. After Mike told his raccoon dream story, we all started eavesdropping on Jimmy, who Trey revealed was playing the album that Phish was performing at Halloween this year. Phish paused and started playing "Beat It." I wasn't fooled at first (hey, I survived 1983, I know that "Beat It" is not the first song on *Thriller*), but then Phish carried on one measure too many and I started sweating. This is not to say that it wouldn't have been an interesting choice, it just wasn't what I was looking for at the time.

The tension mounted as the seconds ticked away to the start of the second set. Then the lights dimmed, the phans yelled, and the distinctive syncopated beat of "You Wanna Be Starting Something" started (which is the first song on *Thriller*). Then I could see the band starting to play and I could hear some piped in noise of some sort but...it wasn't until the horns kicked into the "Real Me" that I realized what was up: *Quadrophe-*

nia, Pete Townshend's tale of a psychotic boy appropriately named Jimmy. The band moved through the album with Page handling most of the vocal duties. "Punk Meets the Godfather," "Doctor Jimmy," and "I've Had Enough" all sounded particularly strong, drawing on the many elements of the band's current lineup, the strength of the original material, and the performance skills and creativity of Phish. The Giant Country Horns added punch to the set, particularly with the addition of the French horn. For me, the finest moment took place with intense interplay of band and brass at five minutes, fifteen seconds. Something interesting occurred during "Bell Boy," when an appropriately dressed figure took the stage with some suitcases, took a long swig from a fifth of booze, and performed the song through a thick British accent. I initially assumed that it was an accented Dude of Life since I had run into him earlier, but as it turns out it was a member of the crew. Finally, the set closed as Fish, who had been chained behind his drum kit, took to center stage to offer a somewhat strained but nonetheless impassioned "Love Reign O'er Me."

After a break, the band returned for a third set that remains one of my all-time favorites. Things started out innocently enough with the opening notes to "YEM," but about a half-hour later it became clear that this was no ordinary "YEM," as the band extended every facet of the song far longer than usual, from Page's segment to "Mike's" featured moments to the vocal jam. Suddenly it occurred to me, maybe this will be the whole set, a forty-five-minute "YEM" as if to say "Okay, here's one set during which we'll perform a double album by the Who, here's the next set during which we'll perform ONE of our songs." But as the "YEM" drew to a close at the forty-three-minute mark, I did not complain when Dave Grippo joined the band for a run through the appropriate "Jesus Just Left Chicago." A standard "Day in the Life" followed and the set came to a brassy close with the horns' pleasing contributions on "Suzy Greenberg."

And then the encore! This one had to be both seen and heard. Before the band came out, the crew set up a replica Keith Moon drum kit with the words The Who on it. We weren't sure what it to make of it. Then Phish came out with their acoustic setup, with Fish sitting behind the toy drum kit as Phish performed "My Generation." On his acoustic guitar, Trey performed his only Pete Townshend windmills of the evening. At the end of the song, Mike and Page continued to vamp on banjo and bass while Fish and Trey lingered for a moment and then systematically destroyed their instruments, kicking them, stepping on them, and throwing them to the ground. This continued for a few minutes or so as Trey and Fish tossed each piece of the drum kit and guitar to the rear of the stage. When this process was complete and the stage was clear of musical shrapnel, an Acme detonator/plunger was brought out and placed in front of Trey and Fish. Trey paused, and then depressed it, setting off an explosion to the rear of the stage where the pieces of the drum kit had been thrown, ending the show in a pyrotechnics flash. Good night Chicago! Exclamation point!

11/14/95 University of Central Florida Arena, Orlando, FL —James Raras, Jr.

Which version of "Stash" is the most experimental? Look no further than the second set of this show. Following an average first set, the "Maze," "Gumbo" combo to open the second offered no warning of what lay ahead. The next forty some-odd minutes of this set would serve as the setting for some of the most inspired Phish jamming ever and would create a precedent to which all "Stashes," past and future, would be judged. From the beginning of this "Stash," the style of play was dif-

ferent. En route to the final "maybe so / maybe not" this version winds its way through the rarely played "Manteca" as well as a version of "Dog Faced Boy" consisting of only vocals over a dissonant backdrop. This "Stash" takes more chances with experimentation than the 8/15/93 Louisville version, has more twists and turns than the rocking 12/29/95 Worcester version, yet still has a harder edge to it as opposed to the transcendent 7/2/97 Amsterdam "Stash." A great "YEM," featuring an "Immigrant Song" jam complete with Trey bellowing, closes the set, and "The Wedge" in the encore was a welcomed treat.

11/25/95 Hampton Coliseum, Hampton, VA—Cory Ferber

It was many years ago now." When the band announced they would play the Hampton Coliseum, excitement rippled through the Phish community. The venue's small capacity of 13,500, plus general-admission seating and a standing-room floor, help foster an indescribable energy between the band and the crowd. Then there is the scene itself: the venue borders on ten hotels, a grocery store, a mall, and restaurants. Throw in stories from some of the most memorable Grateful Dead shows of the '80s, and not even Thanksgiving weekend could keep me from attending this much-anticipated, historic Phish concert.

The band had played in Pittsburgh the night before, so we drove all night long (over four hundred miles and seven hours) to reach Hampton, VA, early in the morning. It was cold outside, and the scene was at an early calm. It appeared that many people had arrived the previous night, and probably had only gotten to bed a few hours earlier. Although there was a small vending scene during Fall '95, the weather did not help the situation. We spent little time in the lot because of the cold and opted to get good seats inside instead.

The show opened with the traditional version of "Poor Heart," somewhat of a surprise since the previous two times on the tour they played a new, slower version of the song. "Poor Heart" segued into the always-trippy cover of the Beatles' "A Day In The Life." I enjoyed "Billy Breathes," as well as my first hybrid "Taste" and "Fog that Surrounds." I really enjoy the vocal layers of these mixed versions. "Wolfman's Brother" is short but fun. The set closes on a high note with a raging "Runaway Jim."

Things continued to heat up in the second set with the recently revived "Timber Ho!" Teases of the controversial "Mind Left Body Jam" can be heard in the opening minutes of the first jam. After the reprise lyrics, the song collapsed into a rare "Gamehendge" narration of "Kung." This version is especially interesting because the band sing the lyrics slowly and without the usual cadence. The familiar closing lines, "Stand up on your feet and call 'From the hills,'" really intensified the energy level between the crowd and the band.

The band then charged into "Mike's Song." Instead of bringing out the tramps, the band jammed an unusually long ten minutes on this section of the song. As Mike and Fish locked in and accentuated the beat, Page and Trey shared the spotlight with quick leads and creative interplay. Eventually, Page took a spotlight solo while Trey entertained himself playing his stand-up drum kit, a frequent situation in '95. He then returned to the guitar and led the band into the short, composed reprise of the song. As soon as the band entered this second section of the song, a "Simple" sound appeared.

To everyone's delight, Trey set down his guitar and walked over to the drums. The place erupted in cheers of the anticipation that Fishman would be coming to the front of the stage. What happened next

"21 in Steel Town"

Andrew Cogan, Ottawa, Ontario, Canada

I think one of the greatest things about Phish is that while most phans can't quite pin down their favorite song or show, most of them can name a favorite experience or moment that left a lasting impression upon them. I definitely have a favorite experience, and it occurred on November 24, 1995, on my twenty-first birthday in Pittsburgh, PA. It was an extraordinary mixing of a great birthday show, being on stage, and meeting the band twice in one evening.

My roommate Andrew, myself, and our friend Nigel had driven down from school (Lennoxville, Quebec) to catch the Landover and Pittsburgh shows and to try and catch MMW in New York at CBGB's Gallery (a club no bigger than Nectar's), to celebrate my 21st birthday, and more importantly, to get away from the worries of school. Landover had been an amazing first show for Andrew and Nigel (to this day, that *Free* still haunts us) and it provided me with idea of approaching the Greenpeace table in Pittsburgh, and asking them if I could make the chess move as a sort of birthday present. So after arriving in Pittsburgh early, we spent some time in the lot and entered the show as early as possible. I rushed to the Greenpeace table immediately, and spoke to Colin, the fellow in charge of the band versus audience chess game.

"Colin," I pleaded, "I've driven five hundred miles from Canada, and it's my twenty-first birthday, can I make the chess move?"

"Dude," he replied, "Let me see your ID…*shit*! Happy Birthday—yeah you can make the chess move, just be back here at the end of first set, and don't get wasted!" I floated down to my seat in time to catch the phenomenal, and currently rare, *Oh Kee Pah> AC/DC Bag* opener. After a ripping first set, I returned to the booth and participated in the "chess move vote," and was escorted stageside to wait until the lights went down.

I barely remember chatting up the stage crew while waiting for the second set, and I faintly remember trying to hum *Bathtub Gin* to one of the sound guys who'd forgotten the tune. What I do remember was that feeling when the lights went down, and I noticed four pairs of feet walking down the divider, towards me. *Total and complete anxiety*. A feeling like this meeting was long overdue. I was nervous and excited at the same time. In that dim light, a sense of arrival—being where I wanted to be—like that feeling when you wake up on a train, plane, car, truck, bus; just as you've reached your destination—a dazed, but thoroughly refreshing moment.

I was on my feet talking to Trey before I knew it. "Trey, it's great to finally meet you," and that was true. I think most phans feel like they know the band, but they just haven't met them yet. Page's face

darted forward. "Hey Andrew!" he said excitedly, and cutting me off before I could say anything else to Trey. I laughed and shook his hand, and chatted both of them up until an unsuspecting Fish came out. As Tubbs stepped forth, I felt, and fulfilled, a *very* spontaneous urge to hug that little guy. I still have no reasoning for that action. (Fish, if you pick up this book and read it, sorry about that, man!). The stagehand grabbed me, not because I was assaulting Fish, but because in my daze, I hadn't heard the chess move announcement. I was spun around and directed towards the stage steps. I felt my eyes widen to the size of baseballs as I gazed outward towards the twenty thousand people packed into the Pittsburgh Civic Arena. An ocean, with waves of people and all kinds of movement everywhere. Total energy permeating the ground, the bodies, and the air. "No wonder they do this a hundred times a year." I thought to myself.

Of the forty-two shows I've seen to this point, of all the clubs, theaters, and arenas with their own superb vantage points, I learned that night, that no matter what venue you're in, the best view is always from the stage. I made the chess move, taking their Bishop with one of ours, and scampered swiftly off the stage. "Nice move!" bellowed Trey as I passed him on the stairs. As I melted into the first row on the way back into the crowd, I heard that unique and raunchy beginning of *Chalkdust*. I smiled. That's what I'd forgotten to request back stage!

That sweet show carried on (BIKE!) and ended as all Phish shows do; with dazical smiles, grins, and a blissful release. We lazily headed back to the lot and decided to hang back near the tour buses. Sure enough, Mike, then Page and Trey came out to chat us up. We exchanged some laughs, and some tales, then they boarded their coach to Hampton. Fish came flying out, late as usual, and apologized for not being able to talk to us. After the buses left, and the lot scene finally faded into nothing, I found myself thinking about how I couldn't have asked for a better birthday, about how much I loved the music of Phish, and about how approachable and down to earth those guys are (for God's sake, Trey and I talked about the perils of being a "rightie" for ten minutes!). A colored piece of paper interrupted my thoughts. It was stuck under my windshield wiper. A note, from that cute couple from Ohio who'd parked beside us, and who we'd hung out with before the show. I read the note, and smiled even harder than before. It read:

"You looked good up there chess king! Happy Birthday! Peace!"

Thanks, Trey, Mike, Page, Jon, Andrew, Nigel, Chris, and that couple from Ohio. I'll never forget that night.

---

was bizarre! Instead of stepping up to the microphone, Fishman walked over to Mike and took the bass from him. Mike then proceeded to pick up Trey's guitar. The band jams out for a few minutes but have no success in developing anything concrete. The rotation continues and Fish is moved over to guitar. It appears that the object is to rotate Fishman straight across the stage. Another rotation lands Fish on piano, where

the rest of the band eventually join him. We would later learn this was Fishman's concert debut on piano.

This is one of the best renditions of "Keyboard Cavalry," an instrumental improvisation piece where all four members play keyboards. It was only played a handful of times in '95, and this version is fast, extended, and focused. Astonishingly, the band is not satisfied ending

"Our Rhombus Story"

Daniel Hobbs, Seattle, MD

It all started on that mystical first day of December, 1995, in the wonderful Land Of Chocolate, known to outsiders as Hershey, PA. Driving into the town you could smell the chocolate in the air and hear the faint voices of the locals gathered to sing carols and rejoice at the spectacle of Santa Claus himself tearing through the streets on top of a huge red fire engine. These people know how to keep what's important. They also know who is their friend. For example, their ancestors believed in the proliferation of cows. These were their friends and prophets. Through time they grew to believe in the proliferation of milk, the nectar of the gods. And across time they grew to believe in the proliferation of…milk chocolate. The energy was crazy that night and flowed throughout the lots like syrup on a sundae.

There were six of us to start with. Hope and I in our car, two in a big green pickup, and two in the Mulemobile. One a phirgin, one a taper, and the rest of us had all seen enough shows to know that we hadn't seen enough shows yet. We all had tickets, energy, and an undying love for Phish. Like I said, you could tell it was gonna be a good one tonight.

I will leave setlists, comparisons, reviews, etc. to others. What I will tell you about is our experience, or at least parts. To get on with the story, I'm gonna first tell you about a time long ago. A time when there was no split between Eastern thought and Western thought. A time when science, religion and philosophy were all one. This time is not now and the place is not the Land Of Chocolate, but Gamehendge itself. This is where we spent the next few hours. While there, we ran across a man on a mission, a sign of things to come. While Colonel Forbin was on his mission, we soon learned of ours. For we were told of the Rhombus that night. The mystical, big, black Rhombus that sits out in the middle of a field in, not Gamehendge, but King of Prussia! Yes, the Rhombus itself was in a city nearby known for a mall that is the largest in all of Prussia.

We listened closely as Trey gave us directions to the Rhombus, each trying to absorb the words as we were simultaneously shaking our collective booties. Unfortunately, it was impossible to piece together the directions after the show. That is, until our taper friend reminded us that the directions were all captured on tape. Listening to the crispy fresh recording, our mission was once again presented to us. "Go to King of Prussia. Find the Rhombus." And like any good adventurers, we couldn't turn it down.

The friend who brought the phirgin couldn't continue on because his adventure lay snowboarding that night. The friend who brought the taper couldn't continue on because the taper's mom had something to say about it. Myself, Hope, and Melissa (the phirgin) surrendered to the phlow and started driving east through the night. We knew that we had to be back in College Park, MD, by morning because that morning New Years Run tickets went on sale. While at a rest stop for coffee and a bathroom Melissa said that she could have sworn she heard Trey quoting *Charlie and the Chocolate Factory*. Something about "I got a golden ticket." In our deliriously worn-out, sleep-deprived mindsets, we envisioned getting to the Rhombus and finding the boys waiting there with tickets in hand for New Year's Eve at MSG. We were getting a little ahead of ourselves. First we had to find the Rhombus.

---

things this way and return to their own instruments for another solid ten-minute jam closing out this one-of-a-kind "Mike's Song."

In a moment of confusion, the band came to the front of stage and performed two acoustic songs, "Two Dollar Bill" and "Blue and Lonesome." They then returned to the keyboard theme with the lovely piano styling of "Strange Design." The sandwich is finally topped with "Weekapaug Groove," highlighted by the trademark rhythm style of Page.

A vibrant version of "Harry Hood" nearly closes out the set. Behind Trey's chord progressions, the other three members methodically developed a complex conversation. The song reaches epic proportions when they explode over Trey, as he holds one note for multiple runs through the main musical sentence.

A perfectly harmonized "Ragtime Gal" follows, in what again appears to be the set closerset-closer. However, the band returned to their instruments again, this time to play a joke on the audience. The band proceeded to play the slower country-blues version "Poor Heart." After the show opener, it was really fun hearing this version to close the show.

When the band returned for the encore, so did the joke. They began playing "Poor Heart" again, this one even slower. They abandon the song, but after about ten seconds they started another version even slower! While my friends and I understood the joke, more than a few people looked confused. After a brief pause, Page starts laughing and said, "Get it?" Trey then remarks, "Do you get it?" A smoking "Fire" closes out this historic night. The tapes can not describe the energy, excitement, and pure pleasure of being at this show.

12/2/95 New Haven Coliseum, New Haven, CT —James Raras, Jr.

This show contained the first "Prince Caspian" opener, with the second to come later in December. A fantastic version of "Possum" (complete with "all fall down" language cue) was the highlight of the first set, and it is well worth seeking the tape for. The "Tweezer" in set two was one of several raging versions from fall '95, and is my favorite of the fall '95 rockers. (The excellent 12/28 version is a more "experimental" version.) The jamming took on a feel that you would be more inclined to hear in "Antelope". The only thing that halted this set from sure legendary status was the four "set-closers" in a row we got to end set two, but sure enough a "Bold as Love" encore sent everyone home happy, with high hopes for the two-night stand at U Mass to come.

12/4/95 Mullins Center, University of Massachusetts, Amherst, MA—Jon Epstein

"Our Rhombus Story" *(continued)*

We got off the highway at the exit for King of Prussia. Step one of the directions complete. Now we just had to find Wilson Drive. Start walking for a long time. When you think you're there, you're not. Keep on walking. Looking to our right we see…Wilson Street. Now we know that Trey said Wilson Drive, not Street. We parked anyway and started looking around. Not too far away we find a gas station and ask the guy working there if he knows of a Wilson Drive or where a big, black Rhombus is. After confusing him and explaining that a rhombus is like a square tilted to the side we decide to try something more reliable. I get on the phone and call 411. I can't quite explain the conversation I had with the operator. Suffice it to say that she didn't know where the Rhombus is, what a rhombus is, or why we came all this way to look for one.

Back to Wilson Street. We start walking. Off in the distance we see a vehicle drive up. Not a car, too big. Could be a bus, maybe even with the boys and tickets in hand for us! No such luck. More kids from the show that night. All in all we probably found about a dozen or so other lost Rhombus hunters in the middle of the night around Wilson Street in King of Prussia. We all walk together for a bit following some train tracks and exploring a new housing development. Could they have torn down the Rhombus to build cookie-cutter houses?! I doubt such blasphemy could take place, even in King of Prussia. To make a long story a little shorter, lets just say that we never did find the Rhombus that night. We did, however, get stopped by the cops while walking back to the car. He asked what we were doing. I started dreaming up all sorts of things to tell him because I figured he never would have believed the truth anyway. He then asks us if we're with the "treasure hunt." Perfect excuse, I wish I had thought of it myself. We told him we were leaving and we went on our merry way.

Back in College Park the next day we flash/redialed the phone until even the most optimistic of us knew the New Year's Run tickets weren't coming that way. We resolved that day to go back to King of Prussia and find the Rhombus, not because we were expecting tickets anymore, but just for the sheer adventure of it all. Two weeks later we were heading up to Philly to see the first Phish Spectrum show. On the way we would make a pit stop and not leave until we were fulfilled.

December 15, we departed in the Mulemobile. Me, Hope, Melissa (no longer the phirgin), and Scott. We parked once again on Wilson Street and started walking. This time we trudged through the snow, across the tracks and kept on walking. At one point we were tired and were losing hope. We thought we saw something, but it wasn't it. Remembering the directions, we kept on walking. Under snowy branches and through tricky ravines we came to a clearing.

The clearing softly held a fresh layer of snow. There was no one around but us adventurers. We walked forward. Looking up we saw *it*! A big, black Rhombus. Sitting on top of the Rhombus was the Famous Mockingbird. We stared in utter disbelief when out of the corner of our eyes we saw a huge *Helping Friendly Book* opened up barely a stone's throw away. Our quest was successful. We jumped and hollered and rolled around in the snow just like the ancient Lizards must have themselves. And all was well again in Gamehendge.

Now, if you like seeing the world through my admittedly warped perception, stop reading now. If you are a stickler for details and need to know more, then read on. The field we were in was really a military cemetery. The Rhombus was a monolithic monument to people who had served and died. On top of the Rhombus was indeed a bird, the most famous mocking/imitation/representational bird in all of the land, a bald eagle. And off in the distance was a stone representation of the *Helping Friendly Book* itself, but it this land it is called a Bible. To us, these were as I first described them to you. You, of course, will have to take your own meaning from this. I wish everyone luck in their quests for their own Rhombuses, and whatever you do, take care of your shoes.

The first set of this show has a great "Stash." I can't think of a "Stash" from all of '95 that is less than great. The second-set "Timber" opener is one of the best "Timbers" I've ever heard—long and quite dark. The workhorse of the night is this "Antelope". This is one of my favorite "Antelopes." It was very intense in the middle. If I had to play one version of one song for someone to get the gist of Phish, I'd play this "Antelope" for them. This is the Phish Machine. I also like the "Ya Mar" and "You Enjoy Myself," featuring a short and scary vocal jam.

12/7/95 Niagara Falls Convention Center, Niagara Falls, NY —Cory Ferber

The NFCC felt more like an airport hanger. It was a huge open space with cement floors and ceiling like a gymnasium. The stage was set up on one end and there was a set of bleachers on the other end. It felt really empty because it was so large. A group of about fifteen of us from Rochester, NY, hung out only a few feet from the left side of the stage. It was a pleasure to have so much room to dance so close to the stage, a rarity at the time.

Although I thoroughly enjoyed the show at the time, I enjoy it even more with repeated listenings to my audience tape. The show opens with a misplaced "My Old Home Place" getting things off to a mellow beginning. I love the lyrics of this song. A rare "Curtain," typically itself an opener, follows and segues directly into "AC/DC Bag!" The first jam of the night had us all grooving. This one is a classic with a well-developed jam. An unusual pairing of "Demand" and "Rift" felt odd, but was soon topped by a mid-set "Slave to the Traffic Light". This was a huge surprise and a great treat. It felt like the perfect song for the atmosphere inside the venue.

The second set opens with a raging "Split Open and Melt," possibly to complete the continuity of "Demand." It's full of energy as they push the jam beyond its limits, and then end it in a rather mellow fashion. "Julius" features Page's colorful piano set against Trey's sharp rhythms.

The "Mike's Song" is a little unusual because it is unfinished. The band opts against the trampolines, and Trey immediately begins a solo. About halfway through the jam, Trey begins playing his small drum kit, something he was doing frequently in '95. Mike then switches the bass line to a somewhat funky sound, reminiscent of a Phil Lesh solo in the '73–74 era. The band ends up never playing the composed reprise section of "Mike's Song" that is usually followed by the sandwich song such as "Simple" or "I Am Hydrogen."

When Trey settles back on guitar, he begins to tease Van Morrison's "Gloria." A very clear "Gloria" jam develops, a song that had been

played six months earlier on 5/16/95. As the jam continues, it suddenly becomes very familiar. In a moment of haze I realized it was "Weeka-paug Groove." The band locked up and dropped the musical scale into the opening riff of the song. This is a very nice "Weekapaug" with a great solo from Trey. As the song enters the reprise section, something unusual happened: no one sang anything.

It soon sounded like the band was going to play "Maze." We were excited! Instead, something weird happened. The look on the band members' faces told me something was wrong. Eventually Trey stopped playing guitar, but Fishman and Page were still playing. He then waved his hand across his throat, giving the universal cut sign, put down his guitar, and walked to the front of the stage. It was an odd moment, and a real buzz kill. Mike soon joined Trey up front, but you could feel and see the tension as Fishman and Page remained at their instruments. I'll never forget watching their facial expressions during this apparent argument. Eventually they gave in and sang "Amazing Grace."

The band came back and encored with a short "Uncle Pen." Although I love this tune, it seemed really strange since it's a song with no jam and has no real musical conversation. This was a little disappointing at the time after being teased with a potential monster show-closing "Maze." This bump in the road does not detract from the rest of the enjoyment. Get a copy and take a listen!

12/9/95 Knickerbocker Arena, Albany, NY—Kim Hannula

December 9 was a Saturday, the day after classes ended. It felt like another rough term, though in retrospect the students I had in both classes were absolutely wonderful and I really enjoyed working with them. But Saturday I was finally really going to be free. "Freeeeeeeeeee!" Jay and I were driving down to Albany to see Phish.

The weather was really ugly. It was snowing hard: a serious, keep-the-truck in four-wheel-drive-and-pray-that-you-don't-have-to-stop-or-turn-fast kind of situation. Low visibility. The kind of snow that, when I'm rational, keeps me home, wearing slippers, and baking bread or grading papers. But Phish was playing, and rationality and Phish obsessions rarely coexist. Actually, I was already exceedingly rational for a Phish fan—I gave up going to shows when I had to lecture the next day after Halloween '94, which left me so tired and grouchy and miserable and barely coherent that I almost gave up seeing Phish altogether. But the term was over, see, and I didn't have to give a final until the middle of next week, since the freshmen had already turned in their final projects. So, weather aside, it was the perfect time and place for me to see Phish. I gave Jay the "puppy-dog eyes" look and he agreed to leave really, really early…before noon. And we really did it, too. And that was probably a good thing, because the drive down was pretty scary. We stayed on the road, though, and got to Albany in plenty of time to check into the hotel and watch TV before going downtown. They had the Discovery channel, which was a treat since we don't have cable at home.

We drove downtown early so we could eat dinner before the show. The roads weren't plowed very well, but we made it to the parking garage with only a little stressful driving around the block and yelling at each other about missing turns. We walked a few blocks from the Knick, trying to get away from the preshow hordes and find a place that was open to eat. It wasn't easy; I think a lot of places closed down early because of the storm. And, of course, we were tromping through pretty thick snow on unplowed sidewalks to get anywhere. We finally found a little Thai place that was open. After some really yummy choco-

late raspberry cake for dessert, we headed back to the Knick to head in.

Our seats were perfect: just off the floor, Page side. And the music…I don't need to talk about it, you've all heard it. I enjoyed the first set, too, though it was a "Yay! I'm at a Phish show! It's been five months!" kind of enjoyment, not an "omyfreakingodwherehasmy-braingone" type of enjoyment. Not that it matters at the show, of course, because enjoyment is enjoyment. I took out my ponytail during "Chalk Dust Torture" because I wanted to feel totally free. Let my hair down. Can't I live while I'm young? Cause I am still young, dammit!

And the second set…why even bother writing about it? I mean, words just cannot do justice to how it felt to be there, listening to that spellbinding "YEM" as it was being created. Jay, who likes Phish but isn't quite sure what the obsession is all about, got "IT" during the "YEM" jam. It was his first time, at his twelfth show. He called the "Gumbo," too. And he was the one (not me) who figured out what the hell was going on at the beginning of "Wilson."

I am way too easily affected by the emotional state of people with me at shows; if I'm with someone who isn't having a very good time, I don't have as good a time, no matter how hard I try to ignore them and just experience the music. But when I'm with someone having the kind of powerful experience Jay was having, especially when I'm as close to that person as I am to Jay, it's incredible. It magnifies my own experience of the music. Damn fine way to spend my twenty-ninth birthday.

12/11/95 Cumberland County Civic Center, Portland, ME —James Raras, Jr.

On this Monday night, Portland was a very cold place. It seemed like an eternity as we waited outside, hoping to get in early for good seats at the general-admission venue. Once we were inside, my friends and I secured some great seats about a third of the way back on Page's side, first row off the floor. We had the entire row to ourselves! The Cumberland County Civic Center is basically an old hockey arena. It probably seats somewhere under ten thousand and is a very nice place to see a show. Once we were all settled, I headed up front to catch the opener. I figured out why the stands were so sparsely filled: everyone was on the floor!

December 1995 was one of the greatest months in the history of Phish, and they always play great shows in Maine, so what follows really shouldn't have surprised anyone. I was about three rows back when the band took the stage and busted into "My Friend." What a great opener! Too bad some people insisted on crowd surfing, but I quickly and politely informed them that it was not how we do things here, and it soon ceased. Flowing out of "My Friend" was "Ha Ha Ha," which I really enjoy live, although it really is not at all musically intricate. "Stash" was next and this was a typically great version, but it was nothing outstanding when compared with the 12/29/95 Worcester and 11/14/95 Orlando versions. This is when I decided that I'd head back to my comfortable seats off the floor, since up front was a little too packed for me.

I walked back during "Prince Caspian," which was a typical 1995 version. The only notable difference was that Trey dedicated it to "Elvis' son, the prince," as this was the venue Elvis was supposed to play his last show. A solid version of "Reba" was next, and I enjoyed it quite a bit, but after "Reba" is when the fun started! Trey began to explain (facetiously) how they have this song "Dog Log" that they play in soundcheck all the time, and they'd like to put out an album consisting solely of various versions of "Dog Log," but they need our help. When Trey gave us

the signal, we were asked to boo really loudly. Trey gave us the signal and we booed heavily (the most booing I've ever heard at a Phish show) until they faded out of the song. Without further ado they cranked into a smoking "Llama," which was slightly jammed out and very enjoyable. After "Llama," Trey, prodded by Fish's insistent playing of the drum beat, announced that we were going to record another track for the "album." This version of "Dog Log" was "lounge lizard" style, à la "Lawn Boy." This time when Trey gave the signal we were to give a high-pitched screech, which we did until the song faded out.

After the screeching halted, Trey said that in order to thank us for our help they would play a song for us that we always wanted to hear, "Tube!" Wow, this was my first "Tube;" my friends and I were all going nuts! Two "Dog Logs" and now "Tube!" We could have driven the three hours home right then and I would have been happy. "Tube" was followed by "McGrupp," "Julius," and "Cavern." These versions were all fairly standard, but Phish had set the tone that this was going to be a special show, and we were eagerly anticipating the second set.

"Curtain" opened the second set in grand fashion, being one of my favorite second-set-openers, and dissolved into an extended spacey intro to "David Bowie." This was an above-average "Bowie," but nothing along the lines of the 12/29/94 Providence monster, or the 6/18/94 UIC masterpiece. After this jammed-out "Bowie," hearing "Mango," another personal first, was like being in the green fields of Gamehendge. This was truly a fantastic experience and is one of the things that keeps me coming back for more, show after show. One minute you're in the murky depths of the abyss with a dark "Bowie" jam and then immediately after the climax, you get enchanted with the beauty and majesty of "The Mango Song." Amazing. "Taste that Surrounds" followed, complete with Fish vocals, and a standard "Scent of a Mule" preceded that. Soon after "Scent" ended, Fish banged out the drum intro to "Harry Hood." This version was very strong and it is hard to say whether I prefer this or the 12/5/95 U Mass version, as far as December 1995 "Hoods" go, but surely 12/30/95 MSG is the top "Hood" of the month!

Following "Hood" I thought we would get one more song, then good night, but I was wrong. What we got was "Suspicious Minds," which adhered to the Elvis theme of the night and featured Fish in his Elvis cape, lined with lights! After "Suspicious Minds," we got the obligatory "HYHU," and then Trey introduced a special guest: Warren Haynes! Witnessing Trey and Warren trade solos on "Funky Bitch" was an amazing experience; a fantastic version of "Bitch" was just the way to end the set. After such a powerful show I was afraid what the encore would bring.

Warren joined the band again in the encore for a version of the Beatles' "While My Guitar Gently Weeps." This would be the last time Phish played this song until February of 1997 in Stuttgart, Germany. As I said, Phish always plays killer shows in Maine, and this was no exception. It was a very special night indeed, and a great venue to do it in. Hopefully they'll play Cumberland County Civic Center again, but I think this was their farewell show to Portland. Was this the best show of December 1995? Many people seem to think so, but personally I like a few of the other ones better (see Hershey, Worcester II, and NYE). However, in terms of fun, I have been to very few Phish shows that rival this gem.

12/29/95 Worcester Centrum, Worcester, MA—James Raras, Jr.

This was my first full New Year's Run, and it had started off quite impressively the prior evening at the same venue, which happened to be a stone's throw from where I grew up. Once inside the Centrum, things were great. We had nice lower-level seats on Page's side, and I was with one of my best friends. After the prior night's great show I didn't really know what to expect, as we figured they'd be holding some of the "big guns" back for the MSG shows to follow. Unknowingly, we stood up when the lights went down to witness one of the stronger shows in Phishtory.

From the first tuning the opener was apparent, "My Friend, My Friend." This was a solid, slightly faster version of one of the staple openers on the fall '95 tour. Following "My Friend" was "Poor Heart," which was standard in placement as well as musically. Out of the "Poor Heart" ending came the spacey dissonance that could mean only one thing: "Down with Disease." This song was not particularly jammed on during the fall '95 tour. In fact, they played the first one of the tour on the first show of December (12/1/95 Hershey Park Arena, PA), and the only version that was really jammed out (i.e., "Type II") was the Providence (12/12/95) version. Nonetheless this was a very upbeat, "Type I Disease" which definitely helped to get things going in the first set. Starting right on the coattails of "Disease" was "Taste that Surrounds," complete with Fish vocals. This was a very nice version for 1995 standards but somewhat pales when compared to many of the present-day versions. (See 11/30/96 Sacramento with Peter Apfelbaum and 7/22/97 Raleigh, to name a couple.) Next up in this high-energy opening set was "NICU", which is always a crowd favorite, and this version was particularly tight. Obviously the band was unaffected by the time off between Fall Tour and the New Year's Run, and it was showing, as they were playing just as well as they had been toward the end of fall '95.

Toward the end of "NICU" we figured that the next song would be a "jam" song that could be used as the centerpiece of the set, as well as for exploratory jamming. We were right. The centerpiece of this set was none other than "Stash." All of the "Stashes" that I heard from December 1995 were very solid, but none compare to this legendary version. This "Stash" is not quite as experimental as 8/15/93 Louisville, 11/14/95 Orlando, or 7/2/97 Amsterdam, but in terms of raw ferocity, this "Stash" is tops in my opinion, despite the flubbed ending. If you like 7/8/94 version (Great Woods), this one will have you playing frisbee with your *ALO* disc. As if the "Stash" had not already completely blown my mind, they followed it up with a monster "Fluffhead," which coincidentally was the one song that eluded me all fall during my touring. For that fact alone, I was particularly psyched to hear this tune, not to mention it still ranks as one of my favorite versions musically, since it just had so much energy. Following "Fluffhead" was a decently jammed "Llama," similar to the 12/11/95 Portland version. Although I thought this would end the set, an a capella "Adeline" proved to be the capper.

During the set break, my friend Tim and I discussed what song we thought would be the "big" song in the second set. Needless to say, we were anticipating a huge second set after the excellent first set, but we knew that some songs were off-limits as they were being saved for MSG on 12/30 and 12/31. We omitted "Mike's Groove" from the possible choices, figuring it would be played on NYE, and "Tweezer" was omitted due to it having been played the night before. The only thing we could think of was "Bowie," but for some reason we had a feeling that wasn't it. We had absolutely no idea what they were going to jam on in the second set. This scenario had us intrigued, because when you don't know what Phish can possibly do now is when they hose you the hardest.

The second set opened with a nice, albeit standard, "Makisupa."

"New Year's Eve 1995 Magic"

Brian Hedden, Old Bridge, NJ

f I live to be a hundred, I'll never forget being inside Madison Square Garden for the 1995 New Year's Eve show. The atmosphere was electric, almost like being there for a playoff hockey or basketball game. But what will linger most is the three-set musical masterpiece that Phish performed that night. The *Punch You in the Eye*, *Sloth* combo was amazing. However, if ever there was a moment that set the stage for what was to be one of the best shows Phish has ever played, it was the jam during *Reba*. Out-of-body, transcendental experiences happen when you allow them to happen, when you're not looking, when you least expect them to. The natural high that I felt during that jam was better than any drug. As the jam reached

toward its crescendo, I felt myself literally soaring over Madison Square Garden, looking down at the band, the fans, the building. Everything was bathed in color and in the most beautiful improvisational music I'd ever heard. No news could bring me down, nothing could touch me. The walls could crumble and I wouldn't have cared. The *Auld Lang Syne>Weekapaug* to kick off the new year might have been one of the most joyful moments of that evening, as well sharing that wonderful new year's kiss with my beautiful wife. But for one night, one moment in particular, Phish made me feel as if I was king of the world. If there was one thing I would want to say to Trey, Mike, Page, and Jon, is thank you for that feeling on that evening.

This flowed smoothly into "Cars Trucks Buses," which at the time was a welcomed new edition to the rotation (and was a bit faster tempo-wise back then). After "CTB" is where the proverbial "stuff" hit the fan; as "Bathtub Gin" began I don't think anyone knew what we were in for. The beginning seemed like just a strong version of "Gin," but as it progressed the Who influence became more and more apparent. This was the first time that I had felt the hose. I had been present at the Providence "Bowie" exactly a year earlier, but I was not open enough to the vast experimentation to feel the effects of the "hose." As Trey began teasing "The Real Me" subtly over and over, I began to dance faster and faster. As the tempo steadily increased, Chris lit up the stage with white windmill-like lights that spun around swiftly until the unbelievably ferocious and smooth segue was complete. I just remember how I felt that I was going to lift from the ground. I was smiling ear to ear as Mike hit Entwistle's bass line and Trey put everything he had into the intense lyrics. After the actual song was over, the jamming still had a Who-ish flavor to it, and I though to myself "if they go back into Gin…." Well, after some fantastic jamming with Page on the clavinet, "The Real Gin" officially became a "Real Me" sandwich as they flawlessly segued back into "Bathtub Gin." Unreal!

Segueing out of the back end of "Gin" (which had no lyrical reprise) was "McGrupp," an excellent song to hear at this point. "Big Black Furry Creature from Mars" started up right on the final notes of "McGrupp" and was an interesting version as Trey ran around stage like a lunatic, wildly thrashing about with his megaphone in hand. Following "BBFCFM," Mike's former bass instructor, Jim Stinnette, came onstage and performed a bass duet with Mike, which segued into the first "La Grange" since 1993. "Bouncin'" followed the "La Grange" breakout, and a nice version of Jimi Hendrix's "Fire" closed a most memorable set. The encore was "Golgi," which hadn't been played much during the fall '95 tour, at least relatively to 1994. It was a nice upbeat encore, which sent everyone home with a smile, while visions of New York City for New Year's danced in our heads.

12/31/95 Madison Square Garden, New York, NY
—Charlie Dirksen

1995 had been the most improvisationally thrilling year of Phishtory, and everyone was excited preshow about what was to come. How could the band top the "Gin"->"Real Me"->"Gin" from 12/29, or the

12/28 "Tweezer", not to mention numerous jams from the Fall Tour? Few, if any, predicted that this New Year's show would—even years later—be glowingly referred to by Phish fans as one of the best Phish shows ever performed.

The "PYITE," "Sloth" opener was the first in history, and was better than any dream opener I could have imagined at the time. "Reba" was fiery with nonstop action from Trey. A great version, up there with fan favorites like Lowell and Halloween '94. "Mockingbird" had some glaring mistakes from Trey (if he only played this more often…), but everyone seemed just as psyched to hear it as I was. "Shine" was hysterical, and I'm glad that the Tom Marshall New Year's Run Tradition continued. "Sparkle" and "Chalk Dust" pleased the crowd even more, and ended the first set powerfully.

The "Drowned"->"Lizards" to open the second set was *awe-inspiring*, and must be heard to be believed (along with the "Fire on the Mountain" tease, which occurs within forty seconds of "Lizards'" first notes). "Drowned" was a dream come true for me, since it was the song I most wanted to hear brought back from *Quadrophenia*. It was passionately and melodiously jammed out, and is still, to this day, a version to hear at all costs. "Runaway Jim" was actually a "Runaway JAM." It was about sixteen minutes long and was the most spectacular version I'd heard since Walnut Creek 6/16, when they first took "Jim" for an experimental run. The "Mike's Song" to close the set contains some of Phish's most brilliant improvisation to date. It also closed with a mellowing digital delay loop jam. A very serene end to an enchanting set of Phish. People were awestruck by what they'd witnessed, and almost afraid of what was to come.

After some Gamehendge Time Lab frolicking, "Weekapaug" segued raucously out of "Auld Lang Syne," starting 1996 out on a GREAT note. The "Weekapaug" went from the high-energy, mellifluous soloing we all know and love into an improvisation so spine-tinglingly good that it charmed people into thinking that it was composed. This jam segued beautifully into a gorgeous "Sea and Sand," masterfully sung by Page. "YEM" contained a haunting, mesmerizing jam segment, which to this day commands respect. "Sanity" was the first version since June '94, and was quite a treat (the band seemed to enjoy it as much as the audience!). "Frankenstein" was an appropriate close to a

frighteningly awesome show. At this point, I couldn't have cared less whether Phish played an encore. But they whipped out "Johnny B. Goode," and performed a version that is still very compelling.

The glorious improvisation at this show profoundly affected thousands of lives, including those of the band. What we believed would be a once-in-a-lifetime experience, though, soon proved to be simply another exalted show in the career of one of rock history's greatest bands.

4/26/96 New Orleans Jazz & Heritage Festival, New Orleans, LA—Saul E. Wertheimer

When it was announced that Phish would be playing a show on the Ray Ban Stage at the N'awlins Jazzfest, it looked like I'd be making my first appearance in the state of Louisiana. Not only that, but tickets were only $10, and that included all-day admission to the Fairgrounds! Of course, there are many reasons to visit N'awlins, but Phish and Jazzfest are the ones that brought me there for the first time.

Phish was scheduled to play one set, starting at 3:25 PM. They opened with "Ya Mar," which is the perfect summer opener, in this fan's opinion. Of course, it wasn't really summer yet, but I had traveled from Chicago, where it was cold and rainy, so this was close enough. The weather that weekend in N'awlins was hot and sunny, with a hundred percent chance of gettin' down! Trey quoted "When the Saints Go Marching In" during the "Ya Mar." This opener really got the crowd in the mood to shake their bones!

The "CTB" featured Michael Ray on trumpet, and was quite a fun version. I only wish that he had stuck around for a few more tunes. This was followed by a "YEM," which is notable for a modulation in the early stages of the jam, which gives way to some fine summery noodling by Trey. His soloing is very mellow, and makes me think of lazy summer evenings, when it's too hot to do anything other than sit on the porch, and have a beer with a friend. Of course, rock 'n roll Trey took over before we knew what was happening. That didn't last for too long, though, as the jam stops abruptly, and jumps into a vocal jam, which turned out to be an a capella version of "Wolfman's Brother." What a surprise! They sang two or three verses before Trey began some wah-wah. The rest of the band joined in soon enough. This was definitely the most interesting version of "Wolfman's" until 12/28/96 Philly.

When this Phish show ended, the party really didn't stop, because we were in N'awlins! The Funky Meters played right after Phish. For those of you keeping track, at 4:20, "Harry "Hood"" was gracing the ears of the sun-soaked crowd.

7/12/96 The Melkweg, Amsterdam, The Netherlands —A.J. Abrams

This was one of the most eagerly anticipated shows of all time. Phish, the biggest psychedelic party band of our generation, was playing Amsterdam, the party and cannabis capital of the world. The announcement of Phish's very first show in Amsterdam was a dream come true for aphishionados everywhere. Unfortunately, what many thought would be one of the best Phish shows of all time turned out to be one of the worst. This show is actually proof of how potent the pot is in Amsterdam. Apparently, the pot is so powerful that it causes the best musicians in the world to forget how to play their own songs. Throughout the show there are many mistakes made both lyrically and musically. Many songs and jam segments remained unfinished or ended in a restrained or quiet manner. All of the jam segments are

short, simple, and mellow. The main reason the jam segments are lame is because Trey appears to be stoned. In fact, in the middle of the show he says the band is going to take a break and go smoke some hash buds. It is hard to hear him during many songs, and there are no spine-tingling guitar solos from him. The endings of so many songs in this show are lame because Trey doesn't "go off" with fiery solos to wrap up the endings like he normally does. In fact, the three words that best sum up this show are mellow, sloppy, and strange. Most of the playing sounds boring and uninspired. Then again, I'm sure the audience was so zonked they never even noticed.

The "Wilson" and "Divided Sky" that open the show sound decent. In fact, the "Divided Sky" is one of the best-played songs of the night, which is surprising giving its complex compositional nature. "Horn" and "Split Open" are next. "Horn" is played normally and "Split" starts off fine, including the jam segment. But eventually the jam begins to get super mellow, and Trey barely plays anything. The volume lowers and the tempo slows down as jam becomes very quiet and hushed. A typical "Split" ends in loud, chaotic, powerful fashion. But the final ending notes of this "Split" are played as though someone was whispering. "Ya Mar" is next and is okay until the end. Trey and Page just keep playing the same boring note over and over again for about ten seconds. Then all of a sudden it sounds like the band is going to bust into "BBFCFM," but instead they opt for "Funky Bitch." In the middle of "Funky Bitch" the band goes into "hush" mode and plays really quietly as Mike whispers instead of sings. Luckily, the band eventually gets louder and they finish up the song in standard fashion. The rest of the set is decent with "Taste" and "Theme" getting honorable mentions as standard versions and sounding fine. "Tweezer" has a nice segue into "Llama" to close out the set.

The second set begins with a series of segues ("Ice">"Caspian"> "Mike's">"Antelope">"Purple Rain") that looks nice on paper, but looks can be deceiving. "Ice" and "Caspian" are okay, but "Mike's Song" is awful and among the worst versions ever because Trey does nothing. He is inaudible during most of this short "Mike's Song" until the segue into "Antelope". This is a lame segue, because at this point the jam dissolved into nothing but Page. As the "Antelope" kicks in over the keyboards, Trey comes back to life. "Antelope" is uptempo and eventually starts to rock out a bit. They play most of "Antelope" fine until they get to the "Rye Rye Rocco" part. At the moment they should go into that part, they instead segue into "Purple Rain." The segue itself is perfect, but an odd and dreadful choice. The "Purple Rain" just absolutely kills all the momentum "Antelope" had achieved. The decision to segue into "Purple Rain" ended "Antelope" prematurely and if I was at the show I would have been horrified.

Next up, the audience gets to create a song. Trey asks them to name a few chords and name a groove. A ska groove is chosen and the band plays this new jam, but Trey cuts it off after only forty seconds and says "We're gonna play our song, yours is too weird." Someone should have reminded Trey that practically every song he was playing that night sounded weird. The "NICU" is a perfect example because it is sloppy both vocally and musically and the jam is completely different than a typical "NICU". However, the segue from "NICU">"Slave" is nice, but the "Slave" is extremely mellow and unfinished. Usually Trey shines during the end of "Slave" with his powerful and emotional solos. But this "Slave" jam just abruptly ends and dies a quick death without ever going anywhere. Just to show you how stoned Trey was, he sounds

amazed when Fishman gets a boring, typical feedback sound from his equipment. "That was Fishman and that was incredible when he plugged his cord in," Trey said excitedly. During the "Suzy Greenberg" that follows Trey sings the first verse but forgets the rest of the lyrics. There are no vocals in this "Suzy Greenberg." Trey jokingly says "Suzie, Suzie, Suzie" where he should be singing an actual verse of the song. Since Trey can't remember any of the words, the band just moved directly into the jam portion. Trey remembers to sing the last verse but as the song ends instead of singing the closing chorus of "Suzy Greenberg" energetically, the band just barely whispers it. The set ends with "Suzie," but for some reason Fishman stays on stage alone and keeps playing drums. He plays a slow, hypnotic beat for about a minute and some audience members don't even realize he is still up there.

The third set begins with a good, normal version of "David Bowie">"Free." The "Bowie" is unfinished as the jam gets real mellow and quiet before segueing into "Free." "Free" is fine, but just like so many jams during this show, this jam just abruptly fades out and ends prematurely. The "Bathtub Gin" during the encore is the exact same way. The jam segment is unfinished and just suddenly ends mysteriously. After "Gin," knowing this Phish performance was lame as hell, Trey whispers "Rock and roll," and they rock out to "Johnny B. Goode." This song is so basic there's no way they can screw it up. And they don't. A solid, rocking version of "Johnny B. Goode" ends one of the sloppiest nights of Phish ever.

8/2/96 Wolf Mountain, Park City, Utah—Charlie Dirksen

The highlights of this show, for me, were the amazing, full rainbows that were visible from the lawn of this quaint outdoor "amphitheater" before Phish took the stage. The brilliantly defined double rainbow lasted for several minutes, and was one of the most spectacular things I've ever seen in the sky. I doubt I will ever be lucky enough to witness something like it ever again. There were also gorgeous mountains serving as the backdrop to these rainbows.

Page opened up this astoundingly short Phish show with an amusing rendition of "Somewhere over the Rainbow" on the Theremin. This would be the other highlight of this show, which featured pretty average playing from the band. "Theme from the Bottom" was strong in the first set. And "Tweezer" had the dying out of the theme ending, which I hadn't heard them play in awhile. Though "Possum" was poorly played at first, it eventually turned into the kind of fiery, tight, and thrilling version you've come to expect. "Hello My Baby" was peformed well, too. The set break, as amazing as it might seem today, was only around 17 mins.

The second set's "Fluffhead"->"Caspian" was easily the show's musical highlight, in my opinion. "Fluffhead" was performed well, and "Caspian" was "new" at this show, in that it featured these gorgeous intro and outro instrumental sections. "Antelope" was good, a contained a tease of the "Star Wars" theme. "PYITE" makes a wonderful encore—even though this version wasn't as tight as you've heard it in the past.

8/4/96-8/7/96 Red Rocks Amphitheater, Morrison, CO —Charlie Dirksen

It was a bad omen when, after pulling into the lot, I got out of the van and stepped on a used syringe. I was wearing shoes, but that, of course, wasn't the point. I hoped it was one used at the Allman Brother's show the night before (a fantastic show, I might add, which I attended thanks to Bill Beach), and not by any Phish fan. But I was disappointed

Red Rocks

all the same to see evidence of such a hard drug at a Phish show.

The shows on this run were good (and at times great), but what was memorable about them, of course, was that they turned out to be the last Red Rocks shows. At least, the last as of this writing. There were some problems (alleged "rioting") with some fans in town, and by August 7, you could sense that Phish's days at Red Rocks were over. People were talking about it. I remember being very sad after the last show of the run—and it wasn't simply because of the forgettable "Bolgi" encore. The scene around these shows had ironically been quite pleasant, though (ironic because of the bullshit in Morrison which ended Phish's Red Rocks gigs). We—I attended these shows with Becky, Bill Beach, Mark Toscano, Scott Carter Eldred, Rob Brooks, Dead Etelson and Dan "Squirrel" Nooter—stayed away from Morrison, and so I can't speak about what went down there. The number of ticketless that I saw between I-70 and the venue day to day paled in comparison to those outside of, say, the 10/31/94 Halloween show. I imagine most of the ticketless were in Morrison, though, based on news coverage. The scene immediately around Red Rocks was actually quite pleasant (and I arrived at all of the shows, except the Allmans show on 8/3, very early).

Musical highlights of the run, in my opinion, were the "Reba" jam segment, "Scent of a Mule" and "Bowie" on 8/4; "Wolfman's," "Down with Disease," "Halley's," and "Mike's Groove" on 8/5; "Tweezer" (with "Norwegian Wood" quoting) and "Harry Hood" (though not musically impressive, it was accompanied by lightning at the show, and it also featured the first "Hood" chants from the audience) on 8/6; "Runaway Jim" (with a "Gypsy Queen" jam!), "Forbin's" (with iguana narration) and "Mockingbird" (worst version ever; check it out) on 8/7.

8/4–8/7/96 Red Rocks Amphitheater, Morrison, CO
—Saul E. Wertheimer

Ah, Red Rocks…I had been waiting two long years to see Phish play at this venue, as one of the first shows I acquired was 8/20/93. I had heard many good things about this place. So, needless to say, I was extremely excited when Phish Mail Order sent me tickets for all four nights. And what nights they would be! We camped at beautiful Mount Evans, at about ten thousand-feet elevation. The drive down to Red Rocks every day was gorgeous.

8/4. What really stands out in my mind from the first show is the "Loving Cup" that closed the first set. It was quite jammed out, but most importantly, this song is one of my fondest memories from a Phish show. I recall gazing in awe at the tremendous place where not only was I with many friends, but I was also seeing the best band ever! All I could think about was, "What a beautiful buzz!" Every "Loving Cup" I have heard since then seems to serve as a time machine of sorts. The second set contained a "Bag," "Reba," "Bowie," and a "Slave," but really wasn't very good.

8/5. The first set of this show was highlighted by a "Julius," which featured Trey pumping his fist twice in the air, right before he took his solo. The second set was the best overall set of the four nights. The "DWD" was long and permagroovin', but the segue into "Ice" made me say, "huh?" Not the smoothest of segues, to say the least. The "Halley's" contained a longer-than-usual, rockin' jam, somewhat reminiscent of 12/14/95 Binghamton, but not as good. The end of the jam featured Page playing the Theremin (for the first time, I think), to the tune of "Somewhere Over the Rainbow." The stage then split apart and another, smaller stage came forward. It was basically a platform on the

stage, and the band played a mini acoustic set on it. This was the first of three occurrences of this style of acoustic set, followed by one at Deer Creek 8/13, and the Clifford Ball 8/16. The old-school "Mike's Groove" to close the set was hot! Ah, "Hydrogen," how elusive art thou!

8/6. Once again, we were at Red Rocks. I know this because Trey made sure to remind us during the "Rift," with an understated U2 jab. Also, I got my first "Dinner and a Movie" at this show, as did many other people, I'm sure. The second set contained what is certainly the musical highlight of the four nights. This "Tweezer" is truly one to remember. As soon as the jam segment began, the intensity didn't let up until the "fading out" section at the end. Trey's soloing was, well, intense, and awe-inspiring at times. The band had "that Sound" during this jam, which had a "Norwegian Wood" segment. Although the "Norwegian Wood Jam" was quite sloppy, it was fun nevertheless. It segued into one of the first "new and improved" "Caspians." I liked this version, but that's probably mostly because the "Tweezer" was so good that I wasn't thinking straight. The "Hood" featured the crowd cheering at the lightning over the Denver skyline, as well as the first time that "HOOD!" accompanied the "HARRY!"

8/7. The first set contains nothing much to speak of; I'm not even sure if I've ever listened to the tape. The "Runaway Jim" that opened the second set was outstanding, and had a severe "Gypsy Queen" jam within it. Hear this! I find that it works pretty well if you get the "Jim" as filler on the second set of the third night. "Mockingbird" was horribly botched, and the encore was poor. The band must have known that they would not be invited back to Red Rocks, which is all the more reason that they should have played a real encore at the last show ever at

Clifford Ball

Kathleen Griffin

Clifford Ball

Red Rocks. Sorry, "Golgi" sucked. Other than the "Jim," the band really didn't seem to have it together that night.

Overall, these four shows were some of the most fun I've ever had. Red Rocks is one of the most amazing places I've ever been. It's a shame that we'll never get to see Phish there again. Kinda sad, actually.

8/14/96 Hershey Park Stadium, Hershey, PA—Craig DeLucia

For some reason, this show gets trashed a bit. Maybe it's because people were expecting a throwaway at the final show before the Clifford Ball. Maybe it's because the monster drive from Noblesville took a lot of energy from the folks on tour. Regardless, this show easily ranks as the show at which I had the most fun and contains some great jams taboot.

This was to be my only show of the summer of 1996. Work was hectic so I couldn't go out west, and the Clifford Ball coincided with the start of my college year so I would be missing that. So, because much of the summer touring was in Europe, I hadn't seen a show in eight months. Damn, was I ready!

During the day, I met up with some old friends and met some new ones, including one (heya Dave!) who would become a frequent show partner. We all walked around Hershey Park, riding some rides and staring at many of the long lines. It was hot that day. In fact it was beyond hot, and the inner tube ride that cooled off our little group was as welcome as those little shower spigots they had placed throughout the park. I remember eating ice cream in the food area and having it melt in my hands. I ate dinner before showtime in that little restaurant just inside the gates of the park, and our table was one of the liveliest in the

joint. Due to an administrative mix-up at the gate, I wound up getting my park admission refunded to me after a conversation with the park manager. So I got to walk around the park with friends for free and know I would be seeing my favorite band that night.

The beginning of the show was fun and danceable, and the little jam between "Wilson" and "Disease" was nice. The musical highlight of the first set, though, was the "Reba." Our group was on the lawn near the security barriers, and we had a great view of the stage. During "Reba," Trey was playing expressly for that little girl who was sitting on her daddy's shoulders in front of the stage. It was truly a beautiful moment, and I wish I knew who that little girl was so I could thank her and her daddy for such a fantastic jam! For most of the first set, we were hosed down with squirt guns from the security guards, who were trying to keep any of us from getting heat stroke.

The "Stash" in the first set remains one of the greatest visual spectacles I have seen at a Phish show, as mother nature provided the best lighting effects this side of Chris Kuroda. The backdrop behind the stage was transparent, and there was a castle-like building atop a huge hill in the distance behind the stage. As the sun began to set during "Stash," a crimson light was slowly cast on that hill. As the "Stash" jam peaked, the sky burst bright red and provided a surreal backdrop to the jam, complete with that castle on the hill.

It was the second set where the jams really kicked in. How can anyone complain about a set with "YEM," "Tweezer", and "Runaway Jim?" Perhaps the perceived problem with this show is that none of these songs stand out as a hundred percent, knock-you-on-your-ass version, but they were all solidly played. The "Theme" was nice, too, and the "Cracklin' Rosie" brought a smile to everyone's faces.

The "Julius" encore was the nightcap to one hell of a day. I remember being surrounded by some of the truly beautiful women whom I had spent the day with (yes, Marcie and Liz, because I know you are both reading this, I still think of the both of you every time I hear this song) and swinging them around to the revival beat. Fact is, I can't think of a better way to spend a day.

Clifford Ball

Michael McNamara

Clifford Ball

8/16–17/96 The Clifford Ball, Plattsburgh, NY
—Jeremy D. Goodwin

The Ball had been a coming of age thing for me, my first real multi-day adventure in which my only implements were a borrowed car filled with camping gear, a good friend, and a future to invent. While I was busy experiencing palpable wonder for several days straight, the thing was simultaneously a coming of age for Phish and all its orbiting planets. It was quite a fortuitous intersection of personal growth and the growth of a community.

The Clifford Ball felt to me like a mass projection of all our playful fantasies about what Phish could be; parts of the mainstream press adopted the term "Phish theme park," and that seems pretty accurate. A theme park or a fantasy camp. A few years later, I would affix a term that I had picked up in a different region of the cultural web that considers itself important enough to coin and assign phrases: Temporary Autonomous Zone.

As if all the fans' and the band's "what if?" daydreams had somehow been projected into reality, the Ball was a capstone Phish experience, the creation of an entire functioning civilization where the landscape (both mental and physical) seemed as improvisational and creative as the most liberating of onstage jams. A plane circling around trailing a banner reading "A dime from here would penetrate"? Sure. Snowboarders doing flips on trampolines during "Tweezer"? Why not. An orchestra playing "Claire de Lune" while a stuntplane does loop-de-loops? Of course. The overwhelming factor, that there were sixty thousand people at a Phish show, hovered constantly in the ether to ensure 'round-the-clock surreality. And all night, the fires burned, the drums beat, and the people danced.

The Clifford Ball was something deeply special to me personally due purely to the logistical and social circumstances. At that time I wasn't used to befriending an endless circle of strangers, chasing adventures for days on end, or seeking transcendence through blaring 4 AM funk under a tent. Counterintuitive as it sounds, it really wasn't that hard to have your life change in Plattsburgh that weekend. What choice did my young psyche have in the face of a swarming mass of unregulated

people who stubbornly insisted on being nice to each other? The effects of a countless procession of benevolent personal encounters and experiences accumulated during the second day's "Antelope", when I felt a sudden jolt of wisdom shake my consciousness and unveil my second-ever epiphany. Due to the nature of epiphanies, my moment of clarity is ineffable, but suffice to say it provided me an entirely new outlook towards general human interaction. After the second night of shows, some of us turned one of the Ball Square houses into a giant drum, and celebrated our bond through dance. It was profoundly moving, and I'm not sure I've experienced anything quite like it since.

Serendipitously, this was also one of those points along the line of Phish's history where both the band and the audience simultaneously got something, and realized that things were changing at that very moment. Sometimes this happens through the music, on a night like 5/7/94. Sometimes it happens through the event, as at the early New Year's shows, or the first show at MSG. The Great Went "Gin" was a time when both of these paths to transcendence collided. On these occasions we all grow up a little, as a community, and for a clear moment achieve a shared consciousness. There are moments sometimes on tour when the room knows…knows that we're all moving forward, in a way, entering ground that neither band nor audience had ever been to before. At least not together. The Clifford Ball was the most obvious of these occasions. It felt like the summation of everything that had happened in the Phish world until then…an enormously exuberant birthday party for the Phish phenomenon as a historical whole. It exploded all concepts of limitation, and brought both band and fans to the profound and crucial conclusion that we just didn't know what this thing might become.

There was a constant feeling of "*Is this really happening?*" that began somewhere around the time you picked up the Clifford Ball radio station on the drive up, and lasted until sometime after your return home. Future summer festivals were inherently less spontaneous, more like an appointed pilgrimage to a spiritual artifact. Yet we trekked back again, in search of something that had already happened…a holy journey to a shooting star.

10/31/96 The Omni, Atlanta, GA
—A.J. Abrams and Brian Lipman

It was evident before this show even started that this third Halloween "musical costume" show was going to be special. To begin with, Phish ended fan voting for the cover album and decided to choose it themselves. They also eliminated the element of surprise because as we walked in they handed us a program revealing the album to be *Remain in Light* by the Talking Heads. However, many fans thought the program was a hoax and just another Phish joke on us. The Phishbill was indeed humorous, but it was also legitimate. *RIL* was the riskiest album choice to date, yet surprisingly it would go on to have more influence on Phish's music than any of the other Halloween choices.

Showing us they meant business on Halloween, this show surprisingly opens up with a rare "Sanity" and the highly appropriate hard-rocker "Highway to Hell." This tune, normally a set closer, had the crowd in a diabolical Halloween frenzy with heads bangin' and fists pumping in celebration of the evil holiday. The opening of the show didn't let up, it continued to rage as "DWD" followed. It had a fast-paced, gorgeous groove and was tight and energetic. While many versions in 1996 were unfinished, this "DWD" deceptively snuck into the closing theme and ended with a strong, solid finish. The "Disease" punched

"10/31/96 The Omni (R.I.P.) Atlanta, GA Set 2"

Trevor Norris, Pine Bluff, AR

As I exited the Omni after the '96 Halloween show, the first thought that entered my mind was, "What just happened in there?" I went to Atlanta hoping to witness a historical performance, as we all know that Halloween is likely to produce something spectacular. At the time, I could not have guessed how much this evening would change things for me and for Phish. I emerged from the show with a fresh perspective on, and a deeper appreciation of, Talking Heads, Phish, and music in general. I must admit that when I saw the Phishbill, I was more than a bit apprehensive concerning the band's choice for the cover album. *Remain in Light* was an album with which I was not very familiar, and one which didn't hold much promise of any recognizable songs, except for *Once in a Lifetime*. Luckily, I opened my mind and let Phish take me on a musical journey. One that has not yet ended for any of us. And that means you, too.

As the first set ended, and I began to think about the musical costume, I found myself warming to the idea of a Talking Heads album. When the boys and guests took the stage, I was ready for anything. From Fish counting it off, the opening drum roll, and "Ha!" of *Born Under Punches*, I was hooked. The interwoven percussive lines played by each instrument produced a tapestry of music that was nearly trance-inducing. Gary Gazaway, Dave Grippo, and especially Karl Perazzo were brilliant. Trey soloed in a style that I had never heard from him, but found intriguing. Page colored the music beautifully with his incredible synth sounds, while Mike, as per usual, looked somewhat bored. Fortunately, his playing belied his countenance, as it was very focused and inspired. And Fish played the intricate rhythms as if they were the most natural thing in the world to him. I think having Karl Perazzo there was really exciting for Fish and Mike (see Mike's comments in his journal on the official Phish homepage). Talk about a dream of a rhythm section! They all were obviously having an incredible time, which usually translates into me having an incredible time. This night was no exception. I was so engrossed in the set that when the boys (and other various people) walked offstage after *The Over-*

load, I felt completely drained. I wasn't sure what I'd just seen. I wasn't even sure that it was over. One thing I was sure of, was that I wanted more of it. Thankfully, the third set was not a letdown, and that was that. Of course, I couldn't wait to get the tapes.

Upon receiving the tapes, I began to wonder what David Byrne and company would think about Phish's interpretation of their masterwork. As I pondered the issue, I came to the realization that there was a means of getting a valid critical review of the set. If ten years from now, a band played a show before twenty thousand screaming fans and devoted an entire set to covering *Junta*, to whom could they go if they wanted an honest review of the performance? As critical as we are concerning Phish's performances of their own material, I'm sure the Phish.Net community would have a harshly discriminating opinion to offer concerning someone else's interpretation of Phish's magnum opus. The only remaining question was whether or not Talking Heads fans had as strong an online presence as we do. I performed a quick search of the Web and found what I was looking for: a Talking Heads fan site, very similar to our beloved gadiel.com. I immediately posted the Parke Puterbaugh article from the Phishbill and an offer for 10/31/96 set two, explaining that there was no charge for the tapes. The only payment I asked, in return for sending the set, was a review of Phish's performance.

And review it they did. I sent tapes to places far (Moscow, London, Sydney…) and near (Dallas, Indianapolis…) and received reviews from each recipient of the set. There were lots of general comments on the performance. Things like, "Phish has done an outstanding job. I'd love to see this live," and "Every time I see David Byrne on tour and he does TH songs, I wish he'd speed them up a bit. Phish has done this to perfection.' The most interesting comments, however, were found in the detailed reviews. Some went so far as to include a song-by-song critique. Here's a sampling:

Born Under Punches—"They captured the energy perfectly." "Trey sorta botches the guitar solo. Great groove though."

into a decent but fairly average "YEM" that featured menacing soloing from Trey. This unbelievable string of crowd favorites was a tremendous way to start the show, as one can't argue with a one-two-three-four punch like this madness. Later in the set the band finished a majestic "Reba" with the now rare whistling and "bag it, tag it" ending. The always fun "Forbin">"Mockingbird" featured a story about David Byrne, giant zoot suit and all, knocking Forbin into outer space. Trey went on to describe how the Mockingbird was coming to save Forbin, but it turned out to be the horrible, evil Mockingbird and it pecked out Forbin's eyes instead of saving him. "Character Zero" and the "Star-Spangled Banner" closed out this ninety-minute all-star Phish interlude and set the tone for set two…that is, if anything could really set the tone for what we were about to witness.

Remain in Light was such a risky choice because very few fans were familiar with it and the music itself was such a radical departure from the Phish sound at the time. Despite the lack of familiarity, fans had no trouble getting down to the Talking Heads' disco/pop/funk/fusion masterpiece. The opening of "Born Under Punches" was a complex yet soothing breath of air following the very intense first set. The smooth, flowing song built up subtly until three vocal tracks combined with Page's techno keyboard sequences and Trey's funk guitar. As the tune wound down, Gary Gazaway and Dave Grippo chimed in a few squawks, warming up for the ensuing mayhem of "Crosseyed and Painless." Yes, this is where all those "C&P" teases to come first originated. The Halloween version introduced us to the driving percussion of Karl Perazzo, and in a sense, to Phish 2000. Fishman was able to pull off Byrne's vo-

"10/31/96 The Omni (R.I.P)" *(continued)*

Crosseyed and Painless—"…the extension of the end adds a lot…." "Fish's drumwork at the end and into *The Great Curve* is excellent."

The Great Curve—"This song is so well done that I now listen to it with a greater appreciation." "….The singer (Page) hits 'The world moves on a woman's hips' *perfectly*."

Once in a Lifetime—"…is an absolute misser." "Hearing how good they can be live, I think they could have done *OiaL* much much better, but TH's live version didn't translate well, either."

Houses in Motion—"This version is very well done….The guitar at the end is fantastic and the lead into *Seen and Not Seen* is one of the highlights of the show." "Phish's bass player shines here."

Seen and Not Seen—"Mike delivered it with the right amount of detachment and thoughtfulness." "I can't believe that they pulled this off. I hear it was performed from a La-Z-Boy? Great idea."

Listening Wind—"…there are great places to add a solo to a song on *RiL* (such as the one he puts at the end of *TGC*), but this is not one of them." "I was impressed with their treatment of this…nice singing."

The Overload—"I love the fact that they made this into a bit of 'performance art'….I hear it was truly bizarre in the best tradition of David Byrne." "I think the singing is awful. Fortunately, they save the song by going into what Phish does best—loopy art music."

All in all, Heads fans applauded Phish for their bravery in tackling such a complex album. There were naysayers (just like on rec.music.phish), but we should take their comments with a huge grain of salt. As one fan intimated, "*Remain in Light* is some sort of holy icon to me." In corresponding with these fans, who are every bit as rabid as we, I gained a new appreciation for Phish.

You have to admire their moxie for choosing such a challenging album, and for meeting the challenge to critical acclaim. When Talking Heads toured in support of *Remain in Light*, they added five musicians to the lineup, still had to rework the songs, and by all accounts did no justice to their own music. The fact that Phish performed songs that even Talking Heads never attempted to play live (*Seen and Not Seen*, *Listening Wind*, and *The Overload*), is further testament to their abilities. Also to their credit is that they made the performance their own, not aping the Heads, but putting their own

Phishy spin on it. From the instrumentation itself, to Mike delivering *Seen and Not Seen* from a Barcalounger, to the unexplainable weirdness that accompanied *The Overload*, there was no mistaking that Phish invested a lot of themselves in the performance.

Prior to Halloween '96, I had heard lots of talk in the community about how each Halloween, the choice of the cover album had tremendous influence on Phish's style thereafter, not only in subsequent setlists, but in the actual manner in which they played. If you listen to many shows from '95 and '96, you can make a plausible case for this statement. However, there is no arguing that *Remain in Light* has been the most influential of the three cover albums. If you've wondered where the genesis of the funk that appeared in '97 can be found, look no further than 10/31/96 set two. We witnessed the birth of the funk that night in Atlanta. If true group improvisation with a collective consciousness and no single leader is the goal, then in *Remain in Light*, Phish found the perfect vehicle for honing their skills.

For all the reasons detailed in this piece, when the uninitiated ask me "Which show is your favorite?" I'm not hesitant to point them toward Halloween '96. The two Phish sets were truly outstanding. When you consider a rare *Sanity* opener, an appropriate *Highway to Hell* followed by *Down with Disease* (a song that grew by leaps and bounds in '96), you have a great start. Follow those with a standardly sick *You Enjoy Myself*, *Prince Caspian*, a moving *Reba*, and *Colonel Forbin's Ascent>Mockingbird* with a crazy Halloween narration involving David Byrne himself, and you've got a meaty middle to the set. Add in a raging *Character Zero*, and the oddly juxtaposed a cappella *Star-Spangled Banner*, and you have a great first set. The third set was full of gems, including the always welcome *Brother*, a funky *Also Sprach Zarathustra*, a nice *Maze*, your typical fall '96 *Simple*, the always surreal *Swept Away>Steep*, *Jesus Just Left Chicago* with horns, and an energetic *Suzie* closer (with *Born Under Punches* teases from Page…listen closely to his fills). The *Frankenstein* encore was perfect for Halloween. I'm not arguing that every song was an incredible version, but as far as song selection goes, that's a pretty potent lineup. All that, plus what I consider to be the most influential single set of music Phish has ever played, and it adds up to be my personal favorite show. I hope if you haven't listened to it, you will. If you have listened to it, listen again. It offers such great insight toward understanding where Phish is taking their music.

---

cals quite accurately and still kept the backbeat going. The horns added another layer to the tune, helping to transform it from an electronic, ultra-produced piece of studio mastery into an onstage rocker.

Perazzo took centerstage at the end of "C&P" with a percussion solo, which exploded into "The Great Curve," one of the highlights of the night. This tune featured intense, almost "Llama"-like chordings and peaked at the end when Trey took a blistering solo, his only one of the *RIL* set. At the song's conclusion the Omni erupted and Fishman let out a shriek. "Once in a Lifetime," the one song everyone knew, was next and ended the upbeat part of the album. From this song the album launches into its darker, somber side.

My only criticism of this album is that the second half loses all the intensity and energy that was established in the first half. The first half

absolutely rages, only to come crashing down into the mellow, occasionally boring second half. The eerie, atmospheric funk tunes begin with "Houses in Motion," which featured a spectacular segue into "Seen and Not Seen." Next, Mike took center stage as he sat in a giant La-Z-Boy rocking chair and turned "Listening Wind" into an almost spoken-word type performance. The album came to a bizarre, dramatic conclusion with "The Overload." As TVs blasted obnoxious video clips, Phish created a massive, eerie, industrial, chaotic wall of sound with real chainsaws, jackhammers, and other power tools. They were illustrating one of the themes of *RIL*, information and media overload. But it was ironic because at the time of this concert, Phish was getting the most media attention they had ever received. After years of ignoring Phish, *Rolling Stone*, MTV, CNN, and other major media outlets finally

caught on and were running feature stories on the band. Was Phish trying to make a statement about their growing popularity and the crush of media and fan attention?

This set ushered in the Phish era of funk-style jamming that would last throughout the next year. The band's improvisations became tighter and more group-oriented. All four musicians began to play as one solid unit and they became a finely tuned groove machine. This new style of jamming was most noticeable in Trey's guitar playing. He began to limit his flashy, fiery solos and became a more rhythm-based, group-oriented guitarist. The *RIL* set was amazing because it was one long, mesmerizing, hypnotic groove. It was an exploration of complicated polyrhythms, textures, and sounds. The set emits a special, swirling, spellbinding aura that still holds up well after repeated listenings. *RIL* is also full of contrasts. It is raging yet soothing, tribal yet futuristic, and psychedelic yet funky. For this album to be pulled off successfully, the rhythm section of Mike and Fishman had to be in top form. Mike, who always has his game face on, looked the most focused I have ever seen him while he pounded away at his bass. His head bobbed furiously as he worked diligently to keep the constant groove flowing throughout the entire album. I did not dance much during this set even though *RIL* is a tremendously funky and easily danceable album. Instead, I just stood there, hypnotized by the groove and soaking in the atmospheric sounds. I was captivated by this sonic masterpiece with layers of textural guitars and polyrhythms enveloping me.

A few people were disappointed with the album choice of *RIL*. However, Phish surely cheered those fans up when they played the rare fan favorite "Brother" to open up the third set. This version was spectacular and more melodic than most versions. Usually, this song is a loud rocker full of monster power chords. Although this version did indeed rock, it was not as quite as heavy-sounding as usual. If there is such a thing as a pretty-sounding "Brother," this is it. Since there were few, if any, guitar solos during *RIL*, Trey was anxious to solo. He was the star of this tune and his solos were high-pitched and melodic. Since this was now the official age of funk, a nice, funky "2001" was next and led into "Maze." This electrifying "Maze" was on fire as Karl Perazzo bashed away on percussion. The musical tension seemed neverending as the "Maze" kept building and building up to an intense peak. Karl Perazzo did his best work during the Talking Heads set. However, out of all the Phish tunes, he sounded best during "Maze" and "Simple." "Simple," a song that drastically improved in 1996, was up next. This song used to be a fairly "simple" rocker. But during the Fall Tour the band began to add on an extended jam section. The "Simple" jam at this show was long and beautiful. It was a mellow, but gorgeous jam that eventually segued into "Jesus Just Left Chicago," which began the horn segment of the set. Now it was Dave "the Truth" Grippo's chance to shine. He came onstage during "Jesus" and remained there for the rest of the set. Grippo belted out some soulful solos, making this a good version, but nothing like the 1995 Halloween masterpiece in Chicago itself. The set ended with "Suzy Greenberg," a song Phish traditionally plays when the horn section is in the house. Gary Gazaway took an atonal solo worthy of his nickname "El Buho." There were a few quick "Born Under Punches" teases so we could get a last tiny dose of Talking Heads before we went home. The horns came back out for an appropriate Frankenstein encore. The horns added another dimension to this classic-rock tune. This unique version was a great way to end the night with a final nod to Halloween, the holiday when some of the best Phish shows of all time occurred. In fact, the show was

so amazing that Atlanta city officials determined that the Omni could never rock so hard again and was not safe enough for any more concerts. Phish had blown the roof off the arena and their power tools had loosened the foundation. A few months later the Omni was demolished. Rumor had it that you could still hear the bizarre feedback from "The Overload" languishing in the rubble.

11/2/96 Coral Sky Amphitheater, West Palm Beach, FL —Saul E. Wertheimer

Ah, the only outdoor show of Fall '96! We spent the day swimming in the Gulf of Mexico, which was a fantastic way to prepare for the show. Still reeling from the "Hotlanta" mayhem of two nights before, my travelling group seriously needed the rejuvenation that was provided by the ocean. The name of the venue served to portend good things for that evening, as certainly the Coral Sky Amphitheater must have something good to offer! The stunning palm trees around its perimeter offset the fact that it was a standard, cookie-cutter outdoor amphitheater.

We staked out our territory on the lawn, and the place seemed empty. I heard that there were only ten thousand people in attendance, which was approximately half of Coral Sky's capacity. That evening was warm and crisp, and having driven from Chicago, our winter blahs were slowly disappearing. Fortunately for us, Karl Perazzo sat in for both sets and helped add to the Talking Heads feel that pervaded the Omni in "Hotlanta." The show opened with an intriguing "Ya Mar," which was the perfect opener, given the warm weather. The "Julius" was quite good, but it's not the first set that people are still talking about.

The second set opened with the best forty minutes of Fall '96 (other than the *Remain in Light* set). "Crosseyed and Painless" was shocking, and it certainly could only have come from another dimension. During this jam, the band sounded as much like One as I have ever heard them—not four mortals, but one Entity. This jam transported us back to the Omni, where nothing was real. The "Antelope" that arose from the closing space of "C&P" contained some interesting work from Trey early on. When it dropped off the sonic cliff, I fell down with it. Really. It was so intense that I fell down onto the lawn, along with one of my travelling companions. The rest of the set was forgettable, although the "Funky Bitch" encore with "Butch Trucks" was fun.

In March '97, portions of the show were broadcast on the radio. There are sparkling pre-FMs of this tape circulating. Get it!

11/8/96 Assembly Hall, Champaign, IL—Jeremy Welsh

Looking back on this cold November Illinois night, my memories are dominated by a ninety-minute period. The drive down, the parking lot, the hall itself, the first set—they are all cloudy visions, made hazy by time and other, more memorable experiences. My clearest memories of this night, though, come from the second set—the only set in six years of Phishing where I have been lucky enough to "ride the rail," stand and dance in the front row. It is amazing how a simple act of "placement" can so completely change an experience.

Champaign was my fourth Phish concert, third show that fall. I had already seen the Pittsburgh/Buffalo run, and after having been very pleased with what I had seen and heard, I was really looking forward to the Champaign/Auburn Hills run. The trip from South Bend to the University of Illinois at Champaign was rather uneventful, and it didn't take long for us to find the Nervi-influenced arena known as Assembly Hall.

Seemingly oblivious of the cold, damp air, a sea of people were milling about the odd, cooling-tower-like building—vending, looking for miracles, just hanging out. And while it took some work by our crew, we were able to find the one extra that we needed.

On entering the arena, I realized I had to split up from my friend Joel—he thought he was somewhere near the front, and while I was on the floor, I was back in the opposite corner, Fishman side. The inside of the Hall is as odd as the outside—the floor is very small, wider than it is deeper, with the bleacher-seats coming directly down. I found my place to the right of the tapers and waited for the show to begin.

I truly wish I remember more of this set. My memories include a pleasant surprise at hearing "Axilla," part one rather than part two (I still enjoy part one over part two—I believe it is because of the cadence of the lyrics), my attempt to come up with the name of "All Things Reconsidered" (which hadn't been played for 108 shows), and my excitement in the "Antelope" closer, which was full of energy. It seemed as though Trey had some problems with his rig, but I really didn't pay much attention. Throughout the set, I took some pictures from my vantage point on the floor—I had gotten my camera in and thought that I could get some nice shots from where my seat was. If I only thought ahead and kept some pictures—I finished off the roll....

Before the first set started, my friend Joel told me that he would come find me during the intermission, and if his seats were decent, I would try to get up with him. So I sat in my seat, enjoying the break, waiting for Joel. As he came up to where I was, I noticed a huge smile on his face. His seat just so happened to be located against the rail, right in front of Page! And guess from where I was going to watch the second set? While it was a little tight up there, I do not think I could stop bobbing up and down and jumping—needless to say, I was a bit excited.

As soon as the lights came down and the band took the stage, I was in a zone. It was amazing to be right in front of Page, looking up at him, and to look across the stage at Trey, Mike, and Fishman. It really was a different world, staring up at the band, watching their feet, watch-

ing the photographers run back and forth in front of me on the other side of the rail. For the first few notes of "2001," my friends and I were scurrying around, trying to make our cameras work—I used up all of my film and Joel's batteries had run out. Damn! Here I am, in the best seats I would ever have, and I used up all of my film. Oh, well, that is what my memory (and tapes) are for, I guess.

The opening "2001" was a quick but fun one. The intro wasn't extended at all as they transitioned directly into the main theme, with Trey moving over to his drum pads for some added texture. The song lasted only about four or five minutes before Fish's repetitive cymbal beats marked the beginning of "Maze." Just like the "Maze" I saw in Pittsburgh a month earlier, this was a rager. Page was all over the keyboards during his section and Trey picked up right where Page left off for his blitzing guitar solo. Great one-two opener. "Bouncing" followed. I didn't mind.

As soon as "Bouncing" finished, Trey launched into "Simple;" one could assume that they knew they were going to play this song next. The band seemed to have this air of confidence as they moved through the opening "What is a band?" section. Maybe they knew that this was going to grow into a must-hear version of "Simple." Trey quickly jumped onto his drum pads and added some high-pitched chime sort of sounds while Page played the piano. They slowly quieted down with the jam becoming a bit atmospheric; Page played very well here, both on the piano and the keyboards (sounds as though he jumped to the Moog at one point). As Mike played some high notes on his bass, Trey kept adding texture with his drums and his guitar (although he wasn't really strumming his guitar, just using pedals and effects). Ten or so minutes in, Trey starts to wrestle out some notes. As Mike and Fishman increase the tempo, Trey joined in with some faster licks. I need to mention that somewhere in here Trey clearly started to have more trouble with his rig. It was actually rather humorous to watch him get so angry—he would jump back towards it and give it this half-assed karate kick. This actually happened a couple times. Kind of amazing, when you think about it, that with all the problems Trey had, this "Simple" ended

"More than Music"

Matthew Solnit

My first Phish concert was something I'd looked forward to for a long time. I'd heard *Junta* for the first time three years before, and had been part of the Phish.Net and trading tapes for over a year. I'd missed them the year before due to lack of transportation, and I was *ready*.

The setting was perfect. I was with my best friends, and because it was general admission we were right in front of the stage. We had about two hours to wait, listen to the Medeski, Martin, and Wood being piped through the speakers, and make friends. Of course, this just sent the suspense into overdrive.

When they hit the stage with *Frankenstein*, it took me the whole song just to get over the fact that I was in the building with them. I know the band discourages raving lunatic fan-dom, but I felt so privileged just to be with them as they did their thing.

The music was, of course, wonderful. For some reason, it's not a very highly rated show (Cow Palace, San Francisco, 11/96), but all I heard was overwhelmingly amazing, perfect music. The highlight was when I predicted *YEM* about forty-five seconds before they played it. Then Chris Kuroda showed me why he's known as the fifth band member during the vocal jam.

But what made that night stand out from every other moment of my life was the feeling of being packed into that beautiful throng of people, who asked nothing of me but to share in the groove. What I felt in there was pure life, flowing within and between us all, filtered through and enhanced by the music of Phish. They put everything they had into their music, and threw it out to us as a gift, only to be whirled back to the stage and augmented, again and again. This wasn't "stage presence." This was the only band that can be on stage and in the audience at the same time.

up being one of the best played (in my opinion). Wow—around fifteen or so minutes into the jam, while Trey rocked out, Fishman just went crazy on his kit. He was all over the place! It was a change, as up until this point he had just helped in keeping the tempo. Fishman might have tired himself out, as before you know it, he slowed the tempo back down, bringing the jam to a close. All I could do was shake my head. Not much in the way of "Type II" jamming, but it seemed to be composed so well, just flowing in and out of tempos and sounds.

"Got to kick it sometime, you know?" Trey exclaimed to the crowd, apologizing for his display—maybe. Fishman added "That song featured Trey's broken guitar rig."

Lightening things up a bit, "Loving Cup" followed. This was a first for me and I just soaked it in, taking drink after drink. With each "Gimme little drink!" Page pounded out more notes on his piano, Trey squeezed out more notes from his guitar. Boy oh boy, what a beautiful buzz.

And the buzz was increased as Trey didn't hesitate to go right into the beginning of "Mike's Song"—my second ever. Next to my friend Pete and his big red wig, I must have looked like a goof, jumping up and down the way I was, holding on to the rail. The tramps section is pretty normal, and Trey followed it up with some interesting repetitions featuring his wah-wah. This "Mike's" became a bit spacey with some nice soaring before the (normal) "Simple" intro. At this point, everyone seems to drop out a bit. Page played around on his organ, and Trey moved over to his drum kit to play some interesting squeak and "water drop" sounds (grouped with backward "water drop" sounds).

At this point, to my surprise, the band left their instruments and headed towards the front of the stage. Trey's remaining loops and effects slowly came to an end. As they became situated at the front of the stage, Trey thanked everyone and announced to the crowd that they were going to be singing the "National Anthem" at an upcoming Timberwolves basketball game (for "those of you who have a TV"), and they needed some practice. A nice treat, with a great crowd reception, but it kind of disrupted the rhythm and groove of the "Mike's," which was just getting interesting.

This must have been Technical Difficulty Night, but this time, it was Mike's turn. As the band prepared to launch into "Mike's Groove," with Fishman starting things off, Mike attempted to start slapping—and nothing happened. For a few seconds, he just couldn't get anything to come out—and then all at once this fast, repetitive pinging came flying out of the speakers. Bu-duh, bu-duh, bu-duh! I guess whatever effect Mike uses at the beginning of "Weekapaug" just wasn't working right, and it came out all at once. Weird. This effect kicked in once or twice more during the "Groove." After the vocals, Trey ripped into a nice soaring solo, with Page (again) on the piano—nice and rocking and drawn out for three or four minutes. Before heading back into the "Trying to make a woman" section, Trey talked over the music, thanking everyone for coming.

I was a bit disappointed with the choice of "Theme" as the encore. I didn't know what to expect, but this really wasn't it. I am not saying it was bad, by any means, as it did take flight and soar for a bit. (Kind of odd to hear the synchronized clapping at the beginning.)

I certainly left that evening more than satisfied—I never thought that I would be against the stage, and to witness that "Simple" from that vantage point was worth the price of the ticket in itself. Coupled with the following evening (Buried Alive opener, "Divided Sky," "Tube," meeting Andy Gadiel, tenth row for "David Bowie"-"Harry Hood" sandwich

second set with "YEM" in between), my second two-show run of 1996 was a success. Even if I don't remember every detail….

12/6/96 Aladdin Theater, Las Vegas, NV—Brian Lipman

Mmmm…Las Vegas, where nothing is what it seems. A tour closer in Las Vegas, Sin City, the desert oasis…this was definitely not to be missed. When we flew in from Austin, TX, on Thursday night we immediately headed to the infamous strip. The Aladdin is in the middle, bisecting the strip between the MGM Grand and Caesar's, right across from the Monte Carlo. The Aladdin was one of the last privately owned and operated casinos, and was smaller and friendlier than many of the new mega-casinos. We easily found it because of the big sign that said "PHISH Friday 8pm—Sold Out." We were definitely in the right place…there were fans in the casino, gambling away.

One blackjack dealer told us that TicketMaster had oversold the show, and that the casino was going to close its doors early the next day and be extra tight on security. She said we should get there really early. This was a funny idea, a casino closing its doors? Hahaha. But it did scare us into getting there at a decent hour.

On Friday the casino was overflowing with Phish fans, who were snagging the slot machine cups to beg for spare change and give their ubiquitous puppies water. Security was being cool, only asking the obvious riff-raff and schwillers to go elsewhere. This was in the days before Wookies became the dominant type of tourscum. The show had a special feel to it: everyone had traveled to get there (not many fans live in Vegas) and it was one of only two shows on the tour to sell out in advance (Halloween being the other). When it got close to showtime the Aladdin high command decided that they were not going to let people enter the theater through the casino: everyone had to go out and around. The reasoning was they didn't want their regular patrons disturbed. The World Rodeo Championship was also in town that week, making Phish fans the second most dominant group, behind rodeo-loving country-music fans (guys drinking bad beer and straddling bulls—never really got that).

The Aladdin was the only theater booked for the whole tour. The main things that set it apart (besides the size: it only held seventy-five hundred) were the size of the stage and the placement of the lights. The stage was small and the band members were much closer to each other than they had been in awhile. Page and Fishman were actually in the same time zone, imagine that! The ceiling behind the stage wasn't too high, and they didn't construct huge light risers, so the lights actually shined on the band and out into the audience. This was one of the only shows in the recent past that was really loud. After taking our seats in the eighth row (which was quite close, compared to eighth row in an arena) we eagerly waited for the show to begin. We knew they had something planned (from a "rare" Fishman leak) and knew that since it was Vegas, and that everyone came here, it wouldn't be a standard tour-closing show. They opened up with "Wilson" and from the beginning it was clear that there was a sense of urgency. This was diametrically opposed to NYE 1996's "Wilson Lite."

The band was clearly on and the rocking began, complete with heavy-metal licks and serious feedback. "Wilson" led directly into a well-played "Peaches En Regalia," which had been exhumed in L.A. just five days before. "Peaches" is a welcome treat and was a great tune for the "2" spot. (Note: it wasn't an old-time "Wilson"->"Peaches" with Trey singing the "blat boom" part of "Wilson" as the intro to "Peaches").

"Poor Heart" followed and actually rocked out. No kidding, really…Trey extended his solo for four extra measures and wailed.

Everyone's friend, egomaniac Trey, was in the house. After "Poor Heart" the space began and "2001" emerged from the murkiness. This was the tour where "2001" came into its own and became a song, not merely a lead-in. This version, clocking in at nearly ten minutes, didn't disappoint as Trey and Page each took multiple groovin' solos. For an added bonus Trey threw in the James Brown lick that he had introduced the previous week in Sacramento.

This was clearly the beginning stages of the funk as we know it these days. The low point of the show followed: a mediocre "Llama," which Trey started by chording out of the post-"2001" space. This was the only tune the whole night that wasn't superb, which is surprising since "Llamas" are usually excellent.

A strong first-set "YEM" came next. It was nothing earth-shattering, but an 8:30 PM "YEM" is always welcomed. It was complete with a "Donuts, I love donuts" vocal jam which melted into a standard but always fun "Cars Trucks and Buses."

Continuing the best set of Fall Tour 1996 was a standout version of "Down with Disease" that seemed to merge the grooviness of the Halloween and Seattle versions with its old-school 1994 roots. The outcome was an energetic and jammed-out "DWD," easily one of my favorites from 1996. The set ended powerfully with a tight "Frankenstein." This first set reminded me of a first set at Halloween, which is so good you expect them to say, "thanks a lot, good night," at the end. It was an all-encompassing set that could have been a second set as well. A "Wilson">"Peaches" opener, "Frank" closer, and some hearty meat in the middle. After a rather lengthy set break (almost an hour) it was time for more action.

Clifford Ball

Liz Kittleman

Set two opened in fitting fashion with a rockin' "Julius" (after all, we were in Vegas) followed by the show's only throwaway song, "Sparkle," which was its usual waste of time. As the "Sparkle" sped up we wondered what was next. They had played "Bowie" and "Mike's" the show before, "YEM" in the first set…maybe "Bathtub Gin?" Then out of left field "Mike's Song" was dropped on our heads. This was the most surprised I had ever been at a Phish show. "Mike's" was the toughest monster jam to get and here it was, twice in a row. Wow! They definitely weren't fucking around tonight. The "Mike's" was twelve minutes long, tight, and evil. It featured the gold lights that were added for the holiday tour and tested in Vegas. The "Mike's" disappointingly segued right into "Simple." There was this guy who draped a huge "Simple" (the shoes company) sign over the balcony. What a schmuck, make a good sign dammit.Luckily my friend Speed Racer prevented me from going up there and strangling him. Nevertheless, the crowed roared with approval from the first notes of "Simple." This "Simple" was actually pretty good, mellowing out to some nice work by Trey and then building gradually. After eight-

een minutes Trey nodded to Fishman, who started up Harry. This Harry is one of my all-time faves and includes some of my favorite intro jamming. The end jam was nice and drawn out, and came to a real peak, which many don't accomplish these days. "Weekapaug" exploded out of the conclusion to Harry and the energy never let up. I am a major fan of "Weekapaug" bursting out of high-energy songs, instead of starting from scratch, like at the following show, 12/28/96 (three "Mike's Grooves" in a row—must be a post-1988 record), where it began after the "Strange Design," which had sucked all the energy out of the whole city. The 1997 New Year's show is a prime example: instead of starting the "'Paug" after "Circus," they threw in the Ween tune, "Roses are Free," which served as a platform for the "Weekapaug." Well, back to Vegas. The "Weekapaug" was masterful and started out with some high-energy jamming, which then out of nowhere came to a dead stop. Fish then started up the "Weekapaug" again and the place exploded.

After doing this a second time, they moved into a pretty section that featured Trey using his watery Leslie effect, and came to another dead stop before punching into the "Weekapaug" finale. This was reminiscent of the hilarious 1991 "Weekapaug" at the Somerville Theater, where Trey ends the "'Paug," and the set, three times! Vegas had a fantastic "Mike's Groove," which was followed by the necessary respite, "Sweet Adeline." Then it was time to "get the Led out." I breathed a sigh of relief as the band started "Good Times, Bad Times." It seemed like they were going to end the show in normal fashion and that everything was going to be a-okay. But then it happened: instead of ending the tune after the requisite Jimmy Page-like solo, Trey's ego took over as he took it through for one more monster chase to end the tour. The dissonance built up, Chris chased the lights, and Fishman banged on the drums, and Trey exploded out of it wailing on "the note." You know, the one you always want but don't get anymore? The one that makes the live album "Slave" melt in your mouth, hands, and brain? Wow! Shortly after, the "GTBT" ended triumphantly and I gave the band the rocking signal…because they absolutely rocked. At this point I will already argue that this was the best two-set show of the tour. The energy and intensity of the playing was unparalleled. It was a shame the tour didn't go on for another week—people would still be talking about it. By the time the holiday run came around they had lost the tightness and intensity. Too bad.

There was an encore that began with, "We'd like to bring up a couple friends to help us out with this one, Larry and Les from Primus." And like all good stories, this encore started with an oom-pah-pah. "Harpua" started out slow and funky…they were playing it in 4/4 as opposed to the usual 7/4. Following the standard beginning, Les chanted the old-time story of the "Wildwood Weed." Then the real story began. You see, Jimmy was getting bored of suburbia and decided to go to Las Vegas… after a full day of walking he realized he wouldn't make it so he set up camp with his favorite feline, Poster Nutbag. They loved each other so much that they stared in each other's eyes and started to yodel. Enter the August Sisters and John McCuen on banjo to play an old-time country tune "Cowboy Sweetheart." Fishman came out from behind the drums to get a better glance at the well-endowed sisters, with a sheepish grin on his face. The next morning, Jimmy and Poster woke up refreshed and realized that they were in fact close to Vegas. When they got there they were confronted by the four Elvii. Fishman proved he was quite a man: with some help from Chris' lights he sang "Suspicious Minds" better than the four Elvii (who did dance better than him, though).

Finally they made it to the Aladdin where Jimmy put his whole

$12 life savings on number seventeen on the roulette wheel (coincidentally, $12 wins $420 in roulette). But just as the wheel started spinning, Harpua appeared across the room. Well you know, big fight, yadda yadda, dead cat, sad kid…."Harpua" finished and launched right into "Suzie," which included Malachi from the movie *Children of the Corn* on percussion, Les and Larry, the yodelers, and the Elvii who were quite pleased to be back onstage. Following the second chorus, Trey pointed at Mike, who gave a "who me?" and then Les stepped up and showed Mike how it was done…beginning the funk breakdown which lead into Elvii madness. Trey played leader firing his megaphone at everyone as the Elvii hammed it up for the crowd, singing "Suzie Q" among many other things! Leaving the show all I could say was "Rock" since that was all that was necessary. Everyone understood. Phish destroyed Vegas…Vegas-style!

Epilogue: in fall 1997 the Aladdin was demolished to make room for the new Planet Hollywood Casino. This marked the end of the independently owned and operated casinos on the strip, and the second venue that had to be razed after Phish played a monumental show there on 1996 fall tour (The Omni in Atlanta being the other).

12/28/96 CoreStates Spectrum, Philadelphia, PA —Jon Epstein

Here's yet another case of a show being overshadowed by the other half of a two-night stand. This is a great show, and outweighs the next night in my opinion, especially the second set. The first set is highlighted by a very good "Split Open and Melt," as well a nice "Jim" opener. And this remains one of my favorite second sets. The "Makisupa">"Maze" opener is phenomenal. The space prior to "TMWSIY" conjures up images of whales, which flows through "Avenu" into a killer "Mike's." To all those who felt '97 was Phish's best year yet, you will love this "Mike's." It foreshadows the year to follow—very loose and funky and featuring a beautiful "Simple"-like jam, before heading into a good "Groove" through "Strange Design." The "Mike's">"Design">"Groove" run makes this show, as well as the Holiday Run itself.

12/28/96 CoreStates Spectrum, Philadelphia, PA —Jonathan Van Schoick

This was quite an historic night for me: the first night of the New Year's Run, my second show, and my eighteenth birthday. I still had not yet gotten into the tape-trading scene, so I was not overly familiar with the unpublished music, which gives a whole new approach to the show. My first show was on 10/21/96 (MSG, New York City), but this was the one that truly sold me on Phish. You appreciate things in the moment, rather then as a comparison to the two dozen other times you've heard the same song. For example, I thought "Frankenstein" was amazing, it totally floored me. Now, after fifteen shows and some 320-plus hours of tape, this song has a "been there, done that" feel. With experience, you really begin to appreciate the nuances of the jam songs and the genius of the improvisations, but at the same time, you tend to lose the excitement of the composed numbers.

The first set is good. The second set smokes because of one man…Page McConnell. If you love Page, you should seek out this show. 1996 is a great year for Page, he really improved. His "mule duel" segments become amazing. This is one of the few shows I've heard that allows Page to shine through, especially compared to later tours. He gets to tear things up on "Maze," then gets a solo from "Mike's Song">

"Strange Design" and then again at the end of "Weekapaug." The man was in rare form. The stuff is beautiful, poetic, pure magic. Like I said, I was sold.

2/23/97 The Fillmore, Cortemaggiore, Italy —Andrew Loewenstern

Even months before the tour started I was worried about Cortemaggiore. Getting around Europe is so easy, the rail system goes to every major city and the train stations are always centrally located. However, Cortemaggiore is not a major city. Unlike every other stop on the spring tour there is no rail station in Cortemaggiore and it isn't located on any maps available to your average American tourist.

It wasn't until we actually were on tour when we got the details. The closest train station was in Piacenza, about fifteen miles away, and there were buses that went back and forth to Cortemaggiore. However, the show was on a Sunday, and there were rumors that the buses weren't going to be running. No problem, many people (including those working for Phish) suggested that the promoter was going to charter some buses to haul all the fans on tour. Other fans were talking about renting a car/van and charging people for rides (a.k.a. "Antelope Express").

We decided to "wing it" as we had been doing all along on tour and went straight to Piacenza by rail. The promoter didn't have buses waiting for us, and the public buses weren't running on Sunday, but there were several taxis at the train station that were eager to take us to Cortemaggiore. When we arrived, we discovered that Cortemaggiore was a tiny town of a few thousand with one hotel (seven rooms total), two cafes, one pizzeria, a movie theater (which doubled as the venue), three churches, and two restaurants. One was about thirty feet from the door to the venue, the other was closed on Sunday. You could walk in a circle around the whole town in about fifteen minutes.

We got to the venue just after the band had finished soundcheck. We heard from others who had watched the soundcheck through the open door that the band had performed a long version of a brand-new song that had only had been played once, in the middle of "Down with Disease" the previous week in Amsterdam. It was later named "Carini Had a Lumpy Head" at the 2/28/97 Berlin show. Someone mentioned that immediately afterward they saw Trey sitting at the console mixing the soundcheck, which was playing back over the PA, a highly unusual event that we soon forgot about.

After a lazy afternoon playing frisbee in the park, we went to the restaurant next to the venue to have dinner, along with seemingly every other American on tour. I had the urge to wash my hands, so I went off in search of the bathroom. The restaurant wasn't very large and was completely filled with Americans going to the show. There was a banquet room off to the side connected by a short hallway. The bathrooms were also off the little hallway so on the way to the bathroom I peeked into the banquet room where the whole Phish crew was having dinner. By this point I was frustrated with trying to find the correct bathroom in each country, and this restaurant didn't have the international symbols printed on the doors. One bathroom door was held open so I assumed it was the men's room and besides, I was only washing my hands. So I went in and started washing my hands when someone came out of the one stall. I turned my head around and sure enough, it was Trey. We quickly exchanged the standard automatic greetings ("How's it going…Fine and you, etc.") and he left to have his dinner. Im-

mediately afterwards an American woman strolled in and exclaimed "What are you doing in the ladies room?"

The venue itself was a movie theater, but the chairs had been removed from the floor in front of the stage. The floor was tri-level and Paul Languedoc's mix position was at the front of the middle section so anyone standing even with or behind the board was well above the heads of everyone in front of the board. The third tier was a cafe/bar setup with tables from which you could watch the show. There was a balcony hanging over the cafe section but it was closed off. I would estimate somewhere between 750 and 1,000 people were there.

Preshow all the tapers were buzzing. It appeared that a Walkman-sized DAT recorder was attached to the soundboard and everyone wanted to know who was lucky enough to get a patch from Paul. We soon found out what was really happening. Just before the lights went out, Chris Kuroda went to the tapers' section and said, "Now would be a good time to start your decks!" Shortly thereafter the lights dimmed, the intermission music faded out, Paul pushed "Play" on the Walkman DAT hooked up to board, and out of the PA came a portion of the "Carini Had a Lumpy Head" the band had recorded and mixed down during soundcheck! The band came out on stage and got into position while the soundcheck was playing and on cue launched into a red-hot version of the song using the prerecorded portion as an intro!

The show was amazing and for the second set Fish wore his dress the only time for the whole tour. After the show there was an Italian bootlegger with a table set up right in front of the crew's tour bus selling bootleg T-shirts and other items with the Phish logo. He literally had his back against the bus! Needless to say, sales were not brisk that night for him. The band had made arrangements for a bus to take everyone back to Piacenza because the town of Cortemaggiore did not want the Phishheads hanging out all night waiting for the public shuttle to start again in the morning. All in all, with the size and intimacy of the town, the mood of the other fans, and the intensity of the show, it was one of the best overall Phish concert experiences I think I will ever have!

6/25/97 L'Aeronef, Lille, France—Ryan Shriver

We arrived in Lille after a three-hour train ride from Strasbourg. It was pouring rain, and after finding no hostels, we found a cheap hotel and an even cheaper bottle of red wine on our way to the venue. L'Aeronef was a disco/rave club located on the third floor of this mall-like structure near the train station. There was a bar right outside the club, and everyone was there drinking before the show. We were all waiting by a set of doors that we thought led into the club when someone looked over and saw people going in another set of doors. Dave, Tom, and I promptly jumped up and ran over. We proceeded to walk right in and were literally the fifth, sixth, and seventh people inside the venue. "I must be in the front row!" There was a railing and the stage was higher (about six feet), but the venue was smaller than Strasbourg. The place gradually filled up, but even fifteen minutes before the show started you could find a seat within twenty feet of the stage!

Phish came on and opened with a roaring "Oblivious Fool." This is a great opening song and a good way to get the crowd moving. We were briefly let down by "Dogs Stole Things," but the "Taste" that followed made up for it. Good God, what a "Taste!" This version reinforced my notion that this song (along with "Theme") will be Phish's next great jamming tune. Trey played his ass off during "Taste," and this version

went for over ten minutes. Then we got "Billy Breathes," a song I had kind of forgotten about but was really glad to hear. And then came "AC/DC Bag." I looked down at my buddy Dave (who, for the first time in his life, was in the front row, dead center) and the smile on his face said it all. Before we left the states for tour, we were talking about songs we'd like to hear. He picked out three, one of which was "AC/DC Bag." I was really glad for him. "AC/DC" was very well played and had an intense build-up jam with Trey going crazy on lead. Right at the end when it got kind of slow, Mike launched in with "My Old Home Place." Of all the bluegrass songs Mike does, this has to be one of my favorites (along with "Uncle Pen").

After this short but sweet number by Mike, we got "Theme." Man, does it get any better than this? "Theme" was, well, extraordinary as usual. The jam out of this "Theme" covered some ground, as I closed my eyes and went along for the ride. After "Theme," the band could have called it a set and I would have been content. But no, they wanted to play more, which was just fine by me. "Wading in the Velvet Sea" followed (did someone sneak them a list of my favorite songs?) and though a little shorter than the previous night, it didn't disappoint. "I Saw it Again" came next (possibly the first minor letdown of the set, but well played nonetheless) and was followed by "Limb by Limb." "My Soul" closed the first set in rockin' fashion, with Trey belting out "My my my my my my my soul, it's my soul…It's my soul people…It's my soul." What a great way to finish the first set.

One thing that was wonderful about the first set was that no one was pushing or shoving and everyone had plenty of room to dance. Even up front on the rail, I had lots of room to move, and people respected your space. Not only was the crowd small (300–350 people tops), but everyone was chilled out and that made for a much better time. I don't even remember seeing a security guard present, which was also nice. It is little things like this that help make a show better, and after that first set I couldn't wait for the second!

Boy, I was not let down. I'm sure that many of you have seen the setlist for this set, and I can tell you it sounded as good as it looks. It

Great Went

was one of the best sets of music I've seen by Phish. Mike opened with his thunderous intro and we were treated to "Down with Disease." I simply love Trey's guitar riff in this song, it's so damn catchy! A twenty-one-plus minute "DWD" segued into "Piper," which was a nice arrangement. The "Piper" was a little longer than usual, but towards the end it started to get a little spacey, and then Trey came back with that "DWD" riff. Piper segued back into "DWD" for a few minutes before heading into a new song sung by Fishman. I'd be tempted to call it "God is My Brain," and it goes "Time for the meat stick / Bury the meat stick / Take out the meat stick / Time. Oh, Oh, God is my brain." This weird number was mostly jamming with a few words thrown in. As of this writing, I'm not sure whether it's officially called "Time" or "Meatstick."

The song flowed into "McGrupp," another treat and the first of tour. "McGrupp" went on and on and was very well played. At one point, Trey would yell, "He looks too much," and then lead the crowd to respond "Like Dave." Trey just kept shaking his fist in the air as he belted out those lines. "McGrupp" finally segued into "Makisupa Policeman." At this point I pinched myself to make sure I wasn't dreaming. This reggae tune had everyone just kind of bobbing up and down with the beat, and toward the end a funny thing started to happen.

I noticed Trey take off his guitar and head over towards Fishman's drums. He then brought a stool out to the front of the stage. Trey took over for Fishman on drums, who came out and sat on the stool. Fishman had a towel on his thigh and proceeded to play the towel with a pair of drumsticks. Trey came back over and adjusted the microphones, so one mic was on the towel and the other mic was Fishman's vocal mic. As the band faded in the background, everyone got quiet as Fishman started playing his towel. The beat seemed obvious, but could it really be? "Oh Cecilia, you're breakin' my heart, you're shakin' my confidence daily...." What the hell was going on? As everyone (including the band) watched, Fishman sang this Simon and Garfunkel classic. The only problem was that Fishman had a tough time with the words and screwed up most of the verses. In fact the crowd knew all the right words and happily sang along. Fishman looked like he was having a good time, and Page, Mike, and Trey were all grins as their buddy was front and center.

Once Fishman got up and took some bows, the rest of the guys launched into the "HYHU" jam. I get a kick every time I hear this, just recently learning the story behind it. But Fishman didn't go back over to his drum set; instead he picked up Trey's guitar and started doodling with it. After about a minute of doodling, Mike put down his bass and headed over to Page. Page let Mike sit down, and Page walked over and put on Mike's bass, which I must admit looked very funny on Page. But hell, Mike looked just as funny on piano! This little switch-instrument jam lasted a little over two minutes, and Mike managed to pull off a nice solo right before they went into "Rocko William."

As Fishman played at the guitar and made this evil-looking face, he sang this bluesy "Rocko William." The band sounded pretty good as a unit, but when Fishman tried to solo he couldn't quite lift off the ground. It was more like tinkering at a solo, but I was having such a good time laughing that it didn't really matter. The whole band looked like they were having a ball, and I know the crowd couldn't believe what they were seeing. After about five minutes, everyone put there instruments down and walked back to their original instruments. What next?

The answer was "Antelope", and quite an "Antelope" it was. Prague's was good, but this one is in a league by itself. As they had done all night long, Phish ascended to new levels while stretching this

one out to fifteen minutes. At the end they kept jamming while saying thanks to the members of the crew and anyone else who happened to pop into Trey's mind at the time. Could this show finally be over? What could they encore with? I must say I wasn't even remotely prepared for the "Guyute" encore. I had heard this song twice before and secretly hoped I'd hear it again. But I never imagined a "Guyute" encore. All I can say is that it was well played.

The second set ran about ninety-one minutes, and was one fine set of Phish. In retrospect, Lille was probably the best show I saw in Europe. It was rock solid from beginning to end. Phish had fun, the fans had fun, and it was truly an intimate experience with the band. Get the tapes of this show!

7/1–2/97 Paradiso, Amsterdam, The Netherlands—Jon Weber

First of all, the Paradiso is an old church that has been converted into a performance space, replete with stained glass windows and an ornate double balcony, all in the confines of a building that holds no more than a thousand people. It was a very intimate place indeed, and the energy of the crowd was intense and intent.

The opener, "Ghost," got things off to an easy, "Wolfman's"-type groove. The jam out of this tune developed significantly, and altogether "Ghost" clocked in just over twenty minutes. At one point, Trey and Fish were singing their favorite brand-new lyric over a jammed groove, "I think you know where you are...you're on the back of a worm!" It was an auspicious start to the show, even shutting up some of the cynics around me that were sick of seeing the new tunes over and over.

Horn was next and then "Ya Mar" followed, with a particularly cool drum segment featuring delicate work by Fishman and a hushed audience. "Limb by Limb" was next, which also proved to be an excellent new song. The vocals are all divergent while at the same time convergent, and the lyrics are actually quite cool. Mike has a really cool background vocal that totally stands out in a killer way. The jam out of this tune was damn impressive; I was finding myself lost in rhythms that are not typical to your standard Phish jam.

After a brief respite in bass space, with Mike doing washes of sound while Page tweaked his Moogs, they segued into the vaguely Celtic lullaby cadence of "Funny as it Seems." Frankly, this song is a disappointment. The J.J. Cale lyrics have just too much of a straight-ahead cheese "lovey-dovey" feel to them, especially coming from a funkster like Mike. Still, it provided some rest for the next selection, "Saw it Again." This tune kicks, with two separate sections. In the first, there are killer "wah" effects from Trey and a totally punchy arrangement of the background vocals. The second section features a slower, harder groove with everyone singing with gospel's conviction, "I saw it again!" An absolutely killer rock and roll song! Trey was yelling about being on the back of the worm again during this one also.

"Dirt" followed, a Beatles sounding-ballad that was maybe placed a little closer to the also-slow "Funny as it Seems" than I would've preferred. "Dirt" has a nice instrumental ending with Trey following the lyric melody. Of all the songs that seem appropriate for the mention of worms, "Dirt" didn't get one.

Next, they broke into the old bag of tricks and pulled out a magical "Reba." Trey was just soaring as Chris Kuroda began involving the stained glass for the first time, lighting up the glass from behind with pulses of light. Full of nuance and melodic expression, this was a truly heavenly "Reba." Which brings me to a digression: is Trey God?

"Dogs Stole Things" closed out the exhaustive eighty-nine-minute set. This is a standard rocker that doesn't seem like it has much room to go anywhere; the groove didn't even seem that cool, kind of stale. Maybe Trey isn't God.

The music of set two was so good, it surpasses my ability to be objective. Being in Amsterdam brings with it certain advantages, and those advantages tend to manifest themselves most intensely during a set break. So take my review with a grain of salt, or whatever else is handy.

To begin set two, Fishman stepped out alone on stage, walked over to Page's electric piano, and started playing a little repetitive ditty. At first I thought that it was actually John Medeski (MMW were playing a week later at a Dutch jazz festival) because Fishman looks like him now, with his crewcut. This is the first time that I've heard Fishman play keyboards in a way that is listenable. Improvement is a good thing.

The rest of the guys then came out, and Trey began the opening to "Timber Ho" while Fishman made his way back to his set. "Timber Ho" was just ridiculous, with Trey busting out otherworldly noises and fat chunks, along with killer support from the Chairman of the Boards.

I was floored that my favorite cover tune of theirs ("Timber") would be followed by one of my favorite originals, "Bathtub Gin!" In forty-five shows, I have only seen "Bathtub" three times, so I'm still totally batty when they start into it. This version is truly a top five of all-time–type affair—full-on "synthoslinky" bass from Mike at one point that will blow your mind when you hear the tape. The syncopated beats that Mike found late in this jam is just further evidence that the man is grounded in his own, uniquely satisfying groove.

The "Bathtub" jam then led into a superslow sex-groove jam version of "Cities," slowed down considerably. In fact, the "Bathtub" jam was just kind of going along, slowing down, and then Trey just kept hammering this one chord slower and slower (it was the "Cities" chord, but with the effects it sounded totally different) and then eventually he just spoke into the mic, "Think of London!" and the roof just about came down.

Aside from playing it at such a slow beat, they were leaving a lot of space around the music (not spacey, but sparse) of the composed part and the initial part of the jam followed this effect. It had sort of a slow blues feel, again, with nice space around the music. The blues feel then sort of absorbed the psychedelic vibe in the room and began mutating into a jam that reminded me of the liquid blues feel that they had in the thirty-five-minute "Free" from 11/22/95 Landover, MD.

Eight minutes into "Cities" the jam loses the more straightforward feeling of the blues jam and sinks down into another wash of sounds, similar to the Mike and Page volume-swell jam from the legendary Providence 12/29/94 "Bowie." There were massive blocks of sound swelling out and in, sometimes with simulated Doppler effect. At one point, when the jam was getting that "weeble-wobble" feel, Trey yelled out, to everyone's bewilderment (once again), "I think you know where you are…you're on the back of the worm!"

So, twenty minutes after "Cities" began, we're still rolling with this whacked jam happening and no clear direction in sight. It was sweet! "Cities" wound up clocking in at twenty-three minutes, but it's hard to tell if the last fifteen minutes might have been something distinct. The "back of the worm jam" perhaps? Raging versions of "Loving Cup" and "Slave" closed out the set. Not a weak link in set two! I could have sworn they were putting more emphasis on "Oh, what a beautiful buzz." Ahh, Amsterdam…

"When the Circus Comes" seemed like an appropriately laid-back

Great Went

encore for such an exhausting evening. Sent home for a night of rest, we were psyched that we still had one more to go.

The second night started out kind of slow (note sarcasm)º.The opening notes of "Mike's Song" are about the last thing you'd expect to begin a show—but I guess we were blessed by our religious surroundings and the vibe of the amazing town that was hosting us. We knew for sure that we were in store for another night of who knows what!

Showing all the outward signs of a man possessed, Trey was ripping the laser sounds (serious chorus processing) and the "Mike's" jam followed suit in a very futuristic fashion—while still staying relatively grounded in terms of the groove and the melody of the jam. Ten minutes in, they launched directly into "Simple," with the vocal harmonies bouncing around the old church in splendid fashion. The "Simple" jam wound down to Trey and Fishman jamming together subtly—with emphatic eye contact between the two as Trey danced close to Fish's set, facing the newly buzzed drummer. Fish was again wearing his all-black Ringo suit (black shirt and tie included), but somehow he still managed to lay down the kind of hard-hitting beats we all know and love.

The fade-out of the "Simple" jam led nicely into the fade-in of "Maze." This "Maze" was particularly nice because it found Page switching frequently between all of his keyboards—synths, Moogs, electric pianos included. It seems that the focus of "Maze" is usually just organ, then piano—not that there's anything wrong with that. In this version, it was cool to hear the bendy notes that he pulls out of the Moog as well some of the other Casio synth noises he taps out of those little tiny synths he now has.

Perhaps as a nod to Page's contribution to a stellar and unique "Maze," they then broke into Page's singing song "Strange Design"— of course nothing unusual here. I found it to be a good time to head up near the front of the stage—an easy thing to do in such a small place. "Ginseng Sullivan" was next with some nice, liquid leads from Trey.

"Vultures" is truly a great new song, and it was a nice way to slide back into the experimental phase from earlier in the set. "Vultures" is absolutely unlike any other Phish song to date. It is very Zappa-esque in terms of the sonic feel and has a very open-ended jam segment that features some truly off-beat work from Mike and Fishman. On top of the awe-inspiring music, the lyrics are killer, and they come at you rapid-fire style—like rounds from an AK47. In addition, the layered vocal effect of this song is also reminiscent of the approach taken by the Talking Heads— the influence of Phish's Halloween '96 show is apparently emerging.

Fully expecting a segue into "Weekapaug" from the killer "Vul-

tures" groove, they instead wound the jam down and next stepped up to play the country shuffle "Water in the Sky." It's kind of a catchy ditty that has a nice varying chorus with pleasing harmonies, a similar feel to the slow version of "Poor Heart" of fall '95.

Finally, they ended the set with a standalone "Weekapaug," with full-on jamming from everyone. Page was stretching all over the place, hammering down different keys (synth and organ, piano, and electric piano, etc.) and Fishman was in a world of his own, bringing out nuances in the beat that I didn't think were possible. On top of it all, Trey and Mike seemed to be feeding off each other, both melodically and spiritually. Mike has rarely looked as intense as he did during the peaking moments of this jam. As "Weekapaug" ended, it was evident that it was a perfect conclusion to a cohesive set of both intense jams and nice-sounding songs.

Set two held much promise as we waited at the set break. They played the entire *Crooked Rain* album by Pavement at the break (the night before was Primus). It was a long set break indeed (not sure if that's why set two was exactly fifty minutes long...).

Set two was short, but it contained no fluff at all—just pure experimentation and exploration. They commenced the set with three minutes of space noises—it seemed that they were considering "2001" before finally dropping into "Stash." The "Stash" jam covered all of the bases. It was a little longer than thirty minutes, ranging from harsh grooves to delicate on-the-spot melodies to raging improvisation. "Stash" did not resolve and conclude; instead the band faded from an intense space segment directly into the opening blasts of "Llama." Page again seemed content experimenting with his Moogs—while we normally can expect a heavy dose of organ from a "Llama" jam, this version found Page standing up, tickling the futuristic noises out of his synthesizers. "Llama," too, was not completed. As the jam really began to rage, they dropped into another sea of space noises. As the space sounds built up, Trey put both his palms down and signaled to "push it down." Page gently continued on piano the chord progression to "Llama," but eventually he gave way to the waves of sound that Mike and Trey were working on. Full-on space ensued.

As the hollowness of the space rung out, Page began playing a familiar little R&B line on the organ, almost sounding like the intro notes to "Cars Trucks and Buses" but to a different groove, in single notes. I did, in fact, think that they were doing an ultra-spacey segue into "CTB." Instead, Trey and Mike followed along on the single-notes that Page was playing, and the groove continued along in a somewhat tweaked manner. Trey then stepped up and sang, tweaked-sounding as well, "Come on and dance...come on and dance...make some romance...because the night is coming and the music's humming and you've got to get down to...WORM TOWN!" We realized it was a play on the Steve Miller tune "Swingtown" and apparently they were continuing the worm theme from the night before.

Trey promptly launched into a story about getting sucked into Amsterdam's canals and having to ride along with the giant worms there. With that, they sunk into a nice rollicking space-worm groove (I don't know any other way to describe it). Eventually they included the ubiquitous new catch phrase, "I think you know where you are...you're on the back of the worm!" with call-and-response vocals between Fish ("I think you know where you are") and Trey ("You're on the back of the worm!"). From there, they again sunk into volume-swell space and Fishman repeated his line over and over ("I think you know where you

are") in a variety of goofy-sounding voices, as we in the audience contemplated whether in fact we did.

The space rung out again and this time led into the slow, yearning piano intro to "Waiting in the Velvet Sea." Sure this song is a bit repetitive and slow, but it has some really nice counter-melody singing from Page. It was certainly, however, a disappointment that they ended the set on this song. As I said, the set clocked in at only fifty minutes. I was sure that the encore would be fat...but why not at least make set two over an hour?

So the encores were fat. In fact, the "Free" is one of the best I've heard in awhile, with some nice, slow funk emphasis from Mike complemented by unusual squelches and squawks from Trey. (Or was that Page?) A bit over ten minutes later they left the stage. The vibe in the air was that there just had to be another encore. Fortunately, we were obliged, and with "David Bowie" no less! The "Bowie" here was killer. Mike made an early reference to the "Maze" bass line (I know we've all been thrown a few times by the hi-hat intro similarity between "Maze" and "Bowie") and he got a burst of laughter from the crowd. Intimate venues are nice. The jam in "Bowie" was great, but hard to describe in the way that "Bowie" jams seem to be. Suffice it to say that it felt like an appropriately experimental way to end the two-night run.

Also appropriate was Chris Kuroda's lighting of the stained glass (lit from the outside in) during the concluding sequence of "Bowie." I'm sure the temptation was there to light up the stained glass all the time, but he did it sparingly over the two nights. Only "Reba" during the first night and "Free" and "Bowie" second night. The effect was that much greater. Less is more. Thank you Phish, for a wonderful time in a wonderful venue in a wonderful town.

7/9/97 Le Transbordeur, Lyon, France—Frances D. Davis

To begin with, I am almost fifty, have raised three sons to maturity, have three granddaughters, have been a musician all of my life, write music of my own, and have been a rock and roll fan since the day I first heard, as a child, some of that rockabilly stuff playing on WMPS and WHBQ in Memphis. My life span has been parallel with that of rock and roll, and the music has influenced me profoundly. I have been through obsessions with Elvis, Gene Pitney, the Beatles (that was a big one), Led Zeppelin, Three Dog Night, Billy Joel, Elton John, Eric Clapton, Tina Turner, and more recently Pink Floyd (another big one), and now Phish. Now, I've gotta tell you, I was bulldozed into the Phish thing. My son John (twenty-one) wouldn't let it rest! He kept shoving it down my throat.

When I first started listening to the Phish music he played for me, I was not very interested. It sounded like repetitive nonsense to me. It was a time when I had lost rock and roll. I just couldn't follow it. It was really fragmenting into a hundred different categories, because rock bands were so determined to be "unique" and original, most of them being neither. It seemed that everything had been done by the end of the '70s, and the Green Day genre of careless, unemotional, I-don't-care-whether-this-does-anything-for-you rock and roll was making a big entrance. I was jaded and unreceptive. But Phish (and John) won out! Given no real choice, I began to listen and receive.

But it was my first Phish concert that really convinced me. I bravely took four students from my music appreciation class (at the private school where I teach) to the Charlotte concert in fall of '96. I was in awe of Trey's incredible skill on the guitar. His playing revealed a very

unique and quixotic personality that smacks of delayed development in the most pleasant and creative way. I was mesmerized by Page's keyboard work. It was on one hand naive and clumsy, and on the other, focused and heart-driven, sometimes revealing measures and measures of hypnotic momentum. Fishman's punky, Animal House style seemed the opposite intellectual extreme and gave a rounding-out effect which saved the group from being too "ozone-layer." And Mike°stable, unflappable Mike°plugging away on the harmonies and the basic beat, never giving us a hint of the man behind the bass line. They seemed the perfect ensemble musically and spiritually.

Since then I have been to the Boston '96 New Year's concert, four concerts in the '97 Summer Tour (that's another story!), the shows in Hampton, VA, in November '97, and the show in Lyon, summer '97. It is this last night to which I hitherto refer.

John, Marie (a German seventeen-year-old whose family relocated to Spartanburg with their business when she was twelve), and I left our dorm in Lyon to head out for the unknown enclave of Americans and a small-venue Phish show in Lyon. We were really psyched! It was Marie's first Phish show. But John and I were coming from huge Phish shows in the U.S. where the individuals on the stage were somewhat impersonal little dots through a haze of smoke and noisy fans.

We came early as all Phish fans know to do. The summer daylight fades very late in France, 9:30 PM in July, so we had lots of visual time in the lot. We were not surprised to see people there in the casual organization that Phish fans usually take before a show, but we were somewhat surprised to see that there were so few there. They were clustered under some trees there doing their usual stuff, and being friendly if approached, but not intrusive to others' personal space.

We could hear the soundcheck, but when John, unable to contain his amazement that he was this close to an open door where the elusive four were actually playing something that he might otherwise be barred from hearing, took his place alone by the door to listen, the few authorities there officiously closed the access! So, we decided to find the entrance and camp out there. There were five guys at the entrance from various parts of the Northeast U.S., drinking a little wine and talking about Phish and life in general. That was one of the best parts of the experience. We had time and something in common. They were a little put off by having a mom there at first, I think. I didn't try to assert myself, but as time went on, sitting on the asphalt together, they offered me a swig du vin, and they relaxed about my presence. That was such a special gift to me of which they were probably unaware.

Finally, the doors opened and the excitement built as it always does. Random cheering and unnecessary but habitual hustling for a place in the relatively small line at the unimpressive entrance to this Transbordeur place proceeded in good order: a sort of microcosm of the bigger venues.

Inside, we found to our delight that this was a stand-where-you-please bar place. People learned of each other and the circumstances of being in such a strange place in the summertime. There was lots of smoking and tossing of the hackey-sack. We were almost first in, delayed by queuing up at the wrong door inside, but we found that we could stand right up under the stage. John was ballistic at the prospect of actually being spat upon by Trey in concert! We struck up a conversation with a "granola-type" male of early age who instantly started making protest about the smoking of tobacco in the club. I decided that I would go to the grandstands in back and smoke my one cigarette that I allowed

myself. I began feeling out-of-place and decided to stay there for a while and observe. Often, people at Phish concerts think I am "event staff" or a journalist or review writer, so I just go with that. I enjoyed watching the various individuals and their pets and personae parading by me. That is always a spectacle that I enjoy about Phish concerts.

They came out with no fanfare. The concert began with some random reference to "Pierre" of Haagen-Dazs. I was bewildered from the beginning with that, but before the concert was over, Trey revealed the mystery of Pierre. I'm still not sure what it was, but everyone else seemed satisfied that Pierre was cool and it was part of the enigma of many Phish references: random, ironic, humorous nonsense that is fun to figure out.

They began with a low-key version of "PYITE." The familiar music was accessible to all and instantly united us all. Cheers rose as a short, happy jam began. The Latin beat and tinkling piano ended the song quickly, and the band and softly segued into "Prince Caspian." Phish has an uncanny knowledge of "programming." The concerts are often like a long story line, which is followed intuitively by those who know their style. Listening experience is required for the full experience. The melancholy, thoughtful idea of "floating on the waves" was a gentle invitation to join in the fantasy. It was a particularly sweet version. We settled in.

"Ginseng Sullivan" shows the penchant for their eclectic style, never wanting to be pigeonholed. Nashville, step back! It was short and probably threw the uninitiated totally off. Then a funky drum beat introduced "Split Open and Melt." The introduction defied a tonality until the lyrics began. It began normally enough, but as the music progressed past the traditional nontonality of the song, it became evident that the jam had begun. I hear John's delighted "whoo-hoo-hoo!" It's right there on the tape! This pulled me back to standing under the stage. It is wonderful how the coming together of a few elements of organized joy in the music can bring one to such a state of well-being. That jam made tears roll down my face. I don't know why. The immersion of the entire essence of one's being in the communal experience of music and fantasy is a powerful thing that Phish can elicit better than any group I've known. They are not media gods. They are ageless, classless fellows in nonreality. We rocked!

Keeping things slow and relaxed with "Dirt," Phish delayed the real excitement. Trey's sweet, epic guitar plays the lead line of the break while he intersperses little soft vocals underneath. A very short version, it could almost be considered a prelude to "Taste," which crescendos in with that running guitar and dampened cymbal pattern. What good musicians these people are! Their often-apologetic vocals put us all in their league, but never obscure their musicality and heart! In this jam, with its soft, fast underpinnings in the bass and percussion, you can hear the excitement of the entire concert begin to build. Masterful in his guitar solo, Trey takes us to the first level. And Page, alternating between duple and triple meters in the background, adds to the ascent. Good golly, we're off and it feels good! The crowd roars and whistles as the jam comes to its inevitable climax.

Then as Phish does so well, it goes from the sublime to the almost, but not quite ridiculous. The crowd was adoringly polite and receptive as the group broke ranks to come way downstage. I heard myself on the tape laughing aloud as they began an a cappella version of "Sweet Adeline." Now, here is where we have bragging rights at this concert! We were looking up their noses as they sang. Wow! Fishman's dramatic solo brought supportive laughter and applause.

Quickly, the boys manned their former positions and began a bumpy, unphrased, noncontinual intro to "Harry Hood." Humorous unpredictability is a definite trademark of Phish programming. Where are we going now? Seemingly, nowhere! Then as we think they have wandered into discombobulated indecision, sounding somewhat like an exhibition of styles and meters, and no one can convincingly boogie, the non-sequitur "Thank you Mr. Minor" makes the conundrum more intense. The experience descends into a very chilled-out guitar and bass duet with a bit of celeste-type diddling on the keyboard. But then you hear it, a gradual perception of building intensity, and you know the jam has begun. It's a code from them to us. There was another mention of Pierre and a corny reference to "AC/DC Baguette" as the little crowd roared!

At the beginning of the second set, they mentioned Pierre again to some surreal synthesizer noises. This gave way to the first watery blurbs of "Down with Disease." This is one of John's favorites, so I was glad to hear it begin. It's a classic, full of "hooks" to grab your memory and keep you wanting more. I love to sing along with this one. But not at this particular concert?

The twelve-bar blues shows up with "My Soul." An unusually fast blues song, this one rocked along almost like a ragtime number with its fast-paced piano breaks. And what was that maniacal laugh near the end?

Next, with no break, comes "Cars Trucks and Buses" to give us a bit of jazz-rock. I love it when Phish cools down and plays in a jazzy style. Page's improv alternated between genius and klutz. I love that about his playing, it's always human enough to make him believable. He really revs up at the end playing chord clusters and thickening the texture. This piece is always a bit of ear-hormone to listen to?too fine.

Now when Béla Fleck and the others came into things, it got a bit complex to gather up. We didn't know for sure that they were coming. We heard rumors going around of all kinds of guests. Béla has played around our parts a lot (the Carolinas), so I recognized his group immediately as they came out, and I was really glad to see them. I can't remember the sequence of things as Fleck and the 'Tones appeared. I know Future Man played with Fishman first. This strange-looking gadget that he plays on is past my comprehension. He presents a really good synthesized percussion performance on it. It seems that he can do a thing or two that a primitive trap-set drummer can't do, but I miss the visual, visceral backdrop power of the drummer. And I have never seen anyone who entertains me more than that incredible bass player, Victor Wooten.

In the "You Enjoy Myself" jam, things get much cooler and thicker in texture with this ensemble. The whole thing spins and spins with little bits of competitive, tandem repetition of ideas with variation according to the artist.

"Ghost" was an awesome collaboration for me. The octave-apart vocal harmony in the slow, funky tempo, combined with those "blatty" low-note interjections by the tenor sax and the insistent, popping and slipping bass part by Wooten made for constant just-short-of-hypnosis involvement. The end of this one is a random, noisy "train wreck" of atonal "spastistism" tripping into the first strains of "Poor Heart." Very fast and ultra-traditional, this song simplifies things for everyone, dispelling any mysticism. Jeff Coffin (special guest of the Flecktones) went wild on tenor sax in this one! He was right in front of me freaking out! It broke the mood, for sure! But Phish never lets you rest, do they?

The finale at the end of "Poor Heart" included several themes and endings from other songs, drawing from snippets of Gershwin to an

Irish jig, radio jingles to stripper closers, rock and roll knock-off riffs, and ended on a grand vaudevillian final chord. This went on for quite a while as each of the musicians on stage tried to one-up the others. The crowd wouldn't let them get off easy. They continued to insist as long as there was any hope for more music.

Trey called up Pierre to the stage. There were the ubiquitous calls for "Freebird" from the audience, who didn't really know what to expect at this point. They brought this Pierre person out on the stage and sang "Hello My Baby" to him and to us all. That was some hot barbershop stuff! We participated with laughing, whooping support. What a celebration! It was an American island in the middle of France, and we were all acting very American!

7/9/97 Le Transbordeur, Lyon, France—John H. Davis

Well, Mom and I took off to study abroad in France for July 1997 and were lucky enough to have Phish come to visit while we were there. We really had no idea what to expect, having only seen shows in the U.S. A week before the show, we practiced the bus route to Le Transbordeur to check it out. I really couldn't believe they would play in a bar, but it appeared as such. The smallest venue I'd ever seen them in was a medium-sized theater in 1994, and Mom only had experience with coliseum/arena Phish.

The lots were just like any Phish show, except there were only about a hundred people out there. There were no French people, all Americans. Someone told me that many people had jumped off tour after the Italian shows. So there ended up being no more than about three hundred people there.

There were rumors going around the lots that Medeski Martin and Wood, Béla Fleck and the Flecktones, and Blues Traveler were all in Europe and that we might get a guest performance. I was pessimistic. I managed to get on front row, which was a first for me. Trey started off the show with a query to the location of Pierre from Haagen Dazs before counting off "PYITE." (Who's Pierre?) The first few songs of the first set were pretty solid. All the songs had a strange new energy to me. Phish in a bar; the way it was created and meant to be! "Caspian" was pretty in a quiet sort of way, compared to U.S. shows. To me, "Caspian" is one of those songs that depends a lot on mood. I still dislike this song at large shows, but it really did seem to fit the vibe of the smaller show. Instead of the soaring Trey solo, there is a more thoughtful and beautiful guitar solo. And Page had an opportunity to draw out the pre-ending with a delicate "Coil"-like solo.

The "Melt" was the gem of the first set. I had heard that Phish had "funked out," as a friend put it. This "Melt" illustrates that trend quite nicely. I knew something great was in the works when they started off much slower than usual, almost ponderous. Trey bobbed his head and strummed the slow groove with a smile. They kept the slow tempo through to the end. It was almost like hearing a completely new song. My only complaint is that they stopped after about thirteen minutes. The whole room was entrenched in the funk and would have been happy to stay that way for much longer! After twenty-three shows and eight "Melts," this remains the most memorable one I've ever seen, mainly because I think "Melt" was meant to be slow and funky.

"Taste" was a good energy builder and got the small group of fans present together with a smile. "Sweet Adeline" (and later, "Amazing Grace") was one of the songs most improved by the small size of the venue. I was standing right in front of Trey's shoes and could hear each

melody line coming from each individual singer. Despite the few yelled requests, the only problem was the multitude of flashing cameras. Trey said, "Chris, if you could just turn on the strobe lights and get 'em back…" Fish sang beautifully.

Like many of the modern ones, the beginning of this "Harry Hood" was fraught with strange sound effects and had minimal playing. The jam segment was pretty and relaxing, as usual. I was hoping that the jam segment would feature a delicate, peaceful interlude, maybe even a silent jam. Trey seemed to be trying to quiet things down, but gave it up for the classic tension-release style, resulting in a very nice "Hood." Mom thought it was much more than nice, though, as she was almost brought to tears. "You can feel good about Fishman, about Haagen Dazs, about Pierre!" While the band drew out the end of Harry, Trey did some quick band introductions (nicknames, of course) and yet another salute to Pierre, and then to "all those people we met in the bar graduating from high school." Then, "You guys like that song 'AC/DC Baguette?'" It's always nice when the boys are in a good mood.

Second set was a blast. I'm still trying to decide if I like this set so much because I was there, or because it was truly great. The answer to that is "yes!" They came out and explained, after yet another salute to Pierre, that they had all gone to a Haagen-Dazs, "the second-best ice cream in the world," before the show and talked with a guy named Pierre who worked there. Trey expressed his hopes that Pierre would work at Ben & Jerry's when they opened a store in Lyon.

"Down with Disease" opened fast and tight. This is the third song that was vastly improved in a smaller venue. They were just on! At the beginning of the jam segment, Trey almost went directly into a solo instead of the "DWD" riff. He was feeling the flow, as he didn't let up for quite a while. Page was chording along like mad, but Trey was in the spotlight for several minutes before I could pay attention to the Phish instead of just Trey. Trey's intensity spread to the rest of the band resulting in one of the best high-energy "Diseases" I've ever heard. All "Type I" jamming, but fire the whole way. This one's underrated, if you ask me! The energy led right into a fast and upbeat "My Soul."

"You Enjoy Myself." Hmmmm…I know some people think that a special guest makes the night twice as good. And others think it just dilutes Phish. Well, je m'en fiche, the rest of this set was incredibly fun!

A very quiet, almost silent jam in the beginning of "YEM," with complete silence from the crowd, save for a couple of hoots and one cough. Gosh, I love that. Pretty standard beginning, other than that. After a few turns on the tramps, Mike and Trey stepped off and Future Man (Roy Wooten) and Jeff Coffin came out and jumped. They dismounted and out came Béla Fleck and Victor Wooten for a couple of bounces. The energy in the crowd immediately went up a notch or two. And thus began the rest of the set.

After the tramps, the four new additions got a chance to solo. Before too long, Trey introduced the musicians to Pierre. (All stage banter was directed to Pierre.) Future Man had the first solo, joined by "The Greazy Troll" soon after. If you have never seen Future Man, he plays a "synth-ax drumitar," which is an electronic drum set in the shape of a guitar. He designed this thing himself. After a few minutes of drums, Victor (one of the best bassists in the world) "lays it down in Lyon for Pierre." Then Jeff (tenor sax) blew himself apoplectic for a good few minutes. Trey really enjoyed this, smiling at him with that goofy grin. Last, but not least, Béla had his turn on the banjo for a few minutes before Trey joined him. Trey and Béla stood facing each other and playing off of each

other. It looked to me like Béla felt a little intimidated or out of his league, maybe. "YEM" isn't really like any song I've ever heard the Flecktones play. But, much like Mike, Béla has a hard face to read. (Trey seemed to be able to draw Jeff out easier than Béla.) But Trey and Béla did produce a beautiful duet, nevertheless. While this was going on, Victor and Mike joined in, both playing Mike's one fretless bass—Vic behind Mike and reaching around. I wonder if that bothered Mike? He was wearing his usual blank face, though.

After the dueling with Béla, all eight of them went into a very intricate and full-bodied jam. (Eight instruments at once is quite an earful.) This descended into a more dissonant, exploratory jam (Type II) for several minutes, becoming kinda funky. "Funky" led into "Ghost," of course, with a smooth key change. At this point, "Ghost" was less than a month old and completely new to my ears. Because of this, I will forever hear a tenor sax in "Ghost," much like I will always hear the Giant Country Horns on songs like "Suzie" and "Cavern."

"Ghost" had some pretty unique jamming, as well. Vic and Mike had a nice duel, and I would have to say that Vic is a little better at soloing. Vic started to play the *Andy Griffith Show* theme when Trey and Mike came back in with the last verse, cutting him off. Oops! The jam started off like most "Ghost" jams, but quickly diverged from the norm when the four Flecktones added their voices. The jam eventually turned toward some really spacey stuff, which is interesting, to say the least, with eight contributors. It was not a very long "Ghost," relative to what it has now become, but still the most unique one of which I know.

"Poor Heart" came out of the fray. Finally, we get to a song where Béla can shine, and he tore it up! Page also had a go, followed by some excellent saxophone. At the end, each person on stage had the opportunity to play a little solo and pass to the next person. Each member had two or three goes. Trey even started a "Freebird" tease during this jam. Trey ended the set, starting a chant of "Pierre! Pierre! Pierre!" which the crowd took up mightily after the stage cleared.

Upon the band's return for the encore, they asked Pierre to come up onstage, which he did. He was a lanky fellow with long, blond hair and a cigarette. They put him up on one of the monitors and stood around him singing "Ragtime Gal" to him. He didn't know what to think and looked quite confused. It was a very good-humored way to end the night.

This show is the most well-rounded show I've seen and also the most fun. There were hardly any bland songs in the whole show, and the three songs with Béla Fleck and the Flecktones are unique and somewhat indescribable. Everyone should give this show a listen. And if you're in Europe when Phish is, it would be worth your while to catch a show!

7/22/97 Walnut Creek Amphitheater, Raleigh, NC
—Craig DeLucia

This show is, by far, the shortest I have ever seen and is one of the shortest I have ever heard on tape. If anyone complains about it, though, I will hunt them down and force them to listen to Fishman impersonating James Brown covering Hanson for hours upon end!

The night before was the U.S. tour opener in Virginia Beach. I was staying at a house in Nag's Head for the weekend, partying down with some fellow fans. One of them had taped the two July Amsterdam shows, so we all got a chance to hear some of the new songs and get prepared. I drove to Raleigh from Nag's Head with those two shows, as well as the night before, lingering in my head.

Pressed up against the gates, I listened to the soundcheck. I knew this would be my last show until the fall, so I wanted it to be a great one. I left a few hours later far from disappointed! I had decided to go to this show at the last minute, so I was on the lawn while my friends were all in the reserved seats. I had found a patch of grass in the front of the lawn near an awesome couple from Texas and a guy named Travis who was at his first show. Prophetically, Travis's last name was Rainwater. We talked and laughed and waited for the show to start.

Honestly, though, the first set was pretty unremarkable. The "Runaway Jim" opener was a surprising call, especially given the monster "Jim" in Raleigh during the summer of 1995. My friend Brian swears he saw Trey pour some water on his hands and rub them together, as if to "wash his hands" of that epic jam. I've heard people corroborate this story, so maybe it happened. The "Stash" was nice, and I knew that Fishman's "Footsteps" poem from the *Schvice* had been turned into a song. Since I thought (and still think) it was a poignant poem, I was glad to hear it. Somewhere about this time is when the rain that had been steadily falling turned into an all-out downpour.

As the band launched into "Taste," we were trying to find ways to stay dry. Travis' girlfriend had some sort of blanket, which had been stretched out over us until it was too soaked to do any good. That's when the thunder and lightning kicked in. Listen to the tapes; the crackles are unmistakable! For a moment, I thought about leaving…hell, I love Phish shows but I certainly didn't want to get electrocuted at one! The lightning crashed down on all sides of the amphitheater, and I realized that I probably had a better chance getting hit while walking to my car than I did standing with thousands of other people!

So, I started to pay attention to the "Taste" jam, and it was simply electrifying. Each crash of thunder and burst of lightning brought a frenzied scream from the crowd, which seemed to further excite the band and deepen the jam. When it ended ten minutes later, I had been hosed in both the literal and metaphoric sense.

I have to say that this is the only show I have ever seen where set break was actually fifteen minutes. Who knows, maybe the band realized how bad the weather was and wanted to finish the show before anyone got hurt. We out on the lawn didn't seem to care anymore, though. Since we were all wet and muddy to begin with, rounds of mudsliding began. It became an all-out pigpen party, and everyone was loving it.

Words can't do the second set justice. All I can do is advise you to get a tape and listen for yourself. The "Disease" starts out really shaky but the set from there is basically flawless. The segue from "Disease" into "Mike's" is perhaps the best, most fluid, most inventive segue the band has ever pulled off. The "Hydrogen" was a treat, and the "Weekapaug" was an all-out dancefest in the mud.

I was excited to hear "When the Circus Comes," and thought it was a sweet way to bring us back to earth after an ethereal show. Little did I realize that we'd get a "Harry Hood" after it to cap an excellent set! Personally, I say get the second set at any cost and have someone throw on the first-set "Taste" as filler. And, if you've got good ears and want goose bumps, pay close attention to the roar of the crowd as they realize that the band is about to break into "Mike's" from "Disease." If you listen closely, you can hear me…cold, wet, tired, and loving every second of it.

7/23/97 Lakewood Amphitheater, Atlanta, GA.—Jeff Leiker

This show was my first of Summer Tour '97. I had not heard any of the previous Europe tour, quite by design; I wanted to hear the new material for the first time live. It was a beautiful day, the sun was out, and there were few clouds in the sky, making the weatherman's prediction of rain look dubious. As always, Lakewood's security force kept to themselves, were courteous to the fans, and even stopped to chat once in a while. As showtime approached and dusk began to creep up on the southern skies, we headed in to grab some nice lawn seats. The sky was beginning to cloud up, but everyone seemed quite energized with anticipation. Apparently the two previous shows had been exceptional.

"Julius" began the set, which was strange to me because my last show (the previous fall) also opened with "Julius." This was a landmark version in my mind. A twelve-minute rocker, no psychedelic side trips, no messing around, just to-the-point, hardcore rock-n-roll. "Dirt" was the first new one for me, a nice song I thought, very catchy and with a great musical backdrop. "NICU" was a live first for me, and we all know what our first "NICU" is like. What a blast of energy. "Dogs Stole Things" was my next new song, it didn't strike me as anything special, just a straight-up funky blues number, well played, but nothing that really shocked the soul. "Ginseng" was well played, with good placement. This set was carrying great continuity even through its many musical style changes. When they finished "Water in the Sky," I was ready for something special. I have never been too thrilled with the old "Water" arrangement even though I loved the lyrics.

"Limb by Limb" really made me step back and listen. This song was the one that got my body movin' and my eyes closed for most of the rest of the set. I loved it from the get-go. The chorus, the complex rhythm, the lyrics which seem to be the epitome of Tom Marshall's style…everything drew me into the song. The "SOAMelt" that followed is one of my all-time favorites. It starts off in the standard way, and the jam even starts off fairly regular, but at about eight minutes in or so, Trey rips into this distorted, Frampton-esque guitar line. It is dark and brooding and just plain bad-ass! "Billy Breathes" was another live first, believe it or not, and I couldn't help but notice how much better it is live than the CD version. I've been in love with this one live for quite a while now.

"Possum" really got the energy level up a notch. Trey laid into this jam like he rarely ever does. For the first time in the show he began to stalk around a bit and do all his little rock-star things like the lunges and little leg kicks. At the conclusion of this raging "Possum," the crowd was in a frenzy and the band left the stage knowing they were on the verge of something special.

For weeks previous to leaving for tour we had been talking about songs we wanted to see live for the first time. "NICU" had been one of those, but the song that always seemed to come up in our conversations was "PYITE." Well, not only did we get it, we got it to open up the second set; a set coming on the heels of one of the most energized jams I had ever seen. Needless to say, this was the best version I've heard to date, a statement I'll stake my reputation on. "Ghost" began—we knew it was called "Ghost" from all the word of mouth, but it was new to my ears. At about three minutes in, I was already lost and dancing, oblivious to the world around me. At about ten minutes I realized that Mike was thundering through a nasty bass line, and Page was just warming up. This monster twitched and twisted and left a wake of destruction in its path, the likes of which I have never heard in any other Phish jam…ever. As Page brought in the clavinet, the energy was shooting out from the stage like a fire hose. Trey picked it up a notch at about thirteen minutes, and Mike followed suit. The snowball was rolling down at a faster rate, and Trey gave it a big shove from behind.

"Isn't it Funny How Everything Works Out When it Comes to Phish?"

Steve Cunningham, Newark, DE

The Great Went. That's where we were headed. After seeing a great show at Darien, NY, we decided after a brief discussion and a consultation with our handy Rand-McNally Atlas that the best route to get to Limestone, ME was through Canada. Most of the others that were making the trek to the Went were opting for the obviously safer route through the U.S.

Mike and I had left Darien several hours before and had put several hundred miles on the van. I was at the wheel at about noon when the trouble began. We had left Darien about eleven hours before, and I was just about at the end of my driving shift before Mike would take over and lead us on into the Went. I don't know if you are familiar with Quebec Autoroute 20, but it is not too friendly. There's not much English to be seen (well, there's not really much of anything). We were about twenty-five miles east of Quebec when the battery light on the van started to flicker.

"That's funny," I said to Mike. "The alternator light is on."

Sleeping in the back, he simply replied, "just keep an eye on it."

"Okay, no problem."

About an hour later, after Mike had taken over the driving, it was obvious that the alternator was not going to get us to Maine. As the charge slowly slipped from the battery, we weighed our options.

"Why don't we try and limp on into the campground and deal with it on Monday morning?" I said. The important thing to realize is that we had no more than fifty miles left to drive. This is after driving several hundred from Darien, New York.

"I don't know if we'll make it that far."

The next alternative that we saw was to stop at the next town and see if we could get a quick repair job. Another ten miles down the road was Edmundston, New Brunswick. As we pulled into town it became obvious that the van was about to die. We pulled into the first gas station that we saw, but they did not have a repair shop. The woman behind the counter told us to try the tire repair shop down the street, they used to work on Volkswagens.

We limped the two hundred yards to the tire shop, and as soon as we pulled into the lot the engine died. It wouldn't be started again until there was a new alternator installed, the manager informed us. He went to see how long it would take to order one and have it shipped.

"You fellows are going to be here until Tuesday at the earliest."

Shit. I honestly felt my entire heart sink. The first notes at the Went were to be played in about twenty-four hours, and this guy is telling me that I'm going to be here for another four days? We went on and explained our situation and he said that he would make a few calls and see what he could do. After an hour of waiting (and becoming increasingly aware that I was going to miss the cornerstone to my summer), he came back with some good news.

As it turns out, the alternator that is used in an '86 Vanagon is the same as the one used in a Jetta of the same year. Also as it turns out, a friend of his had an old Jetta junker sitting around.

"The alternator will be here tomorrow morning."

He told us that there was a campground down the road where we could crash for the night. He wasn't too sure if the van would start in the morning, so he would come by and jump us if need be.

Much relieved, Mike and I headed off to the campground. After making a quick stop to get a case of beer, we settled into our new home for the next eighteen hours. In case you didn't notice, that night was extremely cold for the middle of August. We lit a campfire and talked to the friendly fellow from Ottawa next to us for a few hours before turning in for the night.

At 8 AM, right on schedule, the repair guy came to check on us. As it turned out, the battery had enough juice to start the engine and get us back to the repair shop. Mike and I were quite anxious as the repairs were being made. The campground at the Great Went was undoubtedly bustling with activity at this time, and here we were, broke down in another country, just fifty miles away.

Around eleven, the van was finished. The one thing that we hadn't counted on was paying for the repairs. The total bill came to $75 (pretty cheap for an alternator), but the shop would not accept U.S. dollars. We quickly counted what Canadian currency we had remaining. We were still a few dollars short.

"Just give me what you have there, I've already cut you a big break on the price."

Thankfully, we eagerly handed over what we had left.

Back on the road again, eighteen hours after we broke down. About two hours later (and a *thorough* search by U.S. customs officials) we pulled into the campground. Next to us pulled in a van from Oregon, who also had to stop and get repairs twice on its long journey. They had just barely made it in time, as did we. One of the fellows who was camping in that van pretty much summed up the whole weekend experience with one sentence:

"Isn't it funny how everything works out when it comes to Phish?"

Yeah. It sure is.

He was starting to stalk around the stage again, his riffs getting thicker with each passing minute. I kept feeling like they had hit the peak of the jam, only to realize they were just teasing us. It repeated over and over until at about twenty minutes in, they had hit the most intense, raging, smacking-us-around-and-calling-us-Suzie peak that they had ever achieved. Trey was jumping up and down! As the peak leveled off and I drifted back to Earth, Page led them through a post-apocalyptic, spacey jam that seemed to be a thousand stories all being told. I finally knew what "Story of the Ghost" was about. I could hear all these voices coming from the stage, all lamenting their passing...amazing. "Sam-

ple" followed in strong fashion, clear and concisely played, following the pattern of the show.

"Sample" was followed by a very long break before the boys treated us to my personal favorite, "YEM." As always, it was beautifully performed and spotless throughout the composed section. However, the jam took a weird turn as it slowed down to what I thought signaled an early beginning to the vocal jam. Instead, Trey initiated a sort of Russian folk jam, similar to the klezmer "Mule Duel," but a different melody. This was indeed the most ingenious version of "YEM" I had ever heard, and the band delved further, returning with a sped-up "WUDMTF" over the folk jam instead of returning to it during the vocal jam. As the jam ended, they segued interestingly into a first-time cover; "Rocky Mountain Way." Following that, "Chalk Dust" exploded out of the mix. Trey insisted on ending the vocals short so that he could get a head start on the jams. The rock-star thing was in full bloom here, as Trey was jumping around, lunging back and forth, basically going nuts on his guitar. It was awe-inspiring to see him that energized by a song that frankly has become stale. As he finished, he took off his guitar and played the feedback a bit before setting it on the ground, stepping back, and giving a big hand motion towards it to Fishman's interjection of, "Pépé LePew!" (a reference to the shirt Trey was wearing). "Frankenstein" ended the show on a strong note, simply following the pattern set before them by that second set.

My view on this show is that it was the most cleanly played show I've ever heard. There simply were no screw-ups. The timing was there, the notes were clear, the vocals were on, and the jams were all-out ragers with the exception of "SOAMelt," which was more heady and psychedelic. What makes this show brilliant is the "Ghost." This "Ghost," to me, is the finest piece of improvisation the band had played to date. It did follow the fairly standard tension-release pattern, but was so well conceived and consistent from start to finish that it has no equal. In addition to the musical feats of the band, I felt that this was a very "happy" show. There were so many shining, smiling faces around me. The energy level was way above average, and during the second set, I would classify it as "fever pitch." Since that fateful July night, I have made a commitment to see every show Phish ever plays in Atlanta, a vow I have kept since.

7/30/97 Ventura County Fairground, Ventura, CA—Cory Ferber

There's some good points, and some bad points." I wanted to see a show at the Ventura County Fairgrounds because it was common stomping ground for the Grateful Dead. We were doing the entire tour, and this was one of the mellowest scenes. The energy felt very different from an East Coast show, with a crowd consisting of a much wider age range.

The fairgrounds are a track around a dirt field, which is not very popular with some fans. The stage was on the north side, while a large bleacher stand was on the south side. The stage was a simple platform with speaker stacks on both ends. There was no backdrop to the stage which is what makes the fairgrounds so special. Behind the stage is a breathtaking view of the mountains, with scattered trees in the foreground.

I decided to sit in the bleachers for this show, one of the best decisions I made all tour! Sitting near the top of the bleachers was a surreal experience. Not only could I enjoy the band in the lap of the mountains, I could look to the west and see a view of the Pacific Ocean! Watching the sun set over the beach and water during a Phish show is a very happy

memory. The exhilaration of the venue's natural beauty was even beyond my Red Rocks experience in '96.

Reaching California turned out to be a major celebration for those of us on the bus who had traveled from the tour-opening show in Virginia Beach, VA. We had traveled from the Atlantic to the Pacific in only nine days! The band even rewarded us with the old-school cover of the Talking Heads' "Cities," sandwiched inside a warm and juicy "David Bowie." They had been playing "Cities" in Europe on the last two tours, but this was the first U.S. "Cities" in three years. Other tasty treats included the tour premieres of "Weigh" and Jimi Hendrix's "Fire."

8/6/97 Riverport Amphitheater, Maryland Heights, MO —Saul E. Wertheimer

The first set opened nicely with "NICU". This was only the second time they had ever opened with "NICU", the first being earlier this tour. The "Stash" was solid, but it was nothing outstanding. It doesn't hold a candle to 12/11/95 Portland, ME, for example.

"Beauty of My Dreams" was fun to hear for the first time; it's similar to "Uncle Pen." I really enjoyed "Twist Around." I thought that the jam had a very psychedelic feeling to it, much like Crosby, Stills, Nash & Young tunes have. It segued into "2001," which was a monster of a version. As usual, Chris was dead-on with the lights, but the boys really jammed it out. "2001" is no longer an intro, it is now a full-fledged song. Trey teased a James Brown lick, à la 11/30/96 Sacramento, but I prefer this "2001." "Bag" was all right, but very mellow—good, but not great. "Ya Mar" was also good. Leo (Page) took a nice solo as usual. "YEM" at seventy minutes into the set, and it was great! Both of Trey's attempts at the "Note" were strong, with Trey sustaining very well on the second "Note." The jam segment was different from any other "YEM" jam that I am familiar with. Trey raged for a while, but the bass and drums section stood out. Mike had some weird effect on his bass, because it sounded like we were in outer space. This jam was remarkable!

On to the second set…I had gotten the "Runaway Jim" vibe the day before the show, and I had predicted that it would open the first set. Well, I was one set off. As soon as they started it, I was reminded of the "Jim"->"My Soul" from earlier this tour, and I wondered if they would repeat the segue. They did, but I was certainly not prepared for the monstrosity of this jam. The jam developed into a blues jam, based on the chords to and in the key of "My Soul." This was such a serious "My Soul" jam that I didn't think they would even bother to sing the lyrics! They finally went full-on into "My Soul," and it was a rocker. Very energetic, and very enjoyable! I cannot get over how hot the "Jim" was…it was outstanding, monstrous, fantastic!

I had been personally told that I would really like "Ghost," seeing as how I love the Funk. I've always known that Phish has it in them, but I am so glad to see that they are finally taking advantage of it! "Ghost" is an incredible song. It was probably about twenty minutes long. Mike was laying down a phat bass line the whole time, and I swear, if there had only been a disco ball in Riverport….At the end of the jam, they did a "stop-time" that blew me away, kinda like in the "Weekapaug" from Vegas, 12/6/96. This song is essentially a vehicle for jamming, and I expect that we will be treated to many different and astounding versions of it.

The "Ghost" was so damn good that I even enjoyed the "Caspian!" I really don't like this song, but I enjoyed it on this night. I sat down and laughed most of the time. It just seemed kind of funny that

Phish was following up the last thirty to forty minutes of incredible jamming with "Caspian." The "Cars Trucks and Buses" was fun, and at times reminded me of Jimmy Smith. "Sample" was probably the lowlight of the show for me. I didn't enjoy it at all. "Antelope" set closerset-closer—oh boy! Remember 8/2/93 Tampa? Well forget it! This one blows it away. With the quality of jamming in the recent past, I think I am starting to forget that August '93 ever happened. This "Antelope" was out of control. Right before they segued into a "Makisupa"-esque jam. Anyway, this "Antelope" must be heard to be believed.

The "Julius" encore was the best I've heard. I swear that ever since 10/24/95 Madison, each successive "Julius" that I hear is better than the last one. This one was probably about ten to twelve minutes and was on fire, and put a finishing touch on a tremendous show.

8/10/97 Deer Creek Music Center, Noblesville, IN
—James Raras, Jr.

In a stellar U.S. Summer Tour in 1997, this show remains one of my most listened to, and one of my most regretted misses (I had tickets but I didn't go). The highlight of a solid first set is "Split Open and Melt," and this version is absolutely phenomenal, containing nods to King Crimson as well as several "Third Stone from the Sun" teases. Pay close attention to the jamming just prior to the return to the ending Melt theme…unreal! This is one of my all-time favorite versions (putting the 6/11/94 Red Rocks version to shame) and any "Split" fan who hasn't heard it is missing out. A well-jammed "Hood" also closes set one. The second set opens with "Cities" and the music doesn't stop until the end of the set. The jamming out of "Cities" is particularly awe-inspiring, achieving numerous highs and lows before moving nicely into "Good Times, Bad Times." The whole set flows nicely, although the instrument switch late in the second set doesn't come across on tape very successfully. Overall, this is a very strong show and I highly recommend it.

8-10-97 Deer Creek Music Center, Noblesville, IN—Cory Ferber

Here comes the joker / we all must laugh / cause we're all in this together / and we love to take a bath." Deer Creek is more than just a concert: it's an event. This is a result of many factors, including the numerous places to camp nearby. It feels like you are camping in the middle of nowhere, while many of theses campsites are actually the private homes of kind local Noblesville residents. These camping locations themselves become the scene, with great vibes and few hassles.

The main reason the venue is held in such high esteem is the caliber of shows that have occurred here in the past. A typical Deer Creek show is never typical. I was lucky enough to see Dead play here from '91 through '94, as well as Phish's debut in '95. Inside the pavilion is the best sound, always crisp and clear. While it's great for the audience, it's also a favorite among the musicians who play here.

This is a smoking first set that tops most second sets as far as setlist. Four powerhouse jams carry the set with a rare "Bathtub Gin" opener (only the sixth time ever), "Down with Disease," "Split Open and Melt," and "Harry Hood." The "SOAM" has a large, spacey section, foreshadowing versions played in '99. The "Hood" is one of the best versions of the tour, and one of my all-time favorites. There is a point deep in the jam where Mike's bass becomes prominent, sounding moody and reflective. This mood eventually changes, and as the music converges you will be feeling good.

We were lucky enough to have second-row seats for this one, but by set break everyone had collapsed the seats of the first five rows and it became standing-room only. The set opened with the Talking Heads' "Cities," catching me off guard. We were celebrating, but most people seemed to have no idea what was going on. This song was rare (the first East Coast "Cities" in three years) and after Ventura I didn't expect to see it a second time on the tour, and certainly not as an opener.

The song starts out with a slow groove, and has a very spatial sound. As Trey develops a solo, Mike pushes the jam along. At six minutes, the song takes a turn as Mike changes the tempo and Fishman tightens up. This jam slowly becomes funkier, as Trey weaves in and out of the locked rhythm section. At eleven minutes, Trey begins to layer his guitar with a sound reminiscent of "Free."

At fourteen minutes, the jam collapses. Trey then begins to strum a beautiful rhythm pattern, one that I have subsequently heard at other shows in different songs. It is defiantly a semi-composed jam that the band is familiar with. After Trey's intro, and on cue, Mike starts up a flowing bass line and the rest of the band dive in behind him. Page begins to overlay nicely sparse chords, leading to a long beautiful piano piece over Trey's rhythm. At twenty minutes, the jam begins to peak. As Trey begins to turn up the fuzz, Fishman breaks down the beat and becomes focused on the one.

At twenty-three minutes, the one smoothly becomes the opening notes of Led Zeppelin's "Good Times, Bad Times!" The audience went crazy, and the energy in the pavilion was intense. The jam out of "GTBT" is very similar to the early jam on "Cities," again with laces of "Free." At twenty-nine minutes, Page gets up from the keyboards and takes a solo on the Theremin.

The music then turns spacey as Trey sets a delay loop on his guitar, and instigates an instrument-switch jam! In Page's absence, Trey takes over on keyboards, and Mike takes over on guitar. At thirty-three minutes, Page ends this highly experimental Theremin space jam, and takes over on bass.

Mike soon puts down the guitar and kicks Trey off the keyboards.

Great Went

Ellis Godard

Trey walks over to Fishman, ready to switch instruments. The crowd loved every minute, and the noise built in anticipation of Fishman coming to the front of the stage. But nothing happened! Fishman just kept drumming, acting as if Trey was not even there. It was bizarre, and felt like we had hit a skip in the record. This moment of Trey hovering over Fishman was stuck.

This is when I started to analyze things, mainly because I had all the time in the world. This was going to be Fishman's first time to coming to the front of the stage in the fifteen shows so far this tour. Although he had sung "Bye Bye Foot" three times, that's not a cover song with a vacuum solo! His last cover song performed in the U.S. was Syd Barrett's "Bike" on 11/7/96. Another thought was Fishman's dress. He hadn't worn it all tour. He came out on stage every night in a three-piece suit. Was he looking for respect with this new look? Was he giving up on the goofy cover songs and playing a vacuum?

It is my theory that the band instigated this instrument-switch jam in a sure attempt to get Fishman to the front of the stage. I believe he had no idea this was going to happen, and in retaliation he was contemplating not getting up from the drums. As time passed, I was able to watch the band's facial expressions closely from the front row. Page kept looking over at Mike, both looking annoyed. Their music even begins to convey this sense of annoyance.

"Where I end and you begin / I want to find that line / and cross it back and forth / until it's erased." So how would this deadlock end? Would Fishman get up and sing? What would happen if he didn't get up? How long would Trey wait, and just stand there? Eventually someone would have to give, right? I started to think about how stupid Trey might look if, after standing there all this time, he walks back over to the guitar. These were the things I was thinking about, and vocalizing to my friend. You could feel the tension growing on stage. The audience was confused.

Over seven minutes later (at forty minutes), Fishman bows down from the duel and gets up. What had just happened? My favorite aspect of this sequence is that for one brief moment, Fishman was in total control of the band with the other members at his mercy. Although they may have instigated this switch, they underestimated the ease of ambushing Fishman.

To my delight the band broke into "Rocko William;" this is the first time they played it in the U.S. Fishman picked up the guitar while Mike remained on keyboards and Page on bass. Fishman's humorous singing talents are at their best on this song, and his guitar playing is pretty funny as well. I would give anything for a photo of the band on stage during this song. For most of the song I exaggerated worshiping Fishman to help fulfill his "Johnny B. Goode" fantasy. It was so much fun!

At forty-six minutes, the song comes to a close and the opening beats of "Bowie" begin shortly. I do not remember this, but from the tapes it sounds as if Trey starts the opening drum beat of "Bowie" before handing over the sticks. This would make sense because this is where things get even more peculiar.

Fishman's (and the rest of the band's), first attempt to start the main section of "David Bowie" is purposely flubbed by Trey. I'll never forget the evil look Page gave Trey, as if to say "don't involve us in your games." The main section of "David Bowie" just happens to begin with a sequence that is started by Trey. Suddenly it was clear, Trey turned the tables on the band and now they were eating out of his hand. Fishman made a number of attempts to get the song started, but they were stuck

in the pre-"Bowie" space babble, with Trey nowhere to be found. At fifty-one minutes into the set, it appears that the song is going to start, but Trey fools them again and the music falls apart.

Over nine minutes later (at fifty-six minutes) and suspiciously a few minutes longer than Fishman's previous antics, my theory grows more evidence. In reflecting on these events over two years later, I feel even stronger about my interpretation of the events that happened at this show. Until now, I had never broken down the set by minute and I had no idea that Trey's hold up of the band was longer than Fishman's. The music before "Rocko William" and after "David Bowie" is not like normal Phish space segments. There is essentially nothing going on with the band for seventeen minutes of the set. Why would the band waste so much time on this argument in front of the audience? What statement was Fishman making by not getting up? Who was it directed at? And what was Trey's follow up all about? Was he really getting even with Fishman by outdoing him by a few minutes? Unfortunately, we will probably never have the answers to these questions.

"David Bowie" suffers as a result. Trey sounds uninspired, while Mike and Page carry the song to its end. (The set ends at seventy minutes.) This is one of my favorite songs and this version is still very disappointing. Even more frustrating is the fact that it had the potential to be a monster ending to one of the hottest shows of the year. Although I find the whole shenanigan a little disturbing now that I know they wasted seventeen minutes, at the time of the first incident I was rooting for Fishman and on cloud nine.

The "Cavern" encore seems a little fitting. I have no idea what the song means, or what anything I had just seen means. Oddly, when Trey sang, "Take care of your shoes," someone decided not to take the advice and threw a pair on stage.

8/13/97 Star Lake Amphitheater, Pittsburgh, PA—Cory Ferber

Although I attended this show, my real appreciation has come from listening to the tapes. An odd setlist, energized jams, and perfect sound quality make these tapes ones I return to again and again. Star Lake is a beautiful venue with great sound. I had been there once before in '92, where I saw the Grateful Dead play a memorable "Dark Star"->"Drumz"->"Spanish Jam"->"Other One." Since we were doing the entire Phish tour, I was looking forward to returning to this venue near the end of tour.

The show opens with a one-time version of Elton John's "Amoreena." Page's singing and playing is simply beautiful, followed by a tightly focused Trey solo. The first set is highlighted with extended jams in "Stash," "Gumbo," and the Talking Heads' "Crosseyed and Painless." On this tour "Gumbo" had a long extended jam tacked onto the end the song. This one should not be missed. The "Crosseyed" was the only one of the tour, and a big surprise in the first set. Balancing these solid jams is a bluegrass theme with "Poor Heart," "Water in the Sky," and "Beauty of My Dreams."

The second set starts off with a classic "Runaway Jim" that mixes old and new Phish styles to push the climatic boundaries of the song further. They follow this with a metamorphic "Ghost," which begins funky and turns rock. A beautiful segue occurs when Trey creeps in strands of Hendrix's "Isabella." The first tour performances of old classics "Sleeping Monkey" and "Golgi Apparatus," along with the second playing of "McGrupp," were refreshing and welcomed treats for those of us on the bus.

This show ends with another theme, a unique three-song sequence beginning with an oddly placed "2001" near the end of the set. This was followed by the lyrically zany "Golgi Apparatus," which we thought would be the last song of the second set. It ends in typical concert-ending style fashion as the band began cranking up the noise to the cheers of the crowd. Just when I thought Fishman was beginning a beat sequence to end the show, the next beat is the opening notes of "Frankenstein!" It was wild! We had gone from rock cover to old-school Phish and back to rock again.

8/14/97 Darien Lake Performing Arts Center, Darien, NY —Cory Ferber

When the circus comes to town." The DLPAC is located literally right next to Darien Lake Amusement Park. Its somewhat makeshift and has evolved over the years. Although there is a pavilion, it's unlike most amphitheaters. It's really just a big, flat field, where they laid cement and installed seats. Eventually they covered the seats with a big-top circus tent. There are uncovered lawn seats beyond the cement, all on a flat, even level.

This was essentially a hometown show for me since I was living in Rochester at the time. We had waited out at the venue for our tickets and scored fifth-row seats. The lots opened at 8 AM because of the park, so the scene began early and raged all day. This was one of the finest lot scenes all summer. Near Will Call we ran into the Further bus, the Pranksters, and Ken Kesey signing autographs near the entrance.

The first set begins with five solid jams in "Ya Mar," "Funky Bitch," "Fluffhead," "Limb by Limb," and "Free." This was only the second "Fluffhead" of the tour, and a huge crowd pleaser. I really enjoy this sequence of songs. A rare "Tela" (the first since 11/7/96) and the second "Train Song" of the tour were treats for those of us on tour. The "Antelope" set closerset-closer raged, reaching its peak over and over again.

The second set opens with a wild "Chalk Dust Torture." This song was receiving extra attention that summer, with the band pushing the jam in funky directions all tour. Mike's rendition of "Treat Me Like a Fool" reminds me too much of seeing "Tennessee Waltz" on 11/16/94.

Things begin to get interesting after a nice "Harry Hood." The ending segues into space where Trey and Mike begin trading leads in a dual solo. This leads into a lengthy freeform jam that is beautiful and much different than anything we heard all tour. The jam ends with a subtle "Colonel Forbin" tease by Trey. Fishman continues the tease, and then leads the band into the opening notes. The first "Colonel Forbin" since Halloween '96 was greeted with great enthusiasm from the crowd.

"So here we are again, standing at the base of the mountain, and this is a very different and interesting time for Colonel Forbin here," begins Trey's narration. He continues, "Colonel Forbin realizes on this particular day, he is not going to find the great and knowledgeable Icculus at all, but instead he is going to find [Trey laughs] Ken, Uncle Sam, Bozo, and E-Z-Kesey standing there." The crowd erupted when Kesey strutted on stage dressed as Uncle Sam.

Kesey's narration begins, "My heart is sorely beset because from out amongst the tidbits of these vehicles moving through the nation we have lost an important part of us. For two years no one has seen high nor heard of the bozos. For two years the bozos have been missing. Where are the bozos?" He continues an repeats the curiously interesting lines, "Well, what we heard was they were gonna try to make it here to the Phish concert. We couldn't catch them up at the Further Festi-

val so we decided to come to the Phish concert."

Kesey's then begins a *Wizard of Oz* narration and mentions that ordinarily, his brother in Oz handles finding the bozos. Phish break into what sounds like "Somewhere Over the Rainbow." Kesey welcomes his first helper to the stage to give their "Bozo Report." Out walks the Scarecrow and the band breaks into an instrumental version of "If I Only Had a Brain!" The Scarecrow quietly utters, "We know they were at the Grateful Dead concert and the rumor was they went Phishing." The crowd loved it. The next helper to be introduced was the Tin Man. Kesey and Fishman begin singing the lines "Has anyone seen the Bozos?" as the Tin Man walks out on stage. He goes on to speak a few lines, and tells us he has "a foolish heart."

The third helper to be introduced by Kesey is the Cowardly Lion. Instead of the Lion, out walks Frankenstein with his master! At the same time, the band bust into "Frankenstein!" This is a full version of the song, but the volume of the band is temporarily lowered in the middle. Kesey continues his narration and questions the master as to why he brought him Frankenstein. Kesey utters, "The Cowardly Lion was leading a paramilitary group in northern Idaho and you brought me this? Wonderful!"

At the front of the stage, Kesey and the four Pranksters began to improvise lyrics about the Bozos. The music soon changes from the ending of "Frankenstein" to an unknown funky jam. Fishman can be heard singing "Bozos on the bus," while Kesey sings "There's always room on the bus for you." I was close up enough to really make eye contact with the Pranksters. A large part of the magic for myself was being able to see these five old men dressed up as freaks singing on stage. It made me feel good. About twenty Bozo Clowns suddenly came running through the pavilion! They eventually found their way up on-stage, while Kesey, the Pranksters, and Phish continued to sing and improvise over the funky groove.

Kesey soon mentioned the magic words, "I see a bird. Out comes a bird. Could that possibly be Mockingbird? What kind of bird can it possibly be in the nest when the Pranksters sing? I know it. I see it. I hear it. It's a Mockingbird." The Pranksters then float offstage, and Trey remarks, "See what happens if you take too much acid thirty years later."

Trey goes on to say, "So we're supposed to start the 'Famous Mockingbird' now, but the funk is too deep. We can't stop!" The crowd was ecstatic. The band continues to jam, and then smoothly slides into the opening notes of a rare "Camel Walk," only the third time played since '89! It sounds as if they may have been jamming on "Camel Walk" the entire time.

The show closes with a nice "Taste" that begins with Page flying up and down the piano. I listened to the double-encore "Bouncin'" and "Rocky Top" from the parking lot because we wanted to get a jump on the traffic up to the Great Went. I highly recommend listening to this historic show on tape. Although they can't match the magic of being there, the music is still rewarding and fun.

8/14/97 Darien Lake Performing Arts Center, Darien, NY —Jeremy Welsh

My brother Josh, my friend Brian Zelizo, and I drove up from Pittsburgh that morning, through Erie (saying hi to relatives and dropping a car off), on our way to a theme park outside of Buffalo, NY. The night before, at Star Lake, Phish played a nice show, opening with the only "Amoreena" ever, a great "Gumbo" jam into the only "Horse"-

"Phishin' For Meaning at the Great Went"

Pamela Chodosh, Norway, ME

I've been trying to write about the Phish concert for days now," I tell my son on the phone, weeks after our trip to Limestone. "I just can't seem to get it all into one essay. It's not a five hundred word story. I've written about the crowds, how hard it was to find people, how amazing the scene was, the street vendors, the miles of pitched tents and parked vehicles, and the huge numbers of people milling around everywhere you looked. I've even tried to write about what happened on the last night."

"You mean during Harry Hood, when people started throwing glow sticks?" he says. "Yeah, that was really profound." He, too, remembers the rainbow of glow-in-the-dark oblong light sticks and necklace circles that suddenly flew up into the air and then down and then up again, their numbers growing until the black night that hovered with music over the heads of almost one hundred thousand people was suddenly full of multicolored arcs of light.

"So why was it so profound?" I ask him, looking for the hook I've needed. "Well, first of all it started with just a few glow sticks, maybe five or six, then more and more people started throwing them. But the incredible thing was that the people in the back saw what was happening and they began tossing their sticks up to the people in the front. They voluntarily gave up something that belonged to them. That's the kind of stuff that happens at these concerts. They were caught up in the moment. That's why we go. Yeah, that was really incredible."

"Well if you need any more details about set lists or songs, call me. Just remember," he says before he hangs up, "if you're writing about Phish, it's all about the jam."

So, it's all about the jam, I say to myself afterwards, as I wander from project to project hoping to get a clearer picture of what it is I want to say about being at the Phish concert. Jam, spontaneity, surprise, the unexpected, certainly that was why many of us had traveled all the way to Limestone, ME. That's why we were willing to camp like we were sardines laid in a can, only the can was the big air force base runway. That's why we waited patiently to funnel through the concert gates, pressed through crowds of people in order to find just the right concert spot, danced in place, shoulder to shoulder with our neighbors when we had to, fought rain showers and full-moon crispy temperatures, wrapped in plastic garbage bags or wool blankets to stay warm, waited on neverending lines to use bathrooms that were less than adequate, maneuvered through traffic jams, waving at fellow Phish fans and even drove clear through the night in order to be able to be at this event.

Maybe my son is right. That's why I keep going back to those waves of colored light, why that moment and the feeling of being part of that moment has stayed with me all these weeks. Maybe the music is secondary to the feeling of being there in that place along with all of the other people, being part of the same event. Maybe bound by the experience, no matter what its details, is why we go to any show.

I flash back to the minutes just after the music and the light show ended, when I am standing next to my son. "Was that planned?" I am asking, him. I, myself am still caught in the afterglow of what has just happened. "No that was totally spontaneous," he says with a big broad smile. "That's the euphoria I was telling you about. This is why I've been to seventeen shows. That's why I go to see Phish." His face is as light as if he too were a colored meteor shower glow-in-the-dark stick, having sailed through the moonlit sky.

>"Silent" of the tour, "Crosseyed"->"Wilson" with the "Little Drummer Boy," and "Ghost"->"Isabella." A really fun show.

I wasn't really expecting much out of the Darien Lake show, since it was the last show before the Great Went. I was thinking that the band was going to play some throwaway songs to set themselves up for six sets of strong music with no repeats. But it was a gorgeous day as we drove along, listening to some tapes from earlier that summer in Europe (thanks to Charlie D.), playing "Piper" and "Limb by Limb" for the first time for Brian. Josh and I didn't have tickets, but we weren't too worried, thinking we could snag some there.

When we arrived at the venue, we realized we had some work to do. I was incredibly surprised to find that 'heads didn't want my cash; they wanted nugs or other "kind" things for their extras. But I had lots of cash! It was kind of amazing, if you ask me. Nevertheless, Josh found a lawn seat. After a little more hunting, I actually found a nice mail-order ticket, halfway down on Fishman's side. We headed in close to showtime.

The first set included a fun "Ya Mar" opener, "Fluffhead," a "Limb by Limb"—new for all of our ears, a beautiful "Tela," and to close, a rag-

ing "Antelope". This is a great version, where Trey starts and stops three or four times, building a huge tension and releasing it. They picked it up a notch at the end, and left us wondering what to expect for the next set.

After the "Chalk Dust" opener, they played two songs for Elvis: "Treat Me Like a Fool," and "Elvis' favorite Phish song", "Sparkle." Now is where the weirdness and surprises started. They broke out into "Harry Hood," which caused a huge smile to cross my brother's face. This otherwise normal "Hood" went into a little five-minute jam at the end. Very cool. After the show, some were guessing it was "Blow Wind Blow," but I think it was just a jam all to itself. The jam flowed into "Colonel Forbin's Ascent." As Trey began the story, he said it began just like all of the other stories, except this one was a little different.

That was a definite understatement! Trey introduced Uncle Ken "Easy Greazy" Kesey, and that is where reality stopped. Ken Kesey and His Merry Pranksters (The Bozos!) proceeded to turn Darien Lake on its head. "The Wind doesn't blow—it sucks!" Costumed Birdmen walked through the crowd, midgets and monsters walked the stage (including Frankenstein with accompaniment by the band), all while Phish tried to play along. When they weren't laughing they were playing a low,

funky sort of beat. I couldn't stop laughing myself.

That was surprise number one that night. It really shouldn't have been a surprise though: Ken and his Krewe were making their way east from Cleveland, after the Further bus was "inducted" into the Rock and Roll Hall of Fame. The bus stopped in Erie, and made their way to Darien that afternoon. We could actually see the bus from our seats behind the stage.

As for surprise number two, well, that came as Ken left the stage. Phish's groove started to pick up a little, getting louder and funkier, as Trey started his story back up again. He started talking about going to find the Mockingbird that Ken helped them find, but he realized they couldn't, because "the Funk was too thick!" With that, the band launched into "Camel Walk." I lost it right then and there, listening to one of only three or four "Camel Walks" since the early '90s. Wasn't really a throwaway show after all, eh?

8/16–17/97 The Great Went, Loring Air Force Base, Limestone, ME—David Steinberg

There are four kinds of legendary concerts. There are shows that are renowned for their locale (e.g. Red Rocks or The Gorge), shows that get high praise for being a special event (Halloween or NYE), shows that are exalted for the band's great playing, and the ever-popular great-looking setlist shows. If a show has two or three of these things going for it, it will be remembered forever. The Great Went was the extremely rare show that was legendary in every category.

I first knew that this was a bigger deal for Limestone than the Clifford Ball was for Plattsburgh. There were people parked on overpasses, looking on I-95, watching cars drive by below. Getting off of 95 in Houlton, I stopped in a gas station to see how people were handling the chaos. Everyone seemed to be having fun and enjoying themselves. I bought an ice cream bar and was told that it would take me four and a half hours to get there. That was a lie…by nearly an entire hour.

The first five miles of the drive went great (you know that I had to use the pun somewhere in this review), but then I was stopped. After about five minutes I got bored of sitting there and decided that it was time for auto tag. I got out of the car, ran to the one behind me, hit the hood and said, "Tag. You're it." I then looked in the car. It wasn't filled with Phish fans; rather it was a local mom with her kids. Beet red, I walked back to my car. About two minutes later, still stopped, one of the kids came up to my car, hit it and told me that I was it.

During the next half-hour, while we sat parked by the ironic "Reduced Speed Ahead" sign, I told the family about Phish. I played some tapes for them, and ended up giving them my spare copy of 12/31/96 III and a "Mockingbird" flyer. They gave me their address for tapes. However, I lost that sheet of paper. So guys, if you're reading this, I didn't mean to blow you off.

Traffic finally cleared up a bit and we were able to drive. Going through small town after small town watching the locals sitting in their yards and waving was amazing. I felt that we really were part of the show this time and it was our obligation to perform our tasks properly. The vendors had better have their best veggie burritos and T-shirts, the spinners must spin elegantly, the tapers should produce only A-1 quality tapes, and my timings would have to be perfect.

After an eternity of driving (I had flown into Boston that morning), being able to pick up Went Radio was a relief. I had been listening to the local station that had decided to play all Phish studio albums in

Great Went

shuffle play commercial-free all weekend, but it was getting old; hearing "Fluffhead" stop right before "Fluff's Travels" could begin was amusing though. On Went Radio, Mike revealed that he was singing "Ginseng Sullivan" wrong all these years. Did they fix the version they would play the next afternoon? Umm…no.

There was but one unfortunate occurrence at the Went, and that happened the first night. It rained. Hard. As a result there was a lot of mud throughout the next two days. I ruined a pair of shoes when I misjudged the wisdom of taking a shortcut. Other than that, and the expected high price of food…and the lack of portapotties, I had no complaints about the venue.

I went into the show early the first night to explore the Went Village. It was a lot more surreal than the Clifford Ball's village. The centerpiece was a station wagon, loaded down with suitcases, the Went's logo. The buildings included a free art booth, a bubble house (with mountains of soap bubbles), and a demolition derby between remote-controlled tiny household appliances. I was not the only one wandering the village—I ran into Mike doing the same. I couldn't believe that. Even with seventy-five thousand fans there, the band was still trying to hang out.

Outside of the village, there were other attractions. There was a corn maze with a castle in the middle. However, the corn wasn't quite high enough to make it interesting. There was the portapotty pavilion with a bathtub in the center. All in all, it appeared that they had outdone themselves again.

Around 4 PM, though, it appeared that my body wasn't going to cooperate. Sharp pains through my stomach suddenly appeared. I thought about the first-aid tent, but then I would miss part of the show. Fortunately, right before the show the pain went away. I didn't know it at the time, but this is the second time I had a kidney stone attack at a Phish show. Upon reflection, the thought of trying to get to a hospital from the middle of the show area is quite scary.

Allegedly at exactly 4:20, the band came on and opened with "Makisupa." If I had noticed the time I would have been quite amused. As it was, my amusement began when the jam segued into the end of "Harpua." No more would Phish be chastised for not finishing the Clifford Ball version; there just were a lot of songs played in the middle. "Chalk Dust" followed, at which point we were told that those songs were just the soundcheck (due to the lack of a formal one, allegedly due to a delay in the transit of the equipment from Darien).

Apparently they meant it. With the first three songs, this set lasted close to two hours. Most likely this was the longest set they ever played outside of some one-set shows (and 12/30/97, which was up there as well). While the length was impressive, it's the jams that are the thing. We would get those soon.

Second set opened with "Wolfman's." Earlier this summer I had foolishly assumed that the Gorge "Wolfman's" was the best that they ever had played or ever would play. They were just warming up. This version has an amazing jam that eventually evolves into "Simple." Hmmmm…back-to-back jam songs…that works for me. The "Simple" jam had a long "Odd Couple Theme" tease. The transition between that and the "My Soul" intro was seamless. This is a beautiful segue. I know everyone hates this song, but I sure can't figure out why. I thought it just rocked. They came to a full stop and then started playing a jam that sounded like it was written by Snow White after being up for a week straight. Okay what's next? "Slave?!" No way! Finally they had to try to restore some sanity, but it was too late. It just wasn't meant for them to play a normal song this set; Mike couldn't remember any of the lines of "Rocky Top." Trey added to the amusement by loudly correcting Mike.

The third set has to be a letdown after that, right? Apparently not. The first "Halley's" since the Clifford Ball was to be our opener. This is a unique version of "Halley's Comet." The jam started out like the usual quick jam, but it kept going and going. It took an angry, almost heavy-metal turn that easily could have segued into "BBFCFM." Instead they invented a little vocal reprise, singing "I'm going down, to the central part of town." A happy little jam came out of this that slowed down and funked down until I suddenly realized I was going to get my first "Cities." Never mind the *Slip Stitch and Pass* version. This "Cities" just completely destroys it, not to mention Trey's humorous lyrical substitution of "Fishman sleeps, sleeps in the daytime" and showing us where the "dry ice factory" was, by pointing out into the nothingness to the side of the stage. The funk went on and on until the jam started getting faster and faster and suddenly was "Llama." At the time I thought this might have been the most exciting half-hour I had seen Phish perform. I had no idea how wrong that would be in a mere twenty-four hours.

Even before it started, the second show had an advantage over the first night. Now that the storm was gone, the clothesline was hung. This much-larger-than-life clothing flapped in the breeze (the bra got special attention from the crowd), as the show opened. While no one expected "The Wedge," it made sense after the fact. "…Limestone blocks so large," after all. The arrangement was much closer to the *Rift* version than the one I had seen at Red Rocks. Alas, that was about it for the first set, other than the interesting "Tweezer". Perhaps the first night would be the better of the two. It was at the Ball.

Then again, perhaps not. What to say about this second set. I'm actually nervous writing this review, feeling tempted to just say to listen to the tapes. The "DWD"->"Bathtub Gin" was simply amazing, much better than my meager writing skills could convey. Sure it had the funk common to all of Summer summer '97, but so much more. During "Bathtub Gin," Trey hits this groove and runs with it. It builds and builds and builds until you think you are about to explode with joy. If you notice a weird form in the jam around twenty-four minutes into the "Disease," that's because Jon and Page left their instruments to spray paint on little pieces of wood—similar to the pieces of wood for us to paint in the free art area.

The "Bathtub" led into "Uncle Pen" to give us a chance to reflect and try to assimilate what had gone before. One had to be able to assimilate quickly, because the next song was "2001" and it was a monster version. This is perhaps the definitive Summer '97 song. The funk went on and on. For a bit there Mike and Trey got their chance to spray paint (I liked Mike's the best of the four) and then came back. After nearly twenty-three minutes (!), Trey explained the point of the painting. All of our painted wood had been gathered together in a big structure. They were going to add theirs on top to make it a combined work between us and them. As the wood was passed toward the sculpture on the extreme right-hand side of the field, they played a little jam that some people have taken to calling "Art Jam." If you don't call it a different song, the "2001" clocks at nearly thirty-three minutes, putting it just behind the 12/29/94 "Bowie" for the longest song I have seen.

The art was passed to the sculpture, putting an end to perhaps the best set of live music I have ever seen. Well that's what we thought… until they fired up "Harry Hood." That was it, you should have seen the smiles. During the "Hood" jam, Trey asked Chris to turn off the lights, à la the Gorge. I don't know who was in charge of the video screens, but he or she was making it appear like there were multiple moons in the sky and had them chasing each other. During this jam, a new "Hood" tradition was born. Glowsticks suddenly started flying through the sky. It was beautiful. I know some people don't like the glowstick war and I understand why, but it does put on a good show. The "Hood" came to an end, Trey told us that he liked the glowsticks and we should go get more. We looked around and screamed "And we get another set of this!"

While the raw stats on this set are impressive enough (five songs, ninety-four minutes and fifty-four seconds; excluding the "Uncle Pen" makes four songs, 90:35), it is far from the only measure of this set. The playing was stunning throughout. Only the "Art Jam" doesn't hold up on tape. And when you throw in the painting, the speech about making art together, the moon, the glowsticks, you've got easily the best set I have seen in ages, if not ever. I don't know when I've ever been as happy as I was during the break.

Hopes ran high for the third set, but the band was effectively done for the night and understandably so. We got a cool setlist with the first "Buffalo Bill" since 12/31/94 being followed by the rarities "NICU", "Weigh," and "Guyute." The most surprising moment though came during "Scent." Instead of the usual dueling solos jam, they played almost a "Mind Left Body" theme. A sweet "Prince Caspian" closed the set, and the weekend was almost over.

Phish seem to have this thing now with ending their air force base festivals with controversy. Last year had the unfinished "Harpua." This year had a two-song encore. "Circus Comes to Town" is a good song no matter what the naysayers complain about. During the "Tweezer Reprise" that followed, a giant match was suddenly revealed next to our art. It caught on fire and slowly descended toward the sculpture. Our art burned while Phish fiddled.

Afterwards I heard a lot of theories as to why they did it. A lot of people were just pissed. "They made this big deal about this being what we could accomplish with them and they torched it." Others saw it as a prankster-esque gesture or as a way of celebrating the spontaneity of their jams. Still others were practical. Where could you store a huge tower of painted wood.

My theory is different. Once again Phish have created a moment that no one who was there would ever forget. They did it with the hot dog, they did it with the "DWD" in the sea of balloons, and they did it

with the match. As I walked out the venue (to the strains of "Disco Inferno") and towards the traffic jam to come, I knew that I would never forget this weekend. I think the sheer length of this review attests to that.

11/19/97 Assembly Hall, Champaign, IL—Saul E. Wertheimer

This show opened with a nice, although fairly standard for '97, "Julius." It was a good version, but nothing special. I was happy to hear "Gin" follow this, because who can complain about a "Gin" in the first set! This version was longer and better than the version from 8/10/97 Deer Creek. This "Gin" was well jammed, although it doesn't compare favorably to the best first-set "Gin" of all time, 7/21/97 Virginia Beach. Nevertheless, it was a great version.

The segue into "Llama" was led by Trey. "Llama" was fiery, but the crowd was so loud that I could barely hear Trey's peaks. Assembly Hall does not win the award for being the best-sounding venue I've ever been to.

On the drive down to Champaign, I was talking about how I didn't like "Fee." So naturally, they played it, and I deserved it. The coda to "Fee" segued into "Antelope". This "Antelope" was hot, although clearly not in the realm of Madison 10/24/95 (in my opinion the mother of all "Antelopes"), 11/2/96 West Palm Beach, or the "Antelope" from St. Louis 8/6/97, with the "Makisupa" jam. It was a solid first set with some excellent jamming, which was soon to be forgotten in light of the second set.

Also "Sprach Zarathustra" ("2001") is one of my favorites. If I go more than three days without hearing it, I run the risk of going postal. This version was excellent, although I prefer the 8/6/97 St. Louis version, probably because Trey played some James Brown licks in that one. This song never ceases to put a big grin on my face. I really enjoy watching people who are "Knee Deep in the Funk." This "Also Sprach" clocks in at seventeen minutes. Unfortunately, despite the funk, there is one negative point to this "Also Sprach": Trey missed one of the peaks! I have never heard him do this before, and needless to say, I was quite surprised (and slightly disappointed).

"Wolfman's" was up next. I expected some nice jamming, but I wasn't prepared for something like this! The jam that came out of "Wolfman's" is must-hear improvisation. This is probably some of the finest jamming I have been fortunate enough to have witnessed Phish perform. The jam was long, with numerous valleys and peaks. The "Wolfman's" jam contained some explicit "Crosseyed and Painless" jamming, which at the time sounded more like "Third Stone from the Sun" to me. Listening to the tapes, it is definitely "Crosseyed and Painless." During this jam, the band sounded as much like One as I have ever heard them—not four mortals, but one Entity, capable of doing anything with their instruments. It brought joy to my being. This, undoubtedly, was some mind-numbing "Hose." This "Also Sprach"> "Wolfman's" takes up one entire side of a ninety-minute tape!

"Makisupa" segued out of "Wolfman's," and it was a standard version, up until a portion of the song that I felt compelled to label in my setlist book as "Space Jam." The only thing I can think of that comes even remotely close to serving as a just comparison to this "Space" is the jam that comes out of the "Theme" from 6/22/95 Finger Lakes, especially the minute prior to the segue into "Tweezer." The one word that best sums it up is stunning. My jaw dropped as the "Space" segued back into "Makisupa."

A marvelous "Taste" closed the set and nearly made me wet my

pants. This version was as good as my other favorite version that I've witnessed, 8/9/97 Alpine Valley. It was definitely a very satisfying end to an amazing set.

Now, of course, was the pivotal moment of the show: the encore. I've been getting sick of leaving shows with "Rocky Top" or "Sample" stuck in my head. The other fall '97 show I had seen at this point (11/13/97 Vegas) was very satisfying in this respect. The Champaign "Possum" was quite different from other "Possums," as it never really peaked. However, it was still a rollicking version, leaving me with a fine song ringing through my head as I left the venue.

11/21/97 Hampton Coliseum, Hampton, VA —Jeremy D. Goodwin

Hampton, baby, Hampton! The buzz was high in the weeks leading up to these shows. Coming on the heels of Trey's onstage claim last fall that Hampton was his "favorite room" (add that to the list of "favorite rooms"), the announcement in August of a two-night stand in this cozy, general-admission venue was greeted as a gift from Icculus by anyone who had been to this dandy Coliseum in the past. And over the weekend taboot! So, this clearly wasn't a run-of-the-mill hometown show for anyone; everyone had shown up expecting Hampton to be an event.

The drive from Washington, D.C., was pleasant and calm. I was digging in for two nights in Hampton, followed by a return to classes on Monday (during which I'd hand in a paper on common threads between Woody Allen and Ingmar Bergman), and then a trip home to Massachusetts, from which I'd accomplish the following: see Phish once in Hartford before a decadent three-day wallop of shows in Worcester, and eat a good deal of Thanksgiving turkey in between.

Upon arrival in Hampton, I was overjoyed to find my hotel to be within easy walking distance of the venue, as billed. The lobby of the Holiday Inn was packed with heads checking in late Friday afternoon, and I found that my room was right in the heart of the cluster of hotels

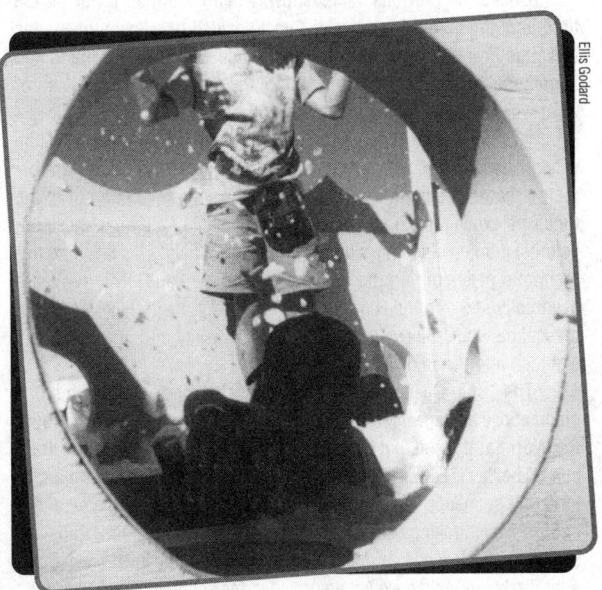

Great Went

segues showed that the band was feeling lively and in a special mood.

"Chalk Dust" was wonderful in light of all past versions: thick, dark, and pleasing. It was nothing outrageous, but very satisfying to my ears. This song has gone from a throwaway to a small treat, in my opinion. "Caspian" was unfinished; during the slow-down at the end, Trey left a ringing chord on delay (like at the end of 12/31/95 New York, set II), and we never got the cheesified hard-rock ending.

Was this the first second-set "Ghost" opener? Definitely the first U.S. one, at least. This "Ghost" was very different from the summer versions. It was not the typical funky, textural playing that marks the least interesting of the '97 jams. Rather, after a brief foray into such jamming, it fell into a quieter, darker mode, propelled by Trey's gravelly soloing, before morphing into an out-of-nowhere segue into "AC/DC Bag." Overall, the "Ghost" was interesting as a stylistic departure and as an opener, but was a throwaway in light of what was to come that night. The jam out of "AC/DC Bag" might have been the best jam I saw all week, and it clearly ranks among the best I've seen personally. After the usual shift to double-time, Trey kept soloing faster and faster until he was no longer in time with the band. Finally, Fishman is the only one who's really playing "Bag," before even he gives up the ghost. Thus, the "Bag" jam melded into improvisation before it could be completed. There was a definite point at which it sneaked out of the "Bag" jam and became pure, unregulated improvisation, and I still get chills when I hear that moment on tape. It was quite stunning and unexpected.

This long jam had many highlights. There was a touch of "Drowned"-like jamming, and The "Real Me" was hinted at briefly. Other teases/near-segues included "Lizards", "Llama," and at one point Fishman was clearly playing the drum part to "Rocko William." Thankfully, there was no instrument switch. This jam picked up where "Emotional Rescue" left off, but it provided more extended peaks and all-around spellbinding jamming. In the midst of this jam I was jumping up and down, amazed to be hearing such exciting improvisation out of a song that had never featured it before. I was convinced at the time that I was hearing some of my favorite Phish, ever…and it was only the beginning of the week.

This was in the days when we still expected to hear major jams only out of the usual list of "jam songs"…an experimental "AC/DC Bag" was just unheard of. After a glorious twenty-eight minutes, it segued smoothly into a typically well-done "Slave." Many folks have listed this among their favorite versions, but I was mainly trying to gather myself from all that had already transpired. "Loving Cup" was very powerful to close the set, moreso than my previous live encounter (at the Went) or the one that would follow later in the week, in Worcester. Trey assumed a very sexual pose during his rip-roaring solo. The energy in that place was just crackling. This is possibly the last time I've seen a "Loving Cup" totally shred a room; starting with this tour, they began playing it much more regularly and it became less of a treat. Another compelling detail was that the show opened and closed with Rolling Stones songs. The "Guyute" encore (back before that song got played into the ground) pushed things way over the top, and solidified the fact that Phish was making a real investment in the weekend.

The crowd at Hampton was fabulous, with an incredible energy level. The positivity came with good reason, of course: the band had clearly dug their heels in for a special weekend. What made it remarkable was that we were aware of how special it was, while allowing ourselves to be being swept into something like a romantic swoon. Phish was better than ever, and we were bearing witness. A part of it.

Page at Jim Pollock's booth, Great Went

Ned Beebe

that make up the Hampton Encampment. It is like a compound: five or so hotels all spilling into the same series of parking lots, basically within sight of the Coliseum itself. While walking around the lots, visiting other hotels, and hanging out in the small wooded area that is tucked in for good measure, there is a palpable feeling of being on the front lines. Frisbees fly, acoustic guitars are strummed, and people wait to see Phish make history.

Before I had time to unpack my socks, my room became a preshow party zone of unforeseen proportions. No complaints there. I would like to thank everyone who helped bring joy and goodwill to me at Hampton. I made friends that night who remain to this day.

Unlike the previous year's show, when I toughed it out on the floor about ten "rows" in front of Trey, I decided to relax in the stands this time around. We settled in on the Page side (but not the fabled Page Zone, which I wouldn't get to until the next night) for the start of what would hopefully be a great weekend.

"Emotional Rescue" was one of the musical highlights of the week. I got the name of the tune from the lyrics, and guessed (correctly) that it was probably a Rolling Stones song. The jam out of the tune was exhilarating; maybe it was the collision of circumstances but I almost jumped out of my skin a few times. The band was reaching tremendous peaks during the first tune of the weekend! This rock jam eventually slid into the Fall fall '97-mode: Trey playing like a troll on mescaline while the rest of the band was low-key and spacey. It was eighteen minutes altogether.

The "Split Open and Melt" was typically good, perhaps a small notch above average. I really thought Trey was yelling something about the Worm at the end, but it was actually a short vocal reprise of "Rescue." The "PYITE" was pretty damn tight, and it dissolved into an interesting sequence where an obviously jovial Trey played some angry chords while looking at Page, as if he was challenging him. Page answered with a few odd chords before gliding smoothly into "Lawn Boy." A similarly interesting exchange provided the segue into "Chalk Dust." Although the song choices at this point were standard, the impromptu

The next night featured an energy level that reminded a lot of people of New Year's Eve. A vigorous wave swept around and around the room before the first set. As I pointed out while happily chattering away preshow in the Page Zone, New Year's Eve has a built-in, automatic energy. The fact that a random stop on the Fall Tour schedule could whip the crowd into a New Year's-like frenzy was a testament to the special efforts of the band onstage, as well as to an appreciative fan base that knew how to enjoy great art after arriving in town for a nonstop party Friday night, with no plans to stop raging and dancing until check-out time Sunday afternoon.

One of the best things about these two-night stands in special venues is that you know the band is also having a great time along with everyone else during the afternoon in between shows. When I think back to that spectacularly sunny day in November '97, digesting the previous night's heroics over lunch at Daryl's while looking forward to another go-round in a few hours, feeling that I was in the midst of my favorite band's creative zenith to date…I think that was indeed a special time in my life and in my Phish career, a still-innocent high point that in some ways will not be surpassed.

In the Hampton Encampment after the first show, I got to visit many friends in assorted hotels, and everyone seemed to be incredibly impressed with the performance. Anticipation for Saturday night was high.

11/22/97 Hampton Coliseum, Hampton, VA—Jim Kittleman

My view from the first row, thanks to arduous waiting all night, was excellent! Discussing what a possible opener might be, trying to endure the long wait for first row, we all chuckled at my sister's vote: "Mike's Song." "Wouldn't that be funny," we all thought.

Well, not only was it funny, it was incredible. Trey started it out much slower than most, giving it a funkier feel. After the lyrics, they started the normal jam, but it was not as funky as the typical summer '97 "Mike's" had been. Mike, however, was solidly laying down the groove throughout. There was never any Type III jamming, if my memory serves me correctly, but there was a lot of Type II exploratory jamming. A spacey jam segued very nicely into "H_2," with Trey starting with the two modulating notes that Mike normally plays. "Hydrogen" was standard, but Trey and Page were really playing off each other's notes, while facing each other.

Then came "Weekapaug." It was powerful throughout, fast and loud, with solid Type I jamming. Then they stopped all together on Trey's count. Phish has gotten really good at this in my opinion. We all thought the song was over. But then out of nowhere, the band came roaring back, much funkier than before, and Trey went off, ripping a jaw-dropping, show-stopping solo. Then, they ended. Whew! The pause was very much like the pause in "Ghost," and the return to "Weekapaug" was really funky, in a "Weekapaugian" kind of way. Needless to say, this was the best show-opener that I've ever seen.

After some banter on what to play, Fish started "Hood." I was astounded by this first set, and they had only played three songs. The composed part of "Hood" was normal, played with no flubs. I must say that I hate how everybody yells "Hood!" these days after the band sings "Harry!" I really wish that had never been started. Anyway, the jam started out beautifully. Fishman kept with the light, spacey feel, as is common with the start of most "Hood" jams, by riding on his rivet cymbal. The lights complimented perfectly with the music; we were all

just floating through space. I don't remember the jam too well after that, but it seemed standard (which means beautiful, melodious jamming) and again Page and Trey really seemed to be working together nicely. They didn't end on one solid note though, which I guess is common these days, but I must say, I really like when they slam the last chord and end it abruptly, like the one on *A Live One*.

"Train Song" followed this incredible start. It mellowed the crowd out a lot, which might have prompted them to play "Billy Breathes." Throughout "Billy," I watched Mike and everyone else basically struggle with the changes, almost as if they had forgotten them. After this, Trey yelled to Fishman, "Frankenstein!" and in they went to the hard-driving Edgar Winter cover. This "Frankenstein" was really funky. That's right, funky! Trey accomplished this by using more staccato notes. Then they ripped into "Izabella." I'd never heard this live, but I couldn't really get into it that much. I was probably still reeling from the first part of the set.

Set break: Now began my quest for Destiny. The night before the show, I printed up about thirty copies of "Destiny Unbound's" first lines, along with an optional chorus. The caption under the header "Destiny Unbound" read: "A pathetic attempt to get Phish to play a song they'll never play again." Anyway, with the help of my new friend Nate (the security guard), I passed out the flyers down the first row. Screaming, trying to let everyone hear, I led everyone in a few practices of the lines, just to warm our voices up. By the way, thank you to all the eager participants (especially my "other side of first row spokesman") who helped carry out my project. I had always wanted to see what I could do with this, and it turned out really well, I thought.

So, at the beginning of the second set, after the crowd died down, all of us (I think a lot more joined in for the real thing) started chanting the lines, at different times, mind you. It was quite loud. My friend, who was sitting well above Page, said he could easily hear it. We got really astonished looks from Page, Trey, and Jon (not Mike of course), and Trey went over and said a few words to Page. Both were laughing in a "caught off guard" sort of way. Then Trey said something to the effect of, "What is that cannibalistic chant? It sounds like, Rah, ror rah oh ror rah" in his best monster voice. Then he said, "What, has human sacrifice become part of the show? Come on then, bring it up here!" Then he started stabbing downward with his guitar as if stabbing the human sacrifice. The band members were all really getting a kick out of this, but we didn't really get anything out of Mike. As good as this attempt was, Mike started singing "Halley's," seemingly unamused by our shenanigans.

I was really psyched when he started up "Halley's" though, because I really enjoyed the one at the Went. My hopes that they would jam this one out were answered tenfold. After the lyrics, Trey yelled to Mike, "Stay in F!" And thus, we entered "porno-funk" land. It did not, however, start out as funky as other songs have this past Summer Tour. It was heavy, groove-oriented Type II jamming with strong hints of Type III. Trey was ecstatic, loving every note that was being released from the stage. His movements throughout the whole show really seemed to be drug- or alcohol-induced, although more likely, musically induced. He appeared to love the jam, and slowly it evolved, although keeping the groove throughout. Little by little, it developed into a more free-flowing, melodious jam. Fishman started laying down a much slower, more flowing beat with a lot of rim shots and cymbal work and the rest followed suit. This part of the jam, definitely twenty-plus minutes, reminded me so much of the "Mike's" from 11/21/95 Winston-Salem, the

slow part with Trey's beautiful melody. If you haven't heard this jam, you really need to check it out. This "Halley's" jam was really good. It fused together the Type II jamming characteristic of, say, '94 "Tweezers", and the Type III jamming of this summer, a groove-oriented ride into funk. (I think the Type III jamming moniker should also incorporate the definition of a groove-oriented jam, not just pure funk.)

Trey then busted into "Tweezer", which I don't remember much of, unfortunately. Then, well along into the jam, Trey said something to Mike which I thought/dreamed was "Let's play Destiny" but wasn't. He then turned and spoke to Page, then to Fish. I assume he was telling them to play "Black-Eyed Katy," because on Trey's count, they all played distinctly rhythmic notes, with Fishman kind of filling in the beats where everyone else wasn't playing. (It was a really fast rhythmic pattern.) I assumed that it was "Black-Eyed Katy" and that it would be funky. Yep, it was funky. Then, they seemed to go back into "Tweezer" and ended again with a spacey fade out, but not before heavily teasing "Cities." "Piper," which I like, was very powerful. With each second, it got faster and more powerful! It seemed longer than other "Pipers" that I heard that summer.

"Antelope"! That's all I have to say. Rather, that's all they have to play to get the crowd incredibly pumped. There was such uproar when they went into the fast part after the beginning that my ears hurt. After a seemingly endless jam, which was like most "Antelopes", they brought it way down. "Rye Rye Rocco...Michael (points) Esquandolas." No reaction from Mike. After "Rye Rye," they flubbed the usual segue into the "You gotta run" part, but they managed to bring it back with even more energy when everything got organized. Trey lit up the crowd with "Set the gearshift for the high gear of your soul!" After they ended, the crowd went totally nuts. My ears were hurting from the thirteen thousand screaming fans. My ears don't normally hurt at shows, so maybe that should tell you something about the show.

This was an awesome way to end the show, and my thoughts for an encore soon enveloped my brain. Having missed the previous night's "Guyute" encore, I was hoping for something special. Although "Bouncin'" wasn't quite what I was looking for, I liked it as I always do. I think it is a really well-written song, unlike a lot of people. Then "Tweezer Reprise" blasted through the speakers, which was nice, but it unfortunately meant the end of the show. Trey was ecstatic, dancing all over the stage, just waiting for Fishman's accompaniment.

It ended an incredible show very nicely, in my opinion. The show had the most jamming I have ever heard at any one Phish concert. Even more than 12/31/95 New York, I think, if you compare the length of the show with the percentage of jamming that occurred. All in all, it was way up there in my list of the greatest that I have seen.

11/23/97 Lawrence Joel Veterans Memorial Coliseum, Winston-Salem, NC—Craig DeLucia

I arrived in Winston-Salem with my friend, Tom, about three hours before showtime. We got lost on our way to the Coliseum and wound up taking some back roads into the parking lot.

The lot scene was a lot different than most that I have experienced. I didn't see a single nitrous tank (thank goodness!). There was a great amount of fun going on, though. I bought a grilled cheese sandwich from some guys from Auburn and stopped for a minute to check out the newlywed couple that was taking in their first show as husband and wife; the groom was still wearing his tuxedo! We checked out the

drum circles and a few other musicians, as well as some bootleg T-shirts. I finally saw and met Antelope Greg, which was fun.

We didn't even try for the floor; I had a feeling that it would be way too chaotic. We settled into the section where the Greenpeace table was on Fishman's side and got ready for the show. As with most Phish concerts, I ran into some friends that I haven't seen in a while. The atmosphere was electric and the crowd was pumped. No doubt, those in attendance who weren't at Hampton had been briefed on how awesome the shows were, so everyone's expectations were high.

On to the show..."My Soul" opened up and was fun. Long solos and a good warm-up. "Theme" was next, and I will never get sick of this song. Typically great "Theme" jam, which built nicely. At the end of "Theme," during the "wall of noise," Trey walked around the stage and signaled something to Mike and Fish. Out of the dissonance they broke into this fat, groovy jam that I figured had to be "Black-Eyed Katy."

Wow! I can't say anything else about this song. I'd like to say that it has "great potential" but it is already starting to realize it! "Sparkle" followed. Even though it wasn't my first choice of a song, it kept the crowd in a frenzy. A strong, solid "Twist Around" (my first) came next. I like this song a lot; anyone else get the feeling that it would sound awesome with horns?

Here is where the set took a huge left turn. The boys broke into "Stash," but it was more like the "Stash of Death," or the "Great Black Stash." The jam was more evil and dark and brooding than anything I have ever heard this band play. They played a bit with tempos and textures but always managed to maintain a strong, evil, dark theme. At one point, they were all locked into a group-groove jam and Chris turned off all of the lights except for a real thick purple. Slowly, he threw on some bright yellow darts behind them, which pierced through the purple veil. It was at this moment that I stopped dancing, shook my head, and realized once again that this band will never cease to amaze me, musically or visually.

After a while, Trey started strumming some familiar chords. I screamed out ""NICU"!" but Trey didn't seem to hear me! He hit the chords a few more times and I started to give up, figuring it was merely a tease. The band locked in, though, and segued beautifully into an outstandingly tight "NICU". "Fluffhead" followed. I hate to say it, but this was a pretty bad "Fluffhead." The entire composed section between "Clod" and "Bundle of Joy" was flubbed awfully. They made up for it with an awfully strong "Arrival," though, which Trey majestically tore through. At this point, I figured the set was over, but they treated us to a nice "Character Zero" to close.

The second set, though, was the absolute meat. I was hoping for a "2001" opener for my friend Tom, but I was more than glad to hear "Bathtub Gin." The jam will knock those liquor bottles off of your shelves! The jam started out like a normal "Gin" jam for several minutes until Fishman challenged the band and kicked in the tempo. The jam rose into a frenzy and went on for a long time. I wish I could describe it, but I probably couldn't do it justice. Rather than feature a lot of individual soloing, it featured band-based chordal jamming that played with tempo and a bit of syncopation. At one point, the style and situation were perfect for a segue into "Crosseyed and Painless," but it didn't happen.

The jam started to dissolve and Trey cued up Mike. Out of the fuzz came the "Disease" bass line. This "Disease" smoked as well! Again, the jam was very band-based as opposed to individually dominated. Out of the jam came the "Low Rider" theme in a different key than the original version. I figured it was just a nice tease and it made me smile, but

excerpt from

"My Five Favorite Phish Moments"

Daniel Nooter, New York, NY

8/17/97 Circus Comes To Town, Tweezer Reprise (E)

During the second set of this show, Trey addresses the audience. He says (approximately), "We think…in fact, we *know* that when we're playing up here, it's not just us playing, but all of you creating the music along with us." He points out the tall wooden sculpture erected along the side of the audience, tells us that it's been constructed from the paintings that we've all done over the weekend of the Went; and then each of the band members add their own painting to that pillar of art. The feeling of intimacy that pervades the air as the audience carries the band's contribution over their heads to the sculpture is out of kilter with the fact that there are 65,000–80,000 of us all gathered together on this clear August evening. A couple of hours later, the band has retreated behind a miasma of feedback and delay loops; all that remains is the smoldering skeleton of burnt art, sending smoke into the now dark night. I remember the shock on some people's faces as *Tweezer Reprise* ended and the flaming baton descended upon the sculpture of art we had all created. Some, I remember, were even angry; but many simply could not understand why the band would burn this unique symbol of the sacred connection between band and audience. For me,

there was nothing it could do *but* burn; and standing there, watching the glowing sculpture collapse into ash, I felt moved to tears. For that sculpture is (or perhaps I should say was) no fetish for the connection between the band and all of us—that will always be there, impervious to anything so pedestrian as fire. Rather, the sculpture represented the amassed energy of those particular nights, created with the audience, to be constantly reburnt and reconstructed every night. Leave the sculpture there? For how long? Forever? No. The circus came to town, and as it must, the circus left—taking with it its magicians and wonders and spectacles and laughter. Where it remains is in our memories—in the will to gather and share these thoughts and experiences and moments which have so moved us, and which allow us to create new and different sculptures of energy and music and beauty at other shows with other people and different circumstances, but with the same love. There was nothing to do but burn that sculpture because it represented the energy and love which can never be crushed and contained in any passive sculpture, but must flow and dance and live. The energy of our shared love was transformed before our eyes into light and heat, to brighten and to warm us; to allow us to flow and dance. And live.

Trey started singing! Then he stopped and cued up Fishman, who swung his mic around and picked up the vocals. After the "take a little trip" lyrics, the band launched into a "Low Rider" jam. From there, Trey started picking up the tempo, and we were suddenly back into the swirling "Disease" ending jam! They stretched it out for another few minutes and then told us they were on their way.

How could they top this? "Bold as Love!" Good-gawd! Chris's lights didn't disappoint, matching the lyrics of the song with bright, punchy colors. I'll never forget the smile that came over my face when those yellow lights came up during the second verse, and then the bright rainbow appeared over the stage. Beautiful vocals from Page and some searing guitar work from Trey closed out the second set.

The "Julius" encore was rocking. I think this song is the perfect encore; it keeps everyone dancing and sends everyone home with a smile. As usual, Trey kicked ass and slowly brought the jam up to infinite levels of happy soloing, and I left with a huge smile on my face. There was a group of fans on the floor and in the bottom seats off Page's side, and Trey looked like he was playing directly to them.

On the way out, we were stuck in a huge traffic jam. Suddenly, we saw the street that we had taken on the way in…the "wrong" way! It turned out to be a great find, because there was no one else on it. We zipped out of the traffic and started on our way home, quite fulfilled after another stellar show.

11/26/97 Hartford Civic Center, Hartford, CT
—Jeremy D. Goodwin

Apparently, Phish specifically scheduled their swing up the East Coast to accommodate my personal schedule. I was primed to gorge on six shows in nine days, with an incredibly easy travel itinerary. After catching Hampton from my school location in Washington, D.C., I arrived home for Thanksgiving just in time for the brief drive south to Hartford for the first New England show since the Great Went. I remember how unseasonably warm and sunny it was that afternoon, as I took the T to Somerville and met up with my friend and travel companion, whom I hadn't seen since August.

Word on the Phish.Net was that Fall Tour had already included breakthrough nights in Denver, Champaign, and Winston-Salem; plus, I had borne witness to the events in Hampton. I had pegged this night as the likely "letdown show," the calm before the storm that would (hopefully) strike in Worcester that weekend. It seemed unlikely that Phish would maintain the momentum of the groundbreaking first week and a half of the tour, considering that the upcoming Massachusetts run was going to leave little space for relaxation. Winston-Salem was ostensibly supposed to be the letdown show, but it ended up becoming another showcase for awe-inspiring improvisation. So Hartford would have to be tame, I reasoned.

All my carefully weighed expectations and predictions for the show were quickly thrown out the window without regret when the band took the stage and opened with "Tweezer".

There was the nagging feeling that another "Tweezer" opener so soon after Denver was something of an abuse, but I trusted that it wouldn't happen again anytime soon, and took it for what it was: a won-

Ellis Godard

Great Went

derful, gutsy communication from the band to the audience that they meant business.

The energy in that room was gushing once everyone realized that a second-set highlight was going to open the show. I remember the lights and the band both exploding into effect simultaneously; it almost took my breath away, particularly since my mail-order seats had put me right behind the tapers' section, in the sweet spot of the venue. The jam was quite enjoyable, and similar to the two "Tweezers" of the summer, but failed to really inspire in all that remarkable a fashion. An excellent show opener, but a ho-hum "Tweezer". As my friend later put it, Trey then "shot 'Tweezer' between the eyes" by segueing into "Sparkle." Oh well.

"Gumbo" was a welcome appearance in the number three slot, having emerging out of nowhere as a credible jam vehicle over the summer. It was shorter than the two monster summer versions, but I thought it was more compelling than at least the 8/13 Star Lake rendition. I've found that the third song of a first set is often provides a sense of the mood of where things will go later.

The rest of the first set had only a few minor highlights, and after a very short set break (thirty minutes), Phish appeared onstage and slid into an ethereal, almost ambient jam. It was fueled largely by Fishman's cymbal work, and lasted for two minutes before Trey emerged on top with the opening riff of "Character Zero".

I had learned a very valuable lesson a few days earlier in Hampton: this band intended to jam on whatever song it opened the second set with. Although "Character Zero" had never before been anything but a brief, upbeat rocker, I for one had confidence that the Fall '97 trend would continue, and this opener would lead to a great, unexpected jam. I gave the song choice the benefit of the doubt, and was richly rewarded.

Indeed, the ensuing musical sequence was straight out of the Fall '97 book: a typical song morphed into a stunning, extended jam. For the

first few minutes of the "Zero" jam segment, the band stayed within the boundaries of the song, but in a blistering, fiery manner. Even if it had ended after a typical length of time, this would have been a surprisingly good "Zero." After several minutes, it appeared that things were headed back towards the end section of the song. Even Chris Kuroda was fooled: the lights shifted to the sequence they usually follow at the end of this tune, when the lyrics return. However, the music kept going without any ending lyrics, and they slid out of "Zero" mode into truly improvisational territory.

The following jam was the obvious highlight of the night, and one of the real highlights of a week of great shows. This was what we came for. At the point when it was clear that this set-opening "Character Zero" was going to become a historic jam, I was as happy as I was at almost any point that week. I savor and truly love that moment when you realize that a song is not going to end like it has a hundred times before, but instead is going to wander into a major jam.

The jamming was very hard and interesting. Eventually, Trey seemed to tease "Foxy Lady" several times, and things got very heavy and crunchy. A very rock-sounding riff was employed repeatedly (and would reappear a few days later near the end of the Worcester "Free"). All in all, this was a very upbeat, sometimes heavy jam that impressed me significantly, especially considering that it emerged from one of the unlikeliest of places.

Twenty minutes into the set, Fishman slithered into the "2001" drum beat. The rest of the band eased into their various parts, and the tune was underway. The intro (pre-theme segment) was very extended and jammed, as in recent versions. The theme was done okay (although a Trey flub unfortunately marred the first run-through), and then the meat of the song was jammed in a typically funky, over-the-top manner. Then Trey began repeating a little funky riff he obviously loves, which originated in James Brown's "Superbad." I had heard this teased on a couple tapes (11/30/96, 12/6/96, 2/22/97), and had been specifically hoping to hear it for myself in person. I was absolutely delighted to hear Trey give me more than just a little tease; Burlington, VT's best attempt at a sex machine proceeded to play the riff over and over, basing a short jam around it. He engaged in a little call-and-response with the rest of the band, as Mike, Page, and Fishman filled in the gaps between repetitions of the riff with incredibly funky measures. Without bothering to finish "2001," the boys slipped effortlessly into the only "Cities" of the tour. The jam was spellbinding for a few short minutes before Trey, for no apparent reason, wrestled it to the ground by dragging the band into "Ya Mar." Until that moment, the potential of the set seemed infinite.

I usually enjoy "Ya Mar," particularly in a first set, but I was much more interested at that point in second-set improvisational heroics, and didn't want to have that interrupted by just another upbeat dance number. "Ya Mar" was unfinished as well, as Trey unexpectedly jump-started "PYITE" in the middle of his solo. By the time a major flub delayed one of the intricate transitions in this song, I felt the momentum of the first three songs had been lost, and in some ways the set was all over.

The very overplayed and unwelcome "Prince Caspian" sealed it, and there was only to be a "Poor Heart" (with a botched intro) and a "Tweezer Reprise" remaining to fill out the set. The usually uneventful "Cavern" was chosen for the encore, but this version was highlighted by a very interesting and odd little jam in the middle during which Trey yelled some of the old, discarded lyrics: "I turned the blade back on the bitch and dropped her in the dung!" This seemed more an expression

of frustration than anything else to me. The song ended in some very heavy noise and strobe lights, and Trey grabbed the megaphone and waved it around, before taking off his guitar and scraping it against one of Page's keyboards.

A very bizarre ending to a show that included some excellent highlights, but many mixed signals as well. In retrospect, I think we should focus on the first forty minutes of the second set, and take this show for what it is: easily above average, complete with some very inspiring jamming, during one of the most inspiring weeks of Phish I've ever heard. There's no need to dwell on the sloppiness or the repeats.

11/26/97 Hartford Civic Center, Hartford, CT—Dan Alford

Anyone who has made live music into a lifestyle choice has secrets. Not secrets like "Can you guess where all my money goes?" or "What do I do every weekend?" The answers to those questions are obvious enough and anyone who has more than a passing acquaintance with a concert junkie doesn't wonder why he or she can't make it to that party when there's a show in town. The secrets I'm talking about are those really personal nights, those nights in smoky rooms that no one else thinks about, but that you know were something special. The Hartford show from '97 is one of those secrets.

This show is understandably underrated. It took place the night before Thanksgiving and was the first show of the northeastern leg of Fall Tour, the southern leg having ended two nights earlier in North Carolina. Also, it preceded the famous Worcester run that boasts myriad highlights, not the least of which was the epic "Runaway Jam" that was literally and metaphorically the centerpiece of all three nights. Nonetheless, Hartford remains one of my most enjoyable evenings of music.

The "Tweezer" opener was the perfect way to send your mind spiraling into a different universe and was a solid showcase for the funk inferno that scorched all of that tour. While the remainder of the set was very song-oriented, it did sport a great "Gumbo" and one of my favorite "McGrupps" ever. I remember having this relaxing haze drop over me.

The second set opened with a short, spacey jam, foreshadowing the place where Phish's funk would land by Summer Tour '98, into a monster "Character Zero." It was one of those songs that just wouldn't quit, and after squirming in all sorts of directions the "Worm" found its way to a nice "2001." A fairly long (but focused) version, the end seemed particularly momentous, and led into the only "Cities" of the tour. The crowd was particularly pleased to hear this very tight version, as *Slip Stitch and Pass* had just come out. The tune was in rotation in the U.S., but only sporadically. A real treat for those in attendance. The jam didn't stop there, though. The slip into "Ya Mar" set off cheers from the crowd who got a huge dose of the start/stop full funk treatment. And then into an oddly placed "PYITE," followed by a "Caspian." The set closed with a "Rocky Top" intro into "Poor Heart" and the full framing effect of a "Tweezer Reprise". The closure that a reprise affords is always nice, but is particularly potent when it bookends an entire show. The "Cavern" encore had the original "Turned the blade back on the bitch" lyrics, although Trey must've decided to use them right then because they were rushed, as though he missed a beat.

12/3/97 CoreStates Spectrum, Philadelphia, PA —Jonathan Van Schoick

The previous night had a smoking second set, so the bar was high for night two. This show is a stellar performance. I had a good seat:

a few rows from the floor, even with Kuroda on Page's side. I had used my previous night's ticket stub to get down to the lower level instead of my nosebleed seat. "PYITE" and "My Soul" were a good team for a high-energy opener, but "Drowned" is where I first got excited. Any music fan worth his salt knows that *Quadrophenia* kicks the crap out of *Tommy*. "Drowned" is one of the best songs off this album and has the best jam potential, as Phish demonstrated. An absolutely awesome jammed-out "Gumbo" came up soon after, similar to the 11/26/97 version. This segued nicely into Also "Sprach Zarathustra." Now, this song is really cool and funky on its own merits, but it's also a chance for Chris Kuroda to solo. If you hear "2001" at an outdoor venue, it's just not nearly as good.

On this night, Chris blew everybody away. I love to hear this song indoors; the only thing that could have made it better would have been a straight-on view of the stage. A fairly straightforward "YEM" ended the set. An incredible "David Bowie" led off set two. This version of "Bowie" is totally different then previous ones in Philly (12/15/95, 12/29/96, and 12/10/97). If this isn't proof of the band checking out old setlists before the show, I don't know what is. It clocks in at around twenty-eight minutes and it flew by for me, always an indication of a good jam. A raging "Possum" follows, and then the real highlight for me, the start/stop funk jam. This was utter musical euphoria. Especially during the first build-up, when they all started hitting the crescendo, Page did the build on the organ, and it all cuts out and the spotlight hits Trey. Wow. Unbelievable. Still probably the best moment for me at any concert. The end of the set was good, the "Harry Hood" was fun, but the real magic was in the first forty-five minutes. A rare Clapton cover ("Crossroads") for an encore topped off the night.

12/6/97 The Palace, Auburn Hills, MI—Saul E. Wertheimer

Auburn Hills certainly isn't my favorite venue, but I left it the night of 12/6/97, rethinking everything I had ever thought about it (and that's saying a lot, because I was a philosophy major!). The "Tweezer" that opened the second set is one of the best I've heard. It contained a long jam, which bring you to Funk Central Station. The segue into "Isabella" is fantastic, and we are treated to an atypical jam that can only be construed as a "licentious funk groove." The segue into "Twist Around" was—once again—fantastic, and then they played the best "Piper" I have ever heard. "Piper" was technically unfinished, as the jam launched off with the power of a space shuttle from Cape Canaveral. This "Piper" took me to another world. It was so intense that Aaron, my traveling companion for the last part of tour, was worried that I would spontaneously combust.

"Sleeping Monkey" was perfectly placed, and the "Tweeprise" that closed the set threatened to bring down the house. I can't remember the encore. This entire set has no regard for accepted rules, morals, or standards. Get this tape…but be very afraid!

12/7/97 Ervin J. Nutter Center, Dayton, OH—Scott Silton

Someone must have told the band it was my fiftieth show; they made sure to keep the setlist fresh and funky! It's hard to imagine becoming jaded with shows like this one around.

Set I: Wow! What a killer set! The "Jesus Just Left Chicago" totally brought the house down, and the "Psycho Killer" was sweet to hear. "My Mind's Got a Mind of Its Own" hasn't been around for a

while—it was the first time I've heard it since '93 I believe. The "Ice" had a few problems but Page was king, and the "Swept/Steep" middle was well placed. The "Theme" included a gorgeous Trey solo. (It sounded to me like he was breathing through the guitar.) Then "Tube!" Whoo! I've been waiting years to catch this, and then they bust out the funky version for me! The middle of "Tube" featured a cool funkified jam, which they launched back into after having wrapped the song up. (It was more or less an untitled funk instrumental, I guess) Then "Slave!" This totally made up for the Cleveland fiasco—this was a momentous "Slave"…and a momentous set.

At set break, I told my neighbor, "They can play shorter sets if they are going to be that good!" Once again the band must have been listening.

Set II: "Timber" was nothing special, but the "Wolfman's"->"Reggae Woman" was phenomenal! Great segue and great tunes! "Boogie On Reggae Woman" is a Stevie Wonder cover. "Reba" and "Guyute" were sweet to hear, although neither version was stellar. "Possum" included a repeated tease of a lick I didn't recognize, and in general was toasty. "A Day in the Life" was a bit of a letdown, I suppose, but even that hasn't been around for a while, and nothing could be a letdown from this fine show. Short but sweet: thirty-five minutes shorter than Cleveland but far more fun! It was especially sweet from the fourteenth row!

12/13/97 Pepsi Arena, Albany, NY—Dan Seideman

Even though this show was on a Saturday night, I found it planted right in the middle of my exam schedule, and I had not one but two exams during the day, not to mention another the next afternoon. (I was quite happy with my exam scores too!) As a result, I had to sell my ticket for the show the night before, but after spending the whole week studying and taking the exams, I left Amherst (MA) for Albany.

I was very excited for the show, even though my brain was still speeding along at a hundred miles an hour, and I couldn't settle down, even during a nice dinner with many Phish.Net friends at the Albany Brew Pub. Getting inside was particularly stressful, as the tapers' line was positioned right in front of a police officer, who was blaring instructions into his megaphone quite rudely. After forcing my way through the mass of people in the street, I found my way to the middle of the tapers' line and proceeded inside. The tapers' section was huge, taking up half of the floor! I found plenty of room to set up my stuff and began waiting in anticipation.

J. Willis Pratt and Weird Bionic opened the show, surprisingly, and I laughed when I saw tapers scrambling for their record buttons. I had seen him play at set break at a Pork Tornado show (Fishman's side project), so I already was familiar with his grungy style of playing. Quite frankly, I don't enjoy his music, and I chose not to tape it.

When the lights finally went down and the band walked onstage, I couldn't wipe the smile off of my face. I stopped thinking about school, stress, and my exams, and even though I had seen four shows just over two weeks ago, I was more excited for this show than I had ever been.

The opening chords of "Ya Mar" sounded through the arena and the show was off and running. The song proceeded as usual for about ten minutes, and just when it looked like it was going to end, Trey reprised the "Ya Mar" guitar theme and the band launched into a spellbinding ten-minute jam. The slow, exploratory jam covered a great deal of new ground and featured some strong work by both Trey and Page.

The band kept the energy high by launching into "Axilla." I like the evil, dissonant sounding lyrics of the original (part one) better than the album lyrics of part two. The white lights on top of the red background lights are also a great effect from Kuroda and company. A strong "Theme from the Bottom" followed, and while the jam certainly soared, it didn't reach the levels of those from 2/26/97 Stuttgart or 8/16/97 Great Went.

"Ginseng Sullivan" was a nice, relaxing song, although I thought the energy level fell when "Strange Design" followed on its heels. "Sample in a Jar" brought the energy back up, and while it's certainly not a rare song, its performance is not as common as it was back in '94. It took me a second to recognize the piano intro to "Vultures," and its placement was excellent. I think the vocal harmonies on this song are quite strong, fast-paced, and complex.

As far as first-set highlights, "Tube" was second only to the "Ya Mar" opener. The jam, like others from fall '97, featured a funky middle section. During the middle of the song, the lighting crew came up with a fantastic effect. Two "eyes" (yellow circles with white ones inside) were put on the white lighting canvas above the stage. They drifted from side to side like eyes looking at both sides of the arena. Soon after they came up, Chris Kuroda turned around to his right-hand lighting guy, laughing. He high-fived the other guy! So, the lighting assistant must have just come up with that new lighting technique on the spot. Hilarious!

The first set closed out with a typically strong "Good Times, Bad Times." While the first set would certainly pale in comparison to what was to come, it was excellent, although it dragged a bit in the middle.

The second set, though (oh, the second set!), was tremendous. If anyone had any doubts after the first set, they were forgotten after the second, because it was fantastic from start to finish. The "NICU", "Punch" combo was well executed, but the set really took off with the opening notes of "Ghost."

The "Ghost" jam went through a strong funk phase, before heading back into traditionally hot machine-gun soloing by Trey. It was definitely a soaring jam segment. The intro to "Mike's" came out of the dissonant jamming at the end of the "Ghost" jam, and it saw me pumping my fist. (No yelling in the tapers' section.) "Mike's Song" is my favorite song because of the complete freedom the band has to take the jam (and the ensuing songs) to completely different places. This "Mike's" was anything but standard. Trey started off the madness by echoing Mike's "Big Dude" line. "Big Dude in the doorway, blockin' his way" was said in a mocking echo tone. It was really funny, and Trey was still laughing two verses later. Then Fish started bantering about Cactus…Gordon. Soon, the band was playing a thick, powerful groove, while chanting, "Bring the Dude!" and they began to break it down, first over a Mike solo or two. Next, Trey yelled, "Fish! Let me bring the Dude!" before playing his own solo. The "Mike's" featured lots of banter from everyone, especially Fishman. Trey took a couple of solos, with no drums, and then the spotlight went to Page, who played a solo on his clavinet that sounds strikingly akin to the theme from TV's *Law & Order*.

The "Mike's" segued cleanly into a really intense "Llama," which mellowed out in a "Possum"-like fashion, before blasting away into the stratosphere. "Circus" was a nice, mellow interlude before a really hot "Weekapaug" with an extended bass intro. "Weekapaug" appeared to be dying out, slowing down more and more, until Mike started singing "Catapult." As I hoped, they then fired back into "Weekapaug," which teased "Can't You Hear Me Knockin'" (by the Rolling Stones) as it often

does. Once again, the jam slowed and quieted down before rocketing into the familiar "Weekapaug" ending. They even closed the song with the ending used in "The Mango Song," a classic blues ending.

Just when I thought the show was going to end, "Hood" started up. A song like "Hood," following such intense jamming is a fantastic way to close out the set. Glowsticks starting flying, and Trey asked Chris to turn out the lights. The glowstick war was visually stunning, although not as tremendous as the war from the Great Went, from what I've heard. (I didn't go). Trey even fired some glowsticks back into the crowd, and at one point, Chris tried to hit the band with a long throw from the lightboard. The band found themselves playing a different type of build, during the crescendo jam during the last segment of "Hood." It wasn't quite as intense as the typical "Hood" jam, but it was unique.

When the band left the stage, I was in awe! I couldn't believe the intensity of their playing and the excitement of the second-set jamming. Unfortunately, the band didn't top the previous night's "Guyute"/"Antelope" encore but rather settled for "My Soul," which was incredibly overplayed over the fall. A second encore song is always welcome, but "Coil" is certainly not my top choice. Even so, I thought Page's solo was a mellow ending to a fantastic show, as well as a calm ending to a tour that was a storm of innovation and exploration.

New Year's Run 1997—Craig DeLucia

Though the 1997 New Years Run started in Maryland, it was viewed by many as a one-night mid-Atlantic warmup followed by a three-night romp through the Big Apple. And what a romp it was!

As with many fans, and as I had done in 1996, I spent the New Years Run traveling with a large group of fans and friends. There was a distinctly different feeling in the air this year, though. The 1996 Run came on the heels of a solid but unspectacular tour, while the 1997 Run came at the close of one of the most exciting Phish years ever. I was lucky enough to catch a few shows earlier in the year (most notably the lightning-inflected Raleigh show in the summer and the underrated Winston-Salem show in the fall), but most of the hose I felt was through tapes of the then-recent

Hampton extravaganza and shows like Rochester and Auburn Hills. None of this prepared me for the four night Run.

Sure enough, Landover was a warm-up. A strong warm-up, mind you, but definitely a warm-up. There were some minor technical problems (the ghost in the machine, according to Trey) and some rough spots, but it was, overall, a solid Phish show. Looking back on it, there were so many songs that were still in their jam infancy it was like a pre-natal Phish show! I had given up on hearing "Cities" so it was great to catch that (remember, at the time, it had only been played on U.S. soil four times since 1994!) and, as a Who fan, the rare "Drowned" was an unexpected treat. Still, my fondest memory of that show was visual rather than musical. My group was scattered around the arena but six of us wound up in the same section on the Page side of the building. During the second set, as we looked across the arena, we saw that some fans had strung a series of glowrings together. The glowrings were being passed around a few rows of that section, bending and gyrating with the music, seemingly under some greater control than the hands that held them. I had gotten somewhat used to seeing and hearing about glowstick wars through the summer and fall of 1997, but this innovative (and harmless) visual spectacle was incredible to watch.

Satisfied, we settled in for the night and then began our trek to

Great Went

New York. And what a trek it was! Overall, with friends, and friends of friends, and the exponential expansion of friends that can only happen on tour (and can only be amplified by a New Years Run), we wound up with a group of almost thirty by the time we got to the city. Our hotel room for eight suddenly became more like fifteen, but the only people who really seemed to mind were the hotel staff!

The show on the 29th was my favorite of the Run musically, and I still listen to it a good bit to this day. Our seats were great second bowl of the Garden but close to parallel to the stage, just a wee bit in front of Fishman. From the reggae "NICU" opener to the rocking "Antelope" closer, I shook my ass, pausing for thought and breath only during "Train Song" and "Dirt." But the second set

Again, this kind of thing became more commonplace from 1997 forward, but go back and look at earlier setlists. To see and hear five solid Phish jamming tunes strung together seamlessly for the duration of the second set blew my mind. No breathers, no real pauses, just ass-kicking jam rock. Hell, the shortest song was "Tube," still in its growth as a jammer, and it may have made me dance harder than any song of the Run!

Post-show, we ventured over to The Wetlands to hear Michael Ray and the Cosmic Krewe. It was a great spot to meet up with folks, and it was a fun excursion for us Mockingbird folks. Even though the project began to come together in the fall of 1996, this New Years Run was the first time that large numbers of the core working groups were together in one spot. We relished the chance to meet some people face-to-face for the first time, and hang out with old friends (many of whom I hadnt seen since the post-show Cubed throwdown in Boston on NYE '96. We even got to meet Moira, but that's another story for another day. And, of course, the music was spectacular and the Krewe kept our tired legs moving.

Woke up on the 30th and ran around the city some. Since I grew up in northern New Jersey, I was no stranger to the area. There was a Phish.net gathering at Mustang Sallys where I got to meet even more

folks interested in Mockingbird, and put faces to names I had seen on-line over the last few years.

And then the show. Have you ever been so tired that you didn't personally enjoy a show, no matter how good it was? You know the feeling—you're on tour, you're running around, you feel run-down, you're grumpy, and you try so very hard to get up but sometimes you don't get there? I was afraid that I was going to be that way when I headed to my seat. I was so tired that I could barely move—we were out all night on the 29th and ran around the city all day.

So I was afraid. And then the show started with something funky, something that I didn't quite recognize—it sounds like—it couldn't be "SNEAKING SALLY"!!! My goodness!! The roar of euphoria for a song that hadn't been played in over eight years (although "Mustang Sally" would have been a lot funnier given the location of the net.gathering earlier that day)! And the show rolled on from there. The movement into "Taste" was fun, as was the set closing "Chalk Dust" /" ADITL" combo. No problems in the world. Wasn't I tired? I didn't remember anymore!

And then the second set. A rocking "AC/DC Bag," with a few teases and a jam of, I am convinced, the bassline and groove to the new "Ghost" (i.e., the album version that we have all become accustomed to). A solid "McGrupp." The longest and most interactive "Harpua" ever, with Tom Marshall and udder balls and pentagrams and olive loafs and fun vocal interplay from Fishman (still my second-favorite "Harpua" behind the 94 Sugarbush hit by a comet Harpua).

After the rocking "Izabella" and the soothing "Hood," I thought for sure the set was done, but we got three more songs. How the hell do they top this in an encore?

They don't. They play, in my opinion, a third set. The first "Carini" in the U.S. (after Mike had told some folks that it was permanently on the shelf). The last "Black-Eyed Katie." A return to "Sneaking Sally" which, after an eight-year absence, had been heard twice in five hours. And, for the cherry on top, a spooky "Frankenstein," complete with Fishman teasing us with the vacuum at center stage.

Anyone who has ever traveled with tapers knows that there's usually some deck-spinning in the hotel room after a show. On this night, there was a daisy chain of DATs rolling into the wee hours of the morning. Where to put the tape flips for analogs? How to best fit this night onto some kind of recording medium. WHAT HAD WE JUST HEARD??

Now, where the 29th and 30th were highly gratifying musically, the 31st was, well, a big party. That's the only way to describe it. The second set stands out as being well-played and well-jammed; the third set found the band trying hard to play loud enough to be heard over the incredibly vocal crowd (so loud that Trey must not have heard his guitar during "Maze"!!). Midnight—well, all I can say is that the fans around me were certainly tripped out by the intense visual display of udder balls and olive loafs and everything from the previous nights "Harpua."

The story goes that they learned the appropriate "New York New York" encore that day kudos to Page for pulling it off! It was one of those moments where I felt like every single fan was on-stage, and the band and its fans were truly one unit, ringing in a new year together the way we have grown accustomed to.

4/2/98 Nassau Coliseum, Uniondale, NY—Jeremy D. Goodwin

I was up all night before Nassau, surging on creative adrenaline. I had to finish a short story for my Experimental Fiction class before leaving for the weekend, and after an extended writing binge, I finally

headed to the campus lab around 4 AM to print it out. Upon arrival I discovered that the lab computers did not have a certain font that my piece required. As this particular stylistic touch was important to the story, I decided to walk back across campus to my room, load the font onto a disc, and returned back to the lab. Finally, I got everything printed out. As it happens, this "short story" was actually just the seedling for what is now my most important creative work: my first novel-in-progress. At the time I knew the piece was a personal breakthrough, and I was very excited about it, but I'm not sure I recognized it for what it was: the defining point in my artistic development to date. It was definitely a thrill already, though.

After printing the master copy, I made a long visit to Mapquest (don't believe the hype, it's not as great as it seems), and finally ended up emerging from the subterranean lab around 7 AM. Much to my surprise, I found that the new morning of April 2 was in full bloom. Not even just the predawn pinkening skies and tentative scurrying of birds. It was full-on, all-out morning. The sun was absolutely glorious and blaring, there were men in suits reading newspapers on park benches, cars headed for work, the whole deal. This is when I realized I wouldn't get a chance to sleep before the trip.

It was okay, though…I was still relatively sprightly, and experienced something of a sublime moment in the deserted school food court, watching bars of sunlight streak across the room, while eating an omelet and hearing "Low Rider" play from the radio. Two hours later, after safely dropping off twenty copies of my story on my professor's doorstep, I was picked up by two of the guys from Liquid Lobster. We had never met but they kindly offered me a ride via e-mail.

The early weather trend continued, and it was a positively glorious Thursday morning. Warm and sunny beyond expectations. The ride north was pleasant and relatively undistinguished…we listened to a crispy tape of Winston-Salem to get in my second "Low Rider" of the day. In Philly we passed the Joker's headquarters, as well as a drab building we nicknamed Ajax Metal Company. So industrial and bleak.

The Nassau Coliseum is an interesting venue in that it apparently has no front door. Consequently, lot-hangers were pretty dispersed, and there was little scene to speak of. As we circled the place, it became evident to me that I was amid a pretty young crowd, even for Phish. On the way into the venue, I had the very strange experience of witnessing an unrelenting chorus of people literally pleading for the chance to bestow free tickets ("Does anyone need a miracle?"). By showtime you literally could not give tickets away. Bizarre. It far surpassed the last time I had seen something remotely similar to this (at 11/30/97, when I heard a guy yelling, "Does anyone have any ketchup so these people can eat their tickets?"). Once inside, I found that the place was so beneath capacity that security was apparently waving kids down onto the floor. I'll note now that I was very pleased with the crowds each night of the Run…the highest energy I've personally seen since Hampton (and this includes the New Year's Run).

Due to an accident of ticketing, I was sitting a few scant rows from R.J. Happily, he scuttled forward to join us, and we settled in for the "Tube" opener. "Nice way to start off these shows." "Tube" was similar in all respects to Dayton, and led into a first-timer for me, the only "Mike kickdown bluegrass tune": "My Mind." I definitely consider this tune a treat, and I believe the band agrees. "Tube," "My Mind," "Sloth"…nice opening sequence, eh? The ubiquitous-in-'97 "NICU" followed, and then we settled in for the first highlight of the Run, "Stash."

Great Went

I've been listening to lots of "Stashes" lately, and this one was fully satisfying! It opened with a quickly repeated phrase from Trey, which gave us the impression of riding a rocket shot to the moon. The intensity in the room was scorching. This led into an unrelated and compelling jam that drifted into a very pretty, un-"Stash" place. A twenty-minute, unfinished "Stash," similar in length to the monster Fall '97 versions.

Then "Horn," "Waste," "Chalk Dust," and a kind of strange postscript to the set. Trey: "That was a low note. Now, for contrast and composition, we will leave you on a high note." And they did so. This high note, in fact, was to last for four days straight.

The second set opened auspiciously with the first "PYITE" I've been able to fully enjoy in person since the Great Went. The opening minutes were stretched out in a way that was quite satisfying, but not necessarily that atypical from most versions since '96. A ten-minute "Simple" followed. Near the beginning, my friend Christian looked over at me and said, "Would you want to be anywhere else?" I didn't need to say anything; we understood each other instantly.

The band teased us with some crazy "Simples" in '96 (the overlooked Charlotte 10/26/96 one is still my favorite), but I've finally learned not to expect exploratory maneuvers during this number. (I usually ruin "Simples" for myself by waiting for the jam that never comes.) Thus, I was able to enjoy the typical, excruciatingly beautiful jam that ensued. Then, a new song. The opening reminded me of "Llama," but the verse part was distinctly reminiscent of "Maze" (particularly Page's part). I very much enjoyed the melody as well as the lyrics, and was pleased at the jam that ensued as well. One section of it began with the now-classic Trey loop, which goes on at the start of dozens of jams from '97 (its on, unaltered, through the entire 8/17 "2001"). It was nice to see that they had basically grabbed a piece of '97 jamming and put it into a song. I specifically hoped that they'd play the tune again in Providence. I timed it at nine minutes.

Then, Trey got talkative. I've noticed that the band seems more willing to specifically talk about how cool they are nowadays, though without putting it as plainly as that. This is a great example. Trey said something along the lines of: "We were bored. We wanted to play some shows…You know those live albums from the '70s, where they're like, 'This song is from our third album.' Well…our new album is from last week's concert!"

Then they dropped into one of the signature tunes of '97, "Wolf-man's Brother." I remember the jam being deliciously, almost uproariously upbeat. R.J. and I both heard premonitions of the segue literally for several minutes before it finally was sealed…and became "Sneakin' Sally!" Wolfman's->"Sneakin' Sally"…how sweet is that?! "Sally" led into what appeared at the time to be the major jam of the night. It spun away, out of upbeat-funky mode into very engaging improvisation. I can't wait to hear this again. The jam finally entered a mode which seemed to me very similar to "Mind Left Body." This led into a piece of jamming that was quite beautiful! I soon began to think that it was so beautiful that it had to composed. Indeed, it soon became clear that we were in fact witnessing another new song debut. If you ask me, it's pretty damn cool that they debuted a new song by segueing into it. Later that weekend, Benji and Jim Raras informed me that the tune's name is "Roget" (according to Marshall). [Note: this turned out to be a misunderstanding on Tom's part, who hadn't been at the show. The song was "Frankie Sez."]

I assumed the great set had already peaked, but apparently I forgot that Phish has been taken over by an extraterrestrial life form. "Twist Around" (another first-timer for me) led into what was easily the most intense jam of the weekend. It was absolutely space-a-tronic 3000. I felt that I was hearing something from Phish that I had never heard before. Picture the best example of fall '97 funk, but genetically mutated and evolved to a higher level of consciousness. The band (particularly Page, probably) was using effects I hadn't heard before. Little squiggles and doodles that make you say "Did I just hear that?" High in this category was a sound that seemed to simulate a DJ scratching a record. It was not just the mood, it was not just the circumstances: I had never before heard Phish create this kind of sensory-numbing, electronic, globular, tornado cone of sound.

As if the sounds were not intense enough, this jam was chosen by Chris Kuroda to demonstrate a new bag of lighting tricks. The jam passed through several waves, each of which seemed, in conjunction with the lights, to be setpieces. It honestly felt like I was watching a play, or some other planned spectacle. The band jammed on some deranged space odyssey theme, which Chris complemented with a unique, frenetic, complex, computer- and joystick-aided onslaught of light that peaked; then the music shifted into a different, similarly pineweasel-on-acid-influenced phase, which Chris complemented with a new array of retina-dazzling lights. A new sound, and new lighting effects to go along with it.

We all know that Kuroda can anticipate changes in jams as if he's a voodoo king, but this was different. I remember this happening at least three or four times, in succession. I still have never seen anything quite this intense at a Phish show again. After the show I theorized that this would be the blueprint for the '98 sound, but it turned out we'd have to wait until 1999 to hear anything along these lines again (see the 12/8/99 "Piper" and the 12/11/99 "Ghost"…the 12/30/99 "Mike's" almost gets there, but doesn't quite reach the same plane of levitational intensity, despite probably the largest amount of fog to ever flood a Phish stage).

This bled into a well-deserved "Sleeping Monkey." I think this is literally the perfect placement for this song…it's a collective sigh of relief for everyone in the room, and when that sigh is deserved, "Monkey" can truly hit the spot. This was followed by the set-closing "Rocky Top." When did this little bluegrass ditty become a full-on rave-up? Well, I guess it's always been like that, since its customary role in the encore,

but I personally have never enjoyed the tune as much as on this night. The "Guyute" encore (before it had been played into the ground) was pretty much as good as it gets, and reminded us of Hampton, as "Sneakin' Sally" had reminded us of the New Year's Run.

4/3/98 Nassau Coliseum, Uniondale, NY—Jeremy D. Goodwin

So yes, it's already been two years. The Spring Run, that unexpected and brilliant "overflow" from Fall/New Year's Run '97, was the culmination of the delirious "we can do anything" feeling that permeated everything related to Phish for over a year. The winter Europe tour had started a headstrong buzz that would only increase throughout the year, and by the end of New Year's '97, the advertising slogan "Phish Destroys America" had been totally fulfilled. And then…four extra shows. Like an extra New Year's Run. A little gift from the band, an unexpected chance to jaunt off into that splendid and friendly Temporary Autonomous Zone that is Phish tour. When Trey joked "this song's from our last week's concert" during the opening night of the Spring Run, it felt like this band could (and would) do anything. The boundaries were disappearing, and the momentum of their swelling oeuvre was growing. It seems obvious now that no creative unit could walk that tightrope indefinitely; this group in particular was destined to crash into mediocrity and vamping through much of the next three tours. The band's abilities had been expanding exponentially from August '93 until early '98, and the train was bound to run off the track. Of course, we didn't know that at the time. Thus the Spring Tour was left as a kind of high point from which we could all view our Phish careers afterwards. At least, it was for me. These particular shows will always stand out to me as a pinnacle of my last unspoiled, unjaded period as a fan. My twenty-fifth show was somewhere in this run; appropriately enough, that stands now as a rough halfway mark in my show-going lifetime. Experiences like Big Cypress continue to demonstrate to me that Phish can still reinvent the show-going experience utterly, and perhaps spur on a domestic version of Ferlinghetti's "rebirth of wonder." The Clifford Ball, the Spring Run, Big Cypress…it is at these unprecedented events that sometimes all of us together, the band included, figure out for ourselves just what this thing is all about, are surprised by the results, and reconsider the horizons. "Carini's gonna get you!"

I don't think I can say anything about the 4/3 show without first saying a few things about the afternoon that preceded it. In the morning we had a pleasant spell of lazing around in the sparse Econolodge room, listening to the earthy acoustic strains of Dylan's John Wesley Harding and a jaunty '91 "Mike's Song." (I periodically thought of the recent Schvice in which Brad, in purposely offhand fashion, discussed the "people who go there early so they wouldn't miss the "Mike's Song" opener" at Hampton this fall.) It was another bright, sunny day, and we took a random drive which serendipitously led to a long bridge stretching out towards an island. The island was a long, narrow wedge of sand with several different park areas. Without meaning to, we had suddenly found ourselves in a very beautiful national park. We wandered toward an elevated wooden walkway that extended into and through a wooded area towards the lighthouse we spied at the edge of the island. We followed this long, curving, wooden walkway through the woods, and noticed the bizarre topography: sand dunes punctuated with pine trees, bushes, various kinds of shrubbery, shells, rocks, and the remnants of giant man-eating crabs. It seemed there were several different ecosystems meshed together. Chris and I were the only ones around. It was

quite serene! There were a few paths to choose from, and we followed one of the forks off of the main walkway, and emerged suddenly onto a beach. It was a little wedge of a beach, strangely absent any shells. There was, however, a deceased horseshoe crab on the sand, which I handled and then posed with. I kicked off my sandals and ran around a little. The sun was brilliant, the sky was a deep blue, and we communed with nature in a delightfully casual way. After meandering some more along the twisting, rambling walkway, we finally found ourselves at the base of the giant, looming lighthouse. We played around on the lighthouse keeper's house (a functioning museum during the week) and took it all in. I gazed for a long time at the ocean, a sight I have grown up with, but am sadly deprived of when away at school.

There were about four hours to go before another Phish show. On the drive back over the bridge, we listened to the "Mike's Song" again while gazing at the dazzlingly blue water, and Chris and I agreed that "Mike's Song" was indeed the Theme Song of the Day. On and off, I considered the prospects of a "Mike's Song" opener at some point that weekend. That evening, after an unnecessarily confusing drive from Hempstead to Uniondale, we arrived at the Nassau Coliseum with only minutes to spare before the forecasted start time. We settled into our seats in the back row of the Page Zone about a minute before the lights went down, and noticed for the first time just how small the venue is. We were literally in the back row of the section, but I had no problem with the seats whatsoever.

"Mike's Song" opener. This was a personal victory for me, as certain factors had prevented me from enjoying the Hampton "Mike's" opener as thoroughly as I could have. I can easily say that this one surpasses the Amsterdam and Hampton openers (I haven't heard the PA one). It was a very solid, fourteen-minute "Mike's." I can't say more than "it was intense." The segue was magnificent though. It was like the Great Went "Gin"->"Uncle Pen" but much better. They stayed in the bluegrass mode maybe thirty seconds, before it finally clicked in to "My Old Home Place." I have absolutely no complaints with a "Mike's"->"MOHP," opener or not…I think it's a great combo. First of all, I can't name any other true segues into bluegrass tunes (other than the aforementioned one at the Went), and I think this tune is the penultimate selection from this genre (with the possible exception of "My Mind," which we got the night before). Phish definitely plays this song to express a sentiment, I believe…and that sentiment is "We're home!" This tune has owned me ever since it opened day two of the Ball.

No fooling around before voyaging off into "Weekapaug." I can't remember anything about the opening bass solo…. The jam, however, was fantastic! It got very intense (there's that vague word again), before settling into a very Talking Heads-eque groove. Upon review of the tapes, I can say that they definitely jammed off of "Crosseyed and Painless," though they did not openly tease the melody (as during the 11/19/97 "Wolfman's," 11/28/97 "YEM," 12/29/98 "2001," and others). Then the Mike and Trey vocal "ahhing," which signals a far-out jam. What a great, extended groove! There might have also been some stop-time tossed in there somewhere. Finally it came around for the usual "'Paug" closing sequence. Eighteen minutes in total.

This was a very good "Mike's Groove," which by itself makes it an above-average first set. The first half-hour of the set was top-notch performance. That's more than I expect from a first set, if you ask me. I'd like to see "Talk" get thrown in there once in a while instead of "Train Song" (which itself is vastly superior to "Waste," however!). Then "Billy

Breathes." I have decided that BB holds its own as a first-set tune if placed properly. No more groans on my part. Then the classic 1997 first-set pairing, "Beauty of My Dogs." I entered this Run with a very healthy attitude toward non-jam tunes. I impressed the hell out of myself the night before by thoroughly getting off on the "Monkey Top" set II finale. Well, I easily surpassed that on Friday night by digging the "Dogs Stole Things." Part of it is that I've been listening to a lot of acoustic, bluesy American heartland-type stuff lately, and I am really appreciating tunes like "Water in the Sky," all the bluegrass stuff, and the like. I think that Phish plays those songs in an affectionate, heartfelt manner (they're not faking it, which I used to suspect sometimes), and we should enjoy them for what they are.

Then a well-deserved "Reba," personally my first since the '96 New Year's Run. My impression was that it was a reasonably long but not necessarily jaw-dropping version. I could easily be underrating it, though. It was enough to revive the second half of the set in any case, before the uneventful "My Soul" closer.

At New Year's, I needed to figure it out from the lyrics, but this time I was immediately cued in to the "Roses Are Free" second-set opener. After MSG as well as the Rochester debut version, I had already been hoping for a jammed-out take on this Ween song. (It includes the lyrics "resist all the urges that make you want to go out and kill…"— sage advice in my opinion). And so, in Nassau, we saw the first jammed "Roses." But is anyone even keeping track of this kind of thing anymore? Phish jams have become so prevalent and so randomly placed this year that statistics like that are losing their relevance. (For example, in '97 I saw a show in which the "Character Zero" was better than the "Tweezer".

It was a real treat and a delight, from an historical as well as purely musical perspective. The jam was the triumphant culmination of all the '97 funking, and featured Trey repeating a deliriously groovy riff over and over. This eventually gave way to some more exploratory work, before segueing into a standard (read: ripping) "Piper." And then, a "Jam." If you leave this out of your setlist, you're wrong, in my opinion. I'm very hard-line when it comes to "Jam," but this fits the exact, specific criteria of a "Jam" in '97 and early '98. "Piper" was played, jammed on in typical fashion, and then completed. From there, they romped off into a new jam. It was not an unfinished "Piper." This meandered into a brief Page solo interlude (nothing so extended as those ones from '95/96), which was the springboard for the opening to "Loving Cup." Then "Antelope".

The antics contained therein have been discussed a lot, but don't overlook the fact that it was altogether a very good "Antelope". When they sang three-part harmony on the theme "Carini's gonna get you" in the opening, it was one of those moments when I felt that this band was perfectly willing to do anything to please all of us special, special people. The jam was very satisfying (the meat of it was played in the dark, in deference to some the meandering glowsticks), and then the last sequence made it a true keeper. They played the end of a phrase, were silent for the intervening seconds, and then jumped on and played the end of the phrase again. Then, during the lyrics, they switched into a mode that was so thickly reggae that I thought for a moment they were segueing into "Makisupa." There were a few more delightful choruses involving Carini before the affair was over.

I doubt I was the only one in the house calling a Carini encore. This version seemed a tad more crisply paced than the previous one at MSG. The addition of "Halley's" to the already formidable encore was

generous, but also meant there'd be no jammed "Halley's" that weekend. Hardly an issue to whine about, though, in the context of such a special night and overly generous encore. Then the "Tweezer Reprise" just sent things over the top. Trey was stomping around the stage, practically headbanging, obviously reluctant to ever get off the stage. As I remember it, the energy in that room for those few minutes was about as intense as I've seen it at a Phish show. The song isn't usually such an inspiration, but in this context (third song of the encore, and no previous "Tweezer" in the show) there was not the initial twinge of disappointment that I at least usually feel, knowing that there's nothing left to come in the set or show. This "Tweeprise" was strictly overtime… one hundred percent a bonus.

So the band headed out of Uniondale positively on fire. My initial impression was that both of these shows were classics…the 4/2 second set, and 4/3 all around. Another note: on one of these two nights, as we drove back after the show, we found a great college radio show called *Echoes*. It was strictly fusion, and it totally blew our overworked music receptors away as we sat numbly in the car. Chris wondered aloud how many other people in our situation found this station as they drove back. We continued listening to the show back in the room, and I quickly fell pleasantly asleep, hearing echoes of the "Sneakin' Sally," with my clothes on.

4/4/98 Providence Civic Center, Providence, RI
—Jeremy D. Goodwin

For the drive to Providence, we decided to take the ferry across what I guess was the Long Island Sound. The altered route brought us through some truly delightful townships…the Hamlet of Northville particularly. I had no idea there were areas with such character, and genuinely rural nature, on Long Island! Along that drive, I had the opportunity to look out the window and see a giant rat-man, holding a picket sign. Apparently, it was a common laboratory rat that had been genetically altered by the AFL-CIO to become a six-foot-tall strike advocate. Either that, or it was a worker dressed in a full-body rat uniform. In any case, it made me doubt my eyes for a few seconds and was actually kind of scary, then of course amusing. The freakish rat-man was holding a sign that said "Rat contractor inside." There were about a dozen other picketers as well (in normal, human garb).

We had a tense little scene at the ferry, waiting on standby with only about five minutes before departure. We knew that if we did not make this ferry, we would not make the show. For some reason, they make you wait for a long time, then finally tell you to buy a ticket back at the ticket stand several hundred yards away. Apparently, it is so they can watch you dash madly through the parking lot, literally racing the other people in line with you. That's exactly what happened. Happily, we beat out the youngish hippies in the lane next to us, and got on the ferry with over two minutes to spare.

The only bad thing about the ferry ride was that they were playing *Sister Act* in the room where Chris and I grabbed a table, and it was way too loud and annoying to either deal with or ignore. So I strapped on some headphones, started up the Worcester "Jim," and explored the boat. I was the only one up on the top deck, in whipping winds, enjoying another experience with nature. I like these kinds of rides quite a bit, actually, having gone on many a whale watch over the years back at home in Massachusetts. It brought back fond memories of the last time I sailed to a Phish show (the Clifford Ball, via Lake Champlain ferry).

Eventually I discovered the presence of other Netters on the ferry, and we fawned over the "Carini" encore in a communal fashion. Upon arrival in Providence, a friendly police officer gave us directions to the Marriott, and I was ready to start Phase Two of the trip. The stark, humble nature of the Econolodge was left behind as I walked into a comfortable room full of Canadians and assorted revelers (and even assorted Canadian revelers). There were about two hours to go before Time to Head Over, and I met a whirlwind of very fine people. Many of them hadn't done Nassau, and so I got to be the smartest guy in the room for a few minutes, as far as recent Phish went.

After a ten-minute drive to the venue, we didn't know exactly where to go. Luckily, a flashing sign ("PARK HERE") was there to help us and provide needed instruction. I was the only one in the group who didn't need to go in and set up taping equipment, so I had a chance to wander around the very crowded streets after a successful and easy visit to Will Call.

It was quite a different scene from Long Island. Whereas 4/2 had been a free show (for those who arrived on the scene without tickets), this time there were many ticketless who had been out in the cold for hours. There is a little park across the street from the venue, and it was very thick with people. Not all that many vendors, to tell the truth. I've seen complaints on the Net about cops giving citations to people in the park, but I encountered no such difficulties. All in all, I thought it created a nice little scene, in absence of a central parking lot…especially if you interpret the activity as buzz and anticipation, rather than hectic and stressful.

The coziness inside the venue made Nassau look like RFK. I was quite happy with our 200-level seats on the Fishman side. After the previous night's encore, I had been calling a "Tweezer" opener all day. There was a sense that the band would rise to the occasion and do the appropriate thing. It was clear that a "Tweezer" opener was the right thing to do, and as I said to Chris, if they would do it at Hartford (or Denver), there was no reason for them not to do it tonight. This was just one of those special weekends. I mean, it was going to be special anyway, due to the uniqueness of the situation…but the first two nights made it clear that Phish was fully interested in meeting and exceeding expectations. "So I guess they have to open with "Tweezer," I kept saying…it was just the right thing to do."

The "Tweezer" opener I had ordered was a treat, though in retrospect much of the jam sludges along before finally achieving an exciting, upbeat sequence right before the end. My nonjadedness was still in effect, and I somehow enjoyed the "Taste" with no complaints, though over the year it has sabotaged more enjoyable jams than I can mention. (For the record, I feel that it's an excellent song with a standard deviation that is just too low to justify the tune's high rate of repetition.) "Bouncing" might have made people who hadn't done Nassau think they were at a normal Phish show…but I knew the surprise would get sprung on them sometime later. Things were different. This was Phish '98—incredibly confident and casual, and in the midst of a capstone four-night romp.

People I spoke with were pretty up and down on the first set, but there was little dead space, as far as standard first-set songs go. It was a higher class of incidental songs than the first set had featured the night before. I was even able to enjoy "Character Zero." After Hartford, I felt that I "owed" that song…so I hung in there for the predictable but searing rock jam at the end. This one was by no means groundbreaking, but I felt that it was an above-average rendition. After the Run was done, the second set of the first night of Providence initially got the most attention and acclaim among Phish circles. There are definitely some impressive setlist shenanigans going on, but I don't think it deserved to so thoroughly bury the Nassau second sets in our collective memory. (In fact, I believe that in the past two years, the 4/3 show sticks out most prominently as not only the show of the Run but an all-time great.)

Somehow, my friend Christian identified Birds of a Feather immediately. I had specifically been hoping for another one in Providence, but I definitely wasn't expecting this ballsy move. Opening the second set with a ripping seventeen-minute version? Indeed! This jam didn't remind me at all of the previous version (a nice sign, I'd say!), and when it went back into a closing round of choruses, I was totally taken aback and impressed. Out of the post-song haze came "2001." This "2001" can only be summed up with: Battlestar Galactafunk. It was a tripsaphonic, hyposonic journey to Planet Nemo. I felt at times like I was listening to a radio transmission from Planet X. You needed a special device to receive some of the sound frequencies being created onstage. I had a RealAudio feed of Trey's effects, and it was funk-diddley-umptious, THX-3000. Literally the most explosively funky thing I had ever experienced.

At one point during the magnificently extended intro, a guy behind me uttered a quiet phrase that totally summed up my feelings at that moment. I had one of those moments of communality that just felt great: when you know everyone else around you is exactly on your wavelength. This guy behind me suddenly chuckled out of nowhere, as if stifling back a laugh, "'98." It took a moment to sink in, but I quickly started laughing joyously, and agreed, "'98!" I started applauding, and all the people around us joined in and started cheering. I think we all felt really great at that moment. '98. We felt jettisoned into the future.

At one point during the too-fucking-good-to-believe "2001," I turned to Christian and joked, "Is it just me?" It seemed that the sounds were jumping up and wriggling around and twisting into contortions previously unimagined in George Clinton's sexual fantasies. I will admit that I was not at all objective at this point, but the Mothership had landed and the aliens were offering to take us on board.

Another interesting tidbit of info: During the intro, people decided to start throwing glowsticks, and the lights went out. It was pretty cool to see all the aforementioned histrionics with the lights out and glowsticks flying about. For some reason, there just weren't that many in the room, though, and it really was not on the level of the previous "glowstick wars" at all.

After the initial "2001" theme, the jam was actually rather pedestrian before making way for the very unexpected Brother. The song included an unprecedented jam segment, and when they went back into the Brother theme and finished the tune, I was once again taken wholly aback. Then there was delicious stage banter about the "radio-friendly version," and the very brief reprise.

Then "Ghost." As someone aptly put it later, in a very rhetorical question, "How huge was the Ghost?" It raged before morphing into a "Can't Turn You Loose" jam.

At some point in Nassau I had said, "I have a fresh attitude now. I'm ready for that "Lizards." I feel that "Lizards" can sometimes be a barometer for how you're receiving a show…it's by all accounts a re-

markably beautiful tune (behold the end solo!), but it is usually viewed as an annoyance by jaded oldbies. If you're in a good frame of mind, willing to invest in the show you're at, however, it can be (and should be) a very rewarding listening experience. I also try to remember how I felt when first blissfully swept up by the chorus ("I come from the land of Gamehendge!") while originallylistening to one of my first Phish tapes, 4/16/92.

I was three years late, but I got to see a Providence "Bowie." At this point in the generous set I wasn't expecting a revelation, and it was indeed one of those upbeat versions I sometimes complain about; but it was about two minutes longer than similar versions, and I found it quite enjoyable and even intense as it was peaking. Enjoyed this one for what it was.

By the time the encore arrived, "Hood" wasn't even surprising. It seemed to slide effortlessly into place, a very special choice for a very special show. I thought the opening section was great. There was lots of stuff going on in there, particularly from Page's various keyboard sounds. And the jam had, to my ears, an almost profound little stretch before the peak. I felt like I was getting the Gravity's Rainbow effect for a while there, as the jam threatened to drift off into the atmosphere. And then, I am quite happy to say, they played the end properly! Yes, they actually jammed on the "You can feel good about Hood" chords at the end (as in most modern versions), rather than going straight to the lyrics (as in all '97 versions, to my knowledge). A nice treat, and a great "Hood!"

Phish in '98. Galactrex THX-3000.

7/28/98—Mike Connors

We arrived in Kansas after a long drive through the night from Chicago. It was a warm day and turned out to be one of the best lot scenes of the summer tour. You could feel the freedom as the boys took the stage to the less then sold out crowd of die-hard fans

By starting off the show with a great "Emotional Rescue" we just knew that this show would be a bit above your average Phish show. This show allowed Phish to relax and have a great all around show in front of a smaller crowd. The "Down with Disease" was nothing spectacular, just a normal version, but the "Moma Dance" that followed turned out to set the mood for the night: funky. Next came "Tela;" I couldn't believe. This "Tela" was the first in a while, and you could tell where the show was heading. "Tela" went right into "Sneakin' Sally," which again let the funk out. "It's Ice" followed, already the third rarity of the first set. The sound at Sandstone is great, probably due to the lack of a shed and the stage setup that is similar to the festival setup, though on a much smaller scale. During the quiet section of Page's piano solo in "It's Ice," Fishman broke out his vacuum and a rare "Lengthwise" emerge. This was the first "Lengthwise" in 295 shows, and it segued right back into "It's Ice." Following an energy packed "Sparkle," they led us into a great version of "Funky Bitch." After the "We'll be back in 15 minutes", they went into a little "Black Eyed Katy" reprise, that finished this fun rare set with some more of that good old funk.

The second set was the tour's halfway point, and it began appropriately with "The Wedge." "Poor Heart," a rare "Mango Song," and "Brother" followed only to give way to a fun filled "Contact." Trey was very talkative during this song, thanking fans that he met last night in a bar for buying the band drinks. The "Contact" even featured a "Mexican Love Style" groove. "Maze," "Prince Caspian" and "You Enjoy Myself"

gave this set a great powerful ending, and put a smile on everyone's face. The encore featured a funky "Camel Walk," followed by a calm and soothing "Squirming Coil." Page's solo to end this "Coil" was accompanied by the crisp night air that brought this amazing show to an end. This show is a must have from the summer of '98, and one of the best Phish has given to us in the recent years.

8/6/98 Lakewood Amphitheater, Atlanta, GA—Peter Broadbent

Everybody who has been to a show knows that the joy is in the total experience. The music draws everybody together, and it is as if all the people are just cells in one big body. I think the friendship felt at Phish shows is a phenomenon unique to the jam-band scene. There really is a wonderful camaraderie that seems to just flow from person to person at a Phish show. I would be content often to just sit in the parking lot and watch the parade of people pass by me. Everybody there is different: different jobs, different families, different cities, but for an afternoon or an evening, they are all feeling the same thing. That is some powerful energy.

I was at Lakewood in Atlanta in August of 1998, and I will take away an image from that show that most others probably didn't even notice, and, really, there was no reason they would have. I guess that is my point: The great thing about a Phish show is that everybody comes away with a different favorite moment.

Here is the moment I took away from Lakewood. "Oh Kee Pah" got things started, and the split second it ended, they broke into a great "Suzy Greenberg." Upon hearing the first note of "Suzie," this guy about ten feet in front of me with long curly hair (in a Fletch, Lakers-style headband) jumped as high as I think a human can possibly jump. One arm clenched in a fist, straight toward the sky. If you've ever seen the *Simpsons* episode that ends in Millhouse (holding a poodle) jumping up as high as he can, then you know what I'm trying to describe. If you haven't seen it, just picture one dude jumping as high as he can because he is so pumped. That is what I am getting at. That guy was so psyched to hear "Suzy Greenberg," that I automatically was as stoked as he was. That is the beauty of a Phish show. The energy just flows from person to person.

Lakewood was an awesome show, thanks to both the band and the crowd. Thanks to Phish for playing "Roses Are Free," my favorite cover. Thanks for playing a killer "Fluffhead." Thanks for taking a chance with "Running with the Devil" (it worked out great). Thanks to the crowd; as long as you are feeling good, so am I. Thanks to the dude with the headband who was so excited to hear "Suzy Greenberg," you made my show. Anyway, it's silly to try and sum up the Phish experience in words, it just doesn't work. So I am gonna stop trying, but thanks for letting me try.

8/8/98 Merriweather Post Pavilion, Columbia, MD —Christian Campagna

Traffic can sometimes be okay. If you're travelling on the high of a great show the night before, and expectations are high, you won't even notice the clock ticking away. I must add though, once the clock starts reading 7:35 and you are still sitting on the highway not knowing how much further you have to go once you get off at your exit, it can be quite unpleasant. Such was the case on this very hot evening in the state of Maryland.

My last Phish show in Maryland (in December of '97) was, to put it bluntly, a personal disaster. I will not go into it here, but I wanted to redeem myself and enjoy this show. Plus, hearing about the venue itself, and some past Dead shows here, I was filled with anticipation bordering on extreme impatience. After sitting on the highway not moving for close to ninety minutes, my car began to move closer to the exit, and I was eventually off and directed to…nowhere! I figured out I was to find my own parking space, so after a few minutes, I made my way to a Sears parking lot and followed the herd. "The herd" is definitely what I felt like, as the crowds had to walk slowly through woods, up hills, down hills, through more woods, and eventually to a roped area that would be the entrance.

My first thought upon entering the venue was of a summer camp. There were trees all over the place, and behind the lawn you could hang out on the hill amid trees and people. There was a barn at the top of the lawn, at the sight of which I immediately called the first-set "Farmhouse."

"The Wedge" opened the show maybe ten minutes after I found an area on the lawn from which I could see the stage. This is the quintessential Phish opener to me, perhaps because of the perfect placement at the Great Went the previous summer. "NICU" followed, and as usual got the crowd smiling, always a pleasure to see this early in a first set. The first funk of the evening came next in the shape of "Sneakin' Sally Through the Alley." This version, although not the longest, is worth hearing as there is some serious, thick funk being laid down. Very similar to the one on Long Island in the spring, except this one eventually made its way to "Guyute." The "Sally" ended with Trey playing the muted counting he normally plays to kick off "Guyute," except he had some heavy delay on his guitar and played it for a bit longer than normal. Rocking as usual. I was unfamiliar with the next song, and learned it was "Ficus" at set break. Although not my favorite song, it was a fine addition to the many personal debuts I got in '98. My predicted "Farmhouse" was next, and I enjoyed it amidst the trees and hot weather. This song is great in the summer for me for some reason. "Possum" followed and was rocking as usual. I thought the set would end, when the band started playing another unfamiliar song to me. As soon as Page started singing I realized it was "Sweet Jane." Perhaps a Halloween tease? Whatever it was, I was happy with it as a set closer.

Set break seemed longer than normal, which gave me time to explore and try to find my friend, who I was supposed to meet at Will Call at 6 PM. This proved a bad idea amongst the thousands of fans, so I settled on the hill behind the lawn. A guy plopped down on his back directly in front of me, and proceeded to "pull a Jimi Hendrix" (vomit while lying on your back). This was my cue to get back on the lawn.

"Cavern" opened the second set in a similar fashion to the version on the Island Tour in the spring, with Trey starting it. I love this song but enjoy it better at the end of a set. Also "Sprach Zarathustra" followed (another prediction of mine, because of the venue) and was, as usual, funky, visually amazing, and all-around fun. Not as great on tape as some versions, but always welcome in my opinion. A beautiful "Tela" was next. After seeing "Forbin"->"Mockingbird" the night prior, this was another great addition to my summer.

Before this show, I still was not sold on "Piper;" it just seemed very loud and cacophonous to me. I will also admit I was not paying much attention during the composed part this particular evening. What eventually happened in the jam, blew me away. Pure jamming, my first "big jam" of the summer so far actually. Immediately following the composed section they start building and building until a bomb goes off, and some rocking Type I jamming. Eventually they lock down a heavy groove thing for a few minutes with Trey busting out some funky licks with his effect made famous in '97 (see jam before Great Went "Gin"). Fishman keeps it interesting on the ride cymbal as Trey starts playing some great melodies that Page picks up immediately. This fades out as Fishman comes out from behind his drum set for my first "Sexual Healing." This is the perfect song for him, and to hear the band sing the backups is hilarious.

What better way to close a solid show than with "Harry Hood?" Call me crazy, but I was never that big a fan of this song, but I always enjoy it when I'm there, and it always seems to end a great show. It's just not my favorite, kill me. I think I enjoy the band/audience bliss during this song more than the actual song.

A glowstick war started, and as usual, seemed useless after the one that took place at the Great Went the summer before. I had no idea what the encore would be, and given the,—quite frankly bizarre—covers debuted this summer, I was ready for anything. I was not ready for "Sabotage" by the Beastie Boys, though. I was very surprised, and even saw some people leaving! It was pretty funny to hear Trey screaming like a little kid. I'm a fan of the Beastie Boys, and I'm not sure what they would think of this, but it was definitely another surprise on what was a great Summer Tour.

Aside from the traffic and parking issues, this show had good song selection, a lot of covers, and a good vibe all around. Phish should make this a two-night Summer Tour venue.

10/15/98 The Fillmore Auditorium, San Francisco, CA —Charlie Dirksen

Excited? I had not been so excited before a Phish show since 10/31/94 Glens Falls! And I was not alone.

It was the most difficult Phish ticket to score since the Third Ball on 6/6/96 (being blessed enough to get one was a miracle of sorts). But unlike that tiny Third Ball gig, which brought back memories of The Early Years in bars, this show's music celebrated the majesty of Phish's more recent musical trends in larger spaces: 1994 leap of faith exploration ("Reba"), 1995 collective, full-band improvisation ("Gumbo"), 1996-98 space-funk-rock-groove ("Ghost," "Wolfman's"). Only weeks before Phish would celebrate 15 years of gigging, everything would be in focus, in alignment and in tune, much as it had been after the 12/31/95 Madison Square Garden show (though the music of tonight's show was not in the same league as much of the music of that legendary NYE).

The pre-show scene outside The Fillmore was not the anarchic circus folks had predicted. Cops were not present, and only a handful of Fillmore security guards were around to tell people what to do (mostly to "keep moving"). There were only about 200 people outside when I arrived around 4pm. By the time I got in, at 6:45pm or so, there were only around 300 people outside and around 300 in. If ever there was a time to be amazed by the spectacle of desperate, pleading, ticketless fans, this was not the time. Things really weren't that bad at all outside (a special thank you to all of you who refrained from showing up ticketless! I'm sure the urge to go without a ticket was enormous!).

In fact, the vast majority of the folks who showed up looking for tickets (maybe 200 or so, tops) were, naturally, that subset of our com-

munity that appears to care the least for the scene we create—and leave behind—at venues. But all were in rare, well-behaved form tonight, in my opinion. One guy had a 1971 Nolan Ryan Topps baseball card which he offered to trade for an extra. Most people, though, were simply using 'ween tickets as tradebait.

If you have never been to the Fillmore, it holds around 1200 people (or so they say). Red carpeted stairs greet you, and take you up into the warmth of a red carpeted, narrow, rectangular hall with walls adorned with gorgeous, framed pictures of some of the musicians who have played here (the Dead, Santana, etc.). The main room features a spacious, freshly polished, wooden dance floor bounded by modest, well-worn carpeting. Chandeliers hang tastefully from a high ceiling, which has a disco ball in the center. A balcony stretches across the room's entire left (stage right) side. Five or so feet off the floor, a huge stage formidably fronts the room.

The vibe as Phish took the stage (about 8:20pm) was unforgettably intense. People were beyond ecstatic, beyond euphoric, beyond enchanted (and beyond the average age of a typical Phish audience, in large part because of the significant number of friends and family of the band in attendance). Everyone was ready for ENLIGHTENMENT with the first notes the band played. The ZONE was already forming before the band would shoot spirits and souls even more heavenward with their music. I was reminded of the vibe before 10/31/94 Glens Falls, and before "The Other Ones" took The Warfield's stage earlier this year on June 4th. Not having the funds to catch Phish in Europe these last several years, I had not seen Phish play in such small room since my first show at the Paradise in 1989. I was a jaded oldbie turned giddy fan boy for the occasion, hell-bent on having a good time, and I did have a great time, despite repeated elbowing in the ribs by savagely euphoric fan boys. And girls.

Phish opened with a predictably powerful "Ghost." It wasn't a monster like 7/3/97 Nuremberg, or a rager like most of the recent summer "Ghosts," but the crowd loved it! It segued masterfully and wondrously into a lovely "Water in the Sky" (the upbeat, latest version). "Wolfman's" and "Gumbo" followed, and were the highlights of the first set, as I heard it. Although "Wolfman's" funked mightily away for the most part, it ended with a whimper. "Gumbo," on the other hand, was awesome from start to finish, with an impressively unusual jam segment that you must hear for yourself. Easily one of my favorite versions and I'm looking forward to hearing it again!

After "Gumbo," Fish began rattling out "Theme's" opening, using the ride instead of the high-hat, but Trey gave him the "Bowie" signal, and Fish promptly started "Bowie's" hi-hat intro. "Bowie's" opening composed section wasn't as tight as you've often heard it, but the jam segment was short and sweet (reminded me of early versions). "Brian & Robert" mellowed out (but did not silence) the typically chatty San Francisco crowd. Trey commented before they launched into it that one of the many things Fish hates is "the yellow light." Trey asked Chris to keep the yellow light on Fish for the entire song (Trey and Page were trying to hold back laughter at times during this non-serious version).

"Reba" featured the only real Type II exploratory improv of the evening. After a somewhat sloppy opening segment, the jam began with help from THE DISCO BALL!! The jam took a predictably "Reba" path for a long, long time (accompanied by the Disco Ball), with heavy noodling from Trey, until something weird clicked in Trey's mind and he forced the groove into a disturbingly dark, twisted form.

Definitely the only real "what the fuck!?" event of the evening, and not an especially pleasing one to my ears, either. It certainly won the award for The Most Queer Type II Jam of the night. No whistling ending; just a leap into a frightening "Character Zero" closer. Set break lasted about 40 minutes. We were treated to a CD's worth of the Afro-Cuban guitar stylings of Marc Ribot.

The second set opened with passionate versions of "My Soul" and "Chalk Dust", two of Phish's most basic songs. As "Chalk Dust" started, the crowd was so crazy with excitement that I thought people would begin slam dancing. I had been hoping for a more memorable Event to kick open the set. But these two typically great (blistering) Phish tunes clearly pleased most in attendance.

"Roggae" was beautiful and perfectly placed. I really needed a good melodious kick in the ass after what I thought were two la-ti-dah openers. It wasn't a flawless version, but it's one of my favorite Phish songs, and I was thrilled! I also love "Moma Dance", which came next, but unfortunately, Phish has apparently decided not to take this tune out there yet. This was a perfectly average "Moma Dance." Sure it was funky. Sure I loved it, but it didn't do anything different from almost all of the versions you have heard.

Fans of "Velvet Sea" will probably really want to hear this version. It was the first time I think I actually enjoyed hearing it live. Trey seemed very into the solo, and, if memory serves, it went on and on and on. I'm not sure how well it will come out on tape, though, because of the (typically) inconsiderate, chatty San Francisco crowd (yes, even at tonight's gig! I couldn't believe it!).

"Fuckerpants" (aka "Prince Caspian") was the highlight of the second set, easily, in my opinion. Fishman kicked open the jam segment with thunderous cymbal and tom work, and everyone else followed suit and played the most balls-to-the-wall version of "Caspian" ever. A must-hear, even for folks who don't like "Caspian." Floating on the waves?!? More like thrashing!

The soothing, gentle, mellifluous and charming "Frankie Says," another of my favorite Phish tunes, came next. Very strange placement. An enormous contrast to the "Caspian." The placement of this version caught me off-guard and didn't sit with me too well.

Like "Moma Dance" earlier in the set, "Birds of a Feather" was basically played the same as it has been all year, with just a bit more of an edge to it. The jam segment sounded more like "Chalk Dust" than "Crosseyed and Painless" to me, this time, though. I'm hoping that they use this tune to go new and different places sometime. Soon.

"Lawn Boy" was perfect for the intimate Fillmore, of course. Page sang very well, and all were amused. Mike took a solo.

"Harry Hood" featured a very eccentric opening segment; lots of toying around from Trey. It wasn't all that tight. The jam segment was… was…was…Original. It opened with Trey briefly teasing Copland's "Fanfare for the Common Man." Strangely and unfortunately, there was no long, Slave-like, bewildering crescendo/build in this version. Rather, Trey seemed to be fighting with ideas. He'd start something and then change direction and then start something again and change direction. I felt that it was aimless, but some folks seemed really into it. I had high hopes in its intro, and was disappointed that nothing even Typically Great (for Harry) seemed to materialize. The version also ended half-heartedly, and many, including Mike Gordon, didn't expect it to close the set.

The encores ("Dirt" and "Limb") were very unusual. As you might

expect, since the band had already played for three hours, they weren't perfect versions. But given the circumstances, they were quite good I thought. The balls it took to close with "Limb by Limb"! Such a complex song, in six, so late in the show. But they ripped out an unusually fierce, somewhat chaotic and *SOAM*-like version.

All things considered, the vibe and the scene of this show won more points than the music, in my opinion obviously. It was wonderful to be so close to the band members again. I have seen bands play The Fillmore for years now, and I never thought I would see Phish perform here. To look up and see them having a good time playing on that stage was the greatest highlight of the evening for me. So even though the music could have been more tight and more magical, it was nevertheless a beautiful, unforgettable evening overall. An excellent Fillmore poster commemorating the evening was available for free post-show (this poster is now being sold by Dry Goods).

10/30/98 Thomas and Mack Center, Las Vegas, NV
—Chris Bertolet

After a homemade breakfast, we lit out to Vegas from L.A. By the time we arrived at the Excalibur, the place was crawling with fans who were drinking and smoking and farting about while waiting to check in. For those of you who've never been to Vegas, take it on my authority that the Excalibur is the cheesiest place in Vegas, which of course makes it the cheesiest place on planet Earth. How marvelously kitschy that a hotel with a medieval theme uses paint colors that didn't even exist until Fermi split the atom. We checked in, snagged a cab, and got online just before five.

Inside, the scene was pretty sedate. The T&M seems very small and intimate to me, given that it's supposed to hold eighteen thousand. It seemed closer to twelve or thirteen thousand. Crowded aisles and spotty ventilation caused a few heat strokes before the lights even went down.

It was the band's fifteenth anniversary, and fittingly, the setlist gave the overall impression of a nostalgic, *Nectar's*-era retrospective. "Wilson" blew the doors off. This was the first time I've heard the new heavy-metal arrangement, and I loved it. I managed to miss one of the highlights of the first set when I bailed to the bathroom during the "Mule" duel—what I could hear of "Chicken Shack" as I returned was nice and bubbly. Clearly, the point of "Long Cool Woman" was to say, "check out how far we've come," and I think in that regard it was hilarious and fitting.

By now the crowd was going crazy, and the first notes of "Antelope" were like a fresh-lit powder keg. Pardon me, but I can't remark on what actually happened during this "Antelope", as the music squirted me through a wormhole and dumped me on some distant orange planet where time ceased to exist. It was a monstrous, remarkable, psychotic version that everyone needs in their collection. Enough said.

I hadn't heard "Guelah" since '96, so I enjoyed it quite a bit. "Lizards" was well delivered, and "Cavern" was high-energy. The crowd loved that three-song stretch, and even though I wouldn't have ever named those songs in a wish list, they seemed perfectly appropriate in the context of the retro set.

The first half of the second set—driving home the *PON* motif—was the hands-down jamming highlight of the evening, and a regular medley in my tape deck ever since. The "Stash" was rather standard, actually, but quickly found its way to the "Manteca" theme. As floored as we were to hear this one emerge, we were even more floored when

Phish absolutely wailed on it. Trey climbed his neck, screaming the "Manteca" phrase and feeding off the crowd's energy as he danced around the stage like a dervish. The theme faded, and the ensuing segue into "Tweezer" unfolded perfectly.

This "Tweezer" was brilliant, and very much a Trey vehicle. Like many '95 "Tweezers" (see 11/30/95), this version just sizzled. I also felt very strongly at this point that the band was making a conscious choice to jam in an "old-school" way this night, almost as if to bring their own evolution full circle. They gave us a bit of everything.

There was another seamless segue from "Tweezer" into "NICU" (already the third of the second set!), and a delicate, tear-jerking little vignette of a jam out of "NICU". Simply beautiful. "Caspian" was a bit of a letdown. Given the song's themes of exploration, I'd sort of prefer more exploration out of the song; less arena-rock bombast and more colors. Nevertheless, "Golgi" was done very well—I'd like to remind all you "Golgi" detractors out there that this is not an easy song to play.

I didn't feel I needed to hear "Driver" again after hearing it at the Greek the night before. I knew we'd get a second song, though, and thought "Freebird" in the far reaches of my mind as the four guys stepped to the mic. Let me tell you, you haven't lived until you've heard an a capella "Freebird" (just kidding—they're all the same). But it was wonderful. I loved it. More importantly, Phish loved it, as both Fishman and Trey left the stage pumping their fists. They knew they'd delivered the goods for three hours.

Overall, this was a generous, interactive, lighthearted, fun show. Highlights were "Wilson," "Antelope", "Stash"->"Manteca"->"Tweezer", the post-"NICU" mini-jam, and "Freebird." A fitting and auspicious warm-up for the following night's festivities.

11/13/98 Cleveland State Convocation Center, Cleveland, OH
—Jeremy Welsh

This was my first show after being lucky enough to see both nights in Prague. I was supposed to go to Star Lake this past summer, but I was sent on a business trip instead. I really wasn't in a position to say no.

I was extremely ready for this show, to put it mildly. I was shut out on my first attempt for NYE tickets, and the week at work was a rough one. My girlfriend, another friend, and I left work early, and raced off for the Ohio turnpike, fighting the Pittsburgh rush-hour traffic (which was not all that bad). We had apple cider, cheese, humus, and a good supply of music (newly acquired Other Ones shows from the summer, Nassau second night, set II, some String Cheese...).

We got to the parking lot right at eight, and rushed our way to the Will Call booth. That line was not a problem; however, the line to get into the show was a pain in the ass. Really clogged, reminiscent of cattle. As we rushed in and looked for our seats, we heard the sounds of a seemingly average "Chalk Dust Torture." As we got to our nice seats (directly behind the floor), we found lots of dancing in the aisles, at least for a while. "Wolfman's Brother" followed, and I was rather excited after hearing about one from Halloween. Oh well, this one didn't go anywhere.

At about this time, I started fearing a less-than-exciting show. I paid a little more attention to "Roggae" than I had in Prague. "Ginseng Sullivan" was the required Mike bluegrass tune (kind of like the "Bobby" country tune, eh?).

"It's Ice" was a really pleasant surprise. Never having been a huge fan, I enjoyed my first live "Ice." The vocals were done rather well, but if I remember right, Fishman came in too early on one of the verses and

made Trey laugh. The spacey jam in the middle of "Ice" was really well done, and could be the best jam of the night. Also, Chris did a great job here, as expected.

It must have been an indecisive night for the boys, as they did a lot of talking before tunes. Trey going to Mike, then to Page, then Mike telling Fishman…got lots of cheering from the crowd, but nothing too spectacular came out of these discussions.

I kind of forgot about "Cars Trucks and Buse*s*," and it was a nice boppy little number, but again, nothing special. "Farmhouse" was a great surprise, at least in my opinion. This was the first time I saw this one live, since that night on *Conan O'Brian*. I really enjoyed this song, and they jammed the end out a bit. I really like the vocals on this song, and they pulled it off really well. "Water in the Sk*y*" has been improved with the new drumming by Fishman, but again, nothing special. "The Sloth" was rocking and got a great reception by the crowd. I felt as though this was more like it, the boys rocking out a bit, and it wasn't "Character Zero." And with the opening sounds of "Antelope," I knew they were bringing this set to a close sixty-five to seventy minutes in. I was keeping my fingers crossed on this one, and I was not disappointed. The opening segment was nice and long, as each of the members took a little solo. I really like when Page pulls out the Moog. A really strong "Antelope" got the crowd up and dancing. Trey changed the lyrics around a bit at the end as well, something about setting the gearshift "to this side of the hole." Huh?

All in all, an extremely average first set. "Ice" was the highlight, as well as "Farmhouse" (at least for me). I tried to get my hopes up thinking of the last show I saw that had "Antelope" close the first set: Darien Lake, where the first set was full of averages, and the second set got crazy.

The hallway was really crowded, and interestingly enough, a lot hotter than inside the arena proper. They were selling beer at the venue, and as my girlfriend pointed out, that really kind of changes the atmosphere of the crowd. Possibly less smoke but certainly loud and obnoxious fans. Also, fans who pass out as two did right next to me. Passing out? What the…?! Why would you do that to yourself at a show? Oh well…

I believe "Olu Dara" was the intermission music.

As the band came out, Trey talked a little bit, telling the crowd how Page got really drunk the night before at the Flats. This got a great cheer out of the crowd, and kind of foreshadowed the "Down with Disease" opener. Starting with a long bass fuzz by Mike, it was easy to guess. This was a really solid twenty-minute or so version of "DWD." I really enjoyed this song, and really got my hopes up. In the middle, Trey started to tease a song, which sounded to me like Velvet Underground's "Rock and Roll," but I may be wrong.

"Sample" was kind of a letdown, as I was hoping for maybe a "Piper" coming out of the end of "DWD." But it was a good "Sample. "Kind of rocked, actually. "Dirt" was really well done, and is one of their more successful slower, emotional songs in my opinion. "Birds of a Feather" really, really surprised me. I did not expect to hear this, as they played it at their last show in Grand Rapids. Although they rocked pretty hard and did a good job, I couldn't get over that this was a repeat. Disappointing. At the beginning of "Meat," I was not too excited, but my feelings would be proven wrong, as this "Meat" is something to hear. It followed a long meeting by Trey and Page, and started off pretty normal. They played it pretty close to the album version before the first reprise,

and had a brief pause. They kicked back into it, played a bit, and stopped for the second time. This time a bit longer pause…and this happened two more times, each time getting longer. About the fourth time, a delay loop had kicked in and they decided to take it out into a nice jam.

The delay loop continued after the song and into the opening notes of "Harry Hood"—although I was excited, as always, to hear "Hood," I realized this was it. I guess it was kind of predictable, with all of the glowsticks that were evident in the crowd. The "Hood" chants were really loud, and the pre-glowstick part was pulled off really well. And as soon as the quiet section began, Chris dimmed the lights and let the glowsticks go to work. My first "war" was really rather impressive; my girlfriend said it was "like giant lightning bugs." It seemed as though most of the tosses were going across the front of the stage, and only one seemed to come close to the band, as it sailed to Page's feet. Looked pretty controlled. I rather enjoyed it, actually, even tough I was tense, hoping none would hit the band. The set was about eighty minutes or so in total.

I was hoping for a unique encore, maybe a "Curtis Loew" breakout to respond to the balloon that made it up onto the stage, or a "Runaway Jim" to acknowledge the fan that ran from the back of the stage and jumped feet first into the front row. But I broke into a huge grin at the beginning of "Good Times, Bad Times." Really well done version! Especially Page's vocals on the "I know what it feels to be alone!" Great stuff!

All in all, a pretty average show. Kind of seemed like a Trey/rock-god show. Lots of posing and soloing, on "The Sloth," "Antelope," "DWD," "BOAF," and "Good Times, Bad Times." My itch certainly was not scratched.

11/24/98 Pepsi Arena, Albany, NY—James Gray

I walked out of the show a few minutes into "Bowie." I was behind the tapers' section mostly bewildered by the dancing and cheering of the crowd around me. I watched them do every variation of the rhythmically challenged, drug-addled hippie jam-band dance: the White Man's Chicken, the White Man's Washboard, the Random Elbow Toss, the Swirl, or any basic movement that may otherwise have been induced by a home remedy for irritable bowel syndrome.

They cheered at the conclusion of each song and they cheered louder still at the beginning of the next. I watched them as they performed this routine between "PYITE," "My Soul," "Roggae," "AC/DC

Oswego

Michael McNamara

Bag." "Lifeboy," and the "Bowie" that finally drove me from the arena. These songs were performed as if by machine, chugging through another New England show for New England fans just grateful the music is loud enough to keep their attention focused for an hour at a time.

The perfunctory nature of the way in which Phish performed reminded me that these guys are merely doing a job. I wasn't watching talented musicians practicing their craft; I was witnessing men at work, bored with their jobs. This point was punctuated by the crazed reaction of the audience. I was bored and they were ecstatic. How could these musicians overcome this gigantic obstacle: the blind devotion of thousands of adoring fans? I suspected they wouldn't dare. They were delivering the goods as promised, filling an order. This may happen to a lot of less talented musicians in boring bands reliant on a single member to focus the energy, but Phish wasn't supposed to be like that. They always said they were more than a band. They said they listened to one another. They said they loved to improvise. They never said they only listened to one another for cues and left all the improvisation to the front man, who instructed the others to take solos as dictated. That wasn't why I was there. I was there because the wonder of a live Phish show was limitless possibility. I watched as those limits grew nearer one another and the possibilities shrank. This thought hit me directly in the "improv" section of "Bowie" when I knew what to expect of this "jam." I was saddened and sickened by the realization that Phish was playing for a different crowd now and the reasons I had for being there evaporated in the frenzied cheers.

I drove the two hours home in silence, mourning a band I loved.

11/27/98 The Centrum, Worcester, MA

The energy in the now fifteen-year-old Centrum was high! The place was very excited and thanks to Phish Tickets By Mail, I had a nice floor seat (with some nice folks around me) from which to observe it all. The ride to the show with Rob Hoffman, and a pleasant conversation at set break with Dan Gardner made the whole evening even that much more enjoyable.

Trey came out on stage excited as well, smiling and pumping his fist, quickly glancing throughout the front rows to see the fans, already making eye contact with many. He was all fired up to play! Mike took some quick peeks but mostly played around adjusting his bass and amp. Fish also checked out those on his side, still wearing the Viking Hat; he must've lost a bet somewhere along the tour and is now relegated to wearing this hat for the remainder of the tour. Page was ready to play, but once he saw what the slight delay in the start was (Trey checking out the crowd) he, too, glanced us over. Throughout the night the band kept in close contact with each other with various glances and hand gestures, very much in sync (unlike the second night, but more on that later).

"Funky Bitch" to start was a nice, standard beginning. Mike did well with the vocals, therefore probably getting himself another song: "Ya Mar." Trey popped a big "Peaches" request balloon with the neck of his guitar. "Ya Mar" contained a nice Hammond organ "Play It Leo" solo from Page with the remaining jam building off of Trey's picking. The jam began to blend into the first chords to "Carini." "Carini Had a Lumpy Head" was strange. It sounded good and strong from where I was sitting, but Trey seemed a little upset. He kept glancing over at Fish either asking for help with the lyrics, and Fish began singing it together with Trey. Or maybe Fish was playing it too fast or whatever; either way, Trey seemed a little

irked. However, somewhere in the middle of the song the band began to arrive at what Trey was looking for, with Mike pounding on the bass, and then Trey's solo ripped through this song and a very worthy version was manufactured. Trey ended the song with a shrug of the shoulders suggesting "at least we finished it off well" and also exchanging small "thank yous" with Fish (something similar to Bobby Weir's small "thank yous" but even smaller). Weird...definitely an inside joke.

"Runaway Jim" was good, very rock and rollish, with the jam containing the "Runaway Jim" melody throughout the whole song. Trey contributed many high, tense notes all along the solo/jam. Mike glanced up in the middle of one of the jams (just before the "by the time he came home he was seventeen" part) to see an oncoming glowstick headed for him, he was able to manage to get his head out of the way, with the glowstick bouncing off his right shoulder. Mike smiled and slightly shook his head, as if to say, "You got me, but come on, take it easy."

"Meat" followed, and since I have never seen them play this song when I was up close (except for Prague, but it was a first for me then and too new to appreciate and understand) I was really never able to follow what goes on. This song is definitely not an arena song; it's more like a jazz-club song. It is amazingly intricate with all four members singing different parts, and playing different complex structures. They are all doing their own thing and at the same time all looking at the others for cues. Amazing! As I said before, this is not an arena song, since the people in the 300 sections probably cannot see the interplay and therefore don't get the song's concept. Trey is constantly looking at Fish. I think Trey has a crush on Fish....After tonight you can really tell why Fish was Trey's best man; these two guys really are close friends and Trey definitely gets off on Fish and his antics. Anyway, a nice job with "Meat!" "Reba's" solo started off as a nice three-beat experiment by Trey, which the band quickly picked up, then abandoned, and then just soared as most good "Reba" jams do. Excellent version! "Plow" (a.k.a. "My Old Home Place") was well done and contained some nice piano work from Page. "Dogs Stole Things" and "Vultures" were normal. After the show a friend thought he heard different lyrics in "Vultures;" if there were, I missed them.

My first "When the Circus Comes" came next, and I really enjoyed it. I am a fan of Los Lobos and like this song. A nice break in the mood and also well done. (Albuquerque the next night had a similar placement and probably is an overall better selection than "Circus" for this spot in the setlist.) "Birds" ended the solid, straightforward set with Trey's solo trying to create one sustaining "bending" note that the rest of the band could jam around. Highlights of set one were "Ya Mar"->"Carini," "Runaway Jim," "Meat," and "Reba".

However next came the monster that was set two. It's been a while since I have seen a more energetic, jammed-out, well-played, all-out set! Maybe never. It was amazing. To put it mildly, they tore the house down. I never say this in my reviews, but every fan must get tapes of this set. Maybe it was just my experience at the show, or maybe it was just the energy achieved between the band and the crowd throughout the night, but I thought they really tore the roof off.

This historic set opened with "Buried Alive." Then came "Wipe Out," allowing for Fish to solo, and for an introduction of "Jon Fishman" at the end. The energy that this "Wipe Out" created moved into..."Chalk Dust Torture!" At the beginning I was thinking, we already heard "BOAF" tonight; by the end I was left just thinking "wow!" "Chalk Dust" started out strong; not with the reckless rock-star abandon like Nassau

4/2/98, but a more cultivated, controlled energy, which the crowd quickly picked up on. This controlled, energetic vibe lasted the whole night. The "Wipe Out" theme poked its head in and out throughout the beginning of this song. The strong jam then blended into a quick two-verse version of The English Beat's "Mirror in the Bathroom." It blended in without a hitch. Out of this new cover came one of the band's most incredible jams I have ever had the pleasure of dancing to. It just didn't stop. It was motoring, sounding like an express train chugging at a million miles per hour down the track. They just kept aggressively hammering on this "pounding" theme. That's all I can say, you will have to listen for yourself. Plus I don't recall them ever going back and singing "Chalk Dust" "Torture after Mirror"—they were just jamming it. In my notes I only have written "Chalk Dust Jam" after this point. Mind you, I was concentrating more on dancing than writing at this point. It definitely lost the "CDT" theme and continued with this motoring theme before finding its way into an aggressive, quick version of "Dog Log." Then, *boom*—back into the "CDT" jam.

"Sanity" was good. The stage was mainly lit up in an evil red glow for a majority of the song, and the ending jam did a quick stop-start that led into "Buffalo Bill." A good portion of the older, more experienced New England crowd picked up on it right away.

"Buffalo Bill" was a rough but happily accepted first-timer for me, and an appropriate fit into this special set. I kept thinking of the irony of the "request balloons" floating around the house all night, none of which had this one on them. The ending tapping jam segued into the first notes of "Mike's Song."

Once again, the "Mike's"->"Weekapaug" was not of the reckless energy one hears in, say, the 10/31/98 Vegas version. It was a harnessed energy. In the middle of the jam, Chris lit up the entire rear seating section, producing that wonderful open space effect of the people behind the band. Eventually, this became a throbbing jam, which I can best describe as an "underwater dolphin sound"; this segued beautifully into "I am Hydrogen."

I checked my personal show files and couldn't believe that I hadn't seen a "Hydrogen" since the 10/8/94 Patriot Center show. That made it even better! The solo was perfect…so sweet and soothing! As with the solos in "Lizards" at 10/31/98 and "Tela" 8/8/98, this solo took me back (to '94 at least), and let the nostalgia flow with it.

Then "Weekapaug!" 10/31/98 may have been better with regard to experimentation, but this one was better with regard to groove. Man, did it groove. The "Wipe Out" teases in this jam went into a "Wipe Out" frenzy with Fish speeding up the tempo with every solo, thus finishing this already fast "Weekapaug Groove" two to three times the speed it should be. This segued into a blend of noise with Trey even rubbing his guitar on the mic stand and then…boom—back into the "Weekapau*g*" theme for a reprise. This theme lasted about a minute and then went into an all-out experimental jam, which mostly consisted of Trey scratching his guitar while Mike continued the "Weekapaug" notes the longest of the four. Once Mike abandoned the theme, the band played an ambient-sounding jam, the majority of which consisted of Trey making sounds extremely similar to the sounds of the Star Wars character R2-D2. At one point, Fish just rolled his drums once or twice. That jolted this soft jam with the continuing energy it needed. He is really great with changing tempo—he knows how to pick his spots.

After all this, at 11:10 PM, we got a fifteen-minute "Antelope." This version was very reminiscent of the one that in the early '90s that

Oswego

contained the "Spider-Man" theme Page had a nice piano part that sounded very similar to something on the "Loaded" album, but I am bad at identifying teases.

The encore, "Wadin*g*," showcased Page singing and included a nice piano intro. It was actually very well done; a nice cooldown after the preceding set. "Golgi" and another "Wipe Out" (one last time for energy's sake) capped it all off nicely.

It really is difficult to describe this show for me, but the least I can say is that the second set definitely tore the house down! The rest is up to the other reviews, the tapes, and time!

By the way, Jerry was in the building: a little Jerry doll was sitting on the back of the soundboard throughout the night.

12/31/98 Madison Square Garden, New York, NY
—Chris Glushko

If you ask most Phish fans what they thought of the shows in 1998, you are likely to get a variety of responses. Many people thought it was one of Phish's finer years as they played high-energy shows, broke out many songs that had seemed to be long forgotten, and continually surprised the audience by learning new and unexpected cover tunes such as the Beastie Boys' "Sabotage" and Van Halen's "Runnin' With the Devil." In addition, the play seemed more focussed and tighter than it did in 1997, a year in which many were critical of the band's often sloppy play and unfocused jamming.

At the same time, many fans found themselves bored in 1998 (at least after the surprise four-show "Island Tour" in April, which seemed more like an extension of fall 1997). The breakouts were fun, the crazy cover tunes were fun, and many of the highly atypical setlists were fun. Yet at the same time, there was something lacking. The long, improvisational groove-oriented jams that brought Phish to new heights in 1997 were becoming few and far between in 1998. Songs like "Down with Disease" that were used at gateways for intense exploration in 1997 were no longer jamming vehicles as the band stuck close to the central theme in powerful, yet relatively uneventful versions. Even some of the band's finest jamming songs such as "Mike's Song" and "David Bowie" became very standard and tame compared to versions of previous years. This isn't to say the band was playing bad, because they were not. They were playing safe.

It was this type of safe play that led me to feel less inspired by the band than in previous years. As stated earlier, the shows had been fun. However, cover tunes and breakouts were not the facets of the

band's play that had brought me so deep into their music. With each show I saw during the summer and fall of 1998 I found myself leaving more and more unfulfilled. This brings us to New Year's Eve, 1998.

Even with all my negative feelings towards the shows that year, it is hard not to get excited for a Phish New Year's Concert. First, there is nothing like the energy of a New Year's crowd, especially in Madison Square Garden. Second, although I had been down on the band's play, I knew that with three sets of music ahead and lots of great songs left in the rotation, even if the show was not an inspirational, jaw-dropping masterpiece, it would at least be satisfying and show everyone a good time.

Before the show, it was practically a known fact among the crowd that the band would cover Prince's "1999" at some point in the evening. The only question was when. Most people, including myself, figured it would be the obvious choice to bring in the new year at midnight. To our surprise, the band took the stage for the first set and immediately jumped into a funked-out version of "1999" complete with dancers in a variety of costumes and some antics by Mike and Trey as they played their instruments laying down with the dancers performing some acrobatic moves above them. "1999" was immediately followed by a "Mike's Song," which effectively set the tone for the evening. The play of the band in the "Mike's Song" was focused and inspired. Over the past year, we had become accustomed to "Mike's">"Simple" with relatively little exploration. However, on this evening, the band chose not to segue into "Simple" out of "Mike's." Instead, they went into a beautiful melodic jam that had Madison Square Garden so mesmerized, one could hear a pin drop. This was followed by a well-received "I Am Hydrogen" and then a blistering "Weekapaug Groove" complete with "1999" teases throughout the intro. As if opening the show with "1999">"Mikes," "Hydrogen">"Weekapaug Groove" wasn't enough of a statement that the band was there to play, a thrilling "Ghost" (with Trey jamming on the theme of "Cold Rain and Snow") followed. "Ghost" segued into the rarely played "Ha Ha Ha," and then "Cavern" closed the set.

Set two opened with "NICU," followed by "Character Zero." "NICU" is always a pleasure to hear and "Character Zero" had the Garden rocking. However, after such a blistering first set, one would have

had higher expectations for the second set. Then came "Tweezer." The "Tweezer" was a glorious improvisational masterpiece. It was a powerful, moving version in which all four band members and twenty thousand people merged into a soaring ball of energy. Then, when it seemed as if the "Tweezer" could not get any better, the band performed a silky-smooth segue into a rare "Cities," leaving twenty thousand fans screaming in ecstasy if they weren't speechless. "Cities" went into "Wading in the Velvet Sea," which provided a much-needed breather before "Run Like an Antelope" built up so much energy the roof of the Garden could have popped off at any moment. "Frankenstein" closed the set, and as the lights went on, a clock appeared, counting down the minutes and seconds until midnight.

With approximately twelve minutes left on the clock the lights went down and the band immediately launched into "Runaway Jim." For the next twelve minutes, the band soared through "Runaway Jim," collecting energy with every minute that went by. As midnight approached, the energy became more and more powerful and the crowd became louder and louder almost to the point where for the last minute before midnight, Phish's PA system could not keep up with the volume of screaming fans in the Garden. A barely audible voice counted down the last ten seconds of 1998, balloons dropped, some mild pyrotechnics exploded around the stage and the band went into the traditional "Auld Lang Syne."" Following "Auld Lang Syne," Phish kicked off the new year with an extended and extremely jammy version of "Simple," which refocused the crowd. "Harry Hood" followed with the band extending the first segment as fans passed around several *enormous* chains of glow rings, creating a visual extravaganza that would be impossible to describe. "Hood" was followed by an expected "Tweezer Reprise," and then "Llama" to close the set. Finally, the night was brought to a close as the band encored with a tasteful version of the Beatles' "While My Guitar Gently Weeps."

The last show of 1998 featured no gimmicks, no crazy, unexpected covers, and essentially no New Year's surprise. Unless maybe the surprise was no surprise, just three sets of Phish at their finest. Either way, I could not have been happier.

7/3/99 Vicki Pennington

Well, they don't call it Hotlanta for nothin', y'all!!
What a great day at Lakewood! My husband and I, together with our one and only Phishing friend still residing in Atlanta, arrived at a few minutes before 6:00 and were literally the last car allowed in the back parking lot before they closed the gate. Whew!. We walked around the lot just long enough to get rid of our extra tickets (we sure made some folks smile!) before we retreated to a shady spot on the grass near the back entrance for a little people-watching. I was positively boiling over with excitement and the anticipation of catching two Phish shows in my hometown over Fourth of July weekend!

Once we made our way inside the venue, we found we had pretty decent seats underneath the pavilion, maybe fifteen or so rows behind those VIP table seats, and we were lucky enough to have relatively quiet neighbors. We were also on the aisle, which I enjoy since the air circulation under the pavilion at Lakewood leaves a lot to be desired. Maybe it was because we were sitting directly in front of them, but Page and Mike both caught a lot of my attention throughout the show. I'm really glad Mike and Trey switched places onstage, since I always dig a positive new element thrown into the pulsating mix of a Phish show.

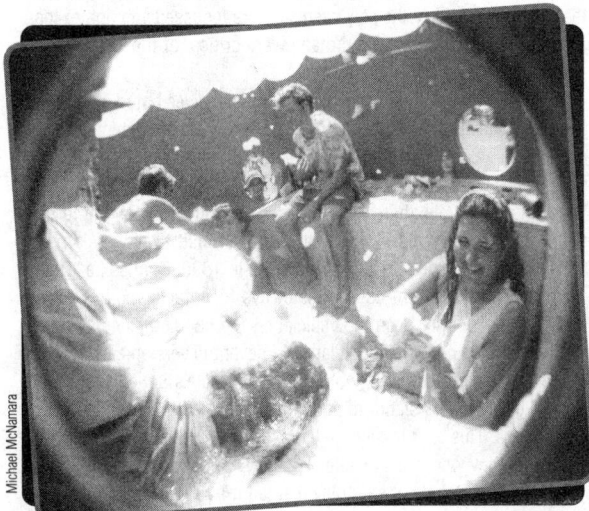

Michael McNamara

Oswego

The show began around 8:15 with a "Chalk Dust" that really got the crowd moving. But then again, don't they all? Serve me up some funky "Gumbo," please! I like mine with extra Mike. This would be the first of four songs in the first set that I would be hearing live for the first time, and that's always a good thing (the others were "Circus," "Tube", and "Meatstick"). After the first two notes of the next song, some guy behind us shouted, "Yay, 'Sparkle!'" and he was indeed correct. This version was nothing really spectacular but, of course, whipped the crowd into a frenzy with the fast ending. Next came "Cavern," which I had heard three times out of my last four shows. But it was "Cavern," so it was also relatively short. Page led the way through "Taste" and a somewhat spacey jam that had a lot of build-up and release. Very, very nice. "Circus" contained a gorgeous jam and lovely vocals from Trey. We then were taken into the stupendous, groovy "Tube", which smoothly segued into "Funky Bitch" and kept the funk turned up. Oh, did I mention Mike? "NICU" is always a crowd pleaser and always good to hear. I had my eyes closed so I completely missed Trey noodling away on his keyboard. I couldn't help it, though: I had to zone in on my dancing groove. "Waste" was a nice way to catch my breath and listen to beautiful harmonies. The set closed with the break-out of "Meatstick," which was very silly, fun, and funky. It was then that I had a premonition: I just knew that we phans should keep a watchful eye on "Meatstick". Something would definitely come of it, but my vision was a little cloudy, and I wasn't able to pinpoint any specifics. I had a distinct feeling it would be memorable, but exactly how special and how memorable was pure speculation at that point. Why is it that no one ever believes that I have a mind connection with Phish?

A spirited "Twist Around" began the second set. It was a much better version than the only other live one I'd heard, at the Gorge in '97. That tune was definitely starting to grow a little. The jam was smoking and then it fell into the "Piper" I'd been waiting to hear. Of course, better versions came later; this one is short, but it's no stinker. Phish spun me around and wrung me out! "Moma Dance" kept the groovy dance beat going (there's that Mike again!) and going. Next we got a much-needed breather with "Mountains in the Mist." Another first-hear for me and I really couldn't make out many of the lyrics, but the vocals were very pretty.

But watch out for that "Antelope!" "Antelope" is on my short list of songs I could hear every show and this version is one of the reasons why. I loved the groovy bass mixed with the spacey keyboards. Simply scrumptious! After that, it was time to grab your powder-blue jacket and a martini for "Contact." What a treat. Very loungy, of course. Trey and Mike led the crowd in swaying our arms above our heads. Too funny. Then somehow or another, "Contact" turned into an instrumental "Little Drummer Boy." Christmas in July? The band really seemed to have a lot of fun with that, but, alas all good things must end.

For the first of two encores, Fishman finally came back onto the stage by himself, grabbed the snare drum from behind his drum kit, and walked up the Trey's mike to sing us his version of "Little Drummer Boy." Classic Fishman. Then the rest of the band came out on the stage and Page said, "As if that wasn't special enough…" and introduced his father, who came out on the stage and, after hugging Mike and Trey, sang "Won't You Come Home, Bill Bailey?" He was a right spry old man with a big, gravelly, ragtime voice. He even did the Charleston during the jam! They all exited the stage, but the lights stayed low. Here comes encore number two: "Harry Hood!" Totally unexpected and just crazy!

Fireworks out in the lot and glowsticks everywhere in the audience. Phabulous show!

7/4/99 Lakewood Amphitheatre, Atlanta, GA

What in the world else should anyone want to be doing on the Fourth of July except grooving to some Phish in their backyard? I couldn't believe I was lucky enough to make just a twenty-five-minute drive to be a part of the magic and debauchery of a Phish show on that hot Atlanta Fourth of July evening. Anticipation amongst phans was very high for this show. Would there be any special guests? Would they play three sets? What type of Phish Fourth of July antics would present themselves?

During this show, as well as the previous evening, I really admired Chris's lights. As we know, lights are such an integral part of a Phish show. I know the lighting rigs must be adjusted to accommodate each different venue, but I saw a big change in the lights since the last time I saw Phish outdoors. For this show, Chris added several new components to his setup, which created a wonderful layered look. The lights seemed to extend farther out into the crowd and they added colorful patterns to the walls and ceiling of the pavilion at the appropriate moments. He still uses what I refer to as the "fall pastels" (blue, brown, yellow, orange) and has added bright, summertime colors that work really well in daylight.

Things got rolling with "My Soul," and I certainly gained a new respect for this tune. I especially love the bluesy piano. Then on to "Ya Mar," which I almost knew was coming at some point or another. Great version, but nothing to compare with *the* version featuring Karl Perazzo on 11/2/96. Then we toured the "Farmhouse," which was remodeled and very beautiful. Always a pleasure. Next we had a little "Oh Kee Pah Ceremony" with all the trimmings and an "AC/DC Bag" taboot! This kicked things into high gear for the rest of the set (for me, at least). Cross another song off of my "need to hear" list with "The Wedge." I love this song and this one was fantastic. "The Wedge" has such a yin and yang feel and always makes me grateful for all of the good things in life, as well as all of the positive aspects of the Phish scene. On to "Vultures," which was quite a treat and really had the crowd moving. Speaking of treats, it was well worth the price of admission to see Fishman in his Fourth of July underpants, shaking his money maker and swinging the vacuum cleaner hose around in front of the people on the front row during "I Didn't Know." I just hope someone got a good picture of that! "Fast Enough for You" came next and was very elegantly crooned. Then, oh my goodness, that extended high-hat intro can only mean one thing…how 'bout a little "Bowie" while the sun goes down? Woo hoo! I'm telling you, Phish can read my mind!

During set break my friend and I were looking at a guy a couple of rows in front of us who had a…well, sort of a ball balanced on his head. It was a little smaller than a tennis ball and he kept it on his head the whole time. We were trying to figure out just what it was and how he could keep it so perfectly balanced, even while he in the process of standing up and sitting down. We joked around about it some and even said that he had a lumpy head.

Then before we knew it, set two began. Has Phish ever told you the story of the "Ghost?" I fear I never tire of hearing it. The jam was spooky and thick and then it segued flawlessly into "Slave". Now that's what I'm talking about! Magnificent! Really gorgeous work on the part of Fishman. "Slave" is always a welcome treat for me; it's one of those tunes I tuck away in the back of my mind since I don't hear it live very

often. The opening vocals were crisp and powerful and the jam went from pounding to delicate and back again. As soon as I heard "Horse" I got really excited because I knew the "Silent in the Morning" coming next would be the bomb. Everyone was really stoked about hearing it and I don't think a soul in the place was disappointed. It was super-tight and showcased beautiful vocals. But it ended somewhat abruptly and "What's the Use" sprung up out of it's wake. It was actually my very first time ever hearing "What's the Use," since I hadn't even listened to the "Siket Disc" yet. I was loving the ambience—it was just what I needed at that particular moment in time. Next thing I know, however, everyone is screaming "Wilson!" and I'm a dancing fool. I believe the fans have dubbed this version the "Heavy Metal Wilson." Seeing Trey swing his guitar up, down and all around really put it over the top. Of course, everyone was excited about "Mike's Song"(including Mike himself). Though I certainly shouldn't complain, I really hear "Mike's Groove" a lot. I always say that I don't want to hear it again for a while (so I won't get sick of it), but then when I do I realize how silly that notion is! "Sleeping Monkey" was very nicely done; gotta give Fishman his props for the great vocals. It was also a welcome chance to stand still and catch my breath. As you might imagine, "Weekapau*g*" was just smokin'! I couldn't believe the show was already over, but I was hoping for a long encore. If there's one thing I've learned in seven years of seeing Phish shows, it is this: Never underestimate.

I completely missed Pete Carini because I was looking at that guy my friend and I saw during set break. He *did* have a lump on his head and it was even glowing! Maybe Phish can read his mind, too.

Time for the "Meatstick" (bury the Meatstick, take out the Meatstick time. Whoa, shocks my brain! Whoa, \ shocks my brain!). Trey told everyone goodnight and what a good time the band always has in Atlanta before introducing the crew and, I honestly understood him to say, some fans they met over the weekend. Then he brought them all out onstage for the debut of the Meatstick Dance. I *knew* there was something special about that song! I don't think I was alone, but "Meatstic*k*" didn't leave my head for quite a while after that night!

I knew it couldn't be over yet because "The Star-Spangled Banner" is just a given on July 4th. Everyone came out in their Uncle Sam outfits (except Mike, who was still wearing his blue jeans and black T-shirt; apparently he had on a bikini top underneath his shirt, which I missed since I was turned around staring at the fireworks). The fireworks were spectacular; certainly better than your run-of-the-mill Lakewood fireworks. What a stellar way to end the weekend!

The first song on the CD that came on after the show ended was (sorry, I don't know the artist): "People all over the world, join hands, get on the love train, love train." What could have been more appropriate?

07/17–18/99 Camp Oswego, Oswego County Airport, Volney, NY—Brian Levine

Could it have been any damn hotter that weekend? When not at the venue for a set, all we did was sit in the shade and hydrate. Still, it was a blast. Besides no official name and no radio station, this was a full-on summerfest.

The first day was highlighted by a funk startup in the opening duo of "Tube" and "Boogie On Reggae Woman." Later, a solid "Tweezer"->"Have Mercy" (first in five years!)->"Taste." The long second set (almost two hours) featured Son Seals on guitar and vocals for his own "Funky Bitch" and "On My Knees." And then it was just the boys again,

and they let loose a solid "Down with Disease" (twenty-plus minutes), a sweet "Wolfman's Brother"->"Sneaking Sally"->"Timber" seguefest, and an always welcome "You Enjoy Myself" to close.

The second day was even better: a great first set with a solid "Bathtub Gin," a sweet bluegrass segment, and solid versions of "Moma Dance" and "Reba". The second had a fantastic "Runaway Jim"->"Free" and a near-flawless "Guyute." The third set included an amazing "Piper" and a crazy segment that you could probably only appreciate fully if you were there ("Wilson"->"Catapult"->"Icculus"->"Smoke On The Water"->"Icculus"), plus the always welcome "Quinn" and "Fluffhead".

7/17-18/99 Oswego County Airport; Volney, New York —Nick Colangelo

Why is it that everything seems the same after a while? Same nine to five job. Same people. Same roads. Same trees. Same band.

What was that last festival? The Great Lemon Ball? Oh, whatever… they all blend together after awhile. Same people, same scenery…but the same improv?! Ahh…the best part about this band is that they never play the same exact thing twice. For better or for worse, as much as the people are the same, the band is the same, the scenery is the same, the food is the same, the life away from the scene is the same, at least there is one redeeming quality.

Though they disappoint us sometimes, the last set on the second say of Oswego was phenomenal and worth waiting through three days of one hundred degree sweltering heat. And then we left in the middle of it.

7/21/99 Star Lake Amphitheater, Burgettstown, PA —Jeremy Welsh

This show was my first since last December's show in Cleveland (I got shut out for NYE), and last year, I was sent away on my first business trip, so I missed "Trenchtown Rock" and "Runaway Jim" here at Star Lake. So needless to say, I was rather excited for last night's show.

The scene seemed rather odd. I can only think that it is at an end of a long and extensive tour; kind of sad, with all the young, lost-looking tour-heads. Lots of ticketless wookies, as the area around the Box Office was very crowded with Heads looking for a miracle. And as for Shakedown Street, well, there really wasn't one. I was hoping to find

Oswego

some nice shirts or stickers or anything, but there were just a few vendors, some food, water, beer, etc. But really nothing to speak of. Maybe the cops were cracking down.

We went inside around 7:15 to find our seats. They were good: left of center, right behind the corporate "boxes." I guess we were even with the tapers, thirty seats to the left. Lots of tapers as the seats filled up. This was my first show with the new configuration onstage, so I pondered that a bit as "Olu Dara" was played over the PA. Thinking of an opener, I had a "Ya Mar" feeling, or maybe a break-out, as they had done the previous two years with "Amoreena" and "Trenchtown Rock."

At around 7:50, the band walked out onto the stage: Trey in a black, long-sleeved T-shirt; Page in a button-down; I think Mike had on a black shirt; and Fish in his muumuu. They opened the show with "AC/DC Bag", which always seems to be a bit slow to my ears. I would certainly not complain if they picked it up a bit. It was nice and funky and really got the crowd into it. "Let's get this show on the road!" The funk was carried out for a bit, with Fishman doing some fun stuff on a wood block. (Fishman stood out the whole night.)

The wood block beats carried right into "Cities," which got a huge roar from the crowd. This version was really nice, with Trey hitting all the lyrics. You could really start to hear how tight the band was with this song as they jammed out the end a bit longer than usual.

After "Cities" ended, the band took a bit of a pause. Trey was talking things over with Fishman and Mike, as Fish banged out some fills. What came next was a quick song that sounded a lot like The Who, or at least Trey's vocalizations did. Fun lyrics, something about a secret…everyone around me held their pens over their setlist books, shrugging their shoulders. It was a nice, quick pop song. After the song, Trey took the time to say the song was a Pavement tune and they have always wanted to play this song (I missed some of what he said, but the song was entitled "Gold Soundz)".

Trey then said the next song will be a cover as well, entitled "Ginseng Sullivan." This token bluegrass song was done rather well , except for a lyric flub by Mike. He seemed to forget one of the verses, and kind of mumbled through. But the musicianship continued to impress me, even on this standard.

Keeping up with the banter, Trey couldn't let Mike's mistake slide and mentioned that they planned on getting all the lyrics correct on the next song, a Phish original. That is when the opening notes of "Limb By Limb" started. Ever since I heard this song on tapes of the '97 European Summer Tour, I was a fan. And this version certainly did not disappoint. At first, I was hesitant of the change made last year on the Island Run, the addition of the "rocking" part near the end (which has appeared on "Story of the Ghost") but I am coming around. It really worked last night, a little edge to an otherwise beautiful song.

"Funky Bitch" quickly started right after "Limb," and it stuck to its name. Mike was given a chance to redeem himself, and he certainly did in this hard and heavy funkfest. It seemed to morph directly into "Black Eyed"…oh sorry, I mean "Moma Dance." I think I am still partial to the instrumental version myself, but who is complaining.

Earlier, in the car, my brother said he hoped to hear "When the Circus Comes to Town," as he really enjoys Phish's version. Well, I wish I was next to him to see his face as they started the opening notes. I think this song takes too much flak, as I really enjoy it as a slow cooldown, and this one ended up being a very nice rendition. And let me use this as a plug to say Los Lobos is very underrated as a band

and as songwriters.

The opening notes of "Taste" started up, and looking at my watch I thought this might be the closer, depending on how hard they raged. And as I mentioned before, and especially in this song, Fishman was *on* last night. I like "Taste," as he can show off his skills as the rhythms are layered, while Trey just wails. And Trey certainly wailed, as I wrote down: "Wow! Wrestling notes out of his guitar!" He got in this stance with his right leg forward, and just worked his axe. It was great to watch. I thought this was turning out to be a great way to end a set that featured lots of nice, tight songs (about seventy-five minutes at this point). In the back of my mind I was hoping for an "Antelope" to close the set, but the "Taste" simply raged in a way that did away with any thoughts of setting the gearshift….

But as the last notes of "Taste" echoed under the pavilion, they did not seem like they were leaving. That is because they wanted to play to the crowd with "Bittersweet Motel." The crowd gave a boisterous applause the two times "Halfway between Erie and Pittsburgh" was sung. A first for me, this nice song left a big smile on my face.

All in all, it was a very strong seventy-eight-minute set. As I said, they were very tight and seemed to be having fun, with even a bit of banter. Nothing spectacular, nothing too out of the ordinary, but a good first set…plus another break-out for Star Lake. I had begun to wonder when Trey was going to sneak a Pavement song into the setlist. Set break approached forty-five to fifty minutes, during which I was thinking of "Ya Mar"(again) or maybe "My Friend," and my girlfriend and I found some different seats a few rows back with more room…and fresh air!

For whatever reason, I wasn't entertaining thoughts of "Mike's Song." I seem to always downplay any hopes of hearing that song, so when I do hear it, I jump and yell and laugh for joy. And that is what happened last night. As soon as the opening notes were strummed by Trey, I lost it, jumping and twisting around. From the new seats that we found, we were able to see the big screens that were showing some great shots of the band. I found myself switching from the stage to the screen. The jam segment out of the opening part was a nice ten minutes long, grooving really deep. About eight minutes in, I could hear a bit of "Simp*e*" coming through. But they wouldn't play it for a couple more minutes, after they "officially" ended "Mike'*s*" and transitioned into "Simple."

And what a "Simple" it was! A cool little noodle at the "Bebop in the band" part seemed to set things off as they jammed out this version for about twenty minutes. As I read this morning, they played "My Left Toe" somewhere in there, but I had yet to hear that instrumental—it all sounded like a jam out of Simple to me, with many parts and themes. Great stuff. One of the closing jams, which could have been "My Left Toe," had the feeling of a plane flying close the ground, over the beautiful landscape of England or Ireland. I don't know if that makes sense, but it was a driving jam that was also full of feeling. Somewhere in there, as I found my brother and sister in another section, I thought to myself of the Champaign "Simple" I witnessed from the front row three years ago (11/8/96); another great "Simple," placed oddly between "Bouncing" and "Loving Cup." That "Simple" was drawn out, but I don't think it had nearly as many "phases."

Near the end of "My Left Toe" (or jam), it almost sounded as they were going to go into "Lizards". It had that high-note repetition series, or so it sounded. But my ears were tricking me as they gradually moved into the grand notes of "Prince Caspian" (or "Prince Fuckerpants", as some like to say). And again, I really enjoyed this song, following the travels of

"Simple." It was grand and big—I wrote "Trey looks lost in himself," as he gazed off, rocking, strumming away. Again, a great picture.

My mind wandered a bit, thinking of what would come next, but everyone seemed to know that "Weekapaug Groove" was going to follow. And Mike made sure you knew, as he slapped the hell out of his 'Doc bass. This "Weekapaug" raged, and lasted for a long time, slipping into a little jam in the middle. All the while, Mike kept his bass work going. Very nice. During the middle jam part, Fish started to work a cow bell, banging it out along a repetitious, almost techno beat. The percussion, along with some keyboard work by Page, reminded my friend Laura of a Talking Heads song, something from "Remain in Light." But no one else really picked up on it. And I really couldn't tell you the last time Phish went out of "Weekapau*g*" into another song….Anyway, it was a great groove.

And although "Golgi Apparatus" is not one of my favorites, it was kind of a nice crowd-pleasing closer, with a ticket stub in everyone's hand. They played "Golgi" at the end of the Star Lake show in '97, as well. I do love when CK turns on the houselights and we can all see the thousands of people dancing and getting down. I kind of had a feeling it would be the closer .

I really had no idea as to what they were going to play as an encore. And I actually wasn't too upset with "Brian & Robert." It is one of my favorite songs off of "Ghost," mostly for the great lyrics. I had a feeling that we were going to get two songs, and "Bold as Love" was a good second song. It gave Page a forum to sing (though he sounded just a bit winded), and Trey a song to show his Hendrix chops. We also got to experience CK's command of the colored lights.

Quick summary: Wednesday's tour-closer at Star Lake was very, very strong. The first set showed a tight band that could jam out songs without getting too spacey. And all they decided to do for the second set was just turn it up a few notches…way up. A thirty-minute "Mike's"->"Simple"->"My Left Toe" was pretty amazing, as was the "Weekapaug." The only downer, in my opinion, was the scene. As mentioned above, lots of Heads seemed lost, or only in search of one thing, and that wasn't music. But I didn't let it get to me as I thoroughly enjoyed my only show of the summer.

9/17/99 Shoreline Amphitheater, Mountain View, CA
—Charlie Dirksen

My girlfriend Becky and I were blessed to receive center box tickets for this show from our friend Mark Young. I had never had a waitress at an outdoor amphitheater Phish show before. It was quite an experience (and an expensive one!). Fish came out on stage wearing his Zeroman frock (if memory serves), but more particularly, the Viking helmet he occasionally wears. I thought for sure things would really smoke from the start, but the first set was pretty tame. "Free Thought" was really cool, and had a "Jingo Va" (Santana) vibe to it which I enjoyed. It was my first time catching this one live. Once the *whole band* starts collectively digging in to this song's jam segment, then it should be a strong opener. "Guyute" was fun, and the "newborn elf" segment of this version was darker and deeper and more dreaded than usual. "Ghost" had a beautiful jam segment, though not profoundly so. "Lawn Boy" was fun, as always. Page the lounge act singer. Page stepped into the darkness, out of the spotlight, for a large part of it, too, very close to the front of the stage, which was highly amusing (or maybe Kuroda just chose not to shine the light on him).

I was psyched to hear "Peaches en Regalia." They played it pretty well, too, though not flawlessly. I still love "Moma Dance", though I don't understand why they (apparently) refuse to really funk this one out. "Water in the Sky" and "Circus" made up the "first set lull" tunes, of course, and lulled the audience they did. I really like "Get Back on the Train", but this version went nowhere. "David Bowie", on the other hand, though not as tight as it once consistently was in its composed section, nevertheless had an inspiring, fired-up jam segment featuring lots of collective improvisation. It was a DELIGHTFUL version of "Bowie," and though it wasn't the 20 min 7/31/99 Japan Monster, it was definitely in that league; it was very strong, especially in light of the last few years of "Bowies." Page stood up at the end of it, as if to say "Let's end the set, Trey, 'Bowie' kicked ass," but it was not to be. They "Coiled" us, and it was flubbed in the composed segment (like all versions of the last few years, right?), and it was obvious to me that Page wasn't that psyched about playing "Coil" at that point. His piano solo was great, as always, but was bereft of the intensity and brilliance of many of his "Coil" solos in past years (hear, e.g., 10/31/94 Glen Falls).

"Runaway Jim" opened the second set well, and was typically awesome in light of all the raging versions of the last few years. "Sand" is an excellent, funky number. This was my first time hearing it, and I loved it, even though this version didn't go anywhere special. Like some of the other new Trey tunes, it has a Santana-esque vibe. But "Sand" is more funkengroovy than the others, and could easily be sandwiched into jam segments of less repetitive, more complex gems like "You Enjoy Myself" or "Bowie" or "Gin." I hope they turn this into a true "Sand"-like number, because it is very versatile and has a catchy hook.

I sat down in the opening seconds of "Piper." "Piper" as you know is virtually "Weekapaug's" main chords repeated o'er and o'er again in a lower octave and different key. And so though I *like* "Piper", of course, since I love "Weekapaug", I nevertheless hadn't been that amused by any but the most amazing versions (e.g., 7/18/99 Oswego, which is awe-inspiring). However, this was the best damn "Piper" that I had ever seen live, and was certainly in the same league as Oswego's. This "Piper" started out typically standard, through the motions. But after the opening five or so minutes, almost all of a sudden, the band clicked in a collective manner and then just skyrocketed off into improvisational rock heaven! Trey became a spectacular, phenomenally talented Rock Star God. Eventually, the version returned to earth, mellowed enchantingly and mystically, and segued somewhat abruptly into "Roggae." Check out this "Piper"!

I love "Roggae," always have, and always will; but this version wasn't anything special. I was happily surprised to get "You Enjoy Myself." Phish really "put it all out on the table" at these Shoreline shows, in a setlist sense. Lots of Big Tunes and lots of New Tunes and well, a LOT OF MUSIC. More than three hours each night I believe.

"YEM's" opening segment was good. Mike's solo section was pretty cool (Mike was, of course, showing off for Phil all night—lots of exceptional Mike at this show!). And Brad Sands brought out three trampolines instead of two during this opening, though, which was a special event.

During the trampolines section, Phil Lesh kinda snorked onto the stage from stage left (audience right) and lept onto a trampoline (on stage right, if I recall correctly). The audience went wild with approval! This was of course the first time that a member of the Grateful Dead performed live with Phish, and the Deadheads in the audience (and there were many)

were going crazy. Phil tried to keep up with Trey and Page, but only lasted about 20 seconds before jumping (falling) off. It was hysterical!

There were some significant monitor sound problems on stage that affected Phil's playing in this "YEM"—at least at first. He had trouble hearing himself (Mike didn't seem to have any sound problems until much later into this very long "YEM," when he spoke to some techs during the version; I don't think I'd ever seen Mike talk to techs during a show before; actually, Phil also, during this "YEM," spoke to some techs, and appeared very annoyed). Phil had his back to the audience, looking at his amps, for much of the first five or so minutes of this version's jam segment. This definitely took some energy out of the jam.

Mike's and Phil's first "bass duet" was a bit hesitant and insecure, but still pleasant. The groove returned markedly after this duet, though, when Fish and Trey lept in and raged for a while. There has never been a more bass-heavy "You Enjoy Myself." Not even the 12/6/96 Vegas version with Claypool. It was insane to have all that bass on that stage. After a strong jam, the second "bass duet" kicked in, lasted for several minutes, and was, for the most part, quite beautiful. Completely improvised, of course. Then it ended. And everyone, including Page, Trey and Fish, applauded Mike and Phil. It was a wonderful moment to see Mike standing up on stage with one of his favorite bassists and strongest influences, Phil Lesh (and both men receiving a great deal of applause from fans).

Eventually, after a lot of warm applause for Phil and Mike, we got "Cold Rain and Snow"! This version was a bit shaky for the first few minutes, since Trey had not rehearsed the song. But it didn't matter (Trey still performed admirably under the circumstances!). Phil sang, and it was fun to hear, and it eventually started to rock. Trey played very well in the jam segment! It was an awesome way to close a well above average Phish set.

I was thinking "Terrapin," or hopefully "Shakedown," for the encore. "Viola Lee Blues" didn't even enter my consciousness, and so I was psyched to hear Phish cover this monster. I was also very happy to see Warren Haynes appear on stage, too! "Viola Lee" had always been one of my favorite Dead tunes. This version was performed well. Warren and Trey accompany each other beautifully. This version had some substantial jamming even though it was short by "Viola Lee" standards. Seek the tapes of this (overall) above-average, and very memorable and historic (ok, at least for Deadheads!), Phish show.

10/1/99 Hilton Coliseum, Ames, IA—Dino Wayne Balocchi

When we found out that this show wasn't sold out in advance, my friend and I decided at about 3 PM to make the drive from Iowa City to Ames. We took off at 5 PM and got in the parking lot at about 7:15. We purchased our tickets at about 7:30, and got first row balcony on Trey's side. Got to our seats at about 7:45 with a couple of drinks and the boys came on at about 7:50.

Right away I was really happy with the sound (despite all the rumors I heard about the sound being subpar this tour) and also with my seats. There were only about ten people in our whole section. This actually provided a weird kind of intimacy and freedom with the band.

"Chalk Dust" opened. This was a strong version. Pretty standard but a good way to get the crowd going. Also, I was having a good time watching Trey play with his pedals, using and perfecting the art of effects and live music. Good work here also by Gordon—he's so loud nowadays. "Moma Dance" was next. The funk was really limited in this

Oswego

version, played very tightly and like the studio version. The end was funny because Fishman kept on singing the ending melody over and over while Trey tried to play different licks in his solo…too bad he was overwhelmed and drowned out by Fish's singing. Its okay, I thought it was entertaining.

You have to be in the right mood to enjoy "Sparkle" and I was in that kind of mood, especially considering the boys were playing so tight. Straightforward version as usual. I heard "First Tube" when Trey opened up the Fillmore and I think this song rocks. To me, this song and "Sand" prove that Phish (or maybe just Trey) are listening to some trance techno these days. This song is high-energy and hypnotic and reminds me of Chemical Brothers. Also, I'm not sure what I think about the backward-guitar effect thing that Trey has been using. It sometimes sounds kind of muddy. And where the hell is Page? Overall though, a great high-energy song.

They followed this with "Bathtub Gin." I will never complain about this song as it is for sure a top-five favorite. There's Page! Thank you. "Faucet Lick" in full effect and I was loving it. The jam took a while to get going but ended up taking off into '98 "Gin" range. Lots of melodic work by Page and Mike and eventually Trey (who took a while as he was doing a lot of screwing around on the effects first). I have seen some great "Gins" (7/29/98 Riverport, UIC '98, and Champaign '97, among others) and this one was great but not historic. Worth getting the tapes and listening to. About eighteen minutes in length, and it included the "Gin" ending.

Next was "Heavy Things." I have two things to say about this song: good time to go to bathroom and get a couple of drinks. It's a boring two-chord pop song that sounds like Hanson. Then "Limb By Limb." I really used to be indifferent about this song, but it's grown on me. Now I like to hear it live and this version was great. Great work by the whole band, especially Mike and Fish. It took on sinister and harmonious tones, due to great band communication. Finally, "Cavern, "and the set was over. While I like the lyrics to this song I sometimes find myself bored when I'm listening to it. Straightforward rock song with wacky lyrics.

Highlights of first set were "Bathtub" and "First Tube". The only improv where they actually took any kind of chance was in "Bathtub"…and even then they seemed reluctant. The song selection was pretty good though, so I couldn't complain.

"NICU" opened the second set. I really dig this song and it makes everyone so happy. Anytime "Play it Leo" gets screamed through an

Kathleen Griffin

Oswego

arena, its cool. Perfectly executed and a great opener. "Antelope" came next. I thought this might branch out into new territory, and it sure did. It wasn't standard by any means. The opening was average length but had a nice bounce to it. No Trey chording, more Trey solo licks: almost like bluegrass. When the jam section began, we got a mellow setting with a distorted chord being looped and Mike laying down the techno bass. The line he put down here was phat as hell. Trey moved to the backward-guitar effect and Page moved to the Moog. Excellent jamming here as the mellow groove was sustained for at least four or five minutes. Then they moved closer and closer to typical "Antelope" land until *boom*: its reggae time. More techno from Trey and hot bass lines from Mike. "Do you have any spike man?" and we're out and runnin' like antelopes. Great version. A must-hear because of the different jam.

Then came "Horse">"Silent." Trey cut off the beginning of "Horse" and just started singing right away. Since when did he start doing this? Is he just too lazy now or does he really think it sounds better? I thought it sounded cheap, but "Silent" was awesome. I have always loved this song, maybe because I love Page's voice. "Silent" soared and glided along with Fish's syncopated ride beat and melted gently into "Gumbo." Yeah! Glad to hear this song. I hadn't heard it since Deer Creek '98. This was a tight jam, but the ending turned into a dark, cloudy Pink Floyd-ish sound. I really liked it because it was completely led by Page on the Moog. I could tell that Mike liked Page's chord progression because he picked up on it right away and stuck with it. However great it was, they definitely took it nowhere and settled, coasting along into the melodic land of "Mountains in the Mist." First time I heard this song and I think it sounds great. Good riff and great melody. Trey sounded the best I have ever heard him, with the exception of the acoustic "Circus" at the Fillmore. Harmony was great and the band worked together in the middle section. No solo really. Pretty cool tune, but I needed something to pick me up.

Then "Julius". This song is cool but I was just not ready for it at all. I was hoping for something funky….Great guitar work here by Trey;

he hit at least three or four peaks before heading out. One thing I always think of when I hear this song is the jammed-out versions of this song in Europe '97…those were the days when nothing was safe from being jammed out. I thought this was the set-closer for sure, but then came "Fluffhead". This song is pretty rare these days, but I seem to catch it at almost half of the shows I go to. After hearing the Alpine sloppiness this summer I was expecting them to butcher it again. I couldn't have been more wrong. Just goes to show, with Phish you never can tell how or what they are going to play. I was very impressed. Probably the tightest version of "Fluff" I have ever heard. "Arrival" was done very well and Trey was soaring. The people in guitar heaven would have been proud as Trey was looking up there for most of the night. I thought for sure the set was over, but with no introduction, "Slave to the Traffic Light." Another one of my top-five Phish songs of all time, and this version was a dandy, played very well in the composed section. During the rock-out parts, Trey was loving the pitch shifter. It sounded okay. The jam section was so beautiful. Mike, I love you for the great lines in this section: you made my night. Mike was the melodic force in the jam and everyone else followed. Great, powerful ending to a long second set that seemed to just keep on going. This was only the third Slave I have heard, but this one takes the cake for sure.

The encore was "Axis: Bold as Love." "An okay version of an okay Hendrix song. Page's voice was again very noteworthy, and Trey also played well. All in all, this seems to be a pretty good show compared to the other shows surrounding it (at least as far as the setlist). I can't help but think that the other shows were played just as tight, but I think this show is worth getting on tape and deserves at least a B or B+.

10/2/99 Target Center, Minneapolis, MN—Ryan J. Nelson

This show was a special one for me, because I got to introduce Phish to a few friends, including one I've known for ten years. It was also the first show I witnessed from as close as ten feet. This was my eighth show overall, which would make me fairly inexperienced by the stan-

dards of many fans, but I am studious, and know my Phish well.

Of course, my fiancée Terri was with me at this show. This was her seventh show, and she had already dragged me across the country to Oswego, Alpine Valley, and Iowa so far in '99. She's really the reason I see as many shows as I do. I can't imagine experiencing Phish without her by my side. But enough of that.

This being a hometown show for us, we managed to secure general-admission floor tickets. Three in our group were first-timers, and the folks around us made sure to let them know just how lucky they were to have general-admission floor tickets for their first show.

My friend Lundo was perturbed by the blue preshow lights; personally, I thought they were dazzling. If I concentrated hard enough on the blue lights, I could forget that I was standing in a basketball arena.

The show began with "Llama:" a great song for pumping up the crowd, but not a great song for reviewing. This was a very high-energy and well-executed version. It gave way to a very slow and groovy version of "Wolfman's Brother." The jam was typical "Wolf" fare, nothing extra special. Mostly Trey- and Fish-oriented. The end of "Wolf" brought on the whok-a-chikah intro of "Punch You in the Eye." This version had a very long intro with Trey experimenting with the "Heavy Things" "beep." It started to sound very "2001"-ish before the initial "hey" section. I hadn't known about the dance Mike and Trey do during the Latin breakdown. My friends and I laughed our collective ass off.

Next up was "Quinn the Eskimo." Terri and I couldn't believe it. We'd shat at Oswego when it happened, and we shat again when it happened at the Target Center. "Quinn" rocked. This is a great sing-along song. Next, we were treated to "Poor Heart" and "Roggae." Poor Heart" was cool, but I could have done without the "Roggae." Luckily, we got "Split Open and Melt" next. This was the jam tune of the set. This version is especially cool because it dropped the "SOAMelt" groove fairly quickly, and while Page kept it in the background, Mike and Trey busted out. They were all over the place during this jam. For a while it sounded like it might not come back around, but eventually Page triumphed, and the outro reared its head. They held the last chords like they were going to end the set, and Trey did intros for the band. He called Page "Stumpy," due to his injured ankle. Mike was "Cactus," Fish was "Manny," and as for himself, he said, "I'm the Good Lieutenant, and don't you forget it." This refers to his Oswego introduction as "The Bad Lieutenant," a reference to a Harvey Keitel movie.

Instead of ending the set, they brought out "The Squirming Coil". This had been Terri's favorite Phish tune for a long time. She always loves Page's beautiful piano solos at the end of the song. Unfortunately, we got no piano solo at Oswego, but this night Page apologized with a long and gorgeous one. It wound and ground and sped, then slowed down, leading into "Loving Cup!" This was a combo I've been dreaming of hearing ever since I was introduced to this song. And since it's a Stones song, I was sure Lundo (who had been appreciating the music thus far, but no real sparks had flown yet) would recognize it. He didn't, but he enjoyed it nonetheless.

Set one was a great set for solid songs but offered little in the jam department. "Wolfman's" had a little, but nothing compared to what it has shown before. "Split Open and Melt" did rage, though.

During set break, we moved a bit back and over towards Page's side of the stage. This was a mistake, but one of the people with us was a wimp and kept complaining about how tired she was, so we didn't have much choice.

This is what I love: a good second-set "Tweezer" opener! This one went in some nasty places (I mean that in a good way), and is a definite highlight of the show. I would've enjoyed it a lot more if there hadn't been some hippie chick in front of me whopping her stinky hair in my face. She was very inconsiderate. Luckily I have the CD-R, so now I can enjoy the show.

"Tweezer" died down and segued into "On Your Way Down." They had just broken this song out at the first Shoreline show, and we felt honored to get to hear it. After "OYWD," we were treated to a sweet "Piper." This is another of Terri's favorites, and this version was killer. It featured a nice, straight build to the chorus, after which Trey dove and the song rumbled. Then Trey made it soar again. The jam raged for a good three minutes before the second chorus, which was very fast. Then it raged for another five minutes at least, before slowly dying down as Trey fell into a little three-note riff; everyone pulsed and Trey quietly soloed. Eventually, Trey walked over to his little keyboard, and emulated his earlier three-note riff. The jam quieted down and followed Trey's rhythm. The pace still raced, but much quieter than before, like a tip-toed footrace. Trey trilled, Page layered, Mike vibroed, Fish swung, fade…fade…and "Piper" died like it birthed, just a few notes on the wind.

Then there was "You Enjoy Myself". I felt very blessed to hear "Tweezer" and "YEM" in the same set, and I was excited about "YEM", since I knew Lundo knew at least part of it. This version stands out for the extra-long spacey part right after the intro; it even went silent for about three seconds (or it would have, if not for all that cheering). During the tramps jam, Page seemed to push at an "Oye Como Va" tease without quite getting there. The jam after the tramps section was all Mike and Page. Very funky. The vocal jam seemed a little tacked on. The song could've easily ended after the final "Wash Uffizi drive me to Firenze," but they went for the vocal jam anyway. It was worth it. A very eerie version.

"Frankenstein" rocked to close the set. A tiny flub in the beginning made it interesting. Lundo knew this one too, so it was cool. Finally the sparks were flying for him. "Waste" was beautiful. This is going to be Terri's and my song at our wedding. We were lucky enough to catch this tune twice in '99.

They seemed to be following a pattern of cover song encores this tour. In Iowa, we got a "Bold As Love", and then in Chicago, we got Son Seals and Sugar Blue. Okay, so the second one doesn't technically count, but I stand by my theory. This was the first time I paid attention while listening to this song, and it's now one of my favorite Beatles tunes. This is why bands should play covers: to expose their fans to new music. Finally, "Tweezer Reprise". I predict this one every time.

I was really hoping to hear a Led Zeppelin cover, since Lundo is such a big Zep fan, but alas, we didn't get it. I'm pleased to say that Lundo really enjoyed the show, and plans on attending Target Center 2000 with us as well.

All in all, this was a great show; not a surprise why this one finds its way onto most people's lists. The "SOAMelt", "Tweezer", and "Piper" are all great jams, and the rest is all played extremely well.

10/7/99 Nassau Coliseum, Uniondale, Long Island, NY
—Dan Alford

I've always hated Nassau and swore I would never return after the Dead broke up, but I ate my words on this Thursday night and they didn't taste all that bad. The whole lot was nothing but mellow. Inside you needed bracelets for the floor, so it was somewhat spacious

there, and there was a continued mellow vibe.

They came on somewhere near eight. Nice "NICU" opener; in my mind this is a tune you can't go wrong with as an opener. Leo [Page] nailed his solo. Organ, then piano, then both. Great. "My Soul" was up next. I actually wanted to see this (can you believe it?). It had a cool intro, not as straightforward as most, and good sustain at the end of Trey's solo. "Dirt", still my favorite of the cheesy ballads, was where I started to get into things. Mike was on the ball and the band crashed down every few measures pushing Ernest's [Trey] solo. Woo hoo!

Then the set got strange. "Bowie", right in the middle of the first set. Mike rolled in on a thundercloud and Fishman raced above like a kite string. One of those "Bowies" that just builds so slowly...I got lost a few times. Plus, Chris' reds and whites were phenomenal. They slowed things back down with "Frankie Says", again with Fish shining. Trey hits an off-key note, but things pick up again with a weird, noodly, and slightly long "Possum". Slow it down again with "Circus". See why the show was weird? Up, down, up, down, up, down, up...

It was definitely time for a new tune. "Gotta Jibboo" is infectious; a looped, funky dreamscape that builds to a fiery earthquake. This one was an instant favorite for me. Then, from way out in left field, "Fluff-head". It had an air of discord. For instance, Trey let out two sets of heavy chords after the first bout of lyrics. Not flubs, just superfluous chords. But the end jam raged and just kept ragin'. Trey was bouncing, leading the crowd, going higher and higher. Wow! Great end to a very strange set.

During set break I saw a really nice security guard asking those without bands to leave the floor. Making "gentleman's agreements." Obnoxious Long Islanders were not obliging. Lights went down again around 10:25 or so and the boys bounced into "Boogie On". A fairly short version, it essentially featured a long solo from Mike and then stopped. "Heavy Things" followed, keeping the vibe alive. I really like this tune, but it needs to develop. The jam has yet to really take shape. Tony held it together a little better on Trey's solo tour.

"Heavy Things" was followed by the heavy funk of "Tube". Slightly strange placement, but a great version. The jam seems to get longer every time I hear it. Page and Trey traded off, everyone churning along, grinding the gears of the machine. "GBOTT" was deeply funkified. It used to be great; now it's awesome, taken to a new level. A happy little steam engine shakin' down the tracks.

A sudden drop into a monster "Mike's" and the vibe is still right there. The jam opened up with a huge tsunami of molten sound from Page: colossal, towering waves that overwhelmed everything else. Trey, having set up a pair of loops, quickly moved to his keys, joining the explosive energy. This segment went on for four or five rounds, and was unique in my experience. Just amazing. A fiery jam followed, one for those who love old-school, loud, and rowdy "Mike's Songs".

After a while the jam wound down into a deep blue ocean, lingering momentarily before segueing into a perfect "McGrupp". Every note was nailed up to the jam, which was somewhat sparse. Page noodled around, responding to slight cues. Trey, then Mike then Trey, then Mike alternated turns pushing things up a notch. It finished up nicely, and the first chords of "Caspian" spewed forth their color. A longtime favorite of mine (I don't care what you say), it had a lavishly painted hot jam at the end. It seemed as though neither Kuroda nor the band knew if it was the closer. Again Chris was spinning the lights but the inevitable "Weeka-paug Groove" had taken effect, wandering about before closing the set.

Oswego

The encore was one of the highlights of the night. A quick "Rocky Top" was fun, a throwback to '92, when it seemed like every encore included a "Rocky Top". But then Trey set right into a flawless "Hydrogen", the first outside of a "Mike's Groove" since '87! "Julius" picked up when the bubble burst, a perfect rollicking encore number. Definitely one for the books. Overall it was a good show, although the theme of the night was discord. A very strange first set, followed by a great second set, followed by a fantastic encore.

December 2, 1999 The Palace, Auburn Hills, MI
—Jesse Jarnow

I got shat upon, quite literally. An auspicious beginning for the mini-tour. I hopped out of my car, over a nicely manicured garden box, with the intention of bopping into the small enclosure housing the cash machine. As I hit the pavement, I felt a glob on my face, atop my eye, between my glasses and skin. The vision in my left eye blurred momentarily. I looked up to see a pack of birds scattering from a tree overlooking the sidewalk. I cleaned my glasses and face, shrugged, and retrieved loot from the automatic teller.

Except for that, and the odorific smellscape of downtown Detroit, the journey was quite uneventful. Quite frankly, it was eerie. For one, we made it to the venue without any hassle. In the miles preceding the exit, though, we saw no signs of tour life. No bumper stickers, microbuses, or compacts with Colorado plates. Arriving in the lot, there didn't seem to be much of a scene either. This, besides some mini-runs, was the first time I'd attended a tour-opener. I'd always enjoyed a vision of hundreds of heads descending from all points onto an unsuspecting locale, somewhere across between a swarm of locusts and an invading army.

Inside the Palace, the vibe was completely nondescript. Again, this confounded expectation. Despite the corporate arena, I fully figured

that the energy would be veritably pulsing, the industrial sterility converted into a crawling organic being. Nope. By showtime, the upper levels were still empty towards the back of the room. The seats behind the stage were completely empty, a giant black backdrop dangling comfortably from the lighting rig behind the band's setup. On one hand, it was slightly discouraging seeing so many empty spots. On the other hand, the backdrop provided for some level of intimacy usually missing at arena gigs. If it is, in fact, a harbinger of things to come, perhaps that'll be a good thing, too. Less people on tour is probably healthy at this point.

Waiting for the show to start, I prepared for the comfortable rush, the oncoming frenzy, when the houselights went off. Coupled with the fact that nobody had seen Phish since the last tour, two months ago, I figured it would be unbearable. It wasn't. There was the intense potential of them being a completely different band than had walked off stage after the Albany tour-closer in October. They weren't. I can't say I was disappointed, but I wasn't surprised. The band walked onstage, Trey casually began strumming the intro to "Runaway Jim" and the show was off and running. Off and walking, actually. The jam pushed tentatively in several directions, but never settled on any one theme.

"Farmhouse" followed and provided the mode the band would follow for their improvisation in the first set. Slightly rearranged, and boasting a new ending refrain, it provided a framework to showcase the band's increasing ability to create improvisations that resemble carefully put together studio arrangements. Here (and in "Heavy Things", "Roggae", and "Velvet Sea") the band wove a delicate balance between clean-sounding Trey soloing, Fish's delicate cymbal work, and measured upper-range contributions from Mike and Page. The quiet sections of "Roggae", in specific, before the majestic power chords signaling the end of the song, were stunning in their dynamic.

Phish, in 1999, is not a band that needs to burn barns, or storm them for that matter. Nor do they want to. Fire is not required and there is little to prove. With that, there are few pyrotechnics. Perhaps this accounts for the empty seats. Instead, the band has elected to erect nearly perfect structures in which to sit and contemplate. Or, for that matter, pay large amounts of money to have two-hundred-year-old barns transported to their property in which to record, as Phish have been doing for the bulk of the past several months. That's not to say that the band can always entirely suppress their exuberant adolescent urges to set things ablaze. It's not that the first set was without energy, it's just that it was a more conservative kind, more along the lines of picking up where they left off sometime ago than starting anew.

The requisite big jam in the first set, "Run Like an Antelope", was a marginal success. Like many versions of late, though, it seemed to amount to not much more than the band running through the motions of the tune. Several times, the band verged on points of no return: dropping into joyous chaos, building and releasing back into the chord progression. Five years ago, the band would've turned the joyous chaos into the bed for the next part of the jam, continuing to build into ecstasy before letting go with an unparalleled precision. Here, the "Antelope" jam in general and the chaos contained therein seemed token signposts to a time long past.

Are they adolescent urges, though? Are jams with monumental releases and shimmering climaxes somehow more immature than textural, ambient explorations with no clear point A or point B other than the moment the music begins and the moment that it ends? This could

be exactly the reason that tension and release jams get a bad rap. They are inherently predictable, in some sense, by the fact that they will ultimately resolve back into a song. The urge to get to this release can be seen as a sort of musical impatience, like a child wanting a clear ending or obvious moral resolution to a troubling story. Sometimes that's okay, though. And sometimes the question of which approach is better or more worthy is completely irrelevant.

The second set this evening focused on grooves, heavy grooves. The grooves weren't tensionless by any stretch of the imagination. Rather, there were occasional releases in the forms of clavinet and bass breakdowns and other spontaneous arrangements. Trey's guitar work on Stevie Wonder's "Boogie On Reggae Woman", the set-opener, was a good example of this. For the duration of the ten-minute jam, he played an A chord. A simple concept. No more. No less. As the jam progressed, with Page and Mike exploring various melodic ideas, Trey played with different voicings, altered his rhythmic attack, and cycled through a variety of guitar tones. There was a logical progression to all of this, and when the band went back into the chorus at the end, it made sense…even leaving the listener wanting more.

Likewise, the sheer funk of "Gotta Jibboo" and "Also Sprach Zarathustra" expanded on the idea of a tensionless tension. Both jams were characterized by an unrelenting groove, Page's work on the Fender Rhodes recalling early '70s Miles Davis. On top of this, Trey and Mike laid down a variety of noises, alternating between gorgeous soloing and ambient noise, with Fish keeping the beat in a completely straightforward yet totally compelling manner. Sandwiched in between the two was a "Bathtub Gin" that featured a more traditional elucidation of the song's theme, culminating in a chaotic build (with numerous reprises of the "Gin" theme), which dissolved into fractured fragments before the "Also Sprach" beat kicked in.

For much of the band's career, up through the mid-'90s, "You Enjoy Myself" was pretty much the band's sole vehicle for funk. Though the song's jam is chameleon-like, often taking on properties of whatever approach the band is focusing on, it has shined particularly for the past several years, seeming tailor-made to the sparse grooves the band so loves to plumb. For all of its chameleon-like qualities, it's one of those songs that can help one get a good idea of what the band is into at the moment. The jam out of "YEM" tonight was a culmination of the evening's improvisations—a combination of deep staccato grooves and more traditional building progressions. All in all, while mining a rock-steady vein, the band morphed the bed into something entirely new—my favorite kind of Phish jam: a completely improvised chord structure on which the band builds the next part of the improvisation to the point where it sounds like they know what they're doing. Midway through the "YEM" jam, Trey and Fish began oohing, integrating in the spontaneous arrangement part of their recent foci.

All of these themes continued as the band wound up the jam, ending it neatly, before starting the vocal jam nearly completely from scratch. What resulted was something genuinely beautiful. Where the band usually moves into scary harmonies and mouth percussion, augmented by vocal delay loops and swirling dark lights via messrs. Languedoc and Kuroda, tonight's vocal jam was straight-up Phish. The band created gorgeous chords, changing them one note at a time in a mature, spontaneous arrangement. It sounded like nothing short of a song Brian Wilson never wrote, gently cascading and carefully twisting with the slightest turn of sound. By the end, it began to sound like a

small choir caroling. When the familiar melody of "Little Drummer Boy" began to take form, a cheer went up from the crowd. From the mesh, Fish began to sing. "I'd like to make love to you, bum-rum-bum-bum-bum…" If I didn't know any better, I would've thought it an outtake from *Pet Sounds*. Soon, Fish was left alone on stage to serenade the crowd.

Now, back in the car, rocketing back towards school and class in the morning and afternoon. Tour, or a collegiate approximation of it, has begun again. Yes, there was mad energy in everything that happened today, preceding the show…but now that it's over, it feels almost like a routine. We've done this before. We'll be home in an hour or so. I'll post the setlist and climb into bed. In the morning, I'll peel myself out of bed and go to class. After my afternoon lecture, we'll pack up the car again and head off to Cincinnati for two more days of fun and high adventure. It's a pattern that I'm sure many are following. It's not new, but that doesn't make it any less exciting: it's a matter of perfecting the dynamic somehow, and understanding it.

12/3/99 Firstar Arena, Cincinnati, OH—Jesse Jarnow

If we're gonna keep cutting it close like this, you should really consider getting a radar detector," Harold suggested as we sliced down I-71, dodging rain, in a beeline for the Firstar Arena.

"Quiet you fool. Drive the goddamn car," I intoned. The ticket time read 7:00. The question was, would anybody bother to tell the band that show was supposed to begin earlier than usual. Harold stepped on the accelerator. "Go the speed limit," I said, not quite believing myself. I looked at the clock. Quarter after seven. "Shit."

"Where the hell is Cincinnati?" Harold asked. "Is there actually a *city*?"

"Who knows what these cretins think of as a metropolis." I glanced out the window. "Watch the Lexus," I said, as Harold sped up in order to avoid a potential calamity involving a merging motorist.

We turned a bend in the road, and there it was, stretched out in front of us. We'd driven from just outside of Cleveland, heading south, skirting Columbus by way of a beltway, and on to Cincinnati. The only signs of life we'd seen had been gross suburban sprawl: strip malls, housing developments, rest stops, and gas station after gas station. Suddenly, a city. A very clean-looking skyline, cloaked in a somewhat drizzly night. The buildings were polished, and the lights colorful. It resembled an enormous Las Vegas theme casino, life-size to the point of surreality.

Somewhere in there, near the riverfront supposedly, was the Firstar Arena. Several wrong turns, however, and we'd be in Kentucky. It was a dangerous line to tread but, hey man, no fear. We made a couple, admittedly, and somehow found ourselves in front of the Firstar Arena. No shit. Parking for $10 and it's almost showtime. Up the ramp, up another…and another. "I've never seen you run before," Harold panted.

"You've never seen me late for a show before," I managed to wheeze in reply. We found ourselves on a walkway, crossing in between Cinergy Field and the Firstar Arena, high above a major street. Seven thirty. Off in the distance, I could see several other skywalks, such as the one we were on, like an architect's design of a futuristic city realized in full. Later, we would learn that one could traverse the majority of downtown Cincinnati by following the path set forth by these walks. We haven't tried it yet, but I wouldn't doubt it.

Rushing through the gates, we made it to our seats just in time for the houselights to go down and the band to take the stage. As Fish and Mike kicked into the intro groove to the still newish "First Tube",

the inadequacies of the venue's sound soon made themselves apparent. From where I was, anyway, it was clear that the evening would be a sonic washout. Going into the tour, I was afraid to hear "First Tube". Supposedly, the band has just recorded a version for release on an upcoming studio album. The band's tendency seems to be to water down song arrangements when they record them. Witness the raw power of fall '97's "Black Eyed Katy" wussified into the "Moma Dance", which is fun in its own right, though not nearly as cool.

Thankfully, "First Tube" seems to be an exception to the rule. It raged. Locked into the groove, the band managed to flex the song into something both deeply funky and fist-pumpingly swell. I'm extremely interested in seeing how the new album turns out. Band members have said that the approach on the new disc is something akin to their live performance. Simultaneously, their live performances of late have been demonstrations of live studio creations, both in terms of the layering effects Trey has been using and the careful, spontaneous arrangements the band has focused on. Either way, where the past several studio Phish albums have focused on the difference between Phish as a live band and Phish as a studio band, whatever comes out of Trey's barn come spring 2000 will surely be a skywalk between the extremes.

The Firstar Arena is pretty old, I gather. It wasn't always the Firstar, though. Last fall, when Phish played the same room, it was called the Crown. Twenty years ago, it was called something else. Exactly twenty years ago tonight, The Who played there. Outside the show, there was a riot in which several fans were trampled to death. The brutal fact of this anniversary made its way around the arena this evening in whispered bits and bites, more folk tale than anything else. It was a grim story to hear. "Which Who song will the band cover tonight?" was an unintentionally perverted question on many lips. No Who song ever came, though the song choices were quite open to interpretation.

"It was many years ago, now," Trey sang in "Wolfman's Brother", "though I really can't be sure"—an unintentional nod to the flying lore, reverberating off the concrete walls. "…and the Wolfman's brother came down on me." Something ominous, to be sure: a dark force. What happened to the counterculture? Was the Who riot in 1979 another ending, an alternate Altamonte? Altamonte was one thing: a couple of rowdy Hell's Angels and some illmatic vibes; hundreds of people stomping, stamping, and crashing was another entirely. When did the counterculture become the culture? Was it some mutated revolution, like the broken rotating stage at Woodstock stuck somewhere in limbo as in *The Fly*? What resulted? This…?

The night had the potential to go full-on into the black. It didn't. There was a glimpse. Or, at least there was on my part, and perhaps that was more mental than anything else, but the "Wolfman's" jam seemed to lurk on the edge of darkness, before pulling back into a somewhat standard groove, which turned into something slightly new just before the ending. Then, happiness. Happy music. The rest of the set seemed, if not celebratory, than (at the very least) somewhat more open to the possibility of life. The song choices were well made, though the executions of most of the songs was somewhat subpar. Of note were the dialogues between Trey and Page in the "Possum" jam, the new edited ending to "Get Back On the Train", and the entirety of the "Slave to the Traffic Light," which (sadly) got mostly eaten up by the echoes.

During set break, we circumnavigated the arena in search of a pay phone. Plastered across every conceivable surface in the venue were advertisements of some ilk. Even the stairs in the arena proper were

painted with small logos and shields. A phone company seemed to be a prominent sponsor, with big, colorful displays featured seemingly every twenty feet. As for phones themselves, they seemed to be infinitely more rare. We located one and, once again, made it to our seats just in time for the beginning of the set.

"Sand" was the evening's exercise in a rock-steady bass line and drum beat. The jam had interesting moments but didn't seem to progress to anything greater. "Limb By Limb", on the other hand, was quite another story. Lyrically, it seemed to be the most direct nod to the events of the past: "trampled by lambs and pecked by the doves." The jam crested in much the same way it has for the past two years, though it quickly dropped into something resembling the ending groove. From there, the band moved into ambient territory. The textural jam, on which Trey played keyboards for a good portion of, was quite different from any "Limb by Limb" so far. For twenty or so minutes, the band explored completely fresh spaces, Fish trying out different drumbeats and tempos, settling, and then moving on again. The entire thing was dark and absolutely spine-melting.

Though the jam could've ended logically without it, Trey forced the band back into the ending and they closed the song. A well-executed "Bug" followed, replete with a slightly rearranged chorus. "Piper" raged in a somewhat predictable manner. For the second run through the vocals, Trey was either completely lost or decided to show off the other three parts of the vocal arrangement. Either way, it was enlightening hearing exactly what the rest of the band is singing during the circular vocals.

"Harry Hood" has been a phoenix of late. The song, completely glorious for much of Phish's career, has grown somewhat stagnant in recent years. Over the course of the first half of Fall Tour, though, it's begun to once again show signs of life. Though nowhere near as monumental as the 10/8/99 Nassau version, this rendition was quite enjoyable. The problem with "Harry's" of late is that the band has been running through the chord changes as if they were no more than that. Step one, the song begins to build; step two, Trey begins to go "deedley-deedley"….It is only when the pattern gets shaken up that things begin to get interesting again. The band seems to have found new ways of shaking it up, specifically at the ground level of the jam, where they can build. While the movement into the song's climax was somewhat hurried and consequentially less than satisfactory, it was at least interesting…which is good.

The encore cover of Velvet Underground's "Rock and Roll" was pure fun. "Despite all the computations / you could just dance to that rock and roll station / it was all right." And it was. Despite any historical heaviness, despite anything Phish has or hasn't been in the past (or is or isn't now), you could just dance. The metaphor of Phish as a DJ can work in many different ways. For one, it describes the way they've come to manipulate their grooves. For the past several years, they've focused on getting good at individual rhythms. When they changed up, it's almost as if they had to pick up the needle and drop it elsewhere on the record. Now, they're getting good at cross-fading between grooves. Likewise, the band also act like DJs in the old radio sense of the word: knowing exactly when to play the right song.

Cries of "Cincinsanity" were heard crossing the skywalk back to the parking garage. While I wouldn't agree with that wholeheartedly, though it certainly works as an amusing piece of wordplay, the show definitely had its moments. The true Cincinsanity began when we invaded the lovely Regal Hotel in downtown Cincinnati. I booked it based

on the fact that they quoted me the cheapest price when I called the hotels listed on the flyer the Mail Order people sent out. Right now, there are six heads sprawled out across the beds and floor, plumb tuckered after an evening of fun.

There is, for example, a player piano in the lobby. It's an all-digital operation. While I was checking in, my friend Daisy sat at it and pretended to play, earning stares from many civilians. Later, I sat at it and attempted to jam with it. The machine's repertoire includes standards like the *Peanuts* theme and "The Dance Of The Sugar Plum Fairies". Adding what bits of piano I knew how to play was ultimately unsuccessful. Finally, I settled on the idea of adding subtle discordance to what was being played. The effect was somewhat disconcerting. The player piano sits next to a large gazebo surrounded by wicker reindeer of varying sizes (a smaller one of which now resides, antler slightly damaged, next to this chair).

After checking in, food became the primary problem. Though it was 12:30 on a Friday night, no place seemed to be open…anywhere in Cincinnati, including the four restaurants and bars right here in the hotel. Pizza-delivery men were accosted in the lobby by hungry heads demanding eats or the phone number they could call to get some. Nobody picked up on the other end. A posse was sent, with no success, to the Hyatt across the street to try and scrounge something up. A story circulated of a head giving a man $20 at the mere mention of the word "pizza." He was confused and scared when the man walked away from it. I'd all but given up on the idea by the time I settled in to write this.

There was a knock on the door. "Who's there?" I called.

"Your fairy godmother," came the reply. The "Frankenknock" (a knock of the intro to Edgar Winter's "Frankenstein") followed. I got up and opened the door. My friend Davey stood in the doorway, pizza box in hand. "Someone just gave me this," he said. He opened the box to reveal a solitary piece of pizza. "We ate a few…this one's all yours." I hugged him.

12/4/99 Firstar Arena, Cincinnati, OH—Jesse Jarnow

There was no distinct beginning to the morning. I faded in and out of sleep as folks wandered in and out of the room. Most everybody was still somewhat famished from the evening before and a sustenance mission was an immediate necessity. Being in the South, Waffle House was the first, logical, and only choice. "There's one at *every* exit," Derek promised. He is a veteran of such roads. And so it came that we ventured into Kentucky. It was my first time in the state, and quite possibly the furthest south I've been in some years. The first Waffle House was brimming with heads, too many to get a table. Several exits later, we located another.

After being gawked at considerably by the locals, and having a long and illuminating conversation about the relative merits of Los Angeles, we consumed our breakfast eats. With nothing much to do, we proceeded to the lot. Shakedown was as active I've ever seen it, occupying a small roadway running under a parking garage. The majority of the vendors had their wares displayed under tents and on tables. Very professional looking. The bazaar aspect of Shakedown is still in full effect, though it's become somewhat more reliable in recent years.

One can go into the lot reasonably expecting to be able to locate certain products with some degree of efficiency. Like society as a whole, once primary food and survival sources have been established, the greater community can get on to more evolved tasks. People selling

books and magazines of their own design have become increasingly common. Likewise, people vending art and photographs (either of the band or of other subjects) have become things to look out for. On the way into the show, I half-considered buying a couple of books (something by Tom Wolfe and the novelization of *2001: A Space Odyssey*) before realizing I had a large pile of unfinished and unstarted ones on my desk.

The rendezvous with friends at Will Call was surprisingly easy, and we wandered into the venue with plenty of time to spare, for once. As we reclined, waiting for the show to begin, we discovered more dates of significance. December 4th holds another somewhat grim anniversary: Frank Vincent Zappa's death from prostate cancer in 1993. The song on everybody's lips (and balloons and signs) was "Peaches En Regalia", busted out several times during the first leg of Fall Tour, though not seen in a bit. Several mentions of Chanukah were made, often with some degree of surprise that the band hadn't played "The Man Who Stepped Into Yesterday" the previous night.

There is a mythological significance invested in many dates involving birthdays, anniversaries of legendary shows, events in world history, and other such bits of arcana. Mostly, it reflects the superstitions of the tour culture, a yearning to be able to foretell the unpredictable. In the real world, everybody seems to have an eye on the future, from street-corner preachers ranting of fire and brimstone to market analysts breaking down the ebb and flow of the stock market. As with pundits of all sorts, predicted setlists are written up with dozens of carefully weighed factors, ranging from the utterly ineffable "the vibe is bouncy in here, they're gonna play 'Fee'," to the utterly scientific "they haven't played "Punch You" in four shows, they're damn well due."

Therefore, it was only with moderate surprise that the band busted into "Heavy Things" to open the first set. They'd played it on opening night in Michigan, though they've been playing it pretty regularly these days. Who's to say, really? It's still the beginning of tour: tabula rasa, man. Calling songs is an interesting proposition. Perhaps there's an art to it, but it's probably more sheer luck than anything else. What drives people to want to predict things? Songs will be played, music will occur, perhaps there will be magic. There certainly seems to be a formula into which things fall, though: bluegrass numbers, ballads, big jams, rock covers. Some people tend to be realistic and observe these tendencies. Others fantasize and throw in what they *want* to hear.

But, to be perfectly honest, there is a way to break things down. With few exceptions, most shows these days don't have a hell of a lot of open jamming. There are second sets like Auburn Hills, with a lot of open-ended material. More, though, there are shows with lots of short songs, interspersed occasionally with heavy improvisation. The first set this evening saw a little bit of jamming, in the forms of "Simple" and "Tweezer". Both of the jams were somewhat nondescript, a mix of funk and loud/quiet dynamic play. The real joys of the set were "Ya Mar " and "Dirt". The former featured some extremely interesting calypso-like rhythm work from Trey behind Page's organ solo.

Mike's recent inclinations to play consistently articulated parts in the upper registers have added a very distinct new twist to the band's sound. This was apparent, too, in "Dirt", which featured the arrangement the band showcased during the first half of the fall. It's nice. The band has finally learned how to play the song (hell, it features a statement of the melody by Mike, surprise, above the twelfth fret) and I really hope they choose to get it down, if only for posterity's sake, for inclusion on the new album.

The single item of distinction in the second set was, without a doubt, "Split Open and Melt". Moving into the jam, the band quickly dropped the telltale measure of 9/8 that distinguishes the song's identity. The improvisation retained the dark vibe of the song, though moved incrementally away from the rhythmic and melodic constrains of it. I once read a post on rec.music.phish that suggested that "Melt" might be a musical tribute to Zappa. I never quite saw what the poster did, but in the context of the evening's performance, it may well be true. The band didn't really need to pay tribute to Frank, they do that every night simply by existing. The jam out of "Melt", rife with experimentation and odd time changes, was an inherited nod to Zappa's fearlessness. More superstition and rationalization.

It also featured one of the most interesting uses yet by Trey of his still relatively new keyboard setup. Normally, Trey's keyboard playing consists of blurps, bleeps, and electronic chirping sounds. Tonight, in the "Melt" jam, he encroached on Page's territory with his application of a synthesized acoustic piano sound. Bashing the keys, he set a strange-sounding loop into action, sounding not entirely unlike a Raymond Scott sample as programmed by Soul Coughing's Mark de Gli Antoni. It introduces the idea of freshly made samples into Phish's music. The complaint of many about the use of samples is that it's somehow cheating, using someone else's musical base as one's own. With this idea, it's not quite the same: calling up one's own previously stated ideas as part of an arsenal of sound. The next step is to build up a collection of sounds over the course of an evening, so parts played in the first set can be recalled during a jam in the second, and so forth.

After "Melt", there was a sudden commotion, as several dudes (possibly, though not necessarily, naked) ran across the stage, dashing from the rear of the stage, around the front, in between Mike's bass stack and Page's baby grand, before being apprehended by security. Whether or not they're to blame in specific, the band seemed to be thrown off for most of the rest of the set. During the "Moma Dance", Fish and Trey couldn't quite hook up for the breakdown between the intro and the chorus. Likewise, the entire band seemed to be just plain *off* for the instrumental preludes of "The Man Who Stepped Into Yesterday", though the Chanukah rendition of "Avenu Malkenu" was admirably tight. The band recovered their momentum by the time "David Bowie" rolled around. The hi-hat intro featured some sparse feedback that didn't seem to amount to much. The jam itself built precisely, not really hitting any new territory, but still managing to sound fresh and exciting (which is a feat after playing the song for thirteen years).

The show, as always, made me happy. Was my head pried open and clamped there for two and a half hours? No, not nearly. Is it necessary to have one's pried open and clamped? Of course, there's no definite answer for that one. Plenty of people go to see Phish for the sheer party of it, and that doesn't (contrary to popular belief) mean going to Phish solely to get trashed. Some people go to dance, participate in ritual, and for pure enjoyment. As Hunter wrote, "Some come to laugh their past away." Is that, in itself, a reason to drive four hours to go see Phish? Why not? If that's the only place where one can find what one needs.

Others go for other reasons. What are the conditions by which they are satisfied? As near as I can tell, there are no set things to fulfill each time, just broad outlines. That's good, because Phish could never do everything at once anyway. On some nights, they can be a big jam band. On others, they could be a stadium-rock band. People's expecta-

tions parallel these in obtuse ways, if only because it's nigh impossible for the band to be any one thing at once. Tonight, I wasn't satisfied. But that doesn't mean that I won't be tomorrow.

I'm tired now. Thankfully, I'm not driving…yet. We use various devices to keep us awake, including, but not limited to *Remain in Light*, riddles, caffeine, and Pop-Tarts. We're just north of Columbus right now, heading back in the direction of home. We're almost at the northernmost edge of Waffle House territory. I'm almost sure I will have one more opportunity to say "hey, let's stop there," before we're out of range.

12/11/99 First Union Spectrum, Philadelphia, PA
—Jesse Jarnow

Driving the knotted interstate's loops winding from New Jersey into Philadelphia and, eventually, into the northern regions of Delaware, was ultimately an overly symbolic affair. Traumatically symbolic, if I may venture a possible overreaction.

Mint was driving my car. We exited off of I-95 to meet up with some friends at a gas station to rendezvous before going to the lot. At the gas station, they gave us directions to the next meeting point, inside of Philadelphia proper. We had to cross the Walt Whitman Bridge (they named a bridge after him?) before entering the city. We pulled onto 295 and headed south…and saw absolutely no signs for said bridge, just indications that we'd soon be entering into Delaware.

So, we turned around. I *knew* we had to be on 95, so getting back to 95 where we got off of it originally seemed like a safe bet. Passing the Mobil station where we had met before, there was absolutely no entrance to 95 in sight. More terrifying was the fact that there was not a single, solitary trace of the exit we had gotten off at before. The path from whence we came had disappeared completely into the night like a fake doorway.

That was where the trauma was rooted. Coming from one place, a relatively safe and known place, and discovering that the path from that point was completely wiped off the face of the map, like it never existed. We stopped at WaWa, only to find out that we had been on exactly the right road for the entire time. Grrr. That was the keynote for the rest of the night, the thing that made the first set of the show so completely horrible for me.

As with driving, all of the trauma could possibly have been avoided if I had simply followed the directions laid out initially and gone to the place where my ticket had told me to. I didn't. The first stop was a seat about four rows off the floor. Then the band started, and we tried to make it down to meet up with our friend. Meanwhile, "Tweezer" was beginning. By the time the band had reached the "Uncle Ebenezer" line, we'd been booted from the floor and were settling into a comfortable spot at the rear of the first section.

With the exception of the fact that my friend Erin was still on the floor, and we were not, I was starting to relax and actually enjoy the music. The previous weekend, I'd sold my ticket to the Rochester show because the Cincinnati shows had done very little for me. On the second night, with the exception of the jam out of "Melt", I'd felt completely unmoved by the music. I described the sensation to one friend, quite cosmically of course, as "soul shrugging." For the entire ride out to Philly from Ohio, I'd fretted that I'd lost my ability to hear Phish's music in a way that had some kind of emotional effect on me.

Phish's music still makes me happy. The same friend managed to hit the nail on the head when she said that the happiness was a "famil-

iar" kind instead of a "this shit really blows my mind and I feel like I'm about to have a musical orgasm." It's a different kind of reaction—perhaps a slightly more mature one, on some levels, but not as easily satisfying. Ultimately what happens is that I end up analyzing the shows to death, trying to glean some joy out of the music produced. At this point, though, that's almost an instinctual reaction. Almost. Is there anything wrong with reacting to music like that? Growing up, one naturally changes.

But…damn, old-school happiness would be nice. Rosebud, I guess. People search for ways to regress, to tap into an older energy source. Some people strive to return to childhood innocence, or at least a more innocent perspective on things. Are there ways to induce that? Or should one not even bother to try?

Meanwhile, the "Tweezer" continued. My problem with the Cincinnati shows is that the band didn't take enough chances with the music— not enough open-ended jamming. Music that I've never heard before (in other words, stuff made up on the spot) has the best odds of producing a reaction in me. For Phish to open up with a big jam song, to me, was a wonderful sign. I danced. I enjoyed it. The jam flowed into a harder-driving groove before dropping into something slightly more ambient. Then they stopped. And then they starting "Bouncing".

I'm not a person who has a problem with "Bouncing Around the Room". I have another friend who disdains the song so much that her friend made her a mix tape of about twenty different versions of the song as a joke. I almost think it'd be interesting to hear the song in all of the band's incarnations; as Page's piano sound improved, as Trey's tone moved from a fat, clean tone to an effects-laden mesh. Nonetheless, it was not something I particularly psyched to hear. I'd truly hoped that the night would be one of those with nothing but open-ended material. There are still sets like that. Set II in Auburn (12/2/99), for instance. This wasn't one of them.

We had been standing in an empty row without seats in the back of the lower section. Occasionally, security guards came around to clear the space. The first time they'd asked me for my ticket, I flashed out a JamBands.com business card. "It's okay," I said, using a mix of Raoul Duke and the Jedi mind trick, "I'm a fully affiliated member of the press."

The security guard squinted and shined his flashlight on the card. "Uh, okay."

He then tapped my friend Harriet on the shoulder. "May I see your ticket?"

"It's okay," I told him. "She's with me." He left us alone.

"Heavy Things" has been in the heaviest of rotation lately, turning up every two or three shows. I'm not getting sick of it. This version began to stretch itself a little bit, moving within the bounds of Trey's ultra-pretty guitar solo into more open territory. It reminded me a little bit of a late-spring '94 version of "Down with Disease", when it first began to stretch itself out a little bit. I do look forward into seeing how this song progresses.

Sometime during the next batch of songs, security showed up again. Again, I flashed the business card. It didn't work. "Press, huh? Then go to the press box." The security guard pushed me in the direction of the aisle.

Then, I screamed something that I've always wanted to scream at someone, reality be damned. "I AM A DOCTOR OF JOURNALISM, GODDAMN IT."

"I don't care who you are!"

"Okay, I'm the Angel of Death."

"Move it."

"I'm Spartacus?" I asked meekly.

By then, we were in the aisle, seatless. Miraculously, as we were regrouping ourselves, Erin came bounding up the steps towards us. She hugged both of us. We tried another set of seats behind the stage, and got booted. And another. The prettiness of "Roggae" was providing a stark contrast to the frustration that was going on in trying to find a place to hang out. As I tried to walk into the next section an angry-looking, dwarfen, bullish security guard chased me. "Let me see your ticket!" I walked away. She chased me briefly away from her post before retreating.

At that point, I was on the verge of a breakdown. "Birds of a Feather" was starting. I like "Birds". The last few versions I'd heard, both live and on tape, had been extremely exciting. I pressed forward towards my section, somewhere in the upper regions of the First Union Spectrum. "They hang on emotions they bottle inside." By the time I got to the stratosphere, the jam was moving towards its conclusion. I was moving further toward bugout. It didn't get very far from the root; more like a traditional Trey solo over a band vamp, like the older versions. Maybe "Birds'" time as a jam song has already come and gone. They needed to prove the song worthy, and now (like "Down with Disease") it can just go back to being itself.

When "Birds" ended, the bottle was opened. The entire trip to Philly, I'd been fretting about lack of emotion. Now, I had 'em in spades; of course, in the wrong direction. The peak of "Guyute" used to make me insanely happy. This time, with each repeated bent note, chills ran through me. "Loving Cup" and "Guyute" are the two songs I am most tired of hearing. Together, they were too much. I took off my glasses and watched Chris's lights blur together. He missed the cue in "Loving Cup" and threw the brights on a full chorus before he was supposed to.

The second set was much better, both musically and emotionally. We found seats and stayed there. The "Gotta Jibboo" continued to test its boundaries. It was one Mike Gordon bass line away from tearing its ass out of its orbit and not returning. Just before the final chorus, it very nearly did. The "Bowie" sequence was where it was at, though. It made me fully happy in a way I hadn't felt in a long time. It didn't just remind me of the happiness I used to get when I heard Phish, it *was* that happiness.

"Bowie" moved into an upbeat jam, both in mood and technique. Trey walked over to Mike and said something to him. A moment later, the jam took on definite form. It took me a second to realize that it was "Have Mercy". The reggae jam out of "Mercy" turned into a breakdown affair: an organ solo and a drum break. During one of the organ breaks, Trey nodded to Page as he walked around the band's setup. Page began playing "HYHU" and Trey switched spots with Fish. What followed was the single event that made the most joyous last night; immature, but absolutely hilarious considering all parties involved. Phish, Fish, Mike, cymbals, and the First Union Spectrum.

Fish stood at the front of the stage, in the spotlight, soloing on his vacuum. Mike walked out from behind his amp with a pair of cymbals in his hand—the "B" "AH" percussion used in "Cracklin' Rosie". He crept slowly up to Fish's side, Fish being occupied with filling an arena with the sound of a home appliance. Mike looked at Fish somewhat quizzically for a few moments, as he assembled the handles on the cymbals. Fish was still oblivious. Then, he slammed them together. Still no reaction. Mike receded back into the darkness. A moment later he was back,

poking Fish in the shoulder. Finally, the band started "Cracklin' Rosie".

It made me happy. Was it a nostalgic happiness? Who gives a shit. I smiled. That counts for a lot, in my book.

12/11/99 First Union Spectrum, Philadelphia, PA—Dan Alford

In Camden, NJ, as you're headin' for the Whatever Bridge that isn't the Walt Whitman Bridge (where incidentally, you can witness the ecstatic beauty that is the life of humanity), there are a lot of porn shops. Or maybe there aren't really that many, it's just that those signs are so huge that they make it seem like there are. Anyway, it looks like most of the shops are closed, but those signs are still there, a constant reminder that this is the best fuckin' country in the world! At least, that's what I think I was thinkin' while we made our way to the home of Liberty, Brotherly Love, and Cheese Steaks.

Philly looks kind of desolate, and the highway structure is weird. On the other hand, it has a ton of really great public art, and the museum had some good stuff that was very recent, including a Scottish artist who I'd keep an eye on if I could remember his name. Anyway Shakedown was hopping. Lots of crystal (rocks, not drugs) vendors. Sierra Nevadas are twist-off. Some nitrous, but not as much as at JGB Rochacha in '94, for those of you who don't remember that night.

We scored floor seats right in front of the soundboard, but there wasn't much room between rows. Luckily, people sometimes can dance in the aisles, like tonight. A pretty chill section.

At quarter after eight or so, we got a "Harry Hood" opener. I knew I was in for a good one. Cool swells in the intro. Mike was sounding great. Page really shined on the end jam. "Mike's Song". Hehehe…I was right. This was a really nice version that fell into a comfortable middle road between the chaos rock of '92 and the deep ambient groove of '98. Definitely a keeper. People into older stuff, like their memories, will enjoy this one. The jam sums up nicely—Trey was a little more playful than usual. A slight change and we're in "Simple". This was an absolutely flawless transition. Really. It was perfect! "Simple" got two stars in my setlist book, which is pretty good. A quick, quiet stroll on a Sunday morning, this version was pretty but moved at a good clip. Very focused. Into "Hydrogen". I was sort of expecting the old leg-lift thing…the vibe was there; after all, the newest song they played all night was "Circus". Into "Weekapaug Groove". Trey hits his groove for the night. He was all over this one, a total barn-burner! It was not a long version, but very tight. What a way to open a show. "Circus"—I like it and don't care what you say.

"Mule" had a cool funky jam in it, and "Cavern" had horribly botched lyrics that Ernest didn't even try to fix. We all had a good chuckle and fell down laughing when he said they'd be back in "about fifteen minutes."

Almost an hour later…

"Boogie On". I'm really only so-so on this tune, but folks enjoy it. CK was kicking ass—I remember a lot of greens. I do really like the way the tune just ends, though. A great way to end a song. Trey starts to play what sort of sounds like "AC/DC Bag" but then it morphs into "Sneakin' Sally", which I really wanted anyway. I don't think it was a tease, just indecision.

"Cause, sometimes, she lets me use her car."

"Sally" rocks, Trey rocks, and I wish it could go on forever, but almost immediately after the last verse they launch into the groove garden. It's deep in here. The groove is threatening to swallow us! So

deep…and then the second absolutely prefect transition of the night. Smooth as silk PJs on silk sheets. "Ghost" is it, man! This is why I love Phish. Mike was slappin' while Page grooved along, the loops are going, and there is this sound structure that spreads out to the sides. Vast. It actually reminded me of a scene in *Moby Dick* where the cabin boy jumps into the water because he is so scared, and he's left there, looking at nothing but this huge expanse of ocean. He is seeing it from eye level, immersed in it. It is totally overwhelming.

The second part of the jam has some spacey Trey noodling over cool work by Page. It doesn't last for too long, though. Instead a wild, extended jamlet starts up. At first it sounds like Steve Austin is about to jump over a fence, but then it stretches and settles in. The smoke starts pouring out and Trey is on the keys, and I see Mike step forward. I was expecting "N_2O", but the jam just kept reverberating until it wound down into a huge "Also Sprach Zarathustra". A very nice version, it wandered all over the night sky and Chris had the flashlight. Finally, the climax hit and it was brighter than daylight. Wooo!

"DWD" was oddly placed, I thought, but offered up another great jam. This was not a jazzy, meandering version *à la* Great Woods '99. It was straight-ahead rock-star Trey leading the pack in a frenzied romp. Short but right on the mark. Definitely a solid closer for a very satisfying show. I'm a pretty positive guy, and have really enjoyed everything I've seen in '99 (five shows at the time, not counting this one), but this was really the best show I've seen in a while. A good setlist with some amazing jamming, and I was totally into it.

12/11/99 First Union Spectrum Philadelphia, PA —Erik Swain

Words cannot describe how awesome this show was. But I will try. Suffice it to say that I have been to well over a hundred concerts by various artists (this was my tenth Phish show), and this was the best show I've ever seen by anyone. And I don't make statements like that if I don't mean it.

I went with a high-school friend, David, who had seen them only once before, way back in 1991. Boy, was he in for a surprise. They're a completely different band now.

The band likes to emphasize how its performance feeds off the audience. There is no better example of that than this night. Sitting in the sixth row directly behind the stage, I got an up-close perspective of how this works.

This was the most electric audience I've ever seen. I guess this is what a Hampton show feels like. A whole bunch of balloons were being bounced around before the show. Then, as the boys hit the stage to a deafening roar, some gigantic orange ones with song names written on them (one had "Windora Bug") were released. Many of these, as well as the smaller balloons, made it onstage, and the band members kicked some away, while Trey popped others with his guitar. The intensity of our greeting, which sounded as loud as the cheering at the *end* of other shows I've seen, seemed to take them a bit by surprise.

Trey had to have been impressed with the crowd's electricity because he went over to Fish to change the game plan, and to the astonishment of everyone, Fish started "Harry Hood!" I knew this was a special moment, but I didn't realize how special until after the show when I learned the last "Hood" opener at a public gig was 10/30/85, *the first time it was ever played*. It started very ambient, with Trey fooling around on the small keyboard, and then became more or less standard. But something very important happened here that isn't picked up on the

tapes. For the first half of the song, the crowd was absolutely hysterical and continued to throw balloons onto the stage. Then the jam section hit and the glowsticks and glowrings started flying, some of which unfortunately made their way to the stage as well. How the band managed to keep their concentration in spite of all this bedlam is beyond me. But I could see that all four of them were extraordinarily calm and locked in a zone. They were feeding off the crowd's energy but not getting overwhelmed by it. And they were perfectly in sync with each other. What they had to do for the first three quarters of the song was equivalent to walking home in a hurricane—and they not only survived but persevered. And in the energetic finale, they displayed all the enthusiasm of a kid after it has stopped raining.

They realized right off the bat they had something special here, and segued into "Mike's Song". Good Lord, I thought, it's like 11/22/97 all over again! That classic show, as you probably know, started "Mike's Groove", then "Hood". At this point I was quite literally fighting back tears, overcome with emotion. I had a feeling this was going to be one of *those* shows.

The "Mike's" was an extremely funky version. They locked into a groove and Page dazzled with an organ solo. Unlike some 1999 versions, there was no dithering around here. They found a path and pursued it directly. This was textbook post-'96 group jamming and ended with a seamless segue into a hard and loud version of "Simple". Toward the end of that, Fish teased "Get Back on the Train" as if he wanted to segue into it, but the others didn't follow. At the end it became very spacey and crawled to a near-stop as the band decided what to do next. I could see that Fish kept tapping his drums as Trey told the others to go into "Hydrogen". This made me very happy, as I consider "Mike's"->"Simple"->"Hydrogen"->"Weekapaug" to be the perfect "Mike's Groove". "Simple" provides the best segue out of "Mike's", but "Hydrogen" provides the best segue into "Weekapaug". "Hydrogen" was pretty standard, which is to say, gorgeous, and Fish hit the final drumbeat more forcefully than usual before going into "Weekapaug". This had great soloing from Mike at first. Then it developed into a very nimble Trey-led jam, darting here and there, more reminiscent of a '93 version than a current one. A great moment occurred when Page cued Kuroda to intensify the lights, Kuroda responded with some fast-moving streams, and Trey responded with a lightning-fast solo. I could also swear the band was feeding off a guy in a mask who climbed atop someone's shoulders and was swaying. What synergy!

After that madness I figured a slow song was coming, and "When the Circus Comes" was the perfect selection. I think Trey's choice here was inspired by the raucous crowd and the balloons. What better way to describe it than a circus? This was another example of the band's performance feeding off the vibe of the audience. It was a particularly emotional version.

Then, just when we thought the set couldn't get any more surprising, they broke out "Scent of a Mule" for the first (and only, as it turned out) time in 1999. Despite the sixty-one-show break it did not sound rusty at all. In lieu of the Trey solo there was a neat little band jam that I hadn't heard them try before.

It was time for a set-closer, and of course they played "Cavern". It follows me around. Six shows out of ten. Trey flubbed the lyrics at one point but laughed at himself. He had nothing to be ashamed of after a set this stellar.

Being behind the stage, I could see them as they came off and

Mark Majewski

Big Cypress

Trey was beaming. He had an extra spring in his step. This confirmed that he shared my feelings about the greatness of this set.

This was the best first set I ever saw. No contest. It may have been the best set, period. It was certainly unmatched for emotion and surprises. "You could not have asked for anything more," people were saying during set break. Indeed, the blueprint was in place for this show to become one of the all-time greats. The only quibble with the first set was the relative lack of envelope-pushing experimentation. If the second set could provide that, we would have a near-perfect show on our hands.

The crowd did the Wave during set break, and remained raucous when the band re-emerged. Trey started chugging out a rhythm that turned out to be "Boogie On Reggae Woman". This was an outstanding groove. The jam here showed why Phish is so far ahead of its competition. Mike plucked out a solo on the bass, Page and Trey handled the rhythm, and Fish timed his fills as a counterpoint to Mike's melody. What other bands could switch roles like that?

This came to a stop and Trey started chording what I and everyone else thought was "AC/DC Bag" but turned out to be "Sneakin' Sally". This was a remarkable version, the best I'd heard since 4/2/98. In tune with the rest of the show so far, there was no meandering here. It was also appropriate for us because David's last name is Palmer and his father's name is Robert. Come to think of it, "AC/DC Bag" would have been equally appropriate. Same with "Tube", for that matter. In any case, they locked into a groove and just ripped. Layer upon layer of cow funk, just heavenly. And then I heard it. Emerging from the stew, Mike plucked out the opening bass line to "Ghost", and my heart just stopped.

This song at this venue holds a very special significance for me. I heard it for the first time, and fell in love with it, the previous time I was at this venue on 12/2/97. It was the first new song in years that I felt was as epic as their old classics, and prompted me to renew my in-

terest in them. If they would segue into it here, I would die. And a few minutes later, they did. What a segue it was. And what a "Ghost". Pure hose. I was once again fighting back tears. It was that good; certainly one of the very best post-'97 "Ghosts". Page was the star of this jam, just tearing up the clavinet and synthesizer. Then the rest of the band dropped out and left Page to fill the hall with eerie synthesizer noises (eventually joined by Trey).

This part of the set was where Kuroda took over. I could not believe what he was doing here. And I was sober. Imagine what it was like for those who were not. I told David that there were only two possible next moves from here, "Also Sprach" or "Disease". I'm not kidding. I was trying to do a mind meld with the band, mentally urging them to take it into one of those two. I don't know why I wanted to hear them at that moment, but that's what my brain (or was it my soul?) was telling me.

Soon, a lot of fog was released, and then a lengthy transition into "Also Sprach"! This became a jam in itself, really led by Kuroda. I can't describe what was going on visually other than to say "Mindf—k." As the jam built into crescendo after crescendo, I figured they would segue into an epic rocker to close the set. Again, I said to David, "Disease" is the choice here. It would be an easy transition because of its spacey bass intro, and it would tear the roof off the place.

I must have been doing the mind-meld thing again, because lo and behold, they segued into "Disease"! This was even better than I could have imagined. Imagine having a set turn out *better* than your wildest dreams! Trey took over and just tore the song apart. The crowd was foaming at the mouth by this point. Phish went for the home run here and just nailed it. They couldn't have continued after this. Just too draining.

All I could say was, "Wow." Remember the zone I was talking about during "Hood"? Well, they were locked in it for the entire second set. I have never seen five people meld into one (including Kuroda, who

was essential to this process) as completely as happened here. Ego-lessness, hose, whatever you want to call it…they achieved it in spades.

At this point I declared to David that we had witnessed a historic show. What struck me about it was how it combined every element they'd introduced since '97: funk, ambient, techno, emotional balladry. I think this show is where they realized what all the summer and fall '99 experiments were building up to.

In shows like this, the encore is beside the point. I would have perfectly understood if they just did "Bouncin'" and/or "Rocky Top". I wondered what was up when Trey left the stage and immediately ran over to Fish, probably proposing an idea. Imagine our surprise when they ripped into "Possum", and then surprised us by playing the "All Fall Down" signal! They fell down, then started up again while still on the ground. You can't blame most of the crowd for not falling down. These signals were conceived when the band was playing small, seat-less halls, not large venues with chairs which we would have crashed into had we attempted to fall. This version was yet another exceptional "Possum" of '99. Trey was providing all these interesting extra fills during the song, and tore up his solos as if it were '95 again. There was no topping this, and off they went, Trey beaming just like before.

Sure, the sets were short, but who cares when they're as packed as these were? Did you ever notice how some of the very best shows (12/31/95 and 11/22/97 come to mind) have short sets, probably because the band was at such a peak that they couldn't possibly have pushed themselves any further? A lot of people after the show were saying it was the best they'd ever seen. Count me in on that, too.

I don't know what else to say. I sincerely believe this will go down as one of the best of '99, and hopefully one of the all-time greats. I'm afraid the tapes won't quite bear out some of the things that made this show so special: Kuroda's contributions, the crowd's energy and how the band fed off of it. Plus the venue's acoustics aren't that great and tapes suffer as a result. But no one will ever be able to convince me that this was not one of *those* shows.

12/12/99 First Union Spectrum, Philadelphia, PA
—Jesse Jarnow

Dedicated to Rick Danko, 1943-1999

God," Erin began. "If I were drinking orange juice right now, I think I'd feel like I was five years old."

I looked at her and took a sip of my "big mama" orange juice, as the waitress had called it. I *love* orange juice. It's probably my favorite drink in the world. I once announced to my literalist, Ayn Rand-loving former roommate that "orange juice is the nectar of the gods."

"No," he had said in return, staring me right in the eye. "It's actually the nectar of oranges." He moved out soon thereafter.

The thing is, though, I've *always* loved orange juice. I drank it nearly every day when I was growing up. In one sense, when I drink it, I feel small twinges of nostalgia. On the other hand…I don't. I never *stopped* loving orange juice, dig? There's a continuum. It never stopped being cool.

All of which made sense while contemplating why I had enjoyed the "Bowie">"Have Mercy">"Cracklin' Rosie" the previous night. Was it nostalgia that made me dance and laugh almost uncontrollably? I never stopped thinking that the kind of music that Phish produced in 1993 and 1994 was cool. It just sort of seems that they did. While it may have been somewhat an act of nostalgia for them to play that se-

quence, it wasn't one for me to appreciate it. At least, that's what I've been telling myself.

From the Bob Evans, we moved across the Walt Whitman Bridge into Philadelphia. As we crossed, we listened to the ethereal "Lazy-bones" by Soul Coughing. The sun was just about setting. The glass and metal skyline glowed golden in the late afternoon. It was quite blinding. To see an entire city illuminated in such a manner was damn near magical. It looked like a CGI-generated metropolis sitting in front of us, each pixel manipulated just perfectly. As the band hit the peak of the song, a flock of birds suddenly emerged from under the bridge, flapping their way in subtle mathematics across our field of vision. Off to the left was the Spectrum.

We explored the scene, sprawled across several lots, meeting up with everybody who needed to be met up with. Inside the venue, the four of us—Erin, Harriet, Mint, and I—headed down to the seats rightfully belonging to Erin and Harriet. From my perspective, they might well have been the best seats I've ever had at a show. They were on the side of the stage, about eight rows up, on what is now the Trey side. The sight line was absolutely gorgeous. Essentially, we saw the show from Trey's perspective as he faced the rest of the band and played.

At that angle, the communication between the band members was both visibly and audibly apparent. Essentially looking over Trey's shoulder, it was easy to tell exactly where he set his gaze. Most of the time, it was on another band member. His attention was divided pretty evenly throughout the night. When he looked at a musician, it was crystal clear what his musical intentions were. In *The Grateful Dead Movie*, filmed in 1974, the volume of each musician went up when he appeared on screen. Watching Trey interact was like that. When he looked over at Fish, suddenly the guitar and drums seemed in perfect synchronization; the rhythmic element of Trey's guitar part relating very distinctly to the melodic element of Fish's drum part. It was the most apparent I've ever witnessed the musical conversation going on between the members of Phish.

It's always there, I assume. I'm not sure if it's always at the level it was on Saturday night, however. The circumstances make it kind of hard to tell. Our seats were amazing, the crowd noise (from where we were) was at a minimum, and there was just an insane amount of open-ended material. In short, it was everything I wanted at a Phish show all fall and never got…until Saturday. From the "Harry" opener, it was clear that the band wanted to go *out*. It took them a good amount of time to even make it to the first lyric section of the song. This was the first place where they engaged in a careful improvisation.

Throughout the whole show, and during the "Harry" intro in specific, I also gained a very new appreciation for Trey's use of effects pedals—often maligned by fans with any number of negative adjectives. Watching Trey dance the dance on Saturday, though, there is very little that he needs to be forgiven for. Just as his hands shape the pitch of the sound coming out of his guitar, his feet shape the tone that comes out of his speakers. People complain that Trey's sound isn't as pure as it once was. While, overall, his playing might not be quite as fluid in some senses as it used to be, the basics of his expression are still there. New things have just been layered atop it. The vibe in the room, both onstage and off, seemed to feel coherent. During the "Harry" jam, for example, the (unfortunately) requisite glowstick war erupted. Thankfully, the bulk of the projectiles were the softer glowrings. Within minutes, though, the bulk of the objects were no longer airborne. Instead, they were linked into a long and flowing chain that extended from one

Mark Majewski

Big Cypress

side of the floor, almost straight across, to the other. It looked like a pulsing neon light, uncoiled and organic. Occasionally, there were breaks in the chain. Following the spaces with my eyes, I could see loose glowsticks being passed atop the crowd in the direction of the gaps. The whole thing looked and felt alive.

Onstage, there was a coherence rarely felt at Phish's shows anymore. "Harry" set the keynote for the first set, kind of like an overture. Bits and pieces of the general ideas stated in the "Harry" jam turned up through the next few songs. The brief jam out of "Mike's Song" recalled the darker spaces of the "thank you, Mr. Minor" composed section of "Harry", injecting it with a Middle-Eastern feel. The improvisation produced by "Simple" followed the broad pattern of many recent versions of the song: loud to soft. By the end of the jam, they'd brought it all the way down. In some ways, it felt like it could've acted as a prelude to the cascading crescendos of "Harry". Finally there came the "Weekapaug Groove" which built into an ecstatic, distinctly un-"Weekapaugy" jam. Instead of blissed-out rock, it was instead a return to the kind of gorgeous melodic peak found in, well, good "Harry's". Did I mention it was beautiful?

The next three songs of the set ("When the Circus Comes", "Scent of a Mule", and "Cavern") seemed conceptually linked in their own way, a kind of return to the root for both band and audience. One hypothesis produced is such: Trey grew up in the Philadelphia area. He definitely attended events at the Spectrum: Flyers games, KISS concerts, who knows? Quite possibly, the circus. In retrospect, this is all quite loony, but it still makes some degree of sense. By word association, Los Lobos' "Circus" was chosen as a song to play. Likewise, "Mule' could've been called for its demented, cartoon-like, circus-sounding middle section; a similar association. Whether or not these decisions were conscious is almost unimportant. Either way, they pro-

vided a thematic tie-in of a return to the root.

The improvisation in the middle of "Mule" was absolutely jaw-dropping. My notes for this section of the show, among other nearly incoherent ravings, read "Klezmer version of the *Popeye* theme." That's one way of describing what happened. Two things could've actually occurred. The first, and most unlikely (in my eyes, anyway) is that the band took the time to learn a traditional Jewish melody in honor of the last night of Chanukah. The other, and more likely, is that they spontaneously composed a very Hebrew-sounding instrumental replete with a repeating melodic line and chorus. Trey shined here.

Towards the end of the instrumental, during the leg-kick dance, Mint suddenly got very excited. Mint is a product of the same kind of conventional Solomon Schecter schooling that produced Mike Gordon. Apparently, for about two steps towards the end of the dance, Mike broke very subtly into a traditional Jewish dance. The reference was, again, probably completely unconscious on Mike's part—perhaps even a stumble. But, the fact that Mike was brought up extremely Jewish, coupled with the fact that Saturday was the last night of Chanukah, was more than enough to tie "Mule" into the idea of a return to the root. Likewise, the foot patterns at the end of the "Cavern" set-closer were linked to "Mule": perhaps the closest thing there is to a traditional dance in Phish lore. With the exception of "Circus", all of the songs in the set existed in Phish's repertoire by 1994. Five years is a long time in Phish history. With the notable exception of "Ghost", the second set was like that too. Unlike the "Bowie">"Have Mercy">"Cracklin' Rosie", though, there wasn't the feeling that the band was doing something to commemorate times gone by. They were just playing. It wasn't nostalgia…it just *was*. It wasn't calling up the ghosts of the past ("but maybe he's still with me…"); it was staying firmly in the present. Any musical references to the past in song choice or approach to improvisation seemed like Trey's

circus and Mike's dance, completely subconscious. In any situation, trying to trace the birth of the present moment is a nearly impossible task. It is only occasionally where pieces of fate fit together. On this particular night, it was clear that the lessons of the past were clearly taken to heart and dealt with in a completely mature manner.

The lyrics to "Ghost" worked on other levels too. Like the "Harry" in the first part of the evening, it provided the keynote for the second set. Over the course of the past semester, I co-taught a class here at Oberlin entitled "Phish For Dorques." As part of the school's Experimental College program, we ran through a history of Phish over the course of thirteen or so weeks, focusing on different periods of the band's development. Following the Cincinnati shows last week, which many of the students attended, a lot of them expressed dissatisfaction (ranging from mild to grave) with Phish's present direction. Some students questioned their love of the band, whether or not the band would ever have the same impact in their lives that they once did. Nothing was resolved by the end of the last class, held on Wednesday, before the Philly shows. In some ways, it almost seemed that the band was left in the past, in a box of tapes and ticket stubs that we had picked apart in the class.

Then Saturday happened. It was both historical and timely. "But maybe he's still with me / The latch was left unhooked / He's waiting in the wind and rain / I simply haven't looked." Saturday, I suppose, I did. All of the jams seemed to take on their own identities, but all of them seemed very much connected to where each song had been in the past—ghosts very much alive and active in the present. The balance between all timestreams on Saturday night was just exactly perfect.

The cover openers (Stevie Wonder's "Boogie On Reggae Woman" and Alan Toussaint's "Sneakin' Sally Through the Alley") brimmed with the bar-band enthusiasm the songs had during their days as band staples at Nectar's, as well as being infused with the energy the band has been riding high on lately. While they may have been nods to the past, it doesn't quite matter. "Ghost" descended into the absolute nether regions of darkness before emerging into a building and blinding "Also Sprach Zarathustra". The entire affair was a class act from top to bottom. The final touch on the cake was the "all fall down" signal during the intro to a sweetly volcanic of the *Gamehendge* rural country-blues, "Possum". Some people fell. Most didn't. It didn't particularly matter. Calling on the secret language was signal enough. To those who didn't care or know what it was, it was just another piece of entertainment from a long evening of such. To those who cared what it was, it highlighted the continuum between drinking orange juice at the age of five, and drinking orange juice at the age of twenty-one. For me, it was a nice end to the tour.

12/16/99 Reynolds Coliseum, Raleigh, NC—Vicki Pennington

Since my husband Lyle and I were a little low on funds, we decided to justify spending the money for tickets and travel to five Phish shows in mid and late December 1999 by declaring those shows as Christmas presents to ourselves. It was the first time since the 1995 Fox Theater shows in Atlanta that we had the chance to see three shows back-to-back, and the only time we had seen five shows in one tour, much less the tour-closers. Big Cypress was to be both our first Phish festival and first New Year's Eve shows. Needless to say, we were ending our year and the decade with quite an unforgettable bang!

We made it to Raleigh in the early afternoon and had plenty of time to check into our hotel and grab some dinner before heading to the show.

It wasn't until we were headed to the venue that I glanced at the tickets and saw that the doors to the venue were scheduled to open at 5:30 PM for this general-admission show, instead of the usual 6:30 PM. It was already 4:50 PM—yipes! After some mild panicking, we rolled onto the NC State University campus at around five-ish. After a quick but unintentional detour, we found a handy parking spot at the entrance of the parking deck, which was about a hundred yards away from the front door.

Thankfully, miracles never cease at Phish shows. Even though it was less than thirty minutes until the doors to venue opened, the line was surprisingly short. We were not out of luck after all. Actually, the doors didn't open until around 6:45, so we had a bit of a wait, but it was not too bad since we had fun listening to the conversations of the excited phans, mostly college kids, all around us.

We found seats in the too-close-together rows of bright red bleacher chairs inside the basketball gym (behind the one guy who was saving literally sixteen seats for all his friends—what's up with that?), Page side, right beside the soundboard. We settled in comfortably and chatted with the friendly folks all around us. I was enjoying the diversity of the crowd, and though the previous night's show in Washington, D.C., snagged my "Reba", I was certainly ready to open up my first Christmas gift (so to speak).

"Wilson" was a great opener that really grabbed the crowd. Nothing outrageous, just "Wilson" in show-opener mode. I've heard a lot of "Chalk Dusts" and this one seemed to rage harder than usual. As long as Phish continues to surprise me, I'll continue to be delighted! It was wonderful to see Page croon "Lawn Boy", but though he stood up and walked out in front of the piano, I thought it was strange that the spotlight never could seem to find him. "Horn" is one of my favorite tunes and this one was beautiful and delicious as always. I was hoping to hear "Limb By Limb" since I haven't in a while. I really dig the Fishman solo at the end. "Roggae" was very ethereal. I love it! "GBOTT" was a first-hear for me and I thought it was a lot of fun. Very catchy, in the best way. I saw some dudes throwin' down some breakdancing moves at the back of the floor, which had gracious plenty of room. I always enjoy scanning the crowd and watching others who are having as much fun as me!

Whoa, where did that "Camel Walk" come from? Right out of nowhere, I'd say! Another first-hear for me and I thought it was fantastic! What a rare gem. The band really seemed to be having a lot of fun in that odd little gymnasium. If that wasn't enough, Phish played another one of my favorites, "Possum"! I love this tune but I seem to keep missing it. A great way to end the set. The energy level during the first set was strong, yet very chill, which I thought was extra cool. I was not a bit disappointed.

Set II got rolling with "Sand"—my first live one and I gushed my toes all in it! Lyle and I both agreed we were hoping they'd save it for Hampton—little did we know! But it was absolutely lovely and at the time I thought it was one for the books. I've been lucky enough to hear several "Mangos", and this version was definitely the finest one. The band seemed to be taking their time with it and playing it carefully. Chills up and down my spine…exquisite! When Page struck the very first cord to "Velvet Sea", three girls behind me (not your typical phan girls, either) all squealed really loud. They sang the "mailed it off to you" part loudly, too, but it was not off-key, so I thought it was cute rather than being irritated by it as I usually am when people feel the need to drown out the band with their own voices. "Tweezer" was jammed out in a way I had never heard before, very solid and phabulous. I love

Overall, this was a great show. I think it's one of the sleeper hits of the tour. The second set is well worth adding to your tape or CD-R collection. I was thinking that the chilly willy energy level was an indicator of things to come and I was more than ready for what awaited me in Hampton and Big Cypress!

12/17/99 Hampton Coliseum, Hampton, VA—Vicki Pennington

Hampton, Baby!!!

Of course, the atmosphere was festive and the anticipation was high. I had fun handing out candy canes to the folks waiting in front of me in the line to get in the Coliseum. Once inside, my husband Lyle and I found seats in our favorite place, which is straight back on the rail at the front of the balcony. Tonight we were a little over to Page's side. Amidst all of the balloons and glowrings, the vibe was kind of strange. I can't really explain it and quite possibly it was my altered state of consciousness, but it was almost a restlessness. It was as if we were expecting too much at Phish's first appearance in Hampton since the *Hampton Comes Alive* album was released just a few weeks earlier. If the Wave was any indicator, the crowd just wasn't into the whole Hampton scene. I was disappointed not to see many holiday costumes, though I saw several other interesting get-ups, most notably some girls with large, crazy sunglasses and feather boas, a guy dressed in a sort of pimp costume, a guy with a big beer mug hat and, of course, "Lawn Boy" (he's my favorite). Mostly, I was extra excited to be back aboard the Mothership!

Things kicked off with a nice "Piper". Though this tune is one of my favorites, it was nothing spectacular, but I thought it was a great way to greet Hampton. "Meat" was cool to hear and I loved the way they totally stopped as if the song was over, then started back up again. Those tricksters! "Sparkle" was nothing really new and exciting. Though I was hoping to hear it during the second set, "Jibboo" came along right when I needed it. This was my first live one. You gotta love that "Jibboo", ya know? And love it I do! The energy level was kept high with "PYITE", which was played very well, then "Circus" brought it down a notch. I thought "Circus" was completely appropriate for the evening and the venue. "Circus" as well as "WITS" are very pretty songs; the "filter out the Everglades" line got lots of cheers in anticipation of the upcoming Big Cypress New Year's Eve festival in Florida. "Twist" was a fun way to end the set. I like it better each time I hear it.

Yes, I am an old softie and I have a real hard time being critical of the band that has brought so much joy into my life, but I will say that the first set left me feeling lukewarm. "Jibboo" and "Twist" were the highlights for me. So, I reflected during the long set break and prepared myself for round two. I also got a kick out of a guy handing out Now and Laters to us chicks in the bathroom line. He was wearing some of those Halloween gross teeth (big, crooked and brown) and he kept telling us that they were not his real teeth. He was a hoot.

Set II started off super strong with a tight "Birds". Now we're talking! "Moma Dance" gave me one of those moments in time which I crave: I was having a ball looking around the room. As far as I could see, every single person was on their feet dancing like no one was watching. No milling about, no chitter-chatter, no sitting down with arms crossed, no worries about firing up the bowl, no worries about anything else at all…just absolute focused groovin'. Shakin' it. Feelin' it. Lovin' it. Yeah! (For the record, the entire second night of Hampton would be that way.)

"Bug" was a fantastic first-hear for me and I totally fell in love with

Big Cypress

when Phish takes an old classic and gives it a new spin. "Runaway Jim" was nice to hear and Trey did the guitar-over-the-head trick, which always makes me smile. To me, that signaled that the boys were definitely having a blast in Raleigh. The "Bittersweet Motel" encore was another surprise; I didn't even recognize it at first but it was great to hear. "Tweeprise" was expected but fun, as usual.

it. I should have been standing up and dancing, but all I could do was sit in my seat and watch in amazement. I could have sworn that the jam at the beginning was nothing more than an opportunity for a light solo. What a beautiful palette of colors! Too bad I was too busy staring at it to think about snapping a photo. Oh, well, it is forever engraved in my memory. What a beautiful song, that "Bug". It really spoke to me.

Unfortunately, "Jennifer Danced" out and broke the spell. I could see that the song has potential, but it hadn't reached it yet and I would have appreciated almost anything else at that moment. It was quite a buzz kill for me. Luckily, "Jennifer Dances" and then she goes away. Afterwards, there was much discussion onstage. What a *long* pause! I was convinced Trey was dragging it out on purpose just to tease us. Finally, "SOAMelt" started up and that groovy vibe was restored. Thank goodness! It think it's fair to say that this version covered some new ground in a spacey kind of way. "Character Zero" brought the set to a rocking close. I don't care what anyone else says, I'm always glad to hear that tune. An odd thing happened at the end of the song, though (at least from my vantage point on the balcony rail): Trey took his bow before anyone else and Mike (and maybe Page) seemed bewildered, like they had planned on playing one more. So, it was no surprise to me when Mike stepped up to the mic for song one of the encore.

"Home Place" is another rare treat for me and I thoroughly enjoyed it. I was also delighted to hear "Squirming Coil" since I haven't in a while and I had been thinking throughout the evening that I needed to hear more of Page. "Loving Cup" was the right way to end the evening—did I mention how terrific it was to be back in Hampton?

As usual, night one of Hampton left me jonesin' for night two. Once we strolled on back to the phabulous Fairfield Inn directly across the street, I was amazed at the complete lack of activity in and around the hotel after the show. Don't misunderstand, I enjoy a good raucous all-night blow-out as much as anyone else, but I mostly engage in quiet reflection after a show. It was just very nice not to be woken up in the middle of the night by a drum circle in the next room. I don't know if it was the "No Party Policy" we all signed upon check-in, strong police presence around the Coliseum or good behavior on the part of the fans. I'm going to say it was the latter, so I'll also say, "Thanks, everyone!" for a fantastic time in Hampton.

12/30/99 -> 1/1/00 Big Cypress Seminole Reservation, FL —Jeremy D. Goodwin

Attending ceremonies and collecting snowflakes

*A*ttending ceremonies and collecting snowflakes
Our tribal ancestors observed the yearly cycle on a community level, observing such events as the planting and harvesting of crops, and the beginning and end of winter, with festivals. On the personal level, the life cycle was celebrated through proscribed rituals at the onset of adulthood, the occasion of a wedding, and the passage from human life into the spectral plane. Without really meaning to, the Phish community had approximated this instinctive process through its own rituals of the life cycle. The summer festivals, Halloween shows, and New Year's Runs serve as a mythological recreation of these ancient customs, which serve to bond a community together through ritual. On a superficial level, they fulfill this role by annually marking the end of summer, the occasion of a holiday, and the passage into a new year. More significant meanings can also be found within the fabric of these Phish rituals.

The Phish community passed from puberty into adulthood with the onset of yearly New Year's gigs (and later, Runs) in 1989, while si-

multaneously planting seeds for a future harvest. After playing in tuxedos in front of a big Boston crowd on the biggest party night of the year, Phish could no longer pass off as merely a fun bar band. They may have been commercially and culturally unknown throughout vast expanses of the uncharted North American wilderness, but at least in their own village, they were adults. Meanwhile, by making New Year's an Event, the group took on a kind of responsibility for the first time. The setting of this yearly engagement may have been the first real obligation (or call it a promise) that Phish took on for its audience. By playing their largest room to date (an accomplishment repeated, on greater scale, at each of the next few New Year's shows), Phish lay the groundwork for future possibilities, hinting at the chance to transcend their current identity and achieve something more.

The ritual of the Halloween costume brought with it all the ribald fun and shared anticipation of an exuberant wedding, where the wine flows and the music plays all night. Phish had moved beyond mere adulthood; now they could schedule their own ceremony at a chosen time. Word was sent through the community, and friends and relatives of all kinds showed up to celebrate together.

While the Clifford Ball was experienced overwhelmingly as a singular event, its success led to the installation of a third and cumulative event in the life cycle of the community. Even while filling amphitheaters and the occasional arena, in summer '96 Phish was still enduring quite legitimately as a cult. To identify a fellow traveler, perhaps by spotting a Phish shirt or sticker, was still a surprise. A sold-out New Year's Eve show at Madison Square Garden in '95 was a revelation, but the sheer size of the Ball exploded all our ideas about remaining culturally camouflaged. We went into the Clifford Ball as fans of a cult phenomenon; we left as citizens of an undiscovered nation. Playing on an enormous stage in front of sixty thousand people, directly across the lake from the tiny bar in which they played their first gigs, Phish passed beyond the realm of poorly kept secret and into a new, as-yet unmapped plane of existence, whose boundaries remain evasive, and where mysteries endure.

By the end of '99 the summer festival thing had become a scheduled routine, but Big Cypress was nevertheless going to be something unprecedented…the first genuinely unprecedented event since the Ball itself. It was a synthesis of two of the explosively energetic, creatively volatile rituals of the yearly Phish life cycle: the summer festival and the New Year's Run. These two rituals were merging, and no one really knew what was going to happen. I pictured a mad chemist in a subversive laboratory, preparing to combine two highly potent chemicals, totally unsure of the effects.

Part of the strange allure of the upcoming Cypress expedition was the purely *vacational* aspect of it. For one thing, I had never been to Florida…or anywhere else really, for that matter, when it comes to classic American vacation spots. (A visit of a week or so with cousins in Los Angeles the summer after fourth grade had provided my only opportunity thus far to see palm trees.) My Phish-induced vacations did not usually prompt such exotic touristry. The bland skylines of Hartford and Albany were more common.

The previous summer we had endured the sunbaked logistical nightmare of Oswego, in which we clung to our lives by alternating between the provisional shade of jury-rigged tarps and the bask of the sluggish air conditioning of our rented car, while eagerly sucking at whatever stray drop of liquid managed to elude the ravenous sun. I was hoping to find more personal comfort at Big Cypress, but still con-

sciously anticipating the hopeful chance that I'd emerge from my New Year's trip with a sunburn; a sunburn to mark and distinguish me upon return to the chilly environs of Boston, MA. Phish had disappointed me musically through much of '98 and parts of '99, but I had no doubts that I'd at least come away from this New Year's show with a sunburn, a sunburn that might possibly even segue into a tan.

As usual, the main logistical issues remained in some doubt as the weeks before the event progressed. First, I had to surmount the thorny issue of the Missing Ticket. My big, shiny, glossy ticket had arrived in the mail, and subsequently secured safely at a location within my home. The ticket was a little smaller (though drastically more aesthetically pleasant) than last year's enormous New Year's Run tickets. These managed, however, to squiggle free from the normally anticipated laws of physics, and somehow disappeared entirely from the realm physical existence. Some theorize that a few visiting Halloween elves from Maine may have accidentally gotten them swept up in their clothes or a doctor's bag after a delirious night of listening to drum-and-bass Miles Davis remixes. In any case, the issue was finally resolved in a delightful manner, with Phish Tickets By Mail [PTBM is the name of the division that conducts mail order] showing remarkable consideration for my condition.

The transportation issue was dodged when a good friend employed his prodigious Internet sleuthing skills on my behalf: an affordable flight/car combo was accumulated about a week before the Southward Ho had to take place. The physical aspects of my transport having been arranged, I mentally prepared for what I was primarily thinking of as a *good time*. New Year's Eve. In Florida. With Phish. I hoped that everything would work out.

As it turned out, pretty much the entire Florida experience worked out with remarkable success. The kind of success you just can't plan, regardless of well-meaning effort. It was fortunate that an appointed rendezvous with a friend in the Delta went down successfully the morning of the thirtieth…but it would have served me little use had the same friend not walked by me in a bright yellow shirt ten minutes before showtime. He then led me to a certain green tarp (even with the soundboard, in front of the stage-left video screen), which would have been enough…even if I hadn't been greeted upon my arrival by one of my best friends from school, who I had totally forgotten was even attending the shows, and who I hadn't seen since graduation the previous spring. That would have been enough…even if I didn't then notice that the entire tarp was packed with wonderful friends, many of whom were currently living on the West Coast, who I also hadn't seen in at least half a year. A lifelong New Englander, I was continually amazed that it was December 30 and yet I was dancing barefoot on a brilliant and sunny day. That would have been enough…even if Phish didn't proceed to play three generous sets, including an incredibly beautiful "Light Up or Leave Me Alone", an inspirationally rocking "Ghost", an enchanting "Tweezer", and a mind-meltingly intense "Mike's Song". Dayenu, indeed.

After enduring what was billed as The Worst Traffic Jam in North America If Not the World, I was rested and anxious to explore the grounds upon our initial arrival in the "Amy's Farm" section. We arrived on-site around 3:30 AM, technically the morning of the thirtieth (though I don't consider it morning until you go to sleep and then wake up). We scoped out the Delta and surrounding areas, amused and pleased to find a blues band rocking out to an appreciative crowd. Strolling along the boardwalk, gazing at the mysterious wooded area across the body of water, it was

clear that the party was in full gear, despite the odd hour. When eighty thousand people find themselves in a surreal landscape with amusements of all kinds provided, I guess there really isn't much down time.

I was glad to locate some funky house beats near the front of the campgrounds, where the Green Crew was shacked. Unfortunately, most of the tracks were unmixed…although there was a DJ (manning dual CD decks), it was more like listening to a compilation tape than a DJ set. *Any* constructive element of the rave scene, however, when integrated into a Phish context, is a positive thing in my view. It was quite a surprise for me to see the continued overlap between these two cultures, a phenomenon I noticed in earnest (after prophesying for some time) at Oswego, where I spent the first few minutes of the "Runaway Jim" across from The Greene watching the needle track across a drum and bass record, and saw prayer flags bearing such messages as "Ravers dig Phish too" and "PLUR." ("Peace love unity respect")

At Big Cypress, there were blatant party kids everywhere and on the loose. For better or worse, they had apparently brought with them the full complement of cutting-edge brain tonics like E and ketamine. Though it's vastly unfair to blame the newfound proliferation of E in the lots on the rave kids (it can just as easily come from the usual enterprising hustlers who cater to the cerebral indulgences of the typical middle-class concert-going crowd), I will tentatively blame (or credit, depending on which way your view is warped) these folks for the fact that you can now apparently purchase K on the same premises that also host the likes of a standard first-set "Golgi."

I needed to get some sleep before the aforementioned morning meeting (scheduled for 11 AM), so I headed back towards the campsite a little before dawn. I was glad to have gotten the layout of the event pretty much understood; at the Ball and the Went I had experienced a painfully slow process of getting my bearings. It was daylight as I walked up Fourth Street, when to my surprise and amusement I saw Chris Glushko (a friend and fellow 'birder') drive by, chattering rapidly into a two-way radio, obviously lost. He and his friend were clearly confused, so I flagged them down and assured them that I knew where everything was. I provided an extra map that I had already acquired, which allowed them to locate their friends' campsite.

I got a few hours of quality sleep before heading to the information booth to find some friends.

That rendezvous was a roaring success, as just about everyone I wanted to see was in attendance. It was Elitist Phish.Net Heaven. It was great to see everyone again. I had last seen most of these folks at the 9:30 Club Trey solo show, a few days before my college graduation. These reunions were sprinkled with a few introductions, as I had my first face-to-face meetings with Bertolet, Zerbo, and others. When Noah told me to meet at the info booth at 11, I had no idea it would turn into an all-out family reunion. There was no official Phish.Net gathering at Big Cypress, but the two 11 AM info booth meetings spontaneously ended up as essentially the same thing…although they were conducted informally among friends, and there was no public solicitation for other folks to come along.

When I returned after a solid hour or more, my friends were still sleeping. The morning was bright, warm, and glorious. The thing was underway.

These were possibly the longest three days of my life, complete with a daily morning appointment that provided a comforting sense of normalcy and continuity. It really feels like a spontaneous (but func-

tioning) civilization at these things, not just a ramshackle lump of partying wanderers. It's easy to be lulled into the feeling that this thing really could hold together indefinitely, if the surrounding outside world would just be so kind as to freeze into perpetual suspension, allowing us our own reality…alas, Temporary Autonomous Zones work because they are indeed *temporary*. It's like collecting snowflakes.

A personal highlight of the first show was the "Weekapaug". Ellis, ever watchful, had informed us all that it was midnight…the months of anticipation and speculation had melted away, and we became acutely aware that we were only twenty-four hours away from *whatever the hell was going to happen in the midnight set*. The realization that it was now New Year's Eve 1999, combined with the insistently propulsive funk of "Weekapaug," gave me the distinct sensation of being hurled into the future…it was New Year's Eve *already?* Only twenty-four hours left before the twentieth century would become past tense? I didn't feel quite ready. I wanted some more 1900s. The calendar didn't seem real.

I managed to adjust, and looked around at the eighty thousand people, most of whom were behind our even-with-board position. Trey continued his "Weekapaugian" flights of glory, Mike jabbed at our sides with spiky bass lines, Page clamored on top of it all, and Fishman propelled us further…further…further into the future, further into the groove…we danced and danced and it was warm and it was New Year's Eve and there were dear friends all around. That green tarp felt like just about the safest place in the world.

The next afternoon, the strong 12/30 show was in the books, but there really was very little room for gloating. Three-set Phish shows in December in the Everglades are certainly not to be discarded lightly, but everyone's mind was occupied with the question: *What the hell are they going to do tonight?* It was easy to make idle predictions like *Gamehendge*, a cover album (to fully integrate the three life-cycle rituals into an inferno of psychic convergence), a "Harpua" or "Forbin's" at the least. I didn't really play any of these games, because I've finally learned enough about Phish to realize that I almost never have any idea of what they're going to do. We did have *some* information to go on, however. Crew members had been seen riding around in the 12/31/94 hot dog in the backstage camping area, and there was a rumor of "no guests." My only prediction, if it can be called that, was an often-repeated assurance that "something really weird is going to happen." In general. In totality. There were too many powerful forces converging. The one thing I totally counted out was normalcy.

During the afternoon set, I had to continually remind myself that, despite the beautiful outdoor setting and perfect weather, I was in fact at the Phish New Year's Eve show, dancing barefoot on a tarp. It literally was thrilling every time I again consciously became aware of these usually incongruent circumstances. After the first set concluded mightily with "After Midnight", and the crowd had started wandering away for a few short minutes, an enormous roar suddenly arose as we walked back towards the campgrounds…the feeling of mutual joy and anticipation gave me chills. Particularly anticipation. It was not a "that was a great set" cheer. It was a "we sure have something in store for us" cheer. After all, the band had just fucking promised us that we were gonna *find out what it's all about*. And that's what I'm in this for in the first place.

For day two, we had staked out our tarp directly in front of the soundboard. I continually marveled at the perfect sound, and we congratulated ourselves for securing such a perfect location. I arrived at that tarp sometime before 11 PM, and did not leave until after 7:30 AM.

I spent the entire Midnight Set within a twenty-foot radius on a green tarp directly in front of the soundboard. I did not need to go to the bathroom, I did not need to eat, I did not need to sleep, I did not need to do anything except take in the most amazing musical performance in the history of rock music.

After attending the previous three NYE shows alone, it was a welcome pleasure to hug upwards of twenty people during "Auld Lang Syne". My friend Jeff summed it up with elegant precision the next morning: "I can't believe *what* I just did, *where* I did it, and *who* I did it with!"

I had come to the ceremony prepared, filling my backpack with such items as a blanket, sweater, camera, electric massager, and psychedelic stuffed dinosaur. The massager got passed around among our group, and the people behind us got in on the fun also. During "DWD", someone lit some sparklers, although that turned out to be a bad idea. I don't think we endangered anyone as much as the flame-breather in front of the board at the Great Went, though.

The set started off at an accelerated pace ("Disease" and "Gin" were standout versions right out of the gate), but nothing Tremendously Weird was happening. The "Heavy Things"/cheesecake episode was enormously amusing. We got primed for "Twist Around", as many in our group had fond memories of the Spring Run version, but it was pretty brief. Had it been a regular set, the "Caspian" probably would have ended it.

And then the unmistakable opening riff of "Rock and Roll". This was the first uproariously brilliant jam of the night, and it features a spellbinding sequence that sounds composed, and no doubt got me jumping up and down. The exuberant chorus provided one of my first peak experiences of the set.

When this Velvet Underground rock gem finally ended thirty minutes later, we got a "YEM". It featured a laugh-out-loud "cheesecake" vocal jam.

And the band leaped into the electrifying rhythm of "Crosseyed and Painless". It was a tremendous thrill to see this live, and the energy surging through the crowd was palpable, at least from my vantage point. It was now nearing the two-hour mark, and I started trying to piece together the fragments of the set in my mind (I wasn't even bothering to attempt to keep a setlist). I realized that the jam was really good, and said to Noah, "You know, I'm beginning to think this is a *really* hot set. Like, if it was just a regular second set. I mean, *really* hot." He agreed, or perhaps just wanted me to stop babbling. I remember getting so utterly lost in this blazing jam that the closing vocals totally surprised me. Listening to the FOBs, it's easy to see why; they really do come out of nowhere.

It was during the ensuing "Minestrone" that I began to adjust to the atypical flow of this unprecedented set. Until now, it had been a total party atmosphere in the crowd. I mean that in the best of ways: it was high-energy, New Year's Eve-type stuff. But our internal clocks were noticing that we had exceeded normal second-set territory. I heard someone say something like, "So this is how you play all night, you have to have the guitarist play acoustic by himself." It wasn't in any way a criticism, just someone thinking out loud, trying like everyone else to comprehend the feat that was just beginning to unfold in front of us.

The short acoustic number was not much of a breather for the band before launching off into "Sand". It was during this very long jam that the mood started to shift, aided no doubt by the very spacey and experimental character of the music. This was basically tied (with "Roses") for

the longest and strangest jam of the night, and during the psychedelic mayhem I believe a lot of people shifted gears, mentally. It was the length of the set, as well as the music, as well as whatever little toys people had put into their heads; the regular trajectory of a set had already been way overshot, and we were left to grasp at the shards of bizarre sounds that bombarded us…with no reference point, floating submissively in the dark improvisational currents. Personally, that's why I go to Phish shows, and I was happy to immerse myself in the space odyssey unfurling from the stage. However, some people were getting cold out there on the raft, and one member of our group finally said, "I want them to play a *song* now."

By the end of this jam, we had traversed beyond all semblance of a normal set's rhythm. The band must have sensed this, because they simulated a normal set-closer by whipping out "Slave". The gentle beauty of that classic song was no doubt the salve that many craved, and it provided a wonderful, thrilling release. I consider this the end of the first internal "set" of the night.

The next string of songs were a bit disjointed ("Albuquerque", "Reba", "Axilla", "Uncle Pen", "David Bowie", "My Soul"), and while boasting a "where did that come from?" brilliantly nailed "Reba", seemed like a transitional stretch. There was a very long pause, during which Trey and Fish appeared to have disappeared from the stage. It was strange, cause we were all just standing around, sort of waiting for something to happen. If they had said, "Okay, we're taking a five-minute break," I don't think anyone would have complained, but I guess they wanted to keep the continuity of the set intact. As Mike and Page hung around onstage, occasionally hitting a stray note, I quipped, "Hello, I'm Mike…I'm not a good public speaker." You had to be there.

Then "Drowned". It's hard to fault the band for working up crowd energy with such excellent cover selections, seeing as they were only the conduit for thrilling improvisation. The "After Midnight" jam is absolutely spine-tingling, and I distinctly remember the surprise and delighted shock I felt when it happened. Those in our group marveled at the fact that, despite the hour being around 5 AM, from our vantage point looking forward, it could as well have been "second song, second set." We were still packed in among a swarming throng of excited concert-goers, up to the gills in energy. I'm sure the energy and pure physical proximity of the revelers dispersed the further you got from the stage, but it was quite intense to experience all this from so close.

It might have been around here that our friend Kaz stretched out on the tarp, rolled up in a blanket, and took a nap. He got in a good thirty-minute power nap, stood up, and resumed dancing. It was that kind of night.

By now, some members of our crew had dispersed…off to expel bodily fluids, acquire food, take refuge in the nearby backstage campgrounds, and otherwise reassemble their internal psychic elements. Eventually it started feeling less like Phish was performing a musical concert for our benefit, and more like we were all subsumed together into a giant, pulsing, organic mass, propelled by the sounds and lights coming from onstage. As Kaz put it, people were living, breathing, sleeping, taking a shit, just *existing*…as the spectacle continued on, like some musical sun that pulled us all along through its gravitational pull and kept our pulses going.

I periodically checked my watch, and Raras and I joked about how fun it was just "whiling away the fours" and then "whiling away the fives" and then…whiling away the sixes." At 6 AM on the dot, "Lawn Boy" started, and only in this context could the lounge number legiti-

mately seem surreal. A friend quite memorably remarked, "It's a little early in the morning for a 'Lawn Boy'."

During Fish's intro to "Love You", eighty thousand of us seemed to experience a brief mental drift…finally punctuated by Fishman's remark, "Oh, are we at a rock concert?" It was a perfect comment, and summed up my feelings precisely. Was this a rock concert? What *was* it? At this moment Sting is probably waking up for his yoga and a morning jog, and Phish is still onstage playing their New Year's Eve show.

"Roses Are Free" seemed to glide up out of the silence slowly, as the band eased back into gear after the Henrietta break. Very casually, apparently at complete ease with themselves as a band and with the eighty thousand people on the premises, at about 6:15 in the morning, Phish proceeded to play what I consider their greatest jam ever. The interplay between the four is astounding, as they seem to pulse and breathe together as one sparkling, inspiring mass. It was as if all conscious barriers and egos had been transcended through sheer exhaustion, all pretenses stripped bare, and all that remained was the music. The glorious, transcendental music. It's like everything that had ever happened in their career, and everything that had happened through the night's marathon project of incessant creative exploration, had accumulated and led up to and enabled this breakthrough. It was a musical (and I suspect, for the band, a personal) epiphany. As they glided along in this aesthetic hyperspace, I kept thinking how damned *improbable* this whole situation was. In fact, I took a picture of the stage, just to prove it was actually happening.

During "Roses", the sky began to lighten. By the end of "Bug" it was already daylight, and I started wondering if and when they were ever going to stop playing. I also noticed the enormous screens, literally for the first time in several hours. There was an extreme close-up of Page's face, with red light streaking through his hair. I quipped, "I am Page…I am the Sun God!" It was pretty strange, honestly. It was sometime around here that a member of our group suddenly produced a still-cold bottle of champagne. The process of handing it around and gulping from it seemed so absurd that it was hilarious, and we started chanting "Happy New Year!" in a kind of hybrid of seriousness, sarcasm, humor, and joy that I cannot describe accurately.

Then "Hood" started, and someone said, "Again? Okay." It was simply an exhausted mistake made by the band, and adds yet more flavor and character to the set. I think Dan Seideman had dozed off briefly, but he staggered to his feet when "2001" sent yet another surge of electricity through the crowd. Okay, this is absurd. Beautifully, triumphantly absurd. The glory of nature had subsumed much of Kuroda's artistic space, but orange, red, and white lights pumped as the band lit into a particularly fiery version of this musical orgasm. Suddenly, everyone was dancing again. I chose this time to mill around the tarp a little more, taking a few pictures, basking in the improbable triumph of it all. Near the end, the band apparently experienced another stream of consciousness moment as they briefly wandered into a reggae flavor, as if to revisit a parallel version of "Hood" that they had accidentally started earlier.

It didn't occur to me that this was the preliminary finale of the set, it just seemed like yet another song. I was absolutely shocked that they next went for "Wading", one of my least favorite Phish originals. This is the only version I ever bother to listen to on tape or CD, out of respect for the coherence of that last hour of the set, but it made our group mutter and scratch our heads.

The resumption of "Meatstick" caused a general wave of joy and

release, as we realized that things were wrapping up. To this day, whenever I hear the beginning of a "Meatstick" it immediately conjures up that feeling of communal triumph, accomplishment, and shared joy that connected us all on that millennial morning in Florida. Trey said a few nice things, and then the band actually slipped into another spacey jam. It was as if they literally could not get off the stage! They were clearly savoring the moment for as long as possible. Finally it ended, and they rather quickly ambled offstage. I believe Trey had his arm around someone's shoulder.

It wasn't until the first George Harrison vocals of "Here Comes the Sun" that everyone realized it was a record playing, and that the event was over. At this point we broke into an enormous ovation, celebrating everything we had heard, lived, learned, and gone through in Big Cypress.

Our group gathered our belongings and took a hurried picture, after which Brian said, "Okay, we're crazy," and headed for bed.

I set off alone, with my backpack and blanket. I made my way into the woods, and proceeded to lounge out in the grass in one of the most beautiful physical environments I have ever seen. I felt that I was experiencing the Transcendental concept of microcosm/macrocosm… while savoring the purely sensual and personal experience in my brain, I simultaneously felt no bigger or more important than the moss on the trees. I felt like I merged into the landscape, an unseen bump on a log. I watched a few people walk by with drums and set up in an open zone in my field of vision. The drum circle slowly grew, people gathered and danced, the rhythmic tones heightened in intensity…and then slowly dissipated, as people wandered off, and finally the last members of the circle said their goodbyes and ambled away, perhaps to start another one somewhere else. And the zone was open again. I had to have been the only person who watched and listened to the entire cycle. I spent a few hours in pretty much the same position, gazing at the trees, listening to the people, contemplating the beautiful blue sky from which I was shaded by tropical trees. I knew that as soon as I left the woods, the spell would be broken, so I remained for as long as I was comfortable.

By the time I wandered back to some friends' campsite, they were waking up. (Along the way I had left a note on Bertolet's camper: "Hi. Jeremy Goodwin, 1/1/00.") I stretched out on the grass, and gazed at the clouds doing their little dance in the sky. We contemplated what we had experienced the night before. I said it felt like we had seen the band *naked*…we had all bound up together and then simultaneously unraveled. It was almost like the band had put their sanity and psyches on display, for us to marvel as they dissipated. It seemed incomprehensible to think about another "normal," two-set show after this. We had just seen the peak of rock musical accomplishment in the twentieth century. I really wanted to go to whatever the next show would be, wherever it was, just to see for myself the first post-Cypress moment and watch the circle become complete.

"I don't know what I could possibly ever need or want this band to do for me again."

They had just jumped through an enormous hoop for us, and I felt one hundred percent satiated. I never needed to see this band play again. What more could I possibly expect them to do for me? I felt like the entire Phish oeuvre had been made complete in a way. Of course, I loved the band, and knew I'd want to see many shows in the future…but I was positive that in all honestly I didn't really *need* any more. They had fulfilled my personal and aesthetic needs like no rock band could possibly ever hope to do again.

And thus, as I lay on the ground lazily chatting and watching the clouds, I felt an unexpected twinge of the bittersweet, realizing that we were gliding atop a plateau, a high point, from which all future Phish happenings would look back and feel the shadow.

12/31/99 Big Cypress Seminole Reservation—Chris Bertolet

The Show.

I believe that years from now (or even sooner) this performance will be known simply as The Show: no one will need to reference a date or place. Which is as it should be, since this evening stood time and space on its ear.

Most Phish-heads know of "Oh Kee Pah Ceremonies," Phish's extended jam-a-thons of legend, and the strange states of mind they produce. The Show (the midnight-to-sunrise set, at least) was like staging an "Oh Kee Pah Ceremony" in a living room, with eighty thousand people looking on. The jams that arose from the inevitable fatigue were the most inspiring and original things I've ever heard Phish play, and extraordinarily connected with the fabric of Creation.

During the "Crosseyed and Painless" jam, I slipped into a waking dream state, where I remained until I fell asleep at 9 AM. From time to time, my limbs went numb, and at several times during the early morning, I went completely out of body for minutes on end. Where I went I can't begin to describe without risking serious credibility damage, but I know I was not alone.

The set started strangely, to be sure. The stage play and pyrotechnics were classic Phish—sandwiching the entire night in the "Meatstick" (much as I despise the tune) was a great way to knock all the bullshit hype down a notch. We spent most of the "Disease" trying to find optimal sound and dance space. By the time we got to our spot behind the second right tower, the fiery jam was smoking its way into a white-hot but short "Llama". The "Gin" that followed was delicate, dreamy, and strange, featuring a full-blown vocal jam. Shades of Murat.

The "Heavy Things" episode was hilarious, and gave everyone a much-needed breather. "Twist" was decent, but no great shakes, so the Best "F@ckerpants" Ever was a welcome surprise. The soaring "Caspian" signaled the arrival of the real meat of The Show: "Rock and Roll", "YEM", and "Crosseyed".

These three jams were all epic in their own right. "Rock and Roll", despite taxing Page vocally, was sweeter than honey. "YEM" was clean and powerful, and the "cheesecake" vocal jam recalled the "donuts" vocal jam from Vegas. The "C&P" jam may have been the runner-up highlight of my evening; it stretched on forever, and in contrast to the benchmark West Palm version, left the groove to explore some eerie, off-kilter places. Inspired jam work. Hose-plus.

After the trance-wonkish "Sand"->"Topplings" (which I was far too out-of-body to even recognize), Jenn and I took a walk for water and food. I danced in the hospitality area to an anti-gravity "Slave" as the amused security people watched, and heard the "Reba" from Phillip Zerbo's VIP RV (H_2O, THC, etc.). We listened to the rocking "Axilla" from the pizza line, and by the time we got back to our crew with the hallowed pie, "Bowie" was in full swing.

This was a driving version with a nice build, though the climax seemed a little tacked on (as it often does when they don't approach it exactly right). By this point, though, it didn't matter. Every note Phish played was infused with something special.

"My Soul" was fun and booty-quakin', but it was "Drowned" that

left me in shambles. *How in God's name can they be playing this hard for this long?* I wondered. Medicated for the cause, or charged by the atmosphere? No matter. The segue into the "After Midnight" jam was seamless, and the "AM" jam was actually better than the one earlier in the evening! "Horse"->"Silent" was gorgeous, per usual, but…

"Piper"…"Piper"…"Piper"…a thousand times "Piper"! I don't know how they do it, but every single "Piper" I hear gets better. I said after the Ventura '97 show that this tune was "the new 'Sparkle'," and I've never been so glad to be so wrong. They actually came back to the verse for the third time in this other-worldly version. Relentless, mind-numbing, awe-inspiring, impossibly electric.

The "Free" was sort of a mess (they were exhausted from the "Piper"), but the night's dose of comedy was close behind as Fishman took his time getting the Electrolux from side stage. Now, I have never seen a vac jam up close, but I can tell you that what I saw on the screens I never need to see again, ever. Truly a hideous sight, especially at five in the morning. That said, this was a spectacular vacuum jam—actually virtuosic—that sent swamp life scurrying for cover in a five-mile radius.

"Roses are Free" catalyzed a long, ambient jam that really encapsulated the mood of the crowd at that point. Trippiest stuff of the evening. The "Bug" that followed was really on-point about the millennium thing—"It doesn't matter…overrated"—and I couldn't help but wish it had been played on ABC instead of "Heavy Things". This tune rawks.

Now, I don't want to start an argument, but I don't think the "Hood" tease was a "Hood" tease. I honestly think that Fishman was so tired that he just plain forgot they'd played it. The "ASZ" they neatly slipped into was very spacey and unique; by this time, Page was nearly asleep on top of his synth. I honestly can't tell you much about it, since I was watching clouds swirl around the crescent moon. I turned around to watch the second "verse" and when I turned around again, the sun was coming up. Oh, my….

The sunrise on January 1, 2000, in Big Cypress was the most unspeakably beautiful thing I have ever seen in my life—a blazing, boiling, holy mirror of the landscape. It was as if Creation was beaming upon all of us, rewarding us for celebrating It with such passion and abandon. Everyone I could see was looking on in silent awe. Though I never really "got" the song until that moment, "Wading in the Velvet Sea" was a letter-perfect accompaniment to the sunrise ("You won't find moments in a box…"), and I wish it had gone on forever. I was breathless.

"Meatstick", and it was over. I could have stood to hear Phish play "Here Comes the Sun" themselves, but it seems ridiculous to wish for more after everything we were blessed with. The Show. I won't ever be the same.

5/20/00 Radio City Music Hall , New York, NY
—Jeremy D. Goodwin

Everyone in the Phish world was feverishly excited about the Radio City thing…except me. From the moment the shows were announced, I thought it was a cool thing, but I assumed I'd never be able to get tickets. Unlike other small-venue events (Fillmore, the Flynn Theatre shows, Joyous Lake Club), this time everyone at least had fair warning and an honest shot to get in the door. The online route seemed the best bet, but I just wasn't interested in independently installing five versions of Netscape on my machine, or commandeering some local college computer lab for an hour and hiring a fleet of trained monkeys to continually hit reload on the "check availability" screen. On the appointed

day, I woke up to my alarm, spent fifteen unsuccessful minutes trying to order tickets, and crawled back into bed. So much for Radio City.

I didn't bother putting out any feelers for extras, since the word on the street was that tickets were extremely scarce. There were stories about Dionysian people asking civilians about extra tickets! For a while it looked like just about the toughest ticket ever. (Apparently there was some miscalculation at some point, because about a week before the show everything loosened up, and those who needed to get hooked up were pretty much taken care of.)

About a week before the shows, I was wasting time on email when something interesting popped up: a fellow Mockingbirder had two extras for the first night. Marty Acaster and I replied at about the same time (instantly), so we each got one. Suddenly, completely out of nowhere, Radio City was on!

I was particularly excited, because I had been hoping for a while for an excuse to go on a New York City adventure. My previous visits to the city had been limited to the '97 and '98 New Year's Runs, and a big mega rave (Boo 4) in November '99. The Phish visits had gone smoothly, but on those visits my exposure to the city was mainly limited to the Long Island Railroad, Penn Station, and the blocks surrounding Madison Square Garden. I was able to navigate that terrain successfully enough, but the more recent, rave-related visit last fall proved more daunting.

When my favorite DJ was nowhere to be found and the main event ended an hour early, we were left to wander through Times Square, and a few hundred of us chose an abandoned street corner to dance to the beats coming from a boom box. Party kids were taking over The City and it felt great! However, by the time we made it in and out of the afterparty (at a local four-level subterranean club) and started wandering the streets again around 11 AM, we were a bit fatigued and agitated. The subway was an ordeal, we walked around forever looking for Lafayette Street, and when we finally made it to our long-awaited destination (a very particular record store), we discovered that it was closed for renovation. All that was available was a super-trendy clothing store that sold tiny cloth dolls for $25.

My friend Nick made me promise to talk him out of any future plans to return to the City, but my reaction was different. While staggering around lost and broke that weekend, I managed to subconsciously fall in love with the place. When the ten-part Ric Burns documentary (*New York*) aired on PBS the next month, I watched each installment avidly, and became entranced by the mystique of the place. I'm a hard-core Bostonian booster, and in the long run I'd much prefer to live in the Olde Towne, but by the time Radio City rolled around I was quite primed for a return engagement in New York. I had a score to settle with the City. Last time, it didn't want me around, and had made that clear. I was ready to take it another round.

I was even able to get a ride to the City from Marty, and the serendipity continued when we somehow found a convenient parking space for the weekend immediately upon arrival. After successfully picking up our tickets from Mockingbird allies in the Sheraton (in a room that came equipped with a fax machine), we made the ten-minute walk to Times Square and located the Marriott Marquis. It was strange to enter a hotel on Phish tour that was not completely subsumed by 'heads. While civilians abounded, some fans identified themselves by approving of the tie-dyed formal wear I was carrying around on a hanger. I had some fun on the escalators and moon rocket-style glass elevators.

There were bright shiny things everywhere, and I had an instant feeling that the weekend was going to be pretty fun.

The two adjoining rooms of our group were pimped out beyond expectations, featuring a view of the heart of Times Square. I find this to be a distinctly American kind of place…one feels intuitively the sense that it is *something* important, some kind of landmark, and yet it is really just a bunch of advertisements and TV screens. A very post-modern kind of landmark that signifies nothing in particular and is composed one hundred percent of superstructural image. Top-notch eye candy, nonetheless!

Not long after arrival at the Marquis, I had one of *those* moments. Everyone else had headed off to the venue, giddy and having taken many pictures (prom style). I was left alone in the rooms, listening to the "2001">"Bowie" from Japan, enjoying the view, and putting on my tie-dye tuxedo shirt. I had a feeling of pretty much total contentment. A serene, calm joy mixed with anticipation. A feeling of all things being in line. I am thankful that Phish has helped facilitate several such moments in my life over the past five years.

It was a very short walk to the unmistakable Radio City marquee, and the scene in front was not too intense. I got some love from random passersby due to my attire, but managed to generally infiltrate the crowd unnoticed. Plenty of people were looking for extras, or looking to trade for the next night, but everything was orderly and didn't even interfere with the traffic. In short, it was not really the zoo I anticipated. They had the orchestra folks enter on one side of the building, the mezzanine ticketholders on another. I was a bit disenchanted by the long line, but it soon started moving quickly, and we passed into the building with nary a frisk from security.

We were elated to find our seats in the third row of the third mezzanine, arguably the sonic and visual sweet spot of the venue. It was apparent that everyone in the room and onstage was pretty damn psyched for the weekend. "First Tube" was sizzling and identical to all previous versions; that's all anybody expected it to be, though, and the energy in the room was very high. There were several Trey windmills, and it looked like he felt like King of the Room.

The opening notes of "Wolfman's" convinced me we were in for a great weekend…the bland, brief jam that ensued was the first cause for doubts. This is probably hands down the least impressive "Wolfman's" since '96. And what did they end it for? "Coil". Third song, first set: first buzz kill. Talk about poor placement. The mid-set Page solo was mercifully brief…I pictured Trey stepping on a button that activates a painful electrode that has been inserted into Page's brain, to let him know when to stop playing.

The balcony was positively rocking during the standard-but-pleasing "Possum". This is one song that I'm still able to get up for, no matter how many similar versions I hear. The crowd always seems to get particularly electrified for this number; I think the reaction is even comparable to that for "Antelope". A standard "Moma" (is there anyone who *still* can get off on this song?) and "Limb", and then…"Character Zero"? Already? That's it? So much for the first set. On the drive into the city, I mock-cynically told Marty to enjoy the first set-closing "Character Zero," sixty-three minutes into the set. As it turned out, "Zero" wrapped things up in a tidy fifty-nine minutes.

Despite the pedestrian song selection, it should be noted that the band definitely sounded tight as far as I could tell. Maybe it was just the excellent, booming sound in the venue, but Phish sounded very precise and energized, though creatively uninspired. This was clearly just a warm-up set. Maybe just early jitters.

At the opening notes of "Zero", I headed out to perform my set break activities. I felt a bit awkward filling up a water bottle at the water fountain wearing a tuxedo, but 'twas all good. I spent most of set break hanging out on the main stairwell, watching the parade of people passing by with mixed drinks in hand. Project Phormal was in full effect: there was creative formalwear of all kinds, plus the standard jacket-and-tie stuff. I chatted up many a wandering interloper during set break, giddily handed out a few pieces of paper with my email on it for some reason, took a few pictures, tried to recruit Mockingbird show reviewers, and generally spread the love, with which I was bubbling over. There was quite a bit around.

Despite the boring first set, the energy in the crowd seemed to pick up right where New Year's had left off…full of community spirit and love (there's that word again). It was like everyone had learned a lesson in Florida, simultaneously, and continued to feel and act in line with the benevolent revelations of that time. (I noted the lack of "cheesecake" activity, pleased. Let's leave that as a special memory, folks…don't make it the next "Hood!")

I don't think anyone was surprised by the "Gotta Jibboo" second-set opener. It worked fine for me; this was nothing outrageous, but the best version I've heard (of only six or so). The "Disease" intro, having appeared *ex nihilo*, seemed longer than usual. The first part of the "Disease" jam was typically shredding; after a bit, Trey started apparently trying to return to the main riff, and cut things off. I pictured him yelling, "Abort! Abort! Radiation has flooded the chamber!" Fortunately, though, either the rest of the band would hear none of it, or he was really just tidying things up by hinting at the main theme before jaunting off into true jam territory, because one of the best jams of the night was to follow. It was very upbeat and rocking, and at one point Fishman was essentially playing "Llama". A few minutes after that, Trey started clearly trying to go into "Llama". Luckily, we avoided that and got to hear more improvisation. They slipped into an irresistibly groovy zone, which many people at the show identified as a "Crosseyed and Painless" tease. Even upon hearing the tapes, however, I still think it was just a "C&P"-like groove, and not a tease. In any case, it's infectiously funky, and everybody's gonna love it on tape. This "DWD" jam deserves credit because, by the time Trey brought things around and finished the song (apparently the trend since '98, after a few years of unfinished "DWD"s), I was taken off guard and had kind of forgotten where we had started.

"Dirt" sounded perfect in the silent theatre. Then a fabulous new chilled-out intro to "Twist"! Most of the crowd didn't catch on until the lyrics, but I thought it was immediately clear that this was going to be "Twist". They basically just vamped around on the "Twist Around" melody for two minutes or so, with Mike playing something damn close to the "Twist" bass line. It was very mellow and slow, and provided a way for the band to ease into the song. I have no doubt that this new intro is going to be the vehicle for some inspired and spine-tingling segues in the future! I love it. I spontaneously threw my "woos" down from the third mezzanine, and I think I heard a few others singing along too. I have loved this song ever since the Spring Run version rudely and unabashedly shredded the fabric of sight and sound, and still consider it a treat. The lyrics, a typically cryptic tale of obsessive-compulsive disorder as it relates to a troubled relationship, are among my favorite in the Marshall oeuvre.

The jam was extremely quiet, and so was the crowd! I found this strangely exhilarating. Many times I've had my hair raised by an exuberant crowd reaction (see the 8/17/97 "Gin" or "Hood" for the most moving example), but on this night I was moved by the pin-drop silence of the crowd, as the band filled the air with subdued, elegantly spacey sounds. The jam reminded me very much of some of the New Year's jamming. This is the new sound. The audience sat in rapt attention as the crystal-clear notes danced out to every corner of the room. Very quiet, very spacey…clearly the best and most important jam of the evening. They've funked out à la "Crosseyed" many times in the past…but "Twist Around" provided the most original and cutting-edge sound currently in the Phish arsenal.

A standard "Piper" followed, during which I escaped into the hallway. "Piper" is usually too much for me to deal with…the screaming lights, the loud and repetitive music, the puzzlingly exuberant crowd reaction. Without much else to do, I chatted up one of the ushers. I asked her how she was, and when she seemed particularly positive, I asked her if it wasn't just another night at work for her. She surprised me by saying that no, she was actually very happy to be working that night, because there hadn't been many events at RCMH lately. "I'm very fortunate that they called me for tonight." I thought that was cool, and asked her opinion of the audience. She said we were great, a lot better than other recent crowds they had had. For instance, when the recent boxing match was there, the crowd was extremely drunk and unruly. She said they were fighting in the atrium and on the stairwells and throwing change around. She had some funny stories to tell, but as I told her, "It sounds like things are getting a little more interesting inside, I have to go back to my seat."

It must have seemed strange to her that I had to leave so abruptly, but it made perfect sense to me…"Piper" had gone through its annoyingly repetitive motions, and the jam part was starting. Everyone I talked to afterwards loved the "Piper", but everyone *always* loves the "Piper". I had been giving "Piper" a chance lately, due to seeing three consecutive jammed-out versions (Portland CCCC, Providence, and Big Cypress), but this was just one of the standard versions that got me so sick of the song in '97 and '98.

Then "Hood". The way things had been going that night, I was very afraid that this would be the last song of the set. By my calculations it seemed that the band had another twenty to thirty minutes available to them for the set, and certainly *should* play an hour-and-a-half set after the incredibly short first set, but who knows. Instead of saying goodnight though, there was yet another in a series of extremely long pauses in between songs, before "Wading". Gag. What exactly were they discussing so thoroughly that led to this song choice?

Then the Trey speech, which was great. One of the main reasons I was excited to see this show was that I wanted to see the band in their first appearance after Big Cypress. It felt like everything had changed on that auspicious weekend in Florida, and I wanted to see the band close the circle by returning to "regular" shows. It was very much like I wanted to witness it with my own eyes just to prove that it was happening, because after that Midnight Set I could barely imagine what it would be like to see a regular two-set show again. It's hard to explain. If you were there at Big Cypress, perhaps you understand.

So, it was really nice to hear what Trey had to say. He openly pledged, on behalf of the band, to do everything they could to keep this thing going as long as possible. I see this as a watershed moment, well

beyond the implications of his various end-of-tour speeches from recent years. It really felt like we were all in this thing together, and that the possibilities for the future are limitless…if no one (onstage or off) fucks it up.

Page also talked about the significance of Radio City itself, so there was a lot of build-up, and then…"Guyute". Uhh…anticlimactic to say the least. Lacking a ticket for the next night, I wanted to savor every minute of being inside, so I danced to "Guyute" for probably the first time in a few years. Danced my ass off, in fact, no doubt to the amusement of some around me. People at Phish shows generally do a slow-paced stoner shuffle, usually involving some wild flagellation of the arms, with very little actual movement of the feet. I thus find it strange to take my rudimentary dancefloor skills (which put me only a notch above the uncoordinated newbies in any club or rave setting), and bring them to a Phish show, where I'm suddenly more like Michael Jackson. It feels nice.

In fact, I continued to dance my ass off at full tilt during the break between second set and encore, and during the acoustic "Minestrone". This was no doubt to the amusement of those around me, who (one must conclude) must have assumed that I was on some kind of drugs or something. Just dancing, folks…sometimes the beat inside your head is all you need.

I was very amused by the applause/"shhh!" exchange during "Minestrone". It's interesting to be among a polite, attentive, etiquette-driven crowd that practices self-policing to the extent of enforcing conformity. It's a lot different from the unruly, vaguely rebellious proceedings at kids' shows and clubs or the staid, subdued aura of boomer arena gigs ("Can you sit down please?"). Is it really that rude or wrong to applaud during "Minestrone"? To yell "wooohoo!" yes, but to applaud? And is it wrong to yell "woohooo!" in the middle of jams? I hope not, because I do it all the time, and consider myself a sparkplug who helps keep the energy high. My slow clap/"woohoo!" routine is well known by anyone who was attended a show with me that included a particularly good jam. As far as I'm concerned this is model behavior. I don't think the band wants us sitting silently, comparing notes and whispering, "*My* this 'Tweezer' is good! I'll e-mail you about it tomorrow."

"Loving Cup" finished things up in particularly ejaculatory fashion, and the show was in the books. Since I wasn't sure I'd be around the next night, I hung around for quite a bit, savoring the beautiful room and chatting people up some more. The crowd lingered like slow death in that place, hanging out in the lobby forever. I finally got my fill and decided to go back to the hotel for the next set of adventures.

Overall, the show was a series of ups and downs. The first set was essentially a tax write-off (though it was a damn "Tweezer"fest compared to Monday's first set), but the second set featured a few minutes of rocking and funking "DWD", and a few minutes of pristine, spacey "Twist Around". Not much to show for the effort of getting tickets and going to the City, and I knew I hadn't had my musical ass kicked as thoroughly as I was hoping…but the overall vibe among the crowd, and the very high energy and positivity circling all around us, helped disguise the fact that I had seen a show that was packed with little disappointments. In the end, it was an important and fun night, and I was glad to be a part of it.

I also continued to learn two lessons. One, it's easy to see that there are people all around who experience a given show in a radically different manner than I do, and that's fine. There's room for all of us. (Well, in this case, six thousand of us.) If you can get down to the umpteenth identical version of "Moma Dance" or "PYITE", go for it. Two, I learned something I had forgotten, that a run of shows is about

the total experience, and that it's not wise to peg *everything* on what happens onstage. I had a wonderful time for myself, despite the fact that I found fully half of the music boring.

Back in the room afterwards, we listened to the night's second set and "Oysterhead," but I paid little attention, concerned instead with attempting to meet and hang out with most of the people who had appeared in the rooms mysteriously. We had fresh fruit to nibble on, and a bathtub full of beers. It was also fun to show off the various views, and generally navigate several simultaneous arenas of camaraderie. There were revelers of all types, including a few unidentified beautiful women. I could do this every week.

5/21/00 Radio City Music Hall, New York, NY
—Jeremy D. Goodwin

I moved to where they hoped I'd be"

Monday morning/afternoon was splendid. I was craving more Phish and really wishing I had a show that night to look forward to, but despite lacking a ticket I nonetheless enjoyed wandering the adjacent streets with some crew members in search of the Soup Nazi. A man dressed and painted entirely in silver gave us directions. Another guy dressed as an angel gave us small cheesecake snacks. We ended up going to one of those places with a ridiculously extensive menu spanning all possible gamuts of culinary genre, apparently including a "veal bar." I found it amusing when the waitress handed me an omelet and bagel, and delivered spinach fettuccini Alfredo with artichoke hearts to the friend sitting beside me.

Breakfast was excellent, and we liberally grabbed the coffee pot from the waitress stand for many a fill-up. The food was good, but the highlight was probably an amusing incident involving me, a cup of coffee, and the effects of sleep deprivation on motor functions. I was deep in conversation, and oblivious to the fact that I was slowly pouring my coffee onto the table in front of me, from chin level. Apparently I had started to take a sip and then forgotten about it somewhere in the process.

When I returned to the room, there was a note for me next to the phone: "Jeremy, Mike called, has ticket for you!"

Woohoo!

I spent the rest of the afternoon casually in our rooms, entertaining a few stray visitors. In the hour or two before showtime, our little suite managed to fill up again almost to capacity. I was particularly pleased that Dan Hantman made it by for my first in-person meeting, and we reveled in his orange corduroy aura. I was able to take a priceless picture of Dan and a nonplussed, cape-wearing, clipboard-wielding ZZYZX. Come to think of it, there were a hell of a lot of people wearing capes in that room. I guess it was our own little fashion statement.

I settled into my second mezzanine seat with some anxiety, as the low roof and safety lights made me feel alienated from the rest of the room. Then the first set was an almost unmitigated train wreck until the "Gin". I really felt like I was watching the VH1 taping, with good reason. In fact, this set could probably work as the Hard Rock special with very little editing. There was just a steady procession of brief, upbeat filler. This may be the first time I've felt that they really weren't playing for *us*...they were playing for some other subset of the audience, maybe radio or label executives, maybe critics, maybe Lorne Michaels...who knows. I have never in my life made this accusation before, but if there's ever been a sell-out Phish show, this first set would have to be it. It was

like "Phish for Dummies." "My Soul", "Billy Breathes", "Heavy Things", "Sparkle"...the song selection speaks for itself. By mid-set I found it positively eerie, and wrote "wtf?" in my setlist book. In an effort to entertain myself, I wrote things like "Get Back on the Pain" and "PIBT" ("Phish is boring tonight") in my book.

Unfortunately, I had yet to abandon my second mezzanine seat by the "SOAM," and (with the rest of the people in the first and second mezzanines) totally missed out on the lighting theatrics. What a shitty place to sit. The proximity to the band is fine, but there's a low ceiling with safety lights turned on, and you have absolutely no physical or visual connection to the rest of the crowd. Thus, Chris turned the houselights on during this song, and I had no idea. I could tell something funky was going on from the crowd reaction, and decided to evacuate ASAP up to the third mezzanine, where things were immeasurably more pleasant. The set-closing "Bathtub Gin" was fabulous, and its discordant last few minutes were among the most experimental of the weekend.

I found some friends during set break, and liberally complained about the first set. One friend tersely reminded me that there were plenty of people outside who would like my ticket. She was missing the point. The point she missed is an important one, and part of a lesson I relearned in New York. Phish had played a mostly listless, boring set, and that was just a fact that I had no control over. Perhaps many people saw it as "energy"; it translated to me as "safe" and "creatively bloated." I was still romping around the place, excited, having a wonderful time, totally thankful to be there. I was still very happy, and aware of how special the show was. I just happen to also have a critical barometer on at the same time. That is to say, I'm aesthetically awake. That doesn't mean I don't deserve to be inside if I'm not interested in lapping up every song on cue.

The *Twilight Zone* theme continued with the "Bouncing" second

Las Vegas

Elise Ryerson

set opener. Was there anyone in the room who was not yet completely clear on the fact that this show was not being played for the fans? It was like Bizarro World. Had we stepped into a 1992 opening set for Santana or something?

Next was "Bowie". The intro was interesting, featuring a variation of the closing "Bouncing" "solo" by Trey. It wasn't one of the eight-minute monster intros from Summer 97, but it was good. Probably about three minutes. People raved about the "Bowie", but I didn't hear anything particularly interesting. It was a "Bowie". Tight, but whatever. I said goodbye to the friends in the first balcony I had visited for the beginning of the set, and headed back to my seat in the middle of it. I remember walking up the broad stairwell alone, listening to the "Bowie" in the background, feeling strangely cold.

Then "Sand", possibly my most anticipated song for the weekend. It was probably the best song of Fall Tour, one of the top-five jams at Big Cypress, and I positively love the eerie album version. Unfortunately, this version was a total throwaway, ending mysteriously after a scant nine minutes. I assume this is the worst-ever version by Phish of "Sand". "Mango Song"…whatever. I was dancing and having fun, but certain lyrics from *The Wall* seemed to apply…"they sent us along as a surrogate band." Where was Phish?

Hanging out with the Ghost in the machine, apparently. This monster "Ghost" totally redeemed the show, and in fact the entire weekend, finally throwing down the improvisational anchor that would ground the shows firmly in the "above average" category. At its outset, I was fearing the worst…another eight- or nine-minute throwaway version meant perhaps to impress the modern-rock program directors in the house. However, somebody had thrown on the switch somewhere, and Phish was back. Throughout this jam, Mike was soloing like a virtuoso, for minutes at a time. Simultaneously, Page had somehow exploded, apparently trying to grab back a huge chunk of the jam space he's evacu-

ated in recent years. These two drove the jam along for several thrilling stretches, and when Trey was soloing melodically *à la* 1995, the band was peaking. This was one of my favorite jams that I've seen in recent years, on first appearance better than anything I saw in '98. The sound was absolutely perfect in the last row (center) of the entire room, and as far as I was concerned the music and lights were designed specifically for us. While grooving relentlessly to this near-thirty-minute "Ghost", I occasionally tilted my head back to watch the lights move around the enormous black and white mosaic that made up the back wall of the theater. *This* is the way to see Phish. I had made friends with the people around me, as I usually try to do, and we were stunned and delighted by this entire jam, hooting and hollering our vociferous approval.

Trey eventually started playing the intro to "Rock and Roll", and the crowd experienced possibly its peak exuberance of the weekend. I was initially hoping for a jammed-out "Rock and Roll" (*à la* Big Cypress), since there seemed to be time left, but I soon got the drift that this was going to be a quick, fiery set-closer, and enjoyed it for what it was. What a great set-closer! Experiencing everything in perfect sound and with perfect sightlines, I cheered along with everyone, literally jumping up and down, enthralled by the music and the energy…in a timeless place, hoping to believe for a moment that everything is indeed alright.

The "Bug" encore seemed appropriate, and I'm now surprised (in retrospect) that it's never been an encore before. I had lately been obsessed with this song and told myself it was a fitting end to the weekend, though it brought us back into Record Release Party world. I didn't expect another song, so the appearance of "Golgi" was fine by me, though by no means a kickdown in the song-selection department. During one of the transitions, the band fell into a silent jam for about five or ten seconds, and then exploded back, all together. Kinda thrilling. It was not until some point during the "Golgi" that I suddenly realized something I had completely forgotten about while in New York: this was

Elise Ryerson

Las Vegas

my fiftieth show.

I was pleased to see Trey giving the "keep going" sign at the end of the song (similar to an umpire's designation of a home run), and there was a little feedback jam. The way Trey was gesturing with his arms, I wondered for a moment if he was playing the Theremin. Then he removed his guitar from his shoulders and waved it around, "throwing" sound into the crowd. It was a nice little extended ending.

After the show I tried to bond with strangers over the "Ghost," but more often than not received only "Dude, it was *all* good!" as a reply. I continued to notice a good number of "cheesecake!" shouts, in marked contrast to the first night. I went around asking people if they had been inside the first night ("no" was by far the predominant answer) and telling them that the "Ghost" was the best thing of either show. Everyone was marveling at the room. I sat in all three mezzanines, and the sound was outstanding everywhere. Throughout the two shows, I greeted strangers with, "Radio City: who knew?" It was a shared sense of mutual discovery and satisfaction.

Several members of our troupe were at the aftershow at the Club Tonic, so things were slightly more subdued post-show. At one point I was being harangued by ZZYZX for my lack of live "Rebas" (only a dozen). I strictly enforced the "keep on drinkin' toooooo" policy, though, and continued my newfound practice of spreading love and minimizing negativity. I have little doubt that this new personal movement was the source of the mysterious NYC subway map that appeared (without explanation) next to my seat while in a mid-show water fountain visit. This was an item I sorely needed, and it proved to be my best friend as I navigated alone through the City the next afternoon. Serendipity.

I had a very humorous episode in one of those random deli/buffet/stores walking back from the show, when a NYC cop came in saying, "Page had a good night, huh? The guy on keyboards? Page was great tonight. Good for Page, I'm happy for him." I'm content to leave that unexplained, as one of the mysteries of the universe.

The next morning I had some Guinness for breakfast, and our two rooms gathered *en masse* once more for a final round of sociability before check-out. My prized subway map was lost and then found again. Somehow there was still more snack food and more beer. And never a shortage of spirited discussions. Finally, the sound of housekeeping approaching inspired us to give up the ghost…a few were heading for new lodging and a show at the Roseland, some were en route to Costa Rica for the SCI fantasy camp, and others merely going home. I regrouped in the semi-surreal lobby of the Marquis and plotted my geographical assault on the City. I still had some unfinished business from my visit to the city for that rave last fall. Tops on my agenda was to visit some "legendary" record stores (in the techno world that means more than five years old), and I perpetrated my only touristy act of the trip: purchasing zero records and one T-shirt at Breakbeat Science. It's a damn good shirt, though. With a spiffy shirt and a couple new records (from the Liquid Sky store) in tow, I grabbed a delicious falafel in the East Village.

6/28/00 PNC Bank Arts Center, Holmdel, NJ—Erik Swain

In my opinion there are two ways in which a Phish show comes to be known as great. The first way is when a show is so musically impressive that it causes you to drop your jaw. The second way is for being a "fun" or "party" or "wacky" show. These are memorable less for their musical performances than for things like antics, banter, breakouts, rar-

ities, or just a raucous good time. The first, in my mind, make for great "concerts"; the second make for great "events." The greatest shows of all, in my book, are those that achieve greatness on both counts.

The caveat is that what comes across most on the tapes is how the show did as a "concert" as opposed to an "event." So the shows that are strong as an "event" but less so as a "concert" are prone to be viewed as overrated by those who weren't there. (Indeed this is how I feel about 7/4/99. It sounds like it was a blast, but I wasn't there and there's not much other than "Ghost"->"Slave" that holds my interest on tape. That is not to say the show didn't achieve greatness, though.)

Given, then, that there are different ways of declaring a show to be great, I have to say that Phish 2000 achieved some form of greatness in all four New Jersey shows on its Summer Tour: June 28 and 29 in Holmdel, and July 3 and 4 in Camden. They differed in how they achieved it, and to what level they achieved it, but it was there throughout. I saw all four (they were my eleventh through fourteenth shows), and had the time of my life.

The first show opened with a very powerful and well-played "Chalk Dust Torture." It had nothing out of the ordinary other than that Trey using his pedals to make something that sounded like a siren. Was this an acknowledgement of the heavy police presence in the lots? Who knows. In any case, the crowd had already worked up an incredible energy level that would not stop all night. Next came "Sloth," which was botched at this venue the previous year. They more than made amends, producing an airtight version with the correct tempo. Trey's playing was strong, which would be a trend for the whole night. "Taste" featured a strong piano solo by Page and a jam that started off a bit noodly but righted itself for a satisfying climax.

The opening strains of "Bathtub Gin" signified that we were now officially in an old-school set, and this was as old-school a jam as you're ever going to hear nowadays. After Fish dragged out the opening beats (it almost seemed like Page wasn't ready), Page ripped up the piano and then the band locked into a tight march. It just kept building and building, getting faster and faster, climaxing in an exhilarating series of runs by Trey. At one point Trey did an extended tease that I'm convinced is "Spill the Wine" by Eric Burdon and War. Anyway, there was no funk and no looping, just four guys doing tension and release and playing as hard as they can with no trickery. I liked this better than almost every "Gin" I heard in 1999.

Do you know how sometimes a burst of insane intensity just seems to come out of nowhere? That's what happened, for example, in the 8/13/93 "Gin" and the 7/6/98 "Piper," and it happened in the "Piper" that came next at this show. Fish quickened the pace really fast, kind of like on the album version, but not as abruptly. Then their playing just kept getting faster and faster and noisier and noisier. Toward the end they got the closest I've ever heard to them doing speed metal. And then after that Trey added a few effects and the band sounded like Santana on the *Lotus* live album (1974)—that is, like a video game. Those who like their "Pipers" to build gradually panned this version, but to me it was simply mind-blowing. I was present for the incredible 8/8/98 version. This to me was better. I think it should be the template for all the post-*Farmhouse* "Pipers."

After two showstoppers in a row I figured we were due for a breather, but they did not give us just *any* breather. It is well known that Trey and Page love to play at this venue, which they frequented as

teenagers. We also know how much the band appreciates raucous, enthusiastic crowds like this one. So as a treat they gave us the first "If I Could" in 120 shows. It may have been a little ragged, but who cares? It had been 120 shows! By the way, this was the second straight show I attended where the band brought back a *Hoist* song after an extended absence. (My previous show was 12/11/99, where they brought "Scent of a Mule" out hibernation after sixty-one shows.) In any case, the band left the stage after "If I Could," making for only an hour-long set. They gave us quite a lot in such a short time.

When they emerged for the second set, Trey began with a huge burst of feedback, almost as if he were going to do "Star-Spangled Banner" Hendrix-style. But as soon as Mike began fiddling with his bass I knew we were going to get "Down with Disease." It began as a typical "shredding Trey" "DWD" but then veered into space (pretty interesting but nothing exceptional) before "shredding Trey" re-emerged for the ending.

As the others wound down, Trey emitted feedback and raised his arm in the air as if to count off something. Then Fish hit the wood block and to everyone's surprise they began "Harry Hood!" December 1999 seemed to have brought a renewed energy to this piece, and that continued here. While this version was not one for the ages, it was fluid and tight. The crowd began an intense glowstick/glowring war, and a few were thrown in Trey's direction. Then more came that way and he tried to catch them. Contrary to some accounts, he did not succeed. But he picked one off the stage floor and threw it back into the audience! So when you hear this huge roar on your tapes for apparently no reason, that's why. Following a raging climax, they started up "Gotta Jibboo," which was standard but maintained the energy level. After that run of three straight jammers we were due for a break, and Trey chose to serenade us with "When the Circus Comes." Then we knew we were heading for the home stretch when they started up "Mike's Song." I had never heard a "Mike's" like this one before. The jam was very groove-oriented: it was as if they had grafted "Mike's" on top of "Sand" or something of that ilk. They were all locked in together with a sense of purpose. And then they started doing tension-and-release exercises with it! A fusion of the new style with the old.

The insistent pace of this and similar jams from this tour reminds me of the "Grindcore" genre, so I've dubbed this hybrid style of playing "Groovecore." If you have a better name for it, go with that. In any case, we would hear this style again at the other New Jersey shows. Eventually they ground this "Mike's" jam to a halt and played with our minds by pausing for about a minute before starting it up again. This version may or may not move you but from a musical-theory perspective I think it was unprecedented, and it sounds great on tape.

After a second stop they started up the chords to "Albuquerque." I worship Neil Young as much as I do Phish, and this was the first Neil cover I had seen Phish do in person. To have it be the middle of "Mike's Groove" was even more mind-blowing for me. It may not sound like much to you, but it was a very emotional moment for me. After it ended Trey continued with some strange figures, slow and countryish. At first I thought it was the intro to "Antelope," but it morphed into the "Weekapaug Groove" chords and off we went. This was a typical hard-charging "Weekapaug" with plenty of "shredding Trey" moments.

Then they left the stage, making this set about seventy minutes. They took the tightness of the first set and added some funk and some of the strange ingredients that cropped up in 1999, making for a truly

impressive event.

After a few minutes Trey rushed back out, unable to contain his excitement. He began "First Tube", its debut as an encore. It was a raw and highly charged version, with Trey producing some abrasive notes and doing his Townshend windmills. But as with "Jibboo," Mike and Fish got the groove just right and Page provided some nice fills on piano and organ. As feedback dripped from Trey's guitar, Page began the piano chords to "Loving Cup," which they absolutely nailed, just like last year at this venue. It was quite a blast to go out on.

I could not believe how tight they were so early into the tour. In particular I had never heard Trey and Fish play better. After retreating into the murk for much of 1999 Trey appeared ready to be the instrumental leader of the band again, and his riffs and solos were always intense and nearly flawless. Fish was driving the band like the great drummers do. Mike was always in sync with them. At this show Page at times got overwhelmed in the mix, but he made his share of strong contributions, and there would be more of those to come in the New Jersey run. Everyone matched the crowd's energy, making for a great time. While not a classic for the ages, this show had its share of great moments, both from a "concert" and an "event" perspective.

It was merely a taste of what New Jersey was about to experience.

6/29/00 PNC Bank Arts Center, Holmdel, NJ—Erik Swain

This, the second show of summer 2000's four-show New Jersey run (or the six-show Northeast run for those who also went to Hartford), is one that is going to be talked about for a while. Not necessarily because of the performance (though it was excellent), but because of all the strange stuff that went on in the second set. In my opinion it was memorable on both counts (the "concert" aspect and the "event" aspect) and has all the ingredients to be considered a classic show. I for one will never forget it.

Of the fourteen shows I have seen through summer 2000, this is one of the two most unusual of the whole bunch, the other being 12/29/96. The boys opened with a hard-rocking and tight "Funky Bitch," picking up where they left off the previous night. "Wilson" was more of the same. They shifted into jamming mode for "Limb By Limb," and ended up with something far superior to their attempt of it at this venue the previous year. At first Trey tried to take the jam into different places than usual. It wound up back in familiar territory but was very satisfying, as was the Fish solo spotlight at the end.

Then the floodgates opened.

"Drowned," at twenty minutes, was shorter than the legendary Hartford 1999 version but every bit as good. They managed to hold a tight groove while getting very exploratory—kind of like the "Groovecore"-style Mike's from the previous night, or like some of the best stuff from 1997. At the apex of the jam I was thinking, "Go to the clav, Page," and soon enough he did! But the clavinet was hard to hear in the mix and Page soon reverted to piano, where he could pound out a rhythmic groove and be heard. No harm, though. The jam was so good that I imagined that this was what it was like to see the Allmans and Derek and the Dominoes back in the day at the Fillmore. And if that wasn't enough, they sprung a segue into "Rock and Roll": two Halloween songs joined together! The "Rock and Roll" was not as extended as the "Drowned," but it provided ten minutes of pure bliss.

And then, like the previous night, they left the stage after less than

an hour. They had hosed us plenty, though, and I figured a long second set was coming.

They emerged for the second set, and an airhorn sounded three times as planned, and we began our "Destiny Unbound" chant:

"Mbrufh blirphr yrulufr ptlifr!"

At least that's what it sounded like to me, and probably to the band as well. People chanted the first line once and then stopped, forcing the airhorn guy to sound it again. The renewed attempts didn't sound any better, though. My theory about the "Destiny" chant turned out to be right. I figured there was no way they would play it, but they might feed off our efforts and produce an exceptional set.

Trey got this puzzled look, shrugged his shoulders and looked at Mike. Mike did nothing. So the band appropriately started up "Birds of a Feather," a song about the fan base. This was like no other "BOAF" I've heard. It was even more out-there than the exploratory 1999 versions. It yet again featured the kind of "Groovecore" jamming we heard in the first set's "Drowned" and the previous night's "Mike's," in which the band establishes a 1999-style groove but augments it with tension-release interplay or something like it. This style is very focused, not drifting like some of the space-groove stuff the previous year, and this "BOAF" was a perfect example of it. And (get this) they teased Coltrane's "A Love Supreme."

As it continued, Trey added some effects, and the jam started to sound like a spaceship descending. It was very appropriate since the ceiling from this venue looks like something out of *Close Encounters of the Third Kind*. Kuroda's lighting played this up perfectly. While in the midst of this madness, Trey walked over to Mike and whispered something. They approached their mikes and started to sing not "Destiny" but "Catapult!"

We knew this was going to be a special set when they pulled this out. The music didn't change at all, we just got the "Catapult" lyrics. This "BOAF"->"Catapult" was the equal of the Big Cypress "SOAMelt"->"Catapult," in my opinion. After the lyrics were over they continued this freaky jam for a few minutes (how it should be noted in a setlist is open to debate) before quieting down. Then Trey fired up "Heavy Things." One might think "buzz kill," but the crowd went nuts! Say what you will, but this served its purpose: to get the crowd excited. The version itself was tight and energetic and it was over soon enough.

They stood around conferencing about what to do next. Finally Trey strummed a familiar riff and off they went into "Sand." This is my favorite of the 1999 batch of songs and I was really hoping to hear this at some point in New Jersey. Little did I know I would be doubly blessed! This version did not disappoint. It was very different from most others I had heard. Trey spent an extended amount of time on the mini-keyboard and created a dark and spooky soundscape with Page. Yet Fish and Mike kept pounding out the groove and there were no delay loops to clutter things up. I think this passage was the closest I've heard to Phish playing straight-up rave music. And when Trey finally picked up the 'doc again, his initial soloing had lots of impact because it came after a long period of no guitar at all. That didn't sustain, as subsequent guitar passages were more meandering, but then the band locked into the "spaceship groove" as they had in "BOAF" and brought it to a fine conclusion.

More conferences and then we heard the chunky first notes of "Meatstick." This was wild and wacky, and has to be heard to be be-

lieved. Not only was there a dance demonstration with Sofi Dillof (during which someone rushed the stage), but we also were treated to altered lyrics commenting on crew members (Carini has a song named after him but the others don't), and the first U.S. performance of the Japanese "Meatstick" lyrics! I especially liked how Trey referenced the 7/15/99 version from the same venue, talking about how they practiced it here to try to break the world record, but lost out to the Macarena… only to find out that in Japan the Macarena never caught on and the "Meatstick" is "a bona fide dance craze!" Lost in all of this was how tight and funky they were playing it, especially toward the end.

Trey was sufficiently impressed that he called for a segue into "Cities." While musically standard, it featured yet more altered lyrics: "A lot of people in…Tokyo…doing the Meatstick…What's that I smell? I smell sushi!" And then for another surprise, they segued into "Walk Away." The crowd went nuts, and the band earned the adulation with a cogent and powerful performance.

Had they ended the set there, it would have been more than satisfying. But they began the opening to "Antelope," and it became a set for the ages. It was fast, furious and flawless. Everyone in sync and raging at full speed. Just total insanity to the ears. Not insanity on the level of 7/16/94, but not too far removed from it either. Unbelievably, they were not done and decided to segue into "Frankenstein." They played it furiously and closed it with a bang. The crowd figured that *had* to be it. Page certainly did, as he stood up. But Trey motioned for him to sit back down and start "Wading in the Velvet Sea."

I have a theory about this decision. Trey's speech during this song was very unusual. He gushed about how much they love playing the venue, and thanked the crew and the fans for making the two shows so great, and the community so special. He never seems to make speeches like that except at tour-closers. My theory is that he desperately would like to return here next year and this was his "goodbye" speech in case they're not allowed to for security reasons. And he called for "Velvet Sea" to evoke the peacefulness of the community at Big Cypress—and maybe to prod everyone to act the same way here. I was quite moved.

The encore is beside the point after a set like that, and you could hear the groans from some corners of the crowd when the band came back out and started "Character Zero." But screw them: I like this song. There, I said it. In fact, I was happy that this version tried to be more than just "wanking Trey." His playing was unusually restrained for this song, as he tried to build up a group jam. Unfortunately, the people on the lawn couldn't hear this very well because the sound up there cut out. In any case, it didn't really work and he went back to "wanking Trey" for the conclusion. But at least they tried; effort was not a problem at these shows.

I thought it was great both as a "concert" and an "event," and every bit fit to be deemed a classic. "Drowned"->"Rock and Roll" is a must-have on tape, and mere words cannot do justice to the second set.

I could not believe how "on" they were for the Holmdel shows. The last time I can remember them playing so in sync with each other and providing so many "Holy Shit!" moments was, I dare say, Fall 1997.

7/4/00 E Centre, Camden, NJ—Erik Swain

Accompanying me was my high-school buddy David, whose first show was 10/17/91 while in college and whose second show was 12/11/99 with me. That amazing show inspired his return trip this night.

Does anyone have a longer gap between their first and second shows?

This was a night of firsts, and here's another one: David must have been the first person to bring an issue of *The Economist* into a Phish show to read beforehand and at set break.

When Phish took the stage, they milled around, eventually going over to the mics for "Star-Spangled Banner." We knew we would get this at some point, but were not expecting it as an opener.

I was expecting something more emphatic than "Farmhouse" to follow. Maybe because of my expectations this seemed a little sluggish until Trey kicked in the wah-wah at the end. But the first "Rift" in sixty shows was emphatic enough. It was a wonderful way to get the crowd going. It was a bit rusty at first, but they upped the intensity at the end and drove it home.

And then they hit us with the first "It's Ice" of the tour. We were so happy to hear this. Page flubbed the lyrics but it was funny. "I love it when they do that!" the guy in front of me exclaimed. There was also a spooky jam segment that provided the show's first taste of the Phish 2000 sound. After a standard "Bouncing" we got the tour's first "Stash!" This was the hottest jam of the set. It was really a tug of war between Phish 2000 and Classic Phish. Page and Fish were doing jazzy flourishes while Trey and Mike were pumping out chugging rhythms and trying to build a groove. This produced some fascinating moments that I would have appreciated more had there not been a vehement dispute between fans and security guards near me.

The oddities kept coming as the band picked "Lizards" next. It featured sublime piano work by Page; this was by far his strongest night of the four New Jersey shows. It was a little late in the set to begin a *Gamehendge* but I'm sure I wasn't the only one thinking "Tela" when "Lizards" wound down and a mellow piece started up. Not quite, but we got another lightly rotated selection in "TMWSIY"->"Avenu"->"TMWSIY." The following "Julius" showcased Blues-Rock Trey in full force. He wailed, the others chugged along with the same intensity, the ending was drawn out a bit longer than normal, and it came to a satisfying close. That was it for the set.

At the end of the six sets I had seen of Phish 2000 I felt mentally and emotionally drained from the musical ass-kicking they had administered. This set did not produce the same feeling. It was lighter, more fun, but not of the same intensity. A "party" set. Nothing wrong with that, just different. "Stash" is probably the only thing that will really hold interest on tape, though parts of "Ice" and "Julius" might also impress.

After a long set break, anticipation in the air was thick, and they came out and started "Gotta Jibboo." While this show overall may be lesser as a "concert," this song may be the most musically impressive part of the whole New Jersey run. If 12/9/95 is the uber "YEM", 7/23/97 is the uber "Ghost," and so on, then this is the uber "Jibboo." That is, a version that goes so far beyond what the song has ever done before that it's almost unfathomable. The first fifteen minutes did what a normal "Jibboo" does, but then things got nuts and we got fifteen minutes of musical heaven. The crowd engaged in the biggest glowring/glowstick war I have ever seen (there were hundreds of them being tossed in the air in bunches somewhere in the middle of the lawn) and erupted to the sound, if not the sight, of the fireworks across the river. The band seemed to play along to the rhythm of all this. Then it got quite spooky, with Trey dropping out on guitar and heading to the mini-keys, with Page producing Moog madness, and Mike and Fish still pumping the groove.

Then Trey went back to guitar and we got this hybrid groove-cum-tension-and-release exercise that I've been calling "Groovecore" for lack of a better word. See also the 6/28 "Mike's," the 6/29 "Drowned" and "BOAF" and the 7/3 "Gin" and "Jim." This got tremendously intense and then they popped a segue out of nowhere into the rare "I Saw It Again!" Damn, I *love* this song! Who else could start a song as funk and then take it to heavy metal? Okay, Funkadelic in the Eddie Hazel years, but who else? This was nailed, and then the song went into an uncharacteristic ambient jam before turning into the even more rare "Magilla!" A jazz tune in the middle of jamming madness? There were some great solo fills from Fish on this one.

After that came "Twist," and here's where things got weird. I love "Twist," and I love it when it stretches out like on 6/20/97 or 4/2/98. And I was excited when they started to do that again. It went "out there," then came back to the main theme, but then went "out there" again. Unfortunately, after a while they just sounded lost, futzing around to no purpose. Lots of neat effects but nothing resembling a coherent beat, which Phish 2000 needs for maximum impact. I dunno, maybe I will like this better when I hear it on tape. These sorts of jams often sound better when you're by yourself listening on headphones than when you're in the midst of an adrenaline-fueled crowd (see the 7/10/99 "Tweezer"). Eventually Trey hit a few familiar notes and the guy behind me called it right away: "Slave!" Whatever had been lost in emotion and intensity was made up here. It was not quite as moving as 8/17/96 or 7/4/99, but few things are. This was the next tier below. A lovely way to end a unique set.

This is one of the more schizophrenic sets you'll hear. It didn't always work but the effort was there and the surprises were there and they produced a moment (the second half of "Jibboo") that will be talked about for years to come. The set is a must-have on tape just for that.

I was hoping for a long encore ("YEM"? "Reba"? "Harpua?") since they left the stage much earlier than they had the previous night. So it was a little surprising to hear "Lawn Boy." Page worked the crowd and Mike took a nice bass solo. Just before the end Page wished us all a happy Fourth and then all of the sudden, onstage sparklers! And then fireworks! KISS? No, Led Zeppelin! Trey ripped "Good Times, Bad Times" to shreds. They sent us off with a great burst of energy.

This last show of the Northeast run may not have lived up to its hype, but that is no reason not to have enjoyed it, especially for the rarities and the "Jibboo." In five years no one will be talking about the unrealized expectations, whatever those may have been. We will be talking about "the historic 7/4/00 'Jibboo.'" And that by itself will have made this night worthwhile.

I consider myself extremely fortunate to have seen four summer shows of Phish 2000. They played extraordinarily well, and you never know when they will get on a roll like this again.

7/21/00 Polaris Amphitheater, Columbus, OH—Jeremy Welsh

During the last song of the second set on Saturday night, I was reminded of what could be my favorite part in all of Phish's music. "That is a pretty bold statement!" my brother said as I tried to explain what I meant. I don't know if it is bold or just overly simple. The part I am referring to is one drum beat played by Fishman, a simple tap of a wood block during in the beginning of "You Enjoy Myself." (I believe the section that follows is fittingly referred to as Nirvana by Mr. Dirksen;

usually around the three-minute mark.) I am always moved by that one tap, and the music to follow…the anticipation, knowing the beauty of "YEM" that is to follow. It is interesting to look back on Saturday, on the fun I had with my family and friends, and think of how the festivities and the music that filled that day in Columbus all led up to one tap of wood.

Saturday unfolded to be a great day from start to finish. What better way to start a day than cooking on a wood fire at a camp, playing cards, relaxing…my brother, his girlfriend Molly, my sister, and I took our time in waking up and getting ready for the show Saturday morning. After the night before, and the rather hard ground at the KOA, it took some time to shake those damp cobwebs from our heads. We headed out to the venue around three or so, hoping to beat the traffic and enjoy the lot for a bit. We had no traffic problems and made it in just fine, under a gorgeous sky. No rain! The only bad thing was that they were parking four cars deep, and we were the second behind a big RV. Might be hanging out late after the show.

I was rather amazed by the hustle and bustle of the lot; I guess everyone wanted to get rid of their excess wares being that it was the last day of the tour. There were some moments when it was so packed I couldn't even move…kind of amazing. And we did our part by handing out as many Mockingbird magnets as we could. My sister was loving it. We ran into David "ZZYZX" Steinberg by way of the magnets; as I handed him one, he introduced himself and said his batch got ruined in the rain on Friday, so I helped replenish his supply. For the most part, everyone was pretty positive. I didn't see any nitrous during the day. Lots of people were looking for miracles but most had smiles. I was a bit surprised/disappointed by the lack of variety in T-shirts (at least four different vendors were selling the same shirts…where is the creativity? By the way, anyone know where I can get a "VWs are People Too" shirt?). I loved the people with the stationary bike-blender for their smoothies: completely organic, no electricity! As 6:30 rolled around, we walked around to the other side of the lot (Fishman side of the amphitheater). It was eerie how quiet and different this section was! I guess it was the VIP parking as we entered the venue through the VIP entrance.

After a few hours of walking around, preshow was relaxing. With the great sounds of Buena Vista Social Club coming out of the PA, we hung out, chatted, and played some cards; we were pretty low on the lawn, just Page of center. My good friends Marc and Barb (and crew) were actually a few feet behind us; it was great to see everyone and spirits were high for the show ahead. I really didn't dwell on the fact that this was going to be my twentieth show (in almost six years of seeing Phish…I guess had paced myself); I was going to let things flow and have fun. And I certainly did that.

"AC/DC Bag" is such a great opener, and kicked things off around 7:45. I was hoping for a "Tweezer," but the "Bag" was good. Slow, building funk under a sunny sky. After the seven-minute "Bag", a nine-minute "First Tube" followed. It was ice and driving, without too much variation. I have always been a fan of "Limb by Limb" and while this version didn't chart any new territory, it was good nonetheless. My brother can't get enough of Trey's spiraling solo in this tune and I have to agree with him. Kind of in the same genre as "Taste" and "Free": piercing and spiraling.

I was pretty excited to hear my first "NICU"—I kind of lump "NICU" with "Timber Ho," "Ya Mar," and "Punch" as songs that are upbeat and very danceable. This was both, albeit quick (four minutes).

They pretty much nailed the "Dirt." After much discussion, Trey sounded off the beginning of "Roses are Free." Along the same lines of "NICU," it put a big smile on my face. The crowd especially loved the "Land of the Great and Free" line. While I was expecting some sort of exploration in this one (maybe comparing a bit too much to Big Cypress or the "Bittersweet Motel" from Rochester '97), it didn't go too far and ended at only five minutes or so. They kept everyone grooving with "Wolfman's Brother." Good version, around ten minutes long. Nothing out of the ordinary, though, as I can remember.

At this point, I got into a bit of a conversation with a guy next to me about placement and reading too much into songs. I said to him that I thought they would wait for the full moon to come out before they played "Wolfman's Brother." But we agreed that we, the fans, probably read into song a bit too much, predicting or analyzing a lot more than the band ever does. I mentioned to him all of my expectations for 11/13/98, thinking they were going to play "Wolfman's" and all these other crazy things, and nothing out of the ordinary happened. I guess Friday night they made a slight reference to the rain in "Punch" ("The Rain had gone, the Storm had passed"). I was just reminded that I read a bit too much into what is played when, and I shouldn't guess what Phish's intentions are…and then I remember the Dead in '95 at Three Rivers when they played four rain songs in a row following a storm, or in Buckeye in '94, right down the road from Polaris, when they played five songs with rain references…oh, well. They are different bands, right? I thought the set would end with the "My Soul" that followed. I was actually impressed with the long, bluesy solo that Page took…Page took a solo and I could actually hear it! I was thinking this might end the set, cutting it close to sixty minutes. But a bit of a discussion followed, and I thought a "YEM" would close out the set (*à la* "YEM" following "Saw It Again" at Shoreline in '97), but they launched into "Julius." This would definitely close the set, and was much better than "My Soul," in my opinion. The last "Julius" I saw was the great jammed-out version from Cleveland '97 and I was happy to hear them jam this out a bit. I would love to see them continue to push the envelope on this song.

The set timed out at just around seventy minutes. Not a bad set. No real complaints, but not much in the way of adventure, either (even with "First Tube", "Roses," and "Wolfman's"). It was a bit different from the night before—the set ended when it was dark outside; Saturday night, it was still rather bright. We made our way up to Marc, joining their crew, wanting to share the second set with some more friends. Why not find more? So I went and found my friends Rich and Dave at set break. Great to see everyone, and gather 'round for the closing set. Macy Gray was over the PA.

I had some hopes for a "Tweezer" to open the second set, and was also thinking we may still get "YEM", or maybe "Ghost." But at 9:30, I was far from disappointed to hear Mike slap out "Down with Disease." Great, great stuff. It was fast from the start and really never let up. It started to take off around five minutes in, with some nice playing by Page. At this point, I had a feeling we were in for a bit of a ride. Fourteen or so minutes in, it got just a bit mellower. That didn't last long, though, as Trey starting playing some reggae licks. Around seventeen minutes, I thought I heard a bit of a "Crosseyed" tease. Did anyone else hear that? Was this the tease/jam that they have been playing all summer? At twenty minutes, Trey added some texture on the keys

as the rest of the band quickened things up. At this point, I wrote down that "Fishman is a machine!" It is amazing as to how long he can keep a beat/rhythm going…does he get tired? (I'm thinking of the DJ Logic jam session down in New Orleans that lasted well into the morning, or the jam I just read about in Indianapolis.) Fishman actually changed things up a bit around twenty-five minutes, playing a bit of a swing beat.

A minute or two later, I heard Page playing something a bit different, teasing a song. I couldn't place it; boy, was that bugging me. And it became clear, just as my brother exclaims "It's the Beatles …": "While My Guitar Gently Weeps!" Wow. Very, very cool. A glow war occurred during this tune, and while it didn't seem to go well with the music, it was pretty cool to watch. This version stretched out for about seven minutes; as my brother described it, it was very "breezy." I thought Trey sang and played very well during this song.

"Makisupa" was fun next, and "Heady Nuggets" received a huge ovation from the crowd. I was surprised at the roar, as was Trey as the screens showed him laughing and smiling. This was actually jammed out a bit, and Trey even moved over the keys for this one. I was rather surprised by this.

I love how the opening notes of "Piper" seem to just float out into the air. I do wish, though, that "Piper" will find its role again as a conduit, floating in and out of jams (see 6/25/97, "DWD">"Piper">"DWD"). But who is complaining? This "Piper" turned out to be rather unique, with a rather different opening, weird rhythms, and an absolutely raging section before the second verse was sung. Don't they usually build through the second verse, and rage afterwards? Page stood out in the beginning of this version on the piano; Kuroda chimed in with those really cool "running" lights, just driving everyone into a frenzy. Around eight minutes into the raging, they sang the verse for the second time, with Trey adding the high "Red red worm." As the jam slowed down, at around twelve minutes or so, I noticed the bright, beautiful full moon, with the clouds passing in front, as they moved into "Mango." Very fun. Page again stood out on the piano. This moved out into a pretty mellow jam, which transitioned into a clear "Have Mercy" tease. I was so happy, along with some friends, to be hearing this song…and then they stopped. WTF? I don't know who was upset, or disagreeing with the song choice, but after the abrupt ending there was long debate. If there ever was a tease in all senses of the word, this was it.

After the debate, I was really hoping for "Have Mercy" to start again, but "Bug" began. I was a bit shocked by the lack of reception. No "Bug" fans in the audience, I guess? And while it wasn't the song I wanted, I was hoping to hear this and was happy with the ten-minute version. I really love the lyrics to this song, and enjoy how the song climaxes with the chorus.

No matter how much I like "Bug," I don't ever think it will make me feel the way the opening notes to "YEM" make me feel (or, as I talked about above, that simple wood block). I was pulling for a "YEM" for three and a half sets, so I was so happy to hear it! This version got very funky, nice and deep, and included some really cool keyboards by Page and Trey. I don't know if I was imagining things, but I thought I heard some "Thank Yous" in the vocal jam, maybe like Peter Frampton's song? What a great way to end the tour, with a "YEM." Trey didn't really give a long talk afterwards, but he did thank everyone.

As for the encore, I thought we might be getting a nice, upbeat "Possum," but I was pleasantly surprised by the "Loving Cup." I always can go for a drink! I just love this song. It was actually the first tune in

my three summer shows that featured Page singing. What were they waiting for! Certainly left me with a beautiful buzz, as the sounds of the Bee Gees over the PA filled the air.

I thought it was a good run to close the tour. Nothing crazy like the Tuesday before (the *Moby Dick* show) but just two days of strong songs. No real throwaways, and nothing too adventurous. Highlights, in my opinion, include: "Timber Ho," "Foam," "Dog Faced Boy," "Mike's"->"jam"->"Frankie Says," the acoustics during "Inlaw," definitely "DWD"->"While My Guitar Gently Weeps," the interesting "Piper," and the "Have Mercy" tease (but come on, play it!).

It was great to share these shows with my brother and sister (and Molly). This made it a family affair. It was fun camping out and braving the monsoon, and it was good to groove and dance and smile with Marc, Barb, Rhett and Pam, Rich, Dave, Dave, and everyone else. Good to meet the Timer, Mr. ZZYZX himself. And happy to see all the smiles and happy faces. I have always said, I will keep wanting to go to Phish as long as they make me smile and dance and groove. So far so good…but I am not ignorant to a bit of ugliness. We all need to work to keep it positive, as I did catch glimpses of the underbelly (the pissing incident and certain dealings in the lawn).

Thanks for reading. Keep spreading the music, and Be Good Family.

10/7/00 Shoreline Ampitheatre, Mountain View, CA——Jeremy Goodwin

My friends and I started singing along to "The Last Time" in a spirit of existential irreverence, prepared to simultaneously celebrate and mourn the fact that this might be the last Phish show ever. However, this song choice really got to me and gave me the chills, in a not entirely positive way. I believed fully that the band really didn't know if this would indeed be the last time. After all, bands don't usually break up because they get together and decide on it; they break up because it just happens.

All week we had been counting down to the bittersweet finale, with reminders like, "Four more shows", "Enjoy the last Stash ever", and the like. Along the way, I had my most fun and rewarding Phish tour ever, making my West Coast debut with auspicious romps through Vegas and Southern California before winding up the state to crash land in San Francisco for a Shoreline weekend. I had seen my first Forbin's from the front of the Page Zone, surrounded by friends I wouldn't see again for an undetermined time. I got to trade lines from Tenacious D songs with Fishman after Irvine. Camped on a cliff overlooking the Pacific Ocean, at a beach north of San Diego. Reunited with scores of old friends, and deepend burgeoning friendships with other folks. And it was all pointing in one direction. It seemed like the candle was burning at both ends onstage, and the ragged, jubilant fans assembled in the enormous Shoreline parking lots for one last family reunion.

At some point during the opening "First Tube," after all the speculation about a third set, special guests, a cover album…after all the hype and anticipation…something very exciting occured to me. I realized that the band likely didn't know what was going to happen. As with Big Cypress, they were just going to go out there and play a Phish show. It was a pleasure to exclaim, "One more 'Mike's Groove' for the road," and Hydrogen seemed sublime.

The vibe at setbreak was quite strange. I was getting a little emotional, and felt a glob of potential tears welling up somewhere in my chest. Was this the last setbreak ever? I managed to locate a few folks

and take some pictures. We hugged, and comforted each other, and wished ourselves good luck. It had been one more tour, eventually it was one more week, and now...one more set.

"Twist Around" felt dark and ominous. "Tweezer" was probably the best Phish jam I had seen in 2000. The "Wading," "Meatstick" combo was an unmistakable nod to Big Cypress, whether the boys were concious of it or not. "YEM" was a benediction, and when the final yelps of the vocal jam died down, we were on our own again.

Well, not yet. The prolonged standing ovation gave me goosebumps, and when "Let It Be" elegantly capped the night, I literally didn't know whether to laugh or cry. It was a gentle poke in the ribs at the fans (who had been liberally predicting a cover of the Beatles' "Abbey Road") as well as a poignant bit of advice to all of us. If this is it, then so be it. If not, another show will come eventually. In the meantime, well...let it be.

By now I was pretty emotional, though I never went beyond the choked up phase. I filtered through the crowd, taking pictures and occasionally chatting up fellow interlopers. The crowd lingered for a long time in the ampitheatre and the adjacent grounds. I walked into several more reunions, took more pictures, and eventually decided it was over. The last notes had been played, the last of the Mockingbird magnets had been handed out, and it was time to go.

Along the long walk back to the car, I sucked up some more ambiance. When I came across a thick crowd dancing to a tape of "Stash" blaring out of a bus, I delighted in the exhuberance, but detected a faint level of despair. I wondered if, by clapping along, I would be merely clinging to the past, trying to recapture something that had run its natural course. I thought of Deadheads who didn't know where to go after Jerry died, and for the first time really empathized with that situation. Would that be me? Soon?

I sat in the back of the car on the ride out of the lot, still filled with joy from a wonderful week, aware that I had grown up a little, and thankful that I have been able to have fun as well as learn things about myself and about the universe, while chasing that ellusive moment around the country... the moment when the music truly reveals the ineffable, and, like a sacred consecration, teaches me a little better how to live. A week later, on a San Francisco dance floor, the lessons of my trip accumulated and I finally realized that it's possible to bring that moment around with you.

Halloween Through the Years

Craig DeLucia / Julia Mordaunt

Phish's Halloween shows have long been fan favorites, from early-day Goddard prank-fests and costume parties to currentday cover albums and marathon shows. Just how important is the Halloween tradition? Fan Jeffrey "Lew" Robert summed it up:

"I've been to three of the four Halloween shows [from 1994 to 1998] and the worst part of them all is the pre-show stress of keeping track of that valuable ticket. I've always felt that the Halloween ticket holds the same value as a winning lottery ticket. I'm always paranoid that I'm going to lose it on the way to the venue. At the Omni in Atlanta, there was a bunch of construction around
the venue so there wasn't much room for people to hang outside. People were packed everywhere. As I approached the entrance it was kind of like walking down a red carpet, the walk-of-fame so to speak. Actually, the walk-of-shame for the ticketless folks crammed around me. They were packed on both sides of the entrance line scrambling for an extra. I felt like the armored truck guy walking from bank to truck. Everyone knew I had the goods. I mean, the crowd is fairly mellow, but the Halloween ticket IS the diggity dank of the fall tour."

From 1986 through 1999 the band played a total of ten Halloween shows, each incorporating a vast array of unique twists and surprises. This chapter will serve as a brief synopsis of each in an attempt to recreate and remember the fright and wonder of Halloweens past.

Friday, October 31, 1986
Sculpture Room, Goddard College, Plainfield, VT

Phish's first Halloween performance together took place in a small sculpture room at Goddard. Musical highlights of this show include early versions of "Sneaking Sally Through the Alley," "Camel Walk," "Slave to the Traffic Light," "AC/DC Bag," "David Bowie" and "Fluffhead."

One thing that makes this show, along with other classic Phish, so enjoyable is the fact that the band seems to truly enjoy jamming and defining their early sound. The jams that come out of "Bowie" and "AC/DC Bag" are noteworthy, along with the rare bluegrass "Back Porch Boogie" and the oft-mentioned "Dave's Energy Guide." True to form, the band has special guests on hand: "Have Mercy" includes Jah Roy as a guest on vocals, and The Joneses were in attendance as well.

And before Trey sent everyone home with the then-anthemic "Alumni Blues," he treated the crowd to a "Skin it Back / Icculus" combo, telling the story of a great man who was (according to this particular narration) born on Halloween in 1935.

Saturday, October 31, 1987
Sculpture Room, Goddard College, Plainfield, VT

The band's second Halloween show opened with a bang and never slowed down. Showing hints of their still-developing jamming abilities, they took the stage in an instrumental free-form and wound through pieces of "Low Rider" before winding up in a soulful rendition of "Whipping Post." Fans of Page will definitely want to seek out this show, as he is clearly the star in the early going.

Other highlights include a four-song "Sneaking Sally" -> "Back Porch Boogie" -> "Halley's Comet" -> "Light Up or Leave Me Alone" combo and a fiery early "You Enjoy Myself." Phish history buffs will want the second set to hear the various pieces of what would become "Fluff's Travels" interspersed among the rest of the songs.

Costumes? The band dressed up as each other this year (be sure to listen to Trey's introductions after "Whipping Post"). Fishman even shaved his body for the occasion! As with 1986, The Joneses were in attendance; this year they performed alongside Phish.

Saturday, October 29, 1988
Sculpture Room, Goddard College, Plainfield, VT

Phish's third Halloween show didn't really happen on Halloween. Played two nights earlier, it was still billed as a Halloween show and was held in the now-hallowed Sculpture Room. The show was packed with musical candy, including a raucous "You Enjoy Myself" -> "Pos-

sum" and a still-developing "Harry Hood." The jammed versions of popular covers "Whipping Post," "La Grange" and "Time Loves a Hero" put the cherry on top. As was becoming (and would continue to become) a Halloween tradition, special guests were the norm. Richard Wright (aka "Nancy") sang on his own "Halley's Comet," Tim Rogers played harmonica on "Curtis Loew," and Russ Remington added saxophone to a good part of the third set.

There are tapes in circulation that are mislabeled "Halloween, 1988." These tapes are actually a mix of some songs from the actual show on the 29th.

Tuesday, October 31, 1989
Goddard College, Plainfield, VT

Halloween 1989 brought Phish back to Goddard. It is believed that this was the first Phish show to be rebroadcast on television; alas, it was only available in Burlington via public access. Musical compadres Ninja Custodian also played—Trey showed his excitement by running around the room and fondling the Madonna-esque strap-on breasts that he was wearing.

Want highlights? Phish played just about every major early original piece. Also evident was a fairly early "Bathtub Gin" and one of the first "Kung" chants. At the time, the "Bowie" (at over twenty minutes long) was one of the longest Phish jams ever. For good measure, the band handed out boxes of macaroni and cheese for the crowd to shake and play along. And, as with many early shows, "Divided Sky" and "You Enjoy Myself" proved to be proud favorites.

Halloween? The band appropriately closed the second set with "Highway to Hell" before returning for the encore. And Trey was obviously having fun, as he invited the crowd back for another "runaway golf cart marathon" the following year.

Wednesday, October 31, 1990
Armstrong Hall, Colorado College, Colorado Springs, CO

This was actually a Halloween double-shot, as it was reborn on Halloween, 1999 as Phish's first full-length MP3 release. Emusic.com added in a web rebroadcast for fans who were distraught over the lack of a live Halloween show in 1999, as well as audio snippets of interviews with the band.

The MP3 release has only made this show more widely available. Listen for a very early pass at the Secret Language with an Oom Pa Pa Signal in "Possum." If you're looking for something a bit frightening, check out the "BBFCFM" encore and the *Munsters* theme tease in "You Enjoy Myself." Jam enthusiasts will want this show to hear seven hardcore jamming Phish tunes all played in one night ("Possum," "Stash," "You Enjoy Myself," "Antelope," "Runaway Jim," "Tweezer," and a classic hard-rocking "Mike's Groove").

Thursday, October 31, 1991
Armstrong Hall, Colorado Springs, CO

Phish made their way back to Colorado Springs for the second Halloween performance in a row. Rocking versions of newer songs were abound (see "Chalk Dust Torture" and "Brother") but the classics were also well-represented (see "You Enjoy Myself," "Runaway Jim," "Bowie," and "Hood"). The band also had a few tricks up their sleeves. When they came out for the second set, Mike's place on the stage was occupied by a woman dressed as Mike, holding his backup bass guitar.

The band cranked out "Landlady," and she pretended to play along while Mike played off-stage. And, when the time came, she even did the Landlady dance with Trey!

In one of the funnier Halloween moments, the band teased "Jesus Just Left Chicago" while a fan dressed as Jesus paraded on the stage. Halloween sacrifice? Trey made the losers stage-dive as a penance. Fans were up to it, though, to grab first prize—free admission to all Phish shows for one year.

Monday, October 31, 1994
Glens Falls Civic Center, Glens Falls, NY

Many would say that this show is where the Halloween tradition became an obsession among fans. Phish had not played on Halloween since 1991, as they were in the studio recording and mixing albums with *Rift* (1992) and *Hoist* (1993). In numerous fan polls, this show is always regarded as one of the best ever, and certainly one of the most ground-breaking.

Halloween 1994 carried as much anticipation as any Phish show ever has. The band announced via the Doniac Schvice that they planned to don a "musical costume" by covering an entire album of another band. Better yet, their decision would be based on fan voting. Speculation was abound, with Pink Floyd's *Dark Side of the Moon*, Frank Zappa's *Joe's Garage*, and The Beatles *The Beatles* (better known as "The White Album") as the leading contenders. Fan Alex Fry penned this poem to recount his feelings:

The Anticipation—by Alex Fry

Road trippin' up to Glens Falls,
Cat calls from Upstate big-n-talls
my Reba costume, the gag,
I'm in drag
and far from home,
I start to groan
as we approach the concert zone.

Joggers, Esthers, and even Fluff-Head,
so glad I opted to be lame instead
of being NORMAL or ORDINARY-
holy smokes that Zappa look-alike is scary
and it takes me back to New Year's Tour
when they dropped "Peaches" from '93 straight into '94, galore!

I'm inside now feeling the tao
ever present,
phish better represent with a phat cover... oh no another
show in the last row, this gots to go!
Man, look at those lucky peops cold chillin in the taping section-

Daring phan just jumped the fence= security interception,
but as they drag him away toward rejection
the infection
spread, 1, 2, 6, 49 heads
up and over the chains,
Lizards regain
control and hold onto the reins, "We All Goin' Fishin'"
in a blink of an eye the whole venue's General Admission!

Phish was up for the task, breaking out a raucous and appropriate Frankenstein to start. Notable versions of "Simple," "Reba," and

"Julius" followed, as well as a fun "Harpua" with a Halloween narration and a tease of Black Sabbath's "War Pigs" taboot.

And then the second set...

As Phish took the stage, fans heard the sound of heartbeats coming through the P.A. It was Floyd's "Speak To Me," the opener to *Dark Side of the Moon*. But the tease soon faded, and soon Ed Sullivan was introducing the crowd to Mike, Jon, Page and Trey. Over the next ninety minutes, the band wove through the entire *White Album*. In keeping with their collective sense of humor, Phish paid tribute by moderately altering several parts of the original composition. Want Phish to put their own unique signature on a song? Listen to the modified barbershop quartet ending of "While My Guitar Gently Weeps." Want references to songs in the Phish lexicon? "Glass Onion" suddenly included a reference to Guyute the pig. Want Fishman at his finest? He got naked as he sang "Revolution 9." And if you're curious as to whether the band acknowledged the connection between The Beatles *White Album* and Phish's *White Tape*, they did: part of the background music playing along to "Revolution 9" is "He Ent to the Bog" (a.k.a. "Hamburger") from Phish's early demo.

Fans would have been content if the show ended then, and it still would have been one of the most discussed evenings in Phishtory. But Phish retook the stage for a classic third set with notable versions of "Bowie," "Slave," and "Antelope." And after a costume contest where many fans were too tired to stand, Phish sent us home with a remarkable "Squirming Coil," featuring a truly emotional piano outro by Page.

Even the uninitiated have to be impressed with Phish's achievement during the second set, covering so many new songs and doing them with remarkable accuracy. "Ob La Di Ob La Da" was the only song that had been jammed on the Phish stage before, and never in its entirety. Only a few songs would ever be heard again: "Back in the USSR," "While My Guitar Gently Weeps," "I'm So Tired," "Blackbird," "Why Don't We Do It in the Road," "Helter Skelter," "Everybody's Got Something To Hide Except Me And My Monkey," and "Cry Baby Cry." And of these, only "While My Guitar Gently Weeps" would endure any sort of longevity in concert rotation (though the rare "Cry Baby Cry" was released on *Hampton Comes Alive*).

10/31/94 Halloween Review —by Lisbeth Trebour Karpman

There was Halloween magic all over the place that night. Sunday night we went in search of the hotel bar, but it had just closed. The owner saw us walking around and basically said "if you're spending money, I'm open!" and we took over the place, literally. By the end of the night (about 2 or 3 hazy hours later), Marcie was behind the bar, mixing concoctions like a mad scientist from hell, and the rest of us were draped across the bar. So there was some serious recovering to do before the show on Monday. We woke up from our naps to cold driving rain outside—we were bummed. But by the time we got it all together and left for the show, the rain had stopped ("Look, the storm's gone"), and turned into a creepy Halloween mist, a perfect backdrop to the night.

We had prepared well, determined to make the most of such a great holiday. Our costumes were fun to do—we were the Jester, Landlady, BBFCFM, My Friend My Friend, Slave, Kitty Malone, and the Armenian Man. We had Halloween treat bags for clever costumers, loose candy for everyone, Silly String and confetti. Dawn had cut this AMAZING Phish logo into a pumpkin (those of you who saw it know how perfect it was!). On our way to the gate, she asked a road crew guy if he

could give it to the band for her. He said he'd make sure they saw it, but that he couldn't guarantee it would get on stage, which wasn't what she cared about anyway—she just wanted to express her appreciation to the guys who made this night possible.

We got in with a minimum of hassle—they really were tearing people's costumes apart. The guy who searched me was actually very nice. I had a duffel bag full of the treat bags, and when he went to search through there I asked him to be careful, and he apologized and left the bag alone! We got our geld (the chocolate foil-covered coins) and headed for the floor. The first thing Dawn and I did was run up to the stage to see if the pumpkin made it, and lo and behold! there it was. (Thank you to whoever made sure it got up there!)

Honorable costume mentions in my eyes: A huge herd of cows as Vermont's Phinest; The Man Who Stepped Into Yesterday (he had a sign on that said October 30, 1994); several angry mobs of joggers, the best ones had shirts that said "Chilly Lake Jogging Club"; Sparkle; Control For Smilers; Dinner & A Movie (a cardboard table hanging around his neck with movies and, you guessed it, dinner); the Helping Phriendly Book.

The floor looked like it was going to be messy and crowded, so when security gave up on it we headed for the stands. We were a few rows up directly on the side of the stage behind Fishman, so we could see all the backstage goings-on, which was an interesting perspective since so many odd things were to follow. "Frankenstein" was perfect— Trey came out wearing this huge weird mask thing, but ditched it after the first song. "Simple" was great in all its grinding relentless glory. Simply the best "Divided Sky" I've ever heard. "Harpua." Poor Poster Nutbag got sucked into The Bowls Of Hell (Poster come back! Poster don't go out there!!) before ever actually meeting Harpua. Barney music played backwards equals "War Pigs" from Black Sabbath (hmmm—I'd always suspected....). During the set break there was a scary sound tape on—a nice touch.

For the second set, THE set, we got a Halloween trick from the band. Out of the speakers came this very "One Of These Days" sound, and I knew it would be Pink Floyd, and I was very psyched (I voted for *Piper At The Gates Of Dawn*). My thoughts were confirmed when they played the beginning to "Dark Side" And then and then and then! Suddenly it switches to Ed Sullivan's introducing the Beatles, and the screaming from the recording is drowned out by the screaming of the audience. I fought back a wave of disappointment that completely disappeared exactly ten bars into "Back In The USSR." The boys were, to be blunt, flawless. I wrote down who sung what for later reference. It was a bit Trey-heavy: I think I would have liked to have seen Mike and Fishman sing a few more. Page had most of the pretty ballads ("Prudence," "Blackbird," "I Will"), but I have to say that Mike singing "Julia" will make this girl's knees weak for a very long time! "Happiness Is A Warm Gun" rocked the house. Mike got creative with "Don't Pass Me By" and went the bluegrass route a la "Foreplay/Long Time." Fishman, of course, did "Why Don't We Do It In The Road?" as only he can. "Helter Skelter" was absolutely evil and demented, and ended with the boys singing "I've got blisters on my fingers!" barbershop-quartet style. Mike's "Honey Pie"—adorable. A creative "Birthday"/not "Birthday"— they played the riffs from the song (somebody mentioned it was dirge-like—absolutely right!) while Fishman gave Brad Sands his birthday cake. And then, "Number Nine, Number Nine, Number Nine" and a cacophony of sound. Trey's up behind the kit, pointing with the drumsticks. Mike's got this cymbal (cause he's in a band), and he's doing this weird

spiral dance with it. Fishman's got all these evil sounds coming from the vac, he starts spouting poetry at the audience. You all know what happened next. All hell breaks loose. Fishman escapes from the dress, literally, that's what he did, yelling the last lines to the Yoko poem—"And we become.... NAKED!!" If I could have one picture in the entire world, it would have to be one of Page's face when this happened. It was priceless—absolute shock. He put his face in his hands and gave up. Trey was cracking up, turned on the bubble machine, which added to the whole weird *Midsummer Night's Dream* thing going down on the stage. Mike just looked pissed—he was like "I want nothing to do with any of this." Fishman put a crown on Mike's head and a banner which said "Good Night" on it, while the original song comes through the speakers. Page leaves the stage, stunned. Mike books off the stage and came over to right underneath where we were sitting for a little while, until, finally, Trey and Fishman go backstage. Utter mayhem.

By this time it's 2 a.m. and we're wondering how we can prop up our exhausted bodies for another set. "David Bowie" was our answer. A great final set, nice encores. The costume contest was in between encores—the finalists were Rutherford the Brave, Fluffhead, Bathtub Gin, Tela & The Multibeast, Mound, Vacuum Boy, AC/DC Bag, and Harry Hood. Third place went to Harry Hood, a girl with this huge cardboard Hood Milk creation, complete with "Missing: (her face) Harry Hood. Where Do You Go When The Lights Go Out?" on the side. Her prize was "THIS!" (I have no idea what it was—an odd sculpture thing). Second place (very close second) went to the Vacuum Boy, who actually looked like a giant blue condom if you can imagine that. He got a beer stein. First prize, a giant bowling trophy, went to Mound, a guy dressed up like a giant Mounds bar. Then Squirming Coil to end the night. It was 3:30 a.m.

10/31/94 Glens Falls Civic Center—by Dean Budnick

Fans had been anticipating this show for weeks. For starters, people were happy to have the date back on the tour docket. Phish hadn't played a Halloween show since Colorado Springs 1991 (the infamous "Wait" show). What's more, Phish had changed the rules a bit this year. Following many weeks of rumor and speculation, the September Schvice confirmed that yes indeed, this show would be a three set affair. Furthermore, the newsletter indicated that in conjunction with an audience costume contest, the band was going to wear a musical costume, performing an album chosen from among the most popular suggestions (although there was some question as to whether or not Phish would perform the album with the highest number of votes or rather would make its selection from among the most popular choices. Before a Bad Hat show in September Fishman indicated that *Thriller* was currently in first place and that the band was not likely to play it). At any rate as the date neared, speculation focused primarily on *Jesus Christ Superstar*, Frank Zappa's *Joe's Garage*, the Stones' *Hot Rocks*, Pink Floyd's *Dark Side of the Moon* and any number of Beatles albums.

The venue itself was an 8,000 seat arena built in the 1970's primarily for hockey. It was nestled in the middle of a mildly decrepit old industrial town, forty miles north of Albany. We made it to Glens Falls long before showtime but since I was taping and I was wearing a goofy costume taboot we decided to head inside early. Although the Schvice had said that the show would start at 10:00, our tickets said 9:30 and we didn't want to chance it. As it turned out, the Schvice was right and we were in the arena long before most people even thought about entering. Still, things could have been worse, as the situation outside de-

teriorated closer to 9:30, with hundreds of the ticketless indulging in the Halloween spirit and antagonizing the crush of people pushing and struggling to get in (the path through security was moving slowly due to everyone's costumes). As an added bonus, because we had entered so early, the Dionysian Production people hadn't had time to see any really cool costumes. So Shelly Culbertson looked me over and handed me a sheet of paper that indicated that I had advanced to the next round of costume judging between the second and third sets.

I abandoned my costume with my friends up at their seats and moved down to the taping section. One nice thing about the Civic Center was that, unlike most northeast venues of this size, while the seats on the side were reserved, the floor was general admission. This offered more room for everyone at the rear of the floor near the tapers. Meanwhile, on the floor, most every conversation turned to the album choice. The familiar speculation continued as the arena slowly filled and expectations rapidly increased. Finally, around 10:15, the houselights dimmed, the band hit the stage and we were underway.

The show started predictably but not unsatisfactorily. Phish stomped into "Frankenstein" and the game was afoot. "Sparkle" was next and it kept the crowd shaking (I can understand why some Phishheads grow a bit tired of this song because the jams don't vary perceptibly from performance to performance, but as far as I'm concerned that complaint is all posture. It's hard to come down hard on a quick tune that gives so many people a big ol' body-twitching, devil-grinning buzz). From here it was an extended version of "Simple," a tune that had evolved nicely since its rough-hewn introduction that past summer. The band then broke into a notable "Divided Sky," as the band deftly moved through the song's complex orchestrations and guitar-sustain exhibitions to some collective improvisations. Many pulses then quickened as fans heard the familiar oom-pah-pah that introduced "Harpua." No one was sure when or how the album would be played and many thought that Jimmy's story might provide the perfect vehicle. This version took place on Halloween and included the familiar "Vibration of Life," with a new twist, the "Vibration of Death." Then when Jimmy moved to his turntable and put on a record, some people in the audience tensed, thinking that this might be the moment. But, no. Instead, Trey indicated that Jimmy had placed a Barney album onto the record player and the band zeroed in on a punch line. Trey explained that Jimmy had accidentally played the album backwards, and Phish then performed the music that Jimmy had heard: twenty seconds of Black Sabbath's "War Pigs,"[[[]] with Fishman doing justice to Ozzy. Trey completed the story, the band sang the Harpua chorus and then it was on to Julius. Phish moved vigorously through this selection which turned out to be the only Hoist song of the evening. A solid version of Horse>Silent came next and while no one could say "I think that this exact thing happened to me just last year," most everyone was thankful that it was happening at all. The set concluded with an exploratory Reba (which included the whistling at the end, always a good sign) and a quick sing-along Golgi. All in all a decent, eighty minute start to the evening.

During the set break all thoughts turned to the impending album. Fans wondered aloud whether it would appear in the next set or in the third. Then, a few minutes before midnight, just after the band members took their places on stage, the sound of a heartbeat pulsed through the speakers. *Dark Side of the Moon*. Some people howled in appreciation. But then the heartbeat ceased and the voice of Ed Sullivan emerged, introducing four lads from Liverpool and...over the thirty-

year old recorded squeals of teenyboppers, Phish broke into Back in the U.S.S.R. The Beatles. *The White Album*. A double album. Wow.

Despite what we knew, I have to admit that it didn't really kick in that they were going to play the entire *White Album* until Page hit the first notes of Dear Prudence. His tender rendition set the tone of the set with Page singing the mellow McCartney tunes (Blackbird, I Will) and Trey providing the vocals on most others, with Mike and Fishman contributing a few takes as well. Glass Onion came next and proved particularly entertaining. First, when Trey sang "the walrus was Paul", a spotlight shined down on soundman extraordinaire Paul Languedoc. Later, Trey changed a few lyrics in the third verse, transforming a Beatles self-reference into a Phish self-reference. Thus, "I told you about the fool on the hill…" became "I told you about Guyute the Pig, you know that he's a-dancing the jig". Phish then presented a faithful cover of Ob-La-Di Ob-La-Da. Of course this wouldn't be a Phish show if the band didn't tweak things a bit, and so as the group moved through the album, Mike offered up a bluegrass interpretation of Don't Pass Me By and Fishman added some Electrolux to his inevitable Why Don't We Do It In the Road. The band completed the first album (or disc, if you prefer) with Mike and Trey's haunting Julia, which rivaled Phish's version of While My Guitar Gently Weeps as the finest of the batch.

Phish paused briefly at the start of side three (disc two). Then, instead of singing Birthday, Fishman stood and announced, "Believe it or not, this is Brad Sands's birthday…we'd like to invite him up here to get his cake". So while Trey, Mike and Page played an instrumental hint of the Beatles' Birthday, big ball boy/trampoline guy Brad Sands walked onstage in his Halloween costume, a Fishman dress, to receive his cake from the drummer. As Brad exited, Phish returned to the action as Mike growled Yer Blues. Page's intonation and phrasing on the subsequent Mother Nature's Son sounded similar to Paul McCartney's original. Trey then assumed vocal duties for much of the set's remainder, contributing two of the finer moments with Revolution (thankfully the slow, loopy version from the album and not the upbeat one later appropriated for a Nike commercial) and Cry Baby Cry (an overlooked Beatles gem). Following the latter tune, the band performed a show-stopping, set-closing Revolution No. 9. Fishman retrieved his vacuum cleaner and started doing his thing while the rest of Phish produced, as best they could, the many voices and sounds of the original. Towards the end of the song, the non-vacuum-soloing members of the band pulled out bubble wands and intermittently blew into them. Then as Revolution No. 9 reached its close with a voice proclaiming "you become naked," Fishman did just that. He pulled his dress over his head and pranced around nude while the Trey, Mike and Page chanted hold that line, hold that line between bubble breaths (a photo of this moment appears on page eleven of the booklet accompanying A Live One, although the letter H modestly covers Fishman's package). At around 1:30 AM the band stepped off-stage to the original taped version of Good Night, the last song on the White Album. Everyone collapsed into seats or onto the floor, exhausted.

But not me. I didn't have time to collapse. I had been a Beatles freak as a kid and as a Phish phreak now I felt like I had to play along, so I threw on my costume. I figured that while I wouldn't be allowed on stage for the finals, at least I would participate in the festivities, and greet the band members during this stage of the judging. Sadly, I was mistaken (Oh yeah, and in case you're wondering, I dressed up as my then-favorite Phish songs, Slave to the Traffic Light. I wore a studded

dog collar with a chain leading up to a facsimile traffic light that I had found at a flea market. Lame yes, but easy to get on and off). Fifteen or so of us were herded into a corner of the hallway which led down towards the band's dressing room. We were told, "Now we're going to separate the wheat from the chaff". I was not surprised to learn that yes, indeed I was chaff (although I did receive a lovely parting gift, a copy of a Surfing magazine from earlier in the year which contained a Trey interview). I returned to my friends who were still ranting excitedly about the set. Their attitudes ranged from the devout ("I think the spirit of John Lennon was with us tonight") to the irreverent ("I don't know about Lennon but I think I saw Ringo at the Greenpeace booth").

Phish returned to the stage around 2:00 AM. Those few people who had dozed off were nudged awake as the band reminded them that the night was by no means at an end, with a massive David Bowie. Next came Bouncing Around the Room, an exercise in calisthenics to keep the adrenaline flowing. The band then launched into Slave To the Traffic Light, which wafted through its Methanyesque progressions and spiraled to a close. A solid Rift followed and most people were sure that this would close out the evening. But no, a real treat came next with the rare Sleeping Monkey. The tune was all the more appropriate on this evening because its ending is unabashedly lifted from Let It Be (if you're curious, yes, one day I'll fix the Sleeping Monkey entry in *The Phishing Manual*). At this point most fans were convinced that Phish would walk. But no, Mike induced square-dance fever with a zippy Poor Heart. Then Trey, Mike, Page and Fishman drop-kicked an exclamation point onto the evening with a savage Antelope. As the song stormed to a close, the band smiled, waved and walked off. Their work was done.

Nearly. The quartet returned to the stage barbershop style and moved through a slightly frayed version of Amazing Grace (Fishman's voice was a bit tired even if the rest of him wasn't). Next it was time for the costume contest, and here my brush with greatness paid off as I rallied the people around me to root for the contestants that had become my favorites during the five minutes we had been corralled together. I lobbied hardest for the woman in the Hood milk carton who ultimately finished third, after she nearly had withdrawn from the competition because someone had danced on her costume during the first set. The winner was dressed as a giant Mounds bar, or rather Mound bar, after the Phish song of that title. The guy who finished second, by the way, appears on page 23 of the *A Live One* booklet. He appeared as a cobalt blue vacuum cleaner and called himself Lawn Boy (although personally I thought it was un-sportsmanlike of him to swing around his hose during the final judging to solicit applause). At any rate Phish then brought the evening to a close with a splendid Squirming Coil. The song concluded with Page on stage alone, ushering us outside with a playful, pleasing piano solo. He wished us goodnight and walked off. It was 3:20 in the morning. We didn't want to go.

Tuesday, October 31, 1995
Rosemont Horizon, Chicago, IL

For the second year in a row, Phish let the fans vote for the musical costume. Unlike 1994, though, the band noted that they would choose an album from fan suggestions, rather than play the album that received the most votes. Legend holds that Frank Zappa's *Joe's Garage* actually received the most votes, but that the band, after rehearsing parts of it, decided that they could not do it justice given the album's complexities that would be difficult to duplicate on the live stage. So, as

the story holds, the band turned to the second-highest vote-getter: The Who's rock opera *Quadrophenia*.

Though *Tommy* is a better known work in the mainstream and garnered several votes of its own, *Quadrophenia* packs a much better story and, musically, rages quite a bit harder. It is the story of Jimmy, a young man schizophrenic twice over, and his attempts to fit in to the early 70's counterculture. Each of Jimmy's four distinct personalities was represented by one of the four members of The Who, which made it even more appropriate for the four distinct members of the Phish quartet.

From the Icculus opener, where Trey urged the crowd to help the Helping Friendly Book ward off the evil Halloween spirits, to the Harpua closer, where Mike told us all a story about raccoons, the first set was a dark precursor to the rest of the evening. See also the Guyute breakout (first in over ten months), a fiery Antelope, and a sinister Free.

As with 1994, the band teased fans with a runner-up album before breaking into the winner. This year, the choice was Michael Jackson's "Beat It," from the best-selling *Thriller* album. It was the last in a string of teases related to The King of Pop that left fans guessing for weeks—see also "Beat It" teases in the 10/29/95 Possum and several teases in the 10/21/95 second set. The most famed tease of the fall, though, was the jam on Pink Floyd's "Breathe" in the 10/22/95 Mike's Song. For the second year in a row, Phish teased a song from *Dark Side of the Moon*, though it would be three years and two days until they played it in its entirety.

The second set included entirely too many highlights to name them all. It can be summed up best using one word: raging. Like the original album, Phish's *Quadrophenia* ranged from complete chaos and excitement into emotional discovery in a matter of seconds. Phish put their own original spin on songs like Helpless Dancer, I'm One, and Sea and Sand, and also delivered rocking versions of The Real Me and Drowned. To cover the horn parts, they called on old friends Dave Grippo (alto saxophone), Don Glasgo (trombone), Joey Somerville (trumpet) and Alan Parshley (French horn). Screaming at times but painfully tender at others, Fishman ended the musical costume with an amazing rendition of Love Reign O'er Me and began to prove that he should be taken seriously as a vocalist, and not just as Henrietta.

Of the *Quadrophenia* songs, only Drowned would have any lasting role in the Phish concert rotation. Though a relative rarity, it has often led to wonderful exploratory jams when played. The Real Me made one cameo (in the famed 12/29/95 "Real Gin") and Sea and Sand has popped up twice. The rest have never again appeared on the Phish stage.

The third set wouldn't be any less intense then the first two. The near-forty minute long You Enjoy Myself, which opened the set, is reason alone to hear this show. The set also included a rather funny Suzy, complete with some Trey lyrical flubs. And who could forget the destruction of the instruments (a la The Who) after an acoustic My Generation—proof of just how much energy was conjured up throughout the show.

10/31/95 Rosemont Horizon—by Dean Budnick

Friends of mine started their campaign in late August after they read the announcement in the Schvice: *Joe's Garage* for Halloween. I could understand their logic, last year was a double album, why not triple it this year? I had my own thoughts however, which focused primarily on the costume contest. Last year I had been so close, but this year I was determined to finally make it onto the stage. I knew that I had to come up with something good, but I just couldn't summon any great

ideas. Meanwhile my pals continued to stuff the ballot box for *Joe's* while I finally decided that maybe it would be better to sit out the contest this year to enjoy the show. Of course that was just a rationalization to cover the fact that I just didn't have any good costume ideas.

As the night before the show approached I made two discoveries. First I learned that the Halloween album would incorporate horns. Next, I concluded that it would inappropriate to show up without a costume. So I brainstormed, came up with a mediocre idea, and harassed some of my friends to do the same. As we met at O'Hare Airport on the morning of the 31st we shared one common goal: we had to go out into the city to buy some stuff to complete our costumes. Following an afternoon that featured a long visit to Woolworth's and the obligatory deep dish pizza, we were back at out hotel and ready for out pre-show prep.

Fortunately, our hotel was just up the street from the Horizon because there was no way that any of us would fit into a car. Manny was dressed as Sleeping Monkey (an ape face with pajamas, furry hands and sleeping cap), Marc was The Curtain (you guessed it: hanging out in the middle of a curtain rod he clipped from his house), Lee was AC/DC Bag, and Rob (of dubious "Dean Budnick for President!" fame) was a total fabrication that he rented from the remainders at a costume shop (I think he said he was a multibeast). I was dressed as the rhombus, trapped in a boxy, bulky foam-core prison. I didn't quite perfect the thing so I had to stick my arms straight out so that I could walk. Oh yeah and to top this off I had this insanely stupid hat in the shape of a rhombus, with a little toy figure emerging from the top to sing Divided Sky.

I waddled over the venue with everyone and somehow bumbled inside (I didn't fit through the turnstile-thankfully they opened a door) only to learn that there was to be no costume contest this year. Eventually I moved into the actual arena, set up my deck and abandoned my costume, convincing some usher to let me place it on an area of floor directly behind the last row of seats.

At some time shortly after 8:00 Phish took the stage (about two hours earlier than the year before). Right off, the band demonstrated that they were going to make this one special, with a Halloween Icculus incantation. Divided Sky came next with some nimble performances both during the scripted parts and the short but captivating improvisational section that followed. My abandoned costume no doubt appreciated the tune. Wilson was third, with some audience participation just as everyone had learned to do from *A Live One*. A quick run through Sparkle followed, eliciting an inordinate number of "yeee-haas" and "wahooos" from the Midwest crowd. Phish moved next into a lengthy Free, a gem of a song with fine harmonies, soaring guitar tone and on this night some fine work by Fish when Trey started on percussion. At the close of this song, Phish paused briefly to consult and then… Guyute! The triumphant return of that ugly old pig with some minor cosmetic surgery. A romping Antelope came next and most of us figured that the set was over. But no, that familiar "oom pah pah" introduced us once again to Harpua. We had discussed the possibility that Phish might play the Halloween album in the middle of Harpua while Jimmy listened to it. After Mike told his raccoon dream story, we all started eavesdropping on Jimmy, who Trey revealed was playing the album that Phish was performing at Halloween this year. Phish paused and started playing Beat It. I wasn't fooled at first, (hey I survived 1983, I know that Beat It is not the first song on *Thriller*) but then Phish carried on one measure too many and I started sweating. This is not to say that it wouldn't have been an interesting choice, it just wasn't what I

was looking for at the time.

The tension mounted as the seconds ticked away to the start of the second set. Then the lights dimmed, the phans yelled, and the distinctive syncopated beat of You Wanna Be Starting Something started (which is the first song on *Thriller*). Then I could see the band starting to play and I could hear some piped in noise of some sort but…it wasn't until the horns kicked into the Real Me that I realized what was up. *Quadrophenia*, Pete Townshend's tale of a psychotic boy appropriately named Jimmy. The band moved through the album with Page handing most of the vocal duties. Punk Meets The Godfather, Doctor Jimmy, and I've Had Enough all sounded particularly strong, drawing on the many elements of the band's current line up, the strength of the original material and the performance skills and creativity of Phish. The Giant Country Horns added punch to the set, particularly with the addition of the French horn. For me, the finest moment took place with intense interplay of band and brass during 5:15. Something interesting occurred during Bell Boy, when an appropriately dressed figure took the stage with some suitcases, took a long swig from a fifth of booze, and performed the song through a thick British accent. I initially assumed that it was an accented Dude of Life since I had run into him earlier, but as it turns out it was a member of the crew. Finally, the set closed as Fish, who had been chained behind his drum kit, took to center stage to offer a somewhat strained but nonetheless impassioned Love Reign O'er Me.

After a break, the band returned for a third set that remains one of my all time favorites. Things started out innocently enough with the opening notes to YEM but about a half hour later it became clear that this is no ordinary YEM, as the band extended every facet of the song far longer than usual, from Page's segment to Mike's featured moments to the vocal jam. Suddenly it occurred to me, maybe this will be the whole set, a 45 minute YEM as if to say "okay, here's one set during which we'll perform a double album by the Who, here's the next set during which we'll perform ONE of our songs." But as the YEM drew to a close at the 43-minute mark, I did not complain when Dave Grippo joined the band for a run through the appropriate Jesus Just Left Chicago. A standard Day in the Life followed and the set came to a brassy close with the horns' pleasing contributions on Suzy Greenberg.

And then the encore! This one both had to be seen and heard. Before the band came out, the crew set up a replica Keith Moon drum kit with the words The Who on it. We weren't sure what it to make of it. Then Phish came out with their acoustic set up, with Fish sitting behind the toy drum kit as Phish performed My Generation. On his acoustic guitar, Trey performed his only Pete Townshend windmills of the evening. At the end of the song, Mike and Page continued to vamp on banjo and bass while Fish and Trey lingered for a moment and then systematically destroyed their instruments, kicking them, stepping on them, and throwing them to the ground. This continued for a few minutes or so as Trey and Fish tossed each piece of the drum kit and guitar to the rear of the stage. When this process was complete and the stage was clear of musical shrapnel, an Acme detonator/plunger was brought out and placed in front of Trey and Fish. Trey paused, and then depressed it, setting off an explosion to the rear of the stage where the pieces of the drum kit had been thrown, ending the show in a pyrotechnics flash. Good night Chicago! Exclamation point!

10/31/95 Rosemont Horizon —by Eric Fleming

*Q*uadrophenia tells a story, but what is it? To boil it down to its most basic elements, it is the story of Jimmy, a rather troubled youth:

Halloween 1995 (Jack and Kat)

he doesn't get along with his parents, he can't hold a job, and all of his money goes towards clothes and pills. He is a mod. OK, fine… but what is a mod? A mod is the antithesis of a rocker, but that doesn't really explain anything; in fact, it complicates it quite a bit. A rocker and a mod listen to the same music. They are both the same age, and might have the same job. They drink the same liquor and do the same drugs. So, how are they different?

Attitude. Pure and simple. Well, attitude and clothes. A rocker, given the choice, will be outside his society, not only indifferent to it, but rather violently against it. A mod, at the other end of the spectrum, wants desperately to be at the height of his society, but rarely has the means to achieve the lofty goal, mainly because of clothes and pills. The mod is very fashion-conscious and is in a constant state of updating his wardrobe to meet the latest trend before it becomes passé.

The Who were a mod band. Not because they were anxious about being accepted (in that respect, they were probably more aligned with the rockers), but because they realized many of their fans were mods, and in their early wardrobe and a few early songs, catered to that audience. And voila! Their fan base was secured.

How does all this relate to *Quadrophenia*, besides being backstory? Of all the members of the Who, Pete Townshend had become the posterboy of the mod culture, and when the Who started gaining notoriety, the mod roots he had worked so hard to cultivate were left behind. *Quadrophenia* was his attempt, years after the mod craze had, in fact, died out, to bring closure to his mod experience. It is not his story, by any means, but it is written with his point of view.

This story is all about cynicism about the world in general, and in particular being let down by a culture. As the story progresses, he is at first enamored with the mod lifestyle, as it gives him a place in so-

ciety he would not normally have. He has status; he has a job; he has the respect of others. But a mod is invariably doomed to self-destruct, as being at the height of fashion (as opposed to actually setting the fashion), means one is always a step behind. As things go along, he realizes that no one really cares, and the leaders of the mod revolution (who in not a small way were the Who themselves) were actually poseurs, and his entire image of the mod culture is ruined. This is further enforced when he finds that one of his mod idols—Ace Face—who had appeared larger than life as he was protesting against the establishment by throwing bottles at a hotel, was actually part of the establishment, working at that very hotel as a bell boy.

After crashing his motor scooter (a mod staple, and a symbol of independence), the narrator steals a boat and heads out on the sea to a rock, in the middle of the bay, to die. He climbs up on it, and as the boat drifts away, leaving him stranded, his life flashes before him, and he sees that in certain ways he has become parts of different people in his life—a dancer he saw and imitated at a party, the posturing group (the Who) that only appeared to lead the revolution, the bell boy, who had once appeared larger than life, but is now a servant, and even his shrink, who had called him schizophrenic.

"Schizophrenic? I'm Bleeding Quadrophenic."

And so *Quadrophenia* does tell a story, just not one that's easy to ascertain from the songs. But I think the explanation goes into the idea behind the story, which is why I find the fact that Phish selected this album as a Halloween costume a bit strange, to be honest.

Out of the many things Phish is as a band, one thing they certainly are not is working class anger. The Who is, and so is *Quadrophenia*. Phish has always seemed to me to be about dexterity, both instrumentally and lyrically. They perform intricate compositions, with incredible harmonies and counter-melodies. And fugues! How many rock bands have been quoted as saying the reason certain songs were not performed on a particular tour is because they hadn't had time to practice the fugues!?! What they do is unique. But they have never struck me as being an incredibly passionate band. Passionate about the music, certainly, but Phish has never been about using the stage as a political platform. Here and there, certainly (Farm Aid comes to mind), but not as a general rule. There just doesn't appear to be the inner need to preach or protest. Which is fine.

But the fact that they did this, when it was truly the biggest stretch of any of their Halloween costumes, is what makes their performance all that much more amazing to me, especially since *Quadrophenia* is really everything Phish is not.

Now, without trying to be overly critical, but simply to try and put this performance in perspective, this is certainly not the best live rendition of *Quadrophenia* I've ever heard, especially when comparing Page's vocals to Roger Daltrey's performance. There is no comparison, and there shouldn't be. Roger Daltrey was a small, insecure tough guy, who always had the cornered animal mentality. Page's voice is simply too pure to really do justice to the throaty vocals Roger was capable of, and that this music demands, but the passion is there. And that is really what made the show for me.

Take away the vocals from Phish's performance, and compare that to what the Who were able to do with it instrumentally, and in my opinion the energy is the same. The power is the same. All things being equal, what's the big deal?

First, covering *Quadrophenia* gives everyone a real chance to shine on some good, old fashioned solos, while keeping them within the structure of the songs, which really aren't built to be split opened for a jam. Fishman in particular would have enjoyed this, I think. Keith Moon of the Who was one of the most unique drummers in rock history, and his style fit in perfectly with the Who. Generally, the rhythm section of a band is held down by the drums and bass, but in the Who, the drums and bass acted more as melody instruments than rhythm, which was carried by Townshend on guitar, who was is fairly judged as one of rock's great rhythm players. But that fact allows the normal rhythm section of Phish to really play out a bit, with some nice fat bass lines and crazy fills on drums, while Trey can chunk along, providing the rhythm along with the keyboards (which the Who only used on a couple songs), with the occasional guitar solo thrown in.

So, the instrumental aspect of this show was first rate. Period. I've played instrumental parts of this show for people before, and always get the same first reaction, You have a copy of the Who live in concert? And it certainly sounds like the real article, but I mentioned the vocals being not quite up to par, so why listen?

Emotion. This performance showed me a side of Phish I hadn't seen before, and I enjoyed it. Phish is generally more playful than this, more teasing, almost as if they're playing hide and seek. Delicate, but with an abundance of technical skill and rhythm that leaves most of us (I feel I can speak for more than just myself here) wanting more. This show just showed me how much more versatile they are, compared to my impressions. So I enjoyed it.

As far as interpreting the songs and making them theirs, to be honest, I didn't hear very much of that going on. It was basically a straight-ahead cover, with the exception of "Helpless Dancer," where I think speed got the best of them, which had the result of turning a very nice song into something else. Only the first couple words of each verse were intelligible, and the speed and sloppiness pretty much ruined the song for me. But other than that, I very much enjoyed the interpretations, or lack thereof. Consider that after the Halloween concert, nearly all the songs from *Quadrophenia* have dropped out of Phish's repertoire, with the exception of "Drowned," which pops up occasionally. It's a pretty hard thing to take a 90 minute piece of someone else's music and make it identifiable as your own when you'll only be doing it once.

The horn section Phish brought in for the concert (Dave Grippo, sax; Don Glasgo, trombone; Joe Somerville Jr., trumpet; Alan Parshley, French horn) really expanded Phish's sound, bringing it more in line with what the Who presented on album.

So, how does this all sum up? Is it as influential on their sound as the Talking Heads cover? Certainly not. Was the concert one of the greatest of all time? I don't know, but I doubt it. But what I get out of this concert was that here is one of my favorite bands, taking a big risk into musical territory not all that familiar, chancing a horrible disaster (both in how they might perform and how the performance would be appreciated by a group of people probably not all that familiar with the music either), and coming out fantastically! And I guess that's what I like about the band the most.

10/31/95 Six Degrees of Halloween—by Cory Ferber

Halloween '95 kicked off what is arguably the greatest two month run of shows in Phish history. An instant classic, this show re-

mains an important Phish concert because it is a major anchor in a mind-boggling demonstration of conceptual continuity. 'Conceptual continuity' is a term used by Frank Zappa to describe the musical and lyrical connections that run through segments, songs, and concerts into a larger and more meaningful experience for the active listener.

The set list is legendary opening in Gamehendge with a rare Icculus, followed by a Divided Sky > Wilson combo. The set then closes with a Harpua that finds Gordon meeting Rocky Raccoon, a nice nod to the Halloween '94 show. It also contains a "Beat It" jam, a costume hint the band had been giving at a string of shows.

The joke continued as the band came on stage for the second set to "Gotta Be Starting Something", the first song on Jackson's Thriller. Trey was even doing the moonwalk. The rock opera *Quadrophenia* is the premier example of musical continuity in and of itself. "Love, Reign O'er Me" remains one of the most climatic moments in Phish history. It's hard to match the goose bump factor of the grand finale of this masterpiece. What truly makes the moment is Fishman, whose entire repertoire previously consisted of cover songs. This was a fitting ending to the album.

The third set continued the continuity with the aptly titled cover songs "Jesus Left Chicago", and "A Day In The Life." The "My Generation" encore is notorious because the band destroyed their instruments on stage in a blend of performance art meets Loony Tunes. The evil Halloween spirits then quickly shifted gears and played the original version of "Ebony and Ivory" over the PA system. This particular song happens to be a duet with Paul McCartney, a weird premeditated gesture to the previous year's Halloween show. This was a fitting ending to the concert.

It's interesting to note the final show of the two months following Halloween '94 became the centerpiece of this demonstration of conceptual continuity. The band's first New Years Eve performance at Madison Square Garden found them mixing elements of Gamehendge with the Halloween tradition. For a band that goes on stage without a set list, the final set is astonishing when carefully analyzed.

The music begins where it actually really did all begin, in the Gamehendge Time Factory. The band then finishes a "Mike's Groove" started earlier in the evening, adding a touch of musical consistency between sets. Page's spur of the moment "Sea and Sand" then weaves in elements of the show that began the madness. This is followed by "YEM," also the improvisational centerpiece of the show that began the madness. An extremely rare "Sanity" follows, and remarkably becomes a connection to the Halloween '96 show where it was the first set opener. The band then closes the climatic set with the first set opener of Halloween '94, "Frankenstein!" "Lost my mind just a couple of times" with a heavy dose of Halloween conceptual continuity.

Quadrophenia Revisited—by Greg Mitchell

I hesitated when I sent in my mail order request for tickets for my local shows on Phish's 2000 Fall Tour. The nearest stops for me are at the Target Center in Minneapolis and Rosemont Arena in Chicago. I almost didn't get the Rosemont tickets as I dislike that venue so much. I saw the Dead many times there, once from behind the band where I only saw the back of one of the drummers and Brent on keyboards all night, and both the sight lines and the sound generally suck. Add onto that its narrow concourses and, like I said, I almost decided to not see Phish there

this fall. But then I thought about Phish's *Quadrophenia* show.

I was lucky enough to be at the Rosemont on 10/31/95. We had great seats—first row of the bleachers right across from the band and when at the beginning of the second set the wind and sea sound effects that open *Quadrophenia* started flowing from the PA, I amp'd out. I went completely out of my mind. I have always loved the Who and have seen them in concert many times over the years. I have studied *Quadrophenia* to the point of compiling my own version of it on tape, combining the original Who record with the extra songs from the movie soundtrack to make a more linear, understandable version of the story. My love of the piece was certainly catalyzed by seeing the Who perform *Quadrophenia* in a 1973 show that turned out to be as legendary as Phish's Halloween show.

On November 20, 1973, I went to the Cow Palace in San Francisco to see the Who. As opposed to rock tours now which have names, back then bands didn't name their tours. Still, on this tour the Who first played *Quadrophenia*. The record had been released earlier that month and I immediately loved it. Complex and deep, I tried to figure out the four sides of the opera's lead character, Jimmy ("I'm not schizophrenic—I'm bleeding quadrophrenic!"). The Cow Palace gig was the second show of the tour—the first had been in Toronto two nights before—and the reports from Canada were good. It was a general admission show (this was before Cincinnati) and we found a spot on the floor half way back. It started out as a typical Who concert with songs like Substitute and I Can't Explain, but soon the band got into *Quadrophenia*. The Who didn't play the whole piece as the instrumentals were too complex to stage and the band played along with tapes in many parts to fill out the instrumentation (while this system failed many nights this tour, it seemingly worked fine in San Francisco). I didn't care. I had Pete Townshend, Roger Daltrey, John Entwistle and Keith Moon playing their new work 100 feet in front of me. After a splendid *Quadrophenia*, the Who went back into performing their hits. In the middle of a song suddenly there were no drums. The problem was there was no Keith Moon. The band quickly finished the song and Townshend said that they'd be taking a short break. That turned into a long break when someone came out and said that Moonie had passed out but was recovering. "Somebody slipped something into Keith's drink," the announcer said. Yeah, I thought, somebody like Moonie. Later it turned out he'd taken some exotic tranquilizer (You have to understand the era. It wasn't "just say no" back then. It was more like, "Just say, 'Humm, OK. I've never done anything purple before.' "). Finally the band came back on stage with Moonie leading the charge, the other three playfully fighting to hold him back. They started playing Magic Bus, for which Moonie initially just had to strike a wood block. So good so far. As the song progressed and he started to play the drums, it was obvious that Keith was still quite out of it. Two big guys stood behind him to keep him from falling off of his stool as Moonie swung wildly for his drums. He'd start falling and the roadies would push him upright so he could swing and sway some more. Finally, there wasn't a roadie big enough to catch him as he fell straight back, off his stool and out cold for the rest of the night. No more Moonie. To my amazement, the band played a few more songs (I can't tell you now what they were) without a drummer. Daltrey got out his tambourine. Townshend, who was having an excellent night (at the next gig in Los Angeles he smashed his guitar for the first time in years), would go over and hit a cymbal with his guitar neck to add in percussion. Entwistle played even more maniacally, hitting bass notes

so fast you didn't miss the drums. Finally, Townshend came up to a mic and said, "I guess this is the end of the show. We're a rock band and we need a drummer. If somebody wants to come up and play with us, fine, but that's our show. Goodbye. Thanks for coming. We'll see you next time," and the band left the stage. The house lights came up. We started walking out. I bitched to my friends about the aborted show, and yet, that was the Who. Crazy Keith. We hadn't quite reached the edge of the floor when the house lights went back off. Whaaat? Unexpectedly, back out came the band, this time with somebody else to play the drums. They announced that their new drummer was just your typical concert-goer who had taken Townshend's request to come up and play with them literally. He had talked his way backstage, saying he was a drummer and a long time Who fan. The band said what the heck. The Who played three basic rock instrumentals with the new kid, with Townshend hanging out by the drums to help him along. He was an OK drummer, not great—it turned out he hadn't played the drums for years—but he was a damn sight better than a passed out Keith Moon. The Who Plus One finished their encore, made their second goodbyes, formed a chorus line and high-kicked their way off stage. There was an article within a few days in the San Francisco Chronicle about our local hero. Imagine—you go to see the Who and end up playing drums with them on stage. What a rush it must have been.

I also saw the Who, or more accurately a supplemented Who with many sidemen, play *Quadrophenia* during their 1997 tour featuring that piece, so you would be right to ask—which band played it better, the Who or Phish? Musically, the best was the 1997 version, with both exquisite playing and staging of the whole opera. But that's like, say, comparing punks and mods. The 1997 Who played the piece every night; in 1995 Phish played it once and with minimal rehearsal. Even discounting that, it's still an unfair comparison. In their glory years nobody rocked harder than the Who, whereas Phish is both strength and finesse. Plus none of Phish's vocalists have the range of Roger Daltrey (surprise, surprise). Still, overall I'll give the nod to Phish. First, the four of them, with a quartet of horn players occasionally filling in, had the guts and the ability to play the whole piece on Halloween and the Who in 1973 didn't. Second, Phish's musical range, from Page's solo performance of Sea and Sand, to the sudden appearance of the Phish Marching Band right before a deliberately butchered Helpless Dancer, through the band's full tilt boogie on The Real Me, show that Phish is the more versatile band of the two. Third, when I hear Love, Reign O'er Me, the final song in Quadrophenia, I no longer picture Daltrey as Adonis, running in place on stage, swinging his microphone while singing the song. Instead I have a vision of a hairy troll in a sundress fronting the band, his legs spread wide while he belts out the song for all he's worth. Phish's 1995 Halloween show was a bravura performance.

Thursday, October 31, 1996
The Omni, Atlanta, GA

For the first time, Phish announced their musical costume before the show. Fans who entered the Omni were handed a mock Playbill, called a "Phishbill," just as if they were entering a Broadway show. In addition to some funny advertisements, it included a write-up of the evening's attraction: The Talking Heads' *Remain in Light*.

For the third year in a row, *Dark Side of the Moon* lobbyists were denied. Some even wandered the Omni in disbelief, convinced that the

Phishbill was a classic Phish psych-out and that there was no way Phish would disclose the costume before they took the stage. These naysayers hung their hats on Phish pulling a huge switcheroo and surprising everyone with something different.

Dark Side fans were not the only ones who were, before show time, a bit skeptical and surprised. Internet rumors in the weeks leading up to the show did include *Remain in Light* (prompting me to buy a copy and listen to it in the days leading up to the show so that I would be familiar with the songs) but also included the usual suspects (*Thriller, Dark Side*) and some oddball choices (Van Halen's *1984*, with David Lee Roth brought in to sing lead vocals). Far fewer fans were familiar with *Remain in Light* than with the 1994 and 1995 Halloween selections—little did any of us realize that this particular Halloween album choice would impact and affect the style of Phish's play more than any other would or could.

The first set include some tasty musical nuggets, including the rare Sanity and a hot Down With Disease / You Enjoy Myself combo. The Forbin's narration only kept some fans guessing—were Trey's references to Talking Heads' frontman David Byrne genuine or just part of the joke?

No one laughed, though, when Phish started the second set with Born Under Punches. And by Crosseyed and Painless, fans were dancing in a way they never had before. The rhythmic grooves of guest percussionist Karl Perazzo augmented Fishman's drumming in ways no one had ever experienced. As with 1995, horns were required. Phish turned to Gary Gazaway and Dave Grippo, whose brass grunts, squawks, and fills further textured the album's sound.

Highlights of the set included The Great Curve and Listening Wind, which Mike performed from a recliner on stage while Trey played the bass. Overload was turned into a piece of bizarre performance art, as multi-media presentations flashed on screens around the stage. The band grabbed new instruments of choice—Trey performed on a skillsaw and Mike on a power drill, while Colonel Bruce Hampton joined in on a jackhammer. Fish, however, called on his trusty old vacuum.

The third set was the cherry on top—with extra whipped cream. A smooth Simple > Swept Away > Steep stands out, as well as Also Sprach Zarathustra > Maze and the brass-enhanced Suzy Greenberg (with a Born Under Punches tease, no less) and Julius. Perhaps the funniest moment of the night came sans horns, though—Dave Grippo teased fans by walking on-stage during Simple, holding up his saxophone during the appropriate lyric, and then exiting quickly.

This show was, and is, as important a night as any in Phishtory. Phish was in the middle of their first-ever arena tour and most fans agree that the early tour shows were not among the band's best performances. This came on the heels of what some fans saw as a lackluster summer tour. The sound that was discovered in *Remain in Light*, though, seeped into the rest of the year. Phish rebounded with stellar performances, starting with the famed "Crosseyed Antelope" at their next show. Most credit *Remain in Light*, along with Mike switching to his Modulus bass, with influencing the band's transition to funkier jamming in 1997 and more groove oriented jamming to close the decade.

10/31/96 Omni—by AJ Abrams and Brian Lipman

It was evident before this show even started that this third Halloween "musical costume" show was going to be special. To begin with,

Phish ended fan voting for the cover album and decided to choose it themselves. They also eliminated the element of surprise because as we walked in they handed us a program revealing the album to be *Remain in Light* by the Talking Heads. However, many fans thought the program was a hoax and just another Phish joke on us. The Phishbill was indeed humorous, but it was also legitimate. *Remain in Light* was the riskiest album choice to date, yet surprisingly it would go on to have more influence on Phish's music than any of the other Halloween choices.

Showing us they meant business on Halloween, this show surprisingly opens up with a rare Sanity and the highly appropriate hard rocker Highway to Hell. This tune, normally a set closer, had the crowd in a diabolical Halloween frenzy with heads bangin' and fists pumping in celebration of the evil holiday. The opening of the show didn't let up, it continued to rage as Down With Disease followed. It had a fast paced, gorgeous groove and was tight and energetic. While many versions in 1996 were unfinished, this DWD deceptively snuck into the closing theme and ended with a strong, solid finish. The Disease punched into a decent, but fairly average YEM that featured menacing soloing from Trey. This unbelievable string of crowd favorites was a tremendous way to start the show, as one can't argue with a 1-2-3-4 punch like this madness. Later in the set the band finished a majestic Reba with the now rare whistling and "bag it, tag it" ending. The always fun Forbid>Mockingbird featured a story about David Byrne, giant zoot suit and all, knocking Forbin into outer space. Trey went on to describe how the Mockingbird was coming to save Forbin, but it turned out to be the horrible, evil Mockingbird and it pecked out Forbin's eyes instead of saving him. Character Zero and the Star Spangled Banner closed out this 90 minute all-star Phish interlude and set the tone for set II…that is if anything could really set the tone for what we were about to witness.

Remain in Light was such a risky choice because very few fans were familiar with it and the music itself was such a radical departure from the Phish sound at the time. Despite the lack of familiarity, fans had no trouble getting down to the Talking Heads' disco/pop/funk/fusion masterpiece. The opening of Born Under Punches was a complex yet soothing breath of air following the very intense first set. The smooth, flowing song built up subtly until three vocal tracks combined with Page's techno keyboard sequences and Trey's funk guitar. As the tune wound down, Gary Gazaway and Dave Grippo chimed in a few squawks, warming up for the ensuing mayhem, Crosseyed and Painless. Yes, this is where all those C&P teases to come first originated. The Halloween version introduced us to the driving percussion of Karl Perazzo, and in a sense, to Phish 2000. Fishman was able to pull off Byrne's vocals quite accurately and still kept the backbeat going. The horns added another layer to the tune, helping to transform it from an electronic, ultra-produced piece of studio mastery into an onstage rocker.

Perazzo took center stage at the end of C&P with a percussion solo, which exploded into the Great Curve, one of the highlights of the night. This tune featured intense, almost Llama-like chordings and peaked at the end when Trey took a blistering solo, his only one of the RIL set. At the song's conclusion the Omni erupted and Fishman let out a shriek. Once in a Lifetime, the one song everyone knew, was next and ended the upbeat part of the album. From this song the album launches into its darker, somber side.

My only criticism of this album is that the second half loses all the intensity and energy that was established in the first half. The first half absolutely rages, only to come crashing down into the mellow, occa-

sionally boring second half. The eerie, atmospheric funk tunes begin with Houses in Motion which featured a spectacular segue into Seen and Not Seen. Next, Mike took center stage as he sat in a giant Lazy Boy rocking chair and turned Listening Wind into an almost spoken-word type performance. The album came to a bizarre, dramatic conclusion with the Overload. As TVs blasted obnoxious video clips Phish created a massive, eerie, industrial, chaotic wall of sound with real chain saws, jackhammers and other power tools. They were illustrating one of the themes of RIL, information and media overload. But it was ironic because at the time of this concert Phish was getting the most media attention they had ever received. After years of ignoring Phish, "Rolling Stone," MTV, CNN and other major media outlets finally caught on and were running feature stories on the band. Was Phish trying to make a statement about their growing popularity and the crush of media and fan attention?

This set ushered in the Phish era of funk style jamming that would last throughout the next year. The band's improvisations became tighter and more group oriented. All four musicians began to play as one solid unit and they became a finely tuned groove machine. This new style of jamming was most noticeable in Trey's guitar playing. He began to limit his flashy, fiery solos and became a more rhythm based, group oriented guitarist. The RIL set was amazing because it was one long, mesmerizing, hypnotic groove. It was an exploration of complicated polyrhythms, textures and sounds. The set emits a special, swirling, spell binding aura that still holds up well after repeated listenings. RIL is also full of contrasts. It is raging yet soothing, tribal yet futuristic, and psychedelic yet funky. For this album to be pulled off successfully, the rhythm section of Mike and Fishman had to be in top form. Mike, who always has his game face on, looked the most focused I have ever seen him while he pounded away at his bass. His head bobbed furiously as he worked diligently to keep the constant groove flowing throughout the entire album. I did not dance much during this set even though RIL is a tremendously funky and easily danceable album. Instead, I just stood there, hypnotized by the groove and soaking in the atmospheric sounds. I was captivated by this sonic masterpiece with layers of textural guitars and polyrhythms enveloping me.

A few people were disappointed with the album choice of RIL. However, Phish surely cheered those fans up when they played the rare fan favorite Brother to open up the third set. This version was spectacular and more melodic than most versions. Usually this song is a loud rocker full of monster power chords. Although this version did indeed rock, it was not as quite as heavy sounding as usual. If there is such a thing as a pretty sounding Brother, this is it. Since there were few, if any, guitar solos during RIL, Trey was anxious to solo. He was the star of this tune and his solos were high pitched and melodic. Since this was now the official age of funk, a nice funky 2001 was next and led into Maze. This electrifying Maze was on fire as Karl Perazzo bashed away on percussion. The musical tension seemed never-ending as the Maze kept building and building up to an intense peak. Perazzo did his best work during the Talking Heads set. However, out of all the Phish tunes, he sounded best during Maze and Simple. Simple, a song that drastically improved in 1996, was up next. This song used to be a fairly "simple" rocker. But during the fall tour the band began to add on an extended jam section. The Simple jam at this show was long and beautiful. It was a mellow, but gorgeous jam that eventually segued into Jesus Left Chicago, which began the horn segment of the set. Now it was Dave "the Truth" Grippo's chance to shine. He came onstage dur-

ing Jesus and remained there for the rest of the set. Grippo belted out some soulful solos, making this a good version, but nothing like the 1995 Halloween masterpiece in Chicago itself. The set ended with Suzy Greenberg, a song Phish traditionally plays when the horn section is in the house. Gary Gazaway took an atonal solo worthy of his nickname "El Buho." There were a few quick Born Under Punches teases so we could get a last tiny dose of Talking Heads before we went home. The horns came back out for an appropriate Frankenstein encore. The horns added another dimension to this classic rock tune. This unique version was a great way to end the night with a final nod to Halloween, the holiday when some of the best Phish shows of all-time occurred. In fact, the show was so amazing that Atlanta city officials determined that the Omni could never rock so hard again and was not safe enough for any more concerts. Phish had blown the roof off the arena and their powertools had loosened the foundation. A few months later the Omni was demolished. Rumor had it that you could still hear the bizarre feedback from the Overload languishing in the rubble.

10/31/96: Remain in Light —by Eric Fleming

When I first heard (a few days after the fact) that Phish's musical costume for 1996 was the album *Remain in Light* by Talking Heads, I suddenly found myself, for the first time in four or five years (the entire span of my being a fan of the group), not all that interested in hearing a tape of the show. Talking Heads just didn't do it for me.

Of course, I should qualify this by saying that I hadn't really heard anything from David Byrne and company for many years. I'd seen their movie, *Stop Making Sense*, around the time of its initial release, and maybe I was too young, or maybe it wasn't the type of music I was into at the time, but for whatever reason, I walked away from my initial Talking Heads experience utterly unimpressed. The same could be said of *Remain in Light*. While I hadn't heard the entire album, I knew a couple of songs, of course, and they were catchy, no doubt, but it just didn't seem the kind of thing I'd want to waste an hour or so listening to, Phish or no Phish.

So I ignored the existence of the concert for a couple months. No desire to hear it; no desire to get a copy; I was happy knowing it existed, but I didn't have any burning need for it. And then I heard that Phish was going to be broadcast nationally on a syndicated, concert-of-the-week radio program. I immediately made plans to listen. As it turns out, the concert selected was from two days after the most recent Halloween show, 11-2-96, from West Palm, FL. I listened, I was impressed, occasionally I was absolutely blown away.

My number one, all-time favorite Phish moment comes from this show…I've heard it referred to as the Crosseyed Antelope. Thirty-five minutes of (for me, at least), pure musical bliss. First comes "Crosseyed and Painless," a tune from *Remain in Light*, which blends directly ands seamlessly into "Run Like an Antelope," a favorite Phish tune I seem to be hearing too infrequently (at least for my tastes), as of late. I was confused though… "Crosseyed and Painless"…this was Talking Heads? This was from the cover set? I wondered how much like the original the version I'd just heard was? I had to find out, so I set up a trade for the Halloween show and went out and bought the original Talking Heads album.

Now, I can't honestly say this changed my life, but… wow!

There is just something about Phish's performance that Thursday night in Atlanta that really gets under my skin. In a good way! This album was (and still is, I think) a bold choice. Unlike the *White Album* and *Quadrophenia*, which are both very well-known albums from very well-known "classic rock" bands, *Remain in Light* is a fairly recent album from a fairly new band. Respected and popular, but still recent. In my case, recent enough that I was young enough when it was first released to ignore it, and too turned off by its mid-'80s release to want to retrace my steps and listen to it later!

I think what I had been assuming about the Halloween costumes was that this was Phish's chance to, at least for one night, don the guise of their musical influences. I think that assumption is, for the most part, correct. Where I had erred was in assuming the band stopped being influenced after they became a band!

Phish has shown, especially in recent years, the ability to continue being influenced, by an astounding variety of musicians. Bluegrass, punk, alternative, and yes, new wave pop… or however you classify Talking Heads.

But, what it is that makes this costume so much better than any of the others, and why is this the most influential cover on the band and how they play music? Of course, these are strictly my opinions, as I do not intend to speak for anyone other than myself (that being an insanely risky proposition), but moving on…

I think the first thing that struck me upon listening to this set was the utter perfection of it. Not to say that all the notes were exactly where they were supposed to be (because they're not, because they never are!), but this costume just seems to fit. Perfectly. One of the things I didn't care for exactly with the first two Halloween costume shows (and I say this was the affirmation that I really LOVED the first two shows!), was they kind of left Page out in the cold. Now, he took most of the lead vocals at the *Quadrophenia* show, but there aren't a whole of keyboard parts (other than banging out chords) in the Beatles show, so this was nice. The textures in this show are just incredible. Unlike the first Halloween, which sounded like a small group, the sound here was simply amazing. The addition of Karl Perazzo (one of Santana's percussionists), was absolutely crucial in that respect. As subsequent shows (11/2/96 in particular) have demonstrated, an additional percussionist can really add to the band's normal, four-piece, experience.

The groove going on during this set is also something I'd not experienced previously. The combination of funky, danceable music, extra percussion, saxophone and all-around incredible playing had my whole body bouncing along with the music.

Something else I noticed during the set was the amazing amount of movement in the music. Occasionally, Phish jams can become static, with the group members getting locked into a groove and sitting there, not moving anywhere, just repeating. That was never the case in this set… the music was always moving, always changing; there was always something happening. A drum fill here, a saxophone riff over there, a keyboard wash or a bass slap, all moving in and around the rhythm of the guitar. It was beautiful!

Here was Phish as I'd always wanted them… exactly how I knew I wanted my music… without ever having had the idea I was unhappy! This was a perfect musical moment, and a true musical costume. Many times, in performing a cover song (especially in a situation like this, where the tune may only be played publicly that one time), the performing band has no time to do anything other than "become" the band who originated the song. Play the same notes and try to sound like the original.

Phish did that (listen to Trey and Fishman doing their best David Byrne impressions on vocals!), but so much more. Unlike previous album covers, Phish jammed on these tunes right away. These are still very identifiable as David Byrne's songs, but "as performed by Phish." The band grabbed these eight songs, and did them justice as Talking Heads tunes, but turned them into Phish songs at the same time. And in the exchange, something else happened, something perhaps more important.

One of the most drastic changes in the band's playing (and compositional) style happened, in my opinion, because of *Remain in Light*. Something I sometimes forget is that this didn't just happen. The band didn't wake up the morning of October 31, 1996, and decide to play this album. They didn't wake up the year before and decide that it might be fun to play *Quadrophenia* that night! This was planned out and re-hearsed… quite a bit, I would imagine. And that is where the transfer took place… from the wailing solos of early Phish and harsh experimentalism of 1994-1995, to the groove-laden playing we_ve been accustomed to the last few years. Sometime in the middle of learning/practicing/perfecting this album, the style took hold. The band decided it liked playing together as equals, something that has been said for many years, but in my opinion has just recently come into being.

Listening to recent shows and recent compositions, those attributes are easy to hear. Group playing and group soloing is more the norm. Songs seem to be written more with the idea of feel than before. Compared to lengthy, through-composed pieces like Guyute and Chalk Dust Torture, which are very rarely different live than they are on album, the newer songs seem almost to have been written as launching pads for extended playing.

The best example of the influence *Remain in Light* had on the band (and compositions in particular) actually has more to do with one of Trey's solo project a year and a half later. Brought together as a one-shot band, the Eight Foot Fluorescent Tubes performed their one-and-only show on April 17, 1998. The purpose of this was a charity event, but also to showcase new songs Trey had written, but didn't think fit into the style of Phish. Listening to this concert, the Talking Heads influence is readily apparent, and it would only be a couple more years until a couple of the songs from that show (First Tube and Sand), plus one that debuted on his solo tour (Jibboo) showed up on the new Phish album. The band's sound had changed so much since 1996, that those very same Talking Heads-influenced songs now fit in perfectly with Phish's current sound.

This is, in my opinion, a much more drastic (and long-lasting) effect on the band than either the *White Album* or *Quadrophenia* has had. Of course, this may change tomorrow. Or in six or seven years, some Halloween night, we may all be treated to that evening's musical costume… the complete cover of a Bjork album, and come to realize over the course of the next year or two exactly how much of a difference her sampling and voice-over techniques have had on Phish. And that's part of the beauty of a musical costume… the ability to turn yourself, if only for one night, into someone else. Or maybe, if you choose… for longer.

Saturday, October 31, 1998
The Thomas and Mack Center, Las Vegas, NV

Viva Las Vegas! For the fourth year, Phish would embark on a musical journey as other performers. This year, the band took the persona of the influential Velvet Underground.

Lisbeth and David Karpman

Halloween (Jeremy Birchman and Elise Ryerson)

For the second year in a row, ushers handed out a Phishbill to the fans. Phillip Zerbo described the program:

"A few words about the Phishbill…the front is just like the Omni [Halloween 1996], with "Phish Halloween" in the place of "The Velvet Underground *Loaded*" that dons the cover of the album. Page 2 is a hysterical mock-ad for "Roggae," "The first and only pill clinically proven to treat pattern dreadlock loss in men." Page 3 is the playbill, program order. Pages 4 and 5 has the back cover of Loaded, a picture of the Velvet Underground, and a narrative of VU history, then on Phish's choice of the album. Pages 6 and 7 are "Who's Who in the Cast" and "Who's Who in the Crew", all of which is very funny! By the way, the picture of Mike and the bird is from 8/15/98 between sets 1 and 2. The bird's name is "Angel" and she is very friendly, and Mike seems quite taken by her, I had the extreme pleasure to be introduced by Mike to this now famous bird at Lemonwheel. The back cover is a insane picture (Mike with the hat and banjo are a riot), a mock ad for "Dirt. Vermont Organic Dirt. Something you can stay with." A HUGE round of applause to Jason Colton and Cynthia Brown from Dionysian and everyone else involved in putting together such a riotous playbill!"

The first set included a funky Sneakin' Sally, which made a sneaky jump into Chalk Dust Torture. Mike's Song > Frankie Says > Weekapaug Groove closed the first set—most were not expecting such a high-octane song so early in the night

Lawn Boy was a highly appropriate tune, given the camp nature of Las Vegas shows.

Phillip Zerbo: "I want to see Page doing this on the bar-top stage in the entrance atrium of the MGM Grand! Man, he'd kill the place! Oh,

and may I take this opportunity to thank our man on the bass guitar, Mister Michael "Cactus" Gordon for that stunning solo! Move over Tom Jones, there is a new act in town!"

Although many fans did not seem too familiar with the music they heard during the second set, it proved to be most enjoyable. Unlike years past, *Loaded* included songs that had been played by Phish before: Sweet Jane (Merriweather, 1998) and Lonesome Cowboy Bill (in Fishman's Henrietta rotation for 1995). The *Loaded* set also included striking versions of Rock 'n Roll (now a familiar tune to see in Phish's sets) and Oh! Sweet Nuthin'.

More so than any other year (with all due respect to *Remain in Light* in 1996), Phish took the opportunity to experiment with their musical costume and weave their own personal touches into its fabric. Witness the following chart prepared by David "ZZYZX" Steinberg, which compares each song's length as originally performed by the Velvets and as performed by Phish:

	Phish Version	VU Version
Who Loves the Sun	3:01	2:50
Sweet Jane	8:13	3:55
Rock 'n Roll	13:11	4:47
Cool it Down	6:58	3:05
New Age	8:07	5:20
Head Held High	4:15	2:52
Lonesome Cowboy Bill	9:17	2:48
Found a Reason	4:28	4:15
Train Round the Bend	6:17	3:20
Oh! Sweet Nuthin'	8:40	7:23

Mitch Goldman gave his thoughts on the *Loaded* set:

"Suffice it to say that...

a. this was the best played and most emotionally resonant of the four Phish "musical costume" shows.

b. these tunes were claimed by Phish as their very own, vehicles for all their old school tension-buildup-release mechanisms, as well as an outpouring of emotion, doubt, anguish, and beauty in nearly every song.

c. Sweet Jane and Rock & Roll were two of the best played performances I've ever heard from Phish.

d. New Age and Oh! Sweet Nuthin' were moving, passionate, and more accurate in their emotional conveyance than even the original VU versions.

I can't say enough about this set...Jane and Rock & Roll were positive rock apocalypses. Jane was NOTHING like the version played at Merriweather; it contained the original extra intro, it built and built and built, and was then totally outdone by Rock & Roll, as convincing a Phish performance as anything I've seen yet. Page did a credible Lou Reed impression, just pouring his heart into the tunes while maintaining that Reed tunelessness so appropriate to the music. Trey sang lead on Sun, Cool It, Head Held High, New Age and Reason (with Mike doing the spoken word bit); Fish sang Cowboy Bill; Page sang Jane, Rock, and an emotional Sweet Nuthin' set closer; Mike sang Train. They took a 40 minute record and turned it into a one hour and 17 minute emotional roller coaster of a set. It was a positive revelation. They could have left then and we still would have witnessed one of the great shows of their career."

The third set proved to be controversial and widely interpreted. Wolfman's Brother, an appropriate choice for Halloween, was over 30 minutes long and included an excellent spacey/airy jam with distinct Roggae and Lifeboy teases, among others. But the jam was dark and unlike anything that fans had heard during a Phish show. The jam eventually morphed into an emotional Piper, and then into Ghost to close the set. But the Ghost seemed to be short, and ended abruptly. Overall, the set left some fans amazed and others disappointed. Chris Bertolet commented on the Wolfman's:

"One of the most polarizing improvisations of Fall, 1998 had to be Phish's marathon "ambient" jam during "Wolfman's Brother" on Halloween in Las Vegas. It's not unusual for this song to spark long, exploratory adventures. But this one was different.

Somewhere around twenty minutes into the jam, sonic ooze and aural smoke began to curl eerily around the crannies of the Thomas and Mack. Much as they did in their ambient jam at the Lemonwheel, Phish was probing new territory. Certainly, I had heard Phish play dark before, but they were always *playing* dark.

No big black furry creatures this night. The music pulsing from the stage was fully pregnant with human doubt, fear, frailty, even despair. It was darkness made sound, and I found myself deeply...unsettled.

I remember looking around to see how others were reacting. Many folks were sitting down, suddenly heavy with some burden. Others were noticeably sighing. A few had tears in their eyes. One or two were fiddling with personal effects, as if to distract themselves. Still others had just tuned out the blackness in favor of muted conversation. Almost no one was dancing.

As for myself, well, I didn't "like it." But I was rapt. As I shifted uncomfortably in my seat, I realized that the music had burrowed inside me. Undeniably, we were listening to art. Unsettling art, disturbing art, and decidedly non-Phishy art, at least in my framework of prior experience. But it was only by shedding the burden of prior experience that I came to appreciate the expression, and to connect with these artists on a new and more meaningful plane. As a fan of Phish and a lover of music, it was a watershed moment for me.

Even today, I can't find it in myself to argue with the many fans who were "repulsed" or "put off" by that jam. I can't find it in myself to criticize those who sat down in their seats, re-arranged their wallets, carried on quiet conversations, thought silently, cried or screamed. We were unsettled, and that's okay. We were unsettled together."

For the only time in the 1990's, Phish's Halloween show was, in part, radio rebroadcast. Selections for the rebroadcast, which ran as a two hour special, included Axilla, Roggae, Birds of a Feather, Frankie Sez, Sweet Jane, Rock and Roll, Cool It Down, New Age, Head Held High, I Found A Reason, and Oh! Sweet Nuthin'. The show was syndicated in over fifty markets nationwide.

Ever wonder what effect the Phish musical costume has on sales of the original album? Note that many fans in search of the album were only able to find the version reissued on Rhino Records. Titled *Fully Loaded*, it also includes an alternate version of the entire album plus ten additional bonus tracks. The original album was believed to be out of print but all signs indicate that this is not true. Regardless, in the week

after Phish's performance, 571 copies of the single-disc version were sold (compared to 157 the previous week, 107 the week before that, and 114 the week before that). Also, 474 copies of the double-disc *Fully Loaded* version were sold (compared to 113 the previous week, 100 the week before, and 67 the week before that).

10/31/98 Thomas and Mack Center, Las Vegas, Nevada
—by Charlie Dirksen

A general admission event, fans were anxiously awaiting the show in line hours before doors. The creativity of the costumes fans were wearing was remarkable. Beautiful and often hysterical costumes everywhere (though there were too many Hunter S. Thompsons and superheroes). Most memorable was a group of at least 5 people dressed as identical aliens.

The show opened with the "real" Axilla. No part II lyrics or ending. It pumped up the audience from the start. PYITE began well with a groovy, somewhat extended opening, but the Trey-flubs later on in the version unfortunately spit it into the weak category. Roggae was wonderful, though it didn't charm me as much as the 7/19/98 Shoreline version, or many other versions from the summer. It is one of my favorite "new" Phish songs, though. The Birds in this set was excellent, and I was reminded of the second version from the Island Tour earlier in the year. Sneaking Sally was a mid-set surprise and treat, and though it funked along well enough, it didn't chart new territory (it wasn't as unique as the Ominous Seapods version that I'd witnessed earlier in the day at Legends Lounge). The segue into Chalk Dust wasn't as smooth as it could have been, but the Chalk Dust itself — like the Birds — was a well-above-average version. The leap into Lawn Boy was impressively swift and clean, taboot. Lawn Boy was really appreciated by the audience (lots of applause), even if the solo that Mike took in it wasn't anything unusually inspired.

A twenty-six minute Mike's Groove!? At this point in the set!? Many of us assumed that we'd get three hour long (i.e., short) sets, and this 'groove smacked some folks upside the head for deigning to predict Phish. The Mike's Song had its moments (repetitive but forceful; not really funky), and Frankie Sez was nice (I love this song), but the real action came in the Weekapaug. Trey clearly lost his mind (and the band, it seemed, did as well) at several points in this all-over-the-place, never-ending 'paug. But everything came around at the end. One hell of a great way to end the set!

The second set was the Velvet Underground's *Loaded*. Get this VU CD, and get the tape of Phish covering it. If you are low on funds, though, get the first Velvet Underground CD, *VU & Nico*. I wish Page

had been higher in the mix for this set, particularly on Train Round the Bend, but it was a well-jammed set nonetheless, and certainly worth hearing — whether you are a fan of Lou Reed's or not. [note: *Loaded* is closer to a Lou Reed album, in my opinion, than a VU album, given the absence of Cale, but whatever]. Sweet Jane, Rock & Roll and New Age were particularly inspired. Many fans think *Loaded* is Phish's finest "cover set," since they phishified an already excellent rock album. Though I agree that Phish improvised more in the *Loaded* set than in any other "cover album set," the *Loaded* set is not my favorite. 10/31/94 will always be one of my favorite Phish shows, though not for its improvisation. The *White Album* was one of my favorites growing up, and I will never forget witnessing Phish cover it live and making rock and roll history. *Remain in Light* was another album I loved when I was in high school. Phish's performance of it in 1996 was very moving and perfect. It is ironically one of my favorite sets of Phish. *Quadrophenia* in 1995 was also well-played and very enjoyable, with some great jams. Unlike the *White Album*, *Quadrophenia* and *Remain in Light* Halloween sets, though, Phish's *Loaded* set was more open, relaxed and free. Phish jammed most of the songs as best they could, not trying to stay within a song's traditional composition. Trey in particular seemed to be having a blast. I will never forget watching them perform this set — and under Chris's magnificent light show, too.

The third set of this Halloween show is still, to this day, controversial. Some people loathed it, while others loved it. The Wolfman's Brother was outrageously improvisational. I thought some of its jamming was good, while the rest was repetitive dogshit — and difficult to tolerate given the little sleep I had in the previous 40 hours. Almost no one was dancing during it. Many people took the opportunity to nap. Things picked up when Piper entered the picture, of course, but there were still a fairly large number of people sitting down (including me). The jamming out of Piper was good, but not as unpredictable and engaging as that on 8/8/98 at Merriweather. Phish was nevertheless improvising in a risky manner in this set, and I respect them for taking the leap (a leap they had only seldom taken since 1995). The Ghost was probably no more than 8-10 minutes or so, and seemed to be going along just fine, when Trey suddenly killed it by sustaining a noise and leaving the stage. Some speculated that he may have been pissed at Mike, since very shortly before he left, he made some motion at Mike with his hand. Whatever happened, the Ghost was very weak, in light of its ending (which was the same sort of b.s. ending that the ending to Halley's was on 7/20 in Ventura). The Monkey encore wasn't anything amazing, even though I have always been amused by this song (just not as amused as I once was). Tweezer Reprise was remarkably powerful and a very strong way to end yet another memorable Phish show.

BEST VERSIONS

by Jeremy D. Goodwin and Chris Glushko

This is probably the most thoroughly and unapologetically subjective feature of The Phish Companion. A crack team of Mockingbird obsessive-compulsive types (essentially Jeremy and Chris) have endevoured to compile the impossible: a list of the ten or so best versions of every Phish jam song. Whereas timings and notes regarding notable versions in the evolution of many songs can be found elsewhere in the book, this list is purely and utterly a matter of opinion. It should, however, provide invaluable assistance to those seeking to hear the best versions their favorite Phish songs.

The reader will note a heavy slant towards material from 1993 and on; this is because we feel that Phish is just a whole lot better nowadays. For instance, to scan a list of notable early versions of Bath-

tub Gin, you'd do best to look at the Jamming Tunes Summary Tables. For our purposes here, there's no need to mention any versions prior to 8/13/93, the first truly breakthrough version.

While none of us can claim to have heard every version of every song, we can assure you that between the two of us we've heard pretty much every major version of these songs from the last six or more years. We're confident that these lists will provide the reader with an informed snapshot of the greatest versions of the most improvisationally inclined songs in the Phish reperetoire.

The Ghost list was compiled by Marty Acaster, and the Tweezer list was compiled from Charlie Dirksen's reviews and ratings. Check the Mockingbird website for information on how to participate in a survey version of this section for the next edition of The Phish Companion.

YEM
10/31/95 Chicago
12/31/95 MSG
7/?/97 Lyon, France
11/28/97 Worcester, MA
7/25/92 Vermont
10/24/95 Madison, WI
11/16/91 Bayou
12/9/95 Albany
11/18/95
7/2/98 Copenhagen
7/15/99
5/5/93

Mike's Song
6/22/94
12/31/95 MSG
12/30/93 Portland
12/1/95 Hershey
8/16/96 Clifford Ball
7/22/97 Walnut Creek
7/31/97 Shoreline
12/13/97 Albany
12/2/97 Philly
12/31/97 MSG
12/7/97 Philly
6/22/95
12/6/96 Vegas

Stash
7/2/97 Amsterdam
11/14/95 Orlando
12/29/95 Worcester
7/1/95 Great Woods
7/8/94 Great Woods
11/19/97 Winstom-Salem
10/10/99 Albany
4/2/98 Nassau
11/30/97 Worcester Centrum
11/13/97 Vegas

DWD
8/17/97 Great Went
6/26/95 SPAC
12/12/95 Providence
11/27/96 Seattle
2/17/97 Amsterdam
7/22/97 Walnut Creek
8/16/96 Clifford Ball
12/31/96 Fleet Center
11/23/97 Winston-Salem
12/31/99 Cypress
12/15/99 MCI Center
         (Wash DC)
7/17/99 Oswego

9/29/97
11/12/94

Weekapaug Groove
12/6/96 Vegas
11/22/97 Hampton
12/31/95 MSG
4/3/98 Nassau
12/28/94 Philly Spectrum
12/31/97 MSG
8/9/97 Alpine Valley
11/27/98 Worcester
12/2/97 Philly
12/13/97 Albany
10/7/99 Nassau
9/16/99 Shoreline

Runaway Jim
11/29/97 Worcester
12/31/95 MSG
6/15/95 Walnut Creek
7/2/95 Sugarbush
7/31/97 Shoreline
8/14/96 Hershey
8/3/93
8/11/98 Star Lake
12/31/98 MSG
7/18/99 Oswego

Reba
5/16/95 Lowell
8/14/96 Hershey
8/17/96 Clifford Ball
4/17/92 Warfield Theatre
2/20/93 Roxy Theatre
12/31/95 MSG
10/31/94 Glenns Falls
8/16/93
12/15/99
12/31/99 Oswego
6/23/95 Waterloo
7/13/99 Great Woods
11/27/98 Worcester

Bathtub Gin
8/17/97 Great Went
12/29/95 Worcester
8/13/93 Muratt Theatre
12/5/95 Amherst
7/25/97 Dallas
7/1/97 Amsterdam
11/23/97 Winston-Salem
7/21/97 VA Beach
12/15/99 MCI Center

(Wash DC)
12/2/99 Detroit
10/1/99 Ames, Iowa
11/28/98 Worcester
11/9/98 Chicago (so bertolet doesn't
         mbitch)
11/7/96 Rupp Arena
9/12/99 Portland, Oregon

Wolfman's
3/1/97 Hamburg
7/25/97
8/2/97 Gorge
8/8/97 Chicago
8/16/97 Great Went
11/19/97 Winston-Salem
11/30/97 Worcester Centrum
11/18/98 Greenville, sc
10/31/98 Vegas
12/28/98 MSG
7/13/99 Great Woods

Ghost
12/11/97 Rochester
         War Memorial
12/13/97 Pepsi Arena;
         Albany, Ny
8/13/97 Starlake
7/2/98 Copenhagen
9/12/99 Potland
9/17/98 Shoreline
7/21/98 Desert Sky
8/16/98 SHE WORE LEMON...
         WHEEL
11/19/98 Winston Salem...
         koool whatever
12/31/98 EMESGEEEEEEE
7/4/99 Lakewood
7/23/97 Lakewood
11/17/97 Denver
7/3/97 Nurnenmenberg

Tweezer
12/28/90
4/27/91
4/21/92
5/06/93
8/12/93
8/15/93
5/07/94
6/10/94
7/06/94
11/02/94
11/23/94
11/28/94

6/14/95
10/22/95
11/30/95
12/02/95
12/14/95
11/03/96
11/27/96
11/26/97
12/06/97
8/01/98
10/30/98
9/18/99
12/16/99
12/30/99
6/24/00

Hood
12/31/93 Worcester Centrum
11/12/94 Kent Center
12/30/94 MSG
10/23/94 Ufla
7/1/95 Great Woods
12/5/95 Amherst
12/30/95 MSG
12/6/96 Vegas
8/10/97 Deer Creek
8/17/97 Great Went
12/31/98 MSG
12/18/99
12/11/99

Simple
10/31/94 Glenns Falls
6/17/94 Milwauke
11/8/96 Champagn
12/6/96 Vegas
10/26/96 Charlotte
12/31/98 MSG
11/29/98 Worcester
8/16/97 Great Went

Soam
7/2/95 Great Woods
8/10/97
12/31/99
8/2/97
PNC 98

THE GUEST BOOK

Written by Craig DeLucia, Charles Franz,
Ellis Godard, Julia Mordaunt, Erik Swain,
Mark Toscano, and Phillip Zerbo

Compiled and Edited by Craig DeLucia

Part of the beauty of the jamband scene is the way that performers welcome each other to the stage. Phish shows have been home to scores of special guests, from accomplished musicians to family members to child trombone prodigies. This chapter will give you some background on every guest that has been documented to appear on-stage with Phish in the last seventeen years.

Thanks to Dean Budnick, Charlie Dirksen, Benji Eisen, Matt King, Mark Lynn, Christian McKee, Michael Preston, Aaron Rosenthal, Jeremy Welsh, Kazimierz O. Wrzenski, and "Fred" for their submissions. Additionally, thanks to Geoff Ecker, who had been maintaining a summary of guest information that served as a basis for parts of this chapter.

Apfelbaum, Peter
● *See Also:* The Cosmic Country Horns
● *Known Appearances:* 11/30/96
● *Notes:* Peter is one of the few artists who can claim to have appeared on-stage with both Phish and the Grateful Dead. A Grammy-nominated musician, he has written for the Kronos Quartet, appeared in studio with trumpeter Don Cherry, and toured with such acts as Jai Uttal. He has also inspired and led his own musical projects, such as the Hieroglyphics Ensemble (which included fellow jazz musicians Benny Green and Josh Redman) and the Peter Apfelbaum Sextet.

Though he also plays piano and percussion, his work with Phish has been on the saxophone. In addition to his membership in The Cosmic Country Horns, Peter joined Phish at The Arco Arena in Sacramento in the fall of 1996. There, he joined in on "Timber Ho!," "Taste," and "Funky Bitch." He later returned with John McEuen to perform an "Amazing Grace" jam and an inspiring "Possum" encore. The "Taste" is often mentioned as a fan-favorite version.

Aquarium Rescue Unit, The
● *Nickname:* "ARU"
● *See Also:* Otiel Burbridge, Jimmy Herring, Colonel Bruce Hampton, Reverend Jeff Mosier
● *Known Appearances:* 11/7/91, 5/5/93
● *Notes:* Aquarium Rescue Unit was founded by the legendary Colonel Bruce Hampton in the early 1990's. The band would receive acclaim in jamband circles throughout the first half of the decade before disbanding to allow its members to pursue other interests, including such offshoots as Frogwings, Jazz is Dead, and Colonel Bruce Hampton's various musical projects.

While the ARU was developing a loyal fan base in the southeast, Phish found themselves attempting to gain ground in the area. The bands entered into a symbiotic relationship, sharing bills around the country. ARU allowed Phish to open for them in the south and spread their music to new audiences; Phish returned the favor by allowing the ARU to open in the northeast. And, of course, the two bands would be integral in planning the first HORDE tour. Phish's affinity for the Colonel Bruce and his ARU has been documented in multiple places. For a fun example on tape, pick up 5/5/92. ARU opened for Phish that night, and Trey referenced them (and chided them) during a hysterical "Icculus," going so far as to remark jokingly that the ARU had been a "feeble bluegrass band" until they read the Helping Friendly Book. Lest Trey's comments be taken seriously, remember that he has commented that the ARU's sound was a distinct influence on his writing the song "Llama."

While individual members of ARU have joined Phish on stage, twice did the two bands get together and jam at once. The first, on 11/7/91 (featuring such songs as "David Bowie"), is not as widely circulated or as memorable as the second. On 5/5/93, to cap an already stellar show, Phish welcomed the ARU during a long "You Enjoy Myself." The resulting jam is one of the most exploratory pieces of music Phish has ever performed.

Artis the Spoonman
● *Known Appearances:* 10/12/91
● *Notes:* Based in Seattle, Washington, Artis the Spoonman is a locally legendary and accomplished spoon player, poet, and songwriter who has toured internationally with his act and made many appearances with other musicians and on television. He claims to have appeared with Frank Zappa, Aerosmith, Pete Seeger, k.d.lang, Bob Weir, Soundgarden, Itzhak Perlman, The Seattle Philharmonic Orchestra, Ani DiFranco, Left Over Salmon, and String Cheese Incident, among others. Artis opened for Phish at several of the Northwestern tour shows in October 1991. He appeared onstage during Set II and the first encore of the 10/12/91 Roseland Theater show and played his spoons on "Brother," "If I Only Had a Brain," "Harry Hood," "Tweezer Reprise," "Lawn Boy," and "Rocky Top."

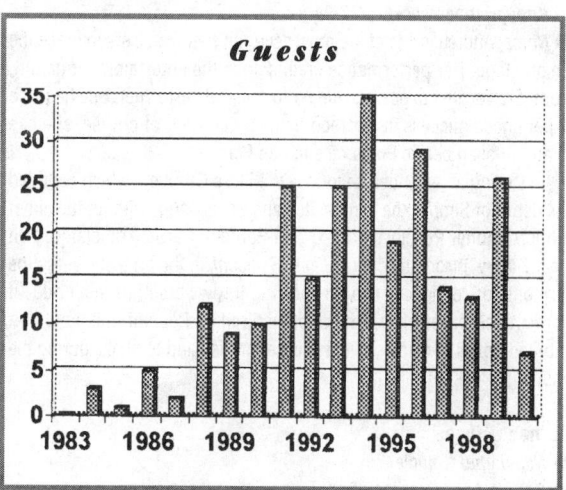

Baby Gramps

● *Known Appearances:* 8/26/93

● *Notes:* Baby Gramps is not so much a man, but a one-man circus act. With a voice like Popeye on helium, Gramps has been known to do tightrope-walking in addition to performing his unique brand of bizarre honky-skronk on a beat-up old guitar. Also a big fan of palindromes and other linguaphiliac absurdities and curiosities, Baby Gramps was the inspiration for the Flecktones' album *UFO Tofu*, which contains a few musical palindromes.

He is often associated with Leftover Salmon, and indeed they helped distribute his first CD, *Same Old Timeously*. Gramps opened extensively for Salmon on their 1998 tours, almost always making an appearance on-stage with them for tunes like "Fairies," "Washington at Valley Forge," and "Ask the Fish." Gramps himself also tours occasionally, either solo or with singing saw and homemade-bass player Curtis Chamberlain. He can be seen most frequently on the West Coast, and plays regular gigs around the Portland and Seattle areas, specializing in fairs and festivals.

Gramps has made three appearances at Phish shows during Summer 1993 when Phish hit his Northwestern U.S. stomping grounds. Gramps opened for Phish at shows in Vancouver, Seattle, and Portland. It was at this third show that Baby Gramps actually shared the stage with Phish, performing the enigmatic "Tea Tray Song" with Fishman on vacuum during the second set. In subsequent solo appearances, he has been known to reference this Portland show (8/26/93), stating that those Phish guys are nice, and they were *almost* able to keep up with his playing!

Baggott, Tom

● *Known Appearances:* 5/11/91

● *Notes:* Add Tom to the list of old-school fans and friends who have guested with Phish. His only known appearance was during the 5/11/91 "You Enjoy Myself," where he jammed along on harmonica. This may have been part of the band's thank-you for Tom organizing the infamous bus trip to the Paradise in Boston for Phish's first show there. Tom currently works with the New York-based jamband Ominous Seapods.

Baker, Andrea

● *Known Appearances:* 5/27/94

● *Notes:* Andrea is one of the most accomplished vocalists to grace the Phish stage. Her performance credits span the entertainment gamut, from jazz vocalist to operatic singer to musical performer. She has also experienced success in her recording career. And, of course, she has sung in Italian before Phish fans in San Francisco.

During an extended second set "Mike's Groove," which included the debut of Simple, the band halted and Baker sang, without the aid of a microphone, Puccini's aria "O Mio Babbino Caro" (translated: "Oh Dear Daddy") from the opera *Gianni Schicchi*. In the aria, she sings the torments of young love and threatens to throw herself from a bridge if her love is not returned. No doubt inspired by Puccini, the band distributed boxes of macaroni and cheese for the band to shake during the ensuing "Possum."

Barnes, Bruce

● *Nickname:* "Sunpie"

● *Known Appearances:* 3/2/93

● *Notes:* Bruce "Sunpie" Barnes, leader of Sunpie & The Louisiana Sunspots, is often hailed as one of the best harmonicists in Louisiana. He is also an accomplished accordionist and vocalist. Sunpie is not just a musician, though. He played professional football with the Kansas City Chiefs and has appeared in several commercials and feature films. And, perhaps most admirably, he spends his days as a Louisiana Park Ranger, protecting the wildlife of the local swamps.

As Bruce is from Louisiana, it was only fitting that Phish called upon his services at Tipitina's in New Orleans in March of 1993. There, the band rocked through blues songs "It's My Life," "Luke-a-Roo," and "Choo Choo Ch' Boogie." Trey returned the favor at Jazzfest in 1996, sitting in with Sunpie and his band.

Beauford, Carter

● *See Also:* The Dave Matthews Band

● *Known Appearances:* 4/21/94, 10/15/94

● *Notes:* Carter Beauford is best known as the drummer for The Dave Matthews Band. The whole band joined Phish on-stage in Winston-Salem for an inspired "All Along the Watchtower" encore on April 21, 1994. Beauford began the festivities by engaging in a interesting drum jam with Fishman before "Watchtower" began. Similarly, he appeared with Fishman in a drum jam that led into the debut of "The Maker" on October 15 of the same year.

Carter is an accomplished musician in his own right. He has also released an instructional video called "Under the Table and Drumming." Interestingly, his involvement in the DMB might not have occurred had he been awarded the job he had auditioned for earlier—drummer in the house band on Arsenio Hall's late-night television show.

Ben and Jerry

● *Known Appearances:* 8/17/96

● *Notes:* These ice cream moguls have two things in common with Phish: they're from Vermont, and they care about the environment. Phish recognized the first at The Clifford Ball in 1996, where Ben and Jerry provided vocals on the first "Brother" in over three years. Then, in 1997, they collaborated again with the release of "Phish Food" ice cream. A portion of the proceeds from sales of "Phish Food" are donated to clean-up efforts at Lake Champlain.

Boston Community Choir

● *Known Appearances:* 12/31/96

● *Notes:* The Boston Community Choir helped Phish ring in a joyous 1997 during the third set and encore of NYE 1996. Wading amidst a sea of balloons that had earlier accumulated on stage, the choir sang during the debut of "Bohemian Rhapsody," a rousing "Julius," and an oh-so-fitting "Amazing Grace." The band seemed to have as much fun performing with the choir as the choir did with them.

Boyle, Karl

● *Known Appearances:* 5/14/88

● *Show Notes:* Karl was Page's music instructor at Goddard. Though they certainly collaborated behind the scenes, Karl only took the stage once: to play sax on "Take the 'A' Train" on 5/14/88.

Bub, Mike

● *See Also:* The Del McCoury Band

● *Known Appearances:* 6/22/00
● *Notes:* Bassist Mike Bub has been a part of the bluegrass community for years. He is best known for his upright bass and baritone vocal talents, and as a member of the Del McCoury Band. Outside of the Oswego appearance with the full Del McCoury Band, Mike's lone stage performance with Phish came during their 2000 Summer Tour opener in Antioch, Tennessee where he played along on bluegrass favorites such as "Uncle Pen" and "I'm Blue I'm Lonesome." In addition to Phish, Bub has played with a slew of renowned artists including Steve Earle, Jerry Douglas, Pete Wernick, Ricky Scaggs and Earle Scruggs.

Buffett, Jimmy
● *Known Appearances:* 11/16/95
● *Notes:* Best known for his radio staple "Margaritaville," Jimmy Buffett has been one of America's most prolific and enduring recording artists over the last thirty years. He is certainly a music icon, though few thought his journey would ever cross paths with Phish. Believe it or not, though, there are a few similarities between the artists. Buffett has a slew of fervent followers who are referred to as "Parrotheads." And lately, some critics have remarked that his long songs on recent albums do not lend themselves to radio airplay.

Buffett was in attendance at the West Palm Beach show on November 16, 1995. The band wanted to bring him out on stage for the encore; he obliged. They could only think of one song that all five musicians knew: Van Morrison's classic "Brown Eyed Girl," which Buffett frequently covers on-stage. And so, for all of eternity, the worlds of Phishheads and Parrotheads became forever entwined.

Burbridge, Oteil
● *See Also:* The Aquarium Rescue Unit
● *Known Appearances:* 6/1/90, 5/2/94
● *Notes:* Oteil has long been involved with the music of Phish. As a member of the Aquarium Rescue Unit, he often shared the stage with Phish in the early 1990's. He has also been a member of The Allman Brothers Band since 1997. And Oteil let his free-form jazz side show as a member of Trey's *Surrender to the Air* project.

In addition to his appearances with the ARU, Otiel has twice graced the Phish stage. On June 1, 1990, he added a second bass guitar to "Run Like an Antelope." And on May 2, 1994, Oteil and fellow bass player Stacy Starkweather joined for an odd "Mike's Song" that saw all the musicians switch instruments on stage.

Bush, Sam
● *Known Appearances:* 6/22/00
● *Notes:* Phish's ties to country music were strengthened when Sam Bush joined them for the better part of the second set in Antioch on 6/22/00. A three-time winner of the National Junior Fiddle Championship in his younger days, Bush delighted the crowd on such Phish standards as "Harry Hood" and "Uncle Pen."

As with many on Nashville's renowned performers, Bush has a resume loaded with credits. As a musician who also plays mandolin and guitar, he is best known as the leader of New Grass Revival, which also starred Bela Fleck, and as a member of the award-winning Nash Ramblers. He has recorded with Trisha Yearwood, Garth Brooks, and Steve Earle. He has toured with Fleck and with Lyle Lovett. He has even produced several albums. But his most impressive credit may be his ded-

ication to the Telluride Bluegrass Festival; as of the 2000 Festival, had appeared at every one since its inception in 1974.

Carlton, John
● *Known Appearances:* 2/24/88
● *Notes:* John is one of a score of old-school guests who were long on talent but on whom we are short on information. From a tape that came into circulation in 1999, it was learned that John guested on drums for "Mustang Sally" and "Sneakin' Sally" on 2/24/88.

Carrey, Jim
● *Known Appearances:* 6/24/99
● *Notes:* Carrey is one of the few non-musicians to appear with Phish, and his appearance was only for a few friends and crew members. Best known as the star of such movies as *Ace Ventura: Pet Detective, The Truman Show,* and *Man on the Moon* and the television series "In Living Color," Carrey was in Vermont shooting his movie *Me, Myself, and Irene* while Phish was rehearsing for their Summer, 1999 tour. Someone hooked the two up and Carrey showed up at Trey's barn for a rehearsal. He added vocals to "Come Together" and "Hey You," neither of which has even been performed before or since. Unfortunately, tapes do not circulate so Carrey's performance of the tunes remains a mystery.

Carter, Jason
● *See Also:* The Del McCoury Band
● *Known Appearances:* 6/22/00
● *Notes:* Carter joined the Del McCoury Band in 1992 as a full time member, playing fiddle and adding baritone vocals. He is known as one of the fastest rising young musicians in bluegrass music and has played with several well-respected musicians in the community, including Ricky Skaggs, Sam Bush and Johnny Cash. His playing has been described as "solid, straight, hard-core bluegrass fiddle style defined by Benny Martin, 'Chubby' Wise, Scotty Stoneman, and Sonny Miller." 1997 saw the release of Carter's first solo effort entitled *On the Move*— an album that features him front and center on fiddle and vocals with the Del McCoury Band backing.

In addition to his appearance with the entire Del McCoury Band in Oswego (1999), Carter joined Phish on 6/22/00 in Antioch, Tennessee. There, he contributed his skills on "Uncle Pen," "I'm Blue I'm Lonesome," and "Freebird," among others.

Chief Jim Billie
● *Known Appearances:* 12/30/99
● *Notes:* Phish did more than perform a legendary set of shows in the swamps of Big Cypress—they met new friends as well. One of these was Chief Jim Billie, Chairman of the Seminole Tribe of Florida since 1979 and singer / songwriter / guitarist. Many of his songs pay homage to the land of his tribe and the people and animals who inhabit it. One of these original compositions, "Big Alligator," is a song about survival and dedication that Billie performed with Phish on 12/30/99. They also collaborated on "Che Hun Ta Mo." Billie's latest album was produced by John McEuen, who also joined on-stage that night.

Claypool, Les
● *Known Appearances:* 5/28/94, 12/6/96
● *Notes:* Few music fans will argue that Les Claypool is one of the

most talented bassists in the world. Imagine the delight of Phish fans at the Laguna Seca Daze festival on May 28, 1994, when Les and Mike Gordon participated in a bass duel during Phish's set! The duel arose from an inspiring "You Enjoy Myself," which also featured Claypool, whose band Primus was also on the bill for the day. In late 1996, Claypool again joined Phish. This time, he brought bandmate Larry Lalonde with him for a bizarre "Harpua" encore that included a long story and other songs sandwiched inside.

Claypool is, of course, best known for his work with Primus. He has also achieved recognition with the Primus side project, Sausage, and his own solo album. He also collaborated on the theme to the television show *South Park* and was instrumental in forming the one-shot power trio Oysterhead.

Cooley, Steve

● *Known Appearances:* 10/10/94
● *Notes:* Steve joined Phish for bluegrass standards "The Old Home Place," "Ginseng Sullivan," and "Nellie Kane" in Louisville, KY on 10/10/94.

Cosmic Country Horns, The

● *See Also:* Peter Apfelbaum, Carl Gerhard, Dave Grippo, The Giant Country Horns, James Harvey, Michael Ray, Tony Tate, Jerome Theriot, Rick Trolsen
● *Known Appearances:* 5/4/94, 12/2/94, 12/3/94
● *Notes:* The name Cosmic Country Horns (or CCH) actually refers to two separate groups of musicians who performed with Phish in 1994. On May 4, the guest horns players were Michael Ray and Carl "Geerz" Gerhard on trumpet, Dave "The Truth" Grippo on alto sax, Tony Tate on tenor sax, Jerome Theriot on baritone sax, and Rick Trolsen on trombone. They joined the band for "You Enjoy Myself," "Buried Alive," "The Landlady," "Julius," "Wolfman's Brother," "Magilla," and "Suzie Greenberg" in the second set, as well as a "Caravan" encore. Then, in December, the CCH joined the band for portions of two California shows. The lineup there featured Grippo on alto sax and percussion, Gerhard and Ray on trumpet, James Harvey on trombone, and Peter Apfelbaum on baritone sax, tenor sax and flute. The song selection on these two nights included "David Bowie," "Buried Alive," "Julius," "The Landlady," "Gumbo," "Caravan," "Suzie Greenberg," "Cavern," "Frankenstein," "Slave to the Traffic Light," "Touch Me," and an "Alumni Blues" jam with introductions.

Stylistically, the CCH were a stark contrast to their predecessors, The Giant Country Horns (GCH). While the GCH had a classical, swing-style to their accompaniment, the CCH had more of a Sun Ra-esque sound, which could be expected given the members of the group and the leadership of Michael Ray. The CCH have not appeared since those two shows in December 1994, but individual members continue to grace the stage. Fans should never rule out a future return; Phish thought enough of the CCH to release a sample of their accompaniment on *A Live One* when they chose to include "Gumbo," recorded on December 2, 1994.

Danforth, Peter

● *Known Appearances:* 7/23/88
● *Notes:* One of the most widely-circulated shows from the 1980's took place at the Underhill, Vermont home of Peter Danforth on July 23, 1988. Tapes of the show often circulate under the title of "Pete's Phabulous Phish Phest." Pete and Dave Grippo joined the band on horns for "Satin Doll" and "Blue Bossa." Currently, Danforth plays sax in the Burlington-based band (sic) with members of Chin Ho!, Dysfunktion, and Currently Nameless.

Daubert, Marc

● *Known Appearances:* 11/3/84, 12/1/84
● *Notes:* Marc Daubert, aka "Daubs," holds an important place in Phish lore. A schoolboy friend of Trey's, Marc would write music with Trey and Tom. As a musical guest, Daubs can be heard adding auxiliary percussion on some early tapes.

Dave Matthews Band, The

● *See Also:* Carter Beauford, LeRoi Moore, Boyd Tinsley, Dave Matthews
● *Known Appearances:* 4/20/94, 4/21/94, 10/15/94
● *Notes:* Phish and the Dave Matthews Band will likely be forever linked in terms of contemporary jambands, despite their varied mainstream appeal. Before the DMB achieved commercial success, though, the two bands shared a kinship. In fact, Phish, who rarely has opening acts at their live shows, allowed the DMB to open on three occasions in 1994. These shows, in Dave's Virginia backyard, allowed the two bands to play to each others' fan bases. And on each occasions where the DMB opened for Phish, fans were treated to full-blown jams involving both bands.

Del McCoury Band, The

● *See Also:* Ronnie McCoury, Jason Carter, Mike Bub
● *Known Appearances:* 7/18/99
● *Notes:* Del McCoury's career began as a member of the Bluegrass Boys with Bill Monroe. Since then, he has become a bluegrass legend, distinguishing himself in several bands and earning the International Bluegrass Music Association's (IBMA) Male Vocalist of the Year honor three consecutive times. He currently leads The Del McCoury Band comprised of Del on rhythm guitar and vocals, his sons Ronnie on mandolin and Rob on banjo, Mike Bub on bass, and Jason Carter on fiddle. The band is a regular at The Grand Ole Opry and has won Album of the Year and Entertainer of the Year awards from the IBMA.

The band's relationship with Phish began at the 1998 Farm Aid concert, where both bands performed. Phish then invited Del's band to perform at the Summer, 1999, Oswego festival; Del's band wowed the crows over at "Echo Lodge" on The Green. Del and company then joined Phish for a rousing "Get Back on the Train," and stayed on for bluegrass numbers such as "I'm Blue I'm Lonesome" and "Beauty of My Dreams."

Dillof, Sofi

● *Known Appearances:* 5/9/89, 8/3/91, 7/9/99, 7/15/99, 10/8/99, 6/29/00
● *Notes:* Sofi Dillof is best known as the wife of Page McConnell and the leader of the Meatstick dance craze. But pick up a few older tapes to hear Sofi actually lend vocals to a few numbers. The first, 5/9/89, was at the release of the original *Junta* cassette. The second was at Amy's Farm on 8/3/91, where Sofi assisted the Dude of Life in performing "Bitchin' Again" with Phish.

Douglas, Jerry

● *Known Appearances:* 7/1/99

● *Notes:* Known as one of the finest dobro players ever, Jerry Douglas has achieved acclaim in country music circles for his amazing finger-picking. His nickname: "Flux," a tribute to his nimble hands and the way

An accomplished studio musician, Douglas has recorded with such bands as Hank Williams, Jr., Reba McIntire, Lyle Lovett, Paul Simon, Bruce Hornsby, The Nitty Gritty Dirt Band, and Maura O'Connell. Douglas also starred in such musical groups as The Whites, Boone Creek (with Ricky Scaggs), and The Country Gentlemen. Jerry is also a member of the select Grammy-winning Guestbook club, as he won in 1983 for "Best Country Instrumental Performance." He has won liter-ally dozens of awards from the International Bluegrass Music Associ-ation and the Academy of Country Music

Douglas, who currently lives in Nashville, joined Phish in Antioch, Tennessee on 7/1/99. He added newfound texture to Wolfman's Brother, not traditionally a guest song, before welcoming Ronnie McCoury and Tim O'Brien for covers of "Beauty of My Dreams" and "Do My Time," as well as Phish originals "Water in the Sky," "Roggae," and "Back on the Train." He then closed out the set by adding Gary Gazaway for "Poor Heart." Unfortunately, Douglas was absent during the summer, 2000 re-turn to Antioch where another lineup of impressive Nashville musicians treated fans to a guest cavalcade.

Drebber, Steven

● *See Also:* The Joneses

● *Known Appearances:* 8/12/89

● *Notes:* Steven Drebber had better have appeared at the Burlington Boat House on August 12, 1989; it was his wedding reception! Steve, the drummer for the 1980's Burlington-based band The Joneses, in-vited Phish to play at the reception. The bands had already shared a his-tory of co-bills and guest appearances. In addition to singing "Blue Sky" to his new bride, Steve played the drums on "Run Like an Antelope" while Fishman played the trumpet and the trombone.

Dude of Life, The

● *Real Name:* Steve Pollak

● *Known Appearances:* 12/1/84, 2/13/87, 9/13/90, 5/12/91, 8/3/91, 11/8/91, 11/20/92, 12/31/92, 5/5/93, 8/9/93, 8/28/93, 7/10/94, 11/24/98

● *Notes:* The Dude of Life, whose real name is Steve Pollak, was once a high school friend of Trey's. The two played together in the band Space Antelope, and collaborated on several songs. When Phish was formed, the two friends kept in touch. The Dude's association with the band stretches as far back as 12/1/84, the first show known to circulate heavily on tape, where he lent his unique vocal stylings to "Skippy the Wondermouse." Some of the Dude's lyrical work, including "Dinner and a Movie," "Fluffhead," "Suzie Greenberg," and "Run Like an Antelope," still appears in Phish's repertoire.

The band responded by backing the Dude on his debut album, *Crimes of the Mind*. The album was recorded in the summer of 1991 but was not released until 1994. When the Dude joins the band on stage it is often to perform one of the songs from the album, including "Dahlia," "TV Show," "Family Picture," "Self," and the title track.

While he usually joins the band to sing one of his songs, or one of the Phish songs he contributed lyrics to, the Dude also has led the

band through an interesting "Mike's Song" (5/12/91, with additional verses) and a fan-favorite, one-time only performance of "Diamond Girl" on New Year's Eve 1992. After more than a four year absence (from July 10, 1994 to November 24, 1998), the Dude rejoined the band for the encore in New Haven. He continues to tour with his own band, which has, in the past, included Fishman on drums.

Ellis, Sydney

● *Known Appearances:* 2/25/97

● *Notes:* As a musician, Sydney Ellis was a late bloomer. She began her career on a session stage in Los Angeles in 1991, a day after her 44th birthday. She continues to record and tour primarily in Europe, both solo and with her Yes Mama Band. Material includes songs culled from her own releases, as well as covers of blues, classic jazz, and folk staples. Sydney joined Phish in Germany on 2/25/97 for three songs, lending vocals to "One Meatball," "Li'l Red Rooster," and "Got My Mojo Workin'."

Eyeburn

● *Known Appearances:* 5/12/89

● *Notes:* An old-school Burlington punk rock outfit, Eyeburn joined Phish at Nectar's for a slamming, mosh-inducing jam inside of "Alumni Blues."

Fishman, Mimi

● *Known Appearances:* 7/19/91, 10/19/91, 5/1/92, 11/23/92, 2/25/93, 4/23/93, 8/20/93, 4/8/94, 10/22/96

● *Notes:* Mimi Fishman currently holds the record for the Phish family member who has made the most on-stage appearances. Given her prowess with Jon's vacuum cleaner and various other musical toys, it seems to be a record well-deserved.

Mimi has substituted for Henrietta on vacuum during "I Didn't Know" (7/19/91), "Terrapin" (10/19/91), "Lengthwise" (11/23/92), "If I Only Had a Brain" (2/25/93), and "Purple Rain" (8/20/93). Mimi also danced in the memorable Madison Square Garden "Freekapaug" on 10/22/96.

Outside of Phish, and her relationship with her famous son, Mimi Fishman is active in raising funds for glaucoma research. An annual concert is held in her honor at The Wetlands Preserve in New York City, with proceeds going to benefit charity. And, in recent years, the website www.jambands.com has conducted an auction of jamband related items to help her raise funds for increased research.

Fichter, Morgan

● *Known Appearances:* 5/27/94

● *Notes:* Bay Area musician Morgan Fichter is best known for her role in the band Camper van Beethoven, whom she joined for their last album. Though Andrea Baker gets the most credit for the Warfield guest slot in 1994, Morgan came out earlier in the set and lend her fiddle to "Nellie Kane" and "My Mind's Got a Mind of Its Own."

Flanagan, Russ

● *Known Appearances:* 2/3/86

● *Notes:* File this one under "M" for "Maybe." An unidentified fiddle player joined along on 2/3/86 and all reports seem to indicate that the guest was Russ, who, at the time, played in The Joneses.

Michael McNamara

Mimi Fishman

Fleck, Bela

- *See Also:* The Flecktones
- *Known Appearances:* 8/21/93, 10/18/94, 11/29/95
- *Notes:* Although best-known as a leader of The Flecktones and as a solo artist, Bela Fleck was creating great music on the banjo long before The Flecktones formation in 1989. His most impressive work outside of his current band came as a member of the famed New Grass Revival. According to his website at www.flecktones.com, Bela is "the only musician to be nominated for Grammys in jazz, bluegrass, pop, country, spoken word, Christian, composition and world music categories." Fleck has appeared on records with artists like Dave Matthews and Bruce Hornsby and has brought such diverse musicians to the live stage as Shawn Colvin, Adrian Belew, and John Medeski.

In addition to his on-stage exploits with The Flecktones, Bela has joined in on "Nellie Kane" (8/21/93, 10/18/94), "Scent of a Mule" (10/18/94), "Lifeboy" (10/18/94), "The Old Home Place" (10/18/94), "Beaumont Rag" (10/18/94), "Llama" (10/18/94), "Taste That Surrounds" (11/29/95), "Poor Heart" (11/29/95), "I'm Blue I'm Lonesome" (11/29/95), "My Long Journey Home" (11/29/95), and "Slave to the Traffic Light" (11/29/95).

Flecktones, The

- *See Also:* Bela Fleck
- *Known Appearances:* 8/21/93, 7/9/97
- *Notes:* The Flecktones are Bela Fleck on banjo, Victor Wooten on bass, Jeff Coffin on saxophone, and Futureman on percussion and Drumitar. Wooten is highly decorated, including the two Bassist of the Year accolades at the Nashville Music Awards and three from Bass Player Magazine. He has also been awarded two Grammys for Best Instrumental Composition and has recorded several solo albums. Coffin has performed and recorded with the Dave Matthews Band, Branford

Marsalis, Bruce Springsteen, Van Morrison, Bruce Hornsby, The Dixie Chicks, and David Grisman, among many others. As a respected session musician, Coffin has appeared on over twenty albums. Add in Fleck himself and Futureman—Roy Wooten, brother of Vic, whose unique Drumitar (a combination of guitar, synthesizer and drum machine) rounds out the quartet's sound.

Individually, each member of The Flecktones is a renowned musician and respected innovator. Together, they have twice appeared on the Phish stage, though Bela Fleck himself has guested on other occasions. On 8/21/93, the Flecktones (in the pre-Coffin days) joined in for the better part of the second set, including "Fee," "Llama," and "David Bowie." Almost four years later, on 7/9/97, the Flecktones (with Coffin) came out during the Tramps Jam in "You Enjoy Myself" and stayed out for a raucous "Ghost" and a set closing "Poor Heart."

Fletcher, Tammy

- *Known Appearances:* 3/18/97
- *Notes:* Tammy Fletcher is a Burlington, Vermont blues singer who fronts The Disciples. She performed with the band at The Flynn Theatre during the March, 1997 benefit, in conjunction with Ben & Jerry's, for the cleanup of Lake Champlain. According to reports, her participation was unplanned—she said Trey spotted her in the audience and plucked her out. She joined the band for "I Told You So" and "Love Me Like a Man." Before jumping on the stage, she was kind enough to calm her date—"Don't worry, Greg," she shouted, "I'm a safe date, baby!"

Fordham, Leigh

- *Known Appearances:* 10/31/95
- *Notes:* Leigh is one of the few non-musicians to make a musical appearance with Phish. He appeared in costume to sing "Bell Boy" during the Quadrophenia musical costume on Halloween, 1995.

Gains, Courtney
● *Known Appearances:* 12/6/96
● *Notes:* Courtney is one of the few guests to have a song lyric reference him: as the actor who played Malachi in *Children of the Corn,* he is forever immortalized in "Rock-a-William." Other popular movies featuring Courtney include *Can't Buy me Love* and *Memphis Belle.* Want more Phishy connections? He appeared in a movie titled *The Landlady* and played Dr. McConnell in *King Cobra.* And, of course, he was part of the bizarre on-stage antics during the 12/6/96 Las Vegas "Harpua." For more stories on Courtney, check out Trey's story in *The Phish Book* about the prank they played together.

Gazaway, Gary
● *Nickname:* "El Buho"; "The Owl"
● *Known Appearances:* 10/31/96, 11/18/96, 7/1/99
Notes: When you think of horns and Phish, the Giant Country Horns immediately jump to mind. Less well-known but of similar stature is Gary "El Buho" Gazaway. Gary sat in on what is widely considered one of the most important sets in Phish history, the *Remain in Light* Halloween costume set on 10/31/96, adding color and texture on trumpet, flugelhorn and trombone. Be sure not to miss the third set of that classic show, which also features Gary (along with Dave Grippo and Karl Perazzo) on "Jesus Just Left Chicago," "Suzie Greenberg," and the powerful "Frankenstein" encore.

Gary has made two subsequent appearances with Phish: On 11/18/96 Gary was the lone guest at the Mid-South Coliseum in Memphis, TN, sitting in on "Tweezer," "Hello My Baby", "Tweezer Reprise," and "Llama." On 7/1/99, Gary joined friends Jerry Douglas, Ronnie Mc-Coury, and Tim O'Brien on the tunes "Doin' My Time" and "Poor Heart."

Most recently, you can find Gary engaged in his own project El Buho; be sure to check out their CD *The Wham Bam Boodle 2000* which features Mike Gordon, as ell as long-time Phish friends Victor Wooten, Oteil Burbridge, and Colonel Bruce Hampton.

Gerhard, Carl
● *Nickname:* "Geerz"
● *See Also:* The Giant Country Horns, The Cosmic Country Horns
● *Known Appearances:* 11/11/88, 2/8/91, 5/17/91, 9/25/91, 11/20/91, 3/24/92, 3/3/93, 4/4/94, 10/14/94, 11/20/98, 11/21/98
● *Notes:* When fans think of horns, they usually think of Geerz. A childhood friend of Page's, Carl has shone as a guest on trumpet for twelve years, including various incarnations of The Giant Country Horns and The Cosmic Country Horns, and is currently a full-time Navy musician who teaches at the Armed Forces School of Music in Virginia Beach, Virginia. His contributions were finally immortalized on the *Hampton Comes Alive* release, where he can be heard on "Cavern" and "Tubthumping."

In addition to his scheduled GCH and CCH appearances, Carl has put his twist on such horn-ready numbers as "Magilla" (2/8/91) and "Take the 'A' Train" (5/17/91), as well as such songs as "La Grange" (2/8/91), But most fans find his repeated work on "Cavern" and "Jesus Just Left Chicago" to be the most delicious of all.

Giant Country Horns, The
● *See Also:* The Cosmic Country Horns, Carl Gerhard, Don Glasgo, Dave Grippo, Mike Hewitt, Chris Peterman, Russ Remington, Joseph Somerville Jr.
● *Known Appearances:* 7/11/91 through 7/27/91, 4/4/94, 4/15/94
● *Notes:* Some Phish songs simply sound like they were written to include horns accompaniment; Cavern and Gumbo immediately come to mind. Even in the early days, fans sometimes got to hear such accompaniment from guests like Carl Gerhard, Dave Grippo, and Russ Remington. In 1991, though, Phish took the concept of "guest horn players" one step further and organized what many fans refer to as "The Horns Tour." From July 11 through July 27, Phish toured with Gerhard on trumpet, Grippo on alto sax, and Remington on tenor sax. They were called The Giant Country Horns, or GCH for short, and they brought new life to many Phish standards. They also allowed the band to cover new songs where horns were integral (such as "Touch Me" and "Moose the Mooche") and play jazz numbers that had been shelved (such as "Caravan" and "Flat Fee"). Even live Phish staples such as "Tweezer," "Mike's Groove," and "You Enjoy Myself" took on a new dimension when augmented with horns.

In April of 1994, the GCH returned, in a new, six-piece lineup, with Don Glasgo (trombone), Mike Hewitt (baritone sax), Chris Peterman (tenor sax), and Joseph Somerville, Jr. (trumpet) joining Grippo and Gerhard. This version of the GCH appeared on 4/4/94 and 4/15/94, accompanying such songs as "Buried Alive," "The Landlady," "Julius," "Magilla," "Split Open and Melt," "Wolfman's Brother," "I Wanna Be Like You," "The Oh Kee Pah Ceremony," "Suzie Greenberg," "Alumni Blues," and "Cavern." As with the original GCH lineup, Phish tried songs that they might not have otherwise played, including "Magilla" (played for the first time since March of 1993) and "Alumni Blues" (unfinished, but still played for the first time since 10/10/91).

Individual members of the group have continued to appear with Phish, so a return of the GCH at some future junction is, like all things Phishy, not impossible. The band has turned to other horn lineups since April of 1994, though, including the Cosmic Country Horns appearances later that year.

Glasgo, Don
● *See Also:* The Giant Country Horns
● *Known Appearances:* 10/31/95
● *Notes:* Glasgo first appeared with Phish as a member of the Giant Country Horns in April of 1994. He also appeared at Halloween 1995, playing trombone throughout the *Quadrophenia* set and on "Suzie Greenberg." Outside of Phish shows, Glasgo can be found accompanying Michael Ray as a member of the northeast version of the Cosmic Krewe. He also teaches music at Dartmouth and Goddard Colleges, serves as director of Dartmouth's Barbary Coast Jazz Ensemble, and is the author of *Jazzlines,* a Dartmouth-based newsletter.

Green, Tim
● *Known Appearances:* 9/26/99
● *Notes:* Friend of Michael Ray, Green joined the Krewe leader in guesting with Phish on 9/26/99. A sax player by trade, Green played on "Cars Trucks Buses," "Funky Bitch," "Free Thought," and "Cavern."

Grippo, Dave
● *Nickname:* "The Truth"
● *See Also:* The Giant Country Horns, The Cosmic Country Horns
● *Known Appearances:* 7/23/88, 10/20/89, 3/9/90, 5/12/91, 11/23/91, 4/4/94, 7/13/95, 10/31/95, 10/31/96, 3/18/97

● *Notes:* Alto saxophonist Dave "The Truth" Grippo has been one of the most frequent guests in Phishtory. He has provided accompaniment to such classic covers as "Satin Doll" and "Blue Bossa" (7/23/88), "Swing Low Sweet Chariot" (10/20/89), "Caravan" and "Donna Lee" (3/9/90). Grippo has also added his talents to many Phish classics, such as "Split Open and Melt" and "Harry Hood" (10/20/89), "Slave to the Traffic Light" and "You Enjoy Myself" (3/9/90), "AC/DC Bag" (5/12/91), "Suzie Greenberg" (4/4/94 and 10/31/96) and "Chalk Dust Torture" (3/18/97). He may be most famous, though, for his inspiring work on "Jesus Just Left Chicago" (see 11/23/91, 10/31/95, and 10/31/96).

Grippo's career as a Phish guest has taken on several historical perspectives that are worth noting. He is the only person to play with both the Giant Country Horns and the Cosmic Country Horns, serving as the bridge between their different styles. He has graced the stage for two Halloween shows, in 1995 and 1996. He assisted Page in recording the score to the movie *Only in America*. And, when Phish rocked *The Late Show* crowd with an inspiring "Julius" on David Letterman's show on 7/13/95, Grippo was by their side.

Grippo is an accomplished musician, having received a degree from the University of Vermont in music education. He has put his degree to good use, teaching at Johnson State College in Vermont. Musically, Grippo has collaborated with Bruce Skalar in a Burlington-based jazz sextet and has been a member of Michael Ray's Cosmic Krewe since 1992.

Guiness, Paul
● *Known Appearances:* 4/16/91
● *Notes:* Not much is known about Paul. His brief but memorable contribution to Phish's live history was a guest appearance on trombone for a version of "Magilla." Paul's band, Ryth McFeud, had opened for Phish on this date in 1991. Many tapes that circulate include Trey joining the band for a ripping "Low Spark of High Heeled Boys."

Gullotti, Bob
● *Known Appearances:* 10/23/96, 7/25/97, 7/26/97
● *Notes:* As many Jazz fans in the northeast will readily attest, Bob Gullotti is one of the most accomplished drummers you will ever encounter. Combining power, subtlety, grace, style, and a virtually unmatched sense of rhythm, Gullotti sets a standard to which most drummers can only imagine reaching.

No wonder, then, that Jon Fishman and Bob Gullotti would hook up on the Phish stage. Bob has sat in with Phish on three occasions: on 10/23/96 at the Hartford Civic Center (check out the extraordinary "Tweezer") for the entire second set and encore, and then for a two-night stint in Texas, 7/25/97 in Dallas (for the entire second set and encore, take special note of the drums duo in "Ya Mar") and 7/26/97 in Austin (for the entire show). Bob was also one of the ensemble members in Trey's "Surrender to the Air" project.

Do yourself a favor: if you are ever in the Boston area on a Monday, you can find Bob performing with the group The Fringe, and on Tuesdays he can be found sitting in with The Hal Crook Group at the AS220 club in Providence.

Hampton, Colonel Bruce
● *See Also:* Aquarium Rescue Unit
● *Known Appearances:* 4/30/92, 4/23/94, 11/28/95, 10/31/96

● *Notes:* Colonel Bruce Hampton is not a colonel. He is THE Colonel. Most fans know his latter-day exploits as front man for the Aquarium Rescue Unit and the Fiji Mariners, two bands that stressed improvisational chops and jamming strength, especially in their live shows. The Colonel has wowed many a crowd with his guitar playing, usually filled with crisp abundant notes and frequent madness and abandon. It was Hampton's appearances with Phish and the rising swell of jam band community that brought the Colonel back into the spotlight. However, the Colonel's origins in the music biz are far more interesting.

Most people don't remember (or have never heard of) the Hampton Grease Band. Formed sometime around 1968, the five-piece featured Glenn Phillips and Harold Kelling on guitars, Mike Holbrook on bass, Jerry Fields on drums, and Hampton, then only in his late teens, on vocals and assorted mayhem. The band's shows were notorious, featuring freaked-out music with lots of on-stage weirdness, such as random people watching TV, friends of the band getting up and walking across the stage during the set, and Hampton's occasionally violent singing (one time he jumpkicked one of his bandmates, who fell into the drum kit in the middle of a song). Buzz was generating around them, and Columbia signed them to record an album. They recorded over 90 minutes of material, most of the songs hitting at around the twenty-minute mark. For some completely mysterious reason, Columbia released the recordings unexpurgated as a double-LP, and it went on to supposedly become the second worst-selling album in Columbia history, beaten only by an obscure yoga recording. The band was dropped and eventually fell apart by 1973, when Hampton auditioned to be Frank Zappa's new lead vocalist.

Though he didn't get that job, the Colonel certainly didn't remain idle. He formed a band, the New Ice Age, followed by the Late Bronze Age. The latter group released a few albums, like *Outside Looking Out* and *One Ruined Life (of a Bronze Tourist)*, but had no commercial success. Seeking to lend his unusual talents and philosophies to a new artistic realm, the Colonel tried his hand at both acting and stand-up comedy, his exploits in the latter field being the stuff of legend; the Colonel did things in his act that would make Andy Kaufman look like a poor man's Henny Youngman. The Colonel appeared in several unusual films, like *Johnny Cash Rides the Rails* (ABC TV movie), *The Slugger's Wife*, *The Bear Bryant Story* (as a football coach), and a "horrible... '80s tit movie" (his words) called *Gettin' It On*. Additionally, he has appeared in several episodes of the police show "Adam-12," and on the Cartoon Network's "Space Ghost" show. His most memorable roles are likely that of "Morris" in the band rehearsal scene in *Sling Blade*, and most recently as the star of Mike Gordon's film *Outside Out*.

Following his questionable '80s exploits, the Colonel formed one his most successful bands, the Aquarium Rescue Unit. Working with such excellent musicians as Jimmy Herring and Oteil Burbridge, the Unit endeared itself to Phish and Dead fans alike, as well as a broader audience of neo-jazz and—blues fans. The Colonel enjoyed moderate commercial success with ARU, but eventually left to work on other projects like the Fiji Mariners, Planet Zambee, and the Code Talkers.

The Colonel officially entered the Phish world on 4/30/92, when he joined the boys on stage to jam on "Tweezer." After an spot with ARU on 5/5/93, he reappeared on 4/23/94 for a "YEM" keyboard jam, and a one-time cover of Leonard Cohen's strange "Who By Fire." On 11/28/95, the Colonel was brought on stage for Fish to serenade him, the drummer belting out a soulful version of "Wind Beneath my Wings" as his hero read a

newspaper. On 10/31/96, the Colonel joined the chaos on stage during "The Overload," the final track of Talking Heads album Remain in Light. He performed on jackhammer for this legendary set closer. Members of Phish have been no stranger to the Colonel's shows either. Fish has appeared with the Colonel on 5/11/93, 7/3/99 (with Mike), and 2/26/00. Mike has also appeared with the man on 3/9/94, and Page (3/21/93) and Trey (3/11/94) have also guested with the Colonel and his bands.

Harvey, James

● *See Also:* The Cosmic Country Horns
● *Known Appearances:* 3/18/97
● *Notes:* James' appearances with Phish have been numerous. As a member of The Cosmic Country Horns, Harvey first played his trombone alongside Trey, Mike, Jon, and Page in 1994. His only appearance without the CCH came at The Flynn Theatre in Burlington on 3/18/97, where he joined Dave Grippo alongside Phish for "Waste," "Character Zero," "Slave," and "Funky Bitch." Harvey has also been a part of side projects (see *Surrender to the Air* and "New York") and projects with which Phish has guested (The Sneakers Jazz Band and the Vermont Jazz All-Stars).

Haynes, Warren

● *Known Appearances:* 12/11/95, 9/16/99, 9/17/99
● *Notes:* Southeast guitar legend Warren Haynes is best-known for his work with The Allman Brothers Band and, later, Government Mule. He has also worked with David Allen Coe, has appeared on albums by artists like Blues Traveler, Jono Manson, The Screamin' Cheetah Wheelies, and Michael McDonald. He also was a part of the infamous Ritz Power Jam in the winter of 1993. In the Phish community, he is known for the searing guitar solos he provided onstage during songs like "Funky Bitch" and "While My Guitar Gently Weeps" on December 11, 1995, "Misty Mountain Hop" on September 16, 1999, and "Viola Lee Blues" (alongside Phil Lesh) one night later.

Herring, Jimmy

● *See Also:* The Aquarium Rescue Unit
● *Known Appearances:* 2/19/93
● *Notes:* Jimmy Herring gained fame as the guitarist alongside Colonel Bruce Hampton in The Aquarium Rescue Unit. After leaving the band, Herring sat in with Day by the River while they auditioned new guitarists in the fall of 1995, led the short-lived supergroup Frogwings, and helped organized Jazz is Dead and The Justice League All-Stars. In the early 90's, Herring made several on-stage appearances with the entire ARU. In fact, many Phish fans jokingly called him their "second favorite red-haired guitarist." Only once has he appeared without the rest of the band; on 2/19/93, he added his blues guitar stylings to "Funky Bitch," "My Sweet One," "Love You," and "Llama."

Hoppe, Sean

● *Know Appearances:* 6/30/94
● *Notes:* Sean is well-known musician in the Richmond, Virginia area, but he became best known to fans as the voice of Jimmy during the 6/30/94 Harpua. Sean sang lead on Phish's brief rendition of "Honkey Tonk Women" before disappearing back into the crowd. Among his musical credits are the bands Headstone Circus and King Solomon's Marbles, as well as a solo project entitled Poppa Hoppe.

Jah Roy

● *Known Appearances:* 10/31/86, 5/25/88, 6/20/88
● *Notes:* Contrary to popular opinion, Jah Roy and Joe Moore are not the same person. The former is a member of Lambs Bread who also contributed vocals on the Phish live stage; the latter is a Burlington-area saxophonist, vocalist, and member of Pork Tornado. Somehow, in the minds of some fans, the two have gotten confused along the way.

Janover, Jamie

● *Known Appearances:* 5/2/91, 8/3/91, 12/30/92
● *Notes:* Jamie holds a place in Phish lore as one of the few long-standing Phish fans who wound up on-stage with the band. He did it by introducing the band to a new instrument, the didgeridoo. In addition to composing his own material, Jamie remains a member of the northeastern music scene and has gained notice for his skills on both the didgeridoo and hammer dulcimer.

Joneses, The

● *See Also:* Russ Flanagan, Steven Drebber
● *Known Appearances:* 4/1/86
● *Notes:* The Joneses were a Burlington contemporary of Phish in the mid- to late-eighties. The bands frequently co-billed shows; for one New Year's Eve performance, a band made up of members of both bands played a show on only a few hours notice! Individual band members have appeared with Phish on other occasions, but the entire band did on April Fools Day, 1986. The bands switched off and each played two short sets, then got together to jam out "Not Fade Away" for the encore.

Jones, Harry

● *Known Appearances:* 3/16/93
● *Notes:* Harry's guest appearance may be the most tender and loving in all of Phishtory. The husband of Trey's grandmother, Harry serenaded his wife with "You Gotta See Mama Every Night" on 3/16/93.

Judd, Wynonna

● *Known Appearances:* 6/22/00
● *Notes:* Considered by some as the queen of current country music, Wynonna Judd joined Phish along with other members of Nashville's finest on 6/22/00. She first gained fame singing alongside her mother, Naomi Judd. The duo racked up four Grammys and eight Country Music Association Awards while releasing ten albums that went either gold or platinum. When Naomi was forced to retire due to health reasons, Wynonna kept on going and going. Surely, the highlight of her career came when she altered the lyrics to "Freebird" to reference a fondness for a certain greasy drummer at the aforementioned show in Antioch.

Kesey, Ken

● *See:* The Merry Pranksters

Khechog, Nawang

● *Known Appearances:* 7/31/99
● *Notes:* Nawang Khechog, a Tibetan-born flutist and composer, is mainly associated with Phish through the Tibet House Benefit Concerts at Carnegie Hall, where he has appeared on stage with Trey. Khechog was born to a nomadic family in Eastern Tibet and, as a child, taught himself the flute. He fled into exile to India in 1959 where he studied

music, meditation and Buddhist philosophy. Eventually, he became a monk for 11 years, studying under His Holiness the Dalai Lama and other Tibetan Masters. In 1986 he moved to Australia where he began to perform and record his own music. He is best known for his instrumental work with the Tibetan Long Horn, the Mayan Ocarinas, and the Australian Aboriginal Didgeridoo. He has recorded several solo albums, including *Sounds of Piece* (1996) and *A Quiet Mind* (1997). Aside from his own musical efforts, he has also appeared in performances and recordings by Kitaro, Carlos Nakai, Peter Kater, Philip Glass, Paul Simon, Natalie Merchant, Baba Olatunji, Beastie Boys, Billy Corgan and Michael Stipe. He continues to play his music worldwide, preserving the Tibetan culture and civilization and speaking out about the current political situation in Tibet.

In 1999 at Carnegie Hall, Khechog accompanied Trey on a memorable version of "Brian and Robert." Along with Foday Musa Suso on kora, Mr. Khechog played the Mayan ocarina with Trey on acoustic guitar. The addition of his flute in this performance of "Brian and Robert" gave the song a beautiful and spiritual calmness and was probably the highlight of Trey's short three song set that evening. In 2000 at Carnegie Hall, Trey returned the favor from the previous year and accompanied Mr. Khechog during his performance. The two were also joined on stage with Carlos Nakai, a Native American flutist. The three performed a wonderful instrumental piece which featured Mr. Khechog again on the Mayan ocarina and Trey first playing ambient sounds on the electric guitar and then switching in the middle of the song to provide an amazing acoustic guitar accompaniment. Only once, though, has Khechog appeared with all of Phish. On 7/31/99, he addressed the plight of Tibet and subsequently guested on an encore-opening jam and the familiar "Brian and Robert."

Kid Rock
● *Known Appearances:* 9/29/00
● *Notes:* It is rare that an artist's guest spot with Phish causes any controversy. Such was not the case in the days after 9/29/00, when the Internet was abuzz with discussion on Kid Rock's four-song guest spot.

The performance was humorous, including some random stage antics from Fishman during an abbreviated "Rapper's Delight." "Walk This Way" and "You Shook Me (All Night Long)" seemed appropriate for Kid's fusion of rap and hard rock. But Kid's altered lyrics to "American Band," though funny to some, summed up the oppositions' viewpoint: inappropriate.

Some wondered why Phish would invite such a vulgar artist on-stage, knowing that his lyrics speak of, among other things, violence against women. Others responded that Kid is merely a character playing in an act that he has created and that it is merely an extension of music as art. Especially in Vegas, fans reasoned—wasn't Phish just making a commentary on "Sin City" as a whole? Like it or hate it, Kid's appearance will at least give fans something new to debate in Phish's touring hiatus.

Going forward, Phish poked fun at Kid's appearance the following night, as "I Didn't Know" included a reference to Kid (real name of Robert) and his sidekick Joe C. Of course, Kid and Phish go back before Vegas—Trey accompanied him for his song "Only God Knows Why" on the television program "Saturday Night Live" on 5/20/00.

Kinchla, Chandler
● *Nickname:* Chan
● *Known Appearances:* 7/27/93
● *See Also:* Blues Traveler
● *Notes:* Chan gained notoriety as the guitarist for Blues Traveler. On several occasions he has joined Phish alongside the rest of his own band, but on one night in the summer of 1993 he joined the band, along with fellow Traveler John Popper, for a "You Enjoy Myself" set-closer.

Krauss, Alison
● *Known Appearances:* 5/3/94
● *Notes:* Few female singers can match the delicious vocals of Grammy award-winning bluegrass artist Allison Krauss, lead singer of the bluegrass band Union Station and the youngest inducted member of The Grand Ole Opry. Phish apparently agreed, as they asked her to help create the studio version of "If I Could." Allison reprised this role on-stage for one night in 1994, adding an unmistakable flourish to one of the band's most heartfelt songs. In addition to her modern accolades, Krauss won the Illinois State Fiddle Championship at age twelve and was once named the Most Promising Fiddler in the Midwest by the Society for the Preservation of Bluegrass in America.

LaLonde, Larry
● *Known Appearances:* 12/6/96
● *Notes:* "Ler" is best known for being the guitar (and banjo) player for Primus, a role he has fulfilled since 1989, a few years after Les Claypool had formed the band. With Larry on guitar, Primus's sound was finally on its way to becoming the ever-evolving freak-funk-a-roll musical jambalaya it has been ever since. Larry has also worked on a side project called Beanpole, opening on occasion for both Mirv and Primus itself. The guitarist appeared on stage with Phish, along with Les, on 12/6/96 for the legendary Las Vegas "Harpua" encore.

Lesh, Phil
● *Known Appearances:* 9/17/99
● *Notes:* What could be said in a few short paragraphs that would in any way due justice to the influence Phil Lesh has had on the members of Phish, so many of their fans, and the world of Rock-and-Roll at large? Phil Lesh was the bassist for the Grateful Dead. If you are not familiar with Phil or the Grateful Dead, please, put down *The Companion*. Go to your nearest bookstore or record store, search the web, ask a friend. A world of magic and discovery await you! If your interest is only in the influence of the Dead on members of Phish, be sure to read the extensive passages on that subject that appear in Richard Gehr's *The Phish Book*.

Fans of both the Grateful Dead and Phish were justifiably ecstatic when in 1999 there began a string of collaborations between Phil Lesh and members of Phish. The first was the historic three-night run of "Phil Lesh and Phriends" shows April 15, 16, and 17, 1999, at the Warfield Theater in San Francisco, CA. This lineup featured Phil Lesh on bass, Steve Kimock on Guitar, John Molo on drums, along with Trey and Page. A meeting of "jam band" heavyweights, these shows were populated mostly by Grateful Dead tunes, but also included "Chalk Dust Torture," "Wolfman's Brother," "Prince Caspian," and "Down with Disease," the latter squeezed in between "Terrapin Station" and "Dark Star!" Do yourself a favor, and seek out tapes of these shows.

After the "Phil and Phriends" run, anticipation was high for a possible guest appearance by Phil at the Phish shows in Phil's neck of the woods, at the Shoreline Amphitheatre in Mountain View, CA. Fans were not disappointed, as Phil joined the Phish stage on 9/17/99. Approaching his 60th birthday and not barely a year after liver transplant surgery, Phil Lesh proved he could still not only jam with the best of them, but that he could *exercise* with the best of them! Phil emerged from the stage wings during "You Enjoy Myself," and joined Mike and Trey on a third trampoline! A glorious bass duet with Mike followed, and then Phil added vocals on "Wolfman's Brother." A rocking "Cold Rain & Snow" ended the set, and then joined by Warren Haynes, Phil led the band through an encore of "Viola Lee Blues." Wow!

Even without members of Phish in tow, Phil Lesh has added both "Wolfman's Brother" and "Sample in a Jar" to the repertoire of his ongoing "Phil Lesh and Friends" project. In addition, Mike Gordon has made two appearances with Phil and his Friends. The first was at the celebration of Phil's 60th birthday on May 10, 2000 in Oakland, CA. Then, a few weeks later on April 8, 2000, Mike joined Phil at the Orpheum Theater in Boston, MA for an encore of "Wolfman's Brother" that also featured a glorious bass duet in the middle. Fans of Phil and Phish can only hope that these instances are only the beginning of a lasting musical collaboration.

Magoo

● *See:* Ninja Custodian

Marley

● *Nickname:* Mar-Mar
● *Known Appearances:* 3/26/92

● *Notes:* Marley (better known as "Mar Mar") is Trey's dog, an adorable mixed breed, primarily golden retriever. Marley has led a long and happy life: she is almost as old as Phish themselves! Trey held up Marley during the "Harpua" encore on 3/26/92 at Ziggy's in Winston Salem, NC. In all fairness, there are probably dozens of Marley "appearances" on or around the Phish stage, especially in the early days (listen to her bark on 8/21/87).

You can catch a glimpse of Marley in the "Down with Disease" video, as well as in the booklet insert for *A Live One*. Marley has been credited and thanked in the liner notes to several of Phish's albums, including her role as "security" in the *Picture of Nectar* notes.

Marley is on stage in spirit at every Phish show: at the end of the neck of Trey's primary Languedoc guitar, there is an inlaid image of Marley saying in bubble "I am the Mar Mar."

Marshall, Tom

● *Known Appearances:* 12/31/93, 12/31/94, 12/31/95, 12/29/96, 12/30/97, 11/21/98, 12/30/98, 7/16/99, 10/8/99, 7/3/00, 9/15/00
● *Notes:* The importance of Tom Marshall in the world of Phish can't be stressed enough. For his role in creating so many of the band's songs, he is seen by many as the fifth member of the band. He is also a musician in his own right; as the keyboardist and singer for Amfibian, he leads a band that plays songs he wrote both for Phish and on his own.

Tom's appearance on the Phish New Year's Run has become an expected and anticipated treat. On New Year's Eve in 1993 and 1994, he sang the lines he wrote for "Run Like an Antelope." He tried his hand at a new number on New Year's Eve 1995, singing the Collective Soul song "Shine" in the middle of a "Colonel Forbin" narration that showcased the band's ability to manipulate time.

Tom Marshall

Michael McNamara

Then, in 1996, the band continued the trend of using Tom to add humor to the New Year's Run. During a rousing "Harpua" on December 29, Trey spoke humorously of "The Uber-demon" and the "evil sound of hell." Marshall came out in time to sing Oasis' pop music hit "Champagne Supernova." The band continued this theme in 1997, as Tom sang the hit "I'm Gonna Be (500 Miles)" during yet another Harpua narration. During the 1998 New Year's Run, Tom returned to singing his own lyrics. He aided in the performance of "Grind," an short original song that was slated for, but cut from, the *Billy Breathes* album.

Not all of Tom's appearances have come on the Run, though. In November of 1998, he showed up at the famous Hampton Coliseum and, along with "Geerz" Gerhard, treated the crowd to a hysterical rendition of the Chumbawumba hit "Tubthumping." Fans can hear this song on the *Hampton Comes Alive* release. Another crowd favorite was Tom's rousing rendition of "Born to Run" in Bruce Springsteen's home state of New Jersey during the summer of 1999. Tom mimicked the "Born in the U.S.A."-era Springsteen, complete with bandana, while Springsteen himself was playing only an hour away. And in 2000, Tom again lent his vocals to the lyrics to "Antelope" (7/3/00 and 9/15/00).

Matthews, Dave
● *See Also:* The Dave Matthews Band
● *Known Appearances:* 6/17/95
● *Notes:* In addition to his appearances with the rest of the DMB, frontman/guitarist Dave Matthews joined Phish on 6/17/95 for their only known rendition of "Three Little Birds."

McConnell, Dr. Jack
● *Known Appearances:* 7/28/93, 4/22/94, 11/18/95, 7/3/99
● *Notes:* He is a renowned physician—some say he was involved in the development of Tylenol. He plays piano and had Phish perform at his Hilton Head home several different times in the early days. And he happens to be the father of Page McConnell. His most frequent contributions are on "Bill Bailey, Won't You Please Come Home." He has played the song in each of his four appearances.

McCoury, Ronnie
● *See Also:* Del McCoury Band, The
● *Known Appearances:* 7/1/99, 6/22/00
● *Notes:* How many young men follow their fathers into a profession and achieve an equal amount of recognition? Ronnie McCoury's father, Del, was named Male Vocalist of the Year by the International Bluegrass Music Association's (IBMA). Ronnie responded by winning the association's Mandolin Player of the Year award twice. He is also a noted vocalist.

While he also appeared with The Del McCoury band onstage during the July 18, 1999, Oswego festival show, Ronnie first appeared with Phish two weeks earlier. The first set of the July 1, Antioch show featured a myriad of special guests, including Ronnie, Jerry Douglas, Tim O'Brien, and Gary Gazaway. Though the show ended a bit prematurely due to inclement weather, Ronnie helped make the show memorable with his work on such Phish originals as "Get Back on the Train" and "Roggae" and such covers as "Beauty of My Dreams" and "Do My Time." Ronnie would reprise many of these songs at Oswego with the Del McCoury Band. Less than a year later, Ronnie was among the special guests in Antioch on 6/22/00 that guested on "Harry Hood," "Blue and Lonesome," "Coming Home," "Uncle Pen," and "Freebird."

McEuen, John
● *Known Appearances:* 11/30/96, 12/6/96, 12/30/99
● *Notes:* Ever think Phish would be within two degrees of separation from Air Supply or Hootie and the Blowfish? Thanks to John McEuen they are, but his work also puts them that much closer to Dolly Parton, The Doors, Kenny Rogers, The Doobie Brothers, Dizzy Gillespie, and Bill Monroe, as well as comedians such as Steve Martin (a high school friend whom McEuen taught to play the banjo) and The Smothers Brothers and actors like Robin Williams, Clint Eastwood, and Sissy Spacek.

McEuen was a founding member of the Nitty Gritty Dirt Band in 1966, and stayed with the group for 21 years and over 22 albums. One of these was the critically-acclaimed and platinum-seller *Will the Circle Be Unbroken*, which included the title song that Phish has covered on a rare few occasions. Interestingly, his first break into show business occurred not as a musician but as a booker who sold out a Bob Dylan show at a Southern California high school in 1965. In the years since, McEuen has, according to his website, flown over two million miles and driven a million more, done over 11,000 interviews and over 300 television performances, produced television shows and interviewed such personalities as Malcolm Forbes and Emmylou Harris, played over 4,600 shows, and, amazingly, "only lost his luggage three times!" Of course, McEuen still writes and releases music, from his solo albums to movie scores.

McEuen's first two Phish appearances were in a one-week span in the fall of 1996. On 11/30, he joined in on banjo for "Uncle Pen" and "The Old Home Place," and came back on lap steel guitar for the "Amazing Grace Jam" and "Possum." He was then part of the Vegas "Harpua" encore on 12/6. McEuen returned at Big Cypress on 12/30 with Chief Jim Billie—McEuen produced Billie's latest album.

McKinney, Cameron
● *Known Appearances:* 5/14/88, 4/18/92, 11/28/94
● *Notes:* How could the life of a kid be any cooler than to appear onstage with Phish? Try appearing three times. McKinney came out with a ukulele for the BBFCFM encore on 4/18/92. Rumored to be only seven years old at the time, Cameron even had the honor of counting out the breaks in the song. Two years later, McKinney added a saxophone to Simple on 11/28/94. Of course, Cameron holds the record for youngest musical guest: at age three, he "played" guitar during "Jesus Jeft Left Chicago" on 5/14/88.

McLachlan, Sarah
● *Known Appearances:* 10/18/98
● *Notes:* Rare are the times when Phish has the chance to collaborate with artists with large mainstream appeal and chart-topping singles. Sarah McLachlan must rank in the pantheon of those guests. She happened to be at the benefits for Neil Young's Bride School when Phish performed in 1998. Sarah added an additional acoustic guitar and vocals to three Phish debuts: "Four Strong Winds," "I Shall Be Released," and "Sad Lisa." Of course, McLachlan was one of the organizers of the Lillith Fair tour, which did for women's musical acts what the Phish-originated HORDE tour did for jambands.

Medeski, Martin, and Wood
● *Known Appearances:* 10/14/95, 10/17/95
● *Notes:* MMW can blame Phish for the infusion of jam-band fans into their acid jazz scene. In the fall of 1995, MMW was still underground in

the Phish scene, until a three day span in October changed everything. They were slated to open for Phish in New Orleans on October 17. But when Phish tour rolled into Austin, Texas three days before, MMW was already in town for a show of their own.

The result was some of the most sought-after tapes ever, as John Medeski (keys), Billy Martin (drums), and Chris Wood (bass) all joined Phish for a ridiculously experimental "You Enjoy Myself." Trey returned the favor later that night, sitting in on guitar with the trio. MMW reprised their avant-garde Phish role three nights later, as expected, with a guest jam out of "Keyboard Cavalry."

Merry Pranksters, The
● *Known Appearances:* 8/14/97
● *Notes:* If you haven't had the pleasure and privilege of reading *Electric Kool-Aid Acid Test* by Tom Wolfe, do yourself a favor and check it out. It chronicles the adventures of The Merry Pranksters and their most famous of vehicles, Furthur. No short description can do this crew sufficient justice; if you don't know about them, find out!

En route to the Rock-and-Roll Hall of Fame in Cleveland, Ken Kesey, The Merry Pranksters and Furthur made a pit stop at the Phish gig on 8/14/97 at Darien Lake in Darien Center, NY. During Phish's performance of "Colonel Forbin," instead of finding the great and knowledgeable Icculus, Colonel Forbin instead finds "Ken Uncle Sam Bozo Kesey." Head Prankster Ken Kesey, dressed as Uncle Sam, appeared on the stage and proclaimed that the Bozos have been missing for two years but are on Phish tour now. What could only be described as "madness" then ensued on stage as Kesey called his fellow Pranksters on-stage to help him find the Bozos, who soon appeared in white costumes. Near the end of this most unusual "Colonel Forbin's," Trey commented "this is what happens after you do too much acid 30 years later..." Indeed!

Miles, Buddy
● *Known Appearances:* 10/22/96
● *Notes:* Among several guest percussionists who accompanied Phish in the Fall of 1996, Buddy Miles is perhaps best known as the drummer with Jimi Hendrix and Band of Gypsys (1969-70) and for his vocal hit "Them Changes" (1970). He and Merle Saunders joined Phish on 10/22/96 at Madison Square Garden for an "All Along the Watchtower" encore, with Miles playing on Fishman's kit, Saunders trading keyboards with Page, and Fishman on Trey's mini-drum kit. Some reviews of the show state that Miles also sang "And she's buying a stairway... to heaven" at the end of the song.

Moore, LeRoi
● *See Also:* The Dave Matthews Band
● *Known Appearances:* 6/17/95, 7/21/97
● *Notes:* LeRoi is best known as the strong-lunged saxophonist from The Dave Matthews Band. Twice he has joined Phish separate from the rest of the band. Along with Dave, LeRoi joined Phish for the "Three Little Birds" encore on 6/17/95. More memorable, though, was Moore's guest shot on 7/21/97. He joined Phish for a jam out of Funky Bitch that turned into a visual spectacle and musical cacophony, with each musician playing multiple instruments and hamming it up.

Mosebee, Dan
● *Known Appearances:* 4/5/90

● *Notes:* Add Dan to the list of one-time harmonica-wielding guests. While we're not sure who he is, we do know that he jammed along to "Jesus Just Left Chicago" during the 1990 Colorado run.

Mosier, Reverend Jeff
● *See Also:* Aquarium Rescue Unit
● *Known Appearances:* 6/1/90, 2/21/93, 11/16/94, 11/17/94, 11/18/94, 11/19/94, 11/20/94
● *Notes:* Perhaps no guest artist has had as great an influence on the band's history as the Reverend Jeff Mosier. His first known appearance with the band was on June 1, 1990. At the time, Mosier was a member of Aquarium Rescue Unit. He added some nifty banjo work to "Run Like an Antelope," "Uncle Pen," and "Rocky Top." When the band was in Atlanta for the infamous Roxy Run in February of 1993, several Aquarium Rescue Unit members again graced the Phish stage. Mosier's contribution helped the band close their three night run with a bang, transforming the usually rocking "Good Times Bad Times" into a rousing bluegrass number and leading them through spirited renditions of "Paul and Silas" and "Pig in a Pen."

Mosier's greatest contribution to Phishtory came in the fall of 1994. The band had begun to experiment more with acoustic songs, including their bluegrass interpretation of Boston's "Foreplay/Long Time." Mosier cemented these experiments from November 16 through November 20. He joined the band on stage during each of these shows and helped perform such covers as "Pig in a Pen," "Tennessee Waltz," "Butter Them Biscuits," "The Old Home Place," and "Dooley," as well as the original "If I Could." Mosier also taught the band "Long Journey Home" and "I'm Blue I'm Lonesome," which he often guested on. These two songs became two of the most frequently played songs of the tour.

More important than the songs he taught, though, were the instruments he brought. Trey learned how to play fiddle. Mike became comfortable on the banjo, and Page mastered the upright bass. Along with Fishman on washboard, these instruments formed the "bluegrass lineup" that the band used for a few songs in the second set of almost every show in the fall of 1994. The band enjoyed this lineup so much that they took to the parking lot in Bloomington, Indiana on November 19 and performed a long set of bluegrass numbers that were forever captured on tape by an alert fan.

Many fans speculate that these songs and instruments, inspired by the addition of Mosier, led to the "Acoustic Army" in 1995, as well as the continued appearance of bluegrass standards. And with the emergence of acoustic numbers like "Driver" and "Sleep" during 1998, we can be sure that Mosier's contributions will not soon be forgotten.

Murawski, Scott
● *Known Appearances:* 7/13/99
● *Notes:* Scott Murawski is the self-taught guitarist and principal songwriter of one of the longest running (longer than Phish!) jambands going, Max Creek. Scott sat in with Phish at Great Woods on 7/13/99 for the set closing "Possum" and the encore of Lynyrd Skynyrd's "Tuesday's Gone." While this was Scott's only appearance with Phish, he also collaborated with Mike Gordon (along with Greg DeGuglielmo on drums and Gordon Stone on Banjo) performing as "The Drop Caps" in early 1997.

Phish actually covered a Max Creek song in the early days, "Back Porch Boogie Blues" Phish also co-billed with Max Creek and Third World at Patrick Gym in Burlington on 11/11/89. Mike Gordon has long

been a fan of Max Creek; you can still occasionally find him in the audience of their shows, and he has made several guest appearances with them, most recently on 1/28/99 at the Higher Ground in Winooski, VT.

Nelson, Willie
- *Known Appearances:* 10/3/98
- *Notes:* Willie Nelson is known as a singer, songwriter, and actor. Above all, though, Nelson is known as a philanthropist and activist. He organized the first Farm Aid concert and still remains active in the event. It was at the 1998 Farm Aid concert that Nelson and Phish crossed paths. In addition to his solo set, Nelson jammed with Phish on such songs as "Moonlight in Vermont" and "Will the Circle Be Unbroken."

To try and sum up Nelson's career is a daunting task. As a solo artist, he is best known for his renditions of country staples and other standards such as "Georgia on My Mind" and "Someone to Watch Over Me." He has long been seen as a representative of country music in general, including his participation (with Kenny Rogers) in USA For Africa's "We Are the World" project. Nelson has recorded with Ray Charles, Neil Young, and Carlos Santana, and even utilized the benefits of modern technology to record a duet with the late Hank Williams. Perhaps most interesting is the number of songs that have been written *about* Willie Nelson, including "Willie" (Hank Cochran and Merle Haggard), "Willy the Wandering Gypsy and Me" (Billy Joe Shaver), and "Willie, Won't You Sing a Song with Me" (George Burns).

Ninja Mike
- *See:* Ninja Custodian

Ninja Custodian
- *See Also:* Ninja Mike, Mr. Magoo
- *Known Appearances:* 3/6/87, 5/28/89, 8/17/92
- *Notes:* Perhaps no late-80's Burlington contemporary was more of a fixture in the Phish scene than Ninja Custodian. Their role in Phishtory is quite significant: the members of the band (including Mike Billington, better known as Ninja Mike) were the ones who convinced John Paluska to see Phish for the first time.

Various members of Ninja Custodian (mostly Magoo and Ninja Mike) appeared with Phish over the years. Such guest slots included 3/6/87 ("Freebird," with Ninja Mike on vocals), 5/28/89 ("Price of Love," plus their own song "Funky (Breakdown)"), and 8/17/92 ("Terrapin"). Ninja Custodian also opened for several Phish shows. See, for example, Halloween, 1989, and the aforementioned 8/17/92. And though they didn't play long on 10/22/89, they were in attendance; listen to the stage banter before the encore and he subsequent modification of the lyrics to "Undun."

O'Brien, Tim
- *Known Appearances:* 8/7/96, 7/1/99
- *Notes:* Tim O'Brien, cofounder of the 80's Colorado based band Hot Rize, is often credited with creating a contemporary hybrid of bluegrass by with blending a modern musical style with traditional bluegrass standards. His compositions and overall musical approach toward bluegrass have been strong influences on Phish's own bluegrass stylings. Tim's bluegrass originals with Hot Rize, in which he played the mandolin and sang lead vocal, plus those as a solo artist have been played by bands such as Phish, Kathy Mattea and The New Grass Revival. Some of Tim's

songs which have made it to the Phish stage are the fan-favorite "Nellie Kane," as well as "Midnight on the Highway" and "Hold to a Dream."

Tim has twice appeared on the Phish stage. On 8/7/96 at Red Rocks he played the mandolin and sang lead vocals for "Hold to a Dream," "99 Years," and "Do My Time." Three summers later, he joined in on 7/1/99 for "Beauty of My Dreams," "Do My Time," "Roggae," "Water in the Sky," and "Back on the Train."

Parshley, Alan
- *Known Appearances:* 10/31/95
- *Notes:* Parshley may be one of the most famous college professors to have a Phish connection. His came on 10/31/95 when he guested (primarily on French horn) for the *Quadrophenia* set with his northeastern neighbors.

Parshley's current title is "Adjunct Teacher of Horn" at Williams College in Williamstown, Massachusetts. He is a member of the Albany Symphony and Vermont Symphony and tours Vermont with the Vermont Brass Quintet and Vermont Symphony Brass. Parshley founded, and serves as director of, The Green Mountain Horn Club, which sponsors workshops and concerts for horn players. Also, he has performed and taught in Austria and is a member of the music faculties at Middlebury College and the University of Vermont

Perazzo, Karl
- *Known Appearances:* 7/25/92, 7/3/96, 10/29/96, 10/31/96, 11/2/96, 11/3/96
- *Notes:* Perazzo, best known as a percussionist with Santana, had a direct influence on the modern Phish sound via his week-long tour stint in late October and early November, 1996. The centerpiece, of course, was the Phishification of the Talking Heads' *Remain in Light* on Halloween, 1996, though other highlights included the famed "Crosseyed Antelope" from 11/2/96. Earlier in the year, he guested on "Taste" and "Llama" during a set where Phish opened for Santana. And, of course, back in 1992 he jammed out on "You Enjoy Myself," "Llama," and "Funky Bitch" along with Santana himself.

Born and raised in San Francisco, Perazzo has long toured with Santana and has appeared on three of Carlos' albums. He has also recorded and played with Malo, Dizzy Gillespie, Pete and Coke Escovedo, Prince, Mariah Carey, and John Lee Hooker, as well as Latino greats Tito Puente and Ruben Blades.

Pierre
- *Known Appearances:* 7/9/97
- *Notes:* It is certainly a rare occasion when the band pulls a fan onstage. The infamous Haagen-Dazs employee Pierre, from Lyon, France, broke the mold on 7/9/97 when the band led him to the stage and serenaded him during the "Hello My Baby" encore. It was the culmination of a day full of references to the most famous ice cream scooper in the annals of Phish.

Pollak, Steve
- *See:* The Dude of Life

Popper, John
- *Known Appearances:* 12/15/89, 3/3/90, 10/6/90, 10/8/90, 11/8/90, 12/28/90, 3/14/92, 7/11/92, 2/6/93, 7/27/93, 6/23/95, 11/15/96

● *Notes:* The relationship between Blues Traveler and Phish has been a long and prosperous one. The bands have organized tours (such as HORDE) together, written a song together, and even collaborated for charity. And, of course, lead Traveler John Popper has appeared on stage with Phish multiple times, and the boys of Phish have often returned the favor.

The first known collaboration between Popper and Phish occurred during a co-bill in New York on 12/15/89. Popper joined in on two songs that would eventually become guest appearance staples, "Jesus Just Left Chicago" and "Funky Bitch." Appearances were fairly common through 1990, with Popper perfecting his harmonica fills on such songs as "My Sweet One," "You Enjoy Myself," and, of course, the three known appearances of the Popper/Anastasio song "Don't Get Me Wrong." Though less common in 1992 and 1993, Popper still managed to fill in on such songs as "Possum," "Fire," "Sleeping Monkey," and "Good Times Bad Times."

Unfortunately, Popper appearances were limited in the second half of the nineties. His last known guest spot was his only time in costume, as he took the persona of "Mean Mr. Mustard" for the song's only appearance. As both bands have achieved fame, their tours have coincided less and less, but Popper still manages to show his Phishy roots from time to time. In 1997, he borrowed part of "Divided Sky" for his track on *A Very Special Christmas 4* and, in 2000, he contributed a track to The Mockingbird Foundation's *Sharing in the Groove* tribute album.

Ray, Michael
● *See Also:* The Cosmic Country Horns
● *Known Appearances:* 10/14/94, 4/26/96, 9/26/99, 9/9/00
● *Notes:* Michael Ray is one of the most accomplished musicians to ever grace the stage at a Phish concert. He is most famous in jazz circles for his work with the legendary Sun Ra. For fifteen years, Ray was Brass Section Leader and a featured trumpet soloist, vocalist and dancer with the Sun Ra Arkestra. He has also worked with several Philadelphia-area soul groups and the popular 70's R&B band Kool & The Gang, as well as Trey's "Surrender to the Air" project.

Ray first appeared as a member of The Cosmic Country Horns in May of 1994. Outside of that lineup, he has appeared three times to lend his skills on trumpet while Phish performed in his hometown of New Orleans: 10/14/94, for "Ya Mar" and "Cavern;" 4/26/96 at Jazzfest, for "Cars Trucks Buses;" and 9/26/99, for "Cars Trucks Buses," "Funky Bitch," "Free Thought," and "Cavern." He crossed paths with Phish again in 2000, as he joined the band in Albany of 9/9/00 for "Sand," "Makisupa Policeman," "Cars Trucks Buses," and "Harry Hood." Phish has returned the favor by appearing several times with Ray's Cosmic Krewe.

Redding, Noel
● *Known Appearances:* 2/6/93
● *Notes:* Best known in rock and roll circles as the bass player for The Jimi Hendrix Experience, Redding is revered in Phish circles for his role in one of the funniest on-stage gags. Phish had long covered Hendrix's "Fire," but Trey chided Mike on 2/6/93 for not getting the song right. Redding came out from backstage to lead the song; Mike moved over to keyboards.

Rekow, Paul
● *Known Appearances:* 7/25/92
● *Notes:* Paul Rekow may be living a musician's dream. A self-pro-

fessed Santana fan, Paul bought his first conga at a pawn shop after seeing Carlos perform live. By age fifteen, he was playing professionally in the Santana cover band Soul Sacrifice. After stints in the bands Malo and Sapo, Rekow joined Carlos in Santana in 1976. Together, along with Karl Perazzo, they added their talents to the memorable 7/25/92 opening set, guesting on "You Enjoy Myself," "Funky Bitch," and "Llama."

Remington, Russ
● *See Also:* The Giant Country Horns
● *Known Appearances:* 10/29/88, 10/20/89
● *Notes:* Saxophonist and founding GCH member Russ Remington also made two appearances without the rest of the horns ensemble. A sample of his woks include "Peaches en Regalia," "Donna Lee," and "Funky Bitch" from 10/29/88 and "Split Open and Melt," "Harry Hood," "Swing Low (Sweet Chariot)," and the short-lived "In a Hole" on 10/20/89.

Rogers, Tim
● *Known Appearances:* 5/3/85, 3/11/88
● *Notes:* Tim "Timber Hole" Rogers was the band's original lighting director. He also played a mean harmonica—announced under the pseudonym "Bobby Brown," Tim would sometimes join the band on-stage during the early years.

Santana, Carlos
● *Known Appearances:* 7/25/92, 7/3/96
● *Notes:* When it comes to lifelong influences, few guitarists have had the impact on Trey as Carlos Santana. See, for example, the 9/13/90 "Landlady," which was dedicated to his spirit, or Trey's remarks about him in *The Phish Book*.

Popular music and mainstream radio caught onto Santana in 1999, with the release of the nine-Grammy-winning, multi-platinum *Supernatural*. The album contained the longest-running number-one single of the year: "Smooth," a famous collaboration with Matchbox 20's Rob Thomas that ruled the airwaves for months. These were not his first Grammys, though: he won in 1988 for Best Rock Instrumental Performance. And this was far from his first album—it was his 36th, in a recording career that began in 1969. As of the summer of 2000, eight of these albums (including *Supernatural*) achieved platinum status, and eight more were certified gold. All told, he has taken rock and roll and blended it with blues and classic Latin styles and sold over fifty million records and played to over thirty million fans.

Among his most famous compositions are "Evil Ways" and "Black Magic Woman," as well as a cover of Tito Puente's "Oye Como Va." In his career, Carlos has recorded albums of his own material with Buddy Miles, John McLaughlin, Herbie Hancock, Willie Nelson, and Booker T. Jones. He scored the film *La Bamba*, participated in both Woodstock (the band's breakthrough show) and the 1987 Rock 'n Roll Summit, and toured in 1988 with renowned jazz saxophonist Wayne Shorter. He has also been a philanthropist, contributing to such causes as Blues for Salvador, San Francisco Earthquake Relief, Tijuana Orphans, and various Latin youth education associations.

In addition to his Grammys, Carlos has been a highly decorated artist. He is a member of both the Rock and Roll Hall of Fame and was an inaugural member of its Bay Music Area counterpart, the Bammy Hall of Fame. He has also received multiple Best Guitarist and Musician

of the Year awards from the Bammy's and has been named Latino Music Legend of the Year by the Chicano Music Awards. In 1996, *Billboard* magazine honored him for his lifetime achievements with their Century Award; in 1998, he was given a star on the Hollywood Walk of Fame. And somewhere in all this, he found the time to influence and play with Phish. Twice he gave Phish the opportunity to tour with and open for his band. While they sometimes joined him on stage, he twice joined them: for "You Enjoy Myself," "Llama," and "Funky Bitch" on 7/25/92 and for "Llama" and "Taste" on 7/3/96.

Saunders, Merl

● *Known Appearances:* 4/23/94, 10/22/96
● *Notes:* Merl Saunders is perhaps best know by his long time collaboration with Jerry Garcia. Merl was the keyboardist on various incarnations of the Jerry Garcia Band in the 1970s (Jerry Garcia Band, Legion of Mary, and Reconstruction), and Jerry has appeared on several of Merl's later albums. Merl is still active in the "jam band" scene, touring often with his own "Merl Saunders and the Rainforest Band" and more recently "Merl and the Funky Friends."

Merl Saunders has sat in with Phish on two occasions. The first was on April 23, 1994 at the Fox Theater in Atlanta, GA, where he joined Page at the keyboards for renditions of Caravan and High-Heel Sneakers. He joined the Phish stage again on October 22, 1996 at Madison Square Garden. Along with Buddy Miles on drums (and joined by the pleasantly outrageous "The Madison Scare Garden dancers"), Merl sat in for the encore of the classic "All Along the Watchtower."

Scaggs, Ricky

● *Known Appearances:* 6/22/00
● *Notes:* Ricky may have been one of a handful of special guests in Antioch on 6/22/00, but his career stands out as one of the best in country and bluegrass music. In the 1970's he played mandolin with both J.D. Crowe and the New South and Boone Creek before turning to country music by the end of the decade. He remained a fixture on *Billboard*'s country music charts through the 1980's, earning a spot as one of the magazine's Top 20 Artists of the Decade. He landed 24 singles in the Top 20, including twelve number one songs. Among his awards are eight from the Country Music Association and four Grammy's. He is still recording and receiving critical acclaim; his most recent album, *Bluegrass Rules*, received ten nominations from the 1999 International Bluegrass Music Association and two Grammys.

Schaffer, Paul

● *Known Appearances:* 10/3/98
● *Notes:* Paul Schaffer gained fame as David Letterman's late night band leader and saw the band play live on the show three times from 1994 through 1997. He happened to be present at Farm Aid and join in the massive guest cavalcade for "Moonlight in Vermont." Phish saw Paul again less than three weeks later, performing on Letterman's show on October 27, but another collaboration (Phish played "Birds of a Feather") was not to be.

Seals, Son

● *Known Appearances:* 7/10/97, 7/17/99, 10/3/99
● *Notes:* Born Frank Seals, Jr., "Son" Seals taught himself to play drums and guitar while living in rural Arkansas. His father owned a club

Son Seals

and Seals honed his chops backing up whomever was playing. He was lucky enough to tour with blues legends Earl Hooker and Albert King before moving to Chicago in 1971 and recording his first album in 1973. In the interim, he played with Junior Wells, James Cotton, and Buddy Guy. In the last 25 years, Seals has played thousands of shows around the world. Long lauded by fans but shunned by critics, Seals finally received the acclaim he deserved when he was named Chicago Blues Entertainer of 1997 at the Chicago Music Awards.

In Phish circles, Seals is best known as the composer of longtime cover "Funky Bitch." Members of Seals' band first joined Phish for the song on 7/10/97. He came back in Oswego on 7/17/99 for another rendition of the song, as well as the debut of "On My Knees." Finally, Seals joined Phish and Sugar Blue for "Funky Bitch" and "Messin' With the Kid."

Smith, Bryant

● *Known Appearances:* 5/16/91
● *Notes:* His origin unknown, Bryant (or perhaps Brian) Smith added a guest trombone shot to "Magilla" on 5/16/91.

Solberg, Dick

● *Known Appearances:* 5/6/93
● *Notes:* Nicknamed the "Sun Mountain Fiddler," Dick is best known as the leader of the Sun Mountain Band. He first played the fiddle at age eight, and has been melding bluegrass, Gaelic, folk, and jazz styles since then. Check out his 1981 release *Riding High* for a fair representation of his sound. Dick's lone Phish guest shot came alongside Jeff Walton on 5/6/93. He augmented such staples as "Rocky Top" and the "HYHU" jam, while also rendering new songs like "I Been to Georgia on a Fast Train."

Somerville Jr., Joseph
● *Known Appearances:* 10/31/95
● *Notes:* Horns were needed for the Halloween, 1995 *Quadrophenia* set. Phish turned to a crew that included Dave Grippo, Don Glasgo, Alan Parshley, and Joseph Somerville, Jr. Somerville, a trumpeter, also helped out on "Suzy Greenberg" later in the show.

Spoonman
● *See:* Artis the Spoonman

Starke, Raiford
● *Known Appearances:* 12/30/99
● *Notes:* Just after releasing his first album *Speak Me*, Raiford Starke joined Phish on guitar at Big Cypress along with Chief Jim Billie and John McEuen for "Che Hun Ta Mo" and "Big Alligator Song." Raiford currently lives in South Florida and plays his own blend of rock and blues guitar, mixing in acoustic ballads for variety.

Starkweather, Stacy
● *Known Appearances:* 5/2/94
● *Notes:* If you were asked the question "who is the most famous bass player in Burlington?" the answer would almost always be Mike Gordon. Unless you lived in Burlington, in which case the answer could well be Stacy Starkweather. A founding member of the Burlington based "The Disciples," Stacy has, at various times, been a member of Jazz Mandolin Project, The "Northeast" Michael Ray & the Cosmic Krewe, the Gordon Stone Trio, and, his own project, Option Anxiety. More directly linking to the Phish world, Stacey was the bass player (with Trey on Guitar, Fishman on drums, and Jamie Masefield on mandolin) for the side project "Bad Hat," which performed several small shows in 1994.

Mike Gordon said of Option Anxiety's *Every November* CD: "I don't always like albums by bass players, but this one I do. Stacy was always a much more agile bass player than myself, so I've looked at him for inspiration and even for a few lessons a while back." Strong praise indeed! Along with Otiel Burbridge, Stacy sat in with Phish on 5/2/94 at the Five Points South Music Hall, Birmingham, AL for the 2nd set closing "Mike's Groove."

Stinnette, Jim
● *Known Appearances:* 12/29/95
● *Notes:* Jim Stinnette is a faculty member at Boston's Berkelee School of Music. He was Mike Gordon's first bass mentor, having been introduced to him by his high school jazz band's guest conductor, Diego Poprokovich. Stinnette sat in with Phish on 12/29/95 at the Worcester Centrum, performing a bass duet with Mike that led in to the classic ZZ Top cover, "La Grange." You can still find Jim Stinnette sitting in with various jazz ensembles in and around Mike's hometown of Sudbury, Massachusetts.

Stone, Gordon
● *Known Appearances:* 11/19/92, 7/22/93
● *Notes:* Banjo and pedal steel player Gordon Stone can be found touring with his very own "Gordon Stone Band." The band, originally known as the Gordon Stone Trio, featured Stone, along with mandolinist Jamie Masefield and bassist Stacy Starkweather—both of Jazz Mandolin Project fame. The later addition of drummer Russ Lawton prompted the

band's name change. The Gordon Stone Band has played at a few of Phish's festivals including The Clifford Ball, The Great Went, and The Lemonwheel. Their most recent release, *Even with the Odds*, was acclaimed as "instrumental album of the year" by the Gannett Press.

In 1992, Gordon Stone got a call from Mike Gordon, requesting banjo lessons. Mike had seen him play bluegrass at clubs around Burlington. While Phish was recording *A Picture of Nectar*, Stone again received a call from Mike inviting him play banjo and pedal steel guitar on "Poor Heart." Stone can also be heard playing pedal steel on "Fast Enough for You," from *Rift*.

In November of 1992, Stone joined Phish on stage at St. Michael's College, where he added some pedal steel to "Fast Enough for You." He would again join them in 1993 in Stowe, Vermont with his banjo on "Paul and Silas," "TMWSIY" and "Rocky Top."

Sugar Blue
● *Known Appearances:* 4/10/93, 8/8/97, 10/3/99
● *Notes:* John Popper isn't the only noted harmonica player to guest with Phish. Sugar Blue is best known for the signature harmonica lick on the Rolling Stones "Miss You." He has even recorded his own interpretation of the song on his album *Blue Blazes*. In addition to his own albums (including a famous take of Sonny Boy Williamson's "Help Me"), Sugar Blue has recorded with Bob Dylan, Stan Getz, and Willie Dixon.

His Phish appearances have usually been memorable late-show and encore slots in the midwest. The first, on 4/10/93, saw Blue punctuate standards "Funky Bitch" and "Cavern," as well as "Hoochie Coochie Man" and the aforementioned "Help Me." He ripped out "Hoochie Coochie Man" again on 8/8/97, along with "Messin' With the Kid." On 10/3/99, blues fans were treated to a dream lineup as both Sugar Blue and Son Seals jammed on "Messin' With the Kid" and "Funky Bitch."

Taube, Nancy
● *See:* Richard Wright

Trucks, Butch
● *Known Appearances:* 11/16/95, 11/2/96
● *Notes:* Along with Jaimoe, Butch Trucks has been the rhythmic backbone of the Allman Brothers Band for over 25 years. He also was instrumental in launching the supergroup Frogwings in 1997, which also featured Marc Quinones, Oteil Burbridge, Jimmy Herring, Derek Trucks, Kofi Burbridge, and Edwin McCain. Butch has twice joined Phish: for "Possum" on 11/16/95 and for "Funky Bitch" on 11/2/96.

Trucks, Derek
● *Known Appearances:* 7/7/99
● *Notes:* Derek Trucks, nephew of Allman Brothers Band legend Butch Trucks, is one of the rising young stars in the world of improvisational rock music. While at first glance he looks like a lost "Hanson" brother, don't let looks deceive you: this guys can rip it up on pace with just about any guitarist alive today. In addition to his own Derek Trucks Band, Derek has toured as a member of Phil Lesh and Friends, The Allman Brothers Band, and the lesser-known but no less rocking Frogwings.

Derek appeared with Phish on 7/7/99 at the Blockbuster Pavilion, Charlotte, NC, adding his slide guitar mastery to the double encore of "Possum" and "Funky Bitch."

Walton, Jeff

● *Known Appearances:* 5/6/93
● *Notes:* We think that the Jeff Walton that appeared on stage with Phish on 5/6/93 is the same Jeff Walton who founded the cult group The Judys and has written many film scores. In any case, Walton played acoustic guitar on "Tennessee Waltz," "I Been to Georgia on a Fast Train," and "That's Allright Mama."

Weir, Bob

● *Known Appearances:* 10/6/00
● *Notes:* Bob Weir became the second member of The Grateful Dead to jam with Phish when he joined them for a three-song encore at Shoreline on 10/6/00. Song selection included a classic Dead cover ("El Paso") and original ("West L.A. Fadeaway"), as well as a rocking "Chalk Dust Torture." Some apparent sound problems limited Weir's involvement in "Chalk Dust" but his vocals and the emotional highlights of the other two songs made it an evening to remember.

Wernick, Pete

● *Known Appearances:* 11/16/97
● *Notes:* Pete Wernick, better known as Dr. Banjo, boasts a resume which includes roles in the famous bluegrass bands Hot Rize (with Tim O'Brien) and Country Cooking, as well as a stint as president of the International Bluegrass Music Association and a prosperous solo career. A scholar with multiple degrees in sociology, he also has written instructional books for the banjo and has led camps and traveling clinics. Currently, Wernick tours as a duo with his wife Joan, as well as with his new band, The Live Five.

Out near his current Colorado home, Wernick joined Phish for "Scent of a Mule" and "Poor Heart" on 11/16/97. Showing Wernick's bluegrass roots, the former included a "Foggy Mountain Breakdown" tease.

Williams, Heloise

● *Known Appearances:* 11/19/98
● *Notes:* Heloise, former singer with the Burlington-area band Viperhouse, joined Phish for a screeching vocal jam out of "You Enjoy Myself." Trey returned the favor later that evening, sitting in with Viperhouse in Winston-Salem. Heloise was also a part of Trey's Eight Foot Fluorescent Tubes side project. Her voice can also be heard on *Story of the Ghost*, as she lent backing vocals to "Shafty" and "Birds of a Feather."

Wright, Richard

● *Nicknames:* Nancy
● *Known Appearances:* 5/17/86, 5/14/88, 10/29/88, 5/26/89, 8/17/89
● *Notes:* Though he had a short-lived nickname of Nancy, Richard Wright has no idea why fans refer to him as "Nancy Taube." There is some speculation that Nancy Taube was an old-school fan and than fans mistook one "Nancy" for another when labeling setlists. On some tapes, Trey refers to Richard as "Nancy," though never "Nancy Taube." Still, fans likely assumed the latter, given earlier errors.

Either way, Richard Wright penned the lyrics to Phish songs "Halley's Comet" and "I Didn't Know." Many early versions of "Halley's" were sung by Richard; for well-circulated versions, see 5/14/88 and 5/26/89. Richard also sang "I Didn't Know" at the former.

Wright, Steven

● *Known Appearances:* 12/30/96
● *Notes:* Steven Wright is a self-professed Phish fan. He even extolled the virtues of the band on *Late Night with Conan O'Brien* after *Billy Breathes* was released in 1996. His lone guest appearance ranks among the oddest moments in Phishtory. Fans recognized him when he appeared on stage during "Scent of a Mule" on 12/30/96 but surely couldn't have guessed that he would add a distinctive bell ring before leaving as conspicuously as he arrived.

Yacovone, Seth

● *Known Appearances:* 11/29/98
● *Notes:* Trey first saw Seth play at a guitar workshop—he took second place in Advance Music's Guitar Summit. When Seth got to join the band on stage in Worcester at the conclusion of the 1998 Fall Tour, they decided on that first song Trey had seen him play: an original composition called "All the Pain Through the Years." He also added guitar licks to the Phish debut of "Layla."

Yodeling Cowgirls, The

● *Known Appearances:* 12/6/96
● *Notes:* Though their real names are Heather August and Anamieke Carrozza, most fans only know these talented musicians as the cowgirls from the infamous 1996 Las Vegas Harpua. Currently, they perform under their stage name onomatopoeia.

Young, Neil

● *Known Appearances:* 10/3/98, 10/17/98, 10/18/98
● *Notes:* Singer-songwriter-guitarist Neil Young has become one of the most important figures in rock over the course of his career. His music may not have many similarities to Phish's in sound, but it does in other ways. In his willingness to take risks, write music that spans a multitude of genres, and play with unfettered passion and intensity every night, he and Phish are kindred spirits.

The Canadian-born Young first came to prominence in the mid-60s as a member of the influential folk-rock combo Buffalo Springfield. After they split up he embarked on a solo career but soon reunited with former Springfield bandmate Stephen Stills in Crosby, Stills, Nash and Young. It was in CSNY that Young became known as a superstar. He soon rejected stardom, though, to follow his muse, which has produced many thrilling and confounding moments. Young has always been ambivalent about fame and has never stayed with one band or style for very long, though he periodically returns to acoustic music, CSNY, and his hard-rock band, Crazy Horse.

While he has profoundly influenced the grunge-rock and acoustic singer-songwriter movements, he has also been willing to try everything from country to blues, from low-fi to synth-pop. He has released scores of influential albums including *Everybody Knows This Is Nowhere* (1969), *After the Gold Rush* (1970), *Tonight's the Night* (1975), *Rust Never Sleeps* (1979), *Freedom* (1989) and *Ragged Glory* (1990).

Young has a gift for writing simple music and making it sound complex, and because of that he has been a major influence on Trey in recent years. "A two-chord Crazy Horse jam is no less transcendent than anyone else's note-filled extravaganza," Trey said in *The Phish Book*. "Neil Young blazes a direct path to the soul without clogging it up with too much thought. I didn't understand him at all in high school, but the older I get, the more he speaks to me."

Trey has also cited (in an interview with www.canoe.ca) the influence of *Tonight's the Night* on the making of Phish's *Farmhouse* album,

and (in *The Phish Book*) the influence of Young's "Thrasher" on Tom Marshall's writing of "The Wedge."

Phish first covered Young on 3/18/97, opening the Lake Champlain benefit with "Cinnamon Girl." That song appeared once more, as the encore of 7/31/97 in Young's home territory of northern California. In 1998 Phish added *Tonight's the Night*'s "Albuquerque" into its regular rotation. It dropped out the following year but re-emerged at The Show on 12/31/99. Also, Marshall's band Amfibian has covered the title track from *Everybody Knows This Is Nowhere*.

Young invited Phish to appear at the 1998 editions of two annual charity events he helps organize, Farm Aid and the Bridge School Benefit. At Farm Aid, after an acoustic set of his own, he borrowed Trey's backup Languedoc to jam with Phish at the end of their set. The highlight was a 20-minute-plus version of "Down By The River" that featured a guitar duel between Trey and Young. To this day many Young die-hards cite that version as one of the song's best performances ever; some even say it turned them on to Phish. Two weeks later at the two-day all-acoustic Bridge benefit, Young joined Phish at the end of their sets each day. They jammed on "Harry Hood" and Phish backed Young on his own "Helpless," Ian Tyson's "Four Strong Winds" and Bob Dylan's "I Shall Be Released."

Trey was in attendance for what many Young fans consider to be the best show of his 1999 solo acoustic tour, 5/1/99 in Chicago. He did not join Young onstage but got some pointers on playing solo sets from Young backstage, which Trey related humorously on 5/8/99 in Madison, WI.

Given the unpredictability of both artists it is impossible to know whether there will be future Young-Phish collaborations. But given Trey's continuing adulation of Young, never rule it out.

Zenzile

● *Known Appearances:* 4/1/86

● *Notes:* Some who have heard Zenzile's guest appearance from 4/1/86 (where he read original poetry) dismissed him as a friend of the band playing a crank or some other staged event. This couldn't be further from the truth; Zenzile is a fighter for South African rights who was exiled from his home for sixteen years. His political stances at Godard led him to leave the school in 1988 after he led the occupation of an administrative building, demanding a Third World Studies program. He has long been active in politics—for example, he publicly protested against Linda Ronstadt when she continued to play Sun City. Now out of exile, he is known by his full name of Zenzile Khoisan and he is one of the key researchers for South Africa's Truth and Reconciliation Committee. Zenzile even served as the assistant to the Coordinator for Human Rights Violations Investigations. Though his 4/1/86 appearance is the only documented occasion of a collaboration with Phish, it is believed that this was one of several.

SIDESHOWS

Craig DeLucia / Ellis Godard

I n addition to hosting others as guests on their own stage, Phish have also shared non-Phish stages with other artists. This section will identify each and every side-show/side-project, and their previous and subsequent associations with Phish, and will list those incarnations both alphabetically and chronologically (by the date at which they appeared, together with setlists for all performances for which setlists are available.)

This chapter documents several kinds of shows, including:

Guest appearances where one or more members of Phish jam with another band. Examples include Page with the Allman Brothers, or Trey with MMW.

Headlining appearances, which are a more specific set of guest appearances. This is when an artist opens for Phish and one or more members of Phish got on stage to jam.

Opening appearances, which are yet another specific set of guest appearances. This is when Phish opens for other artists and joins the other artists during their set.

Side projects developed by band members, like Surrender to the Air, Pork Tornado, or the Trey Anastasio Solo Tour

Miscellaneous appearances that do not fit in any other category, such as open mic nights.

Setlists are listed in chronological order. The first two lines list the date and the venue of the show. The third line notes which members of Phish were involved (**T**rey, **M**ike, **P**age, or **F**ishman), what type of sideshow it was (see listing above), and what artist or band was performing.

While we've tried to make this chapter as comprehensive as possible, there are probably scores of shows that we've missed. Given the band's tendencies to jam with other artists, and the fact that these appearances sometimes go unnoticed (especially in the old days), any attempt to document guest appearances with other bands will forever be incomplete. But we've collected as many as we can confirm.

At best, we've gathered entire setlists. For some shows, we know only the songs that Trey, Mike, Jon, or Page guested on. For some shows, we've included "best-guess titles" for unknown songs. And for some shows, we only know dates. We look to you, our readers, to help this chapter grow.

Also, many times there are prevalent rumors, usually on the Internet, that a member of Phish joined another band on stage. Where we have proven these rumors to be false, we have listed the show in italics for easy reference.

Special thanks, for contributions to this section, to Chris Bertolet, Christian A. Binder, Zeke Bogan, Scott Boyarski, Patrick D. Burke, Troy Colyer, Eric Conko, Anthony Cotton, John B. Dilly, Benjy Eisen, Clay Ellwood, John Fingland, Carl Gerhard, Donald Glasgo, Kristen Godard,

Andy Goodman, Rob Hillard, Jessee Jarnow, Robert G. Johnson, Nick Johnston, Adam Kahan, Erin McKeon, Adam Kurth, Franklin C. Malemud, Heidi Mann, Christian McKee, Dan Mielcarz, Julia Mordaunt, Phil Nazzaro, Michael A. O'Dea, Alex Oliver, Rich Petlock, Dan Schar, Joseph Sirotnak, Jon Smith, Matt Steve, Jimmy T., Jeffrey Trisoliere, Marcie Vogel, Carl Walter, and John J. Wood.

Special thanks are extended to Matthew King, who had been working on a similar document long before this chapter was started and offered it to us as a starting point, Pete Gershon, for his significant contributions, and Erik Swain, for his help in verifying many of these lists.

1980S

April 28, 1984
Slade Hall, University of Vermont, Burlington, VT
M,F   Side   Dangerous Grapes

Sideshows

There were likely many forgotten instances prior to 1992 when members of Phish played side shows, particularly in other bands and sitting in with other bands. And note that data are incomplete for 2000. However, much can be said about the known interim, including a drop in sitting in with opening or headlining acts, since a peak in 1992. Side projects peaked in 1994 (with Trey's Bad Hat tours) and 1999 (with Trey's "solo" tour, plus Fishman joining Jazz Mandolin Project for a tour). Interestingly, guest appearances also peaked during 1994 and 1999—and have outpaced side projects every year except 1999. And both side projects and guest appearances have outpaced other side shows in every year since 1992, when the band's popularity exploded— in years since, when members of Phish have played with other artists, they have done so on other stages, preserving their own stages for primarily united appearances.

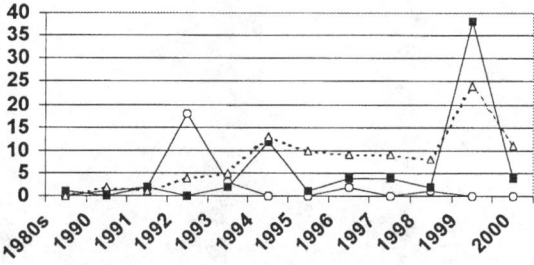

1990

September 8, 1990
The Front, Burlington, VT
T,P   Guest   Blues Traveler
● *Set I:* Rock Me Baby, Mulling it Over, Weird Chick, Out of My Hands > Gina, Optimistic Thought, But Anyway, Slow Change, Mountain Cry, Come Together, Motherfunker
● *Set II:* The Best Part, Love of my Life, 100 Years, Alone
● *ncore:* Gotta Get Mean > Gloria > Gotta Get Mean
Show Notes: Trey and Page sat in for Gotta Get Mean. The show also featured Jerry Gold.

October 6, 1990
Capital Theater, Port Chester, NY
T   Open   Blues Traveler
● Trust in Trust > Sweet Talkin' Hippie, Weird Chick > Mullin it Over, Gina, Gotta Get Mean > Gloria > Gotta Get Mean, Crystal Flame, But Anyway, Mountain Cry
● *Show Notes:* Gloria featured Trey on guitar and vocals during Blues Traveler's opening set.

November 7, 1990
Barrymore Theater, Madison, WI
T,P   Guest   Blues Traveler
● *Show Notes:* Trey and Page sat in for Mother Funker. The setlist is otherwise unknown.

1991

January 20, 1991
Nectar's, Burlington, VT
T,P,M,F   Side   The Johnny B. Fishman Jazz Ensemble

January 27, 1991
Nectar's, Burlington, VT
T,P,M,F   Side   The Johnny B. Fishman Jazz Ensemble
● Mr. P.C., You'd Be So Nice to Come Home To, Sugar, Donna Lee, Moose the Mooch, Take the A-Train, Blue Bossa, Work Song
● *how Notes:* This setlist is incomplete and may not be in order.

January 16, 1991
The Front, Burlington, VT
T   Guest   Blues Traveler
● *Show Notes:* Trey guested during portions of this show. The setlist is unknown.

April 16, 1991
Rick's Cafe, Ann Arbor, MI
T   Head   Ryth McFeud
● *Show Notes:* Ryth McFeud opened for Phish on this night, and Trey

sat in for "Low Spark of Hi-Heeled Boys." The song circulates on many Phish tapes from the evening's show.

November 30, 1991
Colonial Theater, Port Chester, NY
F   Head   Shockra
● Underground People, Tone Clone, Question Air?, Dimension Extention, Stop The Revolution, Don't Let it Stop Ya
● *Show Notes:* Fish sat in on vacuum during Don't Let it Stop Ya.

1992

February 1, 1992
KD Churchill's, Burlington, VT
All   Guest   Shockra
● *Set I;* Tezz, Help Yourself, Question Air, Do What You Want, Stop the Revolution, Let's Go Dancing, No Chagrin, Give It Up
● *Set II;* Spread the Word, Dimension Extension, Tone Clone, Sippin Pipa, Underground People
● *Show Notes:* The last three songs of the second set featured a Phish guest appearance.

February 2, 1992
Queen City Tavern, Burlington, VT
T   Misc   Trey Anastasio and Jamie Masefield
● *Show Notes:* On this night, Trey and Jamie played jazz selections.

Sunday, March 22, 1992
Cultural Center Auditorium, Charleston, WV
T   Open   Buckwheat Zydeco
● Juke Joint Johnny

March 26, 1992
Ziggy's, Winston-Salem, NC
P   Head   Aquarium Rescue Unit
● No One to Blame, Salty Dog, Shoeless Joe, Compared to What, Poor Boy Blues, Temptation, Working on a Building, Peace and Happiness, Sittin on Top of the World, Come on Home
● *Show Notes:* The last three songs, including a notable solo during "Peace and Happiness," featured Page on keys.

July 7, 1992
KD Churchill's, Burlington, VT
T,P,F   Guest   Aquarium Rescue Unit
● *Set I;* Shoeless Joe, Gonna Need Somebody (All Night Long), Sittin on Top of the World, Payday, Time Flack, Basically Frightened > Zambi > Space is the Place, Trondossa, Compared to What
● *Set II;* Jam > Yield Not to Temptaion, Working On a Building, Poor Boy, I Can't Quit You Baby, Time is Free > Jack the Rabbit > Davy Crockett, Elevator to the Moon, Put on Your Shoes, Jazz Bank, Tuxedo Junction, Ain't Nothing You Can Do
● *Encore;* Swing, Believe I…
● *Show Notes:* Dave Grippo, Page McConnel and Jon Fishman guested for the entire show. "Working On a Building" also featured Trey Anastasio.

July 19, 1992
Garden State Arts Center, Holmdel, NJ
T   Guest   Aquarium Rescue Unit
● *Show Notes:* Trey sat in for one song.

July 24, 1992
Jones Beach, Wantagh, Long Island, NY
All   Open   Santana
● *Show Notes:* Phish sat in for part of Santana's set.

July 25, 1992
Stowe Performing Arts Center, Stowe, VT
All   Open   Santana
● *Show Notes:* Phish sat in for part of Santana's set. Santana also sat in for three songs (Runaway Jim, Funky Bitch, and YEM) with Phish.

July 26, 1992
Big Birch Concert Pavilion, Patterson, NY
T,M,P   Open   Santana
● *Show Notes:* Trey, Page and Mike sat in for part of Santana's set.

July 27, 1992
Saratoga Performing Arts Center, Saratoga Springs, NY
All   Open   Santana
● *Show Notes:* Phish joined Santana's band during a jam, and then they all broke into an instrumental "Funky Bitch".

July 28, 1992
Finger Lakes Performing Arts Center, Rochester, NY
All   Open   Santana
● *Show Notes:* Phish sat in for part of Santana's set.

July 30, 1992
Meadow Brook Music Fest, Rochester Hills, MI
All   Open   Santana
● *Show Notes:* Phish sat in for part of Santana's set.

July 31, 1992
Blossom Music Center, Cayahoga Falls, OH
T   Open   Santana
● *Show Notes:* Trey sat in for part of Santana's set.

August 1, 1992
Poplar Creek Music Center, Hoffman Estates, IL
All   Open   Santana
● *Show Notes:* Phish sat in for part of Santana's set.

August 19, 1992
Pema County Fair, Tucson, AZ
T,M,P   Open   Santana
● *Show Notes:* Trey, Page and Mike sat in for part of Santana's set.

August 20, 1992
Pan American Center, Las Cruces, NM
All   Open   Santana
● *Show Notes:* Phish sat in for part of Santana's set.

August 23, 1992
Colorado State Fair, Pueblo State Fairgrounds, Pueblo, CO
All   Open   Santana
● *Show Notes:* Phish was introduced during a rocking jam; Fishman played vacuum, and Mike and Page took brief solos, then Trey and Carlos traded licks, building towards a large jam. No "songs" were played.

August 24, 1992
Gerald Ford Amphitheater, Vail, CO
All   Open   Santana
● *Show Notes:* Phish sat in for part of Santana's set.

August 28, 1992
Concord Pavilion, Concord, CA
All   Open   Santana
● *Show Notes:* Phish sat in for part of Santana's set.

August 29, 1992
Shoreline Amphitheater, Mountain View, CA
All   Open   Santana
● *Show Notes:* Phish sat in for part of Santana's set.

August 30, 1992
Cal Expo Amphitheater, Sacramento, CA
All   Open   Santana
● *Show Notes:* Phish sat in for part of Santana's set.

September 4, 1992
KD Churchills, Burlington, VT
All   Guest   Shockra
● *Set II;* Freaks on Fire, Do What You Want, Elvin Jones, Big Chief > Sippin Pippa > Don't Let It Stop Ya > Jam > Drum Solos > Somewhere over the Rainbow / Wizard of Oz Jam > Don't Let It Stop Ya, Big Chief Reprise, ?
● *Encore;* Underground People
● *Show Notes:* This show featured all four members of Phish. Trey entered for Elvin Jones and Page joined for a piano jam leading into Big Chief. Mike entered during the ensuing jam and then Fishman followed for Sippin Pippa, and Don't Let It Stop Ya.

1993

January 27, 1993
KD Churchills, Burlington, VT
M,F   Guest   Shockra
● Help Yourself, Zero, Gun, Let's Go Dancing, Bass Jam, Dimension Extension, Bass Jam, Tone Clone
● *Encore;* ?, Fire
● *Show Notes:* Mike, introduced as a "special guest from a band called Tuna," joined in from Let's Go Dancing through Tone Clone. Fishman came out during Tone Clone and read a James Joyce selection about hell, after which Mike took a bass solo, and the musicians reprised the song.

February 5, 1993
The Ritz Theater, New York, NY
T,M   Guest   Ritz Power Jam
● *Set I;* Back at the Chicken Shack > Born Under a Bad Sign, Let it Rock, Improv Blues in G, She Caught the Katy, Down the Road, Mess of the Blues, Little Wing, Day Tripper, Escaping, Hey Joe
● *Set II;* Hip Hug-Her, Rock Me Baby, In the Night, Red House, Yonder Wall, She Belongs to Me, Not Fade Away, That's Heaven to Me, Just Before the Bullets Fly, Been Lovin You Too Long, Spanish Moon, All Along the Watchtower
● *Encore;* Gloria
● *Show Notes:* On this historic night, some of the greatest musicians in the history of jam rock joined together in New York City. The root band consisted of Warren Haynes (The Allman Brothers Band) on electric guitar, John Popper (Blues Traveler) on harmonica, Noel Redding (The Jimi Hendrix Experience) on bass and acoustic guitar, Linker Shlyver on bass, Chuck Leavell (sessions player with the Stones, Allmans, ARU, and BT) on piano, Bernie Worrell (Parliament Funkadelic) on clavinet and organ, Jaimoe (Allmans) on drums, Jerome Brailey (Parliament Funkadelic) on drums, and Marc Quinones (Allmans) on percussion. Also possibly in attendence were Paul Schaefer and Anton Fig of the *Late Night wth David Letterman* band and Will Smith, though they did not perform. For most songs, vocals were provided by Haynes, Popper, or Redding. Red House and Yonder Wall featured Dave Tronzo on slide guitar. Spanish Moon featured Trey on guitar and vocals, while Watchtower also saw members of The Dave Matthews Band join the fray while Trey, Dave, and Popper traded vocals. The encore, sung by Popper, featured Trey on guitar and Mike on bass.

February 6, 1993
The Wetlands, New York, NY
F   Guest   Shockra
● *Set II;* Dimension Extension, Zero, Give it up, Tone Clone, I Get High, Big Chief, Underground, People, Confessions of a Man
● *Show Notes:* Dimension Extension featured Fishman on vacuum, while Tone Clone featured Fishman on drums and a reading from Sun Ra's "Book of Information."

May 30, 1993
Laguna Seca Daze, Monterey, CA
P,T   Guest   Blues Traveler
● *Set II;* Sweet Talkin' Hippie, Save His Soul, Defense and Desire, Mulling it Over, Support Your Local Emperor, Whoops, Gina, 100 Years > Sweet Pain, Brother John, Mountain Cry
● *Encore* Gloria
● *Show Notes:* Mountain Cry featured Page on keyboards, while the encore saw Page, Trey and Todd Park Mohr of Big Head Todd and the Monsters join Blues Traveler on-stage.

June 8, 1993
Jazz Trio: Vermont Public Radio Broadcast
T,M   Side   Jazz Mandolin Project
● *Show Notes:* Trey and Mike play with Jamie Masefield.

June 10, 1993
Last Elm Café, Burlington, VT

T,M   Side   Jazz Mandolin Project
● *Show Notes:* Trey and Mike play with Jamie Masefield.

July 5, 1993
National Guitar Summit Workshop, Canterbury School, Milford, CT
T   Misc
● Caravan, Bewitched, Magilla, One Way Out, Why Don't We Do It in the Road, Rock Me Baby, Shaky Ground, Jump Monk, St. Thomas
● *Show Notes:* Trey hosted a guitar seminar and, later, played in the ensuing jam session. Some tapes that circulate are labeled July 13, 1993.

July 9, 1993
JC's, Plattsburgh, NY
T   Misc   Jazz Combo
● *Set I;* C Jam Blues, Magilla, Caravan, Bewitched, ? (Jazz Standard), Billie's Bounce
● *Set II;* The Country Open, Donna Lee, Green Dolphin Street, Jump Monk
● *Show Notes:* Trey played with Jamie Masefield (mandolin), Noel Sagerman (drums), and Justin Rose (upright bass).

September 3, 1993
JC's, Plattsburgh, NY
T   Misc   Jazz Combo
● *Show Notes:* Trey played with Jamie Masefield, Noel Sagerman, and Stacy Starkweather.

November 11, 1993
The Roxy, Los Angeles, CA
T,P   Guest   Widespread Panic
● *Set I:* Pleas, Space Wrangler > Henry Parsons Died > Travelin' Light, Diner > Pilgrims, Hatfield, Walkin' > Holden Oversoul, Love Tractor
● *Set II:* The Take Out > Porch Song, Can't Get High, Worryin', Makes Sense to Me, Little Kin, Chilly Water, New Orleans Fishwater, Pickin up the Pieces, Heroes, Mercy, Wondering, Mr. Soul
● *Encore:* Tipitina's, Low Spark of High-Heeled Boys > Time is Free Jam > Low Spark of High-Heeled Boys
● *Show Notes:* Makes Sense to Me featured T. Lavitz on keyboards. The encore began with T. and Trey playing with Widespread; T. gave way to Page after Tipitina's. Trey also played on an additional, unknown song earlier in the show.

1994

January 14, 1994
Last Elm Cafe, Burlington VT
T,F   Side   Bad Hat
● *Set II:* So What?, Billie's Bounce, The Country Open, Caravan, A-Train.

January 24, 1994
Granny Killiams, Portland, ME
T,F   Side   Bad Hat
● *Set I:* Billie's Bounce, Jump Monk, Lullabye In Birdland, In a Senti-

mental Mood, Magilla, Take The A-Train
● *Set II:* So What?, Milestones In The Sunshine, Caravan, Scrapple From The Apple, Nardis, Au Privave, The Country Open
● *Encore:* St. Thomas

January 27, 1994
Granny Kilian's, Portland, ME
T,F   Side   Bad Hat
● *Set II:* So What?, Milestones in the Sunshine, Caravan, Scrapple by the Apple, Nardis > Sunshine of Your Love Jam > Nardis, Country Open
● *Encore:* St. Thomas

January 28, 1994
JC's, Plattsburgh, NY
T,F   Side   Bad Hat

February 15, 1994
Club Toast, Burlington, VT
F   Guest   Shockra
● *Set I:* Stop The Revolution, Zero, Lila, Do What You Want, Question Air?, Who Do We Think We Are?, Freaks on Fire > Tezz > Underground People
● *Set II:* Cherokee, Don't Let It Stop Ya, 7th Revelation —> Fish's reading re: Bucky domes —> Elvin Jones, Feel Good > Big Chief > Fiyo on the Bayou, Live Wire
● *Encore:* Ma Bitch
● *Encore:* Power of Silence
● *Show Notes:* Fishman read a passage about bucky domes from Robert Anton Wilson's Cosmic Trigger between 7th revelation and Elvin Jones. A "bucky dome", also known as Geodesic dome, is a "sphere" created from a series of triangles, invented by Buckminster Fuller. Fishman lives in a bucky dome.

February 16, 1994
St Michaels College, Colchester, VT
T,F   Side   Bad Hat

February 17, 1994
The Paradise, Boston, MA
M   Guest   Shockra
● *Set I:* Undergorund People, Zero, Freaks On Fire, Do What You Want, 7th Revelation > Bass Jam > Don't Let it Stop Ya
● *Set II:* Cherokee, Question Air, Tezz Jam > What Makes You Feel Good, Elvin Jones, Who Do?, Confessions of a Man
● *Show Notes:* The bass jam and Don't Let it Stop Ya featured Mike on bass.
● *Tape Notes:* Some tape j-cards erroneously report that Mike played for the both sets.

February 23, 1994
Middlebury College, Middlebury, VT
T,F   Side   Bad Hat
● *Set I:* Enrnie's Groove, Jump Monk, Bewitched Bothered and Bewildered, Blues for Ernie, Take the A-Train, Milestones in the Sunshine
● *Set I:* So What?, Magilla, In a Sentimental Mood, The Country Open
Encore: St. Thomas

February 24, 1994
Last Elm Cafe, Burlington, VT
T,F   Side   Bad Hat
● *Set II:* Jump Monk, Magilla, Bewitched, Caravan, Milestones In The Sunshine.

February 25, 1994
JC's, Plattsburgh, NY
T,F   Side   Bad Hat

March 4, 1994
Metronome, Burlington, VT
T,F   Side   Bad Hat

March 8, 1994
Club Toast, Burlington, VT
T,F   Guest   Michael Ray and The Cosmic Krewe
● *Show Notes:* Trey and Fish sat in for the whole show.

March 9, 1994
The Paradise, Boston, MA
M   Guest   Aquarium Rescue Unit
● Plain or Peanut, Payday, Time Flack, No Eggs Underwater, Fixin' to Die, No Reason to Complain, Time is Free, Two Truckloads, Compared

Trey with Michael Ray and the Cosmic Krewe

to What, Salty Dog, Basically Frightened, ?, Elevator to the Moon > Trondossa, Yield Not to Temptation, ?, Peace and Hapiness > Zambi > Space is the Place
● *Encore:* Working on a Building
● *Show Notes:* Fixin' to Die featured Mike, who may have guested on other songs as well. Other guests during the show included Mark and Drew from Leftover Salmon on banjo and mandolin, respectively.

March 9, 1994
Ira Allen Chapel, University of Vermont, Burlington, VT
P   Guest   Widespread Panic
● *Show Notes:* Page sat in on Holden Oversoul and Love Tractor.

March 11, 1994
Club Metronome, Burlington, VT
All   Guest   Aquarium Rescue Unit
● Plain or Peanut > Yield Not To Temptation, Time Flack, Time is Free, Ain't No Reason to Complain, Salty Dog, Pay Day, Tuxedo Junction, Basically Frightened, Zambi > Space is the Place, Trundossa, No Egos Underwater, Two Truckloads
● *Encore:* Working on a Building
● *Encore:* Jam, Jam
● *Show Notes:* Trey, Mike, Fish, and Page sat in for the whole show, along with Michael Ray, Dave Grippo, and Joey Somerville, Jr. Members of Leftover Salmon (who opened) also wandered on and off-stage, contributing occasionally. The second encore was two separate jams, one around 17 minutes long and the second around 8 minutes. Some tapes are missing "Two Truckloads".

March 13, 1994
Lyndon State College, Lyndonville, VT
F   Guest   Aquarium Rescue Unit
● No Egos Underwater, Shoeless Joe, Salty Dog, Two Truckloads, Yield Not to Temptation, Compared to What, Payday, Working on a Building, Basically Frightened, Fixin' to Die, Time Flack
● *Encore:* Plain or Peanut, Jack Rabbit
● *Show Notes:* Fishman played washboard for the entire show.

April 22, 1994
Rockafellas, Columbia, SC
T,F   Guest   Aquarium Rescue Unit
● Plain or Peanut, Two Truckloads, No Egos Underwater, Time Flack, Salty Dog, Spoonful, Time is Free, Fixin' to Die, Lost My Mule in Texas, Jack the Rabbit, Zambi > Space is the Place, Trondossa, Yield Not to Temptation
● *Encore:* Working On a Building
● *Show Notes:* Fixin' to Die featured Fishman and Trey.

April 28, 1994
Sunfest '94, West Palm Beach, FL
T   Guest   Blues Travler
● Alone, Optimistic Thought, Mulling It Over, Should I Stay Or Should I Go, Low Rider > Go Outside and Drive, What's For Breakfast, Sweet Pain, The Good the Bad and the Ugly > Gina, Love and Greed, Crash Burn, Sweet Talking Hippie
● *Encore:* But Anyway

● *Show Notes:* Both Phish and Blues Traveler played one set each for "Sunfest '94". Trey played on "Mulling It Over" and, after the song ended, John Popper exclaimed, "Trey Anastasio! Boy, you know, those Phish guys...*love* that band."

June 3, 1994
Club Toast, Burlington, VT
T   Guest   Michael Ray and The Cosmic Krewe
● *Show Notes:* Trey sat in for the whole show.

June 18, 1994
Post-Show Party: Chicago, IL
F   Guest   Citrus
● *Show Notes:* After the Phish show, Fishman went to a party with some fans and jammed out for a while. Also participating in the jam were Mike Bizar on guitar, Mark Murphy on bass, Pete Herr on percussion, and Scott Bilstad, who, along with Fishman, played drums. A setlist is too difficult to identify, as it was a long jam with many variations on common themes. One of the participants taped a ninety-minute segment of the jam, which circulates. This tape often circulates mislabeled as a parking lot jam.

July 26, 1994
Club Toast, Burlington, VT
T,F   Guest   Michael Ray and The Cosmic Krewe
● *Show Notes:* Trey and Fish sit in for the whole show.

September 10, 1994
Portland Performing Arts Center, Portland, ME
T,F   Side   Bad Hat
● *Set I:* Contois, Turnaround Blues, Airmail Special, Ballad for Gordon, Jump Monk, Milestones in the Sunshine > Blackberry Blossom > Milestones in the Sunshine, Take the A-Train
● *Set II:* Jamie's Cryin' Tease > So What? > Donna Lee, Sentimental Mood, Nosanina, Country Open
● *Encore:* St. Thomas
● *Show Notes:* This venue was not Granny Killian's, as is sometimes reported.

September 11, 1994
Iron Horse Cafe, Northampton, MA
T,F   Side   Bad Hat
● *Set I:*   Contois, Turnaround, Jump Monk, Nozanina, Guyute Jam > Magilla, Milestones In The Sunshine
● *Set II:* Airmail Special, So What? > Donna Lee, Ballad For Trio, The Country Open
● *Encore:* St. Thomas

September 19, 1994
The Flynn Theater, Burlington, VT
T,F   Side   Bad Hat
● *Show Notes:* There was both an early show and a late show.

November 10, 1994
Club Toast, Burlington, VT
P   Guest   Michael Ray and The Cosmic Krewe

● *Show Notes:* Page sat in for the whole show.

1995

January 26, 1995
Memorial Auditorium, Burlington, VT
T   Guest   The Dave Matthews Band
● Seek Up, #36, Dancing Nancies, Best of What's Around, Rhyme and Reason, Jimi Thing, Recently, Water/Wine Jam, Ants Marching
● *Encore:* Nature Intro > Tripping Billies
● *Show Notes:* Trey guested on guitar from Jimi Thing through the end of the show. Tapes are sometimes incorrectly labeled January 27, 1995.

February 3, 1995
Johnson College, VT
T   Guest   Michael Ray and the Cosmic Crewe

February 10, 1995
Club Toast, Burlington, VT
T,F,M   Guest   Michael Ray and the Cosmic Crewe
● *Set I:* Drum Blessing > Second Line, Neverness > Echoes of the Boat People, Saturn, Beans and Rice, Celebrate
● *Set II:* Angels and Demons At Play > You Made a Mistake, "I'll Wait For You" Jam, Dancing Shadows > Pathology, Seven For Neon, Baby Baby, Champions, Shadow World
● *Show Notes:* Trey and Fish played the entire show. Mike Gordon came out during the second set on a one-string bass. This incarnation of the Krewe included Michael Ray, trumpet, vocals, keyboards; Dave Grippo, alto sax; Don Glasgo, valve trombone; Adam Klipple, keyboards; Stacy Starkweather, bass; Bob Gulloti, drums; Steve Ferraris, congas and other percussion.

February 24, 1995
Roseland Ballroom, New York, NY
T   Guest   The Dave Matthews Band
● Seek Up, Warehouse, What Would You Say, Say Goodbye, Minarets, Typical Situation, Granny, The Best of What's Around, All Along the Watchtower, Recently, Two Step > Ants Marching, Pay for What You Get, Halloween
● *Show Notes:* Say Goodbye featured John Popper on harmonica. Trey joined Popper and the DMB for an extended Watchtower.

March 5, 1995
Parimas Thai Restaurant, Burlington, VT
M   Guest   Gordon Stone Trio
● *Set I:* Abdul's, Pachysandra, Time Reel, Ballad For Gordon, Monkey Wrench, Blackberry Blossom
● *Set II:* Blue Monk, Touch and Go, Happy Landings
● *Show Notes:* Mike sat in for Stacy Starkweather the whole show. Other guests included Jamie Masefield and Dave Grippo.

April 8, 1995
East LA, Syracuse, NY
F   Guest   Sons of Papaya

● *Set I:* Rogue Hair, Cherry Pickin Frog, Display of Grace, Rose Hill, Cut the Wave, Trina's Odyssey, Everything is Everything, Self, Big Heart > Pelican Jig, Happy Birthday, Intestinal Fortitude, Pumpkins
● *Set II:* Cabin Fever > Attack of the Rodeo Clown, Route 89, Make You My Bitch, The Bus, Sea Captain, Chooch DeLuke, Leading the Elephants, Stevie's Crib, Go-Kart, Llama
● *Encore:* Weekapaug Jam, Self
● *Show Notes:* This SoP show was played at Mimi Fishman's birthday bash. She joined the band on stage for Make You My Bitch. Later, Fishman himself joined the band for the encore.

April 30, 1995
Jimmy's, New Orleans, LA
T   Guest   Michael Ray and The Cosmic Krewe
● *Show Notes:* Trey sat in for the whole show. It is possible that Fishman may have sat in as well.

July 28, 1995
Club Metronome, Burlington, VT
M   Guest   Leftover Salmon
● *Set I:* Paint it Black, Zombie Jamboree, Big Mamoo, Bosco Stomp, Whispering Waters, Dance on Your Head, Get Me Outta This City, Baby Hold On, Green Thing, Jokester, Cuckoo's Nest, Gold Rush
● *Set II:* Ask the Fish, John Hardy, 99 Years, Madame Rosin, The River's Risin, Hot Burrito Breakdown, Bend in the River, Get Your Ear Off My Floor, Hot Corn Cold Corn, Singing the Blues > Workin on a Building > Singin the Blues, Le Manet, Rueben's Train, Valley of the Full Moon, Cash on the Barrel, Funky Mountain Fogdown, Boogie, 4:20 Polka
● *Encore:* God Save the Queen, Wake and Bake
● *Show Notes:* Cuckoo's Nest and Gold Rush featured young Patrick Ross (13 years old at the time) on fiddle (not bass, as is labelled on some tapes). The first three songs of the second set featured Mike on bass. Mike also sang lead on "John Hardy."

July 24, 1995
Club Toast, Burlington, VT
F   Side   Pork Tornado

July 30, 1995
14th Annual Camp Creek, Indian Lookout Country Club, Duanesburg, NY
M   Guest   Max Creek
● Harmony, Big Boat, Dark Water, Waitin' For You, The Seven, See Things My Way, Life During Wartime, Jones, Tangled Up in Blue, If You Ask Me
● *Encore:* Will the Circle Be Unbroken, One More Saturday Night.
● *Show Notes:* Mike guested on bass for the last four songs of the set (but not the encore). He was joined by Aimon Cronin (vocals) and Bill Constable (fiddle) for Tangled Up in Blue and by Constable and members of Midnight Sun for If You Ask Me.

October 14, 1995
Emo's, Austin, TX
T   Guest   Medeski, Martin, and Wood
● *Show Notes:* Trey guested on Jelly Belly, Does Anybody Love My Jesus?, and Chubb Sub.

1996

January 24, 1996
Carmel's Coffee House, Burlington, VT
T,F   Side   Bad Hat
● Billie's Bounce, Magilla, Caravan, Bewitched, Jump Monk, Airmail Special, In a Sentimental Mood, So What?, Parker's Mood in C, Take The A-Train
● *Encore:* St. Thomas

February 24, 1996
Venue and Location Unknown
M   Guest   Max Creek
● *Set II:* Louisiana Sun, Wild Side, Jessica jam, Season of the Witch, Just a Rose
● *Encore:* 99 Years, Back Porch Boogie
● *Show Notes:* Mike played rhythm guitar because the only bass available was left-handed. He performed for the entire second set and was introduced as "Mike Jones" after "Just a Rose." Mike was asked to come up for the encore, but declined.

March 26, 1996
The Beacon Theater, New York, NY
P   Guest   The Allman Brothers Band
● *Show Notes:* Page filled in for an ailing Greg Allman.

April 1, 1996
The Academy, New York, NY
T,F   Side   Surrender To The Air
● *Set I:* Jam
● *Set II:* Jam

April 2, 1996
The Academy, New York, NY
T,F,P   Side   Surrender To The Air
● *Set I:* Jam
● *Set II:* Jam
● *Show Notes:* Page joined for the second set.

April 11, 1996
Club Toast, Burlington, VT
T   Guest   Merl Saunders and The Rainforest Band
● *Set I:* Opening Jam, Expressway (To Your Heart), The Harder They Come, Built For Comfort, Confusion, Dark Star Jam
● *Set II:* (We All Wanna) Boogie Little Bit, Caravan, Eduardo, Dynamite
● *Encore:* Let's Go Get Stoned > Fire on the Mountain
● *Show Notes:* Trey joined in on guitar from "Built for Comfort" through the end of the show. The highlight was an instrumental, 20+ minute Dark Star jam. The encore was nearly 45 minutes, despite Merl saying at the end of set two, "You know, I stopped using drugs. I have to go to bed!"

April 15, 1996
Club Toast, Burlington, VT
F   Side   Pork Tornado

● *Set I:* Jazz Jam, Pork Tornado -> Shakey Ground -> Pork Tornado, Everything I Play Gonna Be Funky, White Room -> White Wedding -> Play That Funky Music White Boy, Sex Machine, Zero Bag
● *Show Notes:* The second set list is unknown and tapes do not circulate. This version of the song "Pork Tornado" is an early version with minimal lyrics.

April 28, 1996
Jimmy's, New Orleans, LA
T,P   Guest   Michael Ray and The Cosmic Krewe
● *Show Notes:* This incarnation of the Krewe featured sax, trombone, keyboard, two drummers, bass, Michael Ray (trumpet), and a female vocalist, in addition to Trey and Page. This tape is among the most circulated guest appearances and is lauded for its intense jamming.

April 28, 1996
Fais Do-Do Stage, Jazzfest, New Orleans, LA
T   Guest   Bruce "Sunpie" Barnes and the Louisiana Samplers
Garbage Can Woman
● *Show Notes:* This setlist is (obviously) incomplete. Trey sat in for the entire set, playing along with Sunspots' guitarist Jim Kebodeaux. They traded solos first, then jammed later. Garbage Can Woman featured Sunpie (on harmonica), Jim, and Trey sitting on the edge of the stage after Sunpie said "I don't think they can hear us. Let's get out on the porch."

May 2, 1996
Venue Uncertain, Burlington, VT
M   Guest   Leftover Salmon

July 2, 1996
Pista Speedway Stadium, Lonigo, Italy
All   Open   Santana
● ?, Jungle Strut -> Soul Sacrifice -> ? -> Soul Sacrifice, Serpents & Doves, Brotherhood -> Everybody's Everything, Live Together, ?, Exodus -> Get Up Stand Up -> Exodus, Maggot Brain, ?, Mystic Man, Going Home -> (Da Le) Yaleo, Europa, Make Somebody Happy Jam, Black Magic Woman -> Gypsy Queen, Oye Como Va, Europa Reprise
● *Encore:* Evil Ways -> A Love Supreme, Jingo
● *Show Notes:* Phish's opening set was rained out, so they sat in with Santana for an extra-long amount of time. The band joined from the bluesy instrumental (title unknown) before Exodus through Maggot Brain. Black Magic Woman was full of teases, including "I Feel the Earth Move."

July 19, 1996
Les Arenes, Arles, France
All   Open   Santana
● *Show Notes:* Phish sat in with Santana for a few songs.

October 1, 1996
Slade Hall, University of Vermont, Burlington, VT
M   Guest   Gordon Stone Trio
● *Set I:* John Hardy, Slipped Disk, Hold To A Dream, Hubbleville, Midnight on the Highway, Touch and Go, Hard Hearted
● *Set II:* Abdul's, Weekly Time, Tiramisu > I Lied, Caravan > One Way

Rider, Mokey Wrench, Same Old South, Sunday Driver
● *Show Notes:* Mike sat in on bass for the whole show, occasionally lending vocals.

October 3, 1996
Last Elm Cafe, Burlington, VT
M,F   Guest   Gordon Stone Trio
● *Set I:* John Hardy, Slipped Disk, Hold To A Dream, Hubbleville, Backtrackin', Foggy Mountain Breakdown, Midnight on the Highway, Touch and Go
● *Show Notes:* Mike sat in for the whole show. Fishman sat in on washboard during the second set, but the second set list is not known

October 30, 1996
Chameleon Club, Atlanta, GA
M,P   Guest   Aquarium Rescue Unit

1997

January 25, 1997
ARC, Ann Arbor, MI
M   Side   The Drop Cops

April 12, 1997
Chuck's, Syracuse, NY

F   Guest   Stash
● *Show Notes:* Fishman sat in for three songs with this popular Phish cover band. Phish had played this venue in 1988.

May 2, 1997
Venue and Location Unknown
M   Guest   Max Creek

May 5, 1997
Mermaid Lounge, New Orleans, LA
F   Guest   Galactic
● *Show Notes:* Fishman sat in on drums for Sissy Strut.

May 21, 1997
Club Toast, Burlington, VT
T,M,P   Side   New York
● Never Too Late To Spend, Headache, Peter's Dad, Dirt, Big Bird, Only Shallow > Noise of Carpet, She's Not The One, Saw It Again, Melody, Stand > Izabella, 2000
● *Encore:* Hello Violence, New York Groove, Blues Jam
● *Show Notes:* Page joined in for the show-closing Blues Jam.

July 19, 1997
Vermont Brewers Fest, Waterfront Park, Burlington, VT
F   Guest   Mr. Charlie and Blues For Breakfast
● *Show Notes:* Fish sat in for one song.

The Academy: Surrender to the Air

Michael McNamara

September 20, 1997
Club Toast, Burlington, VT
F   Guest   Gordon Stone Trio
● Southwind, Monkey Wrench, Hubbleville, Touch and Go, Time Reel > Crazy Creek > Time Reel > Abdul's, Blackberry Blossom, Dread Banjo, Well, You Needn't, Hog In The Spotlight
● *Encore:* Happy Landings.
● *Show Notes:* Fish played drums for the whole show.

September 25, 1997
Slade Hall, University of Vermont, Burlington, VT
F   Guest   Gordon Stone Trio
● Minor Swing, Hubbleville, Blackberry Blossom, Monkey Wrench, Suthwind, Some Funky Grass, Touch and Go, Time Reel > Abdul's, Dread Banjo, Hoggin' The Spotlight
● *Show Notes:* Fish played drums for the whole show.

October 19, 1997   Toast, Burlington, VT
T,F   Side   Pork Tornado
● *Show Notes:* Trey sat in for part of the show with Fishman's side project.

October 19, 1997
The Flynn Theater, Burlington, VT
T   Guest   Steve Winwood
● *Show Notes:* Trey came out for the final encore number, Give Me Some Lovin'.

November 7, 1997
Club Toast, Burlington, VT
M   Guest   Max Creek
● *Set I:* You Let Me Down Again, I'm A Steady Rollin' Man, The Only One, The Field > When It Comes To You > Blood Red Roses > If You Ask Me
● *Set II:* Louisiana Sun > Thank You (Falettinme Be Mice Elf Agin) > Wild Side > Outside Of Home > Just A Rose
Enc: Lawyers Guns and Money, What I Like About You
● *Show Notes:* Mike joined the band after Louisiana Sun and played through the end of the show.

November 8, 1997
Club Toast, Burlington, VT
M   Guest   Max Creek
● *Set II:* Sailin' Shoes, Something Is Forming, Cecilia > Wild Side > Just A Rose > Season Of The Witch > Just A Rose
● *Show Notes:* This setlist is incomplete and includes only the portion of the second set where Mike appeared. He guested on a a second bass.

December 22, 1997
Variety Playhouse, Atlanta, GA
F   Side   Zambiland Orchestra
● Drum Jam, Old Joe Clark, East Virginia Blues, I Believe to My Soul, Fixin to Die, Eat Some Worms, Christmas Carol Medley, A Love Supreme,
● *Show Notes:* This setlist is incomplete and out of order; there were actually three distinct sets. Fishman played for most of whole show, which featured scores of musicians in rotating jams, including: Derek Trucks on sarod (not sitar), Jeff Sipe (ARU, and mastermind of Zambi-

land) on drums, Khofi Burrbidge (ARU) on flute and keys, Jeff Mosier (ARU) on banjo, Gary "El Buho" Gazaway on trumpet, Michael Ray on trumpet, T. Lavitz on keys, Dr. Dan Matrazzo (Fiji Mariners) on keys, Bob Baglione on guitar, Todd Nance (WSP) on drums, Yonrico Scott (Derek Trucks Band) on drums, Count M'Butu on percussion, Lincoln Metcalf as conductor and on French horn, Jimmy Herring (ARU) on guitar, Todd Smalley (DTB) on bass, someone (of the Virginia disco band Right On) on bass, Ed Nitty on bass, John Cowan (Newgrass Revival) on bass and vocals, two female vocalists, and Fishman, who played drums, tamborine, congas, and vacuum. One memorable jam featured a sarod, standup bass, banjo, and vacuum quartet; a trio jam featured vacuum, a PVC-pipe digeredoo, and an uber-thin clarinet-like reed. There were six horns: 3 trumpets, 2 saxes, a flugelhorn, and the reed. Fixin to Die was led by Colonel Bruce Hampton, who was crowned King of Zambliand.

1998

January 13, 1998
The Iron Horse, Northampton, MA
F   Side   Pork Tornado
● *Set I:* Mary, Who Do You Love, Trouble Every Day, Jazz Instrumental, Everything I Play Gonna Be Funky, She Thinks I Still Care, Jungle Boogie, Guabi Guabi, R&B Instrumental
● *Set II:* Pork Tornado, Maybelline, Dreams to Remember, Disco Inferno, Kiss My Black Ass, Zero Bag, Can't Take My Eyes off You

January 31, 1998
Unknown Venue in the East Village, New York, NY
P   Guest   Gravity

February 1, 1998
Unknown Venue in the East Village, New York, NY
P   Guest   Gravity

February 10, 1998
Sneakers Bar n Grill, Winooski VT
T   Guest   Sneakers Jazz Band

February 14, 1998
Flynn Theater, Burlington, VT
M,F   Guest   Bela Fleck and The Flecktones
● *Show Notes:* The Flecktones played two strong sets, and then Mike and Fish joined them for their encore. Mike appeared to enjoy himself, as he engaged in a bass duel. Fishman also hammed it up on a percussion machine, and everyone else stopped to let him jam.

April 17, 1998
Higher Ground, Winooski, VT
T   Side   Eight Foot Flourescent Tubes
● *Set I:* Bing Bong, Sand, Free Thoughts, Mr. Meat Man, Naturally To Blame, Wighat, The Silicone Fairy, Jam > Higher Ground
● *Set II:* Tore Up, Magilla, Sunny, Stir It Up, Crossroads, Let The Good Times Roll, Soul Power Jam, Drums
● *Show Notes:* The second set included guest appearances from Dave

Grippo, James Harvey, and Bobby Hackney.

September 24, 1998
Middle East, Cambridge, MA
F   Guest   Michael Ray and the Cosmic Krewe
● *Show Notes:* While it was rumored on the internet that Fishman sat in, he did not attend this show.

November 1, 1998
Dead Goat Saloon, Salt Lake City, UT
T,M   Misc
● Driver, Alburquerque, Cortez the Killer, Stir It Up, Bittersweet Motel, Jam -> Teach Your Children
● *Show Notes:* Trey and Mike showed up at an open mic night at The Dead Goat Saloon and treated those in attendance to a few songs. The jam before Teach Your Children included teases of "Summertime" and "While My Guitar Gently Weeps." Joseph Sirotnak guested on guitar and additional vocals from Cortez the Killer through Teach Your Children and his friend "Ken" added guitar and vocals to "Stir It Up." An attempt to close with "Will the Circle Be Unbroken" was aborted when no one could remember enough of the words.

November 10, 1998
Martyr's, Chicago, IL
F   Guest   Dark Star Orchestra
● *Set I:* Wang Dang Doodle > Esau, Peggy-O, Li'l Red Rooster, Brown Eyed Women, Lost Sailor > Saint of Circumstance > Deal
● *Set II:* Help on the Way > Slipknot! > Franklin's Tower, Estimated Prophet > Eyes of the World > Drumz > St. Stephen > Throwing Stones > Not Fade Away
● *Encore:* Revolution
● *Encore:* Blow Away, Terrapin Station
● *Encore:* Playin' in the Band
● *Show Notes:* Dark Star Orchestra plays entire Dead shows, from start to finish, as they originally happened. On this date, they performed October 31, 1983 with Fishman joining the fray midway through Estimated Prophet and remaining through the rest of the show. After that Dead show was played in its entirety, they played some elective encores: a "Blow Away" reprise and "Terrapin Station", then came back for a third encore, "Playing in the Band".

November 19, 1998
Ziggy's, Winston-Salem, NC
T   Guest   Viperhouse

December 4, 1998
The Loft, Tokyo, Japan
F   Guest   Big Frog
● *Show Notes:* While Fishman was on vacation in Japan, he sat in with a Japanese band that plays many Dead and Phish covers. Thought they are hard to find, tapes do circulate.

December 7, 1998
Club Toast, Burlington, VT
M   Guest   Strangefolk
● *Set I:* Stout Hearted, Songs We Sing, New Glock 2, Great Long While, Sweet Libation, Whatever, Step Inside, Alaska, The Night Before

● *Set II:* Udderly Addled, Pawn, Walnut, Mud Spring Draw, Two Boys, Strange Ranger, Heart Blood, Lines and Circles > Strange Ranger Jam > Heart Blood Jam > Lines and Circles, Like You Anyway > Thriller > Like You Anyway
● *Encore:* Casey Jones, Westerly
● *Show Notes:* The "Lines and Circles" sandwich featured Mike on bass.

December 29, 1998
The Wetlands Preserve, New York, NY
M,F   Guest   Viperhouse
● *Show Notes:* While it is known that Mike and Fishman were in attendance, it is not believed that they actually played.

1999

January 26, 1999
Muddy Waters, Burlington, VT
M   Side   ?
● *Show Notes:* Mike joined Jamie Masefield and Doug Perkins (of the Gordon Stone Trio).

February 4, 1999
Slade Hall, University of Vermont, Burlington, VT
M   Side   ?
● Nardis, Devil's Dream, So What?, Yardbird Suite, ?, Red Haired Boy, Airmail Special, Ain't Love Funny > All Blues, Minor Swing, Ballad For Trio, Scrapple From The Apple
● *Encore:* St. Thomas.
● *Show Notes:* Mike joined Jamie Masefield and Doug Perkins (of the Gordon Stone Trio) from Yardbird Suite through the end of the show. After Yardbird Suite, Jamie talked about living in Slade and meeting Mike when they were UVM students.

February 10, 1999
Higher Ground, Winooski, VT
F   Side   Jazz Mandolin Project
● *Set I:* Nimbus, Chapeau, Milliken Way, Flux, The Search, Contois
● *Set II:* Black Market, Full House, Boodha, Johnny's Marching Song, Opera
● *Encore:* The Gourd

February 11, 1999
Sommerville Theatre, Sommerville, MA
F   Side   Jazz Mandolin Project
● *Set I:* Barber's Hint, The Phoenicians, Good & Plenty, The Search, Contois, Mandoneon
● *Set II:* Black Market, Full House, Johnny's Marching Song, Jovan, Chapeau, Opera
● *Encore:* The Gourd

February 12, 1999
Irving Plaza, New York, NY
F   Side   Jazz Mandolin Project
● *Set I:* Flux, Chapeau, Good and Plenty, Nimbus, Jovan, Mandoneon
● *Set II:* Black Market, Full House, Milliken Way, Boodha, Clip, Opera

● *Encore:* The Gourd

February 13, 1999
The 9:30 Club, Washington, DC
F   Side   Jazz Mandolin Project
● *Set I:* Barber's Hint, Milliken Way, Chapeau, Boodha, The Phoenicans, Mandoneon
● *Set II:* Black Market, Full House, Jovan, Contois, Clip, Opera
● *Encore:* The Gourd

February 15, 1999
Higher Ground, Winooski, VT
T   Side   Solo
● *Set I:* Dirt, Dogs Stole Things, Runaway Jim, Brian and Robert, Guyute, Driver, Chalk Dust Torture
● *Set II:* Come On Baby Lets Go Downtown, Gotta Jibboo, Ooh Child, Tops Off, I Can See Clearly Now, Let The Good Times Roll, Free Thought, Bell Bottom Blues, Sand > Drums, Possum, Bing Bong
● *Encore:* Aqui Como Alla, Row Jimmy, Band Intro Jam
● *Show Notes:* This gig was a benefit for Very Special Arts and a warm-up for Trey's Carnegie Hall show. The first set featured Trey solo on acoustic guitar. He performed the second set electric with Russ Lawton on drums and Tony Markellis on bass. Drums featured Trey on a smaller drum set.

February 22, 1999
Carnegie Hall, New York, NY
T   Side   Solo
● Unknown, Brian and Robert, Dirt, Billy Breathes
● *Show Notes:* Trey played an acoustic set at this benefit for the Tibet House. Philip Glass joined on piano for the opener whiile Trey played electric. Brian and Robert featured Nawang Khechog on Tibetan long flute and Foday Musa Suso on kora. Billy Breathes featured Peter Cater on piano. Trey also joined Patti Smith on electric guitar for the show's finale, People Have the Power. Other artists on the bill included Chaksam-Pa, Cibo Matto, Sean Lennon, Shawn Colvin, Phillip Glass, and R.E.M.

The Academy: Surrender to the Air

March 4, 1999
Higher Ground, Winooski, VT
M   Guest   Smokin Grass
● John Hardy, Salt Creek, Hold To A Dream, Caravan, One Way Rider, Midnight Moonlight
● *Show Notes:* Mike joined the band for several songs, as he sang and played his banjo.

March 6, 1999
Tammany Hall, Worcester, MA
F   Guest   The Dude of Life
● Tow Truck Driver, Bullets In The Rainbow
● *Show Notes:* These two songs also featured members of the band Foxtrot Zulu.

March 15, 1999
Johnson State College, Johnson, VT
M   Guest   Glen Schweitzer's Jalapeno Brothers
● *Show Notes:* This show featured special guests Mike Gordon, Vassar Clements, and Buddy Cage.

March 18, 1999
Mad Mountain Tavern, Waitsfield, VT
M   Guest   Glen Schweitzer's Jalapeno Brothers
● *Show Notes:* This show featured special guests Mike Gordon, Vassar Clements, and Buddy Cage.

March 20, 1999
Emerald City, Montpelier, VT
M   Guest   Glen Schweitzer's Jalapeno Brothers
● *Show Notes:* This show featured special guests Mike Gordon, Vassar Clements, and Buddy Cage.

March 21, 1999
The Matterhorn, Stowe, VT
M   Guest   Glen Schweitzer's Jalapeno Brothers
● Goin' Down the Road Feelin' Bad, Love the One You're With, Friend of the Devil, Rocky Top, Turn on Your Lovelight
● *Show Notes:* This setlist is incomplete. This show featured special guests Mike Gordon, Vassar Clements, and Buddy Cage.

March 22, 1999
Higher Ground, Winooski, VT
M   Guest   Glen Schweitzer's Jalapeno Brothers
● *Show Notes:* This show featured special guests Mike Gordon, Vassar Clements, and Buddy Cage.

March 26, 1999
Higher Ground, Winooski, VT
P   Guest   Derek Trucks Band

March 31, 1999
Tuttle Middle School, South Burlington, VT
T   Side   Vermont Jazz All-Stars
● *Show Notes:* The Tuttle Middle School jazz band, led by Dave Grippo,

played their spring concert. Afterwards, Grippo was joined by Trey, Stacy Starkweather, James Harvey, Bruce Skylar, Big Joe Burrell, and Jeff Salisbury. They played two short sets of jazz, including "Caravan," Maceo Parker's "Shake Everything That You Got," and James Harvey's own composition "House of Gold."

April 1, 1999
Higher Ground, Winooski, VT
F   Side   Pork Tornado
● *Set I:* Everything I Play Gonna Be Funky, Pork Tornado, Mary, Do You Know What I Mean, Get Down Tonight, Trouble Every Day -> Who Knows Jam -> Tequilla Jam -> Trouble Every Day
● *Set II:* Jungle Boogie -> Irish Jig, Kiss My Black Ass -> I Don't Mind 'Cause I'm Blind, Sex Machine -> Shake Your Money Maker -> Sex Machine
● *Encore:* Dreams to Remember
● *Show Notes:* Pork Tornado included a "Voodoo Child (Slight Return)" tease. Before Trouble Every Day, Dan Archer did a brief spoof on "If I Had A Hammer."

April 2, 1999
The Pickle Barrel, Killington, VT
F   Side   Pork Tornado

April 3, 1999
Pearl Street, Northampton, MA
F   Side   Pork Tornado

April 5, 1999
Stone Coast Brewery, Portland, ME
F   Side   Pork Tornado

April 6, 1999
The Paradise, Boston, MA
F   Side   Pork Tornado

April 7, 1999
Lupo's, Providence, RI
F   Side   Pork Tornado
● *Set I:* Do You Know What I Mean, Everything I Play Gonna Be Funky, Pork Tornado -> Sing a Simple Song, She Keeps Me Guessin', Trouble Every Day, Zero Bag, Tell Me Something Good
● *Set II:* End of the Line, Mary, Home is Where You Are, I Roll into Town, Jungle Boogie -> Shake Your Money Maker -> Jungle Boogie, Guabi Guabi, Kiss My Black Ass
● *Encore:* Irish Jig, R&B Instrumental, Disco Inferno

April 8, 1999
Toad's Place, New Haven, CT
F   Side   Pork Tornado

April 9, 1999
Higher Ground, Winooski, VT
T   Guest   Jorma Kaoukanen

April 10, 1999
Tramps (Wetlands?), New York City
F   Side   Pork Tornado

April 11, 1999
Tradewinds, Sea Bright, NJ
F   Side   Pork Tornado
● *Set I:* Pork Tornado -> Sing a Simple Song, She Keeps Me Guessin', Home is Where You Are, Mary, Do You Know What I Mean, Jazz Instrumental, Disco Inferno
● *Set II:* Everything I Play Gonna Be Funky, Zero Bag, Jungle Boogie, Tell Me Something Good, End of the Line, ?, Got my Mojo Workin', Guabi Guabi, Kiss My Black Ass
E● *ncore:* Irish Jig, Sex Machine

April 12, 1999
Club Front, San Rafael, CA
T,P   Side   Phil and Friends
● Help on the Way > Slipknot > Franklin's Tower, Shakedown Street, The Wheel, Stella Blue, Ghost, Taste, Waste, Prince Caspian, 2001
● *Show Notes:* This show was not for the public, but was actually a practice session for the upcoming Warfield shows.

April 12, 1999
Sweetwater's, Mill Valley, CA
T   Side   Solo
● Dirt, Brian and Robert, When the Circus Comes
● *Show Notes:* Trey joined the crowd at Sweetwater's for an open mic night.

April 13, 1999
The Trocadero, Philadelphia, PA
F   Side   Pork Tornado
● *Set I:* Mary, Do You Know What I Mean, Everything I Play Gonna Be Funky, Get it On -> Uptime, Home Is Where You Are, Pork Tornado -> Chinatown Jam -> Bring It On Home Jam -> Pork Tornado -> Sing A Simple Song, Tell Me Something Good, She Keeps Me Guessin'
● *Set II:* Disco Inferno, Got My Mojo Workin', Trouble Every Day, It's Your Thing, Zero Bag -> Wipeout, Kiss My Black Ass
● *Encore:* Irish Jig, Jazz Instrumental, Jungle Boogie

April 14, 1999
The 9:30 Club, Washington DC
F   Side   Pork Tornado

April 15, 1999
The Warfield Theatre, San Francisco, CA
T,P   Side   Phil and Friends
● *Pre Set:* Hello Old Friend
● *Set I:* Viola Lee Blues, Big Railroad Blues, Jack-a-Roe, Cosmic Charlie, Wolfman's Brother -> Uncle John's Band
● *Set II:* Alabama Getaway, Sugaree, Like a Rolling Stone -> I Know You Rider, Row Jimmy, Shakedown Street -> Jam -> The Wheel -> Not Fade Away
● *Encore:* Mr. Tambourine Man

● *Show Notes:* Hello Old Friend was played before the show began and included Phil, Steve, and Phil's children. The monster Viola Lee to open the show (first live Viola Lee by Phil since Halloween, 1970) clocked in at just over 32 minutes and the Uncle John's to close was more than 25 minutes long. The encore featured Phil on vocals; prior to the encore, Phil spoke to the crowd about organ donation.

April 16, 1999
The Warfield Theatre, San Francisco, CA
T,P   Side   Phil and Friends
● *Set I:* Help on the Way > Slipknot! > Franklin's Tower, Wish You Were Here, Tennessee Jed, Stella Blue, Alligator
● *Set II:* Bertha, Prince Caspian, St. Stephen -> The Eleven > Unbroken Chain, Chalk Dust Torture > Mountains on the Moon > Scarlet Begonias -> Fire on the Mountain
● *Encore:* Ripple
● *Show Notes:* Phil, Trey, Steve, Page and John continued their practice of opening with long, stron jams; the show-opening triplet was over 37 minutes long. Stella Blue was performed instrumental with Steve on pedal steel. The second set began with teases of Dark Star, St. Stephen, and Mike's Song; one highlight was a long, jammed out Caspian that benefited from Kimock's lead. Alligator was a surprise treat; Phil had not played the song on-stage since April 29, 1971. Ripple was performed acoustic; along with Bertha and Scarlet, it featured Dead alumnus Donna Jean Godchaux on vocals. Prior to the encore, Phil spoke to the crowd about organ donation.

April 17, 1999
The Warfield Theatre, San Francisco, CA
T,P   Side   Phil and Friends
● *Check:* Terrapin Station, Eyes of the World, My Favorite Things
Set I: Dark Star -> It's Up to You, Days Between -> Dark Star -> My Favorite Things, Mississippi Half-step, Bird Song
● *Set II:* Terrapin Station > Down with Disease > Dark Star, Friend of the Devil, Casey Jones, Morning Dew, Goin' Down the Road Feelin' Bad > And We Bid You Goodnight
● *Encore:* Box of Rain
● *Show Notes:* The last two songs of each set featured Donna Jean Godchaux on vocals. The outro jam after the second verse of Dark Star included a brief "Other One" jam. Prior to the encore, Phil spoke to the crowd about organ donation.

April 18, 1999
The Fillmore Auditorium, San Francisco, CA
T,P   Guest   Santana
● Going Home -> Right On Be Free, Migra, Put Your Lights On, Living Space, Serpents & Doves, Day of Celebration, Right On, Everybody's Everything -> Dance Sister Dance, Africa Bamba, Maria Maria, Love of My Life, (Da Le) Yaleo, Make Somebody Happy -> Get It in Your Soul -> Mother Nature's Son, Guajira -> Bacalao Con Pan (drum solo), Singing Wind -> Black Magic Woman -> Gypsy Queen -> Third Stone from the Sun Jam -> Gypsy Queen -> Oye Como Va
● *Encore:* One True Thing, Jingo
● *Show Notes:* While out west for the "Phil and Friends" shows, Trey and Page joined Santana for a few songs (Living Space through Dance

Pork Tornado

Sister Dance) in the middle of his show. Carlos' brother Jorge Santna also sat in on Guajira and Ozomatli joined in for Oye Como through the end of the show.

April 25, 1999
Tipitina's, New Orleans, LA
F   Guest   Jazz Mandolin Project
● *Show Notes:* Fishman sat in on conga for one song.

May 3, 1999
Michigan Theater, Ann Arbor, MI
T   Side   Trey Acoustic/Electric
● *Set I:* Farmhouse, Snowflakes in the Sand, Mist, Bouncing Around the Room, The Inlaw Josie Wales, Guyute, Brian and Robert, Possum
● *Set II:* Ooh Child, Free Thought, Downtown, Gotta Jibboo, Keyboard Solo, Then Came You, First Tube, Sand, I Can See Clearly Now, Will It Go Round in Circles, Drums Jam, Silicon Fairy
● *Encore:* Aqui Como Alla, Voodoo Child
● *Show Notes:* Mist was introduced as "Bake and Boil" at the show. Trey allowed the fans to name the new instrumental now known as The Inlaw Josie Wales. Trey's solo keyboard jam included an "Axel F" tease.

May 4, 1999
Murat Theatre, Indianapolis, IN
T   Side   Trey Acoustic/Electric
● *Set I:* Dirt, Dogs Stole Things, Mist, Snowflakes in the Sand, The Inlaw Josie Wales, Talk, Bathtub Gin, Kissed By Mist, Back on the Train, Wading in the Velvet Sea, Chalk Dust Torture
● *Set II:* Will It Go Round in Circles, First Tube, Ooh Child, Bell Bottom Blues, Heavy Things, Windora Bug, Somanatin, Andre the Giant, I Can See Clearly Now, Sand > Drums Jam, Voodoo Child
● *ncore:* Row Jimmy, Last Tube > Downtown
● *Show Notes:* Bathtub Gin was dedicated to Ali and Jesse (fans Ali McDowell and Jesse Jarnow) for naming The Inlaw Josie Wales as Minestrone. Last Tube included a band intro jam.

May 6, 1999
The Riviera, Chicago, IL
T   Side   Trey Acoustic/Electric
● *Set I:* Back on the Train, Farmhouse, The Inlaw Josie Wales, Sample in a Jar, Driver, Snowflakes in the Sand, Brian and Robert, When the Circus Comes, Mist, Punch You in the Eye > Runaway Jim
● *Set II:* First Tube, Will It Go Round in Circles, Gotta Jibboo, Heavy Things, Tops Off, I Can See Clearly Now, Sand, Aqui Como Alla, Ooh Child, Somanatin, Windora Bug, Come On (Part One)
● *Encore:* Silicon Fairy
● *Show Notes:* During PYITE, Trey whistled the lead guitar lines for the Landlady segment.

May 7, 1999
American Theatre, St. Louis, MO
T   Side   Trey Acoustic/Electric
● *Set I:* Back on the Train, Wolfman's Brother, Farmhouse, Dogs Stole Things, Bouncing Around the Room, Kissed By Mist, Mist, Guyute, Wading in the Velvet Sea, Prince Caspian, Aftermath, AC/DC Bag
● *Set II:* Further On Up the Road, First Tube, Downtown, Gotta Jibboo, Voodoo Child, Aqui Como Alla, Ooh Child, Heavy Thing, Come On (Part One), Sand > Drums Jam, Free Thought, I Can See Clearly Now
● *Encore:* Andre the Giant, Will It Go Round in Circles, Last Tube
● *Show Notes:* Wolfman's Brother included a story about the first time that Trey met Fishman. He compared Fishman's role in Phish to Paul McCartney's role as The Walrus in The Beatles. Before Aftermath (which had never been played live with Phish), Trey talked about his friend Roger Halloway, who got engaged on stage at a Phish show on April 14, 1993. Roger joined Trey for Aftermath (which he helped write) and AC/DC Bag (which carries his name in the lyrics). Last Tube included a Happy Birthday tease after Tony Markellis mentioned that it was a crew member's birthday.

May 8, 1999
Oscar Meyer Theatre, Madison, WI
T   Side   Trey Acoustic/Electric
● *Set I:* Back on the Train, The Inlaw Josie Wales, Farmhouse, Snowflakes in the Sand, Alumni Blues, Billy Breathes, Mist, Chalk Dust Torture, When the Circus Comes, Kissed By Mist, Fluffhead, Brian and Robert
● *Set II:* First Tube, Will It Go Round in Circles, Ooh Child, Gotta Jibboo, Further On Up the Road, Free Thought, Somanatin, Aqui Como Alla, Sand > Drums Jam, Come On (Part One), Bug, Heavy Things
● *Encore:* Windora Bug, Voodoo Child
● *Show Notes:* Alumni was dedicated to the students who were skipping finals to see the show. Billy Breathes was preceded by a story about a conversation Trey had with Neil Young. Neil recommended that Trey move around during the solo set to keep the audience interested! Fluffhead was not followed by Fluff's Travels.

May 10, 1999
Thomas Wolfe Auditorium, Asheville, NC
T   Side   Trey Acoustic/Electric
● *Set I:* Farmhouse, Wading in the Velvet Sea, Back on the Train, You'll Know My Name, The Inlaw Josie Wales, Strange Design, Snowflakes in the Sand, Kissed By Mist, Billy Breathes, Roggae -> The Man Who Stepped Into Yesterday, Possum

● *Set II:* The Wind Cries Mary, Further On Up the Road, Heavy Things, Will It Go Round in Circles, Gotta Jibboo, Ooh Child, Bug, Windora Bug, Free Thought > Drums Jam, Sand
● *Encore:* I Can See Clearly Now
● *Show Notes:* After engaging in a discussion about song titles, Trey announced that he had decided to keep the title "Minstrone," instead of "Purple Hue."

May 11, 1999
The 9:30 Club, Washington, D.C.
T   Side   Trey Acoustic/Electric
● *Set I:* Back on the Train, Farmhouse, Kissed by Mist, Snowflakes in the Sand, Bathtub Gin, Sample in a Jar, Driver, You'll Know My Name, Billy Breathes, Sleep, Blue and Shiny
● *Set II:* Gotta Jibboo, Will It Go Round In Circles, First Tube, Ooh Child, Heavy Things, Sand > Drums Jam, I Can See Clearly Now, Aqui Como Alla, Voodoo Child
● *Encore:* Row Jimmy
● *Show Notes:* Gin was dedicated to Susannah Goodman. As with the night before, Trey played You'll Know My Name after a lengthy introduction of another song. This time, it was Mist. Trey talked about how there were three sets of "duologies," or songs related to each other, on his solo tour. Billy Breathes was played on piano. Tom Marshall guested on Sleep and Blue and Shiny.

May 12, 1999
Graffiti, Pittsburgh, PA
F   Guest   Jazz Mandolin Project

May 13, 1999
SUNY-Binghampton Concert Theatre, Binghampton, NY
T   Side   Trey Acoustic/Electric
● *Set I:* Farmhouse, Back on the Train, Driver, Guyute, Kissed By Mist, You'll Know My Name, Mist, Wading in the Velvet Sea, Brian and Robert, Billy Breathes, Sleep, Blue and Shiny, Waste
● *Set II:* Gotta Jibboo, The Wind Cries Mary, Will It Go Round In Circles, Windora Bug, Further On Up The Road, First Tube -> Sand, Ooh Child > Drums Jam, Smells Like Teen Spirit, Silicon Fairy
● *Encore:* I Can See Clearly Now, Downtown
● *Show Notes:* Kissed by Mist was again dedicated to Julia Butterfly Hill. Trey dedicated You'll Know My Name to the graduating seniors bar-hopping in SUNY—Binghampton's "Pub Crawl." Billy Breathes was played on piano. Blue and Shiny and Waste featured Tom Marshall on vocals. Smells Like Teen Spirit was played jokingly for a fan who screamed out the title after Trey announced that the band would play one more song. They played one verse and then played Silicon Fairy. The graduating seniors were again referenced at the end of the second set and and the end of the encore, which was dedicted to them.

May 13, 1999
Recher Theatre, Towson, MD
F   Guest   Jazz Mandolin Project

May 14, 1999
State Theatre, Portland, ME
T   Side   Trey Acoustic/Electric

● *Set I:* The Inlaw Josie Wales, Back on the Train, When The Circus Comes, Snowflakes In The Sand, Water In The Sky, Farmhouse, Wolfman's Brother, Feel Like Makin' Love, You'll Know My Name, Billy Breathes, Runaway Jim, Kissed By Mist

● *Set II:* First Tube, Will It Go Round in Circles, Gotta Jibboo, Heavy Things, Tops Off, Ooh Child, Sand > Drums Jam, Voodoo Child

● *Encore:* Aqui Como Alla, I Can See Clearly Now, Last Tube

● *Show Notes:* Trey launched into the chorus of Feel Like Makin' Love before You'll Know My Name after discussing the "raunchy" nature of a general admission show. Billy Breathes was played on piano. Kissed By Mist was dedicated to Julia Butterfly Hill. Tony Markellis introduced Tops Off as a blues standard, but admitted that no one knows what the song is really about. Tony also introduced the band at the end of the encore and thanked the crew while indirectly referencing the Chris Kuroda "fan club," CK5.

May 14, 1999
Milestone's, Rochester, NY
F   Guest   Jazz Mandolin Project

May 15, 1999
Palace Theatre, Albany, NY
T   Side   Trey Acoustic/Electric

● *Set I:* The Inlaw Josie Wales, Back on the Train, Farmhouse, Kissed by Mist, Beauty of My Dreams, Wading in the Velvet Sea, Snowflakes

Albany, New York

in the Sand, Possum, Billy Breathes, You'll Know My Name

● *Set II:* Heavy Things, First Tube, Windora Bug, Free Thought, Gotta Jibboo, Bell Bottom Blues, Sand -> Drums Jam, Come On (Part One)

● *Encore:* The Wind Cries Mary, Ooh Child

● *Show Notes:* Kissed by Mist was dedicated to Julia Butterfly Hill. Trey played along with the audience during Possum, picking up a drink while the crowd sustained the chorus. Billy Breathes was played on piano. During Free Thought, Trey introduced the band and then himself as the "Bad Lieutenant." He also got the crowd pumped up for the summer's upcoming Oswego extravaganza.

May 15, 1999
Hobart Folk Festival, Geneva, NY
F   Guest   Jazz Mandolin Project

May 17, 1999
The Flynn Theatre, Burlington, VT
Benefit for the Committee on Temporary Shelter
T   Side   Trey Acoustic/Electric

● *Set I:* Farmhouse, Snowflakes in the Sand, Brian and Robert, Driver, Back on the Train, Mist, Runaway Jim, Billy Breathes

Intermission Featuring Tthe Frederick Tuttle Middle School Jazz Band (conducted by Dave "The Truth" Grippo): In the Mood, Jumpin' at the Woodside, I Feel Good

● *Set II:* The Wind Cries Mary, Heavy Things, First Tube, Ooh Child, Sand > Drums Jam, I Can See Clearly Now, Aqui Como Alla, Free Thought, Downtown, Then Came You, Last Tube

● *Encore:* Further On Up The Road, Voodoo Child

● *Show Notes:* Billy Breathes was played on piano. Trey joined the intermission jazz band on I Feel Good. The band returned the favor on Then Came You and Last Tube. Grippo stayed on stage for Further On Up The Road and was joined by Mike, Page, and Fishman. Grippo left, and the members of Phish stayed on for Voodo Child.

May 19, 1999
The Fillmore Auditorium, Denver, CO
T   Side   Trey Acoustic/Electric

● *Set I:* Taste, Farmhouse, Brian and Robert, Mist, Back on the Train, Wading in the Velvet Sea, Billy Breathes, When The Circus Comes, You'll Know My Name, Guyute

● *Set II:* First Tube, Gotta Jibboo, Heavy Things, Will It Go Round In Circles, Ooh Child, Aqui Como Alla, Sand > Drums Jam, I Can See Clearly Now

● *Encore:* Windora Bug, Voodoo Child

● *Show Notes:* This show marked the opening of the new Fillmore Auditorium.

May 20, 1999
The Boulder Theatre, Boulder, CO
T   Guest   Various

● *Show Notes:* During a benefit at the theatre, Trey joined Tony Furtado and a host of other artists on stage.

June 5, 1999
Higher Ground, Winooski, VT
M   Guest   Leftover Salmon

Salty Dog, High on a Mountaintop
● *Show Notes:* Though the actual show was much longer, the songs listed featured Mike on bass. Also, Jeff Mosier made a guest appearance.

June 8, 1999
Higher Ground, Winooski, VT
T   Side   Vermont Jazz All-Stars
● *Set I:* Take The A-Train, Undecided, Sweet Little Angel, Night In Tunisia, Going Down Slow, Caravan, Jump Monk
● *Set II:* Bright Lights Big City, The Chicken, For The Losers, Cars Trucks Buses, The Jodi Grind, Big Joe Shuffle
● *Encore:* The Landlady, Blues For Cape Verde

June 12, 1999
Club Metronome, Burlington, VT
T   Guest   Big Joe Burrell

July 3, 1999
The Brandyhouse, Atlanta, GA
M,F   Guest   13 Sons

July 5, 1999
Fusion Fest, Shrine Park, Macon, GA
M   Guest   The Derek Trucks Band
● A Love Supreme

August 11, 1999
Higher Ground, Winooski, VT
T   Guest   Los Lobos
● Not Fade Away -> Bertha, She's About a Mover

September 15, 1999
The Last Day Saloon, San Francisco, CA
M   Guest   The Jazz Mandolin Project
● *Set I:* Flux, Spiders, Tuang Guru, Johnny's Marching Blues, The Milliken Way
● *Set II:* Black Market > Fullhouse, Xenoblast -> Blackberry Blossom -> Xenoblast, St. Thomas, The Sabre Dance, The Country Open
● *Show Notes:* The Xenoblast segment of the show featured Mike on bass.

September 20, 1999
Rialto Theatre, Tuscon, AZ
T   Guest   Leftover Salmon
● *Show Notes:* One night before Phish's Tuscon show, Trey joined Salmon for, among other songs, "The Shape I'm In." Apparently, the crowd began doing the Meatstick dance at one point, which prompted Trey to dance along on stage.

October 29, 1999
Higher Ground, Winooski, VT
F   Guest   moe.
● *Set I:* Stranger Than Fiction, Rise, Hi and Lo -> Meat
● *Set II:* The Ghost of Ralph's Mom, Blue Eyed Son, Bring it Back Home, Yodelittle, Opium -> Seat of My Pants -> Rebubla
● *Encore:* San Bernardino, Fire -> I Know You Rider -> Fire

● *Show Notes:* Fishman sat in on drums for Yodelittle and the Fire/Rider/Fire encore combination. Jamie Masefield also guested on these songs, as well as Bring it Back Home.

2000

January 14, 2000
The Meeting House, Starksboro, VT
M   Side
● *Set I:* Scrapple From The Apple, Samba De Orpheus, Little Maggie, Ballad For Trio, Billie's Bounce, Blue Bayou, Devil's Dream
● *Set II:* Red Haired Boy, Aint Love Funny > Hard Time, Cherokee, Black Orpheus, Airmail Special.
● *Show Notes:* Mike played bass and sang, Jamie Masefield playd mandolin, and Doug Perkins played acoustic guitar.

January 28, 2000
M   Guest   Max Creek
Higher Ground, Winooski, VT
● *Set I:* Secrets -> Big Boat, Rainbow -> Double Dare -> Don't Think Twice, It's All Right, I Will Always See Your Face -> Late In The Evening
Set II: Love Makes You Lose Your Mind -> Can't Let Go, I Want To Die Easy -> Cities
● *Encore:* The Bug, Henry -> Just A Rose
● *Show Notes:* Mike played a second bass for the second set and encore.

February 5, 2000
Carnegie Hall, New York, NY
T   Side   Solo
● Farmhouse, The Inlaw Josey Wales, The House Where Nobody Lives
● *Show Notes:* For the second consecutive year, Trey played an acoustic set at this benefit for the Tibet House. At the show, he renamed The Inlaw Josie Wales as The Inlaw Josey Wales and debuted a new song in The House Where Nobody Lives. The latter was played with David Byrne guesting on accordian. Throughout the night, Trey guested with several other artists: with Nawang Khechog and R. Carlos Nakai on an instrumental number; with Rufus Wainwright, Patti Smith, and several others on When Will I Be Loved; with Philip Glass on Third Street; and on the final song of the evening, with Patti Smith, Nawang Khechog, R. Carlos Nakai, and David Byrne on People Have the Power. Third Street was announced as a new Trey original which he had written with Glass earlier in the week. In addition to those mentioned above, performers included Angelique Kidjo, Ashley MacIssac, Virginia Rodrigues, and the Gomang monks.

February 17, 2000
Higher Ground, Winooski, VT
T   Guest   The Dude of Life
Francella, Self, Pete Rose, Dahlia
● *Show Notes:* The listed songs featured Trey on guitar.

February 21, 2000
Patrick Gymnasium, University of Vermont, Burlington, VT
T   Guest   Primus

Blue Collared Tweekers > Communication Breakdown
● *Show Notes:* Trey was reportedly introduced as "Eddie Van Anastasio" before joining the fray.

February 24, 2000
Olympic Auditorium, Los Angeles, CA
T   Guest   B.B. King & the Roots
Soundcheck Jam, Rock Me Baby, Trey Jam, Rock Me Baby, Blues Jam
● *Show Notes:* Trey played along with B.B. King & the Roots as part of the filming of IMAX's *All Access*. Trey also played "Somewhere Over the Rainbow" solo on his guitar during a break in the filming and teased "Happy Birthday."

February 26, 2000
The Brandy House, Atlanta, GA
F   Guest   Colonel Bruce Hampton & The Fiji Mariners
Nash, Turn On Your Lovelight > Time is Free
● *Show Notes:* Fishman joined the Colonel for about an hour, including these two songs.

April 8, 2000
The Orpheum Theatre, Boston, MA
M   Guest   Phil Lesh and Friends
● *Set I:* Jam > St. Stephen > The Eleven > Friend of the Devil > Shakedown Street, Tom Thumb, Bird Song
● *Set II:* Uncle John's Band > In Your Eyes > Mr. Fantasy > My Favorite Things > Mountains of the Moon > In The Midnight Hour
● *Encore:* Wolfman's Brother
● *Show Notes:* Mike guested on the Wolfman's encore on a second bass guitar. The song also featured a bass duet between Mike and Phil.

May 3, 2000
Middlebury College, Middlebury, VT
M   Guest
● *Show Notes:* Mike Gordon played with Vassar Clements, Russ Lawton, Doug Perkins, and Gordon Stone.

May 4, 2000
Saenger Theater, New Orleans, LA
T   Side   Oysterhead
● I am Oysterhead, Mr. Oysterhead, Floyd Jam > Rubbernecking Lions, He Used to be the Owner of the World, Blue Ginger, Happiness in my Pants, Jam > Wildwood Weed, Sinkin' Down, Pseudo Suicide
● *ncore:* Immigrant Song, The Israelites, All Day and All the Night, House of the Rising Sun
● *Show Notes:* Owner of the World was dedicated to Fishman, who ran on stage and bowed. The song began humorously, as Stewart Copeland began playing the wrong song and the band had to regroup. Pseudo Suicide included lyrical quotes from Primus' "Jerry Was a Race Car Driver" and Phish's "Reba." All three musicians were wearing white protective jumpsuits.

May 7, 2000
Howlin' Wolf, New Orleans, LA
F   Guest   Project Logic

● *Show Notes:* This Jazzfest show featured a cavalcade of special guests. In addition to Fishman, the guests included Fuzz (guitar) and Rob Somerville (sax) from Deep Banana Blackout, John Medeski, and Warren Haynes.

May 7, 2000
Cajun Queen Riverboat, New Orleans, LA
F   Guest   Galactic
● *Show Notes:* An exact setlist is not known, but Fishman sat in on Layin' in the Cut and one other song.

May 20, 2000
NBC Studios, New York, NY
T   Guest   Kid Rock
● Only God Knows Why
● *Show Notes:* Trey joined Kid Rock during the television show *Saturday Night Live* and provided a second rhythm guitar to Kid's radio smash.

May 23, 2000
Varieties, Atlanta, GA
M   Guest   Colonel Bruce Hampton and the Code Talkers
● *Set II:* Going Through the Motions, Be My Jelly, No Egos Underwater, Jack the Rabbit, Head on Back to Nashville, Elevator to the Moon, Diggin' Up Bones
● *Encore:* Basically Frightened -> Compared to What -> Basically Frightened -> Have a Bright Tomorrow
● *Show Notes:* Mike played guitar from No Egos Underwater through the end of the show. At one point, Colonel Bruce chided Mike about directing him in *Outside Out*.

July 10, 2000
Private Party, Indianapolis, IN
M,F   Side   Jam Session
● *Show Notes:* Trey's brother-in-law Kevin hosted a private party after that evening's Phish show. Mike and Fish entertained some of the folks in the band practice room by jamming for awhile in the wee hours of the mornings. Mike played guitar for about an hour, while Fish jammed on drums until sunrise.

September 30, 2000
House of Blues, Mandalay Bay, Las Vegas, NV
T   Guest   Les Claypool
● *Set I:* Thela, Shattering Song -> Riders on the Storm -> Shattering Song, Hendershot, Shine On, Riddles -> Jerry Was a Race Cat Driver -> Wynona -> Riddles
● *Set II:* Pink Floyd's *Animals*
● *Encore:* He Used to Be the Owner of the World -> Smoke on the Water -> He Used to Be the Owner of the World, Tomorrow Never Knows
● *Show Notes:* The "Owner of the World" sandwich was performed by Oysterhead (Trey Anastasio, Stewart Copeland, and Les Claypool) while Les's entire Frog Brigade joined for the finale.

VENUE INFORMATION

This section compiles known information about the location and capacity of all the venues at which Phish has performed (since 1993), organized by state (U.S.) or nation (non-U.S.). Selected venues are highlighted following the tables, in narrative entries organized alphabetically by venue name.

This section serves utilitarian purposes, as a reference for information on a venue listed on a coming tour (Phish or otherwise) as well as for venues played in the past. It also provides the reader with an historical framework for Phish's career that is unrelated to their musical de-

velopments, showing progress in terms of venue size and scope. For example, one can glimpse Phish's popularity surge between 1994 and 1996 simply by looking at the stats for Penn State, Pennsylvania. In 1994, Phish performed in the 6,846-capacity Rec Hall, but only two years later, played a venue more than twice as large—the 16,000-capacity Bryce Jordan Center.

Tables compiled by Mark Toscano and Billy Rickards. Highlights compiled by Jeremy Goodwin. Both parts revised and appended by Ellis Godard.

Venue	Location	Phone Number	Seating	I/O	Past Shows
Alabama					
Five Points South Music Hall	1016 20th St. S, Birmingham	205-322-2263		I	5/2/94
Oak Mountain Auditorium	1000 Amphitheatre Dr., Pelham	205-985-9797	reserved/g.a.	O	10/15/94
Arizona					
America West Arena	201 E. Jefferson, Phoenix	602-379-7800	reserved		12/2/96
Buena Vista (Valencia) Theater	265 W. Valencia Rd., Tucson	520-746-1823			5/12/94
Celebrity Theatre	440 N 32nd St., Phoenix	602-267-1600			3/16/93
Compton Terrace	20000 Maricopa Rd., exit 162A off I-10, Phoenix	N/A	g.a.		10/11/95
Desert Sky Pavilion	75th Ave. exit, I-10, Phoenix	602-254-7200	g.a./reserved	O	7/29/97, 10/1/00
Hayden Square	Tempe				5/13/94
Mesa Amphitheatre	263 North Center, Mesa	602-678-2178	g.a.	O	12/9/94
Austria					
Arena	Vienna			?	6/19/97
Belgium					
Le Botanique	Brussels			I	2/14/97
Dour Festival	Dour			O	7/13/96
Ancienne Beguigue	Brussels			?	7/1/92
Canada					
88th Street Music Hall	Vancouver, British Columbia			I	4/3/93
Commodore Ballroom	Vancouver, British Columbia			I	8/24/93
Concert Hall/ Masonic Temple	888 Yonge St., Toronto, Ontario	416-960-0888	1,800 g.a.	I	4/27/93, 8/9/93, 4/6/94
Congress Center	55 Colonel By Dr., Ottawa, Ontario	613-563-1984		I	7/5/94
Le Spectrum	Montreal, Quebec			I	4/29/93
Metropolis	Montreal, Quebec				4/5/94
Molson Amphitheater	Lakeshore Blvd. West at Ontario Place; Ontario		reserved/g.a	O	7/20/99, 7/6/00
Orpheum Theatre	865 Seymour, Vancouver, British Columbia	604-665-3050	reserved	I	10/6/95, 11/26/94
Pacific Coliseum	Hastings & Renfrew, Vancouver, British Columbia	604-253-2311	reserved	I	11/23/96
Theatre St. Denis	Montreal, Quebec				7/6/94
Vogue Theatre	Vancouver, British Columbia			I	5/22/94

Venue	Location	Phone Number	Seating	I/O	Past Shows
California					
Acker Gym at Chico State U.	Warnor at Legion St., Chico	916-898-6005	g.a.	I	12/4/94
ARCO Arena	1 Sports Pkwy., Sacramento	916-928-6900	g.a.	I	11/30/96
Arlington Theatre	1317 State St., Santa Barbara	805-963-4408		I	5/17/94
Cal Expo Amphitheatre	1600 Exposition Blvd., Sacramento	916-263-3066	g.a.	O	9/27/95
Civic Auditorium	1855 Main St., Santa Monica	310-458-8551	g.a.		12/10/94
Coors Amphitheather	2050 Entertainment Circle, Chula Vista	619-671-3600	20,000 10,000 reserved, 10,000 lawn)	O	9/18/99, 10/04/00
The Cow Palace	Geneva & Santos, Daly City	415-469-6063	~14,000 g.a.	I	11/29/96
Crest Theatre	1313 K St., Sacramento			I	3/22/93
East Gym, Humboldt State University	Arcata			I	3/28/93
Event Center at SJSU	7th & San Carlos, San Jose	408-924-6377	g.a.	I	12/3/94
The Fillmore				I	10/15/98
Greek Theatre, UC Berkeley	Gayley Rd., Berkeley	510-642-9988	~8,000 g.a.	O	8/28/93, 10/29/98
Greek Theatre	2700 N. Vermont, Los Angeles	213-665-5857	reserved		9/29/95
Greek Theatre, University of Redlands	Redlands				3/19/93
Laguna Seca Raceway	1025 Monterey Rd., Monterey	408-422-6138		O	5/29/93, 5/30/93, 5/28/94, 5/29/94
Luther Burbank Center	50 Mark West Springs Rd., Santa Rosa	707-527-7006			3/24/93
Montezuma Hall, SDSU	San Diego				5/14/94
The Palace	Hollywood				3/17/93, 3/18/93
Pauley Pavillion, UCLA	405 Hilgard Ave., Los Angeles	310-825-2101	reserved		12/1/96
Recreation Hall, UC Davis	LaRue btwn Russell & Hutchison, Davis	916-752-2571	g.a.	I	12/2/94
Santa Cruz Civic Auditorium	307 Church St., Santa Cruz	408-429-3779		I	3/25/93
Shoreline Amphitheatre	1 Amphitheatre Pkwy, Mountain View	415-967-4040	g.a./reserved	O	9/30/95, 7/31/97, 10/17/98, 10/18/98, 10/6/00, 10/7/00
Sports Arena	3500 Sports Arena Blvd., San Diego	619-225-9813 x300	g.a.		12/4/96
Spreckels Theater	1221 Broadway, San Diego	619-235-0494	reserved	I	12/7/94, 12/8/94
Summer Pops	Embarcadero Marina Park South, San Diego	619-699-4200	g.a.		9/28/95
UCSB Event Center	Ocean Rd., Santa Barbara	805-893-3536	reserved		12/6/94
Ventura County Fairgrounds	Seaside Park, 10 W. Harbor Blvd	805-648-3376	g.a.	O	7/30/97
Ventura Theater	26 S. Chestnut St., Ventura	805-648-1888		I	3/21/93
Verizon Wireless Amphitheatre (was Irvine Meadows Amph.)	8808 Center Drive, Irvine	949-855-6937		O	9/19/99, 10/05/00
The Warfield Theatre	982 Market St., San Francisco	415-567-2060	~2,250 g.a./ reserved	I	3/26/93, 3/27/93, 5/25/94, 5/26/94, 5/27/94
Wiltern Theatre	3790 Wilshire Blvd., Los Angeles	212-380-5005		I	5/16/94
Colorado					
McNichols Arena	1635 Bryant St., Denver	303-640-7300		I	11/16/97, 11/17/97, 11/4/98
El Pomar Great Hall, Pike's Peak Center	190 S. Cascade Ave., Colorado Springs	719-520-7453 or 719-520-7469	2,000 reserved	I	3/9/93

Venue	Location	Phone Number	Seating	I/O	Past Shows
Fiddler's Green	6350 Greenwood Plaza Blvd., Englewood	303-220-7000	17,916 (Reserved: 7,416; Lawn: 10,500)	O	9/27/00
Red Rocks Amphitheatre	16351 Highway 93, Morrison	303-694-1234	g.a.	O	8/20/93, 6/10/94, 6/11/94, 6/9/95, 6/10/95, 8/4/96, 8/5/96, 8/6/96, 8/7/96
Western State College Gym	Gunnison			I	3/14/93
Connecticut					
Hartford Civic Center	One Civic Center Plaza, Hartford	860-727-8010	15,500 reserved	I	10/23/96, 11/26/97
New Haven Coliseum	275 S. Orange St., New Haven	203-772-4200 x211	reserved	I	12/29/93, 12/2/95, 11/24/98
Meadows Music Center	61 Savitt Way, Hartford	860-548-7370	25,000 (7 reserved, 18 lawn)	O	6/30/00, 7/1/00
Sports Center, University of Hartford	West Hartford				4/30/93
Czech Republic					
Lucerna Theatre	Prague			I	7/5/98, 7/6/98
Archa Theater	Prague			I	6/20/97
Delaware					
Bob Carpenter Center, U. of Delaware	S. College Ave., Newark	302-831-4016	~5,000 g.a./reserved	I	2/13/93, 4/18/94
Denmark					
Grey Hall, The	Freetown Christiana, Copenhagen			I	6/30/98, 7/1/98, 7/2/98
Midtifyns Festival	Dyrskuepladsen, Ring, Fyn			O	7/4/98
Pumpehuset	Copenhagen			I	3/2/97
Roskilde Festival	Copehhagen			O	6/27/92
Roskilde Festival	Roskilde			O	6/29/97
District of Columbia.					
Bender Arena, American University	4400 Massachusetts Ave. NW	202-885-3267	5,000 g.a./reserved	I	12/28/93
Lisner Auditorium, GW University	730 21st St. NW	202-994-6800	1,500 g.a./reserved	I	2/7/93
England					
Brixton Academy	Radio One Music Festival, London			I?	7/3/92
Glastonberry Festival	Worthy Farm, Pilton, Somerset			O	6/27/97
Royal Albert Hall	London			I	6/16/97
Shepherd's Bush Empire	London			I	7/11/96, 2/13/97
Florida					
The Band Shell, U. of Florida	Gainesville				10/23/94
Bayfront Park Amphitheatre	Miami			O	8/3/93
The Boatyard Village	Clearwater				4/29/94
The Cameo Theatre	1445 Washington Ave., Miami Beach	305-532-0922		I	2/25/93
Coral Sky Amphitheatre	601-7 Sansbury Way, West Palm Beach	407-795-8883	g.a./reserved	O	11/2/96

Venue	Location	Phone Number	Seating	I/O	Past Shows
Florida *(continued)*					
The Edge Concert Field	100 W. Livingston St., Orlando	407-843-5775	g.a.		2/23/93, 4/30/94, 10/22/94
Florida Theatre	233 W. University Ave., Gainesville	352-375-7361		I	2/27/93
Leon County Civic Center	505 West Pensacola St., Tallahassee	800-322-3602	reserved	I	10/29/96
Mahaffey Theatre	400 First St., St. Petersburg	813-892-5798	reserved	I	10/20/94
The Moon	1105 E. Lafayatte St., Tallahassee	904-878-6900			2/22/93
O'Connell Center	University Ave. and N.S. Dr., Gainesville	904-392-5500	reserved		11/12/95, 11/3/96
The Ritz Theatre	Tampa			I	2/26/93, 8/2/93
The Sundome	4202 E. Fowler Ave., Tampa	813-974-3002	g.a./reserved	I	11/15/95
SunFest	West Palm Beach	N/A	N/A	O	4/28/94
Sunrise Musical Theatre	5555 NW 95th Ave., Sunrise	305-741-7300	reserved	I	10/21/94
U. of Central Florida Arena	Alafaya Trail, Orlando	407-823-3070	g.a./reserved	I	11/14/95
West Palm Beach Auditorium	1610 Palm Beach Lakes Blvd., West Palm Beach	407-683-6010	g.a.	I	11/16/95
France					
Bataclan	Paris			I	2/18/97
Centre International	Deauville			?	7/9/96
Elysee Montmartre	Paris			I	6/30/92
Espace Julien	Marseilles			?	7/10/97
L'Aeronef	Lille			?	6/25/97
La Transbordeur	Lyon/Villeurbanne			I	6/9/97
Les Arenes	Arles			?	7/19/96
La Lairerie	Strasbourg			?	6/24/97
Le Zenith	Paris			I	7/10/96
Theatre Antique	Vienne			I	7/17/96
Theatre de Verdure	Nice			I	7/18/96
Georgia					
Atlanta Civic Center Theatre	395 Piedmont Ave., Atlanta	404-524-7354	reserved	I	10/25/94
Fox Theatre	660 Peachtree St., Atlanta	404-881-2100	4,800 reserved	I	4/23/94, 11/9/95, 11/10/95, 11/11/95
Lakewood Amphitheatre	2002 Lakewood Way, Atlanta	404-627-9704	g.a./reserved	O	6/15/95, 7/23/97 8/6/98, 7/3/99, 7/4/99, 6/23/00, 6/24/00
Masquerade Music Park (adjacent to The Masquerade)	695 North Ave., NE, Atlanta	404-577-8178	~4,000 g.a.	O	7/31/93
The Omni (destroyed 7/27/97)	100 Techwood Dr. NW, Atlanta	N/A	16,510 reserved	I	10/31/96
Roxy Theatre	Atlanta	404-233-7699 or 404-233-1062	1,200– 1,500 g.a.	I	2/19/93, 2/20/93, 2/21/93
Germany					
Forum, The	Nuremberg			I	6/21/96
Hurricane Festival	Scheesal			O	6/21/97
Incognito	Munich			I	2/25/97
Loreley Festival	Loreley			O	6/21/97
Longhorn	Stuttgart-Wangen			I	2/26/97
Huxley's Neue Welt	Berlin			I	2/28/97
Markethalle	Hamburg			I	6/23/96, 3/1/97

Venue	Location	Phone Number	Seating	I/O	Past Shows
Music Hall, The	Hanover			I	6/24/96
Philipshalle	Dusseldorg			I	6/23/92
Resi	Nuremberg			?	6/24/92
Serenadenhof	Nuremberg			O	6/3/97
Stadtpark	Hamburg			O	6/25/96, 6/19/92
Tanzbrunnen	Cologne			?	6/22/96
Waldbuhn	Nordheim			?	6/20/92
Wartesaal	Cologne			I	2/16/97
Idaho					
Boise State U. Pavilion	1910 University Dr., Boise	208-385-1766	g.a./reserved	I	6/7/95
Illinois					
Aragon Ballroom	Chicago		g.a.	I	4/10/93
Assembly Hall, U. of Illinois	1800 S. 1st St., Champaign	217-333-5000	g.a./reserved	I	10/22/95, 11/8/96, 11/19/97
Allstate Arena (was Rosemont Horizon)	6920 North Mannheim Rd., Chicago	847-635-6601	18,500, mix of g.a./reserved	I	10/31/95, 10/03/99, 9/22/00, 9/23/00
UIC Pavilion, U. of Illinois	1140 West Harrison, Chicago	312-413-5700	8,500-9,000 g.a./reserved	I	6/28/94, 11/25/94, 11/7/98, 11/8/98, 11/9/98
World Music Theatre	19100 S. Ridgeland Ave., Tinley Park	708-614-1616	g.a./reserved	O	8/14/93, 8/8/97, 10/3/98
Indiana					
Deer Creek Music Center	12880 E 146th St., Noblesville	317-776-3337	14,000 g.a. 6,000 reserved	O	6/19/95, 8/12/96, 8/13/96, 8/10/97, 8/11/97, 8/2/98, 8/3/98, 7/25/99, 7/26/99, 7/10/00, 7/11/00, 7/12/00
Indiana University Auditorium	1200 E. Seventh, Bloomington	812-855-1103	before renovation: 3,760 reserved after: 3,100	I	11/19/94
Murat Theatre	520 N. New Jersey St., Indianapolis	317-635-2433		I	8/13/93, 6/24/94
Iowa					
Civic Center	Des Moines			I	6/14/94
Five Seasons Arena	370 First Ave. NE, Cedar Rapids	319-362-1729	g.a./reserved	I	10/20/95
Hilton Coliseum, Iowa State University	Elwood Dr. & Lincoln Ave., Ames	515-294-3347	14,000 reserved	I	11/14/96
Student Union Ballroom	Iowa City		g.a.	I	4/12/93
Ireland					
S.F.X. Centre	Dublin			?	6/13/97, 6/14/97
Italy					
Teatro Olimpico	Rome			I	2/22/97
Teatre Smeraldo	Milan			I	2/20/97
Tenax	Florence			I	2/21/97
Fillmore	Cortemaggiore			I	2/23/97
Stadia Bratamsco	Trento			O	7/3/96
Stadio Olimpico	Rome			O	7/5/96
Duomo Square	Pictoia			O	7/6/96
Parco Aquatica	Milan			O	7/7/97

Venue	Location	Phone Number	Seating	I/O	Past Shows
Italy *(continued)*					
La Marna	Sesto Calende			O	7/15/96
Piazza Risorgimento	Cuomo			?	7/5/97
Spiaggia di Rovoltella	Desenzano			?	7/6/97
Japan					
Big Cat	4F Big Step, 1-6-14 Nishi Shinsaibashi, Chuo-ku, Osaka	(06)-6258-5008	750 (est.)	I	6/15/00
Clubb Quattro	3-29-1 Sakae, Naka-ku, Nagoya	(052) 264-8211	550	I	6/13/00
Drum Logos	1-8-25 Maizuru, Chuo-ku, Fukuoka	092-791-0999	650	I	6/14/00
Hibiya Outdoor Theatre	1-5 Hibiya Koen, Chiyoda-ku, Tokyo		2200	O	6/11/00
On Air East	2-14-9 Dogenzaka, Shibuya-ku, Tokyo	(03) 3475-9999	1000 (est.)	I	6/9/00
Zepp Osaka	1-18-31 Minami Kohoku, Suminoe-Ku, Osaka, Japan	06-6361-0313	2180	I	6/16/00
Zepp Toyko	Palette Town 1-Chome, Aomi, Koto-Ku, Tokyo	03-5720-9999	2709	I	6/10/00
Kansas					
Memorial Hall	600 N. 7th St., Kansas City	913-371-7555	3,300 g.a./ reserved	I	4/13/93, 8/17/93, 6/13/94
Sandstone Ampthitheater	633 North 130th St	816.931.3330	14,000	O	7/28/98, 6/30/99, 9/25/00
Kentucky					
Louisville Gardens	525 W. Muhammed Ali Blvd, Louisville	502-574-0060	6,850 g.a. 5,600 reserved	I	10/29/95
Macauley Theatre	315 W. Broadway, Louisville	502-562-0194 or 502-584-7777	1,380 g.a./ reserved (usually reserved)	I	4/16/93, 8/15/93
The Palace Theatre	629 S. 4th Ave., Louisville	502-583-4335	2,700 reserved	I	10/10/94
Rupp Arena	430 W. Vine St., Lexington	606-233-4567	~23,000 reserved	I	11/7/96
Louisiana					
Fairgrounds at 1996 JazzFest	New Orleans	N/A	N/A	O	4/26/96
McAllister Auditorium, Tulane University	McAllister Dr., New Orleans	504-865-5196 or 504-865-5190	1,800 reserved	I	10/14/94
State Palace Theatre	1108 Canal St., New Orleans	504-866-1811	2,800 reserved	I	5/4/94, 10/17/95
Tipitina's	501 Napoleon Ave., New Orleans	504-895-8477	900 g.a.	I	3/2/93, 3/3/93
Maine					
The Ballpark	Old Orchard Beach				7/3/94
Bangor Auditorium	100 Dutton St., Bangor	207-941-9711	g.a.	I	5/7/93, 11/2/94
Cumberland County Civic Center	One Civic Center Square, Portland	207-775-3458	9,000 g.a.	I	12/30/93, 12/11/95
Loring Air Force Base	Alternate Rte. 1, Limestone	207-328-7005	g.a. Lots.	O	8/16/97, 8/17/97, 8/15/98, 8/16/98
Portland Expo	Portland				2/3/93
Maryland					
Meriwether Post Pavillion	10475 Little Patuxent Parkway, Columbia	800.955.5566	10,000 g.a 5,000 reserved	O	8/8/98, 7/9/99, 9/17/00
USAir Arena (formerly The Capital Centre)	1 Harry S Truman Dr., Landover	301-350-3400	19,000 reserved	I	11/22/95, 12/28/97

Venue	Location	Phone Number	Seating	I/O	Past Shows
Massachusetts					
Boston Garden (R.I.P.)	Boston	N/A	15,509 reserved	I	12/31/94
The Fleet Center *	Causeway St., Boston	617-624-1000	19,580 reserved	I	12/30/96, 12/31/96
Tweeter Center (formerly Great Woods Amphitheatre)	885 South Main St., Mansfield	508-339-2331	19,900 g.a./ reserved	O	7/24/93, 7/8/94, 7/9/94, 6/30/95, 7/1/95, 7/12/99, 7/13/99, 9/11/00, 9/12/00
Hard Rock Café	131 Clarendon St., Boston	617-424-7625 or 617-353-1400	~250-500 g.a.	I	1/28/93
Lowell Memorial Auditorium	50 East Merrimack St., Lowell	978-937-8688 or 978-454-2299	2,854 reserved	I	5/16/95
Mullins Center	University of Mass., Amherst	413-545-0505	9,000 reserved	I	4/16/94, 11/3/94, 12/4/95, 12/5/95
Worcester Centrum	50 Foster St., Worcester	508-755-6800	14,800 reserved	I	12/31/93, 12/28/95, 2/29/95, 11/28/97, 11/29/97, 11/30/97, 11/27/98, 11/28/98, 11/29/98
Michigan					
Devos Hall	245 Monroe Ave NW, Grand Rapids	616-456-3922 or 616-742-6600	4,200 reserved	I	11/14/94
Hill Auditorium	825 N. University, U. of Michigan, Ann Arbor	313-763-8587	reserved	I	11/16/94
Meadow Brook Music Theatre	Rochester				8/12/93
Michigan Theatre	Ann Arbor			I	4/17/93, 4/18/93
MSU Auditorium, MSU	East Lansing			I	11/18/94
The Orbit Room (formerly Club Easterbrook)	2525 Lake Easterbrook Blvd., Grand Rapids	616-942-1328	1,500 g.a.	I	8/11/93
The Palace of Auburn Hills	2 Championship Dr., Auburn Hills	810-377-0100	22,076 reserved	I	10/28/95, 11/9/96, 12/6/97
Phoenix Plaza	Pontiac				6/23/94
State Theatre	Kalamazoo			I	6/19/94
Van Andel Arena	130 W. Fulton, Grand Rapids	616-742-6600	12,000 g.a./ reserved	I	11/11/96, 11/11/98
Wing Stadium	3600 Van Rick Dr., Kalamazoo	616-345-5101	g.a.		10/27/95
Minnesota					
Orpheum Theatre	910 Hennepin Ave., Minneapolis	612-339-7007	reserved	I	11/26/94
St. Paul Civic Center Arena	143 West 4th St., St. Paul	612-224-7362	reserved	I	10/25/95
State Theatre	Minneapolis			I	4/9/93, 6/16/94
The Target Center	600 First Ave. North, Minneapolis	612-673-0900	reserved	I	11/13/96, 9/24/00
Mississippi					
Grove Area	U. of Mississippi, Oxford	601-232-7411	g.a.	O	10/13/94
Missouri					
American Theatre	St. Louis			I	4/14/93, 8/16/93
Fox Theatre	527 N. Grand Blvd., St. Louis	314-534-1678	reserved	I	11/23/94
Jesse Auditorium	U. of Missouri, Columbia	314-882-4640	1,755 reserved	I	11/22/94
Kiel Center	1401 Clark Ave., St. Louis	314-622-5435	reserved	I	11/15/96
Municipal Auditorium	301 W. 13th St., Kansas City	816-871-3700	g.a./reserved	I	10/19/95, 11/19/96
Riverport Amphitheatre	14141 Riverport Dr., Maryland Heights	314-298-9944	g.a./reserved	O	6/13/95, 8/6/97 7/29/98

Venue	Location	Phone Number	Seating	I/O	Past Shows
Montana					
Adams Fieldhouse	University of Montana, Missoula	403-243-6661	g.a./reserved	I	10/8/95
Fieldhouse at MSU	Montana State U., Bozeman	406-994-4636	g.a.	I	11/28/94
Nebraska					
Civic Auditorium	1804 Capitol Ave., Omaha	402-444-4750	g.a.	I	11/16/96
Pershing Auditorium, U. of Nebraska	226 Centennial Mall South, Lincoln	402-441-8744	g.a.	I	10/21/95
Netherlands					
Melkweb	Amsterdam			I	6/12/96
Paradiso	Amsterdam			I	2/17/97, 7/1/97, 7/2/97
Nevada					
The Aladdin Theatre	3667 Las Vegas Blvd. S, Las Vegas	702-736-0485	reserved	I	12/6/96
Thomas & Mack Center, UNLV	4505 Maryland Pkwy., Las Vegas	702-895-3761	g.a.	I	11/13/97, 10/30/98, 10/31/98, 9/29/00, 9/30/00
New Hampshire					
Snively Arena, UNH	Durham			I	4/11/94
UNH Fieldhouse, UNH	Durham			I	5/8/93
New Jersey					
E Centre	Route 676 exit 5A		g.a/reserved	O	7/10/99, 7/3/00, 7/4/00
PNC Bank Arts Center (formerly Garden State Arts Center)	Garden State Parkway Exit #116, Holmdel	732-335-0400	4,700 reserved 5,800 g.a.	O	7/2/94, 7/15/99, 7/16/99, 6/28/00, 6/29/00
Waterloo Village Music Center	Rte. 80 Exit 25, Stanhope	201-347-0900	3000 g.a.	I	7/25/93, 6/23/95
New Mexico					
Paolo Soleri Amphitheatre	Santa Fe			O	5/10/94
Sweeney Center	Santa Fe				3/8/93
New York					
Alumni Arena, SUNY Buffalo	Coventry Entrance, Amherst	716-645-2286	8,000 g.a.	I	4/10/94
Auditorium Theatre	875 E. Main St., Rochester	716-325-7760	reserved	I	2/9/93
The Beacon Theatre	2124 Broadway at 74th, New York City	212-496-7070		I	4/13/94, 4/14/94, 4/15/94
Big Birch Concert Pavilion	Rte. 22, Patterson	413-734-5874	g.a./reserved	O	7/13/94
Broome County Arena	1 Stuart Pl., Binghamton	607-778-1528	7,200 g.a.	I	4/9/94, 12/14/95
Cayuga County Fairgrounds	1 Speedway Dr., Weedsport	315-834-6606	12,000 g.a.	O	7/15/93
Cheel Arena, Clarkson University	Potsdam			I	4/24/93
Darien Lake Performing Arts Center	9993 Alleghaney Rd., Darien Center	716-599-4641	15,000 g.a. 5,000 reserved	O	8/7/93, 8/14/97, 9/14/00
Finger Lakes Performing Arts Center	CCFL Campus, Lincoln Hill Rd., Canandaigua	716-222-5000	g.a./reserved	O	7/14/94, 6/22/95
Glens Falls Civic Center	1 Civic Center Plaza, Glens Falls	518-798-0202	4,500 g.a./ reserved	I	10/31/94
Jones Beach Music Theatre	Ocean Drive, Jones Beach State Park, Wantagh, Long Island	516-785-0755	reserved		7/23/93, 7/15/94, 6/28/95, 6/29/95
Joyous Lake	Woodstock				6/6/96
Kuhl Gym, SUNY Genesco	Genesco			I	4/25/93

Venue	Location	Phone Number	Seating	I/O	Past Shows
Madison Square Garden *	2 Pennsylvania Plaza (on Seventh Ave.)	212-465-6000	20,000 reserved	I	12/30/94, 12/30/95, 12/31/95, 10/21/96, 10/22/96, 12/29/97, 12/30/97, 12/31/97, 12/28/98, 12/29/98, 12/30/98, 12/31/98
Marine Midland Arena	1 Main St., Buffalo	716-888-4000	18,000 reserved	I	10/19/96
Mid-Hudson Civic Center	1 Civic Center Plaza, Poughkeepsie	914-454-9800	3,000 g.a.	I	2/12/93
Nassau Coliseum	1255 Hempstead Tpke, Uniondale.	(516) 794-9300		I	4/2/98, 4/3/98
Niagara Falls Convention Center	305 4th St., Niagara Falls	716-286-4781	10,000 g.a./ reserved	I	12/7/95
Olympic Center	216 Main St., Lake Placid	800-447-5224 x122	reserved	I	12/16/95, 12/17/95, 10/16/96
Onondaga County War Memorial	515 Montgomery St., Syracuse	315-435-2121	7,600 reserved	I	11/4/94
Orange County Fairgrounds	239 Wisner Ave., Middletown	914-343-1342	g.a.	O	7/21/93
Oswego County Airport	Volney, NY.		g.a	O	7/17/99, 7/18/99
Palace Theatre	19 Clinton Ave., Albany	518-465-4663	2,801 reserved	I	5/5/93
Pepsi Arena (formerly Knickerbocker Arena)	51 South Pearl St., Albany	518-487-2088	17,500 reserved	I	12/9/95, 12/12/97, 12/13/97, 11/25/98, 9/8/00, 9/9/00
Plattsburgh Air Force Base	exit 36, I-87, Plattsburgh	802-863-5966	g.a. Lots.	O	8/16/96, 8/17/96
Reed Athletic Hall, Colgate University	Clinton			I	4/23/93
Rochester War Memorial	100 Exchange St., Rochester	716-546-2030	14,567		12/11/97
Radio City Music Hall	1260 6th Ave (at 50th St) NYC	212 247-4777	6,000 (approx.)	I	5/21/00, 5/22/00
Roseland Ballroom	239 W 52nd St., New York City	212-249-8870	3,200	I	3/14/92, 2/05/93, 2/06/93, 5/23/00
Saratoga Performing Arts Center	Saratoga Spa State Park, Rte. 50, Saratoga Springs	518-587-3330	25,000 g.a./ reserved	O	7/10/94, 6/26/95
Smith Opera House	82 Seneca St., Geneva	315-781-5483	1,350 reserved	I	2/10/93
Vernon Downs	Stuhlman Road-Route 31, Vernon	315-829-2201	14,000	O	8/12/98
North Carolina					
Benton Convention Center	Winston-Salem			I	2/17/93
Charlotte Blockbuster Pavillion	Interstate 85 exits 46/49		g.a/reserved	O	7/7/99
Charlotte Coliseum	100 Paul Buck Blvd., Charlotte	704-357-4738	reserved	I	11/19/95, 10/26/96
Grady Cole Center	Charlotte				7/28/93, 4/24/94
Lawrence Joel Veterans Memorial Coliseum	2825 University Pkwy., Winston-Salem	910-725-5635	reserved	I	4/21/94, 11/21/95, 11/23/97, 11/19/98
Memorial Hall, UNC	Chapel Hill			I	2/15/93
Varsity Gym, Appalachian State U.	River St., Boone	704-262-3032	g.a.	I	10/26/94
Walnut Creek Amphitheatre (Alltel Pavillion)	3801 Rock Quarry Rd., Raleigh	919-831-6400	g.a./reserved	O	6/29/94, 6/16/95, 7/22/97, 8/7/98, 6/25/00
Ohio					
The Agora Theatre	Cleveland			I	4/22/93
Blossom Music Center	1145 West Steels Corner Rd., Cuyahoga Falls	216-920-8040	g.a./reserved	O	6/20/95, 9/18/00

Venue	Location	Phone Number	Seating	I/O	Past Shows
Ohio *(continued)*					
Cincinnati Music Hall	Cincinnati			I	6/21/94
Cincinnati Zoo Peacock Pavilion	Cincinnati				8/6/93
The Crown	100 Broadway, Cininnati, OH.		reserved	I	11/14/98
CSU Convocation Center, CSU	Cleveland State U., 2000 Prospect Ave., Cleveland	216-687-5555	15,000 g.a./ reserved	I	12/8/95, 12/5/97, 11/13/98
Ervin J. Nutter Center, Wright State U.	3648 Colonel Glenn Hwy, Dayton	513-873-3498	13,000 reserved	I	11/30/95, 12/7/97
Hara Arena	1001 Shiloh Springs Rd., Dayton	513-278-4776	g.a.	I	11/17/94
Mac Center	Janik Dr., Kent State University, Kent	216-672-2338	reserved	I	11/12/94
Nautica Stage	Cleveland				8/8/93, 6/25/94
Polaris Amphitheater	Columbus	614.431.3600	13,000 g.a 6,700 reserved	O	7/31/98, 7/23/99, 7/14/00, 7/15/00
Riverbend Music Center	6295 Kellogg Ave., Cincinnatti	513-232-6220		O	9/20/00
Veterans Memorial Auditorium	Columbus				6/22/94
Oregon					
Ancient Forests Benefit	Portland	N/A	N/A		4/1/93
Arlene Schnitzer Concert Hall	Portland			I	8/26/93
Civic Auditorium	Portland				5/23/94
Hilton Ballroom	Eugene			I	3/30/93
Hult Center	Eugene				5/19/94
Memorial Coliseum	1401 N. Wheeler, Portland	800-992-8499	reserved	I	10/5/95, 11/24/96
Roseland Theatre	Portland			I	4/1/93
Salem Armory	2320 17th St NE, Salem	503-224-8499	g.a.	I	12/1/94
Pennsylvania					
A.J. Palumbo Center	1304 Forbes Ave., Pittsburgh	412-391-1111	reserved		10/9/94
Bryce Jordan Center	127 Bryce Jordan Center, University Park	800-863-3336	16,000 reserved	I	10/17/96, 12/9/97
CoreStates Spectrum	Broad & Pattison, Philadelphia	215-336-3600	reserved	I	12/15/95, 12/28/96, 12/29/96, 12/2/97, 12/3/97
Erie Warner Theatre	811 State St., Erie	814-453-7117	reserved	I	11/13/94
Haas Center for the Arts	Bloomsburg			I	2/11/93
Hershey Park Arena	100 W. Hershey Park Dr., Hershey	717-534-3911	reserved	I	12/1/95
Hershey Park Stadium	100 Hershey Park Dr., Hershey	717-534-3911	g.a./reserved	O	8/14/96, 9/15/00
IC Light Amphitheatre	Pittsburgh			O	7/18/93
Mann Music Center	52nd & Parkside, Philadelphia	215-878-7707	g.a./reserved	O	7/16/93, 7/1/94, 6/24/95, 6/25/95
Philadelphia Civic Center				I	12/28/94
Pittsburgh Civic Arena	300 Auditorium Pl., Pittsburgh	412-642-1800	reserved	I	11/24/95, 10/18/96
Recreation Hall, Penn State U.	Curtin Rd. and Burrowes Rd., University Park	814-863-1000	6,846 probably g.a.	I	4/8/94
Stabler Arena, Lehigh University	Bethlehem			I	10/7/94
Star Lake Amphitheatre	Rte. 18 at Rte. 22W, Burgettstown	412-947-7400	15,500 g.a. 7,183 reserved	O	8/13/97, 8/11/98, 7/21/99, 7/7/00
Tower Theatre	Upper Darby			I	5/1/93, 5/2/93

Venue	Location	Phone Number	Seating	I/O	Past Shows
Rhode Island					
Providence Civic Center	One LaSalle Square, Providence	401-331-6700	reserved	I	12/29/94, 12/12/95, 4/4/98, 4/5/98
Providence Performing Arts Center	Providence			I	2/4/93
Spain					
Zeleste	Barcelona			I	7/8/98, 7/9/98, 7/10/98
Doctor Music Festival	Pyrenees			O	6/11/97
South Carolina					
Bi-Lo Center	650 North Academy St. Greenville	888-386-8497	g.a./reserved	I	11/18/98
Galliard Auditorium	Charleston			I	10/28/94
Spartanburg Memorial Auditorium	385 North Church St., Spartanburg	803-582-8107	reserved	I	10/29/94
North Charleston Coliseum	5001 Coliseum Dr., North Charleston	803-529-5000	reserved	I	11/18/95, 10/27/96
Township Auditorium	Columbia			I	4/22/94
Tennessee					
Amsouth Amphitheatre. (was First American Music Center)	3839 Muffreesboro Road, Antioch (I-24, exit 62)	615-255-9600 (TM)	g.a./reserved	O	7/1/99, 6/22/00
Chattanooga Memorial Auditorium	399 McCallie Ave., Chattanooga	615-757-5042	reserved	I	10/16/94
Civic Coliseum	500 E. Church Ave., Knoxville	615-544-5388	reserved	I	11/28/95, 11/6/96
The Electric Ballroom	Knoxville			I	2/18/93
Knoxville Civic Auditorium	Knoxville			I	4/25/94
Mid South Coliseum	Memphis			I	11/18/96
MTSU Murphy Center	1301 E. Main Street, Mufreesboro.	615-255-9600 (TM)		I	11/15/98
Mud Island Amphitheatre	125 North Front St., Memphis	901-576-7241	reserved	O	6/14/95
Municipal Auditorium	417 4th Ave. North, Nashville	615-862-6390	g.a./reserved	I	11/29/95
Orpheum Theatre	203 South Main St., Memphis	901-525-7800	reserved	I	10/12/94
Tennessee Theatre	Knoxville				7/29/93
Vanderbilt U. Memorial Gym	210 26th Ave. South, Nashville	615-322-2425	reserved/g.a.	I	10/18/94
The Veranda at Starwood Amphitheatre	Antioch			O	7/30/93, 5/3/94
Texas					
Austin Music Hall	208 Nueces, Austin	512-263-4146	g.a.	I	10/14/95, 10/15/95
Backyard Bee Cave	Austin				5/8/94
Bayou City Theatre	Houston				5/6/94
The Bomb Factory	Dallas				5/7/94
Deep Ellum Lodge	Dallas			I	3/5/93
Liberty Lunch	Austin				3/6/93
South Park Meadows	9600 IH-35 So., Austin	512-280-8771	g.a.	O	7/26/97
Starplex Amphitheatre	1818 First Ave., Dallas	214-421-1111	g.a./reserved	O	7/25/97
Will Rogers Auditorium	3401 W. Lancaster, Fort Worth	817-871-8150	reserved	I	10/13/95
Utah					
The Delta Center	Salt Lake City			I	6/8/95
Salt Air	Salt Lake City			O	8/21/93
Triad Amphitheatre	Salt Lake City			O	6/9/94

Venue	Location	Phone Number	Seating	I/O	Past Shows
Utah *(continued)*					
West Valley E Center	West Valley			I	11/14/97, 11/2/98
Wolf Mountain Amphitheatre	4000 Park West Dr., Park City	801-355-5522	g.a./reserved	O	8/2/96
Vermont					
The Flynn Theatre	153 Main St., Burlington	802-652-4500 or 802-86-FLYNN	1,453 reserved	I	4/4/94, 3/18/97
Stowe Performing Arts Center	Stowe				7/22/93
SummerStage at Sugarbush North	Sugarbush North, Mt. Ellen Access Rd., Fayston	802-583-3333	g.a.	O	7/16/94, 7/2/95, 7/3/95
Virginia					
Classic Amphitheatre	Richmond			O	7/27/93, 6/30/94
The Filene Center at WolfTrap	1551 Trap Rd., Vienna	703-255-1860	7,000 g.a./ reserved	O	7/17/93
Hampton Coliseum *	1000 Coliseum Dr., Hampton	804-838-4203	13,800 reserved	I	11/25/95, 10/25/96, 11/21/97, 11/22/97, 11/20/98, 11/21/98
Nissan Pavilion at Stone Ridge (formerly Cellar Door Pavilion)	Wellington Rd. btwn Rte. 66 & Ballsford Rd., Gainesville	703-754-6400	10,000 reserved 12,500– 15,000 g.a.	O	6/17/95
Patriot Center, George Mason U.	4400 University Dr., Fairfax	703.993.3000	~10,000 reserved	I	4/17/94, 10/8/94
University Hall, U. of Virginia	Emmit St./29 North, Charlottesville	804-924-3286	g.a.	I	10/27/94
Virginia Beach Amphitheatre	3550 Cellar Door Wy., Virginia Beach	757-368-3000	7,000 reserved 12,500 g.a.	O	7/21/97, 8/9/98, 7/8/99
Virginia Horse Center	Rte. 39 W, Lexington	540-463-2194	4,000	I	4/20/94
Washington					
Campus Recreation Center, Evergreen College	2700 Evergreen Pkwy NW, Olympia	206-866-6000	g.a.	I	5/20/94, 11/30/94
The Gorge	I-90 Exit 143, Quincy (George)	206-785-6262	g.a.	O	8/2/97, 8/3/97
HUB Ballroom	Seattle			I	4/5/93
Key Arena	305 Harrison St., Seattle	206-684-7200	g.a.	I	11/27/96
Moore Theatre	Seattle			I	5/21/94
Mount Baker Theatre	Bellingham			I	4/2/93
Paramount Theatre	Seattle			I	8/25/93
Seattle Arena	363 Mercer, Seattle	206-628-0888	g.a./reserved	I	10/2/95, 10/3/95
Spokane Arena	720 W. Mallon, Spokane	509-324-7900	reserved	I	11/22/96
Spokane Opera House	334 Spokane Blvd. W., Spokane	800-843-4667	reserved	I	10/7/95
West Virginia					
Municipal Auditroium	Charleston			I	6/26/94
Wisconsin					
Alpine Valley	2699 Highway D, East Troy	414-642-4400	32,500 g.a. 7,500 reserved	O	8/10/96, 8/9/97 8/1/98, 7/24/99, 7/8/00
Dane County Coliseum	1881 Expo Mall East, Madison	608-267-3976	g.a.	I	11/20/94, 10/24/95
Eagles Ballroom	Milwaukee			I	6/17/94
Kohl Center	601 West Dayton St. Madison, WI.	608-263-KOHL	17,300	I	11/6/98

23 East Cabaret (Ardmore, PA)—Erik Swain

This venue, just barely larger than a bar, hosted the first Phish shows in the Philadelphia area. Tucked on the main drag of Ardmore, about 10 minutes west of the city, you could drive right past it without even noticing it. Oddly, the first show, 12/29/89, was the first in the New Year's Run (before anyone was calling it that) of that year. It featured a Divided Sky opener and one of the few performances of In a Hole.

Within four months, the band returned twice, the second time on St. Patrick's Day, in which they opened the second set by improvising a jam with Fishman chanting the words "Killer Joe." They did not come back to Philadelphia until 1992, by which time they were big enough to play the 23 East's larger sister club, the Chestnut Cabaret. The 23 East closed in the mid-1990s but recently reopened under the name "Brownie's at 23 East."

Pre-1993 shows: 12/29/89, 2/10/90, 3/17/90.

Arrowhead Ranch (Parksville, NY) - Phil Nazzaro

Formerly a 'hippie ranch' run by Bill Graham Productions outside of Binghamton NY, Arrowhead Ranch has since closed its doors. However, for two glorious nights Phish and The Giant Country Horns played about as well as they ever have. Maybe it was the pressure of having The Authority and an up and coming NYC band Spin Doctors opening on 7/20, and maybe it was TR3 and the veteran Radiators opening for Phish on the second night. Who knows? It could have been the low pressure of a diminutive turnout on the first day (I couldn't GIVE AWAY an extra ticket in the parking lot) and less then a sellout crowd the second. Or perhaps it was the beautiful New York State surroundings, the feeling of being more or less in the middle of nowhere, the camping on the premises, the friendly staff, seemingly open vending INSIDE the show, Trey publicly inviting everyone to Amy's Farm, having enough open room to play frisbee on the side, or being able to walk up to the stage edge at will. Whatever it was that made this stand so special, RIP Arrowhead. We love you.

The Bayou (Washington DC)—Marcie Vogel

Sadly, this legendary club no longer remains as recent building of high-rise condos has begun where it once stood. The Bayou was legendary for many things: up-and-coming 'jam'bands would play there (Phish, DMB, Hootie, many many others) in the early '90s, the park across the street made for a nice place to 'chill out' before, during and after shows, alcoholic beverages were watered down and over-priced, it was HOT HOT HOT inside and sometimes you could smell the sewage system backing up (and leaking) onto the dance floor. But it didn't matter because everytime I saw a band there (especially Phish) they ripped it up. Nice stage, excellent lights, decent sound system and 2 floors to view the band from made this a specail place to see music. The band knew it too. I fondly remember the "Mrs. Pizza Shit" show there among many others. It was a special place on K street, located at the bottom of Wisconsin Ave in Georgetown across the street from the river. It is missed, at least by this writer.

Berkeley Square (Berkeley, CA)—Mark Toscano

A legendary Berkeley club that served as a pit stop for many then-fledgling local and national bands such as Mr. Bungle and Phish,

the Square was closed down in the mid '90s. Phish performed one show there on their first West Coast tour in 1991.

Cal Expo (Sacramento, CA)—Mark Toscano

Most modest-sized summertime shows in Sacramento occur at this place. Surrounded by the fairgrounds that yearly contain the Cal State Fair, Cal Expo is your standard fairground venue—a dirt circle enclosed partially by aluminum stands. Yuck. The sound was OK, the security was tolerable, but the crowd sucked. Despite some debuts, the show sort of sucked too, though, so who cares.

Capitol Theatre (Port Chester NY)—Marcie Vogel

Ahh, the days of the theater shows. The Capitol Theater is so grand and divine, one can almost feel as if she's entering a movie premiere in Hollywood. The town of Port Chester is made up of huge houses, nice cars and a theater that was in great condition circa 1992. Much excitement filled the air pre-show and as we entered the historic 1,400 seat room we all knew we were in for something special. Two nights of Phish in late November at a beautiful place in a beautiful town... we were all giving thanks indeed.

Chance, The (Poughkeepsie, NY)—Phil Nazzaro

At its inception in 1910, The Chance was a movie theater. But in 1970, new ownership took over, and began promoting concerts. You name it, they've played here. From Twisted Sister to Muddy Waters. And let's not forget Phish's performances. This theater-turned-club in downtown Poughkeepsie has a multi-level floor area, and a balcony upstairs; but not a seat in the house. The old hardwood floors show their age, and evidence of the bar in the back. But the sound is good, and besides the rear section of the balcony, the view is too.

Pre-1993 shows: 10/28/89, 3/2/90, 9/26/90, 12/8/90, 5/2/91

Chestnut Cabaret (Philadelphia, PA)—Erik Swain

The Chestnut Cabaret, located near the campus of the University of Pennsylvania, was Philadelphia's premier club venue in the 1980s and early 1990s, featuring a low stage, a large dance floor, and over-priced drinks. Many up-and-comers of the alternative rock and jamband scenes played there until it folded in the mid '90s. It is a testament to Phish's rapid growth that they played here only once, on 3/21/92.

The band's first visits to the Philadelphia area, in 1989 and 1990, took place at the Chestnut's sister venue, the tiny 23 East Cabaret in nearby Ardmore. They skipped the region in 1991 and were large enough to play the "big" Cabaret when they returned in 1992. But by spring 1993 they had moved on to theaters. The show itself was a fun if not experimental affair, and included a lengthy intro to My Sweet One and a strangely textured Bowie.

Show: 3/21/92

Crest Theatre (Sacramento, CA)—Mark Toscano

This wonderful old Sacramento movie palace was nearly falling apart in the early '90s until money was raised by the city to restore its crumbling facade and interior. Phish played one single show there, but it was a doozy—3/22/93, the most famous Gamehendge show of 'em all. Today, interested folks can check out the Crest, a K Street landmark, for various concerts, revival films, and special events.

E Centre, The (Camden, NJ)—Erik Swain

The E Centre typifies the new breed of outdoor ampitheatre: large size, sparkling cleanliness, plentiful amenities and ridiculously overpriced concessions. It offers quite a contrast in scenery. From the lawn, you have a gorgeous view of the Philadelphia skyline across the Delaware River. From the fragmented lots, you have a dreadful view of downtown Camden, which resembles a war zone.

Transportation to the E Centre is tricky. You have to navigate about 10 city blocks after getting off the highway (Interstate 676), and massive traffic jams often ensue. It is essential to arrive early or budget extra time for your trip. A viable alternative is to park in Center City Philadelphia and take a ferry across the river to the venue. However, the last ferry leaves a half-hour after the show ends, so don't count on doing the post-show lot scene if you use that option. There is also a stop near the venue on the Patco train line, however this is an east-west line and is not accessible from the north or south.

As with the Philadelphia venues, the lot scene here is highly unregulated and features far too many nitrous tanks. But vending is in full force and petty offenses are often ignored. The same cannot be said for the security inside the venue. Those personnel are adamant about clearing the aisles and keeping people in their proper seats. Phish debuted at the venue on 7/10/99 and performed one of the most-maligned shows of the year. Nonetheless it featured a highly experimental "Chalkdust," one of the first jammed "BOAF"s and an energetic "Fluffhead." But the band liked the venue enough to return over the Independence Day holiday in summer 2000. The first show of that run, 7/3/00, was very memorable, featuring the breakouts of "Foam" and "Glide" (the latter with All Fall Down language), a Tom Marshall appearance during "Antelope," an intense "Gin" played in time to the thunderstorm that was drenching fans on the lawn, the funkiest "Sand" to date, and an extremely experimental "Runaway Jim" that lasted 33 minutes. The Independence Day show had its own share of breakouts, including "Rift," "I Saw It Again" and "Magilla," although it will be best remembered for the mold-breaking half-hour "Gotta Jibboo." In 1999 the acoustics were far better in the pavilion than on the lawn.

Shows: 7/10/99, 7/3/00, 7/4/00.

Fillmore Auditorium (San Francisco, CA)—Charlie Dirksen

The Fillmore opened as "The Majestic Hall and Majestic Academy of Dancing" in 1912. Since then, it has primarily been a hall for music and dance, even though in the 1940's it was a roller rink.

As you walk in the doors of this famous museum of psychedelic rock, ruby-red carpeted stairs greet you. They carry you up into the warmth of a narrow, rectangular hall with walls adorned with framed pictures of some of the musicians who have played here (James Brown, Jefferson Airplane, Grateful Dead, Janis, Red Hot Chili Peppers, etc.). The main ballroom features a spacious, freshly polished, wooden dance floor bounded by modest,well-worn, red carpeting. A multitude of chandeliers hang tastefully from a high ceiling with a disco ball in the center. A balcony stretches across the room's entire left (stage right) side. Four or so feet off the floor, an enormous stage formidably fronts the room. There is also a spacious room upstairs with hundreds of colorful Fillmore posters dating back to the 1940s. Visiting The Fillmore to view its poster collection is alone worth the price of admission.

In the late 1960s, in part due to the awe-inspiring energy of pro-

moter Bill Graham, the Fillmore became legendary for its music. The careers of many psychedelic rock bands, including were launched from the Fillmore's enormous stage. Incredible bands and musicians have played the Fillmore, including Jimi Hendrix, Otis Redding, Cream, Muddy Waters, The Who, Chuck Berry, Frank Zappa and the Mothers of Invention, and Miles Davis. As Eric Clapton has said, "There was very much a whole kind of Fillmore energy coming off the audience that combined with the band. When we played the Fillmore for the first time (with Cream) the band was in the light show. If you were in the audience, you didn't know who was playing. Not at all. It was a sensory thing." Carlos Santana launched his U.S. career in the room in 1968, and has played there off and on ever since, most recently in April 1999. The third and final show of his April 1999 run, on April 18, featured many guests including Trey Anastasio and Page McConnell.

Phish played The Fillmore on October 15, 1998. Though to many fans, this show is memorable more for the vibe in the room that night, than for the music, the music's improvisational spirit and energy occasionally hearkened back to the all-hallowed 1993-1995 epoch of Phish's career. Some fans claim to hear the majesty of the Fillmore's soul echoing in the "Gumbo," "Reba" and—believe it or not—the "Velvet Sea" and "Prince Caspian."

Fleet Center (Boston, MA)—Jeremy Goodwin

It only took one visit for the boys to form an impression of the "New Boston Garden". The venue inherited the most high profile gig of Phish's yearly routine because of its location in Boston, the traditional sight for New Year's Eve festivities. Maybe this local tradition would have continued (and not been transplanted to Madison Square Garden) if the boys had found the Fleet more hospitable. Unfortunately though, this venue is pretty much a bland, unimpressive sports arena designed for the sale of corporate luxury boxes. The sixteen Boston Celtics championship banners do their best to impart atmosphere, but few spectators forget that each of these was won in a different room. They at least provide some impressive sports history for fans to gaze at while they wonder why the sound is so bad.

It is located conveniently at the intersection of several subway and commuter rail lines, and the scene on Causeway Street in front of a show is pretty wild (and nostalgic, for those who attended Phish New Year's at the Boston Garden, or any number of Dead shows there over the years). The Boston vibe on New Year's is tough to beat. However, once inside, fans can look forward to stubbing out their cigarettes on command, and watching a parade of uniformed police officers stalk the floor.

After hosting half of a New Year's Run at the Fleet Center (featuring the famous 60,000 balloon drop throughout the first several minutes of 1997), Phish opted to schedule all future Massachusetts dates at the Worcester Centrum or Great Woods/Tweeter Center.

Shows: 12/30/96, 12/31/96

Fly Me to the Moon (Telluride, CO)—Mark Toscano

Also known as The Moon, this is a great club in Telluride, Colorado, known for its eclectic band appearances, cheap drinks, and dark basement setting. Right across the street from the Roma, Phish played one of its shows here on their night off on the first tour in Colorado back in summer 1988. Apparently, most interested Telluridites were boycotting the band's Roma shows because of disagreements with the

place's owner. They suggested Phish play Fly Me to the Moon on the one night off, and the band agreed. To a packed house, Phish made tons of new fans in Colorado, a huge contrast to the one or two people clapping that can be heard on tapes of the Roma shows.

Fox Theater, The(Atlanta, GA)—Ellis Godard

Arguably the most beautiful venue in North America, the "Fabulous Fox" shares little with its namesake in Boulder, CO. Both are theaters, indeed, but Atlanta's gem is much larger, with the plushness that this arty Southern city loves. The most impressive, though most subtle, feature is the vast ceiling which appears as the night sky, with twinkling stars and moving clouds projected on it throughout the show. The area above the stage appears as a bridge, which continues as a turreted walk around the upper edge of every wall, around the perimeter of the room, putting the audience not in a downtown warehouse, but in the depths of some Turkish-looking castle. Even the bathrooms are an exercise in overdone luxury, where any race to relief requires venturing through a series of stairwells and seating rooms.

Glens Falls Civic Center (Glens Falls, NY)—Jack and Kathleen Griffin

The city of Glens Falls is home to about 22,000 fairly conservative "north country" upstate New Yorkers. The city's oval-shaped Civic Center, built in 1977 to host a NHL "triple A" hockey team, is right in what, as the Dead put it, "used to be the heart of town". The arena is sort of your typical minor-league hockey arena, Worchester Centrumesque inside and out, but only about half the size. It can seat about 5000, plus stand about 2000 general admission on the floor. Like Worcester, the small city of Glens Falls was ahead of the minor league hockey arena "curve", but larger, newer venues like the Pepsi Arena in nearby Albany 50 miles south on I-87 make it very unlikely that this venue would ever again see the likes of Phish (or the Dead, who played there twice in the early '80s, or the Who, who did a warm-up show for their 1989 tour).

But probably no event was as illustrious for giving the Glens Falls Civic Center its brief moment in the sun as Phish 10/31/94, Halloween '94, where the venue and the city were for a day the epicenter of all Phishdom. The show itself is widely-acclaimed as one of Phish's best, a blazing first set with an "Antelope" and standout "Simple", followed by the second-set Beatles "White Album" cover, a creditable third set, all ending at 3:20 a.m. with a costume contest won by a guy dressed up like giant Mounds bar. Other than the all-night Big Cypress show on New Years Eve '99, thisshow also holds the record for the latest finish of any show. Note that Glens Falls Civic Center is a non-union venue.

When Phish brought its 1994 Halloween show to the Glens Falls Civic Center, after a several year hiatus in their holiday show tradition, thousands of wookies and costume-clad fans poured into town throughout the day from all points, searching for parking lots and clogging up the city streets. Glens Falls had just a smattering of resident hippy types...mostly high school kids playing dress up. The locals hadn't seen anything like the Phish crowd since the Dead played there. But the Dead crowd was much more low key back then. The 7,000 or so fans who were inside enjoying the show were not joined by about 3,000 disappointed miracle seekers for this long-since sold out show. When the show started about 9:00 and it was becoming clear to those outside

that there would be no miracle that day, the ticketless horde tried a desperate rush at the door, where they were repelled by City police, whereupon a bottle-throwing melee ensued with dozens of arrests. Fans enjoying the show inside were mostly unaware of the troubles at the doors, although a few of the most berzerk gatecrashers were spotted coming through the roof and enjoying the show while dangling from the girders and catwalks above.

The relatively tiny size of this venue was both a visual and audio treat for those of us who were lucky enough to attend (in our own home town, taboot!). The show also produced excellent tapes from a relatively close tapers' section around the "center line" on the arena floor.

Show: 10/31/94

Gorge Amphitheater, The (George, WA)—Charlie Dirksen

The awe-inspiringly beautiful Columbia River Gorge provides the backdrop to the stage at every show at this legendary venue. The natural amphitheater-styled venue is itself carved into basalt cliffs, and also has a spacious, well-maintained lawn. So magnificent that you cannot grasp its majesty without experiencing it first-hand, the view will surely blow you away. If you have never been, it is worth the time and expense of attending a concert here (the traffic in and out can be a nightmare, and be sure not to end up in the dustbowl lot!) regardless of who's playing. This venue has been voted the best large outdoor concert venue by Pollstar for many years, but the hell with Pollstar—Phish fans love this venue, too! It has camping, a General Store and showers. And inside the venue, there are even misting tents to cool down in (the tents are also only a brief skip from the beer garden). Trust me, if you have not experienced this venue, you simply must attend a concert here. Phish has performed five shows at The Gorge and will hopefully play there many more times in the future.

Shows: 8/2/97, 8/3/97, 7/16/98, 7/17/98, 9/10/99, 9/11/99

Great American Music Hall (San Francisco, CA) —Charlie Dirksen

Located in the scenic Tenderloin Heights section of San Francisco, on the same block as the legendary O'Farrell Theater, the Great American Music Hall ("GAMH") is San Francisco's oldest and most beautiful nightclub. As its website perfectly describes, the GAMH "carries guests back to an earlier, more elegant era, one of ornate balconies, soaring marble columns and elaborate ceiling frescoes. Long-time customers and newcomers alike feel at home in the 5,000 square-foot concert hall that symbolized renewal and optimism when it [was built] in 1907. Today a professional sound and lighting system, two full bars, modern kitchen and spacious oak dance floor blend contemporary quality with turn-of-the-century graciousness."

The Hall was constructed after the 1906 San Francisco earthquake by a French architect. Before opening as the GAMH in 1972, the room had been a restaurant/bordello; a dance hall; a jazz club; and a Moose Lodge. The Great American has hosted many legendary shows, particularly the Grateful Dead's August 13, 1975 gig, which is memorialized on the double live CD release, "One from the Vault." West Coast heads were shocked when Phish managed to sell out two gigs at the GAMH on their first visit to the Bay (October 17 and 18, 1991). After these sell outs, though, it was no surprise that Phish would play the considerably larger Warfield Theater only six months later.

Great Woods, aka Tweeter Center (Mansfield, MA)—JDG

Great Woods got lucky. If it was located in East Lansing, Michigan, or Boise, Idaho, it would be just another cookie-cutter shed on the summer circuit. However, it just happens to be *the* summer venue for successful bands in Massachusetts. Since Massachusetts has been the laboratory for each early stage of Phish evolution, Great Woods became a special venue by geographical default.

When Phish made their first visit here in July '93, it became the scene of their first-ever ampitheatre sellout. .Many fans look back at this afternoon as the point they realized that Phish was going to *happen* as, at the least, a regional cultural phenomenon. (By the time they were playing in arenas from coast to coast in Fall '96, they were solidified as a *national* cultural phenomenon).

The band returned for two nights in '94, and dropped a bomb on the local crowd with a first set Gamehendge performance the first night. Some in attendance may have recognized it as a giant "thank you" for about a decade of New England support. It was the first Northeast Gamehendge since the near-mythical debut of the piece at Nectar's, and the final one to date, as of this printing. They weren't finished with Great Woods that year, though, until they had raged through a "YEM"->"Frankenstein"->"YEM" and a torrid "Stash" that showed up on *A Live One*.

Summer '95 wrapped up with a four show, Great Woods/Sugarbush tandem. The band considered Great Woods the last "tour" shows before returning home to play on a Vermont mountain. The first night, fans were greeted by a colossal traffic jam which delayed the start of the show. Things finally started with "AC/DC Bag," a nod to the previous year's "Gamehendge." The second set was packed with special treats, including the first-ever "2001"->"Possum" and the first known "Avenu Malkenu"->"Mike's Song." The following night was broadcast locally on WBCN 104.1, and included a raging "SOAM" and the first truly experimental, second set "Stash."

Great Woods then seemed to drop off the tour map, and at a Spring '97 book signing for *Mike's Corner*, Brad Sands announced that Phish was "banned". This left Massachusetts with no summer Phish shows for a few years, until Great Woods finally saw a return engagement in Summer '99. By now it had succumbed to the omnipresent sponsorship temptation, and been renamed Tweeter Center (can "Tweezer Center" t-shirts be far behind?).

After soundchecking a slew of songs by other local artists, Phish opened the two night stand with their first rendition of Boston's "Foreplay"/"Long Time" in six years. This was also the first time they had played the combo electric. The message was clear..."it's been such a long time", indeed. As if unconsciously summing up the '98/99 touring years in two shows, Phish played a relatively blasé show the first night before knocking everyone's socks off the second. The second night featured a positively sublime Haley's Comet->Roses Are Free-> N2O in the first set. N2O was particularly special, as it had only been played thrice beforehand, including once (you guessed it) at the beginning of the Great Woods "Gamehendge," five years before.

The aforementioned traffic difficulties can be a problem, and once in the lot, fans' partying is often impeded by a formidable security presence. Nevertheless, the Great Woods lot scene is probably one of the biggest around, because "local" shows always seem like a Phish anniversary party. Good thing: plan on spending a few extra *hours* in the lots stuck in traffic after the show, unless you get lucky with parking location. After being in business for almost fifteen years, the venue management still hasn't figured out how to get people out of there in a reasonable timeframe. Lawn patrons who attempt to infiltrate the pavillion encounter a security lockdown reminiscent of Los Alamos (pre-Clinton). Unfortunately, the architects of the lawn apparently didn't think the audience would want to see the stage, so you'll have to settle for watching tv if you get stuck more than half of the way back. And you can at least watch the closed-circuit tvs if you have to wait in line for something mid-set.

Shows: 7/24/93, 7/8/94, 7/9/94, 6/30/95, 7/1/95, 7/12/99, 7/13/99, 9/11/00, 9/12/00

Hampton Coliseum (Hampton, VA)—Jeremy Goodwin

Some venues are automatically "special" because of their geographical location (Boston Garden, Shoreline Ampetheatre, Thomas and Mack Center) while others are distinguished by their architecture (Red Rocks, The Gorge). Hampton doesn't stand out remarkably in either category; nevertheless, it is one of those places that has earned an endearing place in Phishlore through the intrinsic quality of the place itself. It's small (for an arena), fully general admission, and indeed seems to resemble an otherworldly vehicle from outside (thus the "Spaceship Hampton" nickname). It is bordered by several hotels, which string together into one large encampment, puncuated by a nice little wooded area (behind the Red Roof Inn). Plus the blue/green fountain in front is cool to look at, and serves as a meeting place and energy nexus.

Are these external factors the cause for the Hampton Mystique? Who knows...the energy just seems to *happen*. Phish isn't the first band to find something special about the Spaceship...in 1989, the Grateful Dead billed themselves as "Formerly The Warlocks" for a Hampton appearance, and proceeded to play the first "Dark Star" in five years.

Whatever the cause, the Hampton Coliseum has grown into a favorite East Coast tour stop. Phish's first visit in Fall '95 resulted in a very bizarre and noteworthy second set that included "Kung" and the first "Rotation Jam" (out of "Mike's Song"). The visitation the following year saw less jam theatrics, but was studded with several rarer songs, including the atypical set openers ("Ha Ha Ha" and a still-uncommon "Tube"). Before launching into "Stash" in the first set, Trey had this to say: "A lot of people ask me what my favorite room to play in is. And this is pretty much it."

The place really grew into its own with the fabled Fall '97 shows. Scheduling a Friday/Saturday tandem in the midst of one of their greatest tours, the band gave lucky fans the chance to check into Phish fantasy camp for a weekend, and witness legendary, capstone performances in the process. The highlites from that inspired visit include the debut of the Stone's "Emotional Rescue," the first ever experimental "AC/DC Bag," the first "Mike's Song" opener on U.S. soil since 1990, and a sublime twenty minute plus "Haley's Comet" to open the final set.

A similar weekend visit took place almost exactly a year later, and while this go-round lacked some of the improvisational meat of the previous year, the two nights were fueled by high energy and studded with highlites, including the breakout of "Quinn the Eskimo," a made-in-Heaven "Mike's Groove" that encapsulates both "The Wedge" and "The Mango Song," and visits from Dave Grippo and Tom Marshall. The band thought enough of this weekend to release it, in full, on the five cd set *Hampton Comes Alive*.

A month after this live release, Phish ended their Fall '99 tour with another two night visit to the Spaceship. By this point the Hampton Hype was out of control, and while it may have been impossible to meet the skyrocketing expectations of many fans, Phish delivered such fare as an unusually improvisational "SOAM," and a "Do You Feel Like I Do?" jam in "2001" that delighted those who noted the appropriate reference to Peter Frampton. Maybe the band felt they had taken things are far as they could at this place; the lyrical bandbox of an arena was left out of the Fall 2000 tour.

It's probably accurate to say that there's "not a bad seat in the house" at Hampton. The sound is excellent if you avoid the back "corners" of the oval room. Nevertheless, many fans get in line hours before the scheduled opening of the doors, to scramble for the front of the floor, or choice seats in the first level of stands (particularly the "Page Zone", which many discriminating fans select unhesitatingly as the seating location of choice).

Shows: 11/25/95, 10/25/96, 11/21/97, 11/22/97, 11/20/98, 11/21/98, 12/11/99, 12/12/99.

Lisner Auditorium (Washington, D.C.)—Lisner Auditorium —Marcie Vogel

Experiencing Phish at a college venue could always be expected to be a treat just from the campus energy. Most of the campus shows I caught were held in the same type of building: the gym. University of Delaware's Carpenter Center, George Mason's Patriot Center, Penn State, NC State's Reynolds Coliseum: all unremarkable buildings not made with acoustics in mind, however some amazing shows went down inside.

There is one, though, that sticks out in my mind as one of the best sounding college rooms I was lucky enough to be inside: GW's Lisner Auditorium. It was just that, an auditorium built for musical performances and Phish soaked it right up and sprayed us all down with it. The inside is beautiful with a formal arched stage complete with heavy curtains roped off to the sides. The seats are plush and comfy, the admission general and it sounds *so* sweet!

Lisner is part of the GW campus located smack dab in the middle of DC and we spent pre-show at an early RMP gathering across the street at a bar that served some tasty food taboot. Grabbing a spot on the street to park wasn't a problem and there was virtually no traffic leaving after the show. And the show itself was tasty! It was not even close to being sold out, so we all had plenty of room to melt down. Find this show!

Show: 3/17/92

Lucerna Theater (Prague, Czech Republic)—Jeremy.Welsh

Phish has played the mysterious and enchanting city of Prague three times, and in the summer of 1998, Prague occupied the middle spot of a three-city European run. The year before, Phish had played Divaldo Archa in Prague; in 1998, they chose to play the subterranean Lucerna Theater, which holds twice as many people. As if Phish playing Europe was not enough, the Lucerna Theater is a place of dreams.

The entrance to the theater, marked with a large marquee, is located off of Prague's large Wenceslas Square on Stepanska Street. After entering an enclosed arcade, you see the actual entrance to the theater, with its grand staircase—one slowly realizes that the hall is below ground. After winding down what seems to be three stories, you enter

the exquisite hall from the back. The hall itself is rectangular in shape, with the stage at the far end. Architecturally, it is similar to other buildings in this fairy-tale city—untouched, rich Baroque, with cream colored panels and columns with gold tracings and details. To either side, there is a small step up to a hall way that wraps the two sides; above, there are two floors of balconies, the upper-most arched openings bring you close to the coffered ceiling.

While it was incredibly hot and stuffy for both performances, the crowd did not seem to mind as the inexpensive Czech beer flowed freely. A bit too freely as it would seem by Phish's performance the first night. The rough edges were quickly forgotten, though, by the 07.06.98 performance, which featured "AC/DC Bag"->"Ghost">reprise->"Cities" in the first set and a raging "Piper" in the second set that is a must-hear.

07/05/98, 07/06/98

Madison Square Garden (New York City, NY)—Jeremy Goodwin

If any one thing symbolizes the rise of Phish to mainstream arena rock dominance, its their ongoing New Year's residency at MSG. One of the most venerated arenas in the rock world, this place has seen it all, from the Concert for Bangladesh, to John Lennon's last onstage performance (during an Elton John concert), to the American debut of the Who's *Quadrophenia*. When Phish first added "sold out MSG" to their resume, it was yet another milestone in the heady days of '93-95, when the band's popularity exploded, and such anomalies as an appearance on Late Night with David Letterman became feasible.

After one night of the '94 New Year's Run, Phish upped the ante by hosting two nights in '95, and ended the Massachusetts New Year's tradition in the process. Who could complain, seeing as 12/31/95 was universally hailed as the "best Phish show ever"? The band's comfort level is obvious: 1998 signaled the first time they booked an entire four night Holiday Run in one venue.

Fans enjoy the historic room, which somehow manages to seem cozy. There are disagreements over the sound quality, but if you have good enough seats you'll enjoy a clarity absent in many sports arenas. Ticketholders are required to enter one of several designated entrances, but once inside the room, movement is relatively unimpeded. This is also one place you're more likely to see video cameras, champagne bottles, or surfboards...due to a liberal backpack policy.

The Garden was renovated in the '80s and '90s, and thus maintains its vintage aura while offering an extended array of concessionary conveniences. Patrons must traverse a series of escalators to reach the elevated "ground floor"; the band has noted that this results sometimes in a shaking of the floor. On 12/30/97, Trey explained that the mic stands sometimes sway back and forth when everyone is dancing, and promised to try to find "the magic groove" that creates this phenomenon.

Shows: 12/30/94, 12/30/95, 12/31/95, 10/21/96, 10/22/96, 12/29/97, 12/30/97, 12/31/97, 12/28/98, 12/29/98, 12/30/98, 12/31/98

Mann Music Center (Philadelphia, PA)—Erik Swain

A smallish outdoor ampitheater located in Philadelphia's Fairmont Park, the Mann Music Center hosted four summer Phish shows in the mid-1990s. But ever since the larger E Centre opened across the river in Camden, NJ in 1995, the Mann no longer hosts the top-drawing acts. When Phish returned in 1999 for its first summer shows in the Philadelphia area in four years, it went to the E Centre.

Phish's Mann debut on 7/16/93 provided the first performances of "Also Sprach Zarathustra," "Purple Rain" and "Yerushalayim Shel Zahav" (the latter in the middle of "YEM.") The band returned once in 1994 and twice in 1995. The first show of the 1995 run had the last-ever "Spock's Brain" and a fan-favorite "Bowie," while the second featured the unusual "Mikes" -> "Why Don't We Do It In the Road" -> "Weekapaug."

Shows: 7/16/93, 7/1/94, 6/24/95, 6/25/95.

The Marquee, New York, NY—Phil Nazzaro

A typical Lower Manhattan nightclub that mercifully went out of business sometime soon after Phish moved on to bigger and better things. The room basically consisted of a more or less oval shaped dance floor. On the north end was the stage, a bar to the west, and a balcony in the south. If you were up front it was great. The stage was about 2 feet high, with nothing but monitors seperating you from the performers (which led a bunch of girls to jump on stage and dance on 2/16/91). However, the tendency of the management to cram people in like sardines made Phish shows into a sweat-fest (except on 5/18/91 which didn't seem to be sold out). In addition, the sound deadening mass of people did not help attendees in the back hear the PA that was stacked on floor in the front. Due to the crush, and poor sound at least one taper was known to pack it in, and move upstairs before the show even started. If you've been there, you'll understand. And if you've been to the Great Went, did you find the blue 'Contact' shirt I bought from Dry Goods at The Marquee on 12/28/90? It got left in Limestone :(

Masquerade Park (Atlanta, GA)—Ellis Godard

The Masquerade itself is a big black box of angstful noise and youth. But around the left side, in the back, sits a grassy slope facing an outdoor stage, with a view of part of the Atlanta skyline in back. That's where Phish played, *not* in the main (indoor) area.

Matthews Arena (Boston, MA)—Ellis Godard

The best feature of this low-ceiling hockey rink is its close proximity to an enormous YMCA that sits right on a main train line in Boston. The sound is crummy, and the hallways boxy, but (in its favor) the beams were sturdy enough to support Brad Sands in a chicken costume.

Meriwether Post Pavillion (Columbia, MD) —Kristen and Ellis Godard

This is what amphitheaters were going to be, before the mega-sheds such as Nissan Pavillion erupted. Meriwether is an old school shed, and early-generation building that looks a bit like an old hanger, with tent extensions on the sides that purport to keep out rain but invariably keep out the breeze and hold in the humidity. The lawn lacks the treacherous steepness of newer amphitheaters, but is also too flat for a decent view of the stage. Nevertheless, the venue sits in a park-like setting, surrounded by trees and creeks, and the expansive maze of parking lots invariably invites an on-site party well in advance of the show.

Mid-Hudson Civic Center Arena, The (Poughkeepsie, NY) —Phil Nazzaro

The MHCC is essentially a large box with an open floor, and bleachers in the back. Phish played this 3000 person capacity, general ad-

mission venue in a blinding snowstorm on 2/12/93. The security did a nice job of keeping people on their toes; but the one-two punch of Harry Hood-Harpua to end the second set made it all worthwhile. Hint: If the snow is over two feet on the New York Thruway, and you're having trouble keeping it on the road, follow a snowplow.

Shows: 2/12/93

Paradiso (Amsterdam, The Netherlands) —Kristen and Ellis Godard

This converted church sports a balcony that wraps around the large dance floor, all the way to the front of the stage on both sides. Large stained-glass windows behind the stage are typically dark, but Kuroda illuminuated them with different colors for Phish's July 1997 shows.

Philadelphia Civic Centre (Philadelphia, PA)—Erik Swain

The acoustics are horrible, the parking is horrible, and I'm glad it got torn down.

Show: 12/28/94

PNC Bank Arts Center (Holmdel, NJ)—Erik Swain

One of the nation's older outdoor ampitheatres, PNC Bank Arts Center (aka Garden State Arts Center) is located in the scenic hills of suburban central New Jersey, not far from the Shore. It has outstanding acoustics and a ceiling that looks like the bottom of a spaceship. After navigating several parking lots covered in red clay, patrons traverse a field to get to the entrance. Upon entrance, fans are greeted by a large pool with several fountains, and can climb stairs directly up to the back of the lawn. The venue is unusual in that it has its own exit (116) from the Garden State Parkway, and is only accessible in this manner (although a shuttle runs from the nearby New Jersey Transit train station in Matawan). It is part of a complex that includes a Vietnam Veterans memorial and a state police barracks. This police presence, plus the Holmdel community's concern over the multitude of arrests at the 1999 shows, means the lots are heavily patrolled and petty offenses are not tolerated. Security inside the venue is much more lax, and patrons are usually free to dance in the aisles and roam to other seats (provided they are not closer than the seat on your ticket stub.)

Trey remarked on 7/15/99 that he and Page consider it a special venue because they frequented it a lot growing up in the Garden State. Many of the performances at this intimate pavilion reflect that. Phish debuted here with two one-set performances in eight days: 7/11/92 as part of the HORDE festival and 7/19/92 opening for Santana. The former featured Blues Traveler's hefty frontman John Popper "breaking" a trampoline during YEM (it was rigged.)

But Phish did not truly make its mark in Holmdel until its first full show there, 7/2/94, which featured the legendary "Mike's" -> "Simple" -> "Mike's" -> "Yerushalayim" -> "Hydrogen" -> "Weekapaug" in the second set. Unfortunately, the band's following outgrew the venue size, and it did not return for five years.

After the Arts Center underwent an expansion (and got a new corporate name), Phish returned for two shows in 1999. The first, 7/15/99, sported a long first set capped with what some fans thought was the best YEM of the year. Its second set opened with the final "practice" of the Meatstick dance before the record-breaking attempt in Oswego, and

featured a very experimental (and controversial) SOAMelt -> Kung. The next night had an energetic second set and one of Mike's strongest performances in "Weekapaug."

The summer 2000 shows were again memorable. The first night, 6/28/00, had fierce versions of "Gin," "Piper," "DWD" and "Mike's." The second night may have been one of the highlights of the whole tour. The first set brought an awe-inspiring "Drowned" -> "Rock and Roll." The second set had experimental jamming on "BOAF" -> "Catapult" and "Sand," and many other highlites. At the end Trey gushed about how much he loves the venue and how the band hopes to return in the future.

Shows: 7/11/92, 7/19/92, 7/2/94, 7/15/99, 7/16/99, 6/28/00, 6/29/00.

Portland Meadows (Portland, OR)—Mary Acaster

Portland Meadows is a soil-covered horse racing track located in the midst of a bizarre industrialized wasteland indiscriminately strewn between the once pristine banks of the Columbia River and the Columbia Slough in North Portland. When used as a music venue(something which may soon be a thing of the past), a small stage, a set of bleachers, and a beer garden tent are set up near the south end of the oval. The drawback to the presence of the beer tent being that it blocks what could be a spectacular view of Mount Hood. For a venue that could easily hold over 100,000 people (if all available space were used), the crowds at the Meadows are usually quite intimate. Due to the limited availability of parking in the area (especially on nights when there is auto racing at the nearby Portland International Raceway) this is a blessing. Though the added treat of post car race fireworks has been an incredibly electrifying experience on at least one occasion.

Phish opened the 1998 US Summer Tour with their first show at Portland Meadows on 7/15/98, before heading north to the Gorge Amphitheater. In 1999 the show at the Meadows on 9/12/99 followed the two night stand at the Gorge, and the Fall Tour opener in Vancouver BC. Disappointment reigned supreme throughout the Pacific Northwest this year especially for fans who have enjoyed past shows at Portland Meadows, since the entire region was put out to stud, eliminated entirely from the Fall Tour 2000 itinerary.

Red Rocks (Morrison, CO)—Mark Toscano

Fans lucky enough to have caught Phish (no pun intended) at this beautiful Colorado venue may have to attend a show at The Gorge in Washington for a comparable experience, for Phish will likely not be playing Red Rocks again. Due to problems with ticketless "troublemakers" "invading" the small town of Morrison, CO, it has been decided by both venue and band that perhaps Phish has outgrown this 9,200-seat venue set in the middle of the reknowned Red Rocks park, an incredible geological eyeful replete with giant, iron oxide colored sandstone ledges.

Only 15 miles west of Denver, Red Rocks was opened and dedicated in 1941, realizing the dream of George Cranmer, Denver Manager of Parks and Improvements at the time. He had envisioned a glorious, outdoor amphitheatre that combined the surrounding natural splendor with public performances of beautiful music. Since then, it had hosted countless acts, ranging from Blues Traveler to The Beatles, from KISS to U2.

In fact, Trey even humorously references the venue during the 7/25/88 "Icculus" (found on *Junta*), quoting Bono on U2's 1983 *Live*

Under a Blood Red Sky album, which was recorded at the very venue Phish would first play five years later.

The unlikelihood of future concerts at Red Rocks make the ones Phish did play there all the more special. 8/20/93, the debut concert, featured a now-legendary "Harpua" detailing the exploits of a bizarre, behemoth iguana. The iguana made a reappearance in the 8/7/96 "Forbin">"Mockingbird," on the fourth night of the historic four-night run that proved the band's last visit to the venue as performers. Other shows like 6/11/94 and 8/6/96 have entered the pantheon as Phish classics, the latter featuring a near-life-changing interplay of music, fan reaction, and thunder and lightning that made the night a special one for all in attendance.

Shows: 8/20/93, 6/10/94, 6/11/94, 6/9/95, 6/10/95, 8/4/96, 8/5/96, 8/6/96, 8/7/96

Roma (Telluride, CO)—Mark Toscano

Primarily a restaurant specializing in Italian and seafood dishes, this slightly expensive venue was the site of Phish's first western tour, in Telluride, Colorado, back in Summer 1988. During their multi-night gig at the Roma, barely anyone showed up, since most of the town was boycotting any business owned by supposed paycheck defaulter and tax evader Warren Stickney, which included the Roma. After several nights of empty houses, interested Telluride residents suggested Phish play Fly Me to the Moon, across the street, which the band did on their night off to a packed house. Following this triumph, the gigs at Roma continued, with barely anyone in attendance.

Roseland Theater (Portland, OR)—Martin Acaster

Despite being located on the fringe of Portland's drug-infested "Old Town" district, the recently renovated Roseland Theater is still a favorite venue for bands and fans alike. Formerly known as the Starry Night, the Roseland has been the site of performances from a diverse array of bands that ranges from Medeski, Martin, and Wood to the Misfits. The Roseland has all the ambience of a dank cave but boasts stellar acoustics. The floor area is typically swarming with the all-ages crowd, while those 21 and over can seek refuge and a microbrew in the often swelteringly hot balcony. Phish played the Starry Night on 4/5/1991, and the Roseland Theater 10/12/1991, 4/24/1992, 3/31/1993, and 4/1/1993. The recent appearance of the band at the east coast theater of the same name has fueled the local fire clamoring for the band's return to the Roseland west.

Roxy, The (Atlanta, GA)—Ellis Godard

Everyone knows about the show, but no one thinks much about the venue. It is an old theater with the seats ripped out, and floor and walls painted black, rented out to local and regional bands and promoters for cheap. Located in the heart of Buckhead, an upscale area of Atlanta, it is nevertheless as likely to host death rockers or debutantes. Also of note, the Roxy is within walking distance of the Mellow Mushroom, site of one of the earliest net gatherings (2/20/93).

Shoreline Amphitheater (Mountain View, CA)—Mark Toscano

Situated in the middle of Silicon Valley, Shoreline was opened by Bill Graham Presents in 1986 in order to provide a "state-of-the-art" concert-going experience to the people in the Bay Area. Only about a

40-minute drive from San Francisco, Shoreline has hosted innumerable big-name acts, ranging from the Dead to R.E.M. to the Sex Pistols to Santana.

The huge, tent-enclosed venue holds up to 25,000 people, most of whom find a spot for themselves on the impossibly expansive lawn that sits on a hill behind the comparitvely small reserve section (itself pretty sizeable at 6,500 seats). The sound is great, the atmosphere is cordial and loose, and the food is, well, expensive. (What did you expect?)

Though the lawn is nice, beware of severely decreased visibility. The grass is an awful long way from the stage, and the video screens can only capture so much of the on-stage action. Plus, they're usually only turned on when it starts getting dark.

On August 29, 1992, Phish played Shoreline for the first time, opening for Santana on the band's nationwide tour. The guys had previously played Bay Area venues such as the Great American Music Hall, Berkeley Square, and the Warfield, but Shoreline was in an entirely different league.

They made a lot of new fans that night, wowing the largely surprised crowd with bread-and-butter songs like "Rift" and "You Enjoy Myself." The following year, Phish grabbed two nights at the Warfield, and had graduated to THREE in early 1994. They were headlining Shoreline by Fall 1995 (9/30, debuting the band-audience chess game), and have made the venue a necessary stop ever since (7/31/97, 7/19/98, 9/16/99, 9/17/99, 10/6/00, 10/7/00). The band always speaks highly of BGP and the treatment they receive at Shoreline, and fans seem to like it a lot too. They also always plays a fun and worthwhile show there, so check it out if you have the chance.

Shoreline Amphitheater (Mountain View, CA)—Ellis Godard

On the ground, this venue is laid out like a typical new shed. But the shape, location, and ownership set it apart. Owned by Bill Graham Productions, the venue hosts such events as the Bridge School Benefit, and has brought special guests such as Phil Lesh 9/17/99 and Bob Weir 10/6/00.

Shoreline is stuck in a desert area surrounded by mountains and, in more immediate vacinity, scores of power towers. From the right direction on 101, arrival is not bad. But the drive once on site is long and slow—a huge semicircle in the dust and sun year-round. Early arrivals (and carpools of four or more) get closer parking.

From the gravelly dirt of the expansive parking area, one can view the "roof"—not the metal box of Camden, the wood tower of Wolftrap, or the mixed top of Meriwether, but a double-peaked tent top that looks like a circus. Beneath the towering canvas lies a conventional three-section 100s and a well-sloped loge. The lawn above is not as steep as some (e.g. Nissan), and larger than many (compare Chula Vista or Irvine). It also has marked "aisles" of sorts, separating the lawn into three vertical sections, and each of the side sections into top and bottom halves.

Lastly, the garlic fries are highly recommended, as is the Tidehouse Deck, which has a better selection of beer.

Shows: 8/29/92, 9/30/95, 7/31/97, 7/19/98, 9/16/99, 9/17/99, 10/6/00, 10/7/00

Spectrum, The (Philadelphia, PA)—Erik Swain
aka Corestates Spectrum (1996), First Union Spectrum (1998)

When Phish first played at The Spectrum in Philadelphia on 12/15/95, Trey declared it a special occasion, as the venue was the site of the first concert he ever went to: a Jethro Tull show. Fans now consider many of Phish's shows at this venue to be special occasions in their own right.

The aura may not be readily apparent to a first-time visitor. From the outside it resembles nothing so much as a large green sardine can. Its ceiling tends to absorb sound, not making for the best acoustics. Its upper reaches have too many obstructed-view seats. And its parking lots, infiltrated by scores of nitrous vendors, have hosted some of the worst pre- and post-show scenes of any tour. But what it lacks in aesthetics and acoustics, it makes up in atmosphere. It hosted some of the most raucous crowds in all of sports during the '70s and '80s heydays of the Flyers and 76ers, and some would swear you can still smell the blood and sweat of that era's stars such as Bobby Clarke and Julius "Dr. J" Erving. And you can certainly smell the spilled beer from, oh, 1975. It was also one of the Grateful Dead's most favored venues. While they played here over 50 times, it is best known to Deadheads as the site of the breakout of "Unbroken Chain."

That supercharged atmosphere carries over to Phish performances, and the band thinks enough of the venue to have honored it with the first two shows of the 1996 New Year's Run. Perhaps spurred by the exuberance of the crowd, Phish often produces rare and unusual set openers here, such as "Tweezer Reprise" 12/15/95 II, "Makisupa" 12/28/96 II, "Buried Alive" 12/2/97 I, "Tweezer" 12/10/99 I, and most stunning of all, on 12/11/99, the first "Harry Hood" show opener for a paying audience since its 10/30/85 debut. The venue has also hosted two rotation jams (12/11/95 out of "Bathtub Gin" and 12/29/96 out of YEM), and one of the more unusual sets in the band's history, 12/29/96 II. In addition to the "YEM" rotation jam, that set featured Mike's take on "Sixteen Candles" and a Tom Marshall appearance as "the UberDemon" during "Harpua," where he demonstrated "the horrible sounds of hell" by warbling Oasis' "Champagne Supernova."

Other notable musical moments include the 12/11/95 "Hood" and "Maze" -> "Ha Ha Ha" -> "Suspicious Minds;" the 12/28/96 "Maze;" the 12/28/96 and 12/2/97 "Mike's Grooves" (the latter spanning 67 minutes and including the unexpected "Dog-Faced Boy"); the 12/29/96 "Bowie" and "Gin" (featuring perhaps Page's strongest-ever piano intro); the 12/2/97 "Ghost" -> "Divided Sky;" the 12/3/97 "Drowned," "YEM" and "Bowie" (with Simpsons language); the 12/10/99 "Bowie" -> "Have Mercy," and the 12/11/99 "Sneakin' Sally" ->" Ghost" -> "Also Sprach" and "Possum" (with All Fall Down language.)

Despite being located in a charmless neighborhood of warehouses, with Veteran's Stadium literally across the street, the Spectrum is easily accessible by car. It sits at the junction of interstates 76 and 95, and by subway: it is the last stop on the Broad Street line from Center City.

Shows: 12/15/95, 12/28/96, 12/29/96, 12/2/97, 12/3/97, 12/10/99, 12/11/99.

Starwood Amphitheatre Plaza (Nashville, TN)—Ellis Godard

This venue is notable not for the venue itself, but for where in it Phish performed: Not in the amphitheatre itself, which was much too large for Phish's fanbase in the area at the time, but in the entrance plaza, between the concession stand and the men's bathroom. It was about the right amount of space, but the plaza was designed to inter-

rupt strolls with the suggestion of beer and pauses, not to allow a few thousand to focus their attention in the same direction. Trees and picnic tables sat within a hundred feet of the stage, and the PA barely covered off-stage discussions by the band. In fact, they started their set by playing a song of their own over the PA, and slipping on stage to play along with it. And the "stop and have a beer" construction of the "venue" helped conceal the sneak until the song was well underway.

State Theatre (New Brunswick, NJ)—Phil Nazzaro

The State Theater is a beautiful old (but renovated) 1921 vaudville theater in south-central New Jersey. The 1800 seat venue is mostly community minded in its events; but has also hosted world class acts in its time. A Broadway stature stage is second only to the excellent acoustics. Balcony seating is also a plus, although many fans in '93 avoided a bird's eye view by clogging up the aisles. Next to Red Rocks, this may be the "retired venue" I would most like to see Phish perform in again.

Show: 5/3/93.

Sugarbush Resort (Subarbush, VT)—Kristen and Ellis Godard

As one of their early attempts to break from the strictures of venue control over the time and structure of shows, Phish performed several shows on the ski slopes of this ski resort. The plan was to bus people to the top of a mountain, with on-site camping for the first few hundred cars, and camping for everyone else on slopes on the opposite side of the muntain. The 1994 show worked out okay, but the 1995 shows were a sign of times (Red Rocks, anyone?) to come.

The idea of a dozen schoolbuses carrying hoards of fans was kind of fun, in the era of "Chalkdust Torture" and the expanding virus of Phish fandom. But the buses were few, and impatience was high. People walked miles to sneak over the mountain, and eventually trampled every stretch of red tape ambitiously marking (but in now way protecting) the perimeter. By the middle of 7-2-95, the security had given up and were playing Frisbees across the perimeter, long immune to the free-for-all the shows had become. Buses back to the main camping area were a disaster, with fans literally crawling through windows and breaking in the rear emergency doors—purportedly in order to get back quicker, but with the result that bus drivers refused to drive, and many hundreds ended up choosing to walk rather than wait.

Tower Theatre (Upper Darby, PA)—Erik Swain

A converted movie theater, the 3,000-seat Tower has the best acoustics of any venue in the Philadelphia area. That and its gothic architecture make it a place many artists love to frequent. It continues to host major acts (from The Allman Brothers Band to Neil Young) who want to put on intimate shows. Performances for the "King Biscuit Flower Hour" radio show, including ones by Jethro Tull and David Crosby, have been taped there.

Phish has only visited the Tower once, on a two-night stand toward the end of the spring 1993 tour. These two shows, 5/1/93 and 5/2/93, are extraordinarily underrated, probably because of the classic performances that followed them later in the week. The first night is best known for a "Mike's" -> "Great Gig in the Sky" -> "Weekapaug" in which the riff that would become Simple is teased. The second night featured an extraordinarily energetic second set, including a "YEM" and

an "Antelope" for the ages. Unfortunately, Phish's fanbase outgrew the venue's size by the end of the year and they have not returned since.

Shows: 5/1/93, 5/2/93.

Trax (Charlottesville, VA)—Ellis Godard

Phish has played the lovely hamlet of Charlottesville on seven occassions, six of those at this well-known club (and four of those sold out). Trax is situated just around the bend from Thomas Jefferson's historic University of Virginia campus, in an old warehouse (namesake of "Warehouse" by the Dave Matthews Band, who built their loyal following in the room). The clunky ceiling, slanted roof, and gaming sideroom (pool, foosball, and more) prepare concertgoers for a boxy hollowness. However, repeated PA tweaking over two decades, by some of the best soundmen in the business, has resulted in a sound neither boxy nor hollow, but surprisingly crisp. Further, Trax remains perhaps the only club where soundboard tapes accurately capture the live sound. In most clubs, the bass and drums get tuned down so as not to overwhelm, leaving soundboard tapes weak and shallow, but Trax absorbs sound well, and many a soundman has been surprised and impressed by soundboard tapes from this venue.

Though various owners have made attempts at mixed drinks (and food), decent beer is often understocked and the beverage options are often limited. Worse, lack of ventilation keeps the room warm and stuffy with any large crowd, even beyond the warmest summer nights. Finally, younger bands are sometimes frustrated by attempts to get booked in the room. But Phish entered Trax in its (and their) younger days, with good connections established by word-of-mouth after locals heard the band in Grateful Dead parking lots. Phish first arrived in October 1990, brought by the team of Chris Bowman (then booking agent) and Coran Capshaw (then owner, now manager of the Dave Matthews Band). The venue was said to be the first (as well as the second!) to include hotel provisions in Phish's contract. Trax also provided superb cuisine, as had been a house custom for out-of-town acts in that era. Add in a liberally partying student population, and the magic of Phish's six Trax shows is no surprise, including a rhombus narrative, the last "Destiny Unbound" (11/15/91), and an encore which featured Fishman solo, playing vacuum and wearing nothing but a strategically placed red-and-white target.

UC Davis Recreation Center (Davis, CA)—Mark Toscano

A one-night stand for the band whose audience grew exponentially from 1994 to 1995. The show on 12/2/94 was originally supposed to be held in Varsity Hall, but was moved to the Rec Center at the last minute to accommodate more ticket buyers. Still, the show served only a few thousand fans. The center is basically a gymnasium, with stands on either side that were left open during this show for seat-wanting fans. The lack of a barricade at the stage meant that folks (including yours truly) could belly up to the stage and watch not only the band, but the Cosmic Country Horns in full sparkly regalia rip into Landlady, Suzie, and Buried Alive. The downside? Easy. Trough urinals.

USAir Arena (Landover, MD)—JDG

What a shithole. Phish fans weren't the first to figure this out; while local sportscasters abbreviate it as the Cap Centre, Deadheads had been calling it the "Crap Centre" for years. I can't think of why this

sports arena is so disliked, unless it's because of the bad sound, obnoxious security, and oppressive police presence in the lots.

Phish visited the then-home of the Washington Bullets and Washington Capitals once in Fall '95, and unloaded an epic (though controversial) 35 minute version of Free. (During this Free, I was literally in one of the back rows, directly across from the stage, and had to endure flashlight-wielding security guards checking tickets from the same aisle-dancing fans *over and over* again.) The room dropped off the tour schedule altogether until a surprise return to open the 1997 New Year's Run, an appetizer before three nights at MSG (perhaps the Garden was otherwise booked on 12/28?). After fans had been pushed inside the venue by horseback-riding policemen ("It's time to go in" was the universal refrain), they enjoyed another controversial show, studded with special songs but suffering from feedback difficulties and what some perceive as improvisational malaise. It has certainly been forgotten amid an otherwise stellar New Year's Run.

This arena in suburban Landover, Maryland is located within a ten dollar cab ride of the nearest DC Metro stop. Don't expect to see Phish there again, though; since '97 all local touring needs have been met by the Merriweather Post Pavillion and the new MCI Center in downtown DC.

Shows: 11/22/95, 12/28/97

The Warner Theater (Erie, PA)—Charlie Dirksen

If you think Radio City Music Hall is impressive, try visiting this stunningly gorgeous room sometime. Since opening in 1931, the theater

has held around 2500 in plush, upholstered, theatre-styled seats. Upon entering, one is greeted by ornate French mirrors and elaborate, gold and silver leaf columns. You have never seen so much crushed velour in your life. There is also a marble fountain in the lobby immediately outside the interior doors to the hall. I will never forget the face of the beautiful young wookie princess washing her feet in the fountain at setbreak.

Phish performed here on November 13, 1994. The taper's section was practically on top of Paul and the soundboard and, as a result, a naughty front row taper—at the very beginning of the second set opening "Suzie Greenberg"—leaned over and plugged straight into one of Paul's DAT decks. Finding a flat, "mixed for the room and not for you" fully digital soundboard of the second set has been relatively easy ever since.

Wolftrap Park Amphitheare (Vienna, VA)
—Kristen and Ellis Godard

Aka the Filene Center, this fabulous shed sits on National Park Service land that actually contains several venues. The smaller Barns at Wolftrap is a more intimate spot, but even this Amphitheater is a homey place with great sound. A beautiful wood amphitheatre with a fabulous towered roof, and an enormous upper-level balcony that sits *over* a lawn, makes it far from the traditional shed. Further, Wolftrap allows patrons to bring in coolers—although the end result with Phish's visit was an *enormous* mess of trash than embarrassed many fans, and may have hurt chances of a return.

INTERVIEWS

Chris Kuroda

Interviewed by Scott "Seabass" Boyarsky and Hal "Brother" Waterman of CK5 (see Online Resources), backstage prior to the 10/7/00 Shoreline show.

Hal Waterman: The fans want to know about your rig. Can you tell us about your setup?

Chris Kuroda: Sure. The rigs usually come out looking like spaceships, even though that's not my original intent. Originally I'm just trying to place lights where I want them to light the band, or the audience. You know, they have to be in a certain spot. The current rig is set up to look like the Millennium Falcon. But really, on a more technical end, it's designed to set up and break down really quick and easy. It's essentially five pods or five triangles and everything is separate. It's not all interconnected into one giant massive thing that's all bolted together. So, once stage left gear is out of the way you can just bring in stage left piece and break it down and put it on the truck. In a lot of ways it's really designed to be able to get to the venue at 9 am and be able to do a gig by 7 pm.

As far as what's in the setup, there are about 150 par cans (par 64), on 1k lamps, typical standard lights. There are 18 ACL racks. ACL stands for aircraft landing light. Those are the bright white ones that I flash. There are 24 studio spots and 24 studio colors. They are automated lighting made by a company called High End. There are 46 Altstar which is another automated light made by Altman. Those are really cool!

HW: Does Phish own the equipment or do they lease it?

CK: We lease it because there is always new equipment coming out, better lights being made. Just like a car, as soon as you own it, it's obsolete. So lighting companies essentially buy the equipment and lease it out. We have such a good relationship with the lighting companies that we use that we can just literally tell them what gear we want and then we'll lease it from them. We pretty much can have anything we want.

Scott Boyarsky: Do the lighting companies supply you a crew?

CK: Yes, but we always keep the same crew. The lighting crew, even though they are supplied by other lighting companies, I always get the same people because they're the crew!

SB: How many members make up the lighting crew?

CK: There are seven members on the lighting crew.

SB: Who are they?

CK: Myself, Tavi Black, she's the person that climbs up and fixes everything. Julian Watkins, he's the lighting crew chief. He pretty much organizes how the day goes for the crew as far as setup and breakdown. Gary Radkovich (a.k.a. Raco), he sits left of me, and runs the Whole Hog (The lights made by High End). I call cues to him on the left. And on my right is Roger Pujol. He runs the Altstar console. I call cues to him. I run the conventional board in the middle. Brian Dyke (a.k.a. Shoopie), he's what we call a truss monkey. He's also the automated lighting technician. He fixes the moving lights when they break. We have a lot of spares so we're constantly swapping lights in and out of the system.

SB: Are you swapping out lights right in the middle of a show?

CK: We'll either swap a light during the course of the day when we're setting up or at halftime (set break). We can never swap a light that's on the downstage truss because it's over the audience and the danger of a light falling is too great. Due to liability, if a light breaks during a show on the downstage truss we have to live with it. And anything that breaks after halftime you live with, because the show's going on, you can't send people up during the show.

SB: Have you ever had a part of the rig freeze up on you? You know, where the system becomes inoperable?

CK: Oh yes! The rig is so computerized, computers crash, the light show crashes all the time. Lights cause the light board to crash. Sometimes certain lights cause all the other lights to crash because some of them are all wired in series and they're all looped through data. If one light receives bogus data from the console, it will send the bogus data to all the lights. You can fry chips or boards. The disasters are limitless. We've had them all!

SB: What's your course of action if the lights crash in the middle of a show?

CK: Well, years ago I would just freak out and throw my headset and kick things and be really angry, but over the years I've learned that this is the way it is and we try all the time to calmly continue with what we've got. And that is the whole reason why we have three lighting systems. We've got the High End system, the Altstar system, and the Conventional system. So, if one craps out or one fries, you have two more systems to work with. You don't have the full show, but you have a show.

HW: Has the band over the last few years increased your lighting budget? Because the light show has certainly stepped up over the last few years.

CK: Budget is really not the issue. I mean I can pretty much have the budget I want but we try to keep things reasonable. Size of the light show is a different story. This light rig currently is smaller than the last two. It was just getting too big. The last one with all the scrims (those white screens between the lighting trusses) it was too much, too Pink Floydish. It made the band look small, and that's not the idea.

HW: Have you thought about lasers?

CK: Well, we've thought about lasers, but laser technology has come a long way but it's still "lasers", and we want to try and be original, and you know, lots of people use lasers. There's just not a place in Phish for lasers, at least yet. Maybe at a New Years gig for a cool effect, once. Once in a whole night would be pretty cool, but you don't want to spend all that money for a ten second effect and then that's that. Especially with lasers. I mean, on New Years maybe, I mean there's a million things you can do. But in general, no. We try to keep a purist attitude. I'm sure you've noticed there are no more scrims, there's no more backdrops, it's just light. That's the philosophy we're going with.

HW: You have that Escheresque kind of thing going on where you shine the lights on the walls.

CK: Yes, a little bit. I try to only do that a couple times just to kind of-give some different perspective on the lights, some different dimension.

SB: Some of the lights you use have patterns in them. Is that intentional?

CK: Those are built into many of the lights that we use.

HW: Take a song like "Guyute" that Phish plays a lot. Do you just hit a button and let it go?

CK: No, I'm constantly setting up the guys left and right of me on different things. It's a very complicated kind of cue calling.

HW: Is it true you have to be a half second ahead of the band because of the delay?

CK: Yes, between the time that I hit the button and the time the light actually reacts, or between the time that I say the word go and the operators brain hears me say go and physically decides to push the button – that's more time than you think it is. So essentially yes, I'm a half step ahead of the band. So if I say go, the lights are going to even if the band does something different. So if I'm wrong it's going to look stupid and if I'm right it looks great. So I'm pretty much second guessing the whole time.

HW: Have you ever tried to lead the band in a certain direction with the lights?

CK: I would say that's never my intention although sometimes the band members have mentioned to me that the lights have helped. That they've been stuck somewhere and I've helped them out of it. It's never really my intention, I'm just trying to do my job and follow them the best I can. The only time I ever try to get the band to kind of do what I want them to do is during YEM ["You Enjoy Myself"], the vocal jams: If I want to do something crazy with the lights, I'll start doing it and either they'll follow it or they won't. Most of the time they'll follow it. As far as the music is concerned, not that the vocal jam isn't music, I would never even dare do such a thing.

SB: What is your favorite Phish song to light?

CK: "David Bowie". Hands down! There's no question about it! I always like all the worked out stuff, what we call "woked" in the Phish world. For example, "Reba" has a big "woked" section; "Fluffhead" is another with a "woked" section in the middle. "David Bowie" is a "woked" tune and it's just my favorite song. It's a blast to light. The song goes in so many directions. It's got quiet parts, huge parts, worked out parts, it flows nicely. It's just a pleasure to light. It's one of my biggest moments of a night when they play that song.

SB: Does the band know it's you're favorite tune to light?

CK: Yes

HW: What's your least favorite tune to light?

CK: I'll tell you, they're both great songs but after all these years I still haven't figured out what exactly to do with them… They're not tunes I don't like, they're just tunes I don't like to light. "Punch You In The Eye" and "Lizards". I don't know what to do during those songs. You do the best you can.

SB: What was it like to sing "Possum" at your wedding with the Band?

CK: I didn't want to do it, but I got thrown up there and it was a lot of fun! It sure was a lot better then the last time I sang "Possum", which was at the Front in 1989 during "Guest Vocalist Night." I had about ten Bass Ales in me that night, walked away from the light board and yelled, "I'll sing one." People in the crowd singing songs happened way back in the club days. At my wedding, I sounded a lot better.

HW: So, you're married now. What is you're wife's name?

CK: Rhiannon. Her mother named her after the Fleetwood Mac song.

SB: Any little Kurodas on the way?

CK: Ahhhh, ya know. We'll take that one day at a time. We are planning to have a family someday. We're just not exactly sure when we're going to begin. With this time off, who knows! We're about to take all this time off, so one never knows.

HW: Tell us about the Phish hiatus.

CK: Well, there's nothing set in stone. It's a very difficult question to answer because nobody knows. It started out as a year break, and now it's turning into a we're (Phish) going to take a break as long as we feel we need a break and we might go in different directions. We might go into the studio. Essentially what it really boils down to is that they've (Phish) been on the road for 17 years. They're constantly, when they're off the road, being thrown projects. They're overloaded. They need a break to spend time with their families. They need to get off the road. And most importantly, they need to write new music. They all feel that if they take a lot of time, they can really write some good stuff, and get the positive vibes back into what they're doing. In my opinion, I feel like although they're doing great, playing great, and having a great time, they're kind of just going through the motions. Playing the same songs that they've been playing for so long.

HW: Have you ever thought about designing your own lighting system?

CK: No, I haven't really thought about that. I have thought about starting my own lighting company using existing gear. I have had a lot of input in the design of lights like the Altstar. I've had a lot of input on how I wanted that light to work. When we first started using it, it was pretty much just the prototype. Through what I wanted to do I had software specially written for us, parts in the lights specially working for us. So in a way, I've already done that. I've also designed a strobe light for Diversotronics. A few years ago they wrote me a letter and said, "Thank you. We're going to take your strobe light and make it part of our line. Thanks for helping us design a new product." And on the High End stuff that we use currently, we had to have them write us special software because I wasn't able to make the lights do things that I wanted to make them do. There's a lot of special Phish [lighting] software which is why I can make the lights do things that other people can't. They're stuck by the software that they're using.

SB: One of my favorite effects is when you get the lights spinning either sideways or up/down in a 360 degree motion.

CK: That's all Altstar. Altstar is one of the few lights out there that has the ability to do a continuous 360 degree pan and tilt. Essentially, there are two kinds of moving lights. There is the moving mirror, which is what Altstar is. One's called a moving head, which is what a studio spot is. A moving head can only go so far before it hits its yolk, and can only spin so far before it reaches its limit. The Altstar can spin forever. The 360 degree effect is one of those effects that has to be used at just the right time or it looks silly. For an over-obvious statement, if I did it during "[Wading In The] Velvet Sea", it would look silly.

SB: What type of projects might you be working on with your time off?

CK: Already, since we've been on this tour, I've been offered to light about 25 TV shows for international export over the course of the next year. And running lights for the Tito Puente Orchestra for about a week at Roseland [Ballroom, New York City, NY]. That will be just a fun little thing. And the opportunity to light Major League Soccer's championship

halftime show at RFK stadium. And I'm going to LDI, which is the biggest lighting trade show in the world, and I'm going to go down there and talk to some people to see what else I can round up for myself.

HW: Have you thought of running a Kuroda clinic? Teaching young lighting designers how to light?

CK: I've thought about teaching a class at UVM. My wife really wants me to do it. I'm definitely going to look into seeing what it takes to be able to do that. I don't know if it will happen right away, but I'd like to do that someday.

HW: What are your favorite venues to light?

CK: Madison Square Garden, Blossom Music Center, Merriweather, Saratoga Performing Arts Center, and Alpine Valley. MSG is my favorite hands down!

HW: What about least favorite?

CK: Here [Shoreline Amphitheater]. Great room for a concert; horrible room for lights. The big white tent just reflects too much light, washes out everything. I can't even see what it's supposed to look like. And just in general, I prefer indoor venues to outdoors. I know a lot of designers that I thought would have cared for indoor. But they don't care, indoor, outdoor. I guess I'm just really picky about how my stuff looks.

SB: Do you use different color tones depending if the concert is indoors or outdoors? Pastels verses Primaries?

CK: When we do rehearsals for fall tour or spring tour verses rehearsals for summer tour, we use a lot of darker colors because we know we're going to be indoors. We program for a couple of weeks before we go on tour. We set it [the lighting rig] up in an arena, and we basically live there for two weeks or so programming the show. When we know we're going to be doing a summer tour outdoors, we try to use brighter colors. There's still a place for darker colors in the summer, but a lot of them just don't read outside, you can't even see the light.

HW: Do you like when people come up to you, fans who want to meet you?

CK: I'm a little paranoid about it actually.

HW: If a fan is going to say hello, when is the best time?

CK: The best time is probably before the show. Intermission is good too. After the show, I'd love to talk to people, but as soon as those house lights come on it's a crew thing, we're such a well oiled machine. We're pulling plugs, packing up consoles, and if I stop to talk to people, it just slows up the entire operation of getting the band out.

SB: So, do you notice these days a lot more fans coming up to you?

CK: Yes, I do! I like it, it's great!

HW: How does the band feel about it?

CK: I think they're happy for me. I think their main concern is the job that gets done. They want the show to be the best thing. If people think the lights were good, then the show must have been good. It all works together. If they're happy, I'm happy. If I'm happy, they're happy. If the crowd is happy, everybody is happy!

SB: Is Paul [Languadoc] jealous?

CK: No. [Laughs] I am the brunt of some jokes... PL6. Actually, it should be PL5. Actually, now Tom Marshall thinks he's the fifth member.

SB: So do you still check out the CK5 web site?

CK: Oh yes, of course! You bet I do. I spent about ten hours straight one day going through the guestbook one click at a time reading every

single one. That's why we're doing this interview. People want to know what's going on. I want to share.

HW: What's the most rewarding part about this job?

CK: Well, my whole life when I was growing up my Father was thirty years at the same company, Wall Street, New York Stock Exchange, executive guy, got in a suit, commuted on a train everyday. Throughout my whole life growing up, I said to myself, I will not be a "nine-to-fiver." So, when I think back about the whole thing, the fact that I actually accomplished that might have to stand out over everything. The second greatest thing is all the support I get from all the fans. I get a lot of support, and you know, as a human being it just makes you feel so good. And believe it or not, an extremely rewarding thing to me is when I nail a "David Bowie". It brings tears to my eyes sometimes. Doing the job, that's how I express myself to the world. I get to express myself through light and there is a lot of joy to that!

HW: What was it like for you to light Bob Weir?

CK: It was unbelievable!

HW: Were you nervous? Was the band?

CK: No, nobody was nervous. I was excited. You know, I've seen 250 Grateful Dead shows. That El Paso, if you closed your eyes, it almost could have been the Dead, because it's Bob Weir's voice. "West LA [Fadeaway]", well, it sounded like Phish playing "West LA" with Bob Weir singing. For a couple of moments, there it really took me back.

SB: So, you were a big Dead Head?

CK: Yes, I was a Dead Head!

SB: Were you a Bobby fan?

CK: (Laughing) I really liked Jerry a lot better than the rest of the Dead.

SB: How about the Donna years. Do you like listening to shows with Donna singing?

CK: I never saw the Dead during the Donna Years, but Donna drove me nuts. But on tape, she's always off. She's always yelling and screaming. I've met Donna, she's a really wonderful woman. We've connected on a few levels and have had some nice conversations.

SB: How about Phil. Was it exciting to see Phish with Phil?

CK: Phil is the greatest guy in the world! He's just such a nice guy and he's so happy to be alive! He expresses that all the time. I got a Christmas card from him. He's always asking the band to do more Phil And Friends stuff. It's a lot of fun, but the band wants to be Phish. They want to play with Phil too, but their priority is being Phish. This is just my opinion but I think they don't want to be labeled as Phil's friends.

HW: What is you're favorite Phish show ever?

CK: It was 2/7/89 at the Front. A "Possum" to beat all "Possum"s, a "Mike's Song" to beat all "Mike's Song"s. I used to have the cassette, but I think my car ate it. Another favorite of mine, I can't remember the exact date, was at UNH or Dartmouth. I think it was UNH. We did some really cool stuff. We took the lighting truss in the middle of a jam and just brought it in all the way to head level and took it back up. And another favorite would have to be the first time we played the [Madison Square] Garden.

HW: How about your least favorite Phish show?

CK: I can't remember. I mean, there is one, I just can't remember specifics.

SB: How about favorite Grateful Dead shows?

CK: Ones I've attended... Augusta Maine '84. My all time favorite

Dead show which there is no existing soundboard for is Saratoga Performing Arts Center 6/18/83. An amazing Dead show. Merriweather '85 was good. Anything past 1985 just wasn't that great.

HW: Most of us have read about it before but do you mind briefly describing how you got your start?

CK: I was taking guitar lessons from Trey, and he asked me if I knew someone who would want to carry some gear from Nectar's stage to the van after the gig for $20. I said I would do it. I did that for about a week, and the guy who was running the lights at the Stone Church had to take a leak in the middle of the set. He left, I pushed the buttons for a while. Afterwards, I saw Trey walk up to him and say something like, hey man, I thought you were finally getting it during "[Fly Famous] Mockingbird", because the guy really had no rhythm, which just happened to be the song that the kid went to the bathroom. So, I thought to myself, do I want to be carrying gear or do I want to speak up for myself and maybe take a shot at doing lights. So I said something to Trey, and the next week he called me up and said, "Oh, for these gigs this weekend you're doing lights." And I said, "What happened to the other guy?" He said, "Oh, he can't make it." So, I said I didn't even know how to set it up. Trey said, "I'll tell ya what, Chris, we'll figure it out together." I said ok, great. I found out a couple of years later that actually what had happened is they fired the other guy and put me in the slot.

HW: Do you know how many shows you've done since then?

CK: My first show [running lights] was 3/30/89 at the Front. Let's say between 8 and 9 hundred [people].

SB: You can't miss a show. What if a show's going on and you're sick?

CK: I've done shows with a 103 degree fever, with a garbage can next to me, throwing up while running the show. I even tried to call in sick once about eleven years ago. We were playing at Keene State College. We were getting up that morning from Burlington to drive down there, and I was sick as a dog. I called Trey at home, and I said I can't make it. Trey just said, "You have to make it. There's no such thing as calling in sick. You're going no matter what." I said okay, and that day I was setting up lights while dragging a garbage can with me.

HW: Where are you originally from?

CK: I was born in Princeton, New Jersey. I grew up in Chappaqua, New York, which is in Westchester County. When I was about 21, my family moved out to Allentown, PA.

SB: Allentown, home of Dorney Park.

CK: I worked at Dorney Park for one year, operating the roller coaster.

SB: Now you live in the Burlington, Vermont area?

CK: Right outside of Burlington.

SB: Does most of the crew live in Vermont?

CK: Only the Phish crew. Myself, Paul, Brad [Sands], the band, Amy Skelton, John Paluska. It's not a requirement of the band; it's just choice. I lived in New Jersey for a few years, just a few years back, when I should have been in Vermont. I missed meetings all the time, or I'd have to fly in for meetings. It's just better to be there.

HW: What other music do you enjoy other than the Grateful Dead?

CK: I don't really listen to the Dead all that often anymore, I mean I do, when I feel like rocking out. Believe it or not, and I never thought when I was 15 that I would be saying this, I listen to [John] Coltrane, Miles Davis, Illinois Jacquet, a lot of jazz. My wife listens to rap, but she

only does it when I'm not around. She likes the Dead too, and all the jazz. But when I'm not around, she pops in the Dr. Dre, or the Snoop Doggy Dog.

SB: What did you think of the Kid Rock show?

CK: I loved it! I thought it was unbelievable. I've never heard more profanity come off a Phish stage in a ten-minute period in my life.

SB: HW: I think we covered everything, thank you for the time.

CK: My pleasure!

Carl Gerhard

Interviewed by Charlie Dirksen via email in April 2000. See also entry in Dictionary.

Charlie Dirksen: Hi Carl! First off, what's the story behind your first gig on trumpet with Phish, which I believe was on 11/11/88 at the Stone Church in Newmarket, New Hampshire?

Carl Gerhard: I remember it well. I had just moved to Newport, Rhode Island, in September of that year. Page had asked me to come up and sit in that night. I met the band in a pizza place before the show, and we just talked about music and what I might want to play with them that night. I remember it being a blast! I felt right at home up there being with Page. They played with such intensity, and the crowd was totally into it.

CD: When did you first meet Page?

CG: I've known Page since we were about nine or ten. We used to jam together in all kinds of musical settings. We would also sit around and improvise for hours. Absolutely one of the nicest, funniest guys on earth, too!

CD: How and when did the Giant Country Horns begin?

CG: I guess the idea for the horn section spawned from having Russell [Remington] and Dave [Grippo] already in town sitting in with Phish, and then I came up for a "jazz gig" with Phish at Nectar's in January 1991. That's when I met Dave. We played a short rehearsal at the band house and then the gig that night under an assumed name. I think it was something like "The Johnny B. Fishman Jazz Ensemble." I was sick as a dog and spent most of that day in Page's apartment. The next day, Trey asked me if I could get away from work that summer to tour with the band.

CD: Did you rehearse for the summer 1991 Phish tour?

CG: We rehearsed for about two or three days, tops. The ideas and music just seemed to flow and fall right into place. The most amazing thing was seeing the band's reaction when we first added the horn section in rehearsal. I knew right then that this was gonna be something special.

CD: I love it when everything proceeds according to plan. Who wrote the charts for that tour?

CG: We all had a hand in the arranging. Trey had done most of it, I think. I brought up a couple of things that a friend of mine named Rob Vuono wrote after listening to some tapes the band sent me. He wrote the horn lines to "Alumni Blues" and "The Landlady." Some nights, we actually wrote arrangements between soundcheck and the show.

CD: One of the things that got me back into Phish, after several years of not really listening to them, was a copy of the 7/21/91 Arrowhead Ranch show, and particularly the playing of the GCH in that show.

Your trumpet playing in the "Contact" continues to this day to make me smile. Do you have any particular memories of that show? It is probably the most circulated Phish show from 1991.

CG: Thanks for the compliment. I remember that most of my family came from New Jersey to see the show. That was something special. The whole "Arrowhead Ranch experience" helped me realize just how powerful Phish was as a group.

CD: Do you recall any show from that summer in particular?

CG: They were all incredible in their own way. I'd have to say that playing the last gig in Atlanta and sharing the stage with the Aquarium Rescue Unit was very memorable. It was the last show that Russell, Dave, and I played together as the original Giant Country Horns.

CD: What was the travel like on tour in summer 1991, especially the hot run through the south?

CG: Things have changed since '91! Russ, Fish, Dave, and I drove in Fish's Dodge Caravan. No A.C. We had to keep the heat on so the engine wouldn't overheat!

CD: Did the tone of the horns suffer?

CG: I don't think the instruments suffered, but we were hurtin'.

CD: Whose idea was it to wear those white suits, anyway?

CG: I don't know. But I do remember Page coming back from a costume or thrift shop in Burlington the day before the first Burlington show. He picked up three white tuxedo jackets and three pairs of white pants. He took the jackets and put them in a tub of pink dye and the pants in purple dye. They told us to go out and get sneakers that matched. Dave had white and Russell had black, so I wore one black and one white sneaker.

CD: Any wacky road stories from the tour on 1991?

CG: It was really hot at Arrowhead, so we asked Trey if we could do just one gig in shorts and a T shirt. No go. Trey said that the suits were part of the show, the GCH had to look like the GCH, so we had to "tough it out." Our skin was pink for a month!

CD: What was it like being on the road for several weeks?

CG: Being on the road with the band and crew was really fantastic. A few stories though have kept me sworn to secrecy.

CD: Do you recall seeing fans following the whole tour that summer?

CG: I remember a few fans that showed up nearly everywhere we played.

CD: It's been a long time since the Giant Country Horns have played anywhere. Why is that?

CG: It has been a long time. Too long unfortunately. Logistics, probably.

CD: Any hope to see them playing again in the future with Phish?

CG: I really hope so. It's great to go up and sit-in by myself, but there's nothing like being a part of a live horn section!

CD: When did you first start playing trumpet?

CG: I started playing when I was about ten.

CD: How often do you play your trumpet today?

CG: I play quite a bit actually. I'm a full-time Navy musician currently teaching at the Armed Forces School of Music in Virginia Beach, Virginia.

CD: What are your greatest musical influences?

CG: I grew up in a family that totally supported my music. I used to sit in my living room at home for hours and try to play along with every song that came on the radio. That really helped me develop my ear, and from that, I was able to recognize and memorize tunes. I had a great band director in high school (Norris Birnbaum), who loved quality music, regardless of idiom or genre. Our band was always performing the most challenging pieces. He pushed me to be a more well-rounded player. I've been a Navy musician for 14 years, and I've played with some super-talented people who have influenced how I play today. I mean, some really hot musicians. I can't say enough about Phish. You can't help but be positively influenced and motivated by their music and their musicianship. No doubt about it, they are the best at what they do.

CD: What's currently in your CD player, or players?

CG: Nicholas Payton (Gumbo Nouveau). Phenomenal trumpet player. Also, another great trumpet player/singer—Jack Sheldon with Ross Thompkins (On My Own).

CD: As you know, Phish has released a box set of their Hampton 1998 shows, which feature you on the encore, "Tubthumping," with Tom Marshall on vocals, too. Any memories of that evening that you'd like to share?

CG: I had no idea what Trey wanted me to play until after the first set. He told me before the show that he had a surprise in store, and that Tom [Marshall] and I would be doing the encore together. We went into the band rehearsal room (after hearing the CD once!) and fooled around with it during the set break with the band, myself, and Tom. It was a blast, to say the least!

CD: Have any comments on your performance that night?

CG: I'm my own worst critic, Charlie, but I couldn't have enjoyed myself more!

CD: Do you have any favorite Phish songs?

CG: Just about everything we've played horns on.

CD: Do you have a favorite studio Phish release?

CG: *Hoist* was great! Being a part of the tour that promoted that album was cool too! I also love *Rift*. It came out when I lived in Italy, so I was able to turn on my Italian musician friends to Phish—they loved it!

CD: Thanks again, Carl, for taking the time to answer some questions!

Ben "Junta" Hunter

Interviewed by Ellis Godard via email during July 2000. See also entry in Dictionary.

Ellis Godard: How did your association with Phish begin?

Ben "Junta" Hunter: My "official" association with the band began when we rented a nightclub called Molly's in Allston, Massachusetts, on 11/3/88. It was the kind of place that had live music only one night a week. If memory serves, they had Dead cover bands and the like on Sundays, and the rest of the time it was a rather, if you'll excuse the expression, "Euro-trashy" type of dance club.

EG: Had you done other previous bookings or management?

BH: No, although of course I was a big music fan and had seen hundreds of shows at venues all around the east coast. I would say my primary strength was my ability to proselytize—to spread the good Phish word amongst my friends—and act as sort of a "Johnny Appleseed." The band's name was on my lips in nearly every conversation I had during the several years in which I was affiliated with them.

EG: If you earlier or later promoted other early Burlington bands, which ones and what interested you about them?

BH: I was friendly with the band Ninja Custodian and promoted a gig for them at the Paradise in Boston (with not such terrific results), in late 1990 or early 1991. In fact, it was their drummer, Mike Billington (he of the permanent antic disposition), who first turned John Paluska and myself onto Phish. He's from Maine, like John and I, and he's a HUGE music fan and a great drummer. He also, I must say, turned John and I onto a lot of great music in the early days. But to answer the question, I really dug the Ninja boys, both personally and musically. They were a quartet who could rock hard when they wanted to. They had some absolutely amazing original songs and also played some really tasteful, obscure covers. In fact, although I've never seen it reported on any Phish song lists, Phish covered a Ninja tune at a gig, perhaps '90 or '91. They played the Ninja tune "Funky (Breakdown)" in Northhampton, Massachusetts, downstairs at the Pearl Street Nightclub. It really rocked, as I recall.

EG: Phish's early shows were relatively rough, in performance and showmanship. What interested you about them so early on?

BH: I was immediately fascinated by their songs. Their originals sounded so familiar to me that I thought they MUST be covers, and their covers were always interesting and well chosen—often more intense than the original versions, as far as I was concerned.

EG: What did they NOT have early on, that made them hard to book? Or enjoy?

BH: From my perspective, Phish was easy to enjoy from the very beginning. However, I would say that early on they were just a little too weird or sophisticated for many talent bookers to stomach. A good number of them just hadn't heard (or booked) many bands whose music had the complexity of Phish's. I think Phish was one of the first "jam bands" many talent bookers had heard. They were really important groundbreakers in the whole post-Dead (long before the Dead's ultimate demise) movement, which now lives on in an entire generation of young bands. But in those days Phish was quite an anomaly. They weren't doing a set of really straight-ahead tunes, and they weren't easily classifiable, which made them hard to enjoy for people who weren't very forward-thinking or progressive in their musical tastes.

EG: What gave you the idea to rent Molly's on 11/3/88 and 12/2/88?

BH: Tell you the truth, there was a band called Chuck & Helen who used to play a couple of times a week at several Allston (the part of Boston affectionately dubbed "the student slums") bars (they probably still do). They played some Dead songs and all the other predictable covers—"Love the One You're With," "Moondance," etc. . . . Anyway, they always played to a PACKED house, which meant a hundred, maybe a couple of hundred people on Friday and Saturday nights. They were a merely adequate outfit and they did very well in terms of people coming out to see them, so I knew there was a market of hungry music fans just waiting for a quality band like Phish. But since they hadn't played any gigs in the area they weren't an attractive booking for any local clubs. I thought to myself, Why not just rent a room and tell all my friends and basically throw a huge party with great entertainment? As it turned out, at both those shows there were hundreds of people who showed up.

EG: Any shareable stories of the bus ride(s) to Molly's?

BH: I lived in Boston at the time, so all I did was drive over to the club. I certainly rolled another number for the road to the gig, but it was a short road.

EG: What would you have done differently about those shows, knowing what you know now?

BH: Ha! I think I would've had a guy on our team at the door counting how many people came in! As I said, there were a few hundred people in attendance at those first Boston gigs, and I'm sure many more than the club told us had come. As I recall it, we actually took the club's word for how many people were there. That was a pretty naïve way to do things. But by the same token, I don't think anyone has any regrets about those early shows, and no one is too concerned at this point about how much more cash could've been made had we counted heads at the door. At five bucks a ticket no one's gonna get rich anyway. But those shows were pretty heady affairs from my perspective.

EG: Was the scene at early Phish shows different only in degree, or have things changed in other ways?

BH: I think the general vibe is the same, although of course it's now much less intimate than it was back in the old days at small places like The Stone Church or something. But the band, for as long as I've been seeing them, has always had a really strong bond with whatever fans were at the particular gig—whether it's sixty people or sixty thousand people. That obviously hasn't changed. The scale has changed a wee bit, but the vibe is similar. Of course the band was much more hungry for recognition in those days, and you can really hear their burning desire if you listen to those tapes.

EG: Were you at the '88 Telluride gigs? Any good memories of them?

BH: I wasn't there, but heard about 'em. I think for one of those gigs Fishman got, ahem, "lost" and the others had to soldier on as a trio.

EG: What you can you tell us about "the Zoo"?

BH: It was the house Paluska lived in his junior and senior year at Amherst College. It was a communal living situation where like-minded students co-habitated. They had a common kitchen and all took turns cooking meals for the group—stuff like that. It was quite progressive, as you might expect at such a liberal bastion of higher education. Anyway, they would also have rollicking parties every time there was a full moon. It was at one such party Phish was first introduced to the western Massachusetts faithful. I found a "Zoo" tee-shirt recently I used to wear that said "The Zoo" on the front with a Matisse print, and on the back it said, "Every full moon has its dark side."

EG: How did you meet Paluska?

BH: John is my oldest, dearest friend. We grew up in Maine across the street from one another starting at age 2.

EG: What was he like in college?

BH: I'd classify him as a typical boy-genius fuck-up. But seriously, John in college was the same as he is now. He's extremely intelligent and highly regimented, but fun. He likes things a certain way and wants to be in control of every situation—and fully admits these things about himself. Nice thing is, he isn't afraid to laugh about it. But he's got great taste, a great sense of humor, and a great sense of the absurdity of life. All in all, he's a very honorable fellow—a man of his word and a helluva guy to call a "best-friend" type.

EG: Who chose the name Dionysian Productions, and why?

BH: That would have been myself, actually. John and I were driving in my pickup truck, trying to think of provocative names for the company, and Dionysian seemed to fit because we would often talk about

our fondness for "Dionysian reveling." It was actually called Dionysian Productions Limited, originally. We had business cards printed up that had little fish on them. It's pretty funny in retrospect. If I do say so myself, I can't imagine the company being called anything *but* Dionysian Productions. It makes perfect sense given the sensibility of the company's one and only client.

EG: What other choices had you considered for the company's name?

BH: We considered South-of-Perineum Productions, but that was quickly scrapped.

EG: What was the first "office" like?

BH: It was the kitchen table of my junior-year apartment in Boston, at 19 Craig Place. It was actually in Brookline, Massachusetts, to be exact. The toilet in that place made a piercing, high-pitched feedback noise that was loud enough to break glass every time you flushed it. After a while it started happening ALL THE TIME, in the middle of the night, whenever—even when it hadn't been flushed for a long time. It got so bad that one day I bashed the hell out the toilet with a hockey stick trying in vain to make it stop. I don't think we got our security deposit back on that place.

EG: How did you and John share duties?

BH: In the early days, he booked and promoted gigs in western Mass, and I booked and promoted the gigs in Boston.

EG: Did you and John seek advice from managers of other bands? If so, what helpful advice did they provide?

BH: During my tenure I don't remember seeking any advice from managers of other bands. John may have sought some advice later on, but when I was there we really just kind of felt our way along, trying to do what seemed right at the time. One thing I do remember is we always tried to "think big." No matter what small-time club gig we were trying to book at the time, the intention was always to get very popular on the road, and the record deal and everything else would come later.

EG: Mike reportedly handled a lot of the business end at the beginning. How did the transfer to Dionysian take place? E.g., was it gradual or instantaneous? An immediate success or a stressful period?

BH: By the time we took over the band's management they were already very organized and together. They had a whole press packet—promotional materials and the works. Mike had spearheaded a lot of those efforts, but Paul Languedoc also had a hand in the "actual" business (i.e., money handling) side of things. Often times he would collect the money at the end of gigs and he'd write checks to us for our services. Eventually (and incrementally) the band entrusted their precious promo material to Dionysian, and we would dutifully send it out to club owners and talent bookers, hoping to get a positive response and a subsequent booking. When Phish realized Dionysian was going to be the management company for the long haul, they turned over their "stash" of band bios, press photos, demo tapes, and the sacred sheet we'd send to clubs which listed the many, many original and cover songs the band performed. I may have some of that early promo material around somewhere.

EG: What can you recall about early discussions about a record deal?

BH: I remember taking the band's demo to a lawyer in Boston named Jay Fialcov who I believe we'd met in New York at a conference that was then called the New Music Seminar. We played it for him and he loved it. He said he'd had a dream that he'd gotten Phish a record deal. I specifically remember him listening to the jam in one of the songs—"Run Like an Antelope" I think it was—and commenting on the "jazz chords," as he called them, that Page was playing amidst the squall of dissonance and feedback Trey was producing. Fialcov eventually DID help the band get its first deal with Absolute a Go Go, who put out *Lawn Boy*.

EG: Were you around when Phish first made a profit?

BH: A profit? Do you mean in a fiscal year? I'm not sure about that one, though I do know they almost always made a little money on gigs in the early days (but probably not actual PROFIT) because they carried their own production equipment (i.e., lights and sound) and they weren't being given tour support by a record label. As a result, they usually brought enough people into the venue so that they collected some money at least. Of course, there were lots of gigs in the early days that didn't make any money, but almost every time the band went into a new town they'd make an impact. As a result, the next time they came to that town there'd be more people at the gig than there had been the time before. Hence, more money, a better split with the club, etc. . . .

EG: When did you first get a sense that Phish could be successful?

BH: It may sound obvious now, but I'm telling you the honest truth when I say the first time I saw them I thought they could be really successful. They really had their thing together! At that first gig I saw they played "The Lizards" and after the gig I ran breathlessly up to Fishman and said, "What WAS that tune man? I swear I've heard it before." He shrugged and said, "That's our tune, man." I was amazed and, actually, blown away.

I mean, how many times do you see a band and not know any of their songs and still remember hearing (and being totally moved by) one of their originals—enough so you remember it over a dozen years later? Maybe the people who saw Led Zeppelin perform "Stairway to Heaven" live on tour before they released the fourth album, but not many others, I'm willing to bet. I also remember the first time I saw them they played a super-fast version of Hendrix's "Fire." After the gig I was saying to people something like "When I heard they were playing 'Fire' it was cool, but I didn't expect it to turn into a conflagration!" So the short answer is, I knew they had great taste and great songs right away. I believed in their talent immediately, and started a furious search to collect bootleg tapes of gigs they'd done. It's difficult for me to describe how powerful and profound that first experience seeing them live was.

EG: When did you realize just HOW successful they were (are) going to be?

BH: I think I started to get the picture on how successful they could be around 1989, when they started to consistently play venues with hundreds (sometimes thousands) of people in the audience. When I'd see people freaking out the same way I did when I first saw them, I knew the band was on to something special.

EG: Why is your nickname Junta, and how do YOU pronounce it?

BH: My nickname involves a long and mysterious story whose origins I'm not at liberty to discuss. However, I say it "Joon-tah" (the o's sound like they do in "look"). Most of my friends and relations say it that way too, as does the band, with the exception of Page, who says it "June-tah." So you've heard it here first, Phish's first album is called "Joon-tah," not "hoon-tah" as I've often heard it referred to.

EG: Have ever met or been involved with any juntas?

BH: I met a guy called John Giunta (he also pronounces it Joon-tah) the other night. Other than that, no.

EG: Why is the album *Junta* named after you?

BH: I think it was really just intended as a joke by the band, but of course they didn't tell me they were going to call it Junta until I picked up the dubbed cassette tapes of the album and saw "Junta" written on every one of them. It was quite a shock, indeed. They also talked about naming one of their records "Paluska," but that hasn't come to pass yet. "Paluska" doesn't roll off the tongue quite as easily, does it?

EG: What's your favorite tune on *Junta*?

BH: I really like that one called "Sugar Magnolia." Ah, I mean "Y.E.M." would be one of the tunes I really like.

EG: Is *Junta* your favorite Phish album? If not, what is and why?

BH: Actually, it is my favorite, not because it's named after me, but because it evokes a period of time when the band was the most exciting, most important thing in my life. It's also the album that I believe the band's "hunger" to be successful comes through the most resoundingly. The songs are great, very "Phishy" in their complexity, and the performances are a bit raw, but therein lies the charm in my opinion. Having said that, everyone always spends a lot of time mythologizing a band's "early days" as their halcyon period, which I think is kind of lame because it's like looking for something that's already found you. Funny thing is, this happens with every band—every phenomenon really—that gets very popular after a period of time. Everyone always sits around saying, "I remember what this thing was like in the early days, it was so great then, now it's not what it used to be and blah blah blah." What good would things be if they never changed? Pretty boring by my estimation. C'mon, "What's Become of the Baby" is an early Grateful Dead song, but that doesn't mean I EVER need to hear IT played again, live or on record. As far as I'm concerned, Phish is still writing good songs and putting out good albums and playing good shows, so people should be happy they're evolving, not staying in their "Junta" period forever. But let's face it, "Bowie" has a passion and verve that'll be hard for the band to ever match.

EG: Can you think of any ways in which you directly influenced the way Phish does something in their live show?

BH: I taught them how to play their instruments and perform on-stage the exact way they do now—every chord, every riff, every synchronized dance step, the works. But I don't really consider those things to be *really* major aspects of their live show.

EG: What is your current relationship to the band?

BH: We're friendly—no, we're more than friendly. In fact, we often hug and kiss (non-French) and sing "Lovin', Touchin' Squeezin'" in unison when we see each other. I especially dig that adorable little Fishman fellow.

EG: Do you ever freak out at seeing your nickname plastered on albums and tee-shirts?

BH: Yes. I freak out about it so much that when I see someone with a Junta-related product I immediately experience a series of painful bowel contractions and bodily convulsions. I often will go up to the person and command them to divest themselves of the merchandise immediately or else pay me a tariff to wear said garment.

EG: Do you ever wish you had stuck with managing Phish? Why or why not?

BH: I 'm pretty sure band management is not my thing in the final analysis. It would be nice from a monetary perspective to still be involved, but had I continued managing, I know many wonderful things that have transpired in my life wouldn't have happened at all.

EG: Did you continue a career in the music industry? If not, what do you do now (for work)?

BH: I've been writing about music and living in Manhattan for over eight years. I've written a book (*The Midnight Special*) and contributed extensively to many other books (*The Rolling Stone Jazz and Blues Guide*, most recently) and magazines like *Rolling Stone, Spin,* and *Vibe*. I'm currently the editorial director at a company called Limeradio.com. We're assembling THE definitive guide to radio on the Internet. Check us out when we launch, which will be in late August. Internet radio, as most of you know, is an incredible thing, a new frontier, really.

EG: What do you do for fun?

BH: Hang out with my wife and 8-month-old son. Travel. See music and movies. Sniff Drano.

EG: Was Phish ever your favorite band? If not, who? If so, who was until you got "it" with Phish?

BH: I would say they were my favorite band for a while, but I've never had many real "favorite" bands because I've always liked so much DIFFERENT music—from Thelonious Monk to Fela Kuti to Johnny Cash to Compay Segundo to the Kinks to Deep Purple to Jobim and back again.

EG: Do you listen to much Phish these days?

BH: Not much. I guess I primarily listen to them when I see them live.

EG: What was the last Phish show you attended?

BH: Radio City Music Hall [5/22/00].

EG: What was your most memorable show and why?

BH: Those first Paradise shows in Boston were pretty special, just because I felt like I was staking my personal reputation on the fact that Phish was, in fact, a great band. I had told just about every person I knew, literally, about that gig, and most of them came to it!! As a result, I felt personally responsible for everyone's good time and wanted the band to play BETTER than perfectly. I remember cringing and thinking, "C'mon boys, do it right" when they didn't quite perform the initial worked-out section of their opener (I think it may have been "Y.E.M."?) with absolute perfection. In retrospect, I guess it didn't really matter too much, did it? Everyone loved it and had a great time.

EG: After all of these years, are there any Phish songs you'd rather not hear again live?

BH: I haven't seen the band enough in recent years to really comment authoritatively on this one. I do know they have a lot more really good songs than bad ones, That's for sure. The much maligned "Contact" is one that gets a little old, but when it was written I remember loving it, thinking it was hilarious and one of the best things they'd ever written.

EG: What other music are you into?

BH: I'm into music that is "good," regardless of genre. I like a lot of "pop" music (not the stuff that's on the charts, per se), jazz, a lot of what people call "world" music. Stuff from Brazil, Cuba, Africa, the Caribbean. I like traditional Celtic music, I dig Klezmer stuff, funk, classic soul and R&B—name it. If it sounds good, it is good. I believe music is far too classified and explained, poked and prodded these days by people who need to sell it.

EG: What other bands would you like to have been in on the ground floor of?

BH: The Beatles.

EG: Are there any smaller bands now that you would like to be involved with?

BH: I'd rather just go see bands live and enjoy them—it's a lot easier that way—plus you don't get locked into one situation so intimately—I think it's easier to enjoy the product more if you're not so closely involved in the process.

Kevin Shapiro

Interviewed by Charlie Dirksen via email in August and September of 1999. See also entry in Dictionary.

Charlie Dirksen: When did you begin working for Dionysian Productions, and what is your job title and responsibilities?

Kevin Shapiro: I work for Phish not Dionysian Productions, though the distinction is pretty insignificant, since Dionysian only currently manages one artist, Phish. My job title is Phish Archivist and main responsibility is to manage the band's history, information, and creations. I basically keep track of what they do and all their output, track its flow in from the band and organization out to its users, and then back.

CD: Is being the Phish Archivist itself a full-time job for you?

KS: Yes and no. I work full-time for Phish, but my responsibilities for the band are broader than my work in the archives. I also represent the band as In-House Counsel to the degree I am needed in that capacity. I don't take on outside legal or archival work, except to volunteer my time for some local causes.

CD: When was your first Phish show?

KS: September 29, 1991, at the Agora Ballroom in Cleveland, Ohio. It's funny, I just finished reviewing it before writing *This Month in Phish History* (for September, 1991).

CD: What was your first Phish tape?

KS: February 6, 1989, from Nectar's. I'll never forget hearing the fast version of Sanity on that tape. It's like a fourth or fifth generation cassette that's worn nearly to pieces by now.

CD: Do you have any personal favorite shows? A personal favorite Era of Phish?

KS: There are too many greats to list, and a lot of nights have been personally significant for so many reasons. A good example is December 31, 1991. That was my first Phish New Year's show and my first really long road trip to a show. They played tremendously, I went with people I love and met new folks who have grown to be counted among my closest friends in the world. It's even tougher for me to choose a favorite era. I think every era of the band's history reveals something about them, their music and music in general, and the audience. Every point in Phish history has some sort of real value to me, and it's impossible to appraise that value relative to similar thoughts or feelings I had at a different time. Some shows seem like perfect showcases of the group's sound at a certain place or time, and some periods seem dull at the moment compared to some show from "the old days" but in retrospect are very exciting. New favorite shows, songs, and eras arise all the time depending on what I'm listening to and why.

CD: Are you yourself a taper? How long have you been taping?

KS: Yes, my name is Kevin and I am a Taper. It's a strange question since I haven't taped Phish consistently since a couple years before I began my job (my taping fell off during law school), but I have taped the band as recently as this summer. I still tape other shows too, mostly jazz shows and mostly if I think others won't be capturing it. I think I taped my first concert in 1989 or so. I began my taping career by making recordings of bands I played drums in and quickly branched out from there.

CD: I played drums for about eight years or so. The places I've lived for the last ten years of my life haven't been suitable for serious drum practice. Do you play anymore?

KS: I still have my kit and stay in touch with the local music scene. Occasionally I'll get together with friends and jam but my apartment is too small and thinly walled to effectively practice. I sit in with local bands once in a while. A day or two after Dick passed away, I sat in with Blues for Breakfast during their yearly tribute for Garcia. We played "Tangled Up in Blue," and I'm told it sounded all right. I've never developed my drumming skills to a high level. I can play along with most grooves.

CD: Do you tape other bands? What other bands/music do you enjoy?

KS: I enjoy all kinds of bands and music. Phish is my favorite existing musical group, and they have been since I first saw them . . . maybe even before. That said, I catch a lot of jazz, reggae, funk, straight rock and roll, and even some of what would be defined as heavy metal. I love bands like Iron Maiden, Metallica, Led Zeppelin. The psychedelic music scene had a massive impact on me too in terms of Grateful Dead, Hot Tuna, and stuff from the San Francisco and English psychedelic scenes. Later I discovered the Detroit music scene, which included a lot of rock, jazz, and blues. I love just about anything with James Carter or Dennis Chambers. I am definitely a self-professed music fanatic.

CD: What, generally speaking, does the Archives contain? For example, does it have all of the shows from 1992 onward on digital SBD?

KS: The Phish Archives generally contain the band and organization's entire physical history. It's a very broad project encompassing written materials, photographs, audio, video, art, merchandise, stage props and costumes, all kinds of memorabilia from tickets and passes to fan mail, and anything saved and donated by the band, family, or crew through the past sixteen years.

Your question is more specific to audio. We have many formats of audio through the years. In general, we have all of the shows from fall 1992 to present on a digital format, which is typically DAT. The digital soundboard (SBD) distinction is somewhat inaccurate, as most of the reference tapes Paul makes contain some mix of audience from the stage, the mix position, or both. The band has kept so-called digital SBD tapes of every show since November 19, 1992, and of quite a few before then, too. It was November 1992 when Paul permanently added a DAT recorder to the front-of-house equipment.

CD: Is there anything the Archives needs that fans might be able to provide, or help to locate?

KS: We're not seeking submissions, technically, but the answer is a resounding "yes"! We have audio recordings of around sixty to seventy percent of the shows Phish has played and video of far less. We only have those photographs we have shot or commissioned on an "official" basis and there are obviously lots of unofficial images that would be great to add to the Archives. Anything from any of the categories I've listed that is original—or of very high quality or significance—is wel-

Vaults) all were incredibly helpful. The list is too long to thank everyone, but I went after all the information I could get on how to set up an archive of the sort the band wanted. By the time I began serious meetings with the band and management about my vision for the project, I knew a lot more than when I'd started making calls. I also contacted every manufacturer of archival software I could find to see how to go about tracking all the data we had and were about to create.

Since I began, I constantly seek out information about Archival Science, especially as it relates to the entertainment industry and business archives. I attend conferences, read on newsgroups and publications, and stay in touch with as many colleagues as possible. I also have been lucky to have the help of a number of excellent interns and assistants, who have been great in physically digging through and figuring out the collection. I believe the project is worthy of total dedication to preserving and using the material. Without the information contained in our Archives, the ability to communicate what is and was Phish would be very difficult. Phish to me defies accurate description . . . the experience, the music, the culture surrounding all of it can only be understood through its history. I guess that's true of most phenomena.

CD: What did you do this past week, just to put your job in greater perspective?

KS: As always, last week was a busy one. I'm dealing with the Rock and Roll Hall of Fame and Museum about the display of some items, shipped a couple DAT machines out for repair, made all the arrangements with Michael Grace (who engineered 10/31/90), made umpteen different compilations—by track—by set, etc. for the 10/31/90 release, assembled and shipped all the visual content for 10/31/90, made a few changes to some Hampton Comes Alive source tapes, had a number of meetings about humidity in our tape vault, purchased some new duplication equipment, ordered and delivered some equipment and media to the band in the studio, and did some work tracking down some older tape collections . . . oh and I answered a few questions for the Mockingbird Project. Simultaneously, I followed through on international trademark registrations for Phish Stick and Phish Food, dealt with a number of bootleg-selling stores, wrote multiple requests for removal of illegal sales from online auction sites, worked on a licensing agreement for our mail order company, approved some legal bills, and drafted a couple other agreements. Oh, and like any other week, I spent a lot of time answering mail from people with legal and/or archival questions, and supervising my staff. Staying in touch with people in the scene is rewarding and valuable so I try to personally respond to any well-intentioned question. It's daunting to look at in retrospect, but my average week is varied and extremely busy.

CD: What's an example of a Gem that you have on tape that no one else has? Do you have any periods with many shows missing from the Archives?

KS: It's hard to mention a specific Gem. It's like defining the best show or best period, and it's also a loaded question, because I'm not sure what else other people might have. The complete tape of the band's first performance together on October 30, 1983, or their entire first performance with Page, are both Gems that no one else has in any complete sense. The album masters contain myriad Gems of varying degrees and certainly no one else has those. There are so many Gems on tape and the band has traditionally shared a lot of their output with their fans, so it's hard to say. My favorite Gem changes as often as what

comed. I'm sure someday we may seek out specific additions to the collections. So far it's been all I can do to organize, document, and preserve what's already been put away.

CD: When was the Archives first established or started? Did anyone manage it before you?

KS: The Archives were set up as an entity or department when I began my job in January of 1996. I have rough notes about the band's archives and how to separate, store, and use the collection that the band's manager, John Paluska, wrote in around 1990 or so I'd say. Mike (Gordon) and the other band members began keeping notes in journals, photos, articles, and tapes very early in the band's history. . . certainly before they were called "Phish." Mike was the first custodian of all the business records and then Paul Languedoc eventually kind of took that over. Various family members, crew members, and friends kept bits and pieces of things the whole time.

After he started managing Phish in 1988–89, John kept things in pretty good order in terms of trying to get shows documented, though it must have been hard to look forward (as a manager) and backward (as an archivist) at the same time. I think it was when Shelly Culbertson started working for Dionysian in 1992 that the archive project got its first real supervisor. Shelly continued until I arrived, when she was able to turn her attention to ticketing and running our web site. Jason Colton, who also works for Dionysian, and the former head of Phish Mail Order, Cynthia Brown, both helped manage a lot of the band's images when they began work, soon after Shelly. Paul recorded shows and tried to keep them labeled and accounted for, but I get the impression it was pretty loose in the early days, especially early touring days. The mixes, equipment, and his duties varied a lot from day to day from what I can tell. Phish can thank a huge number of dedicated fans who documented the early experience and who were incredibly generous and helpful with piecing together the holes from the early days for the Archives. I turn to those folks more often than not to answer questions about early shows.

CD: How is the Archives organized, in general? What media? Did you seek any outside help in getting it started or organized?

KS: It's set up chronologically by category and tied to relevant events. It is designed with the goal that users can most easily locate the item(s) or information they need, and use/return it with a minimum of difficulty or wear on the collection. I think I already gave a short list of media previously. It's very broad . . . from giant foam and metal hot dogs to every type of magnetic media to the Zero Man jumpsuit. We have the chessboard, old mini-tramps, lots of posters and flyers from shows and events, and everything in between.

I sought a great deal of help setting up the Archives. All the items and information are assessed for value (i.e., keep it or not?), described in a database (which is constantly being updated), and stored in what are hopefully ideal storage conditions. As I began the interview process for the Archivist position, I contacted every "rock and roll" Archivist I could think of and followed all the leads they provided. People like Dick Latvala and Dennis McNally (GD), James Olness (originally with BGP and now his own company, J.O.E.), Rebecca Nichols and Jerry Pompili (also from BGP), Kirk West (Allman Brothers Band), John Scott, David Gans, Joey Helguera (Atlantic Records), Mary Ide (WGBH TV), Jim Henke (Rock and Roll Hall of Fame and Museum), Danny Clinch, Taylor Crothers, Marj Minkin, Jim Pollock, and David Wexler (Hollywood

I'm checking out at the moment. Some of my favorite pieces in the Archives are photographs or posters that are not even anticipated by your question since it focuses on tapes. I really like the HORDE sword given to the bands who participated in the July, 1992, HORDE Tour.

There are lots of periods with many shows missing from the Archives. In general, Mike kept great audio records of shows—and even some practices—from the band's first couple years. Around 1986 and 1987 things get pretty sketchy in terms of the number of master recordings we have in the vault. In the few years from mid-1988 to mid-1991 friends and fans really picked up the slack. That's probably the period from which the most questions arise, since there's been a lot of trading, mislabeling, and embellishing within the Phish community, so it's hard to judge the legitimacy of a purported "master." A number of people have donated large collections of definite masters, and there are many more claiming to have certain shows we lack in Archives.

By fall of 1991, Paul was pretty much recording every show on cassette, so we may lack some recordings from that point through fall of 1992, but not too many. We have never made an attempt to collect or catalog audience recordings of shows that we already have soundboard tapes or mixed tapes of, but I could see it someday happening. Our collection lacks consistently good photographs of the band until the mid-1990s, though those have begun filtering in. There's such a large body of material out there that even considering "filling in the holes" is a daunting task. As people realize we have an archive, original materials seem to sort of find me and we adopt them with open arms.

CD: Who has access to the Archives? Do you often make tapes for VIPs on CD, DAT, and/or analog?

KS: In a physical sense, no one has access except me and my staff. In a larger sense, the Archives exist for the use of the band and organization. The four band members, and anybody who works for Phish or its related companies, are able to "check out" items as they are needed. We ship materials to and from studios, production facilities, design companies, and the road constantly.

As for tape requests, occasionally I get requests from the band to make copies of certain things, depending on what projects are underway. It's basically all for purposes of reviewing their work for public use or some sort. Any project that involves content from any type of media involves the Archives, so album production, movie production, book production, festival production, and merchandise production all require materials for business purposes. Requests for tapes for family members or VIPs occur sometimes, and I try to keep everyone listening to good stuff, but the Archives are really used to support broader projects. We have the ability to make copies on any of the mediums you mentioned.

CD: How are shows being backed up at the present time? Anything on reel?

KS: Some shows exist on reel-to-reel, which is the only real "archival" medium, short of glass masters or something of that sort. Most shows before 1990 or so were on cassettes, which tend to hold up pretty well if not played and if stored properly. We are (slowly) transferring the cassettes to digital formats, like DAT and CDR. From 1990 or so, much of the collection is digital (DAT, DA-88 and DA-38, a couple A-DATs, and some VHS PCM audio). That stuff is slowly being backed onto digital mediums, mostly CDR. The latest research seems to indicate that CDR may not be the archival savior we had all hoped for,

so we're constantly reviewing what to back up and to what mediums it is best migrated.

CD: Are all Phish performances over the past few years now archived in multitrack format? If so, when did Paul start recording shows in multitrack format?

KS: Most are. There are a few that escape multitrack because of space limitations. For example, the recent Japan shows are not on multitrack due to the difficulty of getting all of the machines over there. Paul began doing 32-track DA-88 recording in summer/fall 1994 and has done every show since then on 32-track, with only a few exceptions. Now we're running 40 tracks, which include some backup tracks of the basic 2-track mix that gets run to DAT each night.

CD: Do you foresee releases from the Phish Vault/Archives in the future, similar to what Dick Latvala has done with Grateful Dead vault tapes?

KS: I sincerely hope so. The "White Tape" was the first, being number PA1001, so I guess that leaves a lot of possible releases to come. I don't know if it would ever be a program similar to what Dick has done with the Grateful Dead tapes. Dick tried every trick to get archival releases going after he had a few years to get the collection in some form of order, and he apparently ran into a lot of resistance—or at least a lack of agreement about what to release, and when and how. Eventually, the band decided to forego the decision-making process, and entrusted it to Dick and their studio engineer, John Cutler. That was when a steady flow of releases began. The members of Phish are very hands-on in just about every sense of the organization, so it's really their decision what, when, and if. It's a tough decision, since their current material is so vital and exciting that the thought of archival releases tends to be more of a future vision. I see light at the end of the tunnel and hope the possibilities are someday realized. The level of investment put into the Archives by the band and organization leads me to be confident that they will be.

CD: Are audience tapes made at same time as SBD tapes at shows, analog and digital? What mics are used for the AUD tapes?

KS: Yes, separately and as part of the "SBD" mix DATs that Paul makes as reference tapes. Shows are generally recorded at least three ways. First, there is the 40-track multitrack, which is accomplished using five DA-88 machines, 8 tracks each. They are locked together digitally and can be striped with time code to synch up with video or film.

Second, Paul runs a mix through a simple Mackie mixer of a soundboard feed blended with a small amount of signal from audience mics placed on the stage (AT4033s). He uses a simple delay to match the feeds for a good reference of the show.

Finally, he generally makes audience 2-track cassettes run solely from the mix position microphones, which are AKG414s. Basically what you might make from the taper section. He occasionally will use that to isolate the room sound from one show or another to check out how his mix actually sounded in the house. There are audience feeds to the multitracks from both the on-stage Audio Technicas and the front-of-house mics. There's often BetaCam video run from either a switched feed if a venue has cameras and a film crew for screens or from our camera mounted at the mix position if not. The BetaCam tape receives the same feed as the reference DATs.

CD: As you know, there have been many shows/sets released on SBD>cass>DAT by folks close to the band. Some have been tree'd heavily on the net. There are few SBDs that circulate from 1995 through the

present day, however. What is the reasoning behind this change in policy? Is it true that Page no longer receives an analog master of a show right after it gets played, as he once regularly did?

KS: I don't know if it's really a change in policy. I guess the change correlates in part with me starting to manage the collection, though I don't know if it's a cause and effect situation. The policy as to reference tapes as I said before is that they are for the band's use only. Basically, copies are not run for anyone of any shows no matter how "close to the band" they are, unless the band specifically requests copies be made. There was a period around 1992–1993 when Paul was running DAT masters without an audience mix and running cassette backups of that soundboard mix, as it happened. Those cassette masters were often given to Page, and I suppose he did what he wanted with them. He's recently returned all those cassettes to the Archives and the collection was quite intact, so whatever Page did, he kept them in excellent order and condition. Things find their way into circulation in the most bizarre ways that it's hard to properly answer this question. There is no policy forbidding tape leaks exactly. I think things have just grown to be handled more formally now that the whole collection is under consistent management.

CD: Is there an official policy with respect to the taping of Phish shows from DAT to CD for personal use? A lot of people are backing up their own personal collections on CDR nowadays, and many more are making CDs of *live* Phish for their friends.

KS: No. Our posted taping and duplication policy says it all. It's not media-specific. I will say that DAT to CDR transfers seem to become "bootlegs" for sale or otherwise violating our policy more often than other media, but I don't think people trading music on CDR for personal use is any more harmful than DAT or online transfer, or any other means of trading.

CD: I'm sure some fans would like to know why live video is forbidden (e.g., at shows and on the Internet), while audio taping is allowed. I know what I'd say, but what do you have to say about this?

KS: Live video is forbidden for a few reasons. First, the band and Elektra are the sole copyright holders of the band's performances, and neither wishes to allow video taping at shows. That has always been the policy as far as I know, with very few exceptions. Another reason has to do with commercial bootlegging, which seems to favor video over audio, kind of like the preference for CDR over cassettes. I would hazard a guess that video taping also would require a different level of access (i.e., good sight lines, lighting, etc.) than does audio taping. Can you imagine a huge throbbing section of video techies in front of the front row of each show? Providing live video on the Internet or elsewhere is discouraged because the taping is prohibited and illegal. We don't want to allow people to provide content that they aren't allowed to make. It's inconsistent. That's why we have had to take a stance against unauthorized video distributors online and elsewhere.

CD: I know as an attorney (with some copyright law experience) that it is imperative that copyright holders protect their rights, in order to avoid waiving them. I'm glad that Phish understands the importance of this. Are there 2-track copies of shows from recent years in the vault? Would releasing a SBD for tree'ing on the net, for example, require a mix-down from multitrack to 2-track before it could be released?

KS: I basically answer this above, but there are 2-track copies of es-

sentially every show from the past seven years and of many shows before that. Releasing a reference copy of a show for any reason could theoretically be done without any mix-down, if the band was satisfied with the 2-track mix. For example, all of the music played on the From the Archives radio shows has come direct from 2-track of some form or another. For radio, I try to get out any source noise, "master" the levels to some degree, and make the segues in and out of songs as painless as I can.

CD: How did you go about coming up with all the great music for the Clifford Ball, Great Went, and Lemonwheel Archives shows? Did the band members have any input?

KS: When the idea to do the show came up (thanks to my colleague Jason Colton for the general idea), I approached the band for input of any sort and they basically said, "Run with it." They have given tidbits of feedback at times, while the shows were on, or after they heard them ("Oh god, did we do that tune!?"), but they have given no substantive suggestions of things to include or exclude. It's a realm in which I enjoy almost total freedom, within FCC limits that is. There's an interesting story from Lemonwheel about me trying to showcase the opening song from "The White Tape," which apparently does not fit generally accepted government guidelines for a number of reasons.

CD: I can see the FCC having a problem with "Fuck Your Face."

KS: The story of coming up with the music for the shows is a bit more complicated, but I guess this is my chance to elaborate. I pretty much scan my memory banks, Archive database, friends' suggestions, notes that I get from fans, input from anyone in the organization who's willing to provide it, etc. I come up with initial lists, do a lot of listening, change the lists, refine them, listen some more, try to decide whether there are better or more representative offerings, and eventually pace the Archives for untold hours trying to decide on a good lineup. I try to mix it up a lot, combining soundchecks, outtakes, really old stuff, really new stuff (you mentioned the lack of recent "SBD" releases) and anything that evokes extreme emotion from me. I have been given total freedom with the shows, and it is a very cathartic moment for me when I step up to the mic and decks and start to roll a show.

Perhaps I build it larger than it really is, but it means more to me than I can describe here to "bring the music to the people," and I try to really deliver the goods. I've seen plenty of sunrises from the Archives while trying to piece together the shows, and I've never left one of the broadcasts without thinking, "Was that version good enough?" or similar thoughts. The feedback has been great overall, and I understand that the tapes of some of the shows are still making the rounds, and I look forward to continuing the tradition. It's funny . . . when I'm on the air I try to speak about the music as I would to my girlfriend Kirsten or my buddies, but I inevitably fail, and end up sounding a bit NPR-ish. She has said to me, "Just speak about it like you would to me or to Dick. Tell them it's the royal unbelievable bomb and the best example of a _____ ever done," or words to that effect. I hope everything that I've played has been the royal unbelievable bomb or incredibly hilarious or amazingly instructive about the band's development. That's what I'm after . . . oh and to try not to sound too NPR. Apparently my great excitement and enthusiasm for the music doesn't always travel well via FM.

CD: Well, I was not fortunate enough to have been able to attend the Ball, Went, or Wheel in the flesh, but I have really enjoyed hearing the radio shows, especially the Wheel radio show, which is being circulated

rather well from what I've gathered. It's got some incredible Phish on it. Thank you! Will there be a show in Florida, or can you say? Will you play anything from 10/6/89 Paradise, or any other shows that don't circulate at all?

KS: I too really liked the show I put together for Lemonwheel, and the privilege of changing the station's moniker to "The Love Badger" for a couple hours each day was great. I liked the concept of trying to integrate various others from our organization—who have a strong effect on Phish history—into the program. I am always taking requests and I realize that your first show "does not circulate," but I can't play anything from it, as I have not yet located the master tapes—if there are any. Anyone out there? In the meantime, there was no radio station at Oswego this year, but I understand there will be at the Florida event for New Year's Eve 1999, so I'm getting a solid roster together.

CD: Excellent! Glad to hear it! Let me therefore respectfully request the 12/1/95 Mike's Groove, which is INSANE, and which doesn't circulate on what I'd consider high-quality DAUD. Yet. One last question, Kevin, since I gather he meant a lot to you. What did your friendship with Dick Latvala, the Grateful Dead's archivist, mean to you?

KS: When I started my job as Archivist, I contacted everyone I could and got input from as many professionals in the field as possible. They came from all walks of life and worked in every field of music and media restoration, conservation, preservation, storage, and appreciation. I must say that amongst them all, Dick stood out like a sore thumb. I write this with tears in my eyes, as I still can't believe Dick is not with us. I mean, the phone is ringing and I know it won't be him and that hurts.

Our relationship began when I called him before I started my job, sometime around the end of 1995 or January 1996. Dennis McNally put us in touch. Dick was totally humble and was glad to meet me at my earliest convenience. Apparently he had met with Shelly at some point a couple years before that and had given her a few tips, but I don't think they stayed in close touch. Anyway, we really clicked on the phone, and we made plans for me to visit him in San Francisco during the upcoming fall Phish tour.

I remember him picking me up at my hotel in San Francisco distinctly. He woke up really early as was typical (for him, not me) and drove down from Petaluma to pick me up. I offered to drive up in a rental, but he wouldn't hear of it. When he called from the lobby, he was really funny, saying something like "You'll recognize me immediately . . . I'm the old smelly guy with a GD sweatshirt on." We met and he drove me out to the Club Front studio/rehearsal space, where the GD vault is located. It was a Saturday, the day after the Cow Palace show [November 1996]. I recall he wouldn't go to the Cow Palace show, because it was too late at night and too much driving, but he promised we'd go together someday. We got to the vault and, before entering the building, Dick fed the homeless cats who lived there. It was something he did every day and it was consistent with his sensibilities. Dick had cats at home, too. He really loved cats.

We toured the Club Front facilities (I remember the GD's gear being fully set up in the practice space) and the vault, which was pretty impressive. I believe Dick and his son Richie built it mostly themselves. He ran through some of the design details, as I was looking into moving our magnetic media in-house to a vault, and needed to know what a "vault" for archives consisted of. He blew past the studio material and the video, but when we hit the audio reels (my eyes locked on the Acid Test shows

from 1965–66) his eyes lit up. Dick felt the weight of his job more than anyone that I've ever met, except maybe my dad. The stuff was like gold to him. He walked me up and down each aisle, giving various archival hints and pontificating about eras of GD music. I asked a lot of questions, and took a lot of notes, but we really connected on a personal level, too. He insisted on taking me to his house to "do some real listening," and proceeded to spin some of the sickest material I've ever heard from any band. His house was packed with GD memorabilia and music. Dick showed me his house and personal collection, took me to dinner at his favorite Mexican restaurant, and dropped me off with friends, who took me to the Sacramento Phish show that night. I recall wishing that he had joined me during the Taste with Peter Apfelbaum.

He and I stayed in close touch since that first meeting. He imparted bits of knowledge to me and he slowly warmed up to Phish's music. We corresponded by regular mail and email and spoke pretty regularly by phone. When spring of 1997 came along, I think he was Slip Stitch and Pass's biggest advocate. "That Mike's Song thingy kills me!" he'd say. I remember him claiming to have listened to that track twenty times in a single sitting. I never claimed Dick was not obsessive. Sometime around then I started attending Dick's DP Release Parties on the East Coast. I went to one in Revere, Massachusetts, and was amazed at Dick's patience with autograph seekers and the like. He had tons of friends around, but kept to the task at hand, which was explaining his picks, basically. He absolutely loved his subject and approached it like a scholar more than anything else.

His wife Carol and I went to The Gorge Phish shows together in 1998, and then we flew together back to their little compound, in order to catch the Shoreline Phish show in 1998. With Carol converted by The Gorge and Dick highly excited by Slip Stich's material and some other stuff that I'd primed him with, we hit Shoreline together. I felt honored to sort of "escort" him to the show, and he raved about it from its outset. It was a really smoking show. I recall him posting to a GD Internet forum something to the effect of "It was the best live music I've seen since Derek and the Dominoes and Jimi Hendrix." I think I irritated him during the show by trying too hard to explain it to him. Obviously he got it and didn't need an interpreter. Our relationship flourished and he and [my girlfriend] Kirsten became phone buddies. The Picks kept pouring in, and I have to credit Dick with re-awakening me to the GD's music through his picks. He had copious notes on every tape he had, every tape there was, and a few he thought might exist but he hadn't found them yet. I visited him again in Philadelphia for a Dick's Picks release party, and I took Brad [Sands] and Big Phil with me to meet Dick. We had a great dinner and watched him "perform" in prime fashion at The Electric Factory, giving autographs and analyzing questions.

When the news came out that Trey and Page would join Phil as his Friends this past April, Dick was ecstatic. We made big plans and he intended to go to all three nights. We saw him first at The Warfield on April 15. He was there with Carol and friends and we watched much of the show together. He wouldn't leave his seat in the balcony. Between us, we were beaming side-by-side like the sun. We were perhaps the two proudest people in the world at that moment. We both had tears in our eyes, and he explained that it was the best that he had felt musically since the closing of Winterland. I was wise enough that time not to interpret and I just nodded. He went on to post a glowing review, and to demand that the shows be released in their entirety asap.

Dick was on a life mission to share his love of the music, and he was completely dedicated to it. He skipped the second Warfield show (I never let him live it down), in order to care for his mother who was ill. He gave his tickets to his son Richie, instead, so that he could check it out. His love for Richie was inspiring. He was so proud that his son was a genetic scientist . . . a real job sort of thing. We got together again for night three and watched most of the show together, once again absolutely glowing. We spoke few words those nights, but our emotions could not have been stronger. The day after the Phil and Friends shows, Kirsten and I joined Dick, Carol, and Dick's roommates for a barbecue at his house. We agreed about the epic nature of the shows, though I think I may have viewed them with a more critical eye than he. We had a great time hanging out, and I nearly forgot to leave his place to travel North for some vacation time.

More picks came out and Dick finally got to visit Vermont on Monday, July 12. He called to tell us not to make the huge drive to Brattleboro (it's a couple hours), since he'd just be hanging with fans and wouldn't be good company. We laughed and hopped into the car. I was so excited to have him visit our beautiful state. The release party was at a tiny little place and was poorly attended, but Dick was in prime form. We walked in only to interrupt an interview he was giving. He passed the interviewer deftly to me and bailed out back for a smoke. The night passed with music from Buddy Cage's band and Dick's new Pick. He was happy and optimistic. I recall him wearing a classic Santa Fe 1983 shirt underneath a very loud Hawaiian GD print shirt with a GD hat. The photos are classic. He said DP15 was "in the can" and a better show had never been found, but he hoped to beat it with 16. He couldn't wait for this summer's Shoreline Phish shows and was ready to take his Picks to the next step . . . a serious retrospective by year that was announced last week by his collaborators ["So Many Roads," the Grateful Dead boxed set to be released soon].

I know this is long-winded, but only two weeks later I was at the Naeba Prince Hotel in Niigata, Japan, and Phish's manager popped out of the elevator to sadly deliver the news to me that Dick had suffered a heart attack at home the night before and was in a coma. It was 30 minutes before the band was to go on at The Green Stage, and here I was in paradise and no one could have understood how much it all meant to me . . . except maybe Dick. I broke into tears, somehow knowing it just couldn't work out. I am not religious, but I immediately said a prayer for Dick and his family that their pain would pass swiftly and that he would emerge intact. I felt so helpless and so sad. He was in his absolute prime. He was one of the only people I've ever met doing EXACTLY what he wanted exactly as he wished it done.

I made a quick call to his family to offer any help that might be needed and proceeded to enjoy Phish in Japan. I stayed in touch while over there and found that he'd remained in a coma at the hospital until they discontinued life support and took Dick home, playing his favorite tapes at top volume. I returned from Tokyo jet-lagged on Saturday August 7 and was awoken by a call from Dick's roommate Don giving me the news that he had passed away. I was crushed. I asked what I could do, and his family requested that we come to a celebration of Dick's life in Petaluma. Bad timing that it was, we shot to California for what truly was a celebration of Dick's life. What was left and available of the GD came out, spoke, played Dick's favorite songs to his ashes in front of the Blues for Allah backdrop, which was unfurled for the first time since that tour.

My plans to attend Shoreline with Dick were cancelled, our time together was over, and I am still beside myself with grief. Nonetheless, Dick remains and always will remain a great inspiration to me. His love for the material set him apart from most archivists, and his rapport with the fans was incredible. After all, they were the ultimate users of the collection of which he was in charge. He was never too busy, never anything but polite and loving. I will always remember the words of wisdom Dick left me with, his attitude, his smile, his cough. I miss him and wish him the best, and it may sound selfish, but I wish that we had enjoyed more time together. Dick was my friend and mentor. He was my brother and I hope he has found his peace. Sorry the answer to this one is so rambling, but if I can leave the world with a fraction of the love and admiration he did, I will have been a success.

CD: I think you already have, Kevin. Thank you. You have assisted with the band's releases. What did you have to do with respect to the "Hampton Comes Alive" release?

KS: Like any release, it is entirely a team effort, and my part is no greater or less than anyone on the team. The shows weren't chosen by me, though I constantly (maybe ad nauseum) advocate live releases and have always suggested release of complete shows whenever possible. In this case, the band suggested a release of the November 1998 Hampton shows soon after the fall 1998 tour ended. My part in the beginning process was to make copies for the band, as I would any material that they are considering working with. I think they kicked around various ideas among themselves and with management and considered the possibilities. When they decided they liked the Hampton material enough to release it live on CD, planning and production began.

My role at that point was to make safeties of everything, get the master DATs to the mastering facility, and make a few reclones later in the process to fix a glitch or two that arose in the process. The resulting set is excellent, in my opinion. I also oversaw—with a lot of help from my assistant, Rob—getting the various photos and images to the design team who was creating the packaging. The designers chose the images and integrated them to create the final packaging and inserts, which are impressive. The decision to break the two shows into their distinct pieces using six CDs (as opposed to trying to make it fit another way), the packaging and presentation, and the sheer fact that a live unedited release of any Phish show is coming out are all absolutely mind-blowing to me. I could not be more excited about "Hampton Comes Alive." To me, it is an encouraging signal that the band is able to live with—and even enjoy—their concerts being released as they happened. It has to be hard as an artist to think any canvas is "The One" . . . and Phish paint a lot of canvases. People will always debate the fine points, but Phish concerts live and as they happen are, to me, the essence of Phish. With complete live releases being added to everything else that is happening with the band right now, the future seems unlimited.

Caleb Epstein (cae@home.com) asked about CDR as an archival medium, writing:

I'm a big Phish fan, and have tons of shows on CD-R now. I find myself wondering what research Kevin is talking about, and whether I can expect my recordings to stand the test of time. I'd appreciate any more info you, Charlie, or Kevin, could provide on this.

Kevin responded:

Very briefly, what I was saying is that archivists and others in the world of conservation and archival science do not consider CDR (or any other digital medium) to be "archival" in the sense that it can be reliably used to hold information for the long term. The main reason why is that unlike a piece of film that you can hold up to a light and see the image, digital signals can only be read with proper hardware and software—all of which is variable and prone to becoming outmoded. Therefore, there is no digital archival medium. In the more direct sense, CDR is susceptible to a number of problems, especially if it's not stored in a super-cold, super-dry, dark environment and not played (exactly what Phish and most collectors do not do with their collections). CDR delaminates, scratches very easily, and can be ruined by writing too. Life estimates vary from 100 years (from the marketing departments of some manufacturers, which departments are obviously

assuming perfect storage conditions and likely exaggerating a bit) down to a couple years. A commonly accepted number of years is around 8 or 10 under pretty careful conditions. There's a lot of research to cite on this or you can just watch "the news" where you'll see NASA has already lost data stored on optical disc during the Mars mission, etc. The archival community is struggling to find another medium that lacks the inherent problems of tape and that is more durable than current optical mediums. In addition to all I've said, digital has another big problem (but once you're with DAT you've got it anyway), which is the amount of processing/compression/correction that occurs in the AD/DA conversion(s). A decent place to start that shouldn't put you immediately to sleep is http://www.cd-info.com/CDIC/Technology/CD-R/Media/Longevity.html. Enjoy! -KS

"From the Archives" Shows Playlists

Archivist Kevin Shapiro (see Dictionary entry and Interview) has compiled and DJ-ed a series of shows from backstage at Phish's large

"festival shows". Each show is comprised of his picks from Phish's vault of archived tapes.

(the original) – 89.1 FM, Clifford Ball Radio, 8/15/96

Tweezer >	12/31/91
McGrupp	"
NICU	3/26/92
Brother	3/24/92
Catapult >	6/22/94
Simple >	"
Icculus	"
Setting Sail	7/15/94
Frankenstein	6/23/94
Ride Captain Ride	12/12/92
Big Ball Jam	10/29/94
Split Open and Melt >	"
Buffalo Bill >	"
Makisupa Policeman	"
Cities	7/5/94
Punch You in the Eye	3/26/93
Bathtub Gin >	8/13/93
Yamar	"
Funky Bitch	2/19/93
Curtis Lowe	2/9/90
Landlady >	11/1/91
Destiny Unbound	"
David Bowie >	12/30/92
Timber (Jerry)	"
Magilla	7/14/91
Tube	6/26/94
Alumni Blues >	5/25/88
Light Up or Leave Me...	"

"No. 2", Great Went Radio
Part one, 8/15/97

Bathtub Gin	8/16/96
Halley's Comet >	8/27/89
Alumni Blues	"
Spock's Brain	5/16/95

Reba	"
Fixin' to Die	11/19/94 schk
Dog Log	10/14/95
Swing Low Sweet Chariot	8/29/87
The Curtain With	"
Rhombus narration >	11/15/91
Divided Sky	"
Camel Walk	7/25/88
Harry Hood	4/18/92

Part two, 8/16/97

Carini	3/1/97
Tela	8/27/88
Eliza	11/8/90
Taste	11/30/96
Hurricane	11/19/85
Mike's Song >	6/17/94
Simple >	"
Mile's Song >	"
I Am Hydrogen	"
Weekapaug Groove	"
Shaggy Dog	10/31/86
You Enjoy Myself	5/5/93

Sampler

Selections from both parts of "From the Archives No. 2" circulate as follows:

Alumni Blues	8/17/89
Spock's Brain, Reba	5/16/95
Divided	11/15/91
Camel Walk	7/25/88
Shaggy Dog	10/31/86
Carini	3/1/97
Tela	8/27/88
Eliza	11/8/90
Hurricane	11/19/85
Taste	11/30/96
Harry Hood	4/18/92

"No. 3" –KAZXZA,
"The Badger" Lemonwheel Radio
Part one, 8/15/98

Possum	5/17/92
On Your Way Down	7/23/88
Interview/Harmonica	with
	Danny Clinch
	announcements
Stash > Jam > Manteca	11/15/95
Mike's Song >	5/3/85
Dave's Energyguide	"
Down with Disease >	11/12/94
Jam >	"
Have Mercy >	"
Down with Disease	"
Terrapin Station	8/9/98

Part two, 8/16/98

Stash >	11/14/95
Jam >	"
Manteca >	"
Dog-Faced Boy >	"
Stash	"
Moose the Mootche	7/12/91
Fuck You Face	10/18/91
Brother	"
Abominable Snowman	12/90
Loving Cup	8/8/93
PYITE	8/9/97
The Wedge	?
Runaway Jim ->	6/16/95
Free	"
Tube	10/30/91
Check out the Funk >	4/5/98
Cavern	"
Great Curve	10/31/96

"No. 4" - Thin Air Radio, 91.7FM
Big Cypress
12/29/99, 10-12 p.m. (after schk)

Buried Alive >	12/31/91
Auld Land Syne	"
Llama (w/Gordon Stone)	11/19/92
Drowned >	12/31/95
Lizards	"
Shaggy Dog	12/6/91 schk
Mike's Song >	11/8/91
I Am Hydrogen >	"
Weekapaug Groove	"
Dickie Scotland Song	9/22/99 schk
Col. Forbin's Ascent >	4-16-92
Icculus >	"
Fly Famous Mockingbird	"
Reba	10/1/89
Soul Shakedown Party	2/17/97
Crosseyed & Painless	10/31/96

12/31/99, 7-9 p.m.

Sanity (fast version)	5/26/89
Also Sprach Zarath. >	7/31/99
David Bowie	"
Lushington	8/29/87
Harpua	3/26/92
Magilla > (w. GCH)	7/19/91
Tweezer	"
Possum (Kuroda vocals)	9/4/99
Alumni Blues >	9/14/89
Letter to Jimmy Page >	"
Alumni Blues	"
Cavern >	7/13/94
Wilson >	"
Cavern	"
Destiny Unbound	3/15/91
Highway to Hell	8/13/93

DESCRIPTIVE STATISTICS

Compiled and assembled by David "ZZYZX" Steinberg (aka The Time), based on the information contained in the Mockingbird Foundation's setlists database

Introduction

About 3 years ago I wanted to figure out how to program in Visual Basic. I needed an excuse to learn it, some sort of project. The idea of Phish Stats came to me. I had no idea that within a short time it would be rewritten in Perl, become a website that would be updated daily, get me a job at Microsoft, and eventually be put into this book.

The first part of this section is the raw stats. What is the most frequently played song? What was the 3rd most common second set opener in 1994? Did they play more songs per show in 1993 or 1994? Are songs more overplayed now than they were in 1993 or 1991? To help you answer these burning questions, the total stats, with year by year breakdowns for years after 1988 are provided. The percentage given

after the song is the percentage of times it was played out of the shows selected. In other words, You Enjoy Myself was played in 42% of all shows; in 75% of all shows in 1989, in 59% of all shows in 1990, etc. For the purpose of this section, shows with no known setlist are ignored. Also ignored are shows that arent really shows (such as David Letterman sets). I only counted things that were in some sense really songs. The breakdown is somewhat tenuous; the HYHU or Cold as Ice jams before Fishman songs arent really songs, but the HYHU Jam in the 5/7/94 Tweezerfest is a song. Raps, Trey telling stories, Vibrations of Lifes, and Happy Birthday jamlets are the best examples of songs that werent really considered songs, but I might go back on that in future editions. A list of the songs that stats were computed for along with first and last time played information appears immediately after this introduction.

The Every Time Played section has some headers that might not initally make sense. To explain what they mean, here is the everytime played information for While My Guitar Gently Weeps:

While My Guitar Gently Weeps

DATE	GAP	SET	POS.	SONG BEFORE	SONG AFTER
10/31/94	681	2	8/30	The Continuing Story	Happiness is a Warm
11/2/94	1	1	8/8	Scent of a Mule	***
12/8/94	23	1	10/10	The Lizards	***
6/7/95	8	E	1/1	***	***
6/14/95	5	2	5/5	Acoustic Army	***
6/22/95	6	E	2/2	Acoustic Army	***
6/28/95	5	E	2/2	Sweet Adeline	***
7/2/95	4	1	10/10	Rift	***
10/5/95	8	E	1/1	***	***
10/13/95	5	2	8/10	The Lizards	Sweet Adeline
10/20/95	5	2	6/10	Gumbo	My Long Journey
10/28/95	6	E	1/1	***	***
11/15/95	8	2	8/8	Fee	***
12/4/95	13	1	11/11	Hello My Baby	***
12/11/95	5	E	1/1	***	***
2/26/97	90	1	10/10	Dog Gone Dog	***
8/16/98	103	3	7/7	Bittersweet Motel	***
11/7/98	11	E	2/2	Guyute	***
12/31/98	19	E	1/1	***	***
7/10/99	8	E	1/2	***	Tweezer Reprise
10/2/99	34	E	1/2	***	Tweezer Reprise
7/1/00	40	E	1/1	***	***
7/15/00	10	2	2/7	Down with Disease	Makisupa Policeman
9/20/00	9	1	9/9	Weekapaug Groove	***
10/5/00	10	E	1/1	***	***

While My Guitar Gently Weeps has not been played in the last 2 shows.

Date is the date in which the song had been played. The first time it was played was 10/31/94. Gap is how many shows it was since it was last played. A gap of 0 shows means it was played earlier in the show. A gap of 1 show means it was played in the show before. A gap of 90 shows is fairly impressive. Set is the set in which the song was played. The options are 1, 2, 3, or E. First and second encores are not differentiated. Pos. is where it was played in the set; "7/29" means it was the 7th song played in a 29 song set. Song Before and Song After are the songs played before and after the song in question. If there is a "***" instead of a song title, that means that there was no relevant song. A set opener would have "***" in the Song Before column and a set closer would have "***" for Song After.

Finally, before we get on to the serious matter of statistical analysis, here is a present for Mike Gordon. Mike said in an interview with Free Press, "It's kind of silly when they're making pie graphs about set list openers. But then, I always liked a good graph." I must apologize for having to have an "others" category, but we wanted the graph to be good.

FIRST/LAST TIME SEEN

SONG NAME	FIRST TIME SEEN		LAST TIME SEEN		CURRENT GAP
	Date	Show #	Date	Show #	
1999	12/31/98	1007	12/31/98	1007	113 shows
5:15	10/31/95	760	10/31/95	760	360 shows
99 Years	8/7/96	818	8/7/96	818	302 shows
A Day in the Life	6/10/95	717	9/30/00	1115	5 shows
AC/DC Bag	4/1/86	13	9/30/00	1115	5 shows
Acoustic Army	6/7/95	714	12/8/95	782	338 shows
After Midnight	12/31/99	1071	12/31/99	1071	49 shows
After Midnight Reprise	12/31/99	1071	12/31/99	1071	49 shows
Ain't Love Funny	6/20/97	883	8/9/97	910	210 shows
Albuquerque	7/26/98	963	9/14/00	1104	16 shows
All Along the Watchtower	4/21/94	604	10/22/96	830	290 shows
All Blues	7/30/88	62	2/6/89	81	1039 shows
All Things Reconsidered	9/25/91	313	2/23/97	872	248 shows
All the Pain Through the Years	11/29/98	1003	11/29/98	1003	117 shows
Also Sprach Zarathustra	7/16/93	554	10/7/00	1120	0 shows
Alumni Blues	5/3/85	6	7/24/99	1025	95 shows
Alumni Blues Jam	12/3/94	702	12/3/94	702	418 shows
Amazing Grace	2/3/93	481	10/3/98	978	142 shows
Amazing Grace Jam	5/8/93	550	11/30/96	855	265 shows
Ambient Jam	8/15/98	976	8/15/98	976	144 shows
American Band	11/16/96	847	9/29/100	1114	6 shows
Amoreena	8/13/97	913	8/13/97	913	207 shows
Anarchy	3/4/85	5	10/14/89	122	998 shows
Andy's Chest	9/13/88	68	9/13/88	68	1052 shows
Any Colour You Like	11/2/98	985	11/2/98	985	135 shows
Arc	10/3/98	978	10/3/98	978	142 shows
Auld Lang Syne	12/30/89	145	12/31/99	1071	49 shows
Avenu Malkenu	5/11/87	24	9/20/00	1108	12 shows
Axilla	11/19/92	456	10/5/00	1118	2 shows
Axilla (Part II)	4/16/94	600	12/31/95	793	327 shows
Baby Elephant Walk	12/1/92	465	8/16/98	977	143 shows
Baby Left Me	7/30/88	62	7/30/88	62	1058 shows
Baby Lemonade	3/11/92	362	3/11/92	362	758 shows
Back Porch Boogie Blues	10/31/86	16	10/31/87	34	1086 shows
Back at the Chicken Shack	10/30/98	983	9/24/00	1111	9 shows
Back in the USSR	10/31/94	682	12/6/94	704	416 shows
Back on the Train	6/30/99	1008	10/1/00	1116	4 shows
Bass Jam	5/2/94	612	9/17/99	1038	82 shows
Bathtub Gin	5/26/89	105	10/7/00	1120	0 shows
Beaumont Rag	10/14/94	669	10/18/94	672	448 shows
Beauty of My Dreams	2/16/97	866	10/5/00	1118	2 shows
Been Caught Stealin'	8/1/98	967	12/28/98	1004	116 shows
Bell Boy	10/31/95	760	10/31/95	760	360 shows
Bertha	11/3/84	3	11/3/84	3	1117 shows
Big Alligator Song	12/30/99	1070	12/30/99	1070	50 shows
Big Ball Jam	11/19/92	456	12/9/94	707	413 shows
Big Ball Jam Reprise	3/8/93	506	3/8/93	506	614 shows
Big Black Furry Creature From Mars	8/21/87	28	9/20/00	1108	12 shows

SONG NAME	FIRST TIME SEEN		LAST TIME SEEN		CURRENT GAP
	Date	Show #	Date	Show #	
Big Black Furry Creature from Mars Reprise	6/21/94	643	6/21/94	643	477 shows
Big Leg Emma	5/3/85	6	6/19/88	53	1067 shows
Bike	11/19/87	36	9/12/00	1103	17 shows
Bill Bailey Won't You Please Come Home	7/28/93	563	11/18/95	768	352 shows
Billy Breathes	9/27/95	736	10/1/00	1116	4 shows
Birds of a Feather	4/2/98	942	9/23/00	1110	10 shows
Birthday Jam	10/31/94	682	10/31/94	682	438 shows
Bitchin' Again	8/3/91	312	8/3/91	312	808 shows
Bittersweet Motel	7/21/98	960	9/15/00	1105	15 shows
Black-Eyed Katy	11/13/97	917	12/30/97	940	180 shows
Blackbird	10/31/94	682	11/22/94	694	426 shows
Blister in the Sun	7/9/98	953	7/9/98	953	167 shows
Blister in the Sun Jam	7/26/97	902	7/26/97	902	218 shows
Blue Bayou	7/16/92	427	7/16/92	427	693 shows
Blue Bossa	7/12/88	58	7/23/88	59	1061 shows
Bob Dylan Band	4/15/86	14	4/15/86	14	1106 shows
Bohemian Rhapsody	12/31/96	863	12/31/96	863	257 shows
Bold As Love	7/11/88	57	10/6/00	1119	1 shows
Boogie on Reggae Woman	2/21/87	19	10/6/00	1119	1 shows
Born Under Punches (The Heat goes on)	10/31/96	836	10/31/96	836	284 shows
Born to Run	7/16/99	1019	7/16/99	1019	101 shows
Bouncing Around the Room	1/20/90	147	10/4/00	1117	3 shows
Brain Damage	11/2/98	985	11/2/98	985	135 shows
Breathe	11/2/98	985	11/2/98	985	135 shows
Breathe Jam	10/25/95	756	10/25/95	756	364 shows
Brian and Robert	6/30/98	946	10/6/00	1119	1 shows
Bring it On Home	5/3/85	6	5/3/85	6	1114 shows
Brother	9/25/91	313	9/27/00	1113	7 shows
Brown Eyed Girl	11/16/95	767	11/16/95	767	353 shows
Buffalo Bill	11/21/92	458	7/10/00	1095	25 shows
Bug	6/30/99	1008	10/4/00	1117	3 shows
Bundle of Joy	8/21/87	28	11/3/89	130	990 shows
Buried Alive	5/12/89	101	7/1/00	1089	31 shows
Burning Down the House	8/12/98	975	8/12/98	975	145 shows
Butter Them Biscuits	11/18/94	691	11/22/94	694	426 shows
Bye Bye Foot	6/14/97	880	8/10/97	911	209 shows
Camel Walk	11/3/84	3	10/1/00	1116	4 shows
Can't You Hear Me Knockin'	11/3/84	3	5/3/85	6	1114 shows
Cannonball Jam	5/7/94	616	5/7/94	616	504 shows
Caravan	1/20/90	147	12/29/96	861	259 shows
Carini	2/17/97	867	10/6/00	1119	1 shows
Carolina	1/20/90	147	11/18/98	995	125 shows
Cars Trucks Buses	9/27/95	736	9/20/00	1108	12 shows
Catapult	4/17/92	389	6/29/00	1087	33 shows
Cavern	2/17/90	156	10/4/00	1117	3 shows
Cecilia	6/25/97	887	6/25/97	887	233 shows
Chalk Dust Torture	2/1/91	243	10/6/100	1119	1 shows
Chalk Dust Torture Reprise	12/10/94	708	7/11/00	1096	24 shows
Champagne Supernova	12/29/96	861	12/29/96	861	259 shows
Character Zero	6/6/96	795	10/5/00	1118	2 shows
Che Hun Ta Mao	12/30/99	1070	12/30/99	1070	50 shows
Chess Jam	11/16/95	767	11/16/95	767	353 shows
Choo Choo Ch' Boogie	3/2/93	502	3/2/93	502	618 shows

SONG NAME	FIRST TIME SEEN		LAST TIME SEEN		CURRENT GAP
	Date	Show #	Date	Show #	
Cinnamon Girl	3/18/97	878	7/31/97	905	215 shows
Cities	12/1/84	4	10/6/00	1119	1 shows
Clementine	2/7/93	485	2/7/93	485	635 shows
Clod	10/15/86	15	11/10/89	132	988 shows
Cocaine Jam	8/6/93	569	8/6/93	569	551 shows
Cold Rain and Snow	9/17/99	1038	9/17/99	1038	82 shows
Colonel Forbin's Ascent	3/12/88	43	9/30/00	1115	5 shows
Come On Baby, Let's Go Downtown	9/23/00	1110	10/5/00	1118	2 shows
Come Together	12/8/95	782	12/8/95	782	338 shows
Communication Breakdown	1/27/90	148	9/15/90	210	910 shows
Contact	6/15/88	52	9/17/100	1106	14 shows
Cool it Down	10/31/98	984	9/24/00	1111	9 shows
Corrine Corrina	2/21/87	19	9/15/00	1105	15 shows
Costume Contest	10/31/88	72	10/31/94	682	438 shows
Cowboy's Sweetheart	12/6/96	859	12/6/96	859	261 shows
Cracklin' Rosie	3/7/92	361	12/10/99	1062	58 shows
Crew Football Theme Song	4/16/91	279	5/2/92	400	720 shows
Crimes of the Mind	8/3/91	312	7/10/94	658	462 shows
Crosseyed and Painless	10/31/96	836	9/14/00	1104	16 shows
Crossroads	5/8/93	550	11/28/98	1002	118 shows
Cry Baby Cry	10/31/94	682	11/21/98	998	122 shows
Cryin'	9/29/95	738	9/29/95	738	382 shows
Cut My Hair	10/31/95	760	10/31/95	760	360 shows
Dahlia	9/13/90	208	9/13/90	208	912 shows
Daniel	7/15/93	553	2/23/97	872	248 shows
Dave's Energy Guide	5/3/85	6	6/28/95	730	390 shows
David Bowie	10/31/86	16	10/7/00	1120	0 shows
David Bowie Jam	8/21/87	28	8/21/87	28	1092 shows
Dazed and Confused	5/21/89	104	5/21/89	104	1016 shows
Dear Mrs. Reagan	9/27/85	7	1/18/89	78	1042 shows
Dear Prudence	10/31/94	682	10/31/94	682	438 shows
Demand	4/9/94	594	11/14/96	845	275 shows
Destiny Unbound	9/14/90	209	11/15/91	346	774 shows
Diamond Girl	12/31/92	480	12/31/92	480	640 shows
Digital Delay Loop Jam	4/8/94	593	12/28/96	860	260 shows
Dinner and a Movie	11/19/87	36	9/29/00	1114	6 shows
Dirt	6/14/97	880	9/27/00	1113	7 shows
Divided Sky	8/9/87	26	9/24/00	1111	9 shows
Doctor Jimmy	10/31/95	760	10/31/95	760	360 shows
Dog Faced Boy	4/14/94	598	10/4/00	1117	3 shows
Dog Gone Dog	10/30/85	9	9/17/00	1106	14 shows
Dogs Stole Things	6/13/97	879	9/22/00	1109	11 shows
Doin' My Time	8/7/96	818	7/1/99	1009	111 shows
Don't Get Me Wrong	10/6/90	220	12/28/90	240	880 shows
Don't Pass Me By	10/31/94	682	10/31/94	682	438 shows
Don't Want You No More	12/1/84	4	12/1/84	4	1116 shows
Don't You Wanna Go	5/16/95	713	9/28/95	737	383 shows
Donna Lee	5/5/89	98	7/12/91	299	821 shows
Dooley	11/20/94	693	11/20/94	693	427 shows
Down By the River	10/3/98	978	10/3/98	978	142 shows
Down With Disease	4/4/94	590	10/6/00	1119	1 shows
Down with Disease Jam	12/31/93	589	12/31/93	589	531 shows
Driver	10/17/98	980	10/1/00	1116	4 shows

SONG NAME	FIRST TIME SEEN		LAST TIME SEEN		CURRENT GAP
	Date	Show #	Date	Show #	
Drowned	10/31/95	760	10/5/00	1118	2 shows
Drum Jam	5/2/91	287	7/25/97	901	219 shows
Drums Jam	11/3/84	3	10/15/94	670	450 shows
Earl's Breakdown	11/16/94	689	11/16/94	689	431 shows
Eclipse	11/2/98	985	11/2/98	985	135 shows
El Paso	10/6/100	1119	10/6/100	1119	1 shows
Eliza	9/15/90	210	5/14/92	409	711 shows
Emotional Rescue	11/21/97	922	9/30/100	1115	5 shows
Esther	9/12/88	67	9/30/00	1115	5 shows
Everybody's Got Something to Hide	10/31/94	682	9/25/00	1112	8 shows
Eyes of the World	11/3/84	3	5/3/85	6	1114 shows
Faht	11/22/92	459	12/2/95	778	342 shows
Family Picture	11/8/91	340	11/8/91	340	780 shows
Farmhouse	11/16/97	919	7/14/00	1098	22 shows
Fast Enough for You	11/19/92	456	9/23/00	1110	10 shows
Fee	8/9/87	26	10/7/00	1120	0 shows
Fikus	7/2/98	948	11/7/98	988	132 shows
Fire	12/2/83	1	9/24/100	1111	9 shows
Fire On The Mountain	12/1/84	4	12/1/84	4	1116 shows
Fire up the Ganja	3/4/85	5	3/4/85	5	1115 shows
First Tube	9/9/99	1032	10/7/00	1120	0 shows
Fishing Hole Theme	8/26/89	113	8/26/89	113	1007 shows
Fishman's Gull Poem	10/26/89	126	10/26/89	126	994 shows
Fixin' to Die	11/17/94	690	11/30/94	699	421 shows
Flat Fee	8/9/87	26	7/26/91	310	810 shows
Fluff's Travels	12/6/86	17	6/7/90	204	916 shows
Fluffhead	12/1/84	4	9/29/00	1114	6 shows
Foam	11/3/88	73	7/14/00	1098	22 shows
Fog That Surrounds	9/27/95	736	10/17/95	750	370 shows
Foreplay/Long Time	10/7/94	663	7/12/99	1016	104 shows
Four Strong Winds	10/18/98	981	10/18/98	981	139 shows
Frankenstein	11/11/89	133	9/29/00	1114	6 shows
Frankie Says	4/2/98	942	7/14/00	1098	22 shows
Free	5/16/95	713	9/24/00	1111	9 shows
Freebird	3/6/87	20	6/22/00	1082	38 shows
Freeworld	3/6/87	20	3/6/87	20	1100 shows
Fuck Your Face	4/29/87	23	4/29/87	23	1097 shows
Funky Bitch	3/6/87	20	10/4/00	1117	3 shows
Gettin' Jiggy Wit' It	11/20/98	997	11/20/98	997	123 shows
Ghost	6/13/97	879	9/27/00	1113	7 shows
Ginseng Sullivan	8/11/93	573	9/12/00	1103	17 shows
Glass Onion	10/31/94	682	10/31/94	682	438 shows
Glide	9/27/91	315	10/7/00	1120	0 shows
Glide II	5/16/95	713	5/16/95	713	407 shows
Gloria	5/16/95	713	5/16/95	713	407 shows
Going Down Slow	9/13/90	208	9/14/90	209	911 shows
Gold Soundz	7/21/99	1023	7/21/99	1023	97 shows
Golden Lady	10/20/94	673	10/20/94	673	447 shows
Golgi Apparatus	10/15/86	15	10/6/00	1119	1 shows
Good Times Bad Times	2/13/87	18	9/11/100	1102	18 shows
Got My Mojo Workin'	2/25/97	873	2/25/97	873	247 shows
Gotta Jibboo	9/10/99	1033	10/4/00	1117	3 shows
Grind	12/30/98	1006	12/30/98	1006	114 shows

SONG NAME	FIRST TIME SEEN		LAST TIME SEEN		CURRENT GAP
	Date	Show #	Date	Show #	
Guelah Papyrus	2/1/91	243	9/18/00	1107	13 shows
Gumbo	9/28/90	215	9/27/00	1113	7 shows
Guy Forget	10/1/00	1116	10/1/00	1116	4 shows
Guyute	10/7/94	663	10/5/00	1118	2 shows
Gypsy Queen	8/7/96	818	6/24/97	886	234 shows
HYHU Jam	11/7/91	339	5/7/94	616	504 shows
Ha Ha Ha	5/16/95	713	6/30/00	1088	32 shows
Halley's Comet	10/31/86	16	10/5/00	1118	2 shows
Happiness Is a Warm Gun	10/31/94	682	10/31/94	682	438 shows
Happy Birthday	12/2/83	1	5/17/91	295	825 shows
Harpua	8/9/87	26	11/2/98	985	135 shows
Harry Hood	10/30/85	9	10/4/00	1117	3 shows
Have Mercy	4/1/86	13	12/10/99	1062	58 shows
Head Held High	10/31/98	984	10/31/98	984	136 shows
Heart and soul	11/29/95	775	11/29/95	775	345 shows
Heavy Things	9/11/99	1034	10/6/00	1119	1 shows
Hello My Baby	9/27/95	736	12/5/99	1059	61 shows
Help Me	4/10/93	529	4/10/93	529	591 shows
Help on the Way	4/1/86	13	4/1/86	13	1107 shows
Helpless	10/17/98	980	10/17/98	980	140 shows
Helpless Dancer	10/31/95	760	10/31/95	760	360 shows
Helter Skelter	10/31/94	682	11/17/94	690	430 shows
High-Heel Sneakers	4/23/94	606	4/23/94	606	514 shows
Highway To Hell	10/1/89	117	2/26/97	874	246 shows
Hold Whatcha Got	6/22/00	1082	6/22/00	1082	38 shows
Hold to a Dream	8/7/96	818	8/7/96	818	302 shows
Honey Pie	10/31/94	682	10/31/94	682	438 shows
Honky Tonk Women	6/30/94	650	6/30/94	650	470 shows
Honky Tonk Women Jam	4/12/93	530	4/12/93	530	590 shows
Hoochie Coochie Man	4/10/93	529	8/8/97	909	211 shows
Horn	5/24/90	198	10/5/00	1118	2 shows
Houses in Motion	10/31/96	836	10/31/96	836	284 shows
How High the Moon	4/22/90	184	3/8/93	506	614 shows
Hurricane	11/14/85	10	11/14/85	10	1110 shows
I Am Hydrogen	10/15/86	15	10/7/00	1120	0 shows
I Am the Sea	10/31/95	760	10/31/95	760	360 shows
I Been to Georgia on a Fast Train	5/6/93	548	5/6/93	548	572 shows
I Didn't Know	9/27/87	32	9/30/00	1115	5 shows
I Don't Care	6/16/97	881	6/20/97	883	237 shows
I Found a Reason	10/31/98	984	10/31/98	984	136 shows
I Get a Kick Out of You	8/2/98	968	11/9/98	990	130 shows
I Know a Little	8/10/87	27	8/3/88	63	1057 shows
I Saw it Again	6/14/97	880	9/30/00	1115	5 shows
I Shall Be Released	10/18/98	981	10/18/98	981	139 shows
I Told You So	3/18/97	878	3/18/97	878	242 shows
I Walk the Line	11/19/92	456	3/9/93	507	613 shows
I Wanna Be Like You	4/4/94	590	6/10/94	635	485 shows
I Will	10/31/94	682	10/31/94	682	438 shows
I Wish	10/30/85	9	10/30/85	9	1111 shows
I'll Come Running	5/16/95	713	5/16/95	713	407 shows
I'm Blue I'm Lonesome	11/16/94	689	6/22/00	1082	38 shows
I'm Gonna Be (500 Miles)	12/30/97	940	12/30/97	940	180 shows
I'm One	10/31/95	760	10/31/95	760	360 shows

SONG NAME	FIRST TIME SEEN		LAST TIME SEEN		CURRENT GAP
	Date	Show #	Date	Show #	
I'm So Tired	10/31/94	682	11/18/95	768	352 shows
I've Had Enough	10/31/95	760	10/31/95	760	360 shows
I've Turned Bad	5/9/89	100	5/9/89	100	1020 shows
Icculus	4/1/86	13	7/18/99	1021	99 shows
If I Could	4/4/94	590	6/28/00	1086	34 shows
If I Don't Be There by Morning	5/9/89	100	5/9/89	100	1020 shows
If I Only Had a Brain	3/12/89	89	7/8/99	1013	107 shows
If You Need a Fool	7/29/98	965	7/18/99	1021	99 shows
Immigrant Song Jam	11/14/95	765	11/14/95	765	355 shows
In a Hole	10/20/89	123	12/16/89	143	977 shows
In the Midnight Hour	12/2/83	1	3/4/85	5	1115 shows
Indian War Dance	3/14/93	510	3/14/93	510	610 shows
Is it in my Head	10/31/95	760	10/31/95	760	360 shows
It's Ice	9/25/91	313	10/4/00	1117	3 shows
It's My Life	3/2/93	502	3/2/93	502	618 shows
Izabella	6/13/97	879	7/31/98	966	154 shows
Jagermeister	4/18/90	180	5/6/90	190	930 shows
Jam	11/3/84	3	9/29/00	1114	6 shows
Jennifer Dances	12/5/99	1059	12/17/99	1068	52 shows
Jessica Jam	5/8/93	550	5/8/93	550	570 shows
Jesus Just Left Chicago	8/10/87	27	6/23/00	1083	37 shows
Johnny B. Goode	6/17/95	722	7/8/98	952	168 shows
Julia	10/31/94	682	10/31/94	682	438 shows
Julius	4/4/94	590	9/25/00	1112	8 shows
Jump Monk	3/12/88	43	3/12/88	43	1077 shows
Keyboard Cavalry	9/27/95	736	12/14/95	786	334 shows
Keyboard Cavalry Reprise	10/8/95	745	10/8/95	745	375 shows
Killer Joe	3/17/90	169	3/17/90	169	951 shows
Kung	10/31/89	128	9/29/99	1047	73 shows
La Grange	8/9/87	26	9/22/99	1042	78 shows
La Grange Jam	5/28/89	107	5/28/89	107	1013 shows
Lawn Boy	11/30/89	136	10/1/00	1116	4 shows
Layla	11/29/98	1003	11/29/98	1003	117 shows
Lengthwise	11/19/92	456	7/28/98	964	156 shows
Leprechaun	7/15/93	553	7/31/93	566	554 shows
Let the Good Times Roll	4/29/87	23	4/29/87	23	1097 shows
Letter to Jimmy Page	5/11/87	24	7/15/94	661	459 shows
Li'l Red Rooster	2/25/97	873	2/25/97	873	247 shows
Life on Mars	10/13/95	747	3/2/97	877	243 shows
Lifeboy	2/3/93	481	11/25/98	1000	120 shows
Light Up Or Leave Me Alone	8/9/87	26	12/30/99	1070	50 shows
Limb By Limb	6/13/97	879	10/5/00	1118	2 shows
Listening Wind	10/31/96	836	10/31/96	836	284 shows
Little Drummer Boy	12/6/86	17	12/2/99	1056	64 shows
Lively Up Yourself	4/21/92	392	4/21/92	392	728 shows
Llama	10/30/90	225	10/1/00	1116	4 shows
Lonesome Cowboy Bill	5/16/95	713	10/31/98	984	136 shows
Long Cool Woman in a Black Dress	12/2/83	1	10/30/98	983	137 shows
Long Long Long	10/31/94	682	10/31/94	682	438 shows
Loup Garou	3/2/93	502	3/2/93	502	618 shows
Love Me	2/13/97	864	11/18/98	995	125 shows
Love Me Like a Man	3/18/97	878	3/18/97	878	242 shows
Love Reign O'er Me	10/31/95	760	10/31/95	760	360 shows

SONG NAME	FIRST TIME SEEN		LAST TIME SEEN		CURRENT GAP
	Date	Show #	Date	Show #	
Love You	10/31/87	34	9/24/00	1111	9 shows
Loving Cup	2/3/93	481	10/4/100	1117	3 shows
Low Rider Jam	8/21/87	28	11/23/97	924	196 shows
Lushington	10/15/86	15	8/29/87	29	1091 shows
Magilla	9/13/90	208	7/4/00	1091	29 shows
Maiden Voyage	7/30/88	62	7/30/88	62	1058 shows
Makisupa Policeman	10/23/84	2	9/9/00	1101	19 shows
Makisupa Policeman Jam	8/21/87	28	8/21/87	28	1092 shows
Manteca	11/4/90	229	10/30/98	983	137 shows
Manteca Reprise	4/18/92	390	4/18/92	390	730 shows
Martha My Dear	10/31/94	682	10/31/94	682	438 shows
Maze	3/6/92	360	10/6/00	1119	1 shows
McGrupp and the Watchful Hosemasters	5/3/85	6	9/18/00	1107	13 shows
Mean Mr. Mustard	11/15/96	846	11/15/96	846	274 shows
Meat	7/2/98	948	9/22/00	1109	11 shows
Meat Reprise	6/13/00	1078	6/13/00	1078	42 shows
Meatstick	6/25/97	887	10/7/00	1120	0 shows
Meatstick Reprise	7/4/99	1011	7/4/99	1011	109 shows
Mellow Mood	9/8/00	1100	10/6/00	1119	1 shows
Melt the Guns	9/27/85	7	4/29/87	23	1097 shows
Memories	11/17/90	233	7/6/94	655	465 shows
Merry Pranksters Jam	8/14/97	914	8/14/97	914	206 shows
Messin' With The Kid	8/8/97	909	10/3/99	1050	70 shows
Midnight Rider Jam	6/22/94	644	6/22/94	644	476 shows
Midnight on the Highway	11/23/96	851	11/23/96	851	269 shows
Mike's Song	5/3/85	6	10/7/00	1120	0 shows
Mind Left Body Jam	6/18/94	641	6/18/94	641	479 shows
Minute by Minute	9/13/90	208	9/15/90	210	910 shows
Mirror in the Bathroom	11/27/98	1001	11/27/98	1001	119 shows
Misty Mountain Hop	7/20 /99	1022	10/10/99	1055	65 shows
Moby Dick	11/29/97	927	7/11/00	1096	24 shows
Money	11/2/98	985	11/2/98	985	135 shows
Moonlight in Vermont	10/3/98	978	10/3/98	978	142 shows
Moose the Mooch	7/12/91	299	7/12/91	299	821 shows
Mother Nature's Son	10/31/94	682	10/31/94	682	438 shows
Mound	3/6/92	360	11/19/96	849	271 shows
Mountains in the Mist	7/3/99	1010	12/13/99	1065	55 shows
Mozambique	9/9/99	1032	9/26/99	1045	75 shows
Mr. P.C.	7/30/88	62	11/11/88	75	1045 shows
Mustang Sally	10/15/86	15	6/21/88	55	1065 shows
My Friend My Friend	3/6/92	360	9/27/00	1113	7 shows
My Generation	10/31/95	760	10/31/95	760	360 shows
My Left Toe	6/30/99	1008	10/9/99	1054	66 shows
My Long Journey Home	11/16/94	689	11/29/95	775	345 shows
My Mind's Got a Mind of its Own	3/7/92	361	9/18/00	1107	13 shows
My Soul	2/13/97	864	10/7/00	1120	0 shows
My Sweet One	9/9/89	114	6/24/00	1084	36 shows
NICU	3/6/92	360	10/5/00	1118	2 shows
NO2	6/25/94	647	7/13/99	1017	103 shows
Nellie Kane	7/16/93	554	7/1/00	1089	31 shows
Never	10/17/98	980	10/17/98	980	140 shows
New Age	10/31/98	984	10/31/98	984	136 shows
New York New York	12/31/97	941	12/31/97	941	179 shows

SONG NAME	FIRST TIME SEEN		LAST TIME SEEN		CURRENT GAP
	Date	Show #	Date	Show #	
Night Moves Jam	10/2/95	740	10/2/95	740	380 shows
No Dogs Allowed	7/23/88	59	4/21/90	183	937 shows
No Good Trying	12/7/90	238	12/28/90	240	880 shows
Not Fade Away	4/1/86	13	4/1/86	13	1107 shows
Nowhere Fast	5/9/89	100	5/9/89	100	1020 shows
O Mio Babbino Caro	5/27/94	631	5/27/94	631	489 shows
Ob La Di Ob La Da	10/31/94	682	10/31/94	682	438 shows
Ob La Di Ob La Da Jam	5/6/93	548	5/6/93	548	572 shows
Oblivious Fool	6/13/97	879	11/17/97	920	200 shows
Oh! Sweet Nuthin'	10/31/98	984	10/31/98	984	136 shows
On My Knees	7/17/99	1020	7/17/99	1020	100 shows
On The Run	11/2/98	985	11/2/98	985	135 shows
On Your Way Down	6/24/88	56	10/2/99	1049	71 shows
Once in a Lifetime	10/31/96	836	10/31/96	836	284 shows
One Meatball	2/25/97	873	2/25/97	873	247 shows
Overload	10/31/96	836	10/31/96	836	284 shows
Oye Como Va Jam	8/28/93	585	8/28/93	585	535 shows
Paul and Silas	9/13/90	208	11/29/98	1003	117 shows
Peaches En Regalia	10/15/86	15	9/24/99	1043	77 shows
Phase Dance	9/27/87	32	2/26/88	41	1079 shows
Piano Duet	7/28/93	563	4/22/94	605	515 shows
Pig in a Pen	2/21/93	496	11/16/94	689	431 shows
Piggies	10/31/94	682	10/31/94	682	438 shows
Piper	6/14/97	880	10/5/00	1118	2 shows
Poor Heart	4/22/91	284	9/22/00	1109	11 shows
Poor Heart Reprise	11/25/95	773	11/25/95	773	347 shows
Possum	10/30/85	9	10/5/00	1118	2 shows
Prep School Hippie	9/27/85	7	12/6/86	17	1103 shows
Prince Caspian	6/8/95	715	9/18/00	1107	13 shows
Proud Mary	12/2/83	1	12/2/83	1	1119 shows
Psycho Killer	12/7/97	933	12/7/97	933	187 shows
Psycho Killer Jam	3/30/93	522	3/30/93	522	598 shows
Punch Me in the Eye	4/24/87	22	4/24/87	22	1098 shows
Punch You In The Eye	8/17/89	110	9/24/00	1111	9 shows
Purple Rain	7/16/93	554	7/25/99	1026	94 shows
Pusher Man Jam	11/1/91	337	11/1/91	337	783 shows
Quadrophenia	10/31/95	760	10/31/95	760	360 shows
Quadrophonic Toppling	12/31/99	1071	12/31/99	1071	49 shows
Quinn the Eskimo	4/1/86	13	10/2/99	1049	71 shows
Ramble On	8/1/98	967	8/12/98	975	145 shows
Rapper's Delight	9/29/00	1114	9/29/00	1114	6 shows
Reba	10/1/89	117	10/4/00	1117	3 shows
Revival	10/30/85	9	10/30/85	9	1111 shows
Revolution	10/17/85	8	10/31/94	682	438 shows
Revolution 9	10/31/94	682	10/31/94	682	438 shows
Rhinoceros	8/3/98	969	8/3/98	969	151 shows
Rhombus Narration	11/2/89	129	11/15/91	346	774 shows
Ride Captain Ride	3/23/87	21	12/10/99	1062	58 shows
Rift	2/25/90	160	10/6/00	1119	1 shows
Road Runner	9/11/00	1102	9/11/00	1102	18 shows
Roadhouse Blues	12/2/83	1	12/2/83	1	1119 shows
Rock and Roll	10/31/98	984	10/4/00	1117	3 shows
Rock and Roll All Nite Jam	2/20/93	495	2/20/93	495	625 shows

SONG NAME	FIRST TIME SEEN		LAST TIME SEEN		CURRENT GAP
	Date	Show #	Date	Show #	
Rock and Roll Part Two	11/20/98	997	11/20/98	997	123 shows
Rocko William	2/13/97	864	8/10/97	911	209 shows
Rocky Mountain Way Jam	2/16/91	251	7/23/97	900	220 shows
Rocky Raccoon	10/31/94	682	10/31/94	682	438 shows
Rocky Top	9/21/87	31	9/17/100	1106	14 shows
Roggae	6/30/98	946	9/30/00	1115	5 shows
Roll Like a Cantaloupe	10/15/86	15	11/14/91	345	775 shows
Roses Are Free	12/11/97	935	10/1/00	1116	4 shows
Rotation Jam	11/25/95	773	8/10/97	911	209 shows
Run Like an Antelope	5/3/85	6	10/6/00	1119	1 shows
Runaway Jim	3/28/90	170	10/1/00	1116	4 shows
Running With the Devil	8/6/98	970	8/6/98	970	150 shows
Sabotage	8/8/98	972	11/21/98	998	122 shows
Sad Lisa	10/18/98	981	10/18/98	981	139 shows
Sample in a Jar	2/4/93	482	10/4/00	1117	3 shows
Samson Variation	8/3/97	907	8/3/97	907	213 shows
Sand	9/11/99	1034	10/6/00	1119	1 shows
Sanity	10/15/86	15	11/27/98	1001	119 shows
Satin Doll	6/20/88	54	5/8/93	550	570 shows
Savoy Truffle	10/31/94	682	10/31/94	682	438 shows
Scarlet Begonias	12/2/83	1	5/3/85	6	1114 shows
Scent of a Mule	4/4/94	590	9/23/00	1110	10 shows
Sea and Sand	10/31/95	760	7/20/98	959	161 shows
Secret Language Instructions	3/6/92	360	3/20/92	368	752 shows
Seen and Not Seen	10/31/96	836	10/31/96	836	284 shows
Self	9/13/90	208	11/20/92	457	663 shows
Setting Sail	4/20/91	282	7/15/94	661	459 shows
Sexual Healing	7/20/98	959	11/14/98	993	127 shows
Sexy Sadie	10/31/94	682	10/31/94	682	438 shows
Shafty	4/5/98	945	7/7/00	1093	27 shows
Shaggy Dog	10/15/86	15	10/29/95	759	361 shows
She Caught the Katy and Left Me a Mule to Ride	12/6/86	17	7/21/98	960	160 shows
Shine	12/31/95	793	12/31/95	793	327 shows
Silent in the Morning	3/7/92	361	9/8/00	1100	20 shows
Simple	5/27/94	631	9/30/00	1115	5 shows
Sixteen Candles	12/29/96	861	12/29/96	861	259 shows
Skin It Back	10/15/86	15	7/25/88	61	1059 shows
Skippy the Wondermouse	12/1/84	4	10/30/85	9	1111 shows
Slave to the Traffic Light	12/1/84	4	9/22/00	1109	11 shows
Sleep	10/17/98	980	9/18/00	1107	13 shows
Sleeping Monkey	3/6/92	360	9/23/100	1110	10 shows
Slipknot!	4/1/86	13	4/1/86	13	1107 shows
Smells Like Teen Spirit	11/2/98	985	11/2/98	985	135 shows
Smoke on the Water Jam	7/18/99	1021	7/18/99	1021	99 shows
Sneakin' Sally through the Alley	9/27/85	7	10/5/00	1118	2 shows
So Lonely	11/14/98	993	11/14/98	993	127 shows
Something	10/29/98	982	11/25/98	1000	120 shows
Somewhere Over the Rainbow	8/2/96	814	8/9/98	973	147 shows
Somewhere Over the Rainbow Jam	4/20/94	603	4/20/94	603	517 shows
Soul Shake Down Party	2/17/97	867	2/20/97	869	251 shows
Spanish Flea	12/1/84	4	12/1/84	4	1116 shows
Sparkle	9/25/91	313	9/24/00	1111	9 shows
Sparks	3/23/87	21	11/29/96	854	266 shows

SONG NAME	FIRST TIME SEEN		LAST TIME SEEN		CURRENT GAP
	Date	Show #	Date	Show #	
Speak to Me	10/31/94	682	11/2/98	985	135 shows
Split Open and Melt	2/17/89	84	9/27/00	1113	7 shows
Split Open and Melt Jam	4/14/94	598	6/26/94	648	472 shows
Spock's Brain	5/16/95	713	10/6/00	1119	1 shows
Spooky Jam	3/14/93	510	4/14/93	531	589 shows
Squeeze Box	12/2/83	1	12/2/83	1	1119 shows
St. Stephen Jam	11/3/84	3	11/3/84	3	1117 shows
St. Thomas	5/21/88	50	5/21/88	50	1070 shows
Stand	6/13/97	879	6/13/97	879	241 shows
Stash	9/13/90	208	10/6/00	1119	1 shows
Steep	10/16/96	825	7/1/00	1089	31 shows
Stir It Up Jam	8/21/87	28	8/21/87	28	1092 shows
Strange Design	5/16/95	713	6/24/00	1084	36 shows
Suspicious Minds	9/30/95	739	12/6/96	859	261 shows
Suzy Greenberg	2/13/87	18	9/14/00	1104	16 shows
Sweet Adeline	3/28/90	170	8/1/99	1031	89 shows
Sweet Baby's Arms	11/18/94	691	11/18/94	691	429 shows
Sweet Emotion Jam	3/16/93	511	7/9/99	1014	106 shows
Sweet Jane	8/8/98	972	10/31/98	984	136 shows
Sweet Virginia	9/26/99	1045	9/26/99	1045	75 shows
Swept Away	10/16/96	825	7/1/00	1089	31 shows
Swing Low Sweet Chariot	10/15/86	15	11/16/94	689	431 shows
TV Show	11/8/91	340	11/8/91	340	780 shows
Take Me to the River	11/21/95	770	7/10/97	896	224 shows
Take the A-Train	4/29/87	23	4/13/94	597	523 shows
Talk	8/5/96	816	8/6/98	970	150 shows
Taste	6/7/95	714	9/27/00	1113	7 shows
Taste That Surrounds	10/24/95	755	12/29/95	791	329 shows
Tea Tray Song	8/26/93	584	8/26/93	584	536 shows
Tela	3/12/88	43	11/24/98	999	121 shows
Tell Me Something Good	3/6/87	20	3/6/87	20	1100 shows
Tennessee Waltz	5/6/93	548	11/16/94	689	431 shows
Terrapin	9/21/87	31	7/11/00	1096	24 shows
Terrapin Station	8/9/98	973	8/9/98	973	147 shows
That's Alright Mama	5/6/93	548	5/6/93	548	572 shows
The Asse Festival	5/12/89	101	4/27/91	286	834 shows
The Ballad of Curtis Loew	4/29/87	23	8/2/93	567	553 shows
The Birthday Dub	9/21/87	31	9/21/87	31	1089 shows
The Chase	8/9/87	26	10/26/89	126	994 shows
The Chicken	3/11/88	42	3/11/88	42	1078 shows
The Continuing Story of Bungalow Bill	10/31/94	682	10/31/94	682	438 shows
The Curtain	2/7/88	38	9/9/00	1101	19 shows
The Curtain With	8/9/87	26	9/30/00	1115	5 shows
The Dirty Jobs	10/31/95	760	10/31/95	760	360 shows
The Famous Mockingbird	2/7/88	38	9/30/00	1115	5 shows
The Great Curve	10/31/96	836	10/31/96	836	284 shows
The Great Gig in the Sky	3/14/93	510	11/2/98	985	135 shows
The Happy Whip and Dung Song	7/24/99	1025	7/24/99	1025	95 shows
The Horse	3/7/92	361	9/8/00	1100	20 shows
The Inlaw Josie Wales	9/9/99	1032	10/6/00	1119	1 shows
The Landlady	2/1/90	151	12/3/94	702	418 shows
The Lizards	1/27/88	37	9/25/00	1112	8 shows
The Maker	10/15/94	670	10/15/94	670	450 shows

SONG NAME	FIRST TIME SEEN		LAST TIME SEEN		CURRENT GAP
	Date	Show #	Date	Show #	
The Man Who Stepped Into Yesterday	5/11/87	24	9/20/00	1108	12 shows
The Man Who Stepped Into Yesterday Reprise	5/11/87	24	7/4/00	1091	29 shows
The Mango Song	3/30/89	92	9/27/00	1113	7 shows
The Moma Dance	6/30/98	946	10/6/00	1119	1 shows
The Oh Kee Pa Ceremony	8/17/89	110	9/14/00	1104	16 shows
The Old Home Place	6/26/94	648	6/25/00	1085	35 shows
The Other One	5/3/85	6	5/3/85	6	1114 shows
The Pendulum	4/1/86	13	4/1/86	13	1107 shows
The Practical Song	9/12/88	67	5/26/89	105	1015 shows
The Price of Love	3/30/89	92	5/28/89	107	1013 shows
The Punk Meets the Godfather	10/31/95	760	10/31/95	760	360 shows
The Real Me	10/31/95	760	12/29/95	791	329 shows
The Revolution's Over	9/13/90	208	9/13/90	208	912 shows
The Rock	10/31/95	760	10/31/95	760	360 shows
The Sloth	8/9/87	26	9/24/00	1111	9 shows
The Squirming Coil	1/20/90	147	9/12/100	1103	17 shows
The Star Spangled Banner	10/17/96	826	7/4/00	1091	29 shows
The Vibration of Life	12/7/92	471	11/19/96	849	271 shows
The Wedge	2/3/93	481	9/22/00	1109	11 shows
Them Changes	11/30/97	928	11/30/97	928	192 shows
Theme From The Bottom	5/16/95	713	9/17/00	1106	14 shows
Theme to Star Trek: The Original Series	8/4/96	815	8/4/96	815	305 shows
Three Little Birds	6/17/95	722	6/17/95	722	398 shows
Timber (Jerry)	4/29/87	23	9/30/00	1115	5 shows
Time	11/2/98	985	11/2/98	985	135 shows
Time Loves a Hero	10/31/88	72	8/11/98	974	146 shows
Too Much of Everything	7/26/98	963	8/2/98	968	152 shows
Touch Me	7/11/91	298	12/3/94	702	418 shows
Train Round the Bend	10/31/98	984	10/31/98	984	136 shows
Train Song	7/21/96	809	5/23/00	1074	46 shows
Trenchtown Rock	8/11/98	974	8/11/98	974	146 shows
Tube	9/13/90	208	9/22/00	1109	11 shows
Tube Jam	12/7/97	933	11/2/98	985	135 shows
Tubthumping	11/21/98	998	11/21/98	998	122 shows
Tuesday's Gone	7/13/99	1017	7/13/99	1017	103 shows
Tush	12/6/86	17	8/10/87	27	1093 shows
Tweezer	3/28/90	170	10/7/00	1120	0 shows
Tweezer Reprise	9/21/90	213	10/7/00	1120	0 shows
Twist	6/14/97	880	10/7/00	1120	0 shows
Uncle Pen	3/28/90	170	7/11/00	1096	24 shows
Uncloudy Day	10/3/98	978	10/3/98	978	142 shows
Undun	3/30/89	92	12/7/89	139	981 shows
Us and Them	11/2/98	985	11/2/98	985	135 shows
Vacuum Jam	9/13/88	68	9/13/88	68	1052 shows
Vacuum Solo	3/30/92	376	10/30/92	455	665 shows
Viola Lee Blues	9/17/99	1038	9/17/99	1038	82 shows
Vultures	6/13/97	879	10/1/00	1116	4 shows
Wading in the Velvet Sea	6/13/97	879	10/7/00	1120	0 shows
Wait	10/31/91	336	5/14/92	409	711 shows
Waking Up	6/14/97	880	6/14/97	880	240 shows
Walfredo	2/13/97	864	9/30/00	1115	5 shows
Walk Away	7/23/88	59	10/5/00	1118	2 shows
Walk This Way	9/29/00	1114	9/29/00	1114	6 shows

SONG NAME	FIRST TIME SEEN		LAST TIME SEEN		CURRENT GAP
	Date	Show #	Date	Show #	
Waste	6/6/96	795	10/1/100	1116	4 shows
Water in the Sky	6/13/97	879	9/25/00	1112	8 shows
We're Not Gonna Take It	10/8/99	1053	10/8/99	1053	67 shows
Weekapaug Groove	7/23/88	59	10/7/00	1120	0 shows
Weekapaug Reprise	11/27/98	1001	11/27/98	1001	119 shows
Weigh	3/7/92	361	8/2/98	968	152 shows
West LA Fadeaway	10/6/100	1119	10/6/100	1119	1 shows
What's the Use	7/4/99	1011	9/11/00	1102	18 shows
When Something is Wrong with My Baby	4/24/93	539	4/30/93	543	577 shows
When the Circus Comes	2/13/97	864	10/1/100	1116	4 shows
While My Guitar Gently Weeps	10/31/94	682	10/5/100	1118	2 shows
Whipping Post	11/3/84	3	7/25/99	1026	94 shows
Whipping Post Jam	11/23/85	11	11/23/85	11	1109 shows
White Rabbit Jam	9/30/95	739	9/30/95	739	381 shows
Who By Fire	4/23/94	606	4/23/94	606	514 shows
Who Do? We Do!	4/24/87	22	12/8/89	140	980 shows
Who Knows Jam	10/26/89	126	8/9/93	572	548 shows
Who Loves the Sun	10/31/98	984	10/31/98	984	136 shows
Whole Lotta Love Jam	6/9/90	206	3/22/91	266	854 shows
Why Don't We Do It in the Road	10/31/94	682	2/23/97	872	248 shows
Why Don't You Love Me	3/23/87	21	3/23/87	21	1099 shows
Why You've Been Gone So Long	5/6/93	548	5/6/93	548	572 shows
Wild Child	11/3/84	3	9/8/88	66	1054 shows
Wild Honey Pie	10/31/94	682	10/31/94	682	438 shows
Wild Thing	11/23/85	11	11/23/85	11	1109 shows
Wildwood Weed	12/6/96	859	12/6/96	859	261 shows
Will It Go Round in Circles	9/10/99	1033	9/21/99	1041	79 shows
Will the Circle Be Unbroken	10/3/98	978	10/3/98	978	142 shows
Wilson	10/15/86	15	9/29/00	1114	6 shows
Wind Beneath My Wings	11/28/95	774	11/28/95	774	346 shows
Windora Bug	9/8/00	1100	9/15/00	1105	15 shows
Wipeout	4/15/91	278	11/29/98	1003	117 shows
Wolfman's Brother	4/4/94	590	10/5/00	1118	2 shows
Wormtown Jam	7/2/97	891	7/2/97	891	229 shows
Ya Mar	2/21/87	19	9/24/00	1111	9 shows
Yer Blues	10/31/94	682	10/31/94	682	438 shows
Yerushalayim Shel Zahav	7/16/93	554	12/31/94	712	408 shows
You Enjoy Myself	2/3/86	12	10/7/100	1120	0 shows
You Gotta See Mama Every Night	3/16/93	511	3/16/93	511	609 shows
You Shook Me (All Night Long)	9/29/00	1114	9/29/00	1114	6 shows
You Shook Me All Night Long Jam	4/20/89	94	4/20/89	94	1026 shows

RAW TOTALS

There were 1120 shows played

Shows by day of week

- Sunday- 144
- Monday- 97
- Tuesday- 109
- Wednesday- 140
- Thursday- 170
- Friday- 227
- Saturday- 233

Shows by year

- 1983- 1
- 1984- 3
- 1985- 7
- 1986- 6
- 1987- 19
- 1988- 41
- 1989- 69
- 1990- 96
- 1991- 117
- 1992- 121
- 1993- 109
- 1994- 123
- 1995- 81
- 1996- 70
- 1997- 78
- 1998- 66
- 1999- 64
- 2000- 49

619 songs have been played (100% of songs Phish have played).

The average number of songs per show is 19.2.

The average amount of times each song was played is 34.83.

Total Times Played

You Enjoy Myself - 454 (40%)
Golgi Apparatus - 367 (32%)
Bouncing Around the Room - 365 (32%)
Mike's Song - 362 (32%)
Possum - 358 (31%)
Cavern - 341 (30%)
Weekapaug Groove - 335 (29%)
David Bowie - 328 (29%)
Chalk Dust Torture - 324 (28%)
Stash - 319 (28%)

Run Like an Antelope - 317 (28%)
Suzy Greenberg - 317 (28%)
Divided Sky - 308 (27%)
Reba - 302 (26%)
Runaway Jim - 301 (26%)
Foam - 286 (25%)
The Squirming Coil - 283 (25%)
Sparkle - 279 (24%)
Llama - 269 (24%)
The Lizards - 268 (23%)
I Am Hydrogen - 266 (23%)
Split Open and Melt - 260 (23%)
Poor Heart - 259 (23%)
Fee - 251 (22%)
Tweezer - 243 (21%)
Harry Hood - 237 (21%)
Maze - 236 (21%)
AC/DC Bag - 224 (20%)
Rift - 216 (19%)
I Didn't Know - 203 (18%)
My Sweet One - 202 (18%)
It's Ice - 201 (17%)
Sample in a Jar - 199 (17%)
Uncle Pen - 191 (17%)
Fluffhead - 185 (16%)
Wilson - 183 (16%)
The Landlady - 182 (16%)
The Oh Kee Pa Ceremony - 180 (16%)
Guelah Papyrus - 177 (15%)
Ya Mar - 173 (15%)
Rocky Top - 170 (15%)
Sweet Adeline - 164 (14%)
Tweezer Reprise - 162 (14%)
Good Times Bad Times - 160 (14%)
Bathtub Gin - 154 (13%)
Down With Disease - 143 (12%)
The Sloth - 141 (12%)
Slave to the Traffic Light - 140 (12%)
Julius - 138 (12%)
Lawn Boy - 136 (12%)
Also Sprach Zarathustra - 131 (11%)
Funky Bitch - 131 (11%)
Buried Alive - 129 (11%)
Contact - 128 (11%)
Silent in the Morning - 126 (11%)
The Horse - 123 (10%)
Dinner and a Movie - 120 (10%)
Horn - 119 (10%)
The Curtain - 119 (10%)
Simple - 111 (9%)
Fire - 110 (9%)
Esther - 109 (9%)
Punch You In The Eye - 109 (9%)

Home Grown Music Tent, Shakedown Street.

Amazing Grace - 107 (9%)
Colonel Forbin's Ascent - 105 (9%)
Big Black Furry Creature From Mars - 104 (9%)
Glide - 104 (9%)
My Friend My Friend - 104 (9%)
The Famous Mockingbird - 102 (9%)
Scent of a Mule - 100 (8%)
Big Ball Jam - 96 (8%)
Character Zero - 94 (8%)
Take the A-Train - 92 (8%)
Taste - 92 (8%)
Guyute - 91 (8%)
Theme From The Bottom - 89 (7%)
McGrupp and the Watchful Hosemasters - 88 (7%)
Mound - 88 (7%)
Love You - 86 (7%)
Prince Caspian - 85 (7%)
Free - 83 (7%)
Alumni Blues - 82 (7%)
NICU - 81 (7%)
Wolfman's Brother - 81 (7%)
All Things Reconsidered - 79 (7%)
Paul and Silas - 77 (6%)
The Mango Song - 75 (6%)
Limb By Limb - 74 (6%)
The Man Who Stepped Into Yesterday - 74 (6%)
Avenu Malkenu - 73 (6%)
La Grange - 73 (6%)
Tela - 71 (6%)
Highway To Hell - 70 (6%)
Loving Cup - 69 (6%)
Carolina - 67 (5%)
Cars Trucks Buses - 67 (5%)
Ginseng Sullivan - 67 (5%)
Frankenstein - 66 (5%)
Ghost - 66 (5%)
Makisupa Policeman - 65 (5%)
Peaches En Regalia - 65 (5%)
Tube - 64 (5%)
Gumbo - 63 (5%)

Piper - 62 (5%)
Sleeping Monkey - 62 (5%)
Bold As Love - 61 (5%)
Jesus Just Left Chicago - 60 (5%)
Jam - 59 (5%)
Magilla - 58 (5%)
Axilla - 57 (5%)
Fast Enough for You - 57 (5%)
Halley's Comet - 57 (5%)
Walk Away - 57 (5%)
My Soul - 56 (5%)
Terrapin - 56 (5%)
The Man Who Stepped Into Yesterday
   Reprise - 54 (4%)
Hello My Baby - 53 (4%)
Billy Breathes - 51 (4%)
Brother - 51 (4%)
Harpua - 51 (4%)
Timber (Jerry) - 51 (4%)
The Moma Dance - 50 (4%)
Cracklin' Rosie - 48 (4%)
Beauty of My Dreams - 47 (4%)
If I Could - 47 (4%)
Lifeboy - 47 (4%)
Waste - 47 (4%)
Birds of a Feather - 46 (4%)
Nellie Kane - 46 (4%)
A Day in the Life - 45 (4%)
Roggae - 45 (4%)
Strange Design - 44 (3%)
Dog Faced Boy - 43 (3%)
Dirt - 42 (3%)
When the Circus Comes - 40 (3%)
Caravan - 39 (3%)
My Mind's Got a Mind of its Own - 39 (3%)
Sneakin' Sally through the Alley - 39 (3%)
Axilla (Part II) - 38 (3%)
Twist - 38 (3%)
If I Only Had a Brain - 37 (3%)
Memories - 37 (3%)
Train Song - 37 (3%)
Wading in the Velvet Sea - 37 (3%)
Water in the Sky - 37 (3%)
Whipping Post - 37 (3%)
Farmhouse - 36 (3%)
Back on the Train - 35 (3%)
Cities - 35 (3%)
Bike - 34 (3%)
The Old Home Place - 34 (3%)
Weigh - 33 (2%)
Heavy Things - 32 (2%)
Dogs Stole Things - 31 (2%)
First Tube - 31 (2%)
Purple Rain - 31 (2%)
The Wedge - 31 (2%)
I'm Blue I'm Lonesome - 30 (2%)
Gotta Jibboo - 29 (2%)
Catapult - 28 (2%)

Acoustic Army - 27 (2%)
Kung - 27 (2%)
Destiny Unbound - 26 (2%)
Freebird - 26 (2%)
Sanity - 26 (2%)
Brian and Robert - 25 (2%)
Carini - 25 (2%)
Steep - 25 (2%)
Swept Away - 25 (2%)
The Ballad of Curtis Loew - 25 (2%)
While My Guitar Gently Weeps - 25 (2%)
Boogie on Reggae Woman - 24 (2%)
Sand - 24 (2%)
Bug - 23 (2%)
Johnny B. Goode - 23 (2%)
Lengthwise - 23 (2%)
Vultures - 23 (2%)
Camel Walk - 22 (1%)
Ha Ha Ha - 22 (1%)
Meat - 21 (1%)
The Asse Festival - 21 (1%)
Donna Lee - 20 (1%)
Drowned - 20 (1%)
Eliza - 19 (1%)
Flat Fee - 19 (1%)
Life on Mars - 19 (1%)
Meatstick - 19 (1%)
Dog Gone Dog - 18 (1%)
Driver - 18 (1%)
Frankie Says - 18 (1%)
Foreplay/Long Time - 17 (1%)
Icculus - 17 (1%)
Corrine Corrina - 16 (1%)
Daniel - 15 (1%)
My Long Journey Home - 15 (1%)
Rock and Roll - 15 (1%)
Dave's Energy Guide - 14 (1%)
Demand - 14 (1%)
Taste That Surrounds - 14 (1%)
Bittersweet Motel - 13 (1%)
I Saw it Again - 13 (1%)
Keyboard Cavalry - 13 (1%)
On Your Way Down - 13 (1%)
Suspicious Minds - 13 (1%)
The Inlaw Josie Wales - 13 (1%)
Dear Mrs. Reagan - 12 (1%)
Faht - 12 (1%)
Manteca - 12 (1%)
Roses Are Free - 12 (1%)
Satin Doll - 12 (1%)
Shaggy Dog - 12 (1%)
Sparks - 12 (1%)
Talk - 12 (1%)
The Great Gig in the Sky - 12 (1%)
Yerushalayim Shel Zahav - 12 (1%)
Albuquerque - 11 (0%)
Auld Lang Syne - 11 (0%)
Quinn the Eskimo - 11 (0%)

Phunky Bitches

The Star Spangled Banner - 11 (0%)
Who Do? We Do! - 11 (0%)
Clod - 10 (0%)
Happy Birthday - 10 (0%)
Have Mercy - 10 (0%)
Izabella - 10 (0%)
Sleep - 10 (0%)
The Curtain With - 10 (0%)
What's the Use - 10 (0%)
Anarchy - 9 (0%)
Crossroads - 9 (0%)
I Walk the Line - 9 (0%)
I Wanna Be Like You - 9 (0%)
Love Me - 9 (0%)
Ride Captain Ride - 9 (0%)
Swing Low Sweet Chariot - 9 (0%)
Touch Me - 9 (0%)
Back at the Chicken Shack - 8 (0%)
Buffalo Bill - 8 (0%)
Bundle of Joy - 8 (0%)
Crosseyed and Painless - 8 (0%)
Fog That Surrounds - 8 (0%)
In a Hole - 8 (0%)
Mountains in the Mist - 8 (0%)
Black-Eyed Katy - 7 (0%)
Light Up Or Leave Me Alone - 7 (0%)
Mustang Sally - 7 (0%)
Rhombus Narration - 7 (0%)
Skin It Back - 7 (0%)
Spock's Brain - 7 (0%)
Vacuum Solo - 7 (0%)
Digital Delay Loop Jam - 6 (0%)

Drum Circle at Dusk.

Heidi Mann

Kathleen Griffin

Fluff's Travels - 6 (0%)
Oblivious Fool - 6 (0%)
The Chase - 6 (0%)
The Vibration of Life - 6 (0%)
Back Porch Boogie Blues - 5 (0%)
Been Caught Stealin' - 5 (0%)
Crimes of the Mind - 5 (0%)
Don't You Wanna Go - 5 (0%)
Fikus - 5 (0%)
Lushington - 5 (0%)
Mozambique - 5 (0%)
My Left Toe - 5 (0%)
No Dogs Allowed - 5 (0%)
Prep School Hippie - 5 (0%)
Rocko William - 5 (0%)
Walfredo - 5 (0%)
Butter Them Biscuits - 4 (0%)
Bye Bye Foot - 4 (0%)
Cry Baby Cry - 4 (0%)
Drums Jam - 4 (0%)
Emotional Rescue - 4 (0%)
Letter to Jimmy Page - 4 (0%)
Lonesome Cowboy Bill - 4 (0%)
Mellow Mood - 4 (0%)
Melt the Guns - 4 (0%)
Misty Mountain Hop - 4 (0%)
NO2 - 4 (0%)
Phase Dance - 4 (0%)
Roll Like a Cantaloupe - 4 (0%)
Rotation Jam - 4 (0%)
Self - 4 (0%)
Sexual Healing - 4 (0%)
She Caught the Katy and Left Me a Mule
   to Ride - 4 (0%)
Something - 4 (0%)
Somewhere Over the Rainbow - 4 (0%)
Sweet Emotion Jam - 4 (0%)
Time Loves a Hero - 4 (0%)
Undun - 4 (0%)
Whole Lotta Love Jam - 4 (0%)
Why Don't We Do It in the Road - 4 (0%)
Wipeout - 4 (0%)
Ain't Love Funny - 3 (0%)
Amazing Grace Jam - 3 (0%)
Bass Jam - 3 (0%)
Big Leg Emma - 3 (0%)
Bill Bailey Won't You Please Come Home
   - 3 (0%)
Communication Breakdown - 3 (0%)
Costume Contest - 3 (0%)
Don't Get Me Wrong - 3 (0%)
Drum Jam - 3 (0%)
Eyes of the World - 3 (0%)
Gypsy Queen - 3 (0%)
How High the Moon - 3 (0%)
I Know a Little - 3 (0%)
If You Need a Fool - 3 (0%)
In the Midnight Hour - 3 (0%)

Jennifer Dances - 3 (0%)
Leprechaun - 3 (0%)
Little Drummer Boy - 3 (0%)
No Good Trying - 3 (0%)
Pig in a Pen - 3 (0%)
Sabotage - 3 (0%)
Scarlet Begonias - 3 (0%)
Sea and Sand - 3 (0%)
Secret Language Instructions - 3 (0%)
Setting Sail - 3 (0%)
Shafty - 3 (0%)
Skippy the Wondermouse - 3 (0%)
Wait - 3 (0%)
When Something is Wrong with My Baby
   - 3 (0%)
Wild Child - 3 (0%)
All Along the Watchtower - 2 (0%)
All Blues - 2 (0%)
American Band - 2 (0%)
Baby Elephant Walk - 2 (0%)
Back in the USSR - 2 (0%)
Beaumont Rag - 2 (0%)
Blackbird - 2 (0%)
Blue Bossa - 2 (0%)
Can't You Hear Me Knockin' - 2 (0%)
Chalk Dust Torture Reprise - 2 (0%)
Cinnamon Girl - 2 (0%)
Come On Baby, Let's Go Downtown - 2 (0%)
Cool it Down - 2 (0%)
Crew Football Theme Song - 2 (0%)
Doin' My Time - 2 (0%)
Everybody's Got Something to Hide Except for
   Me and My Monkey - 2 (0%)
Fixin' to Die - 2 (0%)
Going Down Slow - 2 (0%)
HYHU Jam - 2 (0%)
Helter Skelter - 2 (0%)
Hoochie Coochie Man - 2 (0%)
I Don't Care - 2 (0%)
I Get a Kick Out of You - 2 (0%)
I'm So Tired - 2 (0%)
Jagermeister - 2 (0%)
Long Cool Woman in a Black Dress
   - 2 (0%)
Low Rider Jam - 2 (0%)
Messin' With The Kid - 2 (0%)
Minute by Minute - 2 (0%)
Moby Dick - 2 (0%)
Mr. P.C. - 2 (0%)
Piano Duet - 2 (0%)
Ramble On - 2 (0%)
Revolution - 2 (0%)
Rocky Mountain Way Jam - 2 (0%)
Soul Shake Down Party - 2 (0%)
Speak to Me - 2 (0%)
Split Open and Melt Jam - 2 (0%)
Spooky Jam - 2 (0%)
Sweet Jane - 2 (0%)

RMP (Rec. Music Phish) is the Mockingbird's birthplace—this unique face-to-face gathering of online
RMP friends.

Take Me to the River - 2 (0%)
Tennessee Waltz - 2 (0%)
The Practical Song - 2 (0%)
The Price of Love - 2 (0%)
The Real Me - 2 (0%)
Too Much of Everything - 2 (0%)
Tube Jam - 2 (0%)
Tush - 2 (0%)
Who Knows Jam - 2 (0%)
Will It Go Round in Circles - 2 (0%)
Windora Bug - 2 (0%)
1999 - 1 (0%)
5:15 - 1 (0%)
99 Years - 1 (0%)
After Midnight - 1 (0%)
After Midnight Reprise - 1 (0%)
All the Pain Through the Years - 1 (0%)
Alumni Blues Jam - 1 (0%)
Ambient Jam - 1 (0%)
Amoreena - 1 (0%)
Andy's Chest - 1 (0%)
Any Colour You Like - 1 (0%)
Arc - 1 (0%)
Baby Left Me - 1 (0%)
Baby Lemonade - 1 (0%)

Jack Lebowitz, Mbird board member and lawyer, who
collected all these photos and art with his wife Kat.

Bell Boy - 1 (0%)
Bertha - 1 (0%)
Big Alligator Song - 1 (0%)
Big Ball Jam Reprise - 1 (0%)
Big Black Furry Creature from Mars Reprise
  - 1 (0%)
Birthday Jam - 1 (0%)
Bitchin' Again - 1 (0%)
Blister in the Sun - 1 (0%)
Blister in the Sun Jam - 1 (0%)
Blue Bayou - 1 (0%)
Bob Dylan Band - 1 (0%)
Bohemian Rhapsody - 1 (0%)
Born Under Punches (The Heat goes on) - 1 (0%)
Born to Run - 1 (0%)
Brain Damage - 1 (0%)
Breathe - 1 (0%)
Breathe Jam - 1 (0%)
Bring it On Home - 1 (0%)
Brown Eyed Girl - 1 (0%)
Burning Down the House - 1 (0%)
Cannonball Jam - 1 (0%)
Cecilia - 1 (0%)
Champagne Supernova - 1 (0%)
Che Hun Ta Mao - 1 (0%)
Chess Jam - 1 (0%)
Choo Choo Ch' Boogie - 1 (0%)
Clementine - 1 (0%)
Cocaine Jam - 1 (0%)
Cold Rain and Snow - 1 (0%)
Come Together - 1 (0%)
Cowboy's Sweetheart - 1 (0%)
Cryin' - 1 (0%)
Cut My Hair - 1 (0%)
Dahlia - 1 (0%)
David Bowie Jam - 1 (0%)
Dazed and Confused - 1 (0%)
Dear Prudence - 1 (0%)
Diamond Girl - 1 (0%)
Doctor Jimmy - 1 (0%)
Don't Pass Me By - 1 (0%)
Don't Want You No More - 1 (0%)
Dooley - 1 (0%)
Down By the River - 1 (0%)
Down with Disease Jam - 1 (0%)
Earl's Breakdown - 1 (0%)
Eclipse - 1 (0%)
El Paso - 1 (0%)
Family Picture - 1 (0%)
Fire On The Mountain - 1 (0%)
Fire up the Ganja - 1 (0%)
Fishing Hole Theme - 1 (0%)
Fishman's Gull Poem - 1 (0%)
Four Strong Winds - 1 (0%)
Freeworld - 1 (0%)
Fuck Your Face - 1 (0%)
Gettin' Jiggy Wit' It - 1 (0%)
Glass Onion - 1 (0%)

Glide II - 1 (0%)
Gloria - 1 (0%)
Gold Soundz - 1 (0%)
Golden Lady - 1 (0%)
Got My Mojo Workin' - 1 (0%)
Grind - 1 (0%)
Guy Forget - 1 (0%)
Happiness Is a Warm Gun - 1 (0%)
Head Held High - 1 (0%)
Heart and soul - 1 (0%)
Help Me - 1 (0%)
Help on the Way - 1 (0%)
Helpless - 1 (0%)
Helpless Dancer - 1 (0%)
High-Heel Sneakers - 1 (0%)
Hold Whatcha Got - 1 (0%)
Hold to a Dream - 1 (0%)
Honey Pie - 1 (0%)
Honky Tonk Women - 1 (0%)
Honky Tonk Women Jam - 1 (0%)
Houses in Motion - 1 (0%)
Hurricane - 1 (0%)
I Am the Sea - 1 (0%)
I Been to Georgia on a Fast Train - 1 (0%)
I Found a Reason - 1 (0%)
I Shall Be Released - 1 (0%)
I Told You So - 1 (0%)
I Will - 1 (0%)
I Wish - 1 (0%)
I'll Come Running - 1 (0%)
I'm Gonna Be (500 Miles) - 1 (0%)
I'm One - 1 (0%)
I've Had Enough - 1 (0%)
I've Turned Bad - 1 (0%)
If I Don't Be There by Morning - 1 (0%)
Immigrant Song Jam - 1 (0%)
Indian War Dance - 1 (0%)
Is it in my Head - 1 (0%)
It's My Life - 1 (0%)
Jessica Jam - 1 (0%)
Julia - 1 (0%)
Jump Monk - 1 (0%)
Keyboard Cavalry Reprise - 1 (0%)
Killer Joe - 1 (0%)
La Grange Jam - 1 (0%)
Layla - 1 (0%)
Let the Good Times Roll - 1 (0%)
Li'l Red Rooster - 1 (0%)
Listening Wind - 1 (0%)
Lively Up Yourself - 1 (0%)
Long Long Long - 1 (0%)
Loup Garou - 1 (0%)
Love Me Like a Man - 1 (0%)
Love Reign O'er Me - 1 (0%)
Maiden Voyage - 1 (0%)
Makisupa Policeman Jam - 1 (0%)
Manteca Reprise - 1 (0%)
Martha My Dear - 1 (0%)

Mean Mr. Mustard - 1 (0%)
Meat Reprise - 1 (0%)
Meatstick Reprise - 1 (0%)
Merry Pranksters Jam - 1 (0%)
Midnight Rider Jam - 1 (0%)
Midnight on the Highway - 1 (0%)
Mind Left Body Jam - 1 (0%)
Mirror in the Bathroom - 1 (0%)
Money - 1 (0%)
Moonlight in Vermont - 1 (0%)
Moose the Mooch - 1 (0%)
Mother Nature's Son - 1 (0%)
My Generation - 1 (0%)

Phish.net gathering at Great Went

Phish.net gathering at Great Went

Never - 1 (0%)
New Age - 1 (0%)
New York New York - 1 (0%)
Night Moves Jam - 1 (0%)
Not Fade Away - 1 (0%)
Nowhere Fast - 1 (0%)
O Mio Babbino Caro - 1 (0%)
Ob La Di Ob La Da - 1 (0%)
Ob La Di Ob La Da Jam - 1 (0%)
Oh! Sweet Nuthin' - 1 (0%)
On My Knees - 1 (0%)
On The Run - 1 (0%)
Once in a Lifetime - 1 (0%)
One Meatball - 1 (0%)
Overload - 1 (0%)
Oye Como Va Jam - 1 (0%)
Piggies - 1 (0%)

Poor Heart Reprise - 1 (0%)
Proud Mary - 1 (0%)
Psycho Killer - 1 (0%)
Psycho Killer Jam - 1 (0%)
Punch Me in the Eye - 1 (0%)
Pusher Man Jam - 1 (0%)
Quadrophenia - 1 (0%)
Quadrophonic Toppling - 1 (0%)
Rapper's Delight - 1 (0%)
Revival - 1 (0%)
Revolution 9 - 1 (0%)
Rhinoceros - 1 (0%)
Road Runner - 1 (0%)
Roadhouse Blues - 1 (0%)
Rock and Roll All Nite Jam
   - 1 (0%)
Rock and Roll Part Two - 1 (0%)
Rocky Raccoon - 1 (0%)
Running With the Devil - 1 (0%)
Sad Lisa - 1 (0%)
Samson Variation - 1 (0%)
Savoy Truffle - 1 (0%)
Seen and Not Seen - 1 (0%)
Sexy Sadie - 1 (0%)
Shine - 1 (0%)
Sixteen Candles - 1 (0%)
Slipknot! - 1 (0%)
Smells Like Teen Spirit - 1 (0%)
Smoke on the Water Jam - 1 (0%)
So Lonely - 1 (0%)
Somewhere Over the Rainbow
   Jam - 1 (0%)
Spanish Flea - 1 (0%)
Squeeze Box - 1 (0%)
St. Stephen Jam - 1 (0%)
St. Thomas - 1 (0%)
Stand - 1 (0%)
Stir It Up Jam - 1 (0%)
Sweet Baby's Arms - 1 (0%)
Sweet Virginia - 1 (0%)
TV Show - 1 (0%)
Tea Tray Song - 1 (0%)
Tell Me Something Good - 1 (0%)
Terrapin Station - 1 (0%)
That's Alright Mama - 1 (0%)
The Birthday Dub - 1 (0%)
The Chicken - 1 (0%)
The Continuing Story of Bungalow
   Bill - 1 (0%)
The Dirty Jobs - 1 (0%)
The Great Curve - 1 (0%)
The Happy Whip and Dung Song
   - 1 (0%)
The Maker - 1 (0%)
The Other One - 1 (0%)
The Pendulum - 1 (0%)
The Punk Meets the Godfather
   - 1 (0%)

The Revolution's Over - 1 (0%)
The Rock - 1 (0%)
Them Changes - 1 (0%)
Theme to Star Trek: The Original
   Series - 1 (0%)
Three Little Birds - 1 (0%)
Time - 1 (0%)
Train Round the Bend - 1 (0%)
Trenchtown Rock - 1 (0%)
Tubthumping - 1 (0%)
Tuesday's Gone - 1 (0%)
Uncloudy Day - 1 (0%)
Us and Them - 1 (0%)
Vacuum Jam - 1 (0%)
Viola Lee Blues - 1 (0%)
Waking Up - 1 (0%)
Walk This Way - 1 (0%)
We're Not Gonna Take It - 1 (0%)
Weekapaug Reprise - 1 (0%)
West LA Fadeaway - 1 (0%)
Whipping Post Jam - 1 (0%)
White Rabbit Jam - 1 (0%)
Who By Fire - 1 (0%)
Who Loves the Sun - 1 (0%)
Why Don't You Love Me - 1 (0%)
Why You've Been Gone So Long
   - 1 (0%)
Wild Honey Pie - 1 (0%)
Wild Thing - 1 (0%)
Wildwood Weed - 1 (0%)
Will the Circle Be Unbroken
   - 1 (0%)
Wind Beneath My Wings - 1 (0%)
Wormtown Jam - 1 (0%)
Yer Blues - 1 (0%)
You Gotta See Mama Every
   Night - 1 (0%)
You Shook Me (All Night Long) - 1
   (0%)
You Shook Me All Night Long
   Jam - 1 (0%)

First Set Openers

Runaway Jim - 77
Chalk Dust Torture - 70
Buried Alive - 58
Golgi Apparatus - 49
Llama - 47
The Landlady - 38
Suzy Greenberg - 35
Wilson - 34
AC/DC Bag - 28
My Friend My Friend - 27
Ya Mar - 18
Sample in a Jar - 17
The Curtain - 17
The Oh Kee Pa Ceremony - 17
Divided Sky - 16

Rift - 16
Punch You In The Eye - 15
Funky Bitch - 14
Poor Heart - 13
I Didn't Know - 12
Mike's Song - 12
Possum - 12
Julius - 11
Cars Trucks Buses - 10
Down With Disease - 10
First Tube - 10
NICU - 10
Reba - 10
Axilla - 9
Bathtub Gin - 9
Dinner and a Movie - 9
Fee - 9
Maze - 9
Carini - 8
David Bowie - 8
Makisupa Policeman - 8
Split Open and Melt - 8
Carolina - 7
Cavern - 7
My Sweet One - 7
The Sloth - 7
Tube - 7
Limb By Limb - 6
Peaches En Regalia - 6
Slave to the Traffic Light - 6
Sweet Adeline - 6
Theme From The Bottom - 6
Also Sprach Zarathustra - 5

Birds of a Feather - 5
Ghost - 5
Harry Hood - 5
Loving Cup - 5
My Soul - 5
The Moma Dance - 5
Tweezer - 5
Alumni Blues - 4
Bouncing Around the Room - 4
Cities - 4
Farmhouse - 4
Fire - 4
Fluffhead - 4
Foam - 4
Memories - 4
Stash - 4
The Man Who Stepped Into
   Yesterday - 4
Uncle Pen - 4
Wolfman's Brother - 4
You Enjoy Myself - 4
Beauty of My Dreams - 3
Colonel Forbin's Ascent - 3
Don't You Wanna Go - 3
Emotional Rescue - 3
Frankenstein - 3
Glide - 3
Guyute - 3
Halley's Comet - 3
Jam - 3
La Grange - 3
Lengthwise - 3
Piper - 3

James Raras

Phish.net gathering at Great Went

Michael McNamara

Roseland ticket line in NYC.

The first phan from Japan.

Vancouver, B.C.

Rocky Top - 3
Simple - 3
Sneakin' Sally through the Alley - 3
Take the A-Train - 3
Taste - 3
The Squirming Coil - 3
The Wedge - 3
Walk Away - 3
All Things Reconsidered - 2
Bold As Love - 2
Brother - 2
Contact - 2
Ha Ha Ha - 2
Heavy Things - 2
McGrupp and the Watchful
    Hosemasters - 2
Meat - 2
Mellow Mood - 2
Mozambique - 2
Prince Caspian - 2
Satin Doll - 2
The Curtain With - 2
The Lizards - 2
The Old Home Place - 2
The Star Spangled Banner - 2
Tweezer Reprise - 2
Walfredo - 2
Water in the Sky - 2
1999 - 1
All Blues - 1
Amazing Grace - 1
Amoreena - 1
Anarchy - 1
Axilla (Part II) - 1
Back at the Chicken Shack - 1
Back on the Train - 1
Big Black Furry Creature From
    Mars - 1
Bike - 1

Camel Walk - 1
Caravan - 1
Catapult - 1
Cinnamon Girl - 1
Clod - 1
Come On Baby, Let's Go Down-
    town - 1
Daniel - 1
Dear Mrs. Reagan - 1
Demand - 1
Dog Gone Dog - 1
Dogs Stole Things - 1
Don't Get Me Wrong - 1
Esther - 1
Everybody's Got Something to
    Hide Except for Me and My
    Monkey - 1
Fluff's Travels - 1
Foreplay/Long Time - 1
Ginseng Sullivan - 1
Good Times Bad Times - 1
Gumbo - 1
Harpua - 1
Hello My Baby - 1
Helter Skelter - 1
Horn - 1
Hurricane - 1
Icculus - 1
If I Only Had a Brain - 1
In the Midnight Hour - 1
It's Ice - 1
Johnny B. Goode - 1
Kung - 1
Long Cool Woman in a Black
    Dress - 1
Magilla - 1
Mound - 1
Mustang Sally - 1
NO2 - 1

Oblivious Fool - 1
Paul and Silas - 1
Quinn the Eskimo - 1
Ramble On - 1
Rhinoceros - 1
Rhombus Narration - 1
Road Runner - 1
Rock and Roll - 1
Rock and Roll Part Two - 1
Roggae - 1
Roses Are Free - 1
Sanity - 1
Scarlet Begonias - 1
Shaggy Dog - 1
She Caught the Katy and Left Me a
    Mule to Ride - 1
Somewhere Over the Rainbow - 1
Soul Shake Down Party - 1
Sparkle - 1
Sweet Virginia - 1
The Chicken - 1
The Great Gig in the Sky - 1
The Mango Song - 1
Timber (Jerry) - 1
Trenchtown Rock - 1
Whipping Post - 1
Wild Thing - 1

First Set Closers

Run Like an Antelope - 125
David Bowie - 103
Cavern - 70
Golgi Apparatus - 70
Possum - 63
You Enjoy Myself - 42
Weekapaug Groove - 39
Chalk Dust Torture - 37
Character Zero - 36

Good Times Bad Times - 35
Sweet Adeline - 29
Runaway Jim - 26
The Squirming Coil - 26
Sample in a Jar - 25
Suzy Greenberg - 24
Llama - 20
Split Open and Melt - 18
Fire - 14
Rocky Top - 14
Loving Cup - 13
Frankenstein - 12
Julius - 12
Stash - 11
Carolina - 9
Funky Bitch - 9
Hello My Baby - 9
La Grange - 9
Slave to the Traffic Light - 9
Tweezer Reprise - 8
Bold As Love - 7
Divided Sky - 6
Fluffhead - 6
Harry Hood - 6
While My Guitar Gently Weeps - 6
Down With Disease - 5
Harpua - 5
My Soul - 5
The Famous Mockingbird - 5
AC/DC Bag - 4
Amazing Grace - 4
Highway To Hell - 4
I Didn't Know - 4
Alumni Blues - 3
Big Black Furry Creature From
    Mars - 3
Birds of a Feather - 3
Contact - 3
Farmhouse - 3
My Long Journey Home - 3
Prince Caspian - 3
Take the A-Train - 3
Taste - 3
Wilson - 3
A Day in the Life - 2
Bittersweet Motel - 2
Daniel - 2
Foam - 2
Free - 2
Freebird - 2
Guyute - 2
Izabella - 2
Johnny B. Goode - 2
Lushington - 2
Makisupa Policeman - 2
Memories - 2
Oblivious Fool - 2
The Landlady - 2
The Star Spangled Banner - 2

Michael McNamara

Great Woods 1999

Twist - 2
After Midnight - 1
Amazing Grace Jam - 1
Axilla - 1
Axilla (Part II) - 1
Bathtub Gin - 1
Big Leg Emma - 1
Camel Walk - 1
Communication Breakdown - 1
Crimes of the Mind - 1
Crossroads - 1
Dear Mrs. Reagan - 1
Dogs Stole Things - 1
Doin' My Time - 1
Drums Jam - 1
Ghost - 1
Glide - 1
Happy Birthday - 1
Helpless - 1
High-Heel Sneakers - 1
Hurricane - 1
I Been to Georgia on a Fast
    Train - 1
I Shall Be Released - 1
I'm Blue I'm Lonesome - 1
If I Could - 1
In the Midnight Hour - 1
Jam - 1
Lawn Boy - 1
Layla - 1
Life on Mars - 1
McGrupp and the Watchful Hose-
    masters - 1
Meatstick - 1
Melt the Guns - 1
Mike's Song - 1
Mr. P.C. - 1
No Dogs Allowed - 1
Poor Heart - 1
Prep School Hippie - 1
Reba - 1
Rift - 1

Rock and Roll - 1
Setting Sail - 1
Skin It Back - 1
Sleeping Monkey - 1
Sneakin' Sally through the Alley - 1
Sparks - 1
Suspicious Minds - 1
Sweet Jane - 1
Swing Low Sweet Chariot - 1
Tela - 1
Terrapin - 1
The Horse - 1
The Lizards - 1
Theme From The Bottom - 1
Touch Me - 1
Uncloudy Day - 1
Waste - 1
Whipping Post - 1
Wild Thing - 1
Will It Go Round in Circles - 1
Ya Mar - 1

Second Set Openers

Also Sprach Zarathustra - 72
Runaway Jim - 34
Chalk Dust Torture - 32
Suzy Greenberg - 32
Wilson - 32
Mike's Song - 28
Down With Disease - 27
The Curtain - 26
David Bowie - 24
Golgi Apparatus - 24
Llama - 23
Timber (Jerry) - 21
Buried Alive - 19
Possum - 19
The Landlady - 18
AC/DC Bag - 15
Axilla - 15
Tweezer - 15

Dinner and a Movie - 14
Maze - 14
Gotta Jibboo - 13
Rift - 13
Birds of a Feather - 12
Halley's Comet - 12
Julius - 12
Wolfman's Brother - 12
Sample in a Jar - 11
Split Open and Melt - 11
My Sweet One - 10
Peaches En Regalia - 10
The Oh Kee Pa Ceremony - 10
Brother - 9
Ghost - 9
Poor Heart - 9
Glide - 8
Harry Hood - 8
Punch You In The Eye - 8
Stash - 8
The Sloth - 8
Tube - 8
Twist - 8
Drowned - 7
Makisupa Policeman - 7
Reba - 7
The Squirming Coil - 7
Funky Bitch - 6
I Didn't Know - 6
La Grange - 6
My Friend My Friend - 6
Ya Mar - 6
Bathtub Gin - 5
Boogie on Reggae Woman - 5
Divided Sky - 5
Free - 5
NICU - 5
Alumni Blues - 4
Carolina - 4
Fluffhead - 4
Frankenstein - 4
Lengthwise - 4
Limb By Limb - 4

Loving Cup - 4
Piper - 4
Run Like an Antelope - 4
Simple - 4
Theme From The Bottom - 4
Carini - 3
Fire - 3
Foam - 3
Heavy Things - 3
Jam - 3
Rock and Roll - 3
Roses Are Free - 3
Sand - 3
The Lizards - 3
The Man Who Stepped Into
    Yesterday - 3
Walk Away - 3
Axilla (Part II) - 2
Bouncing Around the Room - 2
Cars Trucks Buses - 2
Cavern - 2
Cities - 2
Demand - 2
Dog Gone Dog - 2
Faht - 2
Fee - 2
Ha Ha Ha - 2
Harpua - 2
It's Ice - 2
Meatstick - 2
Sanity - 2
Taste - 2
The Asse Festival - 2
The Old Home Place - 2
The Wedge - 2
You Enjoy Myself - 2
A Day in the Life - 1
All Blues - 1
Anarchy - 1
Back on the Train - 1
Beauty of My Dreams - 1
Bike - 1
Blue Bossa - 1

Arjuna Sundaram

Arjuna Sunderam

Bold As Love - 1
Born Under Punches (The Heat
    goes on) - 1
Caravan - 1
Character Zero - 1
Communication Breakdown - 1
Crew Football Theme Song - 1
Crosseyed and Painless - 1
Daniel - 1
Donna Lee - 1
Farmhouse - 1
First Tube - 1
Fishing Hole Theme - 1
Freebird - 1
Good Times Bad Times - 1
Gumbo - 1
Guyute - 1
Happy Birthday - 1
Help on the Way - 1
How High the Moon - 1
I Am the Sea - 1
I Know a Little - 1
I Saw it Again - 1
Icculus - 1
Jesus Just Left Chicago - 1
Jump Monk - 1
Keyboard Cavalry - 1
Killer Joe - 1
Letter to Jimmy Page - 1
Light Up Or Leave Me Alone - 1
Memories - 1
Mound - 1
Mustang Sally - 1
My Soul - 1
Nellie Kane - 1
No Dogs Allowed - 1
Oblivious Fool - 1
On Your Way Down - 1
Paul and Silas - 1
Ride Captain Ride - 1
Rocky Top - 1
Sabotage - 1

Scarlet Begonias - 1
Sneakin' Sally through the Alley - 1
Speak to Me - 1
Sweet Adeline - 1
Take the A-Train - 1
The Curtain With - 1
The Mango Song - 1
The Moma Dance - 1
Time Loves a Hero - 1
Tweezer Reprise - 1
Uncle Pen - 1
Whipping Post - 1
Who Knows Jam - 1
Who Loves the Sun - 1
Whole Lotta Love Jam - 1
Wipeout - 1

Second Set Closers

Cavern - 67
Tweezer Reprise - 67
Golgi Apparatus - 60
Run Like an Antelope - 53
Possum - 52
Weekapaug Groove - 52
David Bowie - 44
You Enjoy Myself - 39
Slave to the Traffic Light - 37
Good Times Bad Times - 35
Suzy Greenberg - 30
Harry Hood - 25
Chalk Dust Torture - 23
Highway To Hell - 21
Character Zero - 18
The Squirming Coil - 18
Amazing Grace - 17
Big Black Furry Creature From
    Mars - 16
Rocky Top - 14
Sweet Adeline - 14
Frankenstein - 13
Llama - 13

Fire - 10
Hello My Baby - 10
Runaway Jim - 10
A Day in the Life - 9
Julius - 9
Loving Cup - 9
Whipping Post - 9
Sample in a Jar - 8
The Lizards - 8
Contact - 7
Down With Disease - 7
Funky Bitch - 7
Harpua - 7
Divided Sky - 5
Johnny B. Goode - 5
Alumni Blues - 4
Fluffhead - 4
Prince Caspian - 4
AC/DC Bag - 3
Crimes of the Mind - 3

Arjuna Sunderam

Freebird - 3
Ghost - 3
Guyute - 3
Jam - 3
Poor Heart - 3
Amazing Grace Jam - 2
Bathtub Gin - 2
Bold As Love - 2
Bug - 2
Daniel - 2
Dear Mrs. Reagan - 2
Fee - 2
Izabella - 2
La Grange - 2
Lawn Boy - 2
Little Drummer Boy - 2
Meatstick - 2
Misty Mountain Hop - 2
Taste - 2
The Star Spangled Banner - 2
Wading in the Velvet Sea - 2

Waste - 2
While My Guitar Gently Weeps - 2
Wilson - 2
Also Sprach Zarathustra - 1
Bass Jam - 1
Been Caught Stealin' - 1
Bittersweet Motel - 1
Bring it On Home - 1
Camel Walk - 1
Cities - 1
Cold Rain and Snow - 1
Colonel Forbin's Ascent - 1
Corrine Corrina - 1
Cracklin' Rosie - 1
Crossroads - 1
Drowned - 1
Esther - 1
Farmhouse - 1
Foam - 1
Foreplay/Long Time - 1

Free - 1
Going Down Slow - 1
Guelah Papyrus - 1
Gumbo - 1
Halley's Comet - 1
I Didn't Know - 1
If I Only Had a Brain - 1
In a Hole - 1
Jesus Just Left Chicago - 1
Keyboard Cavalry Reprise - 1
Love Reign O'er Me - 1
Maze - 1
McGrupp and the Watchful Hose-
    masters - 1
Memories - 1
Mike's Song - 1
Oh! Sweet Nuthin' - 1
Overload - 1
Peaches En Regalia - 1
Revolution 9 - 1
Rock and Roll - 1
Roll Like a Cantaloupe - 1

Arjuna Sunderam

Self - 1
Simple - 1
Sleeping Monkey - 1
Somewhere Over the Rainbow
   Jam - 1
Split Open and Melt - 1
Stash - 1
Strange Design - 1
Swing Low Sweet Chariot - 1
That's Alright Mama - 1
The Man Who Stepped Into
   Yesterday - 1
The Revolution's Over - 1
The Sloth - 1
The Wedge - 1
Theme From The Bottom - 1
Touch Me - 1
Tweezer - 1
Yerushalayim Shel Zahav - 1
You Shook Me (All Night Long) - 1

Third Set Openers

David Bowie - 3
Jam - 3
La Grange - 3
Mike's Song - 3

Peaches En Regalia - 3
Also Sprach Zarathustra - 2
Auld Lang Syne - 2
Good Times Bad Times - 2
Suzy Greenberg - 2
The Man Who Stepped Into
   Yesterday - 2
The Sloth - 2
Wilson - 2
You Enjoy Myself - 2
AC/DC Bag - 1
Big Black Furry Creature From
   Mars - 1
Big Leg Emma - 1
Brother - 1
Buffalo Bill - 1
Chalk Dust Torture - 1
Fee - 1
Fire - 1
Fluffhead - 1
Halley's Comet - 1
Icculus - 1
Makisupa Policeman - 1
My Soul - 1
My Sweet One - 1
NICU - 1
Paul and Silas - 1
Roll Like a Cantaloupe - 1

Runaway Jim - 1
Sabotage - 1
Sanity - 1
Scarlet Begonias - 1
Skin It Back - 1
Slave to the Traffic Light - 1
Stash - 1
The Birthday Dub - 1
The Oh Kee Pa Ceremony - 1
Wolfman's Brother - 1

Third Set Closers

Run Like an Antelope - 6
Weekapaug Groove - 4
Fluffhead - 3
Good Times Bad Times - 3
Harry Hood - 3
Suzy Greenberg - 3
AC/DC Bag - 2
Corrine Corrina - 2
Llama - 2
Loving Cup - 2
Possum - 2
Slave to the Traffic Light - 2
Tweezer Reprise - 2
Anarchy - 1
Big Black Furry Creature From
   Mars - 1
Dave's Energy Guide - 1
David Bowie - 1
Dear Mrs. Reagan - 1
Fire - 1
Frankenstein - 1
Funky Bitch - 1
Ghost - 1
Hello My Baby - 1
I Am Hydrogen - 1
Jesus Just Left Chicago - 1
Julius - 1
Prince Caspian - 1
Rocky Top - 1
Sanity - 1
She Caught the Katy and Left Me a
   Mule to Ride - 1
Swing Low Sweet Chariot - 1
The Other One - 1
Walk Away - 1
While My Guitar Gently Weeps - 1
Whipping Post - 1

Fourth Set Openers

Ambient Jam - 1

Fourth Set Closers

Ambient Jam - 1

Encores

Rocky Top - 102
Tweezer Reprise - 76
Good Times Bad Times - 63
Amazing Grace - 58
Fire - 57
Sweet Adeline - 57
Contact - 54
Golgi Apparatus - 50
Sleeping Monkey - 41
Big Black Furry Creature From
   Mars - 35
Cavern - 33
Highway To Hell - 32
Possum - 31
Bold As Love - 29
The Squirming Coil - 29
Carolina - 26
Lawn Boy - 26
Suzy Greenberg - 22
Memories - 21
Freebird - 19
Harry Hood - 19
Bouncing Around the Room - 18
Funky Bitch - 16
Chalk Dust Torture - 15
Fee - 15
A Day in the Life - 14
Character Zero - 14
Loving Cup - 13
Sample in a Jar - 13
Frankenstein - 12
Julius - 12
La Grange - 12
While My Guitar Gently Weeps - 12
Hello My Baby - 11
Nellie Kane - 11
Poor Heart - 11
You Enjoy Myself - 11
My Sweet One - 10
AC/DC Bag - 9
Glide - 9
Guyute - 9
Johnny B. Goode - 9
Magilla - 9
Run Like an Antelope - 9
Runaway Jim - 9
Foreplay/Long Time - 8
Slave to the Traffic Light - 8
Take the A-Train - 8
Waste - 8
When the Circus Comes - 8
Brian and Robert - 7
Ginseng Sullivan - 7
Halley's Comet - 7
Jesus Just Left Chicago - 7
Theme From The Bottom - 7
Uncle Pen - 7

Alumni Blues - 6
Caravan - 6
Harpua - 6
I Didn't Know - 6
My Soul - 6
Simple - 6
Whipping Post - 6
Driver - 5
The Inlaw Josie Wales - 5
The Lizards - 5
Ya Mar - 5
Bittersweet Motel - 4
Boogie on Reggae Woman - 4
David Bowie - 4
Horn - 4
Icculus - 4
Love You - 4
Paul and Silas - 4
Punch You In The Eye - 4
Terrapin - 4
The Oh Kee Pa Ceremony - 4
The Old Home Place - 4
Been Caught Stealin' - 3
Bill Bailey Won't You Please Come
    Home - 3
Camel Walk - 3
Carini - 3
Daniel - 3
Divided Sky - 3
I'm Blue I'm Lonesome - 3
Life on Mars - 3
Limb By Limb - 3
Llama - 3
My Long Journey Home - 3
Ride Captain Ride - 3
Rock and Roll - 3
Silent in the Morning - 3
Sparkle - 3
Taste - 3
Walk Away - 3
Wilson - 3
Acoustic Army - 2
All Along the Watchtower - 2
American Band - 2
Auld Lang Syne - 2
Big Ball Jam - 2
Buffalo Bill - 2
Chalk Dust Torture Reprise - 2
Cities - 2
Cracklin' Rosie - 2
Drums Jam - 2
Gumbo - 2
I Am Hydrogen - 2
Jam - 2
Messin' With The Kid - 2
Misty Mountain Hop - 2
Moby Dick - 2
Piano Duet - 2
Reba - 2

Sleep - 2
Something - 2
Split Open and Melt - 2
Stash - 2
The Horse - 2
The Landlady - 2
Touch Me - 2
Wading in the Velvet Sea - 2
When Something is Wrong with
    My Baby - 2
All Things Reconsidered - 1
Anarchy - 1
Axilla - 1
Baby Elephant Walk - 1
Back in the USSR - 1
Bathtub Gin - 1
Beauty of My Dreams - 1
Big Ball Jam Reprise - 1
Billy Breathes - 1
Birds of a Feather - 1
Bitchin' Again - 1
Black-Eyed Katy - 1
Blue Bayou - 1
Born to Run - 1
Brother - 1
Brown Eyed Girl - 1
Bug - 1
Burning Down the House - 1
Cinnamon Girl - 1
Clod - 1
Come Together - 1
Communication Breakdown - 1
Corrine Corrina - 1
Costume Contest - 1
Cowboy's Sweetheart - 1
Crimes of the Mind - 1
Crossroads - 1
Dinner and a Movie - 1
Dirt - 1
Dog Faced Boy - 1
Don't Get Me Wrong - 1
Donna Lee - 1
El Paso - 1
Eliza - 1
Emotional Rescue - 1
Eyes of the World - 1
First Tube - 1
Fixin' to Die - 1
Fluffhead - 1
Free - 1
Gloria - 1
Gotta Jibboo - 1
Grind - 1
Heavy Things - 1
Hoochie Coochie Man - 1
I'll Come Running - 1
If I Only Had a Brain - 1
In a Hole - 1
Izabella - 1

Kung - 1
Lengthwise - 1
Letter to Jimmy Page - 1
Makisupa Policeman - 1
Manteca - 1
McGrupp and the Watchful
    Hosemasters - 1
Meatstick - 1
Meatstick Reprise - 1
Mike's Song - 1
My Friend My Friend - 1
My Generation - 1
New York New York - 1
Not Fade Away - 1
Pig in a Pen - 1
Poor Heart Reprise - 1
Prince Caspian - 1
Pusher Man Jam - 1
Rift - 1
Rocky Mountain Way Jam - 1
Roggae - 1
Running With the Devil - 1
Sabotage - 1
Sanity - 1
Self - 1
Sexual Healing - 1
Smells Like Teen Spirit - 1
Sneakin' Sally through the Alley - 1
So Lonely - 1

Sparks - 1
Stand - 1
Suspicious Minds - 1
Sweet Baby's Arms - 1
Terrapin Station - 1
The Asse Festival - 1
The Curtain - 1
The Maker - 1
The Mango Song - 1
The Practical Song - 1
The Star Spangled Banner - 1
The Wedge - 1
Them Changes - 1
Theme to Star Trek: The Original
    Series - 1
Three Little Birds - 1
Tube - 1
Tubthumping - 1
Tuesday's Gone - 1
Tweezer - 1
Undun - 1
Vacuum Solo - 1
Viola Lee Blues - 1
Weekapaug Groove - 1
Weigh - 1
West LA Fadeaway - 1
Wildwood Weed - 1
Wipeout - 1

Michael Collins

Michael McNamara

Ohio 1999

THE TRAVEL LOG
(AKA TOUR CAPSULES)

By Craig DeLucia and Jeremy Goodwin
Maps by Ellis Godard

Here is a brief tour-by-tour look at the evolution of Phish, focusing on the development of the band's playlist and tour scheduling, plus citations of many important shows along the way, and critical discussion and description of the music found in each era. Also included are comprehensive charts listing which songs debuted, which songs were retired, and which songs reemerged after lengthy absences during each tour. In addition, to trace the band's geographical progress, each tour contains a map showing what states the band visited. Only songs that have been played in full are listed, as jams and teases are apt to pop up anywhere. Due to incomplete data from the earliest days, we have only considered breakouts from 1991 through the present.

1983-1985

"The Early Years"

Most fans know the history of the band, and of how the phenomenon known as "Phish" began as "Blackwood Convention" in the fall of 1983. Few realize, though, how many songs the band used to play. Many of these songs, such as "Proud Mary" and "Bertha," don't exist on tape and will probably never again be heard by fans. Still, they are all listed here to provide a historical perspective on the band's development. And lest fans think that all those early songs were throw-aways, six monster jam vehicles debuted back then: "Slave," "Mike's Song," "McGrupp," "Antelope," "Harry Hood," and "Possum."

Listening to the few tapes that exist from this era provide a snapshot of the early years. You can listen to an older version of "Slave," "Possum," "Makisupa," or "Antelope" and be amazed at how the song has evolved. You can listen to a fun cover like "Wild Child" or "Melt the Guns" and wonder

why it hasn't been played since the 80's. And you can listen to a song like "Prep School Hippie" and laugh at the fun the band has always had on stage. Landmark gigs included 12/1/84 (upstairs at Nectar's) and 10/30/85 (an early Hunt's show with the first known Harry Hood). Perhaps the most important Phishtorical event of this period, though, was the 11/23/85 gig in the cafeteria at Goddard College. It was during this show that Mike had his famous musical epiphany and realized that music was his calling. A close second is 5/3/85, where Page sat in for a few songs and made his first musical contribution to Phish.

Fun is a definite element of these early shows. The band seemingly knew the entire audience at every gig; song dedications and inside jokes were the norm. Stage banter was abound, as the band frequently told stories and kidded amongst themselves. Seek out these early shows. Listen to the band as, in their musical infancy, they began to lay the eggs that would eventually hatch into music history. Know, though, that the "debuts" listed below will probably never be completely verified, as there are many early gigs about which no information can be gleaned. Witness, for example, the early shows at Doolin's, where not a single setlist is known.

DEBUTS (1983 - 1985)

Long Cool Woman in a Black Dress	12/2/1983
Proud Mary	12/2/1983
In the Midnight Hour	12/2/1983
Squeeze Box	12/2/1983
Roadhouse Blues	12/2/1983
Scarlet Begonias	12/2/1983
Fire	12/2/1983
Makisupa Policeman	10/23/1984
Wild Child	11/3/1984
Bertha	11/3/1984
Can't You Hear Me Knockin'	11/3/1984
Camel Walk	11/3/1984
Eyes of the World	11/3/1984
Whipping Post	11/3/1984
Fire on the Mountain	12/1/1984
Spanish Flea	12/1/1984
Don't Want You No More	12/1/1984
Cities	12/1/1984
Skippy the Wondermouse	12/1/1984
Fluffhead	12/1/1984
Slave to the Traffic Light	12/1/1984
Anarchy	3/4/1985
Fire up the Ganja	3/4/1985
Mike's Song	5/3/1985
Dave's Energy Guide	5/3/1985
Big Leg Emma	5/3/1985
Alumni Blues	5/3/1985
Bring it On Home	5/3/1985
McGrupp	5/3/1985
Run Like an Antelope	5/3/1985
The Other One	5/3/1985
Sneakin' Sally	9/27/1985

DEBUTS (1983 - 1985) continued

Prep School Hippie	9/27/1985
Dear Mrs. Reagan	9/27/1985
Melt the Guns	9/27/1985
Revolution	10/17/1985
Harry Hood	10/30/1985
Dog Gone Dog	10/30/1985
Possum	10/30/1985
I Wish	10/30/1985
Revival	10/30/1985
Hurricane	11/14/1985
Wild Thing	11/23/1985

DEPARTURES (1983 - 1985)

	LAST KNOWN	# SHOWS
Proud Mary	12/2/1983	1119
Roadhouse Blues	12/2/1983	1119
Squeeze Box	12/2/1983	1119
Bertha	11/3/1984	1117
Don't Want You No More	12/1/1984	1116
Fire On The Mountain	12/1/1984	1116
Spanish Flea	12/1/1984	1116
Fire up the Ganja	3/4/1985	1115
In the Midnight Hour	3/4/1985	1115
Bring it On Home	5/3/1985	1114
Can't You Hear Me Knockin'	5/3/1985	1114
Eyes of the World	5/3/1985	1114
Scarlet Begonias	5/3/1985	1114
The Other One	5/3/1985	1114
I Wish	10/30/1985	1111
Revival	10/30/1985	1111
Skippy the Wondermouse	10/30/1985	1111
Hurricane	11/14/1985	1110
Wild Thing	11/23/1985	1109

1986

"Hanging at Hunt's"

Although the band's first known appearance at Hunt's was on March 4, 1985, the bulk of the band's gigs there were in 1986. Playing there gave the band a greater legitimacy while allowing them to maintain the intimate relationships they had developed with their fans. Listen to 4/1/86 and 10/15/86 for examples. The former included versions of many future concert staples; the latter was Paul Languedoc's first as soundman and only hinted at the great influence he would eventually have on the band's sound.

Several landmark songs debuted in 1986. Most notable are "You Enjoy Myself," "Golgi Apparatus," and the quirky "Sanity." Among cover songs, "Peaches en Regalia" and the oft-requested "Quinn the Eskimo" made their first appearances. Also, several songs from the not-yet-completed Gamehendge saga, including "Icculus," "AC/DC Bag," and "Wilson," were unveiled.

As the band's fan base grew, so did the nature of their live shows. 1986 brought us the first Halloween show, the first of three known appearances at Goddard's annual SpringFest (5/17/86, with the debut of "Halley's Comet"), a show at a hippie commune (9/26/86), and the first Phish show outside of Vermont (6/1/86, in Boston). Fans also witnessed the first New Year's Eve spectacular – sort of. Short on a band, a club tried to book The Joneses at the last minute and wound up with The Phones, a combination of the two groups!

DEBUTS (1986)

SONG	DEBUT
You Enjoy Myself	2/3/1986
Quinn the Eskimo	4/1/1986
Have Mercy	4/1/1986
The Pendulum	4/1/1986
Icculus	4/1/1986
Help on the Way	4/1/1986
Slipknot!	4/1/1986
AC/DC Bag	4/1/1986
Not Fade Away	4/1/1986
Halley's Comet	5/17/1986
Skin it Back	10/15/1986
I Am Hydrogen	10/15/1986
Lushington	10/15/1986
Peaches en Regalia	10/15/1986
Golgi Apparatus	10/15/1986
Swing Low Sweet Chariot	10/15/1986
Shaggy Dog	10/15/1986
Mustang Sally	10/15/1986
Wilson	10/15/1986
Roll Like a Cantaloupe	10/15/1986
Sanity	10/15/1986
Clod	10/15/1986
Back Porch Boogie Blues	10/31/1986
David Bowie	10/31/1986
Little Drummer Boy	12/6/1986
She Caught the Katy	12/6/1986
Tush	12/6/1986

DEPARTURES (1986)

	LAST KNOWN	# SHOWS
Help on the Way	4/1/1986	1107
Not Fade Away	4/1/1986	1107
Slipknot!	4/1/1986	1107
The Pendulum	4/1/1986	1107
Prep School Hippie	12/6/1986	1103

1987

"The Nectar's Days"

DEBUTS (1987)

SONG	DEBUT
Suzy Greenberg	2/13/1987
Good Times Bad Times	2/13/1987
Boogie On Reggae Woman	2/21/1987
Ya Mar	2/21/1987
Corrine Corrina	2/21/1987
Funky Bitch	3/6/1987
Freebird	3/6/1987
Tell Me Something Good	3/6/1987
Freeworld	3/6/1987
Sparks	3/23/1987
Ride Captain Ride	3/23/1987
Why Don't You Love Me	3/23/1987
Punch Me in the Eye	4/24/1987
Who Do? We Do!	4/24/1987
Fuck Your Face	4/29/1987
Take the A-Train	4/29/1987
Timber (Jerry)	4/29/1987
The Ballad of Curtis Loew	4/29/1987
Let the Good Times Roll	4/29/1987
TMWSIY	5/11/1987
Avenu Malkenu	5/11/1987
Letter to Jimmy Page	5/11/1987
La Grange	8/9/1987
The Chase	8/9/1987
The Curtain With	8/9/1987
The Sloth	8/9/1987
Light Up or Leave Me Alone	8/9/1987
Fee	8/9/1987
Harpua	8/9/1987
Divided Sky	8/9/1987
Flat Fee	8/9/1987

DEBUTS (1987) continued

SONG	DEBUT
I Know a Little	8/10/1987
Jesus Just Left Chicago	8/10/1987
Bundle of Joy	8/21/1987
BBFCFM	8/21/1987
Rocky Top	9/21/1987
Terrapin	9/21/1987
Phase Dance	9/27/1987
I Didn't Know	9/27/1987
Love You	10/31/1987
Dinner and a Movie	11/19/1987
Bike	11/19/1987

DEPARTURES (1987)

	LAST KNOWN	# SHOWS
Freeworld	3/6/1987	1100
Tell Me Something Good	3/6/1987	1100
Why Don't You Love Me	3/23/1987	1099
Punch Me in the Eye	4/24/1987	1098
Fuck Your Face	4/29/1987	1097
Let the Good Times Roll	4/29/1987	1097
Melt the Guns	4/29/1987	1097
Tush	8/10/1987	1093
Lushington	8/29/1987	1091
The Birthday Dub	9/21/1987	1089
Back Porch Boogie Blues	10/31/1987	1086

Having outgrown Hunt's, Phish moved on to regular shows at Nectar's in early 1987. The band's affinity for the venue and its owner would be evident in their 1992 major-label debut, *A Picture of Nectar* (complete with a picture of proprietor Nectar Rorris on the cover).

From a songwriting standpoint, three more of the songs that would comprise Trey's Gamehendge thesis were brought to the Phish stage. They were "The Sloth," "Divided Sky," and "The Man Who Stepped Into Yesterday." Other noteworthy debuts included "Suzie Greenberg," "Fee," "Harpua," "Dinner and a Movie," and most of the pieces that would eventually become "Fluff's Travels." Among long-standing covers, Phish introduced "Good Times Bad Times," "Ya Mar," "Funky Bitch," and "Jesus Just Left Chicago."

The most commonly circulated show from 1987 is 8/21/87, Ian's Farm. It is a wonderful keepsake and photograph of the era because it has a little bit of everything that made these four guys called "Phish": great jams, fun segues, off-the-cuff humor, and a barking dog taboot. Ian's was followed by a three-set show at Eric Larson's house just over a week later. These two shows proved the band's endurance and ability to wow fans with scores of material.

1988

"Welcome to Gamehendge"

The first known-show for 1988 was a sign of things to come: on 1/27/88, the band began a string of Wednesday night gigs at Gallagher's in Waitsfield, VT that continued to expand the fan base in their home state. These Gallagher's gigs were the first regular shows outside of Goddard and Burlington. And though Ian's Farm was in New York, Phish first played a New York bar in 1988 when they played Kenny's Castaways in New York City on 3/31/88.

Phish still played Nectar's, of course; often they played three-night runs. It was there, on 3/12/88, that the Gamehendge saga finally debuted in its entirety. "Tela" and "Colonel Forbin's Ascent" debuted that night; "Lizards" and "Mockingbird" had debuted earlier in the year.

Though we know little details about the show, the seeds of a long-stand standing bond were formed when Phish played at John Paluska's co-op house, The Zoo, at Amherst on 4/2/98. Paluska, of course, went on to co-found Phish's management arm, Dionysian Productions, with Ben Hunter. Later in the year, on 9/24/88, Phish played The Zoo again and even dedicated a song to Paluska.

Phish summer festivals didn't really start until Amy's Farm in 1991, but the band came close in 1988 with a show known as "Pete's Phabulous Phish Phest." Fans first felt the "Weekapaug Groove" on this night (7/23/88); Phish played the then-traditional "Mike's" / "Hydrogen" / "Weekapaug" combination at this show and the following two to get it out there.

The summer brought Phish to Colorado for the first time. It was an infamous trip that has been documented in many places; sadly, though, tapes are hard to come by for most shows and setlists are unknown. The 7/30/88 performance is a classic, though, with Fishman missing most of the first two sets while exploring the mountains nearby. Upon returning, Phish closed the year with famous performances at Penn State (8/27/88) and a few at The Front, as well as their third Halloween show.

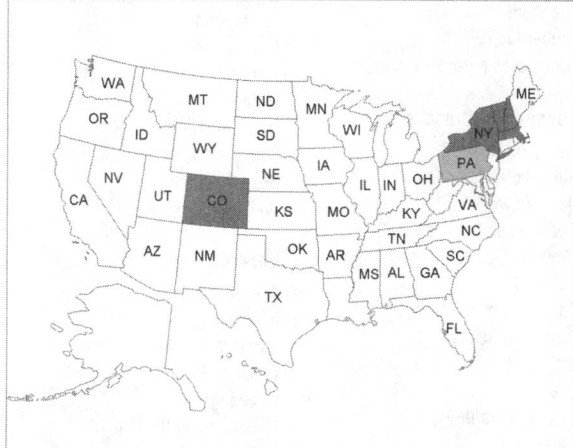

DEBUTS (1988)

SONG	DEBUT
The Lizards	1/27/1988
The Famous Mockingbird	2/7/1988
The Curtain	2/7/1988
The Chicken	3/11/1988
Jump Monk	3/12/1988
Tela	3/12/1988
Colonel Forbin's Ascent	3/12/1988
St. Thomas	5/21/1988
Contact	6/15/1988
Satin Doll	6/20/1988
On Your Way Down	6/24/1988
Bold As Love	7/11/1988
Blue Bossa	7/12/1988
Weekapaug Groove	7/23/1988
Walk Away	7/23/1988

DEBUTS (1988) continued

SONG	DEBUT
No Dogs Allowed	7/23/1988
All Blues	7/30/1988
Mr. P.C.	7/30/1988
Baby Left Me	7/30/1988
Maiden Voyage	7/30/1988
The Practical Song	9/12/1988
Esther	9/12/1988
Andy's Chest	9/13/1988
Time Loves a Hero	10/31/1988
Foam	11/3/1988
Mr. P.C.	11/11/1988

DEPARTURES (1988)

	LAST KNOWN	# SHOWS
Phase Dance	2/26/1988	1079
The Chicken	3/11/1988	1078
Jump Monk	3/12/1988	1077
St. Thomas	5/21/1988	1070
Big Leg Emma	6/19/1988	1067
Mustang Sally	6/21/1988	1065
Blue Bossa	7/23/1988	1061
Skin It Back	7/25/1988	1059
Baby Left Me	7/30/1988	1058
Maiden Voyage	7/30/1988	1058
I Know a Little	8/3/1988	1057
Wild Child	9/8/1988	1054
Andy's Chest	9/13/1988	1052
Mr. P.C.	11/11/1988	1045

There were 41 shows played

Shows by day of week

- Sunday- 4
- Monday- 7
- Tuesday- 3
- Wednesday- 5
- Thursday- 4
- Friday- 6
- Saturday- 12

95 songs have been played (15% of songs Phish have played).

The average number of songs per show is 17.1.

The average amount of times each song was played is 7.41.

Total Times Played

The Lizards - 28 (68%)
You Enjoy Myself - 28 (68%)
Golgi Apparatus - 27 (65%)
Fluffhead - 26 (63%)
Alumni Blues - 23 (56%)
Possum - 21 (51%)
AC/DC Bag - 20 (48%)
Fire - 20 (48%)
Good Times Bad Times - 19 (46%)
Take the A-Train - 19 (46%)

Fee - 17 (41%)
Suzy Greenberg - 17 (41%)
I Didn't Know - 16 (39%)
Peaches En Regalia - 15 (36%)
Wilson - 14 (34%)
David Bowie - 13 (31%)
Funky Bitch - 13 (31%)
Bold As Love - 12 (29%)
La Grange - 12 (29%)
Run Like an Antelope - 12 (29%)
Slave to the Traffic Light - 12 (29%)
Sneakin' Sally through the Alley - 12 (29%)
The Famous Mockingbird - 12 (29%)
Colonel Forbin's Ascent - 11 (26%)
Walk Away - 11 (26%)
Whipping Post - 11 (26%)
McGrupp and the Watchful Hosemasters - 10 (24%)
Big Black Furry Creature From Mars - 9 (21%)
Harry Hood - 9 (21%)
Jesus Just Left Chicago - 9 (21%)
Mike's Song - 9 (21%)
The Ballad of Curtis Loew - 9 (21%)
The Curtain - 9 (21%)
Contact - 8 (19%)
Divided Sky - 8 (19%)

Harpua - 8 (19%)
The Sloth - 8 (19%)
Cities - 7 (17%)
Dinner and a Movie - 7 (17%)
I Am Hydrogen - 7 (17%)
Satin Doll - 7 (17%)
Flat Fee - 6 (14%)
On Your Way Down - 6 (14%)
Timber (Jerry) - 6 (14%)
Weekapaug Groove - 6 (14%)
Corrine Corrina - 5 (12%)
Jam - 5 (12%)
Shaggy Dog - 5 (12%)
Avenu Malkenu - 4 (9%)
Dear Mrs. Reagan - 4 (9%)
Halley's Comet - 4 (9%)
Rocky Top - 4 (9%)
Sanity - 4 (9%)
Tela - 4 (9%)
The Man Who Stepped Into
    Yesterday - 4 (9%)
Bike - 3 (7%)
Camel Walk - 3 (7%)
Dave's Energy Guide - 3 (7%)
Foam - 3 (7%)
Happy Birthday - 3 (7%)
Icculus - 3 (7%)
Light Up Or Leave Me Alone
    - 3 (7%)
Mustang Sally - 3 (7%)
Phase Dance - 3 (7%)
Time Loves a Hero - 3 (7%)
Ya Mar - 3 (7%)
Big Leg Emma - 2 (4%)
Blue Bossa - 2 (4%)
Boogie on Reggae Woman - 2 (4%)
I Know a Little - 2 (4%)
Makisupa Policeman - 2 (4%)
Mr. P.C. - 2 (4%)
Sparks - 2 (4%)
Terrapin - 2 (4%)
The Curtain With - 2 (4%)
The Man Who Stepped Into
    Yesterday Reprise - 2 (4%)
All Blues - 1 (2%)
Anarchy - 1 (2%)
Andy's Chest - 1 (2%)
Baby Left Me - 1 (2%)
Bundle of Joy - 1 (2%)
Clod - 1 (2%)
Costume Contest - 1 (2%)
Esther - 1 (2%)
Jump Monk - 1 (2%)
Maiden Voyage - 1 (2%)
No Dogs Allowed - 1 (2%)
Ride Captain Ride - 1 (2%)
Roll Like a Cantaloupe - 1 (2%)
Skin It Back - 1 (2%)

St. Thomas - 1 (2%)
The Chicken - 1 (2%)
The Practical Song - 1 (2%)
Vacuum Jam - 1 (2%)
Wild Child - 1 (2%)

First Set Openers

Fire - 4
Slave to the Traffic Light - 3
Funky Bitch - 2
I Didn't Know - 2
Satin Doll - 2
Suzy Greenberg - 2
The Curtain - 2
The Curtain With - 2
Walk Away - 2
All Blues - 1
Alumni Blues - 1
Cities - 1
Colonel Forbin's Ascent - 1
Divided Sky - 1
Fluffhead - 1
Golgi Apparatus - 1
Good Times Bad Times - 1
Jam - 1
La Grange - 1
McGrupp and the Watchful
    Hosemasters - 1
Peaches En Regalia - 1
Shaggy Dog - 1
The Chicken - 1
The Lizards - 1
The Sloth - 1

First Set Closers

David Bowie - 6
Bold As Love - 4
Fire - 4
Good Times Bad Times - 4
You Enjoy Myself - 3
I Didn't Know - 2
The Famous Mockingbird - 2
Alumni Blues - 1
Fluffhead - 1
Golgi Apparatus - 1
Harpua - 1
Harry Hood - 1
La Grange - 1
Mr. P.C. - 1
No Dogs Allowed - 1
Possum - 1
Take the A-Train - 1
Tela - 1
Wilson - 1

Second Set Openers

Fluffhead - 2

I Didn't Know - 2
Mike's Song - 2
The Lizards - 2
Wilson - 2
Alumni Blues - 1
Blue Bossa - 1
David Bowie - 1
Funky Bitch - 1
Golgi Apparatus - 1
Good Times Bad Times - 1
Halley's Comet - 1
Happy Birthday - 1
Harpua - 1
I Know a Little - 1
Icculus - 1
Jesus Just Left Chicago - 1
Jump Monk - 1
La Grange - 1
Light Up Or Leave Me Alone - 1
Mustang Sally - 1
Possum - 1
Ride Captain Ride - 1
Sneakin' Sally through the Alley - 1
The Sloth - 1
Timber (Jerry) - 1
Time Loves a Hero - 1

Second Set Closers

Whipping Post - 7
Run Like an Antelope - 4
David Bowie - 3
Good Times Bad Times - 3
Fluffhead - 2
Cities - 1
Corrine Corrina - 1
Dear Mrs. Reagan - 1
Esther - 1
Fire - 1
Golgi Apparatus - 1
Harpua - 1
Harry Hood - 1
Jesus Just Left Chicago - 1
Peaches En Regalia - 1
Roll Like a Cantaloupe - 1

Slave to the Traffic Light - 1
Wilson - 1

Third Set Openers

Suzy Greenberg - 2
The Sloth - 2
Big Leg Emma - 1
Fee - 1
Fluffhead - 1
Good Times Bad Times - 1
Jam - 1
La Grange - 1
Peaches En Regalia - 1
Skin It Back - 1
The Man Who Stepped Into
    Yesterday - 1
You Enjoy Myself - 1

Third Set Closers

Run Like an Antelope - 3
Good Times Bad Times - 2
AC/DC Bag - 1
Big Black Furry Creature From
    Mars - 1
David Bowie - 1
Fire - 1
Fluffhead - 1
Harry Hood - 1
Sanity - 1
Suzy Greenberg - 1
Walk Away - 1

Encores

Fire - 2
Icculus - 2
Camel Walk - 1
Divided Sky - 1
La Grange - 1
McGrupp and the Watchful
    Hosemasters - 1
Run Like an Antelope - 1
Sparks - 1
Suzy Greenberg - 1

1989

"Up at The Front"

As with 1988, Phish kicked off 1989 with a bang. They opened their year with a week-long string of shows in Maine, Massachusetts, and New Hampshire. Outside of the disastrous Colorado run, it was their first real "tour" outside of Vermont. The pinnacle of the trip was the famed Paradise show

in Boston on 1/26/89, where the band rented out the venue from its skeptical managers and proceeded to pack the club with fans who drove in on rented buses.

Several Phish staples first hit the stage in 1989, including "The Mango Song," "My Sweet One," "The Oh Kee Pa Ceremony," and "Lawn Boy." These debuts, though strong, have to be considered second fiddle to the trio of jam monsters that emerged: "Split Open and Melt," "Bathtub Gin," "and "Reba."

Phish continued to play Nectar's, though they turned more and more often to The Front. Once again, Phish outgrew a Burlington bar, and played their last known show at Nectar's on 3/14/89. The early Front shows uphold the Nectar's magic and legacy, though; see 2/7/89 (hot "Sloth" -> "Possum"), 3/30/89 (fun "You Enjoy Myself" to commemorate Chris Kuroda's first full show on lights), and 8/17/89. Phish played the famous Wetlands in New York City for the first time on 3/4/89 and added three more dates during the year, including the well-circulated 10/26/89. Phish also added regular gigs at The Stone Church in Newmarket, NH. Ian threw another grand party on 5/28/89, allowing Phish (along with their friends Ninja Custodian) to play a three-set classic. And Phish ventured north of the border for the first time, playing the Montreal International Jazz Festival on 7/1/89. 1989 closed with the first true New Year's performance, rounding out the decade in Boston.

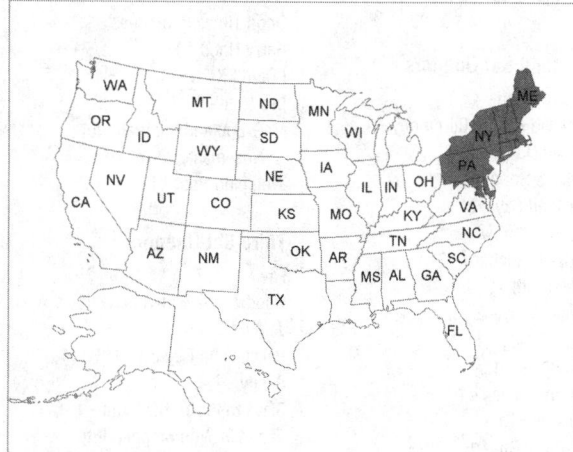

DEBUTS (1989)

SONG	DEBUT
Split Open and Melt	2/17/1989
If I Only Had a Brain	3/12/1989
The Price of Love	3/30/1989
The Mango Song	3/30/1989
Undun	3/30/1989
Donna Lee	5/5/1989
If I Don't Be There by Morning	5/9/1989
Nowhere Fast	5/9/1989
I've Turned Bad	5/9/1989
Buried Alive	5/12/1989
The Asse Festival	5/12/1989
Dazed and Confused	5/21/1989
Bathtub Gin	5/26/1989
The Oh Kee Pa Ceremony	8/17/1989
Punch You in the Eye	8/17/1989
Fishing Hole Theme	8/26/1989

DEBUTS (1989)

SONG	DEBUT
My Sweet One	9/9/1989
Reba	10/1/1989
Highway to Hell	10/1/1989
In a Hole	10/20/1989
Kung	10/31/1989
Frankenstein	11/11/1989
Lawn Boy	11/30/1989
Auld Lang Syne	12/30/1989

DEPARTURES (1989)

	LAST KNOWN	# SHOWS
Dear Mrs. Reagan	1/18/1989	1042
All Blues	2/6/1989	1039
I've Turned Bad	5/9/1989	1020
If I Don't Be There by Morning	5/9/1989	1020
Nowhere Fast	5/9/1989	1020
Dazed and Confused	5/21/1989	1016
The Practical Song	5/26/1989	1015
The Price of Love	5/28/1989	1013
Fishing Hole Theme	8/26/1989	1007
Anarchy	10/14/1989	998
Fishman's Gull Poem	10/26/1989	994
The Chase	10/26/1989	994
Bundle of Joy	11/3/1989	990
Clod	11/10/1989	988
Undun	12/7/1989	981
Who Do? We Do!	12/8/1989	980
In a Hole	12/16/1989	977

There were 69 shows played

Shows by day of week

- Sunday- 8
- Monday- 2
- Tuesday- 4
- Wednesday- 3
- Thursday- 14
- Friday- 18
- Saturday- 20

104 songs have been played (16% of songs Phish have played).

The average number of songs per show is 16.6.

The average amount of times each song was played is 11.03.

Total Times Played

You Enjoy Myself - 50 (72%)
AC/DC Bag - 49 (71%)
Possum - 41 (59%)
I Am Hydrogen - 39 (56%)
Mike's Song - 39 (56%)
Weekapaug Groove - 39 (56%)
Golgi Apparatus - 37 (53%)
Divided Sky - 36 (52%)

The Lizards - 32 (46%)
Run Like an Antelope - 30 (43%)
David Bowie - 29 (42%)
Fee - 28 (40%)
Ya Mar - 27 (39%)
Split Open and Melt - 25 (36%)
Suzy Greenberg - 25 (36%)
The Oh Kee Pa Ceremony
    - 25 (36%)
Foam - 24 (34%)
Bathtub Gin - 23 (33%)
Contact - 23 (33%)
I Didn't Know - 22 (31%)
Alumni Blues - 21 (30%)
Good Times Bad Times - 21 (30%)
Take the A-Train - 20 (28%)
The Sloth - 20 (28%)
Colonel Forbin's Ascent - 18 (26%)
Harry Hood - 17 (24%)
McGrupp and the Watchful
    Hosemasters - 17 (24%)
La Grange - 16 (23%)
My Sweet One - 16 (23%)
The Famous Mockingbird - 16
    (23%)
Fluffhead - 14 (20%)
Reba - 14 (20%)
Wilson - 14 (20%)

Highway To Hell - 13 (18%)
Walk Away - 13 (18%)
Dinner and a Movie - 12 (17%)
Bold As Love - 11 (15%)
Slave to the Traffic Light - 11 (15%)
Esther - 10 (14%)
Fire - 10 (14%)
Lawn Boy - 9 (13%)
If I Only Had a Brain - 8 (11%)
In a Hole - 8 (11%)
The Curtain - 8 (11%)
Who Do? We Do! - 8 (11%)
Funky Bitch - 7 (10%)
Harpua - 7 (10%)
Peaches En Regalia - 7 (10%)
Rocky Top - 7 (10%)
Donna Lee - 6 (8%)
Punch You In The Eye - 6 (8%)
Sanity - 6 (8%)
Whipping Post - 6 (8%)
Avenu Malkenu - 5 (7%)
Big Black Furry Creature From
    Mars - 5 (7%)
Bundle of Joy - 5 (7%)
The Man Who Stepped Into
    Yesterday - 5 (7%)
The Mango Song - 5 (7%)
Frankenstein - 4 (5%)
Makisupa Policeman - 4 (5%)
On Your Way Down - 4 (5%)
Undun - 4 (5%)
Bike - 3 (4%)
Halley's Comet - 3 (4%)
No Dogs Allowed - 3 (4%)
Rhombus Narration - 3 (4%)
Tela - 3 (4%)
The Chase - 3 (4%)
Timber (Jerry) - 3 (4%)
Corrine Corrina - 2 (2%)
Fluff's Travels - 2 (2%)
Happy Birthday - 2 (2%)
Icculus - 2 (2%)
Jesus Just Left Chicago - 2 (2%)
Kung - 2 (2%)
Love You - 2 (2%)
Satin Doll - 2 (2%)
Sneakin' Sally through the Alley
    - 2 (2%)
The Ballad of Curtis Loew - 2 (2%)
The Price of Love - 2 (2%)
All Blues - 1 (1%)
Anarchy - 1 (1%)
Auld Lang Syne - 1 (1%)
Buried Alive - 1 (1%)
Camel Walk - 1 (1%)
Clod - 1 (1%)
Dazed and Confused - 1 (1%)
Dear Mrs. Reagan - 1 (1%)

Dog Gone Dog - 1 (1%)
Fishing Hole Theme - 1 (1%)
Fishman's Gull Poem - 1 (1%)
I've Turned Bad - 1 (1%)
If I Don't Be There by Morning
    - 1 (1%)
Jam - 1 (1%)
La Grange Jam - 1 (1%)
Nowhere Fast - 1 (1%)
Ride Captain Ride - 1 (1%)
Swing Low Sweet Chariot - 1 (1%)
Terrapin - 1 (1%)
The Asse Festival - 1 (1%)
The Man Who Stepped Into
    Yesterday Reprise - 1 (1%)
The Practical Song - 1 (1%)
Who Knows Jam - 1 (1%)
You Shook Me All Night Long Jam
    - 1 (1%)

First Set Openers

AC/DC Bag - 7
I Didn't Know - 7
The Oh Kee Pa Ceremony - 7
Golgi Apparatus - 4
Bathtub Gin - 3
Bold As Love - 2
Dinner and a Movie - 2
Fee - 2
Mike's Song - 2
Take the A-Train - 2
The Curtain - 2
Wilson - 2
You Enjoy Myself - 2
Alumni Blues - 1
Bike - 1
Colonel Forbin's Ascent - 1
David Bowie - 1
Dear Mrs. Reagan - 1
Divided Sky - 1
Esther - 1
Fluff's Travels - 1
Fluffhead - 1
Foam - 1
Funky Bitch - 1
Harpua - 1
Harry Hood - 1
La Grange - 1
Possum - 1
Rhombus Narration - 1
Split Open and Melt - 1
Suzy Greenberg - 1
The Man Who Stepped Into
    Yesterday - 1
The Sloth - 1
Timber (Jerry) - 1
Whipping Post - 1
Ya Mar - 1

First Set Closers

Good Times Bad Times - 12
David Bowie - 9
Run Like an Antelope - 8
Possum - 5
Frankenstein - 4
Golgi Apparatus - 4
Weekapaug Groove - 4
Divided Sky - 3
You Enjoy Myself - 3
Contact - 2
Fluffhead - 2
Foam - 2
La Grange - 2
Big Black Furry Creature From
    Mars - 1
Dear Mrs. Reagan - 1
Harpua - 1
Highway To Hell - 1
Take the A-Train - 1
Terrapin - 1
Whipping Post - 1

Second Set Openers

Harry Hood - 4
The Oh Kee Pa Ceremony - 4
David Bowie - 3
Mike's Song - 3
Divided Sky - 2
I Didn't Know - 2
Suzy Greenberg - 2
The Sloth - 2
Walk Away - 2
AC/DC Bag - 1
All Blues - 1
Alumni Blues - 1
Anarchy - 1
Bathtub Gin - 1
Bike - 1
Bold As Love - 1
Dinner and a Movie - 1
Donna Lee - 1
Fee - 1
Fire - 1
Fishing Hole Theme - 1
Makisupa Policeman - 1
No Dogs Allowed - 1
On Your Way Down - 1
Possum - 1
Reba - 1
Run Like an Antelope - 1
Split Open and Melt - 1
Take the A-Train - 1
The Man Who Stepped Into
    Yesterday - 1
The Mango Song - 1
Who Knows Jam - 1

Wilson - 1
Ya Mar - 1
You Enjoy Myself - 1

Second Set Closers

David Bowie - 8
Golgi Apparatus - 5
Highway To Hell - 4
Possum - 4
Weekapaug Groove - 4
Run Like an Antelope - 3
The Lizards - 3
Bathtub Gin - 2
Contact - 2
Harpua - 2
Camel Walk - 1
Colonel Forbin's Ascent - 1
Divided Sky - 1
Fee - 1
Fire - 1
Fluffhead - 1
Foam - 1
Good Times Bad Times - 1
Harry Hood - 1
I Didn't Know - 1
In a Hole - 1
McGrupp and the Watchful
    Hosemasters - 1
Whipping Post - 1

Third Set Openers

Fire - 1
Good Times Bad Times - 1
Jam - 1
Peaches En Regalia - 1
Sanity - 1
Slave to the Traffic Light - 1
The Man Who Stepped Into
    Yesterday - 1
The Oh Kee Pa Ceremony - 1

Third Set Closers

Run Like an Antelope - 2
Corrine Corrina - 1
Good Times Bad Times - 1
Jesus Just Left Chicago - 1
Possum - 1
Rocky Top - 1
Whipping Post - 1

Encores

Contact - 6
Fire - 4
Golgi Apparatus - 4
Good Times Bad Times - 4
Highway To Hell - 4
Run Like an Antelope - 4

Possum - 3
David Bowie - 2
La Grange - 2
Lawn Boy - 2
The Lizards - 2
AC/DC Bag - 1
Auld Lang Syne - 1
Big Black Furry Creature From
   Mars - 1
Halley's Comet - 1
Harpua - 1
I Am Hydrogen - 1

I Didn't Know - 1
In a Hole - 1
Kung - 1
Makisupa Policeman - 1
Mike's Song - 1
Slave to the Traffic Light - 1
Take the A-Train - 1
The Practical Song - 1
Undun - 1
Weekapaug Groove - 1
Whipping Post - 1
You Enjoy Myself - 1

EARLY 1990

"Venturing South"

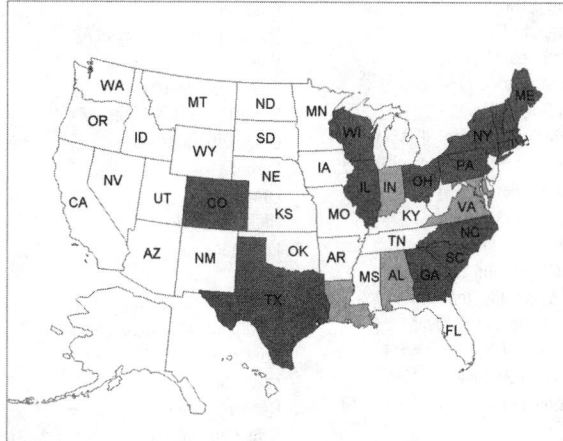

DEBUTS (Early 1990)

SONG	DEBUT
Carolina	1/20/1990
The Squirming Coil	1/20/1990
Caravan	1/20/1990
Bouncing Around the Room	1/20/1990
Communication Breakdown	1/27/1990
The Landlady	2/1/1990
Cavern	2/17/1990
Rift	2/25/1990
Tweezer	3/28/1990
Uncle Pen	3/28/1990
Runaway Jim	3/28/1990
Sweet Adeline	3/28/1990
How High the Moon	4/22/1990
Horn	5/24/1990

DEPARTURES (Early 1990)	LAST KNOWN	# SHOWS
No Dogs Allowed	4/21/1990	937

Goodbye, New England; hello, southeast! Phish first ventured down the Atlantic in early 1990, touring briefly in North and South Carolina, Georgia, and Virginia. Phish leveraged their friendship with jamband Widespread Panic, opening for Widespread (and getting to play to Panic's fanbase) on 2/2/90 and returning the favor for three northeastern shows later in the month. A second Colorado trip was taken in April; afterwards, the band wound through Indiana and Ohio before coming back home. At twenty-four days long, it was their longest "tour" ever. Phish returned south for a string of shows in May and June, building a rapport with Aquarium Rescue Unit, before ringing in the summer with another three-set masterpiece on 6/16/90.

At The Front on 3/9/90, Phish foreshadowed the 1991 horns tour when Dave Grippo guested on eight songs. It was, to date, the longest guest stint at a Phish show. Other notable guests in 1990 included John Popper and, of course, various members of the ARU.

From this era, 3/28/90 stands out as historically significant. Phish debuted four brand-new tunes that night, including fan-favorites "Tweezer" and "Runaway Jim." Other notable 1990 debuts were "Bouncing Around the Room," "The Squirming Coil," "Cavern," and the original "Rift."

FALL 1990

"The First Tour"

Phish had taken extended trips before, but the fall of 1990 seems to stand out as the first true tour in Phishtory. It coincided with the release of Phish's first real album, *Lawn Boy.* It began in earnest, as the band wheeled out nine new songs at the tour opener at The Wetlands. The highlights were "Stash" and "Tube," though other debuts included "Magilla" and "Paul and Silas" (sung, of course, as "Hall in Solace.") Over the rest of the tour, Phish would also introduce fans to "Gumbo," "Tweezer Reprise," and "Llama," as well as the bastard child "Destiny Unbound."

The band went down south for the third time, strengthening their fan base in Athens and Atlanta before heading to Louisiana and Texas for the first time. To reward the loyal Colorado fans, Halloween was held outside of Vermont for the first time. Also, Phish tried their first true New Year's Run, with three shows leading up to the 12/31 blockbuster in Boston.

DEBUTS (Fall 1990)

SONG	DEBUT
Tube	9/13/1990
Minute by Minute	9/13/1990
Paul and Silas	9/13/1990
Magilla	9/13/1990
Stash	9/13/1990
Going Down Slow	9/13/1990
Self	9/13/1990
Dahlia	9/13/1990
The Revolution's Over	9/13/1990
Destiny Unbound	9/14/1990
Eliza	9/15/1990
Tweezer Reprise	9/21/1990
Gumbo	9/28/1990
Don't Get Me Wrong	10/6/1990
Llama	10/30/1990
Manteca	11/4/1990
Memories	11/17/1990
No Good Trying	12/7/1990

DEPARTURES (Fall 1990)	LAST KNOWN	# SHOWS
Dahlia	9/13/1990	912
The Revolution's Over	9/13/1990	912
Going Down Slow	9/14/1990	911
Communication Breakdown	9/15/1990	910
Minute by Minute	9/15/1990	910
Don't Get Me Wrong	12/28/1990	880
No Good Trying	12/28/1990	880

There were 96 shows played

Shows by day of week

- Sunday- 11
- Monday- 7
- Tuesday- 3
- Wednesday- 8
- Thursday- 17
- Friday- 23
- Saturday- 27

108 songs have been played (17% of songs Phish have played).

The average number of songs per show is 18.9.

The average amount of times each song was played is 16.81.

Total Times Played

I Am Hydrogen - 68 (70%)
Mike's Song - 68 (70%)
Possum - 68 (70%)
Weekapaug Groove - 68 (70%)
Bouncing Around the Room - 67 (69%)
You Enjoy Myself - 60 (62%)
The Oh Kee Pa Ceremony - 59 (61%)
Suzy Greenberg - 53 (55%)
Divided Sky - 47 (48%)
Reba - 43 (44%)
The Lizards - 43 (44%)
Uncle Pen - 43 (44%)
Foam - 40 (41%)
Dinner and a Movie - 38 (39%)
Golgi Apparatus - 35 (36%)
My Sweet One - 35 (36%)
Run Like an Antelope - 34 (35%)
The Squirming Coil - 34 (35%)
The Landlady - 33 (34%)
Tweezer - 33 (34%)
AC/DC Bag - 31 (32%)
David Bowie - 28 (29%)
Carolina - 27 (28%)
Esther - 27 (28%)
Good Times Bad Times - 26 (27%)
Contact - 25 (26%)
Fee - 25 (26%)
I Didn't Know - 25 (26%)

Cavern - 24 (25%)
La Grange - 24 (25%)
Caravan - 23 (23%)
Runaway Jim - 23 (23%)
Ya Mar - 23 (23%)
Highway To Hell - 21 (21%)
Lawn Boy - 21 (21%)
Stash - 19 (19%)
Buried Alive - 18 (18%)
The Asse Festival - 18 (18%)
Bathtub Gin - 17 (17%)
Funky Bitch - 17 (17%)
The Sloth - 16 (16%)
Llama - 15 (15%)
Magilla - 15 (15%)
Harry Hood - 14 (14%)
Big Black Furry Creature From Mars - 13 (13%)
Jesus Just Left Chicago - 13 (13%)
Walk Away - 13 (13%)
Donna Lee - 12 (12%)
Fire - 12 (12%)
Fluffhead - 12 (12%)
If I Only Had a Brain - 12 (12%)
Paul and Silas - 12 (12%)
Sweet Adeline - 12 (12%)
Take the A-Train - 12 (12%)
Colonel Forbin's Ascent - 10 (10%)
Love You - 10 (10%)
Rocky Top - 10 (10%)
The Famous Mockingbird - 10 (10%)
Alumni Blues - 9 (9%)
Split Open and Melt - 9 (9%)
Wilson - 9 (9%)
Tela - 8 (8%)
Whipping Post - 8 (8%)
Terrapin - 7 (7%)
The Ballad of Curtis Loew - 7 (7%)
Tube - 7 (7%)
Rift - 6 (6%)
Destiny Unbound - 5 (5%)
Horn - 5 (5%)
Slave to the Traffic Light - 5 (5%)
Avenu Malkenu - 4 (4%)
Eliza - 4 (4%)
Gumbo - 4 (4%)
Harpua - 4 (4%)
McGrupp and the Watchful

Hosemasters - 4 (4%)
The Curtain - 4 (4%)
The Man Who Stepped Into Yesterday - 4 (4%)
Bold As Love - 3 (3%)
Communication Breakdown - 3 (3%)
Don't Get Me Wrong - 3 (3%)
No Good Trying - 3 (3%)
Rhombus Narration - 3 (3%)
Bike - 2 (2%)
Going Down Slow - 2 (2%)
Happy Birthday - 2 (2%)
How High the Moon - 2 (2%)
Jagermeister - 2 (2%)
Makisupa Policeman - 2 (2%)
Manteca - 2 (2%)
Minute by Minute - 2 (2%)
Auld Lang Syne - 1 (1%)
Dahlia - 1 (1%)
Dog Gone Dog - 1 (1%)
Fluff's Travels - 1 (1%)
Jam - 1 (1%)
Killer Joe - 1 (1%)
Memories - 1 (1%)
No Dogs Allowed - 1 (1%)
Ride Captain Ride - 1 (1%)
Roll Like a Cantaloupe - 1 (1%)
Satin Doll - 1 (1%)
Self - 1 (1%)
Sparks - 1 (1%)
The Man Who Stepped Into Yesterday Reprise - 1 (1%)
The Revolution's Over - 1 (1%)
Timber (Jerry) - 1 (1%)
Tweezer Reprise - 1 (1%)
Whole Lotta Love Jam - 1 (1%)

First Set Openers

Golgi Apparatus - 10
Suzy Greenberg - 7
The Landlady - 7
Possum - 6
Reba - 6
Buried Alive - 5
Carolina - 5
Divided Sky - 5
Dinner and a Movie - 4
Mike's Song - 4
Cavern - 2
David Bowie - 2
Foam - 2
I Didn't Know - 2
Runaway Jim - 2
Sweet Adeline - 2
Wilson - 2
AC/DC Bag - 1
Alumni Blues - 1

Bathtub Gin - 1
Colonel Forbin's Ascent - 1
Contact - 1
Don't Get Me Wrong - 1
Fluffhead - 1
Funky Bitch - 1
Harry Hood - 1
If I Only Had a Brain - 1
Llama - 1
Rocky Top - 1
Split Open and Melt - 1
Take the A-Train - 1
The Lizards - 1
The Man Who Stepped Into Yesterday - 1
The Sloth - 1
The Squirming Coil - 1
Uncle Pen - 1
Walk Away - 1

First Set Closers

Possum - 17
Run Like an Antelope - 17
Weekapaug Groove - 12
David Bowie - 10
Good Times Bad Times - 7
Golgi Apparatus - 5
Carolina - 4
Fire - 4
Highway To Hell - 2
La Grange - 2
Llama - 2
Suzy Greenberg - 2
Communication Breakdown - 1
Contact - 1
Lawn Boy - 1
Runaway Jim - 1
Sweet Adeline - 1
The Famous Mockingbird - 1
The Lizards - 1
The Squirming Coil - 1
You Enjoy Myself - 1

Second Set Openers

Golgi Apparatus - 7
Mike's Song - 5
Suzy Greenberg - 5
Possum - 4
Reba - 4
The Landlady - 4
Buried Alive - 3
Carolina - 3
Dinner and a Movie - 3
Funky Bitch - 3
The Squirming Coil - 3
Foam - 2
La Grange - 2
Llama - 2

Split Open and Melt - 2
The Asse Festival - 2
The Oh Kee Pa Ceremony - 2
AC/DC Bag - 1
Caravan - 1
Cavern - 1
Communication Breakdown - 1
David Bowie - 1
Divided Sky - 1
Fee - 1
Harpua - 1
Harry Hood - 1
How High the Moon - 1
I Didn't Know - 1
Killer Joe - 1
My Sweet One - 1
Run Like an Antelope - 1
Stash - 1
Sweet Adeline - 1
The Lizards - 1
The Sloth - 1
Uncle Pen - 1
Whipping Post - 1
Whole Lotta Love Jam - 1
Wilson - 1

Second Set Closers

Weekapaug Groove - 15
Good Times Bad Times - 8
David Bowie - 7
Run Like an Antelope - 7
You Enjoy Myself - 6
Possum - 5
Contact - 4
Divided Sky - 4
Big Black Furry Creature From
    Mars - 3
Golgi Apparatus - 3
Highway To Hell - 3
The Lizards - 3
Fire - 1
Funky Bitch - 1
Going Down Slow - 1
If I Only Had a Brain - 1
La Grange - 1
Lawn Boy - 1

Slave to the Traffic Light - 1
The Revolution's Over - 1
Tweezer Reprise - 1
Whipping Post - 1

Third Set Openers

La Grange - 1
Paul and Silas - 1
Third Set Closers
AC/DC Bag - 1
Weekapaug Groove - 1

Encores

Contact - 14
Good Times Bad Times - 8
Highway To Hell - 8
Big Black Furry Creature From
    Mars - 6
Carolina - 5
Fire - 5
Golgi Apparatus - 5
Lawn Boy - 5
Whipping Post - 5
I Didn't Know - 3
La Grange - 3
AC/DC Bag - 2
Caravan - 2
Jesus Just Left Chicago - 2
Paul and Silas - 2
Suzy Greenberg - 2
The Lizards - 2
Alumni Blues - 1
Bouncing Around the Room - 1
Communication Breakdown - 1
Divided Sky - 1
Don't Get Me Wrong - 1
Donna Lee - 1
Fluffhead - 1
Funky Bitch - 1
Memories - 1
Sweet Adeline - 1
The Asse Festival - 1
The Landlady - 1
The Oh Kee Pa Ceremony - 1
Uncle Pen - 1
You Enjoy Myself - 1

made, though Phish added Tennessee to their resume this time around. And after another Colorado jaunt (see 3/17/91 to hear how much fun the guys had), Phish broke into California with a memorable four night run. They weren't done canvassing the west coast, as they also toured Oregon, Wisconsin, Minnesota, Illinois, and Michigan.

Late April and early May saw Phish back home in the northeast, with ARU opening several shows. Sadly, Phish closed their final Burlington bar when they played their last show at The Front on 5/12/91.

Amid all this, Phish found time to debut new songs. "Chalk Dust Torture" and "Guelah Papyrus" made it out back in February; "Poor Heart" didn't come aboard until April. Also, though it wouldn't become "official" for another year, Phish continued to expand the Secret Language – see 2/19/91.

DEBUTS (Early 1991)

Guelah Papyrus	2/1/1991
Chalk Dust Torture	2/1/1991
Wipeout	4/15/1991
Setting Sail	4/20/1991
Poor Heart	4/22/1991

DEPARTURES (Early 1991)	LAST KNOWN	# SHOWS
The Asse Festival	4/27/1991	834

BREAKOUTS (Early 1991)	SHELVED	BREAKOUT	# SHOWS
The Mango Song	8/19/1989	2/1/1991	132
Slave to the Traffic Light	4/22/1990	3/17/1991	81
Dog Gone Dog	3/9/1990	4/2/1991	105
Icculus	5/1/1989	4/6/1991	178
Harpua	6/9/1990	4/18/1991	74
Bike	11/10/1990	5/17/1991	64

SUMMER 1991

"The Horns Tour"

It was only sixteen days long, but it sure was memorable. Billed as "The Giant Country Horns," Dave Grippo, Russ Remington, and Carl Gerhard joined Phish for fourteen shows that highlighted the band's flexibility. Also, given Trey's arrangement of the horn charts, it further proved their musical capability.

Though no new original songs were played, many old favorites got a facelift. Some, upon being augmented with horns, became songs that few could imagine without the GCH guesting. "Frankenstein" and "Gumbo" immediately come to mind, and both were brought back from brief hiatuses for the tour.

Of course, the cherry on top of the summer was the party at Amy Skelton's farm on 8/3/91. It was billed as a celebration for band and fans alike, and did not disappoint.

DEBUTS (Summer 1991)

Touch Me	7/11/1991
Moose the Mooch	7/12/1991
Bitchin' Again	8/3/1991
Crimes of the Mind	8/3/1991

WINTER 1991

"Expanding Exponentially"

Though more sporadic than the previous fall, Phish continued to expand their tour and explore new areas. The now-common southern swing was

DEPARTURES (Summer 1991)	LAST KNOWN	# SHOWS
Donna Lee	7/12/1991	821
Moose the Mooch	7/12/1991	821
Flat Fee	7/26/1991	810
Bitchin' Again	8/3/1991	808

BREAKOUTS (Summer 1991)	SHELVED	BREAKOUT	# SHOWS
Frankenstein	12/3/1989	7/11/1991	160
Flat Fee	9/13/1988	7/11/1991	230
Gumbo	11/30/1990	7/12/1991	63
Funky Bitch	12/28/1990	7/24/1991	68
Self	9/13/1990	8/3/1991	104

BREAKOUTS (Fall 1991)	SHELVED	BREAKOUT	# SHOWS
Memories	11/17/1990	9/26/1991	81
Eliza	11/24/1990	9/28/1991	82
Walk Away	5/24/1990	10/18/1991	131
Slave to the Traffic Light	3/17/1991	10/24/1991	67
Tube	11/16/1990	10/24/1991	100
Whipping Post	6/5/1990	10/28/1991	131
Roll Like a Cantaloupe	3/11/1990	11/14/1991	177
Bike	5/17/1991	11/20/1991	54

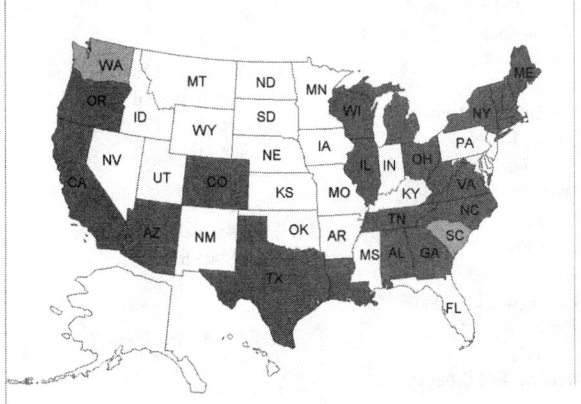

FALL 1991

"Laugh and Laughing"

Another trip to California and Colorado, the latter including another Halloween show. Debuts in Arizona and New Mexico. A southern swing, with more Aquarium Rescue Unit. And tons of great jams and teases. Phish was becoming one hell of a phenomenon – they were now conquering their territory instead of developing it.

Among debuts, "Sparkle" became the most regular rotation song to debut in the fall. It was joined by "Brother," "Sparkle," and "Glide." Development of the Secret Language continued (see 10/24/91 and 10/28/91 for easy examples). The band bid farewell, though, to the always-requested (beyond explanation) "Destiny Unbound."

Musical highlights were abound. Most notable is a fan-favorite "You Enjoy Myself" from 11/16/91.

DEBUTS (Fall 1991)

Brother	9/25/1991
It's Ice	9/25/1991
Sparkle	9/25/1991
All Things Reconsidered	9/25/1991
Glide	9/27/1991
Wait	10/31/1991
TV Show	11/8/1991
Family Picture	11/8/1991

DEPARTURES (Fall 1991)	LAST KNOWN	# SHOWS
Family Picture	11/8/1991	780
TV Show	11/8/1991	780
Roll Like a Cantaloupe	11/14/1991	775
Destiny Unbound	11/15/1991	774

There were 117 shows played

Shows by day of week

- Sunday- 14
- Monday- 5
- Tuesday- 9
- Wednesday- 13
- Thursday- 25
- Friday- 26
- Saturday- 25

115 songs have been played (18% of songs Phish have played).

The average number of songs per show is 22.3.

The average amount of times each song was played is 22.73.

Total Times Played

Cavern - 84 (71%)
The Landlady - 84 (71%)
My Sweet One - 79 (67%)
Llama - 76 (64%)
Bouncing Around the Room - 74 (63%)
The Squirming Coil - 73 (62%)
Golgi Apparatus - 71 (60%)

Foam - 68 (58%)
Chalk Dust Torture - 66 (56%)
Runaway Jim - 64 (54%)
Reba - 59 (50%)
Suzy Greenberg - 56 (47%)
Possum - 55 (47%)
I Am Hydrogen - 54 (46%)
Mike's Song - 54 (46%)
Weekapaug Groove - 54 (46%)
You Enjoy Myself - 53 (45%)
Divided Sky - 52 (44%)
Guelah Papyrus - 51 (43%)
Stash - 50 (42%)
The Oh Kee Pa Ceremony - 50 (42%)
David Bowie - 42 (35%)
Rocky Top - 41 (35%)
The Lizards - 41 (35%)
Fee - 39 (33%)
Buried Alive - 37 (31%)
Split Open and Melt - 37 (31%)
Dinner and a Movie - 36 (30%)
I Didn't Know - 36 (30%)
Tweezer - 36 (30%)
Poor Heart - 33 (28%)
Sparkle - 33 (28%)
The Sloth - 33 (28%)
Lawn Boy - 30 (25%)

Brother - 29 (24%)
Magilla - 27 (23%)
Love You - 26 (22%)
Sweet Adeline - 26 (22%)
Paul and Silas - 25 (21%)
Uncle Pen - 25 (21%)
Big Black Furry Creature From
    Mars - 23 (19%)
Run Like an Antelope - 23 (19%)
The Curtain - 23 (19%)
Fluffhead - 22 (18%)
Harry Hood - 22 (18%)
It's Ice - 22 (18%)
Bathtub Gin - 21 (17%)
Destiny Unbound - 21 (17%)
Esther - 21 (17%)
The Mango Song - 21 (17%)
Horn - 20 (17%)
The Man Who Stepped Into
    Yesterday - 19 (16%)
Tweezer Reprise - 19 (16%)
AC/DC Bag - 18 (15%)
Avenu Malkenu - 18 (15%)
Colonel Forbin's Ascent - 18 (15%)
Take the A-Train - 18 (15%)
The Man Who Stepped Into
    Yesterday Reprise - 18 (15%)
Contact - 17 (14%)
The Famous Mockingbird
    - 17 (14%)
Tela - 16 (13%)
Tube - 16 (13%)
Terrapin - 15 (12%)
Wilson - 15 (12%)
Memories - 12 (10%)
Ya Mar - 12 (10%)
Good Times Bad Times - 11 (9%)
Fire - 10 (8%)
Glide - 10 (8%)
Eliza - 9 (7%)
Jesus Just Left Chicago - 9 (7%)
Flat Fee - 8 (6%)
Touch Me - 8 (6%)
Gumbo - 7 (5%)
Alumni Blues - 6 (5%)
Caravan - 6 (5%)
Carolina - 6 (5%)
Frankenstein - 6 (5%)
Highway To Hell - 6 (5%)
McGrupp and the Watchful
    Hosemasters - 5 (4%)
Harpua - 4 (3%)
If I Only Had a Brain - 4 (3%)
La Grange - 4 (3%)
Funky Bitch - 3 (2%)
Whole Lotta Love Jam - 3 (2%)
Bike - 2 (1%)
Crimes of the Mind - 2 (1%)

Dog Gone Dog - 2 (1%)
Donna Lee - 2 (1%)
Drum Jam - 2 (1%)
Jam - 2 (1%)
Manteca - 2 (1%)
Self - 2 (1%)
Slave to the Traffic Light - 2 (1%)
The Asse Festival - 2 (1%)
Wait - 2 (1%)
Walk Away - 2 (1%)
Whipping Post - 2 (1%)
Wipeout - 2 (1%)
All Things Reconsidered - 1 (0%)
Auld Lang Syne - 1 (0%)
Bitchin' Again - 1 (0%)
Costume Contest - 1 (0%)
Crew Football Theme Song
    - 1 (0%)
Family Picture - 1 (0%)
HYHU Jam - 1 (0%)
Happy Birthday - 1 (0%)
Icculus - 1 (0%)
Moose the Mooch - 1 (0%)
Pusher Man Jam - 1 (0%)
Rhombus Narration - 1 (0%)
Rocky Mountain Way Jam - 1 (0%)
Roll Like a Cantaloupe - 1 (0%)
Setting Sail - 1 (0%)
TV Show - 1 (0%)

First Set Openers

Chalk Dust Torture - 13
Golgi Apparatus - 10
Llama - 10
Runaway Jim - 9
Buried Alive - 8
The Landlady - 7
The Oh Kee Pa Ceremony - 6
Cavern - 4
Memories - 4
My Sweet One - 4
The Curtain - 4
The Sloth - 4
Wilson - 4
AC/DC Bag - 2
Dinner and a Movie - 2
Divided Sky - 2
Possum - 2
Reba - 2
Suzy Greenberg - 2
Sweet Adeline - 2
Bouncing Around the Room - 1
Brother - 1
Carolina - 1
David Bowie - 1
Fluffhead - 1
Foam - 1
Glide - 1

Rocky Top - 1
The Man Who Stepped Into
    Yesterday - 1
The Mango Song - 1
Tube - 1
Uncle Pen - 1

First Set Closers

Golgi Apparatus - 20
David Bowie - 16
Weekapaug Groove - 14
Possum - 8
Llama - 7
Sweet Adeline - 7
Chalk Dust Torture - 5
You Enjoy Myself - 5
Run Like an Antelope - 4
Runaway Jim - 4
Cavern - 3
Rocky Top - 3
Fire - 2
Frankenstein - 2
Suzy Greenberg - 2
Big Black Furry Creature From
    Mars - 1
Divided Sky - 1
Harpua - 1
I Didn't Know - 1
La Grange - 1
Memories - 1
Setting Sail - 1
Take the A-Train - 1
The Famous Mockingbird - 1
The Landlady - 1
Touch Me - 1

Second Set Openers

Chalk Dust Torture - 11
Llama - 9
Golgi Apparatus - 8
Brother - 7
My Sweet One - 6
The Curtain - 6
Buried Alive - 5
Possum - 5
Tube - 5
David Bowie - 4
Suzy Greenberg - 4
The Landlady - 4
Tweezer - 4
Dinner and a Movie - 3
The Oh Kee Pa Ceremony - 3
The Sloth - 3
Divided Sky - 2
Harry Hood - 2
Mike's Song - 2
Runaway Jim - 2

The Squirming Coil - 2
AC/DC Bag - 1
Crew Football Theme Song - 1
Dog Gone Dog - 1
Foam - 1
It's Ice - 1
Paul and Silas - 1
Rocky Top - 1
Split Open and Melt - 1
Stash - 1
The Man Who Stepped Into
    Yesterday - 1
Wilson - 1
Wipeout - 1
Ya Mar - 1

Second Set Closers

Possum - 13
Tweezer Reprise - 12
Weekapaug Groove - 9
Golgi Apparatus - 8
Run Like an Antelope - 8
David Bowie - 7
Rocky Top - 7
Big Black Furry Creature From
    Mars - 5
Chalk Dust Torture - 5
You Enjoy Myself - 5
Cavern - 3
Good Times Bad Times - 3
Llama - 3
Suzy Greenberg - 3
Frankenstein - 2
Harry Hood - 2
Highway To Hell - 2
The Lizards - 2
Contact - 1
Crimes of the Mind - 1
Fire - 1
Guelah Papyrus - 1
Harpua - 1
Lawn Boy - 1
Memories - 1
Runaway Jim - 1
Sweet Adeline - 1
Touch Me - 1
Tweezer - 1

Third Set Openers

AC/DC Bag - 1
Stash - 1
Wilson - 1

Third Set Closers

Harry Hood - 1
Possum - 1
Weekapaug Groove - 1

Encores

Rocky Top - 20
Big Black Furry Creature From
    Mars - 17
Contact - 15
Lawn Boy - 12
Possum - 11
Sweet Adeline - 11
Golgi Apparatus - 9
Suzy Greenberg - 9
Fee - 8
Glide - 8
Good Times Bad Times - 8
Magilla - 8
Fire - 6
Memories - 6
Take the A-Train - 5
The Squirming Coil - 5
Tweezer Reprise - 5
Alumni Blues - 4
Highway To Hell - 4
Jesus Just Left Chicago - 4
Love You - 4
Runaway Jim - 4
Caravan - 3
Harry Hood - 3
Horn - 3
La Grange - 3
Uncle Pen - 3
Bouncing Around the Room - 2
Carolina - 2
Cavern - 2
Llama - 2

Split Open and Melt - 2
Terrapin - 2
The Oh Kee Pa Ceremony - 2
Touch Me - 2
You Enjoy Myself - 2
AC/DC Bag - 1
All Things Reconsidered - 1
Bitchin' Again - 1
Brother - 1
Chalk Dust Torture - 1
Crimes of the Mind - 1
Dinner and a Movie - 1
Eliza - 1
Frankenstein - 1
Gumbo - 1
I Didn't Know - 1
If I Only Had a Brain - 1
Manteca - 1
My Sweet One - 1
Paul and Silas - 1
Poor Heart - 1
Pusher Man Jam - 1
Reba - 1
Rocky Mountain Way Jam - 1
Run Like an Antelope - 1
Self - 1
Sparkle - 1
Stash - 1
The Curtain - 1
The Landlady - 1
Tweezer - 1
Walk Away - 1
Ya Mar - 1

4/16/92 through 4/21/92 as the key stretch, with nary a bad jam from any night, the true run of majesty included such moments as the 4/6/92 "Make Your Own Guacamole Cavern" and the 4/25/92 "Maze." The tide continued in May, with hot shows on 5/2/92 and 5/7/92 before winding up back in Burlington on May 18.

DEBUTS (Spring 1992)

Maze	3/6/1992
My Friend My Friend	3/6/1992
Mound	3/6/1992
NICU	3/6/1992
Sleeping Monkey	3/6/1992
My Mind's Got a Mind of its Own	3/7/1992
The Horse	3/7/1992
Silent in the Morning	3/7/1992
Weigh	3/7/1992
Cracklin' Rosie	3/7/1992
Baby Lemonade	3/11/1992
Catapult	4/17/1992
Lively Up Yourself	4/21/1992

DEPARTURES (Spring 1992)

DEPARTURES (Spring 1992)	LAST KNOWN	# SHOWS
Baby Lemonade	3/11/1992	758
Manteca Reprise	4/18/1992	730
Lively Up Yourself	4/21/1992	728
Eliza	5/14/1992	711
Wait	5/14/1992	711

BREAKOUTS (Spring 1992)

BREAKOUTS (Spring 1992)	SHELVED	BREAKOUT	# SHOWS
Rift	5/19/1990	3/6/1992	164
Sanity	5/28/1989	3/11/1992	255
Setting Sail	4/20/1991	3/25/1992	90
Icculus	4/6/1991	4/16/1992	113
Manteca	3/16/1991	4/18/1992	126
AC/DC Bag	11/1/1991	5/16/1992	74

SPRING 1992

"Speaking the Language"

For the first time since the fall of 1990, Phish had another full bag of brand new songs that they were itching to play. They gave us ten debuts in the first two days of the tour, including staples "Maze," "My Friend My Friend," "NICU," "Sleeping Monkey," "The Horse," "Silent in the Morning," and "Weigh." Also, "Rift" came back in a decidedly new fashion. And, of course, they clued us in to their Secret Language. Get these tapes and hear the band clue fans in on the joke and proceed to drop the Oom Pa Pa, Simpsons, All Fall Down, or Fingerscrape in just about every major jam vehicle.

From this tour forward, tapes of just about every show are available. There is no excuse to not have heard the 3/13/92 "Big Black Furry Antelope," or the 3/24/92 "David Bowie." These highlights, though, were just the prelude to what many continue the strongest stretch of shows in the early 90's: April 1992.

The month began inconspicuously, as the band was still getting comfortable with their new songs and playing along with the Language. By 4/6/92, the stretch of amazing shows was in full force. Though many cite

SUMMER 1992

"Opening Up"

Phish had opened for other bands before, but had never endured a stretch as an opening or supporting act. Phish had also played smaller festivals with other bands, but never huge events with multiple national headliners. And though they had been to Canada, Phish had yet to cross the Atlantic. All that changed in the summer of 1992.

The Phish summer began in Europe, playing festivals with artists ranging from Nirvana to Lou Reed. The 6/19/92 "You Enjoy Myself" stands out, but usually the band played short sets of mostly accessible material. Upon returning home on 7/9/92, the band played four shows on the inaugural HORDE tour before launching a mini-tour of three headlining shows in Virginia.

From there, it was off to play with Santana. 7/25/92 is a date etched in fans memories, as Carlos himself joined Phish during their set that day. Still, it is the six-week period as a whole that as important, as the band learned both music and life lessons from one of the world's most legendary gui-

tarists. Inbetween openers, Phish squeezed in a two-set show in California and an infamous appearance in the MTV studios.

DEBUTS (Summer 1992)

Blue Bayou	7/16/1992

DEPARTURES ((Summer 1992) LAST KNOWN   # SHOWS

	LAST KNOWN	# SHOWS
Blue Bayou	7/16/1992	693

BREAKOUTS (Summer 1992)SHELVED   BREAKOUT # SHOWS

	SHELVED	BREAKOUT	# SHOWS
Funky Bitch	10/15/1991	7/25/1992	107

FALL 1992

"Back on Tour"

Pregnant to jam, Phish returned to headlining in the fall of 1992. Perhaps the summer heat warped their minds; all songs that debuted that fall were just a bit off the beaten path (and more so than usual)! These debuts included "Axilla," "Lengthwise," "Buffalo Bill," and "Faht." The one delicate exception was "Fast Enough for You." Phish also introduced fans to two new participatory concepts: the "Big Ball Jam" and the "Vibration of Life."

Completing their world jaunts, the band wound up in Canada for the first time in over three years and headlined there for the first time. Though, at a month long, the tour was shorter than the summer's Santana festivities, it was packed with strong musical moments. See 11/27/92 and 11/28/92 for back-to-back winners in Port Chester, and 12/7/92 for good examples.

DEBUTS (Fall 1992)

Axilla	11/19/1992
I Walk the Line	11/19/1992
Big Ball Jam	11/19/1992
Fast Enough for You	11/19/1992
Lengthwise	11/19/1992
Buffalo Bill	11/21/1992
Faht	11/22/1992
Baby Elephant Walk	12/1/1992
The Vibration of Life	12/7/1992

DEPARTURES (Fall 1992)   LAST KNOWN   # SHOWS

	LAST KNOWN	# SHOWS
Self	11/20/1992	663

BREAKOUTS (Fall 1992))   SHELVED   BREAKOUT # SHOWS

	SHELVED	BREAKOUT	# SHOWS
Mound	5/8/1992	11/19/1992	51
Bold as Love	4/18/1990	11/19/1992	276
Tube	4/19/1992	11/20/1992	66
Self	11/8/1991	11/20/1992	117
Carolina	5/6/1992	11/21/1992	55
Bathtub Gin	5/12/1992	11/22/1992	51
Tela	5/9/1992	11/22/1992	53
Harpua	5/9/1992	11/28/1992	57
Contact	5/5/1992	11/28/1992	61
Fire	4/13/1992	11/30/1992	78
Whipping Post	12/6/1991	12/5/1992	112
If I Only Had a Brain	6/23/1992	12/12/1992	59
Ride Captain Ride	4/14/1990	12/12/1992	296

NEW YEAR'S 1992

"The First Gag"

Phish played New Year's Eve shows before, and had played extended runs leading up to the big event. But 1992 is usually regarded as the first "New Year's Run," with multiple shows geared around common events and large groups of fans touring to ring in the New Year with their favorite band. Phish rewarded these fans with the first "Timber" in 30 months and the first "Kung" chant in over three years, as well as a famed Dude of Life appearance for "Diamond Girl."

DEBUTS (NYE 1992)

Diamond Girl	12/31/1992

DEPARTURES (NYE 1992))   LAST KNOWN   # SHOWS

	LAST KNOWN	# SHOWS
Diamond Girl	12/31/1992	640

BREAKOUTS (NYE 1992)   SHELVED   BREAKOUT # SHOWS

	SHELVED	BREAKOUT	# SHOWS
Bike	5/7/1992	12/28/1992	73
Timber (Jerry)	6/16/1990	12/30/1992	272
Kung	11/2/1989	12/31/1992	351

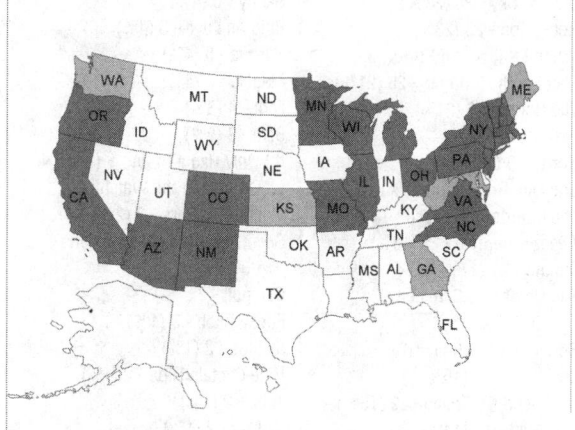

**There were 121 shows played
Shows by day of week**

- Sunday- 16
- Monday- 11
- Tuesday- 16
- Wednesday- 16
- Thursday- 18
- Friday- 22
- Saturday- 22

118 songs have been played (19% of songs Phish have played).

The average number of songs per show is 18.6.

The average amount of times each song was played is 19.10.

Total Times Played

Sparkle - 65 (53%)

Llama - 63 (52%)

Cavern - 58 (47%)

Bouncing Around the Room
   - 55 (45%)

Maze - 55 (45%)

Rift - 54 (44%)

Runaway Jim - 54 (44%)
Stash - 54 (44%)
Foam - 53 (43%)
The Squirming Coil - 51 (42%)
Poor Heart - 48 (39%)
You Enjoy Myself - 46 (38%)
Chalk Dust Torture - 45 (37%)
Reba - 45 (37%)
Suzy Greenberg - 45 (37%)
Guelah Papyrus - 42 (34%)
All Things Reconsidered
  - 41 (33%)
Golgi Apparatus - 41 (33%)
It's Ice - 41 (33%)
Sweet Adeline - 41 (33%)
The Landlady - 40 (33%)
Uncle Pen - 38 (31%)
David Bowie - 37 (30%)
Mike's Song - 35 (28%)
Possum - 35 (28%)
Weekapaug Groove - 35 (28%)
I Am Hydrogen - 34 (28%)
Split Open and Melt - 34 (28%)
Glide - 33 (27%)
Run Like an Antelope - 32 (26%)
My Sweet One - 31 (25%)
Tweezer - 29 (23%)
Divided Sky - 28 (23%)
Rocky Top - 28 (23%)
I Didn't Know - 26 (21%)
Silent in the Morning - 26 (21%)
The Horse - 26 (21%)
Fee - 25 (20%)
Horn - 25 (20%)
Cracklin' Rosie - 24 (19%)
The Lizards - 24 (19%)
Tweezer Reprise - 22 (18%)
Mound - 21 (17%)
The Oh Kee Pa Ceremony
  - 20 (16%)
Buried Alive - 19 (15%)
Love You - 19 (15%)
My Friend My Friend - 19 (15%)
Fluffhead - 18 (14%)
Harry Hood - 18 (14%)
Memories - 18 (14%)
Sleeping Monkey - 17 (14%)
Wilson - 17 (14%)
The Sloth - 16 (13%)
The Curtain - 15 (12%)
Carolina - 14 (11%)
Colonel Forbin's Ascent
  - 14 (11%)
Dinner and a Movie - 14 (11%)
The Famous Mockingbird
  - 14 (11%)
Brother - 13 (10%)
Take the A-Train - 13 (10%)
Terrapin - 13 (10%)

Big Ball Jam - 12 (9%)
Esther - 12 (9%)
Good Times Bad Times - 12 (9%)
Lawn Boy - 12 (9%)
NICU - 12 (9%)
Paul and Silas - 12 (9%)
Big Black Furry Creature From
  Mars - 10 (8%)
Weigh - 10 (8%)
Avenu Malkenu - 9 (7%)
Bathtub Gin - 9 (7%)
Fast Enough for You - 9 (7%)
Tela - 9 (7%)
The Man Who Stepped Into
  Yesterday - 9 (7%)
The Man Who Stepped Into
  Yesterday Reprise - 9 (7%)
Axilla - 8 (6%)
Contact - 8 (6%)
Fire - 8 (6%)
The Mango Song - 8 (6%)
I Walk the Line - 7 (5%)
Vacuum Solo - 7 (5%)
Eliza - 6 (4%)
Lengthwise - 6 (4%)
My Mind's Got a Mind of its
  Own - 6 (4%)
Sanity - 6 (4%)
Bold As Love - 5 (4%)
Harpua - 5 (4%)
Magilla - 5 (4%)
Faht - 4 (3%)
Bike - 3 (2%)
If I Only Had a Brain - 3 (2%)
McGrupp and the Watchful
  Hosemasters - 3 (2%)
Secret Language Instructions
  - 3 (2%)
Catapult - 2 (1%)
Funky Bitch - 2 (1%)
Icculus - 2 (1%)
Ride Captain Ride - 2 (1%)
Tube - 2 (1%)
Ya Mar - 2 (1%)
AC/DC Bag - 1 (0%)
Auld Lang Syne - 1 (0%)
Baby Elephant Walk - 1 (0%)
Baby Lemonade - 1 (0%)
Blue Bayou - 1 (0%)
Buffalo Bill - 1 (0%)
Crew Football Theme Song
  - 1 (0%)
Diamond Girl - 1 (0%)
Jam - 1 (0%)
Kung - 1 (0%)
Lively Up Yourself - 1 (0%)
Manteca - 1 (0%)
Manteca Reprise - 1 (0%)
Self - 1 (0%)

Setting Sail - 1 (0%)
The Vibration of Life - 1 (0%)
Timber (Jerry) - 1 (0%)
Wait - 1 (0%)
Whipping Post - 1 (0%)

First Set Openers
The Landlady - 17
Runaway Jim - 16
Suzy Greenberg - 13
Buried Alive - 11
Chalk Dust Torture - 10
Golgi Apparatus - 9
Llama - 7
Maze - 4
Poor Heart - 4
Rift - 4
The Curtain - 4
Wilson - 4
My Sweet One - 3
Axilla - 2
Glide - 2
All Things Reconsidered - 1
Bouncing Around the Room - 1
Brother - 1
Cavern - 1
Funky Bitch - 1
Reba - 1
Sparkle - 1
Stash - 1
Sweet Adeline - 1
The Oh Kee Pa Ceremony - 1
Uncle Pen - 1

First Set Closers
Run Like an Antelope - 29
David Bowie - 19
You Enjoy Myself - 9
Runaway Jim - 8
Cavern - 7
Golgi Apparatus - 7
Possum - 7
Sweet Adeline - 7
Llama - 6
Rocky Top - 5
Suzy Greenberg - 3
Weekapaug Groove - 3
Stash - 2
Carolina - 1
Chalk Dust Torture - 1
Funky Bitch - 1
Glide - 1
Good Times Bad Times - 1
I Didn't Know - 1
Memories - 1
The Landlady - 1
Tweezer Reprise - 1

Second Set Openers
Glide - 8

Suzy Greenberg - 6
Chalk Dust Torture - 5
Mike's Song - 5
The Curtain - 5
Axilla - 4
Poor Heart - 4
Runaway Jim - 4
The Landlady - 4
Buried Alive - 3
Dinner and a Movie - 3
Golgi Apparatus - 3
Llama - 3
Tweezer - 3
Wilson - 3
Maze - 2
My Sweet One - 2
Rift - 2
Sanity - 2
Brother - 1
Carolina - 1
David Bowie - 1
Memories - 1
My Friend My Friend - 1
Split Open and Melt - 1
The Oh Kee Pa Ceremony - 1
The Sloth - 1

Second Set Closers
Cavern - 18
Golgi Apparatus - 14
Tweezer Reprise - 10
Possum - 9
Runaway Jim - 5
Llama - 4
Suzy Greenberg - 4
Rocky Top - 3
Sweet Adeline - 2
You Enjoy Myself - 2
Cracklin' Rosie - 1
David Bowie - 1
Good Times Bad Times - 1
Maze - 1
Poor Heart - 1
Self - 1
Sleeping Monkey - 1
Weekapaug Groove - 1

Third Set Openers
Mike's Song - 1

Third Set Closers
Llama - 1

Encores
Rocky Top - 20
Sleeping Monkey - 16
Sweet Adeline - 15
Good Times Bad Times - 10
Memories - 10

Tweezer Reprise - 10
Carolina - 9
Fire - 8
Contact - 7
Big Black Furry Creature From
    Mars - 6
Lawn Boy - 6
Bold As Love - 5
Cavern - 4
Golgi Apparatus - 3
Possum - 3
Fee - 2
Ride Captain Ride - 2
Runaway Jim - 2
Suzy Greenberg - 2
The Squirming Coil - 2

Big Ball Jam - 1
Blue Bayou - 1
Bouncing Around the Room - 1
Buffalo Bill - 1
Chalk Dust Torture - 1
Harpua - 1
Harry Hood - 1
Horn - 1
I Didn't Know - 1
My Sweet One - 1
Poor Heart - 1
Sanity - 1
Take the A-Train - 1
The Oh Kee Pa Ceremony - 1
Vacuum Solo - 1
Weigh - 1

WINTER SPRING 1993

"Dusting a Few Off"

The most important debut of early 1993 wasn't a song; it was an instrument. Page wheeled out his new baby grand piano on 2/3/93 and the band debuted the beautiful Stones' classic "Loving Cup" to mark the occasion. Other debuts from this three month winter/spring stretch included "The Wedge," "Lifeboy," and "Sample in a Jar."

    The tour is also noteworthy for the number of songs that were played after extended absences. An amazing fifteen songs were played after being shelved for at least 100 shows; a few others fall just short. Many of these songs are numbers that fans can't imagine the band without, including "Ya Mar," "PYITE," "AC/DC Bag," "Jesus Just Left Chicago," "Halley's Comet," "Makisupa Policeman," and "Gumbo."

    The band was entering a crossroads that would stretch over the next eighteen months. They were playing larger venues and theatres, but trying

DEBUTS (Winter 1993)

Loving Cup	2/3/1993
The Wedge	2/3/1993
Lifeboy	2/3/1993
Amazing Grace	2/3/1993
Sample in a Jar	2/4/1993
Pig in a Pen	2/21/1993
It's My Life	3/2/1993
Loup Garou	3/2/1993
Choo Choo Ch' Boogie	3/2/1993
The Great Gig in the Sky	3/14/1993
You Gotta See Mama Every Night	3/16/1993
Help Me	4/10/1993
Hoochie Coochie Man	4/10/1993
When Something is Wrong	4/24/1993
Why You've Been Gone So Long	5/6/1993
Tennessee Waltz	5/6/1993
I Been to Georgia on a Fast Train	5/6/1993
That's Alright Mama	5/6/1993
Crossroads	5/8/1993

to retain the intimacy they had developed with their fans. Many of these shows are the last with engaging stage banter. With the loss of intimacy, though, came fuller sound and more monster sets. In the midst of a three-night Atlanta run, Phish played their first of many career "segue-fests" on 2/20/93. Landmark sets in Gunnison (3/14/93) and Santa Cruz (3/25/93) flanked the second ever Gamehendge narration (3/22/93). The somewhat forgotten 4/14/93 and 4/29/93 held down April, while the band closed the tour in May with hot shows in Philadelphia (5/2/93) and Albany (5/5/93) before a capstone Durham show on May 8.

DEPARTURES (Winter 1993)	LAST KNOWN	# SHOWS
Choo Choo Ch' Boogie	3/2/1993	618
It's My Life	3/2/1993	618
Loup Garou	3/2/1993	618
How High the Moon	3/8/1993	614
I Walk the Line	3/9/1993	613
You Gotta See Mama Every Night	3/16/1993	609
Help Me	4/10/1993	591
When Something is Wrong	4/30/1993	577
I Been to Georgia on a Fast Train	5/6/1993	572
That's Alright Mama	5/6/1993	572
Why You've Been Gone So Long	5/6/1993	572
Satin Doll	5/8/1993	570
Leprechaun	7/31/1993	554
The Ballad of Curtis Loew	8/2/1993	553

BREAKOUTS (Winter 1993)	SHELVED	BREAKOUT	# SHOWS
Punch You in the Eye	11/9/1989	2/5/1993	352
My Mind's Got a Mind of its Own	5/6/1992	2/7/1993	82
Catapult	4/21/1992	2/10/1993	95
Ya Mar	4/24/1992	2/12/1993	94
AC/DC Bag	5/16/1992	2/19/1993	83
Walk Away	11/2/1991	2/20/1993	157
Have Mercy	10/31/1986	2/20/1993	479
Manteca	4/18/1992	2/21/1993	106
Jesus Just Left Chicago	11/23/1991	3/5/1993	152
How High the Moon	4/26/1990	3/8/1993	320
The Ballad of Curtis Loew	10/30/1990	3/14/1993	285
Halley's Comet	8/17/1989	3/14/1993	400
Magilla	5/8/1992	3/25/1993	113
Icculus	5/2/1992	3/25/1993	118
Caravan	9/25/1991	4/5/1993	214
Tube	11/20/1992	4/12/1993	73
Highway to Hell	11/15/1991	4/12/1993	184
Satin Doll	2/25/1990	4/12/1993	370
Gumbo	7/25/1991	4/16/1993	223
Whipping Post	12/5/1992	4/20/1993	66
Makisupa Policeman	11/26/1990	4/29/1993	307
Take the A-Train	2/12/1993	5/5/1993	58

SUMMER 1993

"Raising the Bar"

Sometimes, a band takes a cover and makes it so identifiably "theirs" that fans can't comprehend that someone else wrote it. Enter "Also Sprach

Zarathustra," added for the summer 1993 tour. Other debuts included the hysterical "Purple Rain" and the short-lived but ridiculously complex "Leprechaun."

Summer 1993 was a tale of two months. July contained fun moments and interesting music, but things changed wholesale in Ybor on 8/2/93. Four incredibly rare songs were dusted off that night ("Brother," "Dog Log," "La Grange," and "Sparks.") A random rocker jumped on stage to belt out vocals. Lyrics were changed. Songs were teased. And, in some minds, a bar was set for the final month and fans continue to use the jams of August 1993 as a yardstick for comparison.

It's been said that every show from August of 1993 has several moments of musical merit. It's not a lie. The band was on fire. Highlights are too numerous to mention; the 8/13/93 Murat "Bathtub Gin," 8/14/93 Tinley Park "Antelope" medley, 8/15/93 "Tweezer," and 8/28/93 "You Enjoy Myself" are just the beginning. Phish also played Red Rocks for the first time, welcomed Bela Fleck and The Flecktones to the stage, and played a show with so many Simpsons Signals (8/11/93) that you would think they were possessed by Homer Simpson himself! All songs became fair game; even such unvarying songs as "It's Ice" were home to teases and Secret Language.

DEBUTS (Summer 1993)

Leprechaun	7/15/1993
Daniel	7/15/1993
Nellie Kane	7/16/1993
Also Sprach Zarathustra	7/16/1993
Yerushalayim Shel Zahav	7/16/1993
Purple Rain	7/16/1993
Bill Bailey Won't You Come Home	7/28/1993
Ginseng Sullivan	8/11/1993
Mice and Bats	8/26/1993

DEPARTURES (Summer 1993)

	LAST KNOWN	# SHOWS
Leprechaun	7/31/1993	554
The Ballad of Curtis Loew	8/2/1993	553
Mice and Bats	8/26/1993	535

BREAKOUTS (Summer 1993)

	SHELVED	BREAKOUT	# SHOWS
My Mind's Got a Mind of its Own	2/20/1993	7/15/1993	58
Faht	12/11/1992	7/15/1993	79
Freebird	3/6/1987	7/15/1993	533
The Mango Song	5/17/1992	7/24/1993	148
Brother	7/14/1992	8/2/1993	142
Dog Gone Dog	5/4/1991	8/2/1993	278
La Grange	3/17/1991	8/2/1993	302
Sparks	9/13/1990	8/2/1993	358
Slave to the Traffic Light	10/24/1991	8/6/1993	237
Memories	3/14/1993	8/9/1993	62
Crimes of the Mind	11/8/1991	8/9/1993	232
Bold As Love	2/26/1993	8/11/1993	73
The Wedge	3/25/1993	8/20/1993	62

NYE 1993

"Inside the Phish Tank"

Phish took their growing New Year's tradition a step further in 1993, adding an aquarium design to the stage. The band used the set as part of their New

Year's gag on 12/31/93 but the best musical present came a night earlier. In a show still regarded as one of the best ever, Phish wowed fans on 12/30/93 with a "Mike's Song" combo for the ages. Listen throughout all four shows as Phish played and teased "Peaches en Regalia" as a tribute to the late Frank Zappa, who passed away not long before the Run. No songs debuted (save the jam that foreshadowed "Down With Disease"), though the aforementioned "Peaches" was played for the first time in four-plus years.

DEBUTS (NYE 1993)

None	N/A

DEPARTURES (NYE 1993)

	LAST KNOWN	# SHOWS
None	N/A	N/A

BREAKOUTS (NYE 1993)

	SHELVED	BREAKOUT	# SHOWS
Peaches en Regalia	6/23/1989	12/28/1993	478

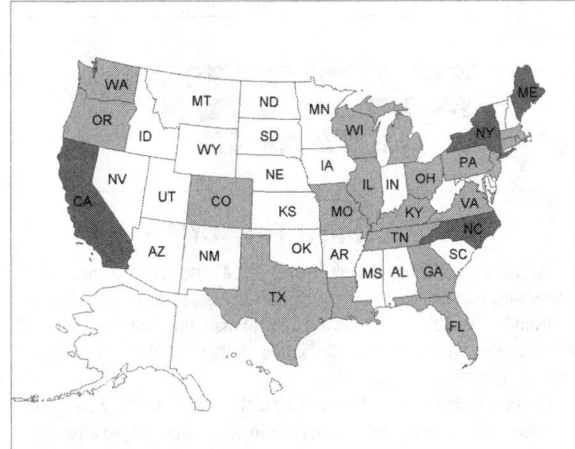

There were 109 shows played

Shows by day of week

- Sunday- 13
- Monday- 10
- Tuesday- 13
- Wednesday- 15
- Thursday- 16
- Friday- 21
- Saturday- 21

163 songs have been played (26% of songs Phish have played).

The average number of songs per show is 23.0.

The average amount of times each song was played is 15.39.

Total Times Played

Rift - 66 (60%)
Big Ball Jam - 62 (56%)
Sparkle - 58 (53%)
Poor Heart - 57 (52%)
It's Ice - 55 (50%)
Stash - 55 (50%)
Maze - 54 (49%)
Amazing Grace - 53 (48%)
You Enjoy Myself - 53 (48%)
Chalk Dust Torture - 51 (46%)
Cavern - 50 (45%)
Bouncing Around the Room - 47 (43%)
Golgi Apparatus - 47 (43%)
Llama - 46 (42%)
Split Open and Melt - 42 (38%)
Runaway Jim - 41 (37%)
The Squirming Coil - 41 (37%)
Guelah Papyrus - 40 (36%)
Mike's Song - 40 (36%)
Silent in the Morning - 39 (35%)
My Friend My Friend - 38 (34%)
Run Like an Antelope - 38 (34%)
Foam - 37 (33%)
The Horse - 37 (33%)
Tweezer - 37 (33%)
Weekapaug Groove - 35 (32%)
Mound - 34 (31%)

David Bowie - 33 (30%)
Fee - 33 (30%)
I Didn't Know - 33 (30%)
Uncle Pen - 33 (30%)
Divided Sky - 31 (28%)
Glide - 30 (27%)
Possum - 30 (27%)
Tweezer Reprise - 30 (27%)
Reba - 29 (26%)
The Lizards - 28 (25%)
Buried Alive - 27 (24%)
All Things Reconsidered - 25 (22%)
Lawn Boy - 24 (22%)
Sample in a Jar - 24 (22%)
I Am Hydrogen - 23 (21%)
Sweet Adeline - 23 (21%)
Also Sprach Zarathustra - 21 (19%)
Suzy Greenberg - 21 (19%)
Fluffhead - 20 (18%)
Horn - 20 (18%)
Paul and Silas - 20 (18%)
Rocky Top - 20 (18%)
Good Times Bad Times - 19 (17%)
Harry Hood - 19 (17%)
My Sweet One - 19 (17%)
Love You - 18 (16%)
Punch You In The Eye - 18 (16%)
Esther - 17 (15%)
Wilson - 17 (15%)
Ya Mar - 17 (15%)
Fast Enough for You - 16 (14%)
Axilla - 15 (13%)
Colonel Forbin's Ascent - 15 (13%)
Lengthwise - 15 (13%)
Purple Rain - 15 (13%)
The Famous Mockingbird - 15 (13%)
The Landlady - 15 (13%)
Contact - 14 (12%)
Daniel - 14 (12%)
Freebird - 14 (12%)
Nellie Kane - 14 (12%)
Weigh - 14 (12%)
The Curtain - 13 (11%)
The Sloth - 13 (11%)
Cracklin' Rosie - 12 (11%)
AC/DC Bag - 11 (10%)
Big Black Furry Creature From Mars - 11 (10%)
My Mind's Got a Mind of its Own - 10 (9%)
Terrapin - 10 (9%)
Highway To Hell - 9 (8%)
Lifeboy - 9 (8%)
Loving Cup - 9 (8%)
The Great Gig in the Sky - 9 (8%)

The Oh Kee Pa Ceremony - 9 (8%)
The Wedge - 9 (8%)
Walk Away - 9 (8%)
Carolina - 8 (7%)
Fire - 8 (7%)
Ginseng Sullivan - 8 (7%)
Bathtub Gin - 7 (6%)
Bike - 7 (6%)
Halley's Comet - 7 (6%)
If I Only Had a Brain - 7 (6%)
Funky Bitch - 6 (5%)
Harpua - 6 (5%)
Kung - 6 (5%)
Avenu Malkenu - 5 (4%)
Caravan - 5 (4%)
Jesus Just Left Chicago - 5 (4%)
McGrupp and the Watchful Hosemasters - 5 (4%)
Memories - 5 (4%)
Sleeping Monkey - 5 (4%)
Tela - 5 (4%)
The Man Who Stepped Into Yesterday - 5 (4%)
Bold As Love - 4 (3%)
Dinner and a Movie - 4 (3%)
Faht - 4 (3%)
Makisupa Policeman - 4 (3%)
Manteca - 4 (3%)
Have Mercy - 3 (2%)
La Grange - 3 (2%)
Leprechaun - 3 (2%)
Peaches En Regalia - 3 (2%)
Slave to the Traffic Light - 3 (2%)
Take the A-Train - 3 (2%)
The Ballad of Curtis Loew - 3 (2%)
The Man Who Stepped Into Yesterday Reprise - 3 (2%)
The Mango Song - 3 (2%)
When Something is Wrong with My Baby - 3 (2%)
Crimes of the Mind - 2 (1%)
Gumbo - 2 (1%)
I Walk the Line - 2 (1%)
Jam - 2 (1%)
Pig in a Pen - 2 (1%)
Satin Doll - 2 (1%)
Sparks - 2 (1%)
Spooky Jam - 2 (1%)
Yerushalayim Shel Zahav - 2 (1%)
Amazing Grace Jam - 1 (0%)
Auld Lang Syne - 1 (0%)
Big Ball Jam Reprise - 1 (0%)
Bill Bailey Won't You Please Come Home - 1 (0%)
Brother - 1 (0%)
Catapult - 1 (0%)
Choo Choo Ch' Boogie - 1 (0%)
Clementine - 1 (0%)

Cocaine Jam - 1 (0%)
Crossroads - 1 (0%)
Dog Gone Dog - 1 (0%)
Down with Disease Jam - 1 (0%)
Help Me - 1 (0%)
Honky Tonk Women Jam - 1 (0%)
Hoochie Coochie Man - 1 (0%)
How High the Moon - 1 (0%)
I Been to Georgia on a Fast Train - 1 (0%)
Icculus - 1 (0%)
Indian War Dance - 1 (0%)
It's My Life - 1 (0%)
Jessica Jam - 1 (0%)
Loup Garou - 1 (0%)
Magilla - 1 (0%)
Ob La Di Ob La Da Jam - 1 (0%)
Oye Como Va Jam - 1 (0%)
Piano Duet - 1 (0%)
Psycho Killer Jam - 1 (0%)
Rock and Roll All Nite Jam - 1 (0%)
Sweet Emotion Jam - 1 (0%)
Tea Tray Song - 1 (0%)
Tennessee Waltz - 1 (0%)
That's Alright Mama - 1 (0%)
The Vibration of Life - 1 (0%)
Tube - 1 (0%)
Whipping Post - 1 (0%)
Who Knows Jam - 1 (0%)
Why You've Been Gone So Long - 1 (0%)
You Gotta See Mama Every Night - 1 (0%)

First Set Openers

Buried Alive - 16
Chalk Dust Torture - 14
Llama - 12
Runaway Jim - 10
Golgi Apparatus - 7
Rift - 6
The Landlady - 6
Suzy Greenberg - 5
Loving Cup - 4
Axilla - 3
David Bowie - 3
Lengthwise - 3
AC/DC Bag - 2
Also Sprach Zarathustra - 2
Maze - 2
Split Open and Melt - 2
Wilson - 2
All Things Reconsidered - 1
Amazing Grace - 1
Big Black Furry Creature From Mars - 1
Contact - 1
Daniel - 1

Divided Sky - 1
Funky Bitch - 1
Peaches En Regalia - 1
Sample in a Jar - 1
Sweet Adeline - 1

First Set Closers

Run Like an Antelope - 26
Cavern - 22
David Bowie - 22
Golgi Apparatus - 13
Possum - 5
Runaway Jim - 5
The Squirming Coil - 5
Chalk Dust Torture - 2
Daniel - 2
Amazing Grace - 1
Crimes of the Mind - 1
Freebird - 1
I Been to Georgia on a Fast Train - 1
La Grange - 1
Suzy Greenberg - 1
You Enjoy Myself - 1

Second Set Openers

Also Sprach Zarathustra - 19
Axilla - 10
Runaway Jim - 7
Wilson - 7
Buried Alive - 5
Chalk Dust Torture - 5
Llama - 5
Rift - 5
My Friend My Friend - 4
Suzy Greenberg - 4
AC/DC Bag - 3
Golgi Apparatus - 3
Lengthwise - 3
Loving Cup - 3
The Landlady - 3
David Bowie - 2
Dinner and a Movie - 2
Maze - 2
Mike's Song - 2
Poor Heart - 2
Possum - 2
The Curtain - 2
Halley's Comet - 1
Punch You In The Eye - 1
Sample in a Jar - 1
Tweezer - 1
Walk Away - 1

Second Set Closers

Tweezer Reprise - 17
Cavern - 14

Golgi Apparatus - 10
Amazing Grace - 7
Good Times Bad Times - 7
Possum - 7
Chalk Dust Torture - 6
Highway To Hell - 6
Big Black Furry Creature From
    Mars - 4
Run Like an Antelope - 4
The Squirming Coil - 4
Daniel - 2
Llama - 2
Rocky Top - 2
Amazing Grace Jam - 1
Crimes of the Mind - 1
David Bowie - 1
Freebird - 1
Gumbo - 1
Harpua - 1
Jam - 1
Runaway Jim - 1
Slave to the Traffic Light - 1
Sweet Adeline - 1
That's Alright Mama - 1
Weekapaug Groove - 1
You Enjoy Myself - 1

Third Set Openers

Auld Lang Syne - 1

Third Set Closers

Tweezer Reprise - 1

Encores

Amazing Grace - 39
Rocky Top - 17
Sweet Adeline - 17
Freebird - 12
Good Times Bad Times - 12
Tweezer Reprise - 12
Carolina - 8

Fire - 8
Golgi Apparatus - 7
Cavern - 6
AC/DC Bag - 5
Contact - 5
My Sweet One - 5
Sleeping Monkey - 5
Big Black Furry Creature From
    Mars - 4
Bold As Love - 4
Chalk Dust Torture - 4
Poor Heart - 4
Daniel - 3
Highway To Hell - 3
Memories - 3
La Grange - 2
Nellie Kane - 2
The Squirming Coil - 2
When Something is Wrong with
    My Baby - 2
Big Ball Jam - 1
Big Ball Jam Reprise - 1
Bill Bailey Won't You Please Come
    Home - 1
Funky Bitch - 1
Gumbo - 1
Halley's Comet - 1
Harry Hood - 1
Lengthwise - 1
Llama - 1
Loving Cup - 1
My Friend My Friend - 1
Paul and Silas - 1
Piano Duet - 1
Pig in a Pen - 1
Possum - 1
Sparkle - 1
Take the A-Train - 1
Terrapin - 1
The Mango Song - 1
Walk Away - 1

SPRING SUMMER 1994

"The Hoist Era"

1994 was home to many firsts for Phish. First video: "Down With Disease." First perceived radio-hit-in-waiting: "Sample in a Jar." First mainstream radio appearances (to support the *Hoist* album). And, from a new song standpoint, the first time Phish hit the stage with songs that had been released on an album but never heard live.

Therefore, we were treated to a barrage of new material in early 1994, the volume of which had not been since in almost two years. "Down With

Disease" led the charge along with the embryonic "Wolfman's Brother," "Julius," and the rest of their *Hoist* companions (save "Lifeboy" and "Sample," which debuted in 1993). The considered but unreleased "Simple" followed later.

As with 1993, breakouts were a popular treat. Eleven songs came back after a hundred shows or more, including "Alumni Blues" (though brief), "Frankenstein" (first since the Horns Tour), "NICU" (reworked), and "Icculus." The champs, though, were "Cities" and "Letter to Jimmy Page," which made their first appearances since 1987-1988. The former went back on the shelf for three more years; the latter has not been heard since.

The band toured continuously, and exhaustively, from April through July to support their largest studio effort. It is difficult to break the tour into direct phases, but distinct differences arose. April brought horns to a few shows, including a legendary run at The Beacon, but the band seemed to be getting comfortable with all the new material they penned. The famous 5/7/94 "Tweezerfest" marked a major change, as the band set out to jam one song to its limits. 5/13/94 and the month-end Warfield run and Laguna Seca Daze appearances also provided strong moments.

But June proved to be the meat of the tour. A return to Red Rocks got things moving, and the band was once again off and running. Segue madness became a trend (6/22/94 and 7/13/94), "Simple" evolved as a viable meat inside "Mike's Song," O.J. Simpson was invoked (6/17/94), and amazing jams were played (most of 6/18/94). The band busted out Gamehendge, among a few other older songs, on 6/26/94 and followed it up with the near-complete *Hoist* album in the second set. They then played the rare Gamehendge again less than two weeks later, and added rocking shows at Great Woods and Sugarbush to close. What started as a tour amid fan concerns of "selling out" became a tour chock-full of tasty highlights.

DEBUTS (Spring 1994)

Scent of a Mule	4/4/1994
Down with Disease	4/4/1994
If I Could	4/4/1994
Julius	4/4/1994
Wolfman's Brother	4/4/1994
I Wanna Be Like You	4/4/1994
Demand	4/9/1994
Split Open and Melt Jam	4/14/1994
Dog Faced Boy	4/14/1994
Axilla (Part II)	4/16/1994
All Along the Watchtower	4/21/1994
High-Heel Sneakers	4/23/1994
Who By Fire	4/23/1994
Simple	5/27/1994
O Mio Babbino Caro	5/27/1994
NO2	6/25/1994
The Old Home Place	6/26/1994

DEPARTURES (Spring 1994)

	LAST KNOWN	# SHOWS
Take the A-Train	4/13/1994	523
High-Heel Sneakers	4/23/1994	514
Who By Fire	4/23/1994	514
O Mio Babbino Caro	5/27/1994	489
I Wanna Be Like You	6/10/1994	485
Honky Tonk Women	6/30/1994	470
Memories	7/6/1994	465
Crimes of the Mind	7/10/1994	462
Letter to Jimmy Page	7/15/1994	459
Setting Sail	7/15/1994	459

BREAKOUTS (Spring 1994)	SHELVED	BREAKOUT	# SHOWS
Magilla	3/25/1993	4/4/1994	72
Alumni Blues	7/18/1991	4/15/1994	296
Sanity	5/17/1992	4/29/1994	198
Catapult	2/10/1993	5/12/1994	132
Carolina	8/7/1993	5/20/1994	55
Dinner and a Movie	9/8/1993	5/21/1994	54
Frankenstein	7/26/1991	6/11/1994	326
Jesus Just Left Chicago	8/26/1993	6/13/1994	53
Terrapin	4/29/1993	6/13/1994	95
Kung	8/7/1993	6/16/1994	69
Gumbo	4/21/1993	6/16/1994	103
Icculus	3/25/1993	6/22/1994	126
NICU	5/1/1992	6/23/1994	246
Yerushalayim Shel Zahav	7/24/1993	6/26/1994	88
Tube	4/12/1993	6/26/1994	118
Cities	9/13/1988	7/5/1994	586
Letter to Jimmy Page	11/19/1987	7/5/1994	618
Memories	12/28/1993	7/6/1994	69
Crimes of the Mind	8/28/1993	7/10/1994	73
Setting Sail	3/25/1992	7/15/1994	289

FALL 1994

"Step Into the Freezer"

Clocking in at 46 shows, this may be the last truly long, sprawling, transcontinetnal odyssey of a tour. It will always be known as the tour in which Phish first donned a musical costume, miraculously covering *The Beatles*. What shouldn't go unnoticed, though, is the full strength of the tour, particularly the stretch from 10/29 through 12/1. Indeed, 11/94 has gone down in the pantheon of the most revered months of Phish tour (with the likes of 8/93, 12/95, and 11/97). Whereas Phish concentrated on new originals in the spring, the band focused on jamming the shit out of whatever they had lying around the canon in the fall. The lyrically mysterious "Guyute" stands as the lone original debut.

As with the previous two years, Phish was rapidly moving into larger venues, especially on the east coast. Regrettably, the Big Ball Jam (12/9/94) was a casualty. But the band still kept that offbeat sense of humor on stage, introducing a bluegrass "Foreplay / Long Time" (10/7/94), a cheer from a girls' soccer team (10/8/94), and memorable guest appearances (including Bela Fleck and Michael Ray).

The most memorable guest came in the form of a week-long "traveling bluegrass clinic" with "The Reverend" Jeff Mosier. Mosier did more than join Phish on stage every night; he also taught them to play new songs and new instruments that they continue to play years later. The short acoustic bluegrass mini-sets helped the band keep their fans guessing as to what the band would try next.

Experimental "Tweezer"s became a hot topic of discussion. Starting in Bangor on 11/2, Phish played two free-form versions of "Tweezer" in the month of November. Each stretched past thirty minutes and included unheard of musical exploration. Sometimes "Tweezer" came in one heavy dose,

other times it was strung throughout an entire set, as on 12/1. Other musical highlights included the 11/12 "Disease" / "Have Mercy" sandwich, the 11/22 jam out of "Funky Bitch," the 11/26 "David Bowie," and the set-long jam of 11/30.

Overall, the jamming was typified by the kind of cacophanous experimentation that had only been hinted at previously. Phish wrapped up on the west coast with another horns appearance and left fans salivating for the New Year's Run. By now, the band was truly flexing its improvisational muscle in ways that hadn't been heard before, and the future seemed more promising than ever. What is particularly notable is that these onstage risks and journeys took place while the venues continued to get larger and the general cultural attention on this once-obscure band continued to intensify.

DEBUTS (Fall 1994)

Guyute	10/7/1994
Foreplay/Long Time	10/7/1994
Beaumont Rag	10/14/1994
The Maker	10/15/1994
Golden Lady	10/20/1994
Speak to Me	10/31/1994
Back in the USSR	10/31/1994
Dear Prudence	10/31/1994
Glass Onion	10/31/1994
Ob La Di Ob La Da	10/31/1994
Wild Honey Pie	10/31/1994
Bungalow Bill	10/31/1994
While My Guitar Gently Weeps	10/31/1994
Happiness is a Warm Gun	10/31/1994
Martha My Dear	10/31/1994
I'm So Tired	10/31/1994
Blackbird	10/31/1994
Piggies	10/31/1994
Rocky Raccoon	10/31/1994
Don't Pass Me By	10/31/1994
Why Don't We Do it in the Road	10/31/1994
I Will	10/31/1994
Julia	10/31/1994
Birthday Jam	10/31/1994
Yer Blues	10/31/1994
Mother Nature's Son	10/31/1994
Everybody's Got Something	10/31/1994
Sexy Sadie	10/31/1994
Helter Skelter	10/31/1994
Long Long Long	10/31/1994
Honey Pie	10/31/1994
Savoy Truffle	10/31/1994
Cry Baby Cry	10/31/1994
Revolution 9	10/31/1994
Earl's Breakdown	11/16/1994
I'm Blue I'm Lonesome	11/16/1994
My Long Journey Home	11/16/1994
Fixin' To Die	11/17/1994
Butter Them Biscuits	11/18/1994
Sweet Baby's Arms	11/18/1994
Dooley	11/20/1994
Chalk Dust Torture Reprise	12/10/1994

DEPARTURES (Fall 1994)	LAST KNOWN	# SHOWS
The Maker	10/15/1994	450
Beaumont Rag	10/18/1994	448
Golden Lady	10/20/1994	447
Birthday Jam	10/31/1994	438
Costume Contest	10/31/1994	438
Dear Prudence	10/31/1994	438
Don't Pass Me By	10/31/1994	438
Glass Onion	10/31/1994	438
Happiness Is a Warm Gun	10/31/1994	438
Honey Pie	10/31/1994	438
I Will	10/31/1994	438
Julia	10/31/1994	438
Long Long Long	10/31/1994	438
Martha My Dear	10/31/1994	438
Mother Nature's Son	10/31/1994	438
Ob La Di Ob La Da	10/31/1994	438
Piggies	10/31/1994	438
Revolution	10/31/1994	438
Revolution 9	10/31/1994	438
Rocky Raccoon	10/31/1994	438
Savoy Truffle	10/31/1994	438
Sexy Sadie	10/31/1994	438
Bungalow Bill	10/31/1994	438
Wild Honey Pie	10/31/1994	438
Yer Blues	10/31/1994	438
Earl's Breakdown	11/16/1994	431
Pig in a Pen	11/16/1994	431
Swing Low Sweet Chariot	11/16/1994	431
Tennessee Waltz	11/16/1994	431
Helter Skelter	11/17/1994	430
Sweet Baby's Arms	11/18/1994	429
Dooley	11/20/1994	427
Blackbird	11/22/1994	426
Butter Them Biscuits	11/22/1994	426
Fixin' to Die	11/30/1994	421
The Landlady	12/3/1994	418
Touch Me	12/3/1994	418
Back in the USSR	12/6/1994	416
Big Ball Jam	12/9/1994	413

BREAKOUTS (Fall 1994))	SHELVED	BREAKOUT	# SHOWS
Axilla	8/16/1993	10/16/1994	93
Lengthwise	8/13/1993	10/20/1994	98
If I Only Had a Brain	12/29/1993	10/25/1994	90
Manteca	5/7/1993	10/28/1994	131
Sparks	5/7/1994	10/29/1994	65
Buffalo Bill	11/21/1992	10/29/1994	223
Loving Cup	5/7/1994	11/4/1994	69
Have Mercy	8/14/1993	11/12/1994	110
Tennessee Waltz	5/6/1993	11/16/1994	141
Pig in a Pen	2/23/1993	11/16/1994	191
Swing Low Sweet Chariot	10/20/1989	11/16/1994	566
Caravan	5/4/1994	12/2/1994	87
Touch Me	7/27/1991	12/3/1994	391

NYE 1994

"A Tale of Two Gardens"

The 1994 New Year's Run can be summed up by two phrases: "Providence 'Bowie'" and "hot dog stunt." The former was played on 12/29 and, coupled with the earlier 11/26/94 version, changed the way fans viewed the song and stunned everyone by the sheer spooky brilliance that contemporary Phish could achieve.. The latter is still the most celebrated New Year's stunt, which was reprised in '99, and provided the first Phish artifact to grace the Rock and Roll Hall of Fame and Museum.

(See the Show Reviews chapter, plus the appropriate Show Notes, for a full discussion of the band's hot dog riding escapade).

Meanwhile, Phish reached a major milestone by selling out Madison Square Garden, the cozy environs that would host many more visits in future tours. Earlier that afternoon, the boys made their first performance for late night tv, playing Chalkdust Torture by request of David Letterman. The party moved to the venerable Boston Garden for the final show of the year, extending the Massachusetts New Year's tradition.

There were no debuts this Run, but the very rare Buffalo Bill popped up out of Mike's Song on 12/31.

DEBUTS (NYE1994)
None   N/A

DEPARTURES ((NYE 1994))	LAST KNOWN	# SHOWS
Yerushalayim Shel Zahav	12/31/1994	408

BREAKOUTS (NYE 1994)	SHELVED	BREAKOUT	# SHOWS
Bold As Love	5/21/1994	12/28/1994	83

There were 123 shows played
Shows by day of week
- Sunday- 16
- Monday- 12
- Tuesday- 11
- Wednesday- 17
- Thursday- 19
- Friday- 24
- Saturday- 24

208 songs have been played (33% of songs Phish have played).

The average number of songs per show is 20.8.

The average amount of times each song was played is 12.30.

Total Times Played

Sample in a Jar - 71 (57%)
Julius - 65 (52%)
Down With Disease - 55 (44%)
Rift - 47 (38%)
Poor Heart - 46 (37%)
Sparkle - 45 (36%)
Maze - 44 (35%)
Scent of a Mule - 44 (35%)
Stash - 44 (35%)
Cavern - 43 (34%)
Golgi Apparatus - 42 (34%)
Run Like an Antelope - 42 (34%)
Suzy Greenberg - 42 (34%)
Bouncing Around the Room - 40 (32%)
It's Ice - 40 (32%)
Split Open and Melt - 40 (32%)
Divided Sky - 39 (31%)
Fee - 39 (31%)
Chalk Dust Torture - 38 (30%)
David Bowie - 38 (30%)
You Enjoy Myself - 38 (30%)
Foam - 36 (29%)
Reba - 36 (29%)
Axilla (Part II) - 34 (27%)
If I Could - 34 (27%)
Runaway Jim - 34 (27%)
Amazing Grace - 31 (25%)
Tweezer - 31 (25%)
Harry Hood - 30 (24%)
Simple - 30 (24%)
Also Sprach Zarathustra - 29 (23%)
Silent in the Morning - 28 (22%)
The Horse - 28 (22%)
The Lizards - 28 (22%)
Mike's Song - 27 (21%)
Wilson - 27 (21%)
Llama - 26 (21%)
Nellie Kane - 26 (21%)
The Squirming Coil - 26 (21%)
Sweet Adeline - 25 (20%)
Tweezer Reprise - 25 (20%)
Lifeboy - 24 (19%)
Dog Faced Boy - 23 (18%)
Big Ball Jam - 22 (17%)
Slave to the Traffic Light - 22 (17%)

Weekapaug Groove - 22 (17%)
Ginseng Sullivan - 20 (16%)
Glide - 20 (16%)
Possum - 20 (16%)
Fluffhead - 19 (15%)
Guyute - 19 (15%)
My Friend My Friend - 19 (15%)
Guelah Papyrus - 18 (14%)
Mound - 18 (14%)
Peaches En Regalia - 17 (13%)
Sleeping Monkey - 17 (13%)
The Curtain - 17 (13%)
Foreplay/Long Time - 16 (13%)
Good Times Bad Times - 16 (13%)
Uncle Pen - 16 (13%)
Highway To Hell - 15 (12%)
I Didn't Know - 15 (12%)
Big Black Furry Creature From Mars - 14 (11%)
I Am Hydrogen - 14 (11%)
My Sweet One - 14 (11%)
Rocky Top - 14 (11%)
The Mango Song - 14 (11%)
AC/DC Bag - 13 (10%)
Buried Alive - 13 (10%)
Contact - 13 (10%)
Fast Enough for You - 13 (10%)
McGrupp and the Watchful Hosemasters - 13 (10%)
The Old Home Place - 13 (10%)
Halley's Comet - 12 (9%)
Horn - 12 (9%)
Tela - 12 (9%)
Ya Mar - 12 (9%)
Bathtub Gin - 11 (8%)
Colonel Forbin's Ascent - 11 (8%)
Esther - 11 (8%)
Frankenstein - 11 (8%)
Punch You In The Eye - 11 (8%)
Purple Rain - 11 (8%)
The Famous Mockingbird - 11 (8%)
NICU - 10 (8%)
The Landlady - 10 (8%)
Yerushalayim Shel Zahav - 10 (8%)
Catapult - 9 (7%)
Demand - 9 (7%)
Fire - 9 (7%)
Gumbo - 9 (7%)
I Wanna Be Like You - 9 (7%)
I'm Blue I'm Lonesome - 9 (7%)
My Long Journey Home - 9 (7%)
The Sloth - 9 (7%)
Wolfman's Brother - 9 (7%)
Avenu Malkenu - 8 (6%)
The Man Who Stepped Into Yesterday - 8 (6%)

The Oh Kee Pa Ceremony - 8 (6%)
Lawn Boy - 7 (5%)
The Man Who Stepped Into Yesterday Reprise - 7 (5%)
Cracklin' Rosie - 6 (4%)
Harpua - 6 (4%)
Love You - 6 (4%)
All Things Reconsidered - 5 (4%)
Bike - 5 (4%)
Bold As Love - 5 (4%)
Carolina - 5 (4%)
Digital Delay Loop Jam - 5 (4%)
Freebird - 5 (4%)
Funky Bitch - 5 (4%)
Jesus Just Left Chicago - 5 (4%)
Kung - 5 (4%)
Magilla - 5 (4%)
Makisupa Policeman - 5 (4%)
My Mind's Got a Mind of its Own - 5 (4%)
Butter Them Biscuits - 4 (3%)
Caravan - 4 (3%)
Paul and Silas - 4 (3%)
Dinner and a Movie - 3 (2%)
Icculus - 3 (2%)
Loving Cup - 3 (2%)
NO2 - 3 (2%)
Terrapin - 3 (2%)
The Vibration of Life - 3 (2%)
While My Guitar Gently Weeps - 3 (2%)
Back in the USSR - 2 (1%)
Beaumont Rag - 2 (1%)
Blackbird - 2 (1%)
Buffalo Bill - 2 (1%)
Cry Baby Cry - 2 (1%)
Drums Jam - 2 (1%)
Faht - 2 (1%)
Fixin' to Die - 2 (1%)
Helter Skelter - 2 (1%)
Jam - 2 (1%)
Letter to Jimmy Page - 2 (1%)
Sanity - 2 (1%)
Sparks - 2 (1%)
Split Open and Melt Jam - 2 (1%)
The Great Gig in the Sky - 2 (1%)
Why Don't We Do It in the Road - 2 (1%)
All Along the Watchtower - 1 (0%)
Alumni Blues - 1 (0%)
Alumni Blues Jam - 1 (0%)
Auld Lang Syne - 1 (0%)
Axilla - 1 (0%)
Bass Jam - 1 (0%)
Big Black Furry Creature from Mars Reprise - 1 (0%)
Bill Bailey Won't You Please Come Home - 1 (0%)

Birthday Jam - 1 (0%)
Cannonball Jam - 1 (0%)
Chalk Dust Torture Reprise - 1 (0%)
Cities - 1 (0%)
Costume Contest - 1 (0%)
Crimes of the Mind - 1 (0%)
Dear Prudence - 1 (0%)
Don't Pass Me By - 1 (0%)
Dooley - 1 (0%)
Earl's Breakdown - 1 (0%)
Everybody's Got Something to Hide Except for Me and My Monkey - 1 (0%)
Glass Onion - 1 (0%)
Golden Lady - 1 (0%)
HYHU Jam - 1 (0%)
Happiness Is a Warm Gun - 1 (0%)
Have Mercy - 1 (0%)
High-Heel Sneakers - 1 (0%)
Honey Pie - 1 (0%)
Honky Tonk Women - 1 (0%)
I Will - 1 (0%)
I'm So Tired - 1 (0%)
If I Only Had a Brain - 1 (0%)
Julia - 1 (0%)
Lengthwise - 1 (0%)
Long Long Long - 1 (0%)
Manteca - 1 (0%)
Martha My Dear - 1 (0%)
Memories - 1 (0%)
Midnight Rider Jam - 1 (0%)
Mind Left Body Jam - 1 (0%)
Mother Nature's Son - 1 (0%)
O Mio Babbino Caro - 1 (0%)
Ob La Di Ob La Da - 1 (0%)
Piano Duet - 1 (0%)
Pig in a Pen - 1 (0%)
Piggies - 1 (0%)
Revolution - 1 (0%)
Revolution 9 - 1 (0%)
Rocky Raccoon - 1 (0%)
Savoy Truffle - 1 (0%)
Setting Sail - 1 (0%)
Sexy Sadie - 1 (0%)
Somewhere Over the Rainbow Jam - 1 (0%)
Speak to Me - 1 (0%)
Sweet Baby's Arms - 1 (0%)
Sweet Emotion Jam - 1 (0%)
Swing Low Sweet Chariot - 1 (0%)
Take the A-Train - 1 (0%)
Tennessee Waltz - 1 (0%)
The Continuing Story of Bungalow Bill - 1 (0%)
The Maker - 1 (0%)
Touch Me - 1 (0%)
Tube - 1 (0%)
Walk Away - 1 (0%)

Weigh - 1 (0%)
Who By Fire - 1 (0%)
Wild Honey Pie - 1 (0%)
Yer Blues - 1 (0%)

First Set Openers

Runaway Jim - 21
Llama - 14
Buried Alive - 9
Chalk Dust Torture - 9
Wilson - 9
My Friend My Friend - 7
Rift - 6
Fee - 5
Golgi Apparatus - 4
Sample in a Jar - 4
Suzy Greenberg - 4
Divided Sky - 3
Down With Disease - 2
Frankenstein - 2
Halley's Comet - 2
Simple - 2
The Curtain - 2
Bouncing Around the Room - 1
Caravan - 1
Catapult - 1
Demand - 1
Funky Bitch - 1
Helter Skelter - 1
I Didn't Know - 1
Kung - 1
Loving Cup - 1
Magilla - 1
Makisupa Policeman - 1
Maze - 1
Mound - 1
NO2 - 1
Peaches En Regalia - 1
Poor Heart - 1
The Great Gig in the Sky - 1
The Landlady - 1

First Set Closers

Cavern - 13
Golgi Apparatus - 12
Sample in a Jar - 10
Run Like an Antelope - 9
Chalk Dust Torture - 8
Sweet Adeline - 8
The Squirming Coil - 7
David Bowie - 5
Julius - 5
Suzy Greenberg - 5
Down With Disease - 4
Possum - 4
AC/DC Bag - 3

Llama - 3
My Long Journey Home - 3
Split Open and Melt - 3
Amazing Grace - 2
Divided Sky - 2
Stash - 2
Tweezer Reprise - 2
While My Guitar Gently Weeps - 2
Axilla (Part II) - 1
Carolina - 1
Frankenstein - 1
Funky Bitch - 1
Good Times Bad Times - 1
High-Heel Sneakers - 1
Rift - 1
Runaway Jim - 1
Slave to the Traffic Light - 1
Swing Low Sweet Chariot - 1
The Horse - 1

Second Set Openers

Also Sprach Zarathustra - 23
Suzy Greenberg - 9
Maze - 6
Peaches En Regalia - 6
The Curtain - 6
David Bowie - 5
Sample in a Jar - 5
Wilson - 5
Rift - 4
Down With Disease - 3
Frankenstein - 3
Halley's Comet - 3
Julius - 3
Mike's Song - 3
Runaway Jim - 3
Split Open and Melt - 3
The Landlady - 3
Axilla (Part II) - 2
Chalk Dust Torture - 2
Demand - 2
Faht - 2
Possum - 2
Run Like an Antelope - 2
The Old Home Place - 2
Dinner and a Movie - 1
Fire - 1
Funky Bitch - 1
Golgi Apparatus - 1
Guyute - 1
Lengthwise - 1
Letter to Jimmy Page - 1
Llama - 1
Loving Cup - 1
My Friend My Friend - 1
Nellie Kane - 1
Poor Heart - 1

Punch You In The Eye - 1
Simple - 1
Speak to Me - 1

Second Set Closers

Cavern - 14
Golgi Apparatus - 12
Suzy Greenberg - 12
Slave to the Traffic Light - 9
Tweezer Reprise - 9
Good Times Bad Times - 7
Possum - 6
Amazing Grace - 5
Highway To Hell - 5
Big Black Furry Creature From
    Mars - 4
Chalk Dust Torture - 4
Run Like an Antelope - 4
Sample in a Jar - 4
The Squirming Coil - 4
You Enjoy Myself - 4
David Bowie - 3
Frankenstein - 2
AC/DC Bag - 1
Bass Jam - 1
Crimes of the Mind - 1
Down With Disease - 1
Foreplay/Long Time - 1
Freebird - 1
Harry Hood - 1
Julius - 1
Llama - 1
Revolution 9 - 1
Runaway Jim - 1
Somewhere Over the Rainbow
    Jam - 1
Sweet Adeline - 1
Yerushalayim Shel Zahav - 1

Third Set Openers

David Bowie - 1
My Sweet One - 1

Third Set Closers

Run Like an Antelope - 1
Slave to the Traffic Light - 1

Encores

Amazing Grace - 14
Rocky Top - 14
Tweezer Reprise - 14
Sleeping Monkey - 12
Golgi Apparatus - 10
Highway To Hell - 10
Cavern - 9
Nellie Kane - 9

Fire - 8
Foreplay/Long Time - 8
Good Times Bad Times - 8
Sweet Adeline - 6
Bold As Love - 5
Ginseng Sullivan - 5
Sample in a Jar - 5
Freebird - 4
The Squirming Coil - 4
Fee - 3
My Sweet One - 3
Poor Heart - 3
Suzy Greenberg - 3
The Old Home Place - 3
Bouncing Around the Room - 2
Chalk Dust Torture - 2
Drums Jam - 2
Funky Bitch - 2
Harry Hood - 2
I'm Blue I'm Lonesome - 2
Icculus - 2
My Long Journey Home - 2
Silent in the Morning - 2
The Horse - 2
Ya Mar - 2
All Along the Watchtower - 1
Auld Lang Syne - 1
Back in the USSR - 1
Big Black Furry Creature From
    Mars - 1
Bill Bailey Won't You Please
    Come Home - 1
Caravan - 1
Carolina - 1
Chalk Dust Torture Reprise - 1
Contact - 1
Costume Contest - 1
Cracklin' Rosie - 1
Fixin' to Die - 1
Frankenstein - 1
Jam - 1
Loving Cup - 1
Magilla - 1
Memories - 1
Piano Duet - 1
Possum - 1
Rift - 1
Runaway Jim - 1
Simple - 1
Slave to the Traffic Light - 1
Sparkle - 1
Sweet Baby's Arms - 1
The Lizards - 1
The Maker - 1
Tube - 1
Uncle Pen - 1
Wilson - 1

SUMMER 1995

"Welcome to Space Camp"

Summer Tour was truly a breakthrough period, featuring a slew of new material and heavy doses of improvisational experimentation. Phish began their year in May, playing a Voters for Choice benefit concert in which they whipped out a stunning selection of ten debuts (six originals and four covers). Two would wind up on *Billy Breathes* a year later ("Theme From the Bottom" and "Free") and one would become a frequently –requested enigma ("Spock's Brain"). Later, the band further previewed the album's eventual roster by introducing "Taste" and "Prince Caspian." The band took to stools and acoustic guitars for "Acoustic Army," and Beatles cover "A Day in the Life" was also introduced. "Camel Walk" came back after 600-plus shows, and "Timber" after over 250. And Phish, by mid-June, was involved in interplanetary exploration of the highest degree, or so it seemed.

The relatively truncated tour began in the midwest, before winding south and eventually up to the East Coast. After a third visit to Red Rocks, Phish hit Mud Island in Memphis and turned out an experimental "Tweezer" that set the tone for the rest of the tour. Songs like "Runaway Jim" (6/16, 7/2), "Bowie" (6/24, 6/29, 7/3) and "Down With Disease" (6/26) produced massive exploration. But the capstone song of the summer was definitely "Tweezer," with additional landmark performances on 6/17, 6/22, and 6/28. New song "Free" also emerged as a potential jammer, with lengthy performances on 6/16 and 6/26. Tour ended with an exhuberant two-day campout in Sugarbush, Vermont, spiced with musical highlights but marred by gatecrashing interlopers.

Summer 1995 was controversial among fans. Some enjoyed the risks Phish was taking on stage. Others had problems stomaching the length and scope of the jams they were hearing. In any case, the band was playing with enormous confidence and defying the easygoing hippy stereotype often applied by lazy critics by providing some of the most experimental rock music this side of Sonic Youth. They offered exciting and groundbreaking exploration with a dedicated consistency that hadn't been seen on Phish tour before. In retrospect, this was the summation of the exploration period of 1994-1995. Fall '95 would be brilliant in its own right, but focused more on soaring, uplifting improvisation often led by a melodious Trey. To borrow a phrase from Mike, the Summer jams were indeed a bit "starved for melody."

DEBUTS (Summer 1995)

Don't You Wanna Go	5/16/1995
Ha Ha Ha	5/16/1995
Spock's Brain	5/16/1995
Strange Design	5/16/1995
Theme From the Bottom	5/16/1995
Lonesome Cowboy Bill	5/16/1995
Free	5/16/1995
Glide II	5/16/1995
I'll Come Running	5/16/1995
Gloria	5/16/1995
Taste	6/7/1995
Acoustic Army	6/7/1995
Prince Caspian	6/8/1995
A Day in the Life	6/10/1995
Johnny B. Goode	6/17/1995
Three Little Birds	6/17/1995

DEPARTURES (Summer 1995)	LAST KNOWN	# SHOWS
Glide II	5/16/1995	407
Gloria	5/16/1995	407
I'll Come Running	5/16/1995	407
Three Little Birds	6/17/1995	398

BREAKOUTS (Summer 1995)	SHELVED	BREAKOUT	# SHOWS
Weigh	5/20/1994	6/7/1995	89
The Wedge	8/20/1993	6/7/1995	134
Ginseng Sullivan	10/10/1994	6/20/1995	58
Camel Walk	2/24/1989	7/2/1995	648
Timber (Jerry)	12/30/1992	7/3/1995	256

FALL 1995

"Out of My Brain on the Train"

Coming off the debated summer, the fall of 1995 started out slowly and charged to the finish line with a huge bang. The Minkin backdrops were totally absent for the first time in years, and a few new additions adorned the stage: Trey's mini percussion setup, and an oversized chess board that hung vertically behind Page.

Much like the *Quadrophenia* cover album itself, Halloween seemed to split the tour into separate personalities. For the first time, Phish began their tour out west and moved east. And fans were treated to a near-tour-long chess match between band and audience that gave us all one more thing to do at setbreak, with fans debating the next move at the Greenpeace table. Each second set was prefaced by monitor man Pete Schall's introduction of the lucky fan who got to move the appropriate Velcro-enhanced piece.

The early tour had its moments, like the 10/7 Hood and the second set of 10/11. And fans were quick to rave about the cross-appearances with Medeski, Martin and Wood (see 10/14 and 10/17). As Halloween approached, the band teased fans more blatantly than they had in 1994, including a jam on Pink Floyd's "Breathe" (10/25) and multiple Michael Jackson teases. The memorable Halloween show in Chicago, featuring an enormous and cathartic "YEM" in addition to the Who costume, marked the midpoint of the tour.

After a week break, Phish returned with three shows at the majestic and medieval Fox Theatre in Atlanta. It would be one of the last times Phish would perform a regular show in so small a venue. Swinging through the southeast, the band picked up special guests like Butch Trucks and Jimmy Buffett (11/16), as well as Bela Fleck (11/29), and broke out a long experimental "Stash" on 11/14 that harkened back to the Tweezerfests of '94. Also, in a move that inspired future jams and original compositions like "Rock-a-William" and "Walfredo," the band participated in their first "Rotation Jam" on 11/25 in Hampton, and another on 12/11 in Philly. November ended with a celebrated show in Dayton, featuring a monster "Tweezer" -> "Makisupa" -> "Antelope."

Although these were memorable moments, the best was yet to come: December '95 is still considered one of the very best months of live Phish. This two-week stretch had it all: humor (see the "Dog Log" show from 12/11), long, strong jams (the 12/9 "You Enjoy Myself," the 12/1 "Mike's Song," the 12/8 "Tweezer" ->"Kung"-> "Tweezer"), and segue fests (the remarkable 12/14/95 set II). Intermixed was a dedication to John Lennon

(12/8/95), hot shows in Hershey (12/1/95) and Providence (12/12/95), and a rare "Tweezer" / "Tweezer Reprise" combination (12/17/95). Fall tour wrapped up in customary fashion, with two upstate New York shows. This strong and triumphant run towards the end of tour left high expectations for the New Year's Run.

DEBUTS (Fall 1995)

Fog that Surrounds	9/27/1995
Cars Trucks Buses	9/27/1995
Billy Breathes	9/27/1995
Keyboard Cavalry	9/27/1995
Hello My Baby	9/27/1995
Cryin'	9/29/1995
Suspicious Minds	9/30/1995
Life on Mars	10/13/1995
Taste That Surrounds	10/24/1995
I Am The Sea	10/31/1995
The Real Me	10/31/1995
Quadrophenia	10/31/1995
Cut My Hair	10/31/1995
The Punk Meets The Godfather	10/31/1995
I'm One	10/31/1995
The Dirty Jobs	10/31/1995
Helpless Dancer	10/31/1995
Is It In My Head	10/31/1995
I've Had Enough	10/31/1995
5:15	10/31/1995
Sea and Sand	10/31/1995
Drowned	10/31/1995
Bell Boy	10/31/1995
Doctor Jimmy	10/31/1995
The Rock	10/31/1995
Love Reign O'er Me	10/31/1995
My Generation	10/31/1995
Brown Eyed Girl	11/16/1995
Take Me to the River	11/21/1995
Wind Beneath My Wings	11/28/1995
Heart and Soul	11/29/1995
Come Together	12/8/1995

DEPARTURES (Fall 1995)

	LAST KNOWN	# SHOWS
Don't You Wanna Go	9/28/1995	383
Cryin'	9/29/1995	382
Fog That Surrounds	10/17/1995	370
Shaggy Dog	10/29/1995	361
5:15	10/31/1995	360
Bell Boy	10/31/1995	360
Cut My Hair	10/31/1995	360
Doctor Jimmy	10/31/1995	360
Helpless Dancer	10/31/1995	360
I Am the Sea	10/31/1995	360
I'm One	10/31/1995	360
I've Had Enough	10/31/1995	360
Is it in my Head	10/31/1995	360
Love Reign O'er Me	10/31/1995	360
My Generation	10/31/1995	360
Quadrophenia	10/31/1995	360
The Dirty Jobs	10/31/1995	360
The Punk Meets the Godfather	10/31/1995	360
The Rock	10/31/1995	360
Brown Eyed Girl	11/16/1995	353
Bill Bailey Won't YouÉ	11/18/1995	352
I'm So Tired	11/18/1995	352
Wind Beneath My Wings	11/28/1995	346
Heart and soul	11/29/1995	345
My Long Journey Home	11/29/1995	345
Faht	12/2/1995	342
Acoustic Army	12/8/1995	338
Come Together	12/8/1995	338
Keyboard Cavalry	12/14/1995	334

BREAKOUTS (Fall 1995)

	SHELVED	BREAKOUT	# SHOWS
Wolfman's Brother	6/26/1994	9/27/1995	88
Fire	10/13/1994	9/28/1995	69
Faht	6/19/1994	10/3/1995	99
Demand	6/26/1994	10/8/1995	97
Crossroads	5/8/1993	10/11/1995	196
Tube	6/26/1994	10/13/1995	99
Kung	10/20/1994	10/14/1995	75
Paul and Silas	11/19/1994	10/24/1995	63
Shaggy Dog	11/3/1988	10/29/1995	686
Jesus Just Left Chicago	12/6/1994	10/31/1995	56
Icculus	11/20/1994	10/31/1995	67
Manteca	10/28/1994	11/14/1995	85
If I Only Had a Brain	10/25/1994	11/16/1995	90
I'm So Tired	10/31/1994	11/18/1995	86
Dinner and a Movie	10/22/1994	11/18/1995	93
Bill Bailey	4/22/1994	11/18/1995	163
The Oh Kee Pa Ceremony	6/9/1995	11/24/1995	56
Bike	12/6/1994	11/24/1995	68
My Sweet One	6/15/1995	12/2/1995	58
Love You	12/28/1994	12/8/1995	73
Dog Gone Dog	8/2/1993	12/11/1995	217

NYE RUN 1995

"The Phish Factory"

This is one of the strongest all around New Year's Runs to date. The band continued its momentum from Fall Tour and cranked out four strong shows in Worcester and New York City. The New Year's show was moved out of Massachusetts for the first time, but Phish atoned with strong performances at the Centrum, including a hot "Tweezer" and the much lauded "Bathtub Gin" -> "The Real Me"-> "Bathtub Gin." The strong 12/29 performance also included a raging "Stash" and a guest appearance from Mike's bass instructor, Jim Stinette.

The New Year's performance itself is generally considered one of the absolute best shows ever, filled with groundbreaking versions of many songs (particularly "Drowned," "Mike's Song," "Runaway Jim," and "Weekapaug Groove"...for starters). And in a nod to the popular radio of the time, Tom

Marshall belted out a rendition of Collective Soul's "Shine" (the lone debut of the run). The first set "Forbin's" laid the stage for the New Year's stunt: a "time factory" which allegedly brought the new year into existence, personified by a freshly bald headed "Baby Fishman," who proceeded to pound out a roaring third set while wearing an enormous bonnet.

There were no original debuts, but "La Grange" resurfaced, as well as "Sanity" and the third-ever "Johnny B. Goode." Also, a few selections from *Quadrophenia* emerged during this Run for the first time since Halloween: "Drowned," "The Real Me," and "Sea and Sand."

DEBUTS (NYE 1995)

Shine	12/31/1995

DEPARTURES (NYE 1995)

	LAST KNOWN	# SHOWS
Taste That Surrounds	12/29/1995	329
The Real Me	12/29/1995	329
Axilla (Part II)	12/31/1995	327
Shine	12/31/1995	327

BREAKOUTS (NYE 1995)

	SHELVED	BREAKOUT	# SHOWS
La Grange	8/14/1993	12/29/1995	215
Johnny B. Goode	7/3/1995	12/31/1995	58
Sanity	6/24/1994	12/31/1995	147

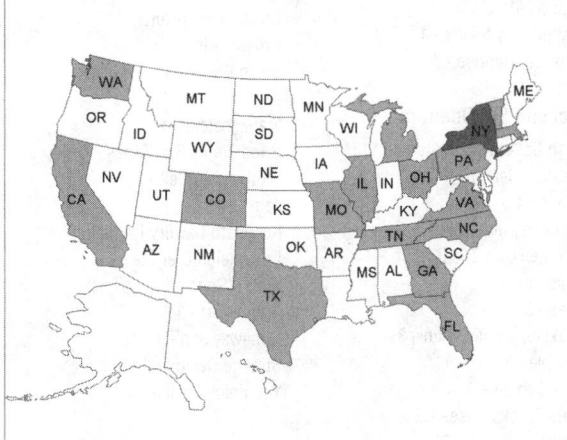

There were 81 shows played Shows by day of week

- Sunday- 10
- Monday- 6
- Tuesday- 12
- Wednesday- 9
- Thursday- 13
- Friday- 15
- Saturday- 16

191 songs have been played (30% of songs Phish have played).

The average number of songs per show is 19.6.

The average amount of times each song was played is 8.32.

Total Times Played

Free - 31 (38%)
Sample in a Jar - 30 (37%)
Strange Design - 28 (34%)
Acoustic Army - 27 (33%)
Theme From The Bottom - 26 (32%)
Maze - 25 (30%)
Poor Heart - 25 (30%)
Run Like an Antelope - 25 (30%)
Sparkle - 25 (30%)

Stash - 25 (30%)
Chalk Dust Torture - 24 (29%)
David Bowie - 24 (29%)
A Day in the Life - 23 (28%)
Cavern - 23 (28%)
Reba - 23 (28%)
Runaway Jim - 23 (28%)
Scent of a Mule - 23 (28%)
You Enjoy Myself - 23 (28%)
Bouncing Around the Room - 22 (27%)
Suzy Greenberg - 22 (27%)
AC/DC Bag - 21 (25%)
Harry Hood - 21 (25%)
Julius - 21 (25%)
Cars Trucks Buses - 20 (24%)
Divided Sky - 20 (24%)
Possum - 20 (24%)
Rift - 20 (24%)
Split Open and Melt - 20 (24%)
Sweet Adeline - 20 (24%)
Simple - 19 (23%)
Slave to the Traffic Light - 19 (23%)
I'm Blue I'm Lonesome - 18 (22%)
It's Ice - 18 (22%)
The Squirming Coil - 18 (22%)
Tweezer - 18 (22%)
Ya Mar - 18 (22%)
Prince Caspian - 17 (20%)
The Lizards - 17 (20%)
Also Sprach Zarathustra - 16 (19%)
Amazing Grace - 16 (19%)
Mike's Song - 16 (19%)
Uncle Pen - 16 (19%)
Hello My Baby - 15 (18%)
Weekapaug Groove - 15 (18%)
Fee - 14 (17%)
Taste That Surrounds - 14 (17%)
Tweezer Reprise - 14 (17%)
Billy Breathes - 13 (16%)
Ha Ha Ha - 13 (16%)
Keyboard Cavalry - 13 (16%)
Llama - 13 (16%)
Wilson - 13 (16%)
My Friend My Friend - 12 (14%)
Timber (Jerry) - 12 (14%)
While My Guitar Gently Weeps - 12 (14%)
Mound - 11 (13%)
Suspicious Minds - 11 (13%)
The Curtain - 11 (13%)
Bathtub Gin - 10 (12%)
Gumbo - 10 (12%)
I Didn't Know - 10 (12%)
Taste - 10 (12%)
Dog Faced Boy - 9 (11%)
Fire - 9 (11%)
Frankenstein - 9 (11%)

If I Could - 9 (11%)
Lifeboy - 9 (11%)
Makisupa Policeman - 9 (11%)
NICU - 9 (11%)
Punch You In The Eye - 9 (11%)
Silent in the Morning - 9 (11%)
The Horse - 9 (11%)
Fluffhead - 8 (9%)
Foam - 8 (9%)
Fog That Surrounds - 8 (9%)
Good Times Bad Times - 8 (9%)
Horn - 8 (9%)
Life on Mars - 8 (9%)
Rocky Top - 8 (9%)
Fast Enough for You - 7 (8%)
Funky Bitch - 7 (8%)
Guyute - 7 (8%)
Kung - 7 (8%)
Tela - 7 (8%)
The Wedge - 7 (8%)
Big Black Furry Creature From Mars - 6 (7%)
Contact - 6 (7%)
Golgi Apparatus - 6 (7%)
Guelah Papyrus - 6 (7%)
Halley's Comet - 6 (7%)
Jam - 6 (7%)
My Long Journey Home - 6 (7%)
Sleeping Monkey - 6 (7%)
The Mango Song - 6 (7%)
Wolfman's Brother - 6 (7%)
Bold As Love - 5 (6%)
Buried Alive - 5 (6%)
Catapult - 5 (6%)
Don't You Wanna Go - 5 (6%)
Down With Disease - 5 (6%)
McGrupp and the Watchful Hosemasters - 5 (6%)
Spock's Brain - 5 (6%)
The Sloth - 5 (6%)
Avenu Malkenu - 4 (4%)
Axilla (Part II) - 4 (4%)
Crossroads - 4 (4%)
Demand - 4 (4%)
Esther - 4 (4%)
Lawn Boy - 4 (4%)
Loving Cup - 4 (4%)
My Mind's Got a Mind of its Own - 4 (4%)
The Man Who Stepped Into Yesterday - 4 (4%)
The Old Home Place - 4 (4%)
Carolina - 3 (3%)
Colonel Forbin's Ascent - 3 (3%)
Cracklin' Rosie - 3 (3%)
Glide - 3 (3%)
Johnny B. Goode - 3 (3%)
Lonesome Cowboy Bill - 3 (3%)

My Sweet One - 3 (3%)
The Famous Mockingbird - 3 (3%)
The Man Who Stepped Into
    Yesterday Reprise - 3 (3%)
Tube - 3 (3%)
All Things Reconsidered - 2 (2%)
Dinner and a Movie - 2 (2%)
Drowned - 2 (2%)
Faht - 2 (2%)
Ginseng Sullivan - 2 (2%)
Harpua - 2 (2%)
Highway To Hell - 2 (2%)
I Am Hydrogen - 2 (2%)
Rotation Jam - 2 (2%)
Sea and Sand - 2 (2%)
The Oh Kee Pa Ceremony - 2 (2%)
The Real Me - 2 (2%)
Weigh - 2 (2%)
5:15 - 1 (1%)
Amazing Grace Jam - 1 (1%)
Auld Lang Syne - 1 (1%)
Bass Jam - 1 (1%)
Bell Boy - 1 (1%)
Bike - 1 (1%)
Bill Bailey Won't You Please
    Come Home - 1 (1%)
Breathe Jam - 1 (1%)
Brown Eyed Girl - 1 (1%)
Camel Walk - 1 (1%)
Chess Jam - 1 (1%)
Come Together - 1 (1%)
Cry Baby Cry - 1 (1%)
Cryin' - 1 (1%)
Cut My Hair - 1 (1%)
Dave's Energy Guide - 1 (1%)
Doctor Jimmy - 1 (1%)
Dog Gone Dog - 1 (1%)
Glide II - 1 (1%)
Gloria - 1 (1%)
Heart and soul - 1 (1%)
Helpless Dancer - 1 (1%)
I Am the Sea - 1 (1%)
I'll Come Running - 1 (1%)
I'm One - 1 (1%)
I'm So Tired - 1 (1%)
I've Had Enough - 1 (1%)
Icculus - 1 (1%)
If I Only Had a Brain - 1 (1%)
Immigrant Song Jam - 1 (1%)
Is it in my Head - 1 (1%)
Jesus Just Left Chicago - 1 (1%)
Keyboard Cavalry Reprise - 1 (1%)
La Grange - 1 (1%)
Love Reign O'er Me - 1 (1%)
Love You - 1 (1%)
Manteca - 1 (1%)
My Generation - 1 (1%)
Night Moves Jam - 1 (1%)

Paul and Silas - 1 (1%)
Poor Heart Reprise - 1 (1%)
Purple Rain - 1 (1%)
Quadrophenia - 1 (1%)
Sanity - 1 (1%)
Shaggy Dog - 1 (1%)
Shine - 1 (1%)
Take Me to the River - 1 (1%)
Terrapin - 1 (1%)
The Dirty Jobs - 1 (1%)
The Punk Meets the Godfather
    - 1 (1%)
The Rock - 1 (1%)
Three Little Birds - 1 (1%)
White Rabbit Jam - 1 (1%)
Why Don't We Do It in the Road
    - 1 (1%)
Wind Beneath My Wings - 1 (1%)

First Set Openers

My Friend My Friend - 11
AC/DC Bag - 7
Ya Mar - 6
Cars Trucks Buses - 5
Sample in a Jar - 5
Buried Alive - 4
Chalk Dust Torture - 3
Don't You Wanna Go - 3
Poor Heart - 3
Runaway Jim - 3
Fee - 2
Julius - 2
Makisupa Policeman - 2
Maze - 2
Prince Caspian - 2
Stash - 2
Tweezer Reprise - 2
Axilla (Part II) - 1
Bouncing Around the Room - 1
Dinner and a Movie - 1
Divided Sky - 1
Halley's Comet - 1
Horn - 1
Icculus - 1
Llama - 1
Possum - 1
Punch You In The Eye - 1
Simple - 1
Split Open and Melt - 1
Suzy Greenberg - 1
The Oh Kee Pa Ceremony - 1
The Old Home Place - 1
Theme From The Bottom - 1
Wolfman's Brother - 1

First Set Closers

Chalk Dust Torture - 9

Sample in a Jar - 8
Cavern - 6
Run Like an Antelope - 6
Split Open and Melt - 6
Suzy Greenberg - 5
The Squirming Coil - 5
Possum - 4
Sweet Adeline - 4
Runaway Jim - 3
David Bowie - 2
Hello My Baby - 2
Slave to the Traffic Light - 2
Stash - 2
While My Guitar Gently Weeps - 2
You Enjoy Myself - 2
Amazing Grace - 1
Amazing Grace Jam - 1
Carolina - 1
Fire - 1
Frankenstein - 1
Free - 1
Funky Bitch - 1
Good Times Bad Times - 1
Harpua - 1
I'm Blue I'm Lonesome - 1
Life on Mars - 1
Suspicious Minds - 1
Tweezer Reprise - 1

Second Set Openers

Also Sprach Zarathustra - 11
Timber (Jerry) - 8
Maze - 4
Runaway Jim - 4
Theme From The Bottom - 4
Wilson - 4
Free - 3
Makisupa Policeman - 3
Simple - 3
The Curtain - 3
Cars Trucks Buses - 2
Halley's Comet - 2
Julius - 2
Poor Heart - 2
Reba - 2
Sample in a Jar - 2
Split Open and Melt - 2
A Day in the Life - 1
AC/DC Bag - 1
Bouncing Around the Room - 1
Chalk Dust Torture - 1
David Bowie - 1
Down With Disease - 1
Drowned - 1
Frankenstein - 1
Golgi Apparatus - 1
Ha Ha Ha - 1
I Am the Sea - 1

Keyboard Cavalry - 1
Mound - 1
My Sweet One - 1
Possum - 1
Rift - 1
Tube - 1
Tweezer Reprise - 1
Ya Mar - 1

Second Set Closers

Cavern - 7
Run Like an Antelope - 7
Slave to the Traffic Light - 7
The Squirming Coil - 7
Tweezer Reprise - 6
A Day in the Life - 5
Amazing Grace - 4
Possum - 4
Suzy Greenberg - 4
Sweet Adeline - 4
Funky Bitch - 2
Golgi Apparatus - 2
Julius - 2
Sample in a Jar - 2
While My Guitar Gently Weeps - 2
Chalk Dust Torture - 1
Crossroads - 1
David Bowie - 1
Fire - 1
Frankenstein - 1
Good Times Bad Times - 1
Highway To Hell - 1
Jam - 1
Keyboard Cavalry Reprise - 1
Love Reign O'er Me - 1
Mike's Song - 1
Poor Heart - 1
Runaway Jim - 1
Strange Design - 1
You Enjoy Myself - 1

Third Set Openers

Auld Lang Syne - 1
You Enjoy Myself - 1

Third Set Closers

Frankenstein - 1
Suzy Greenberg - 1

Encores

A Day in the Life - 11
Rocky Top - 8
Fire - 7
While My Guitar Gently Weeps - 6
Bold As Love - 5
Good Times Bad Times - 5

Tweezer Reprise - 5
Bouncing Around the Room - 4
Sweet Adeline - 4
Amazing Grace - 3
Funky Bitch - 3
Life on Mars - 3
The Squirming Coil - 3
Acoustic Army - 2
Chalk Dust Torture - 2
Frankenstein - 2
Golgi Apparatus - 2
Harry Hood - 2
Hello My Baby - 2
Loving Cup - 2
Simple - 2
Slave to the Traffic Light - 2
Sleeping Monkey - 2
Suzy Greenberg - 2
Theme From The Bottom - 2
Bill Bailey Won't You Please
    Come Home - 1

Brown Eyed Girl - 1
Come Together - 1
Cracklin' Rosie - 1
Fee - 1
Gloria - 1
Halley's Comet - 1
Highway To Hell - 1
I'll Come Running - 1
I'm Blue I'm Lonesome - 1
Johnny B. Goode - 1
Julius - 1
My Generation - 1
My Long Journey Home - 1
Poor Heart - 1
Poor Heart Reprise - 1
Possum - 1
Runaway Jim - 1
The Wedge - 1
Three Little Birds - 1
Uncle Pen - 1

DEBUTS (Summer 1996

Waste	6/6/1996
Character Zero	6/6/1996
Train Song	7/21/1996
Somewhere Over the Rainbow	8/2/1996
Theme to Star Trek	8/4/1996
Talk	8/5/1996
99 Years	8/7/1996
Hold to a Dream	8/7/1996
Do My Time	8/7/1996
Gypsy Queen	8/7/1996

DEPARTURES (Summer 1996)

	LAST KNOWN	# SHOWS
Theme to Star Trek	8/4/1996	305
99 Years	8/7/1996	302
Hold to a Dream	8/7/1996	302

BREAKOUTS (Summer 1996)

	SHELVED	BREAKOUT	# SHOWS
Taste	6/30/1995	7/3/1996	64
Terrapin	6/13/1995	7/11/1996	84
I Am Hydrogen	10/19/1995	7/23/1996	60
Whipping Post	4/20/1993	8/10/1996	284
Weigh	10/22/1995	8/12/1996	66
Glide	11/21/1995	8/13/1996	51
Cracklin' Rosie	11/12/1995	8/14/1996	58
Harpua	10/31/1995	8/17/1996	64
Brother	8/2/1993	8/17/1996	257

SUMMER 1996

"Having a Ball"

Phish followed their legendary 12/31/95 show with one of the longest tour-breaks ever. It would be six full months before they would tour again, though two single shows popped up in the spring. Phish played at Jazzfest in New Orleans on 4/26 and at a small bar in Woodstock, New York on 6/6. The latter allowed the band to road-test two new songs that would end up on *Billy Breathes* ("Waste" and "Character Zero").

In early July, Phish headed back to Europe. The tour was primarily booked as opening act shows with Santana, though Phish did squeeze in a few headlining gigs of their own. The controversial 7/12 Amsterdam show may be the most discussed of the tour. Some fans really like the atypical versions of songs performed on this night (many were unfinished), while others write off the band's performance as loose and incredibly sloppy. Either way, it's evident that the band had a great time at this tiny venue.

A brief two-week American tour followed. The stint included a four night run at Red Rocks (the band's final shows at the beloved venue, due to incidents involving fans and local police) and culminated in a summer festival unprecedented in scope: The Clifford Ball. The Ball had it all: two days, three sets per day, plus a freeform set performed on a moving flatbed truck in the middle of the night. Most impressive was that the band could pull off a festival of this size with no supporting acts, save an afternoon appearance by The Clifford Ball Orchestra. The band treated fans to a breakout of the oft-requested "Brother," (featuring Vermont ice cream entrepenuers Ben and Jerry on vocals), and everyone reveled in the impossible size of the first-ever Phish Fantasy Camp.

FALL 1996

"Arena Rock PermaGroove"

Fresh on the heels of the *Billy Breathes* release, Phish hit the road again in October. Though some moments are endeared, like the 10/18 "Maze" and the 10/22 "Weekapaug," many fans generally regard the first two weeks of this tour as among the weakest (relatively speaking, of course!) in Phishtory. The band was exclusively playing arenas for the first time, and seemed to struggle in converting their sound to the new venues.

Trey continued to use the percussion setup he had introduced the previous Fall, and thus Page was more prominent than ever. Most jams from this tour feature an energetic Page solo, often spiced with the funky sounds of the clavinet. This is the signature Fall 96 sound: a static groove studded with bursts of keyboard. The spacey exploration of 94/95 was all but forgotten, making way for crowd pleasing (but repetitive) dance grooves. Meanwhile, "Simple" and "Down With Disease" emerged for the first time as regular jam vehicles

As with years past, Halloween did not disappoint. The musical costume (*Remain in Light* by Talking Heads) shaped the Phish sound for years to come, pushing the band towards experiments in groove. Guest percussionist Karl Perazzo toured for four shows around the Halloween extravaganza, and contributed to the famed 11/2 "Crosseyed Antelope." Continuing on, the 11/7 "Bathtub Gin" and the 11/13 "Suzy Greenberg" made waves as possi-

ble "best-ever" versions.

Somewhere in the midwest, the band seemed suddenly to loosen up on stage again. In a string of shows from 11/15 to 11/19, the band appeared chattier than they had been in quite awhile, and brought the humor element back to the Phish concert experience. As with many tours, the run to close out the fall was quite strong. The 11/30 performance featured guest saxophonist Peter Apfelbaum on "Taste" and "Timber," and featured perhaps the first repetition of a riff that would continue to pop up over the next year: James Brown's "Superbad." Though the 12/6 Vegas show is deservedly lauded (featuring two members of Primus on "Harpua"), the 11/27 second set (featuring a mighty "Disease" and "Tweezer" -> "Disease Reprise") should not be overlooked. Trey later remarked (in *The Phish Book*) that the band was trying in these last weeks to play a kind of music they hadn't quite invented yet, and by New Year's had to rely on the usual "bag of tricks" to get through a show. It was not a creative high point.

DEBUTS (Fall 1996)

Swept Away	10/16/1996
Steep	10/16/1996
The Star Spangled Banner	10/17/1996
Born Under Punches	10/31/1996
Crosseyed and Painless	10/31/1996
The Great Curve	10/31/1996
Once in a Lifetime	10/31/1996
Houses in Motion	10/31/1996
Seen and Not Seen	10/31/1996
Listening Wind	10/31/1996
Overload	10/31/1996
Mean Mr. Mustard	11/15/1996
American Band	11/16/1996
Midnight on the Highway	11/23/1996
Wildwood Weed	12/6/1996
Cowboy's Sweetheart	12/6/1996

DEPARTURES (Fall 1996)

	LAST KNOWN	# SHOWS
All Along the Watchtower	10/22/1996	290
Born Under Punches	10/31/1996	284
Houses in Motion	10/31/1996	284
Listening Wind	10/31/1996	284
Once in a Lifetime	10/31/1996	284
Overload	10/31/1996	284
Seen and Not Seen	10/31/1996	284
The Great Curve	10/31/1996	284
Demand	11/14/1996	275
Mean Mr. Mustard	11/15/1996	274
Mound	11/19/1996	271
The Vibration of Life	11/19/1996	271
Midnight on the Highway	11/23/1996	269
Sparks	11/29/1996	266
Cowboy's Sweetheart	12/6/1996	261
Suspicious Minds	12/6/1996	261
Wildwood Weed	12/6/1996	261

BREAKOUTS (Fall 1996)

	SHELVED	BREAKOUT	# SHOWS
Ginseng Sullivan	6/23/1995	10/21/1996	103
All Along the Watchtower	4/21/1994	10/22/1996	226
Catapult	12/1/1995	10/27/1996	57
Carolina	11/21/1995	10/27/1996	64
The Wedge	11/14/1995	10/29/1996	70

BREAKOUTS (Fall 1996)

	SHELVED	BREAKOUT	# SHOWS
Jesus Just Left Chicago	10/31/1995	10/31/1996	76
All Things Reconsidered	7/1/1995	11/8/1996	108
Axilla	10/16/1994	11/8/1996	170
Demand	12/7/1995	11/14/1996	64
Kung	12/30/1995	11/16/1996	55
La Grange	12/29/1995	11/16/1996	56
Bold as Love	12/14/1995	11/27/1996	67
Sparks	10/29/1994	11/29/1996	173
Peaches en Regalia	12/31/1994	12/1/1996	144

NYE 1996

"Rhapsody in Boston"

In 1996, Phish continued the trend that they established in 1995 of four shows at two venues. In geographically classic fashion, they booked nights in Philadelphia and Boston, once again celebrating their New England roots.

12/28 provided a mesmerizing digital delay loop jam that bled into "TMWSIY" as well as a raging "Weekapaug" that overflowed into a jaunty Page solo. On 12/29, the band celebrated the anniversaries of the Providence "Bowie" (94) as well as the Worcester "Gin" (95) by providing capable versions of each song. The "Harpua" narration that night featured Tom Marshall (introduced as the "uberdemon"), who revealed that "the horrible sound of hell" was, in fact, Oasis's hit "Champagne Supernova."

The first night at Boston's Fleet Center included a hilarious pantomine jam when the sound went out during "Funky Bitch." The band hammed it up as if to taunt the audience with what they were missing, as Trey played his guitar behind his back and Fishman pounded away silently at the drums. The show was highlighted by a nostalgic "Tweezer" -> "Lifeboy" pairing, as well as an appearance from local comedian Steven Wright (on desk bell) during "Scent of a Mule."

New Year's Eve was fun and featured many popular songs, but came nowhere near the musical majesty of the previous year's edition. It included a rare "Peaches En Regalia" and an out of nowhere "Tweezer Reprise" first set closer. The new year was ushered in by an inspired "Down With Disease" (which clearly foreshadowed the funky grooves that were to come in '97) and an accompanying avalanche of Phish balloons which spanned several minutes and sent tapers scurrying to cover their microphones. The Boston Community Choir put a unique stamp on the night with their guest appearance on the uproarious debut of "Bohemian Rhapsody," as well as a classy "Amazing Grace" encore. Trey later lamented that the show was fun but "intensely planned," and the lack of spontaneity was apparent. A fun but lightweight creative year was capped off by a fun but lightweight New Year's show.

DEBUTS (NYE 1996)

Sixteen Candles	12/29/1996
Champagne Supernova	12/29/1996

DEPARTURES (NYE 1996)

	LAST KNOWN	# SHOWS
Caravan	12/29/1996	259
Champagne Supernova	12/29/1996	259
Sixteen Candles	12/29/1996	259
Bohemian Rhapsody	12/31/1996	257

BREAKOUTS (NYE 1996)	SHELVED	BREAKOUT	# SHOWS
Caravan	12/2/1994	12/29/1996	160

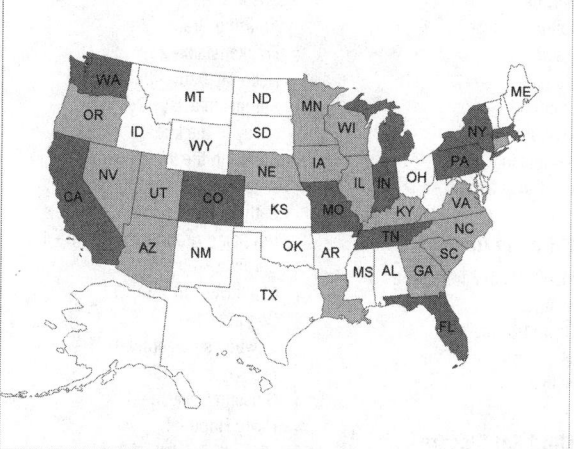

There were 70 shows played

Shows by day of week

- Sunday- 8
- Monday- 9
- Tuesday- 8
- Wednesday- 12
- Thursday- 8
- Friday- 13
- Saturday- 12

166 songs have been played (26% of songs Phish have played).

The average number of songs per show is 17.8.

The average amount of times each song was played is 7.54.

Total Times Played

Taste - 28 (40%)
Sample in a Jar - 26 (37%)
Chalk Dust Torture - 23 (32%)
You Enjoy Myself - 23 (32%)
Character Zero - 21 (30%)
Poor Heart - 21 (30%)
Sparkle - 21 (30%)
Down With Disease - 20 (28%)
Runaway Jim - 20 (28%)
Stash - 20 (28%)
Theme From The Bottom - 20 (28%)
Cars Trucks Buses - 19 (27%)
David Bowie - 19 (27%)
Harry Hood - 19 (27%)
Reba - 19 (27%)
Run Like an Antelope - 19 (27%)
Ya Mar - 19 (27%)
AC/DC Bag - 17 (24%)
Bouncing Around the Room

- 17 (24%)
Cavern - 17 (24%)
Free - 17 (24%)
Hello My Baby - 17 (24%)
Maze - 17 (24%)
Prince Caspian - 17 (24%)
Scent of a Mule - 17 (24%)
Suzy Greenberg - 17 (24%)
Waste - 17 (24%)
Also Sprach Zarathustra - 16 (22%)
Divided Sky - 16 (22%)
Julius - 16 (22%)
Simple - 16 (22%)
Split Open and Melt - 16 (22%)
Tweezer - 16 (22%)
A Day in the Life - 15 (21%)
Mike's Song - 15 (21%)
Punch You In The Eye - 15 (21%)
Train Song - 15 (21%)
Funky Bitch - 14 (20%)
It's Ice - 14 (20%)
Steep - 13 (18%)
Swept Away - 13 (18%)
Weekapaug Groove - 13 (18%)
Slave to the Traffic Light - 12 (17%)
Wilson - 12 (17%)
Guelah Papyrus - 11 (15%)
Rift - 11 (15%)
Bathtub Gin - 10 (14%)
Fee - 10 (14%)
Golgi Apparatus - 10 (14%)
Life on Mars - 10 (14%)
Llama - 10 (14%)
Possum - 10 (14%)
The Lizards - 10 (14%)
Tweezer Reprise - 10 (14%)
Wolfman's Brother - 10 (14%)

Billy Breathes - 9 (12%)
Johnny B. Goode - 9 (12%)
Silent in the Morning - 9 (12%)
Sweet Adeline - 9 (12%)
The Horse - 9 (12%)
Timber (Jerry) - 9 (12%)
Fire - 8 (11%)
Frankenstein - 8 (11%)
Gumbo - 8 (11%)
Talk - 8 (11%)
The Curtain - 8 (11%)
The Star Spangled Banner - 8 (11%)
Makisupa Policeman - 7 (10%)
Rocky Top - 7 (10%)
Strange Design - 7 (10%)
The Squirming Coil - 7 (10%)
Uncle Pen - 7 (10%)
Amazing Grace - 6 (8%)
Fluffhead - 6 (8%)
Foam - 6 (8%)
Ginseng Sullivan - 6 (8%)
Good Times Bad Times - 6 (8%)
Guyute - 6 (8%)
I Didn't Know - 6 (8%)
Loving Cup - 6 (8%)
My Friend My Friend - 6 (8%)
NICU - 6 (8%)
The Sloth - 6 (8%)
Axilla - 5 (7%)
Brother - 5 (7%)
The Old Home Place - 5 (7%)
All Things Reconsidered - 4 (5%)
Contact - 4 (5%)
Fast Enough for You - 4 (5%)
Horn - 4 (5%)
Jam - 4 (5%)
Lawn Boy - 4 (5%)
McGrupp and the Watchful Hosemasters - 4 (5%)
Mound - 4 (5%)
The Mango Song - 4 (5%)
Avenu Malkenu - 3 (4%)
Catapult - 3 (4%)
Esther - 3 (4%)
Harpua - 3 (4%)
Highway To Hell - 3 (4%)
Jesus Just Left Chicago - 3 (4%)
La Grange - 3 (4%)
Peaches En Regalia - 3 (4%)
Purple Rain - 3 (4%)
Somewhere Over the Rainbow - 3 (4%)
The Man Who Stepped Into Yesterday - 3 (4%)
Tube - 3 (4%)
Big Black Furry Creature From Mars - 2 (2%)

Bike - 2 (2%)
Buried Alive - 2 (2%)
Colonel Forbin's Ascent - 2 (2%)
Crosseyed and Painless - 2 (2%)
Glide - 2 (2%)
Ha Ha Ha - 2 (2%)
Halley's Comet - 2 (2%)
I Am Hydrogen - 2 (2%)
If I Could - 2 (2%)
Lifeboy - 2 (2%)
My Mind's Got a Mind of its Own - 2 (2%)
Sleeping Monkey - 2 (2%)
Suspicious Minds - 2 (2%)
Tela - 2 (2%)
The Famous Mockingbird - 2 (2%)
Weigh - 2 (2%)
99 Years - 1 (1%)
All Along the Watchtower - 1 (1%)
Amazing Grace Jam - 1 (1%)
American Band - 1 (1%)
Auld Lang Syne - 1 (1%)
Bohemian Rhapsody - 1 (1%)
Bold As Love - 1 (1%)
Born Under Punches (The Heat goes on) - 1 (1%)
Caravan - 1 (1%)
Carolina - 1 (1%)
Champagne Supernova - 1 (1%)
Cowboy's Sweetheart - 1 (1%)
Cracklin' Rosie - 1 (1%)
Demand - 1 (1%)
Digital Delay Loop Jam - 1 (1%)
Dinner and a Movie - 1 (1%)
Dog Faced Boy - 1 (1%)
Doin' My Time - 1 (1%)
Gypsy Queen - 1 (1%)
Hold to a Dream - 1 (1%)
Houses in Motion - 1 (1%)
Kung - 1 (1%)
Listening Wind - 1 (1%)
Mean Mr. Mustard - 1 (1%)
Midnight on the Highway - 1 (1%)
Once in a Lifetime - 1 (1%)
Overload - 1 (1%)
Rotation Jam - 1 (1%)
Sanity - 1 (1%)
Seen and Not Seen - 1 (1%)
Sixteen Candles - 1 (1%)
Sparks - 1 (1%)
Sweet Emotion Jam - 1 (1%)
Terrapin - 1 (1%)
The Great Curve - 1 (1%)
The Man Who Stepped Into Yesterday Reprise - 1 (1%)
The Oh Kee Pa Ceremony - 1 (1%)
The Vibration of Life - 1 (1%)

The Wedge - 1 (1%)
Theme to Star Trek: The Original
    Series - 1 (1%)
Whipping Post - 1 (1%)
Wildwood Weed - 1 (1%)

First Set Openers

Chalk Dust Torture - 8
Runaway Jim - 8
My Friend My Friend - 5
Wilson - 5
Ya Mar - 5
Poor Heart - 4
Julius - 3
Sample in a Jar - 3
AC/DC Bag - 2
Also Sprach Zarathustra - 2
Cars Trucks Buses - 2
Divided Sky - 2
Punch You In The Eye - 2
Split Open and Melt - 2
Axilla - 1
Buried Alive - 1
Down With Disease - 1
Frankenstein - 1
Funky Bitch - 1
Golgi Apparatus - 1
Ha Ha Ha - 1
It's Ice - 1
Makisupa Policeman - 1
Peaches En Regalia - 1
Rocky Top - 1
Sanity - 1
Somewhere Over the Rainbow - 1
The Curtain - 1
The Old Home Place - 1
The Star Spangled Banner - 1
Theme From The Bottom - 1

First Set Closers

Character Zero - 6
David Bowie - 6
Cavern - 5
Run Like an Antelope - 5
Suzy Greenberg - 5
Frankenstein - 4
You Enjoy Myself - 4
Sample in a Jar - 3
The Squirming Coil - 3
Funky Bitch - 2
Good Times Bad Times - 2
Hello My Baby - 2
Johnny B. Goode - 2
Julius - 2
Llama - 2
Loving Cup - 2
Possum - 2

Tweezer Reprise - 2
Bold As Love - 1
Chalk Dust Torture - 1
Doin' My Time - 1
Golgi Apparatus - 1
Harry Hood - 1
Highway To Hell - 1
La Grange - 1
Runaway Jim - 1
Slave to the Traffic Light - 1
Sweet Adeline - 1
The Star Spangled Banner - 1

Second Set Openers

Also Sprach Zarathustra - 7
AC/DC Bag - 4
Down With Disease - 4
Timber (Jerry) - 4
Wilson - 4
David Bowie - 3
Runaway Jim - 3
The Curtain - 3
Chalk Dust Torture - 2
La Grange - 2
Llama - 2
Makisupa Policeman - 2
Suzy Greenberg - 2
Ya Mar - 2
Born Under Punches (The Heat
    goes on) - 1
Brother - 1
Crosseyed and Painless - 1
Ha Ha Ha - 1
Harry Hood - 1
It's Ice - 1
Julius - 1
Rift - 1
Split Open and Melt - 1
Tube - 1
Tweezer - 1
Wolfman's Brother - 1

Second Set Closers

Slave to the Traffic Light - 6
Weekapaug Groove - 6
Hello My Baby - 5
Harry Hood - 4
Tweezer Reprise - 4
David Bowie - 3
Run Like an Antelope - 3
Suzy Greenberg - 3
A Day in the Life - 2
Fire - 2
Sweet Adeline - 2
The Star Spangled Banner - 2
Amazing Grace - 1
Amazing Grace Jam - 1
Character Zero - 1

Funky Bitch - 1
Golgi Apparatus - 1
Good Times Bad Times - 1
Harpua - 1
Johnny B. Goode - 1
Julius - 1
Llama - 1
Overload - 1
Possum - 1
Sample in a Jar - 1
You Enjoy Myself - 1

Third Set Openers

Also Sprach Zarathustra - 1
Brother - 1
David Bowie - 1
Makisupa Policeman - 1
Wilson - 1

Third Set Closers

Harry Hood - 1
Hello My Baby - 1
Julius - 1
Suzy Greenberg - 1
Tweezer Reprise - 1

Encores

Rocky Top - 6
Fire - 5
Johnny B. Goode - 5
Cavern - 4
Harpua - 4
Julius - 4
Waste - 4

Funky Bitch - 3
Golgi Apparatus - 3
Good Times Bad Times - 3
Possum - 3
Amazing Grace - 2
Frankenstein - 2
Hello My Baby - 2
Sample in a Jar - 2
A Day in the Life - 1
All Along the Watchtower - 1
American Band - 1
Bathtub Gin - 1
Bouncing Around the Room - 1
Carolina - 1
Chalk Dust Torture - 1
Contact - 1
Cowboy's Sweetheart - 1
Fee - 1
Ginseng Sullivan - 1
Harry Hood - 1
Highway To Hell - 1
Jesus Just Left Chicago - 1
Punch You In The Eye - 1
Sleeping Monkey - 1
Stash - 1
Suspicious Minds - 1
Suzy Greenberg - 1
Sweet Adeline - 1
The Squirming Coil - 1
Theme From The Bottom - 1
Theme to Star Trek: The Original
    Series - 1
Tweezer Reprise - 1
Wildwood Weed - 1
Ya Mar - 1

WINTER 1997

"Europe Redux"

For the first time, Phish was booked for a headlining tour in Europe. 3/1 Hamburg was later released in part on *Slip, Stitch and Pass* and came to represent the beginning of the band's transition to more groove-oriented jams. The popular "Carini" was all the rave among new songs, though the short-lived "Rock-a-William" and "Walfredo" also debuted.

The first "Carini" came inside one of the tour's strongest sets, on 2/17. Other fan-favorites include the breakout-fest in Stuttgart (2/26) and the aforementioned Hamburg, which contained the return of the popular "Cities." Though only two weeks long, the tour allowed Phish to finally play regular two-set shows for their European fan base (although, admittedly, a good portion of the crowds consisted of Americans who made the journey overseas). Upon arrival back in the States, the tired band made their second visit to the studios of *Late Night With David Letterman*, to perform "Character Zero."

Fans were once again energized by flashy setlists and inspired play, though this brief tour was only a prelude of things to come. The winter closed with a benefit at Burlington's Flynn Theatre, which included the debut of covers "Love Me Like A Man" and "Cinnamon Girl."

DEBUTS (Winter 1997)

Walfredo	2/13/1997
Love Me	2/13/1997
My Soul	2/13/1997
When the Circus Comes	2/13/1997
Rocko William	2/13/1997
Beauty of My Dreams	2/16/1997
Soul Shake Down Party	2/17/1997
Carini	2/17/1997
One Meatball	2/25/1997
Li'l Red Rooster	2/25/1997
Got My Mojo Workin'	2/25/1997
Cinnamon Girl	3/18/1997
I Told You So	3/18/1997
Love Me Like a Man	3/18/1997

DEPARTURES (Winter 1997)

	LAST KNOWN	# SHOWS
Soul Shake Down Party	2/20/1997	251
All Things Reconsidered	2/23/1997	248
Daniel	2/23/1997	248
Why Don't We Do It in the Road	2/23/1997	248
Got My Mojo Workin'	2/25/1997	247
Li'l Red Rooster	2/25/1997	247
One Meatball	2/25/1997	247
Highway To Hell	2/26/1997	246
Life on Mars	3/2/1997	243
I Told You So	3/18/1997	242
Love Me Like a Man	3/18/1997	242

BREAKOUTS (Winter 1997)

	SHELVED	BREAKOUT	# SHOWS
Why Don't We Do It in the Road	6/25/1995	2/23/1997	144
Daniel	8/28/1993	2/23/1997	287
Dog Gone Dog	12/11/1995	2/26/1997	90
While My Guitar Gently Weeps	12/11/1995	2/26/1997	90
Camel Walk	7/2/1995	2/26/1997	140
Magilla	5/4/1994	2/26/1997	260
Drowned	12/31/1995	2/28/1997	82
Paul and Silas	10/24/1995	2/28/1997	120
Dinner and a Movie	6/8/1996	3/1/1997	59
Cities	7/5/1994	3/1/1997	222

SUMMER 1997

"Riding the Back of the Worm"

It was the tour that changed it all, and set the pace for the next few years. A two night run in Amsterdam seemed to sum it all up best: we were all on the back of the worm, and the worm would groove all summer long.

Phish had, of course, been a jamming band for their entire existence. But the summer of 1997 featured jamming in songs that never stretched out in the past (witness "Gumbo" and "Wolfman's Brother"), introduced a revitalization of the first set, and generally marked a new era in Phishtory. Mike's Modulus bass guitar, noticeably louder and more pronounced, propelled the bus around Europe and the States for six weeks and eventually left everyone speechless, from Dublin to Limestone. Remarkably, many outstanding jams came out of a *new* song, Ghost, which stunned everyone by opening the occasional show with a 10-15 minute version.

The first two nights of the tour included an amazing fifteen debuts. These were not throwaways, either: mostly all stayed in rotation throughout the year, and well more than half are still beloved regulars today. "Ghost," "Twist," "Limb by Limb" and "Piper" may be the best-known, but the group also included the tender "Dirt," the quirky "Vultures," and a rocking cover of "Izabella." And though it wouldn't become an international dance craze for two more summers, the original "Meatstick" debuted in infant form on 6/25.

As with many tours featuring new material, the band spent much of the early tour getting accustomed to their new songs. On 7/1 and 7/2 , the band broke free and started to ride the worm. The show-opening "Ghost" on 7/1 may have been the most unexpected. As it jammed on into the set, fans didn't know if they were witnessing the birth of another jam monster or just the effects of a night in Amsterdam! Thankfully, it was the former…or maybe just a bit of both. This two night stand in a converted church is much circulated, and boasts jaw-dropping second sets, not to mention the first "Mike's Song" show opener in years.

Amsterdam was followed by the hysterical 7/6 soundcheck, as well as strong outings in France on 7/9 and 7/10. The first featured an impressive guest shot from Bela Fleck and all of his Flecktones, including Jeff Coffin on saxophone. The short break between European and American tours left little time for tapes to get out, but the Amsterdam shows were early favorites among those who had a chance to to comprehend the new direction Phish was taking.

Phish made sure to indoctrinate the crowd in Virginia Beach, with U.S. debuts of four of the new bunch to open the first American show, and another reference to "the worm." The following night in Raleigh, a truly electric show kept fans moving and grooving on the worm, delighted by a spine-tingling segue from "Disease" into "Mike's Song." Two shows at the visually spectacular Gorge and two more at the always-popular Deer Creek Amphitheatre followed shortly thereafter, and before fans knew it, the tour was nearly over and headed to Limestone for the second summer festival.

The art sculpture that burned to the ground at The Great Went may have been symbolic: the upcoming fall tour would see Phish divert even further away from the sound that fans had become accustomed to. As our piece of collective art lit up the sky, fans contemplated the events of the Summer: nothing less than a complete renewal and revitalization of the Phish Muse.

DEBUTS (Summer 1997)

Dogs Stole Things	6/13/1997
Limb by Limb	6/13/1997
Wading in the Velvet Sea	6/13/1997
Water in the Sky	6/13/1997
Vultures	6/13/1997
Ghost	6/13/1997
Oblivious Fool	6/13/1997
Stand	6/13/1997
Izabella	6/13/1997
Dirt	6/14/1997
Bye Bye Foot	6/14/1997

DEBUTS (Summer 1997) continued

Twist	6/14/1997
Piper	6/14/1997
I Saw it Again	6/14/1997
Waking Up	6/14/1997
I Don't Care	6/16/1997
Ain't Love Funny	6/20/1997
Meatstick	6/25/1997
Cecilia	6/25/1997
Samson Variation	8/3/1997
Messin' With The Kid	8/8/1997
Amoreena	8/13/1997

DEPARTURES (Summer 1997)	LAST KNOWN	# SHOWS
Stand	6/13/1997	241
Waking Up	6/14/1997	240
I Don't Care	6/20/1997	237
Cecilia	6/25/1997	233
Take Me to the River	7/10/1997	224
Cinnamon Girl	7/31/1997	215
Samson Variation	8/3/1997	213
Hoochie Coochie Man	8/8/1997	211
Ain't Love Funny	8/9/1997	210
Bye Bye Foot	8/10/1997	209
Rocko William	8/10/1997	209
Amoreena	8/13/1997	207

BREAKOUTS (Summer 1997)	SHELVED	BREAKOUT	# SHOWS
Love You	12/8/1995	7/5/1997	111
I Am Hydrogen	8/5/1996	7/22/1997	83
My Mind's Got a Mind of its Own	11/15/1996	8/3/1997	61
Hoochie Coochie Man	4/10/1993	8/8/1997	380
Crossroads	12/9/1995	8/9/1997	127
Tela	11/7/1996	8/14/1997	74
Colonel Forbin's Ascent	10/31/1996	8/14/1997	78
Harpua	12/29/1996	8/16/1997	54
Contact	11/30/1996	8/16/1997	60
Halley's Comet	8/16/1996	8/16/1997	92
The Wedge	10/29/1996	8/17/1997	81
Carolina	10/27/1996	8/17/1997	82
Buffalo Bill	12/31/1994	8/17/1997	204

FALL 1997

"Submerged in Cow Funk"

The fall started with an appearance on Conan O'Brien's late-night television show. *Slip, Stitch and Pass* had just been released and fans debated which track would be played. Phish responded with the ultimate swerve: a new song called "Farmhouse." Then, the Max Weinberg 7 sat silently as Phish played to commercial...with the opening notes of "Mike's Song"! It set the tone for the fall: this band could, and often would, do anything.

As the jams got longer and more frequent, the setlists got shorter (the 11/17 *first* set only had five songs!), and it was not uncommon for half-hour long jams to permeate a show. Songs like "Halley's Comet," "Tube," and "AC/DC Bag" jammed for the first time. The other new tune, "Black-Eyed Katy," spotlighted the self-described "cow funk" jamming that became em-

blematic of the tour. "Wolfman's Brother" continued its newfound role as a jam monster, with capstone versions on 11/19 and 11/30. Even songs like "Character Zero," "Johnny B. Goode," and "Twist" received uncharacteristically extended treatment.

Mike was prominent in the mix; Trey took to playing more chord-based solos and textural tones, Page showed an affinity for spacey flourishes rather than virtuoso piano solos, and Fishman was more springy and aggresive than ever. The result was one of the most consistent tours in Phishtory; it's not hyberbole to say that almost every show contains exciting musical highlights.

The two-night Hampton stand (11/21 and 11/22), followed by an intense second set in Winston-Salem on 11/23, remain among the most circulated shows of the tour. The three night Worcester run made amends for a lack of New England New Year's Run dates, and included the longest ever single song Phish jam, a 59 minute "Runaway Jim." Several set-long segue-fests delighted fans; see the second sets of 11/17 (Denver), 11/19 (Champaign, IL), 12/6 (Auburn Hills), and 12/11/97 (Rochester). At the tour closer in Albany on 12/13, Trey furthered the glowstick trend by asking Chris Kuroda to kill the lights, and the first indoor "glowstick war" occured. This one, during "Harry Hood," signalled an emotional reminder of the Great Went. (In '98, the practice would become routine and perfunctory, especially during "Hood," until Phish was finally forced to include admonishments against glowstick-throwing in the mail order info sheet.)

12/7 deserves mention for one of the most statistically significant breakouts ever: "Boogie On Reggae Woman," after well over 800 shows. The tour also saw the debut of covers "Them Changes" and "Emotional Rescue."

DEBUTS (Fall 1997)

Black-Eyed Katy	11/13/1997
Farmhouse	11/16/1997
Emotional Rescue	11/21/1997
Moby Dick	11/29/1997
Them Changes	11/30/1997
Psycho Killer	12/7/1997
Roses Are Free	12/11/1997

DEPARTURES (Fall 1997)	LAST KNOWN	# SHOWS
Oblivious Fool	11/17/1997	200
Them Changes	11/30/1997	192
Psycho Killer	12/7/1997	187

BREAKOUTS (Fall 1997)	SHELVED	BREAKOUT	# SHOWS
Fast Enough For You	11/22/1996	11/14/1997	68
I Didn't Know	2/22/1997	11/28/1997	55
The Curtain	2/20/1997	11/28/1997	57
The Sloth	2/23/1997	11/29/1997	55
TMWSIY	12/28/1996	11/29/1997	67
Avenu Malkenu	12/28/1996	11/29/1997	67
Buried Alive	2/26/1997	12/2/1997	55
The Star Spangled Banner	12/28/1996	12/2/1997	69
Dog Faced Boy	8/12/1996	12/2/1997	109
Drowned	3/18/1997	12/3/1997	52
My Friend My Friend	2/26/1997	12/5/1997	57
A Day in the Life	2/28/1997	12/7/1997	58
Tube	2/26/1997	12/7/1997	59
Boogie On Reggae Woman	9/13/1988	12/7/1997	865
Axilla	2/28/1997	12/9/1997	59
BBFCFM	8/6/1996	12/11/1997	118
Catapult	3/2/1997	12/13/1997	60

NYE 1997

"Udder Balls and Olive Loafs"

Poor Landover. The Run opener in this city became a mere warm-up for the three Madison Square Garden shows that followed. Starting with ripping versions of "Disease" and "Bowie" on 12/29 and concluding with an appropriate "New York New York" and an exclamatory "Tweezer Reprise," these three nights were the perfect capstone to a wonderful year.

The now-legendary 12/30 show opened with the breakout of "Sneakin' Sally Through the Alley" (the first in over 800 shows) and culminated with one of the strongest encores in recent memory. One of the longest and most involved "Harpua' narrations solidified the myth and lore of this Run, which also included the first "Carini" on U.S. soil, a near set-long "Mike's Groove" combo on New Year's Eve, and an extensively jammed version of "AC/DC Bag."

New Year's featured a large circular screen covering the famous MSG scoreboard, on which many strange images were projected, most referencing the Harpua story from the night before. Steaks, eggs, olive loafs, and clocks swirled around as the crowd danced beneath. At midnight, the "udder ball" itself fell open and dropped oversized balloons on the crowd.

As fans celebrated the birth of 1998 on the streets of New York City, we were satisfied that we had seen a fabulous Run capping a fabulous year. The future seemed untapped. We hoped that the energy would continue into 1998. The only thing we weren't sure of was how we would satisfy our fix in the six months before summer tour.

DEBUTS (NYE 1997)

I'm Gonna Be (500 Miles)	12/30/1997
New York New York	12/31/1997

DEPARTURES (NYE 1997)

	LAST KNOWN	# SHOWS
Black-Eyed Katy	12/30/1997	180
I'm Gonna Be (500 Miles)	12/30/1997	180
New York New York	12/31/1997	179

BREAKOUTS (NYE 1997)

	SHELVED	BREAKOUT	# SHOWS
Carini	3/1/1997	12/30/1997	64
Sneakin' Sally Through The Alley	5/28/1989	12/30/1997	833
My Sweet One	12/14/1995	12/31/1997	155

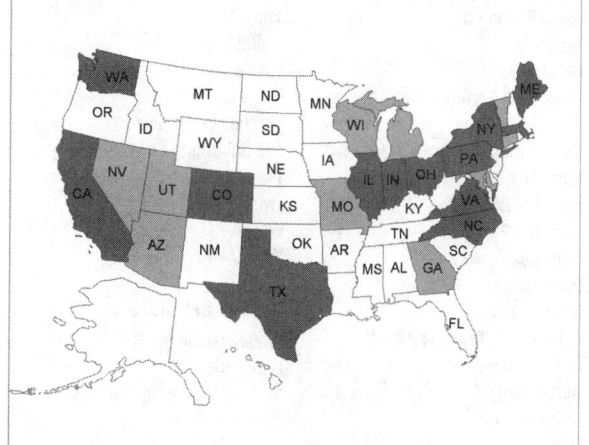

There were 78 shows played
Shows by day of week

- Sunday- 14
- Monday- 6
- Tuesday- 10
- Wednesday- 12
- Thursday- 9
- Friday- 14
- Saturday- 13

194 songs have been played (31% of songs Phish have played).

The average number of songs per show is 17.3.

The average amount of times each song was played is 6.96.

Total Times Played

Character Zero - 32 (41%)
My Soul - 30 (38%)
Taste - 30 (38%)
Ghost - 28 (35%)
Theme From The Bottom - 27 (34%)
Chalk Dust Torture - 26 (33%)
Harry Hood - 23 (29%)
Limb By Limb - 23 (29%)
Stash - 23 (29%)
Prince Caspian - 22 (28%)
Beauty of My Dreams - 21 (26%)
Dirt - 20 (25%)
Dogs Stole Things - 20 (25%)
Bouncing Around the Room - 19 (24%)
You Enjoy Myself - 19 (24%)
Punch You In The Eye - 18 (23%)
Wolfman's Brother - 18 (23%)
Cars Trucks Buses - 17 (21%)
David Bowie - 17 (21%)
Down With Disease - 17 (21%)
Slave to the Traffic Light - 17 (21%)
Loving Cup - 16 (20%)
Maze - 16 (20%)
Run Like an Antelope - 16 (20%)
Runaway Jim - 16 (20%)
Sample in a Jar - 16 (20%)
Water in the Sky - 16 (20%)
Also Sprach Zarathustra - 15 (19%)
Ginseng Sullivan - 15 (19%)
Julius - 15 (19%)
NICU - 15 (19%)
Piper - 15 (19%)
Rocky Top - 15 (19%)
When the Circus Comes - 15 (19%)
Billy Breathes - 14 (17%)
Funky Bitch - 14 (17%)
Free - 13 (16%)
Waste - 13 (16%)

Ya Mar - 13 (16%)
Bathtub Gin - 12 (15%)
Mike's Song - 12 (15%)
Simple - 12 (15%)
Cavern - 11 (14%)
Guyute - 11 (14%)
Jam - 11 (14%)
Poor Heart - 11 (14%)
Split Open and Melt - 11 (14%)
Twist - 11 (14%)
Weekapaug Groove - 11 (14%)
Frankenstein - 10 (12%)
Hello My Baby - 10 (12%)
Johnny B. Goode - 10 (12%)
Reba - 10 (12%)
Sparkle - 10 (12%)
Train Song - 10 (12%)
Tweezer - 10 (12%)
Tweezer Reprise - 10 (12%)
Vultures - 10 (12%)
Wading in the Velvet Sea - 10 (12%)
Cities - 9 (11%)
Steep - 9 (11%)
Swept Away - 9 (11%)
Timber (Jerry) - 9 (11%)
AC/DC Bag - 8 (10%)
Izabella - 8 (10%)
The Squirming Coil - 8 (10%)
Black-Eyed Katy - 7 (8%)
Gumbo - 7 (8%)
I Saw it Again - 7 (8%)
Llama - 7 (8%)
Love Me - 7 (8%)
Possum - 7 (8%)
Scent of a Mule - 7 (8%)
Uncle Pen - 7 (8%)
Wilson - 7 (8%)
Axilla - 6 (7%)
Carini - 6 (7%)
Jesus Just Left Chicago - 6 (7%)
Makisupa Policeman - 6 (7%)
Oblivious Fool - 6 (7%)
Sweet Adeline - 6 (7%)
A Day in the Life - 5 (6%)
Bold As Love - 5 (6%)
Drowned - 5 (6%)
Fire - 5 (6%)
Fluffhead - 5 (6%)
Foam - 5 (6%)
Good Times Bad Times - 5 (6%)
Horn - 5 (6%)
I Am Hydrogen - 5 (6%)
McGrupp and the Watchful Hosemasters - 5 (6%)
Rocko William - 5 (6%)
Silent in the Morning - 5 (6%)
The Horse - 5 (6%)
The Old Home Place - 5 (6%)

Bye Bye Foot - 4 (5%)
Divided Sky - 4 (5%)
Golgi Apparatus - 4 (5%)
Lawn Boy - 4 (5%)
Peaches En Regalia - 4 (5%)
Sleeping Monkey - 4 (5%)
Suzy Greenberg - 4 (5%)
Tube - 4 (5%)
Walfredo - 4 (5%)
Ain't Love Funny - 3 (3%)
Camel Walk - 3 (3%)
Crosseyed and Painless - 3 (3%)
Crossroads - 3 (3%)
Farmhouse - 3 (3%)
Fee - 3 (3%)
Guelah Papyrus - 3 (3%)
Halley's Comet - 3 (3%)
It's Ice - 3 (3%)
Magilla - 3 (3%)
My Friend My Friend - 3 (3%)
Strange Design - 3 (3%)
Talk - 3 (3%)
The Curtain - 3 (3%)
The Lizards - 3 (3%)
The Sloth - 3 (3%)
Weigh - 3 (3%)
Buffalo Bill - 2 (2%)
Buried Alive - 2 (2%)
Catapult - 2 (2%)
Cinnamon Girl - 2 (2%)
Contact - 2 (2%)
Emotional Rescue - 2 (2%)
Gypsy Queen - 2 (2%)
Harpua - 2 (2%)
I Didn't Know - 2 (2%)
I Don't Care - 2 (2%)
My Mind's Got a Mind of its Own
    - 2 (2%)
Roses Are Free - 2 (2%)
Soul Shake Down Party - 2 (2%)
The Oh Kee Pa Ceremony - 2 (2%)
The Wedge - 2 (2%)
All Things Reconsidered - 1 (1%)
Amoreena - 1 (1%)
Auld Lang Syne - 1 (1%)
Avenu Malkenu - 1 (1%)
Big Black Furry Creature From
    Mars - 1 (1%)
Blister in the Sun Jam - 1 (1%)
Boogie on Reggae Woman - 1 (1%)
Carolina - 1 (1%)
Cecilia - 1 (1%)
Colonel Forbin's Ascent - 1 (1%)
Daniel - 1 (1%)
Dinner and a Movie - 1 (1%)
Dog Faced Boy - 1 (1%)
Dog Gone Dog - 1 (1%)
Drum Jam - 1 (1%)

Fast Enough for You - 1 (1%)
Glide - 1 (1%)
Got My Mojo Workin' - 1 (1%)
Ha Ha Ha - 1 (1%)
Highway To Hell - 1 (1%)
Hoochie Coochie Man - 1 (1%)
I Told You So - 1 (1%)
I'm Gonna Be (500 Miles) - 1 (1%)
Kung - 1 (1%)
La Grange - 1 (1%)
Li'l Red Rooster - 1 (1%)
Life on Mars - 1 (1%)
Lifeboy - 1 (1%)
Love Me Like a Man - 1 (1%)
Love You - 1 (1%)
Low Rider Jam - 1 (1%)
Meatstick - 1 (1%)
Merry Pranksters Jam - 1 (1%)
Messin' With The Kid - 1 (1%)
Moby Dick - 1 (1%)
My Sweet One - 1 (1%)
New York New York - 1 (1%)
One Meatball - 1 (1%)
Paul and Silas - 1 (1%)
Psycho Killer - 1 (1%)
Rift - 1 (1%)
Rocky Mountain Way Jam - 1 (1%)
Rotation Jam - 1 (1%)
Samson Variation - 1 (1%)
Sneakin' Sally through the Alley
    - 1 (1%)
Stand - 1 (1%)
Take Me to the River - 1 (1%)
Tela - 1 (1%)
The Man Who Stepped Into
    Yesterday - 1 (1%)
The Man Who Stepped Into
    Yesterday Reprise - 1 (1%)
The Mango Song - 1 (1%)
The Star Spangled Banner - 1 (1%)
Them Changes - 1 (1%)
Tube Jam - 1 (1%)
Waking Up - 1 (1%)
While My Guitar Gently Weeps
    - 1 (1%)
Why Don't We Do It in the Road
    - 1 (1%)
Wormtown Jam - 1 (1%)

First Set Openers

Runaway Jim - 5
Ghost - 4
Julius - 4
NICU - 4
Theme From The Bottom - 4
Beauty of My Dreams - 3
Chalk Dust Torture - 3
Mike's Song - 3

Punch You In The Eye - 3
Bathtub Gin - 2
Carini - 2
Emotional Rescue - 2
Limb By Limb - 2
Makisupa Policeman - 2
My Soul - 2
Taste - 2
The Curtain - 2
The Wedge - 2
Tweezer - 2
Ya Mar - 2
AC/DC Bag - 1
Amoreena - 1
Buried Alive - 1
Camel Walk - 1
Cars Trucks Buses - 1
Cinnamon Girl - 1
Cities - 1
Dogs Stole Things - 1
Down With Disease - 1
Funky Bitch - 1
Golgi Apparatus - 1
Guyute - 1
Johnny B. Goode - 1
Oblivious Fool - 1
Piper - 1
Sample in a Jar - 1
Sneakin' Sally through the Alley - 1
Soul Shake Down Party - 1
Split Open and Melt - 1
The Squirming Coil - 1
Walfredo - 1
Wilson - 1
You Enjoy Myself - 1

First Set Closers

Character Zero - 14
Run Like an Antelope - 7
You Enjoy Myself - 5
Loving Cup - 4
Rocky Top - 4
David Bowie - 3
Taste - 3
Cavern - 2
Chalk Dust Torture - 2
Fire - 2
Good Times Bad Times - 2
Harry Hood - 2
Hello My Baby - 2
Izabella - 2
Oblivious Fool - 2
Possum - 2
Prince Caspian - 2
Slave to the Traffic Light - 2
A Day in the Life - 1
AC/DC Bag - 1
Carolina - 1

Crossroads - 1
Dogs Stole Things - 1
Ghost - 1
Golgi Apparatus - 1
My Soul - 1
Runaway Jim - 1
Split Open and Melt - 1
Sweet Adeline - 1
The Squirming Coil - 1
The Star Spangled Banner - 1
Tweezer Reprise - 1
Weekapaug Groove - 1
While My Guitar Gently Weeps - 1

Second Set Openers

Down With Disease - 7
Timber (Jerry) - 6
Stash - 5
Wolfman's Brother - 5
Runaway Jim - 4
Also Sprach Zarathustra - 3
Chalk Dust Torture - 3
Julius - 3
AC/DC Bag - 2
David Bowie - 2
Ghost - 2
NICU - 2
Punch You In The Eye - 2
Sample in a Jar - 2
Taste - 2
Axilla - 1
Bathtub Gin - 1
Beauty of My Dreams - 1
Buried Alive - 1
Carini - 1
Character Zero - 1
Cities - 1
Daniel - 1
Drowned - 1
Free - 1
Halley's Comet - 1
I Saw it Again - 1
Jam - 1
Limb By Limb - 1
Mike's Song - 1
Oblivious Fool - 1
Peaches En Regalia - 1
The Squirming Coil - 1
Tweezer - 1
Twist - 1
Wilson - 1
Ya Mar - 1

Second Set Closers

Tweezer Reprise - 6
Harry Hood - 5
Slave to the Traffic Light - 5
Character Zero - 4

Frankenstein - 4
Run Like an Antelope - 4
Weekapaug Groove - 4
Cavern - 3
Chalk Dust Torture - 3
Johnny B. Goode - 3
Julius - 3
Prince Caspian - 3
Hello My Baby - 2
Sweet Adeline - 2
Taste - 2
You Enjoy Myself - 2
A Day in the Life - 1
Bold As Love - 1
David Bowie - 1
Fire - 1
Funky Bitch - 1
Ghost - 1
Good Times Bad Times - 1
Guyute - 1
Izabella - 1
Jam - 1
Loving Cup - 1
Poor Heart - 1
Possum - 1
Suzy Greenberg - 1
The Squirming Coil - 1
Theme From The Bottom - 1
Wading in the Velvet Sea - 1

Third Set Openers

Also Sprach Zarathustra - 1
Buffalo Bill - 1
Halley's Comet - 1

Third Set Closers

Funky Bitch - 1
Loving Cup - 1
Prince Caspian - 1

Encores

Rocky Top - 7
Character Zero - 6
My Soul - 6
When the Circus Comes - 6
Bold As Love - 4
Bouncing Around the Room - 4
Loving Cup - 4

Cavern - 3
Guyute - 3
Hello My Baby - 3
Johnny B. Goode - 3
Julius - 3
The Squirming Coil - 3
Theme From The Bottom - 3
Tweezer Reprise - 3
A Day in the Life - 2
David Bowie - 2
Fire - 2
Frankenstein - 2
Funky Bitch - 2
Harry Hood - 2
Possum - 2
Beauty of My Dreams - 1
Billy Breathes - 1
Black-Eyed Katy - 1
Buffalo Bill - 1
Carini - 1
Chalk Dust Torture - 1
Cinnamon Girl - 1
Cities - 1
Contact - 1
Crossroads - 1
Free - 1
Ginseng Sullivan - 1
Good Times Bad Times - 1
Highway To Hell - 1
Hoochie Coochie Man - 1
Izabella - 1
Limb By Limb - 1
Messin' With The Kid - 1
Moby Dick - 1
New York New York - 1
Poor Heart - 1
Prince Caspian - 1
Run Like an Antelope - 1
Sample in a Jar - 1
Slave to the Traffic Light - 1
Sleeping Monkey - 1
Sneakin' Sally through the Alley - 1
Stand - 1
Sweet Adeline - 1
Taste - 1
Them Changes - 1
Waste - 1
You Enjoy Myself - 1

APRIL 1998

"The Island Tour"

An impromptu run of four shows in four nights in the northeast was the answer. Trey noted at the first of the four that the band was "bored" at home

and wanted to play a little bit. Shirts proclaimed it the Island Tour (since it took place in Long Island and Rhode Island), but most fans still refer to it simply as "The Spring Run."

The "cow funk" of 1997 continued, but with a bit more groove and texture. This is one of the most impressive four night stretches in modern Phish, with each night featuring highlights that make it hard to pick a favorite. In Nassau, "Twist" featured an unprecedented space warp jam, "Wolfman's Brother" segued nicely into "Sneakin' Sally" (reminding many of the previous New Year's Run), and Ween's "Roses Are Free" proved an unlikely and impresive jam vehicle. Providence featured possibly the funkiest intro to "Also Sprach Zarathustra" ever, the breakout of "Brother," and a seguefest on 4/5 in which the rollicking "Oblivious Fool" got a facelift, emerging as the dark, grooving "Shafty." "Frankie Sez" and "Birds of a Feather" also debuted during the run, with "Birds" making an appearance in both cities.

These four shows seemed like an extra New Year's Run. Though it lacked the advance excitement of a New Year's Eve performance, the series benefited from the exuberance of a fanbase that was keenly aware it was receiving a special, unprecedented treat: four shows, completely out of nowhere, and completely inspired. The perfomances provided an exclamation mark to the succeses of 1997, and raised anticipation for what '98 was to offer. Affirmed and no longer "bored," the band prepared for Europe.

DEBUTS (Island 1998)

Birds of a Feather	4/2/1998
Frankie Says	4/2/1998
Shafty	4/5/1998

DEPARTURES (Island 1998)

	LAST KNOWN	# SHOWS
None	N/A	N/A

BREAKOUTS (Island 1998)

	SHELVED	BREAKOUT	# SHOWS
Brother	11/30/1996	4/4/1998	89
The Oh Kee Pa Ceremony	3/1/1997	4/5/1998	69

SUMMER 1998

"The Summer of Covers"

The summer began with the briefest European tour to date, lasting only nine shows in four cities. Phish picked up where they left off with The Island Tour, grooving and moving. Strong if not spectacular, the Europe run allowed Phish to debut five new songs that would eventually wind up on *Story of the Ghost*.

The American leg of the summer tour was brief as well, lasting only one month and culminating in the third summer festival, The Lemonwheel. Along the way, Phish debuted fourteen new covers, including a stretch in early August where just about every show featured a new tune. Most were one-shots that were never seen live again, though "Been Caught Stealin'" and "Sabotage" appeared again in the fall. Some were funny, some rocked hard, and some seemed quite odd indeed (Smashing Pumpkins?). There is no doubt that the most sentimental debut was the rendering of "Terrapin Station" on the third anniversary of Jerry Garcia's death (8/9).

Along with the string of debuts came a string of breakouts. "Time Loves a Hero" and "She Caught the Katy" were old-school covers that hadn't been heard since 1987 and 1988. Summer tour also brought us the first "Forbin's" / "Mockingbird" combo since Halloween, 1996 (the 8/14/97 show included the former but not the latter). All told, twenty-seven songs returned after absences of fifty shows or more. While this juxebox mode created a great deal of excitement, some fans eventually grumbled that the flashy setlists were merely covering for a less than spectacular improvisational output. Despite the inconsistency of performance, the band was still able to tap into creative brilliance for such fare as an amazing Runaway Jim on 8/11. The version of "Colonel Forbin's Ascent" is that last one to date (as of the end of Summer Tour 2000).

The Lemonwheel, as had become customary, featured two days with three sets per day. At least. On the first day, Phish returned for a fourth set late night and jammed to the light of the candles surrounding them. Some fans dubbed it "The Ring of Fire Jam," while others called in "The Ambient Set." It foreshadowed a sound Phish would tap into in the future.

DEBUTS (Summer 1998)

Roggae	6/30/1998
The Moma Dance	6/30/1998
Brian and Robert	6/30/1998
Meat	7/2/1998
Fikus	7/2/1998
Blister In The Sun	7/9/1998
Sexual Healing	7/20/1998
Bittersweet Motel	7/21/1998
Too Much of Everything	7/26/1998
Albuquerque	7/26/1998
If You Need a Fool	7/29/1998
Ramble On	8/1/1998
Been Caught Stealin'	8/1/1998
I Get a Kick Out of You	8/2/1998
Rhinoceros	8/3/1998
Running With the Devil	8/6/1998
Sweet Jane	8/8/1998
Sabotage	8/8/1998
Terrapin Station	8/9/1998
Trenchtown Rock	8/11/1998
Burning Down the House	8/12/1998

DEPARTURES (Summer 1998)

	LAST KNOWN	# SHOWS
Johnny B. Goode	7/8/1998	168
Blister in the Sun	7/9/1998	167
Sea and Sand	7/20/1998	161
She Caught the Katy	7/21/1998	160
Lengthwise	7/28/1998	156
Izabella	7/31/1998	154
Too Much of Everything	8/2/1998	152
Weigh	8/2/1998	152
Rhinoceros	8/3/1998	151
Running With the Devil	8/6/1998	150
Talk	8/6/1998	150
Somewhere Over the Rainbow	8/9/1998	147
Terrapin Station	8/9/1998	147
Time Loves a Hero	8/11/1998	146
Trenchtown Rock	8/11/1998	146
Burning Down the House	8/12/1998	145
Ramble On	8/12/1998	145
Baby Elephant Walk	8/16/1998	143

BREAKOUTS (Summer 1998)

	SHELVED	BREAKOUT	# SHOWS
Ha Ha Ha	2/26/1997	6/30/1998	72
Sea and Sand	12/31/1995	7/20/1998	166
She Caught the Katy	8/29/1987	7/21/1998	931
La Grange	2/25/1997	7/26/1998	90
The Mango Song	3/1/1997	7/28/1998	88
Lengthwise	10/20/1994	7/28/1998	291
Glide	7/31/1997	7/29/1998	60
Dog Gone Dog	2/26/1997	7/29/1998	91
Kung	2/26/1997	7/29/1998	91
Rift	2/23/1997	7/31/1998	94
If I Could	8/5/1996	7/31/1998	150
Magilla	7/21/1997	8/1/1998	69
Esther	10/19/1996	8/1/1998	139
Weigh	8/17/1997	8/2/1998	52
Lifeboy	8/3/1997	8/2/1998	61
Bike	11/7/1996	8/3/1998	129
Ride Captain Ride	12/30/1992	8/3/1998	490
Talk	6/24/1997	8/6/1998	84
Cracklin' Rosie	8/14/1996	8/6/1998	148
Colonel Forbin's Ascent	8/14/1997	8/7/1998	57
Wading in the Velvet Sea	8/2/1997	8/7/1998	65
The Famous Mockingbird	10/31/1996	8/7/1998	135
Somewhere Over the Rainbow	8/13/1996	8/9/1998	152
Time Loves a Hero	11/5/1988	8/11/1998	900
Sanity	10/31/1996	8/15/1998	140
While My Guitar Gently Weeps	2/26/1997	8/16/1998	103
Baby Elephant Walk	12/1/1992	8/16/1998	512

FALL 1998

"Starting in Sin City"

Fall tour officially started in Los Angeles on 10/29, though Phish had already played four shows, appeared on *The Late Show With David Letterman*, and taped an appearance for *Sessions*. The four actual gigs showcased an amalgam of Phishy talents: an appearance at Farm Aid (jamming with Neil Young), two acoustic shows for Young's Bridge School Benefits, and a surprise show at The Fillmore. The *Sessions* taping served as a showcase for the *Story of the Ghost* material, as much of the new album was played live.

The tour proper started with a bang: some segue madness in the first two shows, and The Velvet Underground's *Loaded* for Halloween. The band unloaded the longest and most experimental jam of the year (other than the Lemonwheel's fourth set) in the third set's "Wolfman's Brother." But no one was prepared for the Salt Lake City show on 11/2. Some fans were disappointed that Phish had once again neglected to play Pink Floyd's *Dark Side of the Moon* on Halloween. So in front of a half-filled house in Utah, Phish unexpectedly busted out *Dark Side*, but only after a full set and a half of mesmerizing music that included a long "Drowned" / "Jesus" combo and a rocking "Disease." A half baked cover of Nirvana's "Smells Like Teen Spirit" capped off the night, as if things weren't quite surreal enough.

Moving west to east, the tour included a three night stint in Chicago and a strong show in Winston-Salem before moving back to Hampton. Anticipation was high, and the band delivered two exceedingly *fun* shows that un-

fortunately failed to reach the improvisational heights of some previous Hampton appearances. Released in 1999 as *Hampton Comes Alive,* the two night run featured high energy throughout, be it during serious jamming ("Bathtub Gin") or humorous sequences ("Gettin Jiggy Wit It"). It also housed the first "Quinn the Eskimo in over 950 shows; "Nellie Kane" and "Cry Baby Cry" also returned after years on the shelf. On the whole, these shows managed to add to the growing legacy of Hampton among fans, though no specific jams really rank as particualrly noteworthy.

Tour concluded with a swing up the east coast, featuring a string of high energy shows that consistently failed to achieve much improvisational majesty. The upbeat jams were like empty calories, fun at the time but forgotten in the morning. Things wrapped up with three shows in Worcester. The first featured a string of wild segues reminiscent of days past ("Chalk Dust Torture" -> "Mirror in the Bathroom" -> "Chalk Dust Torture" -> "Dog Gone Dog" -> "Chalk Dust Torture") and multiple renditions of the surf rock classic "Wipe Out." The middle show was one of the weakest in recent memory, but the tour finale finally transcended the rocking fluff of the tour with a spacey "Simple" and another strong "Bathtub Gin." The "Roggae" encore, however, left people scratching their heads. Next stop: New York City.

DEBUTS (Fall 1998)

Arc	10/3/1998
Down By the River	10/3/1998
Moonlight in Vermont	10/3/1998
Will the Circle Be Unbroken	10/3/1998
Uncloudy Day	10/3/1998
Sleep	10/17/1998
Never	10/17/1998
Driver	10/17/1998
Helpless	10/17/1998
Sad Lisa	10/18/1998
Four Strong Winds	10/18/1998
I Shall Be Released	10/18/1998
Something	10/29/1998
Back at the Chicken Shack	10/30/1998
Who Loves the Sun	10/31/1998
Rock and Roll	10/31/1998
Cool it Down	10/31/1998
New Age	10/31/1998
Head Held High	10/31/1998
I Found a Reason	10/31/1998
Train Round the Bend	10/31/1998
Oh! Sweet Nuthin'	10/31/1998
Breathe	11/2/1998
On The Run	11/2/1998
Time	11/2/1998
Money	11/2/1998
Us and Them	11/2/1998
Any Colour You Like	11/2/1998
Brain Damage	11/2/1998
Eclipse	11/2/1998
Smells Like Teen Spirit	11/2/1998
So Lonely	11/14/1998
Rock and Roll Part Two	11/20/1998
Gettin' Jiggy Wit' It	11/20/1998
Tubthumping	11/21/1998
Mirror in the Bathroom	11/27/1998
All the Pain Through the Years	11/29/1998
Layla	11/29/1998

DEPARTURES (Fall 1998)

	LAST KNOWN	# SHOWS
Amazing Grace	10/3/1998	142
Arc	10/3/1998	142
Down By the River	10/3/1998	142
Moonlight in Vermont	10/3/1998	142
Uncloudy Day	10/3/1998	142
Will the Circle Be Unbroken	10/3/1998	142
Helpless	10/17/1998	140
Never	10/17/1998	140
Four Strong Winds	10/18/1998	139
I Shall Be Released	10/18/1998	139
Sad Lisa	10/18/1998	139
Long Cool Woman	10/30/1998	137
Manteca	10/30/1998	137
Head Held High	10/31/1998	136
I Found a Reason	10/31/1998	136
Lonesome Cowboy Bill	10/31/1998	136
New Age	10/31/1998	136
Oh! Sweet Nuthin'	10/31/1998	136
Sweet Jane	10/31/1998	136
Train Round the Bend	10/31/1998	136
Who Loves the Sun	10/31/1998	136
Any Colour You Like	11/2/1998	135
Brain Damage	11/2/1998	135
Breathe	11/2/1998	135
Eclipse	11/2/1998	135
Harpua	11/2/1998	135
Money	11/2/1998	135
On The Run	11/2/1998	135
Smells Like Teen Spirit	11/2/1998	135
Speak to Me	11/2/1998	135
The Great Gig in the Sky	11/2/1998	135
Time	11/2/1998	135
Us and Them	11/2/1998	135
Fikus	11/7/1998	132
I Get a Kick Out of You	11/9/1998	130
Sexual Healing	11/14/1998	127
So Lonely	11/14/1998	127
Carolina	11/18/1998	125
Love Me	11/18/1998	125
Gettin' Jiggy Wit' It	11/20/1998	123
Rock and Roll Part Two	11/20/1998	123
Cry Baby Cry	11/21/1998	122
Sabotage	11/21/1998	122
Tubthumping	11/21/1998	122
Tela	11/24/1998	121
Lifeboy	11/25/1998	120
Something	11/25/1998	120
Mirror in the Bathroom	11/27/1998	119
Sanity	11/27/1998	119
Crossroads	11/28/1998	118
All the Pain Through the Years	11/29/1998	117
Layla	11/29/1998	117
Paul and Silas	11/29/1998	117
Wipeout	11/29/1998	117

BREAKOUTS (Fall 1998)

	SHELVED	BREAKOUT	# SHOWS
Amazing Grace	12/31/1996	10/3/1998	115
Carolina	8/17/1997	10/17/1998	64

BREAKOUTS (Fall 1998)	SHELVED	BREAKOUT	# SHOWS
I'm Blue I'm Lonesome	12/12/1995	10/17/1998	195
Freebird	6/19/1994	10/17/1998	338
Walk Away	5/7/1994	10/29/1998	366
Guelah Papyrus	8/11/1997	10/30/1998	71
Manteca	11/14/1995	10/30/1998	218
Long Cool Woman	10/30/1983	10/30/1998	982
Lonesome Cowboy Bill	6/10/1995	10/31/1998	267
The Great Gig in the Sky	7/5/1994	11/2/1998	331
Love Me	11/30/1997	11/8/1998	61
Paul and Silas	2/28/1997	11/8/1998	114
Quinn the Eskimo	8/10/1987	11/20/1998	970
BBFCFM	12/11/1997	11/21/1998	63
Cry Baby Cry	6/16/1995	11/21/1998	277
Nellie Kane	12/8/1994	11/21/1998	292
I Am Hydrogen	12/9/1997	11/27/1998	67
Buffalo Bill	11/29/1997	11/27/1998	74
Wipeout	4/27/1991	11/27/1998	715
Timber (Jerry)	12/31/1997	11/28/1998	61
Crossroads	12/29/1997	11/28/1998	63
Catapult	12/13/1997	11/29/1998	66

though many costumed dancers appeared onstage and in the crowd at each of the shows. On 12/31, these dancers distributed hundreds of glowrings, which some fans attatched into several enormous chains that wormed their way around the venue as the night progressed. The closest thing to a New Year's "stunt" was a small pyrotechnics display onstage at midnight...fun, but nothing compared to the typical visual fare at your average Whitesnake concert. On this night, the band was more concerned with jamming than riding hot dogs or dodging balloons.

In a rare move, a Phish original debuted on a NYE Run, as Tom Marshall showed up to lend vocals to the first-ever "Grind" on 12/30. New Year's was one of the strongest shows of recent years, capped by an elegant "While My Guitar Gently Weeps" encore. Party over; out of time.

DEBUTS (NYE 1998)

Grind	12/30/1998

DEPARTURES (NYE 1998)	LAST KNOWN	# SHOWS
Been Caught Stealin'	12/28/1998	116
Grind	12/30/1998	114
1999	12/31/1998	113

BREAKOUTS (NYE 1998)	SHELVED	BREAKOUT	# SHOWS
None	N/A	N/A	N/A

NYE 1998

"The Madison Square Garden House Band"

Early New Year's Runs featured three or four venues. In 1995 and 1996, the NYE Run consisted of two shows at each of two venues. 1997 saw one in Landover and three at Madison Square Garden. Phish finally went all the way in 1998, playing MSG for four consecutive nights. The Doniac Schivice mistakenly announced that this was the first four night stand in one venue since the eighties, forgetting about the '96 Red Rocks stand.

The first night featured a surprisingly spacey and experimental second set, anchored by the opening "Carini" > "Wolfman's Brother" sequence. The middle shows of the Run were representative of '98 shows, featuring high energy romps (the 12/30 "Disease") and unexpected setlist flourishes (a "Divided Sky" encore on 12/29). An encouraging feature was the appearance of a few short jams that popped up (before 2001 on 12/29, before "Maze" and out of "Coil" on 12/30).

On New Year's Eve, it was clear from the outset that Phish was going to seize the moment appropriately, as the band took the stage to the sound of an electronic voice ("Don't worry, I won't hurt you, I only want you to have some fun") that signalled the beginning Prince's "1999." The audience surged with energy throughout the number, cheering loudly at such lines as "if you didn't come to party, don't bother knocking at my door" and "before that happens I'll dance my life away." As the obviously jubilant band rocked away, they were surrounded by many costumed dancers, who at one point lowered Trey and Mike onto their backs and then lifted them up again. "1999" teases showed up throughout the rest of the show, including "Weekapaug Groove" and "Runaway Jim."

This run was curious from a spectacle standpoint, as a New Year's motif was seemingly discarded after one show. The 12/28 performance included a stage set featuring grass along the sides of the stage and oversized flowers behind the band. These props were absent for the rest of the Run, al-

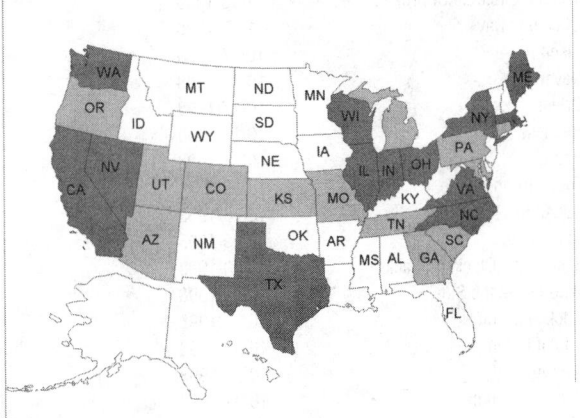

There were 66 shows played

Shows by day of week

- Sunday- 11
- Monday- 6
- Tuesday- 6
- Wednesday- 10
- Thursday- 9
- Friday- 12
- Saturday- 12

238 songs have been played (38% of songs Phish have played).

The average number of songs per show is 17.9.

The average amount of times

each song was played is 4.98.

Total Times Played

Birds of a Feather - 26 (39%)
Roggae - 25 (37%)
The Moma Dance - 25 (37%)
Limb By Limb - 20 (30%)
Chalk Dust Torture - 19 (28%)
Guyute - 19 (28%)
Ghost - 18 (27%)
Piper - 18 (27%)
Brian and Robert - 16 (24%)
Down With Disease - 16 (24%)
Funky Bitch - 16 (24%)
Harry Hood - 16 (24%)
Simple - 16 (24%)
You Enjoy Myself - 16 (24%)

Character Zero - 15 (22%)
David Bowie - 15 (22%)
Mike's Song - 15 (22%)
Run Like an Antelope - 15 (22%)
Weekapaug Groove - 15 (22%)
Possum - 14 (21%)
Frankie Says - 13 (19%)
Loving Cup - 13 (19%)
Reba - 13 (19%)
Sample in a Jar - 13 (19%)
Stash - 13 (19%)
Tweezer - 13 (19%)
Wolfman's Brother - 13 (19%)
Also Sprach Zarathustra
    - 12 (18%)
Cavern - 12 (18%)
Meat - 12 (18%)
My Soul - 12 (18%)
Punch You In The Eye - 12 (18%)
Bathtub Gin - 11 (16%)
NICU - 11 (16%)
Prince Caspian - 11 (16%)
Tweezer Reprise - 11 (16%)
Wading in the Velvet Sea - 11 (16%)
Water in the Sky - 11 (16%)
Beauty of My Dreams - 10 (15%)
Golgi Apparatus - 10 (15%)
Julius - 10 (15%)
Lawn Boy - 10 (15%)
Tube - 10 (15%)
Wilson - 10 (15%)
Driver - 9 (13%)
Maze - 9 (13%)
Sparkle - 9 (13%)
When the Circus Comes - 9 (13%)
Albuquerque - 8 (12%)
Bittersweet Motel - 8 (12%)
Farmhouse - 8 (12%)
Ginseng Sullivan - 8 (12%)
Runaway Jim - 8 (12%)
Slave to the Traffic Light - 8 (12%)
Split Open and Melt - 8 (12%)
Ya Mar - 8 (12%)
AC/DC Bag - 7 (10%)
Axilla - 7 (10%)
Cities - 7 (10%)
Divided Sky - 7 (10%)
Fluffhead - 7 (10%)
Frankenstein - 7 (10%)
Gumbo - 7 (10%)
Halley's Comet - 7 (10%)
Taste - 7 (10%)
Bouncing Around the Room
    - 6 (9%)
Hello My Baby - 6 (9%)
Jam - 6 (9%)
Makisupa Policeman - 6 (9%)
Rocky Top - 6 (9%)
Sleep - 6 (9%)

The Squirming Coil - 6 (9%)
The Wedge - 6 (9%)
Theme From The Bottom - 6 (9%)
Been Caught Stealin' - 5 (7%)
Carini - 5 (7%)
Dogs Stole Things - 5 (7%)
Drowned - 5 (7%)
Fikus - 5 (7%)
Free - 5 (7%)
Freebird - 5 (7%)
Good Times Bad Times - 5 (7%)
Horn - 5 (7%)
Llama - 5 (7%)
Poor Heart - 5 (7%)
Roses Are Free - 5 (7%)
Scent of a Mule - 5 (7%)
Sleeping Monkey - 5 (7%)
The Lizards - 5 (7%)
The Mango Song - 5 (7%)
Train Song - 5 (7%)
Waste - 5 (7%)
Billy Breathes - 4 (6%)
Bold As Love - 4 (6%)
Boogie on Reggae Woman - 4 (6%)
Buried Alive - 4 (6%)
Cars Trucks Buses - 4 (6%)
Dirt - 4 (6%)
Fee - 4 (6%)
Foam - 4 (6%)
Ha Ha Ha - 4 (6%)
McGrupp and the Watchful
    Hosemasters - 4 (6%)
Rift - 4 (6%)
Rock and Roll - 4 (6%)
Sexual Healing - 4 (6%)
Sneakin' Sally through the Alley
    - 4 (6%)
Something - 4 (6%)
Tela - 4 (6%)
The Old Home Place - 4 (6%)
La Grange - 3 (4%)
My Mind's Got a Mind of its
    Own - 3 (4%)
Sabotage - 3 (4%)
The Sloth - 3 (4%)
Vultures - 3 (4%)
While My Guitar Gently Weeps
    - 3 (4%)
Avenu Malkenu - 2 (3%)
Back at the Chicken Shack - 2 (3%)
Big Black Furry Creature From
    Mars - 2 (3%)
Bike - 2 (3%)
Brother - 2 (3%)
Carolina - 2 (3%)
Contact - 2 (3%)
Dog Faced Boy - 2 (3%)
Dog Gone Dog - 2 (3%)
Esther - 2 (3%)

Guelah Papyrus - 2 (3%)
I Am Hydrogen - 2 (3%)
I Get a Kick Out of You - 2 (3%)
If You Need a Fool - 2 (3%)
It's Ice - 2 (3%)
Izabella - 2 (3%)
Jesus Just Left Chicago - 2 (3%)
Kung - 2 (3%)
Lifeboy - 2 (3%)
Love Me - 2 (3%)
My Friend My Friend - 2 (3%)
Paul and Silas - 2 (3%)
Quinn the Eskimo - 2 (3%)
Ramble On - 2 (3%)
Ride Captain Ride - 2 (3%)
Sanity - 2 (3%)
Shafty - 2 (3%)
Silent in the Morning - 2 (3%)
Strange Design - 2 (3%)
Suzy Greenberg - 2 (3%)
Sweet Jane - 2 (3%)
The Curtain - 2 (3%)
The Horse - 2 (3%)
The Man Who Stepped Into
    Yesterday - 2 (3%)
The Oh Kee Pa Ceremony - 2 (3%)
Too Much of Everything - 2 (3%)
Twist - 2 (3%)
Walk Away - 2 (3%)
Wipeout - 2 (3%)
1999 - 1 (1%)
A Day in the Life - 1 (1%)
All the Pain Through the Years
    - 1 (1%)
Amazing Grace - 1 (1%)
Ambient Jam - 1 (1%)
Any Colour You Like - 1 (1%)
Arc - 1 (1%)
Auld Lang Syne - 1 (1%)
Baby Elephant Walk - 1 (1%)
Blister in the Sun - 1 (1%)
Brain Damage - 1 (1%)
Breathe - 1 (1%)
Buffalo Bill - 1 (1%)
Burning Down the House - 1 (1%)
Camel Walk - 1 (1%)
Catapult - 1 (1%)
Colonel Forbin's Ascent - 1 (1%)
Cool it Down - 1 (1%)
Cracklin' Rosie - 1 (1%)
Crossroads - 1 (1%)
Cry Baby Cry - 1 (1%)
Down By the River - 1 (1%)
Eclipse - 1 (1%)
Emotional Rescue - 1 (1%)
Fast Enough for You - 1 (1%)
Four Strong Winds - 1 (1%)
Gettin' Jiggy Wit' It - 1 (1%)
Glide - 1 (1%)

Grind - 1 (1%)
Harpua - 1 (1%)
Head Held High - 1 (1%)
Helpless - 1 (1%)
I Didn't Know - 1 (1%)
I Found a Reason - 1 (1%)
I Shall Be Released - 1 (1%)
I'm Blue I'm Lonesome - 1 (1%)
If I Could - 1 (1%)
Johnny B. Goode - 1 (1%)
Layla - 1 (1%)
Lengthwise - 1 (1%)
Lonesome Cowboy Bill - 1 (1%)
Long Cool Woman in a Black
    Dress - 1 (1%)
Magilla - 1 (1%)
Manteca - 1 (1%)
Mirror in the Bathroom - 1 (1%)
Money - 1 (1%)
Moonlight in Vermont - 1 (1%)
My Sweet One - 1 (1%)
Nellie Kane - 1 (1%)
Never - 1 (1%)
New Age - 1 (1%)
Oh! Sweet Nuthin' - 1 (1%)
On The Run - 1 (1%)
Rhinoceros - 1 (1%)
Rock and Roll Part Two - 1 (1%)
Running With the Devil - 1 (1%)
Sad Lisa - 1 (1%)
Sea and Sand - 1 (1%)
She Caught the Katy and Left Me a
    Mule to Ride - 1 (1%)
Smells Like Teen Spirit - 1 (1%)
So Lonely - 1 (1%)
Somewhere Over the Rainbow
    - 1 (1%)
Speak to Me - 1 (1%)
Steep - 1 (1%)
Sweet Adeline - 1 (1%)
Swept Away - 1 (1%)
Talk - 1 (1%)
Terrapin Station - 1 (1%)
The Famous Mockingbird - 1 (1%)
The Great Gig in the Sky - 1 (1%)
The Man Who Stepped Into
    Yesterday Reprise - 1 (1%)
Timber (Jerry) - 1 (1%)
Time - 1 (1%)
Time Loves a Hero - 1 (1%)
Train Round the Bend - 1 (1%)
Trenchtown Rock - 1 (1%)
Tube Jam - 1 (1%)
Tubthumping - 1 (1%)
Uncloudy Day - 1 (1%)
Us and Them - 1 (1%)
Weekapaug Reprise - 1 (1%)
Weigh - 1 (1%)
Who Loves the Sun - 1 (1%)

Will the Circle Be Unbroken - 1 (1%)

First Set Openers

Birds of a Feather - 4
Punch You In The Eye - 3
The Moma Dance - 3
Axilla - 2
Bathtub Gin - 2
Buried Alive - 2
Chalk Dust Torture - 2
Down With Disease - 2
Funky Bitch - 2
Mike's Song - 2
My Friend My Friend - 2
The Oh Kee Pa Ceremony - 2
Tube - 2
Wilson - 2
1999 - 1
AC/DC Bag - 1
Back at the Chicken Shack - 1
Carini - 1
Carolina - 1
Cities - 1
Emotional Rescue - 1
Ghost - 1
Ginseng Sullivan - 1
Gumbo - 1
Hello My Baby - 1
Julius - 1
La Grange - 1
Limb By Limb - 1
Llama - 1
Makisupa Policeman - 1
My Soul - 1
NICU - 1
Paul and Silas - 1
Possum - 1
Ramble On - 1
Rhinoceros - 1
Rock and Roll - 1
Rock and Roll Part Two - 1
Roggae - 1
Roses Are Free - 1
Stash - 1
Taste - 1
The Squirming Coil - 1
The Wedge - 1
Trenchtown Rock - 1
Tweezer - 1
Water in the Sky - 1
Wolfman's Brother - 1

First Set Closers

Character Zero - 6
Split Open and Melt - 5
Chalk Dust Torture - 4
Run Like an Antelope - 4
Birds of a Feather - 3

Cavern - 3
David Bowie - 3
Good Times Bad Times - 3
My Soul - 3
Weekapaug Groove - 3
Bold As Love - 2
Funky Bitch - 2
Golgi Apparatus - 2
Julius - 2
Loving Cup - 2
Sample in a Jar - 2
A Day in the Life - 1
Carolina - 1
Freebird - 1
Hello My Baby - 1
Helpless - 1
I Shall Be Released - 1
La Grange - 1
Layla - 1
Mike's Song - 1
Possum - 1
Reba - 1
Slave to the Traffic Light - 1
Stash - 1
Sweet Jane - 1
The Famous Mockingbird - 1
Uncloudy Day - 1
You Enjoy Myself - 1

Second Set Openers

Down With Disease - 5
Also Sprach Zarathustra - 3
Bathtub Gin - 3
Julius - 3
Runaway Jim - 3
AC/DC Bag - 2
Birds of a Feather - 2
Buried Alive - 2
Chalk Dust Torture - 2
Drowned - 2
Ghost - 2
Halley's Comet - 2
Mike's Song - 2
Piper - 2
Possum - 2
Roses Are Free - 2
The Wedge - 2
Wolfman's Brother - 2
Carini - 1
Cavern - 1
David Bowie - 1
Free - 1
Gumbo - 1
La Grange - 1
Limb By Limb - 1
Llama - 1
Makisupa Policeman - 1
My Soul - 1

NICU - 1
Punch You In The Eye - 1
Sabotage - 1
Stash - 1
The Curtain - 1
The Moma Dance - 1
Tweezer - 1
Who Loves the Sun - 1
Wilson - 1

Second Set Closers

Harry Hood - 6
Run Like an Antelope - 6
You Enjoy Myself - 5
Character Zero - 4
Weekapaug Groove - 4
Cavern - 3
David Bowie - 3
Down With Disease - 3
Loving Cup - 3
Slave to the Traffic Light - 3
Frankenstein - 2
Hello My Baby - 2
Rocky Top - 2
Been Caught Stealin' - 1
Chalk Dust Torture - 1
Farmhouse - 1
Funky Bitch - 1
Ghost - 1
Golgi Apparatus - 1
Good Times Bad Times - 1
Harpua - 1
Izabella - 1
Johnny B. Goode - 1
Llama - 1
Oh! Sweet Nuthin' - 1
Sample in a Jar - 1
Sweet Adeline - 1
The Squirming Coil - 1
The Wedge - 1

Third Set Openers

NICU - 1
Runaway Jim - 1
Sabotage - 1
Wolfman's Brother - 1

Third Set Closers

Ghost - 1
Llama - 1
Loving Cup - 1
While My Guitar Gently Weeps - 1

Fourth Set Openers

Ambient Jam - 1

Fourth Set Closers

Ambient Jam - 1

Encores

Tweezer Reprise - 10
Harry Hood - 5
Rocky Top - 4
Been Caught Stealin' - 3
Bittersweet Motel - 3
Brian and Robert - 3
Freebird - 3
Funky Bitch - 3
Golgi Apparatus - 3
Guyute - 3
Halley's Comet - 3
Possum - 3
Punch You In The Eye - 3
The Squirming Coil - 3
You Enjoy Myself - 3
Cavern - 2
Hello My Baby - 2
Sample in a Jar - 2
Sleeping Monkey - 2
Something - 2
While My Guitar Gently Weeps - 2
Wilson - 2
Baby Elephant Walk - 1
Birds of a Feather - 1
Bold As Love - 1
Burning Down the House - 1
Camel Walk - 1
Carini - 1
Chalk Dust Torture - 1
Character Zero - 1
Contact - 1
Dirt - 1
Divided Sky - 1
Dog Faced Boy - 1
Driver - 1
Frankenstein - 1
Good Times Bad Times - 1
Grind - 1
Julius - 1
Limb By Limb - 1
Roggae - 1
Run Like an Antelope - 1
Running With the Devil - 1
Sabotage - 1
Sexual Healing - 1
Simple - 1
Slave to the Traffic Light - 1
Sleep - 1
Smells Like Teen Spirit - 1
So Lonely - 1
Suzy Greenberg - 1
Taste - 1
Terrapin Station - 1
Tubthumping - 1
Wading in the Velvet Sea - 1
Waste - 1
When the Circus Comes - 1
Wipeout - 1

SUMMER 1999

"Time for the Meatstick"

For the first time since 1995, Phish did not play in Europe for the summer. Instead, they played a month of shows in the U.S. before venturing to Japan for the first time. As with 1998, Phish took the opportunity to break out a ton of shelved material. Most notable was the fan favorite "Alumni Blues," which hadn't been played since 1994 and had not been played in its entirety since the '91 horns tour. Old Henrietta cover "Whipping Post" emerged in serious guise on 7/25, Boston's "Foreplay/Long Time" made its first electric appearance, and the one-shot "Tuesday's Gone" (with guest Scott Muraski of Max Creek) reminded fans of the previous summer's jukebox antics.

Conspicuously absent in the fall of 1998 were debuts of original material (save the new acoustic songs, and "Grind" on the NYE Run). Phish rebounded with several in the summer of 1999, including "Back on the Train" and "Bug." Both had been played on Trey's solo tour earlier in the year.

The tour consisted primarily of venues that had become Phish summer staples, including The Tweeter Center (formerly Great Woods) and Deer Creek. They also kept Merriweather Post Pavillion in the schedule, and returned to New Jersey's PNC Center (formerly GSAC). For the first time since 1996 there was no tour-ending festival; instead, a mid-tour stop at the Oswego County Airport gave fans their festival fill. In some ways it went beyond the previous festivals (boasting a side stage featuring prominent acts like Son Seals and Del McCourey, as well as late night DJ sets), but it had a smaller attendance, fewer sets, and no special name.

A defining story of the summer was the emergence of Phish's international dance craze, "The Meatstick." Fans tried (unsuccesfully) to enter the *Guinness Book of World Records* with a group dance performance at Oswego, and special guests (like Sofi Dillof) were brought onstage all summer to try to spread the fad. The visit to the former Great Woods seemed to encapsulate the mood of recent tours: paint-by-numbers material one night, brilliant material the next. After the tour's conclusion, a streamlined edition of Phish's touring apparatus travelled to Japan for mutiple appearances at the Fuji Rock Festival.

DEBUTS (Summer 1999)

Back on the Train	6/30/1999
Bug	6/30/1999
My Left Toe	6/30/1999
Mountains in the Mist	7/3/1999
What's the Use	7/4/1999
Tuesday's Gone	7/13/1999
Born to Run	7/16/1999
On My Knees	7/17/1999
Misty Mountain Hop	7/20/1999
Gold Soundz	7/21/1999
The Happy Whip and Dung Song	7/24/1999

DEPARTURES (Summer 1999)

	LAST KNOWN	# SHOWS
Doin' My Time	7/1/1999	111
If I Only Had a Brain	7/8/1999	107
Foreplay/Long Time	7/12/1999	104
NO2	7/13/1999	103
Tuesday's Gone	7/13/1999	103

DEPARTURES (Summer 1999)

	LAST KNOWN	# SHOWS
Born to Run	7/16/1999	101
On My Knees	7/17/1999	100
Icculus	7/18/1999	99
If You Need a Fool	7/18/1999	99
Gold Soundz	7/21/1999	97
Alumni Blues	7/24/1999	95
The Happy Whip and Dung Song	7/24/1999	95
Purple Rain	7/25/1999	94
Whipping Post	7/25/1999	94
Sweet Adeline	8/1/1999	89

BREAKOUTS (Summer 1999)

	SHELVED	BREAKOUT	# SHOWS
Swept Away	6/30/1998	6/30/1999	62
Steep	6/30/1998	6/30/1999	62
Meatstick	6/25/1997	7/3/1999	123
Little Drummer Boy	12/6/1986	7/3/1999	993
Fast Enough For You	7/16/1998	7/4/1999	55
The Star Spangled Banner	12/2/1997	7/4/1999	82
My Mind's Got a Mind of Its Own	7/17/1998	7/7/1999	55
I Saw It Again	12/12/1997	7/8/1999	77
Terrapin	7/11/1996	7/8/1999	211
If I Only Had a Brain	11/16/1995	7/8/1999	246
Foreplay/Long Time	12/9/1994	7/12/1999	309
NO2	7/16/1994	7/13/1999	355
My Sweet One	7/20/1998	7/17/1999	61
Have Mercy	11/12/1994	7/17/1999	334
Icculus	10/31/1995	7/18/1999	261
Fire	12/31/1997	7/23/1999	83
Glide	7/29/1998	7/24/1999	60
Camel Walk	7/28/1998	7/24/1999	61
Alumni Blues	4/15/1994	7/24/1999	426
Whipping Post	8/10/1996	7/25/1999	207
Purple Rain	8/6/1996	7/25/1999	209
Sweet Adeline	7/1/1998	8/1/1999	84

FALL 1999

"I Moved to Where They Hoped I'd Be"

After a few tours that were typified by brilliance sprinkled with malaise (or the reverse, depending on your view), Phish hit the road again not long after the conclusion of Summer Tour. The groove was as thick in 1999 as it had been in 1998, and new bass-oriented songs like "Gotta Jibboo" (which really came into its own towards the end of the tour) and the ominous "Sand" provided fresh outlets for this sound. "Jibboo" opened several second sets, and the jam ballad "Bug" completed a trio that was as frequently employed as "Julius," "Disease" and "Sample" had been in 1994. With "Heavy Things" and "First Tube" also extremely heavy in the rotation, the tour was defined by new material in a way that hadn't been seen since Summer '97.

In each of the past few years the band had harbored a particular brand of spacy jamming to compliment the more prominent "cow funk" (as typified in '97 by the jam before "Hood" on 8/14 and the jam before "Slave" on 8/16, and in '98 by the Halloween "Wolfman's Brother" and 11/29 "Simple"). In Fall '99,

a new form of space began to emerge more prominently as the funk finally began to run its course. The 12/8 "Piper" and 12/11 "Ghost" featured mind-meltingly intense jam styles which, when combined with Chris Kuroda's frantic swirls of light, gave some fans the impression that the stage was about to levetate in front of them. This style had been foreshadowed in the 4/2/98 "Twist," but it was not until Fall '99 that it emerged with any regularity.

The tour itself was actually two short tours in one: a month covering parts of September and October followed by two-plus weeks in December. Although they played both before and after Halloween, Phish chose not to play a show on this hallowed date, apparently ready for another year off from the costume ritual . The first half opened with a debut ("Free Thought") and closed in the familiar environs of Albany, and along the way featured excellent versions of "AC/DC Bag" and "Gumbo" on 9/4, a ripping "Boogie On" in Chula Vista" on 9/18 (a show which also featured a "Tweezer" opener), and a memorable "Mike's"-> "Catapult" ->"Mike's"-> "Kung" ->"Mike's" on 9/29 that reminded many of the crazy seguefests of 1994. Many fans noted a return to form after the sporadic creative production of the previous few tours, but the most notable event from a historical standpoint may have been the appearance of Grateful Dead bassist Phil Lesh during "YEM" on 9/17. He stuck around for a bass-heavy rendition of "Wolfman's Brother," as well as old Dead tunes "Cold Rain and Snow" and "Viola Lee Blues."

As the tour trekked across the continent from Vancouver to New York, many fan favorite venues were visited again, including the Gorge, Shoreline, and Nassau Colliseum, in addition to Pepsi Arena, still known by all as The 'Knick. In addition to the "Free Thought" debut, "Sweet Virginia" was unearthed for the first time to open a show in New Orleans, and covers like "On Your Way Down" and "Peaches en Regalia" were broken out after extended absences. Tom Marshall also made an appearance in Nassau to provide a singing peformance with a straight face for perhaps the first time, as he led the band through the Who's "We're Not Gonna Take It."

The second half of tour featured a return to the cozy Portland CCCC, as well as other familiar Northeast stops like Rochester, Hartford, Providence, and Philadelphia. Portland featured a sublime "Halley's" and an a cappela "Tweezer Reprise" out of "YEM," while Philly upped the ante with a legendary second set on 12/11, only to be answered by a 30 minute second set opening "Drowned" in Hartford. The tour closed with a return to Hampton Colliseum, only a month after the release of *Hampton Comes Alive*. This tour showcased perhaps the most consistent Phish jamming since Fall 97, and while the trance-heavy sound was very different from the classic 93-95 era, fans were optimistic about the ambitious festival planned in the Florida everglades for New Year's.

DEBUTS (Fall 1999)

Mozambique	9/9/1999
The Inlaw Josie Wales	9/9/1999
First Tube	9/9/1999
Will It Go Round in Circles	9/10/1999
Gotta Jibboo	9/10/1999
Heavy Things	9/11/1999
Sand	9/11/1999
Cold Rain and Snow	9/17/1999
Viola Lee Blues	9/17/1999
Sweet Virginia	9/26/1999
We're Not Gonna Take It	10/8/1999
Jennifer Dances	12/5/1999

DEPARTURES (Fall 1999)

	LAST KNOWN	# SHOWS
Cold Rain and Snow	9/17/1999	82

DEPARTURES (Fall 1999)

	LAST KNOWN	# SHOWS
Viola Lee Blues	9/17/1999	82
Will It Go Round in Circles	9/21/1999	79
La Grange	9/22/1999	78
Peaches En Regalia	9/24/1999	77
Mozambique	9/26/1999	75
Sweet Virginia	9/26/1999	75
Kung	9/29/1999	73
On Your Way Down	10/2/1999	71
Quinn the Eskimo	10/2/1999	71
Messin' With The Kid	10/3/1999	70
We're Not Gonna Take It	10/8/1999	67
My Left Toe	10/9/1999	66
Misty Mountain Hop	10/10/1999	65
Little Drummer Boy	12/2/1999	64
Hello My Baby	12/5/1999	61
Cracklin' Rosie	12/10/1999	58
Have Mercy	12/10/1999	58
Ride Captain Ride	12/10/1999	58
Mountains in the Mist	12/13/1999	55
Jennifer Dances	12/17/1999	52

BREAKOUTS (Fall 1999)

	SHELVED	BREAKOUT	# SHOWS
Peaches en Regalia	2/28/1997	9/14/1999	161
On Your Way Down	5/1/1989	9/16/1999	940
Messin' with the Kid	8/8/1997	10/3/1999	141
Uncle Pen	8/17/1997	10/4/1999	135
McGrupp	10/29/1998	10/7/1999	70
Dog Faced Boy	11/18/1998	12/8/1999	66
Ride Captain Ride	11/8/1998	12/10/1999	73
Cracklin' Rosie	8/6/1998	12/10/1999	92
Scent of a Mule	11/28/1998	12/11/1999	61
The Old Home Place	12/30/1998	12/17/1999	62
Dog Gone Dog	11/27/1998	12/18/1999	68
Buffalo Bill	11/27/1998	12/18/1999	68

NYE 1999

"Big Cypress"

Phish had gotten used to planning amibitious summer festivals. Phish had gotten used to planning ambitious New Year's Runs. In 1999, the concepts of Festivals and New Year's were merged into one at Big Cypress, a stretch of the everglades in South Florida that hosted the largest New Year's concert on the planet. It was more than a millenial celebration - it was an event that epitomized all that Phish and their fans were and always would be. The first day featured three sets. The second day featured an early set and a late set, played from before midnight until sunrise, that will forever be known as The Show. ABC television even provided coverage, airing "Heavy Things" live on their celebratory New Year's Eve broadcast. In typical Phish fashion, Trey encouraged the crowd to chant "Cheesecake" to confuse the home audience. The joke, also in true Phishyness, would continue to appear throughout the rest of The Show.

Musical highlights were only outnumbered by spiritual ones; the show was too powerful for the band to even add an encore. The majesty of these two nights can not be capsulized here; one listen to just about any jam from these two nights will have you understanding why many fans called this the greatest Phish concert ever.

DEBUTS (NYE 1999)

Che Hun Ta Mao	12/30/1999
Big Alligator Song	12/30/1999
After Midnight	12/31/1999
Quadrophonic Toppling	12/31/1999

DEPARTURES (NYE 1999)

	LAST KNOWN	# SHOWS
Big Alligator Song	12/30/1999	50
Che Hun Ta Mao	12/30/1999	50
Light Up Or Leave Me Alone	12/30/1999	50
After Midnight	12/31/1999	49
Quadrophonic Toppling	12/31/1999	49

BREAKOUTS (NYE 1999)

	SHELVED	BREAKOUT	# SHOWS
Good Times Bad Times	12/28/1998	12/30/1999	66
Corrine Corrina	2/18/1989	12/30/1999	982
Light Up or Leave Me Alone	7/25/1988	12/30/1999	1009
Auld Lang Syne	12/31/1998	12/31/1999	64
Albuquerque	12/28/1998	12/31/1999	67
Crosseyed and Painless	8/13/1997	12/31/1999	158
Love You	7/5/1997	12/31/1999	178

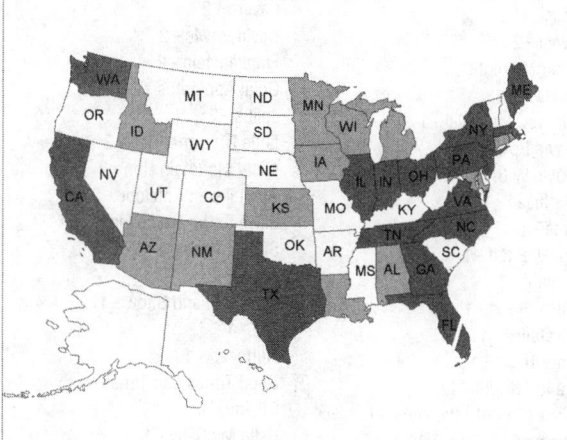

There were 64 shows played
Shows by day of week

- Sunday- 11
- Monday- 4
- Tuesday- 6
- Wednesday- 7
- Thursday- 9
- Friday- 14
- Saturday- 13

201 songs have been played (32% of songs Phish have played).

The average number of songs per show is 18.0.

The average amount of times each song was played is 5.76.

Total Times Played

Back on the Train - 23 (35%)

Chalk Dust Torture - 19 (29%)
Down With Disease - 19 (29%)
Farmhouse - 19 (29%)
Guyute - 19 (29%)
Limb By Limb - 18 (28%)
You Enjoy Myself - 18 (28%)
Heavy Things - 17 (26%)
Piper - 15 (23%)
Wolfman's Brother - 15 (23%)
Also Sprach Zarathustra - 14 (21%)
Character Zero - 14 (21%)
First Tube - 14 (21%)
The Moma Dance - 14 (21%)
Birds of a Feather - 13 (20%)
Free - 13 (20%)
Ghost - 13 (20%)
Mike's Song - 13 (20%)
Possum - 13 (20%)
Punch You In The Eye - 13 (20%)
Roggae - 13 (20%)
Simple - 13 (20%)
Tube - 13 (20%)
Tweezer - 13 (20%)
Tweezer Reprise - 13 (20%)
Weekapaug Groove - 13 (20%)
Bathtub Gin - 12 (18%)
Bug - 12 (18%)
David Bowie - 12 (18%)
Funky Bitch - 12 (18%)
Gotta Jibboo - 12 (18%)
Meatstick - 12 (18%)
Prince Caspian - 12 (18%)
Run Like an Antelope - 12 (18%)
Runaway Jim - 12 (18%)
Sand - 12 (18%)
The Squirming Coil - 12 (18%)
Twist - 12 (18%)
Golgi Apparatus - 11 (17%)
NICU - 11 (17%)
Wilson - 11 (17%)
Bouncing Around the Room - 10 (15%)
Cavern - 10 (15%)
Dirt - 10 (15%)
Loving Cup - 10 (15%)
Split Open and Melt - 10 (15%)
Stash - 10 (15%)
Wading in the Velvet Sea - 10 (15%)
When the Circus Comes - 10 (15%)
Harry Hood - 9 (14%)
Horn - 9 (14%)
Maze - 9 (14%)
Sample in a Jar - 9 (14%)
Taste - 9 (14%)
Ya Mar - 9 (14%)
AC/DC Bag - 8 (12%)
Axilla - 8 (12%)
Beauty of My Dreams - 8 (12%)

Boogie on Reggae Woman - 8 (12%)
Mountains in the Mist - 8 (12%)
Poor Heart - 8 (12%)
Sparkle - 8 (12%)
Waste - 8 (12%)
Water in the Sky - 8 (12%)
Billy Breathes - 7 (10%)
Carini - 7 (10%)
Fluffhead - 7 (10%)
Frankenstein - 7 (10%)
I Am Hydrogen - 7 (10%)
Jam - 7 (10%)
Julius - 7 (10%)
Rocky Top - 7 (10%)
Vultures - 7 (10%)
What's the Use - 7 (10%)
Divided Sky - 6 (9%)
I Didn't Know - 6 (9%)
Lawn Boy - 6 (9%)
Reba - 6 (9%)
Silent in the Morning - 6 (9%)
Slave to the Traffic Light - 6 (9%)
Theme From The Bottom - 6 (9%)
Train Song - 6 (9%)
Brian and Robert - 5 (7%)
Ginseng Sullivan - 5 (7%)
Gumbo - 5 (7%)
Halley's Comet - 5 (7%)
Hello My Baby - 5 (7%)
Llama - 5 (7%)
Makisupa Policeman - 5 (7%)
Meat - 5 (7%)
Mozambique - 5 (7%)
My Left Toe - 5 (7%)
My Soul - 5 (7%)
Rock and Roll - 5 (7%)
Suzy Greenberg - 5 (7%)
The Horse - 5 (7%)
The Wedge - 5 (7%)
Back at the Chicken Shack - 4 (6%)
Catapult - 4 (6%)
Dogs Stole Things - 4 (6%)
Misty Mountain Hop - 4 (6%)
My Mind's Got a Mind of its Own - 4 (6%)
Nellie Kane - 4 (6%)
Sneakin' Sally through the Alley - 4 (6%)
The Inlaw Josie Wales - 4 (6%)
The Lizards - 4 (6%)
The Sloth - 4 (6%)
Avenu Malkenu - 3 (4%)
Bittersweet Motel - 3 (4%)
Bold As Love - 3 (4%)
Cars Trucks Buses - 3 (4%)
Cities - 3 (4%)
Contact - 3 (4%)

Drowned - 3 (4%)
Fast Enough for You - 3 (4%)
Fee - 3 (4%)
I Saw it Again - 3 (4%)
Jennifer Dances - 3 (4%)
On Your Way Down - 3 (4%)
Peaches En Regalia - 3 (4%)
Roses Are Free - 3 (4%)
Sleeping Monkey - 3 (4%)
Strange Design - 3 (4%)
The Curtain - 3 (4%)
The Man Who Stepped Into
    Yesterday - 3 (4%)
Camel Walk - 2 (3%)
Driver - 2 (3%)
Frankie Says - 2 (3%)
Guelah Papyrus - 2 (3%)
Have Mercy - 2 (3%)
Jesus Just Left Chicago - 2 (3%)
Kung - 2 (3%)
Little Drummer Boy - 2 (3%)
My Friend My Friend - 2 (3%)
Quinn the Eskimo - 2 (3%)
Rift - 2 (3%)
Sleep - 2 (3%)
The Man Who Stepped Into
    Yesterday Reprise - 2 (3%)
The Mango Song - 2 (3%)
Uncle Pen - 2 (3%)
Walk Away - 2 (3%)
While My Guitar Gently Weeps
    - 2 (3%)
Will It Go Round in Circles - 2 (3%)
After Midnight - 1 (1%)
After Midnight Reprise - 1 (1%)
Albuquerque - 1 (1%)
Alumni Blues - 1 (1%)
Auld Lang Syne - 1 (1%)
Bass Jam - 1 (1%)
Big Alligator Song - 1 (1%)
Big Black Furry Creature From
    Mars - 1 (1%)
Bike - 1 (1%)
Born to Run - 1 (1%)
Buffalo Bill - 1 (1%)
Che Hun Ta Mao - 1 (1%)
Cold Rain and Snow - 1 (1%)
Corrine Corrina - 1 (1%)
Cracklin' Rosie - 1 (1%)
Crosseyed and Painless - 1 (1%)
Dog Faced Boy - 1 (1%)
Dog Gone Dog - 1 (1%)
Doin' My Time - 1 (1%)
Fire - 1 (1%)
Foreplay/Long Time - 1 (1%)
Glide - 1 (1%)
Gold Soundz - 1 (1%)
Good Times Bad Times - 1 (1%)

Ha Ha Ha - 1 (1%)
I'm Blue I'm Lonesome - 1 (1%)
Icculus - 1 (1%)
If I Only Had a Brain - 1 (1%)
If You Need a Fool - 1 (1%)
La Grange - 1 (1%)
Light Up Or Leave Me Alone
    - 1 (1%)
Love You - 1 (1%)
McGrupp and the Watchful
    Hosemasters - 1 (1%)
Meatstick Reprise - 1 (1%)
Messin' With The Kid - 1 (1%)
My Sweet One - 1 (1%)
NO2 - 1 (1%)
On My Knees - 1 (1%)
Purple Rain - 1 (1%)
Quadrophonic Toppling - 1 (1%)
Ride Captain Ride - 1 (1%)
Scent of a Mule - 1 (1%)
Smoke on the Water Jam - 1 (1%)
Steep - 1 (1%)
Sweet Adeline - 1 (1%)
Sweet Emotion Jam - 1 (1%)
Sweet Virginia - 1 (1%)
Swept Away - 1 (1%)
Terrapin - 1 (1%)
The Happy Whip and Dung Song
    - 1 (1%)
The Oh Kee Pa Ceremony - 1 (1%)
The Old Home Place - 1 (1%)
The Star Spangled Banner - 1 (1%)
Timber (Jerry) - 1 (1%)
Tuesday's Gone - 1 (1%)
Viola Lee Blues - 1 (1%)
We're Not Gonna Take It - 1 (1%)
Whipping Post - 1 (1%)

First Set Openers

Chalk Dust Torture - 5
Farmhouse - 4
First Tube - 4
Punch You In The Eye - 4
Tube - 4
NICU - 3
Runaway Jim - 3
Harry Hood - 2
Heavy Things - 2
Limb By Limb - 2
Mozambique - 2
Piper - 2
Tweezer - 2
Wilson - 2
Ya Mar - 2
AC/DC Bag - 1
Also Sprach Zarathustra - 1
Back on the Train - 1
Bathtub Gin - 1

Birds of a Feather - 1
Carini - 1
Cities - 1
Down With Disease - 1
Foreplay/Long Time - 1
Guyute - 1
Julius - 1
Llama - 1
Meat - 1
My Friend My Friend - 1
My Soul - 1
Poor Heart - 1
Sample in a Jar - 1
Sweet Virginia - 1
Uncle Pen - 1
Water in the Sky - 1
Wolfman's Brother - 1

First Set Closers

Cavern - 6
Character Zero - 6
Loving Cup - 5
Possum - 4
Run Like an Antelope - 4
You Enjoy Myself - 4
Golgi Apparatus - 3
The Squirming Coil - 3
Chalk Dust Torture - 2
Hello My Baby - 2
Rocky Top - 2
Stash - 2
Twist - 2
After Midnight - 1
Axilla - 1
Bittersweet Motel - 1
David Bowie - 1
Down With Disease - 1
Fluffhead - 1
Free - 1
Funky Bitch - 1
Guyute - 1
Harry Hood - 1
Meatstick - 1
Poor Heart - 1
Runaway Jim - 1
Slave to the Traffic Light - 1
Theme From The Bottom - 1
Tweezer Reprise - 1
Waste - 1
Will It Go Round in Circles - 1
Wilson - 1

Second Set Openers

Twist - 6
Also Sprach Zarathustra - 5
Birds of a Feather - 4
Boogie on Reggae Woman - 4
Down With Disease - 4

Ghost - 4
Gotta Jibboo - 4
Wolfman's Brother - 4
Sand - 3
Tweezer - 3
Meatstick - 2
Mike's Song - 2
NICU - 2
Peaches En Regalia - 2
Runaway Jim - 2
Carini - 1
Drowned - 1
Farmhouse - 1
Funky Bitch - 1
Halley's Comet - 1
Jam - 1
Limb By Limb - 1
Possum - 1
Punch You In The Eye - 1
Sample in a Jar - 1
The Squirming Coil - 1
Wilson - 1

Second Set Closers

You Enjoy Myself - 8
Weekapaug Groove - 6
Chalk Dust Torture - 3
Character Zero - 3
Down With Disease - 3
Harry Hood - 3
Cavern - 2
David Bowie - 2
Frankenstein - 2
Golgi Apparatus - 2
Julius - 2
Little Drummer Boy - 2
Misty Mountain Hop - 2
Run Like an Antelope - 2
Slave to the Traffic Light - 2
Suzy Greenberg - 2
Waste - 2
Cold Rain and Snow - 1
Fire - 1
Fluffhead - 1
Good Times Bad Times - 1
Guyute - 1
Hello My Baby - 1
Llama - 1
Loving Cup - 1
Meatstick - 1
Possum - 1
Runaway Jim - 1
Simple - 1
Split Open and Melt - 1
Stash - 1
The Squirming Coil - 1

Third Set Openers

Chalk Dust Torture - 1
My Soul - 1

Third Set Closers

Fluffhead - 1
Weekapaug Groove - 1

Encores

Tweezer Reprise - 12
Character Zero - 5
Rocky Top - 5
Bold As Love - 3
Julius - 3
Rock and Roll - 3
The Squirming Coil - 3
Boogie on Reggae Woman - 2
Bouncing Around the Room - 2
Brian and Robert - 2
Contact - 2
Frankenstein - 2
Golgi Apparatus - 2
Hello My Baby - 2
Misty Mountain Hop - 2
Sample in a Jar - 2
Simple - 2
While My Guitar Gently Weeps - 2
Alumni Blues - 1
Bittersweet Motel - 1
Born to Run - 1
Camel Walk - 1

Carini - 1
Chalk Dust Torture - 1
Cities - 1
Funky Bitch - 1
Glide - 1
Guyute - 1
Halley's Comet - 1
Heavy Things - 1
I Am Hydrogen - 1
Jam - 1
La Grange - 1
Loving Cup - 1
Meatstick - 1
Meatstick Reprise - 1
Messin' With The Kid - 1
Possum - 1
Reba - 1
Ride Captain Ride - 1
Runaway Jim - 1
Silent in the Morning - 1
Slave to the Traffic Light - 1
Sleeping Monkey - 1
Sweet Adeline - 1
Terrapin - 1
The Old Home Place - 1
The Star Spangled Banner - 1
Theme From The Bottom - 1
Tuesday's Gone - 1
Viola Lee Blues - 1
Walk Away - 1
When the Circus Comes - 1
Ya Mar - 1

SPRING SUMMER 2000

"This is a Farmhouse"

Phish released their *Farmhouse* album in May of 2000 and began a promotional blitz the likes of which fans had never seen. The band played television and radio programs from coast to coast and also managed to squeeze in three intimate shows at New York's Radio City Music Hall and Roseland Ballroom that became the hottest Phish tickets ever. Internet-based fans tried one of their most ambitious projects yet at Radio City, encouraging all to come dressed in their best eveningwear for "Project Phormal."

Summer tour proper began with the band's second trip to Japan. Covering four cities with seven shows in eight days, Phish warmed up for their U.S. fans and prepared to come back home a well-oiled jam machine. Shows got stronger as the week drew on; highlights included a jam-laden second set in Fukuoka on 6/14 and a solid second set in Osaka on 6/16. "Down with Disease" reasserted itself as a jam vehicle with two strong renditions.

Phish returned to America and, a week later, swung through the southeast and up the east coast. The tour opener in Antioch on 6/22 featured a variety of special guests. Four shows in New Jersey and two in Connecticut

from 6/28 through 7/4 provided many highlights, including a "Drowned" / "Rock and Roll" combo on 6/29 that combined two Halloween musical costumes, a great all-around show on 6/30, and the first monster Jibboo on 7/4. The band moved west, pausing for a heavy second set on 7/8, and gave us two more legendary Deer Creek shows, including the "Moby Dick"-fest on 7/11. After pausing for torrential rain at Polaris Amphitheatre on 7/14 before closing the tour there the next night, Phish headed to Austin, Texas to tape an episode of *Austin City Limits*.

DEBUTS (Summer 2000)

Coming Home	6/22/2000

BREAKOUTS (Summer 2000)

	SHELVED	BREAKOUT	# SHOWS
It's Ice	11/13/1998	5/23/2000	82
Sleep	7/26/1999	6/14/2000	52
Bike	7/30/1999	6/15/2000	51
I'm Blue I'm Lonesome	7/18/1999	6/22/2000	60
Freebird	12/29/1998	6/22/2000	76
My Sweet One	7/17/1999	6/24/2000	63
If I Could	7/31/1998	6/28/2000	119
Ha Ha Ha	9/9/1999	6/30/2000	55
Swept Away	6/30/1999	7/1/2000	80
Steep	6/30/1999	7/1/2000	80
Buried Alive	11/27/1998	7/1/2000	87
Glide	7/24/1999	7/3/2000	64
Foam	11/28/1998	7/3/2000	87
I Saw It Again	9/10/1999	7/4/2000	57
Rift	8/1/1999	7/4/2000	59
The Star Spangled Banner	7/4/1999	7/4/2000	79
Magilla	8/1/1998	7/4/2000	123
Shafty	7/2/1998	7/7/2000	144
Terrapin	7/8/1999	7/11/2000	82
Moby Dick	11/29/1997	7/11/2000	168
Chalk Dust Torture Reprise	12/10/1994	7/11/2000	387
My Friend My Friend	7/31/1999	7/12/2000	66
The Curtain With	6/19/1988	7/12/2000	1044
Timber (Jerry)	7/17/1999	7/14/2000	78

FALL 2000

"The Last Time?"

Thoughts of the fall tour were clouded by the one thing Phish fans had ignored for years: Phish was taking a break. Rumors had circulated, and word finally broke in late August that Phish had no plans to tour past the 10/7 Shoreline show. It was stated that the hiatus was not a permanent break, but that further tours would not be announced until the band determined what was in their best interests.

A tour with such heavy consequences could only suffer under the weighty expectations that surrounded it. We write this capsule with the tour less than 48 hours old – time will tell how fans perceive it. Surely, great mention will be paid to some of the greatest breakouts in Phishtory. The much-anticipated "Destiny Unbound" appearance never materialized, but the

long-lost "Spock's Brain" was the most notable and "Forbin's" / "Mockingbird" the most sentimental. During the latter, Trey addressed the pending break and tried to quell the fears of fans everywhere, noting (in so many words) that the band had enjoyed the last seventeen years and hoped to enjoy at least seventeen more

Fall 2000 will also be remembered for two interesting special guests: Kid Rock (9/29) and Bob Weir (10/6). Of the tour itself, early favorites included 9/17 and 9/25, with the emotional tour-closing Shoreline shows on 10/6 and 10/7 giving fans a chance to say goodbye for now. The last time? Let it be.

DEBUTS (Fall 2000)

Mellow Mood	9/8/2000
Windora Bug	9/8/2000
Road Runner	9/11/2000
Come On Baby Let's Go Downtown	9/23/2000
Walk This Way	9/29/2000
Rapper's Delight	9/29/2000
You Shook Me (All Night Long)	9/29/2000
Guy Forget	10/1/2000
El Paso	10/6/2000
West L.A. Fadeaway	10/6/2000

BREAKOUTS (Fall 2000)	SHELVED	BREAKOUT	# SHOWS
Fire	7/23/1999	9/8/2000	76
The Oh Kee Pa Ceremony	7/4/1999	9/14/2000	93
McGrupp	10/7/1999	9/18/2000	55
BBFCFM	10/3/1999	9/20/2000	58
Cool it Down	10/31/1998	9/24/2000	127
Everybody's Got Something to Hide	10/31/1994	9/25/2000	430
Brother	7/28/1998	9/27/2000	149
Spock's Brain	6/24/1995	9/29/2000	387
Dinner and a Movie	3/1/1997	9/29/2000	238
American Band	11/16/1996	9/29/2000	267
Walfredo	2/22/1997	9/30/2000	244
Esther	8/9/1998	9/30/2000	142
Colonel Forbins Ascent	8/7/1998	9/30/2000	144
The Famous Mockingbird	8/7/1998	9/30/2000	144
A Day in the Life	7/3/1998	9/30/2000	166
Emotional Rescue	7/28/1998	9/30/2000	151

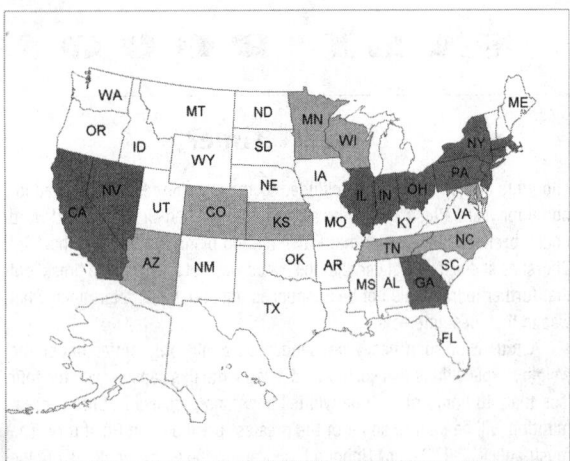

There were 49 shows played

Shows by day of week

- Sunday- 6
- Monday- 6
- Tuesday- 5
- Wednesday- 6
- Thursday- 6
- Friday- 11
- Saturday- 9

188 songs have been played (30% of songs Phish have played).

The average number of songs per show is 17.3.

The average amount of times each song was played is 4.52.

Total Times Played

First Tube - 17 (34%)
Gotta Jibboo - 17 (34%)
Heavy Things - 15 (30%)
Piper - 14 (28%)
Chalk Dust Torture - 13 (26%)
Limb By Limb - 13 (26%)
Twist - 13 (26%)
Back on the Train - 12 (24%)
Character Zero - 12 (24%)
Run Like an Antelope - 12 (24%)
Sand - 12 (24%)
Bathtub Gin - 11 (22%)
Bug - 11 (22%)
David Bowie - 11 (22%)
Down With Disease - 11 (22%)
The Moma Dance - 11 (22%)
Golgi Apparatus - 10 (20%)
Guyute - 10 (20%)
Mike's Song - 10 (20%)
Sample in a Jar - 10 (20%)
Wolfman's Brother - 10 (20%)
You Enjoy Myself - 10 (20%)
Cavern - 9 (18%)
Harry Hood - 9 (18%)
My Soul - 9 (18%)
The Inlaw Josie Wales - 9 (18%)
Weekapaug Groove - 9 (18%)
Also Sprach Zarathustra - 8 (16%)
Beauty of My Dreams - 8 (16%)
Bouncing Around the Room - 8 (16%)
Dirt - 8 (16%)
Funky Bitch - 8 (16%)
Loving Cup - 8 (16%)
Possum - 8 (16%)
Split Open and Melt - 8 (16%)
Taste - 8 (16%)
Axilla - 7 (14%)
Birds of a Feather - 7 (14%)

Boogie on Reggae Woman - 7 (14%)
Carini - 7 (14%)
Driver - 7 (14%)
Ghost - 7 (14%)
Maze - 7 (14%)
NICU - 7 (14%)
Punch You In The Eye - 7 (14%)
Roggae - 7 (14%)
The Squirming Coil - 7 (14%)
Tweezer - 7 (14%)
Tweezer Reprise - 7 (14%)
Wilson - 7 (14%)
Dog Faced Boy - 6 (12%)
Farmhouse - 6 (12%)
Horn - 6 (12%)
It's Ice - 6 (12%)
Meatstick - 6 (12%)
Prince Caspian - 6 (12%)
Rock and Roll - 6 (12%)
Runaway Jim - 6 (12%)
Stash - 6 (12%)
The Mango Song - 6 (12%)
Wading in the Velvet Sea - 6 (12%)
When the Circus Comes - 6 (12%)
Ya Mar - 6 (12%)
AC/DC Bag - 5 (10%)
Drowned - 5 (10%)
Lawn Boy - 5 (10%)
Poor Heart - 5 (10%)
Reba - 5 (10%)
Rift - 5 (10%)
Simple - 5 (10%)
Sparkle - 5 (10%)
The Lizards - 5 (10%)
Billy Breathes - 4 (8%)
Brian and Robert - 4 (8%)
Cars Trucks Buses - 4 (8%)
Cities - 4 (8%)
Divided Sky - 4 (8%)
Fee - 4 (8%)
Frankenstein - 4 (8%)
Free - 4 (8%)
Gumbo - 4 (8%)
Halley's Comet - 4 (8%)
I Am Hydrogen - 4 (8%)
Julius - 4 (8%)
Makisupa Policeman - 4 (8%)
Meat - 4 (8%)
Mellow Mood - 4 (8%)
Slave to the Traffic Light - 4 (8%)
Theme From The Bottom - 4 (8%)
Tube - 4 (8%)
Uncle Pen - 4 (8%)
Walk Away - 4 (8%)
Waste - 4 (8%)
While My Guitar Gently Weeps - 4 (8%)

Bold As Love - 3 (6%)
Contact - 3 (6%)
Fast Enough for You - 3 (6%)
Fluffhead - 3 (6%)
Frankie Says - 3 (6%)
Ginseng Sullivan - 3 (6%)
Glide - 3 (6%)
Good Times Bad Times - 3 (6%)
I Saw it Again - 3 (6%)
Llama - 3 (6%)
My Friend My Friend - 3 (6%)
My Mind's Got a Mind of its
    Own - 3 (6%)
Scent of a Mule - 3 (6%)
Sleeping Monkey - 3 (6%)
The Curtain - 3 (6%)
The Curtain With - 3 (6%)
The Sloth - 3 (6%)
Vultures - 3 (6%)
What's the Use - 3 (6%)
Albuquerque - 2 (4%)
Avenu Malkenu - 2 (4%)
Back at the Chicken Shack
    - 2 (4%)
Bike - 2 (4%)
Bittersweet Motel - 2 (4%)
Come On Baby, Let's Go Down-
    town - 2 (4%)
Crosseyed and Painless - 2 (4%)
Dogs Stole Things - 2 (4%)
Fire - 2 (4%)
Foam - 2 (4%)
Guelah Papyrus - 2 (4%)
I Didn't Know - 2 (4%)
Jam - 2 (4%)
My Sweet One - 2 (4%)
Rocky Top - 2 (4%)
Roses Are Free - 2 (4%)
Silent in the Morning - 2 (4%)
Sleep - 2 (4%)
Sneakin' Sally through the Alley
    - 2 (4%)
Spock's Brain - 2 (4%)
Suzy Greenberg - 2 (4%)
The Horse - 2 (4%)
The Man Who Stepped Into
    Yesterday - 2 (4%)
The Old Home Place - 2 (4%)
Timber (Jerry) - 2 (4%)
Water in the Sky - 2 (4%)
Windora Bug - 2 (4%)
A Day in the Life - 1 (2%)
American Band - 1 (2%)
Big Black Furry Creature From
    Mars - 1 (2%)
Brother - 1 (2%)
Buffalo Bill - 1 (2%)
Buried Alive - 1 (2%)

Camel Walk - 1 (2%)
Catapult - 1 (2%)
Chalk Dust Torture Reprise
    - 1 (2%)
Colonel Forbin's Ascent - 1 (2%)
Cool it Down - 1 (2%)
Corrine Corrina - 1 (2%)
Dinner and a Movie - 1 (2%)
Dog Gone Dog - 1 (2%)
El Paso - 1 (2%)
Emotional Rescue - 1 (2%)
Esther - 1 (2%)
Everybody's Got Something to
    Hide Except for Me and My
    Monkey - 1 (2%)
Freebird - 1 (2%)
Guy Forget - 1 (2%)
Ha Ha Ha - 1 (2%)
Hold Whatcha Got - 1 (2%)
I'm Blue I'm Lonesome - 1 (2%)
If I Could - 1 (2%)
Jesus Just Left Chicago - 1 (2%)
Love You - 1 (2%)
Magilla - 1 (2%)
McGrupp and the Watchful
    Hosemasters - 1 (2%)
Meat Reprise - 1 (2%)
Moby Dick - 1 (2%)
Nellie Kane - 1 (2%)
Rapper's Delight - 1 (2%)
Road Runner - 1 (2%)
Shafty - 1 (2%)
Steep - 1 (2%)
Strange Design - 1 (2%)
Swept Away - 1 (2%)
Terrapin - 1 (2%)
The Famous Mockingbird - 1 (2%)
The Man Who Stepped Into
    Yesterday Reprise - 1 (2%)
The Oh Kee Pa Ceremony - 1 (2%)
The Star Spangled Banner - 1 (2%)
The Wedge - 1 (2%)
Train Song - 1 (2%)
Walfredo - 1 (2%)
Walk This Way - 1 (2%)
West LA Fadeaway - 1 (2%)
You Shook Me (All Night Long)
    - 1 (2%)

First Set Openers

First Tube - 6
Carini - 4
Chalk Dust Torture - 3
Down With Disease - 3
AC/DC Bag - 2
Cars Trucks Buses - 2
Mellow Mood - 2
NICU - 2

Punch You In The Eye - 2
Sample in a Jar - 2
The Moma Dance - 2
Ya Mar - 2
Axilla - 1
Buried Alive - 1
Come On Baby, Let's Go Down-
    town - 1
Everybody's Got Something to
    Hide Except for Me and My
    Monkey - 1
Funky Bitch - 1
Guyute - 1
Ha Ha Ha - 1
Limb By Limb - 1
Meat - 1
My Friend My Friend - 1
My Soul - 1
Possum - 1
Reba - 1
Road Runner - 1
The Star Spangled Banner - 1
Walfredo - 1
Wolfman's Brother - 1

First Set Closers

Run Like an Antelope - 5
Character Zero - 4
Cavern - 3
Chalk Dust Torture - 3
Farmhouse - 3
Julius - 3
Split Open and Melt - 3
Possum - 2
Sample in a Jar - 2
Stash - 2
Weekapaug Groove - 2
You Enjoy Myself - 2
Bathtub Gin - 1
Bittersweet Motel - 1
David Bowie - 1
Golgi Apparatus - 1
Guyute - 1
If I Could - 1
My Soul - 1
Prince Caspian - 1
Rock and Roll - 1
Runaway Jim - 1
Sleeping Monkey - 1
Suzy Greenberg - 1
The Squirming Coil - 1
While My Guitar Gently Weeps - 1
Wilson - 1

Second Set Openers

Gotta Jibboo - 9
Birds of a Feather - 6
Down With Disease - 3

Heavy Things - 3
Rock and Roll - 3
Drowned - 2
Piper - 2
Punch You In The Eye - 2
Runaway Jim - 2
Also Sprach Zarathustra - 1
Back on the Train - 1
Boogie on Reggae Woman - 1
Bouncing Around the Room - 1
Chalk Dust Torture - 1
Cities - 1
Dinner and a Movie - 1
First Tube - 1
Ghost - 1
Halley's Comet - 1
Limb By Limb - 1
Roses Are Free - 1
Timber (Jerry) - 1
Tube - 1
Tweezer - 1
Twist - 1

Second Set Closers

Character Zero - 6
Loving Cup - 4
You Enjoy Myself - 4
Cavern - 3
David Bowie - 3
Bug - 2
Slave to the Traffic Light - 2
Tweezer Reprise - 2
Weekapaug Groove - 2
A Day in the Life - 1
Also Sprach Zarathustra - 1
Bittersweet Motel - 1
Bold As Love - 1
Drowned - 1
Free - 1
Freebird - 1
Funky Bitch - 1
Ghost - 1
Golgi Apparatus - 1
Guyute - 1
Halley's Comet - 1
Harry Hood - 1
Meatstick - 1
Possum - 1
Prince Caspian - 1
Rock and Roll - 1
Run Like an Antelope - 1
Wading in the Velvet Sea - 1
You Shook Me (All Night Long) - 1

Third Set Openers

Mike's Song - 1

Third Set Closers

Weekapaug Groove - 1

Encores

The Inlaw Josie Wales - 5
Driver - 4
Loving Cup - 4
Tweezer Reprise - 4
Cavern - 3
Good Times Bad Times - 3
The Squirming Coil - 3
You Enjoy Myself - 3

Bold As Love - 2
Boogie on Reggae Woman - 2
Brian and Robert - 2
Character Zero - 2
Fire - 2
Guyute - 2
Harry Hood - 2
Possum - 2
Waste - 2
While My Guitar Gently Weeps - 2
American Band - 1
Axilla - 1

Bouncing Around the Room - 1
Bug - 1
Chalk Dust Torture - 1
Chalk Dust Torture Reprise - 1
Contact - 1
El Paso - 1
Emotional Rescue - 1
First Tube - 1
Frankenstein - 1
Golgi Apparatus - 1
Gotta Jibboo - 1
Lawn Boy - 1

Limb By Limb - 1
Moby Dick - 1
Rocky Top - 1
Run Like an Antelope - 1
Sample in a Jar - 1
Sleep - 1
Sleeping Monkey - 1
Suzy Greenberg - 1
Taste - 1
Uncle Pen - 1
Wading in the Velvet Sea - 1
West LA Fadeaway - 1

ANNUAL CHART

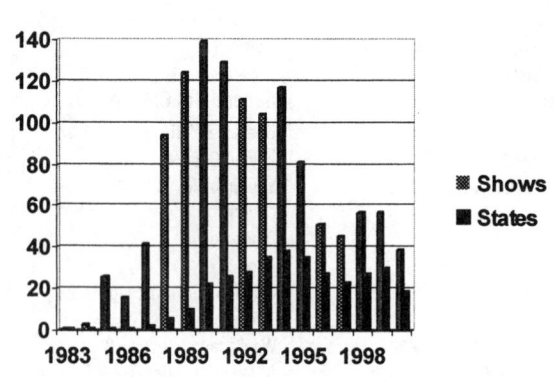

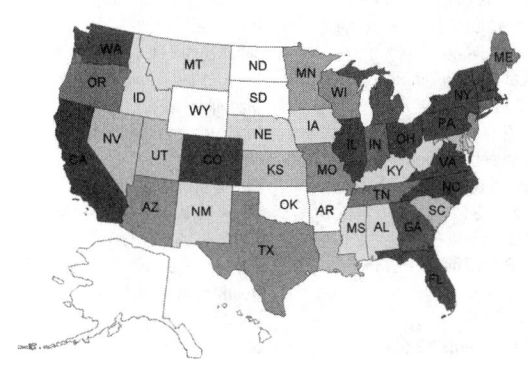

STATE	FIRST	83	84	85	86	87	88	89	90	91	92	93	94	95	96	97	98	99	00	TOTAL	AVG	LAST
AL	10/20/1990								1	2			2					1		6	1.5	9/28/1999
AK	—																			0	—	—
AZ	10/23/1991									2	3	1	3	1	1	1	1	1	1	15	1.5	10/1/2000
AR	—																			0	—	—
CA	3/28/1991									8	13	13	15	4	4	2	5	4	4	72	7.2	10/7/2000
CO	7/28/1988						7		21	14	7	5	2	2	4	2	1		1	66	6	9/27/2000
CT	4/2/1989							2	4	3	3	2		1	1	1	1	1	2	21	1.9	7/1/2000
DE	2/13/1993											1	1							2	1	4/18/1994
DC	12/6/1989							1	3	3	1	2						1		11	1.8	12/15/1999
FL	2/22/1993											6	7	5	3			2		23	4.6	12/31/1999
GA	2/1/1990								8	6	1	4	2	4	1	1	1	2	2	32	2.9	6/24/2000
HI	—																			0	—	—
ID	6/7/1995													1			1			2	1	9/14/1999
IL	3/30/1990								2	4	4	2	2	2	1	2	4	2	2	27	2.5	9/23/2000

STATE	FIRST	83	84	85	86	87	88	89	90	91	92	93	94	95	96	97	98	99	00	TOTAL	AVG	LAST
IN	4/25/1990								1			1	2	1	2	2	2	2	3	16	1.8	6/12/2000
IA	4/12/1993											1	1	1	1			1		5	1	10/1/1999
KS	8/17/1993										1	1	1				1	1	1	6	1	9/25/2000
KY	4/16/1993											2	1	1	1					5	1.3	11/7/1996
LA	10/22/1990								1	2		2	2	1	1			1		10	1.4	9/26/1999
ME	1/20/1989							14	4	5	1	3	2	1		2	2	2		36	3.6	12/8/1999
MD	12/7/1989							1	1		1		1			1	1	1	1	8	1	9/17/2000
MA	6/1/1986						6	25	11	8	7	2	4	7	2	3	3	2	2	82	6.3	9/12/2000
MI	3/7/1991									2	5	4	6	2	2	1	1	1		24	2.7	9/2/1999
MN	11/6/1990									2	1	2	1	1			1		1	9	1.3	9/24/2000
MS	10/13/1994												1							1	1	10/13/1994
MO	3/30/1992										4	2	2	2	2	1	1			14	2	7/29/1998
MT	11/28/1994												1	1						2	1	10/8/1995
NE	10/21/1995													1	1					2	1	11/16/1996
NV	12/6/1996														1	1	2		2	6	1.5	9/30/2000
NH	6/3/1988						5	9	9	9	4	1	1							38	5.4	4/11/1994
NJ	10/7/1990										2	2	1	1				3	4	13	2.2	7/4/2000
NM	10/26/1991										3	1	1					1		6	1.5	9/22/1999
NY	8/21/1987					1	12	16	18	17	20	14	13	12	7	7	9	7	6	159	11.4	9/14/2000
NC	2/7/1990								5	6	2	3	4	2	1	2	2	2	1	30	2.7	7/25/2000
ND	—																			0	—	—
OH	3/27/1990								4	3	6	5	4	3		2	3	3	2	35	3.5	9/20/2000
OK	—																			0	—	—
OR	4/3/1991									5	2	2	3	1	1		1			15	2.1	9/12/1999
PA	8/27/1988						1	3	8		4	4	6	5	5	4	1	3	2	46	3.8	9/15/2000
RI	4/29/1989							8	5	3	1	2	1	1			2	1		24	2.7	12/13/1999
SC	1/31/1990								10	1			3	1	1		1			17	2.8	11/18/1998
SD	—																			0	—	—
TN	2/27/1991									3			4	5	3	2	1	2	1	21	2.6	6/22/2000
TX	10/25/1990								3	2		2	3	3		2	3	2		20	2.5	9/25/1999
UT	8/21/1993											1	1	1	1	1	1			6	1	11/2/1998
VT	10/30/1983	1	3	26	16	41	63	45	16	10	4	1	2	2		1				231	16.5	3/18/1997
VA	2/8/1990								1	5	5	2	5	2	1	3	3	3		30	3	12/18/1999
WA	4/6/1991									1	1	3	3	3	2	2	2	2		19	2.1	9/11/1999
WV	3/22/1992										2	1	1							4	1.3	6/26/1994
WI	3/31/1990								3	3	3	2	1	1	1	1	2	1	1	19	1.7	7/8/2000
WY	—																			0	—	—
U.S.	10/30/1983	1	3	26	16	42	94	124	139	129	111	104	117	81	51	45	57	57	39	1236	68.7	10/7/2000
States	—	1	1	1	1	2	6	10	22	26	28	35	38	35	27	23	27	30	19	42	18.4	—
Avg.	—	1	3	26	16	21	15.7	12.4	6.3	5	4	3	3.1	2.3	1.9	2	2.1	1.9	2.1	29.4	7.1	—

SONGS PLAYED IN CONSECUTIVE SHOWS

You Enjoy Myself was seen in every show from 4/30/89 to 8/17/89 [15 shows].

You Enjoy Myself was seen in every show from 10/14/89 to 11/18/89 [14 shows].

My Sweet One was seen in every show from 11/2/89 to 12/3/89 [10 shows].

Mike's Song was seen in every show from 12/9/89 to 2/17/90 [16 shows].

I Am Hydrogen was seen in every show from 12/9/89 to 2/17/90 [16 shows].

Weekapaug Groove was seen in every show from 12/9/89 to 2/17/90 [16 shows].

The Landlady was seen in every show from 10/4/90 to 11/3/90 11 shows].

Bouncing Around the Room was seen in every show from 10/4/90 to 11/10/90 [14 shows].

Suzy Greenberg was seen in every show from 10/8/90 to 11/24/90 [13 shows].

You Enjoy Myself was seen in every show from 10/31/90 to 11/26/90 [10 shows].

Mike's Song was seen in every show from 10/12/90 to 11/30/90 [14 shows].

I Am Hydrogen was seen in every show from 10/12/90 to 11/30/90 [14 shows].

Weekapaug Groove was seen in every show from 10/12/90 to 11/30/90 [14 shows].

The Landlady was seen in every show from 11/8/90 to 12/28/90 [11 shows].

Runaway Jim was seen in every show from 11/10/90 to 2/1/91 [13 shows].

Llama was seen in every show from 11/3/90 to 12/29/90 [14 shows].

My Sweet One was seen in every show from 2/3/91 to 2/28/91 [13 shows].

Golgi Apparatus was seen in every show from 2/9/91 to 3/13/91 [15 shows].

The Squirming Coil was seen in every show from 2/26/91 to 3/22/91 [12 shows].

The Landlady was seen in every show from 5/19/91 to 7/25/91 [13 shows].

Suzy Greenberg was seen in every show from 7/11/91 to 7/27/91 [14 shows].

Sparkle was seen in every show from 11/22/91 to 3/6/92 [10 shows].

Big Ball Jam was seen in every show from 4/10/93 to 5/2/93 [17 shows].

Also Sprach Zarathustra was seen in every show from 7/16/93 to 7/28/93 [10 shows].

YEAR BY YEAR CHART

	83	84	85	86	87	88	89	90	91	92	93	94	95	96	97	98	99	00	TOTAL
1999	0	0	0	0	0	0	0	0	0	0	0	0	0	0	0	1	0	0	1
5:15	0	0	0	0	0	0	0	0	0	0	0	0	1	0	0	0	0	0	1
99 Years	0	0	0	0	0	0	0	0	0	0	0	0	0	1	0	0	0	0	1
A Day in the Life	0	0	0	0	0	0	0	0	0	0	0	0	23	15	5	1	0	1	45
AC/DC Bag	0	0	0	5	10	20	49	31	18	1	11	13	21	17	8	7	8	5	224
Acoustic Army	0	0	0	0	0	0	0	0	0	0	0	0	27	0	0	0	0	0	27
After Midnight	0	0	0	0	0	0	0	0	0	0	0	0	0	0	0	0	1	0	1
After Midnight Repri	0	0	0	0	0	0	0	0	0	0	0	0	0	0	0	0	1	0	1
Ain't Love Funny	0	0	0	0	0	0	0	0	0	0	0	0	0	0	3	0	0	0	3
Albuquerque	0	0	0	0	0	0	0	0	0	0	0	0	0	0	0	8	1	2	11
All Along Watchtower	0	0	0	0	0	0	0	0	0	0	0	1	0	1	0	0	0	0	2
All Blues	0	0	0	0	0	1	1	0	0	0	0	0	0	0	0	0	0	0	2
All Things Recnsdrd	0	0	0	0	0	0	0	0	1	41	25	5	2	4	1	0	0	0	79
All The Pain Thru	0	0	0	0	0	0	0	0	0	0	0	0	0	0	1	0	0	0	1
Also Sprach	0	0	0	0	0	0	0	0	0	0	21	29	16	16	15	12	14	8	131
Alumni Blues	0	0	4	5	12	23	21	9	6	0	0	1	0	0	0	0	1	0	82
Alumni Blues Jam	0	0	0	0	0	0	0	0	0	0	0	1	0	0	0	0	0	0	1
Amazing Grace	0	0	0	0	0	0	0	0	0	53	31	16	6	0	1	0	0	107
Amazing Grace Jam	0	0	0	0	0	0	0	0	0	0	1	0	1	1	0	0	0	0	3
Ambient Jam	0	0	0	0	0	0	0	0	0	0	0	0	0	0	0	1	0	0	1
American Band	0	0	0	0	0	0	0	0	0	0	0	0	0	1	0	0	1	0	2
Amoreena	0	0	0	0	0	0	0	0	0	0	0	0	0	0	1	0	0	0	1
Anarchy	0	0	3	2	2	1	1	0	0	0	0	0	0	0	0	0	0	0	9

	83	84	85	86	87	88	89	90	91	92	93	94	95	96	97	98	99	00	TOTAL
Andy's Chest	0	0	0	0	0	1	0	0	0	0	0	0	0	0	0	0	0	0	1
Any Colour You Like	0	0	0	0	0	0	0	0	0	0	0	0	0	0	0	1	0	0	1
Arc	0	0	0	0	0	0	0	0	0	0	0	0	0	0	0	1	0	0	1
Auld Lang Syne	0	0	0	0	0	0	1	1	1	1	1	1	1	1	1	1	1	0	11
Avenu Malkenu	0	0	0	0	5	4	5	4	18	9	5	8	4	3	1	2	3	2	73
Axilla	0	0	0	0	0	0	0	0	0	8	15	1	0	5	6	7	9	6	57
Axilla (Part II)	0	0	0	0	0	0	0	0	0	0	0	34	4	0	0	0	0	0	38
Baby Elephant Walk	0	0	0	0	0	0	0	0	0	1	0	0	0	0	0	1	0	0	2
Baby Left Me	0	0	0	0	0	1	0	0	0	0	0	0	0	0	0	0	0	0	1
Baby Lemonade	0	0	0	0	0	0	0	0	0	1	0	0	0	0	0	0	0	0	1
Back Porch Boogie Bl	0	0	0	1	4	0	0	0	0	0	0	0	0	0	0	0	0	0	5
Back @ Chicken Shack	0	0	0	0	0	0	0	0	0	0	0	0	0	0	0	2	4	2	8
Back in the USSR	0	0	0	0	0	0	0	0	0	0	0	2	0	0	0	0	0	0	2
Back on the Train	0	0	0	0	0	0	0	0	0	0	0	0	0	0	0	0	23	12	35
Bass Jam	0	0	0	0	0	0	0	0	0	0	0	1	1	0	0	0	1	0	3
Bathtub Gin	0	0	0	0	0	0	23	17	21	9	7	11	10	10	12	11	12	11	154
Beaumont Rag	0	0	0	0	0	0	0	0	0	0	0	2	0	0	0	0	0	0	2
Beauty of My Dreams	0	0	0	0	0	0	0	0	0	0	0	0	0	0	21	10	8	8	47
Been Caught Stealin'	0	0	0	0	0	0	0	0	0	0	0	0	0	0	0	5	0	0	5
Bell Boy	0	0	0	0	0	0	0	0	0	0	0	0	1	0	0	0	0	0	1
Bertha	0	1	0	0	0	0	0	0	0	0	0	0	0	0	0	0	0	0	1
Big Alligator Song	0	0	0	0	0	0	0	0	0	0	0	0	0	0	0	0	1	0	1
Big Ball Jam	0	0	0	0	0	0	0	0	0	12	62	22	0	0	0	0	0	0	96
Big Ball Jam Reprise	0	0	0	0	0	0	0	0	0	0	1	0	0	0	0	0	0	0	1
BBFCFM	0	0	0	0	6	9	5	13	23	10	11	14	6	2	1	2	1	1	104
BBFCFM Reprise	0	0	0	0	0	0	0	0	0	0	0	1	0	0	0	0	0	0	1
Big Leg Emma	0	0	1	0	0	2	0	0	0	0	0	0	0	0	0	0	0	0	3
Bike	0	0	0	0	1	3	3	2	2	3	7	5	1	2	0	2	1	2	34
Bill Bailey	0	0	0	0	0	0	0	0	0	0	1	1	1	0	0	0	0	0	3
Billy Breathes	0	0	0	0	0	0	0	0	0	0	0	0	13	9	14	4	7	4	51
Birds of a Feather	0	0	0	0	0	0	0	0	0	0	0	0	0	0	0	26	13	7	46
Birthday Jam	0	0	0	0	0	0	0	0	0	0	0	1	0	0	0	0	0	0	1
Bitchin' Again	0	0	0	0	0	0	0	0	1	0	0	0	0	0	0	0	0	0	1
Bittersweet Motel	0	0	0	0	0	0	0	0	0	0	0	0	0	0	0	8	3	2	13
Black-Eyed Katy	0	0	0	0	0	0	0	0	0	0	0	0	0	0	7	0	0	0	7
Blackbird	0	0	0	0	0	0	0	0	0	0	0	2	0	0	0	0	0	0	2
Blister in the Sun	0	0	0	0	0	0	0	0	0	0	0	0	0	0	0	1	0	0	1
Blister in the Sun J	0	0	0	0	0	0	0	0	0	0	0	0	0	0	1	0	0	0	1
Blue Bayou	0	0	0	0	0	0	0	0	0	1	0	0	0	0	0	0	0	0	1
Blue Bossa	0	0	0	0	0	2	0	0	0	0	0	0	0	0	0	0	0	0	2
Bob Dylan Band	0	0	0	1	0	0	0	0	0	0	0	0	0	0	0	0	0	0	1
Bohemian Rhapsody	0	0	0	0	0	0	0	0	0	0	0	0	0	1	0	0	0	0	1
Bold As Love	0	0	0	0	0	12	11	3	0	5	4	5	5	1	5	4	5	1	61
Boogie On Reggae	0	0	0	0	2	2	0	0	0	0	0	0	0	0	1	4	10	5	24
Born Under Punches (	0	0	0	0	0	0	0	0	0	0	0	0	1	0	0	0	0	0	1
Born to Run	0	0	0	0	0	0	0	0	0	0	0	0	0	0	0	0	1	0	1
Bouncing	0	0	0	0	0	0	0	67	74	55	47	40	22	17	19	6	11	7	365
Brain Damage	0	0	0	0	0	0	0	0	0	0	0	0	0	0	0	1	0	0	1
Breathe	0	0	0	0	0	0	0	0	0	0	0	0	0	0	0	1	0	0	1
Breathe Jam	0	0	0	0	0	0	0	0	0	0	0	0	1	0	0	0	0	0	1
Brian and Robert	0	0	0	0	0	0	0	0	0	0	0	0	0	0	0	16	7	2	25
Bring it On Home	0	0	1	0	0	0	0	0	0	0	0	0	0	0	0	0	0	0	1

	83	84	85	86	87	88	89	90	91	92	93	94	95	96	97	98	99	00	TOTAL
Brother	0	0	0	0	0	0	0	0	29	13	1	0	0	5	0	2	0	1	51
Brown Eyed Girl	0	0	0	0	0	0	0	0	0	0	0	0	1	0	0	0	0	0	1
Buffalo Bill	0	0	0	0	0	0	0	0	0	1	0	2	0	0	2	1	1	1	8
Bug	0	0	0	0	0	0	0	0	0	0	0	0	0	0	0	0	13	10	23
Bundle of Joy	0	0	0	0	2	1	5	0	0	0	0	0	0	0	0	0	0	0	8
Buried Alive	0	0	0	0	0	0	1	18	37	19	27	13	5	2	2	4	0	1	129
Burning Down House	0	0	0	0	0	0	0	0	0	0	0	0	0	0	0	1	0	0	1
Butter Them Biscuits	0	0	0	0	0	0	0	0	0	0	0	4	0	0	0	0	0	0	4
Bye Bye Foot	0	0	0	0	0	0	0	0	0	0	0	0	0	0	4	0	0	0	4
Camel Walk	0	1	2	3	4	3	1	0	0	0	0	0	1	0	3	1	2	1	22
Can't You Hear Me Kn	0	1	1	0	0	0	0	0	0	0	0	0	0	0	0	0	0	0	2
Cannonball Jam	0	0	0	0	0	0	0	0	0	0	0	1	0	0	0	0	0	0	1
Caravan	0	0	0	0	0	0	0	23	6	0	5	4	0	1	0	0	0	0	39
Carini	0	0	0	0	0	0	0	0	0	0	0	0	0	0	6	5	7	7	25
Carolina	0	0	0	0	0	0	0	27	6	14	8	5	3	1	1	2	0	0	67
Cars Trucks Buses	0	0	0	0	0	0	0	0	0	0	0	0	20	19	17	4	3	4	67
Catapult	0	0	0	0	0	0	0	0	0	2	1	9	5	3	2	1	4	1	28
Cavern	0	0	0	0	0	0	0	24	84	58	50	43	23	17	11	12	13	6	341
Cecilia	0	0	0	0	0	0	0	0	0	0	0	0	0	0	1	0	0	0	1
Chalk Dust Torture	0	0	0	0	0	0	0	0	66	45	51	38	24	23	26	19	20	12	324
Chalk Dust Reprise	0	0	0	0	0	0	0	0	0	0	0	1	0	0	0	0	0	1	2
Champagne Supernova	0	0	0	0	0	0	0	0	0	0	0	0	0	1	0	0	0	0	1
Character Zero	0	0	0	0	0	0	0	0	0	0	0	0	0	21	32	15	16	10	94
Che Hun Ta Mao	0	0	0	0	0	0	0	0	0	0	0	0	0	0	0	0	1	0	1
Chess Jam	0	0	0	0	0	0	0	0	0	0	0	0	1	0	0	0	0	0	1
Choo Choo Ch' Boogie	0	0	0	0	0	0	0	0	0	0	1	0	0	0	0	0	0	0	1
Cinnamon Girl	0	0	0	0	0	0	0	0	0	0	0	0	0	0	2	0	0	0	2
Cities	0	1	1	1	1	7	0	0	0	0	0	1	0	0	9	7	3	4	35
Clementine	0	0	0	0	0	0	0	0	0	0	1	0	0	0	0	0	0	0	1
Clod	0	0	0	2	6	1	1	0	0	0	0	0	0	0	0	0	0	0	10
Cocaine Jam	0	0	0	0	0	0	0	0	0	0	1	0	0	0	0	0	0	0	1
Cold Rain and Snow	0	0	0	0	0	0	0	0	0	0	0	0	0	0	0	0	1	0	1
Col. Forbin's Ascent	0	0	0	0	0	11	18	10	18	14	15	11	3	2	1	1	0	1	105
Come On Baby, Let's	0	0	0	0	0	0	0	0	0	0	0	0	0	0	0	0	0	2	2
Come Together	0	0	0	0	0	0	0	0	0	0	0	0	1	0	0	0	0	0	1
Communication Brkdwn	0	0	0	0	0	0	0	3	0	0	0	0	0	0	0	0	0	0	3
Contact	0	0	0	0	0	8	23	25	17	8	14	13	6	4	2	2	4	2	128
Cool it Down	0	0	0	0	0	0	0	0	0	0	0	0	0	0	0	1	0	1	2
Corrine Corrina	0	0	0	0	7	5	2	0	0	0	0	0	0	0	0	0	1	1	16
Costume Contest	0	0	0	0	0	1	0	0	1	0	0	1	0	0	0	0	0	0	3
Cowboy's Sweetheart	0	0	0	0	0	0	0	0	0	0	0	0	1	0	0	0	0	0	1
Cracklin' Rosie	0	0	0	0	0	0	0	0	0	24	12	6	3	1	0	1	1	0	48
Crew Football Theme	0	0	0	0	0	0	0	0	1	1	0	0	0	0	0	0	0	0	2
Crimes of the Mind	0	0	0	0	0	0	0	0	2	0	2	1	0	0	0	0	0	0	5
Crosseyed and Painle	0	0	0	0	0	0	0	0	0	0	0	0	0	2	3	0	1	2	8
Crossroads	0	0	0	0	0	0	0	0	0	0	1	0	4	0	3	1	0	0	9
Cry Baby Cry	0	0	0	0	0	0	0	0	0	0	0	2	1	0	0	1	0	0	4
Cryin'	0	0	0	0	0	0	0	0	0	0	0	0	1	0	0	0	0	0	1
Cut My Hair	0	0	0	0	0	0	0	0	0	0	0	0	1	0	0	0	0	0	1
Dahlia	0	0	0	0	0	0	0	1	0	0	0	0	0	0	0	0	0	0	1
Daniel	0	0	0	0	0	0	0	0	0	0	14	0	0	0	1	0	0	0	15
Dave's Energy Guide	0	0	3	3	4	3	0	0	0	0	0	0	1	0	0	0	0	0	14

	83	84	85	86	87	88	89	90	91	92	93	94	95	96	97	98	99	00	TOTAL
David Bowie	0	0	0	2	8	13	29	28	42	37	33	38	24	19	17	15	12	11	328
David Bowie Jam	0	0	0	0	1	0	0	0	0	0	0	0	0	0	0	0	0	0	1
Dazed and Confused	0	0	0	0	0	0	1	0	0	0	0	0	0	0	0	0	0	0	1
Dear Mrs. Reagan	0	0	1	2	4	4	1	0	0	0	0	0	0	0	0	0	0	0	12
Dear Prudence	0	0	0	0	0	0	0	0	0	0	0	1	0	0	0	0	0	0	1
Demand	0	0	0	0	0	0	0	0	0	0	0	9	4	1	0	0	0	0	14
Destiny Unbound	0	0	0	0	0	0	0	5	21	0	0	0	0	0	0	0	0	0	26
Diamond Girl	0	0	0	0	0	0	0	0	0	1	0	0	0	0	0	0	0	0	1
Digital Delay Loop J	0	0	0	0	0	0	0	0	0	0	0	5	0	1	0	0	0	0	6
Dinner and a Movie	0	0	0	0	1	7	12	38	36	14	4	3	2	1	1	0	0	1	120
Dirt	0	0	0	0	0	0	0	0	0	0	0	0	0	0	20	4	10	8	42
Divided Sky	0	0	0	0	10	8	36	47	52	28	31	39	20	16	4	7	6	4	308
Doctor Jimmy	0	0	0	0	0	0	0	0	0	0	0	0	1	0	0	0	0	0	1
Dog Faced Boy	0	0	0	0	0	0	0	0	0	0	0	23	9	1	1	2	1	6	43
Dog Gone Dog	0	0	1	2	4	0	1	1	2	0	1	0	1	0	1	2	1	1	18
Dogs Stole Things	0	0	0	0	0	0	0	0	0	0	0	0	0	0	20	5	4	2	31
Doin' My Time	0	0	0	0	0	0	0	0	0	0	0	0	0	1	0	0	1	0	2
Don't Get Me Wrong	0	0	0	0	0	0	0	3	0	0	0	0	0	0	0	0	0	0	3
Don't Pass Me By	0	0	0	0	0	0	0	0	0	0	0	1	0	0	0	0	0	0	1
Don't Want U No More	0	1	0	0	0	0	0	0	0	0	0	0	0	0	0	0	0	0	1
Don't You Wanna Go	0	0	0	0	0	0	0	0	0	0	0	0	5	0	0	0	0	0	5
Donna Lee	0	0	0	0	0	0	6	12	2	0	0	0	0	0	0	0	0	0	20
Dooley	0	0	0	0	0	0	0	0	0	0	0	1	0	0	0	0	0	0	1
Down By the River	0	0	0	0	0	0	0	0	0	0	0	0	0	0	1	0	0	0	1
Down With Disease	0	0	0	0	0	0	0	0	0	0	0	55	5	20	17	16	19	11	143
Down W Disease Jam	0	0	0	0	0	0	0	0	0	0	1	0	0	0	0	0	0	0	1
Driver	0	0	0	0	0	0	0	0	0	0	0	0	0	0	0	9	6	3	18
Drowned	0	0	0	0	0	0	0	0	0	0	0	0	2	0	5	5	3	5	20
Drum Jam	0	0	0	0	0	0	0	0	2	0	0	0	0	0	1	0	0	0	3
Drums Jam	0	2	0	0	0	0	0	0	0	0	0	2	0	0	0	0	0	0	4
Earl's Breakdown	0	0	0	0	0	0	0	0	0	0	0	1	0	0	0	0	0	0	1
Eclipse	0	0	0	0	0	0	0	0	0	0	0	0	0	0	1	0	0	0	1
El Paso	0	0	0	0	0	0	0	0	0	0	0	0	0	0	0	0	1	0	1
Eliza	0	0	0	0	0	0	0	4	9	6	0	0	0	0	0	0	0	0	19
Emotional Rescue	0	0	0	0	0	0	0	0	0	0	0	0	0	0	2	1	1	0	4
Esther	0	0	0	0	0	1	10	27	21	12	17	11	4	3	0	2	0	1	109
Everybody's Got Some	0	0	0	0	0	0	0	0	0	0	0	1	0	0	0	0	0	1	2
Eyes of the World	0	2	1	0	0	0	0	0	0	0	0	0	0	0	0	0	0	0	3
Faht	0	0	0	0	0	0	0	0	0	4	4	2	2	0	0	0	0	0	12
Family Picture	0	0	0	0	0	0	0	0	1	0	0	0	0	0	0	0	0	0	1
Farmhouse	0	0	0	0	0	0	0	0	0	0	0	0	0	0	3	8	19	6	36
Fast Enough for You	0	0	0	0	0	0	0	0	0	9	16	13	7	4	1	1	3	3	57
Fee	0	0	0	0	7	17	28	25	39	25	33	39	14	10	3	4	3	4	251
Fikus	0	0	0	0	0	0	0	0	0	0	0	0	0	0	0	5	0	0	5
Fire	1	1	0	0	6	20	10	12	10	8	8	9	9	8	5	0	3	0	110
Fire On The Mountain	0	1	0	0	0	0	0	0	0	0	0	0	0	0	0	0	0	0	1
Fire up the Ganja	0	0	1	0	0	0	0	0	0	0	0	0	0	0	0	0	0	0	1
First Tube	0	0	0	0	0	0	0	0	0	0	0	0	0	0	0	0	15	16	31
Fishing Hole Theme	0	0	0	0	0	0	1	0	0	0	0	0	0	0	0	0	0	0	1
Fishman's Gull Poem	0	0	0	0	0	0	1	0	0	0	0	0	0	0	0	0	0	0	1
Fixin' to Die	0	0	0	0	0	0	0	0	0	0	0	2	0	0	0	0	0	0	2
Flat Fee	0	0	0	0	5	6	0	0	8	0	0	0	0	0	0	0	0	0	19

	83	84	85	86	87	88	89	90	91	92	93	94	95	96	97	98	99	00	TOTAL
Fluff's Travels	0	0	0	1	2	0	2	1	0	0	0	0	0	0	0	0	0	0	6
Fluffhead	0	1	1	2	14	26	14	12	22	18	20	19	8	6	5	7	7	3	185
Foam	0	0	0	0	0	3	24	40	68	53	37	36	8	6	5	4	0	2	286
Fog That Surrounds	0	0	0	0	0	0	0	0	0	0	0	0	8	0	0	0	0	0	8
Foreplay/Long Time	0	0	0	0	0	0	0	0	0	0	0	16	0	0	0	0	1	0	17
Four Strong Winds	0	0	0	0	0	0	0	0	0	0	0	0	0	0	0	1	0	0	1
Frankenstein	0	0	0	0	0	0	4	0	6	0	0	11	9	8	10	7	8	3	66
Frankie Says	0	0	0	0	0	0	0	0	0	0	0	0	0	0	0	13	2	3	18
Free	0	0	0	0	0	0	0	0	0	0	0	0	31	17	13	5	13	4	83
Freebird	0	0	0	0	1	0	0	0	0	0	14	5	0	0	0	5	0	1	26
Freeworld	0	0	0	0	1	0	0	0	0	0	0	0	0	0	0	0	0	0	1
Fuck Your Face	0	0	0	0	1	0	0	0	0	0	0	0	0	0	0	0	0	0	1
Funky Bitch	0	0	0	0	7	13	7	17	3	2	6	5	7	14	14	16	12	8	131
Gettin' Jiggy W/ It	0	0	0	0	0	0	0	0	0	0	0	0	0	0	0	1	0	0	1
Ghost	0	0	0	0	0	0	0	0	0	0	0	0	0	0	28	18	13	7	66
Ginseng Sullivan	0	0	0	0	0	0	0	0	0	0	8	20	2	6	15	8	5	3	67
Glass Onion	0	0	0	0	0	0	0	0	0	0	0	1	0	0	0	0	0	0	1
Glide	0	0	0	0	0	0	0	0	10	33	30	20	3	2	1	1	1	3	104
Glide II	0	0	0	0	0	0	0	0	0	0	0	0	1	0	0	0	0	0	1
Gloria	0	0	0	0	0	0	0	0	0	0	0	0	1	0	0	0	0	0	1
Going Down Slow	0	0	0	0	0	0	0	2	0	0	0	0	0	0	0	0	0	0	2
Gold Soundz	0	0	0	0	0	0	0	0	0	0	0	0	0	0	0	0	1	0	1
Golden Lady	0	0	0	0	0	0	0	0	0	0	0	1	0	0	0	0	0	0	1
Golgi Apparatus	0	0	0	2	14	27	37	35	71	41	47	42	6	10	4	10	12	9	367
Good Times Bad Times	0	0	0	0	8	19	21	26	11	12	19	16	8	6	5	5	4	0	160
Got My Mojo Workin'	0	0	0	0	0	0	0	0	0	0	0	0	0	0	1	0	0	0	1
Gotta Jibboo	0	0	0	0	0	0	0	0	0	0	0	0	0	0	0	0	13	16	29
Grind	0	0	0	0	0	0	0	0	0	0	0	0	0	0	0	1	0	0	1
Guelah Papyrus	0	0	0	0	0	0	0	0	51	42	40	18	6	11	3	2	2	2	177
Gumbo	0	0	0	0	0	0	0	4	7	0	2	9	10	8	7	7	5	4	63
Guy Forget	0	0	0	0	0	0	0	0	0	0	0	0	0	0	0	0	0	1	1
Guyute	0	0	0	0	0	0	0	0	0	0	0	19	7	6	11	19	21	8	91
Gypsy Queen	0	0	0	0	0	0	0	0	0	0	0	0	1	2	0	0	0	0	3
HYHU Jam	0	0	0	0	0	0	0	0	1	0	0	1	0	0	0	0	0	0	2
Ha Ha Ha	0	0	0	0	0	0	0	0	0	0	0	0	13	2	1	4	1	1	22
Halley's Comet	0	0	0	1	3	4	3	0	0	0	7	12	6	2	3	7	5	4	57
Happiness Is a Warm	0	0	0	0	0	0	0	0	0	0	0	1	0	0	0	0	0	0	1
Happy Birthday	1	0	0	0	1	3	2	2	1	0	0	0	0	0	0	0	0	0	10
Harpua	0	0	0	0	3	8	7	4	4	5	6	6	2	3	2	1	0	0	51
Harry Hood	0	0	1	3	7	9	17	14	22	18	19	30	21	19	23	16	11	7	237
Have Mercy	0	0	0	4	0	0	0	0	0	0	3	1	0	0	0	0	2	0	10
Head Held High	0	0	0	0	0	0	0	0	0	0	0	0	0	0	0	1	0	0	1
Heart and soul	0	0	0	0	0	0	0	0	0	0	0	0	1	0	0	0	0	0	1
Heavy Things	0	0	0	0	0	0	0	0	0	0	0	0	0	0	0	0	17	15	32
Hello My Baby	0	0	0	0	0	0	0	0	0	0	0	0	15	17	10	6	5	0	53
Help Me	0	0	0	0	0	0	0	0	0	0	0	1	0	0	0	0	0	0	1
Help on the Way	0	0	0	1	0	0	0	0	0	0	0	0	0	0	0	0	0	0	1
Helpless	0	0	0	0	0	0	0	0	0	0	0	0	0	0	0	1	0	0	1
Helpless Dancer	0	0	0	0	0	0	0	0	0	0	0	0	1	0	0	0	0	0	1
Helter Skelter	0	0	0	0	0	0	0	0	0	0	0	0	2	0	0	0	0	0	2
High-Heel Sneakers	0	0	0	0	0	0	0	0	0	0	0	1	0	0	0	0	0	0	1
Highway To Hell	0	0	0	0	0	0	13	21	6	0	9	15	2	3	1	0	0	0	70

	83	84	85	86	87	88	89	90	91	92	93	94	95	96	97	98	99	00	TOTAL
Hold Whatcha Got	0	0	0	0	0	0	0	0	0	0	0	0	0	0	0	0	0	1	1
Hold to a Dream	0	0	0	0	0	0	0	0	0	0	0	0	0	1	0	0	0	0	1
Honey Pie	0	0	0	0	0	0	0	0	0	0	0	1	0	0	0	0	0	0	1
Honky Tonk Women	0	0	0	0	0	0	0	0	0	0	0	1	0	0	0	0	0	0	1
Honky Tonk Women Jam	0	0	0	0	0	0	0	0	0	0	1	0	0	0	0	0	0	0	1
Hoochie Coochie Man	0	0	0	0	0	0	0	0	0	0	1	0	0	0	1	0	0	0	2
Horn	0	0	0	0	0	0	0	5	20	25	20	12	8	4	5	5	9	6	119
Houses in Motion	0	0	0	0	0	0	0	0	0	0	0	0	0	1	0	0	0	0	1
How High the Moon	0	0	0	0	0	0	0	2	0	0	1	0	0	0	0	0	0	0	3
Hurricane	0	0	1	0	0	0	0	0	0	0	0	0	0	0	0	0	0	0	1
I Am Hydrogen	0	0	0	1	4	7	39	68	54	34	23	14	2	2	5	2	7	4	266
I Am the Sea	0	0	0	0	0	0	0	0	0	0	0	0	1	0	0	0	0	0	1
I Been to Georgia on	0	0	0	0	0	0	0	0	0	0	1	0	0	0	0	0	0	0	1
I Didn't Know	0	0	0	0	3	16	22	25	36	26	33	15	10	6	2	1	6	2	203
I Don't Care	0	0	0	0	0	0	0	0	0	0	0	0	0	2	0	0	0	0	2
I Found a Reason	0	0	0	0	0	0	0	0	0	0	0	0	0	0	1	0	0	0	1
I Get a Kick Out of	0	0	0	0	0	0	0	0	0	0	0	0	0	0	2	0	0	0	2
I Know a Little	0	0	0	0	1	2	0	0	0	0	0	0	0	0	0	0	0	0	3
I Saw it Again	0	0	0	0	0	0	0	0	0	0	0	0	0	0	7	0	3	3	13
I Shall Be Released	0	0	0	0	0	0	0	0	0	0	0	0	0	0	0	1	0	0	1
I Told You So	0	0	0	0	0	0	0	0	0	0	0	0	0	1	0	0	0	0	1
I Walk the Line	0	0	0	0	0	0	0	0	0	7	2	0	0	0	0	0	0	0	9
I Wanna Be Like You	0	0	0	0	0	0	0	0	0	0	0	9	0	0	0	0	0	0	9
I Will	0	0	0	0	0	0	0	0	0	0	0	1	0	0	0	0	0	0	1
I Wish	0	0	1	0	0	0	0	0	0	0	0	0	0	0	0	0	0	0	1
I'll Come Running	0	0	0	0	0	0	0	0	0	0	0	0	1	0	0	0	0	0	1
I'm Blue, Lonesome	0	0	0	0	0	0	0	0	0	0	0	0	9	18	0	0	1	1	30
I'm Gonna Be (500 M)	0	0	0	0	0	0	0	0	0	0	0	0	0	1	0	0	0	0	1
I'm One	0	0	0	0	0	0	0	0	0	0	0	0	1	0	0	0	0	0	1
I'm So Tired	0	0	0	0	0	0	0	0	0	0	0	1	1	0	0	0	0	0	2
I've Had Enough	0	0	0	0	0	0	0	0	0	0	0	0	1	0	0	0	0	0	1
I've Turned Bad	0	0	0	0	0	0	0	1	0	0	0	0	0	0	0	0	0	0	1
Icculus	0	0	0	2	1	3	2	0	1	2	1	3	1	0	0	0	1	0	17
If I Could	0	0	0	0	0	0	0	0	0	0	0	34	9	2	0	1	0	1	47
If I Don't Be There	0	0	0	0	0	0	0	1	0	0	0	0	0	0	0	0	0	0	1
If I Only Had a Brai	0	0	0	0	0	0	8	12	4	3	7	1	1	0	0	0	1	0	37
If You Need a Fool	0	0	0	0	0	0	0	0	0	0	0	0	0	0	0	2	1	0	3
Immigrant Song Jam	0	0	0	0	0	0	0	0	0	0	0	0	1	0	0	0	0	0	1
In a Hole	0	0	0	0	0	0	8	0	0	0	0	0	0	0	0	0	0	0	8
In the Midnight Hour	1	1	1	0	0	0	0	0	0	0	0	0	0	0	0	0	0	0	3
Indian War Dance	0	0	0	0	0	0	0	0	0	0	0	1	0	0	0	0	0	0	1
Is it in my Head	0	0	0	0	0	0	0	0	0	0	0	0	1	0	0	0	0	0	1
It's Ice	0	0	0	0	0	0	0	0	22	41	55	40	18	14	3	2	0	6	201
It's My Life	0	0	0	0	0	0	0	0	0	0	1	0	0	0	0	0	0	0	1
Izabella	0	0	0	0	0	0	0	0	0	0	0	0	0	0	0	8	0	2	10
Jagermeister	0	0	0	0	0	0	2	0	0	0	0	0	0	0	0	0	0	0	2
Jam	0	1	3	1	4	5	1	1	2	1	2	2	6	4	11	6	7	2	59
Jennifer Dances	0	0	0	0	0	0	0	0	0	0	0	0	0	0	0	0	3	0	3
Jessica Jam	0	0	0	0	0	0	0	0	0	0	1	0	0	0	0	0	0	0	1
Jesus Just Left	0	0	0	0	2	9	2	13	9	0	5	5	1	3	6	2	2	1	60
Johnny B. Goode	0	0	0	0	0	0	0	0	0	0	0	0	3	9	10	1	0	0	23
Julia	0	0	0	0	0	0	0	0	0	0	0	1	0	0	0	0	0	0	1

	83	84	85	86	87	88	89	90	91	92	93	94	95	96	97	98	99	00	TOTAL
Julius	0	0	0	0	0	0	0	0	0	0	0	65	21	16	15	10	7	4	138
Jump Monk	0	0	0	0	0	1	0	0	0	0	0	0	0	0	0	0	0	0	1
Keyboard Cavalry	0	0	0	0	0	0	0	0	0	0	0	0	13	0	0	0	0	0	13
Keyboard Cavalry Rep	0	0	0	0	0	0	0	0	0	0	0	0	1	0	0	0	0	0	1
Killer Joe	0	0	0	0	0	0	0	1	0	0	0	0	0	0	0	0	0	0	1
Kung	0	0	0	0	0	0	2	0	0	1	6	5	7	1	1	2	2	0	27
La Grange	0	0	0	0	5	12	16	24	4	0	3	0	1	3	1	3	1	0	73
La Grange Jam	0	0	0	0	0	0	1	0	0	0	0	0	0	0	0	0	0	0	1
Lawn Boy	0	0	0	0	0	0	9	21	30	12	24	7	4	4	4	10	7	4	136
Layla	0	0	0	0	0	0	0	0	0	0	0	0	0	0	0	1	0	0	1
Lengthwise	0	0	0	0	0	0	0	0	0	6	15	1	0	0	0	1	0	0	23
Leprechaun	0	0	0	0	0	0	0	0	0	0	3	0	0	0	0	0	0	0	3
Good Times Roll	0	0	0	0	1	0	0	0	0	0	0	0	0	0	0	0	0	0	1
Letter to Jimmy Page	0	0	0	0	2	0	0	0	0	0	0	2	0	0	0	0	0	0	4
Li'l Red Rooster	0	0	0	0	0	0	0	0	0	0	0	0	0	0	1	0	0	0	1
Life on Mars	0	0	0	0	0	0	0	0	0	0	0	0	8	10	1	0	0	0	19
Lifeboy	0	0	0	0	0	0	0	0	0	0	9	24	9	2	1	2	0	0	47
Light Up Or Leave Me	0	0	0	0	3	3	0	0	0	0	0	0	0	0	0	0	1	0	7
Limb By Limb	0	0	0	0	0	0	0	0	0	0	0	0	0	0	23	20	19	12	74
Listening Wind	0	0	0	0	0	0	0	0	0	0	0	0	1	0	0	0	0	0	1
Little Drummer Boy	0	0	0	1	0	0	0	0	0	0	0	0	0	0	0	0	2	0	3
Lively Up Yourself	0	0	0	0	0	0	0	0	0	1	0	0	0	0	0	0	0	0	1
Llama	0	0	0	0	0	0	0	15	76	63	46	26	13	10	7	5	5	3	269
Lonesome Cowboy Bill	0	0	0	0	0	0	0	0	0	0	0	0	3	0	0	1	0	0	4
Long Cool Woman	1	0	0	0	0	0	0	0	0	0	0	0	0	0	0	1	0	0	2
Long Long Long	0	0	0	0	0	0	0	0	0	0	0	1	0	0	0	0	0	0	1
Loup Garou	0	0	0	0	0	0	0	0	0	0	0	1	0	0	0	0	0	0	1
Love Me	0	0	0	0	0	0	0	0	0	0	0	0	0	0	7	2	0	0	9
Love Me Like a Man	0	0	0	0	0	0	0	0	0	0	0	0	0	0	1	0	0	0	1
Love Reign O'er Me	0	0	0	0	0	0	0	0	0	0	0	0	1	0	0	0	0	0	1
Love You	0	0	0	0	1	0	2	10	26	19	18	6	1	0	1	0	1	1	86
Loving Cup	0	0	0	0	0	0	0	0	0	0	9	3	4	6	16	13	14	4	69
Low Rider Jam	0	0	0	0	1	0	0	0	0	0	0	0	0	0	1	0	0	0	2
Lushington	0	0	0	1	4	0	0	0	0	0	0	0	0	0	0	0	0	0	5
Magilla	0	0	0	0	0	0	0	15	27	5	1	5	0	0	3	1	0	1	58
Maiden Voyage	0	0	0	0	0	1	0	0	0	0	0	0	0	0	0	0	0	0	1
Makisupa Policeman	0	2	1	2	6	2	4	2	0	0	4	5	9	7	6	6	5	4	65
Makisupa Policeman J	0	0	0	0	1	0	0	0	0	0	0	0	0	0	0	0	0	0	1
Manteca	0	0	0	0	0	0	0	2	2	1	4	1	1	0	0	1	0	0	12
Manteca Reprise	0	0	0	0	0	0	0	0	0	1	0	0	0	0	0	0	0	0	1
Martha My Dear	0	0	0	0	0	0	0	0	0	0	0	1	0	0	0	0	0	0	1
Maze	0	0	0	0	0	0	0	0	0	55	54	44	25	17	16	9	9	7	236
McGrupp	0	0	2	2	7	10	17	4	5	3	5	13	5	4	5	4	1	1	88
Mean Mr. Mustard	0	0	0	0	0	0	0	0	0	0	0	0	0	1	0	0	0	0	1
Meat	0	0	0	0	0	0	0	0	0	0	0	0	0	0	0	12	5	4	21
Meat Reprise	0	0	0	0	0	0	0	0	0	0	0	0	0	0	0	0	1	0	1
Meatstick	0	0	0	0	0	0	0	0	0	0	0	0	0	0	1	0	12	6	19
Meatstick Reprise	0	0	0	0	0	0	0	0	0	0	0	0	0	0	0	0	1	0	1
Mellow Mood	0	0	0	0	0	0	0	0	0	0	0	0	0	0	0	0	0	4	4
Melt the Guns	0	0	1	1	2	0	0	0	0	0	0	0	0	0	0	0	0	0	4
Memories	0	0	0	0	0	0	0	1	12	18	5	1	0	0	0	0	0	0	37
Merry Pranksters Jam	0	0	0	0	0	0	0	0	0	0	0	0	0	0	1	0	0	0	1

	83	84	85	86	87	88	89	90	91	92	93	94	95	96	97	98	99	00	TOTAL
Messin' With The Kid	0	0	0	0	0	0	0	0	0	0	0	0	0	0	1	0	1	0	2
Midnight Rider Jam	0	0	0	0	0	0	0	0	0	0	0	1	0	0	0	0	0	0	1
Midnight on the High	0	0	0	0	0	0	0	0	0	0	0	0	0	1	0	0	0	0	1
Mike's Song	0	0	3	3	3	9	39	68	54	35	40	27	16	15	12	15	13	10	362
Mind Left Body Jam	0	0	0	0	0	0	0	0	0	0	0	1	0	0	0	0	0	0	1
Minute by Minute	0	0	0	0	0	0	0	2	0	0	0	0	0	0	0	0	0	0	2
Mirror in the Bathro	0	0	0	0	0	0	0	0	0	0	0	0	0	0	0	1	0	0	1
Misty Mountain Hop	0	0	0	0	0	0	0	0	0	0	0	0	0	0	0	0	4	0	4
Moby Dick	0	0	0	0	0	0	0	0	0	0	0	0	0	0	1	0	0	1	2
Money	0	0	0	0	0	0	0	0	0	0	0	0	0	0	1	0	0	0	1
Moonlight In Vt	0	0	0	0	0	0	0	0	0	0	0	0	0	0	1	0	0	0	1
Moose the Mooch	0	0	0	0	0	0	0	0	1	0	0	0	0	0	0	0	0	0	1
Mother Nature's Son	0	0	0	0	0	0	0	0	0	0	0	1	0	0	0	0	0	0	1
Mound	0	0	0	0	0	0	0	0	0	21	34	18	11	4	0	0	0	0	88
Mountains in the Mis	0	0	0	0	0	0	0	0	0	0	0	0	0	0	0	0	8	0	8
Mozambique	0	0	0	0	0	0	0	0	0	0	0	0	0	0	0	0	5	0	5
Mr. P.C.	0	0	0	0	0	2	0	0	0	0	0	0	0	0	0	0	0	0	2
Mustang Sally	0	0	0	2	2	3	0	0	0	0	0	0	0	0	0	0	0	0	7
My Friend My Friend	0	0	0	0	0	0	0	0	0	19	38	19	12	6	3	2	2	3	104
My Generation	0	0	0	0	0	0	0	0	0	0	0	0	1	0	0	0	0	0	1
My Left Toe	0	0	0	0	0	0	0	0	0	0	0	0	0	0	0	0	5	0	5
My Long Journey Home	0	0	0	0	0	0	0	0	0	0	0	9	6	0	0	0	0	0	15
My Mind's Got A Mind	0	0	0	0	0	0	0	0	0	6	10	5	4	2	2	3	4	3	39
My Soul	0	0	0	0	0	0	0	0	0	0	0	0	0	0	30	12	5	9	56
My Sweet One	0	0	0	0	0	0	16	35	79	31	19	14	3	0	1	1	1	2	202
NICU	0	0	0	0	0	0	0	0	0	12	0	10	9	6	15	11	11	7	81
NO2	0	0	0	0	0	0	0	0	0	0	0	3	0	0	0	0	1	0	4
Nellie Kane	0	0	0	0	0	0	0	0	0	0	14	26	0	0	1	4	1	0	46
Never	0	0	0	0	0	0	0	0	0	0	0	0	0	0	1	0	0	0	1
New Age	0	0	0	0	0	0	0	0	0	0	0	0	0	0	1	0	0	0	1
New York New York	0	0	0	0	0	0	0	0	0	0	0	0	0	0	1	0	0	0	1
Night Moves Jam	0	0	0	0	0	0	0	0	0	0	0	0	1	0	0	0	0	0	1
No Dogs Allowed	0	0	0	0	0	1	3	1	0	0	0	0	0	0	0	0	0	0	5
No Good Trying	0	0	0	0	0	0	0	3	0	0	0	0	0	0	0	0	0	0	3
Not Fade Away	0	0	0	1	0	0	0	0	0	0	0	0	0	0	0	0	0	0	1
Nowhere Fast	0	0	0	0	0	1	0	0	0	0	0	0	0	0	0	0	0	0	1
O Mio Babbino Caro	0	0	0	0	0	0	0	0	0	0	0	1	0	0	0	0	0	0	1
Ob La Di Ob La Da	0	0	0	0	0	0	0	0	0	0	0	1	0	0	0	0	0	0	1
Ob La Di Ob La Da Ja	0	0	0	0	0	0	0	0	0	0	1	0	0	0	0	0	0	0	1
Oblivious Fool	0	0	0	0	0	0	0	0	0	0	0	0	0	6	0	0	0	0	6
Oh! Sweet Nuthin'	0	0	0	0	0	0	0	0	0	0	0	0	0	0	1	0	0	0	1
On My Knees	0	0	0	0	0	0	0	0	0	0	0	0	0	0	0	1	0	0	1
On The Run	0	0	0	0	0	0	0	0	0	0	0	0	0	0	1	0	0	0	1
On Your Way Down	0	0	0	0	0	6	4	0	0	0	0	0	0	0	0	0	3	0	13
Once in a Lifetime	0	0	0	0	0	0	0	0	0	0	0	0	0	1	0	0	0	0	1
One Meatball	0	0	0	0	0	0	0	0	0	0	0	0	0	0	1	0	0	0	1
Overload	0	0	0	0	0	0	0	0	0	0	0	0	0	1	0	0	0	0	1
Oye Como Va Jam	0	0	0	0	0	0	0	0	0	0	1	0	0	0	0	0	0	0	1
Paul and Silas	0	0	0	0	0	0	0	12	25	12	20	4	1	0	1	2	0	0	77
Peaches En Regalia	0	0	0	2	11	15	7	0	0	0	3	17	0	3	4	0	3	0	65
Phase Dance	0	0	0	0	1	3	0	0	0	0	0	0	0	0	0	0	0	0	4
Piano Duet	0	0	0	0	0	0	0	0	0	0	1	1	0	0	0	0	0	0	2

	83	84	85	86	87	88	89	90	91	92	93	94	95	96	97	98	99	00	TOTAL
Pig in a Pen	0	0	0	0	0	0	0	0	0	0	2	1	0	0	0	0	0	0	3
Piggies	0	0	0	0	0	0	0	0	0	0	0	1	0	0	0	0	0	0	1
Piper	0	0	0	0	0	0	0	0	0	0	0	0	0	0	15	18	15	14	62
Poor Heart	0	0	0	0	0	0	0	0	33	48	57	46	25	21	11	5	8	5	259
Poor Heart Reprise	0	0	0	0	0	0	0	0	0	0	0	0	1	0	0	0	0	0	1
Possum	0	0	1	1	14	21	41	68	55	35	30	20	20	10	7	14	15	6	358
Prep School Hippie	0	0	2	3	0	0	0	0	0	0	0	0	0	0	0	0	0	0	5
Prince Caspian	0	0	0	0	0	0	0	0	0	0	0	0	17	17	22	11	12	6	85
Proud Mary	1	0	0	0	0	0	0	0	0	0	0	0	0	0	0	0	0	0	1
Psycho Killer	0	0	0	0	0	0	0	0	0	0	0	0	0	1	0	0	0	0	1
Psycho Killer Jam	0	0	0	0	0	0	0	0	0	0	1	0	0	0	0	0	0	0	1
Punch Me in the Eye	0	0	0	0	1	0	0	0	0	0	0	0	0	0	0	0	0	0	1
Punch You In The Eye	0	0	0	0	0	0	6	0	0	0	18	11	9	15	18	12	13	7	109
Purple Rain	0	0	0	0	0	0	0	0	0	0	15	11	1	3	0	0	1	0	31
Pusher Man Jam	0	0	0	0	0	0	0	0	1	0	0	0	0	0	0	0	0	0	1
Quadrophenia	0	0	0	0	0	0	0	0	0	0	0	1	0	0	0	0	0	0	1
Quadrophonic Topplin	0	0	0	0	0	0	0	0	0	0	0	0	0	0	0	0	1	0	1
Quinn the Eskimo	0	0	0	3	4	0	0	0	0	0	0	0	0	0	0	2	2	0	11
Ramble On	0	0	0	0	0	0	0	0	0	0	0	0	0	0	0	2	0	0	2
Rapper's Delight	0	0	0	0	0	0	0	0	0	0	0	0	0	0	0	0	0	1	1
Reba	0	0	0	0	0	0	14	43	59	45	29	36	23	19	10	13	6	5	302
Revival	0	0	1	0	0	0	0	0	0	0	0	0	0	0	0	0	0	0	1
Revolution	0	0	1	0	0	0	0	0	0	0	0	1	0	0	0	0	0	0	2
Revolution 9	0	0	0	0	0	0	0	0	0	0	0	1	0	0	0	0	0	0	1
Rhinoceros	0	0	0	0	0	0	0	0	0	0	0	0	0	0	0	1	0	0	1
Rhombus Narration	0	0	0	0	0	0	3	3	1	0	0	0	0	0	0	0	0	0	7
Ride Captain Ride	0	0	0	0	1	1	1	1	0	2	0	0	0	0	0	2	1	0	9
Rift	0	0	0	0	0	0	0	6	0	54	66	47	20	11	1	4	2	5	216
Road Runner	0	0	0	0	0	0	0	0	0	0	0	0	0	0	0	0	1	0	1
Roadhouse Blues	1	0	0	0	0	0	0	0	0	0	0	0	0	0	0	0	0	0	1
Rock and Roll	0	0	0	0	0	0	0	0	0	0	0	0	0	0	0	4	5	6	15
Rock and Roll All Ni	0	0	0	0	0	0	0	0	0	0	1	0	0	0	0	0	0	0	1
Rock And Roll Part 2	0	0	0	0	0	0	0	0	0	0	0	0	0	0	1	0	0	0	1
Rocko William	0	0	0	0	0	0	0	0	0	0	0	0	0	0	5	0	0	0	5
Rocky Mountain Way J	0	0	0	0	0	0	0	0	1	0	0	0	0	0	1	0	0	0	2
Rocky Raccoon	0	0	0	0	0	0	0	0	0	0	0	1	0	0	0	0	0	0	1
Rocky Top	0	0	0	0	1	4	7	10	41	28	20	14	8	7	15	6	8	1	170
Roggae	0	0	0	0	0	0	0	0	0	0	0	0	0	0	0	25	13	7	45
Roll Like a Cantalou	0	0	0	1	0	1	0	1	1	0	0	0	0	0	0	0	0	0	4
Roses Are Free	0	0	0	0	0	0	0	0	0	0	0	0	0	0	2	5	3	2	12
Rotation Jam	0	0	0	0	0	0	0	0	0	0	0	0	2	1	1	0	0	0	4
Run Like an Antelope	0	0	3	1	3	12	30	34	23	32	38	42	25	19	16	15	13	11	317
Runaway Jim	0	0	0	0	0	0	0	23	64	54	41	34	23	20	16	8	12	6	301
Running With the Dev	0	0	0	0	0	0	0	0	0	0	0	0	0	0	0	1	0	0	1
Sabotage	0	0	0	0	0	0	0	0	0	0	0	0	0	0	0	3	0	0	3
Sad Lisa	0	0	0	0	0	0	0	0	0	0	0	0	0	0	0	1	0	0	1
Sample in a Jar	0	0	0	0	0	0	0	0	0	0	24	71	30	26	16	13	10	9	199
Samson Variation	0	0	0	0	0	0	0	0	0	0	0	0	0	0	1	0	0	0	1
Sand	0	0	0	0	0	0	0	0	0	0	0	0	0	0	0	0	12	12	24
Sanity	0	0	0	2	2	4	6	0	0	6	0	2	1	1	0	2	0	0	26
Satin Doll	0	0	0	0	0	7	2	1	0	0	2	0	0	0	0	0	0	0	12
Savoy Truffle	0	0	0	0	0	0	0	0	0	0	0	1	0	0	0	0	0	0	1

	83	84	85	86	87	88	89	90	91	92	93	94	95	96	97	98	99	00	TOTAL
Scarlet Begonias	1	1	1	0	0	0	0	0	0	0	0	0	0	0	0	0	0	0	3
Scent of a Mule	0	0	0	0	0	0	0	0	0	0	0	44	23	17	7	5	1	3	100
Sea and Sand	0	0	0	0	0	0	0	0	0	0	0	0	2	0	0	1	0	0	3
Secret Language Inst	0	0	0	0	0	0	0	0	0	3	0	0	0	0	0	0	0	0	3
Seen and Not Seen	0	0	0	0	0	0	0	0	0	0	0	0	0	1	0	0	0	0	1
Self	0	0	0	0	0	0	0	1	2	1	0	0	0	0	0	0	0	0	4
Setting Sail	0	0	0	0	0	0	0	0	1	1	0	1	0	0	0	0	0	0	3
Sexual Healing	0	0	0	0	0	0	0	0	0	0	0	0	0	0	0	4	0	0	4
Sexy Sadie	0	0	0	0	0	0	0	0	0	0	0	1	0	0	0	0	0	0	1
Shafty	0	0	0	0	0	0	0	0	0	0	0	0	0	0	0	2	0	1	3
Shaggy Dog	0	0	0	2	4	5	0	0	0	0	0	0	1	0	0	0	0	0	12
She Caught The Katy	0	0	0	1	2	0	0	0	0	0	0	0	0	0	0	1	0	0	4
Shine	0	0	0	0	0	0	0	0	0	0	0	0	1	0	0	0	0	0	1
Silent in the Mornin	0	0	0	0	0	0	0	0	0	26	39	28	9	9	5	2	6	2	126
Simple	0	0	0	0	0	0	0	0	0	0	0	30	19	16	12	16	13	5	111
Sixteen Candles	0	0	0	0	0	0	0	0	0	0	0	0	0	1	0	0	0	0	1
Skin It Back	0	0	0	2	4	1	0	0	0	0	0	0	0	0	0	0	0	0	7
Skippy Wondermouse	0	1	2	0	0	0	0	0	0	0	0	0	0	0	0	0	0	0	3
Slave	0	1	3	4	11	12	11	5	2	0	3	22	19	12	17	8	6	4	140
Sleep	0	0	0	0	0	0	0	0	0	0	0	0	0	0	0	6	3	1	10
Sleeping Monkey	0	0	0	0	0	0	0	0	0	17	5	17	6	2	4	5	4	2	62
Slipknot!	0	0	0	1	0	0	0	0	0	0	0	0	0	0	0	0	0	0	1
Smells Like Teens	0	0	0	0	0	0	0	0	0	0	0	0	0	0	0	1	0	0	1
Smoke on the Water J	0	0	0	0	0	0	0	0	0	0	0	0	0	0	0	0	1	0	1
Sneakin' Sally	0	0	2	3	9	12	2	0	0	0	0	0	0	0	1	4	4	2	39
So Lonely	0	0	0	0	0	0	0	0	0	0	0	0	0	0	0	1	0	0	1
Something	0	0	0	0	0	0	0	0	0	0	0	0	0	0	0	4	0	0	4
Somewhere Over The	0	0	0	0	0	0	0	0	0	0	0	0	0	3	0	1	0	0	4
Somewhere Over Jam	0	0	0	0	0	0	0	0	0	0	0	1	0	0	0	0	0	0	1
Soul Shake Down Part	0	0	0	0	0	0	0	0	0	0	0	0	0	0	2	0	0	0	2
Spanish Flea	0	1	0	0	0	0	0	0	0	0	0	0	0	0	0	0	0	0	1
Sparkle	0	0	0	0	0	0	0	0	33	65	58	45	25	21	10	9	8	5	279
Sparks	0	0	0	0	4	2	0	1	0	0	2	2	0	1	0	0	0	0	12
Speak to Me	0	0	0	0	0	0	0	0	0	0	0	1	0	0	1	0	0	0	2
Split Open and Melt	0	0	0	0	0	0	25	9	37	34	42	40	20	16	11	8	10	8	260
Split Open and Melt	0	0	0	0	0	0	0	0	0	0	0	2	0	0	0	0	0	0	2
Spock's Brain	0	0	0	0	0	0	0	0	0	0	0	0	5	0	0	0	0	2	7
Spooky Jam	0	0	0	0	0	0	0	0	0	0	2	0	0	0	0	0	0	0	2
Squeeze Box	1	0	0	0	0	0	0	0	0	0	0	0	0	0	0	0	0	0	1
St. Stephen Jam	0	1	0	0	0	0	0	0	0	0	0	0	0	0	0	0	0	0	1
St. Thomas	0	0	0	0	0	1	0	0	0	0	0	0	0	0	0	0	0	0	1
Stand	0	0	0	0	0	0	0	0	0	0	0	0	0	0	1	0	0	0	1
Stash	0	0	0	0	0	0	0	19	50	54	55	44	25	20	23	13	10	6	319
Steep	0	0	0	0	0	0	0	0	0	0	0	0	0	13	9	1	1	1	25
Strange Design	0	0	0	0	0	0	0	0	0	0	0	0	28	7	3	2	3	1	44
Suspicious Minds	0	0	0	0	0	0	0	0	0	0	0	0	11	2	0	0	0	0	13
Suzy Greenberg	0	0	0	0	6	17	25	53	56	45	21	42	22	17	4	2	6	1	317
Sweet Adeline	0	0	0	0	0	0	0	12	26	41	23	25	20	9	6	1	1	0	164
Sweet Baby's Arms	0	0	0	0	0	0	0	0	0	0	0	1	0	0	0	0	0	0	1
Sweet Emotion Jam	0	0	0	0	0	0	0	0	0	0	1	1	0	1	0	0	1	0	4
Sweet Jane	0	0	0	0	0	0	0	0	0	0	0	0	0	0	0	2	0	0	2

	83	84	85	86	87	88	89	90	91	92	93	94	95	96	97	98	99	00	TOTAL
Sweet Virginia	0	0	0	0	0	0	0	0	0	0	0	0	0	0	0	0	1	0	1
Swept Away	0	0	0	0	0	0	0	0	0	0	0	0	0	13	9	1	1	1	25
Swing Low Sweet Chrt	0	0	0	2	5	0	1	0	0	0	0	1	0	0	0	0	0	0	9
TV Show	0	0	0	0	0	0	0	0	1	0	0	0	0	0	0	0	0	0	1
Take Me to the River	0	0	0	0	0	0	0	0	0	0	0	0	1	0	1	0	0	0	2
Take the A-Train	0	0	0	0	6	19	20	12	18	13	3	1	0	0	0	0	0	0	92
Talk	0	0	0	0	0	0	0	0	0	0	0	0	0	8	3	1	0	0	12
Taste	0	0	0	0	0	0	0	0	0	0	0	0	10	28	30	7	10	7	92
Taste That Surrounds	0	0	0	0	0	0	0	0	0	0	0	0	14	0	0	0	0	0	14
Tea Tray Song	0	0	0	0	0	0	0	0	0	0	1	0	0	0	0	0	0	0	1
Tela	0	0	0	0	0	4	3	8	16	9	5	12	7	2	1	4	0	0	71
Tell Me Smthg Good	0	0	0	0	1	0	0	0	0	0	0	0	0	0	0	0	0	0	1
Tennessee Waltz	0	0	0	0	0	0	0	0	0	0	1	1	0	0	0	0	0	0	2
Terrapin	0	0	0	0	1	2	1	7	15	13	10	3	1	1	0	0	1	1	56
Terrapin Station	0	0	0	0	0	0	0	0	0	0	0	0	0	0	1	0	0	0	1
That's Alright Mama	0	0	0	0	0	0	0	0	0	0	1	0	0	0	0	0	0	0	1
The Asse Festival	0	0	0	0	0	0	1	18	2	0	0	0	0	0	0	0	0	0	21
Ballad - Curtis Loew	0	0	0	0	4	9	2	7	0	0	3	0	0	0	0	0	0	0	25
The Birthday Dub	0	0	0	0	1	0	0	0	0	0	0	0	0	0	0	0	0	0	1
The Chase	0	0	0	0	3	0	3	0	0	0	0	0	0	0	0	0	0	0	6
The Chicken	0	0	0	0	0	1	0	0	0	0	0	0	0	0	0	0	0	0	1
The Continuing Story	0	0	0	0	0	0	0	0	0	0	0	1	0	0	0	0	0	0	1
The Curtain	0	0	0	0	0	9	8	4	23	15	13	17	11	8	3	2	3	3	119
The Curtain With	0	0	0	0	5	2	0	0	0	0	0	0	0	0	0	0	0	3	10
The Dirty Jobs	0	0	0	0	0	0	0	0	0	0	0	0	1	0	0	0	0	0	1
The Famous Mockingbi	0	0	0	0	0	12	16	10	17	14	15	11	3	2	0	1	0	1	102
The Great Curve	0	0	0	0	0	0	0	0	0	0	0	0	1	0	0	0	0	0	1
The Great Gig in the	0	0	0	0	0	0	0	0	0	0	9	2	0	0	0	1	0	0	12
Happy Whip And Dung	0	0	0	0	0	0	0	0	0	0	0	0	0	0	0	1	0	0	1
The Horse	0	0	0	0	0	0	0	0	0	26	37	28	9	9	5	2	5	2	123
The Inlaw Josie Wale	0	0	0	0	0	0	0	0	0	0	0	0	0	0	0	0	9	4	13
The Landlady	0	0	0	0	0	0	0	33	84	40	15	10	0	0	0	0	0	0	182
The Lizards	0	0	0	0	0	28	32	43	41	24	28	28	17	10	3	5	4	5	268
The Maker	0	0	0	0	0	0	0	0	0	0	0	1	0	0	0	0	0	0	1
T.M.W.S.I.Y.	0	0	0	0	5	4	5	4	19	9	5	8	4	3	1	2	3	2	74
T.M.W.S.I.Y. Reprise	0	0	0	0	4	2	1	1	18	9	3	7	3	1	1	1	2	1	54
The Mango Song	0	0	0	0	0	0	5	0	21	8	3	14	6	4	1	5	2	6	75
The Moma Dance	0	0	0	0	0	0	0	0	0	0	0	0	0	0	0	25	14	11	50
The Oh Kee Pa Ceremo	0	0	0	0	0	0	25	59	50	20	9	8	2	1	2	2	1	1	180
The Old Home Place	0	0	0	0	0	0	0	0	0	0	0	13	4	5	5	4	1	2	34
The Other One	0	0	1	0	0	0	0	0	0	0	0	0	0	0	0	0	0	0	1
The Pendulum	0	0	0	1	0	0	0	0	0	0	0	0	0	0	0	0	0	0	1
The Practical Song	0	0	0	0	0	1	1	0	0	0	0	0	0	0	0	0	0	0	2
The Price of Love	0	0	0	0	0	0	2	0	0	0	0	0	0	0	0	0	0	0	2
The Punk Meets the G	0	0	0	0	0	0	0	0	0	0	0	0	1	0	0	0	0	0	1
The Real Me	0	0	0	0	0	0	0	0	0	0	0	0	2	0	0	0	0	0	2
The Revolution's Ove	0	0	0	0	0	0	0	1	0	0	0	0	0	0	0	0	0	0	1
The Rock	0	0	0	0	0	0	0	0	0	0	0	0	1	0	0	0	0	0	1
The Sloth	0	0	0	0	2	8	20	16	33	16	13	9	5	6	3	3	4	3	141
The Squirming Coil	0	0	0	0	0	0	0	34	73	51	41	26	18	7	8	6	15	4	283
Star Spangled Banner	0	0	0	0	0	0	0	0	0	0	0	0	0	8	1	0	1	1	11
The Vibration of Lif	0	0	0	0	0	0	0	0	0	1	1	3	0	1	0	0	0	0	6

	83	84	85	86	87	88	89	90	91	92	93	94	95	96	97	98	99	00	TOTAL
The Wedge	0	0	0	0	0	0	0	0	0	0	9	0	7	1	2	6	5	1	31
Them Changes	0	0	0	0	0	0	0	0	0	0	0	0	0	0	1	0	0	0	1
Theme From The Botto	0	0	0	0	0	0	0	0	0	0	0	0	26	20	27	6	6	4	89
Star Trek Theme	0	0	0	0	0	0	0	0	0	0	0	0	0	1	0	0	0	0	1
Three Little Birds	0	0	0	0	0	0	0	0	0	0	0	0	1	0	0	0	0	0	1
Timber (Jerry)	0	0	0	0	6	6	3	1	0	1	0	0	12	9	9	1	1	2	51
Time	0	0	0	0	0	0	0	0	0	0	0	0	0	0	0	1	0	0	1
Time Loves a Hero	0	0	0	0	0	3	0	0	0	0	0	0	0	0	0	1	0	0	4
Too Much Of Evrythng	0	0	0	0	0	0	0	0	0	0	0	0	0	0	0	2	0	0	2
Touch Me	0	0	0	0	0	0	0	0	8	0	0	1	0	0	0	0	0	0	9
Train Round the Bend	0	0	0	0	0	0	0	0	0	0	0	0	0	0	0	1	0	0	1
Train Song	0	0	0	0	0	0	0	0	0	0	0	0	0	15	10	5	6	1	37
Trenchtown Rock	0	0	0	0	0	0	0	0	0	0	0	0	0	0	0	1	0	0	1
Tube	0	0	0	0	0	0	0	7	16	2	1	1	3	3	4	10	13	4	64
Tube Jam	0	0	0	0	0	0	0	0	0	0	0	0	0	0	1	1	0	0	2
Tubthumping	0	0	0	0	0	0	0	0	0	0	0	0	0	0	0	1	0	0	1
Tuesday's Gone	0	0	0	0	0	0	0	0	0	0	0	0	0	0	0	0	1	0	1
Tush	0	0	0	1	1	0	0	0	0	0	0	0	0	0	0	0	0	0	2
Tweezer	0	0	0	0	0	0	0	33	36	29	37	31	18	16	10	13	13	7	243
Tweezer Reprise	0	0	0	0	0	0	0	1	19	22	30	25	14	10	10	11	17	3	162
Twist	0	0	0	0	0	0	0	0	0	0	0	0	0	0	11	2	12	13	38
Uncle Pen	0	0	0	0	0	0	0	43	25	38	33	16	16	7	7	0	3	3	191
Uncloudy Day	0	0	0	0	0	0	0	0	0	0	0	0	0	0	0	1	0	0	1
Undun	0	0	0	0	0	0	4	0	0	0	0	0	0	0	0	0	0	0	4
Us and Them	0	0	0	0	0	0	0	0	0	0	0	0	0	0	0	1	0	0	1
Vacuum Jam	0	0	0	0	0	1	0	0	0	0	0	0	0	0	0	0	0	0	1
Vacuum Solo	0	0	0	0	0	0	0	0	0	7	0	0	0	0	0	0	0	0	7
Viola Lee Blues	0	0	0	0	0	0	0	0	0	0	0	0	0	0	0	0	1	0	1
Vultures	0	0	0	0	0	0	0	0	0	0	0	0	0	0	10	3	7	3	23
Wading In Velvet Sea	0	0	0	0	0	0	0	0	0	0	0	0	0	0	10	11	11	5	37
Wait	0	0	0	0	0	0	0	0	2	1	0	0	0	0	0	0	0	0	3
Waking Up	0	0	0	0	0	0	0	0	0	0	0	0	0	0	1	0	0	0	1
Walfredo	0	0	0	0	0	0	0	0	0	0	0	0	0	0	4	0	0	1	5
Walk Away	0	0	0	0	0	11	13	13	2	0	9	1	0	0	0	2	2	4	57
Walk This Way	0	0	0	0	0	0	0	0	0	0	0	0	0	0	0	0	0	1	1
Waste	0	0	0	0	0	0	0	0	0	0	0	0	0	17	13	5	10	2	47
Water in the Sky	0	0	0	0	0	0	0	0	0	0	0	0	0	0	16	11	8	2	37
We're Not Gonna Take	0	0	0	0	0	0	0	0	0	0	0	0	0	0	0	0	1	0	1
Weekapaug Groove	0	0	0	0	0	6	39	68	54	35	35	22	15	13	11	15	13	9	335
Weekapaug Reprise	0	0	0	0	0	0	0	0	0	0	0	0	0	0	1	0	0	0	1
Weigh	0	0	0	0	0	0	0	0	0	10	14	1	2	2	3	1	0	0	33
West LA Fadeaway	0	0	0	0	0	0	0	0	0	0	0	0	0	0	0	0	1	0	1
What's the Use	0	0	0	0	0	0	0	0	0	0	0	0	0	0	0	0	7	3	10
When Something Wrong	0	0	0	0	0	0	0	0	0	0	3	0	0	0	0	0	0	0	3
When Circus Comes	0	0	0	0	0	0	0	0	0	0	0	0	0	0	15	9	10	6	40
While My Guitar Gent	0	0	0	0	0	0	0	0	0	0	0	3	12	0	1	3	4	2	25
Whipping Post	0	1	1	1	3	11	6	8	2	1	1	0	0	1	0	0	1	0	37
Whipping Post Jam	0	0	1	0	0	0	0	0	0	0	0	0	0	0	0	0	0	0	1
White Rabbit Jam	0	0	0	0	0	0	0	0	0	0	0	0	1	0	0	0	0	0	1
Who By Fire	0	0	0	0	0	0	0	0	0	0	0	1	0	0	0	0	0	0	1
Who Do? We Do!	0	0	0	0	3	0	8	0	0	0	0	0	0	0	0	0	0	0	11
Who Knows Jam	0	0	0	0	0	0	1	0	0	0	1	0	0	0	0	0	0	0	2

	83	84	85	86	87	88	89	90	91	92	93	94	95	96	97	98	99	00	TOTAL
Who Loves the Sun	0	0	0	0	0	0	0	0	0	0	0	0	0	0	0	1	0	0	1
Whole Lotta Love Jam	0	0	0	0	0	0	0	1	3	0	0	0	0	0	0	0	0	0	4
Why Don't We Do It i	0	0	0	0	0	0	0	0	0	0	0	2	1	0	1	0	0	0	4
Why Don't U Love Me	0	0	0	0	1	0	0	0	0	0	0	0	0	0	0	0	0	0	1
Why You've Been Gone	0	0	0	0	0	0	0	0	0	0	1	0	0	0	0	0	0	0	1
Wild Child	0	1	1	0	0	1	0	0	0	0	0	0	0	0	0	0	0	0	3
Wild Honey Pie	0	0	0	0	0	0	0	0	0	0	0	1	0	0	0	0	0	0	1
Wild Thing	0	0	1	0	0	0	0	0	0	0	0	0	0	0	0	0	0	0	1
Wildwood Weed	0	0	0	0	0	0	0	0	0	0	0	0	0	1	0	0	0	0	1
Will It Go Round	0	0	0	0	0	0	0	0	0	0	0	0	0	0	0	0	2	0	2
Will The Circle	0	0	0	0	0	0	0	0	0	0	0	0	0	0	0	1	0	0	1
Wilson	0	0	0	1	9	14	14	9	15	17	17	27	13	12	7	10	11	7	183
Wind Beneath Wings	0	0	0	0	0	0	0	0	0	0	0	1	0	0	0	0	0	0	1
Windora Bug	0	0	0	0	0	0	0	0	0	0	0	0	0	0	0	0	0	2	2
Wipeout	0	0	0	0	0	0	0	0	2	0	0	0	0	0	0	2	0	0	4
Wolfman's Brother	0	0	0	0	0	0	0	0	0	0	0	9	6	10	18	13	15	10	81
Wormtown Jam	0	0	0	0	0	0	0	0	0	0	0	0	0	0	1	0	0	0	1
Ya Mar	0	0	0	0	4	3	27	23	12	2	17	12	18	19	13	8	9	6	173
Yer Blues	0	0	0	0	0	0	0	0	0	0	0	1	0	0	0	0	0	0	1
Yerushalayim	0	0	0	0	0	0	0	0	0	0	2	10	0	0	0	0	0	0	12
You Enjoy Myself	0	0	0	5	12	28	50	60	53	46	53	38	23	23	19	16	21	7	454
You Gotta See Mama	0	0	0	0	0	0	0	0	0	0	1	0	0	0	0	0	0	0	1
You Shook Me (All Ni	0	0	0	0	0	0	0	0	0	0	0	0	0	0	0	0	0	1	1
You Shook Me All	0	0	0	0	0	0	1	0	0	0	0	0	0	0	0	0	0	0	1

EVERY TIME PLAYED

DATE	GAP	SET	POS.	SONG BEFORE	SONG AFTER

1999
| 12/31/98 | 1006 | 1 | 1/7 | *** | Mike's Song |

Has not been played in the last 113 shows.

5:15
| 10/31/95 | 759 | 2 | 11/17 | I've Had Enough | Sea and Sand |

Has not been played in the last 360 shows.

99 Years
| 8/7/96 | 817 | 1 | 8/10 | Lawn Boy | Hold to a Dream |

Has not been played in the last 302 shows.

A Day in the Life
6/10/95	716	E	1/1	***	***
6/19/95	6	E	1/1	***	***
6/23/95	3	E	1/1	***	***
6/29/95	5	2	6/6	Acoustic Army	***
7/3/95	4	2	8/10	BBFCFM	Possum
9/27/95	1	2	8/8	Hello My Baby	***
9/29/95	2	2	8/8	Cryin'	***
10/2/95	2	E	1/1	***	***
10/6/95	3	E	2/2	Hello My Baby	***
10/11/95	3	2	11/11	Hello My Baby	***
10/14/95	2	E	1/1	***	***
10/19/95	3	E	1/1	***	***
10/24/95	4	E	1/1	***	***
10/31/95	5	3	3/4	Jesus Just Left	Suzy Greenber
11/11/95	3	1	3/12	Mike's Song	Poor Heart
11/16/95	4	2	1/9	***	David Bowie
11/21/95	3	2	11/11	Carolina	***
11/25/95	3	1	2/9	Poor Heart	David Bowie
11/29/95	2	E	1/1	***	***
12/2/95	3	2	6/9	Tweezer	Golgi Apparat
12/8/95	4	E	2/2	Come Together	***
12/17/95	7	1	3/9	Poor Heart	Run Like Antel
12/30/95	3	E	1/1	***	***
4/26/96	2	1	12/13	Sample in a Jar	David Bowie
7/6/96	4	1	4/6	Poor Heart	Maze
7/11/96	4	E	1/1	***	***
7/22/96	8	1	7/8	Stash	You Enjoy My
8/6/96	7	2	4/8	Prince Caspian	BBFCFM
8/10/96	2	2	8/8	Harry Hood	***
8/17/96	5	3	5/7	Tweezer	Possum
10/17/96	2	1	9/10	Character Zero	Tweezer Repri
11/2/96	11	2	5/6	Harry Hood	Sweet Adeline
11/9/96	5	2	2/7	David Bowie	You Enjoy My
11/14/96	3	2	10/10	Run Like an Antelope	***
11/19/96	4	2	2/7	David Bowie	Bathtub Gin
11/24/96	3	2	4/7	David Bowie	You Enjoy My
12/1/96	4	2	4/10	Simple	Reba
12/29/96	5	2	2/10	David Bowie	Bathtub Gin
2/14/97	4	2	9/9	Scent of a Mule	***
2/20/97	4	2	10/12	Steep	Runaway Jim
2/28/97	6	E	1/1	***	***
12/7/97	58	E	1/1	***	***
12/30/97	7	1	7/7	Chalk Dust Torture	***
7/3/98	9	1	11/11	You Enjoy Myself	***
9/30/00	166	2	7/7	Sand	***

Has not been played in the last 5 shows.

AC/DC Bag
4/1/86	12	2	3/6	Slipknot!	McGrupp
4/15/86	1	1	1/14	***	Dear Mrs. Reagan
10/15/86	1	1	7/9	McGrupp	You Enjoy My
10/31/86	1	2	2/11	Jam	Swing Low Sweet Chrt
12/6/86	1	1	5/14	She Caught The Katy	David Bowie
4/24/87	5	1	2/14	Golgi Apparatus	Possum
4/29/87	1	2	7/7	Quinn the Eskimo	***
8/9/87	3	1	9/11	Good Times Bad Times	Shaggy Dog
8/10/87	1	2	2/10	Fire	Possum
8/29/87	2	1	9/13	Timber (Jerry)	Divided Sky
9/2/87	1	1	1/13	***	Fluffhead
9/21/87	1	1	10/11	Golgi Apparatus	Possum
10/14/87	2	1	9/12	David Bowie	Divided Sky
10/31/87	1	1	8/11	Love You	Possum
11/18/87	1	2	4/4	Fluffhead	***
1/27/88	2	1	3/9	Mustang Sally	Possum
2/7/88	1	2	2/9	Happy Birthday	Timber (Jerry)
2/26/88	3	1	7/13	T.M.W.S.I.Y. Reprise	Possum
3/11/88	1	2	6/8	Harpua	Alumni Blues
3/12/88	1	2	6/11	Wilson	Col. Forbin's A
3/21/88	1	1	10/15	Fire	Possum
3/31/88	1	1	4/14	Fee	Possum

DATE	GAP	SET	POS.	SONG BEFORE	SONG AFTER
4/22/88	2	2	10/13	Ya Mar	Possum
5/15/88	1	1	10/11	Sneakin' Sally	Possum
6/15/88	3	2	2/9	The Lizards	The Sloth
6/20/88	2	1	5/11	Fluffhead	The Lizards
6/21/88	1	2	3/10	I Didn't Know	Flat Fee
7/12/88	3	2	8/9	Slave	Roll Like A Cantalou
7/23/88	1	1	9/13	On Your Way Down	Possum
8/6/88	5	2	2/6	Golgi Apparatus	Satin Doll
9/8/88	2	1	5/8	Wild Child	Col. Forbin's A
9/24/88	4	3	4/4	The Curtain	***
11/5/88	4	2	5/11	The Lizards	Fee
12/2/88	2	2	5/8	The Lizards	Suzy Greenber
12/10/88	1	2	5/7	The Sloth	Possum
1/26/89	3	E	1/2	***	Fire
2/7/89	2	2	3/9	Dinner and a Movie	The Lizards
2/17/89	2	1	1/10	***	You Enjoy My
2/18/89	1	1	4/9	Divided Sky	Fire
2/24/89	1	2	2/4	On Your Way Down	You Enjoy My
3/3/89	1	1	5/11	Foam	The Curtain
3/14/89	3	1	8/12	Contact	Wilson
3/24/89	1	1	7/10	Divided Sky	If I Only Had a Brai
3/30/89	1	3	3/6	Foam	BBFCFM
4/20/89	2	1	1/12	***	Fluffhead
5/1/89	3	1	4/9	Esther	Alumni Blues
5/6/89	2	1	10/13	Bold As Love	Col. Forbin's A
5/12/89	2	1	5/15	Weekapaug Groove	David Bowie
5/13/89	1	1	1/12	***	Alumni Blues
5/20/89	1	1	1/8	***	Alumni Blues
5/21/89	1	1	12/13	Ya Mar	Divided Sky
5/26/89	1	1	2/9	Bold as Love	Mike's Song
5/27/89	1	1	1/11	***	Mike's Song
6/23/89	2	1	1/11	***	You Enjoy My
6/30/89	1	2	2/8	Walk Away	The Curtain
8/17/89	1	2	2/6	Walk Away	The Mango Song
8/19/89	1	1	5/13	Avenu Malkenu	Punch You in
8/23/89	1	2	6/8	You Enjoy Myself	Foam
8/26/89	1	2	5/9	Slave	Donna Lee
9/9/89	1	1	5/11	Divided Sky	McGrupp
9/21/89	2	1	3/9	Ya Mar	My Sweet One
10/1/89	1	2	2/11	***	My Sweet One
10/7/89	2	2	6/9	The Lizards	David Bowie
10/12/89	1	1	2/8	The Oh Kee Pa Ceremo	Col. Forbin's A
10/13/89	1	2	7/8	Weekapaug Groove	Col. Forbin's A
10/14/89	1	1	1/11	***	Divided Sky
10/20/89	1	2	5/10	I Didn't Know	Donna Lee
10/21/89	1	1	7/10	Foam	The Lizards
10/22/89	1	2	6/9	McGrupp	My Sweet One
10/26/89	1	2	4/9	Who Do? We Do!	Reba
10/31/89	2	1	4/9	You Enjoy Myself	Divided Sky
11/2/89	1	2	9/11	Who Do? We Do!	My Sweet One
11/9/89	2	2	2/9	The Oh Kee Pa Ceremo	McGrupp
11/10/89	1	1	6/9	Divided Sky	My Sweet One
11/11/89	1	1	4/8	Bathtub Gin	My Sweet One
11/16/89	1	2	2/4	The Sloth	Tela
11/18/89	1	1	3/11	Take the A-Train	The Lizards
11/30/89	1	1	5/11	The Oh Kee Pa Ceremo	Foam
12/3/89	2	2	3/14	Avenu Malkenu	Esther
12/7/89	1	4	4/11	Take the A-Train	Fee
12/8/89	1	1	6/9	Who Do? We Do!	My Sweet One
12/16/89	3	1	2/9	The Curtain	Lawn Boy
12/29/89	1	1	5/10	The Oh Kee Pa Ceremo	The Lizards
12/31/89	2	1	4/9	The Oh Kee Pa Ceremo	Run Like Antel
1/27/90	2	1	5/13	The Oh Kee Pa Ceremo	My Sweet One
2/9/90	4	1	7/12	Bouncing	The Squirmin
2/10/90	1	2	3/10	Esther	Rocky Top
2/17/90	3	1	3/12	The Oh Kee Pa Ceremo	The Squirmin
2/22/90	1	1	6/9	The Oh Kee Pa Ceremo	Caravan
2/24/90	2	2	3/9	The Oh Kee Pa Ceremo	Fee
3/3/90	4	1	8/12	The Oh Kee Pa Ceremo	Reba
3/7/90	1	2	2/9	The Oh Kee Pa Ceremo	The Squirmin
3/8/90	1	2	4/12	My Sweet One	Caravan
3/9/90	1	2	3/11	The Oh Kee Pa Ceremo	The Curtain
3/10/90	1	1	4/10	McGrupp	Rocky Top

DATE	GAP	SET	POS.	SONG BEFORE	SONG AFTER
3/11/90	1	2	12/13	Slave	David Bowie
3/17/90	1	2	4/6	The Oh Kee Pa Ceremo	Foam
4/5/90	3	2	4/13	Jesus Just Left	Donna Lee
4/7/90	2	1	3/12	My Sweet One	The Squirmin
4/13/90	4	1	8/10	The Oh Kee Pa Ceremo	Reba
4/20/90	4	2	9/11	The Oh Kee Pa Ceremo	Jesus Just Left
5/10/90	10	2	7/8	The Oh Kee Pa Ceremo	Good Time Ba
5/11/90	1	2	2/7	The Oh Kee Pa Ceremo	The Lizards
5/13/90	1	3	1/10	The Oh Kee Pa Ceremo	Dinner and a
5/24/90	4	1	8/9	The Oh Kee Pa Ceremo	Golgi Apparat
6/16/90	9	1	1/10	***	Divided Sky
9/13/90	1	2	8/15	The Oh Kee Pa Ceremo	Buried Alive
9/15/90	2	1	8/14	The Oh Kee Pa Ceremo	The Asse Festival
9/20/90	2	2	2/14	Stash	Bouncing
9/28/90	3	2	1/6	***	Esther
10/19/90	9	E	2/3	Carolina	Paul and Silas
10/30/90	1	3	5/5	Contact	***
11/4/90	4	1	2/10	Carolina	The Curtain
12/8/90	10	1	4/10	Foam	Divided Sky
12/29/90	2	E	2/2	Donna Lee	***
2/7/91	5	E	1/1	***	***
2/8/91	1	1	1/11	***	Reba
2/15/91	3	2	7/10	The Oh Kee Pa Ceremo	Harry Hood
2/26/91	5	1	9/11	The Oh Kee Pa Ceremo	Golgi Apparat
3/15/91	8	1	8/12	The Oh Kee Pa Ceremo	The Lizards
3/23/91	4	2	4/11	The Oh Kee Pa Ceremo	My Sweet One
4/16/91	12	1	7/9	The Oh Kee Pa Ceremo	Tela
4/21/91	4	1	9/14	The Oh Kee Pa Ceremo	Tela
5/3/91	5	2	1/9	***	The Curtain
5/12/91	5	2	12/13	The Oh Kee Pa Ceremo	Rocky Top
5/19/91	4	2	2/10	The Oh Kee Pa Ceremo	Fee
7/12/91	2	1	9/12	Donna Lee	Rocky Top
7/14/91	2	3	1/10	***	The Landlady
7/21/91	5	2	7/9	Esther	Contact
7/25/91	3	1	7/10	Flat Fee	Sweet Adeline
10/6/91	13	1	7/13	The Oh Kee Pa Ceremo	T.M.W.S.I.Y.
10/13/91	4	1	8/13	Tela	The Sloth
11/1/91	11	1	1/11	***	Sparkle
5/16/92	74	2	10/13	The Oh Kee Pa Ceremo	Cracklin' Rosi
2/19/93	83	E	1/1	***	***
3/12/93	14	2	1/11	***	My Friend My
3/22/93	8	2	1/12	Wilson	Col. Forbin's A
3/31/93	7	E	1/2	***	Sweet Adeline
4/14/93	8	2	1/10	***	My Sweet One
4/22/93	6	E	1/2	***	Amazing Grce
5/3/93	2	2	1/11	***	The Curtain
5/8/93	4	E	1/1	***	***
7/31/93	16	E	1/2	***	Freebird
8/12/93	8	1	1/10	***	Reba
8/25/93	1	1	1/11	***	Daniel
4/5/94	8	1	8/8	Rift	***
4/13/94	6	2	10/10	Purple Rain	***
4/18/94	5	1	10/10	The Oh Kee Pa Ceremo	***
5/6/94	13	1	3/9	The Oh Kee Pa Ceremo	Poor Heart
5/20/94	10	1	10/10	Carolina	***
6/18/94	16	1	3/10	Rift	Maze
6/26/94	7	1	6/11	Wilson	Col. Forbin's A
7/8/94	8	1	6/11	Wilson	Col. Forbin's A
7/16/94	6	2	7/11	Harpua	Scent of a Mul
10/22/94	13	2	10/11	Amazing Grace	Highway to Hell
11/18/94	16	1	2/11	Rift	Julius
12/8/94	15	1	3/10	Maze	Scent of a Mul
12/30/94	5	1	3/9	Rift	Sparkle
6/9/95	5	1	5/9	The Oh Kee Pa Ceremo	Theme From the Botto
6/15/95	4	1	3/10	Sparkle	The Old Home
6/19/95	3	1	3/10	Poor Heart	Tela
6/25/95	5	1	2/9	Ya Mar	Taste
6/30/95	4	1	1/9	***	Scent of a Mul
7/3/95	3	2	5/10	David Bowie	The Lizards
9/27/95	1	2	2/8	Cars Trucks Buses	David Bowie
9/29/95	2	1	1/8	***	Sparkle
10/8/95	7	1	1/9	***	Demand

DATE	GAP	SET	POS.	SONG BEFORE	SONG AFTER
10/14/95	3	1	1/11	***	Cars Trucks Buses
10/17/95	2	1	4/10	Uncle Pen	Maze
10/22/95	4	1	1/12	***	My Mind's Got A Mind
10/28/95	4	1	1/10	***	Mound
11/10/95	4	2	8/9	Sparkle	Sweet Adeline
11/15/95	4	1	2/9	Poor Heart	Fast Enough for You
11/18/95	2	2	1/10	***	Sparkle
11/24/95	4	1	2/9	The Oh Kee Pa Ceremo	The Curtain
11/29/95	3	1	1/9	***	Ya Mar
12/7/95	6	1	3/10	The Curtain	Demand
12/16/95	7	1	2/9	Buried Alive	Taste That Surrounds
12/30/95	4	2	4/8	Harry Hood	Lifeboy
4/26/96	2	1	2/13	Ya Mar	Sparkle
6/6/96	1	2	1/10	***	You Enjoy My
7/5/96	2	1	3/6	Chalk Dust Torture	You Enjoy My
7/23/96	14	1	1/9	***	Foam
8/4/96	4	2	1/7	***	Reba
8/10/96	4	1	3/11	Poor Heart	Fee
8/13/96	2	2	1/11	***	The Lizards
8/16/96	2	1	4/8	Ya Mar	Esther
10/19/96	5	2	1/10	***	Sparkle
10/23/96	3	1	3/9	Poor Heart	Foam
10/27/96	3	1	3/11	Punch You in the Eye	Fee
11/11/96	9	1	4/9	Cars Trucks Buses	Sparkle
11/14/96	2	1	1/9	***	Uncle Pen
11/19/96	4	1	2/9	Ya Mar	Foam
11/24/96	2	1	2/11	Poor Heart	All Things Rec
12/2/96	5	1	2/8	Rocky Top	Bouncing
12/30/96	5	2	3/8	Uncle Pen	Guyute
2/14/97	3	2	1/9	***	Ya Mar
2/21/97	5	2	5/9	The Oh Kee Pa Ceremo	Billy Breathes
6/25/97	17	1	5/11	Billy Breathes	The Old Home
7/25/97	14	1	7/7	Makisupa Policeman	***
8/6/97	7	1	6/7	Also Sprach	Ya Mar
11/21/97	14	2	2/4	Ghost	Slave
12/7/97	11	1	1/12	***	Psycho Killer
12/30/97	7	2	1/10	***	McGrupp
7/6/98	11	1	2/9	Buried Alive	Ghost
7/21/98	9	1	1/8	***	Fluffhead
7/29/98	5	2	3/7	If You Need a Fool	The Lizards
9/8/98	8	2	1/11	***	Jam
8/16/98	4	1	7/11	Ya Mar	Frankie Says
11/7/98	11	2	1/4	***	Ghost
11/25/98	12	1	4/9	Roggae	Lifeboy
7/4/99	11	1	5/10	The Oh Kee Pa Ceremo	The Wedge
7/21/99	12	1	1/10	***	Cities
9/14/99	13	2	2/5	Peaches en Regalia	Gumbo
9/26/99	9	1	3/10	First Tube	Dirt
10/4/99	6	2	4/8	The Wedge	Makisupa Policeman
10/8/99	2	1	2/6	Piper	Suzy Greenber
12/3/99	4	1	6/8	Billy Breathes	Possum
12/12/99	7	1	2/8	Heavy Things	Strange Design
5/23/00	10	1	1/12	***	Wilson
6/15/00	6	1	3/8	Chalk Dust Torture	Uncle Pen
6/30/00	8	1	2/10	Ha Ha Ha	Tweezer
7/15/00	11	1	1/9	***	First Tube
9/30/00	16	2	2/7	Timber (Jerry)	Col. Forbin's A

Has not been played in the last 5 shows.

Acoustic Army

DATE	GAP	SET	POS.	SONG BEFORE	SONG AFTER
6/7/95	713	2	6/9	Lonesome Cowboy Bill	Sample in a Ja
6/9/95	2	2	6/8	David Bowie	Sweet Adeline
6/13/95	2	2	5/7	Theme From the Botto	Harry Hood
6/14/95	1	2	4/5	Tweezer	While My Guitar Gent
6/15/95	1	2	7/8	Scent of a Mule	Slave
6/17/95	2	2	8/11	McGrupp	Sweet Adeline
6/19/95	1	2	7/8	You Enjoy Myself	Possum
6/22/95	2	E	1/2	***	While My Guitar Gent

DATE	GAP	SET	POS.	SONG BEFORE	SONG AFTER
6/24/95	2	2	7/9	Harry Hood	Sweet Adeline
6/29/95	4	2	5/6	You Enjoy Myself	A Day in the Life
7/1/95	2	2	7/9	Strange Design	Harry Hood
7/2/95	1	2	7/8	Sleeping Monkey	Slave
9/28/95	3	1	6/9	Fog that Surrounds	Slave
10/2/95	3	1	6/10	Stash	Fog that Surrounds
10/5/95	2	1	9/11	Divided Sky	Julius
10/7/95	2	1	7/9	The Mango Song	Wilson
10/11/95	2	1	7/9	Fog that Surrounds	Julius
10/14/95	2	1	8/11	Catapult	It's Ice
10/19/95	2	1	8/11	Theme From the Botto	Split Open and
10/21/95	2	1	10/12	Strange Design	Good Time Ba
10/24/95	2	1	11/13	Wolfman's Brother	Prince Caspian
10/28/95	3	1	8/10	Billy Breathes	Prince Caspian
11/11/95	5	E	1/2	***	Good Time Ba
11/18/95	5	2	8/8	BBFCFM	BBFCFM
11/24/95	4	2	7/10	Bathtub Gin	Bike
11/29/95	3	1	7/9	Theme From the Botto	Fee
12/8/95	7	1	7/9	It's Ice	Prince Caspian

Has not been played in the last 338 shows.

After Midnight

DATE	GAP	SET	POS.	SONG BEFORE	SONG AFTER
12/31/99	1070	1	14/14	Guyute	***

Has not been played in the last 49 shows.

After Midnight Reprise

DATE	GAP	SET	POS.	SONG BEFORE	SONG AFTER
12/31/99	1070	2	23/35	Drowned	The Horse

Has not been played in the last 49 shows.

Ain't Love Funny

DATE	GAP	SET	POS.	SONG BEFORE	SONG AFTER
6/20/97	882	1	5/8	Horn	Limb by Limb
7/1/97	7	1	5/9	Limb by Limb	I Saw it Again
8/9/97	20	2	4/10	Mike's Song	Simple

Has not been played in the last 210 shows.

Albuquerque

DATE	GAP	SET	POS.	SONG BEFORE	SONG AFTER
7/26/98	962	2	3/6	You Enjoy Myself	Simple
8/1/98	4	2	8/10	Brian and Robert	Chalk Dust Tor
8/7/98	4	2	4/7	Simple	Limb by Limb
10/18/98	10	1	6/12	Loving Cup	The Old Home
10/29/98	1	2	6/7	Simple	David Bowie
11/18/98	13	2	4/7	The Moma Dance	Slave
11/28/98	7	1	5/8	Guyute	Foam
12/28/98	2	1	6/9	Sleep	Driver
12/31/99	67	2	16/35	Slave	Reba
6/10/00	5	2	7/9	Twist	Wading In Velvet Sea
9/14/00	28	1	3/6	Reba	Carini

Has not been played in the last 16 shows.

All Along the Watchtower

DATE	GAP	SET	POS.	SONG BEFORE	SONG AFTER
4/21/94	603	E	3/3	Jam	***
10/22/96	226	E	1/1	***	***

Has not been played in the last 290 shows.

All Blues

DATE	GAP	SET	POS.	SONG BEFORE	SONG AFTER
7/30/88	61	1	1/2	***	Mr. P.C.
2/6/89	19	2	1/7	***	Sanity

Has not been played in the last 1039 shows.

All Things Reconsidered

DATE	GAP	SET	POS.	SONG BEFORE	SONG AFTER
9/25/91	312	E	1/2	***	BBFCFM
3/6/92	47	1	10/11	Reba	David Bowie
3/11/92	2	2	9/11	Baby Lemonade	Harry Hood
3/19/92	5	1	11/12	The Famous Mockingbi	David Bowie
3/21/92	2	2	7/11	Poor Heart	David Bowie
3/22/92	1	1	2/4	Sparkle	Foam
3/25/92	2	2	4/12	Reba	The Squirmin
3/26/92	1	1	3/10	Runaway Jim	Foam

DATE	GAP	SET	POS.	SONG BEFORE	SONG AFTER
3/30/92	3	1	8/11	I Didn't Know	The Sloth
4/1/92	2	1	5/12	Brother	Sparkle
4/3/92	1	1	9/11	Fluffhead	Split Open and
4/5/92	2	2	2/12	Split Open and Melt	You Enjoy My
4/7/92	2	2	2/11	Poor Heart	Tweezer
4/13/92	3	1	7/10	Fee	Foam
4/15/92	1	1	10/11	I Didn't Know	Runaway Jim
4/18/92	3	1	10/11	Sparkle	Run Like Antel
4/22/92	3	1	9/10	Stash	Suzy Greenber
4/25/92	3	2	6/11	Silent in the Mornin	Dinner and a
5/1/92	3	2	4/13	Wilson	My Sweet One
5/5/92	3	2	3/14	Bouncing	Foam
5/6/92	1	2	5/11	You Enjoy Myself	Bouncing
5/8/92	2	2	5/11	Mound	Bouncing
5/12/92	3	1	3/12	Reba	The Sloth
5/14/92	1	1	2/11	Suzy Greenberg	Brother
5/17/92	3	2	5/11	The Squirming Coil	Brother
6/27/92	6	1	6/10	Maze	Chalk Dust Tor
7/14/92	7	2	3/10	Fee	Reba
7/15/92	1	2	7/9	McGrupp	Harry Hood
7/21/92	5	1	1/7	***	Possum
7/27/92	5	1	2/7	Golgi Apparatus	David Bowie
7/30/92	2	1	5/8	It's Ice	Maze
8/17/92	7	1	7/11	Wilson	Foam
8/24/92	4	1	3/7	Poor Heart	Tweezer
11/20/92	8	1	2/12	Axilla	Suzy Greenber
11/22/92	2	1	9/12	Horn	Bathtub Gin
11/28/92	4	1	8/11	Fast Enough for You	Mike's Song
12/1/92	2	2	5/11	My Friend My Friend	Uncle Pen
12/3/92	2	1	3/12	Fee	Split Open and
12/7/92	4	2	8/11	Fast Enough for You	Split Open and
12/10/92	2	1	8/11	I Didn't Know	Reba
12/12/92	2	1	9/11	Poor Heart	Bouncing
12/29/92	3	2	8/14	Fast Enough for You	Mike's Song
2/4/93	4	1	6/14	Fast Enough for You	Stash
2/6/93	2	2	5/14	Sweet Adeline	Mike's Song
2/12/93	5	2	2/11	My Friend My Friend	Reba
2/17/93	3	1	4/11	Weigh	The Sloth
2/20/93	3	1	6/11	Weigh	Divided Sky
2/23/93	3	2	6/13	Punch You in the Eye	Mike's Song
3/2/93	4	1	8/13	Fee	Chalk Dust Tor
3/13/93	7	1	6/11	Fee	Split Open and
3/21/93	6	1	6/11	Esther	Split Open and
3/26/93	4	1	6/10	Fee	Split Open and
3/30/93	1	1	3/11	Poor Heart	Golgi Apparat
4/3/93	4	2	4/10	Mound	The Sloth
4/9/93	2	2	3/10	Suzy Greenberg	Llama
4/17/93	5	1	8/10	My Friend My Friend	Golgi Apparat
4/22/93	4	2	3/10	Bouncing	Tweezer
4/27/93	4	2	3/10	My Friend My Friend	Maze
4/30/93	2	1	11/12	Lawn Boy	Possum
5/6/93	5	1	6/13	Silent in the Mornin	Llama
7/16/93	6	1	7/10	Fast Enough for You	Nellie Kane
7/18/93	2	2	6/10	Fast Enough for You	Fee
7/28/93	7	1	1/11	***	Runaway Jim
8/2/93	4	1	7/12	Suzy Greenberg	Bathtub Gin
8/11/93	6	2	5/10	Esther	Bouncing
8/15/93	4	1	2/10	Sample in a Jar	Caravan
8/24/93	5	1	2/11	Chalk Dust Torture	Bouncing
4/9/94	12	1	8/10	Fee	Stash
4/22/94	11	1	6/11	Sample in a Jar	Nellie Kane
6/24/94	41	1	5/11	Fee	The Sloth
10/13/94	22	1	3/9	Gumbo	Down with Dis
10/28/94	12	1	8/10	Axilla (Part II)	Sample in a Ja
6/14/95	39	1	7/12	Possum	Amazing Grce
7/1/95	14	1	4/9	If I Could	It's Ice
11/8/96	108	1	3/9	Axilla	Mound
11/14/96	4	1	6/9	Free	Bathtub Gin
11/24/96	7	1	3/11	AC/DC Bag	Bouncing
11/30/96	1	3	3/10	Punch You in the Eye	Bouncing
2/23/97	17	1	3/9	Axilla	The Sloth

Has not been played in the last 248 shows.

All along watchtower

DATE	GAP	SET	POS.	SONG BEFORE	SONG AFTER
11/29/98	1002	1	10/11	Maze	Layla

Has not been played in the last 117 shows.

Also Sprach Zarathustra

DATE	GAP	SET	POS.	SONG BEFORE	SONG AFTER
7/16/93	553	2	1/12	***	Split Open and
7/17/93	1	2	1/10	***	Tweezer
7/18/93	1	2	1/10	***	Poor Heart
7/21/93	1	1	1/12	***	Split Open and
7/22/93	1	2	1/11	***	Tweezer
7/23/93	1	2	1/11	***	Poor Heart
7/24/93	1	2	1/12	***	Split Open and
7/25/93	1	2	1/11	***	Suzy Greenber
7/27/93	1	1	1/8	***	Rift
7/28/93	1	2	1/10	***	Axilla
7/30/93	2	2	1/10	***	Tweezer
8/2/93	2	2	1/9	***	Mike's Song
8/7/93	3	2	1/12	***	Mike's Song
8/8/93	1	2	1/11	***	Rift
8/12/93	3	2	1/10	***	The Landlady
8/14/93	2	2	1/13	***	Run Like Antel
8/17/93	3	2	1/10	***	David Bowie
8/20/93	1	2	1/9	***	Slave
8/26/93	4	2	1/8	***	David Bowie
8/28/93	1	2	1/14	***	Rift
12/30/93	1	2	1/9	***	Mike's Song
4/11/94	8	2	1/11	***	Maze
4/14/94	2	2	1/9	***	Run Like Antel
4/18/94	4	2	1/13	***	Sample in a Ja
4/21/94	2	2	1/10	***	Maze
5/8/94	13	2	1/9	***	Run Like Antel
5/12/94	2	2	1/11	***	Run Like Antel
5/16/94	2	1	1/11	***	Run Like Antel
5/20/94	3	2	1/7	***	Run Like Antel
5/26/94	5	2	1/9	***	Run Like Antel
6/11/94	6	2	1/9	***	Run Like Antel
6/17/94	4	2	1/15	***	Sample in a Ja
6/22/94	4	2	1/20	***	Mike's Song
7/2/94	8	2	1/12	***	Mike's Song
7/9/94	5	2	1/10	***	Split Open and
7/14/94	3	2	1/10	***	Sample in a Ja
7/16/94	2	2	5/11	Harpua	Harpua
10/8/94	2	2	1/12	***	Sample in a Ja
10/15/94	6	2	1/11	***	Runaway Jim
10/21/94	6	2	1/11	***	Mike's Song
10/28/94	6	2	1/12	***	David Bowie
11/3/94	4	2	1/8	***	Simple
11/17/94	6	2	1/8	***	David Bowie
11/20/94	3	2	1/10	***	David Bowie
11/25/94	3	2	1/8	***	Mike's Song
11/28/94	2	1	2/9	Chalk Dust Torture	Scent of a Mul
12/2/94	3	1	2/8	Poor Heart	Sparkle
12/6/94	3	2	3/12	Sample in a Jar	Poor Heart
12/10/94	4	2	4/11	Guyute	Mike's Song
12/31/94	4	3	2/8	My Sweet One	Auld Lang Syne
6/14/95	7	2	1/5	***	Poor Heart
6/24/95	8	2	1/9	***	Halley's Comet
6/30/95	5	2	1/10	***	Possum
9/29/95	5	2	1/8	***	Maze
10/5/95	4	2	1/9	***	Runaway Jim
10/13/95	5	1	2/9	Ya Mar	Maze
10/21/95	6	2	1/8	***	David Bowie
10/27/95	4	2	1/9	***	David Bowie
11/11/95	6	2	1/9	***	David Bowie
11/19/95	6	2	2/8	Theme From the Botto	The Curtain
11/28/95	5	2	1/10	***	Maze
12/2/95	4	2	1/9	***	Maze
12/8/95	4	2	1/8	***	Tweezer
12/15/95	5	2	6/8	Rotation Jam	David Bowie
12/17/95	2	2	4/8	Free	Harry Hood
12/30/95	3	1	2/13	Prince Caspian	Suzy Greenber
4/26/96	2	1	9/13	Scent of a Mule	Harry Hood
7/6/96	4	1	1/6	***	Reba
7/11/96	4	2	3/8	Bouncing	Maze
7/23/96	9	2	1/9	***	Runaway Jim
8/5/96	5	2	1/13	***	Down with Dis
8/16/96	7	3	2/6	Makisupa Policeman	Down with Dis

DATE	GAP	SET	POS.	SONG BEFORE	SONG AFTER
10/17/96	3	1	1/10	***	Funky Bitch
10/22/96	4	2	1/10	***	Down with Dis
10/31/96	6	3	2/8	Brother	Maze
11/8/96	5	2	1/8	***	Maze
11/13/96	3	2	1/7	***	Suzy Greenber
11/18/96	4	2	1/9	***	Simple
11/24/96	4	2	1/7	***	Sparkle
11/30/96	3	2	6/11	Contact	Timber (Jerry)
12/6/96	4	1	4/9	Poor Heart	Llama
12/31/96	4	3	1/7	***	Auld Lang Syne
2/13/97	1	1	3/12	Wolfman's Brother	Stash
2/18/97	4	2	2/9	Peaches en Regalia	My Soul
2/22/97	3	2	1/10	Walfredo	Funky Bitch
3/2/97	6	2	1/9	***	Maze
6/21/97	7	1	2/15	Sample in a Jar	Poor Heart
7/10/97	12	2	1/7	***	Julius
8/6/97	12	1	5/8	Twist	AC/DC Bag
8/13/97	5	2	7/9	Sample in a Jar	Golgi Apparat
8/17/97	3	2	4/5	Uncle Pen	Harry Hood
11/14/97	2	1	5/8	Fast Enough For You	Funky Bitch
11/19/97	3	2	1/4	***	Wolfman's Brother
11/26/97	4	2	2/8	Character Zero	Cities
12/3/97	5	1	6/7	Gumbo	You Enjoy My
12/12/97	6	1	2/8	Funky Bitch	Camel Walk
12/31/97	5	3	1/6	***	Auld Lang Syne
4/4/98	3	2	2/6	Birds of a Feather	Brother
7/1/98	3	2	2/5	Tweezer	Loving Cup
7/3/98	2	1	5/11	Guyute	Down with Dis
7/17/98	8	2	1/4	***	Mike's Song
7/24/98	4	2	2/7	Wolfman's Brother	Scent of a Mul
8/1/98	6	2	3/10	Wilson	Magilla
8/8/98	5	2	2/6	Cavern	Tela
8/16/98	5	3	2/7	Sabotage	Wilson
11/4/98	9	2	4/6	Piper	Chalk Dust Tor
11/19/98	10	2	1/8	***	Rock and Roll
11/25/98	4	2	1/8	***	Golgi Apparat
12/29/98	5	2	3/5	Limb by Limb	Boogie On Reggae
7/7/99	7	2	1/7	***	Down with Dis
7/16/99	7	2	1/8	***	Mike's Song
7/20/99	3	2	5/6	Train Song	Misty Mountain Hop
7/31/99	8	2	1/6	***	David Bowie
9/12/99	5	2	4/5	Roggae	You Enjoy My
9/16/99	2	2	1/8	***	Mike's Song
9/22/99	5	1	1/10	***	Chalk Dust Tor
9/25/99	2	2	6/8	Rock and Roll	Frankenstein
9/29/99	3	2	2/12	Gotta Jibboo	Down with Dis
10/9/99	7	2	2/6	Limb by Limb	Down with Dis
12/2/99	2	2	4/6	Bathtub Gin	You Enjoy My
12/11/99	7	2	4/5	Ghost	Down with Dis
12/18/99	6	2	1/10	***	Sand
12/31/99	2	2	33/35	Bug	Wading In Velvet Sea
6/14/00	8	2	5/5	Walk Away	***
6/22/00	3	2	2/10	Gotta Jibboo	Sand
7/6/00	10	2	2/7	Limb by Limb	Bug
7/11/00	4	2	1/13	***	Down with Dis
9/12/00	7	2	5/8	Bike	Mike's Song
9/29/00	11	2	3/9	The Moma Dance	Fluffhead
10/4/00	3	2	2/7	Rock and Roll	Sample in a Ja
10/7/00	3	2	2/7	Twist	Tweezer

Was played in the most recent show.

Alumni Blues

DATE	GAP	SET	POS.	SONG BEFORE	SONG AFTER
5/3/85	5	2	1/6	***	Wild Child
9/27/85	1	1	5/8	Slave	Prep School Hippie
10/17/85	1	1	2/9	Jam	Mike's Song
10/30/85	1	1	8/11	Revival	Prep School Hippie
2/3/86	3	1	5/7	You Enjoy Myself	Prep School Hippie

DATE	GAP	SET	POS.	SONG BEFORE	SONG AFTER
4/1/86	1	2	5/6	McGrupp	Dear Mrs. Reagan
4/15/86	1	1	14/14	Camel Walk	***
10/15/86	1	1	1/9	***	Makisupa Policeman
10/31/86	1	2	11/11	Icculus	***
2/13/87	2	1	6/14	Quinn the Eskimo	Suzy Greenber
2/21/87	1	2	15/15	Dog Gone Dog	***
3/23/87	2	1	3/5	Mike's Song	You Enjoy My
4/24/87	1	1	8/14	Punch Me in the Eye	I Am Hydrgn
4/29/87	1	1	2/2	She Caught The Katy	Golgi Apparat
5/20/87	2	1	9/9	You Enjoy Myself	***
8/10/87	2	1	2/7	Peaches en Regalia	Golgi Apparat
8/29/87	2	2	1/13	***	Ballad - Curtis Loew
9/21/87	2	2	5/5	Suzy Greenberg	***
10/31/87	3	2	15/17	Clod	Fluffhead
11/18/87	1	1	11/12	Divided Sky	Good Time Ba
11/19/87	1	2	6/6	Corrine Corrina	***
1/27/88	1	1	7/9	Sneakin' Sally	Take the A-Trn
2/7/88	1	1	5/10	Golgi Apparatus	Peaches en Regalia
2/8/88	1	3	4/9	Dinner and a Movie	Harry Hood
2/26/88	2	2	8/9	Makisupa Policeman	Whipping Post
3/11/88	1	2	7/8	AC/DC Bag	Run Like Antel
3/31/88	3	1	7/14	Fluffhead	The Lizards
4/22/88	2	1	4/9	Fire	Run Like Antel
5/14/88	1	1	10/11	Fluffhead	Take the A-Trn
5/15/88	1	1	1/11	***	Golgi Apparat
5/21/88	1	1	3/7	Sneakin' Sally	You Enjoy My
5/25/88	1	1	4/9	Funky Bitch	Peaches en Regalia
6/15/88	1	1	2/9	Suzy Greenber	You Enjoy My
6/21/88	3	2	5/10	Flat Fee	Jesus Just Left
6/24/88	1	1	4/11	Jam	On Your Way Down
7/11/88	1	1	11/11	Golgi Apparatus	***
7/23/88	2	2	9/10	La Grange	Peaches en Regalia
7/24/88	1	2	5/8	The Lizards	On Your Way Down
9/24/88	10	1	3/10	On Your Way Down	You Enjoy My
10/29/88	1	2	4/10	Fee	Walk Away
11/3/88	2	1	6/7	Fee	Good Time Ba
11/5/88	1	1	10/11	Fluffhead	David Bowie
12/2/88	2	2	3/8	Good Times Bad Times	The Lizards
12/10/88	1	2	1/7	***	You Enjoy My
1/26/89	3	1	3/10	Golgi Apparatus	You Enjoy My
2/7/89	2	2	7/9	Contact	Fee
2/17/89	2	1	8/10	Take the A-Train	Run Like Antel
3/3/89	3	1	10/11	Divided Sky	Good Time Ba
3/12/89	2	1	5/8	If I Only Had a Brai	Golgi Apparat
3/14/89	1	3	3/7	Sneakin' Sally	The Lizards
4/27/89	5	1	6/8	I Didn't Know	The Lizards
5/1/89	2	1	5/8	AC/DC Bag	Split Open an
5/5/89	1	1	5/8	Fluffhead	Donna Lee
5/13/89	4	1	2/12	AC/DC Bag	You Enjoy My
5/20/89	1	1	2/8	AC/DC Bag	You Enjoy My
8/17/89	7	3	6/8	Halley's Comet	Contact
9/9/89	4	2	3/7	You Enjoy Myself	Split Open and
9/21/89	2	1	4/9	Fee	McGrupp
10/1/89	1	1	1/12	***	McGrupp
10/7/89	2	1	10/11	Makisupa Policeman	Good Time Ba
10/14/89	3	1	8/11	Fee	You Enjoy My
10/31/89	6	2	6/8	The Famous Mockingbi	The Lizards
12/1/89	9	2	1/10	***	Rocky Top
12/7/89	2	1	9/11	Weekapaug Groove	Rhombus Narration
12/9/89	2	2	4/8	Esther	Fee
2/9/90	11	2	6/9	Take the A-Train	Foam
2/23/90	6	1	1/11	***	You Enjoy My
4/6/90	15	2	9/10	I Didn't Know	Good Time Ba
4/13/90	5	2	4/10	You Enjoy Myself	Ballad - Curtis Loew

DATE	GAP	SET	POS.	SONG BEFORE	SONG AFTER
4/20/90	4	1	3/10	Divided Sky	Ya Mar
5/15/90	13	1	2/12	Reba	Foam
5/19/90	1	1	3/8	Ya Mar	Sweet Adeline
10/5/90	23	2	4/8	Ya Mar	Uncle Pen
12/7/90	19	E	1/1	***	***
2/1/91	5	E	1/2	***	Carolina
2/14/91	6	2	8/12	Esther	Bouncing
4/20/91	33	E	2/2	Horn	***
7/13/91	18	1	7/13	Suzy Greenberg	T.M.W.S.I.Y.
7/15/91	2	E	3/3	Contact	***
7/18/91	1	E	1/1	***	***
4/15/94	296	2	8/10	Wolfman's Brother	I Wanna Be Like You
7/24/99	426	E	3/4	Camel Walk	Tweezer Repri

Has not been played in the last 95 shows.

Alumni Blues Jam

DATE	GAP	SET	POS.	SONG BEFORE	SONG AFTER
12/3/94	701	2	8/10	Touch Me	Julius

Has not been played in the last 418 shows.

Amazing Grace

DATE	GAP	SET	POS.	SONG BEFORE	SONG AFTER
2/3/93	480	E	1/2	***	Tweezer Repri
2/4/93	1	E	1/2	***	Good Time Ba
2/5/93	1	E	1/2	***	Loving Cup
2/7/93	2	E	1/3	***	Contact
2/9/93	1	2	12/12	Bike	***
2/10/93	1	E	2/3	Sweet Adeline	Tweezer Repri
2/11/93	1	E	2/2	Bold as Love	***
2/12/93	1	E	1/2	***	Good Time Ba
2/13/93	1	E	1/2	***	Tweezer Repri
2/15/93	1	1	1/12	***	Suzy Greenber
2/18/93	2	2	9/12	Mound	Memories
2/19/93	1	2	12/12	Llama	***
2/22/93	3	E	1/2	***	Fire
2/25/93	1	E	1/2	***	Good Time Ba
2/27/93	2	E	2/3	Sleeping Monkey	Rocky Top
3/2/93	1	2	12/12	Harry Hood	***
3/5/93	2	2	11/11	The Squirming Coil	***
3/8/93	2	2	10/10	The Lizards	***
3/9/93	1	E	1/2	***	Rocky Top
3/13/93	2	E	2/3	My Sweet One	BBFCFM
3/16/93	2	2	15/15	Llama	***
3/17/93	1	1	6/11	Stash	Paul and Silas
3/19/93	2	E	1/2	***	Chalk Dust Tor
3/22/93	2	E	1/2	***	Fire
3/24/93	1	1	8/9	Sample in a Jar	Cavern
3/26/93	2	E	1/2	***	Rocky Top
3/30/93	3	E	2/2	My Sweet One	***
4/2/93	3	E	1/2	***	Rocky Top
4/10/93	4	E	1/2	***	Good Time Ba
4/12/93	1	E	1/3	***	Highway to Hell
4/16/93	2	E	2/2	Gumbo	***
4/18/93	2	E	1/2	***	Rocky Top
4/20/93	1	E	2/2	Funky Bitch	***
4/22/93	2	E	2/2	AC/DC Bag	***
4/24/93	2	E	1/2	***	Good Time Ba
4/27/93	2	E	2/3	My Sweet One	***
4/30/93	2	E	2/3	When Something Wrong	Tweezer Repri
5/2/93	2	E	2/2	Sleeping Monkey	***
5/5/93	2	E	1/4	***	Cavern
5/7/93	2	E	1/2	***	Golgi Apparat
5/8/93	1	2	17/18	Weekapaug Groove	Amazing Grace Jam
5/29/93	1	1	10/10	Runaway Jim	***
7/17/93	4	E	1/3	***	Daniel
7/23/93	4	E	8/10	***	Daniel
7/30/93	6	E	2/2	Walk Away	***
8/2/93	2	E	2/2	Sleeping Monkey	***
8/6/93	2	E	1/1	***	***
8/13/93	6	2	9/9	Suzy Greenberg	***
8/16/93	3	E	1/2	***	Rocky Top
8/21/93	3	E	1/2	***	Nellie Kane
8/25/93	2	1	8/11	Nellie Kane	Stash

DATE	GAP	SET	POS.	SONG BEFORE	SONG AFTER
8/28/93	2	E	2/2	Daniel	***
12/31/93	4	E	2/2	Golgi Apparatus	***
4/5/94	2	2	8/8	Chalk Dust Torture	***
4/9/94	3	E	1/2	***	Highway to Hell
4/11/94	2	2	9/11	You Enjoy Myself	The Oh Kee Pa
4/15/94	3	E	2/2	Magilla	***
4/21/94	5	2	10/10	Possum	***
4/25/94	4	E	1/2	***	Bold as Love
5/7/94	8	E	1/2	***	Sample in a Ja
5/12/94	3	E	1/2	***	Rocky Top
5/16/94	3	2	10/11	BBFCFM	BBFCFM
5/21/94	4	2	9/9	Harry Hood	***
5/23/94	2	E	2/3	Ginseng Sullivan	Highway to Hell
5/26/94	2	2	9/9	You Enjoy Myself	***
6/16/94	9	2	2/3	Ginseng Sullivan	Good Time Ba
6/21/94	4	E	1/1	***	***
6/26/94	5	E	2/4	The Old Home Place	Tube
7/5/94	6	2	10/11	My Sweet One	Golgi Apparat
10/9/94	11	2	5/8	You Enjoy Myself	Julius
10/13/94	3	2	5/12	It's Ice	Mike's Song
10/15/94	2	2	8/11	You Enjoy Myself	Foreplay/Long Time
10/18/94	2	1	10/10	Divided Sky	***
10/22/94	3	2	9/11	Reba	AC/DC Bag
10/26/94	3	E	3/3	Foreplay/Long Time	***
10/31/94	4	E	1/3	***	Costume Contest
11/3/94	2	E	3/4	Nellie Kane	Highway to Hell
11/13/94	3	2	7/8	BBFCFM	The Squirmin
11/16/94	2	E	1/2	***	Suzy Greenber
11/19/94	3	2	6/7	Harry Hood	Good Time Ba
11/23/94	3	1	9/9	Divided Sky	***
11/30/94	4	E	3/3	Silent in the Mornin	***
12/7/94	6	2	8/9	My Long Journey Home	You Enjoy My
12/31/94	7	2	9/9	Weekapaug Groove	***
6/10/95	5	2	7/8	Weekapaug Groove	Sample in a Ja
6/14/95	2	1	8/12	All Things Recnsdrd	The Horse
6/20/95	5	E	2/2	Slave	***
6/25/95	4	2	8/9	Weekapaug Groove	Cavern
6/30/95	4	2	9/10	Weekapaug Groove	The Squirmin
7/3/95	3	E	2/2	Simple	***
9/28/95	2	2	6/8	Keyboard Cavalry	Sample in a Ja
9/30/95	2	E	1/2	***	Good Time Ba
10/5/95	3	2	9/9	Lifeboy	***
10/17/95	8	1	10/10	Strange Design	***
10/20/95	2	1	9/10	Hello My Baby	Amazing Grace Jam
10/29/95	7	2	10/10	Lifeboy	***
11/11/95	4	1	10/12	Stash	Fee
11/16/95	4	2	8/9	If I Only Had a Brai	Possum
11/30/95	9	2	8/8	Strange Design	***
12/7/95	5	2	10/10	Weekapaug Groove	***
8/5/96	35	2	10/13	Strange Design	Mike's Song
8/16/96	7	E	1/1	***	***
11/16/96	24	2	8/8	Suzy Greenberg	***
11/23/96	4	2	9/10	Waste	Harry Hood
11/30/96	4	2	10/11	Funky Bitch	Amazing Grace Jam
12/31/96	8	E	1/1	***	***
10/3/98	115	1	9/10	Will The Circle	Uncloudy Day

Has not been played in the last 142 shows.

Amazing Grace Jam

DATE	GAP	SET	POS.	SONG BEFORE	SONG AFTER
5/8/93	549	2	18/18	Amazing Grace	***
10/20/95	202	1	10/10	Amazing Grace	***
11/30/96	103	2	11/11	Amazing Grace	***

Has not been played in the last 265 shows.

Ambient Jam

DATE	GAP	SET	POS.	SONG BEFORE	SONG AFTER
8/15/98	975	4	1/1	***	***

Has not been played in the last 144 shows.

American Band

DATE	GAP	SET	POS.	SONG BEFORE	SONG AFTER
11/16/96	846	E	1/1	***	***
9/29/00	267	E	1/1	***	***

Has not been played in the last 6 shows.

Amoreena

DATE	GAP	SET	POS.	SONG BEFORE	SONG AFTER
8/13/97	912	1	1/11	***	Poor Heart

Has not been played in the last 207 shows.

Anarchy

DATE	GAP	SET	POS.	SONG BEFORE	SONG AFTER
3/4/85	4	1	1/4	***	Camel Walk
5/3/85	1	E	1/1	***	***
10/17/85	2	1	6/9	Revolution	Camel Walk
4/15/86	6	1	12/14	You Enjoy Myself	Camel Walk
10/15/86	1	3	3/3	Sanity	***
4/29/87	8	3	4/14	Good Times Bad Times	Makisupa Policeman
8/10/87	4	3	5/7	Whipping Post	Tush
7/30/88	35	3	10/13	Fluffhead	Dear Mrs. Reagan
10/14/89	60	2	1/4	***	Highway to Hell

Has not been played in the last 998 shows.

Andy's Chest

DATE	GAP	SET	POS.	SONG BEFORE	SONG AFTER
9/13/88	67	3	2/8	Jam	BBFCFM

Has not been played in the last 1052 shows.

Any Colour You Like

DATE	GAP	SET	POS.	SONG BEFORE	SONG AFTER
11/2/98	984	2	13/16	Us and Them	Brain Damage

Has not been played in the last 135 shows.

Arc

DATE	GAP	SET	POS.	SONG BEFORE	SONG AFTER
10/3/98	977	1	5/10	Runaway Jim	Down By the River

Has not been played in the last 142 shows.

Auld Lang Syne

DATE	GAP	SET	POS.	SONG BEFORE	SONG AFTER
12/30/89	144	E	1/4	***	Mike's Song
12/31/90	97	1	10/12	Weekapaug Groove	Buried Alive
12/31/91	117	2	4/10	Buried Alive	Runaway Jim
12/31/92	121	3	2/9	Mike's Song	Weekapaug Gr
12/31/93	109	3	1/9	***	Down W Disease Jam
12/31/94	123	3	3/8	Also Sprach	Chalk Dust Tor
12/31/95	0	E	2/2	Simple	***
12/31/96	81	3	1/6	***	Weekapaug Gr
12/31/97	78	3	2/7	Also Sprach	Down with Dis
12/31/98	66	3	2/6	Also Sprach	Tweezer
12/31/99	64	2	2/35	Meatstick	Down with Dis

Has not been played in the last 49 shows.

Avenu Malkenu

DATE	GAP	SET	POS.	SONG BEFORE	SONG AFTER
5/11/87	23	1	9/12	T.M.W.S.I.Y.	T.M.W.S.I.Y. Reprise
8/29/87	5	2	12/13	T.M.W.S.I.Y.	T.M.W.S.I.Y.
9/21/87	2	1	2/11	T.M.W.S.I.Y.	T.M.W.S.I.Y. Reprise
10/31/87	3	2	2/17	T.M.W.S.I.Y.	T.M.W.S.I.Y. Reprise
11/18/87	1	1	3/12	T.M.W.S.I.Y.	T.M.W.S.I.Y. Reprise
2/7/88	3	3	3/8	T.M.W.S.I.Y.	T.M.W.S.I.Y. Reprise
2/26/88	3	1	5/13	T.M.W.S.I.Y.	T.M.W.S.I.Y. Reprise
7/24/88	19	3	2/6	T.M.W.S.I.Y.	Peaches en Regalia
9/12/88	7	2	5/10	T.M.W.S.I.Y.	Bundle of Joy
2/24/89	19	1	2/10	T.M.W.S.I.Y.	T.M.W.S.I.Y. Reprise
8/19/89	25	1	4/13	T.M.W.S.I.Y.	AC/DC Bag
8/26/89	2	3	2/5	T.M.W.S.I.Y.	Suzy Greenber
10/13/89	8	2	3/8	T.M.W.S.I.Y.	Mike's Song
12/3/89	17	2	2/14	T.M.W.S.I.Y.	AC/DC Bag
3/9/90	28	1	2/11	T.M.W.S.I.Y.	Caravan
3/11/90	2	1	5/13	T.M.W.S.I.Y.	T.M.W.S.I.Y. Reprise
5/4/90	21	2	4/10	T.M.W.S.I.Y.	Bouncing
6/9/90	17	2	4/14	T.M.W.S.I.Y.	T.M.W.S.I.Y.
2/7/91	40	2	3/14	T.M.W.S.I.Y.	T.M.W.S.I.Y. Reprise
2/9/91	2	1	4/12	T.M.W.S.I.Y.	T.M.W.S.I.Y. Reprise
2/28/91	9	1	10/13	T.M.W.S.I.Y.	T.M.W.S.I.Y. Reprise
3/16/91	7	1	2/14	T.M.W.S.I.Y.	T.M.W.S.I.Y. Reprise
4/11/91	12	2	5/14	T.M.W.S.I.Y.	T.M.W.S.I.Y. Reprise
4/20/91	6	2	8/13	T.M.W.S.I.Y.	T.M.W.S.I.Y. Reprise
4/27/91	4	2	4/13	T.M.W.S.I.Y.	T.M.W.S.I.Y. Reprise
5/3/91	2	1	5/12	T.M.W.S.I.Y.	T.M.W.S.I.Y. Reprise
5/17/91	7	1	10/17	T.M.W.S.I.Y.	T.M.W.S.I.Y. Reprise
7/11/91	3	2	4/10	T.M.W.S.I.Y.	T.M.W.S.I.Y. Reprise
7/13/91	2	1	9/13	T.M.W.S.I.Y.	T.M.W.S.I.Y. Reprise
7/20/91	5	2	9/12	T.M.W.S.I.Y.	T.M.W.S.I.Y. Reprise
7/26/91	5	1	8/12	T.M.W.S.I.Y.	T.M.W.S.I.Y. Reprise
7/27/91	1	1	9/16	T.M.W.S.I.Y.	T.M.W.S.I.Y. Reprise
10/6/91	11	1	9/13	T.M.W.S.I.Y.	T.M.W.S.I.Y. Reprise
10/24/91	10	1	10/12	T.M.W.S.I.Y.	T.M.W.S.I.Y. Reprise
11/2/91	6	2	4/11	T.M.W.S.I.Y.	T.M.W.S.I.Y. Reprise
11/21/91	12	2	8/10	T.M.W.S.I.Y.	T.M.W.S.I.Y. Reprise
3/26/92	23	2	7/13	T.M.W.S.I.Y.	T.M.W.S.I.Y. Reprise
4/8/92	11	2	5/15	T.M.W.S.I.Y.	T.M.W.S.I.Y. Reprise
4/18/92	6	2	12/16	T.M.W.S.I.Y.	T.M.W.S.I.Y. Reprise
5/18/92	23	2	4/13	T.M.W.S.I.Y.	T.M.W.S.I.Y. Reprise
7/16/92	14	2	6/11	T.M.W.S.I.Y.	T.M.W.S.I.Y. Reprise
11/28/92	36	2	5/12	T.M.W.S.I.Y.	Maze
12/6/92	7	2	9/13	T.M.W.S.I.Y.	T.M.W.S.I.Y. Reprise
12/13/92	6	2	8/14	T.M.W.S.I.Y.	T.M.W.S.I.Y. Reprise
12/30/92	3	2	6/12	T.M.W.S.I.Y.	T.M.W.S.I.Y.
2/4/93	3	2	5/13	T.M.W.S.I.Y.	T.M.W.S.I.Y. Reprise
3/27/93	38	2	7/14	T.M.W.S.I.Y.	T.M.W.S.I.Y. Reprise
4/20/93	15	2	6/12	T.M.W.S.I.Y.	T.M.W.S.I.Y. Reprise
7/22/93	23	2	10/11	T.M.W.S.I.Y.	Rocky Top
8/7/93	12	2	6/12	T.M.W.S.I.Y.	The Sloth
4/18/94	32	2	9/13	T.M.W.S.I.Y.	T.M.W.S.I.Y. Reprise
5/14/94	19	2	6/11	T.M.W.S.I.Y.	T.M.W.S.I.Y. Reprise
6/22/94	23	2	13/20	T.M.W.S.I.Y.	T.M.W.S.I.Y. Reprise
7/1/94	7	2	6/11	T.M.W.S.I.Y.	T.M.W.S.I.Y. Reprise

DATE	GAP	SET	POS.	SONG BEFORE	SONG AFTER
7/14/94	9	1	5/11	T.M.W.S.I.Y.	T.M.W.S.I.Y. Reprise
10/16/94	11	1	7/10	T.M.W.S.I.Y.	T.M.W.S.I.Y. Reprise
10/29/94	10	2	3/11	T.M.W.S.I.Y.	T.M.W.S.I.Y. Reprise
11/19/94	11	1	7/11	T.M.W.S.I.Y.	Run Like Antel
6/30/95	40	2	5/10	T.M.W.S.I.Y.	Mike's Song
10/3/95	9	1	8/11	T.M.W.S.I.Y.	T.M.W.S.I.Y. Reprise
11/9/95	20	2	6/10	T.M.W.S.I.Y.	T.M.W.S.I.Y. Reprise
12/30/95	31	1	10/13	T.M.W.S.I.Y.	T.M.W.S.I.Y. Reprise
10/25/96	40	2	5/12	T.M.W.S.I.Y.	T.M.W.S.I.Y. Reprise
11/15/96	14	2	6/11	T.M.W.S.I.Y.	My Mind's Got A Mind
12/28/96	14	2	6/10	T.M.W.S.I.Y.	Mike's Song
11/29/97	67	1	5/12	T.M.W.S.I.Y.	T.M.W.S.I.Y. Reprise
7/31/98	39	2	5/9	T.M.W.S.I.Y.	Twist
11/9/98	24	2	3/7	T.M.W.S.I.Y.	T.M.W.S.I.Y. Reprise
7/24/99	35	1	5/9	T.M.W.S.I.Y.	T.M.W.S.I.Y. Reprise
10/3/99	25	2	4/8	T.M.W.S.I.Y.	BBFCFM
12/4/99	8	2	6/9	T.M.W.S.I.Y.	T.M.W.S.I.Y. Reprise
7/4/00	33	1	9/11	T.M.W.S.I.Y.	T.M.W.S.I.Y. Reprise
9/20/00	17	1	7/9	T.M.W.S.I.Y.	Weekapaug Gr

Has not been played in the last 12 shows.

Axilla

DATE	GAP	SET	POS.	SONG BEFORE	SONG AFTER
11/19/92	455	1	9/12	Esther	The Horse
11/20/92	1	1	1/12	***	All Things Rec
11/22/92	2	2	1/13	***	My Friend My
11/27/92	3	2	1/13	***	Poor Heart
12/1/92	3	2	1/11	***	The Curtain
12/7/92	6	1	1/11	***	Poor Heart
12/11/92	3	2	6/12	Esther	Bouncing
12/30/92	5	2	1/12	***	Rift
2/4/93	3	1	1/11	***	Foam
2/17/93	10	2	1/11	***	The Landlady
2/21/93	4	2	1/10	***	The Curtain
2/23/93	2	2	1/13	***	My Sweet One
3/3/93	5	2	1/13	***	The Curtain
3/9/93	4	2	1/15	***	Rift
3/12/93	1	2	3/11	My Friend My Friend	Sparkle
3/17/93	4	1	1/12	***	Glide
3/25/93	6	2	1/13	***	The Curtain
4/1/93	6	2	1/10	***	The Curtain
4/5/93	3	2	1/9	***	Poor Heart
4/16/93	5	2	1/13	***	The Curtain
5/2/93	13	1	1/11	***	Sparkle
7/28/93	18	2	2/10	Also Sprach	My Sweet One
8/16/93	15	1	1/9	***	Possum
10/16/94	93	1	9/10	T.M.W.S.I.Y. Reprise	Possum
11/8/96	170	1	2/9	Runaway Jim	All Things Rec
11/11/96	2	1	8/9	Theme From the Botto	Runaway Jim
11/16/96	4	2	5/8	Catapult	Harry Hood
11/23/96	4	2	5/10	Makisupa Policeman	Weekapaug Gr
12/31/96	12	1	1/10	***	Peaches en Regalia
2/14/97	2	1	5/9	Sweet Adeline	It's Ice
2/23/97	7	1	2/9	Carini	All Things Rec
2/28/97	3	2	7/9	Love Me	Waste
12/9/97	59	2	5/6	Contact	Harry Hood
12/13/97	3	1	2/9	Ya Mar	Theme From the Botto
12/28/97	1	2	1/9	***	Simple
7/5/98	12	2	4/6	McGrupp	Harry Hood
7/16/98	6	2	4/7	Piper	David Bowie
8/3/98	13	2	2/7	Gumbo	Limb by Limb
10/31/98	15	1	1/10	***	Punch You in
11/20/98	13	2	3/8	Piper	Roses Are Free
11/29/98	6	1	2/11	Paul and Silas	Theme From the Botto
12/28/98	1	1	1/10	***	Stash
7/7/99	8	1	6/10	Sneakin' Sally	Rift
7/15/99	6	1	6/10	Poor Heart	Theme From the Botto
7/18/99	3	2	5/6	Guyute	Llama
7/26/99	6	1	10/11	Mountains in the Mis	Stash
7/30b/99	2	1	8/8	Ghost	***
9/9/99	3	1	2/10	Mozambique	Limb by Limb
9/22/99	10	1	4/10	Guelah Papyrus	My Mind's Got A Mind
12/31/99	29	2	18/35	Reba	Uncle Pen
6/9/00	4	1	1/9	***	Taste
7/1/00	14	1	3/11	Wolfman's Brother	Poor Heart
7/12/00	8	1	8/9	Free	The Squirmin
9/8/00	3	1	10/12	Glide	Taste
9/18/00	7	E	1/2	***	Taste
9/25/00	5	2	5/7	Weekapaug Groove	Harry Hood
10/5/00	6	1	8/10	Beauty of my Dreams	Horn

Has not been played in the last 2 shows.

Axilla (Part II)

DATE	GAP	SET	POS.	SONG BEFORE	SONG AFTER
4/16/94	599	1	3/8	Fee	Rift
4/20/94	3	1	5/7	Bouncing	Stash
4/24/94	4	1	3/8	Ya Mar	Maze
4/30/94	4	2	6/10	Harry Hood	McGrupp
5/4/94	3	2	6/10	Sparkle	Tweezer
5/6/94	1	2	6/9	Reba	Julius
5/8/94	2	1	3/8	Foam	Rift
5/10/94	1	1	5/9	Divided Sky	It's Ice
5/12/94	1	1	6/10	Maze	Foam
5/16/94	3	1	5/10	Divided Sky	Rift
5/20/94	3	2	4/7	Weigh	Wolfman's Brother
5/22/94	2	1	11/11	Dog Faced Boy	***
5/25/94	2	1	7/11	The Famous Mockingbi	Scent of a Mul
5/28/94	3	2	1/8	***	It's Ice
6/10/94	3	2	1/9	***	The Curtain
6/19/94	7	1	4/9	The Lizards	The Curtain
6/23/94	3	2	4/8	The Mango Song	Uncle Pen
6/25/94	2	2	5/9	Bathtub Gin	You Enjoy My
6/26/94	1	2	4/12	If I Could	Lifeboy
6/30/94	2	2	7/15	Sparkle	Harpua
7/3/94	3	1	9/10	Reba	David Bowie
7/6/94	2	1	6/9	Reba	My Mind's Got A Mind
10/22/94	20	1	4/8	Gumbo	Rift
10/25/94	2	2	7/11	Glide	Jesus Just Left
10/26/94	1	2	4/7	Reba	You Enjoy My
10/28/94	2	1	7/10	Glide	All Things Rec
11/2/94	3	2	4/7	The Mango Song	Possum
11/13/94	4	1	5/10	Reba	It's Ice
11/16/94	5	1	5/11	Reba	The Lizards
11/19/94	3	1	4/11	Guyute	Paul and Silas
11/20/94	1	2	4/10	Glide	Reba
12/4/94	10	2	4/7	Reba	You Enjoy My
12/8/94	2	3	3/8	My Mind's Got A Mind	Reba
12/28/94	3	1	6/10	Bouncing	Reba
6/13/95	9	2	3/7	The Lizards	Theme From the Botto
6/28/95	12	1	1/8	***	Foam
12/4/95	49	1	7/11	My Mind's Got A Mind	The Horse
12/31/95	14	2	4/8	The Lizards	Runaway Jim

Has not been played in the last 327 shows.

Baby Elephant Walk

DATE	GAP	SET	POS.	SONG BEFORE	SONG AFTER
12/1/92	464	2	10/11	Dinner and a Movie	David Bowie
8/16/98	512	E	2/2	Harry Hood	***

Has not been played in the last 143 shows.

Baby Left Me

DATE	GAP	SET	POS.	SONG BEFORE	SONG AFTER
7/30/88	61	2	3/6	Suzy Greenberg	Contact

Has not been played in the last 1058 shows.

Baby Lemonade

DATE	GAP	SET	POS.	SONG BEFORE	SONG AFTER
3/11/92	361	2	8/11	Brother	All Things Rec

Has not been played in the last 758 shows.

Back Porch Boogie Blues

DATE	GAP	SET	POS.	SONG BEFORE	SONG AFTER
10/31/86	15	1	9/11	Halley's Comet	Shaggy Dog
2/21/87	3	2	6/15	Camel Walk	Clod
5/20/87	6	1	4/9	Golgi Apparatus	Lushington
8/21/87	3	2	11/12	Low Rider Jam	The Sloth
10/31/87	6	1	4/11	Sneakin' Sally	Halley's Comet

Has not been played in the last 1086 shows.

Back at the Chicken Shack

DATE	GAP	SET	POS.	SONG BEFORE	SONG AFTER
10/30/98	982	1	4/10	Scent of a Mule	Scent of a Mul
11/18/98	12	1	1/9	***	Birds of a Feather
7/10/99	20	1	5/8	Water in the Sky	Sparkle
7/23/99	9	1	3/9	NICU	Punch You in
9/9/99	8	1	7/10	Chalk Dust Torture	Stash
12/18/99	37	1	2/9	Harry Hood	Dog Gone Dog
9/8/00	31	2	4/6	David Bowie	Bathtub Gin
9/24/00	11	1	3/10	Chalk Dust Torture	Sparkle

Has not been played in the last 9 shows.

Back in the USSR

DATE	GAP	SET	POS.	SONG BEFORE	SONG AFTER
10/31/94	681	2	2/30	Speak to Me	Dear Prudence
12/6/94	22	E	1/1	***	***

Has not been played in the last 416 shows.

Back on the Train

DATE	GAP	SET	POS.	SONG BEFORE	SONG AFTER
6/30/99	1007	1	5/8	Horn	Maze
7/1/99	1	1	9/10	Water in the Sky	Poor Heart
7/7/99	3	1	1/10	***	What's the Use
7/9/99	2	1	3/8	Farmhouse	Divided Sky
7/12/99	2	1	3/7	Down with Disease	What's the Use
7/16/99	3	1	7/9	Vultures	Maze
7/18/99	2	1	5/11	Bathtub Gin	If You Need a Fool
7/23/99	3	1	6/9	Fast Enough for You	David Bowie
7/26/99	3	1	2/11	Farmhouse	Vultures
7/31/99	3	1	3/8	Golgi Apparatus	Limb by Limb
9/12/99	5	1	5/10	Bathtub Gin	My Mind's Got A Mind
9/17/99	3	1	9/11	When Circus Comes	David Bowie
9/21/99	3	1	6/9	I Didn't Know	Birds of a Feather
9/24/99	2	1	8/10	Roggae	Guyute
9/29/99	4	2	5/12	Billy Breathes	Mike's Song
10/3/99	3	1	9/12	Ginseng Sullivan	Maze
10/7/99	2	2	4/9	Tube	Mike's Song
12/3/99	5	1	4/8	Bouncing	Billy Breathes
12/5/99	2	1	3/10	Gotta Jibboo	Taste
12/8/99	2	1	2/8	Limb by Limb	Down with Dis
12/16/99	6	1	6/10	Horn	Roggae
12/18/99	2	1	6/9	Heavy Things	First Tube
12/31/99	2	1	11/14	Catapult	Horn
5/22/00	2	1	5/9	Heavy Things	Split Open and
5/23/00	1	1	9/12	When Circus Comes	Gotta Jibboo
6/11/00	3	2	7/8	When Circus Comes	Harry Hood
6/14/00	2	2	1/5	***	Twist
6/16/00	2	1	2/10	Limb by Limb	Sample in a Ja
6/23/00	2	1	5/8	Heavy Things	David Bowie
6/30/00	5	2	5/9	The Inlaw Josie Wale	Makisupa Policeman
7/7/00	5	1	9/11	Maze	The Curtain
7/11/00	3	2	7/13	Moby Dick	Moby Dick

DATE	GAP	SET	POS.	SONG BEFORE	SONG AFTER
7/11/00	0	2	9/13	Moby Dick	Harry Hood
9/17/00	10	1	2/9	Guyute	Bathtub Gin
9/25/00	6	1	5/8	Tweezer	Water in the Sky
10/1/00	4	1	3/10	Wolfman's Brother	Beauty of my Dreams

Has not been played in the last 4 shows.

Bass Jam

DATE	GAP	SET	POS.	SONG BEFORE	SONG AFTER
5/2/94	611	2	9/9	Mike's Song	***
12/29/95	179	2	8/11	BBFCFM	La Grange
9/17/99	247	2	6/8	You Enjoy Myself	Wolfman's Brother

Has not been played in the last 82 shows.

Bathtub Gin

DATE	GAP	SET	POS.	SONG BEFORE	SONG AFTER
5/26/89	104	2	4/6	Split Open and Melt	Run Like Antel
5/27/89	1	1	10/11	Fluffhead	Good Time Ba
5/28/89	1	2	5/16	Weekapaug Groove	Sanity
6/30/89	2	2	5/8	Slave	Mike's Song
8/19/89	2	2	4/4	Divided Sky	***
9/9/89	3	1	7/11	McGrupp	Punch You in
9/14/89	1	2	2/2	Harry Hood	***
9/21/89	1	2	6/9	Possum	You Enjoy My
10/26/89	10	2	7/15	Walk Away	The Sloth
10/31/89	2	1	8/9	Walk Away	Possum
11/2/89	1	1	1/11	***	Foam
11/3/89	1	1	3/10	The Famous Mockingbi	My Sweet One
11/9/89	1	1	6/9	My Sweet One	You Enjoy My
11/10/89	1	2	2/12	Harry Hood	Mike's Song
11/11/89	1	1	3/8	Golgi Apparatus	AC/DC Bag
11/16/89	1	1	4/11	Weekapaug Groove	Foam
11/30/89	2	1	1/11	***	Divided Sky
12/1/89	1	1	6/9	Dinner and a Movie	My Sweet One
12/3/89	1	1	1/9	***	Funky Bitch
12/8/89	2	1	10/11	My Sweet One	Run Like Antel
12/9/89	1	1	9/10	Lawn Boy	Golgi Apparat
12/30/89	4	2	1/9	***	Split Open and
12/31/89	1	1	6/9	Run Like an Antelope	The Lizards
1/20/90	1	1	3/8	Carolina	You Enjoy My
1/27/90	1	2	2/13	Carolina	Ya Mar
1/28/90	1	2	7/10	You Enjoy Myself	Mike's Song
2/10/90	4	1	5/10	You Enjoy Myself	Bouncing
2/15/90	1	1	7/10	Caravan	Mike's Song
2/23/90	4	2	3/11	Reba	Jesus Just Left
2/24/90	1	2	7/9	La Grange	Lawn Boy
3/7/90	5	2	4/9	The Squirming Coil	Split Open and
3/8/90	1	2	2/12	Divided Sky	My Sweet One
4/7/90	9	1	7/12	Walk Away	Possum
4/14/90	5	2	5/11	Tweezer	Bold as Love
4/26/90	7	2	3/11	Esther	The Oh Kee Pa
5/10/90	6	1	7/8	My Sweet One	Possum
5/13/90	2	1	1/10	***	The Oh Kee Pa
6/16/90	13	2	5/8	My Sweet One	You Enjoy My
9/15/90	3	2	4/8	My Sweet One	Foam
10/19/90	14	1	10/15	Possum	The Landlady
2/15/91	26	2	2/10	David Bowie	Ya Mar
3/16/91	14	1	7/14	The Landlady	The Curtain
3/23/91	3	2	2/11	Chalk Dust Torture	The Oh Kee Pa
4/6/91	8	2	7/11	You Enjoy Myself	Icculus
4/22/91	9	2	2/10	Chalk Dust Torture	Uncle Pen
5/10/91	7	1	7/10	The Landlady	Buried Alive
5/12/91	2	2	2/13	David Bowie	Poor Heart
7/12/91	6	1	7/12	The Landlady	Donna Lee
7/14/91	2	3	5/10	Chalk Dust Torture	Mike's Song
7/20/91	4	1	8/10	The Landlady	Gumbo
7/24/91	3	1	6/10	Split Open and Melt	The Landlady
10/13/91	18	2	7/10	Llama	The Squirmin
10/19/91	4	2	2/10	Llama	Sparkle
10/28/91	4	2	6/11	Paul and Silas	You Enjoy My
10/31/91	2	1	8/11	Foam	Paul and Silas
11/13/91	2	2	5/9	Golgi Apparatus	The Squirmin
11/15/91	2	2	2/14	Llama	Poor Heart
11/16/91	1	2	3/9	My Sweet One	Brother
11/20/91	2	1	8/11	Paul and Silas	The Squirmin
11/22/91	2	2	4/10	The Landlady	Run Like Antel
12/5/91	1	1	7/10	Llama	It's Ice
3/11/92	6	2	5/11	The Lizards	My Mind's Got A Mind
3/27/92	12	2	8/13	Rift	Dinner and a
4/6/92	8	2	2/13	Dinner and a Movie	Paul and Silas
4/18/92	8	2	6/16	Manteca	Manteca Reprise
4/25/92	6	2	2/11	Maze	You Enjoy My
5/12/92	12	2	2/9	The Landlady	You Enjoy My
11/22/92	51	1	10/12	All Things Recnsdrd	Sweet Adeline
12/6/92	11	2	6/13	Big Ball Jam	You Enjoy My
12/30/92	9	2	3/12	Rift	You Enjoy My
2/21/93	17	2	7/10	The Lizards	Cracklin' Rosi
3/16/93	15	2	6/15	Tweezer	Esther
3/28/93	10	2	4/9	Mound	Big Ball Jam
4/24/93	18	2	3/10	Foam	Dinner and a
8/2/93	28	1	8/12	All Things Recnsdrd	Makisupa Policeman
8/13/93	8	2	3/9	Rift	Ya Mar
12/30/93	13	1	9/10	Rift	Freebird
4/9/94	6	1	4/10	Rift	Nellie Kane
4/18/94	8	2	4/13	Sparkle	Big Ball Jam
4/24/94	5	1	5/8	Maze	Dog Faced Boy
5/12/94	12	1	8/10	Foam	The Lizards
5/20/94	6	1	5/10	It's Ice	Fast Enough for You
6/17/94	15	1	7/9	Punch You in the Eye	Scent of a Mul
6/25/94	7	2	4/9	Sparkle	Axilla (Part II)
7/5/94	7	2	3/11	Sparkle	Lifeboy
10/14/94	15	1	7/12	Punch You in the Eye	Sweet Adeline
11/18/94	22	2	2/7	Llama	Lifeboy
12/28/94	18	1	4/10	Julius	Bouncing
6/20/95	15	1	5/9	Foam	If I Could
6/26/95	5	1	3/10	Don't You Wanna Go	NICU
10/25/95	11	2	3/10	Cars Trucks Buses	Llama
10/11/95	6	2	2/11	Possum	Mound
11/9/95	15	2	4/10	The Lizards	T.M.W.S.I.Y.
11/24/95	11	2	6/10	Scent of a Mule	Acoustic Army
11/30/95	4	1	6/10	NICU	Rift
12/5/95	4	2	2/8	Poor Heart	Keyboard Cavalry
12/15/95	7	2	4/8	It's Ice	Rotation Jam
12/29/95	4	2	3/11	Cars Trucks Buses	The Real Me
12/29/95	0	2	5/11	The Real Me	McGrupp
7/12/96	12	E	1/2	***	Johnny B. Goode
8/10/96	16	1	10/11	Rift	Cavern
8/16/96	4	1	2/8	Chalk Dust Torture	Ya Mar
10/17/96	3	2	3/8	Chalk Dust Torture	Scent of a Mul
10/27/96	8	2	2/9	Chalk Dust Torture	Rift
11/7/96	6	2	2/4	Suzy Greenberg	Bike
11/14/96	5	1	7/9	All Things Recnsdrd	Talk
11/19/96	4	2	3/7	A Day in the Life	The Vibration of Lif
11/29/96	5	1	6/9	Divided Sky	Life on Mars
12/29/96	7	2	3/10	A Day in the Life	The Lizards
2/17/97	6	1	9/10	Llama	Golgi Apparat
2/22/97	4	2	2/8	Chalk Dust Torture	Sparkle
7/1/97	19	2	3/7	Timber (Jerry)	Cities
7/10/97	6	1	4/8	Ginseng Sullivan	Llama
7/21/97	2	1	6/7	Ginseng Sullivan	Character Zer
7/25/97	3	1	5/7	Water in the Sky	Makisupa Policeman
8/3/97	6	1	1/10	***	Foam
8/10/97	4	1	1/10	***	Sparkle
8/17/97	5	2	2/5	Down with Disease	Uncle Pen
11/19/97	5	1	2/10	Julius	Llama
11/23/97	3	2	1/5	***	Down with Dis
12/6/97	8	1	4/9	Train Song	Foam
4/5/98	13	1	5/8	McGrupp	Cities
7/5/98	5	2	1/6	***	The Moma Dance
7/8/98	2	1	2/7	The Moma Dance	Punch You in
7/20/98	7	1	1/10	***	Dirt
7/29/98	6	1	1/8	***	Dog Gone Dog
8/9/98	8	1	2/9	Punch You in the Eye	The Lizards
8/16/98	4	1	2/11	Ginseng Sullivan	Rift
11/4/98	9	1	4/9	Guyute	Ya Mar
11/9/98	4	2	1/7	***	T.M.W.S.I.Y.
11/20/98	7	2	1/8	***	Piper
11/29/98	6	2	7/8	Possum	You Enjoy My
6/30/99	5	1	1/8	***	Farmhouse
7/10/99	7	1	7/8	Sparkle	Golgi Apparat
7/18/99	6	1	4/11	Water in the Sky	Back on the Train
7/26/99	6	1	8/11	Beauty of My Dreams	Mountains in the Mis
9/12/99	8	1	4/10	Mozambique	Back on the Train
9/22/99	7	1	7/10	Beauty of My Dreams	Mozambique
10/1/99	6	1	5/8	First Tube	Heavy Things
10/10/99	7	2	5/6	Train Song	Character Zer
12/2/99	1	2	3/6	Gotta Jibboo	Also Sprach
12/7/99	4	2	5/8	Bug	Simple
12/15/99	6	1	3/7	Farmhouse	Wolfman's Brother
12/31/99	5	2	5/35	Llama	Heavy Things
5/22/00	2	1	9/9	Horn	***
6/10/00	3	2	5/9	My Soul	Twist
6/23/00	7	1	3/8	My Soul	Heavy Things
6/28/00	3	1	4/6	Taste	Piper
7/3/00	4	1	5/10	Foam	My Soul
7/10/00	5	1	4/10	It's Ice	Buffalo Bill
9/8/00	5	2	5/6	Back @ Chicken Shack	Character Zer
9/17/00	6	1	3/9	Back on the Train	Limb By Limb
9/22/00	3	1	7/9	Dogs Stole Things	Heavy Things
9/29/00	5	1	7/8	Spock's Brain	Character Zer
10/7/00	6	1	6/8	Fee	Glide

Was played in the most recent show.

Beaumont Rag

DATE	GAP	SET	POS.	SONG BEFORE	SONG AFTER
10/14/94	668	2	7/10	Nellie Kane	Foreplay/Long Time
10/18/94	3	2	8/10	The Old Home Place	Nellie Kane

Has not been played in the last 448 shows.

Beauty of My Dreams

DATE	GAP	SET	POS.	SONG BEFORE	SONG AFTER
2/16/97	865	1	1/10	***	Split Open and
2/18/97	2	1	1/10	***	Cavern
2/25/97	5	2	1/10	***	Sample in a Ja
3/1/97	3	1	5/10	Weigh	Wolfman's Brother
3/18/97	2	1	6/10	My Soul	Harry Hood
6/13/97	1	1	3/8	Dogs Stole Things	Billy Breathes
6/16/97	2	1	6/10	Sample in a Jar	Theme From the Botto
6/19/97	1	E	1/3	***	Character Zer
6/24/97	4	1	2/12	Split Open and Melt	Dogs Stole Things
6/29/97	3	1	4/7	Bouncing	Chalk Dust Tor
7/3/97	3	1	4/8	Divided Sky	Taste
7/11/97	5	1	4/7	Stash	Wolfman's Brother
7/25/97	4	1	1/7	***	Wolfman's Brother
7/29/97	2	1	2/9	Theme From the Botto	Gumbo
8/6/97	5	1	3/8	Stash	Twist
8/13/97	5	1	8/11	Silent in the Mornin	Crosseyed and Painle
8/17/97	3	1	2/10	The Wedge	Dogs Stole Things
11/13/97	1	1	6/9	Split Open and Melt	My Soul
11/21/97	5	1	3/8	Split Open and Melt	Dogs Stole Things
12/9/97	12	1	8/10	Dogs Stole Things	Horn
12/31/97	7	1	4/10	My Sweet One	Wolfman's Brother

DATE	GAP	SET	POS	SONG BEFORE	SONG AFTER
4/3/98	2	1	6/9	Billy Breathes	Dogs Stole Things
6/30/98	3	1	10/13	Guyute	Funky Bitch
7/3/98	3	1	2/11	Stash	Sample in a Ja
7/8/98	3	1	4/7	Punch You in the Eye	Frankenstein
7/15/98	3	1	9/13	Brian and Robert	Cars Trucks Buses
7/19/98	3	1	2/8	The Moma Dance	Sample in a Ja
7/25/98	4	1	4/7	Roggae	Ya Mar
8/6/98	8	1	5/12	Roggae	Vultures
8/15/98	6	1	3/12	Simple	Roggae
11/7/98	12	1	9/10	Billy Breathes	Weekapaug Gr
7/1/99	21	1	5/10	Wolfman's Brother	Doin' My Time
7/16/99	10	1	2/9	Sample in a Jar	Dogs Stole Things
7/18/99	2	1	8/11	I'm Blue, Lonesome	The Moma Dance
7/26/99	6	1	7/11	NICU	Bathtub Gin
7/30b/99	2	1	3/8	Sample in a Jar	Stash
9/16/99	8	1	10/14	On Your Way Down	Stash
9/22/99	5	1	6/10	My Mind's Got A Mind	Bathtub Gin
12/12/99	22	1	5/8	Divided Sky	Bug
6/11/00	13	2	3/8	Free	Bug
6/22/00	5	1	3/9	Wolfman's Brother	Golgi Apparat
7/1/00	7	1	7/11	Tube	Roggae
7/12/00	8	1	6/9	Billy Breathes	Free
9/11/00	5	1	7/9	Horn	Ya Mar
9/27/00	11	1	3/10	My Friend My Friend	My Soul
10/1/00	3	1	4/10	Back on the Train	Vultures
10/5/00	2	1	7/10	Come On Baby, Let's	Axilla

Has not been played in the last 2 shows.

Been Caught Stealin'

DATE	GAP	SET	POS	SONG BEFORE	SONG AFTER
8/1/98	966	E	1/2	***	Tweezer Repri
11/8/98	22	E	1/1	***	***
11/19/98	7	2	8/8	Frankenstein	***
11/25/98	4	2	7/8	You Enjoy Myself	Llama
12/28/98	4	E	1/1	***	***

Has not been played in the last 116 shows.

Bell Boy

DATE	GAP	SET	POS	SONG BEFORE	SONG AFTER
10/31/95	759	2	14/17	Drowned	Doctor Jimmy

Has not been played in the last 360 shows.

Bertha

DATE	GAP	SET	POS	SONG BEFORE	SONG AFTER
11/3/84	2	1	4/10	Jam	St. Stephen Jam

Has not been played in the last 1117 shows.

Big Alligator Song

DATE	GAP	SET	POS	SONG BEFORE	SONG AFTER
12/30/99	1069	1	7/12	Che Hun Ta Mao	Possum

Has not been played in the last 50 shows.

Big Ball Jam

DATE	GAP	SET	POS	SONG BEFORE	SONG AFTER
11/19/92	455	2	10/15	Tweezer	Poor Heart
11/22/92	3	2	5/10	Tweezer	Tweezer
11/23/92	1	2	11/14	Jam	Weekapaug Gr
12/3/92	7	2	10/13	My Sweet One	Cracklin' Rosi
12/6/92	3	2	5/13	Paul and Silas	Bathtub Gin
12/8/92	2	2	14/15	My Sweet One	Sleeping Monkey
12/10/92	1	2	9/12	My Sweet One	Maze
12/11/92	1	2	9/12	Paul and Silas	The Squirmin
12/13/92	2	2	11/14	My Sweet One	Cracklin' Rosi
12/29/92	2	2	6/14	My Sweet One	Fast Enough for You
12/29/92	0	E	1/3	***	Carolina
12/30/92	1	2	9/12	Possum	Love You
12/31/92	1	2	7/10	My Sweet One	Stash
2/3/93	1	2	10/11	Terrapin	Possum
2/4/93	1	2	10/13	Uncle Pen	Lengthwise
2/6/93	2	2	11/14	Uncle Pen	Lengthwise
2/7/93	1	2	7/13	Tweezer	Glide
2/9/93	1	2	8/12	Sample in a Jar	Stash
2/11/93	2	2	8/12	Mound	Bouncing
2/12/93	1	2	5/11	Poor Heart	Fast Enough for You
2/13/93	1	2	8/11	You Enjoy Myself	Lengthwise
2/15/93	1	2	9/12	Poor Heart	Bike
2/17/93	1	2	7/11	My Sweet One	Horn
2/19/93	2	2	6/12	Ya Mar	Lawn Boy
2/20/93	1	2	19/22	Fast Enough for You	Terrapin
2/25/93	4	2	7/11	Uncle Pen	Fast Enough for You
2/26/93	1	2	7/11	Mound	You Enjoy My
2/27/93	1	2	5/12	Sample in a Jar	Ya Mar
3/5/93	3	2	8/11	My Sweet One	Love You
3/6/93	1	2	5/9	Paul and Silas	Fast Enough for You
3/8/93	1	2	5/10	Stash	My Friend My
3/9/93	1	2	11/15	Silent in the Mornin	Love You
3/12/93	1	2	7/11	Mound	Chalk Dust Tor
3/13/93	1	2	7/13	Uncle Pen	Mike's Song
3/14/93	1	2	9/11	Rift	The Great Gig in the
3/18/93	3	2	7/10	Uncle Pen	If I Only Had a Brai
3/21/93	2	2	8/12	My Sweet One	Cracklin' Rosi
3/24/93	2	2	6/12	Mound	Fast Enough for You
3/25/93	1	E	2/3	My Sweet One	Sweet Adeline
3/26/93	1	2	7/12	Silent in the Mornin	You Enjoy My
3/28/93	2	2	5/9	Bathtub Gin	You Enjoy My
3/30/93	1	2	5/15	Lifeboy	Weigh
3/31/93	1	2	8/10	Harry Hood	It's Ice
4/1/93	1	2	8/10	Poor Heart	Love You
4/2/93	1	2	11/13	The Lizards	Bike
4/10/93	4	2	6/13	Glide	Mike's Song
4/12/93	1	2	6/10	It's Ice	You Enjoy My
4/14/93	1	2	5/10	Mound	You Enjoy My
4/16/93	1	2	11/13	Uncle Pen	Bike
4/17/93	1	2	10/11	Cracklin' Rosie	The Squirmin
4/18/93	1	2	7/12	Mound	Mike's Song
4/20/93	1	2	4/12	Sample in a Jar	T.M.W.S.I.Y.
4/21/93	1	2	7/11	Silent in the Mornin	Mike's Song
4/22/93	1	2	6/10	The Lizards	You Enjoy My
4/23/93	1	2	6/12	Paul and Silas	Mike's Song
4/24/93	1	2	6/10	Mound	You Enjoy My
4/25/93	1	2	6/11	Uncle Pen	Mike's Song
4/27/93	1	2	6/10	The Lizards	You Enjoy My
4/29/93	1	2	5/13	Mound	Reba
4/30/93	1	2	6/10	Mound	Harry Hood
5/1/93	1	2	5/11	The Squirming Coil	Halley's Comet
5/2/93	1	2	5/10	The Lizards	Uncle Pen
5/5/93	2	2	7/10	Weigh	Ya Mar
5/6/93	1	2	5/11	Uncle Pen	The Squirmin
5/7/93	1	2	5/11	Fee	You Enjoy My
5/8/93	1	2	11/18	Jam	Mike's Song
5/29/93	1	1	8/10	You Enjoy Myself	Runaway Jim
7/17/93	4	2	6/12	Sparkle	Mike's Song
7/21/93	2	1	10/12	Runaway Jim	Purple Rain
7/23/93	2	2	7/11	Uncle Pen	You Enjoy My
8/8/93	12	2	8/11	Possum	Love You
8/12/93	3	2	8/10	Lawn Boy	Golgi Apparat
8/16/93	4	2	8/10	Poor Heart	Take the A-Trn
8/28/93	7	2	8/14	It's Ice	Purple Rain
12/29/93	2	2	8/11	Walk Away	If I Only Had a Brai
4/8/94	6	2	7/9	Bouncing	David Bowie
4/9/94	1	2	4/11	Peaches en Regalia	Demand
4/11/94	2	2	7/11	Sample in a Jar	You Enjoy My
4/13/94	1	2	5/10	Reba	Fee
4/17/94	4	2	6/9	Reba	Maze
4/18/94	1	2	5/13	Bathtub Gin	Ya Mar
4/20/94	1	2	5/11	Sample in a Jar	Harry Hood
4/21/94	1	2	8/10	Scent of a Mule	Possum
4/25/94	4	2	9/10	Bouncing	BBFCFM
5/17/94	15	2	6/9	Uncle Pen	Sample in a Ja
5/19/94	1	2	8/10	Julius	Harry Hood
5/21/94	2	2	5/9	Contact	Julius
5/25/94	3	2	6/9	Contact	Julius
6/13/94	8	2	9/11	Scent of a Mule	Terrapin
6/16/94	2	2	6/11	The Famous Mockingbi	Down with Dis
6/17/94	1	2	13/15	Sparkle	Julius
6/22/94	4	2	18/20	My Sweet One	Jesus Just Left
7/9/94	13	2	8/10	Sparkle	Harry Hood
7/14/94	3	2	8/10	Sparkle	Harry Hood
10/16/94	11	2	5/9	Fluffhead	Run Like Antel
10/25/94	6	2	9/11	Jesus Just Left	If I Only Had a Brai
12/9/94	30	2	6/9	Julius	Cracklin' Rosi

Has not been played in the last 413 shows.

Big Ball Jam Reprise

DATE	GAP	SET	POS	SONG BEFORE	SONG AFTER
3/8/93	505	E	3/3	Chalk Dust Torture	***

Has not been played in the last 614 shows.

Big Black Furry Creature From Mars

DATE	GAP	SET	POS	SONG BEFORE	SONG AFTER
8/21/87	27	3	1/7	***	McGrupp
8/29/87	1	2	5/13	Makisupa Policeman	Flat Fee
9/2/87	1	1	9/13	Possum	Makisupa Policeman
9/21/87	1	2	3/5	The Curtain With	Suzy Greenber
10/31/87	3	1	11/11	You Enjoy Myself	***
11/19/87	2	3	5/14	Divided Sky	Dinner and a
1/27/88	1	3	6/8	Bike	Camel Walk
2/8/88	2	3	9/9	Jesus Just Left	***
4/22/88	8	2	6/13	Shaggy Dog	You Enjoy My
5/14/88	1	1	7/11	The Lizards	Jesus Just Left
5/25/88	3	3	8/11	I Know a Little	Corrine Corrina
7/25/88	10	3	3/4	Harpua	Sanity
8/6/88	3	2	5/6	Sanity	Slave
9/13/88	4	3	3/8	Andy's Chest	Dave's Energy Guide
9/13/88	0	3	5/8	Dave's Energy Guide	Sanity
11/3/88	5	3	4/6	I Didn't Know	Harpua
1/26/89	7	2	8/10	Contact	Foam
2/6/89	1	3	4/9	Harry Hood	Ballad - Curtis Loew
3/30/89	11	3	4/6	AC/DC Bag	Satin Doll
10/6/89	26	1	13/13	Highway to Hell	***
12/9/89	23	E	2/2	Contact	***
1/28/90	8	E	2/2	Lawn Boy	***
2/25/90	11	2	6/6	Fluffhead	***
3/9/90	6	2	11/11	Contact	***
4/7/90	8	2	2/3	Harpua	Contact
4/22/90	10	2	7/9	Esther	Harry Hood
4/28/90	3	E	1/1	***	***
5/11/90	6	E	1/1	***	***
6/1/90	8	1	11/12	Fee	Contact
6/7/90	3	E	2/2	Lawn Boy	***
6/16/90	3	E	2/3	Contact	Good Time Ba
10/31/90	19	E	2/2	Uncle Pen	***
11/8/90	4	2	8/8	You Enjoy Myself	***
11/24/90	4	2	10/12	Good Times Bad Times	Lawn Boy
2/3/91	11	E	2/2	Jesus Just Left	***
2/15/91	5	E	2/4	Caravan	Contact
3/8/91	10	1	11/11	Tweezer	***
3/13/91	2	E	2/2	Take the A-Train	***
3/23/91	5	E	2/2	Take the A-Train	***
3/29/91	2	2	8/8	Bouncing	***
4/4/91	4	2	10/10	Love You	***
4/12/91	4	E	2/3	Contact	The Squirmin
4/19/91	4	E	2/2	Paul and Silas	***
4/25/91	4	2	10/10	Divided Sky	***
5/3/91	5	E	2/2	Take the A-Train	***
5/11/91	4	2		Love You	***
5/17/91	3	2	9/9	Bike	***
7/11/91	3	E	2/2	Contact	***
7/14/91	3	E	2/2	Contact	***
7/19/91	3	2	8/8	The Mango Song	***
7/24/91	4	E	2/2	Contact	***

DATE	GAP	SET	POS.	SONG BEFORE	SONG AFTER
9/25/91	5	E	2/2	All Things Recnsdrd	***
9/28/91	3	E	2/2	Contact	***
10/11/91	8	E	2/2	Sweet Adeline	***
11/2/91	14	E	2/2	Contact	***
11/12/91	5	E	2/4	Ya Mar	Split Open and
11/23/91	9	E	2/2	Jesus Just Left	***
3/13/92	12	1	11/12	Run Like an Antelope	Run Like Antel
3/30/92	12	2	7/13	Vacuum Solo	The Squirmin
4/6/92	6	E	1/1	***	***
4/18/92	8	E	2/2	Contact	***
4/24/92	5	E	2/2	Contact	***
5/2/92	5	E	2/2	Sleeping Monkey	***
5/8/92	5	E	1/1	***	***
6/23/92	11	1	6/8	Uncle Pen	If I Only Had a Brai
11/19/92	40	2	8/15	Tweezer	Tweezer
11/21/92	2	E	2/2	Buffalo Bill	***
2/7/93	27	E	3/3	Contact	***
2/21/93	11	2	10/10	The Squirming Coil	***
2/25/93	3	2	11/11	Golgi Apparatus	***
3/6/93	6	2	9/9	Cracklin' Rosie	***
3/13/93	4	E	3/3	Amazing Grace	***
3/28/93	12	E	2/2	Contact	***
4/17/93	12	E	2/2	Sweet Adeline	***
5/2/93	12	2	10/10	Cracklin' Rosie	***
7/23/93	14	2	9/11	You Enjoy Myself	Chalk Dust Tor
8/8/93	12	1	1/11	***	Foam
12/29/93	16	2	6/11	Contact	Walk Away
4/8/94	6	E	2/2	Contact	***
4/25/94	15	2	10/10	Big Ball Jam	***
4/30/94	3	2	10/10	Purple Rain	***
5/12/94	8	2	11/11	Contact	***
5/16/94	3	2	3/11	Run Like an Antelope	Run Like Antel
5/16/94	0	2	9/11	You Enjoy Myself	Amazing Grce
5/16/94	0	2	11/11	Amazing Grace	***
6/16/94	17	2	9/11	Contact	Purple Rain
6/21/94	4	2	8/16	Chalk Dust Torture	Ginseng Sulli-van
7/6/94	12	2	6/10	Chalk Dust Torture	Sample in a Ja
7/6/94	0	2	8/10	Sample in a Jar	Harry Hood
7/13/94	4	2	9/13	Tweezer	Tweezer
10/27/94	20	2	5/7	Contact	Down with Dis
11/3/94	5	2	6/8	You Enjoy Myself	Harry Hood
11/13/94	3	2	6/8	The Mango Song	Amazing Grce
11/22/94	7	2	8/13	Runaway Jim	I'm Blue, Lonesome
12/1/94	6	2	4/10	Tweezer	Makisupa Po-liceman
7/3/95	35	2	7/10	The Lizards	A Day in the Life
10/19/95	16	2	7/10	Lawn Boy	Kung
10/22/95	3	2	7/11	Makisupa Policeman	Life on Mars
11/18/95	14	2	7/10	Contact	Acoustic Army
11/18/95	0	2	9/10	Acoustic Army	Cavern
11/28/95	6	2	9/10	Contact	Funky Bitch
12/29/95	17	2	7/11	McGrupp	Bass Jam
6/6/96	4	1	6/8	Theme From the Botto	Scent of a Mul
8/6/96	22	2	5/8	A Day in the Life	Purple Rain
11/21/97	118	2	3/6	Roses Are Free	Ghost
11/21/98	63	1	3/9	Wilson	Lawn Boy
12/30/98	8	1	2/12	Chalk Dust Torture	Wilson
10/3/99	44	2	5/8	Avenu Malkenu	David Bowie
9/20/00	58	2	8/9	Guyute	Drowned

Has not been played in the last 12 shows.

Big Black Furry Creature from Mars Reprise

DATE	GAP	SET	POS.	SONG BEFORE	SONG AFTER
6/21/94	642	2	10/16	Ginseng Sullivan	Dog Faced Boy

Has not been played in the last 477 shows.

Big Leg Emma

DATE	GAP	SET	POS.	SONG BEFORE	SONG AFTER
5/3/85	5	1	4/4	Dave's Energy Guide	***
5/21/88	44	3	1/6	***	Rocky Top
6/19/88	3	1	7/8	Suzy Greenberg	You Enjoy My

Has not been played in the last 1067 shows.

Bike

DATE	GAP	SET	POS.	SONG BEFORE	SONG AFTER
11/19/87	35	3	13/14	La Grange	Slave
1/27/88	1	3	5/8	Golgi Apparatus	BBFCFM
2/8/88	2	3	6/9	Harry Hood	Fee
5/21/88	11	2	8/9	Fluffhead	Good Time Ba
2/7/89	32	3	5/6	Slave	Whipping Post
5/12/89	19	1	1/15	***	Mike's Song
10/13/89	20	2	1/8	***	T.M.W.S.I.Y.
4/21/90	62	1	9/10	Suzy Greenberg	Run Like Antel
11/10/90	48	2	7/8	Divided Sky	Possum
5/17/91	64	2	8/9	Cavern	BBFCFM
11/20/91	54	2	7/8	The Landlady	Cavern
4/7/92	34	2	9/11	Maze	My Mind's Got A Mind
5/7/92	21	2	10/12	Fee	The Squirmin
12/28/92	73	2	7/9	The Lizards	Harry Hood
2/9/93	9	2	11/12	The Lizards	Amazing Grce
2/15/93	5	2	10/12	Big Ball Jam	Fee
3/16/93	20	2	10/15	You Enjoy Myself	Lengthwise
3/16/93	0	2	12/15	Lengthwise	Lawn Boy
4/2/93	14	2	12/13	Big Ball Jam	Chalk Dust Tor
4/16/93	7	2	12/13	Big Ball Jam	Highway to Hell
4/24/93	7	2	8/10	You Enjoy Myself	Harry Hood
8/2/93	28	2	8/9	Weekapaug Groove	Run Like Antel
5/6/94	48	2	8/9	Julius	David Bowie
5/21/94	11	2	7/9	Julius	Harry Hood
6/14/94	12	2	8/9	You Enjoy Myself	Possum
10/29/94	43	2	8/11	You Enjoy Myself	Run Like Antel
12/6/94	23	2	9/12	Weekapaug Groove	I'm Blue, Lonesome
11/24/95	68	2	8/10	Acoustic Army	Fee
7/23/96	39	2	8/9	Weekapaug Groove	Slave
11/7/96	29	2	3/4	Bathtub Gin	You Enjoy My Tube
8/3/98	129	2	5/7	Meat	Tube
11/6/98	18	2	6/7	Fluffhead	Harry Hood
7/30b/99	42	2	4/6	Reba	Runaway Jim
6/15/00	51	2	3/4	The Lizards	You Enjoy My
9/12/00	23	2	4/8	Split Open and Melt	Also Sprach

Has not been played in the last 17 shows.

Bill Bailey Won't You Please Come Home

DATE	GAP	SET	POS.	SONG BEFORE	SONG AFTER
7/28/93	562	E	2/2	Piano Duet	***
4/22/94	42	E	2/2	Piano Duet	***
11/18/95	163	E	1/1	***	***

Has not been played in the last 352 shows.

Billy Breathes

DATE	GAP	SET	POS.	SONG BEFORE	SONG AFTER
9/27/95	735	2	4/8	David Bowie	Keyboard Cav-alry
9/28/95	1	1	3/9	Runaway Jim	Scent of a Mul
9/29/95	1	2	6/8	Split Open and Melt	Cryin'
10/3/95	3	2	5/9	Harry Hood	Faht
10/6/95	2	1	3/9	Stash	Reba
10/13/95	4	1	4/9	Maze	I'm Blue, Lonesome
10/19/95	4	1	10/11	Split Open and Melt	Cavern
10/28/95	7	1	7/10	The Lizards	Acoustic Army
11/14/95	7	1	3/9	Foam	Divided Sky
11/19/95	4	2	5/8	Tweezer	Scent of a Mul
11/25/95	4	1	4/9	David Bowie	Taste That Surrounds
12/4/95	6	2	5/9	Run Like an Antelope	Cars Trucks Buses
12/9/95	4	1	8/10	Free	Dog Faced Boy
10/16/96	42	1	6/12	Poor Heart	Mound
10/18/96	2	1	8/10	Divided Sky	Taste
10/25/96	5	1	5/10	Maze	Mound
10/29/96	3	1	8/10	Train Song	Poor Heart
11/3/96	3	1	3/9	Runaway Jim	The Sloth
11/6/96	1	1	8/9	Punch You in the Eye	David Bowie

DATE	GAP	SET	POS.	SONG BEFORE	SONG AFTER
11/18/96	9	1	5/10	Taste	Guelah Pa-pyrus
11/22/96	2	2	4/10	Maze	Swept Away
12/28/96	10	1	5/9	It's Ice	Ginseng Sulli-van
2/14/97	5	1	7/9	It's Ice	Uncle Pen
2/17/97	2	1	7/10	Timber (Jerry)	Llama
2/21/97	3	2	6/9	AC/DC Bag	Reba
2/23/97	2	E	1/2	***	Rocky Top
3/1/97	4	2	7/8	The Mango Song	Theme From the Botto
6/13/97	3	1	4/8	Beauty of My Dreams	Limb by Limb
6/25/97	8	1	4/11	Taste	AC/DC Bag
7/3/97	5	2	3/6	Cars Trucks Buses	Sparkle
7/23/97	8	1	9/10	Split Open and Melt	Possum
7/26/97	2	1	5/9	Stash	Cars Trucks Buses
8/10/97	9	1	6/10	Cars Trucks Buses	Split Open and
8/14/97	3	1	9/10	Train Song	Run Like Antel
11/16/97	5	1	6/11	The Old Home Place	Cars Trucks Buses
11/22/97	4	1	6/8	Train Song	Frankenstein
4/3/98	20	1	5/9	Train Song	Beauty of My Dreams
8/6/98	27	1	8/12	Train Song	Fluffhead
10/18/98	11	1	2/12	Hello My Baby	Piper
11/7/98	7	1	8/10	Fikus	Beauty of My Dreams
7/1/99	21	1	2/10	Punch You in the Eye	Guyute
7/7/99	3	1	3/10	What's the Use	My Mind's Got A Mind
7/16/99	7	1	5/9	Limb by Limb	Vultures
9/11/99	15	1	6/9	Punch You in the Eye	Heavy Things
9/16/99	3	1	13/14	Train Song	Run Like Antel
9/29/99	10	2	4/12	Down with Disease	Back on the Train
12/3/99	10	1	5/8	Back on the Train	AC/DC Bag
5/22/00	16	1	3/9	Chalk Dust Torture	Heavy Things
6/9/00	2	1	3/9	Taste	Poor Heart
7/12/00	22	1	5/9	Heavy Things	Beauty of My Dreams
10/1/00	19	1	7/10	The Inlaw Josie Wale	Llama

Has not been played in the last 4 shows.

Birds of a Feather

DATE	GAP	SET	POS.	SONG BEFORE	SONG AFTER
4/2/98	941	2	3/9	Simple	Wolfman's Brother
4/4/98	2	2	1/6	***	Also Sprach
6/30/98	2	2	2/12	The Moma Dance	Wolfman's Brother
7/2/98	2	1	1/11	***	Cars Trucks Buses
7/5/98	2	1	1/9	***	Taste
7/8/98	2	2	2/7	Wilson	Dirt
7/15/98	3	1	12/13	Roggae	Loving Cup
7/20/98	4	1	6/10	My Sweet One	Theme From the Botto
7/26/98	4	1	1/7	***	Too Much Of Evrythng
7/29/98	2	1	8/8	Glide	***
8/1/98	2	1	7/9	Fikus	Lawn Boy
8/2/98	1	1	9/9	Too Much Of Evrythng	***
8/6/98	2	2	1/7	***	Wolfman's Brother
8/9/98	3	1	5/9	The Moma Dance	Esther
8/16/98	4	1	9/11	Frankie Says	Guyute
10/3/98	1	1	1/10	***	Farmhouse
10/15/98	1	2	8/10	Frankie Says	Lawn Boy
10/29/98	3	1	8/10	Frankie Says	McGrupp
10/31/98	2	1	4/10	Roggae	Sneakin' Sally
11/4/98	2	1	6/9	Ya Mar	Brian and Robert
11/6/98	1	E	1/2	***	Hello My Baby
11/11/98	4	1	6/8	Tela	Theme From the Botto
11/13/98	1	2	4/6	Dirt	Meat

DATE	GAP	SET	POS.	SONG BEFORE	SONG AFTER
11/18/98	3	1	2/9	Back @ Chicken Shack	Farmhouse
11/27/98	6	1	11/11	When Circus Comes	***
12/28/98	3	2	3/6	Wolfman's Brother	When Circus Comes
6/30/99	4	2	3/10	Free	Simple
7/8/99	5	2	1/9	***	If I Only Had a Brai
7/10/99	2	2	3/5	Mountains in the Mis	When Circus Comes
7/17/99	5	1	3/10	Boogie On Reggae	Guelah Papyrus
7/23/99	4	2	3/5	Free	Meatstick
7/25/99	2	2	1/6	***	Walk Away
7/30b/99	3	1	1/8	***	Sample in a Ja
9/9/99	3	2	1/9	***	Ha Ha Ha
9/12/99	3	1	8/10	Frankie Says	Lawn Boy
9/21/99	6	1	7/9	Back on the Train	Theme From the Botto
9/26/99	4	2	5/7	Heavy Things	Meat
12/10/99	17	1	8/10	Roggae	Guyute
12/17/99	6	2	1/6	***	The Moma Dance
6/11/00	9	2	1/8	***	Free
6/24/00	7	2	1/8	***	Bug
6/29/00	3	2	1/10	***	Catapult
7/12/00	10	2	1/5	***	Piper
9/8/00	3	2	1/6	***	Windora Bug
9/15/00	5	1	4/8	Corrine Corrina	Windora Bug
9/23/00	5	2	1/7	***	Tweezer

Has not been played in the last 10 shows.

Birthday Jam

DATE	GAP	SET	POS.	SONG BEFORE	SONG AFTER
10/31/94	681	2	19/30	Julia	Yer Blues

Has not been played in the last 438 shows.

Bitchin' Again

DATE	GAP	SET	POS.	SONG BEFORE	SONG AFTER
8/3/91	311	E	3/5	Self	Crimes of the Mind

Has not been played in the last 808 shows.

Bittersweet Motel

DATE	GAP	SET	POS.	SONG BEFORE	SONG AFTER
7/21/98	959	2	3/8	Simple	Weekapaug Gr
7/26/98	3	E	2/2	Punch You in the Eye	***
7/29/98	2	E	3/3	Golgi Apparatus	***
8/2/98	3	E	2/2	Harry Hood	***
8/7/98	3	1	7/10	Foam	Ghost
8/11/98	3	1	5/11	Time Loves a Hero	Reba
8/16/98	3	3	6/7	Character Zero	While My Guitar Gent
11/2/98	8	1	6/9	Driver	Limb by Limb
7/21/99	38	1	10/10	Taste	***
12/16/99	44	E	1/2	***	Tweezer Repri
12/31/99	4	2	26/35	Silent in the Mornin	Piper
7/3/00	19	2	7/7	Chalk Dust Torture	***
9/15/00	15	1	8/8	Golgi Apparatus	***

Has not been played in the last 15 shows.

Black-Eyed Katy

DATE	GAP	SET	POS.	SONG BEFORE	SONG AFTER
11/13/97	916	1	2/9	Chalk Dust Torture	Theme From the Botto
11/16/97	2	1	3/11	My Soul	Farmhouse
11/22/97	4	2	3/5	Tweezer	Piper
11/23/97	1	1	3/9	Theme From the Botto	Sparkle
11/28/97	2	1	6/8	Farmhouse	Theme From the Botto
12/5/97	5	1	4/10	Funky Bitch	Sparkle
12/30/97	9	E	2/4	Carini	Sneakin' Sally

Has not been played in the last 180 shows.

Blackbird

DATE	GAP	SET	POS.	SONG BEFORE	SONG AFTER
10/31/94	681	2	12/30	I'm So Tired	Piggies
11/22/94	12	2	6/13	The Curtain	Runaway Jim

Has not been played in the last 426 shows.

Blister in the Sun

DATE	GAP	SET	POS.	SONG BEFORE	SONG AFTER
7/9/98	952	2	5/8	Scent of a Mule	Scent of a Mul

Has not been played in the last 167 shows.

Blister in the Sun Jam

DATE	GAP	SET	POS.	SONG BEFORE	SONG AFTER
7/26/97	901	2	4/8	Harry Hood	Harry Hood

Has not been played in the last 218 shows.

Blue Bayou

DATE	GAP	SET	POS.	SONG BEFORE	SONG AFTER
7/16/92	426	E	1/2	***	The Squirmin

Has not been played in the last 693 shows.

Blue Bossa

DATE	GAP	SET	POS.	SONG BEFORE	SONG AFTER
7/12/88	57	2	1/9	***	Take the A-Trn
7/23/88	1	2	7/10	Satin Doll	La Grange

Has not been played in the last 1061 shows.

Bob Dylan Band

DATE	GAP	SET	POS.	SONG BEFORE	SONG AFTER
4/15/86	13	1	8/14	Have Mercy	Dog Gone Dog

Has not been played in the last 1106 shows.

Bohemian Rhapsody

DATE	GAP	SET	POS.	SONG BEFORE	SONG AFTER
12/31/96	862	3	6/7	Run Like an Antelope	Julius

Has not been played in the last 257 shows.

Bold As Love

DATE	GAP	SET	POS.	SONG BEFORE	SONG AFTER
7/11/88	56	1	7/11	Fire	Col. Forbin's A
7/23/88	2	1	12/13	Walk Away	No Dogs Allowed
7/24/88	1	1	10/10	Weekapaug Groove	***
7/25/88	1	2	4/6	Weekapaug Groove	Light Up Or Leave Me
9/8/88	5	1	8/8	The Famous Mockingbi	***
9/12/88	1	1	4/4	Fee	***
9/24/88	3	1	10/10	Divided Sky	***
10/31/88	2	1	8/12	Golgi Apparatus	La Grange
11/3/88	1	2	7/9	Contact	Take the A-Trn
11/5/88	1	2	3/11	Peaches en Regalia	The Lizards
11/11/88	1	2	6/8	Fee	The Lizards
12/2/88	1	1	3/7	Golgi Apparatus	Take the A-Trn
3/12/89	13	1	7/8	Golgi Apparatus	Foam
3/30/89	3	1	1/8	***	McGrupp
5/6/89	7	1	9/13	Possum	AC/DC Bag
5/9/89	1	2	12/14	The Lizards	Harpua
5/13/89	2	2	2/7	Suzy Greenberg	The Lizards
5/20/89	1	2	1/9	***	Mike's Song
5/26/89	2	1	1/9	***	AC/DC Bag
8/17/89	5	3	2/8	The Oh Kee Pa Ceremo	Punch You in
8/19/89	1	1	8/13	Rocky Top	The Mango Song
8/26/89	2	2	2/9	Fishing Hole Theme	Ya Mar
10/6/89	5	1	7/13	Golgi Apparatus	Dinner and a
3/17/90	51	2	2/6	Killer Joe	The Oh Kee Pa
4/14/90	10	2	6/11	Bathtub Gin	Wilson
4/18/90	1	2	8/12	The Oh Kee Pa Ceremo	Lawn Boy
11/19/92	276	E	1/1	***	***
11/22/92	3	E	1/1	***	Carolina
11/27/92	3	E	1/1	***	***
12/3/92	5	E	1/1	***	***
12/10/92	6	E	1/3	***	Carolina
2/11/93	15	E	1/2	***	Amazing Grce
2/26/93	12	E	1/2	***	Sweet Adeline
8/11/93	73	E	2/2	Sweet Adeline	***
8/25/93	10	E	1/2	***	Rocky Top
4/17/94	18	E	2/2	Cracklin' Rosie	***
4/25/94	7	E	2/2	Amazing Grace	***
5/14/94	13	E	1/1	***	***
5/21/94	5	E	1/1	***	***
12/28/94	83	E	1/1	***	***
6/16/95	12	E	1/1	***	***
6/24/95	6	E	1/1	***	***
10/13/95	20	E	1/1	***	***
12/2/95	31	E	1/1	***	***
12/14/95	8	E	1/1	***	***
11/27/96	67	1	9/9	Theme From the Botto	***
2/18/97	15	E	1/1	***	***
11/14/97	50	E	1/1	***	***
11/23/97	6	2	5/5	Down with Disease	***
12/5/97	7	E	1/1	***	***
12/28/97	7	E	1/1	***	***
4/5/98	7	E	1/1	***	***
7/26/98	18	2	5/6	Simple	Sample in a Ja
11/9/98	27	1	10/10	NICU	***
11/21/98	8	1	13/13	Guyute	***
9/21/99	43	E	2/2	Reba	***
10/1/99	7	E	1/1	***	***
12/2/99	8	E	1/1	***	***
6/25/00	29	E	2/2	Uncle Pen	***
9/22/00	24	E	1/1	***	***
10/6/00	10	2	10/10	Brian and Robert	***

Has not been played in the last 1 show.

Boogie on Reggae Woman

DATE	GAP	SET	POS.	SONG BEFORE	SONG AFTER
2/21/87	18	2	11/15	Swing Low Sweet Chrt	Ya Mar
4/29/87	4	3	7/14	Run Like an Antelope	Timber (Jerry)
3/21/88	21	1	6/15	Divided Sky	Timber (Jerry)
9/13/88	24	2	2/6	Ride Captain Ride	Cities
12/7/97	865	2	3/6	Wolfman's Brother	Reba
7/9/98	20	1	2/8	Carini	NICU
8/2/98	15	1	5/9	Silent in the Mornin	Reba
11/21/98	30	1	6/13	Cry Baby Cry	NICU
12/29/98	7	2	4/5	Also Sprach	You Enjoy My
7/17/99	15	1	2/10	Tube	Birds of a Feather
7/25/99	6	1	7/8	I Saw It Again	Cavern
9/18/99	13	2	1/7	***	Meatstick
9/24/99	4	E	1/2	***	Chalk Dust Tor
10/7/99	9	2	1/9	***	Heavy Things
12/2/99	4	2	1/6	***	Gotta Jibboo
12/11/99	7	2	1/5	***	Sneakin' Sally
12/30/99	7	E	1/2	***	Tweezer Repri
5/23/00	4	E	1/2	***	Cavern
7/7/00	19	1	4/11	Divided Sky	Funky Bitch
7/14/00	5	2	4/11	Gotta Jibboo	Stash
9/9/00	3	1	5/8	Maze	Roggae
9/18/00	6	2	1/4	***	Twist
9/25/00	5	E	1/3	***	Driver
10/6/00	7	1	3/7	Stash	Mellow Mood

Has not been played in the last 1 show.

Born Under Punches (The Heat goes on)

DATE	GAP	SET	POS.	SONG BEFORE	SONG AFTER
10/31/96	835	2	1/8	***	Crosseyed and Painle

Has not been played in the last 284 shows.

Born to Run

DATE	GAP	SET	POS.	SONG BEFORE	SONG AFTER
7/16/99	1018	E	1/1	***	***

Has not been played in the last 101 shows.

Bouncing Around the Room

DATE	GAP	SET	POS.	SONG BEFORE	SONG AFTER
1/20/90	146	2	2/10	Suzy Greenberg	Reba
1/27/90	1	1	7/13	My Sweet One	Wilson
1/28/90	1	2	3/10	Run Like an Antelope	Caravan
2/9/90	3	1	6/12	Walk Away	AC/DC Bag
2/10/90	1	1	6/10	Bathtub Gin	Possum
2/15/90	1	2	5/5	Split Open and Melt	Possum
2/16/90	1	2	3/7	Caravan	The Sloth
2/22/90	2	1	3/9	You Enjoy Myself	Ya Mar
2/23/90	1	1	10/11	Walk Away	Run Like Antel
2/25/90	2	1	7/11	The Squirming Coil	David Bowie
3/9/90	6	1	5/11	Ya Mar	Col. Forbin's A
3/11/90	2	2	4/13	My Sweet One	Dinner and a
3/17/90	1	1	4/10	Dinner and a Movie	My Sweet One
4/6/90	4	1	8/11	Dinner and a Movie	The Oh Kee Pa
4/13/90	5	1	3/10	Dinner and a Movie	Fluffhead
4/20/90	4	1	7/10	Dinner and a Movie	Col. Forbin's A
4/22/90	2	2	2/9	Dinner and a Movie	You Enjoy My
4/25/90	1	2	9/12	Dinner and a Movie	Mike's Song
4/26/90	1	1	6/9	Dinner and a Movie	I Didn't Know

DATE	GAP	SET	POS.	SONG BEFORE	SONG AFTER
4/28/90	1	1	6/11	Dinner and a Movie	Possum
4/29/90	1	1	6/13	Dinner and a Movie	Uncle Pen
5/4/90	1	2	5/10	Avenu Malkenu	Possum
5/6/90	1	1	2/8	Possum	Uncle Pen
5/10/90	2	1	3/8	Uncle Pen	Divided Sky
5/11/90	1	1	6/9	Foam	Possum
5/13/90	1	1	5/10	Dinner and a Movie	Runaway Jim
5/15/90	1	1	8/12	Uncle Pen	Split Open and
5/19/90	1	2	7/10	Dinner and a Movie	Rift
5/23/90	1	1	8/10	Uncle Pen	Possum
5/24/90	1	1	2/9	The Sloth	Tweezer
5/30/90	1	1	6/14	Dinner and a Movie	Run Like Antel
5/31/90	1	1	4/12	Dinner and a Movie	Caravan
6/2/90	2	1	3/9	Dinner and a Movie	Reba
6/5/90	1	2	5/10	Dinner and a Movie	My Sweet One
6/7/90	1	2	3/10	Dinner and a Movie	Tweezer
6/8/90	1	1	2/8	Foam	You Enjoy My
6/9/90	1	1	5/10	Dinner and a Movie	Tweezer
6/16/90	1	1	7/10	Uncle Pen	Timber (Jerry)
9/13/90	1	1	10/11	Paul and Silas	Possum
9/14/90	1	1	2/11	Suzy Greenberg	The Landlady
9/16/90	2	1	2/14	Dinner and a Movie	The Sloth
9/20/90	1	2	3/14	AC/DC Bag	The Squirmin
9/22/90	2	2	6/10	Uncle Pen	Stash
9/28/90	1	1	2/10	The Landlady	The Oh Kee Pa
9/29/90	1	1	6/9	Buried Alive	Possum
10/4/90	2	2	2/8	Reba	Foam
10/5/90	1	1	12/13	The Asse Festival	Run Like Antel
10/6/90	1	1	4/13	Dinner and a Movie	Foam
10/7/90	1	2	2/8	Buried Alive	Tweezer
10/8/90	1	1	3/10	The Landlady	Foam
10/12/90	1	1	4/9	Dinner and a Movie	Uncle Pen
10/19/90	1	1	12/15	The Landlady	The Oh Kee Pa
10/30/90	1	1	2/9	The Landlady	Donna Lee
10/31/90	1	1	6/11	Stash	You Enjoy My
11/2/90	1	1	3/14	The Landlady	Divided Sky
11/3/90	1	1	2/11	Dinner and a Movie	Llama
11/4/90	1	1	4/10	The Curtain	Tube
11/8/90	1	2	6/8	Dinner and a Movie	You Enjoy My
11/10/90	1	1	3/11	The Landlady	Runaway Jim
11/17/90	2	1	5/11	Runaway Jim	You Enjoy My
11/24/90	1	2	2/12	Llama	Stash
11/30/90	2	1	7/11	Dinner and a Movie	Tweezer
12/7/90	2	1	3/9	Stash	The Landlady
12/8/90	1	2	4/9	Dinner and a Movie	Run Like Antel
12/28/90	1	E	1/2	***	Highway to Hell
12/29/90	1	2	8/10	Dinner and a Movie	Destiny Unbound
12/31/90	1	1	5/12	The Landlady	My Sweet One
2/1/91	1	1	9/10	Split Open and Melt	David Bowie
2/3/91	2	2	7/9	Split Open and Melt	The Oh Kee Pa
2/7/91	1	1	7/10	Split Open and Melt	Possum
2/8/91	1	2	9/11	Horn	The Lizards
2/9/91	1	2	5/10	The Landlady	Harry Hood
2/14/91	1	2	9/12	Alumni Blues	I Didn't Know
2/16/91	2	1	7/12	The Landlady	Llama
2/19/91	1	2	9/15	Split Open and Melt	Love You
2/20/91	1	1	7/11	My Sweet One	Llama
2/21/91	1	2	4/9	The Landlady	Stash
2/26/91	1	2	5/12	Stash	The Landlady
2/27/91	1	1	9/10	Split Open and Melt	Fire
2/28/91	1	1	2/13	The Landlady	Foam
3/1/91	1	1	8/12	Dinner and a Movie	Buried Alive
3/6/91	1	1	10/11	My Sweet One	David Bowie
3/13/91	3	2	3/12	Split Open and Melt	My Sweet One
3/15/91	1	1	6/12	Dinner and a Movie	The Oh Kee Pa
3/17/91	2	1	2/12	Carolina	The Landlady
3/22/91	1	1	5/11	Destiny Unbound	Split Open and
3/28/91	2	1	5/14	The Landlady	You Enjoy My
3/29/91	1	2	7/8	Tweezer	BBFCFM
3/31/91	1	2	6/7	Guelah Papyrus	Run Like Antel
4/2/91	1	1	5/10	Llama	Foam
4/3/91	1	1	7/10	Dinner and a Movie	Mike's Song
4/5/91	2	1	2/11	The Landlady	Divided Sky
4/11/91	2	1	7/12	Dinner and a Movie	Foam
4/19/91	5	1	2/12	Dinner and a Movie	Divided Sky
4/20/91	1	1	9/11	Chalk Dust Torture	You Enjoy My
4/25/91	3	2	8/10	Dinner and a Movie	Divided Sky
4/27/91	1	E	1/2	***	Good Time Ba
5/2/91	1	1	4/11	Foam	The Landlady
5/3/91	1	1	1/12	***	Foam
5/9/91	2	1	7/10	Llama	Magilla
5/12/91	3	1	2/11	Chalk Dust Torture	Dinner and a
5/16/91	1	2	3/9	Dinner and a Movie	The Landlady
5/19/91	3	1	4/8	Chalk Dust Torture	You Enjoy My
7/12/91	2	1	2/12	Dinner and a Movie	Buried Alive
7/13/91	1	1	12/13	Split Open and Melt	Frankenstein
7/14/91	1	2	6/10	Dinner and a Movie	Split Open and
7/15/91	1	1	6/14	Stash	Mike's Song
7/19/91	2	1	3/10	The Landlady	David Bowie
7/21/91	2	1	8/11	The Landlady	Mike's Song
7/23/91	1	1	9/12	Flat Fee	Mike's Song
7/24/91	1	2	6/10	My Sweet One	Funky Bitch
7/26/91	2	1	11/12	Buried Alive	Golgi Apparat
8/3/91	2	2	4/10	Chalk Dust Torture	Tweezer
9/26/91	2	1	2/10	Llama	Divided Sky
9/28/91	2	1	2/11	The Landlady	Chalk Dust Tor
9/29/91	1	2	2/10	Brother	Eliza
10/2/91	2	1	8/10	Brother	Chalk Dust Tor
10/3/91	1	1	5/10	It's Ice	Llama
10/4/91	1	2	3/11	Brother	Foam
10/6/91	1	1	4/13	Divided Sky	Poor Heart
10/10/91	1	1	5/11	Split Open and Melt	The Landlady
10/11/91	1	1	9/10	Llama	Runaway Jim
10/13/91	2	2	7/9	Jesus Just Left	Love You
10/15/91	1	2	2/12	Brother	Runaway Jim
10/17/91	1	1	3/10	The Landlady	Divided Sky
10/19/91	2	1	7/10	Chalk Dust Torture	My Sweet One
10/23/91	1	1	9/11	Llama	Runaway Jim
10/24/91	1	2	9/11	Dinner and a Movie	Terrapin
10/27/91	1	1	8/10	Brother	Harry Hood
10/30/91	2	2	8/11	The Landlady	Mike's Song
11/2/91	3	1	7/10	Foam	Col. Forbin's A
11/7/91	1	2	2/11	Brother	My Sweet One
11/12/91	4	1	5/11	Brother	Tube
11/14/91	2	E	1/3	***	Good Time Ba
11/15/91	1	2	13/14	Love You	Possum
11/21/91	4	1	2/12	Chalk Dust Torture	Poor Heart
11/23/91	2	1	10/11	Brother	Golgi Apparat
11/30/91	2	2	5/10	It's Ice	My Sweet One
12/4/91	1	1	10/11	Dinner and a Movie	David Bowie
12/5/91	1	1	9/10	It's Ice	Possum
12/31/91	3	2	2/10	Brother	Buried Alive
3/6/92	1	2	7/9	Llama	NICU
3/12/92	3	2	5/11	It's Ice	The Squirmin
3/14/92	2	2	5/10	Split Open and Melt	The Oh Kee Pa
3/17/92	1	1	10/11	Rift	Run Like Antel
3/21/92	3	E	1/2	***	Rocky Top
3/27/92	5	1	9/10	Glide	Run Like Antel
3/28/92	1	1	6/10	Rift	The Landlady
3/30/92	1	2	12/13	Cracklin' Rosie	Tweezer Repri
4/1/92	2	1	3/12	Foam	Brother
4/4/92	2	1	6/10	Chalk Dust Torture	It's Ice
4/7/92	3	1	9/12	Split Open and Melt	Rift
4/12/92	2	2	3/10	Split Open and Melt	Rift
4/16/92	3	1	4/12	It's Ice	Split Open and
4/17/92	1	1	9/13	Maze	The Landlady
4/21/92	3	1	10/11	NICU	David Bowie
4/23/92	2	1	8/11	Llama	It's Ice
4/25/92	2	1	8/11	Chalk Dust Torture	Rift
4/29/92	1	1	8/10	Rift	Take the A-Trn
5/2/92	3	1	8/11	Maze	Stash
5/3/92	1	2	12/14	Dinner and a Movie	The Oh Kee Pa
5/5/92	1	2	2/14	Chalk Dust Torture	All Things Rec
5/6/92	1	2	6/11	All Things Recnsdrd	Uncle Pen
5/8/92	2	1	10/12	All Things Recnsdrd	David Bowie
5/12/92	3	1	8/12	Dinner and a Movie	Buried Alive
5/14/92	1	1	10/11	My Friend My Friend	Run Like Antel
5/15/92	1	1	6/11	Stash	Love You
5/16/92	1	1	5/11	Split Open and Melt	My Sweet One
5/18/92	2	1	3/10	Maze	Divided Sky
6/20/92	2	1	2/8	Buried Alive	Foam
6/27/92	3	1	8/10	Chalk Dust Torture	Uncle Pen
7/10/92	4	1	1/10	***	Llama
7/12/92	2	1	3/11	Chalk Dust Torture	Divided Sky
7/16/92	3	1	7/10	Dinner and a Movie	Rift
7/17/92	1	1	6/7	Maze	Runaway Jim
7/22/92	4	1	3/7	Poor Heart	Maze
7/28/92	5	1	2/6	Chalk Dust Torture	Uncle Pen
7/31/92	2	1	3/6	Chalk Dust Torture	The Oh Kee Pa
8/17/92	6	1	10/11	My Friend My Friend	David Bowie
8/27/92	6	1	2/7	Chalk Dust Torture	The Landlady
8/29/92	2	1	3/5	Rift	Maze
10/30/92	2	1	3/11	Maze	Rift
11/19/92	1	2	4/15	Weekapaug Groove	It's Ice
11/21/92	2	1	7/11	It's Ice	Maze
11/23/92	2	1	9/11	Mound	Memories
11/28/92	3	2	8/12	T.M.W.S.I.Y. Reprise	The Squirmin
11/30/92	1	1	3/10	Foam	Poor Heart
12/1/92	1	1	4/12	Split Open and Melt	Rift
12/3/92	2	1	5/12	Split Open and Melt	Uncle Pen
12/5/92	2	1	3/12	Chalk Dust Torture	Rift
12/7/92	2	1	10/11	Split Open and Melt	You Enjoy My
12/11/92	3	2	7/12	Axilla	Paul and Silas
12/12/92	1	1	10/11	All Things Recnsdrd	Run Like Antel
12/13/92	1	2	3/14	Mound	Llama
12/28/92	1	1	6/10	It's Ice	Rift
12/31/92	3	1	4/11	Maze	Rift
2/4/93	2	1	3/11	Foam	Maze
2/6/93	2	1	10/11	The Wedge	Run Like Antel
2/7/93	1	2	5/13	Reba	Tweezer
2/9/93	1	1	2/10	David Bowie	Poor Heart
2/11/93	2	2	9/12	Big Ball Jam	Love You
2/13/93	2	1	2/10	David Bowie	Poor Heart
2/17/93	2	1	8/11	It's Ice	Fluffhead
2/21/93	4	1	9/10	Dinner and a Movie	Run Like Antel
2/23/93	2	1	4/11	Rift	Split Open and
2/25/93	1	1	9/11	Stash	I Didn't Know
2/27/93	2	1	5/10	Maze	It's Ice
3/3/93	2	1	3/10	Foam	Maze
3/6/93	2	1	7/10	Punch You in the Eye	Maze
3/9/93	2	1	3/10	Foam	Maze
3/13/93	2	1	3/11	Funky Bitch	Maze
3/17/93	3	1	4/11	Foam	Stash
3/19/93	2	1	4/9	Foam	Rift
3/22/93	2	1	5/10	Stash	Rift
3/25/93	2	1	5/11	Possum	Stash
3/27/93	2	2	4/14	It's Ice	Chalk Dust Tor
3/31/93	3	2	3/10	Maze	Uncle Pen
4/2/93	2	1	4/9	Foam	Divided Sky
4/10/93	4	2	3/13	Maze	Rift
4/12/93	1	1	3/11	Tube	Poor Heart
4/14/93	1	1	4/13	Maze	It's Ice
4/17/93	2	1	3/10	Foam	Stash
4/20/93	2	1	5/10	Stash	It's Ice
4/22/93	2	2	2/10	Llama	All Things Rec
4/25/93	3	1	3/11	Possum	It's Ice
4/27/93	1	1	4/10	Foam	Rift
4/30/93	2	1	3/12	Maze	Poor Heart
5/2/93	2	2	7/10	Uncle Pen	Run Like Antel
5/5/93	2	1	6/10	Stash	It's Ice
5/7/93	2	2	2/10	Rift	Maze
5/29/93	2	1	2/10	Chalk Dust Torture	Stash
7/16/93	3	2	5/12	Maze	You Enjoy My
7/21/93	3	1	8/12	Rift	Runaway Jim
7/24/93	3	1	9/10	The Mango Song	The Squirmin
7/29/93	4	2	2/9	Maze	It's Ice
8/3/93	4	2	3/9	Maze	It's Ice
8/7/93	2	1	2/10	Llama	Poor Heart
8/11/93	3	2	6/10	All Things Recnsdrd	Rift
8/15/93	4	2	5/11	The Landlady	Maze
8/20/93	3	1	5/10	Maze	It's Ice
8/24/93	2	1	3/11	All Things Recnsdrd	It's Ice
8/28/93	3	1	2/9	Llama	Foam
12/29/93	2	2	2/11	Maze	Fluffhead
4/5/94	4	1	6/8	Julius	Rift
4/8/94	2	2	6/9	Harry Hood	Big Ball Jam

DATE	GAP	SET	POS.	SONG BEFORE	SONG AFTER
4/10/94	2	E	1/2	***	Golgi Apparat
4/15/94	4	1	7/9	Chalk Dust Torture	It's Ice
4/16/94	1	2	6/9	Julius	You Enjoy My
4/20/94	3	1	4/7	Julius	Axilla (Part II)
4/25/94	5	2	8/10	Divided Sky	Big Ball Jam
4/28/94	1	1	6/11	Down with Disease	It's Ice
5/2/94	3	1	3/10	Split Open and Melt	Down with Dis
5/4/94	2	2	2/9	Run Like an Antelope	You Enjoy My
5/8/94	3	1	6/8	Down with Disease	Stash
5/13/94	3	2	2/9	Chalk Dust Torture	Split Open and
5/16/94	2	1	8/10	Down with Disease	Stash
5/22/94	5	2	2/9	Down with Disease	It's Ice
5/27/94	4	1	4/9	Foam	David Bowie
5/28/94	1	1	4/10	Foam	Stash
6/16/94	7	1	1/10	***	Rift
6/18/94	2	E	1/2	***	Tweezer Repri
6/23/94	4	1	6/10	Foam	Down with Dis
6/30/94	5	1	8/9	Scent of a Mule	Frankenstein
7/3/94	3	2	3/10	The Lizards	It's Ice
7/6/94	2	1	4/9	Julius	Reba
7/10/94	3	2	8/10	Weekapaug Groove	The Squirmin
7/14/94	2	1	2/11	Runaway Jim	Stash
7/15/94	1	2	3/10	David Bowie	Reba
10/9/94	4	2	2/8	David Bowie	Scent of a Mul
10/12/94	2	3	3/9	David Bowie	Scent of a Mul
10/15/94	3	2	10/11	Foreplay/Long Time	Suzy Greenber
10/23/94	6	2	2/9	Runaway Jim	Halley's Comet
10/26/94	2	2	2/7	Rift	Reba
10/31/94	4	3	2/7	David Bowie	Slave
11/4/94	3	1	3/9	It's Ice	David Bowie
11/14/94	3	1	5/9	Split Open and Melt	The Landlady
11/17/94	2	1	4/11	Maze	Wilson
11/22/94	4	1	7/9	I Didn't Know	Down with Dis
11/25/94	2	1	4/8	Reba	Split Open and
11/30/94	3	1	8/10	Down with Disease	I'm Blue, Lonesome
12/4/94	4	2	2/7	Maze	Reba
12/28/94	6	1	5/10	Bathtub Gin	Axilla (Part II)
12/31/94	3	2	3/9	Maze	Mike's Song
6/8/95	3	2	4/8	Free	Tweezer
6/13/95	3	1	3/10	Foam	Stash
6/15/95	2	E	1/2	***	Frankenstein
6/25/95	8	E	1/2	***	Slave
7/1/95	5	1	8/9	Split Open and Melt	Chalk Dust Tor
10/8/95	12	E	1/2	***	Rocky Top
10/20/95	7	2	9/10	I'm Blue, Lonesome	Run Like Antel
10/24/95	3	2	3/8	Theme From the Botto	You Enjoy My
10/27/95	2	2	8/9	Keyboard Cavalry	Possum
11/10/95	5	1	1/9	***	Runaway Jim
11/12/95	2	1	3/10	Llama	Guelah Papyrus
11/18/95	4	1	2/8	Dinner and a Movie	Reba
11/22/95	3	2	4/6	Llama	You Enjoy My
11/25/95	2	1	6/9	Taste That Surrounds	Rift
11/28/95	1	1	3/9	Dinner and a Movie	Foam
12/2/95	4	1	9/10	Taste That Surrounds	Possum
12/4/95	1	E	1/2	***	Rocky Top
12/7/95	2	1	8/10	Guyute	Possum
12/9/95	2	1	6/10	Rift	Free
12/15/95	4	1	8/10	Cars Trucks Buses	Free
12/17/95	2	2	1/8	***	Maze
12/29/95	2	2	10/11	La Grange	Fire
7/7/96	8	1	3/10	Divided Sky	The Curtain
7/9/96	1	1	6/7	Mike's Song	Character Zer
7/11/96	2	2	2/8	Harry Hood	Also Sprach
7/18/96	2	2	3/7	Cars Trucks Buses	Stash
7/22/96	3	1	5/8	Maze	Stash
8/7/96	8	E	1/2	***	Golgi Apparat
10/19/96	10	2	4/7	Slave	Split Open and
10/22/96	2	1	3/9	Runaway Jim	It's Ice
10/29/96	5	1	5/10	Taste	Stash
11/3/96	3	1	8/9	Theme From the Botto	Character Zer
11/8/96	3	2	3/8	Maze	Simple
11/13/96	3	1	2/9	Down with Disease	It's Ice
11/15/96	2	1	3/11	Divided Sky	Character Zer

DATE	GAP	SET	POS.	SONG BEFORE	SONG AFTER
11/24/96	6	1	4/11	All Things Recnsdrd	Reba
11/30/96	3	1	4/10	All Things Recnsdrd	Stash
12/2/96	2	1	3/8	AC/DC Bag	You Enjoy My
12/28/96	3	2	3/10	Maze	Digital Delay
					Loop J
2/16/97	6	1	3/10	Split Open and Melt	Crosseyed and Painle
2/20/97	3	2	6/12	Stash	Free
6/20/97	14	2	7/8	Twist	Julius
6/27/97	5	1	7/8	Taste	Character Zer
6/29/97	1	1	3/7	Taste	Beauty of My Dreams
7/5/97	4	1	2/13	Julius	Uncle Pen
7/11/97	4	1	2/7	Chalk Dust Torture	Stash
7/22/97	2	1	5/8	Stash	Vultures
7/26/97	3	E	1/2	***	Cavern
7/30/97	2	2	6/9	David Bowie	Uncle Pen
8/3/97	3	E	1/2	***	Slave
8/14/97	7	E	1/2	***	Rocky Top
8/17/97	2	1	7/10	Maze	Tweezer
11/13/97	1	2	4/7	Prince Caspian	Mike's Song
11/22/97	6	E	1/2	***	Tweezer Repri
12/2/97	6	2	6/7	Weekapaug Groove	Character Zer
12/5/97	2	2	2/7	Stash	Julius
12/12/97	5	1	5/8	Taste	Tweezer
12/28/97	2	1	10/11	Split Open and Melt	Character Zer
4/4/98	6	1	3/8	Taste	Funky Bitch
6/30/98	2	1	4/13	Water in the Sky	Tube
7/24/98	15	1	3/8	Runaway Jim	Stash
8/9/98	12	1	8/9	Roggae	David Bowie
11/14/98	20	1	4/8	Reba	Tweezer
11/19/98	3	1	5/9	Ginseng Sullivan	Maze
6/30/99	12	E	1/2	***	Sample in a Ja
7/15/99	10	2	5/6	Jam	Chalk Dust Tor
7/23/99	6	E	1/2	***	Rocky Top
8/1/99	7	1	9/10	Poor Heart	Run Like Antel
9/18/99	8	2	4/7	Free	Harry Hood
9/26/99	6	1	6/10	Guyute	Cars Trucks Buses
10/3/99	5	1	11/12	Maze	Guyute
12/3/99	7	1	3/8	Wolfman's Brother	Back on the Train
12/10/99	5	1	2/10	Tweezer	Horn
12/31/99	9	1	6/14	Punch You in the Eye	Poor Heart
5/22/00	2	2	1/6	***	David Bowie
6/9/00	2	2	2/7	Tweezer	The Mango Song
6/16/00	6	E	1/2	***	Harry Hood
6/24/00	3	1	3/6	Runaway Jim	Tweezer
7/4/00	7	1	5/11	It's Ice	Stash
7/14/00	7	2	6/11	Stash	Foam
9/8/00	2	1	4/12	Ghost	The Horse
10/4/00	17	1	3/7	It's Ice	Funky Bitch
Has not been played in the last 3 shows.					

Brain Damage

DATE	GAP	SET	POS.	SONG BEFORE	SONG AFTER
11/2/98	984	2	14/16	Any Colour You Like	Eclipse
Has not been played in the last 135 shows.					

Breathe

DATE	GAP	SET	POS.	SONG BEFORE	SONG AFTER
11/2/98	984	2	7/16	Speak to Me	On The Run
Has not been played in the last 135 shows.					

Breathe Jam

DATE	GAP	SET	POS.	SONG BEFORE	SONG AFTER
10/25/94	755	2	5/9	Mike's Song	Sparkle
Has not been played in the last 364 shows.					

Brian and Robert

DATE	GAP	SET	POS.	SONG BEFORE	SONG AFTER
6/30/98	945	E	1/1	***	***
7/2/98	2	1	4/11	Theme From the Botto	Meat
7/10/98	6	E	1/2	***	Taste
7/15/98	1	1	8/13	Chalk Dust Torture	Beauty of My Dreams
7/21/98	5	2	5/8	Weekapaug Groove	Ghost
8/1/98	7	2	7/10	Fluffhead	Albuquerque

DATE	GAP	SET	POS.	SONG BEFORE	SONG AFTER
8/7/98	4	1	5/10	Stash	Foam
8/9/98	2	2	5/11	Run Like an Antelope	Waste
8/15/98	3	3	5/6	Limb by Limb	Loving Cup
10/15/98	3	1	6/8	David Bowie	Reba
10/18/98	2	1	9/12	Guyute	Sad Lisa
11/4/98	5	1	7/9	Birds of a Feather	Frankie Says
11/7/98	2	1	4/10	Driver	The Wedge
11/18/98	7	E	1/4	***	Sleep
11/24/98	4	1	5/9	Stash	Limb by Limb
12/29/98	6	1	7/10	Split Open and Melt	Guyute
7/15/99	13	E	1/2	***	Frankenstein
7/31/99	12	E	2/3	Jam	Simple
9/18/99	9	1	5/7	Maze	Tube
9/22/99	3	2	4/8	Taste	Mike's Song
12/5/99	17	2	5/7	Weekapaug Groove	Jennifer Dances
6/13/00	19	E	1/2	***	Good Time Ba
6/23/00	5	E	1/2	***	Possum
9/11/00	19	1	4/9	Rift	Vultures
10/6/00	17	2	9/10	Golgi Apparatus	Bold as Love
Has not been played in the last 1 show.					

Bring it On Home

DATE	GAP	SET	POS.	SONG BEFORE	SONG AFTER
5/3/85	5	2	6/6	Cities	***
Has not been played in the last 1114 shows.					

Brother

DATE	GAP	SET	POS.	SONG BEFORE	SONG AFTER
9/25/91	312	1	1/11	***	Poor Heart
9/26/91	1	2	3/11	The Squirming Coil	Sparkle
9/28/91	2	1	9/11	Foam	Golgi Apparat
9/29/91	1	2	1/10	***	Bouncing
10/2/91	2	1	7/10	Reba	Bouncing
10/4/91	2	2	2/11	My Sweet One	Bouncing
10/6/91	1	1	11/13	T.M.W.S.I.Y. Reprise	Terrapin
10/10/91	1	2	1/13	***	Reba
10/12/91	2	2	7/10	Dinner and a Movie	If I Only Had a Brai
10/15/91	2	2	1/12	***	Bouncing
10/18/91	2	2	1/12	***	Uncle Pen
10/23/91	2	1	1/12	***	The Squirmin
10/27/91	2	1	7/10	Fluffhead	Bouncing
10/30/91	2	1	5/7	Sparkle	The Lizards
10/31/91	1	1	2/11	Memories	Ya Mar
11/7/91	3	2	1/11	***	Bouncing
11/8/91	1	1	9/11	The Mango Song	Eliza
11/9/91	1	1	10/11	Horn	Sweet Adeline
11/12/91	2	1	4/11	Uncle Pen	Bouncing
11/14/91	2	1	8/11	Sparkle	The Mango Song
11/16/91	2	2	4/9	Bathtub Gin	You Enjoy My
11/19/91	1	1	6/11	Sparkle	Horn
11/20/91	1	E	2/2	Magilla	***
11/22/91	2	1	4/11	Sparkle	Fee
11/23/91	1	1	9/11	Uncle Pen	Bouncing
11/30/91	2	1	8/11	The Squirming Coil	Paul and Silas
12/4/91	1	1	7/11	Poor Heart	The Squirmin
12/7/91	3	2	5/8	Sparkle	The Lizards
12/31/91	2	1	1/10	***	Bouncing
3/7/92	2	1	1/11	***	My Mind's Got A Mind
3/11/92	1	2	7/11	My Mind's Got A Mind	Baby Lemonade
3/13/92	2	2	2/12	Wilson	The Horse
3/20/92	4	1	3/10	Reba	Glide
3/24/92	3	2	7/13	The Mango Song	Uncle Pen
3/26/92	2	2	5/13	Poor Heart	T.M.W.S.I.Y.
4/1/92	5	1	4/12	Bouncing	All Things Rec
4/6/92	4	1	5/10	Reba	Esther
4/17/92	7	2	1/8	***	You Enjoy My
4/25/92	7	1	5/11	Reba	Tela
5/6/92	7	1	7/11	Tela	Col. Forbin's A
5/17/92	9	2	6/11	All Things Recnsdrd	Sanity
7/14/92	13	1	9/12	Horn	I Didn't Know
8/2/93	142	1	7/11	Poor Heart	The Oh Kee Pa
8/17/96	257	2	4/8	It's Ice	Fluffhead

DATE	GAP	SET	POS.	SONG BEFORE	SONG AFTER
10/23/96	7	2	1/8	***	Ya Mar
10/31/96	5	3	1/8	***	Also Sprach
11/11/96	7	1	6/9	Sparkle	Theme From the Botto
11/30/96	12	2	4/11	Glide	Contact
4/4/98	89	2	3/6	Also Sprach	Ghost
7/28/98	20	2	4/8	The Mango Song	Contact
9/27/00	149	2	6/7	Heavy Things	You Enjoy My

Has not been played in the last 7 shows.

Brown Eyed Girl

DATE	GAP	SET	POS.	SONG BEFORE	SONG AFTER
11/16/95	766	E	1/1	***	***

Has not been played in the last 353 shows.

Buffalo Bill

DATE	GAP	SET	POS.	SONG BEFORE	SONG AFTER
11/21/92	457	E	1/2	***	BBFCFM
10/29/94	223	1	8/10	Split Open and Melt	Makisupa Policeman
12/31/94	31	2	5/9	Mike's Song	Mike's Song
8/17/97	204	3	1/7	***	NICU
11/29/97	11	E	1/3	***	Moby Dick
11/27/98	74	2	9/16	Sanity	Mike's Song
12/18/99	68	2	9/10	Weekapaug Groove	Weekapaug Gr
7/10/00	26	1	5/10	Bathtub Gin	My Mind's Got A Mind

Has not been played in the last 25 shows.

Bug

DATE	GAP	SET	POS.	SONG BEFORE	SONG AFTER
6/30/99	10072	2	8/10	Piper	My Left Toe
7/7/99	4	2	6/7	My Left Toe	You Enjoy My
7/13/99	5	2	3/6	Piper	Mountains in the Mis
9/9/99	15	2	7/9	Tweezer	You Enjoy My
9/21/99	9	2	2/8	Carini	Strange Design
10/8/99	12	2	3/7	Tweezer	Fee
12/3/99	4	2	3/5	Limb by Limb	Piper
12/5/99	2	1	5/10	Taste	Sparkle
12/7/99	1	2	4/8	Heavy Things	Bathtub Gin
12/12/99	4	1	6/8	Beauty of My Dreams	Stash
12/17/99	4	2	3/6	The Moma Dance	Jennifer Dances
12/31/99	3	2	32/35	Roses are Free	Also Sprach
5/22/00	2	E	1/2	***	Golgi Apparat
5/23/00	1	2	8/8	Train Song	***
6/11/00	3	2	4/8	Beauty of My Dreams	David Bowie
6/16/00	4	2	7/7	Julius	***
6/22/00	1	1	6/9	Limb by Limb	Poor Heart
6/24/00	2	2	2/8	Birds of a Feather	My Sweet One
7/1/00	5	2	2/10	Gotta Jibboo	First Tube
7/6/00	3	2	3/7	Also Sprach	Piper
7/15/00	7	2	6/7	The Mango Song	You Enjoy My
9/25/00	13	1	7/8	Water in the Sky	Julius
10/4/00	5	2	5/7	Gotta Jibboo	Harry Hood

Has not been played in the last 3 shows.

Bundle of Joy

DATE	GAP	SET	POS.	SONG BEFORE	SONG AFTER
8/21/87	27	2	3/12	Harpua	Harpua
8/29/87	1	1	12/13	Harpua	Harpua
9/12/88	38	2	6/10	Avenu Malkenu	Camel Walk
9/21/89	49	2	4/9	Dinner and a Movie	Possum
10/1/89	1	2	5/11	Dinner and a Movie	Possum
10/7/89	2	2	2/9	Dinner and a Movie	Possum
10/20/89	4	1	2/10	Harpua	Col. Forbin's A
11/3/89	7	1	6/10	Split Open and Melt	You Enjoy My

Has not been played in the last 990 shows.

Buried Alive

DATE	GAP	SET	POS.	SONG BEFORE	SONG AFTER
5/12/89	100	1	7/15	David Bowie	The Asse Festival
9/13/90	107	1	8/11	Minute by Minute	Paul and Silas
9/13/90	0	2	9/15	AC/DC Bag	Take the A-Trn
9/14/90	1	2	3/10	The Squirming Coil	Tweezer
9/15/90	1	1	1/14	***	Divided Sky
9/21/90	3	2	7/8	Tweezer	Tweezer Repri

DATE	GAP	SET	POS.	SONG BEFORE	SONG AFTER
9/22/90	1	1	1/12	***	Horn
9/29/90	2	1	5/9	Ya Mar	Bouncing
10/7/90	5	2	1/8	***	Bouncing
10/30/90	4	2	11/12	Terrapin	David Bowie
10/31/90	1	1	1/11	***	Possum
11/2/90	1	1	13/14	Possum	Possum
11/10/90	4	1	7/11	My Sweet One	The Lizards
11/16/90	1	1	2/8	Suzy Greenberg	Foam
11/17/90	1	2	1/12	***	Fluffhead
11/24/90	1	1	1/11	***	Possum
11/26/90	1	1	5/11	Reba	You Enjoy My
12/8/90	4	1	1/10	***	Runaway Jim
12/29/90	2	2	1/10	***	Runaway Jim
12/31/90	1	1	11/12	Auld Lang Syne	Possum
2/8/91	5	1	3/11	Reba	Col. Forbin's A
2/9/91	1	2	2/10	Golgi Apparatus	Fluffhead
2/14/91	1	1	3/11	McGrupp	Reba
2/15/91	1	1	6/11	Fee	The Mango Song
2/16/91	1	2	3/9	Reba	Runaway Jim
2/20/91	2	1	1/11	***	Cavern
2/26/91	1	2	1/12	***	Runaway Jim
2/27/91	1	2	2/11	Suzy Greenberg	Cavern
3/1/91	2	1	9/12	Bouncing	Mike's Song
3/9/91	3	2	5/13	The Squirming Coil	Runaway Jim
3/15/91	2	2	1/9	***	Possum
3/16/91	1	2	7/10	Magilla	The Squirmin
3/22/91	2	1	8/11	The Squirming Coil	Cavern
3/31/91	4	1	1/13	***	Cavern
4/2/91	1	2	6/8	Dog Gone Dog	The Squirmin
4/12/91	6	2	7/10	Tela	Reba
4/16/91	2	2	6/11	Magilla	Uncle Pen
4/25/91	6	2	1/10	***	My Sweet One
5/2/91	2	2	9/10	I Didn't Know	Possum
5/4/91	2	2	5/9	The Famous Mockingbi	Harry Hood
5/10/91	2	1	8/10	Bathtub Gin	The Lizards
5/16/91	3	1	1/11	***	Golgi Apparat
5/18/91	2	1	1/9	***	Golgi Apparat
7/12/91	3	1	3/12	Bouncing	Flat Fee
7/20/91	6	2	1/12	***	Reba
7/24/91	3	1	4/10	The Squirming Coil	Split Open and
7/26/91	2	1	10/12	T.M.W.S.I.Y. Reprise	Bouncing
8/3/91	2	3	7/8	The Lizards	Possum
9/27/91	3	1	4/9	Reba	Esther
10/3/91	5	2	8/11	Destiny Unbound	The Squirmin
10/12/91	5	1	1/9	***	Possum
10/27/91	8	1	4/10	The Mango Song	Guelah Papyrus
11/10/91	9	1	1/10	***	The Sloth
11/12/91	1	1	1/11	***	Golgi Apparat
11/20/91	6	1	1/11	***	Possum
12/7/91	9	2	1/8	***	Reba
12/31/91	1	2	3/10	Bouncing	Auld Lang Syne
3/12/92	4	1	7/11	Reba	Rift
3/17/92	3	1	1/11	***	Possum
3/21/92	3	2	1/11	***	The Oh Kee Pa
3/26/92	4	2	1/13	***	The Oh Kee Pa
4/7/92	10	1	1/12	***	Possum
4/16/92	5	1	1/12	***	Possum
4/19/92	3	1	1/11	***	NICU
5/1/92	8	2	2/13	Sanity	Wilson
5/7/92	5	1	3/11	Poor Heart	My Friend My
5/12/92	4	1	9/12	Bouncing	Uncle Pen
6/20/92	7	1	1/8	***	Bouncing
8/17/92	30	1	1/11	***	Poor Heart
8/24/92	1	1	1/7	***	Poor Heart
11/22/92	10	1	1/12	***	The Oh Kee Pa
11/25/92	2	1	1/11	***	Poor Heart
11/30/92	3	2	1/10	***	Runaway Jim
12/13/92	12	1	1/11	***	Wilson
12/28/92	1	1	3/10	Sparkle	Glide
12/31/92	3	1	1/11	***	Poor Heart
2/6/93	4	2	13/14	Lengthwise	Possum
2/7/93	1	1	2/12	Suzy Greenberg	Poor Heart
2/11/93	3	1	2/10	Suzy Greenberg	Poor Heart

DATE	GAP	SET	POS.	SONG BEFORE	SONG AFTER
2/17/93	4	1	1/11	***	Possum
2/21/93	4	1	2/10	Suzy Greenberg	Punch You in
2/25/93	3	1	1/11	***	Poor Heart
3/2/93	1	1	1/13	***	Poor Heart
3/5/93	2	1	1/11	***	Poor Heart
3/12/93	4	1	1/11	***	Poor Heart
3/16/93	3	1	2/11	Sweet Adeline	Poor Heart
3/27/93	9	2	1/14	***	Halley's Comet
3/30/93	2	1	1/11	***	Poor Heart
4/2/93	3	2	1/9	***	Poor Heart
4/9/93	3	2	1/10	***	Suzy Greenber
4/14/93	3	1	1/13	***	Poor Heart
4/21/93	5	1	1/11	***	Poor Heart
4/27/93	5	1	1/10	***	Poor Heart
5/3/93	5	1	1/11	***	Rift
5/7/93	3	1	1/11	***	Poor Heart
7/16/93	5	1	5/10	Ya Mar	Fast Enough for You
7/18/93	2	1	1/9	***	Rift
7/23/93	3	1	1/12	***	Rift
8/6/93	10	2	1/12	***	Tweezer
8/11/93	4	1	1/10	***	Runaway Jim
8/13/93	2	2	1/9	***	Rift
8/21/93	6	1	1/10	***	Poor Heart
8/25/93	2	2	1/8	***	Possum
4/4/94	7	2	3/11	If I Could	The Landlady
4/13/94	7	1	1/8	***	Poor Heart
5/4/94	17	2	4/9	You Enjoy Myself	The Landlady
5/10/94	4	1	1/9	***	Poor Heart
5/16/94	4	1	1/10	***	Poor Heart
5/26/94	8	1	1/10	***	Poor Heart
6/13/94	7	1	1/9	***	Poor Heart
6/23/94	8	1	1/10	***	Poor Heart
7/13/94	14	1	1/11	***	Poor Heart
10/14/94	10	1	1/12	***	Sample in a Ja
11/22/94	25	1	1/9	***	Poor Heart
12/2/94	7	2	3/8	David Bowie	Julius
12/3/94	1	2	3/10	Suzy Greenberg	Gumbo
10/15/94	47	1	1/10	***	Poor Heart
10/29/95	10	1	1/12	***	Poor Heart
12/1/95	18	1	1/10	***	Down with Dis
12/16/95	11	1	1/9	***	AC/DC Bag
12/28/95	2	2	4/8	Wilson	Tweezer
10/16/96	35	1	4/12	Wilson	Poor Heart
11/9/96	17	1	1/10	***	Poor Heart
2/26/97	32	2	1/11	***	Poor Heart
12/2/97	55	1	1/9	***	Down with Dis
7/6/98	22	1	1/9	***	AC/DC Bag
7/29/98	14	2	1/7	***	If You Need a Fool
11/4/98	21	1	1/9	***	Character Zer
11/27/98	15	2	1/16	***	Wipeout
7/1/00	88	1	1/11	***	Wolfman's Brother

Has not been played in the last 31 shows.

Burning Down the House

DATE	GAP	SET	POS.	SONG BEFORE	SONG AFTER
8/12/98	974	E	1/2	***	You Enjoy My

Has not been played in the last 145 shows.

Butter Them Biscuits

DATE	GAP	SET	POS.	SONG BEFORE	SONG AFTER
11/18/94	690	1	9/11	Split Open and Melt	The Old Home
11/19/94	1	1	10/11	I'm Blue, Lonesome	My Long Journey Home
11/20/94	1	1	6/10	If I Could	My Long Journey Home
11/22/94	1	2	10/13	I'm Blue, Lonesome	My Long Journey Home

Has not been played in the last 426 shows.

Bye Bye Foot

DATE	GAP	SET	POS.	SONG BEFORE	SONG AFTER
6/14/97	879	1	8/10	Limb by Limb	Free
6/20/97	3	2	3/8	Ghost	Ginseng Sullivan

DATE	GAP	SET	POS.	SONG BEFORE	SONG AFTER
7/22/97	16	1	7/8	Vultures	Taste
8/10/97	12	1	8/10	Split Open and Melt	Ginseng Sullivan

Has not been played in the last 209 shows.

Camel Walk

DATE	GAP	SET	POS.	SONG BEFORE	SONG AFTER
11/3/84	2	1	7/10	Can't You Hear Me Kn	Eyes of the World
3/4/85	2	1	2/4	Anarchy	Fire up the Ganja
10/17/85	3	1	7/9	Anarchy	Run Like Antel
4/15/86	6	1	13/14	Anarchy	Alumni Blues
10/15/86	1	2	4/14	Swing Low Sweet Chrt	Shaggy Dog
10/31/86	1	1	2/11	Mustang Sally	Golgi Apparat
2/21/87	3	2	5/15	Dear Mrs. Reagan	Back Porch Boogie Bl
3/23/87	2	2	7/9	Why Don't U Love Me	Golgi Apparat
8/21/87	7	1	11/11	Wilson	***
11/19/87	8	3	11/14	Take the A-Train	La Grange
1/27/88	1	3	7/8	BBFCFM	Harry Hood
7/25/88	24	E	2/2	Icculus	***
9/12/88	6	2	7/10	Bundle of Joy	The Practical Song
2/24/89	19	2	4/4	You Enjoy Myself	***
7/2/95	648	1	6/10	Julius	Reba
2/26/97	140	1	1/10	***	Llama
8/14/97	40	2	7/8	Merry Pranksters Jam	Taste
12/12/97	22	1	3/8	Also Sprach	Taste
7/28/98	28	E	1/2	***	The Squirmin
7/24/99	61	E	2/4	Glide	Alumni Blues
12/16/99	42	1	9/10	Heavy Things	Possum
10/1/00	49	2	5/7	When Circus Comes	Driver

Has not been played in the last 4 shows.

Can't You Hear Me Knockin'

DATE	GAP	SET	POS.	SONG BEFORE	SONG AFTER
11/3/84	2	1	6/10	St. Stephen Jam	Camel Walk
5/3/85	3	2	3/6	Wild Child	Jam

Has not been played in the last 1114 shows.

Cannonball Jam

DATE	GAP	SET	POS.	SONG BEFORE	SONG AFTER
5/7/94	615	2	9/12	Walk Away	Purple Rain

Has not been played in the last 504 shows.

Caravan

DATE	GAP	SET	POS.	SONG BEFORE	SONG AFTER
1/20/90	146	1	6/8	The Squirming Coil	The Lizards
1/27/90	1	2	2/7	Communication Brkdwn	You Enjoy My
1/28/90	1	2	4/10	Bouncing	The Squirmin
2/1/90	2	1	5/11	Suzy Greenberg	Divided Sky
2/15/90	3	1	6/10	Dinner and a Movie	Bathtub Gin
2/16/90	1	2	2/7	Golgi Apparatus	Bouncing
2/22/90	2	1	7/9	AC/DC Bag	The Lizards
2/24/90	2	E	2/2	The Lizards	***
3/3/90	2	2	2/7	Dinner and a Movie	Fluffhead
3/7/90	1	1	4/6	Esther	The Lizards
3/8/90	1	2	5/12	AC/DC Bag	I Didn't Know
3/9/90	1	3	3/11	Avenu Malkenu	Ya Mar
4/6/90	7	2	6/10	Harry Hood	Reba
4/13/90	5	2	8/10	Harry Hood	Possum
4/20/90	4	2	1/11	***	Mike's Song
4/28/90	5	2	3/9	Harry Hood	I Didn't Know
5/4/90	2	1	9/12	Weekapaug Groove	If I Only Had a Brai
5/10/90	3	2	4/8	Harry Hood	Reba
5/31/90	8	1	5/12	Bouncing	Esther
6/5/90	3	2	3/10	Divided Sky	Dinner and a
6/16/90	4	3	9/13	Rocky Top	If I Only Had a Brai
11/4/90	22	2	8/13	Manteca	Runaway Jim
11/30/90	7	E	1/3	***	The Oh Kee Pa
2/15/91	14	E	1/4	***	BBFCFM
7/14/91	51	2	2/10	Suzy Greenberg	Divided Sky
7/15/91	1	E	1/3	***	Contact
7/20/91	3	2	3/12	Reba	Dinner and a
7/23/91	2	E	1/2	***	Golgi Apparat
9/25/91	6	1	9/11	The Landlady	Reba

DATE	GAP	SET	POS.	SONG BEFORE	SONG AFTER
4/5/93	214	2	3/9	Poor Heart	Punch You in
4/24/93	12	1	8/11	Rift	When Something Wrong
5/7/93	10	1	5/11	Sparkle	Manteca
7/23/93	10	1	3/12	Rift	Nellie Kane
8/15/93	18	1	3/10	All Things Recnsdrd	Runaway Jim
4/11/94	19	1	1/9	***	Poor Heart
4/23/94	10	1	9/10	Down with Disease	High-Heel Sneakers
5/4/94	8	E	1/1	***	***
12/2/94	87	2	7/8	Gumbo	Suzy Greenber
12/29/96	160	1	2/10	Poor Heart	Cavern

Has not been played in the last 259 shows.

Carini

DATE	GAP	SET	POS.	SONG BEFORE	SONG AFTER
2/17/97	866	2	3/7	Down with Disease	Taste
2/23/97	5	1	1/9	***	Axilla
2/26/97	2	1	7/10	Tube	Rocko William
2/28/97	1	1	1/10	***	Paul and Silas
3/1/97	1	2	1/8	***	Dinner and a
12/30/97	64	E	1/4	***	Black-Eyed Katy
4/3/98	3	E	1/3	***	Halley's Comet
7/9/98	10	1	1/8	***	Boogie On Reggae
11/8/98	36	1	2/10	Taste	Love Me
11/27/98	12	1	3/11	Ya Mar	Runaway Jim
12/28/98	3	2	1/6	***	Wolfman's Brother
7/4/99	7	E	1/3	***	Meatstick Reprise
7/13/99	6	1	8/9	Reba	Funky Bitch
9/10/99	16	1	6/8	Ginseng Sullivan	What's The Use
9/16/99	4	1	5/14	First Tube	Dirt
9/21/99	4	2	1/8	***	Bug
10/3/99	9	1	7/12	Horn	Ginseng Sullivan
12/5/99	9	1	1/8	***	Gotta Jibboo
6/14/00	20	1	1/8	***	The Curtain
6/24/00	5	2	6/8	Frankie Says	The Squirmin
9/14/00	20	1	4/6	Albuquerque	The Oh Kee Pa
9/18/00	3	1	1/10	***	Sparkle
9/24/00	4	2	4/8	Ya Mar	Lawn Boy
9/29/00	3	1	1/8	***	Rift
10/6/00	5	1	1/7	***	Stash

Has not been played in the last 1 show.

Carolina

DATE	GAP	SET	POS.	SONG BEFORE	SONG AFTER
1/20/90	146	1	2/8	Harry Hood	Bathtub Gin
1/27/90	1	1	1/13	***	Bathtub Gin
1/28/90	1	1	6/9	La Grange	Col. Forbin's A
2/9/90	3	1	12/12	Weekapaug Groove	***
2/10/90	1	1	8/10	Possum	Contact
2/15/90	1	1	1/10	***	The Oh Kee Pa
2/16/90	1	E	1/2	***	Whipping Post
2/17/90	1	1	6/12	Harry Hood	Mike's Song
2/23/90	2	1	5/11	Foam	Rocky Top
2/24/90	1	1	1/8	***	You Enjoy My
3/1/90	2	2	6/7	Weekapaug Groove	Slave
3/3/90	2	2	6/7	Funky Bitch	Divided Sky
3/8/90	2	1	6/10	Foam	The Oh Kee Pa
3/10/90	2	1	10/10	Jesus Just Left	***
3/11/90	1	2	1/13	***	Roll Like a Cantalou
3/28/90	2	2	2/16	***	Sweet Adeline
4/4/90	1	1	8/8	Divided Sky	***
4/5/90	1	1	4/9	David Bowie	The Oh Kee Pa
4/6/90	1	2	1/10	***	La Grange
4/8/90	2	E	1/2	***	Fire
4/12/90	2	E	1/1	***	***
4/19/90	4	2	7/8	Highway to Hell	Golgi Apparat
4/29/90	7	1	1/13	***	Possum

DATE	GAP	SET	POS.	SONG BEFORE	SONG AFTER
10/6/90	32	1	13/13	David Bowie	***
10/12/90	3	E	1/2	***	Good Time Ba
10/19/90	1	E	1/3	***	AC/DC Bag
11/4/90	5	1	1/10	***	AC/DC Bag
2/1/91	14	E	2/2	Alumni Blues	***
3/17/91	22	1	1/12	***	Bouncing
4/4/91	8	1	9/10	Possum	Golgi Apparat
4/11/91	3	1	9/12	Foam	You Enjoy My
4/16/91	3	2	10/11	Runaway Jim	Tweezer Repri
10/13/91	47	E	3/3	Uncle Pen	***
3/11/92	36	E	3/4	Memories	Sleeping Monkey
3/28/92	13	2	2/4	Memories	I Didn't Know
4/1/92	3	1	12/12	David Bowie	***
4/30/92	20	E	1/2	***	Cavern
5/6/92	5	E	1/2	***	Good Time Ba
11/21/92	55	2	1/13	***	The Curtain
11/22/92	1	E	2/3	Bold as Love	Tweezer Repri
11/25/92	2	E	2/2	Harry Hood	***
12/4/92	7	2	7/10	The Squirming Coil	Harry Hood
12/6/92	2	2	12/13	Lengthwise	Cavern
12/8/92	2	E	1/2	***	Fire
12/10/92	1	E	1/2	Bold As Love	Tweezer Repri
12/29/92	5	E	2/3	Big Ball Jam	Rocky Top
12/31/92	2	E	1/2	***	Fire
2/17/93	12	E	1/2	***	Good Time Ba
3/12/93	16	E	2/3	Sweet Adeline	Rocky Top
3/24/93	9	E	1/2	***	The Squirmin
3/27/93	3	E	2/2	The Squirming Coil	***
4/1/93	4	E	1/2	***	Tweezer Repri
4/25/93	16	E	2/3	When Something Wrong	Rocky Top
5/1/93	4	E	1/2	***	Rocky Top
8/7/93	26	E	1/2	***	La Grange
5/20/94	55	1	9/10	Dog Faced Boy	AC/DC Bag
6/22/94	19	E	1/2	***	Cavern
6/24/94	2	2	12/13	Cavern	Down with Dis
7/6/94	9	1	8/9	My Mind's Got A Mind	David Bowie
10/28/94	25	1	10/10	Sample in a Jar	***
6/16/95	41	2	3/5	Free	You Enjoy My
6/29/95	10	1	10/10	Split Open and Melt	***
11/21/95	39	2	10/11	Suspicious Minds	A Day in the Life
10/27/96	64	E	2/2	Possum	***
8/17/97	82	1	10/10	Taste	***
10/17/98	64	1	1/10	***	Sleep
11/18/98	15	1	9/9	David Bowie	***

Has not been played in the last 125 shows.

Cars Trucks Buses

DATE	GAP	SET	POS.	SONG BEFORE	SONG AFTER
9/27/95	735	2	1/8	***	AC/DC Bag
9/28/95	1	1	1/9	***	Runaway Jim
9/29/95	1	1	5/8	Strange Design	You Enjoy My
9/30/95	1	1	2/9	My Friend My Friend	White Rabbit Jam
10/2/95	1	2	2/10	Wilson	Bathtub Gin
10/5/95	2	1	6/11	Silent in the Mornin	Strange Design
10/7/95	2	2	2/9	Makisupa Policeman	Split Open and
10/8/95	1	2	2/10	Keyboard Cavalry	Timber (Jerry)
10/14/95	3	1	2/11	AC/DC Bag	Kung
10/19/95	3	1	1/11	***	Runaway Jim
10/21/95	2	1	6/12	Wilson	Kung
10/25/95	3	2	3/9	Life on Mars	Mike's Song
10/29/95	3	1	5/12	Punch You in the Eye	The Horse
11/11/95	4	1	1/12	***	Mike's Song
11/16/95	4	1	1/10	***	Runaway Jim
11/30/95	5	2	1/8	***	Wilson
12/4/95	3	2	6/9	Billy Breathes	You Enjoy My
12/15/95	8	1	7/10	Suspicious Minds	Bouncing
12/29/95	4	2	2/11	Makisupa Policeman	Bathtub Gin
4/26/96	3	1	5/13	Stash	You Enjoy My
7/9/96	6	1	4/7	Taste	Mike's Song
7/18/96	7	1	2/7	Julius	Bouncing
8/14/96	15	2	5/10	Silent in the Mornin	Tweezer

DATE	GAP	SET	POS.	SONG BEFORE	SONG AFTER
8/17/96	2	1	4/10	Reba	The Lizards
10/16/96	1	1	1/12	***	Down with Dis
10/18/96	2	1	4/10	The Old Home Place	Stash
10/21/96	2	1	3/10	Sample in a Jar	The Sloth
10/26/96	4	1	2/9	Julius	Wolfman's Brother
10/29/96	2	1	3/10	Guelah Papyrus	Taste
11/6/96	4	1	2/9	Split Open and Melt	Fast Enough for You
11/11/96	4	1	3/9	Guelah Papyrus	AC/DC Bag
11/14/96	2	1	4/9	Wolfman's Brother	Free
11/18/96	1	1	1/10	***	Timber (Jerry)
11/23/96	3	1	3/9	Guelah Papyrus	Divided Sky
11/29/96	3	1	3/9	NICU	Character Zer
12/1/96	2	1	4/12	Cavern	Character Zer
12/6/96	3	1	7/9	You Enjoy Myself	Down with Dis
12/31/96	4	1	4/10	Punch You in the Eye	Stash
2/13/97	1	2	2/10	Julius	My Soul
2/16/97	2	2	2/11	Sample in a Jar	Free
2/20/97	3	2	2/12	Sample in a Jar	Character Zer
2/28/97	6	1	4/10	My Soul	Peaches en Regalia
3/18/97	3	1	8/10	Harry Hood	Suzy Greenber
6/14/97	2	1	6/10	My Soul	Limb by Limb
7/3/97	12	2	2/6	Ghost	Billy Breathes
7/6/97	2	1	7/9	Silent in the Mornin	Scent of a Mul
7/9/97	1	2	3/6	My Soul	You Enjoy My
7/26/97	7	1	6/9	Billy Breathes	Dirt
7/30/97	2	1	8/9	Piper	Character Zer
8/6/97	4	2	5/7	Prince Caspian	Sample in a Ja
8/8/97	1	1	1/7	***	Gumbo
8/10/97	2	1	5/10	Dirt	Billy Breathes
8/14/97	3	1	6/10	Free	Tela
11/16/97	5	1	7/11	Billy Breathes	Scent of a Mul
12/29/97	20	1	4/9	Crossroads	Train Song
7/2/98	9	1	2/11	Birds of a Feather	Theme From the Botto
7/15/98	7	1	10/13	Beauty of My Dreams	Roggae
8/3/98	14	1	5/8	Ride Captain Ride	The Moma Dance
11/13/98	23	1	6/10	It's Ice	Farmhouse
7/20/99	30	1	3/9	Sample in a Jar	The Sloth
9/26/99	23	1	7/10	Bouncing	Funky Bitch
12/13/99	20	1	2/6	Tube	Gumbo
6/23/00	18	1	7/8	David Bowie	Farmhouse
7/10/00	12	1	1/10	***	Wilson
9/9/00	6	2	5/7	Makisupa Policeman	Funky Bitch
9/20/00	7	1	1/9	***	Wolfman's Brother

Has not been played in the last 12 shows.

Catapult

DATE	GAP	SET	POS.	SONG BEFORE	SONG AFTER
4/17/92	388	1	12/13	David Bowie	David Bowie
4/21/92	3	2	10/13	Weigh	Lively Up Yourself
2/10/93	95	1	9/10	I Didn't Know	Run Like Antel
5/12/94	132	1	1/9	***	Rift
5/26/94	11	1	8/10	It's Ice	Divided Sky
6/22/94	14	2	5/20	Midnight Rider Jam	Simple
6/29/94	5	1	8/11	Silent in the Mornin	David Bowie
7/16/94	13	2	2/11	Run Like an Antelope	Run Like Antel
10/15/94	8	2	6/11	You Enjoy Myself	You Enjoy My
10/23/94	6	1	7/11	Stash	Stash
11/30/94	23	2	8/10	Mike's Song	McGrupp
12/8/94	7	1	7/10	Simple	Simple
6/16/95	15	1	9/10	Dog Faced Boy	Split Open and
10/14/95	27	1	7/11	Stash	Acoustic Army
10/22/95	6	2	3/11	Possum	The Curtain
11/24/95	18	2	4/10	Reba	Scent of a Mul
12/1/95	5	2	8/9	David Bowie	David Bowie
10/27/96	57	1	6/11	Scent of a Mule	Scent of a Mul
11/16/96	13	2	4/8	Kung	Axilla
11/23/96	4	2	7/10	Weekapaug Groove	Waste
3/2/97	26	1	10/13	Run Like an Antelope	Life on Mars
12/13/97	60	2	8/10	Weekapaug Groove	Weekapaug Gr
11/29/98	66	1	7/11	Limb by Limb	Kung

DATE	GAP	SET	POS.	SONG BEFORE	SONG AFTER
7/18/99	18	3	5/9	Wilson	Smoke on the Water J
7/24/99	4	2	2/8	Tweezer	Tweezer
9/29/99	22	2	7/12	Mike's Song	Mike's Song
12/31/99	24	1	10/14	Split Open and Melt	Back on the Train
6/29/00	16	2	2/10	Birds of a Feather	Heavy Things

Has not been played in the last 33 shows.

Cavern

DATE	GAP	SET	POS.	SONG BEFORE	SONG AFTER
2/17/90	155	1	11/12	Jam	You Enjoy My
3/28/90	14	2	14/16	Rift	Highway to Hell
4/5/90	2	2	8/13	Fee	Mike's Song
4/6/90	1	1	1/11	***	You Enjoy My
4/12/90	4	1	8/11	Take the A-Train	Jesus Just Left
4/14/90	2	1	3/10	Uncle Pen	Divided Sky
4/20/90	3	1	5/10	Ya Mar	Dinner and a
4/22/90	2	1	7/12	I Didn't Know	My Sweet One
4/26/90	2	2	6/11	Suzy Greenberg	Sweet Adeline
4/28/90	1	2	1/9	***	Harry Hood
9/14/90	22	2	6/10	Magilla	The Lizards
10/4/90	9	2	7/8	Magilla	You Enjoy My
10/8/90	4	1	5/10	Foam	Reba
10/12/90	1	1	6/9	Uncle Pen	Esther
10/19/90	1	1	8/15	Magilla	Possum
10/30/90	1	1	7/9	Uncle Pen	The Squirmin
10/31/90	1	1	10/11	My Sweet One	Run Like Antel
11/2/90	1	1	10/14	Esther	The Asse Festival
11/10/90	4	1	5/11	Runaway Jim	My Sweet One
11/17/90	2	1	7/11	You Enjoy Myself	Eliza
12/1/90	4	1	1/9	***	The Landlady
12/7/90	1	2	5/11	Donna Lee	Tweezer
12/8/90	1	1	6/10	Divided Sky	The Landlady
12/29/90	2	2	4/10	The Lizards	Stash
2/1/91	2	2	5/5	The Mango Song	***
2/3/91	2	2	4/9	The Landlady	The Mango Song
2/7/91	1	2	9/14	Uncle Pen	Love You
2/8/91	1	2	3/11	The Mango Song	Lawn Boy
2/9/91	1	2	7/10	Harry Hood	Love You
2/14/91	1	1	6/11	Destiny Unbound	The Mango Song
2/16/91	2	1	4/12	Divided Sky	Take the A-Trn
2/20/91	2	1	2/11	Buried Alive	Possum
2/21/91	1	2	2/9	Golgi Apparatus	The Landlady
2/26/91	1	1	1/11	***	Foam
2/27/91	1	2	3/11	Buried Alive	The Squirmin
2/28/91	1	1	8/13	Weekapaug Groove	T.M.W.S.I.Y.
3/1/91	1	1	4/12	Divided Sky	The Squirmin
3/6/91	1	1	6/11	Possum	Divided Sky
3/13/91	3	1	4/9	You Enjoy Myself	Divided Sky
3/15/91	1	2	5/9	Paul and Silas	Destiny Unbound
3/16/91	1	2	9/10	The Squirming Coil	You Enjoy My
3/22/91	2	1	9/11	Buried Alive	Reba
3/23/91	1	2	9/11	Uncle Pen	David Bowie
3/28/91	1	1	3/14	Divided Sky	The Landlady
3/31/91	2	1	2/11	Buried Alive	Runaway Jim
4/2/91	1	2	3/8	Lawn Boy	Fluffhead
4/3/91	1	E	1/2	***	Rocky Top
4/5/91	2	1	4/11	Divided Sky	Take the A-Trn
4/11/91	2	1	2/12	Runaway Jim	Paul and Silas
4/12/91	1	2	5/10	Fluffhead	Tela
4/16/91	2	1	4/9	Paul and Silas	The Mango Song
4/19/91	2	1	4/12	Divided Sky	The Lizards
4/20/91	1	2	6/13	Paul and Silas	T.M.W.S.I.Y.
4/21/91	1	2	9/11	Harry Hood	I Didn't Know
4/25/91	2	1	5/11	The Curtain	Poor Heart
4/27/91	1	1	4/12	Runaway Jim	The Landlady
5/2/91	1	1	9/11	The Squirming Coil	David Bowie
5/4/91	2	1	3/11	Suzy Greenberg	Reba
5/10/91	2	1	2/10	David Bowie	Ya Mar

DATE	GAP	SET	POS.	SONG BEFORE	SONG AFTER
5/16/91	3	1	4/11	Foam	Divided Sky
5/17/91	1	2	7/9	Magilla	Bike
5/18/91	1	1	8/9	Divided Sky	Possum
5/19/91	1	1	6/8	You Enjoy Myself	The Squirmin
7/11/91	1	2	2/10	Dinner and a Movie	T.M.W.S.I.Y.
7/12/91	1	1	11/12	Rocky Top	David Bowie
7/14/91	2	2	9/10	Magilla	Run Like Antel
7/15/91	1	1	12/14	The Lizards	The Squirmin
7/18/91	1	1	8/11	Take the A-Train	Mike's Song
7/19/91	1	1	6/10	Fee	The Squirmin
7/21/91	2	1	1/11	***	Divided Sky
7/23/91	1	2	3/10	Reba	The Lizards
7/24/91	1	1	8/10	The Landlady	Tela
7/25/91	1	1	9/10	Sweet Adeline	Run Like Antel
7/26/91	1	1	6/12	Suzy Greenberg	T.M.W.S.I.Y.
7/27/91	1	1	5/16	Suzy Greenberg	Poor Heart
8/3/91	1	2	7/10	Esther	I Didn't Know
9/25/91	1	2	4/8	Sparkle	Jesus Just Left
9/27/91	2	1	2/9	Runaway Jim	Reba
9/28/91	1	2	4/12	Sparkle	Run Like Antel
9/29/91	1	1	1/10	***	Divided Sky
9/30/91	1	1	1/4	***	Stash
10/2/91	1	1	5/10	Poor Heart	Reba
10/3/91	1	1	9/10	Divided Sky	Possum
10/4/91	1	1	4/10	Poor Heart	Divided Sky
10/6/91	1	2	8/10	I Didn't Know	The Squirmin
10/10/91	1	2	4/13	Poor Heart	Run Like Antel
10/11/91	1	2	2/9	The Curtain	Foam
10/17/91	4	1	5/10	Divided Sky	Poor Heart
10/18/91	1	2	12/12	My Sweet One	***
10/23/91	2	1	11/11	Runaway Jim	***
10/28/91	3	1	2/10	Runaway Jim	Poor Heart
10/30/91	1	1	3/7	Runaway Jim	Sparkle
11/1/91	2	2	11/13	Tela	Poor Heart
11/7/91	2	1	5/11	Sparkle	It's Ice
11/10/91	3	1	10/10	You Enjoy Myself	***
11/12/91	1	2	11/13	Magilla	Love You
11/13/91	1	1	7/10	Esther	Divided Sky
11/15/91	2	1	3/12	Sparkle	The Curtain
11/16/91	1	1	11/11	Ya Mar	***
11/19/91	1	2	10/11	Dinner and a Movie	David Bowie
11/20/91	1	2	8/8	Bike	***
11/22/91	2	1	2/11	Possum	Sparkle
11/24/91	2	2	3/8	Divided Sky	The Mango Song
11/30/91	1	1	6/11	Divided Sky	The Squirmin
12/4/91	1	1	5/11	Runaway Jim	Poor Heart
12/5/91	1	E	2/2	Glide	***
12/7/91	2	1	9/11	The Curtain	The Mango Song
12/31/91	1	2	8/10	Reba	My Sweet One
3/6/92	1	1	2/11	Rift	Sparkle
3/11/92	2	1	10/10	Divided Sky	***
3/12/92	1	2	11/11	My Sweet One	***
3/14/92	2	1	2/13	Runaway Jim	Reba
3/17/92	1	1	3/11	Possum	Sparkle
3/20/92	2	2	7/12	The Mango Song	Uncle Pen
3/24/92	3	2	13/13	Harry Hood	***
3/26/92	2	2	11/13	The Lizards	Cracklin' Rosi
3/28/92	2	1	10/10	Glide	***
3/30/92	1	1	11/11	Runaway Jim	***
3/31/92	1	2	8/13	The Lizards	Dinner and a
4/6/92	5	2	13/13	Uncle Pen	***
4/8/92	2	2	15/15	Terrapin	***
4/12/92	1	2	10/11	Harry Hood	***
4/15/92	2	1	8/11	Uncle Pen	I Didn't Know
4/17/92	2	1	2/11	I Didn't Know	Reba
4/19/92	2	E	2/2	Sleeping Monkey	***
4/21/92	1	E	3/3	Sweet Adeline	***
4/23/92	2	1	1/11	***	The Curtain
4/24/92	1	2	2/12	David Bowie	Ya Mar
4/25/92	1	E	3/3	Sweet Adeline	***
4/30/92	2	E	2/2	Carolina	***
5/2/92	2	2	10/10	Cracklin' Rosie	***
5/5/92	2	2	14/14	The Squirming Coil	***

DATE	GAP	SET	POS.	SONG BEFORE	SONG AFTER
5/6/92	1	1	11/11	Sparkle	***
5/8/92	2	1	2/12	The Curtain	Reba
5/10/92	2	1	6/10	Uncle Pen	Reba
5/12/92	1	2	9/9	Llama	***
5/14/92	1	2	2/13	Glide	Rift
5/15/92	1	1	3/11	Foam	Sparkle
5/16/92	1	1	10/11	The Lizards	David Bowie
5/17/92	2	1	11/11	Harry Hood	***
5/18/92	1	2	11/13	Rift	Love You
6/19/92	1	1	6/7	Sparkle	You Enjoy My
6/24/92	3	2	9/7	Sparkle	Rocky Top
7/1/92	3	1	2/7	The Curtain	Rift
7/10/92	2	1	8/10	The Lizards	Vacuum Solo
7/11/92	1	1	9/11	The Squirming Coil	Vacuum Solo
7/11/92	0	1	7/11	Vacuum Solo	You Enjoy My
7/14/92	2	1	12/12	Poor Heart	***
7/22/92	7	1	6/7	Rift	David Bowie
8/2/92	9	1	7/8	David Bowie	Rocky Top
8/17/92	4	2	11/11	Take the A-Train	***
8/23/92	3	1	4/7	Sparkle	Foam
10/30/92	7	1	5/11	Rift	Vacuum Solo
10/30/92	0	1	7/11	Vacuum Solo	The Squirmin
11/19/92	1	2	15/15	Lengthwise	***
11/23/92	4	2	14/14	Lengthwise	***
11/25/92	1	1	9/11	The Squirming Coil	Sweet Adeline
11/27/92	1	2	13/13	Take the A-Train	***
11/30/92	2	2	10/10	Terrapin	***
12/1/92	1	1	6/12	Rift	Fluffhead
12/3/92	2	2	13/13	Take the A-Train	***
12/4/92	1	1	11/11	The Famous Mockingbi	***
12/6/92	2	2	13/13	Carolina	***
12/10/92	3	1	11/11	Sweet Adeline	***
12/12/92	1	4	4/11	Sparkle	Reba
12/13/92	1	2	14/14	Harry Hood	***
12/28/92	1	2	9/9	Harry Hood	***
12/31/92	3	1	8/11	Divided Sky	Foam
2/4/93	2	2	13/13	Harry Hood	***
2/9/93	4	E	1/2	***	Rocky Top
2/11/93	2	2	12/12	The Lizards	***
2/13/93	2	2	11/11	The Squirming Coil	***
2/18/93	3	1	7/10	Sparkle	Reba
2/20/93	2	1	11/11	Fluffhead	***
2/22/93	2	1	8/10	Fee	I Didn't Know
2/25/93	2	1	3/11	Poor Heart	Maze
2/26/93	1	1	10/10	I Didn't Know	***
3/3/93	3	1	10/10	Lawn Boy	***
3/5/93	1	1	3/11	Poor Heart	Foam
3/8/93	2	2	2/10	Poor Heart	Uncle Pen
3/12/93	2	1	3/11	Poor Heart	Possum
3/16/93	3	1	11/11	McGrupp	***
3/18/93	2	1	10/10	The Squirming Coil	***
3/19/93	1	1	8/9	Fluffhead	Run Like Antel
3/21/93	1	2	12/12	Harry Hood	***
3/24/93	2	1	9/9	Amazing Grace	***
3/26/93	2	1	10/10	Divided Sky	***
3/30/93	3	1	11/11	Divided Sky	***
4/1/93	2	2	10/10	Love You	***
4/3/93	2	2	10/10	Love You	***
4/9/93	2	1	11/11	Divided Sky	***
4/10/93	1	2	13/13	Hoochie Coochie Man	***
4/16/93	3	1	10/10	Harry Hood	***
4/18/93	2	1	10/10	I Didn't Know	***
4/21/93	2	E	2/2	Sweet Adeline	***
4/24/93	3	2	10/10	Harry Hood	***
4/27/93	2	2	10/10	Love You	***
4/30/93	2	1	9/12	Divided Sky	Lawn Boy
5/1/93	1	2	11/11	Weekapaug Groove	***
5/3/93	2	1	11/11	Lawn Boy	***
5/5/93	1	E	2/4	Amazing Grace	Take the A-Trn
5/5/93	0	E	4/4	Take the A-Train	***
5/8/93	3	1	11/11	Satin Doll	***
5/29/93	1	1	6/10	The Squirming Coil	You Enjoy My
7/16/93	3	2	12/12	Harry Hood	***
7/18/93	2	1	9/9	Uncle Pen	***
7/23/93	3	2	12/12	Lawn Boy	***
7/25/93	2	E	1/1	***	***

DATE	GAP	SET	POS.	SONG BEFORE	SONG AFTER
7/28/93	2	1	11/11	Poor Heart	***
7/30/93	2	1	10/10	Reba	***
7/31/93	1	1	9/9	Divided Sky	***
8/3/93	2	1	11/11	Llama	***
8/7/93	2	1	10/10	The Famous Mockingbi	***
8/11/93	3	1	10/10	Sparkle	***
8/14/93	3	1	11/11	Poor Heart	***
8/17/93	3	2	10/10	My Sweet One	***
8/20/93	1	2	9/9	Purple Rain	***
8/25/93	3	1	11/11	Glide	***
12/29/93	4	E	2/2	Nellie Kane	***
4/4/94	3	E	2/2	Harry Hood	***
4/6/94	2	2	9/9	The Squirming Coil	***
4/9/94	2	2	11/11	Slave	***
4/11/94	2	1	9/9	Divided Sky	***
4/15/94	3	2	10/10	I Wanna Be Like You	***
4/17/94	2	1	9/9	My Sweet One	***
4/18/94	1	2	13/13	I Wanna Be Like You	***
4/21/94	2	1	9/9	If I Could	***
4/29/94	6	2	11/11	I Wanna Be Like You	***
5/2/94	2	E	1/1	***	***
5/8/94	5	2	6/9	Julius	You Enjoy My
5/10/94	1	1	9/9	If I Could	***
5/14/94	3	2	11/11	The Lizards	***
5/19/94	3	1	10/10	The Mango Song	***
5/23/94	4	1	10/10	Reba	***
5/26/94	2	1	3/10	Poor Heart	Demand
5/28/94	2	1	10/10	Maze	***
6/10/94	3	1	8/9	The Lizards	Julius
6/13/94	2	2	5/11	Esther	Reba
6/17/94	3	1	9/9	Scent of a Mule	***
6/22/94	4	E	2/2	Carolina	***
6/24/94	2	2	11/13	Poor Heart	Carolina
6/29/94	3	2	8/8	Suzy Greenberg	***
7/1/94	2	2	11/11	Harry Hood	***
7/8/94	5	E	2/2	Nellie Kane	***
7/10/94	2	1	9/9	Julius	***
7/13/94	1	2	2/13	Possum	Wilson
7/13/94	0	2	4/13	Wilson	NICU
7/16/94	3	1	6/11	The Lizards	The Horse
10/7/94	1	E	2/2	Foreplay/Long Time	***
10/13/94	5	2	12/12	Foreplay/Long Time	***
10/14/94	1	2	2/2	Ya Mar	***
10/21/94	5	E	3/3	Foreplay/Long Time	***
10/27/94	5	1	11/11	Poor Heart	***
11/3/94	5	2	8/8	Harry Hood	***
11/14/94	4	1	9/9	Lawn Boy	***
11/20/94	5	2	10/10	Julius	***
11/26/94	4	1	9/9	Poor Heart	***
11/30/94	2	2	10/10	McGrupp	***
12/2/94	2	E	1/1	***	***
12/3/94	1	2	10/10	Julius	***
12/7/94	3	E	1/1	***	***
12/10/94	3	2	11/11	Slave	***
12/30/94	3	1	9/9	Scent of a Mule	***
6/9/95	5	2	4/8	Scent of a Mule	David Bowie
6/14/95	3	1	5/12	Mound	Possum
6/19/95	4	1	9/10	Rift	Run Like Antel
6/22/95	2	1	9/10	Maze	Sweet Adeline
6/25/95	3	2	9/9	Amazing Grace	***
6/29/95	3	1	6/10	Divided Sky	Rift
7/3/95	4	1	11/11	Free	***
9/30/95	4	2	9/9	Suspicious Minds	***
10/5/95	3	2	6/9	Scent of a Mule	David Bowie
10/11/95	4	1	3/9	The Old Home Place	Divided Sky
10/14/95	2	2	6/6	Scent of a Mule	***
10/19/95	3	1	11/11	Billy Breathes	***
10/22/95	3	2	11/11	Slave	***
10/24/95	1	2	8/8	Contact	***
11/10/95	7	1	9/9	Guyute	***
11/14/95	3	1	9/9	I'm Blue, Lonesome	***
11/18/95	3	2	10/10	BBFCBM	***
11/22/95	3	1	6/10	Uncle Pen	Taste That Surrounds
12/1/95	6	1	10/10	Stash	***
12/5/95	3	2	8/8	Harry Hood	***

DATE	GAP	SET	POS.	SONG BEFORE	SONG AFTER
12/11/95	4	1	12/12	Julius	***
12/16/95	4	2	4/8	Scent of a Mule	Mike's Song
12/30/95	4	2	7/8	Scent of a Mule	Run Like Antel
4/26/96	2	E	2/2	Hello My Baby	***
7/7/96	5	1	8/10	Uncle Pen	Run Like Antel
7/11/96	3	1	2/8	Runaway Jim	Reba
7/13/96	2	1	3/10	Runaway Jim	Reba
7/15/96	1	1	8/8	Harry Hood	***
7/22/96	5	1	3/8	Poor Heart	Maze
7/25/96	3	1	8/8	Harry Hood	***
8/5/96	3	E	1/1	***	***
8/10/96	3	1	11/11	Bathtub Gin	***
10/25/96	13	2	11/12	Harry Hood	Star Spangled Banner
11/2/96	5	1	5/9	Taste	Stash
11/11/96	6	E	2/2	Waste	***
11/15/96	3	1	11/11	Taste	***
11/22/96	4	1	10/10	Stash	***
11/24/96	2	E	2/2	Ginseng Sullivan	***
12/1/96	4	1	3/12	Poor Heart	Cars Trucks Buses
12/29/96	5	1	3/10	Caravan	Taste
2/16/97	5	1	9/10	Waste	Chalk Dust Tor
2/18/97	2	1	2/10	Beauty of My Dreams	Punch You in
6/14/97	12	2	8/8	David Bowie	***
6/20/97	3	2	5/8	Ginseng Sullivan	Twist
6/21/97	1	1	15/15	Twist	***
7/3/97	8	2	6/6	Harry Hood	***
7/26/97	10	E	2/2	Bouncing	***
8/10/97	9	E	1/1	***	***
11/26/97	14	E	1/1	***	***
12/6/97	7	1	9/9	Maze	***
12/28/97	6	2	9/9	Rocky Top	***
4/5/98	7	2	8/8	Jam	***
7/5/98	5	1	3/9	Taste	Reba
7/21/98	10	1	6/8	Sparkle	Frankie Says
7/31/98	6	2	9/9	Julius	***
8/8/98	6	2	1/6	***	Also Sprach
8/15/98	4	E	2/3	Halley's Comet	Tweezer Repri
10/30/98	7	1	10/10	The Lizards	***
11/8/98	6	1	10/10	Stash	***
11/15/98	5	1	5/8	Scent of a Mule	Limb by Limb
11/20/98	3	E	1/1	***	***
11/28/98	5	2	9/9	Tweezer	***
12/31/98	5	1	7/7	Ha Ha Ha	***
7/3/99	3	1	4/11	Sparkle	Taste
7/8/99	3	1	8/8	Stash	***
7/16/99	6	1	9/9	Maze	***
7/25/99	7	1	8/8	Boogie On Reggae	***
7/30b/99	3	2	6/6	Runaway Jim	***
9/10/99	4	2	8/9	Split Open and Melt	David Bowie
9/18/99	6	2	7/7	Frankenstein	***
9/26/99	6	1	10/10	Mozambique	***
10/1/99	3	1	8/8	Limb by Limb	***
12/11/99	15	1	8/8	Scent of a Mule	***
5/23/00	11	E	2/2	Boogie On Reggae	***
6/13/00	4	2	9/9	Rocky Top	***
6/24/00	6	1	6/6	Strange Design	***
6/30/00	4	E	1/1	***	***
7/11/00	8	1	8/8	Theme From the Botto	***
9/9/00	5	2	7/7	Funky Bitch	***
9/20/00	7	E	1/1	***	***
9/27/00	5	1	10/10	Taste	***
10/4/00	4	2	7/7	Harry Hood	***

Has not been played in the last 3 shows.

Cecilia

DATE	GAP	SET	POS.	SONG BEFORE	SONG AFTER
6/25/97	886	2	7/9	Makisupa Policeman	Rocko William

Has not been played in the last 233 shows.

Chalk Dust Torture

DATE	GAP	SET	POS.	SONG BEFORE	SONG AFTER
2/1/91	242	2	1/5	***	Reba
2/2/91	1	1	9/9	You Enjoy Myself	***
2/3/91	1	1	8/10	Reba	Foam
2/7/91	1	2	1/14	***	T.M.W.S.I.Y.

DATE	GAP	SET	POS.	SONG BEFORE	SONG AFTER
2/9/91	2	1	12/12	Reba	***
2/15/91	2	2	10/10	Terrapin	***
2/16/91	1	2	1/9	***	Reba
3/15/91	12	2	9/9	Harry Hood	***
3/17/91	2	2	8/8	Slave	***
3/23/91	2	1	1/11	***	Bathtub Gin
3/28/91	1	1	14/14	Love You	***
4/2/91	3	1	10/10	Suzy Greenberg	***
4/3/91	1	2	1/9	***	Take the A-Trn
4/5/91	2	1	7/11	Reba	Foam
4/11/91	2	1	12/12	The Squirming Coil	***
4/15/91	2	1	7/10	Fee	Col. Forbin's A
4/16/91	1	2	4/11	Reba	Magilla
4/20/91	3	1	8/11	Esther	Bouncing
4/22/91	2	2	1/10	***	Bathtub Gin
5/2/91	3	2	1/10	***	Poor Heart
5/3/91	1	1	3/12	Foam	T.M.W.S.I.Y.
5/9/91	2	E	2/2	Fee	***
5/10/91	1	2	7/11	McGrupp	Love You
5/11/91	1	2	1/12	***	You Enjoy My
5/12/91	1	1	1/11	***	Bouncing
5/16/91	1	1	8/11	The Famous Mockingbi	You Enjoy My
5/17/91	1	1	1/17	***	Drum Jam
5/18/91	1	1	3/9	Golgi Apparatus	You Enjoy My
5/19/91	1	1	3/8	The Landlady	Bouncing
7/13/91	3	2	1/9	***	Guelah Pa-pyrus
7/14/91	1	3	4/10	Esther	Bathtub Gin
7/18/91	2	1	1/11	***	Foam
7/20/91	2	1	1/11	***	Foam
7/23/91	2	1	1/12	***	Foam
7/24/91	1	2	2/10	Golgi Apparatus	The Squirmin
7/26/91	2	1	1/12	***	Reba
8/3/91	2	2	3/10	Reba	Bouncing
9/25/91	1	2	8/8	You Enjoy Myself	***
9/26/91	1	2	11/11	Lawn Boy	***
9/28/91	2	1	3/11	Bouncing	The Squirmin
10/2/91	3	1	9/10	Bouncing	Golgi Apparat
10/3/91	1	1	1/10	***	Foam
10/4/91	1	1	1/10	***	Reba
10/10/91	2	1	1/11	***	Foam
10/11/91	1	1	5/10	Guelah Papyrus	You Enjoy My
10/12/91	1	2	4/10	Fluffhead	Take the A-Trn
10/15/91	2	1	1/10	***	Foam
10/17/91	1	1	9/10	Esther	Golgi Apparat
10/19/91	2	1	6/10	Foam	Bouncing
10/23/91	1	1	1/11	***	Reba
10/27/91	2	2	2/10	My Sweet One	The Mango Song
10/31/91	3	1	5/11	The Sloth	Sparkle
11/1/91	1	2	4/13	It's Ice	Eliza
11/7/91	2	1	2/11	Memories	Foam
11/9/91	2	2	1/10	***	Fluffhead
11/12/91	2	2	9/13	Guelah Papyrus	Magilla
11/13/91	1	1	5/10	Sparkle	Esther
11/15/91	2	1	1/12	***	Sparkle
11/16/91	1	2	7/9	Horn	Terrapin
11/19/91	1	1	8/11	Horn	Love You
11/21/91	2	1	1/12	***	Bouncing
11/23/91	2	1	7/11	Sparkle	Uncle Pen
11/24/91	1	2	5/8	The Mango Song	Take the A-Trn
11/30/91	1	2	1/10	***	Uncle Pen
12/4/91	1	2	9/11	The Lizards	Love You
12/7/91	3	2	3/8	Reba	Sparkle
3/7/92	3	2	5/11	Weigh	Horn
3/14/92	4	1	9/13	Fee	Take the A-Trn
3/19/92	2	2	2/10	Glide	NICU
3/25/92	5	2	10/12	My Sweet One	Cracklin' Rosi
3/26/92	1	E	2/3	Sleeping Monkey	Harpua
3/30/92	3	2	10/13	Weigh	Cracklin' Rosi
4/1/92	2	2	8/13	Horn	Cracklin' Rosi
4/2/92	2	1	5/10	Uncle Pen	Bouncing
4/6/92	2	1	7/10	Esther	Guelah Pa-pyrus
4/8/92	2	2	13/15	Silent in the Mornin	Terrapin
4/15/92	3	2	1/8	***	You Enjoy My

DATE	GAP	SET	POS.	SONG BEFORE	SONG AFTER
4/19/92	4	1	9/11	Fee	I Didn't Know
4/25/92	5	1	7/11	Tela	Bouncing
4/30/92	2	2	8/11	Silent in the Mornin	Cracklin' Rosi
5/2/92	2	2	8/10	***	Cracklin' Rosi
5/5/92	2	2	1/14	***	Bouncing
5/6/92	1	2	8/11	Uncle Pen	Terrapin
5/8/92	2	2	9/12	Silent in the Mornin	Terrapin
5/12/92	3	2	5/9	Guelah Papyrus	Terrapin
5/15/92	2	1	8/11	Love You	You Enjoy My
5/17/92	2	1	11/11	Poor Heart	***
6/23/92	4	1	1/8	***	Reba
6/27/92	2	1	7/10	All Things Recnsrd	Bouncing
7/12/92	6	1	2/11	Sweet Adeline	Bouncing
7/15/92	2	1	10/12	Silent in the Mornin	The Lizards
7/17/92	2	1	1/7	***	Sparkle
7/26/92	7	1	1/7	***	It's Ice
7/28/92	2	1	1/6	***	Bouncing
7/31/92	2	1	2/6	***	Suzy Greenberg
8/2/92	2	1	1/8	***	Guelah Pa-pyrus
8/13/92	1	1	1/3	***	Foam
8/19/92	4	1	1/7	***	The Landlady
8/23/92	2	1	1/7	***	Maze
8/27/92	3	1	1/7	***	Bouncing
11/20/92	4	2	1/10	***	Fluffhead
11/25/92	4	2	1/9	***	Foam
11/28/92	2	1	5/11	Esther	Sparkle
12/1/92	2	2	3/11	The Curtain	My Friend My
12/3/92	2	1	7/12	Uncle Pen	The Horse
12/5/92	2	1	2/12	The Landlady	Bouncing
12/7/92	2	2	1/12	***	Reba
12/11/92	3	1	6/11	The Lizards	Guelah Pa-pyrus
12/13/92	2	2	6/14	Fluffhead	T.M.W.S.I.Y.
12/30/92	3	1	5/14	Esther	Fluffhead
2/4/93	3	2	1/13	***	The Wedge
2/6/93	2	2	1/14	***	Mound
2/9/93	2	1	7/10	The Wedge	Esther
2/12/93	3	1	8/11	The Wedge	I Didn't Know
2/15/93	1	1	7/12	Esther	Mound
2/18/93	2	1	1/10	***	Guelah Pa-pyrus
2/21/93	3	1	6/10	Horn	Esther
2/23/93	2	1	8/11	Lawn Boy	The Wedge
2/26/93	2	2	5/11	Glide	Mound
3/2/93	2	1	9/13	All Things Recnsrdrd	The Horse
3/5/93	2	2	2/11	The Landlady	Guelah Pa-pyrus
3/8/93	2	E	2/3	Terrapin	Big Ball Jam Reprise
3/12/93	2	2	8/11	Big Ball Jam	Lengthwise
3/16/93	3	2	8/15	Esther	You Enjoy My
3/18/93	2	1	1/11	***	Guelah Pa-pyrus
3/19/93	1	E	2/2	Amazing Grace	***
3/22/93	2	1	1/10	***	Guelah Pa-pyrus
3/25/93	2	1	1/11	***	Guelah Pa-pyrus
3/27/93	2	2	5/14	Bouncing	T.M.W.S.I.Y.
3/31/93	3	2	10/10	Harpua	***
4/2/93	2	2	13/13	Bike	***
4/9/93	3	1	1/11	***	Sparkle
4/10/93	1	1	8/10	Uncle Pen	Lawn Boy
4/16/93	3	1	1/10	***	Guelah Pa-pyrus
4/20/93	3	2	1/12	***	Fluffhead
4/22/93	2	1	5/10	Reba	Esther
4/23/93	1	1	10/10	Lawn Boy	***
4/24/93	1	1	1/11	***	Guelah Pa-pyrus
4/29/93	3	2	1/13	***	It's Ice
5/1/93	2	2	1/11	***	Fluffhead
5/3/93	2	1	4/11	Weigh	Esther
5/6/93	2	1	1/13	***	Mound

DATE	GAP	SET	POS.	SONG BEFORE	SONG AFTER
5/8/93	2	1	1/12	***	Guelah Pa-pyrus
5/29/93	1	1	1/10	***	Bouncing
7/15/93	2	E	1/2	***	Freebird
7/17/93	2	1	7/11	Reba	The Horse
7/21/93	2	E	1/1	***	***
7/23/93	2	2	10/11	BBFCFM	Highway to Hell
7/28/93	4	2	10/10	The Great Gig in the	***
7/30/93	2	1	7/10	Esther	I Didn't Know
8/2/93	2	1	1/12	***	Guelah Pa-pyrus
8/6/93	2	1	9/10	Nellie Kane	Suzy Greenber
8/9/93	3	1	1/11	***	Who Knows Jam
8/9/93	0	1	3/11	Who Knows Jam	Mound
8/12/93	2	1	3/10	Reba	Guelah Pa-pyrus
8/14/93	2	1	1/11	***	Guelah Pa-pyrus
8/15/93	1	1	10/10	The Famous Mockingbi	***
8/20/93	3	2	6/9	My Friend My Friend	You Enjoy My
8/24/93	2	1	1/11	***	All Things Rec
8/26/93	2	2	8/8	Tea Tray Song	***
8/28/93	1	2	14/14	Contact	***
12/29/93	2	2	11/11	Sweet Adeline	***
4/5/94	4	2	7/8	I Wanna Be Like You	Amazing Grce
4/10/94	4	1	6/9	Esther	I Didn't Know
4/15/94	4	1	6/9	Wilson	Bouncing
4/18/94	3	1	1/10	***	Glide
4/21/94	2	1	1/9	***	Sparkle
4/24/94	3	2	7/9	The Famous Mockingbi	Contact
4/30/94	4	1	1/9	***	Mound
5/3/94	2	2	6/8	Harpua	I Wanna Be Like You
5/6/94	2	1	9/9	Esther	***
5/13/94	5	2	1/9	***	Bouncing
5/20/94	5	E	1/1	***	***
5/23/94	3	1	1/10	***	Sample in a Ja
5/25/94	1	1	11/11	Sweet Adeline	***
5/29/94	4	2	4/10	Esther	Horn
6/11/94	3	1	2/8	Wilson	You Enjoy My
6/18/94	5	2	10/10	You Enjoy Myself	***
6/21/94	2	2	7/16	Esther	BBFCFM
6/25/94	4	1	10/10	Tela	***
6/30/94	3	2	15/15	Love You	***
7/6/94	5	2	5/10	Lawn Boy	BBFCFM
7/10/94	3	1	1/9	***	Horn
7/14/94	2	E	1/1	***	***
7/16/94	2	2	11/11	Contact	***
10/8/94	1	2	1/9	***	Horn
10/10/94	2	1	11/11	Nellie Kane	***
10/14/94	3	2	5/10	Guyute	Nellie Kane
10/20/94	4	2	8/8	Foreplay/Long Time	***
10/23/94	3	1	1/11	***	My Friend My
10/28/94	4	2	9/12	Lifeboy	The Old Home
11/4/94	5	1	9/9	Suzy Greenberg	***
11/12/94	1	1	8/8	Esther	***
11/16/94	3	2	5/7	My Long Journey Home	Fee
11/20/94	4	1	1/10	***	Fee
11/28/94	5	1	1/9	***	Also Sprach
12/2/94	3	2	1/8	***	David Bowie
12/7/94	4	1	8/8	Lifeboy	***
12/10/94	3	1	8/8	Lawn Boy	***
12/31/94	4	3	4/8	Auld Lang Syne	The Horse
6/8/95	3	1	9/9	Prince Caspian	***
6/13/95	3	1	10/10	Sparkle	***
6/20/95	6	2	2/9	Halley's Comet	Prince Caspian
6/23/95	2	1	2/8	Simple	Prince Caspian
6/28/95	4	1	8/8	Fluffhead	***
7/1/95	3	1	9/9	Bouncing	***
9/27/95	3	1	8/9	Strange Design	The Squirmin
9/29/95	2	E	1/1	***	Ha Ha Ha
10/5/95	4	1	1/11	***	Ha Ha Ha

DATE	GAP	SET	POS.	SONG BEFORE	SONG AFTER
10/11/95	4	E	1/1	***	***
10/19/95	5	1	6/11	Esther	Theme From the Botto
10/21/95	2	1	2/12	Tweezer Reprise	Guelah Papyrus
10/25/95	3	1	10/10	I'm Blue, Lonesome	***
10/28/95	2	2	7/7	Frankenstein	***
11/11/95	5	1	12/12	Fee	***
11/14/95	2	1	1/9	***	Foam
11/21/95	5	1	2/10	Fee	Prince Caspian
11/24/95	2	2	1/10	***	Theme From the Botto
12/1/95	5	1	6/10	Wolfman's Brother	Col. Forbin's A
12/5/95	3	1	2/8	Horn	Taste That Surrounds
12/9/95	3	1	10/10	Dog Faced Boy	***
12/15/95	4	1	1/10	***	Harry Hood
12/17/95	2	1	9/9	The Lizards	***
12/31/95	4	1	10/10	Sparkle	***
6/6/96	2	2	3/10	You Enjoy Myself	Sparkle
7/5/96	2	1	2/6	Funky Bitch	AC/DC Bag
7/10/96	4	1	1/7	***	Ya Mar
7/13/96	3	1	9/10	Funky Bitch	You Enjoy My
7/19/96	4	1	5/6	Waste	The Squirmin
7/24/96	4	1	1/5	***	Ya Mar
8/4/96	3	1	1/9	***	Funky Bitch
8/12/96	5	1	4/10	Esther	Weigh
8/16/96	3	1	1/8	***	Bathtub Gin
10/17/96	3	2	2/8	Ya Mar	Bathtub Gin
10/21/96	3	2	2/11	Wilson	Wolfman's Brother
10/23/96	2	E	1/1	***	***
10/27/96	3	2	1/9	***	Bathtub Gin
10/29/96	1	1	1/10	***	Guelah Papyrus
11/7/96	5	1	1/10	***	Weigh
11/11/96	3	1	1/9	***	Guelah Papyrus
11/15/96	3	1	9/11	Train Song	Taste
11/18/96	2	1	7/10	Guelah Papyrus	Ginseng Sullivan
11/23/96	3	1	1/9	***	Guelah Papyrus
11/27/96	2	1	4/9	Ya Mar	The Sloth
11/30/96	2	1	10/10	Prince Caspian	***
12/4/96	3	1	2/11	My Friend My Friend	Horn
12/31/96	5	2	1/9	***	Wilson
2/13/97	1	1	1/12	***	Wolfman's Brother
2/16/97	2	1	10/10	Cavern	***
2/20/97	3	1	4/10	Soul Shake Down Part	Love Me
2/22/97	2	2	1/8	***	Bathtub Gin
2/25/97	2	E	1/1	***	***
3/2/97	4	1	12/13	Life on Mars	Hello My Baby
3/18/97	1	2	9/10	Waste	Slave
6/13/97	1	2	6/9	Slave	Ghost
6/16/97	2	1	8/10	Theme From the Botto	Wolfman's Brother
6/21/97	3	1	12/15	Harry Hood	Jam
6/27/97	4	1	2/8	Wilson	Stash
6/29/97	1	1	5/7	Beauty of My Dreams	Theme From the Botto
7/6/97	5	1	9/9	Scent of a Mule	***
7/11/97	3	1	1/7	***	Bouncing
7/23/97	3	2	6/6	Rocky Mountain Way J	***
7/25/97	1	2	1/6	***	Taste
7/30/97	3	1	3/9	Wolfman's Brother	Water in the Sky
8/8/97	5	2	6/6	Prince Caspian	***
8/14/97	5	2	1/8	***	Love Me
8/16/97	1	1	3/11	Harpua	Theme From the Botto
11/13/97	2	1	1/9	***	Black-Eyed Katy
11/21/97	5	1	7/8	Lawn Boy	Prince Caspian
12/2/97	7	1	4/9	Makisupa Policeman	Ghost
12/5/97	2	2	7/7	Loving Cup	***
12/9/97	3	1	2/10	Mike's Song	My Soul
12/30/97	6	1	6/7	Stash	A Day in the Life
4/2/98	2	1	8/8	Waste	***
7/1/98	5	1	9/9	Waste	***
7/5/98	3	1	9/9	Lawn Boy	***
7/9/98	3	E	1/1	***	***
7/15/98	2	1	7/13	Jam	Brian and Robert
7/24/98	6	2	7/7	Slave	***
8/1/98	6	2	9/10	Albuquerque	Frankenstein
8/7/98	4	2	1/7	***	Mike's Song
8/9/98	2	2	10/11	Frankenstein	Hello My Baby
8/15/98	3	2	8/9	Silent in the Mornin	Slave
10/15/98	3	2	2/10	My Soul	Roggae
10/31/98	5	1	6/10	Sneakin' Sally	Lawn Boy
11/4/98	2	2	5/6	Also Sprach	Loving Cup
11/8/98	3	2	1/8	***	Meat
11/13/98	3	1	1/10	***	Wolfman's Brother
11/19/98	4	2	6/8	Gumbo	Frankenstein
11/24/98	3	1	9/9	Tela	***
11/27/98	2	2	3/16	Wipeout	Mirror in the Bathro
11/27/98	0	2	5/16	Mirror in the Bathro	Dog Gone Dog
11/27/98	0	2	7/16	Dog Gone Dog	Sanity
12/30/98	5	1	1/12	***	BBFCFM
7/3/99	4	1	1/11	***	Gumbo
7/10/99	5	1	2/8	Wilson	Roggae
7/15/99	3	2	6/6	Bouncing	***
7/18/99	3	1	11/11	Reba	***
7/20 /99	1	1	1/9	***	Sample in a Ja
7/24/99	3	2	8/8	Waste	***
7/30a/99	3	1	1/7	***	Guyute
9/9/99	4	1	6/10	Guyute	Back @ Chicken Shack
9/14/99	4	1	1/11	***	The Sloth
9/16/99	1	1	2/14	Ya Mar	Farmhouse
9/22/99	5	1	2/10	Also Sprach	Guelah Papyrus
9/24/99	1	E	2/2	Boogie On Reggae	***
9/28/99	3	2	6/7	Makisupa Policeman	You Enjoy My
10/1/99	2	1	1/8	***	The Moma Dance
10/8/99	5	2	7/7	We're Not Gonna Take	***
12/5/99	6	2	9/10	Fluffhead	Frankenstein
12/12/99	5	1	8/8	Stash	***
12/16/99	3	1	2/10	Wilson	Lawn Boy
12/30/99	3	3	1/9	***	The Moma Dance
5/22/00	3	1	2/9	My Soul	Billy Breathes
6/9/00	2	1	9/9	First Tube	***
6/15/00	5	1	2/8	NICU	AC/DC Bag
6/22/00	2	1	9/9	Roggae	***
6/28/00	4	1	1/6	***	The Sloth
7/3/00	4	2	6/7	Meat	Bittersweet Motel
7/7/00	3	1	1/11	***	Gumbo
7/11/00	3	1	6/8	Chalk Dust Reprise	Theme From the Botto
9/11/00	6	2	1/5	***	Twist
9/17/00	4	1	9/9	The Curtain With	***
9/24/00	5	1	2/10	Mellow Mood	Back @ Chicken Shack
10/5/00	7	1	1/10	***	Guyute
10/6/00	1	E	2/3	El Paso	West LA Fadeaway

Has not been played in the last 1 show.

Chalk Dust Torture Reprise

DATE	GAP	SET	POS.	SONG BEFORE	SONG AFTER
12/10/94	707	E	1/2	***	Good Time Ba
7/11/00	388	1	5/8	Drowned	Chalk Dust Tor
7/11/00	0	E	3/3	Moby Dick	***

Has not been played in the last 24 shows.

Champagne Supernova

DATE	GAP	SET	POS.	SONG BEFORE	SONG AFTER
12/29/96	860	2	9/10	Harpua	Harpua

Has not been played in the last 259 shows.

Character Zero

DATE	GAP	SET	POS.	SONG BEFORE	SONG AFTER
6/6/96	794	2	7/10	Waste	David Bowie
7/9/96	5	1	7/7	Bouncing	***
10/16/96	25	1	12/12	Silent in the Mornin	***
10/17/96	1	1	8/10	Punch You in the Eye	A Day in the Life
10/21/96	3	1	6/10	Divided Sky	Ginseng Sullivan
10/23/96	2	1	6/9	Hello My Baby	Rift
10/26/96	2	1	6/9	Train Song	It's Ice
10/29/96	2	2	7/10	The Wedge	Suspicious Minds
10/31/96	1	1	9/10	The Famous Mockingbi	Star Spangled Banner
11/3/96	2	1	9/9	Bouncing	***
11/7/96	2	1	10/10	Tela	***
11/9/96	2	1	10/10	The Lizards	***
11/13/96	2	1	8/9	Reba	Sweet Adeline
11/15/96	2	1	4/11	Bouncing	Punch You in
11/18/96	2	1	10/10	Reba	***
11/22/96	2	2	7/10	Steep	Theme From the Botto
11/24/96	2	1	6/11	Reba	Strange Design
11/29/96	2	1	4/9	Cars Trucks Buses	Divided Sky
12/1/96	2	1	5/12	Cars Trucks Buses	The Curtain
12/4/96	2	1	9/11	Guyute	The Lizards
12/31/96	5	2	9/9	Prince Caspian	***
2/13/97	1	1	9/12	Poor Heart	Peaches en Regalia
2/14/97	1	E	1/1	***	***
2/18/97	3	1	9/10	Walfredo	Slave
2/20/97	1	2	3/12	Cars Trucks Buses	Uncle Pen
2/21/97	1	E	1/1	***	***
2/22/97	1	1	10/10	I Didn't Know	***
2/28/97	4	1	10/10	Ya Mar	***
3/2/97	2	2	7/9	Waste	Slave
3/18/97	1	1	10/10	Suzy Greenberg	***
6/13/97	1	2	9/9	Oblivious Fool	***
6/19/97	3	E	2/3	Beauty of My Dreams	Hello My Baby
6/22/97	3	1	6/9	Uncle Pen	Theme From the Botto
6/27/97	3	1	8/8	Bouncing	***
6/29/97	1	1	7/7	Theme From the Botto	***
7/3/97	3	E	1/1	***	***
7/5/97	1	1	12/13	Poor Heart	Good Time Ba
7/11/97	4	E	1/1	***	***
7/21/97	1	1	7/7	Bathtub Gin	***
7/25/97	3	2	6/6	Ghost	***
7/30/97	3	1	9/9	Cars Trucks Buses	***
8/3/97	3	1	10/10	Limb by Limb	***
8/8/97	2	1	7/7	Water in the Sky	***
8/11/97	3	2	6/6	You Enjoy Myself	***
8/16/97	3	1	10/11	Train Song	The Squirmin
11/13/97	2	1	9/9	You Enjoy Myself	***
11/17/97	3	E	1/1	***	***
11/23/97	4	1	9/9	Fluffhead	***
11/26/97	1	2	1/8	***	Also Sprach
12/2/97	4	2	7/7	Bouncing	***
12/5/97	2	1	10/10	Limb by Limb	***
12/12/97	5	1	8/8	Train Song	***
12/28/97	2	1	11/11	Bouncing	***
4/4/98	6	1	8/8	Lawn Boy	***
7/2/98	4	1	11/11	Punch You in the Eye	***
7/17/98	9	2	4/4	Weekapaug Groove	***
7/24/98	4	E	1/1	***	***
8/3/98	8	1	8/8	Strange Design	***
8/12/98	6	1	6/8	Roggae	Ramble On

DATE	GAP	SET	POS.	SONG BEFORE	SONG AFTER
8/16/98	2	3	5/7	The Mango Song	Bittersweet Motel
10/15/98	2	1	8/8	Reba	***
10/29/98	3	1	10/10	McGrupp	***
11/4/98	4	1	2/9	Buried Alive	Guyute
11/14/98	7	1	8/8	Sparkle	***
11/18/98	2	2	7/7	Fluffhead	***
11/20/98	2	2	8/8	Harry Hood	***
11/24/98	2	2	6/6	Wading In Velvet Sea	***
12/31/98	8	2	2/7	NICU	Tweezer
7/1/99	2	E	1/1	***	***
7/8/99	4	E	2/2	Terrapin	***
7/12/99	3	1	7/7	Water In the Sky	***
7/17/99	4	1	10/10	Taste	***
7/24/99	5	1	9/9	The Wedge	***
7/31/99	5	1	8/8	Sparkle	***
9/9/99	2	1	10/10	I Didn't Know	***
9/19/99	8	E	2/2	Guyute	***
9/25/99	4	E	1/1	***	***
10/4/99	7	2	8/8	Ya Mar	***
10/10/99	4	2	6/6	Bathtub Gin	***
12/5/99	4	E	1/2	***	Hello My Baby
12/17/99	9	2	6/6	Split Open and Melt	***
12/30/99	2	1	12/12	Ya Mar	***
5/21/00	2	1	7/7	Limb By Limb	***
6/11/00	5	E	1/1	***	***
6/16/00	4	1	10/10	Reba	***
6/23/00	2	2	7/7	Makisupa Policeman	***
6/29/00	4	E	1/1	***	***
7/7/00	6	1	11/11	The Curtain	***
7/11/00	3	2	13/13	Terrapin	***
9/8/00	4	2	6/6	Bathtub Gin	***
9/15/00	5	2	5/5	When Circus Comes	***
9/23/00	5	2	7/7	Piper	***
9/29/00	4	1	8/8	Bathtub Gin	***
10/5/00	4	2	7/7	Piper	***

Has not been played in the last 2 shows.

Che Hun Ta Mao

DATE	GAP	SET	POS.	SONG BEFORE	SONG AFTER
12/30/99	10691		6/12	Limb By Limb	Big Alligator Song

Has not been played in the last 50 shows.

Chess Jam

DATE	GAP	SET	POS.	SONG BEFORE	SONG AFTER
11/16/95	766	1	3/10	Runaway Jim	Horn

Has not been played in the last 353 shows.

Choo Choo Ch' Boogie

DATE	GAP	SET	POS.	SONG BEFORE	SONG AFTER
3/2/93	501	2	10/12	Loup Garou	Harry Hood

Has not been played in the last 618 shows.

Cinnamon Girl

DATE	GAP	SET	POS.	SONG BEFORE	SONG AFTER
3/18/97	877	1	1/10	***	NICU
7/31/97	27	E	1/1	***	***

Has not been played in the last 215 shows.

Cities

DATE	GAP	SET	POS.	SONG BEFORE	SONG AFTER
12/1/84	3	1	8/11	Don't Want U No More	Drums Jam
5/3/85	2	2	5/6	Jam	Bring it On Home
10/15/86	9	1	4/9	Skin it Back	I Am Hydrgn
4/29/87	8	1	7/9	Skin it Back	Fuck Your Face
5/21/88	27	3	3/6	Rocky Top	Take the A-Trn
6/19/88	3	2	2/2	Good Times Bad Times	***
7/12/88	5	1	1/8	***	The Lizards
7/24/88	2	2	7/8	On Your Way Down	David Bowie
8/6/88	4	1	3/9	You Enjoy Myself	Dave's Energy Guide
8/6/88	0	1	5/9	Dave's Energy Guide	Take the A-Trn
9/8/88	2	2	3/8	You Enjoy Myself	Dave's Energy Guide
9/8/88	0	2	5/8	Dave's Energy Guide	Good Time Ba
9/13/88	2	2	3/6	Boogie On Reggae	Dave's Energy Guide

DATE	GAP	SET	POS.	SONG BEFORE	SONG AFTER
7/5/94	586	2	5/11	Lifeboy	You Enjoy My
3/1/97	222	1	1/10	***	The Oh Kee Pa
6/16/97	5	E	1/2	***	Poor Heart
6/20/97	2	1	3/8	Jam	Horn
7/1/97	7	2	4/7	Bathtub Gin	Jam
7/30/97	14	2	4/9	David Bowie	David Bowie
8/10/97	7	2	1/5	***	Good Time Ba
8/16/97	4	3	2/6	Halley's Comet	Llama
11/26/97	10	2	3/8	Also Sprach	Ya Mar
12/28/97	13	1	2/11	Julius	The Curtain
4/5/98	7	1	6/8	Bathtub Gin	Sparkle
6/30/98	1	1	7/13	Stash	Roggae
7/6/98	5	1	4/9	Ghost	Limb by Limb
7/31/98	15	1	5/7	Rift	Water in the Sky
8/15/98	10	1	11/12	Funky Bitch	Weekapaug Gr
11/19/98	20	1	1/9	***	The Curtain
12/31/98	11	2	4/7	Tweezer	Wading In Velvet Sea
7/21/99	16	1	2/10	AC/DC Bag	Gold Soundz
8/1/99	8	1	1/10	***	Rift
9/29/99	16	E	1/1	***	***
6/14/00	32	1	3/8	The Curtain	Gumbo
6/29/00	8	2	6/10	Meatstick	Walk Away
9/24/00	24	2	1/8	***	Free
10/6/00	8	2	6/10	Rift	Sand

Has not been played in the last 1 show.

Clementine

DATE	GAP	SET	POS.	SONG BEFORE	SONG AFTER
2/7/93	484	2	10/13	You Enjoy Myself	The Squirmin

Has not been played in the last 635 shows.

Clod

DATE	GAP	SET	POS.	SONG BEFORE	SONG AFTER
10/15/86	14	E	1/1	***	***
12/6/86	2	1	8/14	Fluff's Travels	David Bowie
2/21/87	2	2	7/15	Back Porch Boogie Bl	Lushington
5/11/87	5	1	6/12	Sneakin' Sally	Peaches en Regalia
8/21/87	4	1	6/11	Harry Hood	The Curtain With
8/29/87	1	1	1/13	***	Slave
9/21/87	2	1	4/11	T.M.W.S.I.Y. Reprise	Slave
10/31/87	3	2	14/17	Who Do? We Do!	Alumni Blues
2/7/88	4	3	5/8	T.M.W.S.I.Y. Reprise	The Curtain
11/10/89	94	2	8/12	Who Do? We Do!	The Sloth

Has not been played in the last 988 shows.

Cocaine Jam

DATE	GAP	SET	POS.	SONG BEFORE	SONG AFTER
8/6/93	568	2	7/12	You Enjoy Myself	You Enjoy My

Has not been played in the last 551 shows.

Cold Rain and Snow

DATE	GAP	SET	POS.	SONG BEFORE	SONG AFTER
9/17/99	10372		8/8	Wolfman's Brother	***

Has not been played in the last 82 shows.

Colonel Forbin's Ascent

DATE	GAP	SET	POS.	SONG BEFORE	SONG AFTER
3/12/88	42	2	7/11	AC/DC Bag	Fam. Mockbrd
3/21/88	1	1	14/15	I Didn't Know	Fam. Mockbrd
3/31/88	1	1	9/14	The Lizards	Fam. Mockbrd
4/22/88	2	1	1/9	***	Fam. Mockbrd
6/21/88	8	1	7/9	The Lizards	Fam. Mockbrd
7/11/88	2	1	8/11	Bold As Love	Fam. Mockbrd
7/23/88	2	1	2/13	Jam	Fam. Mockbrd
7/24/88	1	1	4/10	Funky Bitch	Fam. Mockbrd
9/8/88	6	1	6/8	AC/DC Bag	Fam. Mockbrd
11/11/88	9	1	6/8	Possum	Fam. Mockbrd
12/10/88	2	1	11/12	Wilson	Fam. Mockbrd
1/26/89	3	2	3/10	Icculus	Fam. Mockbrd
2/6/89	1	3	6/9	Ballad - Curtis Loew	Fam. Mockbrd
2/24/89	5	1	6/10	Foam	Fam. Mockbrd
3/3/89	1	2	7/12	Walk Away	Fam. Mockbrd
5/1/89	10	2	7/10	Icculus	Fam. Mockbrd
5/6/89	2	1	11/13	AC/DC Bag	Fam. Mockbrd
5/28/89	8	1	3/9	Run Like an Antelope	Fam. Mockbrd
8/23/89	5	2	2/8	Run Like an Antelope	Fam. Mockbrd

DATE	GAP	SET	POS.	SONG BEFORE	SONG AFTER
8/26/89	1	1	2/8	Fluffhead	Fam. Mockbrd
9/14/89	2	1	5/9	Foam	Fam. Mockbrd
10/12/89	5	1	3/8	AC/DC Bag	Fam. Mockbrd
10/13/89	1	2	8/8	AC/DC Bag	***
10/20/89	2	1	3/10	Bundle of Joy	Fam. Mockbrd
10/22/89	2	1	2/14	La Grange	Fam. Mockbrd
10/28/89	2	1	3/9	You Enjoy Myself	Highway to Hell
10/31/89	1	2	4/8	Reba	Fam. Mockbrd
11/3/89	2	1	1/10	***	Fam. Mockbrd
11/30/89	6	2	3/11	Possum	Fam. Mockbrd
1/28/90	13	1	7/9	Carolina	Fam. Mockbrd
2/25/90	11	1	3/11	My Sweet One	Fam. Mockbrd
3/2/90	2	1	1/2	***	***
3/9/90	4	1	6/11	Bouncing	Fam. Mockbrd
4/14/90	13	1	5/10	Divided Sky	Fam. Mockbrd
4/20/90	1	3	8/10	Bouncing	Fam. Mockbrd
10/7/90	39	1	6/14	Destiny Unbound	Fam. Mockbrd
11/2/90	6	2	2/9	Suzy Greenberg	Fam. Mockbrd
11/26/90	8	2	2/7	Uncle Pen	Fam. Mockbrd
12/28/90	5	1	6/11	Llama	Fam. Mockbrd
2/8/91	7	1	4/11	Buried Alive	Fam. Mockbrd
3/16/91	17	1	10/14	Rocky Top	Fam. Mockbrd
3/23/91	3	1	8/10	Possum	Fam. Mockbrd
3/31/91	3	1	4/13	Runaway Jim	Fam. Mockbrd
4/4/91	3	1	6/10	Llama	Fam. Mockbrd
4/15/91	5	1	8/10	Chalk Dust Torture	Fam. Mockbrd
4/21/91	5	2	4/11	The Landlady	Fam. Mockbrd
5/2/91	4	1	6/11	The Landlady	Llama
5/4/91	2	2	3/9	Llama	Fam. Mockbrd
5/16/91	5	1	6/11	Llama	Fam. Mockbrd
7/14/91	7	1	7/11	My Sweet One	Fam. Mockbrd
9/30/91	17	1	3/4	Stash	Fam. Mockbrd
10/13/91	8	1	5/13	The Landlady	Fam. Mockbrd
10/27/91	7	2	2/13	Llama	Fam. Mockbrd
11/2/91	5	1	8/10	Bouncing	Fam. Mockbrd
11/13/91	6	2	2/9	David Bowie	Fam. Mockbrd
11/20/91	5	1	3/11	Possum	Fam. Mockbrd
12/7/91	9	1	4/11	Foam	Fam. Mockbrd
3/19/92	9	1	9/12	Dinner and a Movie	Fam. Mockbrd
3/24/92	4	1	10/13	Llama	Fam. Mockbrd
3/31/92	6	1	8/10	Llama	Fam. Mockbrd
4/16/92	11	1	9/12	Maze	Icculus
4/21/92	4	2	2/13	Dinner and a Movie	Fam. Mockbrd
4/24/92	3	1	2/11	Runaway Jim	Icculus
5/2/92	5	1	2/11	Runaway Jim	Icculus
5/6/92	3	1	8/11	Brother	Fam. Mockbrd
5/17/92	9	1	3/11	Llama	Fam. Mockbrd
11/21/92	46	1	9/11	Maze	Fam. Mockbrd
11/27/92	4	1	4/12	Divided Sky	Fam. Mockbrd
12/4/92	6	1	9/11	Maze	Fam. Mockbrd
12/8/92	4	1	4/11	Llama	Fam. Mockbrd
12/31/92	8	2	4/10	Sparkle	Fam. Mockbrd
2/7/93	5	1	6/12	Sparkle	Fam. Mockbrd
2/19/93	9	1	6/11	Maze	Fam. Mockbrd
2/25/93	5	1	5/11	Maze	Fam. Mockbrd
3/8/93	7	1	6/12	Llama	How High the Moon
3/18/93	7	1	6/11	Maze	Fam. Mockbrd
3/22/93	3	2	7/13	AC/DC Bag	Fam. Mockbrd
3/25/93	2	2	5/13	Uncle Pen	Kung
4/5/93	9	1	8/10	Stash	Fam. Mockbrd
4/21/93	9	1	6/11	Maze	Fam. Mockbrd
4/25/93	4	1	7/11	Runaway Jim	Fam. Mockbrd
5/3/93	6	1	7/11	Split Open and Melt	Fam. Mockbrd
7/29/93	18	1	8/10	My Mind's Got A Mind	Fam. Mockbrd
8/7/93	6	1	8/10	Maze	Fam. Mockbrd
8/15/93	7	1	8/10	Stash	Fam. Mockbrd
12/30/93	11	1	6/10	Paul and Silas	Fam. Mockbrd
4/11/94	8	2	3/11	Maze	Fam. Mockbrd
4/24/94	1	2	5/9	Julius	Fam. Mockbrd
5/25/94	22	1	5/11	Stash	Fam. Mockbrd
6/16/94	10	2	3/11	Run Like an Antelope	Kung
6/26/94	9	1	7/11	AC/DC Bag	Fam. Mockbrd
7/8/94	8	1	7/11	AC/DC Bag	Fam. Mockbrd
10/14/94	13	1	10/12	Rift	Fam. Mockbrd

DATE	GAP	SET	POS.	SONG BEFORE	SONG AFTER
10/27/94	10	1	4/11	Maze	The Vibration of Lif
11/4/94	6	1	5/9	David Bowie	Fam. Mockbrd
11/17/94	5	1	8/11	Dog Faced Boy	The Vibration of Lif
11/30/94	9	1	5/10	Reba	Fam. Mockbrd
10/5/95	43	2	3/9	Runaway Jim	Fam. Mockbrd
12/1/95	35	1	7/10	Chalk Dust Torture	Fam. Mockbrd
12/31/95	16	1	6/10	Maze	Shine
8/7/96	25	2	5/10	Free	Fam. Mockbrd
10/31/96	18	1	7/10	Reba	Fam. Mockbrd
8/14/97	78	2	5/8	Harry Hood	Merry Pranksters Jam
8/7/98	57	1	9/10	Ghost	Fam. Mockbrd
9/30/00	144	2	3/7	AC/DC Bag	Fam. Mockbrd

Has not been played in the last 5 shows.

Come On Baby, Let's Go Downtown

DATE	GAP	SET	POS.	SONG BEFORE	SONG AFTER
9/23/00	11091		1/6	***	The Moma Dance
10/5/00	8	1	6/10	Limb By Limb	Beauty of my Dreams

Has not been played in the last 2 shows.

Come Together

DATE	GAP	SET	POS.	SONG BEFORE	SONG AFTER
12/8/95	781	E	1/2	***	A Day in the Life

Has not been played in the last 338 shows.

Communication Breakdown

DATE	GAP	SET	POS.	SONG BEFORE	SONG AFTER
1/27/90	147	2	1/7	***	Caravan
1/28/90	1	1	9/9	The Famous Mockingbi	***
9/15/90	61	E	1/2	***	You Enjoy My

Has not been played in the last 910 shows.

Contact

DATE	GAP	SET	POS.	SONG BEFORE	SONG AFTER
6/15/88	51	2	4/9	The Sloth	Dinner and a
6/21/88	3	2	8/10	Good Times Bad Times	Peaches en Regalia
7/23/88	4	3	2/7	You Enjoy Myself	Harry Hood
7/30/88	3	2	4/6	Baby Left Me	Maiden Voyage
10/31/88	10	1	10/12	La Grange	Costume Contest
11/3/88	1	2	6/9	Whipping Post	Bold As Love
12/2/88	3	1	6/7	Divided Sky	You Enjoy My
12/10/88	1	2	3/7	You Enjoy Myself	The Sloth
1/26/89	3	2	7/10	Possum	BBFCFM
2/7/89	2	2	6/9	Timber (Jerry)	Alumni Blues
2/18/89	3	1	9/9	Peaches en Regalia	***
3/4/89	3	2	5/5	Run Like an Antelope	***
3/14/89	2	1	7/12	Fluffhead	AC/DC Bag
4/27/89	5	E	1/2	***	David Bowie
5/1/89	2	2	10/10	David Bowie	***
5/6/89	2	2	3/8	Suzy Greenberg	Fire
5/13/89	2		6/7	If I Only Had a Brai	Fire
5/20/89	1	2	6/9	Foam	Take the A-Trn
5/21/89	1	1	3/13	Foam	Mike's Song
5/28/89	3	2	11/16	Possum	The Price of Love
6/23/89	1	E	1/2	***	Good Time Ba
8/17/89	2	3	7/8	Alumni Blues	Run Like Antel
8/26/89	3	E	1/3	***	The Lizards
10/1/89	4	2	9/11	If I Only Had a Brai	Split Open and
10/7/89	2	2	8/9	David Bowie	Highway to Hell
10/31/89	9	E	1/4	***	Run Like Antel
11/18/89	7	1	11/11	David Bowie	***
11/30/89	1	2	10/11	Suzy Greenberg	David Bowie
12/9/89	5	E	1/2	***	BBFCFM
12/15/89	1	2	7/8	Jesus Just Left	David Bowie
12/31/89	4	E	1/1	***	***
2/10/90	7	1	9/10	Carolina	David Bowie
2/23/90	5	E	1/3	***	I Didn't Know
2/24/90	1	2	9/9	Lawn Boy	***
3/8/90	6	E	1/2	***	Good Time Ba
3/9/90	1	2	10/11	La Grange	BBFCFM
3/11/90	2	1	1/13	***	The Oh Kee Pa
3/28/90	2	2	11/16	Split Open and Melt	La Grange
4/4/90	1	E	1/2	***	Highway to Hell
4/5/90	1	2	13/13	If I Only Had a Brai	***
4/7/90	2	2	3/3	BBFCFM	***
4/25/90	11	E	1/1	***	***
5/4/90	4	E	1/1	***	***
5/19/90	7	E	1/1	***	***
5/24/90	2	2	11/11	Highway to Hell	***
6/1/90	3	1	12/12	BBFCFM	***
6/2/90	1	1	8/9	Fire	Good Time Ba
6/9/90	4	E	2/2	The Landlady	***
6/16/90	1	E	1/3	***	BBFCFM
9/16/90	4	E	1/1	***	***
10/7/90	10	E	1/1	***	***
10/30/90	4	3	4/5	Good Times Bad Times	AC/DC Bag
11/4/90	4	E	1/2	***	Highway to Hell
11/16/90	3	E	1/2	***	Fire
11/26/90	3	E	2/3	Fire	Highway to Hell
12/8/90	4	E	2/3	Funky Bitch	Highway to Hell
2/9/91	9	E	3/4	Suzy Greenberg	Rocky Top
2/15/91	2	E	3/4	BBFCFM	Golgi Apparat
2/27/91	6	E	1/1	***	***
3/23/91	11	2	11/11	David Bowie	***
3/29/91	2	E	1/3	***	Tweezer Repri
4/4/91	4	E	3/4	Highway to Hell	Uncle Pen
4/12/91	4	E	1/3	***	BBFCFM
7/11/91	21	E	1/2	***	BBFCFM
7/14/91	3	E	1/2	***	BBFCFM
7/15/91	1	E	2/3	Caravan	Alumni Blues
7/21/91	4	2	8/9	AC/DC Bag	Tweezer Repri
7/24/91	2	E	1/2	***	BBFCFM
7/27/91	3	E	2/2	Touch Me	***
9/28/91	5	E	1/2	***	BBFCFM
10/12/91	9	E	3/4	Rocky Top	Golgi Apparat
11/2/91	13	E	1/2	***	BBFCFM
11/30/91	16	E	1/2	***	Rocky Top
3/13/92	10	E	1/2	***	Fire
4/1/92	14	2	12/13	Tweezer Reprise	Rocky Top
4/7/92	5	E	1/2	***	Tweezer Repri
4/18/92	7	E	1/2	***	BBFCFM
4/24/92	5	E	1/2	***	BBFCFM
5/5/92	7	E	1/2	***	Rocky Top
11/28/92	61	E	1/2	***	Tweezer Repri
12/11/92	11	E	1/2	***	Good Time Ba
2/7/93	11	E	2/3	Amazing Grace	BBFCFM
2/15/93	6	E	1/2	***	Fire
3/13/93	18	1	8/11	Split Open and Melt	Llama
3/28/93	12	E	1/2	***	BBFCFM
4/14/93	10	E	2/3	Lengthwise	Tweezer Repri
4/25/93	9	2	4/11	Tweezer	Uncle Pen
5/3/93	6	2	6/12	Tweezer	It's Ice
5/6/93	2	E	2/3	Sweet Adeline	Tweezer Repri
5/30/93	4	1	11/13	Split Open and Melt	Llama
7/22/93	6	2	6/11	It's Ice	Possum
7/30/93	7	1	1/10	***	Llama
8/9/93	7	2	7/8	You Enjoy Myself	Crimes of the Mind
8/28/93	13	2	13/14	You Enjoy Myself	Chalk Dust Tor
12/29/93	2	2	5/11	Run Like an Antelope	BBFCFM
4/8/94	2	E	1/2	***	BBFCFM
4/17/94	8	2	8/9	Maze	Golgi Apparat
4/24/94	6	2	8/9	Chalk Dust Torture	Good Time Ba
5/12/94	12	2	10/11	Love You	BBFCFM
5/21/94	7	2	4/9	David Bowie	Big Ball Jam
5/25/94	3	2	5/9	Maze	Big Ball Jam
6/11/94	7	2	8/9	Maze	Frankenstein
6/16/94	3	2	8/11	Down with Disease	BBFCFM
7/16/94	23	2	10/11	Harry Hood	Chalk Dust Tor
10/9/94	3	2	7/8	Julius	Possum
10/27/94	14	2	4/7	Tweezer	BBFCFM
11/18/94	12	2	6/7	Tweezer	Possum
12/28/94	18	2	6/9	Weekapaug Groove	Llama
6/20/95	15	2	6/9	Mike's Song	Weekapaug Gr
6/30/95	8	2	7/10	Mike's Song	Weekapaug Gr
10/7/95	12	2	6/9	It's Ice	Frankenstein
10/24/95	11	2	7/8	Run Like an Antelope	Cavern
11/18/95	13	2	6/10	You Enjoy Myself	BBFCFM
11/28/95	6	2	8/10	Run Like an Antelope	BBFCFM
8/10/96	45	E	1/2	***	Fire
8/16/96	4	2	12/13	Simple	Weekapaug Gr
11/11/96	20	2	10/11	Maze	Slave
11/30/96	12	2	5/11	Brother	Also Sprach
8/16/97	60	E	1/2	***	Loving Cup
12/9/97	19	2	4/6	Timber (Jerry)	Axilla
7/28/98	30	2	5/8	Brother	Maze
11/11/98	27	E	1/3	***	Rocky Top
7/3/99	19	2	6/7	Run Like an Antelope	Little Drummer Boy
9/18/99	29	E	1/2	***	Tweezer Repri
10/10/99	16	E	1/2	***	Misty Mountain Hop
6/13/00	23	2	4/9	Run Like an Antelope	Sand
6/23/00	5	2	5/7	Twist	Makisupa Policeman
9/17/00	23	E	1/2	***	Rocky Top

Has not been played in the last 14 shows.

Cool it Down

DATE	GAP	SET	POS.	SONG BEFORE	SONG AFTER
10/31/98	983	2	4/10	Rock and Roll	New Age
9/24/00	127	2	7/8	Love You	David Bowie

Has not been played in the last 9 shows.

Corrine Corrina

DATE	GAP	SET	POS.	SONG BEFORE	SONG AFTER
2/21/87	18	2	13/15	Ya Mar	Dog Gone Dog
3/6/87	1	1	3/6	Good Times Bad Times	Golgi Apparat
3/23/87	1	2	5/9	Dave's Energy Guide	Why Don't U Love Me
5/11/87	3	E	2/3	Golgi Apparatus	Letter to Jimmy Page
8/9/87	2	3	7/7	McGrupp	***
8/29/87	3	3	2/10	La Grange	Mike's Song
11/19/87	2	2	5/6	Fee	Alumni Blues
1/27/88	1	2	3/10	Slave	Fire
2/24/88	3	1	9/11	Slave	Fee
3/11/88	2	1	10/12	Flat Fee	The Lizards
5/25/88	9	3	9/11	BBFCFM	Harpua
7/30/88	11	2	6/6	Maiden Voyage	***
2/6/89	19	3	9/9	Whipping Post	***
2/18/89	4	1	2/9	Whipping Post	Divided Sky
12/30/99	985	1	4/12	Suzy Greenberg	Limb By Limb
9/15/00	35	1	3/8	Gotta Jibboo	Birds of a Feather

Has not been played in the last 15 shows.

Costume Contest

DATE	GAP	SET	POS.	SONG BEFORE	SONG AFTER
10/31/88	71	1	11/12	Contact	Harry Hood
10/31/91	264	2	2/14	The Landlady	Wait
10/31/94	346	E	2/3	Amazing Grace	The Squirmin

Has not been played in the last 438 shows.

Cowboy's Sweetheart

DATE	GAP	SET	POS.	SONG BEFORE	SONG AFTER
12/6/96	858	E	3/7	Wildwood Weed	Harpua

Has not been played in the last 261 shows.

Cracklin' Rosie

DATE	GAP	SET	POS.	SONG BEFORE	SONG AFTER
3/7/92	360	2	10/11	Weekapaug Groove	Tweezer Repri
3/12/92	2	2	9/11	David Bowie	My Sweet One
3/14/92	2	2	9/10	Harry Hood	Possum
3/19/92	2	2	10/10	The Squirming Coil	***
3/21/92	2	2	10/11	Weigh	You Enjoy My
3/25/92	3	2	11/12	Chalk Dust Torture	Golgi Apparat
3/26/92	1	2	12/13	Cavern	Possum
3/30/92	3	2	11/13	Chalk Dust Torture	Bouncing

DATE	GAP	SET	POS.	SONG BEFORE	SONG AFTER
4/1/92	2	2	9/13	Chalk Dust Torture	The Squirmin
4/6/92	4	2	11/13	Stash	Uncle Pen
4/12/92	3	2	8/10	NICU	Harry Hood
4/15/92	2	2	6/8	NICU	My Sweet One
4/17/92	2	2	7/8	Uncle Pen	Tweezer Repri
4/22/92	4	2	9/11	Poor Heart	Harpua
4/23/92	1	2	12/13	Maze	Golgi Apparat
4/30/92	4	2	9/11	Chalk Dust Torture	Harry Hood
5/2/92	2	2	9/10	Chalk Dust Torture	Cavern
5/3/92	1	2	10/14	The Mango Song	Dinner and a
5/9/92	5	2	7/8	Llama	Golgi Apparat
5/14/92	3	2	12/13	Stash	Possum
5/16/92	2	2	11/13	AC/DC Bag	Poor Heart
11/25/92	50	2	7/9	Tweezer	My Sweet One
12/3/92	6	2	11/13	Big Ball Jam	Take the A-Trn
12/13/92	9	2	12/14	Big Ball Jam	Harry Hood
2/10/93	11	2	10/11	Silent in the Mornin	Possum
2/21/93	9	2	8/10	Bathtub Gin	The Squirmin
3/6/93	9	2	8/9	You Enjoy Myself	BBFCFM
3/21/93	10	2	9/12	Big Ball Jam	Llama
3/27/93	5	2	12/14	Weekapaug Groove	Poor Heart
4/5/93	7	2	8/9	You Enjoy Myself	Tweezer Repri
4/17/93	6	2	9/11	Suzy Greenberg	Big Ball Jam
5/2/93	12	2	9/10	Run Like an Antelope	BBFCFM
5/6/93	3	2	10/11	Rocky Top	That's Alright Mama
8/6/93	21	2	11/12	Slave	Tweezer Repri
8/24/93	13	2	9/10	Rift	Run Like Antel
12/31/93	7	3	7/9	Suzy Greenberg	Harry Hood
4/17/94	12	E	1/2	***	Bold As Love
6/25/94	46	2	7/9	You Enjoy Myself	Harry Hood
10/26/94	31	2	6/7	You Enjoy Myself	David Bowie
11/19/94	14	2	4/7	You Enjoy Myself	Harry Hood
12/9/94	15	2	7/9	Big Ball Jam	You Enjoy My
12/29/94	3	2	6/9	The Lizards	Good Time Ba
6/20/95	14	2	8/9	Weekapaug Groove	Highway to Hell
6/30/95	8	E	1/2	***	Golgi Apparat
11/12/95	32	2	6/8	Slave	Possum
8/14/96	58	2	8/10	Theme From the Botto	Sample in a Ja
8/6/98	148	1	11/12	The Moma Dance	My Soul
12/10/99	92	2	5/7	Have Mercy	Twist

Has not been played in the last 58 shows.

Crew Football Theme Song

DATE	GAP	SET	POS.	SONG BEFORE	SONG AFTER
4/16/91	278	2	1/11	***	My Sweet One
5/2/92	121	2	3/10	David Bowie	David Bowie

Has not been played in the last 720 shows.

Crimes of the Mind

DATE	GAP	SET	POS.	SONG BEFORE	SONG AFTER
8/3/91	311	E	4/5	Bitchin' Again	Harry Hood
11/8/91	28	2	13/13	Family Picture	***
8/9/93	232	2	8/8	Contact	***
8/28/93	13	1	9/9	The Squirming Coil	***
7/10/94	73	2	10/10	The Squirming Coil	***

Has not been played in the last 462 shows.

Crosseyed and Painless

DATE	GAP	SET	POS.	SONG BEFORE	SONG AFTER
10/31/96	835	2	2/8	Born Under Punches (	The Great Curve
11/2/96	1	2	1/6	***	Run Like Antel
2/16/97	29	1	4/10	Bouncing	Guelah Papyrus
2/21/97	4	1	5/6	The Lizards	You Enjoy My
8/13/97	43	1	9/11	Beauty of My Dreams	Wilson
12/31/99	158	2	11/35	You Enjoy Myself	The Inlaw Josie Wale
7/12/00	26	2	3/5	Piper	Prince Caspian
9/14/00	7	2	2/5	Drowned	Dog Faced Boy

Has not been played in the last 16 shows.

Crossroads

DATE	GAP	SET	POS.	SONG BEFORE	SONG AFTER
5/8/93	549	2	13/18	Mike's Song	Mike's Song
10/11/95	196	2	9/11	Suzy Greenberg	Hello My Baby
10/25/95	10	2	9/9	Suzy Greenberg	***
11/10/95	6	2	4/9	You Enjoy Myself	You Enjoy My
12/9/95	21	2	7/8	Slave	Sweet Adeline
8/9/97	127	1	8/8	Lawn Boy	***
12/3/97	20	E	1/1	***	***
12/29/97	9	1	3/9	Golgi Apparatus	Cars Trucks Buses
11/28/98	63	2	7/9	Prince Caspian	Tweezer

Has not been played in the last 118 shows.

Cry Baby Cry

DATE	GAP	SET	POS.	SONG BEFORE	SONG AFTER
10/31/94	681	2	29/30	Savoy Truffle	Revolution 9
11/22/94	12	2	4/13	Yerushalayim	The Curtain
6/16/95	27	1	5/10	Ya Mar	It's Ice
11/21/98	277	1	5/13	Divided Sky	Boogie On Reggae

Has not been played in the last 122 shows.

Cryin'

DATE	GAP	SET	POS.	SONG BEFORE	SONG AFTER
9/29/95	737	2	7/8	Billy Breathes	A Day in the Life

Has not been played in the last 382 shows.

Cut My Hair

DATE	GAP	SET	POS.	SONG BEFORE	SONG AFTER
10/31/95	759	2	4/17	Quadrophenia	The Punk Meets The G

Has not been played in the last 360 shows.

Dahlia

DATE	GAP	SET	POS.	SONG BEFORE	SONG AFTER
9/13/90	207	2	14/15	Self	The Revolution's Ove

Has not been played in the last 912 shows.

Daniel

DATE	GAP	SET	POS.	SONG BEFORE	SONG AFTER
7/15/93	552	2	11/11	Walk Away	***
7/16/93	1	1	1/10	***	Golgi Apparat
7/17/93	1	E	2/3	Amazing Grace	Tweezer Repri
7/21/93	2	1	12/12	Purple Rain	***
7/23/93	2	E	2/2	Amazing Grace	***
7/24/93	2	1	12/12	Purple Rain	Good Time Ba
7/29/93	4	2	8/9	Purple Rain	Good Time Ba
7/31/93	2	2	10/11	Purple Rain	Highway to Hell
8/8/93	5	2	10/11	Love You	Good Time Ba
8/14/93	5	2	10/13	The Squirming Coil	You Enjoy My
8/17/93	3	1	9/9	Fast Enough for You	***
8/21/93	2	2	10/10	Harry Hood	***
8/25/93	2	1	2/11	AC/DC Bag	Sample in a Ja
8/28/93	2	E	1/2	***	Amazing Grce
2/23/97	287	2	1/9	***	Suzy Greenber

Has not been played in the last 248 shows.

Dave's Energy Guide

DATE	GAP	SET	POS.	SONG BEFORE	SONG AFTER
5/3/85	5	1	3/4	Mike's Song	Big Leg Emma
10/17/85	2	1	4/9	Mike's Song	Revolution
11/23/85	3	3	4/4	Run Like an Antelope	***
2/3/86	1	1	3/7	Mike's Song	You Enjoy My
4/1/86	1	1	5/7	The Pendulum	Icculus
10/31/86	3	1	6/11	Melt the Guns	Sneakin' Sally
2/13/87	2	1	12/14	Melt the Guns	Fluffhead
3/23/87	3	2	4/9	Ride Captain Ride	Corrine Corina
4/24/87	1	1	6/14	You Enjoy Myself	Punch Me in the Eye
4/29/87	1	2	3/7	Melt the Guns	Take the A-Trn
8/6/88	41	1	4/9	Cities	Cities
9/8/88	2	2	4/8	Cities	Cities
9/13/88	2	2	4/6	Cities	Run Like Antel
9/13/88	0	3	4/8	BBFCFM	BBFCFM
6/28/95	662	2	4/10	Tweezer	Tweezer

Has not been played in the last 390 shows.

David Bowie

DATE	GAP	SET	POS.	SONG BEFORE	SONG AFTER
10/31/86	15	2	5/11	Peaches en Regalia	Have Mercy
12/6/86	1	1	6/14	AC/DC Bag	Fluff's Travels
12/6/86	0	1	9/14	Clod	You Enjoy My
4/24/87	5	1	12/14	Who Do? We Do!	Dear Mrs. Reagan
8/9/87	4	3	1/7	***	You Enjoy My
8/10/87	1	3	2/7	Icculus	Jesus Just Left
8/29/87	2	3	8/10	Shaggy Dog	Jesus Just Left
9/2/87	1	1	6/13	Wilson	The Chase
9/27/87	2	1	1/9	***	Funky Bitch
10/14/87	1	1	8/12	Possum	AC/DC Bag
10/31/87	1	2	17/17	Fluffhead	***
2/7/88	4	1	10/10	I Didn't Know	***
2/24/88	2	1	11/11	Fee	***
2/26/88	1	2	2/9	The Lizards	Ballad - Curtis Loew
3/11/88	1	1	12/12	The Lizards	***
4/22/88	5	2	13/13	Ballad - Curtis Loew	***
6/20/88	7	2	9/9	Ballad - Curtis Loew	***
7/24/88	6	2	8/8	Cities	***
9/22/88	9	1	5/5	You Enjoy Myself	***
9/24/88	1	2	1/7	***	The Lizards
11/3/88	3	3	6/6	Harpua	***
11/5/88	1	1	11/11	Alumni Blues	***
11/11/88	1	1	8/8	The Famous Mockingbi	***
12/10/88	2	1	3/12	Golgi Apparatus	The Lizards
1/26/89	3	2	10/10	Foam	***
2/6/89	1	E	1/1	***	***
3/3/89	6	2	12/12	Take the A-Train	***
3/24/89	4	1	10/10	Take the A-Train	***
4/20/89	3	1	12/12	Foam	***
4/27/89	1	E	2/2	Contact	***
5/1/89	2	2	9/10	The Famous Mockingbi	Contact
5/6/89	2	1	13/13	The Famous Mockingbi	***
5/12/89	2	1	6/15	AC/DC Bag	Buried Alive
5/13/89	1	1	12/12	Split Open and Melt	***
5/20/89	1	2	8/9	Take the A-Train	Golgi Apparat
5/26/89	2	2	1/6	***	The Mango Song
6/23/89	3	2	7/7	Possum	***
8/26/89	5	2	9/9	Foam	***
9/9/89	1	1	11/11	My Sweet One	***
9/14/89	1	1	9/9	Fee	***
9/21/89	1	1	9/9	Who Do? We Do!	***
10/7/89	3	2	7/9	AC/DC Bag	Contact
10/13/89	2	1	1/4	***	Slave
10/21/89	3	1	10/10	Dog Gone Dog	***
10/26/89	2	2	15/15	No Dogs Allowed	***
10/31/89	2	1	1/8	***	Wilson
11/3/89	2	2	1/5	***	No Dogs Allowed
11/16/89	4	2	4/4	Tela	***
11/18/89	1	1	10/11	Reba	Contact
11/30/89	1	2	11/11	Contact	***
12/9/89	5	1	7/10	Rocky Top	Lawn Boy
12/15/89	1	2	8/8	Contact	***
12/30/89	3	1	2/2	Fluff's Travels	***
2/1/90	6	1	1/11	***	Walk Away
2/9/90	1	2	9/9	Ballad - Curtis Loew	***
2/10/90	1	1	10/10	Contact	***
2/22/90	4	1	9/9	The Lizards	***
2/25/90	3	1	8/11	Bouncing	Satin Doll
3/7/90	4	1	6/6	The Lizards	***
3/11/90	4	2	13/13	AC/DC Bag	***
4/5/90	4	1	3/9	Ya Mar	Carolina
4/7/90	2	1	1/12	***	My Sweet One
4/12/90	3	2	1/11	***	My Sweet One
4/14/90	2	2	11/11	Fee	***
4/18/90	1	2	10/12	Lawn Boy	Jagermeister
4/18/90	0	2	12/12	Jagermeister	***
4/25/90	5	1	4/4	My Sweet One	***
5/6/90	5	2	4/7	Esther	Terrapin

DATE	GAP	SET	POS.	SONG BEFORE	SONG AFTER
5/13/90	4	1	10/10	Lawn Boy	***
6/5/90	9	1	10/12	Take the A-Train	Lawn Boy
9/15/90	7	1	10/14	The Asse Festival	Golgi Apparat
9/22/90	4	1	12/12	I Didn't Know	***
9/29/90	2	1	9/9	Magilla	***
10/6/90	4	1	12/13	If I Only Had a Brai	Carolina
10/30/90	5	2	12/12	Buried Alive	***
11/2/90	2	2	9/9	I Didn't Know	***
11/4/90	2	1	10/10	My Sweet One	***
11/17/90	4	1	11/11	Suzy Greenberg	***
11/24/90	1	1	11/11	Suzy Greenberg	***
11/26/90	1	1	8/11	Paul and Silas	Divided Sky
12/7/90	3	2	11/11	No Good Trying	***
12/29/90	3	1	5/10	Esther	Lawn Boy
2/1/91	2	1	10/10	Bouncing	***
2/3/91	2	2	1/9	***	The Squirmin
2/8/91	2	1	11/11	Guelah Papyrus	***
2/15/91	3	2	1/10	***	Bathtub Gin
2/19/91	2	1	9/9	The Squirming Coil	***
2/21/91	2	2	9/9	The Asse Festival	***
2/27/91	2	2	5/11	The Squirming Coil	Lawn Boy
3/1/91	2	1	11/11	Whole Lotta Love Jam	***
3/6/91	1	1	11/11	Bouncing	***
3/9/91	2	2	8/13	Guelah Papyrus	The Lizards
3/13/91	1	1	9/9	The Squirming Coil	***
3/17/91	3	1	12/12	The Lizards	***
3/23/91	2	2	10/11	Cavern	Contact
3/28/91	1	1	9/14	My Sweet One	The Squirmin
4/3/91	2	2	9/9	Fee	***
4/4/91	1	2	4/10	Guelah Papyrus	Lawn Boy
4/16/91	6	1	9/9	Tela	***
4/21/91	4	2	11/11	I Didn't Know	***
4/25/91	2	1	11/11	Suzy Greenberg	***
5/2/91	2	1	10/11	Cavern	Sweet Adeline
5/10/91	4	1	1/10	***	Cavern
5/12/91	2	1	2/13	***	Bathtub Gin
5/18/91	3	2	8/10	Guelah Papyrus	Terrapin
7/12/91	3	1	12/12	Cavern	***
7/19/91	5	1	4/10	Bouncing	Fee
7/20/91	1	1	10/10	Gumbo	***
7/24/91	3	2	3/10	Guelah Papyrus	Jesus Just Left
9/26/91	6	1	10/10	Foam	***
9/29/91	3	2	10/10	Golgi Apparatus	***
10/4/91	4	1	10/10	Magilla	***
10/11/91	3	2	4/9	Foam	The Mango Song
10/13/91	2	1	9/9	Love You	***
10/17/91	2	2	4/9	Suzy Greenberg	Lawn Boy
10/24/91	4	1	12/12	T.M.W.S.I.Y. Reprise	***
10/28/91	2	1	10/10	Fee	***
10/31/91	2	2	9/14	Wait	Horn
11/7/91	3	2	7/11	Horn	Take the A-Trn
11/10/91	4	1	4/10	Uncle Pen	Fee
11/13/91	2	2	1/9	***	Col. Forbin's A
11/19/91	4	2	11/11	Cavern	***
11/24/91	5	1	9/9	I Didn't Know	***
12/4/91	2	1	11/11	Bouncing	***
3/6/92	5	1	11/11	All Things Recnsdrd	***
3/12/92	3	2	8/11	Uncle Pen	Cracklin' Rosi
3/19/92	1	2	12/12	All Things Recnsdrd	***
3/21/92	2	2	8/11	All Things Recnsdrd	Weigh
3/24/92	2	1	13/13	The Landlady	***
3/26/92	2	1	10/10	NICU	***
3/28/92	2	1	8/10	The Landlady	Glide
4/1/92	3	1	11/12	The Landlady	Carolina
4/5/92	3	2	9/12	The Landlady	Love You
4/8/92	3	2	3/15	Suzy Greenberg	T.M.W.S.I.Y.
4/13/92	2	1	10/10	Take the A-Train	***
4/17/92	3	1	11/13	The Landlady	Catapult
4/17/92	0	1	13/13	Catapult	***
4/21/92	3	1	11/11	Bouncing	***
4/24/92	3	2	1/12	***	Cavern
4/29/92	2	1	10/10	Take the A-Train	***
5/2/92	3	2	2/10	Glide	Crew Football Theme

DATE	GAP	SET	POS.	SONG BEFORE	SONG AFTER
5/2/92	0	2	4/10	Crew Football Theme	Tela
5/8/92	5	1	11/12	Bouncing	Memories
5/12/92	3	1	12/12	Horn	***
5/16/92	3	1	11/11	Cavern	***
6/27/92	7	1	10/10	Uncle Pen	***
7/9/92	3	1	9/12	Guelah Papyrus	Vacuum Solo
7/9/92	0	1	11/12	Vacuum Solo	Glide
7/16/92	1	1	10/10	Guelah Papyrus	***
7/19/92	3	1	4/5	Runaway Jim	Sweet Adeline
7/22/92	2	1	7/7	Cavern	***
7/27/92	4	1	3/7	All Things Recnsdrd	Horn
8/2/92	5	1	6/8	Suzy Greenberg	Cavern
8/17/92	4	1	11/11	Bouncing	***
8/20/92	2	1	5/6	Suzy Greenberg	Sweet Adeline
11/20/92	10	1	12/12	I Walk the Line	***
11/23/92	3	1	11/11	Memories	***
11/27/92	2	2	8/13	I Walk the Line	The Horse
12/1/92	3	2	11/11	Baby Elephant Walk	***
12/4/92	3	2	2/10	Suzy Greenberg	Esther
12/7/92	3	2	9/12	Fee	Love You
12/11/92	3	1	11/11	Memories	***
12/13/92	2	1	11/11	I Didn't Know	***
12/30/92	3	1	12/14	I Didn't Know	Timber (Jerry)
12/30/92	0	1	14/14	Timber (Jerry)	***
2/3/93	2	1	11/11	Guelah Papyrus	***
2/5/93	2	1	11/11	The Vibration of Lif	***
2/9/93	3	1	1/10	***	Bouncing
2/11/93	2	1	10/10	Lawn Boy	***
2/13/93	2	1	1/10	***	Bouncing
2/17/93	2	2	3/11	The Landlady	Glide
2/19/93	2	1	11/11	Poor Heart	***
2/22/93	3	1	10/10	I Didn't Know	***
2/25/93	2	1	11/11	I Didn't Know	***
3/2/93	3	1	13/13	I Didn't Know	***
3/8/93	4	1	12/12	Glide	***
3/12/93	2	1	11/11	Silent in the Mornin	***
3/14/93	2	2	2/11	Halley's Comet	Ballad - Curtis Loew
3/18/93	3	1	11/11	I Didn't Know	***
3/22/93	3	1	10/10	Sparkle	***
3/27/93	4	1	10/10	I Didn't Know	***
3/31/93	3	1	10/10	I Didn't Know	***
4/5/93	4	1	10/10	The Famous Mockingbi	***
4/10/93	2	1	10/10	Lawn Boy	***
4/20/93	6	1	10/10	Lawn Boy	***
4/27/93	6	1	10/10	Sparkle	***
5/1/93	3	1	10/10	Glide	***
5/8/93	6	2	1/18	***	Jessica Jam
5/8/93	0	2	3/18	Jessica Jam	Have Mercy
5/8/93	0	2	5/18	Have Mercy	The Horse
7/15/93	3	2	1/11	***	The Horse
7/17/93	2	1	11/11	The Oh Kee Pa Ceremo	***
7/25/93	6	1	10/10	I Didn't Know	***
7/30/93	4	2	10/10	The Squirming Coil	***
8/8/93	6	1	11/11	I Didn't Know	***
8/13/93	4	1	10/10	Horn	***
8/17/93	4	2	2/10	Also Sprach	The Horse
8/21/93	2	2	7/10	Lawn Boy	If I Only Had a Brai
8/26/93	3	2	2/8	Also Sprach	Lifeboy
12/30/93	4	1	1/10	***	Weigh
4/8/94	5	2	8/9	Big Ball Jam	Suzy Greenber
4/13/94	4	2	8/10	Take the A-Train	Purple Rain
4/17/94	4	2	1/9	***	Wolfman's Brother
4/22/94	4	1	11/11	Silent in the Mornin	***
4/24/94	2	2	2/9	Demand	The Mango Song
4/30/94	4	2	2/10	Wilson	Wolfman's Brother
5/3/94	2	2	1/8	***	If I Could
5/6/94	2	2	9/9	Bike	***
5/10/94	3	2	10/10	Nellie Kane	***
5/14/94	3	1	9/9	Ginseng Sullivan	***
5/21/94	5	2	3/9	Sample in a Jar	Contact
5/27/94	5	1	5/9	Bouncing	If I Could

DATE	GAP	SET	POS.	SONG BEFORE	SONG AFTER
5/29/94	2	1	8/8	I Didn't Know	***
6/10/94	2	1	6/9	Demand	The Lizards
6/14/94	3	2	3/9	Demand	If I Could
6/18/94	3	2	2/10	Peaches en Regalia	Mind Left Body Jam
6/18/94	0	2	4/10	Mind Left Body Jam	Horn
6/23/94	4	2	2/8	Frankenstein	The Mango Song
6/29/94	4	1	9/11	Catapult	I Didn't Know
7/1/94	2	2	1/11	***	If I Could
7/3/94	2	1	10/10	Axilla (Part II)	***
7/6/94	2	1	9/9	Carolina	***
7/10/94	3	2	2/10	Sample in a Jar	Glide
7/15/94	3	2	2/10	Letter to Jimmy Page	Bouncing
10/9/94	4	2	1/8	***	Bouncing
10/12/94	2	2	2/9	Peaches en Regalia	Bouncing
10/18/94	5	2	1/10	***	The Horse
10/22/94	3	2	2/11	Peaches en Regalia	The Horse
10/26/94	3	2	7/7	Cracklin' Rosie	***
10/28/94	2	2	2/12	Also Sprach	Manteca
10/28/94	0	2	4/12	Manteca	The Lizards
10/31/94	2	3	1/7	***	Bouncing
11/4/94	3	1	4/9	Bouncing	Col. Forbin's A
11/14/94	3	2	2/10	Peaches en Regalia	Yerushalayim
11/17/94	2	2	2/8	Also Sprach	Sleeping Monkey
11/20/94	3	2	2/10	Also Sprach	Glide
11/26/94	4	2	2/6	Halley's Comet	Sweet Adeline
12/2/94	4	2	2/8	Chalk Dust Torture	Buried Alive
12/8/94	5	2	7/8	Sweet Adeline	Golgi Apparat
12/29/94	4	2	3/7	Digital Delay Loop J	Halley's Comet
6/9/95	6	2	5/8	Cavern	Acoustic Army
6/13/95	2	2	1/7	***	The Lizards
6/15/95	2	2	3/8	Ha Ha Ha	Strange Design
6/19/95	3	2	2/8	Simple	The Mango Song
6/24/95	4	2	3/9	Halley's Comet	Lifeboy
6/29/95	4	2	2/6	Free	Strange Design
7/3/95	4	2	2/10	Timber (Jerry)	Johnny B. Goode
7/3/95	0	2	4/10	Johnny B. Goode	AC/DC Bag
9/27/95	1	2	3/8	AC/DC Bag	Billy Breathes
10/2/95	4	1	10/10	Tela	***
10/5/95	2	2	7/9	Cavern	Lifeboy
10/8/95	3	2	9/10	Dog Faced Boy	Keyboard Cavalry Rep
10/15/95	4	1	10/10	I'm Blue, Lonesome	***
10/21/95	4	2	2/8	Also Sprach	Lifeboy
10/27/95	4	2	2/9	Also Sprach	Dog Faced Boy
10/29/95	2	2	2/10	Makisupa Policeman	The Mango Song
11/11/95	4	2	2/9	Also Sprach	Suzy Greenber
11/16/95	4	2	2/9	A Day in the Life	Lifeboy
11/21/95	3	2	2/11	Simple	Take Me to the River
11/21/95	0	2	4/11	Take Me to the River	Glide
11/25/95	3	1	3/9	A Day in the Life	Billy Breathes
12/1/95	4	2	7/9	Suspicious Minds	Catapult
12/1/95	0	2	9/9	Catapult	***
12/5/95	3	1	7/8	Esther	I'm Blue, Lonesome
12/11/95	4	2	2/8	The Curtain	The Mango Song
12/15/95	3	2	7/8	Also Sprach	Sweet Adeline
12/30/95	5	1	4/13	Suzy Greenberg	Simple
4/26/96	2	1	13/13	A Day in the Life	***
6/6/96	1	2	8/10	Character Zero	Fee
7/5/96	2	1	6/6	Scent of a Mule	***
7/10/96	4	1	5/7	Waste	Hello My Baby
7/12/96	2	3	1/3	***	Free
7/17/96	3	1	3/5	Sample in a Jar	Ya Mar
8/4/96	9	2	5/7	Sample in a Jar	Sweet Adeline

DATE	GAP	SET	POS.	SONG BEFORE	SONG AFTER
8/13/96	6	2	11/11	Sweet Adeline	***
8/16/96	2	1	8/8	Halley's Comet	***
10/17/96	3	2	8/8	Star Spangled Banner	***
10/21/96	3	2	11/11	Silent in the Mornin	***
10/29/96	6	1	10/10	Poor Heart	***
11/6/96	4	1	9/9	Billy Breathes	***
11/9/96	3	2	1/7	***	A Day in the Life
11/16/96	5	1	8/11	The Old Home Place	Lawn Boy
11/19/96	2	2	1/7	***	A Day in the Life
11/24/96	3	2	3/7	Sparkle	A Day in the Life
12/4/96	6	1	11/11	The Lizards	***
12/29/96	3	2	1/10	***	A Day in the Life
2/13/97	3	1	12/12	Love Me	***
2/16/97	2	2	9/11	Steep	Loving Cup
2/20/97	3	1	9/10	When Circus Comes	Tweezer Repri
2/23/97	3	1	9/9	Frankenstein	***
2/28/97	3	2	5/9	Frankenstein	Love Me
3/18/97	3	2	4/10	Prince Caspian	Love Me
6/14/97	2	2	7/8	Waste	Cavern
6/20/97	3	2	1/8	***	Ghost
7/2/97	8	E	2/2	Free	***
7/21/97	7	2	3/8	Magilla	Wading In Velvet Sea
7/26/97	4	2	2/8	Timber (Jerry)	Harry Hood
7/30/97	2	2	3/9	Free	Cities
7/30/97	0	2	5/9	Cities	Bouncing
8/10/97	7	2	5/5	Rocko William	***
11/16/97	8	E	1/1	***	***
11/29/97	8	1	12/12	Water in the Sky	***
12/3/97	3	2	1/6	***	Possum
12/29/97	9	2	2/5	Down with Disease	Possum
4/4/98	5	2	6/6	The Lizards	***
6/30/98	2	1	13/13	Train Song	***
7/6/98	5	2	5/6	Makisupa Policeman	Loving Cup
7/16/98	5	2	5/7	Axilla	Tube
7/26/98	7	1	3/7	Too Much Of Evrythng	Frankie Says
8/2/98	5	2	4/6	Lifeboy	I Get a Kick Out of
8/9/98	5	1	9/9	Bouncing	***
8/15/98	3	3	2/6	NICU	Strange Design
10/15/98	3	1	5/8	Gumbo	Brian and Robert
10/29/98	3	2	7/7	Albuquerque	***
11/4/98	4	1	9/9	Frankie Says	***
11/14/98	7	2	1/9	***	Something
11/18/98	1		8/9	Love Me	Carolina
11/25/98	5	1	6/9	Lifeboy	Sleep
12/28/98	4	2	6/6	Quinn the Eskimo	***
7/4/99	7	1	10/10	Fast Enough For You	***
7/12/99	5	2	4/6	Makisupa Policeman	The Lizards
7/23/99	8	1	7/9	Back on the Train	Strange Design
7/31/99	6	2	2/6	Also Sprach	Wading In Velvet Sea
9/10/99	3	2	9/9	Cavern	***
9/17/99	5	1	10/11	Back on the Train	The Squirmin
9/25/99	6	2	2/8	NICU	The Squirmin
10/3/99	6	2	6/8	BBFCFM	Wading In Velvet Sea
10/7/99	2	1	4/9	Dirt	Frankie Says
12/4/99	6	2	9/9	When Circus Comes	***
12/10/99	4	2	3/7	The Wedge	Have Mercy
12/31/99	9	2	20/35	Uncle Pen	My Soul
5/22/00	2	2	5/8	Bouncing	Sand
6/11/00	4	2	5/8	Bug	When Circus Comes
6/23/00	6	1	6/8	Back on the Train	Cars Trucks Buses
6/30/00	5	2	9/9	Sleeping Monkey	***
7/10/00	7	1	10/10	Funky Bitch	***
7/14/00	3	3	3/7	Frankie Says	Waste
9/8/00	2	2	3/6	Windora Bug	Back @ Chicken Shack
9/24/00	11	2	8/8	Cool it Down	***
10/1/00	5	2	7/7	Driver	***
10/5/00	2	2	3/7	NICU	Halley's Comet
10/7/00	2	2	6/7	Meatstick	Tweezer Repri

Was played in the most recent show.

David Bowie Jam

DATE	GAP	SET	POS.	SONG BEFORE	SONG AFTER
8/21/87	27	3	5/7	Makisupa Policeman J	Sanity

Has not been played in the last 1092 shows.

Dazed and Confused

DATE	GAP	SET	POS.	SONG BEFORE	SONG AFTER
5/21/89	103	1	8/13	Split Open and Melt	The Sloth

Has not been played in the last 1016 shows.

Dear Mrs. Reagan

DATE	GAP	SET	POS.	SONG BEFORE	SONG AFTER
9/27/85	6	1	7/8	Prep School Hippie	Melt the Guns
4/1/86	6	2	6/6	Alumni Blues	***
4/15/86	1	1	2/14	AC/DC Bag	Prep School Hippie
2/21/87	5	2	4/15	Suzy Greenberg	Camel Walk
4/24/87	3	1	13/14	David Bowie	Slave
8/10/87	5	3	7/7	Tush	***
9/21/87	4	1	8/11	Wilson	Golgi Apparat
2/7/88	7	1	8/10	Phase Dance	I Didn't Know
2/26/88	3	2	6/9	McGrupp	Makisupa Policeman
6/15/88	11	2	9/9	Whipping Post	***
7/30/88	10	3	11/13	Anarchy	Terrapin
1/18/89	16	1	1/1	***	***

Has not been played in the last 1042 shows.

Dear Prudence

DATE	GAP	SET	POS.	SONG BEFORE	SONG AFTER
10/31/94	681	2	3/30	Back in the USSR	Glass Onion

Has not been played in the last 438 shows.

Demand

DATE	GAP	SET	POS.	SONG BEFORE	SONG AFTER
4/9/94	593	2	5/11	Big Ball Jam	Mike's Song
4/14/94	4	1	7/9	Rift	Split Open and
4/24/94	9	2	1/9	***	David Bowie
5/22/94	20	1	1/11	***	The Sloth
5/26/94	3	1	4/10	Cavern	Split Open and
6/10/94	5	1	5/9	Nellie Kane	David Bowie
6/14/94	3	2	2/9	Frankenstein	David Bowie
6/24/94	8	2	1/13	***	Run Like Antel
6/26/94	2	2	10/12	Dog Faced Boy	Split Open and
10/8/95	97	1	2/9	AC/DC Bag	Sparkle
10/15/95	4	1	5/10	I Didn't Know	Llama
10/24/95	6	1	8/13	Silent in the Mornin	Maze
12/7/95	26	1	4/10	AC/DC Bag	Rift
11/14/96	64	2	8/10	Life on Mars	Run Like Antel

Has not been played in the last 275 shows.

Destiny Unbound

DATE	GAP	SET	POS.	SONG BEFORE	SONG AFTER
9/14/90	208	2	8/10	The Lizards	Fire
9/22/90	5	2	3/10	Tweezer	Fee
10/4/90	4	1	7/10	The Lizards	The Sloth
10/7/90	3	1	5/14	The Landlady	Col. Forbin's A
12/29/90	20	2	9/10	Bouncing	Run Like Antel
2/2/91	3	1	7/9	Stash	You Enjoy My
2/3/91	1	1	6/10	Esther	Reba
2/7/91	1	2	13/14	The Sloth	You Enjoy My
2/14/91	3	1	5/11	Reba	Cavern
2/26/91	6	2	7/12	The Landlady	Possum
3/15/91	8	2	6/9	Cavern	I Didn't Know
3/22/91	3	1	4/11	The Landlady	Bouncing
4/3/91	6	2	7/9	The Landlady	Fee
4/11/91	4	2	11/14	The Landlady	Mike's Song
4/19/91	3	2	5/10	The Landlady	My Sweet One
4/22/91	3	2	5/10	The Landlady	The Squirmin
5/12/91	9	1	7/11	The Landlady	Llama
9/26/91	21	2	6/11	The Landlady	Mike's Song
9/29/91	3	1	7/10	The Landlady	You Enjoy My
10/3/91	3	2	7/11	The Landlady	Buried Alive
10/6/91	2	2	5/10	The Landlady	Harry Hood
10/15/91	5	1	8/10	The Landlady	You Enjoy My
10/23/91	4	1	4/11	The Landlady	Paul and Silas
10/27/91	2	2	11/13	The Landlady	Take the A-Trn
11/1/91	4	1	4/11	The Landlady	The Squirmin
11/15/91	9	2	10/14	The Landlady	Harry Hood

Has not been played in the last 774 shows.

Diamond Girl

DATE	GAP	SET	POS.	SONG BEFORE	SONG AFTER
12/31/92	479	3	8/9	The Squirming Coil	Llama

Has not been played in the last 640 shows.

Digital Delay Loop Jam

DATE	GAP	SET	POS.	SONG BEFORE	SONG AFTER
4/8/94	592	1	2/13	Maze	Maze
5/7/94	23	2	6/12	Makisupa Policeman	Sweet Emotion Jam
6/14/94	22	1	4/14	Sweet Adeline	Guelah Papyrus
6/22/94	6	2	15/20	T.M.W.S.I.Y. Reprise	Fluffhead
12/29/94	66	2	2/7	Guyute	David Bowie
12/28/96	150	2	4/10	Bouncing	T.M.W.S.I.Y.

Has not been played in the last 260 shows.

Dinner and a Movie

DATE	GAP	SET	POS.	SONG BEFORE	SONG AFTER
11/19/87	35	3	6/14	BBFCFM	Ballad - Curtis Loew
2/8/88	3	3	3/9	Flat Fee	Alumni Blues
3/11/88	3	2	2/8	Fluffhead	Harry Hood
3/21/88	2	1	12/15	Possum	I Didn't Know
4/22/88	3	1	7/9	Fluffhead	Harry Hood
6/15/88	5	2	5/9	Contact	Take the A-Trn
7/23/88	7	3	4/7	Harry Hood	Slave
8/6/88	5	1	8/9	Funky Bitch	Fire
2/7/89	18	2	2/9	Makisupa Policeman	AC/DC Bag
5/1/89	15	1	1/9	***	You Enjoy My
8/26/89	16	3	4/5	Suzy Greenberg	Run Like Antel
9/21/89	3	2	3/9	The Chase	Bundle of Joy
10/1/89	1	2	4/11	Reba	Bundle of Joy
10/6/89	1	1	8/13	Bold As Love	Happy Birthday
10/7/89	1	2	1/9	***	Bundle of Joy
10/20/89	4	2	3/10	Walk Away	I Didn't Know
10/26/89	3	2	2/15	Who Knows Jam	Who Do? We Do!
10/28/89	1	1	6/9	Good Times Bad Times	Reba
12/1/89	10	1	5/9	The Oh Kee Pa Ceremo	Bathtub Gin
12/9/89	4	1	1/10	***	La Grange
2/9/90	11	2	1/9	***	Ya Mar
2/10/90	1	1	1/10	***	The Oh Kee Pa
2/15/90	1	1	5/10	Divided Sky	Caravan
2/23/90	4	1	7/11	Rocky Top	Ya Mar
3/3/90	5	2	1/7	***	Caravan
3/8/90	2	1	1/10	***	You Enjoy My
3/11/90	3	2	5/13	Bouncing	Take the A-Trn
3/17/90	1	1	3/10	Esther	Bouncing
4/6/90	4	1	7/11	Ya Mar	Bouncing
4/13/90	5	1	2/10	Funky Bitch	Bouncing
4/19/90	3	2	3/8	McGrupp	You Enjoy My
4/20/90	1	1	6/10	Cavern	Bouncing
4/22/90	2	2	1/9	***	Bouncing
4/25/90	1	2	8/12	La Grange	Bouncing
4/26/90	1	1	5/9	Uncle Pen	Bouncing
4/28/90	1	1	5/11	Uncle Pen	Bouncing
4/29/90	1	1	5/13	You Enjoy Myself	Bouncing
5/13/90	6	1	4/10	AC/DC Bag	Bouncing
5/19/90	2	2	6/10	Fee	Bouncing
5/24/90	2	2	2/11	Foam	Possum
5/30/90	1	1	5/14	The Sloth	Bouncing
5/31/90	1	1	3/12	You Enjoy Myself	Bouncing
6/2/90	2	1	2/9	Uncle Pen	Bouncing
6/5/90	1	2	4/10	Caravan	Bouncing
6/7/90	1	2	2/10	My Sweet One	Bouncing
6/9/90	2	1	4/10	Reba	Bouncing
9/14/90	3	1	7/11	Stash	I Didn't Know

DATE	GAP	SET	POS.	SONG BEFORE	SONG AFTER
9/16/90	2	1	1/14	***	Bouncing
9/20/90	1	1	4/12	The Asse Festival	Foam
9/28/90	3	2	4/6	Gumbo	You Enjoy My
9/29/90	1	1	2/9	Divided Sky	The Landlady
10/6/90	4	1	3/13	The Squirming Coil	Bouncing
10/12/90	3	1	3/9	You Enjoy Myself	Bouncing
11/3/90	5	1	1/11	***	Bouncing
11/8/90	2	2	5/8	The Oh Kee Pa Ceremo	Bouncing
11/30/90	6	1	6/11	Esther	Bouncing
12/8/90	3	2	3/9	The Asse Festival	Bouncing
12/29/90	2	2	7/10	Jesus Just Left	Bouncing
2/2/91	3	1	4/9	Guelah Papyrus	Esther
2/15/91	6	1	9/11	The Sloth	Magilla
2/19/91	2	1	5/9	Reba	The Sloth
2/21/91	2	1	2/11	Reba	Ya Mar
2/26/91	1	2	3/12	Runaway Jim	Stash
3/1/91	3	1	7/12	Tweezer	Bouncing
3/15/91	5	1	5/12	Stash	Bouncing
4/3/91	9	1	6/10	Tweezer	Bouncing
4/5/91	2	2	5/9	The Sloth	Harry Hood
4/11/91	2	1	6/12	Magilla	Bouncing
4/19/91	5	1	1/12	***	Bouncing
4/25/91	4	2	7/10	Tela	Bouncing
5/10/91	6	1	4/10	Ya Mar	The Sloth
5/12/91	2	1	3/11	Bouncing	Stash
5/16/91	1	2	2/9	Runaway Jim	Bouncing
5/18/91	2	E	1/2	***	Runaway Jim
5/19/91	1	2	6/10	Reba	The Sloth
7/11/91	1	2	1/10	***	Cavern
7/12/91	1	1	1/12	***	Bouncing
7/14/91	2	2	5/10	Gumbo	Bouncing
7/15/91	1	1	4/14	The Landlady	Stash
7/20/91	3	2	4/12	Caravan	Flat Fee
7/23/91	2	2	8/10	Sweet Adeline	Gumbo
7/26/91	3	2	2/10	Stash	You Enjoy My
9/27/91	5	2	6/10	The Mango Song	The Oh Kee Pa
10/12/91	10	2	6/10	Take the A-Train	Brother
10/18/91	4	2	4/12	Guelah Papyrus	Mike's Song
10/24/91	3	2	8/11	Slave	Bouncing
10/28/91	2	2	3/11	Wilson	Stash
10/31/91	2	2	11/14	Horn	Tube
11/8/91	4	1	3/11	The Landlady	Stash
11/12/91	3	2	1/13	***	Stash
11/14/91	2	2	1/11	***	Roll Like a Cantalou
11/19/91	3	2	9/11	Reba	Cavern
11/22/91	3	1	9/11	Lawn Boy	Stash
12/4/91	4	1	9/11	The Squirming Coil	Bouncing
3/13/92	9	1	6/12	Maze	Divided Sky
3/19/92	3	1	8/12	Silent in the Mornin	Col. Forbin's A
3/21/92	2	1	8/12	Silent in the Mornin	The Squirmin
3/27/92	5	2	9/13	Bathtub Gin	Magilla
3/31/92	3	2	9/13	Cavern	My Friend My
4/6/92	5	2	1/13	***	Bathtub Gin
4/21/92	10	2	1/13	***	Col. Forbin's A
4/25/92	4	2	7/11	All Things Recnsdrd	Harry Hood
5/3/92	5	2	11/14	Cracklin' Rosie	Bouncing
5/12/92	7	1	7/12	It's Ice	Bouncing
7/16/92	19	1	6/10	Wilson	Bouncing
11/20/92	30	2	6/10	Fast Enough for You	Harry Hood
12/1/92	8	2	9/11	Love You	Baby Elephant Walk
12/11/92	9	2	1/12	***	Mike's Song
2/21/93	22	1	8/10	Esther	Bouncing
4/12/93	34	2	1/10	***	Tweezer
4/24/93	9	2	4/10	Bathtub Gin	Mound
8/9/93	33	2	1/8	***	Tweezer
5/21/94	54	2	1/9	***	Sample in a Ja
6/13/94	11	1	6/9	Wolfman's Brother	Stash
10/22/94	38	2	5/11	Silent in the Mornin	Tweezer
11/18/95	93	1	1/8	***	Bouncing
11/28/95	6	1	2/9	Stash	Bouncing
8/6/96	43	1	7/9	The Lizards	Horn
3/1/97	59	2	2/8	Carini	Mike's Song
9/29/00	238	2	1/9	***	The Moma Dance

Has not been played in the last 6 shows.

Dirt

DATE	GAP	SET	POS.	SONG BEFORE	SONG AFTER
6/14/97	879	1	3/10	NICU	Talk
6/16/97	1	2	6/7	Wading In Velvet Sea	Harry Hood
6/21/97	3	1	10/15	Limb by Limb	Harry Hood
6/22/97	1	1	4/9	Stash	Uncle Pen
7/1/97	5	1	7/9	I Saw it Again	Reba
7/9/97	5	1	5/8	Split Open and Melt	Taste
7/21/97	3	1	4/7	Piper	Ginseng Sullivan
7/23/97	2	1	2/10	Julius	NICU
7/26/97	2	1	7/9	Cars Trucks Buses	You Enjoy My
7/29/97	1	1	4/9	Gumbo	Sparkle
7/31/97	2	1	5/9	Limb by Limb	Maze
8/3/97	2	1	4/9	Samson Variation	Vultures
8/8/97	2	1	4/7	The Lizards	It's Ice
8/10/97	2	1	4/10	Down with Disease	Cars Trucks Buses
8/17/97	5	3	5/7	Guyute	Scent of a Mul
11/19/97	5	1	4/10	Llama	Limb By Limb
11/26/97	4	1	6/10	McGrupp	Split Open and
12/2/97	4	1	7/9	Divided Sky	Taste
12/11/97	6	1	4/7	Maze	Limb by Limb
12/29/97	4	1	8/9	Fluffhead	Run Like Antel
7/8/98	13	2	3/7	Birds of a Feather	Piper
7/20/98	7	1	2/10	Bathtub Gin	Poor Heart
10/15/98	20	E	1/2	***	Limb by Limb
11/13/98	13	2	3/6	Sample in a Jar	Birds of a Feather
7/8/99	21	1	5/8	Guyute	Nellie Kane
9/16/99	24	1	6/14	Carini	Vultures
9/21/99	4	2	7/8	Will It Go Round	Run Like Antel
9/26/99	4	1	4/10	AC/DC Bag	Guyute
9/29/99	2	1	5/9	Taste	Nellie Kane
10/7/99	5	1	3/9	My Soul	David Bowie
10/10/99	3	1	5/7	First Tube	Vultures
12/4/99	3	1	6/7	Tweezer	Loving Cup
12/8/99	3	2	2/6	Sand	Piper
12/15/99	5	2	4/7	Free	Reba
5/21/00	6	2	3/8	Down with Disease	Twist
6/11/00	5	1	6/9	Stash	Possum
6/16/00	4	1	7/10	Heavy Things	My Sweet One
6/25/00	4	1	9/10	Heavy Things	Split Open and
7/1/00	4	1	10/11	Vultures	Split Open and
7/15/00	10	1	5/9	NICU	Roses are Free
9/20/00	9	2	3/9	Limb By Limb	It's Ice
9/27/00	5	1	6/10	Limb By Limb	Split Open and

Has not been played in the last 7 shows.

Divided Sky

DATE	GAP	SET	POS.	SONG BEFORE	SONG AFTER
8/9/87	25	3	4/7	Ya Mar	Flat Fee
8/10/87	1	6/7		Quinn the Eskimo	Good Time Ba
8/21/87	1	1	3/11	Peaches en Regalia	Funky Bitch
8/29/87	1	1	10/13	AC/DC Bag	Harpua
9/2/87	1	1	4/13	Sneakin' Sally	Wilson
9/21/87	1	3	6/15	Fee	Dog Gone Dog
10/14/87	2	1	10/12	AC/DC Bag	McGrupp
10/31/87	1	2	11/17	Fee	McGrupp
11/18/87	1	1	10/12	Golgi Apparatus	Alumni Blues
11/19/87	1	3	4/14	Possum	BBFCFM
1/27/88	1	2	6/10	Fluffhead	Ballad - Curtis Loew
2/8/88	2	2	4/6	Peaches en Regalia	The Lizards
3/21/88	5	1	5/15	Sneakin' Sally	Boogie On Reggae
9/24/88	26	1	9/10	Take the A-Train	Bold As Love
10/29/88	1	2	6/10	Walk Away	Ballad - Curtis Loew
11/5/88	3	E	4/4	Sparks	***
11/11/88	1	1	1/8	***	You Enjoy My
12/2/88	1	1	5/7	Take the A-Train	Contact
1/26/89	4	1	8/10	Sanity	Fee

DATE	GAP	SET	POS.	SONG BEFORE	SONG AFTER
2/6/89	1	2	5/7	Golgi Apparatus	On Your Way Down
2/17/89	3	1	4/10	Fee	Split Open and
2/18/89	1	1	3/9	Corrine Corrina	AC/DC Bag
2/18/89	0	1	6/9	Fire	Wilson
3/3/89	2	1	9/11	I Didn't Know	Alumni Blues
3/24/89	4	1	6/10	Golgi Apparatus	AC/DC Bag
3/30/89	1	1	3/8	McGrupp	The Price of Love
4/20/89	2	2	1/10	***	Walk Away
4/27/89	1	1	3/8	The Sloth	Sanity
4/30/89	1	1	5/9	The Lizards	Wilson
5/6/89	3	2	8/8	Slave	***
5/9/89	1	1	9/9	Possum	***
5/20/89	3	1	6/8	Wilson	I Didn't Know
5/21/89	1	1	13/13	AC/DC Bag	***
5/28/89	3	1	1/9	***	Run Like Antel
8/19/89	4	2	3/4	Take the A-Train	Bathtub Gin
8/26/89	2	1	6/8	Split Open and Melt	You Enjoy My
9/9/89	1	1	4/11	Suzy Greenberg	AC/DC Bag
9/21/89	2	2	1/9	***	The Chase
10/12/89	1	1	7/8	Possum	La Grange
10/14/89	1	2	2/11	AC/DC Bag	I Didn't Know
10/20/89	1	1	8/10	Reba	Golgi Apparat
10/22/89	2	1	12/14	Tela	I Didn't Know
10/26/89	1	1	5/11	Fee	I Didn't Know
10/28/89	1	1	8/9	Reba	Harpua
10/31/89	1	1	5/9	AC/DC Bag	Fee
11/2/89	1	2	6/11	Rhombus Narration	McGrupp
11/10/89	3	1	5/9	Fee	AC/DC Bag
11/18/89	3	1	7/11	Possum	Wilson
11/30/89	1	1	2/11	Bathtub Gin	Ya Mar
12/1/89	3	2	3/10	Rocky Top	Walk Away
12/3/89	1	1	5/9	Reba	My Sweet One
12/7/89	1	1	11/11	Rhombus Narration	***
12/15/89	3	2	3/8	Possum	Run Like Antel
12/29/89	2	1	2/10	Rhombus Narration	Ya Mar
12/31/89	2	2	6/7	Split Open and Melt	Fee
1/27/90	2	2	7/7	Terrapin	***
2/1/90	3	1	6/11	Caravan	Possum
2/15/90	3	1	4/10	Suzy Greenberg	Dinner and a
2/24/90	5	1	4/8	Golgi Apparatus	Esther
3/1/90	2	1	4/7	Rhombus Narration	I Didn't Know
3/3/90	2	2	7/7	Carolina	***
3/8/90	2	2	1/12	***	Bathtub Gin
3/10/90	2	1	8/10	Funky Bitch	Jesus Just Left
3/17/90	2	1	7/10	Rhombus Narration	Donna Lee
4/4/90	2	1	7/8	Foam	Carolina
4/6/90	2	1	5/11	Rhombus Narration	Ya Mar
4/8/90	2	1	1/8	***	Funky Bitch
4/9/90	1	2	8/11	Jesus Just Left	Love You
4/12/90	1	1	10/11	Jesus Just Left	Good Time Ba
4/14/90	2	1	4/10	Cavern	Col. Forbin's A
4/20/90	3	1	2/10	Take the A-Train	Alumni Blues
4/22/90	2	1	1/12	***	Uncle Pen
4/25/90	1	1	2/4	If I Only Had a Brai	My Sweet One
4/29/90	3	1	8/13	Uncle Pen	Fluffhead
5/10/90	4	1	4/8	Bouncing	Tweezer
5/13/90	2	1	8/10	Uncle Pen	Lawn Boy
5/23/90	3	1	1/10	***	Ya Mar
5/31/90	3	1	10/12	Uncle Pen	The Oh Kee Pa
6/5/90	3	2	2/10	Sweet Adeline	Caravan
6/7/90	1	2	6/10	Uncle Pen	Love You
6/8/90	1	1	4/8	You Enjoy Myself	Uncle Pen
6/16/90	2	1	2/10	AC/DC Bag	Wilson
9/13/90	1	1	2/11	The Landlady	Foam
9/15/90	2	1	2/14	Buried Alive	Paul and Silas
9/20/90	2	2	5/14	The Squirming Coil	Magilla
9/22/90	2	1	4/12	My Sweet One	Tela
9/28/90	1	2	4/6	You Enjoy Myself	***
9/29/90	1	1	1/9	***	Dinner and a
10/4/90	2	E	1/1	***	***
10/7/90	3	1	1/14	***	Uncle Pen
10/12/90	2	2	5/10	Terrapin	Paul and Silas
11/2/90	4	1	4/14	Bouncing	The Sloth

DATE	GAP	SET	POS.	SONG BEFORE	SONG AFTER
11/8/90	3	2	2/8	Suzy Greenberg	Tweezer
11/10/90	1	2	6/8	Llama	Bike
11/16/90	1	1	7/8	Llama	Golgi Apparat
11/24/90	2	2	12/12	Lawn Boy	***
11/26/90	1	1	9/11	David Bowie	Makisupa Policeman
11/30/90	1	2	7/10	Gumbo	I Didn't Know
12/1/90	1	1	4/9	Llama	Foam
12/8/90	2	1	5/10	AC/DC Bag	Cavern
12/28/90	1	2	9/12	My Sweet One	No Good Trying
12/31/90	2	1	2/12	Suzy Greenberg	I Didn't Know
2/15/91	8	1	3/11	Wilson	Split Open and
2/16/91	1	1	3/12	My Sweet One	Cavern
2/20/91	2	2	2/3	Foam	Guelah Papyrus
2/27/91	3	1	2/10	Golgi Apparatus	I Didn't Know
2/28/91	1	2	5/7	Guelah Papyrus	Love You
3/1/91	1	1	3/12	Foam	Cavern
3/6/91	1	1	7/11	Cavern	Love You
3/13/91	3	1	5/9	Cavern	Esther
3/16/91	2	2	2/10	Llama	Guelah Papyrus
3/23/91	3	1	2/10	The Sloth	Fee
3/28/91	1	1	2/14	Golgi Apparatus	Cavern
4/2/91	3	2	1/8	***	Lawn Boy
4/4/91	2	2	8/10	My Sweet One	Love You
4/5/91	1	1	3/11	Bouncing	Cavern
4/12/91	1	1	3/9	Uncle Pen	Guelah Papyrus
4/19/91	4	1	3/12	Bouncing	Cavern
4/21/91	2	1	4/14	Wilson	Foam
4/25/91	2	2	9/10	Bouncing	BBFCFM
5/2/91	2	2	3/10	Poor Heart	Fee
5/3/91	1	1	7/12	T.M.W.S.I.Y. Reprise	Fee
5/9/91	1	1	1/10	***	Foam
5/16/91	4	1	5/11	Cavern	Col. Forbin's A
5/18/91	2	1	7/9	Foam	Cavern
5/19/91	1	1	1/8	***	The Landlady
7/11/91	1	1	3/8	Suzy Greenberg	Flat Fee
7/13/91	2	2	3/9	Guelah Papyrus	Flat Fee
7/14/91	1	2	3/10	Caravan	Gumbo
7/19/91	2	2	2/8	Suzy Greenberg	I Didn't Know
7/21/91	2	1	2/11	Cavern	Guelah Papyrus
7/25/91	3	1	5/10	Suzy Greenberg	Flat Fee
8/3/91	3	1	10/11	The Sloth	Golgi Apparat
9/26/91	2	1	3/10	Bouncing	Fee
9/29/91	3	1	2/10	Cavern	I Didn't Know
10/3/91	3	1	8/10	Fee	Cavern
10/4/91	1	1	5/10	Cavern	Guelah Papyrus
10/6/91	1	1	3/13	Foam	Bouncing
10/11/91	2	1	3/10	My Sweet One	Guelah Papyrus
10/12/91	1	1	7/9	Esther	Guelah Papyrus
10/17/91	3	1	4/10	Bouncing	Cavern
10/24/91	4	1	7/12	Ya Mar	I Didn't Know
10/28/91	2	2	1/11	***	Wilson
10/30/91	2	2	2/11	Tube	Poor Heart
11/1/91	2	1	10/11	Tube	Sweet Adeline
11/8/91	3	1	6/11	Paul and Silas	Guelah Papyrus
11/13/91	4	1	8/10	Cavern	I Didn't Know
11/15/91	2	1	10/12	Rhombus Narration	Lawn Boy
11/19/91	2	1	11/11	Wilson	***
11/22/91	3	1	7/11	Foam	Lawn Boy
11/24/91	2	2	2/8	Tube	Cavern
11/30/91	1	1	5/11	Sparkle	Cavern
12/6/91	3	2	6/12	Horn	Tela
12/31/91	2	1	7/10	Guelah Papyrus	Esther
3/6/92	1	1	6/11	The Oh Kee Pa Ceremo	Guelah Papyrus
3/11/92	2	1	9/10	Mound	Cavern
3/13/92	2	1	7/12	Dinner and a Movie	Mound
3/17/92	2	1	7/11	I Didn't Know	Guelah Papyrus
3/27/92	8	1	5/10	The Sloth	Guelah Papyrus
3/31/92	3	1	2/10	Wilson	Glide
4/5/92	4	1	3/11	Guelah Papyrus	Wilson
4/7/92	2	1	5/12	Fee	The Horse
4/12/92	2	1	4/11	Guelah Papyrus	The Horse
4/18/92	5	1	2/11	Wilson	Guelah Papyrus
4/22/92	3	1	6/10	Guelah Papyrus	Mound
5/1/92	6	1	7/12	The Sloth	Guelah Papyrus
5/5/92	3	1	7/11	Guelah Papyrus	I Didn't Know
5/9/92	4	2	2/8	Suzy Greenberg	Tela
5/18/92	7	1	4/10	Bouncing	Guelah Papyrus
6/30/92	6	1	2/6	Golgi Apparatus	Guelah Papyrus
7/12/92	5	1	4/11	Bouncing	Fluffhead
7/15/92	2	2	2/9	The Sloth	Esther
7/26/92	9	1	3/7	It's Ice	Weigh
11/19/92	21	1	7/12	Mound	Esther
11/23/92	4	1	7/11	Guelah Papyrus	Mound
11/27/92	2	1	3/12	Wilson	Col. Forbin's A
12/2/92	4	1	3/10	Foam	Fast Enough for You
12/5/92	3	1	9/12	Mound	Sweet Adeline
12/8/92	3	1	8/11	Guelah Papyrus	Mound
12/13/92	4	1	3/11	Wilson	It's Ice
12/29/92	2	1	6/12	My Friend My Friend	Wilson
12/31/92	2	1	7/11	Wilson	Cavern
2/3/93	1	1	6/11	The Wedge	I Didn't Know
2/6/93	3	1	7/11	Horn	Lawn Boy
2/10/93	3	1	6/10	The Sloth	Tela
2/15/93	4	1	5/12	Guelah Papyrus	Esther
2/20/93	4	1	7/11	All Things Recnsdrd	The Horse
2/26/93	5	1	8/10	Horn	I Didn't Know
3/9/93	7	1	6/10	Esther	Glide
3/16/93	4	1	8/11	I Didn't Know	You Gotta See Mama
3/21/93	4	1	4/11	The Sloth	Esther
3/26/93	4	1	9/10	Fluffhead	Cavern
3/30/93	3	1	10/11	Glide	Cavern
4/2/93	3	1	5/9	Bouncing	I Didn't Know
4/9/93	3	1	10/11	It's Ice	Cavern
4/14/93	3	1	11/13	Silent in the Mornin	I Didn't Know
4/18/93	3	1	5/10	Sparkle	Fee
4/23/93	4	1	7/10	My Friend My Friend	Guelah Papyrus
4/30/93	5	1	8/12	Silent in the Mornin	Cavern
5/2/93	2	1	3/11	Sparkle	Mound
5/7/93	4	1	9/11	Horn	I Didn't Know
7/15/93	4	1	3/9	Sample in a Jar	Mound
7/18/93	3	1	7/9	Esther	Uncle Pen
7/22/93	2	1	6/11	Sample in a Jar	Mound
7/24/93	2	1	4/10	Nellie Kane	Guelah Papyrus
7/29/93	4	1	2/10	Funky Bitch	Weigh
7/31/93	2	1	8/9	Nellie Kane	Cavern
8/6/93	3	1	7/10	Horn	Nellie Kane
8/9/93	3	1	9/11	Nellie Kane	Memories
8/14/93	4	1	3/11	Guelah Papyrus	The Horse
8/17/93	3	1	4/9	Guelah Papyrus	Weigh
8/20/93	1	1	1/10	***	Harpua
12/29/93	7	1	5/9	Glide	Wilson
4/4/94	3	1	1/9	***	Sample in a Jar
4/11/94	6	1	8/9	Glide	Cavern
4/13/94	1	1	7/8	Ginseng Sullivan	Golgi Apparat
4/17/94	4	1	4/9	I Didn't Know	Mound
4/22/94	4	1	8/11	Nellie Kane	The Horse
4/25/94	3	2	7/10	The Squirming Coil	Bouncing
4/29/94	2	1	6/12	The Sloth	I Didn't Know
5/2/94	2	1	7/10	Glide	Suzy Greenber
5/7/94	4	1	3/9	Horn	Mound
5/10/94	2	1	4/9	Sample in a Jar	Axilla (Part II)
5/16/94	4	1	4/10	Sample in a Jar	Axilla (Part II)
5/22/94	5	1	3/11	The Sloth	Glide
5/26/94	3	1	9/10	Catapult	Sample in a Ja
5/29/94	3	1	1/8	***	Guelah Papyrus
6/13/94	4	1	4/9	Sample in a Jar	Wolfman's Brother
6/18/94	4	1	9/10	Dog Faced Boy	Sample in a Ja
6/24/94	5	1	1/11	***	Wilson
6/26/94	2	1	11/11	McGrupp	***
6/29/94	1	2	6/8	Lifeboy	Suzy Greenber
7/2/94	3	2	2/9	Golgi Apparatus	Guelah Papyrus
7/8/94	4	1	11/11	McGrupp	***
7/15/94	5	1	3/8	Sample in a Jar	Gumbo
10/7/94	2	1	5/9	Poor Heart	Guelah Papyrus
10/10/94	3	1	2/11	Sample in a Jar	The Horse
10/14/94	3	1	3/12	Sample in a Jar	The Horse
10/18/94	3	1	9/10	Guyute	Amazing Grce
10/22/94	3	1	2/8	Suzy Greenberg	Suzy Greenberg
10/27/94	4	1	7/11	The Famous Mockingbi	The Horse
10/31/94	3	1	4/10	Simple	Harpua
11/3/94	2	1	2/9	Fee	Wilson
11/13/94	3	2	2/8	Suzy Greenberg	The Lizards
11/17/94	3	1	6/11	Wilson	Dog Faced Boy
11/20/94	3	1	9/10	Dooley	Sample in a Ja
11/23/94	2	1	8/9	Suzy Greenberg	Amazing Grce
11/28/94	3	1	8/9	Simple	Sweet Adeline
12/3/94	4	1	2/7	Wilson	Guelah Papyrus
12/7/94	3	2	3/9	Frankenstein	Fee
12/10/94	3	1	6/8	Sample in a Jar	Lawn Boy
12/31/94	4	1	7/8	Peaches en Regalia	Funky Bitch
6/9/95	4	1	2/9	My Friend My Friend	Strange Design
6/17/95	6	1	1/9	***	Suzy Greenber
6/22/95	3	1	4/10	Ha Ha Ha	Guelah Papyrus
6/25/95	3	1	7/9	Sparkle	I Didn't Know
6/29/95	3	1	5/10	Silent in the Mornin	Cavern
7/2/95	3	1	2/10	Sample in a Jar	Gumbo
9/29/95	4	1	3/8	Sparkle	Strange Design
10/5/95	4	1	8/11	Strange Design	Acoustic Army
10/11/95	4	1	4/9	Cavern	If I Could
10/20/95	6	1	4/10	Ha Ha Ha	Fee
10/25/95	4	1	3/10	Sample in a Jar	The Wedge
10/31/95	4	1	2/9	Icculus	Wilson
11/9/95	1	1	1/8	Tweezer Reprise	Prince Caspian
11/14/95	4	1	4/9	Billy Breathes	Esther
11/21/95	5	1	4/10	Prince Caspian	My Long Journey Home
11/28/95	4	1	6/9	I Didn't Know	Guyute
12/4/95	5	1	3/11	Gumbo	Punch You in
12/12/95	6	1	3/10	Sample in a Jar	Lifeboy
12/16/95	3	1	6/9	The Sloth	Dog Faced Boy
12/30/95	4	1	12/13	T.M.W.S.I.Y. Reprise	Sample in a Ja
7/7/96	7	1	2/10	Sample in a Jar	Bouncing
7/12/96	4	1	2/10	Wilson	Horn
7/17/96	3	1	1/5	***	Sample in a Ja
8/5/96	10	1	4/9	Guelah Papyrus	Wolfman's Brother
8/13/96	5	1	1/10	***	Tube
8/16/96	2	1	6/8	Esther	Halley's Comet
10/18/96	4	1	7/10	Strange Design	Billy Breathes
10/21/96	2	1	5/10	The Sloth	Character Zer
11/3/96	9	2	2/8	Timber (Jerry)	Wolfman's Brother
11/9/96	4	1	4/10	The Sloth	Horn
11/11/96	1	2	2/11	Timber (Jerry)	Gumbo
11/15/96	3	1	2/11	Wilson	Bouncing

DATE	GAP	SET	POS.	SONG BEFORE	SONG AFTER
11/23/96	5	1	4/9	Cars Trucks Buses	Punch You in
11/29/96	3	1	5/9	Character Zero	Bathtub Gin
12/2/96	3	2	2/8	Ya Mar	Wolfman's Brother
12/31/96	6	1	8/10	Silent in the Mornin	Sample in a Ja
2/17/97	4	1	2/10	Soul Shake Down Part	Wilson
7/3/97	25	1	3/8	My Soul	Beauty of My Dreams
8/2/97	14	1	5/8	Dogs Stole Things	Wolfman's Brother
12/2/97	23	1	6/9	Ghost	Dirt
7/10/98	25	1	3/4	Dogs Stole Things	Mike's Song
7/17/98	3	1	4/7	Gumbo	Waste
8/2/98	11	1	2/9	Roggae	The Horse
8/15/98	8	1	8/12	The Moma Dance	Water in the Sky
11/9/98	14	1	4/10	I Get a Kick Out of	Frankie Says
11/21/98	8	1	4/13	Lawn Boy	Cry Baby Cry
12/29/98	7	E	1/1	***	***
7/9/99	9	1	4/8	Back on the Train	Train Song
7/20/99	8	1	5/9	The Sloth	Waste
8/1/99	9	1	5/10	The Moma Dance	Horn
9/10/99	2	1	4/8	Twist	Ginseng Sullivan
10/3/99	17	1	4/12	Dogs Stole Things	Heavy Things
12/12/99	14	1	4/8	Strange Design	Beauty of My Dreams
6/15/00	16	1	7/8	Frankie Says	Farmhouse
7/7/00	13	1	3/11	Gumbo	Boogie On Reggae
9/12/00	10	1	6/7	First Tube	Wilson
9/24/00	8	1	6/10	The Sloth	Roggae

Has not been played in the last 9 shows.

Doctor Jimmy

DATE	GAP	SET	POS.	SONG BEFORE	SONG AFTER
10/31/95	759	2	15/17	Bell Boy	The Rock

Has not been played in the last 360 shows.

Dog Faced Boy

DATE	GAP	SET	POS.	SONG BEFORE	SONG AFTER
4/14/94	597	2	8/9	Nellie Kane	Slave
4/18/94	4	1	8/10	Split Open and Melt	The Oh Kee Pa
4/24/94	5	1	6/8	Bathtub Gin	It's Ice
4/25/94	1	1	7/10	Ginseng Sullivan	Tela
4/29/94	2	1	8/12	I Didn't Know	Split Open and
5/10/94	8	2	8/10	Ginseng Sullivan	Nellie Kane
5/17/94	5	1	7/9	Ginseng Sullivan	Split Open and
5/20/94	2	1	8/10	Scent of a Mule	Carolina
5/22/94	2	1	10/11	Ginseng Sullivan	Axilla (Part II)
5/26/94	3	2	7/9	Ginseng Sullivan	You Enjoy My
6/16/94	9	1	8/10	The Curtain	Stash
6/18/94	2	1	8/10	It's Ice	Divided Sky
6/21/94	2	2	11/16	BBFCFM Reprise	Sweet Adeline
6/24/94	3	2	9/13	Llama	Poor Heart
6/26/94	2	2	9/12	Scent of a Mule	Demand
7/15/94	13	2	7/10	Yerushalayim	Julius
10/9/94	4	1	5/7	The Curtain	Split Open and
10/16/94	6	2	7/9	Run Like an Antelope	Sweet Adeline
10/21/94	3	1	8/9	The Lizards	Run Like Antel
10/26/94	4	1	6/10	Guyute	Scent of a Mul
11/3/94	6	1	7/9	Split Open and Melt	Sparkle
11/17/94	6	1	7/11	Divided Sky	Col. Forbin's A
12/28/94	19	1	8/10	Reba	It's Ice
6/16/95	12	1	8/10	My Mind's Got A Mind	Catapult
6/26/95	8	1	8/10	It's Ice	Tela
10/8/95	16	2	8/10	Suspicious Minds	David Bowie
10/27/95	12	2	3/9	David Bowie	Poor Heart
11/10/95	5	1	6/9	It's Ice	Maze
11/14/95	3	2	6/11	Stash	Stash
11/21/95	5	1	9/10	My Friend My Friend	Runaway Jim
12/9/95	13	1	9/10	Billy Breathes	Chalk Dust Tor
12/16/95	5	1	7/9	Divided Sky	Julius
8/12/96	32	1	7/10	It's Ice	Taste
12/2/97	109	2	3/7	Simple	Ya Mar
7/1/98	18	1	6/9	Down with Disease	Piper
11/18/98	48	E	3/4	Sleep	The Squirmin

DATE	GAP	SET	POS.	SONG BEFORE	SONG AFTER
12/8/99	66	2	4/6	Piper	The Lizards
6/16/00	20	2	3/7	Theme From the Botto	Driver
6/22/00	1	2	5/10	Harry Hood	Harry Hood
7/6/00	10	1	4/12	Taste	Heavy Things
7/14/00	6	2	8/11	Foam	Farmhouse
9/14/00	6	2	3/5	Crosseyed and Painle	Prince Caspian
10/4/00	13	1	6/7	Reba	Run Like Antel

Has not been played in the last 3 shows.

Dog Gone Dog

DATE	GAP	SET	POS.	SONG BEFORE	SONG AFTER
10/30/85	1	1	2/11	Harry Hood	Possum
4/15/86	5	1	9/14	Bob Dylan Band	Possum
12/6/86	3	1	11/14	You Enjoy Myself	Tush
2/21/87	2	2	14/15	Corrine Corrina	Alumni Blues
4/29/87	4	2	1/7	***	Melt the Guns
8/21/87	5	1	1/11	***	Peaches en Regalia
9/21/87	3	3	7/15	Divided Sky	Ballad - Curtis Loew
10/21/89	93	1	9/10	The Lizards	David Bowie
3/9/90	42	2	5/11	The Curtain	Slave
4/2/91	105	2	5/8	Fluffhead	Buried Alive
5/4/91	18	2	1/9	***	Llama
8/2/93	278	1	11/12	My Mind's Got A Mind	La Grange
12/11/95	217	1	6/12	Reba	Llama
12/11/95	0	1	8/12	Llama	Tube
2/26/97	90	1	9/10	Rocko William	While My Guitar Gent
7/29/98	91	1	2/8	Bathtub Gin	Foam
11/27/98	36	2	6/16	Chalk Dust Torture	Chalk Dust Tor
12/18/99	68	1	3/9	Back @ Chicken Shack	Tube
9/17/00	37	2	3/5	Theme From the Botto	The Mango Song

Has not been played in the last 14 shows.

Dogs Stole Things

DATE	GAP	SET	POS.	SONG BEFORE	SONG AFTER
6/13/97	878	1	2/8	Theme From the Botto	Beauty of My Dreams
6/14/97	1	2	5/8	Waking Up	Waste
6/16/97	1	1	2/10	The Squirming Coil	Taste
6/19/97	1	1	2/9	Limb by Limb	Theme From the Botto
6/21/97	2	1	5/15	Taste	Theme From the Botto
6/24/97	2	1	3/12	Beauty of My Dreams	Vultures
6/25/97	1	1	2/11	Oblivious Fool	Taste
6/27/97	1	1	4/8	Stash	Poor Heart
7/1/97	2	1	9/9	Reba	***
7/6/97	4	1	3/9	The Old Home Place	Stash
7/10/97	2	1	1/8	***	Limb by Limb
7/21/97	2	1	2/7	Ghost	Piper
7/23/97	2	1	4/10	NICU	Ginseng Sullivan
7/26/97	2	1	2/9	Limb by Limb	Poor Heart
7/31/97	3	1	3/9	Ya Mar	Limb by Limb
8/2/97	1	1	4/8	Ghost	Divided Sky
8/9/97	4	1	5/8	Taste	Reba
8/17/97	6	1	3/10	Beauty of My Dreams	Vultures
11/21/97	6	1	4/8	Beauty of My Dreams	Punch You in
12/9/97	12	1	7/10	Weekapaug Groove	Beauty of My Dreams
4/3/98	9	1	7/9	Beauty of My Dreams	Reba
7/10/98	11	1	2/4	Down with Disease	Divided Sky
11/9/98	36	1	6/10	Frankie Says	Poor Heart
11/21/98	8	1	8/13	NICU	Nellie Kane
11/27/98	3	1	8/11	The Old Home Place	Vultures
7/16/99	18	1	3/10	Beauty of My Dreams	Limb by Limb
9/11/99	15	1	4/9	Limb by Limb	Punch You in
10/3/99	16	1	3/12	Farmhouse	Divided Sky
12/10/99	12	1	5/10	Heavy Things	My Mind's Got A Mind
7/6/00	30	1	2/12	Reba	Taste
9/22/00	17	1	6/9	Slave	Bathtub Gin

Has not been played in the last 11 shows.

Doin' My Time

DATE	GAP	SET	POS.	SONG BEFORE	SONG AFTER
8/7/96	817	1	10/10	Hold to a Dream	***
7/1/99	191	1	6/10	Beauty of My Dreams	Roggae

Has not been played in the last 111 shows.

Don't Get Me Wrong

DATE	GAP	SET	POS.	SONG BEFORE	SONG AFTER
10/6/90	219	E	1/1	***	***
10/8/90	2	1	1/10	***	The Landlady
12/28/90	18	2	11/12	No Good Trying	Funky Bitch

Has not been played in the last 880 shows.

Don't Pass Me By

DATE	GAP	SET	POS.	SONG BEFORE	SONG AFTER
10/31/94	681	2	15/30	Rocky Raccoon	Why Don't We Do it i

Has not been played in the last 438 shows.

Don't Want You No More

DATE	GAP	SET	POS.	SONG BEFORE	SONG AFTER
12/1/84	3	1	7/11	Spanish Flea	Cities

Has not been played in the last 1116 shows.

Don't You Wanna Go

DATE	GAP	SET	POS.	SONG BEFORE	SONG AFTER
5/16/95	712	1	1/12	***	Ha Ha Ha
6/8/95	2	1	1/9	***	Ha Ha Ha
6/14/95	4	1	1/12	***	Gumbo
6/26/95	10	1	2/10	My Friend My Friend	Bathtub Gin
9/28/95	8	2	3/8	Poor Heart	Tweezer

Has not been played in the last 383 shows.

Donna Lee

DATE	GAP	SET	POS.	SONG BEFORE	SONG AFTER
5/5/89	97	1	6/8	Alumni Blues	Fee
5/6/89	1	2	1/8	***	Suzy Greenber
6/23/89	9	1	5/11	Peaches en Regalia	Fee
6/30/89	1	1	5/7	Possum	Fluffhead
8/26/89	4	2	6/9	AC/DC Bag	Funky Bitch
10/20/89	10	2	6/10	AC/DC Bag	Split Open and
2/10/90	30	2	6/10	Happy Birthday	Fee
2/16/90	2	1	6/7	Weekapaug Groove	Run Like Antel
3/9/90	11	1	10/11	Possum	Run Like Antel
3/17/90	3	1	8/10	Divided Sky	The Lizards
4/5/90	3	2	5/13	AC/DC Bag	Tweezer
5/13/90	22	2	5/12	Foam	Tweezer
5/24/90	4	1	4/9	Tweezer	Reba
6/7/90	6	1	3/9	Fluff's Travels	Possum
10/30/90	21	1	3/9	Bouncing	The Asse Festival
11/17/90	8	2	11/12	Rocky Top	Good Time Ba
12/7/90	5	2	4/11	Weekapaug Groove	Cavern
12/29/90	3	E	1/2	***	AC/DC Bag
5/11/91	51	2	5/12	Reba	Mike's Song
7/12/91	7	1	8/12	Bathtub Gin	AC/DC Bag

Has not been played in the last 821 shows.

Dooley

DATE	GAP	SET	POS.	SONG BEFORE	SONG AFTER
11/20/94	692	1	8/10	My Long Journey Home	Divided Sky

Has not been played in the last 427 shows.

Down By the River

DATE	GAP	SET	POS.	SONG BEFORE	SONG AFTER
10/3/98	977	1	6/10	Arc	Moonlight In Vt

Has not been played in the last 142 shows.

Down With Disease

DATE	GAP	SET	POS.	SONG BEFORE	SONG AFTER
4/4/94	589	2	1/11	***	If I Could
4/6/94	2	2	2/9	The Curtain	Wolfman's Brother
4/8/94	1	1	10/13	Silent in the Mornin	If I Could
4/10/94	2	1	9/9	Scent of a Mule	***
4/14/94	3	1	4/9	Sparkle	Glide
4/15/94	1	1	9/9	It's Ice	***
4/17/94	2	1	6/9	Mound	If I Could
4/18/94	1	2	11/13	T.M.W.S.I.Y. Reprise	I Wanna Be Like You
4/21/94	2	1	7/9	The Lizards	If I Could

DATE	GAP	SET	POS.	SONG BEFORE	SONG AFTER
4/23/94	2	1	8/10	Esther	Caravan
4/25/94	2	1	5/10	Foam	Ginseng Sullivan
4/28/94	1	1	5/11	Rift	Bouncing
5/2/94	3	1	4/10	Bouncing	It's Ice
5/3/94	1	2	4/8	Fluffhead	Harpua
5/6/94	2	1	1/9	***	The Oh Kee Pa
5/8/94	2	1	5/8	Rift	Bouncing
5/12/94	2	1	3/10	Rift	Fee
5/14/94	2	1	3/9	Wilson	Fee
5/16/94	1	1	7/10	Rift	Bouncing
5/19/94	2	1	8/10	Silent in the Mornin	The Mango Song
5/21/94	2	1	4/9	Guelah Papyrus	Mound
5/22/94	1	2	1/9	***	Bouncing
5/26/94	3	2	4/9	Fluffhead	Mound
5/29/94	3	1	4/8	Halley's Comet	Sparkle
6/9/94	1	1	4/9	Rift	It's Ice
6/11/94	2	1	5/8	Rift	It's Ice
6/14/94	2	1	7/14	Rift	Fee
6/16/94	1	2	7/11	Big Ball Jam	Contact
6/18/94	2	1	6/10	The Mango Song	It's Ice
6/21/94	2	1	3/16	Poor Heart	My Friend My
6/23/94	2	1	7/10	Bouncing	Silent in the M
6/24/94	1	2	13/13	Carolina	***
6/26/94	2	2	2/12	Julius	If I Could
6/30/94	2	1	1/9	***	Gumbo
7/1/94	1	2	4/11	Fluffhead	T.M.W.S.I.Y.
7/3/94	2	1	3/10	Poor Heart	Fee
7/5/94	1	1	9/10	Esther	Sweet Adeline
7/9/94	3	1	7/10	Scent of a Mule	The Horse
7/13/94	2	1	6/11	The Mango Song	Fee
7/16/94	3	1	2/11	Golgi Apparatus	NO2
10/8/94	2	1	4/9	Sparkle	Guyute
10/10/94	2	2	7/9	Rift	Love You
10/13/94	2	1	4/9	All Things Recnsdrd	I Didn't Know
10/15/94	1	1	7/8	Reba	Golgi Apparat
10/21/94	4	1	2/9	Fee	Foam
10/23/94	2	2	5/9	You Enjoy Myself	Purple Rain
10/27/94	3	2	6/7	BBFCFM	Sweet Adeline
10/29/94	2	2	1/11	***	T.M.W.S.I.Y.
11/3/94	3	1	9/9	Sparkle	***
11/12/94	2	2	3/12	Fluffhead	Have Mercy
11/12/94	0	2	5/12	Have Mercy	Lifeboy
11/17/94	4	1	11/11	The Famous Mockingbi	***
11/19/94	2	1	2/11	Golgi Apparatus	Guyute
11/22/94	2	1	8/9	Bouncing	Sweet Adeline
11/30/94	5	1	7/10	The Famous Mockingbi	Bouncing
12/6/94	5	1	3/8	Mound	Fluffhead
6/16/95	17	1	7/9	Halley's Comet	Esther
6/26/95	8	2	1/6	***	Free
12/1/95	48	1	2/10	Buried Alive	Theme From the Botto
12/12/95	8	2	3/6	Sparkle	The Lizards
12/29/95	6	1	3/9	Poor Heart	Taste That Surrounds
7/15/96	14	2	1/9	***	Maze
7/23/96	6	1	6/9	Scent of a Mule	McGrupp
8/2/96	3	1	3/11	Ya Mar	Guelah Papyrus
8/5/96	2	2	2/13	Also Sprach	It's Ice
8/10/96	3	2	2/8	Wilson	Scent of a Mul
8/14/96	3	1	3/10	Jam	Fee
8/16/96	1	3	3/6	Also Sprach	NICU
10/16/96	2	2	2/12	Cars Trucks Buses	Wilson
10/19/96	3	1	7/9	Gumbo	Prince Caspian
10/22/96	2	2	2/10	Also Sprach	Taste
10/26/96	3	2	1/7	***	You Enjoy My
10/31/96	3	1	3/10	Highway to Hell	You Enjoy My
11/8/96	5	1	5/9	Mound	Prince Caspian
11/13/96	3	1	1/9	***	Bouncing
11/16/96	3	1	2/11	Poor Heart	Guyute
11/22/96	3	2	1/10	***	Prince Caspian
11/27/96	3	2	1/8	***	Jesus Just Left
11/27/96	0	2	6/8	Sweet Emotion Jam	Star Spangled Banner
12/1/96	3	1	7/12	The Curtain	Train Song
12/6/96	3	1	8/9	Cars Trucks Buses	Frankenstein
12/31/96	4	3	3/7	Auld Lang Syne	Suzy Greenber
2/14/97	2	2	3/9	Ya Mar	Funky Bitch
2/17/97	2	2	2/7	The Squirming Coil	Carini
2/17/97	0	2	5/7	Taste	Suzy Greenber
2/21/97	3	1	3/6	Foam	The Lizards
2/25/97	3	2	7/10	My Friend My Friend	Prince Caspian
3/1/97	3	1	3/10	The Oh Kee Pa Ceremo	Weigh
6/14/97	4	1	1/10	***	NICU
6/25/97	7	2	1/9	***	Piper
6/25/97	0	2	3/9	Piper	Meatstick
7/9/97	8	2	1/6	***	My Soul
7/22/97	4	2	1/6	***	Mike's Song
8/2/97	7	2	1/7	***	Tweezer
8/10/97	5	1	3/10	Sparkle	Dirt
8/17/97	5	2	1/5	***	Bathtub Gin
11/17/97	4	2	1/7	***	Oblivious Fool
11/23/97	4	2	2/5	Bathtub Gin	Low Rider Jam
11/23/97	0	2	4/5	Low Rider Jam	Bold as Love
12/2/97	5	1	2/9	Buried Alive	Makisupa Policeman
12/11/97	6	1	2/7	Punch You in the Eye	Ghost
12/11/97	0	2	5/6	Ghost	Johnny B. Goode
12/29/97	4	2	1/5	***	David Bowie
4/5/98	6	2	1/8	***	Ya Mar
7/1/98	2	1	5/9	The Moma Dance	Dog Faced Boy
7/3/98	2	1	6/11	Also Sprach	Limb by Limb
7/10/98	5	1	1/4	***	Dogs Stole Things
7/19/98	4	2	7/7	McGrupp	***
7/25/98	4	1	2/7	Roses Are Free	Roggae
7/28/98	2	1	2/10	Emotional Rescue	The Moma Dance
8/6/98	6	2	7/7	The Mango Song	***
8/11/98	4	2	5/5	When Circus Comes	***
8/16/98	3	2	1/8	***	Piper
11/2/98	8	2	1/16	***	The Mango Song
11/8/98	4	2	4/8	Rock and Roll	Jam
11/13/98	3	2	1/6	***	Sample in a Ja
11/24/98	7	1	1/9	***	The Moma Dance
11/28/98	3	1	3/8	Tube	Guyute
12/30/98	4	2	1/5	***	Piper
7/1/99	3	2	1/3	***	Prince Caspian
7/7/99	3	2	2/7	Also Sprach	My Left Toe
7/12/99	4	1	2/7	Foreplay/Long Time	Back on the Train
7/17/99	4	2	4/8	Jam	Wolfman's Brother
7/26/99	7	2	4/6	Theme From the Botto	Jam
7/30b/99	2	2	1/6	***	My Soul
9/10/99	4	2	1/9	***	The Moma Dance
9/14/99	3	2	4/5	Gumbo	Frankenstein
9/19/99	4	2	6/6	Loving Cup	***
9/24/99	3	1	6/10	The Moma Dance	Roggae
9/26/99	2	2	7/7	Meat	***
9/29/99	2	2	3/12	Also Sprach	Billy Breathes
10/4/99	4	1	8/8	Wilson	***
10/9/99	3	2	3/6	Also Sprach	Wading In Velvet Sea
12/4/99	4	2	1/9	***	Split Open and
12/8/99	3	1	3/8	Back on the Train	Fast Enough For You
12/11/99	2	2	5/5	Also Sprach	***
12/15/99	3	1	1/7	***	Farmhouse
12/31/99	5	2	3/35	Auld Lang Syne	Llama
5/21/00	1	2	2/8	Gotta Jibboo	Dirt
6/10/00	4	1	1/5	***	Sample in a Ja
6/15/00	4	2	1/4	***	The Lizards
6/23/00	3	2	3/7	Jesus Just Left	Twist
7/3/00	7	1	1/10	***	Guelah Papyrus
7/11/00	6	2	2/13	Also Sprach	Moby Dick
7/11/00	0	2	4/13	Moby Dick	Runaway Jim
7/15/00	3	2	1/7	***	While My Guitar Gent
9/12/00	4	2	1/8	***	Heavy Things
9/22/00	6	1	1/9	***	Meat
9/25/00	3	1	2/8	Everybody's Got Some	The Lizards
10/6/00	7	2	2/10	Heavy Things	Spock's Brain

Has not been played in the last 1 show.

Down with Disease Jam

DATE	GAP	SET	POS.	SONG BEFORE	SONG AFTER
12/31/93	588	3	2/9	Auld Lang Syne	Split Open and

Has not been played in the last 531 shows.

Driver

DATE	GAP	SET	POS.	SONG BEFORE	SONG AFTER
10/17/98	979	1	7/10	Freebird	Wading In Velvet Sea
10/29/98	2	1	5/10	Limb by Limb	Sleep
10/30/98	1	E	1/2	***	Freebird
11/2/98	2	1	5/9	Jesus Just Left	Bittersweet Motel
11/7/98	3	1	3/10	Mike's Song	Brian and Robert
11/15/98	6	1	3/8	Ghost	Scent of a Mul
11/20/98	3	1	12/13	Roggae	Split Open and
11/25/98	3	1	8/9	Sleep	Good Time Ba
12/28/98	4	1	7/10	Albuquerque	Tube
7/9/99	10	1	7/8	Llama	Runaway Jim
9/29/99	33	1	3/9	Free	Taste
6/16/00	34	2	4/7	Dog Faced Boy	Slave
6/24/00	3	E	3/4	The Inlaw Josie Wale	Tweezer Repri
7/6/00	8	2	5/7	Piper	Harry Hood
7/14/00	6	E	2/3	The Inlaw Josie Wale	Guyute
9/14/00	6	E	1/3	***	The Inlaw Josie Wale
9/25/00	8	E	2/3	Boogie On Reggae	Tweezer Repri
10/1/00	4	2	6/7	Camel Walk	David Bowie

Has not been played in the last 4 shows.

Drowned

DATE	GAP	SET	POS.	SONG BEFORE	SONG AFTER
10/31/95	759	2	13/17	Sea and Sand	Bell Boy
12/31/95	33	2	1/8	***	Jam
2/28/97	82	2	2/9	Taste	Prince Caspian
3/18/97	3	2	2/10	Taste	Prince Caspian
12/3/97	52	1	3/7	My Soul	The Old Home
12/11/97	5	2	1/6	***	Roses Are Free
12/28/97	3	2	4/9	Ghost	Scent of a Mul
7/9/98	15	2	1/8	***	Theme From the Botto
7/20/98	6	2	1/6	***	Makisupa Policeman
8/7/98	12	1	2/10	Water in the Sky	Frankie Says
11/2/98	14	1	3/9	Tube Jam	Jesus Just Left
11/25/98	15	2	3/8	Golgi Apparatus	Prince Caspian
9/21/99	41	1	4/9	Split Open and Melt	I Didn't Know
12/12/99	23	2	1/5	***	Prince Caspian
12/31/99	7	2	22/35	My Soul	After Midnight Repri
6/29/00	16	1	4/5	Limb by Limb	Rock and Roll
7/11/00	9	1	4/8	Uncle Pen	Chalk Dust Reprise

DATE	GAP	SET	POS.	SONG BEFORE	SONG AFTER
9/14/00	8	2	1/5	***	Crosseyed and Painle
9/20/00	4	2	9/9	BBFCFM	***
10/5/00	10	2	1/7	***	NICU

Has not been played in the last 2 shows.

Drum Jam

DATE	GAP	SET	POS.	SONG BEFORE	SONG AFTER
5/2/91	286	1	2/11	Rocky Top	Foam
5/17/91	8	1	2/17	Chalk Dust Torture	Jam
7/25/97	606	2	4/6	Ya Mar	Ghost

Has not been played in the last 219 shows.

Drums Jam

DATE	GAP	SET	POS.	SONG BEFORE	SONG AFTER
11/3/84	2	1	10/10	Whipping Post	***
12/1/84	1	1	9/11	Cities	Skippy Wondermouse
4/21/94	600	E	1/3	***	Jam
10/15/94	66	E	1/2	***	The Maker

Has not been played in the last 450 shows.

Earl's Breakdown

DATE	GAP	SET	POS.	SONG BEFORE	SONG AFTER
11/16/94	688	1	10/11	Tennessee Waltz	Swing Low Sweet Chrt

Has not been played in the last 431 shows.

Eclipse

DATE	GAP	SET	POS.	SONG BEFORE	SONG AFTER
11/2/98	984	2	15/16	Brain Damage	Harpua

Has not been played in the last 135 shows.

El Paso

DATE	GAP	SET	POS.	SONG BEFORE	SONG AFTER
10/6/00	1118	E	1/3	***	Chalk Dust Tor

Has not been played in the last 1 show.

Eliza

DATE	GAP	SET	POS.	SONG BEFORE	SONG AFTER
9/15/90	209	2	2/8	Split Open and Melt	My Sweet One
9/20/90	2	1	11/12	Weekapaug Groove	La Grange
11/17/90	21	1	8/11	Cavern	The Oh Kee Pa
11/24/90	1	2	4/12	Stash	The Landlady
9/28/91	82	1	7/11	Stash	Foam
9/29/91	1	2	3/10	Bouncing	Foam
10/10/91	6	1	9/11	It's Ice	Llama
10/13/91	3	E	1/3	***	Uncle Pen
11/1/91	11	2	5/13	Chalk Dust Torture	Mike's Song
11/8/91	3	1	10/11	Brother	Golgi Apparat
11/15/91	6	2	7/14	Weekapaug Groove	Tube
11/23/91	6	2	8/13	Tweezer	The Landlady
12/6/91	5	2	2/11	It's Ice	Sparkle
3/12/92	6	2	3/11	Tweezer	It's Ice
3/24/92	8	1	4/13	Foam	Rift
4/7/92	12	2	4/11	Tweezer	You Enjoy My
4/21/92	9	1	8/11	It's Ice	NICU
5/8/92	13	1	6/12	It's Ice	Llama
5/14/92	4	2	5/13	Fluffhead	Mike's Song

Has not been played in the last 711 shows.

Emotional Rescue

DATE	GAP	SET	POS.	SONG BEFORE	SONG AFTER
11/21/97	921	1	1/8	***	Split Open and
12/31/97	19	1	1/10	***	Ya Mar
7/28/98	23	1	1/10	***	Down with Dis
9/30/00	151	E	1/1	***	***

Has not been played in the last 5 shows.

Esther

DATE	GAP	SET	POS.	SONG BEFORE	SONG AFTER
9/12/88	66	2	10/10	Harry Hood	***
2/7/89	15	1	1/9	***	McGrupp
4/20/89	12	1	6/12	Fire	Suzy Greenber
5/1/89	3	1	3/9	You Enjoy Myself	AC/DC Bag
5/6/89	2	1	6/13	Weekapaug Groove	The Sloth
5/9/89	1	2	5/14	Slave	Run Like Antel
5/28/89	7	1	7/9	Slave	Suzy Greenber
10/12/89	13	2	5/7	Weekapaug Groove	Walk Away
11/2/89	9	1	10/11	Split Open and Melt	Good Time Ba
12/3/89	9	2	4/14	AC/DC Bag	The Oh Kee Pa
12/9/89	3	2	3/8	Fluffhead	Alumni Blues
1/20/90	6	2	7/10	Lawn Boy	Mike's Song
2/10/90	6	2	2/10	La Grange	AC/DC Bag
2/16/90	2	1	2/7	Fluffhead	Mike's Song
2/24/90	4	1	5/8	Divided Sky	Possum
3/3/90	4	2	4/7	Fluffhead	Funky Bitch
3/7/90	1	1	3/6	Possum	Caravan
3/10/90	3	1	2/10	Wilson	McGrupp
3/17/90	2	1	2/10	Golgi Apparatus	Dinner and a
4/6/90	4	2	3/10	La Grange	The Sloth
4/9/90	3	2	2/11	Funky Bitch	Uncle Pen
4/13/90	2	1	5/10	Fluffhead	La Grange
4/21/90	5	1	4/10	Funky Bitch	Foam
4/22/90	1	2	6/11	How High the Moon	BBFCFM
4/25/90	1	2	6/12	You Enjoy Myself	La Grange
4/26/90	1	2	2/11	How High the Moon	Bathtub Gin
5/6/90	4	2	3/7	Harry Hood	David Bowie
5/31/90	10	1	6/12	Caravan	Tweezer
6/16/90	7	2	2/8	Golgi Apparatus	Tweezer
9/20/90	5	1	6/12	Foam	The Landlady
9/28/90	3	2	2/6	AC/DC Bag	Gumbo
10/4/90	3	1	3/10	The Landlady	Possum
10/6/90	2	1	3/9	Suzy Greenberg	Possum
10/12/90	3	1	7/9	Cavern	Tweezer
11/2/90	4	1	9/14	Weekapaug Groove	Cavern
11/17/90	6	2	6/12	Weekapaug Groove	Love You
11/30/90	5	1		Weekapaug Groove	Dinner and a
12/29/90	5	1	4/10	You Enjoy Myself	David Bowie
2/2/91	3	1	5/9	Dinner and a Movie	Stash
2/3/91	1	1	5/10	Tweezer	Destiny Unbound
2/14/91	4	2	7/12	Runaway Jim	Alumni Blues
2/19/91	3	2	7/15	The Landlady	Split Open and
2/28/91	5	1	4/13	Foam	Mike's Song
3/13/91	5	1	6/9	Divided Sky	Llama
3/17/91	3	2	2/8	Runaway Jim	My Sweet One
3/31/91	5	1	8/13	My Sweet One	Possum
4/3/91	2	2	5/9	Stash	The Landlady
4/20/91	10	1	7/11	The Landlady	Chalk Dust Tor
5/9/91	8	2	5/8	Stash	Split Open and
7/14/91	11	3	3/10	The Landlady	Chalk Dust Tor
7/21/91	5	2	6/9	The Sloth	AC/DC Bag
8/3/91	6	2	6/10	Tweezer	Cavern
9/27/91	3	1	5/9	Buried Alive	Tweezer
10/3/91	5	2	5/11	Weekapaug Groove	The Landlady
10/12/91	5	1	6/9	Stash	Divided Sky
10/17/91	3	1	8/10	Stash	Chalk Dust Tor
11/13/91	16	1	6/10	Chalk Dust Torture	Cavern
11/21/91	4	1	8/10	Split Open and Melt	Mike's Song
12/31/91	9	1	8/10	Divided Sky	Llama
3/17/92	7	2	6/11	Tweezer	Mike's Song
4/6/92	16	1	6/10	Brother	Chalk Dust Tor
4/18/92	8	1	6/11	Split Open and Melt	Possum
4/30/92	8	1	9/10	Rift	Run Like Antel
5/7/92	6	1	7/11	Runaway Jim	Split Open and
7/15/92	22	2	3/9	Divided Sky	My Sweet One
8/17/92	19	2	4/11	Tweezer	Mike's Song
11/19/92	11	1	8/12	Divided Sky	Axilla
11/28/92	7	1	4/11	Stash	Chalk Dust Tor
12/4/92	5	2	3/10	David Bowie	Possum
12/11/92	6	2	5/12	Weekapaug Groove	Axilla
12/30/92	5	1	4/14	Split Open and Melt	Chalk Dust Tor
2/9/93	7	1	8/10	Chalk Dust Torture	Maze
2/12/93	3	1	6/11	Split Open and Melt	The Wedge
2/15/93	2	1	6/12	Divided Sky	Chalk Dust Tor
2/21/93	5	1	7/10	Chalk Dust Torture	Dinner and a
3/9/93	11	1	5/10	Maze	Divided Sky
3/16/93	4	2	7/15	Bathtub Gin	Chalk Dust Tor
3/21/93	4	1	5/11	Divided Sky	All Things Rec
3/30/93	7	1	7/11	Llama	Stash
4/16/93	10	1	5/10	Split Open and Melt	Llama
4/22/93	5	1	6/10	Chalk Dust Torture	Stash
5/3/93	5	1	5/11	Chalk Dust Torture	Split Open and
7/18/93	10	1	6/10	Maze	Divided Sky
7/30/93	9	1	6/10	Stash	Chalk Dust Tor
8/11/93	8	2	4/10	Weekapaug Groove	All Things Rec
8/14/93	3	1	9/11	Split Open and Melt	Poor Heart
8/26/93	8	1	6/9	Split Open and Melt	It's Ice
12/28/93	2	1	4/10	Split Open and Melt	The Oh Kee Pa
4/10/94	9	1	5/9	Split Open and Melt	Chalk Dust Tor
4/23/94	11	1	7/10	Stash	Down with Dis
5/6/94	9	1	8/9	Stash	Chalk Dust Tor
5/29/94	18	2	3/10	Split Open and Melt	Chalk Dust Tor
6/13/94	4	2	4/11	Weekapaug Groove	Cavern
6/21/94	6	2	6/16	Split Open and Melt	Chalk Dust Tor
7/5/94	11	1	8/10	Stash	Down with Dis
10/10/94	12	2	3/9	Maze	Tweezer
10/20/94	7	1	8/11	Split Open and Melt	Julius
11/12/94	13	1	7/8	Stash	Chalk Dust Tor
11/25/94	10	1	6/8	Split Open and Melt	Julius
6/16/95	25	1	3/10	Down with Disease	Ya Mar
10/19/95	30	1	5/11	Punch You in the Eye	Chalk Dust Tor
11/14/95	14	1	5/9	Divided Sky	Free
12/5/95	15	1	6/8	Free	David Bowie
8/12/96	40	1	3/10	Split Open and Melt	Chalk Dust Tor
8/16/96	3	1	5/8	AC/DC Bag	Divided Sky
10/19/96	1	5	4/9	Free	Llama
8/1/98	139	1	3/9	Mike's Song	Weekapaug Gr
8/9/98	6	1	6/9	Birds of a Feather	Roggae
9/30/00	142	1	9/10	I Saw it Again	Weekapaug Gr

Has not been played in the last 5 shows.

Everybody's Got Something to Hide Except for Me and My Monkey

DATE	GAP	SET	POS.	SONG BEFORE	SONG AFTER
10/31/94	681	2	22/30	Mother Nature's Son	Sexy Sadie
9/25/00	430	1	1/8	***	Down with Dis

Has not been played in the last 8 shows.

Eyes of the World

DATE	GAP	SET	POS.	SONG BEFORE	SONG AFTER
11/3/84	2	1	8/10	Camel Walk	Whipping Post
12/1/84	1	E	1/1	***	***
5/3/85	2	3	2/8	Scarlet Begonias	Whipping Post

Has not been played in the last 1114 shows.

Faht

DATE	GAP	SET	POS.	SONG BEFORE	SONG AFTER
11/22/92	458	2	9/10	You Enjoy Myself	Golgi Apparat
11/27/92	3	2	11/13	Silent in the Mornin	Take the A-Trn
12/4/92	6	2	9/10	Harry Hood	You Enjoy My
12/11/92	6	2	11/12	The Squirming Coil	Possum
7/15/93	79	2	8/11	Possum	The Lizards
7/17/93	2	2	10/12	Weekapaug Groove	Rift
7/23/93	4	2	4/11	Run Like an Antelope	My Friend My
8/16/93	19	2	2/10	Mike's Song	Weekapaug Gr
4/13/94	19	2	1/10	***	The Curtain
6/19/94	45	2	1/8	***	Run Like Antel
10/3/95	99	2	6/9	Billy Breathes	Sweet Adeline
12/2/95	37	2	4/9	Simple	Tweezer

Has not been played in the last 342 shows.

Family Picture

DATE	GAP	SET	POS.	SONG BEFORE	SONG AFTER
11/8/91	339	2	12/13	TV Show	Crimes of the Mind

Has not been played in the last 780 shows.

Farmhouse

DATE	GAP	SET	POS.	SONG BEFORE	SONG AFTER
11/16/97	918	1	4/11	Black-Eyed Katy	The Old Home
11/28/97	7	1	5/8	Maze	Black-Eyed Katy
12/28/97	12	1	7/11	Runaway Jim	Funky Bitch
7/29/98	27	1	5/8	Fikus	Vultures
8/8/98	7	1	6/8	Fikus	Possum
10/3/98	6	1	2/10	Birds of a Feather	The Moma Dance
11/7/98	10	2	4/4	Reba	***
11/13/98	4	1	7/10	Cars Trucks Buses	Water in the Sky
11/18/98	3	1	3/9	Birds of a Feather	My Soul
11/20/98	2	2	5/8	Roses Are Free	Gettin' Jiggy W/ It
12/28/98	7	1	3/10	Stash	Taste

DATE	GAP	SET	POS.	SONG BEFORE	SONG AFTER
6/30/99	4	1	2/8	Bathtub Gin	Tube
7/4/99	3	1	3/10	Ya Mar	The Oh Kee Pa
7/9/99	3	1	2/8	Limb By Limb	Back on the Train
7/15/99	4	1	3/10	Ghost	Horn
7/18/99	3	1	2/11	Punch You in the Eye	Water in the Sky
7/26/99	6	1	1/11	***	Back on the Train
9/10/99	6	1	1/8	***	First Tube
9/14/99	3	1	8/11	Wading In Velvet Sea	Nellie Kane
9/16/99	1	1	3/14	Chalk Dust Torture	First Tube
9/19/99	3	1	6/8	Heavy Things	Stash
9/24/99	3	1	3/10	Punch You in the Eye	Water in the Sky
9/28/99	3	2	1/7	***	Heavy Things
10/3/99	4	1	2/12	First Tube	Dogs Stole Things
10/10/99	5	1	1/7	***	Gotta Jibboo
12/2/99	1	1	2/10	Runaway Jim	Heavy Things
12/4/99	2	2	4/9	The Moma Dance	T.M.W.S.I.Y.
12/7/99	2	1	1/8	***	First Tube
12/15/99	6	1	2/7	Down with Disease	Bathtub Gin
12/30/99	4	1	9/12	Possum	Ghost
6/11/00	7	1	9/9	It's Ice	***
6/15/00	3	1	8/8	Divided Sky	***
6/23/00	3	1	8/8	Cars Trucks Buses	***
6/30/00	5	2	7/9	Makisupa Policeman	Sleeping Monkey
7/4/00	3	1	2/11	Star Spangled Banner	Rift
7/14/00	7	2	9/11	Dog Faced Boy	Taste

Has not been played in the last 22 shows.

Fast Enough for You

DATE	GAP	SET	POS.	SONG BEFORE	SONG AFTER
11/19/92	455	2	12/15	Poor Heart	Llama
11/20/92	1	2	5/10	You Enjoy Myself	Dinner and a
11/25/92	2	2	3/9	Foam	You Enjoy My
11/28/92	2	1	7/11	Sparkle	All Things Rec
12/2/92	3	1	4/10	Divided Sky	Poor Heart
12/4/92	2	1	7/11	Sparkle	Maze
12/7/92	3	1	7/11	Foam	All Things Rec
12/13/92	5	1	9/11	Rift	I Didn't Know
12/29/92	2	2	7/14	Big Ball Jam	All Things Rec
2/4/93	4	1	5/11	Maze	All Things Rec
2/7/93	3	2	2/13	Llama	My Mind's Got A Mind
2/12/93	4	2	6/11	Big Ball Jam	You Enjoy My
2/15/93	2	2	2/12	Rift	Reba
2/20/93	4	2	18/22	Weekapaug Groove	Big Ball Jam
2/25/93	4	2	8/11	Big Ball Jam	If I Only Had a Brai
3/3/93	4	2	10/13	My Sweet One	Terrapin
3/6/93	2	2	6/9	Big Ball Jam	You Enjoy My
3/13/93	4	2	11/13	Weekapaug Groove	Love You
3/24/93	8	2	7/12	Big Ball Jam	You Enjoy My
7/16/93	37	1	6/10	Buried Alive	All Things Rec
7/18/93	2	2	5/10	Mound	All Things Rec
7/29/93	1	1	6/10	The Landlady	My Mind's Got A Mind
8/8/93	7	1	8/11	Punch You in the Eye	Paul and Silas
8/17/93	8	1	8/9	Fluffhead	Daniel
12/28/93	7	2	6/9	The Sloth	Uncle Pen
4/11/94	10	1	4/9	Foam	Magilla
4/29/94	3	1	3/12	You Enjoy Myself	Scent of a Mul
5/7/94	6	1	5/9	Mound	Scent of a Mul
5/14/94	5	2	9/11	Punch You in the Eye	The Lizards
5/20/94	4	1	6/10	Bathtub Gin	Scent of a Mul
6/19/94	17	1	6/9	The Curtain	Scent of a Mul
7/2/94	10	1	4/9	Guelah Papyrus	Scent of a Mul
7/13/94	7	1	9/11	It's Ice	I Didn't Know
10/9/94	6	1	3/7	Foam	The Curtain
10/13/94	3	1	7/9	Foam	Sparkle
10/21/94	6	2	9/11	The Curtain	Scent of a Mul
11/16/94	15	1	3/11	Foam	Reba
12/1/94	11	1	3/8	Uncle Pen	Maze
6/8/95	15	1	6/9	Mound	Reba

DATE	GAP	SET	POS.	SONG BEFORE	SONG AFTER
6/28/95	15	1	3/8	Foam	Reba
10/3/95	11	1	4/11	Foam	I'm Blue, Lonesome
10/22/95	13	1	7/12	NICU	It's Ice
11/15/95	12	1	3/9	AC/DC Bag	Rift
11/30/95	10	1	8/10	Rift	The Lizards
12/28/95	14	1	8/10	Rift	Possum
7/15/96	15	1	3/8	Punch You in the Eye	Guyute
8/13/96	16	1	5/10	Maze	The Old Home
11/6/96	18	1	3/9	Cars Trucks Buses	Taste
11/22/96	11	1	7/10	Sample in a Jar	Train Song
11/14/97	68	1	4/8	Maze	Also Sprach
7/16/98	38	1	5/7	Reba	When Circus Comes
7/4/99	55	1	9/10	I Didn't Know	David Bowie
7/23/99	13	1	5/9	Punch You in the Eye	Back on the Train
12/8/99	37	1	4/8	Down with Disease	Ya Mar
6/13/00	17	1	5/10	Ya Mar	The Old Home
6/25/00	7	2	2/7	Gotta Jibboo	Scent of a Mul
9/23/00	25	2	5/7	Scent of a Mule	Piper

Has not been played in the last 10 shows.

Fee

DATE	GAP	SET	POS.	SONG BEFORE	SONG AFTER
8/9/87	25	2	8/11	Fluffhead	Harry Hood
8/10/87	1	2	5/10	Fluffhead	The Curtain With
8/21/87	1	2	8/12	Flat Fee	Skin it Back
9/21/87	3	3	5/15	Sneakin' Sally	Divided Sky
9/27/87	1	2	5/5	Fire	***
10/31/87	2	2	10/17	The Chase	Divided Sky
11/19/87	2	2	4/6	I Didn't Know	Corrine Corrina
1/27/88	1	3	1/8	***	The Lizards
2/7/88	1	2	5/9	Flat Fee	Possum
2/8/88	1	3	7/9	Bike	Jesus Just Left
2/24/88	1	1	10/11	Corrine Corrina	David Bowie
2/26/88	1	2	4/9	Ballad - Curtis Loew	McGrupp
3/31/88	4	1	3/14	Golgi Apparatus	AC/DC Bag
4/22/88	2	2	4/13	The Lizards	Shaggy Dog
5/25/88	4	3	6/11	La Grange	I Know a Little
6/20/88	3	2	3/9	Tela	Golgi Apparat
6/24/88	2	1	7/11	Golgi Apparatus	Sneakin' Sally
9/12/88	11	1	3/4	Take the A-Train	Bold as Love
9/24/88	3	2	5/7	Possum	Sparks
10/29/88	1	2	3/10	Whipping Post	Alumni Blues
11/3/88	2	1	5/7	Possum	Alumni Blues
11/5/88	1	2	6/11	AC/DC Bag	Mike's Song
11/11/88	1	2	5/6	Mr. P.C.	Bold as Love
12/10/88	1	2	6/12	Foam	Mike's Song
1/25/89	2	1	1/2	***	Fluffhead
1/26/89	1	1	9/10	Divided Sky	Good Time Ba
2/6/89	1	1	5/7	Peaches en Regalia	La Grange
2/7/89	1	2	8/9	Alumni Blues	Run Like Antel
2/17/89	2	1	3/10	You Enjoy Myself	Divided Sky
3/8/89	3	2	4/12	Weekapaug Groove	Possum
3/4/89	1	1	6/8	Weekapaug Groove	Golgi Apparat
5/5/89	10	1	7/8	Donna Lee	Run Like Antel
5/27/89	8	1	6/11	Funky Bitch	You Enjoy My
5/28/89	1	1	5/9	The Famous Mockingbi	Slave
6/23/89	1	1	6/11	Donna Lee	Mike's Song
8/17/89	2	2	4/6	The Mango Song	You Enjoy My
9/14/89	5	1	8/9	La Grange	David Bowie
9/21/89	1	1	5/9	My Sweet One	Alumni Blues
10/7/89	3	1	7/11	Suzy Greenberg	La Grange
10/12/89	1	2	1/7	***	Mike's Song
10/14/89	2	1	7/11	Split Open and Melt	Alumni Blues
10/21/89	2	1	1/10	***	Ya Mar
10/22/89	1	2	8/9	My Sweet One	Possum
10/26/89	1	1	4/11	You Enjoy My	Divided Sky
10/31/89	2	1	6/9	Divided Sky	Walk Away
11/2/89	1	1	6/11	Weekapaug Groove	The Curtain
11/10/89	3	1	4/9	Suzy Greenberg	Divided Sky
11/30/89	4	2	6/11	Undun	Split Open and
12/3/89	2	2	9/14	In a Hole	Possum

DATE	GAP	SET	POS.	SONG BEFORE	SONG AFTER
12/7/89	1	1	5/11	AC/DC Bag	Mike's Song
12/9/89	2	2	5/8	Alumni Blues	Mike's Song
12/31/89	5	2	7/7	Divided Sky	***
2/1/90	5	1	8/11	Possum	Mike's Song
2/10/90	2	2	7/10	Donna Lee	Mike's Song
2/24/90	6	2	4/9	AC/DC Bag	The Squirmin
3/28/90	11	1	3/12	Ya Mar	Walk Away
4/5/90	2	2	7/13	Tweezer	Cavern
4/8/90	3	2	8/10	Weekapaug Groove	My Sweet One
4/14/90	4	2	10/11	Golgi Apparatus	David Bowie
4/18/90	1	2	2/12	La Grange	The Sloth
4/20/90	2	2	7/11	Rift	The Oh Kee Pa
5/6/90	8	2	1/7	***	Harry Hood
5/19/90	6	2	5/10	Suzy Greenberg	Dinner and a
5/24/90	2	2	7/11	Horn	Walk Away
6/1/90	3	1	7/12	Weekapaug Groove	Terrapin
6/1/90	0	1	10/12	Possum	BBFCFM
6/7/90	3	1	5/9	Possum	Reba
6/9/90	2	2	7/14	La Grange	Foam
6/16/90	1	3	7/13	Suzy Greenberg	Rocky Top
9/15/90	3	1	5/14	The Landlady	Tube
9/22/90	4	2	4/10	Destiny Unbound	Uncle Pen
10/1/90	3	1	7/11	Runaway Jim	Gumbo
10/4/90	1	2	4/8	Foam	Tweezer
10/5/90	1	2	7/8	Split Open and Melt	Possum
10/12/90	4	2	2/10	Possum	The Landlady
10/31/90	3	2	6/12	Tweezer	The Oh Kee Pa
11/3/90	2	2	7/12	Stash	Uncle Pen
11/10/90	3	2	4/8	The Asse Festival	Llama
2/15/91	19	1	5/11	Split Open and Melt	Buried Alive
2/21/91	4	1	5/11	Split Open and Melt	Llama
2/27/91	2	1	6/10	You Enjoy Myself	My Sweet One
3/9/91	5	E	2/3	Good Times Bad Times	The Curtain
3/17/91	4	2	6/8	Tweezer	Slave
3/23/91	2	1	3/10	Divided Sky	Llama
4/3/91	5	2	8/9	Destiny Unbound	David Bowie
4/5/91	2	E	1/3	***	The Oh Kee Pa
4/11/91	2	E	1/2	***	Possum
4/15/91	2	1	6/10	Split Open and Melt	Chalk Dust Tor
4/19/91	3	2	2/10	Harry Hood	The Curtain
4/21/91	2	2	2/11	Possum	The Landlady
5/2/91	4	2	4/10	Divided Sky	Split Open and
5/3/91	1	1	8/12	Divided Sky	Paul and Silas
5/9/91	2	E	1/2	***	Chalk Dust Tor
5/12/91	3	1	9/11	Llama	Foam
5/19/91	4	2	3/10	AC/DC Bag	Foam
7/12/91	2	E	1/2	***	Tweezer Repri
7/19/91	5	1	5/10	David Bowie	Cavern
7/21/91	2	E	3/4	Touch Me	Suzy Greenber
7/26/91	4	2	5/10	Flat Fee	Funky Bitch
8/3/91	2	1	6/11	Llama	The Squirmin
9/26/91	2	1	4/10	Divided Sky	It's Ice
10/3/91	6	1	7/10	Llama	Divided Sky
10/6/91	2	2	3/10	Stash	The Landlady
10/10/91	1	2	10/13	Suzy Greenberg	Mike's Song
10/18/91	6	2	9/12	I Didn't Know	Split Open and
10/23/91	2	2	8/10	Love You	You Enjoy My
10/28/91	1	1	5/10	Foam	David Bowie
10/31/91	2	2	5/14	Llama	Wait
11/7/91	3	E	1/4	***	Rocky Top
11/8/91	1	E	1/2	***	Suzy Greenber
11/10/91	2	1	5/10	David Bowie	The Squirmin
11/12/91	1	1	9/11	Harry Hood	Foam
11/14/91	2	2	3/11	Roll Like a Cantalou	Paul and Silas
11/19/91	3	1	4/11	Runaway Jim	Sparkle
11/22/91	3	1	5/11	Brother	Foam
11/23/91	1	2	10/13	The Landlady	Love You
12/5/91	4	2	8/13	Weekapaug Groove	The Sloth
3/11/92	6	1	6/10	Maze	Split Open and
3/14/92	3	1	8/13	Stash	Chalk Dust Tor
3/25/92	7	1	5/10	Rift	Maze
3/31/92	5	2	4/13	Weekapaug Groove	Poor Heart
4/7/92	6	1	4/12	It's Ice	Divided Sky
4/13/92	3	1	6/10	NICU	All Things Rec
4/16/92	2	1	7/12	Rift	Maze
4/19/92	3	1	8/11	Maze	Chalk Dust Tor

DATE	GAP	SET	POS.	SONG BEFORE	SONG AFTER
4/23/92	3	2	10/13	Tweezer	Maze
4/30/92	4	1	3/10	Split Open and Melt	Maze
5/3/92	3	1	5/10	Uncle Pen	Split Open and
5/7/92	3	2	9/12	Weekapaug Groove	Bike
5/9/92	2	1	7/11	Rift	Maze
5/18/92	7	2	9/13	Weekapaug Groove	Rift
7/14/92	12	2	6/12	Tweezer	All Things Rec
11/19/92	31	1	2/12	Maze	Foam
11/22/92	3	1	4/12	Suzy Greenberg	Maze
11/25/92	2	1	4/11	The Landlady	Maze
11/30/92	3	E	1/2	***	Fire
12/3/92	3	2	2/12	Maze	All Things Rec
12/4/92	1	E	1/2	***	Rocky Top
12/6/92	2	1	3/10	Foam	My Friend My
12/7/92	1	2	8/12	It's Ice	David Bowie
12/10/92	2	1	4/11	Foam	Poor Heart
12/13/92	3	1	5/11	It's Ice	Uncle Pen
2/3/93	5	1	3/11	Rift	Llama
2/7/93	4	1	11/12	Split Open and Melt	Runaway Jim
2/11/93	3	1	5/10	Stash	Rift
2/15/93	3	2	11/12	Bike	Llama
2/19/93	3	1	4/11	Split Open and Melt	Maze
2/22/93	3	1	7/10	Foam	Cavern
2/26/93	3	1	3/10	Foam	Split Open and
2/27/93	1	2	11/12	Terrapin	Llama
3/2/93	1	1	7/13	It's Ice	All Things Rec
3/13/93	7	1	5/11	Maze	All Things Rec
3/16/93	2	1	5/11	It's Ice	Maze
3/18/93	2	1	4/11	Rift	Maze
3/24/93	4	1	3/9	Foam	Poor Heart
3/26/93	2	1	5/10	Punch You in the Eye	All Things Rec
3/28/93	2	1	8/11	Maze	It's Ice
4/1/93	3	2	4/10	Possum	Ya Mar
4/5/93	3	1	3/10	It's Ice	Maze
4/12/93	3	2	3/10	Tweezer	Paul and Silas
4/18/93	4	1	6/10	Divided Sky	Maze
4/22/93	3	1	8/10	Stash	Rift
4/25/93	3	2	10/11	Weekapaug Groove	Tweezer Repri
4/29/93	2	1	9/10	Rift	Run Like Antel
5/1/93	5	1	5/10	Split Open and Melt	Rift
5/7/93	5	2	4/10	Maze	Big Ball Jam
7/18/93	7	2	7/10	All Things Recnsdrd	You Enjoy My
7/25/93	5	1	5/10	Stash	Rift
8/3/93	7	1	4/11	Foam	Rift
8/9/93	4	1	5/11	Mound	Split Open and
8/15/93	5	1	5/10	Runaway Jim	Paul and Silas
8/21/93	4	2	4/10	Uncle Pen	Llama
8/26/93	3	1	4/9	Reba	Split Open and
12/28/93	2	1	9/10	It's Ice	Possum
12/31/93	3	2	5/8	It's Ice	Possum
4/4/94	1	1	5/9	Maze	Reba
4/6/94	2	1	8/9	Scent of a Mule	Run Like Antel
4/9/94	2	1	7/10	Julius	All Things Rec
4/13/94	3	2	6/10	Big Ball Jam	Take the A-Trn
4/16/94	3	1	2/8	Runaway Jim	Axilla (Part II)
4/20/94	3	2	7/9	Harry Hood	You Enjoy My
4/23/94	3	1	3/10	Rift	Peaches en Regalia
4/25/94	2	1	3/10	Runaway Jim	Foam
4/29/94	2	2	5/11	Reba	Uncle Pen
5/8/94	7	2	4/9	It's Ice	Julius
5/12/94	2	1	4/10	Down with Disease	Maze
5/14/94	2	1	4/9	Down with Disease	Reba
5/16/94	1	E	1/2	***	Rocky Top
5/20/94	3	1	1/10	***	Maze
5/23/94	3	1	4/10	Foam	Maze
5/28/94	4	2	6/8	Reba	Llama
6/9/94	2	1	8/9	Maze	Suzy Greenber
6/14/94	4	1	8/14	Down with Disease	My Friend My
6/16/94	1	1	4/10	Julius	Maze
6/24/94	7	1	4/11	It's Ice	All Things Rec
7/3/94	7	1	4/10	Down with Disease	NICU
7/13/94	6	1	7/11	Down with Disease	It's Ice
7/15/94	2	1	6/8	Foam	Split Open and
10/8/94	3	1	6/9	Guyute	It's Ice
10/10/94	2	2	5/9	Tweezer	Rift
10/16/94	5	1	4/10	Foam	Split Open and
10/21/94	3	1	1/9	***	Down with Dis
10/23/94	2	2	8/9	Harry Hood	Good Time Ba
10/25/94	1	1	1/9	***	Llama
10/28/94	3	E	1/1	***	Highway to Hell
11/3/94	4	1	1/9	***	Divided Sky
11/16/94	5	2	6/7	Chalk Dust Torture	Run Like Antel
11/20/94	4	1	2/10	Chalk Dust Torture	Scent of a Mul
11/23/94	2	2	2/7	Maze	Scent of a Mul
11/28/94	3	E	1/2	***	Tweezer Repri
12/4/94	5	1	6/9	Tweezer	Mound
12/7/94	2	2	4/9	Divided Sky	Julius
12/10/94	3	1	1/8	***	Rift
12/30/94	3	1	7/9	Stash	Scent of a Mul
6/10/95	6	2	2/8	Maze	Uncle Pen
6/17/95	5	1	4/9	Taste	Uncle Pen
6/24/95	5	1	1/10	***	Rift
6/30/95	5	1	6/9	Mound	Run Like Antel
9/28/95	5	1	6/9	Stash	Fog that Surrounds
10/20/95	15	1	5/10	Divided Sky	Rift
10/24/95	3	1	4/13	Taste That Surrounds	Llama
10/27/95	2	1	8/9	Stash	Suspicious Minds
11/11/95	6	1	11/12	Amazing Grace	Chalk Dust Tor
11/15/95	3	2	7/8	Weekapaug Groove	While My Guitar Gent
11/21/95	4	1	1/10	***	Chalk Dust Tor
11/24/95	2	2	9/10	Bike	Julius
11/29/95	3	1	8/9	Acoustic Army	Split Open and
12/28/95	15	E	1/2	***	Tweezer Repri
6/6/96	5	2	9/10	David Bowie	Sample in a Ja
7/21/96	14	1	12/14	Train Song	Timber (Jerry)
8/4/96	6	1	4/9	Guyute	Split Open and
8/10/96	4	1	4/11	AC/DC Bag	Reba
8/14/96	3	1	4/10	Down with Disease	Poor Heart
8/17/96	2	1	8/10	Taste	Maze
10/19/96	4	E	1/2	***	Rocky Top
10/27/96	6	1	4/11	AC/DC Bag	Scent of a Mul
11/2/96	3	1	3/9	Julius	Taste
11/19/96	12	1	7/9	Stash	Taste
2/25/97	24	2	5/10	Free	My Friend My
11/19/97	48	1	9/13	Ginseng Sullivan	Run Like Antel
12/6/97	11	1	7/9	Sample in a Jar	Maze
7/5/98	18	1	5/9	Reba	Jam
7/25/98	12	2	7/8	Limb By Limb	Run Like Antel
8/11/98	12	1	5/10	Ginseng Sullivan	Maze
11/8/98	15	1	5/10	Ride Captain Ride	Paul and Silas
7/8/99	24	1	2/8	Julius	Jam
9/10/99	20	2	4/9	Piper	Gotta Jibboo
10/8/99	20	2	4/7	Bug	Harry Hood
6/14/00	26	1	6/8	Llama	Heavy Things
7/10/00	16	2	4/7	Twist	What's the Use
9/23/00	15	1	5/6	Halley's Comet	Stash
10/7/00	10	1	5/8	Weekapaug Groove	Bathtub Gin

Was played in the most recent show.

Fikus

DATE	GAP	SET	POS.	SONG BEFORE	SONG AFTER
7/2/98	947	1	6/11	Meat	Shafty
7/29/98	17	1	4/8	Foam	Farmhouse
8/1/98	2	1	6/9	Guyute	Birds of a Feather
8/8/98	5	1	6/9	Guyute	Farmhouse
11/7/98	16	1	7/10	Limb by Limb	Billy Breathes

Has not been played in the last 132 shows.

Fire

DATE	GAP	SET	POS.	SONG BEFORE	SONG AFTER
12/2/83	0	2	2/2	Scarlet Begonias	***
12/1/84	3	1	2/11	Scarlet Begonias	Fire on the Mountain
2/21/87	15	2	2/15	Fluffhead	Suzy Greenber
4/29/87	4	1	5/9	Swing Low Sweet Chrt	Skin it Back
8/10/87	4	2	1/10	***	AC/DC Bag
9/21/87	4	3	12/15	Flat Fee	Terrapin
9/27/87	1	2	4/5	Fluffhead	Fee
11/19/87	4	1	7/7	Harry Hood	***
1/27/88	1	2	4/10	Corrine Corrina	Fluffhead
2/7/88	1	1	1/10	***	McGrupp
2/8/88	1	1	6/7	Phase Dance	You Enjoy My
3/21/88	5	1	9/15	The Lizards	AC/DC Bag
3/31/88	1	1	12/14	Take the A-Train	You Enjoy My
4/2/88	1	1	1/2	***	Good Time Ba
4/22/88	1	1	3/9	The Famous Mockingbi	Alumni Blues
5/14/88	1	1	1/11	***	I Didn't Know
5/15/88	1	E	1/1	***	You Enjoy My
5/21/88	1	1	7/7	Golgi Apparatus	***
5/25/88	1	1	9/9	Suzy Greenberg	***
6/21/88	4	1	9/9	The Famous Mockingbi	***
7/11/88	2	1	6/11	Funky Bitch	Bold As Love
7/23/88	2	2	2/10	The Sloth	The Curtain
7/30/88	3	E	1/1	***	***
8/6/88	2	1	9/9	Dinner and a Movie	***
9/13/88	4	3	8/8	Vacuum Jam	***
10/29/88	3	2	10/10	Take the A-Train	***
11/3/88	2	1	1/7	***	Golgi Apparat
11/5/88	1	1	3/11	Time Loves a Hero	You Enjoy My
1/26/89	6	E	2/2	AC/DC Bag	***
2/7/89	2	E	1/1	***	***
2/18/89	3	1	5/9	AC/DC Bag	Divided Sky
3/14/89	5	3	1/7	***	Sneakin' Sally
4/20/89	4	1	5/12	Fluff's Travels	Esther
5/6/89	5	2	4/8	Contact	Harry Hood
5/13/89	3	2	7/7	Contact	***
5/28/89	5	2	1/16	***	Mike's Song
8/17/89	3	E	2/2	Golgi Apparatus	***
12/8/89	30	E	2/2	Lawn Boy	***
1/29/90	10	1	10/10	Harpua	***
4/5/90	22	1	9/9	The Lizards	***
4/8/90	3	E	2/2	Carolina	***
4/13/90	3	1	10/10	Reba	***
4/22/90	6	2	9/9	Harry Hood	***
4/29/90	4	1	13/13	The Lizards	***
6/2/90	14	1	7/9	The Lizards	Contact
9/14/90	7	2	9/10	Destiny Unbound	Going Down Slow
11/3/90	19	E	2/2	Fluffhead	***
11/8/90	2	E	2/2	Jesus Just Left	***
11/16/90	2	E	2/2	Contact	***
11/26/90	3	E	1/3	***	Contact
2/16/91	16	E	2/5	Lawn Boy	Possum
2/19/91	1	E	2/2	Magilla	***
2/27/91	4	1	10/10	Bouncing	***
3/9/91	5	2	11/13	Love You	Lawn Boy
3/22/91	5	1	11/11	Reba	***
3/28/91	2	E	2/2	Lawn Boy	***
4/15/91	10	2	11/11	Magilla	***
10/10/91	45	E	2/2	The Squirming Coil	***
10/30/91	12	E	1/1	***	***
11/7/91	4	E	4/4	Lawn Boy	***
3/13/92	25	E	2/2	Contact	***
3/20/92	4	E	2/2	Lawn Boy	***
3/24/92	3	E	2/2	Lawn Boy	***
4/13/92	15	E	2/2	Memories	***
11/30/92	78	E	2/2	Fee	***
12/8/92	8	E	2/2	Carolina	***
12/28/92	5	E	2/2	Memories	***
12/31/92	3	E	2/2	Carolina	***
2/6/93	4	E	1/1	***	***
2/15/93	7	E	2/2	Contact	***
2/22/93	6	E	2/2	Amazing Grace	***
3/3/93	6	E	1/1	***	***
3/22/93	13	E	2/2	Amazing Grace	***
4/23/93	22	E	1/1	***	***
8/12/93	36	E	1/2	***	Freebird
8/17/93	5	E	2/2	Memories	***
4/16/94	21	E	1/1	***	***
4/29/94	10	E	1/1	***	***
5/3/94	3	E	2/2	Nellie Kane	***
5/19/94	11	E	4/4	Sweet Adeline	***

DATE	GAP	SET	POS.	SONG BEFORE	SONG AFTER
5/27/94	7	E	1/1	***	***
6/21/94	12	2	1/16	***	Poor Heart
6/26/94	5	E	4/4	Tube	***
7/3/94	5	E	1/1	***	***
10/13/94	15	E	1/1	***	***
9/28/95	69	E	1/1	***	***
10/7/95	7	E	1/1	***	***
10/25/95	12	E	1/1	***	***
11/12/95	8	E	1/1	***	***
11/25/95	9	E	2/2	Poor Heart Reprise	***
11/30/95	3	1	10/10	The Lizards	***
12/12/95	9	E	1/1	***	***
12/16/95	3	E	1/1	***	***
12/29/95	3	2	11/11	Bouncing	***
6/6/96	4	E	2/2	Ya Mar	***
7/13/96	9	1	7/10	Split Open and Melt	Funky Bitch
8/10/96	15	E	2/2	Contact	***
10/26/96	14	E	1/1	***	***
11/3/96	5	E	1/1	***	***
11/19/96	11	2	7/7	Star Spangled Banner	***
11/27/96	4	2	8/8	Star Spangled Banner	***
12/2/96	4	E	1/1	***	***
7/30/97	47	2	9/9	Prince Caspian	***
11/17/97	16	1	5/5	Ghost	***
11/29/97	7	E	3/3	Moby Dick	***
12/9/97	7	E	1/1	***	***
12/31/97	7	1	10/10	The Sloth	***
7/23/99	83	2	5/5	Meatstick	***
9/8/00	76	E	1/1	***	***
9/24/00	11	E	1/1	***	***

Has not been played in the last 9 shows.

Fire On The Mountain

DATE	GAP	SET	POS.	SONG BEFORE	SONG AFTER
12/1/84	3	1	3/11	Fire	Makisupa Policeman

Has not been played in the last 1116 shows.

Fire up the Ganja

DATE	GAP	SET	POS.	SONG BEFORE	SONG AFTER
3/4/85	4	1	3/4	Camel Walk	In the Midnight Hour

Has not been played in the last 1115 shows.

First Tube

DATE	GAP	SET	POS.	SONG BEFORE	SONG AFTER
9/9/99	1031	2	5/9	The Inlaw Josie Wale	Tweezer
9/10/99	1	1	2/8	Farmhouse	Twist
9/12/99	2	1	1/10	***	Poor Heart
9/16/99	2	1	4/14	Farmhouse	Carini
9/19/99	3	1	3/8	Funky Bitch	Gotta Jibboo
9/24/99	3	1	1/10	***	Punch You in
9/26/99	2	1	2/10	Sweet Virginia	AC/DC Bag
9/28/99	1	2	3/7	Heavy Things	Tweezer
10/1/99	2	1	4/8	Sparkle	Bathtub Gin
10/3/99	2	1	1/12	***	Farmhouse
10/10/99	5	1	4/7	Heavy Things	Dirt
12/3/99	2	1	1/8	***	Wolfman's Brother
12/7/99	3	1	2/8	Farmhouse	NICU
12/18/99	9	1	7/9	Back on the Train	The Inlaw Josie Wale
5/21/00	3	1	1/7	***	Wolfman's Brother
5/23/00	2	1	3/12	Wilson	Ya Mar
6/9/00	1	1	8/9	The Moma Dance	Chalk Dust Tor
6/11/00	2	1	1/9	***	Punch You in
6/16/00	4	1	4/10	Sample In a Jar	Golgi Apparat
6/22/00	1	1	1/9	***	Wolfman's Brother
7/1/00	7	2	3/10	Bug	Mike's Song
7/6/00	3	1	7/12	The Moma Dance	I Didn't Know
7/8/00	2	1	6/9	Wolfman's Brother	Llama
7/11/00	2	E	1/3	***	Moby Dick
7/15/00	3	1	2/9	AC/DC Bag	Limb by Limb
9/12/00	4	1	5/7	Ginseng Sullivan	Divided Sky
9/15/00	2	1	1/8	***	Gotta Jibboo
9/20/00	3	2	1/9	***	Limb By Limb
9/24/00	3	1	8/10	Roggae	Punch You in
10/1/00	5	1	1/10	***	Wolfman's Brother
10/7/00	4	1	1/8	***	Mike's Song

Was played in the most recent show.

Fishing Hole Theme

DATE	GAP	SET	POS.	SONG BEFORE	SONG AFTER
8/26/89	112	2	1/9	***	Bold as Love

Has not been played in the last 1007 shows.

Fishman's Gull Poem

DATE	GAP	SET	POS.	SONG BEFORE	SONG AFTER
10/26/89	125	2	13/15	In a Hole	No Dogs Allowed

Has not been played in the last 994 shows.

Fixin' to Die

DATE	GAP	SET	POS.	SONG BEFORE	SONG AFTER
11/17/94	689	E	4/4	My Long Journey Home	***
11/30/94	9	2	5/10	Run Like an Antelope	Ya Mar

Has not been played in the last 421 shows.

Flat Fee

DATE	GAP	SET	POS.	SONG BEFORE	SONG AFTER
8/9/87	25	3	5/7	Divided Sky	McGrupp
8/21/87	2	2	7/12	Sparks	Fee
8/29/87	1	2	6/13	BBFCFM	Lushington
9/21/87	2	3	11/15	Makisupa Policeman	Fire
11/18/87	4	1	5/12	T.M.W.S.I.Y. Reprise	Wilson
2/7/88	3	2	4/9	Timber (Jerry)	Fee
2/8/88	1	3	2/9	The Sloth	Dinner and a
3/11/88	3	1	9/12	Slave	Corrine Corrina
5/15/88	7	2	9/11	I Didn't Know	Whipping Post
6/21/88	6	2	4/10	AC/DC Bag	Alumni Blues
9/13/88	13	1	4/8	You Enjoy Myself	McGrupp
7/11/91	230	1	4/8	Divided Sky	My Sweet One
7/12/91	1	1	4/12	Buried Alive	Reba
7/13/91	1	2	4/9	Divided Sky	Paul and Silas
7/15/91	2	1	10/14	Weekapaug Groove	The Lizards
7/20/91	3	2	5/12	Dinner and a Movie	Golgi Apparat
7/23/91	2	1	8/12	Stash	Bouncing
7/25/91	2	1	6/10	Divided Sky	AC/DC Bag
7/26/91	1	2	4/10	You Enjoy Myself	Fee

Has not been played in the last 810 shows.

Fluff's Travels

DATE	GAP	SET	POS.	SONG BEFORE	SONG AFTER
12/6/86	16	1	7/14	David Bowie	Clod
5/11/87	7	1	2/12	You Enjoy Myself	Possum
10/31/87	10	2	7/17	Timber (Jerry)	I Am Hydrgn
4/20/89	60	1	4/12	You Shook Me All	Fire
12/30/89	51	1	1/2	***	David Bowie
6/7/90	59	1	2/9	Suzy Greenberg	Donna Lee

Has not been played in the last 916 shows.

Fluffhead

DATE	GAP	SET	POS.	SONG BEFORE	SONG AFTER
12/1/84	3	1	11/11	Skippy Wondermouse	***
9/27/85	3	1	2/8	Sneakin' Sally	Skippy Wondermouse
10/15/86	8	2	7/14	Mustang Sally	Sneakin' Sally
10/31/86	1	1	11/11	Shaggy Dog	***
2/13/87	2	1	13/14	Dave's Energy Guide	Harry Hood
2/21/87	1	2	1/15	***	Fire
3/23/87	2	2	1/9	***	Peaches en Regalia
4/24/87	1	1	4/14	Possum	You Enjoy My
4/29/87	1	3	2/14	Peaches en Regalia	Good Time Ba
8/9/87	3	2	7/11	Peaches en Regalia	Fee
8/10/87	1	2	4/10	Possum	Fee
9/2/87	3	1	2/13	AC/DC Bag	Sneakin' Sally
9/21/87	1	3	15/15	La Grange	***
9/27/87	1	2	3/5	I Didn't Know	Fire
10/14/87	1	1	6/12	Slave	Possum
10/31/87	1	2	16/17	Alumni Blues	David Bowie
11/18/87	1	2	3/4	You Enjoy Myself	AC/DC Bag
11/19/87	1	2	2/6	Timber (Jerry)	I Didn't Know
1/27/88	1	2	5/10	Fire	Divided Sky
2/8/88	2	2	1/6	***	Wilson
2/26/88	2	1	11/13	Good Times Bad Times	I Didn't Know
3/11/88	1	2	1/8	***	Dinner and a
3/31/88	3	1	6/14	Possum	Alumni Blues
4/22/88	2	1	6/9	Run Like an Antelope	Dinner and a
5/14/88	1	1	9/11	Jesus Just Left	Alumni Blues
5/15/88	1	1	6/11	Good Times Bad Times	Shaggy Dog
5/21/88	1	2	7/9	Happy Birthday	Bike
5/25/88	1	2	2/3	Jesus Just Left	Whipping Post
6/15/88	1	1	7/9	McGrupp	Golgi Apparat
6/20/88	2	1	4/11	You Enjoy Myself	AC/DC Bag
6/21/88	1	1	1/9	***	Rocky Top
6/24/88	1	1	11/11	Ballad - Curtis Loew	***
7/12/88	2	2	4/9	Timber (Jerry)	Jesus Just Left
7/24/88	2	2	2/8	Light Up Or Leave Me	La Grange
7/25/88	1	2	6/6	Light Up Or Leave Me	***
7/30/88	1	3	9/13	Harpua	Anarchy
8/3/88	1	3	4/8	I Am Hydrogen	Harry Hood
8/27/88	2	1	5/9	Walk Away	Mike's Song
9/13/88	3	2	6/6	Run Like an Antelope	***
9/22/88	1	1	3/5	Take the A-Train	You Enjoy My
9/24/88	1	2	2/4	Good Times Bad Times	The Curtain
10/29/88	1	3	1/1	***	***
11/3/88	2	1	3/7	Golgi Apparatus	Possum
11/5/88	1	1	9/11	Walk Away	Alumni Blues
1/25/89	5	1	2/2	Fee	***
2/7/89	3	3	2/6	Sanity	Suzy Greenber
2/17/89	2	1	10/10	Run Like an Antelope	The Lizards
3/4/89	4	2	2/5	Possum	The Lizards
3/14/89	2	1	6/12	Weekapaug Groove	Contact
3/14/89	0	2	2/2	Wilson	***
3/30/89	2	1	7/8	Ya Mar	Run Like Antel
4/20/89	2	1	2/12	AC/DC Bag	You Shook Me All
5/5/89	4	1	4/8	Ya Mar	Alumni Blues
5/13/89	4	1	6/12	La Grange	Possum
5/27/89	4	1	9/11	Take the A-Train	Bathtub Gin
6/23/89	2	2	2/7	The Sloth	Harry Hood
6/30/89	1	1	6/7	Donna Lee	Run Like Antel
8/26/89	4	1	1/8	***	Col. Forbin's A
12/9/89	28	2	2/8	Take the A-Train	Esther
1/28/90	8	1	4/9	Tela	La Grange
2/16/90	6	1	1/7	***	Esther
2/25/90	5	2	5/6	The Lizards	BBFCFM
3/3/90	3	2	3/7	Caravan	Esther
4/13/90	15	1	4/10	Bouncing	Esther
4/21/90	5	2	5/9	Uncle Pen	Highway to Hell
4/22/90	1	2	4/9	You Enjoy Myself	How High the Moon
4/29/90	4	1	9/13	Divided Sky	Walk Away
5/30/90	11	1	9/14	Lawn Boy	Sweet Adeline
10/30/90	26	2	9/12	Ballad - Curtis Loew	Terrapin
11/3/90	3	E	1/2	***	Fire
11/17/90	5	2	2/12	Buried Alive	Mike's Song
2/9/91	15	2	3/10	Buried Alive	The Landlady
2/16/91	3	2	6/9	Guelah Papyrus	Rocky Top
3/8/91	9	1	3/11	You Enjoy Myself	Stash
3/13/91	2	1	1/9	***	The Landlady
3/17/91	3	1	8/12	Foam	Uncle Pen
3/29/91	4	2	5/8	Rocky Top	Tweezer
4/2/91	2	2	4/8	Cavern	Dog Gone Dog
4/12/91	6	2	4/10	You Enjoy Myself	Cavern
4/20/91	5	1	4/11	Llama	My Sweet One
4/27/91	4	2	9/13	Weekapaug Groove	Tweezer
5/4/91	3	1	8/11	Guelah Papyrus	Mike's Song
5/9/91	1	2	3/8	The Curtain	Stash
5/17/91	5	2	9/9	The Landlady	Magilla
8/3/91	17	3	3/8	Ya Mar	Lawn Boy
10/12/91	13	2	3/10	Uncle Pen	Chalk Dust Tor
10/17/91	3	2	6/9	Lawn Boy	You Enjoy My
10/27/91	5	1	6/10	Guelah Papyrus	Brother
11/1/91	4	1	7/11	Split Open and Melt	Uncle Pen
11/9/91	4	2	2/10	Chalk Dust Torture	Poor Heart

DATE	GAP	SET	POS.	SONG BEFORE	SONG AFTER
11/16/91	6	1	7/11	Sparkle	Foam
11/24/91	6	1	5/9	The Landlady	Sparkle
12/5/91	3	1	5/10	Ya Mar	Llama
3/13/92	8	1	9/12	Mound	Run Like Antel
3/20/92	4	1	6/10	Rift	Maze
3/26/92	5	1	7/10	Stash	Uncle Pen
4/3/92	6	1	8/11	Maze	All Things Rec
4/13/92	7	2	2/11	Llama	Sparkle
4/17/92	3	2	3/8	You Enjoy Myself	The Squirmin
4/24/92	6	1	7/11	The Landlady	Sparkle
5/3/92	6	2	4/14	Silent in the Mornin	Guelah Papyrus
5/7/92	3	2	4/12	Tweezer	Glide
5/14/92	5	2	4/13	Rift	Eliza
7/12/92	15	1	5/11	Divided Sky	Maze
7/16/92	3	2	4/13	The Landlady	T.M.W.S.I.Y.
11/20/92	30	2	2/10	Chalk Dust Torture	Tube
12/1/92	8	1	7/12	Cavern	Maze
12/3/92	2	2	3/13	Guelah Papyrus	Mike's Song
12/6/92	3	1	9/10	Llama	Run Like Antel
12/13/92	6	2	5/14	Llama	Chalk Dust Tor
12/30/92	3	1	6/14	Chalk Dust Torture	Paul and Silas
2/11/93	9	1	7/10	Rift	Llama
2/17/93	4	1	9/11	Bouncing	Maze
2/20/93	3	1	10/11	Silent in the Mornin	Cavern
2/26/93	5	1	6/10	Split Open and Melt	Llama
3/12/93	8	1	8/11	Stash	The Horse
3/19/93	6	1	7/9	Stash	Cavern
3/26/93	5	1	8/10	Split Open and Melt	Divided Sky
4/1/93	5	1	8/10	Paul and Silas	Lawn Boy
4/5/93	3	1	5/10	Maze	Paul and Silas
4/20/93	8	2	2/12	Chalk Dust Torture	Sample in a Ja
4/23/93	3	1	5/10	Split Open and Melt	My Friend My
5/1/93	6	2	2/11	Chalk Dust Torture	My Friend My
5/6/93	4	1	8/13	Llama	Possum
7/24/93	12	2	3/12	Split Open and Melt	Maze
7/30/93	5	2	6/10	Poor Heart	My Friend My
8/8/93	6	2	6/11	It's Ice	Possum
8/13/93	4	1	7/10	Ginseng Sullivan	My Mind's Got A Mind
8/17/93	4	1	7/9	Maze	Fast Enough for You
8/28/93	6	1	6/9	Maze	Stash
12/29/93	2	2	3/11	Bouncing	Run Like Antel
4/5/94	4	1	3/8	Foam	Glide
4/10/94	4	2	4/7	Run Like an Antelope	Ginseng Sullivan
4/16/94	5	1	6/8	Stash	Nellie Kane
4/21/94	4	2	3/10	Maze	Mike's Song
5/3/94	9	2	3/8	If I Could	Down with Dis
5/12/94	6	2	6/11	Uncle Pen	Lifeboy
5/22/94	8	1	7/11	Split Open and Melt	My Sweet One
5/26/94	3	2	3/9	Run Like an Antelope	Down with Dis
6/11/94	6	2	3/9	Run Like an Antelope	Scent of a Mul
6/22/94	8	2	16/20	Digital Delay Loop J	My Sweet One
7/1/94	7	2	3/11	If I Could	Down with Dis
7/6/94	4	1	2/9	Llama	Julius
7/9/94	2	2	3/10	Split Open and Melt	Poor Heart
7/14/94	3	1	8/11	Scent of a Mule	The Horse
10/8/94	4	2	9/12	Weekapaug Groove	Purple Rain
10/16/94	7	2	4/9	Julius	Big Ball Jam
10/22/94	4	1	7/8	Split Open and Melt	Julius
11/12/94	11	2	2/12	Julius	Down with Dis
12/6/94	18	1	4/8	Down with Disease	Jesus Just Left
6/15/95	16	1	9/10	I Didn't Know	Run Like Antel
6/28/95	10	1	7/8	Stash	Chalk Dust Tor
10/13/95	17	1	8/9	Split Open and Melt	Life on Mars
10/27/95	10	1	2/9	Runaway Jim	Taste That Surrounds
11/11/95	6	2	5/9	Uncle Pen	Sleeping Monkey
11/22/95	8	1	4/10	Run Like an Antelope	Uncle Pen
12/8/95	11	1	5/9	Runaway Jim	It's Ice
12/29/95	9	1	7/9	Stash	Llama

DATE	GAP	SET	POS.	SONG BEFORE	SONG AFTER
8/2/96	23	2	5/9	Free	Prince Caspian
8/10/96	5	2	5/8	Free	Whipping Post
8/17/96	5	2	5/8	Brother	Run Like Antel
10/19/96	4	2	6/10	Split Open and Melt	Swept Away
10/27/96	6	2	7/9	Tweezer	Life On Mars
11/30/96	21	1	6/10	Stash	The Old Home
2/23/97	17	1	7/9	Rift	Frankenstein
8/3/97	35	2	3/7	Simple	Lifeboy
8/14/97	7	1	3/10	Funky Bitch	Limb by Limb
11/23/97	10	1	8/9	NICU	Character Zer
12/29/97	15	1	7/9	Theme From the Botto	Dirt
7/2/98	9	1	8/11	Shafty	Ginseng Sullivan
7/21/98	12	1	2/8	AC/DC Bag	Roggae
8/1/98	7	2	6/10	Tweezer	Brian and Robert
8/6/98	3	1	9/12	Billy Breathes	The Moma Dance
8/16/98	7	2	4/8	Ghost	When Circus Comes
11/6/98	10	2	5/7	Prince Caspian	Bike
11/18/98	8	2	6/7	Slave	Character Zer
7/10/99	20	2	5/5	When Circus Comes	***
7/18/99	6	3	9/9	Quinn the Eskimo	***
7/24/99	4	1	2/9	Guyute	Jam
7/31/99	5	2	5/6	Prince Caspian	The Squirmin
10/1/99	18	2	8/9	Julius	Slave
10/7/99	4	1	9/9	Gotta Jibboo	***
12/5/99	7	2	8/10	Maze	Chalk Dust Tor
7/3/00	31	1	8/10	Heavy Things	When Circus Comes
9/17/00	16	1	7/9	Lawn Boy	The Curtain With
9/29/00	8	2	4/9	Also Sprach	Jam

Has not been played in the last 6 shows.

Foam

DATE	GAP	SET	POS.	SONG BEFORE	SONG AFTER
11/3/88	72	3	2/6	Suzy Greenberg	I Didn't Know
11/11/88	2	1	4/8	Slave	Possum
12/10/88	2	1	5/12	The Lizards	Fee
1/26/89	3	2	9/10	BBFCFM	David Bowie
2/7/89	2	1	3/9	McGrupp	The Sloth
2/24/89	4	1	5/10	The Curtain	Col. Forbin's A
3/3/89	1	1	4/11	You Enjoy Myself	AC/DC Bag
3/12/89	2	1	8/8	Bold As Love	***
3/14/89	1	1	12/12	Harpua	***
3/30/89	2	3	2/6	Peaches en Regalia	AC/DC Bag
4/20/89	2	1	11/12	McGrupp	David Bowie
5/13/89	8	1	8/12	Possum	Walk Away
5/20/89	1	2	5/9	Weekapaug Groove	Contact
5/21/89	1	1	2/13	Harry Hood	Contact
8/23/89	8	2	7/8	AC/DC Bag	Good Time Ba
8/26/89	1	2	8/9	Funky Bitch	David Bowie
9/9/89	1	1	1/11	***	The Oh Kee Pa
9/14/89	1	1	4/9	You Enjoy Myself	Col. Forbin's A
10/1/89	2	1	8/12	Wilson	Ya Mar
10/21/89	7	1	6/10	Who Do? We Do!	AC/DC Bag
10/22/89	1	1	8/14	Ya Mar	Rocky Top
11/2/89	4	1	2/11	Bathtub Gin	Mike's Song
11/3/89	1	2	5/5	The Sloth	***
11/16/89	4	1	5/11	Bathtub Gin	The Oh Kee Pa
11/30/89	2	1	6/11	AC/DC Bag	The Lizards
12/9/89	5	1	4/10	The Lizards	In a Hole
12/30/89	4	2	5/9	Suzy Greenberg	My Sweet One
2/9/90	7	2	7/9	Alumni Blues	Ballad - Curtis Loew
2/15/90	2	2	4/5	Possum	Highway to Hell
2/23/90	4	1	4/11	Possum	Carolina
2/25/90	2	1	1/11	***	My Sweet One
3/1/90	1	2	2/7	The Lizards	Mike's Song
3/8/90	4	1	5/10	Ya Mar	Carolina
3/17/90	2	1	5/6	AC/DC Bag	You Enjoy My
4/4/90	2	1	6/8	Possum	Divided Sky

DATE	GAP	SET	POS.	SONG BEFORE	SONG AFTER
4/9/90	5	2	5/11	La Grange	Harry Hood
4/13/90	2	2	2/10	Run Like an Antelope	You Enjoy My
4/18/90	2	1	6/10	The Curtain	You Enjoy My
4/21/90	3	1	5/10	Esther	Walk Away
4/25/90	2	2	1/12	***	Sweet Adeline
4/26/90	1	1	2/9	Possum	You Enjoy My
4/28/90	1	1	10/11	Rift	Run Like Antel
5/11/90	6	1	5/9	Uncle Pen	Bouncing
5/13/90	1	2	4/12	Weekapaug Groove	Donna Lee
5/15/90	1	1	3/12	Alumni Blues	Mike's Song
5/24/90	3	2	1/11	***	Dinner and a
6/8/90	7	1	1/8	***	Bouncing
6/9/90	1	2	8/14	Fee	The Oh Kee Pa
6/16/90	1	3	4/13	Ya Mar	The Oh Kee Pa
9/13/90	1	1	5/12	Divided Sky	Tube
9/15/90	2	2	5/8	Bathtub Gin	Minute by Minute
9/20/90	2	1	5/12	Dinner and a Movie	Esther
10/4/90	6	2	3/8	Bouncing	Fee
10/6/90	2	1	5/13	Bouncing	You Enjoy My
10/8/90	2	1	4/10	Bouncing	Cavern
10/19/90	2	2	2/15	Golgi Apparatus	Uncle Pen
10/30/90	1	2	5/12	Magilla	Reba
10/31/90	1	2	4/12	Runaway Jim	Tweezer
11/2/90	1	2	5/9	My Sweet One	You Enjoy My
11/3/90	1	1	8/11	Magilla	Runaway Jim
11/8/90	2	1	4/12	The Lizards	Uncle Pen
11/16/90	2	1	3/8	Buried Alive	You Enjoy My
11/24/90	2	1	3/11	Possum	Mike's Song
12/1/90	3	1	5/9	Divided Sky	Tweezer
12/7/90	1	1	8/9	Runaway Jim	Llama
12/8/90	1	1	3/10	Runaway Jim	AC/DC Bag
12/28/90	1	1	3/10	Runaway Jim	Horn
2/1/91	3	1	2/10	My Sweet One	Tweezer
2/3/91	2	1	9/10	Chalk Dust Torture	Golgi Apparat
2/7/91	1	1	2/10	Runaway Jim	My Sweet One
2/9/91	2	1	7/12	Runaway Jim	Guelah Papyrus
2/14/91	1	2	4/12	Weekapaug Groove	The Squirmin
2/20/91	4	2	1/3	***	Divided Sky
2/26/91	2	1	2/11	Cavern	The Squirmin
2/28/91	2	1	3/13	Bouncing	Esther
3/1/91	1	1	2/10	Wilson	Divided Sky
3/15/91	5	1	2/12	Llama	My Sweet One
3/17/91	2	1	7/12	Weekapaug Groove	Fluffhead
3/22/91	1	2	4/13	Run Like an Antelope	Paul and Silas
3/29/91	3	2	3/8	I Didn't Know	Rocky Top
4/2/91	2	1	6/10	Bouncing	You Enjoy My
4/3/91	1	1	4/10	The Lizards	Tweezer
4/6/91	2	1	8/11	Chalk Dust Torture	Mike's Song
4/11/91	2	1	8/12	Bouncing	Carolina
4/15/91	2	1	3/10	Ya Mar	Runaway Jim
4/21/91	5	1	5/14	Divided Sky	Jam
5/2/91	4	1	3/10	Drum Jam	Bouncing
5/3/91	1	1	2/12	Bouncing	Chalk Dust Tor
5/9/91	2	1	2/10	Divided Sky	Paul and Silas
5/11/91	1	2	5/11	Poor Heart	McGrupp
5/12/91	2	1	10/11	Fee	Runaway Jim
5/16/91	1	1	3/11	Golgi Apparatus	Cavern
5/18/91	2	1	6/9	Paul and Silas	Divided Sky
5/19/91	1	2	4/10	Fee	Reba
7/13/91	3	1	3/13	Runaway Jim	Llama
7/18/91	3	1	2/11	Chalk Dust Torture	Runaway Jim
7/20/91	2	1	2/10	Chalk Dust Torture	The Squirmin
7/23/91	2	1	2/12	Chalk Dust Torture	The Squirmin
7/25/91	1	2	3/10	The Sloth	Suzy Greenber
7/26/91	1	1	4/12	My Sweet One	Suzy Greenber
7/27/91	1	1	2/16	Llama	The Oh Kee Pa
8/3/91	1	2	2/11	Wilson	Runaway Jim
9/25/91	1	1	3/11	Poor Heart	Llama
9/26/91	1	1	9/10	The Lizards	David Bowie
9/28/91	2	1	8/11	Eliza	Brother
9/29/91	1	2	4/10	Eliza	Reba
10/2/91	2	1	2/10	Llama	The Squirmin
10/3/91	1	1	2/10	Chalk Dust Torture	Uncle Pen
10/4/91	1	2	4/11	Bouncing	Runaway Jim

DATE	GAP	SET	POS.	SONG BEFORE	SONG AFTER
10/6/91	1	1	2/13	Suzy Greenberg	Divided Sky
10/10/91	1	1	2/11	Chalk Dust Torture	Paul and Silas
10/11/91	1	2	3/9	Cavern	David Bowie
10/12/91	1	1	3/9	Possum	My Sweet One
10/15/91	2	1	2/10	Chalk Dust Torture	The Squirmin
10/18/91	2	1	2/9	Runaway Jim	Paul and Silas
10/19/91	1	1	5/10	Runaway Jim	Chalk Dust Tor
10/24/91	2	1	3/12	Suzy Greenberg	Poor Heart
10/28/91	2	1	8/10	The Oh Kee Pa Ceremo	Fee
10/30/91	1	1	1/7	***	Runaway Jim
10/31/91	2	1	7/11	Sparkle	Bathtub Gin
11/2/91	2	1	6/10	Paul and Silas	Bouncing
11/7/91	1	1	3/11	Chalk Dust Torture	Sparkle
11/9/91	2	1	3/11	Runaway Jim	Sparkle
11/12/91	2	1	10/11	Fee	Llama
11/14/91	2	1	5/11	Reba	Tube
11/16/91	2	1	8/11	Fluffhead	Stash
11/19/91	1	1	2/11	Uncle Pen	Runaway Jim
11/21/91	2	1	6/12	Reba	Horn
11/22/91	1	1	6/11	Fee	Divided Sky
11/23/91	1	1	3/11	Reba	Runaway Jim
11/30/91	2	1	3/11	Llama	Sparkle
12/5/91	2	2	4/13	Tube	Mike's Song
12/6/91	1	1	2/9	Memories	Reba
12/7/91	1	1	3/11	Runaway Jim	Col. Forbin's A
12/31/91	1	1	2/10	Possum	Sparkle
3/7/92	2	1	3/11	My Mind's Got A Mind	Runaway Jim
3/12/92	2	1	3/11	Runaway Jim	Sparkle
3/14/92	2	1	5/13	Sparkle	Rift
3/21/92	4	1	3/12	Runaway Jim	Sparkle
3/22/92	1	1	3/4	All Things Recnsrd	The Landlady
3/24/92	1	1	3/13	Poor Heart	Eliza
3/26/92	2	1	4/10	All Things Recnsrd	Sparkle
3/28/92	2	1	2/10	Runaway Jim	Sparkle
3/30/92	1	1	3/11	Llama	Guelah Pa-pyrus
4/1/92	2	1	2/12	Golgi Apparatus	Bouncing
4/4/92	2	1	2/10	Runaway Jim	Reba
4/6/92	2	1	2/10	Suzy Greenberg	Sparkle
4/8/92	2	1	3/11	Sparkle	Guelah Pa-pyrus
4/13/92	2	1	8/10	All Things Recnsrd	Take the A-Trn
4/15/92	1	1	3/11	Suzy Greenberg	Guelah Pa-pyrus
4/17/92	2	1	2/13	Runaway Jim	Sparkle
4/22/92	4	1	2/10	Llama	Reba
4/24/92	2	2	4/12	Ya Mar	Mike's Song
4/29/92	2	1	2/10	Suzy Greenberg	Sparkle
5/2/92	3	2	6/10	Tela	You Enjoy My
5/5/92	2	2	4/14	All Things Recnsrd	Mike's Song
5/6/92	1	1	2/11	Llama	Reba
5/7/92	1	1	5/11	My Friend My Friend	Runaway Jim
5/9/92	2	1	2/11	Runaway Jim	Sparkle
5/15/92	4	1	2/11	Golgi Apparatus	Cavern
5/16/92	1	1	2/11	Maze	Glide
5/18/92	2	1	6/10	Guelah Papyrus	Poor Heart
6/20/92	2	1	3/8	Bouncing	Runaway Jim
6/27/92	3	1	2/10	Runaway Jim	Sparkle
7/11/92	5	1	3/11	Runaway Jim	Sparkle
7/15/92	3	1	4/12	Suzy Greenberg	My Friend My
7/18/92	3	1	2/6	Suzy Greenberg	Llama
7/24/92	4	1	2/6	My Sweet One	Tweezer
7/25/92	1	1	2/8	Runaway Jim	Sparkle
8/1/92	6	1	2/7	Golgi Apparatus	Poor Heart
8/13/92	2	1	2/3	Chalk Dust Torture	You Enjoy My
8/17/92	3	1	8/11	All Things Recnsrd	My Friend My
8/20/92	2	1	2/8	Golgi Apparatus	Stash
8/23/92	1	1	5/7	Cavern	Runaway Jim
8/28/92	4	1	2/7	Poor Heart	Stash
11/19/92	4	1	3/12	Fee	Glide
11/21/92	2	1	3/11	Runaway Jim	Glide
11/23/92	2	1	2/11	Runaway Jim	Glide
11/25/92	1	2	2/9	Chalk Dust Torture	Fast Enough for You
11/28/92	2	1	2/11	My Sweet One	Stash
11/30/92	1	1	2/10	Llama	Bouncing

DATE	GAP	SET	POS.	SONG BEFORE	SONG AFTER
12/2/92	2	1	2/10	Suzy Greenberg	Divided Sky
12/4/92	2	1	2/11	Llama	Poor Heart
12/6/92	2	1	2/10	Runaway Jim	Fee
12/7/92	1	1	6/11	Sparkle	Fast Enough for You
12/10/92	2	1	3/11	Llama	Fee
12/12/92	2	1	2/11	Llama	Sparkle
12/31/92	5	1	9/11	Cavern	I Didn't Know
2/4/93	2	1	2/11	Axilla	Bouncing
2/6/93	2	1	2/11	Golgi Apparatus	Wilson
2/10/93	3	1	2/10	Loving Cup	Guelah Pa-pyrus
2/18/93	6	1	5/10	Tweezer	Sparkle
2/20/93	2	1	2/11	Golgi Apparatus	The Sloth
2/22/93	2	1	6/10	Sparkle	Fee
2/26/93	3	1	2/10	Runaway Jim	Fee
3/3/93	3	1	2/10	Rift	Bouncing
3/5/93	1	1	4/11	Cavern	The Sloth
3/9/93	3	1	2/10	Runaway Jim	Bouncing
3/14/93	3	1	2/11	Loving Cup	Guelah Pa-pyrus
3/17/93	2	1	3/11	Runaway Jim	Bouncing
3/19/93	2	1	3/9	Llama	Bouncing
3/24/93	3	1	2/9	Llama	Fee
3/26/93	2	1	3/10	Sparkle	Punch You in
3/31/93	4	1	2/10	Runaway Jim	Sparkle
4/2/93	2	1	3/9	Poor Heart	Bouncing
4/17/93	8	1	2/10	Llama	Bouncing
4/21/93	3	1	2/11	Poor Heart	Guelah Pa-pyrus
4/24/93	3	2	2/10	Llama	Bathtub Gin
4/27/93	2	1	3/10	Poor Heart	Bouncing
5/1/93	3	1	2/10	Runaway Jim	Guelah Pa-pyrus
5/5/93	3	1	3/10	Guelah Papyrus	Sparkle
5/30/93	5	1	5/13	Poor Heart	Ya Mar
7/18/93	4	1	3/9	Rift	Guelah Pa-pyrus
7/22/93	2	1	2/11	Llama	Horn
7/25/93	3	1	2/10	Wilson	Mound
7/28/93	2	1	5/11	Sample in a Jar	Nellie Kane
7/31/93	3	1	6/9	Mound	Nellie Kane
8/3/93	3	1	3/11	Nellie Kane	Fee
8/8/93	3	1	2/11	BBFCFM	Loving Cup
8/13/93	4	1	4/10	Makisupa Policeman	Stash
8/16/93	3	1	6/9	Sparkle	I Didn't Know
8/21/93	3	1	3/10	Poor Heart	Guelah Pa-pyrus
8/25/93	2	1	5/11	Sparkle	Ginseng Sulli-van
8/28/93	2	1	3/9	Bouncing	Ginseng Sulli-van
12/29/93	2	1	3/9	Peaches en Regalia	Glide
4/5/94	4	1	2/8	Runaway Jim	Fluffhead
4/8/94	2	1	5/13	Glide	I Didn't Know
4/11/94	3	1	3/9	Poor Heart	Fast Enough for You
4/14/94	2	1	2/9	Runaway Jim	Sparkle
4/17/94	3	1	2/9	Loving Cup	I Didn't Know
4/21/94	3	1	3/9	Sparkle	Glide
4/25/94	4	1	4/10	Fee	Down with Dis
4/28/94	1	1	2/11	Runaway Jim	Sample in a Ja
5/2/94	3	1	9/10	Suzy Greenberg	Sample in a Ja
5/4/94	2	1	2/10	Runaway Jim	Sample in a Ja
5/8/94	3	1	2/8	Runaway Jim	Axilla (Part II)
5/12/94	2	1	7/10	Axilla (Part II)	Bathtub Gin
5/21/94	7	1	2/9	Runaway Jim	Guelah Pa-pyrus
5/23/94	2	1	3/10	Sample in a Jar	Fee
5/27/94	3	1	3/9	Runaway Jim	Bouncing
5/28/94	1	1	3/10	Sample in a Jar	Bouncing
6/10/94	3	1	2/9	Runaway Jim	Sample in a Ja
6/17/94	5	1	2/9	Runaway Jim	Glide
6/18/94	5	1	5/10	NICU	Bouncing
7/1/94	6	1	2/10	Runaway Jim	Sample in a Ja
7/9/94	6	1	2/10	Runaway Jim	Gumbo

DATE	GAP	SET	POS.	SONG BEFORE	SONG AFTER
7/13/94	2	1	4/11	Sample in a Jar	The Mango Song
7/15/94	2	1	5/8	Gumbo	Fee
10/9/94	4	1	2/7	Runaway Jim	Fast Enough for You
10/13/94	3	1	6/9	I Didn't Know	Fast Enough for You
10/16/94	3	1	3/10	Horn	Fee
10/21/94	3	1	3/9	Down with Disease	The Mango Song
10/29/94	7	1	5/10	Runaway Jim	Lawn Boy
11/2/94	2	1	2/8	Suzy Greenberg	If I Could
11/12/94	3	1	2/8	Runaway Jim	If I Could
11/16/94	3	1	2/11	Sample in a Jar	Fast Enough for You
11/22/94	5	1	4/9	Horn	Guyute
11/26/94	3	1	5/9	If I Could	The Horse
12/4/94	6	1	2/9	Runaway Jim	If I Could
12/9/94	4	1	2/8	Llama	Guyute
12/29/94	3	1	2/9	Runaway Jim	If I Could
6/13/95	8	1	8/10	Runaway Jim	Bouncing
6/20/95	6	1	4/9	Ginseng Sullivan	Bathtub Gin
6/28/95	6	1	2/8	Axilla (Part II)	Fast Enough for You
10/3/95	11	1	3/11	Guelah Papyrus	Fast Enough for You
10/15/95	8	1	7/10	Llama	Strange De-sign
11/14/95	16	1	2/9	Chalk Dust Torture	Billy Breathes
11/28/95	9	1	4/9	Bouncing	I Didn't Know
12/14/95	12	1	4/10	Horn	Makisupa Po-liceman
7/19/96	22	1	2/6	Runaway Jim	Sweet Adeline
7/23/96	3	1	2/9	AC/DC Bag	Theme From the Botto
8/2/96	3	1	6/11	Poor Heart	Theme From the Botto
8/5/96	2	1	6/9	Wolfman's Brother	If I Could
10/23/96	15	1	4/9	AC/DC Bag	Hello My Baby
11/19/96	18	1	3/9	AC/DC Bag	Theme From the Botto
2/21/97	21	1	2/6	My Soul	Down with Dis
8/3/97	37	1	2/10	Bathtub Gin	Samson Varia-tion
8/9/97	3	2	2/10	Wilson	Mike's Song
11/29/97	17	1	2/12	The Wedge	Simple
12/6/97	5	1	5/9	Bathtub Gin	Sample in a Ja
7/29/98	33	1	3/8	Dog Gone Dog	Fikus
8/7/98	6	1	6/10	Brian and Robert	Bittersweet Motel
11/21/98	27	1	10/13	Nellie Kane	Wading In Vel-vet Sea
11/28/98	4	1	6/8	Albuquerque	The Moma Dance
7/3/00	88	1	4/10	My Mind's Got A Mind	Bathtub Gin
7/14/00	8	2	7/11	Bouncing	Dog Faced Boy

Has not been played in the last 22 shows.

Fog That Surrounds

DATE	GAP	SET	POS.	SONG BEFORE	SONG AFTER
9/27/95	735	1	6/9	I Didn't Know	Strange De-sign
9/28/95	1	1	7/9	Fee	Acoustic Army
9/30/95	2	2	2/9	Runaway Jim	If I Could
10/2/95	1	1	7/10	Acoustic Army	Theme From the Botto
10/5/95	2	1	3/11	Ha Ha Ha	The Horse
10/7/95	2	1	3/9	Gumbo	Mound
10/11/95	2	1	6/9	If I Could	Acoustic Army
10/17/95	4	2	3/6	Prince Caspian	Suzy Greenber

Has not been played in the last 370 shows.

Foreplay/Long Time

DATE	GAP	SET	POS.	SONG BEFORE	SONG AFTER
10/7/94	662	E	1/2	***	Cavern
10/8/94	1	E	1/2	***	Rocky Top

DATE	GAP	SET	POS.	SONG BEFORE	SONG AFTER
10/10/94	2	E	1/2	***	Tweezer Repri
10/12/94	1	2	7/9	Nellie Kane	Harry Hood
10/13/94	1	2	11/12	Weekapaug Groove	Cavern
10/14/94	1	2	8/10	Beaumont Rag	The Squirmin
10/15/94	1	2	9/11	Amazing Grace	Bouncing
10/20/94	3	2	7/8	Nellie Kane	Chalk Dust Tor
10/21/94	1	E	2/3	Sweet Adeline	Cavern
10/25/94	3	E	1/2	***	Golgi Apparat
10/26/94	1	E	2/3	Nellie Kane	Amazing Grce
10/28/94	2	2	12/12	Nellie Kane	***
11/2/94	1	E	2/3	The Old Home Place	Tweezer Repri
11/12/94	3	2	10/12	Nellie Kane	Harry Hood
12/6/94	18	2	11/12	I'm Blue, Lonesome	Run Like Antel
12/9/94	3	E	2/3	I'm Blue, Lonesome	Tweezer Repri
7/12/99	309	1	1/7	***	Down with Dis

Has not been played in the last 104 shows.

Four Strong Winds

DATE	GAP	SET	POS.	SONG BEFORE	SONG AFTER
10/18/98	980	1	11/12	Sad Lisa	I Shall Be Released

Has not been played in the last 139 shows.

Frankenstein

DATE	GAP	SET	POS.	SONG BEFORE	SONG AFTER
11/11/89	132	1	8/8	If I Only Had a Brai	***
11/16/89	1	1	11/11	You Enjoy Myself	***
11/30/89	2	1	11/11	Lawn Boy	***
12/3/89	2	1	9/9	Lawn Boy	***
7/11/91	160	2	10/10	Touch Me	***
7/12/91	1	2	14/14	Sweet Adeline	***
7/13/91	1	1	13/13	Bouncing	***
7/15/91	2	1	14/14	The Squirming Coil	***
7/24/91	6	2	9/10	I Didn't Know	Suzy Greenber
7/26/91	2	E	2/2	Lawn Boy	***
6/11/94	326	2	9/9	Contact	***
6/14/94	2	2	1/9	***	Demand
6/17/94	2	2	15/15	Julius	***
6/23/94	5	2	1/8	***	David Bowie
6/30/94	5	1	9/9	Bouncing	***
7/8/94	6	2	8/11	You Enjoy Myself	You Enjoy My
10/31/94	26	1	1/10	***	Sparkle
11/30/94	17	1	1/10	***	Poor Heart
12/3/94	3	2	1/10	***	Suzy Greenber
12/7/94	3	2	2/9	Rift	Divided Sky
12/30/94	6	E	1/1	***	***
6/15/95	9	E	2/2	Bouncing	***
10/7/95	24	2	7/9	Contact	Harry Hood
10/19/95	7	2	1/10	***	Poor Heart
10/28/95	7	2	6/7	Strange Design	Chalk Dust Tor
11/11/95	5	2	7/9	Sleeping Monkey	Suspicious Minds
11/22/95	8	E	2/2	Poor Heart	***
12/4/95	8	2	9/9	Sample in a Jar	***
12/14/95	7	1	10/10	My Sweet One	***
12/31/95	7	3	6/6	Sanity	***
8/17/96	31	3	2/7	Wilson	Scent of a Mul
10/19/96	4	1	9/9	Prince Caspian	***
10/31/96	8	E	1/1	***	***
11/7/96	4	E	1/1	***	***
11/16/96	7	1	11/11	Sparkle	***
11/29/96	7	1	1/9	***	NICU
12/6/96	5	1	9/9	Down with Disease	***
12/28/96	1	1	9/9	The Mango Song	***
2/13/97	4	2	10/10	Harry Hood	***
2/18/97	4	2	9/9	Harry Hood	***
2/23/97	4	1	8/9	Fluffhead	David Bowie
2/28/97	3	2	4/9	Prince Caspian	David Bowie
7/23/97	25	E	1/1	***	***
8/3/97	7	2	7/7	Hello My Baby	***
8/13/97	6	2	9/9	Golgi Apparatus	***
11/22/97	10	1	7/8	Billy Breathes	Izabella
12/3/97	7	2	5/6	Prince Caspian	Harry Hood
12/30/97	10	E	4/4	Sneakin' Sally	***
7/8/98	12	1	5/7	Beauty of My Dreams	Guyute
7/25/98	10	2	3/8	Wilson	Tweezer
8/1/98	5	2	10/10	Chalk Dust Torture	***

DATE	GAP	SET	POS.	SONG BEFORE	SONG AFTER
8/9/98	6	2	9/11	You Enjoy Myself	Chalk Dust Tor
11/9/98	17	E	1/2	***	Freebird
11/19/98	6	2	7/8	Chalk Dust Torture	Been Caught Stealin'
12/31/98	11	2	7/7	Run Like an Antelope	***
7/15/99	11	E	2/2	Brian and Robert	***
9/14/99	18	2	5/5	Down with Disease	***
9/18/99	3	2	6/7	Harry Hood	Cavern
9/25/99	5	2	7/8	Also Sprach	Julius
10/2/99	5	2	5/6	You Enjoy Myself	Waste
12/5/99	10	2	10/10	Chalk Dust Torture	***
12/15/99	7	E	1/2	***	Rocky Top
6/29/00	21	2	9/10	Run Like an Antelope	Wading In Velvet Sea
7/7/00	6	E	1/1	***	***
9/23/00	17	1	3/6	The Moma Dance	Halley's Comet
9/29/00	4	1	3/8	Rift	Mellow Mood

Has not been played in the last 6 shows.

Frankie Says

DATE	GAP	SET	POS.	SONG BEFORE	SONG AFTER
4/2/98	941	2	6/9	Sneakin' Sally	Twist
6/30/98	4	2	4/12	Wolfman's Brother	Run Like Antel
7/21/98	14	1	7/8	Cavern	Run Like Antel
7/26/98	3	1	4/7	David Bowie	Reba
8/7/98	8	1	3/10	Drowned	Stash
8/16/98	6	1	8/11	AC/DC Bag	Birds of a Feather
10/15/98	2	2	7/10	Prince Caspian	Birds of a Feather
10/29/98	3	1	7/10	Sleep	Birds of a Feather
10/31/98	2	1	9/10	Mike's Song	Weekapaug Gr
11/4/98	2	1	8/9	Brian and Robert	David Bowie
11/9/98	4	1	5/10	Divided Sky	Dogs Stole Things
11/19/98	6	2	4/8	Taste	Gumbo
12/30/98	10	1	9/12	Sample in a Jar	Maze
9/12/99	29	1	7/10	My Mind's Got A Mind	Birds of a Feather
10/7/99	17	1	5/9	David Bowie	Possum
6/15/00	28	1	6/8	Ghost	Divided Sky
6/24/00	4	2	5/8	Run Like an Antelope	Carini
7/14/00	14	3	2/7	Mike's Song	David Bowie

Has not been played in the last 22 shows.

Free

DATE	GAP	SET	POS.	SONG BEFORE	SONG AFTER
5/16/95	712	1	8/12	Lonesome Cowboy Bill	Glide II
6/8/95	2	2	3/8	Rift	Bouncing
6/10/95	2	1	5/9	It's Ice	Rift
6/16/95	4	2	2/5	Runaway Jim	Carolina
6/23/95	5	1	6/8	Ginseng Sullivan	Taste
6/26/95	3	2	2/6	Down with Disease	Poor Heart
6/29/95	2	2	1/6	***	David Bowie
7/3/95	4	1	10/11	Strange Design	Cavern
9/27/95	1	1	3/9	Rift	It's Ice
9/29/95	2	2	3/8	Maze	Ya Mar
10/3/95	3	1	6/11	I'm Blue, Lonesome	T.M.W.S.I.Y.
10/6/95	2	1	7/9	Rift	The Lizards
10/8/95	2	1	9/9	Uncle Pen	***
10/14/95	3	1	4/11	Kung	Sparkle
10/17/95	2	1	8/10	Sparkle	Strange Design
10/20/95	2	1	7/10	Rift	Hello My Baby
10/25/95	4	1	6/10	Scent of a Mule	Strange Design
10/31/95	4	1	6/9	Sparkle	Guyute
11/10/95	2	2	1/9	***	Scent of a Mul
11/14/95	3	1	6/9	Esther	Julius
11/18/95	3	2	3/10	Sparkle	I'm So Tired
11/22/95	3	2	2/6	Rift	Llama
11/28/95	3	2	5/10	Uncle Pen	Wind Beneath Wings
11/30/95	2	2	6/8	Scent of a Mule	Strange Design

DATE	GAP	SET	POS.	SONG BEFORE	SONG AFTER
12/2/95	2	1	7/10	My Sweet One	Taste That Surrounds
12/5/95	2	1	5/8	The Lizards	Esther
12/9/95	3	1	7/10	Bouncing	Billy Breathes
12/12/95	2	2	1/6	***	Sparkle
12/15/95	2	1	9/10	Bouncing	Possum
12/17/95	2	2	3/8	Maze	Also Sprach
12/30/95	3	2	2/8	Ya Mar	Harry Hood
7/12/96	11	3	2/3	David Bowie	Hello My Baby
7/21/96	6	2	5/9	Life on Mars	Run Like Antel
8/2/96	5	2	4/9	Taste	Fluffhead
8/7/96	4	2	4/10	Runaway Jim	Col. Forbin's A
8/10/96	1	2	4/8	Scent of a Mule	Fluffhead
8/16/96	4	2	3/13	Sparkle	The Squirmin
10/17/96	3	2	4/8	Scent of a Mule	The Lizards
10/19/96	2	1	3/9	Rift	Esther
10/22/96	2	1	8/9	Sparkle	You Enjoy My
10/25/96	2	2	8/12	NICU	Strange Design
11/2/96	5	1	8/9	The Lizards	Johnny B. Goode
11/7/96	3	1	8/10	Guyute	Tela
11/14/96	5	1	5/9	Cars Trucks Buses	All Things Rec
11/16/96	2	1	6/11	Rift	The Old Home
11/27/96	6	1	7/9	Uncle Pen	Theme From the Botto
12/2/96	4	2	5/8	Taste	Scent of a Mul
12/29/96	4	1	8/10	Rift	The Squirmin
2/16/97	5	2	3/11	Cars Trucks Buses	Sparkle
2/20/97	3	2	7/12	Bouncing	Swept Away
2/22/97	2	2	7/8	Harry Hood	Hello My Baby
2/25/97	2	2	4/10	Punch You in the Eye	Fee
6/14/97	7	1	9/10	Bye Bye Foot	Prince Caspian
6/24/97	6	1	10/12	Talk	Prince Caspian
7/2/97	5	E	1/2	***	David Bowie
7/6/97	3	2	1/5	***	You Enjoy My
7/26/97	8	2	6/8	Harry Hood	Waste
7/30/97	2	2	2/9	Punch You in the Eye	David Bowie
8/8/97	5	2	2/6	Wolfman's Brother	Limb by Limb
8/14/97	5	1	5/10	Limb by Limb	Cars Trucks Buses
11/30/97	14	2	3/7	Stash	Jam
7/15/98	27	2	4/6	Tweezer	Meat
7/31/98	11	2	2/9	The Curtain	If I Could
11/9/98	24	1	8/10	Poor Heart	NICU
11/21/98	8	2	6/9	The Mango Song	Ha Ha Ha
11/21/98	0	2	8/9	Ha Ha Ha	Weekapaug Gr
12/29/98	7	2	1/5	***	Limb by Limb
6/30/99	3	2	2/10	The Squirming Coil	Birds of a Feather
7/9/99	6	2	2/8	Punch You In the Eye	What's the Use
7/18/99	7	2	2/6	Runaway Jim	Meatstick
7/23/99	3	2	2/5	Ghost	Birds of a Feather
7/31/99	6	1	5/8	Limb by Limb	Roggae
9/11/99	4	1	9/9	Guyute	***
9/18/99	5	2	3/7	Meatstick	Bouncing
9/29/99	8	1	2/9	Runaway Jim	Driver
10/9/99	7	1	6/8	My Left Toe	Sparkle
12/2/99	2	1	9/10	Sample in a Jar	The Squirmin
12/7/99	4	2	7/8	Simple	Suzy Greenber
12/15/99	6	2	3/7	Maze	Dirt
12/31/99	5	2	28/35	Piper	Lawn Boy
6/11/00	6	2	2/8	Birds of a Feather	Beauty of My Dreams
7/12/00	20	1	7/9	Beauty of My Dreams	Axilla
9/17/00	9	2	5/5	The Mango Song	***
9/24/00	5	2	2/8	Cities	Ya Mar

Has not been played in the last 9 shows.

Freebird

DATE	GAP	SET	POS.	SONG BEFORE	SONG AFTER
3/6/87	19	2	1/7	***	Happy Birthday

DATE	GAP	SET	POS.	SONG BEFORE	SONG AFTER
7/15/93	533	E	2/2	Chalk Dust Torture	***
7/16/93	1	E	2/2	Llama	***
7/18/93	2	E	2/2	Rocky Top	***
7/22/93	2	E	1/1	***	***
7/24/93	2	E	2/2	Golgi Apparatus	***
7/29/93	4	E	2/2	Rocky Top	***
7/31/93	2	E	2/2	AC/DC Bag	***
8/3/93	2	E	2/2	Poor Heart	***
8/8/93	3	E	2/2	My Sweet One	***
8/12/93	3	E	2/2	Fire	***
8/15/93	3	2	11/11	Nellie Kane	***
8/20/93	3	E	2/2	The Mango Song	***
8/26/93	4	E	1/1	***	***
12/30/93	4	1	10/10	Bathtub Gin	***
4/23/94	18	E	1/1	***	***
5/6/94	9	E	2/2	Ginseng Sullivan	***
5/13/94	5	E	1/1	***	***
5/29/94	13	2	10/10	Run Like an Antelope	***
6/19/94	9	E	1/1	***	***
10/17/98	338	1	6/10	I'm Blue, Lonesome	Driver
10/30/98	3	E	2/2	Driver	***
11/9/98	7	E	2/2	Frankenstein	***
11/25/98	10	E	3/3	Guyute	***
12/29/98	5	1	10/10	My Soul	***
6/22/00	77	2	10/10	Uncle Pen	***

Has not been played in the last 38 shows.

Freeworld

DATE	GAP	SET	POS.	SONG BEFORE	SONG AFTER
3/6/87	19	2	6/7	Possum	Wilson

Has not been played in the last 1100 shows.

Fuck Your Face

DATE	GAP	SET	POS.	SONG BEFORE	SONG AFTER
4/29/87	22	1	8/9	Cities	Lushington

Has not been played in the last 1097 shows.

Funky Bitc

DATE	GAP	SET	POS.	SONG BEFORE	SONG AFTER
3/6/87	19	1	1/6	***	Good Time Ba
3/23/87	1	1	1/5	***	Mike's Song
8/9/87	5	1	11/11	Shaggy Dog	***
8/21/87	2	1	4/11	Divided Sky	Harry Hood
9/21/87	3	1	6/11	Slave	Wilson
9/27/87	1	1	2/9	David Bowie	Golgi Apparat
11/19/87	4	1	3/7	Sparks	You Enjoy My
1/27/88	1	1	1/9	***	Mustang Sally
2/8/88	2	1	2/7	Slave	Take the A-Trn
3/11/88	3	1	2/12	The Chicken	Sneakin' Sally
5/21/88	8	1	1/7	***	Sneakin' Sally
5/25/88	1	1	3/9	Rocky Top	Alumni Blues
6/19/88	2	1	2/8	The Curtain With	Possum
7/11/88	4	1	5/11	Jam	Fire
7/24/88	3	1	3/10	Golgi Apparatus	Col. Forbin's A
7/30/88	2	2	1/6	***	Suzy Greenber
8/3/88	1	3	7/8	Satin Doll	Walk Away
8/6/88	1	1	7/9	Take the A-Train	Dinner and a
8/27/88	1	1	3/9	You Enjoy Myself	Walk Away
9/13/88	3	1	2/8	Walk Away	You Enjoy My
5/26/89	37	3	2/4	Slave	Ballad - Curtis Loew
5/27/89	1	1	5/11	Weekapaug Groove	Fee
5/28/89	1	2	13/16	The Price of Love	Split Open and
6/30/89	2	1	1/7	***	You Enjoy My
8/26/89	4	2	7/9	Donna Lee	Foam
12/3/89	25	1	2/9	Bathtub Gin	Ya Mar
12/15/89	2	2	5/8	Run Like an Antelope	Jesus Just Left
1/27/90	6	1	10/13	Reba	Mike's Song
2/25/90	12	1	5/11	The Famous Mockingbi	The Squirmin
3/3/90	3	2	5/7	Esther	Carolina
3/10/90	4	1	7/10	The Squirming Coil	Divided Sky
3/28/90	3	2	4/16	Whipping Post	Mike's Song
4/8/90	5	1	2/8	Divided Sky	You Enjoy My
4/9/90	1	2	1/11	***	Esther
4/13/90	2	1	1/10	***	Dinner and a
4/18/90	2	2	4/12	The Sloth	Reba
4/21/90	3	1	3/10	Reba	Esther

DATE	GAP	SET	POS.	SONG BEFORE	SONG AFTER
5/10/90	9	2	1/8	***	Runaway Jim
5/13/90	2	2	9/12	Reba	Sweet Adeline
9/20/90	18	2	10/14	Possum	Stash
9/21/90	1	2	1/8	***	Stash
11/4/90	16	1	7/10	Harry Hood	The Asse Festival
12/8/90	10	E	1/3	***	Contact
12/28/90	1	2	12/12	Don't Get Me Wrong	***
7/24/91	68	2	7/10	Bouncing	I Didn't Know
7/26/91	2	2	6/10	Fee	The Squirmin
10/15/91	7	2	11/12	Love You	Golgi Apparat
7/25/92	107	1	8/8	Llama	***
12/29/92	44	1	1/12	***	Runaway Jim
2/19/93	16	2	8/12	Lawn Boy	My Sweet One
3/13/93	15	1	2/11	The Landlady	Bouncing
3/28/93	12	1	2/11	The Landlady	Sparkle
4/10/93	8	2	10/13	Weekapaug Groove	Help Me
4/20/93	6	E	1/2	***	Amazing Grce
7/29/93	29	1	1/10	***	Divided Sky
4/23/94	42	1	1/10	***	Rift
7/6/94	49	E	4/4	Memories	***
11/13/94	32	E	1/2	***	Tweezer Repri
11/22/94	7	2	1/13	***	Jam
12/31/94	18	1	8/8	Divided Sky	***
6/7/95	2	1	9/10	The Wedge	Slave
7/1/95	19	E	1/1	***	***
10/15/95	16	E	1/1	***	***
10/29/95	10	E	1/1	***	***
11/16/95	8	1	10/10	Guyute	***
11/28/95	7	2	10/10	BBFCM	***
12/11/95	10	2	8/8	Suspicious Minds	***
6/6/96	11	1	4/8	Runaway Jim	Theme From the Botto
7/5/96	2	1	1/6	***	Chalk Dust Tor
7/12/96	6	1	6/10	Ya Mar	Taste
7/13/96	1	1	8/10	Fire	Chalk Dust Tor
7/17/96	2	1	5/5	Ya Mar	***
8/4/96	9	1	2/9	Chalk Dust Torture	Guyute
10/17/96	11	1	2/10	Also Sprach	Sparkle
10/21/96	3	E	1/1	***	***
11/2/96	8	E	1/1	***	***
11/6/96	2	2	9/9	Sample in a Jar	***
11/15/96	7	E	1/1	***	***
11/23/96	5	1	9/9	Rift	***
11/30/96	4	2	9/11	Taste	Amazing Grce
12/30/96	7	1	7/9	Talk	Theme From the Botto
2/14/97	3	2	4/9	Down with Disease	Reba
2/22/97	6	1	3/10	Also Sprach	Theme From the Botto
3/18/97	7	E	2/2	Hello My Baby	***
7/6/97	16	2	5/5	Rocky Top	***
7/10/97	2	E	1/1	***	***
7/21/97	2	2	7/8	Jam	Slave
8/14/97	16	1	2/10	Ya Mar	Fluffhead
8/16/97	1	3	6/6	Limb by Limb	***
11/14/97	3	1	6/8	Also Sprach	Guyute
11/19/97	3	1	6/10	Limb By Limb	Theme From the Botto
11/30/97	7	1	2/6	Guyute	Wolfman's Brother
12/5/97	3	1	3/10	Wilson	Black-Eyed Katy
12/12/97	5	1	1/8	***	Also Sprach
12/28/97	2	1	8/11	Farmhouse	Split Open and
4/4/98	6	1	4/8	Bouncing	Ginseng Sullivan
6/30/98	2	1	11/13	Beauty of My Dreams	Train Song
7/5/98	4	E	1/1	***	***
7/21/98	10	2	8/8	She Caught The Katy	***
7/26/98	3	1	6/7	Reba	Good Time Ba
7/28/98	1	1	10/10	Sparkle	***
8/1/98	3	1	9/9	Lawn Boy	***
8/7/98	4	E	1/1	***	***
8/12/98	1	1	3/8	Makisupa Policeman	Possum
8/15/98	1	1	10/12	Water in the Sky	Cities

DATE	GAP	SET	POS.	SONG BEFORE	SONG AFTER
11/6/98	11	2	2/7	Makisupa Policeman	Simple
11/11/98	4	E	3/3	Rocky Top	***
11/14/98	2	1	1/8	***	My Soul
11/20/98	4	1	4/13	Quinn the Eskimo	Guelah Papyrus
11/27/98	4	1	1/11	***	Ya Mar
12/29/98	4	1	2/10	Rock and Roll	Punch You in
7/3/99	5	1	8/11	Tube	NICU
7/13/99	7	1	9/9	Carini	***
7/17/99	3	2	1/8	***	On My Knees
7/21/99	1	6	6/10	Limb By Limb	The Moma Dance
7/30b/99	6	1	6/8	NICU	Ghost
9/11/99	5	1	2/9	Tube	Limb by Limb
9/19/99	6	1	2/8	NICU	First Tube
9/26/99	5	1	8/10	Cars Trucks Buses	Mozambique
10/3/99	5	E	1/2	***	Messin' with the Kid
10/4/99	1	1	2/8	Uncle Pen	Vultures
12/7/99	9	1	4/8	NICU	Punch You in
12/31/99	11	1	2/14	Runaway Jim	Tube
6/9/00	4	1	6/9	Golgi Apparatus	The Moma Dance
6/25/00	10	1	6/10	Water in the Sky	Horn
6/29/00	2	1	1/5	***	Wilson
7/7/00	6	1	5/11	Boogie On Reggae	Maze
7/10/00	2	1	9/10	Sparkle	David Bowie
9/9/00	6	2	6/7	Cars Trucks Buses	Cavern
9/25/00	11	2	7/7	Harry Hood	***
10/4/00	5	1	4/7	Bouncing	Reba

Has not been played in the last 3 shows.

Gettin' Jiggy Wit' It

DATE	GAP	SET	POS.	SONG BEFORE	SONG AFTER
11/20/98	996	2	6/8	Farmhouse	Harry Hood

Has not been played in the last 123 shows.

Ghost

DATE	GAP	SET	POS.	SONG BEFORE	SONG AFTER
6/13/97	878	2	7/9	Chalk Dust Torture	Oblivious Fool
6/16/97	2	2	2/7	Limb by Limb	I Don't Care
6/19/97	1	2	2/7	Stash	I Saw it Again
6/20/97	1	2	2/8	David Bowie	Bye Bye Foot
6/22/97	2	1	9/9	Hello My Baby	***
6/24/97	1	2	7/7	Wading In Velvet Sea	***
7/1/97	4	1	1/9	***	Horn
7/3/97	2	2	1/6	***	Cars Trucks Buses
7/9/97	3	2	5/6	You Enjoy Myself	Poor Heart
7/10/97	1	2	5/7	Ya Mar	Take Me to the River
7/21/97	2	1	1/7	***	Dogs Stole Things
7/23/97	2	2	2/6	Punch You in the Eye	Sample in a Ja
7/25/97	1	2	5/6	Drum Jam	Character Zer
7/29/97	2	1	6/9	Sparkle	Swept Away
7/31/97	2	1	1/9	***	Ya Mar
8/2/97	1	1	3/8	Ginseng Sullivan	Dogs Stole Things
8/6/97	2	2	3/7	My Soul	Prince Caspian
8/9/97	2	1	3/8	Punch You in the Eye	Taste
8/13/97	3	2	2/9	Runaway Jim	Izabella
8/16/97	2	1	6/11	Punch You in the Eye	Ginseng Sullivan
11/17/97	5	1	4/5	Train Song	Fire
11/21/97	2	2	1/4	***	AC/DC Bag
11/28/97	4	2	4/5	Slave	Johnny B. Goode
12/2/97	3	1	5/9	Chalk Dust Torture	Divided Sky
12/5/97	2	1	1/10	***	Wilson
12/11/97	4	2	4/6	BBFCM	Down with Dis
12/13/97	2	2	3/10	Punch You in the Eye	Mike's Song
12/28/97	1	2	3/9	Simple	Drowned
4/4/98	6	2	4/6	Brother	The Lizards
6/30/98	2	1	2/13	Limb by Limb	Water in the Sky

DATE	GAP	SET	POS.	SONG BEFORE	SONG AFTER
7/2/98	2	2	1/4	***	Runaway Jim
7/6/98	3	1	3/9	AC/DC Bag	Cities
7/8/98	1	2	6/7	Sleeping Monkey	Johnny B. Goode
7/19/98	6	1	5/8	Guyute	Limb by Limb
7/21/98	2	2	6/8	Brian and Robert	She Caught The Katy
8/2/98	8	2	2/6	Possum	Lifeboy
8/7/98	3	1	8/10	Bittersweet Motel	Col. Forbin's A
8/16/98	6	2	3/8	Piper	Fluffhead
10/15/98	2	1	1/8	***	Water in the Sky
10/31/98	5	3	3/3	Piper	***
11/7/98	4	2	2/4	AC/DC Bag	Reba
11/11/98	3	2	6/6	When Circus Comes	***
11/15/98	3	1	2/8	My Friend My Friend	Driver
11/19/98	2	1	8/9	Something	Golgi Apparat
11/24/98	3	2	1/6	***	Halley's Comet
12/31/98	8	1	5/7	Weekapaug Groove	Ha Ha Ha
7/4/99	4	2	1/9	***	Slave
7/15/99	7	1	2/10	Punch You in the Eye	Farmhouse
7/20/99	4	1	7/9	Waste	Wilson
7/23/99	2	2	1/5	***	Free
7/30b/99	5	1	7/8	Funky Bitch	Axilla
9/9/99	3	2	3/9	Ha Ha Ha	The Inlaw Josie Wale
9/12/99	3	2	1/5	***	Runaway Jim
9/17/99	3	1	3/11	Guyute	Lawn Boy
9/22/99	4	2	2/8	Gotta Jibboo	Taste
10/4/99	9	2	1/8	***	Sample in a Ja
10/9/99	3	1	4/8	Guyute	My Left Toe
12/11/99	9	2	3/5	Sneakin' Sally	Also Sprach
12/30/99	7	1	10/12	Farmhouse	Ya Mar
5/22/00	3	2	5/6	The Mango Song	Rock and Roll
6/15/00	7	1	5/8	Uncle Pen	Frankie Says
7/1/00	9	2	10/10	Nellie Kane	***
7/7/00	4	2	1/7	***	Gotta Jibboo
9/8/00	7	1	3/12	Limb By Limb	Bouncing
9/22/00	9	2	3/7	Reba	The Wedge
9/27/00	4	2	3/7	Gumbo	The Mango Song

Has not been played in the last 7 shows.

Ginseng Sullivan

DATE	GAP	SET	POS.	SONG BEFORE	SONG AFTER
8/11/93	572	1	5/10	It's Ice	My Friend My
8/13/93	2	1	6/10	Stash	Fluffhead
8/15/93	2	2	9/11	Sweet Adeline	Nellie Kane
8/20/93	3	1	8/10	The Wedge	Rift
8/24/93	2	2	5/10	Mike's Song	Weekapaug Gr
8/25/93	1	1	6/11	Foam	Nellie Kane
8/28/93	2	1	4/9	Foam	Maze
12/31/93	4	1	4/8	Stash	Reba
4/6/94	3	E	1/3	***	Nellie Kane
4/10/94	3	2	5/7	Fluffhead	I Wanna Be Like You
4/13/94	2	1	6/8	Julius	Divided Sky
4/23/94	9	2	7/10	Harry Hood	You Enjoy My
4/25/94	2	1	6/10	Down with Disease	Dog Faced Boy
4/30/94	3	1	8/9	Rift	Sweet Adeline
5/6/94	4	E	1/2	***	Freebird
5/10/94	3	2	7/10	Harry Hood	Dog Faced Boy
5/14/94	3	1	8/9	My Sweet One	David Bowie
5/17/94	2	1	6/9	Scent of a Mule	Dog Faced Boy
5/19/94	1	E	1/4	***	Nellie Kane
5/22/94	3	1	9/11	My Sweet One	Dog Faced Boy
5/23/94	1	E	1/3	***	Amazing Grce
5/26/94	2	2	6/9	Mound	Dog Faced Boy
6/9/94	4	2	6/10	Scent of a Mule	Mike's Song
6/13/94	3	1	8/9	Stash	Julius
6/16/94	2	E	1/3	***	Amazing Grce

DATE	GAP	SET	POS.	SONG BEFORE	SONG AFTER
6/21/94	4	2	9/16	BBFCFM	BBFCFM Reprise
7/5/94	11	2	8/11	The Great Gig in the	My Sweet One
10/10/94	12	1	9/11	The Old Home Place	Nellie Kane
6/20/95	58	1	3/9	Spock's Brain	Foam
6/23/95	2	1	5/10	Reba	Free
10/21/96	103	1	7/10	Character Zero	Stash
11/15/96	17	1	7/11	Prince Caspian	Train Song
11/18/96	2	1	8/10	Chalk Dust Torture	Reba
11/22/96	2	1	5/10	Taste	Sample in a Ja
11/24/96	2	E	1/2	***	Cavern
12/28/96	8	1	6/9	Billy Breathes	Split Open and
2/16/97	6	1	6/10	Guelah Papyrus	Tweezer
6/20/97	17	2	4/8	Bye Bye Foot	Cavern
7/2/97	8	1	5/8	Strange Design	Vultures
7/9/97	4	1	3/8	Prince Caspian	Split Open and
7/10/97	1	1	3/8	Limb by Limb	Bathtub Gin
7/21/97	2	1	5/7	Dirt	Bathtub Gin
7/23/97	2	1	5/10	Dogs Stole Things	Water in the Sky
8/2/97	6	1	2/8	Theme From the Botto	Ghost
8/10/97	5	1	9/10	Bye Bye Foot	Harry Hood
8/16/97	4	1	7/11	Ghost	You Enjoy My
11/19/97	6	1	8/10	Theme From the Botto	Fee
11/29/97	6	1	8/12	The Sloth	I Saw it Again
12/2/97	2	E	1/2	***	Sample in a Ja
12/5/97	2	1	8/10	My Friend My Friend	Limb by Limb
12/13/97	6	1	4/9	Theme From the Botto	Strange De-sign
4/4/98	7	1	5/8	Funky Bitch	Limb by Limb
7/2/98	4	1	9/11	Fluffhead	Punch You in
8/11/98	26	1	8/11	The Sloth	Fee
8/16/98	3	1	1/11	***	Bathtub Gin
11/13/98	15	1	4/10	Roggae	It's Ice
11/19/98	4	1	4/9	Sample in a Jar	Bouncing
11/24/98	3	1	3/9	The Moma Dance	Stash
12/29/98	6	1	5/10	Horn	Split Open and
7/21/99	18	1	4/10	Gold Soundz	Limb By Limb
9/10/99	10	1	5/8	Divided Sky	Carini
9/28/99	13	1	4/8	Tube	Roggae
10/3/99	4	1	8/12	Carini	Back on the Train
12/5/99	9	1	9/10	Lawn Boy	Twist
6/11/00	18	1	4/9	Horn	Stash
6/30/00	11	1	6/10	Sneakin' Sally	Guyute
9/12/00	15	1	4/7	My Soul	First Tube

Has not been played in the last 17 shows.

Glass Onion

DATE	GAP	SET	POS.	SONG BEFORE	SONG AFTER
10/31/94	681	2	4/30	Dear Prudence	Ob La Di Ob La Da

Has not been played in the last 438 shows.

Glide

DATE	GAP	SET	POS.	SONG BEFORE	SONG AFTER
9/27/91	314	E	1/2	***	Rocky Top
10/27/91	18	E	1/2	***	Possum
10/31/91	3	E	1/2	***	Rocky Top
11/9/91	5	E	1/2	***	Possum
11/14/91	4	2	6/11	It's Ice	Tweezer
11/16/91	2	E	1/2	***	Rocky Top
11/19/91	1	E	1/2	***	Rocky Top
11/22/91	3	E	1/2	***	Suzy Greenber
11/30/91	3	1	1/11	***	Llama
12/5/91	2	E	1/2	***	Cavern
3/17/92	10	2	2/11	Runaway Jim	The Sloth
3/19/92	1	2	1/10	***	Chalk Dust Tor
3/20/92	1	1	4/10	Brother	Rift
3/25/92	4	1	7/10	Maze	Runaway Jim
3/27/92	2	1	8/10	Maze	Bouncing
3/28/92	1	1	9/10	David Bowie	Cavern
3/31/92	2	1	3/10	Divided Sky	Split Open and
4/12/92	8	2	1/10	***	Split Open and
4/18/92	5	2	1/16	***	The Oh Kee Pa
4/22/92	3	2	1/11	***	Run Like Antel
4/24/92	2	2	11/12	Love You	Llama

DATE	GAP	SET	POS.	SONG BEFORE	SONG AFTER
4/30/92	3	2	1/11	***	Tweezer
5/2/92	2	2	1/10	***	David Bowie
5/5/92	2	1	10/11	It's Ice	Run Like Antel
5/7/92	2	2	5/12	Fluffhead	Mike's Song
5/14/92	5	2	1/13	***	Cavern
5/16/92	2	1	3/11	Foam	Split Open and
5/18/92	2	2	1/13	***	Llama
7/9/92	8	1	1/12	***	The Oh Kee Pa
7/9/92	0	1	12/12	David Bowie	***
7/12/92	3	1	8/11	Uncle Pen	Vacuum Solo
7/12/92	0	1	10/11	Vacuum Solo	Possum
7/15/92	2	1	1/12	***	The Oh Kee Pa
7/16/92	1	2	9/13	Llama	Paul and Silas
11/19/92	29	1	4/12	Foam	Split Open and
11/21/92	2	1	4/11	Foam	Poor Heart
11/23/92	2	1	3/11	Foam	Split Open and
11/27/92	2	2	4/13	Possum	It's Ice
11/30/92	2	2	5/10	Maze	Uncle Pen
12/2/92	2	2	7/11	Llama	Lengthwise
12/4/92	2	1	5/11	Stash	Sparkle
12/7/92	3	1	4/11	Maze	Sparkle
12/12/92	4	2	2/10	Maze	The Curtain
12/28/92	2	1	4/10	Buried Alive	It's Ice
12/31/92	3	2	9/10	Stash	Good Time Ba
2/4/93	2	1	10/11	Sample in a Jar	Run Like Antel
2/7/93	3	2	8/13	Big Ball Jam	You Enjoy My
2/13/93	5	1	5/10	It's Ice	Rift
2/17/93	2	2	4/11	David Bowie	My Friend My
2/20/93	3	2	6/22	Tweezer	Mike's Song
2/22/93	2	2	6/11	You Enjoy Myself	The Oh Kee Pa
2/26/93	3	2	4/11	Tweezer	Chalk Dust Tor
3/3/93	2	2	8/13	Weekapaug Groove	My Sweet One
3/8/93	3	1	11/12	It's Ice	David Bowie
3/9/93	1	1	7/10	Divided Sky	Punch You in
3/13/93	2	2	5/13	It's Ice	Uncle Pen
3/17/93	3	2	2/12	Axilla	Reba
3/25/93	6	1	7/11	Stash	Rift
3/30/93	4	1	9/11	Stash	Divided Sky
4/5/93	5	2	6/9	Tweezer	You Enjoy My
4/10/93	2	2	5/13	Rift	Big Ball Jam
4/17/93	4	1	6/10	It's Ice	My Friend My
4/20/93	2	1	7/10	It's Ice	Uncle Pen
4/25/93	5	1	5/11	It's Ice	Runaway Jim
4/29/93	2	1	7/10	Llama	Rift
5/1/93	2	1	9/10	It's Ice	David Bowie
5/5/93	3	1	8/10	It's Ice	Maze
5/8/93	3	1	8/12	Stash	My Friend My
7/16/93	4	2	3/12	Split Open and Melt	Maze
7/21/93	3	1	6/12	Maze	Rift
7/24/93	2	2	5/12	Maze	Sparkle
8/9/93	12	1	7/11	Split Open and Melt	Nellie Kane
8/15/93	3	2	7/10	Maze	Sweet Adeline
8/25/93	6	1	10/11	Stash	Cavern
12/29/93	4	1	4/9	Foam	Divided Sky
4/5/94	4	1	4/8	Fluffhead	Julius
4/8/94	2	1	4/13	Maze	Foam
4/11/94	3	1	7/9	Julius	Divided Sky
4/14/94	2	1	5/9	Down with Disease	Rift
4/18/94	4	1	2/10	Chalk Dust Torture	Poor Heart
4/21/94	2	1	4/9	Foam	Split Open and
5/2/94	8	1	6/10	It's Ice	Divided Sky
5/17/94	11	2	2/9	Runaway Jim	Tweezer
5/22/94	4	1	4/11	Divided Sky	Peaches en Regalia
6/9/94	7	2	2/10	Split Open and Melt	Julius
6/17/94	6	1	3/9	Foam	Split Open and
6/30/94	10	1	6/9	Split Open and Melt	Scent of a Mul
7/10/94	8	2	3/10	David Bowie	Ya Mar
10/7/94	5	1	3/9	Julius	Poor Heart
10/15/94	7	1	5/8	Maze	Reba
10/25/94		2	6/11	Yerushalayim	Axilla (Part II)
10/28/94	3	1	6/10	Stash	Axilla (Part II)
11/20/94	9	2	3/10	Divided Sky	Axilla (Part II)
12/31/94	19	1	4/8	Run Like an Antelope	Mound
6/24/95	15	1	5/10	Julius	Mound

DATE	GAP	SET	POS.	SONG BEFORE	SONG AFTER
10/17/95	23	1	6/10	Maze	Sparkle
11/21/95	20	2	5/11	David Bowie	Ya Mar
8/13/96	51	1	9/10	Llama	Slave
11/30/96	34	2	3/11	It's Ice	Brother
7/31/97	50	1	7/9	Maze	I Saw it Again
7/29/98	60	1	7/8	Vultures	Birds of a Feather
7/24/99	60	E	1/4	***	Camel Walk
7/3/00	65	2	2/7	Runaway Jim	Theme From the Botto
9/8/00	10	1	9/12	NICU	Axilla
10/7/00	20	1	7/8	Bathtub Gin	My Soul

Was played in the most recent show.

Glide II

| 5/16/95 | 712 | 1 | 9/12 | Free | You Enjoy My |

Has not been played in the last 407 shows.

Gloria

| 5/16/95 | 712 | E | 2/2 | I'll Come Running | *** |

Has not been played in the last 407 shows.

Going Down Slow

| 9/13/90 | 207 | 2 | 6/15 | Stash | The Oh Kee Pa |
| 9/14/90 | 1 | 2 | 10/10 | Fire | *** |

Has not been played in the last 911 shows.

Gold Soundz

| 7/21/99 | 1022 | 1 | 3/10 | Cities | Ginseng Sullivan |

Has not been played in the last 97 shows.

Golden Lady

| 10/20/94 | 672 | 1 | 2/11 | Runaway Jim | Poor Heart |

Has not been played in the last 447 shows.

Golgi Apparatus

DATE	GAP	SET	POS.	SONG BEFORE	SONG AFTER
10/15/86	14	2	2/14	Peaches en Regalia	Swing Low Sweet Chrt
10/31/86	1	3	3/11	Camel Walk	Slave
2/13/87	2	1	3/14	Possum	Slave
3/6/87	2	1	4/6	Corrine Corrina	Quinn the Eskimo
3/23/87	1	2	8/9	Camel Walk	Swing Low Sweet Chrt
4/24/87	1	1	1/14	***	AC/DC Bag
4/29/87	1	1	3/9	Alumni Blues	Swing Low Sweet Chrt
5/11/87	1	E	1/3	***	Corrine Corrina
5/20/87	1	1	3/9	Run Like an Antelope	Back Porch Boogie Bl
8/9/87	1	1	1/11	***	Slave
8/10/87	1	1	3/7	Alumni Blues	Wilson
8/21/87	1	2	5/12	Harpua	Sparks
9/21/87	3	1	9/11	Dear Mrs. Reagan	AC/DC Bag
9/27/87	1	1	3/9	Funky Bitch	Peaches en Regalia
10/14/87	1	1	4/12	You Enjoy Myself	Slave
11/18/87	2	1	9/12	Take the A-Train	Divided Sky
1/27/88	2	3	4/8	Suzy Greenberg	Bike
2/7/88	1	1	4/10	Shaggy Dog	Alumni Blues
2/8/88	1	1	4/7	Take the A-Train	Phase Dance
2/24/88	1	1	7/11	Peaches en Regalia	Slave
2/26/88	1	1	13/13	I Didn't Know	***
3/11/88	1	1	7/12	Wilson	Slave
3/21/88	2	1	2/15	Suzy Greenberg	McGrupp
3/31/88	1	2	2/14	I Didn't Know	Fee
4/22/88	2	2	2/13	I Didn't Know	The Lizards
5/15/88	2	1	2/11	Alumni Blues	You Enjoy My
5/21/88	1	1	6/7	St. Thomas	Fire
5/25/88	1	1	6/9	Peaches en Regalia	Sneakin' Sally
6/15/88	1	1	8/9	Fluffhead	La Grange
6/19/88	1	1	4/8	Possum	La Grange
6/20/88	1	2	4/9	Fee	Satin Doll

DATE	GAP	SET	POS.	SONG BEFORE	SONG AFTER
6/21/88	1	2	10/10	Peaches en Regalia	***
6/24/88	1	1	6/11	On Your Way Down	Fee
7/11/88	1	1	10/11	The Famous Mockingbi	Alumni Blues
7/24/88	3	1	2/10	Walk Away	Funky Bitch
8/6/88	4	2	1/6	***	AC/DC Bag
8/27/88	1	1	8/9	Take the A-Train	Tela
9/24/88	5	1	1/10	***	On Your Way Down
10/31/88	2	1	7/12	Time Loves a Hero	Bold as Love
11/3/88	1	1	2/7	Fire	Fluffhead
11/5/88	1	1	7/11	Take the A-Train	Walk Away
12/2/88	2	1	2/7	The Sloth	Bold As Love
12/10/88	1	1	2/12	I Didn't Know	David Bowie
1/26/89	3	1	2/10	I Didn't Know	Alumni Blues
2/6/89	1	2	4/7	Take the A-Train	Divided Sky
2/7/89	1	1	9/9	Weekapaug Groove	***
2/17/89	2	1	6/10	Split Open and Melt	Take the A-Trn
2/24/89	2	1	9/10	Run Like an Antelope	Possum
3/3/89	1	E	1/1	***	***
3/4/89	1	1	7/9	Fee	Good Time Ba
3/12/89	1	1	6/8	Alumni Blues	Bold As Love
3/24/89	2	1	5/10	Weekapaug Groove	Divided Sky
3/30/89	1	2	8/8	La Grange	***
4/27/89	3	1	1/8	***	The Sloth
5/1/89	2	1	8/9	The Lizards	Good Time Ba
5/5/89	1	1	1/8	***	You Enjoy My
5/6/89	1	2	6/8	Harry Hood	Slave
5/13/89	3	1	4/12	You Enjoy Myself	La Grange
5/20/89	1	2	9/9	David Bowie	***
5/26/89	2	2	6/6	Run Like an Antelope	***
8/17/89	5	E	1/2	***	Fire
9/21/89	6	1	1/9	***	Ya Mar
10/1/89	1	1	4/12	Who Do? We Do!	Harry Hood
10/6/89	1	1	6/13	The Sloth	Bold As Love
10/7/89	1	1	1/11	***	Ya Mar
10/14/89	3	1	4/11	I Didn't Know	Ya Mar
10/20/89	1	1	9/10	Divided Sky	Run Like Antel
10/22/89	2	2	3/9	Reba	In a Hole
10/26/89	1	1	2/11	The Oh Kee Pa Ceremo	You Enjoy My
11/2/89	3	2	2/11	The Oh Kee Pa Ceremo	You Enjoy My
11/3/89	1	1	10/10	Reba	***
11/9/89	1	1	2/9	I Didn't Know	Ya Mar
11/11/89	2	1	2/8	The Oh Kee Pa Ceremo	Bathtub Gin
11/30/89	3	E	2/2	In a Hole	***
12/3/89	2	E	2/2	I Didn't Know	***
12/7/89	1	2	11/11	Undun	***
12/9/89	2	1	10/10	Bathtub Gin	***
12/15/89	1	1	2/10	Take The A-Train	Mike's Song
12/16/89	1	1	9/9	In a Hole	***
12/30/89	2	2	9/9	Lawn Boy	***
2/9/90	7	1	1/12	***	The Oh Kee Pa
2/16/90	3	2	1/7	***	Caravan
2/23/90	3	2	1/11	***	Reba
2/24/90	1	1	3/8	You Enjoy Myself	Divided Sky
3/1/90	2	1	1/7	***	Ya Mar
3/8/90	4	2	12/12	Ballad - Curtis Loew	***
3/17/90	1	1	1/10	***	Esther
4/4/90	2	1	1/8	***	You Enjoy My
4/5/90	1	E	1/1	***	***
4/8/90	3	2	1/10	***	Walk Away
4/12/90	2	1	1/11	***	Ya Mar
4/14/90	2	2	9/11	Ride'Captain Ride	Fee
4/19/90	2	2	8/8	Carolina	***
4/22/90	3	E	2/2	Lawn Boy	***
5/19/90	12	1	1/8	***	Ya Mar
5/24/90	2	1	9/9	AC/DC Bag	***
6/5/90	5	E	2/2	Whipping Post	***
6/16/90	4	2	1/8	***	Esther
9/15/90	3	1	11/14	David Bowie	Stash
9/21/90	3	E	1/1	***	***
9/22/90	1	E	2/2	The Asse Festival	***
10/1/90	3	1	9/11	Gumbo	Love You
10/4/90	1	1	1/10	***	The Landlady
10/4/90	0	1	10/10	Uncle Pen	***
10/5/90	1	2	1/8	***	The Curtain
10/7/90	2	2	8/8	Good Times Bad Times	***

DATE	GAP	SET	POS.	SONG BEFORE	SONG AFTER
10/8/90	1	2	4/6	If I Only Had a Brai	Magilla
10/12/90	1	1	9/9	Tweezer	***
10/19/90	1	1	1/15	***	Foam
11/2/90	3	1	1/14	***	The Landlady
11/4/90	2	2	1/13	***	Rocky Top
11/16/90	3	1	8/8	Divided Sky	***
12/7/90	6	1	1/9	***	Stash
12/8/90	1	2	7/9	Tela	No Good Trying
12/28/90	1	1	11/11	Weekapaug Groove	***
12/31/90	2	2	1/9	***	Stash
2/3/91	3	1	10/10	Foam	***
2/7/91	1	1	10/10	The Squirming Coil	***
2/9/91	2	2	1/10	***	Buried Alive
2/14/91	1	1	11/11	The Oh Kee Pa Ceremo	***
2/15/91	1	E	4/4	Contact	***
2/16/91	1	2	9/9	Love You	***
2/19/91	1	1	3/9	The Curtain	Reba
2/20/91	1	1	11/11	Manteca	***
2/21/91	1	2	1/9	***	Cavern
2/26/91	1	1	10/11	AC/DC Bag	La Grange
2/27/91	1	1	1/10	***	Divided Sky
2/28/91	1	1	13/13	My Sweet One	***
3/1/91	2	1	1/11	***	The Landlady
3/6/91	1	1	1/11	***	You Enjoy My
3/8/91	1	1	1/11	***	You Enjoy My
3/9/91	1	2	13/13	Lawn Boy	***
3/13/91	2	2	12/12	The Oh Kee Pa Ceremo	***
3/16/91	2	1	4/14	T.M.W.S.I.Y. Reprise	Reba
3/22/91	2	E	2/2	Magilla	***
3/28/91	2	1	1/14	***	Divided Sky
4/3/91	4	1	1/10	***	Llama
4/4/91	1	1	10/10	Carolina	***
4/12/91	4	1	9/9	Rocky Top	***
4/16/91	1	1	1/9	***	You Enjoy My
4/19/91	2	2	4/10	The Curtain	The Landlady
4/21/91	2	1	1/14	***	Rocky Top
4/27/91	3	1	12/12	Stash	***
5/4/91	3	E	3/3	Runaway Jim	***
5/10/91	2	2	1/11	***	Harry Hood
5/12/91	2	2	5/13	The Curtain	Magilla
5/16/91	1	1	2/11	Buried Alive	Foam
5/17/91	1	E	2/2	Lawn Boy	***
5/18/91	1	1	2/9	Buried Alive	Chalk Dust Tor
5/19/91	1	2	10/10	I Didn't Know	***
7/12/91	2	1	2/14	***	The Squirmin
7/14/91	2	1	4/11	The Squirming Coil	Guelah Papyrus
7/19/91	3	1	1/10	***	The Landlady
7/20/91	1	2	6/12	Flat Fee	Stash
7/23/91	2	E	2/2	Caravan	***
7/24/91	1	1	1/10	***	Chalk Dust Tor
7/25/91	1	2	2/13	The Landlady	The Squirmin
7/26/91	1	1	12/12	Bouncing	***
8/3/91	2	1	11/11	Divided Sky	***
9/26/91	2	2	1/11	***	The Squirmin
9/28/91	2	1	10/11	Brother	Memories
9/29/91	1	2	9/10	My Sweet One	David Bowie
10/2/91	2	1	10/10	Chalk Dust Torture	***
10/4/91	2	E	2/5	Sweet Adeline	Rocky Top
10/6/91	1	1	13/13	Terrapin	***
10/10/91	1	1	11/11	Llama	***
10/12/91	2	E	4/4	Contact	***
10/15/91	2	2	12/12	Funky Bitch	***
10/17/91	1	1	10/10	Chalk Dust Torture	***
10/19/91	2	1	10/10	Stash	***
10/23/91	1	2	4/10	Sparkle	The Mango Song
10/27/91	1	1	10/10	Harry Hood	***
11/2/91	5	2	1/11	***	Run Like Antel
11/8/91	2	1	11/11	Eliza	***
11/12/91	3	1	2/11	Buried Alive	Uncle Pen
11/13/91	1	2	4/9	The Famous Mockingbi	Bathtub Gin
11/14/91	1	1	10/11	The Mango Song	Runaway Jim
11/15/91	1	1	12/12	Lawn Boy	***
11/20/91	3	2	1/8	***	It's Ice

DATE	GAP	SET	POS.	SONG BEFORE	SONG AFTER
11/21/91	1	E	3/3	Sweet Adeline	***
11/23/91	2	1	11/11	Bouncing	***
11/24/91	1	2	8/8	You Enjoy Myself	***
11/30/91	1	2	10/10	Run Like an Antelope	***
12/4/91	1	2	11/11	Love You	***
12/5/91	1	1	1/10	***	Paul and Silas
12/7/91	2	E	2/2	Sweet Adeline	***
12/31/91	1	1	10/10	Llama	***
3/7/92	2	E	2/2	Sweet Adeline	***
3/12/92	2	2	1/11	***	Tweezer
3/14/92	2	2	1/10	***	Llama
3/19/92	2	1	5/12	Sparkle	The Horse
3/21/92	2	1	12/12	Stash	***
3/24/92	2	1	6/13	Rift	The Horse
3/25/92	1	2	12/12	Cracklin' Rosie	***
3/27/92	2	2	13/13	Love You	***
3/30/92	2	2	1/13	***	Uncle Pen
4/1/92	2	1	1/12	***	Foam
4/3/92	1	1	11/11	Split Open and Melt	***
4/7/92	4	2	11/11	My Mind's Got a Mind	***
4/8/92	1	1	11/11	The Squirming Coil	***
4/13/92	2	1	1/10	***	Uncle Pen
4/15/92	1	2	8/8	My Sweet One	***
4/17/92	2	E	1/1	***	***
4/19/92	2	1	11/11	I Didn't Know	***
4/23/92	3	2	13/13	Cracklin' Rosie	***
4/24/92	1	1	11/11	The Squirming Coil	***
4/29/92	2	2	11/11	Love You	***
5/1/92	2	2	13/13	Terrapin	***
5/5/92	3	1	1/11	***	The Curtain
5/6/92	1	2	11/11	Take the A-Train	***
5/8/92	2	2	12/12	Harry Hood	***
5/9/92	1	2	8/8	Cracklin' Rosie	***
5/15/92	4	1	1/11	***	Foam
5/16/92	1	1	8/11	Horn	The Lizards
6/23/92	5	1	8/8	If I Only Had a Brai	***
6/30/92	3	1	1/6	***	Divided Sky
7/10/92	3	1	6/10	Maze	The Lizards
7/15/92	4	2	9/9	Harry Hood	***
7/27/92	10	1	1/7	***	All Things Rec
8/1/92	4	1	1/7	***	Foam
8/20/92	7	1	1/6	***	Foam
11/22/92	12	2	10/10	Faht	***
11/28/92	4	2	12/12	Harpua	***
12/2/92	3	E	1/2	***	Rocky Top
12/5/92	3	1	12/12	Uncle Pen	***
12/10/92	4	1	1/11	***	Llama
12/12/92	2	2	10/10	The Squirming Coil	***
12/28/92	1	2	8/10	Rift	Sweet Adeline
2/6/93	7	1	1/11	***	Foam
2/9/93	2	1	10/10	Maze	***
2/12/93	3	1	1/11	***	Maze
2/13/93	1	1	10/10	Maze	***
2/17/93	2	1	11/11	Maze	***
2/20/93	3	1	1/11	***	Foam
2/23/93	1	1	1/11	***	My Friend My
2/25/93	1	2	10/11	If I Only Had a Brai	BBFCFM
2/27/93	2	1	1/10	***	Rift
3/2/93	1	E	1/2	***	Tweezer Repri
3/6/93	1	3	9/10	Maze	Runaway Jim
3/8/93	1	1	1/12	***	Rift
3/12/93	2	2	11/11	Harry Hood	***
3/14/93	2	E	3/3	Sweet Adeline	***
3/17/93	2	2	12/12	The Great Gig in the	***
3/19/93	2	2	10/10	Love You	***
3/22/93	2	2	1/13	***	It's Ice
3/25/93	2	2	13/13	Weekapaug Groove	***
3/27/93	2	2	14/14	Poor Heart	***
3/30/93	2	1	4/11	All Things Recnsrd	My Friend My
4/2/93	3	1	9/9	Maze	***
4/9/93	3	E	2/2	Sweet Adeline	***
4/12/93	2	2	1/11	***	Tube
4/14/93	1	1	13/13	I Didn't Know	***
4/17/93	2	1	9/10	All Things Recnsrd	Run Like Antel
4/20/93	2	2	12/12	Whipping Post	***
4/22/93	2	1	10/10	Rift	***
4/23/93	1	2	1/12	***	Maze
4/25/93	2	1	11/11	I Didn't Know	***
4/27/93	1	2	1/10	***	My Friend My
4/30/93	2	2	10/10	You Enjoy Myself	***
5/2/93	2	1	11/11	I Didn't Know	***
5/5/93	1	1	10/10	Maze	***
5/7/93	2	E	2/2	Amazing Grace	***
5/30/93	3	1	13/13	Llama	***
7/16/93	2	1	2/10	Daniel	My Friend My
7/18/93	2	2	10/10	Purple Rain	***
7/22/93	2	1	11/11	Stash	***
7/24/93	2	E	1/2	***	Freebird
7/30/93	5	2	8/10	My Friend My Friend	The Squirmin
8/3/93	2	2	9/9	Purple Rain	***
8/12/93	6	2	9/10	Big Ball Jam	Possum
8/14/93	2	2	13/13	Purple Rain	***
8/24/93	6	1	11/11	Maze	***
8/26/93	2	1	9/9	Harry Hood	***
12/28/93	2	E	2/2	Memories	***
12/31/93	3	E	1/2	***	Amazing Grce
4/5/94	2	E	2/2	Nellie Kane	***
4/10/94	4	E	2/2	Bouncing	***
4/13/94	2	1	8/8	Divided Sky	***
4/17/94	4	2	9/9	Contact	***
4/23/94	5	2	10/10	Who By Fire	***
4/28/94	3	E	1/1	***	***
5/2/94	3	2	4/9	Reba	The Lizards
5/4/94	3	2	2/9	Maze	Uncle Pen
5/8/94	2	E	2/2	Sweet Adeline	***
5/19/94	7	2	10/10	Harry Hood	***
5/27/94	7	1	9/9	Harry Hood	***
5/29/94	2	E	2/3	Wilson	Rocky Top
6/9/94	1	2	10/10	Weekapaug Groove	***
6/13/94	3	E	1/1	***	***
6/16/94	2	2	11/11	Purple Rain	***
6/19/94	3	1	9/9	Stash	***
6/22/94	2	1	9/9	Stash	***
6/25/94	3	2	9/9	Harry Hood	***
6/29/94	2	1	11/11	I Didn't Know	***
7/2/94	3	1	1/9	***	Divided Sky
7/5/94	2	2	11/11	Amazing Grace	***
7/8/94	2	2	11/11	Julius	***
7/10/94	2	E	1/2	***	Rocky Top
7/15/94	3	1	8/8	Split Open and Melt	***
7/16/94	1	1	1/11	***	Down with Dis
10/7/94	1	2	9/9	Guyute	***
10/10/94	3	2	1/9	***	Maze
10/15/94	4	1	8/8	Down with Disease	***
10/20/94	3	1	11/11	Guyute	***
10/25/94	4	E	2/2	Foreplay/Long Time	***
10/31/94	5	1	10/10	Reba	***
11/4/94	3	2	8/9	Ya Mar	Slave
11/12/94	1	2	12/12	Harry Hood	***
11/14/94	2	E	1/1	***	***
11/17/94	2	2	8/8	Slave	***
11/19/94	2	1	1/11	***	Down with Dis
11/25/94	4	1	8/8	Julius	***
12/1/94	4	2	10/10	Harry Hood	***
12/3/94	2	E	1/1	***	***
12/4/94	2	2	8/8	Stash	***
12/6/94	2	2	8/8	David Bowie	***
12/31/94	6	1	1/8	***	NICU
6/13/95	6	2	7/7	Harry Hood	***
6/24/95	9	2	9/9	Sweet Adeline	***
6/30/95	5	E	2/2	Cracklin' Rosie	***
10/22/95	22	2	1/11	***	Possum
12/2/95	24	2	7/9	A Day in the Life	The Squirmin
12/29/95	13	E	1/1	***	***
7/15/96	14	E	1/1	***	***
7/21/96	4	1	1/14	***	Guelah Pa-pyrus
7/24/96	3	1	5/5	You Enjoy Myself	***
8/2/96	2	1	8/11	Theme From the Botto	Tweezer
8/7/96	4	E	2/2	Bouncing	***
8/12/96	2	2	8/9	Hello My Baby	Possum
8/17/96	4	2	7/8	Run an Antelope	Slave
10/17/96	2	E	1/1	***	***
11/8/96	15	1	8/9	Reba	Run Like Antel
11/13/96	3	2	7/7	Theme From the Botto	***
2/17/97	23	1	10/10	Bathtub Gin	***
8/13/97	46	2	8/9	Also Sprach	Frankenstein
12/6/97	19	1	1/9	***	Run Like Antel
12/29/97	7	1	2/9	NICU	Crossroads
7/6/98	12	1	9/9	Maze	***
7/24/98	10	1	7/8	Taste	Loving Cup
7/29/98	4	E	2/3	Waste	Bittersweet Motel
8/11/98	9	E	2/2	Wilson	***
10/30/98	9	2	7/7	Prince Caspian	***
11/14/98	10	2	5/9	Guyute	Sexual Healing
11/19/98	3	1	9/9	Ghost	***
11/25/98	4	2	2/8	Also Sprach	Drowned
11/27/98	1	E	2/3	Wading In Velvet Sea	Wipeout
12/28/98	3	1	9/10	Tube	Good Time Ba
6/30/99	4	1	8/8	Limb by Limb	***
7/10/99	7	1	8/8	Bathtub Gin	***
7/16/99	4	2	8/8	Loving Cup	***
7/21/99	4	2	6/6	Weekapaug Groove	***
7/31/99	7	1	2/8	My Friend My Friend	Back on the Train
9/9/99	2	E	2/3	Sample in a Jar	Tweezer Repri
9/21/99	9	1	9/9	Theme From the Botto	***
10/7/99	11	2	8/9	Prince Caspian	Weekapaug Gr
12/8/99	9	E	1/2	***	Tweezer Repri
12/13/99	4	2	7/8	Limb by Limb	Slave
12/30/99	5	2	6/10	Meat	Wolfman's Brother
5/22/00	3	E	2/2	Bug	***
6/9/00	2	1	5/9	Poor Heart	Funky Bitch
6/16/00	6	1	5/10	First Tube	Heavy Things
6/22/00	1	1	4/9	Beauty of my Dreams	Limb by Limb
6/30/00	6	1	8/10	Guyute	Tweezer Repri
7/6/00	4	1	11/12	Prince Caspian	You Enjoy My
7/14/00	6	2	11/11	Taste	***
9/8/00	2	1	12/12	Taste	***
9/15/00	5	1	7/8	Run Like an Antelope	Bittersweet Motel
10/6/00	14	2	8/10	Sand	Brian and Robert

Has not been played in the last 1 show.

Good Time Ba

DATE	GAP	SET	POS.	SONG BEFORE	SONG AFTER
2/13/87	17	1	9/14	Sanity	Wilson
3/6/87	2	1	2/6	Funky Bitch	Corrine Corrina
4/29/87	3	3	3/14	Fluffhead	Anarchy
8/9/87	3	1	8/11	Timber (Jerry)	AC/DC Bag
8/10/87	1	1	7/7	Divided Sky	***
9/21/87	3	2	3/15	The Birthday Dub	Rocky Top
9/27/87	1	1	8/9	Phase Dance	Skin It Back
11/18/87	3	1	12/12	Alumni Blues	***
1/27/88	2	1	9/9	Take the A-Train	***
2/7/88	1	3	8/8	Ballad - Curtis Loew	***
2/26/88	3	1	10/13	Phase Dance	Fluffhead
4/2/88	5	1	2/2	Fire	***
5/15/88	1	3	5/11	Suzy Greenberg	Fluffhead
5/21/88	1	2	9/9	Bike	***
6/15/88	2	2	7/9	Take the A-Train	Whipping Post
6/19/88	1	2	1/2	***	Cities
6/21/88	2	2	7/10	Jesus Just Left	Contact
7/12/88	3	1	4/8	Sneakin' Sally	Happy Birth-day
7/23/88	1	3	7/7	Ballad - Curtis Loew	***
9/8/88	7	2	6/8	Cities	On Your Way Down
9/13/88	2	1	8/8	Peaches en Regalia	***
9/24/88	2	3	1/4	***	Fluffhead
10/31/88	2	1	1/12	***	You Enjoy My
11/3/88	1	1	7/7	Alumni Blues	***
11/5/88	1	2	11/11	I Didn't Know	***

DATE	GAP	SET	POS.	SONG BEFORE	SONG AFTER
12/2/88	2	2	2/8	I Didn't Know	Alumni Blues
12/10/88	1	2	7/7	Possum	***
1/26/89	3	1	10/10	Fee	***
2/6/89	1	3	1/9	***	Walk Away
3/3/89	6	1	11/11	Alumni Blues	***
3/4/89	1	1	8/8	Golgi Apparatus	***
3/14/89	2	3	7/7	You Enjoy Myself	***
5/1/89	7	1	9/9	Golgi Apparatus	***
5/5/89	1	2	3/4	Take the A-Train	McGrupp
5/20/89	5	E	1/1	***	***
5/27/89	3	1	11/11	Bathtub Gin	***
6/23/89	2	E	2/2	Contact	***
8/23/89	4	2	8/8	Foam	***
9/21/89	4	E	1/1	***	***
10/6/89	2	E	1/1	***	***
10/7/89	1	1	11/11	Alumni Blues	***
10/14/89	3	1	11/11	Makisupa Policeman	***
10/22/89	3	1	14/14	I Didn't Know	***
10/28/89	2	1	5/9	Highway to Hell	Dinner and a
11/2/89	2	1	11/11	Esther	***
11/9/89	2	1	9/9	Take the A-Train	***
12/1/89	6	1	9/9	Harry Hood	***
12/15/89	5	1	10/10	You Enjoy Myself	***
2/23/90	16	E	3/3	I Didn't Know	***
3/8/90	7	E	2/2	Contact	***
3/17/90	4	E	1/1	***	***
3/28/90	1	1	12/12	You Enjoy Myself	***
4/4/90	1	2	8/8	I Didn't Know	***
4/6/90	2	2	10/10	Alumni Blues	***
4/12/90	4	1	11/11	Divided Sky	***
5/10/90	15	2	8/8	AC/DC Bag	***
5/11/90	1	2	7/7	Love You	***
5/19/90	3	2	10/10	Jesus Just Left	***
5/24/90	2	E	1/1	***	***
5/30/90	1	1	14/14	Weekapaug Groove	***
5/31/90	1	E	1/1	***	***
6/2/90	2	1	9/9	Contact	***
6/5/90	1	2	10/10	Ballad - Curtis Loew	***
6/7/90	1	1	9/9	The Lizards	***
6/9/90	2	2	14/14	Harpua	***
6/16/90	1	E	3/3	BBFCFM	***
10/5/90	12	E	1/1	***	***
10/7/90	2	2	7/8	The Lizards	Golgi Apparat
10/12/90	2	E	2/2	Carolina	***
10/19/90	1	1	15/15	Suzy Greenberg	***
10/30/90	1	3	3/5	The Lizards	Contact
11/3/90	3	1	11/11	You Enjoy Myself	***
11/17/90	5	2	12/12	Donna Lee	***
11/24/90	1	2	9/12	Love You	BBFCFM
2/26/91	21	E	2/2	Love You	***
3/9/91	6	E	1/3	***	Fee
3/29/91	8	E	3/3	Tweezer Reprise	***
4/5/91	5	2	3/3	My Sweet One	***
4/12/91	3	2	10/10	My Sweet One	***
4/16/91	2	E	2/2	If I Only Had a Brai	***
4/27/91	7	E	2/2	Bouncing	***
5/16/91	8	2	9/9	The Lizards	***
9/30/91	24	E	1/1	***	***
10/19/91	12	E	1/1	***	***
11/14/91	15	E	2/3	Bouncing	You Enjoy My
3/14/92	20	E	2/2	Sleeping Monkey	***
4/1/92	13	E	2/2	Lawn Boy	***
5/1/92	21	E	2/3	Lawn Boy	Rocky Top
5/6/92	4	E	2/2	Carolina	***
5/17/92	9	E	2/2	Lawn Boy	***
6/27/92	6	E	2/2	I Didn't Know	***
7/31/92	21	1	6/6	You Enjoy Myself	***
11/20/92	18	E	2/2	Sweet Adeline	***
12/1/92	8	E	1/1	***	***
12/5/92	4	E	2/2	Memories	***
12/11/92	5	E	2/2	Contact	***
12/31/92	6	2	10/10	Glide	***
2/4/93	2	E	2/2	Amazing Grace	***
2/12/93	7	E	2/2	Amazing Grace	***
2/17/93	3	E	2/2	Carolina	***
2/21/93	4	E	2/4	Sweet Adeline	Paul and Silas

DATE	GAP	SET	POS.	SONG BEFORE	SONG AFTER
2/25/93	3	E	2/2	Amazing Grace	***
3/5/93	5	E	1/1	***	***
3/18/93	9	E	1/1	***	***
3/24/93	4	2	12/12	Terrapin	***
4/3/93	9	E	1/1	***	***
4/10/93	3	E	2/2	Amazing Grace	***
4/24/93	10	E	2/2	Amazing Grace	***
5/29/93	12	E	1/1	***	***
7/17/93	4	2	12/12	Rift	***
7/24/93	5	2	12/12	Daniel	***
7/29/93	4	2	9/9	Daniel	***
8/8/93	7	2	11/11	Daniel	***
8/16/93	7	2	10/10	Take the A-Train	***
8/25/93	5	2	8/8	The Squirming Coil	***
12/30/93	5	E	2/2	Rocky Top	***
4/13/94	9	E	2/2	Sweet Adeline	***
4/18/94	5	E	1/1	***	***
4/24/94	5	2	9/9	Contact	***
4/28/94	2	1	11/11	Julius	***
5/8/94	8	2	9/9	Halley's Comet	***
5/13/94	3	2	9/9	Purple Rain	***
5/26/94	10	E	1/1	***	***
6/16/94	9	E	3/3	Amazing Grace	***
7/5/94	15	E	1/1	***	***
10/12/94	13	E	1/1	***	***
10/23/94	9	2	9/9	Fee	***
11/19/94	16	2	7/7	Amazing Grace	***
11/25/94	4	E	1/1	***	***
12/4/94	7	2	7/7	Purple Rain	***
12/10/94	5	E	2/2	Chalk Dust Reprise	***
12/29/94	2	2	7/7	Cracklin' Rosie	***
6/8/95	5	E	1/1	***	***
6/23/95	11	2	7/7	Llama	***
9/30/95	13	E	2/2	Amazing Grace	***
10/21/95	14	1	11/12	Acoustic Army	Tweezer Repri
11/11/95	10	E	2/2	Acoustic Army	***
11/21/95	7	E	1/1	***	***
12/8/95	12	1	9/9	Prince Caspian	***
12/15/95	5	E	1/2	***	Tweezer Repri
7/10/96	14	1	7/7	Hello My Baby	***
10/29/96	34	E	1/1	***	***
11/13/96	9	E	1/1	***	***
11/23/96	7	E	1/1	***	***
12/6/96	8	2	9/9	Sweet Adeline	***
12/30/96	3	1	9/9	Theme From the Botto	***
2/23/97	10	2	9/9	Why Don't We Do It i	***
7/5/97	21	1	13/13	Character Zero	***
8/10/97	18	2	2/5	Cities	Rotation Jam
12/13/97	26	1	9/9	Tube	***
12/29/97	2	E	1/1	***	***
7/10/98	15	2	8/8	Sample in a Jar	***
7/26/98	9	1	7/7	Funky Bitch	***
11/13/98	29	E	1/1	***	***
11/25/98	8	1	9/9	Driver	***
12/28/98	4	1	10/10	Golgi Apparatus	***
12/30/99	66	2	10/10	Harry Hood	***
6/13/00	8	E	2/2	Brian and Robert	***
7/4/00	13	E	2/2	Lawn Boy	***
9/11/00	11	E	1/1	***	***

Has not been played in the last 18 shows.

Got My Mojo Workin'

DATE	GAP	SET	POS.	SONG BEFORE	SONG AFTER
2/25/97	872	1	5/9	Li'l Red Rooster	Stash

Has not been played in the last 247 shows.

Gotta Jibboo

DATE	GAP	SET	POS.	SONG BEFORE	SONG AFTER
9/10/99	1032	2	5/9	Fee	I Saw it Again
9/19/99	7	1	4/8	First Tube	Heavy Things
9/22/99	2	2	1/8	***	Ghost
9/29/99	5	2	1/12	***	Also Sprach
10/7/99	5	1	8/9	When Circus Comes	Fluffhead
10/10/99	3	1	2/7	Farmhouse	Heavy Things
12/2/99	1	2	2/6	Boogie On Reggae	Bathtub Gin
12/5/99	3	1	2/10	Carini	Back on the Train

DATE	GAP	SET	POS.	SONG BEFORE	SONG AFTER
12/10/99	3	2	1/7	***	The Wedge
12/13/99	3	2	1/8	***	NICU
12/17/99	3	1	4/8	Sparkle	Punch You in
12/30/99	2	2	8/10	Wolfman's Brother	Harry Hood
5/21/00	2	2	1/8	***	Down with Dis
5/23/00	2	1	10/12	Back on the Train	Taste
6/9/00	1	2	5/7	The Squirming Coil	Meatstick
6/13/00	3	2	1/9	***	Wolfman's Brother
6/15/00	2	E	1/1	***	***
6/22/00	2	2	1/10	***	Also Sprach
6/25/00	3	2	1/7	***	Fast Enough For You
7/1/00	4	2	1/10	***	Bug
7/4/00	2	2	1/5	***	I Saw It Again
7/7/00	2	2	2/7	Ghost	Split Open and Sand
7/10/00	2	2	1/7	***	Sand
7/14/00	3	2	3/11	Timber (Jerry)	Boogie On Reggae
9/9/00	3	2	1/7	***	The Curtain
9/15/00	4	1	2/8	First Tube	Corrine Corrina
9/20/00	3	1	3/9	Wolfman's Brother	Mike's Song
9/25/00	4	2	1/7	***	Mike's Song
10/4/00	5	2	4/7	Sample in a Jar	Bug

Has not been played in the last 3 shows.

Grind

DATE	GAP	SET	POS.	SONG BEFORE	SONG AFTER
12/30/98	1005	E	1/2	***	Possum

Has not been played in the last 114 shows.

Guelah Papyrus

DATE	GAP	SET	POS.	SONG BEFORE	SONG AFTER
2/1/91	242	1	6/10	Magilla	Runaway Jim
2/2/91	1	1	3/9	Suzy Greenberg	Dinner and a
2/3/91	1	1	2/10	Runaway Jim	My Sweet One
2/7/91	1	2	7/14	Tweezer Reprise	Uncle Pen
2/8/91	1	1	10/11	Runaway Jim	David Bowie
2/9/91	1	1	8/12	Foam	My Sweet One
2/15/91	2	2	4/10	Ya Mar	My Sweet One
2/16/91	1	2	5/9	Runaway Jim	Fluffhead
2/19/91	1	2	5/15	Weekapaug Groove	The Landlady
2/20/91	1	2	3/3	Divided Sky	***
2/21/91	1	2	6/9	Stash	Uncle Pen
2/26/91	1	1	5/11	Llama	My Sweet One
2/28/91	2	2	4/7	Llama	Divided Sky
3/1/91	1	2	5/11	Llama	Runaway Jim
3/9/91	3	2	7/13	Runaway Jim	David Bowie
3/13/91	1	2	5/12	My Sweet One	Runaway Jim
3/16/91	2	2	3/10	Divided Sky	My Sweet One
3/22/91	2	2	8/13	Runaway Jim	Terrapin
3/28/91	2	1	7/14	You Enjoy Myself	My Sweet One
3/31/91	2	2	5/7	Stash	Bouncing
4/4/91	3	2	3/10	Runaway Jim	David Bowie
4/12/91	4	1	4/9	Divided Sky	The Oh Kee Pa
4/22/91	7	1	7/9	Llama	The Oh Kee Pa
5/4/91	5	1	7/11	Split Open and Melt	Fluffhead
5/9/91	1	1	4/10	Paul and Silas	Reba
5/17/91	5	2	2/9	Possum	Rocky Top
5/18/91	1	2	7/10	My Sweet One	David Bowie
7/13/91	4	2	2/9	Chalk Dust Torture	Divided Sky
7/14/91	1	1	5/11	Golgi Apparatus	My Sweet One
7/18/91	2	1	4/11	Runaway Jim	Suzy Greenber
7/21/91	3	1	3/11	Divided Sky	Poor Heart
7/24/91	2	2	2/10	Possum	David Bowie
8/3/91	4	1	4/11	Runaway Jim	Llama
9/26/91	2	1	7/10	My Sweet One	The Lizards
9/28/91	2	2	2/12	Llama	Sparkle
10/2/91	3	2	4/9	My Sweet One	Runaway Jim
10/4/91	2	1	6/10	Divided Sky	Sparkle
10/11/91	3	1	4/10	Divided Sky	Chalk Dust Tor
10/12/91	1	1	8/9	Divided Sky	You Enjoy My
10/15/91	2	2	4/12	Runaway Jim	Poor Heart
10/18/91	2	3	2/12	Uncle Pen	Dinner and a
10/27/91	4	1	5/10	Buried Alive	Fluffhead
11/2/91	5	2	7/11	Sparkle	Walk Away

DATE	GAP	SET	POS.	SONG BEFORE	SONG AFTER
11/8/91	2	1	7/11	Divided Sky	The Mango Song
11/12/91	3	2	8/13	Weekapaug Groove	Chalk Dust Tor
11/15/91	3	1	8/12	My Sweet One	Rhombus Narration
11/21/91	4	1	4/12	Poor Heart	Reba
11/23/91	2	1	5/11	Runaway Jim	Sparkle
11/30/91	2	1	10/11	Paul and Silas	You Enjoy My
12/6/91	3	1	8/9	The Landlady	I Didn't Know
12/31/91	2	1	6/10	The Lizards	Divided Sky
3/6/92	1	1	7/11	Divided Sky	Maze
3/13/92	4	1	4/12	Poor Heart	Maze
3/17/92	2	1	8/11	Divided Sky	Rift
3/24/92	5	2	5/13	Weekapaug Groove	The Mango Song
3/27/92	3	1	6/10	Divided Sky	Maze
3/30/92	2	1	4/11	Foam	Sparkle
4/3/92	2	1	5/11	Rift	Sparkle
4/5/92	2	1	2/11	Llama	Divided Sky
4/6/92	1	1	8/10	Chalk Dust Torture	The Squirmin
4/8/92	2	1	4/11	Foam	Llama
4/12/92	1	1	3/11	Poor Heart	Divided Sky
4/15/92	2	1	4/11	Foam	Sparkle
4/18/92	3	1	3/11	Divided Sky	Poor Heart
4/21/92	2	1	5/11	Rift	Possum
4/22/92	1	1	5/10	Sparkle	Divided Sky
4/23/92	1	1	5/11	Uncle Pen	The Squirmin
4/29/92	3	1	6/10	Runaway Jim	Rift
5/1/92	2	1	8/12	Divided Sky	It's Ice
5/3/92	2	2	5/14	Fluffhead	Mike's Song
5/5/92	1	1	6/11	Rift	Divided Sky
5/7/92	2	1	10/11	Rift	Possum
5/9/92	2	1	5/11	Split Open and Melt	Rift
5/12/92	2	2	4/9	You Enjoy Myself	Chalk Dust Tor
5/17/92	4	2	3/11	Possum	The Squirmin
5/18/92	1	1	5/10	Divided Sky	Foam
6/24/92	4	1	5/9	Uncle Pen	I Didn't Know
6/30/92	2	1	3/6	Divided Sky	Possum
7/9/92	2	1	8/12	Runaway Jim	David Bowie
7/14/92	4	1	3/12	Rift	Maze
7/16/92	2	1	9/10	Rift	David Bowie
8/2/92	14	1	2/8	Chalk Dust Torture	Rift
8/15/92	3	1	3/5	Sparkle	Maze
8/19/92	2	1	4/7	Runaway Jim	You Enjoy My
11/21/92	12	2	9/13	Uncle Pen	The Squirmin
11/23/92	2	1	6/11	Rift	Divided Sky
11/30/92	4	2	3/10	Runaway Jim	Maze
12/3/92	3	2	2/13	Rift	Fluffhead
12/5/92	2	1	5/12	Rift	Split Open and
12/8/92	2	1	7/11	Uncle Pen	Divided Sky
12/11/92	2	1	7/11	Chalk Dust Torture	Sparkle
12/12/92	1	2	6/10	Rift	You Enjoy My
12/29/92	3	1	3/12	Runaway Jim	Llama
2/3/93	3	1	10/11	Poor Heart	David Bowie
2/5/93	2	1	2/11	Llama	Rift
2/10/93	4	1	3/10	Foam	Reba
2/12/93	3	1	3/11	Maze	Sparkle
2/15/93	2	1	4/12	Sparkle	Divided Sky
2/15/93	0	1	10/12	Stash	I Didn't Know
2/18/93	2	1	3/10	Chalk Dust Torture	Poor Heart
2/22/93	4	1	2/10	Rift	Poor Heart
2/27/93	4	1	3/10	Rift	Maze
3/3/93	2	1	5/10	Maze	Paul and Silas
3/5/93	1	2	3/11	Chalk Dust Torture	Uncle Pen
3/8/93	2	1	3/12	Rift	The Oh Kee Pa
3/12/93	2	1	5/11	Possum	Rift
3/14/93	2	1	3/11	Foam	Sparkle
3/18/93	3	1	2/11	Chalk Dust Torture	Rift
3/22/93	2	1	2/10	Chalk Dust Torture	Uncle Pen
3/25/93	2	1	2/11	Chalk Dust Torture	It's Ice
3/27/93	2	1	2/10	Llama	Rift
4/1/93	4	1	2/10	Llama	Rift
4/3/93	2	1	3/10	Rift	Sparkle
4/9/93	2	1	3/11	Sparkle	Stash
4/16/93	4	1	2/10	Chalk Dust Torture	Sparkle
4/18/93	2	1	2/10	Rift	Split Open and

DATE	GAP	SET	POS.	SONG BEFORE	SONG AFTER
4/21/93	2	1	4/11	Foam	Maze
4/23/93	2	1	8/10	Divided Sky	Lawn Boy
4/24/93	1	1	2/11	Chalk Dust Torture	Poor Heart
4/27/93	2	1	7/10	Stash	It's Ice
5/1/93	3	1	3/10	Foam	Split Open and
5/5/93	3	1	2/10	Rift	Foam
5/8/93	3	1	2/12	Chalk Dust Torture	Rift
5/30/93	2	1	3/13	Maze	Poor Heart
7/18/93	4	1	4/9	Foam	Maze
7/24/93	4	1	5/10	Divided Sky	Rift
8/2/93	7	1	2/12	Chalk Dust Torture	Poor Heart
8/6/93	2	2	3/12	Tweezer	The Squirmin
8/12/93	5	1	4/10	Chalk Dust Torture	Nellie Kane
8/14/93	2	1	2/11	Chalk Dust Torture	Divided Sky
8/17/93	3	1	3/9	Llama	Divided Sky
8/21/93	2	1	4/10	Foam	Rift
8/26/93	3	1	2/9	Runaway Jim	Reba
12/31/93	5	1	2/8	Llama	Stash
4/6/94	3	1	2/9	Llama	Poor Heart
4/15/94	7	1	2/9	Llama	Paul and Silas
5/3/94	14	1	2/9	Rift	Maze
5/21/94	13	1	3/9	Foam	Down with Dis
5/29/94	7	1	2/8	Divided Sky	Halley's Comet
6/9/94	1	1	2/9	Llama	Rift
6/14/94	4	1	2/14	Llama	Sweet Adeline
6/14/94	0	1	5/14	Digital Delay Loop J	Rift
6/22/94	6	1	2/9	Llama	Rift
6/30/94	6	1	4/9	Rift	Split Open and
7/2/94	2	1	3/9	Divided Sky	Fast Enough for You
7/9/94	5	1	5/10	Maze	Scent of a Mul
10/7/94	6	1	6/9	Divided Sky	Stash
10/12/94	4	1	7/9	The Lizards	Julius
10/20/94	6	1	4/11	Poor Heart	Split Open and
10/28/94	7	1	3/10	Llama	Scent of a Mul
11/14/94	8	1	3/9	Scent of a Mule	Split Open and
11/25/94	8	1	2/8	Llama	Reba
12/3/94	6	1	3/7	Divided Sky	Scent of a Mul
6/8/95	13	1	4/9	Runaway Jim	Mound
6/22/95	10	1	5/10	Divided Sky	It's Ice
10/3/95	16	1	2/11	Maze	Foam
10/21/95	12	1	3/12	Chalk Dust Torture	Reba
11/12/95	11	1	4/10	Bouncing	Reba
12/2/95	14	1	4/10	Mound	Reba
7/21/96	31	1	2/14	Golgi Apparatus	Rift
8/2/96	5	1	4/11	Down with Disease	Poor Heart
8/5/96	2	1	3/9	Poor Heart	Divided Sky
10/18/96	11	1	2/10	Runaway Jim	The Old Home
10/25/96	5	1	7/10	Mound	I Didn't Know
10/29/96	3	1	2/10	Chalk Dust Torture	Cars Trucks Buses
11/7/96	5	1	4/10	Rift	Stash
11/11/96	3	1	2/9	Chalk Dust Torture	Cars Trucks Buses
11/18/96	5	1	6/10	Billy Breathes	Chalk Dust Tor
11/23/96	3	1	2/9	Chalk Dust Torture	Cars Trucks Buses
12/29/96	10	1	5/10	Taste	Train Song
2/16/97	5	1	5/10	Crosseyed and Painle	Ginseng Sullivan
6/24/97	20	1	5/12	Vultures	Runaway Jim
8/11/97	26	1	5/8	Guyute	Limb by Limb
10/30/97	71	1	8/10	Run Like An Antelope	The Lizards
11/20/98	14	1	5/13	Funky Bitch	Rift
7/17/99	23	1	4/10	Birds of a Feather	My Sweet One
9/22/99	22	1	3/10	Chalk Dust Torture	Axilla
7/3/00	48	1	2/10	Down with Disease	My Mind's Got A Mind
9/18/00	17	1	5/10	Maze	My Mind's Got A Mind

Has not been played in the last 13 shows.

Gumbo

DATE	GAP	SET	POS.	SONG BEFORE	SONG AFTER
9/28/90	214	2	3/6	Esther	Dinner and a
9/29/90	1	2	3/8	Tweezer	Uncle Pen

DATE	GAP	SET	POS.	SONG BEFORE	SONG AFTER
10/1/90	1	1	8/11	Fee	Golgi Apparat
11/30/90	19	2	6/10	The Lizards	Divided Sky
7/12/91	63	2	6/14	My Sweet One	Mike's Song
7/14/91	2	4	4/10	Divided Sky	Dinner and a
7/19/91	3	1	9/10	You Enjoy Myself	Touch Me
7/20/91	1	1	9/10	Bathtub Gin	David Bowie
7/21/91	1	E	1/4	***	Touch Me
7/23/91	2	1	9/10	Dinner and a Movie	Touch Me
7/25/91	2	2	8/13	The Lizards	Touch Me
4/16/93	223	E	1/2	***	Amazing Grce
4/21/93	4	2	11/11	Weekapaug Groove	***
6/16/94	103	1	6/10	Maze	The Curtain
6/22/94	5	1	4/9	Rift	Maze
6/30/94	6	1	2/9	Down with Disease	Rift
7/9/94	7	1	3/10	Foam	Maze
7/15/94	4	1	4/8	Divided Sky	Foam
10/13/94	7	1	2/9	Llama	All Things Rec
10/22/94	7	1	3/8	Divided Sky	Axilla (Part II)
12/2/94	26	2	6/8	The Landlady	Caravan
12/3/94	1	2	4/10	Buried Alive	Slave
6/14/95	17	1	2/12	Don't You Wanna Go	NICU
6/28/95	11	2	6/10	Tweezer	Sparkle
7/2/95	4	1	3/10	Divided Sky	The Curtain
10/7/95	10	1	2/9	Julius	Fog that Surrounds
10/20/95	8	2	5/10	Maze	While My Guitar Gent
10/29/95	7	1	10/12	NICU	Slave
11/14/95	6	2	2/11	Maze	Stash
12/4/95	14	1	2/11	Julius	Divided Sky
12/9/95	2	3	3/8	Wilson	You Enjoy My
12/28/95	7	1	2/9	Split Open and Melt	The Curtain
7/23/96	21	1	4/9	Theme From the Botto	Scent of a Mul
8/7/96	7	1	5/10	Ya Mar	Taste
8/14/96	4	1	8/10	The Mango Song	Stash
10/19/96	6	1	6/9	Llama	Down with Dis
11/11/96	15	2	3/11	Divided Sky	The Curtain
11/16/96	4	1	4/11	Guyute	Rift
12/2/96	10	1	7/8	Theme From the Botto	Julius
12/30/96	5	1	4/9	Llama	Reba
2/20/97	7	1	7/10	Taste	When Circus Comes
7/29/97	34	1	3/9	Beauty of My Dreams	Dirt
8/8/97	6	1	2/7	Cars Trucks Buses	The Lizards
8/13/97	4	1	5/11	Water in the Sky	The Horse
11/14/97	5	1	2/8	Runaway Jim	Maze
11/26/97	7	1	3/10	Sparkle	My Soul
12/3/97	5	1	5/7	The Old Home Place	Also Sprach
7/17/98	27	1	3/7	Ya Mar	Divided Sky
8/3/98	12	2	1/7	***	Axilla
8/15/98	7	2	3/9	Reba	Sanity
10/15/98	3	1	4/8	Wolfman's Brother	David Bowie
11/11/98	12	1	2/8	Punch You in the Eye	If You Need a Fool
11/19/98	5	2	5/8	Frankie Says	Chalk Dust Tor
11/28/98	6	1	1/8	***	Tube
7/3/99	8	1	2/11	Chalk Dust Torture	Sparkle
7/26/99	17	1	5/11	Sleep	NICU
9/14/99	9	2	3/5	AC/DC Bag	Down with Dis
10/1/99	12	2	5/9	Silent in the Mornin	Mountains in the Mis
12/13/99	17	1	3/6	Cars Trucks Buses	The Moma Dance
6/14/00	14	1	4/8	Cities	Llama
7/7/00	14	1	2/11	Chalk Dust Torture	Divided Sky
9/9/00	8	1	3/8	My Friend My Friend	Maze
9/27/00	12	2	2/7	Piper	Ghost

Has not been played in the last 7 shows.

Guy Forget

DATE	GAP	SET	POS.	SONG BEFORE	SONG AFTER
10/1/00	11152		3/7	Piper	When Circus Comes

Has not been played in the last 4 shows.

Guyute

DATE	GAP	SET	POS.	SONG BEFORE	SONG AFTER
10/7/94	662	1	8/9	Stash	Golgi Apparat
10/8/94	1	1	5/9	Down with Disease	Fee
10/10/94	2	1	7/11	Stash	The Old Home
10/14/94	3	2	4/10	Lifeboy	Chalk Dust Tor
10/18/94	3	1	8/10	It's Ice	Divided Sky
10/20/94	1	1	10/11	Julius	Golgi Apparat
10/26/94	5	1	5/10	Run Like an Antelope	Dog Faced Boy
11/2/94	5	1	5/8	Maze	Stash
11/12/94	3	1	5/8	Maze	Stash
11/19/94	6	1	3/11	Down with Disease	Axilla (Part II)
11/22/94	2	1	5/9	Foam	I Didn't Know
11/26/94	3	1	3/9	Possum	If I Could
11/28/94	1	1	5/9	Stash	Sparkle
12/1/94	2	1	5/8	Maze	I Didn't Know
12/3/94	2	1	6/7	Run Like an Antelope	Sample in a Ja
12/7/94	3	1	6/8	Split Open and Melt	Lifeboy
12/9/94	2	1	3/8	Foam	Sparkle
12/10/94	1	2	3/11	Maze	Also Sprach
12/29/94	2	2	1/7	***	Digital Delay Loop J
10/31/95	50	1	7/9	Free	Run Like Antel
11/10/95	2	1	8/9	Maze	Cavern
11/16/95	5	1	9/10	Timber (Jerry)	Funky Bitch
11/21/95	3	1	7/10	I'm Blue, Lonesome	My Friend My
11/28/95	4	1	7/9	Divided Sky	Hello My Baby
12/7/95	7	1	7/10	Slave	Bouncing
12/28/95	9	1	5/9	Julius	Horn
7/15/96	15	1	4/8	Fast Enough for You	Possum
8/4/96	10	1	3/9	Funky Bitch	Fee
11/7/96	25	1	7/10	Waste	Free
11/16/96	7	1	3/11	Down with Disease	Gumbo
12/4/96	11	1	8/11	Train Song	Character Zer
12/30/96	4	2	4/8	AC/DC Bag	Tweezer
2/17/97	5	1	5/10	My Soul	Timber (Jerry)
3/2/97	10	1	4/13	Sample in a Jar	My Soul
6/25/97	10	E	1/1	***	***
8/11/97	25	1	4/8	Water in the Sky	Guelah Papyrus
8/17/97	4	3	4/7	Weigh	Dirt
11/14/97	2	1	7/8	Funky Bitch	Run Like Antel
11/21/97	4	E	1/1	***	***
11/30/97	6	1	1/6	***	Funky Bitch
12/7/97	5	2	5/6	Reba	Possum
12/12/97	3	E	1/2	***	Run Like Antel
12/30/97	4	2	10/10	Sleeping Monkey	***
4/2/98	2	E	1/1	***	***
6/30/98	4	1	9/13	Roggae	Beauty of My Dreams
7/3/98	3	1	4/11	Sample in a Jar	Also Sprach
7/8/98	3	1	6/7	Frankenstein	Run Like Antel
7/15/98	3	1	4/13	The Moma Dance	Horn
7/19/98	3	1	4/8	Sample in a Jar	Ghost
7/25/98	4	1	6/7	Ya Mar	Julius
8/1/98	5	1	5/9	Weekapaug Groove	Fikus
8/8/98	5	1	4/8	Sneakin' Sally	Fikus
8/16/98	5	1	10/11	Birds of a Feather	Possum
10/18/98	4	1	8/12	The Old Home Place	Brian and Robert
11/4/98	5	1	3/9	Character Zero	Bathtub Gin
11/7/98	2	E	1/2	***	While My Guitar Gent
11/14/98	5	2	4/9	Piper	Golgi Apparat
11/18/98	2	1	5/9	My Soul	Lawn Boy
11/21/98	3	1	12/13	Wading In Velvet Sea	Bold as Love
11/25/98	2	E	2/3	Something	Freebird
11/28/98	2	1	4/8	Down with Disease	Albuquerque
12/29/98	3	1	8/10	Brian and Robert	My Soul
7/1/99	4	1	3/10	Billy Breathes	Wolfman's Brother
7/8/99	4	1	4/8	Jam	Dirt
7/12/99	3	2	6/6	The Lizards	***
7/16/99	3	2	4/6	Simple	Loving Cup
7/18/99	2	2	4/6	Meatstick	Axilla
7/24/99	4	1	1/9	***	Fluffhead
7/30a/99	3	1	2/7	Chalk Dust Torture	Wolfman's Brother
9/9/99	4	1	5/10	Horn	Chalk Dust Tor
9/11/99	2	1	8/9	Heavy Things	Free
9/17/99	4	1	2/11	Mozambique	Ghost
9/19/99	2	E	1/2	***	Character Zer
9/24/99	3	1	9/10	Back on the Train	Loving Cup
9/26/99	2	1	5/10	Dirt	Bouncing
10/3/99	5	1	12/12	Bouncing	***
10/9/99	4	1	3/8	Wilson	Ghost
12/4/99	4	1	4/7	Ya Mar	Tweezer
12/10/99	4	1	9/10	Birds of a Feather	Loving Cup
12/15/99	4	1	5/7	Wolfman's Brother	Train Song
12/31/99	5	1	13/14	Horn	After Midnight
5/21/00	1	2	8/8	Wading In Velvet Sea	***
6/10/00	4	1	5/5	Lawn Boy	***
6/24/00	8	E	1/4	***	The Inlaw Josie Wale
6/30/00	4	1	7/10	Ginseng Sullivan	Golgi Apparat
7/8/00	6	1	8/9	Llama	Run Like Antel
7/14/00	4	E	3/3	Driver	***
9/9/00	3	1	7/8	Roggae	Run Like Antel
9/17/00	5	1	1/9	***	Back on the Train
9/20/00	2	2	7/9	Sand	BBFCM
10/5/00	10	1	2/10	Chalk Dust Torture	Wolfman's Brother

Has not been played in the last 2 shows.

Gypsy Queen

DATE	GAP	SET	POS.	SONG BEFORE	SONG AFTER
8/7/96	817	2	2/10	Runaway Jim	Runaway Jim
3/2/97	59	1	7/13	Runaway Jim	Runaway Jim
6/24/97	9	1	7/12	Runaway Jim	Runaway Jim

Has not been played in the last 234 shows.

HYHU Jam

DATE	GAP	SET	POS.	SONG BEFORE	SONG AFTER
11/7/91	338	2	9/11	Take the A-Train	Love You
5/7/94	277	2	11/12	Purple Rain	Tweezer Repri

Has not been played in the last 504 shows.

Ha Ha Ha

DATE	GAP	SET	POS.	SONG BEFORE	SONG AFTER
5/16/95	712	1	2/12	Don't You Wanna Go	Spock's Brain
6/7/95	1	2	1/9	***	Maze
6/8/95	1	1	2/9	Don't You Wanna Go	Runaway Jim
6/15/95	5	2	2/8	My Sweet One	David Bowie
6/22/95	5	1	3/10	Scent of a Mule	Divided Sky
6/30/95	7	2	3/10	Possum	T.M.W.S.I.Y.
7/2/95	2	2	5/8	Tweezer	Sleeping Monkey
10/5/95	8	1	2/11	Chalk Dust Torture	Fog that Surrounds
10/20/95	10	1	3/10	Ya Mar	Divided Sky
11/16/95	15	2	5/9	Uncle Pen	Harry Hood
11/30/95	9	1	3/10	The Curtain	Julius
12/11/95	8	1	2/12	My Friend My Friend	Stash
12/15/95	3	1	5/10	Maze	Suspicious Minds
10/25/96	45	1	1/10	***	Taste
12/4/96	26	2	1/9	***	Mike's Song
2/26/97	16	2	3/11	Poor Heart	You Enjoy My
6/30/98	72	2	8/12	Ya Mar	Mike's Song
7/24/98	15	2	4/7	Scent of a Mule	Scent of a Mul
11/21/98	37	2	7/9	Free	Free
12/31/98	9	1	6/7	Ghost	Cavern
9/9/99	25	2	2/9	Birds of a Feather	Ghost
6/30/00	56	1	1/10	***	AC/DC Bag

Has not been played in the last 32 shows.

Halley's Comet

DATE	GAP	SET	POS.	SONG BEFORE	SONG AFTER
10/31/86	15	1	8/11	Sneakin' Sally	Back Porch Boogie Bl
4/29/87	7	2	5/7	Take the A-Train	Quinn the Eskimo
8/9/87	3	2	2/11	The Curtain With	The Sloth
10/31/87	8	1	5/11	Back Porch Boogie Bl	Light Up Or Leave Me
5/14/88	14	1	3/11	I Didn't Know	Light Up Or Leave Me
5/25/88	3	3	4/11	Ya Mar	La Grange
6/20/88	3	1	7/11	The Lizards	Wilson
10/29/88	17	2	1/10	***	Whipping Post
3/14/89	19	E	1/1	***	***
5/26/89	15	1	7/9	Sanity	The Sloth
8/17/89	5	3	5/8	Possum	Alumni Blues
3/14/93	400	2	1/11	***	David Bowie
3/27/93	10	2	2/14	Buried Alive	It's Ice
4/17/93	13	2	4/11	The Landlady	You Enjoy My
5/1/93	11	2	6/11	Big Ball Jam	Paul and Silas
8/6/93	25	2	9/12	You Enjoy Myself	Slave
8/24/93	13	E	1/3	***	Poor Heart
12/31/93	7	2	2/8	Tweezer	Poor Heart
4/29/94	21	1	1/12	***	You Enjoy My
5/8/94	7	2	8/9	You Enjoy Myself	Good Time Ba
5/19/94	7	1	1/10	***	Llama
5/29/94	9	1	3/8	Guelah Papyrus	Down with Dis
6/9/94	1	2	4/10	Julius	Scent of a Mul
6/24/94	12	2	3/13	Run Like an Antelope	The Curtain
10/15/94	24	2	3/11	Runaway Jim	Scent of a Mul
10/23/94	6	2	3/9	Bouncing	You Enjoy My
11/2/94	7	2	1/7	***	Tweezer
11/26/94	14	2	1/6	***	David Bowie
11/30/94	2	2	1/10	***	Run Like Antel
12/29/94	11	2	4/7	David Bowie	The Lizards
6/16/95	11	1	1/10	***	Down with Dis
6/20/95	3	2	1/9	***	Chalk Dust Tor
6/24/95	3	2	2/9	Also Sprach	David Bowie
7/2/95	7	E	1/2	***	Tweezer Repri
12/1/95	43	2	1/9	***	Mike's Song
12/14/95	9	2	6/10	Keyboard Cavalry	Jam
8/5/96	30	2	4/13	It's Ice	Somewhere Over The
8/16/96	7	1	7/8	Divided Sky	David Bowie
8/16/97	92	3	1/6	***	Cities
11/22/97	8	2	1/5	***	Tweezer
12/28/97	15	2	6/9	Scent of A Mule	Slave
4/3/98	5	E	2/3	Carini	Tweezer Repri
7/10/98	11	2	1/8	***	Roggae
7/20/98	5	E	2/2	Sexual Healing	***
8/3/98	10	1	2/8	Rhinoceros	I Didn't Know
8/15/98	7	E	1/3	***	Cavern
11/11/98	15	2	1/6	***	Simple
11/24/98	8	2	2/6	Ghost	Tweezer
7/13/99	18	1	3/9	The Curtain	Roses Are Free
9/28/99	29	E	1/2	***	Tweezer Repri
10/8/99	7	2	1/7	***	Tweezer
12/7/99	7	1	7/8	Nellie Kane	The Squirmin
12/15/99	6	2	6/7	Reba	Suzy Greenber
6/30/00	22	2	1/9	***	The Mango Song
9/18/00	19	2	4/4	McGrupp	***
9/23/00	3	1	4/6	Frankenstein	Fee
10/5/00	8	2	4/7	David Bowie	Walk Away

Has not been played in the last 2 shows.

Happiness Is a Warm Gun

DATE	GAP	SET	POS.	SONG BEFORE	SONG AFTER
10/31/94	681	2	9/30	While My Guitar Gent	Martha My Dear

Has not been played in the last 438 shows.

Happy Birthday

DATE	GAP	SET	POS.	SONG BEFORE	SONG AFTER
12/2/83	0	1	6/6	Roadhouse Blues	***
3/6/87	19	2	2/7	Freebird	Harry Hood
2/7/88	18	2	1/9	***	AC/DC Bag
5/21/88	12	2	6/9	Tela	Fluffhead
7/12/88	8	1	5/8	Good Times Bad Times	Peaches en Regalia
10/6/89	60	1	9/13	Dinner and a Movie	Harry Hood

DATE	GAP	SET	POS.	SONG BEFORE	SONG AFTER
10/7/89	1	2	4/9	Possum	The Lizards
2/10/90	34	2	5/10	Rocky Top	Donna Lee
6/16/90	54	3	2/13	La Grange	Ya Mar
5/17/91	88	1	8/17	Suzy Greenberg	T.M.W.S.I.Y.

Has not been played in the last 825 shows.

Harpua

DATE	GAP	SET	POS.	SONG BEFORE	SONG AFTER
8/9/87	25	2	10/11	Harry Hood	Suzy Greenber
8/21/87	2	2	2/12	Mike's Song	Bundle of Joy
8/21/87	0	2	4/12	Bundle of Joy	Golgi Apparat
8/29/87	1	1	11/13	Divided Sky	Bundle of Joy
8/29/87	0	1	13/13	Bundle of Joy	***
3/11/88	13	2	5/8	Ballad - Curtis Loew	AC/DC Bag
4/22/88	5	1	9/9	Harry Hood	***
5/15/88	2	2	11/11	Whipping Post	***
5/25/88	2	3	10/11	Corrine Corrina	Run Like Antel
6/21/88	4	2	1/10	***	I Didn't Know
7/25/88	6	3	2/4	Skin it Back	BBFCFM
7/30/88	1	3	8/13	Sneakin' Sally	Fluffhead
11/3/88	11	3	5/6	BBFCFM	David Bowie
3/14/89	17	1	11/12	You Enjoy Myself	Foam
4/20/89	4	2	10/10	Love You	***
5/9/89	6	2	13/14	Bold as Love	Whipping Post
10/14/89	22	2	4/4	Possum	***
10/20/89	1	1	1/10	***	Bundle of Joy
10/28/89	4	1	9/9	Divided Sky	***
11/10/89	5	E	1/4	***	Highway to Hell
1/29/90	18	1	9/10	Highway to Hell	Fire
3/11/90	18	2	10/13	Split Open and Melt	Slave
4/7/90	6	2	1/3	***	BBFCFM
6/9/90	32	2	13/14	Terrapin	Good Time Ba
4/18/91	74	1	11/11	Possum	***
5/3/91	8	2	8/9	You Enjoy Myself	Tweezer Repri
10/28/91	46	2	9/11	The Squirming Coil	Whipping Post
12/7/91	24	2	8/8	Terrapin	***
3/26/92	15	E	3/3	Chalk Dust Torture	***
4/22/92	20	2	10/11	Cracklin' Rosie	Runaway Jim
5/9/92	13	2	5/8	Tweezer	Llama
11/28/92	57	2	11/12	Terrapin	Golgi Apparat
12/31/92	17	3	4/9	Weekapaug Groove	Kung
12/31/92	0	3	6/9	Kung	The Squirmin
2/12/93	9	2	11/11	Harry Hood	***
3/31/93	34	2	9/10	You Enjoy Myself	Chalk Dust Tor
4/14/93	2	2	9/10	You Enjoy Myself	Runaway Jim
5/7/93	18	2	9/10	Harry Hood	Highway to Hell
7/25/93	12	2	9/10	Purple Rain	Tweezer Repri
8/20/93	19	1	2/10	Divided Sky	Poor Heart
5/3/94	33	2	5/8	Down with Disease	Chalk Dust Tor
6/17/94	27	2	9/15	Weekapaug Groove	Kung
6/17/94	0	2	11/15	Kung	Sparkle
6/30/94	10	2	8/15	Axilla (Part II)	Kung
6/30/94	0	2	10/15	Kung	Honky Tonk Women
6/30/94	0	2	12/15	Honky Tonk Women	Run Like Antel
7/16/94	12	2	4/11	Run Like an Antelope	Also Sprach
7/16/94	0	2	5/11	Also Sprach	AC/DC Bag
10/31/94	20	1	5/10	Divided Sky	Julius
11/25/94	14	2	4/8	Simple	Weekapaug Gr
6/23/95	30	2	5/7	Run Like an Antelope	Llama
10/31/95	34	1	9/9	Run Like an Antelope	***
8/17/96	64	E	1/1	***	***
12/6/96	35	E	1/7	***	Wildwood Weed
12/6/96	0	E	4/7	Cowboy's Sweetheart	Suspicious Minds
12/6/96	0	E	6/7	Suspicious Minds	Suzy Greenber
12/29/96	2	2	8/10	Sixteen Candles	Champagne Supernova
12/29/96	0	2	10/10	Champagne Supernova	***
8/16/97	54	1	2/11	Makisupa Policeman	Chalk Dust Tor
12/30/97	25	2	3/10	McGrupp	I'm Gonna Be (500 M)
12/30/97	0	2	5/10	I'm Gonna Be (500 M)	Izabella
11/2/98	45	2	5/16	You Enjoy Myself	Speak to Me
11/2/98	0	2	16/16	Eclipse	***

Has not been played in the last 135 shows.

Harry Hood

DATE	GAP	SET	POS.	SONG BEFORE	SONG AFTER
10/30/85	8	1	1/11	***	Dog Gone Dog
4/1/86	4	1	3/7	Have Mercy	The Pendulum
10/15/86	2	2	14/14	Have Mercy	***
10/31/86	1	2	7/11	Have Mercy	Sanity
2/13/87	2	1	14/14	Fluffhead	***
3/6/87	2	2	3/7	Happy Birthday	Tell Me Smthg Good
5/20/87	5	1	7/9	Possum	You Enjoy My
8/9/87	1	2	9/11	Fee	Harpua
8/21/87	2	1	5/11	Funky Bitch	Clod
8/29/87	1	1	7/13	Possum	Timber (Jerry)
11/19/87	7	1	6/7	Sneakin' Sally	Fire
1/27/88	1	3	8/8	Camel Walk	***
2/8/88	2	3	5/9	Alumni Blues	Bike
2/24/88	1	2	5/5	La Grange	***
3/11/88	2	2	3/8	Dinner and a Movie	Ballad - Curtis Loew
4/22/88	5	1	8/9	Dinner and a Movie	Harpua
7/23/88	12	3	3/7	Contact	Dinner and a
8/3/88	4	3	5/8	Fluffhead	Satin Doll
9/12/88	4	2	9/10	The Practical Song	Esther
10/31/88	5	1	12/12	Costume Contest	***
2/6/89	9	3	3/9	Walk Away	BBFCFM
5/6/89	18	2	5/8	Fire	Golgi Apparat
5/13/89	3	2	4/7	The Lizards	If I Only Had a Brai
5/21/89	2	1	1/13	***	Foam
5/28/89	3	2	16/16	The Mango Song	***
6/23/89	1	2	3/7	Fluffhead	Ya Mar
8/17/89	2	1	6/9	Rocky Top	Mike's Song
8/26/89	3	1	4/8	The Famous Mockingbi	Split Open and
9/9/89	1	2	5/7	Split Open and Melt	Walk Away
9/13/89	1	2	1/9	***	Bathtub Gin
10/1/89	2	1	5/12	Golgi Apparatus	The Chase
10/6/89	1	1	10/13	Happy Birthday	Possum
10/20/89	5	2	8/10	Split Open and Melt	Swing Low Sweet Chrt
10/22/89	2	2	1/9	***	Reba
11/10/89	7	2	1/12	***	Bathtub Gin
12/1/89	5	1	8/9	My Sweet One	Good Time Ba
12/8/89	3	2	1/7	***	Tela
1/20/90	7	1	1/8	***	Carolina
2/17/90	9	1	5/12	The Squirming Coil	Carolina
4/6/90	17	2	5/10	The Sloth	Caravan
4/9/90	3	2	6/11	Foam	Jesus Just Left
4/13/90	2	2	7/10	The Sloth	Caravan
4/21/90	5	2	1/9	***	Runaway Jim
4/22/90	1	2	8/9	BBFCFM	Fire
4/28/90	3	2	2/9	Cavern	Caravan
5/6/90	3	2	2/7	Fee	Esther
5/10/90	2	2	3/8	Runaway Jim	Caravan
5/24/90	6	2	9/11	Walk Away	Highway to Hell
6/9/90	8	2	2/14	Whole Lotta Love Jam	T.M.W.S.I.Y.
9/15/90	4	2	7/8	Minute by Minute	Possum
11/4/90	19	1	6/10	Tube	Funky Bitch
2/9/91	19	2	6/10	Bouncing	Cavern
2/15/91	2	2	8/10	AC/DC Bag	Terrapin
3/15/91	13	2	8/9	I Didn't Know	Chalk Dust Tor
3/31/91	7	2	1/7	***	***
4/5/91	4	2	6/9	Dinner and a Movie	I Didn't Know
4/19/91	7	2	1/10	***	Fee
4/21/91	2	2	8/11	Uncle Pen	Cavern
5/2/91	4	E	1/1	***	***
5/4/91	2	2	6/9	Buried Alive	Horn
5/10/91	2	2	2/11	Golgi Apparatus	Wilson
7/14/91	10	3	10/10	Touch Me	***
8/9/91	11	E	5/5	Crimes of the Mind	***
10/6/91	10	2	6/10	Destiny Unbound	I Didn't Know
10/12/91	3	2	9/10	If I Only Had a Brai	Tweezer Repri
10/15/91	2	E	2/2	Memories	***
10/19/91	3	2	10/10	Terrapin	***
10/27/91	3	1	9/10	Bouncing	Golgi Apparat
10/31/91	3	2	14/14	I Didn't Know	***
11/12/91	7	1	8/11	The Sloth	Fee
11/15/91	3	2	11/14	Destiny Unbound	Love You
11/21/91	4	2	2/10	Wilson	It's Ice
11/30/91	4	2	3/10	Uncle Pen	It's Ice
3/11/92	8	2	10/11	All Things Recnsdrd	Rocky Top
3/14/92	3	2	8/10	Suzy Greenberg	Cracklin' Rosi
3/20/92	3	2	9/12	Uncle Pen	Terrapin
3/24/92	3	2	12/13	Suzy Greenberg	Cavern
3/27/92	3	2	11/13	Magilla	Love You
4/3/92	5	2	8/9	Llama	Suzy Greenber
4/12/92	6	2	9/10	Cracklin' Rosie	Cavern
4/18/92	5	2	14/16	T.M.W.S.I.Y. Reprise	Love You
4/25/92	6	2	8/11	Dinner and a Movie	Weigh
4/30/92	2	2	10/11	Cracklin' Rosie	Tweezer Repri
5/8/92	7	2	11/12	Terrapin	Golgi Apparat
5/17/92	7	2	10/11	Sparkle	***
7/15/92	14	2	8/9	All Things Recnsdrd	Golgi Apparat
11/20/92	31	2	7/10	Dinner and a Movie	Terrapin
11/25/92	4	E	1/2	***	Carolina
12/4/92	7	2	8/10	Carolina	Faht
12/13/92	8	2	13/14	Cracklin' Rosie	Cavern
12/28/92	1	2	8/9	Bike	Cavern
2/4/93	5	2	12/13	Lengthwise	Cavern
2/12/93	7	2	10/11	Terrapin	Harpua
2/20/93	6	2	21/22	Terrapin	Tweezer Repri
3/2/93	7	2	11/12	Choo Choo Ch' Boogie	Amazing Grce
3/12/93	6	2	10/11	Lengthwise	Golgi Apparat
3/21/93	7	2	11/12	Llama	Cavern
3/31/93	8	2	5/10	Uncle Pen	Big Ball Jam
4/16/93	9	1	9/10	Rift	Cavern
4/24/93	7	2	9/10	Bike	Cavern
4/30/93	4	2	7/10	Big Ball Jam	If I Only Had a Brai
5/7/93	6	2	8/10	The Great Gig in the	Harpua
7/16/93	5	2	11/12	Purple Rain	Cavern
7/28/93	9	2	8/10	My Friend My Friend	The Great Gig in the
8/8/93	8	2	3/11	Rift	Wilson
8/15/93	6	E	1/1	***	***
8/21/93	4	2	9/10	If I Only Had a Brai	Daniel
8/26/93	3	1	8/9	It's Ice	Golgi Apparat
12/28/93	2	2	8/9	Uncle Pen	Highway to Hell
12/31/93	3	3	8/9	Cracklin' Rosie	Tweezer Repri
4/4/94	1	E	1/2	***	Cavern
4/8/94	3	2	5/9	Sparkle	Bouncing
4/10/94	2	2	7/7	I Wanna Be Like You	***
4/15/94	4	1	4/9	Paul and Silas	Wilson
4/20/94	4	2	8/9	Big Ball Jam	Fee
4/23/94	3	2	6/10	Sparkle	Ginseng Sullivan
4/30/94	5	2	5/10	Peaches en Regalia	Axilla (Part II)
5/10/94	7	2	6/10	Scent of a Mule	Ginseng Sullivan
5/19/94	6	2	9/10	Big Ball Jam	Golgi Apparat
5/21/94	2	2	8/9	Bike	Amazing Grce
5/27/94	5	1	8/9	Punch You in the Eye	Golgi Apparat
6/10/94	4	2	8/9	I Wanna Be Like You	Tweezer Repri
6/21/94	8	2	15/16	Sparkle	Suzy Greenber
6/25/94	4	2	8/9	Cracklin' Rosie	Golgi Apparat
7/1/94	4	2	10/11	Terrapin	Cavern
7/6/94	4	2	9/10	BBFCFM	Tweezer Repri
7/9/94	4	2	9/10	Big Ball Jam	Suzy Greenber
7/14/94	3	2	9/10	Big Ball Jam	Highway to Hell
7/16/94	2	2	9/11	Scent of a Mule	Contact
10/8/94	2	2	11/12	Purple Rain	Suzy Greenber
10/12/94	3	2	8/9	Foreplay/Long Time	Sample in a Ja
10/20/94	6	2	5/8	Rift	Nellie Kane
10/23/94	2	2	7/9	Purple Rain	Fee
10/29/94	5	E	1/1	***	***

DATE	GAP	SET	POS.	SONG BEFORE	SONG AFTER
11/3/94	3	2	7/8	BBFCFM	Cavern
11/12/94	2	2	11/12	Foreplay/Long Time	Golgi Apparat
11/19/94	6	2	5/7	Cracklin' Rosie	Amazing Grce
11/22/94	2	2	12/13	My Long Journey Home	Highway to Hell
12/1/94	6	2	9/10	Jesus Just Left	Golgi Apparat
12/30/94	11	2	7/8	Purple Rain	Tweezer Repri
6/7/95	3	2	8/9	Sample in a Jar	Suzy Greenber
6/13/95	4	2	6/7	Acoustic Army	Golgi Apparat
6/17/95	4	2	10/11	Sweet Adeline	Sample in a Ja
6/24/95	5	2	6/9	Suzy Greenberg	Acoustic Army
6/28/95	3	2	9/10	Suzy Greenberg	Tweezer Repri
7/1/95	3	2	8/9	Acoustic Army	Suzy Greenber
9/27/95	3	2	6/8	Keyboard Cavalry	Hello My Baby
10/3/95	5	2	4/9	Sparkle	Billy Breathes
10/7/95	3	2	8/9	Frankenstein	Sweet Adeline
10/15/95	5	2	7/8	Suspicious Minds	Tweezer Repri
10/21/95	4	2	7/8	Purple Rain	Suzy Greenber
11/10/95	9	E	1/1	***	***
11/16/95	5	2	6/9	Ha Ha Ha	If I Only Had a Brai
11/19/95	2	2	7/8	Scent of a Mule	Suzy Greenber
11/25/95	4	2	10/12	Weekapaug Groove	Hello My Baby
11/30/95	3	E	1/1	***	***
12/5/95	4	2	7/8	Lifeboy	Cavern
12/11/95	4	2	6/8	Scent of a Mule	Suspicious Minds
12/15/95	3	1	2/10	Chalk Dust Torture	Wilson
12/17/95	2	2	5/8	Also Sprach	Sparkle
12/30/95	3	2	3/8	Free	AC/DC Bag
4/26/96	2	1	10/13	Also Sprach	Sample in a Ja
7/6/96	4	1	6/6	Maze	***
7/11/96	4	2	1/8	***	Bouncing
7/15/96	3	1	7/8	I Didn't Know	Cavern
7/21/96	4	E	1/1	***	***
7/25/96	4	1	7/8	Life On Mars	Cavern
8/6/96	4	2	7/8	Purple Rain	Tweezer Repri
8/10/96	2	2	7/8	Whipping Post	A Day in the Life
8/16/96	4	3	6/6	Life on Mars	***
10/18/96	4	2	6/6	Waste	***
10/25/96	5	2	10/12	Strange Design	Cavern
11/2/96	5	2	4/6	Waste	A Day in the Life
11/9/96	5	2	7/7	Steep	***
11/16/96	5	2	6/8	Axilla	Suzy Greenber
11/23/96	4	2	10/10	Amazing Grace	***
11/29/96	3	2	10/10	Waste	***
12/2/96	3	2	7/8	Scent of a Mule	Sweet Adeline
12/6/96	2	2	6/9	Jam	Weekapaug Gr
12/31/96	4	2	7/9	Steep	Prince Caspian
2/13/97	1	2	9/10	Rocko William	Frankenstein
2/18/97	4	2	8/9	Train Song	Frankenstein
2/22/97	3	2	6/8	Jesus Just Left	Free
2/26/97	3	1	4/10	My Friend My Friend	My Soul
3/18/97	4	1	7/10	Beauty of My Dreams	Cars Trucks Buses
6/16/97	3	2	7/7	Dirt	***
6/21/97	3	1	11/15	Dirt	Chalk Dust Tor
7/3/97	8	2	5/6	Sparkle	Cavern
7/5/97	1	1	9/13	Piper	Love You
7/9/97	2	1	8/8	Sweet Adeline	***
7/22/97	4	E	2/2	When Circus Comes	***
7/26/97	3	2	3/8	David Bowie	Blister in the Sun J
7/26/97	0	2	5/8	Blister in the Sun J	Free
8/2/97	4	E	1/1	***	***
8/10/97	5	1	10/10	Ginseng Sullivan	***
8/14/97	3	2	4/8	Sparkle	Col. Forbin's A
8/17/97	2	2	5/5	Also Sprach	***
11/16/97	3	2	4/5	Wilson	Izabella
11/22/97	4	1	4/8	Weekapaug Groove	Train Song
11/29/97	4	2	3/5	Strange Design	Prince Caspian
12/3/97	3	2	6/6	Frankenstein	***

DATE	GAP	SET	POS.	SONG BEFORE	SONG AFTER
12/9/97	4	2	6/6	Axilla	***
12/13/97	3	2	10/10	Weekapaug Groove	***
12/30/97	3	2	7/10	Izabella	My Soul
4/4/98	4	E	1/1	***	***
7/1/98	3	E	1/1	***	***
7/5/98	3	2	5/6	Axilla	Rocky Top
7/9/98	3	2	7/8	Scent of a Mule	Izabella
7/15/98	2	2	6/6	Meat	***
7/20/98	4	2	6/6	Prince Caspian	***
7/25/98	3	E	1/2	***	Tweezer Repri
8/2/98	6	E	1/2	***	Bittersweet Motel
8/8/98	4	2	6/6	Sexual Healing	***
8/16/98	5	E	1/2	***	Baby Elephant Walk
10/15/98	2	2	10/10	Lawn Boy	***
10/17/98	1	1	9/10	Wading In Velvet Sea	Helpless
11/6/98	7	2	7/7	Bike	***
11/13/98	5	2	6/6	Meat	***
11/20/98	5	2	7/8	Gettin' Jiggy W/ It	Character Zer
12/31/98	10	3	4/6	Simple	Tweezer Repri
9/11/99	27	2	6/8	Prince Caspian	***
9/18/99	5	2	5/7	Bouncing	Frankenstein
9/28/99	7	1	8/8	Wading In Velvet Sea	***
10/3/99	4	2	8/8	Wading In Velvet Sea	***
10/8/99	3	2	5/7	Fee	We're Not Gonna Take
12/3/99	4	2	5/5	Piper	***
12/11/99	6	1	1/8	***	Mike's Song
12/18/99	6	1	1/9	***	Back @ Chicken Shack
12/30/99	1	2	9/10	Gotta Jibboo	Good Time Ba
5/21/00	2	2	6/8	Piper	Wading In Velvet Sea
6/11/00	5	2	8/8	Back on the Train	***
6/16/00	4	E	2/2	Bouncing	***
6/22/00	1	2	4/10	Sand	Dog Faced Boy
6/22/00	0	2	6/10	Dog Faced Boy	I'm Blue, Lonesome
7/6/00	10	2	6/7	Driver	Loving Cup
7/11/00	4	2	10/13	Back on the Train	Moby Dick
9/9/00	5	E	1/1	***	***
9/25/00	11	2	6/7	Axilla	Funky Bitch
10/4/00	5	2	6/7	Bug	Cavern

Has not been played in the last 3 shows.

Have Mercy

DATE	GAP	SET	POS.	SONG BEFORE	SONG AFTER
4/1/86	12	1	2/7	Quinn the Eskimo	Harry Hood
4/15/86	1	1	7/14	Makisupa Policeman	Bob Dylan Band
10/15/86	1	2	13/14	Mike's Song	Harry Hood
10/31/86	1	2	6/11	David Bowie	Harry Hood
2/20/93	479	2	14/22	Weekapaug Groove	Weekapaug Gr
5/8/93	55	2	4/18	David Bowie	David Bowie
8/14/93	26	2	6/13	Run Like an Antelope	Run Like Antel
11/12/94	110	2	4/12	Down with Disease	Down with Dis
7/17/99	334	1	8/8	Tweezer	Taste
12/10/99	42	2	4/7	David Bowie	Cracklin' Rosi

Has not been played in the last 58 shows.

Head Held High

DATE	GAP	SET	POS.	SONG BEFORE	SONG AFTER
10/31/98	983	2	6/10	New Age	Lonesome Cowboy Bill

Has not been played in the last 136 shows.

Heart and soul

DATE	GAP	SET	POS.	SONG BEFORE	SONG AFTER
11/29/95	774	2	7/11	Taste That Surrounds	Poor Heart

Has not been played in the last 345 shows.

Heavy Things

DATE	GAP	SET	POS.	SONG BEFORE	SONG AFTER
9/11/99	1033	1	7/9	Billy Breathes	Guyute
9/19/99	6	1	5/8	Gotta Jibboo	Farmhouse
9/26/99	5	2	4/7	Mountains in the Mis	Birds of a Feather

DATE	GAP	SET	POS.	SONG BEFORE	SONG AFTER
9/28/99	1	2	2/7	Farmhouse	First Tube
10/1/99	2	1	6/8	Bathtub Gin	Limb by Limb
10/3/99	2	1	5/12	Divided Sky	Horn
10/7/99	2	2	2/9	Boogie On Reggae	Tube
10/10/99	3	1	3/7	Gotta Jibboo	First Tube
12/2/99	1	1	3/10	Farmhouse	Roggae
12/4/99	2	1	1/7	***	Simple
12/7/99	2	2	3/8	Jennifer Dances	Bug
12/10/99	2	1	4/10	Horn	Dogs Stole Things
12/12/99	2	1	1/8	***	AC/DC Bag
12/13/99	1	E	2/2	Silent in the Mornin	***
12/16/99	2	1	8/10	Roggae	Camel Walk
12/18/99	2	1	5/9	Tube	Back on the Train
12/31/99	2	2	6/35	Bathtub Gin	Twist
5/22/00	2	1	4/9	Billy Breathes	Back on the Train
6/10/00	3	2	1/9	***	Sand
6/14/00	3	1	7/8	Fee	Split Open and Dirt
6/16/00	2	1	6/10	Golgi Apparatus	Dirt
6/23/00	2	1	4/8	Bathtub Gin	Back on the Train
6/25/00	2	1	8/10	Horn	Dirt
6/29/00	2	2	3/10	Catapult	Sand
7/3/00	3	1	7/10	My Soul	Fluffhead
7/6/00	2	1	5/12	Dog Faced Boy	The Moma Dance
7/8/00	2	2	1/9	***	Piper
7/12/00	3	1	4/9	Tube	Billy Breathes
9/12/00	6	2	2/8	Down With Disease	Split Open and
9/22/00	6	1	8/9	Bathtub Gin	You Enjoy My
9/27/00	4	2	5/7	The Mango Song	Brother
10/6/00	6	2	1/10	***	Down with Dis

Has not been played in the last 1 show.

Hello My Baby

DATE	GAP	SET	POS.	SONG BEFORE	SONG AFTER
9/27/95	735	2	7/8	Harry Hood	A Day in the Life
10/2/95	4	2	8/10	Slave	The Lizards
10/6/95	3	E	1/2	***	A Day in the Life
10/11/95	3	2	10/11	Crossroads	A Day in the Life
10/14/95	2	2	4/6	You Enjoy Myself	Scent of a Mul
10/20/95	4	1	8/10	Free	Amazing Grce
11/9/95	9	2	9/10	Life on Mars	The Squirmin
11/12/95	3	1	10/10	Split Open and Melt	***
11/19/95	5	1	8/10	It's Ice	Julius
11/25/95	4	2	11/12	Harry Hood	Poor Heart
11/28/95	1	1	8/9	Guyute	Sample in a Ja
12/4/95	5	1	10/11	Silent in the Mornin	While My Guitar Gent
12/7/95	2	1	10/10	Possum	***
12/17/95	8	E	1/2	***	Runaway Jim
12/31/95	4	2	7/8	Strange Design	Mike's Song
4/26/96	1	E	1/2	***	Cavern
7/10/96	7	1	6/7	David Bowie	Good Time Ba
7/11/96	1	2	8/8	You Enjoy Myself	***
7/12/96	1	3	3/3	Free	***
7/18/96	4	1	5/7	Stash	It's Ice
7/23/96	4	1	9/9	Stash	***
8/2/96	3	1	10/11	Tweezer	Possum
8/7/96	4	2	10/10	You Enjoy Myself	***
8/12/96	2	2	7/9	Run Like an Antelope	Golgi Apparat
8/14/96	2	1	10/10	Stash	***
8/16/96	1	2	9/13	Strange Design	Mike's Song
10/19/96	5	2	10/10	Run Like an Antelope	***
10/23/96	3	1	5/9	Foam	Character Zer
10/29/96	4	2	10/10	Slave	***
11/14/96	10	E	2/2	Stash	***
11/18/96	3	2	7/9	Tweezer	Tweezer Repri
11/22/96	2	2	10/10	Slave	***
2/22/97	21	2	8/8	Free	***
3/1/97	5	1	9/10	Reba	Possum
3/2/97	1	1	13/13	Chalk Dust Torture	***

DATE	GAP	SET	POS.	SONG BEFORE	SONG AFTER
3/18/97	1	E	1/2	***	Funky Bitch
6/19/97	4	E	3/3	Character Zero	***
6/22/97	3	1	8/9	Theme From the Botto	Ghost
7/9/97	10	E	1/1	***	***
7/22/97	4	2	6/6	Weekapaug Groove	***
8/3/97	8	2	6/7	Taste	Frankenstein
11/16/97	12	1	11/11	Taste	***
7/9/98	34	1	8/8	Tweezer	***
8/9/98	20	2	11/11	Chalk Dust Torture	***
10/18/98	8	1	1/12	***	Billy Breathes
11/6/98	6	E	2/2	Birds of a Feather	***
11/14/98	6	2	9/9	Julius	***
11/29/98	10	E	2/2	Roggae	***
7/30a/99	25	1	7/7	Waste	***
9/9/99	4	2	9/9	You Enjoy Myself	***
9/14/99	4	E	2/2	Simple	***
9/19/99	4	1	8/8	Stash	***
12/5/99	19	E	2/2	Character Zero	***

Has not been played in the last 61 shows.

Help Me

DATE	GAP	SET	POS.	SONG BEFORE	SONG AFTER
4/10/93	528	2	11/13	Funky Bitch	Hoochie Coochie Man

Has not been played in the last 591 shows.

Help on the Way

DATE	GAP	SET	POS.	SONG BEFORE	SONG AFTER
4/1/86	12	2	1/6	***	Slipknot!

Has not been played in the last 1107 shows.

Helpless

DATE	GAP	SET	POS.	SONG BEFORE	SONG AFTER
10/17/98	979	1	10/10	Harry Hood	***

Has not been played in the last 140 shows.

Helpless Dancer

DATE	GAP	SET	POS.	SONG BEFORE	SONG AFTER
10/31/95	759	2	8/17	The Dirty Jobs	Is It In My Head

Has not been played in the last 360 shows.

Helter Skelter

DATE	GAP	SET	POS.	SONG BEFORE	SONG AFTER
10/31/94	681	2	24/30	Sexy Sadie	Long Long Long
11/17/94	8	1	1/11	***	Scent of a Mul

Has not been played in the last 430 shows.

High-Heel Sneakers

DATE	GAP	SET	POS.	SONG BEFORE	SONG AFTER
4/23/94	605	1	10/10	Caravan	***

Has not been played in the last 514 shows.

Highway To Hell

DATE	GAP	SET	POS.	SONG BEFORE	SONG AFTER
10/1/89	116	E	1/1	***	***
10/6/89	1	1	12/13	Possum	BBFCFM
10/7/89	1	2	9/9	Contact	***
10/12/89	1	E	1/1	***	***
10/14/89	2	2	2/4	Anarchy	Possum
10/21/89	2	2	9/10	You Enjoy Myself	Run Like Antel
10/28/89	3	1	4/9	Col. Forbin's Ascent	Good Time Ba
10/31/89	1	2	8/8	The Lizards	***
11/2/89	1	2	11/11	My Sweet One	***
11/9/89	2	E	1/1	***	***
11/10/89	1	E	2/4	Harpua	Take the A-Trn
12/1/89	5	2	10/10	If I Only Had a Brai	***
12/31/89	9	1	9/9	Satin Doll	***
1/29/90	4	1	8/10	Possum	Harpua
2/10/90	3	E	2/2	I Didn't Know	***
2/15/90	1	2	5/5	Foam	***
2/23/90	4	2	11/11	Weekapaug Groove	***
3/9/90	8	2	7/11	Slave	You Enjoy My
3/28/90	4	2	15/16	Cavern	If I Only Had a Brai
4/4/90	1	E	2/2	Contact	***
4/6/90	2	E	2/2	Jesus Just Left	***
4/13/90	5	2	10/10	Possum	***
4/19/90	3	2	6/8	Terrapin	Carolina
4/21/90	2	2	6/9	Fluffhead	Tela
4/26/90	3	E	1/1	***	***
5/4/90	3	1	11/12	If I Only Had a Brai	Run Like Antel
5/7/90	2	1	2/5	Walk Away	La Grange
5/11/90	2	1	9/9	Reba	***
5/19/90	3	1	8/8	The Lizards	***
5/24/90	2	2	10/11	Harry Hood	Contact
11/4/90	31	E	2/2	Contact	***
11/26/90	6	E	3/3	Contact	***
12/8/90	4	E	3/3	Contact	***
12/28/90	1	E	2/2	Bouncing	***
3/31/91	30	E	2/2	Reba	***
4/4/91	3	E	2/4	Magilla	Contact
4/22/91	11	2	10/10	The Lizards	***
5/10/91	7	E	2/2	Take the A-Train	***
10/28/91	43	2	11/11	Whipping Post	***
11/15/91	12	E	1/1	***	Suzy Greenber
4/12/93	184	E	2/3	Amazing Grace	Rocky Top
4/16/93	2	2	13/13	Bike	***
4/23/93	6	2	12/12	The Squirming Coil	***
5/3/93	8	E	1/1	***	***
5/7/93	3	2	10/10	Harpua	***
7/23/93	10	2	11/11	Chalk Dust Torture	***
7/31/93	7	2	11/11	Daniel	***
8/13/93	9	E	1/1	***	***
12/28/93	11	2	9/9	Harry Hood	***
4/9/94	8	E	2/2	Amazing Grace	***
4/20/94	9	E	1/1	***	***
4/30/94	8	E	2/2	Sleeping Monkey	***
5/17/94	12	E	1/1	***	***
5/23/94	5	E	3/3	Amazing Grace	***
6/9/94	6	E	1/1	***	***
6/19/94	8	2	8/8	My Sweet One	***
6/25/94	5	E	1/1	***	***
7/2/94	5	2	12/12	Slave	***
7/14/94	2	2	8/10	Harry Hood	***
10/16/94	11	E	1/1	***	***
10/22/94	4	2	11/11	AC/DC Bag	***
10/28/94	5	E	2/2	Fee	***
11/3/94	4	E	4/4	Amazing Grace	***
11/22/94	10	2	13/13	Harry Hood	***
6/20/95	30	2	9/9	Cracklin' Rosie	***
10/21/95	29	E	1/1	***	***
6/6/96	42	1	8/8	Scent of a Mule	***
10/31/96	41	1	2/10	Sanity	Down with Dis
12/1/96	20	E	1/1	***	***
2/26/97	18	E	1/1	***	***

Has not been played in the last 246 shows.

Hold Whatcha Got

DATE	GAP	SET	POS.	SONG BEFORE	SONG AFTER
6/22/00	10812	2	8/10	I'm Blue, Lonesome	Uncle Pen

Has not been played in the last 38 shows.

Hold to a Dream

DATE	GAP	SET	POS.	SONG BEFORE	SONG AFTER
8/7/96	817	1	9/10	99 Years	Doin' My Time

Has not been played in the last 302 shows.

Honey Pie

DATE	GAP	SET	POS.	SONG BEFORE	SONG AFTER
10/31/94	681	2	27/30	Revolution	Savoy Truffle

Has not been played in the last 438 shows.

Honky Tonk Women

DATE	GAP	SET	POS.	SONG BEFORE	SONG AFTER
6/30/94	649	2	11/15	Harpua	Harpua

Has not been played in the last 470 shows.

Honky Tonk Women Jam

DATE	GAP	SET	POS.	SONG BEFORE	SONG AFTER
4/12/93	529	2	8/10	You Enjoy Myself	Terrapin

Has not been played in the last 590 shows.

Hoochie Coochie Man

DATE	GAP	SET	POS.	SONG BEFORE	SONG AFTER
4/10/93	528	2	12/13	Help Me	Cavern
8/8/97	380	E	1/2	***	Messin' With The Kid

Has not been played in the last 211 shows.

Horn

DATE	GAP	SET	POS.	SONG BEFORE	SONG AFTER
5/24/90	197	2	6/11	My Sweet One	Fee
6/16/90	9	1	5/10	Reba	Uncle Pen
9/22/90	7	1	2/12	Buried Alive	My Sweet One
12/28/90	26	1	3/11	Foam	Reba
12/29/90	1	1	8/10	Rocky Top	The Oh Kee Pa
2/8/91	6	2	8/11	Weekapaug Groove	Bouncing
3/15/91	16	2	3/9	Possum	Paul and Silas
4/15/91	15	2	5/11	Weekapaug Groove	My Sweet One
4/18/91	2	1	6/11	Paul and Silas	Suzy Greenber
4/20/91	2	E	1/2	***	Alumni Blues
5/4/91	7	2	7/9	Harry Hood	Rocky Top
10/15/91	38	2	7/12	Llama	The Oh Kee Pa
10/19/91	3	2	5/10	Tweezer	Poor Heart
10/23/91	1	1	7/11	It's Ice	Llama
10/28/91	3	E	1/2	***	Rocky Top
10/31/91	2	2	10/14	David Bowie	Dinner and a
11/7/91	3	2	6/11	Tube	David Bowie
11/9/91	2	1	9/11	You Enjoy Myself	Brother
11/13/91	3	E	1/3	***	My Sweet One
11/16/91	3	2	6/9	You Enjoy Myself	Chalk Dust Tor
11/19/91	1	1	7/11	Brother	Chalk Dust Tor
11/21/91	2	1	7/12	Foam	Split Open and
11/23/91	2	2	5/13	Weekapaug Groove	Poor Heart
11/30/91	2	2	7/10	My Sweet One	I Didn't Know
12/6/91	3	2	5/12	You Enjoy Myself	Divided Sky
3/7/92	4	2	6/11	Chalk Dust Torture	Mike's Song
3/25/92	11	2	8/12	Setting Sail	My Sweet One
4/1/92	6	2	7/13	Tweezer	Chalk Dust Tor
4/5/92	3	1	8/11	Rift	It's Ice
4/16/92	2	2	7/12	Weekapaug Groove	Poor Heart
4/23/92	6	2	8/13	NICU	Tweezer
4/24/92	1	2	9/12	The Mango Song	Love You
4/29/92	2	E	1/2	***	Rocky Top
5/1/92	2	1	10/12	It's Ice	I Didn't Know
5/3/92	2	1	9/10	Rift	Runaway Jim
5/12/92	7	1	11/12	Uncle Pen	David Bowie
5/14/92	1		6/11	Maze	Reba
5/16/92	2	1	6/11	My Sweet One	Golgi Apparat
5/18/92	2	1	8/10	Poor Heart	Sparkle
6/20/92	2	1	6/8	It's Ice	Love You
7/1/92	5	1	4/7	Rift	Split Open and
7/14/92	5	1	8/12	Runaway Jim	Brother
7/27/92	11	1	4/7	David Bowie	Suzy Greenber
7/30/92	2	1	2/8	Rift	Sparkle
8/1/92	2	1	6/7	The Squirming Coil	Llama
8/17/92	5	2	8/11	Weekapaug Groove	Terrapin
8/27/92	6	1	4/7	The Landlady	Sparkle
11/22/92	8	1	8/12	Sparkle	All Things Rec
12/2/92	7	1	9/10	Sparkle	You Enjoy My
12/7/92	5	2	4/12	Llama	The Vibration of Lif
2/6/93	13	1	6/11	Maze	Divided Sky
2/17/93	8	2	8/11	Big Ball Jam	You Enjoy My
2/21/93	4	1	5/10	Uncle Pen	Chalk Dust Tor
2/26/93	4	1	7/10	Llama	Divided Sky
3/6/93	5	1	2/10	Llama	The Curtain
3/18/93	8	1	9/11	Sparkle	I Didn't Know
3/25/93	5	1	9/11	Rift	Magilla
4/3/93	8	1	9/10	Reba	Run Like Antel
4/18/93	8	1	9/10	Maze	I Didn't Know
4/29/93	8	1	5/10	Runaway Jim	Llama
5/7/93	7	1	8/11	The Lizards	Divided Sky
7/16/93	5	1	9/11	Nellie Kane	Run Like Antel
7/22/93	4	1	3/11	Foam	My Mind's Got A Mind
7/24/93	2	1	2/10	Llama	Nellie Kane
7/30/93	5	1	3/10	Llama	Uncle Pen
8/6/93	4	1	6/10	Rift	Divided Sky
8/13/93	6	1	9/10	My Mind's Got A Mind	David Bowie
8/16/93	3	1	3/9	Possum	Reba
8/21/93	3	2	2/10	Possum	Uncle Pen
8/24/93	1	2	2/10	Llama	Ya Mar
4/4/94	8	1	7/9	Reba	It's Ice
4/22/94	15	1	2/11	Llama	Uncle Pen

DATE	GAP	SET	POS.	SONG BEFORE	SONG AFTER
5/7/94	11	1	2/9	Llama	Divided Sky
5/29/94	17	2	5/10	Chalk Dust Torture	McGrupp
6/18/94	8	2	5/10	David Bowie	McGrupp
6/24/94	5	1	8/11	Paul and Silas	Reba
7/3/94	7	1	6/10	NICU	The Old Home
7/10/94	5	1	2/9	Chalk Dust Torture	Peaches en Regalia
10/8/94	6	1	2/9	Chalk Dust Torture	Sparkle
10/16/94	7	1	2/10	Rift	Foam
10/25/94	6	1	3/9	Llama	Julius
11/22/94	17	1	3/9	Poor Heart	Foam
6/30/95	38	1	3/9	Scent of a Mule	Taste
9/30/95	7	1	6/9	Uncle Pen	Run Like Antel
10/19/95	12	1	3/11	Runaway Jim	Punch You in
10/27/95	6	1	4/9	Taste That Surrounds	I Didn't Know
11/16/95	10	1	4/10	Chess Jam	Mound
12/5/95	13	1	1/8	***	Chalk Dust Tor
12/14/95	6	1	3/10	Llama	Foam
12/28/95	4	1	6/9	Guyute	Rift
7/12/96	13	1	3/10	Divided Sky	Split Open and
8/6/96	14	1	8/9	Dinner and a Movie	Run Like Antel
11/9/96	25	1	5/10	Divided Sky	Tube
12/4/96	16	1	3/11	Chalk Dust Torture	Uncle Pen
6/20/97	25	1	4/8	Cities	Ain't Love Funny
7/1/97	7	1	2/9	Ghost	Ya Mar
8/11/97	22	1	7/8	Limb by Limb	Run Like Antel
11/29/97	15	1	10/12	I Saw it Again	Water in the Sky
12/9/97	7	1	9/10	Beauty of My Dreams	Loving Cup
4/2/98	8	1	6/8	Stash	Waste
7/15/98	13	1	5/13	Guyute	Jam
11/9/98	35	1	2/10	Llama	I Get a Kick Out of
11/29/98	13	1	5/11	Sparkle	Limb by Limb
12/29/98	2	1	4/10	Punch You in the Eye	Ginseng Sullivan
6/30/99	3	1	4/8	Tube	Back on the Train
7/15/99	10	1	4/10	Farmhouse	Poor Heart
8/1/99	13	1	6/10	Divided Sky	Split Open and
9/9/99	1	1	4/10	Limb by Limb	Guyute
9/25/99	12	1	4/8	Ya Mar	Limb By Limb
10/3/99	6	1	6/12	Heavy Things	Carini
12/10/99	12	1	3/10	Bouncing	Heavy Things
12/16/99	5	1	5/10	Limb by Limb	Back on the Train
12/31/99	4	1	12/14	Back on the Train	Guyute
5/22/00	2	1	8/9	Sparkle	Bathtub Gin
6/11/00	4	1	3/9	Punch You in the Eye	Ginseng Sullivan
6/25/00	8	1	7/10	Funky Bitch	Heavy Things
9/11/00	17	1	6/9	Vultures	Beauty of my Dreams
9/27/00	11	1	8/10	Split Open and Melt	Taste
10/5/00	5	1	9/10	Axilla	Possum

Has not been played in the last 2 shows.

Houses in Motion

DATE	GAP	SET	POS.	SONG BEFORE	SONG AFTER
10/31/96	835	2	5/8	Once in a Lifetime	Seen and Not Seen

Has not been played in the last 284 shows.

How High the Moon

DATE	GAP	SET	POS.	SONG BEFORE	SONG AFTER
4/22/90	183	2	5/9	Fluffhead	Esther
4/26/90	2	2	1/11	***	Esther
3/8/93	320	1	7/12	Col. Forbin's Ascent	The Famous Mockingbi

Has not been played in the last 614 shows.

Hurricane

DATE	GAP	SET	POS.	SONG BEFORE	SONG AFTER
11/14/85	9	1	1/1	***	***

Has not been played in the last 1110 shows.

I Am Hydrogen

DATE	GAP	SET	POS.	SONG BEFORE	SONG AFTER
10/15/86	14	1	5/9	Cities	McGrupp
4/24/87	7	1	9/14	Alumni Blues	Jam
4/29/87	1	3	14/14	Good Times Roll	***
8/29/87	6	3	4/10	Mike's Song	Jam
10/31/87	5	2	8/17	Fluff's Travels	The Chase
7/23/88	25	1	5/13	Mike's Song	Weekapaug Gr
7/24/88	1	1	8/10	Mike's Song	Weekapaug Gr
7/25/88	1	2	2/6	Mike's Song	Weekapaug Gr
8/3/88	2	3	3/8	Mike's Song	Fluffhead
11/5/88	11	2	8/11	Mike's Song	Weekapaug Gr
11/11/88	1	2	2/8	Mike's Song	Weekapaug Gr
12/10/88	2	1	8/12	Mike's Song	Weekapaug Gr
2/7/89	5	1	7/9	Mike's Song	Weekapaug Gr
3/3/89	5	2	2/12	Mike's Song	Weekapaug Gr
3/4/89	1	1	4/8	Mike's Song	Weekapaug Gr
3/12/89	1	1	2/8	Mike's Song	Weekapaug Gr
3/14/89	1	1	4/12	Mike's Song	Weekapaug Gr
3/24/89	1	1	3/10	Mike's Song	Weekapaug Gr
3/30/89	1	2	3/8	Mike's Song	Weekapaug Gr
4/20/89	2	2	7/10	Mike's Song	Weekapaug Gr
5/1/89	3	2	2/10	Mike's Song	Weekapaug Gr
5/6/89	2	1	4/13	Mike's Song	Weekapaug Gr
5/9/89	1	1	5/9	Mike's Song	Weekapaug Gr
5/12/89	1	1	3/15	Mike's Song	Weekapaug Gr
5/20/89	2	2	3/9	Mike's Song	Weekapaug Gr
5/21/89	1	1	5/13	Mike's Song	Weekapaug Gr
5/26/89	1	1	4/9	Mike's Song	Weekapaug Gr
5/27/89	1	1	3/11	Mike's Song	Weekapaug Gr
5/28/89	1	2	3/16	Mike's Song	Weekapaug Gr
6/23/89	1	1	8/11	Mike's Song	Weekapaug Gr
6/30/89	1	2	7/8	Mike's Song	Weekapaug Gr
8/17/89	1	1	8/9	Mike's Song	Weekapaug Gr
8/19/89	1	1	12/13	Mike's Song	Weekapaug Gr
10/6/89	7	1	3/13	Mike's Song	Weekapaug Gr
10/7/89	1	1	4/11	Mike's Song	Weekapaug Gr
10/12/89	1	2	3/7	Mike's Song	Weekapaug Gr
10/13/89	1	2	5/8	Mike's Song	Weekapaug Gr
10/26/89	5	1	10/11	Mike's Song	Weekapaug Gr
11/2/89	3	1	4/11	Mike's Song	Weekapaug Gr
11/9/89	2	2	8/9	Mike's Song	Weekapaug Gr
11/10/89	1	2	4/12	Mike's Song	Weekapaug Gr
11/16/89	2	1	2/11	Mike's Song	Weekapaug Gr
12/1/89	3	2	7/10	Mike's Song	Weekapaug Gr
12/3/89	1	2	13/14	Mike's Song	Weekapaug Gr
12/7/89	1	1	7/11	Mike's Song	Weekapaug Gr
12/9/89	2	2	7/8	Mike's Song	Weekapaug Gr
12/15/89	1	1	4/10	Mike's Song	Weekapaug Gr
12/16/89	1	1	5/9	Mike's Song	Weekapaug Gr
12/29/89	1	1	9/10	Mike's Song	Weekapaug Gr
12/30/89	1	E	3/4	Mike's Song	Weekapaug Gr
12/31/89	1	2	2/7	Mike's Song	Weekapaug Gr
1/20/90	1	2	9/10	Mike's Song	Weekapaug Gr
1/27/90	1	1	12/13	Mike's Song	Weekapaug Gr
1/28/90	1	2	9/10	Mike's Song	Weekapaug Gr
1/29/90	1	1	4/10	Mike's Song	Weekapaug Gr
2/1/90	1	1	10/11	Mike's Song	Weekapaug Gr
2/9/90	1	1	10/12	Mike's Song	Weekapaug Gr
2/10/90	1	2	9/10	Mike's Song	Weekapaug Gr
2/15/90	1	1	9/10	Mike's Song	Weekapaug Gr
2/16/90	1	1	4/7	Mike's Song	Weekapaug Gr
2/17/90	1	1	8/12	Mike's Song	Weekapaug Gr
2/23/90	2	2	9/11	Mike's Song	Weekapaug Gr
3/1/90	3	2	4/7	Mike's Song	Weekapaug Gr
3/3/90	2	1	2/12	Mike's Song	Weekapaug Gr
3/7/90	1	2	8/9	Mike's Song	Weekapaug Gr
3/8/90	1	2	9/12	Mike's Song	Weekapaug Gr
3/11/90	3	1	10/13	Mike's Song	Weekapaug Gr
3/28/90	2	2	6/16	Mike's Song	Weekapaug Gr
4/4/90	1	2	2/8	Mike's Song	Weekapaug Gr
4/5/90	1	2	10/13	Mike's Song	Weekapaug Gr
4/7/90	2	1	11/12	Mike's Song	Weekapaug Gr
4/8/90	1	2	6/10	Mike's Song	Weekapaug Gr
4/12/90	2	2	10/11	Mike's Song	Weekapaug Gr
4/14/90	2	1	9/10	Mike's Song	Weekapaug Gr
4/18/90	1	1	2/10	Mike's Song	Weekapaug Gr
4/20/90	2	2	3/11	Mike's Song	Weekapaug Gr
4/22/90	2	1	11/12	Mike's Song	Weekapaug Gr
4/25/90	1	2	11/12	Mike's Song	Weekapaug Gr
4/26/90	1	2	10/11	Mike's Song	Weekapaug Gr
4/28/90	1	2	8/9	Mike's Song	Weekapaug Gr
5/4/90	2	1	7/12	Mike's Song	Weekapaug Gr
5/6/90	1	1	7/8	Mike's Song	Weekapaug Gr
5/11/90	3	1	2/9	Mike's Song	Weekapaug Gr
5/13/90	1	2	2/12	Mike's Song	Weekapaug Gr
5/15/90	1	1	5/12	Mike's Song	Weekapaug Gr
5/23/90	2	2	10/11	Mike's Song	Weekapaug Gr
5/30/90	2	1	12/14	Mike's Song	Weekapaug Gr
6/1/90	2	1	5/12	Mike's Song	Weekapaug Gr
6/5/90	2	1	4/12	Mike's Song	Weekapaug Gr
6/7/90	1	2	9/10	Mike's Song	Weekapaug Gr
6/8/90	1	2	6/7	Mike's Song	Weekapaug Gr
6/9/90	1	1	9/10	Mike's Song	Weekapaug Gr
6/16/90	1	3	12/13	Mike's Song	Weekapaug Gr
9/13/90	1	2	2/15	Mike's Song	Weekapaug Gr
9/14/90	1	1	10/11	Mike's Song	Weekapaug Gr
9/16/90	2	1	11/14	Mike's Song	Weekapaug Gr
9/20/90	1	1	9/12	Mike's Song	Weekapaug Gr
9/29/90	4	2	7/8	Mike's Song	Weekapaug Gr
10/1/90	1	1	2/11	Mike's Song	Weekapaug Gr
10/5/90	2	1	3/13	Mike's Song	Weekapaug Gr
10/7/90	2	1	11/14	Mike's Song	Weekapaug Gr
10/12/90	2	2	9/10	Mike's Song	Weekapaug Gr
10/19/90	1	1	5/15	Mike's Song	Weekapaug Gr
10/30/90	1	2	2/12	Mike's Song	Weekapaug Gr
10/31/90	1	2	11/12	Mike's Song	Weekapaug Gr
11/2/90	1	1	7/14	Mike's Song	Weekapaug Gr
11/3/90	1	2	3/12	Mike's Song	Weekapaug Gr
11/4/90	1	2	5/13	Mike's Song	Weekapaug Gr
11/8/90	1	1	11/12	Mike's Song	Weekapaug Gr
11/10/90	1	1	10/11	Mike's Song	Weekapaug Gr
11/16/90	1	2	3/11	Mike's Song	Weekapaug Gr
11/17/90	1	2	4/12	Mike's Song	Weekapaug Gr
11/24/90	1	1	5/11	Mike's Song	Weekapaug Gr
11/26/90	1	2	6/7	Mike's Song	Weekapaug Gr
11/30/90	1	1	3/11	Mike's Song	Weekapaug Gr
12/7/90	2	2	2/11	Mike's Song	Weekapaug Gr
12/8/90	1	1	9/10	Mike's Song	Weekapaug Gr
12/28/90	1	1	9/11	Mike's Song	Weekapaug Gr
12/31/90	2	1	8/12	Mike's Song	Weekapaug Gr
2/8/91	5	2	6/11	Mike's Song	Weekapaug Gr
2/14/91	2	2	2/12	Mike's Song	Weekapaug Gr
2/16/91	2	1	11/12	Mike's Song	Weekapaug Gr
2/19/91	1	2	3/15	Mike's Song	Weekapaug Gr
2/21/91	2	1	10/11	Mike's Song	Weekapaug Gr
2/26/91	1	2	11/12	Mike's Song	Weekapaug Gr
2/28/91	2	1	6/13	Mike's Song	Weekapaug Gr
3/1/91	1	1	11/12	Mike's Song	Weekapaug Gr
3/15/91	5	1	11/12	Mike's Song	Weekapaug Gr
3/17/91	2	1	5/12	Mike's Song	Weekapaug Gr
3/22/91	1	2	12/13	Mike's Song	Weekapaug Gr
3/31/91	4	1	12/13	Mike's Song	Weekapaug Gr
4/3/91	2	1	9/10	Mike's Song	Weekapaug Gr
4/5/91	2	1	10/11	Mike's Song	Weekapaug Gr
4/11/91	2	2	13/14	Mike's Song	Weekapaug Gr
4/15/91	2	2	3/11	Mike's Song	Weekapaug Gr
4/19/91	3	1	10/12	Mike's Song	Weekapaug Gr
4/21/91	2	1	12/14	Mike's Song	Weekapaug Gr
4/25/91	2	2	4/10	Mike's Song	Weekapaug Gr
4/27/91	1	2	7/13	Mike's Song	Weekapaug Gr
5/4/91	3	1	10/11	Mike's Song	Weekapaug Gr
5/10/91	2	2	10/11	Mike's Song	Weekapaug Gr
5/11/91	1	2	7/12	Mike's Song	Weekapaug Gr
5/12/91	1	2	8/13	Mike's Song	Weekapaug Gr
5/17/91	2	1	15/17	Mike's Song	Weekapaug Gr
7/11/91	3	2	7/10	Mike's Song	Weekapaug Gr
7/12/91	1	2	8/14	Mike's Song	Weekapaug Gr
7/14/91	2	3	7/10	Mike's Song	Weekapaug Gr
7/15/91	1	1	8/14	Mike's Song	Weekapaug Gr
7/18/91	1	1	10/11	Mike's Song	Weekapaug Gr
7/21/91	3	1	10/11	Mike's Song	Weekapaug Gr
7/23/91	1	1	11/12	Mike's Song	Weekapaug Gr
7/25/91	2	2	12/13	Mike's Song	Weekapaug Gr
7/27/91	2	1	15/16	Mike's Song	Weekapaug Gr

DATE	GAP	SET	POS.	SONG BEFORE	SONG AFTER
9/26/91	3	2	8/11	Mike's Song	Weekapaug Gr
9/28/91	2	2	11/12	Mike's Song	Weekapaug Gr
10/3/91	4	2	3/11	Mike's Song	Weekapaug Gr
10/4/91	1	2	10/11	Mike's Song	Weekapaug Gr
10/10/91	2	2	12/13	Mike's Song	Weekapaug Gr
10/13/91	3	1	12/13	Mike's Song	Weekapaug Gr
10/18/91	3	2	6/12	Mike's Song	Weekapaug Gr
10/24/91	3	2	2/11	Mike's Song	Weekapaug Gr
10/27/91	1	2	7/13	Mike's Song	Weekapaug Gr
10/30/91	2	2	10/11	Mike's Song	Weekapaug Gr
11/1/91	2	2	7/13	Mike's Song	Weekapaug Gr
11/8/91	3	2	7/13	Mike's Song	Weekapaug Gr
11/12/91	3	2	6/13	Mike's Song	Weekapaug Gr
11/15/91	3	2	5/14	Mike's Song	Weekapaug Gr
11/19/91	2	2	4/11	Mike's Song	Weekapaug Gr
11/21/91	2	1	11/12	Mike's Song	Weekapaug Gr
11/23/91	2	2	3/13	Mike's Song	Weekapaug Gr
12/4/91	3	2	5/11	Mike's Song	Weekapaug Gr
12/5/91	1	2	6/13	Mike's Song	Weekapaug Gr
12/31/91	3	3	6/7	Mike's Song	Weekapaug Gr
3/7/92	2	2	8/11	Mike's Song	Weekapaug Gr
3/14/92	4	1	12/13	Mike's Song	Weekapaug Gr
3/17/92	1	2	8/11	Mike's Song	Weekapaug Gr
3/20/92	2	2	2/12	Mike's Song	Weekapaug Gr
3/24/92	3	2	3/13	Mike's Song	Weekapaug Gr
3/27/92	3	2	2/13	Mike's Song	Weekapaug Gr
3/31/92	3	2	2/13	Mike's Song	Weekapaug Gr
4/6/92	5	2	5/13	Mike's Song	Weekapaug Gr
4/8/92	2	2	9/15	Mike's Song	Weekapaug Gr
4/13/92	2	2	5/11	Mike's Song	Weekapaug Gr
4/16/92	2	2	5/12	Mike's Song	Weekapaug Gr
4/19/92	3	2	3/13	Mike's Song	Weekapaug Gr
4/21/92	1	2	7/13	Mike's Song	Weekapaug Gr
4/23/92	2	2	4/13	Mike's Song	Weekapaug Gr
4/24/92	1	2	6/12	Mike's Song	Weekapaug Gr
4/29/92	2	2	8/11	Mike's Song	Weekapaug Gr
5/1/92	2	2	7/13	Mike's Song	Weekapaug Gr
5/3/92	2	2	7/14	Mike's Song	Weekapaug Gr
5/5/92	1	2	6/14	Mike's Song	Weekapaug Gr
5/7/92	2	2	7/12	Mike's Song	Weekapaug Gr
5/14/92	5	2	7/13	Mike's Song	Weekapaug Gr
5/18/92	4	2	7/13	Mike's Song	Weekapaug Gr
7/16/92	14	2	12/13	Mike's Song	Weekapaug Gr
8/17/92	18	2	6/11	Mike's Song	Weekapaug Gr
11/19/92	11	2	2/15	Mike's Song	Weekapaug Gr
11/21/92	2	2	4/13	Mike's Song	Weekapaug Gr
11/23/92	2	2	8/14	Mike's Song	Weekapaug Gr
11/28/92	3	1	10/11	Mike's Song	Weekapaug Gr
12/1/92	2	1	11/12	Mike's Song	Weekapaug Gr
12/3/92	2	2	5/13	Mike's Song	Weekapaug Gr
12/5/92	2	2	10/13	Mike's Song	Weekapaug Gr
12/8/92	3	2	2/15	Mike's Song	Weekapaug Gr
12/11/92	2	2	3/12	Mike's Song	Weekapaug Gr
12/29/92	4	2	10/14	Mike's Song	Weekapaug Gr
2/6/93	6	2	7/14	Mike's Song	Weekapaug Gr
2/9/93	2	2	3/12	Mike's Song	Weekapaug Gr
2/11/93	2	2	5/12	Mike's Song	Weekapaug Gr
2/15/93	3	2	5/12	Mike's Song	Weekapaug Gr
2/18/93	2	2	6/12	Mike's Song	Weekapaug Gr
2/20/93	2	2	10/22	Mike's Song	Kung
2/20/93	0	2	12/22	Kung	Weekapaug Gr
2/23/93	3	2	8/13	Mike's Song	Weekapaug Gr
2/27/93	3	2	8/12	Mike's Song	Weekapaug Gr
3/3/93	2	2	6/13	Mike's Song	Weekapaug Gr
3/9/93	4	2	7/15	Mike's Song	Weekapaug Gr
3/13/93	2	2	9/13	Mike's Song	Weekapaug Gr
3/17/93	3	2	7/12	Mike's Song	Weekapaug Gr
3/19/93	2	2	7/10	Mike's Song	Weekapaug Gr
3/22/93	2	2	12/13	Mike's Song	Weekapaug Gr
3/25/93	2	2	11/13	Mike's Song	Weekapaug Gr
3/27/93	2	2	10/14	Mike's Song	Weekapaug Gr
3/30/93	2	2	8/15	Mike's Song	Weekapaug Gr
4/2/93	3	2	8/13	Mike's Song	Weekapaug Gr
4/16/93	7	2	6/13	Mike's Song	Weekapaug Gr
4/23/93	6	2	8/12	Mike's Song	Weekapaug Gr
4/25/93	2	2	8/11	Mike's Song	Weekapaug Gr

DATE	GAP	SET	POS.	SONG BEFORE	SONG AFTER
4/29/93	2	2	8/13	Mike's Song	Weekapaug Gr
5/8/93	8	2	15/18	Mike's Song	Weekapaug Gr
4/9/94	44	2	7/11	Mike's Song	Weekapaug Gr
4/21/94	10	2	5/10	Mike's Song	Weekapaug Gr
4/29/94	6	2	8/11	Mike's Song	Weekapaug Gr
5/14/94	11	2	3/11	Mike's Song	Weekapaug Gr
5/19/94	3	2	4/10	Mike's Song	Weekapaug Gr
6/9/94	10	2	8/10	Mike's Song	Weekapaug Gr
6/13/94	3	2	2/11	Mike's Song	Weekapaug Gr
6/17/94	3	2	7/15	Mike's Song	Weekapaug Gr
6/22/94	4	2	10/20	Mike's Song	Weekapaug Gr
7/2/94	8	2	6/12	Yerushalayim	Weekapaug Gr
7/10/94	6	2	6/10	Mike's Song	Weekapaug Gr
10/8/94	6	2	7/12	Mike's Song	Weekapaug Gr
10/21/94	10	2	5/11	Mike's Song	Weekapaug Gr
12/10/94	34	2	6/11	Mike's Song	Weekapaug Gr
6/10/95	9	2	5/8	Mike's Song	Weekapaug Gr
10/19/95	34	2	4/10	Mike's Song	Weekapaug Gr
7/23/96	60	2	6/9	Mike's Song	Weekapaug Gr
8/5/96	5	2	12/13	Mike's Song	Weekapaug Gr
7/22/97	83	2	4/6	Simple	Weekapaug Gr
7/31/97	6	2	6/7	Mike's Song	Weekapaug Gr
11/13/97	12	2	6/7	Mike's Song	Weekapaug Gr
11/22/97	6	1	2/8	Mike's Song	Weekapaug Gr
12/9/97	11	1	5/10	Stash	Weekapaug Gr
11/27/98	67	2	11/16	Mike's Song	Weekapaug Gr
12/31/98	6	1	3/7	Mike's Song	Weekapaug Gr
7/16/99	12	2	3/8	Mike's Song	Weekapaug Gr
8/1/99	12	2	5/9	Mike's Song	Weekapaug Gr
9/16/99	6	2	3/8	Mike's Song	Weekapaug Gr
10/7/99	15	E	2/3	Rocky Top	Julius
12/5/99	7	2	3/10	Meatstick	Weekapaug Gr
12/11/99	4	1	4/8	Simple	Weekapaug Gr
12/30/99	7	3	8/9	Simple	Weekapaug Gr
7/1/00	19	2	7/10	Steep	Weekapaug Gr
9/12/00	14	2	7/8	Mike's Song	Weekapaug Gr
9/25/00	9	2	3/7	Mike's Song	Weekapaug Gr
10/7/00	8	1	3/8	Mike's Song	Weekapaug Gr

Was played in the most recent show.

I Am the Sea

DATE	GAP	SET	POS.	SONG BEFORE	SONG AFTER
10/31/95	759	2	1/17	***	The Real Me

Has not been played in the last 360 shows.

I Been to Georgia on a Fast Train

DATE	GAP	SET	POS.	SONG BEFORE	SONG AFTER
5/6/93	547	1	13/13	Tennessee Waltz	***

Has not been played in the last 572 shows.

I Didn't Know

DATE	GAP	SET	POS.	SONG BEFORE	SONG AFTER
9/27/87	31	2	2/5	Wilson	Fluffhead
11/18/87	3	2	1/4	***	You Enjoy My
11/19/87	1	2	3/6	Fluffhead	Fee
2/7/88	2	1	9/10	Dear Mrs. Reagan	David Bowie
2/24/88	2	1	3/11	You Enjoy Myself	The Lizards
2/26/88	1	1	12/13	Fluffhead	Golgi Apparat
3/21/88	3	1	13/15	Dinner and a Movie	Col. Forbin's A
3/31/88	1	1	1/14	***	Golgi Apparat
4/22/88	2	2	1/13	***	Golgi Apparat
5/14/88	1	1	2/11	Fire	Halley's Comet
5/15/88	1	2	8/11	Jesus Just Left	Flat Fee
5/25/88	2	3	2/11	The Sloth	Ya Mar
6/20/88	3	1	11/11	Jam	***
6/21/88	1	2	2/10	Harpua	AC/DC Bag
7/12/88	3	1	8/8	You Enjoy Myself	***
11/3/88	15	3	3/6	Foam	BBFCFM
11/5/88	1	2	10/11	Weekapaug Groove	Good Time Ba
12/2/88	2	2	1/8	***	Good Time Ba
12/10/88	1	1	1/12	***	Golgi Apparat
1/26/89	3	1	1/10	***	Golgi Apparat
2/6/89	1	2	7/7	On Your Way Down	***
3/3/89	6	1	8/11	Run Like an Antelope	Divided Sky
3/4/89	1	1	2/8	Take the A-Train	Mike's Song
4/27/89	7	1	5/8	Sanity	Alumni Blues
4/30/89	1	1	1/9	***	You Enjoy My
5/5/89	2	2	1/4	***	Take the A-Trn
5/6/89	1	1	2/13	You Enjoy Myself	Mike's Song
5/9/89	1	2	7/14	Run Like an Antelope	Nowhere Fast
5/9/89	0	2	10/14	I've Turned Bad	The Lizards
5/20/89	3	1	7/8	Divided Sky	Possum
10/14/89	19	1	3/11	Divided Sky	Golgi Apparat
10/20/89	1	2	4/10	Dinner and a Movie	AC/DC Bag
10/22/89	2	1	13/14	Divided Sky	Good Time Ba
10/26/89	1	1	6/11	Divided Sky	Wilson
10/28/89	1	1	1/9	***	You Enjoy My
11/9/89	4	1	1/9	***	Golgi Apparat
12/1/89	6	1	1/9	***	La Grange
12/3/89	1	E	1/2	***	Golgi Apparat
12/7/89	1	1	1/11	***	You Enjoy My
12/8/89	1	2	5/7	Slave	You Enjoy My
12/15/89	2	2	1/8	***	Possum
12/31/89	4	1	1/9	***	You Enjoy My
2/9/90	6	E	1/1	***	***
2/10/90	1	E	1/2	***	Highway to Hell
2/23/90	5	E	2/3	Contact	Good Time Ba
2/24/90	1	1	7/8	Possum	Run Like Antel
3/1/90	2	1	5/7	Divided Sky	You Enjoy My
3/8/90	4	2	6/12	Caravan	The Lizards
4/4/90	6	2	7/8	The Sloth	Good Time Ba
4/6/90	2	2	8/10	Reba	Alumni Blues
4/14/90	6	2	1/11	***	The Oh Kee Pa
4/22/90	5	1	6/12	Possum	Cavern
4/26/90	2	1	7/9	Bouncing	Run Like Antel
4/28/90	1	2	4/9	Caravan	Reba
5/24/90	11	2	4/11	Possum	My Sweet One
5/31/90	2	1	8/12	Tweezer	Uncle Pen
6/8/90	5	2	4/7	Tweezer	Mike's Song
9/14/90	4	1	8/11	Dinner and a Movie	Mike's Song
9/22/90	5	1	11/12	The Landlady	David Bowie
10/5/90	5	1	1/13	***	Mike's Song
10/7/90	2	2	5/8	My Sweet One	The Lizards
11/2/90	6	2	8/9	The Lizards	David Bowie
11/8/90	3	1	9/12	The Asse Festival	Mike's Song
11/16/90	2	2	10/11	Runaway Jim	Possum
11/30/90	4	2	8/10	Divided Sky	The Sloth
12/29/90	5	1	1/10	***	Llama
12/31/90	1	1	3/12	Divided Sky	The Landlady
2/14/91	7	2	10/12	Bouncing	The Landlady
2/27/91	7	1	3/10	Divided Sky	The Landlady
3/15/91	7	2	7/9	Destiny Unbound	Harry Hood
3/23/91	4	1	5/10	Llama	The Curtain
3/29/91	2	2	2/8	Possum	Foam
3/31/91	1	1	10/13	Possum	Mike's Song
4/5/91	4	2	7/9	Harry Hood	My Sweet One
4/19/91	7	1	7/12	Stash	Rocky Top
4/21/91	2	2	10/11	Cavern	David Bowie
5/2/91	4	2	8/10	My Sweet One	Buried Alive
5/17/91	8	1	13/17	Stash	Mike's Song
5/19/91	2	2	9/10	McGrupp	Golgi Apparat
7/14/91	4	1	10/11	The Sloth	Possum
7/18/91	2	2	7/8	The Landlady	Possum
7/19/91	1	2	3/8	Divided Sky	My Sweet One
7/21/91	2	2	2/9	Tweezer	Runaway Jim
7/24/91	2	2	8/10	Funky Bitch	Frankenstein
7/27/91	3	1	12/16	Possum	The Landlady
8/3/91	1	2	8/10	Cavern	You Enjoy My
9/27/91	3	1	8/9	It's Ice	Llama
9/29/91	2	1	3/10	Divided Sky	It's Ice
10/2/91	2	E	2/3	Possum	Rocky Top
10/6/91	3	2	7/10	Harry Hood	Cavern
10/10/91	1	2	6/13	Run Like an Antelope	Sparkle
10/18/91	6	2	8/12	Weekapaug Groove	Fee
10/24/91	3	1	8/12	Divided Sky	T.M.W.S.I.Y.
10/28/91	2	1	5/10	Reba	Tube
10/31/91	2	2	13/14	Tube	Harry Hood
11/7/91	3	1	10/11	Runaway Jim	Llama
11/8/91	1	2	5/13	The Squirming Coil	Mike's Song
11/13/91	4	1	9/10	Divided Sky	You Enjoy My
11/22/91	7	2	7/10	The Squirming Coil	Llama
11/24/91	2	1	8/9	It's Ice	David Bowie

DATE	GAP	SET	POS.	SONG BEFORE	SONG AFTER
11/30/91	1	2	8/10	Horn	Run Like Antel
12/5/91	2	2	11/13	The Squirming Coil	My Sweet One
12/6/91	1	1	9/9	Guelah Papyrus	***
3/12/92	6	1	5/11	Stash	Reba
3/17/92	3	1	6/11	It's Ice	Divided Sky
3/24/92	5	2	9/13	Uncle Pen	The Oh Kee Pa
3/28/92	4	2	3/4	Carolina	Sweet Adeline
3/30/92	1	1	7/11	Maze	All Things Rec
4/1/92	2	1	9/12	Runaway Jim	The Landlady
4/4/92	2	1	10/10	The Lizards	***
4/15/92	7	1	9/11	Cavern	All Things Rec
4/17/92	2	1	5/13	Stash	Cavern
4/19/92	2	1	10/11	Chalk Dust Torture	Golgi Apparat
4/23/92	3	1	10/11	It's Ice	Possum
5/1/92	5	1	11/12	Horn	Possum
5/3/92	2	1	7/10	Split Open and Melt	Rift
5/5/92	1	1	8/11	Divided Sky	It's Ice
5/9/92	4	1	10/11	The Squirming Coil	Run Like Antel
5/10/92	1	1	8/10	Reba	You Enjoy My
5/17/92	5	1	7/11	Reba	Stash
6/24/92	5	1	8/9	Guelah Papyrus	Sparkle
6/27/92	1	E	1/2	***	Good Time Ba
7/14/92	7	1	10/12	Brother	Poor Heart
7/30/92	13	1	7/8	Maze	Possum
11/30/92	26	1	8/10	It's Ice	Reba
12/10/92	9	1	7/11	Split Open and Melt	All Things Rec
12/13/92	3	1	10/11	Fast Enough for You	David Bowie
12/30/92	3	1	11/14	Reba	David Bowie
12/31/92	1	1	10/11	Foam	Run Like Antel
2/3/93	1	1	7/11	Divided Sky	My Friend My
2/5/93	2	1	7/11	Punch You in the Eye	Poor Heart
2/7/93	2	1	9/12	Rift	Split Open and
2/10/93	2	1	8/10	Tela	Catapult
2/12/93	2	1	9/11	Chalk Dust Torture	Take the A-Trn
2/15/93	2	1	11/12	Guelah Papyrus	Run Like Antel
2/22/93	6	1	9/10	Cavern	David Bowie
2/25/93	2	1	10/11	Bouncing	David Bowie
2/26/93	1	1	9/10	Divided Sky	Cavern
3/2/93	2	1	12/13	Silent in the Mornin	David Bowie
3/5/93	2	1	10/11	It's Ice	Possum
3/9/93	3	1	9/10	Punch You in the Eye	Run Like Antel
3/16/93	4	1	7/11	Maze	Divided Sky
3/18/93	2	1	10/11	Horn	David Bowie
3/24/93	4	1	6/9	Maze	Sample in a Ja
3/27/93	3	1	9/10	Sample in a Jar	David Bowie
3/31/93	3	1	9/10	Reba	David Bowie
4/2/93	2	1	6/9	Divided Sky	Sparkle
4/9/93	3	1	8/11	Maze	It's Ice
4/14/93	3	1	12/13	Divided Sky	Golgi Apparat
4/18/93	3	1	9/10	Horn	Cavern
4/21/93	2	1	10/11	Punch You in the Eye	Run Like Antel
4/25/93	4	1	10/11	Maze	Golgi Apparat
5/2/93	5	1	10/11	Maze	Golgi Apparat
5/7/93	4	1	10/11	Divided Sky	Run Like Antel
5/30/93	3	1	9/13	Run Like an Antelope	Split Open and
7/15/93	1	1	6/9	Stash	My Mind's Got A Mind
7/25/93	8	1	9/10	My Mind's Got A Mind	David Bowie
7/30/93	4	1	8/10	Chalk Dust Torture	Reba
8/8/93	6	1	10/11	Paul and Silas	David Bowie
8/16/93	7	1	7/9	Foam	Split Open and
8/21/93	3	1	9/10	The Landlady	Runaway Jim
12/31/93	8	1	7/8	Peaches en Regalia	Run Like Antel
4/8/94	4	1	6/13	Foam	Punch You in
4/10/94	2	1	7/9	Chalk Dust Torture	Scent of a Mul
4/17/94	6	1	3/9	Foam	Divided Sky
4/29/94	9	1	7/12	Divided Sky	Dog Faced Boy
5/29/94	23	1	7/8	Julius	David Bowie
6/14/94	5	1	11/14	Uncle Pen	My Sweet One
6/14/94	0	1	13/14	My Sweet One	Split Open and
6/29/94	11	1	10/11	David Bowie	Golgi Apparat
7/13/94	10	1	10/11	Fast Enough for You	Split Open and
10/13/94	9	1	5/9	Down with Disease	Foam
10/18/94	4	1	3/10	My Friend My Friend	Poor Heart
10/28/94	8	1	1/10	***	Llama
11/22/94	14	1	6/9	Guyute	Bouncing
12/1/94	6	1	6/8	Guyute	Split Open and
12/9/94	7	1	5/8	Sparkle	It's Ice
12/29/94	3	1	8/10	Uncle Pen	Possum
6/15/95	10	1	8/10	Stash	Fluffhead
6/20/95	4	1	8/9	Taste	Split Open and
6/25/95	4	1	8/9	Divided Sky	Split Open and
7/2/95	6	1	8/10	Reba	Rift
9/27/95	2	1	5/9	It's Ice	Fog that Sur-rounds
10/15/95	13	1	4/10	Slave	Demand
10/27/95	8	1	5/9	Horn	Rift
11/12/95	7	1	6/10	Reba	Taste That Surrounds
11/28/95	10	1	5/9	Foam	Divided Sky
12/28/95	16	2	6/8	Tweezer	Uncle Pen
7/11/96	12	1	4/8	Reba	Sparkle
7/15/96	3	1	6/8	Possum	Harry Hood
8/10/96	14	1	6/11	Reba	The Horse
10/25/96	13	1	8/10	Guelah Papyrus	Stash
11/24/96	20	1	9/11	Taste	Sample in a Ja
12/2/96	5	1	5/8	You Enjoy Myself	Theme From the Botto
2/22/97	14	1	9/10	Split Open and Melt	Character Zer
11/28/97	55	1	3/8	You Enjoy Myself	Maze
8/3/98	43	1	3/8	Halley's Comet	Ride Captain Ride
7/4/99	42	1	8/10	Vultures	Fast Enough For You
7/15/99	7	1	8/10	Theme From the Botto	The Sloth
9/9/99	14	1	9/10	Stash	Character Zer
9/21/99	9	1	5/9	Drowned	Back on the Train
9/29/99	6	2	11/12	Mike's Song	Weekapaug Gr
12/31/99	24	1	4/14	Tube	Punch You in
7/6/00	21	1	8/12	First Tube	The Inlaw Josie Wale
9/30/00	23	1	5/10	Roggae	Mike's Song

Has not been played in the last 5 shows.

I Don't Care

DATE	GAP	SET	POS.	SONG BEFORE	SONG AFTER
6/16/97	880	2	3/7	Ghost	Reba
6/20/97	2	1	7/8	Limb by Limb	Run Like Antel

Has not been played in the last 237 shows.

I Found a Reason

DATE	GAP	SET	POS.	SONG BEFORE	SONG AFTER
10/31/98	983	2	8/10	Lonesome Cowboy Bill	Train Round the Bend

Has not been played in the last 136 shows.

I Get a Kick Out of You

DATE	GAP	SET	POS.	SONG BEFORE	SONG AFTER
8/2/98	967	2	5/6	David Bowie	Loving Cup
11/9/98	22	1	3/10	Horn	Divided Sky

Has not been played in the last 130 shows.

I Know a Little

DATE	GAP	SET	POS.	SONG BEFORE	SONG AFTER
8/10/87	26	2	7/10	The Curtain With	Mustang Sally
5/25/88	24	3	7/11	Fee	BBFCFM
8/3/88	12	2	1/3	***	You Enjoy My

Has not been played in the last 1057 shows.

I Saw it Again

DATE	GAP	SET	POS.	SONG BEFORE	SONG AFTER
6/14/97	879	2	3/8	Piper	Waking Up
6/19/97	2	2	3/7	Ghost	Wading In Vel-vet Sea
6/25/97	5	1	9/11	Wading In Velvet Sea	Limb by Limb
7/1/97	3	1	6/9	Ain't Love Funny	Dirt
7/31/97	15	1	8/9	Glide	You Enjoy My
11/29/97	22	1	9/12	Ginseng Sullivan	Horn
12/12/97	9	2	1/7	***	Piper
7/8/99	77	2	5/9	Jesus Just Left	Sleep
7/25/99	13	1	6/8	Makisupa Policeman	Boogie On Reggae
9/10/99	7	2	6/9	Gotta Jibboo	Split Open and
7/4/00	58	2	2/5	Gotta Jibboo	Magilla
9/8/00	9	1	7/12	Silent in the Mornin	NICU
9/30/00	15	1	8/10	Simple	Esther

Has not been played in the last 5 shows.

I Shall Be Released

DATE	GAP	SET	POS.	SONG BEFORE	SONG AFTER
10/18/98	980	1	12/12	Four Strong Winds	***

Has not been played in the last 139 shows.

I Told You So

DATE	GAP	SET	POS.	SONG BEFORE	SONG AFTER
3/18/97	877	2	6/10	Love Me	Love Me Like a Man

Has not been played in the last 242 shows.

I Walk the Line

DATE	GAP	SET	POS.	SONG BEFORE	SONG AFTER
11/19/92	455	2	6/15	It's Ice	Tweezer
11/20/92	1	1	11/12	Memories	David Bowie
11/23/92	3	2	4/14	The Squirming Coil	Llama
11/27/92	2	2	7/13	McGrupp	David Bowie
12/2/92	4	2	10/11	The Squirming Coil	Runaway Jim
12/5/92	3	2	4/13	Reba	Reba
12/30/92	10	1	9/14	Reba	Reba
2/10/93	8	2	5/11	Tweezer	Sparkle
3/9/93	20	2	13/15	Love You	The Squirmin

Has not been played in the last 613 shows.

I Wanna Be Like You

DATE	GAP	SET	POS.	SONG BEFORE	SONG AFTER
4/4/94	589	2	9/11	Wolfman's Brother	The Oh Kee Pa
4/5/94	1	2	6/8	You Enjoy Myself	Chalk Dust Tor
4/10/94	4	2	6/7	Ginseng Sullivan	Harry Hood
4/15/94	4	2	9/10	Alumni Blues	Cavern
4/18/94	3	2	12/13	Down with Disease	Cavern
4/22/94	3	2	7/8	Runaway Jim	The Squirmin
4/29/94	5	2	10/11	Weekapaug Groove	Cavern
5/3/94	3	2	7/8	Chalk Dust Torture	Slave
6/10/94	22	2	7/9	Possum	Harry Hood

Has not been played in the last 485 shows.

I Will

DATE	GAP	SET	POS.	SONG BEFORE	SONG AFTER
10/31/94	681	2	17/30	Why Don't We Do it i	Julia

Has not been played in the last 438 shows.

I Wish

DATE	GAP	SET	POS.	SONG BEFORE	SONG AFTER
10/30/85	8	1	6/11	Sneakin' Sally	Revival

Has not been played in the last 1111 shows.

I'll Come Running

DATE	GAP	SET	POS.	SONG BEFORE	SONG AFTER
5/16/95	712	E	1/2	***	Gloria

Has not been played in the last 407 shows.

I'm Blue I'm Lonesome

DATE	GAP	SET	POS.	SONG BEFORE	SONG AFTER
11/16/94	688	2	3/7	Simple	My Long Journey Home
11/17/94	1	E	1/4	***	Nellie Kane
11/19/94	2	1	9/11	Run Like an Antelope	Butter Them Biscuits
11/22/94	2	2	9/13	BBFCFM	Butter Them Biscuits
11/30/94	5	1	9/10	Bouncing	My Long Journey Home
12/6/94	5	2	10/12	Bike	Foreplay/Long Time
12/7/94	1	2	6/9	Julius	My Long Journey Home
12/9/94	2	E	1/3	***	Foreplay/Long Time
12/30/94	4	2	4/8	Tweezer	You Enjoy My
9/30/95	28	1	8/9	Run Like an Antelope	Sample in a Ja
10/3/95	2	1	5/11	Fast Enough for You	Free
10/6/95	2	1	5/9	Reba	Rift
10/8/95	2	1	6/9	Reba	Prince Caspian
10/13/95	2	1	5/9	Billy Breathes	Prince Caspian
10/15/95	2	1	9/10	Strange Design	David Bowie
10/17/95	1	E	2/2	My Long Journey Home	***

DATE	GAP	SET	POS.	SONG BEFORE	SONG AFTER
10/20/95	2	2	8/10	My Long Journey Home	Bouncing
10/22/95	2	1	11/12	Sample in a Jar	Stash
10/25/95	2	1	9/10	My Long Journey Home	Chalk Dust Tor
11/14/95	9	1	8/9	Julius	Cavern
11/18/95	3	1	7/8	Slave	Sample in a Ja
11/21/95	2	1	6/10	My Long Journey Home	Guyute
11/24/95	2	1	7/9	Tela	Maze
11/25/95	1	2	7/12	My Long Journey Home	Strange Design
11/29/95	2	2	9/11	Poor Heart	My Long Journey Home
12/5/95	5	1	8/8	David Bowie	***
12/12/95	5	1	9/10	Run Like an Antelope	The Squirmin
10/17/98	195	1	5/10	Possum	Freebird
7/18/99	41	1	7/11	If You Need a Fool	Beauty of My Dreams
6/22/00	61	2	7/10	Harry Hood	Hold Whatcha Got

Has not been played in the last 38 shows.

I'm Gonna Be (500 Miles)

DATE	GAP	SET	POS.	SONG BEFORE	SONG AFTER
12/30/97	939	2	4/10	Harpua	Harpua

Has not been played in the last 180 shows.

I'm One

DATE	GAP	SET	POS.	SONG BEFORE	SONG AFTER
10/31/95	759	2	6/17	The Punk Meets The G	The Dirty Jobs

Has not been played in the last 360 shows.

I'm So Tired

DATE	GAP	SET	POS.	SONG BEFORE	SONG AFTER
10/31/95	681	2	11/30	Martha My Dear	Blackbird
11/18/95	86	2	4/10	Free	You Enjoy My

Has not been played in the last 352 shows.

I've Had Enough

DATE	GAP	SET	POS.	SONG BEFORE	SONG AFTER
10/31/95	759	2	10/17	Is It In My Head	5:15

Has not been played in the last 360 shows.

I've Turned Bad

DATE	GAP	SET	POS.	SONG BEFORE	SONG AFTER
5/9/89	99	2	9/14	Nowhere Fast	I Didn't Know

Has not been played in the last 1020 shows.

Icculus

DATE	GAP	SET	POS.	SONG BEFORE	SONG AFTER
4/1/86	12	1	6/7	Dave's Energy Guide	You Enjoy My
10/31/86	3	2	10/11	Skin it Back	Alumni Blues
8/10/87	11	3	1/7	***	David Bowie
5/15/88	22	2	1/11	***	McGrupp
7/25/88	12	E	1/2	***	Camel Walk
11/5/88	13	E	1/4	***	Suzy Greenber
1/26/89	6	2	2/10	Suzy Greenberg	Col. Forbin's A
5/1/89	17	2	6/10	Possum	Col. Forbin's A
4/6/91	178	2	8/11	Bathtub Gin	Run Like Antel
4/16/92	113	1	10/12	Col. Forbin's Ascent	The Famous Mockingbi
5/2/92	12	1	3/11	Col. Forbin's Ascent	The Famous Mockingbi
3/25/93	118	2	7/13	Kung	The Famous Mockingbi
6/22/94	126	2	7/20	Simple	Simple
10/27/94	35	E	2/3	Slave	Tweezer Repri
11/20/94	14	E	1/1	***	***
10/31/95	67	1	9/9	***	Divided Sky
7/18/99	261	3	7/9	Smoke on the Water J	Quinn the Eskimo

Has not been played in the last 99 shows.

If I Could

DATE	GAP	SET	POS.	SONG BEFORE	SONG AFTER
4/4/94	589	2	2/11	Down with Disease	Buried Alive
4/5/94	1	2	4/8	Tweezer	You Enjoy My
4/8/94	2	1	11/13	Down with Disease	Lawn Boy
4/15/94	6	2	2/10	Maze	The Oh Kee Pa
4/17/94	2	1	7/9	Down with Disease	My Sweet One
4/21/94	3	1	8/9	Down with Disease	Cavern
4/29/94	6	2	3/11	Maze	Reba
5/3/94	3	2	2/8	David Bowie	Fluffhead

DATE	GAP	SET	POS.	SONG BEFORE	SONG AFTER
5/7/94	3	1	8/9	Split Open and Melt	Suzy Greenber
5/10/94	2	1	8/9	Split Open and Melt	Cavern
5/13/94	2	1	6/9	Stash	My Friend My
5/17/94	3	1	4/9	Mound	Scent of a Mul
5/20/94	2	1	3/10	Maze	It's Ice
5/23/94	3	2	3/7	Run Like an Antelope	Sparkle
5/27/94	3	1	6/9	David Bowie	Punch You in
6/9/94	3	1	6/9	It's Ice	Maze
6/14/94	4	2	4/9	David Bowie	It's Ice
6/17/94	2	1	5/9	Split Open and Melt	Punch You in
6/19/94	2	2	3/8	Run Like an Antelope	Reba
6/22/94	2	1	6/9	Maze	Scent of a Mul
6/26/94	4	2	3/12	Down with Disease	Axilla (Part II)
7/1/94	3	2	2/11	David Bowie	Fluffhead
7/5/94	3	1	5/10	Letter to Jimmy Page	Uncle Pen
7/10/94	4	1	6/9	Stash	My Friend My
7/14/94	2	2	4/10	Maze	Uncle Pen
10/13/94	8	2	3/12	Run Like an Antelope	It's Ice
11/2/94	15	1	3/8	Foam	Maze
11/12/94	3	1	3/8	Foam	Maze
11/20/94	7	1	5/10	Stash	Butter Them Biscuits
11/23/94	2	1	5/9	It's Ice	The Oh Kee Pa
11/26/94	2	1	4/9	Guyute	Foam
12/4/94	6	1	3/9	Foam	Rift
12/9/94	4	1	7/8	It's Ice	Run Like Antel
12/29/94	3	1	3/9	Foam	Split Open and
6/7/95	4	1	6/10	Stash	Scent of a Mul
6/20/95	10	1	6/9	Bathtub Gin	Taste
6/25/95	4	1	5/9	Theme From the Botto	Sparkle
7/1/95	5	1	3/9	Llama	All Things Rec
7/3/95	2	1	7/11	It's Ice	Maze
9/30/95	4	2	3/9	Fog that Surrounds	Scent of a Mul
10/11/95	7	1	5/9	Divided Sky	Fog that Surrounds
11/12/95	18	1	8/10	Taste That Surrounds	Split Open and
11/29/95	11	1	4/9	Reba	It's Ice
7/21/96	34	1	5/14	Tweezer	My Mind's Got A Mind
8/5/96	7	1	7/9	Foam	Julius
7/31/98	150	2	3/9	Free	T.M.W.S.I.Y.
6/28/00	120	1	6/6	Piper	***

Has not been played in the last 34 shows.

If I Don't Be There by Morning

DATE	GAP	SET	POS.	SONG BEFORE	SONG AFTER
5/9/89	99	2	3/14	La Grange	Slave

Has not been played in the last 1020 shows.

If I Only Had a Brain

DATE	GAP	SET	POS.	SONG BEFORE	SONG AFTER
3/12/89	88	1	4/8	Weekapaug Groove	Alumni Blues
3/24/89	2	1	8/10	AC/DC Bag	Take the A-Trn
5/13/89	11	2	5/7	Harry Hood	Contact
9/21/89	14	2	8/9	You Enjoy Myself	Run Like Antel
10/1/89	1	2	8/11	You Enjoy Myself	Contact
11/10/89	15	2	11/12	The Lizards	Possum
11/11/89	1	1	7/8	You Enjoy Myself	Frankenstein
12/1/89	4	2	9/10	Weekapaug Groove	Highway To Hell
1/29/90	13	1	2/10	The Lizards	Mike's Song
3/28/90	20	2	16/16	Highway to Hell	***
4/5/90	2	2	12/13	Weekapaug Groove	Contact
4/8/90	3	1	4/8	You Enjoy Myself	The Oh Kee Pa
4/25/90	10	1	1/4	***	Divided Sky
5/4/90	4	1	10/12	Caravan	Highway to Hell
5/7/90	2	1	4/5	La Grange	Possum
5/23/90	6	1	4/10	You Enjoy Myself	The Oh Kee Pa
6/16/90	10	3	10/13	Caravan	Mike's Song
10/6/90	13	1	11/13	Possum	David Bowie
10/8/90	2	2	3/6	Stash	Golgi Apparat
12/31/90	20	2	8/9	Rocky Top	Run Like Antel
4/16/91	37	E	1/2	***	Good Time Ba
7/13/91	21	2	8/9	Stash	You Enjoy My
10/12/91	25	2	8/10	Brother	Harry Hood
11/14/91	20	2	9/11	Take the A-Train	The Lizards

DATE	GAP	SET	POS.	SONG BEFORE	SONG AFTER
4/19/92	46	2	12/13	Lawn Boy	Runaway Jim
6/23/92	25	1	7/8	BBFCFM	Golgi Apparat
12/12/92	59	2	8/10	You Enjoy Myself	The Squirmin
2/7/93	10	2	12/13	The Squirming Coil	Tweezer Repri
2/25/93	14	2	9/11	Fast Enough for You	Golgi Apparat
3/18/93	14	2	8/10	Big Ball Jam	The Squirmin
3/30/93	9	2	14/15	Silent in the Mornin	Tweezer Repri
4/30/93	21	2	8/10	Harry Hood	You Enjoy My
8/21/93	38	2	8/10	David Bowie	Harry Hood
12/29/93	6	2	9/11	Big Ball Jam	Sweet Adeline
10/25/94	90	2	10/11	Big Ball Jam	Possum
11/16/95	90	2	7/9	Harry Hood	Amazing Grce
7/8/99	246	2	2/9	Birds of a Feather	Prince Caspian

Has not been played in the last 107 shows.

If You Need a Fool

DATE	GAP	SET	POS.	SONG BEFORE	SONG AFTER
7/29/98	964	2	2/7	Buried Alive	AC/DC Bag
11/11/98	26	1	3/8	Gumbo	Sleep
7/18/99	30	1	6/11	Back on the Train	I'm Blue, Lonesome

Has not been played in the last 99 shows.

Immigrant Song Jam

DATE	GAP	SET	POS.	SONG BEFORE	SONG AFTER
11/14/95	764	2	10/11	You Enjoy Myself	You Enjoy My

Has not been played in the last 355 shows.

In a Hole

DATE	GAP	SET	POS.	SONG BEFORE	SONG AFTER
10/20/89	122	2	10/10	Swing Low Sweet Chrt	***
10/21/89	1	1	3/10	Ya Mar	McGrupp
10/22/89	1	2		Golgi Apparatus	McGrupp
10/26/89	1	2	12/15	Punch You in the Eye	Fishman's Gull Poem
11/30/89	10	E	1/2	***	Golgi Apparat
12/3/89	2	2	8/14	Split Open and Melt	Fee
12/9/89	3	1	5/10	Foam	Rocky Top
12/16/89	2	1	8/9	The Lizards	Golgi Apparat

Has not been played in the last 977 shows.

In the Midnight Hour

DATE	GAP	SET	POS.	SONG BEFORE	SONG AFTER
12/2/83	0	1	3/6	Proud Mary	Squeeze Box
11/3/84	2	1	1/10	***	Wild Child
3/4/85	2	1	4/4	Fire up the Ganja	***

Has not been played in the last 1115 shows.

Indian War Dance

DATE	GAP	SET	POS.	SONG BEFORE	SONG AFTER
3/14/93	509	1	9/11	Reba	Punch You in

Has not been played in the last 610 shows.

Is it in my Head

DATE	GAP	SET	POS.	SONG BEFORE	SONG AFTER
10/31/95	759	2	9/17	Helpless Dancer	I've Had Enough

Has not been played in the last 360 shows.

It's Ice

DATE	GAP	SET	POS.	SONG BEFORE	SONG AFTER
9/25/91	312	1	7/11	My Sweet One	The Landlady
9/26/91	1	1	5/10	Fee	My Sweet One
9/27/91	1	1	7/9	Tweezer	I Didn't Know
9/29/91	2	1	4/10	I Didn't Know	Poor Heart
10/3/91	3	1	4/10	Uncle Pen	Bouncing
10/10/91	3	1	8/11	Runaway Jim	Eliza
10/13/91	3	2	4/9	The Squirming Coil	My Sweet One
10/19/91	4	1	3/10	Suzy Greenberg	Runaway Jim
10/23/91	1	1	6/11	Paul and Silas	Horn
10/27/91	2	2	5/13	Sparkle	Mike's Song
11/1/91	4	2	3/13	My Sweet One	Chalk Dust Tor
11/7/91	2	1	6/11	Cavern	You Enjoy My
11/9/91	2	2	4/10	Poor Heart	Tweezer
11/13/91	3	1	3/10	Runaway Jim	Sparkle
11/14/91	1	2	5/11	Paul and Silas	Glide
11/16/91	2	1	5/11	Runaway Jim	Sparkle
11/20/91	2	2	2/8	Golgi Apparatus	My Sweet One
11/21/91	1	2	3/10	Harry Hood	The Mango Song

DATE	GAP	SET	POS.	SONG BEFORE	SONG AFTER
11/24/91	3	1	7/9	Sparkle	I Didn't Know
11/30/91	1	2	4/10	Harry Hood	Bouncing
12/5/91	2	1	8/10	Bathtub Gin	Bouncing
12/6/91	1	2	1/12	***	Eliza
3/6/92	3	1	4/11	Sparkle	The Oh Kee Pa
3/12/92	3	2	4/11	Eliza	Bouncing
3/17/92	1	1	5/11	Sparkle	I Didn't Know
3/25/92	6	1	9/10	Runaway Jim	Run Like Antel
4/1/92	6	1	7/12	Sparkle	Runaway Jim
4/4/92	2	1	7/10	Bouncing	Sparkle
4/5/92	1	1	9/11	Horn	Possum
4/7/92	2	1	3/12	Possum	Fee
4/12/92	2	1	7/11	Silent in the Mornin	Sparkle
4/16/92	3	1	3/12	Possum	Bouncing
4/18/92	2	1	8/11	Possum	Sparkle
4/21/92	2	1	7/11	Possum	Eliza
4/23/92	2	1	9/12	Bouncing	I Didn't Know
4/29/92	3	1	4/10	Sparkle	Runaway Jim
5/1/92	2	1	9/12	Guelah Papyrus	Horn
5/3/92	2	1	3/10	Possum	Uncle Pen
5/5/92	1	1	9/11	I Didn't Know	Glide
5/8/92	3	1	5/12	Uncle Pen	Eliza
5/12/92	3	1	6/12	Possum	Dinner and a
5/16/92	3	2	2/13	Runaway Jim	Paul and Silas
6/20/92	4	1	5/8	Runaway Jim	Horn
7/14/92	10	1	6/12	Sparkle	Runaway Jim
7/16/92	2	1	2/10	Poor Heart	Maze
7/21/92	4	1	3/7	Possum	Sparkle
7/26/92	4	1	2/7	Chalk Dust Torture	Divided Sky
7/30/92	3	1	4/8	Sparkle	All Things Rec
8/17/92	7	2	2/11	Suzy Greenberg	Tweezer
8/25/92	5	1	2/7	Runaway Jim	Sparkle
11/19/92	6	2	5/15	Bouncing	I Walk the Line
11/21/92	2	1	6/11	Poor Heart	Bouncing
11/25/92	3	1	7/11	Sparkle	The Squirmin
11/27/92	1	2	5/13	Glide	McGrupp
11/30/92	2	1	7/10	Sparkle	I Didn't Know
12/3/92	3	2	8/13	Lawn Boy	My Sweet One
12/4/92	1	2	5/10	Possum	The Squirmin
12/7/92	3	2	7/12	My Sweet One	Fee
12/8/92	1	2	6/15	Silent in the Mornin	The Lizards
12/11/92	2	1	5/11	Runaway Jim	Uncle Pen
12/13/92	2	1	4/11	Divided Sky	Fee
12/28/92	1	1	5/10	Glide	Bouncing
12/31/92	3	2	2/10	Runaway Jim	Sparkle
2/3/93	1	2	2/11	Runaway Jim	Tweezer
2/5/93	2	2	6/10	Paul and Silas	You Enjoy My
2/7/93	2	1	4/12	Poor Heart	Sparkle
2/10/93	2	2	2/11	Runaway Jim	The Squirmin
2/13/93	3	1	4/10	Poor Heart	Glide
2/17/93	2	1	7/11	Runaway Jim	Bouncing
2/19/93	2	2	2/12	Runaway Jim	Paul and Silas
2/22/93	3	2	3/11	Uncle Pen	Tweezer
2/25/93	2	2	2/11	Suzy Greenberg	Sparkle
2/27/93	2	1	6/10	Bouncing	Sparkle
3/2/93	1	1	6/13	Sparkle	Fee
3/5/93	2	1	9/11	Sparkle	I Didn't Know
3/8/93	2	1	10/12	Sparkle	Glide
3/13/93	3	2	4/13	The Lizards	Glide
3/16/93	2	1	4/10	Poor Heart	Fee
3/17/93	1	1	8/11	Paul and Silas	The Oh Kee Pa
3/19/93	2	2	2/10	Runaway Jim	Uncle Pen
3/22/93	2	2	2/13	Golgi Apparatus	The Lizards
3/25/93	2	1	3/11	Guelah Papyrus	Possum
3/27/93	2	2	3/14	Halley's Comet	Bouncing
3/28/93	1	1	9/11	Fee	Lawn Boy
3/31/93	2	2	7/10	Big Ball Jam	You Enjoy My
4/5/93	2	1	2/10	Llama	Fee
4/9/93	1	1	9/11	I Didn't Know	Divided Sky
4/12/93	2	2	5/10	Paul and Silas	Big Ball Jam
4/14/93	1	1	5/13	Bouncing	Stash
4/17/93	2	1	5/10	Stash	Glide
4/20/93	2	1	6/10	Bouncing	Glide
4/22/93	2	1	3/10	Sparkle	Reba
4/23/93	1	2	4/12	Ballad - Curtis Loew	Paul and Silas
4/25/93	2	1	4/11	Bouncing	Glide
4/27/93	1	1	8/10	Guelah Papyrus	Sparkle
4/29/93	1	2	2/13	Chalk Dust Torture	Ya Mar
5/1/93	2	1	8/10	Sample in a Jar	Glide
5/3/93	2	2	7/12	Contact	McGrupp
5/5/93	1	1	7/10	Bouncing	Glide
5/8/93	3	2	8/18	Silent in the Mornin	The Squirmin
7/15/93	3	2	5/11	Sparkle	Lifeboy
7/17/93	2	2	4/12	The Squirming Coil	Sparkle
7/22/93	3	2	5/11	Sparkle	Contact
7/23/93	1	1	10/12	Runaway Jim	Lawn Boy
7/27/93	3	1	6/8	Sparkle	Purple Rain
7/29/93	2	2	3/9	Bouncing	Lifeboy
7/31/93	2	2	3/11	Runaway Jim	Maze
8/3/93	2	2	4/9	Bouncing	You Enjoy My
8/8/93	3	2	5/11	Wilson	Fluffhead
8/11/93	2	1	4/10	Weigh	Ginseng Sullivan
8/14/93	3	1	6/11	Silent in the Mornin	Sparkle
8/16/93	2	2	5/10	Mound	My Friend My
8/20/93	2	1	6/10	Bouncing	The Wedge
8/24/93	1	1	4/11	Bouncing	Nellie Kane
8/26/93	2	1	7/9	Esther	Harry Hood
8/28/93	1	2	7/14	Sparkle	Big Ball Jam
12/28/93	1	1	8/10	Ya Mar	Fee
12/31/93	3	2	4/8	Poor Heart	Fee
4/4/94	1	1	8/9	Horn	Possum
4/8/94	3	2	3/9	McGrupp	Sparkle
4/10/94	2	1	2/9	Runaway Jim	Sparkle
4/15/94	4	1	8/9	Bouncing	Down with Dis
4/20/94	4	1	2/7	Runaway Jim	Julius
4/24/94	1	4	7/8	Dog Faced Boy	Slave
4/28/94	2	1	7/11	Bouncing	Run Like Antel
5/2/94	3	1	5/10	Down with Disease	Glide
5/4/94	2	1	4/10	Sample in a Jar	Sparkle
5/8/94	3	2	3/9	Run Like an Antelope	Fee
5/10/94	1	1	6/9	Axilla (Part II)	Split Open and
5/13/94	2	1	2/9	Runaway Jim	Julius
5/16/94	2	2	6/11	Sparkle	Julius
5/20/94	3	1	4/10	If I Could	Bathtub Gin
5/22/94	2	2	3/9	Bouncing	McGrupp
5/26/94	3	1	7/10	Sparkle	Catapult
5/28/94	2	2	2/8	Axilla (Part II)	Tweezer
6/9/94	2	1	2/9	Down with Disease	If I Could
6/11/94	2	1	6/8	Down with Disease	Tela
6/14/94	2	2	5/9	If I Could	Sparkle
6/18/94	3	1	7/10	Down with Disease	Dog Faced Boy
6/21/94	2	1	4/5	Sample in a Jar	The Horse
6/24/94	3	1	3/11	Wilson	Fee
6/29/94	3	2	4/8	Tweezer	Lifeboy
7/1/94	2	1	7/10	The Mango Song	Tela
7/3/94	2	2	4/10	Bouncing	The Horse
7/8/94	3	2	5/11	Yerushalayim	Stash
7/13/94	3	1	8/11	Fee	Fast Enough for You
7/15/94	2	2	5/10	Reba	Yerushalayim
10/8/94	3	1	7/9	Fee	Lawn Boy
10/13/94	4	2	4/12	If I Could	Amazing Grce
10/18/94	4	1	7/10	Tela	Guyute
10/26/94	6	1	2/10	Simple	NICU
11/4/94	7	1	2/9	Sample in a Jar	Bouncing
11/13/94	2	1	6/10	Axilla (Part II)	The Vibration of Lif
11/18/94	4	1	6/11	Silent in the Mornin	Tela
11/23/94	4	1	4/9	Simple	If I Could
12/2/94	6	1	5/8	Simple	The Lizards
12/9/94	6	1	6/8	I Didn't Know	If I Could
12/28/94	2	1	9/10	Dog Faced Boy	Run Like Antel
6/10/95	8	1	4/9	Prince Caspian	Free
6/16/95	4	1	6/10	Cry Baby Cry	My Mind's Got A Mind
6/22/95	4	1	6/10	Guelah Papyrus	Strange Design
6/26/95	4	1	7/10	My Mind's Got A Mind	Dog Faced Boy
7/1/95	4	1	5/9	All Things Recnsdrd	Prince Caspian
7/3/95	2	1	6/11	Sparkle	If I Could
9/27/95	1	1	4/9	Free	I Didn't Know
10/3/95	5	2	2/9	Timber (Jerry)	Sparkle
10/7/95	3	2	5/9	Strange Design	Contact
10/14/95	4	1	9/11	Acoustic Army	Tela
10/22/95	6	1	8/12	Fast Enough for You	Poor Heart
10/29/95	5	2	4/10	The Mango Song	Kung
10/29/95	0	2	6/10	Kung	Shaggy Dog
11/10/95	3	1	5/9	The Old Home Place	Dog Faced Boy
11/19/95	7	1	7/10	Strange Design	Hello My Baby
11/29/95	6	1	5/9	If I Could	Theme From the Botto
12/8/95	7	1	6/9	Fluffhead	Acoustic Army
12/15/95	5	2	3/8	Runaway Jim	Bathtub Gin
12/30/95	5	1	6/13	Simple	Kung
12/30/95	0	1	8/13	Kung	T.M.W.S.I.Y.
7/12/96	11	2	1/9	***	Prince Caspian
7/15/96	2	2	5/9	Makisupa Policeman	Julius
7/18/96	2	1	6/7	Hello My Baby	You Enjoy My
7/25/96	6	1	4/8	Sample in a Jar	Run Like Antel
8/5/96	3	2	3/13	Down with Disease	Halley's Comet
8/12/96	4	1	6/10	Weigh	Dog Faced Boy
8/17/96	4	2	3/8	Runaway Jim	Brother
10/16/96	1	1	9/12	Sample in a Jar	The Horse
10/22/96	5	1	4/9	Bouncing	Talk
10/26/96	3	1	7/9	Character Zero	Theme From the Botto
11/13/96	11	1	3/9	Bouncing	Ya Mar
11/22/96	6	1	1/10	***	Runaway Jim
11/30/96	5	2	2/11	La Grange	Glide
12/28/96	5	1	4/9	Wolfman's Brother	Billy Breathes
2/14/97	5	1	6/9	Axilla	Billy Breathes
8/8/97	44	1	5/7	Dirt	Water in the Sky
12/7/97	24	1	5/12	My Mind's Got A Mind	Swept Away
12/7/97	0	1	8/12	Steep	Theme From the Botto
7/28/98	31	1	6/10	Sneakin' Sally	Lengthwise
7/28/98	0	1	8/10	Lengthwise	Sparkle
11/13/98	28	1	5/10	Ginseng Sullivan	Cars Trucks Buses
5/23/00	82	1	7/12	Simple	When Circus Comes
6/11/00	3	1	8/9	Possum	Farmhouse
7/4/00	14	1	4/11	Rift	Bouncing
7/10/00	4	1	3/10	Wilson	Bathtub Gin
9/20/00	13	2	4/9	Dirt	Wading In Velvet Sea
10/4/00	9	1	2/7	The Moma Dance	Bouncing

Has not been played in the last 3 shows.

It's My Life

DATE	GAP	SET	POS.	SONG BEFORE	SONG AFTER
3/2/93	501	2	8/12	Love You	Loup Garou

Has not been played in the last 618 shows.

Izabella

DATE	GAP	SET	POS.	SONG BEFORE	SONG AFTER
6/13/97	878	E	2/2	Stand	***
7/26/97	23	1	9/9	You Enjoy Myself	***
8/13/97	11	2	3/9	Ghost	Sleeping Monkey
11/16/97	6	2	5/5	Harry Hood	***
11/22/97	4	1	8/8	Frankenstein	***
12/6/97	9	2	2/7	Tweezer	Jam
12/12/97	4	2	6/10	Prince Caspian	Tweezer Repri
12/30/97	4	2	6/10	Harpua	Harry Hood
7/9/98	13	2	8/8	Harry Hood	***
7/31/98	13	2	7/9	Twist	Julius

Has not been played in the last 154 shows.

DATE	GAP	SET	POS.	SONG BEFORE	SONG AFTER
Jagermeister					
4/18/90	179	2	11/12	David Bowie	David Bowie
5/6/90	10	2	6/7	Terrapin	You Enjoy My
Has not been played in the last 930 shows.					
Jam					
11/3/84	2	1	3/10	Wild Child	Bertha
5/3/85	3	2	4/6	Can't You Hear Me Kn	Cities
5/3/85	0	3	6/8	Makisupa Policeman	Run Like Antel
10/17/85	2	1	1/9	***	Alumni Blues
10/30/85	1	1	11/11	Skippy Wondermouse	***
10/31/86	7	2	1/11	***	AC/DC Bag
4/24/87	6	1	10/14	I Am Hydrogen	Who Do? We Do!
8/29/87	7	3	5/10	I Am Hydrogen	Who Do? We Do!
10/31/87	5	1	1/11	***	Whipping Post
11/19/87	2	3	1/14	***	Suzy Greenber
6/20/88	18	1	10/11	Ya Mar	I Didn't Know
6/24/88	2	1	3/11	Possum	Alumni Blues
7/11/88	1	1	4/11	The Curtain	Funky Bitch
7/23/88	2	1	1/13	***	Col. Forbin's A
9/13/88	9	3	1/8	***	Andy's Chest
5/28/89	39	3	1/6	***	La Grange Jam
2/17/90	49	1	10/12	Weekapaug Groove	Cavern
4/21/91	127	1	6/14	Foam	My Sweet One
5/17/91	12	1	3/17	Drum Jam	Reba
11/23/92	165	2	10/14	Weekapaug Groove	Big Ball Jam
5/5/93	87	2	10/10	You Enjoy Myself	***
5/8/93	3	2	10/18	The Squirming Coil	Big Ball Jam
4/21/94	54	E	2/3	Drums Jam	All Along Watchtower
11/22/94	90	2	2/13	Funky Bitch	Yerushalayim
6/22/95	31	2	2/4	Theme From the Botto	Tweezer
6/25/95	3	2	6/9	Why Don't We Do It i	Weekapaug Gr
10/17/95	22	2	6/6	Keyboard Cavalry	***
12/5/95	30	2	5/8	Scent of a Mule	Lifeboy
12/14/95	6	2	7/10	Halley's Comet	NICU
12/14/95	0	2	9/10	NICU	Slave
12/31/95	7	2	2/8	Drowned	The Lizards
7/12/96	10	2	6/9	Purple Rain	NICU
8/14/96	19	1	2/10	Wilson	Down with Dis
11/13/96	22	2	3/7	Suzy Greenberg	Prince Caspian
12/6/96	15	2	5/9	Simple	Harry Hood
2/26/97	15	2	8/11	Scent of a Mule	Magilla
6/20/97	9	1	2/8	Taste	Cities
6/21/97	1	1	13/15	Chalk Dust Torture	Twist
7/1/97	6	2	1/7	***	Timber (Jerry)
7/1/97	0	2	2/7	Cities	Loving Cup
7/10/97	6	1	7/8	Wading In Velvet Sea	Oblivious Fool
7/10/97	0	2	7/7	Take Me to the River	***
7/21/97	2	2	6/8	Theme From the Botto	Funky Bitch
8/16/97	17	2	4/7	My Soul	Slave
11/17/97	5	2	4/7	Johnny B. Goode	Jesus Just Left
11/30/97	8	2	4/7	Free	Piper
12/3/97	2	2	3/6	Possum	Prince Caspian
12/6/97	2	2	3/7	Izabella	Twist
4/5/98	13	2	7/8	Possum	Cavern
7/5/98	5	1	6/9	Fee	Water in the Sky
7/15/98	5	1	6/13	Horn	Chalk Dust Tor
8/9/98	18	2	2/11	AC/DC Bag	Sparkle
10/30/98	10	2	5/7	NICU	Prince Caspian
11/8/98	6	2	5/8	Down with Disease	Piper
7/8/99	24	1	3/8	Fee	Guyute
7/15/99	5	2	4/6	Kung	Bouncing
7/17/99	2	2	3/8	On My Knees	Down with Dis
7/24/99	1	1	3/9	Fluffhead	T.M.W.S.I.Y.
7/24/99	0	1	7/9	T.M.W.S.I.Y. Reprise	The Wedge

DATE	GAP	SET	POS.	SONG BEFORE	SONG AFTER
7/24/99	0	2	5/8	The Mango Song	Happy Whip And Dung
7/26/99	2	2	5/6	Down with Disease	Split Open and
7/31/99	3	E	1/3	***	Brian and Robert
10/10/99	25	2	1/6	***	You Enjoy My
6/14/00	24	2	3/5	Twist	Walk Away
9/29/00	35	2	5/9	Fluffhead	Meatstick
Has not been played in the last 6 shows.					
Jennifer Dances					
12/5/99	10582	6/10		Brian and Robert	Maze
12/7/99	1	2	2/8	Wolfman's Brother	Heavy Things
12/17/99	8	2	4/6	Bug	Split Open and
Has not been played in the last 52 shows.					
Jessica Jam					
5/8/93	549	2	2/18	David Bowie	David Bowie
Has not been played in the last 570 shows.					
Jesus Just Left Chicago					
8/10/87	26	3	3/7	David Bowie	Whipping Post
8/29/87	2	3	9/10	David Bowie	She Caught The Katy
1/27/88	8	1	5/9	Possum	Sneakin' Sally
2/8/88	3	3	8/9	Fee	BBFCFM
5/14/88	9	1	8/11	BBFCFM	Fluffhead
5/15/88	1	2	7/11	Take the A-Train	I Didn't Know
5/25/88	2	2	1/3	***	Fluffhead
6/21/88	4	2	6/10	Alumni Blues	Good Time Ba
7/12/88	3	2	5/9	Fluffhead	Makisupa Policeman
7/24/88	2	3	4/6	Peaches en Regalia	McGrupp
8/3/88	3	2	3/3	You Enjoy Myself	***
5/28/89	44	3	6/6	Ya Mar	***
12/15/89	35	2	6/8	Funky Bitch	Contact
1/29/90	8	1	6/10	Weekapaug Groove	Possum
2/23/90	8	2	4/11	Bathtub Gin	Tela
3/10/90	9	1	9/10	Divided Sky	Carolina
3/28/90	3	2	8/16	Weekapaug Groove	The Lizards
4/5/90	2	2	3/13	Uncle Pen	AC/DC Bag
4/6/90	1	E	1/2	***	Highway to Hell
4/9/90	3	2	7/11	Harry Hood	Divided Sky
4/12/90	1	1	9/11	Cavern	Divided Sky
4/20/90	5	2	10/11	AC/DC Bag	You Enjoy My
5/19/90	14	2	9/10	Rift	Good Time Ba
11/4/90	33	2	12/13	Suzy Greenberg	You Enjoy My
11/8/90	1	E	1/2	***	Fire
12/29/90	11	2	6/10	Stash	Dinner and a
2/3/91	4	E	1/2	***	BBFCFM
3/6/91	14	E	1/1	***	***
4/6/91	16	E	1/1	***	***
7/24/91	33	2	4/10	David Bowie	My Sweet One
7/25/91	1	2	6/13	Poor Heart	The Lizards
9/25/91	4	2	5/8	Cavern	Runaway Jim
10/13/91	13	2	6/9	My Sweet One	Bouncing
11/8/91	14	2	9/12	Weekapaug Groove	Self
11/23/91	12	E	1/2	***	BBFCFM
3/5/93	152	2	6/11	Mike's Song	My Sweet One
3/17/93	8	2	4/12	Reba	Mound
4/3/93	14	2	7/10	You Enjoy Myself	My Sweet One
8/11/93	47	2	8/10	Rift	My Sweet One
8/26/93	11	2	5/8	Rift	The Lizards
6/13/94	53	2	7/11	Reba	Scent of a Mul
6/22/94	7	2	19/20	Big Ball Jam	Sample in a Ja
10/25/94	33	2	8/11	Axilla (Part II)	Big Ball Jam
12/1/94	23	2	8/10	Tweezer	Harry Hood
12/6/94	9	1	3/8	Fluffhead	Sparkle
10/31/95	56	3	2/4	You Enjoy Myself	A Day in the Life
10/31/96	76	3	7/8	Steep	Suzy Greenber
11/27/96	17	2	2/8	Down with Disease	Scent of a Mul
12/4/96	5	E	1/1	***	***

DATE	GAP	SET	POS.	SONG BEFORE	SONG AFTER
2/22/97	13	2	5/8	Simple	Harry Hood
3/1/97	5	1	7/10	Wolfman's Brother	Reba
6/19/97	6	2	6/7	Piper	Prince Caspian
8/3/97	25	1	8/10	Twist	Limb by Limb
11/17/97	13	2	5/7	Jam	When Circus Comes
12/7/97	13	1	3/12	Psycho Killer	My Mind's Got A Mind
7/19/98	25	2	5/7	Tweezer	McGrupp
11/2/98	27	1	4/9	Drowned	Driver
7/8/99	28	2	4/9	Prince Caspian	I Saw It Again
10/4/99	38	1	5/8	Runaway Jim	Limb by Limb
6/23/00	32	2	2/7	Rock and Roll	Down with Dis
Has not been played in the last 37 shows.					
Johnny B. Goode					
6/17/95	721	2	5/11	Tweezer	Tweezer
7/3/95	13	2	3/10	David Bowie	David Bowie
12/31/95	58	E	1/1	***	***
7/12/96	10	E	2/2	Bathtub Gin	***
7/21/96	6	1	14/14	Timber (Jerry)	***
8/6/96	8	E	1/1	***	***
10/16/96	8	2	10/10	The Squirming Coil	***
10/25/96	7	E	1/1	***	***
11/2/96	5	1	9/9	Free	***
11/18/96	11	E	2/2	Waste	***
12/1/96	8	2	9/10	Tweezer Reprise	Slave
12/28/96	4	E	1/1	***	***
2/13/97	4	E	2/2	Prince Caspian	***
2/16/97	2	E	2/2	Theme From the Botto	***
2/22/97	5	E	1/1	***	Uncle Pen
3/2/97	6	1	1/13	***	You Enjoy My
7/11/97	20	1	6/7	Wolfman's Brother	You Enjoy My
7/26/97	5	2	8/8	Waste	***
8/2/97	4	2	3/7	Tweezer	Sparkle
11/17/97	14	2	3/7	Oblivious Fool	Jam
11/28/97	6	2	5/5	Ghost	***
12/11/97	9	2	6/6	Down with Disease	***
7/8/98	17	2	7/7	Ghost	***
Has not been played in the last 168 shows.					
Julia					
10/31/94	681	2	18/30	I Will	Birthday Jam
Has not been played in the last 438 shows.					
Julius					
4/4/94	589	2	5/11	The Landlady	Magilla
4/5/94	1	1	5/8	Glide	Bouncing
4/9/94	3	1	6/10	Nellie Kane	Fee
4/11/94	2	1	6/9	Magilla	Glide
4/13/94	1	1	5/8	The Lizards	Ginseng Sullivan
4/15/94	2	2	6/10	The Landlady	Wolfman's Brother
4/16/94	1	2	5/9	The Lizards	Bouncing
4/18/94	2	1	4/10	Poor Heart	My Friend My
4/20/94	1	1	3/7	It's Ice	Bouncing
4/22/94	2	2	2/8	Suzy Greenberg	Reba
4/24/94	2	2	4/9	The Mango Song	Col. Forbin's A
4/28/94	2	1	10/11	The Squirming Coil	Good Time Ba
5/2/94	3	2	6/9	The Lizards	Lawn Boy
5/4/94	2	2	6/9	The Landlady	Wolfman's Brother
5/6/94	1	2	7/9	Axilla (Part II)	Bike
5/8/94	2	2	5/9	Fee	Cavern
5/10/94	1	2	3/9	Wilson	Reba
5/13/94	2	1	3/9	It's Ice	Mound
5/16/94	2	2	7/11	It's Ice	You Enjoy My
5/19/94	2	2	7/10	The Lizards	Big Ball Jam
5/21/94	2	2	6/9	Big Ball Jam	Bike
5/23/94	2	1	8/10	Silent in the Mornin	Reba
5/25/94	1	2	7/9	Big Ball Jam	Purple Rain
5/27/94	2	2	6/12	The Lizards	Nellie Kane
5/29/94	2	1	6/8	Sparkle	I Didn't Know

DATE	GAP	SET	POS.	SONG BEFORE	SONG AFTER
6/9/94	1	2	3/10	Glide	Halley's Comet
6/10/94	1	1	9/9	Cavern	***
6/13/94	2	1	9/9	Ginseng Sullivan	***
6/16/94	2	1	3/10	Rift	Fee
6/17/94	1	2	14/15	Big Ball Jam	Frankenstein
6/19/94	2	1	2/9	Suzy Greenberg	The Lizards
6/21/94	1	2	13/16	Sweet Adeline	Sparkle
6/23/94	2	1	10/10	Punch You in the Eye	***
6/25/94	2	1	3/10	Rift	NICU
6/26/94	1	2	1/12	***	Down with Dis
6/29/94	1	1	5/11	Mound	The Horse
7/1/94	2	1	9/10	Tela	Suzy Greenber
7/3/94	2	2	7/10	Silent in the Mornin	The Squirmin
7/6/94	2	1	3/9	Fluffhead	Bouncing
7/8/94	1	2	10/11	You Enjoy Myself	Golgi Apparat
7/10/94	2	1	8/9	My Friend My Friend	Cavern
7/13/94	1	2	7/13	Tweezer	Tweezer
7/15/94	2	2	8/10	Dog Faced Boy	Setting Sail
10/7/94	2	1	2/9	My Friend My Friend	Glide
10/9/94	2	2	6/8	Amazing Grace	Contact
10/12/94	2	1	8/9	Guelah Papyrus	Sweet Adeline
10/14/94	1	1	12/12	The Famous Mockingbi	***
10/16/94	2	2	3/9	Poor Heart	Fluffhead
10/20/94	2	1	9/11	Esther	Guyute
10/22/94	2	1	8/8	Fluffhead	***
10/25/94	2	1	4/9	Horn	The Horse
10/27/94	2	2	1/7	***	Ya Mar
10/31/94	3	1	6/10	Harpua	The Horse
11/3/94	2	2	4/8	Poor Heart	You Enjoy My
11/12/94	2	2	1/12	***	Fluffhead
11/14/94	2	2	6/10	Poor Heart	The Old Home
11/18/94	3	1	3/11	AC/DC Bag	The Horse
11/20/94	2	2	9/10	Terrapin	Cavern
11/25/94	3	1	7/8	Esther	Golgi Apparat
11/28/94	2	2	5/5	Sleeping Monkey	***
12/2/94	3	2	4/8	Buried Alive	The Landlady
12/3/94	1	2	9/10	Alumni Blues Jam	Cavern
12/7/94	3	2	5/9	Fee	I'm Blue, Lonesome
12/9/94	2	2	5/9	McGrupp	Big Ball Jam
12/28/94	3	1	2/9	Simple	Bathtub Gin
6/8/95	6	2	8/8	Poor Heart	***
6/13/95	3	E	2/2	Sweet Adeline	***
6/17/95	4	1	6/9	Uncle Pen	Lawn Boy
6/24/95	5	1	4/10	Spock's Brain	Glide
7/2/95	7	1	5/10	The Curtain	Camel Walk
10/5/95	8	1	10/11	Acoustic Army	Suzy Greenber
10/7/95	2	1	1/9	***	Gumbo
10/11/95	2	1	8/9	Acoustic Army	Sample in a Ja
10/15/95	3	2	1/8	***	Simple
10/24/95	6	2	1/8	***	Theme From the Botto
10/29/95	4	1	3/12	Poor Heart	Punch You in
11/9/95	2	2	2/10	Theme From the Botto	The Lizards
11/14/95	4	1	7/9	Free	I'm Blue, Lonesome
11/19/95	4	1	9/10	Hello My Baby	The Squirmin
11/24/95	3	2	10/10	Fee	***
11/30/95	4	1	4/10	Ha Ha Ha	NICU
12/4/95	3	1	1/11	***	Gumbo
12/7/95	2	2	5/10	Reba	Sleeping Monkey
12/11/95	3	1	11/12	McGrupp	Cavern
12/16/95	4	1	8/9	Dog Faced Boy	Suzy Greenber
12/28/95	2	1	4/9	The Curtain	Guyute
7/15/96	15	2	6/9	It's Ice	Purple Rain
7/18/96	2	1	1/7	***	Cars Trucks Buses
7/24/96	5	1	3/5	Ya Mar	You Enjoy My
8/5/96	4	1	8/9	If I Could	The Squirmin
8/14/96	6	E	1/1	***	***
10/18/96	5	E	1/1	***	***
10/23/96	4	2	8/8	Slave	***
10/26/96	2	1	1/9	***	Cars Trucks Buses

DATE	GAP	SET	POS.	SONG BEFORE	SONG AFTER
11/2/96	4	1	2/9	Ya Mar	Fee
11/9/96	5	E	1/1	***	***
11/14/96	3	1	9/9	Talk	***
11/22/96	5	E	1/1	***	***
11/27/96	3	1	1/9	***	My Friend My
12/2/96	4	1	8/8	Gumbo	***
12/6/96	2	2	1/9	***	Sparkle
12/31/96	4	3	7/7	Bohemian Rhapsody	***
2/13/97	1	2	1/10	***	Cars Trucks Buses
2/20/97	5	E	1/1	***	***
2/28/97	6	2	9/9	Waste	***
6/20/97	8	2	8/8	Bouncing	***
7/5/97	10	1	1/13	***	Bouncing
7/10/97	3	2	2/7	Also Sprach	Magilla
7/23/97	4	1	1/10	***	Dirt
8/3/97	7	2	1/7	***	Simple
8/6/97	1	E	1/1	***	***
8/16/97	7	2	7/7	Rocky Top	***
11/19/97	6	1	1/10	***	Bathtub Gin
11/23/97	3	E	1/1	***	***
12/5/97	7	2	3/7	Bouncing	Slave
12/9/97	3	2	1/6	***	Simple
12/28/97	4	1	1/11	***	Cities
7/6/98	13	2	1/6	***	Meat
7/8/98	1	E	1/1	***	***
7/16/98	4	2	1/7	***	The Moma Dance
7/25/98	6	1	7/7	Guyute	***
7/31/98	4	2	8/9	Izabella	Cavern
8/11/98	8	1	2/11	Trenchtown Rock	Wolfman's Brother
10/29/98	8	1	1/10	***	Roggae
11/11/98	9	1	8/8	Theme From the Botto	***
11/14/98	2	2	8/9	You Enjoy Myself	Hello My Baby
11/28/98	9	2	1/9	***	Wolfman's Brother
7/8/99	11	1	1/8	***	Fee
7/30b/99	16	E	1/1	***	***
9/16/99	8	2	8/8	Prince Caspian	***
9/25/99	7	2	8/8	Frankenstein	***
10/1/99	4	2	7/9	Mountains in the Mis	Fluffhead
10/7/99	4	E	3/3	I Am Hydrogen	***
12/4/99	6	E	1/2	***	Tweezer Repri
6/16/00	23	2	6/7	Slave	Bug
7/4/00	10	1	11/11	T.M.W.S.I.Y. Reprise	***
7/15/00	8	1	9/9	My Soul	***
9/25/00	13	1	8/8	Bug	***

Has not been played in the last 8 shows.

Jump Monk

DATE	GAP	SET	POS.	SONG BEFORE	SONG AFTER
3/12/88	42	2	1/11	***	McGrupp

Has not been played in the last 1077 shows.

Keyboard Cavalry

DATE	GAP	SET	POS.	SONG BEFORE	SONG AFTER
9/27/95	735	2	5/8	Billy Breathes	Harry Hood
9/28/95	1	2	5/8	Tweezer	Amazing Grce
9/30/95	2	2	6/9	Mike's Song	Weekapaug Gr
10/2/95	1	2	6/10	Simple	Slave
10/6/95	3	2	6/8	Tweezer	Suspicious Minds
10/8/95	2	2	1/10	***	Cars Trucks Buses
10/13/95	2	2	6/10	Run Like an Antelope	The Lizards
10/17/95	3	2	5/6	Suzy Greenberg	Jam
10/27/95	7	2	7/9	McGrupp	Bouncing
11/12/95	7	2	3/8	Tweezer	Sample in a Ja
11/21/95	6	2	8/11	Mike's Song	Suspicious Minds
12/5/95	10	2	3/8	Bathtub Gin	Scent of a Mul
12/14/95	6	2	5/10	Tweezer	Halley's Comet

Has not been played in the last 334 shows.

Keyboard Cavalry Reprise

DATE	GAP	SET	POS.	SONG BEFORE	SONG AFTER
10/8/95	744	2	10/10	David Bowie	***

Has not been played in the last 375 shows.

Killer Joe

DATE	GAP	SET	POS.	SONG BEFORE	SONG AFTER
3/17/90	168	2	1/6	***	Bold As Love

Has not been played in the last 951 shows.

Kung

DATE	GAP	SET	POS.	SONG BEFORE	SONG AFTER
10/31/89	127	E	3/4	Run Like an Antelope	Run Like Antel
11/2/89	1	2	4/11	You Enjoy Myself	Rhombus Narration
12/31/92	351	3	5/9	Harpua	Harpua
2/20/93	15	2	11/22	I Am Hydrogen	I Am Hydrgn
3/8/93	11	2	7/10	My Friend My Friend	You Enjoy My
3/25/93	12	2	6/13	Col. Forbin's Ascent	Icculus
4/14/93	13	1	7/13	Stash	Stash
5/8/93	19	1	6/12	Stash	Stash
8/7/93	20	2	3/12	Mike's Song	Mike's Song
6/16/94	69	2	4/11	Col. Forbin's Ascent	The Famous Mockingbi
6/17/94	1	2	10/15	Harpua	Harpua
6/26/94	8	1	1/11	***	Llama
6/30/94	2	2	9/15	Harpua	Harpua
10/20/94	23	1	6/11	Split Open and Melt	Split Open and
10/14/95	75	1	3/11	Cars Trucks Buses	Free
10/19/95	3	2	8/10	BBFCFM	Suspicious Minds
10/21/95	2	1	7/12	Cars Trucks Buses	The Lizards
10/29/95	6	2	5/10	It's Ice	It's Ice
11/25/95	14	2	2/12	Timber (Jerry)	Mike's Song
12/8/95	9	2	3/8	Tweezer	Tweezer
12/30/95	10	1	7/13	It's Ice	It's Ice
11/16/96	55	2	3/8	Runaway Jim	Catapult
2/26/97	27	2	5/11	You Enjoy Myself	Theme From the Botto
7/29/98	91	2	6/7	Tube	Run Like Antel
11/29/98	38	1	8/11	Catapult	Maze
7/15/99	15	2	3/6	Split Open and Melt	Jam
9/29/99	29	2	9/12	Mike's Song	Mike's Song

Has not been played in the last 73 shows.

La Grange

DATE	GAP	SET	POS.	SONG BEFORE	SONG AFTER
8/9/87	25	1	3/11	Slave	The Chase
8/10/87	1	2	10/10	You Enjoy Myself	***
8/29/87	2	3	1/10	***	Corrine Corrina
9/21/87	2	3	14/15	Terrapin	Fluffhead
11/19/87	5	3	12/14	Camel Walk	Bike
2/24/88	4	2	4/5	Sanity	Harry Hood
5/21/88	10	2	1/9	***	Possum
5/25/88	1	3	5/11	Halley's Comet	Fee
6/15/88	1	1	9/9	Golgi Apparatus	***
6/19/88	1	1	5/8	Golgi Apparatus	Suzy Greenber
7/11/88	4	E	2/2	McGrupp	***
7/23/88	2	2	8/10	Blue Bossa	Alumni Blues
7/24/88	1	2	3/8	Fluffhead	The Lizards
7/30/88	2	3	1/13	***	On Your Way Down
8/6/88	2	1	1/9	***	You Enjoy My
9/24/88	6	1	7/10	Peaches en Regalia	Take the A-Trn
10/31/88	2	1	9/12	Bold as Love	Contact
2/6/89	1	1	6/7	Fee	You Enjoy My
3/14/89	9	3	5/7	The Lizards	You Enjoy My
3/30/89	2	2	7/8	Undun	Golgi Apparat
5/9/89	8	2	2/14	You Enjoy Myself	If I Don't Be There
5/13/89	2	1	5/12	Golgi Apparatus	Fluffhead
8/26/89	11	E	3/3	The Lizards	***
9/14/89	2	1	7/9	The Famous Mockingbi	Fee
10/7/89	4	1	8/11	Fee	Makisupa Policeman
10/12/89	1	1	8/8	Divided Sky	***
10/20/89	3	E	1/2	***	Slave
10/21/89	1	2	7/10	The Sloth	You Enjoy My

DATE	GAP	SET	POS.	SONG BEFORE	SONG AFTER
10/22/89	1	1	1/14	***	Col. Forbin's A
11/10/89	7	1	9/9	You Enjoy Myself	***
12/1/89	5	1	2/9	I Didn't Know	You Enjoy My
12/9/89	4	1	2/10	Dinner and a Movie	The Lizards
12/30/89	4	2	7/9	My Sweet One	Lawn Boy
1/20/90	2	2	5/10	Tela	Lawn Boy
1/27/90	1	E	1/1	***	***
1/28/90	1	1	5/9	Fluffhead	Carolina
2/10/90	4	2	1/10	***	Esther
2/24/90	6	2	6/9	The Squirming Coil	Bathtub Gin
3/9/90	7	2	9/11	You Enjoy Myself	Contact
3/11/90	2	1	8/13	Reba	Mike's Song
3/28/90	2	2	12/16	Contact	Rift
4/6/90	3	2	2/10	Carolina	Esther
4/9/90	3	2	4/11	Uncle Pen	Foam
4/13/90	2	1	6/10	Esther	The Oh Kee Pa
4/18/90	2	2	1/12	***	Fee
4/20/90	2	2	5/11	Weekapaug Groove	Rift
4/25/90	3	2	7/12	Esther	Dinner and a
5/7/90	6	1	3/5	Highway to Hell	If I Only Had a Brai
5/13/90	3	2	12/12	Possum	***
5/19/90	2	1	5/8	Sweet Adeline	You Enjoy My
5/23/90	1	2	5/11	The Lizards	McGrupp
6/9/90	2	2	6/14	T.M.W.S.I.Y.	Fee
6/16/90	1	3	1/13	***	Happy Birth-day
9/13/90	1	E	2/2	The Lizards	***
9/20/90	4	1	12/12	Eliza	***
10/7/90	9	1	14/14	Take the A-Train	***
11/2/90	6	E	2/2	Lawn Boy	***
2/8/91	20	E	2/2	Magilla	***
2/14/91	2	E	2/2	Uncle Pen	***
2/26/91	6	1	11/11	Golgi Apparatus	***
3/17/91	10	E	2/2	Lawn Boy	***
8/2/93	302	1	12/12	Dog Gone Dog	***
8/7/93	3	E	2/2	Carolina	***
8/14/93	6	E	1/1	***	***
12/29/95	215	2	9/11	Bass Jam	Bouncing
11/16/96	56	2	1/8	***	Runaway Jim
11/30/96	8	2	2/11	***	It's Ice
12/29/96	1	6	1/10	The Squirming Coil	***
2/25/97	12	2	9/10	Prince Caspian	Sweet Adeline
7/26/98	90	2	1/6	***	You Enjoy My
8/12/98	12	1	1/8	***	Makisupa Po-liceman
11/15/98	19	1	8/8	Roggae	***
9/22/99	48	E	1/1	***	***

Has not been played in the last 78 shows.

La Grange Jam

DATE	GAP	SET	POS.	SONG BEFORE	SONG AFTER
5/28/89	106	3	2/6	Jam	The Sloth

Has not been played in the last 1013 shows.

Lawn Boy

DATE	GAP	SET	POS.	SONG BEFORE	SONG AFTER
11/30/89	135	1	10/11	Run Like an Antelope	Frankenstein
12/1/89	1	E	1/2	***	Possum
12/3/89	1	1	8/11	Run Like an Antelope	Frankenstein
12/7/89	1	2	8/11	Run Like an Antelope	Possum
12/8/89	1	E	1/2	***	Fire
12/9/89	1	1	8/10	David Bowie	Bathtub Gin
12/16/89	2	1	3/9	AC/DC Bag	Mike's Song
12/29/89	1	1	7/10	The Lizards	Mike's Song
12/30/89	1	2	8/9	La Grange	Golgi Apparat
1/20/90	2	2	8/9	La Grange	Esther
1/28/90	2	E	1/2	***	BBFCFM
2/24/90	10	2	8/9	Bathtub Gin	Contact
4/18/90	21	2	9/12	Bold As Love	David Bowie
4/22/90	4	E	1/2	***	Golgi Apparat
4/26/90	2	1	9/9	Run Like an Antelope	***
5/13/90	8	1	9/10	Divided Sky	David Bowie
5/30/90	5	1	8/14	Run Like an Antelope	Fluffhead
6/5/90	4	1	11/12	David Bowie	Possum
6/7/90	1	E	1/2	***	BBFCFM
6/9/90	2	1	2/10	Possum	Reba

DATE	GAP	SET	POS.	SONG BEFORE	SONG AFTER
6/16/90	1	1	9/10	Timber (Jerry)	Possum
9/20/90	5	2	14/14	Tube	***
9/21/90	1	2	5/8	Tube	Tweezer
9/22/90	1	2	9/10	The Lizards	Possum
9/29/90	2	E	1/1	***	***
11/2/90	11	E	1/2	***	La Grange
11/16/90	5	2	5/11	Weekapaug Groove	Tube
11/17/90	1	2	9/12	Possum	Rocky Top
11/24/90	1	2	11/12	BBFCFM	Divided Sky
12/29/90	7	1	6/10	David Bowie	Rocky Top
2/2/91	3	2	3/3	Run Like an Antelope	***
2/8/91	3	2	4/11	Cavern	Mike's Song
2/9/91	1	E	1/4	***	Suzy Greenber
2/14/91	1	1	9/11	Stash	The Oh Kee Pa
2/16/91	2	E	1/5	***	Fire
2/27/91	5	2	6/11	David Bowie	The Oh Kee Pa
3/9/91	5	2	12/13	Fire	Golgi Apparat
3/17/91	4	E	1/2	***	La Grange
3/28/91	3	E	1/2	***	Fire
4/2/91	3	2	2/8	Divided Sky	Cavern
4/4/91	2	2	5/10	David Bowie	The Landlady
4/11/91	3	2	9/14	Split Open and Melt	The Landlady
4/22/91	8	E	1/4	***	Rocky Top
5/17/91	11	E	1/2	***	Golgi Apparat
7/19/91	9	E	1/2	***	Runaway Jim
7/21/91	2	2	4/9	Runaway Jim	The Sloth
7/26/91	4	E	1/2	***	Frankenstein
8/3/91	2	3	4/8	Fluffhead	My Sweet One
9/26/91	2	2	10/11	Weekapaug Groove	Chalk Dust Tor
9/28/91	2	2	6/12	Run Like an Antelope	The Lizards
10/2/91	3	2	6/9	Runaway Jim	Stash
10/4/91	2	2	9/10	Runaway Jim	Stash
10/12/91	4	E	1/4	***	Rocky Top
10/17/91	3	2	5/9	David Bowie	Fluffhead
10/30/91	7	2	5/11	Run Like an Antelope	Wilson
11/7/91	4	E	3/4	Rocky Top	Fire
11/15/91	7	1	11/12	Divided Sky	Golgi Apparat
11/22/91	5	1	8/11	Divided Sky	Dinner and a
12/6/91	6	E	1/2	***	Rocky Top
12/31/91	2	E	1/3	***	Rocky Top
3/20/92	9	E	1/2	***	Fire
3/24/92	3	E	1/2	***	Fire
4/1/92	7	E	1/2	***	Good Time Ba
4/5/92	3	E	1/2	***	Rocky Top
4/12/92	4	2	6/10	You Enjoy Myself	NICU
4/19/92	6	2	11/13	Llama	If I Only Had a Brai
5/1/92	8	E	1/3	***	Good Time Ba
5/17/92	13	E	1/2	***	Good Time Ba
11/27/92	50	1	7/12	Split Open and Melt	Reba
12/3/92	5	2	7/13	Weekapaug Groove	It's Ice
12/5/92	2	2	8/13	Maze	Mike's Song
12/8/92	3	2	9/15	Run Like an Antelope	Sparkle
2/4/93	10	2	8/13	Weekapaug Groove	Uncle Pen
2/6/93	2	1	8/11	Divided Sky	The Wedge
2/11/93	4	1	9/10	Llama	David Bowie
2/13/93	2	1	8/10	Stash	Maze
2/18/93	3	1	9/10	Reba	Run Like Antel
2/19/93	1	2	7/12	Big Ball Jam	Funky Bitch
2/23/93	4	1	9/10	Reba	Chalk Dust Tor
2/27/93	3	1	9/10	Punch You in the Eye	Run Like Antel
3/3/93	2	1	9/10	Runaway Jim	Cavern
3/9/93	4	2	5/15	Reba	Mike's Song
3/16/93	4	2	13/15	Bike	Llama
3/21/93	4	1	10/11	Punch You in the Eye	Possum
3/28/93	6	1	10/11	It's Ice	Run Like Antel
4/1/93	3	1	9/10	Fluffhead	Run Like Antel
4/10/93	5	1	9/10	Chalk Dust Torture	David Bowie
4/20/93	6	1	9/10	Uncle Pen	David Bowie
4/23/93	3	1	9/10	Guelah Papyrus	Chalk Dust Tor
4/30/93	5	1	10/12	Cavern	All Things Rec
5/3/93	3	1	10/11	Possum	Cavern
5/6/93	2	1	10/13	Possum	Why You've Been Gone
7/23/93	11	1	11/12	It's Ice	Cavern
8/12/93	15	2	7/10	Maze	Big Ball Jam

DATE	GAP	SET	POS.	SONG BEFORE	SONG AFTER
8/21/93	7	2	6/10	Llama	David Bowie
12/31/93	8	2	7/8	Possum	You Enjoy My
4/8/94	4	1	12/13	If I Could	Llama
5/2/94	19	2	7/9	Julius	Mike's Song
7/6/94	43	2	4/10	Tweezer	Chalk Dust Tor
10/8/94	9	1	8/9	It's Ice	Run Like Antel
10/29/94	17	1	6/10	Foam	Split Open and
11/14/94	7	1	8/9	Maze	Cavern
12/10/94	20	1	7/8	Divided Sky	Chalk Dust Tor
6/17/95	14	1	7/9	Julius	The Curtain
10/19/95	29	2	6/10	Weekapaug Groove	BBFCFM
11/18/95	17	1	4/8	Reba	Punch You in
12/9/95	15	2	5/8	You Enjoy Myself	Slave
8/7/96	35	1	7/10	Taste	99 Years
10/22/96	12	2	5/10	The Mango Song	Scent of a Mul
11/16/96	17	1	9/11	David Bowie	Sparkle
12/4/96	11	2	8/9	Reba	Weekapaug Gr
3/1/97	18	2	4/8	Mike's Song	Weekapaug Gr
8/9/97	34	1	7/8	Reba	Crossroads
8/16/97	5	3	4/6	Llama	Limb by Limb
11/21/97	1	1	6/8	Punch You in the Eye	Chalk Dust Tor
4/4/98	22	1	7/8	Limb by Limb	Character Zer
6/30/98	2	2	6/12	Run Like an Antelope	Ya Mar
7/5/98	4	1	8/9	Water in the Sky	Chalk Dust Tor
7/20/98	4	1	4/10	Poor Heart	My Sweet One
8/1/98	8	1	8/9	Birds of a Feather	Funky Bitch
8/16/98	10	1	5/11	Punch You in the Eye	Ya Mar
10/15/98	2	2	9/10	Birds of a Feather	Harry Hood
10/31/98	5	1	7/10	Chalk Dust Torture	Mike's Song
11/18/98	11	1	6/9	Guyute	Love Me
11/21/98	3	1	3/13	BBFCFM	Divided Sky
7/13/99	19	1	6/9	NO2	Reba
9/12/99	18	1	9/10	Birds of a Feather	Possum
9/17/99	3	1	4/11	Ghost	Peaches en Regalia
12/5/99	21	1	8/10	Tube	Ginseng Sulli-van
12/16/99	8	1	3/10	Chalk Dust Torture	Limb by Limb
12/31/99	4	2	29/35	Free	Love You
6/10/00	5	1	4/5	Piper	Guyute
7/4/00	15	E	1/2	***	Good Time Ba
9/17/00	15	1	6/9	The Moma Dance	Fluffhead
9/24/00	2	5	2/8	Carini	Love You
10/1/00	5	1	9/10	Llama	Runaway Jim

Has not been played in the last 4 shows.

Layla

DATE	GAP	SET	POS.	SONG BEFORE	SONG AFTER
11/29/98	1002	1	11/11	All The Pain Thru	***

Has not been played in the last 117 shows.

Lengthwise

DATE	GAP	SET	POS.	SONG BEFORE	SONG AFTER
11/19/92	455	2	14/15	Llama	Cavern
11/20/92	1	2	9/10	Terrapin	Self
11/23/92	3	2	13/14	Weekapaug Groove	Cavern
12/2/92	6	2	8/11	Glide	The Squirmin
12/6/92	4	2	11/13	T.M.W.S.I.Y. Reprise	Carolina
12/8/92	2	2	12/15	Suzy Greenberg	My Sweet One
2/4/93	10	2	11/13	Big Ball Jam	Harry Hood
2/6/93	2	2	12/14	Big Ball Jam	Buried Alive
2/13/93	6	2	9/11	Big Ball Jam	The Squirmin
2/17/93	2	2	10/11	You Enjoy Myself	The Squirmin
2/26/93	8	2	9/11	You Enjoy Myself	The Squirmin
3/12/93	8	2	9/10	Chalk Dust Torture	Harry Hood
3/16/93	3	2	11/15	Bike	Bike
3/31/93	12	2	1/10	***	Maze
4/10/93	6	2	1/13	***	Maze
4/14/93	2	E	1/3	***	Contact
4/23/93	7	2	10/12	Weekapaug Groove	The Squirmin
4/30/93	5	1	1/12	***	Maze
5/30/93	9	1	1/13	***	Maze
8/3/93	16	2	1/9	***	Maze
8/13/93	7	1	1/12	***	Llama
10/20/94	98	2	1/8	***	Maze
7/28/98	291	1	7/10	It's Ice	It's Ice

Has not been played in the last 156 shows.

Leprechaun

DATE	GAP	SET	POS.	SONG BEFORE	SONG AFTER
7/15/93	552	1	8/9	My Mind's Got A Mind	Runaway Jim
7/17/93	2	2	8/12	Mike's Song	Weekapaug Gr
7/31/93	11	2	7/11	Mike's Song	Weekapaug Gr

Has not been played in the last 554 shows.

Let the Good Times Roll

DATE	GAP	SET	POS.	SONG BEFORE	SONG AFTER
4/29/87	22	3	13/14	Ballad - Curtis Loew	I Am Hydrgn

Has not been played in the last 1097 shows.

Letter to Jimmy Page

DATE	GAP	SET	POS.	SONG BEFORE	SONG AFTER
5/11/87	23	E	3/3	Corrine Corrina	***
11/19/87	12	3	9/14	Whipping Post	Take the A-Trn
7/5/94	618	1	4/10	The Curtain	If I Could
7/15/94	7	2	1/10	***	David Bowie

Has not been played in the last 459 shows.

Li'l Red Rooster

DATE	GAP	SET	POS.	SONG BEFORE	SONG AFTER
2/25/97	872	1	4/9	One Meatball	Got My Mojo Workin'

Has not been played in the last 247 shows.

Life on Mars

DATE	GAP	SET	POS.	SONG BEFORE	SONG AFTER
10/13/95	746	1	9/9	Fluffhead	***
10/22/95	7	2	8/11	BBFCFM	Uncle Pen
10/25/95	2	2	2/9	Reba	Cars Trucks Buses
10/27/95	1	E	1/1	***	***
11/9/95	4	2	8/10	T.M.W.S.I.Y. Reprise	Hello My Baby
11/15/95	5	2	5/8	Mike's Song	Weekapaug Gr
11/19/95	3	E	1/2	***	Tweezer Repri
11/24/95	3	E	1/2	***	Rocky Top
7/21/96	37	2	4/9	Reba	Free
7/25/96	4	1	6/8	Run Like an Antelope	Harry Hood
8/7/96	5	2	8/10	Possum	You Enjoy My
8/16/96	5	3	5/6	NICU	Harry Hood
10/21/96	6	2	7/7	Maze	Simple
10/27/96	5	2	8/9	Fluffhead	Tweezer Repri
11/3/96	4	2	6/8	Tweezer	Possum
11/14/96	7	2	7/10	Scent of a Mule	Demand
11/29/96	9	1	7/9	Bathtub Gin	Maze
12/4/96	4	2	6/9	Punch You in the Eye	Reba
3/2/97	19	1	11/13	Catapult	Chalk Dust Tor

Has not been played in the last 243 shows.

Lifeboy

DATE	GAP	SET	POS.	SONG BEFORE	SONG AFTER
2/3/93	480	2	8/11	You Enjoy Myself	Terrapin
2/6/93	3	2	9/14	Weekapaug Groove	Uncle Pen
3/14/93	26	2	7/11	You Enjoy Myself	Rift
3/30/93	12	2	4/15	Tweezer	Big Ball Jam
4/17/93	11	2	6/10	You Enjoy Myself	The Oh Kee Pa
7/15/93	20	2	6/11	It's Ice	Possum
7/29/93	11	2	4/9	It's Ice	Sparkle
8/13/93	11	2	6/9	Mike's Song	The Oh Kee Pa
8/26/93	9	2	3/8	David Bowie	Rift
4/6/94	8	2	6/9	Mike's Song	Weekapaug Gr
4/22/94	13	2	5/8	Tweezer	Runaway Jim
5/4/94	9	1	8/10	Tweezer	Rift
5/12/94	5	2	7/11	Fluffhead	Possum
5/17/94	4	2	4/9	Tweezer	Uncle Pen
5/22/94	4	2	6/9	Tweezer	Rift
5/25/94	2	2	3/9	Tweezer	Maze
5/28/94	3	2	4/8	Tweezer	Reba
6/10/94	3	2	4/9	Tweezer	Sparkle
6/18/94	6	2	8/10	Tweezer	You Enjoy My
6/23/94	4	2	7/8	Tweezer	Slave
6/26/94	3	2	5/12	Axilla (Part II)	Sample in a Ja
6/29/94	1	2	5/8	It's Ice	Divided Sky
7/2/94	3	1	7/9	Tweezer	Sparkle
7/5/94	2	2	4/11	Bathtub Gin	Cities
7/9/94	3	2	6/10	Tweezer	Sparkle
10/7/94	6	2	8/10	Tweezer	My Sweet One
10/14/94	6	2	3/10	Tweezer	Guyote
10/18/94	3	2	6/10	Scent of a Mule	The Old Home
10/28/94	8	2	8/12	Rift	Chalk Dust Tor
11/12/94	6	2	6/12	Down with Disease	Rift
11/18/94	5	2	3/7	Bathtub Gin	Poor Heart
11/23/94	4	2	5/7	Tweezer	You Enjoy My
12/7/94	10	1	7/8	Guyute	Chalk Dust Tor
6/8/95	10	2	6/8	Tweezer	Poor Heart
6/24/95	12	2	4/9	David Bowie	Suzy Greenber
10/5/95	15	2	8/9	David Bowie	Amazing Grce
10/21/95	11	2	3/8	David Bowie	Sparkle
10/29/95	2	2	9/10	Possum	Amazing Grce
11/16/95	8	2	3/9	David Bowie	Uncle Pen
12/5/95	13	2	6/8	Jam	Harry Hood
12/12/95	5	1	4/10	Divided Sky	Punch You in
12/30/95	7	2	5/8	AC/DC Bag	Scent of a Mul
8/13/96	29	2	4/11	Mike's Song	Weekapaug Gr
12/30/96	41	2	6/8	Tweezer	Scent of a Mul
8/3/97	45	2	4/7	Fluffhead	Taste
8/2/98	61	2	3/6	Ghost	David Bowie
11/25/98	32	1	5/9	AC/DC Bag	David Bowie

Has not been played in the last 120 shows.

Light Up Or Leave Me Alone

DATE	GAP	SET	POS.	SONG BEFORE	SONG AFTER
8/9/87	25	2	4/11	The Sloth	Skin it Back
8/21/87	2	1	8/11	The Curtain With	Shaggy Dog
10/31/87	6	1	6/11	Halley's Comet	Love You
5/14/88	14	1	4/11	Halley's Comet	You Enjoy My
7/24/88	12	2	1/8	***	Fluffhead
7/25/88	1	2	5/6	Bold as Love	Fluffhead
12/30/99	1009	1	2/12	Water in the Sky	Suzy Greenber

Has not been played in the last 50 shows.

Limb By Limb

DATE	GAP	SET	POS.	SONG BEFORE	SONG AFTER
6/13/97	878	1	5/8	Billy Breathes	Wolfman's Brother
6/14/97	1	1	7/10	Cars Trucks Buses	Bye Bye Foot
6/16/97	1	2	1/7	***	Ghost
6/19/97	1	1	1/9	***	Dogs Stole Things
6/20/97	1	1	6/8	Ain't Love Funny	I Don't Care
6/21/97	1	1	9/15	Steep	Dirt
6/22/97	1	E	1/1	***	***
6/25/97	2	1	10/11	I Saw it Again	My Soul
7/1/97	3	1	4/9	Ya Mar	Ain't Love Funny
7/10/97	6	1	2/8	Dogs Stole Things	Ginseng Sulli-van
7/23/97	4	1	7/10	Water in the Sky	Split Open and
7/26/97	2	1	1/9	***	Dogs Stole Things
7/31/97	3	1	4/9	Dogs Stole Things	Dirt
8/3/97	2	1	9/10	Jesus Just Left	Character Zer
8/8/97	2	2	3/8	Free	Loving Cup
8/11/97	3	1	6/8	Guelah Papyrus	Horn
8/14/97	2	1	4/10	Fluffhead	Free
8/16/97	1	3	5/6	Lawn Boy	Funky Bitch
11/19/97	6	1	5/10	Dirt	Funky Bitch
11/28/97	5	2	2/5	Timber (Jerry)	Slave
12/5/97	5	1	9/10	Ginseng Sullivan	Character Zer
12/11/97	4	1	5/7	Dirt	Loving Cup
12/31/97	6	1	6/10	Wolfman's Brother	The Horse
4/4/98	3	1	6/8	Ginseng Sullivan	Lawn Boy
6/30/98	2	1	1/13	***	Ghost
7/3/98	3	1	1/9	Down with Disease	Water in the Sky
7/6/98	2	1	5/9	Cities	Train Song
7/15/98	4	2	1/6	***	Simple
7/19/98	3	1	6/8	Ghost	Roggae
7/25/98	4	2	6/8	When Circus Comes	Fee
8/3/98	7	2	3/7	Axilla	Meat
8/7/98	2	2	5/7	Albuquerque	Wading In Velvet Sea
8/11/98	3	2	3/5	Meat	When Circus Comes
8/15/98	2	3	4/6	Strange Design	Brian and Robert
10/15/98	3	E	2/2	Dirt	***
10/29/98	3	1	4/10	Llama	Driver
11/2/98	3	1	7/9	Bittersweet Motel	Wading In Velvet Sea
11/7/98	3	1	6/10	The Wedge	Fikus
11/11/98	3	2	4/6	Walk Away	When Circus Comes
11/15/98	3	1	6/8	Cavern	Roggae
11/24/98	5	1	6/9	Brian and Robert	Sample in a Ja
11/29/98	4	1	6/11	Horn	Catapult
12/29/98	2	2	2/5	Free	Also Sprach
6/30/99	3	1	7/8	Maze	Golgi Apparat
7/9/99	6	1	1/8	***	Farmhouse
7/16/99	5	1	4/9	Dogs Stole Things	Billy Breathes
7/21/99	4	1	5/10	Ginseng Sullivan	Funky Bitch
7/31/99	7	1	4/8	Back on the Train	Free
9/9/99	2	1	3/10	Axilla	Horn
9/11/99	2	1	3/9	Funky Bitch	Dogs Stole Things
9/16/99	3	2	6/8	Mountains in the Mis	Prince Caspian
9/21/99	4	2	5/8	Vultures	Will It Go Round
9/25/99	1	1	5/8	Horn	On Your Way Down
10/1/99	4	1	7/8	Heavy Things	Cavern
10/4/99	3	1	6/8	Jesus Just Left	Wilson
10/9/99	3	2	1/6	***	Also Sprach
12/3/99	3	2	2/5	Sand	Bug
12/8/99	4	1	1/8	***	Back on the Train
12/13/99	4	2	6/8	Mountains in the Mis	Golgi Apparat
12/16/99	2	1	4/10	Lawn Boy	Horn
12/30/99	3	1	5/12	Corrine Corrina	Che Hun Ta Mao
5/21/00	2	1	6/7	The Moma Dance	Character Zer
6/10/00	4	E	2/2	The Inlaw Josie Wale	***
6/16/00	5	1	1/10	***	Back on the Train
6/22/00	1	1	5/9	Golgi Apparatus	Bug
6/29/00	5	1	3/5	Wilson	Drowned
7/6/00	5	2	1/7	***	Also Sprach
7/10/00	3	2	6/7	What's the Use	Loving Cup
7/15/00	4	1	3/9	First Tube	NICU
9/8/00	1	1	2/12	Mellow Mood	Ghost
9/17/00	6	1	4/9	Bathtub Gin	The Moma Dance
9/20/00	2	2	2/9	First Tube	Dirt
9/27/00	5	1	5/10	My Soul	Dirt
10/5/00	5	1	5/10	Sneakin' Sally	Come On Baby, Let's

Has not been played in the last 2 shows.

Listening Wind

DATE	GAP	SET	POS.	SONG BEFORE	SONG AFTER
10/31/96	835	2	7/8	Seen and Not Seen	Overload

Has not been played in the last 284 shows.

Little Drummer Boy

DATE	GAP	SET	POS.	SONG BEFORE	SONG AFTER
12/6/86	16	1	2/14	Mike's Song	Whipping Post
7/3/99	993	2	7/7	Contact	***
12/2/99	46	2	6/6	You Enjoy Myself	***

Has not been played in the last 64 shows.

Lively Up Yourself

DATE	GAP	SET	POS.	SONG BEFORE	SONG AFTER
4/21/92	391	2	11/13	Catapult	Sanity

Has not been played in the last 728 shows.

Llama

DATE	GAP	SET	POS.	SONG BEFORE	SONG AFTER
10/30/90	224	2	7/12	Reba	Ballad - Curtis Loew
11/3/90	3	1	3/11	Bouncing	The Squirmin
11/4/90	1	1	3/13	Rocky Top	Mike's Song
11/8/90	1	1	6/12	Uncle Pen	The Squirmin
11/10/90	1	2	5/8	Fee	Divided Sky

DATE	GAP	SET	POS.	SONG BEFORE	SONG AFTER
11/16/90	1	1	6/8	Magilla	Divided Sky
11/17/90	1	1	1/11	***	The Squirmin
11/24/90	1	2	1/12	***	Bouncing
11/26/90	1		11/11	Makisupa Policeman	***
11/30/90	1	1	10/11	My Sweet One	Possum
12/1/90	1	1	3/9	The Landlady	Divided Sky
12/7/90	1	1	9/9	Foam	***
12/8/90	1	2	1/9	***	The Asse Festival
12/28/90	1	1	5/11	Reba	Col. Forbin's A
12/29/90	1	2	10	I Didn't Know	You Enjoy My
2/8/91	6	2	1/11	***	The Mango Song
2/9/91	1	2	10/10	The Squirming Coil	***
2/15/91	2	1	11/11	Magilla	***
2/16/91	1	1	8/12	Bouncing	The Mango Song
2/19/91	1	1	1/9	***	The Curtain
2/20/91	1	1	8/11	Bouncing	You Enjoy My
2/21/91	1	1	6/11	Fee	The Lizards
2/26/91	1	1	4/11	The Squirming Coil	Guelah Papyrus
2/28/91	2	2	3/7	Reba	Guelah Papyrus
3/1/91	1	2	4/11	Reba	Guelah Papyrus
3/13/91	4	1	7/9	Esther	The Squirmin
3/15/91	1	1	1/12	***	Foam
3/16/91	1	2	1/10	***	Divided Sky
3/22/91	2	1	1/11	***	You Enjoy My
3/23/91	1	1	4/10	Fee	I Didn't Know
4/2/91	4	1	4/10	Reba	Bouncing
4/3/91	1	1	2/10	Golgi Apparatus	The Lizards
4/4/91	1	1	5/10	The Squirming Coil	Col. Forbin's A
4/6/91	2	2	5/11	Magilla	You Enjoy My
4/11/91	1	2	3/14	Reba	T.M.W.S.I.Y.
4/12/91	1	1	1/9	***	Uncle Pen
4/15/91	1	1	10/10	The Famous Mockingbi	***
4/18/91	2	1	1/11	***	Reba
4/20/91	2	1	3/11	Reba	Fluffhead
4/21/91	1	2	6/11	The Famous Mockingbi	Uncle Pen
4/22/91	1	1	6/9	Poor Heart	Guelah Papyrus
4/25/91	1	1	8/11	Reba	The Oh Kee Pa
4/27/91	1	1	8/12	Reba	The Lizards
5/2/91	1	1	7/11	Col. Forbin's Ascent	The Squirmin
5/4/91	2	2	2/9	Dog Gone Dog	Col. Forbin's A
5/9/91	1	1	6/10	Reba	Bouncing
5/12/91	3	1	8/11	Destiny Unbound	Fee
5/16/91	1	1	11/11	Magilla	***
5/19/91	3	1	8/8	The Squirming Coil	***
7/13/91	3	1	4/13	Foam	The Oh Kee Pa
7/14/91	1	1	2/11	Reba	The Squirmin
7/18/91	2	2	1/8	***	Reba
7/20/91	2	1	4/10	The Squirming Coil	The Oh Kee Pa
7/23/91	2	2	1/10	***	Reba
7/25/91	2	2	4/13	The Squirming Coil	Poor Heart
7/27/91	2	1	1/16	***	Foam
8/3/91	1	1	5/11	Guelah Papyrus	Fee
9/25/91	1	1	4/11	Foam	Tela
9/26/91	1	1	1/10	***	Bouncing
9/27/91	1	1	9/9	I Didn't Know	***
9/28/91	1	2	1/12	***	Guelah Papyrus
10/2/91	3	1	1/10	***	Foam
10/3/91	1	1	6/10	Bouncing	Fee
10/4/91	1	E	5/5	Love You	***
10/6/91	1	E	3/3	Possum	***
10/10/91	1	1	10/11	Eliza	Golgi Apparat
10/11/91	1	1	8/10	The Lizards	Bouncing
10/13/91	2	2	1/9	***	Bathtub Gin
10/15/91	1	2	6/12	Poor Heart	Horn
10/18/91	2	1	6/9	Wilson	The Lizards
10/19/91	1	2	1/10	***	Bathtub Gin
10/23/91	1	1	8/11	Horn	Bouncing
10/27/91	2	2	1/13	***	Col. Forbin's A

DATE	GAP	SET	POS.	SONG BEFORE	SONG AFTER
10/31/91	3	2	4/14	Wait	Fee
11/2/91	2	1	3/10	The Curtain	Reba
11/7/91	1	1	11/11	I Didn't Know	***
11/9/91	2	1	5/11	Sparkle	Reba
11/10/91	1	2	4/4	Sweet Adeline	***
11/12/91	1	1	11/11	Foam	***
11/13/91	1	2	7/9	The Squirming Coil	Terrapin
11/14/91	1	1	3/11	Uncle Pen	Reba
11/15/91	1	2	1/14	***	Bathtub Gin
11/16/91	1	2	9/9	Terrapin	***
11/20/91	2	1	10/11	The Squirming Coil	You Enjoy My
11/22/91	2	2	8/10	I Didn't Know	The Lizards
11/23/91	1	1	1/11	***	Reba
11/30/91	1	2	1/11	Glide	Foam
12/4/91	1	1	1/11	***	Reba
12/5/91	1	1	6/10	Fluffhead	Bathtub Gin
12/6/91	1	2	8/12	Tela	Whipping Post
12/31/91	2	1	9/10	Esther	Golgi Apparat
3/6/92	1	2	6/9	Mound	Bouncing
3/11/92	2	2	1/11	***	NICU
3/12/92	1	1	10/11	Magilla	You Enjoy My
3/14/92	2	2	2/10	Golgi Apparatus	The Squirmin
3/17/92	1	2	11/11	Love You	Fluffhead
3/24/92	5	1	9/13	Silent in the Mornin	Col. Forbin's A
3/27/92	3	1	1/10	***	Reba
3/30/92	2	1	2/11	The Landlady	Foam
3/31/92	1	1	7/10	Reba	Col. Forbin's A
4/1/92	1	2	1/13	***	You Enjoy My
4/3/92	1	2	7/9	The Mango Song	Harry Hood
4/5/92	2	1	1/11	***	Guelah Papyrus
4/6/92	1	2	8/13	NICU	Mound
4/8/92	2	1	1/11	Guelah Papyrus	Mound
4/13/92	2	1	1/11	***	Fluffhead
4/16/92	2	2	2/12	Sanity	The Lizards
4/18/92	2	1	10/16	Mound	T.M.W.S.I.Y.
4/19/92	1	2	10/13	The Mango Song	Lawn Boy
4/22/92	2	1	1/10	***	Foam
4/23/92	1	1	7/11	The Squirming Coil	Bouncing
4/24/92	1	2	12/12	Glide	***
4/29/92	2	2	5/11	The Oh Kee Pa Ceremo	The Lizards
5/1/92	2	2	11/13	The Lizards	Terrapin
5/2/92	1	1	11/11	The Squirming Coil	***
5/5/92	2	2	11/14	Poor Heart	Love You
5/6/92	1	1	1/11	***	Foam
5/8/92	2	1	7/12	Eliza	Mound
5/9/92	1	2	6/8	Harpua	Cracklin' Rosi
5/12/92	2	2	8/9	Poor Heart	Cavern
5/17/92	4	1	2/11	The Landlady	Col. Forbin's A
5/18/92	1	2	2/13	Glide	T.M.W.S.I.Y.
6/20/92	2	1	8/8	Love You	***
6/24/92	2	1	2/9	Runaway Jim	Sweet Adeline
7/10/92	5	1	2/10	Bouncing	Reba
7/14/92	3	2	5/10	Reba	The Squirmin
7/16/92	2	2	8/12	T.M.W.S.I.Y. Reprise	Glide
7/18/92	2	1	3/6	Foam	Reba
7/25/92	5	1	7/8	You Enjoy Myself	Funky Bitch
7/26/92	1	1	7/7	The Lizards	***
7/27/92	1	1	6/7	Suzy Greenberg	Sweet Adeline
8/1/92	4	1	7/7	Horn	***
8/14/92	3	1	4/5	The Squirming Coil	Sweet Adeline
8/19/92	3	1	7/7	Uncle Pen	***
8/25/92	4	1	6/7	The Squirming Coil	Sweet Adeline
8/27/92	1	1	7/7	You Enjoy Myself	***
8/30/92	3	1	4/7	Reba	Memories
11/19/92	2	2	13/15	Fast Enough for You	Lengthwise
11/21/92	2	2	13/13	Take the A-Train	***
11/23/92	2	2	5/14	I Walk the Line	Weigh
11/25/92	2	1	3/12	Reba	Mound
11/30/92	2	1	1/10	***	Foam
12/1/92	1	2	7/11	Uncle Pen	Love You
12/2/92	1	2	6/11	Tela	Glide
12/4/92	2	1	1/10	***	Foam
12/6/92	2	1	8/10	The Squirming Coil	Fluffhead
12/7/92	1	2	3/12	Reba	Horn

DATE	GAP	SET	POS.	SONG BEFORE	SONG AFTER
12/8/92	1	1	3/11	Wilson	Col. Forbin's A
12/10/92	1	1	2/11	Golgi Apparatus	Foam
12/12/92	2	1	1/11	***	Foam
12/13/92	1	2	4/14	Bouncing	Fluffhead
12/29/92	2	1	4/12	Guelah Papyrus	My Friend My
12/30/92	1	2	12/12	Take the A-Train	***
12/31/92	1	3	9/9	Diamond Girl	***
2/3/93	1	1	4/11	Fee	The Wedge
2/5/93	2	1	1/11	***	Guelah Papyrus
2/7/93	2	2	1/13	***	Fast Enough for You
2/11/93	3	1	8/10	Fluffhead	Lawn Boy
2/13/93	2	2	6/11	The Lizards	You Enjoy My
2/15/93	1	2	12/12	Fee	***
2/19/93	3	2	11/12	Love You	Amazing Grce
2/22/93	3	2	8/11	The Oh Kee Pa Ceremo	Love You
2/26/93	3	1	6/10	Fluffhead	Horn
2/27/93	1	2	12/12	Fee	***
3/2/93	1	2	5/12	The Lizards	You Enjoy My
3/6/93	3	1	1/10	***	Horn
3/8/93	1	1	5/12	The Oh Kee Pa Ceremo	Col. Forbin's A
3/13/93	3	1	9/11	Contact	Wilson
3/16/93	2	2	14/15	Lawn Boy	Amazing Grce
3/19/93	3	1	2/9	Suzy Greenberg	Foam
3/21/93	1	2	10/12	Cracklin' Rosie	Harry Hood
3/24/93	2	1	1/9	***	Foam
3/27/93	3	1	1/10	***	Guelah Papyrus
3/30/93	2	1	6/11	My Friend My Friend	Esther
4/1/93	2	1	1/10	***	Guelah Papyrus
4/2/93	1	2	4/13	Uncle Pen	The Horse
4/5/93	2	1	1/10	***	It's Ice
4/9/93	1	2	4/10	All Things Recnsrd	Mound
4/12/93	2	1	9/11	Reba	Satin Doll
4/16/93	2	1	6/10	Esther	Sample in a Ja
4/17/93	1	1	1/10	***	Foam
4/20/93	2	2	9/12	My Friend My Friend	You Enjoy My
4/22/93	2	2	1/10	***	Bouncing
4/24/93	2	1	2/10	***	Foam
4/29/93	3	1	6/10	Horn	Glide
5/2/93	3	2	1/10	***	Punch You in
5/6/93	3	1	7/13	All Things Recnsrd	Fluffhead
5/30/93	4	1	12/13	Contact	Golgi Apparat
7/16/93	1	E	1/2	***	Freebird
7/22/93	4	1	1/11	***	Foam
7/24/93	2	1	1/10	***	Horn
7/30/93	5	1	2/10	Contact	Horn
8/3/93	3	1	10/11	Ya Mar	Cavern
8/7/93	2	1	1/10	***	Bouncing
8/13/93	5	1	2/10	Lengthwise	Makisupa Policeman
8/17/93	4	1	2/9	Wilson	Guelah Papyrus
8/21/93	2	2	5/10	Fee	Lawn Boy
8/24/93	1	2	1/10	***	Horn
8/28/93	3	1	1/9	***	Bouncing
12/31/93	4	1	1/8	***	Guelah Papyrus
4/6/94	3	1	1/9	***	Guelah Papyrus
4/8/94	1	1	13/13	Lawn Boy	***
4/15/94	6	1	1/9	***	Guelah Papyrus
4/22/94	6	1	1/11	***	Horn
4/29/94	5	1	12/12	My Mind's Got A Mind	***
5/7/94	6	1	1/9	***	Horn
5/14/94	5	1	1/9	***	Wilson
5/19/94	3	1	2/10	Halley's Comet	My Friend My
5/21/94	2	1	9/9	Tela	***
5/28/94	6	2	7/8	Fee	You Enjoy My
6/9/94	2	1	1/9	***	Guelah Papyrus
6/14/94	4	1	1/14	***	Guelah Papyrus

DATE	GAP	SET	POS.	SONG BEFORE	SONG AFTER
6/22/94	6	1	1/9	***	Guelah Papyrus
6/24/94	2	2	8/13	Sanity	Dog Faced Boy
6/26/94	2	1	2/11	Kung	The Lizards
7/6/94	7	1	1/9	***	Fluffhead
7/8/94	1	1	1/11	***	NO2
10/13/94	12	1	1/9	***	Gumbo
10/18/94	4	2	10/10	Nellie Kane	***
10/25/94	5	1	2/9	Fee	Horn
10/28/94	3	1	2/10	I Didn't Know	Guelah Papyrus
11/18/94	11	2	1/7	***	Bathtub Gin
11/25/94	5	1	1/8	***	Guelah Papyrus
12/6/94	8	1	1/8	***	Mound
12/9/94	3	1	1/8	***	Foam
12/28/94	2	2	7/9	Contact	Love You
6/10/95	8	1	2/9	Makisupa Policeman	Prince Caspian
6/20/95	7	1	1/9	***	Spock's Brain
6/23/95	2	2	6/7	Harpua	Good Time Ba
7/1/95	7	1	2/9	Ya Mar	If I Could
10/2/95	7	2	4/10	Bathtub Gin	Simple
10/11/95	6	2	7/11	Weekapaug Groove	Suzy Greenber
10/15/95	3	1	6/10	Demand	Foam
10/24/95	6	1	5/13	Fee	The Horse
11/12/95	9	1	2/10	My Friend My Friend	Bouncing
11/22/95	7	2	3/6	Free	Bouncing
12/11/95	13	1	7/12	Dog Gone Dog	Dog Gone Dog
12/14/95	2	1	2/10	Suzy Greenberg	Horn
12/29/95	5	1	8/9	Fluffhead	Sweet Adeline
7/3/96	5	1	5/5	Taste	***
7/12/96	7	1	10/10	Tweezer	***
7/21/96	6	2	1/9	***	Theme From the Botto
8/13/96	12	1	8/10	Punch You in the Eye	Glide
10/19/96	7	1	5/9	Esther	Gumbo
10/23/96	3	2	5/8	The Lizards	Suzy Greenber
11/14/96	14	2	1/10	***	Sample in a Ja
11/18/96	3	2	9/9	Tweezer Reprise	***
12/6/96	11	1	5/9	Also Sprach	You Enjoy My
12/30/96	3	1	3/9	The Sloth	Gumbo
2/17/97	5	1	8/10	Billy Breathes	Bathtub Gin
2/26/97	7	1	2/10	Camel Walk	My Friend My
7/2/97	17	2	2/4	Stash	Wormtown Jam
7/10/97	5	1	5/8	Bathtub Gin	Wading In Velvet Sea
8/16/97	19	3	3/6	Cities	Lawn Boy
11/19/97	6	1	3/10	Bathtub Gin	Dirt
12/13/97	16	2	5/10	Mike's Song	When Circus Comes
7/19/98	21	2	1/7	***	Wolfman's Brother
10/29/98	24	1	3/10	Roggae	Limb by Limb
11/9/98	8	1	1/10	***	Horn
11/25/98	12	2	8/8	Been Caught Stealin'	***
12/31/98	7	3	6/6	Tweezer Reprise	***
7/9/99	7	1	6/8	Train Song	Driver
7/18/99	7	2	6/6	Axilla	***
8/1/99	10	2	3/9	Tweezer	Mike's Song
10/2/99	18	1	1/9	***	Wolfman's Brother
12/31/99	22	2	4/35	Down with Disease	Bathtub Gin
6/14/00	8	1	5/8	Gumbo	Fee
7/8/00	15	1	7/9	First Tube	Guyute
10/1/00	22	1	8/10	Billy Breathes	Lawn Boy

Has not been played in the last 4 shows.

Lonesome Cowboy Bill

DATE	GAP	SET	POS.	SONG BEFORE	SONG AFTER
5/16/95	712	1	7/12	Theme From the Botto	Free
6/7/95		2	5/9	Theme From the Botto	Acoustic Army
6/10/95	3	1	8/9	You Enjoy Myself	Suzy Greenber
10/31/98	267	2	7/10	Head Held High	I Found a Reason

Has not been played in the last 136 shows.

Long Cool Woman in a Black Dress

DATE	GAP	SET	POS.	SONG BEFORE	SONG AFTER
12/2/83	0	1	1/6	***	Proud Mary
10/30/98	982	1	6/10	Scent of a Mule	Run Like Antel

Has not been played in the last 137 shows.

Long Long Long

DATE	GAP	SET	POS.	SONG BEFORE	SONG AFTER
10/31/94	681	2	25/30	Helter Skelter	Revolution

Has not been played in the last 438 shows.

Loup Garou

DATE	GAP	SET	POS.	SONG BEFORE	SONG AFTER
3/2/93	501	2	9/12	It's My Life	Choo Choo Ch' Boogie

Has not been played in the last 618 shows.

Love Me

DATE	GAP	SET	POS.	SONG BEFORE	SONG AFTER
2/13/97	863	1	11/12	Peaches en Regalia	David Bowie
2/20/97	5	1	5/10	Chalk Dust Torture	Taste
2/23/97	3	1	5/9	The Sloth	Rift
2/28/97	3	2	6/9	David Bowie	Axilla
3/18/97	3	2	5/10	David Bowie	I Told You So
8/14/97	36	2	2/8	Chalk Dust Torture	Sparkle
11/30/97	14	1	4/6	Wolfman's Brother	The Squirmin
11/8/98	61	1	3/10	Carini	Ride Captain Ride
11/18/98	6	1	7/9	Lawn Boy	David Bowie

Has not been played in the last 125 shows.

Love Me Like a Man

DATE	GAP	SET	POS.	SONG BEFORE	SONG AFTER
3/18/97	877	2	7/10	I Told You So	Waste

Has not been played in the last 242 shows.

Love Reign O'er Me

DATE	GAP	SET	POS.	SONG BEFORE	SONG AFTER
10/31/95	759	2	17/17	The Rock	***

Has not been played in the last 360 shows.

Love You

DATE	GAP	SET	POS.	SONG BEFORE	SONG AFTER
10/31/87	33	1	7/11	Light Up Or Leave Me	AC/DC Bag
4/20/89	60	2	9/10	Weekapaug Groove	Harpua
12/3/89	44	2	11/14	Possum	Mike's Song
4/9/90	38	2	9/11	Divided Sky	Tweezer
4/12/90	1	2	8/11	Runaway Jim	Mike's Song
4/29/90	11	1	11/13	Walk Away	The Lizards
5/11/90	5	2	6/7	Ya Mar	Good Time Ba
6/7/90	11	2	7/10	Divided Sky	Mike's Song
10/1/90	13	1	10/11	Golgi Apparatus	Run Like Antel
10/31/90	9	2	9/12	Suzy Greenberg	Mike's Song
11/3/90	2	2	11/12	Possum	Run Like Antel
11/17/90	5	2	7/12	Esther	Possum
11/24/90	1	2	8/12	You Enjoy Myself	Good Time Ba
2/7/91	12	2	10/14	Cavern	The Lizards
2/9/91	2	2	8/10	Cavern	The Squirmin
2/16/91	3	2	8/9	Rocky Top	Golgi Apparat
2/19/91	1	2	10/15	Bouncing	Whole Lotta Love Jam
2/19/91	0	2	12/15	Whole Lotta Love Jam	The Oh Kee Pa
2/26/91	3	E	1/2	***	Good Time Ba
2/27/91	1	2	9/11	The Sloth	Possum
2/28/91	1	2	6/7	Divided Sky	The Lizards
3/1/91	1	2	9/11	Possum	Whole Lotta Love Jam
3/6/91	1	1	8/11	Divided Sky	My Sweet One
3/9/91	2	2	10/13	The Lizards	Fire
3/28/91	7	1	13/14	Suzy Greenberg	Chalk Dust Tor
4/4/91	5	2	9/10	Divided Sky	BBFCFM
5/10/91	18	2	8/11	Chalk Dust Torture	Mike's Song
5/11/91	1	E	1/2	***	BBFCFM
10/4/91	29	E	4/5	Rocky Top	Llama
10/13/91	5	2	8/9	Bouncing	David Bowie
10/15/91	1	2	10/12	Suzy Greenberg	Funky Bitch
10/17/91	1	2	8/9	You Enjoy Myself	Possum
10/23/91	3	2	7/10	Split Open and Melt	Fee
11/1/91	6	E	1/3	***	Pusher Man Jam
11/7/91	2	2	10/11	HYHU Jam	Possum
11/12/91	4	2	12/13	Cavern	Run Like Antel
11/15/91	3	2	12/14	Harry Hood	Bouncing
11/19/91	2	1	9/11	Chalk Dust Torture	Wilson
11/23/91	4	2	11/13	Fee	My Sweet One
12/4/91	3	2	10/11	Chalk Dust Torture	Golgi Apparat
3/13/92	9	2	10/12	Rift	Secret Language Inst
3/17/92	2	2	10/11	Weekapaug Groove	Llama
3/27/92	8	2	12/13	Harry Hood	Golgi Apparat
3/31/92	3	2	10/12	My Sweet One	Possum
4/5/92	4	2	10/12	David Bowie	Take the A-Trn
4/13/92	5	2	10/11	The Squirming Coil	Possum
4/18/92	4	2	15/16	Harry Hood	Rocky Top
4/24/92	5	2	10/12	Horn	Glide
4/29/92	2	2	10/11	Weekapaug Groove	Golgi Apparat
5/5/92	5	2	12/14	Llama	The Squirmin
5/15/92	8	1	7/11	Bouncing	Chalk Dust Tor
5/17/92	2	2	8/11	Sanity	Sparkle
5/18/92	1	2	12/13	Cavern	Runaway Jim
6/20/92	2	1	7/8	Horn	Llama
11/21/92	43	2	11/13	The Squirming Coil	Take the A-Trn
12/1/92	7	2	8/11	Llama	Dinner and a
12/7/92	6	2	10/12	David Bowie	The Squirmin
12/10/92	2	2	8/10	You Enjoy Myself	The Oh Kee Pa
12/30/92	6	2	10/12	Big Ball Jam	Take the A-Trn
2/5/93	4	2	8/10	You Enjoy Myself	The Squirmin
2/11/93	5	2	10/12	Bouncing	The Lizards
2/19/93	6	2	10/12	My Sweet One	Llama
2/22/93	3	2	9/11	Llama	The Squirmin
3/2/93	5	2	7/12	You Enjoy Myself	It's My Life
3/5/93	2	2	9/11	Big Ball Jam	The Squirmin
3/9/93	3	2	12/15	Big Ball Jam	I Walk the Line
3/13/93	2	2	12/13	Fast Enough for You	Tweezer Repri
3/19/93	5	2	9/10	Weekapaug Groove	Golgi Apparat
3/28/93	7	2	8/9	Paul and Silas	Possum
4/1/93	3	2	9/10	Big Ball Jam	Cavern
4/3/93	2	2	9/10	My Sweet One	Cavern
4/9/93	2	2	9/10	My Sweet One	Possum
4/18/93	6	2	11/12	Walk Away	Tweezer Repri
4/22/93	3	2	9/10	Uncle Pen	Tweezer Repri
4/27/93	4	2	9/10	Silent in the Mornin	Cavern
5/3/93	5	2	10/12	Runaway Jim	My Sweet One
8/8/93	25	2	9/11	Big Ball Jam	Daniel
5/12/94	48	2	9/11	Possum	Contact
5/17/94	4	2	8/9	Sample in a Jar	Slave
6/30/94	27	2	14/15	Run Like an Antelope	Chalk Dust Tor
10/10/94	16	2	8/9	Down with Disease	Slave
11/17/94	24	2	6/8	You Enjoy Myself	Slave
12/28/94	19	2	8/9	Llama	The Squirmin
12/8/95	73	2	5/8	Tweezer	The Squirmin
7/5/97	111	1	10/13	Harry Hood	Poor Heart
12/31/99	178	2	30/35	Lawn Boy	Roses are Free
9/24/00	40	2	6/8	Lawn Boy	Cool it Down

Has not been played in the last 9 shows.

Loving Cup

DATE	GAP	SET	POS.	SONG BEFORE	SONG AFTER
2/3/93	480	1	1/11	***	Rift
2/5/93	2	E	2/2	Amazing Grace	***
2/10/93	4	1	1/10	***	Foam
2/19/93	7	1	1/11	***	Rift
2/26/93	6	2	1/11	***	Paul and Silas
3/14/93	10	1	1/11	***	Foam
3/21/93	5	1	1/12	***	My Friend My
3/30/93	7	2	1/15	***	Rift
8/8/93	49	1	3/11	Foam	Runaway Jim
4/17/94	30	1	1/9	***	Foam
5/7/94	15	2	1/12	***	Sparkle
11/4/94	69	E	1/2	***	Rocky Top
6/19/95	38	2	4/8	The Mango Song	Sparkle
7/3/95	12	1	4/11	Run Like an Antelope	Sparkle
11/9/95	26	E	1/1	***	***

DATE	GAP	SET	POS.	SONG BEFORE	SONG AFTER
12/9/95	22	E	1/1	***	***
7/15/96	22	2	3/9	Maze	Makisupa Policeman
7/23/96	6	2	3/9	Runaway Jim	Sparkle
8/4/96	4	1	9/9	Maze	***
11/8/96	26	2	5/8	Simple	Mike's Song
11/19/96	8	1	9/9	Taste	***
11/24/96	3	2	6/7	You Enjoy Yourself	Suzy Greenber
2/16/97	14	2	10/11	David Bowie	Tweezer Repri
2/25/97	7	1	9/9	Taste	***
6/24/97	13	E	1/1	***	***
7/1/97	4	2	6/7	Jam	Slave
7/21/97	8	E	1/1	***	***
7/29/97	5	1	9/9	Steep	***
8/2/97	3	2	6/7	Wading In Velvet Sea	Tweezer Repri
8/8/97	3	2	4/6	Limb by Limb	Prince Caspian
8/16/97	6	E	2/2	Contact	***
11/13/97	2	E	1/1	***	***
11/21/97	5	2	4/4	Slave	***
11/30/97	6	1	6/6	The Squirming Coil	***
12/5/97	3	2	6/7	The Lizards	Chalk Dust Tor
12/9/97	3	1	10/10	Horn	***
12/11/97	1	1	6/7	Limb by Limb	Rocky Top
12/31/97	6	3	6/6	Prince Caspian	***
4/3/98	2	2	3/4	Piper	Run Like Antel
7/1/98	4	2	3/5	Also Sprach	My Soul
7/6/98	4	2	6/6	David Bowie	***
7/15/98	4	1	13/13	Birds of a Feather	***
7/24/98	6	1	8/8	Golgi Apparatus	***
8/2/98	7	2	6/6	I Get a Kick Out of	***
8/12/98	7	2	4/7	Rift	Sleeping Monkey
8/15/98	1	3	6/6	Brian and Robert	***
10/18/98	5	1	5/12	Roggae	Albuquerque
11/4/98	5	2	6/6	Chalk Dust Torture	***
11/15/98	8	2	6/7	Wading In Velvet Sea	Weekapaug Gr
11/28/98	8	2	4/9	Timber (Jerry)	Scent of a Mul
12/30/98	4	1	11/12	Maze	Reba
7/7/99	6	1	10/10	Maze	***
7/16/99	7	2	7/8	Guyute	Golgi Apparat
9/14/99	17	1	5/11	Waste	What's the Use
9/19/99	4	2	5/6	The Squirming Coil	Down with Dis
9/24/99	3	1	10/10	Guyute	***
10/2/99	6	1	9/9	The Squirming Coil	***
10/9/99	5	2	6/6	Simple	***
12/4/99	4	1	7/7	Dirt	***
12/10/99	4	1	10/10	Guyute	***
12/17/99	6	E	3/3	The Squirming Coil	***
5/21/00	4	E	1/2	The Inlaw Josie Wale	***
6/10/00	4	2	9/9	Wading In Velvet Sea	***
7/6/00	16	2	7/7	Harry Hood	***
7/10/00	3	2	7/7	Limb by Limb	***
7/15/00	4	E	1/1	***	***
9/14/00	5	2	5/5	Prince Caspian	***
9/27/00	9	E	1/1	***	***
10/4/00	4	E	1/1	***	***

Has not been played in the last 3 shows.

Low Rider Jam

DATE	GAP	SET	POS.	SONG BEFORE	SONG AFTER
8/21/87	27	2	10/12	Skin it Back	Back Porch Boogie Bl
11/23/97	896	2	3/5	Down with Disease	Down with Dis

Has not been played in the last 196 shows.

Lushington

DATE	GAP	SET	POS.	SONG BEFORE	SONG AFTER
10/15/86	14	1	9/9	You Enjoy Yourself	***
2/21/87	4	2	8/15	Clod	Peaches en Regalia
4/29/87	4	1	9/9	Fuck Your Face	***
5/20/87	2	1	5/9	Back Porch Boogie Bl	Possum
8/29/87	4	2	7/13	Flat Fee	Suzy Greenber

Has not been played in the last 1091 shows.

Magilla

DATE	GAP	SET	POS.	SONG BEFORE	SONG AFTER
9/13/90	207	2	4/15	Weekapaug Groove	Stash
9/14/90	1	2	5/10	Tweezer	Cavern
9/15/90	1	1	13/14	Stash	The Squirmin
9/16/90	1	1	13/14	Weekapaug Groove	Run Like Antel
9/20/90	1	2	6/14	Divided Sky	The Oh Kee Pa
9/22/90	2	1	8/12	Suzy Greenberg	Wilson
9/29/90	2	1	8/9	Possum	David Bowie
10/4/90	2	2	6/8	Tweezer	Cavern
10/8/90	4	2	5/6	Golgi Apparatus	Run Like Antel
10/12/90	1	2	7/10	Paul and Silas	Mike's Song
10/19/90	1	1	7/15	Weekapaug Groove	Cavern
10/30/90	2	2	4/12	Weekapaug Groove	Foam
11/3/90	3	1	7/11	Suzy Greenberg	Foam
11/16/90	4	1	5/8	You Enjoy Yourself	Llama
12/31/90	10	2	5/9	Runaway Jim	You Enjoy My
2/1/91	1	1	5/10	Tweezer Reprise	Guelah Papyrus
2/8/91	4	E	1/2	***	La Grange
2/15/91	3	1	10/11	Dinner and a Movie	Llama
2/19/91	2	E	1/2	***	Fire
3/16/91	12	2	6/10	Split Open and Melt	Buried Alive
3/22/91	2	E	1/2	***	Golgi Apparat
4/2/91	5	E	1/2	***	Possum
4/4/91	2	E	1/4	***	Highway to Hell
4/6/91	2	2	4/11	Runaway Jim	Llama
4/11/91	1	1	5/12	Tweezer	Dinner and a
4/15/91	2	2	10/11	Possum	Fire
4/16/91	1	2	5/11	Chalk Dust Torture	Buried Alive
5/9/91	11	1	8/10	Bouncing	Runaway Jim
5/12/91	3	2	6/13	Golgi Apparatus	Mike's Song
5/16/91	1	1	10/11	You Enjoy Yourself	Llama
5/17/91	1	2	6/9	Fluffhead	Cavern
7/14/91	6	2	8/10	Split Open and Melt	Cavern
7/19/91	3	2	8/10	My Sweet One	Tweezer
7/25/91	5	2	10/13	Touch Me	Mike's Song
8/3/91	3	E	1/5	***	Self
9/28/91	4	2	9/12	Poor Heart	Mike's Song
10/4/91	5	1	9/10	Suzy Greenberg	David Bowie
10/11/91	2	2	8/9	Poor Heart	Possum
10/17/91	4	E	1/2	***	Rocky Top
11/12/91	15	2	10/13	Chalk Dust Torture	Cavern
11/20/91	5	E	1/2	***	Brother
12/6/91	8	1	6/9	The Squirming Coil	The Landlady
3/12/92	6	1	9/11	Rift	Llama
3/27/92	12	2	10/13	Dinner and a Movie	Harry Hood
4/13/92	12	2	7/11	Weekapaug Groove	Ya Mar
4/25/92	10	1	10/11	Rift	Run Like Antel
5/8/92	9	2	4/12	Stash	Maze
3/25/93	113	1	10/11	Horn	Run Like Antel
4/4/94	72	2	6/11	Julius	Split Open and
4/9/94	4	1	1/10	***	Wilson
4/11/94	2	1	5/9	Fast Enough for You	Julius
4/15/94	3	E	1/2	***	Amazing Grce
5/4/94	15	2	8/9	Wolfman's Brother	Suzy Greenber
2/26/97	260	2	9/11	Jam	Scent of a Mul
7/10/97	2	2	3/7	Julius	Ya Mar
7/21/97	2	2	2/8	Wolfman's Brother	David Bowie
8/1/98	69	2	4/10	Also Sprach	Tweezer
7/4/00	124	2	3/5	I Saw It Again	Twist

Has not been played in the last 29 shows.

Maiden Voyage

DATE	GAP	SET	POS.	SONG BEFORE	SONG AFTER
7/30/88	61	2	5/6	Contact	Corrine Corrina

Has not been played in the last 1058 shows.

Makisupa Policeman

DATE	GAP	SET	POS.	SONG BEFORE	SONG AFTER
10/23/84	1	1	1/1	***	***
12/1/84	2	1	4/11	Fire on the Mountain	Slave
5/3/85	2	3	5/8	McGrupp	Jam
4/15/86	8	1	6/14	Slave	Have Mercy
10/15/86	1	1	2/9	Alumni Blues	Skin it Back
4/29/87	8	3	5/14	Anarchy	Run Like Antel
5/11/87	1	1	11/12	T.M.W.S.I.Y. Reprise	Ya Mar
8/29/87	5	2	4/13	Sneakin' Sally	BBFCFM
9/2/87	1	1	10/13	BBFCFM	Timber (Jerry)
9/21/87	1	1	10/15	Run Like an Antelope	Flat Fee
10/14/87	2	1	12/12	McGrupp	***
2/26/88	8	2	7/9	Dear Mrs. Reagan	Alumni Blues
7/12/88	17	2	6/9	Jesus Just Left	Slave
2/7/89	24	2	1/9	***	Dinner and a
3/30/89	10	E	1/1	***	***
10/7/89	27	1	9/11	La Grange	Alumni Blues
10/14/89	3	1	10/11	You Enjoy Yourself	Good Time Ba
2/25/90	38	2	3/6	McGrupp	The Lizards
11/26/90	75	1	10/11	Divided Sky	Llama
4/29/93	307	2	10/13	Weekapaug Groove	Weekapaug Gr
8/2/93	25	1	9/12	Bathtub Gin	My Mind's Got A Mind
8/7/93	3	1	5/10	Stash	Reba
8/13/93	5	1	3/10	Llama	Foam
5/7/94	41	2	5/12	Sparks	Digital Delay Loop J
6/19/94	26	2	5/8	Reba	The Squirmin
10/29/94	39	1	9/10	Buffalo Bill	Rift
12/1/94	19	2	5/10	BBFCFM	NICU
12/8/94	6	1	1/10	***	Maze
6/10/95	11	1	1/9	***	Llama
7/2/95	17	2	2/8	Runaway Jim	Scent of a Mul
10/7/95	10	2	1/9	***	Cars Trucks Buses
10/22/95	10	2	6/11	Tweezer	BBFCFM
10/29/95	5	2	1/10	***	David Bowie
11/19/95	10	1	1/1	***	Maze
11/30/95	7	2	3/8	Tweezer	Run Like Antel
12/14/95	10	1	5/10	Foam	Split Open and
12/29/95	5	2	1/11	***	Cars Trucks Buses
7/15/96	14	2	4/9	Loving Cup	It's Ice
8/6/96	12	1	1/9	***	Rift
8/16/96	6	3	1/6	***	Also Sprach
10/25/96	9	1	3/10	Taste	Maze
11/15/96	14	2	1/11	***	Maze
11/23/96	5	2	4/10	Simple	Axilla
12/28/96	9	2	1/10	***	Maze
6/25/97	27	2	6/9	McGrupp	Cecilia
7/25/97	14	1	6/7	Bathtub Gin	AC/DC Bag
8/11/97	11	1	1/8	***	Maze
8/16/97	3	1	1/11	***	Harpua
11/19/97	6	2	3/4	Wolfman's Brother	Taste
12/27/97	8	1	3/9	Down with Disease	Chalk Dust Tor
7/6/98	22	2	4/6	Piper	David Bowie
7/17/98	6	1	1/7	***	Ya Mar
7/20/98	2	2	2/6	Drowned	Maze
8/12/98	16	1	2/8	La Grange	Funky Bitch
11/6/98	12	2	1/7	***	Funky Bitch
11/29/98	16	2	3/8	Simple	Possum
7/12/99	13	2	3/6	The Moma Dance	David Bowie
7/25/99	10	1	5/8	Whipping Post	I Saw It Again
9/28/99	20	2	5/7	Tweezer	Chalk Dust Tor
10/4/99	5	2	5/8	AC/DC Bag	Sand
12/12/99	24	2	4/5	The Squirming Coil	Run Like Antel
6/23/00	19	2	6/7	Contact	Character Zer
6/30/00	5	2	6/9	Back on the Train	Farmhouse
7/15/00	11	2	3/7	While My Guitar Gent	Piper
9/9/00	2	2	4/7	Sand	Cars Trucks Buses

Has not been played in the last 19 shows.

Makisupa Policeman Jam

DATE	GAP	SET	POS.	SONG BEFORE	SONG AFTER
8/21/87	27	3	4/7	Stir it Up Jam	David Bowie Jam

Has not been played in the last 1092 shows.

Manteca

DATE	GAP	SET	POS.	SONG BEFORE	SONG AFTER
11/4/90	228	2	7/13	Weekapaug Groove	Caravan
12/28/90	11	2	5/12	Tweezer	Tweezer
2/20/91	13	1	10/11	You Enjoy Yourself	Golgi Apparat

DATE	GAP	SET	POS.	SONG BEFORE	SONG AFTER
3/16/91	11	E	1/2	***	Possum
4/18/92	126	2	5/16	Rift	Bathtub Gin
2/21/93	106	2	4/10	Stash	Stash
5/3/93	50	2	4/12	Tweezer	Tweezer
5/5/93	1	2	3/10	My Friend My Friend	My Friend My
5/7/93	2	1	6/11	Caravan	The Lizards
10/28/94	131	2	3/12	David Bowie	David Bowie
11/14/95	85	2	4/11	Stash	Stash
10/30/98	218	2	2/7	Stash	Tweezer

Has not been played in the last 137 shows.

Manteca Reprise

4/18/92	389	2	7/16	Bathtub Gin	The Lizards

Has not been played in the last 730 shows.

Martha My Dear

10/31/94	681	2	10/30	Happiness is a Warm	I'm So Tired

Has not been played in the last 438 shows.

Maze

3/6/92	359	1	8/11	Guelah Papyrus	Reba
3/7/92	1	1	7/11	Silent in the Mornin	The Mango Song
3/11/92	1	1	5/10	Reba	Fee
3/13/92	2	1	5/12	Guelah Papyrus	Dinner and a
3/20/92	4	1	7/10	Fluffhead	The Lizards
3/25/92	4	1	6/10	Fee	Glide
3/27/92	2	1	6/11	Guelah Papyrus	Glide
3/30/92	2	1	6/11	Sparkle	I Didn't Know
4/3/92	3	1	7/11	Sparkle	Fluffhead
4/5/92	2	2	6/12	Silent in the Mornin	Weigh
4/7/92	2	2	8/11	The Lizards	Bike
4/12/92	2	1	9/11	Sparkle	Reba
4/16/92	3	1	8/12	Fee	Col. Forbin's A
4/17/92	1	1	8/13	Reba	Bouncing
4/19/92	2	1	7/11	Reba	Fee
4/21/92	1	2	13/13	Sanity	***
4/23/92	2	2	11/13	Fee	Cracklin' Rosi
4/25/92	2	2	1/11	***	Bathtub Gin
4/30/92	2	1	4/10	Fee	Reba
5/2/92	2	1	7/11	Reba	Bouncing
5/6/92	3	1	9/11	My Mind's Got A Mind	Tela
5/8/92	2	2	5/12	Magilla	You Enjoy My
5/9/92	1	1	8/11	Fee	The Squirmin
5/14/92	3	1	5/11	Sparkle	Horn
5/16/92	2	1	1/11	***	Foam
5/18/92	2	1	2/10	Suzy Greenberg	Bouncing
6/23/92	3	1	3/8	Reba	Sweet Adeline
6/27/92	2	1	4/10	Reba	All Things Rec
7/10/92	4	1	5/10	Sparkle	Golgi Apparat
7/12/92	2	1	6/11	Fluffhead	Uncle Pen
7/14/92	1	1	4/12	Guelah Papyrus	Sparkle
7/16/92	2	1	3/10	It's Ice	Sparkle
7/17/92	1	1	5/7	The Squirming Coil	Bouncing
7/19/92	2	1	2/5	Poor Heart	Runaway Jim
7/22/92	2	1	4/7	Bouncing	Rift
7/30/92	6	1	6/8	All Things Recnsdrd	I Didn't Know
8/15/92	6	1	4/5	Guelah Papyrus	Runaway Jim
8/23/92	4	1	2/7	Chalk Dust Torture	Sparkle
8/29/92	5	1	4/5	Bouncing	You Enjoy My
10/30/92	2	1	2/11	Runaway Jim	Bouncing
11/19/92	1	1	1/12	***	Fee
11/21/92	2	1	8/11	Bouncing	Col. Forbin's A
11/22/92	1	1	5/12	Fee	Reba
11/25/92	2	1	5/11	Fee	Sparkle
11/28/92	2	2	6/12	Avenu Malkenu	T.M.W.S.I.Y. Reprise
11/30/92	1	2	4/10	Guelah Papyrus	Glide
12/1/92	1	1	8/12	Fluffhead	Sweet Adeline
12/3/92	2	1	1/12	***	Fee
12/4/92	1	1	8/11	Fast Enough for You	Col. Forbin's A
12/5/92	1	2	7/13	Sparkle	Lawn Boy
12/7/92	2	1	3/11	Poor Heart	Glide
12/10/92	2	1	8/11	Big Ball Jam	You Enjoy My
12/12/92	2	2	2/10	***	Glide

DATE	GAP	SET	POS.	SONG BEFORE	SONG AFTER
12/28/92	2	1	1/10	***	Sparkle
12/31/92	3	1	3/11	Poor Heart	Bouncing
2/4/93	2	1	4/11	Bouncing	Fast Enough for You
2/6/93	2	1	5/11	My Friend My Friend	Horn
2/9/93	2	1	9/10	Esther	Golgi Apparat
2/12/93	3	1	2/11	Golgi Apparatus	Guelah Papyrus
2/13/93	1	1	9/10	Lawn Boy	Golgi Apparat
2/17/93	2	1	10/11	Fluffhead	Golgi Apparat
2/19/93	2	1	5/11	Fee	Col. Forbin's A
2/22/93	3	1	4/10	Poor Heart	Sparkle
2/25/93	2	1	4/11	Cavern	Col. Forbin's A
2/27/93	2	1	4/10	Guelah Papyrus	Bouncing
3/3/93	2	1	4/10	Bouncing	Guelah Papyrus
3/6/93	2	1	8/10	Bouncing	Golgi Apparat
3/9/93	2	1	4/10	Bouncing	Esther
3/13/93	2	1	4/11	Bouncing	Fee
3/16/93	2	1	6/11	Fee	I Didn't Know
3/18/93	2	1	5/11	Fee	Col. Forbin's A
3/21/93	2	1	1/11	***	Sparkle
3/24/93	2	1	5/9	Poor Heart	I Didn't Know
3/26/93	2	1	1/10	***	Sparkle
3/28/93	2	1	7/11	The Sloth	Fee
3/31/93	2	2	2/10	Lengthwise	Bouncing
4/2/93	2	1	8/9	Sparkle	Golgi Apparat
4/5/93	2	1	4/10	Fee	Fluffhead
4/9/93	1	1	7/11	Silent in the Mornin	I Didn't Know
4/10/93	1	2	2/13	Lengthwise	Bouncing
4/14/93	2	1	3/13	Poor Heart	Bouncing
4/16/93	1	2	3/13	The Curtain	The Lizards
4/18/93	2	1	7/10	Fee	Horn
4/21/93	2	1	5/11	Guelah Papyrus	Col. Forbin's A
4/23/93	2	2	2/12	Golgi Apparatus	Ballad - Curtis Loew
4/25/93	2	1	9/11	The Famous Mockingbi	I Didn't Know
4/27/93	1	2	4/10	All Things Recnsdrd	The Lizards
4/30/93	2	1	2/12	Lengthwise	Bouncing
5/2/93	2	1	9/11	Poor Heart	I Didn't Know
5/5/93	2	1	9/10	Glide	Golgi Apparat
5/7/93	2	2	3/10	Bouncing	Fee
5/30/93	3	1	2/13	Lengthwise	Guelah Papyrus
7/16/93	2	2	4/12	Glide	Bouncing
7/18/93	2	1	5/9	Guelah Papyrus	Esther
7/21/93	1	1	5/12	The Squirming Coil	Glide
7/23/93	2	1	5/12	Nellie Kane	The Horse
7/24/93	1	2	4/12	Fluffhead	Glide
7/25/93	1	2	6/10	Silent in the Mornin	The Lizards
7/29/93	3	2	1/9	***	Bouncing
7/31/93	2	2	4/11	It's Ice	Sparkle
8/3/93	2	2	2/9	Lengthwise	Bouncing
8/7/93	2	1	7/10	Reba	Col. Forbin's A
8/12/93	4	2	6/10	The Sloth	Lawn Boy
8/15/93	3	2	6/11	Bouncing	Glide
8/17/93	2	1	6/9	Weigh	Fluffhead
8/20/93	1	1	4/10	Poor Heart	Bouncing
8/24/93	2	1	10/11	Uncle Pen	Golgi Apparat
8/28/93	3	1	5/9	Ginseng Sullivan	Fluffhead
12/29/93	2	2	1/11	***	Bouncing
4/4/94	3	1	4/9	Scent of a Mule	Fee
4/8/94	3	1	1/13	***	Digital Delay Loop J
4/8/94	0	1	3/13	Digital Delay Loop J	Glide
4/11/94	3	2	2/11	Also Sprach	Col. Forbin's A
4/15/94	3	2	1/10	***	If I Could
4/17/94	2	2	7/9	Big Ball Jam	Contact
4/21/94	3	2	2/10	Also Sprach	Fluffhead
4/24/94	3	1	4/8	Axilla (Part II)	Bathtub Gin
4/29/94	3	2	2/11	Suzy Greenberg	If I Could
5/3/94	3	1	3/9	Guelah Papyrus	Sparkle
5/6/94	2	2	1/9	***	Golgi Apparat
5/10/94	3	2	1/10	***	Wilson
5/12/94	1	1	5/10	Fee	Axilla (Part II)
5/17/94	1	1	2/9	Suzy Greenberg	Mound

DATE	GAP	SET	POS.	SONG BEFORE	SONG AFTER
5/20/94	2	1	2/10	Fee	If I Could
5/23/94	3	1	5/10	Fee	The Horse
5/25/94	1	2	4/9	Lifeboy	Contact
5/28/94	3	1	9/10	The Sloth	Cavern
6/9/94	2	1	7/9	If I Could	Fee
6/11/94	2	2	7/9	The Squirming Coil	Contact
6/16/94	3	1	5/10	Fee	Gumbo
6/18/94	2	1	4/10	AC/DC Bag	The Mango Song
6/22/94	3	1	5/9	Gumbo	If I Could
6/25/94	3	2	2/9	Suzy Greenberg	Sparkle
6/30/94	3	2	2/15	Wilson	You Enjoy My
7/2/94	2	2	9/12	McGrupp	Sample in a Ja
7/9/94	5	1	4/10	Gumbo	Guelah Papyrus
7/14/94	3	2	3/10	Sample in a Jar	If I Could
7/16/94	2	1	9/11	Silent in the Mornin	Sparkle
10/7/94	1	2	1/10	***	The Horse
10/10/94	3	2	2/9	Golgi Apparatus	Esther
10/15/94	4	1	4/8	Simple	Glide
10/20/94	3	2	2/8	Lengthwise	McGrupp
10/23/94	3	1	10/11	Tela	Sample in a Ja
10/27/94	3	1	3/11	Sparkle	Col. Forbin's A
11/2/94	4	1	4/8	If I Could	Guyute
11/12/94	3	1	4/8	If I Could	Guyute
11/14/94	2	1	7/9	The Landlady	Lawn Boy
11/17/94	2	1	3/11	Scent of a Mule	Bouncing
11/23/94	5	2	1/7	***	Fee
12/1/94	3	1	4/8	Fast Enough for You	Guyute
12/4/94	3	2	1/7	***	Bouncing
12/8/94	3	1	2/10	Makisupa Policeman	AC/DC Bag
12/10/94	2	2	2/11	Simple	Guyute
12/31/94	4	2	2/9	The Old Home Place	Bouncing
6/7/95	2	2	2/9	Ha Ha Ha	Spock's Brain
6/10/95	3	2	1/8	***	Fee
6/17/95	5	2	2/11	Wilson	Mound
6/22/95	3	1	8/10	Strange Design	Cavern
6/25/95	3	2	1/9	***	Sample in a Ja
7/1/95	5	2	2/9	Wilson	Theme From the Botto
7/3/95	2	1	8/11	If I Could	Strange Design
9/29/95	3	2	2/8	Also Sprach	Free
10/3/95	3	1	1/11	***	Guelah Papyrus
10/6/95	2	2	2/8	Poor Heart	Theme From the Botto
10/13/95	4	1	3/9	Also Sprach	Billy Breathes
10/17/95	3	1	5/10	AC/DC Bag	Glide
10/20/95	2	2	4/10	Simple	Gumbo
10/24/95	3	1	9/13	Demand	Wolfman's Brother
10/28/95	3	2	1/7	***	Theme From the Botto
11/10/95	4	1	7/9	Dog Faced Boy	Guyute
11/14/95	3	2	1/11	***	Gumbo
11/19/95	4	1	2/10	Makisupa Policeman	Poor Heart
11/24/95	3	1	8/9	I'm Blue, Lonesome	Suzy Greenber
11/28/95	2	2	2/10	Also Sprach	Suzy Greenber
12/2/95	4	2	2/9	Also Sprach	Simple
12/9/95	5	1	1/10	***	Theme From the Botto
12/15/95	4	1	4/10	Wilson	Ha Ha Ha
12/17/95	2	2	2/8	Bouncing	Free
12/31/95	4	1	5/10	The Squirming Coil	Col. Forbin's A
7/6/96	5	1	5/6	A Day in the Life	Harry Hood
7/11/96	4	2	4/8	Also Sprach	The Lizards
7/15/96	3	2	2/9	Down with Disease	Loving Cup
7/22/96	5	1	4/8	Cavern	Bouncing
8/4/96	5	1	8/9	The Sloth	Loving Cup
8/13/96	6	1	4/10	Tela	Fast Enough for You
8/17/96	3	1	9/10	Fee	Suzy Greenber
10/18/96	3	2	2/6	Suzy Greenberg	You Enjoy My
10/21/96	2	2	6/11	Train Song	Life on Mars
10/25/96	3	1	4/10	Makisupa Policeman	Billy Breathes

DATE	GAP	SET	POS.	SONG BEFORE	SONG AFTER
10/31/96	4	3	3/8	Also Sprach	Simple
11/8/96	5	2	2/8	Also Sprach	Bouncing
11/11/96	2	2	9/11	Steep	Contact
11/15/96	3	2	2/11	Makisupa Policeman	McGrupp
11/22/96	4	2	3/10	Prince Caspian	Billy Breathes
11/29/96	4	1	8/9	Life on Mars	Suzy Greenber
12/28/96	6	2	2/10	Makisupa Policeman	Bouncing
2/13/97	4	2	7/10	When Circus Comes	Rocko William
2/18/97	4	2	4/9	My Soul	Wolfman's Brother
2/23/97	4	2	3/9	Suzy Greenberg	The Horse
3/2/97	5	2	2/9	Also Sprach	Swept Away
6/13/97	2	2	2/9	Stash	Water in the Sky
6/19/97	3	1	6/9	Water in the Sky	Waste
7/2/97	9	1	3/8	Simple	Strange Design
7/25/97	10	1	3/7	Wolfman's Brother	Water in the Sky
7/31/97	4	1	6/9	Dirt	Glide
8/11/97	7	1	2/8	Makisupa Policeman	Water in the Sky
8/17/97	4	1	6/10	Water in the Sky	Bouncing
11/14/97	2	1	3/8	Gumbo	Fast Enough For You
11/28/97	8	1	4/8	I Didn't Know	Farmhouse
12/6/97	6	1	8/9	Fee	Cavern
12/11/97	3	1	3/7	Down with Disease	Dirt
12/31/97	6	3	4/6	Tweezer	Prince Caspian
4/5/98	4	2	4/8	Prince Caspian	Shafty
7/6/98	6	1	8/9	Roggae	Golgi Apparat
7/20/98	8	2	3/6	Makisupa Policeman	Sea and Sand
7/28/98	5	2	6/8	Contact	Prince Caspian
8/11/98	10	1	10/11	Fee	Sample in a Ja
11/6/98	13	1	4/7	Roggae	Meat
11/19/98	9	1	6/9	Bouncing	Something
11/29/98	7	1	9/11	Kung	All The Pain Thru
12/30/98	3	1	10/12	Frankie Says	Loving Cup
6/30/99	2	1	6/8	Back on the Train	Limb by Limb
7/7/99	4	1	9/10	Wolfman's Brother	Loving Cup
7/16/99	7	1	8/9	Back on the Train	Cavern
9/11/99	15	2	4/6	Meatstick	Prince Caspian
9/18/99	5	1	4/7	Wilson	Brian and Robert
9/28/99	7	1	6/8	Roggae	Wading In Velvet Sea
10/3/99	4	1	10/12	Back on the Train	Bouncing
12/5/99	9	2	7/10	Jennifer Dances	Fluffhead
12/15/99	7	2	2/7	Sample in a Jar	Free
6/13/00	12	1	2/10	Meat	Meat Reprise
6/25/00	7	2	5/7	Meat	What's the Use
7/7/00	8	1	6/11	Funky Bitch	Shafty
7/7/00	0	1	8/11	Shafty	Back on the Train
9/9/00	8	1	4/8	Gumbo	Boogie On Reggae
9/18/00	6	1	4/10	The Sloth	Guelah Papyrus
9/30/00	8	1	3/10	The Curtain With	Roggae
10/6/00	4	1	5/7	Mellow Mood	The Moma Dance

Has not been played in the last 1 show.

McGrupp and the Watchful Hosemasters

DATE	GAP	SET	POS.	SONG BEFORE	SONG AFTER
5/3/85	5	3	4/8	Whipping Post	Makisupa Policeman
10/17/85	2	1	9/9	Run Like an Antelope	***
4/1/86	5	2	4/6	AC/DC Bag	Alumni Blues
10/15/86	2	1	6/9	I Am Hydrogen	AC/DC Bag
4/29/87	8	3	11/14	Sparks	Ballad - Curtis Loew

DATE	GAP	SET	POS.	SONG BEFORE	SONG AFTER
8/9/87	3	3	6/7	Flat Fee	Corrine Corrina
8/21/87	2	3	2/7	BBFCFM	Stir it Up Jam
8/29/87	1	1	5/13	The Curtain With	Possum
10/14/87	4	1	11/12	Divided Sky	Makisupa Policeman
10/31/87	1	2	12/17	Divided Sky	Who Do? We Do!
11/19/87	2	1	1/7	***	Sparks
2/7/88	2	1	2/10	Fire	Shaggy Dog
2/26/88	2		5/9	Fee	Dear Mrs. Reagan
3/12/88	2	2	2/11	Jump Monk	The Lizards
3/21/88	1	1	3/15	Golgi Apparatus	Sneakin' Sally
5/15/88	5	2	2/11	Icculus	The Curtain
6/15/88	3	1	6/9	Rocky Top	Fluffhead
7/11/88	5	E	1/2	***	La Grange
7/24/88	3	3	5/6	Jesus Just Left	Run Like Antel
9/13/88	8	1	5/8	Flat Fee	Wilson
9/22/88	1	1	1/5	***	Take the A-Trn
2/7/89	13	1	2/9	Esther	Foam
3/3/89	5	2	5/11	Wilson	You Enjoy My
3/30/89	5	1	2/8	Bold as Love	Divided Sky
4/20/89	2	1	10/12	Possum	Foam
4/30/89	2	1	3/9	You Enjoy Myself	The Lizards
5/5/89	2	2	4/4	Good Times Bad Times	***
6/30/89	11	1	3/7	You Enjoy Myself	Possum
8/17/89	1	1	3/9	Suzy Greenberg	The Sloth
9/9/89	4	1	6/11	AC/DC Bag	Bathtub Gin
9/21/89	2	1	7/9	Alumni Blues	Who Do? We Do!
10/1/89	1	1	2/12	Alumni Blues	Who Do? We Do!
10/21/89	7	1	4/10	In a Hole	Who Do? We Do!
10/22/89	1	2	5/9	In a Hole	AC/DC Bag
11/2/89	4	2	7/11	Divided Sky	Who Do? We Do!
11/9/89	2	2	3/9	AC/DC Bag	Who Do? We Do!
11/10/89	1	2	6/12	Weekapaug Groove	Who Do? We Do!
12/8/89	8	1	6/11	Reba	Who Do? We Do!
2/25/90	20	2	2/6	Reba	Makisupa Policeman
3/10/90	7	1	3/10	Esther	AC/DC Bag
4/19/90	14	2	2/8	Possum	Dinner and a
5/23/90	16	2	6/11	La Grange	Take the A-Trn
2/14/91	52	1	2/11	My Sweet One	Buried Alive
5/10/91	42	2	6/11	Foam	Chalk Dust Tor
5/19/91	6	2	8/10	The Sloth	I Didn't Know
10/13/91	29	1	10/13	The Sloth	Mike's Song
12/31/91	33	1	4/7	Tweezer	Mike's Song
5/14/92	50	2	10/13	Wait	Stash
7/15/92	17	2	6/9	Stash	All Things Rec
11/27/92	36	2	6/13	It's Ice	I Walk The Line
3/16/93	49	1	10/11	You Gotta See Mama	Cavern
3/22/93	5	2	10/13	The Sloth	Mike's Song
5/3/93	30	2	8/12	It's Ice	Runaway Jim
8/7/93	24	2	10/12	My Friend My Friend	Purple Rain
12/30/93	18	2	6/9	Punch You in the Eye	Weekapaug Gr
4/8/94	5	2	2/9	Split Open and Melt	It's Ice
4/30/94	18	2	7/10	Axilla (Part II)	Possum
5/13/94	9	2	4/9	Split Open and Melt	Peaches en Regalia
5/22/94	7	2	4/9	It's Ice	Tweezer
5/29/94	6	2	6/10	Horn	The Oh Kee Pa
6/18/94	8	2	6/10	Horn	Tweezer
6/24/94	5	2	5/13	The Curtain	Simple
6/26/94	2	1	10/11	The Sloth	Divided Sky
7/2/94	4	2	8/12	Weekapaug Groove	Maze
7/8/94	4	1	10/11	The Sloth	Divided Sky
10/20/94	17	2	3/8	Maze	Rift
11/30/94	26	2	9/10	Catapult	Cavern

DATE	GAP	SET	POS.	SONG BEFORE	SONG AFTER
12/9/94	8	2	4/9	Tweezer	Julius
6/17/95	15	2	7/11	Tweezer	Acoustic Army
10/11/95	24	2	5/11	Mike's Song	Weekapaug Gr
10/27/95	11	2	6/9	Simple	Keyboard Cavalry
12/11/95	27	1	10/12	Tube	Julius
12/29/95	7	2	6/11	Bathtub Gin	BBFCFM
7/23/96	20	1	7/9	Down with Disease	Stash
8/12/96	9	2	5/9	Prince Caspian	Run Like Antel
10/26/96	13	2	5/7	Simple	Waste
11/15/96	13	2	3/11	Maze	Split Open and
6/25/97	41	2	5/9	Meatstick	Makisupa Policeman
7/31/97	18	2	4/7	Vultures	Mike's Song
8/13/97	8	2	5/9	Sleeping Monkey	Sample in a Ja
11/26/97	12	1	5/10	My Soul	Dirt
12/30/97	15	2	2/10	AC/DC Bag	Harpua
4/5/98	5	1	4/8	Theme From the Botto	Bathtub Gin
7/5/98	5	2	3/6	The Moma Dance	Axilla
7/19/98	8	2	6/7	Jesus Just Left	Down with Dis
10/29/98	24	1	9/10	Birds of a Feather	Character Zer
10/7/99	70	2	6/9	Mike's Song	Prince Caspian
9/18/00	55	2	3/4	Twist	Halley's Comet

Has not been played in the last 13 shows.

Mean Mr. Mustard

DATE	GAP	SET	POS.	SONG BEFORE	SONG AFTER
11/15/96	845	2	10/11	Sleeping Monkey	Weekapaug Gr

Has not been played in the last 274 shows.

Meat

DATE	GAP	SET	POS.	SONG BEFORE	SONG AFTER
7/2/98	947	1	5/11	Brian and Robert	Fikus
7/6/98	3	2	2/6	Julius	Piper
7/9/98	2	1	5/8	Split Open and Melt	Poor Heart
7/15/98	2	2	5/6	Free	Harry Hood
8/3/98	14	2	4/7	Limb by Limb	Bike
8/11/98	5	2	2/5	Runaway Jim	Limb by Limb
10/30/98	9	1	2/10	Wilson	Scent of a Mul
11/6/98	4	1	5/7	Maze	Sparkle
11/8/98	2	2	2/8	Chalk Dust Torture	Rock and Roll
11/13/98	3	2	5/6	Birds of a Feather	Harry Hood
11/20/98	5	1	7/13	Rift	Stash
11/27/98	4	1	5/11	Runaway Jim	Reba
7/25/99	25	1	1/8	***	My Friend My
9/26/99	19	2	6/7	Birds of a Feather	Down with Dis
10/8/99	8	1	4/6	Suzy Greenberg	Meatstick
12/17/99	15	1	2/8	Piper	Sparkle
12/30/99	2	2	5/10	Taste	Golgi Apparat
6/13/00	8	1	1/10	***	Maze
6/25/00	7	2	4/7	Scent of a Mule	Maze
7/3/00	5	2	5/7	Sand	Chalk Dust Tor
9/22/00	19	1	2/9	Down With Disease	Poor Heart

Has not been played in the last 11 shows.

Meat Reprise

DATE	GAP	SET	POS.	SONG BEFORE	SONG AFTER
6/13/00	1077	1	3/10	Maze	Ya Mar

Has not been played in the last 42 shows.

Meatstick

DATE	GAP	SET	POS.	SONG BEFORE	SONG AFTER
6/25/97	886	2	4/9	Down with Disease	McGrupp
7/3/99	123	1	11/11	Waste	***
7/8/99	3	2	7/9	Sleep	Tube
7/9/99	1	2	4/8	What's the Use	Mike's Song
7/15/99	4	2	1/6	***	Split Open and
7/18/99	3	2	3/6	Free	Guyute
7/23/99	3	2	4/5	Birds of a Feather	Fire
9/11/99	10	2	3/6	Sand	Maze
9/18/99	5	2	2/7	Boogie On Reggae	Free
9/26/99	6	E	1/2	***	Rocky Top
10/8/99	8	1	5/6	Meat	Run Like Antel
12/5/99	6	2	2/10	Mike's Song	I Am Hydrgn
12/31/99	12	1	1/35	***	Auld Lang Syne
12/31/99	0	2	35/35	Wading In Velvet Sea	***

DATE	GAP	SET	POS.	SONG BEFORE	SONG AFTER
6/9/00	4	2	6/7	Gotta Jibboo	Tweezer Repri
6/29/00	12	2	5/10	Sand	Cities
7/12/00	10	2	5/5	Prince Caspian	***
9/22/00	12	2	6/7	When Circus Comes	Run Like Antel
9/29/00	5	2	6/9	Jam	Walk This Way
10/7/00	6	2	5/7	Wading In Velvet Sea	David Bowie

Was played in the most recent show.

Meatstick Reprise

DATE	GAP	SET	POS.	SONG BEFORE	SONG AFTER
7/4/99	1010E		2/3	Carini	Star Spangled Banner

Has not been played in the last 109 shows.

Mellow Mood

DATE	GAP	SET	POS.	SONG BEFORE	SONG AFTER
9/8/00	10991		1/12	***	Limb By Limb
9/24/00	11	1	1/10	***	Chalk Dust Tor
9/29/00	3	1	4/8	Frankenstein	Wilson
10/6/00	5	1	4/7	Boogie On Reggae	Maze

Has not been played in the last 1 show.

Melt the Guns

DATE	GAP	SET	POS.	SONG BEFORE	SONG AFTER
9/27/85	6	1	8/8	Dear Mrs. Reagan	***
10/31/86	9	1	5/11	Slave	Dave's Energy Guide
2/13/87	2	1	11/14	Wilson	Dave's Energy Guide
4/29/87	5	2	2/7	Dog Gone Dog	Dave's Energy Guide

Has not been played in the last 1097 shows.

Memories

DATE	GAP	SET	POS.	SONG BEFORE	SONG AFTER
11/17/90	232	E	1/2	***	Sweet Adeline
9/26/91	81	E	1/3	***	Poor Heart
9/28/91	2	1	11/11	Golgi Apparatus	***
9/29/91	1	E	1/2	***	Rocky Top
10/3/91	3	2	11/11	Tweezer	***
10/15/91	7	E	1/2	***	Harry Hood
10/17/91	1	1	1/10	***	The Landlady
10/24/91	4	E	1/2	***	Sweet Adeline
10/31/91	4	1	1/11	***	Brother
11/7/91	3	1	1/11	***	Chalk Dust Tor
11/12/91	4	E	4/4	Split Open and Melt	***
11/21/91	7	E	1/3	***	Sweet Adeline
12/6/91	7	1	1/9	***	Foam
3/11/92	5	E	2/4	Sanity	Carolina
3/17/92	4	E	1/2	***	Sweet Adeline
3/27/92	8	E	1/2	***	Sweet Adeline
3/28/92	1	2	1/4	***	Carolina
4/13/92	11	E	1/2	***	Fire
4/15/92	1	E	1/3	***	Sweet Adeline
4/16/92	1	2	10/12	Terrapin	Sweet Adeline
4/21/92	4	E	1/3	***	Sweet Adeline
4/25/92	4	E	1/3	***	Sweet Adeline
5/3/92	5	E	1/3	***	Sweet Adeline
5/8/92	4	1	12/12	David Bowie	***
8/30/92	49	1	5/7	Llama	Run Like Antel
11/20/92	3	1	10/12	The Lizards	I Walk the Line
11/23/92	3	1	10/11	Bouncing	David Bowie
11/27/92	1	1	11/12	Mound	Runaway Jim
12/5/92	7	E	1/2	***	Good Time Ba
12/11/92	5	1	10/11	My Friend My Friend	David Bowie
12/28/92	3	E	1/2	***	Fire
2/18/93	16	2	10/12	Amazing Grace	Sweet Adeline
3/14/93	17	E	1/3	***	Sweet Adeline
8/9/93	62	1	10/11	Divided Sky	The Squirmin
8/17/93	7	E	1/2	***	Fire
12/28/93	7	E	1/2	***	Golgi Apparat
7/6/94	69	E	3/4	Nellie Kane	Funky Bitch

Has not been played in the last 465 shows.

Merry Pranksters Jam

DATE	GAP	SET	POS.	SONG BEFORE	SONG AFTER
8/14/97	913	2	6/8	Col. Forbin's Ascent	Camel Walk

Has not been played in the last 206 shows.

Messin' With The Kid

DATE	GAP	SET	POS.	SONG BEFORE	SONG AFTER
8/8/97	908	E	2/2	Hoochie Coochie Man	***
10/3/99	141	E	2/2	Funky Bitch	***

Has not been played in the last 70 shows.

Midnight Rider Jam

DATE	GAP	SET	POS.	SONG BEFORE	SONG AFTER
6/22/94	643	2	4/20	Simple	Catapult

Has not been played in the last 476 shows.

Midnight on the Highway

DATE	GAP	SET	POS.	SONG BEFORE	SONG AFTER
11/23/96	850	1	6/9	Punch You in the Eye	Split Open and

Has not been played in the last 269 shows.

Mike's Song

DATE	GAP	SET	POS.	SONG BEFORE	SONG AFTER
5/3/85	5	1	2/4	Slave	Dave's Energy Guide
10/17/85	2	1	3/9	Alumni Blues	Dave's Energy Guide
11/23/85	3	3	1/4	***	Whipping Post Jam
2/3/86	1	1	2/7	Slave	Dave's Energy Guide
10/15/86	3	2	12/14	Quinn the Eskimo	Have Mercy
12/6/86	2	1	1/14	***	Little Drummer Boy
3/23/87	4	1	2/5	Funky Bitch	Alumni Blues
8/21/87	7	2	1/12	***	Harpua
8/29/87	1	3	3/10	Corrine Corrina	I Am Hydrgen
7/23/88	30	1	4/13	The Famous Mockingbi	I Am Hydrgen
7/24/88	1	1	7/10	Sneakin' Sally	I Am Hydrgen
7/25/88	1	2	1/6	***	I Am Hydrgen
8/3/88	2	3	2/8	Peaches en Regalia	I Am Hydrgen
8/27/88	2	1	6/9	Fluffhead	Take the A-Trn
10/29/88	6	2	8/10	Ballad - Curtis Loew	Take the A-Trn
11/5/88	3	2	7/11	Fee	I Am Hydrgen
11/11/88	1	2	1/8	***	I Am Hydrgen
12/10/88	2	1	7/12	Fee	I Am Hydrgen
2/7/89	5	1	6/9	Possum	I Am Hydrgen
3/3/89	5	2	1/12	***	I Am Hydrgen
3/4/89	1	1	3/8	I Didn't Know	I Am Hydrgen
3/12/89	1	1	1/8	***	I Am Hydrgen
3/14/89	1	1	3/12	Ya Mar	I Am Hydrgen
3/24/89	1	1	2/10	Possum	I Am Hydrgen
3/30/89	1	2	3/8	The Mango Song	I Am Hydrgen
4/20/89	2	2	6/10	The Lizards	I Am Hydrgen
5/1/89	3	2	1/10	***	I Am Hydrgen
5/6/89	2	1	3/13	I Didn't Know	I Am Hydrgen
5/9/89	1	1	4/9	Ya Mar	I Am Hydrgen
5/12/89	1	2	2/15	Bike	I Am Hydrgen
5/20/89	2	2	2/9	Bold as Love	I Am Hydrgen
5/21/89	1	1	4/13	Contact	I Am Hydrgen
5/26/89	1	3	3/9	AC/DC Bag	I Am Hydrgen
5/27/89	1	1	2/11	AC/DC Bag	I Am Hydrgen
5/28/89	1	2	2/16	Fire	I Am Hydrgen
6/23/89	1	1	7/11	Fee	I Am Hydrgen
6/30/89	1	2	6/8	Bathtub Gin	I Am Hydrgen
8/17/89	1	1	7/9	Harry Hood	I Am Hydrgen
8/19/89	1	1	11/13	The Lizards	I Am Hydrgen
10/6/89	7	1	2/13	Timber (Jerry)	I Am Hydrgen
10/7/89	1	1	3/11	Ya Mar	I Am Hydrgen
10/12/89	1	2	2/7	Fee	I Am Hydrgen
10/13/89	1	2	4/8	Avenu Malkenu	I Am Hydrgen
10/26/89	5	1	9/11	The Lizards	I Am Hydrgen
11/2/89	3	1	3/11	Foam	I Am Hydrgen
11/9/89	2	2	7/9	The Lizards	I Am Hydrgen
11/10/89	1	2	3/11	Bathtub Gin	I Am Hydrgen
11/16/89	2	1	1/11	***	I Am Hydrgen
12/1/89	3	2	6/10	The Lizards	I Am Hydrgen
12/3/89	1	2	12/14	Love You	I Am Hydrgen
12/7/89	1	1	6/11	Fee	I Am Hydrgen
12/9/89	2	2	6/8	Fee	I Am Hydrgen
12/15/89	1	1	3/10	Golgi Apparatus	I Am Hydrgen
12/16/89	1	1	4/9	Lawn Boy	I Am Hydrgen
12/29/89	1	1	8/10	Lawn Boy	I Am Hydrgen
12/30/89	1	E	2/4	Auld Lang Syne	I Am Hydrgen
12/31/89	1	2	1/7	***	I Am Hydrgen
1/20/90	1	2	8/10	Esther	I Am Hydrgen
1/27/90	1	1	11/13	Funky Bitch	I Am Hydrgen
1/28/90	1	2	8/10	Bathtub Gin	I Am Hydrgen
1/29/90	1	1	3/10	If I Only Had a Brai	I Am Hydrgen
2/1/90	1	1	9/11	Fee	I Am Hydrgen
2/9/90	1	1	9/12	The Squirming Coil	I Am Hydrgen
2/10/90	1	2	8/10	Fee	I Am Hydrgen
2/15/90	1	1	8/10	Bathtub Gin	I Am Hydrgen
2/16/90	1	1	3/7	Esther	I Am Hydrgen
2/17/90	1	1	7/12	Carolina	I Am Hydrgen
2/23/90	2	2	8/11	Suzy Greenberg	I Am Hydrgen
3/1/90	3	2	3/7	Foam	I Am Hydrgen
3/3/90	2	1	1/12	***	I Am Hydrgen
3/7/90	1	2	7/9	Tela	I Am Hydrgen
3/8/90	1	2	8/12	The Lizards	I Am Hydrgen
3/11/90	3	1	9/13	La Grange	I Am Hydrgen
3/28/90	2	2	5/16	Funky Bitch	I Am Hydrgen
4/4/90	1	2	1/8	***	I Am Hydrgen
4/5/90	1	2	9/13	Cavern	I Am Hydrgen
4/7/90	2	1	10/12	Tweezer	I Am Hydrgen
4/8/90	1	2	5/10	Slave	I Am Hydrgen
4/12/90	2	2	9/11	Love You	I Am Hydrgen
4/14/90	2	1	8/10	Rift	I Am Hydrgen
4/18/90	1	1	1/10	***	I Am Hydrgen
4/20/90	2	2	2/11	Caravan	I Am Hydrgen
4/22/90	2	1	10/12	Slave	I Am Hydrgen
4/25/90	1	2	10/12	Bouncing	I Am Hydrgen
4/26/90	1	2	9/11	Ballad - Curtis Loew	I Am Hydrgen
4/28/90	1	2	7/9	My Sweet One	I Am Hydrgen
5/4/90	2	1	6/12	The Oh Kee Pa Ceremo	I Am Hydrgen
5/6/90	1	1	6/8	Tweezer	I Am Hydrgen
5/11/90	3	1	1/9	***	I Am Hydrgen
5/13/90	1	2	1/12	***	I Am Hydrgen
5/15/90	1	1	4/12	Foam	I Am Hydrgen
5/23/90	2	2	9/11	Run Like an Antelope	I Am Hydrgen
5/30/90	2	1	11/14	Sweet Adeline	I Am Hydrgen
6/1/90	2	1	4/12	Run Like an Antelope	I Am Hydrgen
6/5/90	2	1	3/12	Uncle Pen	I Am Hydrgen
6/7/90	1	2	8/10	Love You	I Am Hydrgen
6/8/90	1	2	5/7	I Didn't Know	I Am Hydrgen
6/9/90	1	1	8/10	Uncle Pen	I Am Hydrgen
6/16/90	1	3	11/13	If I Only Had a Brai	I Am Hydrgen
9/13/90	1	2	1/15	***	I Am Hydrgen
9/14/90	1	1	1/11	I Didn't Know	I Am Hydrgen
9/16/90	2	1	10/14	Paul and Silas	I Am Hydrgen
9/20/90	1	1	8/12	The Landlady	I Am Hydrgen
9/29/90	4	2	6/8	Stash	I Am Hydrgen
10/1/90	1	1	1/11	***	I Am Hydrgen
10/5/90	2	1	2/13	I Didn't Know	I Am Hydrgen
10/7/90	2	1	10/14	The Squirming Coil	I Am Hydrgen
10/12/90	2	2	8/10	Magilla	I Am Hydrgen
10/19/90	1	2	4/15	Uncle Pen	I Am Hydrgen
10/30/90	1	2	1/12	***	I Am Hydrgen
10/31/90	1	2	10/12	Love You	I Am Hydrgen
11/2/90	1	1	6/14	The Sloth	I Am Hydrgen
11/3/90	1	2	2/12	The Landlady	I Am Hydrgen
11/4/90	1	2	4/13	Llama	I Am Hydrgen
11/8/90	1	1	10/12	I Didn't Know	I Am Hydrgen
11/10/90	1	1	9/11	The Lizards	I Am Hydrgen
11/16/90	1	2	2/11	The Landlady	I Am Hydrgen
11/17/90	1	2	3/12	Fluffhead	I Am Hydrgen
11/24/90	1	1	4/11	Foam	I Am Hydrgen
11/26/90	1	2	5/7	Wilson	I Am Hydrgen
11/30/90	1	1	2/11	The Landlady	I Am Hydrgen
12/7/90	2	2	1/11	***	I Am Hydrgen
12/8/90	1	1	8/10	The Landlady	I Am Hydrgen
12/28/90	1	1	8/11	The Famous Mockingbi	I Am Hydrgen
12/31/90	2	1	7/12	My Sweet One	I Am Hydrgen
2/8/91	5	2	5/11	Lawn Boy	I Am Hydrgen
2/14/91	2	1	1/12	***	I Am Hydrgen
2/16/91	2	1	10/12	The Mango Song	I Am Hydrgen
2/19/91	1	2	1/15	My Sweet One	I Am Hydrgen
2/21/91	1	2	9/11	My Sweet One	I Am Hydrgen
2/26/91	1	2	10/12	The Lizards	I Am Hydrgen

DATE	GAP	SET	POS.	SONG BEFORE	SONG AFTER
2/28/91	2	1	5/13	Esther	I Am Hydrgen
3/1/91	1	1	10/12	Buried Alive	I Am Hydrgen
3/15/91	5	1	10/12	The Lizards	I Am Hydrgen
3/17/91	2	1	4/12	The Landlady	I Am Hydrgen
3/22/91	1	2	11/13	Whole Lotta Love Jam	I Am Hydrgen
3/31/91	4	1	11/13	I Didn't Know	I Am Hydrgen
4/3/91	2	1	8/10	Bouncing	I Am Hydrgen
4/5/91	2	1	9/11	Foam	I Am Hydrgen
4/11/91	2	2	12/14	Destiny Unbound	I Am Hydrgen
4/15/91	2	2	2/11	Wipeout	I Am Hydrgen
4/19/91	3	1	9/12	Rocky Top	I Am Hydrgen
4/21/91	2	1	11/14	Tela	I Am Hydrgen
4/25/91	2	2	3/10	My Sweet One	I Am Hydrgen
4/27/91	1	2	6/13	T.M.W.S.I.Y. Reprise	I Am Hydrgen
5/4/91	3	1	9/11	Fluffhead	I Am Hydrgen
5/10/91	2	2	9/11	Love You	I Am Hydrgen
5/11/91	1	2	6/12	Donna Lee	I Am Hydrgen
5/12/91	1	2	7/13	Magilla	I Am Hydrgen
5/17/91	2	1	14/17	I Didn't Know	I Am Hydrgen
7/11/91	3	2	6/10	T.M.W.S.I.Y. Reprise	I Am Hydrgen
7/12/91	1	2	7/14	Gumbo	I Am Hydrgen
7/14/91	2	3	6/10	Bathtub Gin	I Am Hydrgen
7/15/91	1	1	7/14	Bouncing	I Am Hydrgen
7/18/91	1	1	9/11	Cavern	I Am Hydrgen
7/21/91	3	1	9/12	Bouncing	I Am Hydrgen
7/23/91	1	1	10/12	Bouncing	I Am Hydrgen
7/25/91	2	2	11/13	Magilla	I Am Hydrgen
7/27/91	1	1	14/16	The Landlady	I Am Hydrgen
9/26/91	3	2	7/11	Destiny Unbound	I Am Hydrgen
9/28/91	2	2	10/12	Magilla	I Am Hydrgen
10/3/91	4	2	2/11	Paul and Silas	I Am Hydrgen
10/4/91	1	2	9/11	The Squirming Coil	I Am Hydrgen
10/10/91	2	2	11/13	Fee	I Am Hydrgen
10/13/91	3	1	11/13	McGrupp	I Am Hydrgen
10/18/91	3	2	5/12	Dinner and a Movie	I Am Hydrgen
10/24/91	2	1	2/11	***	I Am Hydrgen
10/27/91	1	2	6/13	It's Ice	I Am Hydrgen
10/30/91	2	2	9/11	Bouncing	I Am Hydrgen
11/1/91	2	2	6/13	Eliza	I Am Hydrgen
11/8/91	2	2	6/13	I Didn't Know	I Am Hydrgen
11/12/91	1	2	5/13	Paul and Silas	I Am Hydrgen
11/15/91	3	2	4/14	Poor Heart	I Am Hydrgen
11/19/91	2	2	3/11	My Sweet One	I Am Hydrgen
11/21/91	2	1	10/12	Esther	I Am Hydrgen
11/23/91	2	2	2/13	The Curtain	I Am Hydrgen
12/4/91	3	2	4/11	The Mango Song	I Am Hydrgen
12/5/91	1	2	5/13	Foam	I Am Hydrgen
12/31/91	3	3	5/7	McGrupp	I Am Hydrgen
3/7/92	2	2	2/14	Horn	I Am Hydrgen
3/14/92	4	1	11/13	Take the A-Train	I Am Hydrgen
3/17/92	1	2	7/11	Esther	I Am Hydrgen
3/20/92	2	2	1/12	***	I Am Hydrgen
3/24/92	3	2	2/13	The Curtain	I Am Hydrgen
3/27/92	2	2		***	I Am Hydrgen
3/31/92	3	2	1/13	***	I Am Hydrgen
4/6/92	5	2	4/13	Paul and Silas	I Am Hydrgen
4/8/92	2	2	8/15	My Sweet One	I Am Hydrgen
4/13/92	2	2	4/11	Sparkle	I Am Hydrgen
4/16/92	2	2	4/12	The Lizards	I Am Hydrgen
4/19/92	3	2	2/13	The Curtain	I Am Hydrgen
4/21/92	1	2		Tela	I Am Hydrgen
4/23/92	2	2	3/13	Poor Heart	I Am Hydrgen
4/24/92	1	2	5/12	Foam	I Am Hydrgen
4/29/92	2	2	7/11	The Lizards	I Am Hydrgen
5/1/92	2	2	6/13	My Sweet One	I Am Hydrgen
5/3/92	2	2	6/14	Guelah Papyrus	I Am Hydrgen
5/5/92	1	2	5/14	Foam	I Am Hydrgen
5/7/92	2	2	6/12	Glide	I Am Hydrgen
5/14/92	5	2	6/13	Eliza	I Am Hydrgen
5/18/92	4	2	6/13	T.M.W.S.I.Y. Reprise	I Am Hydrgen
7/16/92	14	2	11/13	Paul and Silas	I Am Hydrgen
8/17/92	18	2	5/11	Esther	I Am Hydrgen
11/19/92	11	2	1/15	***	I Am Hydrgen
11/21/92	2	2	2/14	The Curtain	I Am Hydrgen
11/23/92	2	2	7/14	Weigh	I Am Hydrgen
11/28/92	3	1	9/11	All Things Recnsdrd	I Am Hydrgen
12/1/92	2	1	10/12	Sweet Adeline	I Am Hydrgen
12/3/92	2	2	4/13	Fluffhead	I Am Hydrgen
12/5/92	2	2	9/13	Lawn Boy	I Am Hydrgen
12/8/92	3	2	1/15	***	I Am Hydrgen
12/11/92	2	2	2/12	Dinner and a Movie	I Am Hydrgen
12/29/92	4	2	9/14	All Things Recnsdrd	I Am Hydrgen
12/31/92	2	3	1/9	***	Auld Lang Syne
2/4/93	2	2	3/13	The Wedge	T.M.W.S.I.Y.
2/6/93	2	2	6/14	All Things Recnsdrd	I Am Hydrgen
2/9/93	2	2	2/12	Punch You in the Eye	I Am Hydrgen
2/11/93	2	2	4/12	Uncle Pen	I Am Hydrgen
2/15/93	3	2	4/12	Reba	I Am Hydrgen
2/18/93	2	2	5/12	Punch You in the Eye	I Am Hydrgen
2/20/93	2	2	7/22	Glide	My Mind's Got A Mind
2/20/93	0	2	9/22	My Mind's Got A Mind	I Am Hydrgen
2/23/93	3	2	7/13	All Things Recnsdrd	I Am Hydrgen
2/27/93	3	2	7/12	Ya Mar	I Am Hydrgen
3/3/93	2	2	5/13	Mound	I Am Hydrgen
3/5/93	1	2	5/11	Uncle Pen	Jesus Just Left
3/9/93	3	2	6/15	Lawn Boy	I Am Hydrgen
3/13/93	2	2	8/13	Big Ball Jam	I Am Hydrgen
3/17/93	3	2	6/12	Mound	I Am Hydrgen
3/19/93	2	2	6/10	The Lizards	I Am Hydrgen
3/22/93	2	2	11/13	McGrupp	I Am Hydrgen
3/25/93	2	2	10/13	The Wedge	I Am Hydrgen
3/27/93	2	2	9/14	T.M.W.S.I.Y. Reprise	I Am Hydrgen
3/30/93	2	2	7/15	Weigh	I Am Hydrgen
4/2/93	3	2	7/13	Silent in the Mornin	I Am Hydrgen
4/10/93	4	2	7/13	Big Ball Jam	The Great Gig in the
4/16/93	3	2	5/13	The Lizards	I Am Hydrgen
4/18/93	2	2	8/12	Big Ball Jam	Ya Mar
4/21/93	2	2	8/11	Big Ball Jam	The Great Gig in the
4/23/93	2	2	7/12	Big Ball Jam	I Am Hydrgen
4/25/93	2	2	7/11	Big Ball Jam	I Am Hydrgen
4/29/93	2	2	7/13	Reba	I Am Hydrgen
5/1/93	2	2	8/11	Paul and Silas	The Great Gig in the
5/6/93	4	2	7/11	The Squirming Coil	Ob La Di Ob La Da Ja
5/8/93	2	2	12/18	Big Ball Jam	Crossroads
5/8/93	0	2	14/18	Crossroads	I Am Hydrgen
7/17/93	3	2	7/12	Big Ball Jam	Leprechaun
7/24/93	5	2	7/12	Sparkle	Yerushalayim
7/31/93	6	2	6/11	Sparkle	Leprechaun
8/2/93	1	2	2/9	Also Sprach	Sparks
8/7/93	3	2	2/12	Also Sprach	Kung
8/7/93	0	2	4/12	Kung	T.M.W.S.I.Y.
8/11/93	3	2	1/10	***	The Great Gig in the
8/13/93	2	2	5/9	Ya Mar	Lifeboy
8/16/93	3	2	1/10	***	Faht
8/24/93	4	2	4/10	Ya Mar	Ginseng Sullivan
12/30/93	6	2	2/9	Also Sprach	The Horse
4/6/94	4	2	5/9	Sparkle	Lifeboy
4/9/94	2	2	6/11	Demand	I Am Hydrgen
4/18/94	8	2	7/13	Ya Mar	T.M.W.S.I.Y.
4/21/94	2	2	4/10	Fluffhead	I Am Hydrgen
4/29/94	2	2	7/11	Uncle Pen	I Am Hydrgen
5/2/94	2	2	8/9	Lawn Boy	Bass Jam
5/14/94	9	2	2/11	The Curtain	I Am Hydrgen
5/19/94	3	2	3/10	Sparkle	I Am Hydrgen
5/27/94	7	2	9/12	My Mind's Got A Mind	Simple
6/9/94	3	2	7/10	Ginseng Sullivan	I Am Hydrgen
6/13/94	3	2	1/11	***	I Am Hydrgen
6/17/94	3	2	4/15	Poor Heart	Simple
6/17/94	0	2	6/15	Simple	I Am Hydrgen
6/22/94	4	2	2/20	Also Sprach	Simple
6/22/94	0	2	9/20	Simple	I Am Hydrgen
7/2/94	8	2	2/12	Also Sprach	Simple
7/2/94	0	2	4/12	Simple	Yerushalayim
7/10/94	6	2	5/10	Ya Mar	I Am Hydrgen
10/8/94	6	2	4/12	Rift	Simple
10/8/94	0	2	6/12	Simple	I Am Hydrgen
10/13/94	4	2	6/12	Amazing Grace	Simple
10/13/94	0	2	8/12	Simple	Yerushalayim
10/21/94	6	2	2/11	Also Sprach	Simple
10/21/94	0	2	4/11	Simple	I Am Hydrgen
10/25/94	3	2	1/11	***	Simple
11/4/94	8	2	2/9	The Curtain	Simple
11/4/94	0	2	4/9	Simple	Tela
11/16/94	4	2	1/7	***	Simple
11/25/94	7	2	2/8	Also Sprach	Simple
11/30/94	3	2	7/10	Ya Mar	Catapult
12/6/94	5	2	5/12	Poor Heart	Simple
12/10/94	4	2	5/11	Also Sprach	I Am Hydrgen
12/28/94	1	2	3/9	NICU	The Mango Song
12/31/94	3	2	4/9	Bouncing	Buffalo Bill
12/31/94	0	2	6/9	Buffalo Bill	Yerushalayim
6/10/95	5	2	4/8	Uncle Pen	I Am Hydrgen
6/20/95	7	2	5/9	Uncle Pen	Contact
6/25/95	4	2	4/9	Scent of a Mule	Why Don't We Do It i
6/30/95	4	2	6/10	Avenu Malkenu	Contact
9/30/95	7	2	5/9	Scent of a Mule	Keyboard Cavalry
10/11/95	7	2	4/11	Mound	McGrupp
10/19/95	5	2	3/10	Poor Heart	I Am Hydrgen
10/25/95	5	2	4/9	Cars Trucks Buses	Breathe Jam
11/11/95	7	1	2/12	Cars Trucks Buses	A Day in the Life
11/15/95	3	2	4/8	Scent of a Mule	Life on Mars
11/21/95	4	2	7/11	Ya Mar	Keyboard Cavalry
11/25/95	3	2	3/12	Kung	Rotation Jam
11/25/95	0	2	5/12	Rotation Jam	My Long Journey Home
12/1/95	4	2	2/9	Halley's Comet	Weekapaug Gr
12/7/95	4	2	3/10	Sparkle	Weekapaug Gr
12/16/95	7	2	5/8	Cavern	Simple
12/31/95	5	2	8/8	Hello My Baby	***
7/9/96	7	1	5/7	Cars Trucks Buses	Bouncing
7/12/96	3	2	3/9	Prince Caspian	Run Like Antel
7/23/96	8	2	5/9	Sparkle	I Am Hydrgen
8/5/96	5	2	11/13	Amazing Grace	I Am Hydrgen
8/13/96	5	2	3/11	The Lizards	Lifeboy
8/16/96	2	2	10/13	Hello My Baby	Simple
10/22/96	7	2	7/10	Scent of a Mule	Swept Away
10/29/96	5	2	2/10	Rift	The Horse
11/6/96	4	2	3/9	The Curtain	Swept Away
11/8/96	2	2	6/8	Loving Cup	Star Spangled Banner
11/15/96	5	2	8/11	My Mind's Got A Mind	Sleeping Monkey
11/23/96	5	2	2/10	The Curtain	Simple
12/4/96	7	2	2/9	Ha Ha Ha	Prince Caspian
12/6/96	1	2	3/9	Sparkle	Simple
12/28/96	1	2	7/10	Avenu Malkenu	Strange Design
2/23/97	12	2	7/9	Peaches en Regalia	Why Don't We Do It i
3/1/97	4	2	3/8	Dinner and a Movie	Lawn Boy
7/2/97	15	1	1/8	***	Simple
7/22/97	8	2	2/6	Down with Disease	Simple
7/31/97	6	2	5/7	McGrupp	I Am Hydrgen
8/9/97	5	2	3/10	Foam	Ain't Love Funny
11/13/97	7	2	5/7	Bouncing	I Am Hydrgen
11/22/97	6	1	1/8	***	I Am Hydrgen
12/2/97	6	2	1/7	***	I Am Hydrgen
12/7/97	5	1	1/10	***	Chalk Dust Tor
12/13/97	3	2	4/10	Ghost	Llama
12/31/97	4	2	2/6	Timber (Jerry)	Piper
4/3/98	2	1	1/9	***	The Old Home
6/30/98	3	2	9/12	Ha Ha Ha	Swept Away

DATE	GAP	SET	POS.	SONG BEFORE	SONG AFTER
7/10/98	8	1	4/4	Divided Sky	***
7/10/98	0	2	4/8	Sparkle	Simple
7/17/98	3	2	2/4	Also Sprach	Weekapaug Gr
7/21/98	3	2	1/8	***	Simple
8/1/98	7	1	2/9	Ramble On	Esther
8/7/98	4	2	2/7	Chalk Dust Torture	Simple
8/12/98	4	2	1/7	***	Simple
8/15/98	1	1	1/12	***	Simple
10/31/98	8	1	8/10	Lawn Boy	Frankie Says
11/7/98	4	1	2/10	My Soul	Driver
11/15/98	6	2	3/7	Stash	Simple
11/21/98	4	2	2/9	Sabotage	Simple
11/27/98	3	2	10/16	Buffalo Bill	I Am Hydrgen
12/31/98	6	1	2/7	1999	I Am Hydrgen
7/4/99	4	2	7/9	Wilson	Sleeping Monkey
7/9/99	3	2	5/8	Meatstick	Sweet Emotion Jam
7/16/99	5	2	2/8	Also Sprach	I Am Hydrgen
7/21/99	4	2	1/6	***	Simple
8/1/99	8	2	4/9	Llama	I Am Hydrgen
9/16/99	6	2	2/8	Also Sprach	I Am Hydrgen
9/22/99	5	2	5/8	Brian and Robert	Simple
9/29/99	5	2	6/12	Back on the Train	Catapult
9/29/99	0	2	8/12	Catapult	Kung
9/29/99	0	2	10/12	Kung	I Didn't Know
10/7/99	5	2	5/9	Back on the Train	McGrupp
12/5/99	7	2	1/10	***	Meatstick
12/11/99	4	1	2/8	Harry Hood	Simple
12/18/99	6	2	6/10	Possum	Simple
12/30/99	1	3	6/9	When Circus Comes	Simple
5/23/00	4	1	5/12	Ya Mar	Simple
6/13/00	4	1	8/10	Wilson	Simple
7/1/00	11	2	4/10	First Tube	Swept Away
7/7/00	4	2	5/7	Roggae	Simple
7/14/00	5	3	1/7	***	Frankie Says
9/12/00	5	2	6/8	Also Sprach	I Am Hydrgen
9/20/00	5	1	4/9	Gotta Jibboo	Simple
9/25/00	4	2	2/7	Gotta Jibboo	I Am Hydrgen
9/30/00	3	1	6/10	I Didn't Know	Simple
10/7/00	5	1	2/8	First Tube	I Am Hydrgen

Was played in the most recent show.

Mind Left Body Jam

DATE	GAP	SET	POS.	SONG BEFORE	SONG AFTER
6/18/94	640	2	3/10	David Bowie	David Bowie

Has not been played in the last 479 shows.

Minute by Minute

DATE	GAP	SET	POS.	SONG BEFORE	SONG AFTER
9/13/90	207	1	7/11	Run Like an Antelope	Buried Alive
9/15/90	2	2	6/8	Foam	Harry Hood

Has not been played in the last 910 shows.

Mirror in the Bathroom

DATE	GAP	SET	POS.	SONG BEFORE	SONG AFTER
11/27/98	100	2	4/16	Chalk Dust Torture	Chalk Dust Tor

Has not been played in the last 119 shows.

Misty Mountain Hop

DATE	GAP	SET	POS.	SONG BEFORE	SONG AFTER
7/20/99	1021	2	6/6	Also Sprach	***
9/16/99	15	E	1/1	***	***
9/24/99	6	2	6/6	Sand	***
10/10/99	12	E	2/2	Contact	***

Has not been played in the last 65 shows.

Moby Dick

DATE	GAP	SET	POS.	SONG BEFORE	SONG AFTER
11/29/97	926	E	2/3	Buffalo Bill	Fire
7/11/00	169	2	3/13	Down with Disease	Down with Dis
7/11/00	0	2	6/13	Runaway Jim	Back on the Train
7/11/00	0	2	8/13	Back on the Train	Back on the Train
7/11/00	0	2	11/13	Harry Hood	Terrapin
7/11/00	0	E	2/3	First Tube	Chalk Dust Reprise

Has not been played in the last 24 shows.

Money

DATE	GAP	SET	POS.	SONG BEFORE	SONG AFTER
11/2/98	984	2	11/16	The Great Gig in the	Us and Them

Has not been played in the last 135 shows.

Moonlight in Vermont

DATE	GAP	SET	POS.	SONG BEFORE	SONG AFTER
10/3/98	977	1	7/10	Down By the River	Will The Circle

Has not been played in the last 142 shows.

Moose the Mooch

DATE	GAP	SET	POS.	SONG BEFORE	SONG AFTER
7/12/91	298	2	3/14	The Squirming Coil	Tweezer

Has not been played in the last 821 shows.

Mother Nature's Son

DATE	GAP	SET	POS.	SONG BEFORE	SONG AFTER
10/31/94	681	2	21/30	Yer Blues	Everybody's Got Some

Has not been played in the last 438 shows.

Mound

DATE	GAP	SET	POS.	SONG BEFORE	SONG AFTER
3/6/92	359	2	5/9	Stash	Llama
3/11/92	2	1	8/12	Split Open and Melt	Divided Sky
3/13/92	2	1	8/12	Divided Sky	Fluffhead
3/20/92	4	1	9/10	The Lizards	Run Like Antel
3/25/92	4	2	2/12	Tweezer	Reba
3/30/92	4	2	4/13	Tweezer	You Enjoy My
4/3/92	3	2	4/9	Possum	You Enjoy My
4/6/92	3	2	9/13	Llama	Stash
4/8/92	2	1	6/11	Llama	Reba
4/18/92	6	2	9/16	The Lizards	Llama
4/22/92	3	1	7/10	Divided Sky	Stash
4/29/92	4	2	3/11	Possum	The Oh Kee Pa
5/1/92	2	2	9/13	Weekapaug Groove	The Lizards
5/8/92	6	1	8/12	Llama	All Things Rec
11/19/92	51	1	6/12	Split Open and Melt	Divided Sky
11/23/92	4	1	8/12	Divided Sky	Bouncing
11/27/92	2	1	10/12	Llama	Memories
12/2/92	4	2	3/11	Possum	Tweezer
12/5/92	3	1	8/12	The Lizards	Divided Sky
12/8/92	3	1	9/11	Divided Sky	Sweet Adeline
12/13/92	4	2	2/14	Suzy Greenberg	Bouncing
2/6/93	8	2	2/14	Chalk Dust Torture	Stash
2/11/93	4	2	7/12	Weekapaug Groove	Big Ball Jam
2/15/93	3	1	8/12	Chalk Dust Torture	Stash
2/18/93	2	2	8/12	Weekapaug Groove	Amazing Grce
2/26/93	7	2	6/11	Chalk Dust Torture	Big Ball Jam
3/3/93	3	2	4/13	Split Open and Melt	Mike's Song
3/6/93	2	1	5/10	Split Open and Melt	Punch You in
3/12/93	3	2	6/11	You Enjoy Myself	Big Ball Jam
3/17/93	4	2	5/12	Jesus Just Left	Mike's Song
3/24/93	2	2	5/12	Tweezer	Big Ball Jam
3/26/93	2	2	4/12	Tweezer	The Horse
3/28/93	2	2	3/9	Runaway Jim	Bathtub Jam
3/31/93	2	1	5/10	Split Open and Melt	Punch You in
4/3/93	3	2	3/10	Stash	All Things Rec
4/9/93	2	2	5/10	Llama	My Friend My
4/14/93	3	2	4/10	Tweezer	Big Ball Jam
4/18/93	3	2	6/12	Possum	Big Ball Jam
4/21/93	2	2	2/11	Possum	Split Open and
4/24/93	3	2	5/10	Dinner and a Movie	Big Ball Jam
4/29/93	3	2	4/13	Ya Mar	Big Ball Jam
4/30/93	1	2	5/10	Walk Away	Big Ball Jam
5/2/93	2	1	4/11	Divided Sky	Stash
5/6/93	3	1	2/13	Chalk Dust Torture	Split Open and
5/8/93	2	1	4/12	Rift	Stash
7/15/93	3	1	4/9	Divided Sky	Stash
7/18/93	3	2	4/10	Run Like an Antelope	Fast Enough for You
7/22/93	2	1	7/11	Divided Sky	Ya Mar
7/25/93	3	1	3/10	Foam	Stash
7/28/93	2	2	6/10	The Lizards	My Friend My
7/31/93	3	1	5/9	Split Open and Melt	Foam
8/9/93	6	1	4/11	Chalk Dust Torture	Fee
8/14/93	4	2	8/13	Run Like an Antelope	The Squirmin
8/16/93	2	2	4/10	Weekapaug Groove	It's Ice
8/25/93	5	2	3/8	Possum	My Friend My
4/17/94	18	1	5/9	Divided Sky	Down with Dis

DATE	GAP	SET	POS.	SONG BEFORE	SONG AFTER
4/23/94	5	2	3/10	Run Like an Antelope	Sample in a Ja
4/25/94	2	2	5/10	Run Like an Antelope	The Squirmin
4/30/94	3	1	2/9	Chalk Dust Torture	Stash
5/2/94	1	2	2/9	Runaway Jim	Reba
5/7/94	4	1	4/9	Divided Sky	Fast Enough for You
5/13/94	4	1	4/9	Julius	Stash
5/17/94	3	1	3/9	Maze	If I Could
5/21/94	3	1	5/9	Down with Disease	Stash
5/26/94	4	2	5/9	Down with Disease	Ginseng Sullivan
6/21/94	13	1	2/5	Runaway Jim	Sample in a Ja
6/29/94	6	1	4/11	Reba	Julius
7/13/94	10	2	11/13	Tweezer	Slave
12/1/94	41	2	2/10	Peaches en Regalia	Tweezer
12/4/94	3	1	7/9	Fee	Sweet Adeline
12/6/94	1	1	2/8	Llama	Down with Dis
12/28/94	5	1	1/10	***	Simple
12/31/94	3	1	5/8	Glide	Peaches en Regalia
6/8/95	3	1	5/9	Guelah Papyrus	Fast Enough for You
6/14/95	4	1	4/12	NICU	Cavern
6/17/95	3	2	3/11	Maze	Tweezer
6/24/95	5	1	6/10	Glide	Stash
6/30/95	5	1	7/9	The Lizards	Fee
10/7/95	12	1	4/9	Fog that Surrounds	Possum
10/11/95	2	2	3/11	Bathtub Gin	Mike's Song
10/17/95	4	2	1/6	***	Prince Caspian
10/28/95	8	1	2/10	AC/DC Bag	Timber (Jerry)
11/16/95	9	1	5/10	Horn	Ya Mar
12/2/95	11	1	3/10	Runaway Jim	Guelah Papyrus
10/16/96	47	1	7/12	Billy Breathes	Sample in a Ja
10/25/96	7	1	6/10	Billy Breathes	Guelah Papyrus
11/8/96	9	1	4/9	All Things Recnsdrd	Down with Dis
11/19/96	8	1	5/9	Theme From the Botto	Stash

Has not been played in the last 271 shows.

Mountains in the Mist

DATE	GAP	SET	POS.	SONG BEFORE	SONG AFTER
7/3/99	1009	2	4/7	The Moma Dance	Run Like Antel
7/10/99	5	2	2/5	Tweezer	Birds of a Feather
7/13/99	2	2	4/6	Bug	Run Like Antel
7/26/99	10	1	9/11	Bathtub Gin	Axilla
9/16/99	10	2	5/8	Weekapaug Groove	Limb by Limb
9/26/99	8	2	3/7	Piper	Heavy Things
10/1/99	3	2	6/9	Gumbo	Julius
12/13/99	17	2	5/9	The Inlaw Josie Wale	Limb by Limb

Has not been played in the last 55 shows.

Mozambique

DATE	GAP	SET	POS.	SONG BEFORE	SONG AFTER
9/9/99	1031	1	1/10	***	Axilla
9/12/99	3	1	3/10	Poor Heart	Bathtub Gin
9/17/99	3	1	1/11	***	Guyute
9/22/99	4	1	8/10	Bathtub Gin	Sand
9/26/99	3	1	9/10	Funky Bitch	Cavern

Has not been played in the last 75 shows.

Mr. P.C.

DATE	GAP	SET	POS.	SONG BEFORE	SONG AFTER
7/30/94	61	1	2/2	All Blues	***
11/11/88	13	2	4/8	Weekapaug Groove	Fee

Has not been played in the last 1045 shows.

Mustang Sally

DATE	GAP	SET	POS.	SONG BEFORE	SONG AFTER
10/15/86	14	2	6/14	Shaggy Dog	Fluffhead
10/31/86	1	1	1/11	***	Camel Walk
8/10/87	11	2	8/10	I Know a Little	You Enjoy My
8/29/87	2	2	9/13	Suzy Greenberg	Ya Mar
2/12/88	8	1	2/9	Funky Bitch	AC/DC Bag
2/24/88	3	2	1/5	***	Sneakin' Sally
6/21/88	15	1	3/9	Rocky Top	Suzy Greenber

DATE	GAP	SET	POS.	SONG BEFORE	SONG AFTER

Has not been played in the last 1065 shows.

My Friend My Friend

DATE	GAP	SET	POS.	SONG BEFORE	SONG AFTER
3/6/92	359	2	1/9	***	***
3/11/92	2	1	2/10	Suzy Greenberg	Poor Heart
3/19/92	5	2	8/10	Suzy Greenberg	Paul and Silas
3/21/92	2	2	5/11	Take the A-Train	The Squirmin
3/26/92	4	2	9/13	T.M.W.S.I.Y. Reprise	Poor Heart
3/31/92	4	2	10/13	Dinner and a Movie	The Lizards
4/7/92	6	2	6/11	You Enjoy Myself	My Sweet One
4/19/92	8	1	5/11	Paul and Silas	The Lizards
4/25/92	5	2	5/11	Suzy Greenberg	Reba
5/1/92	3	1	2/12	Suzy Greenberg	Paul and Silas
5/7/92	5	1	4/11	Buried Alive	Poor Heart
5/14/92	5	1	9/11	Poor Heart	Foam
7/15/92	17	1	5/12	Foam	Bouncing
8/17/92	19	1	9/11	Foam	Uncle Pen
11/22/92	14	2	2/10	Axilla	Bouncing
12/1/92	6	2	4/11	Chalk Dust Torture	My Sweet One
12/6/92	5	1	4/10	Fee	All Things Rec
12/11/92	4	1	9/11	Sparkle	My Sweet One
12/29/92	4	1	5/12	Llama	Memories
2/3/93	3	1	8/11	I Didn't Know	Divided Sky
2/6/93	3	1	4/11	Wilson	Poor Heart
2/9/93	2	1	4/10	Poor Heart	Maze
2/12/93	3	2	1/11	***	Rift
2/17/93	3	2	5/11	Glide	All Things Rec
2/19/93	2	1	9/11	Sparkle	My Sweet One
2/23/93	4	1	2/11	Golgi Apparatus	Poor Heart
3/2/93	4	2	1/12	***	Rift
3/8/93	4	2	6/10	Big Ball Jam	Uncle Pen
3/12/93	2	2	2/11	AC/DC Bag	Kung
3/16/93	3	2	1/15	***	Axilla
3/18/93	2	2	1/10	***	The Curtain
3/21/93	2	2	2/12	Loving Cup	Poor Heart
3/27/93	5	1	6/10	Reba	Rift
3/30/93	2	1	5/11	Golgi Apparatus	Uncle Pen
4/1/93	2	1	6/10	The Squirming Coil	Llama
4/3/93	2	1	7/10	The Squirming Coil	Paul and Silas
4/9/93	2	2	6/10	Mound	Reba
4/10/93	1	1	6/10	The Squirming Coil	You Enjoy My
4/17/93	4	1	7/10	Glide	Uncle Pen
4/20/93	2	2	8/12	T.M.W.S.I.Y. Reprise	All Things Rec
4/23/93	3	1	6/10	Fluffhead	Llama
4/27/93	3	2	2/10	Golgi Apparatus	Divided Sky
4/29/93	1	E	1/1	***	All Things Rec
5/1/93	2	2	3/11	Fluffhead	***
5/5/93	3	2	2/10	Runaway Jim	The Squirmin
5/5/93	0	2	4/10	Manteca	Manteca
5/8/93	3	1	9/12	Glide	Poor Heart
7/16/93	4	1	3/10	Golgi Apparatus	Reba
7/23/93	5	2	5/11	Faith	Ya Mar
7/28/93	4	2	7/10	Mound	Uncle Pen
7/30/93	2	2	7/10	Fluffhead	Harry Hood
8/7/93	5	2	9/12	Sparkle	Golgi Apparat
8/9/93	2	2	4/8	Tela	McGrupp
8/11/93	1	1	6/10	Ginseng Sullivan	My Mind's Got A Mind
8/16/93	5	2	6/10	It's Ice	The Mango Song
8/20/93	2	2	5/9	The Squirming Coil	Poor Heart
8/25/93	3	2	4/8	Mound	Chalk Dust Tor
12/28/93	3	2	3/9	You Enjoy Myself	Paul and Silas
4/10/94	9	2	1/7	***	The Lizards
4/18/94	7	1	5/10	Julius	Ya Mar
4/24/94	5	1	1/8	***	Rift
5/6/94	8	1	5/9	Poor Heart	Ya Mar
5/13/94	5	1	7/9	If I Could	Ya Mar
5/19/94	4	1	3/10	Llama	Slave
5/27/94	7	2	3/12	Peaches en Regalia	Poor Heart
6/14/94	7	1	9/14	Fee	Reba
6/21/94	5	2	4/16	Down with Disease	Uncle Pen
7/3/94	10	1	1/10	***	Split Open and
7/10/94	5	1	7/9	If I Could	Poor Heart
10/7/94	5	1	1/9	***	Julius
10/12/94	4	1	1/9	***	Julius

DATE	GAP	SET	POS.	SONG BEFORE	SONG AFTER
10/18/94	5	1	2/10	Simple	I Didn't Know
10/23/94	4	1	2/11	Chalk Dust Torture	Sparkle
10/29/94	5	1	1/10	***	Sparkle
11/14/94	7	1	1/9	***	Scent of a Mul
11/26/94	9	1	1/9	***	Possum
11/30/94	2	1	3/10	Poor Heart	Reba
6/9/95	17	1	1/9	***	Divided Sky
6/15/95	4	1	1/10	***	Sparkle
6/26/95	9	1	1/10	***	Don't You Wanna Go
7/3/95	6	1	1/11	***	Poor Heart
9/30/95	4	1	1/9	***	Cars Trucks Buses
10/20/95	13	1	1/10	***	Ya Mar
10/24/95	3	1	1/13	***	Paul and Silas
11/12/95	9	1	1/10	***	Llama
11/21/95	6	1	8/10	Guyute	Dog Faced Boy
12/11/95	14	1	1/12	***	Ha Ha Ha
12/17/95	5	1	1/9	***	Poor Heart
12/29/95	2	1	1/9	***	Poor Heart
7/15/96	14	1	1/8	***	Punch You in
8/10/96	14	1	1/11	***	Poor Heart
10/19/96	9	1	1/9	***	Rift
11/3/96	10	1	1/9	***	Runaway Jim
11/27/96	15	1	2/9	Julius	Ya Mar
12/4/96	5	1	1/11	***	Chalk Dust Tor
2/25/97	15	2	6/10	Fee	Down with Dis
2/26/97	1	1	3/10	Llama	Harry Hood
12/5/97	57	1	7/10	Runaway Jim	Ginseng Sullivan
7/31/98	35	1	1/7	***	Ya Mar
11/15/98	28	1	1/8	***	Ghost
7/25/99	32	1	2/8	Meat	My Left Toe
7/31/99	4	1	1/8	***	Golgi Apparat
7/12/00	67	1	1/9	***	The Curtain With
9/9/00	4	1	2/8	Possum	Gumbo
9/27/00	12	1	2/10	Sample in a Jar	Beauty of my Dreams

Has not been played in the last 7 shows.

My Generation

DATE	GAP	SET	POS.	SONG BEFORE	SONG AFTER
10/31/95	759	E	1/1	***	***

Has not been played in the last 360 shows.

My Left Toe

DATE	GAP	SET	POS.	SONG BEFORE	SONG AFTER
6/30/99	1007	2	9/10	Bug	Stash
7/7/99	4	2	3/7	Down with Disease	Wading In Velvet Sea
7/7/99	0	2	5/7	Wading In Velvet Sea	Bug
7/21/99	11	2	3/6	Simple	Prince Caspian
7/25/99	3	1	3/8	My Friend My Friend	Whipping Post
10/9/99	28	1	5/8	Ghost	Free

Has not been played in the last 66 shows.

My Long Journey Home

DATE	GAP	SET	POS.	SONG BEFORE	SONG AFTER
11/16/94	688	2	4/7	I'm Blue, Lonesome	Chalk Dust Tor
11/17/94	1	E	3/4	Nellie Kane	Fixin' To Die
11/18/94	1	1	11/11	The Old Home Place	***
11/19/94	1	1	11/11	Butter Them Biscuits	***
11/20/94	1	1	7/10	Butter Them Biscuits	Dooley
11/22/94	1	2	11/13	Butter Them Biscuits	Harry Hood
11/30/94	5	1	10/10	I'm Blue, Lonesome	***
12/7/94	6	2	7/9	I'm Blue, Lonesome	Amazing Grce
12/29/94	5	E	1/2	***	Sleeping Monkey
10/17/95	40	E	1/2	***	I'm Blue, Lonesome
10/20/95	2	2	7/10	While My Guitar Gent	I'm Blue, Lonesome
10/25/95	4	1	8/10	Strange Design	I'm Blue, Lonesome

DATE	GAP	SET	POS.	SONG BEFORE	SONG AFTER
11/21/95	14	1	5/10	Divided Sky	I'm Blue, Lonesome
11/25/95	3	2	6/12	Mike's Song	I'm Blue, Lonesome
11/29/95	2	2	10/11	I'm Blue, Lonesome	Slave

Has not been played in the last 345 shows.

My Mind's Got a Mind of its Own

DATE	GAP	SET	POS.	SONG BEFORE	SONG AFTER
3/7/92	360	1	2/11	Brother	Foam
3/11/92	1	2	6/11	Bathtub Gin	Brother
3/13/92	2	2	7/12	The Lizards	The Sloth
4/7/92	19	2	10/11	Bike	Golgi Apparat
4/30/92	15	2	4/11	The Squirming Coil	You Enjoy My
5/6/92	5	1	4/11	Reba	Maze
2/7/93	82	2	3/13	Fast Enough for You	Reba
2/20/93	10	2	8/12	Mike's Song	Mike's Song
7/15/93	58	1	7/9	I Didn't Know	Leprechaun
7/17/93	2	1	4/11	Sample in a Jar	Stash
7/22/93	3	1	4/11	Horn	Sample in a Ja
7/25/93	3	1	8/10	The Sloth	I Didn't Know
7/29/93	3	1	7/10	Fast Enough for You	Col. Forbin's A
8/2/93	3	1	10/12	Makisupa Policeman	Dog Gone Dog
8/9/93	5	2	5/8	My Friend My Friend	You Enjoy My
8/13/93	3	1	8/10	Fluffhead	Horn
4/25/94	33	2	3/10	Sample in a Jar	Run Like Antel
4/29/94	2	1	11/12	Sanity	Llama
5/27/94	21	2	8/12	Nellie Kane	Mike's Song
7/6/94	24	1	7/9	Axilla (Part II)	Carolina
12/8/94	51	2	2/8	Possum	Axilla (Part II)
6/16/95	15	1	7/10	It's Ice	Dog Faced Boy
6/26/95	8	1	6/10	The Sloth	It's Ice
10/22/95	25	1	2/12	AC/DC Bag	The Sloth
12/4/95	25	1	6/11	Stash	Axilla (Part II)
7/21/96	30	1	6/14	If I Could	Split Open and
11/15/96	37	2	7/11	Avenu Malkenu	Mike's Song
8/3/97	61	1	6/10	Vultures	Twist
12/7/97	26	1	4/12	Jesus Just Left	It's Ice
4/2/98	9	1	2/8	Tube	The Sloth
7/1/98	5	1	3/9	Sample in a Jar	The Moma Dance
7/17/98	10	1	6/7	Waste	My Soul
7/7/99	55	1	4/10	Billy Breathes	Sneakin' Sally
9/12/99	23	1	6/10	Back on the Train	Frankie Says
9/22/99	7	1	5/10	Axilla	Beauty of My Dreams
12/10/99	20	1	6/10	Dogs Stole Things	Roggae
7/3/00	28	1	3/10	Guelah Papyrus	Foam
7/10/00	5	1	6/10	Buffalo Bill	Split Open and
9/18/00	12	1	6/10	Guelah Papyrus	Sample in a Ja

Has not been played in the last 13 shows.

My Soul

DATE	GAP	SET	POS.	SONG BEFORE	SONG AFTER
2/13/97	863	2	3/10	Cars Trucks Buses	Punch You in
2/17/97	3	1	4/10	Wilson	Guyute
2/18/97	1	2	3/9	Also Sprach	Maze
2/21/97	2	1	1/6	***	Foam
2/25/97	3	1	2/9	Runaway Jim	One Meatball
2/26/97	1	1	5/10	Harry Hood	Tube
2/28/97	1	1	3/10	Paul and Silas	Cars Trucks Buses
3/2/97	2	1	5/13	Guyute	Runaway Jim
3/18/97	1	1	5/10	Punch You in the Eye	Beauty of My Dreams
6/14/97	2	1	5/10	Talk	Cars Trucks Buses
6/21/97	4	E	1/1	***	***
6/25/97	3	1	11/11	Limb by Limb	***
6/29/97	2	E	1/1	***	***
7/3/97	3	1	2/8	Piper	Divided Sky
7/6/97	2	E	1/1	***	***
7/9/97	1	2	2/6	Down with Disease	Cars Trucks Buses
7/22/97	4	1	2/8	Runaway Jim	Water in the Sky

DATE	GAP	SET	POS.	SONG BEFORE	SONG AFTER
7/30/97	5	E	1/1	***	***
8/6/97	4	2	2/7	Runaway Jim	Ghost
8/11/97	4	2	4/6	Vultures	You Enjoy My
8/16/97	3	2	3/7	Simple	Jam
11/13/97	2	1	7/9	Beauty of My Dreams	You Enjoy My
11/16/97	2	1	2/11	NICU	Black-Eyed Katy
11/23/97	5	1	1/9	***	Theme From the Botto
11/26/97	1	1	4/10	Gumbo	McGrupp
11/28/97	1	E	1/1	***	***
12/3/97	4	1	2/7	Punch You In The Eye	Drowned
12/9/97	4	1	3/10	Chalk Dust Torture	Stash
12/13/97	3	E	1/2	***	The Squirmin
12/30/97	3	2	8/10	Harry Hood	Sleeping Monkey
4/3/98	3	1	9/9	Reba	***
7/1/98	4	2	4/5	Loving Cup	Sweet Adeline
7/3/98	2	1	9/11	Water in the Sky	You Enjoy My
7/17/98	8	1	7/7	My Mind's Got A Mind	***
7/24/98	4	1	5/8	Stash	Taste
8/6/98	9	1	12/12	Cracklin' Rosie	***
10/15/98	9	2	1/10	***	Chalk Dust Tor
11/7/98	9	1	1/10	***	Mike's Song
11/14/98	5	1	2/8	Funky Bitch	Reba
11/18/98	2	1	4/9	Farmhouse	Guyute
11/25/98	5	1	2/9	Punch You in the Eye	Roggae
12/29/98	5	1	9/10	Guyute	Freebird
7/4/99	6	1	1/10	***	Ya Mar
7/18/99	10	3	1/9	***	Piper
7/30b/99	8	2	2/6	Down with Disease	Reba
10/7/99	23	1	2/9	NICU	Dirt
12/31/99	19	2	21/35	David Bowie	Drowned
5/22/00	2	1	1/9	***	Chalk Dust Tor
6/10/00	3	2	4/9	Sparkle	Bathtub Gin
6/23/00	7	1	2/8	Ya Mar	Bathtub Gin
7/3/00	7	1	6/10	Bathtub Gin	Heavy Things
7/8/00	4	1	3/9	NICU	Poor Heart
7/15/00	5	1	8/9	Wolfman's Brother	Julius
9/12/00	4	1	3/7	Scent of a Mule	Ginseng Sullivan
9/27/00	10	1	4/10	Beauty of my Dreams	Limb By Limb
10/7/00	7	1	8/8	Glide	***

Was played in the most recent show.

My Sweet One

DATE	GAP	SET	POS.	SONG BEFORE	SONG AFTER
9/9/89	113	1	10/11	Wilson	David Bowie
9/21/89	2	1	4/9	AC/DC Bag	Fee
10/1/89	1	2	2/11	AC/DC Bag	Reba
10/22/89	8	2	7/9	AC/DC Bag	Fee
11/2/89	4	2	10/11	AC/DC Bag	Highway to Hell
11/3/89	1	1	4/10	Bathtub Gin	Split Open and
11/9/89	1	1	5/9	The Curtain	Bathtub Gin
11/10/89	1	1	7/9	AC/DC Bag	You Enjoy My
11/11/89	1	1	5/8	AC/DC Bag	You Enjoy My
11/16/89	1	1	8/11	Suzy Greenberg	Reba
11/18/89	1	1	5/11	The Lizards	Possum
11/30/89	1	1	8/11	The Lizards	Run Like Antel
12/1/89	1	1	7/9	Bathtub Gin	Harry Hood
12/3/89	1	1	6/9	Divided Sky	Run Like Antel
12/8/89	2	1	9/11	AC/DC Bag	Bathtub Gin
12/30/89	5	2	6/9	Foam	La Grange
1/27/90	3	1	6/13	AC/DC Bag	Bouncing
2/25/90	12	1	2/11	Foam	Col. Forbin's A
3/3/90	3	1	4/12	Weekapaug Groove	The Squirmin
3/8/90	2	2	3/12	Bathtub Gin	AC/DC Bag
3/11/90	3	2	3/13	Roll Like a Cantalou	Bouncing
3/17/90	1	1	5/10	Bouncing	Rhombus Narration
4/7/90	5	1	2/12	David Bowie	AC/DC Bag
4/8/90	1	2	9/10	Fee	Run Like Antel
4/12/90	2	2	2/11	David Bowie	The Oh Kee Pa
4/18/90	3	1	8/10	You Enjoy Myself	Take the A-Trn
4/22/90	4	1	8/12	Cavern	Slave
4/25/90	1	1	3/4	Divided Sky	David Bowie

DATE	GAP	SET	POS.	SONG BEFORE	SONG AFTER
4/28/90	2	2	6/9	Reba	Mike's Song
5/4/90	2	2	8/10	Reba	You Enjoy My
5/10/90	3	1	6/8	Tweezer	Bathtub Gin
5/13/90	2	2	7/12	Tweezer	Reba
5/24/90	4	2	5/11	I Didn't Know	Horn
6/5/90	5	2	6/10	Bouncing	The Lizards
6/7/90	1	2	1/10	***	Dinner and a
6/8/90	1	2	2/7	Possum	Tweezer
6/16/90	2	2	4/8	Tweezer	Bathtub Gin
9/15/90	3	2	3/8	Eliza	Bathtub Gin
9/22/90	4	1	3/12	Horn	Divided Sky
9/28/90	1	1	6/10	Stash	The Squirmin
10/5/90	4	1	5/13	Weekapaug Groove	The Landlady
10/7/90	2	2	4/8	Tweezer	I Didn't Know
10/8/90	1	1	7/10	Reba	You Enjoy My
10/31/90	4	1	9/11	The Asse Festival	Cavern
11/2/90	1	2	4/9	The Famous Mockingbi	Foam
11/4/90	2	1	9/10	The Asse Festival	David Bowie
11/10/90	2	1	6/11	Cavern	Buried Alive
11/30/90	5	1	9/11	Tweezer	Llama
12/1/90	1	1	7/9	Tweezer	You Enjoy My
12/28/90	3	2	8/12	The Oh Kee Pa Ceremo	Divided Sky
12/31/90	2	1	6/12	Bouncing	Mike's Song
2/1/91	1	1	1/10	***	Foam
2/3/91	2	1	3/10	Guelah Papyrus	Tweezer
2/7/91	1	1	3/10	Foam	The Landlady
2/8/91	1	1	6/11	The Famous Mockingbi	Stash
2/9/91	1	1	9/12	Guelah Papyrus	Tweezer
2/14/91	1	1	1/11	***	McGrupp
2/15/91	1	2	5/10	Guelah Papyrus	The Oh Kee Pa
2/16/91	1	1	2/12	The Sloth	Divided Sky
2/19/91	1	2	1/15	***	Mike's Song
2/20/91	1	1	6/11	Tweezer	Bouncing
2/21/91	1	1	8/11	The Lizards	Mike's Song
2/26/91	1	1	6/11	Guelah Papyrus	Reba
2/27/91	1	1	7/10	Fee	Split Open and
2/28/91	1	1	12/13	T.M.W.S.I.Y. Reprise	Golgi Apparat
3/6/91	2	1	9/11	Love You	Bouncing
3/8/91	1	1	9/11	The Squirming Coil	Tweezer
3/13/91	2	2	4/12	Bouncing	Guelah Papyrus
3/15/91	1	1	3/12	Foam	Stash
3/16/91	1	2	4/10	Guelah Papyrus	Split Open and
3/17/91	1	2	3/8	Esther	The Squirmin
3/23/91	2	2	5/11	AC/DC Bag	Tweezer
3/28/91	1	1	8/14	Guelah Papyrus	David Bowie
3/31/91	1	1	7/13	The Landlady	Esther
4/3/91	2	2	3/9	Take the A-Train	Stash
4/4/91	1	2	7/10	The Landlady	Divided Sky
4/5/91	1	2	8/9	I Didn't Know	Good Time Ba
4/11/91	2	2	1/14	***	Reba
4/12/91	1	2	9/10	Reba	Good Time Ba
4/15/91	1	2	6/11	Horn	The Landlady
4/16/91	1	2	2/11	Crew Football Theme	Reba
4/19/91	2	2	7/10	Destiny Unbound	The Squirmin
4/20/91	1	2	5/11	Fluffhead	The Landlady
4/21/91	1	1	7/14	Jam	The Oh Kee Pa
4/22/91	1	2	8/10	Stash	The Lizards
4/25/91	1	2	2/10	Buried Alive	Mike's Song
4/27/91	1	1	6/12	The Landlady	Reba
5/2/91	1	2	7/10	Tela	I Didn't Know
5/4/91	2	1	5/11	Reba	Split Open and
5/9/91	1	2	1/8	***	The Curtain
5/16/91	4	2	7/9	Tweezer	The Lizards
5/18/91	2	2	6/10	Take the A-Train	Guelah Papyrus
7/11/91	2	1	5/8	Flat Fee	Stash
7/12/91	1	2	5/14	Tweezer	Gumbo
7/14/91	2	1	6/11	Guelah Papyrus	Col. Forbin's A
7/19/91	3	2	4/8	I Didn't Know	Magilla
7/23/91	3	1	4/12	The Squirming Coil	The Oh Kee Pa
7/24/91	1	2	5/10	Jesus Just Left	Bouncing
7/25/91	1	1	1/10	***	The Sloth
7/26/91	1	1	3/12	Reba	Foam
8/3/91	2	3	5/8	Lawn Boy	The Lizards
9/25/91	1	1	6/11	Tela	It's Ice

DATE	GAP	SET	POS.	SONG BEFORE	SONG AFTER
9/26/91	1	1	6/10	It's Ice	Guelah Papyrus
9/28/91	2	1	5/11	The Squirming Coil	Stash
9/29/91	1	2	8/10	The Squirming Coil	Golgi Apparat
10/2/91	2	2	3/9	You Enjoy Myself	Guelah Papyrus
10/4/91	1	2	1/11	***	Brother
10/6/91	1	2	1/10	***	Stash
10/11/91	2	1	2/10	The Landlady	Divided Sky
10/12/91	1	1	4/9	Foam	Stash
10/13/91	1	2	5/9	It's Ice	Jesus Just Left
10/18/91	3	2	11/12	Split Open and Melt	Cavern
10/19/91	1	1	8/10	Bouncing	Stash
10/27/91	3	1	1/10	***	Chalk Dust Tor
10/31/91	3	2	7/14	Wait	Wait
11/1/91	1	2	2/13	Tweezer	It's Ice
11/7/91	2	2	3/11	Bouncing	Reba
11/9/91	2	2	9/10	Terrapin	Tweezer Repri
11/13/91	3	E	2/3	Horn	Sweet Adeline
11/15/91	2	1	7/12	The Squirming Coil	Guelah Papyrus
11/16/91	1	2	2/9	Tube	Bathtub Gin
11/19/91	1	2	2/11	Tube	Mike's Song
11/20/91	1	2	3/8	It's Ice	Run Like Antel
11/22/91	2	2	2/10	Tube	The Landlady
11/23/91	1	2	12/13	Love You	Tweezer Repri
11/30/91	2	2	6/10	Bouncing	Horn
12/4/91	1	2	1/11	***	Stash
12/5/91	1	2	12/13	I Didn't Know	Tweezer Repri
12/7/91	2	1	6/11	The Famous Mockingbi	Stash
12/31/91	1	2	9/10	Cavern	Run Like Antel
3/7/92	2	2	1/11	***	Tweezer
3/12/92	2	2	10/11	Cracklin' Rosie	Cavern
3/19/92	4	2	4/10	NICU	Stash
3/21/92	2	1	10/12	The Squirming Coil	Stash
3/25/92	3	2	9/12	Horn	Chalk Dust Tor
3/27/92	2	2	6/13	Silent in the Mornin	Rift
3/31/92	3	2	3/11/13	My Friend My Friend	Love You
4/8/92	7	2	7/15	T.M.W.S.I.Y. Reprise	Mike's Song
4/15/92	3	2	7/8	Cracklin' Rosie	Golgi Apparat
4/19/92	4	2	7/13	Silent in the Mornin	Tube
5/1/92	8	2	5/13	All Things Recnsdrd	Mike's Song
5/6/92	4	2	1/11	***	Stash
5/8/92	2	2	2/12	Wilson	Stash
5/12/92	3	1	1/12	***	Reba
5/16/92	3	1	6/11	Bouncing	Horn
5/17/92	1	1	5/11	The Famous Mockingbi	Reba
7/10/92	10	E	1/1	***	***
7/15/92	4	2	4/9	Esther	Stash
7/24/92	7	1	1/6	***	Foam
11/22/92	26	2	3/10	My Friend My Friend	Tweezer
11/25/92	2	2	8/9	Cracklin' Rosie	Tweezer Repri
11/28/92	2	1	1/11	***	Foam
12/1/92	2	1	2/12	The Landlady	Split Open and
12/3/92	2	2	9/13	It's Ice	Big Ball Jam
12/6/92	3	1	5/10	My Friend My Friend	The Sloth
12/7/92	1	2	6/12	The Vibration of Lif	It's Ice
12/8/92	1	2	13/15	Lengthwise	Big Ball Jam
12/10/92	1	2	4/10	Tela	Big Ball Jam
12/13/92	3	2	10/14	T.M.W.S.I.Y. Reprise	Big Ball Jam
12/29/92	2	2	5/14	Silent in the Mornin	Big Ball Jam
12/31/92	2	2	6/10	The Famous Mockingbi	Big Ball Jam
2/9/93	6	2	6/12	Weigh	Sample in a Ja
2/17/93	6	2	6/11	My Friend My Friend	Big Ball Jam
2/19/93	2	2	9/12	Funky Bitch	Love You
2/23/93	4	2	2/13	Axilla	Stash
3/3/93	5	2	9/13	Glide	Fast Enough for You
3/5/93	1	2	7/11	Jesus Just Left	Big Ball Jam
3/13/93	5	E	1/3	***	Amazing Grce
3/21/93	6	2	7/12	You Enjoy Myself	Big Ball Jam
3/25/93	3	E	1/3	***	Big Ball Jam
3/30/93	4	E	1/2	***	Amazing Grce
4/3/93	4	2	8/10	Jesus Just Left	Love You
4/9/93	2	2	8/10	You Enjoy Myself	Love You

DATE	GAP	SET	POS.	SONG BEFORE	SONG AFTER
4/14/93	3	2	2/10	AC/DC Bag	Tweezer
4/27/93	10	E	1/2	***	Amazing Grce
5/3/93	5	2	11/12	Love You	Tweezer Repri
7/28/93	17	2	3/10	Axilla	Run Like Antel
8/8/93	8	E	1/2	***	Freebird
8/11/93	2	2	9/10	Jesus Just Left	Run Like Antel
8/17/93	6	2	9/10	Purple Rain	Cavern
4/17/94	22	1	8/9	If I Could	Cavern
5/14/94	20	1	7/9	Sample in a Jar	Ginseng Sullivan
5/22/94	6	1	8/11	Fluffhead	Ginseng Sullivan
5/25/94	2	1	9/11	Scent of a Mule	Sweet Adeline
6/14/94	9	1	12/14	I Didn't Know	I Didn't Know
6/19/94	4	2	7/8	The Squirming Coil	Highway to Hell
6/22/94	2	2	17/20	Fluffhead	Big Ball Jam
7/5/94	10	2	9/11	Ginseng Sullivan	Amazing Grce
7/13/94	5	E	1/2	***	Tweezer Repri
10/7/94	4	2	9/10	Lifeboy	Tweezer Repri
10/18/94	9	E	1/1	***	***
11/3/94	12	E	1/4	***	Nellie Kane
11/30/94	15	2	3/10	Run Like an Antelope	Run Like Antel
12/31/94	13	3	1/8	***	Also Sprach
6/15/95	8	2	1/8	***	Ha Ha Ha
12/2/95	58	1	6/10	Reba	Free
12/14/95	8	1	9/10	Taste That Surrounds	Frankenstein
12/31/97	155	1	3/10	Ya Mar	Beauty of My Dreams
7/20/98	18	1	5/10	Lawn Boy	Birds of a Feather
7/17/99	61	1	5/10	Guelah Papyrus	Roggae
6/16/00	61	1	8/10	Dirt	Reba
6/24/00	3	2	3/8	Bug	Run Like Antel

Has not been played in the last 36 shows.

NICU

DATE	GAP	SET	POS.	SONG BEFORE	SONG AFTER
3/6/92	359	2	8/9	Bouncing	Possum
3/11/92	2	2	2/11	Llama	The Sloth
3/19/92	5	2	3/10	Chalk Dust Torture	My Sweet One
3/26/92	6	1	9/10	Uncle Pen	David Bowie
4/6/92	9	2	7/13	Weekapaug Groove	Llama
4/12/92	3	2	7/10	Lawn Boy	Cracklin' Rosi
4/13/92	1	1	5/10	The Lizards	Fee
4/15/92	1	2	5/8	The Landlady	Cracklin' Rosi
4/19/92	4	1	2/11	Buried Alive	Stash
4/21/92	1	1	9/11	Eliza	Bouncing
4/23/92	2	2	7/13	The Lizards	Horn
5/1/92	5	1	5/12	The Landlady	The Sloth
6/23/94	246	1	4/10	Split Open and Melt	Foam
6/25/94	2	1	4/10	Julius	Stash
7/1/94	4	1	4/10	Sample in a Jar	Stash
7/3/94	2	1	5/10	Fee	Horn
7/13/94	6	2	5/13	Cavern	Tweezer
10/26/94	19	1	3/10	It's Ice	Run Like Antel
11/28/94	20	2	2/5	Suzy Greenberg	Tweezer
12/1/94	2	2	6/10	Makisupa Policeman	Tweezer
12/28/94	9	2	2/9	Suzy Greenberg	Mike's Song
12/31/94	3	2	2/9	Golgi Apparatus	Run Like Antel
6/14/95	7	1	3/12	Gumbo	Mound
6/26/95	10	1	4/10	Bathtub Gin	The Sloth
10/6/95	14	2	4/8	Theme From the Botto	Tweezer
10/22/95	11	1	6/12	Weigh	Fast Enough for You
10/29/95	5	1	9/12	Split Open and Melt	Gumbo
11/30/95	17	1	5/10	Julius	Bathtub Gin
12/9/95	7	1	3/10	Theme From the Botto	The Sloth
12/14/95	3	2	8/10	Jam	Jam
12/29/95	5	1	5/9	Taste That Surrounds	Stash
7/12/96	12	2	7/9	Jam	Slave
8/16/96	20	3	4/6	Down with Disease	Life on Mars
10/25/96	9	2	7/12	T.M.W.S.I.Y. Reprise	Free
11/3/96	6	1	5/9	The Sloth	Sample in a Ja
11/29/96	16	1	2/9	Frankenstein	Cars Trucks Buses
12/28/96	6	1	2/9	Runaway Jim	Wolfman's Brother
2/14/97	5	1	2/9	Runaway Jim	You Enjoy My
2/18/97	3	1	5/10	Runaway Jim	Stash
2/22/97	3	1	5/10	Theme From the Botto	When Circus Comes
3/18/97	7	1	2/10	Cinnamon Girl	Sample in a Ja
6/14/97	2	1	2/10	Down with Disease	Dirt
6/24/97	6	2	3/7	Reba	Twist
7/23/97	14	1	3/10	Dirt	Dogs Stole Things
7/30/97	4	1	1/9	***	Wolfman's Brother
8/6/97	4	1	1/8	***	Stash
8/17/97	8	3	2/7	Buffalo Bill	Weigh
11/16/97	3	1	1/11	***	My Soul
11/23/97	5	1	7/9	Stash	Fluffhead
11/30/97	4	2	1/7	***	Stash
12/13/97	9	2	11/10	***	Punch You in
12/29/97	2	1	1/9	***	Golgi Apparat
4/2/98	3	1	4/8	The Sloth	Stash
7/1/98	5	1	1/9	***	Sample in a Ja
7/9/98	6	1	3/8	Boogie On Reggae	Split Open and
7/16/98	3	1	2/7	The Squirming Coil	Stash
8/6/98	14	2	4/7	Talk	Prince Caspian
8/8/98	2	1	2/8	The Wedge	Sneakin' Sally
8/15/98	4	3	1/6	***	David Bowie
10/30/98	7	2	4/7	Tweezer	Jam
11/9/98	7	1	9/10	Free	Bold as Love
11/21/98	8	1	7/13	Boogie On Reggae	Dogs Stole Things
12/31/98	9	2	1/7	***	Character Zer Waste
7/3/99	3	1	9/11	Funky Bitch	Waste
7/13/99	7	1	1/9	***	The Curtain
7/23/99	7	1	2/9	Ya Mar	Back @ Chicken Shack
7/26/99	3	1	6/11	Gumbo	Beauty of My Dreams
7/30b/99	2	1	5/8	Stash	Funky Bitch
9/19/99	11	1	1/8	***	Funky Bitch
9/25/99	4	2	1/8	***	David Bowie
10/1/99	4	2	1/9	***	Run Like Antel
10/7/99	4	1	1/9	***	My Soul
12/7/99	8	1	3/8	First Tube	Funky Bitch
12/13/99	5	2	2/8	Gotta Jibboo	Sand
6/15/00	15	1	1/8	***	Chalk Dust Tor
6/25/00	5	1	1/10	***	Sample in a Ja
7/8/00	9	1	2/9	Punch You In The Eye	My Soul
7/15/00	5	1	4/9	Limb by Limb	Dirt
9/8/00	1	1	8/12	I Saw it Again	Glide
9/23/00	10	2	3/7	Tweezer	Scent of a Mul
10/5/00	8	2	2/7	Drowned	David Bowie

Has not been played in the last 2 shows.

NO2

DATE	GAP	SET	POS.	SONG BEFORE	SONG AFTER
6/25/94	646	1	1/10	***	Rift
7/8/94	9	1	2/11	Llama	The Lizards
7/16/94	6	1	3/11	Down with Disease	Stash
7/13/99	355	1	5/9	Roses Are Free	Lawn Boy

Has not been played in the last 103 shows.

Nellie Kane

DATE	GAP	SET	POS.	SONG BEFORE	SONG AFTER
7/16/93	553	1	8/10	All Things Recnsdrd	Horn
7/23/93	5	1	4/12	Caravan	Maze
7/24/93	1	1	3/10	Horn	Divided Sky
7/28/93	3	1	6/11	Foam	Split Open and
7/31/93	3	1	7/9	Foam	Divided Sky
8/3/93	2	1	2/11	Runaway Jim	Foam
8/6/93	1	1	8/10	Divided Sky	Chalk Dust Tor
8/9/93	3	1	8/11	Glide	Divided Sky
8/12/93	2	1	5/10	Guelah Papyrus	Split Open and
8/15/93	3	2	10/11	Ginseng Sullivan	Freebird
8/21/93	4	E	2/2	Amazing Grace	***
8/24/93	1	1	5/11	It's Ice	Split Open and
8/25/93	1	1	7/11	Ginseng Sullivan	Amazing Grce
12/29/93	4	E	1/2	***	Cavern
4/5/94	4	E	1/2	***	Golgi Apparat
4/6/94	1	E	2/3	Ginseng Sullivan	Sweet Adeline
4/9/94	2	1	5/10	Bathtub Gin	Julius
4/14/94	4	2	7/9	You Enjoy Myself	Dog Faced Boy
4/16/94	2	1	7/8	Fluffhead	Run Like Antel
4/22/94	5	1	7/11	All Things Recnsdrd	Divided Sky
5/3/94	8	E	1/2	***	Fire
5/10/94	5	2	9/10	Dog Faced Boy	David Bowie
5/19/94	6	E	2/2	Ginseng Sullivan	Sweet Adeline
5/27/94	7	2	7/12	Julius	My Mind's Got A Mind
5/29/94	2	2	1/10	***	Split Open and Demand
6/10/94	2	1	4/9	Sample in a Jar	Demand
7/6/94	20	E	2/4	The Old Home Place	Memories
7/8/94	1	E	1/2	***	Cavern
10/10/94	10	1	10/11	Ginseng Sullivan	Chalk Dust Tor
10/12/94	1	2	6/9	You Enjoy Myself	Foreplay/Long Time
10/14/94	2	2	6/10	Chalk Dust Torture	Beaumont Rag
10/18/94	3	2	9/10	Beaumont Rag	Llama
10/20/94	1	2	6/8	Harry Hood	Foreplay/Long Time
10/26/94	5	E	1/3	***	Foreplay/Long Time
10/28/94	2	2	11/12	The Old Home Place	Foreplay/Long Time
11/3/94	4	E	2/4	My Sweet One	Amazing Grce
11/12/94	2	2	9/12	The Old Home Place	Foreplay/Long Time
11/14/94	2	2	8/10	The Old Home Place	Sweet Adeline
11/17/94	2	E	2/4	I'm Blue, Lonesome	My Long Journey Home
12/8/94	16	2	5/8	Reba	Sweet Adeline
11/21/98	292	1	9/13	Dogs Stole Things	Foam
7/8/99	15	1	6/8	Dirt	Stash
9/14/99	23	1	9/11	Farmhouse	Taste
9/29/99	11	1	6/9	Dirt	Stash
12/7/99	13	1	6/8	Punch You in the Eye	Halley's Comet
7/1/00	29	2	9/10	Weekapaug Groove	Ghost

Has not been played in the last 31 shows.

Never

DATE	GAP	SET	POS.	SONG BEFORE	SONG AFTER
10/17/98	979	1	3/10	Sleep	Possum

Has not been played in the last 140 shows.

New Age

DATE	GAP	SET	POS.	SONG BEFORE	SONG AFTER
10/31/98	983	2	5/10	Cool it Down	Head Held High

Has not been played in the last 136 shows.

New York New York

DATE	GAP	SET	POS.	SONG BEFORE	SONG AFTER
12/31/97	940	E	1/2	***	Tweezer Repri

Has not been played in the last 179 shows.

Night Moves Jam

DATE	GAP	SET	POS.	SONG BEFORE	SONG AFTER
10/2/95	739	1	4/10	Rift	Stash

Has not been played in the last 380 shows.

No Dogs Allowed

DATE	GAP	SET	POS.	SONG BEFORE	SONG AFTER
7/23/88	58	1	13/13	Bold as Love	***
10/20/89	64	2	1/10	***	Walk Away
10/26/89	3	2	14/15	Fishman's Gull Poem	David Bowie
11/3/89	4	2	2/5	David Bowie	The Oh Kee Pa
4/21/90	53	2	3/9	Runaway Jim	Uncle Pen

Has not been played in the last 937 shows.

No Good Trying

DATE	GAP	SET	POS.	SONG BEFORE	SONG AFTER
12/7/90	237	2	10/11	Suzy Greenberg	David Bowie
12/8/90	1	2	8/9	Golgi Apparatus	You Enjoy My
12/28/90	1	2	10/12	Divided Sky	Don't Get Me Wrong

DATE	GAP	SET	POS.	SONG BEFORE	SONG AFTER

Has not been played in the last 880 shows.

Not Fade Away

DATE	GAP	SET	POS.	SONG BEFORE	SONG AFTER
4/1/86	12	E	1/1	***	***

Has not been played in the last 1107 shows.

Nowhere Fast

DATE	GAP	SET	POS.	SONG BEFORE	SONG AFTER
5/9/89	99	2	8/14	I Didn't Know	I've Turned Bad

Has not been played in the last 1020 shows.

O Mio Babbino Caro

DATE	GAP	SET	POS.	SONG BEFORE	SONG AFTER
5/27/94	630	2	11/12	Simple	Possum

Has not been played in the last 489 shows.

Ob La Di Ob La Da

DATE	GAP	SET	POS.	SONG BEFORE	SONG AFTER
10/31/94	681	2	5/30	Glass Onion	Wild Honey Pie

Has not been played in the last 438 shows.

Ob La Di Ob La Da Jam

DATE	GAP	SET	POS.	SONG BEFORE	SONG AFTER
5/6/93	547	2	8/11	Mike's Song	Rocky Top

Has not been played in the last 572 shows.

Oblivious Fool

DATE	GAP	SET	POS.	SONG BEFORE	SONG AFTER
6/13/97	878	2	8/9	Ghost	Character Zer
6/16/97	2	1	10/10	Wolfman's Brother	***
6/25/97	6	1	1/11	***	Dogs Stole Things
7/10/97	9	1	8/8	Jam	***
7/29/97	7	2	1/8	***	Run Like Antel
11/17/97	17	2	2/7	Down with Disease	Johnny B. Goode

Has not been played in the last 200 shows.

Oh! Sweet Nuthin'

DATE	GAP	SET	POS.	SONG BEFORE	SONG AFTER
10/31/98	983	2	10/10	Train Round the Bend	***

Has not been played in the last 136 shows.

On My Knees

DATE	GAP	SET	POS.	SONG BEFORE	SONG AFTER
7/17/99	10192		2/8	Funky Bitch	Jam

Has not been played in the last 100 shows.

On The Run

DATE	GAP	SET	POS.	SONG BEFORE	SONG AFTER
11/2/98	984	2	8/16	Breathe	Time

Has not been played in the last 135 shows.

On Your Way Down

DATE	GAP	SET	POS.	SONG BEFORE	SONG AFTER
6/24/88	55	1	5/11	Alumni Blues	Golgi Apparat
7/23/88	3	1	8/13	The Lizards	AC/DC Bag
7/24/88	1	2	6/8	Alumni Blues	Cities
7/30/88	2	3	2/13	La Grange	Slave
9/8/88	4	2	7/8	Good Times Bad Times	Whipping Post
9/24/88	4	1	2/10	Golgi Apparatus	Alumni Blues
2/6/89	11	2	6/7	Divided Sky	I Didn't Know
2/24/89	5	2	1/4	***	AC/DC Bag
3/30/89	6	1	5/8	The Price of Love	Ya Mar
5/1/89	5	2	4/10	Weekapaug Groove	Possum
9/16/99	940	1	9/14	Sparkle	Beauty of My Dreams
9/25/99	7	1	6/8	Limb By Limb	Sleeping Monkey
10/2/99	5	2	2/6	Tweezer	Piper

Has not been played in the last 71 shows.

Once in a Lifetime

DATE	GAP	SET	POS.	SONG BEFORE	SONG AFTER
10/31/96	835	2	4/8	The Great Curve	Houses in Motion

Has not been played in the last 284 shows.

One Meatball

DATE	GAP	SET	POS.	SONG BEFORE	SONG AFTER
2/25/97	872	1	3/9	My Soul	Li'l Red Rooster

Has not been played in the last 247 shows.

Overload

DATE	GAP	SET	POS.	SONG BEFORE	SONG AFTER
10/31/96	835	2	8/8	Listening Wind	***

Has not been played in the last 284 shows.

Oye Como Va Jam

DATE	GAP	SET	POS.	SONG BEFORE	SONG AFTER
8/28/93	584	2	11/14	You Enjoy Yourself	You Enjoy My

Has not been played in the last 535 shows.

Paul and Silas

DATE	GAP	SET	POS.	SONG BEFORE	SONG AFTER
9/13/90	207	1	9/11	Buried Alive	Bouncing
9/14/90	1	1	5/11	Reba	Stash
9/15/90	1	1	3/14	Divided Sky	The Landlady
9/16/90	1	1	9/14	Tweezer	Mike's Song
9/20/90	1	1	2/12	Reba	The Asse Festival
9/28/90	3	E	1/1	***	***
10/12/90	8	2	6/10	Divided Sky	Magilla
10/19/90	1	E	3/3	.AC/DC Bag	***
10/30/90	1	3	1/5	***	The Lizards
11/3/90	3	2	5/12	Weekapaug Groove	Stash
11/16/90	4	2	7/11	Tube	The Lizards
11/26/90	3	1	7/11	You Enjoy Yourself	David Bowie
3/15/91	28	2	4/9	Horn	Cavern
3/22/91	3	2	5/13	Foam	Stash
4/11/91	10	1	3/12	Cavern	Tweezer
4/16/91	3	1	3/9	You Enjoy Yourself	Cavern
4/18/91	1	1	5/11	The Sloth	Horn
4/19/91	1	E	1/2	***	BBFCM
4/20/91	1	1	5/13	The Squirming Coil	Cavern
5/3/91	6	1	9/12	Fee	Tweezer
5/9/91	2	1	3/10	Foam	Guelah Papyrus
5/18/91	6	1	5/9	You Enjoy Yourself	Foam
7/13/91	4	2	5/9	Flat Fee	The Lizards
10/3/91	20	2	1/11	***	Mike's Song
10/9/91	3	1	3/11	Foam	Split Open and
10/18/91	6	1	3/9	Foam	Reba
10/23/91	2	1	5/11	Destiny Unbound	It's Ice
10/28/91	3	2	5/11	Stash	Bathtub Gin
10/31/91	2	1	9/11	Bathtub Gin	You Enjoy My
11/2/91	2	1	5/10	Reba	Foam
11/8/91	2	1	5/11	Stash	Divided Sky
11/12/91	3	2	4/13	The Squirming Coil	Mike's Song
11/14/91	2	2	4/11	Fee	It's Ice
11/20/91	4	1	7/11	Stash	Bathtub Gin
11/24/91	4	1	2/9	The Sloth	Stash
11/30/91	1	1	9/11	Brother	Guelah Papyrus
12/5/91	2	1	2/10	Golgi Apparatus	Split Open and
3/11/92	6	1	3/10	My Friend My Friend	Reba
3/27/92	12	1	3/10	Reba	The Sloth
4/6/92	8	2	3/13	Bathtub Gin	Mike's Song
4/19/92	9	1	4/11	Stash	My Friend My
4/25/92	5	1	3/11	My Friend My Friend	Reba
5/16/92	15	2	3/13	It's Ice	Tweezer
7/14/92	14	2	7/10	The Squirming Coil	You Enjoy My
7/16/92	2	2	10/13	Glide	Mike's Song
11/28/92	36	2	2/12	Suzy Greenberg	Tweezer
12/6/92	7	2	4/13	Stash	Big Ball Jam
12/11/92	4	2	8/12	Bouncing	Big Ball Jam
12/30/92	5	1	7/14	Fluffhead	Reba
2/5/93	4	2	5/10	Silent in the Mornin	It's Ice
2/19/93	11	2	3/12	It's Ice	You Enjoy My
2/21/93	2	E	3/4	Good Times Bad Times	Pig in a Pen
2/23/93	2	1	10/11	The Wedge	Run Like Antel
2/26/93	2	2	2/11	Loving Cup	Tweezer
3/3/93	3	1	6/10	Guelah Papyrus	Sample in a Ja
3/6/93	2	2	4/9	Reba	Big Ball Jam
3/14/93	5	1	6/11	Stash	Sample in a Ja
3/17/93	2	1	7/11	Amazing Grace	It's Ice
3/28/93	9	2	7/9	You Enjoy Yourself	Love You
4/1/93	3	1	7/10	My Friend My Friend	Fluffhead
4/5/93	3	1	6/10	Fluffhead	Stash
4/12/93	3	2	4/10	Fee	It's Ice
4/23/93	8	2	5/12	It's Ice	Big Ball Jam
5/1/93	6	2	7/11	Halley's Comet	Mike's Song
7/22/93	14	2	8/11	Possum	T.M.W.S.I.Y.
8/8/93	13	1	9/11	Fast Enough for You	I Didn't Know
8/15/93	6	1	6/10	Fee	Stash
8/25/93	6	2	5/8	My Friend My Friend	You Enjoy My
12/30/93	5	1	5/10	Sample in a Jar	Col. Forbin's A
4/15/94	11	1	3/9	Guelah Papyrus	Harry Hood
4/20/94	4	2	3/9	Run Like an Antelope	Sample in a Ja
6/24/94	43	1	7/11	The Sloth	Horn
11/19/94	46	1	5/11	Axilla (Part II)	T.M.W.S.I.Y.
10/24/95	63	1	2/13	My Friend My Friend	Taste That Surrounds
2/28/97	120	1	2/10	Carini	My Soul
11/8/98	114	1	6/10	Fee	Roggae
11/29/98	14	1	1/11	***	Axilla

Has not been played in the last 117 shows.

Peaches En Regalia

DATE	GAP	SET	POS.	SONG BEFORE	SONG AFTER
10/15/86	14	2	1/14	***	Golgi Apparat
10/31/86	1	2	4/11	Swing Low Sweet Chrt	David Bowie
2/21/87	3	2	9/15	Lushington	Swing Low Sweet Chrt
3/23/87	2	2	2/9	Fluffhead	Ride Captain Ride
4/29/87	2	3	1/14	***	Fluffhead
5/11/87	1	1	7/12	Clod	T.M.W.S.I.Y.
8/9/87	2	2	6/11	Skin it Back	Fluffhead
8/10/87	1	1	1/7	***	Alumni Blues
8/21/87	1	1	2/11	Dog Gone Dog	Divided Sky
9/27/87	4	1	4/9	Golgi Apparatus	Take the A-Trn
10/14/87	1	1	1/12	***	Take the A-Trn
10/31/87	2	2	4/17	T.M.W.S.I.Y. Reprise	Take the A-Trn
11/18/87	1	1	7/12	Wilson	Take the A-Trn
2/7/88	3	1	6/10	Alumni Blues	Phase Dance
2/8/88	1	2	3/6	Wilson	Divided Sky
2/24/88	1	1	6/11	Wilson	Golgi Apparat
5/15/88	9	2	5/11	Wilson	Take the A-Trn
5/25/88	2	1	5/9	Alumni Blues	Golgi Apparat
6/20/88	3	1	2/11	Slave	You Enjoy My
6/21/88	1	2	9/10	Contact	Golgi Apparat
7/12/88	3	1	6/8	Happy Birthday	You Enjoy My
7/23/88	1	2	10/10	Alumni Blues	***
7/24/88	1	3	3/6	Avenu Malkenu	Jesus Just Left
8/3/88	3	3	1/8	***	Mike's Song
9/8/88	3	1	1/8	***	Walk Away
9/13/88	2	1	7/8	Wilson	Good Time Ba
9/24/88	2	1	6/10	Wilson	La Grange
11/5/88	4	2	2/11	Wilson	Bold as Love
2/6/89	7	1	4/7	Wilson	Fee
2/18/89	4	1	8/9	Wilson	Contact
3/30/89	7	3	1/6	***	Foam
4/30/89	4	1	7/9	Wilson	Run Like Antel
5/9/89	4	1	2/9	Wilson	Ya Mar
5/28/89	7	2	8/16	Ride Captain Ride	Take the A-Trn
5/28/89	1	1	4/11	Wilson	Donna Lee
12/28/93	478	1	1/10	***	Poor Heart
12/29/93	1	1	2/9	Runaway Jim	Foam
12/31/93	2	1	6/8	Reba	I Didn't Know
4/5/94	2	2	1/8	***	Ya Mar
4/9/94	3	2	3/11	Reba	Big Ball Jam
4/23/94	12	1	4/10	Fee	Poor Heart
4/30/94	5	2	4/10	Wolfman's Brother	Harry Hood
5/13/94	9	2	5/9	McGrupp	Scent of a Mul
5/22/94	7	1	5/11	Glide	Split Open and
5/27/94	4	2	2/12	Suzy Greenberg	My Friend My
6/18/94	10	2	1/10	***	David Bowie
7/10/94	17	1	3/9	Horn	Rift
10/12/94	9	2	1/9	***	David Bowie
10/22/94	8	2	1/11	***	David Bowie
10/28/94	5	2	6/12	The Lizards	Rift

DATE	GAP	SET	POS.	SONG BEFORE	SONG AFTER
11/3/94	4	1	4/9	Wilson	Glide
11/14/94	4	2	1/10	***	David Bowie
12/1/94	12	2	1/10	***	Mound
12/7/94	5	1	1/8	***	Runaway Jim
12/31/94	7	1	6/8	Mound	Divided Sky
12/1/96	144	1	1/12	***	Poor Heart
12/6/96	3	1	2/9	Wilson	Poor Heart
12/31/96	4	1	2/10	Axilla	Punch You in
2/13/97	1	1	10/12	Character Zero	Love Me
2/18/97	4	2	1/9	***	Also Sprach
2/23/97	4	2	6/9	Silent in the Mornin	Mike's Song
2/28/97	3	1	5/10	Cars Trucks Buses	Stash
9/14/99	161	2	1/5	***	AC/DC Bag
9/17/99	2	1	5/11	Lawn Boy	The Moma Dance
9/24/99	5	2	1/6	***	Possum

Has not been played in the last 77 shows.

Phase Dance

DATE	GAP	SET	POS.	SONG BEFORE	SONG AFTER
9/27/87	31	1	7/9	Possum	Good Time Ba
2/7/88	6	1	7/10	Peaches en Regalia	Dear Mrs. Reagan
2/8/88	1	1	5/7	Golgi Apparatus	Fire
2/26/88	2	1	9/13	Possum	Good Time Ba

Has not been played in the last 1079 shows.

Piano Duet

DATE	GAP	SET	POS.	SONG BEFORE	SONG AFTER
7/28/93	562	E	1/2	***	Bill Bailey
4/22/94	42	E	1/2	***	Bill Bailey

Has not been played in the last 515 shows.

Pig in a Pen

DATE	GAP	SET	POS.	SONG BEFORE	SONG AFTER
2/21/93	495	E	4/4	Paul and Silas	***
2/23/93	2	2	10/13	Weekapaug Groove	Weekapaug Gr
11/16/94	191	1	8/11	Stash	Tennessee Waltz

Has not been played in the last 431 shows.

Piggies

DATE	GAP	SET	POS.	SONG BEFORE	SONG AFTER
10/31/94	681	2	13/30	Blackbird	Rocky Raccoon

Has not been played in the last 438 shows.

Piper

DATE	GAP	SET	POS.	SONG BEFORE	SONG AFTER
6/14/97	879	2	2/8	Twist	I Saw it Again
6/19/97	2	2	5/7	Wading In Velvet Sea	Jesus Just Left
6/24/97	4	2	5/7	Twist	Wading In Velvet Sea
6/25/97	1	2	2/9	Down with Disease	Down with Dis
7/3/97	5	1	1/8	***	My Soul
7/5/97	1	1	8/13	Twist	Harry Hood
7/21/97	5	1	3/7	Dogs Stole Things	Dirt
7/30/97	6	1	7/9	Weigh	Cars Trucks Buses
8/11/97	8	2	2/6	Timber (Jerry)	Vultures
11/14/97	6	2	2/4	Wolfman's Brother	Twist
11/22/97	5	2	4/5	Black-Eyed Katy	Run Like Antel
11/30/97	5	2	5/7	Jam	When Circus Comes
12/6/97	4	2	5/7	Twist	Sleeping Monkey
12/12/97	4	2	2/7	I Saw it Again	Swept Away
12/31/97	5	2	3/6	Mike's Song	When Circus Comes
4/3/98	2	2	2/4	Roses Are Free	Loving Cup
7/1/98	4	1	7/9	Dog Faced Boy	Waste
7/6/98	4	2	3/6	Meat	Makisupa Policeman
7/8/98	1	2	4/7	Dirt	Sleeping Monkey
7/16/98	4	2	3/7	The Moma Dance	Axilla
7/19/98	2	2	3/7	Wolfman's Brother	Tweezer
7/25/98	4	2	1/8	***	Wilson
8/1/98	5	2	1/10	***	Wilson
8/8/98	5	2	4/6	Tela	Sexual Healing
8/16/98	5	2	2/8	Down with Disease	Ghost
10/18/98	4	1	3/12	Billy Breathes	Roggae
10/31/98	3	3	2/3	Wolfman's Brother	Ghost
11/4/98	2	2	3/6	The Moma Dance	Also Sprach
11/8/98	3	2	6/8	Jam	Wading In Velvet Sea
11/14/98	4	2	3/9	Something	Guyute
11/20/98	4	2	2/8	Bathtub Gin	Axilla
11/25/98	5	2	5/8	Prince Caspian	You Enjoy My
12/30/98	6	2	2/5	Down with Disease	Prince Caspian
6/30/99	2	2	7/10	Steep	Bug
7/3/99	2	2	2/7	Twist	The Moma Dance
7/13/99	7	2	2/6	Wolfman's Brother	Bug
7/18/99	4	3	2/9	My Soul	Prince Caspian
7/26/99	6	2	2/6	Wolfman's Brother	Theme From the Botto
9/10/99	6	2	3/9	The Moma Dance	Fee
9/17/99	5	2	3/8	Sand	Roggae
9/26/99	7	2	2/7	Twist	Mountains in the Mis
10/2/99	4	2	3/6	On Your Way Down	You Enjoy My
10/8/99	4	1	1/6	***	AC/DC Bag
12/3/99	4	2	4/5	Bug	Harry Hood
12/8/99	4	2	3/6	Dirt	Dog Faced Boy
12/13/99	4	1	5/6	The Moma Dance	Theme From the Botto
12/17/99	3	1	1/8	***	Meat
12/31/99	3	2	27/35	Bittersweet Motel	Free
5/21/00	1	2	5/8	Twist	Harry Hood
5/23/00	2	2	4/8	Waste	You Enjoy My
6/10/00	2	1	3/5	Sample in a Jar	Lawn Boy
6/28/00	10	1	5/6	Bathtub Gin	If I Could
7/6/00	6	2	4/7	Bug	Driver
7/8/00	2	2	2/9	Heavy Things	Rock and Roll
7/12/00	3	2	2/5	Birds of a Feather	Crosseyed and Painle
7/15/00	2	2	4/7	Makisupa Policeman	The Mango Song
9/11/00	3	2	3/5	Twist	What's the Use
9/15/00	3	2	1/5	***	The Lizards
9/23/00	5	2	6/7	Fast Enough For You	Character Zer
9/27/00	3	2	1/7	***	Gumbo
10/1/00	3	2	2/7	Roses are Free	Guy Forget
10/5/00	2	2	6/7	Walk Away	Character Zer

Has not been played in the last 2 shows.

Poor Heart

DATE	GAP	SET	POS.	SONG BEFORE	SONG AFTER
4/22/91	283	1	5/9	Reba	Llama
4/25/91	1	1	6/11	Cavern	Reba
5/2/91	2	2	2/10	Chalk Dust Torture	Divided Sky
5/10/91	4	2	4/11	Wilson	Foam
5/11/91	1	2	3/12	You Enjoy Myself	Reba
5/12/91	1	2	2/13	Bathtub Gin	The Curtain
5/17/91	2	1	5/17	Reba	The Oh Kee Pa
7/18/91	8	2	3/8	Reba	Split Open and
7/21/91	3	1	4/11	Guelah Papyrus	Split Open and
7/25/91	3	2	5/13	Llama	Jesus Just Left
7/27/91	2	1	6/16	Cavern	Stash
8/3/91	1	1	3/8	The Squirming Coil	The Sloth
9/25/91	1	1	2/11	Brother	Foam
9/26/91	1	E	2/3	Memories	Sweet Adeline
9/28/91	2	2	8/12	The Lizards	Magilla
9/29/91	1	1	5/11	It's Ice	The Landlady
10/2/91	2	1	4/10	The Squirming Coil	Cavern
10/4/91	2	1	3/10	Reba	Cavern
10/6/91	1	1	5/13	Bouncing	The Oh Kee Pa
10/10/91	1	2	3/13	Reba	Cavern
10/11/91	1	2	7/9	The Sloth	Magilla
10/15/91	3	2	5/12	Guelah Papyrus	Llama
10/17/91	1	1	6/10	Cavern	Stash
10/19/91	2	2	6/10	Horn	You Enjoy My
10/24/91	2	1	4/12	Foam	Stash
10/28/91	2	1	3/10	Cavern	Reba
10/30/91	1	2	3/11	Divided Sky	Run Like Antel
11/1/91	2	2	12/13	Cavern	Tweezer Repri
11/9/91	4	2	3/10	Fluffhead	It's Ice
11/15/91	5	2	3/14	Bathtub Gin	Mike's Song
11/21/91	4	1	3/12	Bouncing	Guelah Papyrus
11/23/91	2	2	6/13	Horn	Tweezer
12/4/91	3	1	6/11	Cavern	Brother
3/6/92	5	2	2/9	My Friend My Friend	Secret Language Inst
3/13/92	4	1	3/12	Split Open and Melt	Guelah Papyrus
3/17/92	2	2	4/11	The Sloth	Tweezer
3/21/92	3	2	6/11	My Friend My Friend	All Things Rec
3/24/92	2	1	2/13	Stash	Foam
3/26/92	2	2	4/13	Suzy Greenberg	Brother
3/31/92	4	2	5/13	Fee	Stash
4/3/92	2	1	2/11	The Landlady	Stash
4/5/92	2	1	5/11	Wilson	Stash
4/7/92	2	2	1/11	***	All Things Rec
4/12/92	2	1	2/11	Suzy Greenberg	Guelah Papyrus
4/16/92	3	2	8/12	Horn	Terrapin
4/18/92	2	1	4/11	Guelah Papyrus	Split Open and
4/22/92	3	2	8/11	You Enjoy Myself	Cracklin' Rosi
4/23/92	1	2	2/13	The Landlady	Mike's Song
4/25/92	2	1	11/11	Terrapin	***
5/1/92	3	1	3/12	My Friend My Friend	The Landlady
5/5/92	3	2	10/14	Silent in the Mornin	Llama
5/7/92	2	1	2/11	Suzy Greenberg	Buried Alive
5/9/92	2	E	1/2	***	Tweezer Repri
5/12/92	2	2	7/9	Terrapin	Llama
5/14/92	1	1	8/11	Reba	My Friend My
5/16/92	2	2	12/13	Cracklin' Rosie	Tweezer Repri
5/17/92	1	1	10/11	The Mango Song	Chalk Dust Tor
5/18/92	1	1	7/10	Foam	Horn
7/14/92	12	1	11/12	I Didn't Know	Cavern
7/16/92	2	1	1/10	***	It's Ice
7/19/92	3	1	1/5	***	Maze
7/22/92	2	1	2/7	Reba	Bouncing
8/1/92	8	1	3/7	Foam	Stash
8/14/92	1	1	1/5	***	Stash
8/17/92	2	1	2/11	Buried Alive	The Landlady
8/24/92	4	1	2/7	Buried Alive	All Things Rec
8/28/92	3	1	1/7	***	Foam
11/19/92	4	2	11/15	Big Ball Jam	Fast Enough for You
11/21/92	2	1	5/11	Glide	It's Ice
11/23/92	2	2	1/14	***	Stash
11/25/92	1	2	2/11	Buried Alive	The Landlady
11/27/92	1	2	2/13	Axilla	Possum
11/30/92	2	1	4/10	Bouncing	Stash
12/2/92	2	1	5/10	Fast Enough for You	Stash
12/4/92	2	1	3/11	Foam	Stash
12/5/92	1	2	1/13	***	Tweezer
12/7/92	2	1	2/11	Axilla	Maze
12/10/92	2	1	5/11	Fee	Split Open and
12/12/92	2	1	8/11	Split Open and Melt	All Things Rec
12/28/92	2	2	1/9	***	Split Open and
12/31/92	3	1	2/11	Buried Alive	Maze
2/3/93	1	1	9/11	My Friend My Friend	Guelah Papyrus
2/5/93	2	1	8/11	I Didn't Know	Reba
2/7/93	2	1	3/12	Buried Alive	It's Ice
2/9/93	1	1	3/10	Bouncing	My Friend My
2/11/93	2	1	3/10	Buried Alive	Stash
2/12/93	1	2	4/11	Reba	Big Ball Jam
2/13/93	1	1	3/10	Bouncing	It's Ice
2/15/93	1	2	8/12	The Wedge	Big Ball Jam
2/18/93	1	1	3/10	Guelah Papyrus	Tweezer
2/19/93	1	1	10/11	My Friend My Friend	David Bowie

DATE	GAP	SET	POS.	SONG BEFORE	SONG AFTER
2/22/93	3	1	3/10	Guelah Papyrus	Maze
2/23/93	1	E	2/2	Sweet Adeline	***
2/25/93	1	1	2/11	Buried Alive	Cavern
2/27/93	2	2	3/12	Stash	Sample in a Ja
3/2/93	1	1	2/13	Buried Alive	Stash
3/5/93	2	1	2/11	Buried Alive	Cavern
3/6/93	1	E	2/3	Sweet Adeline	Tweezer Repri
3/8/93	1	2	1/10	***	Cavern
3/12/93	2	1	2/11	Buried Alive	Cavern
3/16/93	3	1	3/11	Buried Alive	It's Ice
3/18/93	2	2	2/9	My Friend My Friend	Split Open and
3/21/93	2	1	8/11	Split Open and Melt	Punch You in
3/24/93	2	1	4/9	Fee	Maze
3/27/93	3	2	13/14	Cracklin' Rosie	Golgi Apparat
3/30/93	2	1	2/11	Buried Alive	All Things Rec
4/1/93	2	2	7/10	Tweezer	Big Ball Jam
4/2/93	1	1	2/9	Buried Alive	Foam
4/5/93	2	2	2/9	Axilla	Caravan
4/12/93	3	1	4/11	Bouncing	Stash
4/14/93	1	1	2/13	Buried Alive	Maze
4/18/93	3	2	1/12	***	Tweezer
4/21/93	2	1	2/11	Buried Alive	Foam
4/24/93	3	1	3/11	Guelah Papyrus	Stash
4/27/93	2	1	2/10	Buried Alive	Foam
4/30/93	2	1	4/12	Bouncing	Stash
5/2/93	2	1	8/11	Silent in the Mornin	Maze
5/5/93	2	2	5/10	My Friend My Friend	Weigh
5/7/93	2	1	2/11	Buried Alive	Split Open and
5/30/93	3	1	4/13	Guelah Papyrus	Foam
7/16/93	2	2	9/12	You Enjoy Myself	Purple Rain
7/18/93	2	2	2/10	Also Sprach	Run Like Antel
7/22/93	2	1	9/11	Ya Mar	Stash
7/23/93	1	2	2/11	Also Sprach	Run Like Antel
7/28/93	4	1	10/11	Silent in the Mornin	Cavern
7/30/93	2	2	5/10	Silent in the Mornin	Fluffhead
8/2/93	2	1	3/12	Guelah Papyrus	Brother
8/3/93	1	E	1/2	***	Freebird
8/6/93	1	1	2/10	Split Open and Melt	The Curtain
8/7/93	1	1	3/10	Bouncing	Stash
8/12/93	4	1	9/10	Silent in the Mornin	The Squirmin
8/14/93	2	1	10/11	Esther	Cavern
8/16/93	2	2	7/10	My Friend My Friend	Big Ball Jam
8/20/93	2	1	3/10	Harpua	Maze
8/21/93	1	1	2/10	Buried Alive	Foam
8/24/93	1	E	2/3	Halley's Comet	Sweet Adeline
12/28/93	4	1	2/10	Peaches en Regalia	Split Open and
12/31/93	3	2	3/8	Halley's Comet	It's Ice
4/6/94	3	1	3/9	Guelah Papyrus	Stash
4/11/94	4	1	2/9	Caravan	Foam
4/13/94	1	1	2/8	Buried Alive	Stash
4/16/94	3	2	2/9	Sample in a Jar	Tweezer
4/18/94	2	1	3/10	Glide	Julius
4/20/94	1	2	1/9	***	Run Like Antel
4/23/94	3	1	5/10	Peaches en Regalia	Stash
4/25/94	2	1	9/10	Tela	Split Open and
4/30/94	3	1	4/9	Stash	Sample in a Ja
5/6/94	4	1	4/9	AC/DC Bag	My Friend My
5/10/94	3	1	2/9	Buried Alive	Sample in a Ja
5/16/94	4	1	2/10	Buried Alive	Sample in a Ja
5/19/94	2	1	4/10	My Friend My Friend	Stash
5/26/94	6	1	2/10	Buried Alive	Cavern
5/28/94	2	E	1/1	***	***
6/13/94	5	1	2/9	Buried Alive	Sample in a Ja
6/17/94	3	2	3/15	Sample in a Jar	Mike's Song
6/21/94	3	2	2/16	Fire	Down with Dis
6/23/94	2	1	2/10	Buried Alive	Split Open and
6/24/94	1	2	10/13	Dog Faced Boy	Cavern
6/29/94	2	2	2/8	The Landlady	Tweezer
6/30/94	1	E	2/2	Sleeping Monkey	***
7/3/94	3	1	2/10	My Friend My Friend	Down with Dis
7/6/94	2	2	2/2	The Landlady	Tweezer
7/9/94	2	2	4/10	Fluffhead	Tweezer
7/13/94	2	1	2/11	Buried Alive	Sample in a Ja
10/7/94	4	1	4/9	Glide	Divided Sky
10/9/94	2	E	2/2	Sleeping Monkey	***
10/12/94	2	1	4/9	The Sloth	Split Open and
10/16/94	4	2	2/9	The Landlady	Julius
10/18/94	1	1	4/10	I Didn't Know	Stash
10/20/94	1	1	3/11	Golden Lady	Guelah Papyrus
10/23/94	3	1	5/11	Simple	Stash
10/27/94	3	1	10/11	Silent in the Mornin	Cavern
10/31/94	3	3	6/7	Sleeping Monkey	Run Like Antel
11/3/94	2	2	3/8	Simple	Julius
11/14/94	4	2	5/10	Slave	Julius
11/18/94	3	2	4/7	Lifeboy	Tweezer
11/22/94	3	1	2/9	Buried Alive	Horn
11/26/94	3	1	8/9	Silent in the Mornin	Cavern
11/30/94	2	1	2/10	Frankenstein	My Friend My
12/2/94	2	1	1/8	***	Also Sprach
12/4/94	3	2	4/12	Also Sprach	Mike's Song
12/9/94	3	2	2/9	Wilson	Tweezer
12/10/94	1	2	9/11	Why Don't We Do It i	Slave
12/30/94	3	2	2/8	Sample in a Jar	Tweezer
6/8/95	4	2	7/8	Lifeboy	Julius
6/14/95	4	2	2/5	Also Sprach	Tweezer
6/19/95	4	1	2/10	Theme From the Botto	AC/DC Bag
6/26/95	6	2	3/6	Free	You Enjoy My
6/28/95	1	2	2/10	Sample in a Jar	Tweezer
7/3/95	5	1	2/11	My Friend My Friend	Run Like Antel
9/28/95	2	2	2/8	Theme From the Botto	Don't You Wanna Go
10/2/95	3	1	1/10	***	Wolfman's Brother
10/6/95	3	2	1/8	***	Maze
10/15/95	6	1	2/10	Buried Alive	Slave
10/19/95	2	2	2/10	Frankenstein	Mike's Song
10/22/95	3	1	9/12	It's Ice	Sample in a Ja
10/27/95	3	2	4/9	Dog Faced Boy	Simple
10/29/95	2	1	2/12	Buried Alive	Julius
11/11/95	4	1	4/12	A Day in the Life	Weekapaug Gr
11/15/95	3	1	1/9	***	AC/DC Bag
11/19/95	3	1	3/10	Maze	Rift
11/22/95	2	E	1/2	***	Frankenstein
11/25/95	2	1	1/9	***	A Day in the Life
11/25/95	0	2	12/12	Hello My Baby	***
11/29/95	2	2	8/11	Heart and Soul	I'm Blue, Lonesome
12/1/95	2	1	4/10	Theme From the Botto	Wolfman's Brother
12/5/95	3	2	1/8	***	Bathtub Gin
12/8/95	2	1	2/9	Sample in a Jar	Simple
12/17/95	7	1	2/9	My Friend My Friend	A Day in the Life
12/29/95	2	1	2/9	My Friend My Friend	Down with Dis
6/6/96	4	1	2/8	Split Open and Melt	Runaway Jim
7/6/96	3	1	3/6	Reba	A Day in the Life
7/9/96	2	1	2/7	Theme From the Botto	Taste
7/13/96	4	1	5/10	Reba	Split Open and
7/22/96	6	1	2/8	Sample in a Jar	Cavern
7/25/96	3	1	1/8	***	Punch You in
8/2/96	1	1	5/11	Guelah Papyrus	Foam
8/5/96	2	1	2/9	Wilson	Guelah Papyrus
8/10/96	3	1	2/11	My Friend My Friend	AC/DC Bag
8/14/96	3	1	5/10	Fee	Reba
10/16/96	3	1	5/12	Buried Alive	Billy Breathes
10/23/96	6	1	2/9	Punch You in the Eye	AC/DC Bag
10/29/96	4	1	9/10	Billy Breathes	David Bowie
11/6/96	4	1	6/9	Train Song	Punch You in
11/9/96	3	1	2/10	Buried Alive	The Sloth
11/16/96	5	1	1/11	***	Down with Dis
11/18/96	1	1	3/10	Timber (Jerry)	Taste
11/24/96	4	1	1/11	***	AC/DC Bag
12/1/96	4	1	2/12	Peaches en Regalia	Cavern
12/6/96	3	1	3/9	Peaches en Regalia	Also Sprach
12/29/96	2	1	1/10	***	Caravan
2/13/97	3	1	8/12	Waste	Character Zer
2/26/97	10	2	2/11	Buried Alive	Ha Ha Ha
6/16/97	7	E	2/2	Cities	***
6/21/97	3	1	3/15	Also Sprach	Taste
6/27/97	4	1	5/8	Dogs Stole Things	Taste
7/5/97	5	1	11/13	Love You	Character Zer
7/9/97	2	2	6/6	Ghost	***
7/26/97	7	1	3/9	Dogs Stole Things	Stash
8/13/97	11	1	2/11	Amoreena	Stash
11/16/97	6	1	9/11	Scent of a Mule	Taste
11/26/97	6	2	7/8	Prince Caspian	Tweezer Repri
7/9/98	28	1	6/8	Meat	Tweezer
7/20/98	6	1	3/10	Dirt	Lawn Boy
7/28/98	5	2	2/8	The Wedge	The Mango Song
8/15/98	12	1	6/12	Split Open and Melt	The Moma Dance
11/9/98	14	1	7/10	Dogs Stole Things	Free
7/1/99	19	1	10/10	Back on the Train	***
7/15/99	9	1	5/10	Horn	Axilla
8/1/99	13	1	8/10	Split Open and Melt	Bouncing
9/12/99	4	1	2/10	First Tube	Mozambique
9/21/99	6	1	1/9	***	Sample in a Ja
10/2/99	8	1	5/9	Quinn the Eskimo	Roggae
12/2/99	7	1	7/10	Wading In Velvet Sea	Sample in a Ja
12/31/99	15	1	7/14	Bouncing	Roggae
6/9/00	4	1	4/9	Billy Breathes	Golgi Apparat
6/22/00	7	1	7/9	Bug	Roggae
7/1/00	7	1	4/11	Axilla	Sample in a Ja
7/8/00	5	1	4/9	My Soul	Wolfman's Brother
9/22/00	15	1	3/9	Meat	Wilson

Has not been played in the last 11 shows.

Poor Heart Reprise

11/25/95 772	E	1/2		***	Fire

Has not been played in the last 347 shows.

Possum

DATE	GAP	SET	POS.	SONG BEFORE	SONG AFTER
10/30/85	8	1	3/11	Dog Gone Dog	Slave
4/15/86	5	1	10/14	Dog Gone Dog	You Enjoy My
2/13/87	4	1	2/14	Sneakin' Sally	Golgi Apparat
3/6/87	2	2	5/7	Tell Me Smthg Good	Freeworld
4/24/87	2	1	3/14	AC/DC Bag	Fluffhead
5/11/87	2	1	3/12	Fluff's Travels	Slave
5/20/87	1	1	6/9	Lushington	Harry Hood
8/9/87	1	1	5/11	The Chase	Sneakin' Sally
8/10/87	1	2	3/10	AC/DC Bag	Fluffhead
8/29/87	2	1	6/13	McGrupp	Harry Hood
9/2/87	1	1	8/13	The Chase	BBFCFM
9/21/87	1	1	11/11	AC/DC Bag	***
9/27/87	1	1	6/9	Take the A-Train	Phase Dance
10/14/87	1	1	7/12	Fluffhead	David Bowie
10/31/87	1	1	9/11	AC/DC Bag	You Enjoy My
11/19/87	2	3	3/14	Suzy Greenberg	Divided Sky
1/27/88	1	1	4/9	AC/DC Bag	Jesus Just Left
2/7/88	1	2	6/9	Fee	The Lizards
2/26/88	3	1	8/13	AC/DC Bag	Phase Dance
3/12/88	2	2	10/11	The Sloth	Run Like Antel
3/21/88	1	1	11/15	AC/DC Bag	Dinner and a
3/31/88	1	1	5/14	AC/DC Bag	Fluffhead
4/22/88	2	2	11/13	AC/DC Bag	Ballad - Curtis Loew
5/15/88	1	2	11/11	AC/DC Bag	***
5/21/88	1	2	2/9	La Grange	The Lizards
6/19/88	3	1	3/8	Funky Bitch	Golgi Apparat
6/20/88	1	2	7/9	Take the A-Train	Ballad - Curtis Loew
6/24/88	2	1	2/11	The Lizards	Jam
7/23/88	3	1	10/13	AC/DC Bag	Walk Away
7/30/88	3	3	6/13	Walk Away	Sneakin' Sally
9/8/88	4	2	1/8	***	You Enjoy My
9/24/88	4	2	4/7	Walk Away	Fee
10/31/88	2	1	3/12	You Enjoy Myself	Suzy Greenber
11/3/88	1	1	4/7	Fluffhead	Fee
11/5/88	1	1	5/11	You Enjoy Myself	Take the A-Trn
11/11/88	1	1	5/8	Foam	Col. Forbin's A

DATE	GAP	SET	POS.	SONG BEFORE	SONG AFTER
12/10/88	2	2	6/7	AC/DC Bag	Good Time Ba
1/26/89	3	2	6/10	The Sloth	Contact
2/7/89	2	1	5/9	The Sloth	Mike's Song
2/24/89	4	1	10/10	Golgi Apparatus	***
3/3/89	1	2	5/12	Fee	Walk Away
3/4/89	1	2	1/5	***	Fluffhead
3/24/89	3	1	1/10	***	Mike's Song
4/20/89	3	1	9/12	The Sloth	McGrupp
4/30/89	2	E	1/1	***	***
5/1/89	1	2	5/10	On Your Way Down	Icculus
5/6/89	2	1	8/13	The Sloth	Bold As Love
5/9/89	1	1	8/9	The Sloth	Divided Sky
5/12/89	1	1	12/15	The Sloth	Split Open and
5/13/89	1	1	7/12	Fluffhead	Foam
5/20/89	1	1	8/8	I Didn't Know	***
5/26/89	2	3	4/4	Ballad - Curtis Loew	***
5/28/89	2	2	10/16	Take the A-Train	Contact
6/23/89	1	2	6/7	Split Open and Melt	David Bowie
6/30/89	1	1	4/7	McGrupp	Donna Lee
8/17/89	1	3	4/8	Punch You in the Eye	Halley's Comet
8/26/89	3	1	8/8	You Enjoy Myself	***
9/9/89	1	2	7/7	Walk Away	***
9/21/89	2	2	5/9	Bundle of Joy	Bathtub Gin
10/1/89	1	2	6/11	Bundle of Joy	You Enjoy My
10/6/89	1	1	11/13	Harry Hood	Highway to Hell
10/7/89	1	2	3/9	Bundle of Joy	Happy Birth-day
10/12/89	1	1	6/8	You Enjoy Myself	Divided Sky
10/13/89	1	1	4/4	The Sloth	***
10/14/89	1	2	3/4	Highway to Hell	Harpua
10/21/89	2	2	4/10	Wilson	Reba
10/22/89	1	2	9/9	Fee	***
10/26/89	1	2	10/15	The Chase	Punch You in
10/31/89	2	1	9/9	Bathtub Gin	***
11/10/89	4	2	12/12	If I Only Had a Brai	***
11/18/89	3	1	6/11	My Sweet One	Divided Sky
11/30/89	1	2	2/11	Reba	Col. Forbin's A
12/1/89	1	E	2/2	Lawn Boy	***
12/3/89	1	2	10/14	Fee	Love You
12/7/89	1	2	9/11	Lawn Boy	Undun
12/8/89	1	2	7/7	You Enjoy Myself	***
12/15/89	2	2	2/8	I Didn't Know	Divided Sky
12/16/89	1	E	1/1	***	***
1/29/90	7	1	7/10	Jesus Just Left	Highway to Hell
2/1/90	1	1	7/11	Divided Sky	Fee
2/10/90	2	1	7/10	Bouncing	Carolina
2/15/90	1	2	3/5	Bouncing	Foam
2/16/90	2		5/7	The Sloth	Ballad - Curtis Loew
2/23/90	3	1	3/11	You Enjoy Myself	Foam
2/24/90	1	1	6/8	Esther	I Didn't Know
2/25/90	1	1	11/11	Rift	***
3/1/90	1	1	7/7	You Enjoy Myself	***
3/3/90	2	1	12/12	You Enjoy Myself	***
3/7/90	1	1	2/6	Reba	Esther
3/8/90	1	1	3/10	You Enjoy Myself	Ya Mar
3/9/90	1	1	9/11	The Sloth	Donna Lee
3/11/90	1	1	13/13	The Squirming Coil	***
3/28/90	2	1	1/12	***	Ya Mar
4/4/90	1	1	5/8	Take the A-Train	Foam
4/5/90	1	1	1/9	***	Ya Mar
4/7/90	2	1	8/12	Bathtub Gin	Tweezer
4/8/90	1	1	8/8	Uncle Pen	***
4/12/90	2	1	5/11	Uncle Pen	You Enjoy My
4/13/90	1	2	9/10	Caravan	Highway to Hell
4/18/90	2	1	10/10	Take the A-Train	***
4/19/90	1	2	1/8	***	McGrupp
4/20/90	1	1	10/10	The Famous Mockingbi	***
4/22/90	2	1	5/12	Suzy Greenberg	I Didn't Know
4/26/90	2	1	1/9	***	Foam
4/28/90	1	1	7/11	Bouncing	You Enjoy My
4/29/90	1	1	2/13	Carolina	Ya Mar
5/4/90	1	2	6/10	Bouncing	Reba
5/6/90	1	1	1/8	***	Bouncing
5/7/90	1	1	5/5	If I Only Had a Brai	***
5/10/90	1	1	8/8	Bathtub Gin	***
5/11/90	1	1	7/9	Bouncing	Reba
5/13/90	1	2	11/12	Sweet Adeline	La Grange
5/19/90	2	2	1/10	***	Reba
5/23/90	1	1	9/10	Bouncing	Sweet Adeline
5/24/90	1	2	3/11	Dinner and a Movie	I Didn't Know
5/31/90	2	1	1/12	***	You Enjoy My
6/1/90	1	1	9/12	Terrapin	Fee
6/2/90	1	1	5/9	Reba	The Lizards
6/5/90	1	1	12/12	Lawn Boy	***
6/7/90	1	1	4/9	Donna Lee	Fee
6/8/90	1	2	1/7	***	My Sweet One
6/9/90	1	1	1/10	***	Lawn Boy
6/16/90	1	1	10/10	Lawn Boy	***
9/13/90	1	1	11/11	Bouncing	***
9/15/90	2	2	8/8	Harry Hood	***
9/20/90	2	2	9/14	Suzy Greenberg	Funky Bitch
9/22/90	2	2	10/10	Lawn Boy	***
9/29/90	2	1	7/9	Bouncing	Magilla
10/4/90	2	1	4/10	Esther	The Squirmin
10/5/90	1	2	8/8	Fee	***
10/6/90	1	1	10/13	Esther	If I Only Had a Brai
10/8/90	2	1	10/10	The Oh Kee Pa Ceremo	***
10/12/90	1	2	1/10	***	Fee
10/19/90	1	1	9/15	Cavern	Bathtub Gin
10/30/90	1	1	9/9	The Squirming Coil	***
10/31/90	1	2	2/11	Buried Alive	The Squirmin
11/2/90	1	1	12/14	The Asse Festival	Buried Alive
11/2/90	0	1	14/14	Buried Alive	***
11/3/90	1	2	10/12	Reba	Love You
11/8/90	2	1	2/12	The Landlady	The Lizards
11/10/90	1	2	8/8	Bike	***
11/16/90	1	2	11/11	I Didn't Know	***
11/17/90	1	2	8/12	Love You	Lawn Boy
11/24/90	1	1	2/11	Buried Alive	Foam
11/30/90	2	1	11/11	Llama	***
12/28/90	4	2	2/12	The Landlady	The Squirmin
12/31/90	2	1	12/12	Buried Alive	***
2/7/91	4	1	8/10	Bouncing	The Squirmin
2/14/91	3	2	12/12	The Landlady	***
2/16/91	2	E	3/5	Fire	Rocky Mountain Way J
2/16/91	0	E	5/5	Rocky Mountain Way J	***
2/20/91	2	1	3/11	Cavern	The Squirmin
2/26/91	2	2	8/12	Destiny Unbound	The Lizards
2/27/91	1	2	10/11	Love You	Rocky Top
3/1/91	2	2	8/11	The Sloth	Love You
3/6/91	1	1	5/11	The Squirming Coil	Cavern
3/15/91	4	2	2/9	Buried Alive	Horn
3/16/91	1	E	2/2	Manteca	***
3/23/91	3	1	7/10	The Curtain	Col. Forbin's A
3/29/91	2	2	1/8	***	I Didn't Know
3/31/91	1	1	9/13	Esther	I Didn't Know
4/2/91	1	E	2/2	Magilla	***
4/4/91	2	1	8/10	The Famous Mockingbi	Carolina
4/6/91	2	2	11/11	Terrapin	***
4/11/91	1	E	2/2	Fee	***
4/15/91	2	2	9/11	The Lizards	Magilla
4/18/91	2	1	10/11	The Squirming Coil	Harpua
4/21/91	3	2	1/11	***	Fee
4/27/91	3	2	2/13	The Curtain	T.M.W.S.I.Y.
5/2/91	1	2	10/10	Buried Alive	***
5/4/91	2	2	9/9	Rocky Top	***
5/10/91	2	1	10/10	The Lizards	***
5/17/91	4	2	1/9	***	Guelah Pa-pyrus
5/18/91	1	1	9/9	Cavern	***
5/19/91	1	E	1/1	***	***
7/14/91	4	1	11/11	I Didn't Know	***
7/18/91	2	2	8/8	I Didn't Know	***
7/20/91	2	E	1/1	***	***
7/24/91	3	2	1/10	***	Guelah Pa-pyrus
7/27/91	3	1	11/16	T.M.W.S.I.Y. Reprise	I Didn't Know
8/3/91	1	3	8/8	Buried Alive	***
9/25/91	1	1	11/11	Reba	***
9/27/91	2	2	1/10	***	Tela
10/2/91	4	E	1/3	***	I Didn't Know
10/3/91	1	1	10/10	Cavern	***
10/6/91	2	E	2/3	Sweet Adeline	Llama
10/11/91	2	2	9/9	Magilla	***
10/12/91	1	1	2/9	Buried Alive	Foam
10/17/91	3	2	9/9	Love You	***
10/23/91	2	3	10/10	You Enjoy Myself	***
10/24/91	1	2	11/11	Terrapin	***
10/27/91	1	E	2/2	Glide	***
10/30/91	2	1	7/7	The Lizards	***
11/2/91	3	1	10/10	The Famous Mockingbi	***
11/7/91	1	2	11/11	Love You	***
11/9/91	2	E	2/2	Glide	***
11/13/91	2	2	9/9	Terrapin	***
11/15/91	2	2	14/14	Bouncing	***
11/20/91	3	1	2/11	Buried Alive	Col. Forbin's A
11/22/91	2	1	1/11	***	Cavern
12/5/91	5	1	10/10	Bouncing	***
12/6/91	1	2	10/12	Whipping Post	Wait
12/6/91	0	2	12/12	Wait	***
12/31/91	1	1	1/10	***	Foam
3/6/92	1	2	9/9	NICU	***
3/13/92	4	2	12/12	Secret Language Inst	***
3/14/92	1	2	10/10	Cracklin' Rosie	***
3/17/92	1	1	2/11	Buried Alive	Cavern
3/20/92	2	2	12/12	Secret Language Inst	***
3/26/92	5	2	13/13	Cracklin' Rosie	***
3/31/92	4	2	13/13	Love You	***
4/3/92	2	2	3/9	The Sloth	Mound
4/5/92	2	1	10/11	It's Ice	Sweet Adeline
4/7/92	2	1	2/12	Buried Alive	It's Ice
4/13/92	3	2	11/11	Love You	***
4/16/92	2	1	2/12	Buried Alive	It's Ice
4/18/92	2	1	7/11	Esther	It's Ice
4/21/92	1	2	6/11	Guelah Papyrus	It's Ice
4/23/92	2	1	11/11	I Didn't Know	***
4/29/92	3	2	2/11	The Landlady	Mound
5/1/92	2	1	12/12	I Didn't Know	It's Ice
5/3/92	2	1	2/10	The Landlady	It's Ice
5/7/92	3	1	11/11	Guelah Papyrus	***
5/10/92	3	3	10/10	You Enjoy Myself	***
5/12/92	1	1	5/12	The Sloth	It's Ice
5/14/92	1	2	13/13	Cracklin' Rosie	***
5/17/92	3	2	2/11	The Curtain	Guelah Pa-pyrus
6/30/92	7	1	4/6	Guelah Papyrus	Sweet Adeline
7/12/92	5	1	11/11	Glide	***
7/15/92	2	E	1/3	***	Vacuum Solo
7/15/92	0	E	3/3	Vacuum Solo	***
7/21/92	5	1	2/7	All Things Recnsdrd	It's Ice
7/30/92	7	1	8/8	I Didn't Know	***
11/21/92	20	1	11/11	The Famous Mockingbi	***
11/27/92	4	2	3/13	Poor Heart	Glide
12/2/92	4	2	2/11	Wilson	Mound
12/4/92	2	2	4/10	Esther	It's Ice
12/6/92	2	E	1/1	***	***
12/11/92	4	2	12/12	Faht	***
12/30/92	5	2	8/12	T.M.W.S.I.Y. Reprise	Big Ball Jam
2/3/93	2	2	11/11	Big Ball Jam	***
2/6/93	3	2	14/14	Buried Alive	***
2/10/93	3	2	11/11	Cracklin' Rosie	***
2/17/93	5	1	2/11	Buried Alive	Weigh
2/20/93	3	1	4/11	The Sloth	Weigh
2/23/93	3	2	13/13	Terrapin	***
3/5/93	6	1	11/11	I Didn't Know	***
3/12/93	4	1	4/11	Cavern	Guelah Pa-pyrus
3/21/93	7	1	11/11	Lawn Boy	***
3/25/93	3	1	4/11	It's Ice	Bouncing
3/28/93	3	2	9/9	Love You	***

DATE	GAP	SET	POS.	SONG BEFORE	SONG AFTER
4/1/93	3	2	3/10	The Curtain	Fee
4/9/93	4	2	10/10	Love You	***
4/18/93	6	2	5/12	Silent in the Mornin	Mound
4/21/93	2	2	1/11	***	Mound
4/25/93	4	1	2/11	The Landlady	Bouncing
4/30/93	3	1	12/12	All Things Recnsdrd	***
5/3/93	3	1	9/11	The Famous Mockingbi	Lawn Boy
5/6/93	2	1	9/13	Fluffhead	Lawn Boy
5/30/93	4	E	1/1	***	***
7/15/93	1	2	7/11	Lifeboy	Faht
7/22/93	5	2	7/11	Contact	Paul and Silas
7/29/93	6	1	10/10	The Famous Mockingbi	***
8/8/93	7	2	7/11	Fluffhead	Big Ball Jam
8/12/93	3	2	10/10	Golgi Apparatus	***
8/16/93	4	1	2/9	Axilla	Horn
8/21/93	3	2	1/10	***	Horn
8/25/93	2	2	2/8	Buried Alive	Mound
12/28/93	3	1	10/10	Fee	***
12/31/93	3	2	6/8	Fee	Lawn Boy
4/4/94	1	1	9/9	It's Ice	***
4/11/94	6	E	1/1	***	***
4/21/94	8	2	9/10	Big Ball Jam	Amazing Grce
4/30/94	7	2	8/10	McGrupp	Purple Rain
5/12/94	8	2	8/11	Lifeboy	Love You
5/23/94	9	2	7/7	You Enjoy Myself	***
5/27/94	3	2	12/12	O Mio Babbino Caro	***
6/10/94	4	2	6/9	Sparkle	I Wanna Be Like You
6/14/94	3	2	9/9	Bike	***
7/1/94	13	2	8/11	T.M.W.S.I.Y. Reprise	Terrapin
7/13/94	8	2	1/13	***	Cavern
10/9/94	6	2	8/8	Contact	***
10/16/94	6	1	10/10	Axilla	***
10/25/94	6	2	11/11	If I Only Had a Brai	***
11/2/94	6	2	5/7	Axilla (Part II)	The Lizards
11/18/94	8	2	7/7	Contact	***
11/26/94	6	1	2/9	My Friend My Friend	Guyute
12/4/94	6	1	9/9	Sweet Adeline	***
12/8/94	3	2	1/8	***	My Mind's Got A Mind
12/29/94	4	1	9/9	I Didn't Know	***
6/7/95	4	1	1/10	***	Weigh
6/14/95	5	1	6/12	Cavern	All Things Rec
6/19/95	4	2	8/8	Acoustic Army	***
6/26/95	6	1	10/10	Tela	***
6/30/95	3	2	2/10	Also Sprach	Ha Ha Ha
7/3/95	3	2	9/10	A Day in the Life	The Squirmin
9/27/95	1	E	1/1	***	***
10/7/95	8	1	5/9	Mound	The Mango Song
10/11/95	2	2	1/11	***	Bathtub Gin
10/19/95	5	2	10/10	Suspicious Minds	***
10/22/95	3	2	2/11	Golgi Apparatus	Catapult
10/27/95	3	2	9/9	Bouncing	***
10/29/95	2	2	8/10	Shaggy Dog	Lifeboy
11/12/95	5	2	7/8	Cracklin' Rosie	Tweezer Repri
11/16/95	3	2	9/9	Amazing Grace	***
11/29/95	4	2	4/11	Simple	You Enjoy My
12/2/95	3	1	10/10	Bouncing	***
12/7/95	3	1	9/10	Bouncing	Hello My Baby
12/15/95	6	1	10/10	Free	***
12/28/95	1	1	9/9	Fast Enough for You	***
7/15/96	15	1	5/8	Guyute	I Didn't Know
8/2/96	9	1	11/11	Hello My Baby	***
8/7/96	4	2	7/10	The Famous Mockingbi	Life on Mars
8/12/96	2	2	9/9	Golgi Apparatus	***
8/17/96	4	3	6/7	A Day in the Life	Tweezer Repri
10/21/96	5	1	10/10	Waste	***
10/27/96	5	E	1/2	***	Carolina
11/3/96	4	2	7/8	Life on Mars	Tweezer Repri
11/30/96	17	E	1/1	***	***
12/30/96	7	E	1/1	***	***
3/1/97	14	1	10/10	Hello My Baby	***
7/23/97	24	1	10/10	Billy Breathes	***
7/29/97	3	E	1/1	***	***
11/19/97	18	E	1/1	***	***

DATE	GAP	SET	POS.	SONG BEFORE	SONG AFTER
12/3/97	9	2	2/6	David Bowie	Jam
12/7/97	3	2	6/6	Guyute	***
12/29/97	6	2	3/5	David Bowie	Tube
4/5/98	6	2	6/6	Shafty	Jam
7/6/98	6	E	1/1	***	***
7/19/98	7	E	1/2	***	Tweezer Repri
8/2/98	10	2	1/6	***	Ghost
8/8/98	4	1	7/8	Farmhouse	Sweet Jane
8/12/98	1	4	4/8	Funky Bitch	Roggae
8/16/98	2	1	11/11	Guyute	***
10/17/98	3	1	4/10	Never	I'm Blue, Lonesome
10/29/98	2	2	1/7	***	The Moma Dance
11/6/98	5	1	1/7	***	Wilson
11/20/98	10	1	10/13	Train Song	Roggae
11/24/98	2	2	4/6	Tweezer	Wading In Velvet Sea
11/29/98	4	2	4/8	Makisupa Policeman	Wipeout
11/29/98	0	2	6/8	Wipeout	Bathtub Gin
12/30/98	3	E	2/2	Grind	***
7/13/99	11	2	4/6	Run Like an Antelope	***
7/23/99	7	1	9/9	Strange Design	***
8/1/99	7	2	1/9	***	Tweezer
9/12/99	4	1	10/10	Lawn Boy	***
9/24/99	8	2	2/6	Peaches en Regalia	Wolfman's Brother
10/3/99	7	2	2/8	Twist	T.M.W.S.I.Y.
10/7/99	2	1	6/9	Frankie Says	When Circus Comes
10/9/99	2	1	8/8	Sparkle	***
12/3/99	3	1	7/8	AC/DC Bag	Slave
12/11/99	6	E	1/1	***	***
12/16/99	4	1	10/10	Camel Walk	***
12/18/99	2	2	5/10	Silent In The Mornin	Mike's Song
12/30/99	1	1	8/12	Big Alligator Song	Farmhouse
5/21/00	2	1	4/7	The Squirming Coil	The Moma Dance
6/11/00	5	1	7/9	Dirt	It's Ice
6/23/00	6	E	2/2	Brian and Robert	***
6/30/00	5	1	10/10	Tweezer Reprise	***
7/8/00	6	2	9/9	Silent in the Mornin	***
9/9/00	7	1	1/8	***	My Friend My
9/15/00	4	E	1/1	***	***
10/5/00	13	1	10/10	Horn	***

Has not been played in the last 2 shows.

Prep School Hippie

DATE	GAP	SET	POS.	SONG BEFORE	SONG AFTER
9/27/85	6	1	6/8	Alumni Blues	Dear Mrs. Reagan
10/30/85	2	1	9/11	Alumni Blues	Skippy Wondermouse
2/3/86	3	1	6/7	Alumni Blues	Run Like Antel
4/15/86	2	1	3/14	Dear Mrs. Reagan	Quinn the Eskimo
12/6/86	3	1	14/14	Sneakin' Sally	***

Has not been played in the last 1103 shows.

Prince Caspian

DATE	GAP	SET	POS.	SONG BEFORE	SONG AFTER
6/8/95	714	1	8/9	Reba	Chalk Dust Tor
6/10/95	2	1	3/9	Llama	It's Ice
6/20/95	7	2	3/9	Chalk Dust Torture	Uncle Pen
6/23/95	2	1	3/8	Chalk Dust Torture	Reba
7/1/95	7	1	6/9	It's Ice	Split Open and
10/8/95	12	1	7/9	I'm Blue, Lonesome	Uncle Pen
10/13/95	2	1	6/9	I'm Blue, Lonesome	Split Open and
10/17/95	3	2	2/6	Mound	Fog that Surrounds
10/24/95	5	1	12/13	Acoustic Army	Split Open and
10/28/95	3	1	9/10	Acoustic Army	Run Like Antel
11/9/95	3	1	3/8	Divided Sky	Punch You in
11/15/95	5	1	5/9	Rift	Sparkle
11/21/95	4	1	3/10	Chalk Dust Torture	Divided Sky
12/5/95	8	1	1/10	***	Runaway Jim
12/8/95	4	1	8/9	Acoustic Army	Good Time Ba

DATE	GAP	SET	POS.	SONG BEFORE	SONG AFTER
12/11/95	2	1	4/12	Stash	Reba
12/30/95	8	1	1/13	***	Also Sprach
7/12/96	11	2	2/9	It's Ice	Mike's Song
7/21/96	6	2	8/9	Simple	Suzy Greenber
8/2/96	5	2	6/9	Fluffhead	The Horse
8/6/96	3	2	3/8	Tweezer	A Day in the Life
8/12/96	3	2	4/9	Simple	McGrupp
10/16/96	5	2	7/10	Steep	Run Like Antel
10/19/96	3	1	8/9	Down with Disease	Frankenstein
10/25/96	4	2	2/12	Tube	Timber (Jerry)
10/27/96	2	2	4/9	Rift	Ya Mar
10/31/96	2	1	5/10	You Enjoy Myself	Reba
11/8/96	5	1	6/9	Down with Disease	Reba
11/13/96	2	2	4/7	Jam	You Enjoy My
11/15/96	2	1	6/11	Punch You in the Eye	Ginseng Sullivan
11/22/96	4	2	2/10	Down with Disease	Maze
11/30/96	5	1	9/10	Uncle Pen	Chalk Dust Tor
12/4/96	3	2	3/9	Mike's Song	Sparkle
12/31/96	5	2	8/9	Harry Hood	Character Zer
2/13/97	1	E	1/2	***	Johnny B. Goode
2/17/97	3	2	7/7	Suzy Greenberg	***
2/21/97	3	2	9/9	Waste	***
2/25/97	3	2	8/10	Down with Disease	La Grange
2/28/97	2	2	3/9	Drowned	Frankenstein
3/18/97	3	2	3/9	Drowned	David Bowie
6/14/97	2	1	10/10	Free	***
6/19/97	2	2	7/7	Jesus Just Left	***
6/24/97	4	1	11/12	Free	Rocky Top
7/5/97	7	1	6/13	Theme From the Botto	Twist
7/9/97	2	1	2/8	Punch You in the Eye	Ginseng Sullivan
7/30/97	9	2	8/9	Uncle Pen	Fire
8/6/97	4	2	4/7	Ghost	Cars Trucks Buses
8/8/97	1	2	5/6	Loving Cup	Chalk Dust Tor
8/17/97	7	3	7/7	Scent of a Mule	***
11/13/97	4	1	4/8	Punch You in the Eye	Bouncing
11/21/97	5	1	8/8	Chalk Dust Torture	***
11/26/97	3	2	6/8	Punch You In The Eye	Poor Heart
11/29/97	2	2	4/6	Harry Hood	Suzy Greenber
12/3/97	3	2	4/5	Jam	Frankenstein
12/12/97	6	2	5/7	Steep	Izabella
12/31/97	5	3	5/6	Maze	Loving Cup
4/5/98	4	2	3/8	Ya Mar	Maze
7/2/98	3	2	3/4	Runaway Jim	You Enjoy My
7/20/98	11	2	5/6	Sea and Sand	Harry Hood
7/28/98	5	2	7/8	Maze	You Enjoy My
8/6/98	6	2	5/7	NICU	The Mango Song
10/15/98	9	2	6/10	Wading In Velvet Sea	Frankie Says
10/30/98	4	2	6/7	Jam	Golgi Apparat
11/6/98	4	2	4/7	Simple	Fluffhead
11/25/98	13	2	4/8	Drowned	Piper
11/28/98	2	2	6/9	Scent of a Mule	Crossroads
12/30/98	2	2	3/5	Piper	The Squirmin
7/1/99	3	2	2/3	Down with Disease	You Enjoy My
7/8/99	4	2	3/9	If I Only Had a Brai	Jesus Just Left
7/18/99	8	3	3/9	Piper	Wilson
7/21/99	2	2	4/6	My Left Toe	Weekapaug Gr
7/31/99	7	2	4/6	Wading In Velvet Sea	Fluffhead
9/11/99	4	2	5/6	Maze	Harry Hood
9/16/99	3	2	7/8	Limb by Limb	Julius
9/25/99	7	2	4/8	The Squirming Coil	Rock and Roll
10/7/99	2	2	7/9	McGrupp	Golgi Apparat
10/10/99	3	2	3/6	You Enjoy Myself	Train Song
12/12/99	9	2	2/5	Drowned	The Squirmin
12/31/99	7	2	8/35	Twist	Rock and Roll
6/13/00	7	2	7/9	Roggae	Rocky Top
6/24/00	6	2	8/8	The Squirming Coil	***
7/6/00	8	1	10/12	The Inlaw Josie Wale	Golgi Apparat
7/12/00	5	2	4/5	Crosseyed and Painle	Meatstick
9/14/00	7	2	4/5	Dog Faced Boy	Loving Cup

DATE	GAP	SET	POS.	SONG BEFORE	SONG AFTER
9/18/00	3	1	10/10	Sleep	***

Has not been played in the last 13 shows.

Proud Mary

DATE	GAP	SET	POS.	SONG BEFORE	SONG AFTER
12/2/83	0	1	2/6	Long Cool Woman	In the Midnight Hour

Has not been played in the last 1119 shows.

Psycho Killer

DATE	GAP	SET	POS.	SONG BEFORE	SONG AFTER
12/7/97	932	1	2/12	AC/DC Bag	Jesus Just Left

Has not been played in the last 187 shows.

Psycho Killer Jam

DATE	GAP	SET	POS.	SONG BEFORE	SONG AFTER
3/30/93	521	2	10/15	Weekapaug Groove	Weekapaug Gr

Has not been played in the last 598 shows.

Punch Me in the Eye

DATE	GAP	SET	POS.	SONG BEFORE	SONG AFTER
4/24/87	21	1	7/14	Dave's Energy Guide	Alumni Blues

Has not been played in the last 1098 shows.

Punch You in

DATE	GAP	SET	POS.	SONG BEFORE	SONG AFTER
8/17/89	109	3	3/8	Bold as Love	Possum
8/19/89	1	1	6/13	AC/DC Bag	Rocky Top
9/9/89	3	1	8/11	Bathtub Gin	Wilson
10/26/89	12	2	11/15	Possum	In a Hole
11/3/89	4	1	8/10	You Enjoy Myself	Reba
11/9/89	1	2	5/9	Who Do? We Do!	The Lizards
2/5/93	352	1	6/11	Sparkle	I Didn't Know
2/9/93	3	2	1/12	***	Mike's Song
2/18/93	7	2	4/12	The Lizards	Mike's Song
2/21/93	3	1	3/10	Buried Alive	Uncle Pen
2/23/93	2	2	5/13	The Lizards	All Things Rec
2/27/93	3	1	8/10	Sparkle	Lawn Boy
3/6/93	4	1	6/10	Mound	Bouncing
3/9/93	2	1	8/10	Glide	I Didn't Know
3/14/93	3	1	10/11	Indian War Dance	Runaway Jim
3/21/93	5	1	9/11	Poor Heart	Lawn Boy
3/26/93	4	1	4/10	Foam	Fee
3/31/93	4	1	6/10	Mound	Sample in a Ja
4/5/93	4	2	4/9	Caravan	Tweezer
4/21/93	9	1	9/11	Rift	I Didn't Know
5/2/93	9	2	2/10	Llama	You Enjoy My
7/23/93	14	1	8/12	Silent in the Mornin	Runaway Jim
8/8/93	12	1	7/11	Silent in the Mornin	Fast Enough for You
12/30/93	17	2	5/9	Silent in the Mornin	McGrupp
4/8/94	5	1	7/13	I Didn't Know	The Horse
4/22/94	12	1	4/11	Uncle Pen	Sample in a Ja
4/30/94	6	1	6/9	Sample in a Jar	Rift
5/14/94	10	2	8/11	T.M.W.S.I.Y. Reprise	Fast Enough for You
5/23/94	7	2	5/7	Sparkle	You Enjoy My
5/27/94	3	1	7/9	If I Could	Harry Hood
6/17/94	9	1	6/9	If I Could	Bathtub Gin
6/23/94	5	1	9/10	Silent in the Mornin	Julius
7/5/94	9	2	1/11	***	Sparkle
10/14/94	15	1	6/12	Silent in the Mornin	Bathtub Gin
12/8/94	37	1	5/10	Scent of a Mule	Simple
6/19/95	17	1	5/10	Tela	Reba
6/28/95	7	1	5/8	Reba	Stash
10/19/95	21	1	4/11	Horn	Esther
10/29/95	8	1	4/12	Julius	Cars Trucks Buses
11/9/95	2	1	4/8	Prince Caspian	Simple
11/18/95	7	1	5/8	Lawn Boy	Slave
12/4/95	11	1	4/11	Divided Sky	Stash
12/12/95	6	1	5/10	Lifeboy	The Horse
12/31/95	8	1	1/10	***	The Sloth
7/15/96	12	1	2/8	My Friend My Friend	Fast Enough for You
7/25/96	8	1	2/8	Poor Heart	Sample in a Ja
8/2/96	1	E	1/1	***	***
8/7/96	4	1	1/10	***	Sparkle
8/13/96	3	1	7/10	The Old Home Place	Llama

DATE	GAP	SET	POS.	SONG BEFORE	SONG AFTER
8/17/96	3	1	2/10	The Old Home Place	Reba
10/17/96	2	1	7/10	Talk	Character Zer
10/23/96	5	1	1/9	***	Poor Heart
10/27/96	3	1	2/11	Runaway Jim	AC/DC Bag
11/6/96	5	1	7/9	Poor Heart	Billy Breathes
11/15/96	7	1	5/11	Character Zero	Prince Caspian
11/23/96	5	1	5/9	Divided Sky	Midnight on the High
11/30/96	4	1	2/10	Runaway Jim	All Things Rec
12/4/96	3	2	5/9	Sparkle	Life on Mars
12/31/96	5	1	3/10	Peaches en Regalia	Cars Trucks Buses
2/13/97	1	2	4/10	My Soul	Slave
2/18/97	4	1	3/10	Cavern	Runaway Jim
2/25/97	5	2	3/10	Sample in a Jar	Free
3/2/97	4	2	5/9	Steep	Waste
3/18/97	1	1	4/10	Sample in a Jar	My Soul
6/19/97	4	1	4/9	Theme From the Botto	Water in the Sky
7/9/97	13	1	1/8	***	Prince Caspian
7/23/97	5	2	1/6	***	Ghost
7/30/97	4	2	1/9	***	Free
8/9/97	6	1	2/8	Theme From the Botto	Ghost
8/16/97	5	1	5/11	Theme From the Botto	Ghost
11/13/97	2	2	2/7	Stash	Prince Caspian
11/21/97	5	1	5/8	Dogs Stole Things	Lawn Boy
11/26/97	3	2	5/8	Ya Mar	Prince Caspian
12/3/97	5	1	1/7	***	My Soul
12/11/97	5	1	1/7	***	Down with Dis
12/13/97	2	2	2/10	NICU	Ghost
12/30/97	3	1	4/7	Water in the Sky	Stash
4/2/98	2	2	1/9	***	Simple
7/2/98	6	1	10/11	Ginseng Sullivan	Character Zer
7/8/98	4	1	3/7	Bathtub Gin	Beauty of My Dreams
7/17/98	5	E	1/2	***	Rocky Top
7/26/98	6	E	1/2	***	Bittersweet Motel
7/31/98	3	E	1/2	***	Slave
8/9/98	7	1	1/9	***	Bathtub Gin
8/16/98	4	1	4/11	Rift	Lawn Boy
10/31/98	7	1	2/10	Axilla	Roggae
11/11/98	7	1	1/8	***	Gumbo
11/25/98	9	1	1/9	***	My Soul
12/29/98	5	1	3/10	Funky Bitch	Horn
7/1/99	4	1	1/10	***	Billy Breathes
7/9/99	5	2	1/8	***	Free
7/15/99	4	1	1/10	***	Ghost
7/18/99	3	1	1/11	***	Farmhouse
7/23/99	3	1	4/9	Back @ Chicken Shack	Fast Enough for You
7/30a/99	4	1	5/7	Taste	Waste
9/11/99	6	1	5/9	Dogs Stole Things	Billy Breathes
9/24/99	9	1	2/10	First Tube	Farmhouse
10/2/99	6	1	3/9	Wolfman's Brother	Quinn the Eskimo
10/9/99	5	1	1/8	***	Wilson
12/7/99	6	1	5/8	Funky Bitch	Nellie Kane
12/17/99	8	1	5/8	Gotta Jibboo	When Circus Comes
12/31/99	3	1	5/14	I Didn't Know	Bouncing
5/23/00	3	2	1/8	***	Twist
6/11/00	3	1	2/9	First Tube	Horn
6/25/00	8	1	4/10	The Old Home Place	Water in the Sky
7/8/00	9	1	1/9	***	NICU
7/14/00	4	2	1/11	***	Timber (Jerry)
9/14/00	6	1	1/6	***	Reba
9/24/00	7	1	1/9	First Tube	Sample in a Ja

Has not been played in the last 9 shows.

Purple Rain

DATE	GAP	SET	POS.	SONG BEFORE	SONG AFTER
7/16/93	553	2	10/12	Poor Heart	Harry Hood
7/18/93	2	2	9/10	You Enjoy Myself	Golgi Apparat
7/21/93	1	1	11/12	Big Ball Jam	Daniel
7/24/93	3	2	10/12	Weekapaug Groove	Daniel
7/25/93	1	2	8/10	The Lizards	Harpua
7/27/93	1	1	7/8	It's Ice	You Enjoy My
7/29/93	2	2	7/9	You Enjoy Myself	Daniel
7/31/93	2	2	9/11	Weekapaug Groove	Daniel
8/3/93	2	2	8/9	Sparkle	Golgi Apparat
8/7/93	2	2	11/12	McGrupp	Run Like Antel
8/14/93	6	2	12/13	You Enjoy Myself	Golgi Apparat
8/17/93	3	2	8/10	You Enjoy Myself	My Sweet One
8/20/93	1	2	8/9	You Enjoy Myself	Cavern
8/28/93	5	2	9/14	Big Ball Jam	You Enjoy My
12/30/93	3	2	8/9	Weekapaug Groove	Slave
4/13/94	9	2	9/10	David Bowie	AC/DC Bag
4/30/94	14	2	9/10	Possum	BBFCFM
5/7/94	5	2	10/12	Cannonball Jam	HYHU Jam
5/13/94	4	2	8/9	You Enjoy Myself	Good Time Ba
5/25/94	9	2	8/9	Julius	The Squirmin
6/16/94	10	2	10/11	BBFCFM	Golgi Apparat
10/8/94	25	2	10/12	Fluffhead	Harry Hood
10/23/94	12	2	6/9	Down with Disease	Harry Hood
11/25/94	20	2	7/8	The Mango Song	Run Like Antel
12/4/94	7	2	6/7	You Enjoy Myself	Good Time Ba
12/30/94	8	2	6/8	You Enjoy Myself	Harry Hood
10/21/95	42	2	6/8	You Enjoy Myself	Harry Hood
7/12/96	50	2	5/9	Run Like an Antelope	Jam
7/15/96	2	2	7/9	Julius	Uncle Pen
8/6/96	12	2	6/8	BBFCFM	Harry Hood
7/25/99	209	2	5/6	Suzy Greenberg	You Enjoy My

Has not been played in the last 94 shows.

Pusher Man Jam

DATE	GAP	SET	POS.	SONG BEFORE	SONG AFTER
11/1/91	336	E	2/3	Love You	Stash

Has not been played in the last 783 shows.

Quadrophenia

DATE	GAP	SET	POS.	SONG BEFORE	SONG AFTER
10/31/95	759	2	3/17	The Real Me	Cut My Hair

Has not been played in the last 360 shows.

Quadrophonic Toppling

DATE	GAP	SET	POS.	SONG BEFORE	SONG AFTER
12/31/99	10702	14/35		Sand	Slave

Has not been played in the last 49 shows.

Quinn the Eskimo

DATE	GAP	SET	POS.	SONG BEFORE	SONG AFTER
4/1/86	12	1	1/7	***	Have Mercy
4/15/86	1	1	4/14	Prep School Hippie	Slave
10/15/86	1	2	11/14	Slave	Mike's Song
2/13/87	3	1	5/14	Slave	Alumni Blues
3/6/87	2	1	5/6	Golgi Apparatus	Sneakin' Sally
4/29/87	3	2	6/7	Halley's Comet	AC/DC Bag
8/10/87	4	1	5/7	Wilson	Divided Sky
11/20/98	970	1	3/13	Tube	Funky Bitch
12/28/98	7	2	5/6	When Circus Comes	David Bowie
7/18/99	17	3	8/9	Icculus	Fluffhead
10/2/99	28	1	4/9	Punch You in the Eye	Poor Heart

Has not been played in the last 71 shows.

Ramble On

DATE	GAP	SET	POS.	SONG BEFORE	SONG AFTER
8/1/98	966	1	1/9	***	Mike's Song
8/12/98	8	1	7/8	Character Zero	Slave

Has not been played in the last 145 shows.

Rapper's Delight

DATE	GAP	SET	POS.	SONG BEFORE	SONG AFTER
9/29/00	11132	8/9		Walk This Way	You Shook Me (All Ni

Has not been played in the last 6 shows.

Reba

DATE	GAP	SET	POS.	SONG BEFORE	SONG AFTER
10/1/89	116	2	3/11	My Sweet One	Dinner and a
10/20/89	6	1	7/10	The Oh Kee Pa Ceremo	Divided Sky
10/21/89	1	2	5/10	Possum	The Sloth

DATE	GAP	SET	POS.	SONG BEFORE	SONG AFTER
10/22/89	1	2	2/9	Harry Hood	Golgi Apparat
10/26/89	1	2	5/15	AC/DC Bag	Walk Away
10/28/89	1	1	7/9	Dinner and a Movie	Divided Sky
10/31/89	1	2	3/8	Wilson	Col. Forbin's A
11/2/89	1	1	8/11	The Curtain	Split Open and
11/3/89	1	1	9/10	Punch You in the Eye	Golgi Apparat
11/16/89	4	1	9/11	My Sweet One	You Enjoy My
11/18/89	1	1	9/11	Wilson	David Bowie
11/30/89	1	2	1/11	***	Possum
12/3/89	2	1	4/9	Ya Mar	Divided Sky
12/8/89	2	1	5/11	Ya Mar	McGrupp
1/20/90	7	2	3/10	Bouncing	Tela
1/27/90	1	1	9/13	Wilson	Funky Bitch
2/9/90	4	2	3/9	Ya Mar	Wilson
2/17/90	4	1	1/12	***	The Oh Kee Pa
2/23/90	2	2	2/11	Golgi Apparatus	Bathtub Gin
2/25/90	2	2	1/6	***	McGrupp
3/3/90	3	1	9/12	AC/DC Bag	Rocky Top
3/7/90	1	1	1/6	***	Possum
3/9/90	2	2	1/11	***	The Oh Kee Pa
3/11/90	2	1	7/13	T.M.W.S.I.Y. Reprise	La Grange
4/5/90	4	2	1/13	***	Uncle Pen
4/6/90	1	2	7/10	Caravan	I Didn't Know
4/13/90	5	1	9/10	AC/DC Bag	Fire
4/18/90	2	2	5/12	Funky Bitch	Walk Away
4/21/90	3	1	2/10	Sweet Adeline	Funky Bitch
4/25/90	2	2	3/12	Sweet Adeline	Ya Mar
4/28/90	2	2	5/9	I Didn't Know	My Sweet One
5/4/90	2	2	7/10	Possum	My Sweet One
5/6/90	1	1	4/8	Uncle Pen	Tweezer
5/10/90	2	2	5/8	Caravan	The Oh Kee Pa
5/11/90	1	1	8/9	Possum	Highway to Hell
5/13/90	1	2	8/12	My Sweet One	Funky Bitch
5/15/90	1	1	1/12	***	Alumni Blues
5/19/90	1	2	2/10	Possum	The Oh Kee Pa
5/23/90	1	2	2/11	The Squirming Coil	Tweezer
5/24/90	1	1	5/9	Donna Lee	You Enjoy My
5/30/90	1	1	1/14	***	The Oh Kee Pa
6/2/90	3	1	4/9	Bouncing	Possum
6/7/90	2	1	6/9	Fee	You Enjoy My
6/9/90	2	1	3/10	Lawn Boy	Dinner and a
6/16/90	1	1	4/10	Wilson	Horn
9/13/90	1	2	12/15	Sparks	Self
9/14/90	1	1	4/11	The Landlady	Paul and Silas
9/16/90	2	1	5/14	The Landlady	Ya Mar
9/20/90	1	1	1/12	***	Paul and Silas
10/4/90	6	2	1/8	***	Bouncing
10/8/90	4	1	6/10	Cavern	My Sweet One
10/30/90	3	2	6/12	Foam	Llama
10/31/90	1	2	2/12	The Landlady	Runaway Jim
11/3/90	2	2	9/12	Uncle Pen	Possum
11/10/90	3	1	1/11	***	The Landlady
11/26/90	4	1	4/11	The Sloth	Buried Alive
12/28/90	5	1	4/11	Horn	Llama
2/1/91	3	2	2/5	Chalk Dust Torture	The Landlady
2/3/91	2	1	7/10	Destiny Unbound	Chalk Dust Tor
2/8/91	2	1	2/11	AC/DC Bag	Buried Alive
2/9/91	1	1	11/12	Tweezer	Chalk Dust Tor
2/14/91	1	1	4/11	Buried Alive	Destiny Unbound
2/16/91	2	2	2/9	Chalk Dust Torture	Buried Alive
2/19/91	1	1	4/9	Golgi Apparatus	Dinner and a
2/21/91	2	1	1/11	***	Dinner and a
2/26/91	1	1	7/11	My Sweet One	The Oh Kee Pa
2/28/91	2	2	2/7	The Squirming Coil	Llama
3/1/91	1	2	3/11	The Landlady	Llama
3/13/91	4	2	8/12	The Sloth	Tweezer
3/16/91	2	1	5/14	Golgi Apparatus	The Landlady
3/22/91	2	1	10/11	Cavern	Fire
3/31/91	4	E	1/2	***	Highway to Hell
4/2/91	1	1	3/10	The Landlady	Llama
4/5/91	3	1	6/11	Take the A-Train	Chalk Dust Tor
4/11/91	2	2	2/14	My Sweet One	Llama
4/12/91	1	2	8/10	Buried Alive	My Sweet One
4/16/91	2	2	3/11	My Sweet One	Chalk Dust Tor
4/18/91	1	1	2/11	Llama	The Oh Kee Pa
4/20/91	2	1	2/11	Runaway Jim	Llama
4/22/91	2	1	4/9	The Sloth	Poor Heart
4/25/91	1	1	7/11	Poor Heart	Llama
4/27/91	1	1	7/12	My Sweet One	Llama
5/4/91	3	1	4/11	Cavern	My Sweet One
5/9/91	1	1	5/10	Guelah Papyrus	Llama
5/11/91	2	4	4/12	Poor Heart	Donna Lee
5/17/91	3	1	4/17	Jam	Poor Heart
5/19/91	2	2	5/10	Foam	Dinner and a
7/12/91	2	1	5/12	Flat Fee	The Landlady
7/14/91	2	1	1/11	***	Llama
7/18/91	2	2	2/8	Llama	Poor Heart
7/20/91	2	2	2/12	Buried Alive	Caravan
7/23/91	2	2	2/10	Llama	Cavern
7/26/91	3	1	2/12	Chalk Dust Torture	My Sweet One
8/3/91	2	2	2/10	The Curtain	Chalk Dust Tor
9/25/91	1	1	10/11	Caravan	Possum
9/27/91	2	1	3/9	Cavern	Buried Alive
9/29/91	2	2	5/10	Foam	The Sloth
10/2/91	2	1	6/10	Cavern	Brother
10/4/91	2	1	2/10	Chalk Dust Torture	Poor Heart
10/10/91	2	2	2/13	Brother	Poor Heart
10/13/91	3	1	3/10	Wilson	The Landlady
10/15/91	1	1	6/10	Sparkle	The Landlady
10/18/91	2	1	4/9	Paul and Silas	Wilson
10/23/91	2	1	2/11	Chalk Dust Torture	The Landlady
10/28/91	3	1	4/10	Poor Heart	I Didn't Know
11/2/91	4	1	4/10	Llama	Paul and Silas
11/7/91	1	2	4/11	My Sweet One	Tube
11/9/91	2	1	6/11	Llama	Tube
11/14/91	4	1	4/11	Llama	Foam
11/19/91	3	2	8/11	The Sloth	Dinner and a
11/21/91	2	1	5/12	Guelah Papyrus	Foam
11/23/91	2	1	2/11	Llama	Foam
12/4/91	3	1	2/11	Llama	The Landlady
12/6/91	2	1	3/9	Foam	Uncle Pen
12/7/91	1	2	2/8	Buried Alive	Chalk Dust Tor
12/31/91	1	2	7/10	The Landlady	Cavern
3/6/92	1	1	9/11	Maze	All Things Rec
3/11/92	2	1	4/10	Paul and Silas	Maze
3/12/92	1	1	6/11	I Didn't Know	Buried Alive
3/14/92	2	1	3/13	Cavern	Sparkle
3/20/92	3	1	2/10	Wilson	Brother
3/25/92	4	2	3/12	Mound	All Things Rec
3/27/92	2	1	2/11	Llama	Paul and Silas
3/31/92	3	1	6/10	Rift	Llama
4/4/92	3	1	3/10	Foam	Uncle Pen
4/6/92	2	1	4/10	Sparkle	Brother
4/8/92	2	1	7/11	Mound	Uncle Pen
4/12/92	1	1	10/11	Maze	Run Like Antel
4/15/92	2	2	3/8	You Enjoy Myself	The Landlady
4/17/92	2	1	7/13	Cavern	Maze
4/19/92	2	1	6/11	My Friend My Friend	Maze
4/22/92	2	1	3/10	Foam	Sparkle
4/25/92	3	1	4/11	Paul and Silas	Brother
4/30/92	2	1	5/10	Maze	Uncle Pen
5/2/92	2	1	6/11	Sparkle	Maze
5/6/92	3	1	3/11	Foam	My Mind's Got A Mind
5/8/92	2	1	3/12	Cavern	Uncle Pen
5/10/92	2	1	7/10	Cavern	I Didn't Know
5/12/92	1	1	2/10	My Sweet One	All Things Rec
5/14/92	1	1	7/11	Horn	Poor Heart
5/17/92	3	1	6/11	My Sweet One	I Didn't Know
6/23/92	4	1	2/8	Chalk Dust Torture	Maze
6/27/92	2	1	4/10	Sparkle	Maze
7/10/92	4	1	3/10	Llama	Sparkle
7/14/92	3	2	4/10	All Things Recnsrdrd	Llama
7/18/92	4	1	4/6	Llama	Rift
7/22/92	3	1	1/7	***	Poor Heart
8/17/92	13	1	4/11	The Landlady	Rift
8/24/92	1	1	4/7	The Landlady	You Enjoy My
8/30/92	5	1	3/7	The Landlady	Llama
11/20/92	3	1	6/12	The Sloth	Sparkle
11/22/92	2	1	6/12	Maze	Sparkle
11/27/92	3	1	8/12	Lawn Boy	Llama
11/30/92	2	1	9/10	I Didn't Know	Run Like Antel
12/3/92	3	1	10/12	Silent in the Mornin	Sweet Adeline
12/5/92	2	2	3/13	Tweezer	I Walk The Line
12/5/92	0	2	5/13	I Walk The Line	Sparkle
12/7/92	2	2	2/12	Chalk Dust Torture	Llama
12/10/92	2	1	9/11	All Things Recnsrd	Sweet Adeline
12/12/92	2	1	5/11	Cavern	The Landlady
12/28/92	2		3/9	Split Open and Melt	The Sloth
12/30/92	2	1	8/14	Paul and Silas	I Walk The Line
12/30/92	0	1	10/14	I Walk The Line	I Didn't Know
2/5/93	4	1	9/11	Poor Heart	The Vibration of Lif
2/7/93	2	2	4/13	My Mind's Got A Mind	Bouncing
2/10/93	2	1	4/10	Guelah Papyrus	The Sloth
2/12/93	2	2	3/11	All Things Recnsrd	Poor Heart
2/15/93	2	2	3/12	Fast Enough for You	Mike's Song
2/18/93	2	1	8/10	Cavern	Lawn Boy
2/20/93	2	2	2/22	Wilson	Tweezer
2/23/93	3	1	6/11	Split Open and Melt	Lawn Boy
3/2/93	4	1	4/13	Stash	Sparkle
3/6/93	3	2	3/9	Tweezer	Paul and Silas
3/9/93	2	2	4/15	Tweezer	Lawn Boy
3/14/93	3	1	8/11	Sample in a Jar	Indian War Dance
3/17/93	2	2	3/12	Glide	Jesus Just Left
3/22/93	4	1	8/10	Weigh	Sparkle
3/27/93	4	1	5/10	Stash	My Friend My
3/31/93	3	1	8/10	Sample in a Jar	I Didn't Know
4/3/93	3	1	8/10	My Friend My Friend	Horn
4/12/93	4	1	8/11	Silent in the Mornin	Llama
4/17/93	3	2	2/11	Wilson	The Landlady
4/22/93	4	1	4/10	It's Ice	Chalk Dust Tor
4/29/93	5	2	6/13	Big Ball Jam	Mike's Song
5/8/93	8	1	10/12	My Friend My Friend	Satin Doll
7/17/93	5	1	6/11	Stash	Chalk Dust Tor
7/30/93	10	1	9/10	I Didn't Know	Cavern
8/7/93	5	1	6/10	Makisupa Policeman	Maze
8/12/93	4	1	2/10	AC/DC Bag	Chalk Dust Tor
8/16/93	4	1	4/9	Horn	Sparkle
8/26/93	6	1	3/9	Guelah Papyrus	Fee
12/31/93	5	1	5/8	Ginseng Sullivan	Peaches en Regalia
4/4/94	1	1	6/9	Fee	Horn
4/9/94	4	2	2/11	Sample in a Jar	Peaches en Regalia
4/13/94	3	2	4/10	Sample in a Jar	Big Ball Jam
4/17/94	4	2	5/9	The Sloth	Big Ball Jam
4/22/94	4	2	3/8	Julius	Tweezer
4/29/94	5	2	4/11	If I Could	Fee
5/2/94	2	2	3/9	Mound	Golgi Apparat
5/6/94	3	2	5/9	Sample in a Jar	Axilla (Part II)
5/10/94	3	2	4/10	Julius	Scent of a Mul
5/14/94	3	1	5/9	Fee	Sample in a Ja
5/23/94	7	1	9/10	Julius	Cavern
5/27/94	3	2	4/12	My Friend My Friend	The Lizards
5/28/94	1	2	5/8	Lifeboy	Fee
6/13/94	5	2	6/11	Cavern	Jesus Just Left
6/19/94	5	2	4/8	If I Could	Makisupa Policeman
6/24/94	4	1	9/11	Horn	Sweet Adeline
6/29/94	3	1	3/11	Sample in a Jar	Mound
7/3/94	4	1	8/10	The Old Home Place	Axilla (Part II)
7/6/94	2	1	5/9	Bouncing	Axilla (Part II)
7/8/94	1	2	3/11	Sample in a Jar	Yerushalayim
7/15/94	5	2	4/10	Bouncing	It's Ice
10/7/94	2	2	4/10	Silent in the Mornin	Wilson
10/12/94	4	1	2/9	My Friend My Friend	The Sloth
10/15/94	3	1	6/8	Glide	Down with Dis
10/18/94	2	2	4/8	Silent in the Mornin	Scent of a Mul
10/22/94	3	2	8/11	Wilson	Amazing Grce

DATE	GAP	SET	POS.	SONG BEFORE	SONG AFTER
10/26/94	3	2	3/7	Bouncing	Axilla (Part II)
10/31/94	4	1	9/10	Silent in the Mornin	Golgi Apparat
11/13/94	5	1	4/10	Simple	Axilla (Part II)
11/16/94	2	1	4/11	Fast Enough for You	Axilla (Part II)
11/20/94	4	2	5/10	Axilla (Part II)	Simple
11/25/94	3	1	3/8	Guelah Papyrus	Bouncing
11/30/94	3	1	4/10	My Friend My Friend	Col. Forbin's A
12/4/94	4	2	3/7	Bouncing	Axilla (Part II)
12/8/94	3	2	4/8	Axilla (Part II)	Nellie Kane
12/28/94	3	1	7/10	Axilla (Part II)	Dog Faced Boy
5/16/95	4	1	5/12	Strange Design	Theme From the Botto
6/8/95	2	1	7/9	Fast Enough for You	Prince Caspian
6/13/95	3	1	7/10	Taste	Terrapin
6/19/95	5	1	6/10	Punch You in the Eye	Strange Design
6/23/95	3	1	4/8	Prince Caspian	Ginseng Sullivan
6/28/95	4	1	4/8	Fast Enough for You	Punch You in
7/2/95	4	1	7/10	Camel Walk	I Didn't Know
9/30/95	5	1	4/9	White Rabbit Jam	Uncle Pen
10/6/95	4	1	4/9	Billy Breathes	I'm Blue, Lonesome
10/8/95	2	1	5/9	Wolfman's Brother	I'm Blue, Lonesome
10/14/95	3	2	1/6	***	Rift
10/21/95	5	1	4/12	Guelah Papyrus	Wilson
10/25/95	3	2	1/9	***	Life on Mars
11/9/95	5	1	6/8	Simple	Tela
11/12/95	3	1	5/10	Guelah Papyrus	I Didn't Know
11/18/95	4	1	3/8	Bouncing	Lawn Boy
11/24/95	4	2	3/10	Theme From the Botto	Catapult
11/29/95	3	1	3/9	Ya Mar	If I Could
12/2/95	3	1	5/10	Guelah Papyrus	My Sweet One
12/7/95	3	2	4/10	Taste That Surrounds	Julius
12/11/95	3	1	5/12	Prince Caspian	Dog Gone Dog
12/16/95	4	2	2/8	Sample in a Jar	Scent of a Mul
12/31/95	5	1	3/10	The Sloth	The Squirmin
7/6/96	5	1	2/6	Also Sprach	Poor Heart
7/11/96	4	1	3/8	Cavern	I Didn't Know
7/13/96	2	1	4/10	Cavern	Poor Heart
7/21/96	5	2	3/9	Theme From the Botto	Life on Mars
8/4/96	6	2	2/7	AC/DC Bag	Scent of a Mul
8/10/96	4	1	5/11	Fee	I Didn't Know
8/14/96	3	1	6/10	Poor Heart	The Mango Song
8/17/96	2	1	3/10	Punch You in the Eye	Cars Trucks Buses
10/18/96	3	2	4/6	You Enjoy Myself	Waste
10/21/96	2	2	4/11	Wolfman's Brother	Train Song
10/26/96	4	1	4/9	Wolfman's Brother	Train Song
10/31/96	3	1	6/10	Prince Caspian	Col. Forbin's A
11/8/96	5	1	7/9	Prince Caspian	Golgi Apparat
11/13/96	3	1	7/9	Train Song	Character Zer
11/18/96	4	1	9/10	Ginseng Sullivan	Character Zer
11/24/96	4	1	5/11	Bouncing	Character Zer
12/1/96	4	2	5/10	A Day in the Life	Swept Away
12/4/96	2	2	7/9	Life on Mars	Lawn Boy
12/30/96	4	1	5/9	Gumbo	Talk
2/14/97	3	2	5/9	Funky Bitch	Walfredo
2/18/97	3	2	6/9	Wolfman's Brother	Train Song
2/21/97	2	2	7/9	Billy Breathes	Waste
3/1/97	6	1	8/10	Jesus Just Left	Hello My Baby
6/16/97	5	2	4/7	I Don't Care	Wading In Velvet Sea
6/24/97	5	2	2/7	Wolfman's Brother	NICU
7/1/97	4	1	8/9	Dirt	Dogs Stole Things
8/9/97	20	1	6/8	Dogs Stole Things	Lawn Boy
11/17/97	10	1	2/5	Tweezer	Train Song
12/7/97	13	2	4/6	Boogie On Reggae	Guyute
4/3/98	10	1	8/9	Dogs Stole Things	My Soul
7/5/98	7	1	4/9	Cavern	Fee

DATE	GAP	SET	POS.	SONG BEFORE	SONG AFTER
7/16/98	6	1	4/7	Stash	Fast Enough for You
7/26/98	7	1	5/7	Frankie Says	Funky Bitch
8/2/98	5	1	6/9	Boogie On Reggae	Weigh
8/11/98	6	1	6/11	Bittersweet Motel	The Sloth
8/15/98	2	2	2/9	The Wedge	Gumbo
10/15/98	3	1	7/8	Brian and Robert	Character Zer
10/29/98	3	2	3/7	The Moma Dance	Walk Away
11/7/98	6	2	3/4	Ghost	Farmhouse
11/14/98	5	1	3/8	My Soul	Bouncing
11/27/98	8	1	6/11	Meat	The Old Home
12/30/98	5	1	12/12	Loving Cup	***
7/13/99	11	1	7/9	Lawn Boy	Carini
7/18/99	4	1	10/11	The Moma Dance	Chalk Dust Tor
7/30b/99	8	2	3/6	My Soul	Bike
9/21/99	12	E	1/2	***	Bold as Love
12/15/99	25	2	5/7	Dirt	Halley's Comet
12/31/99	5	2	17/35	Albuquerque	Axilla
6/16/00	10	1	9/10	My Sweet One	Character Zer
7/6/00	11	1	1/12	***	Dogs Stole Things
9/14/00	12	1	2/6	Punch You in the Eye	Albuquerque
9/22/00	5	2	2/7	Tube	Ghost
10/4/00	8	1	5/7	Funky Bitch	Dog Faced Boy

Has not been played in the last 3 shows.

Revival

DATE	GAP	SET	POS.	SONG BEFORE	SONG AFTER
10/30/85	8	1	7/11	I Wish	Alumni Blues

Has not been played in the last 1111 shows.

Revolution

DATE	GAP	SET	POS.	SONG BEFORE	SONG AFTER
10/17/85	7	1	5/9	Dave's Energy Guide	Anarchy
10/31/94	674	2	26/30	Long Long Long	Honey Pie

Has not been played in the last 438 shows.

Revolution 9

DATE	GAP	SET	POS.	SONG BEFORE	SONG AFTER
10/31/94	681	2	30/30	Cry Baby Cry	***

Has not been played in the last 438 shows.

Rhinoceros

DATE	GAP	SET	POS.	SONG BEFORE	SONG AFTER
8/3/98	968	1	1/8	***	Halley's Comet

Has not been played in the last 151 shows.

Rhombus Narration

DATE	GAP	SET	POS.	SONG BEFORE	SONG AFTER
11/2/89	128	2	5/11	Kung	Divided Sky
12/7/89	10	1	10/11	Alumni Blues	Divided Sky
12/29/89	5	1	1/10	***	Divided Sky
3/1/90	17	1	3/7	Ya Mar	Divided Sky
3/17/90	8	1	6/10	My Sweet One	Divided Sky
4/14/90	4	1	4/11	Uncle Pen	Divided Sky
11/15/91	173	1	9/12	Guelah Papyrus	Divided Sky

Has not been played in the last 774 shows.

Ride Captain Ride

DATE	GAP	SET	POS.	SONG BEFORE	SONG AFTER
3/23/87	20	2	3/9	Peaches en Regalia	Dave's Energy Guide
9/13/88	47	2	1/6	***	Boogie On Reggae
5/28/89	39	2	7/16	Sanity	Peaches en Regalia
4/14/90	72	2	8/11	Wilson	Golgi Apparat
12/12/92	296	E	1/2	***	Tweezer Repri
12/30/92	4	E	1/2	***	Sweet Adeline
8/3/98	490	1	4/8	I Didn't Know	Cars Trucks Buses
11/8/98	20	1	4/10	Love Me	Fee
12/10/99	73	E	1/1	***	***

Has not been played in the last 58 shows.

Rift

DATE	GAP	SET	POS.	SONG BEFORE	SONG AFTER
2/25/90	159	1	10/11	Satin Doll	Possum

DATE	GAP	SET	POS.	SONG BEFORE	SONG AFTER
3/28/90	10	2	13/16	La Grange	Cavern
4/14/90	9	1	7/10	The Famous Mockingbi	Mike's Song
4/20/90	3	2	6/11	La Grange	Fee
4/28/90	5	1	9/11	You Enjoy Myself	Foam
5/19/90	9	2	8/10	Bouncing	Jesus Just Left
3/6/92	164	1	1/11	***	Cavern
3/7/92	1	1	10/11	The Landlady	Run Like Antel
3/12/92	2	1	8/11	Buried Alive	Magilla
3/13/92	1	2	9/12	The Sloth	Love You
3/14/92	1	1	6/13	Foam	Stash
3/17/92	1	1	9/11	Guelah Papyrus	Bouncing
3/19/92	1	1	2/12	The Landlady	Split Open and
3/20/92	1	1	5/10	Glide	Fluffhead
3/24/92	3	1	5/13	Eliza	Golgi Apparat
3/25/92	1	1	4/10	Split Open and Melt	Fee
3/27/92	2	2	7/13	My Sweet One	Bathtub Gin
3/28/92	1	1	5/10	Stash	Bouncing
3/31/92	1	1	5/10	Split Open and Melt	Reba
4/3/92	2	1	4/11	Stash	Guelah Papyrus
4/5/92	2	1	7/11	Stash	Horn
4/7/92	2	1	10/12	Bouncing	The Sloth
4/12/92	2	2	4/10	Bouncing	You Enjoy My
4/16/92	3	1	6/12	Split Open and Melt	Fee
4/18/92	2	2	4/16	Suzy Greenberg	Manteca
4/21/92	2	1	4/11	Split Open and Melt	Guelah Papyrus
4/22/92	1	2	5/11	Silent in the Mornin	Wilson
4/25/92	3	1	9/11	Bouncing	Magilla
4/29/92	1	1	7/10	Guelah Papyrus	Bouncing
4/30/92	1	1	8/10	Stash	Esther
5/3/92	3	1	8/10	I Didn't Know	Horn
5/5/92	1	1	5/11	Stash	Guelah Papyrus
5/7/92	2	1	9/11	Split Open and Melt	Guelah Papyrus
5/9/92	2	1	6/11	Guelah Papyrus	Fee
5/14/92	3	2	3/13	Cavern	Fluffhead
5/18/92	4	2	10/13	Fee	Cavern
7/1/92	7	1	3/7	Cavern	Horn
7/14/92	5	1	2/12	The Landlady	Guelah Papyrus
7/16/92	2	1	8/10	Bouncing	Guelah Papyrus
7/18/92	2	1	5/6	Reba	Run Like Antel
7/22/92	3	1	5/7	Maze	Cavern
7/25/92	2	1	5/8	Stash	You Enjoy My
7/30/92	4	1	1/8	***	Horn
8/2/92	3	1	3/8	Guelah Papyrus	The Oh Kee Pa
8/17/92	4	1	5/11	Reba	Wilson
8/29/92	8	1	2/5	Chalk Dust Torture	Bouncing
10/30/92	2	1	4/11	Bouncing	Cavern
11/20/92	2	1	4/12	Suzy Greenberg	The Sloth
11/23/92	3	1	5/11	Split Open and Melt	Guelah Papyrus
11/27/92	2	1	1/12	***	Wilson
12/1/92	3	1	5/12	Bouncing	Cavern
12/3/92	2	2	1/13	***	Guelah Papyrus
12/5/92	2	1	4/12	Bouncing	Guelah Papyrus
12/8/92	3	1	1/11	***	Wilson
12/10/92	1	2	1/10	***	Tweezer
12/12/92	2	2	5/10	Tweezer	Guelah Papyrus
12/13/92	1	1	8/11	Stash	Fast Enough for You
12/28/92	1	1	7/10	Bouncing	Golgi Apparat
12/30/92	2	2	2/12	Axilla	Bathtub Gin
12/31/92	1	1	5/11	Bouncing	Wilson
2/3/93	1	1	2/11	Loving Cup	Fee
2/5/93	2	1	3/11	Guelah Papyrus	Split Open and
2/7/93	2	1	8/12	The Famous Mockingbi	I Didn't Know
2/9/93	1	1	5/10	My Friend My Friend	The Wedge
2/11/93	2	1	6/10	Fee	Fluffhead

DATE	GAP	SET	POS.	SONG BEFORE	SONG AFTER
2/13/93	2	1	6/10	Glide	Stash
2/15/93	1	2	1/12	***	Fast Enough for You
2/18/93	2	2	1/12	***	Stash
2/19/93	1	1	2/11	Loving Cup	Split Open and
2/22/93	3	1	1/10	***	Guelah Papyrus
2/23/93	1	1	3/11	My Friend My Friend	Bouncing
2/25/93	1	1	7/11	The Famous Mockingbi	Stash
2/27/93	2	1	2/10	Golgi Apparatus	Guelah Papyrus
3/3/93	2	1	1/10	***	Foam
3/5/93	1	1	6/11	The Sloth	Stash
3/6/93	1	2	1/9	***	Tweezer
3/8/93	1	1	2/12	Golgi Apparatus	Guelah Papyrus
3/9/93	1	2	2/15	Axilla	Tweezer
3/12/93	1	1	6/11	Guelah Papyrus	Stash
3/14/93	2	2	8/11	Lifeboy	Big Ball Jam
3/18/93	3	1	3/11	Guelah Papyrus	Fee
3/19/93	1	1	5/9	Bouncing	Stash
3/21/93	1	2	3/12	My Friend My Friend	Tweezer
3/22/93	1	1	6/10	Bouncing	Weigh
3/25/93	2	1	8/11	Glide	Horn
3/27/93	2	1	3/10	Guelah Papyrus	Stash
3/30/93	2	2	2/15	Loving Cup	Tweezer
4/1/93	2	1	3/10	Guelah Papyrus	Stash
4/3/93	2	1	2/10	The Landlady	Guelah Papyrus
4/10/93	3	2	4/13	Bouncing	Glide
4/16/93	3	1	8/10	Sample in a Jar	Harry Hood
4/18/93	2	1	1/10	***	Guelah Papyrus
4/21/93	2	1	8/11	The Famous Mockingbi	Punch You in
4/22/93	1	1	9/10	Fee	Golgi Apparat
4/24/93	2	1	7/11	Silent in the Mornin	Caravan
4/27/93	2	1	5/10	Bouncing	Stash
4/29/93	1	1	8/10	Glide	Fee
5/1/93	2	1	6/10	Fee	Sample in a Ja
5/3/93	2	1	2/11	Buried Alive	Weigh
5/5/93	1	1	1/10	***	Guelah Papyrus
5/7/93	2	2	1/10	***	Bouncing
5/8/93	1	1	3/12	Guelah Papyrus	Mound
7/15/93	3	1	1/9	***	Sample in a Ja
7/17/93	2	2	11/12	Faht	Good Time Ba
7/18/93	1	1	2/9	Buried Alive	Foam
7/21/93	1	1	7/12	Glide	Bouncing
7/23/93	2	1	2/12	Buried Alive	Caravan
7/24/93	1	1	6/10	Guelah Papyrus	Stash
7/25/93	1	1	6/10	Fee	The Sloth
7/27/93	1	1	2/8	Also Sprach	Stash
7/29/93	2	1	4/10	Weigh	The Landlady
7/31/93	2	1	1/9	***	Sample in a Ja
8/2/93	1	2	5/9	Ballad - Curtis Loew	The Squirmin
8/3/93	1	1	5/11	Fee	Stash
8/6/93	1	1	5/10	Sample in a Jar	Horn
8/8/93	2	2	2/11	Also Sprach	Harry Hood
8/11/93	2	2	7/10	Bouncing	Jesus Just Left
8/13/93	2	2	2/9	Buried Alive	Bathtub Gin
8/15/93	2	2	1/11	***	Tweezer
8/17/93	2	2	5/10	Silent in the Mornin	Suzy Greenber
8/20/93	1	1	9/10	Ginseng Sullivan	Run Like Antel
8/21/93	1	1	5/10	Guelah Papyrus	Stash
8/24/93	1	2	8/10	Wilson	Cracklin' Rosi
8/26/93	2	2	4/8	Lifeboy	Jesus Just Left
8/28/93	1	2	2/14	Also Sprach	Run Like Antel
12/30/93	3	1	8/10	The Famous Mockingbi	Bathtub Gin
4/5/94	3	1	7/8	Bouncing	AC/DC Bag
4/9/94	3	1	3/10	Wilson	Bathtub Gin
4/14/94	4	1	6/9	Glide	Demand
4/16/94	2	1	4/8	Axilla (Part II)	Stash
4/18/94	2	1	6/10	My Friend My Friend	Split Open and
4/23/94	4	1	2/10	Funky Bitch	Fee

DATE	GAP	SET	POS.	SONG BEFORE	SONG AFTER
4/28/94	3	1	4/11	Sample in a Jar	Down with Dis
4/30/94	2	1	7/9	Punch You in the Eye	Ginseng Sulli-van
5/3/94	2	1	1/9	***	Guelah Papyrus
5/4/94	1	1	9/10	Lifeboy	Tweezer Repri
5/8/94	3	1	4/8	Axilla (Part II)	Down with Dis
5/12/94	2	1	2/10	Catapult	Down with Dis
5/16/94	3	1	6/10	Axilla (Part II)	Down with Dis
5/20/94	3	2	6/7	Wolfman's Brother	You Enjoy My
5/22/94	2	2	7/9	Lifeboy	Slave
5/25/94	2	2	1/9	***	Tweezer
5/28/94	3	1	1/10	***	Sample in a Ja
6/9/94	2	1	3/9	Guelah Papyrus	Down with Dis
6/11/94	2	1	4/8	You Enjoy Myself	Down with Dis
6/14/94	2	1	6/14	Guelah Papyrus	Down with Dis
6/16/94	1	1	2/10	Bouncing	Julius
6/18/94	2	1	2/10	Wilson	AC/DC Bag
6/22/94	3	1	3/9	Guelah Papyrus	Gumbo
6/25/94	3	1	2/10	NO2	Julius
6/30/94	3	1	3/9	Gumbo	Guelah Papyrus
7/2/94	2	E	1/1	***	***
7/5/94	2	1	1/10	***	Sample in a Ja
7/8/94	2	2	1/11	***	Sample in a Ja
7/10/94	2	1	4/9	Peaches en Regalia	Stash
7/15/94	3	1	1/8	***	Sample in a Ja
10/8/94	3	2	3/12	Sample in a Jar	Mike's Song
10/10/94	2	2	6/9	Fee	Down with Dis
10/14/94	3	1	9/12	Sweet Adeline	Col. Forbin's A
10/16/94	2	1	1/10	***	Horn
10/20/94	2	2	4/8	McGrupp	Harry Hood
10/22/94	1	2	5/8	Axilla (Part II)	Split Open and
10/26/94	3	2	1/7	***	Bouncing
10/28/94	2	2	7/12	Peaches en Regalia	Lifeboy
10/29/94	1	1	10/10	Makisupa Policeman	***
10/31/94	1	3	4/7	Slave	Sleeping Monkey
11/12/94	4	2	7/12	Lifeboy	The Old Home
11/18/94	5	1	1/11	***	AC/DC Bag
11/20/94	2	2	7/10	Simple	Terrapin
12/4/94	10	1	4/9	If I Could	Tweezer
12/7/94	2	2	1/9	***	Frankenstein
12/10/94	1	2	1/8	Fee	Stash
12/30/94	3	1	2/9	Wilson	AC/DC Bag
6/8/95	4	2	2/8	Simple	Free
6/10/95	2	1	6/9	Free	You Enjoy My
6/19/95	6	1	8/10	Strange Design	Cavern
6/24/95	4	1	2/10	Fee	Spock's Brain
6/29/95	4	1	7/10	Cavern	Simple
7/2/95	3	1	9/10	I Didn't Know	While My Guitar Gent
9/27/95	2	1	2/9	Wolfman's Brother	Free
10/2/95	4	1	3/10	Wolfman's Brother	Night Moves Jam
10/6/95	3	1	6/9	I'm Blue, Lonesome	Free
10/14/95	5	2	2/6	Reba	You Enjoy My
10/20/95	4	1	6/10	Fee	Free
10/6/95	2	1	6/9	I Didn't Know	Stash
11/15/95	9	1	4/9	Fast Enough for You	Prince Caspian
11/19/95	3	1	4/10	Poor Heart	Stash
11/22/95	2	2	1/6	***	Free
11/25/95	2	1	7/9	Bouncing	Wolfman's Brother
11/30/95	3	1	7/10	Bathtub Gin	Fast Enough for You
12/7/95	5	1	5/10	Demand	Slave
12/9/95	2	1	5/10	The Sloth	Bouncing
12/28/95	7	1	7/9	Horn	Fast Enough for You
7/21/96	19	1	3/14	Guelah Papyrus	Tweezer
8/6/96	8	1	2/9	Makisupa Policeman	Suzy Greenber
8/10/96	2	1	9/11	Silent in the Mornin	Bathtub Gin
10/19/96	9	1	2/9	My Friend My Friend	Free

DATE	GAP	SET	POS.	SONG BEFORE	SONG AFTER
10/23/96	3	1	7/9	Character Zero	Theme From the Botto
10/27/96	3	2	3/9	Bathtub Gin	Prince Caspian
10/29/96	1	2	1/10	***	Mike's Song
11/7/96	5	1	3/10	Weigh	Guelah Papyrus
11/16/96	7	1	5/11	Gumbo	Free
11/23/96	4	1	8/9	Split Open and Melt	Funky Bitch
12/29/96	10	1	7/10	Train Song	Free
2/23/97	11	1	6/9	Love Me	Fluffhead '
7/31/98	94	1	4/7	Roggae	Cities
8/12/98	9	2	3/7	Simple	Loving Cup
8/16/98	2	1	3/11	Bathtub Gin	Punch You in
11/20/98	20	1	6/13	Guelah Papyrus	Meat
7/7/99	15	1	7/10	Axilla	Wolfman's Brother
8/1/99	19	1	2/10	Cities	Wilson
7/4/00	60	1	3/11	Farmhouse	It's Ice
9/11/00	11	1	3/9	The Moma Dance	Brian and Robert
9/18/00	5	1	8/10	Sample in a Jar	Sleep
9/29/00	7	1	2/8	Carini	Frankenstein
10/6/00	5	2	5/10	The Inlaw Josie Wale	Cities

Has not been played in the last 1 show.

Road Runner

9/11/00	11011		1/9	***	The Moma Dance

Has not been played in the last 18 shows.

Roadhouse Blues

12/2/83	0	1	5/6	Squeeze Box	Happy Birth-day

Has not been played in the last 1119 shows.

Rock and Roll

10/31/98	983	2	3/10	Sweet Jane	Cool it Down
11/8/98	5	2	3/8	Meat	Down with Dis
11/19/98	7	2	2/8	Also Sprach	Taste
12/29/98	9	1	1/10	***	Funky Bitch
7/12/99	11	E	1/1	***	***
9/25/99	28	2	5/8	Prince Caspian	Also Sprach
10/4/99	7	E	1/1	***	***
12/3/99	6	E	1/1	***	***
12/31/99	14	2	9/35	Prince Caspian	You Enjoy My
5/22/00	2	2	6/6	Ghost	***
6/23/00	10	2	1/7	***	Jesus Just Left
6/29/00	4	1	5/5	Drowned	***
7/8/00	7	2	3/9	Piper	Tweezer
9/17/00	12	2	1/5	***	Theme From the Botto
10/4/00	11	2	1/7	***	Also Sprach

Has not been played in the last 3 shows.

Rock and Roll All Nite Jam

2/20/93	494	2	16/22	Weekapaug Groove	Weekapaug Gr

Has not been played in the last 625 shows.

Rock and Roll Part Two

11/20/98	996	1	1/13	***	Tube

Has not been played in the last 123 shows.

Rocko William

2/13/97	863	2	8/10	Maze	Harry Hood
2/14/97	1	2	7/9	Walfredo	Scent of a Mul
2/26/97	9	1	8/10	Carini	Dog Gone Dog
6/25/97	13	2	8/9	Cecilia	Run Like Antel
8/10/97	24	2	4/5	Rotation Jam	David Bowie

Has not been played in the last 209 shows.

Rocky Mountain Way Jam

2/16/91	250	E	4/5	Possum	Possum

DATE	GAP	SET	POS.	SONG BEFORE	SONG AFTER
7/23/97	649	2	5/6	You Enjoy Myself	Chalk Dust Tor

Has not been played in the last 220 shows.

Rocky Raccoon

DATE	GAP	SET	POS.	SONG BEFORE	SONG AFTER
10/31/94	681	2	14/30	Piggies	Don't Pass Me By

Has not been played in the last 438 shows.

Rocky Top

DATE	GAP	SET	POS.	SONG BEFORE	SONG AFTER
9/21/87	30	3	3/15	Good Times Bad Times	Sneakin' Sally
5/21/88	19	3	2/6	Big Leg Emma	Cities
5/25/88	1	1	2/9	The Curtain	Funky Bitch
6/15/88	1	1	5/9	Wilson	McGrupp
6/21/88	3	1	2/9	Fluffhead	Mustang Sally
3/30/89	37	3	6/6	Satin Doll	***
8/17/89	18	1	5/9	The Sloth	Harry Hood
8/19/89	1	1	7/13	Punch You in the Eye	Bold As Love
10/22/89	14	1	9/14	Foam	Split Open and
12/1/89	12	2	2/10	Alumni Blues	Divided Sky
12/7/89	2	2	3/11	Suzy Greenberg	Ya Mar
12/9/89	2	1	6/10	In a Hole	David Bowie
2/10/90	12	2	4/10	AC/DC Bag	Happy Birth-day
2/23/90	5	1	6/11	Carolina	Dinner and a
3/3/90	5	1	10/12	Reba	You Enjoy My
3/10/90	4	1	5/10	AC/DC Bag	The Squirmin
6/1/90	34	1	1/12	***	Uncle Pen
6/16/90	6	3	8/13	Fee	Caravan
11/4/90	22	2	2/13	Golgi Apparatus	Llama
11/17/90	4	2	10/12	Lawn Boy	Donna Lee
12/29/90	8	1	7/10	Lawn Boy	Horn
12/31/90	1	2	7/9	You Enjoy Myself	If I Only Had a Brai
2/9/91	6	E	4/4	Contact	***
2/16/91	3	2	7/9	Fluffhead	Love You
2/19/91	1	2	15/15	Suzy Greenberg	***
2/27/91	4	2	11/11	Possum	***
3/16/91	8	1	9/14	The Curtain	Col. Forbin's A
3/23/91	3	1	10/10	The Famous Mockingbi	***
3/29/91	2	2	4/8	Foam	Fluffhead
4/3/91	3	E	2/2	Cavern	***
4/5/91	2	2	1/9	***	Stash
4/12/91	3	1	8/9	Stash	Golgi Apparat
4/15/91	1	E	2/2	The Squirming Coil	***
4/19/91	3	1	8/12	I Didn't Know	Mike's Song
4/21/91	2	1	2/14	Golgi Apparatus	Wilson
4/22/91	1	E	2/4	Lawn Boy	Tweezer
5/2/91	3	1	1/11	***	Drum Jam
5/4/91	2	2	8/9	Horn	Possum
5/9/91	1	2	8/8	The Squirming Coil	***
5/12/91	3	2	13/13	AC/DC Bag	***
5/17/91	2	3	2/9	Guelah Papyrus	The Landlady
7/12/91	4	1	10/12	AC/DC Bag	Cavern
7/20/91	6	2	12/12	You Enjoy Myself	***
8/3/91	7	2	10/10	You Enjoy Myself	***
9/27/91	3	E	2/2	Glide	***
9/29/91	2	E	2/2	Memories	***
10/2/91	2	E	3/3	I Didn't Know	***
10/4/91	2	E	3/5	Golgi Apparatus	Love You
10/6/91	1	2	10/10	The Squirming Coil	***
10/12/91	3	E	2/4	Lawn Boy	Contact
10/15/91	2	1	10/10	You Enjoy Myself	***
10/17/91	1	E	2/2	Magilla	***
10/24/91	4	E	3/3	Sweet Adeline	***
10/28/91	2	E	2/2	Horn	***
10/31/91	2	E	2/2	Glide	***
11/7/91	3	E	2/4	Fee	Lawn Boy
11/16/91	8	E	2/2	Glide	***
11/19/91	1	E	2/2	Glide	***
11/22/91	3	1	11/11	Stash	***
11/24/91	2	E	2/2	Sweet Adeline	***
11/30/91	1	E	2/2	Contact	***
12/6/91	3	E	2/2	Lawn Boy	***
12/31/91	2	E	2/3	Lawn Boy	Tweezer Repri
3/11/92	3	2	11/11	Harry Hood	***
3/19/92	5	E	2/2	Sleeping Monkey	***
3/21/92	2	E	2/2	Bouncing	***
4/1/92	9	2	13/13	Contact	***
4/3/92	1	E	1/1	***	***
4/5/92	2	E	2/2	Lawn Boy	***
4/8/92	3	E	2/2	Sleeping Monkey	***
4/12/92	1	E	2/2	Sweet Adeline	***
4/15/92	2	E	3/3	Sweet Adeline	***
4/18/92	3	2	16/16	Love You	***
4/22/92	3	E	2/2	Take the A-Train	***
4/29/92	4	E	2/2	Horn	***
5/1/92	2	E	3/3	Good Times Bad Times	***
5/5/92	3	E	2/2	Contact	***
5/7/92	2	E	3/3	Sleeping Monkey	***
5/14/92	5	E	2/2	Sleeping Monkey	***
5/15/92	1	1	11/11	Sweet Adeline	***
5/18/92	3	E	1/1	***	***
6/24/92	4	1	9/9	Cavern	***
7/1/92	3	1	7/7	Sweet Adeline	***
7/9/92	1	E	1/1	***	***
8/2/92	20	1	8/8	Cavern	***
8/28/92	11	1	7/7	Runaway Jim	***
11/23/92	8	E	2/2	Sleeping Monkey	***
12/2/92	6	E	2/2	Golgi Apparatus	***
12/4/92	2	E	2/2	Fee	***
12/13/92	8	E	2/2	Sweet Adeline	***
12/29/92	2	E	3/3	Carolina	***
2/9/93	8	E	2/2	Cavern	***
2/18/93	7	2	12/12	Sweet Adeline	***
2/27/93	8	E	3/3	Amazing Grace	***
3/9/93	6	E	2/2	Amazing Grace	***
3/12/93	1	E	3/3	Carolina	***
3/17/93	4	E	2/2	Sweet Adeline	***
3/26/93	7	E	2/2	Amazing Grace	***
4/2/93	6	E	2/2	Amazing Grace	***
4/12/93	5	E	3/3	Highway to Hell	***
4/18/93	4	E	2/2	Amazing Grace	***
4/23/93	6	E	3/3	Carolina	***
5/1/93	4	E	2/2	Carolina	***
5/6/93	4	2	9/11	Ob La Di Ob La Da Ja	Cracklin' Rosi
7/18/93	8	E	1/2	***	Freebird
7/22/93	2	2	11/11	Avenu Malkenu	***
7/29/93	6	E	1/2	***	Freebird
8/9/93	8	E	1/1	***	***
8/16/93	6	E	2/2	Amazing Grace	***
8/25/93	5	E	2/2	Bold as Love	***
12/30/93	5	E	1/2	***	Good Time Ba
4/14/94	10	E	1/1	***	***
5/12/94	21	E	2/2	Amazing Grace	***
5/16/94	3	E	2/2	Fee	***
5/29/94	11	E	3/3	Golgi Apparatus	***
6/10/94	2	E	2/2	Sleeping Monkey	***
6/17/94	5	E	2/2	Sleeping Monkey	***
6/24/94	6	E	1/1	***	***
7/1/94	5	E	1/1	***	***
7/10/94	7	E	2/2	Golgi Apparatus	***
10/8/94	6	E	2/2	Foreplay/Long Time	***
11/4/94	21	E	2/2	Loving Cup	***
11/26/94	12	E	1/1	***	***
12/4/94	6	E	2/2	Sleeping Monkey	***
12/8/94	3	E	3/3	Silent in the Mornin	***
6/14/95	13	E	2/3	Simple	Tweezer Repri
6/26/95	10	E	2/2	Sleeping Monkey	***
10/3/95	12	E	1/1	***	***
10/8/95	4	E	2/2	Bouncing	***
10/20/95	7	E	2/2	Sleeping Monkey	***
11/14/95	13	E	2/2	The Wedge	***
11/24/95	7	E	2/2	Life on Mars	***
12/4/95	7	E	2/2	Bouncing	***
7/23/96	32	E	1/1	***	***
8/4/96	4	E	2/2	Star Trek Theme	***
8/13/96	6	E	2/2	Sleeping Monkey	***
10/19/96	7	E	2/2	Fee	***
11/6/96	11	E	1/1	***	***
12/2/96	18	1	1/8	***	AC/DC Bag
12/29/96	4	E	1/1	***	***
2/17/97	6	E	2/2	Sleeping Monkey	***
2/23/97	5	E	2/2	Billy Breathes	***
6/14/97	8	E	2/2	When Circus Comes	***
6/20/97	3	E	2/2	When Circus Comes	***
6/24/97	3	1	12/12	Prince Caspian	***
7/3/97	6	1	8/8	Theme From the Botto	***
7/6/97	2	2	4/5	Waste	Funky Bitch
7/29/97	9	2	7/8	Sample in a Jar	The Squirmin
8/9/97	7	E	2/2	When Circus Comes	***
8/14/97	4	E	2/2	Bouncing	***
8/16/97	1	2	6/7	Slave	Julius
11/28/97	11	1	8/8	Theme From the Botto	***
12/6/97	6	E	1/1	***	***
12/11/97	3	1	7/7	Loving Cup	***
12/28/97	3	2	8/9	Slave	Cavern
4/2/98	4	2	9/9	Sleeping Monkey	***
7/5/98	8	2	6/6	Harry Hood	***
7/17/98	7	E	2/2	Punch You in the Eye	***
7/21/98	3	E	2/2	Sleeping Monkey	***
11/11/98	31	E	2/3	Contact	Funky Bitch
11/15/98	3	E	1/1	***	***
7/23/99	30	E	2/2	Bouncing	***
9/14/99	12	1	11/11	Taste	***
9/18/99	3	1	7/7	Tube	***
9/26/99	6	E	2/2	Meatstick	***
10/7/99	7	E	1/3	***	I Am Hydrgn
12/7/99	8	E	2/2	Walk Away	***
12/15/99	6	E	2/2	Frankenstein	***
6/13/00	12	2	8/9	Prince Caspian	Cavern
9/17/00	28	E	2/2	Contact	***

Has not been played in the last 14 shows.

Roggae

DATE	GAP	SET	POS.	SONG BEFORE	SONG AFTER
6/30/98	945	1	8/13	Cities	Guyute
7/6/98	5	1	7/9	Train Song	Maze
7/10/98	3	2	2/8	Halley's Comet	Sparkle
7/15/98	1	1	11/13	Cars Trucks Buses	Birds of a Feather
7/19/98	3	1	7/8	Limb by Limb	You Enjoy My
7/21/98	2	1	3/8	Fluffhead	Tube
7/25/98	2	1	3/7	Down with Disease	Beauty of My Dreams
7/31/98	4	1	3/7	Ya Mar	Rift
8/2/98	2	1	1/9	***	Divided Sky
8/6/98	2	1	4/12	Roses Are Free	Beauty of My Dreams
8/9/98	3	1	7/9	Esther	Bouncing
8/12/98	2	1	5/8	Possum	Character Zer
8/15/98	1	1	4/12	Beauty of My Dreams	Split Open and
10/15/98	3	2	3/10	Chalk Dust Torture	The Moma Dance
10/18/98	2	1	4/12	Piper	Loving Cup
10/29/98	1	1	2/10	Julius	Llama
10/31/98	2	1	3/10	Punch You in the Eye	Birds of a Feather
11/6/98	3	1	3/7	Wilson	Maze
11/8/98	2	1	7/10	Paul and Silas	Water in the Sky
11/13/98	3	1	3/10	Wolfman's Brother	Ginseng Sulli-van
11/15/98	2	1	7/8	Limb by Limb	La Grange
11/20/98	3	1	11/13	Possum	Driver
11/25/98	3	1	3/9	My Soul	AC/DC Bag
11/29/98	3	E	1/2	***	Hello My Baby
12/30/98	3	1	4/12	Wilson	Sparkle
7/1/99	3	1	7/10	Doin' My Time	Water in the Sky
7/10/99	6	1	3/8	Chalk Dust Torture	Water in the Sky
7/17/99	5	1	6/10	My Sweet One	Tweezer
7/31/99	10	1	6/8	Free	Sparkle
9/12/99	5	2	3/5	Runaway Jim	Also Sprach
9/17/99	3	2	4/8	Piper	You Enjoy My
9/24/99	5	1	7/10	Down with Disease	Back on the Train
9/28/99	3	1	5/8	Ginseng Sullivan	Maze

DATE	GAP	SET	POS.	SONG BEFORE	SONG AFTER
10/2/99	3	1	6/9	Poor Heart	Split Open and
12/2/99	7	1	4/10	Heavy Things	Run Like Antel
12/10/99	6	1	7/10	My Mind's Got A Mind	Birds of a Feather
12/16/99	5	1	7/10	Back on the Train	Heavy Things
12/31/99	4	1	8/14	Poor Heart	Split Open and
6/13/00	7	2	6/9	Sand	Prince Caspian
6/22/00	4	1	8/9	Poor Heart	Chalk Dust Tor
7/1/00	7	1	8/11	Beauty of My Dreams	Vultures
7/7/00	4	2	4/7	Split Open and Melt	Mike's Song
9/9/00	8	1	6/8	Boogie On Reggae	Guyute
9/24/00	10	1	7/10	Divided Sky	First Tube
9/30/00	4	1	4/10	Maze	I Didn't Know

Has not been played in the last 5 shows.

Roll Like a Cantaloupe

DATE	GAP	SET	POS.	SONG BEFORE	SONG AFTER
10/15/86	14	3	1/3	***	Sanity
7/12/88	43	2	9/9	AC/DC Bag	***
3/11/90	110	2	2/13	Carolina	My Sweet One
11/14/91	177	2	2/11	Dinner and a Movie	Fee

Has not been played in the last 775 shows.

Roses Are Free

DATE	GAP	SET	POS.	SONG BEFORE	SONG AFTER
12/11/97	934	2	2/6	Drowned	BBFCFM
12/31/97	6	2	5/6	When Circus Comes	Weekapaug Gr
4/3/98	2	2	1/4	***	Piper
7/25/98	19	1	1/7	***	Down with Dis
8/6/98	8	1	3/12	Suzy Greenberg	Roggae
11/20/98	27	2	4/8	Axilla	Farmhouse
11/29/98	6	2	1/8	***	Simple
7/13/99	14	1	4/9	Halley's Comet	NO2
9/18/99	22	1	2/7	Tweezer	Wilson
12/31/99	32	2	31/35	Love You	Bug
7/15/00	28	1	6/9	Dirt	Wolfman's Brother
10/1/00	17	2	1/7	***	Piper

Has not been played in the last 4 shows.

Rotation Jam

DATE	GAP	SET	POS.	SONG BEFORE	SONG AFTER
11/25/95	772	2	4/12	Mike's Song	Mike's Song
12/15/95	14	2	5/8	Bathtub Gin	Also Sprach
12/29/96	74	2	6/10	You Enjoy Myself	Sixteen Candles
8/10/97	50	2	3/5	Good Times Bad Times	Rocko William

Has not been played in the last 209 shows.

Run Like an Antelope

DATE	GAP	SET	POS.	SONG BEFORE	SONG AFTER
5/3/85	5	3	7/8	Jam	The Other One
10/17/85	2	1	8/9	Camel Walk	McGrupp
11/23/85	3	3	3/4	Whipping Post Jam	Dave's Energy Guide
2/3/86	1	1	7/7	Prep School Hippie	***
4/29/87	11	3	6/14	Makisupa Policeman	Boogie On Reggae
5/20/87	2	1	2/9	Wilson	Golgi Apparat
9/21/87	6	3	9/15	Ballad - Curtis Loew	Makisupa Policeman
2/8/88	8	2	6/6	The Lizards	***
3/11/88	3	2	8/8	Alumni Blues	***
3/12/88	1	2	11/11	Possum	***
4/22/88	4	1	5/9	Alumni Blues	Fluffhead
5/25/88	4	3	11/11	Harpua	***
7/23/88	8	2	5/10	Terrapin	Satin Doll
7/24/88	1	3	6/6	McGrupp	***
7/30/88	2	3	13/13	Terrapin	***
9/13/88	2	2	5/6	Dave's Energy Guide	Fluffhead
11/3/88	5	2	9/9	Take the A-Train	***
12/2/88	3	2	7/8	Suzy Greenberg	Wilson
12/10/88	1	E	1/1	***	***
2/7/89	5	2	9/9	Fee	***
2/17/89	2	1	9/10	Alumni Blues	Fluffhead
2/24/89	2	1	8/10	The Famous Mockingbi	Golgi Apparat
3/3/89	1	1	7/11	The Curtain	I Didn't Know
3/4/89	1	2	4/5	The Lizards	Contact
3/30/89	4	1	8/8	Fluffhead	***
4/30/89	4	1	8/9	Peaches en Regalia	Terrapin
5/5/89	2	1	8/8	Fee	***
5/9/89	2	2	6/14	Esther	I Didn't Know
5/12/89	1	1	15/15	Ya Mar	***
5/26/89	4	2	5/6	Bathtub Gin	Golgi Apparat
5/28/89	2	1	2/9	Divided Sky	Col. Forbin's A
6/23/89	1	1	11/11	The Lizards	***
6/30/89	1	1	7/7	Fluffhead	***
8/17/89	1	3	8/8	Contact	***
8/23/89	2	2	1/8	***	Col. Forbin's A
8/26/89	1	3	5/5	Dinner and a Movie	***
9/21/89	3	2	9/9	If I Only Had a Brai	***
10/1/89	1	2	12/12	Suzy Greenberg	***
10/20/89	6	1	10/10	Golgi Apparatus	***
10/21/89	1	2	10/10	Highway to Hell	***
10/22/89	1	E	2/2	Undun	***
10/31/89	3	E	2/4	Contact	Kung
10/31/89	0	E	4/4	Kung	***
11/10/89	4	E	4/4	Take the A-Train	***
11/30/89	4	1	9/11	My Sweet One	Lawn Boy
12/3/89	2	1	7/9	My Sweet One	Lawn Boy
12/7/89	1	2	7/11	The Lizards	Lawn Boy
12/8/89	1	1	11/11	Bathtub Gin	***
12/15/89	2	2	4/8	Divided Sky	Funky Bitch
12/31/89	4	1	5/9	AC/DC Bag	Bathtub Gin
1/20/90	1	1	8/8	The Lizards	***
1/27/90	1	2	5/7	The Squirming Coil	Terrapin
1/28/90	1	2	2/10	Wilson	Bouncing
2/16/90	6	1	7/7	Donna Lee	***
2/23/90	3	1	11/11	Bouncing	***
2/24/90	1	1	8/8	I Didn't Know	***
3/8/90	6	1	10/10	Take the A-Train	***
3/9/90	1	1	11/11	Donna Lee	***
3/17/90	3	1	10/10	The Lizards	***
4/6/90	4	1	11/11	Suzy Greenberg	***
4/8/90	2	2	10/10	My Sweet One	***
4/13/90	3	2	1/10	***	Foam
4/21/90	5	1	10/10	Bike	***
4/26/90	3	1	8/9	I Didn't Know	Lawn Boy
4/28/90	1	1	11/11	Foam	***
5/4/90	2	1	12/12	Highway to Hell	***
5/23/90	8	2	8/11	Take the A-Train	Mike's Song
5/30/90	2	1	7/14	Bouncing	Lawn Boy
6/1/90	2	1	3/12	Uncle Pen	Mike's Song
6/8/90	4	1	8/8	Suzy Greenberg	***
6/9/90	1	2	11/14	Suzy Greenberg	Terrapin
6/16/90	1	2	8/8	The Lizards	***
9/13/90	1	1	6/11	The Asse Festival	Minute by Minute
9/16/90	3	1	14/14	Magilla	***
9/28/90	4	1	10/10	The Asse Festival	***
10/1/90	2	1	11/11	Love You	***
10/5/90	2	1	13/13	Bouncing	***
10/8/90	3	2	6/6	Magilla	***
10/31/90	4	1	11/11	Cavern	***
11/3/90	2	2	12/12	Love You	***
11/30/90	8	2	10/10	The Sloth	***
12/8/90	3	2	5/9	Bouncing	Tela
12/29/90	2	1	10/10	Destiny Unbound	***
12/31/90	1	2	9/9	If I Only Had a Brai	***
2/2/91	2	2	2/3	The Sloth	Lawn Boy
2/8/91	3	2	11/11	The Lizards	***
3/16/91	17	1	14/14	Suzy Greenberg	***
3/22/91	2	2	2/13	Suzy Greenberg	Foam
3/31/91	4	2	7/7	Bouncing	***
4/2/91	1	2	8/8	The Squirming Coil	***
4/6/91	4	2	9/11	Icculus	Terrapin
4/19/91	6	2	10/10	Take the A-Train	***
5/12/91	12	E	1/1	***	***
7/14/91	8	2	10/10	Cavern	***
7/25/91	8	1	10/10	Cavern	***
9/28/91	7	2	5/12	Cavern	Lawn Boy
10/10/91	7	2	5/13	Cavern	I Didn't Know
10/18/91	6	1	9/9	Sweet Adeline	***
10/27/91	4	2	13/13	Take the A-Train	***
10/30/91	2	2	4/11	Poor Heart	Lawn Boy
11/2/91	3	2	2/11	Golgi Apparatus	T.M.W.S.I.Y.
11/12/91	5	2	13/13	Love You	***
11/20/91	6	2	4/8	My Sweet One	Tela
11/22/91	2	2	5/10	Bathtub Gin	The Squirmin
11/30/91	3	2	9/10	I Didn't Know	Golgi Apparat
12/7/91	4	1	11/11	The Mango Song	***
12/31/91	1	2	10/10	My Sweet One	***
3/7/92	2	1	11/11	Rift	***
3/13/92	3	1	10/12	Fluffhead	BBFCFM
3/13/92	0	1	12/12	BBFCFM	***
3/17/92	2	1	11/11	Bouncing	***
3/20/92	2	1	10/10	Mound	***
3/25/92	4	1	10/10	It's Ice	***
3/27/92	2	1	10/10	Bouncing	***
3/31/92	3	1	10/10	The Famous Mockingbi	***
4/6/92	5	1	10/10	The Squirming Coil	***
4/12/92	3	1	11/11	Reba	***
4/16/92	3	1	12/12	The Famous Mockingbi	***
4/18/92	2	1	11/11	All Things Recnsdrd	***
4/22/92	3	2	2/11	Glide	The Horse
4/25/92	3	1	11/11	Magilla	***
4/30/92	2	1	10/10	Esther	***
5/5/92	4	1	11/11	Glide	***
5/9/92	4	1	11/11	I Didn't Know	***
5/14/92	3	1	11/11	Bouncing	***
5/18/92	4	1	10/10	Sparkle	***
7/10/92	9	1	10/10	Vacuum Solo	***
7/15/92	4	1	12/12	The Lizards	***
7/18/92	3	1	6/6	Rift	***
8/30/92	25	1	6/7	Memories	Sweet Adeline
11/19/92	2	1	12/12	Silent in the Mornin	***
11/22/92	3	1	12/12	Sweet Adeline	***
11/25/92	2	1	11/11	Sweet Adeline	***
11/30/92	3	1	10/10	Reba	***
12/3/92	2	1	12/12	Sweet Adeline	***
12/6/92	3	1	10/10	Fluffhead	***
12/8/92	2	2	8/15	The Lizards	Lawn Boy
12/12/92	3	1	11/11	Bouncing	***
12/28/92	2	1	10/10	Sweet Adeline	***
12/31/92	3	1	11/11	I Didn't Know	***
2/4/93	2	1	11/11	Glide	***
2/6/93	2	1	11/11	Bouncing	***
2/10/93	3	1	10/10	Catapult	***
2/12/93	2	1	11/11	Take the A-Train	***
2/15/93	2	1	12/12	I Didn't Know	***
2/18/93	2	1	10/10	Lawn Boy	***
2/21/93	3	1	10/10	Bouncing	***
2/23/93	2	1	11/11	Paul and Silas	***
2/27/93	3	1	10/10	Lawn Boy	***
3/9/93	6	1	10/10	I Didn't Know	***
3/13/93	2	1	11/11	Wilson	***
3/17/93	3	1	11/11	Suzy Greenberg	***
3/19/93	2	1	9/9	Cavern	***
3/25/93	4	1	11/11	Magilla	***
3/28/93	3	1	11/11	Lawn Boy	***
4/1/93	3	1	10/10	Lawn Boy	***
4/3/93	2	1	10/10	Horn	***
4/12/93	4	1	11/11	Satin Doll	***
4/17/93	3	1	10/10	Golgi Apparatus	***
4/21/93	3	1	11/11	I Didn't Know	***
4/24/93	3	1	11/11	Sparkle	***
4/29/93	3	1	10/10	Fee	***
5/2/93	3	2	8/10	Bouncing	Cracklin' Rosi
5/7/93	4	1	11/11	I Didn't Know	***
5/30/93	3	1	8/13	Silent in the Mornin	I Didn't Know
7/16/93	2	1	10/10	Horn	***
7/18/93	2	2	3/10	Poor Heart	Mound
7/23/93	3	2	3/11	Poor Heart	Faht
7/28/93	4	2	4/10	My Sweet One	The Lizards
8/2/93	4	2	9/9	Bike	***
8/7/93	3	2	12/12	Purple Rain	***
8/11/93	3	2	10/10	My Sweet One	***
8/14/93	3	2	2/13	Also Sprach	Sparks
8/14/93	0	2	5/13	Walk Away	Have Mercy
8/14/93	0	2	7/13	Have Mercy	Mound

DATE	GAP	SET	POS.	SONG BEFORE	SONG AFTER
8/20/93	4	1	10/10	Rift	***
8/24/93	2	2	10/10	Cracklin' Rosie	***
8/28/93	3	2	3/14	Rift	The Horse
12/29/93	2		4/11	Fluffhead	Contact
12/31/93	2	1	8/8	I Didn't Know	***
4/6/94	3	1	9/9	Fee	***
4/10/94	3	2	3/7	Ya Mar	Fluffhead
4/14/94	3	2	2/9	Also Sprach	The Horse
4/16/94	2	1	8/8	Nellie Kane	***
4/20/94	3	2	2/9	Poor Heart	Paul and Silas
4/23/94	3	2	2/10	Wilson	Mound
4/25/94	2	2	4/10	My Mind's Got A Mind	Mound
4/28/94	1	1	8/11	It's Ice	The Squirmin
5/4/94	5	2	1/9	***	Bouncing
5/8/94	3	2	2/9	Also Sprach	It's Ice
5/12/94	2	2	2/11	Also Sprach	The Horse
5/16/94	3	2	2/11	Also Sprach	BBFCFM
5/16/94	0	2	4/11	BBFCFM	Sparkle
5/20/94	3	2	2/7	Also Sprach	Weigh
5/23/94	3	2	2/7	Wilson	If I Could
5/26/94	2	2	2/9	Also Sprach	Fluffhead
5/29/94	3	2	9/10	Suzy Greenberg	Freebird
6/11/94	3	2	2/9	Also Sprach	Fluffhead
6/16/94	3	2	2/11	Suzy Greenberg	Col. Forbin's A
6/19/94	3	2	2/8	Faht	If I Could
6/24/94	4	2	2/13	Demand	Halley's Comet
6/30/94	4	2	13/15	Harpua	Love You
7/3/94	3	2	9/10	The Squirming Coil	Suzy Greenber
7/9/94	4	1	10/10	Silent in the Mornin	***
7/14/94	3	1	11/11	Silent in the Mornin	***
7/16/94	2	2	1/11	***	Catapult
7/16/94	3	2	3/11	Catapult	Harpua
10/8/94	2	1	9/9	Lawn Boy	***
10/13/94	4	2	2/12	The Old Home Place	If I Could
10/16/94	3	2	6/9	Big Ball Jam	Dog Faced Boy
10/21/94	3	1	9/9	Dog Faced Boy	***
10/26/94	4	1	4/10	NICU	Guyute
10/29/94	3	2	9/11	Bike	Sleeping Monkey
10/29/94	0	2	9/11	Sleeping Monkey	***
10/31/94	1	3	7/7	Poor Heart	***
11/13/94	5	1	10/10	Silent in the Mornin	***
11/16/94	2	2	7/7	Fee	***
11/19/94	3	1	8/11	Avenu Malkenu	I'm Blue, Lonesome
11/25/94	4	2	8/8	Purple Rain	***
11/30/94	3	2	2/10	Halley's Comet	My Sweet One
11/30/94	4	2	4/10	My Sweet One	Fixin' To Die
12/3/94	3	1	5/7	Scent of a Mule	Guyute
12/6/94	2	2	12/12	Foreplay/Long Time	***
12/9/94	3	1	8/8	If I Could	***
12/28/94	2	1	10/10	It's Ice	***
12/31/94	3	1	3/8	NICU	Glide
6/9/95	4	1	9/9	Sparkle	***
6/15/95	1	1	10/10	Fluffhead	***
6/19/95	3	1	10/10	Cavern	***
6/23/95	3	2	4/7	The Wedge	Harpua
6/26/95	3	2	6/6	Strange Design	***
6/30/95	1		9/9	Fee	***
7/3/95	3	1	3/11	Poor Heart	Loving Cup
9/28/95	2	2	8/8	Sample in a Jar	***
9/30/95	2	1	7/9	Horn	I'm Blue, Lonesome
10/2/95	1	2	10/10	The Lizards	***
10/7/95	4	1	9/9	Wilson	***
10/13/95	3	2	5/10	Wilson	Keyboard Cavalry
10/20/95	5	2	10/10	Bouncing	***
10/24/95	3	2	6/8	Sleeping Monkey	Contact
10/28/95	3	1	10/10	Prince Caspian	***
10/31/95	2	1	8/9	Guyute	Harpua
11/11/95	3	2	9/9	Suspicious Minds	***
11/22/95	8	1	3/10	Wilson	Fluffhead
11/28/95	3	2	7/10	Wind Beneath Wings	Contact

DATE	GAP	SET	POS.	SONG BEFORE	SONG AFTER
11/30/95	2	2	4/8	Makisupa Policeman	Scent of a Mul
12/4/95	3	2	4/9	Ya Mar	Billy Breathes
12/8/95	3	2	8/8	Tweezer Reprise	***
12/12/95	3	1	8/10	Silent in the Mornin	I'm Blue, Lonesome
12/17/95	4	1	4/9	A Day in the Life	The Mango Song
12/30/95	3	2	8/8	Cavern	***
7/7/96	7	1	9/10	Cavern	Suzy Greenber
7/12/96	4	2	4/9	Mike's Song	Purple Rain
7/15/96	2	2	9/9	Uncle Pen	***
7/21/96	4	2	6/9	Free	Simple
7/25/96	4	1	5/8	It's Ice	Life On Mars
8/2/96	1	2	9/9	Silent in the Mornin	***
8/6/96	3	1	9/9	Horn	***
8/12/96	3	2	6/9	McGrupp	Hello My Baby
8/17/96	4	2	6/8	Fluffhead	Golgi Apparat
10/16/96	1	2	8/10	Prince Caspian	The Squirmin
10/19/96	3	2	9/10	Steep	Hello My Baby
10/23/96	3	1	9/9	Theme From the Botto	***
10/26/96	2	2	7/7	Waste	***
11/2/96	4	2	2/6	Crosseyed and Painle	Waste
11/8/96	4	1	9/9	Golgi Apparatus	***
11/14/96	4	2	9/10	Demand	A Day in the Life
11/24/96	7	1	11/11	Sample in a Jar	***
12/1/96	4	1	12/12	Sample in a Jar	***
12/31/96	7	3	5/7	Suzy Greenberg	Bohemian Rhapsody
2/14/97	2	1	9/9	Uncle Pen	***
2/21/97	5	2	2/9	Ya Mar	Wilson
3/2/97	7	1	9/13	Runaway Jim	Catapult
6/20/97	6	1	8/8	I Don't Care	***
6/25/97	4	2	9/9	Rocko William	***
7/29/97	16	2	2/8	Oblivious Fool	Wading In Velvet Sea
8/6/97	5	2	7/7	Sample in a Jar	***
8/11/97	4	1	8/8	Horn	***
8/14/97	2	1	8/8	Billy Breathes	***
11/14/97	4	1	8/8	Guyute	***
11/19/97	3	1	10/10	Fee	***
11/22/97	2	2	5/5	Piper	***
11/30/97	2	2	7/7	When Circus Comes	***
12/6/97	4	1	2/9	Golgi Apparatus	Train Song
12/12/97	4	E	2/2	Guyute	***
12/29/97	3	1	9/9	Dirt	***
4/3/98	2	2	4/4	Loving Cup	***
6/30/98	3	2	5/12	Frankie Says	Lawn Boy
7/8/98	6	1	7/7	Guyute	***
7/16/98	4	1	7/7	When Circus Comes	***
7/21/98	4	1	8/8	Frankie Says	***
7/25/98	2	2	8/8	Fee	***
7/29/98	3	2	7/7	Kung	***
8/3/98	4	E	2/2	When Circus Comes	***
8/9/98	4	2	4/11	Sparkle	Brian and Robert
8/16/98	4	2	8/8	Sexual Healing	***
10/30/98	6	1	7/10	Long Cool Woman	Guelah Papyrus
11/8/98	6	2	8/8	Wading In Velvet Sea	***
11/13/98	3	1	10/10	The Sloth	***
11/27/98	9	2	16/16	Weekapaug Reprise	***
12/31/98	6	2	6/7	Wading In Velvet Sea	Frankenstein
7/3/99	3	2	5/7	Mountains in the Mis	Contact
7/13/99	7	2	5/6	Mountains in the Mis	Possum
7/25/99	9	2	3/6	Walk Away	Suzy Greenber
8/1/99	5	1	6/10	Bouncing	***
9/16/99	6	1	14/14	Billy Breathes	***
9/21/99	4	2	8/9	Dirt	***
10/1/99	7	2	2/9	NICU	The Horse
10/8/99	5	1	6/6	Meatstick	***
12/2/99	3	1	5/10	Roggae	Wading In Velvet Sea
12/8/99	5	3	9/9	Silent in the Mornin	***
12/12/99	3	2	5/5	Makisupa Policeman	***
12/30/99	6	3	3/9	The Moma Dance	The Sloth

DATE	GAP	SET	POS.	SONG BEFORE	SONG AFTER
5/23/00	4	2	6/8	You Enjoy Myself	Train Song
6/13/00	4	2	3/9	Wolfman's Brother	Contact
6/24/00	6	2	4/8	My Sweet One	Frankie Says
6/29/00	3	2	8/10	Walk Away	Frankenstein
7/3/00	3	1	10/10	When Circus Comes	***
7/8/00	4	1	9/9	Guyute	***
7/10/00	1	E	1/1	***	***
9/9/00	6	1	8/8	Guyute	***
9/15/00	4	1	6/8	Windora Bug	Golgi Apparat
9/22/00	4	2	7/7	Meatstick	***
10/4/00	8	1	7/7	Dog Faced Boy	***
10/6/00	2	1	7/7	The Moma Dance	***

Has not been played in the last 1 show.

Runaway Jim

DATE	GAP	SET	POS.	SONG BEFORE	SONG AFTER
3/28/93	169	1	10/12	Take the A-Train	You Enjoy My
4/12/90	7	2	7/11	The Lizards	Love You
4/21/90	6	2	2/9	Harry Hood	No Dogs Allowed
5/4/90	6	1	1/12	***	The Sloth
5/10/90	3	2	2/8	Funky Bitch	Harry Hood
5/13/90	2	1	6/10	Bouncing	Uncle Pen
5/15/90	1	1	10/12	Split Open and Melt	The Squirmin
10/1/90	22	1	6/11	Stash	Fee
10/31/90	9	2	3/12	Reba	Foam
11/3/90	2	1	6/12	Foam	You Enjoy My
11/4/90	1	2	9/13	Caravan	The Oh Kee Pa
11/10/90	2	1	4/11	Bouncing	Cavern
11/16/90	1	2	9/11	The Lizards	I Didn't Know
11/17/90	1	1	4/11	The Landlady	Bouncing
11/24/90	1	2	6/12	The Landlady	You Enjoy My
11/26/90	1	1	2/11	The Landlady	The Sloth
11/30/90	3	1	10/10	The Squirming Coil	Stash
12/1/90	1	1	9/9	You Enjoy Myself	***
12/7/90	1	1	7/9	The Asse Festival	Foam
12/8/90	1	1	2/10	Buried Alive	Foam
12/28/90	1	1	1/11	***	Foam
12/29/90	1	2	2/10	Buried Alive	The Lizards
12/31/90	1	2	4/9	The Squirming Coil	Magilla
2/1/91	1	1	7/10	Guelah Papyrus	Split Open and
2/3/91	2	1	1/10	***	Guelah Papyrus
2/7/91	1	1	1/10	***	Foam
2/8/91	1	1	9/11	The Squirming Coil	Guelah Papyrus
2/9/91	1	1	6/12	T.M.W.S.I.Y. Reprise	Foam
2/14/91	1	2	6/12	The Squirming Coil	Esther
2/16/91	2	2	4/9	Buried Alive	Guelah Papyrus
2/19/91	1	1	7/9	The Sloth	The Squirmin
2/26/91	3	2	2/12	Buried Alive	Dinner and a
3/1/91	3	2	6/11	Guelah Papyrus	The Sloth
3/9/91	3	2	6/13	Buried Alive	Guelah Papyrus
3/13/91	1	2	6/12	Guelah Papyrus	The Sloth
3/15/91	1	E	2/2	The Squirming Coil	***
3/17/91	2	2	1/8	***	Esther
3/22/91	1	2	7/13	Stash	Guelah Papyrus
3/31/91	4	1	3/13	Cavern	Col. Forbin's A
4/2/91	1	1	1/10	***	The Landlady
4/4/91	2	2	2/10	The Curtain	Guelah Papyrus
4/6/91	2	2	3/11	Split Open and Melt	Magilla
4/11/91	1	1	1/12	***	Cavern
4/12/91	1	2	2/10	The Landlady	You Enjoy My
4/15/91	1	1	4/10	Foam	Split Open and
4/16/91	1	2	9/11	Tweezer	Carolina
4/20/91	3	1	1/11	***	Reba
4/22/91	2	1	2/9	The Curtain	The Sloth
4/27/91	1	1	3/11	The Landlady	The Curtain
4/27/91	1	1	3/12	The Asse Festival	Cavern
5/3/91	2	2	5/9	The Landlady	Tela
5/4/91	1	E	2/3	Terrapin	Golgi Apparat
5/9/91	1	1	9/10	Magilla	Sweet Adeline
5/12/91	3	1	11/11	Foam	***

DATE	GAP	SET	POS.	SONG BEFORE	SONG AFTER
5/16/91	1	2	1/9	***	Dinner and a
5/18/91	2	E	2/2	Dinner and a Movie	***
7/13/91	4	1	2/13	The Curtain	Foam
7/18/91	3	1	3/11	Foam	Guelah Papyrus
7/19/91	1	E	2/2	Lawn Boy	***
7/21/91	2	2	3/9	I Didn't Know	Lawn Boy
8/3/91	6	1	3/11	Foam	Guelah Papyrus
9/25/91	1	2	6/8	Jesus Just Left	You Enjoy My
9/27/91	2	1	1/9	***	Cavern
10/2/91	4	2	5/9	Guelah Papyrus	Lawn Boy
10/4/91	2	2	5/11	Foam	Lawn Boy
10/10/91	2	1	7/1	The Landlady	It's Ice
10/11/91	1	1	10/10	Bouncing	***
10/13/91	2	1	1/13	***	Wilson
10/15/91	1	2	3/12	Bouncing	Guelah Papyrus
10/18/91	2	1	1/9	***	Foam
10/19/91	1	1	4/10	It's Ice	Foam
10/23/91	1	1	10/11	Bouncing	Cavern
10/28/91	3	1	1/10	***	Cavern
10/30/91	1	1	2/7	Foam	Cavern
10/31/91	1	1	11/11	You Enjoy Myself	***
11/2/91	2	2	10/11	The Landlady	You Enjoy My
11/7/91	1	1	9/11	The Landlady	I Didn't Know
11/9/91	2	1	2/11	The Curtain	Foam
11/13/91	3	1	2/10	The Landlady	It's Ice
11/14/91	1	1	11/11	Golgi Apparatus	***
11/16/91	2	1	4/11	Wilson	It's Ice
11/19/91	1	1	3/11	Foam	Fee
11/21/91	2	2	10/10	T.M.W.S.I.Y. Reprise	***
11/23/91	2	1	4/11	Foam	Guelah Papyrus
12/4/91	3	1	4/11	The Landlady	Cavern
12/7/91	3	1	2/11	Wilson	Foam
12/31/91	1	2	5/10	Auld Lang Syne	The Landlady
3/7/92	2	1	4/11	Foam	The Horse
3/12/92	2	1	1/11	***	Foam
3/14/92	1	1	1/13	***	Cavern
3/17/92	1	2	1/11	***	Glide
3/21/92	3	1	2/12	The Landlady	Foam
3/25/92	3	1	8/10	Glide	It's Ice
3/26/92	1	2	1/10	The Landlady	All Things Rec
3/28/92	2	1	1/10	***	Foam
3/30/92	1	1	10/10	The Sloth	Cavern
4/1/92	2	1	8/12	It's Ice	I Didn't Know
4/4/92	2	1	1/10	***	Foam
4/5/92	1	2	12/12	Take the A-Train	***
4/7/92	2	1	12/12	The Sloth	***
4/15/92	4	1	11/11	All Things Recnsdrd	***
4/17/92	2	1	1/13	***	Foam
4/19/92	2	2	13/13	If I Only Had a Brai	***
4/22/92	2	2	11/11	Harpua	***
4/24/92	2	1	1/11	***	Col. Forbin's A
4/29/92	2	1	5/10	It's Ice	Guelah Papyrus
5/2/92	3	1	1/11	***	Col. Forbin's A
5/3/92	1	1	10/10	Horn	***
5/7/92	3	1	6/11	Foam	Esther
5/9/92	2	1	1/11	***	Foam
5/12/92	2	E	1/1	***	***
5/16/92	3	2	1/13	***	It's Ice
5/18/92	2	2	13/13	Love You	***
6/20/92	2	1	4/8	Foam	It's Ice
6/24/92	2	1	1/9	***	Llama
6/27/92	1	1	1/10	***	Foam
7/9/92	3	1	7/12	The Squirming Coil	Guelah Papyrus
7/11/92	2	1	2/11	The Landlady	Foam
7/14/92	2	1	7/12	It's Ice	Horn
7/16/92	2	2	1/13	***	Weigh
7/17/92	1	1	7/7	Bouncing	***
7/19/92	2	1	3/5	Maze	David Bowie
7/21/92	1	1	7/7	The Squirming Coil	***
7/25/92	3	1	1/8	***	Foam
7/28/92	3	1	6/6	Tweezer	***
8/15/92	7	1	5/5	Maze	***
8/19/92	2	1	3/7	The Landlady	Guelah Papyrus
8/23/92	2	1	6/7	Foam	Stash
8/25/92	2	1	1/7	***	It's Ice
8/28/92	2	1	6/7	The Squirming Coil	Rocky Top
10/30/92	3	1	1/11	***	Maze
11/21/92	3	1	2/11	The Landlady	Foam
11/23/92	2	1	1/11	***	Foam
11/27/92	2	1	12/12	Memories	***
11/30/92	2	2	2/10	Buried Alive	Guelah Papyrus
12/2/92	2	2	11/11	I Walk The Line	***
12/6/92	4	1	1/10	***	Foam
12/7/92	1	E	1/1	***	***
12/11/92	3	1	1/11	***	It's Ice
12/29/92	4	1	2/12	Funky Bitch	Guelah Papyrus
12/31/92	2	2	1/10	***	It's Ice
2/3/93	1	2	1/10	***	It's Ice
2/7/93	4	1	12/12	Fee	***
2/10/93	2	2	1/11	***	It's Ice
2/13/93	3	2	2/11	Wilson	Uncle Pen
2/17/93	2	1	6/11	The Sloth	It's Ice
2/19/93	2	2	1/12	***	It's Ice
2/22/93	3	2	1/11	***	Uncle Pen
2/26/93	3	1	1/10	***	Foam
3/3/93	3	1	8/10	Sample in a Jar	Lawn Boy
3/6/93	2	1	10/10	Golgi Apparatus	***
3/9/93	2	1	1/10	***	Foam
3/14/93	3	1	11/11	Punch You in the Eye	***
3/17/93	2	1	2/11	The Landlady	Foam
3/19/93	2	2	1/10	***	It's Ice
3/26/93	5	2	2/12	Wilson	Tweezer
3/28/93	2	2	2/9	Walk Away	Mound
3/31/93	2	1	1/10	***	Foam
4/2/93	2	2	1/13	***	Sample in a Ja
4/10/93	4	1	1/10	***	Weigh
4/14/93	2	2	10/10	Harpua	***
4/20/93	4	1	1/10	***	Weigh
4/23/93	3	1	1/10	***	Weigh
4/25/93	2	1	6/11	Glide	Col. Forbin's A
4/29/93	2	1	4/10	The Sloth	Horn
5/1/93	2	1	1/10	***	Foam
5/3/93	2	2	9/12	McGrupp	Love You
5/5/93	1	2	1/10	***	My Friend My
5/29/93	4	1	9/10	Big Ball Jam	Amazing Grce
7/15/93	2	1	9/9	Leprechaun	***
7/17/93	2	1	2/11	The Landlady	Sample in a Ja
7/21/93	2	1	9/12	Bouncing	Big Ball Jam
7/23/93	2	1	9/12	Punch You in the Eye	It's Ice
7/28/93	4	1	2/11	All Things Recnsdrd	Ya Mar
7/31/93	3	2	2/11	Wilson	It's Ice
8/3/93	2	1	1/11	***	Nellie Kane
8/8/93	3	1	4/11	Loving Cup	The Horse
8/11/93	2	1	2/11	Buried Alive	Weigh
8/15/93	4	1	4/10	Caravan	Fee
8/21/93	4	1	10/10	I Didn't Know	***
8/26/93	3	1	1/9	***	Guelah Papyrus
12/29/93	3	1	1/9	***	Peaches en Regalia
4/5/94	4	1	1/8	***	Foam
4/10/94	4	1	1/9	***	It's Ice
4/14/94	3	1	1/9	***	Foam
4/16/94	2	1	1/8	***	Fee
4/20/94	3	1	1/7	***	It's Ice
4/22/94	2	2	6/8	Lifeboy	I Wanna Be Like You
4/25/94	3	1	2/10	The Landlady	Fee
4/28/94	1	1	1/11	***	Foam
5/2/94	3	2	1/9	***	Mound
5/4/94	2	1	1/10	***	Foam
5/8/94	3	1	1/8	***	Foam
5/13/94	3	1	1/9	***	It's Ice
5/17/94	3	2	1/9	***	Glide
5/21/94	3	1	1/9	***	Foam
5/27/94	5	1	2/9	Wilson	Foam
6/10/94	4	1	1/9	***	Foam
6/17/94	5	1	1/9	***	Foam
6/21/94	3	1	1/5	***	Mound
7/1/94	8	1	1/10	***	Foam
7/9/94	6	1	1/10	***	Foam
7/14/94	3	1	1/11	***	Bouncing
7/15/94	1	2	10/10	Setting Sail	***
10/9/94	4	1	1/7	***	Foam
10/15/94	5	2	2/11	Also Sprach	Halley's Comet
10/20/94	3	1	1/11	***	Golden Lady
10/23/94	3	2	1/9	***	Bouncing
10/26/94	2	1	10/10	Suzy Greenberg	***
10/29/94	3	1	4/10	Simple	Foam
11/12/94	5	1	1/8	***	Foam
11/18/94	5	E	2/2	Sweet Baby's Arms	***
11/22/94	3	2	7/13	Blackbird	BBFCFM
12/4/94	9	1	1/9	***	Foam
12/7/94	2	1	2/8	Peaches en Regalia	The Sloth
12/29/94	5	1	1/9	***	Foam
6/8/95	5	1	3/9	Ha Ha Ha	Guelah Papyrus
6/13/95	3	1	1/10	***	Foam
6/16/95	3	2	1/5	***	Free
6/23/95	5	2	1/7	***	The Lizards
6/29/95	5	1	1/10	***	Taste
7/2/95	3	2	1/8	***	Makisupa Policeman
9/28/95	3	1	2/9	Cars Trucks Buses	Billy Breathes
9/30/95	2	2	1/9	***	Fog that Surrounds
10/5/95	3	2	2/9	Also Sprach	Col. Forbin's A
10/14/95	6	1	11/11	Tela	***
10/19/95	3	1	2/11	Cars Trucks Buses	Horn
10/22/95	3	1	4/12	The Sloth	Weigh
10/27/95	3	1	1/9	***	Fluffhead
11/10/95	5	1	2/9	Bouncing	Taste That Surrounds
11/16/95	5	1	2/10	Cars Trucks Buses	Chess Jam
11/21/95	3	1	10/10	Dog Faced Boy	***
11/25/95	3	1	9/9	Wolfman's Brother	***
12/2/95	5	1	2/10	Prince Caspian	Mound
12/8/95	4	1	4/9	Simple	Fluffhead
12/12/95	3	2	6/6	Simple	***
12/15/95	2	2	2/8	Tweezer Reprise	It's Ice
12/17/95	2	E	2/2	Hello My Baby	***
12/31/95	4	2	5/8	Axilla (Part II)	Strange Design
6/6/96	2	1	3/8	Poor Heart	Funky Bitch
7/3/96	1	1	1/5	***	Stash
7/11/96	6	1	1/8	***	Cavern
7/13/96	2	1	2/10	Sample in a Jar	Cavern
7/19/96	4	1	1/6	***	Foam
7/23/96	2	2	2/9	Also Sprach	Loving Cup
8/2/96	3	2	1/9	***	Simple
8/7/96	4	2	1/10	***	Gypsy Queen
8/7/96	0	2	3/10	Gypsy Queen	Free
8/14/96	4	2	1/10	***	You Enjoy My
8/17/96	2	2	2/8	The Curtain	It's Ice
10/18/96	3	1	1/10	***	Guelah Papyrus
10/22/96	3	1	2/9	The Curtain	Bouncing
10/27/96	4	1	1/11	***	Punch You in
11/3/96	4	1	2/9	My Friend My Friend	Billy Breathes
11/8/96	3	1	1/9	***	Axilla
11/11/96	2	1	9/9	Axilla	***
11/16/96	4	2	2/8	La Grange	Kung
11/22/96	3	1	2/10	It's Ice	Wolfman's Brother
11/30/96	5	1	1/10	***	Punch You in
12/28/96	5	1	1/9	***	NICU
2/14/97	5	1	1/9	***	NICU
2/18/97	3	1	4/10	Punch You in the Eye	NICU

DATE	GAP	SET	POS.	SONG BEFORE	SONG AFTER
2/20/97	1	2	11/12	A Day in the Life	Sweet Adeline
2/25/97	4	1	1/9	***	My Soul
3/2/97	4	1	6/13	My Soul	Gypsy Queen
3/2/97	0	1	8/13	Gypsy Queen	Run Like Antel
6/19/97	5	1	9/9	Vultures	***
6/24/97	4	1	6/12	Guelah Papyrus	Gypsy Queen
6/24/97	0	1	8/12	Gypsy Queen	Talk
7/6/97	8	1	1/9	***	The Old Home
7/22/97	5	1	1/8	***	My Soul
7/31/97	6	2	1/7	***	When Circus Comes
8/6/97	3	2	1/7	***	My Soul
8/13/97	5	2	1/9	***	Ghost
11/14/97	5	1	1/8	***	Gumbo
11/29/97	9	2	1/5	***	Strange Design
12/5/97	4	1	6/10	Sparkle	My Friend My
12/28/97	7	1	6/11	The Old Home Place	Farmhouse
7/2/98	10	2	2/4	Ghost	Prince Caspian
7/24/98	13	1	2/8	The Moma Dance	Bouncing
8/11/98	13	2	1/5	***	Meat
10/3/98	4	1	4/10	The Moma Dance	Arc
11/4/98	8	2	1/6	***	The Moma Dance
11/15/98	8	2	1/7	***	Stash
11/27/98	7	1	4/11	Carini	Meat
12/31/98	6	3	1/6	***	Auld Lang Syne
7/9/99	7	1	8/8	Driver	***
7/18/99	7	2	1/6	***	Free
7/30b/99	8	2	5/6	Bike	Cavern
9/12/99	6	2	2/5	Ghost	Roggae
9/17/99	3	2	1/8	***	Sand
9/25/99	6	1	2/8	Tube	Ya Mar
9/29/99	3	1	1/9	***	Free
10/4/99	4	1	4/8	Vultures	Jesus Just Left
12/2/99	5	1	1/10	***	Farmhouse
12/12/99	8	E	1/1	***	***
12/16/99	3	2	5/5	Tweezer	***
12/31/99	4	1	1/14	***	Funky Bitch
6/16/00	10	2	1/7	***	Theme From the Botto
6/24/00	3	1	2/6	The Moma Dance	Bouncing
6/30/00	4	1	4/10	Tweezer	Sneakin' Sally
7/3/00	2	2	1/7	***	Glide
7/11/00	6	2	5/13	Down with Disease	Moby Dick
10/1/00	20	1	10/10	Lawn Boy	***

Has not been played in the last 4 shows.

Running With the Devil

DATE	GAP	SET	POS.	SONG BEFORE	SONG AFTER
8/6/98	969	E	1/2	***	You Enjoy My

Has not been played in the last 150 shows.

Sabotage

DATE	GAP	SET	POS.	SONG BEFORE	SONG AFTER
8/8/98	971	E	1/1	***	***
8/16/98	5	3	1/7	***	Also Sprach
11/21/98	21	2	1/9	***	Mike's Song

Has not been played in the last 122 shows.

Sad Lisa

DATE	GAP	SET	POS.	SONG BEFORE	SONG AFTER
10/18/98	980	1	10/12	Brian and Robert	Four Strong Winds

Has not been played in the last 139 shows.

Sample in a Jar

DATE	GAP	SET	POS.	SONG BEFORE	SONG AFTER
2/4/93	481	1	9/11	The Lizards	Glide
2/9/93	4	2	7/12	My Sweet One	Big Ball Jam
2/27/93	15	2	4/12	Poor Heart	Big Ball Jam
3/3/93	2	1	7/10	Paul and Silas	Runaway Jim
3/14/93	7	1	7/11	Paul and Silas	Reba
3/19/93	4	2	4/10	Uncle Pen	The Lizards
3/24/93	3	1	7/9	I Didn't Know	Amazing Grce
3/25/93	1	2	3/13	The Curtain	Uncle Pen

DATE	GAP	SET	POS.	SONG BEFORE	SONG AFTER
3/27/93	2	1	8/10	Uncle Pen	I Didn't Know
3/31/93	3	1	7/10	Punch You in the Eye	Reba
4/2/93	2	2	2/13	Runaway Jim	Uncle Pen
4/16/93	7	1	7/10	Llama	Rift
4/20/93	3	2	3/12	Fluffhead	Big Ball Jam
5/1/93	9	1	7/10	Rift	It's Ice
7/15/93	9	1	2/10	Rift	Divided Sky
7/17/93	2	1	3/11	Runaway Jim	My Mind's Got A Mind
7/22/93	3	1	5/11	My Mind's Got A Mind	Divided Sky
7/28/93	5	1	4/11	Ya Mar	Foam
7/31/93	3	2	2/9	Rift	Ya Mar
8/6/93	3	1	4/10	The Curtain	Rift
8/15/93	8	1	1/10	***	All Things Rec
8/25/93	6	1	3/11	Daniel	Sparkle
12/28/93	3	2	1/9	***	You Enjoy My
12/30/93	2	1	4/10	The Curtain	Paul and Silas
4/4/94	2	1	2/9	Divided Sky	Scent of a Mul
4/6/94	2	1	6/9	The Lizards	Scent of a Mul
4/9/94	2	2	1/11	***	Reba
4/11/94	2	2	6/11	Uncle Pen	Big Ball Jam
4/13/94	1	2	3/10	The Curtain	Reba
4/16/94	3	2	1/9	***	Poor Heart
4/18/94	2	2	2/13	Also Sprach	Sparkle
4/20/94	1	2	4/9	Paul and Silas	Big Ball Jam
4/22/94	2	1	5/11	Punch You in the Eye	All Things Rec
4/23/94	1	2	4/10	Mound	Sparkle
4/25/94	2	2	2/10	The Curtain	My Mind's Got A Mind
4/28/94	1	1	3/11	Foam	Rift
4/30/94	2	1	5/9	Poor Heart	Punch You in
5/2/94	1	1	10/10	Foam	***
5/3/94	1	1	8/9	Scent of a Mule	Sweet Adeline
5/4/94	1	1	3/10	Foam	It's Ice
5/6/94	1	2	4/9	Uncle Pen	Reba
5/7/94	1	E	2/2	Amazing Grace	***
5/10/94	2	1	3/9	Poor Heart	Divided Sky
5/12/94	1	1	10/10	The Lizards	***
5/14/94	2	1	6/9	Reba	My Sweet One
5/16/94	1	1	3/10	Poor Heart	Divided Sky
5/17/94	1	2	7/9	Big Ball Jam	Love You
5/19/94	1	2	1/10	***	Sparkle
5/21/94	2	2	2/9	Dinner and a Movie	David Bowie
5/23/94	2	1	2/10	Chalk Dust Torture	Foam
5/25/94	1	1	2/11	The Curtain	Uncle Pen
5/26/94	1	1	10/10	Divided Sky	***
5/28/94	2	1	2/10	Rift	Foam
6/10/94	3	1	3/9	Foam	Nellie Kane
6/13/94	2	1	3/9	Poor Heart	Divided Sky
6/14/94	1	E	1/1	***	***
6/17/94	2	2	2/15	Also Sprach	Poor Heart
6/18/94	1	1	10/10	Divided Sky	***
6/21/94	2	1	3/5	Mound	It's Ice
6/22/94	1	2	20/20	Jesus Just Left	***
6/24/94	2	1	11/11	Sweet Adeline	***
6/25/94	1	1	7/10	The Mango Song	Scent of a Mul
6/26/94	1	2	6/12	Lifeboy	Wolfman's Brother
6/29/94	1	1	2/11	The Curtain	Reba
7/1/94	2	1	3/10	Foam	NICU
7/2/94	1	2	10/12	Maze	Slave
7/5/94	2	1	2/10	Rift	The Curtain
7/6/94	1	2	7/10	BBFCFM	BBFCFM
7/8/94	1	2	2/11	Rift	Reba
7/10/94	2	2	1/10	***	David Bowie
7/13/94	1	1	3/11	Poor Heart	Foam
7/14/94	1	2	2/10	Also Sprach	Maze
7/15/94	1	1	2/8	Rift	Divided Sky
7/16/94	1	1	11/11	Sparkle	***
10/8/94	2	2	2/12	Also Sprach	Rift
10/10/94	2	1	1/11	***	Divided Sky
10/12/94	1	2	9/9	Harry Hood	***
10/14/94	2	1	2/12	Buried Alive	Divided Sky
10/16/94	2	2	9/9	Sweet Adeline	***
10/20/94	2	E	1/1	***	***
10/23/94	3	1	11/11	Maze	***

DATE	GAP	SET	POS.	SONG BEFORE	SONG AFTER
10/25/94	1	1	9/9	The Lizards	***
10/28/94	3	1	9/10	All Things Recnsdrd	Carolina
11/2/94	3	2	7/7	The Lizards	***
11/4/94	2	1	1/9	***	It's Ice
11/12/94	1	E	1/1	***	***
11/16/94	3	1	1/11	***	Foam
11/20/94	4	1	10/10	Divided Sky	***
11/23/94	2	E	1/1	***	***
11/26/94	2	2	5/6	The Lizards	Slave
12/1/94	3	1	1/8	***	Uncle Pen
12/3/94	2	1	7/7	***	Guyute
12/6/94	2	2	2/12	The Curtain	Also Sprach
12/10/94	4	1	5/8	The Lizards	Divided Sky
12/30/94	3	2	1/8	***	Poor Heart
5/16/95	2	1	12/12	Sweet Adeline	***
6/7/95	1	2	7/9	Acoustic Army	Harry Hood
6/10/95	3	2	8/8	Amazing Grace	***
6/17/95	5	2	11/11	Harry Hood	***
6/22/95	1	1	1/10	***	Scent of a Mul
6/25/95	3	2	2/9	Maze	Scent of a Mul
6/28/95	2	2	1/10	***	Poor Heart
7/2/95	1	1	1/10	***	Divided Sky
9/28/95	3	2	7/8	Amazing Grace	Run Like Antel
9/30/95	2	1	9/9	I'm Blue, Lonesome	***
10/3/95	2	1	10/11	T.M.W.S.I.Y. Reprise	You Enjoy My
10/6/95	2	1	9/9	The Lizards	***
10/8/95	2	2	5/10	Ya Mar	You Enjoy My
10/11/95	1	1	9/9	Julius	***
10/15/95	3	2	5/8	The Lizards	Suspicious Minds
10/17/95	1	1	1/10	***	Stash
10/22/95	4	1	10/12	Poor Heart	I'm Blue, Lonesome
10/25/95	2	1	2/10	Ya Mar	Divided Sky
10/28/95	2	1	5/10	Uncle Pen	The Lizards
11/9/95	3	1	8/8	Tela	***
11/12/95	2	1	4/8	Keyboard Cavalry	Slave
11/18/95	4	1	8/8	I'm Blue, Lonesome	***
11/22/95	3	1	9/10	The Lizards	Sweet Adeline
11/28/95	2	1	9/9	Hello My Baby	***
11/30/95	2	1	1/10	***	The Curtain
12/4/95	3	2	8/9	You Enjoy Myself	Frankenstein
12/8/95	3	1	1/9	***	Poor Heart
12/12/95	3	1	1/9	***	Divided Sky
12/16/95	3	2	1/8	***	Reba
12/30/95	4	1	13/13	Divided Sky	***
4/26/96	2	1	11/13	Harry Hood	A Day in the Life
6/6/96	1	2	10/10	Fee	***
7/7/96	4	1	1/10	***	Divided Sky
7/11/96	3	1	8/8	Scent of a Mule	***
7/13/96	2	1	1/10	***	Runaway Jim
7/17/96	2	1	2/5	Divided Sky	David Bowie
7/22/96	4	1	1/8	***	Poor Heart
7/25/96	3	1	3/8	Punch You in the Eye	It's Ice
8/4/96	2	2	4/7	Scent of a Mule	David Bowie
8/12/96	5	E	1/1	***	***
8/14/96	2	2	9/10	Cracklin' Rosie	Tweezer Repri
8/17/96	2	1	6/10	The Lizards	Taste
10/16/96	1	1	8/12	Mound	It's Ice
10/18/96	2	1	1/10	Taste	***
10/21/96	2	1	2/10	Star Spangled Banner	Cars Trucks Buses
10/26/96	4	1	9/9	Theme From the Botto	***
11/3/96	5	1	6/9	NICU	Theme From the Botto
11/6/96	1	2	8/9	Scent of a Mule	Funky Bitch
11/11/96	4	2	5/11	The Curtain	Tweezer
11/14/96	2	2	2/10	Llama	Taste
11/22/96	5	1	6/10	Ginseng Sullivan	Fast Enough for You
11/24/96	2	1	10/11	I Didn't Know	Run Like Antel
11/29/96	2	E	1/1	***	***
12/1/96	2	1	11/12	Silent in the Mornin	Run Like Antel
12/4/96	2	1	6/11	Timber (Jerry)	Train Song
12/31/96	5	1	9/10	Divided Sky	Tweezer Repri

DATE	GAP	SET	POS.	SONG BEFORE	SONG AFTER
2/16/97	3	2	1/11	***	Cars Trucks Buses
2/20/97	3	2	1/12	***	Cars Trucks Buses
2/25/97	4	2	2/10	Beauty of My Dreams	Punch You in
3/2/97	4	1	3/13	Uncle Pen	Guyute
3/18/97	1	1	3/10	NICU	Punch You in
6/16/97	3	1	5/10	Water in the Sky	Beauty of My Dreams
6/21/97	3	1	1/15	***	Also Sprach
7/5/97	9	1	4/13	Uncle Pen	Theme From the Botto
7/23/97	7	2	3/6	Ghost	You Enjoy My
7/29/97	3	2	6/8	Taste	Rocky Top
8/6/97	5	2	6/7	Cars Trucks Buses	Run Like Antel
8/13/97	5	2	6/9	McGrupp	Also Sprach
12/2/97	16	E	2/2	Ginseng Sullivan	***
12/6/97	3	1	6/9	Foam	Fee
12/13/97	5	1	6/9	Strange Design	Vultures
12/28/97	1	1	4/11	The Curtain	The Old Home
7/1/98	9	1	2/9	NICU	My Mind's Got A Mind
7/3/98	2	1	3/11	Beauty of My Dreams	Guyute
7/10/98	5	2	7/8	Weekapaug Groove	Good Time Ba
7/16/98	2	E	1/1	***	***
7/19/98	2	1	3/8	Beauty of My Dreams	Guyute
7/26/98	5	2	6/6	Bold as Love	***
8/11/98	11	1	11/11	Maze	***
11/2/98	11	1	9/9	Wading In Velvet Sea	***
11/13/98	7	2	2/6	Down with Disease	Dirt
11/19/98	4	1	3/9	The Curtain	Ginseng Sullivan
11/24/98	3	1	7/9	Limb by Limb	Tela
11/28/98	3	E	1/2	***	Tweezer Repri
12/30/98	4	1	8/12	The Old Home Place	Frankie Says
6/30/99	2	E	2/2	Bouncing	***
7/16/99	11	1	1/9	***	Beauty of My Dreams
7/20 /99	3	1	2/9	Chalk Dust Torture	Cars Trucks Buses
7/30b/99	7	1	2/8	Birds of a Feather	Beauty of my Dreams
9/9/99	3	E	1/3	***	Golgi Apparat
9/21/99	9	1	2/9	Poor Heart	Split Open and
10/4/99	10	2	2/8	Ghost	The Wedge
12/2/99	5	1	8/10	Poor Heart	Free
12/15/99	10	2	1/7	***	Maze
6/10/00	10	1	2/5	Down with Disease	Piper
6/16/00	5	1	3/10	Back on the Train	First Tube
6/25/00	4	2	2/10	NICU	The Old Home
7/1/00	4	1	5/11	Poor Heart	Tube
7/14/00	9	1	1/1	***	***
9/14/00	6	E	3/3	The Inlaw Josie Wale	***
9/18/00	3	1	7/10	My Mind's Got A Mind	Rift
9/24/00	4	1	10/10	Punch You in the Eye	***
9/27/00	2	1	1/10	***	My Friend My
10/4/00	4	2	3/7	Also Sprach	Gotta Jibboo

Has not been played in the last 3 shows.

Samson Variation

DATE	GAP	SET	POS.	SONG BEFORE	SONG AFTER
8/3/97	906	1	3/10	Foam	Dirt

Has not been played in the last 213 shows.

Sand

DATE	GAP	SET	POS.	SONG BEFORE	SONG AFTER
9/11/99	1033	2	2/6	Wolfman's Brother	Meatstick
9/17/99	4	2	2/8	Runaway Jim	Piper
9/19/99	2	2	2/6	Twist	Wading In Velvet Sea
9/22/99	2	1	9/10	Mozambique	Waste
9/24/99	1	2	5/6	The Lizards	Misty Mountain Hop
10/4/99	8	2	6/8	Makisupa Policeman	Ya Mar
12/3/99	6	2	1/5	***	Limb by Limb
12/8/99	4	2	1/6	***	Dirt

DATE	GAP	SET	POS.	SONG BEFORE	SONG AFTER
12/13/99	4	2	3/8	NICU	The Inlaw Josie Wale
12/16/99	2	2	1/5	***	The Mango Song
12/18/99	2	2	2/10	Also Sprach	The Horse
12/31/99	2	2	13/35	The Inlaw Josie Wale	Quadrophonic Topplin
5/22/00	2	2	3/6	David Bowie	The Mango Song
6/10/00	3	2	2/9	Heavy Things	Sparkle
6/13/00	2	2	5/9	Contact	Roggae
6/22/00	4	2	3/10	Also Sprach	Harry Hood
6/29/00	5	2	4/10	Heavy Things	Meatstick
7/3/00	3	2	4/7	Theme From the Botto	Meat
7/10/00	5	2	2/7	Gotta Jibboo	Twist
7/14/00	3	3	5/7	Waste	The Lizards
9/9/00	3	2	3/7	The Curtain	Makisupa Policeman
9/20/00	7	2	6/9	Wading In Velvet Sea	Guyute
9/30/00	7	2	6/7	Twist	A Day in the Life
10/6/00	4	2	7/10	Cities	Golgi Apparat

Has not been played in the last 1 show.

Sanity

DATE	GAP	SET	POS.	SONG BEFORE	SONG AFTER
10/15/86	14	3	2/3	Roll Like a Cantalou	Anarchy
10/31/86	1	2	8/11	Harry Hood	Skin it Back
2/13/87	2	1	8/14	Suzy Greenberg	Good Time Ba
8/21/87	10	3	6/7	David Bowie Jam	Swing Low Sweet Chrt
2/24/88	12	2	3/5	Sneakin' Sally	La Grange
7/25/88	21	3	4/4	BBFCFM	***
8/6/88	3	2	4/6	Satin Doll	BBFCFM
9/13/88	4	3	6/8	BBFCFM	Vacuum Jam
1/26/89	12	1	7/10	Take the A-Train	Divided Sky
2/6/89	1	2	2/7	All Blues	Take the A-Trn
2/7/89	1	3	1/6	***	Fluffhead
4/27/89	13	1	4/8	Divided Sky	I Don't Know
5/26/89	10	1	6/9	Weekapaug Groove	Halley's Comet
5/28/89	2	2	6/16	Bathtub Gin	Ride Captain Ride
3/11/92	255	E	1/4	***	Memories
3/20/92	6	2	4/12	Weekapaug Groove	The Sloth
4/16/92	20	2	1/12	***	Llama
4/21/92	4	2	12/13	Lively Up Yourself	Maze
5/1/92	7	2	1/13	***	Buried Alive
5/17/92	13	2	7/11	Brother	Love You
4/29/94	198	1	10/12	Split Open and Melt	My Mind's Got A Mind
6/24/94	36	2	7/13	Simple	Llama
12/31/95	147	3	5/6	You Enjoy Myself	Frankenstein
10/31/96	43	1	1/10	***	Highway to Hell
8/15/98	140	2	4/9	Gumbo	Tweezer
11/27/98	25	2	8/16	Chalk Dust Torture	Buffalo Bill

Has not been played in the last 119 shows.

Satin Doll

DATE	GAP	SET	POS.	SONG BEFORE	SONG AFTER
6/20/88	53	2	5/9	Golgi Apparatus	Take the A-Trn
7/11/88	3	1	1/11	***	Suzy Greenber
7/23/88	2	1	1/10	Run Like an Antelope	Blue Bossa
8/3/88	4	3	6/8	Harry Hood	Funky Bitch
8/6/88	1	2	3/6	AC/DC Bag	Sanity
8/27/88	1	1	1/9	***	You Enjoy My
9/12/88	2	2	2/10	Timber (Jerry)	The Lizards
3/30/89	25	3	5/6	BBFCFM	Rocky Top
12/31/89	54	1	8/9	The Lizards	Highway to Hell
2/25/90	14	1	9/11	David Bowie	Rift
4/12/93	370	1	10/11	Llama	Run Like Antel
5/8/93	20	1	11/12	Reba	Cavern

Has not been played in the last 570 shows.

Savoy Truffle

DATE	GAP	SET	POS.	SONG BEFORE	SONG AFTER
10/31/94	681	2	28/30	Honey Pie	Cry Baby Cry

Has not been played in the last 438 shows.

Scarlet Begonias

DATE	GAP	SET	POS.	SONG BEFORE	SONG AFTER
12/2/83	0	2	1/2	***	Fire
12/1/84	3	1	1/11	***	Fire
5/3/85	2	3	1/8	***	Eyes of the World

Has not been played in the last 1114 shows.

Scent of a Mule

DATE	GAP	SET	POS.	SONG BEFORE	SONG AFTER
4/4/94	589	1	3/9	Sample in a Jar	Maze
4/6/94	2	1	7/9	Sample in a Jar	Fee
4/10/94	3	1	8/9	I Didn't Know	Down with Dis
4/14/94	3	2	5/9	Silent in the Mornin	You Enjoy My
4/21/94	6	2	7/10	Weekapaug Groove	Big Ball Jam
4/29/94	6	1	4/12	Fast Enough for You	The Sloth
5/3/94	3	1	7/9	The Squirming Coil	Sample in a Ja
5/7/94	3	1	6/9	Fast Enough for You	Split Open and
5/10/94	2	2	5/10	Reba	Harry Hood
5/13/94	2	2	6/9	Peaches en Regalia	You Enjoy My
5/17/94	3	1	5/9	If I Could	Ginseng Sullivan
5/20/94	2	1	7/10	Fast Enough for You	Dog Faced Boy
5/25/94	4	1	8/11	Axilla (Part II)	My Sweet One
6/9/94	5	2	5/10	Halley's Comet	Ginseng Sullivan
6/11/94	2	2	4/9	Fluffhead	Split Open and
6/13/94	1	2	8/11	Jesus Just Left	Big Ball Jam
6/17/94	3	1	8/9	Bathtub Gin	Cavern
6/19/94	2	1	7/9	Fast Enough for You	Stash
6/22/94	2	1	7/9	If I Could	Stash
6/25/94	3	1	8/10	Sample in a Jar	Tela
6/26/94	1	2	8/12	Wolfman's Brother	Dog Faced Boy
6/30/94	2	1	7/9	Glide	Bouncing
7/2/94	2	1	5/9	Fast Enough for You	Tweezer
7/9/94	5	1	6/10	Guelah Papyrus	Down with Dis
7/14/94	3	1	7/11	T.M.W.S.I.Y. Reprise	Fluffhead
7/16/94	2	2	8/11	AC/DC Bag	Harry Hood
10/7/94	1	2	6/10	Wilson	Tweezer
10/9/94	2	2	3/8	Bouncing	You Enjoy My
10/12/94	2	2	4/9	Bouncing	You Enjoy My
10/15/94	3	2	4/11	Halley's Comet	You Enjoy My
10/18/94	2	2	5/10	Reba	Lifeboy
10/21/94	2	2	10/11	Fast Enough for You	Slave
10/26/94	4	1	7/10	Dog Faced Boy	The Oh Kee Pa
10/28/94	2	1	4/10	Guelah Papyrus	Stash
11/2/94	3	1	7/8	Stash	While My Guitar Gent
11/4/94	2	1	7/9	The Famous Mockingbi	Suzy Greenber
11/14/94	3	1	2/9	My Friend My Friend	Guelah Papyrus
11/17/94	2	1	2/11	Helter Skelter	Maze
11/20/94	3	1	3/10	Fee	Stash
11/23/94	2	2	3/7	Fee	Tweezer
11/28/94	3	1	3/9	Also Sprach	Stash
12/3/94	4	1	4/7	Guelah Papyrus	Run Like Antel
12/8/94	4	1	4/10	AC/DC Bag	Punch You in
12/30/94	5	1	8/9	Fee	Cavern
6/7/95	3	1	7/10	If I Could	The Wedge
6/9/95	2	2	3/8	The Wedge	Cavern
6/15/95	4	2	6/8	Theme From the Botto	Acoustic Army
6/22/95	5	1	2/10	Sample in a Jar	Ha Ha Ha
6/25/95	3	2	3/9	Sample in a Jar	Mike's Song
6/30/95	4	1	2/9	AC/DC Bag	Horn
7/2/95	2	2	3/8	Makisupa Policeman	Tweezer
9/28/95	3	1	4/9	Billy Breathes	Stash
9/30/95	2	2	4/9	If I Could	Mike's Song
10/5/95	3	2	5/9	The Famous Mockingbi	Cavern
10/14/95	6	2	5/6	Hello My Baby	Cavern
10/20/95	4	2	2/10	Timber (Jerry)	Simple
10/25/95	4	1	5/10	The Wedge	Free

DATE	GAP	SET	POS.	SONG BEFORE	SONG AFTER
10/28/95	2	2	3/7	Theme From the Botto	You Enjoy My
11/10/95	4	2	2/9	Free	You Enjoy My
11/15/95	4	2	3/8	Theme From the Botto	Mike's Song
11/19/95	3	2	6/8	Billy Breathes	Harry Hood
11/24/95	3	2	5/10	Catapult	Bathtub Gin
11/30/95	4	2	5/8	Run Like an Antelope	Free
12/5/95	4	2	4/8	Keyboard Cavalry	Jam
12/11/95	4	2	5/8	Taste That Surrounds	Harry Hood
12/16/95	4	2	3/8	Reba	Cavern
12/30/95	4	2	6/8	Lifeboy	Cavern
4/26/96	2	1	8/13	Wolfman's Brother	Also Sprach
6/6/96	1	1	7/8	BBFCFM	Highway to Hell
7/5/96	2	1	5/6	You Enjoy Myself	David Bowie
7/11/96	5	1	7/8	Stash	Sample in a Ja
7/23/96	9	1	5/9	Gumbo	Down with Dis
8/4/96	4	2	3/7	Reba	Sample in a Ja
8/10/96	4	2	3/8	Down with Disease	Free
8/17/96	5	3	3/7	Frankenstein	Tweezer
10/17/96	2	2	4/8	Bathtub Gin	Free
10/22/96	4	2	6/10	Lawn Boy	Mike's Song
10/27/96	4	1	5/11	Fee	Catapult
10/27/96	0	1	7/11	Catapult	Split Open and
11/6/96	5	2	7/9	Weekapaug Groove	Sample in a Ja
11/14/96	6	2	6/10	Steep	Life on Mars
11/18/96	3	2	5/9	Steep	Tweezer
11/27/96	5	2	3/8	Jesus Just Left	Tweezer
12/2/96	4	2	6/8	Free	Harry Hood
12/30/96	5	2	7/8	Lifeboy	Slave
2/14/97	3	2	8/9	Rocko William	A Day in the Life
2/26/97	9	2	7/11	Theme From the Botto	Jam
2/26/97	0	2	10/11	Magilla	Slave
7/6/97	20	1	8/9	Cars Trucks Buses	Chalk Dust Tor
8/9/97	16	2	8/10	Steep	Slave
8/17/97	6	3	6/7	Dirt	Prince Caspian
11/16/97	3	1	8/11	Cars Trucks Buses	Poor Heart
12/28/97	19	2	5/9	Drowned	Halley's Comet
7/9/98	15	2	4/8	When Circus Comes	Blister In The Sun
7/9/98	0	2	6/8	Blister In The Sun	Harry Hood
7/24/98	8	2	3/7	Also Sprach	Ha Ha Ha
7/24/98	0	2	5/7	Ha Ha Ha	Slave
10/30/98	22	1	3/10	Meat	Back @ Chicken Shack
10/30/98	0	1	5/10	Back @ Chicken Shack	Long Cool Woman
11/15/98	11	1	4/8	Driver	Cavern
11/28/98	8	2	5/9	Loving Cup	Prince Caspian
12/11/99	61	1	7/8	When Circus Comes	Cavern
6/25/00	22	2	3/7	Fast Enough For You	Meat
9/12/00	18	1	2/7	Wolfman's Brother	My Soul
9/23/00	7	2	4/7	NICU	Fast Enough For You

Has not been played in the last 10 shows.

Sea and Sand

DATE	GAP	SET	POS.	SONG BEFORE	SONG AFTER
10/31/95	759	2	12/17	5:15	Drowned
12/31/95	33	3	3/6	Weekapaug Groove	You Enjoy My
7/20/98	166	2	4/6	Maze	Prince Caspian

Has not been played in the last 161 shows.

Secret Language Instructions

DATE	GAP	SET	POS.	SONG BEFORE	SONG AFTER
3/6/92	359	2	3/9	Poor Heart	Stash
3/13/92	4	2	11/12	Love You	Possum
3/20/92	4	2	11/12	Terrapin	Possum

Has not been played in the last 752 shows.

Seen and Not Seen

DATE	GAP	SET	POS.	SONG BEFORE	SONG AFTER
10/31/96	835	2	6/8	Houses in Motion	Listening Wind

Has not been played in the last 284 shows.

Self

DATE	GAP	SET	POS.	SONG BEFORE	SONG AFTER
9/13/90	207	2	13/15	Reba	Dahlia
8/3/91	104	E	2/5	Magilla	Bitchin' Again
11/8/91	28	2	10/13	Jesus Just Left	TV Show
11/20/92	117	2	10/10	Lengthwise	***

Has not been played in the last 663 shows.

Setting Sail

DATE	GAP	SET	POS.	SONG BEFORE	SONG AFTER
4/20/91	281	1	11/11	You Enjoy Myself	***
3/25/92	90	2	7/12	You Enjoy Myself	Horn
7/15/94	289	2	9/10	Julius	Runaway Jim

Has not been played in the last 459 shows.

Sexual Healing

DATE	GAP	SET	POS.	SONG BEFORE	SONG AFTER
7/20/98	958	E	1/2	***	Halley's Comet
8/8/98	13	2	5/6	Piper	Harry Hood
8/16/98	5	2	7/8	Wading In Velvet Sea	Run Like Antel
11/14/98	16	2	6/9	Golgi Apparatus	You Enjoy My

Has not been played in the last 127 shows.

Sexy Sadie

DATE	GAP	SET	POS.	SONG BEFORE	SONG AFTER
10/31/94	681	2	23/30	Everybody's Got Some	Helter Skelter

Has not been played in the last 438 shows.

Shafty

DATE	GAP	SET	POS.	SONG BEFORE	SONG AFTER
4/5/98	944	2	5/8	Maze	Possum
7/2/98	3	1	7/11	Fikus	Fluffhead
7/7/00	145	1	7/11	Maze	Maze

Has not been played in the last 27 shows.

Shaggy Dog

DATE	GAP	SET	POS.	SONG BEFORE	SONG AFTER
10/15/86	14	2	5/14	Camel Walk	Mustang Sally
10/31/86	1	1	10/11	Back Porch Boogie Bl	Fluffhead
8/9/87	10	1	10/11	AC/DC Bag	Funky Bitch
8/21/87	2	1	9/11	Light Up Or Leave Me	Wilson
8/29/87	1	3	7/10	Who Do? We Do!	David Bowie
9/2/87	1	1	12/13	Timber (Jerry)	You Enjoy My
2/7/88	8	1	3/10	McGrupp	Golgi Apparat
4/22/88	9	2	5/13	Fee	BBFCFM
5/15/88	2	1	7/11	Fluffhead	The Lizards
9/12/88	18	1	1/4	***	Take the A-Trn
11/3/88	6	2	4/9	The Lizards	Whipping Post
10/29/95	686	2	7/10	It's Ice	Possum

Has not been played in the last 361 shows.

She Caught the Katy and Left Me a Mule to Ride

DATE	GAP	SET	POS.	SONG BEFORE	SONG AFTER
12/6/86	16	1	4/14	Whipping Post	AC/DC Bag
4/29/87	6	1	1/9	***	Alumni Blues
8/29/87	6	3	10/10	Jesus Just Left	***
7/21/98	931	2	7/8	Ghost	Funky Bitch

Has not been played in the last 160 shows.

Shine

DATE	GAP	SET	POS.	SONG BEFORE	SONG AFTER
12/31/95	792	1	7/10	Col. Forbin's Ascent	The Famous Mockingbi

Has not been played in the last 327 shows.

Silent in the Morning

DATE	GAP	SET	POS.	SONG BEFORE	SONG AFTER
3/7/92	360	1	6/11	The Horse	Maze
3/13/92	3	2	4/12	The Horse	The Landlady
3/19/92	3	1	7/12	The Horse	Dinner and a
3/21/92	2	1	7/12	The Horse	Dinner and a
3/24/92	2	1	8/13	The Horse	Llama
3/27/92	3	2	13/15	The Horse	My Sweet One
4/1/92	4	2	4/13	The Horse	Uncle Pen
4/5/92	3	2	5/12	The Horse	Maze
4/7/92	2	1	7/12	The Horse	Split Open and
4/8/92	1	2	12/15	The Horse	Chalk Dust Tor
4/12/92	1	1	6/11	The Horse	It's Ice

DATE	GAP	SET	POS.	SONG BEFORE	SONG AFTER
4/19/92	6	2	6/13	The Horse	My Sweet One
4/22/92	2	2	4/11	The Horse	Rift
4/25/92	3	2	5/11	The Horse	All Things Rec
4/30/92	2	2	7/11	The Horse	Chalk Dust Tor
5/3/92	3	2	3/14	The Horse	Fluffhead
5/5/92	1	2	9/14	The Horse	Poor Heart
5/8/92	3	2	8/12	The Horse	Chalk Dust Tor
5/16/92	6	2	8/13	The Horse	The Oh Kee Pa
7/15/92	15	1	9/12	The Horse	Chalk Dust Tor
11/19/92	30	1	11/12	The Horse	Run Like Antel
11/21/92	2	2	7/13	The Horse	Uncle Pen
11/27/92	4	2	10/13	The Horse	Faht
12/3/92	5	1	9/12	The Horse	Reba
12/8/92	5	2	5/15	The Horse	It's Ice
12/29/92	6	2	4/14	The Horse	My Sweet One
2/3/93	3	2	5/11	The Horse	Sparkle
2/5/93	2	2	4/10	The Horse	Paul and Silas
2/10/93	4	2	9/11	The Horse	Cracklin' Rosi
2/20/93	8	1	9/11	The Horse	Fluffhead
3/2/93	7	1	11/13	The Horse	I Didn't Know
3/9/93	5	2	10/15	The Horse	Big Ball Jam
3/12/93	1	1	10/11	The Horse	David Bowie
3/17/93	4	2	10/12	The Horse	The Great Gig in the
3/24/93	5	2	10/12	The Horse	Terrapin
3/26/93	2	2	6/12	The Horse	Big Ball Jam
3/30/93	3	2	13/15	The Horse	If I Only Had a Brai
4/2/93	3	2	6/13	The Horse	Mike's Song
4/9/93	3	1	6/11	The Horse	Maze
4/12/93	2	1	7/11	The Horse	Reba
4/14/93	1	1	10/13	The Horse	Divided Sky
4/16/93	1	2	9/13	The Horse	Uncle Pen
4/18/93	2	2	4/12	The Horse	Possum
4/21/93	2	2	6/11	The Horse	Big Ball Jam
4/24/93	3	1	6/11	The Horse	Rift
4/27/93	2	2	8/10	You Enjoy Myself	Love You
4/30/93	2	1	7/12	The Horse	Divided Sky
5/2/93	3	2	7/11	The Horse	Poor Heart
5/6/93	3	1	5/13	The Horse	All Things Rec
5/8/93	2	2	7/18	The Horse	It's Ice
5/30/93	2	1	7/13	Ya Mar	Run Like Antel
7/15/93	1	2	3/11	The Horse	Sparkle
7/17/93	2	1	7/11	The Horse	The Oh Kee Pa
7/23/93	4	1	7/12	The Horse	Punch You in
7/25/93	2	2	5/10	The Horse	Maze
7/28/93	2	1	9/11	The Horse	Poor Heart
7/30/93	2	2	4/10	The Horse	Poor Heart
8/3/93	3	1	8/11	The Horse	Ya Mar
8/8/93	3	1	6/11	The Horse	Punch You in
8/12/93	3	1	8/10	The Horse	Poor Heart
8/14/93	2	1	5/11	The Horse	It's Ice
8/17/93	3	2	4/10	The Horse	Rift
8/24/93	3	1	8/11	The Horse	Uncle Pen
8/28/93	3	2	5/14	The Horse	Sparkle
12/30/93	3	2	4/9	The Horse	Punch You in
4/8/94	5	1	9/13	The Horse	Down with Dis
4/14/94	5	2	4/9	The Horse	Scent of a Mul
4/22/94	7	1	10/11	The Horse	David Bowie
5/12/94	14	2	4/11	The Horse	Uncle Pen
5/19/94	5	1	7/10	The Horse	Down with Dis
5/23/94	4	1	7/10	The Horse	Julius
5/28/94	4	1	7/10	The Horse	The Sloth
6/23/94	13	1	8/10	Down with Disease	Punch You in
6/29/94	4	1	7/11	The Horse	Catapult
7/3/94	4	2	6/10	The Horse	Julius
7/9/94	4	1	6/11	The Horse	Run Like Antel
7/14/94	3	1	10/11	The Horse	Run Like Antel
7/16/94	2	1	8/11	The Horse	Maze
10/7/94	1	2	3/10	The Horse	Reba
10/9/94	3	1	4/11	The Horse	Sparkle
10/14/94	3	1	5/12	The Horse	Punch You in
10/18/94	3	2	3/10	The Horse	Reba
10/22/94	2	2	4/11	The Horse	Dinner and a
10/25/94	2	1	6/9	The Horse	Split Open and
10/27/94	2	1	9/11	The Horse	Poor Heart

DATE	GAP	SET	POS.	SONG BEFORE	SONG AFTER
10/31/94	3	1	8/10	The Horse	Reba
11/13/94	5	1	9/10	The Horse	Run Like Antel
11/18/94	4	1	5/11	The Horse	It's Ice
11/26/94	6	1	7/9	The Horse	Poor Heart
11/30/94	2	E	2/3	The Horse	Amazing Grce
12/8/94	7	E	2/3	The Horse	Rocky Top
12/29/94	4	1	6/9	The Horse	Uncle Pen
12/31/94	2	3	6/8	The Horse	Suzy Greenber
6/14/95	7	1	10/12	The Horse	Spock's Brain
6/24/95	8	1	9/10	The Horse	The Squirmin
6/29/95	4	1	4/10	The Horse	Divided Sky
10/5/95	11	1	5/11	The Horse	Cars Trucks Buses
10/24/95	13	1	7/13	The Horse	Demand
10/29/95	4	1	7/12	The Horse	Split Open and
11/11/95	4	1	7/12	The Horse	Ya Mar
12/4/95	16	1	9/11	The Horse	Hello My Baby
12/12/95	5	1	7/10	The Horse	Run Like Antel
7/21/96	24	1	9/14	The Horse	Taste
8/2/96	5	2	8/9	The Horse	Run Like Antel
8/10/96	5	1	8/11	The Horse	Rift
8/14/96	3	2	4/10	The Horse	Cars Trucks Buses
10/16/96	3	1	11/12	The Horse	Character Zer
10/21/96	4	2	10/11	The Horse	David Bowie
10/29/96	6	2	4/10	The Horse	Weekapaug Gr
12/1/96	21	1	10/12	The Horse	Sample in a Ja
12/31/96	7	1	7/10	The Horse	Divided Sky
2/23/97	9	2	5/9	The Horse	Peaches en Regalia
7/6/97	22	1	6/9	The Horse	Cars Trucks Buses
8/13/97	19	1	7/11	The Horse	Beauty of My Dreams
11/26/97	12	1	9/10	The Horse	Taste
12/31/97	16	1	8/10	The Horse	The Sloth
8/2/98	27	1	4/9	The Horse	Boogie On Reggae
8/15/98	8	2	7/9	The Horse	Chalk Dust Tor
7/4/99	35	2	4/9	The Horse	What's the Use
10/1/99	37	2	4/9	The Horse	Gumbo
12/8/99	13	1	7/8	The Horse	Run Like Antel
12/13/99	4	E	1/2	***	Heavy Things
12/18/99	4	2	4/9	***	Possum
12/31/99	2	2	25/35	The Horse	Bittersweet Motel
7/8/00	23	2	8/9	The Horse	Possum
9/8/00	6	1	6/12	The Horse	I Saw it Again

Has not been played in the last 20 shows.

Simple

DATE	GAP	SET	POS.	SONG BEFORE	SONG AFTER
5/27/94	630	2	10/12	Mike's Song	O Mio Babbino Caro
6/17/94	9	2	5/15	Mike's Song	Mike's Song
6/22/94	4	2	3/20	Mike's Song	Midnight Rider Jam
6/22/94	0	2	6/20	Catapult	Icculus
6/22/94	2	2	8/20	Icculus	Mike's Song
6/24/94	2	2	6/13	McGrupp	Sanity
7/2/94	6	2	3/12	Mike's Song	Mike's Song
10/8/94	12	2	5/12	Mike's Song	Mike's Song
10/13/94	4	2	7/12	Mike's Song	Mike's Song
10/15/94	2	1	3/8	Sparkle	Maze
10/18/94	2	1	1/10	***	My Friend My
10/21/94	2	2	3/11	Mike's Song	Mike's Song
10/23/94	2	1	4/11	Sparkle	Poor Heart
10/25/94	1	2	2/11	Mike's Song	The Mango Song
10/26/94	1	1	1/10	***	It's Ice
10/29/94	3	1	3/10	Sparkle	Runaway Jim
10/31/94	1	1	3/10	Sparkle	Divided Sky
11/3/94	2	2	2/8	Also Sprach	Poor Heart
11/4/94	1	2	3/9	Mike's Song	Mike's Song
11/13/94	2	1	3/10	Sparkle	Reba
11/16/94	2	2	2/7	Mike's Song	I'm Blue, Lonesome
11/20/94	4	2	6/10	Reba	Rift
11/23/94	2	1	3/9	Sparkle	It's Ice
11/25/94	1	2	3/8	Mike's Song	Harpua
11/28/94	2	1	7/9	Sparkle	Divided Sky
12/2/94	3	1	4/8	Sparkle	It's Ice
12/6/94	3	2	6/12	Mike's Song	The Mango Song
12/8/94	2	1	6/10	Punch You in the Eye	Catapult
12/8/94	0	1	8/10	Catapult	The Lizards
12/10/94	2	2	1/11	***	Maze
12/28/94	1	1	2/10	Mound	Julius
12/30/94	2	1	5/9	Sparkle	Stash
12/31/94	1	E	1/2	***	Auld Lang Syne
6/8/95	3	2	1/8	***	Rift
6/14/95	4	E	1/3	***	Rocky Top
6/19/95	4	2	1/8	***	David Bowie
6/23/95	3	1	1/8	***	Chalk Dust Tor
6/29/95	5	1	8/10	Rift	Split Open and
7/3/95	4	E	1/2	***	Amazing Grce
10/2/95	5	2	5/10	Llama	Keyboard Cavalry
10/15/95	9	2	2/8	Julius	Tweezer
10/20/95	3	2	3/10	Scent of a Mule	Maze
10/27/95	5	2	5/9	Poor Heart	McGrupp
11/9/95	4	1	5/8	Punch You in the Eye	Reba
11/16/95	6	1	7/10	Ya Mar	Timber (Jerry)
11/21/95	3	2	1/11	***	David Bowie
11/29/95	5	2	3/11	Sparkle	Possum
12/2/95	3	2	3/9	Maze	Faht
12/8/95	4	1	3/9	Poor Heart	Runaway Jim
12/12/95	3	2	5/6	The Lizards	Runaway Jim
12/16/95	3	2	6/8	Mike's Song	Weekapaug Gr
12/30/95	4	1	5/13	David Bowie	It's Ice
7/21/96	17	2	7/9	Run Like an Antelope	Prince Caspian
8/2/96	5	2	2/9	Runaway Jim	Taste
8/6/96	3	1	4/9	Suzy Greenberg	Theme From the Botto
8/12/96	3	2	3/9	Sparkle	Prince Caspian
8/16/96	3	2	11/13	Mike's Song	Contact
10/16/96	2	2	4/10	Train Song	Swept Away
10/21/96	4	2	8/11	Life on Mars	The Horse
10/26/96	4	2	4/7	Sparkle	McGrupp
10/31/96	3	3	4/8	Maze	Swept Away
11/8/96	5	2	4/8	Bouncing	Loving Cup
11/18/96	7	2	2/9	Also Sprach	Swept Away
11/23/96	3	2	3/10	Mike's Song	Makisupa Policeman
11/29/96	3	2	2/10	Wilson	Sparks
12/1/96	2	2	3/10	Sparkle	A Day in the Life Jam
12/6/96	3	2	4/9	Mike's Song	Jam
12/31/96	3	2	4/9	Sparkle	Swept Away
2/16/97	3	2	5/11	Sparkle	When Circus Comes
2/22/97	5	2	4/8	Sparkle	Jesus Just Left
7/2/97	20	1	2/8	Mike's Song	Maze
7/22/97	8	2	3/6	Mike's Song	I Am Hydrgn
8/3/97	8	2	2/7	Julius	Fluffhead
8/9/97	3	2	5/8	Ain't Love Funny	Swept Away
8/16/97	5	2	2/7	Wolfman's Brother	My Soul
11/16/97	4	2	2/5	Timber (Jerry)	Wilson
11/29/97	8	1	3/12	Foam	T.M.W.S.I.Y.
12/2/97	2	2	2/7	Mike's Song	Dog Faced Boy
12/9/97	5	2	2/6	Julius	Timber (Jerry)
12/28/97	4	2	2/9	Axilla	Ghost
4/2/98	4	2	2/9	Punch You in the Eye	Birds of a Feather
7/2/98	6	E	1/1	***	***
7/10/98	6	2	5/8	Mike's Song	Weekapaug Gr
7/15/98	1	2	2/6	Limb by Limb	Tweezer
7/21/98	5	2	2/8	Mike's Song	Bittersweet Motel
7/26/98	3	2	4/6	Albuquerque	Bold as Love
8/7/98	8	2	3/7	Mike's Song	Albuquerque
8/12/98	4	2	2/7	Mike's Song	Rift
8/15/98	1	1	2/12	Mike's Song	Beauty of My Dreams
10/29/98	6	2	5/7	Walk Away	Albuquerque
11/6/98	5	2	3/7	Funky Bitch	Prince Caspian
11/11/98	4	2	2/6	Halley's Comet	Walk Away
11/15/98	3	2	4/7	Mike's Song	Wading In Velvet Sea
11/21/98	4	2	3/9	Mike's Song	The Wedge
11/29/98	5	2	2/8	Roses Are Free	Makisupa Policeman
12/31/98	4	3	3/6	Auld Lang Syne	Harry Hood
6/30/99	1	2	4/10	Birds of a Feather	Swept Away
7/8/99	5	2	9/9	Tube	***
7/16/99	6	2	5/8	Weekapaug Groove	Guyute
7/21/99	4	2	2/6	Mike's Song	My Left Toe
7/31/99	7	E	3/3	Brian and Robert	***
9/14/99	6	E	1/2	***	Hello My Baby
9/22/99	6	2	6/8	Mike's Song	Train Song
10/9/99	12	2	5/6	Wading In Velvet Sea	Loving Cup
12/4/99	4	1	2/7	Heavy Things	Ya Mar
12/7/99	2	2	6/8	Bathtub Gin	Free
12/11/99	3	1	3/8	Mike's Song	I Am Hydrgn
12/18/99	6	2	7/10	Mike's Song	Weekapaug Gr
12/30/99	1	3	7/9	Mike's Song	I Am Hydrgn
5/23/00	4	1	6/12	Mike's Song	It's Ice
6/13/00	4	1	9/10	Mike's Song	Weekapaug Gr
7/7/00	15	2	6/7	Mike's Song	Weekapaug Gr
9/20/00	15	1	5/9	Mike's Song	T.M.W.S.I.Y.
9/30/00	7	1	7/10	Mike's Song	I Saw it Again

Has not been played in the last 5 shows.

Sixteen Candles

DATE	GAP	SET	POS.	SONG BEFORE	SONG AFTER
12/29/96	860	2	7/10	Rotation Jam	Harpua

Has not been played in the last 259 shows.

Skin It Back

DATE	GAP	SET	POS.	SONG BEFORE	SONG AFTER
10/15/86	14	1	3/9	Makisupa Policeman	Cities
10/31/86	1	2	9/11	Sanity	Icculus
4/29/87	7	1	6/9	Fire	Cities
8/9/87	3	2	5/11	Light Up Or Leave Me	Peaches en Regalia
8/21/87	2	2	9/12	Fee	Low Rider Jam
9/27/87	4	1	9/9	Good Times Bad Times	***
7/25/88	29	3	1/4	***	Harpua

Has not been played in the last 1059 shows.

Skippy the Wondermouse

DATE	GAP	SET	POS.	SONG BEFORE	SONG AFTER
12/1/84	3	1	10/11	Drums Jam	Fluffhead
9/27/85	3	1	3/8	Fluffhead	Slave
10/30/85	2	1	10/11	Prep School Hippie	Jam

Has not been played in the last 1111 shows.

Slave to the Traffic Light

DATE	GAP	SET	POS.	SONG BEFORE	SONG AFTER
12/1/84	3	1	5/11	Makisupa Policeman	Spanish Flea
5/3/85	2	1	1/4	***	Mike's Song
9/27/85	1	1	4/8	Skippy Wondermouse	Alumni Blues
10/30/85	2	1	4/11	Possum	Sneakin' Sally
2/3/86	3	1	1/7	***	Mike's Song
4/15/86	2	1	5/14	Quinn the Eskimo	Makisupa Policeman
10/15/86	1	2	10/14	Wilson	Quinn the Eskimo
10/31/86	1	1	4/11	Golgi Apparatus	Melt the Guns
2/13/87	2	1	4/14	Golgi Apparatus	Quinn the Eskimo
3/6/87	2	E	1/1	***	***
4/24/87	2	1	14/14	Dear Mrs. Reagan	***

DATE	GAP	SET	POS.	SONG BEFORE	SONG AFTER
4/29/87	1	3	9/14	Timber (Jerry)	Sparks
5/11/87	1	1	4/12	Possum	Sneakin' Sally
8/9/87	2	1	2/11	Golgi Apparatus	La Grange
8/29/87	3	1	2/13	Clod	Swing Low Sweet Chrt
9/21/87	2	1	5/11	Clod	Funky Bitch
10/14/87	2	1	5/12	Golgi Apparatus	Fluffhead
11/18/87	2	1	1/12	***	T.M.W.S.I.Y.
11/19/87	1	3	14/14	Bike	***
1/27/88	1	2	2/10	Wilson	Corrine Corrina
2/8/88	2	1	1/7	***	Funky Bitch
2/24/88	1	1	8/11	Golgi Apparatus	Corrine Corrina
3/11/88	2	1	8/12	Golgi Apparatus	Flat Fee
6/20/88	12	1	1/11	***	Peaches en Regalia
7/12/88	4	2	7/9	Makisupa Policeman	AC/DC Bag
7/23/88	1	3	5/7	Dinner and a Movie	Ballad - Curtis Loew
7/30/88	3	3	3/13	On Your Way Down	Timber (Jerry)
8/6/88	2	2	6/6	BBFCFM	***
9/8/88	2	1	3/8	Walk Away	Wild Child
11/5/88	8	1	1/11	***	Time Loves a Hero
11/11/88	1	1	3/8	You Enjoy Myself	Foam
2/7/89	7	3	4/6	Suzy Greenberg	Bike
5/6/89	17	2	7/8	Golgi Apparatus	Divided Sky
5/9/89	1	2	4/14	If I Don't Be There	Esther
5/12/89	1	1	10/15	You Enjoy Myself	The Sloth
5/26/89	4	3	1/4	***	Funky Bitch
5/28/89	2	1	6/9	Fee	Esther
6/30/89	2	2	4/8	The Curtain	Bathtub Gin
8/26/89	4	2	4/9	Ya Mar	AC/DC Bag
10/13/89	1	2	1/4	David Bowie	The Sloth
10/20/89	2	E	2/2	La Grange	***
12/8/89	17	2	4/7	Timber (Jerry)	I Didn't Know
3/1/90	21	2	7/7	Carolina	***
3/9/90	5	2	6/11	Dog Gone Dog	Highway to Hell
3/11/90	2	2	11/13	Harpua	AC/DC Bag
4/8/90	7	2	4/10	The Lizards	Mike's Song
4/22/90	9	1	9/12	My Sweet One	Mike's Song
3/17/91	81	2	7/8	Fee	Chalk Dust Tor
10/24/91	67	2	7/11	Tube	Dinner and a
8/6/93	237	2	10/12	Halley's Comet	Cracklin' Rosi
8/20/93	11	2	2/9	Also Sprach	Split Open and
12/30/93	8	2	9/9	Purple Rain	***
4/9/94	6	2	10/11	Tela	Cavern
4/14/94	2	4	9/9	Dog Faced Boy	***
4/24/94	9	1	8/8	It's Ice	***
5/3/94	6	2	8/8	I Wanna Be Like You	***
5/13/94	7	1	8/9	My Friend My Friend	Suzy Greenber
5/17/94	2	2	8/9	Love You	***
5/22/94	4	2	8/9	Rift	Tweezer Repri
6/13/94	10	2	11/11	Terrapin	***
6/23/94	2	2	8/8	Lifeboy	***
7/2/94	7	2	11/12	Sample in a Jar	Highway to Hell
7/13/94	7	2	12/13	Mound	Suzy Greenber
10/10/94	7	2	9/9	Love You	***
10/21/94	8	2	11/11	Scent of a Mule	***
10/27/94	5	E	1/3	***	Icculus
10/31/94	3	3	3/7	Bouncing	Rift
11/4/94	3	2	9/9	Golgi Apparatus	***
11/14/94	3	2	4/10	Yerushalayim	Poor Heart
11/17/94	2	2	7/8	Love You	Golgi Apparat
11/26/94	7	2	6/6	Sample in a Jar	***
12/3/94	5	2	5/10	Gumbo	The Landlady
12/10/94	6	2	10/11	Poor Heart	Cavern
12/31/94	4	3	8/8	Suzy Greenberg	***
6/7/95	2	1	10/10	Funky Bitch	***
6/9/95	2	2	8/8	Sweet Adeline	***
6/15/95	4	2	8/8	Acoustic Army	***
6/20/95	4	E	1/2	***	Amazing Grce
6/25/95	4	E	2/2	Bouncing	***

DATE	GAP	SET	POS.	SONG BEFORE	SONG AFTER
7/2/95	6	2	8/8	Acoustic Army	***
9/28/95	3	1	9/9	Acoustic Army	***
10/2/95	3	2	7/10	Keyboard Cavalry	Hello My Baby
10/6/95	3	2	8/8	Suspicious Minds	***
10/15/95	6	1	3/10	Poor Heart	I Didn't Know
10/22/95	5	2	10/11	Uncle Pen	Cavern
10/29/95	5	1	11/12	Gumbo	Sweet Adeline
11/12/95	5	2	5/8	Sample in a Jar	Cracklin' Rosi
11/18/95	4	1	6/8	Punch You in the Eye	I'm Blue, Lonesome
11/29/95	7	2	11/11	My Long Journey Home	***
12/7/95	6	1	6/10	Rift	Guyute
12/9/95	2	2	6/8	Lawn Boy	Crossroads
12/14/95	3	2	10/10	Jam	***
12/28/95	4	2	8/8	Uncle Pen	***
7/12/96	13	2	8/9	NICU	Suzy Greenber
7/23/96	8	2	9/9	Bike	***
8/4/96	4	2	7/7	Sweet Adeline	***
8/13/96	6	1	10/10	Glide	***
8/17/96	3	2	8/8	Golgi Apparatus	***
10/19/96	4	2	3/10	Sparkle	Bouncing
10/23/96	2	2	7/8	Suzy Greenberg	Julius
10/29/96	4	2	9/10	Suspicious Minds	Hello My Baby
11/11/96	8	2	11/11	Contact	***
11/22/96	7	2	9/10	Theme From the Botto	Hello My Baby
12/1/96	6	2	10/10	Johnny B. Goode	***
12/30/96	6	2	8/8	Scent of a Mule	***
2/13/97	2	2	5/10	Punch You in the Eye	When Circus Comes
2/18/97	4	1	10/10	Character Zero	***
2/26/97	6	2	11/11	Scent of a Mule	***
3/2/97	3	2	8/9	Character Zero	Tweezer Repri
3/18/97	1	2	10/10	Chalk Dust Torture	***
6/13/97	1	2	5/9	Vultures	Chalk Dust Tor
7/1/97	11	2	7/7	Loving Cup	***
7/21/97	8	2	8/8	Funky Bitch	***
8/3/97	9	E	2/2	Bouncing	***
8/9/97	3	2	9/10	Scent of a Mule	Weekapaug Gr
8/16/97	5	2	5/7	Jam	Rocky Top
11/14/97	3	2	4/4	Twist	***
11/21/97	4	2	3/4	AC/DC Bag	Loving Cup
11/28/97	4	2	3/5	Limb By Limb	Ghost
12/5/97	5	2	4/7	Julius	The Lizards
12/7/97	2	1	12/12	Tube Jam	***
12/28/97	5	2	7/9	Halley's Comet	Rocky Top
7/16/98	18	2	7/7	Tube	***
7/24/98	5	2	6/7	Scent of a Mule	Chalk Dust Tor
7/31/98	5	E	2/2	Punch You in the Eye	***
8/12/98	9	1	8/8	Ramble On	***
8/15/98	1	2	9/9	Chalk Dust Torture	***
11/9/98	14	2	6/7	The Moma Dance	You Enjoy My
11/18/98	5	2	5/7	Albuquerque	Fluffhead
12/30/98	11	2	5/5	The Squirming Coil	***
7/4/99	5	2	2/9	Ghost	The Horse
10/1/99	37	2	9/9	Fluffhead	***
10/9/99	6	E	1/1	***	***
12/3/99	3	1	8/8	Possum	***
12/13/99	8	2	8/8	Golgi Apparatus	***
12/31/99	6	2	15/35	Quadrophonic Topplin	Albuquerque
6/16/00	10	2	5/7	Driver	Julius
6/25/00	4	2	7/7	What's the Use	***
7/4/00	6	2	5/5	Twist	***
9/22/00	18	1	5/9	Wilson	Dogs Stole Things

Has not been played in the last 11 shows.

Sleep

DATE	GAP	SET	POS.	SONG BEFORE	SONG AFTER
10/17/98	979	1	2/10	Carolina	Never
10/29/98	2	1	6/10	Driver	Frankie Says
11/19/98	9	1	4/8	If You Need a Fool	Tela
11/18/98	4	E	2/4	Brian and Robert	Dog Faced Boy
11/25/98	5	1	7/9	David Bowie	Driver
12/28/98	4	1	5/10	Taste	Albuquerque
7/8/99	9	2	6/9	I Saw It Again	Meatstick
7/26/99	14	1	4/11	Vultures	Gumbo

DATE	GAP	SET	POS.	SONG BEFORE	SONG AFTER
6/14/00	52	E	1/2	***	The Squirmin
9/18/00	28	1	9/10	Rift	Prince Caspian

Has not been played in the last 13 shows.

Sleeping Monkey

DATE	GAP	SET	POS.	SONG BEFORE	SONG AFTER
3/6/92	359	E	1/1	***	***
3/11/92	2	E	4/4	Carolina	***
3/14/92	3	E	1/2	***	Good Time Ba
3/19/92	2	E	1/2	***	Rocky Top
3/25/92	5	E	1/2	***	Tweezer Repri
3/26/92	1	E	1/3	***	Chalk Dust Tor
3/30/92	3	E	1/3	***	The Oh Kee Pa
4/8/92	8	E	1/2	***	Rocky Top
4/16/92	4	E	1/1	***	***
4/19/92	3	E	1/2	***	Cavern
4/23/92	3	E	1/2	***	Tweezer Repri
5/2/92	6	E	1/2	***	BBFCFM
5/7/92	4	E	2/3	Sweet Adeline	Rocky Top
5/14/92	5	E	1/2	***	Rocky Top
7/14/92	16	E	1/1	***	***
11/23/92	35	E	1/2	***	Rocky Top
12/8/92	12	2	15/15	Big Ball Jam	***
2/20/93	23	E	1/1	***	***
2/27/93	6	E	1/3	***	Amazing Grce
3/21/93	14	E	1/3	***	Sweet Adeline
5/2/93	30	E	1/2	***	Amazing Grce
8/2/93	22	E	1/2	***	Amazing Grce
4/30/94	44	E	1/2	***	Highway to Hell
5/22/94	16	E	1/1	***	***
5/25/94	5	E	1/2	***	Tweezer Repri
6/10/94	6	E	1/2	***	Rocky Top
6/17/94	5	E	1/2	***	Rocky Top
6/30/94	10	E	1/2	***	Poor Heart
7/9/94	7	E	1/2	***	Tweezer Repri
7/15/94	4	E	1/1	***	***
10/9/94	4	E	1/2	***	Poor Heart
10/21/94	9	2	7/11	Weekapaug Groove	The Curtain
10/29/94	7	2	10/11	Run Like an Antelope	Run Like Antel
10/31/94	1	3	5/7	Rift	Poor Heart
11/17/94	8	2	3/8	David Bowie	Sparkle
11/28/94	8	2	4/5	Tweezer	Julius
12/1/94	2	E	1/2	***	Tweezer Repri
12/4/94	3	E	1/2	***	Rocky Top
12/29/94	7	E	2/2	My Long Journey Home	***
7/2/95	2	E	1/2	***	Rocky Top
7/2/95	5	2	6/8	Ha Ha Ha	Acoustic Army
10/20/95	18	E	1/2	***	Rocky Top
10/24/95	3	2	5/8	You Enjoy Myself	Run Like Antel
11/11/95	8	2	6/9	Fluffhead	Frankenstein
12/7/95	18	2	6/10	Julius	Sparkle
8/13/96	40	E	1/2	***	Rocky Top
11/15/96	25	2	9/11	Mike's Song	Mean Mr. Mustard
2/17/97	21	E	1/2	***	Rocky Top
8/13/97	46	2	4/9	Izabella	McGrupp
8/16/97	19	2	6/7	Piper	Tweezer Repri
12/30/97	2	2	8/9	My Soul	Guyute
4/2/98	2	2	8/9	Twist	Rocky Top
7/8/98	10	2	5/7	Piper	Ghost
7/21/98	8	E	1/2	***	Rocky Top
8/12/98	15	2	5/7	Loving Cup	Weekapaug Gr
10/31/98	9	E	1/2	***	Tweezer Repri
7/4/99	27	2	8/9	Mike's Song	Weekapaug Gr
9/25/99	33	1	7/8	On Your Way Down	Wilson
12/18/99	25	E	2/2	Ya Mar	***
5/23/00	5	1	12/12	Taste	***
6/30/00	14	2	8/9	Farmhouse	David Bowie
9/23/00	22	E	1/2	***	Tweezer Repri

Has not been played in the last 10 shows.

Slipknot!

DATE	GAP	SET	POS.	SONG BEFORE	SONG AFTER
4/1/86	12	2	2/6	Help on the Way	AC/DC Bag

Has not been played in the last 1107 shows.

DATE	GAP	SET	POS.	SONG BEFORE	SONG AFTER

Smells Like Teen Spirit

DATE	GAP	SET	POS.	SONG BEFORE	SONG AFTER
11/2/98	984	E	1/1	***	***

Has not been played in the last 135 shows.

Smoke on the Water Jam

7/18/99	10203		6/9	Catapult	Icculus

Has not been played in the last 99 shows.

Sneakin' Sally through the Alley

9/27/85	6	1	1/8	***	Fluffhead
10/30/85	2	1	5/11	Slave	I Wish
10/15/86	6	2	8/14	Fluffhead	Wilson
10/31/86	1	1	7/11	Dave's Energy Guide	Halley's Comet
12/6/86	1	1	13/14	Tush	Prep School Hippie
2/13/87	1	1	1/14	***	Possum
3/6/87	2	1	6/6	Quinn the Eskimo	***
5/11/87	4	1	5/12	Slave	Clod
8/9/87	2	1	6/11	Possum	Timber (Jerry)
8/29/87	3	2	3/13	Ballad - Curtis Loew	Makisupa Policeman
9/2/87	1	1	3/13	Fluffhead	Divided Sky
9/21/87	1	3	4/15	Rocky Top	Fee
10/31/87	3	1	3/11	Whipping Post	Back Porch Boogie Bl
11/19/87	2	1	5/7	You Enjoy Myself	Harry Hood
1/27/88	1	1	6/9	Jesus Just Left	Alumni Blues
2/24/88	3	2	2/5	Mustang Sally	Sanity
3/11/88	2	1	3/12	Funky Bitch	Take the A-Trn
3/21/88	2	1	4/15	McGrupp	Divided Sky
5/15/88	5	1	9/11	The Lizards	AC/DC Bag
5/21/88	1	1	2/7	Funky Bitch	Alumni Blues
5/25/88	1	1	7/9	Golgi Apparatus	Suzy Greenber
6/20/88	3	2	1/9	***	Tela
6/24/88	2	1	8/11	Fee	You Enjoy My
7/12/88	2	1	3/8	The Lizards	Good Time Ba
7/24/88	2	1	6/10	The Famous Mockingbi	Mike's Song
7/30/88	2	3	7/13	Possum	Harpua
3/14/89	28	3	2/7	Fire	Alumni Blues
5/28/89	17	3	4/6	The Sloth	Ya Mar
12/30/97	833	1	1/7	***	Taste
12/30/97	0	E	3/4	Black-Eyed Katy	Frankenstein
4/2/98	2	2	5/9	Wolfman's Brother	Frankie Says
7/28/98	22	1	5/10	Tela	It's Ice
8/8/98	8	1	3/8	NICU	Guyute
10/31/98	12	1	5/10	Birds of a Feather	Chalk Dust Tor
7/7/99	28	1	5/10	My Mind's Got A Mind	Axilla
7/17/99	8	2	6/8	Wolfman's Brother	Timber (Jerry)
9/28/99	26	1	2/8	Wolfman's Brother	Tube
12/11/99	17	2	2/5	Boogie On Reggae	Ghost
6/30/00	25	1	5/10	Runaway Jim	Ginseng Sullivan
10/5/00	30	1	4/10	Wolfman's Brother	Limb By Limb

Has not been played in the last 2 shows.

So Lonely

11/14/98	992	E	1/2	***	Tweezer Repri

Has not been played in the last 127 shows.

Something

10/29/98	981	E	1/1	***	***
11/14/98	11	2	2/9	David Bowie	Piper
11/19/98	3	1	7/9	Maze	Ghost
11/25/98	4	E	1/3	***	Guyute

Has not been played in the last 120 shows.

Somewhere Over the Rainbow

8/2/96	813	1	1/11	***	Ya Mar
8/5/96	2	2	5/13	Halley's Comet	Waste
8/13/96	5	2	6/11	Weekapaug Groove	Waste
8/9/98	152	2	7/11	Waste	You Enjoy My

Has not been played in the last 147 shows.

Somewhere Over the Rainbow Jam

4/20/94	602	2	9/9	You Enjoy Myself	***

Has not been played in the last 517 shows.

Soul Shake Down Party

2/17/97	866	1	1/10	***	Divided Sky
2/20/97	2	1	3/10	Tweezer	Chalk Dust Tor

Has not been played in the last 251 shows.

Spanish Flea

12/1/84	3	1	6/11	Slave	Don't Want U No More

Has not been played in the last 1116 shows.

Sparkle

9/25/91	312	2	3/8	Stash	Cavern
9/26/91	1	2	4/11	Brother	The Landlady
9/27/91	1	2	3/10	Tela	Split Open and
9/28/91	1	2	3/12	Guelah Papyrus	Cavern
10/4/91	5	1	7/10	Guelah Papyrus	Suzy Greenber
10/10/91	2	7	7/13	I Didn't Know	The Oh Kee Pa
10/15/91	4	1	5/10	Split Open and Melt	Reba
10/18/91	2	E	1/3	***	Walk Away
10/19/91	1	2	3/10	Bathtub Gin	Tweezer
10/23/91	1	2	3/10	The Squirming Coil	Golgi Apparat
10/27/91	2	2	4/13	The Famous Mockingbi	It's Ice
10/30/91	2	1	4/7	Cavern	Brother
10/31/91	1	1	6/11	Chalk Dust Torture	Foam
11/1/91	1	1	2/11	AC/DC Bag	The Landlady
11/2/91	1	2	6/11	T.M.W.S.I.Y. Reprise	Guelah Papyrus
11/7/91	1	1	4/11	Foam	Cavern
11/8/91	1	2	2/13	The Sloth	Split Open and
11/9/91	1	1	4/11	Foam	Llama
11/13/91	3	1	4/10	It's Ice	Chalk Dust Tor
11/14/91	1	1	7/11	Tube	Brother
11/15/91	1	1	2/12	Chalk Dust Torture	Cavern
11/16/91	1	1	6/11	It's Ice	Fluffhead
11/19/91	1	1	5/11	Fee	Brother
11/20/91	1	1	5/11	The Famous Mockingbi	Stash
11/22/91	2	1	3/11	Cavern	Brother
11/23/91	1	1	6/11	Guelah Papyrus	Chalk Dust Tor
11/24/91	1	1	6/9	Fluffhead	It's Ice
11/30/91	1	1	4/11	Foam	Divided Sky
12/4/91	1	2	7/11	Weekapaug Groove	The Lizards
12/5/91	2	2	2/13	Tweezer	Tube
12/6/91	1	2	3/12	Eliza	You Enjoy My
12/7/91	1	2	4/8	Chalk Dust Torture	Brother
12/31/91	1	1	3/10	Foam	Stash
3/6/92	1	1	3/11	Cavern	It's Ice
3/12/92	3	1	3/11	Foam	Stash
3/14/92	2	1	4/13	Reba	Foam
3/17/92	1	1	4/11	Cavern	It's Ice
3/19/92	1	1	4/12	Split Open and Melt	Golgi Apparat
3/21/92	2	1	4/12	Foam	Split Open and
3/22/92	1	1	1/4	***	All Things Rec
3/25/92	2	1	2/10	Wilson	Split Open and
3/26/92	1	1	5/10	Foam	Stash
3/28/92	2	1	5/10	Foam	Stash
3/30/92	1	1	5/11	Guelah Papyrus	Maze
4/1/92	2	1	6/12	All Things Recnsdrd	It's Ice
4/3/92	1	1	6/11	Guelah Papyrus	Maze
4/4/92	1	1	3/10	It's Ice	The Lizards
4/6/92	2	1	3/10	Foam	Reba
4/8/92	1	1	2/11	The Landlady	Foam
4/12/92	1	1	8/11	It's Ice	Maze
4/13/92	1	2	3/11	Fluffhead	Mike's Song
4/15/92	1	1	5/11	Guelah Papyrus	Stash
4/17/92	2	1	3/13	Foam	Stash
4/18/92	1	1	4/11	It's Ice	All Things Rec
4/22/92	3	1	4/10	Reba	Guelah Papyrus
4/24/92	2	1	8/11	Fluffhead	Stash
4/29/92	2	1	3/10	Foam	It's Ice
5/2/92	3	1	5/11	The Famous Mockingbi	Reba
5/5/92	2	1	3/11	The Curtain	Stash
5/6/92	1	1	10/11	The Famous Mockingbi	Cavern
5/7/92	1	2	2/12	The Landlady	Tweezer
5/9/92	2	1	3/11	Foam	Split Open and
5/10/92	1	1	3/10	Suzy Greenberg	Stash
5/14/92	2	1	4/11	The Sloth	Maze
5/15/92	1	1	4/11	Cavern	Stash
5/17/92	2	2	9/11	Love You	Harry Hood
5/18/92	1	1	9/10	Horn	Run Like Antel
6/19/92	1	1	5/7	The Squirming Coil	Cavern
6/24/92	3	1	7/9	I Didn't Know	Cavern
6/27/92	1	1	3/10	Foam	Reba
7/9/92	3	1	4/12	Suzy Greenberg	Stash
7/10/92	1	1	4/10	Reba	Maze
7/11/92	1	1	4/11	Foam	Stash
7/14/92	2	1	5/12	Maze	It's Ice
7/16/92	2	1	4/10	Maze	Wilson
7/17/92	1	1	2/7	Chalk Dust Torture	Stash
7/21/92	3	1	4/7	It's Ice	Stash
7/25/92	3	1	3/8	Foam	Stash
7/30/92	4	1	3/8	Horn	It's Ice
8/15/92	6	1	2/5	The Landlady	Guelah Papyrus
8/23/92	4	1	3/7	Maze	Cavern
8/25/92	2	1	3/7	It's Ice	Stash
8/27/92	1	1	5/7	Horn	You Enjoy My
11/20/92	6	1	7/12	Reba	Stash
11/22/92	2	1	7/12	Reba	Horn
11/25/92	2	1	6/11	Maze	It's Ice
11/28/92	2	1	6/11	Chalk Dust Torture	Fast Enough for You
11/30/92	1	1	6/10	Stash	It's Ice
12/2/92	2	1	8/10	The Lizards	Horn
12/4/92	2	1	6/11	Glide	Fast Enough for You
12/5/92	1	2	6/13	Reba	Maze
12/7/92	2	1	5/11	Glide	Foam
12/8/92	1	2	10/15	Lawn Boy	Suzy Greenber
12/11/92	2	1	8/11	Guelah Papyrus	My Friend My
12/12/92	1	1	3/11	Foam	Cavern
12/28/92	2	1	2/10	Maze	Buried Alive
12/30/92	2	1	2/14	The Landlady	Split Open and
12/31/92	1	2	3/10	It's Ice	Col. Forbin's A
2/3/93	1	2	6/11	Silent in the Mornin	You Enjoy My
2/5/93	2	1	5/11	Split Open and Melt	Punch You in
2/7/93	2	1	5/12	It's Ice	Col. Forbin's A
2/10/93	2	2	6/11	I Walk the Line	You Enjoy My
2/12/93	2	1	4/11	Guelah Papyrus	Split Open and
2/15/93	2	1	3/12	Suzy Greenberg	Guelah Papyrus
2/18/93	2	1	6/10	Foam	Cavern
2/19/93	1	1	8/11	The Famous Mockingbi	My Friend My
2/22/93	3	1	5/10	Maze	Foam
2/25/93	2	2	3/11	It's Ice	Wilson
2/27/93	2	1	7/10	It's Ice	Punch You in
3/5/93	1	1	5/13	Reba	It's Ice
3/5/93	2	1	8/11	Stash	It's Ice
3/8/93	2	1	9/12	The Famous Mockingbi	It's Ice
3/12/93	2	2	4/11	Axilla	You Enjoy My
3/14/93	2	1	4/11	Guelah Papyrus	Stash
3/16/93	1	E	1/2	***	Tweezer Repri
3/18/93	2	1	8/11	The Famous Mockingbi	Horn
3/21/93	2	1	2/11	Maze	The Sloth
3/22/93	1	1	9/10	Reba	David Bowie
3/24/93	1	2	3/12	Split Open and Melt	Tweezer
3/26/93	2	1	2/10	Maze	Foam
3/28/93	2	1	3/11	Funky Bitch	Split Open and
3/31/93	2	1	3/10	Foam	Split Open and
4/2/93	2	1	7/9	I Didn't Know	Maze
4/3/93	1	1	4/10	Guelah Papyrus	Split Open and
4/9/93	2	1	2/11	Chalk Dust Torture	Guelah Papyrus
4/10/93	1	1	3/10	Weigh	Split Open and
4/16/93	3	1	3/10	Guelah Papyrus	Split Open and
4/18/93	2	1	4/10	Split Open and Melt	Divided Sky
4/20/93	1	1	3/10	Weigh	Stash

DATE	GAP	SET	POS.	SONG BEFORE	SONG AFTER
4/22/93	2	1	2/10	Suzy Greenberg	It's Ice
4/23/93	1	1	3/10	Weigh	Split Open and
4/24/93	1	1	10/11	When Something Wrong	Run Like Antel
4/27/93	2	1	9/10	It's Ice	David Bowie
4/30/93	2	2	2/10	Wilson	Tweezer
5/2/93	2	1	2/11	Axilla	Divided Sky
5/5/93	2	1	4/10	Foam	Stash
5/7/93	2	1	4/11	Split Open and Melt	Caravan
5/29/93	2	1	4/11	Stash	The Squirmin
7/15/93	2	2	4/11	Silent in the Mornin	It's Ice
7/17/93	2	2	5/12	It's Ice	Big Ball Jam
7/21/93	2	1	3/12	Split Open and Melt	The Squirmin
7/22/93	1	2	4/11	Walk Away	It's Ice
7/24/93	2	2	6/12	Glide	Mike's Song
7/27/93	2	1	5/8	The Squirming Coil	It's Ice
7/29/93	2	2	5/9	Lifeboy	You Enjoy My
7/31/93	2	2	5/11	Maze	Mike's Song
8/3/93	2	2	7/9	The Lizards	Purple Rain
8/7/93	2	2	8/12	The Sloth	My Friend My
8/11/93	3	1	9/10	Stash	Cavern
8/14/93	3	1	7/11	It's Ice	Split Open and
8/16/93	2	1	5/9	Reba	Foam
8/21/93	3	1	7/10	Stash	The Landlady
8/25/93	2	1	4/11	Sample in a Jar	Foam
8/28/93	2	2	6/14	Silent in the Mornin	It's Ice
12/29/93	2	1	7/9	Wilson	Stash
12/31/93	2	3	5/9	The Lizards	Suzy Greenber
4/6/94	3	2	4/9	Wolfman's Brother	Mike's Song
4/8/94	1	2	4/9	It's Ice	Harry Hood
4/10/94	2	1	3/9	It's Ice	Split Open and
4/14/94	3	1	3/9	Foam	Down with Dis
4/18/94	4	2	3/13	Sample in a Jar	Bathtub Gin
4/21/94	2	1	2/9	Chalk Dust Torture	Foam
4/23/94	2	2	5/10	Sample in a Jar	Harry Hood
5/3/94	7	1	4/9	Maze	Stash
5/4/94	1	1	5/10	It's Ice	Axilla (Part II)
5/7/94	2	2	2/12	Loving Cup	Tweezer
5/16/94	6	2	5/11	Run Like an Antelope	Punch You in
5/19/94	2	2	5/10	Sample in a Jar	Mike's Song
5/23/94	4	2	4/7	If I Could	Punch You in
5/26/94	2	1	6/10	Split Open and Melt	It's Ice
5/29/94	3	1	5/8	Down with Disease	Julius
6/10/94	2	2	5/9	Lifeboy	Possum
6/14/94	3	2	6/9	It's Ice	You Enjoy My
6/17/94	2	2	12/15	Harpua	Big Ball Jam
6/21/94	3	2	14/16	Julius	Harry Hood
6/23/94	2	E	1/2	***	Tweezer Repri
6/25/94	2	2	3/9	Maze	Bathtub Gin
6/30/94	3	2	6/15	You Enjoy Myself	Axilla (Part II)
7/2/94	2	1	8/9	Lifeboy	Tweezer Repri
7/5/94	2	2	2/11	Punch You in the Eye	Bathtub Gin
7/9/94	3	2	7/10	Lifeboy	Big Ball Jam
7/14/94	3	2	7/10	You Enjoy Myself	Big Ball Jam
7/16/94	2	1	10/11	Maze	Sample in a Ja
10/8/94	2	1	3/9	Horn	Down with Dis
10/10/94	2	1	5/11	Silent in the Mornin	Stash
10/13/94	2	1	8/9	Fast Enough for You	Stash
10/15/94	2	1	2/8	Wilson	Simple
10/23/94	6	1	3/11	My Friend My Friend	Simple
10/27/94	2	1	2/11	Wilson	Maze
10/29/94	2	1	2/10	My Friend My Friend	Simple
10/31/94	1	1	2/10	Frankenstein	Simple
11/3/94	2	1	8/9	Dog Faced Boy	Down with Dis
11/13/94	3	1	2/10	Wilson	Simple
11/17/94	3	2	4/8	Sleeping Monkey	You Enjoy My
11/19/94	2	2	2/7	Suzy Greenberg	You Enjoy My
11/23/94	2	1	2/9	Wilson	Simple
11/28/94	3	1	6/9	Guyute	Simple
12/2/94	3	1	3/8	Also Sprach	Simple
12/6/94	3	1	6/8	Jesus Just Left	Stash
12/9/94	3	1	4/8	Guyute	I Didn't Know
12/30/94	4	1	4/9	AC/DC Bag	Simple
6/9/95	5	1	5/8	Taste	Run Like Antel
6/13/95	2	1	9/10	Terrapin	Chalk Dust Tor
6/15/95	2	1	2/10	My Friend My Friend	AC/DC Bag
6/19/95	3	2	5/8	Loving Cup	You Enjoy My
6/25/95	5	1	6/9	If I Could	Divided Sky
6/28/95	2	2	7/10	Gumbo	Suzy Greenber
7/3/95	5	1	5/11	Loving Cup	It's Ice
9/29/95	3	1	2/8	AC/DC Bag	Divided Sky
10/3/95	3	2	3/9	It's Ice	Harry Hood
10/8/95	4	1	3/9	Demand	Wolfman's Brother
10/14/95	3	1	5/11	Free	Stash
10/17/95	2	1	7/10	Glide	Free
10/21/95	3	2	4/8	Lifeboy	You Enjoy My
10/25/95	3	2	6/9	Breathe Jam	Weekapaug Gr
10/31/95	4	1	5/9	Ya Mar	Free
11/10/95	2	2	7/9	Strange Design	AC/DC Bag
11/15/95	4	1	6/9	Prince Caspian	Split Open and
11/18/95	2	2	2/10	AC/DC Bag	Free
11/24/95	4	1	4/9	The Curtain	Stash
11/29/95	3	2	2/11	Timber (Jerry)	Simple
12/4/95	4	2	2/9	Timber (Jerry)	Ya Mar
12/7/95	2	2	7/10	Sleeping Monkey	Mike's Song
12/12/95	4	2	6/8	Free	Down with Dis
12/17/95	4	2	2/6	Harry Hood	Tweezer
12/31/95	4	1	9/10	The Famous Mockingbi	Chalk Dust Tor
4/26/96	1	1	3/13	AC/DC Bag	Stash
6/6/96	1	2	4/10	Chalk Dust Torture	Stash
7/3/96	1	1	3/5	Stash	Taste
7/11/96	6	1	5/8	I Didn't Know	Stash
7/23/96	9	2	4/9	Loving Cup	Suzy Greenber
8/7/96	7	1	2/10	Punch You in the Eye	Stash
8/12/96	2	2	2/9	Timber (Jerry)	Simple
8/16/96	3	2	2/13	Split Open and Melt	Free
10/17/96	3	1	3/10	Funky Bitch	Tweezer
10/19/96	2	2	2/9	AC/DC Bag	Slave
10/22/96	2	1	7/9	Split Open and Melt	Free
10/26/96	3	2	3/7	You Enjoy Myself	Simple
11/3/96	5	2	4/9	Wolfman's Brother	Tweezer
11/11/96	5	1	5/9	AC/DC Bag	Brother
11/16/96	4	1	10/11	Lawn Boy	Frankenstein
11/24/96	5	2	2/7	Also Sprach	David Bowie
11/29/96	2	2	4/10	Sparks	Taste
12/1/96	2	2	2/10	Tweezer	Simple
12/4/96	2	2	4/9	Prince Caspian	Punch You in
12/6/96	1	2	2/9	Julius	Mike's Song
12/31/96	4	2	3/9	Wilson	Simple
2/16/97	3	2	4/11	Free	Simple
2/22/97	5	2	3/8	Bathtub Gin	Simple
7/3/97	21	2	4/6	Billy Breathes	Harry Hood
7/29/97	11	1	5/9	Dirt	Ghost
8/2/97	3	2	4/7	Johnny B. Goode	Wading In Velvet Sea
8/10/97	5	1	2/10	Bathtub Gin	Down with Dis
8/14/97	3	2	3/8	Love Me	Harry Hood
11/23/97	10	1	4/9	Black-Eyed Katy	Twist
11/26/97	1	1	2/10	Tweezer	Gumbo
12/5/97	6	1	5/10	Black-Eyed Katy	Runaway Jim
4/5/98	14	1	7/8	Cities	Split Open and
7/10/98	9	2	3/8	Roggae	Mike's Song
7/21/98	6	1	5/8	Tube	Cavern
7/28/98	4	1	9/10	It's Ice	Funky Bitch
8/9/98	9	2	3/11	Jam	Run Like Antel
11/6/98	14	1	6/7	Meat	Split Open and
11/14/98	6	1	7/8	The Moma Dance	Character Zer
11/29/98	10	1	4/11	Theme From the Botto	Horn
12/30/98	3	1	5/12	Roggae	The Moma Dance
7/3/99	4	1	3/11	Gumbo	Cavern
7/10/99	5	1	6/8	Back @ Chicken Shack	Bathtub Gin
7/31/99	15	1	7/8	Roggae	Character Zer
9/16/99	7	1	8/14	Vultures	On Your Way Down
10/1/99	11	1	3/8	The Moma Dance	First Tube
10/9/99	6	1	7/8	Free	Possum
12/5/99	5	1	6/10	Bug	Tube
12/17/99	9	1	3/8	Meat	Gotta Jibboo
5/22/00	2	1	7/9	Split Open And Melt	Horn
6/10/00	3	2	3/9	Sand	My Soul
7/10/00	19	1	8/10	Split Open and Melt	Funky Bitch
9/18/00	12	1	2/10	Carini	The Sloth
9/24/00	4	1	4/10	Back @ Chicken Shack	The Sloth

Has not been played in the last 9 shows.

Sparks

DATE	GAP	SET	POS.	SONG BEFORE	SONG AFTER
3/23/87	20	1	5/5	You Enjoy Myself	***
4/29/87	2	3	10/14	Slave	McGrupp
8/21/87	5	2	6/12	Golgi Apparatus	Flat Fee
11/19/87	8	1	2/7	McGrupp	Funky Bitch
9/24/88	34	2	6/7	Fee	Whipping Post
11/5/88	4	E	3/4	Suzy Greenberg	Divided Sky
9/13/90	134	2	11/15	Take the A-Train	Reba
8/2/93	359	2	3/9	Mike's Song	Ballad - Curtis Loew
8/14/93	9	2	3/13	Run Like an Antelope	Walk Away
5/7/94	40	2	4/12	Tweezer	Makisupa Policeman
10/29/94	65	2	5/11	T.M.W.S.I.Y. Reprise	Uncle Pen
11/29/96	173	2	3/10	Simple	Sparkle

Has not been played in the last 266 shows.

Speak to Me

DATE	GAP	SET	POS.	SONG BEFORE	SONG AFTER
10/31/94	681	2	1/30	***	Back in the USSR
11/2/98	303	2	6/16	Harpua	Breathe

Has not been played in the last 135 shows.

Split Open and Melt

DATE	GAP	SET	POS.	SONG BEFORE	SONG AFTER
2/17/89	83	1	5/10	Divided Sky	Golgi Apparat
3/3/89	3	2	10/12	The Lizards	Take the A-Trn
4/20/89	7	2	4/10	You Enjoy Myself	The Lizards
5/1/89	3	1	6/9	Alumni Blues	The Lizards
5/12/89	4	1	13/15	Possum	Ya Mar
5/13/89	1	1	11/12	Take the A-Train	David Bowie
5/21/89	2	1	7/13	Weekapaug Groove	Dazed and Confused
5/26/89	1	2	3/6	The Mango Song	Bathtub Gin
5/28/89	2	2	14/16	Funky Bitch	The Mango Song
6/23/89	1	2	5/7	Ya Mar	Possum
8/19/89	3	2	1/4	***	Take the A-Trn
8/26/89	2	1	5/8	Harry Hood	Divided Sky
9/9/89	2	4	4/7	Alumni Blues	Harry Hood
10/1/89	3	2	10/11	Contact	The Lizards
10/14/89	5	1	6/11	Ya Mar	Fee
10/20/89	1	2	7/10	Donna Lee	Harry Hood
10/22/89	2	1	10/14	Rocky Top	Tela
11/2/89	4	1	9/11	Reba	Esther
11/3/89	1	1	5/10	My Sweet One	Bundle of Joy
11/10/89	1	1	1/9	***	The Oh Kee Pa
11/30/89	4	2	7/11	Fee	Take the A-Trn
12/3/89	2	2	7/14	Suzy Greenberg	In a Hole
12/8/89	2	1	3/11	Suzy Greenberg	Ya Mar
12/30/89	5	2	2/9	Bathtub Gin	Ya Mar
12/31/89	1	2	5/7	Ya Mar	Divided Sky
1/28/90	3	1	2/9	Suzy Greenberg	Tela
2/15/90	5	2	1/5	***	Bouncing
3/7/90	10	2	5/9	Bathtub Gin	Tela
3/11/90	4	2	9/13	Ya Mar	Harpua
3/28/90	2	2	10/16	The Lizards	Contact
4/14/90	9	1	1/10	***	Uncle Pen
5/15/90	16	1	9/12	Bouncing	Runaway Jim
9/15/90	15	2	1/8	***	Eliza
10/5/90	9	2	6/8	Uncle Pen	Fee
2/1/91	24	1	8/10	Runaway Jim	Bouncing
2/3/91	2	2	6/9	The Mango Song	Bouncing
2/7/91	1	1	6/10	The Mango Song	Bouncing
2/15/91	4	1	4/11	Divided Sky	Fee
2/19/91	2	2	8/15	Esther	Bouncing
2/21/91	2	1	4/11	Ya Mar	Fee
2/27/91	2	1	8/10	My Sweet One	Bouncing
3/8/91	4	1	7/11	Suzy Greenberg	The Squirmin
3/13/91	2	2	2/12	Suzy Greenberg	Bouncing

DATE	GAP	SET	POS.	SONG BEFORE	SONG AFTER
3/16/91	2	2	5/10	My Sweet One	Magilla
3/22/91	2	1	6/11	Bouncing	The Squirmin
4/6/91	9	2	2/11	Ya Mar	Runaway Jim
4/11/91	1	2	8/14	The Lizards	Lawn Boy
4/15/91	2	1	5/10	Runaway Jim	Fee
4/18/91	2	1	8/11	Suzy Greenberg	The Squirmin
4/20/91	2	2	3/13	Ya Mar	The Squirmin
5/2/91	5	2	5/10	Fee	Tela
5/4/91	2	1	6/11	My Sweet One	Guelah Papyrus
5/9/91	1	2	6/8	Esther	The Squirmin
7/13/91	10	1	11/13	T.M.W.S.I.Y. Reprise	Bouncing
7/14/91	1	2	7/10	Bouncing	Magilla
7/18/91	2	2	4/8	Poor Heart	The Lizards
7/21/91	3	1	5/11	Poor Heart	The Lizards
7/24/91	2	1	5/10	Buried Alive	Bathtub Gin
7/25/91	1	E	1/1	***	***
9/27/91	6	2	4/10	Sparkle	The Mango Song
10/10/91	8	1	4/11	Paul and Silas	Bouncing
10/15/91	4	1	4/10	The Squirming Coil	Sparkle
10/18/91	2	2	10/12	Fee	My Sweet One
10/23/91	2	2	6/10	The Mango Song	Love You
11/1/91	6	1	6/11	The Squirming Coil	Fluffhead
11/8/91	3	2	3/13	Sparkle	The Squirmin
11/10/91	2	2	1/4	***	Terrapin
11/12/91	1	E	3/4	BBFCFM	Memories
11/15/91	3	1	5/12	The Curtain	The Squirmin
11/21/91	4	1	8/12	Horn	Esther
12/5/91	6	1	3/10	Paul and Silas	Ya Mar
3/11/92	6	1	7/10	Fee	Mound
3/13/92	2	1	2/12	The Curtain	Poor Heart
3/14/92	1	2	4/10	The Squirming Coil	Bouncing
3/19/92	2	1	3/12	Rift	Sparkle
3/21/92	2	1	5/12	Sparkle	The Horse
3/25/92	3	1	3/10	Sparkle	Rift
3/31/92	5	1	4/10	Glide	Rift
4/3/92	2	1	10/11	All Things Recnsdrd	Golgi Apparat
4/5/92	2	2	1/12	***	All Things Rec
4/7/92	3	1	8/12	Silent in the Mornin	Bouncing
4/12/92	2	2	2/10	Glide	Bouncing
4/16/92	3	1	5/12	Bouncing	Rift
4/18/92	2	1	5/11	Poor Heart	Esther
4/21/92	2	1	3/11	Uncle Pen	Rift
4/23/92	2	1	3/11	The Curtain	Uncle Pen
4/30/92	4	1	2/10	The Curtain	Fee
5/3/92	3	1	6/10	Fee	I Didn't Know
5/7/92	3	1	8/11	Esther	Rift
5/9/92	2	1	4/11	Sparkle	Guelah Papyrus
5/16/92	5	1	4/11	Glide	Bouncing
7/1/92	9	1	5/7	Horn	Sweet Adeline
7/15/92	6	1	7/12	Uncle Pen	The Horse
7/26/92	9	1	5/7	Weigh	The Lizards
11/19/92	21	1	5/12	Glide	Mound
11/23/92	4	1	4/11	Glide	Rift
11/27/92	2	1	6/12	The Famous Mockingbi	Lawn Boy
12/1/92	3	1	3/12	My Sweet One	Bouncing
12/3/92	2	1	4/12	All Things Recnsdrd	Bouncing
12/5/92	2	1	6/12	Guelah Papyrus	The Lizards
12/7/92	2	1	9/11	All Things Recnsdrd	Bouncing
12/10/92	2	1	6/11	Poor Heart	I Didn't Know
12/12/92	2	1	7/11	The Landlady	Poor Heart
12/28/92	2	2	2/9	Poor Heart	Reba
12/30/92	2	1	3/14	Sparkle	Esther
2/5/93	4	1	4/11	Rift	Sparkle
2/7/93	2	1	10/12	I Didn't Know	Fee
2/12/93	4	1	5/11	Sparkle	Esther
2/19/93	5	1	3/11	Rift	Fee
2/23/93	4	1	5/11	Bouncing	Reba
2/26/93	2	1	4/10	Fee	Fluffhead
3/3/93	3	2	3/13	The Curtain	Mound
3/6/93	2	1	4/10	The Curtain	Mound
3/13/93	4	1	7/11	All Things Recnsdrd	Contact
3/18/93	2	2	3/10	Poor Heart	Tela
3/21/93	2	1	7/11	All Things Recnsdrd	Poor Heart
3/24/93	2	2	2/12	The Landlady	Sparkle
3/26/93	2	1	7/10	All Things Recnsdrd	Fluffhead
3/28/93	2	1	4/11	Sparkle	The Lizards
3/31/93	2	1	4/10	Sparkle	Mound
4/3/93	3	1	5/10	Sparkle	The Squirmin
4/10/93	3	1	4/10	Sparkle	The Squirmin
4/16/93	3	1	4/10	Sparkle	Esther
4/18/93	2	1	3/10	Guelah Papyrus	Sparkle
4/21/93	2	2	3/11	Mound	The Squirmin
4/23/93	2	1	4/10	Sparkle	Fluffhead
4/29/93	4	1	1/10	***	Uncle Pen
5/1/93	2	1	4/10	Guelah Papyrus	Fee
5/3/93	2	1	6/11	Esther	Col. Forbin's A
5/6/93	2	1	3/13	Mound	The Horse
5/7/93	1	1	3/11	Poor Heart	Sparkle
5/30/93	3	1	10/13	I Didn't Know	Contact
7/16/93	2	2	2/12	Also Sprach	Glide
7/21/93	3	1	2/12	Also Sprach	Sparkle
7/24/93	3	2	2/12	Also Sprach	Fluffhead
7/28/93	3	1	7/11	Nellie Kane	The Horse
7/31/93	3	1	4/9	Ya Mar	Mound
8/6/93	3	1	1/10	***	Poor Heart
8/9/93	3	1	6/11	Fee	Glide
8/12/93	2	1	6/10	Nellie Kane	The Horse
8/14/93	2	1	8/11	Sparkle	Esther
8/16/93	2	1	8/9	I Didn't Know	The Squirmin
8/20/93	2	2	3/9	Slave	The Squirmin
8/24/93	2	1	6/11	Nellie Kane	The Horse
8/26/93	2	1	5/9	Fee	Esther
12/28/93	2	1	3/10	Poor Heart	Esther
12/31/93	3	3	3/9	Down W Disease Jam	The Lizards
4/4/94	1	2	7/11	Magilla	Wolfman's Brother
4/8/94	3	2	1/9	***	McGrupp
4/10/94	2	1	4/9	Sparkle	Esther
4/18/94	7	1	7/10	Rift	Dog Faced Boy
4/21/94	2	1	5/9	Glide	The Lizards
4/25/94	4	1	10/10	Poor Heart	***
4/29/94	2	1	9/12	Dog Faced Boy	Sanity
5/2/94	2	1	2/10	The Great Gig in the	Bouncing
5/7/94	4	1	7/9	Scent of a Mule	If I Could
5/10/94	2	1	7/9	It's Ice	If I Could
5/13/94	2	2	3/9	Bouncing	McGrupp
5/17/94	3	1	8/9	Dog Faced Boy	The Squirmin
5/22/94	4	1	6/11	Peaches en Regalia	Fluffhead
5/26/94	3	1	5/10	Demand	Sparkle
5/29/94	3	2	2/10	Nellie Kane	Esther
6/9/94	1	2	1/10	***	Glide
6/11/94	2	2	5/9	Scent of a Mule	The Squirmin
6/14/94	2	1	14/14	I Didn't Know	***
6/17/94	2	1	4/9	Glide	If I Could
6/21/94	3	2	5/16	My Friend My Friend	Esther
6/23/94	2	1	3/10	Poor Heart	NICU
6/30/94	5	1	5/9	Guelah Papyrus	Glide
7/3/94	3	2	2/10	***	The Lizards
7/9/94	4	2	2/10	Also Sprach	Fluffhead
7/13/94	2	1	11/11	I Didn't Know	***
7/15/94	2	1	7/8	Fee	Golgi Apparat
10/9/94	4	1	6/7	Dog Faced Boy	The Squirmin
10/12/94	2	1	5/8	Poor Heart	The Lizards
10/16/94	4	1	5/10	Fee	T.M.W.S.I.Y.
10/20/94	2	1	5/11	Guelah Papyrus	Kung
10/20/94	0	1	7/11	Kung	Esther
10/22/94	2	1	6/8	Rift	Fluffhead
10/25/94	2	1	7/9	Silent in the Mornin	The Lizards
10/29/94	4	1	7/10	Lawn Boy	Buffalo Bill
11/3/94	3	1	6/9	Glide	Dog Faced Boy
11/14/94	4	1	4/9	Guelah Papyrus	Bouncing
11/18/94	3	1	8/11	Tela	Butter Them Biscuits
11/25/94	5	1	5/8	Bouncing	Esther
12/1/94	4	1	7/8	I Didn't Know	Sweet Adeline
12/7/94	5	1	5/8	Ya Mar	Guyute
12/29/94	5	1	4/9	If I Could	The Horse
6/9/95	6	2	1/8	***	The Wedge
6/14/95	3	1	12/12	Spock's Brain	***
6/16/95	2	1	10/10	Catapult	***
6/20/95	3	1	9/9	I Didn't Know	***
6/25/95	4	1	9/9	I Didn't Know	***
6/29/95	3	1	9/10	Simple	Carolina
7/1/95	2	1	7/9	Prince Caspian	Bouncing
9/29/95	5	2	5/8	Ya Mar	Billy Breathes
10/3/95	3	2	8/9	Sweet Adeline	The Squirmin
10/7/95	3	2	3/9	Cars Trucks Buses	Strange Design
10/13/95	3	1	7/9	Prince Caspian	Fluffhead
10/19/95	4	1	9/11	Acoustic Army	Billy Breathes
10/24/95	4	1	13/13	Prince Caspian	***
10/29/95	4	1	8/12	Silent in the Mornin	NICU
11/12/95	5	1	9/10	If I Could	Hello My Baby
11/15/95	2	1	7/9	Sparkle	Sweet Adeline
11/29/95	9	1	9/9	Fee	***
12/7/95	6	2	1/10	***	Strange Design
12/14/95	5	1	6/10	Makisupa Policeman	Tela
12/28/95	4	1	1/9	***	Gumbo
6/6/96	5	1	1/8	***	Poor Heart
7/10/96	6	1	3/7	Ya Mar	Waste
7/12/96	2	1	4/10	Horn	Ya Mar
7/13/96	1	1	6/10	Poor Heart	Fire
7/21/96	5	1	7/14	My Mind's Got A Mind	The Horse
8/4/96	6	1	5/9	Fee	The Mango Song
8/12/96	5	1	2/10	Ya Mar	Esther
8/16/96	3	2	1/13	***	Sparkle
10/19/96	5	2	5/10	Bouncing	Fluffhead
10/22/96	2	1	6/9	Talk	Sparkle
10/27/96	4	1	8/11	Scent of a Mule	Talk
11/6/96	5	1	1/9	***	Cars Trucks Buses
11/9/96	3	1	8/10	Talk	The Lizards
11/15/96	4	2	4/11	McGrupp	T.M.W.S.I.Y.
11/23/96	5	1	7/9	Midnight on the High	Rift
12/28/96	9	1	7/9	Ginseng Sullivan	The Mango Song
2/16/97	6	1	2/10	Beauty of My Dreams	Bouncing
2/22/97	5	1	8/10	Talk	I Didn't Know
6/24/97	15	1	1/12	***	Beauty of My Dreams
7/9/97	9	1	4/8	Ginseng Sullivan	Dirt
7/23/97	5	1	8/10	Limb by Limb	Billy Breathes
8/2/97	6	1	8/8	Water in the Sky	***
8/10/97	5	1	7/10	Billy Breathes	Bye Bye Foot
11/13/97	6	1	5/9	Train Song	Beauty of My Dreams
11/21/97	5	1	2/8	Emotional Rescue	Beauty of My Dreams
11/26/97	3	1	7/10	Dirt	The Horse
12/28/97	13	1	9/11	Funky Bitch	Bouncing
4/5/98	7	1	8/8	Sparkle	***
7/9/98	8	1	4/8	NICU	Meat
7/20/98	6	1	10/10	The Moma Dance	***
8/15/98	17	1	5/12	Roggae	Poor Heart
11/6/98	11	1	7/7	Sparkle	***
11/20/98	10	1	13/13	Driver	***
11/28/98	5	1	8/8	The Moma Dance	***
12/29/98	3	1	6/10	Ginseng Sullivan	Brian and Robert
7/12/99	11	1	5/7	What's the Use	Water In the Sky
7/15/99	2	2	2/6	Meatstick	Kung
7/26/99	9	2	6/6	Jam	***
8/1/99	4	1	7/10	Horn	Poor Heart
9/10/99	2	2	7/9	I Saw it Again	Cavern
9/21/99	8	1	3/9	Sample in a Jar	Drowned
10/2/99	8	1	7/9	Roggae	The Squirmin
12/4/99	9	2	2/9	Down with Disease	The Moma Dance
12/17/99	10	2	5/6	Jennifer Dances	Character Zer
12/31/99	3	1	9/14	Roggae	Catapult

DATE	GAP	SET	POS.	SONG BEFORE	SONG AFTER
5/22/00	2	1	6/9	Back on the Train	Sparkle
6/14/00	6	1	8/8	Heavy Things	***
6/25/00	6	1	10/10	Dirt	***
7/1/00	4	1	11/11	Dirt	***
7/7/00	4	2	3/7	Gotta Jibboo	Roggae
7/10/00	2	1	7/10	My Mind's Got A Mind	Sparkle
9/12/00	8	2	3/8	Heavy Things	Bike
9/27/00	10	1	7/10	Dirt	Horn

Has not been played in the last 7 shows.

Split Open and Melt Jam

DATE	GAP	SET	POS.	SONG BEFORE	SONG AFTER
4/14/94	597	1	8/9	Demand	The Squirmin
6/26/94	50	2	11/12	Demand	Yerushalayim

Has not been played in the last 472 shows.

Spock's Brain

DATE	GAP	SET	POS.	SONG BEFORE	SONG AFTER
5/16/95	712	1	3/12	Ha Ha Ha	Strange Design
6/7/95	1	2	3/9	Maze	Theme From the Botto
6/14/95	5	1	11/12	Silent in the Mornin	Split Open and Ginseng Sullivan
6/20/95	5	1	2/9	Llama	
6/24/95	3	1	3/10	Rift	Julius
9/29/00	387	1	6/8	Wilson	Bathtub Gin
10/6/00	5	2	3/10	Down With Disease	The Inlaw Josie Wale

Has not been played in the last 1 show.

Spooky Jam

DATE	GAP	SET	POS.	SONG BEFORE	SONG AFTER
3/14/93	509	2	5/11	You Enjoy Myself	You Enjoy My
4/14/93	21	2	7/10	You Enjoy Myself	You Enjoy My

Has not been played in the last 589 shows.

Squeeze Box

DATE	GAP	SET	POS.	SONG BEFORE	SONG AFTER
12/2/83	0	1	4/6	In the Midnight Hour	Roadhouse Blues

Has not been played in the last 1119 shows.

St. Stephen Jam

DATE	GAP	SET	POS.	SONG BEFORE	SONG AFTER
11/3/84	2	1	5/10	Bertha	Can't You Hear Me Kn

Has not been played in the last 1117 shows.

St. Thomas

DATE	GAP	SET	POS.	SONG BEFORE	SONG AFTER
5/21/88	49	1	5/7	You Enjoy Myself	Golgi Apparat

Has not been played in the last 1070 shows.

Stand

DATE	GAP	SET	POS.	SONG BEFORE	SONG AFTER
6/13/97	878	E	1/2	***	Izabella

Has not been played in the last 241 shows.

Stash

DATE	GAP	SET	POS.	SONG BEFORE	SONG AFTER
9/13/90	207	2	5/15	Magilla	Going Down Slow
9/14/90	1	1	6/11	Paul and Silas	Dinner and a
9/15/90	1	1	12/14	Golgi Apparatus	Magilla
9/20/90	2	2	1/14	***	AC/DC Bag
9/20/90	0	2	11/14	Funky Bitch	Uncle Pen
9/21/90	1	2	2/8	Funky Bitch	Uncle Pen
9/22/90	1	2	7/10	Bouncing	The Lizards
9/28/90	1	1	5/10	Suzy Greenberg	My Sweet One
9/29/90	1	2	5/8	Uncle Pen	Mike's Song
10/1/90	1	1	5/11	The Asse Festival	Runaway Jim
10/5/90	2	1	10/13	Suzy Greenberg	The Asse Festival
10/7/90	2	1	3/14	Uncle Pen	The Landlady
10/8/90	1	2	2/6	Suzy Greenberg	If I Only Had a Brai
10/31/90	4	1	5/11	The Lizards	Bouncing
11/3/90	2	2	6/12	Paul and Silas	Fee
11/24/90	6	2	3/12	Bouncing	Eliza
11/30/90	2	2	4/10	Runaway Jim	The Lizards
12/7/90	2	1	2/9	Golgi Apparatus	Bouncing
12/29/90	3	2	5/10	Cavern	Jesus Just Left
12/31/90	1	2	2/9	Golgi Apparatus	The Squirmin
2/2/91	2	1	6/9	Esther	Destiny Unbound
2/8/91	3	1	7/11	My Sweet One	The Squirmin
2/14/91	2	1	8/11	The Mango Song	Lawn Boy
2/21/91	5	2	5/9	Bouncing	Guelah Papyrus
2/26/91	1	2	4/12	Dinner and a Movie	Bouncing
3/8/91	5	1	4/11	Fluffhead	The Oh Kee Pa
3/15/91	3	1	4/12	My Sweet One	Dinner and a
3/17/91	2	1	10/12	Uncle Pen	The Lizards
3/22/91	1	2	6/13	Paul and Silas	Runaway Jim
3/31/91	4	2	4/7	The Squirming Coil	Guelah Papyrus
4/3/91	2	2	4/9	My Sweet One	Esther
4/5/91	2	2	2/9	Rocky Top	The Lizards
4/12/91	3	1	7/9	Suzy Greenberg	Rocky Top
4/19/91	4	1	6/12	The Lizards	I Didn't Know
4/22/91	3	2	7/10	The Squirming Coil	My Sweet One
4/27/91	2	1	11/12	Suzy Greenberg	Golgi Apparat
5/9/91	4	2	4/8	Fluffhead	Esther
5/12/91	3	1	4/11	Dinner and a Movie	The Lizards
5/17/91	2	1	12/17	T.M.W.S.I.Y. Reprise	I Didn't Know
5/18/91	1	2	4/10	The Curtain	Take the A-Trn
7/11/91	2	1	6/8	My Sweet One	The Lizards
7/13/91	2	2	7/9	The Lizards	If I Only Had a Brai
7/15/91	2	1	5/14	Dinner and a Movie	Bouncing
7/18/91	1	1	6/11	Suzy Greenberg	Take the A-Trn
7/20/91	2	2	7/12	Golgi Apparatus	T.M.W.S.I.Y.
7/23/91	1	1	7/12	Suzy Greenberg	Flat Fee
7/26/91	3	2	1/10	***	Dinner and a
7/27/91	1	1	7/16	Poor Heart	T.M.W.S.I.Y.
8/3/91	1	3	1/8	***	Ya Mar
9/25/91	1	2	2/8	The Squirming Coil	Sparkle
9/28/91	3	1	6/11	My Sweet One	Eliza
9/30/91	2	1	2/4	Cavern	Col. Forbin's A
10/2/91	1	2	7/9	Lawn Boy	The Oh Kee Pa
10/4/91	2	2	7/11	Lawn Boy	The Squirmin
10/6/91	1	2	5/9	My Sweet One	Fee
10/12/91	3	1	5/9	My Sweet One	Esther
10/17/91	3	1	7/10	Poor Heart	Esther
10/19/91	2	1	9/10	My Sweet One	Golgi Apparat
10/24/91	2	1	5/12	Poor Heart	Ya Mar
10/28/91	2	2	4/11	Dinner and a Movie	Paul and Silas
11/1/91	3	E	3/3	Pusher Man Jam	***
11/8/91	3	1	4/11	Dinner and a Movie	Paul and Silas
11/12/91	3	2	2/13	Dinner and a Movie	The Squirmin
11/16/91	4	1	9/11	Foam	Ya Mar
11/20/91	2	1	6/11	Sparkle	Paul and Silas
11/22/91	2	1	10/11	Dinner and a Movie	Rocky Top
11/24/91	2	1	3/9	Paul and Silas	The Landlady
12/4/91	2	2	2/11	My Sweet One	The Mango Song
12/7/91	3	1	7/11	My Sweet One	The Curtain
12/31/91	1	1	4/10	Sparkle	The Lizards
3/6/92	1	2	4/9	Secret Language Inst	Mound
3/12/92	3	1	4/11	Sparkle	I Didn't Know
3/14/92	2	1	7/13	Rift	Fee
3/19/92	2	2	5/10	My Sweet One	The Oh Kee Pa
3/21/92	2	1	11/12	My Sweet One	Golgi Apparat
3/24/92	2	1	1/13	***	Poor Heart
3/26/92	2	1	6/10	Sparkle	Fluffhead
3/28/92	2	1	4/10	Sparkle	Rift
3/31/92	2	2	3/11	Poor Heart	The Lizards
4/3/92	2	1	3/11	Poor Heart	Rift
4/5/92	2	1	6/11	Poor Heart	Rift
4/6/92	1	2	10/13	Mound	Cracklin' Rosi
4/8/92	2	1	9/11	Uncle Pen	The Squirmin
4/13/92	2	1	3/10	Uncle Pen	The Lizards
4/15/92	1	1	6/11	Sparkle	Uncle Pen
4/18/92	2	1	4/13	Sparkle	I Didn't Know
4/19/92	2	1	3/11	NICU	Paul and Silas
4/22/92	2	1	8/10	Mound	All Things Rec
4/24/92	2	1	9/11	Sparkle	The Squirmin
4/30/92	3	1	7/10	Uncle Pen	Rift
5/2/92	2	1	9/11	Bouncing	The Squirmin
5/5/92	2	1	4/11	Sparkle	Rift
5/6/92	1	2	2/11	My Sweet One	The Squirmin
5/8/92	2	2	3/12	My Sweet One	Magilla
5/10/92	2	1	4/10	Sparkle	Uncle Pen
5/14/92	2	2	11/13	McGrupp	Cracklin' Rosi
5/15/92	1	1	5/11	Sparkle	Bouncing
5/17/92	2	1	8/11	I Didn't Know	The Mango Song
6/19/92	2	1	3/7	Suzy Greenberg	The Squirmin
7/9/92	7	1	5/12	Sparkle	The Squirmin
7/11/92	2	1	5/11	Sparkle	The Squirmin
7/15/92	3	2	5/9	My Sweet One	McGrupp
7/17/92	2	1	3/7	Sparkle	The Squirmin
7/21/92	3	1	5/7	Sparkle	The Squirmin
7/25/92	3	1	4/8	Sparkle	Rift
8/1/92	6	1	4/7	Poor Heart	The Squirmin
8/14/92	3	1	2/5	Poor Heart	The Squirmin
8/20/92	4	1	3/6	Sparkle	The Squirmin
8/23/92	1	1	7/7	Runaway Jim	***
8/25/92	2	1	4/7	Sparkle	The Squirmin
8/28/92	2	1	3/7	Foam	Sweet Adeline
10/30/92	3	1	9/11	The Squirming Coil	Sweet Adeline
11/20/92	2	1	8/12	Sparkle	The Lizards
11/23/92	3	2	2/14	Poor Heart	The Squirmin
11/28/92	3	1	3/11	Foam	Esther
11/30/92	1	1	5/10	Poor Heart	Sparkle
12/2/92	2	1	6/10	Poor Heart	The Lizards
12/4/92	2	1	4/11	Poor Heart	Glide
12/6/92	2	2	3/13	The Curtain	Paul and Silas
12/8/92	2	1	11/11	Sweet Adeline	***
12/11/92	2	1	4/11	Uncle Pen	The Lizards
12/13/92	2	1	7/11	Uncle Pen	Rift
12/29/92	2	1	9/12	Uncle Pen	Tela
12/31/92	2	2	8/10	Big Ball Jam	Glide
2/4/93	2	1	7/11	All Things Recnsdrd	The Lizards
2/6/93	2	2	3/14	Mound	Sweet Adeline
2/9/93	2	2	9/12	Big Ball Jam	The Lizards
2/11/93	2	1	4/10	Poor Heart	Fee
2/13/93	2	1	7/10	Rift	Lawn Boy
2/15/93	1	1	9/12	Mound	Guelah Papyrus
2/18/93	2	2	2/12	Rift	The Lizards
2/21/93	3	2	3/10	The Curtain	Manteca
2/21/93	0	2	5/10	Manteca	The Lizards
2/23/93	2	2	3/13	My Sweet One	The Lizards
2/25/93	1	1	8/11	Rift	Bouncing
2/27/93	2	2	2/12	The Curtain	Poor Heart
3/2/93	1	1	3/13	Poor Heart	Reba
3/5/93	2	1	7/11	Rift	Sparkle
3/8/93	2	2	4/10	Uncle Pen	Big Ball Jam
3/12/93	2	1	7/11	Rift	Fluffhead
3/14/93	2	1	5/11	Sparkle	Paul and Silas
3/17/93	2	1	5/11	Bouncing	Amazing Grce
3/19/93	2	1	6/9	Rift	Fluffhead
3/22/93	2	1	4/11	Uncle Pen	Bouncing
3/25/93	2	1	6/11	Bouncing	Glide
3/27/93	2	1	4/10	Rift	Reba
3/30/93	2	1	8/11	Esther	Glide
4/1/93	2	1	4/10	Rift	The Squirmin
4/3/93	2	2	2/10	Suzy Greenberg	Mound
4/5/93	2	1	7/10	Paul and Silas	Col. Forbin's A
4/9/93	1	1	4/11	Guelah Papyrus	The Horse
4/12/93	2	1	5/11	Poor Heart	The Horse
4/14/93	1	1	6/13	It's Ice	Kung
4/14/93	0	1	8/13	Kung	The Horse
4/17/93	2	1	4/10	Bouncing	It's Ice
4/20/93	2	1	4/10	Sparkle	Bouncing
4/22/93	2	1	7/10	Esther	Fee
4/24/93	2	1	4/11	Poor Heart	The Horse
4/27/93	2	1	6/10	Rift	Guelah Papyrus
4/30/93	2	1	5/12	Poor Heart	The Horse
5/2/93	2	1	5/11	Mound	The Horse

DATE	GAP	SET	POS.	SONG BEFORE	SONG AFTER
5/5/93	2	1	5/10	Sparkle	Bouncing
5/8/93	3	1	5/12	Mound	Kung
5/8/93	0	1	7/12	Kung	Glide
5/29/93	1	1	3/10	Bouncing	Sparkle
7/15/93	2	1	5/9	Mound	I Didn't Know
7/17/93	2	1	5/11	My Mind's Got A Mind	Reba
7/22/93	3	1	10/11	Poor Heart	Golgi Apparat
7/24/93	2	1	7/10	Rift	The Mango Song
7/25/93	1	1	4/10	Mound	Fee
7/27/93	1	1	3/8	Rift	The Squirmin
7/30/93	3	1	5/10	Uncle Pen	Esther
8/3/93	3	1	6/11	Rift	The Horse
8/7/93	2	1	4/10	Poor Heart	Makisupa Policeman
8/11/93	3	1	8/10	The Mango Song	Sparkle
8/13/93	2	1	5/10	Foam	Ginseng Sullivan
8/15/93	2	1	7/10	Paul and Silas	Col. Forbin's A
8/21/93	4	1	6/10	Rift	Sparkle
8/25/93	2	1	9/11	Amazing Grace	Glide
8/28/93	2	1	7/9	Fluffhead	The Squirmin
12/29/93	2	1	8/9	Sparkle	The Squirmin
12/31/93	2	1	3/8	Guelah Papyrus	Ginseng Sullivan
4/6/94	3	1	4/9	Poor Heart	The Lizards
4/9/94	2	1	9/10	All Things Recnsdrd	The Squirmin
4/13/94	3	1	3/8	Poor Heart	The Lizards
4/16/94	3	1	5/8	Rift	Fluffhead
4/20/94	3	1	6/7	Axilla (Part II)	Suzy Greenber
4/23/94	3	1	6/10	Poor Heart	Esther
4/30/94	5	1	3/9	Mound	Poor Heart
5/3/94	2	1	5/9	Sparkle	The Squirmin
5/6/94	2	1	7/9	Ya Mar	Esther
5/8/94	2	1	7/8	Bouncing	The Squirmin
5/13/94	2	1	5/9	Mound	If I Could
5/16/94	2	1	9/10	Bouncing	Sweet Adeline
5/19/94	2	1	5/10	Poor Heart	The Horse
5/21/94	2	1	6/9	Mound	The Squirmin
5/25/94	3	1	4/11	Uncle Pen	Col. Forbin's A
5/28/94	3	1	5/10	Bouncing	The Horse
6/11/94	4	1	8/8	Tela	***
6/13/94	1	1	7/9	Dinner and a Movie	Ginseng Sullivan
6/16/94	2	1	9/10	Dog Faced Boy	The Squirmin
6/19/94	3	1	8/9	Scent of a Mule	Golgi Apparat
6/22/94	3	1	8/9	Scent of a Mule	Golgi Apparat
6/25/94	3	1	5/10	NICU	The Mango Song
7/1/94	4	1	5/10	NICU	The Mango Song
7/5/94	3	1	7/10	Uncle Pen	Esther
7/8/94	2	2	6/11	It's Ice	You Enjoy My
7/10/94	2	1	5/9	Rift	If I Could
7/14/94	2	1	3/11	Bouncing	T.M.W.S.I.Y.
7/16/94	2	1	4/11	NO2	The Lizards
10/7/94	1	1	7/9	Guelah Papyrus	Guyute
10/10/94	3	1	6/11	Sparkle	Guyute
10/13/94	2	1	9/9	Sparkle	***
10/18/94	4	1	5/10	Poor Heart	Tela
10/21/94	2	1	6/9	The Old Home Place	The Lizards
10/23/94	2	1	6/11	Poor Heart	Catapult
10/23/94	0	1	8/11	Catapult	Tela
10/28/94	4	1	5/10	Scent of a Mule	Glide
11/2/94	3	1	6/8	Guyute	Scent of a Mul
11/12/94	3	1	6/8	Guyute	Esther
11/16/94	3	1	7/11	The Lizards	Pig in a Pen
11/20/94	4	1	4/10	Scent of a Mule	If I Could
11/28/94	5	1	4/9	Scent of a Mule	Guyute
12/2/94	3	1	7/8	The Lizards	The Squirmin
12/6/94	3	1	7/8	Sparkle	Golgi Apparat
12/10/94	4	1	3/8	Rift	The Lizards
12/30/94	3	1	6/9	Simple	Fee
6/7/95	3	1	5/10	Strange Design	If I Could
6/13/95	4	1	4/10	Bouncing	Strange Design

DATE	GAP	SET	POS.	SONG BEFORE	SONG AFTER
6/15/95	2	1	7/10	The Wedge	I Didn't Know
6/17/95	2	1	9/9	The Curtain	***
6/24/95	5	1	7/10	Mound	The Horse
6/28/95	3	1	6/8	Punch You in the Eye	Fluffhead
7/1/95	3	2	5/9	Uncle Pen	Strange Design
9/28/95	4	1	5/9	Scent of a Mule	Fee
10/2/95	3	1	5/10	Night Moves Jam	Acoustic Army
10/6/95	3	1	2/9	Ya Mar	Billy Breathes
10/11/95	3	1	1/9	***	The Old Home
10/14/95	2	1	6/11	Sparkle	Catapult
10/17/95	2	1	2/10	Sample in a Jar	Uncle Pen
10/22/95	4	1	12/12	I'm Blue, Lonesome	***
10/27/95	3	1	7/9	Rift	Fee
11/11/95	6	1	9/12	Ya Mar	Amazing Grce
11/14/95	2	3	3/11	Gumbo	Manteca
11/14/95	0	2	5/11	Manteca	Dog Faced Boy
11/14/95	0	2	7/11	Dog Faced Boy	Strange Design
11/19/95	4	1	5/10	Rift	Strange Design
11/24/95	3	1	5/9	Sparkle	Tela
11/28/95	2	1	1/9	***	Dinner and a
12/1/95	3	1	9/10	The Famous Mockingbi	Cavern
12/4/95	2	1	5/11	Punch You in the Eye	My Mind's Got A Mind
12/11/95	5	1	3/12	Ha Ha Ha	Prince Caspian
12/17/95	5	1	7/9	Tube	The Lizards
12/29/95	2	1	6/9	NICU	Fluffhead
4/26/96	3	1	4/13	Sparkle	Cars Trucks Buses
6/6/96	1	2	5/10	Sparkle	Waste
7/3/96	1	1	2/5	Runaway Jim	Sparkle
7/11/96	6	1	6/8	Sparkle	Scent of a Mul
7/18/96	5	1	4/7	Bouncing	Hello My Baby
7/22/96	3	1	6/8	Bouncing	A Day in the Life
7/23/96	1	1	8/9	McGrupp	Hello My Baby
8/7/96	7	1	3/10	Sparkle	Ya Mar
8/9/96	2	1	6/9	Gumbo	Hello My Baby
10/18/96	5	1	5/10	Cars Trucks Buses	Strange Design
10/21/96	2	1	8/10	Ginseng Sullivan	Waste
10/25/96	3	1	9/10	I Didn't Know	The Squirmin
10/29/96	3	1	6/10	Bouncing	Train Song
11/2/96	2	1	6/9	Cavern	The Lizards
11/7/96	3	1	5/10	Guelah Papyrus	Waste
11/14/96	5	E	1/2	***	Hello My Baby
11/19/96	4	1	6/9	Mound	Fee
11/22/96	1	1	9/10	Train Song	Cavern
11/30/96	5	1	5/10	Bouncing	Fluffhead
12/31/96	8	1	5/10	Cars Trucks Buses	The Horse
2/13/97	1	1	4/12	Also Sprach	Walfredo
2/18/97	4	1	6/10	NICU	Waste
2/20/97	1	2	5/12	Uncle Pen	Bouncing
2/25/97	4	1	6/9	Got My Mojo Workin'	Waste
2/28/97	2	1	6/10	Peaches en Regalia	Swept Away
6/13/97	4	2	1/9	***	Maze
6/19/97	3	2	1/7	***	Ghost
6/22/97	3	1	3/9	Water in the Sky	Dirt
6/27/97	3	1	3/8	Chalk Dust Torture	Dogs Stole Things
7/2/97	3	2	1/4	***	Llama
7/6/97	3	1	4/9	Dogs Stole Things	The Horse
7/11/97	3	1	3/7	Bouncing	Beauty of My Dreams
7/22/97	2	1	4/8	Water in the Sky	Bouncing
7/26/97	3	1	4/9	Poor Heart	Billy Breathes
7/30/97	2	1	5/9	Water in the Sky	Weigh
8/6/97	4	1	2/8	NICU	Beauty of My Dreams
8/13/97	5	1	3/11	Poor Heart	Water in the Sky
11/13/97	4	2	1/7	***	Punch You in

DATE	GAP	SET	POS.	SONG BEFORE	SONG AFTER
11/23/97	7	1	6/9	Twist	NICU
11/30/97	4	2	2/7	NICU	Free
12/5/97	3	2	1/7	***	Bouncing
12/9/97	3	1	4/10	My Soul	I Am Hydrgn
12/30/97	6	1	5/7	Punch You in the Eye	Chalk Dust Tor
4/2/98	2	1	5/8	NICU	Horn
6/30/98	4	1	6/13	Tube	Cities
7/3/98	3	1	1/11	***	Beauty of My Dreams
7/16/98	7	1	3/7	NICU	Reba
7/24/98	5	1	4/8	Bouncing	My Soul
7/31/98	5	1	7/7	Water in the Sky	***
8/7/98	5	1	4/10	Frankie Says	Brian and Robert
10/30/98	12	2	1/7	***	Manteca
11/8/98	6	1	9/10	Water in the Sky	Cavern
11/15/98	5	2	2/7	Runaway Jim	Mike's Song
11/20/98	3	1	8/13	Meat	Train Song
11/24/98	2	1	4/9	Ginseng Sullivan	Brian and Robert
12/28/98	5	1	2/10	Axilla	Farmhouse
6/30/99	4	2	10/10	My Left Toe	***
7/8/99	5	1	7/8	Nellie Kane	Cavern
7/26/99	14	1	11/11	Axilla	***
7/30b/99	2	1	4/8	Beauty of my Dreams	NICU
9/9/99	3	1	8/10	Back @ Chicken Shack	I Didn't Know
9/16/99	5	1	11/14	Beauty of My Dreams	Train Song
9/19/99	3	1	7/8	Farmhouse	Hello My Baby
9/29/99	7	1	7/9	Nellie Kane	Theme From the Botto
10/10/99	8	1	7/7	Vultures	***
12/12/99	9	1	7/8	Bug	Chalk Dust Tor
6/11/00	13	1	5/9	Ginseng Sullivan	Dirt
7/4/00	14	1	6/11	Bouncing	The Lizards
7/14/00	7	2	5/11	Boogie On Reggae	Bouncing
9/11/00	4	1	9/9	Ya Mar	***
9/23/00	8	1	6/6	Fee	***
10/6/00	9	1	2/7	Carini	Boogie On Reggae

Has not been played in the last 1 show.

Steep

DATE	GAP	SET	POS.	SONG BEFORE	SONG AFTER
10/16/96	824	2	6/10	Swept Away	Prince Caspian
10/19/96	3	2	8/10	Swept Away	Run Like Antel
10/22/96	2	2	9/10	Swept Away	Weekapaug Gr
10/31/96	6	3	6/8	Swept Away	Jesus Just Left
11/6/96	3	2	5/9	Swept Away	Weekapaug Gr
11/9/96	3	2	6/7	Swept Away	Harry Hood
11/11/96	1	2	8/11	Swept Away	Maze
11/14/96	2	2	5/10	Swept Away	Scent of a Mul
11/18/96	3	2	4/9	Swept Away	Scent of a Mul
11/22/96	2	2	6/10	Swept Away	Character Zer
11/29/96	4	2	7/10	Swept Away	You Enjoy My
12/1/96	2	2	7/10	Swept Away	Tweezer Repri
12/31/96	7	2	6/9	Swept Away	Harry Hood
2/16/97	3	2	8/11	Swept Away	David Bowie
2/20/97	3	2	9/12	Swept Away	A Day in the Life
2/28/97	6	1	8/10	Swept Away	Ya Mar
3/2/97	2	2	4/9	Swept Away	Punch You in
6/21/97	1	1	8/15	Swept Away	Limb by Limb
7/29/97	19	1	8/9	Swept Away	Loving Cup
8/9/97	7	2	7/10	Swept Away	Scent of a Mul
12/7/97	23	1	7/12	Swept Away	It's Ice
12/12/97	3	2	4/7	Swept Away	Prince Caspian
6/30/98	10	2	11/12	Swept Away	Weekapaug Gr
6/30/99	62	2	6/10	Swept Away	Piper
7/1/00	81	2	6/10	Swept Away	I Am Hydrgn

Has not been played in the last 31 shows.

Stir It Up Jam

DATE	GAP	SET	POS.	SONG BEFORE	SONG AFTER
8/21/87	27	3	3/7	McGrupp	Makisupa Policeman J

Has not been played in the last 1092 shows.

Strange Design

DATE	GAP	SET	POS.	SONG BEFORE	SONG AFTER
5/16/95	712	1	4/12	Spock's Brain	Reba
6/7/95	1	1	4/10	Taste	Stash
6/9/95	2	1	3/9	Divided Sky	The Oh Kee Pa
6/13/95	2	1	5/10	Stash	Taste
6/15/95	2	2	4/8	David Bowie	Theme From the Botto
6/19/95	3	1	7/10	Reba	Rift
6/22/95	2	1	7/10	It's Ice	Maze
6/26/95	4	2	5/6	You Enjoy Myself	Run Like Antel
6/29/95	2	2	3/6	David Bowie	You Enjoy My
7/1/95	2	2	6/9	Stash	Acoustic Army
7/3/95	2	1	9/11	Maze	Free
9/27/95	1	1	7/9	Fog that Surrounds	Chalk Dust Tor
9/29/95	2	1	4/8	Divided Sky	Cars Trucks Buses
10/5/95	4	1	7/11	Cars Trucks Buses	Divided Sky
10/7/95	2	2	4/9	Split Open and Melt	It's Ice
10/15/95	5	1	8/10	Foam	I'm Blue, Lonesome
10/17/95	1	1	9/10	Free	Amazing Grce
10/21/95	3	1	9/12	The Lizards	Acoustic Army
10/25/95	3	1	7/10	Free	My Long Journey Home
10/28/95	2	2	5/7	You Enjoy Myself	Frankenstein
11/10/95	4	2	6/9	You Enjoy Myself	Sparkle
11/14/95	3	2	8/11	Stash	You Enjoy My
11/19/95	4	1	6/10	Stash	It's Ice
11/22/95	2	2	6/6	You Enjoy Myself	***
11/25/95	2	2	8/12	I'm Blue, Lonesome	Weekapaug Gr
11/30/95	3	2	7/8	Free	Amazing Grce
12/7/95	5	2	2/10	Split Open and Melt	Taste That Surrounds
12/31/95	12	2	6/8	Runaway Jim	Hello My Baby
8/5/96	23	2	9/13	Train Song	Amazing Grce
8/13/96	5	2	9/11	Train Song	Sweet Adeline
8/16/96	2	2	8/13	Train Song	Hello My Baby
10/18/96	4	1	6/10	Stash	Divided Sky
10/25/96	5	2	9/12	Free	Harry Hood
11/24/96	20	1	7/11	Character Zero	Taste
12/28/96	8	2	8/10	Mike's Song	Weekapaug Gr
7/2/97	31	1	4/8	Maze	Ginseng Sullivan
11/29/97	36	2	2/5	Runaway Jim	Harry Hood
12/13/97	10	1	5/9	Ginseng Sullivan	Sample in a Ja
8/3/98	32	1	7/8	The Moma Dance	Character Zer
8/15/98	7	3	3/6	David Bowie	Limb by Limb
7/23/99	48	1	8/9	David Bowie	Possum
9/21/99	17	2	3/8	Bug	Vultures
12/12/99	23	1	3/8	AC/DC Bag	Divided Sky
6/24/00	20	1	5/6	Tweezer	Cavern

Has not been played in the last 36 shows.

Suspicious Minds

DATE	GAP	SET	POS.	SONG BEFORE	SONG AFTER
9/30/95	738	2	8/9	Weekapaug Groove	Cavern
10/6/95	4	2	7/8	Keyboard Cavalry	Slave
10/8/95	2	2	7/10	You Enjoy Myself	Dog Faced Boy
10/15/95	4	2	6/8	Sample in a Jar	Harry Hood
10/19/95	2	2	9/10	Kung	Possum
10/27/95	6	1	9/9	Fee	***
11/11/95	6	2	8/9	Frankenstein	Run Like Antel
11/21/95	7	2	9/11	Keyboard Cavalry	Carolina
12/1/95	7	2	6/9	Wilson	David Bowie
12/11/95	7	2	7/8	Harry Hood	Funky Bitch
12/15/95	3	1	6/10	Ha Ha Ha	Cars Trucks Buses
10/29/96	48	2	8/10	Character Zero	Slave
12/6/96	24	E	5/7	Harpua	Harpua

Has not been played in the last 261 shows.

Suzy Greenberg

DATE	GAP	SET	POS.	SONG BEFORE	SONG AFTER
2/13/87	17	1	7/14	Alumni Blues	Sanity
2/21/87	1	2	3/15	Fire	Dear Mrs. Reagan
8/9/87	7	2	11/11	Harpua	***
8/29/87	3	2	8/13	Lushington	Mustang Sally
9/21/87	2	2	4/5	BBFCFM	Alumni Blues
11/19/87	5	3	2/14	Jam	Possum
1/27/88	1	3	3/8	The Lizards	Golgi Apparat
2/7/88	1	3	1/8	***	T.M.W.S.I.Y.
2/26/88	3	1	2/13	The Curtain With	You Enjoy My
3/21/88	3	1	1/15	***	Golgi Apparat
4/22/88	3	2	8/13	You Enjoy Myself	Ya Mar
5/15/88	2	1	4/11	You Enjoy Myself	Good Time Ba
5/21/88	1	3	6/6	The Curtain	***
5/25/88	1	1	8/9	Sneakin' Sally	Fire
6/15/88	1	1	1/9	***	Alumni Blues
6/19/88	1	1	6/8	La Grange	Big Leg Emma
6/21/88	2	1	4/9	Mustang Sally	The Curtain
7/11/88	2	1	2/11	Satin Doll	The Curtain
7/30/88	5	2	2/6	Funky Bitch	Baby Left Me
10/31/88	10	1	4/12	Possum	The Lizards
11/3/88	1	3	1/6	***	Foam
11/5/88	1	E	2/4	Icculus	Sparks
12/2/88	2	2	6/8	AC/DC Bag	Run Like Antel
1/26/89	4	2	1/10	***	Icculus
2/6/89	1	1	1/7	***	The Curtain
2/7/89	1	3	3/6	Fluffhead	Slave
4/20/89	12	1	7/12	Esther	The Sloth
5/6/89	5	2	2/8	Donna Lee	Contact
5/13/89	3	2	1/7	***	Bold As Love
5/28/89	5	1	8/9	Esther	You Enjoy My
8/17/89	3	1	2/9	Ya Mar	McGrupp
8/19/89	1	1	2/13	The Oh Kee Pa Ceremo	T.M.W.S.I.Y.
8/26/89	2	3	3/5	Avenu Malkenu	Dinner and a
9/9/89	1	1	3/11	The Oh Kee Pa Ceremo	Divided Sky
9/14/89	1	1	2/9	The Oh Kee Pa Ceremo	You Enjoy My
10/1/89	2	1	11/12	The Oh Kee Pa Ceremo	Run Like Antel
10/7/89	2	1	6/11	Weekapaug Groove	Fee
10/21/89	5	2	2/10	The Oh Kee Pa Ceremo	Wilson
10/22/89	1	1	6/14	The Oh Kee Pa Ceremo	Ya Mar
10/31/89	3	1	2/9	The Oh Kee Pa Ceremo	You Enjoy My
11/10/89	4	1	3/9	The Oh Kee Pa Ceremo	Fee
11/16/89	2	1	7/11	The Oh Kee Pa Ceremo	My Sweet One
11/30/89	2	2	9/11	Take the A-train	Contact
12/3/89	2	2	6/14	The Oh Kee Pa Ceremo	Split Open and
12/7/89	1	2	2/11	The Oh Kee Pa Ceremo	Rocky Top
12/8/89	1	1	2/11	The Oh Kee Pa Ceremo	Split Open and
12/15/89	2	1	8/10	The Oh Kee Pa Ceremo	You Enjoy My
12/30/89	3	2	4/9	Ya Mar	Foam
1/20/90	2	2	1/10	***	Bouncing
1/28/90	2	1	1/9	***	Split Open and
2/1/90	2	1	4/11	The Landlady	Caravan
2/9/90	1	1	3/12	The Oh Kee Pa Ceremo	You Enjoy My
2/10/90	1	1	3/10	The Oh Kee Pa Ceremo	You Enjoy My
2/15/90	1	1	3/10	The Oh Kee Pa Ceremo	Divided Sky
2/23/90	4	2	7/11	The Oh Kee Pa Ceremo	Mike's Song
3/3/90	5	E	1/1	***	***
3/8/90	2	1	8/10	The Oh Kee Pa Ceremo	Take the A-Trn
3/11/90	3	1	3/13	The Oh Kee Pa Ceremo	T.M.W.S.I.Y.
3/28/90	2	1	8/12	The Oh Kee Pa Ceremo	Take the A-Trn
4/5/90	2	1	6/9	The Oh Kee Pa Ceremo	You Enjoy My
4/6/90	1	1	10/11	The Oh Kee Pa Ceremo	Run Like Antel
4/8/90	2	1	6/8	The Oh Kee Pa Ceremo	Uncle Pen
4/12/90	2	2	4/11	The Oh Kee Pa Ceremo	Tweezer
4/14/90	2	2	3/11	The Oh Kee Pa Ceremo	Tweezer
4/21/90	4	1	8/10	The Oh Kee Pa Ceremo	Bike
4/22/90	1	1	4/12	The Oh Kee Pa Ceremo	Possum
4/26/90	2	2	5/11	The Oh Kee Pa Ceremo	Cavern
4/28/90	1	1	3/11	The Oh Kee Pa Ceremo	Uncle Pen
5/10/90	5	1	1/8	***	Uncle Pen
5/19/90	4	2	4/10	The Oh Kee Pa Ceremo	Fee
5/23/90	1	1	6/10	The Oh Kee Pa Ceremo	Uncle Pen
5/30/90	2	1	3/14	The Oh Kee Pa Ceremo	The Sloth
5/31/90	1	1	12/12	The Oh Kee Pa Ceremo	***
6/5/90	3	1	8/12	The Oh Kee Pa Ceremo	Take the A-Trn
6/7/90	1	1	1/9	***	Fluff's Travels
6/8/90	1	1	7/8	The Oh Kee Pa Ceremo	Run Like Antel
6/9/90	1	2	10/14	The Oh Kee Pa Ceremo	Run Like Antel
6/16/90	1	3	6/13	The Oh Kee Pa Ceremo	Fee
9/14/90	2	1	1/11	***	Bouncing
9/20/90	3	2	8/14	The Oh Kee Pa Ceremo	Possum
9/22/90	2	1	7/12	The Oh Kee Pa Ceremo	Magilla
9/28/90	1	1	4/10	The Oh Kee Pa Ceremo	Stash
10/5/90	4	1	9/13	The Oh Kee Pa Ceremo	Stash
10/6/90	1	1	8/13	The Oh Kee Pa Ceremo	Esther
10/8/90	2	2	1/6	***	Stash
10/12/90	1	1	1/9	***	You Enjoy My
10/19/90	1	1	14/15	The Oh Kee Pa Ceremo	Good Time Ba
10/30/90	1	1	5/9	The Asse Festival	Uncle Pen
10/31/90	1	2	8/12	The Oh Kee Pa Ceremo	Love You
11/2/90	1	2	1/9	***	Col. Forbin's A
11/3/90	1	1	6/11	The Oh Kee Pa Ceremo	Magilla
11/4/90	1	2	11/13	The Oh Kee Pa Ceremo	Jesus Just Left
11/8/90	1	2	1/8	***	Divided Sky
11/10/90	1	2	1/8	***	You Enjoy My
11/16/90	1	1	1/8	***	Buried Alive
11/17/90	1	1	10/11	The Oh Kee Pa Ceremo	David Bowie
11/24/90	1	1	10/11	The Oh Kee Pa Ceremo	David Bowie
11/30/90	2	E	3/3	The Oh Kee Pa Ceremo	***
12/7/90	2	2	9/11	The Oh Kee Pa Ceremo	No Good Trying
12/29/90	3	1	10/10	The Oh Kee Pa Ceremo	***
12/31/90	1	1	1/12	***	Divided Sky
2/2/91	2	1	2/9	The Oh Kee Pa Ceremo	Guelah Papyrus
2/3/91	1	2	9/9	The Oh Kee Pa Ceremo	***
2/9/91	3	E	2/4	Lawn Boy	Contact
2/19/91	4	2	14/15	The Oh Kee Pa Ceremo	Rocky Top
2/21/91	2	E	1/1	***	***
2/27/91	2	2	1/11	***	Buried Alive
3/1/91	2	E	2/2	The Oh Kee Pa Ceremo	***
3/8/91	2	1	6/11	The Oh Kee Pa Ceremo	Split Open and
3/9/91	1	2	3/13	The Oh Kee Pa Ceremo	The Squirmin
3/13/91	2	1	1/12	***	Split Open and
3/16/91	2	1	13/14	The Oh Kee Pa Ceremo	Run Like Antel
3/22/91	2	2	2/13	The Oh Kee Pa Ceremo	Run Like Antel
3/28/91	2	1	12/14	The Oh Kee Pa Ceremo	Love You
4/2/91	3	1	9/10	The Oh Kee Pa Ceremo	Chalk Dust Tor
4/4/91	2	1	2/10	The Oh Kee Pa Ceremo	You Enjoy My
4/5/91	1	E	3/3	The Oh Kee Pa Ceremo	***
4/12/91	3	1	6/9	The Oh Kee Pa Ceremo	Stash
4/18/91	3	1	7/11	Horn	Split Open and
4/20/91	2	2	12/13	The Oh Kee Pa Ceremo	Sweet Adeline
4/22/91	2	1	9/9	The Oh Kee Pa Ceremo	***
4/25/91	1	1	10/11	The Oh Kee Pa Ceremo	David Bowie
4/27/91	1	1	10/12	The Lizards	Stash
5/4/91	3	1	2/11	The Oh Kee Pa Ceremo	Cavern
5/11/91	3	2	11/12	The Oh Kee Pa Ceremo	Tweezer Repri
5/17/91	3	1	7/17	The Oh Kee Pa Ceremo	Happy Birthday
5/18/91	1	2	2/10	The Oh Kee Pa Ceremo	The Curtain
7/11/91	2	1	2/8	The Oh Kee Pa Ceremo	Divided Sky
7/12/91	1	2	12/14	The Oh Kee Pa Ceremo	Sweet Adeline
7/13/91	1	1	6/13	The Oh Kee Pa Ceremo	Alumni Blues
7/14/91	1	2	1/10	***	Caravan
7/15/91	1	1	2/14	The Oh Kee Pa Ceremo	The Landlady
7/18/91	1	1	5/11	Guelah Papyrus	Stash
7/19/91	1	2	1/8	***	Divided Sky
7/20/91	1	1	6/10	The Oh Kee Pa Ceremo	The Landlady
7/21/91	1	E	4/4	Fee	***
7/23/91	1	1	6/12	The Oh Kee Pa Ceremo	Stash
7/24/91	1	2	10/10	Frankenstein	***
7/25/91	1	1	4/10	Foam	Divided Sky
7/26/91	1	1	5/12	Foam	Cavern
7/27/91	1	1	4/16	The Oh Kee Pa Ceremo	Cavern
9/27/91	4	2	8/10	The Oh Kee Pa Ceremo	You Enjoy My
9/29/91	2	1	10/10	The Oh Kee Pa Ceremo	***
10/2/91	2	2	9/9	The Oh Kee Pa Ceremo	***
10/4/91	2	1	8/10	Sparkle	Magilla

DATE	GAP	SET	POS.	SONG BEFORE	SONG AFTER
10/6/91	1	1	1/13	***	Foam
10/10/91	1	2	9/13	The Oh Kee Pa Ceremo	Fee
10/15/91	4	2	9/12	The Oh Kee Pa Ceremo	Love You
10/17/91	1	2	3/9	The Oh Kee Pa Ceremo	David Bowie
10/19/91	2	1	2/10	The Landlady	It's Ice
10/24/91	2	1	2/12	The Oh Kee Pa Ceremo	Foam
11/2/91	6	1	1/10	***	The Curtain
11/8/91	2	E	2/2	Fee	***
11/10/91	2	1	8/10	The Oh Kee Pa Ceremo	You Enjoy My
11/15/91	4	E	2/2	Highway to Hell	***
11/22/91	5	E	2/2	Glide	***
12/4/91	4	E	2/2	Sweet Adeline	***
3/11/92	7	1	1/12	***	My Friend My
3/14/92	3	2	7/10	The Oh Kee Pa Ceremo	Harry Hood
3/19/92	2	2	7/10	The Oh Kee Pa Ceremo	My Friend My
3/21/92	2	2	3/11	The Oh Kee Pa Ceremo	Take the A-Trn
3/24/92	2	2	11/13	The Oh Kee Pa Ceremo	Harry Hood
3/26/92	2	2	3/13	The Oh Kee Pa Ceremo	Poor Heart
3/30/92	3	E	3/3	The Oh Kee Pa Ceremo	***
4/3/92	3	2	9/9	Harry Hood	***
4/6/92	3	1	1/10	***	Foam
4/8/92	2	2	2/15	The Oh Kee Pa Ceremo	David Bowie
4/12/92	1	1	1/11	***	Poor Heart
4/15/92	2	1	2/11	The Oh Kee Pa Ceremo	Foam
4/16/92	1	2	12/12	Sweet Adeline	***
4/18/92	2	2	3/16	The Oh Kee Pa Ceremo	Rift
4/21/92	2	1	1/11	***	Uncle Pen
4/22/92	1	1	10/10	All Things Recnsdrd	***
4/25/92	3	1	1/11	***	My Friend My
4/29/92	1	1	1/10	***	Foam
5/1/92	2	1	1/12	***	My Friend My
5/3/92	2	2	14/14	The Oh Kee Pa Ceremo	***
5/7/92	3	1	1/11	***	Poor Heart
5/9/92	2	2	1/8	***	Divided Sky
5/10/92	1	2	1/10	The Landlady	Sparkle
5/14/92	2	1	1/11	***	All Things Rec
5/16/92	2	E	2/2	Sweet Adeline	***
5/18/92	2	1	1/10	***	Maze
6/19/92	1	1	2/7	The Landlady	Stash
7/9/92	7	1	3/12	The Oh Kee Pa Ceremo	Sparkle
7/11/92	2	1	11/11	You Enjoy Myself	***
7/15/92	3	1	3/12	The Oh Kee Pa Ceremo	Foam
7/18/92	3	1	1/6	***	Foam
7/27/92	7	1	5/7	Horn	Llama
7/31/92	3	1	1/6	***	Chalk Dust Tor
8/2/92	2	1	5/8	The Oh Kee Pa Ceremo	David Bowie
8/17/92	4	2	1/11	***	It's Ice
11/20/92	12	1	3/12	All Things Recnsdrd	Rift
11/22/92	2	1	3/12	The Oh Kee Pa Ceremo	Fee
11/28/92	4	2	1/12	***	Paul and Silas
12/2/92	3	1	1/10	***	Foam
12/4/92	2	2	1/10	***	David Bowie
12/6/92	2	2	1/13	***	The Curtain
12/8/92	2	2	11/15	Sparkle	Lengthwise
12/10/92	1	2	10/10	The Oh Kee Pa Ceremo	***
12/13/92	3	2	1/14	***	Mound
12/29/92	1	2	12/12	The Oh Kee Pa Ceremo	***
2/7/93	7	1	1/12	***	Buried Alive
2/11/93	3	1	1/10	***	Buried Alive
2/15/93	3	1	2/12	Amazing Grace	Sparkle
2/21/93	5	1	1/10	***	Buried Alive
2/25/93	3	2	1/11	***	It's Ice
3/13/93	10	2	1/13	***	Tweezer
3/17/93	3	1	10/11	The Oh Kee Pa Ceremo	Run Like Antel
3/19/93	2	1	1/9	***	Llama
3/26/93	5	2	10/12	The Oh Kee Pa Ceremo	The Great Gig in the
4/3/93	7	2	1/10	***	Stash
4/9/93	2	2	2/10	Buried Alive	All Things Rec
4/17/93	5	2	8/11	The Oh Kee Pa Ceremo	Cracklin' Rosi
4/22/93	4	1	1/10	***	Sparkle
5/6/93	11	2	1/11	***	Tweezer
7/25/93	13	2	2/10	Also Sprach	Tweezer
8/2/93	5	2	1/13	***	All Things Rec
8/6/93	2	1	10/10	Chalk Dust Torture	***
8/13/93	6	2	8/9	The Oh Kee Pa Ceremo	Amazing Grce

DATE	GAP	SET	POS.	SONG BEFORE	SONG AFTER
8/17/93	4	2	6/10	Rift	You Enjoy My
12/28/93	7	1	6/10	The Oh Kee Pa Ceremo	Ya Mar
12/31/93	3	3	6/9	Sparkle	Cracklin' Rosi
4/4/94	1	2	11/11	The Oh Kee Pa Ceremo	***
4/8/94	3	2	9/9	David Bowie	***
4/11/94	3	2	11/11	The Oh Kee Pa Ceremo	***
4/15/94	3	2	4/10	The Oh Kee Pa Ceremo	The Landlady
4/20/94	4	1	7/7	Stash	***
4/22/94	2	2	1/8	***	Julius
4/29/94	5	2	1/11	***	Maze
5/2/94	2	1	8/10	Divided Sky	Foam
5/4/94	2	2	9/9	Magilla	***
5/7/94	2	1	9/9	If I Could	***
5/13/94	4	1	9/9	Slave	***
5/17/94	3	1	1/9	***	Maze
5/27/94	8	2	1/12	***	Peaches en Regalia
5/29/94	2	2	8/10	The Oh Kee Pa Ceremo	Run Like Antel
6/9/94	1	1	9/9	Fee	***
6/11/94	2	E	1/1	***	***
6/16/94	3	2	1/11	***	Run Like Antel
6/19/94	3	1	1/9	***	Julius
6/21/94	1	2	16/16	Harry Hood	***
6/25/94	4	2	1/9	***	Maze
6/29/94	2	2	7/8	Divided Sky	Cavern
7/1/94	2	1	10/10	Julius	***
7/3/94	2	2	10/10	Run Like an Antelope	***
7/9/94	4	2	10/10	Harry Hood	***
7/13/94	2	2	13/13	Slave	***
7/16/94	3	E	1/1	***	***
10/8/94	2	2	12/12	Harry Hood	***
10/15/94	6	2	11/11	Bouncing	***
10/22/94	5	1	1/8	***	Divided Sky
10/26/94	3	1	9/10	The Oh Kee Pa Ceremo	Runaway Jim
11/2/94	5	1	1/8	***	Foam
11/4/94	2	1	8/9	Scent of a Mule	Chalk Dust Tor
11/13/94	2	2	1/8	***	Divided Sky
11/16/94	2	E	2/2	Amazing Grace	***
11/19/94	3	2	1/7	***	Sparkle
11/23/94	3	1	7/9	The Oh Kee Pa Ceremo	Divided Sky
11/28/94	3	2	1/5	***	NICU
12/2/94	3	2	8/8	Caravan	***
12/3/94	1	2	2/10	Frankenstein	Buried Alive
12/9/94	5	2	9/9	You Enjoy Myself	***
12/28/94	2	2	1/9	***	NICU
12/31/94	3	3	7/8	Silent in the Mornin	Slave
6/7/95	2	2	9/9	Harry Hood	***
6/10/95	3	1	9/9	Lonesome Cowboy Bill	***
6/17/95	5	1	2/9	Divided Sky	Taste
6/24/95	5	2	5/9	Lifeboy	Harry Hood
6/28/95	3	2	8/10	Sparkle	Harry Hood
7/1/95	3	2	9/9	Harry Hood	***
9/29/95	5	1	8/8	Sweet Adeline	***
10/5/95	4	1	11/11	Julius	***
10/11/95	4	2	8/11	Llama	Crossroads
10/17/95	4	2	4/6	Fog that Surrounds	Keyboard Cavalry
10/21/95	3	2	8/8	Harry Hood	***
10/25/95	3	2	8/9	Weekapaug Groove	Crossroads
10/31/95	4	3	4/4	A Day in the Life	***
11/11/95	3	2	3/9	David Bowie	Uncle Pen
11/15/95	3	E	1/1	***	***
11/19/95	3	2	8/8	Harry Hood	***
11/24/95	3	1	9/9	Maze	***
11/28/95	2	2	3/10	Maze	Uncle Pen
12/1/95	3	E	1/1	***	Llama
12/14/95	9	1	1/10	***	***
12/16/95	2	1	9/9	Julius	***
12/30/95	4	1	3/13	Also Sprach	David Bowie
7/7/96	7	1	10/10	Run Like an Antelope	***
7/12/96	2	2	9/9	Slave	***
7/21/96	6	2	9/9	Prince Caspian	***
8/6/96	8	1	3/9	Rift	Simple
8/12/96	3	1	10/10	The Oh Kee Pa Ceremo	***
8/17/96	3	1	10/10	Maze	***
10/18/96	3	2	1/6	***	Maze

DATE	GAP	SET	POS.	SONG BEFORE	SONG AFTER
10/23/96	4	2	6/8	Llama	Slave
10/27/96	3	1	11/11	Taste	***
10/31/96	2	3	8/8	Jesus Just Left	***
11/7/96	4	2	1/4	***	Bathtub Gin
11/13/96	4	2	2/7	Also Sprach	Jam
11/16/96	3	2	7/8	Harry Hood	Amazing Grce
11/24/96	5	2	7/7	Loving Cup	***
11/29/96	2	1	9/9	Maze	***
12/6/96	5	E	7/7	Harpua	***
12/31/96	4	3	4/7	Down with Disease	Run Like Antel
2/17/97	4	2	6/7	Down with Disease	Prince Caspian
2/23/97	5	2	2/9	Daniel	Maze
3/18/97	6	1	9/10	Cars Trucks Buses	Character Zer
11/29/97	49	2	5/5	Prince Caspian	***
8/6/98	43	1	2/12	The Oh Kee Pa Ceremo	Roses Are Free
11/24/98	29	E	1/2	***	Tweezer Repri
7/25/99	27	2	4/6	Run Like an Antelope	Purple Rain
10/8/99	27	1	3/6	AC/DC Bag	Meat
12/7/99	7	2	8/8	Free	***
12/15/99	6	2	7/7	Halley's Comet	***
12/30/99	4	1	3/12	Light Up Or Leave Me	Corrine Corrina
7/8/00	24	E	1/2	***	Tweezer Repri
9/14/00	10	1	6/6	The Oh Kee Pa Ceremo	***
Has not been played in the last 16 shows.					

Sweet Adeline

DATE	GAP	SET	POS.	SONG BEFORE	SONG AFTER
3/28/90	169	2	2/16	Carolina	Whipping Post
4/21/90	13	1	1/10	***	Reba
4/25/90	2	2	2/12	Foam	Reba
4/26/90	1	2	7/11	Cavern	Ballad - Curtis Loew
4/28/90	1	1	1/11	***	The Oh Kee Pa
5/4/90	2	2	2/10	Whipping Post	T.M.W.S.I.Y.
5/13/90	5	2	10/12	Funky Bitch	Possum
5/19/90	2	1	4/8	Alumni Blues	La Grange
5/23/90	1	1	10/10	Possum	***
5/30/90	2	1	10/14	Fluffhead	Mike's Song
6/5/90	4	2	1/10	***	Divided Sky
11/17/90	30	E	2/2	Memories	***
4/19/91	48	1	12/12	Weekapaug Groove	***
4/20/91	1	2	13/13	Suzy Greenberg	***
4/21/91	1	1	14/14	Weekapaug Groove	***
4/25/91	2	1	1/11	***	The Landlady
4/27/91	1	1	1/12	***	The Asse Festival
5/2/91	1	1	11/11	David Bowie	***
5/3/91	1	1	12/12	The Lizards	***
5/9/91	2	1	10/10	Runaway Jim	***
5/16/91	4	E	1/1	***	***
7/12/91	5	2	13/14	Suzy Greenberg	Frankenstein
7/23/91	8	2	7/10	Tweezer	Dinner and a
7/25/91	2	1	8/10	AC/DC Bag	Cavern
9/26/91	5	E	3/3	Poor Heart	***
10/4/91	7	E	1/5	***	Golgi Apparat
10/6/91	1	E	1/3	***	Possum
10/11/91	2	E	1/3	***	BBFCFM
10/18/91	5	1	8/9	The Lizards	Run Like Antel
10/24/91	3	E	2/3	Memories	Rocky Top
11/1/91	5	1	11/11	Divided Sky	***
11/9/91	4	1	11/11	Brother	***
11/10/91	1	2	3/4	Terrapin	Llama
11/13/91	2	E	3/3	My Sweet One	***
11/21/91	6	E	2/3	Memories	Golgi Apparat
11/24/91	3	E	1/2	***	Rocky Top
12/4/91	2	E	1/2	***	Suzy Greenber
12/7/91	3	E	1/2	***	Golgi Apparat
3/7/92	3	E	1/2	***	Golgi Apparat
3/12/92	2	E	1/3	***	Weigh
3/17/92	3	E	2/2	Memories	***
3/27/92	8	E	2/2	Memories	***
3/28/92	1	2	4/4	I Didn't Know	***
3/31/92	2	E	1/1	***	***

DATE	GAP	SET	POS.	SONG BEFORE	SONG AFTER
4/5/92	4	1	11/11	Possum	***
4/12/92	4	E	1/2	***	Rocky Top
4/15/92	2	E	2/3	Memories	Rocky Top
4/16/92	1	2	11/12	Memories	Suzy Greenber
4/21/92	4	E	2/3	Memories	Cavern
4/25/92	4	E	2/3	Memories	Cavern
5/3/92	5	E	2/3	Memories	Tweezer Repri
5/7/92	3	E	1/3	***	Sleeping Mon-key
5/15/92	6	1	10/11	You Enjoy Myself	Rocky Top
5/16/92	1	E	1/2	***	Suzy Greenber
6/23/92	5	1	4/8	Maze	Uncle Pen
6/24/92	1	1	3/9	Llama	Uncle Pen
6/30/92	2	1	5/6	Possum	You Enjoy My
7/1/92	1	1	6/7	Split Open and Melt	Rocky Top
7/12/92	4	1	1/11	***	Chalk Dust Tor
7/19/92	6	1	5/5	David Bowie	***
7/27/92	6	1	7/7	Llama	***
8/14/92	7	1	5/5	Llama	***
8/20/92	4	1	6/6	David Bowie	***
8/25/92	3	1	7/7	Llama	***
8/28/92	2	1	4/7	Stash	The Squirmin
8/30/92	2	1	7/7	Run Like an Antelope	***
10/30/92	1	1	10/11	Stash	You Enjoy My
11/20/92	2	E	1/2	***	Good Time Ba
11/22/92	2	1	11/12	Bathtub Gin	Run Like Antel
11/25/92	2	1	10/11	Cavern	Run Like Antel
12/1/92	4	1	9/12	Maze	Mike's Song
12/3/92	2	1	11/12	Reba	Run Like Antel
12/5/92	2	1	10/12	Divided Sky	Uncle Pen
12/7/92	2	2	12/12	The Squirming Coil	***
12/8/92	1	1	10/11	Mound	Stash
12/10/92	1	1	10/11	Reba	Cavern
12/13/92	3	E	1/2	***	Rocky Top
12/28/92	1	1	9/10	Golgi Apparatus	Run Like Antel
12/30/92	2	E	2/2	Ride Captain Ride	***
2/6/93	5	2	4/14	Stash	All Things Rec
2/10/93	3	E	1/3	***	Amazing Grce
2/18/93	6	2	11/12	Memories	Rocky Top
2/21/93	3	E	1/4	***	Good Time Ba
2/23/93	2	E	1/2	***	Poor Heart
2/26/93	2	E	2/2	Bold As Love	***
3/3/93	3	2	13/13	The Squirming Coil	***
3/6/93	2	E	1/3	***	Poor Heart
3/12/93	3	E	1/3	***	Carolina
3/14/93	2	E	2/3	Memories	Golgi Apparat
3/16/93	1	1	1/11	***	Buried Alive
3/17/93	1	E	1/2	***	Rocky Top
3/21/93	3	E	2/3	Sleeping Monkey	Tweezer Repri
3/25/93	3	E	3/3	Big Ball Jam	***
3/31/93	5	E	2/2	AC/DC Bag	***
4/9/93	5	E	1/2	***	Golgi Apparat
4/17/93	5	E	1/2	***	BBFCFM
4/21/93	3	E	1/2	***	Cavern
5/6/93	12	E	1/3	***	Contact
8/11/93	25	E	1/2	***	Bold As Love
8/15/93	4	2	8/11	Glide	Ginseng Sulli-van
8/24/93	5	E	3/3	Poor Heart	***
12/29/93	5	2	10/11	If I Only Had a Brai	Chalk Dust Tor
4/6/94	5	2	2/2	Nellie Kane	***
4/13/94	5	E	1/2	***	Good Time Ba
4/24/94	10	E	1/1	***	***
4/30/94	4	1	9/9	Ginseng Sullivan	***
5/3/94	2	1	9/9	Sample in a Jar	***
5/8/94	4	E	1/2	***	Golgi Apparat
5/16/94	5	1	10/10	Stash	***
5/19/94	2	E	3/4	Nellie Kane	Fire
5/25/94	5	1	10/11	My Sweet One	Chalk Dust Tor
6/14/94	9	1	3/14	Guelah Papyrus	Digital Delay Loop J
6/21/94	5	2	12/16	Dog Faced Boy	Julius
6/24/94	3	1	10/11	Reba	Sample in a Ja
7/5/94	8	1	10/10	Down with Disease	***
10/12/94	13	1	9/9	Julius	***
10/14/94	2	1	8/12	Bathtub Gin	Rift

DATE	GAP	SET	POS.	SONG BEFORE	SONG AFTER
10/16/94	2	2	8/9	Dog Faced Boy	Sample in a Ja
10/21/94	3	E	1/3	***	Foreplay/Long Time
10/27/94	5	2	7/7	Down with Disease	***
11/14/94	9	2	9/10	Nellie Kane	You Enjoy My
11/22/94	6	1	9/9	Down with Disease	***
11/26/94	3	2	3/6	David Bowie	The Lizards
11/28/94	1	1	9/9	Divided Sky	***
12/1/94	2	1	8/8	Split Open and Melt	***
12/4/94	3	1	8/9	Mound	Possum
12/8/94	3	2	8/9	Nellie Kane	David Bowie
5/16/95	7	1	11/12	You Enjoy Myself	Sample in a Ja
6/9/95	3	2	7/8	Acoustic Army	Slave
6/13/95	2	E	1/2	***	Julius
6/17/95	4	2	9/11	Acoustic Army	Harry Hood
6/22/95	3	1	10/10	Cavern	***
6/24/95	2	2	8/9	Acoustic Army	Golgi Apparat
6/28/95	3	E	1/2	***	While My Gui-tar Gent
9/29/95	8	1	7/8	You Enjoy Myself	Suzy Greenber
10/3/95	3	2	7/9	Faht	Split Open and
10/7/95	2	2	9/9	Harry Hood	***
10/13/95	3	2	9/10	While My Guitar Gent	The Squirmin
10/22/95	7	E	1/2	***	The Squirmin
10/29/95	5	1	12/12	Slave	***
11/10/95	3	2	9/9	AC/DC Bag	***
11/15/95	4	1	8/9	Split Open and Melt	The Squirmin
11/22/95	5	1	10/10	Sample in a Jar	***
12/5/95	9	E	2/2	Theme From the Botto	***
12/9/95	2	2	8/8	Crossroads	***
12/15/95	4	2	8/8	David Bowie	***
12/29/95	4	1	9/9	Llama	***
7/5/96	6	E	1/1	***	***
7/7/96	2	1	6/10	Tweezer	Uncle Pen
7/19/96	9	1	3/6	Foam	Waste
8/4/96	7	2	6/7	David Bowie	Slave
8/13/96	6	2	10/11	Strange Design	David Bowie
11/2/96	16	2	6/6	A Day in the Life	***
11/13/96	7	1	9/9	Character Zero	***
12/2/96	13	2	8/8	Harry Hood	***
12/6/96	2	2	8/9	Weekapaug Groove	Good Time Ba
2/14/97	6	1	4/9	You Enjoy Myself	Axilla
2/20/97	4	2	12/12	Runaway Jim	***
2/25/97	4	2	10/10	La Grange	***
3/1/97	3	E	2/2	Taste	***
7/9/97	19	1	7/8	Taste	Harry Hood
8/13/97	18	1	11/11	Wilson	***
7/1/98	34	2	5/5	My Soul	***
8/1/99	84	E	1/2	***	Tweezer Repri

Has not been played in the last 89 shows.

Sweet Baby's Arms

DATE	GAP	SET	POS.	SONG BEFORE	SONG AFTER
11/18/94	690	E	1/2	***	Runaway Jim

Has not been played in the last 429 shows.

Sweet Emotion Jam

DATE	GAP	SET	POS.	SONG BEFORE	SONG AFTER
3/16/93	510	2	4/15	Tweezer	Tweezer
5/7/94	105	2	7/12	Digital Delay Loop J	Walk Away
11/27/96	237	2	5/8	Tweezer	Down with Dis
7/9/99	161	2	6/8	Mike's Song	Twist

Has not been played in the last 106 shows.

Sweet Jane

DATE	GAP	SET	POS.	SONG BEFORE	SONG AFTER
8/8/98	971	1	8/8	Possum	***
10/31/98	12	2	2/10	Who Loves the Sun	Rock and Roll

Has not been played in the last 136 shows.

Sweet Virginia

DATE	GAP	SET	POS.	SONG BEFORE	SONG AFTER
9/26/99	1044	1	1/10	***	First Tube

Has not been played in the last 75 shows.

Swept Away

DATE	GAP	SET	POS.	SONG BEFORE	SONG AFTER
10/16/96	824	2	5/10	Simple	Steep
10/19/96	3	2	7/10	Fluffhead	Steep
10/22/96	2	2	8/10	Mike's Song	Steep

DATE	GAP	SET	POS.	SONG BEFORE	SONG AFTER
10/31/96	6	3	5/8	Simple	Steep
11/6/96	3	2	4/9	Mike's Song	Steep
11/9/96	3	2	5/7	Taste	Steep
11/11/96	1	2	7/11	Tweezer	Steep
11/14/96	2	2	4/10	Taste	Steep
11/18/96	3	2	3/9	Simple	Steep
11/22/96	2	2	5/10	Billy Breathes	Steep
11/29/96	4	2	6/10	Taste	Steep
12/1/96	2	2	6/10	Reba	Steep
12/31/96	7	2	5/9	Simple	Steep
2/16/97	3	2	7/11	When Circus Comes	Steep
2/20/97	3	2	8/12	Free	Steep
2/28/97	6	1	7/10	Stash	Steep
3/2/97	2	2	3/9	Maze	Steep
6/21/97	7	1	7/15	Theme From the Botto	Steep
7/29/97	19	1	5/9	Ghost	Steep
8/9/97	7	2	6/10	Simple	Steep
12/7/97	23	1	6/12	It's Ice	Steep
12/12/97	3	2	3/7	Piper	Steep
6/30/98	10	2	10/12	Mike's Song	Steep
6/30/99	62	2	5/10	Simple	Steep
7/1/00	81	2	5/10	Mike's Song	Steep

Has not been played in the last 31 shows.

Swing Low Sweet Chariot

DATE	GAP	SET	POS.	SONG BEFORE	SONG AFTER
10/15/86	14	2	3/14	Golgi Apparatus	Camel Walk
10/31/86	1	2	3/11	AC/DC Bag	Peaches en Regalia
2/21/87	3	2	10/15	Peaches en Regalia	Boogie On Reggae
3/23/87	2	2	9/9	Golgi Apparatus	***
4/29/87	2	1	4/9	Golgi Apparatus	Fire
8/21/87	5	3	7/7	Sanity	***
8/29/87	1	1	3/13	Slave	The Curtain With
10/20/89	94	2	9/10	Harry Hood	In a Hole
11/16/94	566	1	11/11	Earl's Breakdown	***

Has not been played in the last 431 shows.

TV Show

DATE	GAP	SET	POS.	SONG BEFORE	SONG AFTER
11/8/91	339	2	11/13	Self	Family Picture

Has not been played in the last 780 shows.

Take Me to the River

DATE	GAP	SET	POS.	SONG BEFORE	SONG AFTER
11/21/95	769	2	3/11	David Bowie	David Bowie
7/10/97	126	2	6/7	Ghost	Jam

Has not been played in the last 224 shows.

Take the A-Train

DATE	GAP	SET	POS.	SONG BEFORE	SONG AFTER
4/29/87	22	2	4/7	Dave's Energy Guide	Halley's Comet
9/27/87	9	1	5/9	Peaches en Regalia	Possum
10/14/87	1	1	2/12	Peaches en Regalia	You Enjoy My
10/31/87	1	2	5/17	Peaches en Regalia	Timber (Jerry)
11/18/87	1	1	8/12	Peaches en Regalia	Golgi Apparat
11/19/87	1	3	10/14	Letter to Jimmy Page	Camel Walk
1/27/88	1	1	8/9	Alumni Blues	Good Time Ba
2/8/88	2	1	3/7	Funky Bitch	Golgi Apparat
3/11/88	3	1	4/12	Sneakin' Sally	You Enjoy My
3/31/88	3	1	11/14	The Famous Mockingbi	Fire
5/14/88	3	1	11/11	Alumni Blues	***
5/15/88	1	2	6/11	Peaches en Regalia	Jesus Just Left
5/21/88	1	3	4/6	Cities	The Curtain
6/15/88	2	2	6/9	Dinner and a Movie	Good Time Ba
6/20/88	2	2	6/9	Satin Doll	Possum
7/12/88	4	2	2/9	Blue Bossa	Timber (Jerry)
8/6/88	6	1	6/9	Cities	Funky Bitch
8/27/88	1	1	7/9	Mike's Song	Golgi Apparat
9/12/88	2	1	2/4	Shaggy Dog	Fee
9/22/88	2	1	2/5	McGrupp	Fluffhead
9/24/88	1	1	8/10	La Grange	Divided Sky
10/29/88	1	2	9/10	Mike's Song	Fire
11/3/88	2	2	8/9	Bold As Love	Run Like Antel
11/5/88	1	1	6/11	Possum	Golgi Apparat

DATE	GAP	SET	POS.	SONG BEFORE	SONG AFTER
12/2/88	2	1	4/7	Bold As Love	Divided Sky
1/26/89	4	1	6/10	The Lizards	Sanity
2/6/89	1	2	3/7	Sanity	Golgi Apparat
2/11/89	2	1	2/2	The Sloth	***
2/17/89	1	1	7/10	Golgi Apparatus	Alumni Blues
3/3/89	3	2	11/12	Split Open and Melt	David Bowie
3/4/89	1	1	1/8	***	I Didn't Know
3/24/89	3	1	9/10	If I Only Had a Brai	David Bowie
5/5/89	7	2	2/4	I Didn't Know	Good Time Ba
5/13/89	4	1	10/12	Walk Away	Split Open and
5/20/89	1	2	7/9	Contact	David Bowie
5/27/89	3	1	8/11	You Enjoy Myself	Fluffhead
5/28/89	1	2	9/16	Peaches en Regalia	Possum
8/19/89	4	2	2/4	Split Open and Melt	Divided Sky
11/9/89	20	1	8/9	You Enjoy Myself	Good Time Ba
11/10/89	1	E	3/4	Highway to Hell	Run Like Antel
11/18/89	3	1	2/11	You Enjoy Myself	AC/DC Bag
11/30/89	1	2	8/11	Split Open and Melt	Suzy Greenber
12/7/89	3	1	3/11	You Enjoy Myself	AC/DC Bag
12/9/89	2	2	1/8	***	Fluffhead
12/15/89	1	1	1/10	***	Golgi Apparat
2/9/90	10	2	5/9	Wilson	Alumni Blues
3/8/90	13	1	9/10	Suzy Greenberg	Run Like Antel
3/11/90	3	2	6/13	Dinner and a Movie	The Sloth
3/28/90	2	1	9/12	Suzy Greenberg	Runaway Jim
4/4/90	1	1	4/8	Walk Away	Possum
4/12/90	6	1	7/11	You Enjoy Myself	Cavern
4/18/90	3	1	9/10	My Sweet One	Possum
4/20/90	2	1	1/10	***	Divided Sky
5/23/90	15	2	7/11	McGrupp	Run Like Antel
6/5/90	6	1	9/12	Suzy Greenberg	David Bowie
9/13/90	5	2	10/15	Buried Alive	Sparks
10/7/90	13	1	13/14	Weekapaug Groove	La Grange
2/16/91	30	1	5/12	Cavern	The Landlady
3/13/91	11	E	1/2	***	BBFCFM
3/23/91	5	E	1/2	***	BBFCFM
4/3/91	5	2	2/9	Chalk Dust Torture	My Sweet One
4/5/91	2	1	5/11	Cavern	Reba
4/19/91	7	2	9/10	The Squirming Coil	Run Like Antel
5/3/91	7	E	1/2	***	BBFCFM
5/10/91	3	E	1/2	***	Highway to Hell
5/17/91	4	1	17/17	Weekapaug Groove	***
5/18/91	1	2	5/10	Stash	My Sweet One
7/18/91	1	1	7/11	Stash	Cavern
10/12/91	22	2	5/10	Chalk Dust Torture	Dinner and a
10/23/91	6	E	1/1	***	***
10/27/91	2	2	12/13	Destiny Unbound	Run Like Antel
11/1/91	4	2	9/13	Weekapaug Groove	Tela
11/7/91	2	2	8/11	David Bowie	HYHU Jam
11/14/91	6	2	8/11	Tweezer	If I Only Had a Brai
11/24/91	8	2	6/8	Chalk Dust Torture	You Enjoy My
3/14/92	12	1	10/13	Chalk Dust Torture	Mike's Song
3/21/92	4	2	4/11	Suzy Greenberg	My Friend My
4/5/92	12	2	11/12	Love You	Runaway Jim
4/13/92	5	1	9/10	Foam	David Bowie
4/22/92	7	E	1/2	***	Rocky Top
4/29/92	4	1	9/10	Bouncing	David Bowie
5/6/92	6	2	10/11	Terrapin	Golgi Apparat
7/14/92	22	2	9/10	You Enjoy Myself	Tweezer Repri
8/17/92	20	2	10/11	Terrapin	Cavern
11/21/92	13	2	10/13	Love You	Llama
11/27/92	4	2	12/13	Faht	Cavern
12/3/92	5	2	12/13	Cracklin' Rosie	Cavern
12/30/92	12	2	11/12	Love You	Llama
2/12/93	10	1	10/11	I Didn't Know	Run Like Antel
5/5/93	58	E	3/4	Cavern	Cavern
8/16/93	31	2	9/10	Big Ball Jam	Good Time Ba
4/13/94	19	2	7/10	Fee	David Bowie

Has not been played in the last 523 shows.

Talk

DATE	GAP	SET	POS.	SONG BEFORE	SONG AFTER
8/5/96	815	2	7/13	Waste	Train Song
8/16/96	7	2	6/13	Waste	Train Song
10/17/96	3	1	6/10	Theme From the Botto	Punch You in
10/22/96	4	1	5/9	It's Ice	Split Open and
10/27/96	4	1	9/11	Split Open and Melt	Taste
11/9/96	8	1	7/10	Tube	Split Open and
11/14/96	3	1	8/9	Bathtub Gin	Julius
12/30/96	17	1	6/9	Reba	Funky Bitch
2/22/97	9	1	7/10	When Circus Comes	Split Open and
6/14/97	9	1	4/10	Dirt	My Soul
6/24/97	6	1	9/12	Runaway Jim	Free
8/6/98	84	2	3/7	Wolfman's Brother	NICU

Has not been played in the last 150 shows.

Taste

DATE	GAP	SET	POS.	SONG BEFORE	SONG AFTER
6/7/95	713	1	3/10	Weigh	Strange Design
6/9/95	2	1	7/9	Theme From the Botto	Sparkle
6/13/95	2	1	6/10	Strange Design	Reba
6/15/95	2	1	5/10	The Old Home Place	The Wedge
6/17/95	2	1	3/9	Suzy Greenber	Fee
6/20/95	2	1	7/9	If I Could	I Didn't Know
6/23/95	2	1	7/8	Free	You Enjoy My
6/25/95	2	1	3/9	AC/DC Bag	Theme From the Botto
6/29/95	3	1	2/10	Runaway Jim	The Horse
6/30/95	1	1	4/9	Horn	The Wedge
7/3/96	64	1	4/5	Sparkle	Llama
7/9/96	4	1	3/7	Poor Heart	Cars Trucks Buses
7/12/96	3	1	7/10	Funky Bitch	Theme From the Botto
7/21/96	6	1	10/14	Silent in the Mornin	Train Song
8/2/96	5	2	3/9	Simple	Free
8/7/96	4	1	6/10	Gumbo	Lawn Boy
8/12/96	2	1	8/10	Dog Faced Boy	The Oh Kee Pa
8/17/96	4	1	7/10	Sample in a Jar	Fee
10/16/96	1	2	2/10	Wolfman's Brother	Train Song
10/18/96	2	1	9/10	Billy Breathes	Sample in a Ja
10/22/96	3	2	3/10	Down with Disease	The Mango Song
10/25/96	2	1	2/10	Ha Ha Ha	Makisupa Policeman
10/27/96	2	1	10/11	Talk	Suzy Greenber
10/29/96	1	1	4/10	Cars Trucks Buses	Bouncing
11/2/96	2	1	4/9	Fee	Cavern
11/6/96	2	1	4/9	Fast Enough for You	Train Song
11/9/96	3	2	4/7	You Enjoy Myself	Swept Away
11/13/96	2	1	5/9	Ya Mar	Train Song
11/14/96	2	3	2/10	Sample in a Jar	Swept Away
11/15/96	1	1	10/11	Chalk Dust Torture	Cavern
11/18/96	2	1	4/10	Poor Heart	Billy Breathes
11/19/96	1	1	8/9	Fee	Loving Cup
11/22/96	1	1	4/10	Wolfman's Brother	Ginseng Sullivan
11/24/96	2	1	8/11	Strange Design	I Didn't Know
11/29/96	2	2	5/10	Sparkle	Swept Away
11/30/96	1	2	8/11	Timber (Jerry)	Funky Bitch
12/2/96	2	2	4/8	Wolfman's Brother	Free
12/29/96	4	1	4/10	Cavern	Guelah Papyrus
2/13/97	3	1	6/12	Walfredo	Waste
2/17/97	3	2	4/7	Carini	Down with Dis
2/20/97	2	1	6/10	Love Me	Gumbo
2/25/97	4	1	8/9	Waste	Loving Cup
2/28/97	2	2	1/9	***	Drowned
3/1/97	1	E	1/2	***	Sweet Adeline
3/18/97	2	2	1/10	***	Drowned
6/13/97	1	1	8/8	Wading In Velvet Sea	***
6/16/97	2	1	3/10	Dogs Stole Things	Water in the Sky
6/20/97	2	1	1/8	***	Jam
6/21/97	1	1	4/15	Poor Heart	Dogs Stole Things
6/22/97	1	1	1/9	***	Water in the Sky
6/25/97	2	1	3/11	Dogs Stole Things	Billy Breathes
6/27/97	1	1	6/8	Poor Heart	Bouncing
6/29/97	1	1	2/7	You Enjoy Myself	Bouncing
7/3/97	3	1	5/8	Beauty of My Dreams	Train Song
7/9/97	3	1	6/8	Dirt	Sweet Adeline
7/22/97	4	1	8/8	Bye Bye Foot	***
7/25/97	2	2	2/6	Chalk Dust Torture	Ya Mar
7/29/97	2	2	5/8	Twist	Sample in a Ja
8/3/97	4	2	5/7	Lifeboy	Hello My Baby
8/9/97	3	1	4/8	Ghost	Dogs Stole Things
8/14/97	4	2	8/8	Camel Walk	***
8/17/97	2	1	9/10	Tweezer	Carolina
11/16/97	3	1	10/11	Poor Heart	Hello My Baby
11/19/97	2	2	4/4	Makisupa Policeman	***
11/26/97	4	1	10/10	Silent In The Mornin	***
12/2/97	4	1	8/9	Dirt	Star Spangled Banner
12/12/97	7	1	4/8	Camel Walk	Bouncing
12/30/97	4	1	2/7	Sneakin' Sally	Water in the Sky
4/4/98	4	1	2/8	Tweezer	Bouncing
7/5/98	6	1	2/9	Birds of a Feather	Cavern
7/10/98	4	E	2/2	Brian and Robert	***
7/24/98	7	1	6/8	My Soul	Golgi Apparat
11/8/98	28	1	1/10	***	Carini
11/19/98	7	2	3/8	Rock and Roll	Frankie Says
12/28/98	8	1	4/10	Farmhouse	Sleep
7/3/99	6	1	5/11	Cavern	When Circus Comes
7/17/99	10	1	9/10	Have Mercy	Character Zer
7/21/99	3	1	9/10	When Circus Comes	Bittersweet Motel
7/30a/99	5	1	4/7	Wolfman's Brother	Punch You in
9/14/99	8	1	10/11	Nellie Kane	Rocky Top
9/22/99	6	2	3/8	Ghost	Brian and Robert
9/29/99	5	1	4/9	Driver	Dirt
12/5/99	12	1	4/10	Back on the Train	Bug
12/30/99	11	2	4/10	Tweezer	Meat
5/23/00	4	1	11/12	Gotta Jibboo	Sleeping Monkey
6/9/00	1	1	2/9	Axilla	Billy Breathes
6/28/00	11	1	3/6	The Sloth	Bathtub Gin
7/6/00	6	1	3/12	Dogs Stole Things	Dog Faced Boy
7/14/00	6	2	10/11	Farmhouse	Golgi Apparat
9/8/00	2	1	11/12	Axilla	Golgi Apparat
9/18/00	7	E	2/2	Axilla	***
9/27/00	6	1	9/10	Horn	Cavern

Has not been played in the last 7 shows.

Taste That Surrounds

DATE	GAP	SET	POS.	SONG BEFORE	SONG AFTER
10/24/95	754	1	3/13	Paul and Silas	Fee
10/27/95	2	1	3/9	Fluffhead	Horn
11/10/95	5	1	3/9	Runaway Jim	The Old Home
11/12/95	2	1	7/10	I Didn't Know	If I Could
11/22/95	7	1	7/10	Cavern	The Lizards
11/25/95	2	1	5/9	Billy Breathes	Bouncing
11/29/95	2	2	6/11	You Enjoy Myself	Heart and Soul
12/2/95	3	1	8/10	Free	Bouncing
12/5/95	2	1	3/8	Chalk Dust Torture	The Lizards
12/7/95	1	2	3/10	Strange Design	Reba
12/11/95	3	2	4/8	The Mango Song	Scent of a Mul
12/14/95	2	1	4/10	Tela	My Sweet One
12/16/95	2	1	3/9	AC/DC Bag	Ya Mar
12/29/95	3	1	4/9	Down with Disease	NICU

Has not been played in the last 329 shows.

Tea Tray Song

DATE	GAP	SET	POS.	SONG BEFORE	SONG AFTER
8/26/93	583	2	7/8	The Lizards	Chalk Dust Tor

Has not been played in the last 536 shows.

Tela

DATE	GAP	SET	POS.	SONG BEFORE	SONG AFTER
3/12/88	42	2	4/11	The Lizards	Wilson
5/21/88	7	2	5/9	Timber (Jerry)	Happy Birthday

DATE	GAP	SET	POS.	SONG BEFORE	SONG AFTER
6/20/88	4	2	2/9	Sneakin' Sally	Fee
8/27/88	11	1	9/9	Golgi Apparatus	***
10/22/89	60	1	11/14	Split Open and Melt	Divided Sky
11/16/89	9	2	3/4	AC/DC Bag	David Bowie
12/8/89	6	2	2/7	Harry Hood	Timber (Jerry)
1/20/90	7	2	4/10	Reba	La Grange
1/28/90	2	1	3/9	Split Open and Melt	Fluffhead
2/23/90	9	2	5/11	Jesus Just Left	The Oh Kee Pa
3/7/90	6	2	6/9	Split Open and Melt	Mike's Song
4/21/90	19	2	7/9	Highway to Hell	Tweezer
9/22/90	31	1	5/12	Divided Sky	The Oh Kee Pa
10/5/90	5	1	7/13	The Landlady	The Oh Kee Pa
12/8/90	20	2	6/9	Run Like an Antelope	Golgi Apparat
4/12/91	38	2	6/10	Cavern	Buried Alive
4/16/91	2	1	8/9	AC/DC Bag	David Bowie
4/21/91	4	1	10/14	AC/DC Bag	Mike's Song
4/25/91	2	2	6/10	Weekapaug Groove	Dinner and a
5/2/91	2	2	6/10	Split Open and Melt	My Sweet One
5/3/91	1	2	6/9	Runaway Jim	You Enjoy My
5/11/91	4	2	9/12	Weekapaug Groove	The Oh Kee Pa
7/24/91	16	1	9/10	Cavern	You Enjoy My
9/25/91	5	1	5/11	Llama	My Sweet One
9/27/91	2	2	2/10	Possum	Sparkle
10/13/91	11	1	7/13	The Famous Mockingbi	AC/DC Bag
10/27/91	7	2	9/13	Weekapaug Groove	The Landlady
11/1/91	4	2	10/13	Take the A-Train	Cavern
11/9/91	4	2	6/10	Tweezer	The Landlady
11/20/91	8	2	5/8	Run Like an Antelope	The Landlady
12/6/91	8	2	7/12	Divided Sky	Llama
4/21/92	35	2	5/13	Tweezer	Mike's Song
4/25/92	4	1	6/11	Brother	Chalk Dust Tor
5/2/92	4	2	5/10	David Bowie	Foam
5/6/92	3	1	6/11	Maze	Brother
5/9/92	3	2	3/8	Divided Sky	Tweezer
11/22/92	53	2	7/10	Tweezer	You Enjoy My
12/2/92	7	2	5/11	Tweezer	Llama
12/10/92	7	2	3/10	Tweezer	My Sweet One
12/29/92	5	1	10/12	Stash	The Oh Kee Pa
2/10/93	9	1	7/10	Divided Sky	I Didn't Know
3/18/93	26	2	4/10	Split Open and Melt	You Enjoy My
3/22/93	3	2	4/13	The Lizards	Wilson
5/6/93	32	2	3/11	Tweezer	Uncle Pen
8/9/93	24	2	3/8	Tweezer	My Friend My
4/9/94	22	2	9/11	Weekapaug Groove	Slave
4/25/94	14	1	8/10	Dog Faced Boy	Poor Heart
5/21/94	18	1	8/9	The Squirming Coil	Llama
6/11/94	10	1	7/8	It's Ice	Stash
6/25/94	11	1	9/10	Scent of a Mule	Chalk Dust Tor
6/26/94	1	1	4/11	The Lizards	Wilson
7/1/94	3	1	8/10	It's Ice	Julius
7/8/94	5	1	4/11	The Lizards	Wilson
10/18/94	16	1	6/10	Stash	It's Ice
10/23/94	4	1	9/10	Stash	Maze
11/4/94	9	2	5/9	Mike's Song	Weekapaug Gr
11/18/94	6	1	7/11	It's Ice	Split Open and
6/19/95	32	1	4/10	AC/DC Bag	Punch You in
6/26/95	6	1	9/10	Dog Faced Boy	Possum
10/2/95	11	1	9/10	Theme From the Botto	David Bowie
10/14/95	8	1	10/11	It's Ice	Runaway Jim
11/9/95	13	1	7/8	Reba	Sample in a Ja
11/24/95	11	1	6/9	Stash	I'm Blue, Lonesome
12/14/95	14	1	7/10	Split Open and Melt	Taste That Surrounds
8/13/96	35	1	3/10	Tube	Maze
11/7/96	19	1	9/10	Free	Character Zer
8/14/97	74	1	7/10	Cars Trucks Buses	Train Song
7/28/98	50	1	4/10	The Moma Dance	Sneakin' Sally
8/8/98	8	2	3/6	Also Sprach	Piper
11/11/98	19	1	5/8	Sleep	Birds of a Feather
11/24/98	8	1	8/9	Sample in a Jar	Chalk Dust Tor

Has not been played in the last 121 shows.

Tell Me Something Good

DATE	GAP	SET	POS.	SONG BEFORE	SONG AFTER
3/6/87	19	2	4/7	Harry Hood	Possum

Has not been played in the last 1100 shows.

Tennessee Waltz

DATE	GAP	SET	POS.	SONG BEFORE	SONG AFTER
5/6/93	547	1	12/13	Why You've Been Gone	I Been to Georgia on Earl's Break-
11/16/94	141	1	9/11	Pig in a Pen	down

Has not been played in the last 431 shows.

Terrapin

DATE	GAP	SET	POS.	SONG BEFORE	SONG AFTER
9/21/87	3	3	13/15	Fire	La Grange
7/23/88	28	2	4/10	The Curtain	Run Like Antel
7/30/88	3	3	12/13	Dear Mrs. Reagan	Run Like Antel
4/30/89	34	1	9/9	Run Like an Antelope	***
1/27/90	52	2	6/7	Run Like an Antelope	Divided Sky
4/19/90	33	2	5/8	You Enjoy Myself	Highway to Hell
5/6/90	9	2	5/7	David Bowie	Jagermeister
6/1/90	11	1	8/12	Fee	Possum
6/9/90	5	2	12/14	Run Like an Antelope	Harpua
10/12/90	17	2	4/10	The Landlady	Divided Sky
10/30/90	2	2	10/12	Fluffhead	Buried Alive
2/15/91	25	2	9/10	Harry Hood	Chalk Dust Tor
3/13/91	12	2	10/12	Tweezer	The Oh Kee Pa
3/22/91	4	2	9/13	Guelah Papyrus	Whole Lotta Love Jam
4/6/91	9	2	10/11	Run Like an Antelope	Possum
5/4/91	14	E	1/3	***	Runaway Jim
5/18/91	7	2	9/10	David Bowie	The Lizards
10/3/91	24	E	1/2	***	Tweezer Repri
10/6/91	2	1	12/13	Brother	Golgi Apparat
10/19/91	8	2	9/10	The Oh Kee Pa Ceremo	Harry Hood
10/24/91	2	2	10/11	Bouncing	Possum
11/9/91	9	2	8/10	The Landlady	My Sweet One
11/10/91	1	2	2/4	Split Open and Melt	Sweet Adeline
11/13/91	2	2	8/9	Llama	Possum
11/16/91	3	2	8/9	Chalk Dust Torture	Llama
12/7/91	11	2	7/8	The Lizards	Harpua
3/20/92	10	2	10/12	Harry Hood	Secret Language Inst
4/8/92	16	2	14/15	Chalk Dust Torture	Cavern
4/16/92	4	2	9/12	Poor Heart	Memories
4/25/92	8	2	10/11	Weigh	Poor Heart
5/1/92	3	2	12/13	Llama	Golgi Apparat
5/6/92	4	2	9/11	Chalk Dust Torture	Take the A-Trn
5/8/92	2	2	10/12	Chalk Dust Torture	Harry Hood
5/12/92	3	2	6/9	Chalk Dust Torture	Poor Heart
8/17/92	37	2	9/11	Horn	Take the A-Trn
11/20/92	12	2	8/10	Harry Hood	Lengthwise
11/28/92	6	2	10/12	The Squirming Coil	Harpua
11/30/92	1	2	9/10	The Squirming Coil	Cavern
12/29/92	14	2	12/14	Weekapaug Groove	The Squirmin
2/3/93	3	2	9/11	Lifeboy	Big Ball Jam
2/12/93	8	2	9/11	Ya Mar	Harry Hood
2/20/93	6	2	20/22	Big Ball Jam	Harry Hood
2/23/93	3	2	12/13	Weekapaug Groove	Possum
2/27/93	3	2	10/12	Weekapaug Groove	Fee
3/3/93	2	2	11/13	Fast Enough for You	The Squirmin
3/8/93	3	E	1/3	***	Chalk Dust Tor
3/24/93	11	2	11/12	Silent in the Mornin	Good Time Ba
4/12/93	13	2	9/10	Honky Tonk Women Jam	Tweezer Repri
4/29/93	12	2	12/13	Weekapaug Groove	The Squirmin
6/13/94	95	2	10/11	Big Ball Jam	Slave
7/1/94	14	2	9/11	Possum	Harry Hood
11/20/94	4	2	8/10	Rift	Julius
6/13/95	25	1	8/10	Reba	Sparkle
7/11/96	84	2	6/8	The Lizards	You Enjoy My
7/8/99	211	E	1/2	***	Character Zer
7/11/00	83	2	12/13	Moby Dick	Character Zer

Has not been played in the last 24 shows.

Terrapin Station

DATE	GAP	SET	POS.	SONG BEFORE	SONG AFTER
8/9/98	972	E	1/1	***	***

Has not been played in the last 147 shows.

That's Alright Mama

DATE	GAP	SET	POS.	SONG BEFORE	SONG AFTER
5/6/93	547	2	11/11	Cracklin' Rosie	***

Has not been played in the last 572 shows.

The Asse Festival

DATE	GAP	SET	POS.	SONG BEFORE	SONG AFTER
5/12/89	100	1	8/15	Buried Alive	You Enjoy My
9/13/90	107	1	5/11	Tube	Run Like Antel
9/14/90	1	2	1/10	***	The Squirmin
9/15/90	1	1	9/14	AC/DC Bag	David Bowie
9/20/90	2	1	3/12	Paul and Silas	Dinner and a
9/22/90	2	E	1/2	***	Golgi Apparat
9/28/90	1	1	9/10	The Lizards	Run Like Antel
10/1/90	2	1	4/11	Weekapaug Groove	Stash
10/5/90	2	1	11/13	Stash	Bouncing
10/7/90	2	1	8/14	The Famous Mockingbi	The Squirmin
10/30/90	4	1	4/9	Donna Lee	Suzy Greenber
10/31/90	1	1	8/11	You Enjoy Myself	My Sweet One
11/2/90	1	1	11/14	Cavern	Possum
11/4/90	2	1	8/12	Funky Bitch	My Sweet One
11/8/90	1	1	8/12	The Squirming Coil	I Didn't Know
11/10/90	1	2	3/8	You Enjoy Myself	Fee
11/30/90	5	2	1/10	***	The Squirmin
12/7/90	2	1	6/9	You Enjoy Myself	Runaway Jim
12/8/90	1	2	2/9	Llama	Dinner and a
2/21/91	15	2	8/9	Uncle Pen	David Bowie
4/27/91	32	1	2/12	Sweet Adeline	Runaway Jim

Has not been played in the last 834 shows.

The Ballad of Curtis Loew

DATE	GAP	SET	POS.	SONG BEFORE	SONG AFTER
4/29/87	22	3	12/14	McGrupp	Good Times Roll
8/29/87	6	2	2/13	Alumni Blues	Sneakin' Sally
9/21/87	2	3	8/15	Dog Gone Dog	Run Like Antel
11/19/87	5	3	7/14	Dinner and a Movie	Whipping Post
1/27/88	1	2	7/10	Divided Sky	You Enjoy My
2/7/88	1	3	7/8	The Curtain	Good Time Ba
2/26/88	3	2	3/9	David Bowie	Fee
3/11/88	1	2	4/8	Harry Hood	Harpua
4/22/88	5	2	12/13	Possum	David Bowie
6/20/88	7	2	8/9	Possum	David Bowie
6/24/88	2	1	10/11	You Enjoy Myself	Fluffhead
7/23/88	3	3	6/7	Slave	Good Time Ba
10/29/88	12	2	6/7	Divided Sky	Mike's Song
2/6/89	10	3	5/9	BBFCFM	Col. Forbin's A
5/26/89	24	3	3/4	Funky Bitch	Possum
2/9/90	47	2	8/9	Foam	David Bowie
2/16/90	3	2	6/7	Possum	The Lizards
3/8/90	10	2	11/12	Weekapaug Groove	Golgi Apparat
4/13/90	13	2	5/10	Alumni Blues	The Sloth
4/26/90	8	2	8/11	Sweet Adeline	Mike's Song
6/5/90	17	2	9/10	You Enjoy Myself	Good Time Ba
10/30/90	22	2	8/12	Llama	Fluffhead
3/14/93	285	2	3/11	David Bowie	You Enjoy My
4/23/93	28	2	3/12	Maze	It's Ice
8/2/93	29	2	4/9	Sparks	Rift

Has not been played in the last 553 shows.

The Birthday Dub

DATE	GAP	SET	POS.	SONG BEFORE	SONG AFTER
9/21/87	30	3	1/15	***	Good Time Ba

Has not been played in the last 1089 shows.

The Chase

DATE	GAP	SET	POS.	SONG BEFORE	SONG AFTER
8/9/87	25	1	4/11	La Grange	Possum
9/2/87	4	1	7/13	David Bowie	Possum
10/31/87	4	2	9/17	I Am Hydrogen	Fee
9/21/89	82	2	2/9	Divided Sky	Dinner and a
10/1/89	1	2	6/12	Harry Hood	Wilson
10/26/89	9	2	9/15	The Sloth	Possum

Has not been played in the last 994 shows.

The Chicken

DATE	GAP	SET	POS.	SONG BEFORE	SONG AFTER
3/11/88	41	1	1/12	***	Funky Bitch

Has not been played in the last 1078 shows.

The Continuing Story of Bungalow Bill

DATE	GAP	SET	POS.	SONG BEFORE	SONG AFTER
10/31/94	681	2	7/30	Wild Honey Pie	While My Guitar Gent

Has not been played in the last 438 shows.

The Curtain

DATE	GAP	SET	POS.	SONG BEFORE	SONG AFTER
2/7/88	37	3	6/8	Clod	Ballad - Curtis Loew
2/24/88	2	1	1/11	***	You Enjoy My
5/15/88	9	2	3/11	McGrupp	Wilson
5/21/88	1	3	5/6	Take the A-Train	Suzy Greenber
5/25/88	1	1	1/9	***	Rocky Top
6/21/88	4	1	5/9	Suzy Greenberg	The Lizards
7/11/88	2	1	3/11	Suzy Greenberg	Jam
7/23/88	2	2	3/10	Fire	Terrapin
9/24/88	11	3	3/4	Fluffhead	AC/DC Bag
2/6/89	11	1	2/7	Suzy Greenberg	Wilson
2/24/89	5	1	4/9	T.M.W.S.I.Y. Reprise	Foam
3/3/89	1	1	6/11	AC/DC Bag	Run Like Antel
3/14/89	3	1	1/12	***	Ya Mar
6/30/89	19	2	3/8	AC/DC Bag	Slave
11/2/89	20	1	7/11	Fee	Reba
11/9/89	2	1	4/9	Ya Mar	My Sweet One
12/16/89	12	1	1/9	***	AC/DC Bag
3/9/90	23	2	4/11	AC/DC Bag	Dog Gone Dog
4/18/90	14	1	5/10	Uncle Pen	Foam
10/5/90	39	2	2/8	Golgi Apparatus	Ya Mar
11/4/90	10	1	3/10	AC/DC Bag	Bouncing
2/15/91	21	1	1/11	***	Wilson
2/19/91	2	1	2/9	Llama	Golgi Apparat
3/9/91	9	E	3/3	Fee	***
3/16/91	3	1	8/14	Bathtub Gin	Rocky Top
3/23/91	3	1	6/10	I Didn't Know	Possum
4/4/91	6	2	1/10	***	Runaway Jim
4/19/91	8	2	3/10	Fee	Golgi Apparat
4/22/91	3	1	1/9	***	Runaway Jim
4/25/91	1	1	4/11	Runaway Jim	Cavern
4/27/91	1	2	1/13	***	Possum
5/3/91	2	2	2/9	AC/DC Bag	The Sloth
5/9/91	2	2	2/8	My Sweet One	Fluffhead
5/12/91	3	2	3/10	Poor Heart	Golgi Apparat
5/18/91	3	2	3/10	Suzy Greenberg	Stash
7/13/91	4	1	1/13	***	Runaway Jim
8/3/91	12	2	1/10	***	Reba
10/11/91	12	2	1/9	***	Cavern
10/17/91	4	2	1/9	***	The Oh Kee Pa
11/2/91	10	1	2/10	Suzy Greenberg	Llama
11/9/91	3	1	1/11	***	Runaway Jim
11/15/91	5	1	4/12	Cavern	Split Open and
11/23/91	6	2	1/13	***	Mike's Song
12/7/91	6	1	8/11	Stash	Cavern
3/13/92	6	1	1/12	***	Split Open and
3/24/92	7	2	1/13	***	Mike's Song
4/3/92	8	2	1/9	***	The Sloth
4/19/92	12	2	1/13	***	Mike's Song
4/23/92	3	1	2/11	Cavern	Split Open and
4/30/92	4	1	1/10	***	Split Open and
5/5/92	4	1	2/11	Golgi Apparatus	Sparkle
5/8/92	3	1	1/12	***	Cavern
5/17/92	7	2	1/11	***	Possum
7/1/92	8	1	1/7	***	Cavern
11/21/92	38	2	2/13	Carolina	Mike's Song
12/1/92	7	2	2/11	Axilla	Chalk Dust Tor
12/6/92	5	2	2/13	Suzy Greenberg	Stash
12/12/92	5	2	3/10	Glide	Tweezer
12/29/92	3	2	1/14	***	Tweezer
2/5/93	5	2	1/10	***	Tweezer
2/21/93	13	2	2/10	Axilla	Stash
2/27/93	5	2	1/12	***	Stash
3/3/93	2	2	2/13	Axilla	Split Open and
3/6/93	2	1	3/10	Horn	Split Open and
3/16/93	6	2	2/15	My Friend My Friend	Tweezer
3/25/93	7	2	2/13	Axilla	Sample in a Ja
4/1/93	6	2	2/10	Axilla	Possum
4/16/93	8	2	2/13	Axilla	Maze
4/25/93	8	2	2/11	Wilson	Tweezer
5/3/93	6	2	2/12	AC/DC Bag	Tweezer
8/6/93	23	1	3/10	Poor Heart	Sample in a Ja
12/30/93	19	1	3/10	Weigh	Sample in a Ja
4/6/94	4	2	1/9	***	Down with Dis
4/13/94	5	2	2/10	Faht	Sample in a Ja
4/25/94	11	2	1/10	***	Sample in a Ja
5/14/94	13	2	1/11	***	Mike's Song
5/25/94	8	1	1/11	***	Sample in a Ja
6/10/94	6	2	2/9	Axilla (Part II)	Tweezer
6/16/94	4	1	7/10	Gumbo	Dog Faced Boy
6/19/94	3	1	5/9	Axilla (Part II)	Fast Enough for You
6/24/94	4	2	4/13	Halley's Comet	McGrupp
6/29/94	3	1	1/11	***	Sample in a Ja
7/5/94	5	1	3/10	Sample in a Jar	Letter to Jimmy Page
10/9/94	11	1	4/7	Fast Enough for You	Dog Faced Boy
10/14/94	4	2	1/10	***	Tweezer
10/21/94	5	2	8/11	Sleeping Monkey	Fast Enough for You
11/4/94	11	2	1/9	***	Mike's Song
11/22/94	9	2	5/13	Cry Baby Cry	Blackbird
12/6/94	10	2	1/12	***	Sample in a Ja
6/17/95	18	1	8/9	Lawn Boy	Stash
7/2/95	12	1	4/10	Gumbo	Julius
10/22/95	20	2	4/11	Catapult	Tweezer
11/12/95	10	2	1/8	***	Tweezer
11/19/95	5	2	3/8	Also Sprach	Tweezer
11/24/95	3	1	3/9	AC/DC Bag	Sparkle
11/30/95	4	1	2/10	Sample in a Jar	Ha Ha Ha
12/7/95	5	1	2/10	The Old Home Place	AC/DC Bag
12/11/95	3	2	1/8	***	David Bowie
12/14/95	2	2	1/10	***	Tweezer
12/28/95	4	1	3/9	Gumbo	Julius
7/7/96	9	1	4/10	Bouncing	Tweezer
8/6/96	18	2	1/8	***	Tweezer
8/17/96	7	2	1/8	***	Runaway Jim
10/22/96	6	1	1/9	***	Runaway Jim
11/6/96	9	2	2/9	Wilson	Mike's Song
11/11/96	4	2	4/11	Gumbo	Sample in a Ja
11/23/96	8	2	1/10	***	Mike's Song
12/1/96	5	1	6/12	Character Zero	Down with Dis
2/20/97	13	1	1/10	***	Tweezer
11/28/97	57	1	1/8	***	You Enjoy My
12/28/97	12	1	3/11	Cities	Sample in a Ja
7/31/98	28	2	1/9	***	Free
11/19/98	30	1	2/9	Cities	Sample in a Ja
7/13/99	21	1	2/9	NICU	Halley's Comet
9/14/99	19	1	3/11	The Sloth	Waste
12/30/99	34	2	2/10	Wilson	Tweezer
6/14/00	9	1	2/8	Carini	Cities
7/7/00	14	1	10/11	Back on the Train	Character Zer
9/9/00	8	2	2/7	Gotta Jibboo	Sand

Has not been played in the last 19 shows.

The Curtain With

DATE	GAP	SET	POS.	SONG BEFORE	SONG AFTER
8/9/87	25	2	1/11	***	Halley's Comet
8/10/87	1	2	6/10	Fee	I Know a Little Light Up Or Leave Me
8/21/87	1	1	7/11	Clod	Light Up Or Leave Me
8/29/87	1	1	4/13	Swing Low Sweet Chrt	McGrupp
9/21/87	2	2	2/5	You Enjoy Myself	BBFCM
2/26/88	10	1	1/13	***	Suzy Greenber
6/19/88	12	1	1/8	***	Funky Bitch
7/12/00	1044	1	2/9	My Friend My Friend	Tube
9/17/00	9	1	8/9	Fluffhead	Chalk Dust Tor
9/30/00	9	1	2/10	Walfredo	Maze

Has not been played in the last 5 shows.

The Dirty Jobs

DATE	GAP	SET	POS.	SONG BEFORE	SONG AFTER
10/31/95	759	2	7/17	I'm One	Helpless Dancer

Has not been played in the last 360 shows.

The Famous Mockingbird

DATE	GAP	SET	POS.	SONG BEFORE	SONG AFTER
2/7/88	37	2	8/9	The Lizards	Whipping Post
3/12/88	5	2	8/11	Col. Forbin's Ascent	The Sloth
3/21/88	1	1	15/15	Col. Forbin's Ascent	***
3/31/88	1	1	10/14	Col. Forbin's Ascent	Take the A-Trn
4/22/88	2	1	2/9	Col. Forbin's Ascent	Fire
6/21/88	8	1	8/9	Col. Forbin's Ascent	Fire
7/11/88	2	1	9/11	Col. Forbin's Ascent	Golgi Apparat
7/23/88	2	1	3/13	Col. Forbin's Ascent	Mike's Song
7/24/88	1	1	5/10	Col. Forbin's Ascent	Sneakin' Sally
9/8/88	6	1	7/8	Col. Forbin's Ascent	Bold as Love
11/11/88	9	1	7/8	Col. Forbin's Ascent	David Bowie
12/10/88	2	1	12/12	Col. Forbin's Ascent	***
1/26/89	3	2	4/10	Col. Forbin's Ascent	The Sloth
2/6/89	1	3	7/9	Col. Forbin's Ascent	Whipping Post
2/24/89	5	1	7/10	Col. Forbin's Ascent	Run Like Antel
3/3/89	1	2	8/12	Col. Forbin's Ascent	The Lizards
5/1/89	10	2	8/10	Col. Forbin's Ascent	David Bowie
5/6/89	2	1	12/13	Col. Forbin's Ascent	David Bowie
5/28/89	8	1	4/9	Col. Forbin's Ascent	Fee
8/23/89	5	2	3/8	Col. Forbin's Ascent	Ya Mar
8/26/89	1	1	3/8	Col. Forbin's Ascent	Harry Hood
9/14/89	2	1	6/9	Col. Forbin's Ascent	La Grange
10/12/89	5	1	4/8	Col. Forbin's Ascent	You Enjoy My
10/20/89	3	1	4/10	Col. Forbin's Ascent	You Enjoy My
10/22/89	2	1	3/14	Col. Forbin's Ascent	You Enjoy My
10/31/89	3	2	5/8	Col. Forbin's Ascent	Alumni Blues
11/3/89	2	1	2/10	Col. Forbin's Ascent	Bathtub Gin
11/30/89	6	2	4/11	Col. Forbin's Ascent	Undun
1/28/90	13	1	8/9	Col. Forbin's Ascent	Communication Brkdwn
2/25/90	11	1	4/11	Col. Forbin's Ascent	Funky Bitch
3/2/90	2	1	2/2	Col. Forbin's Ascent	***
3/9/90	4	1	7/11	Col. Forbin's Ascent	The Sloth
4/14/90	13	1	6/10	Col. Forbin's Ascent	Rift
4/20/90	3	1	9/10	Col. Forbin's Ascent	Possum
10/7/90	39	1	7/14	Col. Forbin's Ascent	The Asse Festival
11/2/90	6	2	3/9	Col. Forbin's Ascent	My Sweet One
11/26/90	8	2	3/7	Col. Forbin's Ascent	Wilson
12/28/90	5	1	7/11	Col. Forbin's Ascent	Mike's Song
2/8/91	7	1	5/11	Col. Forbin's Ascent	My Sweet One
3/16/91	17	1	11/14	Col. Forbin's Ascent	The Oh Kee Pa
3/23/91	3	1	9/10	Col. Forbin's Ascent	Rocky Top
3/31/91	3	1	5/13	Col. Forbin's Ascent	The Landlady
4/4/91	3	1	7/10	Col. Forbin's Ascent	Possum
4/15/91	5	1	9/10	Col. Forbin's Ascent	Llama
4/21/91	5	2	5/11	Col. Forbin's Ascent	Llama
5/4/91	6	2	4/9	Col. Forbin's Ascent	Buried Alive
5/16/91	5	1	7/11	Col. Forbin's Ascent	Chalk Dust Tor
7/14/91	7	1	8/11	Col. Forbin's Ascent	The Sloth
9/30/91	17	1	4/4	Col. Forbin's Ascent	***
10/13/91	8	1	6/13	Col. Forbin's Ascent	Tela
10/27/91	7	2	3/13	Col. Forbin's Ascent	Sparkle
11/2/91	5	1	9/10	Col. Forbin's Ascent	Possum
11/13/91	6	2	3/9	Col. Forbin's Ascent	Golgi Apparat
11/20/91	5	1	4/11	Col. Forbin's Ascent	Sparkle
12/7/91	9	1	5/11	Col. Forbin's Ascent	My Sweet One
3/19/92	9	1	10/12	Col. Forbin's Ascent	All Things Rec
3/24/92	4	1	11/13	Col. Forbin's Ascent	The Landlady
3/31/92	6	1	9/10	Col. Forbin's Ascent	Run Like Antel
4/16/92	11	1	11/12	Icculus	Run Like Antel
4/21/92	4	2	3/13	Col. Forbin's Ascent	Tweezer
4/24/92	3	1	3/11	Col. Forbin's Ascent	Uncle Pen
5/2/92	5	1	4/11	Icculus	Sparkle
5/6/92	3	1	9/11	Col. Forbin's Ascent	Sparkle
5/17/92	9	1	4/11	Col. Forbin's Ascent	My Sweet One
11/21/92	46	1	10/11	Col. Forbin's Ascent	Possum

DATE	GAP	SET	POS.	SONG BEFORE	SONG AFTER
11/27/92	4	1	5/12	Col. Forbin's Ascent	Split Open and
12/4/92	6	1	10/11	Col. Forbin's Ascent	Cavern
12/8/92	4	1	5/11	Col. Forbin's Ascent	Uncle Pen
12/31/92	8	2	5/10	Col. Forbin's Ascent	My Sweet One
2/7/93	5	1	7/12	Col. Forbin's Ascent	Rift
2/19/93	9	1	7/11	Col. Forbin's Ascent	Sparkle
2/25/93	5	1	6/11	Col. Forbin's Ascent	Rift
3/8/93	7	1	8/12	How High the Moon	Sparkle
3/18/93	7	1	7/11	Col. Forbin's Ascent	Sparkle
3/22/93	3	2	8/13	Col. Forbin's Ascent	The Sloth
3/25/93	2	2	8/13	Icculus	The Wedge
4/5/93	9	1	9/10	Col. Forbin's Ascent	David Bowie
4/21/93	9	1	7/11	Col. Forbin's Ascent	Rift
4/25/93	4	1	8/11	Col. Forbin's Ascent	Maze
5/3/93	6	1	8/11	Col. Forbin's Ascent	Possum
7/29/93	18	1	9/10	Col. Forbin's Ascent	Possum
8/7/93	6	1	9/10	Col. Forbin's Ascent	Cavern
8/15/93	7	1	9/10	Col. Forbin's Ascent	Chalk Dust Tor
12/30/93	11	1	7/10	Col. Forbin's Ascent	Rift
4/11/94	8	2	4/11	Col. Forbin's Ascent	Uncle Pen
4/24/94	11	2	6/9	Col. Forbin's Ascent	Chalk Dust Tor
5/25/94	22	1	6/11	Col. Forbin's Ascent	Axilla (Part II)
6/16/94	10	2	5/11	Kung	Big Ball Jam
6/26/94	9	1	8/11	Col. Forbin's Ascent	The Sloth
7/8/94	8	1	8/11	Col. Forbin's Ascent	The Sloth
10/14/94	13	1	11/12	Col. Forbin's Ascent	Julius
10/27/94	10	1	6/11	The Vibration of Lif	Divided Sky
11/4/94	6	1	6/9	Col. Forbin's Ascent	Scent of a Mul
11/17/94	5	1	10/11	The Vibration of Lif	Down with Dis
11/30/94	9	1	6/10	Col. Forbin's Ascent	Down with Dis
10/5/95	43	2	4/9	Col. Forbin's Ascent	Scent of a Mul
12/1/95	35	1	8/10	Col. Forbin's Ascent	Stash
12/31/95	16	1	8/10	Shine	Sparkle
8/7/96	25	2	6/10	Col. Forbin's Ascent	Possum
10/31/96	18	1	8/10	Col. Forbin's Ascent	Character Zer
8/7/98	135	1	10/10	Col. Forbin's Ascent	***
9/30/00	144	2	4/7	Col. Forbin's Ascent	Twist

Has not been played in the last 5 shows.

The Great Curve

DATE	GAP	SET	POS.	SONG BEFORE	SONG AFTER
10/31/96	835	2	3/8	Crosseyed and Painle	Once in a Lifetime

Has not been played in the last 284 shows.

The Great Gig in the Sky

DATE	GAP	SET	POS.	SONG BEFORE	SONG AFTER
3/14/93	509	2	10/11	Big Ball Jam	The Squirmin
3/17/93	2	2	11/12	Silent in the Mornin	Golgi Apparat
3/26/93	7	2	11/12	Suzy Greenberg	Tweezer Repri
4/10/93	10	2	8/13	Mike's Song	Weekapaug Gr
4/21/93	7	2	9/11	Mike's Song	Weekapaug Gr
5/1/93	8	2	9/11	Mike's Song	Weekapaug Gr
5/7/93	5	2	7/10	You Enjoy Myself	Harry Hood
7/28/93	14	2	9/10	Harry Hood	Chalk Dust Tor
8/11/93	10	2	2/10	Mike's Song	Weekapaug Gr
5/2/94	39	1	1/10	***	Split Open and
7/5/94	42	2	7/11	You Enjoy Myself	Ginseng Sullivan
11/2/98	331	2	10/16	Time	Money

Has not been played in the last 135 shows.

The Happy Whip and Dung Song

DATE	GAP	SET	POS.	SONG BEFORE	SONG AFTER
7/24/99	1024	2	6/8	Jam	Waste

Has not been played in the last 95 shows.

The Horse

DATE	GAP	SET	POS.	SONG BEFORE	SONG AFTER
3/7/92	360	1	5/11	Runaway Jim	Silent in Morni
3/13/92	3	2	3/12	Brother	Silent in Morni
3/19/92	3	1	6/12	Golgi Apparatus	Silent in Morni
3/21/92	2	1	6/12	Split Open and Melt	Silent in Morni
3/24/92	2	1	7/13	Golgi Apparatus	Silent in Morni
3/27/92	3	2	4/13	Weekapaug Groove	Silent in Morni
4/1/92	4	2	3/13	You Enjoy Myself	Silent in Morni
4/5/92	3	2	4/12	You Enjoy Myself	Silent in Morni
4/7/92	2	1	6/12	Divided Sky	Silent in Morni
4/8/92	1	2	11/15	Weekapaug Groove	Silent in Morni
4/12/92	1	1	5/11	Divided Sky	Silent in Morni
4/19/92	6	2	5/13	Weekapaug Groove	Silent in Morni
4/22/92	2	2	3/11	Run Like an Antelope	Silent in Morni
4/25/92	3	2	4/11	You Enjoy Myself	Silent in Morni
4/30/92	2	2	6/11	You Enjoy Myself	Silent in Morni
5/3/92	3	2	2/14	Tweezer	Silent in Morni
5/5/92	1	2	8/14	Weekapaug Groove	Silent in Morni
5/8/92	3	2	7/12	You Enjoy Myself	Silent in Morni
5/16/92	6	2	7/13	You Enjoy Myself	Silent in Morni
7/15/92	15	1	8/12	Split Open and Melt	Silent in Morni
11/19/92	30	1	10/12	Axilla	Silent in Morni
11/21/92	2	2	6/13	Weekapaug Groove	Silent in Morni
11/27/92	4	2	9/13	David Bowie	Silent in Morni
12/3/92	5	1	8/12	Chalk Dust Torture	Silent in Morni
12/8/92	5	2	4/15	Weekapaug Groove	Silent in Morni
12/29/92	6	2	3/14	Tweezer	Silent in Morni
2/3/93	3	2	4/11	Tweezer	Silent in Morni
2/5/93	2	2	3/10	Tweezer	Silent in Morni
2/10/93	4	2	8/11	You Enjoy Myself	Silent in Morni
2/20/93	8	1	8/11	Divided Sky	Silent in Morni
3/2/93	7	1	10/13	Chalk Dust Torture	Silent in Morni
3/9/93	5	2	9/15	Weekapaug Groove	Silent in Morni
3/12/93	1	1	9/11	Fluffhead	Silent in Morni
3/17/93	4	2	9/12	Weekapaug Groove	Silent in Morni
3/24/93	5	2	9/12	You Enjoy Myself	Silent in Morni
3/26/93	2	2	5/12	Mound	Silent in Morni
3/30/93	3	2	12/15	Weekapaug Groove	Silent in Morni
4/2/93	3	2	5/13	Llama	Silent in Morni
4/9/93	3	1	5/11	Stash	Silent in Morni
4/12/93	2	1	6/11	Stash	Silent in Morni
4/14/93	1	1	9/13	Stash	Silent in Morni
4/16/93	1	2	8/13	Weekapaug Groove	Silent in Morni
4/18/93	2	2	3/12	Tweezer	Silent in Morni
4/21/93	2	2	5/11	The Squirming Coil	Silent in Morni
4/24/93	3	1	5/11	Stash	Silent in Morni
4/30/93	4	1	6/12	Stash	Silent in Morni
5/2/93	2	1	6/11	Stash	Silent in Morni
5/6/93	3	1	4/13	Split Open and Melt	Silent in Morni
5/8/93	2	2	6/18	David Bowie	Silent in Morni
7/15/93	3	2	2/11	David Bowie	Silent in Morni
7/17/93	2	1	8/11	Chalk Dust Torture	Silent in Morni
7/23/93	4	1	6/12	Maze	Silent in Morni
7/25/93	2	2	4/10	Tweezer	Silent in Morni
7/28/93	2	1	8/11	Split Open and Melt	Silent in Morni
7/30/93	2	2	3/10	Tweezer	Silent in Morni
8/3/93	3	1	7/11	Stash	Silent in Morni
8/8/93	3	1	5/11	Runaway Jim	Silent in Morni
8/12/93	3	1	7/10	Split Open and Melt	Silent in Morni
8/14/93	2	1	4/11	Divided Sky	Silent in Morni
8/17/93	3	2	3/10	David Bowie	Silent in Morni
8/24/93	3	1	7/11	Split Open and Melt	Silent in Morni
8/28/93	3	2	4/14	Run Like an Antelope	Silent in Morni
12/30/93	3	2	3/9	Mike's Song	Silent in Morni
4/8/94	5	1	8/13	Punch You in the Eye	Silent in Morni
4/14/94	5	2	3/9	Run Like an Antelope	Silent in Morni
4/22/94	7	1	9/11	Divided Sky	Silent in Morni
5/12/94	14	2	3/11	Run Like an Antelope	Silent in Morni
5/19/94	5	1	6/10	Stash	Silent in Morni
5/23/94	4	1	6/10	Maze	Silent in Morni
5/28/94	4	1	6/10	Stash	Silent in Morni
6/21/94	11	1	5/5	It's Ice	***
6/29/94	6	1	6/11	Julius	Silent in Morni
7/3/94	4	2	5/10	It's Ice	Silent in Morni
7/9/94	4	1	8/10	Down with Disease	Silent in Morni
7/14/94	3	1	9/11	Fluffhead	Silent in Morni
7/16/94	2	1	7/11	Cavern	Silent in Morni
10/7/94	1	2	2/10	Maze	Silent in Morni
10/10/94	3	1	3/11	Divided Sky	Silent in Morni
10/14/94	3	1	4/12	Divided Sky	Silent in Morni
10/18/94	3	2	2/10	David Bowie	Silent in Morni
10/22/94	3	2	3/11	David Bowie	Silent in Morni
10/25/94	2	1	5/9	Julius	Silent in Morni
10/27/94	2	1	8/11	Divided Sky	Silent in Morni
10/31/94	3	1	7/10	Julius	Silent in Morni
11/13/94	5	1	8/10	The Vibration of Lif	Silent in Morni
11/18/94	4	1	4/11	Julius	Silent in Morni
11/26/94	6	1	6/9	Foam	Silent in Morni
11/30/94	2	E	1/3	***	Silent in Morni
12/8/94	7	E	1/3	***	Silent in Morni
12/29/94	4	1	5/9	Split Open and Melt	Silent in Morni
12/31/94	2	3	5/8	Chalk Dust Torture	Silent in Morni
6/14/95	7	1	9/12	Amazing Grace	Silent in Morni
6/24/95	8	1	8/10	Stash	Silent in Morni
6/29/95	4	1	3/10	Taste	Silent in Morni
10/5/95	11	1	4/11	Fog that Surrounds	Silent in Morni
10/24/95	13	1	6/13	Llama	Silent in Morni
10/29/95	4	1	6/12	Cars Trucks Buses	Silent in Morni
11/11/95	4	1	6/12	Weekapaug Groove	Silent in Morni
12/4/95	16	1	8/11	Axilla (Part II)	Silent in Morni
12/12/95	6	1	6/10	Punch You in the Eye	Silent in Morni
7/21/96	24	1	8/14	Split Open and Melt	Silent in Morni
8/2/96	5	2	7/9	Prince Caspian	Silent in Morni
8/10/96	5	1	7/11	I Didn't Know	Silent in Morni
8/14/96	3	2	3/10	You Enjoy Myself	Silent in Morni
10/16/96	3	1	10/12	It's Ice	Silent in Morni
10/21/96	4	2	9/11	Simple	Silent in Morni
10/29/96	6	2	3/10	Mike's Song	Silent in Morni
12/1/96	21	1	9/12	Train Song	Silent in Morni
12/31/96	7	1	6/10	Stash	Silent in Morni
2/23/97	9	2	4/9	Maze	Silent in Morni
7/6/97	22	1	5/9	Stash	Silent in Morni
8/13/97	19	1	6/11	Gumbo	Silent in Morni
11/26/97	12	1	8/10	Split Open and Melt	Silent in Morni
12/31/97	16	1	7/10	Limb by Limb	Silent in Morni
8/2/98	27	1	3/9	Divided Sky	Silent in Morni
8/15/98	8	2	6/9	Tweezer	Silent in Morni
7/4/99	35	2	3/9	Slave	Silent in Morni
10/1/99	37	2	3/9	Run Like an Antelope	Silent in Morni
12/8/99	13	1	6/8	Ya Mar	Silent in Morni
12/18/99	8	2	3/10	Sand	Silent in Morni
12/31/99	2	2	24/35	After Midnight Repri	Silent in Morni
7/8/00	23	2	7/9	Twist	Silent in Morni
9/8/00	6	1	5/12	Bouncing	Silent in Morni

Has not been played in the last 20 shows.

The Inlaw Josie Wales

DATE	GAP	SET	POS.	SONG BEFORE	SONG AFTER
9/9/99	1031	2	4/9	Ghost	First Tube
12/13/99	33	2	4/8	Sand	Mountains in the Mis
12/18/99	4	1	8/9	First Tube	You Enjoy My
12/31/99	2	2	12/35	Crosseyed and Painle	Sand
5/21/00	1	E	1/2	***	Loving Cup
6/10/00	4	E	1/2	***	Limb by Limb
6/24/00	8	E	2/4	Guyute	Driver
6/30/00	4	2	4/9	Twist	Back on the Train
7/6/00	4	1	9/12	I Didn't Know	Prince Caspian
7/14/00	6	E	1/3	***	Driver
9/14/00	6	E	2/3	Driver	Sample in a Ja
10/1/00	12	1	6/10	Vultures	Billy Breathes
10/6/00	3	2	4/10	Spock's Brain	Rift

Has not been played in the last 1 show.

The Landlady

DATE	GAP	SET	POS.	SONG BEFORE	SONG AFTER
2/1/90	150	1	3/11	Walk Away	Suzy Greenber
6/9/90	55	E	1/2	***	Contact
9/13/90	2	1	1/11	***	Divided Sky
9/14/90	1	1	3/11	Bouncing	Reba
9/15/90	1	1	4/14	Paul and Silas	Fee
9/16/90	1	1	4/14	The Sloth	Reba
9/20/90	1	1	7/12	Esther	Mike's Song
9/22/90	2	1	10/12	Wilson	I Didn't Know
9/28/90	1	1	1/10	***	Bouncing
9/29/90	1	1	3/9	Dinner and a Movie	Ya Mar
10/4/90	2	1	2/10	Golgi Apparatus	Esther
10/5/90	1	1	6/13	My Sweet One	Tela
10/6/90	1	1	1/13	***	The Squirmin
10/7/90	1	1	4/14	Stash	Destiny Unbound
10/8/90	1	1	2/10	Don't Get Me Wrong	Bouncing

DATE	GAP	SET	POS.	SONG BEFORE	SONG AFTER
10/12/90	1	2	3/10	Fee	Terrapin
10/19/90	1	1	11/15	Bathtub Gin	Bouncing
10/30/90	1	1	1/9	***	Bouncing
10/31/90	1	2	1/12	***	Reba
11/2/90	1	1	2/14	Golgi Apparatus	Bouncing
11/3/90	1	2	1/12	***	Mike's Song
11/8/90	2	1	1/12	***	Possum
11/10/90	1	2	2/11	Reba	Bouncing
11/16/90	1	2	1/11	***	Mike's Song
11/17/90	1	1	3/11	The Squirming Coil	Runaway Jim
11/24/90	1	2	5/12	Eliza	Runaway Jim
11/26/90	1	1	1/11	***	Runaway Jim
11/30/90	1	1	1/11	***	Mike's Song
12/1/90	1	1	2/9	Cavern	Llama
12/7/90	1		4/9	Bouncing	You Enjoy My
12/8/90	1	1	7/10	Cavern	Mike's Song
12/28/90	1	2	1/12	***	Possum
12/31/90	2	1	4/12	I Didn't Know	Bouncing
2/1/91	1	2	3/5	Reba	The Mango Song
2/3/91	2	2	3/9	The Squirming Coil	Cavern
2/7/91	1	1	4/10	My Sweet One	The Mango Song
2/9/91	2	2	4/10	Fluffhead	Bouncing
2/14/91	1	2	11/12	I Didn't Know	Possum
2/16/91	1	1	6/12	Take the A-Train	Bouncing
2/19/91	1	2	6/15	Guelah Papyrus	Esther
2/21/91	2	2	3/9	Cavern	Bouncing
2/26/91	1	2	6/12	Bouncing	Destiny Unbound
2/27/91	1	1	4/10	I Didn't Know	You Enjoy My
2/28/91	1	1	1/13	***	Bouncing
3/1/91	1	2	2/11	Golgi Apparatus	Reba
3/6/91	1	1	3/11	You Enjoy Myself	The Squirmin
3/13/91	3	1	2/9	Fluffhead	You Enjoy My
3/16/91	1	2	6/14	Reba	Bathtub Gin
3/17/91	1	1	3/12	Bouncing	Mike's Song
3/22/91	1	1	3/11	You Enjoy Myself	Destiny Unbound
3/28/91	2	1	4/14	Cavern	Bouncing
3/31/91	2	1	6/13	The Famous Mockingbi	My Sweet One
4/2/91	1	1	2/10	Runaway Jim	Reba
4/3/91	1	2	6/9	Esther	Destiny Unbound
4/4/91	1	2	6/10	Lawn Boy	My Sweet One
4/5/91	1	1	1/11	***	Bouncing
4/11/91	2	2	10/14	Lawn Boy	Destiny Unbound
4/12/91	1	2	1/10	***	Runaway Jim
4/15/91	1	2	7/11	My Sweet One	The Lizards
4/19/91	2	2	5/10	Golgi Apparatus	Destiny Unbound
4/20/91	1	1	6/11	My Sweet One	Esther
4/21/91	1	2	3/11	Fee	Col. Forbin's A
4/22/91	1	2	4/10	Uncle Pen	Destiny Unbound
4/25/91	1	1	2/11	Sweet Adeline	Runaway Jim
4/27/91	1	1	5/12	Cavern	My Sweet One
5/2/91	1	1	5/11	Bouncing	Col. Forbin's A
5/3/91	1	2	4/9	The Sloth	Runaway Jim
5/10/91	3	1	6/10	The Sloth	Bathtub Gin
5/12/91	2	1	6/11	The Lizards	Destiny Unbound
5/16/91	1	2	4/9	Bouncing	The Squirmin
5/17/91	1	2	4/9	Rocky Top	Fluffhead
5/19/91	2	1	2/8	Divided Sky	Chalk Dust Tor
7/11/91	1	1	8/8	The Lizards	***
7/12/91	1	1	6/12	Reba	Bathtub Gin
7/13/91	1	E	1/1	***	***
7/14/91	1	3	2/10	AC/DC Bag	Esther
7/15/91	1	1	3/14	Suzy Greenberg	Dinner and a
7/18/91	1	2	6/8	The Lizards	I Didn't Know
7/19/91	1	1	2/10	Golgi Apparatus	Bouncing
7/20/91	1	1	7/10	Suzy Greenberg	Bathtub Gin
7/21/91	1	1	7/11	The Lizards	Bouncing
7/23/91	1	2	5/10	The Lizards	Tweezer
7/24/91	1	1	7/10	Bathtub Gin	Cavern
7/25/91	1	2	1/13	***	Golgi Apparat
7/27/91	2	1	13/16	I Didn't Know	Mike's Song
9/25/91	2	1	8/11	It's Ice	Caravan
9/26/91	1	2	5/11	Sparkle	Destiny Unbound
9/28/91	2	1	1/11	***	Bouncing
9/29/91	1	1	6/10	Poor Heart	Destiny Unbound
10/2/91	2	2	1/9	***	You Enjoy My
10/3/91	1	2	6/11	Esther	Destiny Unbound
10/6/91	2	2	4/10	Fee	Destiny Unbound
10/10/91	1	1	6/11	Bouncing	Runaway Jim
10/11/91	1	1	1/10	***	My Sweet One
10/13/91	2	1	4/13	Reba	Col. Forbin's A
10/15/91	1	1	7/10	Reba	Destiny Unbound
10/17/91	1	1	2/10	Memories	Bouncing
10/19/91	2	1	1/10	***	Suzy Greenber
10/23/91	1	1	3/11	Reba	Destiny Unbound
10/27/91	2	2	10/13	Tela	Destiny Unbound
10/30/91	2	2	7/11	Wilson	Bouncing
10/31/91	1	2	1/14	***	Costume Contest
11/1/91	1	1	3/11	Sparkle	Destiny Unbound
11/2/91	1	2	9/11	Walk Away	Runaway Jim
11/7/91	1	1	8/11	You Enjoy Myself	Runaway Jim
11/8/91	1	2	1/11	Tube	Dinner and a
11/9/91	1	2	7/10	Tela	Terrapin
11/13/91	3	1	1/10	***	Runaway Jim
11/15/91	2	2	9/14	Tube	Destiny Unbound
11/16/91	1	1	1/11	***	Uncle Pen
11/20/91	2	2	6/8	Tela	Bike
11/22/91	2	2	3/10	My Sweet One	Bathtub Gin
11/23/91	1	2	9/13	Eliza	Fee
11/24/91	1	1	4/9	Stash	Fluffhead
12/4/91	2	1	3/11	Reba	Runaway Jim
12/6/91	2	1	7/9	Magilla	Guelah Papyrus
12/31/91	2	2	6/10	Runaway Jim	Reba
3/7/92	2	1	9/11	The Mango Song	Rift
3/13/92	3	2	5/12	Silent in Morni	The Lizards
3/19/92	3	1	1/12	***	Rift
3/21/92	2	1	1/12	***	Runaway Jim
3/22/92	1	1	4/4	Foam	***
3/24/92	1	1	12/13	The Famous Mockingbi	David Bowie
3/26/92	2	1	1/10	***	Runaway Jim
3/28/92	2	1	7/10	Bouncing	David Bowie
3/30/92	1	1	1/11	***	Llama
4/1/92	2	1	10/12	I Didn't Know	David Bowie
4/3/92	1	1	1/11	***	Poor Heart
4/5/92	2	2	8/12	Weigh	David Bowie
4/8/92	3	1	1/11	***	Sparkle
4/15/92	3	2	4/8	Reba	NICU
4/17/92	2	1	10/13	Bouncing	David Bowie
4/23/92	5	2	1/13	***	Poor Heart
4/24/92	1	1	6/11	The Sloth	Fluffhead
4/29/92	2	2	1/11	***	Possum
5/1/92	2	1	4/12	Poor Heart	NICU
5/3/92	2	1	1/10	***	Possum
5/7/92	3	2	1/12	***	Sparkle
5/10/92	3	1	1/10	***	Suzy Greenber
5/12/92	1	2	1/9	***	Bathtub Gin
5/17/92	4	1	1/11	***	Llama
6/16/92	2	1	1/7	***	Suzy Greenber
7/11/92	9	1	1/11	***	Runaway Jim
7/14/92	2	1	1/12	***	Rift
7/16/92	2	2	3/13	Weigh	Fluffhead
8/15/92	17	1	1/5	***	Sparkle
8/17/92	1	1	3/11	Poor Heart	Reba
8/19/92	1	1	2/7	Chalk Dust Torture	Runaway Jim
8/24/92	3	1	5/7	Tweezer	Reba
8/27/92	2	1	3/7	Bouncing	Horn
8/30/92	3	1	2/7	Uncle Pen	Reba
11/21/92	4	1	1/11	***	Runaway Jim
11/25/92	3	1	3/11	Poor Heart	Fee
12/1/92	4	1	1/12	***	My Sweet One
12/5/92	4	1	1/12	***	Chalk Dust Tor
12/12/92	6	1	6/11	Reba	Split Open and
12/30/92	4	1	1/14	***	Sparkle
2/11/93	9	2	1/12	***	Wilson
2/17/93	4	2	2/11	Axilla	David Bowie
3/5/93	12	2	1/11	***	Chalk Dust Tor
3/13/93	5	1	1/11	***	Funky Bitch
3/17/93	3	1	1/11	***	Runaway Jim
3/24/93	5	2	1/12	***	Split Open and
3/28/93	4	1	1/11	***	Funky Bitch
4/3/93	5	1	1/10	***	Rift
4/17/93	7	2	3/11	Reba	Halley's Comet
4/25/93	7	1	1/11	***	Possum
7/17/93	15	1	1/11	***	Runaway Jim
7/29/93	9	1	5/10	Rift	Fast Enough for You
8/12/93	10	2	2/10	Also Sprach	Tweezer
8/15/93	3	2	4/11	The Lizards	Bouncing
8/21/93	4	1	8/10	Sparkle	I Didn't Know
4/4/94	9	2	4/11	Buried Alive	Julius
4/15/94	9	2	5/10	Suzy Greenberg	Julius
4/25/94	9	1	1/10	***	Runaway Jim
5/4/94	6	2	5/9	Buried Alive	Julius
6/29/94	35	2	1/8	***	Poor Heart
7/6/94	6	2	1/10	***	Poor Heart
10/16/94	16	2	1/9	***	Poor Heart
11/14/94	17	1	6/9	Bouncing	Maze
12/2/94	13	2	5/8	Julius	Gumbo
12/3/94	1	2	6/10	Slave	Touch Me

Has not been played in the last 418 shows.

The Lizards

DATE	GAP	SET	POS.	SONG BEFORE	SONG AFTER
1/27/88	36	3	2/8	Fee	Suzy Greenber
2/7/88	1	2	7/9	Possum	The Famous Mockingbi
2/8/88	1	2	5/6	Divided Sky	Run Like Antel
2/24/88	1	1	4/11	I Didn't Know	Wilson
2/26/88	1	2	1/9	***	David Bowie
3/11/88	1	1	11/12	Corrine Corrina	David Bowie
3/12/88	1	2	3/11	McGrupp	Tela
3/21/88	1	1	8/15	Timber (Jerry)	Fire
3/31/88	1	1	8/14	Alumni Blues	Col. Forbin's A
4/22/88	2	2	3/13	Golgi Apparatus	Fee
5/14/88	1	1	6/11	You Enjoy Myself	BBFCFM
5/15/88	1	1	8/11	Shaggy Dog	Sneakin' Sally
5/21/88	1	2	3/9	Possum	Timber (Jerry)
6/15/88	2	2	1/9	***	AC/DC Bag
6/20/88	2	1	6/11	AC/DC Bag	Halley's Comet
6/21/88	1	1	6/9	The Curtain	Col. Forbin's A
6/24/88	1	1	1/11	***	Possum
7/12/88	2	1	2/8	Cities	Sneakin' Sally
7/23/88	1	1	7/13	Weekapaug Groove	On Your Way Down
7/24/88	1	2	4/8	La Grange	Alumni Blues
9/12/88	7	2	3/10	Satin Doll	T.M.W.S.I.Y.
9/24/88	3	2	2/7	David Bowie	Walk Away
10/31/88	2	1	5/12	Suzy Greenberg	Time Loves a Hero
11/3/88	1	2	3/9	Walk Away	Shaggy Dog
11/5/88	1	2	4/11	Bold as Love	AC/DC Bag
11/11/88	1	2	7/8	Bold as Love	Whipping Post
12/2/88	1	2	4/8	Alumni Blues	AC/DC Bag
12/10/88	1	1	4/12	David Bowie	Foam
1/26/89	3	1	5/10	You Enjoy Myself	Take the A-Trn
2/7/89	2	2	4/9	AC/DC Bag	Timber (Jerry)
3/3/89	5	2	9/12	The Famous Mockingbi	Split Open and

DATE	GAP	SET	POS.	SONG BEFORE	SONG AFTER
3/4/89	1	2	3/5	Fluffhead	Run Like Antel
3/14/89	2	3	4/7	Alumni Blues	La Grange
4/20/89	4	2	5/10	Split Open and Melt	Mike's Song
4/27/89	1	1	7/8	Alumni Blues	Whipping Post
4/30/89	1	1	4/9	McGrupp	Divided Sky
5/1/89	1	1	7/9	Split Open and Melt	Golgi Apparat
5/9/89	3	2	11/14	I Didn't Know	Bold as Love
5/13/89	2	2	3/7	Bold As Love	Harry Hood
5/20/89	1	1	4/8	You Enjoy Myself	Wilson
6/23/89	5	1	10/11	Weekapaug Groove	Run Like Antel
8/17/89	2	2	6/6	You Enjoy Myself	***
8/19/89	1	1	10/13	The Mango Song	Mike's Song
8/26/89	2	E	2/3	Contact	La Grange
10/1/89	4	2	11/11	Split Open and Melt	***
10/7/89	2	2	5/9	Happy Birthday	AC/DC Bag
10/12/89	1	2	7/7	Walk Away	***
10/21/89	4	1	8/10	AC/DC Bag	Dog Gone Dog
10/21/89	0	E	1/1	***	***
10/26/89	2	1	8/11	Wilson	Mike's Song
10/31/89	2	2	7/8	Alumni Blues	Highway to Hell
11/9/89	3	2	6/9	Punch You in the Eye	Mike's Song
11/10/89	1	2	10/12	The Sloth	If I Only Had a Brai
11/18/89	3	1	4/11	AC/DC Bag	My Sweet One
11/30/89	1	1	7/11	Foam	My Sweet One
12/1/89	1	2	5/10	Walk Away	Mike's Song
12/7/89	2	2	6/11	Walk Away	Run Like Antel
12/9/89	2	1	3/10	La Grange	Foam
12/16/89	2	1	7/9	Weekapaug Groove	In a Hole
12/29/89	1	1	6/10	AC/DC Bag	Lawn Boy
12/31/89	2	1	7/9	Bathtub Gin	Satin Doll
1/20/90	1	1	7/8	Caravan	Run Like Antel
1/29/90	3	1	1/10	***	If I Only Had a Brai
2/16/90	5	2	7/7	Ballad - Curtis Loew	***
2/22/90	2	1	8/9	Caravan	David Bowie
2/24/90	2	E	1/2	***	Caravan
2/25/90	1	2	4/6	Makisupa Policeman	Fluffhead
3/1/90	1	2	1/7	***	Foam
3/3/90	2	1	6/12	The Squirming Coil	The Oh Kee Pa
3/7/90	1	1	5/6	Caravan	David Bowie
3/8/90	1	2	7/12	I Didn't Know	Mike's Song
3/17/90	4	1	9/10	Donna Lee	Run Like Antel
3/28/90	1	2	9/16	Jesus Just Left	Split Open and
4/4/90	1	2	4/8	Weekapaug Groove	Uncle Pen
4/5/90	1	1	8/9	You Enjoy Myself	Fire
4/7/90	2	1	5/12	The Squirming Coil	Walk Away
4/8/90	1	2	9/10	Walk Away	Slave
4/12/90	2	2	6/11	Tweezer	Runaway Jim
4/21/90	6	2	9/9	Tweezer	***
4/29/90	5	1	12/13	Love You	Fire
5/4/90	2	1	10/10	You Enjoy Myself	***
5/11/90	4	2	3/7	AC/DC Bag	Tweezer
5/15/90	2	1	12/12	The Squirming Coil	***
5/19/90	1	1	7/8	You Enjoy Myself	Highway to Hell
5/23/90	1	2	4/11	Tweezer	La Grange
6/2/90	5	1	6/9	Possum	Fire
6/5/90	1	2	7/9	My Sweet One	You Enjoy My
6/7/90	1	1	8/9	You Enjoy Myself	Good Time Ba
6/16/90	3	2	7/8	You Enjoy Myself	Run Like Antel
9/13/90	1	E	1/2	***	La Grange
9/14/90	2	2	7/10	Caravan	Destiny Unbound
9/22/90	5	2	8/10	Stash	Lawn Boy
9/28/90	1	1	8/10	The Squirming Coil	The Asse Festival
10/4/90	3	1	6/10	The Squirming Coil	Destiny Unbound
10/7/90	3	2	6/8	I Didn't Know	Good Time Ba
10/30/90	4	3	2/5	Paul and Silas	Good Time Ba
10/31/90	1	1	4/11	The Squirming Coil	Stash
11/2/90	1	2	7/9	You Enjoy Myself	I Didn't Know
11/8/90	3	1	3/12	Possum	Foam

DATE	GAP	SET	POS.	SONG BEFORE	SONG AFTER
11/10/90	1	1	8/11	Buried Alive	Mike's Song
11/16/90	1	2	8/11	Paul and Silas	Runaway Jim
11/24/90	2	1	8/11	The Squirming Coil	The Oh Kee Pa
11/30/90	2	2	5/10	Stash	Gumbo
12/29/90	5	2	3/10	Runaway Jim	Cavern
2/7/91	5	2	11/14	Love You	The Sloth
2/8/91	1	2	10/11	Bouncing	Run Like Antel
2/21/91	7	1	7/11	Llama	My Sweet One
2/26/91	1	2	9/12	Possum	Mike's Song
2/28/91	2	2	7/7	Love You	***
3/9/91	4	2	9/13	David Bowie	Love You
3/15/91	1	2	9/12	AC/DC Bag	Mike's Song
3/17/91	2	1	11/12	Stash	David Bowie
3/23/91	2	2	7/11	Tweezer	Uncle Pen
4/3/91	5	1	3/10	Llama	Foam
4/5/91	2	2	3/9	Stash	The Sloth
4/11/91	2	2	7/14	T.M.W.S.I.Y. Reprise	Split Open and
4/15/91	2	2	8/11	The Landlady	Possum
4/19/91	3	1	5/12	Cavern	Stash
4/22/91	3	2	9/10	My Sweet One	Highway to Hell
4/27/91	2	1	9/12	Llama	Suzy Greenber
5/3/91	2	1	11/12	Tweezer	Sweet Adeline
5/10/91	3	1	9/10	Buried Alive	Possum
5/12/91	2	1	5/11	Stash	The Landlady
5/16/91	1	2	8/9	My Sweet One	Good Time Ba
5/18/91	2	2	10/10	Terrapin	***
7/11/91	2	1	7/8	Stash	The Landlady
7/13/91	2	2	6/9	Paul and Silas	Stash
7/15/91	2	1	11/14	Flat Fee	Cavern
7/18/91	1	2	5/8	Split Open and Melt	The Landlady
7/21/91	3	1	6/11	Split Open and Melt	The Landlady
7/23/91	2	1	4/10	Cavern	The Landlady
7/25/91	2	2	7/13	Jesus Just Left	Gumbo
7/26/91	1	2	9/10	Tweezer	Tweezer Repri
8/3/91	2	3	6/8	My Sweet One	Buried Alive
9/26/91	2	1	8/10	Guelah Papyrus	Foam
9/28/91	2	2	7/12	Lawn Boy	Poor Heart
10/11/91	8	1	7/10	You Enjoy Myself	Llama
10/18/91	5	1	7/9	Llama	Sweet Adeline
10/24/91	3	2	4/11	Weekapaug Groove	Uncle Pen
10/30/91	3	1	3/7	Brother	Possum
11/14/91	10	2	10/11	If I Only Had a Brai	Tweezer
11/22/91	6	2	9/10	Llama	You Enjoy My
12/4/91	4	2	8/11	Sparkle	Chalk Dust Tor
12/7/91	3	2	6/8	Brother	Terrapin
12/31/91	1	1	5/10	Stash	Guelah Papyrus
3/11/92	3	2	4/11	The Sloth	Bathtub Gin
3/13/92	2	2	6/12	The Landlady	My Mind's Got A Mind
3/20/92	4	1	8/10	Maze	Mound
3/26/92	5	2	10/13	My Friend My Friend	Cavern
3/31/92	4	2	7/13	Stash	Cavern
4/4/92	3	1	9/10	Sparkle	I Didn't Know
4/7/92	3	2	7/11	My Friend My Friend	Maze
4/13/92	3	1	4/10	Stash	NICU
4/16/92	2	3	2/12	Llama	Mike's Song
4/18/92	2	2	8/16	Manteca Reprise	Mound
4/23/92	4	2	6/13	Weekapaug Groove	NICU
4/29/92	3	2	6/11	Llama	Mike's Song
5/1/92	2	2	10/13	Mound	Llama
5/16/92	12	1	9/11	Golgi Apparatus	Cavern
7/10/92	11	1	7/10	Golgi Apparatus	Cavern
7/15/92	4	1	11/12	Chalk Dust Torture	Run Like Antel
7/26/92	9	1	6/7	Split Open and Melt	Llama
11/20/92	22	1	9/12	Stash	Memories
11/25/92	4	2	5/9	You Enjoy Myself	Tweezer
12/2/92	5	1	7/10	Stash	Sparkle
12/5/92	3	1	7/12	Split Open and Melt	Mound
12/8/92	3	2	7/15	It's Ice	Run Like Antel
12/11/92	2	1	5/11	Stash	Chalk Dust Tor
12/28/92	3	2	6/9	You Enjoy Myself	Bike
2/4/93	5	1	8/11	Stash	Sample in a Ja
2/9/93	4	2	10/12	Stash	Bike
2/11/93	2	2	11/12	Love You	Cavern

DATE	GAP	SET	POS.	SONG BEFORE	SONG AFTER
2/13/93	2	2	5/11	Tweezer	Llama
2/18/93	3	2	3/12	Stash	Punch You in
2/21/93	3	2	6/10	Stash	Bathtub Gin
2/23/93	2	2	4/13	Stash	Punch You in
3/2/93	4	2	4/12	Tweezer	Llama
3/8/93	4	2	9/10	You Enjoy Myself	Amazing Grce
3/13/93	3	2	3/13	Tweezer	It's Ice
3/19/93	5	2	5/10	Sample in a Jar	Mike's Song
3/22/93	2	2	3/13	It's Ice	Tela
3/28/93	5	1	5/11	Split Open and Melt	The Sloth
4/2/93	4	2	10/13	Weekapaug Groove	Big Ball Jam
4/16/93	7	2	4/13	Maze	Mike's Song
4/22/93	5	2	5/10	Tweezer	Big Ball Jam
4/27/93	4	2	5/10	Maze	Big Ball Jam
5/2/93	4	2	4/10	You Enjoy Myself	Big Ball Jam
5/7/93	4	1	7/11	Manteca	Horn
7/15/93	4	2	9/11	Faht	Walk Away
7/25/93	8	2	7/10	Maze	Purple Rain
7/28/93	2	2	5/10	Run Like an Antelope	Mound
8/3/93	5	2	6/9	You Enjoy Myself	Sparkle
8/12/93	6	2	4/7		The Sloth
8/15/93	3	2	3/11	Tweezer	The Landlady
8/26/93	7	2	6/8	Jesus Just Left	Tea Tray Song
12/28/93	2	2	4/9	My Friend My Friend	The Sloth
12/31/93	3	3	4/9	Split Open and Melt	Sparkle
4/6/94	3	1	5/9	Stash	Sample in a Ja
4/13/94	5	1	4/8	Stash	Julius
4/16/94	3	2	4/9	Tweezer	Julius
4/21/94	4	1	6/9	Split Open and Melt	Down with Dis
5/2/94	8	2	5/9	Golgi Apparatus	Julius
5/12/94	7	1	9/10	Bathtub Gin	Sample in a Ja
5/14/94	2	2	10/11	Fast Enough for You	Cavern
5/19/94	3	2	6/10	Weekapaug Groove	Julius
5/27/94	7	2	5/12	Reba	Julius
6/10/94	4	1	7/9	David Bowie	Cavern
6/19/94	7	1	3/9	Julius	Axilla (Part II)
6/26/94	6	1	3/3	Llama	Tela
7/3/94	5	2	2/10	Split Open and Melt	Bouncing
7/8/94	3	1	3/11	NO2	Tela
7/16/94	6	1	5/10	Stash	Cavern
10/12/94	5	1	6/9	Split Open and Melt	Guelah Papyrus
10/21/94	7	1	7/9	Stash	Dog Faced Boy
10/25/94	3	1	8/9	Split Open and Melt	Sample in a Ja
10/28/94	3	2	5/12	David Bowie	Peaches en Regalia
11/2/94	3	2	6/7	Possum	Sample in a Ja
11/13/94	4	2	3/8	Divided Sky	Tweezer
11/16/94	2	1	6/11	Axilla (Part II)	Stash
11/22/94	5	E	1/1	***	***
11/26/94	3	2	4/6	Sweet Adeline	Sample in a Ja
12/2/94	4	1	6/8	It's Ice	Stash
12/8/94	5	1	9/10	Simple	While My Guitar Gent
12/10/94	2	1	4/8	Stash	Sample in a Ja
12/29/94	2	2	5/7	Halley's Comet	Cracklin' Rosi
6/13/95	8	2	2/7	David Bowie	Axilla (Part II)
6/23/95	8	2	2/7	Runaway Jim	The Wedge
6/30/95	6	1	6/9	The Wedge	Mound
7/3/95	3	2	6/10	AC/DC Bag	BBFCFM
10/2/95	5	2	9/10	Hello My Baby	Run Like Antel
10/6/95	3	1	8/9	Free	Sample in a Ja
10/13/95	4	2	7/10	Keyboard Cavalry	While My Guitar Gent
10/15/95	2	2	4/8	Tweezer	Sample in a Ja
10/21/95	4	1	8/12	Kung	Strange Design
10/28/95	5	1	6/10	Sample in a Jar	Billy Breathes
11/9/95	3	2	3/10	Julius	Bathtub Gin
11/22/95	10	1	8/10	Taste That Surrounds	Sample in a Ja
11/30/95	5	1	9/10	Fast Enough for You	Fire
12/5/95	4	1	4/8	Taste That Surrounds	Free
12/12/95	5	2	4/6	Down with Disease	Simple
12/17/95	4	1	8/9	Stash	Chalk Dust Tor
12/31/95	4	2	3/8	Jam	Axilla (Part II)

DATE	GAP	SET	POS.	SONG BEFORE	SONG AFTER
7/11/96	9	2	5/8	Maze	Terrapin
8/6/96	15	1	6/9	Theme From the Botto	Dinner and a
8/13/96	4	2	2/11	AC/DC Bag	Mike's Song
8/17/96	3	1	5/10	Cars Trucks Buses	Sample in a Ja
10/17/96	2	2	6/8	Free	Star Spangled Banner
10/23/96	5	2	4/8	Tweezer	Llama
11/2/96	6	1	7/9	Stash	Free
11/9/96	5	1	9/10	Split Open and Melt	Character Zer
12/4/96	16	1	10/11	Character Zero	David Bowie
12/29/96	3	2	4/10	Bathtub Gin	You Enjoy My
2/21/97	9	1	4/6	Down with Disease	Crosseyed and Painle
8/8/97	39	1	3/7	Gumbo	Dirt
12/5/97	22	2	5/7	Slave	Loving Cup
4/4/98	13	2	5/6	Ghost	David Bowie
7/29/98	21	2	4/7	AC/DC Bag	Tube
8/9/98	8	1	3/9	Bathtub Gin	The Moma Dance
10/30/98	10	1	9/10	Guelah Papyrus	Cavern
11/18/98	12	2	2/7	Wolfman's Brother	The Moma Dance
7/12/99	21	2	5/6	David Bowie	Guyute
8/1/99	15	2	8/9	The Wedge	You Enjoy My
9/24/99	12	2	4/6	Wolfman's Brother	Sand
12/8/99	18	2	5/6	Dog Faced Boy	You Enjoy My
6/15/00	19	2	2/4	Down with Disease	Bike
7/4/00	11	1	7/11	Stash	T.M.W.S.I.Y.
7/14/00	7	3	6/7	Sand	Weekapaug Gr
9/15/00	7	2	2/5	Piper	Tube
9/25/00	7	1	3/8	Down With Disease	Tweezer

Has not been played in the last 8 shows.

The Maker

DATE	GAP	SET	POS.	SONG BEFORE	SONG AFTER
10/15/94	669	E	2/2	Drums Jam	***

Has not been played in the last 450 shows.

The Man Who Stepped Into Yesterday

DATE	GAP	SET	POS.	SONG BEFORE	SONG AFTER
5/11/87	23	1	8/12	Peaches en Regalia	Avenu Malken
8/29/87	5	2	11/13	Ya Mar	Avenu Malken
8/29/87	0	2	13/13	Avenu Malken	***
9/21/87	2	1	1/11	***	Avenu Malken
10/31/87	3	2	1/17	***	Avenu Malken
11/18/87	1	1	2/12	Slave	Avenu Malken
2/7/88	3	3	2/8	Suzy Greenberg	Avenu Malken
2/26/88	3	1	4/13	You Enjoy Myself	Avenu Malken
7/24/88	19	3	1/6	***	Avenu Malken
9/12/88	7	2	4/10	The Lizards	Avenu Malken
2/24/89	19	1	1/10	***	Avenu Malken
8/19/89	25	1	3/13	Suzy Greenberg	Avenu Malken
8/26/89	2	3	1/5	***	Avenu Malken
10/13/89	8	2	2/8	Bike	Avenu Malken
12/3/89	17	2	1/14	***	Avenu Malken
3/9/90	28	1	1/11	***	Avenu Malken
3/11/90	2	1	4/13	Suzy Greenberg	Avenu Malken
5/4/90	21	2	3/10	Sweet Adeline	Avenu Malken
6/9/90	17	2	3/14	Harry Hood	Avenu Malken
6/9/90	0	2	5/14	Avenu Malken	La Grange
2/7/91	40	2	2/14	Chalk Dust Torture	Avenu Malken
2/9/91	2	1	3/12	The Sloth	Avenu Malken
2/28/91	9	1	9/13	Cavern	Avenu Malken
3/9/91	4	2	1/13	***	The Oh Kee Pa
3/16/91	3	1	1/14	***	Avenu Malken
4/11/91	12	2	4/14	Llama	Avenu Malken
4/20/91	6	2	7/13	Cavern	Avenu Malken
4/27/91	4	2	3/13	Possum	Avenu Malken
5/3/91	2	1	4/12	Chalk Dust Torture	Avenu Malken
5/17/91	7	1	9/17	Happy Birthday	Avenu Malken
7/11/91	3	2	3/10	Cavern	Avenu Malken
7/13/91	2	1	8/13	Alumni Blues	Avenu Malken
7/20/91	5	2	8/12	Stash	Avenu Malken
7/26/91	5	1	7/12	Cavern	Avenu Malken
7/27/91	1	1	8/16	Stash	Avenu Malken
10/6/91	11	1	8/13	AC/DC Bag	Avenu Malken
10/24/91	10	1	9/12	I Didn't Know	Avenu Malken
11/2/91	6	2	3/11	Run Like an Antelope	Avenu Malken
11/21/91	12	2	7/10	Tweezer	Avenu Malken
3/26/92	23	2	6/13	Brother	Avenu Malken
4/8/92	11	2	4/15	David Bowie	Avenu Malken
4/18/92	6	2	11/16	Llama	Avenu Malken
5/18/92	23	2	3/13	Llama	Avenu Malken
7/16/92	14	2	5/13	Fluffhead	Avenu Malken
11/28/92	36	2	4/12	Tweezer	Avenu Malken
12/6/92	7	2	8/13	You Enjoy Myself	Avenu Malken
12/13/92	6	2	7/14	Chalk Dust Torture	Avenu Malken
12/30/92	3	2	5/12	You Enjoy Myself	Avenu Malken
2/4/93	3	2	4/13	Mike's Song	Avenu Malken
3/27/93	38	2	6/14	Chalk Dust Torture	Avenu Malken
4/20/93	15	2	5/12	Big Ball Jam	Avenu Malken
7/22/93	23	2	9/11	Paul and Silas	Avenu Malken
8/7/93	12	2	5/12	Mike's Song	Avenu Malken
4/18/94	32	2	8/13	Mike's Song	Avenu Malken
5/14/94	19	2	5/11	Weekapaug Groove	Avenu Malken
6/22/94	23	2	12/20	Weekapaug Groove	Avenu Malken
7/1/94	7	2	5/11	Down with Disease	Avenu Malken
7/14/94	9	1	4/11	Stash	Avenu Malken
10/16/94	11	1	6/10	Split Open and Melt	Avenu Malken
10/29/94	10	2	2/11	Down with Disease	Avenu Malken
11/19/94	11	1	6/11	Paul and Silas	Avenu Malken
6/30/95	40	2	4/10	Ha Ha Ha	Avenu Malken
10/3/95	9	1	7/11	Free	Avenu Malken
11/9/95	20	2	5/10	Bathtub Gin	Avenu Malken
12/30/95	31	1	9/13	It's Ice	Avenu Malken
10/25/96	40	2	4/12	Timber (Jerry)	Avenu Malken
11/15/96	14	2	5/11	Split Open and Melt	Avenu Malken
12/28/96	14	2	5/10	Digital Delay Loop J	Avenu Malken
11/29/97	67	1	4/12	Simple	Avenu Malken
7/31/98	39	2	4/9	If I Could	Avenu Malken
11/9/98	24	2	2/7	Bathtub Gin	Avenu Malken
7/24/99	35	1	4/9	Jam	Avenu Malken
10/3/99	25	2	3/8	Possum	Avenu Malken
12/4/99	8	2	5/9	Farmhouse	Avenu Malken
7/4/00	33	1	8/11	The Lizards	Avenu Malken
9/20/00	17	1	6/9	Simple	Avenu Malken

Has not been played in the last 12 shows.

The Man Who Stepped Into Yesterday Reprise

DATE	GAP	SET	POS.	SONG BEFORE	SONG AFTER
5/11/87	23	1	10/12	Avenu Malkenu	Makisupa Policeman
9/21/87	7	1	3/11	Avenu Malkenu	Clod
10/31/87	3	2	3/17	Avenu Malkenu	Peaches en Regalia
11/18/87	1	1	4/12	Avenu Malkenu	Flat Fee
2/7/88	3	3	4/8	Avenu Malkenu	Clod
2/26/88	3	1	6/13	Avenu Malkenu	AC/DC Bag
2/24/89	45	1	3/10	Avenu Malkenu	The Curtain
3/11/90	82	1	6/13	Avenu Malkenu	Reba
2/7/91	78	2	4/14	Avenu Malkenu	Tweezer
2/9/91	2	1	5/12	Avenu Malkenu	Runaway Jim
2/28/91	9	1	11/13	Avenu Malkenu	My Sweet One
3/16/91	7	1	3/14	Avenu Malkenu	Golgi Apparat
4/11/91	12	2	6/14	Avenu Malkenu	The Lizards
4/20/91	6	2	9/13	Avenu Malkenu	Tweezer
4/27/91	4	2	5/13	Avenu Malkenu	Mike's Song
5/3/91	2	1	6/12	Avenu Malkenu	Divided Sky
5/17/91	7	1	11/17	Avenu Malkenu	Stash
7/11/91	3	2	5/10	Avenu Malkenu	Mike's Song
7/13/91	2	1	10/13	Avenu Malkenu	Split Open and
7/20/91	5	2	10/12	Avenu Malkenu	You Enjoy My
7/26/91	5	1	9/12	Avenu Malkenu	Buried Alive
7/27/91	1	1	10/16	Avenu Malkenu	Possum
10/6/91	11	1	10/13	Avenu Malkenu	Brother
10/24/91	10	1	11/12	Avenu Malkenu	David Bowie
11/2/91	6	2	5/11	Avenu Malkenu	Sparkle
11/21/91	12	2	9/10	Avenu Malkenu	Runaway Jim
3/26/92	23	2	8/13	Avenu Malkenu	My Friend My
4/8/92	11	2	6/15	Avenu Malkenu	My Sweet One
4/18/92	6	2	13/16	Avenu Malkenu	Harry Hood
5/18/92	23	2	5/13	Avenu Malkenu	Mike's Song
7/16/92	14	2	7/13	Avenu Malkenu	Llama
11/28/92	36	2	7/12	Maze	Bouncing
12/6/92	7	2	10/13	Avenu Malkenu	Lengthwise
12/13/92	6	2	9/14	Avenu Malkenu	My Sweet One
12/30/92	3	2	7/12	Avenu Malkenu	Possum
2/4/93	3	2	6/13	Avenu Malkenu	Weekapaug Gr
3/27/93	38	2	8/14	Avenu Malkenu	Mike's Song
4/20/93	15	2	7/12	Avenu Malkenu	My Friend My
4/18/94	67	2	10/13	Avenu Malkenu	Down with Dis
5/14/94	19	2	7/11	Avenu Malkenu	Punch You in
6/22/94	23	2	14/20	Avenu Malkenu	Digital Delay Loop J
7/1/94	7	2	7/11	Avenu Malkenu	Possum
7/14/94	9	1	6/11	Avenu Malkenu	Scent of a Mul
10/16/94	11	1	8/10	Avenu Malkenu	Axilla
10/29/94	10	2	4/11	Avenu Malkenu	Sparks
10/3/95	60	1	9/11	Avenu Malkenu	Sample in a Ja
11/9/95	20	2	7/10	Avenu Malkenu	Life on Mars
12/30/95	31	1	11/13	Avenu Malkenu	Divided Sky
10/25/96	40	2	6/12	Avenu Malkenu	NICU
11/29/97	95	1	6/12	Avenu Malkenu	The Sloth
11/9/98	63	2	4/7	Avenu Malkenu	The Moma Dance
7/24/99	35	1	6/9	Avenu Malkenu	Jam
12/4/99	33	2	7/9	Avenu Malkenu	When Circus Comes
7/4/00	33	1	10/11	Avenu Malkenu	Julius

Has not been played in the last 29 shows.

The Mango Song

DATE	GAP	SET	POS.	SONG BEFORE	SONG AFTER
3/30/89	91	2	1/8	***	Mike's Song
5/26/89	13	2	2/6	David Bowie	Split Open and
5/28/89	2	2	15/16	Split Open and Melt	Harry Hood
8/17/89	3	2	3/6	AC/DC Bag	Fee
8/19/89	1	1	9/13	Bold As Love	The Lizards
2/1/91	132	2	4/5	The Landlady	Cavern
2/3/91	2	2	5/9	Cavern	Split Open and
2/7/91	1	1	5/10	The Landlady	Split Open and
2/8/91	1	2	2/11	Llama	Cavern
2/9/91	1	1	1/12	***	The Sloth
2/14/91	1	1	7/11	Cavern	Stash
2/15/91	1	1	7/11	Buried Alive	The Sloth
2/16/91	1	1	9/12	Llama	Mike's Song
4/16/91	28	1	5/9	Cavern	The Oh Kee Pa
7/19/91	25	2	7/8	Tweezer	BBFCFM
9/27/91	11	2	5/10	Split Open and Melt	Dinner and a
10/11/91	9	2	5/9	David Bowie	The Sloth
10/23/91	7	2	5/10	Golgi Apparatus	Split Open and
10/27/91	2	1	3/10	Chalk Dust Torture	Buried Alive
11/8/91	7	1	8/11	Guelah Papyrus	Brother
11/14/91	5	1	9/11	Brother	Golgi Apparat
11/19/91	3	2	6/11	Weekapaug Groove	The Sloth
11/21/91	2	2	4/10	It's Ice	Uncle Pen
11/24/91	3	2	4/8	Cavern	Chalk Dust Tor
12/4/91	2	2	3/11	Stash	Mike's Song
12/7/91	3	1	10/11	Cavern	Run Like Antel
3/7/92	3	1	8/11	Maze	The Landlady
3/20/92	7	2	6/12	The Sloth	Cavern
3/24/92	3	2	6/13	Guelah Papyrus	Brother
4/3/92	8	2	6/9	You Enjoy Myself	Llama
4/19/92	12	2	9/13	Tube	Llama
4/24/92	4	2	8/12	Weekapaug Groove	Horn
5/3/92	6	2	9/14	Weekapaug Groove	Cracklin' Rosi
5/17/92	11	1	9/11	Stash	Poor Heart
7/24/93	148	1	8/10	Stash	Bouncing
8/11/93	13	1	7/10	My Friend My Friend	Stash
8/20/93	7	E	1/2	***	Freebird
4/24/94	27	2	3/9	David Bowie	Julius
5/19/94	17	1	9/10	Down with Disease	Cavern
6/18/94	17	1	5/10	Maze	Down with Dis
6/23/94	4	2	3/8	David Bowie	Axilla (Part II)
6/25/94	2	1	6/10	Stash	Sample in a Ja
7/1/94	4	1	6/10	Stash	It's Ice
7/13/94	8	1	5/11	Foam	Down with Dis
10/21/94	15	1	4/9	Foam	The Old Home
10/25/94	3	2	3/11	Simple	Weekapaug Gr
11/2/94	6	2	3/7	Tweezer	Axilla (Part II)

DATE	GAP	SET	POS.	SONG BEFORE	SONG AFTER
11/13/94	4	2	5/8	Tweezer	BBFCFM
11/25/94	9	2	6/8	Weekapaug Groove	Purple Rain
12/6/94	8	2	7/12	Simple	Weekapaug Gr
12/28/94	5	2	4/9	Mike's Song	Weekapaug Gr
6/19/95	14	2	3/8	David Bowie	Loving Cup
10/7/95	21	1	6/9	Possum	Acoustic Army
10/29/95	15	2	3/10	David Bowie	It's Ice
12/1/95	18	2	4/9	Weekapaug Groove	Wilson
12/11/95	7	2	3/8	David Bowie	Taste That Surrounds
12/17/95	5	1	5/9	Run Like an Antelope	Tube
8/4/96	26	1	6/9	Split Open and Melt	The Sloth
8/14/96	7	1	7/10	Reba	Gumbo
10/22/96	8	2	4/10	Taste	Lawn Boy
12/28/96	30	1	8/9	Split Open and Melt	Frankenstein
3/1/97	16	2	6/8	Weekapaug Groove	Billy Breathes
7/28/98	88	2	3/8	Poor Heart	Brother
8/6/98	6	2	6/7	Prince Caspian	Down with Dis
8/16/98	7	3	4/7	Wilson	Character Zer
11/2/98	8	2	2/16	Down with Disease	The Moma Dance
11/21/98	13	2	5/9	The Wedge	Free
7/24/99	27	2	4/8	Tweezer	Jam
12/16/99	42	2	2/5	Sand	Wading In Velvet Sea
5/22/00	6	2	4/6	Sand	Ghost
6/9/00	2	2	3/7	Bouncing	The Squirmin
6/30/00	13	2	2/9	Halley's Comet	Twist
7/15/00	11	2	5/7	Piper	Bug
9/17/00	7	2	4/5	Dog Gone Dog	Free
9/27/00	7	2	4/7	Ghost	Heavy Things

Has not been played in the last 7 shows.

The Moma Dance

DATE	GAP	SET	POS.	SONG BEFORE	SONG AFTER
6/30/98	945	2	1/12	***	Birds of a Feather
7/1/98	1	1	4/9	My Mind's Got A Mind	Down with Dis
7/5/98	3	2	2/6	Bathtub Gin	McGrupp
7/8/98	2	1	1/7	***	Bathtub Gin
7/15/98	3	1	3/13	Water in the Sky	Guyute
7/16/98	1	2	2/7	Julius	Piper
7/19/98	2	1	1/8	***	Beauty of My Dreams
7/20/98	1	1	9/10	Water in the Sky	Split Open and
7/24/98	2	1	1/8	***	Runaway Jim
7/28/98	3	1	3/10	Down with Disease	Tela
8/3/98	5	1	6/8	Cars Trucks Buses	Strange Design
8/6/98	1	1	10/12	Fluffhead	Cracklin' Rosi
8/9/98	3	1	4/9	The Lizards	Birds of a Feather
8/15/98	3	1	7/12	Poor Heart	Divided Sky
10/3/98	2	1	3/10	Farmhouse	Runaway Jim
10/15/98	1	2	4/10	Roggae	Wading In Velvet Sea
10/29/98	3	2	2/7	Possum	Reba
11/2/98	3	2	3/16	The Mango Song	You Enjoy My
11/4/98	1	2	2/6	Runaway Jim	Piper
11/9/98	4	2	5/7	T.M.W.S.I.Y. Reprise	Slave
11/14/98	3	1	6/8	Tweezer	Sparkle
11/18/98	2	2	3/7	The Lizards	Albuquerque
11/24/98	4	1	2/9	Down with Disease	Ginseng Sullivan
11/28/98	3	1	7/8	Foam	Split Open and
12/30/98	4	1	6/12	Sparkle	The Old Home
7/3/99	4	2	3/7	Piper	Mountains in the Mis
7/12/99	6	2	2/6	Twist	Makisupa Policeman
7/18/99	5	1	9/11	Beauty of My Dreams	Reba
7/20/99	1	2	2/6	Twist	What's the Use
7/21/99	1	1	7/10	Funky Bitch	When Circus Comes
8/1/99	8	1	4/10	Wilson	Divided Sky
9/10/99	2	2	2/9	Down with Disease	Piper

DATE	GAP	SET	POS.	SONG BEFORE	SONG AFTER
9/17/99	5	1	6/11	Peaches en Regalia	Water in the Sky
9/24/99	5	1	5/10	Water in the Sky	Down with Dis
10/1/99	5	1	2/8	Chalk Dust Torture	Sparkle
12/4/99	10	2	3/9	Split Open and Melt	Farmhouse
12/13/99	7	1	4/6	Gumbo	Piper
12/17/99	3	2	2/6	Birds Of A Feather	Bug
12/30/99	2	3	2/9	Chalk Dust Torture	Run Like Antel
5/21/00	2	1	5/7	Possum	Limb By Limb
6/9/00	3	1	7/9	Funky Bitch	First Tube
6/24/00	9	1	1/6	***	Runaway Jim
7/6/00	8	1	6/12	Heavy Things	First Tube
7/11/00	4	1	2/8	Ya Mar	Uncle Pen
9/11/00	6	1	2/9	Road Runner	Rift
9/17/00	4	1	5/9	Limb By Limb	Lawn Boy
9/23/00	4	1	2/6	Come On Baby, Let's	Frankenstein
9/29/00	4	2	2/9	Dinner and a Movie	Also Sprach
10/4/00	3	1	1/7	***	It's Ice
10/6/00	2	1	6/7	Maze	Run Like Antel

Has not been played in the last 1 show.

The Oh Kee Pa Ceremony

DATE	GAP	SET	POS.	SONG BEFORE	SONG AFTER
8/17/89	109	3	1/8	***	Bold as Love
8/19/89	1	1	1/13	***	Suzy Greenbe
9/9/89	3	1	2/11	Foam	Suzy Greenbe
9/14/89	1	1	1/9	***	Suzy Greenbe
10/1/89	2	1	10/12	Ya Mar	Suzy Greenbe
10/12/89	3	1	1/8	***	AC/DC Bag
10/20/89	3	1	6/10	You Enjoy Yourself	Reba
10/21/89	1	2	1/10	***	Suzy Greenbe
10/22/89	1	1	5/14	You Enjoy Yourself	Suzy Greenbe
10/26/89	1	1	1/11	***	Golgi Apparat
10/31/89	1	2	1/9	***	Golgi Apparat
11/2/89	1	2	1/11	***	Golgi Apparat
11/3/89	1	2	3/5	No Dogs Allowed	The Sloth
11/9/89	1	2	1/9	***	AC/DC Bag
11/10/89	1	2	2/9	Split Open and Melt	Golgi Apparat
11/11/89	1	1	1/8	***	Golgi Apparat
11/16/89	1	1	6/11	Foam	Suzy Greenbe
11/30/89	2	1	4/11	Ya Mar	AC/DC Bag
12/1/89	1	1	4/9	You Enjoy Yourself	Dinner and a
12/3/89	1	2	5/14	Esther	Suzy Greenbe
12/7/89	1	2	1/11	***	Suzy Greenbe
12/8/89	1	1	1/11	***	Suzy Greenbe
12/15/89	2	1	7/10	Ya Mar	Suzy Greenbe
12/29/89	2	1	4/10	Ya Mar	AC/DC Bag
12/31/89	2	1	3/9	You Enjoy Yourself	AC/DC Bag
1/27/90	2	1	4/13	Ya Mar	AC/DC Bag
2/9/90	4	1	2/12	Golgi Apparatus	Suzy Greenbe
2/10/90	1	1	2/10	Dinner and a Movie	Suzy Greenbe
2/15/90	1	2	2/10	Carolina	Suzy Greenbe
2/17/90	2	1	2/12	Reba	AC/DC Bag
2/22/90	1	1	5/9	Ya Mar	AC/DC Bag
2/23/90	1	2	6/11	Tela	Suzy Greenbe
2/24/90	1	2	2/9	The Sloth	AC/DC Bag
3/3/90	4	1	7/12	The Lizards	Suzy Greenbe
3/7/90	1	2	1/9	***	AC/DC Bag
3/8/90	1	1	7/10	Carolina	Suzy Greenbe
3/9/90	1	2	2/11	Reba	AC/DC Bag
3/11/90	2	1	2/13	Contact	Suzy Greenbe
3/17/90	1	2	3/6	Bold As Love	AC/DC Bag
3/28/90	1	1	7/12	Uncle Pen	Suzy Greenbe
4/5/90	2	1	5/9	Carolina	Suzy Greenbe
4/6/90	1	1	9/11	Bouncing	Suzy Greenbe
4/8/90	2	1	5/8	If I Only Had a Brai	Suzy Greenbe
4/12/90	2	2	3/11	My Sweet One	Suzy Greenbe
4/13/90	1	1	7/10	La Grange	AC/DC Bag
4/14/90	1	2	2/11	I Didn't Know	Suzy Greenbe
4/18/90	1	2	7/12	Walk Away	Bold As Love
4/20/90	2	2	8/11	Fee	AC/DC Bag
4/21/90	1	1	7/10	Walk Away	Suzy Greenbe
4/22/90	1	3	2/12	Uncle Pen	Suzy Greenbe
4/26/90	2	2	4/11	Bathtub Gin	Suzy Greenbe
4/28/90	1	1	2/11	Sweet Adeline	Suzy Greenbe
5/4/90	2	1	5/12	Tweezer	Mike's Song
5/10/90	3	2	6/8	Reba	AC/DC Bag

DATE	GAP	SET	POS.	SONG BEFORE	SONG AFTER
5/11/90	1	2	1/7	***	AC/DC Bag
5/13/90	1	1	2/10	Bathtub Gin	AC/DC Bag
5/19/90	2	2	3/10	Reba	Suzy Greenbe
5/23/90	1	1	5/10	If I Only Had a Brai	Suzy Greenbe
5/24/90	1	1	7/9	You Enjoy Myself	AC/DC Bag
5/30/90	1	1	2/14	Reba	Suzy Greenbe
5/31/90	1	1	11/12	Divided Sky	Suzy Greenbe
6/5/90	3	1	7/12	Ya Mar	Suzy Greenbe
6/8/90	2	1	6/8	Uncle Pen	Suzy Greenbe
6/9/90	1	2	9/14	Foam	Suzy Greenbe
6/16/90	1	3	5/13	Foam	Suzy Greenbe
9/13/90	1	2	7/15	Going Down Slow	AC/DC Bag
9/15/90	2	1	7/14	Tube	AC/DC Bag
9/20/90	2	2	7/14	Magilla	Suzy Greenbe
9/22/90	2	1	6/12	Tela	Suzy Greenbe
9/28/90	1	1	3/10	Bouncing	Suzy Greenbe
10/5/90	4	1	8/13	Tela	Suzy Greenbe
10/6/90	1	1	7/13	You Enjoy Myself	Suzy Greenbe
10/8/90	2	1	9/10	You Enjoy Myself	Possum
10/19/90	2	1	13/15	Bouncing	Suzy Greenbe
10/31/90	2	2	7/12	Fee	Suzy Greenbe
11/3/90	2	1	5/11	The Squirming Coil	Suzy Greenbe
11/4/90	1	2	10/13	Runaway Jim	Suzy Greenbe
11/8/90	1	2	4/8	Tweezer	Dinner and a
11/17/90	3	1	9/11	Eliza	Suzy Greenbe
11/24/90	1	1	9/11	The Lizards	Suzy Greenbe
11/30/90	2	E	2/3	Caravan	Suzy Greenbe
12/7/90	2	2	8/11	The Squirming Coil	Suzy Greenbe
12/28/90	2	2	7/12	Tweezer	My Sweet One
12/29/90	1	1	9/10	Horn	Suzy Greenbe
2/2/91	3	1	1/9	***	Suzy Greenbe
2/3/91	1	2	8/9	Bouncing	Suzy Greenbe
2/14/91	4	1	10/11	Lawn Boy	Golgi Apparat
2/15/91	1	2	6/10	My Sweet One	AC/DC Bag
2/19/91	2	2	13/15	Love You	Suzy Greenbe
2/26/91	3	1	8/11	Reba	AC/DC Bag
2/27/91	1	2	7/11	Lawn Boy	The Sloth
3/1/91	2	E	1/2	***	Suzy Greenbe
3/8/91	2	1	5/11	Stash	Suzy Greenbe
3/9/91	1	2	2/13	T.M.W.S.I.Y.	Suzy Greenbe
3/13/91	1	2	11/12	Terrapin	Golgi Apparat
3/15/91	1	1	7/12	Bouncing	AC/DC Bag
3/16/91	1	1	12/14	The Famous Mockingbi	Suzy Greenbe
3/22/91	2	2	1/13	***	AC/DC Bag
3/23/91	1	2	3/11	Bathtub Gin	AC/DC Bag
3/28/91	1	1	11/14	The Squirming Coil	Suzy Greenbe
4/2/91	3	1	8/10	You Enjoy Myself	Suzy Greenbe
4/4/91	2	1	1/10	***	Suzy Greenbe
4/5/91	1	E	2/3	Fee	Suzy Greenbe
4/12/91	3	1	5/9	Guelah Papyrus	Suzy Greenbe
4/16/91	2	1	6/9	The Mango Song	AC/DC Bag
4/18/91	1	1	3/11	Reba	The Sloth
4/20/91	2	2	11/13	Tweezer	Suzy Greenbe
4/21/91	1	1	8/14	My Sweet One	AC/DC Bag
4/22/91	1	1	8/9	Guelah Papyrus	Suzy Greenbe
4/25/91	1	1	9/11	Llama	Suzy Greenbe
5/4/91	4	1	1/11	***	Suzy Greenbe
5/11/91	3	2	10/12	Tela	Suzy Greenbe
5/12/91	1	2	11/13	The Squirming Coil	AC/DC Bag
5/17/91	2	1	6/17	Poor Heart	Suzy Greenbe
5/18/91	1	2	1/10	***	Suzy Greenbe
5/19/91	1	2	1/10	***	AC/DC Bag
7/11/91	1	1	1/8	***	Suzy Greenbe
7/12/91	1	2	11/14	Touch Me	Suzy Greenbe
7/13/91	1	1	5/13	Llama	Suzy Greenbe
7/15/91	2	1	1/14	***	Suzy Greenbe
7/20/91	3	1	5/10	Llama	Suzy Greenbe
7/23/91	2	1	5/12	My Sweet One	Suzy Greenbe
7/27/91	4	1	3/16	Foam	Suzy Greenbe
9/27/91	4	2	7/10	Dinner and a Movie	Suzy Greenbe
9/29/91	2	1	9/10	You Enjoy Myself	Suzy Greenbe
10/2/91	2	2	8/9	Stash	Suzy Greenbe
10/6/91	3	1	6/13	Poor Heart	AC/DC Bag
10/10/91	1	2	8/13	Sparkle	Suzy Greenbe
10/15/91	4	2	8/12	Horn	Suzy Greenbe
10/17/91	1	2	2/9	The Curtain	Suzy Greenbe

DATE	GAP	SET	POS.	SONG BEFORE	SONG AFTER
10/19/91	2	2	8/10	You Enjoy Myself	Terrapin
10/24/91	2	1	1/12	***	Suzy Greenbe
10/28/91	2	1	7/10	Tube	Foam
11/10/91	8	1	7/10	The Squirming Coil	Suzy Greenbe
3/6/92	18	1	5/11	It's Ice	Divided Sky
3/14/92	5	2	6/10	Bouncing	Suzy Greenbe
3/19/92	2	2	6/10	Stash	Suzy Greenbe
3/21/92	2	2	2/11	Buried Alive	Suzy Greenbe
3/24/92	2	2	10/13	I Didn't Know	Suzy Greenbe
3/26/92	2	2	2/13	Buried Alive	Suzy Greenbe
3/30/92	3	E	2/3	Sleeping Monkey	Suzy Greenbe
4/8/92	8	2	1/15	***	Suzy Greenbe
4/15/92	3	1	1/11	***	Suzy Greenbe
4/18/92	3	2	2/16	Glide	Suzy Greenbe
4/29/92	7	2	4/11	Mound	Llama
5/3/92	4	2	13/14	Bouncing	Suzy Greenbe
5/16/92	10	2	9/13	Silent in the Mornin	AC/DC Bag
7/9/92	10	1	2/12	Glide	Suzy Greenbe
7/15/92	5	1	2/12	Glide	Suzy Greenbe
7/31/92	13	1	4/6	Bouncing	You Enjoy My
8/2/92	2	1	4/8	Rift	Suzy Greenbe
11/22/92	18	1	2/12	Buried Alive	Suzy Greenbe
12/10/92	14	2	9/10	Love You	Suzy Greenbe
12/29/92	5	1	11/12	Tela	Suzy Greenbe
2/22/93	19	2	7/11	Glide	Llama
3/8/93	9	1	4/12	Guelah Papyrus	Llama
3/17/93	6	1	9/11	It's Ice	Suzy Greenbe
3/26/93	7	2	9/12	You Enjoy Myself	Suzy Greenbe
4/17/93	14	2	7/11	Lifeboy	Suzy Greenbe
7/17/93	22	1	10/11	Silent in the Mornin	David Bowie
8/2/93	12	1	5/12	Brother	Suzy Greenbe
8/13/93	8	2	7/9	Lifeboy	Suzy Greenbe
12/28/93	11	1	5/10	Esther	Suzy Greenbe
4/4/94	4	2	10/11	I Wanna Be Like You	Suzy Greenbe
4/11/94	6	2	10/11	Amazing Grace	Suzy Greenbe
4/15/94	3	2	3/10	If I Could	Suzy Greenbe
4/18/94	3	1	9/10	Dog Faced Boy	AC/DC Bag
5/6/94	13	1	2/9	Down with Disease	AC/DC Bag
5/29/94	18	2	7/10	McGrupp	Suzy Greenbe
10/26/94	45	1	8/10	Scent of a Mule	Suzy Greenbe
11/23/94	17	1	6/9	If I Could	Suzy Greenbe
6/9/95	21	1	4/9	Strange Design	AC/DC Bag
11/24/95	56	1	1/9	***	AC/DC Bag
8/12/96	48	1	9/10	Taste	Suzy Greenbe
2/21/97	50	2	4/9	Wilson	AC/DC Bag
3/1/97	6	1	2/10	Cities	Down with Dis
4/5/98	69	1	1/8	***	You Enjoy My
8/6/98	25	1	1/12	***	Suzy Greenbe
7/4/99	41	1	4/10	Farmhouse	AC/DC Bag
9/14/00	93	1	5/6	Carini	Suzy Greenbe

Has not been played in the last 16 shows.

The Old Home Place

DATE	GAP	SET	POS.	SONG BEFORE	SONG AFTER
6/26/94	647	E	1/4	***	Amazing Grce
7/3/94	5	1	7/10	Horn	Reba
7/6/94	2	E	1/4	***	Nellie Kane
10/10/94	11	1	8/11	Guyute	Ginseng Sulli-van
10/13/94	2	2	1/12	***	Run Like Antel
10/18/94	4	2	7/10	Lifeboy	Beaumont Rag
10/21/94	2	1	5/9	The Mango Song	Stash
10/28/94	6	2	10/12	Chalk Dust Torture	Nellie Kane
11/2/94	3	E	1/3	***	Foreplay/Long Time
11/12/94	3	2	8/12	Rift	Nellie Kane
11/14/94	2	2	7/10	Julius	Nellie Kane
11/18/94	3	1	10/11	Butter Them Biscuits	My Long Journey Home
12/31/94	21	2	1/9	***	Maze
6/15/95	8	1	4/10	AC/DC Bag	Taste
10/11/95	26	1	2/9	Stash	Cavern
11/10/95	16	1	4/9	Taste That Surrounds	It's Ice
12/7/95	19	1	1/10	***	The Curtain
8/13/96	40	1	6/10	Fast Enough for You	Punch You in
8/17/96	3	1	1/10	***	Punch You in

DATE	GAP	SET	POS.	SONG BEFORE	SONG AFTER
10/18/96	3	1	3/10	Guelah Papyrus	Cars Trucks Buses
11/16/96	20	1	7/11	Free	David Bowie
11/30/96	8	1	7/10	Fluffhead	Uncle Pen
6/25/97	32	1	6/11	AC/DC Bag	Theme From the Botto
7/6/97	7	1	2/9	Runaway Jim	Dogs Stole Things
11/16/97	25	1	5/11	Farmhouse	Billy Breathes
12/3/97	11	1	4/7	Drowned	Gumbo
12/28/97	8	1	5/11	Sample in a Jar	Runaway Jim
4/3/98	5	1	2/9	Mike's Song	Weekapaug Gr
10/18/98	38	1	7/12	Albuquerque	Guyute
11/27/98	20	1	7/11	Reba	Dogs Stole Things
12/30/98	5	1	7/12	The Moma Dance	Sample in a Ja
12/17/99	62	E	1/3	***	The Squirmin
6/13/00	10	1	6/10	Fast Enough for You	Wilson
6/25/00	7	1	3/10	Sample in a Jar	Punch You in

Has not been played in the last 35 shows.

The Other One

DATE	GAP	SET	POS.	SONG BEFORE	SONG AFTER
5/3/85	5	3	8/8	Run Like an Antelope	***

Has not been played in the last 1114 shows.

The Pendulum

DATE	GAP	SET	POS.	SONG BEFORE	SONG AFTER
4/1/86	12	1	4/7	Harry Hood	Dave's Energy Guide

Has not been played in the last 1107 shows.

The Practical Song

DATE	GAP	SET	POS.	SONG BEFORE	SONG AFTER
9/12/88	66	2	8/10	Camel Walk	Harry Hood
5/26/89	38	E	1/1	***	***

Has not been played in the last 1015 shows.

The Price of Love

DATE	GAP	SET	POS.	SONG BEFORE	SONG AFTER
3/30/89	91	1	4/8	Divided Sky	On Your Way Down
5/28/89	15	2	12/16	Contact	Funky Bitch

Has not been played in the last 1013 shows.

The Punk Meets the Godfather

DATE	GAP	SET	POS.	SONG BEFORE	SONG AFTER
10/31/95	759	2	5/17	Cut My Hair	I'm One

Has not been played in the last 360 shows.

The Real Me

DATE	GAP	SET	POS.	SONG BEFORE	SONG AFTER
10/31/95	759	2	2/17	I Am The Sea	Quadrophenia
12/29/95	31	2	4/11	Bathtub Gin	Bathtub Gin

Has not been played in the last 329 shows.

The Revolution's Over

DATE	GAP	SET	POS.	SONG BEFORE	SONG AFTER
9/13/90	207	2	15/15	Dahlia	***

Has not been played in the last 912 shows.

The Rock

DATE	GAP	SET	POS.	SONG BEFORE	SONG AFTER
10/31/95	759	2	16/17	Doctor Jimmy	Love Reign O'er Me

Has not been played in the last 360 shows.

The Sloth

DATE	GAP	SET	POS.	SONG BEFORE	SONG AFTER
8/9/87	25	2	3/11	Halley's Comet	Light Up Or Leave Me
8/21/87	2	2	12/12	Back Porch Boogie Bl	***
1/27/88	9	2	9/10	You Enjoy Myself	Whipping Post
2/8/88	2	3	1/9	***	Flat Fee
3/12/88	4	2	9/11	The Famous Mockingbi	Possum
5/25/88	8	3	1/11	***	I Didn't Know
6/15/88	1	2	3/9	AC/DC Bag	Contact
7/23/88	7	2	1/10	***	Fire
12/2/88	17	1	1/7	***	Golgi Apparat
12/10/88	1	2	4/7	Contact	AC/DC Bag
1/26/89	3	2	5/10	The Famous Mockingbi	Possum
2/7/89	2	1	4/9	Foam	Possum

DATE	GAP	SET	POS.	SONG BEFORE	SONG AFTER
2/11/89	1	1	1/2	***	Take the A-Trn
4/20/89	11	1	8/12	Suzy Greenberg	Possum
4/27/89	1	1	2/8	Golgi Apparatus	Divided Sky
5/6/89	4	1	7/13	Esther	Possum
5/9/89	1	1	7/9	Weekapaug Groove	Possum
5/12/89	1	1	11/15	Slave	Possum
5/21/89	3	1	9/13	Dazed and Confused	You Enjoy My
5/26/89	1	1	8/9	Halley's Comet	You Enjoy My
5/28/89	2	3	3/6	La Grange Jam	Sneakin' Sally
6/23/89	1	2	1/7	***	Fluffhead
8/17/89	2	1	4/9	McGrupp	Rocky Top
10/6/89	8	1	5/13	Weekapaug Groove	Golgi Apparat
10/13/89	3	1	3/4	Slave	Possum
10/21/89	3	2	6/10	Reba	La Grange
10/26/89	2	2	8/15	Bathtub Gin	The Chase
11/3/89	4	2	4/5	The Oh Kee Pa Ceremo	Foam
11/10/89	2	2	9/12	Clod	The Lizards
11/16/89	2	2	1/4	***	AC/DC Bag
2/16/90	21	2	4/7	Bouncing	Possum
2/24/90	4	2	1/9	***	The Oh Kee Pa
3/9/90	7	1	8/11	The Famous Mockingbi	Possum
3/11/90	2	2	7/13	Take the A-Train	Ya Mar
4/4/90	3	2	6/8	Uncle Pen	I Didn't Know
4/6/90	2	2	4/10	Esther	Harry Hood
4/13/90	5	2	6/10	Ballad - Curtis Loew	Harry Hood
4/18/90	2	2	3/12	Fee	Funky Bitch
5/4/90	9	1	2/12	Runaway Jim	Uncle Pen
5/24/90	9	1	1/9	***	Bouncing
5/30/90	1	1	4/14	Suzy Greenberg	Dinner and a
9/16/90	12	1	3/14	Bouncing	The Landlady
10/4/90	7	1	8/10	Destiny Unbound	Uncle Pen
11/2/90	9	1	5/14	Divided Sky	Mike's Song
11/26/90	8	1	3/11	Runaway Jim	Reba
11/30/90	1	2	9/10	I Didn't Know	Run Like Antel
2/2/91	8	2	1/3	***	Run Like Antel
2/7/91	2	2	12/14	The Lizards	Destiny Un-bound
2/9/91	2	1	2/12	The Mango Song	T.M.W.S.I.Y.
2/15/91	2	1	8/13	The Mango Song	Dinner and a
2/16/91	1	1	1/12	***	My Sweet One
2/19/91	1	1	6/9	Dinner and a Movie	Runaway Jim
2/27/91	4	2	8/11	The Oh Kee Pa Ceremo	Love You
3/1/91	2	2	7/11	Runaway Jim	Possum
3/13/91	4	2	7/12	Runaway Jim	Reba
3/23/91	5	1	1/10	***	Divided Sky
3/31/91	3	2	2/7	Harry Hood	The Squirmin
4/5/91	4	2	4/9	The Lizards	Dinner and a
4/15/91	4	1	1/10	***	Ya Mar
4/18/91	2	1	4/11	The Oh Kee Pa Ceremo	Paul and Silas
4/20/91	2	2	1/13	***	Ya Mar
4/22/91	2	1	3/9	Runaway Jim	Reba
5/3/91	4	2	3/9	The Curtain	The Landlady
5/10/91	3	1	5/10	Dinner and a Movie	The Landlady
5/19/91	6	2	7/10	Dinner and a Movie	McGrupp
7/14/91	4	1	9/11	The Famous Mockingbi	I Didn't Know
7/21/91	5	2	5/9	Lawn Boy	Esther
7/25/91	3	1	2/10	My Sweet One	Foam
8/3/91	3	1	9/11	Poor Heart	Divided Sky
9/29/91	5	2	6/10	Reba	The Squirmin
10/11/91	7	2	6/9	The Mango Song	Poor Heart
10/13/91	2	1	9/13	AC/DC Bag	McGrupp
10/31/91	10	1	4/11	Ya Mar	Chalk Dust Tor
11/8/91	4	2	1/13	***	Sparkle
11/10/91	2	1	2/10	Buried Alive	Uncle Pen
11/12/91	1	1	7/11	Tube	Harry Hood
11/19/91	5	2	7/11	The Mango Song	Reba
11/24/91	5	1	1/9	***	Paul and Silas
12/5/91	3	2	9/13	Fee	The Squirmin
3/11/92	6	2	3/11	NICU	The Lizards
3/13/92	2	2	8/12	My Mind's Got A Mind	Rift
3/17/92	2	2	3/11	Glide	Poor Heart
3/20/92	2	2	5/12	Sanity	The Mango Song
3/27/92	6	1	4/10	Paul and Silas	Divided Sky
3/30/92	2	1	9/11	All Things Recnsdrd	Runaway Jim
4/3/92	3	2	2/9	The Curtain	Possum

DATE	GAP	SET	POS.	SONG BEFORE	SONG AFTER
4/7/92	4	1	11/12	Rift	Runaway Jim
4/24/92	12	1	5/11	Uncle Pen	The Landlady
5/1/92	4	1	6/12	NICU	Divided Sky
5/12/92	9	1	4/12	All Things Recnsrdd	Possum
5/14/92	1	1	3/11	All Things Recnsrdd	Sparkle
7/15/92	17	2	1/9	***	Divided Sky
11/20/92	31	1	5/12	Rift	Reba
12/6/92	13	1	6/10	My Sweet One	The Squirmin
12/28/92	7	2	4/9	Reba	You Enjoy My
2/10/93	10	1	5/10	Reba	Divided Sky
2/17/93	5	1	5/11	All Things Recnsrdd	Runaway Jim
2/20/93	3	1	3/11	Foam	Possum
3/5/93	9	1	5/11	Foam	Rift
3/21/93	11	1	3/11	Sparkle	Divided Sky
3/22/93	1	2	9/13	The Famous Mockingbi	McGrupp
3/28/93	5	1	6/11	The Lizards	Maze
4/3/93	5	2	5/10	All Things Recnsrdd	You Enjoy My
4/29/93	16	1	3/10	Uncle Pen	Runaway Jim
7/25/93	19	1	7/10	Rift	My Mind's Got A Mind
8/7/93	9	2	7/12	Avenu Malkenu	Sparkle
8/12/93	4	2	5/10	The Lizards	Maze
12/28/93	12	2	5/9	The Lizards	Fast Enough for You
4/17/94	15	2	4/9	Uncle Pen	Reba
4/29/94	9	1	5/12	Scent of a Mule	Divided Sky
5/22/94	17	1	2/11	Demand	Divided Sky
5/28/94	5	1	8/10	Silent in the Mornin	Maze
6/24/94	14	1	6/11	All Things Recnsrdd	Paul and Silas
6/26/94	2	1	9/11	The Famous Mockingbi	McGrupp
7/8/94	8	1	9/11	The Famous Mockingbi	McGrupp
10/12/94	11	1	3/9	Reba	Poor Heart
12/7/94	38	1	3/8	Runaway Jim	Ya Mar
6/26/95	24	1	5/10	NICU	My Mind's Got A Mind
10/22/95	25	1	3/12	My Mind's Got A Mind	Runaway Jim
12/9/95	29	1	4/10	NICU	Rift
12/16/95	5	1	5/9	Ya Mar	Divided Sky
12/31/95	5	1	2/10	Punch You in the Eye	Reba
8/4/96	22	1	7/9	The Mango Song	Maze
10/21/96	14	1	4/10	Cars Trucks Buses	Divided Sky
11/3/96	9	1	4/9	Billy Breathes	NICU
11/9/96	4	1	3/10	Poor Heart	Divided Sky
11/27/96	11	1	5/9	Chalk Dust Torture	Uncle Pen
12/30/96	9	1	5/9	Ya Mar	Llama
2/23/97	10	1	4/9	All Things Recnsrdd	Love Me
11/29/97	55	1	7/12	T.M.W.S.I.Y. Reprise	Ginseng Sullivan
12/31/97	14	1	9/10	Silent in the Mornin	Fire
4/2/98	1	1	3/8	My Mind's Got A Mind	NICU
8/11/98	32	1	7/11	Reba	Ginseng Sullivan
11/13/98	18	1	9/10	Water in the Sky	Run Like Antel
7/15/99	26	1	9/10	I Didn't Know	You Enjoy My
7/20/99	4	1	4/9	Cars Trucks Buses	Divided Sky
9/14/99	14	1	2/11	Chalk Dust Torture	The Curtain
12/30/99	34	3	4/9	Run Like an Antelope	When Circus Comes
6/28/00	16	1	2/6	Chalk Dust Torture	Taste
9/18/00	21	1	3/10	Sparkle	Maze
9/24/00	4	1	5/10	Sparkle	Divided Sky

Has not been played in the last 9 shows.

The Squirming Coil

DATE	GAP	SET	POS.	SONG BEFORE	SONG AFTER
1/20/90	146	1	5/8	You Enjoy Myself	Caravan
1/27/90	1	2	4/7	You Enjoy Myself	Run Like Antel
1/28/90	1	2	5/10	Caravan	You Enjoy My
2/9/90	3	1	8/12	AC/DC Bag	Mike's Song
2/17/90	4	1	4/12	AC/DC Bag	Harry Hood
2/24/90	3	2	5/9	Fee	La Grange
2/25/90	1	1	6/11	Funky Bitch	Bouncing
3/3/90	3	1	5/12	My Sweet One	The Lizards
3/7/90	1	2	3/9	AC/DC Bag	Bathtub Gin
3/10/90	3	1	6/10	Rocky Top	Funky Bitch
3/11/90	1	1	12/13	Weekapaug Groove	Possum
4/7/90	6	1	4/12	AC/DC Bag	The Lizards

DATE	GAP	SET	POS.	SONG BEFORE	SONG AFTER
5/15/90	21	1	11/12	Runaway Jim	The Lizards
5/23/90	2	2	1/11	***	Reba
6/5/90	6	1	1/12	***	Uncle Pen
9/14/90	6	2	2/10	The Asse Festival	Buried Alive
9/15/90	1	1	14/14	Magilla	***
9/20/90	2	2	4/14	Bouncing	Divided Sky
9/22/90	2	1	2/10	***	Tweezer
9/28/90	1	1	7/10	My Sweet One	The Lizards
9/29/90	1	2	1/8	***	Tweezer
10/4/90	2	1	5/10	Possum	The Lizards
10/6/90	2	1	2/13	The Landlady	Dinner and a
10/7/90	1	1	9/14	The Asse Festival	Mike's Song
10/30/90	4	1	8/9	Cavern	Possum
10/31/90	1	1	3/11	Possum	The Lizards
11/3/90	2	1	4/11	Llama	The Oh Kee Pa
11/8/90	2	1	7/12	Llama	The Asse Festival
11/17/90	3	1	2/11	Llama	The Landlady
11/24/90	1	1	7/11	Weekapaug Groove	The Lizards
11/30/90	2	2	2/10	The Asse Festival	Runaway Jim
12/7/90	2	2	7/11	Tweezer	The Oh Kee Pa
12/28/90	2	2	3/12	Possum	Tweezer
12/31/90	2	2	3/9	Stash	Runaway Jim
2/3/91	3	2	2/9	David Bowie	The Landlady
2/7/91	1	1	9/10	Possum	Golgi Apparat
2/8/91	1	1	8/11	Stash	Runaway Jim
2/9/91	1	2	9/10	Love You	Llama
2/14/91	1	2	5/12	Foam	Runaway Jim
2/19/91	3	1	8/9	Runaway Jim	David Bowie
2/20/91	1	1	4/11	Possum	Tweezer
2/26/91	2	1	3/11	Foam	Llama
2/27/91	2	1	4/11	Cavern	David Bowie
2/28/91	1	2	1/7	***	Reba
3/1/91	1	1	5/12	Cavern	Tweezer
3/6/91	1	1	4/11	The Landlady	Possum
3/8/91	1	1	8/11	Split Open and Melt	My Sweet One
3/9/91	1	2	4/13	Suzy Greenberg	Buried Alive
3/13/91	1	1	8/11	Llama	David Bowie
3/15/91	1	E	1/2	***	Runaway Jim
3/16/91	1	2	8/10	Buried Alive	Cavern
3/17/91	1	2	4/8	My Sweet One	Tweezer
3/22/91	1	1	7/11	Split Open and Melt	Buried Alive
3/28/91	2	1	10/14	David Bowie	The Oh Kee Pa
3/31/91	2	2	3/7	The Sloth	Stash
4/2/91	1	2	7/8	Buried Alive	Run Like Antel
4/4/91	2	1	4/10	You Enjoy Myself	Llama
4/11/91	3	1	11/12	You Enjoy Myself	Chalk Dust Tor
4/12/91	1	E	3/3	BBFCFM	***
4/15/91	1	E	1/2	***	Rocky Top
4/18/91	2	1	9/11	Split Open and Melt	Possum
4/19/91	1	2	8/10	My Sweet One	Take the A-Trn
4/20/91	1	2	4/13	Split Open and Melt	Paul and Silas
4/22/91	2	2	6/10	Destiny Unbound	Stash
4/27/91	2	2	11/13	Tweezer	Wipeout
5/2/91	1	1	8/11	Llama	Cavern
5/9/91	3	2	7/8	Split Open and Melt	Rocky Top
5/12/91	3	2	10/13	Weekapaug Groove	The Oh Kee Pa
5/16/91	1	2	5/9	The Landlady	Tweezer
5/19/91	3	1	7/8	Cavern	Llama
7/12/91	2	2	2/14	Golgi Apparatus	Moose the Mooch
7/14/91	2	1	3/11	Llama	Golgi Apparat
7/15/91	1	1	13/14	Cavern	Frankenstein
7/19/91	2	1	3/11	Cavern	You Enjoy My
7/20/91	1	1	3/10	Foam	Llama
7/23/91	2	1	3/12	Foam	My Sweet One
7/24/91	1	1	3/10	Chalk Dust Torture	Buried Alive
7/25/91	1	2	3/13	Golgi Apparatus	Llama
7/26/91	1	2	7/10	Funky Bitch	Tweezer
8/3/91	2	1	7/11	Fee	Poor Heart
9/25/91	1	2	1/8	***	Stash
9/26/91	1	2	2/11	Golgi Apparatus	Brother
9/28/91	2	1	4/11	Chalk Dust Torture	My Sweet One
9/29/91	1	2	7/10	The Sloth	My Sweet One
10/2/91	2	1	3/10	Foam	Poor Heart
10/3/91	1	2	9/11	Buried Alive	Tweezer

DATE	GAP	SET	POS.	SONG BEFORE	SONG AFTER
10/4/91	1	2	8/11	Stash	Mike's Song
10/6/91	1	2	9/10	Cavern	Rocky Top
10/10/91	1	E	1/2	***	Fire
10/13/91	1	2	3/9	Bathtub Gin	It's Ice
10/15/91	1	1	3/10	Foam	Split Open and
10/18/91	2	E	3/3	Walk Away	***
10/23/91	2	2	2/10	Brother	Sparkle
10/28/91	3	2	8/11	You Enjoy Myself	Harpua
11/1/91	3	1	5/11	Destiny Unbound	Split Open and
11/8/91	3	2	4/13	Split Open and Melt	I Didn't Know
11/10/91	2	1	6/10	Fee	The Oh Kee Pa
11/12/91	1	2	3/13	Stash	Paul and Silas
11/13/91	1	2	6/9	Bathtub Gin	Llama
11/15/91	2	1	6/12	Split Open and Melt	My Sweet One
11/20/91	3	1	9/11	Bathtub Gin	Llama
11/22/91	2	2	6/10	Run Like an Antelope	I Didn't Know
11/30/91	3	1	7/11	Cavern	Brother
12/4/91	1	1	8/11	Brother	Dinner and a
12/5/91	1	2	10/13	The Sloth	I Didn't Know
12/6/91	1	1	5/9	Uncle Pen	Magilla
12/31/91	2	3	2/7	Wilson	Tweezer
3/7/92	2	3	2/11	Tweezer	Weigh
3/12/92	2	2	6/11	Bouncing	Uncle Pen
3/14/92	2	2	3/10	Llama	Split Open and
3/19/92	2	2	9/10	My Friend My Friend	Cracklin' Rosi
3/21/92	2	1	9/12	Dinner and a Movie	My Sweet One
3/25/92	3	2	5/12	All Things Recnsrdd	You Enjoy My
3/30/92	4	2	8/13	BBFCFM	Weigh
4/1/92	2	2	10/13	Cracklin' Rosie	Tweezer Repri
4/6/92	4	1	9/10	Guelah Papyrus	Run Like Antel
4/8/92	2	1	10/11	Stash	Golgi Apparat
4/13/92	2	2	9/11	Ya Mar	Love You
4/17/92	3	2	4/8	Fluffhead	Tweezer
4/23/92	5	1	6/11	Guelah Papyrus	Llama
4/24/92	1	1	10/11	Stash	Golgi Apparat
4/30/92	3	2	3/11	Tweezer	My Mind's Got A Mind
5/2/92	2	1	10/11	Stash	Llama
5/5/92	2	2	13/14	Love You	Cavern
5/6/92	1	2	3/11	Stash	You Enjoy My
5/7/92	1	2	11/12	Bike	Tweezer Repri
5/9/92	2	1	9/11	Maze	I Didn't Know
5/16/92	2	2	5/13	Tweezer	You Enjoy My
5/17/92	1	2	4/11	Guelah Papyrus	All Things Rec
6/19/92	2	1	4/7	Stash	Sparkle
7/9/92	7	1	6/12	Stash	Runaway Jim
7/11/92	2	1	6/11	Stash	Cavern
7/14/92	2	2	6/10	Llama	Paul and Silas
7/16/92	2	E	2/2	Blue Bayou	***
7/17/92	1	1	4/7	Stash	Maze
7/21/92	3	1	6/7	Stash	Runaway Jim
7/24/92	2	1	4/6	Tweezer	You Enjoy My
7/28/92	4	1	4/6	Uncle Pen	Tweezer
8/1/92	3	1	5/7	Stash	Horn
8/14/92	3	1	3/5	Stash	Llama
8/17/92	2	E	1/1	***	***
8/20/92	2	1	4/6	Stash	David Bowie
8/25/92	3	1	5/7	Stash	Llama
8/28/92	2	1	5/7	Sweet Adeline	Runaway Jim
10/30/92	3	1	8/11	Cavern	Stash
11/21/92	3	2	10/13	Guelah Papyrus	Love You
11/23/92	2	3	3/14	Stash	I Walk the Line
11/25/92	1	1	8/11	It's Ice	Cavern
11/28/92	2	2	9/12	Bouncing	Terrapin
11/30/92	1	2	8/10	You Enjoy Myself	Terrapin
12/2/92	2	2	9/11	Lengthwise	I Walk The Line
12/4/92	2	2	6/10	It's Ice	Carolina
12/6/92	2	1	7/10	The Sloth	Llama
12/7/92	1	2	11/12	Love You	Sweet Adeline
12/11/92	3	2	10/12	Big Ball Jam	Faht
12/12/92	1	2	9/10	If I Only Had a Brai	Golgi Apparat
12/29/92	3	2	13/14	Terrapin	Tweezer Repri
12/31/92	3	3	7/9	Harpua	Diamond Girl
2/5/93	3	2	9/10	Love You	Tweezer Repri

DATE	GAP	SET	POS.	SONG BEFORE	SONG AFTER
2/7/93	2	2	11/13	Clementine	If I Only Had a Brai
2/10/93	2	2	3/11	It's Ice	Tweezer
2/13/93	3	2	10/11	Lengthwise	Cavern
2/17/93	2	2	11/11	Lengthwise	***
2/21/93	4	2	9/10	Cracklin' Rosie	BBFCFM
2/22/93	1	2	9/10	Love You	Tweezer Repri
2/26/93	3	2	10/11	Lengthwise	Tweezer Repri
3/3/93	3	2	12/13	Terrapin	Sweet Adeline
3/5/93	1	2	10/11	Love You	Amazing Grce
3/9/93	3	2	14/15	I Walk the Line	Tweezer Repri
3/14/93	3	2	11/11	The Great Gig in the	***
3/18/93	3	2	9/10	If I Only Had a Brai	Cavern
3/24/93	4	E	2/2	Carolina	***
3/27/93	3	E	1/2	***	Carolina
4/1/93	4	1	5/10	Stash	My Friend My
4/3/93	2	1	6/10	Split Open and Melt	My Friend My
4/10/93	3	1	5/10	Split Open and Melt	My Friend My
4/17/93	4	2	11/11	Big Ball Jam	***
4/21/93	3	2	4/11	Split Open and Melt	The Horse
4/23/93	2	2	11/12	Lengthwise	Highway to Hell
4/29/93	4	2	13/13	Terrapin	***
5/1/93	2	2	4/11	My Friend My Friend	Big Ball Jam
5/6/93	2	2	6/11	Big Ball Jam	Mike's Song
5/8/93	2	2	9/18	It's Ice	Jam
5/29/93	1	1	5/10	Sparkle	Cavern
7/17/93	4	2	3/12	Tweezer	It's Ice
7/21/93	2	1	4/12	Sparkle	Maze
7/24/93	3	1	10/10	Bouncing	***
7/27/93	2	1	4/8	Stash	Sparkle
7/30/93	2	2	9/10	Golgi Apparatus	David Bowie
8/2/93	2	2	6/9	Rift	Weekapaug Gr
8/6/93	2	2	4/12	Guelah Papyrus	Uncle Pen
8/9/93	3	1	11/11	Memories	***
8/12/93	2	1	10/10	Poor Heart	***
8/14/93	2	2	9/13	Mound	Daniel
8/16/93	2	1	9/9	Split Open and Melt	***
8/20/93	2	2	4/9	Split Open and Melt	My Friend My
8/25/93	3	2	7/8	You Enjoy Myself	Good Time Ba
8/28/93	2	1	8/9	Stash	Crimes of the Mind
12/29/93	2	1	9/9	Stash	***
4/6/94	5	2	8/9	Weekapaug Groove	Cavern
4/9/94	2	1	10/10	Stash	***
4/14/94	4	1	9/9	Split Open and Melt	***
4/16/94	2	2	8/9	You Enjoy Myself	Tweezer Repri
4/22/94	5	2	8/8	I Wanna Be Like You	***
4/25/94	2	2	10/10	Mound	Divided Sky
4/28/94	1	1	9/11	Run Like an Antelope	Julius
5/3/94	4	1	6/9	Stash	Scent of a Mul
5/8/94	1	1	8/8	Stash	***
5/10/94	1	E	1/1	***	***
5/17/94	5	1	9/9	Split Open and Melt	***
5/21/94	3	1	7/9	Stash	Tela
5/25/94	3	2	9/9	Purple Rain	***
6/11/94	7	2	6/9	Split Open and Melt	Maze
6/16/94	3	1	10/10	Stash	***
6/19/94	3	2	8/10	Makisupa Policeman	My Sweet One
7/3/94	11	2	8/10	Julius	Run Like Antel
7/10/94	5	2	9/10	Bouncing	Crimes of the Mind
10/9/94	7	1	7/7	Split Open and Melt	***
10/14/94	4	2	9/10	Foreplay/Long Time	Tweezer Repri
10/23/94	7	E	1/1	***	***
10/31/94	6	E	3/3	Costume Contest	***
11/13/94	5	2	8/8	Amazing Grace	***
11/19/94	5	E	1/1	***	***
12/2/94	9	1	8/8	Stash	***
12/28/94	8	2	9/9	Love You	***
6/9/95	7	E	1/1	***	***
6/16/95	5	2	5/5	You Enjoy Myself	***
6/24/95	6	1	10/10	Silent in the Mornin	***
6/30/95	5	2	10/10	Amazing Grace	***
7/3/95	3	2	10/10	Possum	***
9/27/95	1	1	9/9	Chalk Dust Torture	***

DATE	GAP	SET	POS.	SONG BEFORE	SONG AFTER
10/3/95	5	2	9/9	Split Open and Melt	***
10/13/95	6	2	10/10	Sweet Adeline	***
10/22/95	7	E	2/2	Sweet Adeline	***
11/9/95	7	2	10/10	Hello My Baby	***
11/15/95	5	1	9/9	Sweet Adeline	***
11/28/95	3	1	10/10	Julius	***
11/28/95	5	E	1/1	***	***
12/2/95	4	2	8/9	Golgi Apparatus	Tweezer Repri
12/8/95	4	2	6/8	Love You	Tweezer Repri
12/12/95	3	1	10/10	I'm Blue, Lonesome	***
12/16/95	3	2	8/8	Weekapaug Groove	***
12/31/95	5	1	4/10	Reba	Maze
7/19/96	15	1	6/6	Chalk Dust Torture	***
8/5/96	8	1	9/9	Julius	***
8/16/96	7	2	4/13	Free	Waste
10/16/96	2	2	9/10	Run Like an Antelope	Johnny B. Goode
10/25/96	7	1	10/10	Stash	***
11/19/96	17	E	1/1	***	***
12/29/96	10	1	10/10	Free	La Grange
2/17/97	6	2	1/7	***	Down with Dis
6/16/97	14	1	1/10	***	Dogs Stole Things
7/5/97	12	E	1/1	***	***
7/29/97	10	2	8/8	Rocky Top	***
8/11/97	9	E	1/1	***	***
8/16/97	3	1	11/11	Character Zero	***
11/30/97	13	1	5/6	Love Me	Loving Cup
12/13/97	9	E	2/2	My Soul	***
7/16/98	19	1	1/7	***	NICU
7/28/98	8	E	2/2	Camel Walk	***
8/12/98	11	2	7/7	Weekapaug Groove	***
11/4/98	11	E	1/1	***	***
11/18/98	9	E	4/4	Dog Faced Boy	***
12/30/98	11	2	4/5	Prince Caspian	Slave
6/30/99	2	2	1/10	***	Free
7/31/99	22	2	6/6	Fluffhead	***
9/10/99	3	E	1/1	***	***
9/17/99	5	1	11/11	David Bowie	***
9/19/99	2	2	4/6	Wading In Velvet Sea	Loving Cup
9/25/99	4	2	3/8	David Bowie	Prince Caspian
10/2/99	5	1	8/9	Split Open and Melt	Loving Cup
10/8/99	4	E	1/2	***	Tweezer Repri
12/2/99	3	1	10/10	Free	***
12/9/99	4	1	8/8	Halley's Comet	***
12/12/99	4	2	3/5	Prince Caspian	Makisupa Policeman
12/17/99	4	E	2/3	The Old Home Place	Loving Cup
5/21/00	4	1	3/7	Wolfman's Brother	Possum
6/9/00	3	2	4/7	The Mango Song	Gotta Jibboo
6/14/00	4	E	2/2	Sleep	***
6/24/00	5	2	7/8	Carini	Prince Caspian
7/6/00	8	E	1/1	***	***
7/12/00	5	1	9/9	Axilla	***
9/12/00	6	E	1/1	***	***

Has not been played in the last 17 shows.

The Star Spangled Banner

DATE	GAP	SET	POS.	SONG BEFORE	SONG AFTER
10/17/96	825	2	7/8	The Lizards	David Bowie
10/21/96	3	1	1/10	***	Sample in a Ja
10/25/96	3	2	12/12	Cavern	***
10/31/96	4	1	10/10	Character Zero	***
11/8/96	5	2	7/8	Mike's Song	Weekapaug Gr
11/19/96	8	2	6/7	You Enjoy Myself	Fire
11/27/96	4	2	7/8	Down with Disease	Fire
12/28/96	7	2	10/10	Weekapaug Groove	***
12/2/97	69	1	9/9	Taste	***
7/4/99	82	E	3/3	Meatstick Reprise	***
7/4/00	80	1	1/11	***	Farmhouse

Has not been played in the last 29 shows.

The Vibration of Life

DATE	GAP	SET	POS.	SONG BEFORE	SONG AFTER
12/7/92	470	2	5/12	Horn	My Sweet One

DATE	GAP	SET	POS.	SONG BEFORE	SONG AFTER
2/5/93	12	1	10/11	Reba	David Bowie
10/27/94	196	1	5/11	Col. Forbin's Ascent	The Famous Mockingbi
11/13/94	8	1	7/10	It's Ice	The Horse
11/17/94	3	1	9/11	Col. Forbin's Ascent	The Famous Mockingbi
11/19/96	159	2	4/7	Bathtub Gin	You Enjoy My

Has not been played in the last 271 shows.

The Wedge

DATE	GAP	SET	POS.	SONG BEFORE	SONG AFTER
2/3/93	480	1	5/11	Llama	Divided Sky
2/4/93	1	2	2/13	Chalk Dust Torture	Mike's Song
2/6/93	2	1	9/11	Lawn Boy	Bouncing
2/9/93	2	1	6/10	Rift	Chalk Dust Tor
2/12/93	3	1	7/11	Esther	Chalk Dust Tor
2/15/93	2	2	7/12	Weekapaug Groove	Poor Heart
2/23/93	7	1	9/11	Chalk Dust Torture	Paul and Silas
3/25/93	20	2	9/13	The Famous Mockingbi	Mike's Song
8/20/93	62	1	7/10	It's Ice	Ginseng Sullivan
6/7/95	134	1	8/10	Scent of a Mule	Funky Bitch
6/9/95	2	2	2/8	Split Open and Melt	Scent of a Mul
6/15/95	4	1	6/10	Taste	Stash
6/23/95	6	2	3/7	The Lizards	Run Like Antel
6/30/95	6	1	5/9	Taste	The Lizards
10/25/95	24	1	4/10	Divided Sky	Scent of a Mul
11/14/95	9	E	1/2	***	Rocky Top
10/29/96	72	2	6/10	Weekapaug Groove	Character Zer
8/17/97	81	1	1/10	***	Beauty of My Dreams
11/29/97	11	1	1/12	***	Foam
7/28/98	37	2	1/8	***	Poor Heart
8/3/98	5	2	7/7	Tube	***
8/8/98	3	1	1/8	***	NICU
8/15/98	4	2	1/9	***	Reba
11/7/98	12	1	5/10	Brian and Robert	Limb by Limb
11/21/98	10	2	4/9	Simple	The Mango Song
7/4/99	13	1	6/10	AC/DC Bag	Vultures
7/24/99	14	1	8/9	Jam	Character Zer
8/1/99	6	2	7/9	Weekapaug Groove	The Lizards
10/4/99	20	2	3/8	Sample in a Jar	AC/DC Bag
12/10/99	11	2	2/7	Gotta Jibboo	David Bowie
9/22/00	47	2	4/7	Ghost	When Circus Comes

Has not been played in the last 11 shows.

Them Changes

DATE	GAP	SET	POS.	SONG BEFORE	SONG AFTER
11/30/97	927	E	1/1	***	***

Has not been played in the last 192 shows.

Theme From The Bottom

DATE	GAP	SET	POS.	SONG BEFORE	SONG AFTER
5/16/95	712	1	6/12	Reba	Lonesome Cowboy Bill
6/7/95	1	2	4/9	Spock's Brain	Lonesome Cowboy Bill
6/9/95	2	1	6/9	AC/DC Bag	Taste
6/13/95	2	2	4/7	Axilla (Part II)	Acoustic Army
6/15/95	2	2	5/8	Strange Design	Scent of a Mul
6/19/95	3	1	1/10	***	Poor Heart
6/22/95	2	2	1/4	***	Jam
6/25/95	3	1	4/9	Taste	If I Could
6/29/95	3	E	1/1	***	***
7/1/95	2	2	3/9	Maze	Uncle Pen
9/28/95	4	2	1/8	***	Poor Heart
10/2/95	3	1	8/10	Fog that Surrounds	Tela
10/6/95	3	2	3/8	Maze	NICU
10/13/95	4	2	3/10	Uncle Pen	Wilson
10/19/95	4	1	7/11	Chalk Dust Torture	Acoustic Army
10/24/95	4	2	2/8	Julius	Bouncing
10/28/95	3	2	2/7	Maze	Scent of a Mul
11/9/95	3	2	1/10	***	Julius
11/15/95	5	2	2/8	Wilson	Scent of a Mul
11/19/95	3	2	1/8	***	Also Sprach
11/24/95	3	2	2/10	Chalk Dust Torture	Reba

DATE	GAP	SET	POS.	SONG BEFORE	SONG AFTER
11/29/95	3	1	6/9	It's Ice	Acoustic Army
12/1/95	2	1	3/10	Down with Disease	Poor Heart
12/5/95	3	E	1/2	***	Sweet Adeline
12/9/95	3	1	2/10	Maze	NICU
12/28/95	7	2	2/8	Timber (Jerry)	Wilson
6/6/96	5	1	5/8	Funky Bitch	BBFCFM
7/9/96	5	1	1/7	***	Poor Heart
7/12/96	3	1	8/10	Taste	Tweezer
7/21/96	6	2	2/9	Llama	Reba
7/23/96	2	1	3/9	Foam	Gumbo
8/2/96	3	1	7/11	Foam	Golgi Apparat
8/6/96	3	1	5/9	Simple	The Lizards
8/14/96	5	2	7/10	Tweezer	Cracklin' Rosi
10/17/96	4	1	5/10	Tweezer	Talk
10/23/96	5	1	8/9	Rift	Run Like Antel
10/26/96	5	1	8/9	It's Ice	Sample in a Ja
11/3/96	5	1	7/9	Sample in a Jar	Bouncing
11/8/96	3	E	1/1	***	***
11/11/96	2	1	7/9	Brother	Axilla
11/13/96	1	2	6/7	You Enjoy Myself	Golgi Apparat
11/19/96	5	1	4/9	Foam	Mound
11/22/96	1	2	8/10	Character Zero	Slave
11/27/96	3	1	8/9	Free	Bold as Love
12/2/96	4	1	6/8	I Didn't Know	Gumbo
12/30/96	5	1	8/9	Funky Bitch	Good Time Ba
2/16/97	4	E	1/2	***	Johnny B. Goode
2/22/97	5	1	4/10	Funky Bitch	NICU
2/26/97	3	2	6/11	Kung	Scent of a Mul
3/1/97	2	2	8/8	Billy Breathes	***
6/13/97	3	1	1/8	***	Dogs Stole Things
6/16/97	2	1	7/10	Beauty of My Dreams	Chalk Dust Tor
6/19/97	1	1	3/9	Dogs Stole Things	Punch You in
6/21/97	2	1	6/15	Dogs Stole Things	Swept Away
6/22/97	1	1	7/9	Character Zero	Hello My Baby
6/25/97	2	1	7/11	The Old Home Place	Wading In Velvet Sea
6/29/97	2	1	6/7	Chalk Dust Torture	Character Zer
7/3/97	3	1	7/8	Train Song	Rocky Top
7/5/97	1	1	5/13	Sample in a Jar	Prince Caspian
7/21/97	5	2	5/8	Wading In Velvet Sea	Jam
7/25/97	3	E	1/1	***	***
7/29/97	2	1	1/9	***	Beauty of My Dreams
8/2/97	3	1	1/8	***	Ginseng Sullivan
8/9/97	4	1	1/8	***	Punch You in
8/13/97	3	E	1/1	***	***
8/16/97	2	1	4/11	Chalk Dust Torture	Punch You in
11/13/97	2	1	3/9	Black-Eyed Katy	Train Song
11/19/97	4	1	7/10	Funky Bitch	Ginseng Sullivan
11/23/97	3	1	2/9	My Soul	Black-Eyed Katy
11/28/97	2	1	7/8	Black-Eyed Katy	Rocky Top
12/7/97	7	1	9/12	It's Ice	Tube
12/13/97	4	1	3/9	Axilla	Ginseng Sullivan
12/29/97	2	1	6/9	Train Song	Fluffhead
4/5/98	6	1	3/8	You Enjoy Myself	McGrupp
7/2/98	3	1	3/11	Cars Trucks Buses	Brian and Robert
7/9/98	5	2	2/8	Drowned	When Circus Comes
7/20/98	6	1	7/10	Birds of a Feather	Water in the Sky
11/11/98	32	1	7/8	Birds of a Feather	Julius
11/29/98	12	1	3/11	Axilla	Sparkle
7/15/99	15	1	7/10	Axilla	I Didn't Know
7/26/99	9	2	3/6	Piper	Down with Dis
9/12/99	8	E	1/1	***	***
9/21/99	6	1	8/9	Birds of a Feather	Golgi Apparat
9/29/99	6	1	8/9	Stash	Tweezer Repri
12/13/99	18	1	6/6	Piper	***

DATE	GAP	SET	POS.	SONG BEFORE	SONG AFTER
6/16/00	16	2	2/7	Runaway Jim	Dog Faced Boy
7/3/00	9	2	3/7	Glide	Sand
7/11/00	6	1	7/8	Chalk Dust Torture	Cavern
9/17/00	10	2	2/5	Rock and Roll	Dog Gone Dog

Has not been played in the last 14 shows.

Theme to Star Trek: The Original Series

DATE	GAP	SET	POS.	SONG BEFORE	SONG AFTER
8/4/96	814	E	1/2	***	Rocky Top

Has not been played in the last 305 shows.

Three Little Birds

DATE	GAP	SET	POS.	SONG BEFORE	SONG AFTER
6/17/95	721	E	1/1	***	***

Has not been played in the last 398 shows.

Timber (Jerry)

DATE	GAP	SET	POS.	SONG BEFORE	SONG AFTER
4/29/87	22	3	8/14	Boogie On Reggae	Slave
8/9/87	3	1	7/11	Sneakin' Sally	Good Time Ba
8/29/87	3	1	8/13	Harry Hood	AC/DC Bag
9/2/87	1	1	11/13	Makisupa Policeman	Shaggy Dog
10/31/87	4	2	6/17	Take the A-Train	Fluff's Travels
11/19/87	2	2	1/6	***	Fluffhead
2/7/88	2	2	3/9	AC/DC Bag	Flat Fee
3/21/88	6	1	7/15	Boogie On Reggae	The Lizards
5/21/88	6	2	4/9	The Lizards	Tela
7/12/88	2	2	3/9	Take the A-Train	Fluffhead
7/30/88	4	3	4/13	Slave	Walk Away
9/12/88	5	2	1/10	***	Satin Doll
2/7/89	15	2	5/9	The Lizards	Contact
10/6/89	36	1	1/13	***	Mike's Song
12/8/89	22	2	3/7	Tela	Slave
6/16/90	67	1	8/10	Bouncing	Lawn Boy
12/30/92	272	1	13/14	David Bowie	David Bowie
7/3/95	256	2	1/10	***	David Bowie
10/3/95	6	2	1/9	***	It's Ice
10/8/95	4	2	3/10	Cars Trucks Buses	Ya Mar
10/20/95	7	2	1/10	***	Scent of a Mul
10/28/95	6	1	3/10	Mound	Uncle Pen
11/16/95	9	1	8/10	Simple	Guyute
11/25/95	6	2	1/12	***	Kung
11/29/95	2	2	1/11	***	Sparkle
12/4/95	4	2	1/9	***	Sparkle
12/9/95	4	2	1/8	***	Wilson
12/14/95	3	2	3/10	Tweezer	Tweezer
12/28/95	2	1	2/8	***	Theme From the Botto
7/21/96	19	1	13/14	Fee	Johnny B. Goode
8/12/96	11	2	1/9	***	Sparkle
10/25/96	12	2	3/12	Prince Caspian	T.M.W.S.I.Y.
11/3/96	6	2	1/8	***	Divided Sky
11/11/96	2	1	2/11	***	Divided Sky
11/18/96	5	1	2/10	Cars Trucks Buses	Poor Heart
11/30/96	7	2	7/11	Also Sprach	Taste
12/4/96	3	1	5/11	Uncle Pen	Sample in a Ja
12/30/96	4	2	1/8	***	Uncle Pen
2/17/97	5	1	6/10	Guyute	Billy Breathes
7/1/97	23	2	2/7	Jam	Bathtub Gin
7/26/97	12	2	1/8	***	David Bowie
8/11/97	10	2	1/6	***	Piper
11/16/97	7	2	1/5	***	Simple
11/28/97	7	2	1/5	***	Limb By Limb
12/7/97	7	2	1/6	***	Wolfman's Brother
12/9/97	1	2	3/6	Simple	Contact
12/31/97	7	2	1/6	***	Mike's Song
11/28/98	61	2	3/9	Wolfman's Brother	Loving Cup
7/17/99	18	2	7/8	Sneakin' Sally	You Enjoy My
7/14/00	78	2	2/11	Punch You in the Eye	Gotta Jibboo
9/30/00	17	2	1/7	***	AC/DC Bag

Has not been played in the last 5 shows.

Time

DATE	GAP	SET	POS.	SONG BEFORE	SONG AFTER
11/2/98	984	2	9/16	On The Run	The Great Gig in the

Has not been played in the last 135 shows.

Time Loves a Hero

DATE	GAP	SET	POS.	SONG BEFORE	SONG AFTER
10/31/88	71	1	6/12	The Lizards	Golgi Apparat
11/3/88	1	2	1/9	***	Walk Away
11/5/88	1	1	2/11	Slave	Fire
8/11/98	900	1	4/11	Wolfman's Brother	Bittersweet Motel

Has not been played in the last 146 shows.

Too Much of Everything

DATE	GAP	SET	POS.	SONG BEFORE	SONG AFTER
7/26/98	962	1	2/7	Birds of a Feather	David Bowie
8/2/98	5	1	8/9	Weigh	Birds of a Feather

Has not been played in the last 152 shows.

Touch Me

DATE	GAP	SET	POS.	SONG BEFORE	SONG AFTER
7/11/91	297	2	9/10	Weekapaug Groove	Frankenstein
7/12/91	1	2	10/14	Weekapaug Groove	The Oh Kee Pa
7/14/91	2	3	10/14	Weekapaug Groove	Harry Hood
7/19/91	3	1	10/10	Gumbo	***
7/21/91	2	E	2/4	Gumbo	Fee
7/23/91	1	2	10/10	Gumbo	***
7/25/91	2	2	9/13	Gumbo	Magilla
7/27/91	2	E	1/2	***	Contact
12/3/94	391	2	7/10	The Landlady	Alumni Blues Jam

Has not been played in the last 418 shows.

Train Round the Bend

DATE	GAP	SET	POS.	SONG BEFORE	SONG AFTER
10/31/98	983	2	9/10	I Found a Reason	Oh! Sweet Nuthin'

Has not been played in the last 136 shows.

Train Song

DATE	GAP	SET	POS.	SONG BEFORE	SONG AFTER
7/21/96	808	1	11/14	Taste	Fee
8/5/96	7	2	8/13	Talk	Strange Design
8/13/96	5	2	8/11	Waste	Strange Design
8/16/96	2	2	7/13	Talk	Strange Design
10/16/96	2	2	3/10	Taste	Simple
10/21/96	4	2	5/11	Reba	Maze
10/26/96	4	1	5/9	Reba	Character Zer
10/29/96	2	1	7/10	Stash	Billy Breathes
11/6/96	4	1	5/9	Taste	Poor Heart
11/13/96	5	1	6/9	Taste	Reba
11/15/96	2	1	8/11	Ginseng Sullivan	Chalk Dust Tor
11/22/96	4	1	8/10	Fast Enough for You	Stash
12/1/96	6	1	8/12	Down with Disease	The Horse
12/4/96	2	1	7/11	Sample in a Jar	Guyute
12/29/96	3	1	6/10	Guelah Papyrus	Rift
2/18/97	7	2	7/9	Reba	Harry Hood
7/3/97	24	1	6/8	Taste	Theme From the Botto
8/14/97	22	1	8/10	Tela	Billy Breathes
8/16/97	1	1	9/11	You Enjoy Myself	Character Zer
11/13/97	2	1	4/9	Theme From the Botto	Split Open and
11/17/97	3	1	3/5	Reba	Ghost
11/22/97	3	1	5/8	Harry Hood	Billy Breathes
12/6/97	9	1	3/9	Run Like An Antelope	Bathtub Gin
12/12/97	4	1	7/8	Tweezer	Character Zer
12/29/97	3	1	5/9	Cars Trucks Buses	Theme From the Botto
4/3/98	4	1	4/9	Weekapaug Groove	Billy Breathes
6/30/98	3	1	12/13	Funky Bitch	David Bowie
7/6/98	5	1	6/9	Limb by Limb	Roggae
8/6/98	19	1	7/12	Vultures	Billy Breathes
11/20/98	27	1	9/13	Stash	Possum
7/9/99	17	1	5/8	Divided Sky	Llama
7/20/99	8	2	4/6	What's the Use	Also Sprach
9/16/99	15	1	12/14	Stash	Billy Breathes
9/22/99	5	2	7/8	Simple	Weekapaug Gr
10/10/99	13	2	4/6	Prince Caspian	Bathtub Gin

DATE	GAP	SET	POS.	SONG BEFORE	SONG AFTER
12/15/99	11	1	6/7	Guyute	You Enjoy My
5/23/00	8	2	7/8	Run Like an Antelope	Bug

Has not been played in the last 46 shows.

Trenchtown Rock

DATE	GAP	SET	POS.	SONG BEFORE	SONG AFTER
8/11/98	973	1	1/11	***	Julius

Has not been played in the last 146 shows.

Tube

DATE	GAP	SET	POS.	SONG BEFORE	SONG AFTER
9/13/90	207	1	4/11	Foam	The Asse Festival
9/15/90	2	1	6/14	Fee	The Oh Kee Pa
9/16/90	1	1	7/14	Ya Mar	Tweezer
9/20/90	1	2	13/14	Uncle Pen	Lawn Boy
9/21/90	1	2	4/8	Uncle Pen	Lawn Boy
11/4/90	16	1	5/10	Bouncing	Harry Hood
11/16/90	3	2	6/11	Lawn Boy	Paul and Silas
10/24/91	100	2	6/11	Uncle Pen	Slave
10/28/91	2	1	6/10	I Didn't Know	The Oh Kee Pa
10/30/91	1	2	1/11	***	Divided Sky
10/31/91	1	2	12/14	Dinner and a Movie	I Didn't Know
11/1/91	1	1	9/11	Uncle Pen	Divided Sky
11/7/91	2	2	5/11	Reba	Horn
11/8/91	1	1	1/11	***	The Landlady
11/9/91	1	1	7/11	Reba	You Enjoy My
11/12/91	2	1	6/11	Bouncing	The Sloth
11/14/91	2	1	6/11	Foam	Sparkle
11/15/91	1	2	8/14	Eliza	The Landlady
11/16/91	1	2	1/9	***	My Sweet One
11/19/91	2	1	1/11	***	My Sweet One
11/22/91	3	2	1/10	***	My Sweet One
11/24/91	2	2	1/8	***	Divided Sky
12/5/91	3	2	3/13	Sparkle	Foam
4/19/92	35	2	8/13	My Sweet One	The Mango Song
11/20/92	66	2	3/10	Fluffhead	You Enjoy My
4/12/93	73	1	2/11	Golgi Apparatus	Bouncing
6/26/94	118	E	3/4	Amazing Grace	Fire
10/13/95	99	2	1/10	***	Uncle Pen
12/11/95	37	1	9/12	Dog Gone Dog	McGrupp
12/17/95	5	1	6/9	The Mango Song	Stash
8/13/96	32	1	2/10	Divided Sky	Tela
10/25/96	11	2	1/12	***	Prince Caspian
11/9/96	10	1	6/10	Horn	Talk
2/26/97	32	1	6/10	My Soul	Carini
12/7/97	59	1	10/12	Theme From the Botto	Tube Jam
12/13/97	4	1	8/9	Vultures	Good Time Ba
12/29/97	2	2	4/5	Possum	You Enjoy My
4/2/98	3	1	1/8	***	My Mind's Got A Mind
6/30/98	4	1	5/13	Bouncing	Stash
7/16/98	10	2	6/7	David Bowie	Slave
7/21/98	4	1	4/8	Roggae	Sparkle
7/29/98	5	2	5/7	The Lizards	Kung
8/3/98	4	2	6/7	Bike	The Wedge
11/2/98	16	1	1/9	***	Tube Jam
11/20/98	12	1	2/13	Rock And Roll Part 2	Quinn the Eskimo
11/28/98	5	1	2/8	Gumbo	Down with Dis
12/28/98	2	1	8/10	Driver	Golgi Apparat
6/30/99	4	1	3/8	Farmhouse	Horn
7/3/99	2	1	7/11	When Circus Comes	Funky Bitch
7/8/99	3	2	8/9	Meatstick	Simple
7/17/99	7	1	1/10	***	Boogie On Reggae
9/11/99	14	1	1/9	***	Funky Bitch
9/18/99	5	1	6/7	Brian and Robert	Rocky Top
9/25/99	5	1	1/8	***	Runaway Jim
9/28/99	2	1	3/8	Sneakin' Sally	Ginseng Sullivan
10/7/99	6	2	3/9	Heavy Things	Back on the Train
12/5/99	7	1	7/10	Sparkle	Lawn Boy

DATE	GAP	SET	POS.	SONG BEFORE	SONG AFTER
12/13/99	6	1	1/6	***	Cars Trucks Buses
12/18/99	4	1	4/9	Dog Gone Dog	Heavy Things
12/31/99	2	1	3/14	Funky Bitch	I Didn't Know
7/1/00	18	1	6/11	Sample in a Jar	Beauty of My Dreams
7/12/00	8	1	3/9	The Curtain With	Heavy Things
9/15/00	8	2	3/5	The Lizards	When Circus Comes
9/22/00	4	2	1/7	***	Reba

Has not been played in the last 11 shows.

Tube Jam

DATE	GAP	SET	POS.	SONG BEFORE	SONG AFTER
12/7/97	932	1	11/12	Tube	Slave
11/2/98	52	1	2/9	Tube	Drowned

Has not been played in the last 135 shows.

Tubthumping

DATE	GAP	SET	POS.	SONG BEFORE	SONG AFTER
11/21/98	997	E	1/1	***	***

Has not been played in the last 122 shows.

Tuesday's Gone

DATE	GAP	SET	POS.	SONG BEFORE	SONG AFTER
7/13/99	1016	E	1/1	***	***

Has not been played in the last 103 shows.

Tush

DATE	GAP	SET	POS.	SONG BEFORE	SONG AFTER
12/6/86	16	1	12/14	Dog Gone Dog	Sneakin' Sally
8/10/87	10	3	6/7	Anarchy	Dear Mrs. Reagan

Has not been played in the last 1093 shows.

Tweezer

DATE	GAP	SET	POS.	SONG BEFORE	SONG AFTER
3/28/90	169	1	5/12	Walk Away	Uncle Pen
4/5/90	2	2	6/13	Donna Lee	Fee
4/7/90	2	1	9/12	Possum	Mike's Song
4/9/90	2	2	10/11	Love You	Whipping Post
4/12/90	1	2	5/11	Suzy Greenberg	The Lizards
4/14/90	2	2	4/11	Suzy Greenberg	Bathtub Gin
4/21/90	4	2	8/9	Tela	The Lizards
5/4/90	6	1	4/12	Uncle Pen	The Oh Kee Pa
5/6/90	1	1	5/8	Reba	Mike's Song
5/10/90	2	1	5/8	Divided Sky	My Sweet One
5/11/90	1	2	4/7	The Lizards	Ya Mar
5/13/90	1	2	6/12	Donna Lee	My Sweet One
5/23/90	3	2	3/11	Reba	The Lizards
5/24/90	1	1	3/9	Bouncing	Donna Lee
5/31/90	2	1	7/12	Esther	I Didn't Know
6/7/90	4	2	4/10	Bouncing	Uncle Pen
6/8/90	1	2	3/7	My Sweet One	I Didn't Know
6/9/90	1	1	6/10	Bouncing	Uncle Pen
6/16/90	1	2	3/8	Esther	My Sweet One
9/14/90	2	2	4/10	Buried Alive	Magilla
9/16/90	2	1	8/14	Tube	Paul and Silas
9/21/90	2	2	6/8	Lawn Boy	Buried Alive
9/22/90	1	2	2/10	The Squirming Coil	Destiny Unbound
9/29/90	2	2	2/8	The Squirming Coil	Gumbo
10/4/90	2	2	5/8	Fee	Magilla
10/7/90	3	2	3/8	Bouncing	My Sweet One
10/12/90	2	1	8/9	Esther	Golgi Apparat
10/31/90	3	2	5/12	Foam	Fee
11/8/90	4	2	3/8	Divided Sky	The Oh Kee Pa
11/30/90	6	1	8/11	Bouncing	My Sweet One
12/1/90	1	1	6/9	Foam	My Sweet One
12/7/90	1	2	6/11	Cavern	The Squirmin
12/28/90	2	2	4/12	The Squirming Coil	Manteca
12/28/90	0	2	6/12	Manteca	The Oh Kee Pa
2/1/91	3	1	3/10	Foam	Tweezer Repri
2/3/91	2	1	4/10	My Sweet One	Esther
2/7/91	1	2	5/14	T.M.W.S.I.Y. Reprise	Tweezer Repri
2/9/91	2	1	10/12	My Sweet One	Reba
2/20/91	5	1	5/11	The Squirming Coil	My Sweet One
3/1/91	5	1	6/12	The Squirming Coil	Dinner and a
3/8/91	2	1	10/11	My Sweet One	BBFCFM

DATE	GAP	SET	POS.	SONG BEFORE	SONG AFTER
3/13/91	2	2	9/12	Reba	Terrapin
3/17/91	3	2	5/8	The Squirming Coil	Fee
3/23/91	2	2	6/11	My Sweet One	The Lizards
3/29/91	2	2	6/8	Fluffhead	Bouncing
4/3/91	3	1	5/10	Foam	Dinner and a
4/11/91	4	1	4/12	Paul and Silas	Magilla
4/16/91	3	2	8/11	Uncle Pen	Runaway Jim
4/20/91	3	2	10/13	T.M.W.S.I.Y. Reprise	The Oh Kee Pa
4/22/91	2	E	3/4	Rocky Top	Tweezer Repri
4/27/91	2	2	10/13	Fluffhead	The Squirmin
5/3/91	2	1	10/12	Paul and Silas	The Lizards
5/16/91	6	2	6/9	The Squirming Coil	My Sweet One
7/12/91	5	2	4/14	Moose the Mooch	My Sweet One
7/19/91	5	2	6/8	Magilla	The Mango Song
7/21/91	2	2	1/9	***	I Didn't Know
7/23/91	1	2	6/10	The Landlady	Sweet Adeline
7/26/91	3	2	10/11	The Squirming Coil	The Lizards
8/3/91	2	2	5/10	Bouncing	Esther
9/27/91	3	1	6/9	Esther	It's Ice
10/3/91	5	2	10/11	The Squirming Coil	Memories
10/12/91	5	1	1/10	***	Uncle Pen
10/19/91	5	2	4/10	Sparkle	Horn
11/1/91	7	2	1/13	***	My Sweet One
11/9/91	4	2	5/10	It's Ice	Tela
11/14/91	4	2	7/11	Glide	Take the A-Trn
11/14/91	0	2	11/11	The Lizards	***
11/21/91	5	2	6/10	Uncle Pen	Tela
11/23/91	2	2	7/13	Poor Heart	Eliza
12/5/91	4	2	1/13	***	Sparkle
12/31/91	3	3	3/7	The Squirming Coil	McGrupp
3/7/92	2	2	2/11	My Sweet One	The Squirmin
3/12/92	2	2	2/11	Golgi Apparatus	Eliza
3/17/92	3	2	5/11	Poor Heart	Esther
3/25/92	6	2	1/12	***	Mound
3/30/92	4	2	3/13	Uncle Pen	Mound
4/1/92	2	2	6/13	Uncle Pen	Horn
4/7/92	5	2	3/11	All Things Recnsdrd	Eliza
4/17/92	6	2	5/8	The Squirming Coil	Uncle Pen
4/21/92	3	2	4/13	The Famous Mockingbi	Tela
4/23/92	2	2	9/13	Horn	Fee
4/30/92	4	2	2/11	Glide	The Squirmin
5/3/92	3	2	1/14	***	The Horse
5/7/92	2	2	3/12	Sparkle	Fluffhead
5/9/92	2	2	4/8	Tela	Harpua
5/16/92	5	2	4/13	Paul and Silas	The Squirmin
7/14/92	14	2	1/10	***	Fee
7/24/92	8	1	3/6	Foam	The Squirmin
7/28/92	4	1	5/6	The Squirming Coil	Runaway Jim
8/17/92	8	2	3/11	It's Ice	Esther
8/24/92	4	1	4/7	All Things Recnsdrd	The Landlady
11/19/92	7	2	7/15	I Walk the Line	BBFCFM
11/19/92	0	2	9/15	BBFCFM	Big Ball Jam
11/22/92	3	2	4/10	My Sweet One	Big Ball Jam
11/22/92	0	2	6/10	Big Ball Jam	Tela
11/25/92	2	2	6/9	The Lizards	Cracklin' Rosi
11/28/92	2	2	3/12	Paul and Silas	T.M.W.S.I.Y.
12/2/92	3	2	4/11	Mound	Tela
12/5/92	3	2	2/13	Poor Heart	Reba
12/10/92	4	2	2/10	Rift	Tela
12/12/92	2	2	2/14	The Curtain	Rift
12/29/92	3	2	2/14	The Curtain	The Horse
2/3/93	3	2	3/11	It's Ice	The Horse
2/5/93	2	2	2/10	The Curtain	The Horse
2/7/93	2	2	6/13	Bouncing	Big Ball Jam
2/10/93	2	2	4/11	The Squirming Coil	I Walk the Line
2/13/93	3	2	4/11	Uncle Pen	The Lizards
2/18/93	3	1	4/10	Poor Heart	Foam
2/20/93	2	2	3/22	Reba	Walk Away
2/20/93	0	2	5/22	Walk Away	Glide
2/22/93	2	2	4/11	It's Ice	You Enjoy My
2/26/93	3	2	3/11	Paul and Silas	Glide
3/2/93	2	2	2/12	Uncle Pen	The Lizards
3/6/93	3	2	2/9	Rift	Reba
3/9/93	2	2	3/15	Rift	Reba

DATE	GAP	SET	POS.	SONG BEFORE	SONG AFTER
3/13/93	2	2	2/13	Suzy Greenberg	The Lizards
3/16/93	2	2	3/15	The Curtain	Sweet Emotion Jam
3/16/93	0	2	5/15	Sweet Emotion Jam	Bathtub Gin
3/21/93	4	2	4/12	Rift	Ya Mar
3/24/93	2	2	4/12	Sparkle	Mound
3/26/93	2	2	3/12	Runaway Jim	Mound
3/30/93	3	2	3/15	Rift	Lifeboy
4/1/93	2	2	6/10	Ya Mar	Poor Heart
4/5/93	3	2	5/9	Punch You in the Eye	Glide
4/12/93	3	2	2/10	Dinner and a Movie	Fee
4/14/93	1	2	3/10	My Sweet One	Mound
4/18/93	3	2	2/12	Poor Heart	The Horse
4/22/93	3	2	4/10	All Things Recnsdrd	The Lizards
4/25/93	3	2	3/11	The Curtain	Contact
4/30/93	3	2	3/10	Sparkle	Walk Away
5/3/93	3	2	3/12	The Curtain	Manteca
5/3/93	0	2	5/12	Manteca	Contact
5/6/93	2	2	2/11	Suzy Greenberg	Tela
7/17/93	7	2	2/12	Also Sprach	The Squirmin
7/22/93	3	2	2/11	Also Sprach	Walk Away
7/25/93	3	2	2/11	Suzy Greenberg	The Horse
7/30/93	4	2	2/10	Also Sprach	The Horse
8/6/93	4	2	2/12	Buried Alive	Guelah Papyrus
8/9/93	3	2	2/8	Dinner and a Movie	Tela
8/12/93	2	2	3/10	The Landlady	The Lizards
8/15/93	3	2	2/11	Rift	The Lizards
12/31/93	12	2	1/8	***	Halley's Comet
4/5/94	2	2	3/8	Ya Mar	If I Could
4/16/94	9	2	3/9	Poor Heart	The Lizards
4/22/94	5	2	4/8	Reba	Lifeboy
5/4/94	9	1	7/10	Axilla (Part II)	Lifeboy
5/7/94	2	2	3/12	Sparkle	Sparks
5/17/94	7	2	3/9	Glide	Lifeboy
5/22/94	4	2	5/9	McGrupp	Lifeboy
5/25/94	2	2	2/9	Rift	Lifeboy
5/28/94	3	2	3/9	It's Ice	Lifeboy
6/10/94	3	2	3/9	The Curtain	Lifeboy
6/18/94	6	2	7/10	McGrupp	Lifeboy
6/23/94	4	2	6/8	Uncle Pen	Lifeboy
6/29/94	4	2	3/8	Poor Heart	It's Ice
7/2/94	3	1	6/9	Scent of a Mule	Lifeboy
7/6/94	3	2	3/10	Poor Heart	Lawn Boy
7/9/94	2	2	5/10	Poor Heart	Lifeboy
7/13/94	2	2	6/13	NICU	Julius
7/13/94	0	2	8/13	Julius	BBFCFM
7/13/94	0	2	10/13	BBFCFM	Mound
10/7/94	4	2	7/10	Scent of a Mule	Lifeboy
10/10/94	3	2	4/9	Esther	Fee
10/14/94	3	2	2/10	The Curtain	Lifeboy
10/22/94	6	2	6/11	Dinner and a Movie	Wilson
10/27/94	4	2	3/7	Ya Mar	Contact
11/2/94	4	2	2/7	Halley's Comet	The Mango Song
11/13/94	4	2	4/8	The Lizards	The Mango Song
11/18/94	4	2	5/7	Poor Heart	Contact
11/23/94	4	2	4/7	Scent of a Mule	Lifeboy
11/28/94	3	2	3/5	NICU	Sleeping Monkey
12/1/94	2	2	3/10	Mound	BBFCFM
12/1/94	0	2	7/10	NICU	Jesus Just Left
12/4/94	3	1	5/9	Rift	Fee
12/9/94	4	2	3/9	Poor Heart	McGrupp
12/30/94	4	2	3/8	Poor Heart	I'm Blue, Lonesome
6/8/95	4	2	5/8	Bouncing	Lifeboy
6/14/95	4	2	3/5	Poor Heart	Acoustic Army
6/17/95	3	2	4/11	Mound	Johnny B. Goode
6/17/95	0	2	6/11	Johnny B. Goode	McGrupp
6/22/95	3	2	3/4	Jam	Tweezer Repri

DATE	GAP	SET	POS.	SONG BEFORE	SONG AFTER
6/28/95	5	2	3/10	Poor Heart	Dave's Energy Guide
6/28/95	0	2	5/10	Dave's Energy Guide	Gumbo
7/2/95	4	2	4/8	Scent of a Mule	Ha Ha Ha
9/28/95	3	2	4/8	Don't You Wanna Go	Keyboard Cavalry
10/6/95	6	2	5/8	NICU	Keyboard Cavalry
10/15/95	6	2	3/8	Simple	The Lizards
10/22/95	5	2	5/11	The Curtain	Makisupa Policeman
11/12/95	10	2	2/8	The Curtain	Keyboard Cavalry
11/19/95	5	2	4/8	The Curtain	Billy Breathes
11/30/95	7	2	2/8	Cars Trucks Buses	Makisupa Policeman
12/2/95	2	2	5/9	Faht	A Day in the Life
12/8/95	4	2	2/8	Also Sprach	Kung
12/8/95	0	2	4/8	Kung	Love You
12/14/95	4	2	2/10	The Curtain	Timber (Jerry)
12/14/95	0	2	4/10	Timber (Jerry)	Keyboard Cavalry
12/17/95	3	2	7/8	Sparkle	Tweezer Repri
12/28/95	1	2	5/8	Buried Alive	I Didn't Know
7/7/96	9	1	5/10	The Curtain	Sweet Adeline
7/12/96	4	1	9/10	Theme From the Botto	Llama
7/21/96	6	1	4/14	Rift	If I Could
8/2/96	5	1	9/11	Golgi Apparatus	Hello My Baby
8/6/96	3	2	2/8	The Curtain	Prince Caspian
8/14/96	5	2	6/10	Cars Trucks Buses	Theme From the Botto
8/17/96	2	3	4/7	Scent of a Mule	A Day in the Life
10/17/96	2	1	4/10	Sparkle	Theme From the Botto
10/23/96	5	2	3/8	Ya Mar	The Lizards
10/27/96	3	2	6/9	Ya Mar	Fluffhead
11/3/96	4	2	5/8	Sparkle	Life on Mars
11/11/96	5	2	6/11	Sample in a Jar	Swept Away
11/18/96	5	2	6/9	Scent of a Mule	Hello My Baby
11/27/96	5	2	4/8	Scent of a Mule	Sweet Emotion Jam
12/1/96	3	2	1/10	***	Sparkle
12/30/96	6	2	5/8	Guyute	Lifeboy
2/16/97	4	1	7/10	Ginseng Sullivan	Waste
2/20/97	1	2	1/10	The Curtain	Soul Shake Down Part
8/2/97	37	2	2/7	Down with Disease	Johnny B. Goode
8/17/97	10	1	8/10	Bouncing	Taste
11/17/97	4	1	1/5	***	Reba
11/22/97	3	2	2/5	Halley's Comet	Black-Eyed Katy
11/26/97	2	1	1/10	***	Sparkle
12/6/97	7	2	1/7	***	Izabella
12/12/97	4	1	6/8	Bouncing	Train Song
12/31/97	5	3	3/6	Auld Lang Syne	Maze
4/4/98	3	1	1/8	***	Taste
7/1/98	3	2	1/5	***	Also Sprach
7/9/98	6	1	7/8	Poor Heart	Hello My Baby
7/15/98	2	2	3/6	Simple	Free
7/19/98	3	2	4/7	Piper	Jesus Just Left
7/25/98	4	2	4/8	Frankenstein	When Circus Comes
8/1/98	5	2	5/10	Magilla	Fluffhead
8/15/98	2	2	5/9	Sanity	The Horse
10/30/98	7	2	3/7	Manteca	NICU
11/14/98	10	1	5/8	Bouncing	The Moma Dance
11/24/98	6	2	3/6	Halley's Comet	Possum
11/28/98	3	2	8/9	Crossroads	Cavern
12/31/98	5	2	3/7	Character Zero	Cities

DATE	GAP	SET	POS.	SONG BEFORE	SONG AFTER
7/10/99	8	2	1/5	***	Mountains in the Mis
7/17/99	5	1	7/10	Roggae	Have Mercy
7/24/99	5	2	1/8	***	Catapult
7/24/99	0	2	3/8	Catapult	The Mango Song
8/1/99	6	2	2/9	Possum	Llama
9/9/99	1	2	6/9	First Tube	Bug
9/18/99	7	1	1/7	***	Roses Are Free
9/28/99	7	2	4/7	First Tube	Makisupa Policeman
10/2/99	3	2	1/6	***	On Your Way Down
10/8/99	4	2	2/7	Halley's Comet	Bug
12/4/99	5	1	5/7	Guyute	Dirt
12/10/99	4	1	1/10	***	Bouncing
12/16/99	5	2	4/5	Wading In Velvet Sea	Runaway Jim
12/30/99	3	2	3/10	The Curtain	Taste
6/9/00	5	2	1/7	***	Bouncing
6/24/00	9	1	4/6	Bouncing	Strange Design
6/30/00	4	1	3/10	AC/DC Bag	Runaway Jim
7/8/00	6	2	4/9	Rock and Roll	Walk Away
9/23/00	16	2	2/7	Birds of a Feather	NICU
9/25/00	2	1	4/8	The Lizards	Back on the Train
10/7/00	8	2	3/7	Also Sprach	Wading In Velvet Sea

Was played in the most recent show.

Tweezer Reprise

DATE	GAP	SET	POS.	SONG BEFORE	SONG AFTER
9/21/90	212	2	8/8	Buried Alive	***
2/1/91	30	1	4/10	Tweezer	Magilla
2/7/91	3	2	6/14	Tweezer	Guelah Papyrus
3/29/91	23	E	2/3	Contact	Good Time Ba
4/16/91	10	2	11/11	Carolina	***
4/22/91	5	E	4/4	Tweezer	***
4/27/91	2	2	13/13	Wipeout	***
5/3/91	2	2	9/9	Harpua	***
5/11/91	4	2	12/12	Suzy Greenberg	***
7/12/91	7	E	2/2	Fee	***
7/21/91	7	2	9/9	Contact	***
7/26/91	4	2	10/10	The Lizards	***
9/27/91	5	2	10/10	You Enjoy Myself	***
10/3/91	5	E	2/2	Terrapin	***
10/12/91	5	2	10/10	Harry Hood	***
11/1/91	12	2	13/13	Poor Heart	***
11/9/91	4	2	10/10	My Sweet One	***
11/23/91	11	2	13/13	My Sweet One	***
12/5/91	4	2	13/13	My Sweet One	***
12/31/91	3	E	3/3	Rocky Top	***
3/7/92	2	2	11/11	Cracklin' Rosie	***
3/12/92	2	E	3/3	Weigh	***
3/25/92	9	E	2/2	Sleeping Monkey	***
3/30/92	4	2	13/13	Bouncing	***
4/1/92	2	2	11/13	The Squirming Coil	Contact
4/7/92	5	E	2/2	Contact	***
4/17/92	2	E	8/8	Cracklin' Rosie	***
4/23/92	5	E	2/2	Sleeping Monkey	***
4/30/92	4	2	11/11	Harry Hood	***
5/3/92	3	E	3/3	Sweet Adeline	***
5/7/92	3	2	12/12	The Squirming Coil	***
5/9/92	2	E	2/2	Poor Heart	***
5/16/92	5	2	13/13	Poor Heart	***
7/14/92	14	2	10/10	Take the A-Train	***
7/24/92	8	1	6/6	You Enjoy Myself	***
11/22/92	26	E	3/3	Carolina	***
11/25/92	2	2	9/9	My Sweet One	***
11/28/92	2	E	2/2	Contact	***
12/5/92	6	2	13/13	Whipping Post	***
12/10/92	4	E	3/3	Carolina	***
12/12/92	2	E	2/2	Ride Captain Ride	***
12/29/92	3	2	14/14	The Squirming Coil	***
2/3/93	3	E	2/2	Amazing Grace	***

DATE	GAP	SET	POS.	SONG BEFORE	SONG AFTER
2/5/93	2	2	10/10	The Squirming Coil	***
2/7/93	2	2	13/13	If I Only Had a Brai	***
2/10/93	2	E	3/3	Amazing Grace	***
2/13/93	3	E	2/2	Amazing Grace	***
2/20/93	5	2	22/22	Harry Hood	***
2/22/93	2	2	11/11	The Squirming Coil	***
2/26/93	3	2	11/11	The Squirming Coil	***
3/2/93	2	E	2/2	Golgi Apparatus	***
3/6/93	3	E	3/3	Poor Heart	***
3/9/93	2	2	15/15	The Squirming Coil	***
3/13/93	2	2	13/13	Love You	***
3/16/93	2	E	2/2	Sparkle	***
3/21/93	4	E	3/3	Sweet Adeline	***
3/26/93	4	2	12/12	The Great Gig in the	***
3/30/93	3	2	15/15	If I Only Had a Brai	***
4/1/93	2	E	2/2	Carolina	***
4/5/93	3	2	9/9	Cracklin' Rosie	***
4/12/93	2	2	10/10	Terrapin	***
4/14/93	1	E	3/3	Contact	***
4/18/93	3	2	12/12	Love You	***
4/22/93	3	2	10/10	Love You	***
4/25/93	3	2	11/11	Fee	***
4/30/93	3	E	3/3	Amazing Grace	***
5/3/93	3	2	12/12	My Sweet One	***
5/6/93	2	E	3/3	Contact	***
7/17/93	7	E	3/3	Daniel	***
7/25/93	6	2	10/10	Harpua	***
8/6/93	8	2	12/12	Cracklin' Rosie	***
12/31/93	20	3	9/9	Harry Hood	***
4/16/94	11	2	9/9	The Squirming Coil	***
5/4/94	14	1	10/10	Rift	***
5/7/94	2	2	12/12	HYHU Jam	***
5/22/94	11	2	9/9	Slave	***
5/25/94	2	E	2/2	Sleeping Monkey	***
6/10/94	2	2	9/9	Harry Hood	***
6/18/94	6	E	2/2	Bouncing	***
6/23/94	4	E	2/2	Sparkle	***
6/29/94	4	E	2/2	Ya Mar	***
7/2/94	3	1	9/9	Sparkle	***
7/6/94	3	2	10/10	Harry Hood	***
7/9/94	2	E	2/2	Sleeping Monkey	***
7/13/94	2	E	2/2	My Sweet One	***
10/7/94	4	2	10/10	My Sweet One	***
10/10/94	3	E	2/2	Foreplay/Long Time	***
10/14/94	3	2	10/10	The Squirming Coil	***
10/22/94	6	E	2/2	Uncle Pen	***
10/27/94	4	E	3/3	Icculus	***
11/2/94	4	E	3/3	Foreplay/Long Time	***
11/13/94	4	E	2/2	Funky Bitch	***
11/23/94	8	2	7/7	You Enjoy Myself	***
11/28/94	3	E	2/2	Fee	***
12/1/94	2	E	2/2	Sleeping Monkey	***
12/9/94	7	E	3/3	Foreplay/Long Time	***
12/30/94	4	2	8/8	Harry Hood	***
6/14/95	8	E	3/3	Rocky Top	***
6/22/95	6	2	4/4	Tweezer	***
6/28/95	5	2	10/10	Harry Hood	***
7/2/95	4	E	2/2	Halley's Comet	***
10/15/95	15	2	8/8	Harry Hood	***
10/21/95	4	1	1/12	***	Chalk Dust Tor
10/21/95	0	1	12/12	Good Times Bad Times	***
11/9/95	8	1	1/8	***	Divided Sky
11/12/95	3	2	8/8	Possum	***
11/19/95	5	E	2/2	Life on Mars	***
12/2/95	9	2	9/9	The Squirming Coil	***
12/8/95	4	2	7/8	The Squirming Coil	Run Like Antel
12/15/95	5	2	1/8	***	Runaway Jim
12/15/95	0	E	2/2	Good Times Bad Times	***
12/17/95	2	2	8/8	Tweezer	***
12/28/95	1	E	2/2	Fee	***
8/6/96	27	2	8/8	Harry Hood	***
8/14/96	5	2	10/10	Sample in a Jar	***
8/17/96	2	3	7/7	Possum	***
10/17/96	2	1	10/10	A Day in the Life	***
10/27/96	8	2	9/9	Life On Mars	***
11/3/96	4	2	8/8	Possum	***

DATE	GAP	SET	POS.	SONG BEFORE	SONG AFTER
11/18/96	10	2	8/9	Hello My Baby	Llama
11/27/96	5	E	2/2	Waste	***
12/1/96	3	2	8/10	Steep	Johnny B. Goode
12/31/96	7	1	10/10	Sample in a Jar	***
2/16/97	3	2	11/11	Loving Cup	***
2/20/97	3	1	10/10	David Bowie	***
3/2/97	8	2	9/9	Slave	***
8/2/97	29	2	7/7	Loving Cup	***
8/17/97	10	E	2/2	When Circus Comes	***
11/22/97	7	E	2/2	Bouncing	***
11/26/97	2	2	8/8	Poor Heart	***
12/6/97	7	2	7/7	Sleeping Monkey	***
12/12/97	4	2	7/7	Izabella	***
12/31/97	5	E	2/2	New York New York	***
4/3/98	2	E	3/3	Halley's Comet	***
7/15/98	12	E	2/2	Wilson	***
7/19/98	3	E	2/2	Possum	***
7/25/98	4	E	2/2	Harry Hood	***
8/1/98	5	E	2/2	Been Caught Stealin'	***
8/15/98	9	E	3/3	Cavern	***
10/31/98	8	E	2/2	Sleeping Monkey	***
11/14/98	9	E	2/2	So Lonely	***
11/24/98	6	E	2/2	Suzy Greenberg	***
11/28/98	3	E	2/2	Sample in a Jar	***
12/31/98	5	3	5/6	Harry Hood	Llama
7/10/99	8	E	2/2	While My Guitar Gent	***
7/24/99	10	E	4/4	Alumni Blues	***
8/1/99	6	E	2/2	Sweet Adeline	***
9/9/99	1	E	3/3	Golgi Apparatus	***
9/18/99	7	E	2/2	Contact	***
9/28/99	7	E	2/2	Halley's Comet	***
9/29/99	1	1	9/9	Theme From the Botto	***
10/2/99	2	E	2/2	While My Guitar Gent	***
10/8/99	4	E	2/2	The Squirming Coil	***
12/4/99	5	2	2/2	Julius	***
12/8/99	3	E	2/2	Golgi Apparatus	***
12/16/99	6	E	2/2	Bittersweet Motel	***
12/30/99	3	E	2/2	Boogie On Reggae	***
6/9/00	5	2	7/7	Meatstick	***
6/24/00	9	E	4/4	Driver	***
6/30/00	4	1	9/10	Golgi Apparatus	Possum
7/8/00	6	E	2/2	Suzy Greenberg	***
9/23/00	16	E	2/2	Sleeping Monkey	***
9/25/00	2	E	3/3	Driver	***
10/7/00	8	2	7/7	David Bowie	***

Was played in the most recent show.

Twist

DATE	GAP	SET	POS.	SONG BEFORE	SONG AFTER
6/14/97	879	2	1/8	***	Piper
6/20/97	3	2	6/8	Cavern	Bouncing
6/21/97	1	1	14/15	Jam	Cavern
6/24/97	2	2	2/2	NICU	Piper
7/5/97	7	1	7/13	Prince Caspian	Piper
7/29/97	10	2	4/8	Wading In Velvet Sea	Taste
8/3/97	4	1	7/10	My Mind's Got A Mind	Jesus Just Left
8/6/97	1	1	4/8	Beauty of My Dreams	Also Sprach
11/14/97	10	2	3/4	Piper	Slave
11/23/97	6	1	5/9	Sparkle	Stash
12/6/97	8	2	4/7	Jam	Piper
4/2/98	10	2	7/9	Frankie Says	Sleeping Monkey
7/31/98	24	2	6/9	Avenu Malkenu	Izabella
7/3/99	44	2	1/7	***	Piper
7/9/99	4	2	7/8	Sweet Emotion Jam	Weekapaug Gr
7/12/99	2	2	1/6	***	The Moma Dance
7/20/99	6	2	1/6	***	The Moma Dance
9/10/99	11	1	3/8	First Tube	Divided Sky
9/19/99	7	2	1/6	***	Sand
9/26/99	5	2	1/7	***	Piper
10/3/99	5	2	1/8	***	Possum
12/5/99	9	1	10/10	Ginseng Sullivan	***
12/10/99	3	2	6/7	Cracklin' Rosie	Waste

DATE	GAP	SET	POS.	SONG BEFORE	SONG AFTER
12/17/99	6	1	8/8	Water in the Sky	***
12/31/99	3	2	7/35	Heavy Things	Prince Caspian
5/21/00	1	2	4/8	Dirt	Piper
5/23/00	2	2	2/8	Punch You In The Eye	Waste
6/10/00	2	2	6/9	Bathtub Gin	Albuquerque
6/14/00	3	2	2/5	Back on the Train	Jam
6/23/00	4	2	4/7	Down with Disease	Contact
6/30/00	5	2	3/9	The Mango Song	The Inlaw Josie Wale
7/4/00	3	2	4/5	Magilla	Slave
7/8/00	3	2	6/9	Walk Away	The Horse
7/10/00	1	2	3/7	Sand	Fee
9/11/00	7	2	2/5	Chalk Dust Torture	Piper
9/18/00	5	2	2/4	Boogie On Reggae	McGrupp
9/30/00	8	2	5/7	The Famous Mockingbi	Sand
10/7/00	5	2	1/7	***	Also Sprach

Was played in the most recent show.

Uncle Pen

DATE	GAP	SET	POS.	SONG BEFORE	SONG AFTER
3/28/90	169	1	6/12	Tweezer	The Oh Kee Pa
4/4/90	1	2	5/8	The Lizards	The Sloth
4/5/90	1	2	2/13	Reba	Jesus Just Left
4/6/90	1	1	3/11	You Enjoy Myself	Rhombus Narration
4/8/90	2	1	7/8	Suzy Greenberg	Possum
4/9/90	1	2	3/11	Esther	La Grange
4/12/90	1	1	4/11	Walk Away	Possum
4/14/90	2	1	2/10	Split Open and Melt	Cavern
4/18/90	1	1	4/10	Weekapaug Groove	The Curtain
4/21/90	3	2	4/9	No Dogs Allowed	Fluffhead
4/22/90	1	1	2/12	Divided Sky	The Oh Kee Pa
4/26/90	1	1	4/9	You Enjoy Myself	Dinner and a
4/28/90	1	1	4/11	Suzy Greenberg	Dinner and a
4/29/90	1	1	7/13	Bouncing	Divided Sky
5/4/90	1	1	3/12	The Sloth	Tweezer
5/6/90	1	1	3/8	Bouncing	Reba
5/10/90	2	1	2/8	Suzy Greenberg	Bouncing
5/11/90	1	1	4/9	Weekapaug Groove	Foam
5/13/90	1	1	7/10	Runaway Jim	Divided Sky
5/15/90	1	1	7/12	Weekapaug Groove	Bouncing
5/23/90	2	1	7/12	Suzy Greenberg	Bouncing
5/31/90	3	1	9/12	I Didn't Know	Divided Sky
6/1/90	1	1	2/12	Rocky Top	Run Like Antel
6/2/90	1	1	1/9	***	Dinner and a
6/5/90	1	1	2/12	The Squirming Coil	Mike's Song
6/7/90	1	2	5/10	Tweezer	Divided Sky
6/8/90	1	1	5/8	Divided Sky	The Oh Kee Pa
6/9/90	1	1	7/10	Tweezer	Mike's Song
6/16/90	1	1	6/10	Horn	Bouncing
9/20/90	5	2	12/14	Stash	Tube
9/21/90	1	2	3/8	Stash	Tube
9/22/90	1	1	4/8	Fee	Bouncing
9/29/90	2	2	4/8	Gumbo	Stash
10/4/90	2	1	9/10	The Sloth	Golgi Apparat
10/5/90	1	1	4/10	Alumni Blues	Split Open and
10/7/90	2	1	2/14	Divided Sky	Stash
10/12/90	2	1	5/9	Bouncing	Cavern
10/19/90	1	1	3/15	Foam	Mike's Song
10/30/90	1	1	6/9	Suzy Greenberg	Cavern
10/31/90	1	E	1/2	***	BBFCFM
11/3/90	2	2	8/12	Fee	Reba
11/8/90	1	1	5/12	Foam	Llama
11/26/90	5	2	1/7	***	Col. Forbin's A
2/7/91	11	2	8/14	Guelah Papyrus	Cavern
2/14/91	3	E	1/2	***	La Grange
2/21/91	2	2	7/9	Guelah Papyrus	The Asse Festival
3/17/91	11	1	9/12	Fluffhead	Stash
3/23/91	2	2	8/11	The Lizards	Cavern
4/4/91	6	E	4/4	Contact	***
4/12/91	4	1	2/9	Llama	Divided Sky
4/16/91	2	2	7/11	Buried Alive	Tweezer
4/21/91	2	2	7/11	Llama	Harry Hood
4/22/91	1	2	3/10	Bathtub Gin	The Landlady

DATE	GAP	SET	POS.	SONG BEFORE	SONG AFTER
10/3/91	36	1	3/10	Foam	It's Ice
10/12/91	5	2	2/10	Tweezer	Fluffhead
10/13/91	1	E	2/3	Eliza	Carolina
10/18/91	3	2	2/12	Brother	Guelah Papyrus
10/24/91	3	2	5/11	The Lizards	Tube
11/1/91	5	1	8/11	Fluffhead	Tube
11/10/91	5	1	3/10	The Sloth	David Bowie
11/12/91	1	1	3/11	Golgi Apparatus	Brother
11/14/91	2	1	2/11	Wilson	Llama
11/16/91	2	1	2/11	The Landlady	Wilson
11/19/91	1	1	1/11	***	Foam
11/21/91	2	2	5/10	The Mango Song	Tweezer
11/23/91	2	1	8/11	Chalk Dust Torture	Brother
11/30/91	2	2	2/10	Chalk Dust Torture	Harry Hood
12/6/91	3	1	4/9	Reba	The Squirmin
3/12/92	6	2	7/11	The Squirming Coil	David Bowie
3/20/92	5	2	8/12	Cavern	Harry Hood
3/24/92	3	2	8/13	Brother	I Didn't Know
3/26/92	2	1	8/10	Fluffhead	NICU
3/30/92	3	2	2/13	Golgi Apparatus	Tweezer
4/1/92	2	2	5/13	Silent in the Mornin	Tweezer
4/4/92	2	1	4/10	Reba	Chalk Dust Tor
4/6/92	2	2	12/13	Cracklin' Rosie	Cavern
4/8/92	2	1	8/11	Reba	Stash
4/13/92	2	1	2/10	Golgi Apparatus	Stash
4/15/92	1	1	7/11	Stash	Cavern
4/17/92	2	2	6/8	Tweezer	Cracklin' Rosi
4/21/92	3	1	2/11	Suzy Greenberg	Split Open and
4/23/92	2	1	4/11	Split Open and Melt	Guelah Papyrus
4/24/92	1	1	4/11	The Famous Mockingbi	The Sloth
4/30/92	3	1	6/10	Reba	Stash
5/3/92	3	1	4/10	It's Ice	Fee
5/6/92	2	2	7/11	Bouncing	Chalk Dust Tor
5/8/92	2	1	4/12	Reba	It's Ice
5/10/92	2	1	5/10	Stash	Cavern
5/12/92	1	1	10/12	Buried Alive	Horn
6/23/92	1	5	5/8	Sweet Adeline	BBFCFM
6/24/92	1	1	4/9	Sweet Adeline	Guelah Papyrus
6/27/92	1	1	9/10	Bouncing	David Bowie
7/12/92	6	1	7/11	Maze	Glide
7/15/92	2	1	6/12	My Friend My Friend	Split Open and
7/28/92	11	1	3/6	Bouncing	The Squirmin
8/19/92	9	1	6/7	You Enjoy Myself	Llama
8/30/92	8	1	1/7	***	The Landlady
11/21/92	4	2	8/13	Silent in the Mornin	Guelah Papyrus
11/30/92	6	2	6/10	Glide	You Enjoy My
12/1/92	1	2	6/11	All Things Recnsdrd	Llama
12/3/92	2	1	6/12	Bouncing	Chalk Dust Tor
12/5/92	2	1	11/12	Sweet Adeline	Golgi Apparat
12/8/92	3	1	6/11	The Famous Mockingbi	Guelah Papyrus
12/11/92	2	1	3/11	It's Ice	Stash
12/13/92	2	1	6/11	Fee	Stash
12/29/92	2	1	8/12	Wilson	Stash
2/4/93	4	2	9/13	Lawn Boy	Big Ball Jam
2/6/93	2	2	10/14	Lifeboy	Big Ball Jam
2/11/93	4	2	3/11	Wilson	Mike's Song
2/13/93	2	2	3/11	Runaway Jim	Tweezer
2/21/93	6	1	4/10	Punch You in the Eye	Horn
2/22/93	1	2	2/11	Runaway Jim	It's Ice
2/25/93	2	2	6/11	You Enjoy Myself	Big Ball Jam
3/2/93	3	2	2/12	My Friend My Friend	Tweezer
3/5/93	2	2	4/11	Guelah Papyrus	Mike's Song
3/8/93	2	2	3/10	Cavern	Stash
3/13/93	3	2	6/13	Glide	Big Ball Jam
3/18/93	4	2	6/10	You Enjoy Myself	Big Ball Jam
3/19/93	1	2	3/10	It's Ice	Sample in a Ja
3/22/93	2	2	3/10	Guelah Papyrus	Stash
3/25/93	2	2	4/13	Sample in a Jar	Col. Forbin's A
3/27/93	2	1	7/10	My Friend My Friend	Sample in a Ja
3/31/93	2	2	4/10	Bouncing	Harry Hood
4/2/93	2	2	3/13	Sample in a Jar	Llama

DATE	GAP	SET	POS.	SONG BEFORE	SONG AFTER
4/10/93	4	1	7/10	My Friend My Friend	Chalk Dust Tor
4/16/93	3	2	10/13	Silent in the Mornin	Big Ball Jam
4/20/93	3	1	8/10	Glide	Lawn Boy
4/22/93	2	2	8/10	You Enjoy Myself	Love You
4/25/93	3	2	5/11	Contact	Big Ball Jam
4/29/93	2	1	2/10	Split Open and Melt	The Sloth
5/2/93	3	2	6/10	Big Ball Jam	Bouncing
5/6/93	3	2	4/11	Tela	Big Ball Jam
7/18/93	8	1	8/9	Divided Sky	Cavern
7/23/93	3	2	6/11	My Friend My Friend	Big Ball Jam
7/30/93	6	1	4/10	Horn	Stash
8/6/93	4	2	5/12	The Squirming Coil	You Enjoy My
8/21/93	12	2	3/10	Horn	Fee
8/24/93	1	1	9/11	Silent in the Mornin	Maze
12/28/93	4	2	7/9	Fast Enough for You	Harry Hood
4/11/94	10	2	5/11	The Famous Mockingbi	Sample in a Ja
4/17/94	5	2	3/9	Wolfman's Brother	The Sloth
4/22/94	4	1	3/11	Horn	Punch You in
4/29/94	5	2	6/11	Fee	Mike's Song
5/6/94	5	2	3/9	Golgi Apparatus	Sample in a Ja
5/12/94	4	2	5/11	Silent in the Mornin	Fluffhead
5/17/94	2	2	5/9	Lifeboy	Big Ball Jam
5/25/94	6	1	3/11	Sample in a Jar	Stash
6/14/94	9	1	10/14	My Friend My Friend	I Didn't Know
6/23/94	7	2	5/8	Axilla (Part II)	Tweezer
7/5/94	9	1	6/10	If I Could	Stash
7/14/94	6	2	5/10	If I Could	You Enjoy My
10/22/94	15	E	1/2	***	Tweezer Repri
10/29/94	6	2	6/11	Sparks	You Enjoy My
12/1/94	19	1	2/8	Sample in a Jar	Fast Enough for You
12/29/94	10	1	7/9	Silent in the Mornin	I Didn't Know
6/10/95	7	2	3/8	Fee	Mike's Song
6/17/95	5	1	5/9	Fee	Julius
6/20/95	2	2	4/9	Prince Caspian	Mike's Song
7/1/95	9	2	4/9	Theme From the Botto	Stash
9/30/95	6	1	5/9	Reba	Horn
10/8/95	6	1	8/9	Prince Caspian	Free
10/13/95	2	2	2/10	Tube	Theme From the Botto
10/17/95	3	1	3/10	Stash	AC/DC Bag
10/22/95	4	2	9/11	Life on Mars	Slave
10/28/95	4	1	4/10	Timber (Jerry)	Sample in a Ja
11/11/95	5	2	4/9	Suzy Greenberg	Fluffhead
11/16/95	4	2	4/9	Lifeboy	Ha Ha Ha
11/22/95	4	1	5/10	Fluffhead	Cavern
11/28/95	3	2	4/10	Suzy Greenberg	Free
12/7/95	7	E	1/1	***	***
12/28/95	9	2	7/8	I Didn't Know	Slave
7/7/96	9	1	7/10	Sweet Adeline	Cavern
7/15/96	6	2	8/9	Purple Rain	Run Like Antel
11/14/96	40	1	2/9	AC/DC Bag	Wolfman's Brother
11/27/96	8	1	6/9	The Sloth	Free
11/30/96	2	1	8/10	The Old Home Place	Prince Caspian
12/4/96	3	1	4/11	Horn	Timber (Jerry)
12/30/96	4	2	2/8	Timber (Jerry)	AC/DC Bag
2/14/97	3	1	8/9	Billy Breathes	Run Like Antel
2/20/97	4	2	4/12	Character Zero	Stash
3/2/97	8	1	2/13	Johnny B. Goode	Sample in a Ja
6/22/97	8	1	5/9	Dirt	Character Zer
7/5/97	8	1	3/13	Bouncing	Sample in a Ja
7/30/97	11	2	7/7	Bouncing	Prince Caspian
8/17/97	12	2	3/5	Bathtub Gin	Also Sprach
10/4/99	135	1	1/8	***	Funky Bitch
12/31/99	20	2	19/35	Axilla	David Bowie
6/15/00	9	1	4/8	AC/DC Bag	Ghost
6/22/00	2	2	9/10	Hold Whatcha Got	Freebird
6/25/00	3	E	1/2	***	Bold as Love
7/11/00	11	1	3/8	The Moma Dance	Drowned

Has not been played in the last 24 shows.

Uncloudy Day

DATE	GAP	SET	POS.	SONG BEFORE	SONG AFTER
10/3/98	977	1	10/10	Amazing Grace	***

Has not been played in the last 142 shows.

Undun

DATE	GAP	SET	POS.	SONG BEFORE	SONG AFTER
3/30/89	91	2	6/8	You Enjoy Myself	La Grange
10/22/89	33	E	1/2	***	Run Like Antel
11/30/89	11	2	5/11	The Famous Mockingbi	Fee
12/7/89	3	2	10/11	Possum	Golgi Apparat

Has not been played in the last 981 shows.

Us and Them

DATE	GAP	SET	POS.	SONG BEFORE	SONG AFTER
11/2/98	984	2	12/16	Money	Any Colour You Like

Has not been played in the last 135 shows.

Vacuum Jam

DATE	GAP	SET	POS.	SONG BEFORE	SONG AFTER
9/13/88	67	3	7/8	Sanity	Fire

Has not been played in the last 1052 shows.

Vacuum Solo

DATE	GAP	SET	POS.	SONG BEFORE	SONG AFTER
3/30/92	375	2	6/13	You Enjoy Myself	BBFCFM
7/9/92	45	1	10/12	David Bowie	David Bowie
7/10/92	1	1	9/10	Cavern	Run Like Antel
7/11/92	1	1	8/11	Cavern	Cavern
7/12/92	1	1	9/11	Glide	Glide
7/15/92	2	E	2/3	Possum	Possum
10/30/92	29	1	6/11	Cavern	Cavern

Has not been played in the last 665 shows.

Viola Lee Blues

DATE	GAP	SET	POS.	SONG BEFORE	SONG AFTER
9/17/99	1037	E	1/1	***	***

Has not been played in the last 82 shows.

Vultures

DATE	GAP	SET	POS.	SONG BEFORE	SONG AFTER
6/13/97	878	2	4/9	Water in the Sky	Slave
6/19/97	3	1	8/9	Waste	Runaway Jim
6/24/97	4	1	4/12	Dogs Stole Things	Guelah Papyrus
7/2/97	5	1	6/8	Ginseng Sullivan	Water in the Sky
7/22/97	8	1	6/8	Bouncing	Bye Bye Foot
7/31/97	6	2	3/7	When Circus Comes	McGrupp
8/3/97	2	1	5/10	Dirt	My Mind's Got A Mind
8/11/97	5	2	3/6	Piper	My Soul
8/17/97	4	1	4/10	Dogs Stole Things	Water in the Sky
12/13/97	21	1	7/9	Sample in a Jar	Tube
7/29/98	28	1	6/8	Farmhouse	Glide
8/6/98	5	1	6/12	Beauty of My Dreams	Train Song
11/27/98	31	1	9/11	Dogs Stole Things	When Circus Comes
7/4/99	10	1	7/10	The Wedge	I Didn't Know
7/16/99	8	1	6/9	Billy Breathes	Back on the Train
7/26/99	8	1	3/11	Back on the Train	Sleep
9/16/99	10	1	7/14	Dirt	Sparkle
9/21/99	4	2	4/8	Strange Design	Limb by Limb
10/4/99	10	1	3/8	Funky Bitch	Runaway Jim
10/10/99	4	1	6/7	Dirt	Stash
7/1/00	34	1	9/11	Roggae	Dirt
9/11/00	13	1	5/9	Brian and Robert	Horn
10/1/00	14	1	5/10	Beauty of my Dreams	The Inlaw Josie Wale

Has not been played in the last 4 shows.

Wading in the Velvet Sea

DATE	GAP	SET	POS.	SONG BEFORE	SONG AFTER
6/13/97	878	1	7/8	Wolfman's Brother	Taste
6/16/97	2	2	5/7	Reba	Dirt
6/19/97	1	2	4/7	I Saw it Again	Piper
6/24/97	4	2	6/7	Piper	Ghost
6/25/97	1	1	8/11	Theme From the Botto	I Saw it Again
7/2/97	4	2	4/4	Wormtown Jam	***
7/10/97	5	1	6/8	Llama	Jam

DATE	GAP	SET	POS.	SONG BEFORE	SONG AFTER
7/21/97	2	2	4/8	David Bowie	Theme From the Botto
7/29/97	5	2	3/8	Run Like an Antelope	Twist
8/2/97	3	2	5/7	Sparkle	Loving Cup
8/7/98	65	2	6/7	Limb by Limb	Weekapaug Gr
8/16/98	6	2	6/8	When Circus Comes	Sexual Heal-ing
10/15/98	2	2	5/10	The Moma Dance	Prince Caspian
10/17/98	1	1	8/10	Driver	Harry Hood
11/2/98	5	1	8/9	Limb by Limb	Sample in a Ja
11/8/98	4	2	7/8	Piper	Run Like Antel
11/15/98	5	2	5/7	Simple	Loving Cup
11/21/98	4	1	11/13	Foam	Guyute
11/24/98	1	2	5/6	Possum	Character Zer
11/27/98	2	E	1/3	***	Golgi Apparat
12/31/98	6	2	5/7	Cities	Run Like Antel
7/7/99	5	2	4/7	My Left Toe	My Left Toe
7/31/99	18	2	3/6	David Bowie	Prince Caspian
9/14/99	6	1	7/11	What's the Use	Farmhouse
9/19/99	4	2	3/6	Sand	The Squirmin
9/28/99	6	1	7/8	Maze	Harry Hood
10/3/99	4	2	7/8	David Bowie	Harry Hood
10/9/99	4	2	4/6	Down with Disease	Simple
12/2/99	2	1	6/10	Run Like an Antelope	Poor Heart
12/16/99	11	2	3/5	The Mango Song	Tweezer
12/31/99	4	2	34/35	Also Sprach	Meatstick
5/21/00	1	2	7/8	Harry Hood	Guyute
6/10/00	4	2	8/9	Albuquerque	Loving Cup
6/29/00	11	2	10/10	Frankenstein	***
7/12/00	10	E	1/1	***	***
9/20/00	11	2	5/9	It's Ice	Sand
10/7/00	12	2	4/7	Tweezer	Meatstick

Was played in the most recent show.

Wait

DATE	GAP	SET	POS.	SONG BEFORE	SONG AFTER
10/31/91	335	2	3/14	Costume Contest	Llama
10/31/91	0	2	6/14	Fee	My Sweet One
10/31/91	0	2	8/14	My Sweet One	David Bowie
12/6/91	21	2	11/12	Possum	Possum
5/14/92	52	2	9/13	Weekapaug Groove	McGrupp

Has not been played in the last 711 shows.

Waking Up

DATE	GAP	SET	POS.	SONG BEFORE	SONG AFTER
6/14/97	879	2	4/8	I Saw it Again	Dogs Stole Things

Has not been played in the last 240 shows.

Walfredo

DATE	GAP	SET	POS.	SONG BEFORE	SONG AFTER
2/13/97	863	1	5/12	Stash	Taste
2/14/97	1	2	6/9	Reba	Rocko William
2/18/97	3	1	8/10	Waste	Character Zer
2/22/97	3	1	1/10	***	Also Sprach
9/30/00	244	1	1/10	***	The Curtain With

Has not been played in the last 5 shows.

Walk Away

DATE	GAP	SET	POS.	SONG BEFORE	SONG AFTER
7/23/88	58	1	11/13	Possum	Bold as Love
7/24/88	1	1	1/10	***	Golgi Apparat
7/30/88	2	3	5/13	Timber (Jerry)	Possum
8/3/88	1	3	8/8	Funky Bitch	***
8/27/88	2	1	4/9	Funky Bitch	Fluffhead
9/8/88	1	1	2/8	Peaches en Regalia	Slave
9/13/88	2	1	1/8	***	Funky Bitch
9/24/88	2	2	3/7	The Lizards	Possum
10/29/88	1	2	5/10	Alumni Blues	Divided Sky
11/3/88	2	2	2/9	Time Loves a Hero	The Lizards
11/5/88	1	1	8/11	Golgi Apparatus	Fluffhead
2/6/89	7	3	2/9	Good Times Bad Times	Harry Hood
3/3/89	6	2	6/12	Possum	Col. Forbin's A
4/20/89	7	2	2/10	Divided Sky	You Enjoy My
5/13/89	8	1	9/12	Foam	Take the A-Trn
6/30/89	7	2	1/8	***	AC/DC Bag

DATE	GAP	SET	POS.	SONG BEFORE	SONG AFTER
8/17/89	1	2	1/6	***	AC/DC Bag
9/9/89	4	2	6/7	Harry Hood	Possum
10/12/89	6	2	6/7	Esther	The Lizards
10/20/89	3	2	2/10	No Dogs Allowed	Dinner and a
10/26/89	3	2	6/15	Reba	Bathtub Gin
10/31/89	2	1	7/9	Fee	Bathtub Gin
12/1/89	9	2	4/10	Divided Sky	The Lizards
12/7/89	2	2	5/11	Ya Mar	The Lizards
2/1/90	12	1	2/11	David Bowie	The Landlady
2/9/90	1	1	5/12	You Enjoy Myself	Bouncing
2/23/90	6	1	9/11	Ya Mar	Bouncing
3/28/90	12	1	4/12	Fee	Tweezer
4/4/90	1	1	3/8	You Enjoy Myself	Take the A-Trn
4/7/90	3	1	6/12	The Lizards	Bathtub Gin
4/8/90	1	2	2/10	Golgi Apparatus	The Lizards
4/12/90	2	1	3/11	Ya Mar	Uncle Pen
4/18/90	3	2	6/12	Reba	The Oh Kee Pa
4/21/90	1	1	6/10	Foam	The Oh Kee Pa
4/29/90	5	1	10/13	Fluffhead	Love You
5/7/90	3	1	1/5	***	Highway to Hell
5/24/90	7	2	8/11	Fee	Harry Hood
10/18/91	131	E	2/3	Sparkle	The Squirmin
11/2/91	9	2	8/11	Guelah Papyrus	The Landlady
2/20/93	157	2	4/22	Tweezer	Tweezer
3/28/93	26	2	1/9	***	Runaway Jim
4/18/93	13	2	10/12	Ya Mar	Love You
4/30/93	9	2	4/10	Sweet One	Mound
7/15/93	10	2	10/11	The Lizards	Daniel
7/22/93	5	2	3/11	Tweezer	Sparkle
7/30/93	7	E	1/2	***	Amazing Grce
8/14/93	11	2	4/13	Sparks	Run Like Antel
12/29/93	11	2	7/11	BBFCM	Big Ball Jam
5/7/94	29	2	8/12	Sweet Emotion Jam	Cannonball Jam
10/29/98	366	2	4/7	Reba	Simple
11/11/98	9	2	3/6	Simple	Limb by Limb
7/25/99	35	2	2/6	Birds of a Feather	Run Like Antel
12/7/99	34	E	1/2	***	Rocky Top
6/14/00	19	2	4/5	Jam	Also Sprach
6/29/00	8	2	7/10	Cities	Run Like Antel
7/8/00	7	2	5/9	Tweezer	Twist
10/5/00	24	2	5/7	Halley's Comet	Piper

Has not been played in the last 2 shows.

Walk This Way

DATE	GAP	SET	POS.	SONG BEFORE	SONG AFTER
9/29/00	11132	2	7/9	Meatstick	Rapper's De-light

Has not been played in the last 6 shows.

Waste

DATE	GAP	SET	POS.	SONG BEFORE	SONG AFTER
6/6/96	794	2	6/10	Stash	Character Zer
7/10/96	6	1	4/7	Split Open and Melt	David Bowie
7/19/96	7	1	4/6	Sweet Adeline	Chalk Dust Tor
8/5/96	8	2	6/13	Somewhere Over The	Talk
8/13/96	5	2	7/11	Somewhere Over The	Train Song
8/16/96	2	2	5/13	The Squirming Coil	Talk
10/16/96	2	E	1/1	***	***
10/18/96	2	2	5/6	Reba	Harry Hood
10/21/96	2	1	9/10	Stash	Possum
10/26/96	4	2	6/7	McGrupp	Run Like Antel
11/2/96	4	2	3/8	Run Like an Antelope	Harry Hood
11/7/96	3	1	6/10	Stash	Guyute
11/11/96	3	E	1/2	***	Cavern
11/18/96	5	E	1/2	***	Johnny B. Goode
11/23/96	3	2	8/10	Catapult	Amazing Grce
11/27/96	2	E	1/2	***	Tweezer Repri
11/29/96	1	2	9/10	You Enjoy Myself	Harry Hood
2/13/97	10	1	7/12	Taste	Poor Heart
2/16/97	2	1	8/10	Tweezer	Cavern
2/18/97	2	1	7/10	Stash	Walfredo
2/21/97	2	2	8/9	Reba	Prince Caspian
2/25/97	3	1	7/9	Stash	Taste

DATE	GAP	SET	POS.	SONG BEFORE	SONG AFTER
2/28/97	2	2	8/9	Axilla	Julius
3/2/97	2	2	6/9	Punch You in the Eye	Character Zer
3/18/97	1	2	8/10	Love Me Like a Man	Chalk Dust Tor
6/14/97	2	2	6/8	Dogs Stole Things	David Bowie
6/19/97	2	1	7/9	Maze	Vultures
7/6/97	12	2	3/5	You Enjoy Myself	Rocky Top
7/26/97	8	2	7/8	Free	Johnny B. Goode
12/11/97	33	E	1/1	***	***
4/2/98	7	1	7/8	Horn	Chalk Dust Tor
7/1/98	5	1	8/9	Piper	Chalk Dust Tor
7/17/98	10	1	5/7	Divided Sky	My Mind's Got A Mind
7/29/98	8	E	1/3	***	Golgi Apparat
8/9/98	8	2	6/11	Brian and Robert	Somewhere Over The
7/3/99	37	1	10/11	NICU	Meatstick
7/20/99	12	1	6/9	Divided Sky	Ghost
7/24/99	3	2	7/8	Happy Whip And Dung	Chalk Dust Tor
7/30a/99	3	1	6/7	Punch You in the Eye	Hello My Baby
9/14/99	8	1	4/11	The Curtain	Loving Cup
9/22/99	6	1	10/10	Sand	***
10/2/99	7	2	6/6	Frankenstein	***
12/10/99	13	2	7/7	Twist	***
5/23/00	12	2	3/8	Twist	Piper
7/3/00	16	E	1/1	***	***
7/14/00	3	4	3/7	David Bowie	Sand
10/1/00	18	E	1/1	***	***

Has not been played in the last 4 shows.

Water in the Sky

DATE	GAP	SET	POS.	SONG BEFORE	SONG AFTER
6/13/97	878	2	3/9	Maze	Vultures
6/16/97	2	1	4/10	Taste	Sample in a Ja
6/19/97	1	1	5/9	Punch You in the Eye	Maze
6/22/97	3	1	2/9	Taste	Stash
7/2/97	6	1	7/8	Vultures	Weekapaug Gr
7/22/97	8	1	3/8	My Soul	Stash
7/23/97	1	1	6/10	Ginseng Sullivan	Limb by Limb
7/25/97	1	1	4/7	Maze	Bathtub Gin
7/30/97	3	1	4/9	Chalk Dust Torture	Stash
8/2/97	2	1	7/8	Wolfman's Brother	Split Open and
8/8/97	3	1	6/7	It's Ice	Character Zer
8/11/97	3	1	3/8	Maze	Guyute
8/13/97	1	1	4/11	Stash	Gumbo
8/17/97	3	1	5/10	Vultures	Maze
11/29/97	11	1	11/12	Horn	David Bowie
12/30/97	13	1	3/7	Taste	Punch You in
6/30/98	6	1	3/13	Ghost	Bouncing
7/3/98	3	1	8/11	Limb by Limb	My Soul
7/5/98	1	1	7/9	Jam	Lawn Boy
7/15/98	5	1	2/13	Wolfman's Brother	The Moma Dance
7/20/98	4	1	8/10	Theme From the Botto	The Moma Dance
7/31/98	7	1	6/7	Cities	Stash
8/7/98	5	1	1/10	***	Drowned
8/15/98	5	1	9/12	Divided Sky	Funky Bitch
10/15/98	3	1	2/8	Ghost	Wolfman's Brother
11/8/98	10	1	8/10	Roggae	Stash
11/13/98	3	1	8/10	Farmhouse	The Sloth
7/1/99	17	1	8/10	Roggae	Back on the Train
7/10/99	6	1	4/8	Roggae	Back @ Chicken Shack
7/12/99	1	1	6/7	Split Open and Melt	Character Zer
7/18/99	5	1	3/11	Farmhouse	Bathtub Gin
9/17/99	17	1	7/11	The Moma Dance	When Circus Comes
9/24/99	5	1	4/10	Farmhouse	The Moma Dance
12/17/99	25	1	7/8	When Circus Comes	Twist
12/30/99	2	1	1/12	***	Light Up Or Leave Me
6/25/00	15	1	5/10	Punch You in the Eye	Funky Bitch
9/25/00	27	1	6/8	Back on the Train	Bug

DATE	GAP	SET	POS.	SONG BEFORE	SONG AFTER
Has not been played in the last 8 shows.					

We're Not Gonna Take It

DATE	GAP	SET	POS.	SONG BEFORE	SONG AFTER
10/8/99	10522		6/7	Harry Hood	Chalk Dust Tor
Has not been played in the last 67 shows.					

Weekapaug Groove

DATE	GAP	SET	POS.	SONG BEFORE	SONG AFTER
7/23/88	58	1	6/13	I Am Hydrogen	The Lizards
7/24/88	1	1	9/10	I Am Hydrogen	Bold As Love
7/25/88	1	2	3/6	I Am Hydrogen	Bold as Love
11/5/88	13	2	9/11	I Am Hydrogen	I Didn't Know
11/11/88	1	2	3/8	I Am Hydrogen	Mr. P.C.
12/10/88	2	1	9/12	I Am Hydrogen	Wilson
2/7/89	5	1	8/9	I Am Hydrogen	Golgi Apparat
3/3/89	5	2	3/12	I Am Hydrogen	Fee
3/4/89	1	1	5/8	I Am Hydrogen	Fee
3/12/89	1	1	3/8	I Am Hydrogen	If I Only Had a Brai
3/14/89	1	1	5/12	I Am Hydrogen	Fluffhead
3/24/89	1	1	4/10	I Am Hydrogen	Golgi Apparat
3/30/89	1	2	4/8	I Am Hydrogen	You Enjoy My
4/20/89	2	2	8/10	I Am Hydrogen	Love You
5/1/89	3	2	3/10	I Am Hydrogen	On Your Way Down
5/6/89	2	1	5/13	I Am Hydrogen	Esther
5/9/89	1	1	6/9	I Am Hydrogen	The Sloth
5/12/89	1	1	4/15	I Am Hydrogen	AC/DC Bag
5/20/89	2	2	4/9	I Am Hydrogen	Foam
5/21/89	1	1	6/13	I Am Hydrogen	Split Open and Sanity
5/26/89	1	1	5/9	I Am Hydrogen	Funky Bitch
5/27/89	1	1	4/11	I Am Hydrogen	Bathtub Gin
5/28/89	1	2	4/16	I Am Hydrogen	The Lizards
6/23/89	1	1	9/11	I Am Hydrogen	***
6/30/89	1	2	8/8	I Am Hydrogen	***
8/17/89	1	1	9/9	I Am Hydrogen	***
8/19/89	1	1	13/13	I Am Hydrogen	The Sloth
10/6/89	7	1	4/13	I Am Hydrogen	Suzy Greenber
10/7/89	1	1	5/11	I Am Hydrogen	Esther
10/12/89	1	2	4/7	I Am Hydrogen	AC/DC Bag
10/13/89	1	2	6/8	I Am Hydrogen	***
10/26/89	5	1	11/11	I Am Hydrogen	Fee
11/2/89	3	1	5/11	I Am Hydrogen	***
11/9/89	2	2	9/9	I Am Hydrogen	McGrupp
11/10/89	1	2	5/12	I Am Hydrogen	Bathtub Gin
11/16/89	2	1	3/11	I Am Hydrogen	If I Only Had a Brai
12/1/89	3	2	8/10	I Am Hydrogen	***
12/3/89	1	2	14/14	I Am Hydrogen	***
12/7/89	1	1	8/11	I Am Hydrogen	Alumni Blues
12/9/89	2	2	8/8	I Am Hydrogen	***
12/15/89	1	1	5/10	I Am Hydrogen	Ya Mar
12/16/89	1	1	6/9	I Am Hydrogen	The Lizards
12/29/89	1	1	10/10	I Am Hydrogen	***
12/30/89	1	E	4/4	I Am Hydrogen	***
12/31/89	1	2	3/7	I Am Hydrogen	Ya Mar
1/20/90	1	2	10/10	I Am Hydrogen	***
1/27/90	1	1	13/13	I Am Hydrogen	***
1/28/90	1	2	10/10	I Am Hydrogen	***
1/29/90	1	1	5/10	I Am Hydrogen	Jesus Just Left
2/1/90	1	1	11/11	I Am Hydrogen	***
2/9/90	1	1	11/12	I Am Hydrogen	Carolina
2/10/90	1	2	10/10	I Am Hydrogen	***
2/15/90	1	1	10/10	I Am Hydrogen	***
2/16/90	1	1	5/7	I Am Hydrogen	Donna Lee
2/17/90	1	1	9/12	I Am Hydrogen	Jam
2/23/90	2	2	10/11	I Am Hydrogen	Highway to Hell
3/1/90	3	2	5/7	I Am Hydrogen	Carolina
3/3/90	2	1	3/12	I Am Hydrogen	My Sweet One
3/7/90	1	2	9/9	I Am Hydrogen	***
3/8/90	1	2	10/12	I Am Hydrogen	Ballad - Curtis Loew
3/11/90	3	1	11/13	I Am Hydrogen	The Squirmin
3/28/90	2	2	7/16	I Am Hydrogen	Jesus Just Left
4/4/90	1	2	3/8	I Am Hydrogen	The Lizards
4/5/90	1	2	11/13	I Am Hydrogen	If I Only Had a Brai
4/7/90	2	1	12/12	I Am Hydrogen	***
4/8/90	1	2	7/10	I Am Hydrogen	Fee
4/12/90	2	2	11/11	I Am Hydrogen	***
4/14/90	2	1	10/10	I Am Hydrogen	***
4/18/90	1	1	3/10	I Am Hydrogen	Uncle Pen
4/20/90	2	2	4/11	I Am Hydrogen	La Grange
4/22/90	2	1	12/12	I Am Hydrogen	***
4/25/90	1	2	12/12	I Am Hydrogen	***
4/26/90	1	2	11/11	I Am Hydrogen	***
4/28/90	1	2	9/9	I Am Hydrogen	***
5/4/90	2	1	8/12	I Am Hydrogen	Caravan
5/6/90	1	1	8/8	I Am Hydrogen	***
5/11/90	3	1	3/9	I Am Hydrogen	Uncle Pen
5/13/90	1	2	3/12	I Am Hydrogen	Foam
5/15/90	1	1	6/12	I Am Hydrogen	Uncle Pen
5/23/90	2	2	11/11	I Am Hydrogen	***
5/30/90	1	1	13/14	I Am Hydrogen	Good Time Ba
6/1/90	2	1	6/12	I Am Hydrogen	Fee
6/5/90	2	1	5/12	I Am Hydrogen	Ya Mar
6/7/90	1	2	10/10	I Am Hydrogen	***
6/8/90	1	2	7/7	I Am Hydrogen	***
6/9/90	1	1	10/10	I Am Hydrogen	***
6/16/90	1	3	13/13	I Am Hydrogen	***
9/13/90	1	2	3/15	I Am Hydrogen	Magilla
9/14/90	1	1	11/11	I Am Hydrogen	***
9/16/90	1	2	12/14	I Am Hydrogen	Magilla
9/20/90	1	1	10/12	I Am Hydrogen	Eliza
9/29/90	4	2	8/8	I Am Hydrogen	***
10/1/90	1	1	3/11	I Am Hydrogen	The Asse Festival
10/5/90	2	1	4/13	I Am Hydrogen	My Sweet One
10/7/90	2	1	12/14	I Am Hydrogen	Take the A-Trn
10/12/90	2	2	10/10	I Am Hydrogen	***
10/19/90	1	1	6/5	I Am Hydrogen	Magilla
10/30/90	1	2	3/12	I Am Hydrogen	Magilla
10/31/90	1	2	12/12	I Am Hydrogen	***
11/2/90	1	1	8/14	I Am Hydrogen	Esther
11/3/90	1	2	4/12	I Am Hydrogen	Paul and Silas
11/4/90	1	2	6/13	I Am Hydrogen	Manteca
11/8/90	1	1	12/12	I Am Hydrogen	***
11/10/90	1	1	11/11	I Am Hydrogen	***
11/16/90	1	2	4/11	I Am Hydrogen	Lawn Boy
11/17/90	1	2	5/12	I Am Hydrogen	Esther
11/24/90	1	1	6/11	I Am Hydrogen	The Squirmin
11/26/90	1	2	7/7	I Am Hydrogen	***
11/30/90	1	1	4/11	I Am Hydrogen	Esther
12/7/90	2	2	3/11	I Am Hydrogen	Donna Lee
12/8/90	1	1	10/10	I Am Hydrogen	***
12/28/90	1	1	10/11	I Am Hydrogen	Golgi Apparat
12/31/90	2	1	9/12	I Am Hydrogen	Auld Lang Syne
2/8/91	5	2	7/11	I Am Hydrogen	Horn
2/14/91	2	2	3/12	I Am Hydrogen	Foam
2/16/91	2	1	12/12	I Am Hydrogen	***
2/19/91	1	2	4/15	I Am Hydrogen	Guelah Papyrus
2/21/91	2	1	11/11	I Am Hydrogen	***
2/26/91	1	2	12/12	I Am Hydrogen	***
2/28/91	1	2	7/13	I Am Hydrogen	Cavern
3/1/91	1	1	12/12	I Am Hydrogen	***
3/15/91	5	1	12/12	I Am Hydrogen	***
3/17/91	1	2	6/12	I Am Hydrogen	Foam
3/22/91	1	2	13/13	I Am Hydrogen	***
3/31/91	4	1	13/13	I Am Hydrogen	***
4/3/91	2	1	10/10	I Am Hydrogen	***
4/5/91	2	1	11/11	I Am Hydrogen	***
4/11/91	2	2	14/14	I Am Hydrogen	***
4/15/91	2	2	4/11	I Am Hydrogen	Horn
4/19/91	3	1	11/12	I Am Hydrogen	Sweet Adeline
4/21/91	2	1	13/14	I Am Hydrogen	Sweet Adeline
4/25/91	2	2	5/10	I Am Hydrogen	Tela
4/27/91	1	2	8/13	I Am Hydrogen	Fluffhead
5/4/91	3	1	11/11	I Am Hydrogen	***
5/10/91	2	2	11/11	I Am Hydrogen	***
5/11/91	1	2	8/12	I Am Hydrogen	Tela
5/12/91	1	2	9/13	I Am Hydrogen	The Squirmin
5/17/91	2	1	16/17	I Am Hydrogen	Take the A-Trn
7/11/91	3	2	8/10	I Am Hydrogen	Touch Me
7/12/91	1	2	9/14	I Am Hydrogen	Touch Me
7/14/91	2	3	8/10	I Am Hydrogen	Touch Me
7/15/91	1	1	9/14	I Am Hydrogen	Flat Fee
7/18/91	1	1	11/11	I Am Hydrogen	***
7/21/91	3	1	11/11	I Am Hydrogen	***
7/23/91	1	1	12/12	I Am Hydrogen	***
7/25/91	2	2	13/13	I Am Hydrogen	***
7/27/91	2	1	16/16	I Am Hydrogen	***
9/26/91	3	2	9/11	I Am Hydrogen	Lawn Boy
9/28/91	2	2	12/12	I Am Hydrogen	***
10/3/91	4	2	4/11	I Am Hydrogen	Esther
10/4/91	2	1	11/11	I Am Hydrogen	***
10/10/91	2	2	13/13	I Am Hydrogen	***
10/13/91	3	1	13/13	I Am Hydrogen	***
10/18/91	3	2	7/12	I Am Hydrogen	I Didn't Know
10/24/91	3	2	3/11	I Am Hydrogen	The Lizards
10/27/91	1	2	8/13	I Am Hydrogen	Tela
10/30/91	2	2	11/11	I Am Hydrogen	***
11/1/91	2	2	8/13	I Am Hydrogen	Take the A-Trn
11/8/91	3	2	8/13	I Am Hydrogen	Jesus Just Left
11/12/91	3	2	7/13	I Am Hydrogen	Guelah Papyrus
11/15/91	3	2	6/14	I Am Hydrogen	Eliza
11/19/91	2	2	5/11	I Am Hydrogen	The Mango Song
11/21/91	2	1	12/12	I Am Hydrogen	***
11/23/91	2	2	4/13	I Am Hydrogen	Horn
12/4/91	3	2	6/11	I Am Hydrogen	Sparkle
12/5/91	1	2	7/13	I Am Hydrogen	Fee
12/31/91	3	3	7/7	I Am Hydrogen	***
3/7/92	2	2	9/11	I Am Hydrogen	Cracklin' Rosi
3/14/92	4	1	13/13	I Am Hydrogen	***
3/17/92	1	2	9/11	I Am Hydrogen	Love You
3/20/92	2	2	3/12	I Am Hydrogen	Sanity
3/24/92	3	2	4/13	I Am Hydrogen	Guelah Papyrus
3/27/92	3	2	3/13	I Am Hydrogen	The Horse
3/31/92	3	2	3/13	I Am Hydrogen	Fee
4/6/92	5	2	6/13	I Am Hydrogen	NICU
4/8/92	2	2	10/15	I Am Hydrogen	The Horse
4/13/92	2	2	6/11	I Am Hydrogen	Magilla
4/16/92	2	2	6/12	I Am Hydrogen	Horn
4/19/92	2	2	4/13	I Am Hydrogen	The Horse
4/21/92	1	2	8/13	I Am Hydrogen	Weigh
4/23/92	2	2	5/13	I Am Hydrogen	The Lizards
4/24/92	1	2	7/12	I Am Hydrogen	The Mango Song
4/29/92	2	2	9/11	I Am Hydrogen	Love You
5/1/92	2	2	8/13	I Am Hydrogen	Mound
5/3/92	2	2	8/14	I Am Hydrogen	The Mango Song
5/5/92	1	2	7/14	I Am Hydrogen	The Horse
5/7/92	2	2	8/12	I Am Hydrogen	Fee
5/14/92	5	2	8/13	I Am Hydrogen	Wait
5/18/92	4	2	8/13	I Am Hydrogen	Fee
7/16/92	14	2	13/13	I Am Hydrogen	***
8/17/92	18	2	7/11	I Am Hydrogen	Horn
11/19/92	11	2	3/15	I Am Hydrogen	Bouncing
11/21/92	2	2	5/13	I Am Hydrogen	The Horse
11/23/92	2	2	9/14	I Am Hydrogen	Jam
11/23/92	0	2	12/14	Big Ball Jam	Lengthwise
11/28/92	3	1	11/11	I Am Hydrogen	***
12/1/92	2	1	12/12	I Am Hydrogen	***
12/3/92	2	2	6/13	I Am Hydrogen	Lawn Boy
12/5/92	2	2	11/13	I Am Hydrogen	Whipping Post
12/8/92	3	2	3/15	I Am Hydrogen	The Horse
12/11/92	2	2	4/12	I Am Hydrogen	Esther

DATE	GAP	SET	POS.	SONG BEFORE	SONG AFTER
12/29/92	4	2	11/14	I Am Hydrogen	Terrapin
12/31/92	2	3	3/9	Auld Lang Syne	Harpua
2/4/93	2	2	7/13	T.M.W.S.I.Y. Reprise	Lawn Boy
2/6/93	2	2	8/14	I Am Hydrogen	Lifeboy
2/9/93	2	2	4/12	I Am Hydrogen	Weigh
2/11/93	2	2	6/12	I Am Hydrogen	Mound
2/15/93	3	2	6/12	I Am Hydrogen	The Wedge
2/18/93	2	2	7/12	I Am Hydrogen	Mound
2/20/93	2	2	13/22	I Am Hydrogen	Have Mercy
2/20/93	0	2	15/22	Have Mercy	Rock and Roll All Ni
2/20/93	0	2	17/22	Rock and Roll All Ni	Fast Enough for You
2/23/93	3	2	9/13	I Am Hydrogen	Pig in a Pen
2/23/93	0	2	11/13	Pig in a Pen	Terrapin
2/27/93	3	2	9/12	I Am Hydrogen	Terrapin
3/3/93	2	2	7/13	I Am Hydrogen	Glide
3/9/93	4	2	8/15	I Am Hydrogen	The Horse
3/13/93	2	2	10/13	I Am Hydrogen	Fast Enough for You
3/17/93	3	2	8/12	I Am Hydrogen	The Horse
3/19/93	2	2	8/10	I Am Hydrogen	Love You
3/22/93	2	2	13/13	I Am Hydrogen	***
3/25/93	2	2	12/13	I Am Hydrogen	Golgi Apparat
3/27/93	2	2	11/14	I Am Hydrogen	Cracklin' Rosi
3/30/93	2	2	9/15	I Am Hydrogen	Psycho Killer Jam
3/30/93	0	2	11/15	Psycho Killer Jam	The Horse
4/2/93	3	2	9/13	I Am Hydrogen	The Lizards
4/10/93	4	2	9/13	The Great Gig in the	Funky Bitch
4/16/93	3	2	7/13	I Am Hydrogen	The Horse
4/21/93	4	2	10/11	The Great Gig in the	Gumbo
4/23/93	2	2	9/12	I Am Hydrogen	Lengthwise
4/25/93	2	2	9/11	I Am Hydrogen	Fee
4/29/93	2	2	9/13	I Am Hydrogen	Makisupa Policeman
4/29/93	0	2	11/13	Makisupa Policeman	Terrapin
5/1/93	2	2	10/11	The Great Gig in the	Cavern
5/8/93	6	2	16/18	I Am Hydrogen	Amazing Grce
7/17/93	5	2	9/12	Leprechaun	Faht
7/24/93	5	2	9/12	Yerushalayim	Purple Rain
7/31/93	6	2	8/11	Leprechaun	Purple Rain
8/2/93	1	2	7/9	The Squirming Coil	Bike
8/11/93	6	2	3/10	The Great Gig in the	Esther
8/16/93	5	2	3/10	Faht	Mound
8/24/93	4	2	6/10	Ginseng Sullivan	Wilson
12/30/93	6	2	7/9	McGrupp	Purple Rain
4/6/94	4	2	7/9	Lifeboy	The Squirmin
4/9/94	2	2	8/11	I Am Hydrogen	Tela
4/21/94	10	2	6/10	I Am Hydrogen	Scent of a Mul
4/29/94	6	2	9/11	I Am Hydrogen	I Wanna Be Like You
5/14/94	11	2	4/11	I Am Hydrogen	T.M.W.S.I.Y.
5/19/94	3	2	5/10	I Am Hydrogen	The Lizards
6/9/94	10	2	9/10	I Am Hydrogen	Golgi Apparat
6/13/94	3	2	3/11	I Am Hydrogen	Esther
6/17/94	3	2	8/15	I Am Hydrogen	Harpua
6/22/94	4	2	11/20	I Am Hydrogen	T.M.W.S.I.Y.
7/2/94	8	2	7/12	I Am Hydrogen	McGrupp
7/10/94	6	2	7/10	I Am Hydrogen	Bouncing
10/8/94	6	2	8/12	I Am Hydrogen	Fluffhead
10/13/94	4	2	10/12	Yerushalayim	Foreplay/Long Time
10/21/94	6	2	6/11	I Am Hydrogen	Sleeping Monkey
10/25/94	3	2	4/11	The Mango Song	Yerushalayim
11/4/94	8	2	6/9	Tela	Ya Mar
11/25/94	11	2	5/8	Harpua	The Mango Song
12/6/94	8	2	8/12	The Mango Song	Bike
12/10/94	4	2	7/11	I Am Hydrogen	Why Don't We Do It i
12/28/94	1	2	5/9	The Mango Song	Contact
12/31/94	3	2	8/9	Yerushalayim	Amazing Grce
6/10/95	5	2	6/8	I Am Hydrogen	Amazing Grce
6/20/95	7	2	7/9	Contact	Cracklin' Rosi
6/25/95	4	2	7/9	Jam	Amazing Grce
6/30/95	4	2	8/10	Contact	Amazing Grce
9/30/95	7	2	7/9	Keyboard Cavalry	Suspicious Minds
10/11/95	7	2	6/11	McGrupp	Llama
10/19/95	5	2	5/10	I Am Hydrogen	Lawn Boy
10/25/95	5	2	7/9	Sparkle	Suzy Greenber
11/11/95	7	1	5/12	Poor Heart	The Horse
11/15/95	3	2	6/8	Life on Mars	Fee
11/25/95	7	2	9/12	Strange Design	Harry Hood
12/1/95	4	2	3/9	Mike's Song	The Mango Song
12/7/95	4	2	9/10	Mike's Song	Amazing Grce
12/16/95	7	2	7/8	Simple	The Squirmin
12/31/95	5	3	2/6	Auld Lang Syne	Sea and Sand
7/23/96	18	2	7/9	I Am Hydrogen	Bike
8/5/96	5	2	13/13	I Am Hydrogen	***
8/13/96	5	2	5/11	Lifeboy	Somewhere Over The
8/16/96	2	2	13/13	Contact	***
10/22/96	7	2	10/10	Steep	***
10/29/96	5	2	10/10	Silent in the Mornin	The Wedge
11/6/96	4	2	6/9	Steep	Scent of a Mul
11/8/96	2	2	8/8	Star Spangled Banner	***
11/15/96	5	2	11/11	Mean Mr. Mustard	***
11/23/96	5	2	6/10	Axilla	Catapult
12/4/96	7	2	9/9	Lawn Boy	***
12/6/96	1	2	7/9	Harry Hood	Sweet Adeline
12/28/96	1	2	9/10	Strange Design	Star Spangled Banner
3/1/97	16	2	5/8	Lawn Boy	The Mango Song
7/2/97	15	1	8/8	Water in the Sky	***
7/22/97	8	2	5/6	I Am Hydrogen	Hello My Baby
7/31/97	6	2	7/7	I Am Hydrogen	***
8/9/97	5	2	10/10	Slave	***
11/13/97	7	2	7/10	I Am Hydrogen	***
11/22/97	6	1	3/8	I Am Hydrogen	Harry Hood
12/2/97	6	2	5/7	Ya Mar	Bouncing
12/9/97	5	1	6/10	I Am Hydrogen	Dogs Stole Things
12/13/97	3	2	7/10	When Circus Comes	Catapult
12/13/97	0	2	9/10	Catapult	Harry Hood
12/31/97	4	2	6/6	Roses Are Free	***
4/3/98	2	1	3/9	The Old Home Place	Train Song
6/30/98	3	2	12/12	Steep	***
7/10/98	8	2	6/8	Simple	Sample in a Ja
7/17/98	3	2	3/4	Mike's Song	Character Zer
7/21/98	3	2	4/8	Bittersweet Motel	Brian and Robert
8/1/98	7	1	4/9	Esther	***
8/7/98	4	2	7/7	Wading In Velvet Sea	***
8/12/98	4	2	6/7	Sleeping Monkey	The Squirmin
8/15/98	1	1	12/12	Cities	***
10/31/98	8	1	10/10	Frankie Says	***
11/7/98	4	1	10/10	Beauty of My Dreams	***
11/15/98	6	2	7/7	Loving Cup	***
11/21/98	4	2	9/9	Free	***
11/27/98	3	2	12/16	I Am Hydrogen	Wipeout
11/27/98	0	2	14/16	Wipeout	Weekapaug Reprise
12/31/98	6	1	4/7	I Am Hydrogen	Ghost
7/4/99	4	2	9/9	Sleeping Monkey	***
7/9/99	3	2	8/9	Twist	***
7/16/99	5	2	4/8	I Am Hydrogen	Simple
7/21/99	4	2	5/6	Prince Caspian	Golgi Apparat
8/1/99	4	2	6/9	I Am Hydrogen	The Wedge
9/16/99	6	2	4/9	I Am Hydrogen	Mountains in the Mis
9/22/99	5	2	8/8	Train Song	***
9/29/99	5	2	12/12	I Didn't Know	***
10/7/99	5	2	9/9	Golgi Apparatus	***
12/5/99	7	2	4/10	I Am Hydrogen	Brian and Robert
12/11/99	4	1	5/8	I Am Hydrogen	When Circus Comes
12/18/99	6	2	8/10	Simple	Buffalo Bill
12/18/99	0	2	10/10	Buffalo Bill	***
12/30/99	1	3	9/9	I Am Hydrogen	***
6/13/00	8	1	10/10	Simple	***
7/1/00	11	2	8/10	I Am Hydrogen	Nellie Kane
7/7/00	4	2	7/7	Simple	***
7/14/00	5	3	7/7	The Lizards	***
9/12/00	5	2	8/8	I Am Hydrogen	***
9/20/00	5	1	8/9	Avenu Malkenu	While My Guitar Gent
9/25/00	4	2	4/7	I Am Hydrogen	Axilla
9/30/00	3	1	10/10	Esther	***
10/7/00	5	1	4/8	I Am Hydrogen	Fee

Was played in the most recent show.

Weekapaug Reprise

DATE	GAP	SET	POS.	SONG BEFORE	SONG AFTER
11/27/98	1000	2	15/16	Weekapaug Groove	Run Like Antel

Has not been played in the last 119 shows.

Weigh

DATE	GAP	SET	POS.	SONG BEFORE	SONG AFTER
3/7/92	360	2	4/11	The Squirming Coil	Chalk Dust Tor
3/12/92	2	E	2/3	Sweet Adeline	Tweezer Repri
3/21/92	2	2	9/11	David Bowie	Cracklin' Rosi
3/30/92	7	2	9/13	The Squirming Coil	Chalk Dust Tor
4/5/92	5	2	7/12	Maze	The Landlady
4/21/92	11	2	9/13	Weekapaug Groove	Catapult
4/25/92	4	2	9/11	Harry Hood	Terrapin
7/16/92	31	2	2/13	Runaway Jim	The Landlady
7/26/92	8	1	4/7	Divided Sky	Split Open and
11/23/92	25	2	6/14	Llama	Mike's Song
2/9/93	26	2	5/12	Weekapaug Groove	My Sweet One
2/17/93	6	1	3/11	Possum	All Things Rec
2/20/93	3	1	5/11	Possum	All Things Rec
3/22/93	21	1	7/10	Rift	Reba
3/30/93	6	2	6/15	Big Ball Jam	Mike's Song
4/10/93	7	1	2/10	Runaway Jim	Sparkle
4/20/93	6	1	2/10	Runaway Jim	Sparkle
4/23/93	3	1	2/10	Runaway Jim	Sparkle
5/3/93	8	1	3/11	Rift	Chalk Dust Tor
5/5/93	1	2	6/10	Poor Heart	Big Ball Jam
7/29/93	17	1	3/10	Divided Sky	Rift
8/11/93	9	1	3/10	Runaway Jim	It's Ice
8/17/93	6	1	5/9	Divided Sky	Maze
12/30/93	9	1	2/10	David Bowie	The Curtain
5/20/94	37	2	3/7	Run Like an Antelope	Axilla (Part II)
6/7/95	89	1	2/10	Possum	Taste
10/22/95	40	1	5/12	Runaway Jim	NICU
8/12/96	66	1	9/10	Chalk Dust Torture	It's Ice
11/7/96	20	1	2/10	Chalk Dust Torture	Rift
3/1/97	36	1	4/10	Down with Disease	Beauty of My Dreams
7/30/97	28	1	6/9	Stash	Piper
8/17/97	12	3	3/7	NICU	Guyute
8/2/98	52	1	7/9	Reba	Too Much Of Evrythng

Has not been played in the last 152 shows.

West LA Fadeaway

DATE	GAP	SET	POS.	SONG BEFORE	SONG AFTER
10/6/00	1118	E	3/3	Chalk Dust Torture	***

Has not been played in the last 1 show.

What's the Use?

DATE	GAP	SET	POS.	SONG BEFORE	SONG AFTER
7/4/99	1010	2	5/9	Silent in the Mornin	Wilson
7/7/99	1	1	2/10	Back on the Train	Billy Breathes
7/9/99	2	2	3/8	Free	Meatstick
7/12/99	2	1	4/7	Back on the Train	Split Open and
7/20/99	2	3	2/6	The Moma Dance	Train Song
9/10/99	11	1	7/8	Carini	Will It Go Round
9/14/99	3	1	6/11	Loving Cup	Wading In Velvet Sea
6/25/00	49	2	6/7	Maze	Slave
7/10/00	10	2	5/7	Fee	Limb by Limb
9/11/00	12	2	4/5	Piper	You Enjoy My

Has not been played in the last 18 shows.

When Something is Wrong with My Baby

DATE	GAP	SET	POS.	SONG BEFORE	SONG AFTER
4/24/93	538	1	9/11	Caravan	Sparkle
4/25/93	1	E	1/3	***	Carolina
4/30/93	3	E	1/3	***	Amazing Grce

Has not been played in the last 577 shows.

When the Circus Comes

DATE	GAP	SET	POS.	SONG BEFORE	SONG AFTER
2/13/97	863	2	6/10	Slave	Maze
2/16/97	2	2	6/11	Simple	Swept Away
2/20/97	3	1	8/10	Gumbo	David Bowie
2/22/97	2	1	6/10	NICU	Talk
6/14/97	9	E	1/2	***	Rocky Top
6/20/97	3	E	1/2	***	Rocky Top
7/1/97	7	E	1/1	***	***
7/22/97	9	E	1/2	***	Harry Hood
7/31/97	6	2	2/7	Runaway Jim	Vultures
8/9/97	5	E	1/2	***	Rocky Top
8/17/97	6	E	1/2	***	Tweezer Repri
11/17/97	4	2	6/7	Jesus Just Left	You Enjoy My
11/30/97	8	2	6/7	Piper	Run Like Antel
12/13/97	9	2	6/10	Llama	Weekapaug Gr
12/31/97	4	2	4/6	Piper	Roses Are Free
7/9/98	12	2	3/8	Theme From the Botto	Scent of a Mul
7/16/98	3	1	6/7	Fast Enough for You	Run Like Antel
7/25/98	6	2	5/8	Tweezer	Limb By Limb
8/3/98	7	E	1/2	***	Run Like Antel
8/11/98	5	2	4/5	Limb by Limb	Down with Dis
8/16/98	2	2	5/8	Fluffhead	Wading In Velvet Sea
11/11/98	14	2	5/6	Limb by Limb	Ghost
11/27/98	10	1	10/11	Vultures	Birds of a Feather
12/28/98	3	2	4/6	Birds of a Feather	Quinn the Eskimo
7/3/99	6	1	6/11	Taste	Tube
7/10/99	5	2	4/5	Birds of a Feather	Fluffhead
7/21/99	8	1	8/10	The Moma Dance	Taste
9/11/99	11	E	1/1	***	***
9/17/99	4	1	8/11	Water in the Sky	Back on the Train
10/7/99	14	1	7/9	Possum	Gotta Jibboo
12/4/99	6	2	8/9	T.M.W.S.I.Y. Reprise	David Bowie
12/11/99	5	1	6/8	Weekapaug Groove	Scent of a Mul
12/17/99	5	1	6/8	Punch You in the Eye	Water in the Sky
12/30/99	2	3	5/9	The Sloth	Mike's Song
5/23/00	4	1	8/12	It's Ice	Back on the Train
6/11/00	3	2	6/8	David Bowie	Back on the Train
7/3/00	13	1	9/10	Fluffhead	Run Like Antel
9/15/00	15	2	4/5	Tube	Character Zer
9/22/00	4	2	5/7	The Wedge	Meatstick
10/1/00	7	2	4/7	Guy Forget	Camel Walk

Has not been played in the last 4 shows.

While My Guitar Gently Weeps

DATE	GAP	SET	POS.	SONG BEFORE	SONG AFTER
10/31/94	681	2	8/30	The Continuing Story	Happiness is a Warm
11/2/94	1	1	8/8	Scent of a Mule	***
12/8/94	23	1	10/10	The Lizards	***
6/7/95	8	E	1/1	***	***
6/14/95	5	2	5/5	Acoustic Army	***
6/22/95	6	E	2/2	Acoustic Army	***
6/28/95	5	E	2/2	Sweet Adeline	***
7/2/95	4	1	10/10	Rift	***
10/5/95	8	E	1/1	***	***
10/13/95	5	2	8/10	The Lizards	Sweet Adeline
10/20/95	5	2	6/10	Gumbo	My Long Journey Home
10/28/95	6	E	1/1	***	***
11/15/95	8	2	8/8	Fee	***
12/4/95	13	1	11/11	Hello My Baby	***

Whipping Post

DATE	GAP	SET	POS.	SONG BEFORE	SONG AFTER
12/11/95	5	E	1/1	***	***
2/26/97	90	1	10/10	Dog Gone Dog	***
8/16/98	103	3	7/7	Bittersweet Motel	***
11/7/98	11	E	2/2	Guyute	***
12/31/98	19	E	1/1	***	***
7/10/99	8	E	1/2	***	Tweezer Repri
10/2/99	34	E	1/2	***	Tweezer Repri
7/1/00	40	E	1/1	***	***
7/15/00	10	2	2/7	Down with Disease	Makisupa Policeman
9/20/00	9	1	9/9	Weekapaug Groove	***
10/5/00	10	E	1/1	***	***

Has not been played in the last 2 shows.

Whipping Post

DATE	GAP	SET	POS.	SONG BEFORE	SONG AFTER
11/3/84	2	1	9/10	Eyes of the World	Drums Jam
5/3/85	3	3	3/8	Eyes of the World	McGrupp
12/6/86	11	1	3/14	Little Drummer Boy	She Caught The Katy
8/10/87	10	3	4/7	Jesus Just Left	Anarchy
10/31/87	7	1	2/11	Jam	Sneakin' Sally
11/19/87	23	3	8/14	Ballad - Curtis Loew	Letter to Jimmy Page
1/27/88	1	2	10/10	The Sloth	***
2/7/88	1	2	9/9	The Famous Mockingbi	***
2/26/88	3	2	9/9	Alumni Blues	***
5/15/88	8	2	10/11	Flat Fee	Harpua
5/25/88	2	2	3/3	Fluffhead	***
6/15/88	1	2	8/9	Good Times Bad Times	Dear Mrs. Reagan
9/8/88	14	2	8/8	On Your Way Down	***
9/24/88	4	2	7/7	Sparks	***
10/29/88	1	2	2/10	Halley's Comet	Fee
11/3/88	2	2	5/9	Shaggy Dog	Contact
11/11/88	2	2	8/8	The Lizards	***
2/6/89	6	3	8/9	The Famous Mockingbi	Corrine Corrina
2/7/89	1	3	6/6	Bike	***
2/18/89	3	1	1/9	***	Corrine Corrina
4/27/89	10	1	8/8	The Lizards	***
5/9/89	5	2	14/14	Harpua	***
5/13/89	2	E	1/1	***	***
2/16/90	53	E	2/2	Carolina	***
3/7/90	9	E	1/1	***	***
3/9/90	2	E	1/1	***	***
3/28/90	4	2	3/16	Sweet Adeline	Funky Bitch
4/9/90	6	2	11/11	Tweezer	***
5/4/90	13	2	1/1	***	Sweet Adeline
5/10/90	3	E	1/1	***	***
6/5/90	11	E	1/2	***	Golgi Apparat
10/28/91	131	2	10/11	Harpua	Highway to Hell
12/6/91	23	2	9/12	Llama	Possum
12/5/92	112	2	12/13	Weekapaug Groove	Tweezer Repri
4/20/93	66	2	11/12	You Enjoy Myself	Golgi Apparat
8/10/96	284	2	8/8	Fluffhead	Harry Hood
7/25/99	207	1	4/8	My Left Toe	Makisupa Policeman

Has not been played in the last 94 shows.

Whipping Post Jam

DATE	GAP	SET	POS.	SONG BEFORE	SONG AFTER
11/23/85	10	3	2/4	Mike's Song	Run Like Antel

Has not been played in the last 1109 shows.

White Rabbit Jam

DATE	GAP	SET	POS.	SONG BEFORE	SONG AFTER
9/30/95	738	1	3/9	Cars Trucks Buses	Reba

Has not been played in the last 381 shows.

Who By Fire

DATE	GAP	SET	POS.	SONG BEFORE	SONG AFTER
4/23/94	605	2	9/10	You Enjoy Myself	Golgi Apparat

Has not been played in the last 514 shows.

Who Do? We Do!

DATE	GAP	SET	POS.	SONG BEFORE	SONG AFTER
4/24/87	21	1	11/14	Jam	David Bowie

Who Knows Jam

DATE	GAP	SET	POS.	SONG BEFORE	SONG AFTER
8/29/87	7	3	6/10	Jam	Shaggy Dog
10/31/87	5	2	13/17	McGrupp	Clod
9/21/89	82	1	8/9	McGrupp	David Bowie
10/1/89	1	1	3/12	McGrupp	Golgi Apparat
10/21/89	7	1	5/10	McGrupp	Foam
10/26/89	2	2	3/15	Dinner and a Movie	AC/DC Bag
11/2/89	3	2	8/11	McGrupp	AC/DC Bag
11/9/89	2	2	4/9	McGrupp	Punch You in
11/10/89	1	2	7/12	McGrupp	Clod
12/8/89	8	1	7/11	McGrupp	AC/DC Bag

Has not been played in the last 980 shows.

Who Knows Jam

DATE	GAP	SET	POS.	SONG BEFORE	SONG AFTER
10/26/89	125	2	1/15	***	Dinner and a
8/9/93	446	1	2/11	Chalk Dust Torture	Chalk Dust Tor

Has not been played in the last 548 shows.

Who Loves the Sun

DATE	GAP	SET	POS.	SONG BEFORE	SONG AFTER
10/31/98	983	2	1/10	***	Sweet Jane

Has not been played in the last 136 shows.

Whole Lotta Love Jam

DATE	GAP	SET	POS.	SONG BEFORE	SONG AFTER
6/9/90	205	2	1/14	***	Harry Hood
2/19/91	46	2	11/15	Love You	Love You
3/1/91	6	2	10/11	Love You	David Bowie
3/22/91	8	2	10/13	Terrapin	Mike's Song

Has not been played in the last 854 shows.

Why Don't We Do It in the Road

DATE	GAP	SET	POS.	SONG BEFORE	SONG AFTER
10/31/94	681	2	16/30	Don't Pass Me By	I Will
12/10/94	26	2	8/11	Weekapaug Groove	Poor Heart
6/25/95	20	2	5/9	Mike's Song	Jam
2/23/97	144	2	8/9	Mike's Song	Good Time Ba

Has not been played in the last 248 shows.

Why Don't You Love Me

DATE	GAP	SET	POS.	SONG BEFORE	SONG AFTER
3/23/87	20	2	6/9	Corrine Corrina	Camel Walk

Has not been played in the last 1099 shows.

Why You've Been Gone So Long

DATE	GAP	SET	POS.	SONG BEFORE	SONG AFTER
5/6/93	547	1	11/13	Lawn Boy	Tennessee Waltz

Has not been played in the last 572 shows.

Wild Child

DATE	GAP	SET	POS.	SONG BEFORE	SONG AFTER
11/3/84	2	1	2/10	In the Midnight Hour	Jam
5/3/85	3	2	2/6	Alumni Blues	Can't You Hear Me Kn
9/8/88	60	1	4/8	Slave	AC/DC Bag

Has not been played in the last 1054 shows.

Wild Honey Pie

DATE	GAP	SET	POS.	SONG BEFORE	SONG AFTER
10/31/94	681	2	6/30	Ob La Di Ob La Da	The Continuing Story

Has not been played in the last 438 shows.

Wild Thing

DATE	GAP	SET	POS.	SONG BEFORE	SONG AFTER
11/23/85	10	1	1/1	***	***

Has not been played in the last 1109 shows.

Wildwood Weed

DATE	GAP	SET	POS.	SONG BEFORE	SONG AFTER
12/6/96	858	E	2/7	Harpua	Cowboy's Sweetheart

Has not been played in the last 261 shows.

Will It Go Round in Circles

DATE	GAP	SET	POS.	SONG BEFORE	SONG AFTER
9/10/99	10321	2	8/8	What's The Use	***
9/21/99	8	2	6/8	Limb by Limb	Dirt

Has not been played in the last 79 shows.

Will the Circle Be Unbroken

DATE	GAP	SET	POS.	SONG BEFORE	SONG AFTER
10/3/98	977	1	8/10	Moonlight In Vt	Amazing Grce

Has not been played in the last 142 shows.

Wilson

DATE	GAP	SET	POS.	SONG BEFORE	SONG AFTER
10/15/86	14	2	9/14	Sneakin' Sally	Slave
2/13/87	3	1	10/14	Good Times Bad Times	Melt the Guns
3/6/87	2	2	7/7	Freeworld	***
5/20/87	5	1	1/9	***	Run Like Antel
8/10/87	2	1	4/7	Golgi Apparatus	Quinn the Eskimo
8/21/87	1	1	10/11	Shaggy Dog	Camel Walk
9/2/87	2	1	5/13	Divided Sky	David Bowie
9/21/87	1	1	7/11	Funky Bitch	Dear Mrs. Reagan
9/27/87	1	2	1/5	***	I Didn't Know
11/18/87	3	1	6/12	Flat Fee	Peaches en Regalia
1/27/88	2	2	1/10	***	Slave
2/8/88	2	2	2/6	Fluffhead	Peaches en Regalia
2/24/88	1	1	5/11	The Lizards	Peaches en Regalia
3/11/88	2	1	6/12	You Enjoy Myself	Golgi Apparat
3/12/88	1	2	5/11	Tela	AC/DC Bag
3/31/88	2	1	14/14	You Enjoy Myself	***
5/15/88	4	2	4/11	The Curtain	Peaches en Regalia
6/15/88	3	1	4/9	You Enjoy Myself	Rocky Top
6/20/88	2	1	8/11	Halley's Comet	Ya Mar
9/13/88	14	1	6/8	McGrupp	Peaches en Regalia
9/24/88	2	1	5/10	You Enjoy Myself	Peaches en Regalia
11/5/88	4	2	1/11	***	Peaches en Regalia
12/2/88	2	2	8/8	Run Like an Antelope	***
12/10/88	1	1	10/12	Weekapaug Groove	Col. Forbin's A
2/6/89	4	1	3/7	The Curtain	Peaches en Regalia
2/18/89	4	1	7/9	Divided Sky	Peaches en Regalia
3/3/89	2	1	1/11	***	McGrupp
3/14/89	3	1	9/12	AC/DC Bag	You Enjoy My
3/14/89	0	2	1/2	***	Fluffhead
4/30/89	6	1	6/9	Divided Sky	Peaches en Regalia
5/9/89	4	1	1/9	***	Peaches en Regalia
5/20/89	3	1	5/8	The Lizards	Divided Sky
6/23/89	5	1	3/11	You Enjoy Myself	Peaches en Regalia
9/9/89	6	1	9/11	Punch You in the Eye	My Sweet One
10/1/89	3	1	7/12	The Chase	Foam
10/21/89	7	2	3/10	Suzy Greenberg	Possum
10/26/89	2	1	7/11	I Didn't Know	The Lizards
10/31/89	2	2	2/8	David Bowie	Reba
11/18/89	7	1	8/11	Divided Sky	Reba
1/27/90	13	1	8/13	Bouncing	Reba
1/28/90	1	2	1/10	***	Run Like Antel
2/9/90	3	2	4/9	Reba	Take the A-Trn
2/22/90	5	1	1/9	***	You Enjoy My
3/10/90	10	1	1/10	***	Esther
4/14/90	12	2	7/11	Bold as Love	Ride Captain Ride
6/16/90	28	1	3/10	Divided Sky	Reba
9/22/90	7	1	9/12	Magilla	The Landlady
11/26/90	21	2	4/7	The Famous Mockingbi	Mike's Song
2/15/91	15	1	2/11	The Curtain	Divided Sky
3/1/91	8	1	1/12	***	Foam
4/21/91	25	1	3/14	Rocky Top	Divided Sky
5/10/91	8	2	3/11	Harry Hood	Poor Heart
8/3/91	21	1	1/11	***	Foam
10/13/91	14	1	2/13	Runaway Jim	Reba
10/18/91	3	1	5/9	Reba	Llama
10/28/91	5	2	2/11	Divided Sky	Dinner and a
10/30/91	1	2	6/11	Lawn Boy	The Landlady
11/14/91	10	1	1/11	***	Uncle Pen
11/16/91	2	1	3/11	Uncle Pen	Runaway Jim
11/19/91	1	1	10/11	Love You	Divided Sky
11/21/91	2	2	1/10	***	Harry Hood
12/7/91	8	1	1/11	***	Runaway Jim
12/31/91	1	3	1/7	***	The Squirmin
3/13/92	5	2	1/12	***	Brother
3/20/92	4	1	1/10	***	Reba
3/25/92	4	1	1/10	***	Sparkle
3/31/92	5	1	1/10	***	Divided Sky
4/5/92	4	1	4/11	Divided Sky	Poor Heart
4/18/92	9	1	1/11	***	Divided Sky
4/22/92	3	2	6/11	Rift	You Enjoy My
5/1/92	6	2	3/13	Buried Alive	All Things Rec
5/8/92	6	2	1/12	***	My Sweet One
7/16/92	22	1	5/10	Sparkle	Dinner and a
8/17/92	18	1	6/11	Rift	All Things Rec
11/27/92	17	1	2/12	Rift	Divided Sky
12/2/92	4	2	1/11	***	Possum
12/8/92	6	1	2/11	Rift	Llama
12/13/92	4	1	2/11	Buried Alive	Divided Sky
12/29/92	2	1	7/12	Divided Sky	Uncle Pen
12/31/92	2	1	6/11	Rift	Divided Sky
2/6/93	4	1	3/11	Foam	My Friend My
2/11/93	4	2	2/12	The Landlady	Uncle Pen
2/13/93	2	2	1/11	***	Runaway Jim
2/20/93	5	2	1/22	***	Reba
2/25/93	4	2	4/11	Sparkle	You Enjoy My
3/13/93	10	1	10/11	Llama	Run Like Antel
3/22/93	7	2	5/13	Tela	AC/DC Bag
3/26/93	3	2	1/12	***	Runaway Jim
4/17/93	14	2	1/11	***	Reba
4/25/93	7	2	1/11	***	The Curtain
4/30/93	3	2	1/10	***	Sparkle
7/25/93	18	1	1/11	***	Foam
7/31/93	5	2	1/11	***	Runaway Jim
8/8/93	5	2	4/11	Harry Hood	It's Ice
8/17/93	8	1	1/9	***	Llama
8/24/93	3	2	7/10	Weekapaug Groove	Rift
12/29/93	5	1	6/9	Divided Sky	Sparkle
4/9/94	7	1	2/10	Magilla	Rift
4/15/94	5	1	5/9	Harry Hood	Chalk Dust Tor
4/23/94	7	2	1/10	***	Run Like Antel
4/30/94	5	2	1/10	***	David Bowie
5/10/94	7	2	2/10	Maze	Julius
5/14/94	3	1	2/9	Llama	Down with Dis
5/23/94	7	2	1/7	***	Run Like Antel
5/27/94	3	1	1/9	***	Runaway Jim
5/29/94	2	E	1/3	***	Golgi Apparat
6/11/94	3	1	1/9	***	Chalk Dust Tor
6/18/94	5	1	1/10	***	Rift
6/24/94	5	1	2/11	Divided Sky	It's Ice
6/26/94	2	1	5/11	Tela	AC/DC Bag
6/30/94	2	2	1/15	***	Maze
7/8/94	6	1	5/11	Tela	AC/DC Bag
7/13/94	3	2	3/13	Cavern	Cavern
10/7/94	4	2	5/10	Reba	Scent of a Mul
10/15/94	7	1	1/8	***	Sparkle
10/22/94	5	2	7/11	Tweezer	Reba
10/27/94	4	1	1/11	***	Sparkle
11/3/94	5	1	3/9	Divided Sky	Peaches en Regalia
11/13/94	3	1	1/10	***	Sparkle
11/17/94	3	1	5/11	Bouncing	Divided Sky
11/23/94	5	1	1/9	***	Sparkle
12/3/94	7	1	1/7	***	Divided Sky
12/9/94	5	2	1/9	***	Poor Heart
12/30/94	4	1	1/9	***	Rift
6/17/95	11	2	1/11	***	Maze
7/1/95	11	2	1/9	***	Maze
10/2/95	7	2	1/10	***	Cars Trucks Buses
10/7/95	4	1	8/9	Acoustic Army	Run Like Antel
10/13/95	3	2	4/10	Theme From the Botto	Run Like Antel
10/21/95	6	1	5/12	Reba	Cars Trucks Buses
10/31/95	7	1	3/9	Divided Sky	Ya Mar
11/15/95	6	2	1/8	***	Theme From the Botto
11/22/95	5	1	2/10	Cars Trucks Buses	Run Like Antel
12/1/95	6	2	5/9	The Mango Song	Suspicious Minds
12/9/95	6	2	2/8	Timber (Jerry)	Gumbo
12/15/95	4	1	3/10	Harry Hood	Maze
12/28/95	3	2	3/8	Theme From the Botto	Buried Alive
7/12/96	13	1	1/10	***	Divided Sky
8/5/96	13	1	1/9	***	Poor Heart
8/10/96	3	2	1/8	***	Down with Dis
8/14/96	3	1	1/10	***	Jam
8/17/96	2	3	1/7	***	Frankenstein
10/16/96	1	1	3/12	Down with Disease	Buried Alive
10/21/96	4	2	1/11	***	Chalk Dust Tor
11/6/96	10	2	1/9	***	The Curtain
11/15/96	7	1	1/11	***	Divided Sky
11/29/96	8	2	1/10	***	Simple
12/6/96	5	1	1/9	***	Peaches en Regalia
12/31/96	4	2	2/9	Chalk Dust Torture	Sparkle
2/17/97	4	1	3/10	Divided Sky	My Soul
2/21/97	3	2	3/9	Run Like an Antelope	The Oh Kee Pa
6/27/97	18	1	1/8	***	Chalk Dust Tor
8/9/97	22	2	1/10	***	Foam
8/13/97	3	1	10/11	Crosseyed and Painle	Sweet Adeline
11/16/97	6	2	3/5	Simple	Harry Hood
12/5/97	12	1	2/10	Ghost	Funky Bitch
7/8/98	21	2	1/7	***	Birds of a Feather
7/15/98	3	E	1/2	***	Tweezer Repri
7/25/98	7	2	2/8	Piper	Frankenstein
8/1/98	5	2	2/10	Piper	Also Sprach
8/11/98	7	E	1/2	***	Golgi Apparat
8/16/98	3	3	3/7	Also Sprach	The Mango Song
10/30/98	6	1	1/10	***	Meat
11/6/98	4	1	2/7	Possum	Roggae
11/21/98	11	1	1/13	***	BBFCFM
12/30/98	8	1	3/12	BBFCFM	Roggae
7/4/99	5	2	6/9	What's the Use	Mike's Song
7/10/99	4	1	1/8	***	Chalk Dust Tor
7/18/99	6	3	4/9	Prince Caspian	Catapult
7/20/99	1	1	8/9	Ghost	You Enjoy My
8/1/99	9	1	3/10	Rift	The Moma Dance
9/18/99	8	1	3/7	Roses Are Free	Maze
9/25/99	5	1	8/8	Sleeping Monkey	***
10/4/99	7	1	7/8	Limb by Limb	Down with Dis
10/9/99	3	1	2/8	Punch You In the Eye	Guyute
12/16/99	13	1	1/10	***	Chalk Dust Tor
12/30/99	3	2	1/10	***	The Curtain
5/23/00	4	1	2/12	AC/DC Bag	First Tube
6/13/00	4	1	7/10	The Old Home Place	Mike's Song
6/29/00	9	1	2/5	Funky Bitch	Limb by Limb
7/10/00	8	1	2/10	Cars Trucks Buses	It's Ice
9/12/00	8	1	7/7	Divided Sky	***
9/22/00	6	1	4/9	Poor Heart	Slave
9/29/00	5	1	5/8	Mellow Mood	Spock's Brain

Has not been played in the last 6 shows.

Wind Beneath My Wings

DATE	GAP	SET	POS.	SONG BEFORE	SONG AFTER
11/28/95	773	2	6/10	Free	Run Like Antel

Has not been played in the last 346 shows.

Windora Bug

DATE	GAP	SET	POS.	SONG BEFORE	SONG AFTER
9/8/00	1099	2	2/6	Birds of a Feather	David Bowie
9/15/00	5	1	5/8	Birds of a Feather	Run Like Antel

Has not been played in the last 15 shows.

Wipeout

DATE	GAP	SET	POS.	SONG BEFORE	SONG AFTER
4/15/91	277	2	1/11	***	Mike's Song
4/27/91	8	2	12/13	The Squirming Coil	Tweezer Repri
11/27/98	715	2	2/16	Buried Alive	Chalk Dust Tor
11/27/98	0	2	13/16	Weekapaug Groove	Weekapaug Gr

DATE	GAP	SET	POS.	SONG BEFORE	SONG AFTER
11/27/98	0	E	3/3	Golgi Apparatus	***
11/29/98	2	2	5/8	Possum	Possum

Has not been played in the last 117 shows.

Wolfman's Brother

DATE	GAP	SET	POS.	SONG BEFORE	SONG AFTER
4/4/94	589	2	8/11	Split Open and Melt	I Wanna Be Like You
4/6/94	2	2	3/9	Down with Disease	Sparkle
4/15/94	7	2	7/10	Julius	Alumni Blues
4/17/94	2	2	2/9	David Bowie	Uncle Pen
4/30/94	10	2	3/10	David Bowie	Peaches en Regalia
5/4/94	3	2	7/9	Julius	Magilla
5/20/94	11	2	5/7	Axilla (Part II)	Rift
6/13/94	12	1	5/9	Divided Sky	Dinner and a
6/26/94	11	2	7/12	Sample in a Jar	Scent of a Mul
9/27/95	88	1	1/9	***	Rift
10/2/95	4	1	2/10	Poor Heart	Rift
10/8/95	5	1	4/9	Sparkle	Reba
10/24/95	10	1	10/13	Maze	Acoustic Army
11/25/95	18	1	8/9	Rift	Runaway Jim
12/1/95	4	1	5/9	Poor Heart	Chalk Dust Tor
4/26/96	17	1	7/13	You Enjoy Myself	Scent of a Mul
8/5/96	22	1	5/9	Divided Sky	Foam
10/16/96	9	2	1/10	***	Taste
10/21/96	4	2	3/11	Chalk Dust Torture	Reba
10/26/96	4	1	3/9	Cars Trucks Buses	Reba
11/3/96	5	2	3/8	Divided Sky	Sparkle
11/14/96	7	1	3/9	Uncle Pen	Cars Trucks Buses
11/22/96	5	1	3/10	Runaway Jim	Taste
12/2/96	7	2	3/8	Divided Sky	Taste
12/28/96	3	1	3/9	NICU	It's Ice
2/13/97	4	1	2/12	Chalk Dust Torture	Also Sprach
2/18/97	4	2	5/9	Maze	Reba
3/1/97	8	1	6/10	Beauty of My Dreams	Jesus Just Left
6/13/97	3	1	6/8	Limb by Limb	Wading In Velvet Sea
6/16/97	2	1	9/10	Chalk Dust Torture	Oblivious Fool
6/24/97	5	2	1/7	***	Reba
7/11/97	11	1	5/7	Beauty of My Dreams	Johnny B. Goode
7/21/97	1	2	1/8	***	Magilla
7/25/97	3	1	2/7	Beauty of My Dreams	Maze
7/30/97	3	1	2/9	NICU	Chalk Dust Tor
8/2/97	2	1	6/8	Divided Sky	Water in the Sky
8/8/97	3	2	1/6	***	Free
8/16/97	6	2	1/7	***	Simple
11/14/97	3	2	1/4	***	Piper
11/19/97	3	2	2/4	Also Sprach	Makisupa Policeman
11/30/97	7	1	3/6	Funky Bitch	Love Me
12/7/97	5	2	2/6	Timber (Jerry)	Boogie On Reggae
12/31/97	8	1	5/10	Beauty of My Dreams	Limb by Limb
4/2/98	1	2	4/9	Birds of a Feather	Sneakin' Sally
6/30/98	4	2	3/12	Birds of a Feather	Frankie Says
7/15/98	9	1	1/13	***	Water in the Sky
7/19/98	3	2	2/7	Llama	Piper
7/24/98	3	2	1/7	***	Also Sprach
8/6/98	9	2	2/7	Birds of a Feather	Talk
8/11/98	4	1	3/11	Julius	Time Loves a Hero
10/15/98	5	1	3/8	Water in the Sky	Gumbo
10/31/98	5	3	1/3	***	Piper
11/13/98	8	1	2/10	Chalk Dust Torture	Roggae
11/18/98	3	2	1/7	***	The Lizards
11/28/98	7	2	2/9	Julius	Timber (Jerry)
12/28/98	2	2	2/6	Carini	Birds of a Feather
7/1/99	5	1	4/10	Guyute	Beauty of My Dreams
7/7/99	3	1	8/10	Rift	Maze

DATE	GAP	SET	POS.	SONG BEFORE	SONG AFTER
7/13/99	5	2	1/6	***	Piper
7/17/99	3	2	5/8	Down with Disease	Sneakin' Sally
7/26/99	7	2	1/6	***	Piper
7/30a/99	1	1	3/7	Guyute	Taste
9/11/99	6	2	1/6	***	Sand
9/17/99	4	2	7/8	Bass Jam	Cold Rain and Snow
9/24/99	5	2	3/6	Possum	The Lizards
9/28/99	3	1	1/8	***	Sneakin' Sally
10/2/99	3	1	2/9	Llama	Punch You in
12/3/99	8	1	2/8	First Tube	Bouncing
12/7/99	3	2	1/8	***	Jennifer Dances
12/15/99	6	1	4/7	Bathtub Gin	Guyute
12/30/99	4	2	7/10	Golgi Apparatus	Gotta Jibboo
5/21/00	2	1	2/7	First Tube	The Squirmin
6/13/00	6	2	2/9	Gotta Jibboo	Run Like Antel
6/22/00	4	1	2/9	First Tube	Beauty of my Dreams
7/1/00	7	1	2/11	Buried Alive	Axilla
7/8/00	5	1	5/9	Poor Heart	First Tube
7/15/00	5	1	7/9	Roses are Free	My Soul
9/12/00	4	1	1/7	***	Scent of a Mul
9/20/00	5	1	2/9	Cars Trucks Buses	Gotta Jibboo
10/1/00	8	1	2/10	First Tube	Back on the Train
10/5/00	2	1	3/10	Guyute	Sneakin' Sally

Has not been played in the last 2 shows.

Wormtown Jam

DATE	GAP	SET	POS.	SONG BEFORE	SONG AFTER
7/2/97	890	2	3/4	Llama	Wading In Velvet Sea

Has not been played in the last 229 shows.

Ya Mar

DATE	GAP	SET	POS.	SONG BEFORE	SONG AFTER
2/21/87	18	2	12/15	Boogie On Reggae	Corrine Corrina
5/11/87	5	1	12/12	Makisupa Policeman	***
8/9/87	2	3	3/7	You Enjoy Myself	Divided Sky
8/29/87	3	2	10/13	Mustang Sally	T.M.W.S.I.Y.
4/22/88	18	2	9/13	Suzy Greenberg	AC/DC Bag
5/25/88	4	3	3/11	I Didn't Know	Halley's Comet
6/20/88	3	1	9/11	Wilson	Jam
3/14/89	36	1	2/12	The Curtain	Mike's Song
3/30/89	2	1	6/8	On Your Way Down	Fluffhead
5/5/89	6	1	3/8	You Enjoy Myself	Fluffhead
5/9/89	2	1	3/8	Peaches en Regalia	Mike's Song
5/12/89	1	1	14/15	Split Open and Melt	Run Like Antel
5/21/89	3	1	11/13	You Enjoy Myself	AC/DC Bag
5/28/89	3	3	5/6	Sneakin' Sally	Jesus Just Left
6/23/89	1	2	4/7	Harry Hood	Split Open and
8/17/89	2	1	1/9	***	Suzy Greenber
8/23/89	2	2	4/8	The Famous Mockingbi	You Enjoy My
8/26/89	1	2	3/9	Bold as Love	Slave
9/9/89	1	2	1/7	***	You Enjoy My
9/21/89	2	1	2/9	Golgi Apparatus	AC/DC Bag
10/1/89	1	1	9/12	Foam	The Oh Kee Pa
10/7/89	2	2	2/11	Golgi Apparatus	Mike's Song
10/14/89	3	1	5/11	Golgi Apparatus	Split Open and
10/21/89	2	1	2/10	Fee	In a Hole
10/22/89	1	1	7/14	Suzy Greenberg	Foam
11/9/89	6	1	3/9	Golgi Apparatus	The Curtain
11/30/89	5	1	3/11	Divided Sky	The Oh Kee Pa
12/3/89	2	1	3/9	Funky Bitch	Reba
12/7/89	2	4	4/11	Rocky Top	Walk Away
12/8/89	1	1	4/11	Split Open and Melt	Reba
12/15/89	1	1	6/10	Weekapaug Groove	The Oh Kee Pa
12/29/89	2	1	3/10	Divided Sky	The Oh Kee Pa
12/30/89	1	2	3/9	Split Open and Melt	Suzy Greenber
12/31/89	1	2	4/7	Weekapaug Groove	Split Open and
1/27/90	2	1	3/13	Bathtub Gin	The Oh Kee Pa
2/9/90	4	2	3/9	Dinner and a Movie	Reba
2/22/90	5	1	4/9	Bouncing	The Oh Kee Pa

DATE	GAP	SET	POS.	SONG BEFORE	SONG AFTER
2/23/90	1	1	8/11	Dinner and a Movie	Walk Away
3/1/90	3	1	2/7	Golgi Apparatus	Rhombus Narration
3/8/90	4	1	4/10	Possum	Foam
3/9/90	1	1	4/11	Caravan	Bouncing
3/11/90	2	2	8/13	The Sloth	Split Open and
3/28/90	2	1	2/12	Possum	Fee
4/5/90	2	1	2/9	Possum	David Bowie
4/6/90	1	1	6/11	Divided Sky	Dinner and a
4/12/90	4	1	2/11	Golgi Apparatus	Walk Away
4/20/90	5	1	4/10	Alumni Blues	Cavern
4/25/90	3	2	4/12	Reba	You Enjoy My
4/29/90	3	1	3/13	Possum	You Enjoy My
5/11/90	5	2	5/7	Tweezer	Love You
5/19/90	3	1	2/8	Golgi Apparatus	Alumni Blues
5/23/90	1	1	2/10	Divided Sky	You Enjoy My
6/5/90	6	1	6/12	Weekapaug Groove	The Oh Kee Pa
6/16/90	4	3	3/13	Happy Birthday	Foam
9/16/90	4	1	6/14	Reba	Tube
9/29/90	5	1	4/9	The Landlady	Buried Alive
10/5/90	3	2	3/8	The Curtain	Alumni Blues
2/15/91	31	2	3/10	Bathtub Gin	Guelah Papyrus
2/21/91	4	1	3/11	Dinner and a Movie	Split Open and
4/6/91	21	2	1/11	***	Split Open and
4/15/91	3	1	2/10	The Sloth	Foam
4/20/91	4	2	2/13	The Sloth	Split Open and
5/10/91	9	1	3/10	Cavern	Dinner and a
8/3/91	21	3	2/8	Stash	Fluffhead
10/24/91	20	1	6/12	Stash	Divided Sky
10/31/91	4	1	3/11	Brother	The Sloth
11/12/91	7	E	1/4	***	BBFCFM
11/16/91	4	1	10/11	Stash	Cavern
12/5/91	9	1	4/10	Split Open and Melt	Fluffhead
4/13/92	30	2	8/11	Magilla	The Squirmin
4/24/92	3	2	3/12	Cavern	Foam
2/13/93	94	2	8/11	You Enjoy Myself	Terrapin
2/19/93	5	2	5/12	You Enjoy Myself	Big Ball Jam
2/27/93	7	2	6/12	Big Ball Jam	Mike's Song
3/21/93	14	2	5/12	Tweezer	You Enjoy My
4/1/93	9	2	5/10	Fee	Tweezer
4/18/93	10	2	9/12	Mike's Song	Walk Away
4/29/93	8	2	3/13	It's Ice	Mound
5/5/93	5	2	8/10	Big Ball Jam	You Enjoy My
5/30/93	5	1	6/13	Foam	Silent in the M
7/16/93	2	1	4/10	My Friend My Friend	Buried Alive
7/22/93	4	1	8/11	Mound	Poor Heart
7/28/93	5	1	3/11	Runaway Jim	Sample in a Ja
7/31/93	3	1	3/9	Sample in a Jar	Split Open and
8/3/93	2	1	9/11	Silent in the Mornin	Llama
8/13/93	7	2	4/9	Bathtub Gin	Mike's Song
8/24/93	7	2	3/10	Horn	Mike's Song
12/28/93	4	1	7/10	Suzy Greenberg	It's Ice
4/5/94	5	2	2/8	Peaches en Regalia	Tweezer
4/10/94	4	2	2/7	My Friend My Friend	Run Like Antel
4/18/94	7	2	6/13	Big Ball Jam	Mike's Song
4/24/94	5	1	2/8	My Friend My Friend	Axilla (Part II)
5/6/94	8	1	6/9	My Friend My Friend	Stash
6/29/94	34	E	1/2	***	Tweezer Repri
7/10/94	9	2	4/10	Glide	Mike's Song
10/14/94	11	E	1/2	***	Cavern
10/27/94	10	2	2/7	Julius	Tweezer
11/4/94	6	2	7/9	Weekapaug Groove	Golgi Apparat
11/30/94	14	2	6/10	Fixin' To Die	Mike's Song
12/7/94	6	1	4/8	The Sloth	Split Open and
6/16/95	16	1	4/10	Esther	Cry Baby Cry
6/25/95	7	1	1/9	***	AC/DC Bag
7/1/95	5	1	1/9	***	Llama
9/29/95	5	2	4/8	Free	Split Open and
10/6/95	5	1	1/9	***	Stash
10/8/95	2	2	4/10	Timber (Jerry)	Sample in a Ja
10/13/95	2	1	1/9	***	Also Sprach
10/20/95	5	1	2/10	My Friend My Friend	Ha Ha Ha
10/25/95	4	1	1/10	***	Sample in a Ja
10/31/95	4	1	4/9	Wilson	Sparkle
11/11/95	3	1	8/12	Silent in the Mornin	Stash

DATE	GAP	SET	POS.	SONG BEFORE	SONG AFTER
11/16/95	4	1	6/10	Mound	Simple
11/21/95	3	2	6/11	Glide	Mike's Song
11/29/95	5	1	2/9	AC/DC Bag	Reba
12/4/95	4	2	3/9	Sparkle	Run Like Antel
12/12/95	6	1	1/10	***	Sample in a Ja
12/16/95	3	1	4/9	Taste That Surrounds	The Sloth
12/30/95	4	2	1/8	***	Free
4/26/96	2	1	1/13	***	AC/DC Bag
6/6/96	1	E	1/2	***	Fire
7/10/96	6	1	2/7	Chalk Dust Torture	Split Open and
7/12/96	2	1	5/10	Split Open and Melt	Funky Bitch
7/17/96	3	1	4/5	David Bowie	Funky Bitch
7/24/96	6	1	2/5	Chalk Dust Torture	Julius
8/2/96	2	1	2/11	Somewhere Over The	Down with Dis
8/7/96	4	1	4/10	Stash	Gumbo
8/12/96	2	1	1/10	***	Split Open and
8/16/96	3	1	3/8	Bathtub Gin	AC/DC Bag
10/17/96	3	2	1/8	***	Chalk Dust Tor
10/23/96	5	2	2/8	Brother	Tweezer
10/27/96	3	2	5/9	Prince Caspian	Tweezer
11/2/96	3	1	1/9	***	Julius
11/13/96	7	1	3/9	It's Ice	Taste
11/19/96	5	1	1/9	***	AC/DC Bag
11/27/96	4	1	3/9	My Friend My Friend	Chalk Dust Tor
12/2/96	4	2	1/8	***	Divided Sky
12/30/96	5	1	1/9	***	The Sloth
2/14/97	3	2	2/9	AC/DC Bag	Down with Dis
2/21/97	5	2	1/9	***	Run Like Antel
2/28/97	5	1	9/10	Steep	Character Zer
7/1/97	15	1	3/9	Horn	Limb by Limb
7/10/97	6	2	4/7	Magilla	Ghost
7/25/97	5	2	3/6	Taste	Drum Jam
7/31/97	4	1	2/9	Ghost	Dogs Stole Things
8/6/97	3	1	7/8	AC/DC Bag	You Enjoy My
8/14/97	6	1	1/10	***	Funky Bitch
11/26/97	11	2	3/9	Cities	Punch You in
12/2/97	4	2	4/7	Dog Faced Boy	Weekapaug Gr
12/13/97	8	1	1/9	***	Axilla
12/31/97	4	1	2/10	Emotional Rescue	My Sweet One
4/5/98	4	2	2/8	Down with Disease	Prince Caspian
6/30/98	1	2	7/12	Lawn Boy	Ha Ha Ha
7/17/98	11	1	2/7	Makisupa Policeman	Gumbo
7/25/98	5	1	5/7	Beauty of My Dreams	Guyute
7/31/98	4	1	2/7	My Friend My Friend	Roggae
8/16/98	11	1	6/11	Lawn Boy	AC/DC Bag
11/4/98	9	1	5/9	Bathtub Gin	Birds of a Feather
11/27/98	15	1	2/11	Funky Bitch	Carini
7/4/99	10	1	2/10	My Soul	Farmhouse
7/23/99	13	1	1/9	***	NICU
9/16/99	13	1	1/14	***	Chalk Dust Tor
9/25/99	7	1	3/8	Runaway Jim	Horn
10/4/99	7	2	7/8	Sand	Character Zer
12/4/99	1	1	3/7	Simple	Guyute
12/8/99	3	1	5/8	Fast Enough For You	The Horse
12/18/99	8	E	1/2	***	Sleeping Monkey
12/30/99	1	1	11/12	Ghost	Character Zer
5/23/00	4	1	4/12	First Tube	Mike's Song
6/13/00	4	1	4/10	Meat Reprise	Fast Enough for You
6/23/00	5	1	1/8	***	My Soul
7/11/00	13	1	1/8	***	The Moma Dance
9/11/00	6	1	8/9	Beauty of my Dreams	Stash
9/24/00	9	2	3/8	Free	Carini

Has not been played in the last 9 shows.

Yer Blues

DATE	GAP	SET	POS.	SONG BEFORE	SONG AFTER
10/31/94	681	2	20/30	Birthday Jam	Mother Nature's Son

Has not been played in the last 438 shows.

Yerushalayim Shel Zahav

DATE	GAP	SET	POS.	SONG BEFORE	SONG AFTER
7/16/93	553	2	7/12	You Enjoy Myself	You Enjoy My
7/24/93	6	2	8/12	Mike's Song	Weekapaug Gr
6/26/94	88	2	12/12	Split Open and Melt	***
6/30/94	2	2	4/15	You Enjoy Myself	You Enjoy My
7/2/94	2	2	5/12	Mike's Song	I Am Hydrgn
7/8/94	4	2	4/11	Reba	It's Ice
7/15/94	5	2	6/10	It's Ice	Dog Faced Boy
10/13/94	7	2	9/12	Mike's Song	Weekapaug Gr
10/25/94	9	2	5/11	Weekapaug Groove	Glide
11/14/94	11	2	3/10	David Bowie	Slave
11/22/94	6	2	3/13	Jam	Cry Baby Cry
12/31/94	18	2	7/9	Mike's Song	Weekapaug Gr

Has not been played in the last 408 shows.

You Enjoy Myself

DATE	GAP	SET	POS.	SONG BEFORE	SONG AFTER
2/3/86	11	1	4/7	Dave's Energy Guide	Alumni Blues
4/1/86	1	1	7/7	Icculus	***
4/15/86	1	1	11/14	Possum	Anarchy
10/15/86	1	1	8/9	AC/DC Bag	Lushington
12/6/86	2	1	10/14	David Bowie	Dog Gone Dog
3/23/87	4	1	4/5	Alumni Blues	Sparks
4/24/87	1	1	5/14	Fluffhead	Dave's Energy Guide
5/11/87	2	1	1/12	***	Fluff's Travels
5/20/87	1	1	8/9	Harry Hood	Alumni Blues
8/9/87	1	3	2/7	David Bowie	Ya Mar
8/10/87	1	2	9/10	Mustang Sally	La Grange
9/2/87	3	1	13/13	Shaggy Dog	***
9/21/87	1	2	1/5	***	The Curtain With
10/14/87	2	1	3/12	Take the A-Train	Golgi Apparat
10/31/87	1	1	10/11	Possum	BBFCFM
11/18/87	1	2	2/4	I Didn't Know	Fluffhead
11/19/87	1	1	4/7	Funky Bitch	Sneakin' Sally
1/27/88	1	2	8/10	Ballad - Curtis Loew	The Sloth
2/8/88	2	1	7/7	Fire	***
2/24/88	1	1	2/11	The Curtain	I Didn't Know
2/26/88	1	1	3/13	Suzy Greenberg	T.M.W.S.I.Y.
3/11/88	1	1	5/12	Take the A-Train	Wilson
3/31/88	3	1	13/14	Fire	Wilson
4/22/88	2	2	7/13	BBFCFM	Suzy Greenber
5/14/88	1	1	5/11	Light Up Or Leave Me	The Lizards
5/15/88	1	1	3/11	Golgi Apparatus	Suzy Greenber
5/21/88	1	1	4/7	Alumni Blues	St. Thomas
6/15/88	2	1	3/9	Alumni Blues	Wilson
6/19/88	1	1	8/8	Big Leg Emma	***
6/20/88	1	1	3/11	Peaches en Regalia	Fluffhead
6/24/88	2	1	9/11	Sneakin' Sally	Ballad - Curtis Loew
7/12/88	2	1	7/8	Peaches en Regalia	I Didn't Know
7/23/88	1	3	1/7	***	Contact
8/3/88	4	2	2/3	I Know A Little	Jesus Just Left
8/6/88	1	1	2/9	La Grange	Cities
8/27/88	1	1	2/9	Satin Doll	Funky Bitch
9/8/88	1	2	2/8	Possum	Cities
9/13/88	2	1	3/8	Funky Bitch	Flat Fee
9/22/88	1	1	4/7	Fluffhead	David Bowie
9/24/88	1	1	4/10	Alumni Blues	Wilson
10/31/88	2	1	2/12	Good Times Bad Times	Possum
11/5/88	2	1	4/11	Fire	Possum
11/11/88	1	1	2/8	Divided Sky	Slave
12/2/88	1	1	7/7	Contact	***
12/10/88	1	2	2/7	Alumni Blues	Contact
1/26/89	3	1	4/10	Alumni Blues	The Lizards
2/6/89	1	1	7/7	La Grange	***
2/17/89	3	1	2/10	AC/DC Bag	Fee
2/24/89	2	2	3/4	AC/DC Bag	Camel Walk
3/3/89	1	1	3/11	McGrupp	Foam
3/14/89	3	1	10/12	Wilson	Harpua
3/14/89	0	3	6/7	La Grange	Good Time Ba
3/30/89	2	2	5/8	Weekapaug Groove	Undun
4/20/89	2	2	3/10	Walk Away	Split Open and
4/30/89	2	1	2/9	I Didn't Know	McGrupp
5/1/89	1	1	2/9	Dinner and a Movie	Esther
5/5/89	1	1	2/8	Golgi Apparatus	Ya Mar
5/6/89	1	1	1/13	***	I Didn't Know
5/9/89	1	2	1/14	***	La Grange
5/12/89	1	1	9/15	The Asse Festival	Slave
5/13/89	1	1	3/12	Alumni Blues	Golgi Apparat
5/20/89	1	1	3/8	Alumni Blues	The Lizards
5/21/89	1	1	10/13	The Sloth	Ya Mar
5/26/89	1	1	9/9	The Sloth	***
5/27/89	1	1	7/11	Fee	Take the A-Trn
5/28/89	1	1	9/9	Suzy Greenberg	***
6/23/89	1	1	2/11	AC/DC Bag	Wilson
6/30/89	1	1	2/7	Funky Bitch	McGrupp
8/17/89	1	2	5/6	Fee	The Lizards
8/23/89	2	2	5/8	Ya Mar	AC/DC Bag
8/26/89	1	1	7/8	Divided Sky	Possum
9/9/89	1	2	2/7	Ya Mar	Alumni Blues
9/14/89	1	1	3/9	Suzy Greenberg	Foam
9/21/89	1	2	7/9	Bathtub Gin	If I Only Had a Brai
10/1/89	1	2	7/11	Possum	If I Only Had a Brai
10/7/89	2	E	1/1	***	***
10/12/89	1	1	5/8	The Famous Mockingbi	Possum
10/14/89	2	1	9/11	Alumni Blues	Makisupa Policeman
10/20/89	1	1	5/10	The Famous Mockingbi	The Oh Kee Pa
10/21/89	1	2	8/10	La Grange	Highway to Hell
10/22/89	1	1	4/14	The Famous Mockingbi	The Oh Kee Pa
10/26/89	1	3	3/11	Golgi Apparatus	Fee
10/28/89	1	1	2/9	I Didn't Know	Col. Forbin's A
10/31/89	1	1	3/9	Suzy Greenberg	AC/DC Bag
11/2/89	1	2	3/11	Golgi Apparatus	Kung
11/3/89	1	1	7/10	Bundle of Joy	Punch You in
11/9/89	1	1	7/9	Bathtub Gin	Take the A-Trn
11/10/89	1	1	8/9	My Sweet One	La Grange
11/11/89	1	1	6/8	My Sweet One	If I Only Had a Brai
11/16/89	1	1	10/11	Reba	Frankenstein
11/18/89	1	1	11/11	***	Take the A-Trn
12/1/89	2	1	3/9	La Grange	The Oh Kee Pa
12/7/89	2	1	2/11	I Didn't Know	Take the A-Trn
12/8/89	1	2	6/7	I Didn't Know	Possum
12/15/89	2	1	9/10	Suzy Greenberg	Good Time Ba
12/31/89	4	1	2/9	I Didn't Know	The Oh Kee Pa
1/20/90	1	1	4/8	Bathtub Gin	The Squirmin
1/27/90	1	2	3/7	Caravan	The Squirmin
1/28/90	1	2	6/10	The Squirming Coil	Bathtub Gin
2/9/90	3	1	4/12	Suzy Greenberg	Walk Away
2/10/90	1	1	4/10	Suzy Greenberg	Bathtub Gin
2/17/90	3	1	12/12	Cavern	***
2/22/90	1	1	2/9	Wilson	Bouncing
2/23/90	1	1	2/11	Alumni Blues	Possum
2/24/90	1	1	2/8	Carolina	Golgi Apparat
3/1/90	1	1	6/7	I Didn't Know	Possum
3/3/90	2	1	11/12	Rocky Top	Possum
3/8/90	2	1	2/10	Dinner and a Movie	Possum
3/9/90	1	2	8/11	Highway to Hell	La Grange
3/17/90	3	2	6/6	Foam	***
3/28/90	1	1	11/12	Runaway Jim	Good Time Ba
4/4/90	1	1	2/8	Golgi Apparatus	Walk Away
4/5/90	1	1	7/9	Suzy Greenberg	The Lizards
4/6/90	1	2	2/11	Cavern	Uncle Pen
4/8/90	2	1	3/8	Funky Bitch	If I Only Had a Brai
4/12/90	2	1	6/11	Possum	Take the A-Trn
4/13/90	1	2	3/10	Foam	Alumni Blues
4/18/90	2	1	7/10	Foam	My Sweet One
4/19/90	1	2	4/8	Dinner and a Movie	Terrapin
4/20/90	2	1	11/11	Jesus Just Left	***
4/22/90	2	2	3/9	Bouncing	Fluffhead
4/25/90	1	2	5/12	Ya Mar	Esther
4/26/90	1	1	3/9	Foam	Uncle Pen
4/28/90	1	1	8/11	Possum	Rift

DATE	GAP	SET	POS.	SONG BEFORE	SONG AFTER
4/29/90	1	1	4/13	Ya Mar	Dinner and a
5/4/90	1	2	9/10	My Sweet One	The Lizards
5/6/90	1	2	7/7	Jagermeister	***
5/19/90	6	1	6/8	La Grange	The Lizards
5/23/90	1	1	3/10	Ya Mar	If I Only Had a Brai
5/24/90	1	1	6/9	Reba	The Oh Kee Pa
5/31/90	2	1	2/12	Possum	Dinner and a
6/5/90	3	2	8/10	The Lizards	Ballad - Curtis Loew
6/7/90	1	1	7/9	Reba	The Lizards
6/8/90	1	1	3/8	Bouncing	Divided Sky
6/16/90	2	2	6/8	Bathtub Gin	The Lizards
9/15/90	3	E	1/2	Communication Brkdwn	***
9/28/90	5	2	5/6	Dinner and a Movie	Divided Sky
10/4/90	3	2	8/8	Cavern	***
10/6/90	2	1	6/13	Foam	The Oh Kee Pa
10/8/90	2	1	8/10	My Sweet One	The Oh Kee Pa
10/12/90	1	1	2/9	Suzy Greenberg	Dinner and a
10/31/90	3	1	7/11	Bouncing	The Asse Festival
11/2/90	1	2	6/9	Foam	The Lizards
11/3/90	1	1	10/11	Runaway Jim	Good Time Ba
11/4/90	1	2	13/13	Jesus Just Left	***
11/8/90	1	2	7/8	Bouncing	BBFCFM
11/10/90	1	2	7/8	Suzy Greenberg	The Asse Festival
11/16/90	1	1	4/8	Foam	Magilla
11/17/90	1	1	6/11	Bouncing	Cavern
11/24/90	1	2	7/12	Runaway Jim	Love You
11/26/90	1	1	6/11	Buried Alive	Paul and Silas
12/1/90	2	1	8/9	My Sweet One	Runaway Jim
12/7/90	1	1	5/9	The Landlady	The Asse Festival
12/8/90	1	2	9/9	No Good Trying	***
12/29/90	2	1	3/10	Llama	Esther
12/31/90	1	2	6/9	Magilla	Rocky Top
2/2/91	2	1	8/9	Destiny Unbound	Chalk Dust Tor
2/7/91	2	2	14/14	Destiny Unbound	***
2/20/91	7	1	9/11	Llama	Manteca
2/27/91	3	1	5/10	The Landlady	Fee
2/28/91	1	E	1/1	***	***
3/6/91	1	2	2/11	Golgi Apparatus	The Landlady
3/8/91	1	1	2/11	Golgi Apparatus	Fluffhead
3/13/91	2	1	3/9	The Landlady	Cavern
3/16/91	2	2	10/10	Cavern	***
3/22/91	2	1	2/11	Llama	The Landlady
3/28/91	2	1	6/14	Bouncing	Guelah Papyrus
4/2/91	3	1	7/10	Foam	The Oh Kee Pa
4/4/91	2	1	3/10	Suzy Greenberg	The Squirmin
4/6/91	2	2	6/11	Llama	Bathtub Gin
4/11/91	1	1	10/12	Carolina	The Squirmin
4/12/91	1	1	2/9	Runaway Jim	Fluffhead
4/16/91	2	1	2/9	Golgi Apparatus	Paul and Silas
4/20/91	3	1	10/11	Bouncing	Setting Sail
5/3/91	6	2	7/9	Tela	Harpua
5/11/91	4	2	2/12	Chalk Dust Torture	Poor Heart
5/16/91	2	1	9/11	Chalk Dust Torture	Magilla
5/18/91	2	1	4/9	Chalk Dust Torture	Paul and Silas
5/19/91	1	1	5/8	Bouncing	Cavern
7/13/91	3	2	9/9	If I Only Had a Brai	***
7/19/91	4	1	8/10	The Squirming Coil	Gumbo
7/20/91	1	2	11/12	T.M.W.S.I.Y. Reprise	Rocky Top
7/24/91	3	1	10/10	Tela	***
7/26/91	2	3	3/10	Dinner and a Movie	Flat Fee
8/3/91	2	2	9/10	I Didn't Know	Rocky Top
9/25/91	1	2	7/8	Runaway Jim	Chalk Dust Tor
9/27/91	2	2	9/10	Suzy Greenberg	Tweezer Repri
9/29/91	2	1	8/10	Destiny Unbound	The Oh Kee Pa
10/2/91	2	2	2/9	The Landlady	My Sweet One
10/11/91	5	1	6/10	Chalk Dust Torture	The Lizards
10/12/91	1	1	9/9	Guelah Papyrus	***
10/15/91	1	2	9/10	Destiny Unbound	Rocky Top
10/17/91	1	2	7/9	Fluffhead	Love You
10/19/91	2	2	7/10	Poor Heart	The Oh Kee Pa
10/23/91	1	2	9/10	Fee	Possum
10/28/91	3	2	7/11	Bathtub Gin	The Squirmin
10/31/91	2	1	10/11	Paul and Silas	Runaway Jim
11/2/91	2	2	11/11	Runaway Jim	***
11/7/91	1	1	7/11	It's Ice	The Landlady
11/9/91	2	1	8/11	Tube	Horn
11/10/91	1	1	9/10	Suzy Greenberg	Cavern
11/13/91	2	1	10/10	I Didn't Know	***
11/14/91	1	E	3/3	Good Times Bad Times	***
11/16/91	2	2	5/5	Brother	Horn
11/20/91	2	1	11/11	Llama	***
11/22/91	2	2	10/10	The Lizards	***
11/24/91	2	2	7/8	Take the A-Train	Golgi Apparat
11/30/91	1	1	11/11	Guelah Papyrus	***
12/6/91	3	2	4/12	Sparkle	Horn
3/12/92	6	1	11/11	Llama	***
3/21/92	2	1	11/11	Cracklin' Rosie	***
3/25/92	3	2	6/12	The Squirming Coil	Setting Sail
3/30/92	4	2	5/13	Mound	Vacuum Solo
4/1/92	2	2	2/13	Llama	The Horse
4/3/92	1	2	5/9	Mound	The Mango Song
4/5/92	2	2	3/12	All Things Recnsrd	The Horse
4/7/92	2	2	5/11	Eliza	My Friend My
4/12/92	2	2	5/10	Rift	Lawn Boy
4/15/92	2	2	2/8	Chalk Dust Torture	Reba
4/17/92	2	2	2/8	Brother	Fluffhead
4/22/92	4	2	7/11	Wilson	Poor Heart
4/25/92	3	2	3/11	Bathtub Gin	The Horse
4/30/92	2	2	5/11	My Mind's Got A Mind	The Horse
5/2/92	2	2	7/10	Foam	Chalk Dust Tor
5/6/92	3	2	4/11	The Squirming Coil	All Things Rec
5/8/92	2	2	6/12	Maze	The Horse
5/10/92	2	1	9/10	I Didn't Know	Possum
5/12/92	1	2	3/9	Bathtub Gin	Guelah Papyrus
5/15/92	2	1	9/11	Chalk Dust Torture	Sweet Adeline
5/16/92	1	2	6/13	The Squirming Coil	The Horse
6/19/92	3	1	7/7	Cavern	***
6/30/92	5	1	6/6	Sweet Adeline	***
7/11/92	4	1	10/11	Cavern	Suzy Greenber
7/14/92	2	2	8/10	Paul and Silas	Take the A-Trn
7/24/92	8	1	5/6	The Squirming Coil	Tweezer Repri
7/25/92	1	1	6/8	Rift	Llama
7/31/92	5	1	5/6	The Oh Kee Pa Ceremo	Good Time Ba
8/13/92	3	1	3/3	Foam	***
8/19/92	4	1	5/10	Guelah Papyrus	Uncle Pen
8/24/92	3	1	7/7	Reba	***
8/27/92	2	1	6/7	Sparkle	Llama
8/29/92	2	1	6/5	Maze	***
10/30/92	2	1	11/11	Sweet Adeline	***
11/20/92	2	2	4/10	Tube	Fast Enough for You
11/22/92	2	2	8/10	Tela	Faht
11/25/92	2	2	4/9	Fast Enough for You	The Lizards
11/30/92	3	2	7/10	Uncle Pen	The Squirmin
12/2/92	2	1	10/10	Horn	***
12/4/92	2	2	10/10	Faht	***
12/6/92	2	2	7/13	Bathtub Gin	T.M.W.S.I.Y.
12/7/92	1	1	11/11	Bouncing	***
12/10/92	2	2	7/10	Maze	Love You
12/12/92	2	2	7/10	Guelah Papyrus	If I Only Had a Brai
12/28/92	2	2	5/9	The Sloth	The Lizards
12/30/92	2	2	4/12	Bathtub Gin	T.M.W.S.I.Y.
2/3/93	2	2	7/11	Sparkle	Lifeboy
2/5/93	2	2	7/10	It's Ice	Love You
2/7/93	2	2	9/13	Glide	Clementine
2/10/93	2	2	7/11	Sparkle	The Horse
2/12/93	2	2	7/11	Fast Enough for You	Ya Mar
2/13/93	1	2	7/11	Llama	Big Ball Jam
2/17/93	2	2	9/11	Horn	Lengthwise
2/19/93	2	2	4/12	Paul and Silas	Ya Mar
2/22/93	3	2	5/11	Tweezer	Glide
2/25/93	2	2	5/11	Wilson	Uncle Pen
2/26/93	1	2	8/11	Big Ball Jam	Lengthwise
3/2/93	2	2	6/12	Llama	Love You
3/6/93	3	2	7/9	Fast Enough for You	Cracklin' Rosi
3/8/93	1	2	8/10	Kung	The Lizards
3/12/93	2	2	5/11	Sparkle	Mound
3/14/93	2	2	4/11	Ballad - Curtis Loew	Spooky Jam
3/14/93	0	2	6/11	Spooky Jam	Lifeboy
3/16/93	1	2	9/15	Chalk Dust Torture	Bike
3/18/93	2	2	5/10	Tela	Uncle Pen
3/21/93	2	2	6/12	Ya Mar	My Sweet One
3/24/93	2	2	8/12	Fast Enough for You	The Horse
3/26/93	2	2	8/12	Big Ball Jam	The Oh Kee Pa
3/28/93	2	2	6/9	Big Ball Jam	Paul and Silas
3/31/93	2	2	8/10	It's Ice	Harpua
4/3/93	2	2	6/10	The Sloth	Jesus Just Left
4/5/93	1	2	7/9	Glide	Cracklin' Rosi
4/9/93	1	2	7/10	My Friend My Friend	My Sweet One
4/12/93	2	2	7/10	Big Ball Jam	Honky Tonk Women Jam
4/14/93	1	2	6/10	Big Ball Jam	Spooky Jam
4/14/93	0	2	8/10	Spooky Jam	Harpua
4/17/93	2	2	5/11	Halley's Comet	Lifeboy
4/20/93	2	2	10/12	Llama	Whipping Post
4/22/93		2	7/10	Big Ball Jam	Uncle Pen
4/24/93		2	7/10	Big Ball Jam	Bike
4/27/93		2	7/10	Big Ball Jam	Silent in the M
4/30/93	2	2	9/10	If I Only Had a Brai	Golgi Apparat
5/2/93	2	2	3/10	Punch You in the Eye	The Lizards
5/5/93	2	2	9/10	Ya Mar	Jam
5/7/93	2	2	6/10	Big Ball Jam	The Great Gig in the
5/29/93	2	1	7/10	Cavern	Big Ball Jam
7/16/93	3	2	6/12	Bouncing	Yerushalayim
7/16/93	0	2	8/12	Yerushalayim	Poor Heart
7/18/93	2	2	8/10	Fee	Purple Rain
7/23/93	3	2	8/11	Big Ball Jam	BBFCFM
7/27/93	3	1	8/8	Purple Rain	***
7/29/93	2	2	6/9	Sparkle	Purple Rain
8/3/93	4	2	5/9	It's Ice	The Lizards
8/6/93	1	2	6/12	Uncle Pen	Cocaine Jam
8/6/93	0	2	8/12	Cocaine Jam	Halley's Comet
8/9/93	3	2	6/8	My Mind's Got A Mind	Contact
8/14/93	4	2	11/13	Daniel	Purple Rain
8/17/93	3	2	7/10	Suzy Greenberg	Purple Rain
8/20/93	1	2	7/9	Chalk Dust Torture	Purple Rain
8/25/93	3	2	6/8	Paul and Silas	The Squirmin
8/28/93	2	2	10/14	Purple Rain	Oye Como Va Jam
8/28/93	0	2	12/14	Oye Como Va Jam	Contact
12/28/93	1	2	2/9	Sample in a Jar	My Friend My
12/31/93	3	2	8/8	Lawn Boy	***
4/5/94	2	2	5/8	If I Could	I Wanna Be Like You
4/11/94	5	2	8/11	Big Ball Jam	Amazing Grce
4/14/94	2	2	6/9	Scent of a Mule	Nellie Kane
4/16/94	2	2	7/9	Bouncing	The Squirmin
4/20/94	3	2	8/9	Fee	Somewhere Over Jam
4/23/94	3	2	8/10	Ginseng Sullivan	Who By Fire
4/29/94	4	1	2/12	Halley's Comet	Fast Enough for You
5/4/94	4	2	3/9	Bouncing	Buried Alive
5/8/94	3	2	7/9	Cavern	Halley's Comet
5/13/94	3	2	7/9	Scent of a Mule	Purple Rain
5/16/94	2	2	8/11	Julius	BBFCFM
5/20/94	3	2	7/7	Rift	***
5/23/94	3	2	6/7	Punch You in the Eye	Possum
5/26/94	2	2	8/9	Dog Faced Boy	Amazing Grce
5/28/94	2	2	8/8	Llama	***
6/11/94	4	1	3/8	Chalk Dust Torture	Rift
6/14/94	2	2	7/9	Sparkle	Bike
6/18/94	3	2	9/10	Lifeboy	Chalk Dust Tor
6/25/94	6	2	6/9	Axilla (Part II)	Cracklin' Rosi

DATE	GAP	SET	POS.	SONG BEFORE	SONG AFTER
6/30/94	3	2	3/15	Maze	Yerushalayim
6/30/94	0	2	5/15	Yerushalayim	Sparkle
7/5/94	4	2	6/11	Cities	The Great Gig in the
7/8/94	2	2	7/11	Stash	Frankenstein
7/8/94	0	2	9/11	Frankenstein	Julius
7/14/94	4	2	6/10	Uncle Pen	Sparkle
10/9/94	5	2	4/8	Scent of a Mule	Amazing Grce
10/12/94	2	2	5/9	Scent of a Mule	Nellie Kane
10/15/94	3	2	5/11	Scent of a Mule	Catapult
10/15/94	0	2	7/11	Catapult	Amazing Grce
10/23/94	6	2	4/9	Halley's Comet	Down with Dis
10/26/94	2	2	5/7	Axilla (Part II)	Cracklin' Rosi
10/29/94	3	2	7/11	Uncle Pen	Bike
11/3/94	3	2	5/8	Julius	BBFCFM
11/14/94	4	2	10/10	Sweet Adeline	***
11/17/94	2	2	5/8	Sparkle	Love You
11/19/94	2	2	3/7	Sparkle	Cracklin' Rosi
11/23/94	3	2	6/7	Lifeboy	Tweezer Repri
12/4/94	8	2	5/7	Axilla (Part II)	Purple Rain
12/7/94	2	2	9/9	Amazing Grace	***
12/9/94	2	2	8/9	Cracklin' Rosie	Suzy Greenber
12/30/94	4	2	5/8	I'm Blue, Lonesome	Purple Rain
5/16/95	2	1	10/12	Glide II	Sweet Adeline
6/10/95	4	1	7/9	Rift	Lonesome Cowboy Bill
6/16/95	4	2	4/5	Carolina	The Squirmin
6/19/95	2	2	6/8	Sparkle	Acoustic Army
6/23/95	3	1	8/8	Taste	***
6/26/95	3	2	4/6	Poor Heart	Strange De-sign
6/29/95	2	2	4/6	Strange Design	Acoustic Army
9/29/95	7	1	6/8	Cars Trucks Buses	Sweet Adeline
10/3/95	3	1	11/11	Sample in a Jar	***
10/8/95	4	2	6/10	Sample in a Jar	Suspicious Minds
10/14/95	3	2	3/6	Rift	Hello My Baby
10/21/95	5	2	5/8	Sparkle	Purple Rain
10/24/95	2	2	4/8	Bouncing	Sleeping Monkey
10/28/95	3	2	4/7	Scent of a Mule	Strange De-sign
10/31/95	2	3	1/4	***	Jesus Just Left
11/10/95	2	2	3/9	Scent of a Mule	Crossroads
11/10/95	0	2	5/9	Crossroads	Strange De-sign
11/14/95	3	2	9/11	Strange Design	Immigrant Song Jam
11/14/95	0	2	11/11	Immigrant Song Jam	***
11/18/95	3	2	5/10	I'm So Tired	Contact
11/22/95	3	2	5/6	Bouncing	Strange De-sign
11/29/95	4	2	5/11	Possum	Taste That Surrounds
12/4/95	4	2	7/9	Cars Trucks Buses	Sample in a Ja
12/9/95	4	2	4/8	Gumbo	Lawn Boy
12/31/95	10	3	4/6	Sea and Sand	Sanity
4/26/96	1	1	6/13	Cars Trucks Buses	Wolfman's Brother
6/6/96	1	2	2/10	AC/DC Bag	Chalk Dust Tor
7/5/96	2	1	4/6	AC/DC Bag	Scent of a Mul
7/11/96	5	2	7/8	Terrapin	Hello My Baby
7/13/96	2	1	10/10	Chalk Dust Torture	***
7/18/96	3	1	7/7	It's Ice	***
7/22/96	3	1	8/8	A Day in the Life	***
7/24/96	2	1	4/5	Julius	Golgi Apparat
8/7/96	6	2	9/10	Life on Mars	Hello My Baby
8/14/96	4	2	2/10	Runaway Jim	The Horse
10/18/96	5	2	3/6	Maze	Reba
10/22/96	3	1	9/9	Free	***
10/26/96	3	2	2/7	Down with Disease	Sparkle
10/31/96	3	1	4/10	Down with Disease	Prince Caspian
11/7/96	4	2	4/4	Bike	***
11/9/96	2	2	3/7	A Day in the Life	Taste

DATE	GAP	SET	POS.	SONG BEFORE	SONG AFTER
11/13/96	2	2	5/7	Prince Caspian	Theme From the Botto
11/19/96	5	2	5/7	The Vibration of Lif	Star Spangled Banner
11/24/96	3	2	5/7	A Day in the Life	Loving Cup
11/29/96	2	2	8/10	Steep	Waste
12/2/96	3	1	4/8	Bouncing	I Didn't Know
12/6/96	2	1	6/9	Llama	Cars Trucks Buses
12/29/96	2	2	5/10	The Lizards	Rotation Jam
2/14/97	4	1	3/9	NICU	Sweet Adeline
2/21/97	5	1	6/6	Crosseyed and Painle	***
2/26/97	4	2	4/11	Ha Ha Ha	Kung
3/2/97	3	E	1/1	***	***
6/29/97	12	1	1/7	***	Taste
7/6/97	5	2	2/5	Free	Waste
7/9/97	1	2	4/6	Cars Trucks Buses	Ghost
7/11/97	2	1	7/7	Johnny B. Goode	***
7/23/97	3	2	4/6	Sample in a Jar	Rocky Mountain Way J
7/26/97	2	1	8/9	Dirt	Izabella
7/31/97	3	1	9/9	I Saw it Again	***
8/6/97	3	1	8/8	Ya Mar	***
8/11/97	4	2	5/6	My Soul	Character Zer
8/16/97	3	1	8/11	Ginseng Sullivan	Train Song
11/13/97	2	1	8/9	My Soul	Character Zer
11/17/97	3	2	7/7	When Circus Comes	***
11/28/97	6	1	2/8	The Curtain	I Didn't Know
12/3/97	4	1	7/7	Also Sprach	***
12/29/97	9	2	5/5	Tube	***
4/5/98	6	1	2/8	The Oh Kee Pa Ceremo	Theme From the Botto
7/2/98	3	2	4/4	Prince Caspian	***
7/3/98	1	1	10/11	My Soul	A Day in the Life
7/19/98	9	1	8/8	Roggae	***
7/26/98	5	2	2/6	La Grange	Albuquerque
7/28/98	1	2	8/8	Prince Caspian	***
8/6/98	6	E	2/2	Running With the Dev	***
8/9/98	3	2	8/11	Somewhere Over The	Frankenstein
8/12/98	2	E	2/2	Burning Down House	***
11/2/98	10	2	4/16	The Moma Dance	Harpua
11/9/98	5	2	7/7	Slave	***
11/14/98	3	2	7/9	Sexual Healing	Julius
11/19/98	3	E	1/1	***	***
11/25/98	4	2	6/8	Piper	Been Caught Stealin'
11/29/98	3	2	8/8	Bathtub Gin	***
12/29/98	2	2	5/5	Boogie On Reggae	***
7/1/99	4	2	3/3	Prince Caspian	***
7/7/99	3	2	7/7	Bug	***
7/15/99	6	1	10/10	The Sloth	***
7/17/99	2	2	8/8	Timber (Jerry)	***
7/20/99	2	1	9/9	Wilson	***
7/25/99	4	2	6/6	Purple Rain	***
8/1/99	5	2	9/9	The Lizards	***
9/9/99	1	2	8/9	Bug	Hello My Baby
9/12/99	3	2	5/5	Also Sprach	***
9/17/99	3	2	5/8	Roggae	Bass Jam
9/28/99	8	2	7/7	Chalk Dust Torture	***
10/2/99	3	2	4/6	Piper	Frankenstein
10/10/99	6	2	2/6	Jam	Prince Caspian
12/2/99	1	2	5/6	Also Sprach	Little Drummer Boy
12/8/99	5	2	6/6	The Lizards	***
12/15/99	5	1	7/7	Train Song	***
12/18/99	3	1	9/9	The Inlaw Josie Wale	***
12/31/99	2	2	10/35	Rock and Roll	Crosseyed and Painle
5/23/00	3	2	5/8	Piper	Run Like Antel
6/9/00	1	E	1/1	***	***
6/15/00	5	2	4/4	Bike	***
6/22/00	2	E	1/1	***	***
7/6/00	10	1	12/12	Golgi Apparatus	***
7/15/00	7	2	7/7	Bug	***

DATE	GAP	SET	POS.	SONG BEFORE	SONG AFTER
9/11/00	3	2	5/5	What's the Use	***
9/22/00	7	1	9/9	Heavy Things	***
9/27/00	4	2	7/7	Brother	***
10/7/00	7	E	1/1	***	***

Was played in the most recent show.

You Gotta See Mama Every Night

DATE	GAP	SET	POS.	SONG BEFORE	SONG AFTER
3/16/93	510	1	9/11	Divided Sky	McGrupp

Has not been played in the last 609 shows.

You Shook Me (All Night Long)

DATE	GAP	SET	POS.	SONG BEFORE	SONG AFTER
9/29/00	11132		9/9	Rapper's Delight	***

Has not been played in the last 6 shows.

You Shook Me All Night Long Jam

DATE	GAP	SET	POS.	SONG BEFORE	SONG AFTER
4/20/89	93	1	3/12	Fluffhead	Fluff's Travels

Has not been played in the last 1026 shows.

Part IV

Taping

Taping

TAPE GUIDE

Written by Jack R. Lebowitz

Amateur tape trading has various levels, a certain logic, and its own set of rules. The process will be unfamiliar to newcomers, and may seem intimidating. This section explains the variables, and provides hints that will allow readers to find and acquire recordings of performances described elsewhere in this book.

1.0 Introduction

Chances are, since you're reading this, that you may already have or be interested in building a collection of tapes of Phish or other bands. Perhaps you just have a casual interest in simply getting a few high-quality tapes or recordable CDs (CD-Rs) of shows. Maybe you're just curious about what's up with that group you've noticed at shows crouching beneath a forest of microphone stands behind the soundboard. This guide to trading and recording live music will point you in the right direction in how to hook up with tapes/CDs and other traders, as well as comprehending the whole taping phenomenon and its revolutionary implications for music distribution.

Some background on this phenomenon is helpful to understand the following sections, which cover the nuts and bolts of taping and trading. A good starting place is the novel role that trading band-authorized "audience tapes" occupies in the world of recorded music. From the time the phonograph was invented by Thomas Edison in 1877, the production and distribution of recorded music has been controlled by the recording industry as a function of audio recording technology. Although the technology of record manufacture has changed a lot in 125 years, from shellac cylinders to vinyl LPs to CDs, all of those media had to be factory-manufactured. The music on those recordings was recorded by professionals, usually in studios, and authorized by the artists' management. Prior to the 1980s, only the occasional unauthorized "bootleg" of performances by popular artists like Bob Dylan or the Grateful Dead—often a surreptitiously taped live show or collection of "leaked" studio outtakes—would be independently pressed and distributed. However, the extensive equipment needed to manufacture records and the risky, illegal nature of that activity meant that bootlegs were not widely available. Rabid fans might have a bootleg record or two, but they were not typically the cornerstone of anyone's collection. They were also usually of inferior sound quality to the authorized goods.

Economists would describe the recording industry's structure in its first hundred years as a "vertically integrated oligopoly," with a handful of record labels controlling the recording, manufacture, and distribution of most recorded music from the studio to the retail store and, ultimately, the consumer. However, about twenty years ago, the first cracks in that wall began to appear, spurred by technological improvements in battery-powered tape decks and microphones, and by "jam bands," particularly the Grateful Dead, who were willing to allow their fans to make audience tapes of their unique performances for noncommercial home use and trading. (Jerry Garcia got the idea from having seen decks on the edge of bluegrass stages.) Later, the evolution of computer-based conferencing systems, e-mail, and, in the '90s, the Internet and personal computers

with CD recorders ("burners") allowed for digital audio tapes (DATs) and CD-Rs to be freely and widely disseminated totally outside of the commercial system of music distribution. This evolution facilitated a departure from oligopoly.

The taping scene has snowballed from its modest beginnings in the murky days of bootlegging. As important as the technological improvements that allow for state-of-the-art digital recordings, many bands such as Phish have seen fit not only to tolerate but to expressly encourage audience taping. This enlightened attitude speaks to the generosity (and some might also say shrewd marketing) of bands and their management to allow their fans to spread the music and the accompanying buzz. Because taping is legal within the bounds of the bands' noncommercial home-use policies, most tapers and traders do not refer to their legitimate audience tapes as "bootleg" recordings or "boots." (Such recordings might, however, *become* "bootleg" tapes or CDs when they are manufactured offshore and come back to second-hand CD or independent record stores as illegal recordings for sale at hefty prices.)

Given how widespread tapes of popular bands are, it is rare that a taper or trader is involved in manufacturing commercial bootlegs. Tapers often remark that the best defense against bootleggers is to make audience recordings so easy to get "for free" through trading that no one would think of paying $50 for a mediocre CD (often with pirated images and incorrect song titles) just for convenience's sake. Tapers' ethics and their understanding of bands' noncommercial home-use polices allows tapes to be sold, if at all, only for the cost of blank media. Tapers who have tried to justify charging any premium on spinning tapes (such as asking for two blanks for each tape spun, or $5 per tape) routinely get "flamed" (that is, harshly criticized) in taping discussion forums on the Internet, even though they may seek to recover the cost of expensive taping equipment or labor.

Amateur live recordings are available in three major formats: analog cassette, DAT, and CD-R (typically from a DAT source). The analog cassette is the familiar "compact cassette" introduced by Phillips in the 1960s and made ubiquitous by the Sony Walkman, car and home tape decks, and portable boom-boxes. DAT tapes are a digital medium equivalent in technical quality to CDs. Today, most shows are originally taped in DAT format, then spread to others through digital "clones" of the DAT tape, then digital-to-analog (D>A) transfers to cassette tapes, or (hopefully digital) transfers to CD-Rs.

In collecting and trading live recordings, you can either go analog, DAT, CD-R, or all three. As I'll explain later in comparing the three technologies, the depth of your interest in taping and how much you are willing to commit to the hobby of collecting live music recordings will help define what kind of equipment you will need.

1.1 Tape technology: Digital vs. Analog
CD-Rs, DATs, and analog tapes are all used to record and trade live music. Each format has advantages and disadvantages, and it's helpful to understand how these media work and differ.

Analog taping uses the familiar stereo compact cassette format, which is a magnetic tape similar to the old reel-to-reel tape machines. A thin strip of magnetic tape is mechanically pulled past recording heads, which encode a magnetic pattern representing an analog of the sound energy (voltage fluctuations) gathered by microphones.

It is theoretically possible to get a fairly good-sounding tape with the analog cassette format, but the medium has some inherent limita-

tions. One is that the dynamic range, or amount of information which can be captured from the live sound source is limited compared to a digital medium. Another, more significant limitation is that when analog recordings are copied to a later "generation" of tape, not all of the information is transferred—some will be lost to hiss, which is cumulative from generation to generation.

On the other hand, when a digital tape is copied, every bit of data on the tape is copied to the later generation, and (ideally) no quality is lost. Copying, or "cloning," a digital tape is similar to copying a digital file on a computer: The copy is the same, bit for bit, as the original. When there is an error in this process, however, "dropouts" (no sound) or "diginoise" (static fuzz) occur. Analog cassette tapes have the advantages of being more durable and insensitive to environmental conditions, as well as playable on more ubiquitous types of audio players. But they are typically shorter (90 to 110 minutes), and longer tapes risk thinning and breakage, whereas DATs can be two hours without comparable risks. CD-Rs offer a good compromise, though their digital quality is offset by the seventy-four-minute limit of that medium (though eighty-minute CD-Rs are available).

The advantages of each type of taping equipment has led to a two-tier system for taping most live shows: DAT taping is used at the show to make extremely high-quality master tapes, which are later cloned to perfect digital copies and then "spun down" to analog or burned to CD-R for everyday listening and further reproduction. A first-generation analog tape is the first analog recording made from a digital tape (D>A) or analog master, if an analog deck was used for the initial recording. If that tape is copied to another analog tape, the copy is referred to as "second generation." Generally, a first-generation analog tape sounds virtually the same as the digital master; the effects are subtle, even on good playback equipment. A second-generation tape typically sounds less crisp and detailed than the master. After two or more generations, the quality is significantly degraded from that of the digital (or analog) masters.

The DAT technology used to make audience tape masters at shows is a modern miracle. While the DAT recorder may look outwardly like a small cassette player, it is actually a special-purpose computer using modern digital interfaces and tape-storage technologies. The DAT recorder uses a miniature VCR-like cassette with four-millimeter tape, which is about half the thickness (but two or three times the capacity) of analog cassette tape. The DAT tape cassette's operation is similar to a miniature VCR cassette in that the tape travels only in one direction and thereby does not have two "sides" which are flipped halfway through. Although the DAT cassette is smaller, the DAT medium is capable of storing mind-boggling amounts of digital information on either a two-hour (sixty-meter) or three hour (ninety-meter) tape.

The DAT deck also uses a similar type of recording technology as a VCR, where two tiny heads on a small drum spin diagonally (helical) along the tape, encoding stripes of digital information. DAT works by capturing a large number of samples of a sound-wave pattern and saving them as digital information. Similar in concept to a motion picture's twenty-four frames (or samples) per second, the DAT medium takes approximately 48,000 samples/second x two stereo channels x 16-bit word length per sample, which equates to a bitstream of about 1.2 megabytes of data per second. This provides an ear-popping maximum bandwidth, or "signal-to-noise" ratio, of ninety-two decibels for the DAT technology, compared to about sixty-four decibels theoretically possi-

ble for analog cassette tape (using metal tapes with a high-quality analog tape deck).

The downside to the DAT medium is cost, durability, and everyday usability. While DAT decks have overtaken the taping sections at shows, the approximately $600 cost (at the time of this writing) of the least-expensive portable DAT deck is still more than double the cost of a high-end three-head analog recorder (currently $150–300). DAT decks also tend not to stand up as well to heavy use over time and require more frequent maintenance, especially head replacement, which can be expensive. It is also hard to find (and afford) car-mountable DAT tape players. For these reasons, many tapers and traders do not use DAT, CD-R, or analog media exclusively: They use DAT for making and trading master recordings, and CD-Rs or analog cassettes for everyday listening.

1.2 Live show taping and the taping "food chain"

A list of bands known to allow taping is maintained and updated monthly on the DAT-Heads web site and published to the DAT Heads e-mail list (see Sections 7.1 and 7.2). The taping scenes for various bands and venues range from highly organized to very casual. At Phish shows, there is a designated taping section (or simply "the section"), usually just behind the soundboard. Some bands, usually smaller acts playing in clubs, allow tapers to plug into the PA soundboard. Most venues at which large acts like Phish play do *not* allow soundboard access, but require tapers to bring their own microphones and mic stands to the taping section. Some bands, including Phish, also require tapers to purchase special tapers' tickets allowing them to bring taping equipment into the venue and to get access to the tapers' section.

Tapers use a wide variety of microphones, from electronics chain-store microphones costing less than $100 to professional-quality studio microphones costing upwards of $3,000 (often with high-quality outboard preamplifiers or digital-to-analog converters). One of the major advantages of the DAT format is that, like the ability to clone flawless digital copies by playing from one DAT deck to another, a DAT deck is able to pass a digital bitstream of what is being recorded. This means that it is possible to tape shows without owning any microphones by simply plugging one's DAT deck into another deck that already has mic access (known as "patching"). Since each recording deck passes the digital bitstream being recorded, it is possible to "daisy chain" a bunch of DAT decks together, with as many as a dozen decks in the section getting a digital signal from a single pair of microphones. Thus, DAT technology allows perfect recordings made with excellent microphones to circulate widely through the taping community. Beyond Phish and the Grateful Dead, a surprisingly large number of improvisation-oriented rock and jazz acts are documented on high-quality digital tape, which are available as a kind of distributed archive among the taping community. The following section describes how you can gain access to that archive for your own listening enjoyment.

1.3 How to get tapes

Here are some suggestions on how you can go about obtaining some tapes, perhaps even start a collection. If you're simply interested in getting a few tapes (of Phish or another band), the best way is to ask around and find a friend or friend-of-a-friend who collects recordings to make you a few copies for "blanks and postage" (or "B&P"). This means that you buy the blank tapes or CD-Rs of the proper length and

a stamped return envelope and your friend will fill them for you with material from either a DAT, CD-R, or early-generation analog master.

If you want more than a few tapes or even wish to get hooked up with a potentially limitless supply, there are some further steps you could take. First, get Internet access with a stable, at least semipermanent e-mail address. (Keep in mind that fan tape distribution substitutes a fan network for a corporate-commercial structure, and the Net makes that social networking possible for little or no cost.) This enables you to participate in a large number of public offers to distribute music through "tape trees" and public "B&P offers." On public Internet Usenet newsgroups such as rec.music.phish, mailing lists such as DAT-Heads, and the mailing lists of individual jam bands, there is a steady diet of such offers, more than most sane people could ever participate in.

Joining tape trees is an excellent way to hook up with some fine, usually current, tapes of Phish and other bands. A tape tree is an organized method of distributing a single high-quality "seed" to hundreds or even thousands of fans in both digital and analog form, typically through a hierarchical branching structure in which each participant makes multiple copies. Some trees are *ad hoc* offers by a fan who wishes to spread a certain show; other trees are semipermanent or permanent arrangements, like the DooDah tree or Operation Everyshow where a whole Phish tour might be "treed."

Here's how it works. First, the tree administrator (tree admin, for short) posts an offer to a newsgroup or list such as rec.music.phish or DAT-Heads. A sign-up form will be provided which must be e-mailed back to the tree admin by the announced deadline, usually a week or two after the initial tree announcement. After the sign-up period closes, the admin posts a tree structure, which is a family tree–like diagram of everyone's e-mail addresses in the tree showing how the single "seed" will be duplicated to everyone on the tree. Usually, the DAT master will be cloned for several levels of DAT tree branches, who make additional DAT clones and pass them to the DAT leaves, who will in turn make first-generation D>A analog tapes to be copied in analog branches and leaves (those unable to make copies for others). The goal of a well-designed tree is to distribute the tape as widely as possible with as few as possible analog generations at the leaves, hopefully no more than two or three. This allows even the analog leaves to get very good-quality, early-generation tapes.

When the tree structure is posted, you find your name on the structure to see who is above you (your parent) and below you (your children). After an initial e-mail contact, you arrange to send blanks and postage (or trade) to your parent, and (if you are not a leaf) for your children to send blanks and postage to you. Then, your parent copies the tape for you and sends it in a padded mailing envelope in the mail. When you receive it, if you have children you copy the tape for them on their blanks and send it to them. If you don't have children, you're a leaf and you don't need to copy the tape further. Either way, you enjoy a great new tape for the cost of blanks and postage!

In filling out your tree sign-up application, you'll see that questions are usually asked about the type and quality of your duplicating equipment (if you have any). The reason for this is that the tree admins need to know who on the tree can copy DAT or analog tapes so that they can create the tree structure and prioritize use of the best equipment. An advantage of being a branch, as opposed to a leaf, is that you will get a copy usually weeks or even months sooner. If a number of people have duplicating ability and want to be branches, the admin will

usually choose among applicants by choosing the ones with the highest-quality duplicating equipment, on the reasonable premise that this will preserve the quality of the tapes as they are duplicated at each step, particularly in the degradation-prone analog realm.

The next logical step for those interested in collecting analog tapes is to invest in good analog duplication equipment. The typical tree application shows a hierarchy of equipment in terms of generally perceived quality. At the top is a three-head analog deck for recording, with a separate analog machine used as the "play" machine directly cabled into the inputs of the three-head "record" machine. A three-head deck, with separate heads for erase, record, and play, is a superior recording system to the two-head decks where the record and play functions are combined into a single head. The three-head deck also allows for the tape being recorded to be monitored as it is being recorded to check the quality of the original. A new three-head analog deck generally costs in the $250–800 range, though high-quality used equipment is also available. An inexpensive "play" deck can usually be had for around $100, and many taping beginners may be able to use their existing deck as the "play" deck. Dual-well automatic dubbing decks are less favored than the separate record and play decks for three reasons: noise levels usually cannot be adjusted in the automatic dual-well decks; single-well decks are generally higher-quality; and high-speed dubbing and automatic-reverse features substitute convenience for quality. Thus, taping etiquette and tree rules often frown on the use of dubbing decks. A good and fairly current orientation to cassette decks and their various features can be found in the November 1996 issue of *Stereo Review*, which should be available from most public and university library reference collections.

Because the distribution of fan-produced tapes is an informal, social endeavor, customs and expectations have emerged under the heading of "netiquette," similar to participation in Internet groups. I'll touch on some of these important, unwritten rules to help you avoid some "newbie" (first-time user) errors and help you start trading with as few problems as possible.

One question is what analog blanks to use. You'll want to use high-quality blanks, since you'd be cheating yourself and probably confusing your tree parent or friend by sending poor-quality blanks. Analog cassette tape is formulated in several types: normal-bias (Type I), chrome or high-bias (Type II), and metal (Type IV) tapes. Normal tapes are cheap but low quality and not really suitable for copying good live show recordings (even though these types of tape are used by the record companies for the commercial cassette tapes sold in record shops!).

The analog tape used in 99 percent of trades and B&P deals is a high-bias/chrome/Type II tape, and the brand which is used 95 percent of the time is the Maxell XL-II or XL-IIS tapes. Although other companies, such as TDK and Fuji, make Type II tapes, for reasons of custom, price, and consistency, the Maxell XL-II is the common currency of the analog world.

The Maxell XL-II and XL-IIS tapes are very similar, except that the XL-IIS has a better shell and (it is rumored) slightly better tape. The XL-IIS is usually available only from specialized suppliers that sell primarily to the taping community, such as Terrapin Tapes, Cassette House, and American-Digital (see Section 7.2 for info on how to find these and other vendor phone numbers). However, the normal XL-IIs will work just fine and are widely available at most record stores and discount chain stores. However, if you are going to buy a lot of tapes, you should

check out one of the specialized tapers' vendors, which offer great bulk prices on tapes.

If you ultimately end up going digital, you'll find that DAT tapers are equally persnickety about what tapes they will accept in trades and B&P offers. Poor-quality tapes can "shed" particles on the heads of the DAT machines they're used in, which can lead to head clogging, requiring an expensive trip to the repair shop.

Most traders stick to agreed-upon media brands as being universally acceptable and many avoid unlabeled (non-brand name) or "one-pass" (computer backup) tapes. Currently, the acceptable brands of DAT tapes seem to be Sony DG, Maxell HS-4, Fuji, and KAO Gold (the latter are probably best but have been discontinued).

A great boon to DAT tapers (and part of the reason for the growth of the medium) is that the four-millimeter tape used in the audio DAT format and its helical-scan tape-recording technology is the same as the DDS computer tape used for personal computer backups. Since the market for economical computer backup tapes is vastly larger than that for digital audio tapes, demand has driven the price for these tapes way down. While audio DAT tapes made by Sony, Panasonic, or Ampex (for instance) are more than acceptable in trade, they are significantly more expensive, running around $5–10 as opposed to $3–4 for DDS tapes. Virtually all traders believe the DDS tapes are equivalent to tapes branded as audio DAT tapes, although the tape manufacturers (but sometimes not their own engineers) "officially" deny that DDS tapes are the same as their DAT tapes.

One peculiarity of DDS tapes is that their length is noted in meters, not minutes like audio DAT or audio cassette tapes. A meter is two minutes of tape. Therefore a sixty-meter DDS tape is two hours, and a ninety-meter tape is three hours. While a ninety-meter DDS tape will accommodate the typical two-set Phish or Dead show, many traders believe that the thinner ninety-meter tapes cause excessive wear on their tape deck heads and transport mechanisms, so use them as little as possible. The DAT trading community seems fairly divided on the issue of whether to use ninety-meter tapes, so tape length is a very important item to be agreed upon when setting up a DAT trade.

Similarly, in the CD-R world, many brands of blank CD-Rs are agreed upon to work well with CD burners, but many others are shunned as being problematic (i.e., incompatible with a particular burner, resulting in a "coaster," a failed CD-R burn) and the list of acceptable brands is constantly changing. For analog trades, as previously noted, most traders have traditionally agreed upon the Maxell XL-II (or XL-IIS) brand as a universal currency. However, the situation is far more complicated with respect to blank DAT and CD-R media. For this reason, if you trade DATs or CD-Rs, it is best to indicate on your tape list the exact brands and lengths of tapes or CD-Rs you will accept.

When communicating with your trading partner, also be sure to ask what length blanks you'll need. Analog cassette tapes come in both ninety-minute and hundred-minute lengths (among others, but these are the only ones used for trading). You will need supplies of both tape lengths. A two-set Phish show usually requires two tapes, but their lengths may be different, even for the same show. Make sure to send the right length blanks so that your partner doesn't have to substitute tapes. Send only brand new, shrink-wrapped tapes—previously recorded tapes are unacceptable. Also send the correct amount of return postage and an adhesive return label so your partner will have to do as little extra work as possible. Some of these details (like whether

to send postage loose or affixed) may differ with your partner, so it's good taping etiquette to ask (via e-mail) exactly what to do, while the deal is being set up. You should also confirm turnaround times; most people expect the trade to be a month or so at the outset, but expectations differ, so communication is good.

Copying tapes is fairly easy to do, but attention to a few details helps to get the best possible copies. A DAT to DAT digital transfer, or "clone", is the easiest and most foolproof method, as compared to copying analog tapes or digital to analog (D>A) transfers. A DAT deck has no knobs and requires no settings for digital transfers. You just need to set up one deck as your "play" deck and the other as the "record" deck. Connect the two decks with a single coaxial cable (of the sort discussed in Section 6.0, "Taping at shows"). Before making the copy, place a fresh tape in the recording deck and "unpack" it by fast forwarding to the end, then rewinding back to the "top" of the tape. Then hit "record" on the record deck, and "play" on the play deck, and you're off. You can either listen to the show as it's recording, or do something else. The rest of the recording process is automatic, much like copying a computer file. The DAT to DAT recording will transfer not just the audio information (the music) but also "subcode" data, including a digital time code called "A"-(for absolute) time, as well as whatever track numbers might have also been put on the master tape. DAT machines otherwise require little maintenance. Most manufacturers just recommend the use of a special "dry" head cleaning tape which you run for ten seconds every twenty to fifty hours of deck use. DAT's it!

Digital to Analog ("D>A") recording requires more work, but excellent results may be had, especially with "first generation" D>A masters. The play and record decks are best connected by a pair of coaxial-type audio interconnects which terminate in RCA type stereo plugs. These cables insure that the relatively low "line levels" coming from the play deck are not degraded. Good interconnect cables are available at audio or electronics chain stores. You can get by in a pinch with the flat plastic ribbon cables that probably came with your tape deck, but if you're going to do much copying, get a good pair of coaxial audio interconnects. For their analog outputs, Sony portable DAT decks use the relatively sketchy one-eighth inch stereo "miniplug", which is a relatively undesirable type of connection because of its small size and fragility. It will work, but if you're going to be doing much D>A, you will probably want a non-portable, "home" type DAT deck as your play deck, which also has the preferable type of audio outputs: a pair of normal stereo RCA jacks.

To set up to make D>A copies, cable the decks together directly, with the DAT deck's analog outputs patched into the analog tape deck's inputs. If you want to listen when recording, run the analog deck's outputs into to your amp or receiver. In other words, try to avoid any extra amplification or connection stages between the two tape decks, such any internal "tape in/out" feature your preamp or receiver might have. Because analog tapes are much shorter than DAT tapes and have two sides which must be "flipped" halfway through, making a D>A copy requires somewhat more effort and attention than the simple DAT cloning process. You can plan the tape flips by first "timing" the tapes. Fast forward the DAT tape and listen to the portion of the tape around 46 to 51 minutes (half of a 90 minute and 100 minute-length analog tape, respectively), and figure out where best in that segment of the tape to do the tape flip, hopefully between songs. When you figure out the best analog blank lengths to use and places to do the flips, make a note of

the DAT tape's exact "A"-time at the cut. When doing the actual copying, knowing the "A-time" of the cut beforehand will allow you to anticipate the flip and cut or fade "on cue". I use a Sharpie-type marker pen to write the "A-time" for the flip in big numbers on a Post-it Note, for instance, "44:39", and slap it on the tape deck. Then you can start the copying onto the analog deck and attend to your other business, just remembering to come back to do your tape flip at the end of "David Bowie", or after about forty minutes or so.

Timing tapes for D>A is a bit of extra work and hassle, so make sure you keep good records of the tape lengths used and "A-times" where you did the flips so you don't repeat the same work when you make additional copies of that show. I use a print-out of the setlist with flips indicated by slashes and an arrow to the corresponding DAT "A-time". And, luckily for those who trade tapes of Phish or other widely-traded bands, fans have created websites which "collect" and post analog tape flip information, which is an obvious timesaver for anyone doing D>A. For current information on such Phish "tape flip info" sites, use the search phrase "tape flips" on the www.Phish.net site or some of the other taping or band-related sites discussed in Section 7.0, Internet Resources.

One additional complication in copying onto analog tapes involves "setting levels". A DAT clone has identical levels to the master; the levels can't be adjusted during copying. There is no "level" knob for digital input on a DAT machine. Not so with an analog tape deck, which usually has a large "input level" knob and a VU-level meter which shows tape signal levels on a decibel ("dB") scale. Settling optimal recording levels on the analog record deck requires a bit of practice and observation. If you're using a Type II tape such as the typical Maxell XL-II, you should set the levels so the record deck's VU meter's levels peak at about +3 dB and the "average" levels of music bump up around the 0 dB level. You may have to listen to some of the tape you're recording to see where the levels "fit" these target peaks you're aiming for. Setting levels is the aural equivalent of adjusting exposures for photo film. You don't want "overexposure", with muddy distortion from too-high levels, but you also don't want "underexposure" which makes tapes recorded with too low levels sound "hissy" when the tape is over-amplified to needed playback volume.

While most home analog decks have a Dolby or similar special noise reduction encoding option, most analog tapes traded are made *without* noise reduction, out of long-standing custom and perhaps compatibility issues. If your analog deck has a "noise reduction" setting, turn it to "No reduction" or "off", rather than the Dolby-on setting. Other than the added chores of setting levels and planning tape flips, copying D>A is otherwise much the same as DAT cloning. Hit "record", "play" and walk away, until a tape needs to be flipped. There is, however, a bit more routine "user maintenance" which affects analog tape copy quality and which probably should be done on your analog decks, as compared to DAT decks. You should clean your analog recording heads frequently. by swabbing them with a commercial tape head cleaning solution or isopropyl alcohol. The latter is equal to the head cleaning solutions, but is much less expensive (~$3/pint). Isopropyl alcohol be found, or ordered, at any pharmacy. Ask for "anhydrous isopropyl alcohol, USP", which is 99% alcohol. You can use Q-tip type swabs to clean the tape deck heads, or better yet, special lintless foam swabs available at electronics parts stores.

In addition to frequent head cleaning, periodic head demagnetization of your analog decks' tape heads is also recommended to optimize the recording process. Don't bother with the suspect combo cleaner-demagnetizers tapes in cassette shells. Get a "wand" type, plug-in demagnetizer such as the Teac E-3 (~$40). Feel free to clean analog heads and demagnetize as much as you like. More is apparently better, as many professional recording studios do this maintenance <u>every</u> time a tape recorder is used. While this level of housekeeping might be overkill for home taping purposes, it's probably worthwhile to clean and demag your heads as often as you can find time to do it, hopefully at least every thirty hours of use.

2.0 Making and maintaining a tape list.

Having some sort of organized list of your tapes is essential if you want to accumulate more than a few. When you have two tape decks or a CD-R burner, you can trade. This is most often done by first trading tape lists so each person in the trade can see what the other has to offer. Even before you are able to trade, when you are "groveling" tapes from another kind trader, maintaining your tape list is helpful so your friend can quickly see what you have to trade.

Tape lists are fairly easy to make and maintain, and can be done in a variety of different ways. You can create a simple list with a word processor or text editor. Specialized tape cataloging programs such as TapeTracker for Windows or WinTaper generate standardized tape lists automatically using preformatted, modifiable templates.

Lists are sometimes exchanged in the proprietary formatted output of the word processors or spreadsheet programs with which they are created (e.g., Microsoft Word .doc files). To be useful to the largest number of recipients and transmittable in the widest variety of platforms, including e-mail attachments and your personal web site, tape lists are best exported and exchanged as plain ASCII text files or in tasteful HTML files.

To create your initial, simple tape list with a word-processing program, you should use a fixed-width typeface font (like Courier New 10 pt., which has a fixed width of twelve characters per inch). Use a maximum line length of seventy-four characters, which works out to approximately one-inch margins on an 8 1/2 x 11-inch "virtual" page. This allows you to keep the information for each tape in a "tabbed table" format, which avoids jumbling of columns because of potential line breaks or wrapping problems. A fixed-width table looks like this:

```
05/05/93 Albany, NY _ Palace Theater   A:D 136 AKG451 ck61

05/06/93 Albany, NY _ Palace Theater   A:D 165 AKG461 ck60
Reba cut

05/30/93 Monterey, CA _ Laguna Seca Raceway   A:D 154
SchoepsMK461

08/09/93 Toronto, ON, Canada _ The Masonic   S:D 160 Hot!

08/13/93 Indianapolis, IN _ Murat Theater   S:D 170
```

Here's what a variable-width table looks like:

```
05/05/93 Albany, NY _ Palace Theater    A:D 136 AKG451 ck61

05/06/93 Albany, NY _ Palace Theater    A:D 165 AKG461 ck60
Reba cut
```

```
05/30/93 Monterey, CA _ Laguna Seca Raceway   A:D 154
SchoepsMK461

08/09/93 Toronto, ON, Canada _ The Masonic   S:D 160 Hot!

08/13/93 Indianapolis, IN _ Murat Theater   S:D 170
```

An additional benefit of this common format is that it prints out nicely in hard copy in the default page format (8 1/2 x 11 inches, portrait mode). Although using automatic tape-cataloging programs like TapeTracker makes the list-keeping chore a breeze (including such snazzy features as a virtual librarian for loaning tapes, and a trade-tracking system), many traders maintain huge lists with even hundreds of tapes using standard word processors like Microsoft Word or Word Perfect. To export the files for use as your current tape list export it in ASCII DOS text (.txt) or HTML format. By using the fixed-width fonts, tabbed columns, and margins (as shown above), without any fancy and proprietary formatting information, the files can be opened by any universal, generic text reader such as Windows Notepad, and they will remain properly formatted.

A tape list is most commonly (and best) divided by the various bands or musicians in the owner's collection, arranged alphabetically by artist. Each band or artist is a separate section of the list; in HTML format, the artist's name is a section heading displayed in larger type. Within each band or artist section, the shows or tapes are arranged chronologically.

This most common format for tape lists are those output automatically by tape-collection management programs such as Tape-Tracker or WinTaper. Typically, the date (in MM/DD/YY format) in the left column is followed by a column with the venue or event. These first two columns for date and venue are pretty standardized for just about all traders, but the next columns vary widely by trader. For DAT traders, the next columns typically have information on the source (audience or soundboard, digital or analog) and "rig" used (microphones, preamps, etc.) to record the master tape.

At the top of each list, TapeTracker generates an abbreviation key for every possible permutation of source information. Under the Tape-Tracker abbreviation scheme, for instance, "A:D" stands for an audience-recorded tape digitally recorded on a portable DAT machine. The TapeTracker scheme is even robust enough to allow for properly cataloging a "Betty Board" tape of a 1970 Grateful Dead show. ("Betty Boards" are a legendary source of widely traded Grateful Dead tapes. Originally taped by the Dead's then recording engineer Betty Cantor, Betty's personal archive ended up after her accidental death being auctioned off as "abandoned property" at a self-storage locker for the cost of the overdue rentals. The locker contents, including many reel-to-reel tapes of vintage Grateful Dead tapes from the 1970's era, was bought by a group of tapers who took up a collection to acquire them). Tape-Tracker's abbreviation for a "Betty Board" sourced tape is "S:bR,P,D," which stands for Soundboard-"Betty Board" copied to PCM, then to DAT.

As in the above tape list example, the fourth column usually indicates the actual length of the show in minutes (for those who are into accuracy) or the total length of the tapes or CDs used, for those who are lazy (like me). This is sometimes followed by information about the type of microphone used, as well as brief comments about the show.

Analog traders most often use the columns to the right of the venue columns to convey information about the sound quality of the

tape. In analog technology, unlike cloning DATs, a perfect copy of a tape cannot be made. Since analog tapes degrade a bit each time they are copied, analog traders traditionally rate the sound quality on an "academic" scale of "A" or "A+" for outstanding, to "C" for the least desirable, but still tradable grade, where tapes may have a hissy, muddy, or boomy sound. (The grade a tape is given relates to the tape's technical sound quality, not the quality of the show itself.) Many analog traders refuse to trade with other analog traders who do not grade the sound quality of their tapes, and this requirement is often stated on the trader's tape list.

If you have followed the above formatting suggestions, you can exchange tape lists in a wide variety of ways. You can, for instance, simply print out the list in hardcopy on 8 1/2 x 11-inch pages in normal portrait orientation. You can also attach the .txt files to an e-mail message, or even incorporate the list in the body of the e-mail message.

Most traders put their tape lists on a personal web site or tape-trading web site as simple .txt files or equivalent HTML pages. Then a trader can simply reference the location of his tape list web page as a URL (e.g., http://home.hawaii.rr.com/ptj/file/datlist.html). When you are posting to a public list such as DAT-Heads or Digiphish in search of a trade, putting your entire list in the e-mail message rather than simply listing a web URL reference is often considered a "waste of bandwidth" and thus "bad netiquette." Therefore, it's best to find a web site to maintain your list for easy access by potential trading partners.

Many Internet service providers (ISPs), including AOL, provide their subscribers with limited (but sufficient) server disk space and a personal URL to allow you to upload and publish HTML pages, such as your current tape list. Other providers such as GeoCities, Xoom, and Tripod offer an equivalent free service, paid for by banner advertisements. Until recently, several other providers offered specialized sites for the taping community to post their tape lists, such as tapetrading.com. These tape-trading sites offered additional functionality to tape traders, such as allowing tape lists to be interactively searched on the site to identify particular traders who might have a particular show or band of interest. However, several of these sites have recently shut down as of this writing because of uncertainties over whether the recent revisions to the Grateful Dead and Phish audio-taping policies regarding advertiser-sponsored sites violate the applicable legal restrictions of taping and trading "for noncommercial home use only." Despite the problems caused by these recent restrictions on taping web sites, it is still fairly easy to find free personal web site space elsewhere on the Web to post your tape list. A current reference to free web site providers for tape lists can be found on the taping-related PauseRecord site at www.pauserecord.com.

3.0 Trading tapes.

At first blush, it would seem that because DAT tapes and CD-Rs are digital media, the most efficient, computer-age way of trading tapes might be electronically, through e-mail attachments, web sites or file transfer protocol (FTP). While this may be the way that future traders do most of their trades, today's relatively slow dial-up connections and vast file sizes for the CD-quality, uncompressed DAT or CD formats (~1.2 megabytes per second or over one gigabyte for the average Phish set) prevent this method from being practical for most. However, this is changing a bit: Those with cable modems or DSL can download a full 44.1-kHz DAT/CD in several hours from a site like Etree.org. However,

for most of us, the most practical and cheapest way of trading is the low-tech method that analog traders have always used: padded envelopes carried by the United States Postal Service.

Tapes (analog and DAT) and CD-Rs of live music are usually traded under two different types of arrangements: outright trading and blanks-and-postage (B&P) offers. Both methods involve common netiquette techniques and understandings. Trading occurs between two tapers who each have capabilities to duplicate tapes, either through having two tape decks or by having CD burners or PCs with an appropriate sound card or DAT interface to make CD-Rs from DAT tapes. B&P offers are typically done between a trader without duplication capabilities (such as DAT "unideckers") and another trader who can clone or copy tapes. B&P offers are also common on tape trees between "parents" and their "children," as well as in situations where one partner wants to offer a tape in his collection to others who are in search of (ISO, for short) that tape, but who may not be interested in receiving another tape from the recipient's list in trade.

In a trade offer, one person initiates the trade by posting his ISO request to an e-mail list such as Digiphish or DAT-Heads. The trader who responds and offers to spin that tape then asks (by e-mail) for the tape list or tape list URL of the recipient. The trader then selects a tape of similar length on the recipient's list and e-mails back his choice, after which both traders confirm by e-mail the acceptability of the type, brand, and lengths of tape or media that each will be using. Each trader then spins the tape or burns the CD-R his trading partner has selected within a reasonable, agreed-upon period (usually one to two weeks) and mails his tapes to the other trader after they are spun. In an outright trade, each traders pays for his own postage and mailing envelope and spins the tape on his own blank media. In a trade, both sides exchange their trades by return mail simultaneously within the agreed-upon turnaround time.

In a B&P offer, by contrast, the person in search of a particular show or a tree "child" sends the appropriate amount of blank media and return postage to the person who has agreed to fill his blank tape (or burn his blank CD-Rs). Like a trade, the details of these arrangements should be agreed upon beforehand by e-mail before the B&P packages are sent off. Often, for instance, the trader spinning the tapes may be picky about the brands of tapes he will accept.

In a B&P offer, when you send your blanks off, make sure to enclose a note with the shows you are asking for, as well as your name, e-mail address, and return postal address. This is most often done by printing out a copy of the e-mail message that you exchanged about the trade with a short note. Although most remember to do this, it will not surprise veteran tapers to receive an envelope with blank tapes inside and nothing else, without any indication of who sent the tapes or why they were sent. While busy traders may ultimately figure out what the tapes are for, usually after some "where are my tapes?" follow-ups, doing so is a pain and does not make the tape spinner's life easier.

4.0 Postage & Mailing =

The U.S. Postal Service offers two popular services which are used for most tape trades: Priority Mail, which currently costs a fixed $3.20 for up to two pounds, and First Class Mail. Since DAT tapes have roughly double the capacity, while being much smaller and lighter than audio cassette tapes, first class mail is the most popular and economical mail service for sending DATs. A typical DAT trade weighs three to six ounces

($.77–1.44 in postage). A typical one-show trade of two 60m DAT tapes, a one-page note, and a bubble-padded envelope weighs a bit less than four ounces, and costs the sender only $0.99 in First Class postage. Although Priority Mail is sometimes slightly faster than First Class Mail (perhaps two rather than two to three days to most U.S. destinations), it is *not* a guaranteed delivery service and often takes about the same time to ship as the much less expensive First Class Mail.

On the other hand, for heavier audio cassette tapes and DAT trades of over six tapes, fixed-rate Priority Mail service may make more sense, particularly because the Postal Service provides free shipping materials such as a small, self-sealing cardboard box the size of a video cassette, which holds six DAT tapes or four audio cassette tapes. Another nice Priority Mail "freebie" is an untearable Tyvek (tm) envelope, which makes a nice outer envelope for an analog B&P trade.

The average DAT tape trade fits nicely into a size #0 or #00 (CD-size) padded envelope. The padded envelopes of choice are self-sealing, plastic "bubblepack" envelopes, not the older-style, heavier "padded" envelopes with the grayish, dusty padding requiring staples for closing. The recommended mailing envelopes are made by several different manufacturers but use a common sizing scheme. Larger #5 envelopes work well for four to eight audio cassette tapes. They also happen to fit exactly inside the Tyvek Priority Mail courier-type envelope (USPS Envelope Form EP-14).

While the bubblepack envelopes are more expensive than the older "padded" type, they are also much lighter, and their increased cost is more than offset in the postage savings. The self-seal bubblepack envelopes also do not use staples or an opening tear strip which destroys the envelope, and can therefore be more easily recycled for a second or third use. Lastly, the paper stuffing in the old padded envelopes contains huge amounts of lint and dust particles which usually raises an unwanted dust cloud when the envelope is opened—reason enough for many DAT tapers to hate them.

To keep overall mailing costs as low as possible, it helps to buy bubblepack envelopes in bulk. Buying in single quantities at the Post Office or at stores like Kinko's, Staples, or a shipping center can be a huge rip-off as envelopes are often sold for as much as fifty cents apiece in single "convenience" quantities. Even office discount stores such as Staples do not offer much better prices in the shrink-wrapped six-packs when purchased in less than carton lots. The least expensive way of getting envelopes is buying in bulk quantities from shipping supply companies such as ULINE (www.uline.com) or MANCO, where envelopes in a 250-quantity case may cost as little as 15¢ apiece. (Consider splitting the cost of a case of envelopes with a taping friend or two.)

If you're mailing someone blank tapes in a B&P offer, as the name suggests, you should include the correct postage for return of the finished tapes to you. Loose postage stamps in the correct amount are best. If you must use a postage meter strip, be sure to turn the date off for the return postage strip (per postal regulations). As of now, you can't use the new PC "e-postage" from stamps.com or e-stamp.com for return postage. You may want to put the loose stamps in a small envelope or folded sheet of paper. The glassine stamp envelopes which are given out free with stamp purchases at the post office are best. Just ask the clerk to put the stamps in a glassine envelope when you buy them at the counter.

Many B&P tapers also prefer the person sending the blanks to include their return address on an adhesive label. That way, all they have to do is throw in the finished tapes, slap the return label over the old label, paste the new stamps on, and drop the envelope in the mail. Obviously, anything you can do to make the B&P offer more convenient for the trader who's spinning the music on your blanks is karmically correct.

One additional custom that may accompany a B&P deal is what's sometimes referred to as a "hose," a small gift of nominal value, like a postcard, sticker, small plastic doodad, or a particularly nice note included with the blanks as a way of saying "thank you" to the person doing the spinning.

The delivery of tape trades by mail is one of the things I like best about the taping hobby. I'm probably like most adults in that the bulk of our household's daily mail is a dreary accumulation of bills to be paid and solicitations for stuff we're not interested in. But coming home to see the telltale brown envelope puts me back in that childhood zone where the mailman's visit is a happy event because it's bringing some long-awaited thing I've sent away for. Yay, a new tape!

5.0 Tape trees

Tape "trees, weeds, bushes, twigs, seeds, and vines" are a botanical analogy to the popular way, in which particular shows or tapes become widely distributed within the trading community. A single high-quality seed tape can be duplicated to several trunks or branches, who in turn can duplicate and spread the tapes to many more twigs and leaves. The size and shape of the tree or vine will differ according to how it is structured by the tree admin who makes the offer of organizing a tree, or "treeing" the particular show. Participating in organized tape trees requires that you have web access, a valid e-mail account that will be good for at least the next several months, since the offer, sign-up and tree-posting steps, and later "parent-child" communication, all require reliable online access.

As mentioned earlier, trees are either "permanent" for many shows or "ad hoc" for a particular show. Permanent trees can be like the former Operation Everyshow Phish tree or Ken Sorce's excellent DooDah Trees site, which allows for both per-tree and permanent sign-ups for monthly trees, tracks a tree's status and progress, and automatically sends out follow-up e-mails and status requests to move the tapes along through the tree structure.

Individual trees for both analog and DAT tapes are often posted to rec.music.phish and the Digiphish list (see Section 7.4). Trees will be either analog cassette, DAT, CD-R, or a combination of those media. The trend today is for most trees to be either entirely digital (DAT and perhaps a CD-R branch or two) or entirely analog. Unfortunately, analog trees or analog sections of trees tend to have the most newbies and most substantial follow-up problems, so that it is much harder to run analog trees than digital trees. If a tree is listed as DAT and not analog, don't sign up for it if you're only an "analogger," and don't send someone cassette media or ask the tree admin to run an analog section—it won't be well received. It's also not good netiquette to "grovel" the tree admin or someone listed as a branch on a digital tree (or e-mail trading list like Digiphish) for them to do D>A to cassette for you individually when you see a DAT tree or offer posted online somewhere.

That warning about "grovels" doesn't mean that an analogger can't get access to first-generation digital sources. Many DAT tapers will do D>A for you if you become friendly with them, but in limited doses, as the copying, with tape flips, is much more work than cloning DATs. There's also a tradition within the taping community to make those rel-

ative DAT newbies without digital duplication capabilities ("unideckers") pay back those who provided them with DAT clones by spinning D>A for those lower on the taping "food chain" with only analog cassette decks. Therefore, many offers and trees on Digiphish commit a trader receiving a tape to make a D>A offer on rec.music.phish to a few takers. In such a case, it wouldn't be at all out of line for you to e-mail that person about your interest in having the show and ask if he would do D>A for you.

One more hint for analoggers just starting out: First-generation analogs from DATs make excellent analog masters for *you* to spread the music further. (Consider using a metal Type IV analog tape like the Maxell MX-S for this purpose.) The hypothetical DAT taper discussed above will be very impressed by your offer to spread the tape further within the analog community if you are in turn able and willing to copy the tapes received. It also shows that you understand the karmic web of giving and getting, which is essential to the whole mission of "spreading the music" and not "hoarding" it, a sentiment that resonates with most experienced tapers and traders. I have found that one of the best ways to get music is to offer to spread it (and then to follow through).

Here's how the typical tree works. An offer is posted to a list or newsgroup, which will usually give the basic details about the show, setlist (if not widely available), length (number and length of tapes needed), microphone data, and similar recording info, as well as a sign-up form. There is usually a cutoff time for sign-ups, so submit your sign-up application by the deadline. There are often particular instructions about how to set the reply line of your reply so that the tree admin can instantly see from your e-mail subject line where you should be put in the tree without having to plow through the rest of the stuff in your sign-up form. Many tree admins also use these subject line to automatically filter and sort the e-mail by type of participant. For example: "Subject: Alpine 8/1/98 60m branch 5" means that the tree admin has directed me to put the tree name "Alpine 8/1/98" as a flag for his e-mail client's filter, together with my preference for being a branch or leaf, lengths of blanks preferred, and number of copies I'm willing to spin.

Here are a couple of tips about how to maximize your satisfaction with trees. The first is to follow the tree admin's sign up instructions *exactly*. Try to be as careful as you would be in filling out, for example, a Phish mail-order ticket order form. In particular, make sure you set the "mail to" and "subject" lines correctly when you prepare the e-mail reply with your tree application. Many tree admins use the mailbox-filtering features of e-mail clients such as Eudora Pro to sort the 20–150 responses typically received into groups from which branches and leaves are automatically sorted. Many admins are hard-nosed about their "roolz." If you cause them inconvenience by sending the reply to the wrong reply address or your sign-up didn't go through their automatic filter, their attitude may be similar to Phish Mail Order's for those who can't follow instructions: There were plenty of people able to do it right who took your place in line.

And even if you run across a kind-hearted tree admin who finds your wayward or late application and adds you to a tree manually, you still may have run afoul of that admin's almost certain "Bozo filter." For a tree to work reliably, the tree admin must know that the people he picks from among the tree applications as the trunk and top branches of his tree are reliable traders. The admin will try to get people who will perform responsibly by getting their tapes from their parent quickly and spinning them for their children fast to keep the tree rolling.

Many trees don't work, or become "stalled," often lower in the tree structure for the obvious reason that some people will flake on their tree responsibilities to move and spin their tapes when required. And to a surprising degree, tree sign-ups even among moderately to well-experienced DAT traders indicate many people, perhaps 25 percent in my entirely nonscientific poll, can't follow a half-dozen ludicrously simple directions. We're not talking about completing Federal Tax Form Schedules or anything too difficult. Perhaps this e-mail stuff just *seems* too easy and casual, and people make careless mistakes to whip that e-mail sign-up off. Thus, when a tree admin is looking over a whole bunch of sign-ups while assembling a tree, those who didn't take the time to fill out a form correctly are not going to be placed as the main branches that the tree admin wants to put higher on the tree.

Besides being kind to tree admins, there are some good selfish reasons why you want to take care to send in a good sign-up and thus get as high on the tree as possible. As a higher-level branch, you'll get the tapes sooner. Moreover, the higher on the tree you are, the better the probability of the tree reliably delivering for you, since the possibility of people "flailing" and "broken links" multiplies in a cumulative fashion as the tree spreads. Even DAT clones, which in theory should be identical to the thousandth generation, are a better source from someone higher in the tree. There's less chance for glitches in the form of diginoise and/or dropouts, which appear to come from electronic or mechanical errors in the DAT copying process.

So, fill out the tree sign-up form completely and honestly. Completely means including regular postal (snail) addresses and phone numbers if they are requested on the form. Be specific about your duplication equipment if you're signing up as a branch, and be fair in rating its quality where required (for analog trees). Most forms ask you to "clip out" *only* the reply portion of the sign-up form in your message. Do exactly that, using "cut-and-paste" or "block reply" functions. Don't bounce back the entire sign-up message with all of the instructions. (That instruction is an obvious trigger for a Bozo filter.) Following the above instructions carefully will put you above at least the 15 percent of the bozos who couldn't manage that, and will thus get you higher on the tree. Finally, just as in grade school, neatness in filling out and formatting the form counts. Reliable and successful people who can manage such skills in our modern, information-based society are what tree admins look for in choosing branch leaders.

Tree admins are betting their tree's success on people who will be *reliable*. The tree admin will usually recognize a bunch of names from his own personal experience as being reliable traders or longtime Netters and tend to put them higher up on the tree as main branches. But he'll still need reliable "underbranches" as children to those main branches and parents for the next-level branches. These will most often be distributed to people whom the admin might not personally know but who have filled out the sign-up forms properly. The more doubtful, residual Bozos tend to get put on last, at the bottom of the tree. This principle also is relevant to having the appropriate and reliable patching gear at shows if you want to tape or patch (see Section 6.0).

Here's an example: Let's say you've signed up for a tree for Phish 12/31/95. The offer will usually say whether the tree structure will be posted on a web site or whether it will be e-mailed to all participants. If the former, check the web site when the tree structure posting is announced.

The usual tree structure looks something like this—in our simple example for this tutorial, a very small tree with only three branches and a few leaves:

1.0 Moe Schmoe <moes@well.com>
1.1 Jack Lebowitz <jack@jackleen.com>
1.1.1 Esteemed Reader <you@yourdomain.com>
1.1.2 Joe Blough <mango44@aol.com>
1.2 Renee Roe <funky4033@funkybitches.com>
1.3 Harbour Clough <djclough4@mindspring.com>
2.0 Larry Doe <ltd404@panther.middlebury.edu>
 3.0 Curly Hough <cyclops420@seanet.com>

In this example, there are three main branch leaders, Moe for Branch 1 (our branch), and Larry and Curly for the other two branches. When the tree structure is posted, Moe, Larry, and Curly get in touch with the tree admin and arrange to get copies of the master tape, or seed. I am one of three children of Moe, in tree position 1.1, and I have two children: you ("Esteemed Reader" in my example) in tree position 1.1.1 and Joe Blough in tree position 1.1.2. In the tape-tree convention shown above, each succeeding branch or generation of the tree is indented one tab to the right. Your parents (and their siblings) will be one level up and to the left. One's children (and their siblings) will be listed one level down and to the right.

As Moe's child, I am obligated to get in touch with Moe (at his e-mail address listed on the above tree structure) and discuss how I will get the tape from him: either by trade or blanks and postage. In a tree situation, it is generally acceptable for me to simply send Moe the proper amount of blanks and postage and have Moe copy the treed show and send it back to me for further treeing. Or, if both Moe and I agree on this by e-mail, we can trade tapes. Moe will request a tape he'd like from my tape list and I will copy it and send it back to him at about the same time he's copying the treed tape on his own new blanks (on a tape brand and length acceptable to me). Thereby we'll exchange a clone of the treed tape for a clone of a tape from my list "in trade."

Either way, within a few weeks, I should have a clone of the treed tape from Moe. In the meantime, my two tree children, you and Joe, have gotten in touch with me by e-mail and gotten my snail mail address and other necessary information, such as the type of tapes needed. You've then quickly mailed me the proper amount and type of blanks and postage. Because neither of you has tape duplication capabilities, the tree admin put you on the tree as leaves, who have no further children to copy tapes for. So within a week or so after Moe's master tape shows up in my mailbox, I'll have copied them and mailed them to you. Thus you will be playing them about ten days after Moe sent them to me.

That's how a successful tree works and demonstrates how organized trees have resulted in many tapes being spread. Unfortunately, sometimes trees "break down" for reasons that may now be fairly obvious. Hopefully, the above suggestions will be help you to benefit from the many excellent trees that are run within the online trading community. If you do have problems on a tree and really want the tape, ask the tree admin (via e-mail) to follow up and help you out, or to reassign you to another, more reliable parent who would be willing to take on another child. This will usually solve any problems.

6.0 Taping at shows.

I've left the most obvious way of getting new tapes—taping with your own rig at shows—for last. Presumably by the time you are considering this option, you will be familiar with the mechanics of taping and trading. If you have a battery-powered tape deck (analog, minidisc, or DAT) and the right connecting cables, you can make master tapes at shows as long as there are other tapers you can connect or "patch" into. If you have microphones or soundboard connecting cables (where soundboard access is permitted), you can tape even if there are no other tapers present and you can allow other tapers to patch into you.

Most tapers taping at shows begin by patching, because they lack the often expensive microphone rigs or soundboard cables. It is also easier to let an experienced "lead deck" set the proper levels, which will also be automatically set for the downstream (digital) patching decks. This is a good way to learn about how live show taping works, especially those details well beyond this elementary overview of taping and trading.

Tapers use microphones as the source of audience tapes at most larger shows for a variety of reasons, the main one being that soundboard access is generally not permitted at larger venues. "Front-of-house" (FOH) engineers that run the soundboard at a typical Phish show in a venue with fifteen thousand in attendance will not risk a taper unplugging some vital PA cabling in an effort to tap into the board. An episode pretty much like this happened in the early 1990s which led to Phish soundman Paul Languadoc banishing tapers from the soundboard area and the band's subsequent "no SBD access" policy. Unfortunately, many other soundmen and FOH engineers have had similar bad experiences with tapers, and soundboard access is therefore common only at smaller, taper-friendly venues. Lack of soundboard access has not really been a problem, despite the novice trader's popular perception that soundboard tapes are the best.

Many tapers, if not most, prefer audience shows made with good microphones to soundboard tapes. Soundboard sources are often poor for taping since they are predominantly mixed for the in-house PA, where louder self-amplified instruments like guitar, drums, and bass are unnaturally low in the mix, as they need less PA reinforcement. Moreover, the better microphone rigs present in the taping section often provide sound recordings that rival "commercial" quality, and are a far more natural-sounding source for taping than the typical soundboard mix.

Today, the recording hardware in the "tapers' pit" at most Phish shows, and even club gigs of smaller acts, is usually of superb quality. In recent years, it has become commonplace for many tapers in the section to run rigs of professional field-recording gear: externally powered ("phantom" power) pairs of stereo microphones with interchangeable directional "capsules," such as Schoeps, Neumanns, and B&K (now DPA) microphones. The mics and their associated battery-powered preamps or external analog-to-digital converters can cost in the $1,500–5,000 range for new equipment, including mic stands, cables, heavy-duty battery packs, and other necessities or extravagances.

It's possible to get into owning mics for less money, and many tapers do so for the fun of taping the shows themselves. There are several microphones available in the $200–300 range that are popular among some tapers. However, most would agree that shows taped with low-end "stealth" mics (like Sonic Sense or Core Sound) or single-point mics like the Audio Technica AT822 mic usually are not going to be as good (or tradable) as the widely available tapes made by the German and Danish microphone rigs mentioned above.

Probably the best reason not to bother getting a low-end microphone rig is that it is fairly easy and common for tapers to be allowed to patch into the primo rigs and record the identical signal being provided to the mic owner's lead deck. Because DAT machines are miniature computers optimized to record an audio-derived digital bitstream, these little computers can be "networked" together at shows with coaxial or optical connecting cables. The lead deck or a digital "patch bay" can feed a small network of DAT machines which are synchronized or "daisy-chained" together. As many as a dozen battery-powered DAT machines or minidisc recorders can be synchronized to a common signal at the "CD-quality" audio digital standard (44.1 or 48 kHz). Therefore, one need not own microphone rigs to have fairly easy access to "signal" from those rigs. You only need a battery-powered DAT deck (or minidisc or analog recorder, with some limitations which I'll mention later), proper cables, and of course a sense of etiquette.

The most popular battery-powered DAT recorders today in the "section" are Sony D7s and D8s, and their newer brethren the Sony D-100/M-1s (virtually identical consumer/pro models) introduced in the mid-'90s. These Walkman-sized devices, costing $500–800, run on two AA batteries. The Sony units are truly the "Volkswagens" of digital taping, because their low price point, full features, and durability make them the entry-level favorite, as well as a good choice for a second or third deck. Next in price and popularity is the notebook-sized Tascam DA-P1 ($1,300), the most widespread lead deck used with microphone rigs, and the HHb Portadat, a similar DAT deck for about twice the price of the Tascam DA-P1.

Patching is easy and usually produces a successful recording to take home if you have the right gear and know the rules. There are basically only two (related) rules. The first is to show up fairly early with the proper patching gear. The other is to be considerate in your approach to the lead-deck person from whom you're looking to patch. The proper patching gear means a reliable battery-powered recorder, with adequate battery power to run at least two hours without changing. It also means reliable cables, which can be a much less obvious requirement.

The main problem with patching the Sony units stems from the fact that popular machines do not come with a built-in digital interface or provide the required coaxial connector cables. Worse, the Sony seven-pin digital interface is not a standard plug type and also uses a nonstandard voltage level for digital signals, which varies between the older Sony D-8s and newer D-100/M-1 models. The upshot of this confusion is that if you want to patch with Sonys, you need to own both a suitable seven-pin-to-coax adapter cable and a built-in or separate seventy-five-ohm coaxial connecting cable with two RCA-type ends for input and output. You can expect to spend about $100–150 for these. If you don't have proper connecting cables, you risk being unable to reliably acquire or pass signal and that your patch will fail. Worse, because of the daisy-chain nature of connecting machines digitally in patching, you risk everyone connected to you downstream losing signal because of your weak link in the chain. Therefore, in setting up a patch, you want to be able to demonstrate to whomever you're "groveling" the patch from that you have the required equipment to reliably acquire and pass the digital signal in the mini-network he's setting up.

For the required Sony seven-pin-to-coax interface cables, the most common and best choices are the Oade Brothers I/O cables ($100–150) or the Plotnick Cables ($120). The Plotnick cables come with built-in coaxial connector cables terminating in the required RCA-

type phono jack plugs, which connect to a DA-P1's digital output jacks, or to another coax cable. If you use the Oade interface or another interface that uses separate coax cables, make sure the coax cable you're using is true seventy-five-ohm cable designed for *digital*, not analog, feed. A good choice and value is the Apogee WydeEye digital audio cable (approximately $30) in one-half-meter or one-meter length (about $30 from Musicians Interstate Supply, 1-800-IN-A-BAND). The Apogee WydeEye cables are nicely made and have a distinctive purple sheath which announces to whomever you're handing the cable off to that you just might have a clue. In a hobby where the ownership and display of $3,000 Apogee AD1000 analog-to-digital converters is common, it's nice to know you can get at least some respect from "those in the know" by owning the right kind of $25 cable. In a pinch, if you're lacking coax, you can use a video interconnect cable (available at most audio stores that sell home-theater stuff) as your coax digital audio cable. These video interconnects usually have the requisite impedance and high-bandwidth capabilities, as well as relatively tight connections. When it comes to home use of coax cables for connecting DAT machines in DAT cloning, good-quality digital interconnections equals flawlessly copied clones.

There are various lower-cost and "homebrew" seven-pin-to-coax adapters available. These adapters however have well-known reliability problems, such as exposed pins, which don't tolerate the jostling of equipment common in "the section," or a lack of required active electronics in the seven-pin plug needed to convert the Sony input or output to the correct DAT standard voltages. Thus these inferior connecting cables are not recommended.

Aside from having the proper patching equipment, a bit of taper's etiquette is helpful to arrange your patch smoothly. You don't have to "grovel" or prearrange a patch by e-mail before a show, although it doesn't hurt if you can agree to meet someone you know from whom you can patch. The trick is to show up and set up early, even before the half-hour immediately preceding the lights go down and the start of the show.

At a Phish or similar show, you should plan on getting to the venue a half hour to forty-five minutes *before* doors open, and find the tapers waiting in line to get in. Usually, they'll be clustered at one particular entrance, up front and ready to go in with their gear. The gear is very recognizable: mic stands, backpacks and hardshell camera cases containing microphones, preamps, and similar equipment. Most taping sections are expressly or de facto "general admission" even where seat numbers are assigned on tickets. "Real estate" is scarce in the taping section, and the coveted positions towards the front rail are traditionally first come, first served. The more serious tapers are "early birds" and will be among the first to enter the arena. You'll want to be right behind them. As a side benefit, the security search getting in the door is also usually easier and more perfunctory when the doors first open and fifty audio tapers go through *en masse*. Usually, when you go in with the tapers, all you have to do is show your deck in your pack and say "audio tape recorder," and you'll be quickly waved through with no further hassles. At some events, you must have a taper's ticket to bring in a deck, although venues vary enforcement of this rule and it's usually not a problem.

After you get through the doors and are in "the section," another piece of etiquette is helpful: Give those with microphones a few minutes to break out their gear and set up *before* "groveling" your patch. There will still be plenty of time for you to get set up. Watch the tapers

setting up and look for the bigger rigs towards the front with paired microphones. Approach a taper who's done getting his mic stand up and setting up his mics and ask if you can "have a patch" or "if he has a digital patch or coax-out available." It's okay to ask what kind of microphone rig he's running to help you decide who to patch out of, if there are multiple choices. A good response is anything with Schoeps (pronounced "shepps"), Neumanns (pronounced "NOY-mens"), B&K (now DPA), AKG480s, Earthworks (or rigs using an Apogee AD1000 converter), or a patch bay.

When someone's agreed to patch you, he will ask that you hand him your coax cable's RCA input jack. He'll find a place to plug it in somewhere in the daisy chain he's setting up. If he's well-equipped for organized patching, he may even run a "patch bay" to allow multiple decks to plug directly into a junction box without a daisy chain. You should be prepared to hand off your DAT deck with freshly charged batteries and blank tape all queued up and ready to start recording. Because physical space in the tapers' section is scarce, most often the taper will want to run your deck for you during the show. It's much easier for one person (the taper and perhaps a helper) to start and stop a dozen small tape decks than to have a dozen people crawling over each other in a few square feet trying to accomplish the same result.

If the taper offers to run your deck, you should leave after you're patched in. Come back at setbreak to change tapes and batteries, and again immediately after the show to claim your gear. It helps to have some unique identifying sticker or nametag on your deck and cables and a small flashlight, such as a mini-Maglite. When in "the section," be careful and avoid knocking into someone's gear or cables as you pick your way through to your deck.

Having your rig in order when "groveling" a patch will help make things go smoothly, since the biggest concern of most tapers in setting up a daisy chain is making sure it works, so that hopefully no one's deck in the chain is "beebed out" and disappoints with a spoiled tape. Because of the weakest-link nature of all chains, everyone downstream of the lead deck needs cables that can pass signal upstream and downstream. If your gear seams reliable, you will probably be placed higher up in the chain, which gives you a better shot at getting a good signal and avoiding being behind other potential weak links. If your gear seems doubtful or isn't set up to provide a coax digital output, you'll most likely be put at the end of a chain, where it's less likely you'll go home with a good tape.

At club shows, the drill of groveling patches is much the same, although typically less intimidating than the frenetic scene at Phish shows. Get there early and look for the action in the vicinity of the soundboard or where any floor mic stand is being set up. Check the BTAT list (see Section 7.1) for what's allowed and who to talk to.

One last hint about patching and cloning while "on tour" for national acts such as Phish: Tapers often congregate in several hotel rooms at the larger hotels near the venue. After the show, bring your deck, connecting cables, and power supplies to the taping parties where that night's show or other recent shows will be duplicated on many a hotel-room dresser.

7.0 Internet resources

Taping and the Internet have been intertwined since the earliest days of computer conferencing systems in the mid-'80s on private bulletin boards and "timeshare" computers. These primitive conferencing systems evolved into today's Internet newsgroups and e-lists. Tapers adapted early to communicating via computer by participating in trades, trees, and listservs organized on computer networks. It is rumored that tape-trading Deadheads and other chatting Dead fans sustained the pioneering BBS WELL (now well.com) during its lean start-up years when few people saw much need to pay for computer-conferencing services by the hour. Engineers and other "wired" geeks and students at universities (.edu domains) also tended to be well-represented among the ranks of those into live music and trading.

Phish fans have much to be proud of in the historic co-evolution of computer geeks and zealous music fans. The Usenet newsgroup rec.music.phish (a.k.a. RMP) was one of the first newsgroups devoted to taping. Phish.Netters were also involved in the development of the Netspace project at Brown University, which runs a server for many bands and music mailing lists (in this case, listservs) including the Phish.Net and DAT-Heads Digests, among others.

DAT tapers and traders are, not surprisingly, well-represented on the Internet. As a result, you can easily find as much information as you require online, presented in a fairly well-organized way. You can also make connections with other traders online. It would be a futile effort to catalogue all of the hundreds of DAT and taping-related sites out there, much less decide which ones you might find most useful for your own trading needs. New sites and services come and go every day. Rather than attempt an encyclopedic approach, let me just point out the most useful sites of widespread interest. You can use these sites and resources as "portals," through which you can link to the particular site or resource you need.

The best portal site for DAT tapers is the DAT-Heads Digests listserv and web site. The DAT-Heads list has been around since the early '90s. Over the years the list's archive site has evolved into an encyclopedic, searchable database of past discussions about all things related to taping. The archive site also serves as a portal with its array of well-organized links to other taping resources. Other useful resources you may want to check out are also briefly described below. From these half-dozen or so core sites, you can find all the help and community you need. For those interested in getting and trading DAT-sourced material on CD-Rs, there are many Frequently Asked Questions files (FAQs) and sites devoted to the arcana of CD duplication. Those include not only DAT-Heads but sites and lists targeted to CD burning, like People for a Clearer Phish (PCP).

In the past year especially, it seems the Web has spawned a major branch of sites that can serve as an efficient distribution medium for DAT/CD-quality digital bitstreams, as well as a means to exchange text messages about tape trading. For those with cable modems or other fast Internet connections, it is now possible to download whole concerts (derived from audience DAT tapes) from server sites such as Etrees.org.

However, until the day comes when we can easily e-mail gigabyte files of any show to one another, it's likely that tapes will continue to be made on DAT machines and traded the old-fashioned way. These sites and lists provide a good starting point for finding web-based listservs and sites.

7.1 The DAT-Heads Mailing List.

DAT-Heads is both a listserv and a searchable archive site. The DAT-Heads listserv has been around since the early '90s and is the basic web resource on DAT taping. The listserv, maintained by long-time Phish.Net-

ter Sean Kennedy, is unmoderated and sends its e-mail subscribers between one and three digests of about ten to thirty e-mails daily. The e-mails are a mix of technical questions about DAT taping (and digital media in general), "grovels," and offers for tapes of a wide variety of music.

Reading the DAT-Heads listserv for a while will give you a basic education in DAT taping tips and goings-on. Although it is an unmoderated mailing list, there is a high "signal-to-noise" ratio there, compared to many other electronic public forums—most posters stay basically on topic. Lurk awhile to get a feel for what and how to post to the list, then join in. If you're considering asking the list a question that you think might have been asked before, check out the FAQ and the searchable archives at the DAT-Heads archive site.

To subscribe to the DAT-Heads listserv, send an e-mail message from the mail account to which you want the digests sent. Your sign-up message should be sent to the subscription address: dat-heads-subscribe@datheads.phish.net, and the subject line and body of the message should say "subscribe". If your effort to subscribe is successful, you'll receive a confirming message, which includes instructions for posting, and you'll start receiving the Digests later that day.

Every few months, the DAT-Heads listserv posts a "Market Posting," maintained and updated by Seth Breidbart, which has recent vendor and mail order prices for DAT tape decks and other equipment. A quick check of the "Market Posting" before buying equipment will tell you the models' features and lowest street prices at various vendors. This information is especially useful since DAT equipment tends to be sold by a relatively few specialized vendors and is generally not available (at competitive street prices, anyway) from mid-fi chain audio retailers like Best Buy or Circuit City.

Another feature on the DAT-Heads listserv is a useful reference compendium of Bands that Allow Taping (BTAT), a list maintained by Kurt Andrew Kemp. BTAT is an alphabetized listing of hundreds of bands that allow taping, as well as other known, verified information about their exact taping policies, such as what type of taping access is allowed (soundboard, microphone stands, etc.) and the band person to talk to at the venue if there are problems getting in with taping equipment or setting up. The most recently updated BTAT list is available at the DAT-Heads archive site, as well as being mirrored in HTML-ized browser format by Mike Wagner at www.enteract.com/~wagner/btat. If you're interested in taping or trading a particular artist, checking BTAT is a must. BTAT also has good links to many bands' or fans' own web sites and listservs.

In the past several years, list maintainer Kemp has also ended each BTAT digest with a separate (and mercifully brief) listing of Bands That Are *Against* Taping (BTAAT). This listing is a sometimes humorous, sometimes scary, litany of anti-taper bias among bands and/or their management or record labels. Many musicians or managers seem disposed to feel that audience taping eats into the livelihoods they would otherwise earn through recording royalties from official releases. If you're even thinking of taping a band whose official anti-taping policy has landed them on the BTAAT listing, it pays to read the BTAAT entry carefully before attempting to tape to find out whether "stealthing" is tolerated despite the official line, or whether tapers will be harassed or hunted down by house security.

7.2 The DAT-Heads archive site and links

The DAT-Heads archive home page is located at www.eklektix.com/dat-heads/. In addition to the previously mentioned searchable archives of past DAT-Heads discussion threads, there is a Frequently Asked Questions file (FAQ), which is worth downloading and at least skimming so you know what it covers, if you need it. There is also a microphone FAQ, somewhat in need of updating, but still helpful for those interested in microphones. The most recent BTAT/BTAAT lists and "Market Posting" is linked to the DAT-Heads archive page. A list of vendors of tape decks, tapes, and other gear is also linked to the home page.

Lastly, the DAT-Heads home page has links to dozens of other taping sites of interest, including web sites dealing with the foibles of popular tape decks, such as Victor Liu's pages on the Sony decks whose affordable ($600) price point has brought taping to the masses. Those with other widely used decks such as the Tascam DA–20, DA–30, and DA-P1 portables will find similar pages documenting maintenance tips and "easter-egg" features such as error counters, which are not documented in the manufacturer's official Owner's Manual.

7.3 Other taping sites worth checking out

Several other sites are worth looking at or subscribing to. John Procopio's PauseRecord listserv at www.pauserecord.com offers a periodic digest of taping and music-related news and links to more detailed articles, similar to Internet newspapers like InfoBeat. For information about how to subscribe to the PauseRecord mailing list, send an e-mail to PauseRecord.com-help@listbot.com. A similar web site with good taping information and links is Jeff Tiedrich's Resources for Tapers site at www.resourcesfortapers.com.

7.4 Digiphish

In a book about mostly about Phish and only incidentally about DAT taping, I'd be remiss in not singling out Digiphish as a listserv that deserves particular mention. Digiphish, as its name suggests, is a list devoted to the taping and trading of digital Phish recordings. Unlike DAT-Heads, e-mail messages posted to the list are sent individually (actually, usually several times daily in groups of a half-dozen messages), rather than automatically pasted together into a lengthy digest. This means the trading offers and "weeds" (small, informal trees) on Digiphish happen fast and furious, making it a good place to hang out if you want access to trading Phish recordings, including the latest and hottest shows. Messages on Digiphish are mostly oriented to DAT taping and trading, including trading of taping tickets and groveling for patches before and during Phish tour. Discussion of DAT>CD-R techniques or CD-R trading is okay too, as long as the topic is about the trading of Phish on digital media. The list is moderated, so grovels for D>A dubs will usually be deemed "off-topic" by the moderator and won't get posted.

The rules of the Digiphish list and subscription information are listed on the list's host, the open Internet listserv service, Onelist. Sign-ups for the Digiphish list on a web-based subscription form and further information on the list can be found at the listserv's site www.one-list.com. Once logged on to Onelist, follow the links or search the site to get information on Digiphish.

7.5 Music sites

If you're interested in taping live music, there are several sites that will let you know who's playing when and where. The best of the breed is Jambands.com, founded by long-time Phish.Netter and author Dean Budnick. The site is located at www.jambands.com and features a searchable database that lists upcoming shows you may be interested in seeing or collecting. Jambands.com's homepage has a weekly magazine format that links to news features and music columns and reviews by Dean and many others. For upcoming dates, you should also check out Tourdate.com at www.tourdate.com and Pollstar at http://pollstar.com. As to most any particular band or artist which is typically taped, any band barely out of the garage these days will have its own web site, and often a listserv, where the band's rabid fan corps can plan their upcoming convocation at that roadhouse bar in West Nowhere. A general web search for the name of the band or artist ought to be enough to find the sites and lists that are out there for followers of a particular music.

Of course, for those who follow Phish, web resources are abundant. The official web site at www.phish.com has up-to-the-minute tour dates and mail-order ticket information. Phish.Net, the unofficial fan web site (www.phish.net) and its associated Usenet newsgroup rec.music.phish is one of the Internet's first and still most widely acclaimed fan sites. The Phish.Net hosts show reviews, a comprehensive FAQ maintained by Mockingbird Foundation director Ellis Godard, a searchable archive of Phish setlists called the *Helping Phriendly Book*, and links to David "ZZYZX" Steinberg's interactive "stats" pages, which will tell you such critical information as when a song was first and last played and how many times its been played, both in total and in the shows you've attended. The Phish.Net discussions and materials were contributed out of love and respect for the music, and many of the earliest and most prolific Phish.Netters have contributed to the book you are now holding.

Phish.Net also hosts several listservs to keep you up to the minute with things you need to know if you're following Phish. Phish-news, a low-traffic, one-way e-mail listserv of important (and official) band announcements such as upcoming tours and ticket purchase information, is a must. During Phish tour, the Phish-news list will send you the official setlist of the last evening's show, usually within hours of the encore. To subscribe to the Phish-news list, e-mail listserv@netspace.org from the e-mail account you want to subscribe, with a message body of "subscribe phish-news". If you have problems subscribing or unsubscribing, e-mail a helpful human being at phish-news-request@netspace.org.

Lastly, there's the Phish.Net discussion newsgroup, rec.music.phish, which is one of the Internet's longest-running discussion groups. Phish.Net evolved from an e-mail list to one of the earliest Usenet newsgroups, rec.music.phish. From its earliest days, Phish.Net helped fans share their thoughts about the music and the scene, and has led to many face-to-face friendships when people hung out with Netters they'd communicated with, or maybe traded tapes with, between tours. Luckily, just as the newsgroup was becoming a victim of its own success, with a volume of postings no sane person could read, along came a series of editors—Rosemary Spano, Benji Eisen, and Phil Zerbo—who put out a "digestified" list of the best messages posted. This list delivers an interesting digest of the newsgroup almost every day, pro-

viding a welcome five-minute diversion into matters Phishy. To subscribe to the digestified e-mail list, send an e-mail from the account you want subscribed to listserv@netspace.org. The message body should say "subscribe phishnet-digest".

The Phish.Net Digest is a two-way list by virtue of the ability to post responses to messages in the Digest or start new discussion threads by posting to the Usenet newsgroup through an e-mail gateway. To post to the list, e-mail your message to rmp@www.phish.net. According to the editors of the Digest, you can expect that if your posting is of general interest to the newsgroup, it will be posted within a day or so of your sending it to the list moderator through the e-mail link.

Aside from the digestifed newsgroup e-mails, you can also access the raw, unedited newsgroup rec.music.phish through a web browser or newsgroup reader. Aside from more off-topic, teen rant, and spam stuff you'll find there, which will make you value the Digest editors' efforts, you'll find other, perhaps useful information of less than universal import which won't end up on the Digest. This might include informal selling of extra tickets before and during tour, as well as tape-trading activity, particularly for analog tape traders.

7.6 Tape tree and trading sites

There are numerous sites where tapes are treed or traded, and many of these are listed from a main link at the DAT-Heads archives tapes site at www.eklektix.com/dat-heads. My favorite tape tree site is "Ken the DooDah Man's" site at www.webjams.com. Unlike most tape tree sites, which simply post the tree structure for everyone to follow, Ken's site automatically tracks the progress of the tape tree and sends out friendly follow-up reminders to send blanks or arrange trades to keep the tree moving. Later, if Ken's "DooDah code" detects that the tree is "stalled" because someone's not duplicating and sending their tapes on a timely basis, more insistent follow-up e-mails will be automatically sent, followed by human intervention from tree admins Ken or Sue, if necessary. This combination of timely e-mail nudges with more serious follow-up seems to work well. I have participated in many trees on the DooDah site and have never had any problems with tree parents or children. The progress of the tree is trackable on the site for all to see, and everyone therefore seems to behaves more reliably. The site is down as of this writing for upgrading to the DooDah code which will feature a less clunky user interface to an SQL database that will recognize returning visitors and return only the information relevant to that subscriber's trees, as well as quicker tree sign-ups and progress report entry screens.

Many tape-trading sites such as www.tapetrading.com sprung up in 1997–1999 and featured searchable tape-list databases where you could seek a certain tape in traders' collections and match it with lists of traders who might be seeking trades. Many of these sites are now in legal limbo as a result of more detailed conditions outlined by the management of Phish and the Grateful Dead's archives about the "noncommercial use" restrictions of audience taping. Since Phish and Grateful Dead tapes are well represented in a majority of tape lists, the new band policies have greatly restricted the operation of many of these tape-trading sites which often offset their operation costs with banner advertising revenues.

8.0 A few thoughts about stereos and other music playback systems

Today's high-bandwidth digital recordings raise the bar by providing a huge dynamic range of audio signal to the downstream components. Digital recordings are free from the mushy-sounding analog "noise floor" of unwanted hum, wow, and flutter. Played back through high-quality equipment, digital recordings not only can have a "you are there" realism when played loud, but will still sound full and detailed at reasonable living-room listening levels. After listening to hundreds of shows on DAT, I am still captivated by the details of the ambient concert hall sound and the crowd murmurs between sets, and how, on DATs, the sound is detailed and sharp enough that you can distinguish between different voices in the crowd.

Audiophiles have their own lingo for discussing this, including words like "soundscape," "presence," and "imaging." They're describing a kind of "close your eyes and you're there" feeling, which has been the goal of audio engineers since the beginning of sound recording. But good audio reproduction is no simple matter. A $700 DAT deck will solve the problem of providing a good audio source, but the downstream parts of the audio chain—the amplifier and loudspeakers—must be up to the challenge of providing a pure, powerful signal to speakers that can faithfully change those analog voltage changes to sound waves.

Sadly, most mid-range, modern "component" systems and compact "bookshelf" speakers are not up to this task. The amplifiers lack sufficient power, and the speakers lack sufficient size to reproduce the encoded signal, especially at mid-range and high frequencies. Even headphone listening through output jacks in both portable and home amps is not very good quality, because you are not listening to the signal coming through the amplifier and going to the speakers but rather through a cheap, separate "op amp," which may be a small integrated circuit costing less than a dollar.

Therefore, it pays to consider the quality and limitations of your downstream playback system. Some perspective can be provided by reference to "audiophile" standards, which are discussed in such print magazines as *Stereophile* and its web site (www.stereophile.com) and in Internet newsgroups such as rec.music.audio.hi-end. In the audiophile world, a high-end amplifier or speaker can run into the thousands of dollars, sometimes up to $100,000. A mid-range component is something of quality at a more reasonable price point, typically $800–2,000. With rare exceptions, low-end stuff is banished from the audiophile's world. Anything you might have bought at a department or electronics chain store, or made in Japan and branded Sony, Pioneer, Onkyo, etc. (other than certain tape-recording equipment), is considered certifiably low end. Lower still is mass-market consumer junk, producing sound which is acceptable to those used to listening to a pair of three-inch speakers inside their TVs, car radios, or portable boomboxes. To the extent that today's consumers are being induced to buy expensive audio equipment, it's in the context of delivering five-channel "home-theater" systems, complete with subwoofer for reproducing realistic explosions and helicopter noises from film soundtracks.

Once you get beyond the inherently off-putting consumerism and snobbery of some of the audiophile take on things, it's worthwhile to think about the nub of their critique: For the most part, a mass-market audio system delivered at a $379 price point is not going to do justice to your digital recordings. Luckily, there are a lot of systems out there that can, and at a fairly reasonable price and good value. Particularly in the mid-range market, there are a number of engineers and manufacturers who are looking to deliver great "bang for the buck" and build equipment from good, rather than cheap, components. Some of these components may cost as little as $300–500, but they are listed semi-annually in *Stereophile*'s "Recommended Audio Components" issues and in the ads and web sites of the robust used equipment market for those who can afford to "trade up" to the latest toys.

So listen carefully to your stereo system and ask yourself if you should move the speakers to improve the sound or upgrade your amplifier or speakers. If you like to listen through headphones, the "mass market = junk" rule applies with a vengeance. Not only is the internal "op amp" of an amplifier junky, but in a portable system run on batteries, the built-in headphone amp is designed to minimize battery drain, not to provide sufficient current to run headphone speakers efficiently. The sound is therefore harsh and distorted, especially when played loud. The answer, again from geeky high-end audio engineers, is a separate, high-quality headphone amplifier like Headroom Corporation's Headroom Supreme www.headphone.com, which is a miniaturized one-half-watt amplifier optimized to provide a beefy, high-quality signal to headphones. Because only small amounts of air need to be moved with headphones, you can get a lot of "bang for the buck" and hear what a gazillion-dollar reference power amp or loudspeaker system would sound like with a good amp and reference-quality headphones (like the Sennheiser HD600s) for less than $800. The Headroom amp can also run portably on four D cells or can use a wall power "wart" for home use.

TAPING NOTES

Compiled by Craig Delucia

This chapter includes known information about tapes for every show in the Setlists section. (Show notes are included within the Setlists chapter.) The Scarcity and GHI rankings are on a scale of 1 to 5; a 1 is extremely rare or a poor show (respectively), and a 5 should be easy to find and was a superb show (respectively). A blank cell indicates that tapes are believed to exist, but that an assessment has not been made; an "n/a" indicates that no tapes are believed to exist.

This data is based on input from a core group of Mockingbird supporters. It is thus based on a purposive sample of informants, rather than a statistically significant sample of fans, an approach that seemed appropriate for this edition. The Foundation encourages readers to request, via email or "snail mail", a spreadsheet template with which to submit your own Availability and GHI scores so that we can incorporate a wider body of data in the next edition.

Date	Location	Scarcity	GHI	Comments	Medium
1983–1986					
10/30/1983	UVM (Burlington)	n/a	n/a		
12/2/1983	UVM (Burlington)	n/a	n/a	Confirmed in interview to exist; does not circulate	
12/3/1983	UVM (Burlington)	n/a	n/a		
10/23/1984	Burlington	n/a	n/a		
11/3/1984	Slade Hall	2.00	2.50		
12/1/1984	Nectar's	4.00	4.17	Two versions circulate; one complete and one partial	SBD > Cass1 > DAT
2/1/1985	Doolin's	n/a	n/a		
2/15/1985	Doolin's	n/a	n/a		
2/22/1985	Doolin's	n/a	n/a		
2/25/1985	Doolin's	n/a	n/a		
2/25/1985	Private Party	n/a	n/a		
3/2/1985	Hunt's	n/a	n/a		
3/4/1985	Hunt's	2.00	2.00		SBD > Cass1 > DAT
3/9/1985	Doolin's	n/a	n/a		
3/16/1985	Doolin's	n/a	n/a		
3/29/1985	Doolin's	n/a	n/a		
4/6/1985	Finbar's	n/a	n/a		
4/19/1985	Hunt's	n/a	n/a		
4/21/1985	Goddard	n/a	n/a		
5/1/1985	Fraternity Party	n/a	n/a		
5/1/1985	Fraternity Party	n/a	n/a		
5/1/1985	Fraternity Party	n/a	n/a		
5/1/1985	Private Party	n/a	n/a		
5/3/1985	UVM (Burlington)	3.00	3.98	"Only Set III circulates heavily, some report having seen others"	SBD > Cass? > DAT
5/7/1985	Finbar's	n/a	n/a		
5/31/1985	Slade Hall	n/a	n/a		
9/26/1985	WRUV Radio	1.00			
9/27/1985	Slade Hall	n/a	n/a		
10/17/1985	Finbar's	1.50	2.67		SBD > Cass? > DAT
10/20/1985	Slade Hall	n/a	n/a		
10/26/1985	Goddard	n/a	n/a		
10/30/1985	Hunt's	1.50	2.94		SBD > Cass? > DAT
11/2/1985	Slade Hall	n/a	n/a		

Date	Location	Scarcity	GHI	Comments	Medium
11/14/1985	Memorial Auditorium	n/a	n/a	"SBD copies of 'Hurricane' circulate; remainder not known to exist"	Partial SBD
11/23/1985	Goddard	3.00	4.25	Tapes that circulate include only the third set	SBD > Cass2 > DAT
12/13/1985	Burlington	n/a	n/a		
2/3/1986	Hunt's	2.00	2.25		
2/28/1986	Slade Hall	n/a	n/a		
4/1/1986	Hunt's	2.00	2.92		
4/15/1986	UVM (Burlington)	2.00	3.00		SBD > Cass? > DAT
4/29/1986	UVM (Burlington)	n/a	n/a		
5/16/1986	Memorial Auditorium	n/a	n/a		
5/17/1986	Goddard	n/a	n/a		
6/1/1986	Boston	n/a	n/a		
9/3/1986	Hunt's	n/a	n/a		
9/10/1986	Finbar's	n/a	n/a		
9/26/1986	Johnson	n/a	n/a		
10/12/1986	Goddard	n/a	n/a		
10/15/1986	Hunt's	3.50	3.38		SBD > Cass0 > DAT
10/31/1986	Goddard	3.00	3.50	Only Set I circulates as a soundboard	SBD > Cass? > HiFi > DAT
11/7/1986	UVM (Burlington)	n/a	n/a		
11/14/1986	Slade Hall	n/a	n/a		
11/18/1986	Nectar's	n/a	n/a		
12/6/1986	South Burlington	n/a	n/a		
1987					
1/19/1987	Hunt's	n/a	n/a		
1/21/1987	Hunt's	n/a	n/a		
2/1/1987	Nectar's	n/a	n/a		
2/2/1987	Nectar's	n/a	n/a		
2/7/1987	Monkton	n/a	n/a		
2/13/1987	Johnson		2.50		
2/21/1987	Burlington		2.50	Tapes that circulate cut during the second set; first set does not circulate	
3/6/1987	Goddard		2.12		SBD > Cass0 > DAT
3/22/1987	Nectar's	n/a	n/a		
3/23/1987	Nectar's		3.25		SBD > Cass? > DAT
4/24/1987	Burlington		3.11		
4/28/1987	Nectar's	n/a	n/a		
4/29/1987	Nectar's		4.06		SBD > Cass0 > DAT
5/10/1987	Nectar's	n/a	n/a		
5/11/1987	Nectar's		3.12	Tapes that circulate include only the first set and encore	
5/12/1987	Nectar's	n/a	n/a		
5/16/1987	Goddard	n/a	n/a		
5/20/1987	South Burlington	n/a	n/a	Show is not known to exist on audio tape	Partial video
8/9/1987	Nectar's		3.00	Most tapes that circulate only include the first set and part of the second	
8/10/1987	Nectar's		3.93		SBD > Cass1 > DAT
8/21/1987	Ian's Farm		4.50		
8/22/1987	Vergennes	n/a	n/a		
8/29/1987	South Burlington		3.95		SBD > Cass? > DAT
9/2/1987	Hunt's		2.25		
9/3/1987	Hunt's	n/a	n/a		

Date	Location	Scarcity	GHI	Comments	Medium
1987 *(continued)*					
9/4/1987	Goddard	n/a	n/a		
9/19/1987	Goddard	n/a	n/a		
9/20/1987	Nectar's	n/a	n/a		
9/21/1987	Nectar's		3.00		
9/27/1987	Burlington		2.75	Tapes that circulate cut during the second set	
10/10/1987	Shelburne	n/a	n/a		
10/14/1987	Hunt's				
10/18/1987	Nectar's	n/a	n/a		
10/19/1987	Nectar's	n/a	n/a		
10/23/1987	Cork's	n/a	n/a		
10/24/1987	Cork's	n/a	n/a		
10/31/1987	Goddard		3.45		
11/18/1987	Hunt's		2.55	Tapes that circulate cut during the second set	
11/19/1987	Hunt's		2.80		
11/22/1987	Nectar's	n/a	n/a		
11/23/1987	Nectar's	n/a	n/a		
11/24/1987	Nectar's	n/a	n/a		
1988					
1/27/1988	Waitsfield		3.00		
2/3/1988	Waitsfield	n/a	n/a		
2/7/1988	Nectar's		2.80		
2/8/1988	Nectar's		3.08		
2/10/1988	Waitsfield	n/a	n/a		
2/20/1988	Canton	n/a	n/a		
2/24/1988	Waitsfield		3.44	Tapes that circulate cut during the second set	
2/26/1988	Burlington				
3/9/1988	Waitsfield	n/a	n/a		
3/11/1988	Johnson		2.75		
3/12/1988	Nectar's		4.38	Tapes that circulate include only the second set	
3/20/1988	Nectar's	n/a	n/a		
3/21/1988	Nectar's				
3/22/1988	Nectar's	n/a	n/a		
3/31/1988	New York				
4/2/1988	Amherst	n/a	n/a	Filler labeled this date circulates but no full sets	
4/6/1988	Waitsfield	n/a	n/a		
4/17/1988	Nectar's	n/a	n/a		
4/18/1988	Nectar's	n/a	n/a		
4/19/1988	Nectar's	n/a	n/a		
4/22/1988	Burlington		3.25		
4/27/1988	Waitsfield	n/a	n/a		
4/30/1988	Hamilton	n/a	n/a		
5/2/1988	Haunt	n/a	n/a		
5/3/1988	Haunt	n/a	n/a		
5/5/1988	Slade Hall	n/a	n/a		
5/12/1988	New York	n/a	n/a		
5/14/1988	Goddard		3.37		
5/15/1988	Hinesburg		3.28	Higher quality copies containing only Possum through the end circulate	SBD > Cass? > DAT
5/21/1988	Nectar's		3.45		

Date	Location	Scarcity	GHI	Comments	Medium
5/22/1988	Nectar's	n/a	n/a		
5/23/1988	Nectar's	n/a	n/a		
5/24/1988	Nectar's	n/a	n/a		
5/25/1988	Nectar's		3.77		SBD > Cass? > DAT
5/27/1988	The Front	n/a	n/a		
5/28/1988	Waitsfield	n/a	n/a		
6/3/1988	Squam Lake	n/a	n/a		
6/4/1988	Squam Lake	n/a	n/a		
6/15/1988	The Front		2.25		SBD > Cass1 > DAT (Set II Only)
6/17/1988	Morrisville	n/a	n/a		
6/19/1988	Nectar's		3.88	Tapes that circulate cut during the second set	SBD > Cass? > DAT
6/20/1988	Nectar's		4.42		SBD > Cass4 > DAT
6/21/1988	Nectar's			Some tapes circulate with the Harpua and I Didn't Know out of order	SBD > Cass? > DAT
6/23/1988	New York	n/a	n/a		
6/24/1988	Burlington	0.50			
6/27/1988	Coyasuna	n/a	n/a		
7/7/1988	The Front	n/a	n/a		
7/8/1988	The Front	n/a	n/a		
7/11/1988	Burlington		3.10	Most copies that circulate have a cut in The Curtain	SBD > Cass? > DAT
7/12/1988	Burlington		2.85		SBD > Cass2 > DAT
7/23/1988	Underhill (Pete's Show)		4.30		

"Why is Phish So Great, Anyway?"

Jesse Appelman, Palo Alto, CA

Unenlightened people often ask me what makes Phish so special. They wonder why someone would spend so much money and travel great distances just to see a band. When they see my tape collection, they want to know why I would ever want to have so many tapes of concerts from this one band. To them, I offer this as an answer.

When I got home from school one afternoon in December, there was a padded envelope at the door. I dashed to the door from my car, grabbed it, rushed inside, and tore it open. Finding six tapes from the soon-to-be-legendary fall tour of 1997, I grabbed one and headed off to my room. I glanced at the tape's label. It was the second set of the 11/19/97 show in Champaign, IL. I popped the tape into my Walkman and pressed play.

As I got my homework from my backpack and set it on the floor in front of me, the opening notes of Phish's funky version of *Also Sprach Zarathustra* entered my ears. I immediately knew I was in for a ride. The song was an extended funk jam, as Trey noodled endlessly on top of Fish's steady funk beat. The instantly recognizable theme from 2001 was played only two or three times throughout the ten-plus-minute song. Eventually, the song ended, melting into a spacey, bubbling mass from which something was sure to emerge.

What emerged was *Wolfman's Brother*. "Mmmmm…*Wolfman's*," I said in my best Homer Simpson voice. If the previous song was any indication of this show's direction, this *Wolfman's Brother* was sure to be epic. As the song began, I remembered the homework sitting in front of me on the floor. I grabbed a pen and started working.

As the *Wolfman's* jam began, the music changed. It was still funky at first, much like the version on *Slip, Stitch, and Pass*, but as time passed the jam became fluid and melodic. Each note, rather than sharply accentuating the rest, blended in seamlessly with the bed of sound. Musical bliss. The jam had a hypnotic quality, becoming spacey and formless as the rhythm disappeared. Around this point, my ears stopped paying conscious attention to the music as I sat in a trance-like state. As the music washed over me, I became disconnected from everything going on around me. All that existed was the music. All of a sudden, the tape came to an end and the Walkman clicked off, jerking me from my trance.

I looked at my watch and saw that forty-five minutes had passed. I looked at the homework in front of me. It had my name in the upper right corner. Nothing else. That is what makes Phish so special. Try it sometime.

Date	Location	Scarcity	GHI	Comments	Medium
1988 (continued)					
7/24/1988	Nectar's		3.38		SBD > Cass? > DAT
7/25/1988	Nectar's		3.18	"Tapes that circulate include sets two and three, plus the encore"	SBD > Cass2 > DAT
7/28/1998	Telluride	n/a	n/a		
7/29/1998	Telluride	n/a	n/a		
7/30/1988	Telluride		3.50	Tapes that circulate include Harpua through Antelope	SBD > Cass3 > DAT (Partial Set III)
8/3/1988	Telluride		3.55	Tapes that circulate include partial second set plus the third set	
8/4/1988	Telluride	n/a	n/a		
8/5/1988	Telluride	n/a	n/a		
8/6/1988	Aspen		3.50		SBD > Cass0 > DAT
8/11/1988	The Front	n/a	n/a		
8/12/1988	The Front	n/a	n/a		
8/13/1988	The Front	n/a	n/a		SBD > Cass? > DAT
8/17/1988	Waitsfield	n/a	n/a		
8/18/1988	Burlington	n/a	n/a		
8/21/1988	Nectar's	n/a	n/a		
8/22/1988	Nectar's	n/a	n/a		
8/24/1988	"Unknown, VT"	n/a	n/a		
8/27/1988	Penn State		2.93		SBD > Cass? > DAT
8/29/1988	Burlington	n/a	n/a		
8/30/1988	Burlington	n/a	n/a		
9/8/1988	The Front		2.93		SBD > Cass0 > DAT
9/9/1988	The Front	n/a	n/a		
9/10/1988	The Front	n/a	n/a		
9/12/1988	Burlington		3.28	Tapes that circulate include an incomplete first set	
9/13/1988	Burlington		3.18		
9/16/1988	Durham	n/a	n/a		
9/22/1988	Binghamton	n/a	n/a		
9/24/1988	Amherst		2.81	Most tapes that circulate are cut during Golgi	SBD > Cass0 > DAT
10/28/1988	Middlebury	n/a	n/a		
10/29/1988	Goddard		3.76		SBD > Cass? > DAT
11/3/1988	Molly's		3.23		SBD > Cass? > DAT
11/4/1988	Clinton	n/a	n/a		
11/5/1988	Hamilton		3.38		SBD > Cass0 > DAT
11/11/1988	Newmarket		1.93	Most tapes include mislabeled filler from 10/29/88	SBD > Cass? > DAT
12/2/1988	Boston				
12/9/1988	Northampton	n/a	n/a		
12/10/1988	Amherst		2.35	Often mislabeled 10/12/88	
12/11/1988	The Front	n/a	n/a		
12/12/1988	The Front	n/a	n/a		
12/15/1988	The Front	n/a	n/a		
12/16/1988	UVM (Burlington)	n/a	n/a		
12/17/1988	Newmarket	n/a	n/a		
1989					
1/18/1989	Waitsfield	n/a	n/a		
1/20/1989	Bar Harbor	n/a	n/a		
1/21/1989	Oronoko	n/a	n/a		
1/25/1989	Old Town	n/a	n/a		

Date	Location	Scarcity	GHI	Comments	Medium
1/26/1989	Boston		2.90		
1/28/1989	Dartmouth	n/a	n/a		
2/1/1989	Bennington	n/a	n/a		
2/5/1989	The Front	n/a	n/a		
2/6/1989	The Front		3.38	SBD copies in circulation are cut after Lizards	SBD > Cass1 > DAT
2/7/1989	The Front		4.13		SBD > Cass? > DAT
2/10/1989	Amherst	n/a	n/a		
2/11/1989	Northhampton	n/a	n/a		
2/17/1989	Newmarket				
2/18/1989	Newmarket				
2/23/1989	The Front	n/a	n/a		
2/24/1989	The Front		2.00		SBD > Cass? > DAT
2/25/1989	The Front	n/a	n/a		
3/1/1989	Waitsfield	n/a	n/a		
3/3/1989	Burlington		3.32		
3/4/1989	Wetlands			Tapes that circulate cut during the second set	
3/11/1989	Northampton	n/a	n/a		
3/12/1989	Nectar's		2.08	Partial set circulates	
3/13/1989	Nectar's	n/a	n/a		
3/14/1989	Nectar's				
3/24/1989	Boston	0.50		Partial set circulates	
3/25/1989	Portland	n/a	n/a		
3/30/1989	The Front		4.63		SBD > Cass? > DAT
3/31/1989	The Front	n/a	n/a		
4/1/1989	Northhampton	n/a	2.12		
4/2/1989	Naugatuck	n/a	2.80		
4/7/1989	Newmarket	n/a	3.25		
4/13/1989	Rutland	n/a			
4/14/1989	Johnson		2.12		SBD > Cass1 > DAT
4/15/1989	Burlington		2.80		
4/19/1989	Somerville	n/a			
4/20/1989	Amherst		3.25	Most copies that circulate are cut during Harpua	SBD > Cass? > DAT
4/21/1989	The Front	n/a	4.12		
4/22/1989	The Front	n/a	3.00		
4/27/1989	Durham				
4/28/1989	Brunswick	n/a	2.85		
4/29/1989	Providence	n/a			
4/30/1989	Cambridge		2.15		
5/1/1989	Northhampton		4.00		
5/3/1989	Lancaster	n/a	n/a		
5/5/1989	Clinton		4.00		
5/6/1989	Hanover				SBD > Cass1 > DAT
5/7/1989	The Front	n/a	n/a		
5/8/1989	The Front	n/a	n/a		
5/9/1989	Nectar's		3.19		SBD > Cass1 > DAT
5/11/1989	Albany	n/a	4.12		
5/12/1989	Syracuse	n/a	3.00		
5/13/1989	Syracuse		4.12		SBD > Cass? > DAT
5/14/1989	Amherst	n/a	n/a		
5/18/1989	Portland	n/a	n/a		

Date	Location	Scarcity	GHI	Comments	Medium
1989 *(continued)*					
5/19/1989	Newport	n/a	n/a		
5/20/1989	Northfield		3.00		
5/21/1989	Burlington		2.12		
5/26/1989	Rutland		2.85		
5/27/1989	West Hartford			Tapes that circulate include only the first set	
5/28/1989	Hebron		3.78		SBD > Cass0 > DAT
5/30/1989	Northampton	n/a	n/a		
6/3/1989	Wetlands	n/a	n/a		
6/8/1989	Geneva	n/a	n/a		
6/10/1989	Providence	n/a	n/a		
6/14/1989	Burlington	n/a	n/a		
6/16/1989	Portland	n/a	n/a		
6/17/1989	Portland	n/a	n/a		
6/23/1989	Boston				
6/29/1989	The Front	n/a	n/a		
6/30/1989	Northampton				SBD > Cass? > DAT
7/1/1989	Montreal	n/a	n/a		
8/11/1989	Portland	n/a	n/a		
8/12/1989	Burlington		3.03	Only the first set is in heavy circulation	
8/13/1989	Martha's Vineyard	n/a	3.75		
8/17/1989	The Front		3.75		SBD > Cass? > DAT
8/18/1989	Northampton	n/a	n/a		
8/19/1989	Hanover		3.13	Tapes that circulate cut during the second set	SBD > Cass2 > DAT
8/23/1989	Providence			Tapes that circulate include only the second set	
8/25/1989	Newport	n/a	n/a		
8/26/1989	Townshend		4.02		
9/1/1989	Brunswick	n/a	n/a		
9/2/1989	Wetlands	n/a	n/a		
9/6/1989	Providence	n/a	n/a		
9/7/1989	The Front	n/a	n/a		
9/8/1989	The Front	n/a	n/a		
9/9/1989	Bennington				SBD > Cass1 > DAT
9/13/1989	Providence	n/a	n/a		
9/14/1989	Medford			Tapes that circulate cut during the second set	
9/16/1989	Portland	n/a	n/a		
9/20/1989	Providence	n/a	n/a		
9/21/1989	Northampton		4.26		SBD > ? > Cass? > DAT
10/1/1989	The Front		2.52		SBD > Cass? > DAT
10/6/1989	Boston		2.55		
10/7/1989	Lewiston		3.60		SBD > Cass1 > DAT
10/10/1989	The Front	n/a	n/a		
10/12/1989	Keene	n/a	n/a		
10/13/1989	Syracuse	n/a	n/a		
10/14/1989	Geneva			Tapes that circulate cut during the second set	
10/20/1989	The Front		3.83		SBD > Cass0 > DAT
10/21/1989	The Front				SBD > Cass? > DAT
10/22/1989	The Front		2.35	Tapes that circulate cut into La Grange and during Antelope	SBD > Cass? > DAT
10/26/1989	Wetlands		3.28		SBD > Cass? > DAT
10/28/1989	Poughkeepsie	n/a	n/a		

"On the Roof"

Darius Zelkha, Palo Alto, CA

It has been said that a lot of odd things happen in Morocco. I offer this story as proof:

I was on the rooftop terrace of the building I was living in at the time. It was around five in the evening, and the sun had just begun its descent towards the horizon. (A lot has been written about the Moroccan sky, and it's all true: It is truly glorious.) I had my headphones on, and Phish was playing a rendition of *Taste* performed about four and a half months (on August 3, 1997, to be exact) prior to this very moment that I happened to be on the roof in Morocco, watching the sunset and listening to them play it. Although Phish had performed this music more than four months before, the world around me had evidently waited until this very moment to jam with them.

Though I had my headphones on, I could still hear the five o'clock sounds of the neighborhood: there was a traffic jam (I use the word "jam" loosely in this case, of course; the traffic was definitely not "jamming" in a manner that fit my musical tastes) that began during the piano solo, the haphazard horn blasts falling into place aside Page's own rhythmic runs and bounces. In the neighborhood, such a ruckus was not uncommon, but on this particular evening, the hubbub lasted an uncommonly long time. I mention the noise of the traffic for the sole reason that the racket ended precisely the same second as the piano solo reached its furious peak and then dropped to nothing—it was as if the final horn blast served to both announce the beginning of the guitar build and inform me of the current musical collaboration I was witnessing. The horn died out, and suddenly it was only Page, Mike, Fish, and a lone sustained note from Trey; the world around me laid out for the compulsory four measures.

As the first notes of guitar introduced themselves into the groundwork of the jam, the wind decided to get involved, and I saw the clouds shift slowly towards the East, a movement marked only by the birds that passed over the roof in patterns that, it seemed, were loosely choreographed to the rising and falling guitar lines flowing through the headphones and into my ears. The sounds on tape steadily grew, and nature, not to be drowned out, countered with a series of dog barks, which repeatedly landed in a haphazard (though not what I would classify as "random") pile around each off-beat offered by Fishman's hi-hat. At that moment, a woman washing clothing on a nearby roof made her entrance, slapping the laundry against the rooftop in an odd (though not unpleasant) triplet pattern, which, when placed against Fishman's pulse and the dogs' cries, built a rhythmic canvas which Trey immediately seized and complemented gracefully.

Of course, the sun was still falling toward the horizon, though now a bit faster than before; it could be said that the sun was actually the leader of this jam, as each section of the musical collaboration seemed to rise in intensity in direct relation to the sky's color. Now, at what seemed to be nearly the peak of the jam, the sky turned a deep maroon, and, all at once, the true soloist emerged from a distance, as the *mouzzen* voiced the evening call to prayer. The call approached from the horizon and effortlessly cut through Trey's trills and Mike's thumps with a virtuosity which Phish could not counter but, instead, merely hope to sustain and inspire by furiously maintaining the current intensity of the jam. The sky was suddenly an odd shade of purple; I say "odd" because it was a color that only hung in the air a second (as soon as I noticed it, it wasn't quite the same color any longer), a second in which the combined music reached its glorious climax, and, precisely as the four voices of Phish were brought together in unison for the final chords of the jam, the sun dropped below the horizon, the woman and her laundry went inside, the call to prayer silenced the dogs and faded, along with the clouds, into the sky itself, and it was quiet. I took my headphones off and went inside.

Date	Location	Scarcity	GHI	Comments	Medium
10/31/1989	Plainfield		3.85		Pro-Shot Video
11/2/1989	Durham		2.95		
11/3/1989	Portland		2.75	Tapes that circulate cut during the second set	SBD > Cass? > DAT
11/4/1989	Bar Harbor	n/a	n/a		
11/9/1989	Williamstown		2.50		SBD > Cass? > DAT
11/10/1989	Clinton		2.10	Tapes that circaulte are cut during Suzy and Fee	SBD > Cass? > DAT
11/11/1989	Burlington		3.06		
11/16/1989	Northampton		2.82		
11/18/1989	Ardmore	n/a			
11/30/1989	Boston				SBD > Cass0 > DAT
12/1/1989	Boston	0.25			SBD > Cass0 > DAT
12/3/1989	The Front				
12/4/1989	Burlington	n/a	n/a		
12/6/1989	"Washington, D.C."	n/a	n/a		

Date	Location	Scarcity	GHI	Comments	Medium
1989 *(continued)*					
12/7/1989	Baltimore		2.33		SBD > Cass1 > DAT
12/8/1989	Poultney		3.00		SBD > Cass1 > DAT
12/9/1989	Castleton		2.00		SBD > Cass? > DAT
12/15/1989	New York				SBD > Cass? > DAT
12/16/1989	Burlington				
12/29/1989	Philadelphia			Tapes that circulate include only the first set	
12/30/1989	Wetlands			Tapes that circulate include only the second set and encore	
12/31/1989	Boston				
Early 1990					
1/2/1990	Durham	n/a	n/a		
1/13/1990	Exeter	n/a	n/a		
1/19/1990	Worcester	n/a	n/a		
1/20/1990	Hannover	1.50	2.00		DSBD
1/25/1990	Oronoko	n/a	n/a		
1/26/1990	Portland	n/a	n/a		
1/27/1990	The Front	1.50			
1/28/1990	The Front	1.67	3.00		
1/29/1990	Ithaca	1.00			
1/31/1990	Charleston	n/a	n/a		
2/1/1990	Athens	1.00			Video
2/2/1990	Athens	n/a	n/a		
2/3/1990	Atlanta	n/a	n/a		
2/4/1990	Columbia	n/a	n/a		
2/5/1990	Charleston	n/a	n/a		
2/6/1990	Hilton Head	n/a	n/a		
2/7/1990	Chapel Hill	n/a	n/a		
2/8/1990	Richmond	n/a	n/a		
2/9/1990	Lancaster	1.17	3.00		SBD > Cass0 > DAT
2/10/1990	Philadelphia	1.50	3.00		DSBD
2/15/1990	Providence	2.33		Tapes that circulate include the first set and part of the second	DSBD
2/16/1990	Boston	1.17			SBD > Cass0 > DAT
2/17/1990	Amherst	1.17			
2/22/1990	Keene	1.17		Tapes that circulate include only the first set	
2/23/1990	Haverford	1.92	3.33		SBD > Cass0 > DAT
2/24/1990	"Washington, D.C."	2.00			SBD > Cass1 > DAT
2/25/1990	Baltimore	1.67	4.00		
3/1/1990	New Haven	2.67	2.00		SBD > Cass? > DAT
3/2/1990	Poughkeepsie	n/a	n/a		
3/3/1990	Wetlands	1.50	4.00		
3/5/1990	Ithaca	n/a	n/a		
3/7/1990	Durham	1.17		Tapes that circulate cut during Lizards	SBD > Cass1 > DAT
3/8/1990	Saratoga Springs	2.42			SBD > Cass0 > PCM > DAT
3/9/1990	The Front	2.17			SBD > Cass1 > DAT
3/10/1990	The Front	1.00		Tapes that circulate include only the first set	
3/11/1990	The Front	2.50			SBD > Cass? > DAT
3/16/1990	Ardmore	n/a	n/a		
3/17/1990	Ardmore	1.00			SBD Matrix > Cass0 > DAT

Date	Location	Scarcity	GHI	Comments	Medium
3/27/1990	Columbus	n/a	n/a		
3/28/1990	Granville	1.67			
3/29/1990	Dayton	n/a	n/a		
3/30/1990	Chicago	n/a	n/a		
3/31/1990	Madison	n/a	n/a		
4/4/1990	Boulder	1.17			
4/5/1990	Boulder	2.29			SBD > Cass0 > DAT
4/6/1990	Crested Butte	1.17			SBD > Cass? > DAT (Set II)
4/7/1990	Crested Butte	1.17		Tapes that circulate cut during the second set	
4/8/1990	Telluride	1.00			
4/9/1990	Telluride	1.00		Tapes that circulate include only the second set	
4/11/1990	Telluride	n/a	n/a		
4/12/1990	Steamboat Springs	1.00			
4/13/1990	Steamboat Springs	1.00			
4/14/1990	Steamboat Springs	1.00			
4/18/1990	Denver	1.83	2.80		SBD > Cass0 > DAT
4/19/1990	Boulder	1.17		Tapes that circulate include only the second set	
4/20/1990	Fort Collins	1.67			
4/21/1990	Fort Collins	1.17			
4/22/1990	Colorado Springs	3.17	3.38		DSBD
4/25/1990	South Bend	2.00	2.50		
4/26/1990	Oberlin	1.83			
4/28/1990	Boston	1.67			
4/29/1990	Woodbury	1.83	1.50		Pro-Shot Video
5/3/1990	Keene	n/a	n/a		
5/4/1990	Keene	1.67			
5/6/1990	New Haven	1.50			
5/7/1990	Ithaca	n/a	n/a		
5/9/1990	Portland	n/a	n/a		
5/10/1990	Northampton	1.17	3.00		
5/11/1990	Providence	1.00			
5/12/1990	The Front	n/a	n/a		
5/13/1990	The Front	1.33	3.00		SBD > Cass2 > DAT
5/15/1990	Clinton	1.33			
5/19/1990	Concord	1.17			
5/23/1990	Richmond	1.00	3.00		SBD > Cass1 > DAT
5/24/1990	Raleigh	1.33	2.00		SBD > Cass0 > DAT
5/25/1990	Hilton Head	n/a	n/a		
5/26/1990	Hilton Head	n/a	n/a		
5/28/1990	Hilton Head	n/a	n/a		
5/30/1990	Athens	1.00			
5/31/1990	Athens	1.00			SBD Matrix > PCM > DAT (Partial)
6/1/1990	Atlanta	1.50	3.95		
6/2/1990	Columbia	1.17			
6/5/1990	Chapel Hill	1.83	3.00		SBD > Cass? > DAT
6/6/1990	Salem	n/a	n/a		
6/7/1990	"Washington, D.C."	1.17			
6/8/1990	Philadelphia	1.17			
6/9/1990	Wetlands	1.83	4.00		SBD > Cass1 > DAT
6/16/1990	Townshend	3.00	4.33		DSBD (Set II)

Date	Location	Scarcity	GHI	Comments	Medium
Early 1990 *(continued)*					
6/17/1990	Wendell Studios	2.00	4.00		
7/8/1990	Ardmore	n/a	n/a		
8/4/1990	Hinesburg	n/a	n/a		
9/2/1990	Shelburne	n/a	n/a		
Fall, 1990					
9/13/1990	Wetlands	3.58	3.93	Some copies that circulate are missing the encore	DSBD
9/14/1990	Providence	1.17			
9/15/1990	Keene	1.17			
9/16/1990	Middletown	2.42			
9/17/1990	The Front	n/a	n/a		
9/18/1990	The Front	n/a	n/a		
9/20/1990	Somerville	1.67			
9/21/1990	Somerville	1.67		Tapes that circulate include only the second set	
9/22/1990	Amherst	1.17			
9/27/1990	The Front	n/a	n/a		
9/28/1990	Poughkeepsie	1.00			
9/29/1990	Ardmore	1.50			
10/1/1990	Ithaca	1.50			
10/3/1990	Portland	n/a	n/a		
10/4/1990	Durham	1.17			SBD > Cass? > DAT
10/5/1990	Saratoga Springs	1.33			
10/6/1990	Port Chester	2.00			DSBD
10/7/1990	Sayreville	1.00			
10/8/1990	"Washington, D.C."	1.17			
10/10/1990	Charlottesville	n/a	n/a		
10/11/1990	Richmond	n/a	n/a		
10/12/1990	Chapel Hill	1.33			
10/13/1990	Columbia	n/a	n/a		
10/14/1990	Hilton Head	n/a	n/a		
10/17/1990	Charlotte	n/a	n/a		
10/18/1990	Athens	n/a	n/a		
10/19/1990	Atlanta	n/a	n/a		
10/20/1990	Tuscaloosa	n/a	n/a		
10/22/1990	New Orleans	n/a	n/a		
10/25/1990	Austin	n/a	n/a		
10/26/1990	Houston	n/a	n/a		
10/27/1990	Dallas	n/a	n/a		
10/30/1990	Crested Butte	3.64	2.00		SBD > Multitrack Reel > DAT
10/31/1990	Colorado Springs	4.29	3.75		Official MP3 Release
11/2/1990	Boulder	3.56	3.42		SBD > Multitrack Reel > DAT
11/3/1990	Boulder	3.21	2.75		SBD > Multitrack Reel > DAT
11/4/1990	Fort Collins	3.88	3.88		SBD > Multitrack Reel > DAT
11/6/1990	Minneapolis	n/a	n/a		
11/8/1990	Madison	1.50	4.00		SBD > Cass1 > DAT (Check + Set I)
11/9/1990	Chicago	n/a	n/a		
11/10/1990	Richmond	1.17			
11/16/1990	Providence	1.33			

Date	Location	Scarcity	GHI	Comments	Medium
11/17/1990	Somerville	1.33	5.00		SBD > Cass? > DAT (No Encore)
11/24/1990	Port Chester	2.75	2.50		DSBD
11/26/1990	Ithaca	1.17			DSBD
11/28/1990	Syracuse	n/a	n/a		
11/30/1990	Keene	1.67			
12/1/1990	The Front	1.43		Tapes that circulate include only the first set	
12/2/1990	The Front	n/a	n/a		
12/7/1990	Amherst	1.57			
12/8/1990	Poughkeepsie	1.17			
12/28/1990	New York	3.25	3.67		DSBD
12/29/1990	Providence	1.67			DSBD
12/31/1990	Boston	2.14	3.00		
Winter/Spring, 1991					
2/1/1991	Providence	1.60		Two versions circulate; one complete and one partial	
2/2/1991	Lewiston	1.00			
2/3/1991	Burlington	2.40			
2/4/1991	Burlington	n/a	n/a		
2/7/1991	Killington	2.44	4.00		
2/8/1991	Portsmouth	2.11			
2/9/1991	Northhampton	1.78			
2/14/1991	Ithaca	1.67			
2/15/1991	Keene	2.67	3.00		
2/16/1991	New York	1.67	3.25		
2/19/1991	"Washington, D.C."	1.90	3.00		
2/20/1991	Richmond	1.89		Tapes that circulate are missing most of the 2nd set	
2/21/1991	Charlottesville	2.00	2.50		SBD > Cass0 HiFi > DAT
2/22/1991	Chapel Hill	n/a	n/a		
2/23/1991	Charlotte	n/a	n/a		
2/26/1991	Salem	1.44			
2/27/1991	Knoxville	1.56			
2/28/1991	Nashville	1.80		Most tapes that circulate end after Divided Sky	
3/1/1991	Athens	1.90			
3/2/1991	Atlanta	n/a	n/a		
3/6/1991	Memphis	1.50			
3/7/1991	Oxford	n/a	n/a		
3/8/1991	Tuscaloosa	1.44		Tapes that circulate include only the first set	
3/9/1991	New Orleans	2.00		Tapes that circulate include only the second set	
3/13/1991	Boulder	3.94	3.00		DSBD
3/15/1991	Denver	4.45	4.08		DSBD
3/16/1991	Breckenridge	3.73	4.00		DSBD
3/17/1991	Aspen	3.59	3.57		SBD > Cass0 > DAT
3/19/1991	Durango	n/a	n/a		
3/22/1991	Steamboat Springs	3.25	4.62		DSBD
3/23/1991	Steamboat Springs	2.60			DSBD
3/25/1991	Durango	n/a	n/a		
3/28/1991	Santa Cruz	2.40	4.00		
3/29/1991	San Francisco	2.44		Tapes that circulate include only the second set	
3/31/1991	Berkley	2.20			

Date	Location	Scarcity	GHI	Comments	Medium
Winter/Spring, 1991 *(continued)*					
4/2/1991	Arcata	1.55			
4/3/1991	Ashland	1.45			
4/4/1991	Eugene	2.22			SBD > Cass0 > DAT
4/5/1991	Portland	2.39	3.96		SBD > Cass0 > DAT
4/6/1991	Olympa	2.00		Tapes that circulate include only the second set	SBD > Cass0 > DAT
4/11/1991	Northfield	3.65	3.75		DSBD
4/12/1991	Madison	2.78			SBD > Cass0 > DAT
4/13/1991	Chicago	n/a	n/a		
4/15/1991	Evanston	1.89			
4/16/1991	Ann Arbor	2.67	3.50		SBD > DAT > Cass0 > DAT
4/18/1991	Oberlin	1.56		Tapes that circulate include only the first set	
4/19/1991	Buffalo	2.00			
4/20/1991	Rochester	2.33			SBD > Cass3 > DAT
4/21/1991	Potsdam	1.67			
4/22/1991	Burlington	2.20			
4/25/1991	Durham	1.45			
4/27/1991	Portchester	3.70	3.95		DSBD
5/2/1991	Poughkeepsie	1.67	3.00		
5/3/1991	Somerville	3.67	3.60		DSBD
5/4/1991	Somerville	2.72	3.50		SBD > Cass? > DAT
5/9/1991	Portland	1.00			
5/10/1991	Waterville	2.61	3.00		SBD > Cass? > DAT
5/11/1991	The Front	2.30		Tapes that circulate include only the second set	
5/12/1991	Burlington	2.50			
5/16/1991	New Britain	1.56			

"India Introduced"

Darius Zelkha, Palo Alto, CA

When I spent the month of January 1997 in India, studying percussion, I packed everything I needed for the month in a single backpack: a bundle of underwear and socks, three t-shirts, a few pairs of pants, a sweatshirt, my journal, and, of course, my Walkman and some music, including two Phish tapes: *Billy Breathes* and a soundboard of the first set of the April 17, 1992, show at the Warfield Theater in San Francisco (the *Reba* has a jam segment for the record books, and the *Bowie* makes my palms sweat).

While in India, I spent most of my time in Madras (now officially called Chennai), a large city in the southeastern region of the continent. Just in case you've never been to Madras, allow me to set the scene: While home to millions of people, it's hard to think of Madras as a "big city." It's really just a cluster of large villages with a few big buildings thrown in, and life there is an eclectic mix of rural village traditions and modern-day hustle and bustle. Compared to some of India's other large metropolitan areas, such as Bombay and Bangalore, Madras is far from Westernized. As of my visit, there was no McDonald's, no cybercafés, and certainly no visible Phish fan base.

Then me, my Walkman, *Billy Breathes*, and 4/17/92 set one arrived.

Much of my average day was spent traveling to and from my percussion teacher's house, so I logged a lot of hours on the Madras city buses. Taking the bus in India is an experience in and of itself, a routine most foreigners avoid, for good reason: the buses, while cheap to ride (they cost around three cents each way), are in dangerously high demand by locals as a mode of transportation. In fact, the buses are so crowded that between the mass of people crammed inside the bus ("standing room only" takes on a new meaning) and the handful of fearless youngsters that grasp on the outside railing, the vehicles have been known to actually tip over on occasion. In this way, riding the bus in India is a lot like being in the front row of a Phish show: it's very hot and very crowded, there's a lot of gentle pushing going on, and you see a lot of the same people there day after day.

Anyway, I spent a good amount of time riding the bus each day, and since I got on at the beginning of the route, I usually got a seat. In the beginning, I was content to read, see the city, and chat with the

Date	Location	Scarcity	GHI	Comments	Medium
5/17/1991	Providence	1.70			
5/18/1991	New York	1.67	2.50		
5/19/1991	Salisbury	1.56			
Summer, 1991					
7/11/1991	Burlington	4.20	4.00		DSBD
7/12/1991	Keene	4.28	3.25		DSBD
7/13/1991	Lenox	3.30	3.33		
7/14/1991	Townshend	4.35	4.17		DSBD
7/15/1991	New York	4.22	3.00		DSBD
7/16/1991	New York	n/a	n/a		
7/18/1991	Hampton Beach	2.44	2.00		
7/19/1991	Somerville	3.72	3.00		
7/20/1991	Arrowhead Ranch	3.46	4.25		Pro-Shot Video
7/21/1991	Arrowhead Ranch	4.92	4.54		DSBD
7/23/1991	Washington D.C.	3.41	3.00		DSBD
7/24/1991	Charlottesville	3.60	3.88		DSBD
7/25/1991	Chapel Hill	2.70	3.33		SBD > Cass0 > DAT
7/26/1991	Athens	2.56	4.05		
7/27/1991	Athens	2.56	2.50		
8/3/1991	Amy's Farm	4.58	4.37		DSBD
8/19/1991	Dartmouth	n/a	n/a		
Fall, 1991					
9/25/1991	Keene	2.33			
9/26/1991	Ithaca	2.20	4.00		
9/27/1991	Rochester	1.78	2.00		

"India Introduced" (continued)

people around me during these hours of transport. Towards the end of my stay, though, I had read all my books, had seen all of the city, and had met most of the daily bus-goers. To fend off the growing forces of boredom, I began taking my Walkman on the bus with me.

For the historical record, it's possible (though not likely) that on these bus trips the Phish fan base of southern India was born.

Because I was a foreigner, I attracted a good amount of attention on the bus, and the sight of my Walkman fueled the curiosity and encouraged the stares. I didn't mind. If I caught people staring, or I just felt like making conversation, I'd say hello and offer them a listen of whatever tape was currently in the player. On many of these bus rides, that tape was either *Billy Breathes* or 4/17/92 set one.

Out of courtesy, my fellow bus patrons would usually decline my initial offer, but, when offered a second time, more often than not they would cautiously apply the foreign frequencies of Phish to their previously untainted ears.

The music was almost always greeted with an initial look of surprise, which was often followed by a polite smile. (In all honesty, though, I admit that in many cases the music was acknowledged by a yelp which never developed into anything even remotely resembling a smile or any other indication of pleasure.)

See for yourself. Here are a few actual responses to the music:

"Very nice guitar songs. Very soft." (an eighteen-year-old Indian student after hearing *Talk*, *Theme from the Bottom*, and *Bliss* from *Billy Breathes*)

". . . . ." (silence, accompanied by a big grin and mild headbobbing, from a twenty-three-year-old Indian textile merchant, while listening to the 4/17/92 *Stash*)

". . . . ." (silence, accompanied by a furrowed brow and no headbobbing, from a twenty-five-year-old Indian engineer while hearing *Sparkle* from 4/17/92; after giving my Walkman back to me, the man quickly changed seats, occasionally glancing back at me with a confused look on his face) [Editor's Note: maybe the man realized that *Sparkle* was about masturbation.]

"I don't like it. Do you have any Michael Jackson?" (twenty-two-year-old Indian student after hearing the final few minutes of the 4/17/92 *Bowie>Catapult>Bowie*)

So, there you have it. In my estimation, it may take a few more albums and a world tour or two, but when Phish have finally "sold out" in India—and are playing the large auditoriums instead of the small clubs—well, you can blame some of it on me.

Date	Location	Scarcity	GHI	Comments	Medium
Fall, 1991 *(continued)*					
9/28/1991	Buffalo	1.89	3.00		
9/29/1991	Cleveland	1.55			
9/30/1991	Athens	n/a	n/a		
10/2/1991	Chicago	1.56			
10/3/1991	Champaign	1.70			
10/4/1991	Madison	1.67			SBD > Cass2 > DAT
10/5/1991	Minneapolis	n/a	n/a		
10/6/1991	St. Paul	1.56	3.00		SBD > Cass? > DAT
10/10/1991	Eugene	2.00			SBD > Cass1 > DAT
10/11/1991	Seattle	1.78			SBD > Cass1 > DAT (Set I)
10/12/1991	Portland	1.67			SBD > Cass1 > DAT
10/13/1991	Olympia	3.67	5.00		DSBD
10/15/1991	Arcata	1.89			
10/17/1991	San Francisco	2.44	3.00		
10/18/1991	San Francisco	2.78	5.00		SBD > Cass2 > DAT
10/19/1991	Santa Cruz	3.60	3.33		DSBD
10/23/1991	Tempe	1.42			
10/24/1991	Prescott	1.78			
10/26/1991	Santa Fe	n/a	n/a		
10/27/1991	Telluride	2.10			
10/28/1991	Telluride	2.50	3.25		SBD > Cass2 > DAT
10/30/1991	Boulder	2.08			
10/31/1991	Colorado Springs	3.55			
11/1/1991	Denver	3.75	3.00		DSBD
11/2/1991	Fort Collins	2.50			
11/4/1991	Dallas	n/a	n/a		
11/5/1991	Austin	n/a	n/a		
11/7/1991	New Orleans	2.00	2.25		
11/8/1991	Tuscaloosa	1.89			
11/9/1991	Atlanta	2.00			
11/10/1991	Charleston	1.00			
11/12/1991	Athens	1.56	4.00		
11/13/1991	Davidson	1.60	3.00		
11/14/1991	Chapel Hill	2.20			DSBD
11/15/1991	Charlottesville	2.91	5.00		
11/16/1991	"Washington, DC"	2.59	4.00		
11/19/1991	New Britain	1.56			
11/20/1991	Providence	2.30			
11/21/1991	Somerville	3.00			DSBD (Set I)
11/22/1991	Portland	2.00			
11/23/1991	Barre	1.89			
11/24/1991	Hannover	1.67			
11/30/1991	Port Chester	2.95	3.33		DSBD
12/4/1991	Plattsburgh	1.44			
12/5/1991	Greenfield	2.30	4.00		
12/6/1991	Middlebury	3.00			SBD > ? > DAT
12/7/1991	Portsmouth	2.89			SBD > Cass4 > DAT
12/31/1991	Worcester	4.00	4.50		DSBD

Date	Location	Scarcity	GHI	Comments	Medium
Spring, 1992					
3/6/1992	Portsmouth	3.50	3.75		
3/7/1992	Portsmouth	3.00	4.00		
3/11/1992	Keene	3.00			
3/12/1992	Burlington	3.08		Soundboard copies in circulation have cuts in Jim and Rift	SBD > Cass0 > DAT
3/13/1992	Providence	4.46	4.13		DSBD
3/14/1992	Roseland	4.15	3.63		DSBD (Set I)
3/17/1992	"Washington, D.C."	2.13			
3/19/1992	New Haven	2.96	2.00		SBD > Cass0 > DAT (Set II)
3/20/1992	Binghamton	3.62	3.50		SBD > ? > DAT
3/21/1992	Philadelphia	3.79	3.00	Soundboard copies iinclude a complete first set and partial second	DSBD
3/22/1992	Charleston	2.00	1.50		FM > Cass? > DAT (four songs)
3/24/1992	Richmond	2.42	3.33		
3/25/1992	Charlottesville	2.58	5.00		DSBD (Set II)
3/26/1992	Winston-Salem	2.33	3.00		
3/27/1992	Charlotte	2.17	3.00		
3/28/1992	Atlanta	2.63	2.00		
3/30/1992	St. Louis	2.83	4.00		
3/31/1992	Columbia	2.00			
4/1/1992	Lawrence	1.67			
4/3/1992	Beaver Creek	2.08			
4/4/1992	Boulder	2.21			
4/5/1992	Boulder	3.12	2.67		DSBD
4/6/1992	Gunnison	3.46	2.60		SBD > Cass? > DAT
4/7/1992	Durango	2.33			SBD > Cass3 > DAT
4/8/1992	Albuquerque	2.08			
4/12/1992	Tucson	2.25			SBD > Cass1 > DAT (Set I)
4/13/1992	Tempe	3.00			SBD > Cass2 > DAT
4/15/1992	Los Angeles	3.13			SBD > Cass0 > DAT
4/16/1992	Santa Barbara	4.96	4.21		DSBD
4/17/1992	Warfield	4.00	4.00		DSBD
4/18/1992	Palo Alto	4.31	4.22		DSBD
4/19/1992	Santa Cruz	3.29	3.25		SBD > ? > DAT
4/21/1992	Eureka	3.75	3.40	Soundboard copies have a cut in Maze	DSBD > Cass0 > DAT
4/22/1992	Eugene	2.17	4.00		SBD > Cass0 > DAT
4/23/1992	Seattle	2.08			
4/24/1992	Portland	1.96			SBD > ? > DAT
4/25/1992	Olympia	2.42			SBD > Cass3 > DAT
4/29/1992	Minneapolis	2.46	2.00		SBD > Cass1 > DAT (Set II)
4/30/1992	Madison	2.42			SBD > Cass3 > DAT
5/1/1992	Milwaukee	3.25	3.00		SBD > Cass0 > DAT (Set I)
5/2/1992	Chicago	3.29	4.00		
5/3/1992	East Lansing	2.13	2.00		SBD > Cass1 > DAT
5/5/1992	Cincinnati	2.33			
5/6/1992	Detroit	2.92	4.00		DSBD (Set I)
5/7/1992	Cleveland	2.83			
5/8/1992	North Tonowanda	2.63			
5/9/1992	Syracuse	3.17	3.00		DSBD

"untitled"

Bradley Lonard, Sydney, Australia

I'm a Phish fan—have been since 1993. I listen to 'em daily, I collect live tapes, I read excerpts from *Mike's Corner* to friends ("very good" they say, moving in the general direction of Away). I even have the T-shirts. There's just one little difference between me and you:

I have never seen Phish live.

I live in Sydney, Australia, about half a planet away from the band. They've never come down here (and with what I can only describe as a nonexistent profile, seem unlikely to do so in the future). I, despite the best-laid plans, have yet to make it to the U.S.A. So, I've never seen Phish play. Hell, for a couple of years I didn't even have any tapes.

I occasionally get strange reactions from U.S. correspondents when I tell them this. The most extreme came from one argumentative bloke who told me I had no right to call myself a Phish fan if I hadn't seen 'em. Most don't go that far, but there does seem to be a general consensus, and it goes like this:

"Hey man, are you missing out or what? Phish is a live experience!"

Well, yes and no. There's no doubt in my mind that Phish live at

their best (fill in the date of your favorite tape here) is a truly beautiful thing. But there seems to be another general consensus out there:

"Phish's studio albums are crap. Freeze-dried versions of songs they play much better live. And there's not enough jamming." (This consensus seems to be shared by some of the band members.)

I'd argue strongly against this one. Perhaps out of necessity— all I knew of Phish for a few years were their albums. Yes, live shows (and tapes) offer improvisation, jams, spur of the moment lunacy, high energy, and, most obviously, a repertoire about five times larger than the one on disc. But does that mean one can't love Phish long-distance through their studio stuff? I say thee nay!

Everyone has a moment when they discovered Phish. Mine came in February 1993 in an import record store in Sydney. Flicking through the racks of new releases, I came across *A Picture of Nectar*. "Phish?" I thought. "Crazy name…." I idly remembered reading of them in an American magazine a few months before. I scanned the sleeve. "Hmmm…*Chalkdust Torture? Guelah Papyrus? Tweezer?*" I made a spur-of-the-moment decision. Who cares what the music sounds like? Any band that named their songs things like *Chalkdust*

Date	Location	Scarcity	GHI	Comments	Medium
Spring, 1992 *(continued)*					
5/10/1992	Amherst	2.00			
5/12/1992	Canton	2.75	2.00		SBD > Cass? > DAT (Set II)
5/14/1992	Port Chester	3.96	5.00		SBD > Cass? > DAT
5/15/1992	New York	2.17			
5/16/1992	Boston	3.17	2.00		SBD > Cass? > DAT
5/17/1992	Schenectady	3.00	5.00		
5/18/1992	Burlington	3.00	2.00		
Summer, 1992 Europe Tour					
6/19/1992	Hamburg	2.00	2.00		SBD > Cass? > DAT
6/20/1992	Nordheim	1.87	1.67		
6/23/1992	Dusseldorf	1.93	2.00		SBD > Cass? > DAT
6/24/1992	Nuremberg	2.00	2.00		
6/27/1992	Copenhagen	1.64			
6/30/1992	Paris	1.43			
7/1/1992	Belgium	1.43			
7/3/1992	London	n/a	n/a		
Summer, 1992 U.S. Tour					
7/9/1992	Portland	1.56			
7/10/1992	Syracuse	1.78	2.50		
7/11/1992	Holmdel	1.89	2.50		
7/12/1992	Jones Beach	1.44	2.50		
7/14/1992	Norfolk	1.22			
7/15/1992	Charlottesville	2.60			SBD > Cass0 > DAT

"untitled" (continued)

Torture sounded okay by me! As it turned out, I loved *Nectar*—loved its eccentricity, its eclecticism, its "anything goes" attitude. So when *Rift* appeared, I was an eager customer.

I don't think *Rift* left my CD player in six months, and I'd still call it both my favorite Phish on record and the most successful. Where *Nectar* changed directions every few minutes, *Rift* is more consistent. Without knowing of the "concept" behind it, I think you can tell that it works as a song cycle—that it all adds up to more than the sum of its parts. Even minor songs like *The Wedge* or *Mound* work in this context. Yes, I've heard "better" versions of *Rift*, "hotter" versions of *Maze* on tapes. But, strewn as they are amongst a set, they've never given me the emotional punch that comes from listening to the *Rift* album as a whole.

That's also the case, of course, with *Billy Breathes*, particularly what we might think of as "side two" (if such things hadn't been made obsolete by CD—still, ever notice how many acts seem to sequence an album so it falls into two parts?). *Train Song* to *Prince Caspian* form to me a kind of suite, unified in sound and context, if not quite in theme. I'm not surprised that so many fans complain that these songs "don't work" in concert (although *Caspian* seems to be taking on a life of its own). Actually, I'm surprised Phish hasn't played the "suite" in concert as a whole. Between *Billy* and *Caspian*, *Swept Away>Steep* makes an oddly beautiful connection; live, it's

just a way to get from one place to another, maybe freak out a bit, throw in a scream or two, let the audience catch its breath while the band works up to bigger things.

I don't want to intellectualize this too much. I just want to make the point that Phish in concert—"being there"—is one side of the equation, and for those of us separated from that experience by the tyranny of distance, Phish's studio albums—so often dismissed by people on "the scene"—seem equally important and admirable. (They're also *available*, although they take some hunting out, whereas I had to get hooked up to the Net, lurk on rec.music.phish and grovel for quite a while before I could begin collecting tapes.)

So, do I think I've missed anything by not catching Phish in concert? Yeah, a couple of things. Firstly, Chris Kuroda at work ("hot lights by a hot guy!"). Somewhat more seriously, what I've missed is the sense of community that I so often read about on rec.music.phish. I'm a lone voice here; my love of Phish is shared by practically no one I've met in this country. To be part of the crowd at the Went, at Shoreline, at Madison Square Garden on New Year's Eve is something I can only dream about—to be with thousands of people who, like me, know the lyrics to *Suzie Greenberg* or *Halley's Comet*.

Still, one day I might just make it. And when I do, I know it's gonna be the gig where Mike revives *Destiny Unbound*.

Date	Location	Scarcity	GHI	Comments	Medium
7/16/1992	Richmond	2.00	2.75		
7/17/1992	Columbia	1.00			
7/18/1992	Philadelphia	1.00			
7/19/1992	Holmdel	1.00			
7/21/1992	Great Woods	1.22			DSBD
7/22/1992	Nashua	1.11			
7/23/1992	MTV Studios	0.70	3.00		Television Broadcast
7/24/1992	Jones Beach	1.50			DSBD
7/25/1992	Stowe	4.83	4.41		DSBD
7/26/1992	Big Birch	1.30			
7/27/1992	SPAC	1.00			
7/28/1992	FLPAC	1.00			
7/30/1992	Rochester Hills	1.00			
7/31/1992	Cuyahoga	1.20			
8/1/1992	Hoffman Estates	1.00			
8/2/1992	Marilyn Heights	1.00			
8/13/1992	Los Angeles	1.67			DSBD
8/14/1992	Los Angeles	1.67			DSBD
8/15/1992	Los Angeles	1.44			DSBD
8/17/1992	San Juan Capistrano	3.18	3.13		SBD > Cass1 > DAT
8/19/1992	Tucson	1.11			
8/20/1992	Las Cruces	1.11			
8/23/1992	Pueblo	1.11			
8/24/1992	Vail	1.11			
8/25/1992	Santa Fe	1.11			

Date	Location	Scarcity	GHI	Comments	Medium
Summer, 1992 U.S. Tour *(continued)*					
8/27/1992	Santa Barbara	1.11			
8/28/1992	Concord	1.00			
8/29/1992	Shoreline	1.89			DSBD; Pro-Shot Video
8/30/1992	Sacramento	1.22			
Fall, 1992					
10/30/1992	Boston	2.00			
11/19/1992	Colchester	3.50	3.50		SBD > Cass1 > DAT
11/20/1992	Albany	3.42	3.50		SBD > Cass1 > DAT
11/21/1992	Stony Brook	2.75	2.50		
11/22/1992	Ithaca	2.83	3.33		
11/23/1992	Binghamton	3.67	2.00		
11/25/1992	Glenside	2.17	3.00		
11/27/1992	Port Chester	3.83	4.00		
11/28/1992	Port Chester	4.08	3.63		
11/30/1992	Pittsburgh	2.33			
12/1/1992	Granville	1.83			
12/2/1992	Columbus	2.42	2.00		SBD > Cass0 > DAT
12/3/1992	Cincinnati	2.13			SBD > Cass? > DAT (Set I)
12/4/1992	St. Louis	2.00			
12/5/1992	Chicago	2.67			SBD > Cass0 > DAT
12/6/1992	Chicago	2.42			
12/7/1992	Minneapolis	2.08			
12/8/1992	Madison	1.92			
12/10/1992	Kalamazoo	2.17			
12/11/1992	Ann Arbor	2.33			
12/12/1992	Ontario	2.33			SBD > Cass0 > DAT
12/13/1992	Quebec	1.67			
Holiday Run, 1992					
12/28/1992	New Haven	2.93	3.00		
12/29/1992	New Haven	3.43	4.17		
12/30/1992	Springfield	3.80	3.83		
12/31/1992	Boston	4.27	3.55		Pre-FM > DAT; FM Broadcast
Spring/Summer, 1993					
1/28/1993	Hard Rock	n/a	n/a		
2/3/1993	Portland	2.81	5.00		
2/4/1993	Providence	2.94	3.00		
2/5/1993	Roseland	2.81	2.00		
2/6/1993	Roseland	3.31	3.17		
2/7/1993	"Washington, D.C."	2.72	2.00		
2/9/1993	Rochester	2.31			
2/10/1993	Geneva	2.38			
2/11/1993	Bloomsburg	2.22			
2/12/1993	Poughkeepsie	2.75	4.00		
2/13/1993	Newark	2.69			
2/15/1993	Chapel Hill	2.69	3.00		
2/17/1993	Winston-Salem	2.47			
2/18/1993	Lexington	2.50			
2/19/1993	Roxy	3.59	3.00		SBD > Cass? > DAT

Date	Location	Scarcity	GHI	Comments	Medium
2/20/1993	Roxy	4.86	4.35		DSBD; DSBD > Cass 0 > DAT
2/21/1993	Roxy	3.59	3.00		
2/22/1993	Tallahasse	2.13			
2/23/1993	Orlando	2.38			
2/25/1993	Miami Beach	2.25			
2/26/1993	Tampa	2.13			
2/27/1993	Gainesville	2.53			SBD > DAT > Cass1 > SBM > DAT
3/2/1993	New Orleans	2.71			
3/3/1993	New Orleans	2.71			
3/5/1993	Dallas	2.31			
3/6/1993	Austin	2.31	3.00		
3/8/1993	Santa Fe	1.94			
3/9/1993	Colorado Springs	2.15			
3/12/1993	Vail	2.53	3.00		
3/13/1993	Boulder	2.74			
3/14/1993	Gunnison	4.13	3.83		SBD > Cass? > DAT
3/16/1993	Phoenix	2.38			
3/17/1993	Hollywood	2.50			
3/18/1993	Hollywood	2.50			
3/19/1993	Redlands	2.25			
3/21/1993	Ventura	2.38			DSBD
3/22/1993	Sacramento	4.69	4.07		SBD > Cass0 > DAT
3/24/1993	Santa Rosa	2.69			
3/25/1993	Santa Cruz	2.66	4.00		
3/26/1993	Warfield	3.22	3.00		
3/27/1993	Warfield	3.34	3.00		
3/28/1993	Arcata	2.38			
3/30/1993	Eugene	2.94			
3/31/1993	Portland	3.06	3.00		
4/1/1993	Portland	2.63			
4/2/1993	Bellingham	2.28			
4/3/1993	Vancouver	2.13			
4/5/1993	Seattle	2.50			
4/9/1993	Minneapolis	2.75			SBD > Cass0 > DAT
4/10/1993	Chicago	3.34			SBD > Cass0 > DAT
4/12/1993	Iowa City	2.29			
4/14/1993	St. Louis	2.91	4.00		
4/16/1993	Louisville	2.63	4.00		
4/17/1993	Ann Arbor	2.81	4.00		
4/18/1993	Ann Arbor	3.06	2.50		SBD > Cass0 > DAT
4/20/1993	Columbus	2.69	2.00		
4/21/1993	Columbus	3.19	4.00		
4/22/1993	Cleveland	2.72			
4/23/1993	Hamilton	2.59	4.00		SBD > Cass1 > DAT
4/24/1993	Potsdam	2.56			
4/25/1993	Geneseo	2.47			
4/27/1993	Toronto	2.56			
4/29/1993	Montreal	3.06	3.60	Some tapes that circulate are missing the encore	SBD > Cass1 > DAT
4/30/1993	Hartford	3.12			
5/1/1993	Philadelphia	3.69	2.83		

Date	Location	Scarcity	GHI	Comments	Medium
Spring/Summer, 1993 *(continued)*					
5/2/1993	Philadelphia	3.38	4.00		
5/3/1993	New Brunswick	3.19	3.00		SBD > Cass1 > DAT (Set II)
5/5/1993	Albany	3.94	4.60		SBD > Cass1 > DAT (Set II)
5/6/1993	Albany	3.69	3.00		
5/7/1993	Bangor	2.94			SBD > Cass1 > DAT
5/8/1993	Durham	4.00	4.00		SBD > Cass? > DAT
5/29/1993	Laguna Seca	2.94	2.50		
5/30/1993	Laguna Seca	3.00	2.00		SBD > Cass0 > DAT
Summer, 1993					
7/15/1993	Weedsport	2.71	2.88		
7/16/1993	Philadelphia	3.53	2.25		SBD > Cass0 > DAT
7/17/1993	Vienna	3.47	3.00		
7/18/1993	Pittsburgh	2.75	3.00		
7/21/1993	Middletown	2.69	1.50		
7/22/1993	Stowe	3.58	2.25		SBD > Cass1 > DAT
7/23/1993	Wantagh	3.50	1.67		
7/24/1993	Great Woods	4.16	4.17		
7/25/1993	Waterloo	3.84	3.00		SBD > Cass0 > DAT (I); DSBD (II)
7/27/1993	Richmond	2.53	2.50		
7/28/1993	Charlotte	2.59	4.00		
7/29/1993	Knoxville	2.17	4.50		
7/30/1993	Antioch	2.41	4.50		
7/31/1993	Atlanta	3.00	3.00		DSBD
8/2/1993	Ybor	3.79	4.00		
8/3/1993	Miami	2.44	4.00		
8/6/1993	Cincinnati	4.14	4.00		SBD > Cass1 > DAT (Set II)
8/7/1993	Darien	4.11	3.94		
8/8/1993	Cleveland	3.56	3.00		
8/9/1993	Toronto	3.42	3.40		
8/11/1993	Grand Rapids	3.44	3.50		
8/12/1993	Rochester	3.50	2.67		
8/13/1993	Murat	4.39	4.71		SBD > Cass0 > DAT
8/14/1993	Tinley Park	3.88	3.31		SBD > Cass1 > DAT (Set II)
8/15/1993	Louisville	3.38	3.50		
8/16/1993	St. Louis	3.15	4.00		
8/17/1993	Kansas City	3.26	3.00		
8/20/1993	Red Rocks	4.63	4.21		DSBD > Cass0 > DAT
8/21/1993	Salt Lake City	3.65	3.76		
8/24/1993	Vancouver	2.88	4.50		SBD > Cass0 > DAT
8/25/1993	Seattle	2.71	2.90		
8/26/1993	Portland	3.15	3.00		
8/28/1993	Berkley	3.97	3.45		
Holiday Run, 1993					
12/28/1993	Washington	3.53	3.00		
12/29/1993	New Haven	3.45	2.50		
12/30/1993	Portland	4.58	4.50		SBD > DAT > Cass0 > DAT
12/31/1993	Worcester	4.45	3.50		Pre-FM Matrix > DAT; FM Broadcast

"The Agents of Good Nature"

Kenneth Williford, Orlando, FL

What of the connection between Phish and *organic* evolution? You know, Darwinian stuff—natural selection, etc. It is *this* connection that has made Phish my favorite band. It is *this* connection that sends me shivering with fright, weeping with joy, and floating in brain-space, leaving body behind.

The Vibration of Life

About three billion years ago, there was a "primordial soup" floating around in a salty sea under methane skies. The soup was full of organic chemicals, becoming increasingly complex as the millennia wore on, until one day (or night) something replicated itself. A bulbous blob broke in two, pulled apart like bubbly gum and split again. The primordial soup began to stir itself, so to speak.

What did all this sound like? I imagine a deep, soft, liquid rumble-ooze—approximately seven hertz (cycles/second) with probing tones that sprout gently from the background, reach out into the surrounding medium, and then recede again.

Applied Vibe

Upon further examination (and with a little patient acceptance) we find that nearly everything natural operates under similar conditions. At one scale or another the vibration of life is evident. Of course, it helps to be able to think not only in seconds, minutes, and hours, but in geologic, and even "universal" time scales (by the latter I mean the coalescence of galaxies, cosmic expansion and contraction). Imagine yourself a detached observer, and fast-forward the events on earth's surface (proliferations to extinctions of species, mountain building and erosion) from the origin of life, to the present, to the distant future…

Evolution by Natural Selection (quite loosely):

Life fills every available niche as "archaic" RNA rings and later the double helix (and later…) replicate furiously, competing for scarce resources. Branches "sprout gently" from the background, trying different mechanisms: reaching out in success, receding in failure, sometimes blossoming intensely in a wide-open burst of accomplishment that dissipates in magnesium sparkles. which brings me at long last to…

The Jam

Tweezer. Mike's Song (>jam 12/31/95!!!). *YEM. Reba*…

The above process seems to be operating through the members of Phish whenever they turn away from the conscious note-playing of a *Bouncing* to the utter hosary of (insert your favorite example here). When our favorite red-head turns his heavy-lidded eyes to the heavens and you can almost see the music coming in from above—*this is the applied vibe*. The band members link up and begin to explore uncharted territory. Phrases sprout gently (from the silence/static/rumble) and either recede, expand-recede, or burst forth in ecstatic accomplishment, often dissipating in tonal sparkles. It is a fractalline exploration, a multidimensional dendrite. Seemingly reflexive movements on the part of the four animals on stage (subconscious reactions to evolving stimuli?) are transformed by the tools at their finger- (or toe-) tips and assault the dead air, causing it to jump to life in meaningful patterns.

This is what the Vibration of Life has become. It has refined Itself from a resonant ooze-pulse to a sharp and glimmering explosion of meaning. This is my magic, and the members of Phish, in my humble opinion, are the closest things to magicians that exist today. They can harness the Vibration and expose it on demand. They can rip open the fabric of perception and show us what lies beneath the surface. The otherworldly jams are *always* there—right now, right now, and right now—Phish plugs into them and sprays them onto us in a meaningful way. This is why we attend their performances. This is why we record their performances.

They are the agents of good nature.

Save your complaints, and silence your whimpers, fans. Listen harder—as hard as you can. Look for what Phish shows you in the world at large, because it is there every day, everywhere.

Date	Location	Scarcity	GHI	Comments	Medium
Spring / Summer, 1994					
4/4/1994	Burlington	4.39	2.75		DSBD
4/5/1994	Montreal	2.71	2.50		
4/6/1994	Toronto	2.68			
4/8/1994	Penn State	3.14			SBD > Cass? > DAT (Set I)
4/9/1994	Binghamton	4.04	3.49		SBD > Cass0 > DAT
4/10/1994	Buffalo	3.32	4.00		
4/11/1994	Durham	2.75			
4/13/1994	Beacon	3.69	2.90		
4/14/1994	Beacon	3.69	2.63		

Date	Location	Scarcity	GHI	Comments	Medium
Spring/Summer, 1994 *(continued)*					
4/15/1994	Beacon	4.20	3.34		
4/16/1994	Amherst	3.70	2.00		
4/17/1994	Fairfax	3.21	3.00		SBD > ? > DAT
4/18/1994	Newark	3.36	2.00		
4/20/1994	Lexington	3.71	2.50		
4/21/1994	Winston-Salem	3.81	3.75		
4/22/1994	Columbia	3.29	3.00		
4/23/1994	Atlanta	4.20	3.75		SBD > ? > DAT
4/24/1994	Charlotte	3.57	3.00		SBD > Cass? > DAT (Set I)
4/25/1994	Knoxville	2.87	3.00		
4/26/1994	"Purple Dragon, Atlanta"	3.00	2.00		
4/28/1994	West Palm Beach	2.70	3.50		
4/29/1994	Clearwater	3.13	3.58		
4/30/1994	Orlando	3.14			SBD > Cass0 > DAT (Set II)
5/2/1994	Birmingham	2.93	4.00		SBD > ? > DAT (Set II)
5/3/1994	Antioch	3.36	3.50		
5/4/1994	New Orleans	3.93	3.30		
5/6/1994	Houston	2.64			
5/7/1994	Bomb Factory	4.91	4.31		SBD > DAT > Cass0 > DAT
5/8/1994	Austin	3.07			
5/10/1994	Santa Fe	2.93			
5/12/1994	Tucson	2.64			
5/13/1994	Tempe	3.29	3.50		
5/14/1994	San Diego	3.21	3.00		SBD > Cass? > DAT (Set II)
5/16/1994	Los Angeles	3.14			
5/17/1994	Santa Barbara	3.07			
5/19/1994	Eugene	3.53	2.50		
5/20/1994	Olympia	3.00			
5/21/1994	Seattle	3.00			
5/22/1994	Vancouver	3.13			SBD > Cass0 > DAT
5/23/1994	Portland	2.93	2.00		
5/25/1994	Warfield	3.56	3.00		
5/26/1994	Warfield	3.75	3.50		
5/27/1994	Warfield	4.41	3.50	Soundboard copies in circulation lack the acoustic songs	SBD > ? > DAT
5/28/1994	Laguna Seca	3.33	3.00	Soundboard copies in circulation lack the last three songs	DSBD
5/29/1994	Laguna Seca	3.27	3.00	Soundboard copies in circulation lack the last two songs	SBD > ? > DAT
6/9/1994	Salt Lake City	3.29			
6/10/1994	Red Rocks	4.30			
6/11/1994	Red Rocks	4.43	4.16		FM Rebroadcast
6/13/1994	Kansas City	3.29			
6/14/1994	Des Moines	3.29	3.00		SBD > Cass? > DAT
6/16/1994	Minneapolis	3.67	3.38	Soundboard copies in circulation lack Ginseng and Amazing Grace	DSBD
6/17/1994	Milwaukee	4.33	3.50		SBD > Cass0 > DAT
6/18/1994	Chicago	4.41	4.21	Some soundboard copies have cuts in Tweezer	SBD > Cass1 > DAT
6/19/1994	Kalamazoo	3.50	2.00		
6/21/1994	Cincinnati	3.20	3.25		

Date	Location	Scarcity	GHI	Comments	Medium
6/22/1994	Columbus	4.67	4.43		DSBD > Cass0 > DAT
6/23/1994	Pontiac	3.13	3.00		SBD > Cass0 > DAT
6/24/1994	Murat	3.93	4.00		
6/25/1994	Cleveland	3.29	2.50		
6/26/1994	Charleston	4.47	4.15		SBD > Cass? > DAT
6/29/1994	Raleigh	3.47	2.75		
6/30/1994	Richmond	4.00	3.35		
7/1/1994	Philadelphia	3.43	2.06		
7/2/1994	Holmdel	3.79	4.00		
7/3/1994	Old Orchard Beach	3.57	2.10		
7/5/1994	Ottawa	3.07	2.83		
7/6/1994	Montreal	3.20	3.00		
7/8/1994	Great Woods	4.57	4.25		
7/9/1994	Great Woods	4.37	3.50		
7/10/1994	SPAC	4.00	2.20		
7/13/1994	Big Birch	4.53	4.09		DSBD
7/14/1994	FLPAC	3.60	3.00		
7/15/1994	Jones Beach	3.87	3.25		
7/16/1994	Sugarbush	4.63	4.14		
Fall, 1994					
10/7/1994	Bethlehem	3.29	2.50		
10/8/1994	Fairfax	4.14	3.13		
10/9/1994	Pittsburgh	3.14	2.25		
10/10/1994	Louisville	3.00	2.75		
10/12/1994	Memphis	2.93	2.54		
10/13/1994	Oxford	2.50	2.87		
10/14/1994	New Orleans	3.64	3.30		SBD > Cass1 > DAT (Set I)
10/15/1994	Pelham	3.75	3.50		SBD > Cass1 > DAT (Set II)
10/16/1994	Chattanooga	3.46	3.00		
10/18/1994	Nashville	3.75	3.00		SBD > Cass0 > DAT
10/20/1994	St. Petersburg	3.29	4.00		
10/21/1994	Sunrise	3.29	3.33		
10/22/1994	Orlando	3.21	2.00		
10/23/1994	Gainesville	3.61	3.21		
10/25/1994	Atlanta	3.86	3.50		
10/26/1994	Boone	3.29	2.50		
10/27/1994	Charlottesville	3.71	3.50		
10/28/1994	Charleston	3.43	3.50		
10/29/1994	Spartanburg	4.35	4.25		SBD > Cass0 > DAT (Set I)
10/31/1994	Glens Falls	5.00	4.68		
11/2/1994	Bangor	3.82	3.33		SBD > Cass0 > DAT (Set II)
11/3/1994	Amherst	3.93	2.50		
11/4/1994	Syracuse	4.21	2.94		SBD > Cass1 > DAT
11/12/1994	Kent	3.82	4.05		SBD > Cass0 > DAT (partial)
11/13/1994	Erie	3.21	2.67		DSBD
11/14/1994	Grand Rapids	3.54	3.00		
11/16/1994	Ann Arbor	3.86	3.50		
11/17/1994	Dayton	4.14	3.17		
11/18/1994	East Lansing	3.39	2.07		
11/19/1994	Bloomington	3.73	2.47		

Date	Location	Scarcity	GHI	Comments	Medium
Fall, 1994 *(continued)*					
11/19/1994	Bloomington (lot)	3.04	2.00		
11/20/1994	Madison	3.64	3.00		
11/22/1994	Columbia	3.71	4.04		
11/23/1994	St. Louis	3.50	4.00		
11/25/1994	Chicago	4.11	3.37		
11/26/1994	Minneapolis	3.88	3.00		
11/28/1994	Bozeman	3.68	4.25		
11/30/1994	Olympia	4.14	4.39		
12/1/1994	Salem	4.00	4.55		
12/2/1994	Davis	3.71	3.00		SBD > Cass0 > DAT (partial)
12/3/1994	San Jose	3.73	3.00	Soundboard copies in circulation lack the encore	DSBD > Cass0 > DAT
12/4/1994	Chico	3.14	2.00		
12/6/1994	Santa Barbara	3.21	2.50		
12/7/1994	San Diego	3.71	3.00		
12/8/1994	San Diego	4.07	3.50	Soundboard copies in circulation lack Makisupa	DSBD
12/9/1994	Mesa	2.94	2.59		
12/10/1994	Santa Monica	3.21	3.00		
Holiday Run, 1994					
12/28/1994	Philadelphia	4.16	3.75		SBD > ? > DAT (Set II)
12/29/1994	Providence	4.44	4.13		
12/30/1994	MSG	4.72	3.39	Full soundboard copies of set I also circulate	Matrix > Cass0 > DAT
12/30/1994	Letterman	2.71	2.73		Television Broadcast
12/31/1994	Boston	4.69	2.93		

"I Don't Get It—
What's So Good About These Guys?"

Casey Logan, Omaha, NE

The question might as well be a kick to the crotch. It's one Phish fans dread hearing from their non-Phish fan friends (the unfortunates, that is). It usually comes up in the car—the Phish fan is driving, something comparable to musical bliss is playing on the tape deck (say, the 12/9/95 *You Enjoy Myself*), and the passenger has had enough. He or she asks the dreaded question.

"So, I don't get it. What's so good about these guys?"

Meanwhile the Phish fan has broken out into a fierce sweat and driving a Toyota Corolla has become as challenging as manning a monster truck through a sea of gelatin. Whether the question has caused this reaction, or simply the intense re-entry from the silent jam pouring from the sweet-sounding factory speakers, remains to be seen.

Okay, cut out of third person (it was, after all, for literary effect): the Phish fan is me. I have no clue if fellow Phish fans have had similar experiences trying to explain the majesty of their favorite band, or even if others allow non-fans into their lives. As for me, the painful experience of this question seeps through a crack in the earth and smacks me in the face at my most vulnerable of moments.

The first time I was forced to verbally explain why Phish is so good was at a bar in Lawrence, KS. I was visiting my former girlfriend and some friends. At this time I was still dating her; we had a very good relationship (still do), and pretty much knew each other like we knew ourselves. Which is precisely why it hurt so much when she questioned the band I love.

"I don't get it," she said. "They just don't seem that good to me—I mean, listen."

Even I will admit that at that exact millisecond in time, she had the slightest, tiniest, inkling of a point. You see, a joke me and some friends play when we find a bar which actually has *A Live One* on the jukebox is to play the thirty-minute *Tweezer*. It's childish and stupid, but the looks it gets from some people are priceless. So we were about twenty minutes into the quite experimental *Tweezer* when the question arose. That fact dulled the hurt a little. Now had the question arisen around the 3:43 mark of *Harry Hood* on the same CD, my heart would have been broken. Check that. Obliterated.

Date	Location	Scarcity	GHI	Comments	Medium
Summer, 1995					
5/14/1995	Burlington	n/a	n/a		
5/16/1995	Lowell	4.31	3.45		
6/7/1995	Boise	3.22	2.67		
6/8/1995	Salt Lake City	3.00	3.00		
6/9/1995	Red Rocks	4.08	2.67		
6/10/1995	Red Rocks	4.14	3.42		
6/13/1995	Mayland Heights	3.06	2.81		
6/14/1995	Memphis	3.83	3.00		
6/15/1995	Atlanta	3.44	2.67		
6/16/1995	Walnut Creek	4.39	4.00		
6/17/1995	Nissan	3.97	3.10		
6/19/1995	Deer Creek	4.08	2.67		
6/20/1995	Cuyahoga Falls	3.83	2.92		
6/22/1995	FLPAC	3.75	3.63		
6/23/1995	Waterloo	4.39	3.00		SBD > ? > DAT
6/24/1995	Philadelphia	3.75	3.25		
6/25/1995	Philadelphia	3.81	2.96		
6/26/1995	Saratoga Springs	4.11	3.67		
6/28/1995	Jones Beach	4.00	3.33		
6/29/1995	Jones Beach	4.00	3.13		
6/30/1995	Great Woods	4.39	2.90		
7/1/1995	Great Woods	4.61	2.75		FM Broadcast
7/2/1995	Sugarbush	4.50	3.81		SBD > ? > DAT

"I Dont't Get It" (continued)

"Well, I mean…its just that, you gotta…." My mind was blank. Here I was, perfectly sober, staring my loved one in the face and I couldn't put into words exactly what it is that makes me get in a car and drive hundreds of miles to see a band, no matter how important a test I have the next day. I couldn't even mumble a few compounded syllables which might explain the inane fact that if I swallowed poison and could buy an antidote for $25, yet Phish tickets went on sale that day, I'd take my chances with the ole immune system God gave me and head for the box office.

But I couldn't. She asks me what seems like a simple question and I turn out to be the vocal equivalent of a garden hoe.

The second time I was asked the question was a little bit scary. I was driving back to school with a couple of friends. We were listening to the 7/23/97 *You Enjoy Myself*, a fabulous ditty in which the band breaks free from the standard funk jam to entertain us with a little Hebrew-style playing. So choice, so very choice. My shotgun companion didn't exactly concur. Almost mimicking the wrenching query that had given me a painful mind-wedgy back in Lawrence, she reached into her purse of questions and threw the inquisitive sand in my eyes.

"I don't understand what's so good about these guys." Oh the agony. Wait, what—is that the vocal jam now arising and morphing with the Hebrew jam? And she's asking me what? "It all sounds the same."

To this day I'm still proud of myself for not undoing her seatbelt and racing for the nearest concrete wall. All sounds the same? I tried my best to explain to her that if Phish is one thing, it is eclectic.

Few bands around encompass such a variety of style as the boys from Vermont—from blues to jazz to Latin to funk to bluegrass, to barbershop for crissakes.

But my mini-sermon on Phish's musical diversity was without merit. And when I really thought about it, I couldn't blame her for her stance. I will always readily admit that Phish is not for everyone. However, what I try so desperately to do each time that poke-in-the-eye question rears its ugly, lazy-eyed face is describe what it is that makes me love the music so much. But my mouth usually turns to mush and I end up just pointing to the stereo, mouth agape, pleading the questioner to listen, just listen. And perhaps that is the closest I can come to describing it: demonstrating my inability to describe it verbally. Because as hokey as it sounds, there is a feeling I get from the music that transcends my speaking capacity.

On a day where I feel particularly eager to bridge the gap between myself and a non-Phish fan friend, I will attempt at describing this personal phenomenon; I will let them see a part of me that I usually keep hidden (that's figurative of course, not literal).

But I admit, on most days I will be less ambitious. And so I'll simply bridge the gap the best way I know how. By no means is it ideal, but in the closest way possible, it allows us both to simultaneously enjoy the music of my favorite band.

I'll fast-forward to *Bouncin'*.

Date	Location	Scarcity	GHI	Comments	Medium
Summer, 1995 (continued)					
7/3/1995	Sugarbush	4.39	3.40		
7/13/1995	Letterman	2.63	2.50		Television Broadcast
Fall, 1995					
9/27/1995	Sacramento	3.22	1.50		SBD > ? > DAT
9/28/1995	San Diego	2.78	1.00		
9/29/1995	Los Angeles	3.14	1.50		
9/30/1995	Shoreline	3.92	3.00		SBD > ? > DAT
10/2/1995	Seattle	3.06	1.63		
10/3/1995	Seattle	3.06	1.75		
10/5/1995	Portland	3.00	2.00		
10/6/1995	Vancouver	2.78	3.00		
10/7/1995	Spokane	3.44	3.17		SBD > ? > DAT
10/8/1995	Missoula	3.06	1.86		
10/11/1995	Tempe	3.14	2.50		
10/13/1995	Fort Worth	3.11	2.00		
10/14/1995	Austin	4.00	2.50		
10/15/1995	Austin	3.78	2.75		
10/17/1995	New Orleans	3.72	2.75		
10/19/1995	Kansas City	3.28	1.95		
10/20/1995	Cedar Rapids	3.05	1.44		
10/21/1995	Lincoln	3.94	2.86		
10/22/1995	Champaign	3.89	3.60		
10/24/1995	Madison	3.69	3.80		
10/25/1995	St. Paul	3.24	2.87		
10/27/1995	Kalamazoo	3.44	2.33		
10/28/1995	Auburn Hills	3.61	3.00		
10/29/1995	Louisville	3.61	3.25		
10/31/1995	Chicago	4.84	4.38		
11/9/1995	Atlanta	4.03	4.04		
11/10/1995	Atlanta	4.03	2.95		
11/11/1995	Atlanta	4.08	3.71		
11/12/1995	Gainesville	3.26	2.24		
11/14/1995	Orlando	3.76	4.20		
11/15/1995	Tampa	3.11	2.95		
11/16/1995	West Palm Beach	3.74	2.33		
11/18/1995	Charleston	3.33	3.35		
11/19/1995	Charlotte	3.31	3.25		
11/21/1995	Winston-Salem	3.89	3.33		
11/22/1995	Landover	3.81	3.87		
11/24/1995	Pittsburgh	3.63	2.50		
11/25/1995	Hampton	4.17	3.50		
11/28/1995	Knoxville	3.14	2.85		
11/29/1995	Nashville	3.69	3.75		
11/30/1995	Dayton	3.72	3.87		
12/1/1995	Hershey	3.97	4.16		
12/2/1995	New Haven	3.84	3.21		
12/4/1995	Amherst	3.74	2.65		
12/5/1995	Amherst	3.89	3.00		
12/7/1995	Niagra Falls	3.83	4.50		

Date	Location	Scarcity	GHI	Comments	Medium
12/8/1995	Cleveland	3.72	3.23		
12/9/1995	Albany	4.53	4.01		
12/11/1995	Portland	4.28	3.57		
12/12/1995	Providence	3.78	4.33		
12/14/1995	Binghampton	4.31	4.66		
12/15/1995	Philadelphia	4.11	3.61		
12/16/1995	Lake Placid	3.81	3.00		
12/17/1995	Lake Placid	4.03	3.50		
Holiday Run, 1995					
12/28/1995	Worcester	4.03	2.86		SBD > ? > DAT
12/29/1995	Worcester	4.58	4.32		
12/30/1995	MSG	4.50	3.12		
12/31/1995	MSG	5.00	4.88		
Spring, 1996					
4/26/1996	Jazzfest	3.98	2.34		
6/6/1996	Third Ball	3.85	2.61		DSBD
Summer, 1996 European Tour					
7/3/1996	Trento	2.19	2.50		
7/5/1996	Rome	2.39	1.00		
7/6/1996	Pictoia	2.36	1.00		
7/7/1996	Milan	2.50	1.00		
7/9/1996	France	2.61	2.17		
7/10/1996	Paris	2.73	1.50		
7/11/1996	London	3.05	1.00	Soundboard copies in circulation include bad cuts and dropouts	DSBD
7/12/1996	Amsterdam	4.00	2.17		
7/13/1996	Dour	2.25	1.05		
7/15/1996	Sesto Calende	2.44	1.00		
7/17/1996	Vienne	2.47	1.00		
7/18/1996	Nice	2.25	1.00		
7/19/1996	Arles	2.19	1.00		
7/21/1996	Nuremberg	2.84	2.00		
7/22/1996	Cologne	2.65	3.08		
7/23/1996	Hamburg	2.93	2.50		
7/24/1996	Hannover	2.36	1.62		
7/25/1996	Hamburg	2.73	1.93		
Summer, 1996 U.S. Tour					
8/2/1996	Park City	3.05	1.50		
8/4/1996	Red Rocks	4.43	2.17		
8/5/1996	Red Rocks	4.33	3.20		
8/6/1996	Red Rocks	4.53	2.90		
8/7/1996	Red Rocks	4.38	2.63		
8/10/1996	Alpine Valley	3.95	2.40		
8/12/1996	Deer Creek	4.21	3.25		
8/13/1996	Deer Creek	4.38	3.92		
8/14/1996	Hershey	3.83	3.40		
8/16/1996	The Clifford Ball	4.90	4.05		DSBD
8/17/1996	The Flatbed Jam	2.24	2.63		
8/17/1996	The Clifford Ball	4.90	3.78		DSBD; Pro-Shot Video

Date	Location	Scarcity	GHI	Comments	Medium
Fall, 1996 Tour					
10/16/1996	Lake Placid	3.21	1.67		
10/17/1996	Penn State	3.42	1.25		
10/18/1996	Pittsburgh	3.58	3.25		
10/19/1996	Buffalo	3.53	2.75		
10/21/1996	MSG	4.18	2.00		
10/22/1996	MSG	4.38	2.93		
10/23/1996	Hartford	4.11	2.60		
10/25/1996	Hampton	4.20	3.58		
10/26/1996	Charlotte	3.71	3.14		
10/27/1996	Charleston	3.58	2.94		
10/29/1996	Tallahasse	3.63	3.42		
10/31/1996	Atlanta	5.00	4.72		Pro-Shot Video
11/2/1996	West Palm Beach	4.73	4.15		Partial FM
11/3/1996	Gainesville	3.45	2.88		
11/6/1996	Knoxville	3.50	2.65		
11/7/1996	Lexington	4.05	3.79		
11/8/1996	Champaign	3.84	3.25		
11/9/1996	Auburn Hills	3.79	2.40		
11/11/1996	Grand Rapids	3.42	2.00		
11/13/1996	Minneapolis	3.68	2.50		
11/14/1996	Ames	3.23	2.00		
11/15/1996	St. Louis	4.12	3.58		
11/16/1996	Omaha	3.53	3.50		
11/18/1996	Memphis	3.48	2.25		
11/19/1996	Kansas City	3.34	2.50		
11/22/1996	Spokane	3.18	4.50		
11/23/1996	Vancouver	3.55	2.75		
11/24/1996	Portland	3.45	3.50		
11/27/1996	Seattle	3.92	3.58		
11/29/1996	Cow Palace	3.55	2.33		
11/30/1996	Sacramento	3.97	3.69		
12/1/1996	Los Angeles	3.83	3.75		
12/2/1996	Phoenix	3.20	2.85		
12/4/1996	San Diego	3.53	2.50		
12/6/1996	Las Vegas	4.64	4.62		
Holiday Run, 1996					
12/28/1996	Philadelphia	4.15	3.31		
12/29/1996	Philadelphia	4.40	3.31		
12/30/1996	Boston	4.43	2.77		
12/31/1996	Boston	4.83	3.46		FM Broadcast
Winter, 1997 European Tour					
2/13/1997	London	3.62	2.50		
2/14/1997	Brussels	3.22	2.00		
2/16/1997	Cologne	3.97	2.71		Television and FM Broadcast
2/17/1997	Amsterdam	4.36	4.05		
2/18/1997	Paris	3.56	2.00		
2/20/1997	Milan	3.31	1.50		
2/21/1997	Florence	3.38	3.25		

"Bye Bye Foot"
Clay, Myerstown, PA

Where I end and you begin.
I want to know where that line is
so that I can cross it
back and forth
until it disappears from the erosion of our
footsteps

Phish is a band that relies on bridging the gap between minds, a group that proves individuals can move as one unit. The music swirls and unifies, only to fracture apart…and congregates again. It seems somewhat profound that the scene, *our* scene, reflects most of the traits that the band itself embodies. Many of our lives are intimately connected through the noodlings of four extraordinary musicians, connected in endless chains of invisible coincidence and inconceivable fate. I have seen more magic thanks to this band than anywhere else in my life. I truly believe that Phish somehow encourages *connectiveness*.

Every one of us has been touched by the taping phenomenon, whether you're a selective trader or an indiscriminate junkie. At the root of our passion lies music, and to be without shows is to be without soulfood. The Tapers Section and the world of DAT trickle down the sounds of every mystical concert. Many friends are made by tape circulation, as Heads seem to stick together on college grounds or cross-country. We mail packages to waiting hands never shaken, to faces never seen. Ripples quickly expand into huge circles. Connectiveness happens.

Beyond the simple enjoyment of the music there are so many examples of this sort of sharing…it would take pages to list them all. Connectiveness is being in a far away city and being able to find a room with total strangers. Connectiveness is a spontaneous cheer. Connectiveness is asking someone for a ride, and becoming best friends between shows. Connectiveness is sharing food with a brother or sister who hasn't eaten all day. Connectiveness is Phish.Net. Connectiveness is dancing alone to *Reba* in a darkened room, and suddenly realizing that wherever your friends are, whenever they hear this music, that they are sharing the experience with you, and you reach out your arms and realize you're touching their souls. You are part of each other forever. Connectiveness is completing a song that was started a year ago. Connectiveness is the lunatic grin we all wear during the beginning of *YEM*. Connectiveness is a Big Ball Jam, connectiveness is *Kung*. Connectiveness is language signals. Connectiveness is thousands of voices paying homage to the night sky. Connectiveness is seeing a loved one's face during connectiveness. Connectiveness is seeing a Phish sticker on the highway and knowing that person is like you. Connectiveness is a miracle ticket. Connectiveness is falling backwards over a cooler at 3 AM before the Clifford Ball, and discovering the cooler belongs to some of your best friends in the world. Connectiveness is the Great Went Glowstick Jam.

One final example of connectiveness: Just before the beginning of New Year's Eve '97, I was standing in front of Madison Square Garden giving out Uno cards to whoever wanted to play. A guy came up and watched me for a minute or two before approaching. When I asked him if he wanted a card, he sort of just looked at me in disbelief. "You're the same as me, man," he said. "We're on the same path, I can tell just by seeing you stand here giving out these cards, you're just like me. I can't believe it." I didn't know what to say for a moment. Looking at him, at the truth in his eyes, I knew he was right. I can't really explain it, but somehow, across the colossal void that is the space between minds, this kid had bridged our realities for one moment. He had seen past the shells of our bodies and into my heart. For lack of a better response, I just walked over and hugged the guy. "You're right, you're right. I wish I would have met you before, I know we'd have been friends." He shook his head excitedly, and simply said, "Don't worry about it, we already are."

A month later I discovered Adam goes to my college, and lives less than three miles from my house. Before New Year's Eve, I'd never seen him before in my life.

They are Phish. You are Phish. We are Phish together.

Date	Location	Scarcity	GHI	Comments	Medium
2/22/1997	Rome	3.21	2.83		
2/23/1997	Cortemaggiore	3.92	3.92		
2/25/1997	Munich	3.21	2.13		
2/26/1997	Stuttgart	4.50	3.76		
2/26/1997	Badeu-Badeu	2.15	1.20		
2/28/1997	Berlin	3.03	2.38		
3/1/1997	Hamburg	4.50	3.99	"A multitrack soundboard copy also circulates, albeit with many cuts"	FM Broadcast
3/2/1997	Copenhagen	3.72	2.40		

Date	Location	Scarcity	GHI	Comments	Medium
Spring, 1997 Miscellaneous U.S.					
3/5/1997	Letterman	2.94	1.60		Television Broadcast
3/18/1997	Burlington	4.00	2.42		FM Broadcast
Summer, 1997 European Tour					
6/6/1997	Bradstock	3.18	2.70		
6/13/1997	Dublin	3.35	3.33		
6/14/1997	Dublin	3.29	3.00		
6/16/1997	London	3.32	2.00		
6/19/1997	Vienna	3.38	3.00		
6/20/1997	Prague	3.88	3.79		
6/21/1997	Scheesal	2.68	2.50		
6/22/1997	Loreley	2.97	3.35		Television Broadcast; DSBD
6/24/1997	Strasbourg	3.00	2.50		
6/25/1997	Lille	4.12	4.00		
6/27/1997	Somerset	2.59	2.50		
6/29/1997	Roskilde	2.72	3.00		
7/1/1997	Amsterdam	4.36	3.97		
7/2/1997	Amsterdam	4.42	4.57		
7/3/1997	Nuremberg	3.06	2.83		
7/5/1997	Como	3.32	3.08		
7/6/1997	Desenzano Soundcheck	3.59	4.33		
7/6/1997	Desenzano	3.38	3.00		
7/9/1997	Lyon	4.18	4.32		
7/10/1997	Marseilles	3.50	3.50		
7/11/1997	Pyrenees	2.71	2.80		
Summer, 1997 U.S. Tour					
7/21/1997	Virginia Beach	4.42	3.26		
7/22/1997	Raleigh	4.14	3.90		
7/23/1997	Atlanta	4.19	3.15		
7/25/1997	Dallas	3.82	3.69		
7/26/1997	Austin	3.72	3.36		
7/29/1997	Phoenix	3.36	2.75		
7/30/1997	Ventura	4.03	3.85		
7/31/1997	Shoreline	4.34	4.22		
8/2/1997	Gorge	4.39	3.27		
8/3/1997	Gorge	4.39	2.56		
8/6/1997	Maryland Heights	3.67	3.67		
8/8/1997	Tinley Park	3.86	2.58		
8/9/1997	Alpine Valley	4.28	3.58		
8/10/1997	Deer Creek	4.42	4.08		
8/11/1997	Deer Creek	4.42	2.90		
8/13/1997	Star Lake	4.15	3.12		
8/14/1997	Darien Center	4.28	3.45		
8/16/1997	The Great Went	4.76	3.96		
8/17/1997	The Great Went	4.82	4.55		
Fall, 1997 Tour					
11/7/1997	Conan	2.81	1.91		Television Broadcast
11/13/1997	Las Vegas	3.95	2.87		
11/14/1997	West Valley	3.94	2.71		

Date	Location	Scarcity	GHI	Comments	Medium
11/16/1997	Denver	4.21	3.30		
11/17/1997	Denver	4.47	4.18		
11/19/1997	Champaign	4.18	4.29		
11/21/1997	Hampton	4.85	4.30		
11/22/1997	Hampton	4.85	4.85		
11/23/1997	Winston-Salem	4.34	4.45		
11/26/1997	Hartford	4.28	3.21		
11/28/1997	Worcester	4.58	3.79		
11/29/1997	Worcester	4.63	4.29		
11/30/1997	Worcester	4.58	3.80		
12/2/1997	Philadelphia	4.31	3.79		
12/3/1997	Philadelphia	4.36	3.50		
12/5/1997	Cleveland	3.83	2.10		
12/6/1997	Auburn Hills	4.33	4.14		
12/7/1997	Dayton	4.68	4.39		
12/9/1997	State College	3.86	2.27		
12/11/1997	Rochester	4.22	4.04		
12/12/1997	Albany	4.50	2.85		
12/13/1997	Albany	4.56	3.60		
Holiday Run, 1997					
12/28/1997	Landover	3.94	2.85		
12/29/1997	MSG	4.47	3.89		
12/30/1997	MSG	4.74	4.12		
12/31/1997	MSG	4.71	3.19		
The Island Tour, 1998					
4/2/1998	Nassau	4.87	4.24		
4/3/1998	Nassau	4.91	4.63		
4/4/1998	Providence	4.91	3.93		
4/5/1998	Providence	4.91	3.68		
Summer, 1998 European Tour					
6/30/1998	Copenhagen	4.20	4.67		
7/1/1998	Copenhagen	3.95	4.00		
7/2/1998	Copenhagen	4.05	4.35		
7/3/1998	Fyn	1.95	2.10		
7/5/1998	Prague	3.80	3.33		SBD > Cass0 > DAT
7/6/1998	Prague	4.15	3.60		
7/8/1998	Barcelona	3.95	2.96	Soundboard copies that circulate are only complete through Guyute	Matrix > Cass0 > DAT
7/9/1998	Barcelona	4.00	3.88		
7/10/1998	Barcelona	3.60	3.50		
Summer, 1998 U.S. Tour					
7/15/1998	Portland	4.57	3.20		
7/16/1998	The Gorge	4.76	3.20		
7/17/1998	The Gorge	4.81	3.79		
7/19/1998	Shoreline	4.86	3.31		
7/20/1998	Ventura	4.76	3.29		
7/21/1998	Phoenix	4.57	3.08		
7/24/1998	Houston	4.43	2.60		
7/25/1998	Austin	4.57	2.44		

Date	Location	Scarcity	GHI	Comments	Medium
Summer, 1998 U.S. Tour *(continued)*					
7/26/1998	Dallas	4.52	2.25		
7/28/1998	Bonner Springs	4.71	3.57		
7/29/1998	Maryland Heights	4.62	3.57		
7/31/1998	Columbus	4.57	3.00		
8/1/1998	Alpine Valley	4.83	4.06		
8/2/1998	Deer Creek	4.91	2.67		
8/3/1998	Deer Creek	4.86	3.49		
8/6/1998	Lakewood	4.61	2.42		
8/7/1998	Walnut Creek	4.71	2.92		
8/8/1998	Merriweather	4.82	2.50		
8/9/1998	Virginia Beach	5.00	4.01		Matrix > ? > DAT (Encore only)
8/11/1998	Star Lake	4.71	3.70		
8/12/1998	Vernon Downs	4.73	3.69		
8/15/1998	Lemonwheel	4.91	4.00		
8/16/1998	Lemonwheel	4.91	3.81		
Fall, 1998 Miscellaneous U.S.					
10/3/1998	Farm Aid	4.05	3.81	Complete AUD tapes circulate; FM copies have cuts	FM Available; Television Broadcast

"Hot Dog in Hindsight: Jams Past, Present, and Future"

Travis Vande Berg, Chicago, Illinois

This morning I woke up a little earlier than usual, and instead of getting up or going back to sleep, I put on the first disc of the 12/31 midnight set (*Meatstick>Bathtub Gin*) and listened to the entire thing with my eyes closed. As I listened to the pre-recorded *Meatstick* that starts out the set, my mind wandered around the whole Big Cypress experience until it settled on the return of the Hot Dog from 12/31/94. Even with all the rumors flying weeks and months prior to the Big Cypress New Year's celebration, no one predicted the Hot Dog's triumphant return to Phish history. Gamehendge, *Harpua*, and *Destiny* predictions all bounced around rec.music.phish and among phans everywhere, but no mention was made of the Hot Dog. Of course, this makes sense. No one could have possibly expected the Hot Dog. It was definitely unthinkable which is why it was such an amazing, exciting thing to have witnessed that night.

However, as I listened to the pre-recorded *Meatstick*, it occurred to me that, in hindsight, nothing made more sense about New Years Eve 1999 than the reappearance of the Hot Dog.

While Phish had indeed played New Years Eve many times prior to 1994, 12/31/94 was really the first "big" New Years show the band played. Yes, there was the "Phishtank" in 1993, but in '94 the band made the ultimate physical connection with the phans by using the giant Hot Dog, not only as an elaborate prop for their mischief, but

also as a means by which to make the worst seats in the house the best seats, even if only for a song. From that moment on, the Hot Dog has had an important place in the history of the band.

The second half of 1994 and 1995 also marked a key time in the musical development of the band. It was in mid/late 1994 that Phish began to really push their jamming to its absolute limits as shown particularly well in many of the *Tweezers* from the era. This trend of "epic jamming" continued into 1995 with amazing results (see 10/31 *YEM*, 11/14 *Stash*, etc, etc). A listen through *A Live One* (which was recorded during this period) provides a good example of the band's sound at the time. I believe that New Years Eve 1994 served as an important landmark for Phish's sound by separating the pre-1995 era of the band really *learning* about each other musically and becoming truly comfortable with each other's playing from the era of expanded musical boundaries in 1995 where the band pushed the envelope of what they could do on stage. "Epic jamming" was the style of the time, and it reached its culmination a year later on New Years Eve 1995 with one of the greatest shows in Phish history.

Phish seemed to spend much of 1996 trying to figure out where to go next. They were comfortable with each other musically and seemed to have pushed the "epic jamming" of 1995 as far as it could go. The band seemed to find guidance in the form of their rendition

Date	Location	Scarcity	GHI	Comments	Medium
10/15/1998	Fillmore	4.09	2.33		
10/17/1998	Bridge	4.27	3.00		
10/18/1998	Bridge	4.27	3.21		
10/20/1998	Sessions	3.95	2.75		Television Broadcast (Partial); DSBD
10/27/1998	Letterman	2.86	1.30		Television Broadcast
Fall, 1998 U.S. Tour					
10/29/1998	Greek	4.48	3.38		
10/30/1998	Las Vegas	4.82	3.88		
10/31/1998	Las Vegas	4.95	4.55		FM Broadcast (partial)
11/2/1998	Salt Lake City	4.95	4.66		
11/3/1998	"KBCO, Boulder"	2.71	1.50		FM Broadcast
11/4/1998	Denver	4.55	2.25		
11/6/1998	Madison	4.55	3.00		
11/7/1998	Chicago	4.62	2.50		
11/8/1998	Chicago	4.67	2.50		
11/9/1998	Chicago	4.76	3.64		
11/11/1998	Grand Rapids	4.40	2.00		
11/13/1998	Cleveland	4.65	2.50		
11/14/1998	Cincinnatti	4.60	3.80		

"Hot Dog in Hindsight" *(continued)*

of the Talking Heads *Remain in Light* album on Halloween 1996. From this point on, Phish began a new musical undertaking—the "cow funk" characteristic of much of 1997 and 1998. A couple of trips through Europe and the recording of *Story of the Ghost* further solidified this new "cow funk jamming" style.

Much of 1999 seemed to be a period of "jam indecision" and musical experimentation for the band after having apparently reached the peak of their "cow funk jamming" with such songs as *Ghost* and *Wolfman's Brother*. Summer tour '99 was interesting and somewhat controversial from the point of view of many phans. Unfinished jams, new songs from Trey's solo tour, an increase in My Bloody Valentine-esque jamming, and the rise of a silly little song called *Meatstick* (complete with its own *Macarena*-inspired dance) all raised questions and concerns about the band as they seemed to be trying to establish a new musical/jamming direction. Fall tour relieved some phans' fears, and the December tour did a lot to raise hopes and expectations for the big New Years show in Florida.

On December 30, Trey confirmed that Phish would indeed be playing the entire eight or so hours from midnight to sunrise on the 31st/1st—an amazing feat of musicianship by any standards. Finally, it came—the big set—which brings me back to the Hot Dog.

I believe that the Hot Dog represents Phish's experimentation with different types of jamming from late-1994 through the end of 1999. It marked the beginning of the period of "epic jamming" and "cow funk jamming" and all of the transition periods before, during, and after each of these—all of which were illustrated beautifully in at least one song during that midnight set. The set itself served as a musical recap of the last six years of Phish, and the Hot Dog served

as a sort of physical representation of the same thing. Of course, even more conveniently, the Hot Dog also fits nicely with the band's musical and comical explorations of *Meatstick* in 1999.

In addition to this physical representation of Phish's musical development and the *Meatstick* tie-in, I think that the Hot Dog also brings this era of exploratory jamming (represented best by the "epic jamming" of 1995 and the "cow funk jamming" of 1997/98) full circle—providing closure. I believe that the era of exploratory jamming is over for the time being, and the band will become and continue to develop as, in Fish's words, "Phish 2000". What will this mean as far as the Phish's musical direction is concerned? Of course, it doesn't necessarily mean the end of the "epic jamming" or "cow funk jamming" of particular songs, but I do think that the band will find a new musical style—perhaps marking the beginning of a new jamming era.

In the few shows that I have seen or heard since Big Cypress, Phish seems to be experimenting with a tighter, more straight-ahead rock and roll sound. Whether this will continue or not remains to be seen. I do, however, think that the band will begin to place a greater emphasis on songwriting—on words more than jams—in the near future, especially with new material. (This already seems apparent to me on much of *Farmhouse*.) I would also not be surprised to hear Phish take a stab at writing longer more orchestral/composed pieces or to embark on an acoustic tour or two (something which, I believe, may have been mentioned by at least one band member). Regardless of what musical direction the band takes in the future, I think that the journey and its results will mark another exciting era in Phish history for both the band and the phans.

Date	Location	Scarcity	GHI	Comments	Medium
Fall, 1998 U.S. Tour *(continued)*					
11/15/1998	Murfreesboro	4.40	2.50		
11/18/1998	Greenville	4.35	3.13		
11/19/1998	Winston-Salem	4.55	3.00		
11/20/1998	Hampton	4.95	3.66		Official Release
11/21/1998	Hampton	5.00	3.55		Official Release
11/24/1998	New Haven	4.55	3.30		
11/25/1998	Albany	4.75	2.69		
11/27/1998	Worcester	4.86	4.25		
11/28/1998	Worcester	4.90	2.57		
11/29/1998	Worcester	4.95	3.65		
Holiday Run, 1998					
12/28/1998	MSG	4.73	3.12		
12/29/1998	MSG	4.82	3.38		
12/30/1998	MSG	4.86	2.87		
12/31/1998	MSG	4.95	4.20		
Summer, 1999					
6/24/1999	Westford	n/a	n/a		
6/30/1999	Bonner Springs	4.40	1.67		
7/1/1999	Antioch	4.65	3.14		
7/3/1999	Atlanta	4.95	3.09		
7/4/1999	Atlanta	4.95	3.44		
7/7/1999	Charlotte	4.75	2.50		
7/8/1999	Virginia Beach	4.75	2.75		
7/9/1999	Merriweather	4.79	3.33		
7/10/1999	Camden	4.74	2.70		
7/12/1999	Tweeter Center	4.79	2.77		
7/13/1999	Tweeter Center	4.84	3.48		
7/15/1999	Holmdel	4.80	3.00		
7/16/1999	Holmdel	4.80	3.07		
7/17/1999	Oswego	4.90	3.61		
7/18/1999	Oswego	4.90	4.32		
7/20/1999	Toronto	4.55	2.57		
7/21/1999	Star Lake	4.53	3.36		
7/23/1999	Columbus	4.68	2.50		
7/24/1999	Alpine Valley	4.95	2.67		
7/25/1999	Deer Creek	4.95	4.38		
7/26/1999	Deer Creek	4.80	3.19		
7/30/1999	Japan (Early)	3.32	1.93		
7/30/1999	Japan (Late)	3.68	2.38		SBD > Cass1 > DAT (partial)
7/31/1999	Japan	3.95	3.25		Satellite > VHS > Cass0 > DAT
8/1/1999	Japan	4.18	3.93		Satellite > VHS > Cass0 > DAT
Fall, 1999					
9/9/1999	Vancouver	4.55	2.75		
9/10/1999	Gorge	4.74	2.95		
9/11/1999	Gorge	4.79	3.43		
9/12/1999	Portland	4.53	3.71		
9/14/1999	Boise	4.85	4.04		

Date	Location	Scarcity	GHI	Comments	Medium
9/16/1999	Shoreline	4.70	3.81		
9/17/1999	Shoreline	5.00	4.38		
9/18/1999	Chula Vista	4.68	3.81		
9/19/1999	Irvine	4.47	2.50		
9/21/1999	Tucson	4.11	2.00		
9/22/1999	Las Crusces	4.53	3.70		
9/24/1999	Austin	4.47	3.00		
9/25/1999	Houston	4.45	3.17		
9/26/1999	New Orleans	4.65	3.77		
9/28/1999	Pelham	4.58	3.36		
9/29/1999	Memphis	4.85	4.25		
10/1/1999	Ames	4.25	2.08		
10/2/1999	Minneapolis	4.65	3.66		
10/3/1999	Chicago	4.70	2.00		
10/4/1999	Normal	4.50	2.80		
10/7/1999	Nassau	4.90	3.22		
10/8/1999	Nassau	4.84	3.81		
10/9/1999	Albany	4.89	3.22		
10/10/1999	Albany	4.89	3.57		
12/2/1999	Auburn Hills	4.68	3.38		
12/3/1999	Cincinnati	4.65	1.63		
12/4/1999	Cincinnati	4.75	2.75		
12/5/1999	Rochester	4.75	3.20		
12/7/1999	Portland	4.75	3.57		
12/8/1999	Portland	4.74	3.50		
12/10/1999	Philadelphia	4.90	3.42		
12/11/1999	Philadelphia	4.95	4.25		
12/12/1999	Hartford	4.60	3.50		
12/13/1999	Providence	4.74	3.29		
12/15/1999	"Washington, D.C."	4.63	2.33		
12/16/1999	Raleigh	4.79	2.94		
12/17/1999	Hampton	4.80	2.67		
12/18/1999	Hampton	4.90	4.12		
Holiday Run, 1999: Big Cypress					
12/30/1999	Big Cypress	4.91	4.20		
12/31/1999	Big Cypress	4.91	4.95		
Spring, 2000 Farmhouse Promos					
5/15/2000	"Y100, Philadelphia"				FM Broadcast
5/15/2000	"WXPN, Philadelphia"		1.00		FM Broadcast
5/17/2000	Letterman		1.50		Television Broadcast
5/18/2000	"KFOG, San Francisco"				FM Broadcast
5/19/2000	Key Club				FM Broadcast
5/19/2000	Key Club (Late)				FM Broadcast
5/21/2000	Radio City		3.03		
5/22/2000	Radio City		3.00		
5/23/2000	Roseland		4.17		Television Broadcast (Partial)
Summer, 2000 Japan Tour					
6/9/2000	Tokyo	2.00	2.50		Television Broadcast
6/10/2000	Tokyo	2.00	3.50		

Date	Location	Scarcity	GHI	Comments	Medium
Summer, 2000 Japan Tour *(continued)*					
6/11/2000	Tokyo	2.00	1.50		
6/13/2000	Nagoya	2.00	4.00		
6/14/2000	Fukuoka	2.00	3.93		
6/15/2000	Osaka	2.00	3.00		
6/16/2000	Osaka	2.00	4.40		
Summer, 2000 U.S. Tour					
6/22/2000	Antioch		4.50		
6/23/2000	Atlanta		3.00		
6/24/2000	Atlanta		5.00		
6/25/2000	Raleigh		2.00		
6/27/2000	Conan				Television Broadcast
6/28/2000	Holmdel		4.00		
6/29/2000	Holmdel		5.00		
6/30/2000	Hartford				
7/1/2000	Hartford		3.00		
7/3/2000	Camden		5.00		
7/4/2000	Camden		4.00		
7/6/2000	Toronto		3.00		
7/7/2000	Star Lake				
7/8/2000	Alpine		3.00		
7/10/2000	Deer Creek		1.25		
7/11/2000	Deer Creek		4.38		
7/12/2000	Deer Creek		2.75		
7/14/2000	Columbus		3.25		
7/15/2000	Columbus		3.50		
7/17/2000	Austin				Television Broadcast (Partial)
Fall, 2000					
9/8/2000	Albany				
9/9/2000	Albany				
9/11/2000	Tweeter Center				
9/12/2000	Tweeter Center				
9/14/2000	Darien				
9/15/2000	Hershey				
9/17/2000	Merriweather				
9/18/2000	Blossom				
9/20/2000	Cincinatti				
9/22/2000	Rosemont				
9/23/2000	Rosemont				
9/24/2000	Minneapolis				
9/25/2000	Bonner Springs				
9/27/2000	Englewood				
9/29/2000	Las Vegas				
9/30/2000	Las Vegas				
10/1/2000	Phoenix				
10/4/2000	Chula Vista				
10/5/2000	Irvine				
10/6/2000	Shoreline				
10/7/2000	Shoreline				

Part V

DICTIONARY

This section defines common Phish fan jargon including names, places, and events in Phish history as well as common slang, particularly terms and phrases used by the band on stage and in interviews. While serving as both a glossary of terms and answers to frequently asked questions, this is not meant to be a comprehensive list of all Phish-related verbiage. Many terms appear on too many pages to make this an index, but there are implicit and explicit pointers to other chapters for information about specific songs, shows, albums, etc.

Written by Ellis Godard, based on an initial draft by Craig DeLucia and with the assistance of hundreds of contributors either directly to this chapter or to the Phish.Net Frequently Asked Questions file. (See Online Resources chapter).

2001: A Space Odyssey   Arthur C. Clarke and Stanley Kubrick movie for which the theme song was the "Dawn" portion of Richard Strauss' "Also Sprach Zarathustra", which was named after Frederick Nietsche's *Thus Spoke Zarathustra* and reworked as funky disco in Emir Deodato's "Also Sprach Zarathustra", a key song for the Peter Sellar's movie *Being There*. Phish performs Deodato's version; see those Song Histories.

420   colloquially, refers to marijuana, either specifically as a call to imbibe or generally in celebration of the herb. Embues snickering significance on 4:20 a.m. or p.m., April 20th, State Route 420, and any other use of the number.

Despite legend, there is no police or criminal code 420 for having observed use or possession. (The closest is the Illinois Department of Revenue, which classifies the Cannabis and Controlled Substances Tax Act under Part 428.) Possible origin seems to be the Waldos, an early 1970s San Rafael (CA) High School student group who met at that time at a campus statue of Louis Pasteur, saluted each other at other times with, "420 Louis!", and spread the term from the Bay Area via Grateful Dead fans. Other purported explanations precede the Waldos, and range in the hundreds, from Bob Dylan's "Rainy Day Women #12 and 35" (12x35=420) and CSNY's "4+20" back to the nursery rhyme line "four and twenty black birds" back to the King James Bible on "the four and twenty elders" (in Revelation 5:14). To note, there are 315 known chemicals in marijuana, not 420; tea time is typically 5:30, not 4:20; and Jamaican workers are more likely to get home at 5:45 than at 4:20. Appropriately, however, Salmon Rushdie wrote (in *Midnight's Children*), "420 has been, since time immemorial, the number associated with fraud, deception, and trickery." The number's appearance in Indian history, and the popularity of Eastern religion in the 1960s, could account for its emergeance in the Bay Area.

Phish performed on April 20th in 1989, 1990, 1991, 1993, and 1994, and have started several shows at 4:20, including the first day of the Great Went (which is 420 miles from Boston, once home to Phish). The number also appears suspiciously in a number of other places, including releases (*Lawnboy* has 420 megabytes of information), lyrics (such as the "Vibration of Life's" seven beats per second, which makes 420 beats per minute), Ticketmaster service charges (summer 1997), Dry Goods orders (Fall 1997 limited edition Pollock

poster printed on 100% hemp), mail order ticket sections (NYE 1997), and the band's logo (which has 4 gills and 20 bubbles). An uproar during the 12/31/96 "2001" (audible on tapes) was in response to an enormous digital clock which was counting down to midnight and reached "4:20" (at 11:55:40 p.m.).

8 number of recurring insignificance among fans. At 7/16/94, someone near the stage handed out hundreds of green 3"x3" stickers with the number 8 printed on them. Years earlier, on Phish.Net, there was a bit of "phishlosophy" about the import of "2^3" espoused by Mark Goldberg, soon after nicknamed "Cubed".

8 Foot Florescent Tubes one of Trey's side projects, with only one show to date; see Side Shows chapter.

A capella singing without accompanying instrumentation. Phish performs a capella improvisations at the end of "You Enjoy Myself" (see also the vocal jam between YEM and "Woflman's" on 4/26/96), and a capella arrangements in the style of barbershop quartets including traditional selections such as "Carolina", "Memories", "Hello My Baby", and "Amazing Grace" (though 5/8/93 and 10/20/95 were not a capella), as well as original arrangements such as for "The Star-Spangled Banner" and even "Freebird". The band has taken barbershop quartet lessons, and Trey (in particular) has mentioned the complexities in interviews.

Aaron Wolfe see "Wolfe, Aaron" and "Errand Wolfe".

AB microphone placement in which they are parallel to each other, and spaced apart according to the distance from the sound source. Also known as "Spaced".

Abrahams, Dave a friend of Trey's since childhood. His mother, Geulah, is the subject of "Guelah Papyrus" and his father, Elihu, dances on the bed in "Sample in a Jar." He has contributed to such Phish songs as "Slave to the Traffic Light," "Runaway Jim," and "Glide." Dave is also the inspiration for his and Trey's "Dave's Energy Guide., and is the "looks too much like Dave" mentioned in "McGrupp and the Watchful Hosemasters".

AC/DC Bag the robot in Gamehendge who kills Mr. Palmer.

After Show name for the pass (an "after show pass", a sticker not a laminate) which allows access to a backstage area following the show. Depending on the venue and event, that area may or may not feature beer (sometimes for sale towards charity), music (such as the backstage performances at the Great Went), and/or the band (who more frequently remain in areas deeper backstage).

Aisle Monkeys fans who leave their seats and congregate in the aisles and halls to dance.

Alligator Alley nickname for the portion of I-75 that runs from east to west in Florida, and which hosted a 20-mile traffic jam en route to Big Cypress on 12/29/00.

Almanac see *Pharmer's Almanac, The*

ALO *A Live One*, a two-disc release from Phish. See discography.

American Recording Company Woodland Hills, CA, location where *Hoist* was recorded.

American Road seven-minute film which sets most of "You Enjoy Myself" (from *Junta*) to a series of clips from the 48 contiguous U.S. states. Director and producer Peter Shapiro (later owner of the Wetlands Preserve in New York) shot the footage during a 30-day trip

covering 13,254 miles and combining Phish tour with sightseeing. The final product premiered at the Sundance Music Festival and was televised on MSNBC's *Edgewise* (four times each on 7/12&13/97).

Amfibian Tom Marshall's band; see Sharing in the Groove section.

Amy's Farm Phish's first festival show (not counting the co-billed Arrowhead Ranch shows), held 8/3/91 at the farm of Amy Skelton (see "Skelton, Amy" entry.)

Anastasio, Trey lead guitarist, lyricist, and personality in Phish. See entry for guitar, and Biography chapter.

Animation Phish's music has been set to animation on at least four occasions: An early 1990s group of fans used early graphics software to compose a film for "Esther", which was shown during the setbreak of one show. The 12/31/98 New Year's Eve show featured four-way projections of an animated sequence leading up to midnight. "You Enjoy Myself" and "First Tube" were set to animation during summer 2000, in multimedia installations by www.bullseyeart.com.

Aquarium Stage setup decorations designed by Chris McGregor and used for the 12/28-31/93 NYE run, which outlined the stage as though it was an aquarium. Around the edge of the stage itself was a broken rim of glass walls, a bit higher in the corners. A similar rectangle hung above and outlined the top of the aquarium. Behind Mike and Trey, at center back of stage, was a large clam. Surrounding the drums and keys were large replicas of coral, aquarium plants, and gravel. Eight or so large colorful fish hung from the rafters, down into the "aquarium". At the close of the second set, the band changed into diving outfits as the vocal jam died down. Trey announced "We're going on one last adventure" and they left stage. During the break, the PA played not the water-related tunes (Take Me to the River, Red Rain, Here Comes the Flood, Black Water, The Flood) of earlier setbreaks, but new age noises and bubbling water. (See song history for "Faht".) To start the third set, the band, in wet suits, entered the aquarium from a platform above, "diving" in, exploring, and entering the clam, which by this point had opened. Once all were in, the clam shut, rose 10 or so feet into the air, opened, burped, counted down the last 10 seconds of the year, and shot lights and confetti into the air, at which time the band returned (sans wetsuits), entering from stage right.

Archer Studios location where *Lawn Boy* and *Crimes of the Mind* were recorded.

Archives shows radio broadcasts put together and DJ-ed by Phish archivist Kevin Shapiro (see Interview) for broadcast at festival shows, featuring highlights of past shows. There was once each at the Clifford Ball and Lemonwheel, and two each at the Great Went and Big Cypress. (See sidebars [WHERE IN BOOK?] for playlists.)

Arrowhead Ranch site of the first camping/festival shows at which Phish performed, 7/21&22/91.

Asbell, Paul Trey's college guitar teacher at UVM.

Asse Festival middle part of the Phish original "Guelah Papyrus", though once a separate song in its own right.

ASZ "Also Sprach Zarathustra", aka "2001". See *2001* entry, above.

Atonal see fugues

AUD Audience tape recording. See Taping Guide chapter.

Audience participation Phish fans have become part of the show in a number of ways, including (and see the entries for) clapping, wav-

ing, dancing, chanting, secret language, flyers, marshmallow and glowstick/glowring "wars", and humming; see entries for each.

Avenu Malkenu Hebrew prayer performed within "TMWSIY", a Phish original.

B&J see Ben and Jerry's.

B&P or **B and P** see Blanks and Postage

Back of the Worm see Wormtown.

Backdrops, Stage see Minkins.

Backstage see After Show, Betty Ford Clinic, and Laminate.

Bad Hat Trey side project, which toured twice in 1994 and helped birth Jazz Mandolin Project. See Side Shows entries.

Bad Lieutenant Trey's nickname from his 1999 solo tour. (See Side Shows chapter.) Refers to a movie title in which Harvey Keitel plays a self-destructive NYC policeman dealing with his family problems, religious beliefs, gambling and drug addiction, while tracking a pair of men who raped a nun on a Bronx church altar.

Badger, The Lemonwheel radio station, KAZXZA. See Archive Show Playlists. Named for host, and band archivist, Kevin Shapiro, aka "The Love Badger."

Bag-Vacuum also known as the "bag-vac", Fishman's simultaneous use of bagpipes and his vacuum (see that entry) on March 11, 17, 20, 21, 24, 28, and 30 and May 1, 1992.

Ball All the Time the slogan of the Clifford Ball radio station.

Ball Radio Clifford Ball radio station.

Balloons 79,627 of them dropped on 12/31/96, breaking a record held by the Democratic National Convention (est. 65,000). The balloons each had a design related to the event, with four designs total.

Bangor Tweezer, The the version of "Tweezer" performed on 11/28/94.

Barrett, Syd former member of Pink Floyd, and author of several songs Phish has covered, including "Baby Lemonade", "No Good Trying", "Bike" and "Love You" (a.k.a. "Terrapin" and "Honey Love"). Fishman has called Barrett rock's "greatest lyricist".

Baseball on several occasions, baseball players have been credited with songwriting, including Carl "Yaz" Yastrzemski, Boston Red Sox outfield who Mike credited on 4/18/92; and Pete Rose, who Trey credited in 1989 for, along with God, writing "Avenu Malkenu."

Bass From 1989 (when it was built) through mid-1997, Mike had used the "Dragon bass", a five-string built by Paul Languedoc with a mother-of-pearl inlay of an Asian dragon on the headstock. He started using a five-string graphite Modulus Quantum 5 on the February/March European tour in 1997, contributing heavily to the "pornofunk" sound.

Bathroom song a song which never changes from version to version, and thus during which a fan can feel safe running to the bathroom without worrying about missing anything. Although any potential bathroom song may also hold a place in any particular fan's heart, typical examples include "Squirming Coil", "Prince Caspian", and, for some, "Esther". Except for the end of "Coil", each is long enough to allow even for the bathroom lines which form during them, and typically without variation that fans would not want to miss.

BATR "Bouncing Around the Room", a Phish original.

BBFCFM "Big Black Furry Creature From Mars", a Phish original.

BBJ "Big Ball Jam", a Phish original. See also, that entry below.

Bearsville Outtakes unused leftovers from production of *Story of a Ghost*, of which some portions circulate in trading circles, and others were used for *The Siket Disc.*

Bearsville Studios Bearsville, NY, location where *Billy Breathes* and *Story of a Ghost* were recorded and where *A Live One* and *Slip Stitch and Pass* were engineered and mastered.

Beavis and Butthead see MTV.

Being There movie starring Peter Sellars. See listing for *2001.*

Ben and Jerry fellow Vermont residents who appeared onstage at the Clifford Ball to sing a verse of "Brother" and whose ice cream company created and distributes a flavor called "Phish Food" ice cream, also available in "Phish Stick" ice cream bars, from which proceeds benefit the cleanup of Lake Champlain. See Phish Food.

Benefits include 4/6/85 for Oxfam (Central American humanitarian aid via the Tools for Peace and Justice in Central America); 12/10/88 for NORML (the National Organization for the Reform of Marijuana Laws); 4/15/89 for VPIRG (Vermont Public Interest Research Group); 5/16/95 for Voters for Choice (who support candidates who support abortion rights); 7/2/95 in part for King Street (an after-school program in Burlington); 10/17-18/98 at the Bridge School Benefit (for "children with severe speech and physical impairments"); and 10/3/98 for Farm Aid (for family farmers, and against agribusiness lobbying). Additionally, at a number of shows, Phish has encouraged people to bring canned goods. Also, Trey performed without the rest of the band at two Tibet House benefits, 2/22/99 and 2/5/00 (see Sideshows). See also Waterwheel Foundation, Greenpeace, and Green Crew; also, Organizations.

Betty see Frost, Betty

Betty Ford Clinic nickname for a backstage area (a.k.a. "the Clinic") for band guests before the show and during setbreak (contrast with After Show and Laminate) featuring alcohol, notably tequila, at shows from circa 1997 until mid-1999.

Big Ball Jam stage antic in which Brad Sands throws beach balls into the audience, after which the band bases their improvisation on the movement of the balls, playing when the balls are touched and holding a frenzied note when the balls are grabbed and held by one or more audience members. Typically ended with the balls being tossed back into a "hoop" made by the arms of Trey, Mike, Page, and Brad Sands. See also, Song History.

Big Phil veteran fan known by strangers for his size and location (typically 11th row center), and by friends for his wit and taping skills, who established a rapport with the band in the early 1990s by providing them with videotapes of every episode of the "Simpsons".

Billy's Groove song series, frequent in 1997 and resurfaced in 2000, that inserts "Swept Away" and "Steep" (two songs from *Billy Breathes*) between "Mike's Song" and "Weekapaug Groove" (i.e. replacing "I Am Hydrogen" in "Mike's Groove").

Birthdays *Band:* Page 5/17/63, Trey 9/30/64, Jon 2/19/65, and Mike 6/3/65.—*Crew:* Brad Sands 10/31/69, Pete Carini 12/30/69, Chris Kuroda 7/26/65.—*Also:* Marley, fall 1984; Mimi Fishman 4/5/?.

Bittersweet Motel documentary directed by Todd Phillips, debuted 3/12/00 at the South-by-Southwest (SXSW) Film Festival in Austin,

TX, and released to theaters in 8/25/00, which profiles much of 1997 (including Europe, the Great Went, Rochester, and New Year's Eve).

Bivouac Jaun see Discography. Jaun, not Juan.

Blacklight test holding a black light to the back of a ticket to check for Ticketmaster logos. Novelty stores sell small pocket blacklights. See also entry for Counterfeits.

Blackwood Convention band's monicker for their first show, probably 10/30/83. See setlists; 12/2/83 may have been the first show under the name Phish. The name Blackwood Convention had previously been the name of a band whose leader was the brother of the Paul who played in the Tombstone Blues Band and The Edge (see those entries), and was later used by a band featuring Paul and Mike.

Blank a cassette tape (typically Maxell XLII 100 min.) or CDR purchased with nothing on it, to be used for duplicating traded shows.

Blanks and postage a process for getting live tapes when you do not have any to trade. Practice in tape trading in which a person sends the taper enough blank tapes to cover the shows and a self-addressed stamped envelope. The taper then makes the copies and sends them back. The taper makes no profit, but makes copies of their tapes out of the goodness of their heart for another person who sends them blank tapes and return postage. See also, Taping Guide chapter.

Blastoplasts explosive devices used by revolutionary Lizards in Gamehendge, as mentioned in the lyrics to "Llama", and see liner notes to *Rift*.

Blob, The process attempted by the band which involved rotating turns in which each member added or subtracted pieces, beginning with individual notes. Parts of The Blob were extracted and became tracks on *Billy Breathes*.

BOAF "Birds of a Feather", a Phish original.

Book of Phriends one of several volumes circulated among fans for the recording of thoughts, memories, and artwork. Originally intended as a hardcopy solidarity resource among netters who meet on tour, there are now perhaps 12 volumes, most of unknown whereabouts. Each book starts as a bound collection of blank pages, typically with an envelope (or other container) of crayons or pencils or markers attached; with decorations on the inside, outside, and/or binding; and occasionally in a bag or box to protect it and ease passage. Each is taken to a Phish show and passed to another fan (usually but not necessarily someone from the Phish.Net) in the lot or at pre- or post-event gatherings. That person holds it for the night (or so, maybe more or less) and reads and enjoys whatever's in it, adds his/her comments/thoughts/art/additions, and takes it to the next show (or tour, if received at the end of a tour). The actual mechanics and additional guidelines for passage may be ad hoc, but rely upon the trust and solidarity which preserve this net. The primary requirement is intent to attend the next announced show. Volume status and progress is tracked online in the Frequently Asked Questions file (see Online Resources).

Books about Phish see listings for *The Phish Book*, *The Phishing Manual*, *The Pharmer's Almanac*, and *Go Phish*.

Bootleg historically has referred to any recording of a live show (Phish or otherwise), often sold for profit. Introduces confusion where acts (such as Phish) allow not-for-profit taping and tape trading, such that tapers distance themselves from the word's negative connotations by using other words, such as "tapes". Sales (and pur-

chase) of for-profit bootlegs threaten the taping practices and environment. For-profit bootlegs are typically of low sound quality, and typically include theft of artwork, photography, and other content. They are also typically sold for outrageous prices, whereas the large trading community allows fans to acquire recordings for the mere cost of blanks and postage. (See B&P entry and Tape Guide chapter.)

Boyle, Karl Page's advisor at Goddard College, under whom he wrote his thesis "The Art of Improvisation".

Bozeman Tweezer, The the version of "Tweezer" performed on 11/28/94.

Brad see Sands, Brad

Breakout any song revived after a long absence. Alternately, any new song (cover or original) previously unplayed. See Statistics chapter. See also, Rarity.

BRTR "Bouncing (A)round the Room", a Phish original.

Bruho see El Bruho entry. See also, Gary Gazaway in Guest Book.

Bruno nickname for monitor engineer (since Fall 1996) Mark Bradley.

BTP Back To Paul (Languedoc, the soundman), an acronym alternative to FOB (see that entry).

Bubble machine used only once so far, on 10/31/94.

Budnick, Dean Harvard graduate who studied American Civilization, authored *The Phishing Manual* and *Jam Bands*, and founded and heads jambands.com.

Bugtown see The Screw.

Bustout see Breakout or Rarity.

Cactus nickname for Mike Gordon.

Cardioid microphone configuration involving more than one omnidirectional microphone in a 90-degree pattern.

Carini, Pete Henrietta's drum tech, and namesake of the Phish original "Carini" (aka "Lucy with a Lumpy Head"). Appeared on stage 7/9/98 wearing a protective helmet.

CDR compact disc recordable, a technology which allows individuals to produce their own CDs.

CDRW compact disc re-writable, a technology which allows CDRs to be recorded multiple times (like an analog cassette) rather than once (like a photographic negative).

CDT "Chalkdust Torture", a Phish original.

Chairman of the Boards nickname for Page, combining Frank Sinatra's alias "Chairman of the Board" (particularly appropriate if you see or hear Page sing "Lawnboy") with the fact that he plays keyboards.

Chanting most commonly during the opening of "Wilson", as Trey and Mike together play two pairs of low notes (duh-dun… duh-dun), and the audience responds "Wiiiil-son!" Initially notable 4/9/94, and repeated 12/30/94 with Trey throwing his fist into the air stirring enough frenzy to put the version on *A Live One*. See also, entry for Singing. Also, Trey started a "cheesecake" chant at 12/31/99, just before and after the segment aired on ABC.

Charities see Benefits, Waterwheel Foundation, and Mockingbird Foundation.

Cheesecake word Trey instructed the crowd at Big Cypress 12/31/99 to chant for the television broadcast, rather than applauding; appeared again throughout the seven-hour set.

Chess Match   band-audience contest during Fall 1995, beginning 9/30/95 and including two complete chess games. Each night, Phish would make their move at the beginning of the show, on a large board hung above the stage on Page's side (left facing, stage right). During the setbreak, interested fans would vote on the next move at the Greenpeace table, and a duly selected fan (initially "Pooh") would go onstage at the beginning of set two to make the elected move.

Chocolate   at several shows, including Halloween 1994, fans received chocolate coins as souvenirs.

Chris Kuroda   band lighting director, lauded as the "fifth member of Phish". See CK5 in Online Resources chapter.

Cigarette test   most common test for whether or not a ticket is real. According to legend, carefully hold a cigarette or match to the back of the ticket and, on a legit ticket, a small disc-shaped spot will turn blank on the front rather than burning through. Try at your own risk, as no test is sanctioned; see entry for Counterfeits. This only works on Ticketmaster tickets, not on mail order tickets. Further, it may be reproducible by counterfeiters. Worse, someone may not know their ticket is counterfeit and may not trust the test; burning the ticket may create a problem. You should be relying on reputable sources (known persons, including Phish and Ticketmaster) to get tickets anyway. However, this test is so commonly regarded that those who refuse the cigarette test are often regarded (even without the test) as knowingly selling a counterfeit.

Circus of Light   fan-produced video by E.R. Silverbush, sold via the Internet, about the Phish fan scene. Includes extensive interviews as the filmmaker follows the summer 1999 tour.

Michael McNamara

Pete Carini (Guitar tech and Song namesake).

CK5   group of fans promoting recognition of Chris Kuroda as the "fifth member" of the band. See Online Resources chapter.

Clapping   frowned upon during jams. Works better with some songs—for example "Dogs Stole Things" rather than "Character Zero". The band encourages clapping in particular rhythms along with "Mound" (initially to help Fishman). Additionally, a five-beat riff by Fishman in "Stash" was originally mimicked by audience members, though has been supplanted by a four-beat clap which sounds to many like two claps on *A Live One,* such that many now only clap twice at that point in the song.

Clifford Ball Orchestra   afternoon performance on 8/17/96, between the first and second sets, featuring gliders flying overhead to the music and then off into the sunset as the music came to an end. Tapes do exist and circulate. The setlist was as follows: Debussy: Nocturnes (2 movements), Ravel: Pavane Pour une Enfante Defunte, Debussy: Claire de Lune, Ravel: Tombeau de Couperin (2 movements), Chavrier: Joyeux Muse, Faure: Pelleas et Mellisandre (2 movements), and Stravinsky: The Firebird (2 movements)

Clifford Ball, The   not the first (see Amy's Farm), but the preeminent Phish festival (setting the stage for the Lemonwheel and Great Went), held August 15-17, 1996, at the former Air Force Base in Plattsburgh, New York.

    Named for a once-famed aviator who held fabulous balls for other aviators such as Amelia Earheart. The band purportedly learned of Ball from a plaque in a Pittsburgh-area airport, with the epitaph "a beacon of light in the world of flight". Trey used that phrase to introduce Page at 3/26/92 (during the Harpua encore), and at 3/24/92 he called Fishman "Clifford O'Sullivan…a beacon of light in the world of flight!"

    Phish performed three sets and an encore on each of the two show days, where some 70-80,000 fans camped on site and enjoyed overhead entertainment by bombers, fighters, gliders, and other aerial vehicles, including two planes pulling banners with silly sayings (e.g. "Help… We're out of fuel… Seriously…"); carnival rides; wandering jugglers and stilters; a string quartet, a blues quartet, a choral quintet, guitar soloists, and a full orchestra; fireworks; scores of food vendors, a general store with basic necessities, and wandering ice vendors; 900 portable johns, cleaned regularly; and large fresh water tanks, filled regularly; on stage guests, including Ben and Jerry, two trampolinists, and a woman swinging on a rope; three huge video screens, and four sound towers; a central village ("Ball Square") built on a hill; and movies in the camping area (Fantasia on Thursday night; cartoons and Rocky Horror Picture Show on Friday). The audience was four times the size of host Clinton County, and temporarily made Plattsburgh the ninth largetst city in New York State. See also, Flatbed Truck Jam and Clifford Care Bears entries, and Archive Show Playlists ([sidebars where?]).

    Listed as the venue for the Phish live double album *A Live One*, which includes tracks from a dozen different venues in 1994, nearly two years before the Clifford Ball event.

Clifford Care Bears   effort organized by Ali and David Balter to help maintain the scene at the Clifford Ball by keeping it a "clean, happy, and safe" place. Through a concerted effort and effective pre-planning, the group helped control trash and collect recycling (both of which the Green Crew also do), keep an eye out against problems (like a Neighborhood Watch for on-tour Phish fans), and promote glee and fun (like Merry Pranksters with a tangible purpose). See also Organizations.

Clinic, the   see Betty Ford Clinic.

Colonel Forbin   pivotal character in the Gamehendge story (TMWSIY), who enters Gamehendge when the Lizards are living in bondage. Forbin spends time with Tela and Rutherford (revolutionaries) and then retrieves the stolen Helping Friendly Book from the evil King Wilson by climbing a mountain to seek Icculus with the help of the Famous Mockingbird. Forbin then becomes Wilsonian himself in a twist reminiscent of George Orwell's *Animal Farm*.

Colton, Jason   assistant to John Paluska, Phish's manager

Conan   Phish have performed on *The Late Show with Conan O'Brian* twice, playing "Farmhouse" 11/19/97 (the song's debut) and "Get Back on the Train" 6/27/00. Conan has also mentioned Phish several other times, including 1/5/99 talking about attending 12/31/98 and saying "it's a scene baby" and that he "became a hepster"; 2/11/99, mentioning being at a Phish concert when Fred Savage tapped him on the shoulder; and 2/24/99, with Fred Savage as a guest and the first subject was how Fred and Conan saw each other at the 12/31/98 Phish show. (Fred said he was freaked out by it, like seeing one of your teachers at the mall.)

Coop, The   bookstore in Harvard Square (the Harvard University bookstore, a.k.a. Harvard Coop) at which Mike had a book signing for *Mike's Corner*, which turned into a question-and-answer session. Brad Sands, wearing a green suit and standing somewhat stiffly, answered several questions on behalf of Mike, and insisted that Phish was banned from Great Woods forever. He also prevented Mike from signing a Phish Food container.

Cosmic Country Horns   Combination of the Giant Country Horns and the Cosmic Krewe. See any of these listings in the Guest Book chapter.

Costumes   Fishman wore a lime-green shirt with Pork Tornado on 1/26/97, but more typically wears a dress (see entry for Dress). Mike has worn lime-green pants and shirt, but typically rolls his pants up to his knees regardless of color. The band has on occasion worn masks. See also Musical Costumes.

Counterfeit tickets   fake tickets sold which may (to some degree) appear real but probably won't get you in (and may get your arrested and fined.) Note that "ticket brokers" often sell counterfeits. You are advised to purchase tickets only from reputable sources: Ticketmaster, venue box offices, or Phish mail order.

Counterfeiters have kept pace with attempts to foil their efforts, such as replicating colored layers in paper. Complex images and black-light techniques have not been successfully duplicated and help identify what's real, but for many years were found only on mail order tickets. Several methods are used in lots to determine whether tickets are real. Try them at your own risk, as none are officially sanctioned; see entries for Blacklight test, Cigarette test, and Fingernail test. Most effective is the Bozo test: the images are usually sloppy, the text is often muddled, and the entire design is usually off-balance.

Creek Jam   Many 1986 tapes circulate with "Creek Jam" as the name of the Max Creek song "Back Porch." Some tapes even label it "Back Porch Boogie".

Crispy   used to describe either a high-quality live recording or a stoned (i.e. high on marijuana) person.

CTB   "Cars Trucks Buses", a Phish original.

Culbertson, Shelly   longtime fan of the band, who joined Dionysian

as an Internet liaison in 1993 and then helped develop Phish's mail order and ticket distribution system, which she now manages.

Cymbals   played by Fishman during "Cracklin' Rosie", with a "b" on the underside of one and "ah" on the underside of the other.

D'oh   exclamation of frustration used by Homer Simpson on the animated series *The Simpsons*. Yell it when Phish teases the theme to the show. (See Secret Language.)

Dancing, band   Trey and Mike dance in "Cavern", "Manteca", "Moma Dance", "Guelah Papyrus" (a swaying hop), "PYITE" and "Landlady" (the "storm dance"; see 2/5/93), "It's Ice" (back-and-forth; see also entry for Glide), "Meatstick" (introduced 7/4/98), "Stash" (robotic staccato) and "Hydrogen" (lying on their backs with their feet in the air as if peddling bikes). Fishman stands on his stool and wiggles his butt during "It's Ice". The only one commonly mimicked by the audience is the "Meatstick" dance.

Dangerous Grapes   band in which Mike and Fishman played in early 1984, while Trey was expelled from UVM.

DAT   The preferred medium in the Phish taping scene, DAT stands for Digital Audio Tape. A DAT recorder stores the music on a DAT tape in binary code (1's and 0's). This produces crystal clear (though some would say sterile) audio sound, rivaling that of a CD. See also the Taping Guide chapter.

Daubert, Marc   Princeton Day School pal of Trey and Tom Marshall, a member of Space Antelope and an early guest with Phish. Also known as Daubs, and Marc "the Rites of Spring" Daubert. See also Chronology, Guest Book, and Interview.

Daubs   see Marc Daubert.

DAUD   digital recording made in the audience (Digital AUDience) using microphones, as opposed to an analog recording (AUD) or a digital recording from the soundboard (DSBD).

Dave, Looks too Much Like   see Abrahams, Dave

Dave's Energy Guide   See listing in Song Histories chapter.

DCC   digital compact cassette, an ill-fated technology for archiving digital sound for analog prices, made by Phillips and comparable (in lousy compression quality) to Sony's Minidiscs.

Dean   see Budnick, Dean.

DEG   "Dave's Energy Guide", a Phish original.

Demo releases   see Discography.

Deodato   see 2001.

Destiny Chant   effort to get everyone to sing the lyrics to "Destiny Unbound", a popular rarity not played since 11/15/91. Trey once joked that if the entire audience sang the song as the band came on stage, they'd play it again. A fan distributed flyers promoting the idea at 8/6/96, and the loudest chant was probably 8/16/98, where it was loud enough to be picked up by the mics and broadcast to the event. (Trey only grinned. The band played "Sabotage" instead.) An 11/24/97 attempt included distributing flyers to the first six rows of the show, organization during the set break, and band recognition of the effort: Fishman looked surprised, Mike was stoic, Trey and Page laughed; listen for Trey's "death chant" comments… but then they played "Halley's Comet".

Digests   one of a number of attempts to distribute content from the Usenet newsgroup rec.music.phish to a list of subscribers via email.

The original Phish.Net Digest included all content from the newsgroup, through a gateway managed by Shelly Culbertson; that stopped when the volume got too high, with some 50,000 people reading the newsgroup weekly. Rosemary's Digest, managed by Rosemary Macintosh, followed and contained her picks of the best content of rec.music.phish. This Digest was followed by Beny's Digest, nicknamed "The Eigest," which was managed by Benjy Eisen. Following the Eigest and as of this writing, the new Phish.Net Digest—a digest of rec.music.phish messages—is managed by a team of fans in order to ensure stability and thoroughness. See Online Resources chapter.

Dionysian Productions   Phish's management company, co-founded by Ben "Junta" Hunter (see Interview) and John Paluska; now run by Paluska, his assistant Jason Colton, and with the key (and historical) assistance of Shelly Culbertson (ticketing), Amy Skelton (merchandising), and Kevin Shapiro (archivist and in-house counsel).

Disco set   2 a.m. performance by the band (featuring 1970s keyboards, particularly Moogs and Korgs) on a flatbed truck (decorated with strobe lights and disco balls) parked at the entrance to the concert grounds of the Great Went. See also Flatbed Truck Jam.

DMB   Dave Matthews Band. See listings in Guest Book and Sideshows chapters.

Documentary   see *Bittersweet Motel.*

Dogs   appear in many Phish lyrics ("Dog Log", "Runaway Jim", "Harpua", "McGrupp", and "Dogs Stole Things") and covers (such as "Shaggy Dog"), shows and stage banter (e.g. Trey cooing at Marley repeatedly on 5/28/89), and even equipment (see Guitars). Space Antelope attempted to cover Pink Floyd's "Dogs" (rumored to have happened at a Taft School assembly). Trey and his mother Dina wrote a children's musical "Gus the Christmas Dog", from which Phish has played "No Dogs Allowed." (Other pieces from the work birthed "Lizards" and "The Divided Sky.") See also, Marley.

Dogs on tour   are a bad idea. Some people routinely bring animals on tour—dogs and, yes, even cats. Some even purchase (or otherwise acquire) a pet just *for* tour. They may be fun to have around, they might miss you while you're gone, and they might give you a sense of security. But they don't enjoy being locked in or to a vehicle in a parking lot. Instructions from Phish and venues clearly and routinely indicate that dogs are not allowed, and have on occasion said that Health Department and/or Humane Society personnel would break into vehicles to release and impound animals. Owners often permit their animals to urinate and defecate freely in parking lots, and rarely do anything to clean up or cover up the refuse. It would go a long way to cleaning up our scene—literally *and* figuratively—if animals were left at home.

DOL   see Dude of Life, and Chronology and Guest Book chapters.

Dolls   Sometimes thrown onstage, e.g. Clifford the Big Red Doll (held in the air near the rail for every show on Summer 93 tour and then thrown onstage at the tour closer, also appeared onstage at fall 93 shows) and Tickle Me Elmo (the item that was thrown onstage to Trey before the start of 12/28/96; based on a *Sesame Street* character, Elmo; see also, listing for *Sesame Street*)

Doniac Schvice   current name of Phish's newsletter. Mike Gordon answered a letter (in *Doniac Schvice* Tiny Edition Volume 1, the insert to *A Live One*), "Doniac Schvice is the feeling you get when you're

fidgeting with your keys to get in your house, and the phone rings, and then stops ringing." The creative and distinctive layout has primarily been the responsibility and accomplishment of Jason Colton.

Dress   Fishman is known for several dresses worn onstage, and almost always performs in one. The most common is blue with orange-colored donut shapes (a.k.a. the "Zeroman dress"). Less common is one covered with holes and eyes. Both are actually sleeveless frocks, not dresses. The former was found in a dumpster.

Drums   Since 1996, Fishman has played a custom-made drum kit (jade green with blonde hoops) crafted by Ayotte Drums of Vancouver, B.C.

Dry Goods   official merchandise arm of the Phish enterprise, which sells both through the Phish website as well as *Doniac Schvice*, the band's newsletter. Dry Goods has sold Phish posters, hats, stickers, t-shirts, and CDs for years. It has recently added such odd items as lyric magnets to its line. This past summer, Phish offered a CD unaffiliated with Elektra exclusively through Dry Goods (the original Phish demo tape, the *White Album*) and hope to offer more such special releases in the future.

Dry Ice   pumped in insane amounts beginning in 1987 (esp. at the Living Room), and later during heavy jams such as in "Simple", though also in "Kung" (e.g. on 10/20/94) and "2001" (e.g. on 12/30/95). The substance is purportedly mixed with mineral oil in order to intensify the atmospheric effects of Kuroda's lights.

DSBD   Digital Soundboard, signifying a recording (tape, CD, or otherwise) for which the original source was a digital recording directly fed from show's soundboard output, as opposed to an analog recording or an audience (microphone) recording.

Dude of Life   Steve Pollak (*not* Steve Volato, Tom Marshall, or Jim Pollock), a long-time friend of the band; lyricist for "Slave to the Traffic Light", "Suzy Greenberg", "Dinner and a Movie", and "Fluffhead"; and occasional on-stage guest, including 12/1/84, 2/13/87, 9/13/90, 5/12/91, 8/3/91, 11/8/91, 11/20/92, 12/31/92, 5/5/93, 8/9/93, 8/28/93, and 7/10/94. He is known for odd attire, throwing rubber chickens (see that entry), and other shenanigans (such as pushing a lawnmower on stage 12/31/92), and has been profiled in the *Doniac Schvice*. He was summoned in a chant 12/13/97, but did not appear. Phish played on his albums, *Crimes of the Mind* and *Under the Sound Umbrella* (see Discography). Fishman played in the Dude's band during its 1994 tour and on 3/6/99; Trey performed with the Dude on 2/17/00. See also, entries for DOL and rubber chickens, and Guest Book and Side Shows chapters.

Edge, The   Mike's second high school band. Included all of the members of the Tombstone Blues Band except Kerrie Kaffe, who founded that predecessor. See Biographies chapter.

El Bruho   nickname of Gary Gazaway, trumpet player with the Giant Country Horns. Spanish for "the Owl". By contract, "El Brujo" is a male witch, warlock, or voodoo doctor.

Electrolux   brand of vacuum that Fishman "plays". See Vacuum.

Eliza   title of a Phish original, Trey's wife's middle name, and first name of Trey and Sue's daughter born 8/21/95.

Ernie (Stires)   see Stires, Ernie

Errand Wolfe   character in Gamehendge (named after Trey's friend Aaron Wolfe) to whom Colonel Forbin presents the retrieved Helping

Friendly Book, but who then uses it to his own advantage. He conquers Gamehendge, captures the Famous Mockingbird, and has the Sloth kill Wilson. See also, Aaron Wolfe entry and Interview.

Esther Video, The   animated film shown during the setbreak 7/19/91, accompanying the studio version of "Esther" from *Junta* with sketches by Scott Nybakken animated by CoSa (a graphics company) and directed by John Greene. Circulates lightly on videotape, both a direct filming of a computer screen with overdubbed sound, and in an amateur video of the 7/19/91 show. CoSa, headed by Paluska acquaintance Greg DeoCampo, planned to do the Gamehendge CD-ROM which never came to pass, first due to lack of funding and later by Phish's disinterest in profiting from the tale.

E-Tree   created by People for a Clearer Phish (PCP) to distribute electronic music files of authorized concert recordings via high-speed Internet connections (and FTP servers) in a "tree"-like format, bypassing the "snail mail" snag of conventional trading. These files are then used immediately to burn CDRs, so that distribution of recordings is now measured in minutes or hours rather than days or weeks. See Online Resources.

Euphoria Studios   Revere, MA, location where *Junta* was recorded.

Europe   Phish has done five European tours, in support of the Violent Femmes and Lou Reed in 1992 and Santana in 1996, in Spring 1997, Summer 1997, and Summer 1998. There is a small but growing population of fans and Phish tape traders in Europe, although attention is more evident in Israel and Japan.

Fall tour   string of shows typically occurring during September through November. See Setlists beginning fall 1991 (though not 1993). Note that the December 1999 tour is typically called the Winter Tour of that year.

Famous Mockingbird   Gamehendge character who assisted Colonel Forbin in retrieving the stolen Helping Friendly Book from the evil King Wilson. See also, Song History for that title.

Fan Club   none official, but see entries for Phish.net and Phunky Bitches, and chapter of Online Resources.

Fan Groups   see Organizations.

FAQ   Frequently Asked Questions, typically in reference to a FAQ File, a resource commonly offered on web sites or within online communities in order to level the discussions and weed out repeated discussions about basic matters. See entry in Online Resources.

Fatty   in older usage, referred to a joint, aka hogleg. Also, Phatty. For contemporary use, see listing for Phat.

FEFY   "Fast Enough For You", a Phish original.

Finger in the air   signal used by ticketless fans to indicate that they are in search of an extra ticket as they walk around the lots prior to a show.

Fingernail test   instead of burning your ticket (see entry for Cigarette test), some suggest that if you run a fingernail quickly across the front of a ticket that the friction will leave a black line if it the ticket is real. (See entry for Counterfeits).

Firenze   Florence, to Italians. See also, entry for WATSIYEM and Song History for "You Enjoy Myself".

Fireworks   during "Antelope" 7/18/93 and 7/3/94; during the encores 8/16/96, 8/16/97, 7/4/98, and 7/4/99; as well as 10/22/94, from a Disney anniversary party a few blocks away, during "Julius" and ac-

counting for the extended jam in the setlist.

Fish   nickname for Jon Fishman. See also Henrietta.

Fishbeck, Andrew   former road manager, replaced around 1992 by roadie Brad Sands.

Fishman, Jon   drummer for Phish. See entries for drums and Henrietta, and Biographies chapter.

Fishman, Mimi   Adoptive mother of Phish's drummer, Jon. She attends as many shows as she can, is actively involved in raising money for charities such as glaucoma and diabetes, and is highly visible in the "jambands" community. See also Guest Book.

Flatbed Truck Jam (aka "Flatbed Jam", "Flatbed Set")   ambient, improvisational performance by Phish at 3:30a.m.—in the wee hours after the first Clifford Ball show—on a flatbed truck, which slowly drove the length of the parking lots, from the venue to the entry/exit and back.". See Setlists, 8/16/96. Tapes exist, the first 20 minutes or so from Audio Technica 822 mics attached to bicycle handlebars, and the last 15 minutes or so from Neumann KM-140 mics attached to a stick. See also Disco Set.

Fleezer, The   the version of "Tweezer" performed on 6/22/95, a.k.a. the Canandaigua Tweezer.

Flyers   distributed at various times at shows for purposes ranging from marketing to performance.

First, by the band on 12/31/92 to play with audiences of the WBCN radio broadcast, including eight reactions (such as everyone stomping their feet or screaming "eggplant") mostly triggered by signs held up by Trey.

Later, by fans, including Andrew Croke on 11/13/94 (listen for the "tomahawk chop" before the second set), Darius Zelkha on 12/8/95 (listen for the first line of "Destiny Unbound" sung by some before the second set) and at the 8/96 Red Rocks shows (listen for "Hood!" during the opening segment of "Harry Hood", and see entry for Hairy Balls), and Todd Kennedy (the "Helping Friendly Flyer", circa 1998).

More recently, by the Mockingbird Foundation (to solicit material for this book) and the *Pharmer's Almanac Tour Update* (a newsletter distributed in show lots and including recent setlists, news, and marketing). See also entry for 'Zines.

Flyers, The   Philadelphia hockey team, whose jerseys Trey sometimes wears. Chris Kuroda was forced to wear one on 12/30/97 after losing a bet with Trey. Phish has sung national anthem to open several Flyers games, including 5/5/97 and 12/1/97. After the latter (which was televised), commentator Linda Cohn (who grew up in Vermont and went to UVM with Mike) said, "Nobody, nobody, belts out Run Like An Antelope better than Trey!"

FM   Frequency Modulation, a means of radio transfer, occasionally seen as a source for a Phish recording (such as when the New Year's or West Palm Beach shows were broadcast on typical commercial FM radio), and occasionally the source for on-site recordings, either through simulcast (as at the Lemonwheel) or by stealth reception of local low-frequency technical uses (e.g. through listening devices for the hard-of-hearing).

FOB   see entry for Front-of-Board

Forbin   see entry for Colonel Forbin

Frakes, Jonathan   portrays Captain Riker on *Star Trek: The New Generation*. Performed trombone on "Riker's Mailbox" on *Hoist*, and is the neighbor of the album's producer. The track is an outtake from a seven-minute experiment with "Buffalo Bill".

Frodo   Fishman's first band. Trey dedicated the 8/12/98 "Possum" to Frodo.

Front-of-Board (FOB)   recordings made from microphones which are placed forward of the soundboard (facing the stage), rather than behind or to the side of the board, where the designated tapers' section is typically situated. Phish's taping policy bars FOB taping, which arguably interferes with others' enjoyment of the show through obstructed view, obstructed row space, or the need for respectful noise levels. However, some tapers persist, insisting that the resulting sound quality is much higher, particularly at outdoor shows where winds are problematic and the taping section is far from stage.

Frost, Betty   Band employee who answers fan mail sent to the band and its members. Mike used to deal with all of the mail, and answered most of it, usually on postcards. (Trey also occasionally sent postcards, in response to mail directed specifically to him.) But as the volume of mail increased, answering it became a full-time job.

Fugues   composition in which a theme is introduced by one "voice", which then plays a contrapuntal (playing notes that ascend or descend interactively with another voice) harmony mimicking that original theme. The second voice enters immediately after the first voice has finished the theme and repeats the theme, while the first voice is mimicking the theme with counterpoint, creating interweaving harmony based on the original theme. Note that this overlap is not the same as in a circular canon, or round (such as "Row Your Boat"). A fugue is usually limited to only four voices, but each adds further complexity. The voices are not performing the same melody in turns, but separate parts   the first homophonic, the others chordal.

Trey learned about fugues, and developed his early fugue work, under the auspices of Ernie Stires. Phish has fugues in the middle section (the "Asse Festival") of "Guelah Papyrus", the opening prejam segment of "Reba", part of "All Things Reconsidered", the horn parts before the all-vocals segment in "Split Open and Melt", and the third part of Tela (which is an atonal fugue with an eight-measure theme divided into two parts). "The Chase" section of "Fluffhead" (1:09 to 2:21 from the start of track 2 on *Junta*) involves Trey, Mike, and Page playing melodies that race around each other, but that does not make a fugue. Although these and other parts of Phish songs are said to be "fugue-like", a fugure is a very specific thing, as much a science as an art.

Gala Event, The   early label/name of "McGrupp and the Watchful Hosemasters" on tapes from the 80's. Trey announces it as such on one or more occasions (8/21/87 or 11/9/89).

Gamehendge   mythical land in *The Man Who Stepped Into Yesterday*, and the nickname of that story and compilation, written by Trey as his senior study at Goddard College. The story concerns the aging Colonel Forbin, in a suburban town in Long Island, who one day finds a door to another land while walking his faithful dog McGrupp. Stepping through this door, he finds himself in a land of vast green forests and a huge mountain. But the land is sociologically vibrant; see entries for Lizards, Tela, Rutherford the Brave, Errand Wolfe, Roger, Mr. Palmer, AC/DC Bag, Helping Friendly Book, and Rhombus.

Gamehendge, Live   The songs that are considered part of the Gamehendge mythology have been played either on their own (see Statistics for the constituent songs) or together as part of a near-complete version of TMWSIY, on five occasions: 3/12/88 (the entire original project, though most left during "Col. Forbin"), 10/13/91 (with "Reba" and "Landlady" inserted, and other songs in odd order), 3/22/93 (via ice imagery, and possibly in response to audience attentiveness; "McGrupp" replaced "Possum", and Tela no longer a spy), 6/26/94 (via the "Kung" chant, and see Gamehoist entry), and 7/8/94 ("McGrupp" instead of "Possum", and followed by "Divided Sky"). The latter two were recorded, as the band at the time was considering releasing the story commercially; they have since expressly decided not to do so.

Gamehoist   alias for the 6/26/94 show, which featured the Gamehendge songs as the first set and *Hoist*, in its entirety, as the second set.

GCH   Giant Country Horns. See Guest Book chapter.

Geerz   nickname of Carl Gerhard; see that entry.

Generation   used to designate how far removed a live recording is from the master. Each successive analog copy from the master is one higher generation. (Digital copies are exact duplicates of the master, with no generational loss or degradation.)

Some traders call the first analog tape (from microphones, soundboard, or a DAT tape) a "zero" generation or "analog master", akin to a digitally perfect recording. They only call the *second* analog tape a "first generation", contending that the first one cannot "be" a generation. However, many regard this as incorrect and deceptive, and contend that any analog is a step away from ambient sound, and is therefore the first analog generation. While this dispute is often sidetracked into tangential issues such as sound degradation and even quality ratings, the pivotal issue is what to label the master.

Gerhard, Carl "Gears"   trumpeter with the Giant Country Horns when Phish toured with them in Summer 1991, and has played with Phish on many other occasions over the years (most recently in "Tubthumping" at Hampton on 11/21/98). Nicknamed Geerz. See Interview.

Giant Country Horns   Phish's original touring horn section for the Summer 1991 tour. See Guest Book chapter.

Glides   alias for "Phish heads" (see that entry) as well as for the rubber mats on which Trey and Mike slid back-and-forth during "It's Ice" and (occasionally) "Glide" during 1993. The mats were sold via early 1990s infomercials as exercise equipment, and included rubber socks that facilitate sliding.

Glowstick wars   refers to the now common practice of audience members tossing "glowsticks" and/or "glowrings" into the air during the musical jams, resulting in one of the most interesting, vibrant, continuous, and controversial aspects of audience participation at Phish shows. See also "Harry Hood" song history, and entries for Marshmallows and Tortillas.

Origin: Though most known from the Great Went (and photographs taken of them there, such as one used as the band's 1997 Christmas card), glowsticks were first thrown by the band into the audience during the 11/25/94 "Harpua". A few were thrown on 8/2/97 during "Harry Hood", when Trey asked Chris "Topher" Kuroda to cut the house lights so the band could play while watching the stars. But when Trey gave Topher the same request on 8/17/97, hundreds of glowsticks began flying through the air. Trey threw back some that

landed on the stage, and said after the song "Go get some more of those things, man!", and glowing arcs have been tossed in most "Harry Hood"s since (especially other times Trey has asked Topher to cut the lights such as on 12/30/97). By the end of 1998, they were also appearing in such songs as "Down with Disease" and "Piper". And now their placement is nearly random, such as a 7/4/99 glow event during "Silent in the Morning"!

Glowrings vs. Glowsticks: The visual result is a collage of fluorescent arcs above and across the crowd, but another result has been occasional injuries (and at least one lawsuit, against the band and the Hampton Coliseum). There is now a movement in favor of glowrings rather than glowsticks, and the band distributed thousands of the former to the 12/31/98 audience, although use of the word "glowsticks" persists regardless of which are thrown. Phish's intense lighting makes it difficult to see thing in the air, or coming at your face. Sticks are heavy, hard, and pointed, while rings are lighter, softer, pliable, entirely rounded, and bouncy. The heavier glowsticks can also interfere with or harm equipment, including both recording equipment in the tapers' section as well as band rigs on stage.

Go Phish   widely disparaged book about Phish which purportedly contains a great deal of fiction, inaccuracies, and exaggerations. Nonetheless interesting for its attempt at riveting (though laughable) behind-the-scenes narrative.

Goddard College   free-spirited institution of higher learning in Vermont, located in the woods and ascribing no grades. Page went to Goddard first, and recruited Trey and Fish from UVM after Trey was expelled and during a recruitment drive which netted Page $100 (fifty bucks each).

Golfcart   means of transportation in and around lots by band members, especially during the summer 1998 tour and at the festival shows (Clifford Ball, Great Went, Lemonwheel). Mike also uses one (or sometimes a mountain bike) to wander through the lots prior to shows, talking to fans and exploring the crowd. The band was delivered to stage on one 7/30/93, arriving as "Contact" was broadcast over the PA. There was one onstage 7/3/00. Also mentioned in "Kung" ("we can stage a runaway golfcart marathon").

Goo Balls   brown clumps combining primarily healthy items (granola, wheat germ, nuts, grains), sweets (chocolate or carob chips, caramel chips), and sticky stuff (peanut butter or, if baked, butter/margarine), and typically alleged to include marijuana extract or content. Trey has mentioned them in "Makisupa Policeman", and they are frequently sold in the lots at Phish shows.

Gordon, Mike   bassist for Phish, a.k.a. "Cactus". See entry for bass, and Biographies chapter.

Greasy Fizeek   nickname of Fishman during 1993, and his name as listed in the liner to *Hoist*. Fans were panicked that Phish had gotten a new drummer when the newsletter talked of ousting the old drummer Jon Fishman, while welcoming in their new drummer "Greasy Fizeek."

Great Went, The   sequel to the Clifford Ball, held 8/16&17/99 at the decommissioned Loring Air Force Base in Limestone, ME. In addition to over 500 minutes of music (six sets and two encores), the event featured the world's largest firetruck, a 2 a.m. electronica performance by the band (see "Disco Set"), sidestages with the Gordon Stone Trio and the Beatroots Gypsy Caravan, a photography posing by a

thousand nude fans, an afternoon set by a string quartet (playing Debussy) and the Bangor Symphony Orchestra (playing Stravinsky's "Histoire du Soldat" and Debussy's "Claire de Lune"), and a radio station (89.1 FM WENT).

The event's name came from a drunken scene in the David Lynch movie *Fire Walk With Me*, in a line which itself references a restaurant critic mentioned in an episode of Lynch's television series *Twin Peaks*.

Green Crew, The   a loosely organized collection of volunteers who make a special effort to keep parking lots and entry areas clean, and thereby help keep venues and locals happy, Mother Nature stronger, and the history of Phish longer. At each show, between dozens (sometimes scores) of volunteers collect bags of trash and recyclables before and after shows, and are provided with bags to help clean up after tens of thousands. The group was started in the spring of 1994, informally associated with the Greenpeace tables (see that entry). The Green Crew (not affiliated with Waterwheel, and never affiliated with Greenpeace) has since been headed by Shane Johnson. See also Recycling.

Greenpeace   tables featured on Phish tour from sometime in 1992/ 1993 through early 1996, then replaced by tables for the Waterwheel Foundation (see that entry). The tables raised money for Greenpeace,

Michael McNamara

circulated petitions about national issues as well as issues local or regional to the show, and raised awareness about national and regional issues. The tables were manned and managed by "Greenpeace Henry" Schwab and "Greenpeace Mike" Hayes. Henry also managed the Green Crew (see that entry), later helped start the Waterwheel Foundation, and currently mans that table at shows.

GTBT   "Good Times Bad Times".

Guest Pass   see After Show.

Guitar   The first guitar Trey got made by Paul was a short-scale travel guitar he took to Europe with Pete and Dudley (both also of Space Antelope). Prior to that, he used a pearl-white solidbody Ibanez (which he used to write "I Am Hydrogen" in his father's basement), last seen at his bachelor party jam session. In 1987, Paul built the "blonde beauty" from spruce and maple, with two humbuckers and a piece of plastic filling the middle pickup hole; this became the backup until the koa was built in 1996. His main guitar, built in 1990, has the same (blonde) finish as the main one but is made from padauk, with a different inlay on the headstock, a large inlay from fres 11-13, and two chrome soapbars. The koa hollowbody built in 1996 has a darker, redder finish, almost like mahogany, with different inlays and two soapbars. Mainly a backup, it was used increasingly throughout 1996 and 1997, though the padauk remains Trey's main axe. The acoustic guitar (see Biographies) was made by Michael Wentzell of quilted hon, larch, flamed maple, quilted mahogany, and ebony.

Guy Forget *(gee for-ZHAY)*   French tennis player in the late 1980s to early 1990s. ESPN Sportscenter anchors used to refer to him as "the unforgettable Guy Forget". Trey and Dave sang a short ditty about him during a radio promotion, the band sang it during some 1993 soundchecks, and the band performed it on 10/1/00: "I never met a man I could not forget like Guy Forget."

Hairy Balls   joke implied by efforts to supplant audience members screaming during "Harry Hood". As one suggestion distributed by flyer to audience members (See entry for Flyers), fans were instructed to yell "Hood!" after each "Harry" in the "Harry... Harry... where do you go when the lights go out?" part of the song. In response, some opposed to the practice tried to shift the "fun" to something more likely to die out, creating the call-and-response "Harry ... balls!".

Hampton Comes Alive   six-disc live release. See Discography chapter.

Handicapped seating   Tickets themselves do not include or allow a handicapped designation. If you contact a venue in advance, you can sometimes get assistance which may include a special entrance, use of an elevator, and designated seating (though sometimes in an aisle and/or at a loge or balcony portal). Most venues use the term "handicapped/special needs accessible" seating. Each venue is different, with some making little or no accommodation for handicapped seating and others providing special areas for both the handicapped and their companions. (Hampton Coliseum is one of the most accommodating.) Some venues sell tickets to the handicapped directly, so it may behoove you to call them first and early.

Hebrew   appears in Phish shows in their covers of "Avenu Malkenu" (as the middle of "TMWSIY"), and "Jerusalem City of Gold" (the end of "Demand" on *Hoist* and performed independently live). Mike did a "Happy Passover Bass Solo" on 4/18/92. Mike and Fishman are Jewish, and one group has claimed (though without supporting data)

that Phish audiences may be 30% Jewish.

Other foreign languages in Phish lyrics include Italian (part of the chorus to "You Enjoy Myself"), and possibly Russian ("Reba") and Spanish ("Yamar").

Helping Friendly Book   item in the Gamehendge story which contains all the knowledge of the universe and "the ancient secrets of eternal joy and never-ending splendor", everything needed to keep the Lizards happy. Stolen by Wilson and retrieved by Colonel Forbin and the Famous Mockingbird, with the warning from Icculus that "all knowledge seeming innocent and pure becomes a deadly weapon in the hands of avarice and greed." Also taken as the name of the first online collection of Phish setlists which, incidentally and ironically (in light of the Book's title), were printed out without permission, copied, and distributed by the *Pharmer's Almanac* founders in Fall 1995 to fund their touring. (They reportedly got the idea after the second Sugarbush show, at which Charlie Dirksen distributed 100 three-hole-punched copies for free.) Though these same setlists founded the Almanac's setlists file, the Almanac editors have since apologized, and thankfully given credit to those to whom credit is due. see introduction to Setlists chapter.

Helping Phriendly Phanzine   'zine started by Jason Kaczorowsky, which sold out 1,000 issues at $2 each during the summer 1997 tour. No known issues since.

Henrietta   nickname of Fishman, who has also been called Jon the Fishman (1984); Moses Brown, Moses Heaps, and Moses Dewitt (5/15/88 and 3/15/91, and he wears a "Moses Brown" t-shirt on the cover of the "Free" single and in *Billy Breathes* promo photos); Moses Yastrzemski (2/7/89); J. Edgar Hoover (12/7/89); Vinnie Barbarito (2/23/90); Phil Collins (2/25/90); Tubbs (*Rift* liner notes); Zero man (initially 9/13/90); Johnnie B. Fishman (10/20/89); Hankrietta, the shortest man in rock and roll (3/19/91); Sultan of Swat (7/21/91); the fourth member of the Giant Country Horns and Phish's multi-instrumentalist (7/21/91); Hankrietta, the shortest man in show business (10/13/91); Showboat Gertrude and Peter Shaw (10/19/91); Hankrietta (11/13/91); the hardest man in show business (after a photo from the front center of a show as he tossed the front of his dress into the air); the Yo Yo Ma of Vacuum Cleaners (4/17/92); Tommy Dorsey (4/19/92); the Piper (5/1/92); Sans Bag the Piper (5/2/92); Tubbs the Beast Boy (11/19/92); Eye Ball man (after the white dress); Tubbs, the little hairy beast-man (2/20/93, introducing himself); Little Jon and Friar Tubbs (3/5/93); Jon, Friar Tubbs, and Henrietta Fieldberg (3/9/93); Henrietta Tubman (4/5/93); Chuck Norris (8/8/93); Greasy Fizeek (beginning 12/31/93 and in *Hoist* liner notes); Marco Esquandolas (11/13/94); Luke Skywalker (12/29/94); Sneezeblood Eyeball (6/13/95); Forrest Gump (11/24/95); Morton Charleton Heston (10/25/96 and 11/2/96); Barn Boy (*Billy Breathes* liner); the orchestral Greasy Troll (7/10/97); the inhuman computer drumbeat (7/21/97); Bob Weaver (throughout the U.S. summer 1998 tour); Sammy Hagar the Horrible Horn Section (11/13/98, in a horned Viking helmet worn for most of the fall 1998 tour); Russell Crow (7-11-00); and Joe C. (9/29/00).

Other nicknames (dates unknown) include Tubman; Missing Link; Central Scrutinizer; Showboat Gertrude (esp. with the trombone); the man with the high hat (regarding Trey's conveyance of one of Fishman's hobbies); second best trombone player in Vermont and

parts of New Hampshire; and Captain Caveman.

    As drummer for the Jazz Mandolin Project's Tour de Flux incarnation (see Sideshows), he was the Abominable Shitstutski (1/27/98); Edgar Finnegan from Kinneymanport, Maine (1/29/98); all the way from Bombay Curry, Mr. Stanley Hindustan (2/7/98); Igor Spewshitzki (2/8/98); Aardvark von Doozer (2/13/99); Vajona (e.g. 7/17/99); and Ralph Boringsteen (7/6/00)

Hey hole technique used by the band to practice improvisation; "musical communication exercises" as Trey has called them, with several loose variations (such as "filling the hey hole" and "including your own hey"). In the original version, one person varies their contribution to a solid melody bed, the other three change theirs to match, and when each member senses a new united bed he says "Hey!", with the goal of all four saying it at the same time with each transition; then the next person initiates change, and the process continues in rotation.

HFB see Helping Friendly Book. Also, HPB for Helping Phriendly Book, the online resource. See also, Project History and introduction to the Setlists chapter.

High schools Trey went to Taft, in Watertown, CT; Fishman went to Jamesville-Dewitt in Dewitt, NY; Page went to Lawrence Academy, Groton, MA (for his senior year); and Mike went to Sudbury High School, Sudbury, MA.

Hockey see Flyers.

Holdsworth, Jeff original rhythm guitarist with Trey, Mike, and Fishman, who reportedly found religion and left the band to complete a chemistry degree. His last date with Phish is unknown, sometimes reported as 5/3/85 but also possibly 2/3/86.

Holiday Run, or Holiday Tour See New Year's Run

HORDE festival series in the mid-1990s featuring up-and-coming mid-range acts. An acronym for Horizons of Rock Developing Everywhere, HORDE was the hippie precursor to Lollapalooza and other harder-edged festivals, and was organized by Blues Traveler frontman John Popper. Phish performed at the first ever HORDE Tour in 1992 with Widespread Panic, Blues Traveler, Spin Doctors, and Colonel Bruce Hampton and Aquarium Rescue Unit. They headlined both the first show (at Cumberland County Civic Center in Portland, Maine) and Phish's final show (at Jones Beach Theater in New York), as well as on several HORDE shows the following year.

Horn Tour refers to Summer 1991 tour which featured the Giant Country Horns. See Setlists and Guest Book.

Horns have appeared onstage with Phish in various forms, including the Giant Country Horns (esp. Summer 1991), the Cosmic Country Horns, and solo horns (Carl Gerhard, Russell Remmington, and Gary Gazaway; see Guest Book chapter, and the constituent setlists. Also, Fishman has played a trombone, such as during "Touch Me". In the studio, "Julius" on *Hoist* featured the Tower of Power Horns, with fluglehornist Greg Adams (as well as The Ricki Grundy Chorale, Rose Stone, and Jenn McClain).

    Songs particularly known for being played with horns include "Buried Alive" (normally without horns), "Gumbo" (original, rarely played since but picked up late summer '97 when it became very spacey/groovy), "Frankenstein" (great cover), "Split Open and Melt" (10-20-89 is a classic favorite), "Suzy" (frequently played without horns, before and after the horn tour, but a perennial favorite when

horns are present), "AC/DC Bag" (originally on *TMWSIY* without horns), and "Julius" (in particular on Dave Letterman, also with Dave Grippo).

Hose, the euphemism for deep and powerful improvisational jamming, frequently borne of intense interaction between the band and the audience (e.g. the 8/13/93, 12/29/95, and 8/17/98 versions of "Bathtub Gin"). Also used in adjective form, as in "we got hosed tonight", meaning that improvisation during the show was especially transcendent.

    Originates in a Marvin Gaye expression related by Carlos Santana in telling Phish, after seeing them perform, that he pictured "the audience as a sea of flowers, the music was the water, and you guys were the hose" making the audience blossom. Incorporated into Phish's philosophy of "surrendering to the flow", as when Trey talks about music as rushing through a musician and out into the air. Also, the portion of the vacuum which Fish uses to "play".

Hot Dog enormous prop used on 12/31/94 and 12/31/99, which looks like a hot dog-shaped roller coaster car. In the debut, the band rode the hot dog across Boston Garden, above the fans, playing "Auld Lang Syne" and then throwing out goodies while "Tropical Hot Dog Night" played over the PA; in the return, the band rode in for the third (long and late) set, riding the hot dog on the back of a truck from the back left of the crowd to the stage while "Meatstick" played over the PA. The hot dog now hangs in the atrium of the Rock and Roll Hall of Fame in Cleveland.

Hotline official source for tour dates and ticket information. See Online Resources chapter.

HQ high-quality, as in tapes, referring to the sound quality, including preservation of the original sound, degradation from successive generations, and/or "digi-noise" (see entry, or Tape Guide chapter).

Humming "Bathtub Gin" garnered some interaction during the Spring 1999 Trey solo tour. From early in the tour, the audience was humming to fill space left by the missing three members of the band. At the Indianapolis show, Trey repeated that part of the song.

Hunter, Ben a.k.a. Junta, co-founded Dionysian Productions with John Paluska. As a Boston University student, Ben had rented out Molly's for 11-3-88 and 12-2-88 to rave success—the latter was the first "sold out" Phish show—and then the Paradise on 1/26/89. See Interview.

HYHU "Hold Your Head Up", an Argent song Phish covers as Fishman comes to and from stage front-and-center.

Hypercardioid microphone configuration, with a pattern thinner than cardioids (i.e. less than 90 degrees) and variable.

Icculus great and knowledgeable being—prophet, wizard, god, genius, and/or shaman (we do not know)—who lives atop a mountain in Gamehendge, and wrote the Helping Friendly Book. Icculus gets the Famous Mockingbird to assist Colonel Forbin in retrieving the Book from the evil Wilson.

IDK "I Didn't Know", a Phish original written by Richard Wright, aka "Nancy Taube".

Inside Out informal group of fans formed in summer 1997 by Phish. Netters (particularly Chris Bertolet and Greg Starks) to combat the perceived scourge of "hard" drugs at Phish shows. Although the group has never flyered concerts, their online efforts created significant dis-

cussion on RMP about changing dynamics in the lots at Phish shows.

Instruments   the main instruments are guitar (Trey Anastasio), bass (Mike Gordon), drums (Jon Fishman), and keyboards (Page McConnell). See those entries and, for other instruments, the Biographies chapter.

Island Tour, The   a four-show series (4/2-6/98) in Long Island and Rhode Island, and not part of any other tour.

Jamming   improvisational performance within or beyond a song. See also entries for Segue, Type II Jamming, Pornofunk, Silent Jamming, Start/Stop Jamming, Themes, Overtures, and Hey Hole.

J-Cards   paper insert in a cassette case, which is bent twice and therefore looks like the letter "j" from the side.

Jim   see Pollock, Jim

Jimmy's Dream   an unofficial documentary about the Clifford Ball produced by fan Bruce Carlin, which includes amateur film footage as well as footage shot professionally for the Ball's video screens during the second set of 8/17/96. Includes the entire second set, and circulates privately among fans. Jimmy is a character in "Harpua", the last song of the event (see Setlists and Show Reviews).

JMP   Jazz Mandolin Project; see Side Projects.

Jon   see Fishman, Jon.

Junta   nickname of Ben Hunter (see entry and Interview) and name of an early Phish album (see Discography). Pronounced *JOON-tuh*.

Karma Crew   seeks "to improve the life and face of the lot community". Begun by Jay "Kid" Archibald with flyers ("Top Ten Ways to Save the Scene") distributed at the Clifford Ball, and then by his 5/6/97 post to RMP about "preserving the vitality of the Phish scene, creating a harmonious environment between fans, venues, and local communities, and educating the people who do not know what it takes to make this work." Though without organizational structure or activities, the group/effort had many supporters and generated discussions about education (rather than enforcement efforts) about litter, beggars, and "bad drugs" such as nitrous oxide, a.k.a. "hippie crack". See also Organizations.

Kayaker   Gamehendge character who "parks [his] kayak on a stone" and then yells at Wilson in "Punch You in the Eye", a song not part of *TMWSIY* but connected with it lyrically and temporally.

Keyboards   Page plays a Hammond B3 with a Leslie 122 speaker (see that entry), a Fender Rhodes, a Yamaha C7 "baby grand" (7'6") piano (since 2/3/93), a Hohner D2 Clavinet (on top of the piano), a Moog Source (on top of the Clav; formerly on the B3), and a Yamaha CS50 polyphonic synthesizer (on top of the B3; formerly between he and the audience). Note that there has been some changes in the synthesizers, with some shows possibly including a Yamaha CS80, a flatpanel Moog, a MiniMoog, and a Korg Prophecy. Additionally, Trey plays a Yamaha AN1-X keyboard, notably during "Sand" but also, for example, during the 10/5/00 "Guyute" and "Chalkdust".

KFOG   San Francisco radio station (known for webcasts as much as for their DJs) that held a May 2000 contest, the winners of which got to attend a small studio performance by Phish, recorded for later airplay.

Kick down   to give away, purportedly to the less fortunate. Used in request (or expectation) of a ticket, spare change, or beer. The phrase "kick down so I can get down" seeks a "miracle" (i.e. free) ticket, a

term borrowed from Grateful Dead fans.

Kids   term used by common lot go-ers, to greet and describe each other. Also used to describe a group of friends or "family", as in "my kids."

Kind   top of the line/extremely good, though definitions and expectations of "kind" objects vary significantly. Typically refers to potent marijuana, but also used more broadly. See also entry for Phat.

King of the Hill   animated series which included "Free" coming from a VW bus full of hippies on a fall 1996 episode set at a camp, and a neon sign flashing "Phish" in a fall 1998 episode set in Vegas.

Kuroda, Chris   Phish's lighting designer and board operator, aka Topher or just Toph (*Toe-ff*). Chris has been the lighting designer (and director) for Phish since 1989. As LD, Chris is responsible for the visual aspects of a Phish concert, taking care of the audiences' eyes while the band entertains our ears. Because of the reactions that his spectacular lightings evoke, Kuroda is often called the fifth member of the band, fulfilling the role sought in the March 1989 Phish newsletter, which included an ad seeking a "creative light person to run new light show for PHISH on a salaried, permanent basis. This very valuable partner will travel with the band as a 5th member." See also, listing for CK5.

Laguna Seca Daze   event at the Laguna Seca Raceway. See {dates} in the Setlists.

Lamb's Bread   a reggae band from the northeast US; see entry in Guest Book. Also, used throughout history by the Rastafarian culture as another word for marijuana, a reference to "king's bread" meaning the gift of the Almighty Father that was bestowed upon the earth for its use as sacrament and a directive to a higher level of consciousness.

Laminate   shorthand for the laminated "All Access" passes reserved for the band, production staff, and close associates. (Compare entries for After Show and Betty Ford Clinic.) In recent years, several informal fan groups have developed their own "lammys" to wear at shows, partly to help find others known only through cyberspace, and partly for the fun of mischief.

Language Signals   see Secret Language

Languedoc, Paul   Phish's Front of House (FOH) manager ("soundman") since sometime circa 1989. His first Phish show was 5/15/85, and he first ran sound 10/15/86. Prior to working for Phish, he made hundreds of instruments, and is known for using European hardwoods and fantastic inlays. He worked at the shop that built Trey's earliest custom guitar, and started making them himself in the summer of 1985. By that fall, he was building a bass for Mike. He has since built two of Trey's guitars (see that entry), two of Mike's basses (see that entry), the band's stage risers, and their monitors. No known nickname other than one introduction as "the Root Doc".

Late Show, The   see Letterman.

LemonWheel   sequel to the Clifford Ball and the Great Went, held 8/15&16/98 at the Loring Air Force Base in Limestone, ME. Events included three sets and an encore each day, to a crowd of around 60,000, as well as a fourth set on the 16th ambient jamming surrounded by hundreds of candles, an elephant float that paraded out of the concert grounds, a Garden of Infinite Pleasantries, and side stages with the Gordon Stone Trio, Miracle Orchestra, Keller Williams, and Manic Mule. See also Setlists.

Length   varies greatly from performance to performance, for many

Phish songs. Longest versions include the 11/29/97 "Runaway Jim" (60 minutes), the 6/14/95 "Tweezer" (50 minutes), the 6/22/95 "Tweezer" (45 minutes), and the 10/31/95 "You Enjoy Myself" (45 minutes). Other songs that have reached notable length include "Antelope", "Bathtub Gin", "David Bowie", "Down with Disease", "Free", "Ghost", "Simple", "Stash", and "Wolfman's Brother"; see those Song Histories. See also the Jamming Tune Summary Charts chapter for lengths of particular note, for the core group of songs for which length is most of interest.

Also of interest has been the longest note sustained by Trey, e.g. during "Divided Sky".

Leno   see *Tonight Show.*

Leslie   speaker behind Page's organs with the vertical spinning piece on the front inside (a built-in tube amplifier) which sits behind Page's organs. The tweeter (the horn speaker on top of the woofer) is controlled by a draw bar at knee level and spins, deflecting the sound from the woofer in a 90-degree elbow, creating a vibrato effect on the bend and frequency of the tone as the sound goes a small distance further away and closer to the back of the cabinet. There is thus a Doppler effect, and no "sound deflector", although the Leslie has a built-in tube amplifier. At a concert, the sound from the speaker is picked up by anywhere from one to four microphones before being sent through the PA system. Even with today's digital technology, it's difficult to create just the right organ sound without a Leslie speaker.

Letterman   Phish performed on the *Late Show with David Letterman* on four occasions: "Chalkdust Torture" 12/30/94, "Julius" 7/13/95, "Character Zero" 3/5/97, "Birds of a Feather" 10/27/98, and "Heavy Things" 5/15/00. Phish has appeared in Letterman's Top Ten lists at least twice: 9/1/98's Top Ten Things that Average Americans think NASDAQ is: #4. "Something you bake in brownies and sell at Phish concerts"; and 4/5/99's Top Ten Historical Inaccuracies in Peter Jennings' The Century; #10. Lincoln was not assassinated at a "Phish show".

Lizards   inhabitants of Gamehendge, a simple people who lived in harmony with nature and each other, as taught by the Helping Friendly Book. Since they were trusting people, they welcomed Wilson, who betrayed them and stole the Book. See also, entries for Wilson, Gamehendge, Helping Friendly Book.

Llamas   ridden by the Lizards in Gamehendge after setting blastoplasts, as suggested in the liner notes to *Rift.*

Loaded   Velvet Underground album that Phish covered on 10/31/98. See Setlists and Halloween chapters.

Logo   the mix of the word "phish" and the outline of a fish, drawn by Trey in high school and the primary iconic emblem of the band and its following. The logo is owned by Phish, and Dionysian Productions vigorously control and protects its commercial use.

There has been some argument that the image is not a fish, but a dog. The dot on the front, just above what appears to be a mouth, might very well be a nose, except that fish don't have noses. It could also be the actual mouth or an eye, hairlip, tumor, intake valve/jet, decoration, or missing dot from the 'i'. And the top of the 'h' could be a fin. Alternately, how about a left-handed guitar player, facing his left? (Turn the logo clockwise ninety degrees. The fish face is a turban, the slit in the top of the H becomes a mouth, the space between the P's and H's tops is the nose, the hole in the P is the eye, the dot

on the I becomes a goatee, the tail becomes feet, and the S becomes arms holding an invisible guitar.) There are four gills and 20 bubbles (4:20). There are also four potential images of pipes/bowls, and several hidden words. (Flip the logo upside down, cover the bottom half, and read from the "h" to the "h", you can make out the word "acid".)

Note that the logo, which had previously appeared on all things Phish, appears nowhere in or on *Billy Breathes*, *Slip Stitch and Pass*, or *Ghost*, and is on *The Phish Book* only embossed on the hardback cover, underneath the jacket, and that only for the first printing.

Love Badger, The   nickname for band archivist Kevin Shapiro during his "From the Archive" radio shows. See also The Badger.

Love Goat   Page's R&B band that opened on 5/3/85.

Lucy   purportedly the son of an Elektra official. See entry for Carini and song history for "Carini".

LXL   "Limb by Limb", a Phish original released on *Ghost*.

Lyricists   include primarily Tom Marshall and Trey (lyrics and music, respectively, though Trey has also written many on his own), but also Mike (inc. "Foam", "Mound", "Mike's Song", "BBFCFM", "Simple", "Contact"), Page ("Cars Trucks Buses" and "Magilla"), Fishman ("My Sweet One", "Dog-Faced Boy", "Faht"), Susannah Goodman ("Bathtub Gin"), Marc Daubert ("Curtain"), Richard Wright ("I Didn't Know", "Haley's Comet"), Dude of Life (inc. "She's Bitchin' Again"), J. Linitz ("Train Song"), Scott Herman ("Cavern", "Limb by Limb", and the second verse of "Squirming Coil"), and Bob Szuter and Aaron Wolfe ("Golgi Apparatus").

M Set, The   set two of 11/15/96, in which all the songs had an M in the title and after which Trey said "this set was brought to you by the letter M and the number 420."

Macaroni and cheese (aka Mac and Cheese)   distributed to the audience at the 9/28/85 Slade Hall show (hundreds of boxes) and at the 5/27/94 Warfield show (thousands of boxes) and shaken en masse as percussion during "Possum".

Machine Gun Trey   nickname for guitar style in which Trey fires off a rapid series of pyrotechnic notes. For example, listen to early versions of "You Enjoy Myself", such as 5/28/89.

Mail-order   Phish-run service (Phish Tickets By Mail) for fans, created by Shelly Culbertson with help from Grateful Dead Ticket Sales, which allows lower-hassle ordering of tickets directly from the band via an order form available in the *Doniac Schvice* or on the band's website (see Online Resources chapter). Allows fans to circumvent ticket agency costs and to receive often artistic tickets. Also, the only source for tapers tickets (see that entry, and the Tape Guide chapter) for shows with reserved seating.

Makisupa   locality of the legal officer in "Makisupa Policeman". See Song History.

Man With A Plan   mock documentary (available on video) about farmer Fred Tuttle's campaign for Senate in Vermont, for which the motto was "Spread Fred"; see that entry.

Marley   Trey's loyal dog, a mixed breed of mostly golden retriever, who was the source of inspiration for "Dog Log" and traveled with the band before slowing with age. Trey has referred to her during numerous shows—the 12/7/91 Dog Log, for example, is repeatedly dedicated to Marley—and has even occasionally brought her on

stage. She and many canine friends can be best heard on tapes of the 8/21/87 show at Ian's farm, complemented by Phish playing many dog-related songs. Marley was profiled in the May 1992 Phish newsletter, and appears on both of Trey's guitars: an inlaid bubble saying "I am the Mar Mar" above the headstock on his main guitar, and an inlay of a younger Marley on his other guitar. She can also be seen in the liner notes to *Billy Breathes*, *Picture of Nectar* (listed as "security"), *Slip Stitch and Pass*, and *A Live One* (listed as the last thank you), and in the "Down with Disease" video (barking "stop"). Note that Paul McCartney's "Martha" (on the *White Album*, and which Trey sang on 10/31/94) was about his own dog.

Marshall, Tom the lyricist for most of Phish's music, Tom combines depth, imagery, sense and nonsense to create songs that are often very flexible in terms of interpretation, yet very structured and cohesive both verbally and rhythmically. His lyrics often sound very playful when spoken aloud, and some contend that when they are pondered *slowly*, they make perfect sense. See Guestbook and Discography (for 10/00 Trey/Tom release).

Marshmallows thrown by fans at 8/6/96, 8/9/97 (starting with 20 bags), 7/98, 8/1/98, 8/2/98, 11/8/98, and 7/24&25/99, all in or near Chicago. The practice reportedly follows from Grateful Dead shows in the 1980s at the Saratoga Performing Arts Center (SPAC) in New York, where there were marshmallow feuds between the lawn and loge.

Master original tape onto which a taper records a show.

McConnell, Page keyboardist for the band. See entry for keyboards, and Biographies chapter.

MD mini-disc, an ill-fated technology for quickly achieving DAT sound for analog prices, made by Phillips and comparable (in lousy compression quality) to Sony's Minidiscs.

Meade Ranch   See "Ranch, The"

Meatstick dance series of movements (see diagram) to accompany the Phish original "Meatstick". It was introduced to the public on 7/4/99, when the band was joined by about thirty crew members. Mike and Trey have also led the audience in the dance on several other occasions, sometimes joined by Page's wife Sofi, and explained the instructions on other occasions, such as 9/18/99 when four fans

Tom Marshall and Benjy Eisen (of "Benjy's Digest").

Michael McNamara

were invited on stage to join in the dance.

Phish aimed to break the record for the most people doing a dance simultaneously. Trey announced 7/4/99 that the "Meatstick" dance would be "bigger than the Macarena", which was the dance that was done for some previous records (50K at a Yankee's game in 1996 and 65,000 in Kosice in 1997). While some sources (including CNN) have reported that Phish actually broke the record, they did not: The current record was set by 74,000 doing the "Chicken Dance" at a county fair in Akron, Ohio. Phish's first attempt was at Oswego 7/16/99, with lessons given on the side stage and Guinness officials on hand to film the event (as Trey announced on 7/15/99), but only about 60,000 people attended and not all participated. Trey reported during a later show that a second attempt would be made on 12/31/99, but there is not indication that the attempt was either successful or officially validated. (See also, entry for World Records.)

The dance existed in early 1998: A studio version of the song has a spoken break in it when Mike laughs and declares "that could be the next cha-cha"; and Page responds in *The Phish Book*, "though you won't see me doing it".

Meatstick, Japanese lyrics—The Japanese lyrics, taught to the band by The Boredoms (see Song History), are: Meatosticku Jiuando, Meatosticku Kakushite, Meatosticku Toridashta, Jiuan, Do Do Atamaga Shock, Do Do Atamaga Shock.

MFMF "My Friend, My Friend", a Phish original released on *Rift*.

Mike see Gordon, Mike.

Mike's Groove originally trio of songs ("Mike's Song", "I Am Hydrogen", and "Weekapaug Groove") which John Paluska said (circa 1992) would always be played together and only together, but which started to separate as early as 12/31/92. Now often used to any musical event (or "sandwich") which starts with "Mike's Song" and ends with "Weekapaug Groove", such as at 11/11/95. See also, entry for Billy's Groove, and component listings in the Song Histories chapter.

Mike's Corner book by Mike Gordon of 55 short pieces, mostly compiled from his columns (of the same title) in the Doniac Schvice and its precursor, with illustrations by his wife Cilla.

Mimi see Fishman, Mimi

Minkin, Marjorie Mike's mother, who painted several backdrops for the stage, including the famous Minkins, see below. Also featured in the *White Tape* song "Minkin".

Minkins, The stage backdrop crafted by Marjorie Minkin and used 1991 to 1994. Originally canvas and later on glass, they are loved for being so moving, yet abstract enough (enormous pastel swashes, arguably spelling Phish and arguably about absolutely nothing particular) that any two viewers see different things. Fishman described them as "big translucent weird shape things that the light plays with and stuff." (*Rockline*, 3/22/94) Nonetheless, they reportedly distracted from the band's presence and also with the way the lights integrated with the show, and so are no longer used.

Miracle a free ticket, often sought non-verbally with one finger extended into the air. The "miracle"-seeking practice is a residue of the Grateful Dead scene. Despite repeated attempts from Phish and Dionysian to attend Phish concerts only with tickets secured in advance, some fans continue to seek miracles out of financial hardship, real or imagined.

MLB or MLBJ "Mind Left Body (Jam)"; see Song History.

MMGAMOIO or MMGMO "My Mind's Got a Mind of Its Own".

MMW Medeski Martin and Wood. See Guest Book.

MO see Mail Order.

Moby Dick Show, the 7/11/00; see Setlists and entry for Themes.

Mockingbird see Famous Mockingbird

Mockingbird Foundation founded in 1997 to produce charitable funds from Phish fandom. For complete information, see www.phish.net/ mockingbird . See also Organizations.

Molly short for Molecule, initially (summer 1996) purported to be a new variation on "ecstasy" beyond the original chemical structures (MDA and then MDMA), and now colloquially any substance sold as ecstasy (aka "X" or "E").

Mood Ranch See "Ranch, The".

Morello, Joe Fishman's drum instructor circa 1995. Previously, he had taken only three formal lessons, in 1978 at age 13.

Movie see *Bittersweet Motel, Outside Out, Jimmy's Dream*.

MP3 file format used to trade music electronically via the Internet. Castigated for its lousy compression technology, which results in lower quality sound and high error rates, MP3s are gaining popularity and media attention ,but hardcore traders are (at this writing) focused aggressively on SHNs.

Mr. Palmer accountant in Gamehendge who is executed by the AC/DC Bag, a robot.

Andy English

The Mockingbird Foundation.

Mr. Sausage vendor at the Clifford Ball. Trey whispers "Mr. Sausage" ominously near the beginning of the third set on 8/16/96. Mr. Sausage went on to grace several other Phish festivals.

Mrs. Pizza Shit band moniker used throughout the 11/15/91 show at Trax.

MSO "My Sweet One".

MTV have not provided Phish the backing that other large, popular acts receive, in part because Phish have not sought the visibility the network provides. The only video Phish has made, for "Down with Disease", was aired late-night perhaps four times during the spring of 1994, then used that fall as the butt of humor in an episode of "Beavis and Butt-head".

Phish was the house band for the 7/23/92 episode of *Hangin' with MTV*, which featured dancing, interviews, and live music. This episode featured a battle of the bands, in which Metallica beat out Megadeath. Phish performed for about 10 minutes, doing part of "Divided Sky" and instrumentals of "Buried Alive", "Landlady", and "BBFCFM" before and after commercial breaks. Elektra mailed pre-labeled (but blank) video tapes to various people in the music industry, to tape the performance.

They also appeared in the MTV studios in 1993 in support of *Picture of Nectar*, performing "Poor Heart" and "Stash" (the latter with trampolines).

The network's "Year in Review" for 1995 spent a full minute on the band, including John Popper raving about the band, as well as a short clip of the band's one video. Other mentions have been brief, such as of 10/31/96, or host Matt Pinfield recommending *Slip Stitch and Pass* as "a great Christmas gift for hippie friends or relatives" on 12/18/97.

MTV did not send any cameras or crew to the historic Clifford Ball, but five months later (in November 1996) they twice aired a 22-minute montage produced by Dionysian, including some footage also in "Henrietta's Dream" (see that entry).

Phish has used clips of Phish as background music in promotional ads, such as the main riff from "Possum" as background to two guys in camouflage, and in several shows, including "Landlady" and "Tweezer" on a spring 1992 episode of Cindy Crawford's "House of Style", and ""Down with Disease" on the summer 1994 "Sex in the '90s" special as well as on "Real World IV" (Los Angeles) and the first "Road Rules". They have also been mentioned, for example, on the 3/3/97 episode of the game show "Singled Out", in which potential dates had to choose "some other band or Phish". (The guy and two of the three girls said Phish, and the host turned to the musician and asked, "Have you ever seen those guys? They're great!"). And for the 2000 Video Music Awards promotional ads, a guy wearing a green "Camp Oswego" shirt set up camp across the street from Radio City Music Hall.

Mud Island Tweezer, The the version of "Tweezer" performed on 6/14/95.

Mug beginning fall 1997, there was a mug, then a phone, then a rubber chicken, and then a plastic cup on Page's piano. For summer 1998, it was again a white phone. Each device concealed a microphone with which Trey communicated to an earpiece Page wore.

Mulcahey name spoken in "Character Zero".

Multibeast character(s) in Gamehendge, described in *TMWSIY* narration as "an enormous shaggy horse-like creature covered from head to tail with alternating blotches of brown and white." After the Unit Monster rescued Rutherford the Brave from drowning, Tela appeared on the shore upon a ("two-toned") multibeast.

Musical Costume Phish's term for covering an entire album by another band for Halloween, including the Beatles' *White Album* 10/31/94, the Who's *Quadrophenia* 10/31/95, the Talking Heads' *Remain in Light* 10/31/96, and the Velvet Underground's *Loaded* 10/31/98. They also covered Pink Floyd's *Dark Side of the Moon* in its entirety during the 11/2/98 second set.

Nakedness Fishman has displayed it several times, including 4/89 (lowered from the rafters playing an unamplified vacuum) and 10/31/94 (during "Revolution #9"). The entire band stripped for a 2/97 issue of *Rolling Stone*.

Nancy Taube see Wright, Richard.

National Guitar Summer Workshop annual institute at the New School in New Middlebury, CT. Trey attended the first NGSW in July 1983, prior to his sophomore year at UVM, and returned ten years later for a question-and-answer session followed by a jam session with friends and other former students. Tapes of both sessions circulate, typically labeled Trey Speaks and Trey Plays, and selections have been filtered widely as fillers and as part of volume I of an interviews collection known as the Tank Talk Tapes; see separate entries for these traded collections.

Net Gathering pre-planned meeting of Phish.netters prior to or following a show, typically at a nearby bar or restaurant. Good place to meet new faces, find fellow tape traders, and set or celebrate the mood. The first known Phish.Net Gathering was held on 2/20/93; some successful ones in recent years include 8/17/97, 11/22/97, 12/30/97, and 12/30/99.

Net Shirt see Phish.net Shirt.

Net, the see entry for Phish.net and chapter of Online Resources.

Netiquette appropriate behavior on the Internet, including not writing messages in all capitals (hard on the eyes and seen as SHOUTING); not posting commercial messages in noncommercial locations; "lurking" in a group before actively participating or, further, seeking anything from it. Violations of netiquette are said to attract "flames", outspoken rebuke and, on occasion, condemnation.

New Year's Eve Run series of shows (typically four) leading up to and including New Year's Eve. This practice began 1989 and continued through 1999. The "official" name for these shows has been the Holiday Tour. See the appropriate Setlists.

New York band name assumed by Trey, Mike, James Harvey, Paul Jaffe (aka Pistol Stamen), and Tom Lawson for a show at Club Toast, in Burlington, VT, on 5/21/97. Paul Jaffe and Tom Lawson are both from "The Pants". Page joined the group during the jam in the encore. They performed originals by various members, including new songs later played by Phish, along with covers by artists including the Pants, Frank Black, My Bloody Valentine, Stereo Lab, Sly and the Family Stone, and Jimi Hendrix. See entry in Side Projects.

Newsletter originally called simply *The Phish Newsletter*, later renamed *Doniac Schvice* (see that entry).

Nicknames Mike is Cactus, Page is Chairman of the Boards, Trey has

referred to himself as "the good Lieutenant" (and the '96 *Phishbill* called him "Leadership Qualities"), and Jon has dozens of nicknames—see entry for Henrietta. See also entry for Root Doc.

Ninja Custodians Burlington band that was a contemporary of Phish's in the early days. They have been referenced onstage, most notably during the 4/17/92 "You Enjoy Myself" vocal jam. See Guest Book.

Nipple slicing activity mentioned in several songs ("Fee" and "Punch", e.g.), and possibly referring to the Oh Kee Pa ceremonies; see that Song History, and entry for "Triple Nipple".

Nitrous the only drug so unwelcome in Phish lots that it is specifically outlawed on mail order flyers and tickets. This is also an early song; see listing for "Nitrous" in Song Histories chapter.

Nonmusical Projects see Biographies for each band member. See also entries for *Mike's Corner* and *Outside Out*.

NOS A method of placing microphones in which they are not crossed, but pointed away from each other and towards each stack of amplifiers or at a predetermined angle.

Nugs or Nuggets buds of cannabis (marijuana), typically high-quality and high-potency, well-manicured during growth and harvest to be small balls rather than long dongs, and dried on a flat surface rather than hung upside down.

NYE New Year's Eve. See Special Shows section, and appropriate Setlists and Show Reviews.

OE see Operation Everyshow.

Official releases see Discography.

OJ Show, The 6/17/94, the night of O.J. Simpson's nationally televised ride in a white Ford Bronco. Show named so because Phish mentioned the former football superstar throughout the second set (esp. in "Also Spracht", "Poor Heart", "Mike's Song', and "Simple) after having seen footage of the chase during the setbreak.

Okipa misspelling; see Song History for "Oh Kee Pa Ceremony".

Omni (Omnidirectional) a microphone with a 360 degree pickup pattern. Records sound coming from all directions.

On the Back of the Worm see Wormtown.

Operation Everyshow (a.k.a. OE) tape-distribution system (see Tape Tree entry) started by James Gray in the summer of 1995 (after "tiring of inferior sources and slow tape trees") by which a large number of people would receive an entire tour's tapes in a single structure. Some participants signed up for a week of tour at a time, others joined the "permastructure" and committed to spreading an entire tour. Gray persisted in spite of complaints about the success of the trees and—supported by the recording contributions of Don "Team Schoeps" Wright and Stan Lobitz—organized tape trees of every Phish show performed for five years. OE eventually branched into a few early Pink Floyd trees before folding after a couple successful years.

Organizations Phish fans, concerned about larger crowds, more trash, and "hard drugs", have initiated many efforts to improve and preserve the Phish scene,. See entries for Inside Out, Karma Crew, Clifford Care Bears, Phunky Bitches, the Phellowship, and the Green Crew. See also, entries for the Waterwheel Foundation, Greenpeace, Mockingbird Foundation, and Benefits. Not all organizations are totally serious or charitable; see People for A Louder Mike and CK5.

Organs see Keyboards.

Orlando Stash, The   the version of "Tweezer" performed on 11/14/95.

Orpheum Bowie, The   the version of "David Bowie" performed on 11/26/94.

ORTF   A method of placing microphones in which they criss-cross eachother approximately in the middle of the bodies.

Oswego   Phish's fourth annual summer festival, held in July 1999 at the Oswego County Airport in Volney, NY, and following to a degree the model set by the Clifford Ball, Great Went, and Lemonwheel. This event, however, was in the middle of a tour, did not have a name, and was originally scheduled for the usual two sets per day (though a third set was added to 7/18). As an omen of Big Cypress (12/30/99-1/1/00), the festival area was concentrated outside the concert gates, allowing it to be enjoyed throughout the event. Like Lemonwheel, there was a side stage, but in the lot and with bigger billing, including some of Phish's greatest influences such as Son Seals and the Del McCoury Band, as well as several guest DJs who led an all night rave in which Fishman also participated.

Outside Out   Mike's film, originally called the *Outstructional Video*, starring Colonel Bruce Hampton as guitar teacher who attempts to unteach his student. Debuted 3/12/00 at the South-by-Southwest (SXSW) Film Festival in Austin, TX.

Outstructional Video, The   early working title of Mike's movie *Outside Out*; see above.

Overtures   series of teases by Trey (in particular) of setlists from a previous set (as in the second sets of 2/20/93 and 4/30/94).

Oysterhead   one-time Trey side project with Les Claypool (of Primus) and Stuart Copeland (of the Police).

Page   see McConnell, Page

Palmer   the accountant in Gamehendge who is killed by the AC/DC Bag, a robot.

Paluska, John   Phish's manager, co-founder of Dionysian Productions and credited with strong early promotion of the band. In March of his junior year at Amherst College (of which he is a 1989 graduate), while on a skiing vacation, Paluska saw Phish at Nectar's (reportedly for 3/12/88). He called the band the next day and booked them for an all-campus party at Humphries House (aka The Zoo), a housing cooperative of which John was the social director. It was the band's highest-paying gig and their first professional out-of-state gig.

Patching in   connecting a recording device (such as a DAT or analog tape recorder) to the soundboard or to another recording device, via cables, in order to capture the soundboard's output signal.

Paul   see Languedoc, Paul.

PBs   Phunky Bitches. See entry in Online Resources chapter.

PCP   People for a Clearer Phish, the premier online organization set up to spread the music of Phish clearly and freely on CD-R and other digital media. Founded in March 1998 by Mike Pelletier, the PCP was responsible for the first ever Phish CD-R tree, making digital recordings available for everyone. Its primary purpose is to digitally clone authorized audience recordings and soundboards of live concerts. Cloning is performed for free; money or any material profit is strictly prohibited. A variety of members play key roles in the entire process, ensuring a long life for the organization. The PCP has been strategically positioned to deliver the highest quality recordings, to the most

fans, faster than anyone else.

PCP Compliant   designation (perhaps tongue-in-cheek) for a recording which meets the standards created by the People for a Clearer Phish to assure an excellent level of quality for the creation, cloning and distribution of digital concert recordings.

People For A Louder Mike   A lighthearted organization started by Chris Glushko prior to Summer Tour '97, urging that Mike's bass be turned up in the mix. Miraculously, Summer Tour provided the birth of the "funk" era, and boasted a noticeably louder Mike. PLM hosts a website, which has assisted in a "permanent" tree structure (compare Operation Everyshow). The group also distributed a limited number of t-shirts in 1997.

Petras, Henry   a hard-core Phish fan in the early 1990's who reportedly traveled the farthest to see the Amy's Farm 8/3/91 show (from Palo Alto, CA, to Auburn, ME). Just before the second set of the 9/28/91 show at The Rink, Henry was awarded a trophy by the band for this feat. (He was also wished a happy birthday, since 9/28/91 was his birthday.)

Phat   like kind and fatty (or "phatty"), used to describe or sell everything being sold in the parking lot of a Phish show (from food to drugs), often regardless of its quality (actual or relative). Also used to refer to other acquisitions, such as a superb hotel room or ride; to a situation, such as being in the HOV lane when all other traffic is stopped; or to a song, set, or show, such as 2/20/93 seemed to those in attendance. (Note, then, that phatness is relative and may not convey across time.) Fatty is superficially beyond kind, though perhaps without depth. See also, listings for Kind, Trustafarian.

Phellowship   According to its charter, "The Phellowship is a group of Phish Heads who choose to remain drug and alcohol free. We are not affiliated with Alcoholics Anonymous, Narcotics Anonymous, Phish, or The Wharf Rats. The Phellowship has absolutely no opinion on the issue of drugs and alcohol, and neither condemns nor condones it. Our simple purpose is to provide 'phellowship', support, and information to those who seek the comfort and camaraderie of other clean and sober people at shows. The only requirement for membership is a desire to stay substance-free at shows. Though The Phellowship consists primarily of those recovering from addiction, we are open to anyone who wishes to remain clean and sober at shows".

The Phellowship has had a presence on the Phish.Net since early 1996. The first official meeting of the group occurred at the 10/31/96 show. It was there that a fledgling group of clean and sober fans were allowed to set up a table inside the venue to serve as a meeting place for those who choose to remain clean and sober at shows. After a few more gatherings met with success that fall, the group came back in the summer of 1997 and has been on Phish tour ever since. In that time, membership has blossomed and thousands of people have come to know the Phellowship, several calling themselves members. Whether recovering from addiction or just choosing to refrain, teams of clean and sober fans gather at the table each night of tour and share in the freedom and joy that seeing Phish is all about. Having absolutely no opinion on issues relating to drugs or alcohol, The Phellowship wishes to simply make itself available to those who seek a clean and sober environment at shows.

Phil and Phriends   4/15-17/99 variation on Phil and Friends (a musical project by Grateful Dead bassist Phil Lesh) involving Trey and

Page from Phish, as well as Steve Kimock (Zero, KVHW, Steve Kimock Band, and the Other Ones) and John Molo (the Other Ones).

Phish 2000 moniker under which the band was introduced by Trey on 11/2/90 and by Fishman on 12/31/99 (just before "Roses are Free"). The name also surfaced sporadically in audience discussions during the fall 1997 tour, particularly at Hampton.

Phish Book, The the first official book on Phish, written by Richard Gehr with assistance from the band and others close to the band.

Phish Food flavor of Ben & Jerry's ice cream—with chocolate ice cream, caramel and marshmallow swirls, and inch-long fudge fish—originally called Moby Dick, as conceived by Tad Van Leer. Launched on 2/20/97, it is reportedly the company's third most popular flavor and sells an estimated 3.5 million gallons per year. Phish's proceeds support cleanup of Lake Champlain, and spurred the creation of the Waterwheel Foundation. See also, Setlist for 3/18/97.

Phish Tickets by Mail official distribution service for Phish's mail order ticket service, created by Shelly Culbertson with help from Grateful Dead Ticket Sales. See Mail Order.

Phish.Net Shirt one of three designs (1992, 1993, and 1994) produced and distributed by Phish.Netters for the promotion of the online community and its volunteer-maintained resources, and to assist Phish.netters in meeting each other at Phish shows. See also, Net Gathering.

Phish.Net, The originally a mailing list with fourteen members, then a Usenet newsgroup (RMP), and now primarily a web site which houses the resources created in earlier eras, together with current news and other information. In earlier days, designation as a "Phish netter" meant membership in a small and narrowly defined group. (There was even a "Netter's list" circulated in 1993 to help people get in touch). With the explosion of internet use and the deluge of posts to RMP, this is now less of a cohesive community and more of a network of working groups and their volunteer-produced resources. Although the term originated with RMP and www.phish.net, it can be used broadly to refer to the vast network of mailing lists, newsgroups, web pages, and chat rooms which discuss Phish, their music, and related issues. See Online Resources chapter.

Phishbill pamphlets distributed upon entry to the 10/31/96 and 10/31/98 shows, modeled after the theatre program *Playbill*, to give some background on the musical costumes (*Remain in Light* and *Loaded*). The bills included witty humor from the band, such as mock advertisements, a "Who's who in the cast", and some serious commentary about the band's interest in the album being performed. See also Musical Costumes.

PhishCast originally, a channel on the PointCast news network (an Internet-based "push" technology) extended from the Phish.Net FAQ (see Online Resources). More recently re-appropriated for some official streaming and for an unofficial chat room.

Phishing Manual, The book by Dean Budnick, subtitled "A Compendium to the Music of Phish", which details one fan's memories and anecdotes on Phish history through 1994.

Phunky Bitches organization dedicated to improving the scene, especially for women. At shows, they have distributed (for free) condoms, tampons, earplugs, small bandages, disinfectant, aspirin and other useful items, as well as fliers with listings of local hospitals, women's shelters and crisis hotline numbers. When not touring, much of their activity takes place on their mailing list, which was initially announced as a sort of training for women to get onto RMP, but almost immediately became a discussion forum of its own, featuring both male and female subscribers. See also Online Resources.

Ping Pong Balls dropped from the Hot Dog during 12/31/94, and imprinted with the band's official logo and the date.

Planes featured at the Clifford Ball and the Great Went, most notably a biplane with trailing banners (e.g. "Seriously, Help me—No more gas!", "Evan Dando", and "A Dime From Here Would Penetrate") and a glider caressing the sky during the sunset as the Clifford Ball symphony ended.

PLM see People for a Louder Mike.

Pollak, Steve see Dude of Life.

Pollock, Jim—artist known for his artwork for Phish, including posters, tour shirts, liner notes (esp. *Junta*), mail order tickets, and a cartoon ("Bob Chin" and "Grungy Dudes") in the *Doniac Schvice*. He can also been seen at festival shows (such as Great Went and Lemonwheel) manning a structure in the concert grounds, and selling limited-edition prints.

Though sometimes confused, he is *not* the Dude of Life. (That's Steve Pollak.)

PON *Picture of Nectar*, a Phish album. See Discography chapter.

Pond, The 'zine announced on RMP on 1/22/99 by Brian Kirk, purportedly distributed in the summer of 1999 for $5 per issue, and advertised as supporting artists (poets, painters, and photographers) of the Phish community, but not heard of since.

Pork Tornado Fishman's side band. See Side Shows.

Pornofunk euphemism for the funkified sound that Phish evolved

James Raras

throughout 1997, particularly on the summer and fall U.S. tours, and especially in "Also Sprach", "Cities", "Ghost", "Gumbo", and "Wolfman's Brother". Particularly evident during the April 1998 "Island Tour"; see also, the "Bathtub Gins" from 7/29/98 and 11/9/98. Lauded as a strong new direction for Phish, though also bemoaned by its omnipresence and the disappearance of high-powered, guitar-heavy wailing.

Some consider this not a "type" of jamming but something closer to a genre, and argue that Type II jamming (see that entry) can occur within various contexts which Phish adopts, including funk, rock, jazz, reggae, folk, bluegrass, and even a capella. Pornofunk, then, is not a third type of jamming, but just Type II funk.

Prison Joke   told by Fishman 4/11/91, and best heard by his telling on tapes.

Providence Bowie, The   refers to the version of "David Bowie" played in the second set of 12/29/94 at the Providence Civic Center.

PTBM   see Phish Tickets By Mail, Mail Order.

PYITE   "Punch You in the Eye", a Phish original.

Quadrophenia   Who album which Phish covered 10/31/95. See Setlists and Halloween chapters.

Rail, The   the front row of a Phish concert, usually in the form of "on the rail". Area inhabited by habitually determined fans who prefer the proximity to the band, the sound near the monitors, and the community which they have built among themselves.

Ranch, The   ranch-style house on Lake Champlain in Shelburne, VT, in which Page and many college friends lived during the mid- to late-1980s. The Joneses had a close circle of friends who referred to themselves as The Moodsters (derived from Ken Kesey's Merry Pranksters) and who referred to The Ranch as The Mood Ranch. Through the years some of the tapes that were labeled The Mood Ranch were miscopied as The Mead Ranch or even Meade.

Rarity   rarely played song, or song just performed that had previously been rare (aka Breakout or Bustout). The most popular and highly prized rarity, for over eight years, has been "Destiny Unbound".

Real Gin, The   Refers to a trio of segued songs (Bathtub Gin -> The Real Me -> Bathtub Gin) that Phish preformed on 12/29/95 at the Worcester Centrum (aka "The Worcester Gin").

Recycling   crucial on tour, where tens of thousands produce tons of waste in a few hours and then leave the area. Even though glass, alcohol, and vending are not allowed, trash abounds in lots. Help out by keeping your trash bagged, bringing extra bags for others, encouraging others to bag their trash, and picking up a few bottles or cans before you leave any lot. If starting a fresh trash bag, put a few items in first to help withstand wind, then put the bag somewhere easily visible but not likely to be tripped or driven over. Where bags and bins are not available, or are full, confine refuse to an organized pile.

Relatives   on stage have included Mimi Fishman (Henrietta's mother; see Guest Book), Mike's grandmother (12/31/94 during "Chalkdust Torture"), and Dr. Jack McConnell (Page's father; see Guest Book). See also, Minkins (created by Mike's mom, Marjorie Minkin).

Phish lyrics mention only Eliju Abrahams (Dave's father, in "Sample in a Jar".) However, Phish plays "Eliza" (an original) and "Izabella" (a Hendrix cover), songs with the same names as Trey's daughters. Eliza

is also Trey's wife Sue's middle name. Page and Sofie's daughter is named Delia Edna McConnell.

Remain in Light   Talking Heads' album that Phish covered on 10/31/96. See Setlists and Halloween chapters.

Rhombus   sculpture in a clearing in some woods near Trey's hometown where he and friends would hang out, sing songs, and grow; therefore also a place where the early kernels of Phish grew, including lyrics. The sculpture and location served as inspiration for Trey and Tom Marshall's songwriting. The rhombus has been featured in Gamehendge narration as the place the Lizards went to chant Divided Sky (11/15/91).

Riker   see Frakes, Jonathan.

RLA   "Run Like an Antelope", a Phish original.

RMP   rec.music.phish, a Usenet newsgroup devoted entirely to Phish. For information, see the Phish.Net web site and FAQ; see Online Resources.

Rockpalast   German television program which broadcast the 2/16/97 and 6/22/97 shows.

Rollerblading   done by Trey during the "Weekapaug Groove" on 9/28/91. He changed to a wireless setup during "I Am Hydrogen", jumped off the stage during the jam in "Weekapaug", and rollerbladed around the venue, out in the crowd. Just before the encore, he apologized for knocking over a woman near the back.

Root Doc, The   see entry for Languedoc.

Rotation Jams   where the band swaps instruments while jamming, including 12/29/96 and 2/13/97. The rotation does not lend itself to quality jamming, but is a novelty and is a testament to the multi-talented nature of the group. Some songs, such as "Walfredo", were written intentionally to be performed by the band members in rotation.

Rubber chicken   thrown into audiences by the Dude of Life (see that entry), e.g. on 8/9/93. Each has band signatures, quotations, and a story part. The Dude has also thrown them at his own shows (see Side Shows), such as 2/5/95 (labelled #8).—See also, entry for Telephone.

Rutherford the Brave   character in Gamehendge, a revolutionary like Tela, who jumps into a lake—"forgetting that his suit of armor" was on—and drowns.

Sands, Brad   road manager, formerly known merely as stage hand; also the "Balloon Tech" for 12/31/93, and the Famous Mockingbird (in a Big Bird costume) on 12/31/92. Aka Sandsio, and babysitter.

Sandsio   see Sands, Brad

Sandwich   bookending of a string of shows by a pair of related songs, such as "Tweezer" and "Tweezer Reprise" (a "Tweezer sandwich", including everything in the middle) or "Mike's Song" and "Weekapaug Groove" (loosely a "Mike's Groove", sandwhiching whatever comes in between.)

SBD   recording from the soundboard; see Tape Guide.

Schall, Pete   monitor man until fall 1996 (i.e. prior to Mark "Bruno" Bradley). Introduced the fan chess players in 1995 (see Chess entry). Credited as "stage sound" in the liner notes to *Picture of Nectar* and *A Live One*.

Schwag   low-quality marijuana, typically brown and little (if any noticeable) potency.

Schwilly   cheap beer. Also, the intentionally assumed mental state of some concert goers before entering a show.

Screw, The (a.k.a. Bugtown)   the area in many outdoor venues between the pavilion seating and the lawn. While intended for walking, this area is often used by fans to dance.

Seating Choice   For shows not general admission, all methods of getting tickets (mail order, ticketmaster outlets, phone sales, and, when available, online sales) reportedly get the same ratio allotments of various ticket quality (e.g. floor, loge, balcony, obstructed). All methods are first-come, first-served, but everyone gets the same shot at the same time, sometimes with little notice. Unfortunately, there are of course illicit and unethical ways to get better seats.

Secret Language   set of musical signals crafted to elicit certain responses from other band members or from the audience. These cues evolved from a set of signals the band would make to each other, such as pointing out and commenting on someone in the front row. The signals eventually became a spectacular paradigm of interaction between and and audience, with prompts for fans to scream "Doh!" (after the theme to *The Simpsons*), fall to the floor (after a series of four descending notes), face the back of the room (after a quote from "Turn Turn Turn"), laugh (after six fast notes), sing a random note (signal obscure), or scream "Aw, fuck!" (e.g. 4/21/92). See page 85 of *The Phish Book* for the band's listing of component signals.

Signals are announced before they arrive by a high trill of two notes since 1992, but by a quote from the Vapors' "Turning Japanese" prior to that year. They are most frequently heard in "Possum", "Wilson", "Antelope", "Maze", or "David Bowie" (during the hi-hat introduction).

Trey first explained "the language" to audiences on 3/6/92, and again on 3/12/92, 3/13/92, 3/14/92, 3/20/92, 4/22/92, 4/29/92, 5/14/92, 12/29/94, and 12/31/94. See also entry for Flyers.

Section, The   nickname for the taper's section, the area of seats reserved for those who make live recordings of Phish shows. Typically requires a special ticket.

Segue   smooth musical transition ("flow") from one song into another, pronounced SEHG-way and denoted on setlists by > or ->; see introduction to the Setlists chapter for this distinction.

Seminole   native American tribe residing in Central Florida. During the Big Cypress NYE2000 event, the tribe's Chief, Jim Billie, inducted the fans in attendance at Cypress into the tribe as honorary members.

Sesame Street   popular children's television show, the affiliated namesake magazine of which Trey's mother Dina was a writer/editor. She has written a number of children's books, mostly published in Ireland, and has written stories and songs with Trey. They put out at least three albums together: *Quentin the Quackless Duck*, *Timothy Tatter's Sad Gloomy Day*, and *Large Motor Skills*. The September 1996 issue's cover features a suspicious looking guitarist, and lettered blocks spelling out both "fish" and Trey.

Sessions on West 54th   PBS show originally hosted by David Byrne on which Phish performed a one-hour set, broadcast 1/9-16/99 (depending on local broadcast schedules) and including three songs ("Birds of a Feather", "Ghost", and "Taste") interspersed with clips of interviews with Byrne.

Shakedown Street   the main vending/commerce area the parking lot,

typically a particular aisle, row, street, runway, road, path, or walkway. Derived directly from the Grateful Dead song and (subsequently) the Dead parking lot culture. Some refer to it as "Fakedown Street," not simply for the low-brow tie dyes and schwag wares that often get sold on it, but because of the (mis?)appropriation of the label "Shakedown Street" from the Dead scene and Dead fans.

Shapiro, Kevin   archivist for the band, responsible for collecting, cataloguing and tracking audio and video recordings, press clippings, and all other manner of archived and vaulted materials. Kevin also acts as Dionysian's in-house counsel. See also, Interview.

Shelly   see Culbertson, Shelly.

Shepherd, the   character (possibly narrator) in "McGrupp and the Watchful Hosemasters", in which he "tends his shores by the Baltic sea".

Shotgun   A microphone with a very narrow pickup pattern. Normally used to record a source from large distances. Minimizes crowd noise.

Signals   see Secret Language

Silent Jam   technique Phish employs by which they continue improvising without continuing to make sounds with their instruments, i.e. improvisation without amplification. Each band member slowly lowers their volume of their playing to complete silence but maintains the facial expressions, body language, and appearance with their instrument as if they were also maintaining full-throttle improvisation. Fans typically react as if the jam had gotten louder or more intense. The improvisational sequence is retained between the band and audience, and in the ideal is regained and re-entered by all present, in roughly perfect timing, as though there had been sound the entire time. See 12/9/95 "You Enjoy Myself", and compare to entry for Start/Stop Jamming.

Simpsons, The   Phish teases the theme song (see entry for Secret Language), and many episodes of the show contain arguable references to Phish antics (a picture of J. Edgar Hoover in something akin to Henrietta's dress, and a school band using glowsticks), covers (Principal Skinner singing "Hello My Baby" over the PA; Homer dancing to "Baby Elephant Walk"; a wild performance of "Revolution #9"; and various appearances of "Frankenstein" and "We're an American Band"; plus a horse being *hoist*ed, remarkably similar to the cover of *Hoist*), and originals (Homer bootlegging "bathtub gin"; Homer standing on a box of Mr. Sparkle detergent while Bart joked about changing a "fishbulb"; an "antelope crossing" sign; Jasper and Lisa stepping into a freezer; Moe's Tavern being renamed Moe's Cavern; Bart calling both Millhouse and Willie "Lawn Boy"; Homer saying, "Barney, I could punch you in the nose"; and Lisa's evil twin being named Eliza).

The idea that the show would reference Phish is ridiculed by many. (For example, Lawnboy is a mower brand.) However, the show has made explicit references to various other bands, including Sonic Youth, Smashing Pumpkins, Peter Frampton, Michael Jackson, Cypress Hill, Steve Miller Band, Bob Marley, The Ramones, Red Hot Chilli Peppers, Spinal Tap, Pink Floyd, Grand Funk Railroad (Homer's favorite band), and the Beatles.

Singing   done by the band, onstage. When done by fans, it may interfere with others' enjoyment, and may get picked up by mics and alter the show for hundreds or thousands of people who'll hear it later on tape. Some obvious exceptions include "Wilson" (see Chanting),

"Destiny Unbound" (see "Destiny Chant"), and "Harry Hood" (see "Hairy Balls"), as well as "Col. Forbin's Ascent" ("so slowly") and Fluffhead ("powerful pills, oh yeah"), Bathtub Gin ("we love to take a bath") "Twist Around" ("woo").

SITM   "Silent in the Morning", a Phish original.

Singles   see notes in Discography.

Skelton, Amy   a devotee in the early Nectar's days, owner of the horse (Molly) on the front of Phish's 1994 release *Hoist*, and merchandising manager for Phish. She owns a barn in Vermont where Molly lives, and where Phish played many early shows. Amy has long been known as "Phish's first fan", although Brian Long has been acknowledged as an earlier fan.

Slip Stitch and Pass   Elektra album release involving threaded tracks from the 3/1/97 Copenhagen show. See Discography and Setlist chapters.

SOAM   "Split Open and Melt" or "Scent of a Mule", both Phish originals, although Scent of a Mule is more properly and widely abbreviated as either Scent or SOAMule, since SOAM has been Split Open and Melt longer than Scent has even been a song.

Soundboard   production console at which the soundman (see Languedoc, Paul) mixes the sounds the band is making, for broadcast to the venue. Also recorded on five synchronized eight-track DATs (40 tracks total) via a submixer, as well as directly to a two-track DAT, and archived (see Shapiro, Kevin). Access to tapers is no longer allowed, and has generally not been granted since 6/16/90. (Crucial equipment was unplugged during "Horn" at that show.) See also, Taping Guide, and entry for Patching In.

Space Antelope   Trey's second high school band at Taft. In his junior year, seven of the eleven-member Red Tide graduated. The remaining four—Rob "Flash" Gordon (on lead guitar), Doug Taft (bass), Doug Parsons (drums), and Trey (on rhythm guitar, now self-taught), with occasional appearances by Steve ("the Dude of Life") Pollak—reformed as a quartet. For the band's keynote song, "Run Like a Space Antelope", Tom Marshall wrote the verse and Steve wrote the chorus: "run like space antelopes, out of control."

Spark   slang expression for putting fire to a marijuana cigarette, or to a pipe or "bowl" fueled with marijuana. Also the title of a song by The Who which Phish has played and teased.

Spinning   twirling dance pattern seen at Phish shows, which was also routinely practiced by a group known as The Spinners at Grateful Dead shows. Also, the dubbing of a live recording (as in spinning tapes—see Tape Guide).

Spliff, Splif, or Spleef   marijuana cigarette, as mentioned in "Makisupa Policeman". In Jamaica, "spliff" (pronounced "spleef") is an alternate name for a blunt, a cigarette of marijuana and tobacco blended together and rolled in the outer layer of a cigar. In England, a "spliff" (pronounced as it is spelled) refers to the same blend, but typically is rolled in cigarette papers.

Spread Fred   button Mike was wearing on 8/17/96. See *Man with a Plan*.

Spun   under the influence of LSD, particularly in liquid form.

SSTTA   "Sneakin' Sally through the Alley", originally by Robert Palmer.

Stage banter   things said during or between tunes, often interesting for their arbitrariness, e.g. the "Prison Joke" on 4/11/91. Sometimes stretches across several shows, for example, the "back of the worm" banter at 7/1&2/97

Stage Order   Page has always been on the far left, facing the stage. Originally, Fishman was on the far right, with Mike beside him and Trey between Page and Mike. Circa 1997, Fishman's drum stand moved behind Mike. Beginning 6/30/99, Trey and Mike had swapped so that Trey is in front of Fishman and Mike is centered, between Trey and Page.

Start/Stop   sometimes used to refer to a > (as opposed to ->) segue. See entry for Segue and introduction to Setlists chapter.

Start/Stop Jamming   which occurs when the band stops playing and then—after waiting in silence for a few beats or even measures—comes back in playing together. Incorporated in the composition of "Black-Eyed Katy" (debuted on 11/13/97); evident in "Ghost" 11/28/97, "Possum" 12/3/97, "Izabella" 12/6/97, "Tube" 12/7/97, and "Run Like an Antelope" 12/12/97; and audible during more than half the songs of 7/19/98, even including "YEM" and "Sample in a Jar". See also entry for Jamming; and compare to entry for Silent Jamming.

Stinette, Jim   Mike's one-time bass instructor, who appeared onstage with Phish for a bass duet on "La Grange" 12/29/95.

Stink, Stank, Stunk   words Trey used in "Antelope" on 12/28/96, referring to high-quality marijuana, said to be "stinky" and sometimes called "skunk".

Stires, Ernie   UVM composition mentor to Trey (as well as Jamie Masefield of Jazz Mandolin Project), a jazz composer and pianist with a penchant for 1930s and '40s big band and neoclassical composition, who specializes in atonal sonorous composition. Bad Hat, which includes both Jamie and Trey, performed two tribute tunes, "Blues for Ernie" and "Ernie's Groove". In late 1997, Stires released a CD featuring one track by Trey; see Discography.

STTA   Surrender to the Air.

Summer tour   string of shows occurring during the summer months, typically during July and August (though 1995, for example, was June-July, and some years have had European tours in June.)

Surrender to the Air   improvisational jazz project, and album release of the same name, organized by Trey, and featuring Trey and Fishman, as well as John Medeski, Oteil and Kofi Burbridge, James Harvey, Marc Ribot, and others. Inspired by eclectic jazz artist Sun Ra, the group made two live appearances and one studio session. See Discography and Side Shows entries.

Tackle Box, The   Phish fan 'zine which circulated for a few issues in 1995-1996.

Tank Talk Tapes   collection of interviews with members of Phish, assembled in late 1993 by Ellis Godard. Originally on three analog tapes (labeled Volumes 1–3), now traded on two DAT tapes (labeled Tapes 1 and 2), the collection includes 270 minutes, 13 interviews, and various musical snippets interspersed throughout.

Tape Trade   The exchange of duplicated concert recordings without the exchange of money. See Taping Guide.

Tape Tree   hierarchical, branching distribution system for disseminating live recordings, whereby most participants ("branches") duplicate shows for several others ("leaves"), in order to spread a show quickly and efficiently. (See also, E-tree entry, and Tape Guide chapter.)

Tapers' Tickets special tickets that allow access to the tapers' section, where equipment can be set up to record Phish shows live. Not all shows have tapers' tickets or a tapers' section, although those that do require having one to bring equipment in or to tape the show. Most general admission Phish shows simply require tapers to get to the show and set up early in whatever area is provided as the show's tapers' section. Available only through Phish Tickets By Mail.

TapeTracker popular (and probably leading) software used for tracking live tape/CD collections, including features to track trades, loans, wants, and more. Written and distributed by Steve Zimmerman. See Tape Guide. See also entry for WinTaper.

Tela character in Gamehendge, a revolutionary like Rutherford and "the jewel" of the land, who befriends Rutherford and Roger but who may in fact be a spy for either Wilson or Errand Wolfe.

Telephone beginning fall 1997, there was a mug, then a phone, then a rubber chicken, and then a plastic cup on Page's piano. For summer 1998, it was again a white phone. Each device concealed a microphone with which Trey communicated to an earpiece Page wore.

Television Phish has been televised in entire performance (the 10/3/98 Farm Aid show broadcast on CMT), edited performance (e.g. *Austin City Limits* 10/15/00, and see entry for *Sessions on West 54th*), short performances (see entries for Flyers, Letterman, and Conan); and selections (such as the 7/1/95 "Bouncing Around the Room" on ABC's *In Concert* 6/7/96; and various pieces on CNN's *Showbiz Today* 11/13/98 and *World Beat* 2/13/99). Additionally, Trey accompanied Kid Rock on "Only God Knows Why" on the 5/20/00 episode of *Saturday Night Live*.

Phish has frequently appeared as background music, including "Weigh" during some WNYT (channel 6, NYC) weather commercials in 1993; "The Mango Song" during the 1996 Olympics; "You Enjoy Myself" in a story about the Zendik Farm community on the 5/21/97 *Rolling Stone State of the Union*; "Cars Trucks Busses" on ABC's *NFL Air It Out* on 8/24/97, and again during a segment on the best unknown college football players during the Nebraska vs. Colorado football game on 11/28/97; "Sparkle" during a story on Japanese supermarkets during the Olympics 2/10/98; "Cities" during the *Road to the Final Four* show 3/21/98, over clips of Arizona's championship the previous year; "Stash" during the weather report on KOMU (channel 8, Columbia, MO) 7/3/98; "Weigh" during some summer 1998 news promos for WRGB (upstate NY); "Chalkdust Torture" as the theme to the Denver PBS show *Colorado Inside and Out* in August 1998; "Birds of a Feather" on the 10/7/98 episode of *Dawson's Creek* (less than a week after the single was sent to radio stations and nearly three weeks before its release on album); "Bliss" during CNN and MSNBC coverage of JFK Jr.'s missing plane in August 1999; "Free" during a dirtbike segment on NBC's "Gravity Games" 10/31/99 ; "Twist Around" on the daytime drama "As the World Turns" 7/24/00; "Rift" during the 2000 Olympics on 9/26/00; and "Down with Disease" various times on *The Howard Stern Show*.

Several sports videos include Phish music, including "Chalkdust Torture" on the Tony Roberts extreme skiing video, and on the skiing and snowboarding video *Continuium*; "Free" on a free-skiing video entitled *Harvest* and a ski/snowboard movie called *Uprising*; and "You Enjoy Myself" on the surfing video entitled *Jacked*.

Other Phish sightings on TV include Trey Anastasio during broadcast of the September 1996 Hockey world championships (U.S.

vs. Canada, in Montreal); a "Trey 420" sign held up by a fan during an 11/23/97 football game; a stack of discs in a pulled-over Volvo on the 11/17/97 *Real Stories of the Highway Patrol*; two questions on *Jeopardy*, 3/11/98 ("Phish Food and Cherry Garcia are both flavors of this company's ice cream") and 7/24/00 ("Ben and Jerry's has a flavor named after this Vermont band"); when one character loses his friend during "The Mango Song" on a fall 1998 episode of *Boston Common*; a poster of 7/30/97 on the school courtyard bulletin board in an August 1998 episode of "Buffy the Vampire Slayer", and a poster for an MSG show in the coffeeshop on two episodes, aired 9/29/98 and 10/1/98; in Letterman's Top 10 list (see Letterman entry); and on an October 1998 episode of *Viva Variety* (during which host Mr. Laupin said Jenine Gerafalo "dresses like she just got kicked out of a Phish concert".) Also, in 1998, the cover of *Ghost* was shown on *Early Edition*, a short-lived series in which the main character found a newspaper each morning that would have that day's news in it.

See also entries for *American Road*, Conan, Flyers, *King of the Hill*, Leno, Letterman, MTV, *Rockpalast, Sessions on West 54th,* and *Simpsons*.

TFTB "Theme from the Bottom", though not an often used abbreviation.

The Man Who Stepped Into Yesterday (aka TMWSIY) Trey's senior project at Goddard College, consisting of a written essay and a 90-minute tape, recorded on a four-track tape recorder, of an eight-song composed series including "Lizards", "Tela", "Wilson", "AC/DC Bag", "Colonel Forbin's Ascent", "Famous Mockingbird", "Sloth", and "Possum", interlaced by pieces of narration. The project described a fictional land called Gamehendge, and is sometimes known by that name. Also refers to an instrumental that resembles the music that serves as background to the narration segments. See also, any of these individual Song Histories, including the one for "TMWSIY".

Theme Songs Phish teases and plays various theme songs. See entry for Secret Language, and Song Histories of, for example, "Fishin' Hole Theme" (the theme to *The Andy Griffith Show*).

Themes single riff, song, banter, or feel throughout a particular show, especially evident in its jamming (see that entry). Best examples include 7/22/00 (the "Moby Dick" show), 7/1&2/99 (the "Wormtown" shows), 11/27/98 (the "Wipe Out" Show), 4/30/94 (with "The Lion Sleeps Tonight" teased throughout set II), 12/31/98 (with frequent teases of "1999" in the first set), 7/16/92 (with "Blue Bayou" teases), and 11/29/92 (with "On Broadway" teases). Though sometimes mentioned in the same conversation, 2/20/93 doesn't really count, as that was a meld of things that had already been played, or were about to be. See also entries for Jamming and Wormtown.

Theremin one of the first electronic instruments, and the only instrument played without being touched. Pronounced TAYR-uh-min and invented in 1918 by Russian physicist Leon Theremin. First sold to RCA in 1929, the lead manufacturer today is Robert Moog's company Big Briar. Page used the theremin in summer 1996, and only off and on since then (e.g., on 8/6/97).

How it works: The device is a complex interaction of two pairs of measurements. What the audience sees is Page moving his hand to interrupt an electromagnetic field. That field is monitored by two antennae forming a right angle: One measures change in amplitude and produces changes in volume, and the other reads changes in frequency and produces changes in pitch. Within the device, an elec-

tronic oscillator creates a high-pitched tone as a reference tone, while a second oscillator is affected by the combined measurements of Page's hand movements. The pulsed frequency between these two oscillators' tones is the sound you hear.

Other appearances: Most often used in early "B" science fiction movies, such as The Lost Weekend and The Day the Earth Still, and in Ed Wood. Also featured in the Beach Boys' "Good Vibrations (at the end), in Led Zeppelin's "Whole Lotta Love" (in the middle), and in the original Star Trek theme; frequently by 1960s acid rock band Lothar and the Hand People, and occasionally by Jon Spencer and the Blues Explosion. Contrary to popular fan belief, the Beatles did not use a theremin.

Third Ball, The held 6/6/96 in a small bar in Woodstock, NY, following the recording of *Billy Breathes* at Bearsville Studios. The event was advertised unofficially by a fan on rec.music.phish just a few hours before showtime. There were approximately 200 people in attendance, and about 300 folks outside. Completely unrelated to the Clifford Ball.

This Month in Phish History a regular feature on www.phish.com, written by Kevin Shapiro, which documents a single month through narrative and photos, with an emphasis on shows and setlists but which also touches on lives, releases, and side projects.

Tickets see Mail Order and Hotline.

Time Science nickname for the 12/31/95 New Year's Eve event involving smoke, equipment, and the transformation of Fishman from Father Time to the Baby New Year, but which was introduced as being necessary to move the world into the next year.

Timer, The nickname for David "ZZYZX" Steinberg, for his practice for many years of carrying a stopwatch and clipboard, and timing the length of each individual song, then making explicit and detailed (and occasionally disparaging) comments about the lengths of performances just completed. More widely known for his web-based statistical resource; see the Online Resources chapter.

TMWSIY see The Man Who Stepped Into Yesterday.

Tombstone Blues Band Mike's first high school band. See Biographies chapter.

Tonight Show Phish made their debut appearance on *The Tonight Show* on 10/3/00, performing "Twist Around".

Tortillas thrown by a few dozen audience members on 8/7/96, in greater quantity on 12/30/99, and during the final tour at the 10/5/00 and 10/7/00 setbreaks, though with greatest effect on 9/10/99 and 9/11/99, where the Gorge's wind currents carried them gliding much further. (Hint: It doesn't really work inside.)

Tour chronologically close and connected series of shows, typically announced, ticketed, and sold together or in blocks. See also, Summer Tour, Holiday Tour, *et al.*

Tour Rats see Wookies.

Tracking Mike's documentary about the making of *Hoist*. Available from Dry Goods.

Trampolines used by Trey and Mike, at least as early as 3/10/90, bouncing in rhythm with the music, particularly in segments of "YEM" (e.g. 4/29/90) and "Mike's Song" (e.g. 5/6/90, and usually just before "I Am Hydrogen"), but also occasionally in "Run Like an An-

telope", "Runaway Jim", "Wilson", "Divided Sky", "Walk Away" (4/29/90), "Scent of a Mule" (11/23/94), "Bouncing Round the Room" (12/2/96), and "Stash" (in 1993 on MTV; see that entry). The bouncing (though not the choreography) is often mimicked by many in the audience. Note that the choreography rarely changes, although Trey might spin 270 degrees left instead of 90 degrees right to face Page. Tapes reflect audience reactions to the synchronized bouncing, but the antics are somewhat diversionary, since Page is typically the only one jamming during the segment.

The small, one-person props are delivered to stage by the Brad Sands, add fun to the entertainment, and may also assist with difficult timings (see also, entry for Clapping). In early club venues, typically long flat halls, the bouncing also helped those in the back see the band. Also at early gigs, as the tramps became worn and replaced, they were given away to audience members, including on 12/7/91 and 4/5/93. Guests have occasionally filled in, including Dave Matthews on 4/21/94 when Trey had a broken leg.

The 7/27/93 HORDE encore poked fun at John Popper's having broken a tramp on 3/14/92: A giant trampoline was brought on stage after Phish's second set, and surrounded by musicians from throughout the day. A stuffed figure in a wheelchair was slowly lowered from the rafters, then suddenly dropped, breaking the trampoline. After the other musician left the stage, Popper's voice could be heard pleading, "Wait, guys—come back!"

Tree see Tape Tree.

Trey see Biography for Trey Anastasio.

Trey Plays / Trey Speaks pair of moderately circulated 90-minute tapes of the lecture and performance portions, respectively, of the 1993 National Guitar Summer Workshop; see that entry, above.

Triple Nipple the appearance in one show of any three of the four Phish originals which reference nipple slicing: "Fee", "Sloth", "Punch You In The Eye", and "Sanity". For example, 12/31/95 included "Punch", "Sloth", and "Sanity", a solid Triple Nipple. Additionally, "The Oh Kee Pa Ceremony" may refer to nipple pain (see that Song History). Only one show (10/26/89) is known to have featured four of these songs, and no show has yet featured all five.

Trustafarian financially secure hippie, who may or may not actually have a trust fund, but who gives the impression of pretending to be freewheeling and down-and-out, even while charging the Volvo's gas to dad's Visa. Reminiscent of Glen Fry's early 1980s line "Deadhead sticker on a Cadillac", but typically updated with late-1990s dreadlocks and Y2K-compliant cell phones. Symptoms include overuse of the adjective "phat" (i.e. good, cheap, and/or powerful), the verb "kick down" (i.e. share, often with a stranger of lesser fortune), the noun "custies" (non-freaks who buy beers, art, and lot shirts), and the phrase "it's all good" (particularly when it clearly isn't).

Tuttle, Fred main character in *Man with a Plan*; see that entry. He was at the Clifford Ball campaigning.

Type II Jamming name given by Phish.netter John Flynn to distinguish variations on notes and tempo fixed around similar chord progressions and time signature within a song's typical structure ("Type I jamming", as in practically every version of "Chalkdust", "Sample", "Character Zero", and "Possum") from improvised variations in chord progressions, rhythms, keys, and song structure. "Pornofunk" (see

that entry) is also sometimes (though much less often) called "Type III jamming". See also Jamming.

Unfinished   increasingly, Phish has left songs "unfinished", meaning that they have not completed the song's ending as it is typically known. Usually, but not always, this happens when a song segues into a jam which does not return to the song, but some of those jams themselves have died out rather than segueing into something new. Particularly notable are unfinished versions of "Harry Hood" (especially fall 1995), since that song has such as distinctive and triumphant ending; see that Song History. Note that songs being "unfinished" were of more interest prior to 1997—such as the 11/30/94 "Antelope" or 8/13/93 "Bathtub Gin"—after which song endings have more often given way to segues.

Unit Monster   Tela's partner, a beast who saves Rutherford from drowning in "Lizards".

Uno cards   distributed by fans at shows (particularly in the fall of 1997) and through tape trades, largely for nonsensical fun. Ascribed meanings include use to find a ticket, to find or meet friends, to attract vendors, and as a new form of currency. Occasionally displayed tucked into a hat or belt, or pinned or otherwise attached to a shirt or skirt.

Vacuum   1965 baby blue Electrolux which Fishman plays by holding the tube to his mouth, varying the opening against his cheek (and thus air flow through the tube) to affect the sound. An earlier, 1967 model was donated to the Hard Rock Café 1/29/93. A frequent part of Fishman's stage-front bits since circa 1989, it has appeared twice in several shows, including 2/20/93, 4/10/94, 7/11/96, and 8/10/96. Also used in conjunction with a bagpipe to produce the Bag-Vac (see that entry).

Veggie Burrito   typical lot fare, sold by fans and filled with some combination of beans, rice, lettuce, and other vegetables. The better ones are fresher, warm (on cold nights), and filled with better ingredients. Don't be fooled by size or price.

Videos   Phish has made only one video, in the sense of a filmed accompaniment to a single song; see entry for MTV. However, see entries for *Tracking*, *Bittersweet Motel*, *Circus of Light*, *American Road*, and *Esther Video*.

Elektra distributed a promotional video in 1992 pushing *Rift*, including footage from 11/28/92 as well as the band explaining their melding of styles as a making soup.

Some professionally filmed ("pro shot" or just "pro") videos circulate. The band videotaped a number of shows in 1993, and has filmed or videotaped most shows (including every U.S. show) for at least the last three years. Some professionally filmed videos of shows circulate, including 4/29/90 Waterbury (still marketed for sale, legally though not by Phish), 8/21/92 Shoreline (the in-venue closed circuit video captures, sold illegally), and various television appearances (see that entry), esp. 2/16/97 and 6/22/97 from German broadcast.

While prohibited at Phish shows, amateur bootleg videos nevertheless have been made and are sometimes traded, despite their typically poor quality. There are amateur videos of at least 91 shows through the end of 1997, of which few are both watchable and traded: 12/29/93, 10/31/94, 12/30/94, 6/28/95, 12/31/95, 11/11/95, 11/15/96, and 11/22/97. Two shows (5/20/87 and 10/31/89) were videotaped by amateurs with band assistance, but are more rare (although the lat-

ter was once broadcast on a public-access cable station in Burlington.)

Vocal jams   typically extend from "You Enjoy Myself", utilizing *a capella* techniques to improvise as a group, usually without any preset structure though often around a particular word or phrase, such as "Hamburger" or "White boys, attack!". See Song History for "You Enjoy Myself".

Voters for Choice   beneficiary of the 5/16/95 Phish show, which raised $30,000 and is said to have been orchestrated by John Paluska, who lived near a clinic targeted during the January 1995 anti-abortion shootings.

Wars   audience members have engaged en masse in repeated throwing into the air of glowsticks, glowrings, marshmallows, and tortillas; see those entries.

WaterWheel Foundation, The   organization started by Phish to disburse a charitable portion of merchandise sales, proceeds from Phish Food, and money collected at each show.

WATSIYEM   "What are they saying in You Enjoy Myself", the most frequently asked lyrics question, which has come to stand for what it means to be clueless about Phish, as in "That's such a WATSIYEM question." Mocked by Mike in the newsletter, where he provided a half-dozen farcical answers, such as "Water your team, in a beehive, I'm a sent you". The "correct" answer (or at least what they're singing most of the time) is "Wash Uffizi, drive me to Firenze".

Waving   typically done by audience members, swaying their arms back and forth above their head, in time to the last chorus of "Contact". The band used to lead the audience in doing this, and some fans persist without their lead.

WBCN   Boston radio station best known for a series of January 1 airings of night-before New Year's Eve shows, for several on-air inter-

Michael McNamara

views with band members, and for airplay of early Phish albums, which had received little exposure elsewhere.

Wedding Band, The movie, billed as "the Spinal Tap of wedding receptions", about a Jewish/Catholic wedding and starring Dom DeLuise & Debbie Gibson. Fishman plays in the band (in a pink dress) with James Montgomery on blues harp, Barrow Goodrow (formerly of Boston) on guitar, Chad Hollister (as Hebber Stebber) on percussion and vocals, Aaron Hersey on bass, Joe Moore on saxophone, Martin GuiGui on keyboard, and other special guests, including members of the Dude of Life's band. The movie was filmed in 1997, premiered 12/17/98 at Higher Ground, and distributed to video April 2000. It won "Audience Favorite" at the Palm Springs International Film Festival, Ft. Lauderdale International Film Festival, and San Diego Film Festival in 1999.

Wendell Studios location where a July 1990 demo was recorded.

White Album, The nickname for an early and untitled Phish demo tape, as well as for the Beatles' album that Phish covered 10/31/94. See the Discography and Halloween chapters, respectively.

White Crow Studios Burlington, VT, location where *Rift* and *Picture of Nectar* were recorded.

White Tape, The arguably more accurate and appropriate title for Phish's *White Album*.

Wilson the evil king in the Gamehendge story (*TMWSIY*). Wilson arrived and lived among the Lizards, but took advantage of them, eventually took the Helping Friendly Book, used it to enslave the Lizards, and hid it away in a mountaintop castle tower.

WinTaper popular software used for tracking live tape/CD collections, designed and distributed by Dan Tepper. Predated TapeTracker (see that entry). See also Tape Guide.

Wipe Out Show, the 11/27/98; see Setlists and entry for Themes.

Wolfe, Aaron childhood friend of Trey and Tom, and name of a character in Gamehendge. Listed as Woolf in the liner to *Hampton Comes Alive*.

Wookies (aka Tour Rats) an arguably unflattering but nevertheless not always mean-spirited moniker which refers to the often unshowered, dreadlocked fans who frequent the lots and venues of shows. Though like other species of fan (e.g., frat boy, taper, Internet geek, etc.) many wookies are friendly, articulate and kind, others expect something (spare change, tickets, beer, drugs, etc.) for free and can be indignant when they don't get it.

Worcester Jim, The refers to the version of "Runaway Jim" that opened the second set 11/29/97 at the Worcester, MA, Centrum. Known for its length; see Timing Chart.

World records Phish has broken several records, including the largest concert in North America in 1996 (the Clifford Ball, 8/16&17/96), the largest balloon drop ever (12/31/96), and the largest nude photograph (1500 people simultaneously at the Great Went, 8/17/97). However, despite repeated attempts, they are not yet in the *Guinness Book of World Records*. The most recent attempt was with the Meatstick Dance; see that entry.

Wormtown originally, a theme developed on 7/1/97 and carried into 7/2/97, (both at the Paradiso in Amsterdam). The word now sometimes refers to having experienced the Hose (see that entry).

At the first Paradiso show, Trey yelled "You're on the back of the worm" during "Ya Mar" and "Saw It Again" in the first set, and then Trey and Jon repeated "I think you know where you are....you're on the back of the worm!" during "Ghost" and "Cities". At the second show, "Llama" segued into a variation on the Steve Miller Band's "Swingtown", followed by some explanatory narration about the city's canals, and then repeated during chanting returns of Trey's line from the previous night.

Both "Wormtown" and "riding on the back of the worm" became associated with the funky style of jamming that debuted on that tour—deep, nasty, wobbly funk. Indeed, the jam out of "Stash" from 7/2/97 had four parts, but the fourth (based on a series four measures long) has reappeared at least three other occasions: in Germany later the same week; 7/21/97 Virginia Beach (where Trey said "don't do anything I wouldn't do… or you may end up on the back of the worm!"); and during the second set of 8/16/97.

Wright, Richard writer of "Halley's Comet" and "I Didn't Know", previously known as Nancy Taube although "Nancy" was an old nickname and "Taube" has no known source. See Interview.

XY A method of placing microphones in which they crisscross each other only at the very end (at the diaphragms), and at a 90 degree angle.

YEM "You Enjoy Myself", a Phish original.

Zarathustra see 2001.

ZZYZX original nickname for "The Timer" (see that entry), taken from the name of a highway to a research facility in the southwest.

'Zines There have been several periodicals devoted to Phish, though none have lasted. *The Tackle Box* and *Helping Friendly Phanzine* are best known. *The Pond* and *The Phish Forum* were announced but are not known to have materialized. *Signal to Noise* (formerly *Soundboard;* Burlington-based, edited by Pete Gershon) and *Fantastic Voyage System* (New Jersey-based, edited by Paul Parietti) are devoted to the wider "jam band" scene, but early issues (in particular) devoted heavy coverage to Phish. *Relix, Dupree's Diamond News*, and *Unbroken Chain* (which ceased in 1998) are focused on the Grateful Dead, but have paid increasing attention to Phish.

ONLINE RESOURCES

Compiled by Ellis Godard.

There is a wide variety of information about Phish available on the Internet. This section lists the most stable of those resources. Additional URLs are given throughout the book, usually at the end of the introduction to most chapters.

Official Web Sites

Official Phish Site

http://www.phish.com/

Official site for the band and their management company, Dionysian, including current hotline (/hotline.html) and tourdates (/tourdates.html), news (/news2.html), and periodic "This Month in Phish History" features.

Elektra

http://www.elecktra.com

The official site of Phish's label, although other sites are better for information such as tour dates (Phish.com) and soundclips (SugarMegs, next page).

Fan-Managed Web Resources

Newbie Central

http://www.phish.net/newbie/

A great first-stop, all-directions place for someone first getting into Phish, tape trading, and the online world.

Frequently Asked Questions File

http://www.phish.net/faq

This 350-webpage site includes answers to thousands of questions (organized into five sections) about the band, their music, their live shows, tapes of their shows, and the online community of their fans. Navigable in at least six ways.

Helping Friendly Book, The

http://www.phish.net/hfb/

The original source for Phish setlists, and still the most comprehensive and current source online, soon to be updated by the Mockingbird Foundation's collection.

ZZYZX's PhishStats

http://www.ihoz.com/PhishStats.html

Compute your *personal* statistics, or run any of a dozen features designed, implemented, and maintained by board member and programming/math hobbyist David Steinberg

Andy Gadiel's Page

http://www.gadiel.com/phish/

A widely popular site—no doubt the most successful of any individual fan—Andy's includes rumors, chat rooms, and access to a database of shows by other "jambands"

LivePhish

http://www.livephish.org

Formerly phishtapes.com and traders-corner.org, a center for trading and listing trades

Organization Web Sites

The Mockingbird Foundation Site

http://www.phish.net/mockingbird

Not only the focal point for submissions to the Project and announcements from the foundation, but also the storehouse for more than a dozen web-based crossword puzzles about Phish and Phish lore.

CK5

http://members.home.net/ck5/

Effort to make fans aware who Chris Kuroda (lighting director) is, and to emphasize his impact upon Phish shows.

A legit and recognized movement, CK has their stickers on *all* of Chris' equipment.

People for a Louder Mike

http://www.netspace.org/~dan/plm/

Organized to encourage that Mike's bass be turned up in the mix, PLM has a fun site and the best unofficial t-shirt ever

The Phunky Bitches

http://phunky.com

This community by, of, and for female Phish fans provides social support and basic concert needs, such as tampons and band aids, and serves as an online discussion group

Brian/Robert

http://brianrobert.com

Gathering place for gay and lesbian fans, responding to common feelings of "I know I'm not the only one, but sometimes at shows I feel that way."

The Phellowship

http://www.phellowship.org

A group of Phish Heads who choose to remain drug and alcohol free and who help provide a clean and sober environment at Phish shows to those who seek one there.

Phish.Net, The

http://www.phish.net/

Central site of, by, and for the 50,000+-person online community that is The Phish.Net. This homepage provides direction to current setlists and news, upcoming news and tourdates, frequently asked questions, introductions for "newbies", indices of fan sites, and much more. Plus lyrics, artwork, a powerful search engine, and more.

Other Fan Phish Web Sites

Phans.com

http://www.phans.comAnother leading site by a solo effort, phans.com includes an extensive archive of past news stories and Phishtory even

DigiPhish

http://www.digiphish.com

Founded in 1996, DigiPhish is both a website and a mailing list, dedicated exclusively to the trading and distribution of DAT tapes.

Nugs.Net

http://www.nugs.net

Great source of quality MP3s and little minifeature sites on specific shows.

Phantasy Phish

http://phantasyphish.com

Enter your expectations for songs to be played (including specifying openers, closers, breakouts, and more), then see how your predictions rank against other prophetic fans.

Other Fan pages

http://www.phish.net/online/www/

Moderated list of some of the best of the hundreds of individually-maintained Phish fan web pages.

Web Resources, Non-Phish

The Dude of Life

http://dudeoflife.com

See Sideshows, Guestbook, and Dictionary.

Amfibian

http://dudeoflife.com

See Dictionary and *Sharing in the Groove*

E-Trees

http://www.etree.org

Online communal effort to digitally trade live recordings with maximum retention of sound quality, currently using Shorten to create highly compressed files of CD quality

Jambands.com

http://www.jambands.com

Monthly webzine with critical commentary, exclusive interviews, and much other original content

Jambase

http://www.jambase.com

Database-driven engine for marketing and locating local shows by growing bands enjoyed by Phish fans and others

SugarMegs

http://eyes.jeffdell.com/

One of the most bandwidth-rich sites on the net, SugarMegs includes RealAudio and MPEG3 sound files of Phish, Grateful Dead, and others, available via ftp or live feeds

Mailing Lists

Phish News

send email to phish-news@phish.net

http://www.phish.net/online/phishnet-news.html

A just-the-facts-ma'am mailing list: important tour date changes, mail order updates, setlist of each show (once verified), ticket release information, and selected ancillary information such as important updates to www.phish.net

Phishnet Digest, The

email listserv@netspace.org with "subscribe phishnet-digest" as subject http://www.phish.net/online/phishnet-digest.html

Digestified collections of the best reviews, essays, discussions, and tape offers on the Usenet newsgroup rec.music.Phish (see below)

Phish.Net Workers' List

email listserv@netspace.org with "subscribe phish-www" as subject Discussion list for the folks who manage the world wide web resources of the Phish.Net, and who work to develop those resources. Your help—graphical, design, conception, corrections, additions, submissions, or whatever—would be most appreciated.

The Phunky Bitches

email listserv@netspace.org with "subscribe phish-women" as subject Discussion list for the Phunky Bitches (see website description above

Faht Harpua's Updates

email fahtharpua@aol.comwith

"Subscribe Faht's Updates" as subject, and "emailaddress firstname lastname" in body Discussion list for the Phunky Bitches (see website description above)

Usenet Newsgroups

rec.music.phish

One of the largest and most evolved newsgroups on the Usenet, with nearly a decade of history and dozens of connected side-niches in other parts of cyberspace.

SHARING IN THE GROOVE

In December 1999, more than three years after first organizing what would become this book, Craig Delucia had the idea to extend the work of the Foundation to a cover album, also for charity...

It's about COMPLETION, since a *printed* guide to the band and their music could be encyclopedic but not complete.

It's about PHISH, the Vermont-based quartet that has become the world's biggest and most consistent touring act, with legions of devoted fans .

It's about TIME, given their dozen releases which include hundreds of originals that combine compositional brilliance and improvisational delivery.

It's about TIMING, with Phish taking their first "extended hiatus" after seventeen years, a break of unknown length and purpose.

It's about FAMILY, with more than a dozen acts covering the original music of Phish, including parts of the Phish musical family as well as family of some of their greatest influences.

It's about DIVERSITY, with blues, bluegrass, rock, jazz, barbershop quartet, and folk; careful compositions, integrative improvisations, loose extrapolations, and a capella vocalizations.

It's about INFLUENCES, including those who have performed with Phish, those whose songs Phish have performed, and those who typify genres which have come to bear on Phish's music.

It's about INVERSION, taking Phish songs back to Phish influences and looking forward to what the band has become, and has yet to be.

It's about CHANGE, with an instrumental version of a song with heavy lyrics, a funk version of a jazz tune, a newgrass version of a rock tune, and an industrial version of a new age ballad.

It's about CHARITY, with everyone involving donating their time, services, and expense, and all of the Foundation's proceeds providing non-profit support in music education.

It's about *SHARING IN THE GROOVE*, with artists sharing in Phish's music just as Phish in some way shares theirs, available soon from the Mockingbird Foundation.

For more information about the tracks and artists, and for ordering information, keep an eye on http://www.phish.net/mockingbird/album/